LE LOGICIEL = SOFTWARE
EPLURER = DEBUG
À LA PAGE = UP-TO-DATE
LES JAMBIÈRES = LEGWARMERS
LES GÉNÉRIQUES = FILM CREDITS
LE DÉCOLLAGE = LIFTOFF
L'EMBOUTEILLAGE = TRAFFIC JAM

Are you a student reading classic or contemporary novels? Do you enjoy French films? Are you a business person studying newspapers, magazines, or technical publications filled with slang, jargon, and mysterious abbreviations? Or are you a tourist taking in the sights and doing some shopping?

If you want to pronounce French correctly, know precisely what a word means and exactly how to use it, have rapid, easy reference to an extensive French and English vocabulary, *Kettridge* is the only bilingual French and English dictionary for you.

STANLEY AND ELEANOR HOCHMAN are professional editors, writers, and translators. Among their French translations, done both separately and as a team, are works ranging from such nineteenth-century classics as Zola's *Germinal* and the one-act plays of Jules Renard to books of contemporary interest in the fields of political science, film criticism, Latin American history, and science fiction. They have graduate degrees from Columbia University and have done postgraduate study at the Sorbonne and the University of Florence.

KETTRIDGE'S
FRENCH–ENGLISH
ENGLISH–FRENCH
DICTIONARY

NEW REVISED EDITION

*Edited, revised, and
updated by*
Stanley and Eleanor Hochman

A SIGNET BOOK

NEW AMERICAN LIBRARY

A DIVISION OF PENGUIN BOOKS USA INC., NEW YORK
PUBLISHED IN CANADA BY
PENGUIN BOOKS CANADA LIMITED MARKHAM, ONTARIO

Copyright ©1968, 1984 by New American Library,
a division of Penguin Books USA Inc.

Library of Congress Catalog Card Number: 83-63045

SIGNET, SIGNET CLASSIC, MENTOR, ONYX, PLUME, MERIDIAN
and NAL BOOKS are published by New American Library, a division of
Penguin Books USA Inc., 1633 Broadway, New York, New York 10019

First Signet Printing, November, 1968
Tenth Signet Printing (First Printing, Revised Edition), July, 1984

17 18 19 20 21 22 23 24 25

PRINTED IN CANADA

CONTENTS

KEY TO INTERNATIONAL PHONETIC TRANSCRIPTION

VOWELS

a   papa, femme, roi (papa, fam, rwa)

ɑ   passer, bâiller, bas, (pɑse, baje, bɑ)

ɑ̃   rampant, encan, temps (rɑ̃pɑ̃, ɑ̃kɑ̃, tɑ̃)

e   récréer, fée, chez (rekree, fe, ʃe)

ə   de, que, recevoir (də, kə, rəsəvwaːr)

ɛ   frais, près, rets, bel (frɛ, prɛ, rɛ, bɛl)

ɛ̃   bien, bain, vin, oint (bjɛ̃, bɛ̃, vɛ̃, wɛ̃)

i   civilité, nihiliste, y (sivilite, niilist, i)

o   gros, tôt, peau, aux (gro, to, po, o)

ɔ   colonne, opossum (kɔlɔn, ɔpɔsɔm)

ɔ̃   componction, mont (kɔ̃pɔ̃ksjɔ̃, mɔ̃)

œ   œuf, cueillir, seul (œf, kœjiːr, sœl)

œ̃   un, parfum, défunt (œ̃, parfœ̃, defœ̃)

ø   bleu, creux, vœu (blø, krø, vø)

u   trou, goût, courroux (tru, gu, kuru)

y   vu, une, murmurer (vy, yn, myrmyre)

ː indicates that the sound represented by the preceding symbol is long; thus:

aː   car, bail, soir (kaːr, baːj, swaːr)

ɑː   passe, âme, paille (pɑːs, ɑːm, pɑːj)

ɑ̃ː   ambre, antre, centre (ɑ̃ːbr, ɑ̃ːtr, sɑ̃ːtr)

ɛː   faire, ère, guerre (fɛːr, ɛːr, gɛːr)

ɛ̃ː   sainte, linge, peintre (sɛ̃ːt, lɛ̃ːʒ, pɛ̃ːtr)

iː   fille, lyre, abîme (fiːj, liːr, abiːm)

oː   dôme, rose, haute (doːm, roːz, oːt)

ɔː   fort, bord, corps (fɔːr, bɔːr, kɔːr)

ɔ̃ː   fondre, pompe, onze (fɔ̃ːdr, pɔ̃ːp, ɔ̃ːz)

œː   œil, deuil, beurre (œːj, dœːj, bœːr)

œ̃ː   humble, défunte (œ̃ːbl, defœ̃ːt)

øː   creuse, aqueuse (krøːz, akøːz)

uː   tour, cours, bourre (tuːr, kuːr, buːr)

yː   murmure, usure (myrmyːr, yzyːr)

CONSONANTS

g   gangue, gué, exil (gɑ̃ːg, ge, egzil)

j   fiancé fouille, ayant (fjɑ̃se, fuːj, ɛjɑ̃)

ɲ   cognac, baigner (kɔɲak, bɛɲe)

ʃ   chat, chiche, hache (ʃa, ʃiʃ, aʃ)

ʒ   je, juge, géologie (ʒə, ʒyːʒ, ʒeɔlɔʒi)

ɥ   cuir, huile, fruit (kɥiːr, ɥil, frɥi)

vi

The following consonants have their usual values:

b	bonbon, bimbelot (bɔ̃bɔ̃, bɛ̃blo)	n	nonne, inanition (nɔn, in-anisjɔ̃)
d	dedans, demande (dədɑ̃, də-mɑ̃ːd)	p	papier, obscur (papje, ɔpskyːr)
f	fifre, graphique (fifr, grafik)	r	rare, bizarrerie (raːr, bizarri)
h	=h aspirated about as in English (chiefly French interjections)	s	si, ceci, stoïcisme (si, səsi, stɔisism)
k	kaki, caquet, extra (kaki, kakɛ, ɛkstra)	t	quantité, théâtre (kɑ̃tite, teɑːtr)
l	lilas, parallèle (lila, paralɛl)	v	vive, verve, wagon (viːv, vɛrv, vagɔ̃)
m	momie, minimum (momi, minimɔm)	w	ouest, gloire, allouer (wɛst, glwaːr, alwe)
		z	zigzag, magasin (zigzag, mag-azɛ̃)

The sounds of the symbols to be learned can only be acquired by hearing them spoken, just as colors must be seen to be appreciated.

NOTE

The author considers himself fortunate in having at his disposal the International Phonetic System, and if the reader will take the trouble to learn it, he will, the author feels sure, hold himself equally blessed.

Gone forever for all practical purposes are the fantastic "imitated" pronunciations. Every language has certain sounds which are peculiar to itself and have no equivalents in another. For this reason, imitated pronunciations, although capable of transcribing French into French phonetically, English into English, and so on, are inherently incapable of transliterating one language into another, and are responsible in large measure for many people's bad pronunciation of foreign languages.

Pronunciation of French is very difficult for the foreigner. Exceptions to rule, silent letters, and other peculiarities abound. Therefore, every time he refers to a word in the French vocabulary, the English reader is advised to compare, and correct if necessary, his notion of how it should be pronounced.

ARRANGEMENT

As far as is reasonably possible, set or inseparable word groups are entered under the first word of the group.

ABBREVIATIONS USED IN THIS DICTIONARY

†

ADVERBS

Most French adverbs of manner are formed by adding **-ment** to the feminine singular of the adjective, corresponding to the English suffix -ly (-le being changed into -ly, -ic into -ically, and -y into -ily); thus,

naturel (natyrɛl)	**correct** (kɔrɛkt)	**relatif** (rəlatif)
naturelle (rɛl)	**correcte** (rɛkt)	**relative** (ti;v)
naturellement (rɛlmɑ̃)	**correctement** (təmɑ̃)*	**relativement** (tivmɑ̃‡)
natural; naturally	correct; correctly	relative; relatively

So also with adjectives ending in e of identical form in both genders; as,

énergique (enɛrʒik); **énergiquement** (ʒikmɑ̃), energetic; energetically.
admirable (admirabl); **admirablement** (bləmɑ̃*), admirable; admirably.
ordinaire (ɔrdinɛ;r); **ordinairement** (nɛrmɑ̃‡), ordinary; ordinarily.

Adjectives whose masculine form ends in **-ai** (as **vrai**), **-é** (as **modéré**), **-i** (as **hardi**), and **-u** (as **absolu**), add the suffix **-ment** to the masculine form; thus,

modéré (mɔdere)	**modérée** (re)	**modérément** (remɑ̃)
	moderate;	moderately

In order to economize space (most adverbs of manner being long words), French and English adverbs ending regularly as above, and with no appreciable change of meaning, are not given in the dictionary. Instead, the adjectives are marked † (e.g, **naturel, le**†, **modéré**†, e), in reference hereto. Adverbs not formed according to these rules, particularly those presenting peculiarity or difficulty, are given in the ordinary way.

* Note:—When two pronounced consonants immediately precede the ending **-ement**, the e of ement is pronounced (ə). Otherwise it is silent.

‡ Note that the vowel sound is short here, rəlati;v, tivmɑ̃; ɔrdinɛ;r, nɛrmɑ̃.

It may be observed that most ordinary English adverbs of manner for which no French form ending in **-ment** exists can be translated by *d'une manière*, plus the corresponding feminine adjective, as **satisfactorily**, *d'une manière satisfaisante*.

The swing dash (~) signifies repetition in the singular of a leading vocabulary word (word printed in **times roman type**). Followed by *s* (~s), it signifies the like repetition in the plural.

The paragraph (¶) also signifies repetition of a leading vocabulary word, but indicates the commencement of a different part of speech. This symbol is used to make the point of transition conspicuous.

An initial letter followed by a period signifies repetition of a translation.

[Brackets] enclose words, or parts of words, which can be used or omitted at will.

SUBJECT INDICATIONS

Avn.	Aviation	*Mach.*	Machinery; Machine
Agric.	Agriculture	*Math.*	Mathematics
Anat.	Anatomy	*Meas.*	Measurement;
Arch.	Architecture		Measure
Arith.	Arithmetic	*Mech.*	Mechanics
Artil.	Artillery	*Med.*	Medicine; Medical
Astr.	Astronomy	*Metall.*	Metallurgy
Bil.	Billiards	*Meteor.*	Meteorology
Biol.	Biology	*Mil.*	Military
Bkkpg.	Bookkeeping	*Min.*	Mining
Boat.	Boating	*Miner.*	Mineralogy
Bookb.	Bookbinding	*Mol.*	Mollusc
Bot.	Botany	*Motor.*	Motoring; Motor car
Box.	Boxing	*Mus.*	Music
Build.	Building	*Myth.*	Mythology
Carp.	Carpentry	*Nat. Hist.*	Natural History
Chem.	Chemistry	*Naut.*	Nautical
Com.	Commerce	*Nav.*	Navy; Naval
Conch.	Conchology, Shell-	*Need.*	Needlework
	fish, Shells	*Opt.*	Optics
Cook.	Cookery	*Path.*	Pathology
Crust.	Crustacea(n)	*Phar.*	Pharmacy
Cust.	Customs	*Philos.*	Philosophy
Danc.	Dancing	*Phot.*	Photography
Eccl.	Ecclesiastical	*Phys.*	Physics
Elec.	Electricity; Electric	*Phys. Geog.*	Physical Geography
Emb.	Embroidery	*Poet.*	Poetry; Poetic
Engin.	Engineering	*Pol.*	Politics
Fenc.	Fencing	*Post*	Post Office; Postal
Fin.	Finance	*Pros.*	Prosody
Fish.	Fishing	*Radio*	Wireless
Foot.	Football	*Relig.*	Religion
Geog.	Geography	*Rhet.*	Rhetoric
Geol.	Geology	*Rly.*	Railway(s)
Geom.	Geometry	*Sch.*	School
Gram.	Grammar	*Ship.*	Shipping
Gym.	Gymnastics	*Shipbldg.*	Shipbuilding
Her.	Heraldry	*Stk Ex.*	Stock Exchange
Hist.	History; Historical	*Surg.*	Surgery
Horol.	Horology, Clocks	*Surv.*	Surveying
	& Watches	*Swim.*	Swimming
Hort.	Horticulture	*Teleg.*	Telegraphy
Hunt.	Hunting	*Teleph.*	Telephony
Hyd.	Hydraulics	*Ten.*	Tennis
Inc. Tax	Income Tax	*Theat.*	Theater; Theatrical
Insce.	Insurance	*Theol.*	Theology
Join.	Joinery	*Typ.*	Typography;
Jump.	Jumping		Printing
Knit.	Knitting	*Univ.*	University
Lit.	Liturgy	*Vet.*	Veterinary
Log.	Logic	*Zool.*	Zoology

a	adjective
abb	abbreviation
abs	absolutely, i.e, (verb) used without its object
ad	adverb or adverbial phrase (see also †ADVERBS, page viii)
a.f	adjective feminine only, i.e, not masculine also
a.m	adjective masculine only, i.e, not feminine also
art	article
att	attributively, i.e, (noun) used as adjective
aux	auxiliary (verb)
c	conjunction or conjunctive phrase
Cf.	Compare
col	collectively, collective noun
comps	compounds; in combination
e.g	for example
Eng.	England; English
&	and, et (The sign & is used in the dictionary only to save space)
etc.	et cetera
f	feminine. In the French-English section, *f* = noun feminine
fig.	figuratively
f.pl.	feminine plural. In the French-English section, *f.pl* = noun feminine plural
Fr.	France; French
f.s	feminine singular. In the French-English section, *f.s* = noun feminine singular
i	interjection
i.e	that is to say
imp	impersonal
inv	invariable
ir	irregular (verb)
lit.	literally
m	masculine. In the French-English section, *m* = noun masculine
m,f	masculine & feminine (noun)
m.pl	masculine plural. In the French-English section, *m.pl* = noun masculine plural
m.s	masculine singular. In the French-English section, *m.s* = noun masculine singular
n	noun. In the French-English section, *n* = noun masculine & feminine (of persons)
neg.	negative; (used) negatively
oft.	often
opp.	opposed to
p.a	participial adjective
pers.	person(s)
pl	plural
pn	pronoun
p.p	participle past
p.pr	participle present
pr	preposition or prepositional phrase
s	singular
v.i	verb intransitive
v.i. & t	verb intransitive & verb transitive
v.pr.	verb pronominal
v.t	verb transitive
v.t. & i	verb transitive & verb intransitive

FRENCH-ENGLISH DICTIONARY

FRENCH-ENGLISH DICTIONARY

A

a *see* **avoir.**

à (a) (**à le** *is contracted into* **au, à les** *into* **aux**) *pr,* to; at; in; within; into; on; by; with; for; of; after; from; under; according to; between; till, until; and. *When coupled with noun, often rendered in English by noun used attributively,* as, *canne à sucre,* sugar cane. *un homme ~ craindre,* a man to be feared *or* to fear. *~ prendre après les repas,* to be taken after meals. *~ ne pas confondre avec . . .,* not to be confused with *. . . de 2 ~ 3 fois par jour,* 2 or 3 times a day.

abaissement (abɛsmã) *m,* lowering; sinking; fall; humiliation. **abaisser** (se) *v.t,* to lower, let down; humble, abase. **s'~,** to subside; sink; humble oneself.

abandon (abãdɔ̃) *m,* abandonment, dereliction, desertion; unconstraint. *à l'~,* in confusion, at random, anyhow; derelict. **abandonnement** (dɔnmã) *m,* profligacy. **abandonner** (ne) *v.t,* to abandon, leave, desert, forsake; give up, relinquish, surrender; concede. **s'~ à,** to give way to, indulge in.

abaque (abak) *m,* abacus; diagram.

abasourdir (abazurdi:r) *v.t,* to dumbfound, stun.

abâtardir (s') (abɑtardi:r) *v.pr,* to degenerate.

abat-jour (abaʒu:r) *m,* shade, lampshade. **abats** (ba) *m.pl.* Same as *abattis.* **abat-son** (abasɔ̃) *m,* louvers. **abattage** (bata:ʒ) *m,* felling; slaughtering. **abattant** (tã) *m,* flap. **abattement** (tmã) *m,* prostration, depression, dejection, despondency; deductions (*for dependents, Inc. Tax*). **abatteur** (tœ:r) *m,* feller; slaughterman. **abattis** (ti) *m,* demolitions; fell; kill; giblets. **abattoir** (twa:r) *m,* slaughterhouse, abattoir. **abattre** (tr) *v.t.ir,* to knock down; bring down; cut down; lay; fell; slaughter, kill; mine; deject. **s'~,** to fall down; become depressed; subside. **abattu, e** (ty) *a,* depressed, low-spirited, downcast. **abat-vent** (abavã) *m,* windshield. **abat-voix** (abavwa) *m,* sounding board.

abbaye (abɛi) *f,* abbey. **abbé** (be) *m,* abbot; priest. **abbesse** (bɛs) *f,* abbess.

abcès (apsɛ) *m,* abscess, gathering. *~ aux gencives,* gumboil.

abdication (abdikasjɔ̃) *f,* abdication. **abdiquer** (ke) *v.t. & abs,* to abdicate; surrender, waive.

abdomen (abdɔmɛn) *m,* abdomen.

abeille (abɛ:j) *f,* bee. *~ ouvrière,* worker b.

aberration (abɛrasjɔ̃) *f,* aberration.

abêtir (abɛti:r) *v.t,* to make dull.

abhorrer (abɔre) *v.t,* to abhor, loathe, detest.

abîme (abi:m) *m,* abyss, gulf, chasm. **abîmer** (bime) *v.t,* to swallow up; ruin, spoil. **s'~,** to bury (*or* immerse) oneself, welter; get spoiled.

abject, e (abʒɛkt) *a,* abject, mean. **abjection** (sjɔ̃) *f,* abjectness, etc.

abjurer (abʒyre) *v.t,* to abjure, forswear, renounce.

ablatif (ablatif) *m,* ablative [case].

abnégation (abnegasjɔ̃) *f,* abnegation, self-denial.

aboiement (abwamã) *m,* bark[ing], bay[ing]. **aux abois** (bwa), at bay; hard pressed, at one's wit's end.

abolir (abɔli:r) *v.t,* to abolish. **abolition** (lisjɔ̃) *f,* abolition; repeal. **abolitioniste** (lisjɔnist) *m,* freetrader.

abominable† (abɔminabl) *a,* abominable, nefarious. **abomination** (sjɔ̃) *f,* abomination. **abominer** (ne) *v.t,* to abominate.

abondance (abɔ̃dã:s) *f,* abundance, plenty, galore; fullness. *parler d'~,* to speak extempore. **abondant, e** (dã, ã:t) *a,* abundant,

plentiful, plenteous. profuse.
abondamment (damɑ̃) *ad*, abundantly, etc. **abonder** (de) *v.i*, to abound. ~ *dans le sens de*, to quite agree with, chime in with.
abonné, e (abɔne) *n*, subscriber; commuter; consumer (*gas, elec.*). **abonnement** (nmɑ̃) *m*, subscription, season ticket; commutation ticket. **abonner** (ne) *v.t*, to subscribe for. s'~, to subscribe.
abonnir (abɔni:r) *v.t*, to improve.
abord (abɔ:r) *m*, landing; approach, access. [*tout*] *d'~, au premier ~, de prime ~*, at first, first of all, to begin with. **abordable** (bɔrdabl) *a*, accessible, approachable. **abordage** (da:ʒ) *m*, landing; collision, fouling. **aborder** (de) *v.i. & t*, to land; approach; broach; board; collide with, foul.
aborigène (abɔriʒɛ:n) *a. & m*, aboriginal; (*m.pl.*) aborigines.
abortif, ive (abɔrtif, i:v) *a*, abortive (*of premature birth*).
aboucher (abuʃe) *v.t*, to bring together; join up.
aboutir (abuti:r) *v.i*, to end, lead; eventuate, materialize; come to a head, culminate.
aboutissement (abutismɑ̃) *m*, result, issue, outcome, effect.
aboyer (abwaje) *v.i*, to bark, bay; be in full cry; cry out. **aboyeur** (jœ:r) *m*, barker (*circus, etc.*).
abrégé (abreʒe) *m*, abridgement, epitome, abstract, summary. *en ~*, shortly, briefly; abbreviated. **abréger** (ʒe) *v.t*, to abridge, epitomize; abbreviate.
abreuver (abrœve) *v.t*, to water; season; soak, steep, drench; prime (*pump*). s'~, to drink, soak, fill oneself, wallow, bathe. **abreuvoir** (vwa:r) *m*, watering place, horse pond, drinking trough.
abréviation (abrevjasjɔ̃) *f*, abbreviation; contraction.
abri (abri) *m*, shelter, cover, dugout; cab (*locomotive*). *à l'~ de*, under cover of, sheltered from. ~ *blindé*, bombshelter.
abricot (abriko) *m*, apricot; vagina (*obscene*). **abricotier** (kɔtje) *m*, apricot tree.

abriter (abrite) *v.t*, to shelter, shield, screen.
abrivent (abrivɑ̃) *m*, shelter, hut; matting, screen.
abrogation (abrɔgasjɔ̃) *f*, abrogation, repeal. **abroger** (ʒe) *v.t*, to abrogate.
abrupt, e (abrypt) *a*, abrupt, sheer.
abruti, e (abryti) *p.a*, brutish, besotted, sottish; stupefied (*alcohol, fatigue*). ¶ *m*, beast (*pers.*). **abrutir** (ti:r) *v.t*, to brutalize, besot. **abrutissement** (tismɑ̃) *m*, brutishness.
absence (apsɑ̃:s) *f*, absence. ~ [*d'esprit*], absence of mind. **absent, e** (sɑ̃, ɑ̃:t) *a*, absent, away [from home], out, not at home. ~ *par congé*, away on holiday. ¶ *m*, absentee. s'**absenter** (sɑ̃te) *v.pr*, to absent oneself, keep away.
abside (apsid) *f*, apse.
absinthe (apsɛ̃:t) *f*, wormwood; absinth.
absolu†, e (apsɔly) *a*, absolute; hard & fast; positive; peremptory.
absolution (apsɔlysjɔ̃) *f*, absolution; acquittal.
absorbant, e (apsɔrbɑ̃, ɑ̃:t) *a*, absorbent, bibulous; absorbing, engrossing. **absorber** (be) *v.t. & abs*, to absorb, drink in, imbibe; engross. **absorption** (psjɔ̃) *f*, absorption.
absoudre (apsudr) *v.t.ir*, to absolve.
abstème (apstɛ:m) *a*, abstemious. ¶ *n*, abstainer. s'**abstenir** (stəni:r) *v.pr*, to abstain, refrain, forbear. **abstention** (stɑ̃sjɔ̃) *f*, abstention. **abstinence** (stinɑ̃:s) *f*, abstinence, temperance.
abstinent (apstinɑ̃) *m*, teetotaller.
abstraction (apstraksjɔ̃) *f*, abstraction. ~ *faite de*, apart from, setting aside. **abstraire** (strɛ:r) *v.t.ir*, to abstract. **abstrait, e** (strɛ, ɛ:t) *a*, abstract. l'**abstrait**, *m*, the abstract (opp. *concrete*).
abstrus, e (apstry, y:z) *a*, abstruse, recondite.
absurde† (apsyrd) *a*, absurd, preposterous. l'**absurde**, *m*, the absurd, an absurdity. **absurdité** (dite) *f*, absurdity, nonsense.

abus (aby) *m*, abuse, misuse; breach. **abuser** (ze) *v.t*, to deceive, delude, mislead, misguide. ~ *de*, to abuse, misuse, trespass on. *s'~*, to delude oneself. **abusif, ive†** (zif, i:v) *a*, abusive, improper.

abysse (abis) *m*, abyss.

Abyssinie (**l'**) (abisini) *f*, Abyssinia. **abyssinien, ne** (njɛ̃, ɛn) *a*. & A~, *n*, ou **abyssin, e** (sɛ̃, in) *a*. & A~, *n*, Abyssinian.

acabit (akabi) *m*, stamp, sort, nature. *de même* ~, of the same sort or type.

acacia (akasja) *m*, acacia.

académicien, ne (akademisjɛ̃, ɛn) *n*, academician. **académie** (mi) *f*, academy, college; academy figure. **académique** (mik) *a*, academic(al).

acagnarder (akaɲarde) *v.t*, to make lazy.

acajou (akaʒu) *m*, mahogany. ~*des Antilles*, Spanish mahogany.

acare (aka:r) *m*, mite, tick.

acariâtre (akarjɑ:tr) *a*, peevish, sour[-tempered].

accablant (akɑblɑ̃) *a*, crushing; overwhelming.

accablement (akɑbləmɑ̃) *m*, despondency, dejection; prostration; great pressure (*of business*). **accabler** (ble) *v.t*, to overwhelm, crush, overcome.

accalmie (akalmi) *f*, lull.

accaparer (akapare) *v.t*, to corner, buy up, monopolize. **accapareur, euse** (rœ:r, ø:z) *n*, monopolist.

accéder à (aksede) *v.t*, to accede to, consent to; reach.

accélérateur (akseleratœ:r) *m*, accelerator. **accélérer** (re) *v.t*, to accelerate, quicken. *pas accéléré*, on the double, quick march.

accent (aksɑ̃) *m*, accent; stress; tone, pronunciation; (*pl.*) strains. **accentuer** (tɥe) *v.t*, to accent, accentuate, emphasize, stress. *s'~*, to become more noticeable, grow stronger, increase.

acceptable (aksɛptabl) *a*, acceptable. **acceptation** (sjɔ̃) *f*, acceptance, accepter (te) *v.t abs*, to accept; undertake. **accepteur** (tœ:r) *m*, acceptor. **acception** (psjɔ̃) *f*, respect, acceptation (*of a word*).

accès (aksɛ) *m*, access, approach; fit, attack, flush. ~ *direct*, direct access (*computers*). ~ *séquentiel*, serial access (*computers*). **accessible** (sɛsibl) *a*, accessible, approachable.

accession (aksɛsjɔ̃) *f*, accession; consent.

accessoire† (aksɛswa:r) *a*, accessory. ¶ *m*, accessory, adjunct; (*pl.*) fittings, furniture; properties (*Theat.*). **accessoiriste** (ist) *n*, property manager (*Theat.*). ~ *de plateau*, property manager (*cinema*).

accident (aksidɑ̃) *m*, accident; smash; unevenness; hazard (*Golf*); accidental (*Mus.*). **accidenté, e** (te) *a*, hilly, broken; checkered, eventful. **accidentel, le†** (tɛl) *a*, accidental, casual.

acclamation (aklamasjɔ̃) *f*, acclamation, cheering. **acclamer** (me) *v.t*, to acclaim, hail, cheer.

acclimatation (aklimatasjɔ̃) *f*, acclimatization. *jardin d'~*, zoo. **acclimater** (te) *v.t*, to acclimatize. *s'~*, to become accustomed to.

accointance (akwɛ̃tɑ̃:s) *f. oft. pl*, intimacy; dealings.

accolade (akɔlad) *f*, embrace, hug; brace, bracket (*Typ.*). **accoler** (le) *v.t*, to brace, bracket.

accommodation (akɔmɔdasjɔ̃) *f*, accommodation. **accommodement** (dmɑ̃) *m*, compromise, arrangement, settlement, terms. **accommoder** (de) *v.t*, to suit; please; reconcile; adapt; prepare (*food*); arrange, settle. *s'~à*, to adapt oneself to. *s'~ de*, to put up with.

accompagnateur trice (akɔ̃paɲatœ:r, tris) *n*, accompan[y]ist. **accompagnement** (ɲmɑ̃) *m*, accompaniment; concomitant. **accompagner** (ɲe) *v.t*, to accompany, attend, escort.

accompli, e (akɔ̃pli) *a*, accomplished, thorough. **accomplir** (pli:r) *v.t*, to accomplish, achieve, perform, carry out. *s'~*, to happen. **accomplissement** (plismɑ̃) *m*, accomplishment, etc.

accord (akɔ:r) *m*, accord, agreement; harmony, concord; consent; chord (*Mus.*); tune; (*pl.*) betrothal. *d'~*, agreed, granted; in tune. *d'un commun ~*, with one accord. **accordage** (kɔrda:ʒ) *m*, tuning. **accordailles** (da:j) *f.pl*, betrothal. **accordéon** (deɔ̃) *m*, accordion. **accorder** (de) *v.t*, to accord, grant, bestow, allow, afford; spare; reconcile; tune; attune. *s'~*, to agree; accord; tune [up]. accordeur (dœ:r) *m*, tuner.

accort, e (akɔ:r, ɔrt) *a*, amiable, pleasing.

accostage (akɔsta:ʒ) *m*, docking (*ships, spaceships*). **accoster** (kɔste) *v.t*, to accost; come alongside.

accotement (akɔtmɑ̃) *m*, side path, greensward, verge. **accoter** (te) *v.t*, to hold up; lean, rest. **accotoir** (twa:r) *m*, rest, arm.

accouchement (akuʃmɑ̃) *m*, confinement, lying-in, childbirth. **accoucher** (ʃe) *v.i*, to be confined, give birth, deliver, bring forth; speak out. **accoucheur** (ʃœ:r) *m*, maternity doctor. **accoucheuse** (jøːz) *f*, midwife.

accouder (s') (akude) *v.pr*, to rest (*or* lean) on one's elbow(s). **accoudoir** (dwa:r) *m*, arm; rail.

accouple (akupl) *f*, leash. **accoupler** (ple) *v.t*, to couple, connect, yoke; pair, mate.

accourcie (akursi) *f*, shortcut. **accourcir** (si:r) *v.t*, to shorten.

accourir (akuri:r) *v.i.ir*, to run [up], rush.

accoutrement (akutrəmɑ̃) *m*, trappings, garb, rig. **accoutrer** (tre) *v.t*, to rig out.

accoutumance (akutymɑ̃:s) *f*, habit, use. **accoutumer** (me) *v.t*, to accustom, inure.

accréditer (akredite) *v.t*, to accredit, open a credit for. *s'~*, to gain credence.

accroc (akro) *m*, rent, tear; snag, hitch; stain.

accroche-coeur (akrɔʃkœ:r) *m*, lovelock, kiss-curl. **accrocher** (ʃe) *v.t*, to hook; grapple; hang [up]; run against; catch. *s'~*, to hang on.

accroire (akrwa:r) *v.t*: *faire ~ à*, to cause to believe. *en faire ~ à*, to impose [up]on. *s'en faire ~*, to be conceited.

accroître (akrwa:tr) *v.t. & i. ir*, to increase, grow, accrue. **accroissement** (krwasmɑ̃) *m*, increase, etc.

accroupir (s') (akrupi:r) *v.pr*, to squat, crouch, cower.

accueil (akœ:j) *m*, reception, welcome; honor (*bill*). **accueillir** (kœji:r) *v.t.ir*, to receive, welcome, greet; entertain; honor, meet (*bill*).

accul (akyl) *m*, cove, creek; lair. **acculer** (akyle) *v.t*, to [drive into a] corner. *s'~*, to stand at bay; jib. *s'~ contre*, to set one's back against.

accumulateur (akymylatœ:r) *m*, accumulator, [storage] battery. **accumulation** (sjɔ̃) *f*, accumulation. **accumuler** (le) *v.t. & abs. & s'~*, to accumulate; gather.

accusateur, trice (akyzatœ:r, tris) *n*, accuser. ¶ *a*, accusing. **accusatif** (tif) *m*, accusative [case]. **accusation** (sjɔ̃) *f*, accusation, charge; indictment. **accusé, e** (ze) *n*, accused, prisoner at the bar. **accusé de réception**, *m*, acknowledgment. **accuser** (ze) *v.t*, to accuse, charge; indict; impeach; blame; show, betray; bring out; complain of (*medically*). *~ réception de*, to acknowledge receipt of. *s'~ de*, to avow, acknowledge, confess. *s'~ soi-même*, to plead guilty.

acerbe (asɛrb) *a*, sour, sharp, harsh.

acéré, e (asere) *a*, steeled, sharp, keen, cutting. **acérer** (re) *v.t*, to steel.

acétique (asetik) *a*, acetic.

achalandage (aʃalɑ̃da:ʒ) *m*, bringing custom; custom, connection, patronage. **achalandé, e** (de) *p.a*, patronized. **achalander** (de) *v.t*, to bring custom; commercialize. *s'~*, to get custom.

acharné, e (aʃarne) *a*, rabid, furious, fierce, desperate, relentless, ruthless; obstinate, bitter, inveterate, confirmed; intense, eager; fleshed. **acharnement** (nəmɑ̃) *m*, rabidness, etc. **acharner** (ne) *v.t*, to set on, set against; flesh. *s'~*, to attack furiously; be set, be bent, be insatiable, be inveterate.

achat (aʃa) *m*, purchase, buying.

acheminement (aʃminmã) *m*, way; progress; forwarding; routing; step. **acheminer** (ne) *v.t*, to direct; expedite; forward, dispatch, route. **s'~**, to proceed.

acheter (aʃte) *v.t*, to buy, purchase. **acheteur, euse** (tœːr, ØːZ) *n*, buyer, purchaser.

achevé, e (aʃve) *a*, accomplished, perfect, thorough, out & out, arrant. **achèvement** (ʃevmã) *m*, finishing, completion. **achever** (ʃve) *v.t*, to finish, perfect, end. *achevez donc!* out with it!

achopper (aʃɔpe) *v.i*. & **s'~**, to stumble.

achromatique (akrɔmatik) *a*, achromatic.

acide (asid) *a*, acid, sour, sharp, tart. ¶ *m*, acid. **acidité** (dite) *f*, acidity, etc. **aciduler** (dyle) *v.t*, to acidulate.

acier (asje) *m*, steel. ~ *sur sole*, open hearth s.; ~ *Thomas*, basic Bessemer s.; ~ *trempé et revenu*, tempered s. **aciérer** (sjere) *v.t*, to steel, caseharden. **aciérie** (ri) *f*, steel works.

acné (akne) *f*, acne.

acolyte (akɔlit) *m*, acolyte.

acompte (akɔ̃ːt) *m*, installment; cover, margin. ~ *de dividende*, interim dividend. ~ *de préférence*, option money (*on a property*).

aconit (akɔnit) *m*, aconite, monk's-hood, wolfsbane.

acoquinant, e (akɔkinã, ɑ̃ːt) *a*, enticing. **s'acoquiner à, auprès** (ne), to get fond of, become attached to.

Açores (les) (asɔːr) *f.pl*, the Azores.

à-coup (aku) *m*, jerk, shock; (*pl.*) backlash (*gears*).

acoustique (akustik) *a*, acoustic. ¶ *f*, acoustics.

acquéreur (akerœːr) *m*, purchaser, buyer. **acquérir** (riːr) *v.t.ir*, to acquire, get, win, purchase; (*abs.*) to improve. **s'~**, to accrue.

acquêts (akε) *m.pl*, acquisition; windfall.

acquiescement (akjɛsmã) *m*, acquiescence. **acquiescer (se)** *v.i*, to acquiesce.

acquis, e (aki, iːz) *p.a*, acquired; earned; devoted; vested (*rights*). ¶ *m. s.* & *pl*, acquirements, attainments, experience. **acquisition** (kizisjɔ̃) *f*, acquisition, purchase; haul.

acquit (aki) *m*, receipt, discharge. [*pour*] ~, received [with thanks], paid. *à l'~ de*, on behalf of, on account of. **acquit-à-caution** (kitakosjɔ̃) *m*, bond note, transhipment bond. **acquitté, e** (te) *a*, duty-paid (*Cust.*).à l'acquitté, *ad*, duty paid, ex bond. **acquittement** (tmã) *m*, discharge, acquittal. **acquitter** (te) *v.t*, to acquit, discharge; receipt (*bill*). **s'~**, to acquit oneself, perform; be quits, catch up (*games*).

âcre (ɑːkr) *a*, acrid, tart, sour, sharp, pungent. **âcreté** (ɑkrəte) *f*, acridity, etc.

acrimonie (akrimɔni) *f*, acrimony. **acrimonieux, euse** (njØ, Øːz) *a*, acrimonious.

acrobate (akrɔbat) *n*, acrobat, tumbler. **acrobatie** (si) *f*, acrobatics; stunt. **acrobatique** (tik) *a*, acrobatic.

acrostiche (akrɔstiʃ) *m*. & *a*, acrostic.

acte (akt) *m*, act, action; deed, indenture, instrument, document, agreement, contract; bond; certificate; licence; (*pl.*) transactions (*of a society*). ~ *d'accusation*, indictment. ~ *de dernière volonté*, last will & testament. ~ *de naissance, de mariage, de décès*, certificate of birth, of marriage, of death. ~ *dommageable*, tort (*law*). ~ *sous seing privé* (sẽ), simple contract. [*pièce en un*] ~, one-act play. *prendre* ~ *de*, to take note of. **acteur, trice** (tœːr, tris) *n*, actor, actress, player. ~ *à transformations*, quick-change artist. ~ *de composition*, character actor.

acter (akte) *v.i*, to take action.

actif, ive (aktif, iːv) *a*, active, brisk; busy. ¶ *m*, active voice; assets.

action (aksjɔ̃) *f*, action, act, deed;

effect, agency; share, (*pl.*) stock. ~s *au porteur*, bearer shares, b. stock. ~[*s*] *de grâce*, thanksgiving. ~s *de priorité*, ~s *privilégiées*, preference shares, preferred stock. ~s *nominatives*, registered shares, r. stock. ~s *gratuites*, bonus shares. ~s [*entièrement*] *libérées*, fully paid shares. ~s *non libérées*, partly paid shares. *par* ~s, joint-stock (*att.*). **actionnaire** (ɔnɛːr) *n*, shareholder, stockholder. **actionnariat** (ɔnarja) *f*, employee shareholding.

actionner (aksjone) *v.t*, to drive, actuate, run, work; bring an action against, sue.

activement (aktivmã) *ad*, actively, briskly. **activer** (ve) *v.t*, to quicken, urge, press, rouse, stir up, speed up, hurry. **activité** (vite) *f*, activity, briskness. *en* ~ [*de service*], on active service. *en pleine* ~, in full operation, in full swing.

actuaire (aktɥɛːr) *m*, actuary.

actualité (aktɥalite) *f*, actuality, present state; (*pl.*) passing (*or* current) events, questions of the hour; news (*movies*). ~s *de la mode*, present-day fashions. **actuel, le** (tɥɛl) *a*, present, for the time being. **actuellement** (lmã) *ad*, now, at present.

acuité (akɥite) *f*, sharpness, acuteness, keenness; shrillness.

adage (adaːʒ) *m*, adage, saying, saw. ~ *de droit*, legal maxim.

adaptation (adaptasjɔ̃) *m*, adaptation, adjustment. ~ *à l'usager*, customization.

adapter (adapte) *v.t*, to adapt, fit, suit. **adapteur** (tœːr) *m*, adapter (*Phot.*).

addition (adisjɔ̃) *f*, addition, cast, tot; bill (*at restaurant*). **additionnel, le** (ɔnɛl) *a*, additional. **additionner** (ne) *v.t*, to add [up], cast, tot up.

adénoïde (adenɔid) *a*, adenoid.

adepte (adɛpt) *n*, adept.

adhérence (aderãːs) *f*, adherence, adhesion. **adhérent, e** (rã, ãːt) *n*, adherent, supporter, member. **adhérer** (re) *v.i*, to adhere, cohere, stick. **adhésion** (zjɔ̃) *f*,

adhesion, adhesiveness; membership.

adieu (adjø) *i. & m*, good-bye, farewell, adieu; parting.

adipeux, euse (adipø, øːz) *a*, adipose, fatty.

adjacent, e (adʒasã, ãːt) *a*, adjacent, adjoining.

adjectif (adʒɛktif) *a.m*, adjectival. ¶ *m*, adjective. ~ *attribut*, predicative a. ~ *épithète*, attributive a. ~ *verbal*, participial a. (*present*). **adjectivement** (tivmã) *ad*, adjectivally, attributively.

adjoindre (adʒwɛːdr) *v.t.ir*, to join, associate. **adjoint, e** (ʒwɛ̃, ɛ̃t) *a. & n*, assistant.

adjudant (adʒydã) *m*, sergeant major. ~ *major*, adjutant.

adjudicataire (adʒydikatɛːr) *n*, purchaser; contractor. **adjudication** (sjɔ̃) *f*, adjudication; award of contract; auction. **adjuger** (ʒe) *v.t*, to adjudge, adjudicate; award; award the contract for; knock down.

adjurer (adʒyre) *v.t*, to adjure, beseech.

admettre (admɛtr) *v.t.ir*, to admit, allow, grant; pass (*at exam*).

administrateur, trice (administratœːr, tris) *n*, director; administrator, trix. ~ *délégué*, ~ *directeur*, managing director. **administration** (sjɔ̃) *f*, administration, management, direction; board, directorate; authorities. ~ *publique*, civil service. *conseil d'*~, board of directors. **administrer** (tre) *v.t*, to administer, manage, direct.

admirable† (admirabl) *a*, admirable, wonderful, capital. **admirateur, trice** (tœːr, tris) *n*, admirer. **admiration** (sjɔ̃) *f*, admiration, wonder. **admirer** (re) *v.t*, to admire, wonder at.

admis (admi) *a*, admitted; accepted; conventional.

admissible (admisibl) *a*, admissible. **admission** (sjɔ̃) *f*, admission, admittance; intake; entrance.

admonester (admɔnɛste) *v.t*, to admonish, reprimand. **admonestation** (tasjɔ̃) *f*, **admonition** (nisjɔ̃) *f*, admonition, etc.`

adolescence (adɔlɛsɑ̃:s) *f*, adolescence, youth. **adolescent, e** (sɑ̃, ɑ̃:t) *a*, adolescent. ¶ *n*, adolescent, youth, girl.

adonner (s') (adɔne) *v. pr*, to give (*or* apply) oneself, addict oneself, take.

adopter (adɔpte) *v.t*, to adopt, carry, pass, confirm. **adoptif, ive** (tif, i;v) *a*, adoptive, adopted. **adoption** (sjɔ̃) *f*, adoption, etc.

adorable (adɔrabl) *a*, adorable, charming, lovely, delightful. **adorateur, trice** (tœ:r, tris) *n*, adorer, worshiper, votary. **adoration** (sjɔ̃) *f*, adoration, worship. **adorer** (re) *v.t*, to adore, worship.

adosser (adose) *v.t*, to back, lean. s'~, to lean one's back against.

adoucir (adusi;r) *v.t*, to sweeten; soften; smooth, temper, subdue, allay, alleviate, soothe, ease, appease, assuage, mollify, qualify.

adresse (adrɛs) *f*, address, direction; skill, dexterity, craft, deftness; shrewdness; handiness; clever move. **adresser** (se) *v.t*, to address, direct, send. s'~ à, to address, apply to; inquire of; cater for.

Adriatique (adriatik) *a. & f*, Adriatic.

adroit, e† (adrwa, at) *a*, adroit, dext[e]rous, deft, handy, skillful, clever, neat; shrewd.

adulateur, trice (adylatœ:r, tris) *a*, adulatory. **adulation** (sjɔ̃) *f*, adulation. **aduler** (le) *v.t*, to adulate.

adulte (adylt) *a. & n*, adult, grown-up.

adultère (adyltɛ:r) *n*, adulterer, ess; (*m.*) adultery. ¶ *a*, adulterous.

advenir (advəni;r) *v.i.ir*, to happen, occur, befall, come to pass. *advienne que pourra*, come what may, whate'er betide.

adverbe (advɛrb) *m*, adverb. ~ *de quantité*, a. of number. **adverbial, e†** (bjal) *a*, adverbial.

adversaire (advɛrsɛ:r) *m*, adversary, opponent, foe. **adverse** (vɛrs) *a*, adverse, opposing. **adversité** (site) *f*, adversity, misfortune.

aérage (aera:ʒ) *m*, **aération** (rasjɔ̃) *f*, ventilation, airing; draft; aeration. **aérer** (re) *v.t*, to ventilate, air; aerate.

aérien, ne (aerjɛ̃, ɛn) *a*, aerial, airy, air (*att.*); overhead.

aérodrome (aerɔdro:m) *m*, airport, aviation ground.

aérodynamique (aerɔdinamik) *a*, aerodynamic; streamlined. ¶ *f,*, aerodynamics. **aérodynamisme** (mism) *m*, streamlining.

aérogare (aeroga:r) *f*, air terminal.

aéroglisseur (aerɔglisœ:r) *m*, hovercraft.

aérolithe (aerɔlit) *m*, aerolite, meteorite.

aéronaute (aerɔno:t) *n*, aeronaut. **aéronautique** (notik) *a*, aeronautic(al), air (*att.*). ¶ *f*, aeronautics.

aéronef (aerɔnɛf) *m*, aircraft.

aéroplane (aerɔplan) *m*, [air]plane.

aéroport (aerɔpɔ:r) *m*, airport.

aérospatial (aerɔspajal) *a*, aerospatial.

aérostat (aerɔsta) *m*, lighter than air machine; balloon. **aérostation** (sjɔ̃) *f*, lighter than air aviation *or* branch (*army*); ballooning. **aérostier** (tje) *m*, balloonist.

affabilité (afabilite) *f*, affability. **affable** (bl) *a*, affable.

affacturage (afaktyraʒ) *m*, factoring (*Fin.*).

affadir (afadi;r) *v.t*, to sicken; make insipid, flatten. **affadissement** (dismɑ̃) *m*, loss of flavor; nauseousness.

affaiblir (afɛbli:r) *v.t*, to weaken, enfeeble; reduce (*Phot.*). **affaiblissement** (blismɑ̃) *m*, weakening, diminution, fading.

affaire (afɛ:r) *f*, affair, matter, case, thing, job, proposition, business, piece of business, concern; transaction, dealing, bargain; lawsuit; re (*law*); engagement (*Mil.*). ~*s par correspondance*, mail order business. ~ *roulante*, going concern. *ce malade est hors d'*~, this patient is out of danger. *son* ~ *est faite*, he's done for. **affairé, e** (fɛre) *a*, busy. ¶ *n*, busy man, woman.

affaissement (afɛsmɑ̃) *m*, subsidence, sinking; collapse. **affaisser (se)** *v.t*, to cause to subside; weigh down. **s'~**, to subside, sink, collapse.

affaler (afale) *v.t*, to haul down. **affale!** lower away! **s'affaler**, to sink, drop, down.

affamé, e (afame) *a*, famished, hungry, starving, craving. ¶ *n*, starveling. **affamer (me)** *v.t*, to famish, starve.

affecté, e (afɛkte) *a*, affected; prim. **affecter (te)** *v.t*, to assign, design, charge, apply, set aside; aspire to; assume; affect; move. **affectation** (tasj5) *f*, assignment (*Mil.*); affectation; appropriation. **affection** (afɛksj5) *f*, affection, liking; complaint (*Med.*). **affectionné, e** (ɔne) *a*, **affectueux, euse†** (tɥø, ø:z) *a*, affectionate, fond, loving. **affectionner** (ɔne) *v.t*, to be fond of, like.

afférent (aferɑ̃) *a*, relating, pertaining, to.

affermer (afɛrme) *v.t*, to lease, let out, farm [out], rent.

affermir (afɛrmi:r) *v.t*, to strengthen.

affété, e (afete) *a*, affected, mincing. **afféterie** (tri) *f*, affectation.

affiche (afiʃ) *f*, poster, bill, placard; sign. **~ lumineuse**, electric sign. **afficher** (ʃe) *v.t*, to post, bill, placard, stick (*bills*); proclaim, advertise, show up. **s'~**, to show off. **afficheur** (ʃœ:r) *m*, bill-poster, billsticker.

affilé, e (afile) *a*, sharp (*tongue*). **d'affilée**, *ad*, at a stretch. **affiler (le)** *v.t*, to sharpen (*tools*).

affilier (afilje) *v.t*, to affiliate.

affiloir (afilwa:r) *m*, steel; strop.

affinage (afina3) *m*, refining. **affiner (ne)** *v.t*, to refine. **affinerie** (nri) *f*, refinery. **affineur** (nœ:r) *m*, refiner.

affinité (afinite) *f*, affinity.

affiquets (afikɛ) *m.pl*, getup, finery.

affirmatif, ive† (afirmatif, i:v) *a. & f*, affirmative. **affirmation** (sj5) *f*, affirmation. **affirmer (me)** *v.t*, to affirm, assert, aver, vouch.

affixe (afiks) *m*, affix.

affleurement (aflœrmɑ̃) *m*, lev-eling; outcrop (*Geol.*). **affleurer (re)** *v.t*, to level, flush; (*v.i.*) to crop out.

affliction (afliksj5) *f*, affliction. **affliger** (3e) *v.t*, to afflict, distress, grieve; mortify; curse.

affluence (aflyɑ̃:s) *f*, affluence; crowd; flow, flood; concourse. **affluent** (ɑ̃) *m*, tributary, affluent, feeder. **affluer (e)** *v.i*, to flow; run; abound, flock.

affolement (afɔlmɑ̃) *m*, panic; distraction. **affoler** (afole) *v.t*, to infatuate; madden; distract.

affouiller (afuje) *v.t*, to undermine, wash away.

affourché, e (afurʃe) *a*, astride, astraddle.

affranchi, e (afrɑ̃ʃi) *n*, emancipated slave. **affranchir** (ʃi:r) *v.t*, to [set] free, liberate; relieve; prepay, stamp (*Post*). **affranchissement** (ʃismɑ̃) *m*, emancipation, enfranchisement; prepayment.

affres (afr) *f.pl*, pangs, throes.

affrètement (afrɛtmɑ̃) *m*, freighting, chartering. **affréter** (frete) *v.t*, to charter. **affréteur** (tœ:r) *m*, charterer.

affreux, euse† (afrø, ø:z) *a*, frightful, fearful, ghastly. ¶ *m*, dangerous person, mercenary (*soldier*).

affriander (afriɑ̃de) **& affrioler** (ɔle) *v.t*, to allure, tempt; make attractive.

affront (afr5) *m*, affront; slight, cut.

affronter (afr5te) *v.t*, to front, confront, face, brave.

affubler (afyble) *v.t*, to dress up.

affût (afy) *m*, hiding place; stand; [gun] carriage. *à l'~*, on the watch, on the lookout. **affûter** (afyte) *v.t*, to sharpen, grind.

afghan, e (afgɑ̃, an) *a. & A~*, *n*, Afghan.

afin de (afɛ̃) *pr*, in order to, so as to, to. **afin que**, *c*, in order that, so that, that.

africain, e (afrikɛ̃, ɛn) *a. & A~*, *n*, African. **l'Afrique** (frik) *f*, Africa.

agacer (agase) *v.t*, to set on edge, irritate, annoy; provoke, excite.

agacement (smã) *m*, setting on edge, etc. **agacerie** (sri) *f*, provocation.

agate (agat) *f*, agate.

âge (ɑːʒ) *m*, age. *l'~ de raison*, years of discretion. *l'~ ingrat*, the awkward age. *l'~ viril*, man's estate. *troisième ~*, the "golden years"; senior citizens. *d'un certain ~*, no longer young. *quel ~ a-t-il?* how old is he? *il n'est pas en ~*, he is not of (*or* is under) age. **âgé, e** (aʒe) *a*, aged, old. *~ de 20 ans*, 20 years old.

agence (aʒãːs) *f*, agency, bureau. *~ d'information*, news agency, press a. *~ de presse*, wire service, news agency. *~ de renseignements*, mercantile office, m. agency. *~ immobilière*, real estate agency.

agencé, e (aʒãse) *p.p*, dressed, got up. **agencement** (smã) *m*, arrangement; fittings & fixtures. **agencer (se)** *v.t*, to arrange, fit [up].

agenda (aʒɛ̃da) *m*, diary; agenda; memorandum book.

agenouiller [(s')] (aʒnuje) *v.pr*, to kneel [down]. **agenouilloir** (jwaːr) *m*, hassock.

agent (aʒã) *m*, agent; broker; officer; medium. *~ comptable*, accountant. *~ de change*, stockbroker (*nominated by the government*). *~ de la douane*, customs officer. *~ de liaison*, liaison officer. *~ [de police]*, policeman. *~ de police des côtes à terre*, coastguard. *~ de recouvrements*, debt collector, dun. *~ du service sanitaire*, health officer. *~ en douane*, customs agent. *~ maritime*, shipping agent. *~s s'abstenir*, no agents.

aggloméré (aglɔmere) *m*, briquet[te], compressed fuel; conglomerate. **agglomérer (re)** *v.t*, to agglomerate.

agglutiner (aglytine) *v.t*, to agglutinate.

aggraver (agrave) *v.t*, to aggravate; increase.

agile† (aʒil)*a*, agile, nimble, lithe, active. **agilité** (lite) *f*, agility, etc.

agio (aʒjo) *m*, exchange [premium]; agio; discount charges.

agiotage (ʒjɔtaːʒ) *m*, gambling, jobbery, rigging; exchange business. **agioter** (te) *v.i*, to speculate, gamble. **agioteur** (tœːr) *m*, speculator, gambler.

agir (aʒiːr) *v.i*, to act, operate, work, do; proceed (*law*). *s'~*, *v.imp*, to be the matter, be in question. **agissant, e** (ʒisã, ãːt) *a*, active. **agissements** (smã) *m. pl*, goings-on, doings (*underhand*).

agitateur (aʒitatœːr) *m*, agitator (*Pol*.); stirrer (*rod*). **agiter** (te) *v.t*, to agitate, perturb, shake, stir; wag; wave; debate, discuss, *nuit agitée* restless night. *mer agitée*, rough sea. **agitation** (tasjɔ̃) *f*, agitation; unrest

agneau (aɲo) *m*, lamb. *~femelle*, ewe lamb. **agneler** (nəle) *v.i*, to lamb, yean. **agnelet** (lɛ) *m*, lambkin.

agonie (agɔni) *f*, [death] agony, death struggle. *à l'~*, dying. **agonir** (niːr) *v.t*, to load (*with abuse*). **agonisant, e** (nizã, ãːt) *a*, dying. **agoniser** (ze) *v.i*, to be dying.

agrafe (agraf) *f*, hook, clasp, fastener, snap, staple, cramp. *~ & porte*, hook & eye. **agrafer** (fe) *v.t*, to hook, etc; do up (*dress*); grab, nab. **agrafeuse** (føːz) *f*, stapler.

agraire (agrɛːr) *a*, agrarian, land (*att*.).

agrandir (agrãdiːr) *v.t*, to enlarge. **agrandisseur** (disœːr) *m*, enlarger (*Phot*.).

agréable† (agreabl) *a*. & *m*, agreeable, pleasant, nice, congenial; acceptable, palatable.

agréé (agree) *m*, lawyer (at *tribunal de commerce*). **agréer** (gree) *v.t*, to accept, approve, agree; (*v.i*) to please, suit. *agréez, monsieur, mes salutations empressées*, yours faithfully.

agrégation (agregasjɔ̃) *f*, admission; aggregation. **agréger** (ʒe) *v.t*, to admit (*as member*).

agrément (agremã) *m*, consent, approval; agreeableness, pleasantness, amenity; pleasure, charm; trimming (*dress*). (*pl*.) amenities (*housing*). **agrémenter**

(te) *v.t*, to adorn, ornament, trim.

agrès (agrɛ) *m.pl*, tackle, gear, rigging.

agresseur (agrɛsœːr) *m*, aggressor. **agressif, ive** (sif, iːv) *a*, aggressive. **agression** (sjɔ̃) *f*, aggression.

agreste (agrɛst) *a*, rustic; uncouth.

agricole (agrikɔl) *a*, agricultural. **agriculteur** (kyltœːr) *m*, agricultur[al]ist, farmer. **agriculture** (tyːr) *f*, agriculture, farming, husbandry.

agriffer (s') (agrife) *v.pr*, to claw, cling, lay hold.

agripper (agripe) *v.t*, to lay hold of, clutch, grab, grip.

agronome (agrɔnɔm) *m*, agronomist. **agronomie** (mi) *f*, agronomy, husbandry.

aguerrir (agɛriːr) *v.t*, to harden to war; inure, season.

aguets (être aux) (agɛ), to be on the watch *or* lookout.

aguicher (agiʃe) *v.t*, to excite, tease (*intellectually, sexually*); give the eye to.

aheurtement (aœrtəmɑ̃) *m*, obsession. **s'aheurter** (te) *v.pr.*, to cling, be obsessed, be bent.

ahurir (ayriːr) *v.t*, to flurry, fluster, bewilder, daze.

aide (ɛːd) *f*, aid, help, assistance. *à l'~!* help! ¶ *n*, assistant, helper, mate. *~ de camp, m,* aide-de-camp. **aider** (ɛde) *v.t*, to aid, help, assist. **s'~ de**, to make use of.

aide-mémoire (ɛdmemwaːr) *m*, handbook, manual; aide-mémoire (*diplomatic*).

aïe (aːj) *i*, ow!, ouch!

aïeul, e (ajœl) *n*, grandfather, -mother. **aïeux** (ajø) *m.pl*, forefathers.

aigle (ɛgl) *m*, eagle (*male bird*); genius, mastermind; (*f.*) eagle (*hen bird & standard*). **aiglon, ne** (glɔ̃, ɔn) *n*, eaglet.

aigret† (ɛːgr) *a*, sour, tart; bitter; sharp; churlish; shrill. ¶ *m*, sourness, etc; chill (*in the air*). **~-doux, ce** (ɛgrədu, us) *a*, bittersweet, sub-acid. **aigrefin** (fɛ̃) *m*, sharper; haddock. **aigrelet, te** (lɛ, ɛt) *a*, sourish, tart. **aigret, te** (grɛ, ɛt) *a*, sourish, tartish.

aigrette (ɛgrɛt) *f*, aigrette, egret, plume. **aigretté, e** (te), *a*, tufted, crested.

aigreur (ɛgrœːr) *f*, sourness, acerbity. **aigrir** (griːr) *v.t*, to sour, embitter.

aigu, ë (egy) *a*, acute, sharp, pointed; shrill. ¶ *m*, upper register (*Mus.*).

aigue-marine (ɛgmarin) *f*, aquamarine.

aiguière (ɛgjɛːr) *f*, ewer.

aiguillade (egɥijad) *f*, goad.

aiguille (egɥiːj) *f*, needle; hand, pointer; switch (*Rly.*). *~ à coudre*, sewing needle. *~ à passer*, bodkin. *~ à repriser*, darning needle. *~ à tricoter*, knitting n., k. pin. *~ de glace*, icicle. **aiguillée** (gɥije) *f*, needleful. **aiguiller** (egɥije) *v.t*, to shunt; switch (*Rly.*).

aiguillon (egɥijɔ̃) *m*, goad; sting; prickle; spur, stimulus, incentive. **aiguillonner** (jɔne) *v.t*, to goad, spur on, stimulate.

aiguiser (egɥize) *v.t*, to sharpen, grind, whet; stimulate.

ail (aːj) *m*, garlic. *gousse d'~*, garlic clove. **ailloli** (ajɔli), *m*, garlic mayonnaise.

aile (ɛl) *f*, wing; aisle; flange; blade, vane; fender. **ailé, e** (le) *a*, winged. **aileron** (lrɔ̃) *m*, pinion; fin; paddle board; aileron.

ailleurs (ajœːr) *ad*, elsewhere, somewhere else. *par ~*, incidentally. *d'~, ad*, besides, moreover.

aimable† (ɛmabl) *a*, amiable, pleasant; kind; lovable. **aimant, e** (mɑ̃, ɑ̃ːt) *a*, loving, affectionate.

aimant (ɛmɑ̃) *m*, magnet. **aimanter** (te) *v.t*, to magnetize.

aimer (ɛme) *v.t. & abs*, to love; be fond of; like.

aine (ɛn) *f*, groin (*Anat.*).

aîné, e (ɛne) *a. & n*, elder; eldest; senior. **aînesse** (nɛs) *f*, seniority.

ainsi (ɛ̃si) *ad*, so, thus. *~soit-il*, so be it. *~ que, c*, [just] as; as also.

air (ɛːr) *m*, air; look, likeness; manner; way; mien; aria; tune, song. *en l'~*, in the air, airy (*schemes*); idle (*tales*); groundless (*fears*); empty (*threats*). *de plein ~*, outdoor (*as games*). *en plein ~*, in the open air, alfresco.

airain (ɛrɛ̃) (*Poet.*) *m*, bronze, brass.

aire (ɛːr) *f*, area, floor; eyrie; threshing floor. *~ de lancement*, launching pad. *~ de vent*, point of the compass.

airelle (ɛrɛl) *f*, blueberry, huckleberry.

aisance (ɛzɑ̃ːs) *f*, ease; freedom; affluence, sufficiency, competence. **aise** (ɛːz) *a*, glad, pleased. ¶ *f*, ease, comfort; joy, pleasure; (*pl.*) creature comforts. **aisé, e** (ɛze) *a*, easy; comfortable; well-off, affluent. **aisément** (mɑ̃) *ad*, easily; comfortably; readily.

aisselle (ɛsɛl) *f*, armpit.

ajonc (aʒɔ̃) *m*, furze, gorse, whin.

ajouré, e (aʒure) *a*, perforated, pierced; open-work (*att.*).

ajourner (aʒurne) *v.t*, to adjourn, postpone, put off; subpoena; defer (*draft*).

ajouté (aʒute) *m*, rider, addition. **ajouter** (te) *v.t*, to add; implement.

ajustage (aʒystaːʒ) *m*, fitting, setting up. **ajustement** (təmɑ̃) *m*, adjustment; arrangement; settlement. **ajuster** (te) *v.t*, to adjust, fit [up]; lay out; deck out, array; set straight; aim at (*with gun*). *s'~*, to tidy oneself up. **ajusteur** (tœːr) *m*, fitter, artificer.

ajutage (aʒytaːʒ) *m*, nozzle, jet.

alambic (alɑ̃bik) *m*, still. **alambiquer** (ke) *v.t*, to puzzle; spin out, wiredraw (*fig.*).

alanguir (alɑ̃giːr) *v.t*, to make languid.

alarmant, e (alarmɑ̃, ɑ̃ːt) *a*, alarming. **alarme** (larm) *f*, alarm. **alarmer** (me) *v.t*, to alarm; startle.

albâtre (albɑːtr) *m*, alabaster.

alcali (alkali) *m*, alkali. **alcalin, e** (lɛ̃, in) *a*, alkaline.

alchimie (alʃimi) *f*, alchemy. **alchimiste** (mist) *m*, alchemist.

alcool (alkɔl) *m*, alcohol, spirit[s]. *~ ammon aromatique*, sal volatile. *~ dénaturé*, *~ à brûler*, methylated spirit. **alcoolique** (kɔɔlik) *a. & n*, alcoholic.

alcootest (alkɔtɛst) *m*, breathalyzer test.

alcôve (alkoːv) *f*, alcove, recess. *~ de dortoir*, cubicle.

alcyonien (alsjɔnjɛ̃) *a.m*, halcyon.

aléa (alea) *m*, chance. **aléatoire** (twaːr) *a*, uncertain, contingent, aleatory.

alène (alɛːn) *f*, awl.

alentour (alɑ̃tuːr) *ad*, around, round about. *d'~*, surrounding. *~s*, *m.pl*, surroundings.

alerte (alɛrt) *a*, alert, wide-awake. ¶ *i*, up! look out! ¶ *f*, alarm, alert.

aléser (aleze) *v.t*, to ream, broach, bore [out]. **alésage** (zaːʒ) *m*, reaming, etc; bore. **alésoir** (zwaːr) *m*, reamer, broach.

alevin (alvɛ̃) *m*, fry, young fish.

Alexandrie (alɛksɑ̃dri) *f*, Alexandria. **alexandrin, e** (drɛ̃, in) *a*, Alexandrian; Alexandrine.

alfa (alfa) *m*, alfa [grass], esparto [grass].

algarade (algarad) *f*, storm of abuse, blowing up.

algèbre (alʒɛbr) *m*, algebra; Greek (*fig.*).

Alger (alʒe) *m*, Algiers. **l'Algérie** (ʒeri) *f*, Algeria. **algérien, ne** (rjɛ̃, ɛn) *a. & A~*, *n*, Algerian.

algue (alg) *f*, seaweed, alga.

alibi (alibi) *m*, alibi.

aliboron (alibɔrɔ̃) *m*: *un maître ~*, an ass, a blockhead.

aliéné, e (aljene) *n*, mental patient, lunatic. **aliénation d'esprit**, *~ mentale* (nasjɔ̃), insanity, lunacy, madness. **aliéner** (ne) *v.t*, to alienate, estrange; derange, unhinge (*mind*); transfer (*property*).

aligner (aliɲe) *v.t*, to align, range; finish off (*phrases*). **alignement** (ɲmɑ̃) *m*, alignment, etc; building line.

aliment (alimɑ̃) *m*, food; nutriment; fuel (*fig.*); (*pl.*) sustenance; (*pl.*) cud. **alimentaire** (tɛːr) *a*, alimentary, feeding, feed, food (*att.*). **alimentation** (tasjɔ̃) *f*, feeding; feed. **alimenter** (te) *v.t*, to feed, supply.

alinéa (alinea) *m*, [fresh] paragraph, new par[agraph]; subsection.

alité, e (alite) *a*, laid up, bedridden. **aliter** (te) *v.t*, to keep in bed.

alizé (alize) *a*, trade (*wind*).

allaiter (alɛte) *v.t*, to suckle, nurse.

allant, e (alɑ̃, ɑ̃:t) *a*, active. ¶ *m*, activity; go; initiative. ~*s* & *venants*, passersby, comers & goers.

allécher (aleʃe) *v.t*, to allure, entice.

allée (ale) *f*, walk, lane, path; drive; passage. ~ *en berceau*, covered walk. ~*s* & *venues*, coming & going, running about.

allégation (alegasjɔ̃) *f*, allegation.

allège (alɛ:ʒ) *f*, lighter, barge, craft. **alléger** (leʒe) *v.t*, to lighten; thin; alleviate. **allégement** (lɛʒmɑ̃) *m*, lightening, etc.

allégorie (allegɔri) *f*, allegory. **allégorique†** (rik) *a*, allegoric(al).

allègre (allɛ:gr) *a*, lively, cheerful, brisk. **allégresse** (allegrɛs), *f*, joy[fulness], cheerfulness.

alléguer (alege) *v.t*, to allege, adduce; plead, urge; quote, cite.

Alléluia (alleluija), hallelujah.

Allemagne (l') (almaɲ) *f*, Germany. **allemand, e** (mɑ̃, ɑ̃:d) *a*. & A~, *n*, German. **l'allemand**, *m*, German (*language*).

aller (ale) *m*, going, outward journey. *l'*~ & *retour*, roundtrip ticket. *l'*~ & *le venir*, the come-&-go. ~ *à la dérive*, to drift. ¶ *v.i.ir*, to go; run; be (*well, ill, etc.*); get; do; fare; fit, suit. ~ *à bicyclette*, to cycle. ~ *à cheval*, to ride. ~ *en auto*, ~ *en voiture*, to drive. **s'en** ~, to go [away], be off.

alliage (aljaːʒ) *m*, alloy. **alliance** (jɑ̃:s) *f*, alliance, union; match; intermarriage; wedding ring. *cousin, par* ~, cousin by marriage. **allié, e** (je) *n*, ally; relation [by marriage]. **allier** (je) *v.t*, to ally, unite; match; alloy. **s'**~, to unite; marry; intermarry.

alligator (aligatɔːr) *m*, alligator.

allô (alo) (*Teleph.*) *i*, hello!

allocation (allɔkasjɔ̃) *f*, allocation, allowance.

allocution (allɔkysjɔ̃) *f*, speech, address.

allonge (alɔ̃:ʒ) *f*, lengthening

piece; rider (*to bill of exchange*).. **allonger** (lɔ̃ʒe) *v.t*, to lengthen, elongate; eke out; stretch [out]; deal (*blow*).

allotissement (alɔtismɑ̃) *m*, apportionment, allotment; grouping into lots.

allouer (alwe) *v.t*, to allocate, allow, grant.

allumage (alymaːʒ) *m*, lighting, ignition. *couper l'*~, to switch off the ignition. **allumer** (me) *v.t*, to light, ignite; kindle; fire, stir up. ~ *la lumière*, ~ *l'électricité*, to switch (*or* turn) on the light. **allumette** (mɛt) *f*, match. ~ *bougie*, wax vesta. ~*s de sûreté*, safety matches. ~*s en carnet*, book matches. **allumeur** (mœːr) *m*, lighter. **allumeuse** (møːz) *f*, flirt.

allure (alyːr) *f*, walk, gait, pace; demeanor, carriage; trim; way. *à toute* ~, at top speed. *d'*~ *louche*, suspicious-looking.

allusion (allyzjɔ̃) *f*, allusion; hint, innuendo.

almanach (almana; *in liaison*, -nak) *m*, almanac.

aloès (alɔɛs) *m*, aloe. [*suc d'*] ~, aloes.

aloi (alwa) *m*, standard, quality; legal tender. *de bon* ~, genuine.

alors (alɔːr) *ad*, then. ~ *que*, *a*, when.

alouette (alwɛt) *f*, lark. ~ *des champs*, skylark.

alourdir (alurdiːr) *v.t*, to make heavy.

aloyau (alwajo) *m*, sirloin (*beef*).

alpaga (alpaga) *m*, alpaca.

Alpes (les) (alp) *f.pl*, the Alps. **alpestre** (pɛstr) *a*, Alpine.

alpha (alfa) *m*, alpha. **alphabet** (bɛ) *m*, alphabet; A B C, primer. **alphabétique†** (betik) *a*, alphabetical.

alphabétisation (alfabetizasjɔ̃) *f*, instruction of nation or group (*not individual*) in literacy.

alpin, e (alpɛ̃, in) *a*, Alpine. **l'alpinisme** (pinism) *m*, mountaineering. **alpiniste** (nist) *n*, Alpinist, mountaineer.

Alsace (l') (alzas) *f*, Alsace. **alsacien, ne** (sjɛ, ɛn) *a*. & A~, *n*, Alsatian.

altérant, e (alterɑ̃, ɑ̃:t) *a*, thirst-creating.

altération (alterasjɔ̃) *f*, alteration, change; adulteration; faltering voice; heavy thirst.

altercation (altɛrkasjɔ̃) *f*, altercation.

altérer (altere) *v.t*, to change; debase, adulterate; garble; weather (*Geol.*); make thirsty. *altéré de sang*, bloodthirsty.

alternatif, ive† (altɛrnatif, iːv) *a*, alternative; alternate; alternating. ¶ *f*, alternative; option. **alterner** (ne) *v.i. & t*, to alternate.

altesse (altɛs) *f*, highness (*title*).

altier, ère (altje, ɛːr) *a*, haughty, lofty, lordly.

altitude (altityd) *f*, altitude, height, elevation.

alto (alto) *m*, alto; tenor violin, viola; alto saxhorn.

altruiste (altryist) *n*, altruist. ¶ *a*, altruistic.

aluminium (alyminjɔm) *m*, aluminum.

alun (alœ̃) *m*, alum.

alunir (alyniːr) *v.i*, to land on the moon.

alvéole (alveɔl) *m*, cell; socket (*tooth*).

amabilité (amabilite) *f*, amiability, kindness.

amadou (amadu) *m*, tinder, touchwood. **amadouer** (dwe) *v.t*, to coax, wheedle, cajole.

amaigrir (amɛgriːr) *v.t*, to [make] thin, emaciate.

amalgame (amalgam) *m*, amalgam; mixture. **amalgamer** (me) *v.t*, to amalgamate.

amande (amɑ̃ːd) *f*, almond. **amandier** (mɑ̃dje) *m*, almond [tree].

amant (amɑ̃) *m*, paramour; lover.

amariner (amarine) *v.t*, to make a sailor of; man (*prize ship*).

amarrage (amaraːʒ) *m*, mooring; docking (*spacecraft*).

amarre (amaːr) *f*, [mooring] rope, fast, line; hawser. **amarrer** (mare) *v.t*, to make fast, moor; lash, seize; berth; belay.

amas (amɑ) *m*, heap, pile, mass; collection; drift (*snow*); hoard. **amasser** (se) *v.t*, to amass, heap [up], pile up, lay up, hoard.

amateur (amatœːr) *m*, lover (*devotee*); amateur; fancier. *il est*

[*grand*] ~ *de . . .*, he is [very] fond of . . . (*e.g, art, collecting, gardening*); . . . is his hobby.

amazone (amazoːn) *f*, Amazon; horsewoman. [*habit d'*]~, riding habit. l'A~, *m*, **le fleuve des** A~s, the Amazon (*river*).

ambages (ɑ̃baːʒ) *f.pl*, circumlocution. *sans* ~, candidly.

ambassade (ɑ̃basad) *f*, embassy; errand. **ambassadeur, drice** (dœːr, dris) *n*, ambassador, dress; messenger. *l'*~ *de France*, the French ambassador.

ambiance (ɑ̃bjɑ̃ːs) *f*, environment. **ambiant, e** (ɑ̃, ɑ̃ːt) *a*, surrounding, ambient.

ambigu†, **ë** (ɑ̃bigy) *a*, ambiguous. ¶ *m*, mixture. **ambiguité** (gɥite) *f*, ambiguity.

ambitieux, euse† (ɑ̃bisjø, øːz) *a*, ambitious. **ambition** (sjɔ̃) *f*, ambition. **ambitionner** (ɔne) *v.t*, to be eager for, aspire to.

ambre (ɑ̃ːbr) *m*, amber. ~ *gris*, ambergris.

ambroisie (ɑ̃brwazi) *f*, ambrosia.

ambulance (ɑ̃bylɑ̃ːs) *f*, ambulance. **ambulant, e** (lɑ̃, ɑ̃ːt) *a*, itinerant, strolling; traveling.

âme (ɑːm) *f*, soul, mind, spirit, ghost, life, heart; mainstay; soundpost; core; web; bore (*gun*); motto. *dans l'*~, at heart. ~ *damnée*, [mere] tool (*pers.*).

améliorer (ameljɔre) *v.t, & s'*~, to ameliorate, better, improve, mend; appreciate.

aménager (amenaʒe) *v.t*, to lay out, fit; harness (*waterfall*); reclaim (*submerged land*). **aménagement** (ʒmɑ̃) *m*, layout; accommodation, appointments. **aménageur** (aʒœr) *m*, urban planner.

amende (amɑ̃ːd) *f*, fine. ~ *honorable*, apology.

amender (amɑ̃de) *v.t*, to amend; improve.

amène (amɛːn) *a*, pleasing, agreeable.

amener (amne) *v.t*, to bring, lead; lead up to; haul down; strike (*colors*). *amené de loin*, farfetched. *s'*~, to arrive, turn up.

aménité (amenite) *f*, amenity, graciousness.

amenuiser (amənɥize) v.t, to thin.

amer, ère† (amɛːr) a, bitter; briny. ¶ m, bitter, bitterness; (pl.) bitters; gall; sea mark, landmark (Naut.).

américain, e (amerikɛ̃, ɛn) a. & A~, n, American. avoir l'œil ~, to keep a sharp lookout. idiotisme ~, Americanism. l'Amérique (rik) f, America.

Amerlo, Amerloque (amerlo, lɔk) m, an American (slang).

amerrir (ameriːr) v.i, to alight [on the water] (seaplane).

amertume (amɛrtym) f, bitterness.

ameublement (amœbləmɑ̃) m, [suite of] furniture.

ameuter (amøte) v.t, to train in a pack (dogs); stir up (mob). s'~, to assemble.

ami, e (ami) a, friendly; kindly. ¶ n, friend; lover. ~ de cœur, bosom friend. amis & parents, kith & kin; petite ~e, mistress.

amiable† (mjabl) a, **amical, e†** (mikal) a, amicable, friendly, kind. amiable compositeur, arbitrator (law). à l'amiable, amicably; by private treaty (sale).

amidon (amidɔ̃) m, starch. **amidonner** (dɔne) v.t, to starch.

amincir (amɛ̃siːr) v.t, to thin.

amiral (amiral) m, admiral; flagship. ~ commandant d'escadre, admiral of the fleet.

amirauté (rote) f, admiralty; admiralship.

amitié (amitje) f, friendship, kindness, love, liking; (pl.) kind regards.

ammoniaque (amɔnjak) f, ammonia.

amnistie (amnisti) f, amnesty, oblivion.

amodiation (amɔdjasjɔ̃) f, leasing (land, fishing, mining rights). amodier, (ɔdje) v.t, to farm out, lease, sublease.

amoindrir (amwɛ̃driːr) v.t, to lessen, decrease.

amollir (amɔliːr) v.t, to soften, mollify; enervate.

amonceler (amɔ̃sle) v.t, to heap [up], pile up, drift.

amont (amɔ̃) m, headwaters; up-

per part. en ~, ad, upstream, up. en ~ de, pr, above, up.

amorçage (amɔrsaːʒ) m, priming; starting (Elec.); baiting (fish).

amorce (amɔrs) f, bait; allurement; [percussion] cap; priming; beginning, start; leader (tape, etc.). amorcer (se) v.t, to bait, etc.; energize (Elec.). ~ un arc, to strike an arc.

amorphe (amɔrf) a, amorphous.

amortir (amɔrtiːr) v.t, to deaden, damp; redeem, amortize, sink, pay off; write off, depreciate. amortisseur (tisœːr) m, shock absorber (motor); damper (Radio).

amour (amuːr) m, love; passion; idol; (pl.) love affairs, amours. ~ intéressé, cupboard love. ~ vache, brutal lovemaking. mal d'~, lovesickness. pour l'~ de, for the sake (or love) of. amouracher (muraʃe) v.t, to enamor. amoureux, euse† (rø, øːz) a, in love, enamored; loving, amorous; tender, soft. ¶ n, lover, sweetheart. amour-propre (amurprɔpr) m, self-respect; pride; self-esteem.

amovible (amɔvibl) a, removable, detachable.

ampère (ɑ̃pɛːr) m, ampere.

amphibie (ɑ̃fibi) a, amphibious. ¶ m, amphibian.

amphithéâtre (ɑ̃fiteaːtr) m, amphitheater.

ample† (ɑ̃ːpl) a, ample, full; wide. **ampleur** (ɑ̃plœːr) f, ampleness, etc. **ampliation** (pliasjɔ̃) f, duplicate, office copy. pour ~, [certified] a true copy. **amplificateur** (fikatœːr) m, enlarger (Phot.); amplifier (Radio). **amplifier** (fje) v.t, to amplify. **amplitude** (tyd) f, amplitude.

ampoule (ɑ̃pul) f, phial; blister; bulb (elec. lamp, thermometer). **ampoulé, e** (le) a, inflated, bombastic, high-flown.

amputer (ɑ̃pyte) v.t, to amputate, cut off.

amulette (amylɛt) f, amulet, charm.

amure (amyːr) f, tack (sail).

amuse-gueule (amyːzgœl) m, tidbit, cocktail snack.

amuser (amyze) v.t, to amuse, entertain; beguile, fool, trifle with. **s'~**, to amuse (*or* enjoy) oneself; dally, loiter. **amusement** (zmɑ̃) *m*, amusement, etc. **amusette** (zɛt) *f*, plaything.

amygdale (amigdal) *f*, tonsil. **amygdalite** (lit) *f*, tonsillitis.

an (ɑ̃) *m*, year. *il a 10 ~s*, he is 10 years old. *le jour de l'~*, New Year's day.

anachorète (anakɔrɛt) *m*, anchoret, anchorite.

anachronisme (anakrɔnism) *m*, anachronism.

analogie (analɔʒi) *f*, analogy. **analogue** (lɔg) *a*, analogous, like.

analyse (anali:z) *f*, analysis. *~ grammaticale*, parsing. **analyser** (lize) *v.t*, to analyze; parse. **analyseur** (lizœ:r) *m*, analyzer; scanner (*TV*). **analyste** (list) *m*, analyst. **analytique†** (tik) *a*, analytic(al).

ananas (ananɑ) *m*, pineapple.

anarchie (anarʃi) *f*, anarchy. **anarchique†** (ʃik) *a*, anarchic(al). **anarchiste** (ʃist) *n. & a*, anarchist.

Anastasie (anastazi) *f*, censorship (*slang*).

anatomie (anatɔmi) *f*, anatomy. **anatomique†** (mik) *a*, anatomical.

ancestral, e (ɑ̃sɛstral) *a*, ancestral. **ancêtre** (sɛ:tr) *m*, ancestor.

anche (ɑ̃:ʃ) *f*, reed (*Mus.*).

anchois (ɑ̃ʃwa) *m*, anchovy.

ancien, ne (ɑ̃sjɛ̃, ɛn) *a*, ancient, old; of long standing; former; bygone; quondam; late, ex-; senior. *ancien combattant*, ex-service man. ¶ *m*, ancient; elder (*Eccl.*). **anciennement** (ɛnmɑ̃) *ad*, anciently, of old, formerly. **ancienneté** (nte) *f*, ancientness, antiquity; seniority. *de toute ~*, from time immemorial.

ancolie (ɑ̃kɔli) *f*, columbine (*Bot.*)

ancrage (ɑ̃kra:ʒ) *m*, anchorage; anchoring. **ancre** (ɑ̃:kr) *f*, anchor. *~ à jet, kedge* [a.]. *~ de veille* (*Naut.*) *& ~ de salut* (*fig.*), sheet anchor. **ancrer** (ɑ̃kre) (*Build.*) *v.t*, to anchor, fix.

andain (ɑ̃dɛ̃) *m*, swath, wind row.

andouille (ɑ̃du:j) *f*, chitterlings (*sausage*); fool, boob. *~ de calcif*, penis (*obscene*).

andouiller (ɑ̃duje) *m*, tine, antler.

âne (ɑ:n) *m*, ass, jackass, donkey; dunce, dolt.

anéantir (aneɑ̃ti:r) *v.t*, to annihilate, crush; prostrate. **s'~**, to humble oneself.

anecdote (anɛgdɔt) *f*, anecdote.

anémie (anemi) *f*, anemia. **anémique** (mik) *a*, anemic.

ânerie (ɑnri) *f*, gross stupidity.

anéroïde (anerɔid) *a*, aneroid.

ânesse (ɑnɛs) *f*, [she] ass, jenny.

anesthésie (anɛstezi) *f*, anesthesia. *~ à la reine*, twilight sleep. **anesthésique** (zik) *a. & m*, anesthetic.

anfractueux, euse (ɑ̃fraktɥø, ø:z) *a*, winding; craggy.

ange (ɑ̃:ʒ) *m*, angel. *~ déchu*, fallen a. *être aux ~s*, to be in raptures. **angélique†** (ɑ̃ʒelik) *a*, angelic(al). ¶ *f*, angelica. **Angélus** (ly:s) *m*, angelus [bell].

angine (ɑ̃ʒin) *f*, angina, quinsy. *~ de poitrine*, angina pectoris.

anglais, e (ɑ̃glɛ, ɛ:z) *a*, English; British; imperial. **A~**, *n*, Englishman, -woman, Briton. *l'anglais*, *m*, English (*language*). *avoir ses ~, les ~ sont débarqués*, to be menstruating (*slang*).

angle (ɑ̃:gl) *m*, angle, corner.

Angleterre (l') (ɑ̃glətɛ:r) *f*, England. **anglicisme** (glisism) *m*, Anglicism. **anglomanie** (glɔmani) *f*, Anglomania. **les îles Anglo-Normandes**, the Channel Islands. **anglophile** (fil) *a. & n*, Anglophile, pro-British. **anglophobe** (fɔb) *a. & n*, Anglophobe, anti-British. **anglo-saxon, ne** (saksɔ̃, ɔn) *a. & A~-S~*, *n*, Anglo-Saxon.

angoisse (ɑ̃gwas) *f*, anguish, pang. **angoisser** (se) *v.t*, to distress, pain. *poire d'~*, choke pear.

angora (ɑ̃gɔra) *m*, Persian [cat].

anguillade (ɑ̃gijad) *f*, lash, cut. **anguille** (ɑ̃gi:j) *f*, eel. *~ de caleçon*, penis (*obscene*). *~ de mer*, conger [eel]. *quelque ~ sous roche* (*fig.*), something in the wind.

angulaire (ɑ̃gylɛ:r) *a*, angular, corner (*att.*). *pierre ~*, cornerstone.

anicroche (anikrɔʃ) *f*, hitch, snag.

ânier, ère (ɑnje, ɛːr) *n*, donkey driver.

animal, e (animal) *a*, animal. ¶ *m*, animal, dumb animal, beast, brute; creature.

animateur, trice (animatœːr, tris) *n*, animator, moving spirit; disk jockey (*Radio*); host, emcee (*TV, Radio*); cartoonist (*cinema*).

animation (sjɔ̃) *f*, animation, liveliness, bustle, life. **animé, e** (me) *a*, animate; animated, lively, buoyant, spirited, brisk, bustling, agog, astir; instinct. **animer** (me) *v.t*, to animate, quicken, brighten, enliven, inspirit; actuate, impel.

animosité (animozite) *f*, animosity, animus, spite.

anis (ani) *m*, anise. [*graine d'*]~, aniseed.

ankylose (ɑ̃kiloːz) *f*, anchylosis; cramp. **ankyloser** (lose) *v.t*, to stiffen.

annales (anal) *f.pl*, annals.

anneau (ano) *m*, ring; coil (*snake*); ringlet; link.

année (ane) *f*, year, twelvemonth. ~ *à millésime*, vintage year.

annexe (anɛks) *f*, annex; dependency (*country*); schedule; enclosure; tender (*boat*). *lettre* ~, covering letter. **annexer** (kse) *v.t*, to annex, attach. **annexion** (ksjɔ̃) *f*, annexation.

annihiler (aniile) *v.t*, to annihilate; annul.

anniversaire (anivɛrsɛːr) *a & m*, anniversary. *l'*~ *de ma naissance*, my birthday.

annonce (anɔ̃ːs) *f*, announcement, advertisement; bans. ~-*article*, *f*, puff paragraph. ~ *de fantaisie*, ~ *courante*, display advertisement. *petite annonce*, classified ad. **annoncer** (nɔ̃se) *v.t*, to announce, advertise, proclaim, herald; give out; betoken, foreshadow; inform; state; show in, usher in; preach; foretell. *ça s'annonce bien*, that's promising. **annonceur** (sœːr) *m*, advertiser; announcer. **l'Annonciation** (sjasjɔ̃) *f*, the Annunciation, Lady Day.

annoter (anɔte) *v.t*, to annotate.

annuaire (anɥɛːr) *m*, annual, year book, directory (*telephone*); list (*Army, Navy, etc.*). **annuel,**

le† (nɥɛl) *a*, annual, yearly. **annuité** (nɥite) *f*, annuity.

annulaire (anylɛːr) *a*, annular. [*doigt*] ~, *m*, ring finger, third f.

annulation (anylasjɔ̃) *f*, annulment; cancellation.

annuler (anyle) *v.t*, to annul, nullify, quash, cancel; contra.

anoblir (anɔbliːr) *v.t*, to ennoble.

anode (anɔd) *f*, anode.

anodin, e (anɔdɛ̃, in) *a*, anodyne, soothing; harmless, mild, tame. ¶ *m*, anodyne.

anomal, e (anɔmal) *a*, anomalous. **anomalie** (li) *f*, anomaly.

ânon (ɑnɔ̃) *m*, young ass, foal. **ânonner** (nɔne) *v.i*, to falter, hem & haw.

anonyme (anɔnim) *a*, anonymous; unnamed.

anormal, e (anɔrmal) *a*, abnormal.

anse (ɑ̃ːs) *f*, handle; bow; cove. *faire le pot à deux* ~*s*, to set one's arms akimbo.

anspect (ɑ̃spɛk) *m*, handspike.

antagonisme (ɑ̃tagɔnism) *m*, antagonism. **antagoniste** (nist) *m*, antagonist, opponent.

antan (ɑ̃tɑ̃) *m*, yesteryear.

antarctique (ɑ̃tar[k]tik) *a*, antarctic.

antécédent, e (ɑ̃tesedɑ̃, ɑ̃ːt) *a. & m*, antecedent.

antédiluvien, ne (ɑ̃tedilyvjɛ̃, ɛn) *a*, antediluvian.

antenne (ɑ̃tɛn) *f*, antenna, feeler, horn; aerial (*Radio*); branch line (*Rly.*). ~ *d'appartement*, indoor aerial. *droit à l'*~, right to broadcast time.

antérieur, e† (ɑ̃terjœːr) *a*, anterior, prior, previous. **antériorité** (rjɔrite) *f*, priority.

anthère (ɑ̃tɛːr) *f*, anther.

anthologie (ɑ̃tɔlɔʒi) *f*, anthology.

anthracite (ɑ̃trasit) *m*, anthracite.

anthrax (ɑ̃traks) *m*, carbuncle. (*Med.*)

anthropophage (ɑ̃trɔpofaːʒ) *a*. & *m*, cannibal.

anti-aérien, ne (ɑ̃tiaerjɛ̃, ɛn) *a*, antiaircraft.

antialcoolique (ɑ̃tialkɔɔlik) *a*, teetotal.

anti-aveuglant (ɑ̃tiavœglɑ̃) *a*, antiglare, antidazzle.

antichambre (ãtiʃãːbr) *f*, ante-chamber, anteroom. *faire~chez*, to dance attendance on.

antichar (ãtiʃaːr) *m*, antitank weapon.

anticipation (ãtisipasjɔ̃) *f*, anticipation, advance. **anticiper** (pe) *v.t*, to anticipate, forestall. *~ sur*, to encroach on.

antidater (ãtidate) *v.t*, to ante-date.

antidérapant, e (ãtiderapã, ãːt) *a*, nonskid.

antidote (ãtidɔt) *m*, antidote.

antienne (ãtjɛn) *f*, anthem.

antigel (ãtiʒel) *m*, antifreeze.

Antilles (les) (ãtiːj) *f.pl*, the West Indies, the Antilles. *la mer des ~*, the Caribbean sea.

antilope (ãtilɔp) *f*, antelope.

antimoine (ãtimwan) *m*, anti-mony.

antipathie (ãtipati) *f*, antipathy, dislike. **antipathique** (tik) *a*, anti-pathetic.

antipatriotique (ãtipatriɔtik) *a*, unpatriotic.

antipodes (ãtipɔd) *m.pl*, anti-podes.

antiquailles (ãtikɑːj) *f.pl*, worthless antiques. **antiquaire** (kɛːr) *n*, antiquary, -rian. **antique** (tik) *a*, ancient, antique. ¶ *m*, antique (*style*); (*f.*) antique (*relic*). *magasin d'~s*, antique shop. **antiquité** (kite) *f*, antiquity.

antiseptique (ãtiseptik) *a. & m*, antiseptic; preservative (*for perishable foodstuffs*).

antithèse (ãtiteːz) *f*, antithesis.

antivol (ãtivɔl) *m*, ignition lock; theft-proof device (*bicycle, etc.*).

antre (ãːtr) *m*, cave, den, lair.

anus (anyːs) *m*, anus.

Anvers (ãvɛːr, -vɛrs) *m*, Antwerp. **anversois, e** (vɛrswa, aːz) *a*, of Antwerp.

anxiété (ãksjete) *f*, anxiety. **anxieux, euse** (ksjø, øːz) *a*, anxious.

aorte (aɔrt) *f*, aorta.

août (u) *m*, August. **aoûtien, ne** (jẽ, jɛn) *n*, person who vacations in August.

apache (apaʃ) *m*, Apache, desper-ado; hooligan, rough.

apaiser (apɛze) *v.t*, to appease, allay, assuage, quiet, quell, quench. *s'~*, to abate.

aparté (aparte) *m*, aside, stage whisper.

apathie (apati) *f*, apathy, **apa-thique** (tik) *a*, apathetic, lacka-daisical.

apatride (apatrid) *m*, stateless person.

apercevoir (apɛrsəvwaːr) *v.t*, to perceive, see, espy. **s'~**, to per-ceive, find. **apercu** (sy) *m*, out-line, summary; rough estimate; insight.

apéritif (aperitif) *m*, appetizer.

à-peu-près (apøprɛ) *m*, approxi-mation, rough estimate.

aphone (afɔn) *a*, voiceless, aphonic.

aphorisme (afɔrism) *m*, aphor-ism.

apiculture (apikyltyːr) *f*, bee-keeping.

apitoyer (apitwaje) *v.t*, to move to pity.

aplanir (aplaniːr) *v.t*, to level; smooth.

aplatir (aplatiːr) *v.t*, to flat[ten]; squash; smooth; plane. **aplatisse-ment** (tismã) *m*, flatt[en]ing; flat-ness.

aplomb (aplɔ̃) *m*, perpendicular-ity, plumb; self-possession. **d'~**, plumb, upright.

Apocalypse (apɔkalips) *f*, Rev-elation, Apocalypse.

apogée (apɔʒe) *m*, apogee; height; zenith, acme, high-water mark (*fig.*).

apologétique (apɔlɔʒetik) *a*, apologetic. **apologie** (ʒi) *f*, apolo-gia, justification.

apoplectique (apɔplɛktik) *a. & m*, apoplectic. **apoplexie** (ksi) *f*, apoplexy.

apostasie (apɔstazi) *f*, apostasy, defection. **apostat** (ta) *m. & att*, apostate.

aposter (apɔste) *v.t*, to station, post, set.

apostille (apɔstiːj) *f*, marginal note, side note; recommendation. **apostiller** (tije) *v.t*, to make a note on.

apostolat (apɔstɔla) *m*, aposto-late, apostleship. **apostolique†** (lik) *a*, apostolic(al).

apostrophe (apɔstrɔf) *f*, apos-trophe; reproach. **apostropher**

(fe) *v.t*, to apostrophize; up-braid.

apothéose (apoteo:z) *f*, apotheosis.

apôtre (apo:tr) *m*, apostle. *bon ~*, hypocrite.

apparaître (aparɛ:tr) *v.i.ir*, to appear.

apparat (apara) *m*, state, show, pomp.

appareil (aparɛ:j) *m*, array; apparatus, appliance, plant, gear, tackle, rig; telephone; attachment (*to machine*); dressing (*on wound*); camera. *~ dentaire*, dental brace. *~ réflex*, reflex camera. *~ à sous*, coin-operated or slot machine. **appareillage** (ja:ʒ) *m*, installation; equipment; preparation; accessories; matching (colors, etc.); getting under weigh (*Naut.*). **appareiller** (rɛje) *v.t. & i*, to match, pair, mate; fit; get under weigh. **appareilleur** (jœ:r) *m*, fitter.

apparemment (aparamɑ̃) *ad*, apparently. **apparence** (rɑ̃:s) *f*, appearance, look; guise; likelihood. **apparent, e** (rɑ̃, ɑ̃:t) *a*, apparent, seeming.

apparenté, e (apparɑ̃te) *a*, related, akin, connected. **apparenter** (te) *v.t*, to connect, ally. *s'~*, to marry (*à = into*); blend.

apparier (aparje) *v.t*, to match, pair.

appariteur (aparitœ:r) *m*, usher; beadle.

apparition (aparisjɔ̃) *f*, appearance, advent; apparition.

appartement (apartəmɑ̃) *m*, [suite of] rooms, apartment.

appartenir (apartəni:r) *v.i.ir*, to belong, [ap]pertain, concern. *s'~*, to be one's own master *or* mistress.

appas (apɑ) *m.pl*, attractions, charms. **appât** (pɑ) *m*, bait, allurement, lure, draw. **appâter** (te) *v.t*, to bait; allure; cram (*poultry*).

appauvrir (apovri:r) *v.t*, to impoverish, beggar; thin (*wine*).

appeau (apo) *m*, bird call.

appel (apɛl) *m*, call, calling [up]; appeal; invitation; muster; challenge. *~ telephonique*, phone call. *~ de fonds*, call. *~[nominal]*, roll call, muster, call over. *en ~ à*, to appeal to. **appelant** (plɑ̃) *m*, decoy bird. **appeler** (ple) *v.t. & i*, to call; term; appeal; invite; challenge. *s'~*, to be called. *je m'appelle Adam*, my name is Adam.

appendice (apēdis) *m*, appendage, appendix. **appendicite** (sit) *f*, appendicitis.

appendre (apɑ̃:dr) *v.t*, to hang up.

appentis (apɑ̃ti) *m*, lean-to, penthouse; outhouse.

appesantir (apəzɑ̃ti:r) *v.t*, to make heavy, dull, weigh down.

appéter (appete) *v.t*, to crave for, long for.

appétissant, e (apetisɑ̃, ɑ̃:t) *a*, appetizing, tempting. **appétit** (ti) *m*, appetite; desire; lust.

applaudir (aplodi:r) *v.t. & i*, to applaud, cheer. *~ à*, to commend. *s'~ de*, to congratulate oneself on. **applaudissement** (dismɑ̃) *m. oft. pl*, applause, cheer, plaudit.

application (aplikasjɔ̃) *f*, application; infliction; diligence. *[dentelle d']~*, appliqué lace. **applique** (plik) *f*, appliqué [work] (*metal*); sconce, bracket. **appliqué, e** (ke) *p.a*, applied; close, studious. **appliquer** (ke) *v.t*, to apply, put, lay on; give charge; inflict. *s'~ à*, to apply oneself to.

appoint (apwē) *m*, addition; small coin, [small] change, odd money; help. **appointements** (tmɑ̃) *m.pl*, salary. **appointer** (te) *v.t*, to put on a salary basis (*in p.p*, salaried); point; sew up, stitch together.

appontement (apɔ̃tmɑ̃) *m*, wharf.

apport (apɔ:r) *m*, bringing; transfer, assignment; capital brought in; assets transferred *or* taken over; contribution; collection (*of goods by Rly. Co.*); drift (*Geol.*). *valeurs d'~*, vendor's assets. **apporter** (pɔrte) *v.t*, to bring, fetch; transfer, assign; give; waft. **apporte!** fetch it! (*to dog*). **apporteur** (tœ:r) *m*, vendor.

apposer (apoze) *v.t*, to affix, put,

append, set. **apposition** (zisjɔ̃) f, affixture, etc; apposition. **en ~** (*Gram.*), in apposition; attributively.

appréciable (apresjabl) a, appreciable; measurable. **appréciation** (sjɔ̃) f, valuation, estimate; appreciation. **apprécier** (sje) v.t, to value; estimate; esteem.

appréhender (apreɑ̃de) v.t, to apprehend; arrest. **appréhension** (sjɔ̃) f, apprehension; arrest.

apprendre (aprɑ̃:dr) v.t. & abs. ir, to learn, hear, understand; teach; inform, tell. *mal appris*, ill-bred.

apprenti, e (aprɑ̃ti) n, apprentice; learner; novice, tyro. **apprentissage** (sa:ʒ) m, apprenticeship; articles. *mettre en ~*, to apprentice.

apprêt (aprɛ) m, dressing; affectation; editing (*computers*); (*pl.*) preparations. **apprêté, e** (te) a, affected. **apprêter** (te) v.t, to prepare, dress prime.

apprivoiser (aprivwaze) v.t, to tame. **s' ~**, to grow tame; become sociable.

approbation (aprɔbasjɔ̃) f, approbation, approval, confirmation.

approchant, e (aprɔʃɑ̃, ɑ̃:t) a, approximating, like. **approche** (prɔʃ) f, approach. **approcher** (ʃe) v.t. & i, to approach, draw near; resemble, border on.

approfondi, e (aprɔfɔ̃di) p.a, thorough, exhaustive. **approfondir** (di:r) v.t, to deepen; dive into.

approprier (aprɔprie) v.t, to adapt, suit. **s'~**, to appropriate.

approuver (apruve) v.t, to approve, countenance, confirm, pass.

approvisionner (aprɔvizjɔne) v.t, to supply, store, stock, provision. **s' ~ de**, to lay in [a stock of]. **approvisionnement** (nmɑ̃) m, supplying, etc; supply, etc.

approximatif, ive† (aprɔksimatif, i:v) a, approximate, rough. **approximation** (sjɔ̃) f, approximation.

appui (apɥi) m, support, rest; fulcrum; stress (*Gram.*); windowsill. *à hauteur d'~*, elbow-high, breast-high. **~-bras**, armrest. **~-**

tête, headrest. **~-main**, maulstick. **appuyer** (pɥije) v.t. & i, to support; back; second; hold up; lean, rest; bear; press; lay stress. **s'~**, to rest, lean; rely, depend.

âpre† (ɑ:pr) a, rough, harsh; sharp; ruthless; greedy, grasping.

après (aprɛ) pr, after. *ap. J.-C.*, A.D. ¶ad, after[wards]. **~ que**, c, after, when. **d'~**, pr, according to, after, from. **~ coup**, ad, too late, after the event, a day after the fair. **~-demain**, ad. & m, the day after tomorrow. **d'~-guerre**, a, postwar. **~-midi**, m, afternoon. *de l'~-midi*, post meridiem, p.m.

âpreté (aprəte) f, roughness, etc, as *âpre*; asperity.

à-propos (aprɔpo) m, aptness; opportuneness.

apte (apt) a, fit[ted], competent, qualified; apt. **aptitude** (tityd) f, aptitude, aptness, etc; faculty, flair.

apurer (apyre) v.t, to agree, reconcile; wipe off (*debt, etc.*); audit; get discharged, get canceled.

aquafortiste (akwafɔrtist) m, etcher.

aquaplane (akwaplan) m, surfboard.

aquarelle (akwarɛl) f, watercolor.

aquarium (akwarjɔm) m, aquarium.

aquatique (akwatik) a, aquatic, water (*att.*).

aqueduc (akdyk) m, aqueduct.

aqueux, euse (akø, ø:z) a, aqueous, watery.

à quia (kɥia), nonplussed.

aquilin (akilɛ̃) a.m, aquiline, hook[ed], Roman (*nose*).

ara (ara) m, macaw, ara.

arabe (arab) a, Arab; Arabian; Arabic. ¶m, Arabic (*language*). **A~**, n, Arab[ian] (*pers.*). **arabesque** (bɛsk) f, arabesque, **l'Arabie** (bi) f, Arabia. **Arabique** (bik) a, Arabian (*gulf*).

arable (arabl) a, arable, tillable.

arachide (araʃid) f, groundnut, peanut, monkey nut.

araignée (arɛɲe) f, spider.

aratoire (aratwa:r) *a*, agricultural, farming.

arbitrage (arbitra:ʒ) *m*, arbitration; arbitrament; arbitrage. **arbitraire†** (trɛ:r) *a*, arbitrary; highhanded. **arbitre** (tr) *m*, arbitrator, arbiter; referee, umpire. *libre ~*, freewill. *~ de lignes*, linesman (*Ten.*). **arbitrer** (tre) *v.t*, to arbitrate; arrange; referee, umpire.

arborer (arbɔre) *v.t*, to raise, hoist, set up; flaunt.

arbre (arbr) *m*, tree; shaft, axle, spindle, mandrel, -il, arbor. *~ de haute futaie*, timber tree. *~ de plein vent*, standard. *~ en espalier*, wall tree. *~ moteur*, *~ de couche*, driving shaft. *~ toujours vert*, evergreen. **arbrisseau** (briso) *m*, shrub.

arbuste (arbyst) *m*, bush.

arc (ark) *m*, bow; arc; arch. **arcade** (kad) *f*, archway; arch; (*pl.*) arcade.

arc-boutant (arkbutɑ̃) *m*, [flying] buttress; raking shore; strut, spur, brac. **arc-bouter** (te) *v.t*, to buttress.

arceau (arso) *m*, arch; hoop; cradle (*Surg.*).

arc-en-ciel (arkɑ̃sjɛl) *m*, rainbow.

archaïque (arkaik) *a*, archaic.

archange (arkɑ̃:ʒ) *m*, archangel.

arche (arʃ) *f*, arch; ark. *l'~ d'alliance*, the Ark of the Covenant. *l'~ de Noé* (nɔe), Noah's ark.

archéologie (arkeɔlɔʒi) *f*, archaeology. **archéologique** (ʒik) *a*, archaeologic(al). **archéologue** (lɔg) *m*, archaeologist.

archer (arʃe) *m*, archer, bowman. **archet** (ʃɛ) *m*, bow, fiddlestick.

archevêché (arʃəvɛʃe) *m*, archbishopric; palace. **archevêque** (vɛ:k) *m*, archbishop.

archidiacre (arʃidjakr) *m*, archdeacon.

archipel (arʃipɛl) *m*, archipelago.

architecte (arʃitɛkt) *m*, architect. **architectural, e** (tyral) *a*, architectural. **architecture** (ty:r) *f*, architecture.

archives (arʃi:v) *f.pl*, archives, records.

arçon (arsɔ̃) *m*, saddle bow; bow.

arctique (arktik) *a*, arctic.

ardent, e (ardɑ̃, ɑ̃:t) *a*, burning, hot, fiery, raging, blazing, live; ardent, keen, fervent, fervid, eager, earnest, spirited; passionate. **ardemment** (damɑ̃) *ad*, ardently, etc. **ardeur** (dœ:r) *f*, ardor, heat, etc; zest. *~ d'estomac*, heartburn.

ardoise (ardwa:z) *f*, slate. **ardoisé, e** (dwaze) *a*, s.-colored. **ardoisière** (zjɛ:r) *f*, s. quarry.

ardu, e (ardy) *a*, steep; arduous, hard, uphill.

are (a:r) *m*, are = 100 square meters *or* 119.60 sq. yards.

arène (arɛn) *f*, arena, lists, ring; cockpit; sand (*Poet.*).

arête (arɛt) *f*, [fish]bone; ridge, edge, arris; arête; groin, hip (*Arch.*); awn, beard (*Bot.*). *~ vive*, sharp edge.

argent (arʒɑ̃) *m*, silver; money, cash. *~ comptant*, ready money, spot cash. *~ doré*, silver-gilt. *un ~ fou*, a mint of money. *~ liquide*, ready money. *~ mignon*, small savings (*to spend on pleasure*). *~sec*, hard cash. *~ sur table*, cash down. **argenter** (te) *v.t*, to silver[-plate], [electro]plate. **argenterie** (tri) *f*, silver, [s.] plate. **argentin, e** (tɛ̃, in) *a*, argentine, silvery, silvern. ¶ *a. &* A~, *n*, Argentine (*Geog.*). l'**Argentine**, *f*, the Argentina.

argile (arʒil) *f*, clay. *~ réfractaire*, fire clay. **argileux, euse** (lø, ø:z) *a*, clayey, argillaceous.

argot (argo) *m*, slang.

arguer (argɥe) *v.t*, to infer, deduce. **argument** (gymɑ̃) *m*, argument; synopsis. **argumenter** (te) *v.t*, to argue.

argutie (argysi) *f*, quibble, cavil, hairsplitting.

aria (arja) *m*, bother, ado, to-do.

aride (arid) *a*, arid, dry, barren. **aridité** (dite) *f*, aridity, etc.

aristocrate (aristɔkrat) *n*, aristocrat. ¶ *att. &* **aristocratique†** (tik) *a*, aristocratic(al). **aristocratie** (si) *f*, aristocracy.

arithméticien, ne (aritmetisjɛ̃, ɛn) *n*, arithmetician. **arithmétique†** (tik) *a*, arithmetical. ¶ *f*, arithmetic.

arlequin (arləkɛ̃) *m*, harlequin;

turncoat (*pers.*); scraps, leavings, leftovers, orts, hash. **arlequinade** (kinad) *f*, harlequinade.

armateur (armatœːr) *m*, [ship]-owner, [registered] manager (*ship's*).

armature (armatyːr) *f*, trussing; bracing; fastening, strap; reinforcement; armor, sheathing, plating; gear (*pump*); armature (*Phys.*); key signature (*Mus.*); framework (*fig.*).

arme (arm) *f*, arm, weapon; (*pl.*) arms (*Mil.*); branch of the service; [coat of] arms, [armorial] bearings. ~ *à feu*, firearm. ~ [*à feu*] *portative*, small arm. ~ *blanche*, side arm; cold steel. *sans* ~*s*, unarmed. *faire* (ou *tirer*) *des* ~*s*, to fence. *faire ses premières* ~*s*, to participate in one's first battle; make one's debut.

armée (arme) *f*, army, force[s]; host. ~ *active*, regular army. *A~ du Salut*, Salvation Army. *zone des* ~*s*, theater of operations.

armeline (armɛlin) *f*, ermine (*fur*).

armement (armɛmɑ̃) *m*, arming; armament; fitting out, equipment; manning; shipping; shipowners.

Arménie (l') (armeni) *f*, Armenia. **arménien, ne** (njɛ̃, ɛn) *a.* & A~, *n*, Armenian.

armer (arme) *v.t*, to arm; fit out, equip; man; commission (*ship*); truss, brace; reinforce, armor, sheathe; set (*Phot. shutter*); cock (*gun*), sign (*clef*); dub (*knight*); (*v.i.*) to arm.

armoire (armwaːr) *f*, cupboard, cabinet, wardrobe. ~ *à pharmacie*, medicine cabinet. ~ *vitrée*, display cabinet, china cabinet.

armoiries (armwari) *f.pl*, [coat of] arms, [armorial] bearings. **armorial, e** (mɔrjal) *a.* & *m*, armorial. **armorier** (rje) *v.t*, to [em]blazon.

armure (armyːr) *f*, armor, sheathing; armature (*Phys.*). ~ *complète*, suit of armor. **armurier** (myrje) *m*, gunsmith; armorer.

arnaque (arnak) *f*, swindle, trickery, sting. **arnaquer** (ke) *v.t*, to swindle.

arnica (arnika) *f*, arnica.

aromatique (arɔmatik) *a*, aromatic. **arôme** (roːm) *m*, aroma.

arpège (arpɛːʒ) *m*, arpeggio.

arpent (arpɑ̃) *m*, acre.

arpentage (arpɑ̃taːʒ) *m*, land measuring, surveying. **arpenter** (te) *v.t*, to measure, survey; pace, tramp. **arpenteur** (tœːr) *m*, [land] surveyor.

arquer (arke) *v.t. & i. & s'~*, to arch, curve, bend.

arrache-clou (araʃklu) *m*, nail extractor. **d'arrache-pied**, *ad*, without intermission; on end, at a stretch. **arracher** (ʃe) *v.t*, to pluck, pull, tear, draw; drag; uproot, dig up; extract; wring; snatch; squeeze, extort, screw out. **arracheur, euse** (ʃœːr, ø:z) *n*, drawer, puller; (*f.*) grubber.

arraisonner (arɛzɔne) *v.t*, to visit. (*Cust.*).

arrangeant, e (arɑ̃ʒɑ̃, ɑ̃:t) *a*, accommodating, obliging. **arrangement** (ʒmɑ̃) *m*, arrangement; settlement. **arranger** (ʒe) *v.t*, to arrange; settle (lawsuit). *s'~*, to agree, come to terms; settle down; get on, manage. *arrangez-vous!* do the best you can! do as you like!

arrenter (arɑ̃te) *v.t*, to lease.

arrérager (areraʒe) *v.i*, to get (*or* fall) into arrear[s]. **arrérages** (raːʒ) *m.pl*, interest (*on Government stocks or the like*); rent, pension, or the like, accrued & due.

arrestation (arɛstasjɔ̃) *f*, arrest, custody. **arrêt** (rɛ) *m*, stoppage, stop; arrest; seizure, detention; standstill; catch; tackle (*Foot.*); judgment, sentence; decree. ~ *en cours de route*, break of journey. ~ *facultatif*, cars stop here if requested. ~ *fixe*, all cars stop here. *aux* ~*s*, under arrest (*Mil.*); kept in (*Sch.*). ~ *d'urgence*, emergency shutdown, scram (*atomic physics*). ~ *sur l'image*, freeze frame (*cinema*). *chien d'*~, setter, pointer. *prononcer un* ~, to pass sentence. **arrêté, e** (te) *p.a*, decided, settled, preconcerted. ¶ *m*, order, decree; making up, closing, ruling off, rest

(*Bkkpg.*). **arrêter** (te) *v.t. & i*, to stop; arrest; seize, detain; fix; retain, engage; conclude; make up, close, rule off (*Bkkpg.*); fasten off (*Need.*); agree upon; decide on; (*v.t. & abs.*) point, set (*dog*). s'~, to stop, stay, call; draw up (*car*). **arrhes** (aːr) *f.pl*, deposit, earnest [money].

arrière (arjɛːr) *m*, back [part]; back (*Foot.*); rear; tail; stern. **en ~**, behind; behind-hand; back, at the back, in the rear; astern; with one's back to the engine. *Note: arrière in comps is pronounced* arjer, *thus*, ~*-bouche* (arjɛrbuʃ) *f*, fauces. ~*-garde*, *f*, rear guard. *arrière-grand-mère*, *f*, *arrière-grand-père*, *m*, great-grandmother, -father. ~*-main*, *m*, backhand (*Ten.*). ~*-neveu*, *m*, ~*-nièce*, *f*, grandnephew, -niece. ~*-pensée*, *f*, ulterior motive, mental reservation. ~*-petite-fille*, *f*, great-granddaughter. ~*-petit-fils*, *m*, g.-grandson. ~*-petits-enfants*, *m.pl*, g.-grandchildren. ~*-plan*, *m*, background. ~*-point*, *m*, backstitch (*Need.*). ~*-port*, *m*, inner harbor. **arriéré**, **e** (rjere) *a*, overdue, in arrear[s]; outstanding, owing; behindhand; backward (*child*); old-fashioned. ¶ *m*, arrears. **arriérer** (re) *v.t*, to put off, defer, hold over. s'~, to fall behind; get into arrears.

arrimer (arime) *v.t*, to stow, trim. **arrimeur** (mœːr) *m*, stower, trimmer; stevedore.

arrivage (arivaːʒ) *m*, arrival. **arrivée** (ve) *f*, arrival, coming; finish[ing] (*sport*), [winning] post; home (*running*); inlet. **à l'~ & d'~**, incoming; at the finish, finishing. **arriver** (ve) *v.i*, to arrive, come; get; finish; happen, come about, c. to pass, occur, befall; be due (*train*); succeed. ~ *à égalité*, to tie (*sport*). *arrive que pourra*, come what may. *en ~ à*, to come to, be reduced to. **arriviste** (arivist) *m.f*, pusher, social climber.

arrogamment (arɔgamɑ̃) *ad*, arrogantly. **arrogance** (gɑ̃ːs) *f*, arrogance, assumption. **arrogant**, **e** (gɑ̃, ɑ̃ːt) *a*, arrogant, overbearing. **s'arroger** (ɔʒe)

v.pr, to arrogate [to oneself], assume.

arroi (arwa) *m*, plight, pickle.

arrondir (arɔ̃diːr) *v.t*, to round [off]. **arrondissement** (dismɑ̃) *m*, rounding; ward, district.

arroser (arɔze) *v.t*, to water, [be]sprinkle, bedew, wet; baste; stand treat. *ça s'arrose*, that calls for a drink. **arrosoir** (zwaːr) *m*, watering can.

arsenal (arsənal) *m*, arsenal. ~ *maritime*, naval dockyard.

art (aːr) *m*, art, skill; artfulness, artifice. ~*s d'agrément*, accomplishments. *septième ~*, cinema. *huitième ~*, television.

artère (artɛːr) *f*, artery; thoroughfare; feeder (*Elec.*). **artériel, le** (terjɛl) *a*, arterial.

artésien, ne (artezjɛ̃, ɛn) *a*, Artesian.

arthrite (artrit) *f*, arthritis.

artichaut (artiʃo) *m*, artichoke; spikes.

article (artikl) *m*, article, subject, matter; section, clause, item, entry; requisite, material, commodity, (*pl.*) wares. ~ *à côté*, side line. ~ *de fond*, leading article, leader. ~ *de tête*, lead story (*newspaper*). ~[s] *de Paris*, artistic novelties, fancy goods. ~*s dépareillés*, oddments.

articulation (artikylasjɔ̃) *f*, articulation, joint; deployment; knuckle; utterance. **articuler** (le) *v.t. & i. & s'~*, to articulate, joint, link; utter.

artifice (artifis) *m*, artifice, artfulness, craft; contrivance; art. ~*s de théâtre*, stage effects. **artificiel, le**† (sjɛl) *a*, artificial. **artificier** (sje) *m*, pyrotechnist. **artificieux, euse**† (sjø, øːz) *a*, artful, cunning, crafty.

artillerie (artijri) *f*, artillery, ordnance; gunnery. ~ *de place*, garrison artillery. **artilleur** (jœːr) *m*, artilleryman, gunner.

artimon (artimɔ̃) *m*, mizzen mast; m. sail.

artisan, e (artizɑ̃, an) *n*, artisan; craftsman; operative; (*fig.*) author, originator, artificer, architect. ~ *en bois*, woodworker. **artison** (artizɔ̃) *m*, wood worm;

clothes moth. **artisonné, e** (zɔne) *a*, worm-eaten; moth-eaten.

artiste (artist) *n*, artist; artiste, performer. **artiste†** & **artistique** (tik) *a*, artistic.

aryen, ne (arjɛ̃, ɛn) *a*, Aryan.

as (ɑ:s) *m*, ace. ~ *de l'aviation*, flying ace. ~ *de pique*, ace of spades (*Cards*); rump, parson's nose (*fowl*).

asbeste (azbɛst) *m*, asbestos.

ascendance (asɑ̃dɑ̃:s) *f*, ancestry.

ascendant, e (asɑ̃dɑ̃, ɑ̃:t) *a*, ascending, upward. ¶ *m*, ascendant, -ent; ascendancy, -ency; (*pl.*) ancestry. **ascenseur** (sœ:r) *m*, elevator. **ascension** (sjɔ̃) *f*, ascent, climb, rising, ascension. *l'A~*, Ascension day. **ascensionniste** (ɔnist) *n*, climber, mountaineer.

ascète (asɛt) *n*. & **ascétique** (setik) *a*, ascetic.

asiatique (azjatik) *a*. & A~, *n*, Asiatic. **l'Asie** (zi) *f*, Asia. *l'~ Mineure*, Asia Minor.

asile (azil) *m*, asylum, shelter; home; haven, sanctuary. ~ *d'aliénés*, mental institution.

aspect (aspɛ) *m*, aspect, sight, appearance, look, bearing; complexion.

asperge (aspɛrʒ) *f*, asparagus.

asperger (aspɛrʒe) *v.t*, to [be]sprinkle, asperse.

aspérité (asperite) *f*, asperity, roughness.

aspersion (aspɛrsjɔ̃) *f*, aspersion, sprinkling.

asphalte (asfalt) *m*, asphalt.

asphyxie (asfiksi) *f*, asphyxia, suffocation, gassing. **asphyxier** (sje) *v.t*, to asphyxiate, etc.

aspic (aspik) *m*, asp; slanderer, backbiter; aspic.

aspirail (aspira:j) *m*, air hole, vent, flue.

aspirant, e (aspirɑ̃, ɑ̃:t) *n*, aspirant, suitor; candidate. ~ [*de marine*], midshipman. **aspirateur** [*de poussières*] (ratœ:r) *m*, vacuum cleaner. **aspiration** (sjɔ̃) *f*, aspiration; inspiration; yearning. **aspirer** (re) *v.t*, to inspire, inhale, exhaust, suck, draw; aspirate; (*v.i.*) to aspire.

aspirine (aspirin) *f*, aspirin.

assagir (asaʒi:r) *v.t*, to make wiser; sober; steady.

assaillant (asajɑ̃) *m*, assailant. **assaillir** (ji:r) *v.t.ir*, to assail, assault.

assainir (asɛni:r) *v.t*, to cleanse, sanitate.

assaisonnement (asɛzɔnmɑ̃) *m*, seasoning, flavoring; dressing (*salad*); condiment, relish. **assaisonner** (ne) *v.t*, to season, etc. leaven (*fig.*).

assassin, e (asasɛ̃, in) *n*, assassin, murderer, ess. *à l'~!* murder! ¶ *a*, bewitching, killing (*looks, eyes*). **assassinat** (sina) *m*, assassination, murder. **assassiner** (ne) *v.t*, to assassinate, murder, kill; tire to death, bore, plague.

assaut (aso) *m*, assault, storming, onset, onslaught; match, bout. ~ *d'armes*, assault of (*or* at) arms, fencing match. ~ *de démonstration*, sparring match.

assèchement (asɛʃmɑ̃) *m*, drainage; drying. **assécher** (seʃe) *v.t*. & *i*, to drain, dry.

assemblage (asɑ̃bla:ʒ) *m*, assemblage, congregation; joint (*in wood, metal, etc.*). **assemblée** (ble) *f*, meeting, assembly, conclave, congregation; meet (*Hunt.*). **assembler** (ble), *v.t*, to assemble, collect, gather, summon; join. *s'~*, to meet, assemble, congregate, flock.

assener (asəne) *v.t*, to strike, deal (*blow*).

assentiment (asɑ̃timɑ̃) *m*, assent.

asseoir (aswa:r) *v.t.ir*, to seat, set, bed, base, fix, secure, establish; pitch (*camp, tent*). *s'~*, to sit [down].

assermenter (asɛrmɑ̃te) *v.t*, to swear in.

assertion (asɛrsjɔ̃) *f*, assertion.

asservir (asɛrvi:r) *v.t*, to enslave.

assez (ase) *ad*, enough, rather, pretty, fairly.

assidu, e (asidy) *a*, assiduous, sedulous, industrious; regular. **assiduité** (dɥite) *f*, assiduity, etc. **assidûment** (dymɑ̃), *ad*, assiduously, etc.

assiégeant (asjeʒɑ̃) *m*, besieger. **assiéger** (ʒe) *v.t*, to besiege, beleaguer, beset, crowd round, throng; dun.

assiette (asʃɛt) *f*, plate; seat, seating, bed, base, foundation; basis; set, firmness, steadiness, stability, security; trim (*ship*). **assiettée** (te) *f*, plateful.

assignation (asiɲasjɔ̃) *f*, assignation; assignment; charge; summons; writ; subpoena. **assigner** (ɲe) *v.t*, to assign; charge; summon; cite; subpoena.

assimiler (asimile) *v.t*, to assimilate, liken, compare.

assis (asi) *p.a*, seated, sitting; established.

assise (asiːz) *f*, bed, foundation; course (*Build.*); (*pl.*) assize[s] (*law*).

assistance (asistɑ̃ːs) *f*, assistance, aid, help; attendance, audience. ~ *judiciaire*, legal aid. ~ *privée*, private charity. ~ *publique*, public assistance *or* relief. ~ *sociale*, social welfare work. **assistant, e** (tɑ̃, ɑ̃ːt) *n*, assistant; bystander, onlooker. **assister** (te) *v.t*, to assist, aid, help. ~ *à*, to attend, be present at, witness.

association (asɔsjasjɔ̃) *f*, association; society; g[u]ild; partnership. **associé, e** (sje) *n*, associate, member, partner. **associer** (sje) *v.t*, to associate; take into partnership. s'~ *avec*, to go into partnership with; join with; sympathize with.

assoiffé (aswafe) *a*, thirsty.

assolement (asɔlmɑ̃) *m*, rotation (*crops*).

assombrir (asɔ̃briːr) *v.t*, to darken, gloom, cloud.

assommant, e (asɔmɑ̃, ɑ̃ːt) *a*, killing, oppressive, overwhelming, tiresome, wearisome, boring. **assommer** (me) *v.t*, to knock down, fell, strike dead; beat, thrash, nearly kill; overwhelm, weary to death, bore. **assommoir** (mwaːr) *m*, bludgeon, life preserver, lethal weapon; pole-axe; deadfall; dram shop.

assomption (asɔ̃psjɔ̃) *f*, Assumption (*Eccl.*).

assortiment (asɔrtimɑ̃) *m*, assortment; set; blend; match. **assortir** (tiːr) *v.t. & i*, to assort, supply; stock; blend; match; suit.

assortissant, e (tisɑ̃, ɑ̃ːt) *a*, suitable, becoming.

assoupir (asupiːr) *v.t*, to make drowsy, send to sleep, lull, deaden; hush up. s'~, to doze; die down. **assoupissant, e** (pisɑ̃, ɑ̃ːt) *a*, dull, humdrum. **assoupissement** (pismɑ̃) *m*, drowsiness; lethargy.

assouplir (asupliːr) *v.t*, to make supple; make tractable; soften.

assourdir (asurdiːr) *v.t*, to deafen, muffle; tone down.

assouvir (asuviːr) *v.t*, to satiate, glut.

assujettir (asyʒɛtiːr) *v.t*, to subject, subdue; bind, tie down; fix, fasten.

assumer (asyme) *v.t*, to assume.

assurance (asyrɑ̃ːs) *f*, assurance; confidence; security; pledge; insurance. ~ *contre les accidents du travail*, workmen's compensation i. ~ *maritime*, marine i., sea i. ~*s sociales*, social security. ~ *sur la vie*, life i. **assuré†, e** (re) *a*, assured, sure, safe; confident, bold. *mal* ~, insecure, unsafe. ¶ (*pers.*) *n*, insured, assured. **assurer** (re) *v.t*, to assure, ensure, insure, secure, guarantee; make fast, steady, set, strengthen; affirm; confirm. s'~, to make sure; trust; insure (*Insce.*). **assureur** (rœːr) *m*, insurer, underwriter.

Assyrie (l') (asiri) *f*, Assyria. **assyrien, ne** (rjɛ̃, ɛn) *a. & A~, n*, Assyrian.

aster (astɛːr) *m*, aster.

astérisque (asterisk) *m*, asterisk, star.

astéroïde (asterɔid) *m*, asteroid.

asthmatique (asmatik) *a. & n*, asthmatic. **asthme** (asm) *m*, asthma.

asticot (astiko) *m*, gentle, maggot.

asticoter (astikɔte) *v.t*, to tease.

astigmate (astigmat) *a*, astigmatic.

astiquer (astike) *v.t*, to polish.

astre (astr) *m*, star, luminary.

astreindre (astrɛ̃ːdr) *v.t.ir*, to bind, tie down, compel. **astreinte** (trɛ̃ːt) *f*, penalty.

astringent, e (astrɛ̃ʒɑ̃, ɑ̃ːt) *a. & m*, astringent.

astrologie (astrɔlɔʒi) *f*, astrology. **astrologue** (lɔg) m, astrologer.

astronaute (astronoːt) m, astronaut.

astronef (astronɛf) m, spacecraft, spaceship.

astronome (astronɔm) m, astronomer. **astronomie** (mi) f, astronomy. **astronomique†** (mik) a, astronomic(al).

astuce (astys) f, astuteness, artfulness, craftiness, guile. **astucieux, euse†** (sjø, øːz) a, astute, etc.

atelier (atəlje) m, [work]shop, mill, house, workroom, studio; staff; students.

atermoiement (atɛrmwamɑ̃) m, delay, procrastination, evasion. **atermoyer** (je) v.i, to procrastinate.

athée (ate) m, atheist. ¶ a, atheistic. **athéisme** (teism) m, atheism. **Athènes** (atɛn) f, Athens. **athénien, ne** (tenje, ɛn) a. & A~, n, Athenian.

athlète (atlɛt) m, athlete. **athlétique** (letik) a, athletic. **athlétisme** (letism) m, athletics.

atlantique (atlɑ̃tik) a, Atlantic. **l'[océan] A~**, m, the A. [ocean]. **atlantiste** (tist) m, person favoring inclusion of France in NATO.

atlas (atlɑːs) m, atlas; [book of] plates.

atmosphère (atmɔsfɛːr) f, atmosphere; medium (ether). **atmosphérique** (ferik) a, atmospheric(al), air (att.).

atome (atoːm) m, atom; mote. **atomique** (tɔmik) a, atomic(al). **atomiser** (tɔmize) v.t, to atomize, pulverize.

atone (atoːne) a, atonic, toneless, lackluster, dull; unstressed (Gram.).

atours (atuːr) m.pl, finery.

atout (atu) m, trump [card], trumps.

âtre (ɑːtr) m, hearth, fireplace.

atroce† (atrɔs) a, atrocious, heinous, outrageous; excruciating. **atrocité** (site) f, atrocity, etc.

atrophie (atrɔfi) f, atrophy, wasting away.

attabler (s') (atable) v.pr, to sit down [to table].

attachant, e (ataʃɑ̃, ɑ̃ːt) a, in-

teresting; engaging, winning. **attache** (taʃ) f, tie, fastening, leash, binder, bond, band, clip, paper fastener; attachment. **attaché** (ʃe) m, attaché. **attachement** (ʃmɑ̃) m, attachment; fondness; devotion. **attacher** (ʃe) v.t, to attach, tie, fasten, bind; rivet (attention). s'~, to fasten, devote oneself, cling, stick.

attaque (atak) f, attack, onset, onslaught, raid; fit, stroke, seizure, **attaquer** (ke) v.t, to attack, set on, assault; spur on; impugn. ~ en justice, to bring an action against. s'~à, to attack; tackle, grapple with.

attardé (atarde) a, belated; backward, old-fashioned.

attarder (s') (atarde) v.pr, to loiter, linger.

atteindre (atɛ̃ːdr) v.t.ir, to reach, attain; strike; hit; overtake, catch [up]; affect. **atteinte** (tɛːt) f, reach, etc.; blow, stroke, cut; reflection, slur.

attelage (atlaːʒ) m, harnessing; coupling; team. **atteler** (tle) v.t, to harness, yoke, attach, couple. **attelle** (atɛl) f, splint; (pl.) hames.

attenant, e [à] (atnɑ̃, ɑ̃ːt) a, adjoining.

attendant (en) (atɑ̃dɑ̃) ad, meanwhile, in the mean time. ¶ pr, pending. **en attendant que**, c, till, until. **attendre** (tɑ̃ːdr) v.t. & i, to wait for, wait, stay, expect, await, bide, look forward to. s'~à, to expect, look for; rely on.

attendrir (atɑ̃driːr) v.t, to soften, move, melt, affect. s'~, to be moved.

attendu (atɑ̃dy) pr, considering. ~ que, c, seeing that, whereas.

attentat (atɑ̃ta) m, (criminal) attempt, assault, outrage. **attentatoire** (twaːr) a, prejudicial.

attente (atɑ̃ːt) f, waiting, expectation.

attenter à (atɑ̃te), to make an attempt on.

attentif, ive† (atɑ̃tif, iːv) a, attentive, careful, mindful. **attention** (sjɔ̃) f, attention; notice; care[fulness], heed; kindness. faire ~, to pay attention, mind.

atténuer (atenɥe) v.t, to attenuate, weaken; minimize; extenuate.

atterrer (atɛre) *v.t,* to overwhelm, dumbfound.

atterrir (atɛri:r) *v.i,* to land, alight. **atterrissage** (risa:ʒ) *m,* landing (*plane, spacecraft*); making land (*ship*). ~ *plané,* glide landing.

attestation (atɛstasjɔ̃) *f,* attestation; certificate, testimonial. **attester** (te) *v.t,* to attest, testify, vouch, certify, witness.

attiédir (atjedi:r) *v.t,* to cool; warm; make lukewarm.

attifer (atife) *v.t,* to dress up.

attique (atik) *a,* Attic.

attirail (atira:j) *m,* appliances, apparatus, implements, habiliment; string; baggage, paraphernalia; show, pomp.

attirance (atirɑ̃:s) *f,* attraction. **attirer** (re) *v.t,* to attract, draw; lure; win. **s'~,** to incur, win.

attiser (atize) *v.t,* to stir, poke; fan (*fig.*).

attitré, e (atitre) *a,* accredited, recognized; by appointment.

attitude (atityd) *f,* attitude, posture.

attouchement (atuʃmɑ̃) *m,* touching, contact.

attractif, ive (atraktif, i:v) *a,* attractive (*Phys.*). **attraction** (ksjɔ̃) *f,* attraction; draw; loadstone; (*pl.*) varieties (*Theat.*); (*pl.*) cabaret [show].

attrait (atrɛ) *m,* attraction; draw; appeal; inclination, bent; (*pl.*) charms; amenities (*housing*).

attrape (atrap) *f,* trap, catch, hoax. **~-nigaud,** *m,* booby trap. **~-plats,** potholder. **attraper** (pe) *v.t,* to [en]trap, [en]snare, catch, take in, hoax; draw (*in lottery*); hit; tell off, scold (*slang*); hit off. **s'~,** to get caught.

attrayant, e (atrɛjɑ̃, ɑ̃:t) *a,* attractive, engaging, winning.

attribuer (atribɥe) *v.t,* to attribute, ascribe, predicate; father; allot. **attribuable** (abl) *a,* attributable, etc. **attribut** (by) *m,* attribute; predicate. **attributaire** (tɛ:r) *n,* allottee. **attribution** (sjɔ̃) *f,* attribution; allotment. *les ~s,* powers, duties.

attrister (atriste) *v.t,* to sadden.

attrition (atrisjɔ̃) *f,* attrition, abrasion.

attroupement (atrupmɑ̃) *m,* unlawful assembly; mob; riot.

aubade (obad) *f,* aubade; cat-calling.

aubaine (obɛn) *f,* windfall, godsend.

aube (o:b) *f,* dawn; alb; blade, vane, paddle, float.

aubépine (obepin) *f,* hawthorn.

auberge (obɛrʒ) *f,* inn; hostel. ~ *de jeunesse,* youth hostel. *vous n'êtes pas encore sorti de l'~,* you're still in trouble. **aubergiste** (ʒist) *n,* innkeeper, landlord, -lady.

aubergine (obɛrʒin) *f,* eggplant.

aubier (obje) *m,* sapwood.

aucun, e (okœ̃, yn) *a. & pn,* any; anyone; (*neg.*) no, none; no one. **aucunement** (kynmɑ̃) *ad,* in any way; (*neg.*) not at all, by no means, nowise.

audace (odas) *f,* audacity, boldness, daring. *payer d'~,* to face the music. **audacieux, euse†** (sjø, ø:z) *a,* audacious, etc.

au-delà, au-dessous see delà, dessous.

au-devant (odvɑ̃) *ad,* forward, ahead. *aller ~ de,* to go to meet.

audience (odjɑ̃:s) *f,* audience, hearing; court. **auditeur, trice** (ditœ:r, tris) *n,* hearer, listener, auditor; prosecutor. **audition** (sjɔ̃) *f,* hearing, audition; concert; recital. **auditoire** (twa:r) *m,* audience; auditorium; congregation.

auge (o:ʒ) *f,* **auget** (oʒɛ) *m,* trough, bucket. **augée** (oʒe) *f,* troughful, bucketful.

augmenter (ɔgmɑ̃te) *v.t. & i,* to increase, augment, enlarge, enhance; supplement. **augmentation** (tasjɔ̃) *f,* increase; raise (*in salary*).

augure (ogy:r) *m,* augury, omen; prophet, augur. **augurer** (gyre) *v.t,* to augur, make.

auguste (ogyst) *a,* august.

aujourd'hui (oʒurdɥi) *ad. & m,* today. *d'~ en huit, en quinze,* a week from today, fortnight.

aumône & **l'aumône** (omo:n) *f,* alms, charity. **aumônier** (monje) *m,* chaplain.

aune (o:n) *m*, alder.

auparavant (oparavã), *ad*, before[hand].

auprès (oprɛ) *ad*, near, close [by], [near] at hand. ~ **de**, *pr*, near, close to *or* by, by; [attached] to; with; in.

auquel *see* **lequel**.

auréole (oreol) *f*, aureole, halo; halation (*Phot*.).

auriculaire (orikylɛ:r) *a*, auricular, ear (*att.*). [**doigt**] ~, *m*, little (*or* fourth) finger.

aurifère (orifɛ:r) *a*, auriferous, gold (*att.*).

aurore (oro:r) *f*, dawn, daybreak, morn; aurora. ~ **boréale**, aurora borealis, northern lights.

ausculter (oskylte) *v.t*, to sound (*Med*.).

auspice (ospis) *m*, auspice, omen.

aussi (osi) *ad*, also, too, likewise; so; as. ¶ *c*, therefore, consequently, so. ~ **bien**, besides, moreover. ~ **bien que**, *c*, as well as. **aussitôt** (to) *ad*, directly, at once. ~ **dit**, ~ **fait**, no sooner said than done. ~ **que**, *c*, as soon as.

austère† (ostɛ:r) *a*, austere, stern. **austérité** (terite) *f*, austerity, etc.

austral, e (ostral) *a*, austral, southern. **l'Australasie** (lazi) *f*, Australasia. **l'Australie** (li), Australia. **australien, ne** (ljɛ̃, ɛn) *a*. & A~, *n*, Australian.

autan (otã) (*Poet*.) *m*, storm, blast.

autant (otã), *ad*, as (*or* so) much, as many, as far; as well, as good, as often. ~ **que**, as much as, as far as. **d'**~ **que**, *c*, especially as.

autel (otɛl) *m*, altar.

auteur (otœ:r) *m*, author; writer; composer; originator; founder (*race*); progenitor; perpetrator (*crime*); party at fault (*accident*); inventor; designer; informant; doer. *les* ~*s de nos jours*, our progenitors. ~ *dramatique*, playwright.

authentique† (otãtik) *a*, authentic, genuine. **authenticité** (site) *f*, authenticity, etc.

auto (oto, oto) *préfixe*, auto,

self-, *e.g. papier* ~*vireur*, self-toning paper (*Phot*.).

auto (oto, oto)*f*, auto, car.

autobiographie (otobiografi) *f*, autobiography.

autobus (otoby:s) *m*, bus.

autocar (otoka:r) *m*, interurban bus.

auto-caravane (otokaravan) *f*, camper, mobile home.

autochenille (otoʃni:j) *f*, caterpillar tractor.

autocrate, trice (otokrat, tris) *n*, autocrat. **autocratie** (si) *f*, autocracy. **autocratique** (tik) *a*, autocratic(al).

autocuisseur (otokɥizœ:r) *m*, pressure cooker.

autodidacte (otodidakt) *a*, self-taught.

autogène (otoʒɛ:n) *a*, autogenous.

autogestion (otoʒɛstjõ) *f*, management of a firm by its employees.

autographe (otograf) *m*. & *a*, autograph.

automate (otomat) *m*, automaton. **automatique†** (tik) *a*, automatic(al), self-acting.

automnal, e (otomnal) *a*, autumnal. **automne** (ton) *m*, autumn, fall.

automobile (o- *ou* otomobil) *a*, self-propelling, motor (*att.*). ¶ *f*, automobile. **automobilisme** (lism) *m*, motoring. **automobiliste** (list) *n*, motorist.

automotrice (otomotris) *f*, railcar, self-propelling railway car.

autonome (otonom) *a*, autonomous, self-governing; off line (*computers*). **autonomie** (mi) *f*, autonomy, self-government.

autopsie (otopsi) *f*, postmortem, autopsy.

autorisation (otorizasjõ) *f*, authorization, leave; warrant. **autoriser** (ze) *v.t*, to authorize, empower, allow. **autoritaire** (tɛ:r) *a*, authoritative. **autorité** (te) *f*, authority; power. *faire* ~, to be regarded as an authority.

autoroute (otorut) *f*, express highway.

auto-stop (otostop) *m*, hitchhiking. **auto-stoppeur, euse** (pœ:r, ø:z) *n*, hitchhiker.

autour (otu:r) *m*, goshawk.

autour (otu:r) *ad.* & **autour de**, *pr*, round, around, about.

autre (o:tr) *a* & *pn*, other; another; next (*world*); else. **un ~ soi-même**, one's second self. **~ part**, elsewhere. **à d'~s!** nonsense! **autrefois** (otrəfwa) *ad*, formerly; once [upon a time]. **d'~**, of old, of yore; bygone. **autrement** (otrəmã) *ad*, otherwise; differently; [or] else.

Autriche (l') (otriʃ) *f*, Austria. **autrichien, ne** (ʃjẽ, ɛn) *a.* & **A~**, *n*, Austrian.

autruche (otryʃ) *f*, ostrich.

autrui (otrɥi) *pn*, others, other people.

auvent (ovã) *m*, penthouse; weatherboard; porch roof; hood.

auxiliaire (oksiljɛ:r) *a.* & *m*; auxiliary.

avachi, e (avaʃi) *a*, flabby, baggy; out of shape.

aval (aval) *m*, lower part; tail; guarantee, backing; endorsement. **en ~**, *ad*, downstream, down. **en ~ de**, *pr*, down, below.

avalanche (avalã:ʃ) *f*, avalanche; shower (*fig.*).

avaler (avale) *v.t*, to swallow, devour; stomach; lower; (*v.i.*) to go downstream.

avaliser (avalize) *v.t*, to guarantee, back.

à-valoir (avalwa:r) *m.inv*, advance payment.

avaloire (avalwa:r) *f*, gullet, throat.

avance (avã:s) *f*, advance, start; lead; projection; fast (*on clock*). **à l'~, d'~, en ~, par ~**, *ad*, in advance, beforehand. **avancé, e** (vãse) *p.a*, advance[d]; projecting; late (*hour, etc.*); high (*meat*). **avancer (se)** *v.t*, to advance, put forward, push, hasten; help; promote, further; set ahead (*clock*); (*v.i.*) to advance; project, jut out; gain (*of clock*). **avancement** (smã) *m*, advancement; feed (*Mach.*). **recevoir de l'~**, to be promoted.

avanie (avani) *f*, affront, insult.

avant (avã) *pr*, before; till, until. **av. J.C.**, B.C. **avant terme**, premature(ly) (*childbirth*). **~ [que] de**, *pr*, **~ que**, *c*, before. ¶ *ad*,

forward, before, far, deep[ly]. **de l'~ à l'arrière**, fore & aft (*Naut.*). **en ~**, *ad*, forward, on, onward[s], ahead, before. **en ~!** forward! go ahead! on! **en ~, marche!** quick march! ¶ *m*, front, forepart; fore; head, bow (*Naut.*); steerage; forward (*Foot.*). **~ [du] centre**, center forward. **~-bras**, *m*, forearm. **~-coureur**, *m*, forerunner, harbinger, herald; (*att.*) premonitory. **~-dernier, ère**, *a.* & *n*, last but one. **~-garde**, *f*, van[guard]. **~-goût**, *m*, foretaste, earnest. **d'~-guerre**, *a*, prewar. **~-hier**, *ad.* & *m*, the day before yesterday. **~-hier soir**, the night before last. **~-main**, *m*, forehand (*Ten.*). **~-port**, *m*, outer harbor. **~-poste**, *m*, outpost. **~-première**, *f*, dress rehearsal; private view (*art*). **~-projet**, *m*, rough draft. **~-propos**, *m*, foreword, preface. **~-scène**, *f*, proscenium; stage box. **~-toit**, *m*, eaves. **l'~-veille**, *f*, two days before.

avantage (avãta:ʒ) *m*, advantage, benefit; odds; leverage; upper hand, pull. **~ [de jeu]**, [ad]vantage [game] (*Ten.*). **avantager** (taʒe) *v.t*, to benefit, favor, endow. **avantageux, euse†** (ʒø, ø:z) *a*, advantageous, good, beneficial.

avare† (ava:r) *a*, avaricious; miserly, sparing, chary. ¶ *n*, miser, screw. **avarice** (varis) *f*, avarice. **avaricieux, euse** (sjø, ø:z) *a*, avaricious.

avarie (avari) *f*, damage; average (*Marine Law*). **avarier** (rje) *v.t*, to damage. **s'~**, to deteriorate, go bad (*meat, etc.*).

avec (avɛk) *pr*, with. **d'~**, from.

aveline (avlin) *f*, filbert, cob[nut]. **avelinier** (nje) *m*, filbert [tree].

avenant (avnã) *m*, endorsement (*Insce.*). **à l'~ de**, *pr*, in keeping with.

avenant, e (avnã, ã:t) *a*, prepossessing, comely. **à l'~**, in keeping, accordingly. ¶ *m*, codicil, rider (*contract, treaty, etc.*).

avènement (avɛnmã) *m*, accession; advent, coming (*of Christ*).

avenir (avni:r) *m*, future, pros-

pect, outlook; promise. **à P~,
ad,** in future, hereafter; henceforth.

avent (l') (avã) *m,* advent (*Eccl.*).

aventure (avãty:r) *f,* [ad]ven-
ture. *dire la bonne ~,* to tell
fortunes. **à P~, ad,** haphazard,
at random. **d'~, par ~,** by
chance, perchance. **aventurer**
(tyie) *v.t,* to [ad]venture. **aventureux, euse** (rø, ø:z) *a,* [ad]ven-
turous. **aventurier, ère** (rje, ɛ:r)
n, adventurer, ess.

avenu (avny) *a,* in modern French
used exclusively in phrase **nul et
non ~,** null and void.

avenue (avny) *f,* avenue; drive.

avéré, e (avere) *p.a,* established,
proved. **avérer** (avere) *v.t,* to
establish; authenticate.

avers (avɛ:r) *m,* obverse (*coin*).

averse (avɛrs) *f,* shower.

aversion (avɛrsjɔ̃) *f,* aversion,
dislike.

avertir (avɛrti:r) *v.t,* to notify,
[fore]warn, caution. **avertissement** (tismã) *m,* notification;
warning; demand note (*taxes*).
avertisseur (sœ:r) *m,* call boy;
alarm; hooter; horn. *~ d'incendie,* fire alarm.

aveu (avø) *m,* avowal, admission,
confession; consent.

aveugle (avœ:gl) *a,* blind. ¶ *n,*
blind man, woman. *les ~s, m.pl,*
the blind. **aveuglement** (glǝmã)
m, blindness (*fig.*). **aveuglément** (glemã) *ad,* blindly. **aveugler** (gle) *v.t,* to blind; stop
(*leak*). **à l'aveuglette** (glɛt),
blindly.

aviateur, trice (avjatœr, tris)
a, flying, flight (*att.*). ¶ *n,* aviator, flier. **aviation** (sjɔ̃) *f,* aviation, flying.

aviculture (avikylty:r) *f,* aviculture; poultry farming.

avide† (avid) *a,* greedy, grasping,
eager, athirst, avid. **avidité** (dite)
f, avidity, greed[iness].

avilir (avili:r) *v.t,* to degrade,
debase; depreciate.

aviné, e (avine) *a,* intoxicated;
smelling of drink; tipsy (*walk*).

avion (avjɔ̃) *m,* airplane. *~ à réaction,* jet. *par ~,* by airmail.

aviron (avirɔ̃) *m,* oar. *~ de*

couple, scull. *~ de pointe,* single
oar (opp. *scull*). *l'~,* rowing.

avis (avi) *m,* opinion; mind; [way
of] thinking; judgment; advice;
notice, intimation. *jusqu'à nouvel
~,* until further notice. **avisé, e**
(ze) *a,* prudent, circumspect,
canny. **aviser** (ze) *v.t,* to advise,
notify, warn; espy. *s'~ de,* to bethink oneself of, dare to. **aviso**
(zo) *m,* dispatch boat.

aviver (avive) *v.t,* to revive,
brighten; sharpen (*tool*).

avocasserie (avɔkasri) *f,* pettifoggery. **avocat, e** (ka, kat) *n,*
counsel, lawyer; advocate. *~
général,* attorney general.

avoine (avwan) *f,* oats.

avoir (avwa:r) *m,* possessions,
property, holding(s); credit[or],
Cr (*Bkkpg.*). *tout son ~,* one's all.
¶ *v.t.ir,* to have; hold, keep; get;
be; measure; have on; be the matter with, ail. *en ~,* to have some
or any. *il y a,* there is, there are;
it is; ago; for. *il y en a,* there is
(are) some. *il n'y en a plus,* there
is none left. *se faire ~,* to be
taken in.

avoisinant, e (avwazinã, ã:t) *a,*
neighboring, bordering on. **avoisiner** (ne) *v.t,* to border on.

avortement (avɔrtǝmã) *m,* abortion; miscarriage (*fig.*). **avorter**
(te) *v.i,* to abort; miscarry. **avorton** (tɔ̃) *m,* abortion (*creature*).

avoué, e (avwe) *p.a,* acknowl-
edged; ostensible. ¶ *m,* lawyer.
avouer (we) *v.t,* to avow, confess; acknowledge, own. *s'~ coupable,* to plead guilty.

avril (avril) *m,* April. *donner un
poisson d' ~ à,* to make an April
fool of.

axe (aks) *m,* axis; spindle; axle.
~ de manivelle, crankshaft.

axiome (aksjo:m) *m,* axiom.

ayant cause (ɛjã) *m,* assign.
ayant droit, *m,* party [entitled].

azalée (azale) *f,* azalea.

azimut (azimyt) *m,* azimuth.
prendre un ~, to take a bearing.
direction tous les ~s, facing all directions.

azotate (azɔtat) *m,* nitrate. **azote**
(zɔt) *m,* nitrogen. **azoteux, euse**

(tø, ø:z) a, nitrous. **azotique** (tik) a, nitric.

azur (azy:r) m, azure. **azuré, e** (zyre) a, azure.

azyme (azim) a, unleavened.

B

baba (baba) a.inv, dumbfounded. ¶ m, rum-soaked cake.

babeurre (babœ:r) m, buttermilk; churn dash[er].

babil (babi) m, chatter, tattle, prattle, babble. **babillard, e** (bija:r, ard) n, chatterbox. **babiller** (je) v.i, to chatter, etc.

babine (babin) f, lip, chap, chop.

babiole (babjɔl) f, toy, plaything; trifle, bauble, gewgaw.

bâbord (babɔ:r) m, port [side] (Naut.).

babouches (babuʃ) f.pl, mules (slippers).

babouin (babwɛ̃) m, baboon. petit ~, petite babouine (win), young monkey (child).

babylonien, ne (babilɔnjɛ̃, ɛn) a, Babylonian.

bac (bak) m, ferry[boat]; vat, trough. ~ aérien, air ferry. ~ d'éléments, cell jar (Elec.). ~ de batterie, battery case. ~ transbordeur, train ferry.

baccalauréat (bakalɔrea) m, bachelor's degree.

bacchanal (bakanal) m, row; orgy. **bacchanales** (nal) f.pl, Bacchanalia.

bâche (ba:ʃ) f, sheet; cloth; tilt; tank; forcing frame. ~ goudronnée, tarpaulin.

bachelier, ère (baʃəlje, ɛ:r) n, bachelor (science).

bachique (baʃik) a, Bacchic; drinking (song).

bachot (baʃo) m, wherry; punt; bachelor's degree.

bacille (basil) m, bacillus.

bâcler (bakle) v.t, to bar, bolt; scamp.

bactéries (bakteri) f.pl, bacteria.

badaud, e (bado, o:d) n, saunterer, idler, gaper.

badigeon (badiʒɔ̃) m, distemper; whitewash (paint).

badin (badɛ̃, in) a, playful, jocose. ¶ n, wag. **badine** (din) f, switch, cane; (pl.) tongs. ba-

diner (ne) v.i, to jest, poke fun, banter, play, toy; flutter.

bafouer (bafwe) v.t, to scoff at.

bafouiller (bafuje) v.t, to stammer; talk foolishness.

bâfrer (bafre) v.i, to guzzle, gormandize.

bagage (baga:ʒ) m. oft. pl, luggage, baggage.

bagarre (baga:r) f, fray, brawl, broil, scuffle.

bagatelle (bagatɛl) f, trifle, bagatelle.

bagne (baɲ) m, convict prison.

bagnole (baɲɔl) f, cart; automobile.

bagou (bagu) m, gift of gab.

bague (bag) f, ring; collar; bush (Mach.).

baguenauder (bagnode) v.i, to trifle, fiddle, peddle, fool about.

baguer (bage) v.t, to tack, baste (Need.).

bagues sauves (bag so:v), safe & sound, without a scratch.

baguette (bagɛt) f, rod, stick, wand; loaf of bread; ramrod; bead (Arch., etc.). ~s à jour, open clocks or clox (stockings). ~ divinatoire (divinatwa:r), dowsing rod, divining rod.

bahut (bay) m, chest, trunk.

bai, e (bɛ) a. & m, bay (horse).

baie (bɛ) f, bay (Geog.); berry (Bot.); opening (in wall). ~ de porte, doorway.

baignade (bɛɲad) f, bathing; dip; bathing place. **baigner** (ɲe) v.t. & i. se ~, to bathe, dip; wash; steep; suffuse; welter. **baigneur, euse** (ɲœ:r, ø:z) n, bather; bathman, bath attendant. **baignoire** (ɲwa:r) f, bath (tub); box (Theat.).

bail (ba:j) m, lease.

bâiller (baje) v.i, to yawn, gape; be ajar.

bailleur, eresse (bajœ:r, jrɛs) n, lessor. bailleur de fonds, money lender; silent partner; financial backer.

bâillon (bajɔ̃) m, gag. **bâillonner** (jɔne) v.t, to gag.

bain (bɛ̃) m, bath; (pl. & s.) bathing; (pl.) watering place, spa. ~ de développement, ~ révélateur, developing bath (Phot.). ~ douche, shower bath. ~ de siège,

sitz b., hip b. ~ *de soleil*, sun-
bath. ~*s de soleil*, sunbathing. ~
de virage-fixage, fixing & toning
bath (*Phot.*). ~*-marie* (*mari*) *m*,
water bath; double boiler; boiler
(*in range*). ~ *mixte*, mixed bathing.

baïonnette (bajɔnɛt) *f*, bayonet.
baisemain (bɛzmɛ̃) *m*, kissing
[of] hands. **baiser** (ze) *m*, kiss.
¶ *v.t*, to kiss. *Note:* (*slang*) to
have sexual intercourse. I kissed
my sister, is in French *j'ai em-
brassé ma sœur*. **baisoter** (zɔte)
v.t, to smother with kisses, kiss
& cuddle.

baisse (bɛs) *f*, fall, drop. **baisser**
(se) *v.t. & i*, to lower, let down,
put down; drop; cast down; fall;
sink. **se ~**, to stoop, bend. **baissier** (sje) (*Stk Ex.*) *m*, bear, short.
baisure (bɛzyːr) *f*, kissing crust.
bajoue (baʒu) *f*, chop, chap.
bal (bal) *m*, ball, dance; d. hall.
~ *costumé*, ~ *travesti*, fancy dress
ball. ~ *masqué*, masked ball. ~
par souscription, subscription
dance.

balader (balade) *v.i*, to stroll; take
a walk. *envoyer ~*, to get rid of
(*person or thing*). **baladeur** (dœːr)
m, stroller, saunterer; selector
rod (*auto*); portable radio or cassette player with headphone. **baladeuse** (dØːz) *f*, trailer; handcart;
portable lamp.

baladin, e (baladɛ̃, ĩn) *n*,
mountebank, clown; buffoon.
balafre (balafr) *f*, gash, slash;
scar. **balafrer** (fre) *v.t*, to gash,
etc.

balai (balɛ) *m*, broom; brush;
windshield wiper. ~ *d'âtre*, hearth
brush. ~ *de bouleau*, birch
broom, besom. ~ *de tapis*, carpet
broom. ~ *garde-robe*, lavatory
brush. ~ *mécanique pour tapis*,
carpet sweeper.

balance (balɑ̃ːs) *f*, balance; poise;
scale; [pair of] scales; suspense.
~ *de vérification*, ~ *d'ordre*, trial
balance (*Bkkpg.*). *faire pencher la
~*, to turn the scale. **balancer**
(lɑ̃se) *v.t. & i*, to balance, poise,
weigh, offset; swing, sway, rock;
hold in suspense, be in suspense,
waver, halt; dismiss, fire; throw

away. **se ~**, to swing, sway, rock;
seesaw; hover. **balancement**
(smɑ̃) *m*, balancing. **balancier**
(sje) *m*, balancing pole (*tight
rope*); beam, bob (*Mach.*); fly
press; balance wheel (*Horol.*);
pendulum (*Horol.*); scale maker.
~ *monétaire*, coining press. **balançoire** (swaːr) *f*, seesaw; swing
(*child's*); twaddle.

balayage (balɛjaːʒ) *m*, sweeping;
picture scanning (*TV*). **balayer**
(je) *v.t*, to sweep [out, up]; scavenge. **balayette** (jɛt) *f*, whisk
[brush, broom], flick; penis (*obscene*). **balayeur, euse** (jœːr,
Øːz) *n*, sweeper, scavenger. **balayeuse**,
f, street sweeper (*Mach.*). ~
mécanique pour tapis, carpet
sweeper. **balayures** (jyːr) *f.pl*,
sweepings.

balbutier (balbysje) *v.t. & i*, to
stammer, mumble.

balcon (balkɔ̃) *m*, balcony. [*premier*] ~, dress circle; woman's
breasts (*slang*).

baldaquin (baldakɛ̃) *m*, canopy;
tester.

baleine (balɛn) *f*, whale; whalebone; steel (*corset*); rib (*umbrella*). **baleineau** (no) *m*, whale
calf. **baleinier** (nje) *m*, whaler
(*ship*). **baleinière** (njɛːr) *f*, whale-
boat.

balise (baliːz) *f*, beacon; sea
mark; tow path. **baliser** (lize) *v.t*,
to beacon; buoy.

baliverne (balivɛrn) *f*. oft. *pl*,
twaddle.

Balkans (les) (balkɑ̃) *m.pl*, the
Balkans. **balkanique** (kanik) *a*,
Balkan.

ballade (balad) *f*, ballad (*poem*).

ballant, e (balɑ̃, ɑ̃ːt) *a*, swinging, dangling.

ballast (balast) *m*, ballast (*road,
Rly*).

balle (bal) *f*, ball; franc (*slang*);
bullet, shot; bale; pack; husk,
chaff; glume; fore! (*Golf*). ~ *à la
volée*, trap ball. ~ *au but*, ~ *mise*,
hit.

ballerine (balrin) *f*, ballet girl.
ballet (lɛ) *m*, ballet (*Theat.*).
balloches (balɔʃ) *m.pl*, balls, testicles (*obscene*).
ballon (balɔ̃) *m*, balloon; ball;

flask, bulb (*Chem.*). ~ *au panier*, basketball. ~ *d'enfant*, toy balloon. ~ *d'essai*, pilot balloon; feeler (*fig.*). ~ *de boxe*, punching bag. ~ [*de football*], [foot]ball. **balloné, e** (lone) *p.a*, distended; ballooned (*dress*). **ballonner** (ne) *v.t*, to distend (*stomach*).

ballot (balo) *m*, bale; pack; pack (*Mil.*). **ballotter** (lɔte) *v.t. & i*, to toss, shake, rattle; bob; send from pillar to post; bandy [about].

balnéaire (balnɛːr) *a*, bathing, watering (*place*), seaside (*resort*).

balourd, e (baluːr, urd) *n*, lumpish person, hulking fellow. **balourdise** (lurdiːz) *f*, stupidity; blunder.

balsamier (balzamje) *m*, balsam [tree]. **balsamine** (min) *f*, garden balsam (*plant*). **balsamique** (mik) *a*, balsamic; balmy.

Baltique (la) [mer] (baltik), the Baltic sea [sea].

balustrade (balystrad) *f*, balustrade; railing. **balustre** (tr) *m*, baluster, banister; railing.

bambin, e (bãbɛ̃, in) *n*, kid, youngster.

bamboche (bãbɔʃ) *f*, spree.

bambou (bãbu) *m*, bamboo.

ban (bã) *m*, ban. ~*s de mariage*, banns. *mettre aux ~s*, to outlaw, banish. *en rupture de ~*, to have broken parole, be on a spree. *le ~ et l'arrière ~*, everybody; both regulars and reserves (*Mil.*).

banal, e (banal) *a*, banal, common[place], trite, hackneyed, humdrum. *voiture banalisée*, unmarked car (*police*). **banaliser** (lize) *v.t*, to vulgarize.

banane (banan) *f*, banana. **bananier** (nje) *m*, banana [plant, tree].

banc (bã) *m*, bench, form, seat, settle; box (*jury*); bank, bed, reef; shoal (*sand, fish*); school (*fish*); floe (*ice*). ~ *à coulisses*, sliding seat (*rowboat*). ~ [*d'église*], pew, ~ *des prévenus*, dock. *sur les ~s*, at school (*fig.*).

bancal, e (bãkal) *a*, bandy[-legged]; rickety.

bandage (bãdaːʒ) *m*, bandage; tire; stretching. ~ [*herniaire*] (ɛrnjeːr), truss. **bande** (bãːd) *f*,

band, strip, slip, tape, belt, strap, bandage; streak; wrapper; heel; list (*Naut.*); cushion (*Bil.*); blurb; troop, company, pack, gang, crew, party, set; ring; flock, flight. ~ *civile*, citizens' band (*CB Radio*). ~ *dessinée*, comic strip. ~ *molletière*, puttee. ~ *noire*, terrorist band. ~ *sonore*, sound track. ~-*amorce*, leader (*film, tape*). ~-*annonce*, trailer (*cinema*). ~-video, video tape. **bandeau** (bãdo) *m*, headband, bandeau; bandage (*over eyes*); veil (*fig.*), **bander** (de) *v.t*, to bandage, bind, tie up; stretch, tense, bend, key up; brace; tire (*wheels*). ~ [*les yeux à, de*], to blindfold; hoodwink. *v.i*, to have an erection (*obscene*); strain; touch cushion (*billiards*).

banderole (bãdrɔl) *f*, banderol[e], streamer.

bandit (bãdi) *m*, bandit, robber; ruffian.

bandoulière (bãduljɛːr) *f*, bandolier, shoulder strap. *en ~*, slung [over shoulder].

banlieue (bãljø) *f*, suburbs, outskirts. *de ~*, suburban.

banne (ban) *f*, sheet; tilt; awning; blind (*shop*); hamper.

bannière (banjɛːr) *f*, banner.

bannir (baniːr) *v.t*, to banish; expel.

banque (bãːk) *f*, bank; banking; workbench. ~ *de données*, data bank. *carnet, livret, de ~*, passbook. *faire sauter la ~*, to break the bank.

banqueroute (bãkrut) *f*, bankruptcy. *faire ~*, to go bankrupt. **banqueroutier, ère** (tje, ɛːr) *n*, bankrupt.

banquet (bãkɛ) *m*, banquet.

banquette (bãkɛt) *f*, bench, seat; bunker (*golf*).

banquier (bãkje) *m*, banker; broker. ~ *en valeurs*, stockbroker. ¶ *a*, banking.

banquise (bãkiːz) *f*, ice floe.

banquiste (bãkist) *m*, humbug, charlatan.

baptême (batɛːm) *m*, baptism, christening. ~ *du tropique*, ~ *de la ligne*, crossing the line ducking. **baptiser** (tize) *v.t*, to baptize, christen; bless (*bell*, *etc.*); nickname, dub; water, dilute. **baptismal, e** (tismal) *a*, baptismal. **baptistère** (tɛːr) *m*, baptistry.

baquet (bakɛ) *m*, bucket, tub, trough. ~-**baignoire**, *m*, bathtub.

bar (baːr) *m*, bar (*drinking*); bass (*fish*).

baragouin (baragwẽ) *m*, gibberish, jargon, lingo. **baragouiner** (gwine) *v.i. & t*, to gibber; jabber.

baraque (barak) *f*, hut; booth; hovel.

baraterie (baratri) *f*, barratry.

baratin (baratẽ) *m*, patter, sweet talk, line. **baratiner** (tine) *v.i. & t*, to sweet-talk, spin a yarn.

baratte (barat) *f*, churn. **baratter** (te) *v.t*, to churn.

Barbade (**la**) (barbad), Barbado[e]s.

barbare (barbaːr) *a*, barbaric; barbarian; barbarous. ¶ *m*, barbarian. **barbarie** (bari) *f*, barbarism; barbarity. **barbarisme** (rism) *m*, barbarism (*Gram.*).

barbe (barb) *f*, beard; shaving; shave; barb (*feather*); awn; whiskers (*cat*); wattle; (*pl.*) burr; mold (*fungi*). *B*~-*Bleue*, m, Bluebeard. ~ *de bouc*, goatee. *la* ~-*!*, enough! *vivre dans sa* ~, to laugh up one's sleeve. *se faire faire la* ~, to get shaved. **barbelé, e** (bəle) *a*, barbed, spiked. **barbiche** (biʃ) *f*, goatee. **barbier** (bje) *m*, barber. **barbifier** (fje) *v.t*, to shave. **barbon** (bɔ̃) *m*, [old] fog[e]y. **barbouse** (buz) *m*, bearded man; secret agent (*slang*).

barboter (barbɔte) *v.i*, to dabble, paddle, splash about; flounder; wade; mumble. **barbotage** (taːʒ) *m*, dabbling, etc; mash (*for cattle*). **barboteur** (tœːr) *m*, paddler; mudlark; muddler; flounderer; duck (*tame*). **barboteuse** (tøːz) *f*, rompers.

barbouiller (barbuje) *v.t*, to daub, [be]smear; blur; scribble; bungle; mumble.

barbu, e (barby) *a*, bearded. ¶ *f*, brill.

Barcelone (barsəlɔn) *f*, Barcelona.

bardane (bardan) *f*, burdock, bur[r].

barde (bard) *m*, bard, poet; (*f.*) packsaddle; slice of bacon.

bardot (bardo) *m*, hinny.

barème (barɛːm) *m*, ready reckoner; scale; graph.

barguigner (bargiɲe) *v.t*, to shilly-shally, haggle.

baril (bari) *m*, barrel, cask. **barillet** (rijɛ) m, keg; cylinder, barrel, drum.

bariolage (barjɔlaːʒ) *m*, medley, motley. **bariolé** (le) *p.a*, motley, particolored, pied.

barnum (barnɔm) *m*, showman.

baromètre (barɔmɛtr) *m*, barometer, glass. **barométrique** (metrik) *a*, barometric(al).

baron, ne (barɔ̃, ɔn) *n*, baron, ess.

baroque (barɔk) *a*, odd, queer, quaint.

barque (bark) *f*, boat, smack, bark.

barrage (baraːʒ) *m*, barrier; dam; weir; barrage; closing (*street*); playing off (*tie*). **barre** (baːr) *f*, bar, rod, rail; stroke; stripe; cross (*on letter t*); helm, tiller, wheel (*Naut.*). ~ *à sphères*, barbell. ~ *de commande*, control rod (*nuclear reactor*). ~ *d'eau*, [tidal] bore. ~ *de dopage*, booster rod (*nuclear reactor*). ~ *de flot*, tidal wave. ~ *de pilotage*, regulating rod (*nuclear reactor*). ~ *de plage*, surf. ~ *fixe*, horizontal bar. [*jeu de*] ~*s*, prisoner's base. **barreau** (baro) *m*, bar (*lit. & law*); rung. **barrer** (re) *v.t*, to bar, rail, fence off; close; dam; cross out, strike out, blue-pencil. ~ *un chèque*, to mark a check "for deposit only." **barrette** (rɛt) *f*, (small) bar; bar brooch; biretta; cardinal's cap. **barreur** (rœːr) *m*, man at the wheel; helmsman; coxswain.

barricade (barikad) *f*, barricade. **barricader** (de) *v.t*, to barricade.

barrière (barjɛːr) *f*, barrier, fence; bar; gate; toll gate; starting post; lists (*Hist.*).

barrique (barik) *f*, cask, hogshead.

barrir (bariːr) *v.i*, to trumpet (*elephant*).

baryton (baritɔ̃) *m*, baritone; b. saxhorn.

bas, se (ba, a:s) *a,* low, lower, nether, down; shallow; cloudy; mean, vile, base, degrading; vulgar; cheap. *bas âge,* infancy. *avoir la vue basse,* to be shortsighted. *faire main basse sur,* to lay violent hands on. bas, *ad,* low, low down; down; off. ¶ *m,* bottom, foot; lower notes (*Mus.*); stocking; (*pl.*) hose. à ~, *ad,* down [with] . . . ! *bas les mains!* hands off! en ~, *ad,* at the bottom; below; down; downward; downstairs.

basalte (bazalt) *m,* basalt.

basane (bazan) *f,* sheepskin, roan, basan, basil. **basané, e** (ne) *a,* tanned, tawny, swarthy, sunburnt.

bas-bleu (bablø) *m,* bluestocking.

bas-côté (bakote) *m,* aisle.

bascule (baskyl) *f,* balanced lever; rocker; seesaw. [*balance à*] ~, weighing machine, scale[s]. ~ *romaine,* platform scales. à ~, flip-flop (*computers*). **basculer** (le) *v.i,* to seesaw, swing, rock, tip [up], tilt. *faire* ~, to dip (*auto headlights*).

base (ba:z) *f,* base, bottom, foot; basis, groundwork; group of militants in a political party or union. ~ *de lancement,* launching base, range (*missiles, spacecraft*). *jeter les* ~*s,* to lay foundations.

bas-fond (bafɔ̃) *m,* lowland, flat, bottom; shallows (*Naut.*). ~*s de la société,* underworld.

basilic (bazilik) *m,* [sweet] basil; basilisk.

basilique (bazilik) *f,* basilica.

basique (bazik) *a,* basic, basal.

basque (bask) *f,* skirt, tail.

bas-relief (barəljɛf) *m,* low relief, bas-relief.

basse (ba:s) *f,* bass [voice, singer, string, tuba]; cello; reef, flat (*Naut.*)

basse-cour (basku:r) *f,* farmyard, barnyard, poultry yard, stable yard.

bassement (basmɑ̃) *ad,* meanly, basely. **bassesse** (sɛs) *f,* meanness, etc; humbleness (*birth*).

basset (basɛ) *m,* basset. ~ *allemand,* dachshund.

bassin (basɛ̃) *m,* basin, bowl, pan; scale (*pan*); [collection] plate; ornamental lake; dock; pelvis. ~ *à flot,* wet dock. ~ *à sec,* dry dock. ~ [*de garde-robe*], ~ *pour malade,* = *de lit,* bedpan. **bassine** (sin) *f,* pan, copper. **bassinet** (nɛ) *m,* buttercup. **bassinoire** (nwa:r) *f,* warming pan.

basson (basɔ̃) *m,* bassoon.

bastonnade (bastɔnad) *f,* cudgeling.

bas-ventre (bavɑ̃:tr) *m,* lower part of the abdomen.

bât (ba) *m,* packsaddle.

bataclan (bataklɑ̃) *m,* traps, hamper.

bataille (bata:j) *f,* battle, fight, fray. **batailler** (taje) *v.i,* to battle, fight; struggle; wrangle. **batailleur, euse** (jœ:r, ø:z) *a,* combative, pugnacious. **bataillon** (tajɔ̃) *m,* battalion, host; heap. ~ *de travailleurs,* labor battalion.

bâtard, e (ba:ta:r, ard) *a. & n,* bastard, mongrel; loaf of bread. **bâtardise** (tardi:z) *f,* bastardy.

bateau (bato) *m,* boat, ship, vessel, smack. ~ *à rames,* row[ing] boat. ~ *à roues,* paddle b. ~ *à vapeur,* steamboat. ~ *à voiles,* sailing b. ~-*citerne,* tanker. ~ *d'habitation,* houseboat. ~ *de passage,* ferryboat. ~ *de promenade,* row[ing] b. (*pleasure*). ~ *de sauvetage,* lifeboat. ~-*feu,* lightship. ~ *omnibus,* ~-*mouche,* water [omni]bus. ~-*porte, m,* caisson (*dock*). *mener quelqu'un en* ~, to trick someone. *monter un* ~ *à quelqu'un,* to pull a trick on someone. **batelage** (tla:ʒ) *m,* lighterage; acrobatic tricks. **batelée** (tle) *f,* boatload. **bateleur** (tlœ:r) *m,* knock-about comedian. **batelier** (təlje) *m,* bargeman, bargee, lighterman. **batellerie** (tɛlri) *f,* inland navigation; small craft.

bâti (bati) *m,* tacking, basting (*Need.*); frame[work], casing. ~ [*d'assise*], bed plate. ~ *de forge,* smith's hearth.

batifoler (batifɔle) *v.i,* to romp, frolic, skylark; dally (*amorously*).

bâtiment (batimɑ̃) *m,* building; house; vessel, ship. ~ *de guerre,* man-of-war. **bâtir** (ti:r) *v.t, & abs,* to build; tack, baste (*Need.*). **bâtisse** (tis) *f,* masonry.

batiste (batist) *f*, cambric, batiste.

bâton (batɔ̃) *m*, stick; cudgel; tinglestick; staff; truncheon; baton; pole; perch; support (*fig.*). ~ *d'or*, wallflower. ~ *de rouge* [*pour les lèvres*], lipstick. *à* ~*s rompus*, by fits & starts, desultorily. **bâtonner** (tɔne) *v.t*, to beat; cudgel. **bâtonnet** (nɛ) *m*, [tip]cat; chopstick.

battage (bata:ʒ) *m*, beating; threshing; churning. **battant** (tɑ̃) *m*, clapper (*bell*); leaf (*door*). ~ *neuf*, brand-new. *pluie battante*, pelting rain. **batte** (bat) *f*, beater. ~ *à beurre*, churn dash[er]. **battement** (tmɑ̃) *m*, beating, beat, etc, as *battre*. **batterie** (tri) *f*, fight, scuffle; battery; beat[ing]; set, utensils; percussion instruments; (*s. & pl.*) plan(s), tactics. ~ *de tambour*, roll of the drum. **batteur** (tœ:r) *m*, beater; whisk. ~ *de pavé*, lounger, loafer. ~ *en grange*, thresher (*pers.*). **batteuse** (tø:z) *f*, threshing machine. **battoir** (twa:r) *m*, beater; battledore. **battre** (tr) *v.t. & i. ir*, to beat, strike, batter; scour (*country*); thrash; thresh; churn; hammer; ram; coin, mint; raise (*money*); fly (*national flag*); shell (*Mil.*); clap (*hands*); shuffle (*cards*); bang; flap; jar; throb, pulsate, pant; tick (*clock*). ~ *contrevapeur*, to reverse steam. *se* ~, to fight. *se* ~ *les flancs*, to lash its tail. **battu, e** (ty) *p.a*, beaten. ¶ *f*, drive, battue, beat (*Hunt.*); tramp (*of horse*).

bau (bo) *m*, beam (*ship's timber*).

baudet (bodɛ) *m*, donkey.

baudrier (bodrie) *m*, cross belt.

baudruche (bodryʃ) *f*, goldbeater's skin.

baume (bo:m) *m*, balsam, balm. **baumier** (bomje) *m*, balsam [tree].

bavarder (bavarde) *v.i*, to prate, blab; gossip.

bavarois, e (bavarwa, a:z) *a. & B*~, *n*, Bavarian.

bave (ba:v) *f*, drivel; slobber; slime. **baver** (bave) *v.i*, to drivel; slobber. **bavette** (vɛt) *f*, **bavoir**

(vwa:r) *m*, bib, feeder. **bavure** (vy:r) *f*, smear; burr; seam.

Bavière (la) (bavjɛ:r), Bavaria.

bayer aux corneilles (bɛje), to stargaze, gape [at the moon].

bayette (bɛjɛt) *f*, baize.

bazar (baza:r) *m*, bazaar, arcade (*of shops*); (*cheap*) stores.

béant, e (beɑ̃, ɑ̃:t) *a*, gaping, yawning, open.

béat, e† (bea, at) *a*, sanctimonious; blissful; smug, self-satisfied. ¶ *n*, saint. **béatifier** (tifje) *v.t*, to beatify. **béatitude** (tyd) *f*, beatitude, blessedness, bliss.

beau, bel, belle (bo, bɛl) *a*, beautiful, fine, handsome, fair, pretty, comely, lovely, good, nice; graceful; fashionable; smart; bright; palmy (*days*). *le beau monde*, fashionable society. *avoir beau dire*, to speak in vain. *bel esprit*, [man of] wit; witling. *bel & bien*, ad, fairly; plainly. *à la belle étoile*, in the open [air]. **beau**, *m*, beautiful; beau, Adonis. *au* ~, *au* ~ *fixe*, at fair, at set fair (*barometer*). *faire le* ~, to beg (*dog*). *tout* ~!, careful!, hold it! **beaucoup** (ku) *ad. & m*, a great (*or* good) deal, a good (*or* great) many, very much; much, many, greatly. *de* ~, by far. **beau-fils**, *m*, stepson. **beau-frère**, *m*, brother-in-law. **beau-père**, *m*, father-in-law; stepfather.

beaupré (bopre) *m*, bowsprit.

beauté (bote) *f*, beauty, fairness, loveliness, comeliness; belle.

beaux-arts (boza:r) *m.pl*, fine arts, art.

bébé (bebe) *m*, baby; [baby] doll. ~ *dormeur*, sleeping doll.

bec (bɛk) *m*, beak, bill; nose, nozzle, snout; jaw; spout; mouthpiece; mouth; lip, tip; burner, jet; nib; point; cutwater. ~ *de gaz*, gas burner; lamppost. *le* ~ *dans l'eau*, in a fix, mess.

bécarre (beka:r) (*Mus.*) *m. & a*, natural, cancel.

bécasse (bekas) *f*, woodcock. **bécasseau** (so) *m*, sandpiper. **bécassine** (sin) *f*, snipe.

bec-de-cane (bɛkdəkan) *m*, slide bolt; lever handle; flat-nosed pliers.

bec-de-corbeau (bɛkdəkɔrbo) *m*, wire cutter.

bec-de-lièvre (bɛkdəljɛːvr) *m*, harelip.

bêche (bɛʃ) *f*, spade. **bêcher** (ʃe) *v.t*, to dig, spade.

becquetance (bɛktɑ̃ːs) *f*, food, grub (*slang*).

becqueter (bɛkte) *v.t*, to peck, pick. **se ~**, to bill.

bedeau (bədo) *m*, beadle; verger.

beffroi (befrwa) *m*, belfry; gantry.

bégayer (begɛje) *v.i. & t*, to stutter, stammer, lisp, falter. **bégaiement** (gɛmɑ̃) *m*, stuttering, etc.

bègue (bɛːg) *n*, stutterer, stammerer.

bégueule (begœl) *f*, prude. ¶ *a*, prudish, squeamish, straitlaced. **bégueulerie** (lri) *f*, prudery, etc.

beignet (bɛɲɛ) *m*, fritter (*Cook.*).

bêlement (bɛlmɑ̃) *m*, bleat[ing], baa[ing]. **bêler** (le) *v.i*, to bleat, baa.

belette (bəlɛt) *f*, weasel.

belge (bɛlʒ) *a. & B~*, *n*, Belgian. **la Belgique** (ʒik), Belgium.

bélier (belje) *m*, ram, tup; battering ram.

belladone (bɛladɔn) *f*, belladonna, deadly nightshade.

bellâtre (bɛlɑːtr) *a*, dandified, foppish.

belle (bɛl) *f*, beauty; deciding game, rubber. *la B~ au bois dormant*, the Sleeping Beauty. *la B~ & la Bête*, Beauty & the Beast. **~-de-jour**, *f*, convolvulus. **~-fille**, *f*, stepdaughter; daughter-in-law. **bellement** (lmɑ̃) *ad*, softly, gently. **belle-mère**, *f*, stepmother; mother-in-law. **belles-lettres**, *f.pl*, polite letters *or* literature. **belle-sœur**, *f*, sister-in-law.

belligérant, e (bɛliʒerɑ̃, ɑ̃ːt) *a. & n*, belligerent. **belliqueux, euse** (bɛlikø, øːz) *a*, warlike, bellicose.

bellot, te (bɛlo, ɔt) *a*, pretty; dapper.

belvédère (bɛlvedɛːr) *m*, belvedere, lookout.

bémol (bemɔl) *m. & att*, flat (*Mus.*).

bénédicité (benedisite) *m*, grace, blessing (*before meals*). **bénédiction** (ksjɔ̃) *f*, consecration, blessing; benediction. *qûe c'est une ~*, with a vengeance, & no mistake.

bénéfice (benefis) *m*, advantage, benefit; profit; living, benefice (*Eccl.*). **bénéficiaire** (sjɛːr) *a*, [showing a] profit; in credit. ¶ *n*, beneficiary, payee. **bénéficier** (sje) *v.i*, to [make a] profit, benefit.

benêt (bənɛ) *a.m*, silly, simple, foolish. ¶ *m*, booby, simpleton, noodle.

bénévole† (benevɔl) *a*, kind; voluntary.

Bengale (le) (bɛ̃gal), Bengal **bengali** (li) *a.inv. & (bird) m. & B~ (pers.) m*, Bengali.

béni, e (beni) *p.p*, blessed, blest. **bénin, igne†** (benɛ̃, iɲ) *a*, benign, benignant, kind; mild. **bénir** (niːr) *v.t*, to consecrate; bless; thank. **bénit, e** (ni, ite) *p.p*, consecrated, holy (*bread, water*). **bénitier** (tje) *m*, holy-water basin, stoup.

benjoin (bɛ̃ʒwɛ̃) *m*, benzoin, benjamin.

benne (bɛn) *f*, hamper, basket; bucket, kibble, tub (*Min.*).

benzine (bɛzin) *f*, benzine.

benzol (bɛzɔl) *m*, benzol, benzene.

béquille (bekiːj) *f*, crutch; crutch handle; crutch key; spud (*Agric.*).

bercail (bɛrkaːj) *m*, fold (*Relig.*).

berceau (bɛrso) *m*, cradle; cot; arbor, bower. **bercelonnette** (səlɔnɛt) *f*, bassinet, cot. **bercer** (se) *v.t*, to rock, dandle; lull; bring up; cherish. **berceuse** (søːz) *f*, rocker (*pers.*); rocking chair; lullaby.

béret [basque] (berɛ) *m*, beret.

bergamote (bɛrgamɔt) *f*, bergamot (*orange, pear*). **bergamotier** (tje) *m*, bergamot [tree] (*orange*).

berge (bɛrʒ) *f*, bank (*river, road*); year (*usually plural*).

berger (bɛrʒe) *m*, shepherd; swain. **bergère** (ʒɛːr) *f*, shepherdess; nymph; easy chair. **bergerie** (ʒəri) *f*, [sheep]fold, pen. **bergeronnette** (rɔnɛt) *f*, wagtail.

berline (bɛrlin) *f*, four-door sedan.

berlue (bɛrly) *f*, faulty vision. *avoir la ~*, to get it all wrong.

Bermudes (les) (bɛrmyd) *f.pl*, the Bermudas.

bernacle (bɛrnakl) *f*, barnacle (*Crust.*). **bernard-l'ermite** (narlɛrmit) *m*, hermit crab.

berne (bɛrn) *f*, banter. *en ~*, at half-mast (*flag*). **berner** (ne) *v.t*, to make fun of; chaff.

bernique (bɛrnik) *i*, nothing doing!

béryl (beril) *m*, beryl.

besace (bəzas) *f*, scrip, wallet (*beggar's*). *réduit à la ~*, reduced to beggary.

besicles (bəzikl) *f.pl*, eyeglasses.

besogne (bəzɔɲ) *f*, [piece of] work, task, job. *~ alimentaire*, potboiler. **besogneux, euse** (ɲø, ø:z) *a*, needy, impecunious. **besoin** (zwɛ̃) *m*, need; requirement; pinch; [referee in] case of need (*Com.*).

bestial, e† (bɛstjal) *a*, bestial; beastly; hoggish. **bestiaux** (tjo) *m.pl*, cattle. **bêta** (bɛta) *m*, blockhead, fool. **bétail** (beta:j) *m*, cattle. **bête** (bɛ:t) *f*, beast, animal; creature; fool. *~ à bon Dieu*, ladybird. *~ noire*, pet aversion. *~s fauves*, deer; wild beasts (*big felines*). *chercher la petite ~*, to look for trouble. ¶ †, *a*, stupid, foolish, silly. **bêtise** (beti:z) *f*, stupidity; nonsense.

béton (betɔ̃) *m*, concrete. *~ armé*, reinforced concrete.

bette (bɛt) *f*, white beet. **betterave** (tra:v) *f*, beetroot, beet. *~ à sucre*, sugar beet. *~ fourragère*, mangel[-wurzel].

beugler (bøgle) *v.i. & t*, to bellow, low, moo; bawl.

beurre (bœ:r) *m*, butter. *~ d'anchois*, anchovy paste. *un oeil au ~ noir*, a black eye. **beurrée** (bœre) *f*, slice of bread & butter. **beurrer** (re) *v.t*, to butter. **beurrier** (rje) *m*, butter dish.

bévue (bevy) *f*, blunder; howler.

biais (bjɛ) *m*, slant; skew; bias; bent; dodge, shift. **biaiser** (ze) *v.i*, to slant; dodge, shuffle, shift.

bibelot (biblo) *m*, curio, knickknack.

biberon, ne (bibrɔ̃, ɔn) *n*, tippler; (*m.*) feeding bottle.

Bible (bibl) *f*, Bible. **bibliographie** (bliɔgrafi) *f*, bibliography. **bibliophile** (fil) *m*, bibliophile, booklover. **bibliothécaire** (tekɛ:r) *n*, librarian. **bibliothéconomie** (tekɔnɔmi) *f*, library science. **bibliothèque** (tek) *f*, library; bookcase; bookstall. *~ circulante*, circulating library. *~ de prêt*, lending l. *~ où les livres se consultent sur place & ~ d'ouvrages à consulter*, reference library. **biblique** (blik) *a*, biblical; Bible (*Society*). **biblorhapte** (blɔrapt) *m*, binder.

bic (bik) *m*, ballpoint pen.

biceps (bisɛps) *m*, biceps.

biche (biʃ) *f*, hind (*deer*).

bichon, ne (biʃɔ̃, ɔn) *n*, Maltese [dog, bitch], lap dog. **bichonner** (ʃɔne) *v.t*, to curl; titivate.

bicot (biko) *m*, kid (*goat*); Arab (*pejorative*).

bicoque (bikɔk) *f*, shanty.

bicycle (bisikl) *m*, bicycle. **bicyclette** (klɛt) *f*, [safety] bicycle, cycle. *~ de course*, racer. **bicycliste** (klist) *n*, [bi]cyclist.

bidasse (bidas) *m*, private (*soldier*).

bidet (bidɛ) *m*, nag, cob; bidet.

bidon (bidɔ̃) *m*, canteen, water bottle (*Mil.*); drum (*gasoline*, etc.), can. **bidonville** (vil) *m*, hooverville, shantytown.

bidule (bidyl) *m*, thing, gadget, thingamabob.

bief (bjɛf) *m*, race[way] (*mill*); pond (*canal*).

bielle (bjɛl) *f*, [connecting] rod; strut, brace.

bien (bjɛ̃) *ad*, well; right, proper; nicely, all right; clearly; fully; thoroughly; much; very; far; fast; fain; indeed; duly; really, quite. *~ de*, much, many. *~ que*, *c*, [al]though. ¶ *m*, good; weal; blessing; endowment; mercy; (*oft. pl.*) possessions, property, chattel, estate, substance. *~ immeubles*, real property. *~s mal acquis*, ill-gotten gains. *~s [transmissibles par voie de succession]*, hereditament.

bien-aimé, e *ou* **bienaimé,** ‹ (bjɛ̃neme) *a. & n*, [well-]beloved, darling.

bien-dire (bjɛ̃di:r) *m*, fine speaking. **bien-disant, e** (dizɑ̃, ɑ̃:t) *a*, well-spoken, fair-spoken.

bien-être (bjɛ̃nɛːtr) *m*, well-being; welfare.

bienfaisance (bjɛ̃fəzãːs) *f*, beneficence; benevolence; bounteousness; charity; donations. **bienfaisant, e** (zã, ãːt) *a*, beneficent, etc. **bienfait** (fɛ) *m*, kindness, benefaction, benefit, boon; mercy. **bienfaiteur, trice** (tœːr, tris) *n*, benefactor, tress.

bienheureux, euse (bjɛ̃nœrø, øːz) *a*, blessed; blissful.

biennal, e (bjɛnal) *a*, biennial.

bienséant, e (bjɛ̃seã, ãːt), *a*, proper, becoming, decorous.

biens-fonds (bjɛ̃fɔ̃) *m.pl*, real estate.

bientôt (bjɛ̃to) *ad*, soon, shortly.

bienveillant, e (bjɛ̃vɛjã, ãːt) *a*, kind[ly], friendly.

bienvenue (bjɛ̃vny) *f*, welcome; footing.

bière (bjɛːr) *f*, beer; coffin. *~ au tonneau*, *~ à la pompe*, draught beer. *~ blonde*, pale ale. *~ brune*, dark ale.

biffer (bife) *v.t*, to strike out, cross out, delete, rule out, cancel.

bifteck (biftɛk) *m*, [beef]steak.

bifurcation (bifyrkasjɔ̃) *f*, bifurcation, fork; junction.

bigame (bigam) *a*, bigamous. ¶ *n*, bigamist. **bigamie** (mi) *f*, bigamy.

bigarade (bigarad) *f*, Seville orange.

bigarré, e (bigare) *p.a*, variegated, particolored, pied, motley. **bigarrer** (re) *v.t*, to variegate, medley; [inter]lard.

bigorneau (bigɔrno) *m*, [peri]winkle (*Crust.*).

bigot, e (bigo, ɔt) *a*, bigoted. ¶ *n*, bigot. **bigoterie** (gɔtri) *f*, bigotry.

bigoudi (bigudi) *m*, hair curler.

bijou (biʒu) *m*, jewel, gem; darling. **bijouterie** (tri) *f*, jewelry. **bijoutier, ère** (tje, ɛːr) *n*, jeweler.

bilan (bilã) *m*, balance sheet; statement of affairs. *déposer son ~*, to file a petition in bankruptcy.

bilboquet (bilbɔkɛ) *m*, cup & ball.

bile (bil) *f*, bile. *se faire de la ~*, to get upset, worry. **bilieux, euse** (ljø, øːz) *a*, bilious.

billard (bijaːr) *m*, billiards. [*salle de*] *~*, billiard room.

bille (biːj) *f*, ball; billiard ball; marble (*games*); sawlog; bar.

billet (bijɛ) *m*, note, bill; ticket. *~ à ordre*, note of hand, promissory note. *~ à prix réduit*, cheap ticket. *~ d'aller & retour*, round-trip ticket. *~ de banque*, bank note. *~ de complaisance*, accommodation note. *~ de faire-part*, wedding or funeral announcement. *~ de faveur*, free pass, complimentary ticket. *~ de quai*, platform ticket. *~ de logement*, billet (*Mil.*). *~ doux*, love letter. *~ garde-place*, *~ de location de place*, reserved seat ticket. *~ global*, through ticket (*sea-land-sea*). *~ perdant*, blank (*lottery*).

billevesée (bilvəze) *f*, nonsense.

billion (biljɔ̃) *m*, billion.

billon (bijɔ̃) *m*, ridge (*Agric.*); copper &/or nickel [coin].

billot (bijo) *m*, [chopping] block.

bimbelot (bɛ̃blo) *m*, fancy article. **bimbeloterie** (blɔtri) *f*, fancy goods.

bimensuel, le (bimãsɥɛl) *a*, semimonthly, twice monthly. **bimestriel, le** (mɛstriɛl) *a*, bimonthly, [in] alternate months.

binaire (binɛːr) *a*, binary. *chiffre ~*, binary digit (*computers*). *nombre ~*, binary number. *notation ~*, binary notation.

biner (bine) *v.t*, to hoe. **binette** (nɛt) *f*, hoe.

binocle (binɔkl) *m*, eyeglasses.

biographe (biɔgraf) *m*, biographer. **biographie** (fi) *f*, biography.

biologie (biɔlɔʒi) *f*, biology. **biologiste** (ʒist), **biologue** (lɔg) *m*, biologist.

bipasse (bipas) *m*, bypass, shunt.

bipède (bipɛd) *a*, biped[al]. ¶ *m*, biped.

biplan (biplã) *m*, biplane.

bique (bik) *f*, nanny [goat]. *vieille ~*, unpleasant old woman.

birman, e (birmã, an) *a.* & **B~**, *n*, Burmese. **la Birmanie** (mani), Burma.

bis, e (bi, iːz) *a*, brownish gray; brown (*bread*).

bis (bis) *ad*, bis, repeat (*Mus.*).

encore. ¶ *m*, encore. ¶ *a*, ᴬ, ½ (*house number*).

bisaïeul, e (bizajœl) *n*, great-grandfather, -mother.

bisannuel, le (bizanɥɛl) *a*, biennial.

bisbille (bizbi:j) *f*, squabble. **en ~**, at loggerheads.

biscornu, e (biskɔrny) *a*, misshapen; queer, odd.

biscotte (biskɔt) *f*, rusk. **biscuit** (kɥi) *m*, biscuit; zwieback. **~ de Savoie**, sponge cake.

bise (bi:z) *f*, north wind, chilly blast of wind; kiss on the cheek. **se faire la ~**, to kiss each other on the cheek. **biser** (ze) *v.t*, to kiss.

biseau (bizo) *m*, bevel. **biseauter** (te) *v.t*, to bevel.

bismuth (bismyt) *m*, bismuth.

bison (biz5) *m*, bison.

bissac (bisak) *m*, wallet, bag.

bissection (bisɛksj5) *f*, bisection.

bisser (bise) *v.t*, to encore.

bissextile (bisɛkstil) *a*, leap (*year*).

bistourner (bisturne) *v.t*, to twist, wrench.

bit (bit) *m*, bit (*Min.*); bit (*computers, Math.*).

bite (bit) *f*, penis (*obscene*).

bitume (bitym) *m*, bitumen, pitch, asphalt. **bitumineux, euse** (minø, ø:z) *a*, bituminous; tarry.

bivalve (bivalv) *a. & m*, bivalve.

bivouac (bivwak) *m*, bivouac. **bivouaquer** (ke) *v.i*, to bivouac, camp out.

bizarre† (biza:r) *a*, odd, queer, peculiar, freakish, outlandish. **bizarrerie** (zarri) *f*, oddness, etc.

blackbouler (blakbule) *v.t*, to blackball.

blafard, e (blafa:r, ard) *a*, pale, pallid, wan; lurid.

blague (blag) *f*, [tobacco] pouch; gammon, bunkum, rubbish, humbug, blarney, chaff; bounce, brag. **sans ~**, you don't say. **blaguer** (blage) *v.i*, to joke; rib. **blagueur** (gœ:r) *m*, joker; humbug.

blaireau (blɛro) *m*, badger; shaving brush.

blâme (bla:m) *m*, blame, reprimand. **blâmer** (blame) *v.t*, to blame.

blanc, che (blɑ̃, ɑ̃:ʃ) *a*, white;

hoary; blank, clean; fair (*skin*). **le mont Blanc**, Mont Blanc. **~ de lessive**, fresh from the wash. ¶ *m*, white (*color, man, etc.*); blank; margin (*book page*), chalk (*Bil.*); breast (*fowl*). **~ de baleine**, spermaceti. **~ de céruse**, white lead. **~ de champignon**, mushroom spawn. **~ de chaux**, whitewash. **~ de craie**, whiting. **~ de grand fond**, front margin. **~ de petit fond**, back margin, (*pl. col.*) gutter. **~ de pied**, bottom margin. **~ de terre à pipe**, pipe clay. **~ de tête**, top margin. **nuit blanche**, sleepless night.

blanc-bec (blɑ̃bɛk) *m*, callow youth.

blanchaille (blɑ̃ʃa:j) *f*, fry; whitebait.

blanchâtre (blɑ̃ʃɑ:tr) *a*, whitish. **blanche** (blɑ̃:ʃ) *f*, white (*woman, ball*); minim (*Mus.*). **blancheur** (blɑ̃ʃœ:r) *f*, whiteness. **blanchir** (ʃi:r) *v.t. & i*, to whiten; blanch; bleach; whitewash; wash; wash for; launder; clean up; scald. **~ à la chaux**, to whitewash. **blanchisserie** (ʃisri) *f*, laundry. **blanchisseuse** (sø:z) *f*, washerwoman. **~ [de fin]**, [fine] laundress.

blanc-manger (blɑ̃mɑ̃ʒe) *m*, blancmange.

blanc-seing (blɑ̃sɛ̃) *m*, blank signature.

blaser (blɑze) *v.t*, to blunt, surfeit, pall on.

blason (blɑz5) *m*, coat of arms, armorial bearings; blazon[ry], heraldry. **blasonner** (zɔne) *v.t*, to [em]blazon; malign.

blasphémateur, trice (blasfematœ:r, tris) *n*, blasphemer. **blasphématoire** (twa:r) *a*, blasphemous. **blasphème** (fɛ:m) *m*, blasphemy; profanity. **blasphémer** (feme) *v.i. & t*, to blaspheme, curse.

blatte (blat) *f*, cockroach, black beetle.

blé (ble) *m*, wheat. [**champ de**] **~**, wheatfield. **~ à moudre**, grist. **~ de Turquie**, Indian corn, maize. **~ noir**, buckwheat.

bled (blɛd) *f*, inland country (*in North Africa*); burg, one-horse town. **quelle ~**, what a dump!

blême (blɛːm) *a*, pale, pallid, wan, ghastly. **blêmir** (blemiːr) *v.i*, to [turn] pale.

bléser (bleze) *v.i*, to lisp.

blesser (blɛse) *v.t*, to wound, hurt, injure, gall; grate upon (*ear*); shock, offend; pinch (*shoes*). ~ *à mort*, to injure fatally. ~ *quelqu'un au cœur*, to hurt someone's feelings. **blessure** (syːr) *f*, wound, etc.

blet, te (blɛ, ɛt) *a*, overripe, soft.

bleu, e (blø) *a*, blue; underdone (*meat*); ¶ *m*, blue; blue mark (*bruise*); blueprint; recruit (*Mil.*); ~ *de ciel*, ~ *céleste*, sky blue. ~ *marine*, navy b. *conte* ~, fairy tale. **bleuâtre** (ɑːtr) *a*, bluish. **bleuet** (ɛ) *m*, cornflower. **bleuir** (iːr) *v.t. & i*, to blue.

blindage (blɛ̃daːʒ) *m*, armor-plating; armor; sheeting; shield (*atomic physics*).

bloc (blɔk) *m*, block, lump; coalition (*Pol.*); guardroom. ~ *journalier*, block calendar.

blocage (blɔkaːʒ) , rubble[work]; clamping, as *bloquer;* locking (*screw, etc.*); price &/or wage freeze. **blocaille** (kɑːj) *f*, rubble[stone], ballast.

bloc-film (blɔkfilm) *m*, film pack.

blockhaus (blɔkoːs) *m*, blockhouse; conning tower.

bloc-mémorandum (blɔkmemɔrɑ̃dɔm) *m*, scribbling block. **bloc-notes** (nɔt) *m*. ou **bloc de correspondance**, [*writing*] pad. **bloc-sténo** (steno) *m*, shorthand notebook.

blocus (blɔkyːs) *m*, blockade.

blond, e (blɔ̃, ɔ̃ːd) *a*, fair, flaxen, blond, e; light. ¶ *n*, fair-haired person, blond, e. ¶ *m*, blond, e, flaxen (*color*). ~ *ardent*, auburn. ~ *cendré*, ash blonde. ~ *doré*, golden (*hair*). ~ *hasardé*, reddish (*hair*). ~ *platine*, platinum blonde. ~ *roux*, sandy (*hair*).

bloquer (blɔke) *v.t*, to clamp, lock; tie up; lump; blockade; block.

blottir (se) (blɔtiːr) *v.pr*, to squat, crouch, couch, cower; lie hid; cuddle up, nestle, snuggle, nuzzle, huddle.

blouse (bluːz) *f*, smock; blouse. ~[-*paletot*], *f*, overalls. **blouser**

(bluze) *v.t*, to take in, dupe. **blouson** (zɔ̃) *m*, lumber-jacket. ~ *doré*, spoiled rich kid. ~ *noir*, black leather jacket, juvenile delinquent.

bluette (blyɛt) *f*, literary trifle.

bluter (blyte) *v.t*, to bolt, sift.

boa (bɔa) *m*, boa (*wrap*). ~ *constrictor* (kɔ̃striktɔːr), boa constrictor.

bobine (bɔbin) *f*, bobbin, drum, reel, spool; coil (*Elec.*). ~ *débitrice*, supply reel. ~ *d'enroulement*, take-up reel. **bobiner** (ne) *v.t*, to wind, coil.

bobo (bɔbo) *m*, slight injury; bump.

bocage (bɔkaːʒ) *m*, grove. **bocager, ère** (kaʒe, ɛːr) *a*, sylvan, wood (*nymph*).

bocal (bɔkal) *m*, bottle, jar; globe, fishbowl.

bocard (bɔkaːr) *m*, stamp [mill]. **bocarder** (karde) *v.t*, to mill, stamp (*ore*).

bock (bɔk) *m*, glass (*for, or of, beer*).

bœuf (bœf) *m*, ox, bullock; beef. ~ *salé*, corned beef.

bohème (bɔɛːm) *n. & a*, Bohemian (*n. & a.*), free & easy. *la* ~, Bohemia (*fig.*). **bohémien, ne** (emjɛ̃, ɛn) *n*, gypsy.

boire (bwaːr) *v.t. & i. ir*, to drink; absorb; imbibe; swallow, pocket (*insult*); drown. ~ *un coup*, to have a drink.

bois (bwa) *m*, wood; park; horns, antlers, head (*stag*); stock (*rifle, plane*); stuff (*one is made of*); (*pl.*) wood[-wind] (*Mus.*). ~ *à brûler*, ~ *de chauffage*, firewood. ~ *contreplaqué*, plywood. ~ [*de charpente*], timber, lumber. ~ *de lit*, bedstead. ~ *de placage*, veneer. ~ *de rose*, tulip wood. ~ *de satin*, satin w. ~ *plaqué triplé*, 3-ply w. **boisage** (zaːʒ) *m*, timbering. **boisement** (zmɑ̃) *m*, afforestation. **boiser** (ze) *v.t*, to timber; wainscot; afforest. **boiserie** (zri) *f*, woodwork; wainscoting.

boisseau (bwaso) *m*, bushel.

boisson (bwasɔ̃) *f*, drink, beverage, liquor.

boîte (bwaːt) *f*, box, case, chest, caddy, canister, can; a place of work: ~ *noire*, black box (*airplane*). *une grosse* ~, important business firm. ~ [*à conserves*], [preserving] can. ~ *à musique*, music box. ~ *de nuit*, nightclub. ~ *de vitesses*, gear box. *mettre en* ~, to pull somebody's leg.

boiter (bwate) *v.i*, to limp, halt, hobble. **boiterie** (tri) *f*, lameness. **boiteux, euse** (tø, ø:z) *a*, lame; halting; rickety.

boitier (bwatje) *m*, box with divisions; case (*watch*).

bol (bɔl) *m*, bowl, basin; bolus. ~ *rince-doigts*, finger bowl.

bolduc (bɔldyk) *m*, ribbon for gift wrapping; red tape.

Bolivie (la) (bɔlivi), Bolivia. **bolivien, ne** (vjɛ̃, ɛn) *a. & B~, n*, Bolivian.

Bologne (bɔlɔɲ) *f*, Bologna.

bombance (bɔ̃bɑ̃:s) *f*, feasting, junketing.

bombardement (bɔ̃bardəmɑ̃) *m*, bombardment, shelling, bombing. **bombarder** (de) *v.t*, to bombard. ~ *quelqu'un à une place*, to pitchfork someone into an office. **bombe** (bɔ̃:b) *f*, bomb; ball (*signal*); bombshell (*fig.*). *faire la* ~, to paint the town red.

bomber (bɔ̃be) *v.t. & i. & se* ~, to bulge, swell, camber, belly; bend.

bon, ne (bɔ̃, ɔn) *a*, good; sound; kind; nice; fine; boon (*companion*); palatable; fit; right; proper; safe; fast (*color*). **bon**, *comps:* ~ *enfant*, good-natured. [*à*] ~ *marché, a*, cheap, *à* ~ *marché, ad*, cheap[ly]. ~ *sens* (sɑ̃), [common] sense, [right] senses. **bonne**, *comps: la* ~ *année*, a happy New Year. ~ *bouche*, tidbit. ~ *femme*, simple good-natured woman. ~ *fin*, meeting (*engagement, bills*), protection (*bills*). ~ *maman*, grandmama, granny. **bon**, stet (*Typ.*). **bon à tirer**, [for] press (*Typ.*). ¶ *m*, good; cream (*of story*); order; note; license; voucher; bond; draft; scrip; profit. (*un*) ~ *à rien, m. & a*, (a) good-for-nothing, (a) ne'er-do-well. ~ *d'ouverture*, inspection order (*Cust.*). ~ *de bord*, mate's receipt. ~ *d'échange*, voucher.

bonasse (bɔnas) *a*, good-hearted; easy-going; simple-minded.

bonbon (bɔ̃bɔ̃) *m*, candy; (*pl.*) confectionery. ~*s de chocolat*, chocolates. **bonbonnière** (bɔ̃bɔnjɛ:r) *f*, confectionery box, chocolate box; sweet bowl; pretty little place (*house*).

bond (bɔ̃) *m*, bound, bounce, spring; rebound; spurt.

bonde (bɔ̃:d) *f*, bung[hole]; bung, plug. **bonder** (bɔ̃de) *v.t*, to fill to the bung, cram.

bondir (bɔ̃di:r) *v.i*, to bound, etc, as *bond*.

bondon (bɔ̃dɔ̃) *m*, bung; bondon. **bondonner** (dɔne) *v.t*, to bung.

bonheur (bɔnœ:r) *m*, happiness, welfare; [good] luck; blessing. *le* ~ *du célibat*, single blessedness. *au petit* ~, haphazardly.

bonhomie (bɔnɔmi) *f*, good nature, geniality; credulity. **bonhomme** (nɔm) *m*, simple good-natured man. *le* ~ *Noël*, Santa Claus.

bonification (bɔnifikasjɔ̃) *f*, improvement; allowance. **bonifier** (fje) *v.t*, to improve; allow, credit.

boniment (bɔnimɑ̃) *m*, patter (*showman's*); claptrap.

bonjour (bɔ̃ʒu:r) *m*, good morning, good afternoon, good day.

bonne (bɔn) *f*, [maid]servant, servant[girl]; waitress. ~ *à tout faire*, general servant, maid-of-all-work. [*d'enfant*], nurse[maid].

bonnement (bɔnmɑ̃) *m*, candidly, plainly.

bonnet (bɔnɛ) *m*, cap, hat. ~ *de police*, forage cap. ~ *magique*, wishing cap. *gros* ~, bigwig.

bonneterie (bɔntri) *f*, hosiery.

bonneteur (bɔntœ:r) *m*, card-sharper.

bonnetier (bɔntje) *m*, hosier.

bonniche (bɔniʃ) *f*, maid, female domestic (*pejorative*).

bonsoir (bɔ̃swa:r) *m*, good evening, good night.

bonté (bɔ̃te) *f*, goodness, kindness.

bookmaker (bukmekɛ:r) *m*, bookmaker. ~ *marron*, welsher.

booléen, ne (buleɛ̃, ɛɛn) *a*, Boolean. *algèbre booléen*, Boolean algebra. *opérateur booléen*, Boolean connective. *opération booléenne*, Boolean operation.

boom (bum) *m*, boom (*Fin.*); party or dance for young people.

borax (boraks) *m*, borax.

bord (bo:r) *m*, edge, border, brink, verge, fringe, rim, margin; brim; flap; edging, binding, hem; bank, side, shore, coast, strand; board, side (*ship*); tack (*Naut.*); ship. *à* ~, on board, aboard. *à grands* ~*s*, broad-brimmed (*hat*). *à pleins* ~*s*, brimful. *par-dessus* ~, overboard.

bordé (borde) *m*, braid; gimp; planking; plating (*ship*).

bordeaux (bordo) *m*, Bordeaux, claret.

bordée (borde) *f*, broadside; volley (*fig.*); board, tack (*ship*); watch (*Naut.*).

bordel (bordɛl) *m*, brothel; general disorder.

border (borde) *v.t*, to border, edge, hem, bind; flange; tuck in (*bed*); line; plate (*ship*); ship (*oars*); run along, fringe; curb.

bordereau (bordəro) *m*, memorandum, list, schedule, statement, slip, note, contract [note].

bordier (bordje) *a.m. & m*, lopsided (*boat*).

bordure (bordy:r) *f*, border, edge, edging, binding, hem, skirt, rim; curb; front (*sea, river*). ~ *de fleurs vivaces*, herbaceous border.

bore (bo:r) *m*, boron (*Chem.*).

boréal, e (boreal) *a*, boreal, north[ern].

borgne (borɲ) *a. & n*, one-eyed (person); blind; dark, dingy; frowsy; low, of ill fame. *rue* ~, blind alley, dead end.

borique (borik) *a*, boric, boracic.

borne (born) *f*, bound[ary], landmark, post; spur; terminal (*Elec.*). ~ *kilométrique*, milestone. ~ *postale*, pillar box. *dépasser les* ~*s*, to go too far. **borner** (ne) *v.t*, to bound, confine, mark out; restrict; stint.

bornoyer (bornwaje) *v.t*, to squint over (*an alignment*).

Bosphore (le) (bosfo:r), the Bosphorus.

bosquet (boskɛ) *m*, grove, spinney, thicket, shrubbery.

bosse (bos) *f*, hunch, hump; bump; dent, dint, bruise; mound; painter (*boat*). *avoir la* ~ *de*, to have a talent for. **bosseler** (sle) *v.t*, to [em]boss; dent, dint, bruise, batter. **bossoir** (swa:r) *m*, davit; cathead. **bossu, e** (sy) *a*, hunchbacked, humpbacked. ¶ *n*, hunchback, humpback. **bossuer** (sɥe) *v.t*, to dent, dint, bruise, batter.

bosser (bose) *v.i*, to work like a dog.

bot (bo) *a.m*, club (*foot*).

botanique (botanik) *a*, botanic(al). ¶ *f*, botany. **botaniste** (nist) *m*, botanist.

botte (bot) *f*, bundle, bunch; truss; coil; clump; thrust, lunge, pass; [high] boot. ~*s à genouillère*, jackboots. ~*s à l'écuyère*, riding boots. ~*s à revers*, top boots. ~*s cuissardes* (kɥisard) thigh boots; waders. ~*s montant aux genoux*, Wellingtons. **botteler** (tle) *v.t*, to bundle, bunch; truss (*hay*). **botter** (te) *v.t*, to boot, fit, put boots on. **bottier** (tje) *m*, bootmaker. **bottine** (tin) *f*, [half] boot. ~*s d'escalade*, climbing boots.

bottin (botɛ̃) *m*, directory; who's who.

bouc (buk) *m*, he-goat, billy g. ~ *émissaire*, scapegoat.

boucan (bukɑ̃) *m*, noise, racket, etc.

boucanier (bukanje) *m*, buccaneer.

boucaut (buko) *m*, cask, hogshead.

bouche (buʃ) *f*, mouth; muzzle (*gun*); nozzle; hydrant, plug, flue; living. ~ *à feu*, piece of ordnance. ~ *béante*, ~ *bée*, open-mouthed. ~ *close!* not a word! mum['s the word]! ~ *d'incendie*, fire hydrant. **bouchée** (ʃe) *f*, mouthful, bite; patty, pasty. **boucher** (ʃe) *v.t*, to stop, obstruct; shut; close; plug, seal; bung; stopper, cork: *se* ~ *le nez*, to hold one's nose. *bouché à l'émeri*, stoppered (*bottle*).

boucher (buʃe) *m*, butcher. **boucherie** (ʃri) *f*, butcher's shop; butchery; slaughter.

bouche-trou (buʃtru) *m*, stopgap.

bouchon (buʃɔ̃) *m*, stopper, cork; plug, cap, bung; wisp; bundle;

tavern; float. ~ *de vapeur*, airlock. *goût de* ~, corky taste. **bouchonner** (ʃɔne) *v.t*, to bundle up, rub down (*horse*).

boucle (bukl) *f*, buckle, ring, shackle; loop; sweep; eye, bight; curl, lock, ringlet; handle. ~ *d'amarrage*, ringbolt. **boucler** (kle) *v.t*, & *i*, to buckle; ring (*bull, etc.*); curl; loop; bulge; lock up; put away; balance (*budget*). ~ *la boucle*, to loop the loop. **bouclier** (klie) *m*, shield, buckler; shield (*atomic physics*). ~ *thermique*, heat shield.

bouddhique (budik) *a*, buddhist. **bouddhiste** (dist) *m*, buddhist.

bouder (bude) *v.i*, to sulk; shirk.

boudin (budɛ̃) *m*, blood-sausage; corkscrew curl; saddlebag; flange. ~ *d'air*, inner tube.

boue (bu) *f*, mud, dirt, mire; slime, sludge, swarf.

bouée (bue) *f*, buoy. ~ *de sauvetage*, life b.

boueux, euse (buø, ø:z) *a*, muddy, dirty, miry, mud (*spring*). ¶ *m*, scavenger.

bouffe (buf) *a*, comic.

bouffée (bufe) *f*, puff, breath, fume, whiff, gust; fit. **bouffer** (fe) *v.i*, to puff, swell; rise; bulge; *v.t*, to puff out; eat greedily (*slang*). ~ *de la vache enragée*, to have a hard time, be very poor. *se* ~ *le nez*, to have a bitter argument. **bouffi, e** (fi) *a*, puffy, swollen, bloated; turgid, bombastic. **bouffir** (fi:r) *v.t*, to swell, bloat.

bouffon, ne (bufɔ̃, ɔn) *a*, comic(al), clownish, farcical. ¶ *m*, buffoon, jester, clown; laughingstock, butt. **bouffonnerie** (fɔnri) *f*, buffoonery, foolery.

bouge (bu:ʒ) *m*, hole, hovel, den; bulge; bilge (*cask*).

bougeoir (buʒwa:r) *m*, candlestick.

bouger (buʒe) *v.i*, to budge, move, stir.

bougie (buʒi) *f*, candle. ~ *d'allumage*, spark plug. ~ *de préchauffage*, glow plug (*diesel*). *une lampe de 60* ~*s*, a 60 candlepower lamp.

bougonner (bugɔne) *v.i*, to grumble, grouse.

bougran (bugrɑ̃) *m*, buckram.

bougre (bu:gr) *m*, fellow, guy.

bouillant, e (brijɑ̃, ɑ̃:t) *a*, boiling; fiery, hotheaded. **bouillie** (ji) *f*, pap; porridge, gruel; pulp; mush. **bouilleur** (jœ:r) *m*, brandy distiller. ~ *de cru*, legal home distiller. **bouillir** (ji:r) *v.i.ir*, to boil. *faire* ~, to boil, *v.t*, ~ *à demi*, to parboil. **bouilloire** (jwa:r) *f*, kettle. ~ *à sifflet*, singing k. **bouillon** (jɔ̃) *m*, bubble; gush, spirt, spurt; broth, soup, bouillon, cup of broth, tea (*beef, etc.*); slops (*liquid diet*); restaurant; blow[hole]; puff, returns (*newspaper*). **bouillonner** (jɔne) *v.i*, to bubble, boil, seethe. **bouillotte** (jɔt) *f*, kettle; foot warmer. ~ *à eau chaude*, hot-water bottle.

boujaron (buʒarɔ̃) *m*, tot (*of rum, etc.*).

boulanger, ère (bulɑ̃ʒe, ɛ:r) *n*, baker. **boulangerie** (ʒri) *f*, baking; bakery.

boule (bul) *f*, ball; bowling ball; head (*slang*). ~ *d'eau chaude*, hot-water bottle. ~ *de neige*, snowball; guelder rose. [*jeu de*] ~*s*, [game of] bowls.

Boule (bul) *m*, buhl[work].

bouleau (bulo) *m*, birch [tree]. ~ *blanc*, silver birch. [*verge de*] ~, birch [rod].

bouledogue (buldɔg) *m*, bulldog.

bouler (bule) *v.t*, to send rolling; swell; blunder.

boulet (bulɛ) *m*, cannon ball; ball. **boulette** (lɛt) *f*, pellet.

boulevard (bulva:r) *m*, boulevard, avenue; bulwark (*fig.*).

bouleverser (bulvɛrse) *v.t*, to convulse, wreck, upset, overthrow.

boulier (bulje) *m*, ball frame, abacus; scoring board, string (*Bil.*).

boulin (bulɛ̃) *m*, pigeonhole (*in dovecot*); putlog.

boulingrin (bulɛ̃grɛ̃) *m*, lawn, grass plot.

boulon (bulɔ̃) *m*, bolt, pin. **boulonner** (lɔne) *v.t*, to bolt.

boulot, te (bulo, ɔt) *a*, dumpy, squat, squab[by], stumpy. ¶ *m*, work. *métro,* ~*, dodo*, subway, work, sleep.

bouquet (bukɛ) *m*, bouquet, nosegay, posy, bunch, cluster, tuft, clump; aroma; crowning piece; climax; prawn. *c'est le ~*, that's the last straw. **bouquetière** (ktjɛːr) *f*, flower girl.

bouquetin (buktɛ̃) *m*, ibex.

bouquin (bukɛ̃) *m*, old he-goat; buck hare; buck rabbit; [old] book (*of little value*). **bouquineur** (kinœːr) *m*, book hunter; lover of old books. **bouquiniste** (nist) *m*, secondhand bookseller.

bourbe (burb) *f*, mud. **bourbeux, euse**, (bø, øːz) *a*, muddy. **bourbier** (bje) *m*, slough, quag[mire]; scrape, fix.

bourde (burd) *f*, fib; blunder. *débiter des ~s*, to fib. *donneur* (*ou conteur*) *de ~s*, fibber.

bourdon (burdɔ̃) *m*, pilgrim's staff; bumblebee; great bell; drone (*Mus.*); drone [bee] out[, see copy] (*Typ.*). **bourdonner** (dɔne) *v.i. & t*, to hum, buzz, drone, boom, din, sing (*in ears*).

bourg (buːr) *m*, market town, borough. **bourgade** (burgad) *f*, small town, straggling village.

bourgeois, e (burʒwa, aːz) *a*, middle-class; homely, plain (*cooking, etc.*); private (*house*). *en bourgeois*, in plain clothes, in mufti. ¶ *n*, middle-class man, woman. **bourgeoisie** (ʒwazi) *f*, middle class[es]; bourgeoisie.

bourgeon (burʒɔ̃) *m*, bud; shoot; pimple. **bourgeonner** (ʒɔne) *v.i*, to bud, etc.

bourgogne *ou* **vin de B~** (burgɔɲ) *m*, burgundy.

bourlinguer (burlɛ̃ge) *v.i*, to wallow; strain (*Naut.*); rough it.

bourrade (burad) *f*, blow, thump.

bourrage (buraːʒ) *m*, stuffing, padding; cramming (*exam, etc.*); card or paper jam (*computers*). *~ de crâne*, eyewash, tripe, foolish ideas.

bourrasque (burask) *f*, squall; gust; tantrum.

bourratif (buratif) *a*, filling (*food*).

bourre (buːr) *f*, hair, flock, waste, down, fluff, floss; padding, stuffing, wad.

bourreau (buro) *m*, executioner, headsman, hangman; tyrant; tormentor. *~ d'argent*, spendthrift.

~ des cœurs, lady-killer. **bourreler** (rle) *v.t*, (*of conscience*) to torment, prick, sting. *avoir une conscience bourrelée de remords*, to be conscience-stricken.

bourrelet (burlɛ) *m*, cushion; pad; flange. **bourrelier** (rəlje) *m*, harness maker.

bourrer (bure) *v.t*, to stuff, pad; cram, choke; tamp, ram, pack; snap at; belabor, thrash.

bourriche (buriʃ) *f*, basket, frail.

bourrique (burik) *f*, she-ass; donkey.

bourru, e (bury) *a*, surly, churlish, crusty, grumpy, gruff; rough; downy. ¶ *m*, churl, bear, curmudgeon.

bourse (burs) *f*, purse, bag, pouch; scholarship; exhibition; stock exchange, market, house; session, business day, working day (*stock market*). *~ à pasteur*, shepherd's-purse (*Bot.*). *~ [des valeurs]*, stock exchange. *~ de marchandises*, *~ de commerce*, produce exchange, commercial sale rooms. **boursicoter** (sikɔte) *v.i*, to dabble on the stock exchange. **boursier, ère** (sje, ɛːr) *n*, scholarship holder; speculator.

boursouflé, e (bursufle) *p.a*, inflated, turgid, bombastic. **boursoufler** (fle) *v.t. & se ~*, to swell, puff, bloat.

bousculade (buskylad) *f*, scrimmage, hustle, rush. **bousculer** (le) *v.t*, to upset; push about, jostle, hustle; ride out (*polo*).

bouse (buːz) *f*, dung (*cattle*).

bousillage (buzijaːʒ) *m*, cob, daub, mud; bungle, botch.

bousiller (buzije) *v.t*, to ruin, botch, bungle; smash. *~ une voiture*, smash a car. *se faire ~*, to get killed.

boussole (busɔl) *f*, [magnetic] compass, dial; (*fig.*) head, wits; guide. *~ marine*, mariner's compass. *perdre la ~*, go mad.

boustifaille (bustifaːj) *f*, food, grub (*slang*). **boustifailler** (faje) *v.i*, to stuff oneself with food.

bout (bu) *m*, end; finish; extremity; tip; cap; bottom; bit, stump; ferrule; button. [*petit*] *~ d'homme*, midget, chit, manikin. *~ de lettre*,

line or two. ~ *de rôle*, small part
(*Theat.*). *au* ~ *de son rouleau*, at
the end of one's rope. *faire un* ~
de toilette, to tidy oneself up. ~
de vergue, yardarm. ~ *du sein*,
nipple, teat. *à* ~ *portant*, point-
blank. *être à* ~, to be exhausted.

boutade (butad) *f*, whim, crotchet, fancy, fit; sally (*wit*).
par ~*s*, in fits & starts.

boute-en-train (butãtrɛ̃) *m*,
life [& soul] (*of the party*).

boutefeu (butfø) (*fig.*) *m*, firebrand, mischief-maker.

bouteille (butɛːj) *f*, bottle, flask,
jar. ~ *thermos*, thermos. ~ *à
gaz*, gas cylinder.

bouteur (butœr) *m*, bulldozer. ~
biais, angledozer.

boutique (butik) *f*, shop, stall,
booth, stand; stock (*in shop*);
shady concern; concern. ~
franche, duty-free shop. **boutiquier, ère** (kje, ɛːr) *n*, shopkeeper, tradesman, -woman.

boutoir (butwaːr) *m*, snout (*boar*).

bouton (butɔ̃) *m*, bud; pimple; button; stud (*collar*); knob, handle.
~ *poussoir*, push button. ~ *à
pression*, snap fastener. ~ *d'or*,
buttercup. ~*s de manchettes*,
cuff links. ~ *de manivelle*, crank
pin. ~ *de sonnette*, bell push. ~
du sein, nipple, teat. **boutonner**
(tɔne) *v.t*, button [up] (*v.i.*) to
bud; break out in pimples. se ~,
to button oneself up. **boutonnière**
(njeːr) *f*, buttonhole; cut, gash.

bouture (butyːr) *f*, slip, cutting
(*Hort.*).

bouverie (buvri) *f*, cattle pen,
ox stall. **bouvier, ère** (vje, ɛːr) *n*,
cowherd, herdsman. **bouvillon**
(vijɔ̃) *m*, steer.

bouvreuil (buvrœːj) *m*, bullfinch.

bovin, e (bɔvɛ̃, in) *a*, bovine, neat,
cattle (*att.*).

box (bɔks) *m*, box stall (*horse*); garage space.

boxe (bɔks) *f*, boxing. ~ *à poings
nus*, bare-fist boxing, knuckle
fighting. ~ *contre son ombre*,
shadowboxing. **boxer** (kse) *v.i.
& t*, to box, spar. **boxeur** (ksœːr)
m, boxer. ~ *professionnel*, prize-
fighter.

boyau (bwajo) *m*, gut; hose

(*pipe*); tubular [tire] (*bicycle*);
passageway. ~ *de tranchée*, communication trench.

bracelet (braslɛ) *m*, bracelet,
wristlet, strap, bangle. ~*-montre*,
wristwatch.

braconner (brakɔne) *v.i*, to
poach. **braconnier** (nje) *m*,
poacher.

brader (brade) *v.t*, to sell merchandise cheaply. **braderie** (dri) *f*,
clearance sale; surplus sale.

braguette (bragɛt) *f*, fly (*trousers*).

brahmane (braman) *m*, brahmin.

brai (brɛ) *m*, pitch, tar.

brailler (braje) *v.i*, to bawl,
squall.

braiment (brɛmã) *m*, bray[ing].
braire (brɛːr) *v.i.ir*, to bray.

braise (brɛːz) *f*, embers; breeze,
cinders; money (*slang*). **braiser**
(brɛze) *v.t*, to braise. **braisière**
(zjeːr) *f*, stew-pan.

bramer (brame) *v.i*, to bell, troat.

brancard (brãkaːr) *m*, stretcher;
shaft; wheelbarrow. **brancardier**
(kardje) *m*, stretcher-bearer.

branchage (brãʃaːʒ) *m*,
branches; horns. **branche** (brãːʃ)
f, branch; leg (*compass, tripod*);
prong, tooth, tine; shank; stick. ~
de tranchée, communication
trench. ~ *gourmande*, sucker
(*Hort.*). *vieille* ~, old fellow.
branchement (brãʃmã) *m*,
branch[ing]; branch pipe; branch,
tap (*Elec.*); lead (*Elec. service*);
turnout (*Rly.*). **brancher** (ʃe) *v.t*,
to branch; connect, plug in; (*v.i.*)
to perch. **branchette** (ʃɛt) *f*, twig.
branchies (ʃi) *f.pl*, gills (*fish*).

brande (brãːd) *f*, heather; heath,
moor[land].

brandiller (brãdije) *v.t*, to
swing, dangle.

brandir (brãdiːr) *v.t*, to brandish, flourish.

brandon (brãdɔ̃) *m*, [fire]brand,
spark (*from conflagration*).

branlant, e (brãlã, ãːt) *a*, shaky,
loose, rocking. **branle** (brãːl) *m*,
swing[ing]; jangle; impulse, impetus; (*fig.*) dance, running, lead,
example. en ~*-bas* (brãlbɑ), astir,
agog. **branler** (brãle) *v.t. & i*, to
swing, shake, wag[gle], be loose,

dance, bob. *se* ~, to masturbate.

braque (brak) *m*, hound; madcap. **braquer** (ke) *v.t*, to aim (*gun*); point (*telescope*); fix (*eyes*).

bras (brɑ) *m*, arm; flipper; (*pl.*) hands (*workmen*); handle (*oar, etc.*); brace (*Naut.*); (*pl.*) jaws (*of death*). *en* ~ *de chemise*, in shirt sleeves. ~ *de mer*, arm of sea, sound. ~ *dessus*, ~ *dessous*, arm in arm. *à [force de]* ~, [by] hand[-power], manual.

braser (brɑze) *v.t*, to braze, hard-solder.

brasero (brɑzero) *m*, brazier; fire basket. **brasier** (zje) *m*, bright fire; inferno. **brasiller** (zije) *v.t*, to broil; (*v.i.*) to sparkle.

brassage (brasa:ʒ) *m*, brewing; stirring.

brassard (brasa:r) *m*, armlet, brassard, badge, band.

brasse (bras) *f*, fathom (Fr. *brasse marine* = 1 meter 62; Eng. *fathom* = 6 feet); stroke (*distance covered at one swimming movement*); breaststroke.

brassée (brase) *f*, armful; stroke (*one swimming movement*).

brasser (brase) *v.t*, to brew, mash; stir; dispatch; brace (*Naut.*). **brasserie** (sri) *f*, brewery, restaurant. **brasseur** (sœ:r) *m*, brewer. ~ *d'affaires*, man with many irons in the fire; shady financier.

brassiage (brasja:ʒ) *m*, fathoming, sounding.

brassière (brasjɛ:r) *f*, vest (*baby's*); shoulder strap; (*pl.*) leading strings. ~ *de sauvetage*, life jacket, cork j.

brasure (brɑzy:r) *f*, brazing; braze (*joint*).

bravache (bravaʃ) *m*, blusterer, swaggerer, bully, hector. **bravade** (vad) *f*, bravado, bluster. **brave** (bra:v) *a*, brave, gallant, bold, stout; honest, good, worthy. ¶ *m*, brave man. *mon* ~, my good man. **bravement** (bravmɑ̃) *ad*, bravely, etc; ably. **braver** (ve) *v.t*, to brave, face; dare, defy. **bravo** (vo) *ad*, bravo! hurrah, -ray! well done! hear! hear! ¶ *m*, cheer. **bravoure** (vu:r) *f*, bravery, gallantry.

brayer (brɛje) *m*, truss (*Surg.*).

break (brɛk) *m*, break, brake; station wagon.

brebis (brəbi) *f*, ewe, sheep. ~ *galeuse*, plague, nuisance (*pers.*); black sheep (*fig.*).

brèche (brɛʃ) *f*, breach, gap; nick.

bredouille (brədu:j) *a*, empty-handed. **bredouiller** (duje) *v.i*, to stammer, mumble.

bref, ève (brɛf, ɛ:v) *a*, brief, curt. [*syllabe*] **brève**, *f*, short [syllable]. **bref**, *ad*, briefly, in short, in fine.

breloque (brələk) *f*, charm (*seal, etc.*). *battre la* ~, to sound the all-clear; be nutty (*pers.*).

brème (brɛm) *f*, bream (*fish*); identity or playing card (*slang*). *taper les* ~*s*, to play cards.

Brême (brɛ:m) *f*, Bremen.

Brésil (le) (brezil), Brazil. **brésilien, ne** (ljɛ̃, ɛn) *a. & B~, n,* Brazilian.

Bretagne (la) (brətaɲ), Brittany.

bretelle (brətɛl) *f*, brace, suspender, sling; (*pl.*) suspenders, (*men's*); shoulder straps (*women's*).

breuil (brœ:j) *m*, covert (*game*).

breuvage (brœva:ʒ) *m*, beverage, drink; draught.

brevet (brəvɛ) *m*, diploma, certificate; patent, license. indentures (*apprenticeship*). **breveter** (vte) *v.t*, to patent; license.

bréviaire (brevjɛ:r) *m*, breviary; favorite author (*book*).

bribes (brib) *f.pl*, scraps, leavings; odds & ends; excerpts; snatches.

bric, *ad* : *de* ~ & *de broc* (brik, brɔk), here a little & there a little. **bric-à-brac** (kabrak) *m*, bric-à-brac.

brick (brik) *m*, brig (*Naut.*).

bricole (brikɔl) *f*, breast strap; (*pl.*) odd jobs. **bricoler** (le) *v.i*, to do odd jobs (*repairs, etc.*). **bricoleur** (lœ:r) *m*, do-it-yourselfer.

bride (brid) *f*, bridle; rein[s]; curb, check; clamp, cramp; flange; treble (*crochet*). *à toute* ~, *à* ~ *abattue*, at full speed. **brider** (de) *v.t. & i*, to bridle; check, curb; bind; pinch, be tight; clamp. *des yeux bridés*, slit (*or* almond) eyes.

bridge (bridʒ) *m*, bridge (*cards*). ~ *aux enchères*, auction b. ~ *plafond*, ~ *contrat*, contract b.

brièvement (brievmã) *ad*, briefly, shortly. **brièveté** (vte) *f*, brevity.

brigade (brigad) *f*, brigade; party, posse, gang. **brigadier** (dje) *m*, colonel commandant; bombardier; corporal (*cavalry*); sergeant (*police*); bowman (*boat*).

brigand (brigã) *m*, brigand, highwayman, robber; scamp. **brigandage** (daːʒ) *m*, brigandage, highway robbery.

brigue (brig) *f*, intrigue; faction. **briguer** (ge) *v.i. & t*, to intrigue; intrigue for; canvass, court, aspire to.

brillamment (brijamã) *ad*, brilliantly, brightly. **brillant, e** (jã, ãːt) *a*, brilliant, bright, shining, glittering; blooming; splendid; glossy (*phot. paper*). ¶ *m*, brilliant (*diamond*). **brillantine** (jãtin) *f*, brilliantine. **briller** (je) *v.i*, to shine, brighten; glitter, glisten; glow.

brimade (brimad) *f*, practical joke (*on newcomer*).

brimbale (brẽbal) *f*, pump handle. **brimbaler** (le) *v.i*, to dangle; wobble.

brimborion (brẽbɔrjɔ̃), *m*, knick-knack, bauble.

brin (brẽ) *m*, blade; slip, sprig; shoot; strand (*rope*); joint (*fishing rod*); bit. ~ *d'osier*, withe, withy. *un beau* ~ *d'homme, de fille*, a fine youth, girl. **brindille** (diːj) *f*, sprig, twig.

brioche (briɔʃ) *f*, brioche; blunder; potbelly (*slang*).

brique (brik) *f*, brick; bar (*soap, etc.*); 10,000 francs (*slang*). *bouffer des* ~*s*, to have nothing to eat.

briquet (brikɛ) *m*, lighter (*gasoline, etc.*); tinder box, [flint &] steel.

briquetage (briktaːʒ) *m*, brickwork. **briqueterie** (ktri) *f*, brickfield. **briquetier** (ktje) *m*, brickmaker. **briquette** (kɛt) *f*, briquet[te].

bris (bri) *m*, breaking; wreck-

[age]. **brisant** (zã) *m*, reef; breakwater; breaker (*wave*); (*pl.*) broken water.

brise (briːz) *f*, breeze (*wind*).

brise-bise (brizbiːz) *m*, draft protector; short curtain, brise-bise. **brisées** (ze) *f.pl*, footsteps (*fig.*). **brise-jet** (brizʒe) *m*, anti-splash tap nozzle. **brise-lames** (lam) *m*, breakwater. **brisement** (zmã) *m*, breaking, etc, as *briser*. ~ *de cœur*, contrition (*Theol.*); heartbreak. **briser** (ze) *v.t. & i*, to break, smash, shatter, shiver, dash; exhaust. se ~, to break; come apart (*be detachable*), fold [up]. **brise-tout** (ztu) *m*, destructive person. **briseur** (zœːr) *m*, breaker (*pers.*). **brisure** (zyːr) *f*, break; wristband; neckband.

bristol (bristɔl) *m*, visiting or business card.

britannique (britanik) *a*, British, Britannic. *les îles B~s*, the British Isles.

broc (bro) *m*, jug, pitcher. ~ *de toilette*, water jug, ewer.

brocanter (brɔkãte) *v.i*, to deal in works of art, curios, bargains, used goods.

brocard (brɔkaːr) *m*, gibe, lampoon.

brocart (brɔkaːr) *m*, brocade.

brochant sur le tout (brɔʃã), to cap all. **broche** (brɔʃ) *f*, spit, broach; knitting needle; spindle, arbor; spike; pin, pintle; drift[pin]; brooch; (*pl.*) tusks (*wild boar*). **brochée** (ʃe) *f*, spitful. **brocher** (ʃe) *v.t*, to brocade; stitch, sew (*books*); drift (*rivets*); scamp (*work*). *un livre broché*, a paperback book. **brochet** (ʃɛ) *m*, pike, jack (*fish*). **brochette** (ʃɛt) *f*, skewer. **brochure** (ʃyːr) *f*, interwoven pattern (*fabrics*), stitching, sewing; pamphlet, booklet, brochure; paperback binding.

brocoli (brɔkɔli) *m*, broccoli.

brodequin (brɔdkẽ) *m*, lace boot; buskin; sock (*comedy*).

broder (brɔde) *v.t*, to embroider. **broderie** (dri) *f*, embroidery. ~ *à fils couchés*, couching. ~*-application*, appliqué (*or* applied) work. **brodeur, euse** (dœːr, øːz) *n*, embroiderer, ess.

brome (brɔːm) *m*, bromine. **bromure** (brɔmyːr) *m*, bromide.

broncher (brɔ̃ʃe) *v.i*, to stumble, trip; flinch, falter.

bronches (brɔ̃ʃ) *f.pl*, bronchia. **bronchite** (brɔ̃ʃit) *f*, bronchitis.

bronze (brɔ̃ːz) *m*, bronze. ~ [*industriel*] gun metal. **bronzer** (brɔ̃ze) *v.t*, to bronze; (*fig.*) steel, [*case*]harden; tan.

broquette (brɔkɛt) *f*, tack(s).

brosse (brɔs) *f*, brush. ~ *à barbe*, shaving b. ~ *à cheveux*, ~ *à tête*, hairbrush. ~ *à cirer*, shoe b. ~ *à dents*, toothbrush. ~ *à habits*, clothes b. ~ *à laver*, scrubbing b. ~ *à miettes* [*pour la table*], crumb b. ~ *rude, douce*, hard, soft, b. *cheveux en* ~, crew cut. **brossée** (se) *f*, brushing; beating, drubbing. **brosser** (se) *v.t*, to brush; scrub (*floor*); thrash, drub. ~ *un tableau*, to sketch in a situation (*verbally*). *se* ~ *la tête, les dents*, to brush one's hair, teeth. **brosserie** (sri) *f*, brush making; b. works. **brossier, ère** (sje, ɛːr) *n*, brush maker.

brou (bru) *m*, husk (*walnut, almond*); juice (*of walnut husk*).

brouette (bruɛt) *f*, [*wheel*]barrow.

brouhaha (bruaa) *m*, hubbub, din, pother.

brouillamini (brujamini) *m*, disorder, muddle.

brouillard (brujaːr) *m*, fog, mist, haze; rough book. **brouillasse** (jas) *f*, [Scotch] mist. **brouille** (bruːj) *f*, discord, misunderstanding. **brouiller** (bruje) *v.t*, to jumble, muddle, blur, embroil; shuffle (*cards*); scramble (*eggs*). se ~, to break up (*weather*); fall out; get confused, be at loggerheads. **brouilleur** (jœːr) *m*, jammer (*Radio*), scrambler (*code*). **brouillon, ne** (jɔ̃, ɔn) *n*, muddler; (*m.*) [rough] draft; rough copy; scratch pad.

brouir (bruiːr) *v.t*, to wither, blast, blight. **brouissure** (isyːr) *f*, blight.

broussailles (brusaːj) *f.pl*, brushwood, undergrowth, scrub. *en* ~, unkempt. **brousse** (brus) *f*, bush (*scrub*).

broussin (brusɛ̃) *m*, gnarl (*on tree*).

brout (bru) *m*, browse. **brouter** (te) *v.t. & abs*, to browse (on); nibble; chatter (*tool*). ~ *le cresson*, to perform cunnilingus (*obscene*).

broutilles (brutiːj) *f.pl*, twigs; trifles.

broyer (brwaje) *v.t*, to crush, grind, mill.

bruant (bryɑ̃) *m*, bunting (*bird*).

brucelles (brysɛl) *f.pl*, tweezers.

brugnon (brynɔ̃) *m*, nectarine.

bruine (bruin) *f*, drizzle, mizzle. **bruiner** (ne) *v.imp*, to drizzle, mizzle.

bruire (bruiːr) *v.i.ir*, to murmur, rustle, sough. **bruissement** (ismɑ̃) *m*, murmur, etc.

bruit (brui) *m*, noise, row, racket, din, clatter, ado, fuss; rumor, report, news. ~ *de pas*, tramp. **bruiteur** (tœːr) *m*, sound effects man.

brûlant, e (brylɑ̃, ɑ̃ːt) *a*, burning, hot, scorching, broiling; afire. **brûle-gueule** (bryl) *m*, short tobacco pipe. **brûle-parfum**, *m*, incense burner. **à brûle-pourpoint** (purpwɛ̃) *ad*, point-blank, to one's face. **brûlé** (le) *m*, burning (*smell, taste*). **brûler** (le) *v.t. & i*, to burn, scorch, parch, sear; singe; nip; roast; mull (*wine*). *je me suis brûlé le bras*, I have burnt my arm. *se* ~ *la cervelle*, to blow one's brains out. ~ *un feu*, to go through a red light. **brûleur** (lœːr) *m*, burner. **brûlure** (lyːr) *f*, burn; scald.

brume (brym) *f*, fog, mist, haze. **brumeux, euse** (mø, øːz) *a*, foggy; wintry.

brun, e (brœ̃, yn) *a*, brown; dark, dusky. ¶ *m*, brown; (*f.*) dusk, gloaming. **brunâtre** (brynɑːtr) *a*, brownish. **brunet** (nɛ) *m*, dark man, dark boy. **brunette** (nɛt) *f*, brunette. **brunir** (niːr) *v.t*, to brown; tan; burnish. **brunissage** (nisaːʒ) *m*, burnishing.

brusque† (brysk) *a*, blunt, bluff, brusque, offhand, curt, abrupt, gruff. **brusquer** (ke) *v.t*, to treat abruptly; precipitate, rush. ~ *l'aventure*, to chance it. **brusquerie** (kəri) *f*, bluntness, etc.

brut, e (bryt) *a,* raw, crude; uncut (*gem*); unmanufactured; unpolished; unsweetened (*wine*); rough; gross (*Com.*); inorganic; brute (*beast, force*). *art* ~, instinctive art. **brutal, e†** (tal) *a,* brutal; brutish, coarse, rough. ¶ *f,* brute, bully. **brutaliser** (lise) *v.t,* to maltreat; bully. **brutalité** (te) *f,* brutality, etc. **brute** (bryt) *f,* brute.

Bruxelles (brysɛl) *f,* Brussels.

bruyant, e (bryjɑ̃, ɑ̃:t) *a,* noisy, boisterous, rollicking, clamorous, loud, blatant; hoydenish. **bruyamment** (jamɑ̃) *ad,* noisily.

bruyère (bryjɛ:r) *f,* heather; heath, moor; brier, briar (*pipe wood*).

buanderie (byɑ̃dri) *f,* washhouse, laundry. **buandier, ère** (dje, ɛ:r) *n,* bleacher.

buccin (byksɛ̃) *m,* whelk (*Mol.*).

bûche (by:ʃ) *f,* log, billet, chump; Swiss roll; blockhead. ~ *de Noël,* yule log. *ramasser une* ~, to take a tumble. **bûcher** (byʃe) *m,* woodshed; pile, stack (*firewood*); pyre; stake (*for burning alive*). ¶ *v.t. & i,* to rough-hew, dress, trim; swot. **bûcheron** (ʃrɔ̃) *m,* woodman, lumberman. **bûchette** (ʃet) *f,* stick. **bûcheur, euse** (ʃœ:r, ø:z) *n,* plodder, brain worker.

bucolique (bykɔlik) *a. & f,* bucolic.

budget (bydʒɛ) *m,* budget; estimates (*parliamentary*).

buée (bye) *f,* steam, moisture; fumes.

buffet (byfɛ) *m,* cupboard; sideboard, buffet; refreshment bar *or* room; running buffet.

buffle (byfl) *m,* buffalo. [*peau de*] ~, buff [leather].

bugle (bygl) *m,* flügel horn; (*f.*) bugle (*Bot.*).

buire (bɥi:r) *f,* beaker, flagon, jug.

buis (bɥi) *m,* box [tree]; boxwood.

buisson (bɥisɔ̃) *m,* bush. **buissonneux, euse** (sɔnø, ø:z) *a,* bushy. **faire l'école buissonnière** (njɛ:r), to play hooky.

bulbe (bylb) *f,* bulb (*Bot.*); (*m.*) bulb (*Anat.*). **bulbeux, euse** (bø, ø:z) *a,* bulbous.

bulgare (bylga:r) *a. & B~,* *n,* Bulgarian. **la Bulgarie** (gari), Bulgaria.

bulle (byl) *f,* bubble; blister; bleb; bull (*Pope's*).

bulletin (byltɛ̃) *m,* paper, note, bulletin, letter; ticket; voucher; form; list; report. ~ *de la cote,* stock exchange daily official list. ~ *de vote,* ballot. ~ *météorologique,* weather forecast.

buraliste (byralist) *n,* in *France,* keeper of a state-owned tobacco shop (*bureau de tabac*), where also postage stamps are sold, & licenses are issued. *Also,* clerk, tax collector. **bureau** (ro) *m,* writing table; table, desk; bureau; office; counting house; agency; exchange; committee, executive. ~ *américain,* ~ *à rideau,* rolltop desk. ~ [*central téléphonique*], [telephone] exchange. ~ *d'esprit,* coterie of wits. ~ [*de location*], box office. ~ *de garantie,* government assay office. ~ *de plâcement,* employment agency, registry office. ~ *de police,* police station. ~ *de poste,* post office. ~ *de scrutin,* polling station. ~ *de tabac,* tobacconist's shop. ~ *des objets trouvés,* lost property office. ~ *des rebuts,* dead letter office. ~ *ministre,* pedestal desk, kneehole d. ~ *municipal de placement gratuit,* labor exchange. *à* ~[*x*] *ouvert*[*s*], on demand, on presentation. ~ *restant,* to be called for. *sur le* ~, (*matter*) under consideration. *le deuxième* ~ Intelligence Dept. (*Mil.*). **bureaucrate** (krat) *m,* bureaucrat. **bureaucratie** (si) *f,* bureaucracy.

burette (byrɛt) *f,* bottle (*oil, vinegar*); cruet (*Eccl.*). ~ [*à huile*], oil can; (*pl.*) testicles (*obscene*).

burin (byrɛ̃) *m,* graver; chisel. ~ [*à froid*], cold chisel. **buriner** (rine) *v.t,* to engrave; chisel, chip.

burlesque (byrlɛsk), *a. & m,* burlesque, farcical; comic(al).

buse (by:z) *f,* buzzard; air pipe; nozzle; blockhead.

buste (byst) *m,* bust.

but (by; *in liaison,* byt) *m,* butt, mark; target; goal; winning post; aim, object, end, intention, pur-

pose, point. ~ *de transformation*, converted goal. *de ~ en blanc*, point-blank, bluntly. ~ *à ~*, even (*games*).
butée (byte) *f*, abutment (*bridge*); shore (*prop*); thrust (*Mech.*); stop. **buter** (te) *v.i. & t*, to butt; stumble; shore. *se ~ à* (*fig.*), to be bent on; be up against.
butin (bytɛ̃) *m*, booty, spoil, loot, plunder. **butiner** (tine) *v.i. & t*, to pillage, plunder, loot.
butoir (bytwaːr) *m*, stop; stop blocks; buffer.
butor (bytoːr) *m*, bittern; dolt.
butte (byt) *f*, mound, knoll, hillock; butts (*behind target*). **butter** (te) *v.t*, to ridge; earth, hill.
buvable (byvabl) *a*, drinkable; acceptable. **buvard** (vaːr) *m*, blotter, blotting pad *or* case. **buvette** (vɛt) *f*, refreshment bar *or* room; pump room (*spa*). **buveur, euse** (vœːr, øːz) *n*, drinker. *~ d'eau*, teetotaller. **buvoter** (vɔte) *v.i*, to sip; tipple.

C

ça (sa) *pn*. Contraction of *cela*.
çà (sa) *ad:* ~ *& là*, here & there, hither & thither, this way & that. *~ va?*, how are you? is that all right? *~ va*, all right, okay. *~ y est*, that's all right, that does it. *ah! çà, i*, now then! come now!
cabale (kabal) *f*, cabal; caucus. **cabaler** (le) *v.i*, to plot, intrigue.
cabane (kaban) *f*, cabin, hut; kennel; hutch. *~ de bois*, log cabin, 1. hut. **cabanon** (nɔ̃) *m*, padded cell.
cabaret (kabarɛ) *m*, wine shop *or* cellar; tavern, public house; restaurant; set *or* service (*china, liqueur, etc.*). **cabaretier, ère** (bartje, ɛːr) *n*, innkeeper; publican.
cabas (kabɑ) *m*, frail; shopping basket.
cabestan (kabɛstɑ̃) *m*, capstan; winch.
cabillaud (kabijo) *m*, cod[fish].
cabine (kabin) *f*, cabin; box; cage, car; telephone booth. *~ de projection*, projection booth (*cinema*). *opérateur de ~*, projectionist (*cinema*).

cabinet (kabinɛ) *m*, room, closet; chambers; den; practice (*professional*); cabinet (*ministerial*); collection (*curiosities*). *~s* ou *~ [d'aisances]*, toilet. *~ de consultation*, consulting room, surgery. *~ de débarras*, lumber room. *~ de lecture*, reading room, newsroom; lending library. *~ de toilette*, dressing room, toilet. *~ de travail*, study. *~ de verdure*, arbor, bower. *~ noir*, darkroom (*Phot.*). *vie de ~*, indoor life.
câble (kɑːbl) *m*, rope, cable, line, wire, cord. **câbler** (kɑble) *v.t*, to cable (*Teleg.*). **cabliste** (list) *m*, cableman (*TV*).
caboche (kabɔʃ) *f*, pate, noddle; head; hobnail. **cabochon** (ʃɔ̃) *m*, cabochon; brass nail.
cabosser (kabɔse) *v.t*, to dent, batter.
cabotage (kabɔtaːʒ) *m*, coasting; coasting trade, home trade. **caboter** (te) *v.i*, to coast. **caboteur** (tœːr) *m*, coaster.
cabotin, e (kabɔtɛ̃, in) *n*, strolling player; ham actor; theatrical person (*affected*).
caboulot (kabulo) *m*, dive, seamy café.
cabrer (se) (kabre) *v.pr*, to rear; jib (*fig.*), take offense. **cabri** (kabri) *m*, kid (*goat*). **cabriole** (ɔl) *f*, leap. **cabrioler** (le) *v.i*, to caper. **cabriolet** (lɛ) *m*, gig, cabriolet; handcuffs (*of cord*).
caca (kaka) *m*, excrement (*children's term*). *~ d'oie*, gosling green.
cabrer (se) (kabre) *v.pr*, to rear; jib (*fig.*), take offense. **cabri** (kabri) *m*, kid (*goat*). **cabriole** (ɔl) *f*, leap. **cabrioler** (le) *v.i*, to caper. **cabriolet** (lɛ) *m*, gig, cabriolet; handcuffs (*of cord*).
cacahuète (kakawɛt) *f*, peanut.
cacao (kakao) *m*, cacao, cocoa. **cacaoyer** (ɔje) *ou* **cacaotier** (ɔtje) *m*, cacao [tree].
cacatoès (kakatɔɛs) *m*, cockatoo, parakeet.
cachalot (kaʃalo) *m*, sperm whale, cachalot.
cache (kaʃ) *f*, hiding place; mask (*Phot.*). **~-ampoule**, *m*, bulb shade (*Elec.*). **~-cache**, *m*, hide-

&-seek. **~-corset,** *m,* camisole, underbodice.

cachemire (kaʃmiːr) *m,* cashmere.

cache-nez (kaʃne) *m,* muffler, comforter, scarf. **cache-pot** (po) *m,* jardinière (*pot*). **cache-poussière** (pusjeːr) *m,* dust coat. **cache-sex** (sɛks) *m,* bikini, G-string. **cacher** (ʃe) *v.t,* to hide, conceal, secrete; mask. **~** *son jeu,* to be underhanded. **cachet** (ʃɛ) *m,* seal, signet; cachet; ticket, voucher; stamp (*fig.*); fee, salary. **cacheter** (ʃte) *v.t,* to seal, do up. **cachette** (ʃɛt) *f,* hiding place. **en ~,** secretly, stealthily, covertly, on the sly. **cachot** (ʃo) *m,* dungeon, cell. **cachotter** (ʃɔte) *v.t,* to make a mystery of it. **cachottier, ère** (tje, ɛːr) *n,* sly-boots; (*att.*) secretive.

cachou (kaʃu) *m,* cachou.

cacochyme (kakɔʃim) *a,* sensitive [to illness]; queer.

cacophonie (kakɔfɔni) *f,* cacophony.

cactus (kaktyːs) *m,* cactus.

cadastre (kadastr) *m,* cadastral survey; valuation list (*basis for taxes*). **cadastrer** (tre) *v.t,* to survey [& value]; enter (*in valuation list*).

cadavéreux, euse (kadaverø, øːz) *a,* cadaverous, corpselike. **cadavre** (daːvr) *m,* corpse; carcass; skeleton.

cadeau (kado) *m,* present, gift.

cadenas (kadnɑ) *m,* padlock. **cadenasser** (dnase) *v.t,* to padlock; fasten.

cadence (kadãːs) *f,* cadence, rhythm, time, step; tune (*fig.*). *aller en* ~, to keep time.

cadet, te (kadɛ, ɛt) *a. & n,* younger (brother, sister); cadet, junior, minor; caddie (*golf*); least (*fig.*).

Cadix (kadiks) *m,* Cadiz.

cadrage (kadraʒ) *m,* framing (*cinema*).

cadran (kadrã) *m,* dial [plate], face [plate]. ~ [*solaire*], [sun] dial.

cadre (kaːdr) *m,* frame, framework; frame aerial; limits, scheme, scope, compass; upper echelon employee, administrator. *les* ~*s,* commissioned and noncommissioned officers (*Mil.*). **cadrer** (kadre) *v.i,* to square, agree, tally, suit, fit, match; to frame (*cinema*). **cadreur** (rœr) *m,* cameraman (*cinema*).

caduc, uque (kadyk) *a,* broken, decrepit, declining, frail; lapsed, statute barred. **caducité** (dysite) *f,* dilapidated state; decrepitude, senile decay; lapsing, nullity.

cafard, e (kafaːr, ard) *n,* canter, hypocrite; tell-tale, sneak; (*m.*) cockroach, black beetle; desert madness. *avoir le* ~, to have the blues.

café (kafe) *m,* coffee; café. ~ *complet,* coffee, roll & butter. **caféier** (feje) *m,* coffee tree; c. planter. **cafetier, ère** (ftje, ɛːr) *n,* café keeper, caterer; (*f.*) coffeepot.

cage (kaːʒ) *f,* cage; case, housing; shaft (*lift*). ~ *à poulets,* chicken coop. ~ *d'escalier,* staircase, stairway.

cagnard, e (kaɲaːr, ard) *a,* lazy, slothful. ¶ *n,* lazybones. **cagnardise** (ɲardiːz) *f,* laziness, sloth.

cagneux, euse (kaɲø, øːz) *a,* knock-kneed; crooked (*legs*).

cagnotte (kaɲɔt) (*cards*) *f,* pool, kitty, pot.

cagot, e (kago, ɔt) *n,* hypocrite; (*att.*) sanctimonious.

cagoule (kagul) *f,* (monk's) hooded cloak; penitent's hood.

cahier (kaje) *m,* notebook. ~ *de dessin,* sketch book. ~ *des charges,* specification.

cahin-caha (kaɛ̃kaa) *ad,* so so, middling. *aller* ~, to jog on.

cahot (kao) *m,* jolt, bump; vicissitude. **cahoter** (ɔte) *v.t. & i,* to jolt, bump; toss about.

cahute (kayt) *f,* hovel; hut.

caïd (kaid) *m,* Arab chief; gang leader; expert.

caille (kaːj) *f,* quail.

caillé (kaje) *m,* **caillebotte** (kajbɔt) *f,* curd[s]. **cailler** (kaje) *v.t. & se* ~, to curd[le]; clot.

cailletage (kajtaːʒ) *m,* gossip. **caillette** (jɛt) *f,* gossip (*pers.*).

caillot (kajo) *m*, clot.
caillou (kaju) *m*, pebble; flint; stone; boulder (*Geol.*). **caillouteux, euse** (tø, ø:z) *a*, pebbly; stony, flinty. **cailloutis** (ti) *m*, pebblestone, roadstones.

Caire (le) (kɛ:r), Cairo.

caisse (kɛs) *f*, case, box; tub (*for shrub*); body (*vehicle*); drum; cash; cash box, cash register; till; coffer, chest; cashier's office *or* desk *or* counter, pay office; bank, treasury, fund, association. **en ~**, in (*or* on) hand, in the till. **~ à eau**, tank. **~ à médicaments**, medicine chest. **~ claire**, snare drum. **~ d'amortissement**, sinking fund. **~ de dépôts**, safe deposit (*institution*). **~ de retraites pour la vieillesse**, old-age pension fund. **~ doublée de ferblanc**, tin-lined case. **~ enregistreuse**, **~ contrôleuse**, cash register. **~ d'épargne**, savings bank.
caissier, ère (kɛsje, ɛ:r) *n*, cashier; teller (*bank*). **~-comptable**, cashier & bookkeeper. **~ des titres**, securities clerk.
caisson (kɛsɔ̃) *m*, caisson, pontoon; bin, bunker, box, locker.
cajoler (kaʒɔle) *v.t*, to cajole, wheedle, coax. **cajolerie** (lri) *f*, cajolery, etc.
cake (kɛk) *m*, fruitcake (*other cake: "gateau"*).
cal (kal) *m*, callosity, callus.
calaison (kalɛzɔ̃) *f*, load draught (*ship*.)
calamité (kalamite) *f*, calamity. **calamiteux, euse** (tø, ø:z) *a*, calamitous.
calandre (kalɑ̃:dr) *f*, calender; mangle; weevil. **calandrer** (lɑ̃dre) *v.t*, to calender; mangle.
calcaire (kalkɛ:r) *m*, limestone. ¶ *a*, calcareous, lime[stone] (*att.*)
calciner (kalsine) *v.t*, to calcine, burn.
calcium (kalsjɔm) *m*, calcium.
calcul (kalkyl) *m*, calculation, reckoning; arithmetic; sum; calculus, stone (*Med.*). **calculer** (le) *v.t. & abs*, to calculate, reckon; compute. **calculateur** (atœ:r) *m*,

calculator; computer (*small one for simple mathematical functions*). **~ électronique**, electronic computer. **~ numérique**, digital computer. **calculatrice** (atris) *f*, calculator (*desk size*).

cale (kal) *f*, hold (*of ship*); wedge, key, scotch. **~ [de construction]**, stocks, slip[s] (*Shipbldg.*). **~ de halage**, slipway. **~ sèche, ~ de radoub**, dry dock.
calebasse (kalbas) *f*, calabash, gourd.
caleçon (kalsɔ̃) *m*, pants, drawers. **~ de bain**, swimming trunks.
calembour (kalɑ̃bu:r) *m*, pun. **faire des ~s**, to pun. **faiseur de ~s**, punster.
calembredaine (kalɑ̃brədɛn) *f*. oft. pl, nonsense, foolery.
calendes (kalɑ̃:d) *f.pl*, calends. **~ grecques** (*fig.*), doomsday. **calendrier** (lɑ̃drie) *m*, calendar.
calepin (kalpɛ̃) *m*, notebook; working drawing.
caler (kale) *v.t. & i*, to wedge, key; scotch; draw (*so much water—ship*); strike (*sail*); stall (*motor*). **~ [la voile]**, to give in, knuckle under. **être calé en**, to be well up in (*subject*). **calé (le)** *a*, well-informed; clever; difficult.
calfater (kalfate) *v.t*, to calk.
calfeutrage (kalføtra:ʒ) *m*, weatherstripping.
calfeutrer (kalføtre) *v.t*, to list (*door*). **se ~**, to make oneself cosy, shut oneself in.
calibre (kalibr) *m*, caliber, bore; standing (*fig.*); gauge; template, pattern, shape; calliper[s]. **calibrer** (bre) *v.t*, to gauge, calliper, calibrate.
calice (kalis) *m*, chalice, communion cup; cup; calyx.
calicot (kaliko) *m*, calico.
calife (kalif) *m*, caliph.
Californie (la) (kaliforni), California. **californien, ne** (njɛ̃, ɛn) *a. & C~*, *n*, Californian.
califourchon (à) (kalifurʃɔ̃) *ad*, astride, astraddle.
câlin, e (kɑlɛ̃, in) *a*, caressing, wheedling. ¶ *n*, pet, darling; wheedler. **câliner** (line) *v.t*, to

fondle, pet, cuddle; wheedle. **câ-linerie** (nri) *f*, fondling; wheedling.

calleux, euse (kalø, ø:z) *a*, callous, horny.

calligraphie (kaligrafi) *f*, calligraphy, penmanship.

callosité (kalozite) *f*, callosity.

calmant (kalmɑ̃) *m*, sedative, soother.

calmar (kalma:r) *m*, calamary, squid.

calme (kalm) *a*, calm, quiet, still; composed, collected, cool. ¶ *m*, calm, calmness. ~ *plat*, dead calm. **calmer** (me) *v.t.* & *i.* & se ~, to calm; soothe, salve; subside, abate.

calomnie (kalɔmni) *f*, calumny, slander. **calomnier** (nje) *v.t*, to calumniate, slander. **calomnieux, euse** (njø, ø:z) *a*, calumnious, slanderous.

calorie (kalɔri) *f*, calorie. **calorifère** (rifɛ:r) *m*, heater. ~ *à feu continu*, slow-combustion stove. **calorique** (rik) (*Phys.*), *m*, caloric, heat.

calot (kalo) *m*, forage cap. **calotte** (lɔt) *f*, skull cap; cap; calotte; canopy (*heaven*); cuff (*blow*). **calotter** (te) *v.t*, to cuff.

calque (kalk) *m*, tracing; copy (*fig.*). **calquer** (ke) *v.t*, to trace; copy.

calus (kaly:s) *m*, callus, callosity.

Calvaire (kalvɛ:r) *m*, Calvary (*place*). **calvaire**, (*representation*); cross (*fig.*).

calvitie (kalvisi) *f*, baldness.

camarade (kamarad) *n*, comrade, fellow, mate, chum, companion. ~ *d'atelier*, fellow workman. ~ *d'école*, schoolfellow, schoolmate. ~ *de bord*, shipmate. ~ *de bouteille*, boon companion. ~ *de collège*, fellow student. ~ *de jeu*, playfellow, playmate. ~ *de lit*, ~ *de chambrée*, bedfellow, roommate. ~ *de malheur*, fellow sufferer. ~ *de plat*, messmate. ~ *de promotion*, class mate. **camaraderie** (dri) *f*, comradeship, fellowship, friendship.

camard, e (kama:r, ard) *a*, snubnosed. *la camarde*, [grim] death (*fig.*).

cambouis (kɑ̃bwi) *m*, cart grease.

cambrer (kɑ̃bre) *v.t.* & se ~, to camber, arch, bend, curve.

cambriolage (kɑ̃briɔla:ʒ) *m*, housebreaking, burglary. **cambrioler** (le) *v.t*, to burgle. **cambrioleur** (lœ:r) *m*, burglar, cracksman. ~ *chat*, cat burglar.

cambrure (kɑ̃bry:r) *f*, camber. ~-*support*, *f*, arch support (*for foot in shoe*).

cambuse (kɑ̃by:z) *f*, steward's room (*ship*). **cambusier** (byzje) *m*, steward's mate; storekeeper (*Naut.*).

came (kam) *f*, cam, wiper, lifter; drugs (*heroin, etc.*).

camé, e (kame) *a*, drugged. ¶ *m*, drug addict, junkie.

camée (kame) *m*, cameo.

caméléon (kamele5) *m*, chameleon, trimmer, time server.

camélia (kamelja) *m*, camellia.

camelot (kamlo) *m*, hawker, street vender (*as newsboy*), handbill distributor. **camelote** (lɔt) *f*, rubbish, trash.

camera (kamera) *m*, movie camera.

camion (kamjɔ) *m*, wagon, truck; ~-*citerne*, *m*, tank truck. ~ *à benne basculante*, dump truck. **camionnage** (ɔna:ʒ) *m*, cartage. **camionnette** (nɛt) *f*, light truck. **camionneur** (nœr) *m*, truck driver, carter, carman; van horse, vanner.

camisole (kamizɔl) *f*, vest (*woman's*). ~ *de force*, straitjacket.

camomille (kamɔmi:j) *f*, camomile.

camouflage (kamufla:ʒ) *m*, camouflage. **camoufler** (fle) *v.t*, to disguise, camouflage.

camouflet (kamuflɛ) *m*, snub.

camp (kɑ̃) *m*, camp, field; side. ~ *de concentration* (civil), ~ *de prisonniers* (Mil.), internment camp. ~ *volant*, temporary camp; flying column.

campagnard, e (kɑ̃paɲa:r, ard) *n*, countryman, -woman. **campagne** (paɲ) *f*, country, countryside, fields; field (*Mil.*); campaign; run; cruise (*Nav.*). *faire une bonne* ~, to have a good year (*business*).

campagnol (kăpaɲɔl) *m*, vole.

campanile (kăpanil) *m*, campanile, bell tower.

campanule (kăpanyl) *f*, campanula, bell [flower]. ~ *à grandes fleurs*, Canterbury Bell.

campêche (kăpeʃ) *m*, logwood.

campement (kăpmã) *m*, encampment; camping [out]. **camper** (pe) *v.i.* & *t*, to [en]camp; lodge, ensconce; put, clap, stick. ~ *là*, to leave in the lurch. ~ *un personnage*, to play a theatrical role (*well*).

camphre (kã:fr) *m*, camphor. **camphrer** (kăfre) *v.t*, to camphorate.

campos (kăpo) *m*, holiday.

camus, e (kamy, y:z) *a*, flat-nosed, snub-nosed; pug-nosed.

Canada (le) (kanada), Canada. **canadien, ne** (djɛ̃, ɛn) *a.* & C~, *n*, Canadian; sheepskin jacket.

canaille (kanɑːj) *f*, rabble, mob, riffraff, ragtag [& bobtail]; blackguard, scoundrel, rascal.

canal (kanal) *m*, canal, channel, duct, pipe, passage, race[way], ditch, sluice[way]. ~ *de dérivation*, leat. ~ *banalisé*, citizens' band (*CB radio*). ~ *maritime*, ship canal. **canalisation** (lizasjɔ̃) *f*, canalization, piping; pipeline; mains. **canaliser** (ze) *v.t*, to canalize, pipe; (*fig.*) concentrate, focus, centralize.

canapé (kanape) *m*, sofa, couch, lounge. ~-*divan*, chesterfield. ~-*lit*, sofa bed.

canard (kanaːr) *m*, duck, drake; canard, hoax; rag (*worthless newspaper*). *bâtiment* ~, pitching ship. **canarder** (narde) *v.t*, to snipe (*Mil.*); pepper (*with shot*); (*v.i.*) to pitch (*ship*). **canardière** (djɛːr) *f*, duck pond; decoy (*place*); fowling piece.

canari (kanari) *m*, canary (*bird*). **les [îles] Canaries**, *f.pl*, the Canary Islands, the Canaries.

cancan (kãkã) *m*, cancan (*dance*); tattle, scandal, backbiting.

cancer (kɑsɛːr) *m*, cancer (*Med.*),

le ~, crab (*Astr.*). **cancéreux, euse** (serø, ø:z) *a*, cancerous.

cancre (kã:kr) *m*, crab (*Crust.*); dunce, duffer.

cancrelat (kãkrəla) *m*, cockroach.

candélabre (kãdelɑːbr) *m*, candelabrum; multi-light fixture.

candeur (kãdœːr) *f*, guilelessness, ingenuousness.

candidat, e (kãdida, at) *n*, candidate; examinee. ~ *à la députation*, parliamentary candidate. **candidature** (ty:r) *f*, candidature. *poser sa* ~, to apply for a job; announce one's candidacy.

candide† (kãdid) *a*, guileless, ingenuous.

candir (se) (kãdiːr) *v.pr*, to candy. *fruits candis* (di), crystalized fruits. [**sucre**] **candi** (di), *m*, [sugar] candy.

cane (kan) *f*, duck (*female*). **caner** (ne) *v.i*, to run away, show the white feather. **caneton** (ntɔ̃) duckling (*male*). **canette** (nɛt) *f*, duckling (*female*); [spring-stoppered] bottle (*for, or of, beer*); bobbin.

canevas (kanva) *m*, canvas; sketch; groundwork, outline, skeleton.

caniche (kaniʃ) *n.* & *a*, poodle.

canicule (kanikyl) *f*, dog days.

canif (kanif) *m*, penknife.

canin, e (kanɛ̃, in) *a*, canine, dog (*att.*).

caniveau (kanivo) *m*, gutter, gully, kennel [stone]; conduit.

canne (kan) *f*, cane; stick; walking stick; singlestick. ~ *à épée*, sword stick. ~ *à lancer*, casting rod (*Fish.*). ~ *à mouche*, fly rod (*Fish.*). ~ *à pêche*, fishing rod. ~ *à sucre*, sugarcane. ~ *plombée*, loaded stick. ~-*siège*, sportsman's seat, stick s.

canneberge (kanbɛrʒ) *f*, cranberry.

canneler (kanle) *v.t*, to channel, flute, groove, corrugate, rifle.

cannelle (kanɛl) *f*, cinnamon; butt cock.

cannelure (kanlyːr) *f*, channel-[ling], etc. as *canneler*.

canner (kane) *v.t*, to cane (*chairs*).

cannibale (kanibal) *m*, cannibal, man-eater; savage (*fierce man*).

canoë (kanɔe) *m*, canoe.

canon (kanɔ̃) *m*, gun, cannon; cañon, canyon; barrel, pipe, tube; canon (*rule—Eccl.*). ~ *d'amarrage*, bollard. ~ *de campagne à tir rapide*, quick-firing field gun. *droit* ~, canon law. **canonicat** (nɔnika) *m*, canonicate, canonry; sinecure. **canoniser** (ze) *v.t*, to canonize. **canonnade** (nad) *f*, cannonade. **canonnage** (naːʒ) *m*, gunnery. **canonner** (ne) *v.t*, to cannonade, bombard, shell. **canonnier** (nje) *m*, gunner. **canonnière** (njɛːr) *f*, gunboat; pop gun (*toy*).

canot (kano) *m*, boat; dinghy; cutter. ~ *à rames*, rowboat. ~ *de sauvetage*, lifeboat. **canotage** (nɔtaːʒ) *m*, boating, rowing. **canoter** (te) *v.i*, to boat, row. **canotier** (tje) *m*, rower, oarsman; boatman, waterman; boat keeper. [*chapeau*] ~, boater.

cantate (kɑ̃tat) *f*, cantata. **cantatrice** (tris) *f*, professional singer (*woman*), vocalist.

cantharide (kɑ̃tarid) *f*, Spanish fly.

cantine (kɑ̃tin) *f*, canteen. **cantinier, ère** (nje, ɛːr) *n*, canteen keeper.

cantique (kɑ̃tik) *m*, canticle, song, hymn.

canton (kɑ̃tɔ̃) *m*, canton, district. **cantonade** (tɔnad) *f*, wings (*Theat.*). **cantonnement** (nmɑ̃) *m*, cantonment, quarters; billets. ~ *de pêche*, stretch of fishing. **cantonner** (ne) *v.t. & i*, to canton, quarter, billet. *se* ~ *dans*, to withdraw to; keep oneself to. **cantonnier** (nje) *m*, roadman, road mender.

canular (kanylaːr) *m*, hoax, practical joke; tall tale.

canule (kanyl) *f*, nozzle; butt cock.

caoutchouc (kautʃu) *m*, rubber, elastic; [rubber] tire; waterproof, mackintosh; galosh, golosh, overshoe. ~ *durci*, vulcanite. **caoutchouter** (ʃute) *v.t*, to rubber[ize], waterproof; rubber-tire.

cap (kap) *m*, cape, headland, foreland; head. ~ *à pic*, bluff. *le* ~ *de Bonne-Espérance*, the Cape of Good Hope. *le* ~ *Vert*, Cape Verde. *mettre le* ~ *sur*, to head for.

capable (kapabl) *a*, capable; able, fit; efficient, qualified. **capacité** (site) *f*, capacity, capability, etc.

caparaçonner (kaparasɔne) *v.t*, to caparison.

cape (kap) *f*, hooded cape; hood; bowler [hat]. *rire sous* ~, to laugh up one's sleeve, chuckle. **capeline** (plin) *f*, hood.

capharnaüm (kafarnaɔm) *m*, jumble shop.

capillaire (kapillɛːr) *a*, capillary. ¶ *m*, maidenhair [fern].

capilotade (kapilɔtad) *f*, hash; pulp.

capitaine (kapitɛn) *m*, captain; master, skipper. ~ *au long cours*, deep-sea captain, master of foreign-going vessel. ~ *d'armement*, marine superintendent. ~ *d'entraînement*, coach. ~ *de corvette*, lieutenant commander (*Nav.*). ~ *de frégate*, commander (*Nav.*). ~ *de port*, harbor master. ~ *de vaisseau*, captain (*Nav.*). ~ *marchand*, captain of merchant ship, master mariner.

capital, e (kapital) *a*, capital, principal, main, essential; deadly (*sins*). ¶ *m. oft. pl*, principal, capital, capital sum; capital stock; money; assets. ~*-actions, m*, share capital. ~ *de roulement*, working c. ~ *engagé*, trading c. ~*-risque*, venture c. *le* ~ *& le travail*, Capital & Labor. *peine* ~, death penalty. ¶ *f*, capital (*town, letter*); metropolis. **capitaliser** (lize) *v.t*, to capitalize. **capitaliste** (list) *n*, capitalist.

capitan (kapitɑ̃) *m*, blusterer.

capitation (kapitasjɔ̃) *f*, poll tax.

capiteux, euse (kapitø, øːz) *a*, heady.

capitonner (kapitɔne) *v.t*, to upholster; quilt.

capituler (kapityle) *v.i*, to capitulate; compromise (*with conscience*).

capon, ne (kapɔ̃, ɔn) *n*, coward; sneak (*Sch.*).

caporal (kapɔral) *m*, corporal; caporal (*tobacco*).

capot (kapo) *m*, bonnet, hood, cover. être ~, to be defeated. faire ~, to capsize. **capote** (pɔt) *f*, greatcoat, overcoat (*Mil.*); hood, bonnet, cowl; top of convertible automobile. ~ *anglaise*, condom. ~ *pliante*, collapsible top (*auto*). **capoter** (te) *v.i*, to capsize, overturn.

câpre (kɑːpr) *f*, caper (*Bot.*).

caprice (kapris) *m*, caprice, whim, freak; [passing] fancy; vagary. **capricieux, euse,†** (sjø, øːz) *a*, capricious; temperamental; wayward.

capsule (kapsyl) *f*, capsule; seal (*bottle*); [percussion] cap.

capter (kapte) *v.t*, to catch, collect, save, recover; obtain by undue influence. *vouloir* ~, to make a bid for. ~ *les suffrages de*, win the votes of. **capteur** (tœːr) *m*, captor; sensor, gauge. ~ *de pression*, pressure gauge.

captieux, euse (kapsjø, øːz) *a*, captious.

captif, ive (kaptif, iːv) *a. & n*, captive. **captiver** (tive) *v.t*, to captivate. **captivité** (vite) *f*, captivity, bondage. **capture** (tyːr) *f*, capture. **capturer** (tyre) *v.t*, to capture, take; catch.

capuce (kapys) *m*, **capuchon** (ʃ5) *m*, hood, cowl.

capucin, e (kapysɛ̃, in) *n*, Capuchin friar, nun; (*f.*) nasturtium. **capucinade** (sinad) *f*, dull discourse.

caque (kak) *f*, barrel, keg. **caquer** (ke) *v.t*, to cure (*herrings*); barrel.

caquet (kakɛ) *m*, cackle; chatter. **caqueter** (kte) *v.i*, to cackle; chatter.

car (kaːr) *c*, for, because. ¶ *m*, bus.

carabin (karabɛ̃) *m*, medical student; saw-bones. **carabine** (bin) *f*, carbine, rifle. **carabiné, e** (ne) *a*, strong, stiff.

caracole (karakɔl) *f*, caracole.

caractère (karaktɛːr) *m*, character; characteristic, property, nature; complexion; authority; temper; type, (*pl.*) print. *écrire en* ~*s* *d'imprimerie*, to write in block letters. *jeu de* ~*s*, character set (*computers*). **caractériser** (terize) *v.t*, to characterize. **caractéristique** (ristik) *a*, characteristic. ¶ *f*, characteristic, feature.

carafe (karaf) *f*, water bottle, jug, decanter. **carafon** (f5) *m*, [small] decanter.

carambolage (karɑ̃bɔlaːʒ) *m*, cannon (*Bil.*).

caramel (karamɛl) *m*, caramel.

carapace (karapas) *f*, carapace, shell.

carat (kara) *m*, carat; carat goods; year (*age*). *sot à vingt-quatre* (ou *à trente-six*) ~*s*, champion idiot, out & out fool.

caravane (karavan) *f*, caravan. **caravansérail** (vɑ̃seraːj) *m*, caravanserai.

carbonate (karbɔnat) *m*, carbonate. **carbone** (bɔn) *m*, carbon. **carbonifère** (nifeːr) *a*, carboniferous, coal[-bearing]. **carbonique** (nik) *a*, carbonic. **carboniser** (ze) *v.t*, to carbonize, char. **carbonnade** (nad) *f*, grill[ed meat]. *à la* ~, grilled.

carburant (karbyrɑ̃) *m*, motor fuel.

carburateur (karbyratœːr) *m*, carburetor. **carbure** (byːr) *m*, carbide.

carcan (karkɑ̃) *m*, carcan (*Hist.*); yoke.

carcasse (karkas) *f*, carcass, carcase, body, skeleton, shell, frame[work]; shape (*hat, etc.*).

cardiaque (kardjak) *a*, cardiac. *crise* ~, heart attack. ¶ *n*, heart case (*pers.*).

cardinal, e (kardinal) *a*, cardinal. ¶ *m*, cardinal (*Eccl.*).

cardiogramme (kardjɔgram) *m*, cardiogram. **cardiograph** (graf) *m*, cardiographer; cardiogram. **cardiologue** (lɔg) *m*, cardiologist.

carême (karɛːm) *m*, lent.

carence (karɑ̃ːs) *f*, assets nil; insolvency.

carène (karɛn) *f*, bottom (*of ship*). **caréner** (rene) *v.t*, to careen.

caresse (karɛs) *f*, caress, endearment; blandishment. **caresser** (se) *v.t*, to caress; fondle; stroke; pat; cherish; flatter; indulge.

cargaison (kargɛzɔ̃) *f*, cargo, lading.

cargo (kargo) *m*, cargo-boat.

cari (kari) *m*, curry.

caricature (karikaty:r) *f*, caricature; cartoon; sight. **caricaturer** (tyre) *v.t*, to caricature. **caricaturiste** (rist) *n*, caricaturist, cartoonist.

carie (kari) *f*, caries, decay; rot. **carier** (rje) *v.t*, & se ~, to rot, decay.

carillon (karijɔ̃) *m*, chime[s]; carillon; peal; racket, row. **carillonner** (jone) *v.i*. & *t*, to chime, ring a peal; clatter; noise abroad. **carillonneur** (nœ:r) *m*, [bell] ringer.

carlin (karlɛ̃) *m*, pug [dog].

carlingue (karlɛ̃:g) *f*, ke[e]lson (*Naut*.); cockpit (*Avn*.).

carme (karm) *m*, Carmelite [friar]. **carmélite** (melit) *f*, Carmelite [nun].

carmin (karmɛ̃) *m*, carmine.

carnage (karna:ʒ) *m*, carnage, slaughter, bloodshed. **carnassier, ère** (nasje, ɛ:r) *a*, carnivorous. ¶ *m*, carnivore; (*f*.) game bag.

carnaval (karnaval) *m*, carnival.

carné, e (karne) *a*, flesh-colored; meaty (*food*); meat (*diet*).

carneau (karno) *m*, flue.

carnet (karnɛ) *m*, notebook, memorandum book; book. ~ *de bal*, dance program. ~ *de chèques*, checkbook. ~ *de compte*, ~ *de banque*, [bank] pass book. ~*-répertoire*, address book.

carnier (karnje) *m*, game bag. **carnivore** (nivɔ:r) *a*, carnivorous. ~**s**, *m.pl*, carnivora.

caroncule (karɔ̃kyl) *f*, wattle (*turkey*).

carotte (karɔt) *f*, carrot; bore core; plug, twist (*tobacco*); trick. *des cheveux* ~, carroty hair, ginger hair.

caroube (karub) *f*, carob [bean], locust [bean].

Carpathes (les) (karpat) *m.pl*, the Carpathians.

carpe (karp) *f*, carp (*fish*). *m*, wrist.

carpette (karpɛt) *f*, bordered [& seamless] carpet; rug.

carquois (karkwa) *m*, quiver (*for arrows*).

carre (ka:r) *f*, cross section; corner.

carré, e (kare) *a*, square. ¶ *m*, square; bed, patch (*Hort*.); landing, floor. ~ *des officiers*, ward room; mess room. ~ *long*, rectangle, oblong. **carreau** (ro) *m*, tile; floor; squab, cushion; hassock; diamonds (*cards*); pane, square. **carrefour** (karfu:r) *m*, crossroads; intersection (*in city*). *de* ~, street (*musician*); gutter (*language*). **carrelage** (rla:ʒ) *m*, tile floor[ing]. ~ *en briques*, brick paving. **carrelet** (rlɛ) *m*, square ruler; square file; plaice. **carrément** (remɑ̃) *ad*, square[ly], outright, flat[ly], straightforwardly. **carrer** (re) *v.t*, to square. se ~, to strut, swagger; settle oneself.

carrier (karje) *m*, quarryman. **carrière** (ɛ:r) *f*, career, course, scope, play, vent, head; walk of life; quarry, pit.

carriole (karjɔl) *f*, light cart.

carrosse (karɔs) *m*, coach. **carrosserie** (sri) *f*, coachbuilding; (*car*) body; bodywork. **carrossier** (sje) *m*, coachbuilder; motor body builder; coach horse.

carrousel (karuzɛl) *m*, tournament; merry-go-round; turntable, carousel (*air terminal baggage*).

carrure (kary:r) *f*, breadth of shoulders.

cartable (kartabl) *m*, satchel (*Sch*.).

carte (kart) *f*, card; ticket; map, chart. ~*s à jouer*, playing cards. ~ *blanche*, free hand, full discretionary power. ~ *céleste*, star map, map of the heavens. ~ *d'abonnement*, season ticket. ~ *d'adresse*, address card, business c. ~ *d'État-major*, ordnance [survey] map. ~ *de résultats*, scoring card (*golf*). ~ [*de visite*], [visiting] card. ~ *des vins*, wine list. ~ *du jour*, bill of fare, menu. ~ *en courbes de niveau*, contour map. ~ *grise*, registration (*auto*). ~ *orange*, monthly subway or bus pass. ~ *perforée*, punched card. ~ *postale illustrée*, picture postcard. ~ *vermeil*, senior citizen's reduction card.

cartel (kartɛl) *m*, challenge; cartel; coalition.

carter (kartɛːr) *m*, gear case.

cartilage (kartila:ʒ) *m*, cartilage, gristle.

cartographe (kartɔgraf) *m*, cartographer, map producer.

cartomancien, ne (kartɔmãsjɛ̃, ɛn) *n,* fortuneteller (*by cards*).

carton (kartɔ̃) *m*, cardboard, pasteboard, millboard; [cardboard] box *or* case, carton; mount (*Phot.*); cartoon; offcut (*Bookb.*); cancel (*Bookb.*). ~ *à chapeau*, hat box. ~ *de débarquement*, landing ticket. ~ *de dessins*, portfolio of drawings. ~ *de modiste*, bandbox. ~*paille*, *m*, strawboard. ~*-pâte*, *m*, papier-mâché. **cartonné, e** (tɔne) *p.a*, in boards (*book*). **cartonnier** (nje) *m*, cardboard [box] maker; file case.

cartouche (kartuʃ) *f*, cartridge, round [of ammunition]; case (*firework*); (*m.*) cartouche. ~ *à balle*, ball cartridge. ~ *à blanc*, blank c. **cartoucherie** (ʃri) *f*, cartridge factory. **cartouchière** (ʃjɛːr) *f*, cartridge pouch.

carvi (karvi) *m*, caraway.

cas (kɑ) *m*, case, event, circumstance, instance; matter; cause (*law*). ~ *limite*, borderline case. *faire* ~ *de*, to think highly of.

casanier, ère (kazanje, ɛːr) *a*. & *n*, stay-at-home.

casaque (kazak) *f*, jumper (*woman's*). *tourner* ~, to sell out (*Pol.*).

cascade (kaskad) *f*, cascade, waterfall, fall[s]; prank, spree; gag (*actor's*). **cascadeur** (œːr) *m*, stuntman (*cinema*); trapeze artist; reveller. **cascatelle** (tɛl) *f*, cascade.

case (kɑːz) *f*, compartment, division, pigeon hole; square (*chessboard*); frame, space (*on printed form*); locker; bin; native hut, cabin.

casemate (kazmat) *f*, casemate.

caser (kɑze) *v.t*, *t*o put away; find a situation for, settle.

caserne (kazɛrn) *f*, barrack[s]. **caserner** (ne) *v.t*, to barrack.

casier (kɑzje) *m*, cabinet, nest of drawers, [set of] pigeon holes; bin; rack. ~ *judiciaire*, police records.

casino (kazino) *m*, casino.

Caspienne (la mer) (kaspjɛn), the Caspian sea.

casque (kask) *m*, helmet; headphones, earphones. ~ *blindé*, crash helmet. ~ *de soleil*, sun helmet. ~ *en moelle*, pith helmet. ~ *respiratoire*, smoke helmet, gas mask (*fire*). **casquette** (kɛt) *f*, (*man's or boy's*) [peak] cap.

cassant, e (kɑsã, ãːt) *a*, brittle, crisp, short, hard; blunt, curt. **cassation** (sasjɔ̃) *f*, cassation, quashing, reduction to the ranks. **casse** (kɑːs) *f*, breakage, breakages; cassia; case (*Typ.*); ladle, scoop. ¶ (kɑs) *comps:* ~*-cou*, *m*, breakneck [place], death trap; dare-devil; roughrider; (*i.*) look out! mind! ~*-couilles*, *m*, ball-breaker (*obscene*). ~*-croûte*, *m*, snack; s. bar. ~*-noisettes*, *m*, nutcrackers; nuthatch. ~*-noix*, *m*, nutcrackers; nutcracker (*bird*). ~*-pieds*, *m*, bore (*person*). ~*-pierres*, *m*, stone breaker (*Mach.*). ~*-pipes*, *m*, war (*slang*). ~*-tête*, *m*, club, life preserver; puzzle, teaser. **casser** (kɑse) *v.t*. & *i*, to break, crack, snap; shatter; quash, set aside (*law*); cashier; reduce to the ranks. ~ *les prix*, to bring prices down. ~ *aux gages*, to pay off. *se* ~ *la tête*, to break one's head; puzzle (*or* rack) one's brains. *se* ~, to take off, leave (*slang*).

casserole (kasrɔl) *f*, saucepan, stewpan. ~ [*en terre cuite*], casserole.

cassette (kasɛt) *f*, casket, case; money box; privy purse; cassette (*magnetic tape*).

casseur (kɑsœːr) *m*, breaker. ~ *d'assiettes*, brawler.

cassier (kasje) *m*, cassia tree.

cassine (kasin) *f*, country cottage.

cassis (kɑsis) *m*, black currant(s); b. c. bush; b. c. cordial; water bar (*across road*).

cassonade (kasɔnad) *f*, moist sugar, brown s.

cassure (kɑsyːr) *f*, break, crack, fracture.

castagnette (kastaɲɛt), *f*, castanet.

caste (kast) *f*, caste. *esprit de ~*, class consciousness.

castor (kastɔːr) *m*, beaver. *~ du Canada*, musquash (*fur*).

castration (kastrasjɔ̃) *f*, castration; gelding.

casuel, le (kɑzɥel) *a*, casual; case (*ending—Gram.*). ¶ *m*, casual profits; perquisites.

casuistique (kɑzɥistik) *f*, casuistry.

cataclysme (kataklism) *m*, cataclysm, disaster.

catacombe (katakɔ̃b) *f*, catacomb.

catafalque (katafalk) *m*, catafalque.

catalogue (katalɔg) *m*, catalog, list. *~ par ordre de matières*, subject catalog. *~ raisonné*, descriptive c. **cataloguer** (ge) *v.t*, to catalog, list.

cataplasme (kataplasm) *m*, poultice.

catapulte (katapylt) *f*, catapult (*Hist. & Avn.*).

cataracte (katarakt) *f*, cataract (*falls & Med.*); (*pl.*) sluice gates (*of heaven*).

catarrhe (kataːr) *m*, catarrh.

catastrophe (katastrof) *f*, catastrophe.

catch (katʃ) *m*, wrestling (*sport*). **catcheur** (ʃœːr) *m*, wrestler.

catéchiser (kateʃize) *v.t*, to catechize; reason with, try to persuade. **catéchisme** (ʃism) *m*, catechism.

catégorie (kategɔri) *f*, category, class; predicament (*Log.*). **catégorique†** (rik) *a*, categorical; flat (*refusal*).

caténation (katenasjɔ̃) *f*, concatenation, series.

cathédrale (katedral) *f*, cathedral, minster.

cathode (katɔd) *f*, cathode.

catholicisme (katɔlisism) *m*, catholicism, Roman Catholicism. **catholique** (lik) *a*, catholic, Roman Catholic; orthodox. ¶ *n*, catholic, Roman Catholic.

catimini (en) (katimini) *ad*, stealthily, on the sly.

catin (katɛ̃) *f*, whore; slut (*slang*).

Caucase (le) (kokɑːz), the Caucasus. **caucasien, ne** (kɑzjɛ̃, ɛn) *a. & C~*, *n*, Caucasian.

cauchemar (koʃmaːr) *m*, nightmare, incubus; bugbear.

caudataire (kodatɛːr) *m*, train bearer; toady, toadeater, lickspittle.

cause (koːz) *f*, cause, occasion, ground[s]; case, action (*law*); brief (*law*); consideration (*equivalent, law*). *~ célèbre*, famous case. *à ~ de*, on account of, because of, for; for the sake of, through. *en tout état de ~*, in any case. *& pour ~*, & for good reasons, & very properly. *sans ~*, briefless (*lawyer*). **causer** (koze) *v.t*, to cause, occasion.

causer (koze) *v.i*, to talk, converse, chat; talk of; sit out (*a dance*). *assez causé!* that'll do! **causerie** (zri) *f*, talk, chat, chitchat; causerie. **causette** (zɛt) *f*, little chat. **causeur, euse** (zœːr, øːz) *n*, talker, conversation[al]ist; (*f.*) settee.

caustique (kostik) *a*, caustic, biting, cutting. ¶ *m*, caustic (*Phar.*).

cauteleux, euse (kotlø, øːz) *a*, cunning, crafty.

cautère (kotɛːr) *m*, cautery. **cautériser** (terize) *v.t*, to cauterize, sear.

caution (kosjɔ̃) *f*, surety, security, guarantee, -ty, guarantor, indemnity, bail. *se rendre ~ pour*, to go bail for. *sujet à ~*, unreliable. **cautionnement** (ɔnmɑ̃) *m*, security, indemnity, deposit, bail, surety (*or indemnity*) bond, qualification (*in shares*). **cautionner** (ne) *v.t*, to become security for, guarantee, bail; give security for, answer for.

cavalcade (kavalkad) *f*, cavalcade; pageant; ride.

cavalerie (kavalri) *f*, cavalry; horse (*troop*); stable (*horses*). **cavalier, ère†** (lje, ɛːr) *a*, offhand, cavalier; free & easy; riding (*track*); bridle (*path*). ¶ *m*,

horseman, rider, equestrian; trooper; gentleman, man; cavalier, escort; partner (*at dance*); knight (*chess*); [wire] staple. ¶ *f*, horsewoman, rider, equestrian.
cave (ka:v) *a*, hollow, sunk[en]. ¶ *f*, cellar, vault; pool (*cards*). ~ à liqueurs, liqueur case *or* set; tantalus. ~ *forte*, strong room. ¶ *m*, square (*person*); john (*prostitute's client*). caveau (kavo) *m*, [small] cellar; vault (*family grave*). **caver** (ve) *v.t*, to hollow, scoop out, [under]mine, wear away *or* hollow; put up (*money at cards*). **caverne** (vɛrn) *f*, cavern, cave; den. **caverneux, euse** (nø, ø:z) *a*, cavernous, hollow.
caviar (kavja:r) *m*, caviar[e].
cavité (kavite) *f*, cavity, hollow.
cawcher, ère (kauʃe, ɛ:r) *a*, kosher.
ce, cet, cette, *pl.* **ces** (sə, sɛt, sɛt, se) *a*, this; that; such [a]; (*pl.*) these; those; such. *cette rue-ci* & *non cette rue-là*, this street & not that street. *ce soir*, this evening, tonight. *cette nuit*, last night.
ce (sə), *c'* ou *ç'* *as in c'est,* *ç'a été*, *pn*, it; this, that; he, she; they; those. *c'est-à-dire* (*abb.* c.-à-d.) that is to say, i.e., viz. *ce que*, what, that which.
cébiste (sebist) *m*, one who uses CB radio.
ceci (səsi) *pn*, this.
cécité (sesite) *f*, blindness. ~ *des neiges*, snow b. ~ *pour les couleurs*, color b.
cédant, e (sedɑ̃, ɑ̃:t) *n*, transferor, assignor. **céder** (de) *v.t. & i. & abs*, to cede, yield, give up; give in, surrender, cave in; assign, transfer; dispose of, give way. [*le*] ~ *à*, to yield [the palm] to, be second to.
cédille (sedi:j) *f*, cedilla.
cédrat (sedra) *m*, citron.
cèdre (sɛ:dr) *m*, cedar. ~ *du Liban* (libɑ̃), c. of Lebanon.
cédule (sedyl) *f*, schedule (*Inc. Tax*).
ceindre (sɛ̃:dr) *v.t.ir*, to surround, [en]compass, [en]circle, gird[le], belt, wreathe. **ceinture** (sɛ̃ty:r) *f*, belt, girdle, sash, waistband; waist, middle; waist lock (*wres-*

tling); enclosure. ~ *cartouchière*, cartridge belt. ~ *de sauvetage*, life b. ~ *porte-jarretelles*, suspender b. ~ *de sécurité*, safety b. (*auto*). ceinturer (tyre) *v.t*, to grasp round the body. **ceinturon** (rɔ̃) *m*, belt (*sword, etc.*).
cela (səla) *pn*, that; it; so. *c'est* ~, that is it; that's right, just so.
célèbre (selɛbr) *a*, celebrated, famous, noted. **célébrer** (lebre) *v.t*, to celebrate; solemnize, hold (*funeral*); sing (*praises of*). **célébrité** (brite) *f*, celebrity.
celer (səle) *v.t*, to conceal, hide.
céleri (selri) *m*, celery.
célérité (selerite) *f*, celerity, swiftness, dispatch.
céleste (selɛst) *a*, celestial, heavenly; of the heavens (*map*), star (*map*); sky (*blue*).
célibat (seliba) *m*, celibacy, single life. **célibataire** (tɛ:r) *n*, bachelor, celibate, single man, woman.
cellérier (selerje) *m*, cellarer. **cellier** (lje) *m*, storeroom (*wines*).
cellulaire (selylɛ:r) *a*, cellular. *voiture* ~, police van. **cellule** (lyl) *f*, cell; light meter. **celluloïd** (lɔid) *m*, celluloid. **cellulose** (lo:z) *f*, cellulose.
Celte (sɛlt) *n*, Celt, Kelt. **celtique** (tik) *a. & m.* (*language*), Celtic, Keltic.
celui, celle, *pl.* **ceux, celles** (səlɥi, sɛl, sø, sɛl) *pn*, he, she; those; the one. *celui-ci, celle-ci*, this one, this, the latter. *celui-là, celle-là*, that one, that, the former.
cémenter (semɑ̃te) *v.t*, to cement (*metal*); caseharden.
cénacle (senakl) *m*, group, coterie (*especially literary*).
cendre (sɑ̃:dr) *f. oft. pl*, ash[es]; dust; embers. **cendré, e** (sɑ̃dre) *a*, ash[-colored], ashen, ashy; gray (*brain matter*). ¶ *f*, cinders (*track*). **cendrier** (drie) *m*, ash pan; ash tray. ~ *sur pied*, smokers' stand.
Cendrillon (sɑ̃drijɔ̃) *f*, Cinderella.
Cène (sɛ:n) *f*, Last Supper; Lord's supper.
cenelle (sənɛl) *f*, haw; holly berry.

cénotaphe (senɔtaf) *m*, cenotaph.

censé, e (sɑ̃se) *a*, deemed, reputed, supposed. **censément** (mɑ̃) *ad*, supposedly, virtually. **censeur** (sœːr) *m*, censor; critic; auditor; vice principal (*college*); examiner (*plays*). **censure** (syːr) *f*, censorship; [vote of] censure; [board of] censors. **censurer** (syre) *v.t*, to censure, criticize, find fault with, reprehend.

cent (sɑ̃) *a. & m*, hundred. **centaine** (tɛn) *f*, hundred [or so], about a hundred.

centaure (sɑ̃toːr) *m*, centaur.

centenaire (sɑ̃tnɛːr) *n*, centenarian; (*m.*) centenary.

centième (sɑ̃tjɛm) *a. & m*, hundredth.

centigrade (sɑ̃tigrad) *a*, centigrade. Water freezes 0° Cent. = 32 Fahr. Water boils 100° C. = 212 F. *To convert* :—F. = ⅘ C. + 32 [thus, 100 C. × 9 = 900 ÷ 5 = 180 + 32 = 212 F.]. C. = ⅝ (F. — 32) [thus, 212 F. — 32 = 180 × 5 = 900 ÷ 9 = 100 C.].

centigramme (sɑ̃tigram) *m*, centigram = ¹⁄₁₀₀ gram *or* 0.154 grain.

centilitre (sɑ̃tilitr) *m*, centiliter = ¹⁄₁₀₀ liter *or* 0.070 gill.

centime (sɑ̃tim) *m*, centime = ¹⁄₁₀₀ of franc.

centimètre (sɑ̃timɛtr) *m*, centimeter = ¹⁄₁₀₀ meter *or* 0.3937 inch; tape measure (divided into cms, 1½ meters long). ~ *carré*, square centimeter = 0.15500 sq. inch. ~ *cube*, cubic centimeter = 0.0610 cub. inch.

central, e (sɑ̃tral) *a*, central. ¶ *m*, telephone exchange. **centraliser** (lize) *v.t*, to centralize. **centre** (sɑ̃tr) *m*, center, middle; hub (*fig.*). ~ *de direction*, control center. ~ *de table*, table center. ~ *de villégiature*, holiday resort. **centrer** (sɑ̃tre) *v.t*, to center. **centrifuge** (trify:ʒ) *a*, centrifugal. **centripète** (pɛt) *a*, centripetal.

centuple (sɑ̃typl) *m*, centuple, hundredfold.

cep (sɛp) *m*, stock (*vine*); (*pl.*) stocks (*Hist.*). **cépée** (sepe) *f*, head of shoots (*willow, etc.*).

cependant (səpɑ̃dɑ̃) *ad*, in the mean time, meantime, meanwhile. ¶ *c*, yet, still, nevertheless, though.

céramique (seramik) *f*, ceramics.

cerceau (sɛrso) *m*, hoop; cradle (*Surg.*).

cercle (sɛrkl) *m*, circle; ring, hoop, band; club (*of people*). ~ *des fées*, fairy ring. *en* ~*s*, in the wood (*wine*). **cercler** (kle) *v.t*, to hoop (*casks*).

cercueil (sɛrkœ:j) *m*, coffin, shell; cocktail made of beer, Picon, and grenadine.

céréale (sereal) *a.f. & f*, cereal.

cérébral, e (serebral) *a*, cerebral, brain (*att.*).

cérémonial (seremɔnjal) *m*, ceremonial. **cérémonie** (ni) *f*, ceremony, circumstance, fuss, ado. *visite de* ~, formal visit. **cérémonieux, euse†** (njø, ø:z) *a*, ceremonious, formal.

cerf (sɛːr & sɛrf) *m*, stag, hart, deer.

cerfeuil (sɛrfœ:j) *m*, chervil.

cerf-volant (sɛrvɔlɑ̃) *m*, stag beetle; kite (*paper*).

cerisaie (sərizɛ) *f*, cherry orchard. **cerise** (riːz) *f*, cherry. ¶ *a. & m*, cherry-red; cerise. **cerisier** (rizje) *m*, cherry [tree].

cerne (sɛrn) *m*, ring (*tree, eyes, moon*), circle. **cerner** (ne) *v.t*, to surround, [en]circle, [en]compass, ring, hem in; invest (*Mil.*); shell (*nuts*); dig round (*tree*). *les yeux cernés*, rings under the eyes.

certain, e (sɛrtɛ̃, ɛn) *a*, certain; sure; stated; some. *le certain*, fixed (*rate of*) exchange. **certainement** (tɛnmɑ̃) *ad*, certainly, of course, by all means. **certes** (sɛrt) *ad*, most certainly, indeed.

certificat (sɛrtifika) *m*, certificate, scrip; testimonial, character. ~ *d'action(s)*, stock certificate. **certifier** (fje) *v.t*, to certify; witness.

certitude (sɛrtityd) *f*, certainty.

céruse (sery:z) *f*, ceruse, white lead.

cerveau (sɛrvo) *m*, brain; brains, intellect, mind, head. ~ *brûlé*, madcap, hothead. ~ *creux*, dreamer. **cervelle** (vɛl) *f*, brain[s], mind, head; pith (*palm tree*); (*s. & pl. Cook.*) brains. *rompre la ~ à quelqu'un*, to drive someone crazy.

cervelas (sɛrvəla) *m*, cervelat sausage.

Cervin (le mont) (sɛrvɛ̃), the Matterhorn.

cessation (sɛsasjɔ̃) *f*, cessation, discontinuance; suspension. **sans cesse** (sɛs), without cease, unceasingly. **cesser (se)** *v.i. & t*, to cease, leave off, break off, stop. *faire ~*, to put a stop to.

cessible (sɛsibl) *a*, transferable. **cession** (sjɔ) *f*, transfer, assignment. *~ d'intérêt*, farming out, leasing out, subleasing. **cessionbail** (ba:j) *f*, lease-back. **cessionnaire** (ɔnɛ:r) *n*, transferee.

Ceylan (selɑ̃) *m*, Ceylon.

chablis (ʃabli) *m*, windfall (*tree*); Chablis (*wine*).

chabot (ʃabo) *m*, chub (*fish*).

chacal (ʃakal) *m*, jackal.

chacun, e (ʃakœ̃, yn) *pn*, each, each one, every one. ¶ *m*, everybody, everyone, every one.

chafouin, e (ʃafwɛ̃, in) *a. & n*, sorry (fellow), poor (creature).

chagrin, e (ʃagrɛ̃, in) *a*, sorrowful, glum, moody, grieved, vexed, fretful. ¶ *m*, grief, sorrow, vexation, fret[fulness], chagrin; shagreen. *~ d'amour*, disappointment in love. **chagriner** (grine) *v.t*, to grieve, afflict; vex. *se ~*, to grieve, fret, repine.

chah (ʃa) *m*, shah.

chahut (ʃay) *m*, uproar; prank. **chahuter** (te) *v.t. & i*, to behave in an undisciplined manner; heckle. *vol chahuté*, rough flight (*Avn.*).

chaîne (ʃɛ:n) *f*, chain; range (*hills*); channel (*TV*). (*pl.*) fetters, bonds; warp. *~ de mailles*, chain of stitches, casting off (*Knit.*). *faire une ~ de mailles*, to cast off. *travail à la ~*, assembly-line work. **chaînette** (ʃɛnɛt) *f*, chain (*small*). **chaînon** (nɔ̃) *m*, link. *~ manquant*, missing link.

chair (ʃɛ:r) *f. sometimes pl*, flesh; meat; pulp (*of fruit*). *~ à pâté*, mincemeat. *~s baveuses*, proud flesh. *~ de poule*, gooseflesh (*fig.*). *cela fait venir la ~ de poule*, it makes one's flesh creep.

chaire (ʃɛ:r) *f*, pulpit; desk; throne (*bishop's*); chair, professorship; mastership; see.

chaise (ʃɛ:z) *f*, chair, seat; stall (*choir*); hanger (*Mach.*). *~ à porteurs*, sedan [chair]. *~ de pont*, deck chair. *~ paillée*, rushseat chair. *~ [percée]*, [night] commode.

chaland (ʃalɑ̃) *m*, barge, lighter, scow.

chaland, e (ʃalɑ̃, ɑ̃:d) *n*, customer, patron.

chalandage (ʃalɑ̃daʒ) *m*, window shopping, browsing (*in stores*).

châle (ʃɑ:l) *m*, shawl, wrap.

chalet (ʃalɛ) *m*, chalet, cottage. *~ de nécessité*, public convenience.

chaleur (ʃalœ:r) *f*, heat, warmth, glow. **chaleureux, euse†** (lœrø, ø:z) *a*, warm (*fig.*), cordial.

chaloupe (ʃalup) *f*, launch, longboat. *~ canonnière*, gunboat.

chalumeau (ʃalymo) *m*, blowpipe; reed; drinking straw; [shepherd's] pipe.

chalut (ʃaly) *m*, trawl [net]. **chalutier** (tje) *m*, trawler.

chamade (ʃamad) *f*, parley, chamade. *battre la ~*, to signal for a parley; be in a panic.

chamailler (se) (ʃamaje) *v.pr*, to bicker, wrangle, squabble, brawl.

chamarrer (ʃamare) *v.t*, to bedizen, bedeck; lard (*fig.*).

chambranle (ʃɑ̃brɑ̃:l) *m*, frame (*door, window*).

chambre (ʃɑ̃:br) *f*, room, chamber, apartment, lodging; cabin (*ship's*); house; committee; court. *~ à air*, inner tube (*tire*). *~ [à coucher]*, [bed]room. *~ à deux lits*, double[-bedded] room. *~ à un lit*, single r. *~ d'ami*, guest room, spare [bed]room. *~ d'enfants*, nursery. *~ d'explosion*, combustion chamber (*motor*). *~ de chauffe*, stokehole; boiler room. *~ de compensation*, clearing house. *~ de [mise à] mort*, death chamber. *C~ des communes, des pairs*, House of Commons, of Lords. *C~ des députés*,

Chamber of Deputies. ~ *des valeurs*, strong room (*ship*). ~*s en enfilade*, suite of rooms. ~ *sur le derrière*, ~ *sur la cour*, back room. ~ *sur le devant*, ~ *sur la rue*, front r. ~ *syndicale des agents de change*, stock exchange committee. ~ *noire*, darkroom (*Phot*.); camera obscura. **chambrée** (ʃɑ̃bre) *f*, roomful; house (*audience*); barrack room. **chambrer** (bre) *v.t*, to confine, closet; chamber, hollow out; take the chill off (*wine*).

chameau (ʃamo) *m*, camel; rascal; brute; s.o.b. (*slang*). **chamelier** (məlje) *m*, c. driver. **chamelle** (mɛl) *f*, she camel.

chamois (ʃamwa) *m*, chamois. [*peau de*] ~, wash leather, chamois [leather].

champ (ʃɑ̃) *m*, field, ground; scope, range; shot (*cinema*); edge. ~*s communs*, common [land]. ~ *d'aviation*, airfield. ~ *de courses*, racecourse. ~ *de manœuvres*, drill ground, parade g., ~ *de massacre*, shambles. ~ *de tir*, rifle range, shooting r. ~ *du repos*, churchyard. ~ *visuel*, field of vision. *hors* ~, off camera, screen. *dans le champ*, on screen, in (*sound*). *profondeur de* ~, depth of field (*cinema*). ~*contre* ~, angle/reverse angle (*cinema*).

champagne *ou* **vin de C**~ (ʃɑ̃paɲ) *m*, champagne. ~ *frappé* [*de glace*], iced c.

champêtre (ʃɑ̃pɛ:tr) *a*, rural, country (*att*.), rustic, sylvan.

champignon (ʃɑ̃piɲɔ̃) *m*, mushroom, wigstand. ~ [*vénéneux*], fungus, toadstool. **champignonnière** (ɲɔnjɛ:r) *f*, mushroom bed.

champion (ʃɑ̃pjɔ̃) *m*, champion. **championnat** (ɔna) *m*, championship.

chance (ʃɑ̃:s) *f*, chance; luck.

chanceler (ʃɑ̃sle) *v.i*, to totter, reel, stagger; waver, falter.

chancelier (ʃɑ̃səlje) *m*, chancellor. **chancelière** (lje:r) *f*, foot muff. **chancellerie** (sɛlri) *f*, chancellery.

chanceux, euse (ʃɑ̃sø, ø:z) *a*, lucky; hazardous.

chancre (ʃɑ̃:kr) *m*, canker; ulcer.

chandail (ʃɑ̃da:j) *m*, sweater (*dress*).

chandelier (ʃɑ̃dəlje) *m*, chandler; candlestick. **chandelle** (dɛl) *f*, candle; prop, post, shore; lob (*Ten*.). *je lui dois une fière* ~, I have reason to be grateful to him.

chanfrein (ʃɑ̃frɛ̃) *m*, chamfer; forehead (*horse*).

change (ʃɑ̃:ʒ) *m*, exchange (*Fin*.). *bureau de* ~, foreign exchange office. **changeant, e** (ʃɑ̃ʒɑ̃, ɑ̃:t) *a*, changeable, variable; fitful; fickle; shot (*fabrics*). **changement** (ʒmɑ̃) *m*, change, alteration; turn (*tide*); shift (*wind*); amendment (*to document*). ~ *à vue*, transformation scene. ~ *de décor*[*ation*], scene shifting. ~ *de marche*, reversing; r. gear. ~ *de vitesse*, gear shift. ~ [*de voie*], switch points (*Rly*.). **changer** (ʒe) *v.t. & abs. & i*, to change, alter; turn; exchange; shift; amend. ~ *d'avis, de linge*, to change one's mind, one's linen. ~ *de pas*, to change step. **changeur** (ʒœ:r) *m*, money changer.

chanoine (ʃanwan) *m*, canon (*Eccl*.).

chanson (ʃɑ̃sɔ̃) *f*, song, ballad, ditty; lay; story. ~ [*de bord*], [sea] chanty. ~ *de circonstance*, topical song. ~ *de route*, marching song. ~*s*, [~*s*]! nonsense! humbug! fiddlesticks! **chansonner** (sɔne) *v.t*, to lampoon. **chansonnette** (nɛt) *f*, ditty; comic song. **chansonnier, ère** (nje, ɛ:r) *n*, song writer; (*m*.) song book; small revue-theater.

chant (ʃɑ̃) *m*, singing, song, lay, chant; melody; canto; warbling, crowing, chirp. ~ *d'allégresse*, carol. ~ *du coq*, cockcrow[ing]. ~ *du cygne*, swan song. ~ *funèbre*, ~ *de mort*, dirge, lament. *de* ~, edgeways, edgewise, on edge.

chantage (ʃɑ̃ta:ʒ) *m*, blackmail.

chantant, e (ʃɑ̃tɑ̃, ɑ̃:t) *a*, musical, tuneful; singsong.

chanteau (ʃɑ̃to) *m*, [c]hunk; cutting (*snip of cloth*).

chanter (ʃɑ̃te) *v.i. & t*, to sing, chant, play the air; warble, crow, chirp; talk [about], say, cry. ~

toujours la même antienne, to be always harping on the same string. ~ *victoire sur,* to crow over. *faire ~ quelqu'un,* to blackmail someone. *si ça vous chante,* if that suits you. **chanterelle** (trɛl) *f,* highest string; call bird. **chanteur, euse** (tœːr, ɸːz) *n,* singer, vocalist; songster, songstress; *(att.)* song *(bird).*

chantier (ʃɑ̃tje) *m,* yard; floor *(foundry);* shipyard; dockyard dunnage; gantry, scantling *(for cask).* sur le ~, work in hand.

chantonner (ʃɑ̃tɔne) *v.i,* to hum *(tune).*

chantourner (ʃɑ̃turne) *v.t,* to jig-saw.

chantre (ʃɑ̃ːtr) *m,* cantor; Bard.

chanvre (ʃɑ̃ːvr) *m,* hemp; hash *(drug).*

chaos (kao) *m,* chaos. **chaotique** (ɔtik) *a,* chaotic.

chaparder (ʃaparde) *v.t,* to steal, swipe; scrounge.

chape (ʃap) *f,* cope; chape; cover, cap, lid; shell; strap; bearings; coating, covering.

chapeau (ʃapo) *m,* hat, bonnet; cap, cover, hood. ~ *à cornes,* cocked hat. ~ *claque,* crush h., opera h. ~ *haut de forme,* ~ *de soie,* high hat, silk h. ~ *melon,* bowler [h.]. ~ *rabattu,* slouch h. ~ *souple,* felt h. ~ *bas,* hat in hand. ~x *bas!,* hats off. (In student circles, the cry "*chapeau!*" warns offender to remove his/her hat.)

chapechute (ʃapʃyt) *f,* godsend, windfall.

chapelain (ʃaplɛ̃) *m,* chaplain.

chapelet (ʃaplɛ) *m,* rosary; [string of] beads; string, rope.

chapelier (ʃapəlje) *m,* hatter. [malle] **chapelière** (ɛːr) *f,* Saratoga [trunk].

chapelle (ʃapɛl) *f,* chapel; meeting house; [church] plate; coterie, set. ~ *ardente,* mortuary chapel. ~ *de la Vierge,* Lady chapel. ~ *sépulcrale,* mortuary chapel. *petite* ~, artistic clique or coterie.

chapellerie (ʃapɛlri) *f,* hat trade; h. shop.

chapelure (ʃaplyːr) *f,* grated bread crumbs.

chaperon (ʃaprɔ̃) *m,* chaperon;

coping. **chaperonner** (prɔne) *v.t,* to chaperon; cope *(wall).*

chapiteau (ʃapito) *m,* capital *(Arch.);* head, cap, top.

chapitre (ʃapitr) *m,* chapter *(book, canons);* head[ing]; item; subject, matter, point. **chapitrer** (tre) *v.t,* to lecture, reprimand.

chapon (ʃapɔ̃) *m,* capon.

chaque (ʃak) *a,* each, every; either.

char (ʃaːr) *m,* chariot; wagon. ~ *à bancs,* charabanc *(horse).* ~ *d'assaut,* tank *(Mil.).* ~ [de deuil], ~ *funèbre,* hearse.

charade (ʃarad) *f,* charade; conundrum.

charançon (ʃarɑ̃sɔ̃) *m,* weevil.

charbon [ʃarbɔ̃] *m,* coal[s]; charcoal; carbon; embers; carbuncle *(Med.);* anthrax; blight *(Agric.).* ~ *à dessin,* charcoal [pencil]. *en* ~, burnt to a cinder *(meat). faire du* ~, to coal. *sur des* ~s [*ardents*], on tenterhooks. **charbonnage** (bonaːʒ) *m,* coal mining; *(pl.)* coal mines. **charbonner** (ne) *v.t,* to black *(face, etc.).* se ~, *v.pr. ou* ~, *v.i,* to char, carbonize; *(v.i.)* to smoke *(lamp).* **charbonnerie** (nri) *f,* coal yard. **charbonnier** (nje) *m,* charcoal burner; coal merchant; coalman; coal cellar; collier *(ship).*

charcuter (ʃarkyte) *v.t,* to hack, mangle *(in carving).* **charcuterie** (tri) *f,* pork butchery; [dressed] pork, pig meat. **charcutier, ère** (tje, ɛːr) *n,* pork butcher.

chardon (ʃardɔ̃) *m,* thistle; spikes. ~ *à bonnetier,* ~ *à foulon,* teasel. **chardonneret** (dɔnrɛ) *m,* goldfinch.

charge (ʃarʒ) *f,* load, burden; charge, encumbrance, onus; expense; stress; pressure; head [of water]; loading; shipment; cargo; trust, care, custody; cure *(of souls);* duty, office; practice; membership, seat; instructions, directions; caricature; overacting; impersonation *(Theat.);* joke. ~ *à la cueillette,* general cargo. *à* [*la*] ~ *de,* on condition that, provided that. *à la* ~ *de,* chargeable to, payable by, at the expense of; dependent on. *en* ~, live *(Elec.);* load *(water line);* [now] loading (*ship*). ~ *de pointe*, peak load (*computers*). ~ *utile*, payload. **chargé, e** (ʒe) *a*, loaded; full; live (*shell*); furred (*tongue*); overcast, heavy (*weather*); insured (*Post*). **chargé d'affaires,** *m*, chargé d'affaires. **chargement** (ʒəmɑ̃) *m*, loading, lading; charging; filling; shipping, shipment; cargo; consignment; insurance (*Post*); registered package. ~ *en plein jour*, daylight loading (*Phot.*). **charger** (ʒe) *v.t*, to load, lade, burden, charge, fill; stress; inflate (*account*); clog, saddle; lie heavy on; ship; instruct, order, direct; entrust; overact; overdo; overdraw; overcharge; caricature; [in]criminate; insure (*Post*). se ~ **de**, to undertake, take charge of, attend to. **chargeur** (ʒœːr) *m*, charger, loader; shipper; stoker (*Mach.*).

chariot (ʃarjo) *m*, truck, wagon, wain, trolley, car; go-cart; carriage, carrier; dolly (*cinema*).

charitable† (ʃaritabl) *a*, charitable, benevolent. **charité** (te) *f*, charity; alms; dole.

charivari (ʃarivari) *m*, charivari, hubbub.

charlatan (ʃarlatɑ̃) *m*, charlatan, quack. **charlatanerie** (tanri) *f*, quackery.

charmant, e (ʃarmɑ̃, ɑ̃ːt) *a*, charming, fascinating, delightful. **charme** (ʃarm) *m*, charm, spell; attraction; allurement; hornbeam, yoke elm. *sous le* ~, spellbound. **charmer** (me) *v.t*, to charm, delight, bewitch; beguile, while away. **charmeur, euse** (mœːr, øːz) *n*, charmer. **charmille** (miːj) *f*, hedge *or* bower (*of hornbeam*).

charnel, le† (ʃarnɛl) *a*, carnal, sensual. **charnier** (nje) *m*, charnel house, ossuary.

charnière (ʃarnjɛːr) *f*, hinge. *à* ~, *à* ~s, hinged.

charnu, e (ʃarny) *a*, fleshy, brawny. **charnure** (nyːr) *f*, flesh (*of pers.*). **charogne** (rɔɲ) *f*, carrion.

charpente (ʃarpɑ̃ːt) *f*, frame[work]. ~ [*en bois*], timber work. ~ *en fer*, ironwork. ~ *métallique*, iron & steel construc-

tional work. **charpenter** (pɑ̃te) *v.t*, to carpenter, frame, put together. *bien charpenté*, well-knit, well-built, of sturdy build. **charpenterie** (tri) *f*, carpentry; (*ship's*) timber yard. **charpentier** (tje) *m*, carpenter. ~ *de vaisseau*, shipwright. ~ *en fer*, ironworker.

charpie (ʃarpi) *f*, lint; shreds.

charretée (ʃarte) *f*, cartload. **charretier, ère** (tje, ɛːr) *n*, carter. **charrette** (rɛt) *f*, cart. ~ *anglaise*, dogcart, trap. **charrier** (rje) *v.t*, to cart, carry, convey; drift; make fun of. **charroi** (rwa) *m*, cartage. **charroyer** (rwaje) *v.t*, to cart. **charron** (rɔ̃) *m*, wheelwright.

charrue (ʃary) *f*, plow. ~ *multiple*, gang p.

charte (ʃart) *f*, charter; deed (*ancient*). ~-**partie**, *f*, charter [party]. ~ *de grain*, grain charter.

chartreuse (ʃartrøːz) *f*, Carthusian monastery; lone cottage; chartreuse (*liqueur*). **chartreux** (trø) *m*, Carthusian [monk].

chas (ʃa) *m*, eye (*needle, etc.*).

chasse (ʃas) *f*, chase, hunt, hunting; shooting; shoot; pursuit; kill (*of game*); play, clearance (*Mech.*); set (*of saw teeth*); (*pl.*) squares (*bookbinding*). ~ *à courre* (kuːr), hunt[ing] (*riding to hounds*). ~ *à la grosse bête*, big-game hunting. ~ *au cerf à l'affût*, deer stalking. ~ *au lévrier*, coursing. ~ *aux oiseaux*, fowling. ~ *d'air*, blast (*or* rush) of air. ~ [*d'eau*], flush. ~ *gardée*, ~ *réservée*, [game] preserves. ~ *aux sorcières*, witch-hunt.

châsse (ʃɑːs) *f*, reliquary, shrine; frame (*spectacles*); scales (*lancet*).

chassé (ʃase) *m*, chassé (*Danc.*).

chasse-mouches (ʃasmuʃ) *m*, fly whisk; fly net. **chasse-neige** (nɛːʒ) *m*, snow squall; snowplow.

chasser (ʃase) *v.t. & abs. & i*, to drive, drive away *or* out *or* off *or* in; expel; chase, chevy, chivy; hound out; hunt; shoot; course; pursue; dismiss; dispel; drift; drag (*anchor*); chassé (*Danc.*). ~ *à l'affût*, to stalk. **chasseur, euse** (sœːr, øːz) *n*, hunter, huntress, huntsman; -catcher (*butter-*

flies, etc.); messenger, commissionaire, page[boy]; chaser (*Nav.*). fighter (*Avn.*).

chassieux, euse (ʃasjø, ø:z) *a*, gummy (*eyes*), blear-eyed.

châssis (ʃasi) *m*, frame; sash; chassis (*motor*); panel (*radio*); chase (*Typ.*); flat (*Theat.*); stretcher (*for painter's canvas*). ~ *à fiches*, casement, French sash.

chaste† (ʃast) *a*, chaste. **chasteté** (təte) *f*, chastity.

chasuble (ʃazybl) *f*, chasuble.

chat (ʃa) *m*, **chatte** (ʃat) *f*, cat, tom [cat]; he-cat, she-cat, puss, pussy [cat]; female sex organ (*slang*). (*m.*) tag (*game*). *le Chat botté*, Puss in Boots. *cambrioleur* ~, cat burglar. ~ *d'Espagne*, tortoiseshell cat. ~ *de Siam*, Siamese c. ~ *de gouttières*, stray c. ~ *persan*, ~ *angora*, Persian c.

châtaigne (ʃatɛɲ) *f*, [sweet] chestnut. **châtaignier** (nje) *m*, chestnut [tree]. **châtain, e** (tɛ̃, ɛn) *a*, [chestnut-]brown (*hair*).

château (ʃato) *m*, castle; palace; manor [house], [country] seat, mansion, hall. ~ *d'eau*, water tower. ~ *de cartes*, house of cards. ~*x en Espagne*, castles in the air *or* in Spain. **châtelain** (tlɛ̃) *m*, lord of the manor, squire. **châtelaine** (tlɛn) *f*, lady of the manor; chatelaine, key chain.

chat-huant (ʃayɑ̃) *m*, tawny owl, brown o.

châtier (ʃatje) *v.t*, to chastise, castigate; chasten. **châtiment** (timɑ̃) *m*, chastisement, etc.

chatoiement (ʃatwamɑ̃) *m*, shimmer; sheen; play of light.

chaton (ʃatɔ̃) *m*, kitten; bezel; setting (*jewel*).

chatouiller (ʃatuje) *v.t*, to tickle; touch up. **chatouilleux, euse** (tujø, ø:z) *a*, ticklish; touchy, sensitive; punctilious.

chatoyant, e (ʃatwajɑ̃, ɑ̃:t) *a*, iridescent; shot (*fabrics*). **chatoyer** (je) *v.i*, to shimmer; sparkle.

châtrer (ʃatre) *v.t*, to castrate, geld; prune, thin.

chattemite (ʃatmit) *f*, unctuous hypocrite, Chadband.

chatteries (ʃatri) *f.pl*, blandishments; delicacies, dainties.

chaud, e† (ʃo, o:d) *a*, hot, warm. *à chaud*, [while] hot. *pleurer à chaudes larmes*, to cry bitterly. *avoir chaud*, to be warm (*of pers.*). *faire* ~, to be warm (*weather*).

chaudière (ʃodjɛ:r) *f*, boiler; copper. **chaudron** (dr5) *m*, caldron, pot. **[petite] chaudronnerie** (drɔnri) *f*, coppersmith's [& brazier's] trade. **[grosse] chaudronnerie**, boiler-making *or* works. **chaudronnier** (nje) *m*, coppersmith, brazier; boiler maker. ~ *ambulant*, tinker.

chauffage (ʃofa:ʒ) *m*, heating, warming; stoking; firing. ~ *central*, central heating. **chauffard** (fa:r) *m*, reckless driver, etc. **chauffe** (ʃo:f) *f*, fire chamber; stoking, firing; heat, melt; heating. ~*-bain* (ʃof) *m*, water heater. ~*-lit*, *m*, warming pan. ~*-pieds*, *m*, foot warmer. ~*-plats*, *m*, chafing dish. **chauffer** (ʃofe) *v.t*, to heat, warm; air (*linen*); stoke, fire, fuel; push on with; urge on; cram (*exam*); (*v.i.*) to heat, get hot; run hot; get up steam. *se* ~, to warm oneself, bask. *se* ~ *les pieds*, to warm one's feet. **chaufferette** (frɛt) *f*, foot warmer. **chaufferie** (fri) *f*, chafery; stokehole; boiler room. **chauffeur** (fœ:r) *m*, stoker, fireman; driver (*auto*), chauffeur. ~*-mécanicien*, engineman. **chauffeuse** (fø:z) *f*, woman driver, fireside chair.

chaufour (ʃofu:r) *m*, lime kiln. **chaufournier** (furnje) *m*, lime burner.

chauler (ʃole) *v.t*, to lime.

chaume (ʃo:m) *m*, culm (*Bot.*); stubble; s. field; thatch; cottage (*fig.*). *couvrir en* ~, to thatch. **chaumière** (ʃomjɛ:r) *f*, [thatched] cottage.

chaussée (ʃose) *f*, bank; causeway, road[way].

chausse-pied (ʃospje) *m*, shoehorn. **chausser** (se) *v.t*, to put on (*shoes, stockings*); shoe, boot, make shoes for; suit, fit (*of footwear*); hill, earth up. *se* ~ *d'une opinion*, to get an opinion into one's head. **chaussettes** (sɛt) *f.pl*, socks, half-hose. **chausson** (sõ) *m*, slipper (*list*); shoe; bootee; bed sock; savate; turnover (*Cook.*). **chaussure** (sy:r) *f*, footwear; shoe. ~ [*montante*], boot. ~s de marche, de ski, walking, ski, boots. ~s vernies, patent leather shoes; dress shoes.

chauve (ʃoːv) *a*, bald. ¶ *m*, baldhead (*pers.*). **~-souris** (ʃovsuri) *f*, bat.

chauvinisme (ʃovinism) *m*, chauvinism, jingoism.

chaux (ʃo) *f*, lime. ~ vive, quicklime.

chavirer (ʃavire) *v.i*, to capsize, overturn; upset; fail. [faire] ~, *v.t*, to capsize, etc; tip, dump, shoot.

chef (ʃɛf) *m*, head, chief; chieftain; commander, commanding officer; general (*Mil.*); leader; principal; master; superior; superintendent; manager; foreman; head, heading; authority; right. ~ d'accusation, count of indictment. ~ d'atelier, shop foreman. ~ d'attaque, leader (violin, chorus). ~ d'émeute, ringleader. ~ d'équipe, foreman. ~ d'orchestre, conductor. ~ de bataillon, major. ~ [de cuisine], head cook, chef. ~ de file, leader; file leader; fugleman; leading ship. ~ de gare, station master. ~ de maison, householder. ~ de musique, bandmaster (*Mil.*). ~ de nage, stroke (oarsman). ~ de pièce, gun captain. ~ de rayon, floorwalker. ~ de salle, headwaiter. ~ de théâtre, musical director. ~ du jury, foreman of the jury. ~ du service des ateliers, works manager. ~ éclaireur, scout master. de ce ~, under this head[ing], hereunder. de mon propre ~, on my own authority.

chef-d'œuvre (ʃɛdœːvr) *m*, masterpiece; mess.

chef-lieu (ʃɛfljø) *m*, capital (department, county), county seat; headquarters, seat.

cheik (ʃɛk) *m*, sheikh.

chelem (ʃlɛm) *m*, slam (cards).

chemin (ʃəmɛ̃) *m*, way, road, lane, path, track; headway. ~ d'escalier, stair carpet. ~ de fer, railway, railroad. ~ de kalage, tow[ing] path. ~ des écoliers, longest way round, roundabout way. ~ de la croix, stations of the Cross. ~ de traverse, crossroad. ~ faisant, on the way. faire son ~, to make one's way. il n'y va pas par quatre ~s, he doesn't beat about the bush.

chemineau (ʃəmino) *m*, tramp, hobo.

cheminée (ʃəmine) *f*, chimney, smoke stack, shaft, funnel; fireplace, chimney piece, mantelpiece; chimney pot; vent; chute, shoot.

cheminer (ʃəmine) *v.i*, to tramp, walk; trudge; move along, proceed; meander, creep.

cheminot (ʃəmino) *m*, railwayman.

chemise (ʃəmiːz) *f*, shirt (man's); chemise (woman's); jacket (water, steam); cover, lining, case, wrapper. ~ de nuit, nightshirt (man's); n. dress, n. gown (woman's). ~ de soirée, dress shirt. ~ de ville, tunic s. ~ [pour dossier], folder. **chemiserie** (mizri) *f*, shirt making, hosiery. **chemisier, ère** (zje, ɛːr) *n*, shirtmaker, hosier.

chenal (ʃənal) *m*, channel, race, course; fairway; gutter.

chenapan (ʃnapã) *m*, scamp, rogue.

chêne (ʃɛn) *m*, oak. **~-liège**, *m*, cork tree.

chéneau (ʃeno) *m*, gutter (eaves).

chenet (ʃənɛ) *m*, [fire]dog, andiron.

chènevis (ʃɛnvi) *m*, hemp seed.

chenil (ʃəni) *m*, kennel (hounds); hovel.

chenille (ʃəniːj) *f*, caterpillar; track.

chenu, e (ʃəny) *a*, snow-capped; snow-clad; bare at the top (trees).

cheptel (ʃətɛl) *m*, livestock, cattle.

chèque (ʃɛk) *m*, check. ~ sans provision, worthless c.

cher, ère† (ʃɛːr) *a*, dear, high [-priced], expensive, costly; precious, scarce (time). ma chère, my dear. mon cher, my dear fellow. **cher**, *ad*, dearly; much.

chercher (ʃɛrʃe) *v.t*, to look for, try to find, search for, hunt for, seek; beg; pick (*quarrel*). aller ~, to go for, [go &] fetch, go to look for. venir ~, to come for, come & fetch, come to look for. **chercheur, euse** (ʃœːr, øːz) *n*, seeker, searcher, inquirer, investigator, research worker. ~ d'aventures, adventurer. ~d'or, gold digger. ¶ att, inquiring (*mind, etc.*).

chère (ʃɛːr) *f*, living, fare, cheer. faire bonne ~, to fare (*feed*) well. faire maigre ~, to fare badly.

chérir (ʃeriːr) *v.t*, to cherish, hold dear; cling to, hug (*as error*). mon chéri, ma chérie, my love, my darling, dearest.

cherté (ʃɛrte) *f*, dearness, costliness.

chérubin (ʃerybɛ̃) *m*, cherub.

chester (ʃɛsteːr) *m*, in France, Cheddar *or* Cheshire cheese.

chétif, ive† (ʃetif, iːv) *a*, mean, miserable, sorry, paltry, puny, stunted, sickly, wretched.

cheval (ʃəval) *m*, horse. ~ à bascule, rocking h. ~ côtier, ~ de renfort, trace h. ~ d'attelage, carriage h. ~ de bât, packhorse, drudge. ~ de bataille, war horse, charger; pet argument. chevaux de bois, merry-go-round. ~ de charrette, cart h. ~ de chasse, hunter. ~ de course, racehorse. ~ de louage, hack. ~ de race, ~ pur sang, thoroughbred [horse]. ~ de retour, old offender, jail bird. ~ de volée, leader (*horse*). ~ [vapeur], horse power (Fr. h.p. = 75 kilogrammeters per second; Eng. h.p. = 550 foot pounds per sec.). une [automobile de] 10 chevaux, a 10 horse [power] car. à ~, on horseback. **chevalement** (ʃəvalmɑ̃) *m*, trestle shore; [pit-]headframe; derrick. **chevaler** (ʃəvale) *v.t*, to shore. **chevaleresque** (ʃrɛsk) *a*, chivalrous, knightly. **chevalerie** (ʃrī) *f*, knighthood, chivalry. ~ errante, knight errantry. **chevalet** (ʃlɛ) *m*, horse, trestle; easel; rest (Bil., *etc.*); bridge (*violin, etc.*). **chevalier** (ʃlje) *m*, knight, chevalier. ~ d'industrie, adventurer, swindler. **chevalière** (ʃljeːr) *f*, signet ring. **chevalin, e** (ʃlɛ̃, in)

a, equine, horsy; horse (*species*). **chevauchée** (ʃoʃe) *f*, ride. **chevaucher** (ʃe) *v.i. & t*, to ride; straddle; span; overlap.

chevelu, e (ʃəvly) *a*, long-haired; hairy; bearded. **chevelure** (vlyːr) *f*, [head of] hair, locks; scalp (*trophy*); coma (Bot. & comet); foliage.

chevet (ʃəvɛ) *m*, bolster, pillow; bedhead; bedside.

cheveu (ʃəvø) *m*, (a single human) hair. les ~x, the hair. ~x en brosse, crewcut. couper un ~ en quatre, to split hairs.

cheville (ʃəviːj) *f*, pin, peg; treenail; bolt; pintle; spike; expletive (*in verse*). ~ [du pied], ankle. ~ ouvrière, king bolt, center pin; mainspring (*fig.*), master mind, prime mover. se fouler la ~, to sprain one's ankle. **cheviller** (vije) *v.t. & i*, to pin, peg, bolt; pad (*verses*).

chèvre (ʃɛːvr) *f*, goat (*in general*); she-goat; nanny [goat]; gin (Mech.); sawhorse; jack. ~ de carrossier, carriage jack. ~ [verticale], derrick [crane]. **chevreau** (ʃəvro) *m*, kid; kid [leather]. **chèvrefeuille** (ʃɛvrəfœːj) *m*, honeysuckle, woodbine. **chevrette** (ʃəvrɛt) *f*, kid; she-goat; roe-doe; shrimp, prawn; trivet. **chevreuil** (vrœːj) *m*, roebuck; venison. **chevrier, ère** (vrie, ɛːr) *n*, goatherd. **chevron** (vrɔ̃) *m*, rafter; chevron; stripe (long Mil. service). **chevroter** (vrote) *v.i*, to bleat (*goat & fig.*); quaver, shake; kid. **chevrotin** (tɛ̃) *m*, fawn; musk deer; kid [leather]. **chevrotine** (tin) *f*, buckshot.

chez (ʃe) *pr*, at; at (*or* to) (*or* in) the house, etc, of; care of, c/o; of, stocked by; with; among, in. ~ moi, ~ lui, ~ vous, at home. mon ~moi, my home. ~ soi, [at] home. un ~soi, a home of one's own.

chialer (ʃjale) *v.i*, to weep; snivel; complain.

chiasse (ʃjas) *f*, speck (*fly*); cast (*worm*); scum, dross (*metal*).

chic (ʃik) *a*, stylish, chic, smart. ~ type, a good fellow. ¶ *m*, stylishness.

chicane (ʃikan) *f*, chicanery, quibble, pettifoggery, cavil, shuffle; baffle [plate]. **chicaner** (kane) *v.i.* to chicane; (*v.t.*) to cavil at, carp at; dispute every inch of (*ground*); hug (*wind, Naut.*). **chicanerie** (nri) *f*, chicanery, etc.

chiche† (ʃiʃ) *a*, stingy, mean, niggardly, chary, sparing. ¶ *pois* ~, *n*, chickpea. ¶ *int*, chiche!, I dare you! You're on!

chicorée (ʃikɔre) *f*, chicory.

chicot (ʃiko) *m*, stump, snag. **chicoter** (kɔte) *v.i.* to wrangle (*about trifles*).

chien, ne (ʃjɛ̃, ɛn) *n*, dog, bitch, hound; (*m.*) hammer, cock (*of gun*); dog, pawl, catch. ~ *couchant*, setter. *faire le* ~ *couchant*, to toady, cringe. ~ *courant*, ~ *de chasse*, hound. ~ *d'arrêt*, pointer. ~ *de berger*, sheep dog. ~ *de garde*, ~ *d'attache*, watch d. ~ *de luxe*, fancy d. ~ *de mer*, dog fish. ~ *de Saint-Bernard* (sɛ̃bɛrnaːr), St. Bernard dog. ~ *de salon*, lap d. ~*loup*, Alsatian. ~ *savant*, performing dog. *entre chien & loup*, at dusk.

chiendent (ʃjɛ̃dɑ̃) *m*, couch [grass]; problem, difficulty.

chier (ʃje) *v.i.* to defecate (*obscene*). *faire* ~, to annoy, disturb. ~ *du poivre*, shake off the police.

chiffe (ʃif) *f*, rag. **chiffon** (f5) *m*, bit of stuff (*old or new*); rag, clout; scrap; fallal; chiffon; (*pl.*) dress, finery. **chiffonner** (fɔne) *v.t*, to [c]rumple; ruffle, annoy, vex, bother; (*v.i.*) to do needlework, use one's needle. **chiffonnier, ère** (nje, ɛːr) *n*, rag picker *or* merchant, rag [& bone] man; (*m.*) chiffonier.

chiffre (ʃifr) *m*, figure, number, numeral, cipher; amount; monogram; colophon. *un* [*seul*] ~, a digit (*0-9*). *en* ~*s connus*, in plain figures. ~ *d'affaires*, turnover. ~*indice*, index number. **mot en chiffré** (fre), word in cipher. **chiffrer** (fre) *v.i.* to reckon, cipher; figure, appear; (*v.t.*) to number, figure, cipher. *se* ~, to figure out, work out, amount.

chignon (ʃiɲ5) *m*, chignon.

Chili (le) (ʃili), Chile, -li. **chilien, ne** (ljɛ̃, ɛn) *a*. & **C**~, *n*, Chilean.

chimère (ʃimɛːr) *f*, chimera. **chimérique** (merik) *a*, chimerical; visionary, fanciful.

chimie (ʃimi) *f*, chemistry. **chimique†** (mik) *a*, chemical; actinic (*rays*). **chimiste** (mist) *n*, chemist (*scientist*).

chimpanzé (ʃɛ̃pɑ̃ze) *m*, chimpanzee.

Chine (la) (ʃin), China. **chinois, e** (nwa, aːz) *a*. & **C**~ (*pers.*), *n*, Chinese. **le chinois**, Chinese (*language*); penis (*obscene*); Maoist. **chinoiserie** (nwazri) *f*, Chinese curio; (*pl.*) red tape, complicated formalities.

chiner (ʃine) *v.i.* to shop flea markets or secondhand stores. ¶ *v.t*, to mock; to cadge.

chiourme (ʃjurm) *f*, galley slaves; gang of convicts.

chiper (ʃipe) *v.t*, to swipe, filch, pilfer.

chipie (ʃipi) *f*, ill-natured woman. **chipoter** (pɔte) *v.i.* to nibble; haggle.

chique (ʃik) *f*, quid, chew (*of tobacco*); jigger (*insect*).

chiqué (ʃike) *m*, pretense, sham, fuss.

chiquenaude (ʃiknoːd) *f*, fillip, flip, flick; snap of fingers.

chiquer (ʃike) *v.t*. & *i*, to chew (*tobacco*).

chirographaire (kirɔgrafɛːr) *a*, unsecured (*creditors, debts*); simple, naked (*debentures*).

chiromancie (kirɔmɑ̃si) *f*, palmistry, chiromancy. **chiromancien, ne** (sjɛ̃, ɛn) *n*, palmist, chiromancer.

chiropraxie, chiropractie (ʃirɔpraksi, prakti) *f*, chiropractic.

chirurgical, e (ʃiryrʒikal) *a*, surgical. **chirurgie** (ʒi) *f*, surgery. **chirurgien** (ʒjɛ̃) *m*, surgeon.

chiure (ʃjyːr) *f*, flyspeck.

chlorate (klɔrat) *m*, chlorate. **chlore** (klɔːr) *m*, chlorine. **chlorhydrique** (klɔridrik) *a*, hydrochloric, muriatic (*acid*). **chloroforme** (rɔform) *m*, chloroform. **chloroformer** (me) *v.t*, to chloroform. **chlorure** (ryːr) *m*, chloride. ~ *de chaux*, c. of lime.

choc (ʃɔk) *m*, shock, impact, brunt, onset, onslaught, clash;

clink (*glasses*). *prix de ~*, drastically cut prices; big sale.

chocolat (ʃɔkɔla) *m*, chocolate. *~ au lait*, c. with milk; milk c. *~s fourrés à la crème*, c. creams. *~ lacté*, milk c. **chocolatier, ère** (latje ɛ:r) *n*, c. manufacturer; c. seller; (*f.*) c. pot.

chœur (kœ:r) *m*, choir, quire; chorus; chancel. *faire ~ au refrain*, to join in the chorus.

choir (ʃwa:r) *v.i.ir*, to fall.

choisi, e (ʃwazi) *a*, select, choice. **choisir** (zi:r) *v.t*, to choose, select, pick. **choix** (ʃwa) *m*, choice, selection; pick; option; quality. *au ~*, all at the same price.

choléra (kɔlera) *m*, cholera.

chômage (ʃomɑ:ʒ) *m*, closing, idleness, standing [idle], shutting down, unemployment; demurrage (*Rly.*); lying up (*ship*). *~ du dimanche*, Sunday closing. **chômer** (me) *v.i*, to close, lie idle; lie fallow; shut down, stop work, be out [of work]; be short; (*v.t.*) to keep (*une fête = a saint's day*). **chômeur, euse** (mœ:r, ø:z) *n*, unemployed person. *les chômeurs*, the unemployed.

chope (ʃɔp) *f*, glass (*for, or of, beer*). **chopine** (pin) *f*, pint (about ½ liter). **chopiner** (ne) *v.i*, to tipple.

chopper (ʃɔpe) *v.i*, to stumble; blunder.

choquant, e (ʃɔkɑ̃, ɑ̃:t) *a*, shocking; offensive. **choquer** (ke) *v.t*, to shock, strike, clash with; clink, chink; offend.

choral, e (kɔral) *a*, choral. [*société*] *chorale*, *f*, choral society.

chorégraphie (kɔregrafi) *f*, choreography.

choriste (kɔrist) *n*, chorister; chorus singer (*opera*). **faire chorus** (ry:s), to [repeat in] chorus.

chose (ʃo:z) *f*, thing; matter; fact; chattel; property; compliment. *la ~ publique*, the common weal, the public welfare. *~ qui va sans dire*, matter of course. *où en sont les ~s?* how do things stand?

chott (ʃɔt) *m*, salt lake (*N. Africa*).

chou (ʃu) *m*, cabbage; cream puff (*pastry*). *~ de Bruxelles*, Brussels sprouts. *~ de Milan* (milɑ̃),

savoy. *~-fleur*, *m*, cauliflower. *frisé*, kale. *~ marin*, sea kale. *~-navet*, rutabaga. *~-rave*, *m*, kohlrabi. **chou[chou]**, *m*, darling, ducky, honey. *le chouchou*, the pet.

choucas (ʃuka) *m*, jackdaw.

choucroute (ʃukrut) *f*, sauerkraut; dish of sauerkraut, sausages, ham hocks, etc.

chouette (ʃwɛt) *f*, owl. ¶ *a. & int*, great! *~ alors!*, that's great! *c'est ~!*, it's great!

choyer (ʃwaje) *v.t*, to pamper, pet, coddle; cherish.

chrétien, ne (kretjɛ̃, ɛn) *a. & n*, Christian. **chrétiennement** (ɛnmɑ̃) *ad*, christianly. **chrétienté** (ēte) *f*, Christendom. **le Christ** (krist), Christ. **christ**, *m*, crucifix. **christianiser** (tjanize) *v.t*, to christianize. **christianisme** (nism) *m*, Christianity.

chromate (krɔmat) *m*, chromate.

chromatique (krɔmatik) *a*, chromatic.

chrome (kro:m) *m*, chromium, chrome. **chromé e** (krome) *a*, chrome (*steel, leather*); chromium (*steel*); chromium-plated.

chronique (krɔnik) *a*, chronic. ¶ *f*, chronicle; gossip; intelligence, notes (*in newspaper*). **chroniqueur** (kœ:r) *m*, chronicler; reporter (*news*).

chronographe (krɔnɔgraf) *m*, chronograph; stop-watch.

chronologie (krɔnɔlɔʒi) *f*, chronology. **chronologique†** (ʒik) *a*, chronological.

chronométrage (krɔnɔmetra:ʒ) *m*, timing (*race*). **chronomètre** (metr) *m*, chronometer. **chronométrer** (metre) *v.i*, to time. **chronométreur** (trœ:r) *m*, timekeeper (*Sport*). *~-analyseur*, time-study analyst.

chrysalide (krizalid) *f*, chrysalis, pupa.

chrysanthème (krizɑ̃tɛ:m) *m*, chrysanthemum.

chuchoter (ʃyʃɔte) *v.i. & t*, to whisper. **chuchoterie** (tri) *f*, whispering. **chuchoteur, euse** (tœ:r, ø:z) *n*, whisperer.

chuinter (ʃɥēte) *v.i*, to hoot (*owl*).

chut (ʃyt, ʃt) *i*, hush!

chute (ʃyt) *f*, fall, drop; downfall, collapse, smash, crash; failure (*of a play*); spray (*flowers, Need.*). ~ [*d'eau*], [water]fall, falls. ~ *des reins*, the small of the back. *la* ~ *du jour*, the close of day, nightfall, eventide.

chuter (ʃyte) *v.t*, to hiss (an *actor*).

Chypre (ʃipr) *f*, Cyprus.

ci (si) *ad*, here. ~*-après*, hereinafter, further on, below. ~*-contre*, opposite. ~*-dessous*, below, undermentioned, hereunder. ~*-dessus*, above[-mentioned]. ~*-devant*, formerly, late. ~*-gît*, here lies (*grave*). ~*-inclus*, *e* & *ci-joint*, *e*, enclosed, herewith, subjoined. ¶ *pn*, this.

cible (sibl) *f*, target; butt (*fig.*).

ciboire (sibwa:r) *m*, ciborium, pyx.

ciboule (sibul) *f*, spring onion, scallion. **ciboulette** (lɛt) *f*, chive.

cicatrice (sikatris) *f*, scar, mark. **cicatriser** (ze) *v.t.* & *se* ~, to scar; mark; heal, skin over.

cicerone (siseron) *m*, cicerone, guide.

cidre (si:dr) *m*, cider.

ciel (sjɛl) *m*, heaven, heavens, sky; air; climate, clime; tester, canopy; roof. *à* ~ *ouvert*, in the open air; open-cast, daylight (*Min.*).

cierge (sjɛrʒ) (*Eccl.*) *m*, [wax] candle, taper.

cigale (sigal) *f*, cicada, grasshopper.

cigare (siga:r) *m*, cigar. ~ *de la Havane*, Havana c. **cigarette** (garɛt) *f*, cigarette.

cigogne (sigɔɲ) *f*, stork.

ciguë (sigy) *f*, hemlock.

cil (sil) *m*, eyelash; hair (*Bot.*). **ciller** (sije) *v.i*, to blink; move an eyelid.

cime (sim) *f*, top, summit, peak.

ciment (simã) *m*, cement. **cimenter** (te) *v.t*, to cement.

cimeterre (simtɛ:r) *m*, scimitar.

cimetière (simtjɛ:r) *m*, cemetery, burial ground, graveyard, churchyard.

cimier (simje) *m*, crest; haunch (*venison*); buttock (*beef*).

cinabre (sina:br) *m*, cinnabar.

cinéaste (sineast) *m*, filmmaker.

ciné-actualités (sineaktyalite) *f*, newsreel theater.

ciné-club (sineklœb) *m*, film society.

cinégramme (sinegram) *m*, kinescope (*TV*).

cinémathèque (sinematɛk) *f*, film library; museum offering film showings.

cinématographe (sinematograf), **cinéma**, *abb, m*, movie theater; movies. ~ *d'essai*, art theater. ~ *d'exclusivité*, first-run theater. ~ *permanent*, continuous-show theater.

cinéphile (sinefil) *m*. & *f*, film enthusiast, fan.

cinéprojecteur (sineprɔʒɛktœ:r) *m*, film projector.

cinéraire (sinerɛ:r) *a*, cinerary. ¶ *f*, cineraria (*Bot.*).

ciné-roman (sinerɔmã) *m*, film serial; novelized & illustrated story of a film.

cinéscope (sineskɔp) *m*, kinescope (*TV*).

cinétique (sinetik) *a*, kinetic.

cingalais, e (sɛ̃galɛ, ɛ:z) *a*. & C~, *n*, Cingalese.

cinglé, e (sɛ̃gle) *a*, nutty, crazy, etc.

cingler (sɛ̃gle) *v.t*, to lash, cut, whip; shingle (*Metall.*); to sail, scud.

cinq (sɛ̃[:]k; *before a consonant*, sɛ̃) *a*. & *m*, five; fifth; cinq[ue]. **cinquantaine** (sɛ̃kɑ̃tɛn) *f*, fifty [or so]; golden wedding. **cinquante** (kɑ̃:t) *a*. & *m*, fifty. **cinquantenaire** (kɑ̃tnɛ:r) *m*, fiftieth anniversary. **cinquantième** (tjɛm) *a*. & *n*, fiftieth. **cinquième**† (kjɛm) *a*. & *n*, fifth.

cintre (sɛ̃:tr) *m*, arch, curve; center (*for arch*); clothes hanger. **cintrer** (sɛ̃tre) *v.t*, to arch, bend, curve.

cipaye (sipa:j) *m*, sepoy.

cirage (sira:ʒ) *m*, waxing; polishing; shoe polish.

circoncire (sirkɔ̃si:r) *v.t.ir*, to circumcise.

circonférence (sirkɔ̃ferɑ̃:s) *f*, circumference, girth.

circonflexe (sirkɔ̃flɛks) *a*. & *m*, circumflex.

circonlocution (sirkɔ̃lɔkysjɔ̃) *f*, circumlocution.

circonscription (sirkɔ̃skripsjɔ̃) *f*, circumscription; area. ~ *électorale*, constituency. **circonscrire** (skri:r) *v.t.ir*, to circumscribe; locate.

circonspect, e (sirkɔ̃spɛ[k], ɛkt) *a*, circumspect, cautious, wary, guarded.

circonstance (sirkɔ̃stɑ̃:s) *f*, circumstance; occasion; nonce. *de* ~, for the occasion. **circonstancié, e** (stɑ̃sje) *p.a*, circumstantial, detailed (*account*). **circonstancier** (sje) *v.t*, to detail.

circonvenir (sirkɔ̃vni:r) *v.t.ir*, to circumvent, outwit, overreach.

circonvoisin, e (sirkɔ̃vwazɛ̃, in) *a*, surrounding.

circuit (sirkɥi) *m*, circuit, round. ~ *de paroles*, circumlocution.

circulaire† (sirkylɛ:r) *a*. & *f*, circular. **circulant, e** (lɑ̃, ɑ̃:t) *a*, circulating, floating. **circulation** (lasjɔ̃) *f*, circulation, running, traveling, working; traffic; currency; turnover, sales. **circuler** (le) *v.i*, to circulate, run, travel. *circulez!* move on! pass along!

cire (si:r) *f*, wax. ~ *à cacheter*, sealing wax. **ciré** (sire) *m*, oilskin. **cirer** (re) *v.t*, to wax; polish (*shoes*). **cireur** (rœ:r) *m*, bootblack. **cireuse** (rø:z) *f*, floor polisher (*Mach.*). **cirier** (rje) *m*, wax chandler.

ciron (sirɔ̃) *m*, mite (*insect*).

cirque (sirk) *m*, circus; corrie.

cirrhose (siro:z) *f*, cirrhosis.

cirrus (sir[r]y:s) *m*, cirrus (*Meteor.*).

cisailler (sizaje) *v.t*, to shear, clip. **cisailles** (zɑ:j) *f.pl*, shears, shearing machine. **ciseau** (zo) *m*, chisel. ~ *à déballer*, case opener. ~ *à froid*, cold chisel. **~x**, *pl*, [pair of] scissors; shears, clippers. **ciseler** (zle) *v.t*, to chisel; chase. **ciselet** (zlɛ) *m*, graver. **ciselure** (zly:r) *f*, chiseling; chasing.

citadelle (sitadɛl) *f*, citadel; stronghold.

citadin, e (sitadɛ̃, in) *n*, townsman, citizen.

citation (sitasjɔ̃) *f*, citation, quotation; summons, subpoena. ~ *à l'ordre de l'armée*, mention in dispatches.

cité (site) *f*, city., ~-*dortoir*, bedroom community.

citer (site) *v.t*, to cite, quote; mention; instance; summon; summons; subpoena.

citérieur, e (siterjœ:r) *a*, hither (*Geog.*).

citerne (sitɛrn) *f*, tank, cistern.

cithare (sita:r) *f*, zither.

citoyen, ne (sitwajɛ̃, ɛn) *n*, citizen.

citrique (sitrik) *a*, citric. **citron** (trɔ̃) *m*, lemon; citron. ~ *pressé*, lemon squash. **citronnade** (trɔnad) *f*, lemonade. **citronnier** (nje) *m*, lemon tree; citron tree.

citrouille (sitru:j) *f*, pumpkin.

cive[tte] (siv[ɛt]) *f*, chive.

civet de lièvre (sivɛ) *m*, jugged hare.

civette (sivɛt) *f*, civet [cat].

civière (sivjɛ:r) *f*, handbarrow; stretcher, litter; bier.

civil, e† (sivil) *a*, civil; calendar (*month, year*). ¶ *m*, civilian; noncombatant. *en* ~, in plain clothes, in mufti. **civilisateur, trice** (lizatœ:r, tris) *a*, civilizing. **civilisation** (sjɔ̃) *f*, civilization. **civiliser** (ze) *v.t*, to civilize. **civilité** (te) *f*, civility; (*pl.*) compliments.

civique (sivik) *a*, civic.

clabauder (klabode) *v.i*, to babble (*of hound*); backbite.

claie (klɛ) *f*, hurdle; fence. *passer à la* ~, to screen.

clair, e† (klɛ:r) *a*, clear; bright; light; thin; plain, explicit. *sabre au clair*, with drawn sword. *tirer au clair*, *v.t*, to clear up. **clair**, *ad*, clearly, plainly; thinly. ¶ *m*, light; plain language (*Teleg.*). ~ *de lune*, moonlight. **clairet** (klɛrɛ) *a.m*, pale (*wine, precious stone*).

claire-voie (klɛrvwa) *f*, grating. *à* ~, openwork, lattice (*att.*).

clairière (klɛrjɛ:r) *f*, glade; clearing; lane.

clair-obscur (klɛrɔpsky:r) *m*, chiaroscuro, light & shade.

clairon (klɛr5) *m*, bugle; bugler; clarion. **claironner** (rɔne) *v.t*, to noise abroad.

clairsemé, e (klɛrsəme) *a*, thinly sown; sparse, few & far between.

clairvoyance (klɛrvwajã:s) *f*, clear-sightedness, shrewdness.

clameur (klamœ:r) *f*, clamor, outcry.

clampin (klɑ̃pɛ̃) *m*, slowcoach.

clan (klɑ̃) *m*, clan, set.

clandestin, e† (klɑ̃dɛstɛ̃, in) *a*, clandestine, underhand.

clapet (klapɛ) *m*, clack [valve], flap.

clapier (klapje) *m*, rabbit burrow, r. hutch.

clapoter (klapɔte) *v.i*, to plash, swash. **clapoteux, euse** (tø, ø:z) *a*, choppy (*water*).

clapper (klape) *v.i*, to smack (*tongue*).

claque (klak) *f*, slap, smack; claque (*Theat.*). ¶ *m*, crush hat, opera hat.

claquedent (klakdɑ̃) *m*, starveling; brothel; gambling den.

claquemurer (klakmyre) *v.t*, to coop up, immure, closet.

claquer (klake) *v.i. & t*, to clap, clatter, slap, snap, crack, chatter, slam; die; go to pieces. **claquet** (kɛ) *m*, **claquette** (kɛt) *f*, **claquoir** (kwa:r) *m*, clapper. **claquettes**, *f.pl*, step dance, tap d.

clarifier (klarifje) *v.t*, to clarify, fine.

clarine (klarin) *f*, cowbell.

clarinette (klarinɛt) *f*, clarinet.

clarté (klarte) *f*, clearness; brightness; light.

classe (klɑ:s) *f*, class, order; rate; grade (*at school*); school; contingent (*of recruiting year*). ~ *moyenne*, middle class[es]. [*salle de*] ~, classroom. **classement** (klɑsmɑ̃) *m*, classing, classification; rating; filing; order, position (*running, etc.*). **classer** (se) *v.t*, to class, classify; sort, grade; file (*letters, etc.*); position; marshal. **classeur** (sœ:r) *m*, file; filing cabinet; stationery rack. **classification** (klasifikasj5) *f*, classification. **classique†** (sik) *a*, classic; classical; class, school

(*att.*); educational; standard. ¶ *m*, classic.

claudication (klodikasj5) *f*, lameness.

clause (klo:z) *f*, clause, term, provision, stipulation.

claustral, e (klostral) *a*, claustral, cloistral.

claveau (klavo) *m*, arch-stone, voussoir; sheep pox.

clavecin (klavsɛ̃) *m*, harpsichord.

clavelée (klavle) *f*, sheep pox.

clavette (klavɛt) *f*, key, cotter, pin. ~ *d'essieu*, axle pin, linchpin. ~ *fendue*, split pin.

clavicule (klavikyl) *f*, collar bone.

clavier (klavje) *m*, keyboard; manual; (*musical*) compass, range.

clayonnage (klɛjɔna:ʒ) *m*, wattling; mat[tress].

clef, *sometimes* **clé** (kle) *f*, key; clue (*puzzle*); wrench; plug, spigot; clef. ~ *à marteau*, screw hammer; adjustable wrench. ~ *anglaise*, monkey wrench. ~ *de contact*, (*allumage*), ignition key switch. ~ *d'ut*, C (*or tenor*) (*or alto*) clef. ~ *de fa*, F (*or bass*) c. ~ *de sol*, G (*or treble*) c. ~ *de voûte*, keystone. *sous* ~, locked up, under lock & key.

clématite (klematit) *f*, clematis.

clémence (klemɑ̃:s) *f*, clemency, mercy, leniency; mildness. **clément, e** (mɑ̃, ɑ̃:t) *a*, clement, etc.

clémentine (klemɑ̃tin) *f*, tangerine; clementine.

cleptomane (klɛptoman) *n*, kleptomaniac. **cleptomanie** (ni) *f*, kleptomania.

clerc (klɛ:r) *m*, clerk (*Relig., law*). *pas de* ~, false step, error. **clergé** (klɛrʒe) *m*, clergy; priesthood. **clérical, e** (klerikal) *a. & m*, clerical.

cliché (kliʃe) *m*, plate (*Typ.*); negative (*Phot.*); stock phrase, hackneyed p., tag. ~ *au trait*, linecut, line engraving. ~ *simili*, ~ *tramé*, half-tone engraving. **clicher** (ʃe) *v.t*, to stereotype.

client, e (kliɑ̃, ɑ̃:t) *n*, client, customer; patient. **clientèle** (ɑ̃tɛl) *f*, clientele, public, connection, custom; goodwill, practice.

cligner (kliɲe) *v.i*, to wink; blink; wince. **clignotant** (ɲɔtɑ̃) *a*, blinking. ¶ *m*, flashing traffic light. *les ~s*, direction signal-lights. **clignoter** (ɲɔte) *v.i*, to blink, twinkle; twitch.

climat (klima) *m*, climate. **climatérique** (materik) *a*, climacteric (*Med.*); climatic. **climatique** (tik) *a*, climatic. **climatiser** (tize) *v.t*, to air-condition.

clin d'œil (klɛ̃dœːj) *m*, wink; twinkling of an eye, trice.

clinicien (klinisjɛ̃) *m*, clinician. **clinique** (nik) *a*, clinical. ¶ *f*, clinic; nursing home; surgery (*room*).

clinquant (klɛ̃kɑ̃) *m*, tinsel; foil; showiness.

clique (klik) *f*, clique, set, gang; drums & bugles (*Mil. band*).

cliquet (klikɛ) *m*, pawl, click, catch. ~ [*à canon*], engineer's ratchet brace. ~ [*simple*], ratchet. **cliqueter** (kte) *v.i*, to click, clank, clash, rattle, jingle. **cliquetis** (kti) *m*, click[ing], *etc.* **cliquettes** (kɛt) *f.pl*, bones, castanets.

clisser (klise) *v.t*, to wicker (*bottles*).

clivage (klivaːʒ) *m*, cleavage (*Miner.*); separation of social strata.

cloaque (klɔak) *m*, cesspool; sink (*fig.*).

clochard (klɔʃaːr) *m*, tramp, hobo. **cloche** (klɔʃ) *f*, bell; bell glass; bell jar; dish cover; cloche. ~ *à fromage*, cheese cover. ~ *à plongeur*, diving bell.

clochement (klɔʃmɑ̃) *m*, hobble, limp.

cloche-pied (à) (klɔʃpje) *ad*, on one leg. *sauter à ~*, to hop.

clocher (klɔʃe) *m*, belfry. ~ [*pointu*], steeple. *de ~* (*fig.*), parish (*att.*), parochial.

clocher (klɔʃe) *v.i*, to hobble, limp, halt, be lame. *il y a quelque chose qui cloche*, something's wrong.

clocheton (klɔʃtɔ̃) *m*, bell turret. **clochette** (klɔʃɛt) *f*, hand bell; bell [flower]. ~ *d'hiver*, snowdrop.

cloison (klwazɔ̃) *f*, partition; bulkhead; septum. ~ *étanche*, watertight bulkhead. [*émail*] **cloisonné** (zɔne) *m*, cloisonné [enamel]. **cloisonner** (ne) *v.t*, to partition [off].

cloître (klwaːtr) *m*, cloister. **cloîtrer** (watre) *v.t*, to cloister, immure.

clopin-clopant (klɔpɛ̃klɔpɑ̃) *ad*, hobbling along. **clopiner** (pine) *v.i*, to hobble.

cloporte (klɔpɔrt) *m*, wood louse.

cloque (klɔk) *f*, blister; rust (*Agric.*).

clore (klɔːr) *v.t. & i. ir*, to close, shut; enclose; conclude. **clos** (klo) *m*, enclosure. **clôture** (kloty:r) *f*, enclosure, fence, fencing; screen (*choir*); closure; closing; conclusion (*sessions, sittings*). *cours de ~*, closing price. *date de ~*, closing date. ~ *à claire-voie*, paling.

clou (klu) *m*, nail; boil (*Med.*). *les ~s*, studded crossing (*pedestrian*). ~ *à crochet*, tenterhook. ~ *à dessin*, drawing pin. ~ *à deux pointes*, [wire] staple. ~ *de girofle*, clove. ~ *de la fête*, chief attraction, star turn. ~ *de Paris*, French nail. wire n. ~ *découpé*, cut n. *mettre au ~*, to pawn something. (*pl.*) crosswalk. **clouer** (klue) *v.t*, to nail [up, down]; pin; tie. ~ *la bouche à quelqu'un*, to shut someone up (*silence*). **clouter** (te) *v.t*, to stud. *passage clouté*, studded crossing (*pedestrian crossing*). **clouterie** (tri) *f*, nailmaking; n. works. **cloutier** (tje) *m*, nailmaker.

clovisse (klɔvis) *f*, cockle (*Mol.*).

clown (klun) *m*, clown. **clownerie** (nri) *f*, clownery.

club (klyb) *m*, club. ~ *de golf*, golf club (*people & stick*).

coaguler (koagyle) *v.t*, to coagulate.

coaliser (se) (koalize) *v.pr*, to combine. **coalition** (sjɔ̃) *f*, coalition; combine, ring.

coaltar (kɔltaːr) *m*, coal tar.

coasser (koase) *v.i*, to croak (*frog*).

coaxial (kɔaksjal) *m*, feeder cable.

cobalt (kɔbalt) *m*, cobalt.

cobaye (kɔbaːj) *m*, guinea pig.

cobra (kɔbra) *m*, cobra.

cocaïne (kɔkain) *f*, cocaine.

cocarde (kɔkard) *f*, cockade, rosette.

cocasse (kɔkas) *a*, droll, comical.

coccinelle (kɔksinɛl) *f*, ladybird.

coche (kɔʃ) *f*, sow; notch, score. ¶ *m*, stagecoach.

cochenille (kɔʃniːj) *f*, cochineal.

cocher (kɔʃe) *m*, coachman, driver. ~ *de fiacre*, cabman.

cocher (kɔʃe) *v.t*, to notch, score.

cochet (kɔʃe) *m*, cockerel.

cochon (kɔʃɔ̃) *m*, hog, pig, porker, swine; dirty pig (*man*). ~ *d'Inde*, guinea pig. ~ *de lait*, sucking pig. **cochonnée** (ʃɔne) *f*, farrow, litter. **cochonner** (ne) *v.i*, to farrow, pig. **cochonnerie** (nri) *f*, filthiness, obscenity.

coco (kɔko) *m*, coco[nut].

coco (kɔko) *m*, **cocotte** (kɔt) *f*, darling.

cocon (kɔkɔ̃) *m*, cocoon.

cocorico (kɔkɔriko) *m*, cock-a-doodle-doo.

cocotier (kɔkɔtje) *m*, coco[nut] palm.

cocotte (kɔkɔt) *f*, stew pot; kept woman, loose w.; darling (*endearment*). ~-*minute* (minyt), pressure cooker.

code (kɔd) *m*, code; statute book; law; canons (*taste*). ~ *de la route*, highway code, road code, code of the road. *mettre en* ~, to dim (*auto lights*). Cf. *phare-code*.

codétenteur, trice (kodetɑ̃tœːr, tris) *n*, joint holder.

codex [pharmaceutique] (kɔdɛks) *m*, pharmacopoeia.

codicille (kɔdisil) *m*, codicil.

codifier (kɔdifje) *v.t*, to codify.

codirecteur, trice (kodirɛktœːr, tris) *n*, joint manager, ess.

coefficient (koefisjɑ̃) *m*, coefficient.

cœur (kœːr) *m*, heart; courage; feelings; core; height (*of summer*); depth (*of winter*); hearts (*cards*). *à* ~ *joie*, as much as you want. *de bon* ~, willingly, gladly.

coffre (kɔfr) *m*, chest, box, trunk, bin, locker, coffer; case. ~-*fort* (frəfoːr) *m*, safe. **coffrer** (fre) *v.t*, to lock up (*pers.*). **coffret**

(frɛ) *m*, casket, box, chest. ~ *à monnaie*, cash box. ~ *de pharmacie*, medicine chest.

cogérant, e (kɔʒerɑ̃, ɑ̃ːt) *n*, joint manager, ess.

cogestion (kɔʒɛstjɔ̃) *f*, joint management.

cognac (kɔɲak) *m*, cognac, brandy.

cognassier (kɔɲasje) *m*, quince [tree].

cognée de bûcheron (kɔɲe) *f*, felling axe. **cogner** (ɲe) *v.t. & i*, to drive in; knock, bump, thump.

cohabiter (koabite) *v.i*, to cohabit.

cohérence (kɔerɑ̃ːs) *f*, coherence. **cohérent, e** (rɑ̃, ɑ̃ːt) *a*, coherent, connected; cohesive. **cohésion** (zjɔ̃) *f*, cohesion.

cohorte (kɔɔrt) *f*, cohort.

cohue (kɔy) *f*, crowd, crush.

coi, te (kwa, at) *a*, still, quiet.

coiffe (kwaf) *f*, headdress; cap; lining (*hat*); nosecone. **coiffer** (fe) *v.t*, to hat; cap; fit, suit (*hat*); dress (*or do*) [the hair of]. *se* ~ *de* (*fig.*), to be infatuated with. **coiffeur, euse** (fœːr, øːz) *n*, hairdresser. ¶ *f*, dressing table. ~ *psyché*, cheval d. t. **coiffure** (fyːr) *f*, headdress, headgear; style of hairdressing. ~ *à la Ninon* (ninɔ̃), ~ *à la Jeanne d'Arc* (ʒɑ̃ndark) bob[bed hair]. ~ *de cotillon*, paper hat (*Danc.*).

coin (kwɛ̃) *m*, corner, angle; wedge, key, quoin; die; stamp; mark; plot, patch (*land*). ~ *du feu*, fireside, chimney corner. **coincer** (kwɛ̃se) *v.t*, to wedge; key; jam.

coïncidence (kɔɛ̃sidɑ̃ːs) *f*, coincidence. **coïncider** (de) *v.i*, to coincide.

coing (kwɛ̃) *m*, quince (*fruit*).

coïntéressé, e (kɔɛ̃terɛse) *n*, co-adventurer.

coke (kɔk) *m*, coke.

col (kɔl) *m*, collar; neck (*bottle*); pass, col, saddle. ~ *rabattu*, double collar, turndown c. (*attached*). ~ *souple*, soft c. ~ *tenant*, c. attached (*to shirt*). ~ *transformable*, two-way c. *faux* ~, [shirt] collar (*detached*). *faux* ~ *cassé*, wing c. *faux* ~ *montant*, *faux* ~ *droit*, high c., stand-up c.

faux ~ rabattu, double c., turn-down c. *~ roulé*, turtleneck c.

col-blanc (kɔlblɑ̃) *m*, white-collar worker.

col-bleu (kɔlblø) *m*, blue-collar worker; bluejacket (*Nav.*).

coléoptère (kɔleɔptɛːr) *a*, cole-opterous. ¶ *m*, coleopter[an], beetle.

colère (kɔlɛːr) *f*, anger, rage, passion, temper, fume. *~ bleue*, towering rage. **colère & colérique** (lerik) *a*, quick-tempered, hasty, peppery, choleric.

colibri (kɔlibri) *m*, humming bird.

colifichet (kɔlifiʃɛ) *m*, knick-knack; (*pl.*) frippery.

colimaçon (kɔlimasɔ̃) *m*, snail. *en ~*, spiral.

colin-maillard (kɔlɛ̃majaːr) *m*, blindman's buff.

colique (kɔlik) *f*, colic, gripes.

colis (kɔli) *m*, parcel, package; article [of luggage]. *~ à livrer par exprès*, express parcel (*Post*). *~-avion*, air p. *~ contre remboursement*, cash on delivery p. *par ~ postal*, by parcel post.

collaborateur, trice (kɔlabɔratœːr, tris) *n*, collaborator, contributor. **collaborer** (re) *v.i*, to collaborate. *~ à*, to contribute to, write for (*journal*).

collage (kɔlaːʒ) *m*, sticking, pasting; gluing; sizing; hanging (*paper*); fining (*wine*); free union of a couple; splicing (*film*). *~ à sec*, drymounting (*Photo.*). **collant, e** (lɑ̃, ɑ̃ːt) *a*, sticky; tacky; tight, close-fitting. ¶ *m*, pantyhose.

collatéral, e (kɔlateral) *a*, collateral, side (*att.*).

collation (kɔlasjɔ̃) *f*, collation; light meal, snack. **collationner** (ɔne) *v.t*, to collate, compare, read over; repeat; (*v.i.*) to have a snack.

colle (kɔl) *f*, glue, paste; oral test (*exams*); detention (*Sch.*); difficult question. *~ [de poisson]*, isinglass; fish glue. *~ forte*, glue.

collecte (kɔlɛkt) *f*, collection (*money*); collect. **collecteur** (tœːr) *m*, collector; main (*drain*). *~ d'impôts*, tax collector. **collec-**

tif, ive† (tif, iːv) *a*, collective, joint. **collection** (sjɔ̃) *f*, collection; file (*newspapers*). **collectionner** (ɔne) *v.t*, to collect. **collectionneur, euse** (nœːr, øːz) *n*, collector.

collège (kɔlɛːʒ) *m*, college, high school. *~ électoral*, electoral college. **collégial, e** (leʒjal) *a*, collegiate. **collégien, ne** (ʒjɛ̃, ɛn) *n*, collegian, schoolboy -girl.

collègue (kɔlɛg) *m*, colleague.

coller (kɔle) *v.t*, to stick; paste; glue; size; hang (*paper*); fine (*wine*); fix, fasten; cushion (*Bil.*); to fail (*exam*); (*v.i.*) to fit tightly, cling; to be punished (*Sch.*). **se ~**, to stick, cling, cleave.

collerette (kɔlrɛt) *f*, collaret[te]; flange.

collet (kɔlɛ) *m*, collar; collet; neck; scrag (*mutton*); scruff of the neck; flange. *~ monté* (fig.), straitlaced; prim. **colleter** (lte) *v.t*, to collar, grapple with.

colleur (kɔlœːr) *m*, paperhanger; billposter, billsticker; examiner (*Sch.*).

colleuse (kɔløːz) *f*, splicer (*film*).

collier (kɔlje) *m*, necklace; collar; strap; ring. *~ de misère*, drudgery.

colline (kɔlin) *f*, hill.

collision (kɔlizjɔ̃) *f*, collision, clash.

collocation (kɔlɔkasjɔ̃) *f*, settling the list of creditors; dividend (*to creditors*). *bordereau de ~*, list of creditors.

colloque (kɔlɔk) *m*, colloquy, conversation.

colloquer (kɔlɔke) *v.t*, to collocate; foist.

collusion (kɔlysjɔ̃) *f*, collusion.

colombe (kɔlɔ̃ːb) *f*, dove.

Colombie (la) (kɔlɔ̃bi), Columbia.

colombier (kɔlɔ̃bje) *m*, dovecote.

colon (kɔlɔ̃) *m*, colonist, settler.

colonel (kɔlɔnɛl) *m*, colonel.

colonial, e (kɔlɔnjal) *a*, colonial. **colonie** (ni) *f*, colony, settlement. *la ~ du Cap*, Cape Colony. **coloniser** (nize) *v.t*, to colonize.

colonnade (kɔlɔnad) *f*, colonnade. **colonne** (lɔn) *f*, column, pillar; post. ~ *vertébrale*, spinal column.

colophane (kɔlɔfan) *f*, resin (*violin*).

colorer (kɔlɔre) *v.t*, to color; stain (*glass*). **colorier** (rje) *v.t*, to color. **coloris** (ri) *m*, color[ing], hue.

colossal, e† (kɔlɔsal) *a*, colossal. **colosse** (lɔs) *m*, colossus; giant.

colporter (kɔlpɔrte) *v.t*, to hawk, peddle; spread (*news, gossip*). **colporteur** (tœːr) *m*, peddler.

coltineur (kɔltinœːr) *m*, porter (*dock*); heaver (*coal*).

colza (kɔlza) *m*, colza.

coma (kɔma) *m*, coma (*Med.*). **comateux, euse** (tø, øːz) *a*, comatose.

combat (kɔ̃ba) *m*, combat, fight, battle, action; war (*elements*); contest, bout, match. ~ *de boxe*, boxing match. ~ *de boxe professionel*, prize fight[ing]. ~ *de près*, infighting (*Box.*). *hors de* ~, disabled. **combativité** (tã) *f*, combativeness. **combattant** (tã) *m*, combatant, fighter. *ancien* ~, veteran. **combattre** (tr) *v.t. & i. ir*, to fight; oppose; combat; contend with; strive; vie.

combe (kɔ̃ːb) *f*, coomb, combe, dale.

combien (kɔ̃bjɛ̃) *ad*, how much; how many; how far; how. ~ *de fois?* how many times? how often? ~ *de temps?* how long?

combinaison (kɔ̃binɛzɔ̃) *f*, combination; plan, contrivance, scheme; lady's slip; overalls. **combine** (bin) *f*, trick, scheme (*generally not quite legal or moral*). **combiner** (ne) *v.t*, to combine; contrive, devise.

comble (kɔ̃ːbl) *a*, full, crowded. ¶ *m*, heaping; top, height, highest pitch; acme, summit, sum; last straw; roof. ~ *brisé*, mansard roof. *salle* ~, full house (*Theat.*). **combler** (kɔ̃ble) *v.t*, to heap, shower, fill, load, overwhelm; make up, make good.

combustible (kɔ̃bystibl) *a*, combustible; fuel (*att.*). ¶ *m*, fuel, firing. **combustion** (tjɔ̃) *f*, combustion; burning; conflagration, fire (*fig.*); burnup (*nuclear*).

Côme (**le lac de**) (koːm), Lake Como.

comédie (kɔmedi) *f*, comedy; theatricals; players; sham. **comédien, ne** (djɛ̃, ɛn) *n*, comedian, enne, actor, tress, player.

comestible (kɔmestibl) *a*, edible. ~**s**, *m.pl*, eatables, provisions.

comète (kɔmɛt) *f*, comet; headband (*Bookb.*).

comice agricole (kɔmis) *m*, agricultural show, cattle show.

comique† (kɔmik) *a*, comic; comical; funny, ludicrous. ¶ *m*, comedy; c. writer; comic actor; funny part, joke. ~ *de la troupe* (*fig.*), funny man.

comité (kɔmite) *m*, committee. *en petit* ~, select group; insiders only.

commandant (kɔmãdã) *m*, commander, commanding officer; commandant; major (*Mil.*); commodore (*Naut.*); squadron leader (*Avn.*). **commande** (mãːd) *f*, order; indent; driving; drive; driving gear; control. *de* ~, [arranged] to order; feigned. *sur* ~, (*made*) to order, commissioned. *bulletin de* ~, order form. *touche de* ~, command key (*computers*). **commandement** (mãdmã) *m*, command, order; commandment; behest; word of command. **commander** (de) *v.t. & i*, to command, order, bespeak; govern; demand; drive (*Mach.*).

commanditaire (kɔmãditɛːr) *m*, silent partner; sponsor. **commandite** (dit) *f*, limited liability; finance, interest. **commandité** (te) *m*, acting partner. **commanditer** (te) *v.t*, to finance, take an interest in; sponsor.

comme (kɔm) *ad*, as, like, such as; how. ~ *ci*, ~ *ça*, so so, middling. ¶ *c*, as, since.

commémorer (kɔmemɔre) *v.t*, to commemorate.

commençant, e (kɔmãsã, ãːt) *n*, beginner, tyro, learner. **commencement** (smã) *m*, beginning, start, commencement, inception, outset. **commencer** (se) *v.t. & i*, to begin, commence, start.

commensal, e (kɔmãsal) *n*, messmate, fellow boarder.

comment (kɔmã) *ad*, how; what! why! ~*!*, of all the nerve! how

dare you! ~?, what? I don't understand. *et* ~!, and how!

commentaire (kɔmãtɛːr) *m*,
commentary; comment. **commentateur** (tatœːr) *m*, narrator; anno-
tator; news commentator (*TV*).
commenter (te) *v.t*, or ~ *sur*, to
comment on.

commérage (kɔmeraːʒ) *m*, gossip, tittle-tattle.

commerçant, e (kɔmersɑ̃, ɑ̃ːt)
a, commercial, trading, business
(*att.*). ¶ *n*, trader, merchant.
commerce (mɛrs) *m*, commerce,
trade, trading, business; traders;
intercourse, dealings. ~ *de détail*, retail trade. *d'un* ~ *agréable*, easy to get on with. **com-
mercer** (mɛrse) *v.i*, to trade,
deal; hold intercourse. **commercial, e†** (sjal) *a*, commercial,
business, trade, trading (*att.*);
produce (*market*).

commère (kɔmɛːr) *f*, fellow
sponsor; gossip; busybody;
shrewd woman; leading lady (*revue*).

commettant (kɔmɛtɑ̃) *m*, principal (*law*); (*pl.*) constituents
(*Pol.*). **commettre** (mɛtr) *v.t.ir*,
to commit; perpetrate; appoint;
entrust; compromise. **commis**
(mi) *m*, clerk. ~ *aux vivres*,
ship's steward. ~ *d'entreprise*,
clerk of [the] works. ~ *de magasin*, shop assistant. ~ *voyageur*, traveling salesman. **commissaire** (sɛːr) *m*, commissioner;
officer (*emigration*); steward
(*fête, race meeting, etc.*); purser
(*ship*); paymaster (*navy*); superintendent (*police*). ~ *des* (ou
aux) *comptes*, auditor. ~ *priseur*, auctioneer. **commissariat**
(sarja) *m*, the status *or* office
(rooms) of a *commissaire*; thus,
~ *de police*, central police station. ~ *des comptes*, auditorship.

commission (kɔmisjɔ̃) *f*, commission; errand; committee.
commissionnaire (ɔnɛːr) *m*,
agent, commission agent, factor;
messenger; porter. ~ *chargeur*,
shipping agent. ~ *de transport*[*s*], forwarding a. ~ *en
douane*, customs a. **commission-
ner** (ne) *v.t*, to commission.

commode (kɔmɔd) *f*, [chest of]
drawers. ¶ *a*, convenient, handy; commodious, pleasant;
easy, easy-going. **commodément**
(demɑ̃) *ad*, conveniently. **commodité** (dite) *f*, convenience;
commodiousness; (*pl.*) toilet.

commotion (kɔmosjɔ̃) *f*, commotion, upheaval; shock; shell
shock. ~ *au cerveau*, concussion
of the brain.

commuer (kɔmɥe) *v.t*, to commute.

commun, e (kɔmœ̃, yn) *a*, common; usual; general; ordinary;
commonplace; vulgar; average.
peu ~, uncommon. ¶ *m*, generality, run. *en, hors du*, ~, in, out
of the, common. **communal, e**
(mynal) *a*, communal; parish
(*att.*). ¶ *m*, common [land].
communauté (note) *f*, community; commonwealth; sisterhood.
la C~ *d'Australie*, the Commonwealth of Australia. **commune**
(myn) *f*, commune, parish (*civil*).
communément (nemɑ̃) *ad*, commonly, generally.

communiant, e (kɔmynjɑ̃, ɑ̃ːt)
n, communicant.

communicatif, ive (kɔmynika-
tif, iːv) *a*, communicative. **communication** (sjɔ̃) *f*, communication; touch; intercourse; interchange; discovery; access (*of, to,
documents*); call (*Teleph.*).

communier (kɔmynje) *v.i. & t*,
to communicate (*Eccl.*). **communion** (njɔ̃) *f*, communion; sacrament; fellowship; persuasion,
faith, denomination.

communiqué (kɔmynike) *m*, official statement (*to press*);
communiqué. **communiquer** (ke)
v.t. & i, to communicate; impart, convey; produce (*documents*).

communisme (kɔmynism) *m*,
communism. **communiste** (nist)
n, communist.

commutateur (kɔmytatœːr) *m*,
switch; commutator. ~ *code*,
dimmer (*auto*). **commutation** (sjɔ̃)
f, commutation.

compacité (kɔ̃pasite) *f*, com-
pactness, closeness. **compact, e**
(pakt) *a*, compact, dense; concise, compendious.

compagne (kɔ̃paɲ) *f*, companion; mate; partner (*wife*). ~ *de voyage*, fellow passenger, f. traveler. **compagnie** (ɲi) *f*, company; companionship; bevy; covey. *de bonne* ~, well-bred, gentlemanly, ladylike. *de mauvaise* ~, ill-bred, ungentlemanly, unladylike. **& Cie** (e kɔpaɲi), & Co. **compagnon** (ɲɔ̃) *m*, companion; mate; journeyman. ~ *de malheur*, fellow sufferer. ~ *de voyage*, fellow passenger, f. traveler.

comparable (kɔparabl) *a*, comparable. **comparaison** (rɛzɔ̃) *f*, comparison; simile.

comparaître (kɔparɛ:tr) *v.i.ir*, to appear (*law*).

comparatif, ive† (kɔparatif, i:v) *a*, comparative. ¶ *m*, comparative (*Gram.*). **comparé, e** (re) *p.a*, comparative (*sciences*). **comparer** (re) *v.t*, to compare, liken.

comparse (kɔpars) *n*, supernumerary (*Theat.*); (*m.*) cipher (*pers.*).

compartiment (kɔpartimɑ̃) *m*, compartment.

comparution (kɔparysjɔ̃) *f*, appearance (*law*).

compas (kɔpɑ) *m*, [pair of] compasses; compass. **compassé** (se) *a*, formal, stiff; regular. **compasser** (se) *v.t*, to measure.

compassion (kɔpasjɔ̃) *f*, compassion. **compatible** (tibl) *a*, compatible, consistent. **compatir** (ti:r) *v.i*, to sympathize, bear. **compatissant, e** (tisɑ̃, ɑ̃:t) *a*, compassionate.

compatriote (kɔpatriɔt) *n*, compatriot, [fellow] countryman, -woman.

compendieusement (kɔpɑ̃djøzmɑ̃) *ad*, briefly. **compendium** (pɛ̃djɔm) *m*, compendium.

compensateur, trice (kɔpɑ̃satœ:r, tris) *a*, compensating; countervailing (*duty*). **compensation** (sjɔ̃) *f*, compensation; set off, offset; quid pro quo; making up (*Stk Ex.*); clearing (*banking*). **compenser** (se) *v.t*, to compensate, offset; make up; clear. ~ *les dépens*, to order each party to pay its own costs.

compère (kɔpɛ:r) *m*, fellow sponsor; fellow; crony; confederate; leading man (*revue*); compère. ~**-loriot**, *m*, sty (*eye*).

compétence (kɔpetɑ̃:s) *f*, competence; jurisdiction; province. **compétent, e** (tɑ̃, ɑ̃:t) *a*, competent.

compétiteur, trice (kɔpetitœ:r, tris) *n*, competitor. **compétition** (sjɔ̃) *f*, competition.

compiler (kɔpile) *v.t. & abs*, to compile.

complainte (kɔplɛ̃:t) *f*, ballad, lay.

complaire à (kɔplɛ:r) *v.ir*, to gratify, humor. **se complaire**, to take pleasure, [take] delight, fancy oneself, pat oneself on the back. **complaisamment** (plɛzamɑ̃) *ad*, complacently; obligingly. **complaisance** (zɑ̃:s) *f*, complaisance; deference; kindness; willingness; complacence, -cy; accommodation (*Fin.*). **complaisant, e** (zɑ̃, ɑ̃:t) *a*, obliging, willing; complaisant, accommodating, compliant; complacent. ¶ *n*, time server.

complément (kɔplemɑ̃) *m*, complement. ~ *de poids*, makeweight. **complémentaire** (tɛ:r) *a*, complementary, fuller.

complet, ète (kɔplɛ, ɛt) *a*, complete, total, whole, full; unabridged; utter; wholemeal (*bread*). *wagon complet*, *charge complète*, truckload. *complet*, full house (*Theat.*) *c'est* ~!, that's the last straw. ¶ *m*, complement; suit [of clothes] (*man's*). *au* ~, complete, full. **complètement** (plɛtmɑ̃) *ad*, completely; quite; thoroughly. ¶ *m*, completion. **compléter** (plete) *v.t*, to complete.

complexe (kɔplɛks) *a*, complex; many-sided; compound. ¶ *m*, complex. ~ *d'infériorité*, inferiority c. *être bourré de* ~*s*, to be extremely inhibited.

complexion (kɔplɛksjɔ̃) *f*, constitution; disposition.

complexité (kɔplɛksite) *f*, complexity.

complication (kɔplikasjɔ̃) *f*, complication; intricacy.

complice (kɔplis) *a*, accessory,

privy, a party (*de* = to). ¶ *n*, accomplice, confederate. ~ *en adultère*, co-respondent. **complicité** (site) *f*, complicity.

complies (kɔ̃pli) *f.pl*, complin[e] (*Eccl.*).

compliment (kɔ̃plimɑ̃) *m*, compliment, congratulation; (*pl.*) kind regards. **complimenter** (te) *v.t*, to compliment. **complimenteur, euse** (tœːr, øːz) *a*, overcivil. ¶ *n*, flatterer.

compliquer (kɔ̃plike) *v.t*, to complicate.

complot (kɔ̃plo) *m*, plot. **comploter** (plɔte) *v.t*, to plot.

componction (kɔ̃pɔ̃ksjɔ̃) *f*, compunction.

comporter (kɔ̃pɔrte) *v.t*, to admit of; call for, require. se ~, to behave.

composant, e (kɔ̃pozɑ̃, ɑ̃ːt) *a.* & *m*, component, constituent. **composé, e** (ze) *a*, compound, composite; composed, demure. *bien composée*, select (*company of people*). ¶ *m*, compound. **composer** (ze) *v.t. & i*, to compose; compound; settle; set (*Typ.*); dial (*Teleph.*). se ~, to be composed, consist. **compositeur, trice** (pozitœːr, tris) *n*, composer; compositor, [type] setter. **composition** (sjɔ̃) *f*, composition; settlement; [type] setting; essay; examination (*Sch.*); paper (*Sch.*). **composteur** (postœːr) *m*, composing stick; office printing outfit.

composter (kɔ̃pɔste) *v.t*, to date or punch (*railway ticket, etc.*). *compostez vos billets*, have your tickets punched.

compote (kɔ̃pɔt) *f*, compote, stewed fruit. ~ *de pommes*, stewed apples. *en* ~, overdone (*meat*); to a jelly (*face injury*). **compotier** (tje) *m*, fruit bowl.

compréhensif, ive (kɔ̃preɑ̃sif, iːv) *a*, comprehensive. **compréhension** (sjɔ̃) *f*, comprehension, understanding. **comprendre** (prɑ̃ːdr) *v.t.ir*, to comprehend, understand, make out; comprise, include, cover. *y compris*, including. *non compris*, not including, exclusive of.

compresse (kɔ̃prɛːs) *f*, compress

(*Med.*). **compresseur** (prɛsœːr) *m*, compressor. **compression** (sjɔ̃) *f*, compression; repression; cut (*in expenditure*). **comprimer** (prime) *v.t*, to compress; repress; restrain.

comprimé (kɔ̃prime) *m*, pill, tablet; pack (*computers*).

compromettre (kɔ̃prɔmɛtr) *v.t. & i. ir*, to compromise; impair. se ~, to compromise (*or commit*) oneself. **compromis** (mi) *m*, compromise; bond.

comptabilité (kɔ̃tabilite) *f*, bookkeeping; accountancy; accounts. **comptable** (bl) *a*, accountable, responsible; book (*entry, value*); accounting *or* bookkeeping (*machine*). ¶ *n*, accountant, bookkeeper. **comptant** (tɑ̃) *m*, cash, prompt (*or* spot) cash. ready money. [*au*] ~, in (*or* for) cash, cash down. **compte** (kɔ̃ːt) *m*, counting, count, reckoning; account. ~*-gouttes* (kɔ̃t-gut) *m* dropper. ~*-pas*, *m*, pedometer. ~ *rendu*, report; review. ~ *à rebours*, countdown. ~ *rond*, round figures, r. numbers; even money *à* ~, on account. *tout* ~ *fait*, all told. *se rendre* ~ *de*, to realize. **compter** (kɔ̃te) *v.t. & i*, to count. reckon; number; rely, depend; calculate; intend, mean. **compteur** (tœːr) *m*, meter, counter; taximeter, clock; computer. ~ *de bicyclette*, cyclometer. ~ *de sport* stopwatch, recorder. ~ *de tours* speed (*or* revolution) counter. ~ *de vitesse*, speedometer. **comptoir** (twaːr) *m*, counter; bar branch, agency; office.

compulser (kɔ̃pylse) *v.t*, to go through, examine.

comte (kɔ̃ːt) *m*, count (*title*). **comté** (kɔ̃te) *m*, county, shire. **comtesse** (tɛs) *f*, countess.

con (kɔ̃) *m*, cunt. *con, ne* (ɔn) *n* imbecile. *le roi des* ~*s*, the king of fools, *conard* (naːr) *m*, idiot fool, etc. **conasse** (nas) *f*, stupid woman; slut. **connerie** (kɔnri) *f* imbecility. *faire une* ~, to do something foolish.

concasser (kɔ̃kɑse) *v.t*, to pound break, crush.

concave (kɔ̃kaːv) *a*, concave **concavité** (kavite) *f*, concavity

concéder (kɔ̃sede) *v.t*, to concede, grant.

concentration (kɔ̃sɑ̃trasjɔ̃) *f*, concentration. **concentrer** (tre) *v.t*, to concentrate; center (*fig.*); repress. **concentrique** (trik) *a*, concentric.

concepteur (kɔ̃sɛptœːr) *m*, idea man. **~-projecteur**, author of a project.

conception (kɔ̃sɛpsjɔ̃) *f*, conception.

concernant (kɔ̃sɛrnɑ̃) *pr*, concerning. **concerner** (ne) *v.t*, to concern, affect.

concert (kɔ̃sɛːr) *m*, concert; chorus (*fig.*). **concertant, e** (sɛrtɑ̃, ɑ̃ːt) *n*, concert performer. **concerter** (te) *v.t*, to concert, plan. **concerto** (sɛrto) *m*, concerto.

concession (kɔ̃sɛsjɔ̃) *f*, concession, grant, claim, license. **concessionnaire** (ɔnɛːr) *n*, concession[n]aire, grantor, claimholder.

concevable (kɔ̃s[ə]vabl) *a*, conceivable. **concevoir** (səvwaːr) *v.t. & abs*, to conceive; entertain; understand; word; couch.

concierge (kɔ̃sjɛrʒ) *n*, doorkeepper, [hall] porter, caretaker, housekeeper; keeper (*prison*).

concile (kɔ̃sil) *m*, council (*Eccl.*).

conciliabule (kɔ̃siljabyl) *m*, secret meeting; confabulation.

concilier (kɔ̃silje) *v.t*, to conciliate, reconcile; win.

concis, e (kɔ̃si, iːz) *a*, concise, terse, crisp, brief. **concision** (sizjɔ̃) *f*, conciseness, brevity.

concitoyen, ne (kɔ̃sitwajɛ̃, ɛn) *n*, fellow citizen.

concluant, e (kɔ̃klyɑ̃, ɑ̃ːt) *a*, conclusive. **conclure** (klyːr) *v.t. & i. ir*, to conclude, end; clinch; infer. **conclusion** (klyzjɔ̃) *f*, conclusion, inference; (*pl.*) pleas (*law*).

concombre (kɔ̃kɔ̃ːbr) *m*, cucumber.

concordance (kɔ̃kɔrdɑ̃ːs) *f*, agreement, reconciliation; concordance; concord. **concordat** (da) *m*, composition; concordat. **concorde** (kɔrd) *f*, concord, harmony. **concorder** (de) *v.i*, to agree, tally.

concourir (kɔ̃kuriːr) *v.i.i.ir*, to

concur; compete; rank. **concours** (kuːr) *m*, concurrence; assistance, help; concourse; confluence; competition, contest; meeting; show; [competitive] examination; equality. **~ orthographique**, spelling bee.

concret, ète (kɔ̃krɛ, ɛt) *a*, concrete. **le concret**, the concrete (opp. *abstract*).

conçu, *p.p*, concevoir.

concubine (kɔ̃kybin) *f*, concubine.

concupiscence (kɔ̃kypisɑ̃ːs) *f*, concupiscence.

concurrence (kɔ̃kyrɑ̃ːs) *f*, competition; equality [of rank]. *à ~ de*, amounting to. *jusqu'à ~ de*, up to, not exceeding. **concurrent, e** (rɑ̃, ɑ̃ːt) *a*, concurrent. ¶ *n*, competitor.

concussion (kɔ̃kysjɔ̃) *f*, misappropriation.

condamnation (kɔ̃dɑnasjɔ̃) *f*, condemnation; sentence; judgment; conviction. **condamné, e** (ne) *n*, convict. **~ à mort**, condemned man, woman. **condamner** (ne) *v.t*, to condemn; doom; convict; sentence; mulct; give up (*patient*); block up (*door*); board up (*window*); batten down (*Naut.*).

condé (kɔ̃de) *m*, a tacit agreement with the police; a police detective.

condensateur (kɔ̃dɑ̃satœːr) *m*, condenser (*Phys., Elec., Opt.*). **condensation** (sjɔ̃) *f*, condensation. **condenser** (dɑ̃se) *v.t*, to condense; boil down; pack (*computers*). **condenseur** (sœːr) *m*, condenser (*steam*).

condescendance (kɔ̃dɛsɑ̃dɑ̃ːs) *f*, condescension. **condescendre** (dr) *v.i*, to condescend; comply.

condiment (kɔ̃dimɑ̃) *m*, condiment.

condisciple (kɔ̃disipl) *m*, fellow student, schoolfellow.

condition (kɔ̃disjɔ̃) *f*, condition; (*pl.*) terms; position. **~provisionnelle**, proviso. *à ~*, on approval. *en ~*, in (*domestic*) service. **conditionnel, le**† (ɔnɛl) *a*, conditional. **conditionner**(ne) *v.t*, to condition; make up.

condoléance (kɔ̃dɔleɑ̃ːs) *f*, condolence.

conducteur, trice (kɔ̃dyktœːr, tris) *n*, conductor, tress; driver; drover; guard (*Rly*.). ~ *des travaux*, foreman of job, factory foreman (*Build*.). ~ *principal*, main, lead (*Elec*.). **conduire** (dɥiːr) *v.t. & abs. ir*, to conduct, lead, guide, show; direct, manage, run; drive; steer; take, carry, convey; conduce. *se* ~, to behave. **conduit** (dɥi) *m*, pipe, conduit, duct. **conduite** (dɥit) *f*, conduct, behavior, bearing; management; lead; care; driving; pipe. ~ [*maîtresse*], main.

cône (koːn) *m*, cone; taper.

confection (kɔ̃fɛksjɔ̃) *f*, making up; ready-made clothes, *or* business; outfitting. **confectionner** (ɔne) *v.t*, to make up; concoct. **confectionneur, euse** (nœːr, øːz) *n*, clothier, outfitter.

confédération (kɔ̃federasjɔ̃) *f*, confederation, confederacy. *se* **confédérer** (re) *v.pr*, to confederate.

conférence (kɔ̃ferɑ̃ːs) *f*, conference; lecture; debating society. **conférencier, ère** (rɑ̃sje, ɛːr) *n*, lecturer. **conférer** (re) *v.i. & t*, to confer; bestow; compare.

confesse (kɔ̃fɛs) *f*, confession (*to priest*). **confesser** (se) *v.t*, to confess, own. *se* ~, to confess [one's sins]. **confesseur** (sœːr) *m*, confessor. **confession** (sjɔ̃) *f*, confession. **confessionnal** (ɔnal) *m*, confessional [box]. **confessionnel, le** (nɛl) *a*, confessional; denominational.

confiance (kɔ̃fjɑ̃ːs) *f*, confidence, trust, faith, reliance, dependence. **confiant, e** (ɑ̃, ɑ̃ːt) *a*, confident, sanguine, hopeful; confiding. **confidemment** (fidamɑ̃) *ad*, confidentially. **confidence** (dɑ̃ːs) *f*, confidence, secrecy. **confident, e** (dɑ̃, ɑ̃ːt) *n*, confidant, e. **confidentiel, le†** (sjɛl) *a*, confidential. **confier** (fje) *v.t*, to entrust, confide; trust, commit; vest. *se* ~, to confide in, rely.

configuration (kɔ̃figyrasjɔ̃) *f*, configuration, lie, lay.

confiner (kɔ̃fine) *v.i*, to border; (*v.t*.) to confine. **confins** (fɛ̃) *m.pl*, confines; ends.

confire (kɔ̃fiːr) *v.t.ir*, to preserve; pickle.

confirmer (kɔ̃firme) *v.t*, to confirm.

confiscation (kɔ̃fiskasjɔ̃) *f*, confiscation.

confiserie (kɔ̃fizri) *f*, confectionery; confectioner's shop. **confiseur, euse** (zœːr, øːz) *n*, confectioner.

confisquer (kɔ̃fiske) *v.t*, to confiscate; impound.

confiture (kɔ̃fityːr) *f*. oft. pl, preserve, jam. ~ *d'oranges*, [orange] marmalade.

conflagration (kɔ̃flagrasjɔ̃) *f*, conflagration.

conflit (kɔ̃fli) *m*, conflict, clash, strife.

confluent (kɔ̃flyɑ̃) *m*, confluence, meeting. **confluer** (flye) *v.i*, to join, meet.

confondre (kɔ̃fɔ̃ːdr) *v.t*, to confound; mingle; blend; confuse; mistake; discomfit; overwhelm.

conformation (kɔ̃fɔrmasjɔ̃) *f*, conformation. **conforme** (fɔrm) *a*, conformable; according; in harmony; agreeable. *pour copie* ~, [certified] a true copy. **conformé, e** (me) *p.a*, (*well, ill*) formed. **conformément** (mɑ̃) *ad*, conformably, according. **conformer** (me) *v.t. & se* ~, to conform. **conformité** (mite) *f*, conformity, compliance.

confort (kɔ̃fɔːr) *m*, comfort(s). **confortable†** (fɔrtabl) *a*, comfortable, snug.

confraternité (kɔ̃fraternite) *f*, confraternity, brotherhood. **confrère** (frɛːr) *m*, colleague, confrere, brother; contemporary. **confrérie** (freri) *f*, brotherhood, sisterhood; confraternity.

confronter (kɔ̃frɔ̃te) *v.t*, to confront; compare.

confus, e (kɔ̃fy, yːz) *a*, confused; jumbled; indiscriminate; embarrassed. **confusément** (fyzemɑ̃) *ad*, confusedly; dimly. **confusion** (zjɔ̃) *f*, confusion; embarrassment.

congé (kɔ̃ʒe) *m*, leave; vacation; furlough; dismissal, discharge notice [to quit]; permission; clearance (*ship*); cart note (*Cust.*); fillet (*Arch.*). donner ~, to fire (*employee*). **congédier** (dje) *v.t*, to dismiss, discharge; pay off.

congélation (kɔ̃zelasjɔ̃) *f*, congelation, freezing; frostbite. **congeler** (ʒle) *v.t.* & **se** ~, to congeal, freeze.

congénital, e (kɔ̃zenital) *a*, congenital.

congère (kɔ̃ʒɛːr) *f*, snowdrift. ~ de sable, sand drift.

congestion (kɔ̃zɛstjɔ̃) *f*, congestion. ~ cérébrale, pulmonaire, sanguine, c. of the brain, of the lungs, of the blood. **congestionner** (ɔne) *v.t*, to congest (*Med.*).

conglomérat (kɔ̃glɔmera) *m*, conglomerate.

congratulation (kɔ̃gratylasjɔ̃) *f*, congratulation. **congratuler** (le) *v.t*, to congratulate.

congre (kɔ̃ːgr) *m*, conger [eel].

congrégation (kɔ̃gregasjɔ̃) *f*, congregation (*Eccl.*).

congrès (kɔ̃grɛ) *m*, congress. **congressiste** (sist) *n*, member of the (*or* a) congress.

congru, e (kɔ̃gry) *a*, congruous, fitting. à la portion congrue, on short pay, on a meager income. **congrûment** (grymɑ̃) *ad*, congruously.

conifère (kɔnifɛːr) *a*, coniferous. ¶ *m*, conifer.

conique (kɔnik) *a*, conic(al); taper[ing].

conjectural, e† (kɔ̃zɛktyral) *a*, conjectural. **conjecture** (ty:r) *f*, conjecture, surmise, guess. **conjecturer** (tyre) *v.t*, to conjecture.

conjoindre (kɔ̃zwɛ̃:dr) *v.t.ir*, to [con]join, unite. **conjoint, e†** (ʒwɛ̃, ɛ̃:t) *a*, [con]joint. ¶ *n*, party to a (*or* the) marriage (*law*). **conjonction** (ʒɔ̃ksjɔ̃) *f*, conjunction, union. **conjoncture** (ʒɔ̃kty:r) *f*, conjuncture.

conjugaison (kɔ̃zygɛzɔ̃) *f*, conjugation.

conjugal, e† (kɔ̃zygal) *a*, conjugal, connubial, matrimonial, marriage (*tie*), married (*life*).

conjuguer (kɔ̃zyge) *v.t*, to conjugate. machines conjuguées, twin engines.

conjuration (kɔ̃zyrasjɔ̃) *f*, conspiracy; conjuration. **conjuré (re)** *m*, conspirator. **conjurer** (re) *v.t.* & *i*, to conspire; conjure.

connaissance (kɔnɛsɑ̃ːs) *f*, knowledge; ken; acquaintance; consciousness, senses; cognizance; (*pl.*) learning, attainments, acquirements. avoir sa ~, to be conscious (*awake*). en ~ de cause, advisedly. figure de ~, familiar face. prendre ~ de, to take note of. sans ~, unconscious, insensible, senseless.

connaissement (kɔnɛsmɑ̃) *m*, bill of lading.

connaisseur, euse (kɔnɛsœːr, øːz) *n*, connoisseur, judge. **connaître** (nɛːtr) *v.t.* & *abs. ir*, to know, be acquainted with; be aware of; take cognizance. se ~ à (ou en), to be a [good] judge of. se faire ~ , to introduce oneself, make oneself known; become known.

connexe (kɔnɛks) *a*, connected, allied, like. & ~s, & the like. **connexion** (ksjɔ̃), **connexité** (ksite) *f*, connection.

connivence (kɔnivɑ̃ːs) *f*, connivance. être de ~ pour, to connive at.

connu (le) (kɔny), the known.

conque (kɔ̃ːk) *f*, conch.

conquis, *p.p.*, **conquérir**.

conquérant, e (kɔ̃kerɑ̃, ɑ̃ːt) *n*, conqueror, ess. **conquérir** (riːr) *v.t.ir*, to conquer. **conquête** (kɛːt) *f*, conquest.

consacrer (kɔ̃sakre) *v.t*, to consecrate, hallow; dedicate; devote; appropriate, set apart; sanction. consacré (à la mémoire de), sacred. terme consacré, accepted term.

consanguinité (kɔ̃sɑ̃ginite) *f*, consanguinity, blood relationship.

conscience (kɔ̃sjɑ̃ːs) *f*, conscience; conscientiousness; consciousness. se faire ~ de, to be reluctant to. avoir ~ de, to be aware of. **consciencieux, euse†** (ɑ̃sjø, øːz) *a*, conscientious. **conscient, e** (sjɑ̃, ɑ̃ːt), *a*, conscious (*aware*); sentient (*being*).

conscription (kɔ̃skripsjɔ̃) *f*, conscription. **conscrit** (skri) *m*, conscript, draftee; tyro; freshman (*Sch.*).

consécration (kɔ̃sekrasjɔ̃) *f*, consecration; dedication; sanction.

consécutif, ive† (kɔ̃sekytif, i:v) *a*, consecutive.

conseil (kɔ̃sɛ:j) *m*, advice, counsel; board; council; court; counsel (*pers. law*). ~ **de prud'hommes**, conciliation board. **C~ des ministres, C~ de Cabinet**, cabinet council. ~ **d'administration**, board [of directors]. ~ **de guerre**, council of war; court martial. **conseiller** (sɛje) *v.t*, to advise, counsel. **conseiller, ère** (je, ɛ:r) *n*, adviser, councilor. **conseilleur, euse** (jœ:r, ø:z) *n*, officious adviser.

consentement (kɔ̃sɑ̃tmɑ̃) *m*, consent; assent. **consentir** (ti:r) *v.i.ir*, to consent, agree.

conséquemmant (kɔ̃sekamɑ̃) *ad*, consequently, accordingly. ~ **à**, consistently with. **conséquence** (kɑ̃:s) *f*, consequence; outcome, sequel; inference. **conséquent, e** (kɑ̃, ɑ̃:t) *a*, consistent, rational; consequent. *par conséquent*, consequently, accordingly, therefore.

conservateur, trice (kɔ̃sɛrvatœ:r, tris) *n*, conservator, keeper; warden; ranger; curator, trix; conservative (*Pol.*); registrar (*mortgages*). **conservation** (sjɔ̃) *f*, preservation; care; registry. ~ **par le froid**, cold storage. **conservatoire** (twa:r) *m*, school, academy (*music, etc.*); museum. **conserve** (sɛrv) *f*, preserve; (*pl.*) canned food; (*pl.*) dark glasses; consort (*Naut.*). ~s **au vinaigre**, pickles. **conserver** (ve) *v.t. & abs*, to preserve; pickle; conserve, keep. ~ **la composition**, to keep the type standing.

considérable† (kɔ̃siderabl) *a*, considerable; eminent; large. **considérant** (rɑ̃) *m*, preamble. **considération** (rasjɔ̃) *f*, consideration; regard. **considérer** (re) *v.t*, to consider; esteem; regard, deem.

consignataire (kɔ̃siɲatɛ:r) *m*, trustee; consignee. **consignateur** (tœ:r) *m*, consignor. **consignation** (sjɔ̃) *f*, deposit; consignment. **con-**

signe (siɲ) *f*, orders (*to sentry*); confinement to barracks; checkroom, baggage room; deposit (*bottles, etc.*). **consigner** (ɲe) *v.t*, to deposit; consign; record, chronicle; confine [to barracks]. ~ **à la porte**, to refuse admittance.

consistance (kɔ̃sistɑ̃:s) *f*, consistence, -cy; stability; credit, standing. **consistant, e** (tɑ̃, ɑ̃:t) *a*, firm, set. **consister** (te) *v.i*, to consist. **consistoire** (twa:r) *m*, consistory.

consolateur, trice (kɔ̃sɔlatœ:r, tris) *n*, consoler, comforter. **consolation** (sjɔ̃) *f*, consolation, comfort, solace, cheer. **console** (sɔl) *f*, bracket; console; console table. **consoler** (le) *v.t*, to console.

consolider (kɔ̃sɔlide) *v.t*, to consolidate, strengthen; unify, fund (*debt*); exercise, take up (*option*). **consolidation** (dasjɔ̃) *f*, consolidation.

consommateur (kɔ̃sɔmatœ:r) *m*, consumer; customer (*at café*). **consommation** (sjɔ̃) *f*, consumption, use; drink; consummation. **consommé, e** (me) *a*, consummate. ¶ *m*, stock (*Cook.*); clear soup. **consommer** (me) *v.t*, to consume; use; drink, spend (*money in café*); consummate. **consomption** (sɔ̃psjɔ̃) *f*, consumption (*destruction & Med.*).

consonance (kɔ̃sɔnɑ̃:s) *f*, consonance. **consonant, e** (nɑ̃, ɑ̃:t) *a*, consonant. **consonne** (sɔn) *f*, consonant.

consorts (kɔ̃sɔ:r) *m.pl*, confederates. **consortium** (sɔrsjɔm) *m*, syndicate, consortium.

conspirateur, trice (kɔ̃spiratœ:r, tris) *n*, conspirator, plotter. **conspiration** (sjɔ̃) *f*, conspiracy, plot. **conspirer** (re) *v.i. & t*, to conspire, plot; tend.

conspuer (kɔ̃spɥe) *v.t*, to conspue; hoot, boo, barrack. *conspuez-le!* down with him!

constamment (kɔ̃stamɑ̃) *ad*, constantly. **constance** (stɑ̃:s) *f*, constancy; steadfastness; persistence, perseverance; patience. *avec* ~, steadfastly. **constant, e** (stɑ̃, ɑ̃:t) *a*, constant; steadfast;

enduring; obvious. ¶ *f*, constant.

constater (kõstate) *v.t*, to ascertain; verify, prove, establish; declare; attest; evidence; record; note; show; mention; be of opinion. **constatation** (tasjõ) *f*, ascertainment, etc.

constellation (kõstɛllasjõ) *f*, constellation; galaxy (*fig.*). **constellé, e** (stɛlle) *a*, constellated; studded.

consternation (kõstɛrnasjõ) *f*, consternation, dismay. **consterner** (ne) *v.t*, to dismay, stagger.

constipation (kõstipasjõ) *f*, constipation, costiveness. **constiper** (pe) *v.t*, to constipate, bind.

constituant, e (kõstitɥɑ̃, ɑ̃:t) *a*, constituent, component. **constituer** (tɥe) *v.t*, to constitute; form, incorporate; settle; instruct; brief; appoint. *se ~ prisonnier*, to give oneself up [to the police]. **constitution** (tysjõ) *f*, constitution; composition. *~ de dot*, marriage settlement. **constitutionnel, le†** (ɔnɛl) *a*, constitutional; temperamental.

constructeur (kõstryktœ:r) *m*, builder, maker, constructor. **construction** (sjõ) *f*, construction; building; making; build; engineering; erection; structure. **construire** (strɥi:r) *v.t.ir*, to construct; build, erect; make; construe.

consul (kõsyl) *m*, consul. *le C~ britannique*, the British c. *le ~ de France*, the French c. **consulaire** (lɛ:r) *a*, consular. **consulat** (la) *m*, consulate; consulship.

consultant, e (kõsyltɑ̃, ɑ̃:t) *a*, consulting. **consultation** (tasjõ) *f*, consultation; opinion (*legal*), advice. **consulter** (te) *v.t. & i*, to consult; refer to.

consumer (kõsyme) *v.t*, to consume; waste, spend.

contact (kõtakt) *m*, contact; touch; connection (*Elec.*).

contagieux, euse (kõtaʒjø, ø:z) *a*, contagious, infectious, catching. **contagion** (ʒjõ) *f*, contagion; contagiousness.

contamination (kõtaminasjõ) *f*, contamination. **contaminer** (ne) *v.t*, to contaminate.

conte (kõ:t) *m*, story; tale, yarn; short story; fable. *~ de bonne femme*, *~ de vieille*, *~ à dormir debout*, nonsense. *~ de fées*, *~ bleu*, fairy tale. *~ rimé*, nursery rhyme. *~s en l'air*, cock-&-bull story, moonshine.

contemplatif, ive (kõtɑ̃platif, i;v) *a*, contemplative. **contemplation** (sjõ) *f*, contemplation; gazing. **contempler** (ple) *v.t*, to contemplate, view; gaze on; meditate upon.

contemporain, e (kõtɑ̃porɛ̃, ɛn) *a*, contemporaneous, contemporary. ¶ *n*, contemporary.

contempteur, trice (kõtɑ̃ptœ:r, tris) *n*, scorner.

contenance (kõtnɑ̃:s) *f*, capacity, content; countenance, demeanor, bearing. *perdre ~*, to lose face. **contenant** (tnɑ̃) *m*, container. **contenir** (tni:r) *v.t.ir*, to contain, hold; accommodate; comprise; restrain, control.

conteneur (kõtnœr) *m*, container. **conteneurisation** (izasjõ) *f*, containerization. **conteneuriser** (ize) *v.t*, to containerize.

content, e (kõtɑ̃, ɑ̃:t) *a*, content; contentedly; satisfied; pleased; glad. ¶ *m*, fill; heart's content. **contentement** (tɑ̃tmɑ̃) *m*, content[ment]; satisfaction. **contenter** (te) *v.t*, to content, satisfy, gratify.

contentieux, euse (kõtɑ̃sjø, ø:z) *a*, contentious, law (*att.*). ¶ *m*, law department or office; contentious business. **contention** (sjõ) *f*, application, intentness.

contenu (kõtny) *m*, contents.

conter (kõte) *v.t*, to tell, relate.

contestable (kõtɛstabl) *a*, questionable, debatable, moot. **contestation** (sjõ) *f*, dispute, contestation. **contestataire** (tatɛ:r) *a*, tending to challenge. ¶ *m*, challenger; social militant. **sans conteste** (tɛst), indisputably. **contester** (te) *v.t. & abs*, to contest, challenge, question, dispute.

conteur, euse (kõtœ:r, ø:z) *n*, narrator; storyteller.

contexte (kõtɛkst) *m*, context.

contexture (kõtɛksty:r) *f*, [con]texture.

contigu, ë (kɔ̃tigy) *a*, contiguous, adjoining. **contiguité** (gɥite) *f*, contiguity.

continence (kɔ̃tinɑ̃:s) *f*, continence. **continent, e** (nɑ̃, ɑ̃:t) *a*, continent; modest.

continent (kɔ̃tinɑ̃) *m*, continent, mainland. *le c~*, the Continent (*Europe*). **continental, e** (tal) *a*, continental.

contingence (kɔ̃tɛ̃ʒɑ̃:s) *f*, contingency. **contingent, e** (ʒɑ̃, ɑ̃:t) *a*, contingent. ¶ *m*, contingent, share; quota. **contingentement** (ʒɑ̃tmɑ̃) *m*, curtailment. **contingenter** (te) *v.t*, to fix quotas for.

continu, e (kɔ̃tiny) *a*, continuous; direct (*Elec. current*). **continuation** (nɥasjɔ̃) *f*, continuation; continuance. **continuel, le†** (nɥel) *a*, continual, unceasing. **continuer** (nɥe) *v.t. & i*, to continue; carry on; go on; proceed; keep on. **continuité** (nɥite) *f*, continuity; ceaselessness. **continûment** (nymɑ̃) *ad*, continuously.

contondant, e (kɔ̃tɔ̃dɑ̃, ɑ̃:t) *a*, blunt (*instrument*).

contorsion (kɔ̃tɔrsjɔ̃) *f*, contortion; twist.

contour (kɔ̃tu:r) *m*, contour, outline. *~ de hanches, de poitrine*, hip, bust, measurement. **contourner** (turne) *v.t*, to contort, twist; encircle.

contractant, e (kɔ̃traktɑ̃, ɑ̃:t) *a*, contracting. ¶ *n*, contractant. **contracter** (te) *v.t. & abs*, to contract; enter into; take out, effect (*Insce. policy*). **contraction** (sjɔ̃) *f*, contraction, shrinkage. **contractuel, le** (tɥel) *a*, contractual.

contradiction (kɔ̃tradiksjɔ̃) *f*, contradiction; discrepancy. **contradictoire** (twa:r) *a*, contradictory; conflicting; after trial; check, control (*att.*), joint. *examen ~*, cross-examination.

contraindre (kɔ̃trɛ̃:dr) *v.t.ir*, to constrain, compel, force, coerce, drive; restrain. *~ par saisie de biens*, to distrain upon (*pers.*). **contrainte** (trɛ̃:t) *f*, constraint, compulsion.

contraire (kɔ̃trɛ:r) *a*, contrary, converse, opposed; unfavorable. ¶ *m*, contrary, reverse, converse, opposite. *au ~*, on the contrary.

contrairement (trɛrmɑ̃) *ad*, contrarily, contrary, counter.

contralto (kɔ̃tralto) *m*, contralto.

contrariant, e (kɔ̃trarjɑ̃, ɑ̃:t) *a*, trying, provoking. **contrarier** (rje) *v.t. & abs*, to thwart, interfere with, impede, cross; vex. **contrariété** (rjete) *f*, contrariety; annoyance, nuisance.

contraste (kɔ̃trast) *m*, contrast. **contraster** (te) *v.i. & t*, to contrast.

contrat (kɔ̃tra) *m*, contract; agreement; deed, indenture; articles; letter; bond. *dresser un ~*, to draw up a deed.

contravention (kɔ̃travɑ̃sjɔ̃) *f*, contravention; breach; infringement; offense; ticket or fine (*auto*). *dresser une ~ à* to summons (*legal*).

contre (kɔ̃:tr) *pr. & ad*, against; contrary to; to (*as* 3 to 1); by, close to; versus. *~ nature*, unnatural.

contre-allée (kɔ̃trale) *f*, side walk.

contre-amiral (kɔ̃tramiral) *m*, rear admiral.

contre-attaque (kɔ̃tratak) *f*, counterattack.

contre-avions (kɔ̃travjɔ̃) *a*, antiaircraft.

contrebalancer (kɔ̃trəbalɑ̃se) *v.t*, to counterbalance, counterpoise.

contrebande (kɔ̃trəbɑ̃:d) *f*, smuggling, contraband. *de ~* (*fig.*), counterfeit. **contrebandier, ère** (bɑ̃dje, ɛ:r) *n*, smuggler.

contrebas (en) (kɔ̃trəba) *ad*, below, lower down; downwards.

contrebasse (kɔ̃trəba:s) *f*, double bass, contrabass.

contrecarrer (kɔ̃trəkare) *v.t*, to thwart, cross; counteract.

contre-champ (kɔ̃trəʃɑ̃) *m*, reverse angle shot (*cinema, TV*).

contrecœur (à) (kɔ̃trəkœ:r) *ad*, reluctantly.

contrecoup (kɔ̃trəku) *m*, rebound; recoil; reaction.

contredanse (kɔ̃trədɑ̃:s) *f*, quadrille; ticket (*parking, traffic, etc.*).

contredire (kɔ̃trədi:r) *v.t. & abs. ir*, to contradict, gainsay.

se~, to contradict oneself; conflict. **sans contredit** (di), unquestionably.

contrée (kɔ̃tre) *f*, country, region.

contre-écrou (kɔ̃trekru) *m*, locknut.

contre-expertise (kɔ̃trɛkspɛrtiːz) *f*, countervaluation.

contrefaçon (kɔ̃trəfasɔ̃) *f*, counterfeit; forgery; infringement; piracy; imitation. ~ *littéraire*, ~ *de librairie*, infringement of copyright. **contrefacteur** (faktœːr) *m*, counterfeiter, etc. **contrefaire** (fɛːr) *v.t.ir*, to counterfeit; mimic, take off; pretend to be; disguise; deform. **contrefaiseur, euse** (fəzœːr, øːz) *n*, mimic.

contre-fiche (kɔ̃trəfiʃ) *f*, strut, brace; raking shore.

contre-fil (à) (kɔ̃trəfil) *ad*, against the grain.

contrefort (kɔ̃trəfɔːr) *m*, buttress; spur.

contre-haut (en) (kɔ̃trəo) *ad*, above, higher up; upwards.

contre-jour (kɔ̃trəʒuːr) *m*, unfavorable light; backlighting. *à ~,* against the light; with one's back to the light.

contremaître (kɔ̃trəmɛːtr) *m*, foreman; first mate (*Naut.*).

contremander (kɔ̃trəmɑ̃de) *v.t,* to countermand; call off.

contremarque (kɔ̃trəmark) *f*, countermark; pass-out check (*Theat.*).

contrepartie (kɔ̃trəparti) *f*, counterpart; contra; contrary [opinion]; other side *or* party; another dealer; running stock (*against one's client*).

contrepasser (kɔ̃trəpɑse) *v.t,* to write back, reverse, contra; endorse back.

contre-pédaler (kɔ̃trəpedale) *v.i,* to back-pedal.

contre-petterie (kɔ̃trəpɛtri) *f*, Spoonerism.

contre-pied (kɔ̃trəpje) *m*, opposite (*course, view*).

contreplaqué (kɔ̃trəplake) *m*, plywood. ~ *en trois*, three-ply [wood].

contre-plongée (kɔ̃trəplɔ̃ʒe) *f*, low-angle shot (*cinema, TV*).

contrepoids (kɔ̃trəpwa) *m*, counterweight, counterpoise, counterbalance, balance weight.

contre-poil (à) (kɔ̃trəpwal), the wrong way.

contrepoint (kɔ̃trəpwɛ̃) *m*, counterpoint.

contre-pointe (kɔ̃trəpwɛ̃ːt) *f*, loose headstock, tailstock.

contrepoison (kɔ̃trəpwazɔ̃) *m*, antidote.

contre-porte (kɔ̃trəpɔrt) *f*, screen door.

contreseing (kɔ̃trəsɛ̃) *m*, counter signature.

contresens (kɔ̃trəsɑ̃ːs) *m*, misconstruction; mistranslation; misinterpretation; bull; wrong way *or* sense.

contresigner (kɔtrəsiɲe) *v.t,* to countersign.

contretemps (kɔ̃trətɑ̃) *m*, mishap, unfortunate occurrence, awkward incident, hitch. *à ~,* inopportunely.

contre-torpilleur (kɔ̃trətɔrpijœːr) *m*, [torpedo-boat] destroyer.

contretype (kɔ̃trətip) *m*, duplicate (*film*). ~ *négatif*, internegative.

contrevenir à (kɔ̃trəvəniːr) *v.ir,* to contravene, infringe, transgress.

contrevent (kɔ̃trəvɑ̃) *m*, outside shutter.

contrevérité (kɔ̃trəverite) *f*, untruth.

contribuable (kɔ̃tribɥabl) *n*, taxpayer. *¶ a,* taxable. **contribuer** (bɥe) *v.i,* to contribute; conduce. **contribution** (bysjɔ̃) *f*, contribution; tax; excise.

contrister (kɔ̃triste) *v.t,* to sadden, grieve.

contrit, e (kɔ̃tri, it) *a,* contrite. **contrition** (sjɔ̃) *f*, contrition.

contrôle (kɔ̃troːl) *m*, control; supervision; roster; hallmark; inspection; check; ticket office; box office. ~ *de présence*, timekeeping. **contrôler** (trole) *v.t,* to control; inspect; supervise; check; hallmark. **contrôleur** (lœːr) *m*, controller, comptroller; supervisor; examiner; ticket collector; inspector; checker; timekeeper; telltale (*Mach.*). ~ *des tours*, lap scorer.

contrordre (kɔ̃trɔrdr) *m*, counter instructions.

controuvé, e (kɔ̃truve) *p.p*, fabricated, invented.

controverse (kɔ̃trɔvɛrs) *f*, controversy. **controversé, e** (se) *p.p*, debated.

contumace (kɔ̃tymas) *f*, contumacy.

contus, e (kɔ̃ty, y:z) *a*, bruised. **contusion** (tyzjɔ̃) *f*, bruise, contusion. **contusionner** (ɔne) *v.t*, to bruise, contuse.

convaincant, e (kɔ̃vɛ̃kɑ̃, ɑ̃:t) *a*, convincing, cogent. **convaincre** (vɛ̃:kr) *v.t.ir*, to convince; convict.

convalescence (kɔ̃valesɑ̃:s) *f*, convalescence. **convalescent, e** (sɑ̃, ɑ̃:t) *a. & n*, convalescent.

convenable† (kɔ̃vnabl) *a*, proper, fit, [be]fitting, becoming, decorous; suitable, convenient; expedient. **convenance** (vnɑ̃:s) *f*, propriety, fitness, congruity; harmony; convenience; expedience, -cy. **convenir** (vni:r) *v.i.ir*, to agree; own; suit; befit; be expedient; become, do. *mot convenu*, code word. *rédiger en langage convenu*, to code. **convention** (vɑ̃sjɔ̃) *f*, covenant; agreement, contract; convention. **de ~ & conventionnel, le** (ɔnɛl) *a*, conventional.

converger (kɔ̃verʒe) *v.i*, to converge.

convers, e (kɔ̃vɛ:r, ɛrs) *a*, lay (*brother, sister*). **converse, a.f. & f**, converse. conversation, talk; call (*Teleph.*).

conversation (kɔ̃vɛrsasjɔ̃) *f*, **converser** (se) *v.i*, to converse, talk, commune; wheel (*Mil.*). **conversion** (sjɔ̃) *f*, conversion; change. **convertible** (tibl) *a*, convertible. **converti, e** (ti) *n*, convert. **convertir** (ti:r) *v.t*, to convert, change, turn. se ~, to become converted (*Relig.*). **convertissable** (tisabl) *a*, convertible (*Fin.*). **convertissement** (smɑ̃) *m*, conversion (*Fin.*). **convertisseur** (sœ:r) *m*, converter.

convexe (kɔ̃vɛks) *a*, convex. **convexité** (ite) *f*, convexity.

conviction ((kɔ̃viksjɔ̃) *f*, conviction.

convié, e (kɔ̃vje) *n*, guest. **convier** (vje) *v.t*, to invite; (*fig.*), urge. **convive** (vi:v) *n*, guest; table companion.

convocation (kɔ̃vɔkasjɔ̃) *f*, convocation, calling; notice [of meeting]; calling-up (*Mil.*).

convoi (kɔ̃vwa) *m*, convoy; train (*Rly.*); funeral [procession].

convoiter (kɔ̃vwate) *v.t*, to covet, lust after. **convoiteux, euse** (tø, (ø):z) *a*, covetous. **convoitise** (ti:z) *f*, covetousness; lust.

convoler (kɔ̃vɔle) *v.i. & abs*, to marry again. ~ *en secondes, en troisièmes, noces*, to marry a second, a third, time.

convoquer (kɔ̃vɔke) *v.t*, to convoke, call, summon, convene; call together.

convoyer (kɔ̃vwaje) *v.t*, to convoy; escort.

convulsif, ive† (kɔ̃vylsif, i:v) *a*, convulsive. **convulsion** (sjɔ̃) *f*, convulsion; upheaval.

coopératif, ive (kɔɔperatif, i:v) *a*, cooperative. [*société*] *coopérative*, cooperative society. **coopération** (sjɔ̃) *f*, cooperation. **coopérer** (re) *v.i*, to cooperate.

coordonné (kɔɔrdɔne) *a*, coordinated. **coordonnées** (kɔɔrdɔne) *f. pl*, coordinates. *donner ses ~*, to give one's name, address, & phone number.

coordonner (kɔɔrdɔne) *v.t*, to coordinate.

copain (kɔpɛ) *m*, buddy, pal.

copeau (kɔpo) *m*, shaving; chip.

Copenhague (kɔpɛnag) *f*, Copenhagen.

copie (kɔpi) *f*, copy; paper (*Sch.*). ~ *en clair*, hard copy, printout (*computers*). **copier** (pje) *v.t. & abs*, to copy; transcribe; imitate.

copieux, euse† (kɔpjø, ø:z) *a*, copious, full; hearty (*meal*).

copine (kɔpin) *f*, friend (*female*).

copiste (kɔpist) *n*, copyist; fraudulent copier of fashion designs presented by couturiers.

copropriétaire (koprɔprietɛ:r) *n*, joint owner.

copulation (kɔpylasjɔ̃) *f*, copulation.

coq (kɔk) *m*, cock, rooster; weathercock; bantam (*Box.*); cook (*ship's*). ~-à-l'âne, *m*, cock-&-bull story. ~ *d'Inde*, turkey-cock. ~ *d bruyère*, heathcock, blackcock, moor cock. ~ *de combat*, game c. ~ *du village*, cock of the walk. *comme un* ~ *en pâte*, sitting pretty. [~] *faisan*, cock pheasant.

coque (kɔk) *f*, shell; hull (*ship*); husk; pod; cocoon; cockle (*Mol.*); loop (*of ribbon, hair*). œuf à la ~, boiled egg.

coquelicot (kɔkliko) *m*, poppy.

coqueluche (kɔklyʃ) *f*, whooping cough; darling.

coquemar (kɔkma:r) *m*, kettle, pot.

coquerico (kɔkəriko) *m*, cock-a-doodle-doo.

coquet, te† (kɔkɛ, ɛt) *a*, coquettish, skittish; stylish, smart, natty, trim. ¶ *n*, flirt, coquette. **coqueter** (kte) *v.i*, to coquet, flirt.

coquetier (kɔktje) *m*, egg cup; egg merchant.

coquetterie (kɔkɛtri) *f*, coquetry; as *coquet, te*.

coquillage (kɔkija:ʒ) *m*, shellfish; shell, conch. **coquille** (ki:j) *f*, shell; bush (*Mach.*); misprint, literal [error]; demy (*paper*).

coquin, e (kɔkɛ̃, in) *n*, rogue, rascal, knave, scamp; (*f.*) hussy, jade, minx. **coquinerie** (kinri) *f*, knavery, roguery, rascality.

cor (kɔ:r) *m*, horn (*Mus.*); corn (*on foot*); antler, tine. ~ *d'harmonie*, French horn. *à* ~ *& à cri*, clamorously.

corail (kɔra:j) *m*, coral. **corailleur** (rajœ:r) *m*, coral fisher. **banc corallifère** (ralifɛ:r), coral reef.

Coran (kɔrɑ̃) *m*, Koran.

corbeau (kɔrbo) *m*, raven; crow; corbel.

corbeille (kɔrbɛ:j) *f*, basket; dress circle (*Theat.*). ~ *à papiers*, wastepaper b. ~ [*de mariage*], (*bridegroom's*) wedding presents.

corbillard (kɔrbija:r) *m*, hearse.

cordage (kɔrda:ʒ) *m*, rope; (*pl.*) cordage. **corde** (kɔrd) *f*, rope, cord, line; band; thread; string;

halter (*hanging*); chord. *les* ~*s*, the strings (*orchestra*). *à* ~*s*, string[ed] (*Mus.*). ~ *à boyau*, catgut. ~ *à linge*, clothes line. ~ *à piano*, piano wire. ~ *à sauter*, skipping rope. ~ *sensible*, sensitive spot. **cordeau** (do) *m*, line; string; chalk-line (*cord*); fuse. **cordelette** (dəlɛt) *f*, cord, string. **cordelière** (ljɛ:r) *f*, girdle. **corder** (de) *v.t*, to twist; cord, rope. **corderie** (dri) *f*, rope works; r. making.

cordial, e† (kɔrdjal) *a*, cordial, hearty. ¶ *m*, cordial. **cordialité** (lite) *f*, cordiality, etc.

cordier (kɔrdje) *m*, rope maker; drifter (*boat*). **cordon** (dɔ̃) *m*, strand, twist; string; cord; lace (*shoe*); pull (*bell*); border; milled edge; row; cordon, ribbon. ~ *sanitaire*, quarantine line. **cordonner** (dɔne) *v.t*, to twist, twine. **cordonnerie** (nri) *f*, shoemaker's shop; boot & shoe trade. **cordonnet** (nɛ) *m*, braid, cord, twist; milled edge; overcast (*Emb.*). **cordonnier, ère** (nje, ɛ:r) *n*, boot & shoe repairer, shoemaker.

Corée (la) (kɔre), Korea. **cōréen, ne** (reɛ̃, ɛn) *a*. & C~, *n*, Korean.

coriace (kɔrjas) *a*, leathery, tough.

corindon (kɔrɛ̃dɔ̃) *m*, corundum.

Corinthe (kɔrɛ̃:t) *f*, Corinth. **corinthien, ne** (rɛ̃tjɛ̃, ɛn) *a*. & C~, *n*, Corinthian.

cormoran (kɔmɔrɑ̃) *m*, cormorant.

cornac (kɔrnak) *m*, mahout; keeper; guide.

cornaline (kɔrnalin) *f*, carnelian.

corne (kɔrn) *f*, horn; dog['s] ear; gaff (*spar*). ~ *d'abondance*, horn of plenty, cornucopia. ~ *de cerf*, deerhorn. **corné, e** (ne) *a*, horny.

corneille (kɔrnɛ:j) *f*, crow; rook. *bayer aux* ~*s*, to rubberneck.

cornemuse (kɔrnəmy:z) *f*, bagpipe[s].

corner (kɔrne) *v.i*, to sound a horn; hoot (*auto*); speak in ear trumpet; din; ring (*ears*); (*v.t.*) to trumpet, din; dog ear, turn down. **cornet** (nɛ) *m*, cornet (*cone*). ~ [*à dés*], dice box. ~ *à pistons*, cornet (*Mus.*). ~

[*acoustique*], ear trumpet. ~ [*avertisseur*], horn (*auto*).

corniche (kɔrniʃ) *f*, cornice; ledge.

cornichon (kɔrniʃ5) *m*, gherkin.

cornier, ère (kɔrnje, ɛːr) *a*, corner, angle (*att.*). ¶ *f*, angle iron.

Cornouailles (la) (kɔrnwɑːj), Cornwall.

cornu, e (kɔrny) *a*, horned; absurd. ¶ *f*, retort, still.

corollaire (kɔrɔlɛːr) *m*, corollary.

coron (kɔrɔ̃) *m*, (*coal*) miner's dwelling; mining village.

corporation (kɔrpɔrasjɔ̃) *f*, corporation, guild. **corporel, le†** (rɛl) *a*, corporeal; corporal; bodily. **corps** (kɔːr) *m*, body; substance; corps, brigade; bodice; barrel, cylinder; hull (*ship*). ~ 6, 8 ou ~ de 6, de 8, points, 6, 8, point [size] (*Typ.*). ~ à ~, hand to hand (*fight*); clinch (*Box.*). ~ *composé*, compound (*Chem.*). ~ *de garde*, guard-house, guardroom. ~ *de logis*, ~ *de bâtiment*, main [portion of] building. ~ *de métier*, guild. ~ *électoral*, electorate, country. ~ *& biens*, crew & cargo, life & property. ~ [*mort*], [dead] body, corpse. ~ *mort*, dolphin, moorings (*Naut.*). *à* ~ *perdu*, recklessly. ~ *simple*, element (*Chem.*). *prendre* ~, to take shape.

corpulence (kɔrpylɑ̃ːs) *f*, stoutness, corpulence, -ency, portliness, burliness. **corpulent, e** (lɑ̃, ɑ̃ːt) *a*, corpulent.

corpuscule (kɔrpyskyl) *m*, corpuscle.

correct, e† (kɔrɛkt) *a*, correct. **correcteur, trice** (tœːr, tris) *n*, corrector. ~ *d'imprimerie*, proof-reader. **correctif** (tif) *m*, corrective. **correction** (sjɔ̃) *f*, correction; correctness; propriety; punishment. ~ *des épreuves*, proofreading. **correctionnel, le†** (ɔnɛl) *a*, correctional. *tribune* ~, police court.

corrélatif, ive (kɔrelatif, iːv) *a*, correlative.

correspondance (kɔrɛspɔ̃dɑ̃ːs) *f*, correspondence; letters; connection, transfer point, inter-

change. **correspondant, e** (dɑ̃, ɑ̃ːt) *a*, corresponding. ¶ *n*, correspondent; friend acting for parents (*to pupil*). **correspondre** (pɔːdr) *v.i*, to correspond; tally; communicate.

corridor (kɔridɔːr) *m*, corridor, passage.

corrigé (kɔriʒe) *m*, fair copy (*Sch.*); pony (*book*). **corriger** (ʒe) *v.t*, to correct; compensate for; chastise.

corroborer (kɔrɔbɔre) *v.t*, to corroborate.

corroder (kɔrɔde) *v.t*, to corrode.

corroi (kɔrwa) *m*, currying (*leather*); puddle (*clay*).

corrompre (kɔrɔ̃ːpr) *v.t*, to corrupt, taint, spoil; bribe.

corrosif, ive (kɔrozif, iːv) *a. & m*, corrosive. **corrosion** (zjɔ̃) *f*, corrosion.

corroyer (kɔrwaje) *v.t*, to curry (*leather*); puddle, pug; weld; trim, dress.

corruptible (kɔryptibl) *a*, corruptible. **corruption** (sjɔ̃) *f*, corruption; bribery.

corsage (kɔrsaːʒ) *m*, bust; bodice, corsage.

corsaire (kɔrsɛːr) *m*, corsair, privateer; shark (*Fin.*). *pantalon* ~, pedal pushers.

Corse (la) (kɔrs), Corsica. **corse**, *a. & C~*, *n*, Corsican.

corsé, e (kɔrse) *p.a*, full-bodied (*wine*); strong, forcible (*language*). **corser (se)** *v.t*, to fortify, strengthen. *se*~, to become serious.

corset (kɔrsɛ) *m*, corset, stays. **corseter** (səte) *v.t*, to corset. **corsetier, ère** (tje, ɛːr) *n*, corset maker.

cortège (kɔrtɛːʒ) *m*, retinue, train; procession; pageant.

corvée (kɔrve) *f*, statute (*or* forced) labor, corvée; fatigue (*Mil.*); drudgery.

cosmétique (kɔsmetik) *a. & m*, cosmetic.

cosmique (kɔsmik) *a*, cosmic.

cosmonaute (kɔsmɔnot) *n*, astronaut.

cosmopolite (kɔsmɔpɔlit) *m. & a*, cosmopolite; cosmopolitan.

cosse (kɔs) *f*, pod, cod, shell,

husk, hull; thimble, eye[let] (*Naut.*).

cosser (kɔse) *v.i,* to butt (*rams*).

cossu, e (kɔsy) *a,* well off; rich.

costard (kɔsta:r) *m,* man's business suit (*slang*).

costaud (kɔsto) *a,* hefty, sturdy. ¶ *m,* muscleman.

costume (kɔstym) *m,* costume, dress, garb; suit; frock. ~ *marin,* sailor suit. **costumer** (me) *v.t,* to dress (*in fancy dress*). **costumier, ère** (mje, ɛ:r) *n,* theatrical & fancy costumer; wardrobe keeper (*Theat.*).

cote (kɔt) *f,* quota, share, contribution; assessment, rating; quotation(s), price(s), rates, mark(s), marking, call, list; due dating (*bill*); character, class (*ship*); odds, betting; reading (*survey*). ~ *d'amour,* favoritism, backstairs influence. ~ *de la bourse,* stock exchange daily official list. ~ *des changes,* [foreign] exchange rates. ~ *mal taillée,* rough & ready settlement, compromise.

côte (ko:t) *f,* rib; slope; hill; [sea]coast, shore, seaboard. *à* ~*s,* ribbed, corded. ~ *à* ~, side by side, alongside. *de la* ~ *de,* descended from. *faire* ~, to run ashore. *la C*~ *d'Azur,* the Riviera. *la C*~ *d'Ivoire,* the Ivory Coast. *la C*~ *de l'Or,* the Gold Coast.

côté (kote) *m,* side; way, direction; [broad]side (*Naut.*); beam ends (*Naut.*). ~ *du vent,* weather side. ~ *faible,* weak spot (*fig. of pers.*). ~ *sous le vent,* lee [side]. *à* ~, *ad,* near, to one side. *à* ~ *de, pr,* by the side of; next to; next door to; beside. *de*~, *ad,* sideways; sidelong; aside, apart, on one side, by. *de l'autre* ~, on the other side *or* hand; over the way.

coteau (kɔto) *m,* hill, hillside, slope.

côtelé, e (kotle) *a,* ribbed, corduroy.

côtelette (kotlɛt) *f,* chop, cutlet. ~ *de filet,* loin chop.

coter (kɔte) *v.t,* to letter; number; mark; page; assess, rate; quote;

class; rank. *croquis coté,* dimensioned sketch.

coterie (kɔtri) *f,* set, clique, circle.

cothurne (kɔtyrn) *m,* buskin, cothurnus.

côtier, ère (kotje, ɛ:r) *a,* coast[ing]; inshore. [*bateau*] *côtier,* coaster. [*cheval*] *côtier,* trace horse.

cotillon (kɔtijɔ̃) *m,* petticoat; cotillion.

cotisation (kɔtizasjɔ̃) *f,* quota, share, contribution; subscription; fee; assessment. **cotiser** (ze) *v.t,* to assess. **se** ~, to club together; subscribe.

coton (kɔtɔ̃) *m,* cotton; c wool; down, fluff. ~ *hydrophile, m,* absorbent cotton. ~*-poudre, m,* guncotton. *c'est* ~, it's difficult. *filer un mauvais* ~, to be in trouble (*health, financial*). **cotonnade** (tɔnad) *f,* cotton [cloth, goods]. **cotonneux, euse** (nø, ø:z) *a,* cottony; downy; fluffy; wooly. **cotonnier, ère** (nje, ɛ:r) *a,* cotton (*att.*). ¶ *m,* cotton plant.

côtoyer (kotwaje) *v.t. & abs,* to run along, hug (*shore*); skirt; coast; border upon.

cotre (kɔtr) *m,* cutter (*boat*). ~ *de la douane,* revenue cutter.

cotret (kɔtrɛ) *m,* fagot, stick.

cotte (kɔt) *f,* petticoat; overalls. ~ *de mailles,* coat of mail.

cou (ku) *m,* neck.

couard, e (kua:r, ard) *a,* coward[ly]. ¶ *n,* coward. **couardise** (kuardi:z) *f,* cowardice.

couchant (kuʃɑ̃) *m,* setting; west; wane, decline. **couche** (kuʃ) *f,* bed, couch; hotbed; layer; stratum; seam; sheet; coat[ing]; course; lap[ping]; diaper; ring (*in tree*); (*pl.*) confinement, lying-in, childbed; delivery, birth. **coucher** (kuʃe) *m,* going to bed; setting (*sun, etc.*); night's lodging, board; bed[ding]. ~ *de soleil,* sunset. *au* ~ *du soleil,* at sunset, at sundown. ¶ *v.t,* to lay; lay down; put to bed; lay low; beat down, slope. ~ *en joue,* to aim (at). ~ *par écrit,* to commit to (*or* put in) (*or* set down in) writing. ¶ *v.i,* to lie, lie down; spend the night, sleep. **se** ~, to lie down, go to bed; couch; set, go down (*sun, moon*). **couchette** (ʃɛt) *f*, crib, cot; berth, bunk, couchette.

couci-couça (kusikusa), **couci-couci**, *ad*, so so, middling.

coucou (kuku) *m*, cuckoo; cowslip. [*pendule à*] ~, cuckoo clock.

coude (kud) *m*, elbow; bend; crank. *jouer des* ~*s*, to elbow one's way. *huile de* ~, elbow grease. **coudées franches** (kude) *f.pl*, elbowroom (*fig.*); scope.

cou-de-pied (kudpje) *m*, instep.

couder (kude) *v.t*, to bend, crank. **coudoyer** (dwaje) *v.t*, to elbow, jostle; run up against; come very near to.

coudre (kudr) *v.t. & abs. ir*, to sew; s. up; s. on; stitch; piece, tack (*fig.*).

coudrier (kudrie) *m*, hazel (*bush*).

couenne (kwan) *f*, rind (*bacon*); crackling (*pork*); mole (*Med.*).

couguar (kugwaːr) *m*, cougar, puma.

couille (kuj) *f*, testicle (*slang*). ~ *molle*, sissy, milksop. **couillon** (jɔ̃) *m*, idiot, fathead.

coulage (kulaːʒ) *m*, running; pouring, casting; leakage. **coulant, e** (lɑ̃, ɑ̃ːt) *a*, flowing, easy, liquid, running, loose; accommodating. ¶ *m*, runner (*Hort. & Mech.*); slide. **coulé** (le) *m*, slur (*Mus.*); follow [shot] (*Bil.*); casting. **coulée** (le) *f*, running; flow; cast[ing]; tapping; run (*animal track*); running hand. **couler** (le) *v.t*, to pour, tap, cast; strain; sink, slide; slur (*Mus.*); (*v.i.*) to flow, run; trickle; gutter; leak; glide, slide, slip. ~ *ou* ~ *à fond ou* ~ *à pic ou* ~ *bas*, to sink, founder, go down. *faire* ~, to spill, shed; slip, turn on water. *se* ~, to slide, slip.

couleur (kulœːr) *f*, color; coloring; paint; dye; complexion; suit (*cards*); (*pl.*) colors (*flag*). *sous* ~ *de*, under color of (*fig.*).

couleuvre (kulœːvr) *f*, snake; bitter pill (*fig.*). ~ *à collier*, common snake. *avaler une* ~, to swallow an insult.

coulis (kuli) *m*, grout[ing].

coulisse (kulis) *f*, slide; slideway; heading, hem (*for tape*); link (*Mach.*); link motion; side scene (*Theat.*); (*pl.*) slips, wings (*Theat.*); coulisse (*unofficial or free market on Paris Bourse*). *dans la* ~, behind the scenes. *à* ~, sliding. *regard en* ~, sidelong glance. **coulissier** (sje) *m*, coulissier (*broker on Paris coulisse market*).

couloir (kulwaːr) *m*, passage, corridor; lobby.

couloire (kulwaːr) *f*, strainer.

coup (ku) *m*, blow; stroke; hit; chop; coup; knock; thrust; poke; cut, slash; nip; prick; dig; whack; slap; stab; shock; clap, peal; flap; rap; wave, sweep; touch; shot; report; rush; beat; blast; gust; move (*chess, etc.*); knack; glass, drink; time, moment; try, go; pitch (*angler's*). ~ *au but*, hit. ~ *d'air*, rush of air; chill (*Med.*). ~ *d'amende*, penalty stroke (*golf*). ~ *d'assommoir*, knock-down blow (*fig.*). ~ *d'envoi*, kick-off (*Foot.*). ~ *d'épaule*, lift. ~ *d'épingle*, pin prick. ~ *d'éponge* (*fig.*), clean slate. ~ *d'essai*, first attempt, trial shot. ~*s d'essai*, practice (*Ten.*). ~ *d'œil*, glance, twinkling; look; judgment; view. ~ *d'ongle*, scratch. *à* ~*s de*, with (*blows from*). ~ *de balai*, sweep. ~ *de bec*, peck. ~ *de brosse*, brush. ~ *de chapeau*, salute, bow. ~ *de chiffon*, wipe, rub with a cloth. *à* ~*s de ciseaux*, with scissors & paste (*fig.*). ~ *de collier*, tug. ~ *de corne*, butt. ~ *de coude*, nudge. ~ *de dents*, bite. *traduire à* ~*s de dictionnaire*, to translate by looking up every other word in the dictionary. ~ *de feu*, shot. ~ *de filet*, cast; haul; catch. ~ *de fleuret*, pass (*Fenc.*). ~ *de force*, feat of strength. ~ *de foudre*, thunderbolt. ~ *de fouet*, lash; fillip. ~ *de froid*, cold snap; chill (*Med.*). ~ *de grâce*, finishing stroke, quietus. ~ *de griffe*, scratch. *à* ~*s de hache*, in a rough & ready fashion. ~ *de hasard*, fluke. ~ *de l'étrier*, stirrup cup. ~ *de lumière*, burst of light.

~ [de lunette], sight. ~ de main, surprise attack; swift bold stroke (action), lightning move; helping hand. ~ de marteau, knock (at the door). ~ de massue, stunning blow. un ~ de mer, a great wave, a heavy sea. ~ de patte, dig (fig.). ~ [de pied], kick. ~ de poing, punch; fisticuffs; knuckle-duster. ~ de sang, [apoplectic] stroke. ~ de sifflet, [blast of a] whistle. ~ de soleil, sunstroke. ~ de sonnette, ring [of a bell]. ~ de téléphone, ring [of the telephone]. ~ de tête, butt; rash act. ~ de théâtre, stage trick; sensation[al event]. ~ de tonnerre, thunderclap, peal of t. ~ de vent, squall, gust of wind; flurry; blast; gale. ~ déloyal, foul (Box.). ~s & blessures, assault & battery. ~ manqué, miss, failure. ~ monté, put-up job. ~ sur ~, one after another. à ~ sûr, assuredly. sur le~, at the time.

coupable (kupabl) a, guilty, culpable; sinful. ¶ n, culprit, offender.

coupage (kupa:ʒ) m, blending (wines). **coupant, e** (pɑ̃, ɑ̃:t) a, cutting, sharp; edge[d]. ¶ m, [cutting] edge. **coupe** (kup) f, cutting; cutting out (clothes); cut; division; section; length (piece of a stuff); overarm stroke (swim.); cup, chalice, goblet, glass; bowl, dish; cup (sport); plate (turf). **coupé** (pe) m, brougham; coupé. **coupe-cigares,** m, cigar cutter. **coupe-circuit,** m, cut-out (Elec.). **coupe-gorge,** m, cutthroat place. **coupe-jarret,** m, cutthroat (pers.). **coupe-verre à molette,** m, wheel glass cutter. **coupé-lit,** m, sleeping compartment (Rly.). **coupelle** (pɛl) f, cupel. **coupeller** (le) v.t, to cupel. **coupe-papier,** m, paper knife. **couper** (pe) v.t & abs, to cut; c. off; c. down; c. in (on road, etc.); c. out; chop off; intersect, cross; slice (ball); blend (wines); dilute, water; interrupt; switch off. se ~, to cut oneself; cut; contradict oneself; intersect. se faire ~ les cheveux, to have one's hair cut. **couperet** (prɛ) m, cleaver, chopper; knife.

couperose (kuprɔ:z) f, copperas, vitriol; acne; blotched face.

coupeur, euse (kupœ:r, ø:z) n, cutter. ~ de bourses, pickpocket.

couple (kupl) f, couple, two; brace; yoke; leash. ¶ m, couple (pers.); pair; cell (Elec.); timber (ship). ~ [moteur], torque, couple. **coupler** (ple) v.t, to couple, connect. **couplet** (plɛ) m, verse; strap hinge.

coupole (kupɔl) f, cupola, dome.

coupon (kupɔ̃) m, remnant; short length; coupon; half (Rly. ticket). **coupure** (py:r) f, cut; clipping (newspaper); denomination; power cut (Elec.).

cour (ku:r) f, court; [court]yard; courtship, suit. ~ de cassation, supreme court of appeal. ~ de l'église, churchyard. faire la ~ à, to court, woo, make love to.

courage (kuraʒ) m, courage, fortitude, spirit, pluck, nerve. ~ arrosé, Dutch courage. ¶ i, courage! cheer up! **courageux, euse†** (raʒø, ø:z) a, courageous, game.

couramment (kuramɑ̃) ad, fluently; usually, commonly. **courant, e** (rɑ̃, ɑ̃:t) a, current; running; instant, present; run (measurement). ¶ m, current; stream; tide; course; current (or present) month. ~ alternatif, alternating current (Elec.). ~ continu, direct c. ~ d'affaires, turnover. ~ d'air, draft; blast. ~ de jusant, ebb tide. ~ de palan, tackle fall. fin ~, at end of the month. au ~, up-to-date. se mettre au ~ de, to become informed about. ~ de pointe, peak current. ~-jet, jet stream (Meteor.). ¶ f, diarrhea.

courbatu, e (kurbaty) a, tired out; stiff in the joints. **courbature** (ty:r) f, stiffness, tiredness.

courbe (kurb) a, curve[d]. ¶ f, curve, bend, sweep. ~ de niveau, contour line. **courber** (be) v.t & i. & se ~, to bend, curve, bow. **courbette** (bɛt) f, curvet. faire des ~s, to curvet; bow & scrape. faire une ~, to duck. **courbure** (by:r) f, curvature, bend.

coureur, euse (kurœ:r, ø:z) n, runner; racer; wanderer, rover; gadabout; frequenter; rake. ~ cycliste, racing cyclist. ~ de bals, dancing man. ~ *de spectacles*, playgoer. ~ *de vitesse*, sprinter.

courge (kurʒ) *f*, pumpkin; gourd. ~ *à la moelle*, vegetable marrow.

courir (kuri:r) *v.i. & t. ir*, to run; go; run about; hurry; slip (*or* pass) away; race; sail; circulate, go round; be in fashion; be rife; accrue; tramp up & down; run after; pursue; frequent; hunt; course; hunt after; incur; go through; travel. *le bruit court que . . .*, it is reported that . . , there is a rumor abroad that . . .

courlis (kurli), **courlieu** (ljø) *m*, curlew.

couronne (kurɔn) *f*, crown; wreath; coronet; corona; circlet; ring; tonsure. ~ [*mortuaire*], wreath (*funeral*). **couronnement** (nmɑ̃) *m*, coronation; crowning; crowning piece; coping; taffrail. **couronner** (ne) *v.t*, to crown; wreathe; cap; cope; award a prize to; reward; surround.

courrier (kurje) *m*, mail, post, letters; courier, messenger; news, intelligence; mail coach. **courriériste** (rjerist) *m*, par writer.

courroie (kurwa) *f*, belt, band; strap. ~*s* [*de transmission*], belting. ~ *de ventilateur*, fanbelt. ~ *trapézoïdal*, V-belt.

courroucer (kuruse) *v.t*, to incense, anger. **courroux** (ru) *m*, wrath, anger, ire, rage.

cours (ku:r) *m*, course; flow; run; stream; way; class (*Sch.*); currency; tender (*legal*); price, rate, quotation; avenue. ~ *authentique & officiel*, stock exchange daily official list. ~ *d'eau*, stream, watercourse. ~ *de danse*, dancing class, school of dancing. en ~, current; present, instant; in progress.

course (kurs) *f*, run; race; (*pl.*) running, racing; outing; trip; errand; way; course; career; fare; stroke, travel; privateering. **de** ~, racing (*as cycle*, *ski*); race (*as horse*); speed (*skates*). **en** ~, out [on business]. ~ *aux armements*, arms race. ~ *à pied*, foot race. ~ *d'obstacles*, steeplechase; obstacle race. ~ *de barrage*, runoff (*from dead heat*). ~ *de chars*,

chariot race. ~ *de côte*, hill climb. ~ *de demifond*, middle-distance race. ~ *de fond*, long-distance r.; distance swim. ~ *de haies*, hurdle race. ~*s de lévriers*, greyhound racing, dog r., dogs. ~ *de* (*or à*) *relais*, relay r. ~ *de taureaux*, bullfight. ~ *en sacs*, sack race. ~ *nulle*; ~ *à égalité*, dead heat. ~ *par équipes*, team race. ~ *sur piste*, track r., ~ *sur route*, road race. ~*s sur route*, road racing. **coursier** (sje) *m*, charger (*horse*), steed, courser.

court, e (ku:r, urt) *a*, short; limited. *à courtes vues*, short-sighted (*fig.*). *à court de*, short of; out of stock of. **court**, *ad*, short.

court (kɔrt *ou* ku:r) *m*, court (*Ten.*).

courtage (kurta:ʒ) *m*, broking; brokerage; commission.

courtaud, e (kurto, o:d) *n*, thickset (*or* dumpy) person. **courtauder** (tode) *v.t*, to crop the tail of.

court-circuit (kursirkɥi) *m*, short [circuit].

courte-botte (kurtəbɔt) *m*, shrimp (*pers.*).

courtement (kurtəmɑ̃) *ad*, shortly.

courtepointe (kurtəpwɛ̃:t) *f*, [down] quilt.

courtier, ère (kurtje, ɛ:r) *n*, broker.

courtisan (kurtizɑ̃, an) *a*, flattering, obsequious. ¶ *m*, courtier. ¶ *f*, courtesan. **courtiser** (ze) *v.t*, to court; woo; fawn on. **courtois, e†** (twa, a:z) *a*, courteous; courtly, urbane. **courtoisie** (twazi) *f*, courtesy, etc.

couseur, euse (kuzœ:r, ø:z), *n*, sewer (*Need.*).

cousin, e (kuzɛ̃, in) *n*, cousin; friend. ~ *germain, e*, first cousin. ~ *issu(e) de germain*, second c. ¶ *m*, gnat, midge. **cousiner** [**ensemble**] (zine) *v.i*, to get on well [together].

coussin (kusɛ̃) *m*, cushion; hassock; bolster; pillow; pad. **coussinet** (sinɛ) *m*, [small] cushion; pad; bearing, brass, bush; [screwing] die; [rail] chair (*Rly.*).

cousu (kuzy) *a*, sewn. ~ *main*,

handsewn. *du ~ main*, a sure thing, no problem, easy.

coût (ku) *m*, cost. **coûtant** (tɑ̃) *a*, *au prix ~*, at cost price.

couteau (kuto) *m*, knife; cutter; knife edge. *~ à découper*, carving knife, [meat] carver. *~ à dessert*, cheese knife. *~ à virole*, *~ à cran d'arrêt*, clasp k., jackknife. *à ~*, eating (*apples, etc.*). *à~x tirés*, at daggers drawn (*fig.*). *le ~ à la gorge*, a pistol [held] at one's head (*fig.*). **coutelas** (tlɑ) *m*, big kitchen knife. **coutelier**, **ère** (təlje, ɛːr) *n*, cutler. **coutellerie** (tɛlri) *f*, cutlery; c. works *or* shop.

coûter (kute) *v.i*, to cost; (*abs.*) to cost money. *coûte que coûte*, at all costs. **coûteusement** (təzmɑ̃) *ad*, expensively. **coûteux**, **euse** (tø, ø ̞ːz) *a*, costly, expensive.

coutil (kuti) *m*, [canvas] tick-[ing]; drill; duck.

coutume (kutym) *f*, custom, usage, habit, practice, wont. *de ~*, usual. **coutumier**, **ère** (mje, ɛːr) *a*, accustomed, in the habit; customary; common, unwritten (*law*). *~ du fait*, in the habit of doing so.

couture (kutyːr) *f*, seam; sewing; needlework; scar; pock, pit. *~ [à la main]*, plain sewing. *battre à plate ~*, to beat hollow (*or* soundly). **couturer** (tyre) *v.t*, to scar, seam (*with wounds*); pock, pit. **couturier** (rje) *m*, costum[i]er, mantlemaker. **couturière** (rjeːr) *f*, dressmaker; seamstress, needlewoman.

couvain (kuvɛ̃) *m*, nest of (*insects'*) eggs. **couvaison** (vɛzɔ̃) *f*, brooding time, sitting t. **couvée** (ve) *f*, brood, hatch, clutch; progeny.

couvent (kuvɑ̃) *m*, convent, monastery, nunnery; convent school.

couver (kuve) *v.t*, to sit on (*eggs*); hatch; incubate; (*abs.*) to brood, sit; mother (*fig.*); (*v.i.*) to smolder; brew. *~ des yeux*, to gaze at; gloat over. *mettre ~*, to set (*hen*).

couvercle (kuvɛrkl) *m*, cover, lid, cap, head.

couvert, **e** (kuvɛːr, ɛrt) *p.a*, covered; clad; overgrown; wooded; shady; overcast; covert. ¶ *m*, table [things]; knife, fork, & spoon; spoon & fork; cover; shady retreat. *le ~*, shelter, lodging. *mettre, ôter, le ~*, to lay, clear, the table. *à ~*, under cover, sheltered; covered; packed (*consignment*). ¶ *f*, blanket; glaze (*on pottery*). **couverture** (vɛrtyːr) *f*, covering; cover; margin; roofing; blanket; counterpane; rug (*traveling*); cloth (*horse*).

couveuse (kuvøːz) *f*, brood hen, sitting hen; incubator. **couvi** (vi) *a.m*, addle[d].

couvre-chef (kuvrəʃef) *m*, headgear. **couvre-engrenages** (vrɑ̃grənaːʒ) *m*, gearcase. **couvre-feu** (vrə) *m*, lights out (*Mil.*); curfew. **couvre-joint**, *m*, welt, butt strap. **couvre-lit**, *m*, bedspread. **couvre-livre**, *m*, jacket, dust cover (*book*). **couvre-pied**, *m*, down quilt. **couvre-théière**, *m*, tea cosy. **couvreur** (vrœːr) *m*, slater; tiler; thatcher. **couvrir** (vriːr) *v.t.ir*, to cover; roof; load (*with praise, abuse*); drown (*sounds*). *se ~*, to cover oneself, wrap up; put one's hat on; become overcast.

crabe (krab) *m*, crab (*Crust.*).

crac (krak) *m*, crack, snap; (*i.*) before you could say Jack Robinson.

crachat (kraʃa) *m*, spit[tle], star (*decoration*). **crachement** (ʃmɑ̃) *m*, spitting. **cracher** (ʃe) *v.i*, to spit; spit out; splutter; splash (*tap*); spout; pay unwillingly, cough up. *tout craché*, to a tee. **crachoir** (ʃwaːr) *m*, spittoon. *tenir le ~*, to monopolize the conversation.

crack (krak) *m*, crack (*racehorse*).

Cracovie (krakɔvi) *f*, Krakow.

crado (krado) *a*, filthy (*slang*).

crack (krak) *m*, crack (*racehorse*).

Cracovie (krakɔvi) *f*, Krakow.

craie (krɛ) *f*, chalk.

craindre (krɛ̃ːdr) *v.t. & abs. ir*, to fear, be afraid of, dread; cannot stand. *craint l'humidité, la* *chaleur,* to be kept dry, cool *or* in a dry, cool, place. **crainte** (krɛ̃:t) *f,* fear, dread, awe. **craintif, ive†** (krɛ̃tif, i:v) *a,* timid, timorous, fearful, afraid.

cramoisi, e (kramwazi) *a. & m,* crimson.

crampe (krɑ̃:p) *f,* cramp (*Med.*); staple. **crampon** (krɑ̃pɔ̃) *m,* cramp [iron], clamp, holdfast; fastener, catch; staple; [dog] spike; crampon, stud; bore (*pers.*). **cramponner** (pɔne) *v.t,* to cramp, clamp, fasten; pester. se ~, to cling, fasten.

cran (krɑ̃) *m,* notch, nick; peg (*fig.*); pluck, mettle. ~ *d'arrêt,* safety catch.

crâne (krɑ:n) *m,* skull, cranium. ¶†, *a,* plucky, jaunty. **crâner** (krɑne) *v.i,* to swagger; brazen it out.

crapaud (krapo) *m,* toad; low easy chair; baby grand; fire-cracker; flaw. *laid comme un ~,* [as] ugly as sin. **crapaudière** (djɛ:r) *f,* toad hole. **crapaudine** (din) *f,* toadstone; strainer, grating; plug hole; center casting.

crapoussin, e (krapusɛ̃, in) *n,* shrimp (*pers.*).

crapule (krapyl) *f,* debauchery; debauchee. **crapuleux, euse†** (lø, ø:z) *a,* debauched, lewd; filthy.

craque (krak) *f,* fib, cram.

craquelin (kraklɛ̃) *m,* cracknel.

craquelure (krakly:r) *f,* crack(s) (*in enamel, etc.*). **craquer** (ke) *v.i,* to ˙crack, crackle, crunch, creak. **craqueter** (kte) *v.i,* to crackle.

craqueur (krakœ:r) *m,* liar (*slang*), cracker (*oil production*).

crasse (kras) *a.f,* crass. ¶ *f,* dirt, filth, grime, squalor; scum, dross, slag, clinker; scale; gutter (*fig.*); sordidness. **crasseux, euse** (sø, ø:z) *a,* dirty, filthy, grimy, grubby, unwashed, foul, squalid.

cratère (kratɛ:r) *m,* crater.

cravache (kravaʃ) *f,* riding whip, horsewhip, crop. **cravacher** (ʃe) *v.t,* to flog; horsewhip.

cravan (kravɑ̃) *m,* barnacle (*on ship*).

cravate (kravat) *f,* [neck]tie; bow & tassels (*of color staff*). ~ *de soirée,* dress bow.

crayeux, euse (krɛjø, ø:z) *a,* chalky. **crayon** (jɔ̃) *m,* pencil; sketch, outline. ~ *à mine de plomb,* lead pencil. ~ *pastel,* crayon. **crayonner** (jɔne) *v.t,* to pencil; sketch, outline.

créance (kreɑ̃:s) *f,* credence, belief, trust; credit; [book] debt; indebtedness; claim. **créancier, ère** (ɑ̃sje, ɛ:r) *n,* creditor. ~ *hypothécaire,* mortgagee.

créateur, trice (kreatœ:r, tris) *n,* creator, tress, maker; founder, foundress; (*att.*) creative. **création** (sjɔ̃) *f,* creation; founding. **créature** (ty:r) *f,* creature.

crécelle (kresɛl) *f,* rattle (*toy, etc.*).

crécerelle (kresrɛl) *f,* kestrel.

crèche (krɛʃ) *f,* crib, manger; day nursery, crèche.

crédence (kredɑ̃:s) *f,* sideboard; credence [table].

crédibilité (kredibilite) *f,* credibility. **crédit** (di) *m,* credit; trust; influence; repute; creditor; bank; (*pl.*) supplies (*parliamentary*). *au comptant ou à ~,* cash or terms (*sales*). ~ *foncier,* loan, building society (*government controlled*). ~ *municipal,* mortgage loan office & pawnshop. **créditer** (te) *v.t,* to credit. **créditeur** (tœ:r) *m. & att,* creditor.

credo (kredo) *m,* creed, credo; gospel (*fig.*). **crédule** (kredyl) *a,* credulous, gullible. **crédulité** (lite) *f,* credulity.

créer (kree) *v.t. & abs,* to create, make; establish, found; make out, write out (*check*).

crémaillère (kremajɛ:r) *f,* pothook; rack (*toothed*). *pendre la ~,* to give a housewarming.

crémation (kremasjɔ̃) *f,* cremation.

crème (krɛm) *f,* cream; custard. ~ *chocolatée,* chocolate cream. ~ *glacée,* ice cream, cream ice. **crémerie** (mri) *f,* dairy; creamery; tea shop. **crémeux, euse** (kremø, ø:z) *a,* creamy. **crémier, ère** (mje, ɛ:r) *n,* dairyman, -woman; (*m.*) cream jug.

Crémone (kremɔn) *f,* Cremona. c~, *f,* espagnolette.

créneau (kreno) *m,* battlement; loophole; gap (*in time schedule*);

parking space between two cars. *faire un ~*, to squeeze into a parking space. **créneler** (nle) *v.t*, to crenellate, castellate, battlement, embattle; tooth, ratchet; mill (*coin*).

créole (kreɔl) *n. & a*, creole.

créosote (kreɔzɔt) *f*, creosote.

crêpe (krɛ:p) *m*, crape, crêpe; (*f.*) pancake. **crêper** (krɛpe) *v.t*, to crimp, crisp, frizz[le].

crépi (krepi) *m*, roughcast (*Build.*).

crépine (krepin) *f*, fringe; strainer, rose.

crépins (krepɛ̃) *m.pl*, grindery.

crépir (krepi:r) *v.t*, to roughcast; grain (*leather*).

crépiter (krepite) *v.i*, to crackle, patter (*rain*); crepitate.

crépu, e (krepy) *a*, woolly, fuzzy (*hair*).

crépuscule (krepyskyl) *m*, twilight, gloaming; decline.

crescendo (krɛsɛ̃do) *ad. & m*, crescendo.

cresson (krəsɔ̃) *m*, cress, watercress. **cressonnière** (sɔnjɛ:r) *f*, watercress bed.

Crésus (krezy:s) *m*, Croesus.

Crète (la) (krɛ:t), Crete.

crête (krɛ:t) *f*, comb; crest; ridge. *~-de-coq*, cockscomb (*Bot.*). **crêté, e** (krɛte), *a*, crested.

crétin, e (kretɛ̃, in) *n*, cretin; idiot; dunce.

cretonne (krətɔn) *f*, cretonne.

creuser (krøze) *v.t. & abs*, to dig; hollow; excavate; scoop; sink; deepen. *se ~*, to grow hollow; rise (*sea*). *~ la tête*, to rack one's brains. **creusage** (za:ʒ), **creusement** (zmɑ̃) *m*, digging.

creuset (krøze) *m*, crucible, [melting] pot.

creux, euse (krø, ø:z) *a*, hollow, deep; sunken; shallow, empty. *heures creuses*, off-peak hours. *saison creuse*, slack season. ¶ *m*, hollow, cavity; hole; pit; trough (*wave*); space; hollowness; mold.

crevaison (krəvɛzɔ̃) *f*, death (*animals*); bursting; puncture (*tire, balloon*).

crevasse (krəvas) *f*, crevice, chink, crack, fissure, rift, crevasse; chap (*skin*). **crevasser** (se) *v.t*, to crack; chap.

crève-cœur (krɛvkœ:r) *m*, keen disappointment, wrench (*fig.*).

crever (krəve) *v.i. & t*, to burst; break; crack; split; puncture; put out (*eyes*); die. **à crevés** (ve), slashed, slit (*dress*).

crevette (krəvɛt) *f*: *~ [grise]*, shrimp. *~ [rose]*, prawn.

cri (kri) *m*, cry, snout; scream; shriek; screech; squeal; halloo; chirp; outcry; opinion. *~ de guerre*, war cry; slogan (*Pol.*). **criailler** (ɑje) *v.i*, to squeal; scold, nag. **criant, e** (ɑ̃, ɑ̃:t) *a*, crying, glaring. **criard, e** (a:r, ard) *a*, squealing, squalling, screaming, clamorous; blatant; pressing (*debts*).

crible (kribl) *m*, sieve, riddle, screen. **cribler** (ble) *v.t*, to sift, riddle, screen; honeycomb. **criblure** (bly:r) *f*, siftings, screenings.

cric (kri) *m*, [lifting] jack. *~ crac!* (krikkrak) crack! snap!

cricri (krikri) *m*, chirp; cricket (*insect*).

criée (krie) *f*, auction. **crier** (e) *v.i. & t*, to cry, shout; scream, shriek, screech; call out, clamor, protest; halloo; chirp; creak; keep telling. **crieur, euse** (œ:r, ø:z) *n*, crier; hawker. *~ de journaux*, newsboy.

crime (krim) *m*, crime; felony; offense; sin. *~ d'État*, treason. *~ de faux*, forgery. *~ passionnel* (pɑsjɔnɛl), love tragedy.

Crimée (la) (krime), the Crimea.

criminel, le† (kriminɛl) *a*, criminal; felonious; guilty. ¶ *n*, criminal; felon.

crin (krɛ̃) *m*, [horse]hair; (*vegetable*) fiber; (*pl.*) mane [& tail]. *à tous ~s*, out & out.

crincrin (krɛ̃krɛ̃) *m*, (*bad*) fiddle.

crinière (krinjɛ:r) *f*, mane; horsetail plume; abundant crop (*hair*).

crique (krik) *f*, creek, inlet (*sea*).

criquet (krikɛ) *m*, locust; cricket.

crise (kri:z) *f*, crisis; shortage, slump; attack, fit. *~ du logement*, housing problem.

crispation (krispasjɔ̃) *f*, shriveling; twitching; (*pl.*) fidgets. **crisper** (pe) *v.t*, to clench. *se ~*, to shrivel [up].

crisser (krise) *v.t. & i,* grate; squeak (*brakes*).

cristal (kristal) *m,* crystal; [crystal] glass. ~ *taillé,* cut [crystal] glass. *cristaux de soude,* [washing] soda. **cristallerie** (lri) *f,* crystal glass[ware] making or works. **cristallin, e** (lɛ̃, in) *a,* crystalline. ¶ *m,* crystalline lens (*eye*). **cristalliser** (lize) *v.t. & i. & se* ~, to crystallize. **cristallomancie** (talɔmɑ̃si) *f,* crystal gazing.

critère (kritɛːr), **criterium** (terjɔm) *m,* criterion, standard; eliminating test, preliminary trial.

critiquable (kritikabl) *a,* criticizable, open to criticism, exceptionable. **critique** (tik) *a,* critical, censorious; crucial; ticklish. ¶ *m,* critic; reviewer. ¶ *f,* criticism, critique; review; critics (*pers.*); censure, stricture. **critiquer** (ke) *v.t,* to criticize, censure.

croasser (krɔase) *v.i,* to caw, croak.

croc (kro) *m,* hook; boat hook; fang; tusk (*walrus, etc.*). en ~, curled, turned up (*moustache*). ¶ (krɔk) *i,* [s]crunch! **—en-jambe** (krɔkɑ̃ʒɑ̃ːb) *m,* trip [up]; leg lock; dirty trick. **croche** (krɔʃ) *a,* crooked. ¶ *f,* quaver (*Mus.*). **crochet** (ʃɛ) *m,* hook; crook; crank tool; tenterhook; crochet (*Need.*); c. hook; picklock, skeleton key; sudden turn, swerve; detour; fang; [square] bracket; hook (*Box.*). ~ *à la fourche,* hairpin crochet. ~ *de suspension,* hanger, hook. *aux* ~*s de,* at the expense of. **crocheter** (ʃte) *v.t,* to pick, force the lock of. **crochu, e** (ʃy) *a,* hooked, crooked.

crocodile (krɔkɔdil) *m,* crocodile.

croire (krwaːr) *v.t. & abs. ir,* to believe; trust; think; take for.

croisade (krwazad) *f,* crusade. **croisé, e** (ze) *p.a,* crossed; cross; double-breasted (*coat*). *mots croisés,* crossword puzzle. ¶ *m,* crusader; twill. ¶ *f,* crossing; casement [window]. **croisement** (zmɑ̃) *m,* crossing; cross; cross-breeding; frog (*Rly.*). **croiser** (ze) *v.t,* to cross; fold; pass; thwart; twill; (*v.i.*) to lap over; cruise. se ~, to intersect; fold (*one's arms*). **croiseur** (zœːr) *m,* cruiser. ~ *cuirassé de combat,* battle c. **croisière** (zjɛːr) *f,* cruise; cruising ground; cruising fleet. **croisillon** (zijɔ̃) *m,* cross [piece]; arm (*of cross*); bar (*window*).

croissance (krwasɑ̃ːs) *f,* growth. **croissant, e** (sɑ̃, ɑ̃ːt) *a,* growing, increasing. ¶ *m,* crescent; billhook; pruning hook; horseshoe roll. **croître** (krwaːtr) *v.i. ir,* to grow; increase; rise; draw out (*days*); wax (*moon*).

croix (krwa) *f,* cross; rood; dagger, obelisk (*Typ.*). ~ *de Malte,* Maltese cross. *la C~ Rouge,* the Red Cross.

croquant, e (krɔkɑ̃, ɑ̃ːt) *a,* crisp. ¶ *m,* peasant, hick (*slang*).

croque-mitaine (krɔkmitɛn) *m,* bog[e]y [man]; bugbear. **croque-mort,** *m,* undertaker's man.

croquer (krɔke) *v.i. & t,* to [s]crunch; munch; gobble up; sketch; croquet. **croquet** (kɛ) *m,* croquet (*game*). **croquette** (kɛt) *f,* croquette (*Cook.*). **croquis** (ki) *m,* sketch.

crosse (krɔs) *f,* crosier, crook; butt (*rifle*); crosshead (*piston*); crutch (*or* hook) stick; stick (*hockey*); club (*golf*); crosse (*lacrosse*). *la* ~ *canadienne,* lacrosse. **crossée** (se) *f,* drive (*golf*). **crosser** (se) *v.t,* to strike (*ball*); spurn.

crotte (krɔt) *f,* (*street*) mud, dirt; gutter (*fig.*); dung, droppings. **crotté, e** (te) *p.a,* muddy, dirty. **crotter** (te) *v.t,* to dirty, bespatter. **crottin** (tɛ̃) *m,* dung (*horse*).

crouler (krule) *v.i,* to collapse; sink; crumble.

croup (krup) *m,* croup (*Med.*). **croupe** (krup) *f,* croup[e], crupper, rump; ridge (*hill*); hip (*roof*). **croupier** (pje) *m,* croupier (*gaming*). **croupière** (pjɛːr) *f,* crupper (*harness*); sternfast. **croupion** (pjɔ̃) *m,* rump; parson's nose (*fowl*). **croupir** (piːr) *v.i,* to wallow; stagnate. **crou-**

pissant, e (pisɑ̃, ɑ̃ːt) *a*, stagnant.
croustillant, e (krustijɑ̃, ɑ̃ːt) *a*, crisp, crusty, short. **croustille** (tiːj) *f*, (*bit of*) crust (*bread*). **croustilleux, euse** (tijø, øːz) *a*, spicy, smutty. **croûte** (krut) *f*, crust; rind (*cheese*); scab; daub. *casser la* ~, to have a snack. *vieille* ~, a has-been (*sports journalism*). **croûton** (tɔ̃) *m*, crust[y] end; sippet; [old] fogy.
croyable (krwajabl) *a*, credible, believable; trustworthy. **croyance** (jɑ̃ːs) *f*, belief; credit; creed; faith; persuasion. **croyant, e** (jɑ̃, ɑ̃ːt) *a*, believing. ¶ *n*, believer; (*pl.*) the faithful.
cru, *p.p,* **croire.**
crû, *p.p,* **croître.**
cru (kry) *m*, growth; vintage; invention.
cru, e (kry) *a*, raw, crude; garish, indigestible; hard (*water*); blunt; free, broad. **à cru,** next the skin; bareback[ed] (*riding*).
cruauté (kryote) *f*, cruelty.
cruche (kryʃ) *f*, pitcher, jug; dolt, dunce.
crucial, iaux (krysjal, jo) *a*, cross-shaped (*surg.*); crucial (*situation, argument, etc.*).
crucifiement (krysifimɑ̃) *m*, crucifixion. **crucifier** (fje) *v.t*, to crucify. **crucifix** (fi) *m*, crucifix. **crucifixion** (fiksjɔ̃) *f*, crucifixion.
crudité (krydite) *f*, rawness, raw food; crudity, crudeness; hardness (*water*); belching. *les* ~s, raw vegetables (*on a menu*).
crue (kry) *f*, rising, flood, spate, freshet; advance (*glacier*).
cruel, ȴeṭ (kryɛl) *a*, cruel; grievous; sore; bitter.
crûment (krymɑ̃) *ad*, crudely, bluntly.
crustacé, e (krystase) *a. & m*, crustacean.
crypte (kript) *f*, crypt; follicle.
cubage (kybaːʒ) *m*, cubic content; measurement; yardage.
cubain, e (kybɛ̃, ɛn) *a. &* **C~,** *n*, Cuban.
cube (kyb) *m*, cube. ¶ *a*, cubic, cube (*root*). **cuber** (be) *v.t*, to cube; measure, gauge.
cubilot (kybilo) *m*, cupola [furnace].

cubique (kybik) *a*, cubic(al); cube (*root*). **cubisme** (bism) *m*, cubism. **cubiste** (bist) *n*, cubist.
cueillette (kœjɛt) *f*, gathering, picking; crop. **cueilleur, euse** (jœːr, øːz) *n*, picker. **cueillir** (jiːr) *v.t.ir*, to gather, pick, cull, pluck; snatch (*kiss*); buttonhole (*pers.*).
cuiller *ou* **cuillère** (kɥijɛːr) *f*, spoon; ladle; scoop; spoon [bait]. ~ *à café,* ~ *à moka,* coffee spoon. ~ *à dessert,* ~ *à entremets,* dessert s. ~ *à potage,* soup ladle. ~ *à ragoût,* gravy spoon. ~ *à soupe,* tablespoon. ~ *à thé,* teaspoon. **cuillerée** (jre) *f*, spoonful. ~ *à bouche,* tablespoonful.
cuir (kɥiːr) *m*, leather; hide, skin; strop; incorrect liaison (*in speaking*). ~ *chevelu,* scalp (*Anat.*). ~ *de porc,* pigskin. ~ *de vache,* cowhide. ~ *verni,* patent leather.
cuirasse (kɥiras) *f*, cuirass; armor [plating]; sheathing; saddle (*lathe*). **cuirassé, e** (se) *a*, armored, ironclad; (*fig.*) steeled; [case]hardened; proof. [*navire*] *cuirassé,* battleship, ironclad. **cuirassier** (sje) *m*, cuirassier.
cuire (kɥiːr) *v.t. & i. ir*, to cook; roast; bake; burn, fire (*bricks*); boil; ripen; smart. **cuisant, e** (kɥizɑ̃, ɑ̃ːt) *a*, smarting, burning; biting (*cold*); bitter. **cuisine** (zin) *f*, kitchen; galley, caboose; cookery, cooking; food; machination. **cuisiner** (ne) *v.i*, to cook; (*v.t.*) to cook; (*fig.*) concoct, fudge; pump (*pers.*). **cuisinette** (net) *f*, kitchenette. **cuisinier, ère** (nje, ɛːr) *n*, cook. ¶ *m*, cookery book. ¶ *f*, cooker, cooking range; Dutch oven.
cuisse (kɥis) *f*, thigh; leg (*fowl*).
cuisson (kɥisɔ̃) *f*, cooking; baking; burning, firing; smarting.
cuissot (kɥiso) *m*, haunch (*venison*).
cuistre (kɥistr) *m*, self-conceited pedant; ill-mannered man.
cuit (kɥi) *a*, cooked; baked; done. *trop* ~, overdone. ~ *à point,* done to a turn. **cuite** (kɥit) *f*, baking. *prendre une* ~, to get drunk.

cuivre (kɥiːvr) *m*, copper; copperplate; copper bit (*soldering*). ~ [*jaune*], brass. ~ [*rouge*], copper. les ~s, the brass (*Mus.*). **cuivré, e** (kɥivre) *a*, copper-colored; metallic (*voice*); brassy; lurid. **cuivrer** (vre) *v.t*, to copper.

cul (ky) *m*, backside; tail (*cart*). **culasse** (las) *f*, breech (*gun*). se chargeant par la ~, breech-loading. **culbutage** (bytaːʒ) *m*, somersaulting; knocking over; dumping. **culbutant** (kylbytā) *m*, tumbler (*pigeon*). **culbute** (byt) *f*, somersault; tumble; fall. **culbuter** (te) *v.i. & t*, to tumble, topple over; tip, tilt, dump, shoot; overthrow; rout. **cul-de-jatte** (kydʒat) *m*, legless cripple. **cul-de-lampe** (kydlā:p) *m*, cul-de-lampe; tailpiece (*Typ.*). **cul-de-sac** (kydsak) *m*, blind alley, dead end. **culée** (kyle) *f*, abutment (*bridge*).

culinaire (kylinɛːr) *a*, culinary. **culminant, e** (kylminā, ā:t) *a*, culminating. **culminer** (ne) *v.i*, to culminate (*Astr.*).

culot (kylo) *m*, container (*lamp*); base; cap; plug; youngest; nerve. avoir du ~, to have a lot of nerve. **culotte** (lɔt) *f*, breeches; knee b—s; knickerbockers; knickers; rump (*beef*). ~ *courte*, shorts, trunks. ~ *de cheval*, riding breeches. ~ *de peau*, buckskins. ~ *pour le golf*, plus-fours. **culotté, e** (te) *p.p*, trousered. **culotter** (te) *v.t*, to put trousers on; season (*pipe*).

culpabilité (kylpabilite) *f*, culpability, guilt.

culte (kylt) *m*, worship; cult, creed. le ~ *des scientistes chrétiens*, Christian science. **cultivateur, trice** (kyltivatœːr, tris) *n*, cultivator, grower, agricultur[al]ist, farmer, husbandman. **cultiver** (ve) *v.t*, to cultivate, grow; raise; farm, till. **culture** (tyːr) *f*, culture, cultivation, farming; (*pl.*) land [under cultivation]. ~ *maraîchère*, market gardening.

cumul (kymyl) *m*, plurality (*of offices*). **cumulatif, ive** (latif, i:v) *a*, cumulative. **cumulus** (lyːs) *m*, cumulus.

cunéiforme (kyneifɔrm) *a*, cuneiform.

cupide (kypid) *a*, covetous, grasping. **cupidité** (ite) *f*, greed.

Cupidon (kypidɔ̃) *m*, Cupid.

curable (kyrabl) *a*, curable.

curage (kyraːʒ) *m*, cleansing; flushing.

curatelle (kyratɛl) *f*, guardianship, trusteeship. **curateur, trice** (tœːr, tris) *n*, guardian, trustee; administrator, trix.

curatif, ive (kyratif, i:v) *a. & m*, curative. **cure** (kyːr) *f*, cure; vicarship, rectorship; vicarage, rectory. **curé** (kyre) *m*, parish priest; vicar, rector.

cure-dent (kyrdā) *m*, toothpick. venir en ~, to be invited after dinner.

curée (kyre) *f*, quarry (*given to hounds*); scramble.

curer (kyre) *v.t*, to cleanse, clean; flush; pick (*teeth*). **curette** (rɛt) *f*, scraper, cleaner. **cureur** (rœːr) *m*, cleaner; sewerman.

curieux, euse† (kyrjø, ø:z) *a*, curious; interested; odd; quaint; inquisitive, prying. ¶ *n*, curious (*or inquisitive*) person; sightseer; onlooker; bystander; (*m.*) curious part *or* thing; collector (*art, books*). **curiosité** (ozite) *f*, curiosity; quaintness; curio; (*pl.*) sights (*of a city*).

curseur (kyrsœːr) *m*, runner, slide[r] (*Mech.*); cursor (*computers*). **cursif, ive** (sif, i:v) *a*, cursive, running.

curviligne (kyrviliɲ) *a*, curvilinear.

cutané, e (kytane) *a*, cutaneous, skin (*att.*). **cuticule** (tikyl) *f*, cuticle.

cuve (kyːv) *f*, vat. ~-*matière*, mash tub. **cuvée** (kyve) *f*, vatful; vintage. **cuveler** (vle) *v.t*, to tub, case (*Min.*).

cuver (kyve) *v.i*, to ferment (*wine*). ~ *son vin*, to sleep off a drunk. **cuvette** (vɛt) *f*, washbasin; basin; dish; tray; bowl; cup, cistern (*barometer*). **cuvier** (vje) *m*, washtub.

cyanure (sjanyːr) *m*, cyanide.

cyclamen (siklamɛn) *m*, cyclamen.

cycle (sikl) *m*, cycle; cycle trade.

cyclisme (klism) *m*, cycling.
cycliste (klist) *n*, cyclist.
cyclomoteur (siklɔmɔtœr) *m*, motorbike.
cyclone (siklon) *m*, cyclone.
cygne (siɲ) *m*, swan.
cylinder (silɛ͂ːdr) *m*, cylinder; roller; roll; barrel, drum. ~ **compresseur à vapeur**, steamroller. **cylindrer** (lɛ͂dre) *v.t*, to roll; mangle; calender; round. **cylindrique** (drik) *a*, cylindrical; parallel (*drill shank*).
cymbales (sɛ͂bal) *f.pl*, cymbals.
cynique† (sinik) *a*, cynic, cynical. ¶ *m*, cynic. **cynisme** (nism) *m*, cynicism.
cyprès (siprɛ) *m*, cypress.
cytise (sitiːz) *m*, laburnum.

D

dac, d'ac (dak) *i*, ok, agreed (*short for "d'accord"*).
dactylographe (daktilɔgraf) *n*, typist. **dactylographie** (fi) *f*, typewriting, typing.
dada (dada) *m*, gee-gee; hobby horse; pet subject, fad.
dadais (dadɛ) *m*, booby, ninny.
dague (dag) *f*, dagger, dirk.
dahlia (dalja) *m*, dahlia.
daigner (dɛɲe) *v.i*, to deign to, be pleased to, vouchsafe.
daim (dɛ͂) *m*, [fallow] deer, buck. [peau de] ~, buckskin, doeskin. **daine** (dɛn) *f*, doe.
dais (dɛ) *m*, canopy; hood (*car*).
dallage (dalaːʒ) *m*, flagging, pavement. **dalle** (dal) *f*, flag[stone]; slab. **daller** (le) *v.t*, to pave, flag.
dalmate (dalmat) *a*, Dalmatian. **la Dalmatie** (si), Dalmatia.
dalot (dalo) *m*, scupper.
daltonisme (daltɔnism) *m*, color-blindness.
dam (dɑ͂) *m*, injury, prejudice; displeasure. *peine du* ~, eternal damnation.
damas (damɑ) *m*, damask; damson. **D~**, *m*, Damascus. **damasquiner** (maskine) *v.t*, to damascene.
dame (dam) *f*, lady; dame; partner (*dance*); queen (*cards, chess*);

king (*checkers*); beetle, rammer. *la* ~, Mrs. (*law*). *les* ~*s*, checkers (*game*). ~ *d'onze heures*, star of Bethlehem. ~ *de compagnie*, lady companion. ~ [*de nage*], rowlock. ~*jeanne* (ʒaːn), *f*, demijohn. ¶ *i*, why! indeed! well! **damer** (me) *v.t*, to crown (*checkers*); queen (*chess*); tamp, ram. **damier** (mje) *m*, checkerboard.
damnable† (dɑnabl) *a*, damnable. **damnation** (sjɔ͂) *f*, damnation. **damné, e** (ne) *a. & n*, damned. **damner** (ne) *v.t*, to damn.
damoiseau (damwazo) *m*, galant.
dandiner (se) (dɑ͂dine) *v.pr*, to waddle.
dandy (dɑ͂di) *m*, dandy.
Danemark (le) (danmark), Denmark.
danger (dɑ͂ʒe) *m*, danger, jeopardy; fear. **dangereux, euse†** (ʒrø, øːz) *a*, dangerous.
danois, e (danwa, aːz) *a. & (language) m*, Danish. **D~** (*pers.*) *n*, Dane.
dans (dɑ͂) *pr*, in; into; within; during; among; about; out of; with; hence. ~ *les présentes*, herein (*law*). ~ *œuvre*, inside, in the clear (*Meas.*). ~ *le temps*, in earlier days, formerly.
dansant, e (dɑ͂sɑ͂, ɑ͂ːt) *a*, dancing; dance (*tea*). **danse** (dɑ͂ːs) *f*, dance; dancing. ~ *de Saint-Guy* (gi), St. Vitus's dance. **D~** *macabre*, Dance of Death, Dance Macabre. **danser** (dɑ͂se) *v.i. & t*, to dance. **danseur, euse** (sœːr, øːz) *n*, dancer; partner; ballet dancer. ~ *mondain, e*, ballroom dancer.
dard (daːr) *m*, dart; sting (*insect's*); pistil; dace (*fish*). **darder** (darde) *v.t*, to dart, hurl, fling, shoot; spear.
dare-dare (darda:r) *ad*, quickly (*slang*).
dartre (dartr) *f*, herpes, skin disease.
date (dat) *f*, date (*time*). *de longue* ~, of long standing. **dater** (te) *v.t*, to date. *à* ~ *de*, from, on & after.
datif (datif) *m*, dative [case].

datte (dat) *f*, date (*fruit*). **dattier** (tje) *m*, date palm.

dauber (dobe) *v.t*, to drub, thump; jeer at. ~ *sur*, to jeer at.

dauphin (dofɛ̃) *m*, dolphin (*Zool.*).

davantage (davɑ̃taːʒ) *ad*, more, further; longer.

davier (davje) *m*, forceps (*dentist's*); davit (*Naut.*).

de (də), **d'** (d) (**de le** *is contracted into* **du**, **de les** *into* **des**) *pr*, of; from; by; for; in; on; some; any; than; between; with; to. *When coupled with Fr. noun, often rendered in Eng. by noun used attributively, as, mine de charbon, coal mine.*

dé (de) *m*, thimble; die (*gaming & Mach.*); bearing (*Mach.*); tee (*golf*).

déambuler (deɑ̃byle) *v.i*, to stroll, saunter, walk up and down.

débâcle (debɑːkl) *f*, breaking up (*ice*); crash, collapse; landslide (*Pol.*). **débâcler** (bɑkle) *v.t*, to clear; (*v.i.*) to break up.

déballage (debalaːʒ) *m*, unpacking; show (*of wares*). **déballer** (le) *v.t*, to unpack.

débandade (debɑ̃dad) *f*, stampede, rout. *à la* ~, helter-skelter; anyhow. **débander** (de) *v.t*, to relax, unbend; unbandage; to disband (*Mil.*). **se** ~, to break ranks in disorder.

débaptiser (debatize) *v.t*, to change the name of, rename.

débarbouiller (debarbuje) *v.t*, to wash (*someone's*) face; extricate.

débarcadère (debarkadɛːr) *m*, landing [place *or* stage], wharf; platform (*Rly.*).

débarder (debarde) *v.t*, to unload. **débardeur** (dœːr) *m*, docker; longshoreman; sleeveless undershirt.

débarquer (debarke) *v.t. & i*, to land, disembark; detrain; discharge; get rid of; alight. **débarquement** (kəmɑ̃) *m*, landing, etc. *au* ~, ex ship, ex steamer (*sales*).

débarras (debarɑ) *m*, riddance; lumber room; storeroom. **dé-** **barrasser** (rase) *v.t*, to clear, rid, extricate, disburden, relieve. *se* ~ *de*, to get rid of, scrap.

débat (deba) *m*, discussion; debate; (*pl.*) proceedings; (*pl.*) trial, hearing; dispute. **débattre** (tr) *v.t.ir*, to debate, discuss, argue; arrange. **se** ~, to struggle; flounder; wriggle.

débauche (deboːʃ) *f*, debauch[ery]; carousal; riot (*fig.*); treat. ~ *de boisson*, drunken bout. **débauché, e** (boʃe) *n*, debauchee, rake. **débaucher** (ʃe) *v.t*, to debauch, corrupt; induce to strike; seduce from duty; lead astray; reduce the staff.

débecqueter *or* **débecter** (debɛkte) *v.t*, to disgust (*slang*).

débile† (debil) *a*, weakly; weak; feeble. **débilité** (lite) *f*, debility; weakness. **débiliter** (te) *v.t*, to debilitate, enfeeble.

débit (debi) *m*, sale (*retail*); market, demand; (*government*) license to sell; (*licensed*) shop; flow, discharge, yield, output, capacity, feed; delivery (*pump, speech*); cutting up, chopping; debit [side], debtor [side]. ~ *de tabac*, license to sell tobacco; tobacconist's shop. **débitant, e** (tɑ̃, ɑ̃ːt) *n*, dealer, retailer. ~ *de spiritueux*, licensed victualler. ~ *de tabac*, tobacconist. **débiter** (te) *v.t*, to retail, sell; discharge, yield; deliver, utter; spread (*news*); spin (*yarns*); cut up; saw; chop (*firewood*); debit. **débiteur, euse** (tœːr, øːz) *n*, utterer (*lies*); -monger (*news, scandal*); (*f.*) (*also* **débitrice**) (*In Fr. stores*) girl who conducts customers to cash desk to see that they pay. **débiteur, trice** (tœːr, tris) *n. & att*, debtor, debit (*att.*). ~ *hypothécaire*, mortgagor.

déblai (deblɛ) *m*, cut[ting], excavation; (*s. & pl.*) waste, rubbish, spoil.

déblatérer contre (deblatere), to abuse.

déblayer (deblɛje) *v.t*, to clear, c. out, c. away.

débloquer (deblɔke) *v.t*, to free, relieve, unblock, unlock; rave, speak incoherently.

déboire (debwa:r) *m*, (*nasty*) aftertaste; disappointment.

déboiser (debwaze) *v.t*, to deforest.

déboîtement (debwatmã) *m*, dislocation (*limb*). **déboîter** (te) *v.t*, to dislocate; disjoint.

débonder (debõde) *v.t*, to unstop; open the sluice gates of; open, relax (*Med.*). [se] ~, to burst forth, break out, escape.

débonnaire† (debonε:r) *a*, meek; easy-going; accommodating.

débordement (debordǝmã) *m*, overflow; outburst; excess, licentiousness. ~ *inférieure*, underflow (*computers*). **déborder** (de) *v.i*, to overflow, brim over, run over; slop [over]; break out; (*v.t.*) to overlap; outflank; untuck; trim the edges of; unship (*oars*). *être débordé*, to be overwhelmed (*by work or events*).

débotter (debote) *v.t*, to take (*someone's*) boots off. se ~, to take one's boots off. **au débotté** (te), immediately upon arrival.

débouché (debuʃe) *m*, opening, outlet; issue; waterway; prospects; market sale. **déboucher** (ʃe) *v.t*, to open, unstop, uncork; (*v.i.*) to open, emerge, debouch; lead into.

déboucler (debukle) *v.t*, to unbuckle; uncurl.

débouler [dans] (debule) *v.i*, to tumble down (*as stairs*).

déboulonner (debulone) *v.t*, to unrivet; debunk.

débourber (deburbe) *v.t*, to clean out, cleanse; extricate.

débourrer (debure) *v.t*, to ream (*pipe*); unstop; break in (*horse*).

débours (debu:r) & **déboursé** (burse) *m*, both mostly *pl*, disbursement, out of pocket expense, outlay. **débourser** (se) *v.t*, to disburse, lay out, spend.

debout (dǝbu) *ad*, on end, erect; standing; up; head (*wind*). *mourir* ~, to die in harness.

débouter (debute) *v.t*, to nonsuit, dismiss (*law*).

déboutonner (debutone) *v.t*, to unbutton. se ~ (*fig.*), to open out, speak one's mind.

débraillé, e (debraje) (*fig.*) *a*, dissolute. se **débrailler** (je) *v.pr*, to unbutton oneself (*unbecomingly*).

débrayer (debreje) (*Mech.*) *v.t*, to throw out of gear, disconnect; let out the clutch (*auto*); go on strike.

débrider (debride) *v.t*, to unbridle. *sans* ~, without stopping.

débris (debri) *m.pl*, remains, debris, litter; scrap; wreck[age].

débrouillard, e (debruja:r, ard) *a*, resourceful. ¶ *n*, resourceful person.

débrouiller (debruje) *v.t*, to unravel, disentangle, clear up. se ~, to extricate oneself; manage.

débucher (debyʃe) *v.i*, to break cover.

débusquer (debyske) *v.t*, to dislodge, drive out; oust.

début (deby) *m*, beginning, opening, outset, outbreak, start; first appearance; f. work; coming out (*in society*). **débutant, e** (tã, ã:t) *n*, beginner; débutant, e. **débuter** (te) *v.i*, to begin, start, make one's first appearance; lead (*cards*).

deçà (dǝsa) *ad*, on this side. ~, *delà* ou ~ & *delà*, here & there, to & fro. *en* ~ *de*, *pr*, on this side of.

décacheter (dekaʃte) *v.t*, to unseal, open.

décade (dekad) *f*, ten days; decad-[e] (*books*).

décadence (dekadã:s) *f*, decadence, decline, decay. **décadent, e** (dã, ã:t) *a*, decadent.

décaféiner (dekafeine) *v.t*, to decaffeinate.

décagone (dekagon) *m*, decagon.

décaisser (dekεse) *v.t*, to unpack; withdraw (*money*).

décalage (dekala:ʒ) *m*, unwedging; staggering; gap, lag; setback (*fig*). **décaler** (kale) *v.t*, to unwedge; shift; stagger; readjust.

décalcomanie (dekalkomani) *f*, transfer (*for china & as a toy*); decal.

décalitre (dekalitr) *m*, decaliter = 10 liters *or* 2.200 gallons.

décalotter (dekalote) *v.t*, to uncap; remove the end of (*lemon*, *egg*, *etc.*); circumcize.

décalque (dekalk) *m*, transfer (*Emb.*); tracing. **décalquer** (ke) *v.t*, to transfer, trace.

décamètre (dekamɛːtr) *m*, decameter = 10 meters *or* 10.936 yards. ~ *d'arpenteur*, measuring tape.

décamper (dekăpe) *v.i*, to decamp, make off.

décanat (dekana) *m*, deanery (*office*).

décanter (dekăte) *v.t*, to decant.

décaper (dekape) *v.t*, to scour.

décapiter (dekapite) *v.t*, to behead, decapitate.

décapotable (dekapɔtabl) *m*, convertible (*auto*).

décatir (dekatiːr) *v.t*, to sponge, steam (*fabrics*); take gloss off. se ~, to become worn, show one's age.

décéder (desede) *v.i*, to decease.

déceler (desle) *v.t*, to reveal, betray.

décembre (desãːbr) *m*, December.

décemment (desamã) *ad*, decently. **décence** (sãːs) *f*, decency, propriety.

décennal, e (desɛnal) *a*, decennial.

décennie (deseni) *f*, decade.

décent, e (desã, ãːt) *a*, decent; proper.

décentraliser (desãtralize) *v.t*, to decentralize.

déception (desɛpsjɔ̃) *f*, disappointment.

décerner (desɛrne) *v.t*, to award.

décès (desɛ) *m*, death, decease, demise.

décevant, e (desvã, ãːt) *a*, deceptive, misleading. **décevoir** (s[ə]vwaːr) *v.t*, to deceive; disappoint.

déchaîner (deʃɛne) *v.t*, to unchain, let loose. se ~, break loose; break out.

déchanter (deʃãte) *v.i*, to sing small, change one's tone.

décharge (deʃarʒ) *f*, discharge; unloading; outflow; outfall; volley; release; relief; composition (*to creditors*); waste heap. **décharger** (ʒe) *v.t. & abs*, to discharge; unload; empty; relieve; disburden, ease; deal (*blow*); come off (*ink*). **déchargeur** (ʒœːr) *m*, stevedore; lightning rod.

décharné, e (deʃarne) *p.a*, emaciated, gaunt, skinny, scraggy.

déchausser (deʃose) *v.t*, to take off (*someone's*) shoes; [lay] bare; dislodge.

dèche (dɛʃ) *f*, tightened straits, poverty, want. *être dans la* ~, to be down and out.

déchéance (deʃeãːs) *f*, [down] fall; loss, forfeiture; lapse, expiration.

déchet (deʃɛ) *m. oft. pl*, waste, loss; scrap, refuse.

déchiffrer (deʃifre) *v.t.* & *abs*, to decipher, decode, make out, read (*or* play) at sight.

déchiqueter (deʃikte) *v.t*, to slash; jag; shred.

déchirant, e (deʃirã, ãːt) *a*, heartrending, harrowing. **déchirer** (re) *v.t*, to tear, rend, rip, lacerate; tear up; break up; harrow; split (*ears with noise*). **déchirure** (ryːr) *f*, tear, rent, rip.

déchoir (deʃwaːr) *v.i.ir*, to fall, decline. ~ *de*, to forfeit.

décibel (desibɛl) *m*, decibel (*Phys.*).

décidé, e (deside) *a*, decided; settled, determined. **décidément** (mã) *ad*, decidedly; definitely. **décider** (de) *v.t. & abs*, to decide, settle, resolve, determine; induce, persuade, prevail upon. se ~, to decide, make up one's mind.

décidu, e (desidy) *a*, deciduous.

décigramme (desigram) *m*, decigram = ¹⁄₁₀ gram *or* 1.543 grains.

décilitre (desilitr) *m*, deciliter = ¹⁄₁₀ liter *or* 0.176 pint.

décimal, e (desimal) *a. & f*, decimal.

décime (desim) *m*, 10 centimes; 10% surtax. **décimer** (me) *v.t*, to decimate.

décimètre (desimɛtr) *m*, decimeter = ¹⁄₁₀ meter *or* 3.937 inches; decimeter rule. *double* ~, 2-decimeter rule. ~ *carré*, square d. = 15.500 sq. ins. ~ *cube*, cubic d. = 61.024 cub. ins.

décisif, ive† (desizif, iːv) *a*, decisive; critical; positive. **décision** (zjɔ̃) *f*, decision; conclusion; resolution; ruling, award.

déclamateur (deklamatœːr) *m*, stump orator, spouter. **déclamation** (sjɔ̃) *f*, declamation, elocution; delivery; rant. **déclamer** (me) *v.t. & abs. & i*, to declaim; recite; spout, rant.

déclaration (deklarasjɔ̃) *f*, declaration; statement; return; proclamation; finding (*jury*). ~ *sous serment*, affidavit. **déclarer** (re) *v.t*, to declare, state, report; proclaim; certify; disclose; find (*juries*). se ~, to declare oneself; show itself; break out.

déclassé, e (deklɑse) *n*, [social] outcast. **déclasser** (se) *v.t*, to degrade; transfer from one class to another.

déclencher (deklɑ̃ʃe) *v.t*, to trip, release; disengage (*Mech.*); launch (*attack*). **déclencheur** (ʃœːr) *m*, [shutter] release (*Phot.*).

déclic (deklik) *m*, trigger, catch, trip, release.

déclin (deklɛ̃) *m*, decline, wane. **déclinaison** (klinɛzɔ̃) *f*, declination; declension (*Gram.*). **décliner** (ne) *v.i. & t*, to decline; wane; give, state (*name, etc.*).

déclive (dekliːv) *a*, sloping. **déclivité** (klivite) *f*, declivity, slope.

décocher (dekɔʃe) *v.t*, to let off, let fly.

décoction (dekɔksjɔ̃) *f*, decoction.

décoiffer (dekwafe) *v.t*, to take off the hat of; uncork, crack (*a bottle*); disarrange (*hair*).

décollage (dekɔlaːʒ) *m*, unsticking, ungluing; liftoff (*missiles, spacecraft*). **décoller** (kɔle) *v.t*, to unglue, unstick; *v.i*, take off (*Avn.*); lift o. (*spacecraft*). se ~, to come unstuck, part.

décolleté, e (dekɔlte) *a*, low-necked; free, licentious. ¶ *m*, low-necked dress; court shoes.

décoloniser (dekɔlɔnize) *v.t*, to decolonize; liberate (*women, minorities, etc.*).

décolorer (dekɔlɔre) *v.t*, to discolor.

décombres (dekɔ̃ːbr) *m.pl*, demolitions, rubbish.

décommander (dekɔmɑ̃de) *v.t*, to countermand, cancel; call off; ask not to come.

décomposer (dekɔ̃poze) *v.t*, to decompose; distort.

décompte (dekɔ̃ːt) *m*, deduction;

working out; table, sheet. *éprouver du ~ dans*, to be disappointed in. **décompter** (kɔ̃te) *v.t. & abs*, to deduct; work out; suffer disappointment.

déconcerter (dekɔ̃sɛrte) *v.t*, to disconcert; upset.

déconfire (dekɔ̃fiːr) *v.t.ir*, to nonplus. **déconfiture** (fityːr) *f*, insolvency.

déconner (dekɔne) *v.i*, to talk nonsense, babble (*slang*).

déconseiller (dekɔ̃sɛje) *v.t*, to dissuade.

déconsidérer (dekɔ̃sidere) *v.t*, to discredit.

décontenancement (dekɔ̃tnɑ̃smɑ̃) *m*, surprise, shock (*at a movie, book, etc.*).

décontenancer (dekɔ̃tnɑ̃se) *v.t*, to abash.

décontracter (dekɔ̃trakte) *v.t*, to relax (*physically, mentally*). *un type décontracté*, a laid-back guy.

déconvenue (dekɔ̃vny) *f*, discomfiture.

décor (dekɔːr) *m*, decoration; set (*Theat.*); (*pl.*) scenery; (*pl.*) regalia (*freemasons'*). **décorateur** (kɔratœːr) *m*, decorator; scene painter, stage designer. **décoratif, ive** (tif, iːv) *a*, decorative. **décoration** (sjɔ̃) *f*, decoration; order, medal; scenery. **décorer** (re) *v.t*, to decorate; dignify.

décortiquer (dekɔrtike) *v.t*, to bark; peel.

décorum (dekɔrɔm) *m*, decorum; etiquette.

découcher (dekuʃe) *v.i*, to sleep out.

découdre (dekudr) *v.t.ir*, to unstitch; rip.

découler (dekule) *v.i*, to trickle, run down; proceed, issue.

découpage (dekupaːʒ) *m*, shooting script, continuity script. ~ *technique*, final shooting script, shot list.

découper (dekupe) *v.t. & abs*, to carve (*meat*); cut up; cut out; fretsaw; punch [out]. se ~, to stand out. **découpeur, euse** (pœːr, øːz) *n*, carver (*pers.*).

découpler (dekuple) *v.t*, to slip, uncouple.

découpoir (dekupwaːr) *m*, [hollow] punch. **découpure** (py:r) *f*, cutting out; fretwork.

découragement (dekuraʒmɑ̃) *m*, discouragement, despondency. **décourager** (ʒe) *v.t*, to discourage, dishearten, depress, dispirit; daunt; deter. se ~, to lose heart, despond.

décousu, e (dekuzy) (*fig.*) *a*, loose, disconnected, disjointed, rambling, desultory. ¶ *m*, looseness.

découvert, e (dekuvɛ:r, ɛrt) *a*, uncovered, bare, open, unprotected. à découvert, *ad*, uncovered, open; unpacked; unsecured (*loan*); overdrawn. **découvert**, *m*, overdraft; bear account, bears (*Stk Ex.*). **découverte**, *f*, discovery; find; detection; disclosure; background note (*cinema*). aller à la ~, to scout. **découvrir** (vri:r) *v.t.ir*, to uncover, bare, open; discover, detect; descry, espy; find; f. out. se ~, to expose oneself; take one's hat off; come to light.

décrasser (dekrase) *v.t*, to cleanse, clean, scour.

décréditer (dekredite) *v.t*, to discredit.

décrépit, e (dekrepi, it) *a*, decrepit. **décrépitude** (tyd) *f*, decrepitude, senile decay.

décret (dekrɛ) *m*, decree, fiat, ordinance, order, enactment. **décréter** (krete) *v.t*, to decree, enact, ordain.

décri (dekri) *m*, disrepute. **décrier** (krie) *v.t*, to decry, run down.

décrire (dekri:r) *v.t. & abs. ir*, to describe.

décrocher (dekrɔʃe) *v.t*, to unhook; take down.

décroître (dekrwɑ:tr) *v.i.ir*, to decrease, shorten, dwindle, wane.

décrotter (dekrɔte) *v.t*, to clean, brush, scrape. **décrotteur** (tœ:r) *m*, bootblack (*pers.*). **décrottoir** (twa:r) *m*, scraper [mat].

décrue (dekry) *f*, fall (*river*); retreat (*glacier*). **déçu, p.p**, décevoir.

décuple (dekypl) *a. & m*, tenfold. **décupler** (ple) *v.t. & i*, to increase tenfold.

dédaigner (dedɛɲe) *v.t*, to disdain, scorn, despise. **dédaigneux,**

euse† (ɲø, ø:z) *a*, disdainful, scornful, supercilious. **dédain** (dɛ̃)*m*, disdain, disregard, scorn.

dédale (dedal) *m*, maze, labyrinth.

dedans (dədɑ̃) *ad*, inside, in. de ~, from within. (*rire*) en ~, *ad*, inwardly. en ~ de, *pr*, within. ¶ *m*, inside, interior.

dédicace (dedikas) *f*, dedication; inscription. **dédier** (dje) *v.t*, to dedicate; devote; inscribe.

dédire (dedi:r) *v.t.ir*, to gainsay. se ~ de, to retract, unsay. **dédit** (di) *m*, retractation; penalty, forfeit.

dédouaner (dedwane) *v.t*, to clear, take out of bond (*Cust.*).

dédommagement (dedɔmaʒmɑ̃) *m*, indemnity, compensation, damages. **dédommager** (ʒe) *v.t*, to compensate, recoup, indemnify.

dédoubler (deduble) *v.t*, to divide into two; duplicate (*train*); unline. ~ les rangs, to form single file.

déductif, ive (dedyktif, i:v) *a*, deductive, inferential. **déduction** (ksjɔ̃) *f*, deduction; allowance; relief; inference. **déduire** (dɥi:r) *v.t.ir*, to deduct; deduce, infer.

déesse (dees) *f*, goddess.

défaillance (defajɑ̃:s) *f*, swoon, fainting [fit]; lapse; failing; default; eclipse. **défaillant, e** (jɑ̃, ɑ̃:t) *a*, failing; drooping; defaulting. ¶ *n*, defaulter. **défaillir** (ji:r) *v.i.ir*, to faint; fail; flinch; falter.

défaire (defɛ:r) *v.t.ir*, to undo; take off; defeat, rout. se ~, to come undone. se ~ de, to get rid of; unload (*stocks*); make away with. **défait, e** (fɛ, ɛt) *a*, undone; defeated; drawn (*look*). **défaite**, *f*, defeat; shuffle, evasion.

défalcation (defalkasjɔ̃) *f*, deduction. **défalquer** (ke) *v.t*, to deduct.

défaut (defo) *m*, defect, fault, flaw, blemish; default, failure, want, lack, deficiency.

défaveur (defavœ:r) *f*, disfavor. **défavorable**† (vɔrabl) *a*, unfavorable, inauspicious. **défavoriser** (ize) *v.t*, to disadvantage.

défectif, ive (defɛktif, i:v) *a*, defective. **défection** (sjɔ̃) f, defection. **défectueux, euse†** (tɥø, ø:z) a, defective, faulty, deficient. **défectuosité** (tɥozite) f, defect, fault, flaw.

défendable (defɑ̃dabl) a, defensible. **défendeur, eresse** (dœ:r, drɛs) n, defendant; respondent (law). **défendre** (fɑ̃:dr) v.t, to defend; protect, shield; forbid, prohibit. se ~, to defend oneself; deny; excuse oneself; manage somehow; engage in prostitution. **défense** (fɑ̃:s) f, defense; (pl.) plea; protection; prohibition; tusk; fender (Naut.). ~ d'afficher, post no bills. ~ d'entrer [sans autorisation], no admittance [except on business], private. ~ d'entrer sous peine d'amende, trespassers will be prosecuted. ~ de circuler sur l'herbe, [please] keep off the grass. ~ de fumer, no smoking. ~ de passer, no thoroughfare. ~ de toucher, [please] do not touch. ~ expresse (ou absolue) de fumer, smoking strictly prohibited. ~ passive, civil defense. ~ légitime, self-defense. **défenseur** (fɑ̃sœ:r) m, defender; advocate; counsel for the defense. **défensif, ive** (sif, i:v) a. & f, defensive.

déféquer (defeke) v.t. & i, to defecate.

déférence (deferɑ̃:s) f, deference, respect. **déférent, e** (rɑ̃, ɑ̃:t) a, deferential. **déférer** (re) v.t, to confer, bestow; refer (to court); hand over (to justice); administer (oath); (v.i.) to defer (submit).

déferler (defɛrle) v.t, to unfurl; (v.i.) to break (waves).

déferrer (defɛre) v.t, to unshoe (horse); disconnect.

défi (defi) m, challenge; defiance. **défiance** (fjɑ̃:s) f, distrust, mistrust. ~ de soi-même, diffidence. **défiant, e** (ɑ̃, ɑ̃:t) a, distrustful, mistrustful; wary.

déficit (defisi) m, deficit, deficiency, short[age], minus quantity. **déficitaire** (tɛ:r) a, debit (att.), showing a loss, adverse; short.

défier (defje) v.t, to challenge; brave; dare; defy, baffle. se ~ de,

to distrust, mistrust; beware of.

défigurer (defigyre) v.t, to disfigure; deface; distort.

défilé (defile) m, defile; march past; procession; parade. **défiler** (le) v.t, to unthread; (v.i.) to defile; file off; march past. se ~ (fig.), to make off.

défini, e (defini) p.a, definite; finite (mood, Gram.). **définir** (ni:r) v.t, to define; describe; determine; decide. **définissable** (nisabl) a, definable. **définitif, ive†** (tif, i:v) a, definitive; absolute (decree); final; ultimate; standard (edition). **en définitive**, ad, finally, in short. **définition** (sjɔ̃) f, definition; decision.

déflation (deflasjɔ̃) f, deflation (Fin.).

défléchir (defleʃi:r) v.t, to deflect.

défleurir (deflœri:r) v.i, to shed its blossoms; (v.t.) to deflower, strip of flowers. **défloraison** (florɛzɔ̃) f, defloration (stripping). **défloration** (rasjɔ̃) f, defloration (ravishment). **déflorer** (re) v.t, to deflower (strip of flowers or ravish); take the freshness off (news).

défoncer (defɔ̃se) v.t, to stave [in]; break up.

déformer (deforme) v.t, to deform; distort; strain (Mech.).

défouler (defule) v.t, to eliminate complexes. **défoulement** (mɑ̃) m, liberation (from inhibitions).

défourner (defurne) v.t, to take out of the oven.

défraîchi, e (defrɛʃi) p.a, shopworn. **défraîchir** (ʃi:r) v.t. & se ~, to fade.

défrayer (defrɛje) v.t, to defray; entertain; keep up (conversation).

défricher (defriʃe) v.t, to clear, grub, reclaim.

défriser (defrize) v.t, to uncurl; disconcert.

défroncer (defrɔ̃se) v.t, to iron out; smooth.

défroque (defrɔk) f, cast-off clothing. **défroquer** (ke) v.t, to unfrock.

défunt, e (defœ̃, œ̃:t) a. & n, deceased, defunct, departed, late (a.).

dégagé, e (degaʒe) a, free, easy, unconstrained; perky. **dégagement** (ʒmã) m, redemption; clearing; disengagement, evolution; exit. **dégager** (ʒe) v.t, to redeem; make out (*meaning*); relieve; extricate; free, disengage, give off, evolve, emit; clear; set off (*figure*).

dégaine (degɛ:n) f, awkwardness. **dégainer** (gene) v.t. & abs, to unsheathe, draw.

déganter (se) (degãte) v.pr, to take off one's gloves.

dégarnir (degarni:r) v.t, to strip, dismantle.

dégât (dega) m. oft. pl, damage, havoc.

dégauchir (degoʃi:r) v.t, to true, straighten.

dégel (deʒɛl) m, thaw. **dégeler** (ʒle) v.t. & i. & se ~, to thaw.

dégénérer (deʒenere) v.i, to degenerate. **dégénérescence** (resã:s) & **dégénération** (rasjɔ̃) f, degeneration, degeneracy.

dégingandé, e (deʒẽgãde) a, ungainly, gawky.

dégivrer (deʒivre) v.t, to de-ice; defrost (*refrigerator*). **dégivreur** (rœ:r) m, de-icing device.

dégoiser (degwaze) v.t, to spout (*abuse*).

dégommer (degɔme) v.t, to ungum; oust.

dégonfler (degɔ̃fle) v.t, to deflate; relieve. se ~, to collapse; back down.

dégorger (degɔrʒe) v.t, to disgorge; unstop. [se] ~, to discharge; overflow.

dégouliner (deguline) v.i, to trickle, drip.

dégourdi, e (degurdi) p.a, wide-awake, alive. **dégourdir** (di:r) v.t, to revive. *faire* ~, to take the chill off (*water*).

dégoût (degu) m, want of appetite; distaste, dislike, disrelish; disgust, loathing, aversion; disappointment. **dégoûtant, e** (tã, ã:t) a, disgusting, loathsome; disheartening. **dégoûter** (te) v.t, to make one sick of; disgust. *faire le dégoûté*, to be fastidious, be squeamish.

dégoutter (degute) v.i. & abs, to drip, trickle, dribble.

dégradateur (degradatœ:r) m, vignetter (*Phot.*). **dégradation** (sjɔ̃) f, degradation; defacement; dilapidation. **dégrader** (de) v.t, to degrade; deface; dilapidate; damage; shade [off], vignette.

dégrafer (degrafe) v.t, to unhook, unfasten.

dégraisser (degrese) v.t, to take off the grease (*or* fat) from; skim; scour.

dégras (degra) m, dubbin[g].

degré (degre) m, degree; step, stair; grade; stage; pitch; extent.

dégrèvement (degrevmã) m, relief, reduction, cut (*taxes*). **dégrever** (grəve) v.t, to relieve; cancel; disencumber (*from mortgage*).

dégringolade (degrẽgɔlad) f, tumble; collapse, slump. **dégringoler** (le) v.t, to rush down. ~ *dans*, to tumble (*or* fall) down *or* into.

dégriser (degrize) v.t, to sober; disillusion.

dégrossir (degrosi:r) v.t, to rough down; rough-hew; sketch out; break in.

déguenillé, e (degnije) a, tattered, ragged.

dégueulasse (degølas) a, disgusting (*food, person, etc.*). **dégueuler** (le) v.i, to vomit; spew out.

déguerpir (degɛrpi:r) v.i, to move out; pack off.

déguisement (degizmã) m, disguise; fancy dress. **déguiser** (ze) v.t, to disguise; conceal; change (*name*). se ~, to disguise oneself, masquerade.

dégustateur (degystatœ:r) m, taster. **dégustation** (sjɔ̃) f, tasting. **déguster** (te) v.t, to taste, sample.

déhanchement (deãʃmã) m, waddle.

déharnacher (dearnaʃe) v.t, to unharness.

dehors (dəɔ:r) ad, out; outside; out of doors; in the offing. ¶ ~! out! (*Box., etc.*). *de* ~, from without. *en* ~, ad, outside, outward; frank. *en* ~ *de*, pr, outside, without. ¶ m, outside, exterior; (*pl.*) outworks (*Mil.*); (*pl.*) grounds (*of mansion*); (*pl.*) appearances.

déifier (deifje) *v.t*, to deify. **dé-ité** (te) *f*, deity.

déjà (deʒa) *ad*, already; before.

déjection (deʒɛksjɔ̃) *f*, evacuation (*bowels*).

déjeter (deʒte) *v.t.* & se ~, to warp (*wood*); buckle.

déjeuner (deʒœne) *v.i*, to breakfast; lunch. ¶ *m*, breakfast set, b. service. *petit ~*, breakfast.

déjouer (deʒwe) *v.t*, to baffle, thwart, frustrate, foil, outwit, outmaneuver.

déjucher (deʒyʃe) (*fig.*) *v.i*, to come down; (*v.t.*) to bring down.

delà (dəla) *pr*, beyond. *au-~*, beyond; more. *au-~ de*, beyond; more. [*plus*] *en ~*, farther [off]. *par-~*, beyond. *l'au-~*, *m*, the beyond (*future life*).

délabré, e (delabre) *p.a*, dilapidated; brokendown; tumbledown; ramshackle, gimcrack. **délabrement** (brəmɑ̃) *m*, dilapidation; wreck. **délabrer** (bre) *v.t*, to dilapidate, shatter.

délacer (delase) *v.t*, to unlace.

délai (delɛ) *m*, time, extension [of time]; delay. *~ de congé*, [term of] notice.

délaissement (delɛsmɑ̃) *m*, abandonment, desertion; destitution. **délaisser** (se) *v.t*, to forsake; abandon, desert; jilt.

délassement (delɑsmɑ̃) *m*, relaxation, recreation. **délasser** (se) *v.t.* & *abs*, to refresh, relax.

délateur, trice (delatœːr, tris) *n*, informer.

délateur, trice (delatœːr, tris) *n*, informer. **délation** (sjɔ̃) *f*, denunciation, squealing.

délaver (delave) *v.t*, to soak; dilute.

délayer (delɛje) *v.t*, to add water to, thin; spin out.

deleatur (deleatyːr) *m*, delete (*sign, Typ.*).

délecter (delɛkte) *v.t.* & se ~, to delight.

délégation (delegasjɔ̃) *f*, delegation, deputation. **délégué, e** (ge) *n*, delegate; deputy. **déléguer** (ge) *v.t*, to delegate, depute.

délester (delɛste) *v.t*, to unballast; relieve.

délétère (deletɛːr) *a*, deleterious.

délibération (deliberasjɔ̃) *f*, deliberation, consideration, proceedings; transaction, business; decision, resolution. **délibéré†, e** (re) *a*, deliberate. **délibérer** (re) *v.i*, to deliberate, consult; (*v.t.*) to decide, resolve on. *~ sur*, to consider, transact (*business at meeting*).

délicat, e† (delika, at) *a*, delicate; nice; refined; dainty, fastidious, squeamish; tender; ticklish, tricky. **délicatesse** (tɛs) *f*, delicacy.

délice (delis) *m*, delight, pleasure, luxury. *~s, f.pl*, delight(s), pleasure(s), delectation. **délicieux, euse†** (sjø, øːz) *a*, delicious; delightful; charming.

délictueux (deliktyø) *a*, unlawful, illegal, felonious.

délié, e (delje) *a*, thin, slender, slim; glib. ¶ *m*, thin stroke, up stroke. **délier** (lje) *v.t*, to untie; loose[n]; release.

délimiter (delimite) *v.t*, to delimit.

délinéation (delineasjɔ̃) *f*, delineation.

délinquant, e (delɛ̃kɑ̃, ɑ̃ːt) *n*, delinquent, offender.

déliquescence (delikɥɛsɑ̃ːs) *f*, deliquescence; corruption (*fig.*).

délirant, e (delirɑ̃, ɑ̃ːt) *a*, delirious; frenzied; raving. **délire** (liːr) *m*, delirium; frenzy. **délirer** (lire) *v.i*, to be delirious.

délit (deli) *m*, offense, misdemeanor. *en flagrant ~*, in the act.

délivrance (delivrɑ̃ːs) *f*, deliverance; rescue; release; delivery; issue. **délivrer** (vre) *v.t*, to deliver; rescue; release; hand [over]; issue (*tickets*).

déloger (deloʒe) *v.i*, to [re]move; (*v.t.*) to turn out; dislodge.

déloyal, e† (delwajal) *a*, disloyal; unfair; dishonest. **déloyauté** (jote) *f*, disloyalty.

delta (dɛlta) *m*, delta.

déluge (delyːʒ) *m*, deluge, flood; [down]pour.

déluré, e (delyre) *a*, wide-awake; knowing.

démagogue (demagɔg) *m*, demagogue.

démailler (demaje) *v.t.* to undo (*knitting*). se ~, to run (*stocking*).

demain (dəmɛ̃) *ad.* & *m*, tomorrow. ~ *matin*, tomorrow morning.

démancher (demɑ̃ʃe) *v.t.* to unhandle; dislocate.

demande (dəmɑ̃:d) *f*, request, desire; application; inquiry; demand; call; indent; claim; bid; instance; suit; proposal (*marriage*); question. ~ *d'emploi*, situation wanted. **demander** (mɑ̃de) *v.t.* to ask, a. for, request; charge; inquire; apply for; claim; want; bid [for]; beg; sue for. ~ *par voie d'annonces*, to advertise for. *on demande un . . .*, wanted a . . . se ~, to ask onself, wonder. **demandeur, euse** (dœ:r, ∅:z) *n*, petitioner; applicant. **demandeur, eresse** (dœ:r, drɛs) *n*, plaintiff.

démangeaison (demɑ̃ʒɛzɔ̃) *f*, itch[ing]; urge; longing. **démanger** (ʒe) *v.i.* to itch; long. *le bras me démange*, my arm itches. *la langue lui démange*, he is itching (*or* longing) to speak.

démanteler (demɑ̃tle) *v.t.* to dismantle.

démantibuler (demɑ̃tibule) *v.t.* to break to pieces.

démarcation (demarkasjɔ̃) *f*, demarcation.

démarche (demarʃ) *f*, gait, walk, bearing; step, measure. **démarcheur** (ʃœ:r) *m*, canvasser, runner, share pusher.

démarier (demarje) *v.t.* to unmarry; thin (*plants*).

démarquer (demarke) *v.t.* to mark down (*prices*); remove identification; plagiarize.

démarrage (demara:ʒ) *m*, unmooring; starting. ~ *à chaud, à froid*, warm start, cold start (*computers*). **démarrer** (re) *v.t.* to unmoor; (*v.i.*) to leave her moorings; cast off; start; stir. **démarreur** (œ:r) *m*, starter (*auto*).

démasquer (demaske) *v.t.* to unmask; uncover; show up.

démâter (demɑte) *v.t.* to dismast.

démêlé (demɛle) *m*, contention. **démêler** (le) *v.t.* to disentangle, unravel; comb out; quarrel about. *se* ~ *de*, to get out of. **démêloir** (lwa:r) *m*, rake comb.

démembrer (demɑ̃bre) *v.t.* to dismember.

déménagement (demenaʒmɑ̃) *m*, removal, moving. **déménager** (ʒe) *v.t.* & *abs*, to remove, move [out] (*house*); (*v.i.*) to be off; go off one's head. **déménageur** (ʒœ:r) *m*, removal contractor, [furniture] remover.

démence (demɑ̃:s) *f*, insanity, madness, dementia.

démener (se) (demne) *v.pr*, to throw oneself about; strive hard.

dément, e (demɑ̃, ɑ̃:t) *a.* & *n*, crazy, mad (person).

démenti (demɑ̃ti) *m*, denial, contradiction, lie; failure, disappointment. **démentir** (ti:r) *v.t.ir*, to give the lie to; contradict; belie.

démerder (se) (demerde) *v.i.* to manage somehow, figure something out; hurry up, get a move on (*slang*).

démérite (demerit) *m*, demerit, unworthiness. **démériter** (te) *v.i.* & *abs*, to deserve censure, offend.

démesuré†, e (dem[ə]zyre) *a*, inordinate; enormous, huge.

démettre (demɛtr) *v.t.ir*, to dislocate, put out of joint. se ~ *de*, to resign, retire.

demeurant (au) (dəmœrɑ̃), after all, in other respects. **demeure** (mœ:r) *f*, residence, dwelling, abode; delay. *à* ~, fixed, stationary, set. *en* ~, in arrears. **demeurer** (mœre) *v.i.* to reside, live, dwell; stay, remain, stop; lie.

demi, e (dəmi) *a*, half. demi, *ad*, half. ¶ *m*, half; halfback (*Foot.*); a beer (*ordered in a café*). *à* ~, *ad*, half, by halves.

demi (dəmi) *comps*: *~-bas, m.pl*, half-hose. *~-cercle, m*, semicircle. *~-dieu, m*, demigod. *~-finale, f*, semi-final. *~-frère, m*, half-brother, stepbrother. *~-gros, m*, small wholesale trade. *une* ~-*heure*, half an hour. *~-jour, m*, half-light, twilight. *~-lune, f*, crescent (*of buildings*). *~-mot*, *m*, hint. ~*-pensionnaire*, *n*, day boarder. ~*-place*, *f*, half fare, half price. ~*-relief*, *m*, mezzo-relievo. ~*-sœur*, *f*, half-sister, stepsister. *en* ~*-solde*, on half pay (*Mil.*). ~*-ton*, *m*, semitone. *à* ~*-voix*, in an undertone.

demie (dəmi) *f*, (a) half; half-hour; half past. *une heure &* ~, an hour & a half; half-past one.

démission (demisjɔ̃) *f*, resignation. **démissionner** (ɔne) *v.i*, to resign.

démobiliser (demɔbilize) *v.t*, to demobilize.

démocrate (demɔkrat) *m*, democrat. **démocratie** (si) *f*, democracy. **démocratique** (tik) *a*, democratic.

démodé, e (demɔde) *a*, old-fashioned; out of date.

demoiselle (dəmwazɛl) *f*, young lady; girl; single woman, maiden [lady]; spinster; miss; damsel; dragon fly; beetle, rammer; rowlock. ~ *de compagnie*, lady companion. ~ *d'honneur*, bridesmaid.

démolir (demɔliːr) *v.t*, to demolish, break up; explode (*fig.*). **démolisseur** (lisœːr) *m*, breaker (*house, ship*); iconoclast. **démolition** (sjɔ̃) *f*, demolition; (*pl.*) demolitions.

démon (demɔ̃) *m*, demon, devil; fiend; demon, genius; imp. ~ *familier*, familiar [spirit].

démonétiser (demonetize) *v.t*, to demonetize, call in; discredit.

démoniaque (demɔnjak) *a*, demoniac(al). ¶ *n*, demoniac.

démonstrateur (demɔ̃stratœːr) *m*, demonstrator. **démonstratif, ive** (tif, iːv) *a*, conclusive; demonstrative. **démonstration** (sjɔ̃) *f*, demonstration; proof. ~ *par l'absurde*, reduction to absurdity, reductio ad absurdum.

démontable (demɔ̃tabl) *a*, sectional. **démonter** (te) *v.t*, to dismount; unhorse, throw; take to pieces; upset, nonplus.

démontrer (demɔ̃tre) *v.t*, to demonstrate, prove; show.

démoraliser (demɔralize) *v.t*, to demoralize.

démordre (demɔrdr) *v.i*, to let go; desist.

démoscopie (demɔskɔpi) *f*, science of opinion-sounding of masses.

démunir (se) de (demyniːr), to part with.

démuseler (demyzle) *v.t*, to unmuzzle.

dénaturer (denatyre) *v.t*, to denature; pervert, render unnatural; distort; misrepresent.

dénébulateur (denebylatœːr) *m*, fog-dispersal device. **dénébulation** (lasjɔ̃) *f*, fog dispersal. **dénébuler** (le) *v.t*, to disperse fog.

dénégation (denegasjɔ̃) *f*, denial; disclaimer.

déni (deni) *m*, denial; refusal.

déniaiser (denjɛze) *v.t*, to sharpen (*wits*).

dénicher (deniʃe) *v.t*, to take out of the nest; ferret out; (*v.i.*) to fly [away]. **dénicheur** (ʃœːr) *m*, birds'-nester; hunter (*curios*).

denier (dənje) *m*: ~ *à Dieu*, earnest money; key money. *le* ~ *de la veuve*, the widow's mite. *le* ~ *de Saint-Pierre*, Peter's pence. ~*s*, *pl*, money, funds.

dénier (denje) *v.t*, to deny; disclaim.

dénigrer (denigre) *v.t*, to disparage, run down; detract from.

dénombrement (denɔ̃brəmɑ̃) *m*, count; census.

dénominateur (denɔminatœːr) *m*, denominator. **dénommer** (me) *v.t*, to name, denominate.

dénoncer (denɔ̃se) *v.t*, to proclaim, declare; denounce, inform against. **dénonciation** (sjasjɔ̃) *f*, denunciation; information.

dénoter (denɔte) *v.t*, to denote, betoken.

dénouement (denumɑ̃) *m*, upshot; ending. **dénouer** (nwe) *v.t*, to untie, undo; loosen; unravel.

dénoyauter (denwajote) *v.t*, to pit (*fruit*).

denrée (dɑ̃re) *f*, *oft. pl*, commodity, produce. ~ *alimentaire*, foodstuff.

dense (dɑ̃ːs) *a*, dense, close; thick. **densité** (dɑ̃site) *f*, density.

dent (dɑ̃) *f*, tooth; prong; cog; tusk; serration; [jagged] peak.

~s *de dessous, de dessus, de devant, du fond, de lait, de sagesse,* lower, upper, front, back, milk, wisdom, teeth. **dentaire** (tɛːr) *a,* dental (*Anat.*). **dental, e** (tal) *a,* dental (*Anat. & phonetics*). ¶ *f,* dental (*phonetics*). **denté, e** (te) *a,* toothed, cogged; dentate. ~ *en scie,* serrate. **denteler** (tle) *v.t,* to indent, notch, jag, serrate. **dentelle** (tɛl) *f,* lace; laced paper; tracery. ~ *à l'aiguille,* needle-made lace. ~ *au point à l'aiguille,* needle-point l. ~ *aux fuseaux,* pillow l. **dentelure** (tlyːr) *f,* indentation, serration. **dentier** (tje) *m,* set of (*artificial*) teeth, denture, [dental] plate. **dentifrice** (tifris) *m,* toothpaste; tooth powder. **dentiste** (tist) *m,* dentist; (*att.*) dental (*surgeon*). **dentition** (sjɔ̃) *f,* dentition, teething. **denture** (tyːr) *f,* set of (*natural*) teeth; teeth (*cogs*). ~ *artificielle,* denture, [dental] plate.

dénuder (denyde) *v.t,* to denude, bare, strip.

dénué, e (denɥe) *a,* devoid, destitute. **dénuement** (nymɑ̃) *m,* destitution, penury. **se dénuer de** (nɥe), to part with.

dépannage (depanaːʒ) *m,* auto repairs. **dépanner** (ne) *v.t,* to repair, help. **dépanneuse** (nøːz) *f,* tow truck.

dépaqueter (depakte) *v.t,* to unpack.

dépareillé, e (depareje) *a,* odd (*pair or set*). **dépareiller** (je) *v.t,* to break (*a set*).

déparer (depare) *v.t,* to strip; spoil, mar; pick out the best.

déparler (deparle) *v.i,* with *neg,* to stop talking.

départ (depaːr) *m,* departure, sailing; start; parting (*Chem.*). *faire le* ~ *entre, de,* to discriminate between. ~ *arrêté,* standing start. ~ *lancé,* flying start. ~ *usines,* ex works, ex mill (*sales*).

départager (departaʒe) *v.t,* to decide between. ~ *les voix,* to give the casting vote.

département (departəmɑ̃) *m,* department; county; province; line. **départemental, e** (tal) *a,* departmental.

départir (departiːr) *v.t.ir,* to divide; part (*metals*); distribute, dispense, endow. **se** ~, to desist, swerve (*fig.*).

dépassement (depasmɑ̃) *m,* going beyond; excess.

dépasser (depase) *v.t,* to go beyond, go over, exceed, be above, top; turn (*a certain age*); pass, leave behind, overshoot, overreach; be longer; project beyond.

dépaver (depave) *v.t,* to unpave.

dépaysé, e (depeize) *p.a,* lost; among strangers; out of one's element. **dépayser** (ze) *v.t,* to remove from usual surroundings.

dépecer (depəse) *v.t,* to cut up; break up.

dépêche (depɛːʃ) *f,* dispatch; message; telegram. **dépêcher** (pɛʃe) *v.t,* to dispatch. **se** ~, to make haste, be quick, hurry up; look sharp.

dépeindre (depɛ̃ːdr) *v.t.ir,* to depict, portray, delineate, picture.

dépenaillé, e (depnaje) *a,* in rags; ill-dressed.

dépendance (depɑ̃dɑ̃ːs) *f,* dependence; subjection; dependency; outbuilding, outhouse; annex[e]. **dépendant, e** (dɑ̃, ɑ̃ːt) *a,* dependent. **dépendre** (pɑ̃ːdr) *v.i,* to depend, belong; be a dependency (*de* = of); to take down, to unhang.

dépens (depɑ̃) *m.pl,* expense; [law] costs. **dépense** (pɑ̃ːs) *f,* expense, charge, cost, expenditure; efflux; steward's room. ~ *de bouche,* living expenses. **dépenser** (pɑ̃se) *v.t,* to spend, expend. **dépensier, ère** (sje, ɛːr) *a,* extravagant, thriftless. ¶ *n,* spendthrift; bursar.

déperdition (depɛrdisjɔ̃) *f,* waste, loss.

dépérir (deperiːr) *v.i,* to dwindle, pine away, wither, decay.

dépêtrer (depɛtre) *v.t,* to extricate.

dépeupler (depœple) *v.t,* to depopulate; unstock.

déphasage (defazaːʒ) *m,* phase displacement (*Elec.*); lag (*cultural, social, etc.*). **déphasé** (ze) *a,* disoriented.

dépiler (depile) *v.t*, to depilate, pluck; unhair.

dépiquer (depike) *v.t*, to unquilt; transplant; thresh (*grain*); cheer up.

dépister (depiste) *v.t*, to track down, run to earth; throw off the scent, foil.

dépit (depi) *m*, spite, spleen, despite. **dépiter** (te) *v.t*, to vex; spite.

déplacé, e (deplase) *a*, out of place, ill-timed; uncalled for. **déplacement** (smã) *m*, displacement, removal, shift[ing]; traveling. **déplacer** (se) *v.t*, to displace; [re]move, shift.

déplaire (deplɛːr) *v.i.ir*, to be displeasing, offend. ~ **à**, to displease. **se ~**, to be unhappy; not to thrive. **déplaisant, e** (plɛzã, ãːt) *a*, unpleasing, unpleasant. **déplaisir** (zi:r) *m*, displeasure.

déplanter (deplãte) *v.t*, to take up. **déplantoir** (twaːr) *m*, trowel (*Hort.*).

dépliant (depliã) *m*, folder. **déplier** (plie) *v.t*, to unfold.

déplisser (deplise) *v.t*, to unpleat, iron out.

déploiement (deplwamã) *m*, unfolding; deployment.

déplorable† (deplɔrabl) *a*, deplorable. **déplorer** (re) *v.t*, to deplore, bewail.

déployer (deplwaje) *v.t*, to unfold; unfurl; deploy; spread [out]; expand; display.

déplumer (deplyme) *v.t*, to pluck, deplume. **se ~**, to molt.

déplu, *p.p*, **déplaire**.

dépolir (depɔliːr) *v.t*, to take the surface off. *verre dépoli*, ground glass, frosted glass.

dépolitisation (depɔlitizasjɔ̃) *f*, depoliticization. **dépolitiser** (tize) *v.t*, to depoliticize.

dépolluer (depɔlye) *v.t*, to cleanse, depollute.

déportements (depɔrtəmã) *m.pl*, misconduct.

déporter (depɔrte) *v.t*, to deport; transport (*convict*). **se ~**, to withdraw claims (*law*).

déposant, e (depozã, ãːt) *n*, deponent; depositor; customer (*bank*). **dépose** (poːz) *f*, taking

up; t. down; t. off. **déposer** (poze) *v.t*, to lay down; l. aside; deposit; place, lodge, hand in; file, lay; depose; register (*trade mark*); prefer; take up, t. down, t. off. **se ~**, to settle. **dépositaire** (pozitɛːr) *n*, depositary; trustee; storer (*furniture warehouseman*). **déposition** (sjɔ̃) *f*, deposition; evidence.

déposséder (deposede) *v.t*, to dispossess, oust.

dépôt (depo) *m*, deposit; deposition; trust; handing in; filing; depot, store[house], warehouse, repository; depository; shed; yard; cells (*prison*); sediment. *en ~*, on sale [or return]; in bond.

dépoter (depɔte) *v.t*, to plant out; decant.

dépotoir (depɔtwaːr) *m*, refuse dump; refuse disposal plant.

dépouille (depuːj) *f*, slough (*serpent, worm*); skin (*wild beast*); spoil; remains (*mortal*). **dépouiller** (puje) *v.t*, to skin; cast (*skin*); strip, divest, despoil; go through; analyze; count (*votes*). **se ~**, to slough, cast its skin; shed its leaves.

dépourvoir (depurvwaːr) *v.t.ir*, to deprive. **dépourvu, e** (vy) *p.a*, destitute, bereft, devoid. *au dépourvu*, *ad*, unawares, napping.

dépravation (depravasjɔ̃) *f*, depravation; depravity. **dépraver** (ve) *v.t*, to deprave, vitiate.

dépréciation (depresjasjɔ̃) *f*, depreciation. **déprécier** (sje) *v.t*, to depreciate, underrate, undervalue, disparage.

déprédation (depredasjɔ̃) *f*, depredation.

déprendre (se) (deprãːdr) *v.pr. ir*, to break away, part.

dépression (depresjɔ̃) *f*, depression. ~ *nerveuse*, nervous breakdown. **déprimer** (prime) *v.t*, to depress; dispirit.

depuis (dəpɥi) *pr. & ad*, since, for, from. ~ *quand?* how long? since when? ~ *que*, *c*, since.

députation (depytasjɔ̃) *f*, deputation; membership (*parliament*). **député (te)** *m*, deputy; congressman; delegate. **députer** (te) *v.t.* to depute.

déraciné, e (derasine) (*pers.*) *n*, fish out of water. **déraciner** (ne) *v.t*, to uproot, eradicate.

déraidir (se) (deredi:r) (*fig.*) *v.pr*, to unbend, thaw.

dérailler (deraje) *v.i*, to derail; go astray (*fig.*). **dérailleur** (rajœ:r) *m*, bicycle gearshift; shifting track (*Rly.*).

déraison (derezɔ̃) *f*, unreason-[ableness]. **déraisonnable†** (zɔnabl) *a*, unreasonable, preposterous. **déraisonner** (ne) *v.i*, to talk nonsense.

dérangement (derɑ̃ʒmɑ̃) *m*, derangement; disturbance; fault. **déranger** (ʒe) *v.t*, to disarrange; disturb; upset; trouble; put out of order; derange, unsettle.

déraper (derape) *v.t. & i*, to trip (*anchor*); skid; side-slip.

déréaliser (derealize) *v.t*, to strip of psychological reality.

déréglé, e (deregle) *a*, out of order; lawless. **dérèglement** (rɛglǝmɑ̃) *m*, disordered state; irregularity; derangement; profligacy. **dérégler** (regle) *v.t*, to put out of order; derange; disorder.

dérider (deride) *v.t*, to smooth, unwrinkle; cheer up.

dérision (derizjɔ̃) *f*, derision. **dérisoire** (zwa:r) *a*, derisory, laughable.

dérivation (derivasjɔ̃) *f*, derivation; deflection; loop [line]; flume; shunt (*Elec.*). **dérive** (ri:v) *f*, leeway; drift; breakaway. **en ~, à la ~**, adrift **dérivé** (ve) *m*, derivative. **dériver** (ve) *v.t*, to divert; shunt (*Elec.*); unrivet; (*v.i.*) to be derived; spring, originate; drift, drive (*Naut.*).

dernier, ère (dɛrnje, ɛ:r) *a*, last; hindmost; latter; late; latest; final; closing; junior (*partner*); highest; utmost; extreme; dire; lowest, worst. *dernier cri*, latest [thing out]. *dernier jugement*, crack of doom. *dernières galeries*, gallery (*Theat.*) *dernière main*, finishing touches. **dernièrement** (njɛrmɑ̃) *ad*, lately, latterly, not long ago.

dérobé, e (derɔbe) *a*, secret, hid-

den, concealed; spare (*time*). **à la dérobée**, *ad*, by stealth, on the sly. **dérober** (be) *v.t*, to steal, rob; snatch; conceal, hide. *se ~ à*, to shirk. *se ~ de*, to steal away from. *se ~ sous*, to give way under.

déroger (derɔʒe) *v.i*, to derogate.

dérouiller (deruje) *v.t*, to rub off the rust from; beat up, punish. *se ~*, to stretch (*muscles, legs*).

déroulement (derulmɑ̃) *m*, unfolding; development; passing. **dérouler** (rule) *v.t*, to unroll, unfold; evolve.

déroute (derut) *f*, rout; ruin. *mettre en ~*, to rout. **dérouter** (te) *v.t*, to lead astray; baffle, nonplus.

derrière (dɛrjɛ:r) *pr. & ad*, behind; aft; astern. ¶ *m*, back; rear; hinder part; tail (*cart*).

derviche (dɛrviʃ) *ou* **dervis** (vi) *m*, dervish.

des *see* **de**.

dès (dɛ) *pr*, from; since. *~ à présent*, from now onward. *~ lors*, ever since then; consequently. *~ que*, *c*, as soon as.

désabonner (se) (dezabɔne) *v.pr*, to discontinue one's subscription *or* season ticket.

désabuser (dezabyze) *v.t*, to disabuse, undeceive.

désaccord (dezakɔ:r) *m*, disagreement; discord (*Mus.*). **désaccorder** (kɔrde) *v.t*, to put out of tune. *se ~*, to break their engagement (*marriage*).

désaccoupler (dezakuple) *v.t*, to uncouple.

désaccoutumer (dezakutyme) *v.t*, to break of the habit.

désaffection (dezafɛksjɔ̃) *f*, disaffection.

désagréable† (dezagreabl) *a*, disagreeable, unpleasant. *~ au goût*, distasteful; unpalatable.

désagréger (dezagreʒe) *v.t*, to disintegrate, weather.

désagrément (dezagremɑ̃) *m*, source of annoyance; unpleasantness; vexation.

désajuster (dezaʒyste) *v.t*, to derange; disarrange.

désaltérer (dezaltere) *v.t*, to quench (*someone's*) thirst.

désamorcer (dezamɔrse) *v.t*, to unprime.

désappointement (dezapwɛ̃tmɑ̃) *m*, disappointment. **désappointer** (te) *v.t*, to disappoint.

désapprendre (dezaprɑ̃:dr) *v.t.* & *abs. ir*, to forget; unlearn.

désapprobation (dezaprɔbasjɔ̃) *f*, disapprobation, disapproval. **désapprouver** (pruve) *v.t*, to disapprove [of], frown [up]on.

désarçonner (dezarsɔne) *v.t*, to unseat, unhorse, throw; silence, floor.

désarmement (dezarməmɑ̃) *m*, disarmament; laying up (*ship*). **désarmer** (me) *v.t.* & *i*, to disarm, unarm; uncock (*gun*); lay up.

désarroi (dezarwa) *m*, disarray, disorder.

désassembler (dezasɑ̃ble) *v.t*, to take to pieces, disconnect, disjoint.

désastre (dezastr) *m*, disaster. **désastreux, euse** (trø, ø:z), *a*, disastrous.

désavantage (dezavɑ̃ta:ʒ) *m*, disadvantage, drawback. **désavantager** (taʒe) *v.t*, to place at a disadvantage, handicap. **désavantageux, euse†** (ʒø, ø:z) *a*, disadvantageous.

désaveu (dezavø) *m*, disavowal, denial, disclaimer. **désavouer** (vwe) *v.t*, to disavow; disown; disclaim; disapprove.

desceller (desele) *v.t*, to unseal.

descendance (desɑ̃dɑ̃:s) *f*, descent, lineage; descendants. **descendant, e** (dɑ̃, ɑ̃:t) *a*, descending, downward; down (*train, etc.*); outgoing (*tide*). ¶ *n*, descendant; (*pl.*) progeny. **descendre** (sɑ̃:dr) *v.i.* & *t*, to descend, go down; alight, dismount, get down; stay, stop, put up (*at a hotel*); lower; drop; fall; sink; make a descent; kill (*slang*). ~ [à terre], to land. ~ *en vol plané*, to plane down. **descente** (sɑ̃:t) *f*, descent; fall; lowering; slope, incline; downpipe; raid; run (*of depositors on bank*). ~ *de bain*, bath mat. ~ *de justice*, domiciliary visit. ~ *de lit*, bedside rug.

description (dɛskripsjɔ̃) *f*, description; inventory.

désemparer (dezɑ̃pare) *v.t*, to disable (*ship*); quit, leave. *sans* ~, on the spot, there & then; without intermission, continuous(ly).

désemplir (dezɑ̃pli:r) *v.t*, to partly empty; (*v.i.*) to empty. *ne pas* ~, to be always full.

désenchanter (dezɑ̃ʃɑ̃te) *v.t*, to disenchant; disillusion.

désencombrer (dezɑ̃kɔ̃bre) *v.t*, to disencumber, clear.

désenfiler (dezɑ̃file) *v.t*, to unthread.

désenfler (dezɑ̃fle) *v.t*, to deflate; (*v.i.*) to go down (*swelling*).

désenivrer (dezɑ̃nivre) *v.t*, to sober. *il ne désenivre point*, he is never sober.

désennuyer (dezɑ̃nɥije) *v.t*, to divert, amuse.

désenrhumer (dezɑ̃ryme) *v.t*, to cure of a cold. **désenrouer** (rwe) *v.t*, to cure of hoarseness.

déséquilibré, e (dezekilibre) *a*, unbalanced.

désert, e (deze:r, ɛrt) *a*, desert; deserted, empty, desolate. ¶ *m*, desert, wilderness. **déserter** (zerte) *v.t.* & *abs*, to desert, forsake. ~ *de*, to leave. **déserteur** (tœ:r) *m*, deserter. **désertion** (sjɔ̃) *f*, desertion. **désertique** (tik) *a*, desert.

désespérance (dezɛspera:s) *f*, despair. **désespérant, e** (rɑ̃, ɑ̃:t) *a*, heartbreaking. **désespéré†, e** (re) *a*, desperate, hopeless. ¶ *n*, desperate man, woman, madman. **désespérer** (re) *v.i.* & *abs*, to despair; (*v.t.*) to drive to despair. **désespoir** (pwa:r) *m*, despair; desperation.

désétatiser (dezetatize) *v.t*, to return to the private sector.

déshabillé, e (dɛzabije) *m*, undress, dishabille; wrap; true colors (*fig.*). **déshabiller** (je) *v.t*, to undress, disrobe, strip; lay bare (*fig.*).

déshabituer (dezabitɥe) *v.t*, to break of the habit.

déshérence (dezerɑ̃:s) *f*, escheat.

déshériter (dezerite) *v.t*, to disinherit.

déshonnête† (dezɔnɛːt) *a*, indecent, immodest.

déshonneur (dezɔnœːr) *m*, dishonor, disgrace. **déshonorant, e** (nɔrɑ̃, ɑ̃ːt) *a*, dishonorable, discreditable. **déshonorer** (re) *v.t*, to dishonor, disgrace.

déshydrater (dezidrate) *v.t*, to dehydrate. **déshydrateur** (tœːr) *m*, dehydrator.

desiderata (deziderata) *m.pl*, desiderata, wants.

désigner (deziɲe) *v.t*, to designate; indicate, point out; describe; nominate; appoint. **désignation** (ɲasjɔ̃) *f*, designation.

désillusionner (dezilyzjɔne) *v.t*, to disillusion, undeceive.

désincorporer (dezɛ̃kɔrpɔre) *v.t*, to disincorporate, disembody.

désinence (dezinɑ̃ːs) *f*, ending (*word*).

désinfectant (dezɛ̃fɛktɑ̃) *m*, disinfectant. **désinfecter** (te) *v.t*, to disinfect, deodorize. **désinfection** (sjɔ̃) *f*, disinfection.

désintegration (dezɛ̃tegrasjɔ̃) *f*, disintegration, breaking up; splitting (*atom*). **désintegrer** (gre) *v.t*, to crush, break up; split, smash (*atom*).

désintéressé, e (dezɛ̃terɛse) *a*, not implicated; disinterested, candid; unselfish. **désintéressement** (smɑ̃) *m*, disinterestedness; unselfishness. **désintéresser** (se) *v.t*, to buy out, satisfy, pay off. *se ~ de*, to take no further interest in.

désinviter (dezɛ̃vite) *v.t*, to ask not to come.

désinvolte (dezɛ̃vɔlt) *a*, easy. **désinvolture** (tyːr) *f*, unconstraint; free & easy manner.

désir (deziːr) *m*, desire, wish. **désirable** (zirabl) *a*, desirable. **désirer** (re) *v.t. & abs*, to desire, want, be desirous of, wish, wish for. **désireux, euse** (rø, øːz) *a*, desirous, wishful, anxious.

désistement (dezistəmɑ̃) *m*, waiver (*law*); withdrawal. **se désister de** (te), to waive; withdraw from; stand down from (*candidacy*).

désobéir (dezɔbeiːr) *v.i. & abs*, to disobey. *~ à*, to disobey (*v.t.*). **désobéissance** (isɑ̃ːs) *f*, disobedience. **désobéissant, e** (sɑ̃, ɑ̃ːt) *a*, disobedient.

désobligeance (dezɔbliʒɑ̃ːs) *f*, disobligingness, unkindness. **désobligeant, e** (ʒɑ̃, ɑ̃ːt) *a*, disobliging, unkind, ungracious. **désobliger** (ʒe) *v.t*, to disoblige.

désobstruer (dezɔpstrye) *v.t*, to clear.

désoccupé, e (dezɔkype) *a*, unoccupied.

désœuvré, e (dezøvre) *a*, idle, at a loose end. ¶ *n*, idler. **désœuvrement** (vrəmɑ̃) *m*, idleness.

désolation (dezɔlasjɔ̃) *f*, desolation. **désolé, e** (le) *p.a*, desolate; disconsolate, forlorn, distressed, extremely sorry. **désoler** (le) *v.t*, to desolate, distress, grieve.

désopilant, e (dezɔpilɑ̃, ɑ̃ːt) *a*, highly amusing.

désordonné, e (dezɔrdɔne) *a*, untidy; disorderly; inordinate. **désordre** (dr) *m*, disorder; disorderliness. *~s*, riots.

désorganiser (dezɔrganize) *v.t*, to disorganize.

désorienter (dezɔrjɑ̃te) *v.t*, to disconcert, bewilder.

désormais (dezɔrmɛ) *ad*, henceforth; hereafter.

désosser (dezɔse) *v.t*, to bone; take apart (*mechanism, etc.*).

despote (dɛspɔt) *m*, despot. **despotique†** (tik) *a*, despotic. **despotisme** (tism) *m*, despotism.

desquels, desquelles, *see* lequel.

dessaisir (desɛziːr) *v.t*, to release; dispossess, deprive; unlash (*Naut.*).

dessaler (dɛsale) *v.t*, to unsalt; soak (*meat*); sharpen wits.

dessécher (deseʃe) *v.t*, to desiccate; dry up, drain; wither, parch. **dessèchement** (sɛʃmɑ̃) *m*, desiccation, etc.

dessein (dɛsɛ̃) *m*, design, plan, project; purpose. *à ~*, on purpose, designedly.

desseller (desɛle) *v.t*, to unsaddle.

desserrer (desɛre) *v.t*, to loosen, slack[en]; open.

dessert (desɛːr) *m*, dessert (*dessert, cheese, fruit*).

desserte (desɛrt) *f*, duties. **desservir** (viːr) *v.t.ir*, to serve; minister to (*Eccl.*). ~ [*la table*], to clear the table.

dessiccation (dɛsikasjɔ̃) *f*, desiccation.

dessiller (desije) *v.t*, to open (*eyes*) (*fig.*).

dessin (desɛ̃) *m*, drawing, sketching; design, pattern; sketch; cartoon; plan. ~ *à carreaux*, check [pattern]. ~ *à main levée*, freehand drawing. ~ *au trait*, outline d. ~ *industriel*, mechanical d. ~ *ombré*, shaded d. ~ *animé*, animated cartoon. **dessinateur, trice** (sinatœːr, tris) *n*, sketcher, drawer; draftsman; cartoonist; designer. ~ *de jardins*, landscape gardener. **dessiner** (sine) *v.t*, to draw, sketch; design; show; outline. se ~, to stand out; show up; loom; take shape.

dessoûler (desule) *v.t*, to sober. *il ne dessoûle jamais*, he is never sober.

dessous (dəsu) *ad. & pr*, under; under it, them; underneath; beneath, below. *au*~ (otsu) *ad*, under[neath], below. *au*~ *de*, *pr*, below, under, beneath. *en* ~, *ad*, underneath; underhand; stealthily; sly. *là*~, *ad*, under there, under that, underneath. *par*~, *pr. & ad*, under[neath], beneath. ¶ *m*, under part, underside, bottom; face (*card*); wrong side (*fabric*); worst of it (*fig.*); (*pl.*) underclothing, underwear (*women's*). ~ *de plat*, table mat.

dessus (dəsy) *ad*, over, above; on, upon, [up]on it, them. *au*~ (otsy) *ad*, above [it], over it; upwards. *au*~ *de*, *pr*, above, over; beyond. *en* ~, *ad*, on [the] top. *là*~, *ad*, on that, thereon; thereupon. *par*~, *pr. & ad*, over; into. *par*~ *bord*, overboard. ¶ *m*, upper part; top; back (*hand*); treble (*Mus.*), soprano; right side (*fabric*); *prendre le* ~, to get the upper hand, mastery, whip hand; best of it. ~ *de coussin*, cushion cover. ~ *de fourneau*, top of grate. ~ *de plateau*, tray cloth. ~

de lit, bedspread. ~ *du panier*, pick of the basket.

destin (dɛstɛ̃) *m*, destiny, fate, lot, doom. **destinataire** (tinatɛːr) *n*, consignee; receiver, recipient; addressee. *aux risques & périls du* ~, at owner's risk. **destination** (sjɔ̃) *f*, destination; purpose. *à* ~ *de*, [bound] for. **destinée** (ne) *f*, destiny, lot. **destiner** (ne) *v.t*, to destine, design, intend, mean; allot, assign; fate, doom.

destitué, e (dɛstitɥe) *p.a*, devoid, lacking. **destituer** (tɥe) *v.t*, to dismiss, remove, displace. **destitution** (tysjɔ̃) *f*, dismissal; removal.

destructeur, trice (destryktœːr, tris) *a*, destructive. ¶ *n*, destroyer. **destructif, ive** (tif, iːv) *a*, destructive. **destruction** (sjɔ̃) *f*, destruction.

désuet, te (desɥe, ɛt) *a*, obsolete. ~ *calculée*, planned obsolescence. **désuétude** (sɥetyd) *f*, disuse.

désunion (dezynjɔ̃) *f*, disunion. **désunir** (niːr) *v.t*, to disunite.

détachement (detaʃmɑ̃) *m*, detachment; detail (*men*). **détacher** (ʃe) *v.t*, to detach, untie, undo, unfasten; take off, t. down; detail (*Mil.*). se ~, to come away; break off; b. away; stand out.

détail (detaːj) *m*, detail, particular; retail. **détaillant, e** (tajɑ̃, ɑ̃ːt) *n*, retailer. **détailler** (je) *v.t*, to cut up; retail, peddle; detail.

détaler (detale) *v.i*, to make off, scamper away.

détaxer (detakse) *v.t*, to return (*or remit*) the duties (*or charges*) on; untax.

détecteur (detɛktœːr) *m*, detector (*radio*). **détective** (tiːv) *m*, detective.

déteindre (detɛ̃ːdr) *v.t. & i. ir*, to fade. ~ *sur*, to come off on (*dye*); influence.

dételer (detle) *v.t. & abs*, to unharness; unyoke; ease off, stop.

détendre (detɑ̃ːdr) *v.t, & abs. & se* ~, to unbend, slack[en], relax, expand; take down.

détenir (detniːr) *v.t.ir*, to hold; detain.

détente (detɑ̃ːt) *f*, relaxation; expansion; trigger.

détenteur, trice (detɑ̃tœːr, tris) *n*, holder (*pers.*). **détention** (sjɔ̃) *f*, holding; detention, detainment. **détenu, e** (tny) *n*, prisoner.

détergent (deterʒɑ̃) *a*, detergent (*Med.*). ¶ *m*, detergent, cleansing product.

détérioration (deterjɔrasjɔ̃) *f*, deterioration, impairment, damage, dilapidation. **se détériorer** (re) *v.pr*, to deteriorate.

détermination (detɛrminasjɔ̃) *f*, determination; resolution; resolve. **déterminé, e** (ne) *a*, determinate, definite; determined, resolute; keen; specific. **déterminer** (ne) *v.t*, to determine; fix; decide (upon); resolve; bring about. **se ~**, to resolve, make up one's mind.

déterrer (detɛre) *v.t*, to unearth, dug up; disinter, exhume.

détestable (detɛstabl) *a*, detestable. **détester** (te) *v.t*, to detest, hate.

détonation (detɔnasjɔ̃) *f*, detonation, report. **détoner** (ne) *v.i*, to detonate.

détonner (detɔne) *v.i*, to be (*or* sing) (*or* play) out of tune; sing flat; jar; be out of keeping; be out of one's element.

détordre (detɔrdr) *v.t*, to untwist. **détors, e** (tɔːr, ɔrs) *a*, untwisted. **détortiller** (tɔrtije) *v.t*, to untwist; disentangle.

détour (detuːr) *m*, winding; turn-[ing]; detour; dodge. **sans ~**, straightforwardly. **détourné, e** (turne) *a*, by (*road*); roundabout, circuitous, devious. **détourner** (ne) *v.t*, to divert, deflect, distract, turn aside, avert; deter; twist; dissuade; make away with, misappropriate, misapply, embezzle, peculate; abduct. **détournement** (nəmɑ̃) *m*, diversion, etc.

détracteur (detraktœːr) *m*, detractor.

détraquer (detrake) *v.t*, to derange.

détrempe (detrɑ̃ːp) *f*, distemper (*paint*); softening (*steel*). **peindre à la ~**, to distemper. **détremper** (trɑ̃pe) *v.t*, to soak, sodden, dilute; soften.

détresse (detrɛs) *f*, distress; straits.

détriment (detrimɑ̃) *m*, detriment, prejudice.

détritus (detrityːs) *m*, detritus; litter, rubbish.

détroit (detrwa) *m*, strait, straits, sound. *le ~ de Gibraltar, du Pas de Calais*, the Straits of Gibraltar, of Dover.

détromper (detrɔ̃pe) *v.t*, to undeceive.

détrôner (detrone) *v.t*, to dethrone.

détrousser (detruse) *v.t*, to rob. **détrousseur** (sœːr) *m*, footpad.

détruire (detrɥiːr) *v.t. & abs. ir*, to demolish; destroy; ruin. •

dette (dɛt) *f*, debt; indebtedness. **~ [active]**, assets. **~ [passive]**, liabilities.

deug or D.E.U.G. (døg) *m*, diploma (*diplôme d'études universitaires générales*); similar to that of community or junior college.

deuil (dœːj) *m*, mourning; bereavement; mourners. *conduire le ~*, to be chief mourner. *~ de veuve*, widow's weeds.

Deutéronome (døterɔnɔm) *m*, Deuteronomy.

deux (dø; *in liaison* døz) *a*, two; second; a (*word, line*); a few (*steps*). *tous les ~ jours*, every other day. *~ jumeaux, elles*, twins. ¶ *m*, two; deuce (*cards, dice*). **deuxième**† (døzjɛm) *a. & n*, second. *~ de change, f*, second of exchange.

deux-points (døpwɛ̃) *m*, colon.

dévaler (devale) *v.i. & t*, to go down.

dévaliser (devalize) *v.t*, to rifle, strip, rob.

dévaluation (devalɥasjɔ̃) *f*, devaluation.

devancer (dəvɑ̃se) *v.t*, to get the start of; precede; forestall; outstrip, outdo, outrival. **devancier, ère** (sje, ɛːr) *n*, predecessor.

devant (dəvɑ̃) *ad*, before, in front, ahead. ¶ *pr*, before, in front of, ahead of. *aller au-de*, to go to meet; anticipate. *par-~, ad. & pr*, in front, before, in the presence of. ¶ *m*, front; fore; frontage; (*pl.*) foreground.

devanture (d[ə]vãty:r) *f*, front (*store, etc.*); window (*store*).

dévastateur, trice (devasta- tœ:r, tris) *n*, devastator. **dé- vastation** (sjɔ̃) *f*, devastation. **dévaster** (te) *v.t*, to devastate.

déveine (devɛn) *f*, bad luck.

développateur (devlɔpatœ:r) *m*, developer (*proper*) (*Phot.*). **dé- veloppement** (pmɑ̃) *m*, opening out; spread; growth; develop- ment; evolution (*Geom.*); gear (*bicycle*). **développer** (pe) *v.t*, to open out; unwrap; develop.

devenir (dəvni:r) *v.i.ir*, to be- come; grow; wax; go; get.

dévergondage (devɛrgɔ̃da:ʒ) *m*, licentiousness; extravagance (*fig.*). **dévergondé, e** (de) *a. & n*, licentious, shameless, profli- gate (*person*).

déverrouiller (devɛruje) *v.t*, to unbolt.

devers (dəvɛ:r): *par~, pr*, by, before.

dévers, e (devɛ:r, ɛrs) *a*, out of plumb, out of true. ¶ *m*, cant. **déverser** (vɛrse) *v.t*, to warp; in- cline; discharge; pour. **déversoir** (swa:r) *m*, weir.

dévêtir (se) (devɛti:r) *v.pr.ir*, to strip, undress; leave off some of one's (*warm*) clothes.

déviation (devjasjɔ̃) *f*, deviation; deflection; detour. ~ *de la co- lonne vertébrale*, curvature of the spine.

dévider (devide) *v.t*, to wind, reel; unwind. **dévidoir** (dwa:r) *m*, reel, spool.

dévier (devje) *v.i*, to deviate, swerve; curve (*spine*); (*v.t.*) to deflect, curve.

devin, ineresse (dəvɛ̃, vinrɛs) *n*, diviner, soothsayer. **deviner** (vine) *v.t, & abs*, to divine; guess. **devinette** (nɛt) *f*, riddle, conundrum.

devis (dəvi) *m*, chat, talk; esti- mate; specification; manifest (*stowage*).

dévisager (devizaʒe) *v.t*, to stare at.

devise (dəvi:z) *f*, device; motto. ~ [*étrangère*], [foreign] currency, [f.] bill, [f.] exchange. ~ *publi- citaire*, slogan.

deviser (dəvize) *v.i*, to chat.

dévisser (devise) *v.t*, to unscrew.

dévoiement (devwamɑ̃) *m*, looseness (*bowels*).

dévoiler (devwale) *v.t*, to un- veil; reveal, disclose.

devoir (dəvwa:r) *m*, duty; exer- cise; (*pl.*) homework; (*pl.*) re- spects. ¶ *v.t. & abs. ir*, to owe. *Followed by infinitive*: should, ought; must, have to; am to.

dévolu, e (devɔly) *a*, devolved, vested.

dévorant, e (devɔrɑ̃, ɑ̃:t) *a*, ravenous; consuming; wasting; devouring. **dévorer** (re) *v.t*, to devour, lap up; swallow; sti- fle.

dévot, et (devo, ɔt) *a*, devout, devotional; religious; sancti- monious. ¶ *n*, devout person; devotee. **dévotion** (vosjɔ̃) *f*, de- votion, devoutness.

dévouement (devumɑ̃) *m*, de- votion, self-sacrifice. **dévouer** (vwe) *v.t*, to dedicate; devote.

dévoyer (se) (devwaje) *v.pr*. (*Conjugated like envoyer, ex- cept Future je dévoierai*), to go astray (*fig.*).

dextérité (dɛksterite) *f*, dexter- ity, skill.

dextrine (dɛkstrin) *f*, dextrin.

diabète (djabɛt) *m*, diabetes.

diable (dja:bl) *m*, devil, deuce; dolly, truck. ¶ *i*, the devil! the deuce! the dickens! *au* ~ *vauvert*, a long way off, to hell and gone. **diablerie** (djablǝri) *f*, devilry, devilment. **diablesse** (blɛs) *f*, she- devil. **diablotin** (blɔtɛ̃) *m*, little devil, imp. **diabolique†** (bɔlik) *a*, diabolic(al), devilish, fiendish.

diabolo (djabɔlo) *m*, dolly, twin- wheel assembly (*automotive*).

diacre (djakr) *m*, deacon.

diacritique (djakritik) *a*, dia- critical.

diadème (djadɛm) *m*, diadem.

diagnostic (djagnɔstik) *m*, diag- nosis. **diagnostiquer** (ke) *v.t*, to diagnose.

diagonal, e† (djagɔnal) *a. & f*, diagonal.

diagramme (djagram) *m*, dia- gram, chart.

dialecte (djalɛkt) *m*, dialect.

dialectique (djalɛktik) *f*, dialectics.

dialogue (djalɔg) *m*, dialogue. **dialoguer** (ge) *v.i*, to converse; write in dialogue. **dialogiste** (gist) *m*, scriptwriter, screenwriter.

diamant (djamɑ̃) *m*, diamond.

diamétral, e† (djametral) *a*, diametric. **diamètre** (mɛtr) *m*, diameter.

diane (djan) *f*, reveille (*Mil.*).

diantre (djɑ̃:tr) *m*, the deuce.

diapason (djapazɔ̃) *m*, diapason, pitch; compass, range. ~ *à bouche*, pitch pipe. ~ *à branches*, tuning fork. ~ *normal*, concert pitch.

diaphane (djafan) *a*, diaphanous.

diaphragme (djafragm) *m*, diaphragm; stop.

diapositive (djapozitiv) *f*, color slide, transparency. (*sometimes* **diapo** (djapo) *f*.).

diaprer (djapre) *v.t*, to diaper, variegate. *étoffe diaprée*, diaper.

diarrhée (djare) *f*, diarrhea.

diatonique (djatɔnik) *a*, diatonic.

diatribe (djatrib) *f*, diatribe.

dictateur (diktatœ:r) *m*, dictator. **dictatorial**, e (tɔrjal) *a*, dictatorial. **dictature** (ty:r) *f*, dictatorship.

dictée (dikte) *f*, dictation. **dicter** (te) *v.t. & abs*, to dictate. **diction** (sjɔ̃) *f*, diction, delivery. **dictionnaire** (ɔnɛ:r) *m*, dictionary. ~ *géographique*, gazetteer. **dicton** (tɔ̃) *m*, saying, dictum; saw, byword.

didactique (didaktik) *a*, didactic.

dièse (djɛ:z) *m*, sharp (*Mus.*).

diète (djɛt) *f*, diet. ~ *absolue*, starvation d. **mettre à la** ~, *v.t*, **faire** ~, *v.i*, to diet.

Dieu (djø) *m*, God; goodness! **d~**, god.

diffamation (difamasjɔ̃) *f*, defamation, libel, slander. **diffamatoire** (twa:r) & **diffamant**, e (mɑ̃, ɑ̃:t) *a*, defamatory, etc. **diffamer** (me) *v.t*, to defame, malign.

différé (difere) *a*, deferred; off-line (*computers*). *émission en* ~, prerecorded broadcast.

différemment (diferamɑ̃) *ad*, differently. **différence** (rɑ̃:s) *f*, difference; odds. **différencier** (rɑ̃sje) *v.t*, to differentiate. **différend** (rɑ̃) *m*, difference, dispute. **différent**, e (rɑ̃, ɑ̃:t) *a*, different, various. **différentiel, le** (rɑ̃sjɛl) *a. & m*, differential. **différer** (re) *v.t. & abs*, to defer, delay, put off, postpone, hold over, tarry; (*v.i.*) to differ; be at variance.

difficile (difisil) *a*, difficult, hard; fastidious; trying. **difficilement** (lmɑ̃) *ad*, with difficulty. **difficulté** (kylte) *f*, difficulty; tiff. **difficultueux, euse** (tɥø, ø:z) *a*, troublesome; fussy.

difforme (difɔrm) *a*, deformed, misshapen, unshapely. **difformité** (mite) *f*, deformity.

diffus, e (dify, y:z) *a*, diffused; diffuse; long-winded, wordy. **diffuser** (fyze) *v.t*, to diffuse; broadcast. **diffusion** (zjɔ̃) *f*, diffusion; broadcasting; long-windedness, wordiness.

digérer (diʒere) *v.t. & abs*, to digest; brook, stomach. *je ne digère pas la viande*, meat does not agree with me. **digestible** (ʒɛstibl) *a*, digestible. **digestif, ive** (tif, i:v) *a. & m*, digestive. **digestion** (tjɔ̃) *f*, digestion.

digicode (diʒikɔd) *m*, coded pushbutton system for controlling access to buildings, rooms, etc.

digital, e (diʒital) *a*, digital, finger (*att.*). ¶ *f*, foxglove; digitalis (*Phar.*).

digne (diɲ) *a*, worthy; deserving; dignified. **dignement** (ɲimɑ̃) *ad*, worthily, with dignity; adequately. **dignitaire** (ɲitɛ:r) *m*, dignitary. **dignité** (te) *f*, dignity; rank.

digression (digrɛsjɔ̃) *f*, digression.

digue (dig) *f*, dike, dam; sea wall; barrier (*fig.*).

dilapider (dilapide) *v.t*, to squander; misappropriate.

dilater (dilate) *v.t*, to dilate; expand; swell.

dilemme (dilɛm) *m*, dilemma.

dilettante (dilettɑ̃:t) *m*, dilettante, amateur.

diligemment (diliʒamɑ̃) *ad*,

diligently. **diligence** (3ɑ̃:s) *f*, diligence; industry; despatch; proceedings, suit (*law*); stage coach. **diligent, e** (3ɑ̃, ɑ̃:t) *a*, diligent; industrious; expeditious.

diluer (dilɥe) *v.t*, to dilute; water (*stock, Fin.*).

diluvien, ne (dilyvjɛ̃, ɛn) *a*, diluvial; torrential (*rain*).

dimanche (dimɑ̃:ʃ) *m*, Sunday, sabbath. ~ *des Rameaux*, Palm Sunday.

dime (di:m) *f*, tithe.

dimension (dimɑ̃sjɔ̃) *f*, dimension, size, measurement; particularity, aspect.

diminuer (diminɥe) *v.t. & i*, to diminish, decrease, reduce, abate, lower; taper; get thin. *aller en diminuant*, to taper. *entièrement diminué*, fully fashioned (*stocking*). **diminutif, ive** (nytif, i:v) *a*, diminutive (*Gram.*). ¶ *m*, diminutive (*Gram.*); miniature. **diminution** (sjɔ̃) *f*, diminution, etc., as *diminuer*.

dinanderie (dinɑ̃dri) *f*, brasswares; kitchen utensils. **dinandier** (dje) *m*, brazier.

dinatoire (dinatwa:r) *a*, substantial (*lunch*).

dinde (dɛ̃:d) *f*, turkey [hen]; goose (*fig.*). **dindon** (dɛ̃dɔ̃) *m*, turkey [cock]; goose (*fig.*); dupe. **dindonneau** (dɔno) *m*, turkey poult.

diner (dine) *m*, dinner. ¶ *v.i*, to dine. **dinette** (nɛt) *f*, little dinner; doll's dinner party. **dineur, euse** (nœ:r, ø:z) *n*, diner.

dingue (dɛ̃:g) *a*, loony, cracked (*slang*). ¶ *m*, a loony, madcap, nut (*person*).

diocésain, e (djɔsezɛ̃, ɛn) *a*, diocesan. **diocèse** (sɛ:z) *m*, diocese.

dioptrie (diɔptri) *f*, diopter.

diphtérie (difteri) *f*, diphtheria.

diphtongue (diftɔ̃:g) *f*, diphthong.

diplomate (diplɔmat) *m*, diplomat[ist]; (*att.*) diplomatic. **diplomatie** (si) *f*, diplomacy. **diplomatique** (tik) *a*, diplomatic. **diplôme** (plo:m) *m*, diploma, certificate. **diplômé, e** (plome) *a. & n*, certified (*teacher, etc.*).

dire (di:r) *m*, saying, assertion; allegation. ¶ *v.t.ir*, to say; tell;

speak; bid (*adieu, etc.*); mean. ~ *son fait à quelqu'un*, to give someone a piece of one's mind. *dites donc!* look here!

direct, e (dirɛkt) *a*, direct; straight; through (*Rly.*); flat (*contradiction*). *un direct du droit, du gauche*, a straight right, left (*Box.*). *en* ~, live (*TV, etc.*); on-line (*computers*). **directement** (təmɑ̃) *ad*, directly, direct; straight; due; through.

directeur, trice (dirɛktœ:r, tris) *n*, manager; principal, headmaster, headmistress; editor; director; warden; leader. [*arbitre*] ~ *de combat*, referee (*Box.*). ~ *de conscience*, spiritual director. ~ *général des postes, télégraphes & téléphones*, postmaster general. ~ *de production*, production manager, associate producer (*cinema*). ~ *de salle*, movie theater manager. **direction** (sjɔ̃) *f*, direction; strike (*lode*); way; management; manager's office; guidance; lead[ership]; mastership; steering. **Directoire** (twa:r) *m*, Directory; Directoire. **dirigeable** (riʒabl) *a*, dirigible. ¶ *m*, airship, dirigible. **diriger** (ʒe) *v.t*, to direct; manage; steer; train (*gun*). *se* ~, to make, steer (*vers* = for). **dirigisme** (ʒism) *m*, planning; state control. ~ *économique*, planned economy.

discernement (disɛrnəmɑ̃) *m*, discrimination; discernment. **discerner** (ne) *v.t*, to discern; distinguish; discriminate.

disciple (disipl) *m*, disciple, follower. **disciplinaire** (plinɛ:r) *a*, disciplinary. ¶ *m*, disciplinarian. **discipline** (plin) *f*, discipline. **discipliner** (ne) *v.t*, to discipline.

discontinuer (diskɔ̃tinɥe) *v.t*, to discontinue.

disconvenance (diskɔ̃vnɑ̃:s) *f*, dissimilarity, disparity. **disconvenir** (vni:r) *v.i.ir*, to deny. ~ *de*, to gainsay.

discordance (diskɔrdɑ̃:s) *f*, discordance, disagreement; lack of harmony, difference. **discorde** (kɔrd) *f*, discord, strife, contention.

discourir (diskuri:r) *v.i. & abs. ir*, to discourse, descant. **discours**

(ku:r) *m*, talk; discourse, speech, oration, address. ~ *d'apparat*, set speech.

discourtois, e (diskurtwa, a:z) *a*, discourteous. **discourtoisie** (twazi) *f*, discourtesy.

discrédit (diskredi) *m*, discredit, disrepute. **discréditer** (te) *v.t*, to discredit.

discret, ète† (diskrɛ, ɛt) *a*, discreet; unobtrusive; unpretentious; discrete. **discrétion** (kresjɔ̃) *f*, discretion; secrecy. *à* ~, as much as you want.

discrimination (diskriminasjɔ̃) *f*, discrimination.

disculper (diskylpe) *v.t*, to exculpate.

discursif, ive (diskyrsif, i:v) *a*, discursive. **discussion** (kysjɔ̃) *f*, discussion; debate; question, dispute. **discutable** (tabl) *a*, debatable, arguable, moot. **discuter** (te) *v.t. & abs. & v.i*, to discuss, debate, argue; controvert; auction off to pay debts.

disert, e (dizɛ:r, ɛrt) *a*, fluent.

disette (dizɛt) *f*, dearth, scarcity. ~ *d'argent*, penury. ~ *d'eau*, drought.

diseur, euse (dizœ:r, ø:z) *n*, talker. ~ *de bonne aventure*, fortune teller. ~ *de bons mots*, wit. ~ *de chansonnettes*, entertainer, humorist (*at concert*).

disgrâce (disgra:s) *f*, disgrace, disfavor; misfortune. **disgracier** (grasje) *v.t*, to dismiss from favor, disgrace. **disgracieux, euse** (sjø, ø:z) *a*, uncouth, ungraceful.

disjoindre (disʒwɛ̃:dr) *v.t.ir*, to disjoin.

disjoncteur (dizʒɔ̃ktœ:r) *m*, switch, circuit-breaker.

dislocation (dislɔkasjɔ̃) *f*, dislocation; dismemberment; dispersal (*troops, convoy*).

disloquer (dislɔke) *v.t*, to dislocate, put out of joint; dismember; break up; dislodge. **dislocation** (kasjɔ̃) *f*, dislocation; breakaway.

dispache (dispaʃ) *f*, average adjustment (*Insce.*).

disparaître (disparɛ:tr) *v.i.ir*, to disappear, vanish.

disparate (disparat) *a*, disparate,

ill-assorted. ¶ *f*, incongruity. **disparité** (rite) *f*, disparity.

disparition (disparisjɔ̃) *f*, disappearance. **les disparus** (ry) *m.pl*, the missing (*soldiers*).

dispendieux, euse (dispɑ̃djø, ø:z) *a*, expensive, costly.

dispensaire (dispɑ̃sɛ:r) *m*, dispensary. **dispensateur, trice** (satœ:r, tris) *n*, dispenser. **dispense** (pɑ̃:s) *f*, dispensation; exemption. ~ *de bans*, marriage license. **dispenser** (pɑ̃se) *v.t*, to dispense, exempt, excuse, spare.

disperser (dispɛrse) *v.t*, to disperse, scatter. *ordre dispersé*, extended order (*Mil.*). **dispersion** (sjɔ̃) *f*, dispersion, dispersal.

disponibilité (dispɔnibilite) *f*, availability; (*pl.*) available funds, liquid assets. *en* ~, unattached (*Mil.*). **disponible** (bl) *a*, available, spare, disposable; liquid; on hand; unattached; in print.

dispos, e (dispo, o:z) *a*, fit, well, hearty; good (*humor*). **disposer** (poze) *v.t*, to dispose; arrange; lay out; incline; provide; draw (*bill*). **dispositif** (pozitif) *m*, purview (*law*); device, arrangement, contrivance, gear. ~ *à 3 vitesses*, 3-speed gear. ~ *de fortune*, ~ *de circonstance*, makeshift. ~*s de mines*, preparatory work (*Min.*). ~ *passe-vues*, slide changer. **disposition** (sjɔ̃) *f*, disposition, ordering, arrangement; lie; layout; tendency; tone; frame of mind; state; humor; aptitude, flair; disposal; provision (*of a law*); dispensation (*of Providence*); draft (*Fin.*).

disproportion (disprɔpɔrsjɔ̃) *f*, disproportion. **disproportionné, e** (ɔne) *a*, disproportionate.

disputailler (dispytaje) *v.i*, to wrangle, bicker. **dispute** (pyt) *f*, dispute; contest; contention. **disputer** (te) *v.i. & t*, to dispute; contend; vie; contest. **se** ~, to wrangle.

disqualifier (diskalifje) *v.t*, to disqualify (*sport*).

disquaire (diskɛ:r) *m*, phonograph record dealer. **disque** (disk) *m*, disk, disc, discus; wheel; phonograph record. ~ *de sta*-

tionnement, parking disk (*for use in a* zone bleue—*limited parking area*). **disquette** (ɛt) *f*, floppy disk, diskette (*computers*).

dissection (disɛksjɔ̃) *f*, dissection.

dissemblable (disɑ̃blabl) *a*, dissimilar. **dissemblance** (blɑ̃:s) *f*, dissimilarity.

disséminer (disemine) *v.t*, to disseminate; scatter.

dissension (disɑ̃sjɔ̃) *f*, dissension.

dissentiment (disɑ̃timɑ̃) *m*, dissent, disagreement.

disséquer (diseke) *v.t*, to dissect.

dissertation (disɛrtasjɔ̃) *f*, dissertation, disquisition, essay.

dissidence (disidɑ̃:s) *f*, dissidence, dissent. **dissident, e** (dɑ̃, ɑ̃:t) *a*, dissentient; dissenting. ¶ *n*, dissentient; dissenter.

dissimilaire (disimilɛ:r) *a*, dissimilar.

dissimulé, e (disimyle) *a*, secretive. **dissimuler** (le) *v.t. & abs*, to dissimulate; dissemble; conceal.

dissipateur, trice (disipatœ:r, tris) *n. & a*, spendthrift. **dissipation** (sjɔ̃) *f*, dissipation; extravagance. **dissiper** (pe) *v.t*, to dissipate; dispel; disperse; scatter; fritter away.

dissocier (disɔsje) *v.t*, to dissociate.

dissolu, e (disɔly) *a*, dissolute, profligate. **dissolution** (sjɔ̃) *f*, dissolution; solution; dissoluteness. **dissolvant, e** (vɑ̃, ɑ̃:t) *a. & m*, [dis]solvent.

dissonance (disɔnɑ̃:s) *f*, dissonance; discord. **dissonant, e** (nɑ̃, ɑ̃:t) *a*, dissonant, discordant.

dissoudre (disudr) *v.t.ir*, to dissolve.

dissuader (disɥade) *v.t*, to dissuade.

dissuasion (disɥazjɔ̃) *f*, dissuasion. *la force de* ~, dissuasive military power. *arme de* ~, military deterrent.

dissyllabe (disilab) *m*, disyllable.

dissymétrique (disimetrik) *a*, unsymmetrical.

distance (distɑ̃:s) *f*, distance; range; way [off]. *garder ses* ~*s* (*fig.*), to keep one's distance. *commande à* ~, remote control. **distancer** (tɑ̃se) *v.t*, to [out] distance. **distanciation** (tɑ̃sjasjɔ̃) *f*, alienation effect (*Theat.*). **distant, e** (tɑ̃, ɑ̃:t) *a*, distant; aloof.

distendre (distɑ̃:dr) *v.t*, to distend.

distillateur (distilatœ:r) *m*, distiller. **distillation** (sjɔ̃) *f*, distillation; distillate. **distiller** (le) *v.t*, to distil; exude. **distillerie** (lri) *f*, distillery.

distinct, e† (distɛ̃:kt) *a*, distinct; clear, plain. **distinctif, ive** (tɛ̃ktif, i:v) *a*, distinctive. **distinction** (sjɔ̃) *f*, distinction. **distingué, e** (tɛ̃ge) *a*, distinguished; refined; gentlemanly; ladylike. **distinguer** (ge) *v.t*, to distinguish; discriminate; make out; single out.

distique (distik) *m*, distich; couplet.

distorsion (distɔrsjɔ̃) *f*, distortion.

distraction (distraksjɔ̃) *f*, distraction; absence of mind; appropriation; severance; amusement, hobby. **distraire** (trɛ:r) *v.t.ir*, to distract; appropriate; set aside; take away, t. off; amuse. **distrait, e†** (trɛ, ɛt) *a*, absentminded; listless, vacant.

distribuer (distribɥe) *v.t*, to distribute; give out; deal out; issue; deliver (*letters*); arrange; cast (*actors' parts*). **distributeur, trice** (bytœ:r, tris) *n*, distributor; gasoline pump. *distributeur automatique*, automatic [delivery] machine, slot machine. **distribution** (sjɔ̃) *f*, distribution; issue; allotment; delivery (*post*); valve gear; arrangement, layout. ~ *de prix*, prize giving; speech day. ~ *des aumônes*, almsgiving. ~ [*des rôles*], cast[ing] (*Theat.*). ~ *par coulisse*, link motion.

district (distrikt) *m*, district, field.

dito (dito) (*abb.* dᵒ) *ad*, ditto, do.

diurne (djyrn) *a*, diurnal.

diva (diva) *f*, prima donna, diva.

divagation (divagasjɔ̃) *f*, digression; wandering, rambling. **divaguer** (ge) *v.i*, to digress.

divan (divɑ̃) *m*, divan; settee.

divergence (diverʒãːs) *f*, divergence. **divergent, e** (ʒã, ãːt) *a*, divergent. **diverger** (ʒe) *v.i*, to diverge.

divers, e† (diveːr, ɛrs) *a*, different, diverse; sundry, miscellaneous; various, many. **diversifier** (versifje) *v.t*, to diversify, vary. **diversion** (sjɔ̃) *f*, diversion. **diversité** (site) *f*, diversity, variety, difference. **divertir** (tiːr) *v.t*, to divert; amuse, entertain. *se ~ aux dépens de*, to make fun of, make merry over. **divertissement** (tismã) *m*, diversion; amusement, entertainment; divertissement.

divette (divɛt) *f*, variety actress.

dividende (dividãːd) *m*, dividend.

divin, e† (divɛ̃, in) *a*, divine; godlike. **divination** (vinasjɔ̃) *f*, divination. **diviniser** (nize) *v.t*, to deify. **divinité** (te) *f*, divinity, godhead; deity.

diviser (divize) *v.t*, to divide; part. **diviseur** (zœːr) *m*, divisor. **division** (zjɔ̃) *f*, division; department; hyphen (*end of line*).

divorce (divɔrs) *m*, divorce. **divorcer** (se) *v.i*, to be divorced. *~ d'avec*, to divorce.

divulguer (divylge) *v.t*, to divulge, blab.

dix (*in liaison*, diz; *before consonant or 'h,'* di) *a*, ten. ¶ (dis) *m*, ten; 10th. *~-huit* (dizɥit) *bef. cons. or 'h,'* ɥi) *a. &*, eighteen; 18th. *~-huitième* (tjɛm) *a. & n*, eighteenth. **dixième†** (dizjɛm) *a. & n*, tenth; tenth of a lottery ticket. **dix-neuf** (dizncɛf; *in liaison*, nœv; *bef. cons. or 'h,'* nœ) *a. & m*, nineteen; 19th. **dix-neuvième** (vjɛm) *a. & n*, nineteenth. **dix-sept** (disset) *bef. cons. or 'h,'* sɛ) *a. & m*, seventeen; 17th. **dix-septième** (tjɛm) *a. & n*, seventeenth.

dizain (dizɛ̃) *m*, ten-line stanza. **dizaine** (zɛn) *f*, ten [or so], about ten; ten; decade.

do (do) (*Mus.*) *m*, C.

docile† (dɔsil) *a*, docile, amenable, ductile. **docilité** (lite) *f*, docility.

dock (dɔk) *m*, dock; dock warehouse, warehouse, store. *~ fri-*

gorifique, cold store. **docker** (kɛːr) *m*, docker. .

docte† (dɔkt) *a*, learned. **docteur** (tœːr) *m*, doctor. **doctoral, e†** (tɔral) *a*, doctoral; pompous; grandiloquent. **doctorat** (ra) *m*, doctorate.

doctrinaire (dɔktrinɛːr) *m. & a*, doctrinaire. **doctrine** (trin) *f*, doctrine, tenet.

document (dɔkymã) *m*, document. *~s à l'appui*, supporting documents. **documentaire** (tɛːr) *a*, documentary. **documenter** (te) *v.t*, to document.

dodeliner (dɔdline) *v.t*, to rock, dandle. *~ de*, to wag (*head*).

dodo (dɔdo) *m*, bye-bye; cot.

dodu, e (dɔdy) *a*, plump, rotund.

dogmatique† (dɔgmatik) *a*, dogmatic. **dogmatiser** (ze) *v.i*, to dogmatize. **dogme** (dɔgm) *m*, dogma; tenet.

dogue (dɔg) *m*, watchdog; mastiff. bear (*fig., pers.*).

doigt (dwa) *m*, finger; digit; thimbleful, nip (*liquor*). *~ [de pied]*, toe. *à deux ~s de*, within an ace of. **doigté** (dwate) *m*, fingering (*Mus.*); diplomacy, tact. **doigter** (te) *v.i. & t*, to finger (*Mus.*). **doigtier** (tje) *m*, fingerstall.

doit (dwa) *m*, debit [side], debtor [side].

dol (dɔl) *m*, wilful misrepresentation.

doléance (dɔleãːs) *f*, complaint, grievance. **dolent, e** (lã, ãːt) *a*, doleful; painful; out of sorts.

dollar (dɔlaːr) *m*, dollar.

domaine (dɔmɛn) *m*, domain, demesne, estate; property; land; province.

dôme (doːm) *m*, dome; canopy.

domesticité (dɔmɛstisite) *f*, service; [staff of] servants, household; domesticity. **domestique** (tik) *a*, domestic, home. ¶ *n*, servant, domestic; man[servant]; maid[servant]. **domestiquer** (ke) *v.t*, to domesticate.

domicile (dɔmisil) *m*, residence, abode, house, premises, domicile. *franco à ~*, free delivery. **domicilier** (lje) *v.t*, to domicile.

dominant, e (dɔminã, ãːt) *a*, dominant, ruling; prevailing. ¶

f, dominant (*Mus.*). **dominateur, trice** (natœːr, tris) *n*, ruler; (*att.*) ruling; domineering. **domination** (sjɔ̃) *f*, domination; dominion; rule, sway. ~ *de la lie du peuple*, mob law. **dominer** (ne) *v.i. & t*, to dominate; overlook; tower above; rule; domineer.

dominicain, e (dɔminikɛ̃, ɛn) *n*, Dominican.

dominical, e (dɔminikal) *a*, dominical; Sunday (*rest*); Lord's (*prayer*).

domino (dɔmino) *m*, domino.

dommage (dɔmaːʒ) *m*, damage, injury, loss; pity (*regret*). ~*s-intérêts*, damages (*law*).

dompter (dɔ̃te) *v.t*, to tame; break in; subdue. **dompteur, euse** (tœːr, øːz) *n*, tamer.

don (dɔ̃) *m*, bestowal; gift; present; donation; dower; knack. **donataire** (dɔnatɛːr) *n*, donee. **donateur, trice** (tœːr, tris) *n*, donor. **donation** (sjɔ̃) *f*, donation, gift.

donc (dɔ̃; *in liaison or emphatically*, dɔ̃ːk) *c*, therefore, then, hence, so; to be sure.

dondon (dɔ̃dɔ̃) *f*, bouncing girl; plump woman.

donjon (dɔ̃ʒɔ̃) *m*, keep (*castle*).

donnant, e (dɔnɑ̃, ɑ̃ːt) *a*, generous. **donnant donnant**, *ad*, give & take, tit for tat. **donne** (dɔn) *f*, deal (*cards*). **donnée** (ne) *f*, datum; fundamental idea, motif. **donner** (ne) *v.t*, to give, bestow; impart, afford; tender; make; let; yield, give up; show; teach (*someone a lesson*); set (*task*); perform (*play*); deal (*cards*); (*v.i.*) to strike, hit; fall; run; sag. ~ *sur*, to face, front, look on, give on, overlook (*street, etc.*). ~ *dans le piège*, to fall into the trap. **donneur, euse** (nœːr, øːz) *n*, giver; donor; dealer (*cards*). ~ *d'ordre*, principal.

Don Quichotte (dɔ̃kiʃɔt) *m*, Quixote, champion (*of lost causes*).

dont (dɔ̃) *pn*, whose; of whom; of *or* from *or* by whom *or* which; whereof; as per.

donzelle (dɔ̃zɛl) *f*, wench.

doper (dɔpe) *v.t*, to dope; boost (*Elec.*); add power to.

dorade (dɔrad) *f*, dorado, dolphin; goldfish. **doré, e** (re) *a*, gilt, gilded; golden. ~ *sur tranche*, gilt-edged. **dorée,** *f*, [John] dory.

dorénavant (dɔrenavɑ̃) *ad*, henceforth.

dorer (dɔre) *v.t*, to gild; block (*Bookb.*); glaze (*pastry*). **doreur, euse** (rœːr, øːz) *n*, gilder; blocker.

dorique (dɔrik) *a. & m*, Doric.

dorloter (dɔrlɔte) *v.t*, to coddle; pamper.

dormant, e (dɔrmɑ̃, ɑ̃ːt) *a*, sleeping, dormant, still, standing, stagnant. ¶ *m*, casing, frame. **dormeur, euse** (mœːr, øːz) *n*, sleeper. ¶ *f*, lounge chair; stud earring; sleeping suit. **dormir** (miːr) *v.i.ir*, to sleep, be asleep; lie dormant. ~ *comme une souche*, to sleep like a log. **dormitif** (mitif) *m*, sleeping draft.

dorsal, e (dɔrsal) *a*, dorsal.

dortoir (dɔrtwaːr) *m*, dormitory.

dorure (dɔryːr) *f*, gilding; blocking (*Bookb.*); gilt; glazing (*pastry*).

dos (do) *m*, back; back, spine (*book*); bridge (*nose*). *en* ~ *d'âne*, hogbacked.

dose (doːz) *f*, dose, measure. **doser** (doze) *v.t*, to proportion, measure out, dose.

dossier (dosje) *m*, back; bundle (*papers*); dossier; brief (*law*); record.

dot (dɔt) *f*, dowry, dower, [marriage] portion. **dotal, e** (tal) *a*, dowral, dotal. **dotation** (sjɔ̃) *f*, endowment. **doter** (te) *v.t*, to dower, portion; endow.

douairière (dwɛrjɛːr) *f*, dowager.

douane (dwan) *f*, customs; custom house. **douanier, ère** (nje, ɛːr) *a*, customs (*att.*). ¶ *m*, customs officer.

doublage (dublaːʒ) *m*, doubling; lining; sheathing (*ship*). **double** (bl) *a*, double; twofold; dual; double-dealing. ~ *croche*, *f*, semiquaver. ~ *emploi*, *m*, duplication. *à* ~ *face*, double-faced. ~ *fond*, *m*, false bottom. ¶ *ad*, double; in duplicate. ¶ *m*, double; duplicate, counterpart. ~ *messieurs*, *dames, mixte,* men's, women's, mixed, doubles (*Ten.*). **doublement** (bləmᾶ) *ad,* doubly. ¶ *m,* doubling. **doubler** (ble) *v.t,* to double; understudy; overtake; line; sheathe; weather (*cape*); dub (*movies*); (*v.i.*) to double. *noɳ doublé, e,* unlined. *doublé or,* rolled gold. **doublure** (bly:r) *f,* lining; understudy; stunt person (*cinema*).

douceâtre (dusɑ:tr) *a,* sweetish.
doucement (smᾶ) *ad,* gently; softly; sweetly; slowly; gingerly; quietly; peacefully; smoothly, easily; so-so; pretty well. **doucereux, euse** (srø, ø:z) *a,* mawkish, sickly; mealy-mouthed, smooth-tongued. **douceur** (sœ:r) *f,* sweetness; softness; gentleness; mildness; meekness; pleasure; (*pl.*) dainties, sweets; soft nothings.
douche (duʃ) *f,* shower (*bath*); douche. **doucher** (ʃe) *v.t,* to shower; douche.
doucine (dusin) *f,* ogee.
douer (dwe) *v.t,* to endow, endue, gift.
douille (du:j) *f,* socket, holder; case (*cartridge*).
douillet, te† (duje, ɛt) *a,* soft, downy; cosy.
douleur (dulœ:r) *f,* pain, ache; throe; sorrow, grief, woe. **douloureux, euse†** (lurø, ø:z) *a,* painful; sore; mournful, grievous, sad.
doute (dut) *m,* doubt, misgiving. **douter** (te) *v.i. & abs,* to doubt, question. ~ *de,* to doubt, question (*v.t.*). *se* ~ *de,* to suspect. **douteux, euse†** (tø, ø:z) *a,* doubtful, dubious, questionable.
douve (du:v) *f,* stave (*cask*); ditch (*Agric.*); moat (*castle*); water jump (*turf*); water hazard (*golf*).
Douvres (du:vr) *m,* Dover.
doux, ouce (du, us) *a,* sweet; soft; dulcet; gentle; mild; meek; quiet (*horse*); smooth; easy; pleasant; fresh (*water*). *tout doux,* gently. *en douce,* on the q.t. *le doux,* the sweet (*opp.* the bitter).
douzaine (duzɛn) *f,* dozen. **douze** (du:z) *a. & m,* twelve;

12th. **douzième†** (duzjɛm) *a. & n,* twelfth.
doyen, ne (dwajɛ, ɛn) *n,* dean; doyen; senior. **doyenné** (jɛne) *m,* deanery.
drachme (drakm) *f,* drachma.
dragage (draga:ʒ) *m,* dredging; dragging; sweeping (*for mines*).
dragée (draʒe) *f,* sugar almond; pill; birdshot.
drageon (draʒɔ̃) *m,* sucker (*Bot., Hort.*).
dragon (dragɔ̃) *m,* dragon; dragoon; termagant, virago.
drague (drag) *f,* dredge[r]; drag; d. net; grains, draff. **draguer** (ge) *v.t,* to dredge, drag, sweep; to go looking for women; cruise for sexual partners. **dragueur** (gœ:r) *m,* dredger (*pers. & boat*). ~ *de mines,* mine sweeper.
drain (drɛ̃) *m,* drain; d. pipe. **drainage** (drɛna:ʒ) *m,* drainage; drain (*demand*). **drainer** (ne) *v.t,* to drain.
dramatique† (dramatik) *a,* dramatic; operatic. **dramatiser** (ze) *v.t,* to dramatize. **dramatiste** (tist) *m,* **dramaturge** (tyrʒ) *n,* dramatist, playwright, dramaturge. **drame** (dram) *m,* drama; tragedy, sensational affair. ~ *pleureur,* sob-stuff.
drap (dra) *m,* cloth; sheet; pickle (*fig.*). ~ *mortuaire,* pall. ~ *vert,* green baize. *être dans le beau* ~*s,* to be in a nasty situation. **drapeau** (po) *m,* flag, colors. **draper** (pe) *v.t,* to drape; pillory (*fig.*). **draperie** (pri) *f,* drapery; cloth trade; bunting. **drapier** (pje) *m,* draper, clothier, cloth merchant; cloth manufacturer.
drastique (drastik) *a,* drastic.
drawback (drobak) *m,* drawback (*Cust.*).
drêche (drɛʃ) *f,* grains, draff.
drelin-drelin (drəlɛ̃) tinkle! tinkle!
drenne (drɛn) *f,* missel thrush.
Dresde (drɛzd) *f,* Dresden.
dresser (drɛse) *v.t,* to erect, raise, set up, rear; prick up (*ears*); pitch (*tent*); set (*trap*); draw up, make out, prepare; make (*bed,* etc.); lay (*table*); trim; dish up; true, straighten, dress, face; train; drill; break in. **dresseur**

(sœːr) *m*, trainer (*animals*). **dressoir** (swaɪr) *m*, sideboard.

drille (driːj) *m*, fellow. ¶ *f*, drill, brace; (*pl.*) rags (*for paper-making*).

drisse (dris) *f*, halyard.

drogman (drɔgmɑ̃) *m*, dragoman.

drogue (drɔg) *f*, drug; nostrum; trash; worthless person. **droguer** (ge) *v.t*, to physic; drug; (*v.i.*) to wait, cool one's heels. **droguerie** (gri) *f*, druggist's business; drugstore.

droguet (drɔgɛ) *m*, drugget.

droguiste (drɔgist) *m*, druggist (*wholesale*); drysalter.

droit, e (drwa, at) *a*, straight; upright, erect, plumb; straightforward, honest; right, right-hand[ed]; single-breasted. **droit**, *ad*, straight; s. on; due (*south, etc.*) **droit**, *m*, right; due, duty, fee; law; reason. ~*s d'adaptation au cinéma*, film rights. ~ *d'aînesse*, ~ *du sang*, birthright. ~ *d'auteur*, copyright; royalty. ~ *de cité*, citizenship. ~*s de douane*, customs duties. ~*s de reproduction dans les journaux & périodiques*, serial rights. ~ *de rétention*, lien. ~*s de succession*, inheritance taxes. ~ *de vendre*, license to sell. *de* ~, de jure. *faire son* ~, to study law. **droite**, *f*, right hand, r. side; right. *à* ~, on (*or* to) the right. **droitement** (tmɑ̃) *ad*, uprightly, righteously. **droitier, ère** (tje, ɛːr) *n*, right-handed person *or* player; rightist (*Pol.*). **droiture** (tyːr) *f*, uprightness, straightforwardness, rectitude.

drolatique (drɔlatik) *a*, comic, humorous. **drôle†** (droːl) *a*, funny, humorous, droll; queer, odd. *un ~ de corps*, a queer fellow, an oddity. ¶ *m*, funny (*queer*) man; rascal. **drôlerie** (drolri) *f*, drollery, fun. **drôlesse** (lɛs) *f*, hussy.

dromadaire (drɔmadɛːr) *m*, dromedary.

drome (drɔm) *f*, raft.

dru, e (dry) *a*, thick; sturdy. **dru**, *ad*, thick[ly].

drugstore (drœgstɔr) *m*, store selling a variety of items (*books, cosmetics, records*) and often in-cluding a bar or restaurant. Not a "drugstore" in the American sense ("*pharmacie*").

druide (drɥid) *m*, Druid.

dryade (driad) *f*, dryad.

dû, due (dy) *p.p. & p.a*, due; owing; forward (*carriage*); proper. ¶ *m*, due (*right*).

dualité (dyalite) *f*, duality.

duo (dyk) *m*, duke. **ducal, e** (kal) *a*, ducal. **duché** (ʃe) *m*, duchy; dukedom. **duchesse** (ʃɛs) *f*, duchess.

ductile (dyktil) *a*, ductile.

duègne (dɥɛɲ) *f*, duenna.

duel (dɥel) *m*, duel. **duelliste** (list) *m*, duellist.

dûment (dymɑ̃) *ad*, duly, properly.

dune (dyn) *f*, dune, sand hill, down.

dunette (dynɛt) *f*, poop; poop deck.

Dunkerque (dœ̃kɛrk) *m*, Dunkirk.

duo (dyo) *m*, duet.

duodécimal, e (dyɔdesimal) *a*, duodecimal.

dupe (dyp) *f*, dupe, gull. **duper** (pe) *v.t*, to dupe, gull, take in, fool. **duperie** (pri) *f*, dupery, trickery, take-in. **dupeur, euse** (pœːr, øːz) *n*, trick[st]er.

duplicata (dyplikata) *m*, duplicate.

duplicité (dyplisite) *f*, duplicity; double dealing.

duquel *see* **lequel**.

dur, e (dyːr) *a*, hard; tough; hardened, inured; dire; harsh; hardboiled (*egg*).

durable (dyrabl) *a*, durable, lasting, abiding.

durant (dyrɑ̃) *pr*, during, for.

durcir (dyrsiːr) *v.t. & i. & se* ~, to harden. **durcissement** (sismɑ̃) *m*, hardening.

dure (dyːr) *f*, bare ground.

durée (dyre) *f*, duration, length, life.

durement (dyrmɑ̃) *ad*, hard; harshly.

durer (dyre) *v.i. & abs*, to last; hang heavy (*time*); hold out, stand; live.

dureté (dyrte) *f*, hardness; tough-

ness; harshness. ~ *d'oreille*, hardness of hearing.

durillon (dyrijɔ̃) *m*, callus, hard
skin.

duvet (dyvɛ) *m*, down; nap.
duveté, e (vte) *a*, downy, fluffy.

dynamique (dinamik) *a*, dynamic. ¶ *f*, dynamics.

dynamite (dinamit) *f*, dynamite.

dynamo (dinamo) *f*, dynamo.
~-électrique (mɔ) *a*, dynamo-
electric.

dynastie (dinasti) *f*, dynasty.

dysenterie (disɑ̃tri) *f*, dysentery.

dyspepsie (dispɛpsi) *f*, dyspepsia.

E

eau (o) *f*, water; rain. ~ *bénite de
cour*, fair promises, empty words.
~ *de boudin* (odbudɛ̃), thin air,
smoke (*fig.*). ~ *de cale*, bilge
water. ~-*de-vie* (odvi), brandy. ~
douce, fresh water. ~ *dentifrice*,
mouthwash. ~-*forte*, aqua fortis;
etching. ~ *minérale* [*artificielle*],
mineral [water]. ~ *minérale* [*naturelle*], mineral w.; table w. *de la
plus belle* ~, of the finest water
(*gem*); of the deepest dye (*fig.*).
être en ~, to be in a sweat. *faire*
~, to make water, leak. *faire de
l'*~, to [take in] water.

eaux (o) *f.pl*, waters, water; fountains; watering place, spa; tide;
wake (*ship*). *marcher dans les*
~ *de*, to follow in the wake of
(*Naut. & fig.*). ~ *à marée*, tidal
water. ~ *d'égout*, sew[er]age. ~
ménagères, slops. ~-*vannes*,
waste water; sewage [water]. ~
vives, spring tide.

ébahir (ebaiːr) *v.t*, to dumbfound, amaze.

ébarber (ebarbe) *v.t*, to take the
burr off; trim (*edges*); wipe
(*joint*).

ébattre (s') (ebatr) *v.pr.ir.* ou
prendre ses ébats (eba), to frolic,
gambol; hop about.

ébaubi, e (ebobi) *a*, dumbfounded.

ébauche (eboːʃ) *f*, [rough] sketch,
draft, outline. **ébaucher** (boʃe)
v.t, to sketch [out], draft; rough
out; rough down.

ébène (ebɛn) *f*, ebony. **ébénier**
(benje) *m*, ebony [tree]. **ébéniste**
(nist) *m*, cabinetmaker. **ébénisterie** (tri) *f*, cabinetmaking; cab-
inetwork.

éberluer (eberlye) *v.t*, to amaze,
astound; hoodwink.

éblouir (ebluiːr) *v.t. & abs*, to
dazzle, glare.

ébonite (ebɔnit) *f*, ebonite, vulcanite.

éborgner (ebɔrɲe) *v.t*, to blind in
one eye; disbud; shut out view
from.

éboueur (ebuœːr) *m*, streetcleaner; scavenger.

ébouillanter (ebujɑ̃te) *v.t*, to
plunge into boiling water; scald.

éboulement (ebulmɑ̃) *m*, falling
in, caving in; fall, slip. **ébouler**
(le) *v.i*, to fall in, cave in, slip.
éboulis (li) *m*, fall (*earth*).

ébourgeonner (eburʒɔne) *v.t*, to
disbud.

ébouriffer (eburife) *v.t*, to di-
shevel, ruffle, tousle; stagger.

ébouter (ebute) *v.t*, to cut off
the end of.

ébrancher (ebrɑ̃ʃe) *v.t*, to lop.

ébranlement (ebrɑ̃lmɑ̃) *m*,
shaking; shock, concussion; tottering; jangle. **ébranler** (le) *v.t*,
to shake; jangle. *s'*~, to shake,
totter; move off.

ébraser (ebraze) *v.t*, to splay.

ébrécher (ebreʃe) *v.t*, to chip,
jag; break (*jaw*); make a hole in
(*fortune*).

ébriété (ebriete) *f*, drunkenness.

ébrouer (s') (ebrue) *v.pr*, to
sneeze (*animals*); snort.

ébruiter (ebrɥite) *v.t*, to noise
abroad.

ébullition (ebylisjɔ̃) *f*, boiling,
ebullition; turmoil; whirl.

écacher (ekaʃe) *v.t*, to crush; flatten.

écaille (ekaːj) *f*, scale; flake;
chip; shell. ~ [*de tortue*], tortoise shell. **écailler** (kaje) *v.t*, to
scale; open (*oysters*). *s'*~, to
scale, flake; peel [off]. **écailler,
ère** (je, ɛːr) *n*, oysterman,
-woman. **écailleux, euse** (jø, øːz)
a, scaly, flaky.

écale (ekal) *f*, shell; pod. **écaler**
(le) *v.t*, to shell.

écarbouiller (ekarbuje) *v.t*, to crush, squash.

écarlate (ekarlat) *f. & a*, scarlet.

écarquiller (ekarkije) *v.t*, to open wide (*eyes*). ~ *les yeux*, to stare.

écart (eka:r) *m*, variation, difference; error; digression; flight; straddling; strain (*Vet.*). *faire un* ~, to side-step; (*horse*) shy. *à l'*~, aside, on one side; aloof. *à l'*~ *de*, at some distance from. **écarté, e** (karte) *p.a*, out-of-the-way, remote, secluded, lonely. **écarté**, *m*, écarté (*cards*).

écarteler (ekartəle) *v.t*, to quarter.

écartement (ekartəmɑ̃) *m*, spreading; distance apart; d. between; gauge (*Rly.*). ~ *des essieux*, wheelbase. **écarter** (te) *v.t*, to separate, spread, open; turn (*or* push) aside *or* out of the way; avert, ward off; divert; discard (*cards*). **s'**~, to stand aside; deviate; wander, stray, swerve.

Ecclésiaste (l') (ɛklezjast) *m*, Ecclesiastes. **ecclésiastique**† (tik) *a*, ecclesiastical, clerical. ¶ *m*, ecclesiastic, clergyman, cleric. l'**E**~, Ecclesiasticus.

écervelé, e (esɛrvəle) *a*, giddy, hare-brained. ¶ *n*, madcap.

échafaud (eʃafo) *m*, scaffold, stage. **échafaudage** (da:ʒ) *m*, scaffolding; structure, fabric (*fig.*). **échafauder** (de) *v.i*, to erect a scaffold; (*v.t.*) to build up (*fig.*).

échalas (eʃalɑ) *m*, pole (*hop, etc.*); prop, stick. **échalasser** (se) *v.t*, to pole, prop.

échalier (eʃalje) *m*, stile; hurdle fence.

échalote (eʃalɔt) *f*, shallot, eschalot.

échancrer (eʃɑ̃kre) *v.t*, to cut away (*neck of garment*); notch, indent. *col très échancré*, very low neck. **échancrure** (kry:r) *f*, (*neck*) opening; notch; indentation.

échange (eʃɑ̃:ʒ) *m*, exchange, barter; interchange. *quelques* ~s, practice (*Ten.*). **échanger** (ʃɑ̃ʒe) *v.t*, to exchange; barter.

échanson (eʃɑ̃sɔ̃) *m*, cupbearer.

échantillon (eʃɑ̃tijɔ̃) *m*, sample; dimension, size, section; pattern (*of stuff, etc.*), specimen, taste. **échantillonner** (ɔne) *v.t*, to sample, cut of a pattern from; gauge; tram (*tapestry work*).

échappatoire (eʃapatwa:r) *f*, loophole; evasion. **échappé, e** (pe) *n*, runaway. ~ *de prison*, escaped prisoner. **échappée** (pe) *f*, prank; snatch; spell; turning space; headroom. ~ [*de vue*], vista; glimpse, peep. **échappement** (pmɑ̃) *m*, exhaust, release (*steam*); escape, leak (*gas, etc.*); escapement (*Horol.*); turning space, headroom. **échapper** (pe) *v.i. & abs*, to escape, run away; slip; (*v.t.*) to escape. *l'*~ *belle*, to have a narrow escape. *laisser* ~, to overlook. **s'**~, to escape; leak; fly off; vanish; forget oneself.

écharde (eʃard) *f*, splinter, prickle.

écharpe (eʃarp) *f*, scarf; stole; sash; sling. *en* ~, scarfwise; aslant; in a sling. **écharper** (pe) *v.t*, to cut to pieces, hack; lynch.

échasse (eʃa:s) *f*, stilt; pole (*scaffold*). **échassier** (ʃasje) *m*, wader (*bird*).

échauder (eʃode) *v.t*, to scald. **s'**~, (*fig.*), to burn one's fingers.

échauffé, e (eʃofe) *n*, hothead (*pers.*). **échauffement** (fmɑ̃) *m*, heating; overheating. **échauffer** (fe) *v.t*, to heat; overheat; warm; parboil (*fig.*); excite. **s'**~, to get warm *or* heated *or* overheated *or* excited. **échauffourée** (fure) *f*, affray, brush.

échéance (eʃeɑ̃:s) *f*, due date; date [payable]; maturity; tenor; term, currency; expiration. *à courte* ~, short-term loan. *venir à* ~, to fall due. *le cas échéant* (ʃeɑ̃), in that case, should it so happen.

échec (eʃek) *m*, check, failure, repulse; (*pl.*) chess; chessmen. ¶ *i*, check! ~ & *mat*, checkmate. *faire quelqu'un* ~ & *mat*, to checkmate someone.

échelle (eʃel) *f*, ladder; scale. ~ *à coulisse*, extension ladder. ~ *de sauvetage*, fire escape. ~ *double*, [pair of] steps. ~ *mobile*, sliding scale. ~s *du Levant*, Levantine ports. *faire la courte* ~, to give a helping hand. **éche-**

lori (ʃlɔ̃) *m*, rung, round; step, stepping stone (*fig.*); echelon (*Mil.*). **échelonner** (ʃlɔne) *v.t*, to spread; echelon.

écheniller (eʃnije) *v.t*, to clear of caterpillars; remove undesirables (*things, people*); polish (*text, etc.*).

écheveau (eʃvo) *m*, skein, hank.

échevelé, e (eʃəvle) *a*, disheveled (*hair*).

échine (eʃin) *f*, spine, backbone; chine. **échinée** (ne) *f*, chine (*Cook.*). **échiner** (ne) *v.t*, to break (*someone's*) back; belabor. **s'~**, to break one's back; slave.

échiquier (eʃikje) *m*, chessboard; intricacies.

écho (eko) *m*, echo; (*pl.*) news items (*in paper*). **faire ~**, to echo (*v.i.*). **se faire l'~ de**, to echo (*v.t.*).

échoir (eʃwaːr) *v.i.ir*, to fall, devolve; fall due, mature; expire. *intérêts à ~*, accruing interest.

échoppe (eʃɔp) *f*, stall, booth.

échotier (ekɔtje) *m*, gossip columnist.

échouer (eʃwe) *v.i. & t. & s'~*, to strand, ground, beach; fail; miscarry, fall through. *échoué à sec*, high & dry (*Naut.*).

échu, e (eʃy) *p.a*, due, outstanding, owing; matured.

éclabousser (eklabuse) *v.t*, to splash, [be]spatter. **éclaboussure** (syːr) *f*, splash, spatter.

éclair (eklɛːr) *m*, flash [of light]; [flash of] lightning; flash; glint, gleam. *~ au chocolat*, chocolate éclair. *~[s] de chaleur*, heat lightning, summer l. *~ diffus*, *~ en nappes*, sheet l. *~ ramifié*, forked l. **éclairage** (klɛraːʒ) *m*, lighting, illumination; light. *~ par projection*, flood lighting. **éclairant, e** (rɑ̃, ɑ̃ːt) *a*, lighting.

éclaircie (eklɛrsi) *f*, break, opening, rift; bright interval (*Meteor.*); clearing, glade; thinning out. **éclaircir** (siːr) *v.t*, to clear, c. up; brighten; thin, t. out; elucidate, enlighten.

éclairé, e (eklɛre) *p.p*, enlightened. **éclairer** (re) *v.t. & abs*, to light [up], lighten, illuminate, illumine; throw light upon; clear up; enlighten; reconnoiter (*Mil.*);

(*v.i.*) to shine; (*v.imp.*) to lighten (*emit lightning*). **éclaireur** (rœːr) *m*, scout; boy scout. **éclaireuse** (røːz) *f*, girl scout.

éclanche (eklɑ̃ːʃ) *f*, shoulder of mutton.

éclat (ekla) *m*, splinter; chip; fragment; burst, roar, shout; peal, clap; noise, scandal; shake (*timber*); brilliancy, radiancy, brightness; flash; glare; glamour. *faire un ~*, to make a stir. *rire aux ~s*, to laugh heartily. **éclatant, e** (tɑ̃, ɑ̃ːt) *a*, bright, brilliant, shining; piercing, shrill; splendid; striking, glaring, signal. **éclatement** (tmɑ̃) *m*, bursting, explosion. **éclater** (te) *v.i*, to burst, explode, blow up; fly; split; splinter; break out; burst out; shine, flash.

éclectique (eklɛktik) *a*, eclectic. **éclectisme** (tism) *m*, eclecticism.

éclipse (eklips) *f*, eclipse. **éclipser** (se) *v.t*, to eclipse; outshine, overshadow. **s'~**, to become eclipsed; vanish. **écliptique** (tik) *a. & f*, ecliptic.

éclisse (eklis) *f*, split-wood; splint (*Surg.*); fish[plate] (*Rly.*). **éclisser** (se) *v.t*, to fish[plate].

éclopé, e (eklɔpe) *a*, footsore, lame, crippled.

éclore (eklɔːr) *v.i.ir*, to hatch; open (*flower*); come to light. **éclosion** (klozjɔ̃) *f*, hatching; opening.

écluse (eklyːz) *f*, (*canal*) lock; lock gate; floodgate (*fig.*). **éclusée** (klyze) *f*, (*lock*) feed; locking, lockage. **écluser** (ze) *v.t*, to lock; shut off. **éclusier, ère** (zje, ɛːr) *n*, lock keeper.

écœurer (ekœre) *v.t*, to sicken, nauseate.

école (ekɔl) *f*, school, college; drill, training; blunder. *~ de peloton*, squad drill. *~ maternelle*, nursery school. *~ normale*, normal school, training college (*teachers*). *~ pratique*, technical school. *~ professionelle*, training center (*trade*). **écolier, ère** (lje, ɛːr) *n*, schoolboy, -girl, pupil, scholar; tyro.

écologie (ekɔlɔʒi) *f*, ecology. **écologique** (ʒik) *a*, ecologic.

éconduire (ekɔ̃dɥiːr) *v.t.ir*, to show out; put off (*with excuse*).

économat (ekɔnɔma) *m*, stewardship, bursarship; bursar's office; store. **économe** (nɔm) *a*, economical, thrifty, sparing. ¶ *n*, steward; bursar; housekeeper. **économie** (mi) *f*, economy, thrift, saving; management; arrangement. ~ *de bouts de chandelle*, cheeseparing. ~ *domestique*, domestic economy, housekeeping. ~ *politique*, political economy. ~ *rurale*, husbandry. **économique†** (mik) *a*, economical; economic. **économiser** (ze) *v.t. & abs.*, to economize, save. **économiste** (mist) *m*, economist.

écope (ekɔp) *f*, scoop, bailer. **écoper** (pe) *v.t*, to bail (*or* bale) [out]; (*v.i.*) to catch it (*suffer*).

écoperche (ekɔperʃ) *f*, scaffold pole.

écorce (ekɔrs) *f*, bark; peel, rind, skin; crust (*earth's*); surface (*fig.*). **écorcer** (se) *v.t*, to bark; peel.

écorcher (ekɔrʃe) *v.t*, to flay, skin; abrade, graze, scrape, gall, chafe; grate on (*ears*); fleece (*fig.*). **écorcheur, euse** (ʃœːr, øːz) *n*, shark, extortioner; (*m.*) knacker. **écorchure** (ʃyːr) *f*, abrasion, gall, graze, scrape.

écorner (ekɔrne) *v.t*, to break off a horn *or* corner; chip; dogear; curtail.

écornifler (ekɔrnifle) *v.t*, to cadge; sponge on.

écornure (ekɔrnyːr) *f*, chip.

écossais, e (ekɔsɛ, ɛːz) *a*, Scotch, Scottish. **É~**, *n*, Scotchman, -woman, Scot. **l'Écosse** (kɔs) *f*, Scotland, North Britain.

écosser (ekɔse) *v.t*, to shell, hull.

écot (eko) *m*, share; score; reckoning; lopped tree; stick, fagot.

écoulement (ekulmɑ̃) *m*, flow, outflow; drainage; discharge; gleet; passing; placing, sale. **écouler** (le) *v.t*, to place, sell. **s'~**, to flow out *or* away, run off; disperse; pass (*or* slip) away, elapse; sell.

écourter (ekurte) to cut short; crop, dock; curtail.

écoute (ekut) *f*, sheet (*Naut.*); listening post. **aux écoutes**, on the watch *or* lookout. **écouter**

(te) *v.t. & abs*, to listen to, listen, hearken; listen in; hear. ~ *aux portes*, to eavesdrop. *s'~ trop*, to coddle oneself. **écouteur, euse** (tœːr, øːz) *n*, listener. ~ *aux portes*, eavesdropper. ¶ *m*, receiver, earpiece (*Teleph.*). **écouteux** (tø) *a.m*, skittish (*horse*).

écoutille (ekutiːj) *f*, hatch[way].

écouvillon (ekuvijɔ̃) *m*, mop; sponge (*gun*); swab (*Med.*).

écrabouiller (ekrabuje) *v.t*, to crush, squash.

écran (ekrɑ̃) *m*, screen; filter (*Phot.*); shade. ~ *à pied*, fire screen. ~ *fumigène* (fymiʒɛn), smoke screen.

écrasé, e (ekrɑze) *p.a*, squat. **écraser** (ze) *v.t*, to crush; squash; run over; overwhelm. *en ~*, to sleep very soundly. *s'~*, to collapse, crumple up, crash.

écrémer (ekreme) *v.t*, to cream, skim.

écrevisse (ekrəvis) *f*, crayfish, crawfish (*river*).

écrier (s') (ekrie) *v.pr*, to exclaim, cry; c. out.

écrin (ekrɛ̃) *m*, case, jewel case, casket. ~ *manucure*, manicure set.

écrire (ekriːr) *v.t. & abs. ir*, to write; spell. ~ *à la machine*, to type. **écrit** (kri) *m*, writing; document. **écrit, e** (kri, it) *p.p*, written; w. on; statute (*law*). **écriteau** (to) *m*, bill, notice; n. board. **écriture** (tyːr) *f*, writing; handwriting. ~ *à la machine*, typewriting, typing. ~ *de pattes de mouche*, crabbed handwriting. *l'Écriture* [*sainte*] *ou les* [*saintes*] *Écritures*, [Holy] Scripture, the Scriptures, Holy Writ. **écrivailler** (vɑje) *ou* **écrivasser** (vase) *v.i*, to scribble (*of author*). **écrivailleur, euse** (vɑjœːr, øːz) *ou* **écrivassier, ère** (vasje, ɛːr) *n*, scribbler, hack, penny-a-liner. **écrivain** (vɛ̃) *m*, writer, author.

écrou (ekru) *m*, nut; entry (*in prison register*). ~ *à huit pans*, octagonal nut. ~ *à oreilles*, ~ *papillon*, wing n. ~ *à six pans*, hexagonal n. **écrouer** (krue) *v.t*, to enter (*in prison register*).

écroulement (ekrulmɑ̃) *m*, collapse. **s'écrouler** (le) *v.pr*, to collapse, give way.

écru, e (ekry) *a*, raw; unbleached.

écu (eky) *m*, shield; escutcheon; (*pl.*) money.

écueil (ekœːj) *m*, reef, rock, shelf; pitfall; cause of downfall.

écuelle (ekyɛl) *f*, bowl; porringer. **écuellée** (le) *f*, bowlful.

éculer (ekyle) *v.t*, to wear down (*shoe*) at heel.

écume (ekym) *f*, foam; froth; lather; scum, dross, skimmings. ~ **de mer**, [sea] wrack; meerschaum. **écumer** (me) *v.i*, to foam, froth; (*v.t.*) to skim [off], scum; scour, rove (*seas*); pick up (*news*). **écumeux, euse** (mø, øːz) *a*, foamy, frothy. **écumoire** (mwaːr) *f*, skimmer.

écurer (ekyre) *v.t*, to scour, cleanse, clean out.

écureuil (ekyrœːj) *m*, squirrel.

écurie (ekyri) *f*, stable, (*pl.*) mews; stud (*racing*).

écusson (ekysɔ̃) *m*, [e]scutcheon, shield, hatchment.

écuyer, ère (ekɥije, ɛːr) *n*, riding master; horseman, -woman; rider; equestrian; equerry; [e]squire (*Hist.*).

eczéma (egzema) *m*, eczema.

édelweiss (edɛlvajs *ou* -vɛs) *m*, edelweiss.

éden (edɛn) *m*, Eden (*fig.*). l'É~, [the Garden of] Eden.

édenté, e (edɑ̃te) *a*, toothless.

édicter (edikte) *v.t*, to decree, enact.

édicule (edikyl) *m*, kiosk, shelter; public convenience.

édification (edifikasjɔ̃) *f*, erection; edification. **édifice** (fis) *m*, edifice, building, structure. **édifier** (fje) *v.t*, to erect, build; b. up; edify; enlighten.

édile (edil) *m*, magistrate; aedile (*Hist.*). **édilité** (lite) *f*, magistrature.

Edimbourg (edɛ̃buːr) *m*, Edinburgh.

édit (edi) *m*, edict.

éditer (edite) *v.t*, to publish; edit. **éditeur, trice** (tœːr, tris) *n*, publisher; editor, tress. **édition** (sjɔ̃) *f*, edition; publishing. ~ **à tirage restreint**, limited edition.

édredon (edrədɔ̃) *m*, eiderdown.

éducateur, trice (edykatœːr, tris) *n*, educator. **éducation** (sjɔ̃) *f*, education; training; upbringing; rearing; nurture. **sans** ~, ill-bred. **éduquer** (ke) *v.t*, to bring up; train.

éfaufiler (efofile) *v.t*, to unravel.

effacé, e (efase) *p.a*, unobtrusive. **effacer** (se) *v.t*, to efface, obliterate, delete; erase, rub out, blot out, wipe out, expunge; outshine. **s'**~, to wear away; keep in the background; stand aside. **effaçure** (syːr) *f*, obliteration, deletion; erasure.

effarement (efarmɑ̃) *m*, fright. **effarer** (re) *v.t*, to scare, frighten. **effaroucher** (ruʃe) *v.t*, to startle, frighten away. **s'**~, to take fright.

effectif, ive† (efɛktif, iːv) *a*, effective; real; actual; in cash, in coin; paid up (*capital*). ¶ *m*, effective, strength, complement, force (*men*). **effectuer** (tɥe) *v.t*, to effect, carry out, make, execute.

efféminé, e (efemine) *a*, effeminate, womanish, unmanly, ladylike. ¶ *m*, effeminate [man]. **efféminer** (ne) *v.t*, to [make] effeminate.

effervescence (efɛrvesɑ̃ːs) *f*, effervescence, -ency; ferment (*fig.*), unrest. **effervescent, e** (sɑ̃, ɑ̃ːt) *a*, effervescent.

effet (efɛ) *m*, effect; action; purpose, avail; impression; screw, break, spin (*on ball*); negotiable instrument; bill [of exchange], bill or note, draft; (*pl.*) effects, goods, belongings, things; securities, stock[s & shares]. ~ **à payer**, **à recevoir**, bill payable, receivable. **à** ~, intended for effect. **en** ~, in fact, indeed.

effeuiller (efœje) *v.t*, to thin out, pluck (*leaves, petals, hopes*).

efficace† (efikas) *a*, efficacious; effectual; efficient; able; adequate. **efficacité** (site) *f*, efficacy; efficiency.

effigie (efiʒi) *f*, effigy.

effilé, e (efile) *a*, slender; slim; tapering, streamlined. ¶ *m*, fringe. **effiler** (le) *v.t*, to unravel. **s'effilocher** (lɔʃe) *v.pr*, to fray. **effilure** (lyːr) *f*, ravelings.

efflanqué, e (eflɑ̃ke) *p.a*, emaciated; lank[y].

effleurer (eflœre) *v.t*, to touch, t. on; graze; glance, skim; scratch.

effleurir (eflœri:r) *v.i. & s'~,* to effloresce. **efflorescence** (eflɔresɑ̃:s) *f*, efflorescence.

effluve (efly:v) *m*, effluvium.

effondrement (efɔ̃drəmɑ̃) *m*, fall; subsidence; collapse, downfall; slump. **effondrer** (dre) *v.t*, to break open, stave in. **s'~,** to fall in, cave in; collapse, slump. **effondrilles** (dri:j) *f.pl*, grounds, sediment.

efforcer (s') (eforse) *v.pr. & abs*, to endeavor, strive, do one's utmost. **effort** (fo:r) *m*, effort, exertion, endeavor; force; stress (*Mech*.); strain. *~ de traction*, pull.

effraction (efraksjɔ̃) *f*, housebreaking.

effraie (efrɛ) *f*, barn owl, screech owl.

effranger (efrɑ̃ʒe) *v.t*, to fray.

effrayant, e (efrɛjɑ̃, ɑ̃:t) *a*, dreadful, frightful. **effrayer** (je) *v.t*, to frighten, scare.

effréné, e (efrene) *a*, unbridled, unrestrained; frantic.

effriter (efrite) *v.t*, to exhaust. **s'~,** to crumble.

effroi (efrwɑ) *m*, fright, terror.

effronté, e (efrɔ̃te) *a*, shameless, brazen, impudent, barefaced. **effrontément** (mɑ̃) *ad*, shamelessly. **effronterie** (tri) *f*, effrontery.

effroyable† (efrwajabl) *a*, frightful; awful.

effusion (ɛfyzjɔ̃) *f*, effusion, outpouring; shedding; overflowing; effusiveness. *~ de sang*, bloodshed.

égal, e (egal) *a*, equal; even, level; equable; alike; [all] the same, all one. ¶ *n*, equal (*of pers.*). *à l'égal de*, like. **également** (lmɑ̃) *ad*, equally, alike. **égaler** (le) *v.t*, to equalize, make equal; equal; match. **égaliser** (lize) *v.t*, to equalize; level. **égalité** (te) *f*, equality; evens (*betting*); evenness; smoothness. *~ à rien*, love all (*Ten.*). *~ de points*, tie (*sport*). *~ de voix*, tie (*voting*). *à ~,* deuce (*40 all*) (*Ten.*).

égard (ega:r) *m*, regard, consid-

eration, respect; sake. *à l'~ de*, with regard (*or* respect) (*or* reference) to. *en ~ à*, considering.

égaré, e (egare) *a*, lost, stray[ed]; erring; wild (*eyes*). **égarer** (re) *v.t*, to mislead, misguide, lead astray; bewilder; mislay. **s'~,** to go astray, lose one's way; miscarry.

égayer (egɛje) *v.t*, to enliven, cheer [up], exhilarate. **s'~,** to make merry.

Égée (la mer) (eʒe), the Aegean sea.

égide (eʒid) *f*, aegis, wing.

églantier (eglɑ̃tje) *m*, wild (*or* dog) rose (*bush*). *~ odorant*, sweetbriar. **églantine** (tin) *f*, wild (*or* dog) rose (*flower*). *~ odorante*, sweetbriar, eglantine.

église (egli:z) *f*, church. *l'É~ anglicane* (ɑ̃glikan), the Church of England. *l'É~ d'État*, the established Church. *~ de monastère, ~ abbatiale* (abasjal), minster.

égoïsme (egɔism) *m*, egoism, selfishness. **égoïste†** (ist) *a*, egoistic(al), selfish. ¶ *n*, egoist.

égorger (egɔrʒe) *v.t*, to cut the throat of; butcher, slaughter; ruin.

égosiller (s') (egozije) *v.pr*, to shout (*or* sing) oneself hoarse.

égotisme (egɔtism) *m*, egotism. **égotiste** (tist) *a*, egotistic(al). ¶ *n*, egotist.

égout (egu) *m*, drainage (*surplus water*); drip[pings]; sewer, drain. **égoutier** (tje) *m*, sewerman. **égoutter** (te) *v.t. & i. & s'~,* to drain; drip. **égouttoir** (twa:r) *m*, drainer, draining rack; plate rack. **égoutture** (ty:r) *f*, drainings; drippings.

égratigner (egratiɲe) *v.t*, to scratch. **égratignure** (ɲy:r) *f*, scratch.

égrener (egrəne) *v.t*, to pick off; shell; gin (*cotton*); tell (*beads*). **s'~,** to seed.

égrillard, e (egrija:r, ard) *a*, ribald.

Égypte (l') (eʒipt) *f*, Egypt. **égyptien, ne** (sjɛ̃, ɛn) *a. & É~, n*, Egyptian. **égyptologie** (tɔlɔʒi) *f*, Egyptology. **égyptologue** (lɔg) *m*, Egyptologist.

eh (e) *i*, [h]ehl ~ *bienl* now then! well!

éhonté, e (eõte) *a*, shameless, barefaced.

eider (edɛːr) *m*, eider [duck].

éjaculation (eʒakylasjɔ̃) *f*, ejaculation (*fluid*); fervent prayer. **éjaculer** (le) *v.t.* & *i*, to ejaculate (*fluid*).

éjecteur (eʒɛktœːr) *m*, ejector.

élaborer (elabɔre) *v.t*, to elaborate; work out, evolve.

élagage (elagaːʒ) *m*, lopping; pruning; prunings. **élaguer** (ge) *v.t.*, to lop; prune.

élan (elɑ̃) *m*, bound, spring; dash, dart, rush, run[-up] (*jump.*); [out]burst; impetus, momentum; flight; glow; elk, moose, eland. *avec ~*, running (*jump, dive*). *sans ~*, standing (*j., d.*). **élancé, e** (se) *a*, slender, slim. **élancements** (smɑ̃) *m.pl*, shooting pains, twinges; yearning (*soul*). **élancer** (se) *v.i*, to throb, shoot. **s'~**, to bound, spring, leap, dash, dart.

élargir (elarʒiːr) *v.t*, to enlarge; broaden; widen; let out; extend; release (*prisoner*).

élasticité (elastisite) *f*, elasticity, spring[iness], resilience. **élastique** (tik) *a*, elastic, spring[y], resilient; bouyant. ¶ *m*, elastic.

Elbe(l'île d') (ɛlb) *f*, the Island of Elba. **l'Elbe**, *m*, the Elbe (*river*).

eldorado (ɛldɔrado) *m*, El Dorado.

électeur, trice (elɛktœːr, tris) *n*, elector, constituent. **élection** (sjɔ̃) *f*, election, polling. *~ de remplacement*, *~ partielle*, by-election. **électorat** (tɔra) *m*, franchise.

électricien (elɛktrisjɛ̃) *m*, electrician. **électricité** (site) *f*, electricity. **électrification** (fikasjɔ̃) *f*, electrification. **électrifier** (fje) *v.t*, to electrify. **électrique** (trik) *a*, electric(al). **électriser** (ze) *v.t*, to electrify, electrize; thrill. **électro-aimant** (trɔɛmɑ̃) *m*, electromagnet. **électrocuter** (kyte) *v.t*, to electrocute. **électrode** (trɔd) *f*, electrode. **électrolyse** (liːz) *f*, electrolysis. **électron** (trɔ̃) *m*,

electron. **électrotype** (tip) *m*, electrotype.

élégamment (elegamɑ̃) *ad*, elegantly, stylishly. **élégance** (gɑ̃ːs) *f*, elegance, stylishness. **élégant, e** (gɑ̃, ɑ̃ːt) *a*, elegant, stylish, fashionable. ¶ *n*, man, woman, of fashion.

élégie (eleʒi) *f*, elegy.

élément (elemɑ̃) *m*, element; (*pl.*) rudiments (*of a science, an art*); unit; cell (*Phys.*). **élémentaire** (tɛːr) *a*, elementary.

éléphant (elefɑ̃) *m*, elephant.

élevage (elvaːʒ) *m*, breeding, rearing, stock farming. **élévateur** (elevatœːr) *m*, elevator. **élévation** (sjɔ̃) *f*, elevation; raising; rise; eminence; height; loftiness; altitude. **élévatoire** (twaːr) *m*, elevator (*Surg.*). **élève** (elɛːv) *n*, pupil, student; rearing (*animal reared*). *~ de l'école navale*, naval cadet. ¶ *f*, breeding, rearing (*act*). **élevé, e** (elve) *p.a*, high; lofty; bred, brought up. **élever** (ve) *v.t*, to elevate, raise, lift; erect; bring up, rear, breed. **s'~**, to rise; arise. *s'~ à*, to reach, amount to. **éleveur** (lvœːr) *m*, grazier; breeder.

elfe (ɛlf) *m*, elf, brownie.

élider (elide) *v.t*, to elide.

éligible (eliʒibl) *a*, eligible.

élimer (elime) *v.t*, to wear threadbare.

éliminatoire (eliminatwaːr) *a*. & *f*, eliminating *or* trial (*heat*). **éliminer** (ne) *v.t*, to eliminate; weed out.

élingue (elɛ̃ːg) *f*, sling.

élire (eliːr) *v.t.ir*, to elect; return.

élision (elizjɔ̃) *f*, elision.

élite (elit) *f*, elite.

élixir (eliksiːr) *m*, elixir.

elle (ɛl) *pn*, she; her; it; herself. *~-même*, herself; itself. *~s, pl*, they; them. *~-mêmes*, themselves.

ellipse (elips) *f*, ellipse; ellipsis. **elliptique†** (tik) *a*, elliptic(al).

élocution (elɔkysjɔ̃) *f*, elocution.

éloge (elɔːʒ) *m*, eulogy, praise, encomium. **élogieux, euse†** (lɔʒjø, øːz) *a*, eulogistic.

éloigné, e (elwaɲe) *p.a*, distant, outlying, far [off *or* away], remote. **éloignement** (ɲmɑ̃) m, removal; estrangement; distance, remoteness; dislike. **éloigner** (ɲe) v.t, to remove; keep away; defer; estrange; disincline. s'~, to withdraw, go away; differ; swerve.

éloquemment (elɔkamɑ̃) ad, eloquently. **éloquence** (kɑːs) f, eloquence, oratory. **éloquent, e** (kɑ̃, ɑ̃ːt) a, eloquent.

Elseneur (elsənœːr) f, Elsinore.

élu, e (ely) n, elected member. *les élus*, the elect (*Relig.*).

élucider (elyside) v.t, to elucidate.

élucubration (elykybrasjɔ̃) f, lucubration.

éluder (elyde) v.t, to elude, evade, shirk.

élyme (elim) m, lyme-grass.

élysée & (*Myth.*) É~ (elize) m, Elysium. *l'É~*, the Élysée; Paris residence of French president. **élyséen, ne** (zeɛ̃, ɛn) a, Elysian.

émacié, e (emasje) a, emaciated.

émail (emaːj) m, enamel; e. ware; glaze. **émaillage** (majaː3) m, enameling. **émailler** (je) v.t, to enamel; glaze; stud; intersperse.

émanation (emanasjɔ̃) f, emanation, efflux, effluence.

émanciper (emɑ̃sipe) v.t, to emancipate. s'~, to overstep the mark (*fig.*), forget oneself.

émaner (emane) v.i, to emanate, issue.

émarger (emar3e) v.t, to sign [in the margin]; draw (*salary*); trim the margins of.

émasculer (emaskyle) v.t, to emasculate.

emballage (ɑ̃balaː3) m, packing; spurt, burst (*speed*). **emballement** (lmɑ̃) m, bolting (*horse*); racing (*Mach.*); boom (*Stk Ex.*); excitement. **emballer** (le) v.t, to pack [up], wrap [up]; pack off, bundle off; carry away (*fig.*). s'~, to bolt; race; be carried away. **emballeur** (lœːr) m, packer.

embarcadère (ɑ̃barkadɛːr) m, landing [place or stage]; wharf; platform (*Rly.*). **embarcation** (sjɔ̃) f, craft, boat, launch.

embardée (ɑ̃barde) f, lurch,

[sudden] swerve; yaw. *faire une* ~, to yaw; swerve; catch a crab (*boating*).

embargo (ɑ̃bargo) m, embargo.

embarquement (ɑ̃barkəmɑ̃) m, embarkation; shipment; entrainment. **embarquer** (ke) v.t. & s'~, to embark; ship; entrain; (*v.i.*) to ship water, ship a sea. s'~ *clandestinement*, to stow away.

embarras (ɑ̃bara) m, obstruction, block, jam; traffic jam; encumbrance; inconvenience; superfluity; airs (*affectation*); perplexity, fix, quandary, embarrassment; straits; difficulty; scrape. ~ *de la langue*, impediment of speech, i. in one's s. *faire des* ~, to be fussy. **embarrassant, e** (sɑ̃, ɑ̃ːt) a, cumbersome; awkward, embarrassing. **embarrasser** (se) v.t, to obstruct, block [up]; [en]cumber, hamper; be in the way of; entangle; embarrass, perplex, nonplus.

embâter (ɑ̃bɑte) v.t, to saddle.

embaucher (ɑ̃boʃe) v.t, to engage, take on (*workmen*). *bureau d'embauche*, hiring office. **embauchoir** (ʃwaːr) m, shoe tree.

embaumer (ɑ̃bome) v.t, to embalm; perfume, scent.

embéguiner (ɑ̃begine) v.t, to muffle up; infatuate.

embellie (ɑ̃bɛli) f, lull. **embellir** (liːr) v.t, to embellish, beautify; improve; (*v.i.*) to grow more beautiful.

emberlificoter (ɑ̃bɛrlifikɔte) v.t, to entangle.

embesogné, e (ɑ̃bəzɔɲe) a, very busy.

embêtant, e (ɑ̃bɛtɑ̃) a, annoying, boring.

embêter (ɑ̃bɛte) v.t, to annoy; bore.

emblée (d') (ɑ̃ble) ad, at the very outset, right away, straight off.

emblématique (ɑ̃blematik) a, emblematic(al). **emblème** (blɛːm) m, emblem; attribute.

embob[el]iner (ɑ̃bɔb[l]ine) v.t, to wheedle, coax.

emboîter (ɑ̃bwate) v.t, to fit

in[to], box, nest, house; socket.
embolie (ăbɔli) *f*, embolism.
embonpoint (ăbɔ̃pwɛ̃) *m*, stoutness, plumpness, flesh.
emboucher (ăbuʃe) *v.t*, to put to one's mouth; blow. *mal embouché*, foul-mouthed. **embouchoir** (ʃwaːr) *m*, mouthpiece; shoe tree. **embouchure** (ʃyːr) *f*, mouthpiece; mouth.
embouer (ăbwe) *v.t*, to muddy.
embourber (ăburbe) *v.t*, to bog, mire; involve. s'~, to stick in the mud.
embourgeoiser (s') (ăburʒwaze) *v.pr*, to marry into (*or* mix with) the middle classes.
embout (ăbu) *m*, ferrule; capping.
embouteillage (ăbutejaːʒ) *m*, bottling (*wine, etc*.); bottling up (*harbor*); traffic jam. **embouteiller** (eje) *v.t*, to bottle; b. up; block.
embouter (ăbute) *v.t*, to ferrule, tip.
emboutir (ăbutiːr) *v.t*, to shape, stamp, press; ferrule.
embranchement (ăbrɑ̃ʃmɑ̃) *m*, branching [off]; junction (*Rly*.). ~ *particulier*, private siding (*Rly*.). **embrancher** (ʃe) *v.t*, to branch off.
embrasement (ăbrazmɑ̃) *m*, conflagration, burning; illumination. **embraser** (ze) *v.t*, to [set on] fire; illuminate (*festively*).
embrassade (ăbrasad) *f*, embrace, hug. **embrasse** (bras) *f*, curtain holder. **embrassement** (smɑ̃) *m*, embrace. **embrasser** (se) *v.t*, to embrace, hug; kiss (Cf. *baiser*); take in; take up; espouse. *je vous embrasse* [*de tout cœur*], [with] [best] love (*letter*).
embrasure (ăbrazyːr) *f*, recess; embrasure.
embrayer (ăbrεje) *v.t*, to engage (*Mach.*), throw into gear. **embrayage** (jaːʒ) *m*, engaging; clutch.
embrever (ăbrəve) *v.t*, to joggle.
embrigader (ăbrigade) *v.t*, to brigade; enroll.
embrocation (ăbrɔkasjɔ̃) *f*, embrocation.
embrocher (ăbrɔʃe) *v.t*, to spit; run through, impale.

embrouillamini (ăbrujamini) *m*, confusion. **embrouiller** (je) *v.t*, to ravel, tangle; embroil, muddle, confuse.
embroussaillé, e (ăbrusaje) *a*, brushy; bushy; matted.
embrumer (ăbryme) *v.t*, to fog, shroud, darken. **embrun** (brœ̃) *m*, spray, spindrift.
embryon (ăbriɔ̃) *m*, embryo. **embryonnaire** (ɔnεːr) *a*, embryonic.
embûche (ăbyʃ) *f*, trap. **embuscade** (byskad) *f*, ambush, ambuscade. *se tenir en* ~, to lie in wait. **embusqué** (ke) *m*, shirker. **embusquer** (ke) *v.t*, to place in ambush. s'~, to ambush, lie in wait; shirk.
émeraude (emroːd) *f*, emerald.
émerger (emεrʒe) *v.i*, to emerge; loom; peep.
émeri (emri) *m*, emery.
émerillon (emrijɔ̃) *m*, merlin (*bird*); swivel. **émerillonné, e** (jone) *a*, bright, sparkling.
émérite (emerit) *a*, experienced; confirmed; emeritus.
émerveiller (emεrveje) *v.t*, to astonish. s'~, to marvel.
émétique (emetik) *a.* & *m*, emetic.
émetteur (emεtœːr) *m*, issuer; (*att.*) transmitter (*Teleg.*). **émettre** (tr) *v.t.ir*, to emit, utter; express; issue; broadcast; transmit.
émeute (emøːt) *f*, riot, disturbance, outbreak. **émeutier** (møtje) *m*, rioter.
émietter (emjεte) *v.t.* & s'~, to crumble.
émigrant, e (emigrɑ̃, ɑ̃ːt) *n*, emigrant. **émigration** (grasjɔ̃) *f*, emigration. **émigré, e** (gre) *n*, refugee; émigré (*Hist.*). **émigrer** (gre) *v.i*, to emigrate; migrate.
émincé, e (emɛ̃se) *p.p*, cut into thin slices. ¶ *m*, hash.
éminemment (eminamɑ̃) *ad*, eminently, highly. **éminence** (nɑ̃ːs) *f*, eminence; height; ball (*thumb*). *Son E~*, *f*, His Eminence (*cardinal*). **éminent, e** (nɑ̃, ɑ̃ːt) *a*, eminent; distinguished; prominent. **éminentissime** (nɑ̃tisim) *a*, most eminent.
émir (emiːr) *m*, emir; ameer, amir.

émissaire (emisɛːr) *m*, emissary.
émission (sjɔ̃) *f*, emission; issue;
uttering; broadcasting, transmission. ∼ *en différé*, prerecorded
broadcast. ∼ *en direct*, live
broadcast.
emmagasiner (ãmagazine) *v.t*,
to store, s. up; warehouse.
emmailloter (ãmajɔte) *v.t*, to
swathe; bandage.
emmancher (ãmãʃe) *v.t*, to handle; fix; set about. **emmanchure**
(ʃyːr) *f*, armhole.
emmêler (ãmɛle) *v.t*, to [en]tangle; muddle.
emménagement (ãmenaʒmã)
m, moving in (*house*); accommodation, appointments (*ship*).
emménager (ʒe) *v.t*, to install,
settle; move into; (*v.i.*) to move
in.
emmener (ãmne) *v.t*, to take
away.
emmerdant (ãmɛrdã) *a*, annoying, irritating. **emmerdement**
(dmã) *m*, nuisance, irritation;
problem; difficulty. **emmerder**
(de) *v.t*, to annoy, irritate. *s'*∼, to
be bored.
emmiellé, e (ãmjɛle) *a*, honeyed.
emmitoufler (ãmitufle) *v.t*, to
muffle up.
emmortaiser (ãmɔrtɛze) *v.t*, to
mortise.
émoi (emwa) *m*, emotion, agitation, flutter.
émollient, e (emɔljã, ãːt) *a. &
m*, emollient.
émoluments (emɔlymã) *m.pl*,
emoluments.
émonder (emɔ̃de) *v.t*, to prune.
émondes (mɔːd) *f.pl*, prunings.
émotion (emosjɔ̃) *f*, emotion;
thrill; excitement.
émoucher (emuʃe) *v.t*, to drive
away the flies from.
émouchet (emuʃɛ) *m*, kestrel.
émouchette (emuʃɛt) *f*, fly net.
émouchoir (ʃwaːr) *m*, fly whisk.
émoulu, e (emuly) *a: frais ∼ de*,
fresh from (*college*); well up in
(*subject*).
émousser (emuse) *v.t*, to blunt,
dull; remove the moss from.
émoustiller (emustije) *v.t*, to exhilarate.
émouvant (emuvã) *a*, moving,
touching, thrilling.

émouvoir (emuvwaːr) *v.t.ir*, to
move; stir [up], rouse.
empailler (ãpaje) *v.t*, to cover
(*or* pack) (*or* stuff) with straw;
stuff (*dead animal*). **empailleur,
euse** (jœːr, øːz) *n*, chair caner,
taxidermist.
empanacher (ãpanaʃe) *v.t*, to
plume; adorn.
empaqueter (ãpakte) *v.t*, to
pack [up]. *s'*∼, to wrap [oneself] up.
emparer (s') **de** (ãpare) *v.pr*,
to seize, take possession of;
monopolize, engross.
empâter (ãpate) *v.t*, to paste;
make sticky; fatten, force-feed
(*poultry*); impaste.
empattement (ãpatmã) *m*,
footing (*Build.*); wheelbase;
serif.
empaumer (ãpome) *v.t*, to strike
(*ball*); manipulate (*pers.*).
empêché, e (ãpeʃe) *p.p*, puzzled,
at a loss. **empêchement** (ʃmã)
m, hindrance, impediment, obstacle, bar; prevention. **empêcher** (ʃe) *v.t*, to prevent, hinder, impede; keep from; preclude. *s'*∼, to forbear, refrain,
help.
empeigne (ãpɛɲ) *f*, vamp, upper (*shoe*).
empereur (ãprœːr) *m*, emperor.
empesé, e (ãpəze) *a*, starchy,
stiff. **empeser** (ze) *v.t*, to starch.
empester (ãpɛste) *v.t*, to infect;
corrupt; (*abs.*) to stink.
empêtrer (ãpɛtre) *v.t*, to entangle, hamper; embarrass; involve.
emphase (ãfaːs) *f*, bombast,
pomposity, fustian; magniloquence; emphasis. **emphatique†**
(fatik) *a*, bombastic, pompous;
magniloquent; emphatic.
empiècement (ãpjɛsmã) *m*,
yoke (*dress*).
empierrer (ãpjɛre) *v.t*, to pave,
macadamize; fill with stones
(*drainage ditch*).
empiètement (ãpjɛtmã) *m*, encroachment, trespass. **empiéter
sur** (pjete), to encroach on; trespass on (*fig.*).
empiffrer (ãpifre) *v.t*, to stuff,
gorge.

empiler (ãpile) *v.t*, to pile [up]; stack; herd together.

empire (ãpi:r) *m*, dominion, sway; hold; mastery; rule; empire. *~ sur soi-même*, self-control.

empirer (ãpire) *v.t*, to make worse; (*v.i.*) to grow worse.

empirique (ãpirik) *a*, empiric(al), rule-of-thumb. ¶ *m*, empiric[ist]. **empiriquement** (kmã) *ad*, empirically, by rule of thumb. **empirisme** (rism) *m*, empiricism.

emplacement (ãplasmã) *m*, site, position, location.

emplâtre (ãpla:tr) *m*, plaster (*Phar.*); futile person. *~ adhésif*, adhesive plaster.

emplette (ãplɛt) *f*, purchase, shopping; bargain.

emplir (ãpli:r) *v.t. & s'~*, to fill; (*v.i.*) to be swamped (*boat*).

emploi (ãplwa) *m*, employment; job; use; entry (*Bkkpg.*); part, line (*of actor*). *plein ~*, full employment. **employé, e** (je) *n*, employee; clerk. *~ d'administration*, civil servant. *~ du gaz*, gas man. **employer** (je) *v.t*, to employ; use. *s'~*, to occupy (*or* exert) (*or* busy) oneself. **employeur, euse** (jœ:r, ø:z) *n*, employer.

emplumé, e (ãplyme) *p.a*, feathered. **emplumer** (me) *v.t*, to feather; tar & feather.

empocher (ãpɔʃe) *v.t*, to pocket.

empoignant, e (ãpwaɲã, ã:t) *a*, thrilling, poignant. **empoigner** (ɲe) *v.t*, to grasp; grip; clutch; grab; take to task, abuse; thrill.

empois (ãpwa) *m*, starch [paste].

empoisonnement (ãpwazɔnmã) *m*, poisoning. **empoisonner** (ne) *v.t*, to poison; infect; corrupt; (*abs.*) to be poisonous; stink. **empoisonneur, euse** (nœ:r, ø:z) *n*, poisoner; bad cook.

empoissonner (ãpwasɔne) *v.t*, to stock (*pond*) with fish.

emporté, e (ãpɔrte) *a*, hasty, quick-tempered, fiery, passionate. **emportement** (təmã) *m*, transport (*fig.*); outburst, fit of anger.

emporte-pièce (ãpɔrtəpjɛs) *m*, [hollow] punch. *à l'~* (*fig.*), trenchant.

emporter (ãpɔrte) *v.t*, to carry (*or* take) (*or* sweep) (*or* wash) away (*or* off) (*or* out); (*Mil.*) carry (*place*). *l'~ sur*, to surpass, outdo; overrule; prevail over, preponderate over. *s'~*, to get angry, fire up; bolt (*horse*).

empoté, e (ãpɔte) *a*, clumsy. **empoter** (te) *v.t*, to pot.

empourprer (ãpurpre) *v.t*, to purple; crimson.

empreindre (ãprɛ̃:dr) *v.t.ir*, to imprint, impress, stamp. **empreinte** (prɛ̃:t) *f*, impress[ion], [im]print; stamp (*fig.*); mold (*Typ.*). *~ de pas*, *~ du pied*, footprint. *~ digitale*, fingerprint. *~ du doigt*, fingermark.

empressé, e (ãprese) *a*, eager, zealous; attentive. **empressement** (smã) *m*, eagerness, alacrity, readiness. **s'empresser** (se) *v.pr*, to hasten; be eager. *~ auprès de*, to dance attendance on.

emprise (ãpri:z) *f*, hold, ascendancy.

emprisonnement (ãprizɔnmã) *m*, imprisonment. *~ cellulaire*, separate cell system. **emprisonner** (ne) *v.t*, to imprison, confine.

emprunt (ãprœ̃) *m*, borrowing, loan; [making] use. *~ de la Défense nationale*, war loan. *d'~* (*fig.*), artificial, sham, assumed. **emprunté, e** (te) *p.a*, borrowed; assumed (*name*); awkward. **emprunter** (te) *v.t*, to borrow; assume (*name*); use, make use of. **emprunteur, euse** (tœ:r, ø:z) *n*, borrower.

empuantir (ãpɥãti:r) *v.t*, to infect.

empyrée (ãpire) *m*, empyrean.

ému, *p.p*, **émouvoir**.

émulation (emylasjɔ̃) *f*, emulation. **émule** (myl) *n*, emulator, rival.

émulsion (emylsjɔ̃) *f*, emulsion.

en (ã) *pr*, in; into; within; on; to; at; with; in the; in a; like [a]; as [a]; by; while; of; under. *~ voiture!* all aboard!

en (ã) *pn. & ad*, of it, its, of them, their, of him, of her; about it, about them, etc.; for (*or* by) (*or* with) (*or* from) it *or* them, etc.;

some, any. ~ *sus*, or *plus*, in addition. ~ *venir là*, to come (*sink*) to that point. *je n'*~ *ai pas*, I don't have any. *si le cœur vous* ~ *dit*, if you feel like doing it.

enamourer (s') (ãnamure) *v.pr*, to fall in love.

énarque (enark) *m*, civil service administrator, student or graduate of the École Nationale d'Administration.

encadrement (ãkadramã) *m*, framing; officering (*Mil.*); frame; framework. ~ *de credit*, credit regulation.

encadrer (ãkadre) *v.t*, to frame; surround; incorporate; officer.

encager (ãkaʒe) *v.t*, to [en]cage.

encaisse (ãkɛs) *f*, cash [in hand]. ~ *métallique*, cash & bullion in hand. **encaisser** (se) *v.t*, to [en]case; cash; collect; put in the cash box; embank (*river, road*); put up with. *il ne peut pas l'*~, he can't stand him.

encan (ãkã) *m*, auction.

encanailler (s') (ãkanaje) *v.i*, to contract low habits.

encaquer (ãkake) *v.t*, to barrel. *encaqués comme des harengs*, packed like sardines (*people*).

encart (ãkaːr) *m*, insert (*Bookb.*). **encarter** (karte) *v.t*, to inset (*Bookb.*); insert (*Bookb.*); card; card index; register.

en-cas (ãka) *m*, something (*ready to eat*) in case of need; umbrella-sunshade.

encastrer (ãkastre) *v.t*, to house; embed.

encaustique (ãkostik) *a. & f*, encaustic. ~ *pour meubles*, furniture polish. **encaustiquer** (ke) *v.t*, to polish (*furniture*).

encaver (ãkave) *v.t*, to cellar.

enceindre (ãsɛ̃ːdr) *v.t.ir*, to enclose, gird, surround. **enceinte** (sɛ̃t) *a.f*, pregnant, with child, expectant. ¶ *f*, enclosure; precinct; ring (*Box.*); fencing; wall; hall. ~ *du pesage*, paddock (*turf*). ~ *de confinement*, containment (*reactor*).

encens (ãsã) *m*, incense. ~ *mâle*, frankincense. **encenser** (se) *v.t*, to [in]cense, burn i. to; flatter. **encensoir** (swaːr) *m*, censer.

encercler (ãsɛrkle) *v.t*, to hoop; encircle.

enchaînement (ãʃɛnmã) (*fig.*) *m*, chain, series, train. **enchaîner** (ne) *v.t*, to chain [up]; enchain, fetter, manacle; bind; link; enslave; enthrall.

enchantement (ãʃãtmã) *m*, enchantment, magic, spell; glamour, witchery; delight. **enchanter** (te) *v.t*, to enchant, bewitch; delight, enrapture. **enchanteur, eresse** (tœːr, trɛːs) *n*, enchanter, tress; (*att.*) enchanting, bewitching.

enchâsser (ãʃase) *v.t*, to set, mount; enshrine; incorporate. **enchâssure** (syːr) *f*, setting.

enchère (ãʃɛːr) *f*, bid[ding]; auction, sale. **enchérir** (ʃeriːr) *v.t*, to raise the price of; (*v.i.*) to rise in price; bid. ~ *sur*, to outbid; outdo. **enchérisseur** (risœːr) *m*, bidder.

enchevêtrer (s') (ãʃvɛtre) *v.pr*, to get [en]tangled (*or* confused).

enchifrènement (ãʃifrɛnmã) *m*, cold in the head, snuffles.

enclave (ãklaːv) *f*, land-locked property (*law*); enclave (*international*); recess (*Build.*). **enclaver** (klave) *v.t*, to enclose, shut in, fit in.

enclin, e (ãklɛ̃, in) *a*, inclined, prone, minded, given.

enclore (ãklɔːr) *v.t.ir*, to enclose, fence in. **enclos** (klo) *m*, enclosure; paddock.

enclouer (ãklue) *v.t*, to spike (*gun*). **enclouure** (kluyːr) (*fig.*) *f*, rub.

enclume (ãklym) *f*, anvil.

encoche (ãkɔʃ) *f*, notch, nick, slot. ~*s*, thumb index (*books*). **encocher** (ʃe) *v.t*, to notch.

encodage (ãkɔdaːʒ) *m*, encoding (*computer, etc.*). **encoder** (de) *v.t*, to encode. **encodeur** (dœːr) *m*, encoder (*computers*).

encoignure (ãkɔɲyːr) *f*, corner; corner cupboard.

encollage (ãkɔlaːʒ) *m*, sizing; size (*glue*). **encoller** (le) *v.t*, to size.

encolure (ãkɔlyːr) *f*, neck; neck measurement, [neck] size; look (*fig.*).

encombrant, e (ãkɔ̃brã, ã:t) *a*, bulky; cumbersome, in the way; embarrassing. **sans encombre** (kɔ̃:br), without hindrance. **encombrement** (kɔ̃brəmã) *m*, block, congestion, [over]crowding; glut[ting]; litter; space occupied, floor space; measurement (*Ship.*). **encombrer** (bre) *v.t*, to block, congest, overcrowd; glut, overstock; encumber, litter.

encontre (à l'~ de) (ãkɔ̃:tr), in opposition to. **aller à l'~ de**, to run counter to.

encorbellement (ãkɔrbɛlmã) *m*, cantilever.

encore (ãkɔ:r) *ad*, still; yet; again; also; moreover; too; more; else. ~ **un, une**, one more, another. ~ **un coup**, once again, once more. ~ **un peu**, a little more *or* longer. ~ **que**, *c*, although.

encourager (ãkuraʒe) *v.t*, to encourage, hearten; foster; promote; countenance, abet; halloo (*dogs*).

encourir (ãkuri:r) *v.t.ir*, to incur, run.

encrasser (ãkrase) *v.t*, to foul, dirty, grime; clog.

encre (ã:kr) *f*, ink. ~ **à marquer le linge**, marking i. ~ **de Chine**, Indian i. ~ **stylographique** (stilɔgrafik), fountain pen i. **encrer** (ãkre) *v.t*, to ink. **encrier** (krie) *m*, inkstand, inkpot. ~ **d'écolier**, inkwell.

encroûté, e (ãkrute) (*fig.*) *a*, crusted, fogyish.

enculer (ãkyle) *v.t*, to sodomize; get the better of (*obscene*).

encuver (ãkyve) *v.t*, to vat; put in the tub.

encyclique (ãsiklik) *a. & f*, encyclic(al).

encyclopédie (ãsikləpedi) *f*, [en]cyclopedia.

endémique (ãdemik) *a*, endemic.

endenter (ãdãte) *v.t*, to tooth, cog.

endetté, e (ãdɛte) *p.a*, in debt. **endetter** (te) *v.t*, to involve in debt. **s'~**, to run into d.

endeuiller (ãdœje) *v.t*, to put into mourning; make gloomy.

endêvé, e (ãdeve) *a*, exasperated. **endêver** (ve) *v.i*, to be furious.

endiablé, e (ãdjable) *a*, (*as if*) possessed; wild, frenzied. **endiabler** (ble) *v.i*, to be furious.

endiguer (ãdige) *v.t*, to dike; dam.

endimancher (s') (ãdimãʃe) *v.pr*, to put on one's Sunday best.

endive (ãdi:v) *f*, chicory; endive.

endoctriner (ãdɔktrine) *v.t*, to indoctrinate; coach.

endolorir (ãdɔlɔri:r) *v.t*, to make ache.

endommager (ãdɔmaʒe) *v.t*, to damage, injure.

endormant, e (ãdɔrmã, ã:t) *a*, soporific; wearisome. **endormeur** (mœ:r) *m*, bore. **endormi, e** (mi) *p.a*, asleep; sleepy; drowsy. ¶ *n*, sleepyhead. **endormir** (mi:r) *v.t.ir*, to send to sleep; lull. **s'~**, to fall asleep, go to sleep.

endos[sement] (ãdo[smã]) *m*, endorsement. **endosser** (se) *v.t*, to put on, don; take on, shoulder; endorse. **endosseur** (sœ:r) *m*, endorser.

endroit (ãdrwa) *m*, place, spot, part; right side, face (*fabric*). **à l'~ de**, towards, regarding.

enduire (ãdɥi:r) *v.t.ir*, to smear; coat; render. **enduit** (dɥi) *m*, coat[ing]; rendering.

endurance (ãdyrã:s) *f*, endurance. **endurant, e** (rã, ã:t) *a*, patient. **rendre ~**, to harden. **endurcir** (si:r) *v.t. & s'~**, to harden. **endurcissement** (sismã) *m*, hardness, callousness, obduracy. **endurer** (re) *v.t*, to endure.

énergétique (enɛrʒetik) *f*, energetics (*Phys.*). **énergie** (ʒi) *f*, energy, power; emphasis; efficacy (*remedy*); backbone. **énergique†** (ʒik) *a*, energetic, powerful, strong; forcible, emphatic; strenuous.

énergumène (enɛrgymɛn) *m.f*, fanatic; ranter.

énerver (enɛrve) *v.t*, to enervate; exasperate.

enfance (ãfã:s) *f*, childhood; infancy; second childhood, dotage; A B C (*of an art*). **enfant** (fã) *n*, child; infant; boy; girl; fellow, lad. ~ **de chœur**, choir boy, chorister. ~**s perdus**, forlorn hope (*Mil.*). ~ *prodige*, infant prodigy. ~ *prodigue*, prodigal son. ~ *trouvé*, foundling; stowaway. **enfantement** (tmã) *m*, birth (*fig.*). **enfanter** (te) *v.t*, to give birth to (*fig.*). **enfantillage** (tijaːʒ) *m*, childishness, **enfantin**, **e** (tɛ̃, in) *a*, infantile; childish; infant (*class*); nursery (*language*).

enfariner (ãfarine) *v.t*, to [cover with] flour.

enfer (ãfɛːr) *m*, hell, inferno. *les* ~*s*, the nether regions, the underworld, Hades. *d'*~, infernal; blazing (*fire*).

enfermer (ãfɛrme) *v.t*, to shut up; lock up; enclose; impound; contain.

enferrer (ãfɛre) *v.t*, to run through (*with sword*). *s'*~, to become involved. *s'*~ *soi-même*, to give oneself away.

enfieller (ãfjɛle) *v.t*, to embitter, sour.

enfiévrer (ãfjevre) *v.t*, to make feverish.

enfilade (ãfilad) *f*, suite; series; string; row; enfilade. **enfiler** (le) *v.t*, to thread; string; run (*or* go) through; go along; enfilade, rake; draw in (*person to reckless gaming*).

enfin (ãfɛ̃) *ad*, at last, lastly, after all; in short, in fine; in fact; come now!

enflammer (ãflame) *v.t*, to [set on] fire, ignite; inflame. *s'*~, to catch (*or* take) fire, ignite, fire up.

enfler (ãfle) *v.t. & i. & s'*~, to swell, inflate. **enflure** (flyːr) *f*, swelling, etc.

enfoncer (ãfɔ̃se) *v.t*, to drive [in]; sink, bury, immerse; break open, b. in; b. up; stave in; (*v.i. & abs.*) to sink. **enfoncement** (smã) *m*, driving [in]; hollow, depression; recess; background. **enfonçure** (syːr) *f*, hole; bottom (*cask*).

enfouir (ãfwiːr) *v.t*, to bury, hide.

enfourcher (ãfurʃe) *v.t*, to bestride; ride to death (*fig.*).

enfourner (ãfurne) *v.t*, to put in the oven.

enfreindre (ãfrɛ̃ːdr) *v.t.ir*, to infringe, break.

enfuir (s') (ãfɥiːr) *v.pr*, to flee; escape; run away; elope; leak; fly; vanish.

enfumer (ãfyme) *v.t*, to smoke; s. out.

engageant, **e** (ãgaʒã, ãːt) *a*, engaging, winning; inviting. **engagement** (ʒmã) *m*, engagement; booking; entry (*sporting event*); enlistment; signing on; commitment; liability, undertaking; pledging, pledge, pawning, hypothecation. **engager** (ʒe) *v.t*, to engage; book; enter; enlist; sign [on]; betroth; bind; plight; pledge, pawn; mortgage, hypothecate; invite, urge, induce; foul (*ropes*). **engagé**, *p.p*, on her beam ends; waterlogged (*boat*). **s'engager**, to undertake, covenant; enlist; enter; foul.

engainer (ãgɛne) *v.t*, to sheathe, case.

engeance (ãʒãːs) *f*, brood, lot (*of despicable people*).

engelure (ãʒlyːr) *f*, chilblain.

engendrer (ãʒãdre) *v.t*, to beget; sire; engender; breed; generate.

engerber (ãʒɛrbe) *v.t*, to sheaf, bind.

engin (ãʒɛ̃) *m*, appliance, contrivance, gear, tackle; engine (*of war*); missile. ~ *spatiale*, spacecraft.

englober (ãglɔbe) *v.t*, to include, embody.

engloutir (ãglutiːr) *v.t*, to swallow; s. up; bolt (*food*); engulf, swamp.

engluer (ãglye) *v.t*, to [bird] lime; ensnare; take in.

engoncé (ãgɔ̃se) *a*, stiff, awkward; bundled up; bound up in.

engorger (ãgɔrʒe) *v.t*, to choke [up], stop up.

engouer (s') (ãgue) *v.pr*, to become infatuated.

engouffrer (ãgufre) *v.t*, to engulf, swallow up.

engourdir (ãgurdiːr) *v.t*, to [be] numb, dull. **engourdissement** (dismã) *m*, numbness (*physical or mental*); sluggishness (*Com.*).

engrais (ãgrɛ) *m*, fattening food; manure. ~ *chimique*, fertilizer.

engraisser (se) v.t, to fatten; manure.

engranger (ãgrãʒe) v.t, to garner, get in.

engraver (ãgrave) v.t, to strand; (v.i.) to ground (boat).

engrenage (ãgrəna:ʒ) m, gear[ing]; meshes, toils (fig.). **engrener** (ne) v.t, to [throw into] gear, mesh, engage; set going.

engrosser (ãgrose) v.t, to make pregnant.

engrossir (ãgrosi:r) v.i, to become pregnant.

engueulade (ãgœlad) m, bawling out, angry reproof. **engueuler** (le) v.t, to bawl out, scold. s'~ avec, to argue angrily with. se faire ~, to be bawled out.

engrumeler (ãgrymle) v.t, to clot, curdle.

enguirlander (ãgirlãde) v.t, to garland, wreathe; wheedle.

enhardir (ãardi:r) v.t, to embolden.

énigmatique† (enigmatik) a, enigmatic(al). **énigme** (nigm) f, riddle, conundrum, puzzle, enigma.

enivrer (ãnivre) v.t, to intoxicate, inebriate; elate.

enjambée (ãʒãbe) f, stride. **enjamber** (be) v.t. & abs, to stride [over or along]; (v.i.) to encroach, project.

enjeu (ãʒø) m, stake (wager).

enjoindre (ãʒwɛ̃:dr) v.t.ir, to enjoin.

enjôler (ãʒole) v.t, to wheedle, inveigle, bamboozle.

enjoliver (ãʒolive) v.t, to embellish; set off.

enjolivure (ãʒolivy:r) m, hubcap.

enjoué, e (ãʒwe) a, playful, jocular, vivacious. **enjouement** (ʒumã) m, playfulness.

enlacer (ãlase) v.t, to [en]lace; entwine; clasp, fold.

enlaidir (ãlɛdi:r) v.t, to make ugly; disfigure.

enlevage (ãlva:ʒ) m, spurt (rowing). **enlever** (lve) v.t, to lift, raise; carry (or take) (or clear) (or sweep) away (or off); remove, collect; kidnap; abduct, rape, buy up; take up (shares); snap up (bargain). être enlevé par la mer ou par les lames, to be washed overboard. se faire ~ par, to elope with. **enlèvement** (levmã) m, lifting, etc.; elopement; kidnapping; storming (military position).

enliser (s') (ãlize) v.pr, to sink [into the sand or mud].

enluminer (ãlymine) v.t, to color, illuminate (MS.); flush, redden. **enluminure** (ny:r) f, coloring; illumination; high color.

ennemi, e (ɛnmi) n, enemy, foe. ¶ a, enemy, inimical, hostile; averse; clashing.

ennoblir (ãnobli:r) v.t, to ennoble, uplift, dignify.

ennui (ãnɥi) m, wearisomeness, tedium, boredom; bother, nuisance; worry, trouble. **ennuyer** (nɥije) v.t, to weary, tire, bore; annoy, worry. **ennuyeux, euse†** (jø, ø:z) a, tiresome, tedious, irksome; prosy.

énoncé (enɔ̃se) m, statement. **énoncer (se)** v.t, to state, enunciate, express, specify. **énonciation** (sjasjɔ̃) f, stating, enunciation.

enorgueillir (ãnɔrgœji:r) v.t, to make proud, elate. s'~, to pride oneself.

énorme (enɔrm) a, enormous, huge, mountainous, tremendous; outrageous. **énormément** (memã) ad, enormously. **énormité** (mite) f, enormousness; enormity.

enquérir (s') (ãkeri:r) v.pr.ir, to inquire, ask. **enquête** (kɛ:t) f, inquiry, investigation; inquest.

enraciner (ãrasine) v.t. & s'~, to take root.

enragé, e (ãraʒe) p.a, mad; rabid; enraged, infuriated; raging; wild. ¶ m, madman, fiend (fig.). **enrageant, e** (ʒã, ã:t) a, maddening. **enrager** (ʒe) v.i, to fume. faire ~, to madden, infuriate.

enrayer (ãreje) v.t, to drag, skid, lock (wheel); spoke (wheel); brake; stop, check (fig.).

enrégimenter (ãreʒimãte) (fig.) v.t, to enroll.

enregistrer (ãrəʒistre) v.t, to register; file; score; record; book; chronicle. **enregistrement** (trəmã) m, registration; registry; recording. ~ magnétophonique, tape recording. ~ *fractionné,* rerecording, duoplay (*sound recording*). enregistreur (trœːr) *m,* recording instrument. ~ *de vol,* flight recorder.

enrhumer (ɑ̃ryme) *v.t,* to give (*someone*) a cold. s'~, to catch [a] cold.

enrichi, e (ɑ̃riʃi) *n,* one who has become rich. **enrichir** (jiːr) *v.t,* to enrich. s'~, to make money.

enrober (ɑ̃rɔbe) *v.t,* to encase.

enrôler (ɑ̃role) *v.t,* to enroll, enlist.

enrouer (ɑ̃rwe) *v.t,* to make hoarse *or* husky.

enrouler (ɑ̃rule) *v.t,* to wind, coil, wrap, roll [up].

ensablement (ɑ̃sabləmɑ̃) *m,* sandbank. **ensabler** (ble) *v.t,* to sand [up]; run aground.

ensacher (ɑ̃saʃe) *v.t,* to bag, sack.

ensanglanter (ɑ̃sɑ̃glɑ̃te) *v.t,* to stain with blood.

enseigne (ɑ̃sɛɲ) *f,* sign; sign [board]; ensign. *à bonnes* ~*s,* on sure grounds; on good security. *à telles* ~*s que,* in proof of which. ~ *de vaisseau, m,* ensign (*Nav.*).

enseignement (ɑ̃sɛɲmɑ̃) *m,* teaching, tuition, training, education; (*pl.*) teachings, lessons. ~ *programmé,* programmed instruction. **enseigner** (ɲe) *v.t,* to show; tell of; teach, teach how.

ensellé, e (ɑ̃sɛle) *a,* saddle-backed.

ensemble (ɑ̃sɑ̃ːbl) *ad,* together. ¶ *m,* whole; aggregate; general effect; unity, harmony. ~ *deux pièces,* two-piece set, ensemble; suit. ~ *de données,* data set (*computers*). ~ *spécialisé,* dedicated system (*computers*). *dans l'*~, on the whole. *vue d'*~, overall view.

ensemencer (ɑ̃smɑ̃se) *v.t,* to sow (*land*).

enserrer (ɑ̃sɛre) *v.t,* to encompass, enclose; tie up (*fig.*); put under glass (*Hort.*).

ensevelir (ɑ̃səvliːr) *v.t,* to bury, entomb; plunge; shroud.

ensoleillé, e (ɑ̃sɔlɛje) *a,* sunny; sunlit. **ensoleiller** (je) *v.t,* to sun; light up, brighten.

ensommeillé, e (ɑ̃sɔmɛje) *a,* sleepy, drowsy.

ensorceler (ɑ̃sɔrsəle) *v.t,* to bewitch.

ensuite (ɑ̃sɥit) *ad,* afterwards, then, next. s'**ensuivre** (sɥiːvr) *v.pr.ir,* to follow, ensue.

entablement (ɑ̃tabləmɑ̃) *m,* entablature.

entacher (ɑ̃taʃe) *v.t,* to taint; vitiate.

entaille (ɑ̃taːj) *f,* notch, nick, groove, slot; gash, hack. **entailler** (taje) *v.t,* to notch.

entame (ɑ̃tam) *f,* first cut, outside [cut]. **entamer** (me) *v.t,* to cut [into] (*slightly*); injure; penetrate; break into, broach; shake (*one's faith*); fathom; begin, open, initiate.

entasser (ɑ̃tase) *v.t,* to heap up, pile up, stack, huddle.

ente (ɑ̃ːt) (*Hort.*) *f,* graft; stock.

entendement (ɑ̃tɑ̃dmɑ̃) *m,* understanding; intelligence. **entendre** (tɑ̃ːdr) *v.t. & abs,* to hear; listen to; understand; mean; require. *laisser* ~, to hint. ~ *à,* to consent to. s'~, to understand; u. each other; come to an understanding; get on; be subject to. **entendu, e** (tɑ̃dy) *a,* capable, businesslike; versed; arranged; conceived. *bien entendu,* clearly understood; of course. *entendu!* agreed! okay! **entente** (tɑ̃ːt) *f,* understanding. *mot, phrase, à double* ~, word, phrase, with a double meaning, double entendre.

enter (ɑ̃te) *v.t,* to [en]graft.

entériner (ɑ̃terine) *v.t,* to ratify, confirm; rubber-stamp.

entérique (ɑ̃terik) *a,* enteric.

enterrement (ɑ̃tɛrmɑ̃) *m,* burial, interment; funeral. **enterrer** (re) *v.t,* to bury, inter; sink (*money, a fortune, en* = in); outlive.

en-tête (ɑ̃tɛːt) *m,* head[ing] (*letter, bill, ledger*).

entêté, e (ɑ̃tɛte) *p.a,* obstinate, headstrong, stubborn. **entêtement** (tmɑ̃) *m,* obstinacy. **entêter** (te) *v.t. & abs,* to make giddy; go to the head; infatuate. s'~, to be obstinate.

enthousiasme (ãtuzjasm) *m*, enthusiasm; rapture. **enthousiasmer** (me) *v.t*, to enrapture, carry away. **s'~**, to go into raptures. **enthousiaste** (ast) *a*, enthusiastic, ¶ *n*, enthusiast.

enticher (ãtiʃe) *v.t*, to taint; infatuate.

entier, ère (ãtje, ɛːr) *a*, entire, whole; full; the same, as it was; headstrong, self-willed. ¶ *m*, entirety. [*nombre*] ~, whole number, integer. **en ~**, entirely, in full, right through. **entièrement** (tjɛrmã) *ad*, entirely, wholly; fully; quite; clean (*shaven*).

entité (ãtite) *f*, entity.

entoiler (ãtwale) *v.t*, to mount [on calico *or* linen]; bind in cloth.

entomologie (ãtɔmɔlɔʒi) *f*, entomology. **entomologiste** (ʒist) *m*, entomologist.

entonner (ãtɔne) *v.t. & abs*, to intone, intonate; strike up (*tune*); barrel.

entonnoir (ãtɔnwaːr) *m*, funnel; hollow; shell hole; mine crater.

entorse (ãtɔrs) *f*, sprain, strain, twist, wrench. **entortiller** (tije) *v.t*, to twist, [en]twine, wind, wrap; get round (*someone*).

entour (ãtuːr) *m*: **à l'~**, around, round about. **~s**, *pl*, environs, outskirts, purlieus; associates; aspects. **entourage** (turaʒ) *m*, setting, surroundings; environment, associates. **entourer** (re) *v.t*, to surround, beset, hedge.

entournure (ãturnyːr) *f*, armhole (*garment*). **être gêné aux ~s**, to be in a financial bind.

en-tout-cas (ãtuka) *m*, umbrella-sunshade.

entracte (ãtrakt) *m*, interval, entr'acte; interlude.

entraide (ãtrɛːd) *f*, helpfulness to each other. **s'entraider** (trɛde) *v.pr*, to help one another.

entrailles (ãtraːj) *f.pl*, entrails, bowels, inwards; compassion, heart.

entr'aimer (s') (ãtrɛme) *v.pr*, to love one another.

entrain (ãtrɛ̃) *m*, liveliness, spirit, go, gusto. **entraînant, e** (trɛnã, ãːt) *a*, inspiriting, stirring. **entraînement** (nmã) *m*, impulse;

force; ~ enthusiasm; training (*sport*); sparring; coaching; pace making; feed (*Mach*.). **entraîne** (ne) *v.t*, to carry (*or* draw) (o wash) away *or* along; drift; in volve, entail; lead; train; coach pace. **s'~ à la boxe**, to spar. **en traîneur** (nœːr) *m*, trainer; coach pacemaker. **entraîneuse** (nøːz) j bargirl, shill.

entrait (ãtrɛ) *m*, tie beam; ti rod.

entrant, e (ãtrã, ãːt) *a*, ingo ing; insinuating.

entrave (ãtraːv) *f*, fetter, shackle trammel, clog, obstacle; hobble **entraver** (trave) *v.t*, to fetter impede, hinder, hamper.

entre (ãːtr) *pr*, between; in, into among[st]; of. **~ deux**, *ad*, i between; middling. **~ deux âges** middle-aged. **~ deux eaux**, un der water.

entrebâillé, e (ãtrəbaje) *a* half-open, ajar. **entrebâilleur d fenêtre** (jœːr) *m*, casement stay

entrechat (ãtrəʃa) *m*, entrechat caper.

entrechoquer (ãtrəʃɔke) *v.t*, tc strike against each other. **s'~**, tc clash, collide.

entrecôte (ãtrəkoːt) *f*, rib steak **entrecouper** (ãtrəkupe) *v.t*, tc intersect; break.

entrecroiser (s') (ãtrəkrwaze) *v.pr*, to intersect; criss-cross.

entre-déchirer (s') (ãtrəde ʃire) *v.pr*, to tear one another tc pieces.

entre-deux (ãtrədø) *m*, space [between]; parting; trough (*sea*)

entrée (ãtre) *f*, entrance, entry ingress; admittance, admission [admission] ticket; way in; ac cess; entrée; beginning; mouth inlet; gate. **~ dans le monde** birth; coming out (*in society*). le **~s de faveur**, the free lis (*Theat.*). **~ de serrure**, keyhole **~ en douane**, clearance (*or* entry .inwards. **~ en séance**, opening o the sitting. [*droit d'*]~, impor duty. **~ des artistes**, stage door anus (*obscène*).

entrefaite (ãtrəfɛt) *f*: **sur ce ~s**, in the midst of all this.

entrefilet (ãtrəfilɛ) *m*, [short paragraph (*newspaper*).

entregent (ãtrəʒã) *m*, tact; gumption.

entrelacer (ãtrəlase) *v.t*, to interlace, intertwine, interweave.

entrelardé, e (ãtrəlarde) *p.a*, streaky (*meat*). **entrelarder** (de) *v.t*, to lard; interlard.

entre-ligne (ãtrəliɲ) *m*, interlineation.

entremêler (ãtrəmɛle) *v.t*, to [inter]mix, intermingle; intersperse.

entremets (ãtrəmɛ) *m*, side dish; dessert (*dinner course*).

entremetteur, euse (ãtrəmɛtœːr, ɸːz) *n*, go-between. **s'entremettre** (tr) *v.pr.ir*, to intervene. **entremise** (miːz) *f*, intervention; agency; medium.

entrepont (ãtrəpɔ̃) *m*, betweendecks.

entreposer (ãtrəpoze) *v.t*, to warehouse, store; bond. **entreposeur** (zœːr) *m*, warehouse keeper; bonded storekeeper. **entrepositaire** (zitɛːr) *n*, bonder. **entrepôt** (po) *m*, warehouse, store; emporium, mart. ~ *frigorifique*, cold storage. ~ [*légal*], ~ *de douane*, bond[ed warehouse]. *en* ~ ou *à l'*~ ou *en E.*, in bond[ed warehouse].

entreprenant, e (ãtrəprənã, ãːt) *a*, enterprising, pushing. **entreprendre** (prãːdr) *v.t.ir*, to undertake; contract for; tackle (*pers.*) ~ *sur*, to encroach on. **entrepreneur** (prənœːr) *m*, contractor. ~ *de monuments funéraires*, ~ *de pompes funèbres*, undertaker. ~ *de transports*, ~ *de roulage*, haulage contractor, carrier. **entreprise** (priːz) *f*, undertaking; enterprise; concern; business; contract; encroachment.

entrer (ãtre) *v.i*, to enter; come in; go in; walk in; march in; step in; get in; go; come. ~ *en déchargement*, to break bulk (*Ship.*). X. *entre* [*en scène*], enter X. (*Theat.*). ¶ *v.t*, to introduce. ~ *en fraude*, to smuggle in.

entresol (ãtrəsɔl) *m*, mezzanine [floor].

entrée-sortie (ãtresɔrti) *f*, inputoutput (*computers*).

entre-temps (ãtrətã) *ad*, meanwhile. ¶ *m*, interval.

entretenir (ãtrətniːr) *v.t.ir*, to maintain; keep in repair; keep up; support, keep; speak to, report to. *s'*~, to last; hold together; converse. *s'* ~ *la main*, to keep one's hand in. **entretien** (tjɛ̃) *m*, maintenance; upkeep; support, keep; clothes, dress; talk; interview.

entretoile (ãtrətwal) *f*, lace insertion.

entretoise (ãtrətwaːz) *f*, brace, strut, cross-piece; stay-bolt.

entrevoir (ãtrəvwaːr) *v.t.ir*, to catch a glimpse of; see indistinctly; sense. *s'*~, to see each other, meet. **entrevue** (vy) *f*, interview.

entrouvrir (ãtruvriːr) *v.t.ir*, to half-open.

énumérer (enymere) *v.t*, to enumerate, rehearse; recite.

envahir (ãvaiːr) *v.t*, to invade, break into; overrun; flood; overgrow; encroach on, trench on. **envahissement** (ismã) *m*, invasion; inrush; encroachment. **envahisseur** (sœːr) *m*, invader.

envaser (s') (ãvaze) *v.pr*, to silt up; sink in the mud.

enveloppe (ãvlɔp) *f*, envelope; wrapper; cover[ing]; jacket[ing]; sheath[ing]; lagging; casing; exterior (*fig.*). ~ *à panneau*, ~ *à fenêtre*, window envelope. ~ *affranchie pour la réponse*, stamped addressed e. **envelopper** (vlɔpe) *v.t*, to envelop; wrap [up]; enfold; [en]shroud; cover; case; jacket; lag; involve.

envenimer (ãvnime) *v.t*, to poison; envenom, embitter.

envergure (ãvɛrgyːr) *f*, spread, span; wing spread, w. span; stretch; expanse; breadth.

envers (ãvɛːr) *m*, wrong side, back, reverse; seamy side. *à l'*~, inside out; topsy-turvy. ¶ *pr*, towards, to. ~ *& contre tous*, through thick & thin.

envi (à l') (ãvi), in emulation, vying.

envie (ãvi) *f*, envy; wish, desire, mind, longing, fancy; birthmark; agnail, hang-nail. **envier** (vje) *v.t*, to envy, begrudge. **envieux, euse** (vjø, ∅ːz) *a*, envious.

environ (ãvirɔ̃) *ad*, about, thereabouts. ~**s**, *m.pl*, environs, outskirts, purlieus, neighborhood.

environner (rɔne) *v.t*, to environ, surround; beset.

envisager (ãvizaʒe) *v.t*, to look in the face; look on; envisage; contemplate, view.

envoi (ãvwa) *m*, sending, forwarding, dispatch; sending in, s. out; remittance; consignment; parcel, package; article (*Post*). ~ *contre remboursement*, cash on delivery.

envol (ãvɔl) *m*, flight; taking off (*Avn.*). **envolée** (le) *f*, flight (*fig.*). **s'envoler** (le) *v.pr*, to fly [away]; take off (*Avn.*).

envoûter (ãvute) *v.t*, to bewitch.

envoyé, e (ãvwaje) *n*, envoy; messenger. ~ *spécial*, special correspondent. **envoyer** (je) *v.t*, to send, forward, dispatch; send in, s. out; remit; tender. **envoyeur, euse** (jœːr, ∅ːz) *n*, sender.

éolien, ne (eɔljɛ̃, ɛn) *a*, Aeolian, wind (*att.*).

épagneul, e (epaɲœl) *n*, spaniel.

épais, e (epɛ, ɛːs) *a*, thick, dense. ~ *de*, thick (*Meas.*). **épais**, *ad*, thick[ly]. ¶ *m*, thickness. **épaisseur** (pɛsœːr) *f*, thickness; ply; thick; density. **épaissir** (siːr) *v.t*, to thicken. ~, *v.i.* & *s'*~, to thicken; get stout.

épanchement (epãʃmã) *m*, effusion, outpouring. ~ *de synovie* (sinɔvi), water on the knee. **épancher** (ʃe) *v.t*, to pour out; vent; open (*heart*). *s'*~, to overflow.

épandre (epãːdr) *v.t*, to spread; shed.

épanoui (epanwi) *a*, in full bloom; beaming, cheerful, etc. **épanouir** (epanwiːr) *v.t.* & *s'*~, to open, expand; brighten; blossom. **épanouissement** (wismã) *m*, blooming, beaming.

épargne (eparɲ) *f*, saving, economy, thrift. *la petite* ~, the small investor. **épargner** (ɲe) *v.t*, to save [up], lay by, economize, husband; spare, grudge, stint.

éparpiller (eparpije) *v.t*, to scat-ter; fritter away. **épars, e** (paːr, ars) *a*, scattered, straggling.

épatant (epatã) *a*, fine, wonderful, terrific.

épaté, e (epate) *p.a*, amazed; with crippled foot; flat (*nose*). **épater** (te) *v.t*, to astonish.

épaulard (epolaːr) *m*, grampus, orc.

épaule (epoːl) *f*, shoulder. **épaulée** (pole) *f*, push with the shoulder. **épaulement** (lmã) *m*, shoulder (*Carp.*). **épauler** (le) *v.t*, to splay; shoulder; bring (*rifle*) to the shoulder; back up. **épaulette** (lɛt) *f*, yoke (*dress*); shoulder strap; epaulet[te].

épave (epaːv) *a*, stray[ed]. ¶ *f*, stray; derelict, wreck; (*pl.*) wreckage; jetsam; flotsam; lagan; remnant.

épée (epe) *f*, sword. ~ *de chevet*, fallback; ruling passion.

épeler (eple) *v.t*, to spell. **épellation** (pɛlasjɔ̃) *f*, spelling.

éperdu†, e (epɛrdy) *a*, distracted; desperate.

éperlan (epɛrlã) *m*, smelt (*fish*).

éperon (eprɔ̃) *m*, spur; buttress; ram (*battleship*). **éperonne** (prɔne) *v.t*, to spur; s. on.

épervier (epɛrvje) *m*, sparrow hawk; sweep net; cast net.

éphélide (efelid) *f*, freckle.

éphémère (efemɛːr) *a*, ephemeral, mushroom. ¶ *m*, ephemera-ron, Mayfly. **éphéméride** (merid) *f*, ephemeris; block calendar.

épi (epi) *m*, ear (*grain*); col (*corn*); spike (*flower*); spra (*jewels*).

épice (epis) *f*, spice. **épicé, e** (se *a*, spicy. **épicer** (se) *v.t*, to spice **épicerie** (sri) *f*, grocery; grocer shop; spices. **épicier, ère** (sje ɛːr) *n*, grocer.

épicurien, ne (epikyrjɛ̃, ɛn) *a* & *m*, epicurean.

épidémie (epidemi) *f*, epidemic outbreak (*disease*). **épidémiqu** (mik) *a*, epidemic.

épiderme (epidɛrm) *m*, epider mis. *avoir l'*~ *sensible*, to b thin-skinned (*fig.*).

épier (epje) *v.t*, to spy [on] watch.

épieu (epjø) *m*, boar spear.

épiglotte (epiglɔt) *f*, epiglottis

épigramme (epigram) *f*, epigram; skit.

épigraphe (epigraf) *f*, epigraph, quotation, motto (*prefixed to book or chapter*).

épilepsie (epilɛpsi) *f*, epilepsy. **épileptique** (tik) *a.* & *n*, epileptic.

épiler (epile) *v.t*, to depilate, pluck [out hairs].

épilogue (epilɔg) *m*, epilogue. **épiloguer** (ge) *v.i*, to find fault. **épilogueur, euse** (gœːr, øːz) *n*, faultfinder.

épinard (*Bot.*) *m.* & ~**s** (*Cook.*) *pl.* (epinaːr), spinach. ~**s en branches**, leaf s.

épine (epin) *f*, thorn [bush]; thorn; spine (*Bot.*). ~ **blanche**, hawthorn, whitethorn. ~ **noire**, blackthorn. ~ **dorsale**, spine, backbone. **épineux, euse** (nø, øːz) *a*, thorny, spiny, prickly; knotty. **épine-vinette** (vinɛt) *f*, barberry, berberry.

épingle (epɛ̃ːgl) *f*, pin. ~ **à friser**, hair curler. ~ **à linge**, clothespin. ~ **de sûreté**, ~ **de nourrice**, ~ **anglaise**, safety pin. ~**s**, pin money. *tiré à quatre* ~**s**, spic & span. **épingler** (pêgle) *v.t*, to pin.

épinoche (epinɔʃ) *f*, stickleback.

Épiphanie (epifani) *f*, Epiphany.

épique (epik) *a*, epic.

épiscopal, e (episkɔpal) *a*, episcopal. **épiscopat** (pa) *m*, episcopate; episcopacy.

épisode (epizɔd) *m*, episode.

épisser (epise) *v.t*, to splice (*rope*). **épissoir** (swaːr) *m*, marline spike, marlinspike. **épissure** (syːr) *f*, splice.

épistolaire (epistɔlɛːr) *a*, epistolary. **épistolier, ère** (lje, ɛːr) *n*, letter writer (*pers.*).

épitaphe (epitaf) *f*, epitaph.

épithète (epitɛt) *f*, epithet.

épitomé (epitɔme) *m*, epitome.

épître (epiːtr) *f*, epistle; letter.

éploré, e (eplɔre) *a*, tearful, in tears, weeping.

éplucher (eplyʃe) *v.t*, to prepare, clean; peel, pare; preen, prink; sift (*fig.*), scan. **s'**~, to plume (*or* preen) (*or* prink) its feathers. **épluchures** (ʃyːr) *f.pl*, parings, peelings.

épointer (epwɛ̃te) *v.t*, to break the point off; point (*sharpen*).

éponge (epɔ̃ːʒ) *f*, sponge. **éponger** (pɔ̃ʒe) *v.t*, to sponge; mop; mop up; dab; blot.

épontille (epɔ̃tiːj) *f*, stanchion (*ship*).

épopée (epɔpe) *f*, epic, epopee, epos.

époque (epɔk) *f*, epoch; era, age; time, date, period.

époumoner (epumɔne) *v.t*, to puff.

épouse (epuːz) *f*, wife, spouse, consort. **épouser** (puze) *v.t*, to marry, wed; espouse. ~ [*la forme de*], to correspond (*or* conform) in shape to; adapt itself to, fit.

épousseter (epuste) *v.t*, to dust; rub down.

épouvantable† (epuvɑ̃tabl) *a*, frightful, fearful, dreadful. **épouvantail** (taːj) *m*, scarecrow; bugbear. **épouvante** (vɑ̃ːt) *f*, terror, fright. **épouvanter** (vɑ̃te) *v.t*, to terrify, frighten, scare.

époux (epu) *m*, husband, spouse, consort; (*pl.*) husband & wife, [married] couple.

épreindre (eprɛ̃ːdr) *v.t.ir*, to press [out], squeeze [out].

éprendre (s') (eprɑ̃ːdr) *v.pr.ir*, to be smitten, be enamored, be taken, fall in love. **épris (epri)** *a*, smitten; in love.

épreuve (eprœːv) *f*, test[ing]; trial; ordeal; proof (*Typ.*); heat (*sport*); event (*sport*). ~ **de force**, showdown. ~**s de tournage**, rushes (*TV, cinema*). ~ **d'imprimerie**, printer's proof. ~ **en placard**, galley proof. [~] **finale**, final [heat]. ~ **négative**, negative (*Phot.*). ~ **nulle**, dead heat. ~ [*positive*], print, pòsitive (*Phot.*). *à l'* ~ **de**, proof against. *à l'* ~ **du feu, des intempéries, des maladresses**, fireproof, weather-p., fool-p. *à toute* ~, unflinching; trusty. **éprouver** (pruve) *v.t*, to test, prove, try; experience, meet with, sustain, undergo; suffer; feel. **éprouvette** (vɛt) *f*, test glass; t. tube; t. piece; probe (*Surg.*).

épris (epri) *a*, smitten, enamoured, infatuated.

épuisé, e (epɥize) *p.a*, exhausted, spent; effete; out of print. **épuisement** (mɑ̃) *m*, *arrêt par* ~, burnout. **épuiser** (ze) *v.t*, to exhaust;

drain; empty. **épuisette** (zɛt) f, landing net; scoop, bailer.

épuration (epyrasjɔ̃) f, purification; refining. **épure** (py:r) f, working drawing; diagram. **épurer** (pyre) v.t, to purify; refine; weed out; debug (*computers*).

équarrir (ekari:r) v.t, to square; quarter, cut up (*dead animal*).

équateur (ekwatœ:r) m, equator. l'E~ (*Geog.*), Ecuador.

équation (ekwasjɔ̃) f, equation.

équatorial, e (ekwatɔrjal) a, equatorial. ¶ m, equatorial [telescope].

équerre (ekɛ:r) f, square (*instrument & at right angles*).

équestre (ekɛstr) a, equestrian.

équilibre (ekilibr) m, equilibrium; [equi]poise; balance; b. of power (*Pol.*). **équilibrer** (bre) v.t, to equilibrate, poise, balance, counterbalance.

équinoxe (ekinɔks) m, equinox. **équinoxial, e** (ksjal) a, equinoctial.

équipage (ekipa:ʒ) m, crew (*ship*); outfit, rig; set; train; equipage, turnout; plight. ~ de chasse, hunt. **équipe** (kip) f, train (*of boats*); shift, gang, corps, squad; crew (*boat*); team, side (*sport*). ~ de tournage, film unit. chef d'~, foreman. **équipée** (pe) f, escapade, lark. **équipement** (pmɑ̃) m, equipment; outfit. ~ de survie, survival kit. ~ de vie, life-support system. **équiper** (pe) v.t, to equip, fit out, rig [out].

équitable† (ekitabl) a, equitable, fair, just.

équitation (ekitasjɔ̃) f, riding, horsemanship.

équité (ekite) f, equity, fairness.

équivalent, e (ekivalɑ̃, ɑ̃:t) a. & m, equivalent. **équivaloir** (lwa:r) v.i.ir, to be equivalent; be tantamount.

équivoque (ekivɔk) a, equivocal; ambiguous, dubious, questionable. ¶ f, equivocation, ambiguity, prevarication. **équivoquer** (ke) v.i, to equivocate, prevaricate.

érable (erabl) m, maple. ~ madré, bird's-eye maple.

éradication (eradikasjɔ̃) f, eradication.

érafler (erafle) v.t, to scratch, graze. **éraflure** (fly:r) f, scratch.

éraillé, e (eraje) p.a, frayed; husky, hoarse; bloodshot. **érailler** (je) v.t, to fray.

ère (ɛ:r) f, era, epoch.

Érèbe (l') (ereb) m, Erebus.

érection (erɛksjɔ̃) f, erection; raising.

éreinter (erɛ̃te) v.t, to break the back of; tire out; lash (*fig.*), slate, pull to pieces.

ergol (ɛrgɔl) m, propellant.

ergot (ɛrgo) m, spur (*bird*); snug, lug; pin; ergot (*Bot. & Med.*). **ergoté, e** (gɔte) a, spurred (*bird*). **ergoter** (te) v.i, to cavil, quibble.

Érié (le lac) (erje), Lake Erie.

ériger (eriʒe) v.t, to erect, put up; raise, set up.

ermitage (ɛrmita:ʒ) m, hermitage. **ermite** (mit) m, hermit.

éroder (erɔde) v.t, to erode. **érosion** (zjɔ̃) f, erosion.

érotique (erɔtik) a, erotic; amatory. **érotisme** (tism) m, eroticism.

errant, e (ɛrɑ̃, ɑ̃:t) a, wandering; roving; stray; errant. **erratique** (ratik) a, erratic (*Geol., Med., etc.*).

erratum (eratɔm) m, erratum.

erre (ɛ:r) f, [head]way (*Naut.*); (pl.) track, spoor; (pl.) footsteps (*fig.*). **errements** (ɛrmɑ̃) m.pl, ways, methods. **errer** (ɛre) v.i, to wander, roam, rove, stroll, stray; err. **erreur** (rœ:r) f, error, mistake; fallacy. ~ de calcul, miscalculation. ~ de nom, misnomer. ~ de (ou sur la) personne, mistaken identity. ~ typographique, misprint. **erroné, e** (rone) a, erroneous, wrong, mistaken.

éructation (eryktasjɔ̃) f, eructation, belch[ing]. **éructer** (te) v.i, to eruct, belch.

érudit, e (erydi, it) a, erudite, scholarly, learned. ¶ m, scholar, learned man. **érudition** (disjɔ̃) f, erudition, learning, scholarship.

éruption (erypsjɔ̃) f, eruption; rash; blowout (*well*).

ès (ɛs) pr, of; in.

escabeau (ɛskabo) m. & **escabelle** (bɛl) f, stool.

escadre (ɛska:dr) f, squadron

(*Nav.*). **escadrille** (kadri;j) *f*, flotilla (*Nav.*); squadron (*air*). **escadron** (dr5) *m*, squadron (*cavalry*).

escalade (ɛskalad) *f*, scaling; escalation (*Mil.*). ~ *militaire & diplomatique*, military & diplomatic escalation. **escalader** (de) *v.t*, to scale, climb [over].

escale (ɛskal) *f*, call (*Ship.*); port of call. *faire* ~, to call.

escalier (ɛskalje) *m*, stair[s], staircase. ~ *d'honneur*, grand staircase. ~ *roulant*, escalator. ~ *tournant*, spiral (*or* winding) stairs.

escalope (ɛskalɔp) *f*, cutlet.

escamotage (ɛskamɔta;ʒ) *m*, juggling, conjuring. **escamoter** (te) *v.t*, to conjure away, spirit away; filch; (*abs.*) to juggle, conjure. **escamoteur** (tœ;r) *m*, juggler, conjuror, -er; pickpocket.

escampette (ɛskɑ̃pɛt) *f*: *prendre la poudre d'*~, to bolt, skedaddle. **escapade** (kapad) *f*, escapade, prank, lark.

escarbille (ɛskarbi;j) *f*, [coal] cinder.

escarbot (ɛskarbo) *m*, dung beetle.

escargot (ɛskargo) *m*, (*edible*) snail.

escarmouche (ɛskarmuʃ) *f*, skirmish. **escarmoucher** (ʃe) *v.i*, to skirmish.

escarpe (ɛskarp) *f*, [e]scarp. ¶ *m*, cutthroat, desperado. **escarpé, e** (pe) *a*, precipitous, steep, bluff. **escarpement** (pəmɑ̃) *m*, steepness; escarpment; slope.

escarpin (ɛskarpɛ̃) *m*, pump (*dress shoe*).

escarpolette (ɛskarpɔlɛt) *f*, swing (*child's*).

escarre (ɛska;r) *f*, scab (*Med.*).

Escaut (l') (ɛsko) *m*, the Scheldt.

escient (ɛsjɑ̃) *m*, knowledge. *à bon* ~, knowingly, wittingly.

esclaffer (s') (ɛsklafe) *v.pr*, to burst out laughing.

esclandre (ɛsklɑ̃;dr) *m*, scandal, scene.

esclavage (ɛsklava;ʒ) *m*, slavery, bondage, thraldom. **esclave** (kla;v) *n*, slave, thrall.

escobarder (ɛskɔbarde) *v.i*, to shuffle.

escogriffe (ɛskɔgrif) *m*, gawk, lout.

escompte (ɛskɔ̃;t) *m*, discount; discounting. **escompter** (kɔ̃te) *v.t*, to discount; cash (*a check for someone*); anticipate; bank on.

escorte (ɛskɔrt) *f*, escort; convoy. **escorter** (te) *v.t*, to escort; convoy.

escouade (ɛskwad) *f*, squad, gang.

escrime (ɛskrim) *f*, fencing, swordsmanship. **s'escrimer** (me) *v.pr*, to try hard.

escroc (ɛskro) *m*, swindler, sharper, crook. **escroquer** (krɔke) *v.t. & abs*, to swindle, swindle out of.

espace (ɛspɑs) *m*, space; room; (*f.*) space (*Typ.*). ~*s verts*, open *or* green spaces (*city planning*). ~ *lointain*, deep space. ~ *extra-atmosphérique*, outer space. **espacer** (se) *v.t.*, to space.

espadon (ɛspadɔ̃) *m*, swordfish.

espadrille (ɛspadri;j) *f*, canvas shoe with hempen sole.

Espagne (l') (ɛspaɲ) *f*, Spain. **espagnol, e** (nɔl) *a. & (language) m*, Spanish. **E**~, *n*, Spaniard. **espagnolette** (lɛt) *f*, window hasp.

espalier (ɛspalje) *m*, espalier.

espar (ɛspa;r) *m*, spar (*Naut.*); handspike (*Mil.*).

espèce (ɛspɛs) *f*, kind, sort, species; case in point (*law*); (*pl.*) cash, coin, specie. *l'*~ *animale*, the brute creation. *l'*~ *humaine*, mankind. ~*s sonnantes*, hard cash.

espérance (ɛsperɑ̃;s) *f*, hope, expectation; (*pl.*) promise. **espérer** (re) *v.t. & abs*, to hope for, expect; trust; hope.

espiègle (ɛspjɛgl) *a*, roguish, mischievous, impish, elfish; arch. ¶ *n*, rogue (*playfully*). **espièglerie** (glɛri) *f*, roguishness, mischief, prank.

espion, ne (ɛspjɔ̃, ɔn) *n*, spy. **espionnage** (ɔna;ʒ) *m*, espionage, spying. **espionner** (ne) *v.t. & abs*, to spy upon, watch; spy.

esplanade (ɛsplanad) *f*, esplanade, parade.

espoir (ɛspwaːr) *m*, hope, expectation.

esprit (ɛspri) *m*, spirit; ghost; mind; nous; feeling; sense; head; wit; temper. *l'~ de caste*, class consciousness. *~ de corps*, esprit de corps; team spirit. *~ fort*, free thinker. *le Saint-Esprit ou l'Esprit-Saint*, the Holy Ghost, the Holy Spirit.

esquif (ɛskif) *m*, skiff.

esquille (ɛskiːj) *f*, splinter (*of bone*).

ésquimau (ɛskimo) *a*, Eskimo. ¶ *m*, Eskimo; child's snowsuit; chocolate ice-cream pop.

esquinter (ɛskɛ̃te) *v.t*, to exhaust, tire; kill (*slang*).

esquisse (ɛskis) *f*, sketch; outline. **esquisser** (se) *v.t*, to sketch.

esquive (ɛskiːv) *f*, slip (*Box.*), dodging. **esquiver** (kive) *v.t*, to avoid, evade; dodge, slip. *s'~*, to slip away.

essai (ɛsɛ) *m*, test[ing], trial; attempt; assay[ing]; essay. *coup d'~*, first try.

essaim (ɛsɛ̃) *m*, swarm (*bees*). **essaimer** (ɛsɛme) *v.i*, to swarm; branch out (*fig.*).

essanger (ɛsɑ̃ʒe) *v.t*, to soak (*dirty linen*).

essarter (ɛsarte) *v.t*, to clear; grub up.

essayage (ɛsejaːʒ) *m*, testing; fitting; trying on.

essayer (ɛseje) *v.t*, to try, essay, endeavor, attempt; try on (*clothes*); test, essay. *s'~ à*, to try one's hand (*or* skill) at. **essayeur, euse** (jœːr, øːz) *n*, essayer; fitter (*clothes*). **essayiste** (jist) *n*, essayist.

esse (ɛs) *f*, S; S hook; linchpin.

essence (ɛsɑ̃ːs) *f*, essence; spirit; gasoline; kind *or* species (*of tree or wood*). *~ de bergamote*, bergamot oil. *~ de roses*, otto of roses, attar [of roses]. *poste d'~*, filling station. **essentiel, le†** (sɑ̃sjɛl) *a*, essential, material. ¶ *m*, essential, main point.

esseulé, e (ɛsœle) *p.p*, lone[some].

essieu (ɛsjø) *m*, axle, axletree.

essor (ɛsɔːr) *m*, flight, soaring, wing; play, scope; progress, strides.

essorer (ɛsɔre) *v.t*, to dry; wring (*washing*). **essoreuse** (røːz) *f*, wringer.

essoriller (ɛsɔrije) *v.t*, to crop.

essouffler (ɛsufle) *v.t*, to blow, wind.

essuie-glace (ɛsɥi) *m*, windshield wiper. **essuie-main,** *m*, [hand] towel. **essuie-plume,** *m*, penwiper. **essuie-verres,** *m*, glass cloth. **essuyer** (sɥije) *v.t*, to wipe [up], dry; mop up; endure, go through; experience, meet with.

est (ɛst) *m*, east.

estacade (ɛstakad) *f*, wing dam; jetty; boom (*harbor*); coal stage.

estafette (ɛstafɛt) *f*, courier; dispatch rider.

estafilade (ɛstafilad) *f*, gash, rent.

estame (ɛstam) *f*, worsted (*fabric*).

estaminet (ɛstaminɛ) *m*, small café & bar.

estampe (ɛstɑ̃ːp) *f*, print, engraving; swage. **estamper** (tɑ̃pe) *v.t*, to stamp; emboss; swage; dropforge; rub (*inscription*).

estampille (ɛstɑ̃piːj) *f*, stamp; trademark. **estampiller** (pije) *v.t*, to stamp; mark.

esthétique (ɛstetik) *a*, aesthetic.

estimation (ɛstimasjɔ̃) *f*, estimate, valuation; dead reckoning (*Naut.*). **estime** (tim) *f*, esteem, estimation; dead reckoning (*Naut.*). **estimer** (me) *v.t*, to estimate; value; esteem; deem; reckon.

estival, e (ɛstival) *a*, summer (*att.*). **estiver** (ve) *v.t*, to summer (*cattle*).

estoc (ɛstɔk) *m*, point (*sword*); stock (*tree*). **estocade** (kad) *f*, thrust (*Fenc.*). **estocader** (de) *v.t*, to thrust.

estomac (ɛstɔma) *m*, stomach; pluck. **estomaquer** (make) *v.t*, to take (*someone's*) breath away; offend.

estompe (ɛstɔ̃ːp) *f*, stump (*art*). **estomper** (tɔ̃pe) *v.t*, to stump; tone down (*fig.*).

Estonie (l') (ɛstɔni) *f*, Estonia.

estouffade (ɛstufad) *f*, steaming (*Cook.*).

estrade (ɛstrad) *f*, platform, stage; dais.

estragon (ɛstragɔ̃) *m*, tarragon.

estropié, e (ɛstrɔpje) *n*, cripple.
estropier (pje) *v.t*, to cripple,
lame; maim; murder (*language*).
estuaire (ɛstɥɛːr) *m*, estuary,
firth.
esturgeon (ɛstyrʒɔ̃) *m*, sturgeon.
et (e) *c*. (*abb. &*), and, &. ~ . . . ~
. . ., both . . . and . . . ~ *ainsi
de suite*, and so on; and so forth.
~ *patati*, ~ *patata* (patati, ta),
and so on, and so forth. ~*/ou*,
and/or.
étable (etabl) *f*, (*cattle*) shed,
house; sty. **établer** (ble) *v.t*, to
stable, stall; sty.
établi (etabli) *m*, [work] bench,
stand. **établir** (bliːr) *v.t*, to establish; set up; set (*a sail*); lay
down; settle; draw [up], make
out; strike (*balance*); prove; substantiate. **établissement** (blismɑ̃)
m, establishment, etc; institution;
capital expenditure.
étage (etaːʒ) *m*, floor, stor[e]y;
stage, level; step; tier; rank, degree; measures (*Geol.*). **étager**
(taʒe) *v.t*, to range; terrace;
spread. **étagère** (ʒɛːr) *f*, [set of]
shelves; whatnot; dresser. ~ *de
cheminée*, mantelpiece.
étai (etɛ) *m*, shore, prop, post;
stay.
étain (etɛ̃) *m*, tin; pewter. *feuille
d'*~, tinfoil.
étal (etal) *m*, butcher's shop.
étalage (laːʒ) *m*, (*shop*) window
[show]; window dressing; show;
display; stall. **étalagiste** (laʒist)
n, frontsman; stall holder; window dresser.
étale (etal) *a.inv*, slack (*water*)
(*Naut.*).
étaler (etale) *v.t*, to expose for
sale; show; show off, flaunt, air;
display; lay out; spread [out];
stem (*the tide*). **s'**~, to sprawl.
étalon (etalɔ̃) *m*, stallion, stud
horse; standard (*of values*). **éta-
lonner** (lone) *v.t*, to stamp
(*weights, etc.*); rate; standardize.
étambot (etɑ̃bo) *m*, sternpost
(*ship*).
étamer (etame) *v.t*, to tin; silver
(*mirror*).
étamine (etamin) *f*, bolting
cloth; filter cloth; stamen (*Bot.*).
~ *à pavillon*, bunting.

étamper (etɑ̃pe) *v.t*, to stamp,
press; swage; drop-forge.
étanche (etɑ̃ːʃ) *a*, tight; watertight; impervious. **étancher**
(tɑ̃ʃe) *v.t*, to staunch, stop; make
watertight; dry; quench, slake.
étançon (etɑ̃sɔ̃) *m*, shore; stanchion. **étançonner** (sɔne) *v.t*, to
shore [up].
étang (etɑ̃) *m*, pond, pool.
étape (etap) *f*, stage, stopping
place.
état (eta) *m*, state; condition;
frame (*of mind*); plight; repair;
order; fettle, trim; status; position, posture; profession, occupation; statement, account, return, list; state (*stage of engraved
or etched plate*). en [*bon*] ~ *de
navigabilité*, seaworthy; airwor-
thy. ~ *de siège*, state of siege. ~
des malades, sick list. ~ *civil*,
legal or civil status. ~*-major*,
general staff. *en* ~ *de*, fit for. *hors
d'*~, useless. État, *m*, State government. *les* ~*s-Unis* [*d'Amérique*], the United States [of
America]. **étatisme** (tism) *m*, State
socialism, nationalism. **État-
major** (maʒɔːr) *m*, staff (*Mil.*);
[staff] headquarters; senior officers, executive.
étau (eto) *m*, vise (*tool*). ~*-limeur*
(limœːr), shaping machine.
étayer (etɛje) *v.t*, to shore [up];
prop, support.
et cætera (etsetera) *phrase & m*.
(*abb. etc.*), et cetera, etc.
été (ete) *m*, summer; prime [of
life]. ¶ *p.p*, **être**.
éteignoir (etɛɲwaːr) *m*, extinguisher (*light*); damper, wet blanket (*fig., pers.*). **éteindre** (tɛ̃ːdr)
v.t.ir, to extinguish, put out; silence (*enemy's fire*); slake, slack;
quench; pay off; soften. ~ *la lumière*, ~ *l'électricité*, to switch
off (*or turn off*) the light. **s'**~,
to go out (*light*); pass away; die
[out]. **éteint, e** (tɛ̃, ɛ̃ːt) *p.a*, extinct; out; dull.
étendage (etɑ̃daːʒ) *m*, hanging
out (*washing*); spreading; clothes-
lines; lying at full length. **étan-
dard** (daːr) *m*, standard, flag,
colors. **étendoir** (dwaːr) *m*,
clothesline; drying yard. **étendre**
(tɑ̃ːdr) *v.t*, to spread, extend;

expand; widen; stretch [out]; reach [out]; lay [out]; hang out; dilute. **s'~**, to extend; spread; stretch; reach; expatiate, enlarge. **étendu, e** (tãdy) *a*, extensive, wide, far-reaching; outspread; outstretched. **étendue** (dy) *f*, extent; area; compass; stretch, expanse, sweep, tract; reach; range; scope; length.

éternel, le† (etɛrnɛl) *a*, eternal, everlasting; never-ending. **éterniser** (nize) *v.t*, to eternalize; protract. **s'~**, to last (*or* stay) forever. **éternité** (te) *f*, eternity.

éternuement (etɛrnymã) *m*, sneezing; sneeze. **éternuer** (nɥe) *v.i*, to sneeze.

étêter (etɛte) *v.t*, to top, poll; take the head off.

éteule (etœl) *f*, stubble.

éther (etɛːr) *m*, ether. **éthéré, e** (tere) *a*, ethereal.

Éthiopie (l') (etjɔpi) *f*, Ethiopia. **éthiopien, ne** (pjɛ̃, ɛn) *a. & É~*, *n*, Ethiopian.

éthique (etik) *a*, ethical. ¶ *f*, ethics.

ethnie (ɛtni) *f*, ethnos, ethnic group.

ethnographie (ɛtnɔgrafi) *f*, ethnography. **ethnologie** (lɔʒi) *f*, ethnology. **ethnologique** (ʒik) *a*, ethnologic(al). **ethnologue** (lɔg) *m*, ethnologist.

éthyle (etil) *m*, ethyl.

étiage (etjaːʒ) *m*, low water; low-water mark (*river*).

étinceler (etɛ̃sle) *v.i*, to sparkle, glitter, glisten, flash. **étincelle** (sɛl) *f*, spark; sparkle, flash.

étioler (etjole) *v.t*, to etiolate, blanch. **s'~**, to droop, wilt.

étique (etik) *a*, emaciated, skinny.

étiqueter (etikte) *v.t*, to label; ticket. **étiquette** (kɛt) *f*, label; tally; ticket; etiquette. *~ volante*, tie-on label; tag label.

étirer (etire) *v.t*, to stretch, draw [out].

étoffe (etɔf) *f*, stuff; fabric; material; grit (*fig.*); establishment charges (*printer's*). *~ à carreaux, ~ en damier*, check [material]. **étoffé, e** (fe) *p.a*, stuffed; stocky. **étoffer** (fe) *v.t*, to use sufficient material in; stuff; fill out.

étoile (etwal) *f*, star; asterisk. *~ de mer*, starfish. *~ du matin*, *~ matinière* (matinjɛːr), morning star. *~ tombante, ~ filante*, shooting s., falling s. *à la belle ~*, in the open. **étoilé, e** (le) *a*, starry; starli[gh]t; starred.

étole (etɔl) *f*, stole.

étonnant, e (etɔnã, ãːt) *a*, astonishing, amazing, surprising; wonderful. **étonnamment** (namã) *ad*, astonishingly. **étonnement** (nmã) *m*, astonishment. **étonner** (ne) *v.t*, to astonish, amaze, surprise. **s'~**, to be astonished, wonder, marvel.

étouffant, e (etufã, ãːt) *a*, stifling, sultry; stuffy.

étouffée (etufe) *f*, steaming (*Cook.*).

étouffer (etufe) *v.t. & i*, to choke, stifle; smother; quell; hush up. **étouffoir** (fwaːr) *m*, charcoal extinguisher; damper (*piano*).

étoupe (etup) *f*, tow, junk, oakum. **étouper** (pe) *v.t*, to caulk.

étoupille (etupiːj) *f*, friction tube; fuse.

étourderie (eturdəri) *f*, thoughtlessness. **étourdi, e** (di) *a*, thoughtless, heedless; flighty. ¶ *m*, scatterbrain. **à l'étourdie & étourdiment** (dimã) *ad*, thoughtlessly. **étourdir** (diːr) *v.t*, to stun; deafen; din; make dizzy; daze; deaden. **s'~**, to forget (*or* drown) one's troubles. **étourdissement** (dismã) *m*, dizziness, giddiness; stupefaction.

étourneau (eturno) *m*, starling (*bird*); foolish youth.

étrange† (etrãːʒ) *a*, strange, odd, queer; quaint. **étranger, ère** (trãʒe, ɛɪr) *a*, foreign; strange; unfamiliar; extraneous; alien, irrelevant. ¶ *n*, foreigner, alien; stranger. ¶ *m*, foreign parts. **à l'~**, *ad*, abroad. **de l'~**, from abroad. **étrangeté** (ʒte) *f*, strangeness, oddness; quaintness.

étranglement (etrãglemã) *m*, strangulation. **étrangler** (gle) *v.t*, to strangle, throttle, choke; narrow; squeeze; strangulate; (*v.i.*) to choke.

étrave (etraːv) *f*, stem (*ship*).

être (ɛːtr) *m*, being; creature; thing; reality; stock (*tree*); (*pl.*)

arrangements or disposition of a building. ¶ *v.i.ir*, to be; belong; come; have. y ~, to get it, understand. *où en êtes-vous?*, how far have you got?

étrécir (etresi:r) *v.t. & i. & s'~*, to narrow, shrink, contract.

étreindre (etrɛ̃:dr) *v.t.ir*, to clasp, hug, grip; wring; bind. **étreinte** (trɛ̃:t) *f*, grip, grasp; hug, embrace.

étrenne (etrɛn) *f*, first use; (*pl.*) New Year's gift, handsel; Christmas present. (*In Fr. presents are given on or about Jan. 1*). **étrenner** (trɛne) *v.t*, to be the first customer of; use (*or wear*) for the first time; handsel.

étrésillon (etrezijɔ̃) *m*, strut, brace; flying shore.

étrier (etrie) *m*, stirrup; U bolt; strap.

étrille (etri:j) *f*, currycomb. **étriller** (trije) *v.t*, to curry; drub; fleece.

étriper (etripe) *v.t*, to gut.

étriqué, e (etrike) *a*, scant[y], narrow; cramped. **étriquer** (ke) *v.t*, to skimp.

étrivière (etrivjɛ:r) *f*, stirrup leather; (*pl.*) thrashing.

étroit, e† (etrwa, at) *a*, narrow; limited; close; tight; strict. **étroitesse** (tɛs) *f*, narrowness, etc.

étude (etyd) *f*, study; preparation (*Sch.*); survey; (*lawyer's*) office; practice. **étudiant, e** (djɑ̃, ɑ̃:t) *n*, student. **étudier** (dje) *v.i. & t*, to study; read; survey. *s'~*, to try hard, be careful.

étui (etɥi) *m*, case, box; cover.

étuve (ety:v) *f*, drying stove; oven (*fig.*). *~ humide*, steam room (*bath*). *~ sèche*, hot room, sweating r. (*bath*). **étuvée** (tyve) *f*, steaming (*Cook.*). **étuver** (ve) *v.t*, to stove; stew; foment (*Med.*).

étymologie (etimɔlɔʒi) *f*, etymology. **étymologique†** (ʒik) *a*, etymologic(al).

eucalyptus (økalipty:s) *m*, eucalyptus.

Eucharistie (økaristi) *f*, Eucharist, holy communion.

eugénie (øʒeni) *f*, eugenics. **eugénique** (nik) *a*, eugenic.

euh (ø) *i*, hem! hum! h'm!

eunuque (ønyk) *m*, eunuch.

euphémique (øfemik) *a*, euphemistic. **euphémisme** (mism) *m*, euphemism.

euphonie (øfɔni) *f*, euphony. **euphonique** (nik) *a*, euphonic, euphonious.

Euphrate (l') (øfrat) *m*, the Euphrates.

Europe (l') (ørɔp) *f*, Europe. **européen, ne** (peɛ̃, ɛn) *a. & E~*, *n*, European.

eux (ø) *pn.m.pl*. See *lui*.

évacuer (evakɥe) *v.t & abs*, to evacuate, void, clear out.

évader (s') (evade) *v.pr*, to escape, get away.

évaluation (evalɥasjɔ̃) *f*, valuation, estimate; casting off (*Typ.*). **évaluer** (lɥe) *v.t*, to value, estimate; cast off.

évanescent, e (evanɛsɑ̃, ɑ̃:t) *a*, evanescent.

évangélique† (evɑ̃ʒelik) *a*, evangelic(al). **évangéliste** (list) *m*, evangelist. **évangile & É~** (ʒil) *m*, gospel.

évanouir (s') (evanwi:r) *v.pr*, to faint, swoon; vanish, fade away. **évanouissement** (wismɑ̃) *m*, fading (*radio, sound, etc.*); fainting fit.

évaporation (evaporasjɔ̃) *f*, evaporation. **évaporé, e** (re) *n*, feather-brained creature. **évaporer** (re) *v.t*, to evaporate; vent. *s'~*, to evaporate.

évaser (evase) *v.t*, to flare, bell-mouth.

évasif, ive† (evazif, i:v) *a*, evasive. **évasion** (zjɔ̃) *f*, escape, flight.

évêché (eveʃe) *m*, bishopric; see; bishop's house.

éveil (evɛ:j) *m*, alert, guard; warning; awakening (*fig.*). **éveillé, e** (veje) *a*, wide-awake; perky. **éveiller** (je) *v.t*, to wake [up]. *s'~*, to awaken (*fig.*).

événement (evɛnmɑ̃) *m*, event, occurrence, incident; emergency; outcome, issue.

évent (evɑ̃) *m*, [open] air; vent; air hole; flaw; flatness (*liquor*). **éventail** (ta:j) *m*, fan. **éventaire** (tɛ:r) *m*, peddler's tray; street stand or stall. **éventé, e** (te) *p.a*, stale, flat, dead; giddy, flighty. **éventer** (te) *v.t*, to fan; air; turn over; flatten;

fill (*sail*); open; get wind of; let out.

éventrer (evɑ̃tre) *v.t*, to rip open, r. up; disembowel, eviscerate.

éventualité (evɑ̃tɥalite) *f*, eventuality, contingency. **éventuel, le†** (tɥɛl) *a*, contingent.

évêque (evɛːk) *m*, bishop.

évertuer (s') (evɛrtɥe) *v.pr*, to exert oneself, strive.

éviction (eviksjɔ̃) *f*, eviction.

évidence (evidɑ̃ːs) *f*, evidence. *en ~*, in e., conspicuous. **évident, e** (dɑ̃, ɑ̃ːt) *a*, evident, obvious, plain. **évidemment** (damɑ̃) *ad*, evidently.

évider (evide) *v.t*, to hollow out; cut away; groove, flute.

évier (evje) *m*, sink (*kitchen*).

évincer (evɛ̃se) *v.t*, to evict; oust, turn out.

évitable (evitabl) *a*, avoidable. **évitage** (taːʒ) *m*, ou **évitée** (te) *f*, sea room; swinging. **évitement** (tmɑ̃) *m*, ou **voie d'~** (*Rly.*), passing place, turnout, shunting loop. **éviter** (te) *v.t*, to avoid, shun; eschew; evade, dodge, steer clear of; help; (*v.i. & abs.*) to swing (*Naut.*). *~ de la tête*, to duck.

évocation (evɔkasjɔ̃) *f*, evocation, calling up, raising.

évoluer (evɔlɥe) *v.i*, to perform evolutions, maneuver, evolve. **évolution** (lysjɔ̃) *f*, evolution.

évoquer (evɔke) *v.t*, to evoke, conjure up.

ex- (ɛks) *pr*, ex-; ex; late.

exacerber (ɛgzasɛrbe) *v.t*, to exacerbate.

exact, e† (ɛgzakt) *a*, exact, accurate, correct; punctual. **exaction** (ksjɔ̃) *f*, exaction. **exactitude** (tityd) *f*, exactness, exactitude, accuracy; punctuality.

exagération (ɛgzaʒerasjɔ̃) *f*, exaggeration. **exagérer** (re) *v.t. & abs*, to exaggerate; overstate; overdo.

exalter (ɛgzalte) *v.t*, to exalt; extol; excite.

examen (ɛgzamɛ̃) *m*, examination; scrutiny. **examinateur, trice** (minatœːr, tris) *n*, examiner. **examiner** (ne) *v.t*, to examine; overhaul; look into.

exaspérer (ɛgzaspere) *v.t*, to exasperate; aggravate (*Med.*).

exaucer (ɛgzose) *v.t*, to hear (*prayer*), grant.

excavateur (ɛkskavatœːr) *m*, excavator, digger, shovel, navvy. **excavation** (sjɔ̃) *f*, excavation; pothole.

excédant (ɛksedɑ̃) *a*, surplus; excessive; exasperating; overwhelming (*odor*). **excédent** *m*, excess, surplus. *~ de bagages*, surplus baggage. **excéder (de)** *v.t*, to exceed; tire, weary; importune.

excellemment (ɛksɛlamɑ̃) *ad*, excellently. **excellence** (lɑ̃ːs) *f*, excellence; choiceness. *par ~*, preëminently. *Son E~*, *f*, His Excellency. **excellent, e** (lɑ̃, ɑ̃ːt) *a*, excellent. **exceller (le)** *v.i*, to excel.

excentricité (ɛksɑ̃trisite) *f*, eccentricity; throw; remoteness. **excentrique** (trik) *a*, eccentric; outlying. ¶ (*Mech.*) *m*, eccentric, cam.

excepté (ɛksɛpte) *pr*, except[ing], save, but, barring. **excepter (te)** *v.t*, to except. **exception** (sjɔ̃) *f*, exception; plea (*law*). *~ péremptoire*, demurrer. **exceptionnel, le†** (ɔnɛl) *a*, exceptional.

excès (ɛksɛ) *m*, excess; abuse; violence. **excessif, ive†** (sɛsif, iːv) *a*, excessive; fulsome; undue.

excitant (ɛksitɑ̃) *m*, stimulant. **excitation** (tasjɔ̃) *f*, excitation; incitement; excitement. **exciter (te)** *v.t*, to excite; incite; stir up; urge; rouse; stimulate, fan.

exclamation (ɛksklamasjɔ̃) *f*, exclamation; ejaculation. **s'exclamer (me)** *v.pr*, to exclaim against.

exclure (ɛksklyːr) *v.t.ir*, to exclude; shut out, debar. **exclusif, ive†** (klyzif, iːv) *a*, exclusive; sole. **exclusion** (zjɔ̃) *f*, exclusion. **exclusivité** (zivite) *f*, exclusive (*or* sole) right(s); scoop (*journalism*). *en ~*, first-run (*movie*).

excommunier (ɛkskɔmynje) *v.t*, to excommunicate.

excrément (ɛkskremɑ̃) *m*, excrement; scum (*fig.*).

excroissance (ɛkskrwasɑ̃ːs) *f*, excrescence.

excursion (ɛkskyrsjɔ̃) *f*, excursion, trip, tour, outing. ~ à pied, walking tour, hike. ~ accompagnée, conducted tour. excursionniste (ɔnist) n, excursionist.

excuse (ɛkskyːs) f, excuse; (pl.) apology. excuser (kyze) v.t, to excuse.

exeat (ɛgzeat) m, exeat; dismissal.

exécrable† (ɛgzekrabl) a, execrable. exécrer (kre) v.t, to execrate.

exécutable (ɛgzekytabl) a, workable, practicable. exécutant, e (tã, ãːt) n, performer (Mus.). exécuter (te) v.t, to execute; carry out; perform; fulfil; enforce; expel; buy in against, sell out against (Stk Ex.); distrain upon, sell up. s'~, to pay up; yield. exécuteur (trice) testamentaire, executor, trix. exécution (sjɔ̃) f, execution, etc. exécutoire (twaːr) a, executory; enforceable.

exemplaire (ɛgzãplɛːr) a, exemplary. ¶ m, copy, specimen. ~ du souffleur, prompt book. exemple (zãːpl) m, example; lead; illustration; instance; copy. par ~!, you don't say!, it can't be true!

exempt, e (ɛgzã, ãːt) a, exempt, free. exempter (zãte) v.t, to exempt, free; excuse. s'~ de, to abstain from, get out of. exemption (zãpsjɔ̃) f, exemption; immunity; freedom.

exercer (ɛgzɛrse) v.t, to exercise; train; drill; practice; ply (trade); exert; wield (power); try (patience); inspect (excise). exercice (sis) m, exercise; drill[ing]; practice; office; tenure (of office); inspection; trading; [financial] year, [accounting] period. ~ de doigté, five-finger exercise. ~s de tir, musketry (Mil.).

exfolier (s') (ɛksfɔlje) v.pr, to exfoliate.

exhalaison (ɛgzalɛzɔ̃) f, exhalation (mist). exhalation (lasjɔ̃) f, exhalation (act). exhaler (le) v.t, to exhale; vent; reek with, reek of.

exhausser (ɛgzose) v.t, to raise.

exhiber (ɛgzibe) v.t, to exhibit, produce, show. exhibition (bisjɔ̃) f, exhibition.

exhorter (ɛgzɔrte) v.t, to exhort, urge.

exhumer (ɛgzyme) v.t, to exhume, disinter; rake up.

exigeant, e (ɛgziʒã, ãːt) a, particular, exacting, hard to please. exigence (ʒãːs) f, unreasonableness; requirement; exigence, -cy. exiger (ʒe) v.t, to exact, require, demand; call for. exigibilité (ʒibilite) f, [re]payability; demand; current liability. exigible (bl) a, [re]payable; claimable, exigible.

exigu, ë (ɛgzigy) a, exiguous, scanty, jejune, small, diminutive. exiguïté (gqite) f, exiguity.

exil (ɛgzil) m, exile. exilé, e (le) n, exile. exiler (le) v.t, to exile.

existence (ɛgzistãːs) f, existence; life; stock (Com.). exister (te) v.i, to exist, be; be extant.

existentialisme (egzistãsjalism) m, existentialism (Philos.).

ex-libris (ɛkslibriːs) m, bookplate, ex-libris.

exode (ɛgzɔd) m, exodus, flight. l'E~, Exodus (Bible).

exonérer (ɛgzɔnere) v.t, to exonerate, exempt.

exorbitamment (ɛgzɔrbitamã) ad, exorbitantly. exorbitant, e (tã, ãːt) a, exorbitant, extravagant.

exorciser (ɛgzɔrsize) v.t, to exorcise.

exorde (ɛgzɔrd) m, exordium; beginning.

exotique (ɛgzɔtik) a, exotic; foreign.

expansif, ive (ɛkspãsif, iːv) a, expansive; effusive. expansion (sjɔ̃) f, expansion.

expatrier (ɛkspatrie) v.t, to expatriate.

expectant, e (ɛkspɛktã, ãːt) a, expectant; wait-&-see. expectative (tatiːv) f, expectation, expectancy.

expectorer (ɛkspɛktɔre) v.t. & abs, to expectorate.

expédient, e (ɛkspedjã, ãːt) a, expedient. ¶ m, expedient, resource, shift.

expédier (ɛkspedje) v.t, to expedite; dispose of; bolt (food); dispatch, send, forward, ship; copy & authenticate (law). ~

[*en douane*] to clear (*a ship*) [outwards]. **expéditeur, trice** (ditœːr, tris) *n*, sender; (*m.*) shipper; consignor; forwarding agent. **expéditif, ive** (tif, iːv) *a*, expeditious. **expédition** (sjɔ̃) *f*, expedition; disposal; dispatch, sending, forwarding; shipment, consignment; transit; adventure; clearance [outwards]; copy; (*pl.*) [ship's clearance] papers. **expéditionnaire** (ɔnɛːr) *a*, expeditionary. ¶ *m*, sender; dispatch clerk; shipping clerk; copying clerk.

expérience (ɛksperjɑ̃ːs) *f*, experiment; experience. **expérimental, e†** (rimɑ̃tal) *a*, experimental. **expérimenter** (te) *v.t*, to try; (*abs.*) to experiment.

expert, e (ɛkspɛːr, ɛrt) *a*, expert, skilled. ¶ *m*, expert; surveyor. ~-**comptable**, professional accountant. **expertise** (pɛrtiːz) *f*, survey; examination; report. **expertiser** (tize) *v.t*, to survey.

expier (ɛkspje) *v.t*, to expiate, atone for.

expiration (ɛkspirasjɔ̃) *f*, expiration; expiry. **expirer** (re) *v.t. & i*, to expire.

explétif, ive (ɛkspletif, iːv) *a*, expletive.

explicatif, ive (ɛksplikatif, iːv) *a*, explanatory. **explication** (sjɔ̃) *f*, explanation; construction, rendering. **explicite†** (sit) *a*, explicit. **expliquer** (ke) *v.t*, to explain; account for; construe, render.

exploit (ɛksplwa) *m*, exploit, achievement, feat; writ. **exploitable** (tabl) *a*, workable; payable. **exploitant** (tɑ̃) *m*, operator, owner or [his] agent (*mine, etc.*). **exploitation** (tasjɔ̃) *f*, work[ing], operation; mining; exploitation; workings; farming; trading. ~ **agricole**, farm. **exploiter** (te) *v.t*, to work, run, operate; farm; mine; exploit. **exploiteur, euse** (tœːr, øːz) *n*, exploiter.

explorateur, trice (ɛksplɔratœːr, tris) *n*, explorer. **explorer** (re) *v.t*, to explore.

exploser (ɛksploze) *v.i*, to explode. **explosif** (zif) *m*, explosive.

¶ *a*, explosive; sensational. **explosion** (zjɔ̃) *f*, explosion; [out]burst.

exportateur (ɛkspɔrtatœːr) *m*, exporter. **exportation** (sjɔ̃) *f*, export[ation]. **exporter** (te) *v.t*, to export.

exposant, e (ɛkspozɑ̃, ɑ̃ːt) *n*, exhibitor; petitioner (*law*); (*m.*) exponent, index (*Math.*). **exposé** (ze) *m*, statement; account. **exposer** (ze) *v.t. & abs*, to expose; show, display, exhibit; open; expound; explain; state. **exposition** (zisjɔ̃) *f*, exposition; exposure; exhibition, show; aspect, frontage (*of house*).

exprès, esse (ɛksprɛ, ɛs) *a*, express. **exprès**, *ad*, on purpose, purposely. ¶ *m*, express messenger. [**train**] **express** (prɛs) *m*, express [train]. *bateau express*, fast boat. **expressément** (prɛsemɑ̃) *ad*, expressly.

expressif, ive (ɛkspresif, iːv) *a*, expressive. **expression** (sjɔ̃) *f*, expression; phrase. **exprimer** (prime) *v.t*, to express; squeeze out; voice.

exproprier (ɛksprɔprie) *v.t*, to expropriate.

expulser (ɛkspylse) *v.t*, to expel, drive out, eject.

expurger (ɛkspyrʒe) *v.t*, to expurgate, bowdlerize.

exquis, e (ɛkski, iːz) *a*, exquisite. ¶ *m*, exquisiteness. **exquisément** (kizemɑ̃) *ad*, exquisitely.

exsangue (ɛksɑ̃ːg) *a*, bloodless, anemic; corpse-like.

exsuder (ɛksyde) *v.i*, to exude.

extase (ɛkstɑːz) *f*, ecstasy; trance. **s'extasier** (tɑzje) *v.pr*, to go into ecstasies. **extatique** (tatik) *a*, ecstatic, rapturous.

extenseur (ɛkstɑ̃sœːr) *m*, extensor (*muscle*); chest expander; trouser stretcher. **extensible** (sibl) *a*, extensible, expanding; open-ended (*computers*). **extension** (sjɔ̃) *f*, extension. *par ~*, in a wider sense..

exsuder (ɛksyde) *v.i*, to exude.

extase (ɛkstɑːz) *f*, ecstasy; trance. **s'extasier** (tɑzje) *v.pr*, to go into ecstasies. **extatique** (tatik) *a*, ecstatic, rapturous.

extenseur (ɛkstɑ̃sœːr) *m*, extensor (*muscle*); chest expander; trouser stretcher. **extension** (sjɔ̃) *f*, extension. **par ~**, in a wider sense.

exténuer (ɛkstenɥe) *v.t*, to tire out, wear out.

extérieur, e† (ɛksterjœ:r) *a*, exterior, external, outer, outside; outward; foreign. ¶ *m*, exterior, outside; foreign countries, abroad.

exterminer (ɛkstɛrmine) *v.t*, to exterminate.

externat (ɛkstɛrna) *m*, day school. **externe** (tɛrn) *a*, external, exterior. *pour l'usage ~*, for outward application, not to be taken (*Med.*). ¶ *n*, day scholar; nonresident assistant to hospital surgeon.

exterritorialité (ɛksteritɔrjalite) *f*, extraterritoriality.

extincteur [d'incendie] (ɛkstɛ̃ktœ:r) *m*, [fire] extinguisher. **extinction** (sjɔ̃) *f*, extinction; slaking; quenching; paying off; loss (*of voice*). **~ des feux**, lights out (*Mil.*).

extirper (ɛkstirpe) *v.t*, to extirpate, eradicate.

extorquer (ɛkstɔrke) *v.t*, to extort, wring. **extorsion** (sjɔ̃) *f*, extortion.

extra (ɛkstra) *ad. & m*, extra; top quality (*food, etc.*).

extraction (ɛkstraksjɔ̃) *f*, extraction; winning (*Min.*); quarrying; birth, parentage.

extrader (ɛkstrade) *v.t*, to extradite. **extradition** (disjɔ̃) *f*, extradition.

extraire (ɛkstrɛ:r) *v.t.ir*, to extract, take out; excerpt; get, win; quarry. **extrait** (trɛ) *m*, extract; excerpt. **~s d'auteurs**, extracts (*or* selections) from [the writings *or* works of] authors. **~ de naissance**, birth certificate. **~ mortuaire**, death c.

extraordinaire† (ɛkstraɔrdinɛːr) *a. & m*, extraordinary; special; unusual.

extravagance (ɛkstravagɑ̃:s) *f*, extravagance; exorbitance; folly. **extravagant, e** (gɑ̃, ɑ̃:t) *a*, extravagant, wild. **extravaguer** (ge) *v.i*, to rave.

extrême (ɛkstrɛːm) *a. & m*, extreme (*a. & m.*); utmost; drastic; dire. **~onction**, *f*, extreme unction. *l'E~Orient*, *m*, the Far East. **extrêmement** (trɛmmɑ̃) *ad*, extremely; exceedingly; intensely. **extrémiste** (tremist) *n*, extremist. **extrémité** (te) *f*, extremity; end; tip.

extrinsèque (ɛkstrɛ̃sɛk) *a*, extrinsic.

exubérance (ɛgzyberɑ̃:s) *f*, exuberance; luxuriance. **exubérant, e** (rɑ̃, ɑ̃:t) *a*, exuberant; luxuriant.

exulter (ɛgzylte) *v.i*, to exult.

F

fa (fa) *m*, F (Mus.).

fable (fa:bl) *f*, fable; story; byword, laughing stock. **fablier** (fablie) *m*, fabulist; book of fables.

fabricant (fabrikɑ̃) *m*, manufacturer, maker. **fabricateur, trice** (katœ:r, tris) *n*, fabricator; forger. **~ de fausse monnaie**, counterfeiter. **fabrication** (sjɔ̃) *f*, manufacture; make; work; fabrication. **fabrique** (brik) *f*, [manu]factory, works, mill; fabric (*edifice*); vestry, church council; invention (*fig.*). **fabriquer** (ke) *v.t*, to manufacture, make; fabricate, invent, trump up.

fabuleux, euse† (fabylø, ø:z) *a*, fabulous, fabled. **fabuliste** (list) *m*, fabulist.

façade (fasad) *f*, front, frontage, façade, frontispiece (*Arch.*).

face (fas) *f*, face; front; frontage (*extent of front*); side (*record*); obverse, head (*coin*); aspect. **~ à** facing. **en ~**, to one's face. **en ~ de**, *pr*, opposite, facing. *faire ~ à*, to face; keep pace with; front; meet.

face-à-main (fasamɛ̃) *m*, lorgnette.

facétie (fasesi) *f*, joke, jest. **facétieux, euse** (sjø, ø:z) *a*, facetious, waggish, jocular.

facette (fasɛt) *f*, facet. **facetter** (te) *v.t*, to facet.

fâché, e (faʃe) *p.a*, angry; sorry. **fâcher** (ʃe) *v.t*, to make angry, anger; grieve, pain. se ~, to get (*or* be) angry. **fâcherie** (ʃri) *f*, bad feeling; tiff. **fâcheux, euse†** (ʃø, øːz) *a*, unfortunate, tiresome, troublesome; sad. ¶ *m*, unfortunate part; bore, nuisance (*pers.*).

facial, e (fasjal) *a*, facial; face (*att.*). **faciès** (sjɛːs) *m*, facies; cast of features.

facile† (fasil) *a*, easy; facile; ready; fluent. **facilité** (lite) *f*, easiness, ease; facility; fluency; aptitude. **faciliter** (te) *v.t*, to facilitate.

façon (fasɔ̃) *f*, make; workmanship; making; labor; manner, fashion, way, wise, style, pattern; (*pl.*) manners; (*pl.*) ceremony, fuss. *de ~ à*, so as to. *de toute ~*, in any case. *en aucune ~*, by no means. *de ~ que*, so that. *faire des ~s*, to stand on ceremony.

faconde (fakɔ̃ːd) *f*, flow of language.

façonné, e (fasɔne) *p.a*, figured (*textiles*). **façonner** (ne) *v.t*, to make; shape, fashion, form, mold; dress. **façonnier, ère** (nje, ɛːr) *a*, [over-]ceremonious, fussy.

fac-similé (faksimile) *m*, facsimile.

factage (faktaːʒ) *m*, parcels delivery; porterage. **facteur** (tœːr) *m*, maker (*instruments*); postman; porter (*Rly.*); salesman; agent; factor, element. ~ *des télégraphes*, telegraph messenger, t. boy.

factice (faktis) *a*, imitation (*att.*), artificial; factitious; forced; meretricious.

factieux, euse (faksjø, øːz), *a*, factious.

faction (faksjɔ̃) *f*, sentry duty, guard; faction. **factionnaire** (ɔnɛːr) *m*, sentry.

factorerie (faktɔrri) *f*, [foreign *or* colonial] agency.

factotum (faktɔtɔm) *m*, factotum, man Friday.

factrice (faktris) *f*, postwoman.

factum (faktɔm) *m*, diatribe; statement of claim (*law*).

facture (faktyːr) *f*, invoice, bill;

note; treatment (*music, art*); workmanship. ~ *fictive*, pro forma invoice. ~ *générale*, statement [of account]. **facturer** (tyre) *v.t*, to invoice.

facultatif, ive† (fakyltatif, iːv) *a*, optional. **faculté** (te) *f*, faculty; option; right; power; leave; liberty; property; branch [of study]; (*pl.*) means; (*pl.*) cargo, goods (*marine Insce.*).

fadaise[s] (fadɛːz) *f.[pl.]*, twaddle, flummery, rubbish, stuff & nonsense.

fadasse (fadas) *a*, sickly, insipid. **fade†** (fad) *a*, insipid, tasteless, flat; mawkish; namby-pamby. **fadeur** (dœːr) *f*, insipidity.

faffe (faf) *m*, piece of paper; banknote. (*pl.*) **fafiots** (jo) identity papers (*slang*).

fagot (fago) *m*, fagot; bundle. **fagoter** (gɔte) *v.t*, to fagot; bundle; dress like a swell.

faiblard, e (fɛblaːr, ard) *a*, weakly. ¶ *n*, weakling. **faible†** (bl) *a*, weak; feeble; low; faint; shallow; slight; thin; light; small; scant[y]; slack; bare. ¶ *m*, weak point; weakness, partiality, sneaking fondness; foible; failing. *les ~s*, the weak. **faiblesse** (blɛs) *f*, weakness; swoon. **faiblir** (bliːr) *v.i*, to weaken; slacken; give way; flag, fail.

faïence (fajɑ̃ːs) *f*, earthenware, pottery, crockery, china. **faïencerie** (jɑ̃sri) *f*, pottery [works]; earthenware. **faïencier, ère** (sje, ɛːr) *n*, earthenware; manufacturer *or* dealer.

faille (faːj) *f*, faille (*fabric*); fault (*Geol.*). **failli** (faji) *m*, bankrupt, insolvent. **faillibilité** (bilite) *f*, fallibility. **faillible** (bl) *a*, fallible. **faillir** (jiːr) *v.i.ir*, to fail; to nearly . . .; to err. **faillite** (jit) *f*, failure; bankruptcy; insolvency.

faim (fɛ̃) *f*, hunger; starvation. *avoir ~*, *grand~*, to be hungry, very hungry.

faine (fɛːn) *f*, beechnut; (*pl.*) beechmast.

fainéant, e (feneɑ̃, ɑ̃ːt) *a*, idle, do-nothing. ¶ *n*, idler, lazybones, loafer. **fainéanter** (ɑ̃te) *v.i*, to idle, loaf. **fainéantise** (tiːz) *f*, idleness, etc.

faire (fɛːr) *m*, technique (*art, etc.*). ¶ *v.t. & i. ir*, to make; do; create; form; perform; effect; write; play; commit; go; run; be; matter; have; get; keep; mind; get ready; lay; put; offer; o. up; give; take; take in (*provisions, etc.*); deal (*cards*); cut (*teeth*); make up (*face, the cash*); make out (*pretend*); wage (*war*); pay; ejaculate; say; charge; quote; accustom; call; turn. *cela fait mon affaire*, that suits me. *faites attention*, be careful. ~ *savoir*, to inform. *se* ~, to be done; be made; happen, take place; be; be getting; become; grow; make oneself; get; gain; turn. *ne vous en faites pas*, don't worry. **faire-part** (fɛrpaːr) *m*, announcement of betrothal, wedding, birth, death. **faisable** (fəzabl) *a*, feasible, practicable.

faisan, e (fɛzɑ̃, an) *n*, pheasant. **faisandé, e** (zɑ̃de) *a*, high, gamy; tainted. **faisandeau** (do) *m*, young pheasant. **se faisander** (de) *v. pr*, to get high. **faisanderie** (dri) *f*, pheasantry.

faisceau (fɛso) *m*, bunch, bundle, cluster, sheaf, nest; beam (*Opt.*); pencil (*Opt.*); pile, stack (*arms*); (*pl.*) fasces (*Hist.*).

faiseur, euse (fəzœːr, øːz) *n*, maker; doer; -monger; bluffer.

fait (fɛ; *in liaison*, fɛt) *m*, act, deed; feat; fact; point; occurrence, happening. ~*s divers*, news items. ~*s & dits*, sayings & doings. ~*s & gestes*, doings, exploits. *dans* (or *par*) *le* ~ or *en* ~, as a matter of fact. *de* ~, de facto, actual. *prendre sur le* ~, to catch redhanded.

faite, e (fɛ, ɛt) *p.p. & p.a*: ~ *de boue & de crachat*, jerry-built. ~ *par tailleur*, tailormade. *un homme fait*, a full-grown man.

faitage (fɛtaːʒ) *m*, roofing; ridge pole; ridge capping. **faîte** (fɛt) *m*, top, apex, summit, zenith. **faîtière** (fɛtjɛːr) *a.f*, ridge (*att.*). ¶ *f*, ridge tile; ridge pole (*tent*).

fait-tout (fɛtu) *m*, stewpan.

faix (fɛ) *m*, burden, load, weight, incubus.

fakir (fakiːr) *m*, fakir.

falaise (falɛːz) *f*, cliff (*on seashore*).

falbalas (falbala) *m.pl*, furbelows.

fallacieux, euse† (falasjø, øːz) *a*, fallacious, misleading.

falloir (falwaːr) *v.imp.ir*, to be necessary, must, should, ought, shall, to have to, shall (*or* will) have to; to want; to require; to take. *s'en* ~, to be wanting; be far, fall short. *comme il faut*, proper (*behavior*). *il s'en faut de beaucoup*, far from it.

falot (falo) *m*, lantern.

falot, e (falo, ɔt) *a*, funny little (*pers.*).

falourde (falurd) *f*, bundle of firewood logs.

falsifier (falsifje) *v.t*, to adulterate; debase; falsify; tamper with; forge.

famé, e (fame) *a*, -famed.

famélique (famelik) *a*, starveling.

fameux, euse† (famø, øːz) *a*, famous; notorious; capital; first-rate; rare; champion (*att.*).

familial, e (familjal) *a*, family (*att.*). **familiariser** (ljarize) *v.t*, to familiarize, accustom. **familiarité** (te) *f*, familiarity; intimacy; (*pl.*) liberties. **familier, ère** (lje, ɛːr) *a*, familiar; intimate; habitual; colloquial; household (*gods*). ¶ *m*, familiar. **famille** (miːj) *f*, family; people. *en* ~, at home.

famine (famin) *f*, famine, starvation.

fanage (fanaːʒ) *m*, tedding; fallen leaves.

fanal (fanal) *m*, light, lamp.

fanatique (fanatik) *a*, fanatic(al); obsessed. ¶ *n*, fanatic; devotee. **fanatiser** (ze) *v.t*, to fanaticize. **fanatisme** (tism) *m*, fanaticism.

fanchon (fɑ̃ʃɔ̃) *f*, kerchief.

fane (fan) *f*, fallen leaf; top (*turnip, etc.*).

faner (fane) *v.t*, to ted, toss (*hay*); fade. **faneur, euse** (nœːr, øːz) (*pers.*) *n. & (Mach.) f*, haymaker; tedder.

fanfare (fãfa:r) f, flourish of trumpets, fanfare; brass band. **fanfaron, ne** (farõ, ɔn) a, blustering, swaggering, hectoring, bragging. **fanfaronnade** (rɔnad) & **fanfaronnerie** (nri) f, bluster, swagger, brag.

fanfreluches (fãfrəlyʃ) f.pl, fallals, frills & furbelows.

fange (fã:ʒ) f, mire, mud, filth, muck; gutter (fig.). **fangeux, euse** (fãʒø, ø:z) a, miry.

fanion (fanjõ) m, flag, banner. (Mil.) pennon.

fanon (fanõ) m, dewlap; whalebone; fetlock; (Eccl.) maniple.

fantaisie (fãtɛzi) f, fancy, notion, whim; fantasy; fantasia. [objet de] ~, fancy [article]. **fantaisiste** (zist) a, fantastic, whimsical. **fantasmagorie** (tasmagori) f, phantasmagoria; fabrication. **fantasque** (task) a, whimsical, odd; temperamental.

fantassin (fãtasɛ̃) m, infantryman. ~ de la flotte, marine.

fantastique (fãtastik) a. & m, fantastic, fanciful; weird, eerie, uncanny.

fantoche (fãtɔʃ) m, puppet (pers.).

fantomatique (fãtomatik) a, ghostly, unearthly. **fantôme** (to:m) m, phantom, ghost.

faon (fã) m, fawn. **faonner** (fane) v.i, to fawn (of deer).

faquin (fakɛ̃) m, scurvy fellow, cad. **faquinerie** (kinri) f, scurvy trick.

faroud, e (faro, o:d) n, fop, dandy.

farce (fars) f, stuffing, forcemeat; farce; foolery; joke; practical joke; antic. faire ses ~s, to sow one's wild oats. ~s et attrapes, practical jokes, tricks. **farceur, euse** (sœ:r, ø:z) n, joker; humorist; practical joker; comedian. **farcir** (si:r) v.t, to stuff; cram.

fard (fa:r) m, paint, grease p., make-up; disguise, guile.

fardage (farda:ʒ) m, dunnage; top hamper; hamper.

fardeau (fardo) m, burden, load, weight, onus.

farder (farde) v.t, to paint, make up (face); gloss, varnish (fig.);

dunnage (ship); (v.i.) to weigh [heavy]; sink. se ~, to make up.

fardier (fardje) m, trolley.

farfadet (farfadɛ) m, goblin, sprite.

farfelu (farfely) a, strange, bizarre. ¶ m, someone who behaves strangely.

farfouiller (farfuje) v.i, to rummage [about], fumble.

faribole[s] (faribɔl) f.[pl.], twaddle.

farinacé, e (farinase) a, farinaceous. **farine** (rin) f, flour, meal, farina. ~ de lin, linseed meal. ~ de riz, ground rice. ~ lactée, malted milk. **farineux, euse** (nø, ø:z) a, floury, mealy; farinaceous. **farinier, ère** (nje, ɛ:r) n, flour dealer; miller.

farouch[e] (faruʃ) m, crimson clover.

farouche (faruʃ) a, wild, savage, fierce; grim; surly; unapproachable, shy, coy.

farrago (farago) m, mixture (fodder); farrago; hotchpotch.

fascicule (fasikyl) m, fascicle; number, part, instalment (publication).

fascinateur, trice (fasinatœ:r, tris) a, fascinating. **fascination** (sjõ) f, fascination; witchery.

fascine (fasin) f, fascine; fagot.

fasciner (fasine) v.t, to fascinate.

fascisme (fasism) m, fascism. **fasciste** (sist) m, fascist.

faste (fast) m. no pl, pomp, pageantry; show, ostentation; (m.pl.) fasti; annals.

fastidieux, euse† (fastidjø, ø:z) a, tedious, wearisome, irksome, dull.

fastueux, euse† (fastyø, ø:z) a, given to display; ostentatious, showy, gaudy.

fat (fat) a.m, foppish. ¶ m, fop, coxcomb, jackanapes.

fatal, e† (fatal) a, fatal; fateful; latest, final. **fatalisme** (lism) m, fatalism. **fataliste** (list) n, fatalist. **fatalité** (te) f, fate, fatality; mischance.

fatidique (fatidik) a, fatidical, prophetic.

fatigant, e (fatigã, ã:t) a, fatiguing, tiring; tiresome; tedious.

fatique (tig) *f*, fatigue, tiredness, fag; stress, [over]strain. *de ~*, working (*clothes*). **fatiguer** (ge) *v.t*, to fatigue, tire; stress, [over]strain, task, wear out; (*v.i.*) to labor (*ship*).

fatras (fatrɑ) *m*, jumble, medley. **fatrasser** (trase) *v.i*, to potter.

fatuité (fatɥite) *f*, self-conceit.

fauber[t] (fobɛ:r) *m*, swab (*Naut.*).

faubourg (fobu:r) *m*, suburb; quarter (*town*). **faubourien, ne** (burjɛ̃, ɛn) *a. & n*, working-class suburban (dweller).

faucard (foka:r) *m*, river weeding shear.

fauchage (foʃa:ʒ) *m*, mowing. **faucher** (ʃe) *v.t*, to mow; m. down. **fauchet** (ʃɛ) *m*, hay rake. **faucheur** (ʃœ:r) *m*, mower (*pers.*). *~ ou* **faucheux** (ʃø) *m*, daddy longlegs. **faucheuse** (ʃø:z) *f*, mower (*Mach.*). **faucille** (si:j) *f*, sickle, reaping hook.

faucon (fokɔ̃) *m*, falcon, hawk. *~ pèlerin*, peregrine [falcon]. **fauconnerie** (kɔnri) *f*, falconry; hawking. **fauconnier** (nje) *m*, falconer. **fauconnière** (jɛ:r) *f*, saddle bag.

faufiler (fofile) *v.t*, to tack, baste (*Need.*); slip in, insinuate. **faufilure** (ly:r) *f*, tacking, basting.

faune (fo:n) *m*, faun; (*f.*) fauna.

faussaire (fosɛ:r) *n*, forger. **faussement** (smɑ̃) *ad*, falsely; wrongfully. **fausser** (se) *v.t*, to bend; buckle; warp; strain; upset; derange; foul; falsify, pervert. **fausset** (sɛ) *m*, falsetto (*voice*); spigot, vent peg. **fausseté** (ste) *f*, falseness, falsity; falsehood, untruth.

faute (fo:t) *f*, fault; mistake, error; blame; foul (*Foot.*); want, lack. *~ d'orthographe*, misspelling. *~ d'impression*, printer's error, misprint. *~ de copiste*, *~ de plume*, clerical error. *~ de*, failing, in default of, for want of. *sans ~*, without fail.

fauteuil (fotœ:j) *m*, armchair, easy chair; chair; seat; orchestra seat (*Theat.*). *~ à bascule*, rocking chair. *~ [de la présidence]*, chair (*at meeting*).

fautif, ive (fotif, i:v) *a*, faulty, at fault, offending.

fauve (fo:v) *a*, fawn[-colored], fallow; fulvous, tawny; buff; lurid (*light*). ¶ *m*, fawn; buff (*color*); (*pl.*) deer; wild beasts (*big felines*).

fauvette (fovɛt) *f*, warbler (*bird*). *~ à tête noire*, blackcap. *~ des haies*, hedge sparrow.

faux (fo) *f*, scythe; falx.

faux, fausse (fo, o:s) *a*, false; wrong; untrue; base, counterfeit; forged; spurious; bogus; unjust (*weight*); improper (*navigation*); blank, blind (*window*); attempted (*suicide*). **faux**, *comps:* *~ bourdon*, drone [bee]. *~ brillant*, imitation [stone], paste; tinsel (*fig.*). *~ col*, see col. *~ coup de queue*, miscue. *~ ébénier*, laburnum. *~ frais*, incidental expenses; untaxed costs (*law*). *~-fuyant*, *m*, evasion, shift. *~-monnayeur*, *m*, counterfeiter. *~ nom*, alias. *~ numéro [d'appel]*, wrong number (*Teleph.*). *~ pas*, mistake, slip. *~ témoignage*, false evidence, perjury. **fausse**, *comps:* *~ boîte*, dummy [box]. *~ couche*, miscarriage. *~ déclaration*, misstatement, misrepresentation. *~ équerre*, bevel [square]. *~ honte*, false shame; bashfulness. *~ manche*, sleeve protector. **faux**, *ad*, falsely, wrongly; out of tune. *à ~*, wrongly, unjustly. ¶ *m*, forgery. *le ~*, the false.

faveur (favœ:r) *f*, favor; boon; goodwill. *billet de ~*, complimentary ticket. **favorable**† (vɔrabl) *a*, favorable. **favori, ite** (ri, it) *a. & n*, favorite; pet; minion; (*m.pl.*) [side] whiskers. **favoriser** (ze) *v.t*, to favor, befriend; foster, promote. **favoritisme** (tism) *m*, favoritism.

fébrile† (febril) *a*, febrile, feverish.

fécond, e (fekɔ̃, ɔ̃:d) *a*, fruitful, fecund, fertile, prolific; life-giving; bountiful. **féconder** (kɔ̃de) *v.t*, to fertilize, fecundate, impregnate; milt; fructify. **fécondité** (dite) *f*, fecundity, fertility, fruitfulness.

fécule (fekyl) *f*, starch, farina.

féculent, e (lã, ã:t) *a*, starchy (*food*).

fédéral, e (federal) *a*, federal. **fédération** (sj5) *f*, federation, union. **fédérer** (re) *v.t*, to federate.

fée (fe) *f*, fairy, pixy, -xie. **féerie** (feri) *f*, fairyhood; Fairyland; fairy scene. **féerique** (ferik) *a*, fairylike.

feindre (fɛ̃:dr) *v.t. & abs. ir*, to feign, pretend, sham; feint. **feint, e** (fɛ̃, ɛ̃:t) *p.a*, feigned, sham; false, blind (*door, etc.*). ¶ feint, pretence, sham.

fêler (fɛle) *v.t*, to crack.

félicitation (felisitasj5) *f*, congratulation. **félicité** (te) *f*, happiness, felicity. **féliciter** (te) *v.t*, to congratulate.

félidés (felide) *m.pl*, Felidae. **félin, e** (lɛ̃, in) *a. & m*, feline, cat (*att.*).

félon, ne (fel5, ɔn) *a*, disloyal. **félonie** (lɔni) *f*, disloyalty.

fêlure (fɛly:r) *f*, crack, split.

femelle (fəmɛl) *f. & a*, female, she; hen; cow (*elephant, etc.*). **féminin, e** (feminɛ̃, in) *a*, feminine; womanish (*voice*); female. ¶ *m*, feminine (*Gram.*). **féminiser** (nize) *v.t*, to feminize. **féminisme** (nism) *m*, feminism. **féministe** (nist) *a. & n*, feminist. **femme** (fam) *f*, woman; female; wife. **~-caoutchouc, ~-serpent**, *f*, contortionist. **~ de chambre**, lady's maid; housemaid; chambermaid; stewardess (*ship*). **~ de journée**, cleaning woman. **~ de ménage**, cleaning woman. **femmelette** (mlɛt) *f*, silly little woman; effeminate (*man*).

fémur (femy:r) *m*, femur.

fenaison (fənɛz5) *f*, haymaking.

fendant (fãdã) *m*, swaggerer.

fendiller (fãdije) *v.t*, to crack, fissure. **fendre** (fã:dr) *v.t*, to split, cleave; rend; rive; crack; slot, nick, slit; break (*heart*). **~ un cheveu en quatre**, to split hairs. **fendu, e** (fãdy) *a*, split, cleft. **bien fendu**, longlegged (*man*).

fenêtrage (fənɛtra:ʒ) *m*, windows (*col.*). **fenêtre** (nɛ:tr) *f*, window. **~ à guillotine**, sash w. **~ à tabatière**, skylight. **~ en**

saillie, bay window. **~ [ordinaire]**, casement [window].

fenil (fəni) *m*, hayloft.

fenouil (fənu:j) *m*, fennel; f. seed.

fente (fã:t) *f*, crack, cleft, split, slit; fissure, crevice, cranny; slot; nick.

féodal, e (feɔdal) *a*, feudal. **féodalité** (lite) *f*, feudalism, feudality.

fer (fɛ:r) *m*, iron; bar; section; shoe; bit; head (*lance, etc.*); tag (*laces*); sword, weapon; (*pl.*) irons, chains, shackles; fetters, manacles; obstetrical forceps. **~ à friser**, curling irons. **~ à repasser**, [flat] iron. **~ à souder**, soldering iron, soldering bit. **~[s] cavalier[s]**, horseshoe bars, h. iron, h. sections. **~ de (ou à) cheval**, horseshoe. **~ de fonte**, cast iron. **~ de lance**, spear head. **~s dorés**, gilt tooling (*Bookb.*). **~ en barre[s]**, bar iron. **~ en lame**, sheet i. **~ [forgé]**, wrought i.

fer-blanc (fɛrblã) *m*, tin [plate], tinned [sheet] iron. **ferblanterie** (blãtri) *f*, tin plate working *or* trade; tinware. **ferblantier** (tje) *m*, tinsmith.

férié (ferje) *a*, **jour ~**, holiday (*not a working day*).

férir (feri:r) *v.t*: **sans coup ~**, without striking a blow.

ferler (fɛrle) *v.t*, to furl (*sail*).

fermage (fɛrma:ʒ) *m*, rent (*farm, land*); tenant farming.

fermant, e (fɛrmã, ã:t) *a*, lockup; closing.

ferme† (fɛrm) *a*, firm, solid, steady, steadfast, staunch. ¶ *ad*, firmly, firm, fast, hard. ¶ *i*, steady! ¶ *f*, lease; farm; farmhouse; homestead; truss, girder (*Build.*); set piece (*Theat.*).

ferment (fɛrmã) *m*, ferment; leaven. **fermentation** (tasj5) *f*, fermentation; ferment (*fig.*). **fermenter** (te) *v.i*, to ferment; to [be at] work (*fig.*).

fermer (fɛrme) *v.t. & i*, to shut, s. up, s. down, close, c. up, c. down; do up; turn off, shut off; switch off; stop up; enclose. **~ [à clef]** *v.t. & i*, to lock [up]. **~ la marche**, to bring up the rear.

fermeté (fɛrmǝte) *f,* firmness, steadfastness, steadiness, strength.

fermeture (fɛrmǝty:r) *f,* shutting; closing; fastening; fastener. ~ *éclair,* zipper. ~ *pression,* snap fastener.

fermier, ère (fɛrmje, ɛ:r) *n,* farmer; tenant (*farm*); lessee; tenant farmer; (*att.*) leasing.

fermoir (fɛrmwa:r) *m,* clasp, fastener, snap; double-beveled chisel.

féroce (ferɔs) *a,* ferocious, fierce, savage, wild. **férocité** (site) *f,* ferocity.

ferrage (fɛra:ʒ) *m,* shoeing; tiring; tagging. **ferraille** (rɑ:j) *f,* old iron, scrap iron. **ferrailler** (rɑje) *v.i,* to slash about. **ferrailleur** (jœ:r) *m,* dealer in old iron; sword rattler. **ferré, e** (re) *p.a,* ironshod; shod; hobnailed; versed, conversant. ~ *à glace,* roughshod, frost-nailed. **ferrement** (fɛrmã) *m,* ironwork; shoeing; putting in irons. **ferrer** (re) *v.t,* to iron, bind (*with any metal*); shoe; tire; tag; strike (*fish*). **ferret** (rɛ) *m,* tag (*lace*). **ferreux** (rø) *a.m,* ferrous. **ferronnerie** (rɔnri) *f,* ironworks; iron warehouse; ironmongery. **ferronnier, ère** (nje, ɛ:r) *n,* iron worker; ironmonger. **ferrugineux, euse** (ryʒinø, ø:z) *a,* ferruginous, **ferrure** (ry:r) *f,* ironwork; binding; shoeing; fitting, mounting.

ferroutage (feruta:ʒ) *m,* piggyback transportation of truck trailers. **ferrouter** (te) *v.t,* to transport truck trailers piggyback.

fertile (fɛrtil) *a,* fertile, fruitful; prolific; fat (*land*). **fertiliser** (lize) *v.t,* to fertilize. **fertilité** (te) *f,* fertility.

féru, e (fery) *a,* struck; smitten (*love*).

férule (feryl) *f,* ferula (*Bot.*); bondage; cane (*Sch.*); lash (*fig.*).

fervent, e (fɛrvã, ã:t) *a,* fervent, earnest. ¶ *n,* enthusiast, devotee. **ferveur** (vœ:r) *f,* fervor, earnestness.

fesse (fɛs) *f,* buttock. *serrer les* ~*s,* to be afraid. **fessée** (se) *f,* spanking. **fesse-mathieu** (matjø) *m,* miser. **fesser** (se) *v.t,* to spank; birch.

festin (fɛstɛ̃) *m,* feast, banquet. **festiner** (tine) *v.t. & abs,* to feast. **festival** (val) *m,* musical festival. **feston** (fɛstɔ̃) *m,* festoon; scallop (*edging*). **festonner** (tɔne) *v.t,* to festoon; scallop. ¶ *v.i,* to reel about (*drunk*).

festoyer (fɛstwaje) *v.t. & i,* to feast.

fête (fɛt) *f,* feast, festivity; festival; fête; holiday; saint's day; birthday; entertainment, treat. *la* ~ *de* [*l'anniversaire de*] *l'Armistice,* Armistice Day. *la Fête-Dieu,* Corpus Christi. ~ *foraine,* fête (*at a fair*). ~ *légale,* legal holiday. **fêter** (fɛte) *v.t,* to keep [as a holiday], celebrate; fête, entertain.

fétiche (fetiʃ) *m,* fetish; mascot (*as on car*); charm. **fétichisme** (ʃism) *m,* fetishism.

fétide (fetid) *a,* fetid, foul. **fétidité** (dite) *f,* fetidness, foulness.

fétu (fety) *m,* straw; (*fig.*) straw, rush, rap, fig, pin.

feu, (fø) *m,* fire; flame; flare; flash; light; lamp; firing (*Mil.*); heat (*fig.*); home, hearth. ~ *à éclipses,* intermittent light (*Naut.*). ~ *concentré,* group firing (*Mil.*). ~ *d'artifice,* firework. ~ *de bengale,* Bengal light. ~ *de bivouac,* campfire. ~ *de cheminée,* chimney on fire. ~*x de circulation,* traffic lights, stop & go lights. ~ *de joie,* bonfire. ~ *de paille* (*fig.*), flash in the pan. ~ *de peloton,* volley firing (*Mil.*). ~ *follet,* ignis fatuus, will-o'-the-wisp. ~ *roulant,* running fire. ~*!* fire! (*Mil.*). *au* ~*!* (*house, etc, on*) fire! *faire long* ~, to hang fire. *ni* ~ *ni lieu,* neither house nor home. *avez-vous du* ~*?,* do you have a light? (*for cigarette*).

feu, e (fø) *a,* late, the late (*deceased*).

feuillage (fœja:ʒ) *m,* foliage, leafage, leaves. **feuillaison** (jezɔ̃) *f,* leafing, foliation. **feuillard** (ja:r) *m,* hoop wood. ~ *de fer,* hoop iron, strap iron, strip iron. **feuille** (fœ:j) *f,* sheet; leaf; slip; list; roll (*pay*); [news]paper; blade; flake; foil. ~ *d'appel,* muster roll. ~ *de chou,* rag (*worthless newspaper*). ~*-document,* data sheet. ~ *de* *garde*, endpaper. ~*s de placage*, veneer. ~ *de présence*, time sheet, attendance s. ~ *de rose*, rose leaf (*petal*). ~ *de route*, waybill. ~ *de tirée*, proof (*Typ.*). ~ *de transfert*, transfer deed, [deed of] transfer. ~ *de vigne*, fig leaf (*art*). ~ *mobile*, looseleaf (*book*). ~ *volante*, loose sheet (*paper*). **feuillé**, e (fœje) *a*, leafy, foliate. ¶ *f*, greenwood, trees. **feuillet** (jɛ) *m*, leaf (*book*); thin sheet, t. plate; lamina. **feuilleter** (fœjte) *v.t*, to run through, thumb (*book*); roll out (*pastry*); flake. **feuilleton** (tɔ̃) *m*, serial [story]. **feuillu**, e (jy) *a*, leafy. **feuillure** (jy:r) *f*, rabbet, rebate, fillister.

feutre (fø:tr) *m*, felt. ~ *mou*, ~ *souple*, soft felt (*hat*). ~ *velours*, velours. **feutrer** (føtre) *v.t*, to felt, pad. *à pas feutrés*, stealthily.

fève (fɛ:v) *f*, bean. ~ *de marais*, broad bean. **féverole** (fɛvrɔl) *f*, horse bean.

février (fevrie) *m*, February.

fez (fɛ:z) *m*, fez.

fi (fi) *i*, ughl fiel ~ *doncl* for shamel *faire* ~ *de*, to pooh-pooh.

fiabilité (fjabilite) *f*, reliability. *essai de* ~, reliability test.

fiacre (fjakr) *m*, cab, four-wheeler.

fiançailles (fjɑ̃sɑ:j) *f.pl*, engagement, betrothal. **fiancé**, e (se) *n*, fiancé, e, betrothed. **fiancer** (se) *v.t*, to betroth, engage, affiance.

fiasco (fjasko) *m*, fiasco, failure, breakdown.

fibre (fibr) *f*, fiber; string (*fig.*). ~ *de coco*, coir. **fibreux**, **euse** (brø, ø:z) *a*, fibrous, stringy. **fibrille** (bril) *f*, fibril.

ficelé, e (fisle) *p.a*, dressed (*badly*). **ficeler** (sle) *v.t*, to [tie with] string, tie up. **ficelle** (sɛl) *f*, string, twine; packthread; dodge, trick, game.

fiche (fiʃ) *f*, hinge; peg, pin, stake; plug, key; slip (*paper*); card (*loose index*); ticket; ~ *de consolation*, booby prize; some slight consolation. ~ *de tournage*, dope sheet (*TV, cinema*). **ficher** (ʃe) *v.t*, to drive in, stick. **se** ~ *de*, to laugh at; not care about. **fichier**

(ʃje) *m*, card index; file (*computers*).

fichtre (fiʃtr) *i*, good gracious!

fichu (fiʃy) *m*, neckerchief, fichu. ¶ *a*, done for. *mal* ~, out of sorts.

fictif, **ive†** (fiktif, i:v) *a*, fictitious, sham. **fiction** (sj5) *f*, fiction, figment.

fidéicommis (fideikɔmi) *m*, trust (*law*).

fidèle† (fidɛl) *a*, faithful; loyal; true; reliable, trustworthy; fast; retentive. **les** ~**s**, *m.pl*, the faithful. **fidélité** (delite) *f*, fidelity, faithfulness; truthfulness; reliability; retentiveness.

fidibus (fidiby:s) *m*, spill, pipe light.

fiduciaire (fidysjɛ:r) *a*, fiduciary.

fief (fjɛf) *m*, fief, feud, fee (*Hist.*); preserve (*fig.*). **fieffé**, e (fe) *a*, arrant, downright, unmitigated, egregious, regular, outright, rank, out & out, of the deepest dye.

fiel (fjɛl) *m*, gall; rancor. **fielleux**, **euse** (lø, ø:z) *a*, rancorous.

fiente (fjɑ̃:t) *f*, dung, droppings.

fier (fje) *v.t*, to entrust. **se** ~, to trust, rely.

fier, **ère†** (fjɛ:r) *a*, proud, haughty; lofty; stately; lordly; rare, fine; arrant. **fier-à-bras** (fjɛrabra) *m*, swaggerer. **fierté** (fjɛrte) *f*, pride; boldness (*touch*).

fièvre (fjɛ:vr) *f*, fever; heat (*fig.*). ~ *aphteuse* (aftø:z), foot-&-mouth disease. ~ *des foins*, hay fever. ~ *paludéenne*, malaria, marsh fever; ague. **fiévreux**, **euse†** (evrø, ø:z) *a*, feverish. ¶ *n*, fever case (*pers.*).

fifre (fifr) *m*, fife; fifer.

figé, e (fiʒe) *a*, frozen (*fig.*); set. **figer** (ʒe) *v.t. & se* ~, to congeal, coagulate, set.

fignoler (fiɲɔle) *v.t. & abs*, to overelaborate.

figue (fig) *f*, fig. ~ *de Barbarie*, prickly pear. **figuier** (gje) *m*, fig tree.

figurant, e (figyrɑ̃, ɑ̃:t) *n*, supernumerary; one who takes no prominent part. **figuratif**, **ive†** (ratif, i:v) *a*, figurative; pictorial (*plan*, *map*); picture (*writing*).

figure (gy:r) *f*, figure; form, shape; face (*of pers.*), countenance; show[ing]; (*pl.*) court cards. ~ *de cire*, waxwork. ~ *de mots*, ~ *de rhétorique*, figure of speech. ~ *de proue*, figurehead (*ship*). ~ *en lame de couteau*, hatchet face. **figuré, e** (gyre) *p.a*, pictorial (*plan, map*); figure (*dance, stone*); figurative (*sense*). ¶ *m*, figurative sense. **figurément** (mã) *ad*, figuratively (*sense*). **figurer** (re) *v.t*, to figure, represent, picture, show; (*v.i.*) to appear, figure, show. se ~, to imagine, fancy, picture to oneself. **figurine** (rin) *f*, figurine, statuette.

fil (fil) *m*, thread; yarn; wire; filament; string (*pearls, etc.*); [cutting] edge; grain (*wood, etc.*); flaw. ~ *à plomb*, plumb line. ~ *carcasse des fleuristes*, flower wire. ~ *de fer barbelé*, barb[ed] wire. ~*s de la Vierge*, gossamer. ~ [*de lin*], linen [thread]. ~ *souple*, flex[ible wire] (*Elec.*). **filage** (la:3) *m*, spinning; pouring (*oil on waves*). **filament** (lamã) *m*, filament; thread. **filandres** (lã:dr) *f.pl*, gossamer; strings. **filandreux, euse** (lãdrø, ø:z) *a*, stringy; long-drawn; diffuse. **filant, e** (lã, ã:t) *a*, ropy (*liquid*); falling, shooting (*star*). **filasse** (las) *f*, tow (*flax, hemp*).

filateur, trice (filatœ:r, tris) *n*, spinner (*pers.*); (*m.*) spinner (*owner*). **filature** (ty:r) *f*, cotton mill; spinning; shadowing (*a pers.*).

file (fil) *f*, file, line. ~ *d'attente*, queue. **filé** (file) *m*, thread. **filer** (le) *v.t*, to spin; draw (*into wire*); pay out (*cable*); pour (*oil on waves*); shadow (*a pers.*); handle (*fig.*); (*v.i.*) to run; be off; make off; file off; flare (*lamp*). ~ *à l'anglaise*, to take French leave. ~ *doux*, to obey without a word.

filet (filε) *m*, thread; string; filament; fillet; undercut; loin (*mutton*); worm (*screw*); trickle, stream; dash (*admixture*); rule (*Typ.*); net; netting. ~ *à bagage*, luggage rack (*Rly.*). ~ *à provisions*, string bag, net b. ~*s de*

sole, filleted sole. **filetage** (lta:3) *m*, screw cutting. **fileter** (lte) *v.t*, to thread, screw, **fileur, euse** (lœ:r, ø:z) *n*, spinner, net maker; shadower (*detectives, etc.*).

filial, e† (filjal) *a*, filial. **[société] filiale,** *f*, subsidiary [company]. **filiation** (sjɔ̃) *f*, filiation; relationship.

filière (filjε:r) *f*, draw plate; die [plate]; screw plate; [screw] stock; wire gauge; purlin; regular channel[s] (*fig.*). ~ *garnie*, stock & dies.

filigrane (filigran) *m*, filigree [work]; watermark (*paper*).

fille (fi:j) *f*, girl; maid; maiden; daughter; whore (*familiar*). ~ *de ferme*, dairy maid, milkmaid. ~ *de service*, maidservant, housemaid. **fillette** (fijεt) *f*, little girl. **filleul, e** (fijœl) *n*, godchild, godson, god-daughter; protégé.

film (film) *m*, film; movie. ~ *interdit*, banned movie. ~ *muet*, silent m. ~ *parlant*, sound m. ~*-annonce*, trailer. ~ *à recette*, box-office success. ~ *en relief*, 3-D movie. *grand* ~, main feature.

filon (filɔ̃) *m*, lode; mine (*fig.*).

filoselle (filɔzεl) *f*, floss silk.

filou (filu) *m*, pickpocket; sharper; swindler. **filouter** (te) *v.t*, to rob, filch; cheat. **filouterie** (tri) *f*, robbery; swindle.

fils (fis) *m*, son; junior. ~ *de ses œuvres*, self-made man. ~ *de son père*, chip off the old block. ~ *à papa*, well-connected young man; playboy.

filtrage (filtra:3) *m*. & **filtration** (trasjɔ̃) *f*, filtration, straining; percolation. **filtre** (tr) *m*, filter; percolator (*coffee*). **filtrer** (tre) *v.t. & i*, to filter, strain; percolate, leach.

fin (fε̃) *f*, end, close, finish, last; finis; object, aim, purpose. ~ *d'alerte*, all clear (*Mil.*).

fin (fε̃) *m*, fine metal; fine linen. *or à tant de grammes de* ~, gold so many grams fine.

fin, e (fε̃, in) *a*, fine; delicate; choice; slender; small; keen, sharp; subtle; smart. *fin fond*, farthest end, very depths. *fin matois*, artful dodger. *le fin mot*, the last word; the long & the

short of it, the upshot. *fine à
l'eau,* brandy & soda. *fine champagne,* liqueur brandy. *fines
herbes,* savory herbs.

final, e† (final) *a,* final; last; ultimate. **¶** *f,* final (*sport*). **final[e],**
m, finale (*Mus.*). **finalité** (lite)
f, finality.

finance (finã:s) *f,* finance; (*pl.*)
finances, cash, money. **financer**
(nãse) *v.i,* to find money, finance.
financier, ère† (sje, ε:r) *a,* financial. **¶** *m,* financier.

finasser (finase) *v.i,* to finesse.
finasserie (sri) *f,* trickery; cunning; (*pl.*) wiles. **finassier, ère**
(sje, ε:r) *n,* trickster.

finaud, e (fino, o:d) *a,* sly, wily.
¶ *n,* artful dodger, slyboots. **finauderie** (odri) *f,* sly dodge.

fine (fin) *f,* liqueur brandy.

finement (finmã) *ad,* finely;
shrewdly. **finesse** (nɛs) *f,* fineness.

fini, e (fini) *a,* finished; over;
consummate; finite (*being*). **¶** *m,*
finish; (the) finite. **finir** (ni:r)
v.t. & abs. & i, to finish, end. ~
de parler, to finish (*or* leave off)
speaking. *en* ~, to finish.

Finlande (la) (fẽlã:d), Finland.
finnois, e (finwa, a:z) & **finlandais, e** (fẽlãde, ε:z) *a,* Finnish.
Finnois, e & **Finlandais, e,** *n,*
Finn, Finlander. *le finnois,* Finnish (*language*).

fiole (fjɔl) *f,* flask, phial.

floriture (fjority:r) *f,* grace [note];
flourish.

firmament (firmamã) *m,* firmament.

firme (firm) *f,* firm (*industrial,
commercial*).

fisc (fisk) *m,* Treasury; taxes; Internal Revenue Service. **fiscal, e**
(kal) *a,* fiscal (*att.*). **fiscalité** (lite)
f, fiscal system; piling up of taxation; methods of [tax] collection.

fissa (fisa) *ad,* quick, sharp.

fissure (fisy:r) *f,* fissure, crack,
cleft; hiatus.

fiston (fistɔ̃) *m,* son; youngster.

fistule (fistyl) *f,* fistula.

fixage (fiksa:ʒ) *m.* & **fixation**
(asjɔ̃) *f,* fixing, fixation; fastening. **fixatif** (tif) *m,* fixing [solu-
tion] (*Phot.*). **fixe†** (fiks) *a,*
fixed, fast, stationary; intent; set.
¶ *i,* eyes front! **¶** *m,* fixed salary.

~*cravate, m,* tie clip. **fixer** (kse)
v.t, to fix, fasten, secure; set;
settle; rivet (*fig.*). ~ *dans la mémoire,* to commit to memory,
memorize. **fixité** (ksite) *f,* fixity,
steadiness.

flaccidité (flaksidite) *f,* flaccidity, flabbiness.

flacon (flakɔ̃) *m,* bottle, flask,
flagon. ~ *à couvercle vissé,*
screw-capped bottle. ~ *à odeur,*
scent b., smelling b.

flageller (flaʒɛle) *v.t,* to scourge,
flagellate.

flageoler (flaʒɔle) *v.i,* to tremble,
shake. **flageolet** (lɛ) *m,* flageolet
(*Mus. & bean*).

flagorner (flagɔrne) *v.t,* to fawn
[up]on, toady to. **flagornerie**
(nəri) *f,* toadyism, soft soap. **flagorneur, euse** (nœ:r, ∅:z) *n,*
toady.

flagrant, e (flagrã, ã:t) *a,* flagrant, glaring. *en flagrant délit,*
in the [very] act, redhanded.

flair (flɛ:r) *m,* scent, smell; nose;
acumen; keenness. **flairer** (flɛre)
v.t. & abs, to scent, smell, scent
out, nose [out].

flamand, e (flamã, ã:d) *a.* &
(*language*) *m,* Flemish. **F~,** *n,*
Fleming (*pers.*).

flamant (flamã) *m,* flamingo.

flambant, e (flãbã, ã:t) *a,* flam-
ing, blazing; smart. *tout flambant
neuf, toute flambante neuve,*
brand new. **flambeau** (bo) *m,*
torch; candlestick. **flambé, e** (be)
p.p, lost, gone; done for. **flambée**
(be) *f,* blaze. ~ *des prix,* runaway
inflation. **flamber** (be) *v.i,* to
flame, blaze, flare; (v.t.) to flame
(*needle, Surg.*); singe. **flamberge**
(bɛrʒ) *f,* sword (*jocularly*). **flamboyer** (bwaje) *v.i,* to blaze; flame,
flare, flash.

flamme (flɑ:m) *f,* flame; blaze,
flare, light; passion; pennant,
pendant, pennon, streamer. ~ *de
bengale,* Bengal light. **flammèche**
(flamɛʃ) *f,* spark, flake (*ignited
matter*).

flan (flã) *m,* flan; custard; blank
(*metal*); mold (*Typ.*). *c'est du* ~,
it's baloney.

flanc (flã) *m,* side, flank; womb.

flancher (flãʃe) *v.i,* to flinch;
give in; break down (*auto*).

Flandre (la) (flɑ̃ːdr), Flanders.

flandrin (flɑ̃drɛ̃) *m*, lanky fellow.

flanelle (flanɛl) *f*, flannel. **~ de coton**, flannelette.

flâner (flɑne) & **flânocher** (nɔʃe) *v.i*, to saunter; stroll; lounge; loaf. **flânerie** (nri) *f*, sauntering. **flâneur, euse** (nœːr, øːz) *n*, saunterer.

flanquer (flɑ̃ke) *v.t*, to flank; fling, throw, chuck; land (*blow*).

flaque (flak) *f*, puddle; pool, plash. **une flaquée d'eau** (ke) some water (*thrown*).

flasque (flask) *a*, flabby, limp, flaccid. ¶ *m*, cheek, side.

flatter (flate) *v.t. & abs*, to flatter; stroke; pat; humor; please. **flatterie** (tri) *f*, flattery. **flatteur, euse** (tœːr, øːz) *n*, flatterer. ¶ *a*, flattering.

flatulence (flatylɑ̃ːs) *f*, flatulence, -cy. **flatuosité** (tчozite) *f*, flatus, wind.

fléau (fleo) *m*, flail; scourge, plague, bane, curse; beam (*scale*); bar.

flèche (flɛʃ) *f*, arrow, shaft; spire; jib, boom (*crane*); beam (*plow*); trail (*gun carriage*); flitch (*bacon*); sag, dip. **~ littorale**, spit (*Phys. Geog.*). **fléchette** (fleʃɛt) *f*, dart.

fléchir (fleʃiːr) *v.t. & i*, to bend, bow, flex; sag; move; flag, yield; give way; relent. **fléchisseur** (ʃisœːr) *a.m. & m*, flexor.

flegmatique (flɛgmatik) *a*, phlegmatic; stolid. **flegme** (flɛgm) *m*, coolness, phlegm (*fig.*), stolidity.

flet (flɛ) *m*, flounder (*fish*). **flétan** (fletɑ̃) *m*, halibut.

flétrir (fletriːr) *v.t*, to fade, wither, wilt, blight; brand. **flétrissure** (trisyːr) *f*, fading, withering; blight; stigma.

fleur (flœːr) *f*, flower; blossom; bloom; pick; prime, heyday, blush, flush. **~ de la Passion**, passion flower. **~s des bois, ~s des champs, ~s des prés**, wild flowers. **la ~ des pois**, the pick of the bunch. **à ~ de**, level (*or* even) (*or* flush) with. **fleurer** (flœre) *v.i*, to smell.

fleuret (flœrɛ) *m*, foil (*Fenc.*); drill.

fleurette (flœrɛt) *f*, floweret. **conter ~**, to make love. **fleuri, e** (ri) *a*, in bloom; flowery; florid. **fleurir** (riːr) *v.i*, to flower, blossom, bloom; flourish; (*v.t.*) to deck with flowers. **fleuriste** (rist) *n*, florist; (*att.*) floral, flower. **fleuron** (rɔ̃) *m*, flower work; flower; floret; colophon.

fleuve (flœːv) *m*, river.

flexible (flɛksibl) *a*, flexible, pliant, pliable. **flexion** (ksjɔ̃) *f*, flection; deflection; inflection, ending (*Gram.*)

flibustier (flibystje) *m*, filibuster, freebooter; swindler.

flic (flik) *m*, cop.

flic flac (flikflak), crack, smack.

flingue (flɛ̃ːg) *m*, piece (*firearm*), gun. **flinguer** (ge) *v.t*, to bump off, kill, shoot.

flirt (flœrt) *m*, flirtation. **flirter** (te) *v.i*, to flirt.

floc (flɔk) *m*, thud; slash.

flocon (flɔkɔ̃) *m*, flock, tuft; flake. **floconneux, euse** (kɔnø, øːz) *a*, fleecy; flaky.

flonflon (flɔ̃flɔ̃) *m*, blare.

floraison (flɔrɛzɔ̃) *f*, flowering, blossoming, blooming. **floral, e** (ral) *a*, floral, flower (*att.*). **flore** (flɔːr) *f*, flora.

florence (flɔrɑ̃ːs) *m*, sarsenet; [silkworm] gut.

florès (flɔrɛːs): **faire ~**, to make a stir.

Floride (la) (flɔrid), Florida.

florissant, e (flɔrisɑ̃, ɑ̃ːt) *a*, flourishing, thriving.

flot (flo) *m. oft. pl*, wave, billow; surge; rush; stream, flood; flood tide. **~ de la marée**, tidal wave. **à ~**, afloat. **à ~s**, in torrents. **flottage** (flɔtaːʒ) *m*, floating (*lumber*), rafting. **flottant, e** (tɑ̃, ɑ̃ːt) *a*, floating; flowing, waving; baggy; wavering; evasive, elusive. **flotte** (flɔt) *f*, fleet; float; floater. **flottement** (tmɑ̃) *m*, swaying; wavering. **flotter** (te) *v.i*, to float; waft; wave; hang; waver, fluctuate. **flotteur** (tœːr) *m*, raftsman; float; floater; ball. **flotille** (tiːj) *f*, flotilla.

flou, e (flu) *a*, fuzzy; woolly; hazy, blurry. **flou**, *ad*, fuzzily. ¶ *m*, fuzziness.

flouer (flue) *v.t*, to swindle.

fluctuation (flyktɥasjɔ̃) *f*, fluctuation.

fluet, te (flyɛ, ɛt) *a*, slender, thin.

fluide (flyid) *a*, fluid, flowing. ¶ *m*, fluid (*imponderable*). **fluidité** (dite) *f*, fluidity.

fluor (flyɔːr) *m*, fluorine. **fluorescent, e** (ɔrɛsɑ̃, ɑ̃ːt) *a*, fluorescent.

flûte (flyt) *f*, flute; flute [glass]; baton (*bread*). ~ **de Pan**, Pan's pipes. **flûté, e** (te) *a*, fluty. **flûter** (te) *v.i*, to flute, pipe. **flûtiste** (tist) *n*, flutist.

fluvial, e (flyvjal) *a*, fluvial, river (*att*.). **fluviatile** (atil) *a*, fluviatile.

flux (fly) *m*, flux; flow; flood; flush (*cards*). **le ~ et le re~**, the ebb and flow. **fluxion** (ksjɔ̃) *f*, swelling (*face*).

foc (fɔk) *m*, jib (*sail*).

focal, e (fɔkal) *a*, focal.

fœtus (fetyːs) *m*, fetus.

foi (fwa) *f*, faith; troth; belief; reliance, trust; witness. *ajouter* ~ **à**, to credit, believe in. *ma* ~ *non!* O dear no!

foie (fwa) *m*, liver (*Anat*.). *avoir les* ~*s blancs*, to be afraid.

foin (fwɛ̃) *m. oft. pl*, hay.

foire (fwaːr) *f*, fair, market.

foirer (fware) *v.i*, to have diarrhea; fail (*slang*).

fois (fwa) *f*, time. *à la* ~, at a time; at the same t., both; together.

foison (fwazɔ̃) *f*, plenty. *à* ~, galore. **foisonner** (zɔne) *v.i*, to abound, be plentiful; swarm; increase.

fol, folle, *see* **fou**.

folâtre (fɔlaːtr) *a*, playful, skittish, sportive, wanton. **folâtrer** (latre) *v.i*, to play about, romp, frolic.

foliacé, e (fɔljase) *a*, foliaceous. **foliation** (sjɔ̃) *f*, foliation; leafing.

folichon, ne (fɔliʃɔ̃, ɔn) *a*, wanton, unchaste.

folie (fɔli) *f*, madness; folly, foolishness; mania, passion, hobby. *à la* ~, to distraction.

folio (fɔljo) *m*, folio. **foliole** (ɔl) *f*, leaflet (*Bot*.). **folioter** (ɔte) *v.t*, to folio.

folk-lore (fɔlklɔːr) *m*, folklore.

follement (fɔlmɑ̃) *ad*, madly; foolishly. **follet, te** (lɛ, ɛt) *a*, frolicsome; downy, fluffy (*hair*). [*esprit*] **follet**, *m*, sprite, [hob] goblin, puck. **follette**, *f*, playful creature.

folliculaire (fɔlikylɛːr) *m*, scribbler, hack (*writer*). **follicule** (kyl) *m*, follicle; leaflet.

fomentation (fɔmɑ̃tasjɔ̃) *f*, fomentation (*Med. & fig*.). **fomenter** (te) *v.t*, to foment.

foncé, e (fɔ̃se) *a*, dark, deep (*color*). **foncer** (se) *v.t*, to bottom (*cask, etc*.); sink (*well, etc*.); (*v.i*.) to rush; charge.

fonceur (fɔ̃sœːr) *m*, dynamic capitalist; financial "whiz kid."

foncier, ère (fɔ̃sje, ɛːr) *a*, landed, land, ground, property (*att*.); deep-seated, fundamental. **foncièrement** (ɛrmɑ̃) *ad*, thoroughly.

fonction (fɔ̃ksjɔ̃) *f. oft. pl*, function, duty, office. *faire* ~ *de*, to act as. **fonctionnaire** (ɔnɛːr) *n*, official, officer, functionary. ~ *public, ique*, civil servant. **fonctionnarisme** (narism) *m*, officialdom; officialism. **fonctionnel, le** (nɛl) *a*, functional. **fonctionner** (ne) *v.i*, to function, run, work, act.

fond (fɔ̃) *m*, bottom; ground; substratum; crown (*hat*); depth; floor; back; head; groundwork; background; seat (*trousers, chair*); heart; substance; main issue (*law*); undertone; undercurrent; staying power, stamina. ~ **de cale**, bilge (*ship*). *à* ~, thoroughly; home. *au* ~, after all, in reality. *de* ~ *en comble*, from top to bottom. *faire* ~ *sur*, to rely on.

fondamental, e† (fɔ̃damɑ̃tal) *a*, fundamental, basic; foundation (*stone*).

fondant, e (fɔ̃dɑ̃, ɑ̃ːt) *a*, melting (*ice*); that melts in the mouth, luscious, juicy. ¶ *m*, flux; fondant.

fondateur, trice (fɔ̃datœːr, tris) *n*, founder, foundress; promoter. **fondation** (sjɔ̃) *f*, foundation; bed; establishment.

fondé de pouvoir(s) (fɔ̃de) *m*, attorney; proxy; duly authorized representative.

fondement (fɔ̃dmɑ̃) *m. oft. pl,* foundation, ground, base, basis; fundament. **fonder** (de) *v.t,* to found; base, ground. **se ~,** to take one's stand; be based.

fonderie (fɔ̃dri) *f,* foundry; [smelting] works; founding. **fondeur** (dœːr) *m,* founder.

fondre (fɔ̃:dr) *v.t,* to melt, dissolve; smelt; fuse; cast, found; merge; blend; (*v.i.*) to melt, dissolve, fuse; blow, go (*fuse*). **~ sur,** to fall [up]on, pounce on, swoop down on. **fondu** (dy) *m,* fade-out (*TV & cinema*); shunt (*sound, TV, etc.*). **~ au noir,** fade to black. **~ enchaîné,** lap dissolve. **~ ouvert,** fade-in.

fondrière (fɔ̃driɛːr) *f,* pit, hollow, hole (*in road*); quagmire, morass.

fonds (fɔ̃) *m. oft. pl,* fund; funds; money, cash; capital; stock; security. **~ d'amortissement,** sinking fund. **~** [*de commerce*], goodwill, business. **~ de prévoyance,** contingency fund. **~ de roulement,** working capital. **~** [*de terre*], estate, [piece of] land. **à ~ perdu,** with capital sunk (*as in an annuity*).

fongueux, euse (fɔ̃gø, øːz) *a,* fungous. **fongus** (gyːs) *m,* fungus.

fontaine (fɔ̃tɛn) *f,* fountain, spring, well; cistern (*house*). **~ de Jouvence,** fountain of youth. **fontainier** (nje) *m,* maker of (*or* dealer in) domestic water appliances (*cisterns, filters, etc.*); plumber; turncock; well sinker.

fonte (fɔ̃:t) *f,* melting; smelting; casting, founding; melt; font (*Typ.*); holster. **~ d'acier,** cast steel. **~** [*de fer*], [cast] iron. **~** [*en gueuses*], **~ en saumons,** pig [iron].

fonts (fɔ̃) *m.pl,* font (*Eccl.*).

football (futbɔl) *m,* football (*game*). [**~**] *rugby,* Rugby [f.].

for (fɔːr) *m:* **~ intérieur,** conscience.

forage (fɔraːʒ) *m,* boring, drilling.

forain, e (fɔrɛ̃, ɛn) *a,* nonresident; traveling, itinerant. ¶ *m,* [traveling] showman. [*marchand*] *fo-rain,* peddler or boothkeeper at a fair.

forban (fɔrbɑ̃) *m,* [sea] rover; pirate; shark (*fig.*).

forçage (fɔrsaːʒ) *m,* forcing (*Hort.*); overweight (*coin*).

forçat (fɔrsa) *m,* convict.

force (fɔrs) *f,* force; power; strength; potency; might; press (*of sail*); many, plenty of; (*pl.*) shears. **~ d'âme,** fortitude. **~ d'inertie,** inertia. **~ de bras,** hand power. **~ de cheval, ~ en chevaux,** horsepower. **~ de l'âge,** prime of life. **~ de levier,** leverage. **~ des choses,** force of circumstances. **~ du pouls,** pulse rate. **~ du sang,** call of the blood (*fig.*). **~ majeure,** force majeure, cause beyond control. **à ~ de,** by dint of. **à toute ~,** at all costs.

forcé, e (fɔrse) *p.a,* forced, compulsory; farfetched; strained. **forcément** (mɑ̃) *ad,* perforce, necessarily.

forcené, e (fɔrsəne) *n,* madman; fury.

forceps (fɔrsɛps) *m,* obstetrical forceps.

forcer (fɔrse) *v.t,* to force; wrench open; compel; make; drive; obtrude; strain; constrain; overcome; overwork; crowd; run down (*Hunt.*). **forcerie** (səri) *f,* forcing bed (*Hort.*).

forclore (fɔrklɔːr) *v.t.ir,* to debar by time (*law*). **forclusion** (klyzjɔ̃) *f,* debarment by time.

forer (fɔre) *v.t,* to bore, drill.

forestier, ère (fɔrɛstje, ɛːr) *a,* forest (*att.*). ¶ *m,* forester.

foret (fɔre) *m,* drill; bit. **~ hélicoïdal,** twist drill.

forêt (fɔre) *f,* forest; shock (*hair*). **la F~-Noire,** the Black Forest.

foreur (fɔrœːr) *m,* driller (*pers.*). **foreuse** (røːz) *f,* boring machine, drilling m.

forfaire à (fɔrfɛːr) *v.ir,* to fail in (*duty*); forfeit (*honor*). **forfait** (fɛ) *m,* crime; contract; fixed price, agreed sum. **à ~ ou forfaitaire** (tɛːr) *a,* on contract, contractual, at an agreed price; through (*rate*); standard (*charge*). **forfaiture** (tyːr) *f,* breach of trust.

forfanterie (fɔrfɑ̃tri) *f*, boasting, bragging.

forge (fɔrʒ) *f*, forge; smithy; blacksmith's shop; ironworks. **forger** (ʒe) *v.t*, to forge; fabricate; coin (*word*). **se ~**, to conjure up. **forgeron** (ʒərɔ̃) *m*, [black]smith. **forgeur, euse** (ʒœːr, øːz), *n*, fabricator, inventor (*stories, lies*); (*m.*) forgeman.

formaliser (se) (fɔrmalize) *v.pr*, to take exception, t. offense, t. amiss. **formaliste** (list) *a*, formal, precise. **formalité** (te) *f*, formality.

format (fɔrma) *m*, size (*book*), format; gauge. **~ de l'image**, frame size. **formation** (sjɔ̃) *f*, formation; structure; training. **forme** (fɔrm) *f*, form, shape; block (*hat*); last (*shoe*); (*pl.*) manners; form (*Typ.*). **rester en ~**, to keep fit, keep in form. **formel, le†** (mɛl) *a*, formal; express; strict; flat. **former** (me) *v.t*, to form, shape, fashion; frame; make; train. **~ les faisceaux**, to stack arms (*Mil.*). **~ une liste de jurés, ~ un tableau**, to impanel a jury.

formidable† (fɔrmidabl) *a*, formidable.

Formose (fɔrmoːz) *f*, Formosa.

formulaire (fɔrmylɛːr) *m*, formulary. **formule** (myl) *f*, formula; form; prescription (*Med.*). **formuler** (le) *v.t*, to draw up; write out; formulate.

fornication (fɔrnikasjɔ̃) *f*, fornication.

fort, e (fɔːr, ɔrt) *a*, strong; powerful; heavy; stout; stiff; fortified; steep; large; great; big; high; good; bad; full; loud; well up; overweight (*coin*); hard (*solder*). **~ se faire fort** (*fort* is inv.), to undertake. **fort**, *ad*, hard; loud[ly]; very. **~ avant dans la nuit**, far into the night. **¶** *m* (the) strong (*pers.*); market porter; strongest part; thick[est]; height; depth; strong point, forte; lair, fort, stronghold. **au plus ~ du combat**, in the thick of the fight. **forte** (fɔrte) *ad*, forte (*Mus.*). **fortement** (təmɑ̃) *ad*, strongly; highly; hard.

forteresse (fɔrtərɛs) *f*, fortress, stronghold.

fortification (fɔrtifikasjɔ̃) *f*, fortification. **fortifier** (fje) *v.t*, to strengthen, brace, invigorate; fortify.

fortin (fɔrtɛ̃) *m*, small fort.

fortuit, e† (fɔrtɥi, it) *a*, fortuitous, chance, casual, accidental.

fortune (fɔrtyn) *f*, fortune; luck, chance. **~ de mer**, perils of the sea. **dîner à la ~ du pot**, to take pot luck. **de ~**, makeshift; chance (*att.*). **fortuné, e** (ne) *a*, fortunate, lucky; well-to-do, moneyed.

forum (fɔrɔm) *m*, forum.

forure (fɔryːr) *f*, bore, hole; pipe (*key*).

fosse (foːs) *f*, pit, hole; den; grave; deep (*ocean*); fosse. **~ [d'aisances]**, cesspool. **~ septique**, septic tank.

fossé (fose) *m*, ditch, trench; moat; rift (*fig.*). **sauter le ~**, to take the plunge (*fig.*). **fossette** (fosɛt) *f*, dimple.

fossile (fɔsil) *a. & m*, fossil.

fossoyeur (foswajœːr) *m*, gravedigger.

fou, fol, folle (fu, fɔl) *a*, mad, insane; wild, frantic; foolish; passionately fond; uncontrollable; tremendous. **~ à lier**, raving mad, stark m. **folle de son corps**, wanton (*woman*). **fou, folle**, *n*, madman, -woman, lunatic; homosexual (*slang*). (*m.*) fool; jester (*court*); bishop (*chess*).

fouailler (fwaje) *v.t*, to whip; castigate (*fig.*).

foucade (fukad) *f*, fit; start.

foudre (fudr) *f*, lightning; thunder, [thunder]bolt; (*m.*) thunderbolt (*fig. & Myth.*); tun. **coup de ~**, love at first sight. **foudroyer** (drwaje) *v.t*, to strike with lightning, blast; (*in. p.p.*) thunderstruck; crushed.

fouet (fwɛ) *m*, whip; whipcord; whisk (*egg*); tip (*wing*). **le ~**, a flogging. **fouetter** (te) *v.t. & i*, to whip, flog, lash; beat; whisk; stir (*the blood*).

fougère (fuʒɛːr) *f*, fern. **~ [à l'aigle]**, bracken, brake. **~ arborescente**, tree fern.

fougue (fug) *f*, fire (*fig.*), spirit, mettle. **fougueux, euse†** (gø, ∅:z) *a*, fiery, spirited, mettlesome.

fouille (fu:j) *f*, excavation, cut, trench, pit. **fouille-au-pot** (fujopo) *m*, cook's boy. **fouiller** (fuje) *v.t. & abs. & i*, to excavate; dig; mine; burrow in[to]; burrow; nuzzle; root; rummage, ransack; search, dive, peer into; fumble, grope; pry. **fouilleur** (jœ:r) *m*, searcher. **fouillis** (ji) *m*, jumble, muddle, litter.

fouine (fwin) *f*, beech marten (*Zool.*); pitchfork; fish spear, grains. **fouiner** (ne) *v.i*, to slink away; nose about.

foulage (fula:ʒ) *m*, fulling; pressing (*grapes*); impression (*Typ.*).

foulard (fula:r) *m*, foulard.

foule (ful) *f*, crowd, throng; mob.

fouler (fule) *v.t*, to press; full, mill (*cloth*); give an impression (*Typ.*); tread [on], trample [on]; harass; sprain, wrench; gall. ~ *aux pieds*, to tread underfoot; ride roughshod over. **foulon** (lɔ̃) *m*, fuller.

foulque (fulk) *f*, coot.

foulure (fuly:r) *f*, sprain, wrench.

four (fu:r) *m*, oven; kiln; furnace; failure, fiasco. ~ *crématoire* (krematwa:r), crematorium.

fourbe (furb) *a*, knavish. ¶ *m*, knave, cheat. ¶ *f. &* **fourberie** (bəri) *f*, knavery, cheating.

fourbi (furbi) *m*, kit (*Mil.*) *tout le* ~, the whole kit and caboodle.

fourbir (furbi:r) *v.t*, to furbish, rub up.

fourbu, e (furby) *a*, foundered (*Vet.*); tired out.

fourche (furʃ) *f*, fork; pitchfork. **fourcher** (ʃe) *v.i*, to fork; branch off. **fourchette** (ʃet) *f*, fork (*table*); trencherman; bracket (*Mil. & statistics*); wishbone. **fourchon** (ʃɔ̃) *m*, prong; fork (*tree*). **fourchu, e** (ʃy) *a*, forked; cleft; cloven.

fourgon (furgɔ̃) *m*, wagon; truck; van; poker, rake. ~ *de déménagements*, moving van. ~ *des bagages*, baggage car. **fourgonner** (gɔne) *v.i*, to poke [about].

fourmi (furmi) *f*, ant, emmet; (*pl.*) pins & needles (*fig.*). **fourmilier** (milje) *m*, anteater. **fourmilière** (lje:r) *f*, ant's nest. **fourmi-lion** (ljɔ̃) *m*, ant lion. **fourmiller** (mije) *v.t*, to swarm; teem; abound; tingle.

fournaise (furnɛ:z) *f*, furnace, inferno. **fourneau** (no) *m*, stove; furnace; bowl (*pipe*). ~ *à gaz, à pétrole*, gas, oil, stove. *haut* ~, blast furnace. *philanthropique*, soup kitchen. **fournée** (ne) *f*, batch.

fourni, e (furni) *p.a*, stocked; thick, bushy.

fournier, ère (furnje, ɛːr) *n*, baker (*for public*). **fournil** (ni) *m*, bakehouse.

fourniment (furnimɑ̃) *f*, equipment (*soldier's*). **fournir** (ni:r) *v.t. & abs*, to furnish, supply, provide; afford, adduce; give; find; lodge, deposit; produce; follow (*cards*); (*v.i.*) to provide, contribute. ~ *la carrière*, to stay the course. ~ [*à*] *la couleur demandée*, to follow suit. **fournissement** (nismɑ̃) *m*, contribution. **fournisseur, euse** (sœ:r, ∅:z) *n*, supplier; dealer; contractor; tradesman. ~ *de l'armée*, army contractor. ~ *de navires*, ship chandler, marine store dealer. **fourniture** (ty:r) *f*, supply, store; requisite; (*pl.*) stationery; material; supplying; trimmings (*tailor's*); seasoning (*for salad, i.e. savory herbs*).

fourrage (fura:ʒ) *m*, fodder, provender, forage; fur lining. **fourrager** (raʒe) *v.i. & t*, to forage; rummage; ravage. **fourrageur** (ʒœ:r) *m*, forager.

fourré (fure) *m*, thicket, brake; cover (*game*); jungle. **fourré, e** (re) *p.a*, fur-lined; stuffed (*Cook.*); wooded; jungly.

fourreau (furo) *m*, scabbard, sheath; case; cover; sleeve, cylinder.

fourrer (fure) *v.t*, to thrust, poke, shove; stuff, cram; line [with fur]. **fourre-tout** (rtu) *m*, hold-all. **fourreur, euse** (rœ:r, ∅:z) *n*, furrier.

fourrier (furje) *m*, quartermaster; harbinger.

fourrière (furjɛːr) *f*, pound (*dogs*, etc.). *mettre à la* ~, to impound.

fourrure (furyːr) *f*, fur, skin; welt, strap.

fourvoyer (furvwaje) *v.t*, to lead astray; mislead.

foutre (futr) *m*, sexual discharge (*obscene*). ¶ *v.t*, to fuck (*archaic*). *fous le camp*, scram. *fousmoi la paix*, let me be (*obscene*). *se foutre*, not give a damn. *je m'en fous*, I don't give a damn (*obscene*).

foutu (futy) *a*, done for; lousy. *mal* ~, out of sorts, luck; badly dressed; badly put together.

fox-terrier (fɔkstɛrje) *m*, fox terrier.

fox-trot (fɔkstrɔt) *m*, fox trot.

foyer (fwaje) *m*, hearth; furnace; fire box; stoker (*mechanical*); fireside; home; seat; hotbed; focus. ~ *d'étudiants*, hospice. ~ *des artistes*, greenroom. ~ [*du public*], foyer (*Theat.*). [*pierre de*] ~, hearthstone.

frac (frak) *m*, dress coat.

fracas (frakɑ) *m*, crash; roar; din, row, noise, bluster. **fracasser** (kase) *v.t*, to smash, shatter, shiver.

fraction (fraksjɔ̃) *f*, fraction; group (politics); breaking (*holy bread*). ~ *périodique*, recurring (*or* circulating) decimal. **fractionnaire** (ɔnɛːr) *a*, fractional. **fractionner** (ne) *v.t*, to split.

fracture (fraktyːr) *f*, fracture, breaking. **fracturer** (tyre) *v.t*, to fracture, break.

fragile (fraʒil) *a*, fragile; brittle; frail; [on parcels] with care. **fragilité** (lite) *f*, fragility, etc.

fragment (fragmɑ̃) *m*, fragment, piece, scrap; snatch. **fragmentaire** (tɛːr) *a*, fragmentary. **fragmenter** (te) *v.t*, to break [up].

frai (frɛ) *m*, spawning; spawn.

fraîchement (frɛʃmɑ̃) *ad*, in the cool; coolly; freshly, newly, lately. **fraîcheur** (ʃœːr) *f*, freshness; cool[ness]; chill; bloom (*fig.*). **fraîchir** (ʃiːr) *v.i*, to freshen. **frais, aîche** (frɛ, ɛːʃ) *a*, fresh; cool; chilly; new (*bread*,

etc.); recent; new-laid; wet (*paint, ink, fish*). *frais & gaillard, frais & dispos*, hale & hearty, fit & fresh. **frais, aîche** (*with p.p.*) *ad*, fresh[ly], newly, e.g, *des roses fraîches cueillies*, fresh[ly] gathered roses. **frais**, *m*, cool. *au* ~ *ou à la fraîche*, in the cool.

frais (frɛ) *m.pl*, expenses; expense; charges; cost; costs (*law*); efforts, pains. ~ *d'école*, ~ *scolaires*, tuition fees. ~ *de constitution*, preliminary expenses (*company*). ~ *de contentieux*, legal charges. ~ *divers*, general (*or* sundry) expenses. ~ *généraux*, standing (*or* establishment) (*or* overhead) expenses (*or* charges). *faux* ~, incidental expenses. *se mettre en* ~, to go to some expense.

fraise (frɛːz) *f*, strawberry; countersink [bit]; [milling] cutter; ruff (*Hist., dress*). ~ *des bois*, wild strawberry. **fraiser** (frɛze) *v.t*, to crimp; countersink; mill. **fraisier** (zje) *m*, strawberry plant.

fraisil (frɛzi) *m*, breeze (*cinders*).

framboise (frɑ̃bwaːz) *f*, raspberry. **framboisier** (bwazje) *m*, raspberry bush.

franc (frɑ̃) *m*, franc = 100 centimes. ~*s-or*, ~*s-argent*, ~*s-papier*, gold, silver, paper, francs. *le nouveau* ~, the franc since 1960, when it was substituted for 100 *anciens francs*.

franc, anche (frɑ̃, ɑ̃ːʃ) *a*, free; frank, candid, outspoken; open, open-hearted; aboveboard; clear (*complete, of days*); clean (*break, jump*); downright, out & out, regular, arrant; volunteer (*corps*); ungrafted (*tree*). *franc arbitre*, free will. *franc* (*anche*) *de port* ou *franc le port* (*inv.*), carriage free; post free. **franc**, *ad*, frankly, candidly.

français, e (frɑ̃sɛ, ɛːz) *a*, French. **F~,** *n*, Frenchman -woman. *les Français*, the French. *le français*, French (*language*).

franc-bord (frɑ̃bɔːr) *m*, freeboard (*ship*); open space.

France (la) (frɑ̃ːs), France.

Francfort (frãkfoːr) *m*, Frankfort.

franchement (frãʃmã) *ad*, frankly, candidly, openly; downright; heartily; boldly.

franchir (frãʃiːr) *v.t*, to jump over, leap o., pass o., get o.; pass through; clear; pass; cross; overstep; shoot (*rapids*); bridge, span; turn (*a certain age*); make (*hoop, croquet*).

franchise (frãʃiːz) *f*, exemption; franking (*Post*); frankness, outspokenness; plain dealing; freedom; immunity (*diplomatic*). ~ *de poids,* ~ *de bagages,* weight allowed free, free allowance of luggage.

francisation (frãsizasjɔ̃) *f*, Frenchification; registration (*ship*).

franciscain (frãsiskɛ̃) *m*, Franciscan, gray friar.

franciser (frãsize) *v.t*, to Frenchify, gallicize.

francité (frãsite) *f*, overall characteristics of French civilization.

franc-jeu (frãʒø) *m*, fair play.

franc-maçon (frãmasɔ̃) *m*, freemason. **franc-maçonnerie** (sɔnri) *f*, freemasonry.

franco (frãko) *ad*, free, f. of charge. ~ [à] *bord*, free on board. ~ *à quai*, free at wharf, ex wharf. ~ *de port*, carriage paid; post p. ~ *wagon,* ~ *gare*, free on rail, f. on truck.

francophile (frãkɔfil) *a. & n*, Francophile. **francophobe** (fɔb) *a. & n*, Francophobe.

franc-tireur (frãtirœːr) *m*, sniper; free-lance.

frange (frãːʒ) *f*, fringe. **franger** (frãʒe) *v.t*, to fringe.

franquette (à la bonne) frãkɛt), simply, without ceremony.

frappant, e (frapã, ãːt) *a*, striking. **frappe** (frap) *f*, stamp; minting; set of matrices (*Typ.*). *Force de* ~, striking force. **frapper** (pe) *v.t. & abs. & v.i*, to strike; hit; smite; tap; knock; slap; stamp; mint; impose, levy; be secured on; ice, chill (*bottle, etc.*). ~ [*de glace*], to ice. ~ *de nullité*, to render void.

frasque (frask) *f*, escapade.

frater (fratɛːr) *m*, lay brother. **fraternel, le†** (tɛrnɛl) *a*, fraternal, brotherly. **fraterniser** (nize) *v.i*, to fraternize. **fraternité** (te) *f*, fraternity, brotherhood. **fratricide** (trisid) *m*, fratricide; (*att.*) fratricidal.

fraude (froːd) *f*, fraud; smuggling. *la* ~ *fiscale*, evasion of tax. **frauder** (frode) *v.t*, to defraud, cheat; evade [payment of]. **fraudeur, euse** (dœːr, øːz) *n*, defrauder; smuggler. ~ *des droits du fisc*, tax dodger. **frauduleux, euse†** (dylø, øːz) *a*, fraudulent.

frayer (frɛje) *v.t. & i*, to open up, clear, blaze; rub; spawn; rub shoulders, associate. se ~, to force (*a passage*); fight (*or* grope) (*one's way*).

frayeur (frɛjœːr) *f*, fright, fear, dread.

fredaine (frədɛn) *f*, prank.

fredonner (frədone) *v.i. & t*, to hum (*tune*).

frégate (fregat) *f*, frigate.

frein (frɛ̃) *m*, brake; curb, check (*fig.*); frenum (*Anat.*). ~ *à ruban,* ~ *à bandé*, band brake. ~ *à vide*, vacuum b. ~ *sur jantes*, rim b. ~ *sur les quatre roues*, four-wheel b. ~ *sur moyeux*, hub b. ~ *sur pneu*, spoon b. **freiner** (frɛne) *v.i*, ou *serrer les freins*, to [put on (*or* apply) the] brake.

frelater (frəlate) *v.t*, to adulterate, doctor.

frêle (frɛːl) *a*, frail; weak.

frelon (frəlɔ̃) *m*, hornet.

freluche (frəlyʃ) *f*, tassel; tuft. **freluquet** (kɛ) *m*, whippersnapper, puppy (*man*); coxcomb.

frémir (fremiːr) *v.i*, to rustle, murmur, simmer; vibrate, quiver, shudder. **frémissement** (fremismã) *m*, quivering, shivering, shuddering, etc.

frêne (frɛːn) *m*, ash [tree, timber].

frénésie (frenezi) *f*, frenzy. **frénétique†** (tik) *a*, frantic, frenzied.

fréquemment (frekamã) *ad*, frequently, repeatedly, often. **fréquence** (kãːs) *f*, frequency; prevalence. **fréquent, e** (kã, ãːt) *a*, frequent; rapid (*pulse, etc.*). **fréquentation** (kãtasjɔ̃) *f*, fre-

quentation; (*pl.*) companionship.
fréquenté, e (te) *p.p,* crowded.
fréquenter (te) *v.i,* to frequent;
resort to; associate with.
frère (frɛːr) *m,* brother; (*pl.*)
brethren (*Eccl.*); friar; sister
[ship]. ~ *de lait,* foster brother.
frérot (frero) *m,* [dear] little
brother.
fresaie;(frəzɛ) *f,* barn owl, screech
owl.
fresque (frɛsk) *f,* fresco.
fressure (frɛsyːr) *f,* innards
(*butchery*).
fret (frɛ) *m,* freight. *prendre à*
~, to charter. **fréter** (frete) *v.t,*
to freight; charter. **fréteur** (tœːr)
m, [ship]owner.
frétiller (fretije) *v.i,* to frisk;
wriggle; fidget; itch. ~ *de la*
queue, to wag its tail (*dog*).
fretin (frətɛ̃) *m,* fry (*fish*); small
fry (*pers.*).
frette (frɛt) *f,* hoop, collar, band,
ring, ferrule; fret (*Arch., Her.*).
fretter (te) *v.t,* to hoop, bind.
freux (frø) *m,* rook (*bird*).
friable (friabl) *a,* friable, crumbly.
friand, e (friɑ̃, ɑ̃ːd) *a,* dainty.
~ *de,* fond of. **friandise** (ɑ̃diːz)
f, dainty, delicacy, sweet.
Fribourg (fribuːr) *m,* Fribourg,
Freiburg (*Switzerland*). **F~-en-**
Brisgau (brizgo) *m,* Freiburg
(*Baden*).
fric (frik) *m,* dough, bread, money
(*slang*).
fricassée (frikase) *f,* fricassee.
fricasser (se) *v.t,* to fricassee;
fritter away. **fricasseur, euse**
(sœːr, øːz) *n,* bad cook; squand-
erer.
friche (friʃ) *f,* waste land, fallow
[land]. *en* ~, fallow; undeveloped.
fricot (friko) *m,* stew. **fricoter**
(kɔte) *v.i.,* to stew; cook badly;
(*v.t.*) to squander.. **fricoteur, euse**
(tœːr, øːz) *n,* jobber; shirker.
friction (friksjɔ̃) *f,* friction; rubbing; dry shampoo; scalp mas-
sage. **frictionner** (ɔne) *v.t,* to
rub, chafe.
frigidité (friʒidite) *f,* frigidity,
coldness. **frigorifier** (gɔrifje) *v.t,*
to refrigerate,.freeze (*meat, etc.*).
frigorifique (fik) *a,* refrigerating,

freezing, cold (*att.*). ¶ *m,* cold
store.
frileux, euse (frilø, øːz) *a,*
chilly (*pers.*).
frimas (frima) *m,* icy mist, rime.
frime (frim) *f,* sham, pretense.
frimousse (frimus) *f,* phiz, little
face.
fringale (frɛ̃gal) *f,* hunger; craving. *avoir la* ~, to be famishing.
fringant, e (frɛ̃gɑ̃, ɑ̃ːt) *a,* frisky,
lively; smart. **fringuer** (ge) *v.i,*
to frisk, skip about.
friper (fripe) *v.t,* to [c]rumple,
crease. **friperie** (pri) *f,* cast-off
clothes; second-hand furniture;
frippery, trumpery; secondhand
dealer's shop. **fripier, ère** (pje,
ɛːr) *n,* secondhand dealer.
fripon, ne (fripɔ̃, ɔn) *n,* knave,
rogue, rascal; hussy, minx; thief.
¶ *a,* knavish, roguish, rascally.
friponner (pɔne) *v.t. & abs,* to
cheat out of; steal from; cheat.
friponnerie (nri) *f,* knavery,
roguery, rascality.
friquet (frikɛ) *m,* tree sparrow.
frire (friːr) *v.t. & i. ir,* to fry.
frise (friːz) *f,* frieze. **la F~,**
Friesland.
friser (frize) *v.t. & i,* to curl,
frizzle, frizz, crimp; graze; border on. **frison** (zɔ̃) *m,* curl.
frison, ne (frizɔ̃, ɔn) *a. & F~, n,*
Frisian.
frisotter (frizɔte) *v.t,* to frizz[le].
frisquet (friskɛ) *a.m. & a.f,*
chilly.
frisquette (friskɛt) *f,* frisket
(*Typ.*).
frisson (frisɔ̃) *m,* shiver, shudder, quiver; thrill. **frissonner**
(sɔne) *v.i,* to shiver, etc.
frisure (frizyːr) *f,* curling; curliness; (*pl.*) curls.
frites (frit) *pl.f,* French fries.
friture (frityːr) *f,* frying; crackling
(*Teleph.*); fry; frying oil, frying
fat; fried fish.
frivole (frivɔl) *a,* frivolous,
flighty; trivial, fiddling, trumpery;
flimsy, frothy. **frivolité** (lite) *f,* frivolity, trifle; tatting.
froc (frɔk) *m,* cowl; frock (*monk's*);
monkery, monkhood; trousers
(*slang*). *baisser son* ~, to accept
humiliation.
froid, e† (frwa, ad) *a,* cold; fri-

gid; cool, chill[y]. *en* ~, to be on unfriendly terms. à **froid,** *ad,* cold, when cold; in cold blood. ¶ *m,* cold; c. weather; frost (*degrees of*); coldness; chill[iness]; coolness. **froideur** (dœːr) *f,* coldness; chilliness; coolness; frigidity. **froidure** (dyːr) *f,* coldness, cold.

froisser (frwase) *v.t,* to bruise; crush; [c]rumple; offend, hurt, wound.

frôler (frole) *v.t,* to graze, brush [against]; come very near to (*fig.*).

fromage (frɔmaːʒ) *m,* cheese; soft job, a snap. ~ *à la crème,* double-cream cheese. ~ *blanc,* cream cheese. ~ *de porc,* brawn. **fromager, ère** (maʒe, ɛːr) *n,* cheese maker; cheesemonger; (*att.*) cheese. **fromagerie** (ʒri) *f,* cheese dairy.

froment (frɔmɑ̃) *m,* wheat.

fronce (frɔ̃ːs) *f,* gather; pucker. ~*s smock* (smɔk), smocking. **froncer** (frɔ̃se) *v.t,* to wrinkle; purse, pucker (*lips*); gather (*Need.*). ~ *le*[*s*] *sourcil*[*s*], to frown, knit one's brows.

frondaison (frɔ̃dɛzɔ̃) *f,* foliation, leafing; foliage.

fronde (frɔ̃ːd) *f,* sling; catapult (*boy's*); frond (*Bot.*); obstruction (*fig.*). **fronder** (frɔ̃de) *v.i,* to catapult; obstruct; (*v.t.*) to find fault with. **frondeur** (dœːr) *m,* slinger; faultfinder; critic. ~, **euse** (øːz) *att,* fault-finding.

front (frɔ̃) *m,* front; front [line] (*Mil.*); forehead; brow; face; head; impudence, cheek. *de* ~, abreast; frontal; front. *faire* ~ *à,* to face.

frontière (frɔ̃tjɛːr) *f. & att,* frontier, border.

frontispice (frɔ̃tispis) *m,* frontispiece (*book*); title page. **fronton** (tɔ̃) *m,* fronton, pediment.

frottage (frɔtaːʒ) *m,* polishing (*floors*). **frottée** (te) *f,* drubbing, thrashing. **frottement** (tmɑ̃) *m,* rubbing; friction; contact, intercourse. **frotter** (te) *v.t. & i,* to rub; polish; scumble; drub, pommel; box (*ears*); strike (*match*). *se* ~ *à* (*fig.*), to rub shoulders with. *se* ~ *les mains,* to rub one's hands. **frotteur** (tœːr) *m,* floor polisher (*pers.*). **frottis** (ti) *m,* scumble; rubbing (*copy*). **frottoir** (twaːr) *m,* rubber, polisher.

frou-frou (frufru) *m,* rustling, swish.

frousse (frus) *f,* fear, funk.

fructifier (fryktifje) *v.i,* to fructify. **fructueux, euse†** (tɥø, øːz) *a,* fruitful (*fig. & Poet.*), profitable.

frugal, e† (frygal) *a,* frugal. **frugalité** (lite) *f,* frugality.

fruit (frɥi) *m,* fruit; profit; benefit; batter (*Build.*). ~ *tombé,* windfall. **fruiterie** (tri) *f,* fruit shop; f. trade. **fruitier, ère** (tje, ɛːr) *n,* fruiterer, greengrocer; (*att.*) fruit.

frusques (frysk) *f.pl,* clothes.

frusquin (fryskɛ̃) *m,* worldly goods.

fruste (fryst) *a,* defaced, worn.

frustrer (frystre) *v.t,* to deprive; defraud; frustrate, balk.

fuchsia (fyksja) *m,* fuchsia.

fugace (fygas) *a,* fleeting; unretentive (*memory*). **fugitif, ive** (ʒitif, iːv) *a,* fugitive, fleeting, transitory, short-lived. ¶ *n,* fugitive, runaway.

fugue (fyg) *f,* fugue (*Mus.*); flight, bolt; elopement.

fuir (fɥiːr) *v.i.ir,* to flee, fly, flit, run away; escape; recede; vanish; leak; (*v.t.ir.*) to flee [from], run away from; shun; eschew. **fuite** (fɥit) *f,* flight; escape; leak[age].

fulguration (fylgyrasjɔ̃) *f,* heat (*or* summer) lightning.

fulmicoton (fylmikɔtɔ̃) *m,* guncotton.

fulminer (fylmine) *v.i. & t,* to fulminate, thunder, storm.

fumage (fymaːʒ) *m,* smoking (*meat, fish*); manuring. **fume-cigarette,** *m,* cigarette holder. **fumée** (me) *f. oft. pl,* smoke; fume; steam, vapor; reek; phantom, vanity; (*pl.*) dung. **fumer** (me) *v.i. & t,* to smoke; cure; steam; reek; fume; manure. *cheminée qui fume,* smoky chimney. **fumerie** (mri) *f,* opium den. **fumet** (mɛ) *m,* smell; bouquet; scent. **fumeur, euse** (mœːr, øːz) *n,* smoker. **fumeux, euse** (mø, øːz) *a,* smoky;

heady; hazy. **fumier** (mje) *m*, litter (*straw & dung*), dung, manure; muck; dunghill; contemptible person.

fumigation (fymigasjɔ̃) *f*, fumigation.

fumiste (fymist) *m*, heating engineer; practical joker. **fumisterie** (tri) *f*, heating engineering; practical joke. **fumivore** (vɔːr) *a*, smoke-consuming. ¶ *m*, s. consumer, s. preventer. **fumoir** (mwaːr) *m*, smoke house; smoking room.

fumure (fymyːr) *f*, manuring; manure.

funambule (fynɑ̃byl) *n*, funambulist; rope walker. **funambulesque** (lɛsk) *a*, funambulatory; fantastic.

funèbre (fynɛːbr) *a*, funeral; funereal; dead (*march*); illomened (*birds*). **funérailles** (nerɑːj) *f.pl*, funeral. **funéraire** (rɛːr) *a*, funeral.

funeste (fynɛst) *a*, deadly, baneful, baleful, fatal.

funiculaire (fynikylɛːr) *a. & m*, funicular, cable railway.

fur (fyːr) *m*: *au ~ & à mesure*, in proportion. *au ~ & à mesure des besoins*, as [& when] required. *au ~ & à mesure que*, as [& when].

furet (fyrɛ) *m*, ferret. **fureter** (ɾte) *v.i. & t*, to ferret, f. about, pry. **fureteur, euse** (rtœːr, øːz) *n*, ferreter, rummager; collector, hunter; nosybody.

fureur (fyrœːr) *f*, fury, rage, wrath; passion; distraction; craze; frenzy; furore. *faire ~*, to be the rage. **furibond, e** (ribɔ̃, ɔːd) *a*, furious. ¶ *n*, madman; fury. **furie** (ri) *f*, fury. F~, Fury (*Myth.*). **furieux, euse†** (rjø, øːz) *a*, furious, raging, mad, raving; tremendous. ¶ *n*, madman, -woman.

furoncle (fyrɔ̃ːkl) *m*, boil (*Med.*).

furtif, ive† (fyrtif, iːv) *a*, furtive, stealthy, sly.

fusain (fyzɛ̃) *m*, spindle tree; charcoal [pencil]; c. drawing.

fuseau (fyzo) *m*, spindle (*spinning*); pintle.

fusée (fyze) *f*, rocket, fuse; fusee (*Horol.*); (*axle*) journal; [out]burst (*fig.*). ~ *volante*, sky rocket. ~ *éclairante, de signalisation*, flare. **fusée-sonde** (fyzeɔ̃ːd) probe, sounding rocket.

fuselage (fyzlaːʒ) *m*, fuselage. **fuselé, e** (zle) *a*, spindle-shaped; tapering; streamlined.

fuser (fyze) *v.i*, to spread, run (*colors*); fuse, melt; burn slowly.

fusible (fyzibl) *a*, fusible.

fusil (fyzi) *m*, gun, rifle; steel (*sharpener*). ~ *à vent*, air gun. ~ *à deux coups*, double-barrelled g. ~ *mitrailleur*, machine g. ~ *pour le tir à plomb*, shotgun. ~ *se chargeant par la culasse*, breech-loader. *coup de ~*, gunshot; an unexpectedly high bill. **fusilier** (zilje) *m*, ~ *marin*, marine. ~ *mitrailleur*, machine gunner. **fusillade** (zijad) *f*, fusillade. **fusiller** (je) *v.t*, to shoot (*spy, deserter*); bombard (*fig.*).

fusion (fyzjɔ̃) *f*, fusion, melting, smelting. **fusionner** (ɔne) *v.t. & i*, to amalgamate, merge.

fustiger (fystiʒe) *v.t*, to flog; rebuke.

fût (fy) *m*, stock (*rifle, plane*); handle; shank; shaft (*of column*); post; cask; drum.

futaie (fytɛ) *f*, timber-tree forest.

futaille (fytaːj) *f*, cask, barrel.

futaine (fytɛn) *f*, fustian.

futé, e (fyte) *a*, crafty; sly; sharp.

futile (fytil) *a*, futile, nugatory; trifling, idle. **futilité** (lite) *f*, futility; (*pl.*) trifles; (*pl.*) trash (*worthless contents of book*).

futur, e (fytyːr) *a*, future. ¶ *n*, intended (*husband, wife*). ¶ *m*, future; futurity. ~ *antérieur*, future perfect (*Gram.*). ~ [*simple*], future [tense].

fuyant, e (fɥijɑ̃, ɑ̃ːt) *a*, receding, retreating; vanishing (*perspective*); shifty. **fuyard, e** (jaːr, ard) *n*, fugitive, runaway.

G

gabardine (gabardin) *f*, gabardine; raincoat.

gabare (gabaːr) *f*, lighter, barge; dragnet.

gabarit (gabari) *m*, gauge, templet; mold (*ship*).

gabegie (gabʒi) *f*, mismanagement & dishonesty.

gabier (gabje) *m*, top[s]man (*Naut.*).

gâche (gɑːʃ) *f*, staple (*lock, wall*). **gâcher** (gaʃe) *v.t*, to temper (*mortar*); spoil, botch, mess up. **gâchis** (ʃi) *m*, (*wet*) mortar; slush, sludge; mess.

gâchette (gaʃɛt) *f*, trigger; catch; pawl (*Mech.*).

gadoue (gadu) *f*, night soil, sewage.

gaffe (gaf) *f*, boat hook; gaff (*Fish.*); blunder, howler. **gaffer** (fe) *v.t*, to hook, gaff; (*v.i.*) to blunder.

gage (gaːʒ) *m*, pledge, pawn, security, gage; hostage; forfeit (*at play*); token, proof; (*pl.*) wages, pay; forfeits (*game*). **à ~s**, paid, hired. **gager** (gaʒe) *v.t*, to pay; bet. **gageure** (ʒyːr) *f*, wager. **gagiste** (ʒist) *m*, employee.

gagnage (gɑɲaːʒ) *m*, pasturage.

gagnant, e (gɑɲɑ̃, ɑ̃ːt) *n*, winner; (*att.*) winning. **gagne-pain** (ɲpɛ̃) *m*, livelihood; breadwinner. **gagne-petit** (ɲpəti) *m*, knife grinder; one who earns (*or* makes) very little. **gagner** (ɲe) *v.t. & abs. & i*, to gain; be the gainer; get; make; earn; win; gain over; reach, get to; overtake; spread. **~ à être connu**, to improve on acquaintance. **se ~,** to be catching; spread.

gai, e† (ge) *a*, gay, merry; lively; blithe; bright, cheerful. **gai, i,** merrily!

gaieté (gete) *f*, gaiety; cheerfulness; liveliness; merriment, mirth, glee. **de ~ de cœur**, out of sheer wantonness. **gaillard, e†** (gajaːr, ard) *a*, jolly, merry; hearty; free, ribald. ¶ *m*, fellow, fine f., jolly f. ¶ *f*, strapping gay wench. **gaillardise** (jardiːz) *f*, gaiety, jollity; broad humor.

gailletin (gajtɛ̃) *m*. ou **gaillette** (jɛt) *f*, cobbles, nuts (*coal*).

gain (gɛ̃) *m*, gain, profit, lucre; earnings; winning; winnings. **~ de cause**, decision in one's favor; right, justification. **en ~,** in pocket, to the good.

gaine (gɛːn) *f*, sheath, case; girdle; pedestal.

gala (gala) *m*, gala.

galamment (galamɑ̃) *ad*, courteously, gallantly; skillfully. **galant, e** (lɑ̃, ɑ̃ːt) *a*, gallant (*to women*); amatory; stylish. **galant homme**, gentleman. ¶ *m*, gallant; spark; philanderer; lover; slippery gentleman. **galanterie** (lɑ̃tri) *f*, politeness, gallantry (*to women*); love affair.

galbe (galb) *m*, contour, outline.

gale (gal) *f*, itch; mange; scab.

galée (gale) *f*, composing galley.

galène (galɛn) *f*, galena.

galère (galɛːr) *f*, galley (*Hist.*).

galerie (galri) *f*, gallery; arcade; level, drive, drift, road[way] (*Min.*); (*pl, Theat.*) balcony. **~ à écho**, whispering gallery. **~ à flanc de coteau**, adit. **faire ~,** to sit out.

galérien (galerjɛ̃) *m*, galley slave.

galerne (galɛrn) *f*, northwester (*wind*).

galet (galɛ) *m*, pebble; (*pl. or s.*) shingle; roller, wheel, runner; castor, caster.

galetas (galtɑ) *m*, garret, attic.

galette (galɛt) *f*, ship biscuit, hardtack; money, loot (*slang*).

galeux, euse (galø, øːz) *a*, itchy; scabby; mangy; scurfy.

galhauban (galobɑ̃) *m*, backstay (*Naut.*).

galimafrée (galimafre) *f*, hash, hotchpotch.

galimatias (galimatjɑ) *m*, balderdash, gibberish.

galion (galjɔ̃) *m*, galleon (*Hist.*).

galle (gal) *f*, gall [nut].

Galles (le pays de) (gal), Wales. **la Galles du Nord, du Sud**, North, South, Wales.

gallican, e (galikɑ̃, an) *a. & n*, Gallican. **gallicisme** (sism) *m*, gallicism.

gallois, e (galwa, aːz) *a*, Welsh. **G~,** *n*, Welshman, -woman. **le gallois**, Welsh (*language*).

gallophobe (galɔfɔb) *a. & n*, Gallophobe, anti-French.

galoche (galɔʃ) *f*, rubber, overshoe.

galon (galɔ̃) *m*, braid, galloon; gimp; stripe (*N.C.O.'s, & Navy*); band (*officer's*). **galonner** (lɔne) *v.t*, to braid, lace.

galop (galo) *m*, gallop; galop

(*dance*); hot haste; scolding. **galoper** (lɔpe) *v.i*, to gallop; run, career. **galopin** (pɛ̃) *m*, urchin.

galuchat (galyʃa) *m*, shagreen.

galvanique (galvanik) *a*, galvanic. **galvaniser** (ze) *v.t*, to galvanize. **galvanisme** (nism) *m*, galvanism.

galvauder (galvode) *v.t*, to misuse; botch; (*v.i.*) to loiter. se ~, to sully one's name.

gambade (gɑ̃bad) *f*, gambol, frisk; (*pl.*) antics, capers. **gambader** (de) *v.i*, to gambol, etc.

gamberger (gɑ̃berʒe) *v.i. & t*, to imagine; understand; stroll.

Gambie (la) (gɑ̃bi), Gambia.

gambiller (gɑ̃bije) *v.i*, to skip about.

gambit (gɑ̃bi) *m*, gambit (*chess*).

gamelle (gamɛl) *f*, mess kit; mess (*Nav.*).

gamin, e (gamɛ̃, in) *n*, urchin; youngster; (*f.*) hoyden, romp. ~ *des rues*, street child, s. arab. ¶ *a*, saucy. **gaminer** (mine) *v.i*, to play about. **gaminerie** (nri) *f*, child's prank; [tom]foolery.

gamme (gam) *f*, scale; gamut; range; tone, tune (*fig.*). *haut de* ~, high quality, first class.

ganache (ganaʃ) *f*, lower jaw (*horse*); duffer, fogey.

Gand (gɑ̃) *m*, Ghent.

Gange (le) (gɑ̃:ʒ), the Ganges.

ganglion (gɑ̃gliɔ̃) *m*, ganglion.

gangrène (gɑ̃grɛn) *f*, gangrene. **gangrener** (grəne) *v.t*, to gangrene; corrupt, canker.

gangue (gɑ̃:g) *f*, gangue, matrix.

ganse (gɑ̃:s) *f*, cord (*braided*); gimp; loop.

gant (gɑ̃) *m*, glove; gauntlet (*fig.*); (*pl.*) credit. ~*s de peau glacée*, glacé kid gloves. ~*s de Suède*, suède g. ~ *de toilette*, washcloth in shape of glove or mitt. **gantelée** (tle) *f*, foxglove. **gantelet** (tlɛ) *m*, gauntlet. **ganter** (te) *v.t*, to glove. se ~, to put on one's gloves. **ganterie** (tri) *f*, glove trade. **gantier, ère** (tje, ɛ:r) *n*, glover.

garage (gara:ʒ) *m*, shunting (*Rly.*); garage, parking (*motor*); shed (*cycle*); docking (*boat*); hangar (*Avn.*).

garance (garɑ̃:s) *f*, madder.

garant, e (garɑ̃, ɑ̃:t) *n*, guaran-

tor, surety (*pers.*); (*m.*) authority; warrant; [tackle] fall (*Naut.*). **garantie** (rɑ̃ti) *f*, guarantee, guaranty, warranty; security; indemnity; safeguard; underwriting (*Fin.*). **garantir** (ti:r) *v.t*, to guarantee; warrant; secure; keep, protect, shield; vouch for; underwrite (*Fin.*).

garce (gars) *f*, bitchy woman.

garcette (garsɛt) *f*, gasket; rope end.

garçon (garsɔ̃) *m*, boy, lad; son; [young] man; fellow, chap; bachelor, single man. ~ *d'écurie*, stableboy. ~ *d'honneur*, best man. ~ *de bureau*, messenger, commissionaire. ~ *de cabine*, steward. ~ [*de café*], waiter. ~ *de course*, errand boy. ~ *manqué*, tomboy, hoyden, romp. **garçonne** (sɔn) *f*, bachelor girl. **garçonnet** (sɔnɛ) *m*, little boy. **garçonnier, ère** (nje, ɛ:r) *a*, (*of girl*) mannish, masculine; fond of men's society. ¶ *f*, bachelor flat.

garde (gard) *f*, guardianship; guard; keeping, charge, [safe] custody; watch; heed, care; protection; notice; hilt; covering card; endpaper. ~ *blanche*, flyleaf. ~ *descendante*, old guard (*Mil.*). ~ *montante*, new guard.

garde (gard) *m*, guard (*pers.*); keeper; watchman; watcher (*Cust.*); warder; ranger. ~-*barrière*, *n*, gatekeeper (*level crossing*). ~-*boue*, *m*, fender (*auto*). ~-*cendre*, *m*, fender (*fireplace*). ~ *champêtre*, *m*, rural policeman. ~-*chasse*, *m*, gamekeeper. ~-*chiourme*, *m*, prison guard; slave driver; foreman. ~-*corps*, *m*, rail (*ship*). ~-*côte*, *m*, coastguard ship. ~-*crotte*, *m*, fender (*auto*). ~-*fou*, *m*, handrail, railing. ~-*frein*, *m*, brakesman. ~-*malades*, *n*, [sick] nurse. ~-*manger*, *m*, pantry, larder. ~-*meuble*, *m*, furniture warehouse. ~-*robe*, *f*, wardrobe; privy. ~-*vue*, *m*, eyeshade.

gardénia (gardenja) *m*, gardenia.

garder (garde) *v.t*, to keep; retain; harbor; tend, look after, mind; guard, protect. se ~ *de*, to take care not to; beware of; refrain from. **garderie** (dəri) *f*, day nursery. **gardeur, euse** (dœːr, ∅ːz) *n*, keeper, -herd (*cow, swine*). **gardien, ne** (djɛ̃, ɛn) *n*, guardian; keeper, caretaker, custodian, attendant, warder, dress. ~ *de but*, goal keeper. ~ *de la paix*, policeman.

gardon (gardɔ̃) *m*, roach (*fish*).

gare (gaːr) *i*, look out! take care! mind. ¶ *f*, station (*Rly.*). ~ *d'embranchement*, ~ *de bifurcation*, junction. ~ *d'évitement*, sidings. *chef de* ~, stationmaster. ~ *maritime*, harbor station. *en* ~, ~ *restante*, [at railway station,] to be called for.

garenne (garɛn) *f*, [rabbit] warren.

garer (gare) *v.t*, to shunt, switch (*train*); garage (*car*). se~, to shunt; pull to one side; get out of the way, take cover; park a car.

gargariser (se) (gargarize) *v.pr. & abs*, to gargle; gloat on. **gargarisme** (rism) *m*, gargle.

gargote (gargɔt) *f*, beanery.

gargouille (garguːj) *f*, gargoyle; waterspout (*rain*). **gargouiller** (guje) *v.i*, to gurgle; rumble (*bowels*).

gargousse (gargus) *f*, cartridge (*cannon*).

garnement (garnəmɑ̃) *m*. ou *mauvais* ~, scapegrace, scamp.

garni (garni) *m*, furnished room. ¶ *a*, furnished, trimmed.

garnir (garniːr) *v.t. & abs*, to furnish; stock; fill; line; lag; stuff; trim; garnish; decorate. **garnison** (nizɔ̃) *f*, garrison. **garniture** (tyːr) *f*, fittings; furniture; trimmings; packing, lagging, gasket; lining; garnish; seasoning (*of salad, i.e, savory herbs*); set. ~ *de foyer*, fire irons. ~ *de table*, luncheon set.

garrot (garo) *m*, withers; tourniquet; garrote. **garrotter** (rɔte) *v.t*, to pinion; strangle.

gars (ga) *m*, lad, boy; fellow. *allez les* ~, let's go, boys.

gascon, ne (gaskɔ̃, ɔn) *n*, braggart, Gascon. **gasconnade** (kɔnad) *f*, boasting, gasconade.

gaspillage (gaspijaːʒ) *m*, waste, squandering. **gaspiller** (pije) *v.t*, to waste, squander; spoil.

gastéropode (gasterɔpɔd) *m*, gastropod. **gastrique** (trik) *a*, gastric. **gastrite** (trit) *f*, gastritis. **gastronome** (trɔnɔm) *m*, gastronome. **gastronomie** (mi) *f*, gastronomy. **gastronomique** (mik) *a*, gastronomic(al).

gâté, e (gɑte) *p.a*, spoiled; damaged, rotten.

gâteau (gɑto) *m*, cake; comb (*honey*); spoils. ~ *sec*, cookie. *c'est du* ~, it's easy. *papa* ~, sugar daddy.

gâte-métier (gɑtmetje) *m*, [price] cutter; rat. **gâter** (te) *v.t*, to spoil, mar; soil; corrupt; taint; indulge, pamper. **gâterie** (tri) *f*, overindulgence (*to pers.*), spoiling.

gauche (goːʃ) *a*, left; crooked; awkward, clumsy; tactless. *tenir à* ~, to keep left. ¶ *f*, left. ¶ *le* [poing] gauche, the left (*Box.*) **gauchement** (goʃmɑ̃) *ad*, awkwardly, clumsily. **gaucher, ère** (ʃe, ɛːr) *a*, left-handed. ¶ *n*, left-hander (*pers. or player*). **gaucherie** (ʃri) *f*, awkwardness. **gauchir** (ʃiːr) *v.i. & t*, to turn aside; shuffle; buckle, bend; warp, wind.

gaudriole (godfiɔl) *f*, broad joke.

gaufre (goːfr) *f*, comb (*honey*); waffle; wafer. **gaufrer** (gofre) *v.t*, to goffer, crimp; emboss; figure; tool (*Bookb.*). **gaufrette** (frɛt) *f*, wafer [biscuit] (*flat*).

gaule (goːl) *f*, pole; fishing rod; switch (*stick*).

gaulois, e (golwa, aːz) *a*, Gallic; joyous, broad, free. G~, n, Gaul. **gauloiserie** (lwazri) *f*, broadness; broad humor.

gausser (se) de (gose), to poke fun at.

gavage (gavaːʒ) *m*, cramming; forcible feeding.

gave (gaːv) *m*, mountain torrent.

gaver (gave) *v.t*, to cram (*poultry, pupil for exam*); feed forcibly; stuff.

gavotte (gavɔt) *f*, gavotte.

gaz (gaːz) *m*, gas; flatus, wind. ~ *lacrymogène* (lakrimɔʒɛn), tear gas. ~ *moutarde*, mustard g.

gaze (gaːz) *f*, gauze.

gazéifier (gazeifje) *v.t*, to gasify; aerate.

gazelle (gazɛl) *f*, gazelle.

gazer (gɑze) *v.t,* to cover with gauze; veil, tone down; gas (*war*); to speed ahead.

gazette (gazɛt) *f,* gazette; newsmonger, gossip.

gazeux, euse (gazø, øːz) *a,* gaseous; gassy; aerated; effervescing. **gazier** (zje) *m,* gas worker; gas fitter. **gazogène** (zɔʒɛn) *m,* gazogene, seltzogene; [gas] producer. **gazomètre** (mɛtr) *m,* gasometer.

gazon (gazɔ̃) *m,* grass; turf, sod; lawn, [green]sward. **gazonner** (zɔne) *v.t,* to turf.

gazouiller (gazuje) *v.i,* to warble, chirp, twitter; purl, babble; prattle.

geai (ʒe) *m,* jay (*bird*).

géant, e (ʒeɑ̃, ɑ̃ːt) *n,* giant, ess; (*att.*) giant.

géhenne (ʒeɛn) *f,* Gehenna, hell.

geignard, e (ʒeɲaːr, ard) *a,* whining, fretful. **geindre** (ʒɛ̃dr) *v.i.ir,* to whine, fret.

gel (ʒɛl) *m,* frost, freezing; freeze (*in diplomatic relations*).

gélatine (ʒelatin) *f,* gelatin[e]. **gélatineux, euse** (nø, øːz) *a,* gelatinous.

gelé, e (ʒele) *a,* frozen; frostbitten. **gelée** (le) *f,* frost; jelly. ~ *blanche,* hoar frost, white f. ~ *noire,* ~ *à glace,* black f. **geler** (le) *v.t. & i. & imp. & se* ~, to freeze.

gémir (ʒemiːr) *v.i,* to groan, moan; complain. **gémissement** (mismɑ̃) *m,* groan[ing].

gemme (ʒɛm) *f,* gem; bud; (*att.*) gem (*stone*); rock (*salt*).

gênant, e (ʒɛnɑ̃, ɑ̃ːt) *a,* in the way; awkward; troublesome.

gencive (ʒɑ̃siːv) *f,* gum (*Anat.*).

gendarme (ʒɑ̃darm) *m,* gendarme, policeman; Amazon; martinet; spark; flaw; red herring. **se gendarmer** (me) *v.pr,* to be up in arms, fire up. **gendarmerie** (məri) *f,* state police force; headquarters of state police.

gendre (ʒɑ̃ːdr) *m,* son-in-law.

gêne (ʒɛn) *f,* discomfort; inconvenience; constraint; want; straits, straitened circumstances. *sans* ~, indifferent (*to other people's convenience*), unconcerned, cool; unconventional, free & easy.

généalogie (ʒenealɔʒi) *f,* genealogy; pedigree. **généalogique** (ʒik) *a,* genealogical, family (*tree*).

gêner (ʒɛne) *v.t,* to hinder, hamper, cramp; pinch (*shoes, etc.*); interfere with; inconvenience.

général, e† (ʒeneral) *a,* general; common; prevailing. **le** ~, the general (*fig.*). ~ *de corps d'armée,* lieutenant general. ~ *de division,* major general. ~ *en chef,* (*full*) general. ¶ *f,* general's wife; dress rehearsal; alarm call. **généralat** (la) *m,* generalship. **généraliser** (lize) *v.t. & abs,* to generalize. **se** ~, to become general. **généralissime** (sim) *m,* generalissimo, commander-in-chief. **généralité** (te) *f,* generality.

générateur, trice (ʒeneratœːr, tris) *a,* generating. ¶ *m,* generator. **génération** (sjɔ̃) *f,* generation. *les appareils de troisième* ~, technically advanced equipment (*electronics*).

généreux, euse† (ʒenerø, øːz) *a,* generous, bounteous, bountiful.

générique (ʒenerik) *a,* generic. ¶ *m,* credits (*cinema*).

générosité (ʒenerozite) *f,* generosity, bounteousness; (*pl.*) acts of generosity.

Gênes (ʒɛn) *f,* Genoa.

genèse (ʒənɛiz) *f,* genesis. *la G*~, Genesis (*Bible*).

genet (ʒənɛ) *m,* jennet (*horse*).

genêt (ʒənɛ) *m,* broom (*Bot.*). ~ *épineux,* furze, gorse, whin.

genette (ʒənɛt) *f,* genet (*civet*).

gêneur (ʒɛnœːr) *m,* nuisance (*pers.*).

Genève (ʒənɛːv) *f,* Geneva.

genévrier (ʒənevrie) *m,* juniper (*genus*).

génial, e (ʒenjal) *a,* [full] of genius. **génie** (ni) *m,* genius; spirit; Muse; bent; engineering.

genièvre (ʒənjɛːvr) *m,* juniper tree, berry; gin.

génisse (ʒenis) *f,* heifer.

génital, e (ʒenital) *a,* genital.

génitif (ʒenitif) *m*, genitive [case].

génois, e (ʒenwa, aːz) *a. & G~*, *n*, Genoese.

genou (ʒənu) *m*, knee; (*pl.*) lap. *à ~x*, on one's knees, kneeling. **genouillère** (ʒɛːr) *f*, kneepad; knuckle [joint] (*Mech.*).

genre (ʒãːr) *m*, kind; sort; line; type; description; genus; manner; way; style; fashion; genre (*real life picture*); gender (*Gram.*). *le ~ humain*, mankind.

gens (ʒã) *m.pl. & f.pl*, people, folk, men; servants, *les ~ du commun*, *m.pl*, [the] common people. **gent** (ʒã) *f*, tribe, race, folk.

gentiane (ʒãsjan) *f*, gentian.

gentil (ʒãti) *m. & a.m*, gentile.

gentil, le (ʒãti, iːj) *a*, nice, pretty, sweet; kind, good. *~ à croquer*, perfectly sweet (*pers.*). **gentilhomme** (tijɔm) *m*, nobleman; gentleman. *~ campagnard*, gentleman farmer. **gentilhommerie** (mri) *f*, gentility; gentlemanliness. **gentilhommière** (mjɛːr) *f*, country seat.

gentilité (ʒãtilite) *f*, pagandom; paganism.

gentillâtre (ʒãtijaːtr) *m*, obscure gentleman.

gentillesse (ʒãtijɛs) *f*, prettiness; gracefulness; (*pl.*) pretty speeches; (*pl.*) pretty tricks; nasty trick. **gentillet, te** (jɛ, ɛt) *a*, rather nice. **gentiment** (mã) *ad*, nicely, prettily.

gentleman (dʒɛntləman) *m*, gentleman; (*att.*) gentlemanly.

génuflexion (ʒenyflɛksjɔ̃) *f*, genuflexion.

géodésie (ʒeɔdezi) *f*, geodesy. **géognosie** (ɔgnozi) *f*, geognosy. **géographe** (graf) *m*, geographer. **géographie** (fi) *f*, geography. **géographique**† (fik) *a*, geographic(al).

geôle (ʒoːl) *f*, jail; jailer's lodge. **geôlier, ère** (ʒolje, ɛːr) *n*, jailer; wardress.

géologie (ʒeɔlɔʒi) *f*, geology. *~ sur le terrain*, field g. **géologique** (ʒik) *a*, geologic(al). **géologue** (lɔg) *m*, geologist.

géométral, e† (ʒeɔmetral) *a*, flat, plane. **géomètre** (mɛtr) *m*,

geometer, geometrician; surveyor. *~ du cadastre*, ordnance surveyor. **géométrie** (metri) *f*, geometry. **géométrique**† (trik) *a*, geometric(al); mathematical (*precise*).

Georgie (la) (ʒɔrʒi), Georgia (*U.S.A.*).

Géorgie (la) (ʒeɔrʒi), Georgia (*Asia*).

gérance (ʒerãːs) *f*, management; board of directors.

géranium (ʒeranjɔm) *m*, geranium.

gérant, e (ʒerã, ãːt) *n*, manager, ess; (*att.*) managing.

gerbe (ʒɛrb) *f*, sheaf; shower; spray (*flowers*). *~ d'eau*, spray of water; splash. **gerber** (be) *v.t*, to bind, sheaf, pile.

gerboise (ʒɛrbwaːs) *f*, jerboa.

gerce (ʒɛrs) *f*, crack; clothes moth. **gercer** (se) *v.t*, to chap; crack. **gerçure** (syːr) *f*, chap; crack; shake (*timber*).

gérer (ʒere) *v.t*, to manage. *mal ~*, to mismanage.

germain, e (ʒɛrmɛ̃, ɛn) *a*, germane, own, full (*brother, sister*). *cousin ~*, first cousin. *issu de ~*, second cousin.

germe (ʒɛrm) *m*, germ; eye (*potato*); tread (*egg*); sprout; bud (*fig.*); seed (*fig.*). **germer** (me) *v.i*, to germinate; shoot, sprout; spring up, germ. **germination** (minasjɔ̃) *f*, germination.

gérondif (ʒerɔ̃dif) *m*, gerund.

géronte (ʒerɔ̃ːt) *m*, old man (*in comedy*); old fool.

gésier (ʒezje) *m*, gizzard.

gésir (ʒeziːr) *v.i.ir*, to lie (*sick, dead*).

gesse (ʒɛs) *f*, vetch, pea.

gestation (ʒɛstasjɔ̃) *f*, gestation.

geste (ʒɛst) *m*, gesture; motion, movement; action; wave, flourish, lift (*of the hand*); (*f*.) epic. **gesticuler** (tikyle) *v.i*, to gesticulate.

gestion (ʒɛstjɔ̃) *f*, management, administration; care.

geyser (ʒezɛːr) *m*, geyser.

ghetto (ɡeto) *m*, ghetto.

gibecière (ʒipsjeːr) *f*, game bag; pouch; satchel, knapsack. **gi-**

berne (bɛrn) *f*, pouch (*cartridge*); knapsack.

gibet (ʒibɛ) *m*, gibbet, gallows.

gibier (ʒibje) *m*, game (*Hunt.*). ~ **à poil**, ground g. ~ **de potence**, gallows bird.

giboulée (ʒibule) *f*, shower; hailstorm.

giboyer (ʒibwaje) *v.i*, to go shooting. **giboyeux, euse** (jø, øːz), *a*, full of game, gamy.

gicler (ʒikle) *v.i*, to spirt, squirt, splash. **gicleur** (klœːr) *m*, jet; nozzle.

gifle (ʒifl) *f*, slap, smack. **gifler** (fle) *v.t*, to slap, smack.

gigantesque (ʒigɑ̃tɛsk) *a*, gigantic.

gigot (ʒigo) *m*, leg (*of lamb, etc.*). **gigoter** (gɔte) *v.t*, to fidget; jerk about.

gigue (ʒig) *f*, jig (*Mus., dance*).

gilet (ʒilɛ) *m*, waistcoat, vest; cardigan; woolly coat. ~ **de sauvetage**, life vest.

Gille (ʒil) *m*, clown, fool.

gingembre (ʒɛ̃ʒɑ̃ːbr) *m*, ginger.

girafe (ʒiraf) *f*, giraffe; microphone boom (*cinema*).

girandole (ʒirɑ̃dɔl) *f*, girandole; epergne.

giration (ʒirasjɔ̃) *f*, gyration. **giratoire** (twaːr) *a*, gyratory; traffic circle.

girofle (ʒirɔfl) *m*, clove (*spice*). **giroflée** (fle) *f*, stock (*Bot.*). ~ **jaune**, wallflower. **giroflier** (flie) *m*, clove tree.

giron (ʒirɔ̃) *m*, lap (*of pers.*); bosom, pale (*of the church*); tread (*of stair step*).

girouette (ʒirwɛt) *f*, vane, weathercock (*lit. & fig.*).

gisant, e (ʒizɑ̃, ɑ̃ːt) *a*, lying. ¶ *n*, recumbent figure (*statue*). **gisement** (zmɑ̃) *m*, lie, bearing (*Naut.*); bed, seam, deposit, stratum (*Geol.*).

gitane (ʒitan) *m, f*, gypsy.

gîte (ʒit) *m*, home, shelter, lodging; form (*hare*); bed, seam, deposit (*Geol.*); leg of beef. ~ **rural**, vacation lodging on a farm.

givre (ʒiːvr) *m*, hoarfrost rime.

glabre (glɑːbr) *a*, glabrous, hairless; cleanshaven.

glace (glas) *f. sometimes pl. in sense of ice*, ice; ice cream. (*pl.*)

frost, chill (*fig., of age*); glass; [looking] glass, mirror; icing (*sugar*); flaw. ~ **de vitrage**, plate glass, ~[*s*] *flottante*[*s*], ice floe. **glacé, e** (se) *p.a*, frozen; icy; chill; iced; stony (*look*); glacé. **glacer** (se) *v.t*, to freeze, chill; ice; glaze; gloss; scumble. **se** ~, to freeze; glaze. **glaciaire** (sjɛːr) (*Geol.*) *a*, glacial, glacier, ice (*att.*). **glacial, e** (sjal) *a*, glacial, icy; frozen; frosty; frigid. **glacier** (sje) *m*, ice-cream vender; confectioner; glacier. **glacière** (sjɛːr) *f*, ice house; freezer, icebox. **glacis** (si) *m*, slope; glacis; glaze; scumble. **glaçon** (sɔ̃) *m*, floe; piece of ice; icicle; ice cube.

gladiateur (gladjatœːr) *m*, gladiator.

glaïeul (glajœl) *m*, gladiolus.

glaire (glɛːr) *f*, glair, white of egg.

glaise (glɛːz) *f*, clay; pug, puddle. **glaiser** (gleze) *v.t*, to clay, pug, puddle. **glaisière** (zjɛːr) *f*, clay pit.

glaive (glɛːv) (*Poet.*) *m*, sword, brand.

glanage (glanaːʒ) *m*, gleaning. **gland** (glɑ̃) *m*, acorn; (*pl.*) tassel. **glande** (glɑ̃ːd) *f*, gland; tumor. **des** ~**s au cou**, swollen glands. **glandée** (glɑ̃de) *f*, acorn crop.

glane (glan) *f*, gleaning; rope (*of onions, etc.*). **glaner** (ne) *v.t. & abs*, to glean. **glaneur, euse** (nœːr, øːz) *n*, gleaner. **glanure** (nyːr) *f*, gleanings.

glapir (glapiːr) *v.i*, to yelp, yap, bark.

glas (glɑ) *m*, knell, passing bell.

glauque (gloːk) *a*, glaucous.

glèbe (glɛːb) *f*, glebe, soil.

glène (glɛːn) *f*, socket (*bone*); coil (*rope*).

glissade (glisad) *f*, slide, sliding, slip; glissade. **glissant, e** (sɑ̃, ɑ̃ːt) *a*, slippery. **glissé** (se) *m*, glide (*Danc.*). **glissement** (smɑ̃) *m*, sliding, slide, slip[ping]; slump; glide; gliding. **glisser** (se) *v.i. & t*, to slide; skid; slip; glide; slur. **glisseur, euse** (sœːr, øːz) *n*, slider (*pers.*). ¶ *m*, hydroplane, speed boat; glider (*Avn.*). ~ **de course**, racing boat. ~ **de croisière**, fast cruiser (*speedboat*). **glissière** (sjɛːr) *f*, slide, guide (*Mach.*). **glissoire** (swaːr) *f*, slide (*track on ice*).

global, e† (glɔbal) *a*, total, inclusive, aggregate (*sum*); grand, sum (*total*). **globe** (glɔb) *m*, globe; ball; orb. **globulaire** (bylɛːr) & **globuleux, euse** (lø, øːz) *a*, globular. **globule** (byl) *m*, globule.

gloire (glwaːr) *f*, glory; fame; pride; boast. *se faire ~ de*, to glory in, pride oneself on. **glorieux, euse†** (glɔrjø, øːz) *a*, glorious; proud; conceited. **glorifier** (rifje) *v.t*, to glorify, praise. *se ~ de*, to glory in, boast of. **gloriole** (rjɔl) *f*, vainglory, vanity; kudos.

glose (gloːz) *f*, gloss, commentary; criticism. **gloser** [**sur**] (gloze) *v.t. & i*, to find fault with. **glossaire** (glɔsɛːr) *m*, glossary. **glossateur** (satœːr) *m*, commentator.

glotte (glɔt) *f*, glottis.

glouglou (gluglu) *m*, gurgle, bubbling. **glouglouter** (te) *v.i*, to gobble (*of turkey*).

glousser (gluse) *v.i*, to cluck; chuckle; giggle; titter.

glouton, ne† (glutɔ̃, ɔn) *a*, gluttonous. ¶ *n*, glutton. **gloutonnerie** (tɔnri) *f*, gluttony.

glu (gly) *f*, birdlime; glue (*marine*). **gluant, e** (ɑ̃, ɑ̃ːt) *a*, gluey, sticky. **gluau** (o) *m*, (*bird*) lime twig.

glucose (glykoːz) *f*, glucose.

glume (glym) *f*, glume; chaff.

gluten (glytɛn) *f*, gluten. **glutineux, euse** (tinø, øːz) *a*, glutinous.

glycérine (gliserin) *f*, glycerin[e].

glycine (glisin) *f*, wistaria.

gnangnan (nɑ̃nɑ̃) *n. & a*, lackadaisical (*person*).

gneiss (gnɛs) *m*, gneiss.

gnome (gnoːm) *m*, gnome.

gnostique (gnɔstik) *m*, gnostic.

go (tout de) (go) *ad*, straight off, there & then.

gobelet (gɔblɛ) *m*, goblet; tumbler. *joueur des ~s*, shell game swindler.

gobelin (gɔblɛ̃) *m*, [hob]goblin, imp.

gobe-mouches (gɔbmuʃ) *m*, flycatcher (*bird*); flytrap (*plant*);

simpleton, gaper. **gober** (be) *v.t*, to bolt, gulp down; swallow (*fig.*).

goberger (se) (gɔbɛrʒe) *v.pr*, to do oneself well.

godailler (gɔdaje) *v.i*, to carouse.

godelureau (gɔdlyro) *m*, country bumpkin.

goder (gɔde) *v.i*, to pucker; bag (*trousers*); have an erection (*slang*). **godet** (dɛ) *m*, cup; noggin; bucket (*elevator*); saucer (*artist's*); pucker, ruck.

godiche (gɔdiʃ) *a. & n*, awkward (person), hobbledehoy.

godille (gɔdiːj) *f*, scull (*stern oar*). **godiller** (dije) *v.t*, to scull.

goéland (gɔelɑ̃) *m*, sea gull.

goélette (gɔelɛt) *f*, schooner.

goémon (gɔemɔ̃) *m*, seaweed, wrack.

gogo (gɔgo) *m*, simpleton, gull. *à ~*, in plenty; in clover.

goguenarder (gɔgnarde) *v.i*, to banter, crack jokes; jeer; sneer.

goguette (être en) (gɔgɛt), to be jolly (*in drink*).

goinfre (gwɛ̃ːfr) *m*, guzzler. **goinfrer** (gwɛ̃fre) *v.i*, to guzzle, gorge.

goitre (gwaːtr) *m*, goiter, wen.

golf (gɔlf) *m*, golf; golf course, golf links. *~ miniature, ~ réduit*, miniature golf.

golfe (gɔlf) *m*, gulf, bay, bight. *~ Arabique*, Arabian Gulf. *~ de Gascogne* (gaskɔɲ). Bay of Biscay. *~ Persique* (pɛrsik), Persian Gulf.

gommage (gɔmaːʒ) *m*, gumming. **gomme** (gɔm) *f*, gum. *~ [à effacer]*, eraser. *~ à mâcher*, chewing gum. *~ arabique*, g. arabic, *~ [élastique]*, [india] rubber. **gommer** (me) *v.t*, to gum; erase; eliminate. **gommeux, euse** (mø, øːz) *a*, gummy. **gommier** (mje) *m*, gum tree.

gond (gɔ̃) *m*, (*gate*) hook. *~ & penture*, hook & hinge.

gond (gɔ̃) *m*, hinge (*door, etc.*) *sortir de ses ~s*, to fly off the handle.

gondole (gɔ̃dɔl) *f*, gondola.

gondoler (gɔ̃dɔle) *v.i*, to swell; warp.

gondolier (gɔ̃dɔlje) *m*, gondolier.

gonfler (gɔ̃fle) *v.t. & i. & se ~*, to swell, inflate, pump up (*tire*). **gonfleur** (flœːr) *m*, pump (*air*).

gong (gɔ̃g) *m*, gong.

gonzesse (gɔ̃zɛs) *f*, woman, broad, wife (*familiar, tending to be pejorative*); cowardly or weak man (*slang*).

gord (gɔːr) *m*, weir (*Fish.*).

goret (gɔrɛ) *m*, piglet, porker; pig (*child*).

gorge (gɔrʒ) *f*, throat, gullet; bosom, bust; neck; mouth (*of tunnel*); gorge; groove; tumbler (*lock*). **gorgée** (ʒe) *f*, mouthful, gulp. **gorger** (ʒe) *v.t*, to gorge, cram, load.

gorille (gɔriːj) *m*, gorilla.

gosier (gozje) *m*, throat, gullet.

gosse (gɔs) *m*, *f*, kid, brat, youngster, etc.

gothique (gɔtik) *a*, Gothic; old-fashioned.

goton (gɔtɔ̃) *f*, slut.

gouache (gwaʃ) *f*, gouache (*art*).

gouailler (gwaje) *v.t. & i*, to chaff, banter.

goudron (gudrɔ̃) *m*, tar. **goudronner** (drɔne) *v.t*, to tar, spray with tar. **toile goudronnée**, tarpaulin.

gouffre (gufr) *m*, gulf, abyss, chasm; whirlpool.

gouge (guːʒ) *f*, gouge (*tool*).

gouine (gwin) *f*, lesbian. (*slang*).

goujat (guʒa) *m*, cad, blackguard. **goujaterie** (tri) *f*, dirty trick.

goujon (guʒɔ̃) *m*, gudgeon (*fish & Mech.*); dowel, joggle, stud. **goujonner** (ʒɔne) *v.t*, to dowel; joggle, stud.

goule (gul) *f*, ghoul.

goulée (gule) *f*, mouthful, gulp. **goulet** (lɛ) *m*, narrows, gut (*Naut.*). **goulot** (lo) *m*, neck (*bottle*). ~ **d'étranglement**, bottleneck. **goulotte** (lɔt) *f*, spout. **goulu, e** (ly) *a*, greedy. **goulûment** (lymɑ̃) *ad*, greedily.

goupille (gupiːj) *f*, pin; bolt. ~ *fendue*, split pin; cotter. **goupillon** (pijɔ̃) *m*, holy-water sprinkler; bottle brush; penis (*slang*).

gourbi (gurbi) *m*, hut; hovel; dugout.

gourd, e (guːr, urd) *a*, numb. **gourde** (gurd) *f*, gourd; flask; fool.

gourdin (gurdɛ̃) *m*, cudgel.

gourmade (gurmad) *f*, punch, blow.

gourmand, e (gurmɑ̃, ɑ̃ːd) *a*, gourmand; greedy. ~ *de*, fond of. ¶ *n*, gourmand; glutton. **gourmander** (mɑ̃de) *v.t*, to scold, chide; lard (*Cook.*). **gourmandise** (diːz) *f*, gluttony.

gourme (gurm) *f*, strangles (*Vet.*); wild oats (*fig.*). *jeter sa ~*, to sow one's wild oats.

gourmé, e (gurme) *p.a*, stiff, formal. **gourmer** (me) *v.t*, to curb (*horse*); punch, pommel.

gourmet (gurmɛ) *m*, gourmet, epicure; connoisseur, judge.

gourmette (gurmɛt) *f*, curb (*harness*). *lâcher la gourmette à*, to give a free rein to (*horse, pers.*).

gousse (gus) *f*, pod, shell. ~ *d'ail*, clove of garlic. ~ *de plomb*, net sinker, n. weight.

gousset (gusɛ) *m*, pocket (*vest*); fob; gusset.

goût (gu) *m*, taste; relish; flavor; tang; liking, fondness; style. **goûter** (te) *m*, afternoon snack. ¶ *v.t*, to taste; try; relish; like.

goutte (gut) *f*, drop; drip; dram; sip; spot, splash; gout (*Med.*). **gouttelette** (tlɛt) *f*, tiny drop. **goutteux, euse** (tø, øːz) *a*, gouty. **gouttière** (tjɛːr) *f*, roof gutter; (*pl.*) caves.

gouvernail (guvɛrnaːj) *m*, rudder; helm (*fig.*).

gouvernante (guvɛrnɑ̃ːt) *f*, governess; housekeeper. **gouvernants** (nɑ̃) *m.pl*, government in power. **gouverne** (vɛrn) *f*, guidance; steering. **gouvernement** (nəmɑ̃) *m*, government; management; care. **gouverner** (ne) *v.t. & abs*, to steer (*Naut.*); govern, rule; look after. **gouverneur** (nœːr) *m*, governor.

goyave (gɔjaːv) *f*, guava. **goyavier** (javje) *m*, gauva [tree].

grabat (graba) *m*, pallet, mean bed. **grabataire** (tɛːr) *a. & n*, bedridden (person).

grabuge (grabyːʒ) *m*, row, brawl.

grâce (grɑːs) *f*, grace; gracefulness; favor; mercy; pardon; thanks; (*pl.*) grace (*after meal*). *les [trois] G~s*, the Graces. *de ~*, *ad*, pray, please, for goodness' sake. **gracier** (grasje) *v.t*, to pardon, reprieve. **gracieusement**

(sjøzmã) *ad*, graciously; gratu-itously, free. **gracieuseté** (zte) *f*, graciousness; kindness; gratuity. **gracieux, euse** (søj, ∅;z) *a*, grace-ful, pleasing; gracious. *à titre ~,* free of charge.

gracile (grasil) *a*, slender, slim. **gracilité** (lite) *f*, slenderness.

gradation (gradasjõ) *f*, grada-tion. ~ [*ascendante*], climax (*Rhet.*). ~ *descendante*, anticli-max. **grade** (grad) *m*, grade; rank; rating; degree (*Univ.*). *prendre ses ~s,* to graduate. *en prendre pour son ~.* to get bawled out. **gradé** (de) *m*, noncommissioned officer. ~*s & soldats*, rank & file. **gradin** (dɛ̃) *m*, tier; step; stope (*Min.*). **gradué, e** (dɥe) *n*, gradu-ate (*Univ.*). **graduel, le†** (dɥɛl) *a*, gradual. **graduer** (dɥe) *v.t*, to graduate; grade.

graillon (grɑjõ) *m*, burning (*smell, taste, of burned meat, fat*). **graillonner** (jone) *v.i*, to catch fire (*Cook.*); hawk (*with throat*).

grain (grɛ̃) *m*, grain; seed; berry, bean; bead; speck; dash; spice; modicum; squall (*Naut.*). ~ *de beauté,* beauty spot; mole (*on skin*). ~ *de grêle,* hailstone. ~ *de plomb,* pellet. ~ *de raisin,* grape.

graine (grɛ:n) *f*, seed; silkworms' eggs. ~ *d'anis,* aniseed. ~ *de lin,* linseed. ~ *des canaris,* canary seed. **grainier, ère** (nje, ɛ:r) *n*, seedsman.

graissage (grɛsa:ʒ) *m*, greasing, lubrication, oiling. **graisse** (grɛ:s) *f*, fat; grease; blubber; ropiness (*wine*). ~ *de rognon,* suet. ~ *de rôti,* dripping. **graisser** (grɛse) *v.t*, to grease, lubricate. ~ [*à l'huile*], to oil. **graisseur** (sœ:r) *m*, greaser; oiler; lubricator. **graisseux, euse** (sø, ∅;z) *a*, greasy, oily; fatty; messy.

gramen (gramɛn) *m*, lawn grass. *une graminée* (mine) a grass (*plant*).

grammaire (grammɛ:r) *f*, gram-mar. *contre la ~,* ungram-matical. **grammairien, ne** (mɛrjɛ̃, ɛn) *n*, grammarian. **grammatical, e†** (matikal) *a*, grammatical.

gramine (gram) *m*, gram = 15.432 grains.

gramophone (gramɔfɔn) *m*, phonograph.

grand, e (grã, ã;d) *a*, great, large, big; noble; major (*prophet, etc.*); high; tall; grown-up; long; broad; wide; open (*air*); deep (*mourning*); full (*dress, orches-tra*); high-class (*wine*); loud; heavy (*rain*); grand; main; trunk (*line*); general (*public*); much, many. **grand,** *comps:* ~ *canot,* launch, pinnace. ~ *chemin,* high-way, main road. ~ *danois,* great Dane (*dog*). *un ~ homme manqué,* a might-have-been. *un homme ~,* a tall man. *au ~ jour,* in broad daylight; publicly. ~ *jour* [*de la publicité*], limelight. ~ *livre,* ledger; register (*share, stock*). ~ *magasin* [*de nouveautés*], big stores, department store. *le ~ monde,* [high] society, high life, the upper crust. *le ~ nettoyage,* the spring cleaning. ~ *rabbin,* chief rabbi. **grande,** *comps:* ~*s eaux,* spate, freshet; fountains. *à ~s journées,* by forced marches. ~ *largeur,* double width (*cloth*). ~ *marée,* spring tide. ~ *multipli-cation,* high gear. ~ *pêche,* deep-sea fishing (*whale & cod*). ~ *pé-dale,* loud pedal. ~ *personne,* grown-up. *à* [*la*] ~ *pluie,* at much rain (*barometer*). ~ *tenue &* ~ *toilette,* full dress. ~*s vacances,* summer holidays.

grand (grã) *m*, great man; adult, grown-up. (*the*) *great;* (*pl.*) (*the*) *great ones* (*of the earth*). ~ *de l'eau,* high-water mark. ~*s & petits,* old & young. *en ~,* on a large scale; life-size.

grand-chose (grãʃo;z) *pn. usu-ally with neg,* much.

grand-crosse (grãkrɔs) *f*, driver (*golf club*).

Grande-Bretagne (la) (grãd-brətaɲ), [Great] Britain.

grandelet, te (grãdlɛ, ɛt) *a*, growing (*big*); rather tall. **grande-ment** (dmã) *ad*, grandly; nobly; greatly; altogether; ample, amply. **grandeur** (dœ:r) *f*, size; magni-tude; height; greatness; mighti-ness; nobility; grandeur. ~ *na-*

turelle, life-size. *Votre Ḡ~*, your Grace; your Lordship.

grand-fer (grãfɛːr) *m*, driving iron (*golf*).

grandiloquence (grãdilɔkãːs) *f*, grandiloquence. **grandiloquent, e** (kã, ãːt) *a*, grandiloquent.

grandiose (grãdjoːz) *a*, grandiose, imposing.

grandir (grãdiːr) *v.i*, to grow taller; grow up; grow; (*v.t.*) to make taller *or* bigger; magnify. **grandissime** (disim) *a*, very great.

grand-maman (grãmamã) *f*, grandmamma, granny. **grand-mère** (grãmɛːr) *f*, grandmother.

grand-messe (grãmɛs) *f*, high mass.

grand-oncle (grãtɔ̃ːkl) *m*, great-uncle.

grand-père (grãpɛːr) *m*, grandfather.

grand-route (grãrut) *ou* **grande route** (ãːd) *f*, highway, main road.

grand-tante (grãtãːt) *f*, great-aunt.

grand-voile (grãvwaːl) *f*, mainsail.

grange (grãːʒ) *f*, barn.

granit (grani[t]) *m*, granite.

granule (granyl) *m*, granule. **granuler** (le) *v.t*, to granulate.

graphique† (grafik) *a*, graphic. ¶ *m*, diagram, chart, graph.

graphite (grafit) *m*, graphite, plumbago, black lead.

grappe (grap) *f*, bunch, cluster. **grappiller** (pije) *v.i. & t*, to glean (*grapes*); pick up, scrape up.

grappin (grapɛ̃) *m*, grapnel; creeper (*well*).

gras, se (grɑ, ɑːs) *a*, fat; fatty; oily; oil (*varnish*); ropy (*wine*); plump (*chicken*); fatted (*calf*); greasy; thick; rich (*food, etc.*); meat (*diet, day, etc.*); full-face, bold-faced (*type*); smutty, ribald, broad (*story*). **gras**, *m*, fat. *~ de la jambe*, calf. *~ du bras*, fleshy part of the arm. **grassement** (grasmã) *ad*, (*to live*) on the fat of the land; handsomely. **grasset, te** (sɛ, ɛt) *a*, fattish. **grasseyer** (sɛje) *v.i*, to burr (*speaking*). **grassouillet, te** (suje, ɛt) *a*, plump; chubby.

gratification (gratifikasjɔ̃) *f*, bonus, gratuity. **gratifier** (fje) *v.t*, to bestow, confer.

gratinˑ (gratɛ̃) *m*, brown crust (*in pot*); gratin. *le ~*, the 400. **gratiner** (tine) *v.t*, to gratinate (*Cook.*).

gratis (gratis) *ad*, gratis, free.

gratitude (gratityd) *f*, gratitude.

gratte (grat) *f*, scrapings (*savings*); pickings, graft. **gratte-ciel**, *m*, skyscraper. **gratte-cul**, *m*, hip (*Bot.*). **gratte-miettes**, *m*, crumb scoop. **gratte-papier**, *m*, penpusher. **gratter** (te) *v.t*, to scrape; scratch; s. out, erase. **grattoir** (twaːr) *m*, knife eraser; scraper.

gratuit, e† (gratɥi, it) *a*, gratuitous, free; unpaid (*no salary*); wanton (*insult*). **gratuité** (te) *f*, gratuitousness.

grave (graːv) *a*, grave; solemn; serious; weighty; severe; grievous; deep (*sound*); heavy. ¶ *m*, lower register (*Mus.*).

graveleux, euse (gravlø, øːz) *a*, gravelly, gritty; smutty, ribald. **gravelle** (vɛl) *f*, gravel (*Med.*). **gravelure** (vlyːr) *f*, smuttiness, ribaldry.

gravement (gravmã) *ad*, gravely; seriously; rather slowly (*Mus.*).

graver (grave) *v.t*, to engrave; grave; cut; inscribe; impress (*on memory*). *~ à l'eau-forte*, to etch. *~ en relief*, to emboss. **graveur** (vœːr) *m*, engraver.

gravier (gravje) *m*, gravel, grit.

gravir (graviːr) *v.i. & t*, to climb, clamber.

gravitation (gravitasjɔ̃) *f*, gravitation. **gravité** (te) *f*, gravity; weight (*fig.*); depth (*sound*). **graviter** (te) *v.i*, to gravitate.

gravure (gravyːr) *f*, engraving; cut; print; illustration. *~ à l'eau-forte*, etching. *~ à la manière noire*, mezzotint. *~ au trait*, line engaving. *~ dans le texte*, illustration in text. *~ de mode*, fashion plate. *~ en creux*, die sinking. *~ hors texte*, illustration outside text. *~ sur bois*, wood engraving; woodcut.

gré (gre) *m*, will; free will; wish; pleasure; liking; taste. *au ~ de*, according to; at the mercy of. *bon* ~, *mal* ~, willynilly. *de* ~ *ou de force*, by fair means or foul. *de* ~ *à* ~, by negotiation; by private treaty. *savoir* ~ *de*, to be grateful for.

grèbe (grɛb) *m*, grebe.

gree, ecque (grɛk) *a*, Greek, Grecian. G~, *n*, Greek (*pers.*). *le grec*, Greek (*language*). *la Grèce* (grɛːs), Greece. **grecque**, *f*, Greek fret (*Arch.*).

gredin, e (grədɛ̃, in) *n*, villain, scoundrel, miscreant. **gredinerie** (dinri) *f*, villainy.

gréement (gremɑ̃) (*Naut.*) *m*, rigging; gear. **gréer** (gree) *v.t*, to rig.

greffe (grɛf) *m*, registry (*legal*); (*f.*) graft (*Hort. & Surg.*), scion; grafting. **greffer** (fe) *v.t*, to graft. **greffier** (fje) *m*, clerk (*of court*); registrar. **greffon** (fɔ̃) *m*, graft, scion.

grégaire (gregɛːr) *a*, gregarious, herd (*att.*).

grège (grɛːʒ) *a*, raw (*silk*).

grégorien, ne (gregɔrjɛ̃, ɛn) *a*, Gregorian.

grêle (grɛːl) *a*, slender, thin (*legs, voice*); small (*intestine*). ¶ *f*, hail, shower (*fig.*). **grêlé, e** (grɛle) *p.a*, pockmarked, pitted; most unfortunate. **grêler** (le) *v.imp*, to hail; (*v.t.*) to damage by hail.

grelin (grəlɛ̃) *m*, hawser.

grêlon (grɛlɔ̃) *m*, (*big*) hailstone.

grelot (grəlo) *m*, bell (*spherical with ball inside*). **grelotter** (lɔte) *v.i*, to shiver (*cold*).

grenade (grənad) *f*, pomegranate; grenade. G~, *f*, Granada (Spain). *la* G~, Grenada (*W. Indies*). **grenadier** (dje) *m*, pomegranate [tree]; grenadier; virago. **grenadille** (diːj) *f*, granadilla (*Bot.*). **grenadin** (dɛ̃) *m*, grenadine (*Cook.*). **grenadine** (din) *f*, grenadine (*cordial, fabric*).

grenaille (grənɑːj) *f*, tailings (*grain*); shot.

grenat (grəna) *m*, garnet. ~ ~ *cabochon*, carbuncle.

greneler (grənle) *v.t*, to grain (*leather*). **grené** (ne) *m*, stipple (*art*). **grener** (ne) *v.i*, to seed;

(*v.t.*) to granulate; grain. **grènetis** (grɛnti) *m*, milling (*on coin*).

grenier (grənje) *m*, granary; loft; garner; garret; attic. *en* ~, in bulk.

grenouille (grənuːj) *f*, frog; money box; funds (*club, society*). *manger, bouffer, la* ~, to make off with entrusted funds. **grenouillère** (nujɛːr) *f*, froggery; swamp

grenu, e (grəny) *a*, grainy, seedy; grained. ¶ *m*, graining (*on leather*).

grès (grɛ) *m*, sandstone; grit; stoneware. ~ *meulier* (mœlje), millstone grit.

grésil (grezi) *m*, (*tiny hard pellets of*) hail. **grésiller** (je) *v.imp*, to hail; (*v.t.*) to shrivel [up].

gresserie (grɛsri) *f*, sandstone quarry; sandstone (*work*); stoneware.

grève (grɛːv) *f*, beach, shore, (*Poet.*) strand; strike. ~ *patronale*, lockout. ~ *perlée*, slowdown. ~ *sur le tas*, sitdown strike. ~ *sauvage*, wildcat s. ~ *thrombose*, partial s. ~ *surprise*, lightning s. *se mettre en* ~, *faire* ~, to [go on] strike.

grever (grəve) *v.t*, to burden, weight, encumber, saddle. [put] on, [put] upon.

gréviste (grevist) *n*, striker; (*att.*) strike.

grianneau (griano) *m*, young grouse.

gribouiller (gribuje) *v.t. & abs*, to scrawl; daub.

grief (grief) *m*, grievance; complaint. **grièvement** (ɛvmɑ̃) *ad*, seriously (*injured*).

griffe (grif) *f*, claw, talon; clutch; clip; grip; jaw; dog; tendril; facsimile signature; autograph stamp; stamp. *coup de* ~, scratch. **griffer** (fe) *v.t*, to claw, scratch; blaze (*tree*). **griffon** (fɔ̃) *m*, griffin, griffon. **griffonner** (fɔne) *v.t. & abs*, to scrawl; scribble. **griffure** (fyːr) *f*, scratch.

grignon (griɲɔ̃) *m*, crust[y] end (*bread*).

grignoter (griɲɔte) *v.t. & abs*, to nibble; get a few pickings (*profit*).

grigou (grigu) *m*, miser, screw, hunks.

gril (gri) *m*, gridiron; grill; grating. *sur le* ~, on tenterhooks (*fig.*). **grillade** (grijad) *f*, grilling; broiling; grill (*meat*). **grillage** (ja:ʒ) *m*, roasting (*ore*); grating; [wire] netting; grillage. **grille** (gri:j) *f*, grating; grill[e], grid; screen; wire guard; grate; railing[s]. ~*pain* (grijpɛ̃) *m*, toaster. **griller** (grije) *v.t. & i*, to grill; broil; toast; roast; scorch; burn; long, itch; grate, rail in.

grillon (grijɔ̃) *m*, cricket (*insect*).

grimace (grimas) *f*, grimace, wry face, grin; sham. **grimacer** (se) *v.i*, to grimace, make faces, grin; pucker, crease. **grimacier, ère** (sje, ɛːr) *a*, grinning; mincing; sham.

grime (grim) *m*, dotard (*of comedy*). **se grimer** (me) *v.pr*, to make up (*Theat.*).

grimoire (grimwa:r) *m*, gibberish; scrawl.

grimper (grɛ̃pe) *v.i*, to climb, clamber; creep.

grincer (grɛ̃se) *v.i*, to grind, grate, creak. ~ *des* (ou *les*) *dents*, to grind (*or* gnash) one's teeth.

grincheux, euse (grɛ̃ʃø, øːz) *a*, churlish, crabbed.

gringalet (grɛ̃galɛ) *m*, shrimp (*pers.*).

grippe (grip) *f*, influenza; dislike. *prendre en* ~, to take a dislike to. **gripper** (pe) *v.t*, to snatch (*steal*); (*v.i.*) to seize (*Mach.*). *être grippé, e*, to have influenza. se ~, to pucker. **grippe-sou**, *m*, money grubber.

gris, e (gri, i:z) *a*, gray; brown (*paper*); grizzly; dull; tipsy, fuddled. ¶ *m*, gray. **grisaille** (griza:j) *f*, grisaille. **grisailler** (zaje) *v.t*, to [paint] gray. **grisâtre** (zɑ:tr) *a*, grayish. **griser** (ze) *v.t*, to fuddle, muddle, intoxicate. **grisette** (zɛt) *f*, grisette (*girl*); white-throat (*bird*).

grisbi (grizbi) *m*, money, dough, bread (*slang*).

grisoller (grizɔle) *v.i*, to carol (*lark*).

grison, ne (grizɔ̃, ɔn) *a*, grayish,

grizzled (*hair*). ¶ *m*, graybeard; donkey. **grisonner** (zɔne) *v.i*, to gray.

grisou (grizu) *m*, firedamp.

grive (gri:v) *f*, thrush. ~ *chanteuse*, song t., throstle.

grivois, e (grivwa, a:z) *a*, broad, ribald.

Groenland (le) (grɔɛlɑ̃[:d]), Greenland.

grog (grɔg) *m*, grog.

grogner (grɔɲe) *v.i*, to grunt; grumble. **grognon** (ɲɔ̃) *m*, grumbler.

groin (grwɛ̃) *m*, snout (*pig*).

grommeler (grɔmle) *v.i*, to grumble at, g. about.

gronder (grɔ̃de) *v.i*, to growl, snarl; roar; rumble, mutter, peal; howl (*wind*); grumble; (*v.t.*) to scold.

groom (grum) *m*, groom; page boy.

gros, se (gro, o:s) *a*, big; large; great; broad; stout; loud; strong; hearty; pregnant; fraught; swollen; coarse; gross; thick; deep; high; heavy; structural (*repairs*). **gros**, *comps*: ~ *bonnet*, bigwig. ~ *boulet*, heavy weight (*throwing*). ~ *galet*, boulder. ~ *morceau*, lump. ~ *mots*, bad language, foul words. ~ *murs*, main walls. ~ *œuvre*, main structure (*of a building*). ~ *plan*, close-up (*Phot.*). ~ *poisson*, heavy fish. **grosse**, *comps*: ~ *caisse*, bass drum, big drum. ~ *pièce*, heavy casting, heavy fish, etc. **gros**, *ad*, a great deal, much. ¶ *m*, bulk, body, mass; main part; large (*coal*). **en** ~, *ad*, roughly, broadly. [commerce de (*ou* en)] ~, wholesale [trade].

gros-bec (grobɛk) *m*, hawfinch, grosbeak.

groseille (grozɛ:j) *f*, currant (*red, white*). ~ *verte*, ~ *à maquereau*, gooseberry. **groseillier** (zeje) *m*, currant bush. ~ *à maquereau*, gooseberry bush.

gros-porteur (grɔpɔrtœ:r) *m*, jumbo jet.

grosse (gro:s) *f*, large hand, text hand (*writing*); engrossment (*law*); gross (*144*). **grossesse** (grosɛs) *f*, pregnancy. **grosseur** (sœ:r) *f*, size; swelling. ~ *de* *ceinture, de poitrine,* waist, chest, measurement.

grossier, **èret** (grosje, ɛır) *a,* coarse; rough; gross; rude; rank, crass; glaring; unmannerly, boorish; ribald. **grossièreté** (ɛrte) *f,* coarseness, etc.

grossir (grosiːr) *v.t. & i,* to make bigger, enlarge; magnify; swell, inflate; exaggerate.

grossiste (grosist) *m,* wholesaler.

grosso-modo (grosomodo) *ad,* roughly.

grossoyer (groswaje) *v.t,* to engross *(law).*

grotesque† (grotɛsk) *a,* grotesque. ¶ *m,* grotesque[ness]; clown; *(f.)* grotesque *(art).*

grotte (grot) *f,* grotto.

grouiller (gruje) *v.i,* to swarm, be alive *(with vermin);* seethe; move.

groupe (grup) *m,* group, batch, knot, cluster; company; party; unit *(Mil.);* pool *(typists, etc.).* **groupement** (pmã) *m,* grouping; pool *(Fin.).* **grouper** (pe) *v.t,* to group. **groupiste** (pist) *m,* groupman *(technical).*

grouse (gruːz) *f,* grouse (bird).

gruau (gryo) *m,* meal; groats; gruel. ~ *d'avoine,* oatmeal.

grue (gry) *f,* crane *(bird & hoist);* whore. *faire le pied de* ~, to wait patiently.

gruger (gryʒe) *v.t,* to bleed *(fig.).*

grume (grym) *f,* bark *(left on felled tree).* en ~, in the log.

grumeau (grymo) *m,* clot, curd. **se grumeler** (mle) *v.pr,* to clot, curdle.

gruyère (gryjɛːr) *m,* gruyère [cheese].

guano (gwano) *m,* guano.

gué (ge) *m,* ford. **gréable** (abl) *a,* fordable. **guéer** (gee) *v.t,* to ford *(river);* water *(horse);* rinse *(linen).*

guelte (gɛlt) *f,* commission *(on sales).*

guenille (gəniːj) *f,* rag, tatter.

guenon (gɔnɔ̃) & **guenuche** (nyʃ) *f,* she-monkey; fright *(woman).*

guêpe (gɛːp) *f,* wasp. **guêpier** (gɛpje) *m,* wasps' nest; hornets' nest *(fig.);* bee eater.

guère (ne . . .) (ne . . . gɛːr) *ad,* hardly, h. any; barely; not much;

not many; but little; only; hardly ever.

guéret (gerɛ) *m,* plowed land; fallow land; *(poet.)* field.

guéridon (geridɔ̃) *m,* occasional table; coffee t., cocktail t.

guérilla (gerilla) *f,* guerrilla.

guérillero (gerijero) *m,* guerrilla *(Mil.).*

guérir (geriːr) *v.t. & abs. & i. & se* ~, to cure; heal; recover; get better. **guérison** (rizɔ̃) *f,* cure, healing, recovery. **guérisseur, euse** (sœr, øːz) *n,* healer; quack doctor, medicine man.

guérite (gerit) *f,* sentry box; signal box; lookout; hooded wicker chair.

Guernesey (gɛrnəze) *f,* Guernsey.

guerre (gɛːr) *f,* war, warfare; strife; feud. ~ *d'usure,* war of attrition. ~ *de mouvement,* open warfare. ~ *de plume,* paper warfare. ~ *sociale,* class war. *de bonne* ~ *(fig.),* fair [play]. **guerrier, ère** (gɛrje, ɛːr) *a,* warlike; martial, war *(att.).* ¶ *n,* warrior. **guerroyer** (rwaje) *v.i,* to [wage] war.

guet (gɛ) *m,* watch. *faire le* ~, to be on the alert; lookout. ~-**apens** (getapɑ̃) *m,* ambush; trap; trick.

guêtre (gɛːtr) *f,* gaiter. ~*s de ville,* spats.

guetter (gete) *v.t,* to watch. **guetteur** (tœːr) *m,* lookout [man].

gueule (gœl) *f,* mouth *(animal);* trap *(mouth).* *faire la* ~, sulk. *se casser la* ~, to suffer injury *(physical, social, etc.).* *ta* ~!, shut up! ~-*de-loup,* snapdragon; exhaust muffler. **gueuler** (le) *v.i,* to shout.

gueuler (gœle) *v.i,* to yell, bawl, etc.

gueules (gœl) *m,* gules *(Her.).*

gueuse (gøːz) *f,* pig *(iron);* heavy weight.

gueuser (gøze) *v.i,* to beg. **gueuserie** (zri) *f,* beggary. **gueux, euse** (gø, øːz) *n,* beggar; rascal. ¶ *a,* beggarly.

gui (gi) *m,* mistletoe.

guichet (giʃe) *m,* wicket [gate]; shutter; counter *(cashier's).* ~

[de distribution des billets], ticket office; ticket window. à ~ ouvert, on demand. ~ automatique, automatic teller machine (banks). guichetier (ʃtje) m, turnkey.

guide (gid) m, guide; conductor; guide [book]; (f.) [driving] rein. ~âne, m, manual, handbook. **guider** (de) v.t, to guide, conduct; steer. **guiderope** (rɔp) m, guide rope, trail r. (Avn.). **guidon** (dɔ) m, pennant; handlebar (cycle); foresight (gun). ~ de renvoi, reference [mark].

guigne (giɲ) f, black cherry; bad luck.

guigner (giɲe) v.t. & abs, to peep at; peep; have an eye to.

guignier (giɲje) m, black cherry [tree].

guignol (giɲɔl) m, Punch & Judy [show]; puppet.

guignon (giɲɔ̃) m, bad luck.

guillaume (gijoːm) m, rabbet plane.

guillemeter (gijmete) v.t, to put in quotes. **guillemets** (mɛ) m.pl, quotation marks, (in Fr. printed thus « »; written thus « » or thus " ").

guilleret, te (gijrɛ, ɛt) a, lively, gay; broad (story).

guilleri (gijri) m, chirp[ing] (sparrow).

guillochis (gijoʃi) m, guilloche; engine turning; checkering.

guillotine (gijotin) f, guillotine. fenêtre à ~, sash window. **guillotiner** (ne) v.t, to guillotine.

guimauve (gimoːv) f, marshmallow (Bot. & candy); sentimental person, song, etc.

guimbarde (gɛ̃bard) f, covered wagon; rattletrap (vehicle); Jew's harp.

guimpe (gɛ̃ːp) f, wimple; blouse front.

guindé, e (gɛ̃de) p.a, strained, stiff; stilted. **guinder** (de) v.t, to hoist; strain, force (fig.).

guinée (gine) f, guinea (21/-). la G~, Guinea (Geog.).

guingan (gɛ̃gã) m, gingham (fabric).

guingois (gɛ̃gwa) m, crookedness, wryness. de ~, awry, askew.

guinguette (gɛ̃gɛt) f, tavern with gardens & dance hall.

guipure (gipyːr) f, guipure.

guirlande (girlãːd) f, garland, wreath.

guise (giːz) f, way. en ~ de, by way of.

guitare (gitaːr) f, guitar; repetition, (same) old story. ~ hawaïenne, ukulele.

Gulf-Stream (gylfstriːm) m, Gulf Stream.

gustation (gystasjɔ̃) f, tasting.

gutta-percha (gytapɛrka) f, gutta-percha.

guttural, e (gytyral) a. & f, guttural.

Guyane (la) (gɥijan) Guiana.

gymnase (ʒimnaːz) m, gymnasium. **gymnasiarque** (nazjark) & **gymnaste** (nast) m, gymnast. **gymnastique** (tik) a, gymnastic. ¶ f, gymnastics, drill (Swedish); gymnastic (of mind, etc.). **gymnique** (nik) f, gymnastics.

gymnote (ʒimnɔt) m, electric eel.

gynécologie (ʒinekɔlɔʒi) f, gynecology.

gypse (ʒips) m, gypsum; plaster of Paris. **gypseux, euse** (søˌ øˌz) a, gypseous.

gyroscope (ʒirɔskɔp) m, gyroscope.

H

The sign ' denotes that the h is aspirate in the French sense, i.e, no liaison or elision.

habile† (abil) a, able, clever, skillful, cunning, skilled. **habileté** (lte) f, ability, skill.

habilité (abilite) f, competency (law). **habiliter** (te) v.t, to enable, capacitate.

habillement (abijmã) m, clothing; dress, raiment, habiliments. **habiller** (je) v.t, to dress, clothe; suit; abuse. **habilleuse** (jøːz) f, dresser (Theat.). **habit** (bi) m. mostly pl, clothes, suit; garb; habit; (men's evening) dress; vestment. ~ d'arlequin, motley. ~s de tous les jours, everyday clothes. ~ de soirée, dress coat; (pl.) dress [suit], dress clothes.

habitable (abitabl) *a*, [in]habitable.

habitacle (abitakl) *m*, abode; binnacle.

habitant, e (abitã, ã:t) *n*, inhabitant, dweller; occupier; resident, occupant, inmate; denizen. **habitat** (ta) *m*, habitat. **habitation** (sjɔ̃) *f*, habitation, dwelling, residence, abode, house. **habiter** (te) *v.t*, to inhabit, occupy, live in, l. at; (*v.i.*) to live, dwell.

habitude (abityd) *f*, habit; use; practice; wont. **habitué, e** (tɥe) *n*, frequenter. **habituel, le†** (tɥɛl) *a*, habitual, usual, wonted. **habituer** (tɥe) *v.t*, to habituate, accustom, inure.

'hâblerie (ɑbləri) *f*, brag. **'hâbleur, euse** (blœ:r, ø:z) *n*, braggart.

'hache (aʃ) *f*, axe. ~ *à main*, hatchet. ~ *coupe-gazon*, edging knife. ~ *d'armes*, battle-axe, pole-axe. **'hacher** (ʃe) *v.t*, to chop [up]; hack; cut to pieces; hash, mince; hatch (*engrave*). **'hachis** (ʃi) *m*, hash, mince. **'hachoir** (ʃwa:r) *m*, mincer; chopping board.

'hagard, e (aga:r, ard) *a*, haggard, wild; drawn (*face*).

'haie (ɛ) *f*, hedge[row]; hurdle; line, row (*people*); beam (*plow*). ~ *vive*, quickset hedge. *faire la* ~, to line up on both sides.

'haillon (ajɔ̃) *m*, rag, tatter.

'haine (ɛ:n) *f*, hatred; odium; dudgeon. **'haineux, euse** (ɛnø, ø:z) *a*, full of hatred. **'haïr** (ai:r) *v.t*, to hate, loathe.

'haire (ɛ:r) *f*, hair shirt.

'haïssable (aisabl) *a*, hateful.

Haïti (aiti) *f*, Haiti.

'halage ([h]ala:ʒ) *m*, towing.

'halbran (albrɑ̃) *m*, young, wild duck.

'hâle (ɑ:l) *m*, [heat of the] sun, sunburn. **'hâlé, e** (ɑle) *p.a*, sunburned, tanned, weather-beaten.

haleine (alɛn) *f*, breath, wind; training (*fig.*); suspense. *de longue* ~, (*work, etc.*) of time, requiring long persistent effort.

'haler ([h]ale) *v.t*, to tow, haul, pull, heave; set on (*dog*).

'hâler (ɑle) *v.t*, to burn, tan. *se* ~, to get sunburned.

'haletant, e (altɑ̃, ɑ̃:t) *a*, panting; breathless. **'haleter** (te) *v.i*, to pant, gasp [for breath].

'hall ([h]ɔl) *m*, hall; lounge (*hotel*).

'halle (al) *f*, [covered] market; shed (*goods*).

'hallebarde (albard) *f*, halberd (*Hist.*).

'hallier (alje) *m*, covert (*game*).

hallucination (alysinasjɔ̃) *f*, hallucination.

'halo (alo) *m*, halo (*Astr., Anat.*); halation (*Phot.*).

'halot (alo) *m*, rabbit hole.

'halte (alt) *f*, halt, stop. ¶ ([h]alt) *& ~-là i*, halt! stop!

'halte-garderie (altgardəri) *m*, babysitting facility in a supermarket.

haltère (altɛ:r) *m*, dumbbell.

hamac (amak) *m*, hammock.

Hambourg (ɑ̃bu:r) *m*, Hamburg.

hameau (amo) *m*, hamlet.

hameçon (amsɔ̃) *m*, [fish] hook; bait (*fig.*).

hampe (ɑ̃:p) *f*, staff, shaft, handle; scape (*Bot.*).

'hanche (ɑ̃:ʃ) *f*, hip; haunch. *les poings sur les* ~*s*, arms akimbo.

'handicap (ɑ̃dikap) *m*, handicap (*sport*). **'handicaper** (pe) *v.t*, to handicap. **'handicapeur** (pœ:r) *m*, handicapper.

'hangar (ɑ̃ga:r) *m*, shed, outhouse. ~ [*d'aviation*], hangar.

'hanneton (antɔ̃) *m*, cockchafer; scatterbrain. *pas piqué des* ~*s*, up to snuff, what it should be.

Hanovre (anɔ:vr) *m*, Hanover (*town*). *le H~*, Hanover (*province*).

'hanter (ɑ̃te) *v.t*, to frequent, haunt; keep (*bad company*). **'hantise** (ti:z) *f*, haunting; obsession.

'happe (ap) *f*, cramp [iron]; cramp, clamp. **'happer** (pe) *v.t*, to snap up; catch.

'haquet (akɛ) *m*, dray.

'harangue (arɑ̃:g) *f*, harangue, speech. **'haranguer** (rɑ̃ge) *v.t. & i*, to harangue.

'haras (arɑ) *m*, stud farm; stud.

'harasse (aras) *f*, crate.
'harasser (arase) *v.t*, to tire out, weary.
'harceler (arsəle) *v.t*, to harass, harry, bait; worry, pepper; heckle.
'harde (ard) *f*, herd (*deer*); leash (*set of dogs*). **'harder** (de) *v.t*, to leash.
'hardes (ard) *f.pl*, clothes (*worn*).
'hardi†, e (ardi) *a*, bold, daring; hardy; rash; forward, pert. **'hardiesse** (djɛs) *f*, boldness, daring, hardihood; forwardness, pertness; liberty.
'hardware (ardwɛːr) *m*, hardware (*computers*).
'harem (arɛm) *m*, harem.
'hareng (arɑ̃) *m*, herring. ~ *bouffi*, bloater. ~ *salé & fumé*, kipper. ~ *saur* (sɔːr), red herring. **'harengaison** (gɛzɔ̃) *f*, herring season; h. fishery. **'harengère** (ʒɛːr) *f*, fishwife. **'harenguier** (gje) *m*, herring boat.
'hargneux, euse (arɲø, øːz) *a*, surly, peevish, ill-tempered, nagging, snappy, fractious; snarling.
'haricot (ariko) *m*, kidney bean, haricot. ~ *d'Espagne*, scarlet runner, runner bean. ~*s secs*, beans (*dried*). ~*s verts*, stringbeans. *la fin des* ~*s*, the end of everything.
'haridelle (aridɛl) *f*, jade (*horse*).
harmonica (armɔnika) *m*, harmonica; musical glasses. ~ *à bouche*, mouth organ. **harmonie** (ni) *f*, harmony; (*in*) keeping; band. **harmonieux, euse†** (njø, øːz) *a*, harmonious, tuneful. **harmonique†** (nik) *a. & m*, harmonic. **harmoniser** (ze) *v.t*, to harmonize; attune. **s'~**, to harmonize, tone. **harmonium** (njɔm) *m*, harmonium.
'harnachement (arnaʃmɑ̃) *m*, harnessing; harness; trappings, rig. **'harnacher** (ʃe) *v.t*, to harness; rig out. **'harnais** (nɛ) *m*, harness; gear, tackle. **blanchir sous le harnois** (nwa), to grow old in the service.
'haro (aro) *m*, hue & cry; outcry.
harpagon (arpagɔ̃) *m*, miser, skinflint.

'harpe (arp) *f*, harp; toothing (*Build.*).
'harpie (arpi) *f*, harpy; hellcat.
'harpiste (arpist) *n*, harpist.
'harpon (arpɔ̃) *m*, harpoon. **'harponner** (pone) *v.t*, to harpoon.
'hart (aːr) *f*, withe, withy; halter; hanging.
'hasard (azaːr) *m*, chance, luck, risk, venture; hazard. *au* ~, at random. **'hasarder** (zarde) *v.t*, to hazard, risk, venture. **'hasardeux, euse†** (dø, øːz) *a*, venturesome; hazardous, risky.
'hase ([h]aːz) *f*, doe hare.
'hâte (ɑːt) *f*, haste, hurry. *avoir* ~, to be in a hurry. **'hâter** (ɑte) *v.t*, to hasten, hurry; quicken; expedite; force (*Hort.*). *se* ~, to make haste, hurry. **'hâtif, ive†** (tif, iːv) *a*, hasty, hurried; cursory; forward, early (*fruit, etc.*). **'hâtiveau** (vo) *m*, early pear, apple, pea, etc.
'hauban (obɑ̃) *m*, shroud (*Naut.*); guy, stay.
'hausse (oːs) *f*, raise; flashboard; wedge (*to pack up to level*); elevator (*in shoe*); backsight (*gun*); leaf (*rifle*). *à la* ~, on the rise. **'haussement d'épaules** (osmɑ̃) *m*, shrug[ging] [of the shoulders]. **'hausser (se)** *v.t*, to raise, lift; shrug; (*v.i.*) to raise. **'haussier** (sje) *m*, bull (*Stk Ex.*).
'haussière (osjɛːr) *f*, hawser.
'haut, e (o, oːt) *a*, high; tall; lofty; upper; top; up; high-class; loud; deep; remote (*antiquity*); big. *le haut commerce*, [the] big traders, the merchant class. *haut enseignement*, higher education. *haut fait* [*d'armes*], feat of arms. *de hauts faits*, doughty deeds. *haut fourneau*, blast furnace. *haute mer*, high seas, open sea. *haute taille*, tallness (*pers.*). **'haut**, *ad*, high; h. up; loudly, aloud. ~ *les mains!* hands up! ¶ *m*, top, head; higher notes (*Mus.*); perch (*fig.*). ~ *de casse*, upper case (*Typ.*). ~ *du pavé*, wall (*side of pavement*). *de* ~, high, in height. *des* ~*s & des bas* or *du* ~ *& du bas*, ups & downs. *en* ~, [up] above; aloft; upstairs.

'hautain, e (otɛ̃, ɛn) *a*, haughty, lordly; lofty, proud.

'hautbois (obwɑ) *m*, oboe, hautboy. **'hautboïste** (bɔist) *m*, oboist.

'hautement (otmɑ̃) *ad*, boldly, openly. **'hauteur** (tœːr) *f*, height; elevation; tallness (*steeple, etc.*); loftiness; altitude; level; hill; depth; haughtiness. *être à la ~ de*, to be equal to. *~ de marche*, rise (*of step*). *~ [musicale]*, pitch (*of a sound*).

'haut-fond (ofɔ̃) *m*, shoal.

'haut-le-cœur (olkœːr) *m*, heave, retch, nausea.

'haut-le-corps (olkɔːr) *m*, start, jump.

'haut-parleur (oparlœːr) *m*, loudspeaker.

'havane (avan) *m*, Havana (*cigar*). ¶ *a*, brown, tan (*boots*). **la H~**, Havana (*Geog.*).

'hâve (ɑːv) *a*, wan, emaciated.

'havre (ɑːvr) *m*, haven. **le H~**, Havre (*Geog.*).

'havresac (ɑvrəsak) *m*, knapsack.

Hawaï (avai) *m*, Hawaii. **hawaïen, ne** (iɛ̃, ɛn) *a*. & **H~**, *n*, Hawaiian.

'Haye (la) (ɛ), the Hague.

'hé (e) *i*, hi! hoy! hey! hallo[a]! *~ là-bas!* hallo[a] there!

hebdomadaire (ɛbdɔmadɛːr) *a*, weekly.

héberger (ebɛrʒe) *v.t*, to harbor; lodge, entertain, put up.

hébéter (ebete) *v.t*, to dull; stupefy, daze.

hébraïque (ebraïk) *a*, Hebraic, Hebrew. **l'hébreu** (brø) *m*, Hebrew (*language*); Greek (*jargon*).

hécatombe (ekatɔ̃b) *f*, hecatomb.

hectare (ɛktaːr) *m*, hectare = 100 ares *or* 2.4711 acres.

hectique (ɛktik) *a*, hectic (*fever*).

hectogramme (ɛktɔgram) *m*, hectogram = 100 grams *or* 3.527 ozs avoirdupois. **hectolitre** (litr) *m*, hectoliter = 100 liters *or* 2.75 imperial bushels *or* 22.01 imperial gallons. **hectomètre** (mɛtr) *m*, hectometer = 100 meters *or* 109.36 yards.

hégémonie (eʒemɔni) *f*, hegemony.

'hein ([h]ɛ̃) *i*, eyl what [do you say]?

hélas (elɑːs) *i*, alas!

'héler ([h]ele) *v.t*, to hail, call; speak (*ship*).

hélianthe (eljɑ̃t) *m*, helianthus.

hélice (elis) *f*, helix, spiral; screw, propeller; spinner (*Fish.*). **en ~ & hélicoïdal, e** (kɔidal) *a*, spiral, helical, twist (*drill*). **hélicoptère** (kɔptɛːr) *m*, helicopter.

héligare (eligaːr) *f*, helicopter terminal. **héliport** (elipɔːr) *m*, heliport.

héliotrope (eljɔtrɔp) *m*, heliotrope; cherry-pie; bloodstone.

hélium (eljɔm) *m*, helium.

hélix (eliks) *m*, helix (*ear*).

hellénisme (ɛlenism) *m*, Hellenism.

hémisphère (emisfɛːr) *m*, hemisphere.

hémorragie (emɔraʒi) *f*, hemorrhage. **hémorroïdes** (rɔid) *f.pl*, hemorrhoids, piles.

'henné (ɛnne) *m*, henna.

'hennir ([h]ɛniːr) *v.i*, to neigh, whinny.

'hep (hɛp) *i*, fore! (*golf*).

héraldique (eraldik) *a*, heraldic. ¶ *f*, heraldry. **'héraut** (ro) *m*, herald (*Hist.*).

herbacé, e (ɛrbase) *a*, herbaceous. **herbage** (baːʒ) *m*, grass, pasture (*uncut*); herbage; green vegetables, green stuff, greens. **herbe** (ɛrb) *f*, herb; plant; grass; weed; wort (*Bot.*); marijuana. *l'~*, grass court (*Ten.*). *fines ~s*, herbs (*seasoning*). *l'~ longue*, the rough (*golf*). *~ menue*, fine grass. *~s menues*, fine herbs (*fine in texture, as savory herbs*). *en ~*, green; unripe; budding (*fig.*); in embryo (*fig.*). **herbette** (bɛt) (*poet.*) *f*, [green]sward. **herbeux, euse** (bø, øːz) *a*, grassy. **herbier** (bje) *m*, herbal, herbarium. **herbivore** (bivɔːr) *a*. & *m*, herbivorous (*animal*). **herboriser** (bɔrize) *v.i*, to botanize, herborize. **herboriste** (rist) *n*, herbalist. **herbu, e** (by) *a*, grassy.

hercule (ɛrkyl) *m*, Hercules,

strong man. **herculéen, ne** (leɛ̃, ɛn) a, Herculean.

'hère (ɛːr) m, wretch, wight; young stag.

héréditaire† (ereditɛːr) a, hereditary. **hérédité** (te) f, heirship, inheritance (*right*); heredity.

hérésie (erezi) f, heresy. **hérétique** (tik) a, heretical. ¶ n, heretic.

'hérissé, e (erise) p.a, bristly; prickly; on end (*hair*); bristling, beset. **'hérisser (se)** v.i. & se ~, to bristle [up], stand on end; (v.t.) to bristle, erect; stud. **'hérisson** (s5) m, hedgehog; (*sea*) urchin; clod crusher; sprocket wheel.

héritage (eritaːʒ) m, inheritance; heritage. **hériter** (te) v.i. & t, to inherit. **héritier, ère** (tje, ɛːr) n, heir, heiress.

hermaphrodite (ɛrmafrɔdit) m, hermaphrodite.

hermétique† (ɛrmetik) a, hermetic.

hermine (ɛrmin) f, ermine, stoat. **herminette** (ɛrminɛt) f, adze.

'hernie (ɛrni) f, hernia, rupture.

héroï-comique (erɔikɔmik) a, heroicomic, mock-heroic. **héroïne** (in) f, heroine. **héroïque†** (ik) a, heroic. **héroïsme** (ism) m, heroism.

'héron (erɔ̃) m, heron. **'héronnière** (rɔnjɛːr) f, heronry.

héros (ero) m, hero.

herpès (ɛrpɛs) m, herpes.

'herse (ɛrs) f, harrow; portcullis. **'herser (se)** v.t, to harrow

hésitation (ezitasjɔ̃) f, hesitation. **hésiter** (te) v.i, to hesitate, waver; falter.

hétaïre (etaiːr) f, hetaera, courtesan.

hétéroclite (eterɔklit) a, freak[ish], odd, queer; heteroclite. **hétérodoxe** (dɔks) a, heterodox, unorthodox. **hétérodoxie** (ksi) f, heterodoxy. **hétérogène** (ʒɛn) a, heterogeneous; mixed.

'hêtre (ɛːtr) m, beech [tree, wood]. ~ *rouge*, copper beech.

heure (œːr) f. oft. pl, hour; time; moment; present; o'clock. *l'* ~ *du coucher*, bedtime. ~ *du lieu*, local time. *l'* ~ *du repas*, meal t. ~ *s de bureau*, ~ *s d'ouverture*, business hours. ~ *s de pointe*, ~ *s d'affluence*, peak h—s, rush h—s. ~ *s supplémentaires*, overtime. *à la bonne* ~, well & good, all right. *de bonne* ~, ad, early, betimes, in good time. *c'est l'* ~, the time has come, is up. *à tout à l'* ~, see you soon. *l'* ~ *H*, zero hour.

heureux, euse† (œrø, øːz) a, happy; pleased; fortunate; prosperous; blissful; blessed; successful; lucky; safe (*arrival*).

'heurt (œːr) m, shock, knock, bump. **'heurté, e** (œrte) a, contrasty. **'heurter** (te) v.t. & i, to run (against); knock; shock. **'heurtoir** (twaːr) m, stop blocks (*Rly.*); buffer.

hexagone (ɛgzagɔn) m, hexagon. *le* H—~, continental France. ¶ a, hexagonal. **hexamètre** (mɛtr) m, hexameter.

hiatus (jatyːs) m, hiatus (*Gram.*).

hiberner (ibɛrne) v.t, to hibernate.

'hibou (ibu) m, owl; recluse; unsociable person.

'hic (ik) m, rub (*difficulty*).

'hideur (idœːr) f, hideousness. **'hideux, euse†** (dø, øːz) a, hideous.

'hie (i) f, beetle, rammer; pile driver.

hiemal, e (jemal) a, winter (*att.*).

hier (iɛːr) ad, yesterday. ~ [*au*] *soir*, last night.

'hiérarchie (jerarʃi) f, hierarchy.

hiéroglyphe (jerɔglif) m, hieroglyph.

hilare (ilaːr) a, hilarious, laughing. **hilarité** (larite) f, hilarity, merriment, laughter.

hindou, e (ɛ̃du) a. & H—~, n, Hindu, -doo. **l'hindoustani** (stani) m, Hindustani.

hippique (ippik) a, horse (*show*, *etc.*), equine. **hippocampe** (ippɔkɑ̃ːp) m, hippocampus, sea horse. **hippodrome** (drɔːm) m, hippodrome, circus. **hippopotame** (pɔtam) m, hippopotamus.

hirondelle (irɔ̃dɛl) f, swallow. ~ *de fenêtre*, [house] martin. ~ *de rivage*, sand martin.

hirsute (irsyt) *a*, hirsute, shaggy; rough; boorish.

hisser ([h]ise) *v.t*, to hoist; raise.

histoire (istwa:r) *f*, history; story, tale, yarn; fib; (*pl.*) fuss. *le plus beau de l'~*, the best of the story. *faire des ~s*, to make a fuss. *s'attirer des ~s*, to get into trouble. **historié, e** (tɔrje) *p.a*, illuminated, ornamental. **historien** (rjɛ̃) *m*, historian. **historier** (rje) *v.t*, to ornament. **historiette** (rjet) *f*, anecdote. **historique†** (rik) *a*, historical, historic. ¶ *m*, history, account. *~ du régiment*, regimental records.

histrion (istriɔ̃) *m*, histrion.

hiver (ivɛ:r) *m*, winter. **hivernage** (verna:ʒ) *m*, wintering. **hivernal, e** (nal) *a*, winter (*att.*), wintry. **hiverner** (ne) *v.i. & t*, to winter.

ho (ho) *i*, hi! *~, du navire!* ship ahoy!

hobereau (ɔbro) *m*, hobby (*bird*); petty country gentleman.

hoche (ɔʃ) *f*, notch, nick (*on tally*).

hochement (ɔʃmɑ̃) *m*, shake; toss (*head*). **hochepot** (ʃpo) *m*, hodgepodge. **hochequeue** (kø) *m*, wagtail. **hocher** (ʃe) *v.t. & i*, to shake; toss; notch, nick. **hochet** (ʃe) *m*, rattle, coral; bauble, plaything.

hockey (ɔke) *m*, hockey. *~ sur glace*, ice h.

hoir (wa:r) *m*, heir. **hoirie** (wari) *f*, inheritance.

holà ([h]ɔla) *i*, hallo[a]! Hallo! enough!

hollandais, e (ɔlɑ̃dɛ, ɛ:z) *a*, Dutch. **H~,** *n*, Dutchman, -woman. *le h~*, Dutch (*language*). **la Hollande** (lɑ̃:d), Holland.

holocauste (ɔlɔko:st) *m*, holocaust, burnt offering; sacrifice.

hom ([h]ɔm) *i*, hum! humph!

homard (ɔma:r) *m*, lobster.

homélie (ɔmeli) *f*, homily.

homéopathe (ɔmeɔpat) *m*, homoeopath[ist]. **homéopathie** (ti) *f*, homoeopathy. **homéopathique** (tik) *a*, homoeopathic.

homérique (ɔmerik) *a*, Homeric.

homicide (ɔmisid) *a*, homicidal. ¶ *n*, homicide (*pers.*); (*m.*) homicide (*act*). *~ excusable*, justifiable h. *~ involontaire*, manslaughter. *~ volontaire*, willful murder.

hommage (ɔma:ʒ) *m*, homage; (*pl.*) respects, compliments; token, tribute.

hommasse (ɔmas) *a*, mannish, masculine (*woman*). **homme** (ɔm) *m*, man; (*pl.*) mankind. *~ à bonnes fortunes*, lady-killer. *~ à femmes, ~ galant*, ladies' (*or* lady's*) man. *~ à projets*, schemer. *~ à tout faire*, man of all work, jack of all trades, handyman. *~ calé*, man of substance; well-informed man. *~ -caoutchouc, ~-serpent*, contortionist. *~ d'affaires*, business man; business agent; steward. *~ d'État*, statesman. *~ d'exécution*, man of deeds. *~ dans les affaires*, business man. *~ de barre*, helmsman, steersman. *~ de couleur*, mulatto. *~ de foyer*, family man. *l'~ de la rue*, the man in the street. *~ de lettres*, man of letters, literary m. *~ de métier*, craftsman. *~ de mer*, seaman, seafaring man. *~ de paille*, strawman. *~ de peine*, [common] laborer. *~ de science*, scientist. *~ l' ~ intérieur*, the inner man. *~-orchestre*, one-man band. *~-sandwich*, sandwich man. *~ sans aveu*, vagrant, outcast.

homogène (ɔmɔʒɛ:n) *a*, homogeneous.

homologuer (ɔmɔlɔge) *v.t*, to ratify; prove (*will*); accept (*a sport record*).

homonyme (ɔmɔnim) *m*, homonym, namesake.

hongre (ɔ̃:gr) *a.m*, gelded. ¶ *m*, gelding. **hongrer** (ɔ̃gre) *v.t*, to geld.

Hongrie (la) (ɔ̃gri) Hungary. **hongrois, e** (grwa, a:z) *a. & H~,** *n*, Hungarian. *le hongrois*, Hungarian (*language*).

honnête† (ɔnɛ:t) *a*, honest, honorable, upright; respectable, straight, decent; well-bred, civil, courteous; fair, reasonable. **honnêteté** (nɛtte) *f*, honesty; decency, propriety; courtesy; fairness, reasonableness; recompense.

honneur (ɔnœːr) *m*, honor; mettle; justice (*as to a meal*); credit; pleasure (*e.g, of seeing you*). **jouer pour l'~**, to play for love. **faire ~ à** (*Com.*), to honor, meet.

'honnir (ɔniːr) *v.t*, to disgrace.

honorable† (ɔnɔrabl) *a*, honorable; reputable; respectable. **honoraire** (rɛːr) *a*, honorary. **~s**, *m.pl*, fee[s], honorarium. **honorariat** (rarja) *m*, honorary membership. **honorer** (re) *v.t*, to honor; respect; favor; grace; dignify; do credit to. **honorifique** (rifik), *a*, honorary.

'honte (ɔ̃ːt) *f*., shame, disgrace; reproach, scandal. **avoir ~**, to be ashamed. **faire ~ à**, to put to shame, make ashamed. **'honteux, euse** (ɔ̃tø, ø:z) *a*, ashamed; bashful, shamefaced; sheepish; shameful, disgraceful, inglorious; uncomplaining (*poor*).

hôpital (opital) *m*, hospital. **~ de contagieux**, isolation h.

'hoquet (ɔkɛ) *m*, hiccup; gasp.

horaire (ɔrɛːr) *m*, timetable; person paid by the hour.

'horde (ɔrd) *f*, horde.

'horion (ɔrjɔ̃) *m*, thump, whack.

horizon (ɔrizɔ̃) *m*, horizon. **horizontal, e** (tal) *a*, horizontal. **horizontalement** (lmɑ̃) *ad*, horizontally; across (*crossword clues*).

horloge (ɔrlɔːʒ) *f*, clock (*big*). **~ à carillon**, chiming c., musical c. **~ à sonnerie**, striking c. **~ de la mort**, deathwatch [beetle]. **~ de parquet**, grandfather's clock. **horloger** (lɔʒe) *m*, clockmaker, watchmaker. **horlogerie** (ʒri) *f*, horology; clock & watch making; clocks & watches.

hormis (ɔrmi) *pr*, except, but, save.

horoscope (ɔrɔskɔp) *m*, horoscope, nativity; fortune.

horreur (ɔrrœːr) *f*, horror, fright; object. **horrible†** (ɔrribl) *a*, horrible, frightful; horrid. **horripiler** (ɔrripile) *v.t*, to exasperate.

horrifier (ɔrrifje) *v.t*, to horrify.

'hors (ɔːr) & **~ de**, *pr*, out; out of; without; besides; over; be-

yond; beside; except; save. **~ bord, a. & ad**, outboard. **~ concours**, not competing [for prize]. **~ courant**, dead (*wire*). **~ -d'œuvre**, *m*, addition (*to a building*); hors-d'œuvre (*Cook.*); extra, digression. **hors d'œuvre, att**, (*part*) added (*to a building*); outside (*Meas.*); unmounted (*stone*); extra, digressive. **~ de combat**, out of action; disabled. **~ des limites**, out of bounds. **~ ligne**, out of the common, exceptional. **~ texte**, outside text (*plate, illustration, map, etc.*). **~-texte**, *m*, plate [outside text]. **~ tout**, over all (*Meas.*).

hortensia (ɔrtɑ̃sja) *m*, hydrangea.

horticole (ɔrtikɔl) *a*, horticultural. **horticulteur** (kyltœːr) *m*, horticulturist. **horticulture** (tyːr) *f*, horticulture, gardening.

hosanna (ɔzanna) *m*, hosanna; hurrah.

hospice (ɔspis) *m*, asylum, home; almshouse; hostel; hospice. **hospitalier, ère** (talje, ɛːr) *a*, hospitable; hospital (*att.*). ¶ *f*, sister of mercy, s. of charity. **hospitalisé, a** (lize) *n*, inmate; in-patient. **hospitalité** (te) *f*, hospitality.

hostie (ɔsti) *f*, host (*Eccl.*).

hostile† (ɔstil) *a*, hostile, unfriendly, inimical. **hostilité** (lite) *f*, hostility.

hôte, esse (oːt, oːtɛs) *n*, host, hostess; guest, visitor; inmate; denizen.

hôtel [*pour voyageurs*] (ɔtɛl) *m*, hotel. **~** [*particulier*], mansion; town house. **~ de la Monnaie, ~ des Monnaies**, mint. **~ de ville**, town hall. **~ des postes**, general post office. **~ des ventes**, auction rooms. **~-Dieu**, hospital. **~ garni**, rooming house. **~ meublé**, furnished apartments. **hôtelier, ère** (təlje, ɛːr) *n*, hotelkeeper. **hôtellerie** (tɛlri) *f*, fashionable restaurant; (*archaic*) hostelry.

hotte (ɔt) *f*, basket, hod.

'houblon (ublɔ̃) *m*, hop [plant]; hops. **'houblonner** (blɔne) *v.t*, to hop (*beer*). **'houblonnière** (njɛːr) *f*, hop field.

'houe (u) *f*, hoe. **'houer** (ue) *v.t*, to hoe.

'houille (u:j) *f*, coal. ~ *blanche*, water power. **'houiller, ère** (uje, ɛ:r) *a*, coal (*att.*), carboniferous. ¶ *f*, coal mine. **'houilleur** (jœ:r) *m*, coal miner.

'houle (ul) *f*, swell, surge. ~ *de fond*, ground swell. ~ *longue*, roller.

'houlette (ulɛt) *f*, shepherd's crook; trowel (*Hort.*).

'houleux, euse (ulø, ø:z) *a*, swelling (*sea*); surging tumultuous.

'houper (upe) *v.t*, to halloo, hollo (*Hunt.*).

'houppe (up) & **'houpette** (pɛt) *f*, tuft, tassel; (*powder*) puff.

'hourder (urde) *v.t*, to roughcast; pug.

'hourra (hurra) *m*, hurrah, hurray.

'hourvari (urvari) *m*, hullabaloo.

'houspiller (uspije) *v.t*, to maul; mob; taunt, abuse.

'housse (us) *f*, horse cloth; hammer cloth; dust sheet; furniture cover; dust cover (*computers*). **'housser** (se) *v.t*, to dust; put loose cover(s) on (*furniture*). **'houssine** (sin) *f*, switch. **'houssiner** (ne) *v.t*, to switch. **'houssoir** (swa:r) *m*, whisk, flick; feather duster.

'houx (u) *m*, holly.

'hoyau (wajo) *m*, mattock.

'hublot (yblo) *m*, scuttle, port [hole].

'huche (yʃ) *f*, trough, bin.

'hue (hy) *i*, gee up! **'huée** (ɥe) *f*, whoop; hoot[ing]. **'huer** (ɥe) *v.t*, to whoop, halloo; hoot, boo, barrack.

'huette (ɥɛt) *f*, wood owl, tawny owl.

'huguenote (ygnɔt) *f*, pipkin, casserole.

huilage (ɥila:ʒ) *m*, oiling. **huile** (ɥil) *f*, oil. ~ *à mécanisme*, machine o. ~ *d'éclairage*, lamp o. ~ *de coude*, elbow grease (*fig.*). ~ *de foie de morue*, cod-liver oil. ~ *de table*, ~ *comestible*, salad o. *c'est une* ~, he's a big shot. **huiler** (le) *v.t*, to oil. **huilerie** (lri)

f, oil mill; oil shop. **huileux, euse** (lø, ø:z) *a*, oily. **huilier** (lje) *m*, cruet; oil can.

huis clos (à) (ɥi), in camera; behind closed doors. **huissier** (sje) *m*, usher; bailiff.

'huit (ɥit; *before a consonant*, ɥi) *a*. & *m*, eight; eighth. ~ [*jours*] ou **'huitaine [de jours]** (tɛn) *f*, week (e.g, *Friday to Friday*). **'huitième**† (tjɛm) *a*. & *n*, eighth.

huître (ɥitr) *f*, oyster; booby, fool. ~*s du pays*, natives. ~ *perlière* (pɛrljɛ:r), pearl oyster.

'hulotte (ylɔt) *f*, wood owl, tawny owl.

humain, e† (ymɛ̃, ɛn) *a*, human; humane. **humaniser** (manize) *v.t*, to humanize. **humanitaire** (tɛ:r) *a*. & *m*, humanitarian. **humanité** (te) *f*, humanity (all senses).

humble† (œ̃:bl) *a*, humble, lowly.

humecter (ymɛkte) *v.t*, to moisten, damp, wet.

'humer (yme) *v.t*, to suck in; sip; inhale.

humérus (ymery:s) *m*, humerus.

humeur (ymœ:r) *f*, humor, mood; temper; ill-humor, [ill-] temper, petulance.

humide† (ymid) *a*, damp, moist, humid; watery, wet. **humidifier** (difje) *v.t*, to damp. **humidité** (te) *f*, damp[ness].

humilier (ymilje) *v.t*, to humiliate, humble. **humilité** (lite) *f*, humility, lowliness.

humoriste (ymɔrist) *m*, humorist. ¶ ~ & **humoristique** (tik) *a*, humorous. **humour** (mu:r) *m*, humor.

humus (ymy:s) *m*, humus, mold.

'hune (yn) *f*, top (*Naut.*). ~ *de vigie*, crow's nest. **'hunier** (nje) *m*, topsail.

'huppe (yp) *f*, hoopoe; crest. **'huppé, e** (pe) *a*, crested, tufted; smart (*moving in high society*); clever.

'hure (y:r) *f*, head (*boar*, *etc.*); jowl (*fish*); brawn.

'hurler (yrle) *v.i*, to howl, yell. **hurluberlu** (yrlybɛrly) *m*, harum-scarum.

'hutte (yt) *f*, hut, shanty.

hyacinthe (jasɛ̃:t) *f*, hyacinth, jacinth.

hybride (ibrid) *a. & m*, hybrid.
hydrate (idrat) *m*, hydrate.
hydraulique (idrolik) *a*, hydraulic, water (*att.*). ¶ *f*, hydraulics.
hydravion (idravjɔ̃) *m*, seaplane. ~ *à coque*, flying boat.
hydre (i:dr) *f*, hydra.
hydrobase (idrɔba:z) *f*, seaplane base.
hydrocarbure (idrɔkarby:r) *m*, hydrocarbon. **hydrogène** (ʒɛn) *m. & att*, hydrogen. **hydrophile** (fil) *a*, absorbent (*cotton wool*). **hydrophobie** (fɔbi) *f*, hydrophobia, rabies. **hydropique** (pik) *a*, dropsical. **hydropisie** (pizi) *f*, dropsy. **hydroscope** (skɔp) *m*, water-diviner, dowser. **hydroscopie** (pi) *f*, water-divining, dowsing. **hydrothérapie** (terapi) *f*, hydropathy. **hydrothérapique** (pik) *a*, hydropathic.
hydroglisseur (idrɔglisœ:r) *m*, hydroglider; hydroplane.
hydroptère (idrɔptɛ:r) *m*, hydrofoil.
hyène (jɛn) *f*, hyena.
hygiène (iʒjɛn) *f*, hygiene, hygienics, health, sanitation. **hygiénique†** (ʒjenik) *a*, hygienic, healthy, sanitary; toilet (*paper*).
hymen (imɛn) *ou* **hyménée** (mene) *m*, hymen; wedlock. **hyménoptères** (nɔptɛ:r) *m.pl*, hymenoptera.
hymne (imn) *m*, hymn, song, anthem (*national*). ¶ *f*, hymn (*in church*).
hyperbole (ipɛrbɔl) *f*, hyperbole; hyperbola.
hypermarché (ipɛrmarʃe) *m*, outsized supermarket (*generally in suburbs of big city*).
hypnotiser (ipnɔtize) *v.t*, to hypnotize. **hypnotisme** (tism) *m*, hypnotism.
hypocondriaque (ipɔkɔ̃driak) *a. & n*, hypochondriac. **hypocrisie** (krizi) *f*, hypocrisy, cant. **hypocrite†** (krit) *a*, hypocritical. ¶ *n*, hypocrite. **hypodermique** (dɛrmik) *a*, hypodermic. **hypothèque** (tɛk) *f*, mortgage. **hypothéquer** (ke) *v.t*, to mortgage. **hypothèse** (tɛ:z) *f*, hypothesis. **hypothétique†** (tetik) *a*, hypothetic(al).

hystérie (isteri) *f*, hysteria. **hystérique** (rik) *a*, hysteric(al).

I

iambe (jɑ̃:b) *m. & **iambique** (jɑ̃bik) *a*, iambic.
ibis (ibis) *m*, ibis.
iceberg (isbɛrg) *m*, iceberg.
ichtyologie (iktjɔlɔʒi) *f*, ichthyology.
ici (isi) *ad*, here; this; now. ~*-bas*, here below. ~ *X.*, X. speaking (*Teleph.*). *d'*~ *là*, between now & then.
icône (iko:n) *f*, icon. **iconoclaste** (kɔnɔklast) *m*, iconoclast.
ictère (iktɛ:r) *m*, jaundice.
idéal, e† (ideal) *a. & m*, ideal. **idéaliste** (list) *n*, idealist. **idée** (de) *f*, idea, notion; thought; mind; impression; view. ~ *directrice*, guiding principle.
idem (idɛm) *ad*, idem, ditto.
identifier (idɑ̃tifje) *v.t*, to identify. **identique†** (tik) *a*, identical. **identité** (te) *f*, identity, sameness.
idiome (idjo:m) *m*, language, dialect.
idiosyncrasie (idjɔsɛ̃krazi) *f*, idiosyncrasy.
idiot, e (idjo, ɔt) *a*, idiotic. ¶ *n*, idiot; imbecile, natural. **idiotie** (jɔsi) *f*, idiocy.
idiotisme (idjɔtism) *m*, idiom, locution.
idolâtre (idɔlɑ:tr) *a*, idolatrous. ¶ *n*, idolater, tress. **idolâtrer** (latre) *v.t*, to idolize. **idolâtrie** (tri) *f*, idolatry. **idolâtrique** (trik) *a*, idolatrous. **idole** (dɔl) *f*, idol.
idylle (idil) *f*, idyll; romance (*love*).
if (if) *m*, yew [tree].
igname (iɲam) *f*, yam.
ignare (iɲa:r) *a*, ignorant. ¶ *n*, ignoramus.
igné, e (igne) *a*, igneous. **ignifuge** (nify:ʒ) *a*, fireproof. **ignifuger** (fyʒe) *v.t*, to fireproof. **ignition** (nisjɔ̃) *f*, ignition.
ignoble† (iɲɔbl) *a*, ignoble, base; filthy.
ignominie (iɲɔmini) *f*, ignominy. **ignominieux, euse†** (njø, ø:z) *a*, ignominious, inglorious.

ignorance (iɲɔrɑ̃:s) f, ignorance; blunder. **ignorant, e** (rɑ̃, ɑ̃:t) a, ignorant; unacquainted. ¶ n, ignoramus, dunce. **ignoré, e** (re) p.a, unknown. **ignorer** (re) v.t. & abs, to be ignorant (or unaware) of, not to know.

iguane (igwan) m, iguana.

il (il) pn, he; it; she (of ship); there; (pl.) they.

île (i:l) f, island, isle. les îles Britanniques, les îles du Vent, etc. See under britannique, vent, etc.

illégal, e† (illegal) a, illegal, unlawful. **illégitime†** (ʒitim) a, illegitimate; unlawful; spurious. **illégitimité** (mite) f, illegitimacy.

illettré, e (illɛtre) a. & n, illiterate.

illicite† (illisit) a, illicit, unlawful.

illico (illiko) ad, directly, at once.

illimité, e (illimite) a, unlimited, unbounded, boundless; indefinite (leave).

illisible† (illizibl) a, illegible; unreadable.

illogique (illɔʒik) a, illogical. **illogisme** (ʒism) m, illogicality.

illumination (illyminasjɔ̃) f, illumination; inspiration. ~ par projection, floodlighting. **illuminé** (ne) m, visionary, madman. **illuminer** (ne) v.t, to illuminate; light up.

illusion (illyzjɔ̃) f, illusion; phantasm; delusion. ~ d'optique, optical illusion. **illusionner** (illyzjone) v.t, to fool, trick, deceive. **illusoire** (zwa:r) a, illusory, illusive.

illustration (illystrasjɔ̃) f, luster (fig.); celebrity (pers.); illustration. **illustre** (tr) a, illustrious. **illustrer** (tre) v.t, to make illustrious; illustrate. **illustrissime** (trisim) a, most illustrious.

îlot (ilo) m, islet; island, block (houses).

îlote (ilɔt) m, helot. **îlotisme** (tism) m, helotry.

image (ima:ʒ) f, image; reflection; picture; likeness; idea; (pl.) imagery. ~ d'écran, soft copy (computers). ~s-par-seconde, frames

per second (cinema). **imagé, e** (maʒe) p.a, picturesque, ornate. **imaginaire** (ʒinɛ:r) a, imaginary, fancied, fictive. **imagination** (nasjɔ̃) f, imagination, fancy. **imaginer** (ne) v.t, to imagine; fancy; devise, invent. s'~, to imagine, think.

imbécile† (ɛbesil) a, silly, stupid, imbecile, fatuous. ¶ n, fool. **imbécillité** (silite) f, stupidity, fatuity.

imberbe (ɛbɛrb) a, beardless; raw, callow.

imbiber (ɛbibe) v.t, to soak, imbue, wet. s'~ (de), to imbibe, sink in.

imbriquer (ɛbrike) v.t, to imbricate, overlap; interleave (computers).

imbrisable (ɛbrizabl) a, unbreakable.

imbroglio (ɛbrɔljo) m, imbroglio.

imbu, e (ɛby) a, imbued.

imbuvable (ɛbyvabl) a, undrinkable.

imitateur, trice (imitatœ:r, tris) n, imitator, mimic. ¶ a, imitative, mimic. **imitation** (sjɔ̃) f, imitation. **imiter** (te) v.t, to imitate; mimic; resemble, be like.

immaculé, e (immakyle) a, immaculate.

immanent, e (immanɑ̃, ɑ̃:t) a, immanent.

immangeable (imm- ou ɛmɑ̃-ʒabl) a, uneatable.

immanquable† (imm- ou ɛmɑ̃-kabl) a, sure [to happen]; unmistakable.

immatériel, le† (immaterjɛl) a, immaterial.

immatriculer (immatrikyle) v.t, to register, enter, enroll.

immédiat, e† (immedja, at) a, immediate; proximate; direct.

immémorial, e (immemɔrjal) a, immemorial.

immense (immɑ̃:s) a, immense, huge, vast; boundless. **immensément** (mɑ̃semɑ̃) ad, immensely. **immensité** (site) f, immensity; vastness; infinitude. **immensurable** (syrabl) a, immeasurable.

immerger (immɛrʒe) v.t, to immerse, plunge, dip.

immérité, e (immerite) *a*, un-merited, undeserved, unearned.

immersion (immɛrsjɔ̃) *f*, im-mersion.

immeuble (immœbl) *m*. *oft*. *pl*, real estate, realty; premises.

immigration (immigrasjɔ̃) *f*, immigration.

imminence (imminɑ̃ːs) *f*, im-minence. **imminent, e** (nɑ̃, ɑ̃ːt) *a*, imminent, impending.

immiscer (s') (immise) *v.pr*, to meddle, interfere. **immixtion** (mikstjɔ̃) *f*, interference.

immobile (immɔbil) *a*, immo-bile, set, unmovable, motionless, still; unmoved. **immobilier, ère** (lje, ɛːr) *a*, real (*estate*—*law*); property (*market*); estate (*agen-cy*); building (*society*). **immobi-lisations** (lizasjɔ̃) *f.pl*, capital ex-penditure. **immobiliser** (ze) *v.t*, to immobilize; lock up, tie up; capitalize.

immodéré†, e (immɔdere) *a*, immoderate; excessive; unre-strained.

immodeste† (immɔdɛst) *a*, im-modest.

immolation (immɔlasjɔ̃) *f*, im-molation, sacrifice; holocaust. **immoler** (le) *v.t*, to immolate, sacrifice; slay.

immonde (immɔ̃ːd) *a*, unclean, foul. **immondice** (mɔ̃dis) *f*, *oft*. *pl*, dirt, refuse, rubbish, litter.

immoral, e (immɔral) *a*, im-moral. **immoralité** (lite) *f*, im-morality.

immortaliser (immɔrtalize) *v.t*, to immortalize. **immortalité** (te) *f*, immortality. **immortel, le†** (tɛl) *a*, immortal; everlasting, un-dying. ¶ *m*, immortal.

immuable† (immyabl) *a*, im-mutable, unchangeable; hard-&-fast.

immunité (immynite) *f*, immu-nity.

impair, e (ɛpɛːr) *a*, uneven, odd (*number*). ¶ *m*, blunder.

impalpable (ɛpalpabl) *a*, im-palpable.

impardonnable (ɛpardɔnabl) *a*, unpardonable, unforgivable.

imparfait, e† (ɛparfɛ, ɛt) *a*, un-finished; imperfect. ¶ *m*, imper-fect [tense].

imparité (ɛparite) *f*, unevenness, oddness.

impartial, e† (ɛparsjal) *a*, im-partial, unbiased.

impartir (ɛpartiːr) *v.t*, to im-part, bestow.

impasse (ɛpɑːs) *f*, blind alley, dead end; deadlock, cleft stick.

impassible (ɛpasibl) *a*, impas-sible; impassive.

impatiemment (ɛpasjamɑ̃) *ad*, impatiently. **impatience** (sjɑ̃ːs) *f*, impatience; (*pl*.) fidgets. **im-patient, e** (ɑ̃, ɑ̃ːt) *a*, impatient; agog. **impatientant, e** (dtɑ̃, ɑ̃ːt) *a*, provoking, tiresome. **impa-tienter** (te) *v.t*, to put out of pa-tience, provoke. **s'~**, to grow impatient.

impatroniser (s') (ɛpatrɔnize) *v.pr*, to become master (*in a household*).

impayable (ɛpɛjabl) *a*, impay-able; invaluable, priceless; highly amusing. **impayé, e** (je) *a*, un-paid; dishonored (*bill*).

impeccable (ɛpɛkabl) *a*, impec-cable; infallible.

impedimenta (ɛpedimɛta) *m*. *pl*, impedimenta.

impénétrable† (ɛpenetrabl) *a*, impenetrable; impervious; in-scrutable.

impénitence (ɛpenitɑ̃ːs) *f*, im-penitence; obduracy. **impénitent, e** (tɑ̃, ɑ̃ːt) *a*, impenitent; obdu-rate.

impératif, ive† (ɛperatif, iːv) *a*. & *m*, imperative. **impératrice** (ɛperatris) *f*, em-press.

imperceptible† (ɛpɛrsɛptibl) *a*, imperceptible. **~** [*à l'ouïe*], in-audible.

imperfection (ɛpɛrfɛksjɔ̃) *f*, im-perfection; incompletion.

impérial, e (ɛperjal) *a*, imperial. ¶ *f*, imperial (*beard*); top, upper deck, outside (*bus*) **impérialiste** (list) *m*, imperialist; (*att*.) impe-rialistic.

impérieux, euse† (ɛperjø, øːz) *a*, imperious.

impérissable (ɛperisabl) *a*, im-perishable; undying.

impéritie (ɛperisi) *f*, incapacity.

imperméabiliser (ɛpɛrmeabil-ize) *v.t*, to [water]proof. **imper-**

méable (bl) *a*, impermeable, impervious, -proof; -tight (*air, etc.*); waterproof. ¶ *m*, raincoat.

impersonnel, le† (ɛ̃pɛrsɔnɛl) *a*, impersonal.

impertinemment (ɛ̃pɛrtinamɑ̃) *ad*, impertinently, pertly. **impertinence** (nɑ̃:s) *f*, [piece of] impertinence, pertness. **impertinent, e** (nɑ̃, ɑ̃:t) *a*, impertinent, pert; irrelevant (*law*).

imperturbable† (ɛ̃pɛrtyrbabl) *a*, imperturbable, unruffled.

impétrant, e (ɛ̃petrɑ̃, ɑ̃:t) *n*, grantee.

impétueux, euse† (ɛ̃petɥø, ø:z) *a*, impetuous; hot-headed; gusty (*wind*). **impétuosité** (tɥozite) *f*, impetuosity.

impie (ɛ̃pi) *a*, impious, ungodly, godless; unholy. **impiété** (pjete) *f*, impiety.

impitoyable† (ɛ̃pitwajabl) *a*, pitiless, merciless, ruthless, relentless.

implacable† (ɛ̃plakabl) *a*, implacable.

implanter (ɛ̃plɑ̃te) *v.t*, to implant.

implicite† (ɛ̃plisit) *a*, implicit; implied. **impliquer** (ke) *v.t*, to implicate; involve; imply.

implorer (ɛ̃plɔre) *v.t*, to implore, beseech, crave.

impoli†, e (ɛ̃pɔli) *a*, impolite. **impolitesse** (tɛs) *f*, impoliteness, rudeness.

impolitique (ɛ̃pɔlitik) *a*, impolitic.

impondérable (ɛ̃pɔ̃derabl) *a*. & *m*, imponderable.

impopulaire (ɛ̃pɔpylɛ:r) *a*, unpopular.

importance (ɛ̃pɔrtɑ̃:s) *f*, importance, moment; extent, magnitude. **d'~,** *ad*, soundly. **important, e** (tɑ̃, ɑ̃:t) *a*, important. *faire l'~,* to give oneself airs. ¶ *m*, main thing.

importateur (ɛ̃pɔrtatœ:r) *m*, importer. **importation** (sjɔ̃) *f*, import[ation]. **importer** (te) *v.t*, to import; (*v.i.*) to matter, signify. *n'importe*, no matter. *n'importe où*, anywhere. *n'importe quoi*, no matter what. *qu'importe*, what's the difference.

importun, e (ɛ̃pɔrtœ̃, yn) *a*, im-portunate, tiresome, troublesome. ¶ *n*, intruder; nuisance. **importuner** (tyne) *v.t*, to importune, worry, molest, pester. **importunité** (nite) *f*, importunity, molestation.

imposable (ɛ̃pozabl) *a*, taxable, assessable, dutiable. **imposant** (zɑ̃) *a*, imposing, commanding, dignified. **imposé, e** (ze) *n*, taxpayer. **imposer** (ze) *v.t. & abs*, to impose; enforce; lay [on]; thrust; tax, rate, assess; [over]awe. *en ~ à,* to impose [up]on, deceive. **imposition** (zisjɔ̃) *f*, imposition; tax; assessment.

impossibilité (ɛ̃pɔsibilite) *f*, impossibility. **impossible** (bl) *a*, impossible. **l'~,** *m*, impossibilities; one's [very] utmost.

imposte (ɛ̃pɔst) *f*, impost (*Arch.*).

imposteur (ɛ̃pɔstœ:r) *m*, impostor, humbug. **imposture** (ty:r) *f*, imposture, imposition.

impôt (ɛ̃po) *m*, tax; duty; taxes; taxation. *~ du timbre*, stamp duty. *~ foncier*, land tax, property tax. *~ général (ou global) sur le revenu*, surtax. *~ sur le revenu* ou *~[s] cédulaire[s]* (sedylɛ:r), income tax.

impotent, e (ɛ̃pɔtɑ̃, ɑ̃:t) *a*, helpless, crippled. ¶ *n*, cripple.

impraticable (ɛ̃pratikabl) *a*, impracticable; impassable.

imprécation (ɛ̃prekasjɔ̃) *f*, imprecation, curse.

imprécis, e (ɛ̃presi, i:z) *a*, vague. **imprécision** (sizjɔ̃) *f*, vagueness.

imprégner (ɛ̃prepe) *v.t*, to impregnate.

imprenable (ɛ̃prənabl) *a*, impregnable. *vue ~,* unspoilable view.

impresario (ɛ̃prezarjo) *m*, impresario.

impression (ɛ̃presjɔ̃) *f*, impression; impress; printing, machining, striking off (*Typ.*); print; issue; priming (*paint*); sensation. *~ de mémoire*, core dump (*computers*). **impressionnant, e** (ɔnɑ̃, ɑ̃:t) *a*, impressive. **impressionner** (ne) *v.t*, to impress, affect. **impressionnisme** (nism) *m*, impressionism.

imprévisible (ɛ̃previzibl) *a*, unforeseeable; unpredictable.

imprévoyance (ẽprevwajã:s) *f*, shortsightedness, improvidence. **imprévu, e** (vy) *a. & m*, unforeseen; unexpected; contingency (*n.*).

imprimante (ẽprimã:t) *f*, printer (*computers*). ~ à grande vitesse, high-speed printer.

imprimé (ẽprime) *m*, printed book, p. form; p. paper; (*pl.*) p. matter, literature; handbill, leaflet. **imprimer** (me) *v.t*, to imprint; impress; print; prime (*paint*); impart. **imprimerie** (mri) *f*, printing (*art*); p. plant; p. works, p. office. **imprimeur** (mœ:r) *m*, printer.

improbable (ẽprɔbabl) *a*, improbable.

improbation (ẽprɔbasjɔ̃) *f*, disapproval.

improbe (ẽprɔb) *a*, dishonest.

improductif, ive (ẽprɔdyktif, i:v) *a*, unproductive.

impromptu (ẽprɔ̃[p]ty) *ad, a. inv. & m*, impromptu; extempore; offhand.

impropre† (ẽprɔpr) *a*, wrong; inappropriate; unsuitable; unfit. **impropriété** (ẽprɔpriete) *f*, impropriety, incorrectness.

improuver (ẽpruve) *v.t*, to disapprove [of].

improvisateur, trice (ẽprɔvizatœ:r, tris) *n*, improvisator. **improviser** (ze) *v.t. & abs*, to improvise, extemporize; vamp (*Mus.*). à l'improviste (vist) *ad*, unexpectedly, unawares.

imprudemment (ẽprydamã) *ad*, imprudently. **imprudence** (dã:s) *f*, imprudence. **imprudent, e** (dã, ã:t) *a*, imprudent, incautious.

impubliable (ẽpybliable) *a*, unprintable.

impudence (ẽpydã:s) *f*, shamelessness; impudence. **impudent, e** (dã, ã:t) *a. & n*, shameless, etc, (person). **impudemment** (damã) *ad*, impudently, etc.

impudeur (ẽpydœ:r) *f*, immodesty; indecency. **impudicité** (disite) *f*, impudicity, lewdness. **impudique†** (dik) *a*, unchaste, lewd.

impuissance (ẽpɥisã:s) *f*, powerlessness; inability; impotence.

-cy. **impuissant, e** (sã, ã:t) *a*, powerless; impotent.

impulsif, ive (ẽpylsif, i:v) *a*, impulsive. **impulsion** (sjɔ̃) *f*, impulse; impetus; impulsion; spur (*of the moment*).

impunément (ẽpynemã) *ad*, with impunity. **impuni, e** (ni) *a*, unpunished, scot-free. **impunité** (te) *f*, impunity.

impur, e† (ẽpy:r) *a*, impure; unclean. **impureté** (pyrte) *f*, impurity.

imputer (ẽpyte) *v.t*, to impute, ascribe; charge.

inabordable (inabɔrdabl) *a*, inaccessible.

inacceptable (inaksɛptabl) *a*, unacceptable.

inaccessible (inaksɛsibl) *a*, inaccessible.

inaccordable (inakɔrdabl) *a*, irreconcilable; inadmissible.

inaccoutumé, e (inakutyme) *a*, unaccustomed; unusual.

inachevé, e (inaʃve) *a*, unfinished.

inactif, ive (inaktif, i:v) *a*, inactive; dull, flat. **inaction** (sjɔ̃) *f*, inaction, drift. **inactivité** (tivite) *f*, inactivity, dullness.

inadapté (inadapte) *a*, maladjusted; misfitted. ¶ *n*, maladjusted person, misfit.

inadmissible (inadmisibl) *a*, inadmissible.

inadvertance (inadvɛrtã:s) *f*, inadvertence, oversight.

inaliénable (inaljenabl) *a*, inalienable.

inaltérable (inalterabl) *a*, unalterable.

inamical, e (inamikal) *a*, unfriendly.

inamovible (inamɔvibl) *a*, irremovable.

inanimé, e (inanime) *a*, inanimate, lifeless.

inanité (inanite) *f*, inanity, futility.

inanition (inanisjɔ̃) *f*, inanition, starvation.

inaperçu, e (inapɛrsy) *a*, unseen, unnoticed.

inappétence (inapetã:s) *f*, loss of appetite.

inapplicable (inaplikabl) *a*, inapplicable. **inappliqué, e** (ke) a, inattentive; unapplied.

inappréciable (inapresjabl) a, inappreciable; inestimable, priceless.

inapte (inapt) a, inapt, unfit.

inarticulé, e (inartikyle) a, inarticulate.

inattaquable (inatakabl) a, unassailable.

inattendu, e (inatɑ̃dy) a, unexpected.

inattention (inatɑ̃sjɔ̃) f, inattention.

inaugurer (inogyre) v.t, to inaugurate; unveil, open; usher in (fig.).

incalculable (ɛ̃kalkylabl) a, incalculable.

incandescence (ɛ̃kɑ̃dɛsɑ̃:s) f, incandescence, glow, white heat. **incandescent, e** (sɑ̃, ɑ̃:t) a, incandescent, glowing, white-hot.

incantation (ɛ̃kɑ̃tasjɔ̃) f, incantation.

incapable (ɛ̃kapabl) a, incapable; unfit; unable, unequal; incompetent; inefficient. **les ~s,** m.pl, the unemployable. **incapacité** (site) f, incapacity, etc; disablement, disability.

incarcérer (ɛ̃karsere) v.t, to incarcerate.

incarnadin, e (ɛ̃karnadɛ̃, in) a, incarnadine. **incarnat, e** (na, at) a, rosy, pink, roseate. **incarnation** (sjɔ̃) f, incarnation, embodiment. **incarné, e** (ne) p.a, incarnate; ingrowing (nail).

incartade (ɛ̃kartad) f, prank, indiscretion, lapse; outburst, tirade.

incassable (ɛ̃kɑsabl) a, unbreakable.

incendiaire (ɛ̃sɑ̃djɛ:r) a. & n, incendiary. **incendie** (di) m, [outbreak of] fire. ~ **volontaire,** arson, incendiarism. **incendié, e** (dje) n, sufferer by a fire. **incendier** (dje) v.t, to [set on] fire, set f. tq.

incertain, e (ɛ̃sɛrtɛ̃, ɛn) a, uncertain, unsettled. **incertitude** (tityd) f, uncertainty; suspense.

incessamment (ɛ̃sɛsamɑ̃) ad, incessantly; forthwith. **incessant, e** (sɑ̃, ɑ̃:t) a, incessant, unceasing, ceaseless.

incessible (ɛ̃sɛsibl) a, inalienable; not transferable.

inceste (ɛ̃sɛst) m, incest. **incestueux, euse†** (tɥø, ø:z) a, incestuous.

incidemment (ɛ̃sidamɑ̃) ad, incidentally. **incident, e** (dɑ̃, ɑ̃:t) a, incidental; incident (ray). ¶ m, incident; point of law; difficulty.

incinérateur (ɛ̃sineratœ:r) m, incinerator, destructor. **incinérer** (re) v.t, to incinerate; cremate.

incirconcis, e (ɛ̃sirkɔ̃si, i:z) a, uncircumcised.

inciser (ɛ̃size) v.t, to incise, cut; lance. **incisif, ive** (zif, i:v) a, incisive. [dent.] **incisive f,** incisor. **incision** (zjɔ̃) f, incision; lancing.

incitation (ɛ̃sitasjɔ̃) f, incitement. **inciter** (te) v.t, to incite, instigate.

incivil, e† (ɛ̃sivil) a, uncivil. **incivilité** (lite) f, incivility.

inclément, e (ɛ̃klemɑ̃, ɑ̃:t) a, inclement.

inclinaison (ɛ̃klinɛzɔ̃) f, inclination; gradient; slope; slant; cant; tilt; dip; pitch; rake. **inclination** (nasjɔ̃) f, inclination; leaning, bent; bow, nod; attachment, love, sweetheart. **incliner** (ne) v.t. & i. & s'~, to incline; lean; slope, slant; cant; tilt; dip; pitch; rake; bow [down]; nod; bank (Avn.).

inclure (ɛ̃kly:r) v.t.ir, to enclose. **inclusivement** (klyzivmɑ̃) ad, inclusively; inclusive (dates).

incognito (ɛ̃kɔɲito ou ɛ̃kɔgnito) ad. & m, incognito.

incohérence (ɛ̃koerɑ̃:s) f, incoherence. **incohérent, e** (rɑ̃, ɑ̃:t) a, incoherent; rambling.

incolore (ɛ̃kɔlɔ:r) a, colorless.

incomber (ɛ̃kɔ̃be) v.i, to be incumbent, devolve, rest.

incombustible (ɛ̃kɔ̃bystibl) a, incombustible, fireproof.

incommensurable (ɛ̃kɔmɑ̃syrabl) a, incommensurable.

incommode (ɛ̃kɔmɔd) a, inconvenient; uncomfortable; tiresome. **incommodé, e** (de) p.a, poorly (health); crippled, disabled; embarrassed. **incommodément** (demɑ̃) ad, uncomfortably. **incommoder** (de) v.t, to inconvenience,

incommode. **incommodité** (dite)
f, inconvenience; nuisance (*law*);
(*ship in*) difficulties (*navigation*).
incomparable† (ēkɔparabl) *a*,
incomparable.
incompatible (ēkɔpatibl) *a*, incompatible.
incompétent, e (ēkɔpetã, ã:t)
a, incompetent.
incomplet, **ète†** (ēkɔple, ɛt) *a*,
incomplete.
incompréhensible (ēkɔpreã-
sibl) *a*, incomprehensible. **incom-
préhension** (sjɔ̃) *f*, obtuseness.
incompris, e (ēkɔpri, i:z) *a*, misunderstood; unappreciated.
inconcevable (ēkɔsvabl) *a*, inconceivable.
inconciliable (ēkɔsiljabl) *a*, irreconcilable.
inconduite (ēkɔdчit) *f*, misconduct, misbehavior.
incongru, e (ēkɔgry) *a*, incongruous; uncouth. **incongruité**
(gryite) *f*, incongruity; malaprop-
ism; impropriety.
inconnu, e (ēkɔny) *a*, unknown.
¶ *n*,. unknown person; stranger;
nobody . P~, *m*, the unknown.
[**quantité**] **inconnue**, *f*, unknown
[quantity].
inconsciemment (ēkɔsjamã)
ad, unconsciously. **inconscience**
(sjã:s) *f*, unconsciousness. **inconscient**, e (ã, ã:t) *a*, unconscious; irresponsible.
inconséquent, e (ēkɔsekã, ã:t)
a, inconsistent; inconsequent[ial];
flighty.
inconsidéré†, e (ēkɔsidere) *a*,
inconsiderate; thoughtless.
inconsistant, e (ēkɔsistã, ã:t) *a*,
inconsistent.
inconsolable† (ēkɔsɔlabl) *a*, inconsolable. **inconsolé**, e (le) *a*,
unconsoled, forlorn.
inconstant, e (ēkɔstã, ã:t) *a*, inconstant; changeable; fickle.
inconstitutionnel, **le†** (ēkɔsti-
tysjɔnɛl) *a*, unconstitutional.
incontestable† (ēkɔtestabl) *a*,
undeniable. **incontesté**, e (te) *a*,
undisputed.
incontinent, e (ēkɔtinã, ã:t) *a*,
incontinent, unchaste.
inconvenance (ēkɔvnã:s) *f*, impropriety. **inconvenant**, e (vnã,

ã:t) *a*, unbecoming, unseemly,
indecorous.
inconvénient (ēkɔvenjã) *m*, inconvenience; drawback.
incorporer (ēkɔrpɔre) *v.t*, to
incorporate; blend.
incorrect, e (ēkɔrɛkt) *a*, incorrect; inaccurate; unbusinesslike.
incorrectement (təmã) *ad*, incorrectly, etc; ungrammatically. **incorrection** (ksjɔ̃) *f*, incorrectness,
etc.
incorrigible† (ēkɔriʒibl) *a*, incorrigible, irreclaimable, hopeless.
incorruptible (ēkɔryptibl) *a*,
incorruptible.
incrédibilité (ēkredibilite) *f*,
incredibility. **incrédule** (dyl) *a*,
incredulous. ¶ *n*, unbeliever. **incrédulité** (lite) *f*, incredulity; unbelief.
incréé, e (ēkree) *a*, uncreated.
incriminer (ēkrimine) *v.t*, to incriminate; challenge.
incroyable† (ēkrwajabl) *a*, incredible.
incrustation (ēkrystasjɔ̃) *f*, incrustation; inlay, inlaid work;
scale. **incruster** (te) *v.t*, to incrust; inlay; scale.
incubation (ēkybasjɔ̃) *f*, incubation.
inculpé, e (ēkylpe) *n*, accused.
inculper (pe) *v.t*, to inculpate,
charge.
inculquer (ēkylke) *v.t*, to inculcate, instill.
inculte (ēkylt) *a*, uncultivated,
waste; wild; unkempt; uncultured, untutored.
incurable† (ēkyrabl) *a*. & *n*, incurable.
incurie (ēkyri) *f*, carelessness.
incursion (ēkyrsjɔ̃) *f*, incursion,
raid, inroad, foray.
inde (ē:d) *m*. ou *bleu d'~*, indigo
blue. **l'I~**, *f*, India.
indébrouillable (ēdebrujabl) *a*,
inextricable.
indécemment (ēdesamã) *ad*, in-
decently. **indécence** (sã:s) *f*, indecency. **indécent**, e (sã, ã:t) *a*,
indecent.
indéchiffrable (ēdeʃifrabl) *a*,
undecipherable; illegible; unintelligible.
indécis, e (ēdesi, i:z) *a*, unde-

cided; unsettled; drawn (*battle*, *game*). **indécision** (sisjɔ̃) *f*, indecision.

indécrottable (ɛ̃dekrɔtabl) *a*, uncleanable; incorrigible.

indéfendable (ɛ̃defɑ̃dabl) *a*, indefensible.

indéfini†, e (ɛ̃defini) *a*, indefinite; undefined. **indéfinissable** (sabl) *a*, indefinable; unaccountable; nondescript.

indéfrisable (ɛ̃defrizabl) *a*, that which will not uncurl (*hair*, *etc.*) ¶ *f*, permanent wave.

indélébile (ɛ̃delebil) *a*, indelible.

indélicat, e† (ɛ̃delika, at) *a*, indelicate; tactless; unscrupulous, sharp. **indélicatesse** (tɛs) *f*, indelicacy.

indémaillable (ɛ̃demajabl) *a*, (*stocking*) runproof.

indemne (ɛ̃dɛmn) *a*, unscathed, scatheless, unhurt, scot-free. **indemniser** (nize) *v.t*, to indemnify, compensate. **indemnité** (te) *f*, indemnity, compensation; claim, loss (*Insce.*); allowance, remuneration, bonus. ~ *de chômage*, unemployment benefit. ~ *de vie chère*, cost-of-living bonus. ~ *de licenciement*, severance pay.

indéniable (ɛ̃denjabl) *a*, undeniable.

indépendamment (ɛ̃depɑ̃damɑ̃) *ad*, independently. ~ *de*, irrespective of. **indépendance** (dɑ̃:s) *f*, independence. **indépendant**, e (dɑ̃, ɑ̃:t) *a*, independent; free; self-contained.

indéracinable (ɛ̃derasinabl) *a*, ineradicable.

indéréglable (ɛ̃dereglabl) *a*, foolproof.

indescriptible (ɛ̃dɛskriptibl) *a*, indescribable.

indésirable (ɛ̃dezirabl) *a*, undesirable; objectionable. ¶ *n*, undesirable.

indestructible (ɛ̃dɛstryktibl) *a*, indestructible.

indéterminé, e (ɛ̃detɛrmine) *a*, undetermined; indeterminate.

indévot, e (ɛ̃devo, ɔt) *a*, irreligious.

index (ɛ̃dɛks) *m*, index; pointer; first finger, forefinger; blacklist. ~ [*expurgatoire*] (ɛkspyrgatwa:r), index [expurgatorius].

indicateur, trice (ɛ̃dikatœ:r, tris) *n*, informer; (*m.*) timetable, time book; guide [book] (*Rly.*, *street*, *post*); indicator, gauge. ~ *universel des P.T.T.* (= *Postes, Télégraphes & Téléphones*), post office guide. **indicatif, ive** (tif; i:v) *a*, indicative. [mode] **indicatif**, *m*, i. [mood]; area code (*phone*). **indication** (sjɔ̃) *f*. *oft. pl*, indication; clue; information; particular; instruction, stage directions. ~ *de nom & de lieu de résidence de l'imprimeur*, printer's imprint. ~ *de nom* (ou *de firme*) *de l'éditeur*, publisher's imprint. **indice** (dis) *m*, indication; sign; index; figure; number. ~ *du coût de la vie*, cost-of-living index. ~ *inférieur, superieur*, subscript, superscript. **indicible** (sibl) *a*, unspeakable, unutterable.

indien, ne (ɛ̃djɛ̃, ɛn) *a*. & I~, *n*, Indian. ¶ *f*, print[ed cotton fabric].

indifféremment (ɛ̃diferamɑ̃) *ad*, indifferently; indiscriminately. **indifférence** (rɑ̃:s) *f*, indifference; unconcern. **indifférent**, e (rɑ̃, ɑ̃:t) *a*, indifferent; unconcerned.

indigène (ɛ̃diʒɛ:n) *a*, native, indigenous. ¶ *n*, native.

indigent, e (ɛ̃diʒɑ̃, ɑ̃:t) *a*. & *n*, indigent, poor, pauper (*n.*). ~ *de passage*, casual.

indigeste (ɛ̃diʒɛst) *a*, indigestible; undigested (*fig.*); crude. **indigestion** (tjɔ̃) *f*, indigestion.

indignation (ɛ̃diɲasjɔ̃) *f*, indignation. **indigne†** (diɲ) *a*, unworthy; undeserving; disqualified (*law*); outrageous. **indigné**, e (ɲe) *p.a*, indignant. **indigner** (ɲe) *v.t*, to exasperate. **indignité** (ɲite) *f*, unworthiness; indignity; outrage.

indigo (ɛ̃digo) *m*, indigo. **indigotier** (gɔtje) *m*, indigo plant.

indiquer (ɛ̃dike) *v.t*, to indicate, show, point out; mark; mention; state.

indirect, e† (ɛ̃dirɛkt) *a*, indirect; consequential (*damages*); crooked (*fig.*).

indiscipliné, e (ɛ̃disipline) *a*, unruly.

indiscret, ète† (ɛ̃diskrɛ, ɛt) *a*,

indiscreet; forward; prying. indiscrétion (kresj5) *f*, indiscretion.
indiscutable† (ɛ̃diskytabl) *a*, indisputable.
indispensable† (ɛ̃dispɑ̃sabl) *a*, indispensable.
indisponible (ɛ̃disponibl) *a*, inalienable; unavailable; not available.
indisposé, e (ɛ̃dispoze) *a*, indisposed, unwell, poorly, out of sorts. **indisposer** (ze) *v.t*, to upset; set against. **indisposition** (zisj5) *f*, indisposition.
indissoluble† (ɛ̃disolybl) *a*, indissoluble.
indistinct, e (ɛ̃distɛ̃ːkt) *a*, indistinct. **indistinctement** (tɛktəmɑ̃) *ad*, indistinctly; indiscriminately.
individu (ɛ̃dividy) *m*, individual; fellow. **son ~,** oneself, number one. **individualité** (dɥalite) *f*, individuality. **individuel, le†** (dɥɛl) *a*, individual; several (law).
indivis, e (ɛ̃divi, iːz) *a*, undivided; joint. **par indivis** *ou* **indivisément** (vizemɑ̃) *ad*, jointly. **indivisible†** (zibl) *a*, indivisible.
Indochine (l') (ɛ̃doʃin) *f*, Indo-China (*Cambodia, Laos, Vietnam*).
indocile (ɛ̃dosil) *a*, intractable.
indolemment (ɛ̃dolamɑ̃) *ad*, indolently; lazily. **indolence** (lɑ̃ːs) *f*, indolence, sloth; apathy, indifference. **indolent, e** (lɑ̃, ɑ̃ːt) *a*, indolent, slothful; apathetic, indifferent, lackadaisical.
indolore (ɛ̃doloːr) *a*, painless.
indomptable (ɛ̃d5tabl) *a*, untamable; indomitable; uncontrollable. **indompté, e** (te) *a*, untamed; unconquered; unsubdued.
indu, e (ɛ̃dy) *a*, untimely (*hour*).
indubitable† (ɛ̃dybitabl) *a*, indubitable, undoubted.
induction (ɛ̃dyksj5) *f*, induction; inference. **induire** (dɥiːr) *v.t.ir*, to lead; infer; induce. **~ en erreur,** to mislead. **induit** (dɥi) *m*, armature (*dynamo*).
indulgence (ɛ̃dylʒɑ̃ːs) *f*, indulgence; forbearance, leniency. **indulgent, e** (ʒɑ̃, ɑ̃ːt) *a*, indulgent, lenient.
indûment (ɛ̃dymɑ̃) *ad*, unduly.

industrialiser (ɛ̃dystrialize) *v.t*, to industrialize. **industrialisme** (lism) *m*, industrialism. **industrie** (tri) *f*, ingenuity; industry; manufacture, trade. **~-clef,** key industry. **~ d'art,** handicraft. **industriel, le†** (ɛl) *a*, industrial; manufacturing. ¶ *m*, manufacturer; millowner; industrialist. **industrieux, euse†** (ø, øːz) *a*, industrious, busy.
inébranlable† (inebrɑ̃labl) *a*, unshakable; immovable; unyielding; steadfast.
inédit, e (inedi, it) *a*, unpublished (*book*); unusual.
ineffable (inefabl) *a*, ineffable, unutterable.
ineffaçable (inefasabl) *a*, ineffaceable.
inefficace† (inefikas) *a*, inefficacious; ineffectual; ineffective; nugatory.
inégal, e† (inegal) *a*, unequal; uneven. **inégalité** (lite) *f*, inequality; unevenness.
inélégant, e (inelegɑ̃, ɑ̃ːt) *a*, inelegant.
inéligible (ineliʒibl) *a*, ineligible.
inemployable (inɑ̃plwajabl) *a*, unusable (*tool, etc.*). **inemployé, e** (je) *a*, unemployed (*resources, etc.*).
inénarrable (inenarabl) *a*, indescribable.
inepte† (inɛpt) *a*, inept, inane, silly. **ineptie** (si) *f*, ineptitude.
inépuisable† (inepɥizabl) *a*, inexhaustible.
inerte (inɛrt) *a*, inert, sluggish. **inertie** (si) *f*, inertia; listlessness.
inespéré†, e (inɛspere) *a*, unhoped for, unexpected.
inestimable (inɛstimabl) *a*, inestimable, priceless.
inévitable† (inevitabl) *a*, inevitable; unavoidable.
inexact, e† (inɛgzakt) *a*, inexact, inaccurate, incorrect; unpunctual. **inexactitude** (tityd) *f*, inexactitude.
inexcusable (inɛkskyzabl) *a*, inexcusable.
inexécutable (inɛgzekytabl) *a*, unworkable; inexecutable. **inexécution** (sj5) *f*, nonperformance.
inexercé, e (inɛgzɛrse) *a*, unskilled.

inexigible (inεgziʒibl) *a*, not due, undue.

inexistant, e (inεgzistã, ã:t) *a*, nonexistent. **inexistence** (tã:s) *f*, nonexistence.

inexorable† (inεgzɔrabl) *a*, inexorable.

inexpérience (inεksperjã:s) *f*, inexperience. **inexpérimenté, e** (rimãte) *a*, inexperienced, unskilled.

inexplicable (inεksplikabl) *a*, inexplicable. **inexpliqué, e** (ke) *a*, unexplained.

inexploré, e (inεksplɔre) *a*, unexplored.

inexprimable (inεksprimabl) *a*, inexpressible.

inexpugnable (inεkspygnabl) *a*, impregnable.

in extenso (inεkstēso) *ad*, in extenso, in full.

inextinguible (inεkstēgɥibl) *a*, inextinguishable; unquenchable; irrepressible, uncontrollable.

inextricable (inεkstrikabl) *a*, inextricable.

infaillible† (ɛfajibl) *a*, infallible; unerring.

infaisable (ɛfəzabl) *a*, unfeasible; impracticable.

infamant, e (ɛfamã, ã:t) *a*, defamatory; opprobrious; infamous (*law*). **infâme** (fɑ:m) *a*, infamous, foul. **infamie** (fami) *f*, infamy.

infanterie (ɛfãtri) *f*, infantry.

infanticide (ɛfãtisid) (*act*) *m*. & (*pers.*) *n*, infanticide. **infantile** (til) *a*, infant[ile] (*Med.*).

infatigable† (ɛfatigabl) *a*, indefatigable, tireless.

infatuation (ɛfatɥasjɔ̃) *f*, infatuation. **s'infatuer** (tɥe) *v.pr*, to become infatuated.

infécond, e (ɛfekɔ̃, ɔ̃:d) *a*, barren.

infect, e (ɛfεkt) *a*, stinking, foul. **infecter** (te) *v.t*, to infect, taint; (*v.i.*) to stink. **infectieux, euse** (sjø, ø:z) *a*, infectious (*Med.*). **infection** (sjɔ̃) *f*, infection; stench.

inférence (ɛferã:s) *f*, inference. **inférer** (re) *v.t*, to infer.

inférieur, e (ɛferjœ:r) *a*, lower, bottom, under, nether; inferior, less. ¶ *m*, inferior (*pers.*). **in-**

fériorité (rjɔrite) *f*, inferiority.

infernal, e (ɛfεrnal) *a*, infernal, hellish.

infertile (ɛfεrtil) *a*, infertile, barren.

infester (ɛfεste) *v.t*, to infest, overrun.

infidèle† (ɛfidεl) *a*, unfaithful; faithless; inaccurate; dishonest; infidel. ¶ *n*, unfaithful person; infidel. **infidélité** (delite) *f*, infidelity; unfaithfulness; dishonesty; breach of trust.

infiltrer (s') (ɛfiltre) *v.pr*, to infiltrate, percolate.

infime (ɛfim) *a*, lowest; insignificant; tiny.

infini, e (ɛfini) *a*, infinite. **l'infini,** *m*, the infinite; infinity (*Math., Phot.*). **à l'infini,** *ad*, ad infinitum. **infiniment** (mã) *ad*, infinitely. **infinité** (te) *f*, infinity, infinitude. *une ~ de*, no end of. **infinitésimal, e** (tezimal) *a*, infinitesimal. **[mode] infinitif** (tif) *m*, infinitive [mood].

infirme (ɛfirm) *a*, infirm, invalid. ¶ *n*, invalid. **infirmer** (me) *v.t*, to invalidate; quash; weaken. **infirmerie** (məri) *f*, infirmary, sick room (*Sch., etc.*). **infirmier, ère** (mje, ε:r) *n*, hospital attendant, h. orderly, h. nurse, male n., sick n. *infirmière en chef*, head nurse, matron. **infirmité** (mite) *f*, infirmity; frailty, weakness.

inflammable (ɛflamabl) *a*, inflammable. **inflammation** (sjɔ̃) *f*, ignition; inflammation.

inflation (ɛflasjɔ̃) *f*, inflation (*Fin.*).

infléchir (ɛfleʃi:r) *v.t*, to inflect, bend. **inflexible†** (flεksibl) *a*, inflexible. **inflexion** (ksjɔ̃) *f*, inflection.

infliger (ɛfliʒe) *v.t*, to inflict.

influence (ɛflyã:s) *f*, influence, sway. **influencer** (ãse) *v.t*, to influence, sway. **influent, e** (ã, ã:t) *a*, influential. **influer sur** (e), to influence.

infographie (ɛfɔgrafi) *f*, computer graphics.

in-folio (ɛfɔljo) *a.m.* & *m*, folio (*book*).

informateur, trice (ɛfɔrma-tœ:r, tris) *n*, informant. **informa-**

tion (sjɔ̃) *f. mostly pl,* inquiry; (*pl.*) newscast (*radio*).

informatique (ɛ̃fɔrmatik) *f,* data processing. ~ *absolue,* integrated d. p. ~ *commercial,* business d. p. *cours d'*~, computer training course. *reseau* ~, c. network. **informatiser** (tize) *v.t,* to computerize.

informe (ɛ̃fɔrm) *a,* shapeless, formless; informal (*law*).

informé (ɛ̃fɔrme) *m,* inquiry (*law*). **informer** (me) *v.t,* to inform, acquaint. **s'** ~, to inquire.

infortune (ɛ̃fɔrtyn) *f,* misfortune; adversity; mischance. **infortuné, e** (ne) *a. & n,* unfortunate.

infraction (ɛ̃fraksjɔ̃) *f,* infraction, infringement, breach; offense.

infranchissable (ɛ̃frɑ̃ʃisabl) *a,* impassable; insuperable.

infréquenté, e (ɛ̃frekɑ̃te) *a,* unfrequented.

infroissable (ɛ̃frwasabl) *a,* wrinkle-proof, uncrushable.

infructueux, euse† (ɛ̃fryktɥø, øːz) *a,* fruitless (fig.).

infus, e (ɛ̃fy, yːz) *a,* inborn, innate. **infuser** (fyze) *v.t,* infuse; instill. [s'] ~, to draw (*tea*). **infusible** (zibl) *a,* infusible. **infusion** (zjɔ̃) *f,* infusion; tea. **infusoires** (zwaːr) *m.pl,* infusoria.

ingambe (ɛ̃gɑ̃ːb) *a,* nimble.

ingénier (**s'**) (ɛ̃zenje) *v.pr,* to try, contrive.

ingénierie (ɛ̃zenjəri) *f,* project study & development; engineering.

ingénieur (ɛ̃zenjœːr) *m,* engineer. ~**conseil,** consulting e.

ingenieux, euse† (ɛ̃zenjø, øːz) *a,* ingenious. **ingéniosité** (jozite) *f,* ingenuity.

ingénu†, e (ɛ̃zeny) *a,* ingenuous, artless; unsophisticated. ¶ *f,* ingénue (*Theat.*). **ingénuité** (nɥite) *f,* ingenuousness, etc.

ingérer (**s'**) (ɛ̃zere) *v.pr,* to interfere, meddle.

ingouvernable (ɛ̃guvɛrnabl) *a,* ungovernable; uncontrollable.

ingrat, e (ɛ̃gra, at) *a,* ungrateful; thankless; unpromising; unpleasing. **ingratitude** (tityd) *f,* ingratitude.

ingrédient (ɛ̃gredjɑ̃) *m,* ingredient, constituent.

inguérissable (ɛ̃gerisabl) *a,* incurable; inconsolable.

ingurgiter (ɛ̃gyrʒite) *v.t,* to swallow, wolf down; be made to swallow.

inhabile† (inabil) *a,* incapable.

inhabitable (inabitabl) *a,* uninhabitable. **inhabité, e** (te) *a,* uninhabited, untenanted.

inhabitué (inabitye) *a,* unaccustomed.

inhaler (inale) *v.t,* to inhale.

inharmonieux, euse (inarmɔnjø, øːz) *a,* inharmonious; unmusical.

inhérent, e (inerɑ̃, ɑ̃ːt) *a,* inherent.

inhospitalier, ère (inɔspitalje, ɛːr) *a,* inhospitable.

inhumain, e† (inymɛ̃, ɛn) *a,* inhuman. **inhumanité** (manite) *f,* inhumanity.

inhumer (inyme) *v.t,* to inter, bury.

inimaginable (inimaʒinabl) *a,* unimaginable.

inimitable (inimitabl) *a,* inimitable.

inimitié (inimitje) *f,* enmity, ill feeling.

ininflammable (inɛ̃flamabl) *a,* uninflammable.

inintelligent, e (inɛ̃teliʒɑ̃, ɑ̃ːt) *a,* unintelligent. **inintelligible†** (ʒibl) *a,* unintelligible.

ininterrompu, e (inɛ̃tɛrɔ̃py) *a,* uninterrupted, unbroken.

inique† (inik) *a,* iniquitous, nefarious, unrighteous. **iniquité** (kite) *f,* iniquity, sin.

initial, e† (inisjal) *a,* initial; opening. ¶ *f,* initial [letter]. **initiation** (sjɔ̃) *f,* initiation. **initiative** (tiːv) *f,* initiative; push, drive. **initié, e** (sje) *n,* initiate. **initier** (sje) *v.t,* to initiate.

injecté, e (ɛ̃zɛkte) *a,* bloodshot; flushed; impregnated (*wood*). **injecter** (te) *v.t,* to inject. **injecteur** (tœːr) *m,* injector. **injection** (ksjɔ̃) *f,* injection.

injonction (ɛ̃zɔ̃ksjɔ̃) *f,* injunction.

injure (ɛ̃zyːr) *f,* injury, wrong; insult; (*pl.*) abuse; (*s. or pl.*) ravages. **injurier** (zyrje) *v.t,* to abuse, insult, revile. **injurieux, euse†** (rjø, ø:z) *a*, abusive, insulting, offensive, opprobrious, injurious.

injuste† (ɛ̃ʒyst) *a. & m*, unjust; unrighteous; unfair; inequitable; wrong. **injustice** (tis) *f*, injustice; unrighteousness; unfairness; wrong. **injustifiable** (tifjabl) *a*, unjustifiable.

inlassable (ɛ̃lasabl) *a*, untiring, unflagging.

inné, e (inne) *a*, innate, inborn, inbred. **innéité** (ite) *f*, innateness.

innocemment (inɔsamɑ̃) *ad*, innocently. **innocent, e** (sɑ̃, ɑ̃:t) *a*, innocent; guiltless, not guilty; sinless, blameless; guileless, artless; harmless. ¶ *n*, innocent; simpleton. **innocence** (sɑ̃:s) *f*, innocence, etc. **innocenter** (sɑ̃te) *v.t*, to find not guilty.

innocuité (innɔkɥite) *f*, harmlessness.

innombrable (innɔ̃brabl) *a*, innumerable, numberless, countless, untold.

innommé, e (innɔme) *a*, unnamed. **innommable** (mabl) *a*, unnamable.

innovation (innɔvasjɔ̃) *f*, innovation, [new] departure.

inobservance (inɔpsɛrvɑ̃:s) & **inobservation** (vasjɔ̃) *f*, inobservance, disregard. **inobservé, e** (ve) *a*, not complied with (*rules*).

inoccupé, e (inɔkype) *a*, unoccupied, idle; vacant.

inoculation (inɔkylasjɔ̃) *f*, inoculation. **inoculer** (le) *v.t*, to inoculate.

inodore (inɔdɔ:r) *a*, odorless.

inoffensif, ive (inɔfɑ̃sif, i:v) *a*, innocuous; innoxious; inoffensive; harmless.

inondation (inɔ̃dasjɔ̃) *f*, inundation, flood. **inonder** (de) *v.t*, to inundate, flood, deluge.

inopérant, e (inɔperɑ̃, ɑ̃:t) *a*, inoperative.

inopiné†, e (inɔpine) *a*, unexpected, sudden.

inopportun, e (inɔpɔrtœ̃, yn) *a*, inopportune.

inorganique (inɔrganik) *a*, inorganic.

inoubliable (inubliabl) *a*, unforgettable.

inouï, e (inwi) *a*, unheard of.

inoxydable (inɔksidabl) *a*, stainless, rustless.

inquiet, ète (ɛ̃kjɛ, ɛt) *a*, uneasy; troubled; restless, fidgety. **inquiéter** (jete) *v.t*, to make uneasy; disquiet; disturb; trouble; molest. **inquiétude** (tyd) *f*, uneasiness, disquiet[ude]; restlessness.

inquisiteur, trice (ɛ̃kizitœ:r, tris) *a*, inquisitive. **inquisition** (sjɔ̃) *f*, inquisition.

insaisissable (ɛ̃sɛzisabl) *a*, not distrainable; difficult to catch, elusive; imperceptible.

insalubre (ɛ̃salybr) *a*, unhealthy; insanitary.

insanité (ɛ̃sanite) *f*, insanity (*folly*), nonsense.

insatiable† (ɛ̃sasjabl) *a*, insatiable.

insciemment (ɛ̃sjamɑ̃) *ad*, unknowingly.

inscription (ɛ̃skripsjɔ̃) *f*, inscription; writing; epitaph; registration, registry; entry; matriculation; quotation (*in Stk Ex. list*). ~ *de* (ou *en*) *faux*, pleading of forgery. *prendre des* (*ses*) ~*s*, to matriculate. **inscrire** (skri:r) *v.t.ir*, to inscribe; register; enter; write; quote. *s'inscrire en faux*, to plead forgery (*law*); deny the truth (*contre* = of). *s'*~, to register.

inscrutable (ɛ̃skrytabl) *a*, inscrutable.

insecte (ɛ̃sɛkt) *m*, insect. **insecticide** (tisid) *a. & m*, insecticide. **insectivore** (vɔ:r) *a*, insectivorous. ~*s*, *m.pl*, insectivora.

insécurité (ɛ̃sekyrite) *f*, insecurity.

insensé, e (ɛ̃sɑ̃se) *a*, insensate, mad; senseless. ¶ *n*, madman, -woman. **insensible†** (sibl) *a*, insensible; unfeeling, callous.

insensibiliser (ɛ̃sɑ̃sibilize) *v.t*, to anesthetize.

inséparable† (ɛ̃separabl) *a*, inseparable. ~*s*, *n.pl*, inseparables (*pers*.); love birds.

insérer (ɛ̃sere) *v.t*, to insert, put in. **insert** (sɛrt) *m*, cut-in, insert, inlay (*cinema*). ~ *filmé*, film insert. **insertion** (sersjɔ̃) *f*, insertion.

insidieux, euse† (ɛ̃sidjø, ø:z) *a*, insidious.

insigne (ēsiɲ) *a*, signal, conspicuous; distinguished; arrant, rank, notorious. ¶ *m*, badge; (*pl.*) insignia. ~*s de la royauté*, regalia.

insignifiant, e (ēsiɲifjã, ã:t) *a*, insignificant, trifling, trivial, vacuous.

insinuation (ēsinɥasjɔ̃) *f*, insinuation; innuendo. **insinuer** (nɥe) *v.t*, to insinuate; hint at; introduce.

insipide (ēsipid) *a*, insipid; tasteless, vapid.

insistance (ēsistã:s) *f*, insistence. **insister** (te) *v.i*, to insist.

insociable (ēsɔsjabl) *a*, unsociable.

insolation (ēsɔlasjɔ̃) *f*, insolation; sun bathing; sunstroke.

insolemment (ēsɔlamã) *ad*, insolently. **insolence** (lã:s) *f*, insolence. **insolent, e** (lã, ã:t) *a*, insolent; overbearing; extraordinary.

insolite (ēsɔlit) *a*, unusual, unwonted.

insoluble (ēsɔlybl) *a*, insoluble.

insolvabilité (ēsɔlvabilite) *f*, insolvency. **insolvable** (bl) *a*, insolvent.

insomnie (ēsɔmni) *f*. *oft. pl*, insomnia, sleeplessness.

insondable (ēsɔ̃dabl) *a*, unfathomable, fathomless.

insonore (ēsɔnɔ:r) *a*, soundproof.

insouciant, e (ēsusjã, ã:t) *a*, careless, unconcerned; jaunty. **insoucieux, euse** (sjø, ø:z) *a*, heedless, regardless.

insoumis, e (ēsumi, i:z) *a*, unsubdued. ¶ *m*, absentee (*Mil.*).

insoutenable (ēsutnabl) *a*, untenable, indefensible; insufferable.

inspecter (ēspɛkte) *v.t*, to inspect, examine. **inspecteur, trice** (tœ:r, tris) *n*, inspector; examiner; floorwalker. ~ *du travail*, factory inspector. **inspection** (ksjɔ̃) *f*, inspection, examination; inspectorship.

inspiration (ēspirasjɔ̃) *f*, inspiration. **inspirer** (re) *v.t*, to inspire (*air & fig.*); prompt.

instabilité (ēstabilite) *f*, insta-

bility. **instable** (bl) *a*, unstable, unsteady.

installation (ēstalasjɔ̃) *f*, installation; induction (*Eccl.*). **installer** (le) *v.t*, to install; induct; settle.

instamment (ēstamã) *ad*, earnestly; urgently. **instance** (stã:s) *f*, (*pl.*) entreaties; (*law*) instance. **instant, e** (stã, ã:t) *a*, urgent, instant. ¶ *m*, instant, moment. *à l'*~, a moment ago; at once. **instantané†, e** (stãtane) *a*, instantaneous. ¶ *m*, snapshot.

instar de (à l') (ēsta:r) *pr*, like, as in.

instigation (ēstigasjɔ̃) *f*, instigation.

instiller (ēstille) *v.t*, to instill (*liquid*).

instinct (ēstē) *m*, instinct. **instinctif, ive†** (stēktif, i:v) *a*, instinctive.

instituer (ēstitɥe) *v.t*, to institute; appoint. **institut** (ty) *m*, institute, institution. **instituteur, trice** (tœ:r, tris) *n*, teacher; governess. **institution** (sjɔ̃) *f*, institution; school; hostel.

instructeur (ēstryktœ:r) *m*, instructor; drill sergeant. **instructif, ive** (tif, i:v) *a*, instructive. **instruction** (sjɔ̃) *f*, instruction; education; schooling; tuition; training; lesson; pleading (*law*). ~ *par écrit*, pleadings (*law*). *sans* ~, uneducated. **instruire** (strɥi:r) *v.t.ir*, to instruct; teach; educate; train; inform; plead (*law*). *s'*~, to learn.

instrument (ēstrymã) *m*, instrument; implement; tool. **instrumental, e** (tal) *a*, instrumental. **instrumentiste** (tist) *n*, instrumentalist.

insu de (à l') (ēsy) *pr*, unknown to. *à mon insu*, without my knowledge.

insubmersible (ēsybmɛrsibl) *a*, unsinkable.

insubordonné, e (ēsybɔrdɔne) *a*, insubordinate.

insuccès (ēsyksɛ) *m*, failure, miscarriage.

insuffisamment (ēsyfizamã) *ad*, insufficiently. **insuffisance** (zã:s) *f*, insufficiency, shortage.

~ **d'imposition**, underassessment.
insuffisant, e (ɛ̃zã, ã;t) *a*, insufficient, inadequate; incompetent.
insulaire (ɛ̃syluɛ;r) *a*, insular. ¶ *n*, islander.
Insulinde (ɛ̃sylɛ̃;d) *f*, Indian Archipelago.
insulte (ɛ̃sylt) *f*, insult. **insulter** (te) *v.t*, to insult. ~ **à**, to jeer at; be an insult to.
insupportable† (ɛ̃syportabl) *a*, insupportable; unbearable; insufferable.
insurgé, e (ɛ̃syrʒe) *a*. & *n*, insurgent. **s'insurger** (ʒe) *v.pr*, to revolt.
insurmontable (ɛ̃syrmɔ̃tabl) *a*, insurmountable, insuperable.
insurrection (ɛ̃syrɛksjɔ̃) *f*, insurrection.
intact, e (ɛ̃takt) *a*, intact; whole; unblemished.
intaille (ɛ̃tɑ;j) *f*, intaglio.
intangible (ɛ̃tɑ̃ʒibl) *a*, intangible.
intarissable† (ɛ̃tarisabl) *a*, unfailing, perennial, inexhaustible. *il est* ~, he never stops talking.
intégral, e† (ɛ̃tegral) *a*, integral, whole, entire, [in] full; unexpurgated. **l'intégralité** (lite) *f*, the whole, the entirety.
intègre (ɛ̃tegr) *a*, upright; honest. **intégrité** (tegrite) *f*, integrity.
intégrer (ɛ̃tegre) *v.t*, to integrate, incorporate. **s'~**, to combine with, join with.
intellect (ɛ̃tɛlɛkt) *m*, intellect. **intellectuel, le†** (tɥɛl) *a*. & *m*, intellectual; brain, *att*.
intelligemment (ɛ̃teliʒamɑ̃) *ad*, intelligently. **intelligence** (ʒɑ̃;s) *f*, intelligence, intellect; understanding; knowledge; (*on good*) terms; (*pl.*) correspondence; (*pl.*) dealings. **intelligent, e** (ʒɑ̃, ɑ̃;t) *a*, intelligent. **intelligible†** (ʒibl) *a*, intelligible; audible.
intempérance (ɛ̃tɑ̃perɑ̃;s) *f*, intemperance; insobriety; excess. **intempérant, e** (rɑ̃, ɑ̃;t) *a*, intemperate. **intempérie** (ri) *f. usually pl*, [inclemency of the] weather.
intempestif, ive† (ɛ̃tɑ̃pɛstif, i;v) *a*, unseasonable, untimely, ill-timed.

intenable (ɛ̃tnabl) *a*, untenable.
intendance (ɛ̃tɑ̃dɑ̃;s) *f*, stewardship. ~ *militaire*, commissariat. **intendant** (dɑ̃) *m*, steward, bailiff.
intense (ɛ̃tɑ̃;s) *a*, intense; strenuous. **intensif, ive†** (tãsif, i;v) *a*, intensive. **intensifier** (fje) *v.t*, to intensify. **intensité** (te) *f*, intensity; strength, depth (*color*). ~ *lumineuse en bougies*, candlepower.
intenter (ɛ̃tɑ̃te) *v.t*, to enter, bring, institute (*action at law*).
intention (ɛ̃tɑ̃sjɔ̃) *f*, intention; intent, purpose; meaning; will. *à l'~ de*, for [the sake of]. **intentionné, e** (ɔne) *a*, -intentioned, -meaning, -disposed. **intentionnel, le†** (nɛl) *a*, intentional.
inter (l') (ɛ̃tɛ;r) *abb*, long distance (*Teleph.*).
intercaler (ɛ̃tɛrkale) *v.t*, to intercalate.
intercéder (ɛ̃tɛrsede) *v.i*, to intercede.
intercepter (ɛ̃tɛrsɛpte) *v.t*, to intercept.
intercesseur (ɛ̃tɛrsɛsœ;r) *m*, intercessor. **intercession** (sjɔ̃) *f*, intercession.
interchangeable (ɛ̃tɛrʃɑ̃ʒabl) *a*, interchangeable.
interclasser (ɛ̃tɛrklɑse) *v.t*, to collate (*computers*). **interclassement** (mɑ̃) *m*, collation (*computers*). **interclasseuse** (ø;z) *f*, collator (*computers*).
interdiction (ɛ̃tɛrdiksjɔ̃) *f*, interdiction; prohibition; ban; deprivation (*rights*). **interdire** (di;r) *v.t.ir*, to interdict, prohibit; forbid; ban; taboo; inhibit; deprive (*Eccl.*); disconcert, nonplus. **interdit** (di) *m*, person under judicial interdiction; interdict (*Eccl.*). *sens* ~, no thoroughfare.
intéressé, e (ɛ̃terese) *n*, interested party. ¶ *a*, selfish. **intéresser** (se) *v.t*, to interest; concern. **intérêt** (rɛ) *m*, interest; stake.
interférence (ɛ̃tɛrferɑ̃;s) *f*, interference (*Phys.*).
interfolier (ɛ̃tɛrfɔlje) *v.t*, to interleave.
intérieur, e† (ɛ̃terjœ;r) *a*, inte-

rior; internal; inner; inward; inside; inland; home, domestic. ¶ m, interior, inside; home; home life, private life.

intérim (ĕterim) m, interim. *faire l'~*, to deputize. **intérimaire** (mɛːr) a, interim; acting.

interjection (ĕtɛrʒɛksjɔ̃) f, interjection; ejaculation; lodging (*appeal*). **interjeter** (ʒəte) v.t, to lodge (*appeal*).

interligne (ĕtɛrliɲ) m, space between lines; space (*Mus.*); (f.) lead (*Typ.*). **interligner** (ɲe) v.t, to lead. **interlinéaire** (lineɛːr) a, interlinear.

interlocuteur, trice (ĕtɛrlɔkytœːr, tris) n, interlocutor.

interlope (ĕtɛrlɔp) a, dubious, suspect.

interloquer (ĕtɛrlɔke) v.t, to take aback.

interlude (ĕtɛrlyd) m, interlude (*Mus., etc.*); voluntary (*organ*).

intermède (ĕtɛrmɛd) m, intermezzo; interlude. **intermédiaire** (medjɛːr) a, intermediate. ¶ m, intermission; intermediary; middleman, go-between; instrumentality, medium.

interminable (ĕtɛrminabl) a, interminable.

intermittent, e (ĕtɛrmitɑ̃, ɑ̃ːt) a, intermittent.

internat (ĕtɛrna) m, boarding school; boarding-in, living-in; internship.

international, e (ĕtɛrnasjɔnal) a, international; foreign (*postal system*). ¶ f, international (*association*); internationale (*hymn*). **internationaliste** (list) n. & a, internationalist.

interne (ĕtɛrn) a, internal; inward. [*élève*] ~, n, boarder. ¶ m, intern. **interné, e** (ne) n, internee; inmate (*asylum*). **interner** (ne) v.t, to intern (*war, etc.*); place under restraint (*lunatic*).

interpeller (ĕtɛrpɛlle) v.t, to interpellate; to challenge, call upon, heckle, accost (*someone*).

interphone (ɛtɛrfɔn) m, intercom.

interplanétaire (ĕtɛrplanetɛːr) a, interplanetary.

interpoler (ĕtɛrpɔle) v.t, to interpolate.

interposer (ĕtɛrpoze) v.t, to interpose. *s'~*, to interpose, mediate.

interprétation (ĕtɛrpretasjɔ̃) f, interpretation; construction; rendering. **interprète** (prɛt) n, interpreter; exponent. **interpréter** (prete) v.t, to interpret; render.

interrègne (ĕtɛrrɛɲ) m, interregnum.

interrogateur, trice (ĕtɛrɔgatœːr, tris) n, interrogator, questioner; examiner. **interrogatif, ive†** (tif, iːv) a, interrogative. **interrogation** (sjɔ̃) f, interrogation; question, query. **interrogatoire** (twaːr) m, interrogatory. **interroger** (ʒe) v.t, to interrogate.

interrompre (ĕtɛrɔ̃ːpr) v.t, to interrupt, break, stop. **interrupteur, trice** (ryptœːr, tris) n, interrupter; (m.) switch; circuit breaker. **interruption** (sjɔ̃) f, interruption, break.

intersection (ĕtɛrsɛksjɔ̃) f, intersection.

interstice (ĕtɛrstis) m, interstice.

interurbain, e (ĕtɛryrbɛ̃, ɛn) a, interurban; long distance (*Teleph.*). Cf. *inter* (l').

intervalle (ĕtɛrval) m, interval; space; gap; interlude.

intervenant (ĕtɛrvənɑ̃) m, acceptor for honor (*Com.*). **intervenir** (vəniːr) v.i.ir, to intervene, interfere; happen. **intervention** (vɑ̃sjɔ̃) f, intervention.

interversion (ĕtɛrvɛrsjɔ̃) f, inversion. **intervertir** (tiːr) v.t, to invert.

interview (ĕtɛrvju) f, interview (*for news*). **interviewer** (vjuve) v.t, to interview.

intestat (ĕtɛsta) a.inv, intestate.

intestin, e (ĕtɛstɛ̃, in) a, intestine; internal. ¶ m, intestine, bowel, gut. **intestinal, e** (tinal) a, intestinal.

intime† (ĕtim) a, intimate; in[ner]most; inward; close, near; private. ¶ m, intimate. **intimer** (me) v.t, to notify.

intimider (ĕtimide) v.t, to intimidate, cow, overawe.

intimité (ĕtimite) f, intimacy, closeness.

intitulé (ɛ̃tityle) *m*, title, name; premises (*deed*). **intituler** (le) *v.t*, to entitle, call, name.

intolérable† (ɛ̃tɔlerabl) *a*, intolerable, insufferable. **intolérance** (rɑ̃:s) *f*, intolerance. **intolérant, e** (rɑ̃, ɑ̃:t) *a*, intolerant.

intonation (ɛ̃tɔnasjɔ̃) *f*, intonation.

intoxication (ɛ̃tɔksikasjɔ̃) *f*, poisoning. **intoxiquer** (ke) *v.t*, to poison.

intraduisible (ɛ̃traɥizibl) *a*, untranslatable.

intraitable (ɛ̃trɛtabl) *a*, intractable; unreasonable.

intransigeant, e (ɛ̃trɑ̃ziʒɑ̃, ɑ̃:t) *a*, intransigent, uncompromising. ¶ *n*, intransigent, diehard.

intransitif, ive† (ɛ̃trɑ̃zitif, i:v) *a*, intransitive.

intrépide† (ɛ̃trepid) *a*, intrepid, fearless, dauntless. **intrépidité** (dite) *f*, intrepidity, etc.

intrigant, e (ɛ̃trigɑ̃, ɑ̃:t) *a*, intriguing, designing. ¶ *n*, intriguer, schemer, wirepuller. **intrigue** (trig) *f*, intrigue; plot. **intriguer** (ge) *v.t*, to rouse the interest (*or* curiosity) of, intrigue, puzzle; (*v.i.*) to intrigue, plot, scheme, pull the wires.

intrinsèque† (ɛ̃trɛ̃sɛk) *a*, intrinsic.

introducteur, trice (ɛ̃trɔdyktœ:r, tris) *n*, introducer. **introduction** (ksjɔ̃) *f*, introduction; opening (*law case*). **introduire** (dɥi:r) *v.t.ir*, to introduce; show in, usher in. s'~, to get in, gain admittance; intrude.

introït (ɛ̃trɔit) *m*, introit.

introniser (ɛ̃trɔnize) *v.t*, to enthrone.

introspection (ɛ̃trɔspɛksjɔ̃) *f*, introspection.

introuvable (ɛ̃truvabl) *a*, undiscoverable; peerless.

intrus, e (ɛtry, y:z) *n*, intruder, interloper; trespasser. (*law*). **intrusion** (tryzjɔ̃) *f*, intrusion; trespass.

intuitif, ive (ɛ̃tɥitif, i:v) *a*, intuitive. **intuition** (sjɔ̃) *f*, intuition.

inusable (inyzable) *a*, hard-wearing; for hard wear. **inusité, e**

(zite) *a*, uncustomary; obsolete.

inutile† (inytil) *a*, useless; unprofitable; unnecessary, needless. **inutilisable** (lizabl) *a*, unusable; unserviceable. **inutilisé, e** (ze) *a. & p.p*, unutilized. **inutilité** (te) *f*, uselessness; (*pl.*) useless things.

invalide† (ɛ̃valid) *a*, invalid; invalided. ¶ *m*, old *or* disabled soldier; pensioner. **invalider** (de) *v.t*, to invalidate; unseat. **invalidité** (dite) *f*, invalidity; disablement, disability.

invariable† (ɛ̃varjabl) *a*, invariable, unchangeable.

invasion (ɛ̃vazjɔ̃) *f*, invasion; inrush; influx.

invective (ɛ̃vɛkti:v) *f*, invective. **invectiver** (tive) *v.i*, to inveigh, rail.

invendable (ɛ̃vɑ̃dabl) *a*, unsalable. **invendu, e** (dy) *a*, unsold.

inventaire (ɛ̃vɑ̃tɛ:r) *m*, inventory; list; stock-taking; valuation; accounts, balance sheet & schedules. **inventer** (te) *v.t*, to invent; devise; trump up. **inventeur, trice** (tœ:r, tris) *n*, inventor; discoverer; finder; author (*fig.*). **inventif, ive** (tif, i:v) *a*, inventive. **invention** (sjɔ̃) *f*, invention. **inventorier** (tɔrje) *v.t*, to inventory; list; take stock of; value.

inversable (ɛ̃vɛrsabl) *a*, uncapsizable (*boat*); unspillable (*ink bottle*).

inverse† (ɛ̃vɛrs) *a*, inverse; reciprocal; reverse; contrary; contra. ¶ *m*, inverse; reverse; reciprocal. **inverser** (se) *v.t*, to reverse. **inversion** (sjɔ̃) *f*, inversion; reversal.

invertébré, e (ɛ̃vɛrtebre) *a. & m*, invertebrate.

invertir (ɛ̃vɛrti:r) *v.t*, to invert; reverse.

investigation (ɛ̃vɛstigasjɔ̃) *f*, investigation.

investir (ɛ̃vɛsti:r) *v.t*, to invest (*all Eng. senses*); vest; dignify; blockade; invest. **investissement** (tismɑ̃) *m*, investment (*Mil.*). **investiture** (ty:r) *f*, investiture.

invétéré, e (ɛ̃vetere) *p.a*, inveterate, ingrained. **s'invétérer** (re) *v.pr*, to become inveterate.

invincible† (ēvẽsibl) a, invincible; insurmountable.
inviolable† (ēvjɔlabl) a, inviolable. **inviolé, e (le)** a, inviolate.
invisible† (ēvizibl) a, invisible; never to be seen. *devenir ~*, to vanish.
invitation (ēvitasjɔ̃) f, invitation. **invite** (vit) f, call (*cards*). **invité, e (te)** n, guest. **inviter (te)** v.t, to invite, ask; court; request; tempt; call for (*trumps*).
invocation (ēvɔkasjɔ̃) f, invocation.
involontaire† (ēvɔlɔ̃tɛːr) a, involuntary; unintentional.
invoquer (ēvɔke) v.t, to invoke, call upon.
invraisemblable† (ēvrɛsãblabl) a, unlikely; improbable. **invraisemblablement** (blɛmã) ad, unlikely, improbably. **invraisemblance** (blã:s) f, unlikelihood, improbability.
invulnérable (ēvylnerabl) a, invulnerable.
iode (jɔd) m, iodine.
ion (iɔ̃) m, ion.
ionien, ne (iɔnjẽ, ɛn), **Ionique** (nik) a, Ionian, Ionic.
iota (jɔta) m, iota, jot, tittle, whit.
irascible (irasibl) a, irascible, testy.
iridium (iridjɔm) m, iridium.
iris (iris) m, iris; rainbow. *~ des marais*, yellow iris, flag. **irisation** (zasjɔ̃) f, iridescence. **irisé, e (ze)** a, iridescent.
irlandais, e (irlãdɛ, ɛːz) a, Irish. **I~**, n, Irishman, -woman. **l'Irlandais**, m, Irish (*language*). **l'Irlande** (lã:d) f, Ireland. *mer d'Irlande*, Irish Sea.
ironie (irɔni) f, irony. **ironique†** (nik) a, ironic(al).
irrachetable (irraʃtabl) a, irredeemable (*Fin.*).
irradiation (irradjasjɔ̃) f, irradiation.
irraisonnable (irrɛzɔnabl) a, irrational, unreasoning. **irrationnel, le** (irrasjɔnɛl) a, irrational.
irréalisable (irrealizabl) a, unrealizable.
irrecevable (irrəsəvabl) a, inadmissible (*evidence*); unacceptable.

irréconciliable (irrekɔ̃siljabl) a, irreconcilable.
irrécouvrable (irrekuvrabl) a, irrecoverable.
irrécupérable (irrekypɛrabl) a, unrecoverable; irretrievable.
irrécusable (irrekyzabl) a, unimpeachable, unexceptionable.
irrédentisme (irredãtism) m, irredentism.
irréductible (irredyktibl) a, irreducible; indomitable (*will*).
irréel, le (irreɛl) a, unreal.
irréfléchi, e (irrefleʃi) a, unconsidered. **irréflexion** (flɛksjɔ̃) f, thoughtlessness.
irréfutable† (irrefytabl) a, irrefutable. **irréfuté, e (te)** a, unrefuted.
irrégularité (irregylarite) f, irregularity. **irrégulier, ère†** (lje, ɛːr) a, irregular; erratic.
irréligieux, euse† (irreliʒjø, øːz) a, irreligious.
irrémédiable† (irremedjabl) a, irremediable.
irremplaçable (irrãplasabl) a, irreplaceable.
irréparable† (irreparabl) a, irreparable, irretrievable.
irréprochable† (irreprɔʃabl) a, irreproachable.
irrésistible† (irrezistibl) a, irresistible.
irrésolu, e (irrezɔly) a, irresolute.
irrespectueux, euse† (irrespɛktɥø, øːz) a, disrespectful.
irrespirable (irrɛspirabl) a, unbreathable.
irresponsable (irrɛspɔ̃sabl) a, irresponsible.
irrétrécissable (irretresisabl) a, unshrinkable.
irrévérencieux, euse (irreverãsjø, øːz) a, disrespectful. **irrévérent, e** (rã, ã:t) a, irreverent.
irrévocable† (irrevɔkabl), a, irrevocable.
irrigateur (irrigatœːr) m, irrigator; garden hose, etc. **irrigation** (sjɔ̃) f, irrigation. **irriguer** (ge) v.t, to irrigate.
irritable (irritabl) a, irritable, testy. **irritation** (sjɔ̃) f, irritation. **irriter (te)** v.t, to irritate; anger; excite. **s'~**, to grow angry; fret, chafe.

irruption (irrypsjɔ̃) *f*, irruption, inroad, inrush.
Islam (islam) *m*, Islam.
islandais, e (islɑ̃dɛ, ɛ:z) *a.* & (*language*) *m*, Icelandic. **I~,** *n*, Icelander. **l'Islande** (lɑ̃:d) *f*, Iceland.
isolateur (izɔlatœ:r) *m*, insulator. **isolé, e** (le) *a*, isolated; detached; unattached (*Mil.*); lonely; alone; aloof. **isolement** (lmɑ̃) *m*, isolation; loneliness; insulation. **isolément** (lemɑ̃) *ad*, separately; singly. **isoler** (le) *v.t*, to isolate; insulate. **isoloir** (lwar) *m*, insulator; voting booth.
isoloir (lwar) *m*, insulator; voting booth.
israélien, ienne, (israeljɛ̃, ɛn) *a.* & *n*, Israeli.
israélite (iz- ou israelit) *n*, Israelite, Jew. ¶ *a*, Jewish.
issu, e (isy) *a*, descended, born, sprung. **issue** (sy) *f*, issue; end; solution; egress, exit, way out; outlet; outcome, upshot; (*pl.*) offal, garbage; by-products. **à l'~ de,** *ad*, at the end of, on leaving.
isthme (ism) *m*, isthmus.
Italie (l') (itali) *f*, Italy. **italien, ne** (ljɛ̃, ɛn) *a,* & **I~,** *n*, Italian. **l'italien,** Italian (*language*).
italique (italik) *a*, italic. ¶ *m*, italics.
item (itɛm) *ad*, item, likewise; ditto.
itinéraire (itinerɛ:r) *m*, itinerary, route.
ivoire (ivwa:r) *m*, ivory.
ivraie (ivrɛ) *f*, cockle, darnel; tares (*fig.*).
ivre (i:vr) *a*, drunk[en], intoxicated, inebriate[d], tipsy. **~ à pleurer,** maudlin. **~ mort,** dead drunk. **ivresse** (ivrɛs) *f*, drunkenness, intoxication; frenzy, rapture. **ivrogne** (vrɔɲ) *a*, drunken. ¶ *m*, drunkard, toper, inebriate, sot. **ivrognerie** (ɲri) *f*. drunkenness. **ivrognesse** (ɲɛs) *f*, drunkard, inebriate, sot.

J

jabot (ʒabo) *m*, crop (*bird*); frill. **jaboter** (bɔte) & **jacasser** (kase) *v.i*, to jabber, chatter.
jachère (ʒaʃɛ:r) *f*, fallow [land]. **jachérer** (ʃere) *v.t*, to fallow.
jacinthe (ʒasɛ̃t) *f*, hyacinth (*Bot.*); jacinth (*Miner.*). **~ des bois,** wild hyacinth, bluebell.
jacobée (ʒakɔbe) *f*, ragwort.
jacobin (ʒakɔbɛ̃) *m*, jacobin.
jactance (ʒaktɑ̃:s) *f*, boasting. *avoir de la ~,* to have the gift of gab.
jade (ʒad) *m*, jade (*Miner.*).
jadis (ʒadis) *ad*, formerly, once. *au temps ~,* in the olden time.
jaguar (ʒagwa:r) *m*, jaguar.
jaillir (ʒaji:r) *v.i*, to gush, spout, spurt, squirt, jet; fly; splash; spring; well; flash. **jaillissant** (sɑ) *a*, gushing, shouting. **jaillissement** (smɑ̃) *m*, gushing, spurt. **~ d'éloquence,** burst of eloquence.
jais (ʒɛ) *m*, jet (*lignite*).
jalon (ʒalɔ̃) *m*, peg, stake, picket; range pole; landmark (*fig.*). **jalonner** (lɔne) *v.t*, to peg, stake [out]. **dot. jalonneur** (nœ:r) *m*, marker (*Mil.*).
jalouser (ʒaluze) *v.t*, to be jealous of. **jalousie** (zi) *f*, jealousy; Venetian blind; jalousie. **jaloux, ouse†** (lu, u:z) *a*, jealous; anxious.
Jamaïque (la) (ʒamaik), Jamaica.
jamais (ʒamɛ) *ad*, ever; never. *à ~ ou pour ~,* forever. *ne . . . ~,* never, ne'er (*Poet.*).
jambage (ʒɑ̃ba:ʒ) *m*, pier (*Build.*); jamb; down stroke; pothook. **jambe** (ʒɑ̃:b) *f*, leg; shank. **~ de force,** strut. **~ deçà, ~ delà,** astride, astraddle. **jambière** (ʒɑ̃bjɛ:r) *f*, legging; shin guard; legwarmer. **jambon** (bɔ̃) *m*, ham (*hog, boar*).
jante (ʒɑ̃:t) *f*, felloe, felly; rim. **jantille** (ʒɑ̃ti:j) *f*, paddle [board] (*waterwheel*).
janvier (ʒɑ̃vje) *m*, January.
Japon (ʒapɔ̃) *m*, Japanese porcelain; J. paper. **le ~,** Japan (*Geog.*) **japonais, e** (pɔnɛ, ɛ:z) *a.* & **J~** (*pers.*) *n*, Japanese. *le japonais,* Japanese (*language*). **japonerie** (nri) *f*, Japanese curio, etc.

japper (ʒape) *v.i,* to yap, yelp.

jaquette (ʒakɛt) *f,* morning coat, tail c. (*man's*); short c. (*woman's*). *être de la* ~, to be a homosexual (*male*).

jard (ʒaːr) *m,* river gravel.

jardin (ʒardɛ̃) *m,* garden. ~ *de rocaille,* ~ *alpestre,* rock g. ~ *anglais,* landscape g. ~ *d'enfants,* kindergarten. ~ *de fenêtre,* window box. ~ *de l'église,* churchyard. ~ *des plantes,* botanical gardens. ~ *maraîcher,* market garden. ~ *potager,* kitchen garden. **jardinage** (dina:ʒ) *m,* gardening; garden plots. **jardiner** (ne) *v.i,* to garden. **jardinet** (nɛ) *m,* small garden. **jardinier, ère** (nje, ɛːr) *n,* gardener; (*f.*) flower stand, jardinière.

jargon (ʒargɔ̃) *m,* jargon; lingo; slang, cant; jargoon (*Miner.*). **jargonner** (ɡɔne) *v.i. & t,* to jabber.

jarre (ʒaːr) *f,* jar (*pot*).

jarret (ʒarɛ) *m,* bend of the knee; ham (*in man*); hock, hough (*horse*); knuckle (*veal*); shin (*beef*). **jarretelles** (rtɛl) *f.pl,* [sock and stocking] suspenders. **jarretière** (rtjɛːr) *f,* garter; gunsling.

jars (ʒaːr) *m,* gander.

jas (ʒɑ) *m,* stock (*anchor*).

jaser (ʒɑze) *v.i,* to chatter; blab. **jaserie** (zri) *f,* chatter. **jaseur, euse** (zœːr, øːz) *n,* chatterer.

jasmin (ʒasmɛ̃) *m,* jasmine.

jaspe (ʒasp) *m,* jasper. ~ *sanguin,* bloodstone. **jasper** (pe) *v.t,* to marble; mottle. **jaspure** (pyːr) *f,* marbling.

jatte (ʒat) *f,* bowl.

jauge (ʒoːʒ) *f,* gauge; gauging rod; register[ed tonnage] (*ship*). ~ *à huile,* dipstick. **jauger** (ʒoʒe) *v.t,* to gauge; measure (*ship*); size up (*pers.*).

jaunâtre (ʒonɑːtr) *a,* yellowish; sallow. **jaune** (ʒoːn) *a,* yellow; sallow; [light] brown (*boots*). *la mer Jaune,* the Yellow Sea. *rire* ~, to give a sickly smile. ¶ *m,* yellow; yolk (*egg*); strikebreaker; (*pl.*) yellow races. **jaunir** (ʒoniːr) *v.t. & i,* to yellow. **jaunisse** (nis) *f,* jaundice.

Java (ʒava) *m,* Java. **javanais, e** (nɛ, ɛːz) *a. & J*~, *n,* Javan[ese].

javelle (ʒavel) *f,* swath; chlorinated water; javel w. **javelliser** (lize) *v.t,* to chlorinate.

javelot (ʒavlo) *m,* javelin.

je, j' (ʒə, ʒ) *pn,* I.

jean-foutre (ʒɑ̃futr) *m,* good-for-nothing (*strong slang*).

jérémiade (ʒeremjad) *f,* jeremiad.

jersey (ʒɛrze) *m,* stockinet; jersey. **J**~, *f,* Jersey (*Geog.*). **jersiais, e** (zjɛ, ɛːz) *a,* Jersey (*cattle*).

Jérusalem (ʒeryzalɛm) *f,* Jerusalem.

jésuite (ʒezɥit) *m,* Jesuit. **jésuitique** (tik) *a,* Jesuitical.

Jésus (ʒezy) *m,* Jesus. **Jésus-Christ** (kri) *m,* Jesus Christ.

jet (ʒɛ) *m,* throw[ing]; cast[ing]; toss[ing]; fling; pouring (*metal*); catch (*fish*); folds (*drapery*); flash (*light*); spurt; burst; jet (*aircraft*); stream; nozzle, spout; shoot, sprout; attempt, go. ~ [*à la mer*], jettison. ~ *d'eau,* spray; ornamental fountain. *du premier* ~, at first try. **jeté** (ʒəte) *m,* over (*Knit.*). ~ *de lit,* bedspread, overlay. **jetée** (te) *f,* jetty, pier; finger (*air terminal*). ~ *promenade,* pier (*seaside*). **jeter** (te) *v.t. & abs,* to throw; cast; dash; fling; hurl; toss; pitch; splash; put; lay (*foundations*); shed (*light*); heave (*sigh*); utter (*cry*); run, discharge (*of abscess*); sprout; strike (*root*); pour, run (*metal*). ~ [*à la mer*], to jettison. *se* ~, to throw oneself; jump; fall, run. **jeton** (tɔ̃) *m,* counter; tally; token. ~*s de présence,* directors' fees; fees. *avoir les* ~*s,* to be afraid. *faux* ~, hypocrite.

jeu (ʒø) *m,* play; game; sport; pastime; gaming; gambling; speculation; execution; acting, trick; play (*Mech.*); slack; clearance; lash; stroke (*piston, etc.*); blowing [out] (*fuse*); set, assortment; stop (*organ*); pack (*cards*); hand (*cards*); stake[s]. ~ *d'adresse,* game of skill. ~ *d'anneaux,* ship quoits, ring quoits. ~ *d'esprit,* witticism. ~ *de baquet,* tipping (*or* tilting) the bucket. ~ *de boules*, [game of] bowls. ~ *de chat*, touch [last], tag. ~ *de fléchettes*, darts. ~ *de jambes*, foot work (*sport*). ~ [*bizarre*] *de la nature*, freak [of nature]. ~ *de la scie*, cat's-cradle. ~*x de main*, horseplay, rough & tumble. ~ *de mots*, play on words, pun. ~ *de patience*, jigsaw puzzle. ~ *de paume*, real tennis (*ancient game*). ~*x de physionomie*, play of features. ~*x de salon*, ~*x de société*, parlor games, indoor games. ~ *de scène*, stage trick. ~ *de tennis*, game of tennis; t. court. ~ *de volant*, badminton. ~ *du cochonnet*, [game of] bowls. ~*x innocents*, parlor games, forfeits. ~, *manche*, & *partie*, game-set-match (*Ten.*). ~ *muet*, dumb show. *pas du* (ou *de*) ~, not fair.

jeudi (ʒ∅di) *m*, Thursday.

jeun (à) (ʒœ̃) *ad*, fasting; on an empty stomach.

jeune (ʒœn) *a*, young; youthful; juvenile; rising (*generation*); younger; minor. ~ *personne*, *f*, young lady; young person, juvenile. [le] ~, junior, the younger. ¶ *n*, young person.

jeûne (ʒ∅:n) *m*, fast[ing]; abstinence. **jeûner** (ʒ∅ne) *v.i*, to fast.

jeunement (ʒœnmã) *ad*, youthfully. **jeunesse** (nɛs) *f*, youth; childhood; youthfulness; boyhood; girlhood; girl. **jeunet, te** (nɛ, ɛt) *a*, [very] young.

jiu-jitsu (ʒyʒitsy) *m*, ju-jutsu, ju-jitsu, judo.

joaillerie (ʒwajri) *f*, jewelry. **joaillier, ère** (je, ɛːr) *n*, jeweler.

jobard, e (ʒɔbaːr, ard) *n*, simpleton, fool.

jockey (ʒɔkɛ) *m*, jockey (*turf*).

jocko (ʒɔko) *m*, orangutan.

jocrisse (ʒɔkris) *m*, simpleton.

joie (ʒwa) *f*, joy[fulness], glee; mirth, merriment; pleasure; gaiety.

joignant, e [à] (ʒwaɲã, ãːt) *a*, adjoining. **joindre** (ʒwɛ:dr) *v.t. & i. ir. & se* ~, to join; unite; fold (*hands*); combine; adjoin; attach; add; meet. **joint** (ʒwɛ̃) *n*, joint, join. **jointif, ive** (tif,

iːv) *a*, close. **jointoyer** (twaje) *v.t*, to point (*masonry*). **jointure** (tyːr) *f*, juncture; joint; knuckle.

joli, e (ʒɔli) *a*, pretty; good-looking; nice; fine. **joliment** (mã) *ad*, prettily; very well.

jonc (ʒ5) *m*, rush; bulrush; cane; hoop ring. **joncher** (ʃe) *v.t*, to strew, litter.

jonction (ʒ5ksj5) *f*, junction, meeting.

jongler (ʒ5gle) *v.i*, to juggle. **jonglerie** (glɛri) *f*, juggling; juggle, trick. **jongleur** (glœːr) *m*, juggler; trickster.

jonque (ʒ5:k) *f*, junk (*Chinese*).

jonquille (ʒ5kiːj) *f*, jonquil.

jouailler (ʒuaje) *v.i*, to play [for] low [stakes]; play a little (*music*).

joubarbe (ʒubarb) *f*, houseleek.

joue (ʒu) *f*, cheek; jowl; flange. *mettre* (ou *coucher*) *en* ~, to [take] aim at.

jouée (ʒwe) *f*, reveal (*Arch.*).

jouer (ʒwe) *v.i. & t. & abs*, to play; sport; toy; move (*chess*, *etc.*); gamble; be on the gamble; speculate; operate; work; perform; act (*Theat.*); trifle; trick, fool; stake; back (*horse*); feign; look like; blow [out] (*fuse*). ~ *sur le(s) mot(s)*, to play on words, pun. *à qui à* ~? whose move is it? *se* ~ *de*, to make light of. **jouet** (ʒwɛ) *m*, toy; plaything; sport, butt. **joueur, euse** (ʒwœːr, ø:z), *n*, player; performer; gambler; speculator; operator; (*good, bad*) loser; (*att.*) fond of play. ~ *un de plus*, odd player (*golf*).

joufflu, e (ʒufly) *a*, chubby.

joug (ʒu[g]) *m*, yoke.

jouir de (ʒwiːr) *v.t*, to enjoy; e. the company of; avail oneself of the services of; use; have. **jouissance** (ʒwisã:s) *f*, enjoyment; pleasure, delight; use; possession; tenure; fruition; due date of coupon, interest payable (*date*).

joujou (ʒuʒu) *m*, plaything, toy.

jour (ʒuːr) *m*, day; daytime; [day]light; opening, gap; day, surface, grass (*Min.*); (*pl.*) openwork (*Need.*). *le* ~ *de l'an*, New Year's Day. *son* ~ [*de réception*], her at-home day. *le ~ des Cendres*, Ash Wednesday. *le ~ des morts*, All Soul's Day. *le ~ des propitiations*, the day of atonement. ~ *du terme*, quarter day. ~ *férié* (ferje), [public] holiday; holy day. ~ *gras*, meat day (*Eccl.*). *les ~s gras*, Shrovetide. ~ *maigre*, fast day. *à ~*, open; openwork[ed]; through; up to date. *à ce ~*, to date. *au ~ le ~*, from day to day; from hand to mouth. *à la ~*, by the day. *femme de ~*, cleaning woman.

Jourdain (le) (ʒurdɛ̃), the Jordan.

journal (ʒurnal) *m*, journal; diary; log [book]; book; register; [news]paper; gazette. ~ *parlé*, weather & news (*radio*). ~ *de bord*, log book, flight log. ~ *des transmissions*, transmission log (*computers*). **journalier, ère** (lje, ɛːr) *a*, daily; inconstant; fickle. ¶ *m*, day laborer. **journalisme** (lism) *m*, journalism; press. **journaliste** (list) *m*, journalist, reporter, columnist.

journée (ʒurne) *f*, day; daytime; day's work; day's pay. ~ *de chemin*, day's journey. **journellement** (nɛlmɑ̃) *ad*, daily.

joute (ʒut) *f*, joust; tilt[ing]; contest; fight. ~ *sur l'eau*, water tournament. **jouter** (te) *v.i*, to joust.

jouvenceau, elle (ʒuvɑ̃so, ɛl) *n*, youth, damsel.

jovial, e† (ʒɔvjal) *a*, jovial, merry, jolly.

joyau (ʒwajo) *m*, jewel.

joyeux, euse† (ʒwajø, øːz) *a*, joyful, joyous, jolly, genial, convivial, merry, jocund. ¶ *f.pl*, testicles (*slang*).

jubilaire (ʒybilɛːr) *a*, jubilee, holy (*year*). **jubilation** (lasjɔ̃) *f*, jubilation, jollification, jollity. **jubilé (le)** *m*, jubilee.

jucher (ʒyʃe) *v.i.* & se ~, to roost, perch. **juchoir** (ʃwaːr) *m*, roost, perch.

judaïque† (ʒydaik) *a*, Judaic.

Judas (ʒyda) *m*, Judas (*traitor*). **j~**, spyhole, peephole, judas; window mirror.

judiciaire† (ʒydisjɛːr) *a*, judicial; legal.

judicieux, euse† (ʒydisjø, øːz) *a*, judicious, discerning.

juge (ʒyːʒ) *m*, judge; justice; magistrate; umpire. *les Juges*, Judges (*Bible*). ~ *d'instruction*, examining magistrate. **jugement** (ʒyʒmɑ̃) *m*, judgment; trial; estimation; discernment; sentence; decree. **juger** (ʒe) *v.t.* & *abs*, to judge; try (*case*); pass judgment; think, deem.

jugulaire (ʒygylɛːr) *f*, chin strap. [*veine*] ~, *f*, jugular [vein]. **juguler** (le) *v.t*, to strangle.

juif, ive (ʒɥif, iːv) *n*, Jew, Jewess. *Juif errant*, Wandering Jew. ¶ *a*, Jewish.

juillet (ʒɥijɛ) *m*, July.

juin (ʒɥɛ̃) *m*, June.

juiverie (ʒɥivri) *f*, ghetto.

jujube (ʒyʒyb) *m*, jujube. **jujubier** (bje) *m*, jujube [shrub].

julep (ʒylɛp) *m*, julep.

jules (ʒyl) *m*, husband; pimp; chamberpot. **julie** (li) *f*, wife, girlfriend. *faire sa ~*, to be goodygoody.

jumeau, elle (ʒymo, ɛl) *a*, twin; semidetached. ¶ *n*, twin; (*f.*) binocular [glass], glass[es]; upright, standard, housing. ~[*s*] *de théâtre*, opera glass[es]. **jumeler** (mle) *v.t*, to pair.

jument (ʒymɑ̃) *f*, mare.

jungle (ʒɔ̃ːgl) *f*, jungle.

jupe (ʒyp) *f*, skirt. ~-*culotte*, divided s. **jupier, ère** (pje, ɛːr) *n*, skirt maker. **jupon** (pɔ̃) *m*, petticoat.

juré, e (ʒyre) *a*, sworn. ¶ *m*, juryman, juror. **jurer** (re) *v.t.* & *abs*, to swear; s. by; blaspheme; vow; (*v.i.*) to clash, jar. **jureur** (rœːr) *m*, swearer.

juridiction (ʒyridiksjɔ̃) *f*, jurisdiction; province, line. **juridique†** (dik) *a*, juridical, law (*att.*). **jurisconsulte** (riskɔ̃sylt) *m*, jurist. **jurisprudence** (prydɑ̃ːs) *f*, jurisprudence, law. **juriste** (rist) *m*, jurist.

juron (ʒyrɔ̃) *m*, (*profane*) oath.

jury (ʒyri) *m*, jury; selection committee. ~ *d'admission*, hanging committee (*art*). ~ *d'examen*, board of examiners.

jus (ʒy) *m*, juice; gravy; coffee; electric current. *c'est le même ~,* it's the same thing. ~ de réglisse, licorice.

jusant (ʒyzɑ̃) m, ebb.

jusque & poet. **jusques** (ʒysk) pr, to; as (or so) far as; till, until; even; up to. *jusqu'à ce que*, till, until. *jusqu'à concurrence de*, up to, not exceeding. *jusqu'à quand?* till when? how long? *jusqu'ici*, so far, thus far; till now, hitherto. *jusqu'où?* how far? *jusque-là*, so far; till then.

juste (ʒyst) a, just; right; fair; legitimate; correct; accurate; exact; proper; true; condign; upright; righteous; tight (fit). ~ milieu, happy medium, golden mean. à ~ titre, fairly, rightly. le ~, the right. les ~s, m.pl, the just, the righteous. ¶ ad, just; right; barely. **justement** (təmɑ̃) ad, justly; exactly, just. **justesse** (tɛs) f, accuracy; correctness. **justice** (tis) f, justice; equity; right; rights; righteousness; justness; fairness; judicature; court of law; law; law officers. *Palais de J~*, law courts. **justiciable** (sijabl) a, under the jurisdiction; amenable. **justicier** (sje) m, justiciary. **justifiable** (fjabl) a, justifiable, warrantable. **justificatif, ive** (fikatif, i:v) a, justificative; voucher (att.). **justifier** (fje) v.t, to justify; warrant; vindicate; prove.

jute (ʒyt) m, jute.

juter (ʒyte) v.i, to be juicy. **juteux, euse** (tø, ø:z) a, juicy.

juvénile (ʒyvenil) a, juvenile, youthful.

juxtaposer (ʒykstapoze) v.t, to juxtapose.

K

kakatoès (kaktɔɛs) m, cockatoo.

kaki (kaki) a, khaki.

kaléidoscope (kaleidɔskɔp) m, kaleidoscope.

kangourou (kɑ̃guru) m, kangaroo.

kaolin (kaɔlɛ̃) m, kaolin, china clay.

Kénia (le) (kenja), Kenya.

képi (kepi) m, cap (peaked).

kermesse (kɛrmɛs) f, kermis, fête, fair.

khédive (kediːv) m, Khedive.

kif (kif) m, dope (drug). ~-~, a, the same, likewise.

kilogramme (kilɔgram) m, kilogram = 1000 grams or 2.2046 (about 2⅕) lbs.

kilomètre (kilɔmɛtr) m, kilometer = 1000 meters or 0.62137 (about ⅝) mile. **Kilométrique** (metrik) a, kilometric(al).

kimono (kimɔno) m, kimono.

kiosque (kjɔsk) m, kiosk; stall; bookstall; conning tower (submarine). ~ à musique, bandstand. ~ de jardin, summer house.

klaxon (klaksɔn) m, horn (auto). **klaxonner (ne)** v.t & i, to honk a horn.

krach (krak) m, crash, smash (Fin.).

kyrielle (kirjɛl) f, string, rigmarole.

kyste (kist) m, cyst (Med.).

L

la (la) m, A (Mus.). *donner le ~* (fig.), to set the fashion.

là (la) ad, there; then; that. ~-bas, [over] yonder, over there. ~dedans, in there; within. ~-dehors, outside, without. ~-dessous, under there, underneath. ~-dessus, on that, thereon; thereupon. ~-haut, up there. de ~, away, off; out of there; from then. par ~, that way; through there, thereby. ¶ i, there [now]! oh ~ ~! wow!

labeur (labœːr) m, labor, toil; book work (Typ.).

labial, e (labjal) a. & f, labial.

laboratoire (labɔratwaːr) m, laboratory.

laborieux, euse† (labɔrjø, ø:z) a, laborious, hard-working; working (class); arduous, toilsome, hard; labored.

labour (labuːr) m, plowing, tillage. **labourable** (burabl) a, arable, plow (land). **labourage** (raːʒ) m, plowing, tillage. **labourer (re)** v.t. & abs, to plow, till; plow up; drag (anchor); graze (sea bottom). **laboureur** (rœːr) m, plowman.

labyrinthe (labirɛ̃:t) *m*, labyrinth, maze.

lac (lak) *m*, lake, mere. *Note.—*
For named lakes, see under proper name, e.g, *le lac Léman*, under *Léman*. ~ *de cirque*, tarn. ~ *salé*, salt lake.

lacer (lase) *v.t*, to lace [up].

lacérer (lasere) *v.t*, to lacerate, tear.

lacet (lasɛ) *m*, lace (*shoe, etc.*); winding (*road*); nosing (*of locomotive*); snare, noose; (*pl.*) toils.

lâche† (lɑ:ʃ) *a*, loose; slack; lax; faint-hearted, cowardly, unmanly, dastardly, mean. **lâcher** (lɑʃe) *v.t*, to loose[n]; slacken; let out; relax; let fly; release; liberate; let go; let down; jilt; drop; [let] slip; blurt out; open, turn on (*tap*); utter; fire (*shot*). ~ *pied*, to give way. ~ *prise*, to let go. **lâcheté** (ʃte) *f*, cowardice; meanness.

lacis (lasi) *m*, network; plexus.

laconique† (lakɔnik) *a*, laconic.

lacrymal, e (lakrimal) *a*, lachrymal, tear (*att.*).

lacrymogène (lakrimɔʒɛn) *a*, tear-inducing. *gaz* ~, tear gas.

lacs (lɑ) *m*, toils (*fig.*). ~ *d'amour*, love knot, true-love[r's] knot.

lacté, e (lakte) *a*, lacteal; milk (*att.*); milky.

lacune (lakyn) *f*, lacuna; gap; hiatus; blank.

lacustre (lakystr) *a*, lacustrine, lake (*att.*).

lad (lad) *m*, stable boy (*turf*).

ladre (lɑ:dr) *n*, miser, niggard, skinflint. ¶ *a*, stingy, mean, niggardly. **ladrerie** (lɑdrəri) *f*, stinginess.

lagune (lagyn) *f*, lagoon.

lai (lɛ) *a.m*, lay (*brother*). ¶ *m*, lay (*poem*).

laïc see **laïque**.

laîche (lɛʃ) *f*, sedge.

laid, e (lɛ, ɛd) *a*, ugly, plain, ill-favored, unsightly; naughty. **laideron** (drɔ̃) *m*, plain girl. **laideur** (dœ:r) *f*, ugliness.

laie (lɛ) *f*, wild sow.

lainage (lɛna:ʒ) *m*, woolen goods, woolens; teaseling. **laine** (lɛn) *f*, wool. ~ *peignée*, worsted.

lainer (lɛne) *v.t*, to teasel. **lainerie** (nri) *f*, woolen mill; ʍ, trade; wool shop. **laineux, euse** (nø, ø:z) *a*, woolly. **lainier, ère** (nje, ɛ:r) *a*, wool (*trade, etc.*) ¶ *m*, woolen manufacturer.

laïque (laik) *a. & m*, laic, lay(man); undenominational.

laisse (lɛs) *f*, leash, slip; sea ware; watermark (*tidal*).

laissé-pour-compte (lɛse) *m*, returned or rejected article.

laissées (lɛse) *f.pl*, droppings, dung.

laisser (lɛse) *v.t*, to leave; let; allow; let have. ~ *aller* & ~ *échapper*, to let go. ~ *courre* (ku:r), to slip (*hounds*). ~ *tomber*, to drop; let fall. *laissez donc!* leave off! laisser-aller, *m*, unconstraint; carelessness. laisser-faire, *m*, noninterference, drift. laissez-passer, *m*, pass; 500-franc note (*slang*).

lait (lɛ) *m*, milk. ~ *condensé*, ~ *concentré*, ~ *conservé*, condensed m. ~ *de beurre*, buttermilk. ~ *de chaux*, whitewash. **laitage** (ta:ʒ) *m*, milk food. **laitance** (tɑ̃:s) *ou* **laite** (lɛt) *f*, soft roe, milt. **laité, e** (te) *a*, soft-roed. **laiterie** (tri) *f*, dairy. **laiteux, euse** (tø, ø:z) *a*, milky.

laitier (lɛtje) *m*, slag, scoria[e].

laitier, ère (lɛtje, ɛ:r) *m*, milkman, milkmaid, dairyman. ¶ *f*, milker (*cow*).

laiton (lɛtɔ̃) *m*, brass.

laitue (lɛty) *f*, lettuce. ~ *pommée*, cabbage l. ~ *romaine*, Romaine lettuce.

laize (lɛ:z) *f*, width (*of cloth*).

lama (lama) *m*, lama (*pers.*); llama (*Zool.*).

lamaneur (lamanœ:r) *m*, branch pilot.

lamantin (lamɑ̃tɛ̃) *m*, manatee, sea cow.

lambeau (lɑ̃bo) *m*, rag, tatter; shred; remnant.

lambin, e (lɑ̃bɛ̃, in) *n*, dawdler, slowcoach; (*att.*) dawdling, slow, dilatory, leisurely. **lambiner** (bine) *v.i*, to dawdle, lag.

lambourde (lɑ̃burd) *f*, joist; wall-plate.

lambris (lɑ̃bri) *m*, wainscot; paneling. ~ *d'appui*, dado. ~

dorés, gilded apartments. **lambrisser (se)** *v.t*, to wainscot; panel; line.

lame (lam) *f*, [thin] sheet; plate; lamina; flake; blade; cutter; lath, slat (*blind*); spangle; wave, sea, billow; swordsman. **lamé**, e (lame) *a. & m*, lamé. **lamelle** (mɛl) *f*, lamina, flake.

lamentable† (lamãtabl) *a*, lamentable, deplorable, pitiful, pitiable; woeful. **lamentation** (sjɔ̃) *f*, lament[ation], wail[ing]. **se lamenter (te)** *v.pr*, to lament, wail. *se ~ sur*, to bewail, deplore.

laminer (lamine) *v.t*, to roll (*metal*); laminate. **laminoir** (nwaːr) *m*, rolling mill.

lampadaire (lãpadɛːr) *m*, lamp standard.

lampas (lãpɑ) *m*, lampas (*silk & Vet.*).

lampe (lãːp) *f*, lamp; radio tube. *~ à alcool*, spirit lamp. *~ à pied*, floor l. *~ de poche*, *électrique*, flashlight. *~ de travail*, reading lamp. *~éclair*, *f*, flashbulb.

lamper (lãpe) *v.t*, to toss off, swill, swig.

lampion (lãpjɔ̃) *m*, fairy light, f. lamp. *~ en papier*, paper lantern. **lampiste** (pist) *m*, lampman. **lampisterie** (təri) *f*, lamp room.

lamproie (lãprwa) *f*, lamprey.

lampyre (lãpiːr) *m*, glowworm.

lance (lãːs) *f*, spear; lance; [hose] branch. **~-flamme**, *m*, flamethrower. **~-torpille**, *m*, torpedo launcher. **lancement** (lãsmã) *m*, throwing; launch[ing]; floating, promotion. *~ du javelot*, *du disque*, *du gros boulet*, *du marteau*, throwing the javelin, the discus, the heavy weight, the hammer. *~ du poids*, putting the shot. *base de ~*, *f*, launching base. **lancer** (se) *m*, release (*pigeons*); starting (*Hunt.*). ¶ *v.t*, to throw; cast; put (*the shot*); fling; hurl; shy; drop (*bombs*); dart; shoot; fire; toss; pitch; let off; ejaculate; initiate; launch; catapult (*airplane*); float; promote; issue; set (*dog on*, *fashion*); deliver (*ball*, Ten.); fly (*kite*); start (*stag*, *game*). **lancette** (sɛt) *f*, lancet. **lanceur** (sœːr) *m*, pitcher (*baseball*); launcher,

launch vehicle. **lanciers** (sje) *m.pl*, lancers (*Danc.*). **lancinant**, e (sinã, ãːt) *a*, shooting (*pain*).

landau (lãdo) *m*, landau. *~ [pour enfant]*, baby carriage, perambulator. *~ pliant*, folding carriage. **landaulet** (lɛ) *m*, landaulet.

lande (lãːd) *f*, heath, moor- [land]) links.

langage (lãgaːʒ) *m*, language, speech, parlance. *~ de poissarde*, *~ des halles*, abusive language.

lange (lãːʒ) *m*, diaper; (*pl*, *lit. & fig.*) swaddling clothes.

langoureux, euse† (lãgurø, øːz) *a*, languorous.

langouste (lãgust) *f*, spiny lobster, (*sea*) crayfish. **langoustine** (stin) *f*, prawn.

langue (lãːg) *f*, tongue; language, speech. *~ verte*, slang. *~ vulgaire*, vernacular. *mauvaise ~*, backbiter. *donner sa ~ au chat*, to give up (*riddle*, *etc.*). **languette** (lɔgɛt) *f*, tongue; pointer, feather (*as on a board—Carp.*, *& Mach.*); strip; cleat.

langueur (lãgœːr) *f*, languor; listlessness; languishment. **languir** (giːr) *v.i*, to languish, pine [away]; mope; long, weary; droop, flag, drag. **languissant**, e (gisã, ãːt) *a*, languishing; languid; lackadaisical; flat, dull.

lanière (lanjɛːr) *f*, thong, lash; strip; lace (*leather*).

lanterne (lãtɛrn) *f*, lantern; lamp; (*pl.*) nonsense. *~ sourde*, dark l. *~tempête*, hurricane lamp. *~ vénitienne*, paper lantern. **lanterner** (ne) *v.i*, to shilly-shally; trifle; (*v.t.*) to humbug. **lanternier** (nje) *m*, lantern maker; lamplighter; shilly-shallier.

lapalissade (lapalisad) *f*, truism.

laper (lape) *v.i. & t*, to lap [up], lick up.

lapereau (lapro) *m*, young rabbit.

lapidaire (lapidɛːr) *a. & m*, lapidary. **lapider** (de) *v.t*, to stone; throw stones at; pelt; set on (*someone*).

lapin, e (lapɛ̃, in) *n*, [buck, doe] rabbit, coney. *~ bélier*, lop-ear[ed r.]. *~ domestique*, *~ de* *clapier,* ~ *de choux,* tame r. ~ *de garenne,* wild r. *chaud* ~, a skirt chaser. *poser un* ~ *à quelqu'un,* to stand somebody up. **lapinière** (pinjɛːr) *f,* rabbitry.

lapis[-lazuli] (lapis[lazyli]) *m,* lapis lazuli.

lapon, one (lapɔ̃, ɔn) *a. & L~, n,* Lapp, Laplander (*n.*). **la Laponie** (pɔni) Lapland.

laps de temps (laps) *m,* lapse of time. **lapsus** (syːs) *m,* lapsus, lapse, slip.

laquais (lakɛ) *m,* lackey, flunkey, menial.

laque (lak) *f,* lac; lake (*paint*). ~ *en écailles,* shellac. ¶ *m,* lacquer, l. work; japan. **laquer** (ke) *v.t,* to lacquer, japan, enamel.

larbin (larbɛ̃) *m,* flunkey.

larcin (larsɛ̃) *m,* larceny; crib, plagiarism.

lard (laːr) *m,* bacon; fat; blubber. *faire du* ~, to grow fat in idleness. *tête de* ~, pigheaded person. **larder** (larde) *v.t,* to lard (*Cook.*); [inter]lard; load; pierce. **lardon** (dɔ̃) *m,* lardoon, gibe; young child (*slang*).

lares (laːr) *m.pl,* home. [dieux] ~, Lares.

largage (largaːʒ) *m,* parachute dropping of troops or materiel; release of bombs from plane.

large† (larʒ) *a,* broad, wide; large; loose; extensive; sweeping; free; liberal. ¶ *m,* room, space; open sea; offing. *au* ~, in the offing; out at sea; well off. *au ~l* keep off! *de* ~, wide, broad (*Meas.*). **largesse** (ʒɛs) *f,* liberality; bounty, largess[e]. **largeur** (ʒœːr) *f,* breadth; width; beam (*ship*); gauge (*Rly. track*).

larguer (large) *v.t,* to let go, cast off, slip.

larix (lariks) *m,* larch [tree].

larme (larm) *f,* tear; drop (*of drink*). **larmier** (mje) *m,* drip-[stone]. **larmoiement** (mwamɑ̃) *m,* watering of the eyes. **larmoyant, e** (jɑ̃, ɑ̃ːt) *a,* weeping; in tears; tearful; maudlin. **larmoyer** (je) *v.i,* to water; weep, shed tears.

larron (larɔ̃) *m,* thief.

larve (larv) *f,* larva, grub.

laryngite (larɛ̃ʒit) *f,* laryngitis. **larynx** (rɛ̃ːks) *m,* larynx.

las, asse (lɑ, ɑːs) *a,* tired, weary.

lascar (laskaːr) *m,* fellow, guy. *drôle de* ~, funny, strange, guy.

lascif, ive† (lasif, iːv) *a,* lascivious, wanton.

lasser (lɑse) *v.t,* to tire; weary.

lasso (laso) *m,* lasso.

latent, e (latɑ̃, ɑ̃ːt) *a,* latent, hidden.

latéral, e† (lateral) *a,* lateral, side (*att.*).

latex (latɛks) *m,* latex.

latin, e (latɛ̃, in) *a. & m,* Latin. ~ *de cuisine,* dog Latin.

latitude (latityd) *f,* latitude; scope.

latte (lat) *f,* lath. **latter** (te) *v.t,* to lath. **lattis** (ti) *m,* lathing.

laudanum (lodanɔm) *m,* laudanum.

laudatif, ive (lodatif, iːv) *a,* laudatory.

lauréat (lɔrea) *a.m,* laureate. ¶ *m,* prizeman; prize winner. **laurier** (rje) *m,* laurel, bay; (*pl, fig.*) laurels. ~*-rose, m,* oleander.

lavable (lavabl) *a,* washable. **lavabo** (bo) *m,* washstand; bathroom. **lavage** (vaːʒ) *m,* washing, w. out.

lavallière (lavaljɛːr) *f,* Lavallière [neck]tie.

lavande (lavɑ̃ːd) *f,* lavender.

lavasse (lavas) *f,* slops.

lave (laːv) *f,* lava.

lavement (lavmɑ̃) *m,* enema; washing (*hands, feet*).

laver (lave) *v.t,* to wash; w. out; scrub. ~ *la vaisselle,* to wash the dishes. **laverie** (vri) *f,* washhouse. **lavette** (vɛt) *f,* dish mop; dish cloth. **laveur, euse** (vœːr, øːz) *n,* washer. *laveuse de linge,* washerwoman. *laveuse mécanique,* washing machine. **lavis** (vi) *m,* wash (*art*); wash drawing. **lavoir** (vwaːr) *m,* washhouse, scullery; washer (*Mach.*).

lawn-tennis (lɔntɛnis) *m,* lawn tennis.

laxatif, ive (laksatif, iːv) *a. & m,* laxative, aperient, opening (*medicine*).

layetier (lɛjtje) *m,* box maker. ~*emballeur,* packing-case maker. **layette** (jɛt) *f,* baby linen, layette.

lazaret (lazarɛ) *m*, lazaret[to].

lazzi (lazi) *m*, buffoonery.

le, l'; la, l'; les (lə, l; la, l; le) *art*, the; a, an (*weight, etc.*). Often untranslated, as in *le paradis*, paradise. *l'enfer*, hell. *le Japon*, Japan. *la nature*, nature. *l'histoire*, history. *la France;* France. *les enfers*, Hades.

le, l'; la, l'; les (lə, l; la, l; le) *pn*, him; her; it; them; he; she; they; so.

lé (le) *m*, width(*of cloth*).

leader (lidœːr) (*pers.*) *m*, leader (*political*).

lèche (lɛʃ) *f*, thin slice. ~*-botte*, ~*-cul*, bootlicker, flatterer. **lèche-frite** (frit) *f*, dripping pan. **lécher** (leʃe) *v.t*, to lick; overelaborate. ~ *les vitrines*, to go window-shopping.

lèche-vitrines (lɛʃvitrin) *m*, window shopping.

leçon (ləsɔ̃) *f*, lesson; lecture; reading (*text*); story. ~ *de choses*, object lesson.

lecteur, trice (lɛktœːr, tris) *n*, reader. ~ *optique*, optical character reader (*computers*). **lecture** (tyːr) *f*, reading; perusal.

ledit, ladite, lesdits, lesdites (lədi, ladit, ledi, ledit) *a*, the said (*law*).

légal, e† (legal) *a*, legal; statutory; lawful. **légaliser** (lize) *v.t*, to legalize.

légat (lega) *m*, legate. **légataire** (tɛːr) *n*, legatee. ~ *particulier*, specific l. ~ *universel*, residuary l. **légation** (sjɔ̃) *f*, legation.

lège (lɛːʒ) *a*, light (*Naut.*).

légendaire (leʒɑ̃dɛːr) *a*, legendary, fabled. **légende** (ʒɑ̃ːd) *f*, legend; characteristics, reference note, explanatory note, signs & symbols (*on map*).

léger, ère† (leʒe, ɛːr) *a*, light; flighty, frivolous; fast; slight; mild; weak (*tea, etc.*). ~ *à la course*, fleet of foot. *à la légère*, lightly, scantily; without due consideration. **légèreté** (ʒɛrte) *f*, lightness; levity.

légiferer (leʒifere) *v.i*, to legislate (*with* sur).

légion (leʒjɔ̃) *f*, legion. *ils s'appellent ~*, their name is legion.

législateur, trice (leʒislatœːr, tris) *n*, legislator, lawgiver. **législatif, ive** (tif, iːv) *a*, legislative; parliamentary (*election*). **législation** (sjɔ̃) *f*, legislation. **législature** (tyːr) *f*, legislature. **légiste** (ʒist) *m*,. legist, lawyer. **légitime†** (ʒitim) *a*, legitimate; lawful; rightful. ~ *défense*, self-defense. **légitimer** (me) *v.t*, to legitimatize; legitimate; justify. **légitimité** (mite) *f*, legitimacy, lawfulness.

legs (lɛg *ou* lɛ) *m*, legacy, bequest. **léguer** (lege) *v.t*, to bequeath, will,. devise,. leave.

légume (legym) *m*, vegetable. *les grosses ~s*, bigshots. **légumier** (mje) *m*, vegetable dish. **légumineux, euse** (minø, øːz) *a*, leguminous. ¶ *f*, legume[n], pulse.

leitmotiv (laitmɔtif) *m*, leitmotiv, -if.

Léman (le lac) (lemɑ̃), the Lake of Geneva, Lake Leman.

lendemain (lɑ̃dmɛ̃) *m*, next day, day after, morrow; future. *sans ~*, short-lived.

Léningrad (leningrad) *m*, Leningrad.

lent, e† (lɑ̃, ɑ̃ːt) *a*, slow; dilatory; lingering; low (*fever, speed*). ¶ *f*, nit. **lenteur** (lɑ̃tœːr) *f*, slowness.

lenticulaire (lɑ̃tikylɛːr) *a*, lenticular. **lentille** (lɑ̃tij) *f*, lentil; lens; freckle; bob, ball. ~ *d'eau*, ~ *de marais*, duckweed.

lentisque (lɑ̃tisk) *m*, lentisk, mastic [tree].

léonin, e (leɔnɛ̃, in) *a*, leonine; one-sided.

léopard (leɔpaːr) *m*, leopard.

lépas (lepɑs) *m*, limpet.

lépidoptères (lepidɔptɛːr) *m.pl*, Lepidoptera.

lèpre (lɛpr) *f*, leprosy. **lépreux, euse** (leprø, øːz) *a*, leprous. ¶ *n*, leper. **léproserie** (prozri) *f*, leper hospital.

lequel, laquelle, lesquels, lesquelles (ləkɛl, lakɛl, lekɛl) *pn*, who; whom; which.

lèse-majesté (lɛzmaʒɛste) *f*, [high] treason; lese-majesty. **léser** (leze) *v.t*, to injure; wrong.

lésiner (lezine) *v.i*, to be stingy, haggle. **lésinerie** (nri) *f*, stinginess, meanness.

lésion (lezjɔ̃) *f*, lesion, injury, hurt.

lessive (lɛsiːv) *f*, washing, wash; lye; detergent. **lessiver** (sive) *v.t*, to wash; scrub, swill; leach. *être lessivé*, to be exhausted (*slang*). **lessiveuse** (vøːz) *f*, wash boiler.

lest (lɛst) *m*, ballast.

leste† (lɛst) *a*, nimble; smart; flippant; free, indecorous.

lester (lɛste) *v.t*, to ballast. *se ~ l'estomac*, to line one's stomach.

léthargie (letarʒi) *f*, lethargy. **léthargique** (ʒik) *a*, lethargic. **Léthé** (lete) *m*, Lethe.

léthifère (letifɛːr) *a*, deadly, lethal.

letton, onne (lɛtɔ̃, ɔn) *a*. & **L~**, *n*, Lett; Latvian. **la Lettonie** (tɔni), Latvia.

lettrage (lɛtraːʒ) *m*, lettering. **lettre** (tr) *f*, letter; note. *~ avion*, airmail letter. *~ close* (*fig.*), sealed book. *~ d'un autre œil*, wrong font. *~ de change*, bill of exchange. *~ de crédit*, *de créance*, letter of credit. *~s de créance*, credentials. *~ de [faire] part*, notice announcing a birth, marriage, or death. *~s de naturalisation*, naturalization papers. *~[s] de service*, commission (*officer's*). *~ de voiture*, consignment note. *~ missive*, letter missive. *~ moulée*, block letter. *~ recommandée*, registered letter. *en toutes ~*, in full, fully. **lettré, e** (tre) *a*. & *n*, lettered, literate, well-read (*person*). **lettrine** (trin) *f*, drop letter (*Typ.*); catchword (*at head of dictionary page*).

leur (lœːr) *a*, their. **le ~, la ~, ~ les ~s**, *pn*, theirs.

leurre (lœːr) *m*, lure; catch (*fig.*). **leurrer** (lœre) *v.t*, to lure. **se ~**, to delude oneself.

levain (ləvɛ̃) *m*, leaven, yeast, barm. *sans ~*, unleavened.

levant (ləvɑ̃) *a.m*, rising (*sun*). ¶ *m*, east. *du ~ au couchant*, from east to west. **L~**, *m*, Levant. **levantin, e** (tɛ̃, in) *a*. & **L~**, *n*, Levantine.

levé [de plans] (ləve) *m*, survey[ing]. **levée** (ve) *f*, raising; lifting; lift; levy, removal; close (*sitting*); collection (*letters*); clearing (*letter box*); trick (*cards*); embankment; causeway. **lever** (ve) *m*, rising, getting up (*from bed*); rise (*sun*). *~ [de plans]*, survey[ing]. *~ de rideau*, curtain raiser. ¶ *v.t*, to lift; hoist; raise; take up; remove; cut off; levy; clear (*letter box*); close (*sitting*); break up (*camp*); weigh (*anchor*); plot (*plan*); (*v.i.*) to rise; shoot (*plant*). *faire ~*, to raise, leaven (*dough*). *se~*, *v.pr.* & *abs*, to rise, get up; stand up.

léviathan (levjatɑ̃) *m*, leviathan.

levier (ləvje) *m*, lever; handspike.

lévite (levit) *m*, Levite; priest; satellite. **le Lévitique** (tik), Leviticus.

levraut (ləvro) *m*, leveret, young hare.

lèvre (lɛːvr) *f*, lip.

levrette (ləvrɛt) *f*, greyhound [bitch]. **lévrier** (levrie) *m*, greyhound. *~ de la mer*, ocean greyhound (*fig.*). *~ russe*, borzoi.

levure (ləvyːr) *f*, yeast, barm.

lexicographe (lɛksikɔgraf) *m*, lexicographer. **lexique** (sik) *m*, lexicon.

Leyde (lɛd) *f*, Leyden.

lézard (lezaːr) *m*, lizard.

lézarde (lezard) *f*, crack, crevice, chink. **lézarder** (de) *v.i*, to sun oneself. *v.t*, to crack, split (*plaster*). **se ~**, to crack, split.

liais (ljɛ) *m*, kind of Portland stone.

liaison (ljɛzɔ̃) *f*, connection; bond; liaison; slur (*Mus.*); tie (*Mus.*); thickening (*Cook.*). **liaisonner** (zɔne) *v.t*, to bond (*masonry*).

liane (ljan) *f*, liana, liane.

liant, e (ljɑ̃, ɑ̃ːt) *a*, pliant; sociable, responsive. ¶ *m*, pliancy.

liard (ljaːr) *m*, farthing (*fig.*), rap. **liarder** (arde) *v.i*, to haggle.

lias (ljɑ) *m*, lias (*Geol.*). **liasique** (azik) *a*, liassic.

liasse (ljas) *f*, bundle; file.

libation (libasjɔ̃) *f*, libation; drinking.

libelle (libɛl) *m*, libel.

libellé (libɛlle) *m*, drawing [up]; wording; particulars. **libeller** (le) *v.t*, to draw [up], make; word.

libelliste (libɛllist) *m*, libeler.

libellule (libɛlyl) *f*, dragonfly.

libéral, e† (liberal) *a*, liberal, open-handed; learned (*profession*, in France such as médicin, avocat, notaire, not in the pay of the State, or under its control). ¶ *m*, liberal. **libéralisme** (lism) *m*, liberalism. **libéralité** (te) *f*, liberality.

libérateur, trice (liberatœːr, tris) *n*, liberator, deliverer. **libération** (sjɔ̃) *f*, liberation; discharge; release; paying up. **libérer** (re) *v.t*, to liberate. **liberté** (berte) *f*, liberty, freedom. ~ [*de langage*], ~ *de parole*, outspokenness. ~ *de parler*, free-[dom of] speech.

libertin, e (libertɛ̃, in) *a*, libertine, rakish; wayward. ¶ *m*, libertine, rake. **libertinage** (tinaːʒ) *m*, licentiousness; waywardness.

libraire (librɛːr) *m*, bookseller. ~*-éditeur*, b. & publisher. **librairie** (brɛri) *f*, book trade; bookstore; publishing house.

libre† (libr) *a*, free; at liberty, disengaged; available; vacant; spare; open; welcome; clear (*way*); unstamped (*paper*). ~ *arbitre*, *m*, free will. ~*-échange*, *m*, f. trade. ~*-échangiste* (eʃɑ̃ʒist) *m*, f. trader. ~ *parole*, f. speech. ~ *penseur*, freethinker. ~*-service*, self-service.

librettiste (librɛtist) *m*, librettist.

lice (lis) *f*, lists, arena; bitch hound; warp.

licence (lisɑ̃ːs) *f*, license; licentiate's degree; leave; licentiousness. **licencié, e** (sɑ̃sje) *n*, licentiate, bachelor (*laws, arts*); dismissed employee. **licencier** (sje) *v.t*, to disband (*troops*); dismiss, discharge. **licencieux, euse**† (sjø, øːz) *a*, licentious, ribald.

lichen (likɛn) *m*, lichen.

licher (liʃe) *v.t*, to lick; drink; tipple.

licite† (lisit) *a*, licit, lawful.

licorne (likɔrn) *f*, unicorn.

licou (liku) *or poet.*, *before vowel*, **licol** (kɔl) *m*, halter (*harness*).

licteur (liktœːr) *m*, lictor.

lie (li) *f*, lees, dregs; offscourings, scum. **faire chère lie**, to live well.

lié, e (lje) *p.a*, bound, tied; intimate, thick.

liège (ljɛːʒ) *m*, cork.

lien (ljɛ̃) *m*, bond; tie; link; binder; strap. **lier** (lje) *v.t*, to bind; tie

[up]; join; link; knit; connect; enter into; tie (*Mus.*); slur (*Mus.*); thicken (*sauce*).

lierre (ljɛːr) *m*, ivy. ~ *terrestre*, ground i.

lieu (ljø) *m*, place; stead; ground[s], occasion; (*s. & pl.*) spot; (*pl.*) premises. ~*x* [*d'aisance*] ou *petit* ~, watercloset, privy, latrine, john. ~*x communs*, commonplaces (*Rhet. & platitudes*). ~*x de pêche*, where to fish. *au* ~ *de*, instead of, in lieu of. *au* ~ *que*, whereas. *avoir* ~, to take place.

lieue (ljø) *f*, league (= 4 kilometers); mile(s) (*long way*). *d'une* ~, a mile off.

lieur (ljœːr) (*pers.*) *m*. & **lieuse** (øːz) (*Mach.*) *f*, binder (*sheaf*).

lieutenant (ljøtnɑ̃) *m*, lieutenant; mate (*ship*). ~*-colonel*, lieutenant colonel. ~ *de vaisseau*, [naval] lieutenant.

lièvre (ljɛːvr) *m*, hare.

ligament (ligamɑ̃) *m*, ligament. **ligature** (tyːr) *f*, ligature.

lige (liːʒ) *a*. & **vassal** ~, *m*, liege.

lignage (liɲaːʒ) *m*, lineage, descent; linage (*Typ.*).

ligne (liɲ) *f*, line; rank. ~ *d'autobus*, bus route. ~ *de but*, *de touche*, goal, touch, l. (*Foot.*). ~ *de départ*, starting l.; scratch l. ~ *de faite*, watershed. ~ *de flottaison* (flɔtɛzɔ̃), water line (*ship*). ~ *de fond*, *de côté*, *de service*, médiane *de service*, base, side, service, center service, l. (*Ten.*). ~ *supplémentaire*, ledger l. (*Mus.*). *à la* ~, new paragraph. *en* ~, on line (*computers*).

lignée (liɲe) *f*, issue, line, stock.

ligneux, euse (liɲø, øːz) *a*, ligneous, woody. **lignite** (ɲit) *m*, lignite.

ligoter (ligɔte) *v.t*, to bind, lash.

ligue (lig) *f*, league. **liguer** (ge) *v.t*, to l.

lilas (lila) *m*. & *att*, lilac.

lilliputien, ne (lilipysjɛ̃, ɛn) *a*, Lilliputian.

limace (limas) *f*, slug (*Mol.*); Archimedean screw. **limaçon** (sɔ̃) *m*, snail (*Mol.*). *en* ~, spiral, winding.

limaille (limaːj) *f*, filings, dust.

limande (limɑ̃ːd) *f*, dab (*fish*).
limbe (lɛ̃ːb) *m*, limb (*Math*.); (*pl*.) limbo.
lime (lim) *f*, file (*tool*). **limer** (me) *v.t*, to file; polish (*fig*.).
limier (limje) *m*, bloodhound; sleuth-hound.
liminaire (liminɛːr) *a*, prefatory.
limitation (limitasjɔ̃) *f*, limitation. *~des naissances*, birth control. **limite** (mit) *f*, limit; bound-[ary]. *~ des neiges éternelles*, snow line. **limiter** (te) *v.t*, to limit; bound; restrict. **limitrophe** (trɔf) *a*, bordering.
limoger (limɔʒe) *v.t*, to fire (*job*).
limon (limɔ̃) *m*, mud, slime, ooze, silt; clay (*fig*.); string (*stairs*); shaft, thill (*cart*); lime (*citrus*). **limonade** (mɔnad) *f*, lemonade. *~ gazeuse*, carbonated lemonade. *~ non gazeuse*, still lemonade. **limonadier, ère** (dje, ɛːr) *n*, light refreshment caterer, café keeper. **limoneux, euse** (nø, øːz) *a*, muddy, slimy. **limonier** (nje) *m*, lime [tree] (*citrus*).
limousine (limuzin) *f*, limousine.
limpide (lɛ̃pid) *a*, limpid, clear, pellucid.
limure (limyːr) *f*, filing; filings.
lin (lɛ̃) *m*, flax; linen.
linceul (lɛ̃sœl *ou* œːj) *m*, shroud, winding sheet.
linéaire (lineɛːr) *a*, linear; lineal. **linéament** (neamɑ̃) *m*, lineament, feature; outline.
linge (lɛ̃ːʒ) *m*, linen; cloth. *~ à thé*, tea cloth. *~ de table*, table linen. **linger, ère** (lɛ̃ʒe, ɛːr) *n*, lingerie maker; fancy draper; (*f*.) wardrobe keeper. **lingerie** (ʒri) *f*, fancy drapery, lingerie; linen room.
lingot (lɛ̃go) *m*, ingot; slug (*bullet & Typ*.).
lingual, e (lɛ̃gwal) *a. & f*, lingual. **linguiste** (gɥist) *m*, linguist. **linguistique** (tik) *f*, linguistics.
linière (linjɛːr) *a.f*, linen (*industry*). ¶ *f*, flax field.
liniment (linimɑ̃) *m*, liniment.
linoléum (linɔleɔm) *m*, linoleum. *~ imprimé*, printed linoleum, oilcloth. *~ incrusté*, inlaid linoleum.
linon (linɔ̃) *m*, linon; lawn (*fabric*).

linot (lino) *m*, ou **linotte** (nɔt) *f*, linnet.
linotype (linɔtip) *a. & f*, linotype.
linteau (lɛ̃to) *m*, lintel, transom.
lion (ljɔ̃) *m*, lion. *~ marin*, sea l. **lionceau** (so) *m*, l. cub, l. whelp. **lionne** (ɔn) *f*, lioness; fury.
lippe (lip) *f*, thick underlip. *faire la ~*, to pout. **lippu, e** (py) *a*, thick-lipped.
liquéfaction (likefaksjɔ̃) *f*, liquefaction. **liquéfier** (fje) *v.t*, to liquefy. **liqueur** (kœːr) *f*, liquor, drink; solution (*Chem*.). *~ d'ammoniaque*, liquid ammonia, hartshorn. *~ [de dessert]*, liqueur. *~ de ménage*, homemade wine. *~s fortes*, strong drink. *~s fraîches*, nonalcoholic drinks. *~ [spiritueuse]*, spirit.
liquidateur (likidatœːr) *m*, liquidator. **liquidation** (sjɔ̃) *f*, liquidation, winding up; closing; settlement, account (*Stk Ex*.); [liquidation] sale, closing-down sale, selling off.
liquide (likid) *a*, liquid; wet (*goods*). *argent ~*, ready cash. ¶ *m*, liquid; fluid; liquor (*alcoholic*); (*f*.) liquid (*Gram*.).
liquider (likide) *v.t*, to liquidate, wind up; close; settle; pay off; sell off.
liquoreux, euse (likɔrø, øːz) *a*, sweet (*wine*). **liquoriste** (rist) *n*, wine & spirit merchant.
lire (liːr) *v.t. & abs. ir*, to read; hear from.
lis (lis) *m*, lily. *~ tigré*, tiger lily.
Lisbonne (lizbɔn) *f*, Lisbon.
liseré (lizere) *m*, piping (*braid*); border.
liseron (lizrɔ̃) *ou* **liset** (ze) *m*, bindweed.
liseur, euse (lizœːr, øːz) *m*, reader. *~ de pensées*, mind r. ¶ *f*, reading stand; bed jacket. **lisible†** (zibl) *a*, legible; readable (*interesting*).
lisière (lizjɛːr) *f*, selvedge, list; leading-strings; border, edge, skirt.
lisse (lis) *a*, smooth; sleek; plain; flush. ¶ *f*, warp; rail (*ship*). **lisser** (se) *v.t*, to smooth. **lissoir** (swaːr) *m*, smoother.
listage (listaːʒ) *m*, listing (*com-*

puters). **lister** (te) *v.t*, to list (*computers*).

liste (list) *f*, list, roll; panel (*jury*). ~ **des admis**, pass list (*exams*). ~ **électorale**, register of voters.

lit (li) *m*, bed; bedstead; layer; marriage; set (*of tide, etc.*). ~ **à colonnes**, four-poster. ~ **de douleur**, sick bed. **être exposé sur un** ~ **de parade**, to lie in state.

litanie (litani) *f*, rigmarole; (*pl.*) litany.

liteau (lito) *m*, stripe (*on cloth*); runner (*for shelf*); haunt (*wolves'*).

litée (lite) *f*, group (*collection of animals in the same den or lair*).

literie (litri) *f*, bedding.

litharge (litarʒ) *f*, litharge.

lithine (litin) *f*, lithia. **lithium** (tiɔm) *m*, lithium.

lithographe (litɔgraf) *m*, lithographer. **lithographie** (fi) *f*, lithography; lithograph. **lithographier** (fje) *v.t*, to lithograph. **lithographique** (fik) *a*, lithographic.

litière (litjɛːr) *f*, litter (*straw & dung; also palanquin*).

litige (litiːʒ) *m*, litigation; dispute. **litigieux, euse** (tiʒjø, øːz) *a*, litigious; contentious.

litorne (litɔrn) *f*, fieldfare.

litre (litr) *m*, liter. = 1.75980 (about 1¾) pints; liter measure; liter bottle.

littéraire† (literɛːr) *a*, literary. **littéral, e**† (literal) *a*, literal. **littérateur** (literatœːr) *m*, literary man. **littérature** (tyːr) *f*, literature; learning; empty talk.

littoral, e (litɔral) *a*, littoral. ¶ *m*, littoral, seaboard.

Lit[h]uanie (la) (lituani), Lithuania.

liturgie (lityrʒi) *f*, liturgy.

liure (ljyːr) *f*, cart rope.

livide (livid) *a*, livid, ghastly.

Livourne (livurn) *f*, Leghorn.

livrable (livrabl) *a*, deliverable. ¶ (*Com.*) *m*, forward, terminal, [for] shipment; futures, options. **livraison** (vrɛzɔ̃) *f*, delivery; part, number (*publication*).

livre (liːvr) *f*, pound = ½ kilogram; franc. *Note*.—The word *livre* (meaning a present-day

French franc) is still sometimes used, but almost exclusively in literature. ~ (*sterling*), pound [sterling]. **la** ~, sterling, the £.

livre (liːvr) *m*, book; journal; register; diary; day book. **grand** ~, ledger. ~ **à feuille[t]s mobiles**, looseleaf book. ~ **à succès**, ~ **à grand tirage**, bestseller. ~ **s d'agrément**, light reading. ~ **d'exemples**, copybook. ~ **d'images**, picture b. ~ **d'office**, ~ **d'église**, ~ **de prières**, prayer b. ~ **de bord** & ~ **de loch**, log [b.]. ~ **de chevet**, favorite b. ~ **de lecture**, reader. ~ **de signatures**, autograph book. ~ **feint**, dummy book (*for bookshelf*). ~ **généalogique**, stud b.; herd b. ~ **de poche**, paperback book. **à** ~ **ouvert**, at sight. **faire un** ~, to make book (*betting*).

livrée (livre) *f*, livery; servants; badge.

livrer (livre) *v.t*, to deliver; d. up; surrender; consign; commit; confide; join, give (*battle*). ~ **par erreur**, to misdeliver.

livret (livrɛ) *m*, book (*small register*); handbook; libretto. ~ **militaire**, service record.

livreur, euse (livrœːr øːz) *n*, delivery man *or* boy *or* girl.

lobe (lɔb) *m*, lobe.

lobélie (lɔbeli) *f*, lobelia.

local, e† (lɔkal) *a*, local. ¶ *m. oft. pl*, premises. **localiser** (lize) *v.t*, to place; localize. **localité** (te) *f*, locality, place. **locataire** (tɛːr) *n*, tenant, occupier; leaseholder; lodger; renter; hirer. **locatif, ive** (tif, iːv) *a*, tenant's (*repairs*); rental, letting (*value*). **location** (sjɔ̃) *f*, letting, renting, hire; reservation, booking; tenancy.

loch (lɔk) *m*, log (*float—ship's*).

loche (lɔʃ) *f*, loach (*fish*); slug (*Mol.*).

lock-out (lɔkaut) *m*, lockout.

locomobile (lɔkɔmɔbil) *f*, agricultural engine, traction e. **locomoteur, trice** (tœːr, tris) *a*, locomotive. **locomotion** (sjɔ̃) *f*, locomotion. **locomotive** (tiːv) *f*, locomotive, [railway] engine; a hit movie which a theater can acquire only if it also accepts less successful films; an influential person capa-

ble of drawing customers to res-
taurants, clubs, etc.

locuste (lɔkyst) *f*, locust; shrimp,
prawn.

locution (lɔkysjɔ̃) *f*, phrase.

lof (lɔf) *m*, windward side (*ship*);
luff. **lofer** (fe) *v.t*, to luff.

logarithme (lɔgaritm) *m*, logarithm.

loge (lɔ:ʒ) *f*, lodge (*porter's, freemasons'*); loggia; box (*Theat.*);
dressing room (*actor's*); cage
(*menagerie*); loculus. **logeable**
(lɔʒabl) *a*, tenantable, [in]habit-
able. **logement** (ʒmɑ̃) *m*, lodging, housing, billeting; accommodation, quarters. **loger** (ʒe) *v.i.*
& *t*, to lodge, live; stay; accommodate; house; billet; stable. **logeur, euse** (ʒœ:r, ø:z) *n*, landlord, -lady, lodging-house keeper.

logiciel (lɔʒisjɛl) *m*, software
(*computers*).

logicien (lɔʒisjɛ̃) *m*, logician.
logique† (ʒik) *a*, logical. ¶ *f*,
logic.

logis (lɔʒi) *m*, house, home.

loi (lwa) *f*, law; enactment; statute; act; standard (*of coin*). **hors
la ~,** outlaw.

loin (lwɛ̃) *ad*, far, f. away, f. off;
f. back; afar; afield; a long way.
~ de compte, out of one's reckoning, wide of the mark. **lointain, e** (tɛ̃, ɛn) *a*, remote, far off,
distant. ¶ *m*, distance.

loir (lwa:r) *m*, dormouse.

loisible (lwazibl) *a*, permissible.
loisir (zi:r) *m. oft. pl*, leisure,
[spare] time. **à ~,** *ad*, at leisure.

lolo (lolo) *m*, milk (*babytalk*). **les
~s,** women's breasts (*slang*).

lombaire (lɔ̃bɛ:r) *a*, lumbar.

Lombardie (la) (lɔ̃bardi), Lombardy.

lombes (lɔ̃:b) *m.pl*, loins.

londonien, ne (lɔ̃dɔnjɛ̃, ɛn) *a*,
London. **L~,** *n*, Londoner. **Londres** (lɔ̃:dr) *m*, London.

long, ue (lɔ̃, ɔ̃:g) *a*, long; lengthy;
slow, dilatory. *long échange,*
rally (*Ten.*). *à la longue,* in the
long run, in the end. ¶ *m*, length.
au ~, at length, at large. *au ~ &
au large,* far & wide. *de ~,* long
(*Meas.*). *de ~ en large,* to & fro,
up & down. *en ~,* lengthways. *le*

~ de, along; alongside. [*syllabe*]
longue, f, long [syllable].

longanimité (lɔ̃ganimite) *f*,
long-suffering, forbearance.

long-courrier (lɔ̃kurje) *m*,
ocean-going ship. **long cours,** *m*,
deep-sea navigation; ocean (*or
foreign*) voyage.

longe (lɔ̃:ʒ) *f*, lead rope (*attached
to halter*); leading rein; tether;
loin (*veal*).

longer (lɔ̃ʒe) *v.t*, to run along,
skirt.

longévité (lɔ̃ʒevite) *f*, longevity.

longitude (lɔ̃ʒityd) *f*, longitude.
longitudinal, e† (dinal) *a*, longitudinal.

longtemps (lɔ̃tɑ̃) *ad*, long; a
long while. **longuement** (lɔ̃gmɑ̃)
ad, long; lengthily. **longuet, te**
(gɛ, ɛt) *a*, longish. **longueur**
(gœ:r) *f*, length; lengthiness; delay. *en ~,* lengthways; slowly.
longue-vue (lɔ̃gvy) *f*, telescope,
spyglass.

lopette (lɔpɛt) *m*, homosexual
(*slang*).

lopin (lɔpɛ̃) *m*, patch, plot (*of
ground*), allotment.

loquace (lɔkwas) *a*, loquacious,
talkative, garrulous. **loquacité**
(site) *f*, loquacity.

logue (lɔk) *f*, rag, tatter.

loquet (lɔkɛ) *m*, latch (*door*).
loqueteau (kto) *m*, catch (*window*).

loqueteux, euse (lɔktø, ø:z) *a*.
& *n*, ragged (person).

lord (lɔ:r) *m*, lord (*Eng.*).

lorgner (lɔrɲe) *v.t*, to quiz; eye;
ogle, leer at. **lorgnette[s] de spectacle** (ɲɛt) *f*. [*pl*.], opera glass-
[es]. **lorgnon** (ɲɔ̃) *m*, eyeglasses,
pince-nez.

loriot (lɔrjo) *m*, [golden] oriole.

lors (lɔ:r) *ad*, then. **~ de,** at the
time of. **~ même que,** even
though. **lorsque** (lɔrskə) *c*,
when.

losange (lɔzɑ̃:ʒ) (*Geom.*) *m*,
lozenge, rhomb[us]; diamond.

lot (lo) *m*, lot; portion; prize (*lottery*); consignment; kit. **~ de réparation,** repair kit. *gros ~,* jack-
pot. **loterie** (lɔtri) *f*, lottery;
sweepstake[s]; raffle, draw; gamble.

lotion (losjɔ̃) *f*, lotion; washing.

lotir (lɔti:r) *v.t*, to allot, parcel out. *bien loti*, lucky. **lotissement** (tismɑ̃) *m*, allotment; development (*land*).

loto (lɔto) *m*, lotto (*game*).

lotus (lɔty:s) *ou* **lotos** (tɔs) *m*, lotus.

louable (lwabl) *a*, laudable, praiseworthy; deserving of praise.

louage (lwa:ʒ) *m*, letting, renting, hiring; hire.

louange (lwɑ̃:ʒ) *f*, praise; commendation. **louanger** (ɑ̃ʒe) *v.t*, to laud [to the skies].

louche (luʃ) *a*, cross-eyed, squint-[ing]; cloudy; shady, suspicious. ¶ *f*, soup ladle. **loucher** (ʃe) *v.i*, to squint.

louer (lwe) *v.t*, to let [out], rent, hire; reserve, book; praise, laud. *à ~*, to [be] let; for hire. *se ~ de*, to be pleased with. **loueur** (euse) *de chaises* (lwœ:r, ø:z), chair attendant.

loufoque (lufɔk) *a*, screwball, loony. ¶ *m*, screwball, crackpot.

lougre (lu:gr) *m*, lugger (*Naut.*).

louis (lwi) *m*, louis (*old gold coin = 20 present-day francs*).

Louisiane (lwizjan) *f*, Louisiana.

loulou (lulu) *m*, Pomeranian [dog], pom.

loup (lu) *m*, wolf; waster. *loup-cervier* (servje) *m*, [common] lynx (*N. Europe*). *~ de mer* (*pers.*). hard-bitten sailor, old salt, [jack] tar.

loupe (lup) *f*, wen (*Med.*); bur[r] (*on tree*); lens, [magnifying] glass. **louper** (pe) *v.i*, to slack; (*v.t.*) to botch.

loup-garou (lugaru) *m*, werewolf; bugbear; bear (*pers.*).

lourd, e† (lu:r, urd) *a*, heavy; weighty; dull; sluggish; close (*weather*). **lourdaud, e** (lurdo, o:d) *n*, lubber, lout, bumpkin, dolt, fathead, oaf. **lourdeur** (dœ:r) *f*, heaviness.

loustic (lustik) *m*, wag, funny man.

loutre (lutr) *f*, otter.

louve (lu:v) *f*, [she-]wolf; lewis. **louveteau** (luvto) *m*, wolf cub (*Zool. & scouting*).

louvoyer (luvwaje) *v.i*, to tack [about].

lover (lɔve) *v.t*, to coil (*rope*).

loyal, e† (lwajal) *a*, honest, straight[forward]; fair; true, loyal. **loyalisme** (lism) *m*, loyalty, allegiance (*to sovereign*); loyalism. **loyaliste** (list) *a. & n*, loyalist. **loyauté** (jote) *f*, honesty, etc.

loyer (lwaje) *m*, rent; hire; price; wages.

lubie (lybi) *f*, whim, crotchet, vagary, fad, kink.

lubricité (lybrisite) *f*, lubricity, lewdness. **lubrifier** (fje) *v.t*, to lubricate, grease. **lubrique** (brik) *a*, lewd, wanton.

lucarne (lykarn) *f*, dormer [window].

lucide (lysid) *a*, lucid, clear. **lucidité** (dite) *f*, lucidity.

luciole (lysjɔl) *f*, firefly; glowworm.

Lucques (lyk) *f*, Lucca.

lucratif, ive (lykratif, i:v) *a*, lucrative. **lucre** (lykr) *m*, lucre, pelf, gain.

luette (lɥɛt) *f*, uvula.

lueur (lɥœ:r) *f*, glimmer; gleam; glimpse; spark.

luge (ly:ʒ) *f*, luge. **luger** (lyʒe) *v.i*, to luge.

lugubre† (lygy:br) *a*, lugubrious, doleful, gloomy.

lui, leur (lɥi, lœ:r) *pn*, [to] him, her, it, them; at him, etc.

lui, eux (lɥi, ø) *pn.m*, he, it, they; him, it, them. *lui-même, eux-mêmes*, himself, itself, themselves.

luire (lɥi:r) *v.i.ir*, to shine, gleam. **luisant, e** (lɥizɑ̃, ɑ̃:t) *a*, shining, gleaming; bright; glossy. ¶ *m*, shine, gloss, sheen.

lumbago (lɔ̃bago) *m*, lumbago.

lumière (lymjɛ:r) *f*, light; luminary (*pers.*); [port] hole; oil hole; spout hole; hole; vent; mouth; throat; (*pl.*) understanding, insight; (*pl.*) enlightenment. *~-éclair*, flash (*Phot.*). *~ magnésique* (maɲezik), magnesium light. **lumignon** (miɲɔ̃) *m*, snuff (*wick*); candle end; dim light. **luminaire** (nɛ:r) *m*, luminary; light; lights; lights. **lumineux,**

euseɣ (nø, ǿːz) *a*, luminous; bright.

lunaire (lynɛːr) *a*, lunar. ¶ *f*, honesty (*Bot.*).

lunatique (lynatik) *a*. & *n*, whimsical (person).

lundi (lœ̃di) *m*, Monday.

lune (lyn) *f*, moon; arse (*slang*). ~ *de miel*, honeymoon; threshold (*fig.*). *clair de* ~, moonlight.

lunetier (lyntje) *m*, spectacle maker, optician. **lunette** (nɛt) *f*, (*pl.*) glasses, goggles; wishing bone; rim (*watch*). ~ [*d'approche*], [refracting] telescope. ~ *de repère*, finder. ~*s en écaille*, horn-rimmed spectacles. ~ *arrière*, rear window (*auto*).

lupin (lypɛ̃) *m*, lupin[e] (*Bot.*).

lupus (lypyːs) *m*, lupus.

lurette (lyrɛt) *f*: *il y a belle* ~ *que*, it is ages since.

luron (lyrɔ̃) *m*, jolly sturdy fellow. **luronne** (rɔn) *f*, jovial stout-hearted woman.

lusin (lyzɛ̃) *m*, marline.

lustre (lystr) *m*, luster; gloss; foil (*fig.*); chandelier. **lustrer** (tre) *v.t*, to luster; gloss; glaze.

lut (lyt) *m*, lute (*cement*). **luter** (te) *v.t*, to lute.

luth (lyt) *m*, lute (*Mus.*). **lutherie** (tri) *f*, musical instrument making.

luthérien, ne (lyterjɛ̃, ɛn) *a*. & *n*, Lutheran.

luthier (lytje) *m*, musical instrument maker.

lutin, e (lytɛ̃, in) *a*, roguish, impish. ¶ *m*, [hob]goblin, sprite, elf, imp. **lutiner** (tine) *v.t*. & *i*, to plague, tease.

lutrin (lytrɛ̃) *m*, lectern, reading desk.

lutte (lyt) *f*, wrestling; struggle; fight, contest, tussle, fray. ~ *à la corde*, tug of war. ~ *libre*, no holds barred. **lutter** (te) *v.i*, to wrestle; struggle, fight, contend; vie. **lutteur** (tœːr) *m*, wrestler.

luxation (lyksasjɔ̃) *f*, dislocation (*Surg.*).

luxe (lyks) *m*, luxury; sumptuousness; profusion.

Luxembourg (lyksɑ̃buːr) *m*, Luxemburg.

luxer (lykse) *v.t*, to dislocate.

luxueux, euse (lyksɥø, ǿːz) *a*, luxurious. **luxure** (ksyːr) *f*, lust. **luxuriant, e** (ksyrjɑ̃, ɑ̃ːt) *a*, luxuriant, lush, rank. **luxurieux, euse** (rjø, ǿːz) *a*, lustful, lewd.

luzerne (lyzɛrn) *f*, alfalfa.

lycée (lise) *m*, secondary school. **lycéen, ne** (seɛ̃, ɛn) *n*, student (*at a lycée*), schoolboy, -girl.

lymphe (lɛ̃ːf) *f*, lymph; sap.

lyncher (lɛ̃ʃe) *v.t*, to lynch.

lynx (lɛ̃ːks) *m*, lynx.

lyophiliser (ljɔfilize) *v.t*, to freeze-dry.

Lyon (ljɔ̃) *m*, Lyons.

lyre (liːr) *f*, lyre. & *toute la* ~, & all the rest of it. **lyrique** (lirik) *a*, lyric; lyrical; opera (*house*). ¶ *m*, lyric poet. **lyrisme** (rism) *m*, lyricism.

M

ma *see* **mon**.

maboul, e (mabul) *a*, nutty, cracked. ¶ *n*, loon, madman, idiot.

mac (mak) *m*, pimp (*slang*).

macab (makab) *m*, corpse (*slang*).

macabre (makɑːbr) *a*, macabre; grim, gruesome, ghastly.

macadam (makadam) *m*, macadam. **macadamiser** (mize) *v.t*, to macadamize.

macaque (makak) *m*, macaco, macaque.

macareux (makarø) *m*, puffin.

macaron (makarɔ̃) *m*, macaroon.

macaroni (makarɔni) *m*, macaroni.

macchabée (makabe) *m*, corpse (*slang*).

macédoine (masedwan) *f*, macédoine, salad (*fruit*); medley.

macérer (masere) *v.t*, to macerate.

mâchefer (mɑʃfɛːr) *m*, clinker.

mâcher (mɑʃe) *v.t*, to chew; masticate; champ (*bit*). *ne pas le* ~, not to mince matters. **mâcheur, euse** (ʃœːr, ǿːz) *n*, chewer.

machiavélique (makjavelik) *a*, Machiavellian.

machin (maʃɛ̃) *m*, thing, gadget; what's-his-name.

machinal, e† (maʃinal) *a*, mechanical (*fig.*). **machination** (sjɔ̃) *f*, machination. **machine** (ʃin) *f*, machine; (*pl.*) machinery; engine; gadget. ~ *à coudre*, sewing machine. ~ *à écrire*, typewriter. ~ *à vapeur*, steam engine. ~*-outil*, *f*, machine tool. ~ *routière*, traction engine. **machiner** (ne) *v.t*, to scheme, plot. **machinerie** (nri) *f*, machinery; engine room, e. house. **machinisme** (nism) *m*, mechanization. **machiniste** (nist) *m*, scene shifter; engineer; bus driver; stagehand, grip, dolly man.

mâchoire (maʃwaːr) *f*, jaw.

mâchonner (maʃɔne) *v.t*, to chew; mumble.

mâchurer (maʃyre) *v.t*, to black, smudge.

macis (masi) *m*, mace (*spice*).

macle (makl) *f*, twin (*crystal*).

maçon (masɔ̃) *m*, mason; bricklayer. **maçonnage** (sɔnaːʒ) *m*, masonry; brickwork. **maçonner** (ne) *v.t*, to mason; brick up. **maçonnerie** (nri) *f*, masonry; stonework; brickwork. **maçonnique** (nik) *a*, masonic.

macule (makyl) *f*, spot, stain; sun spot, macula. **maculer** (lɘ) *v.t. & i*, to stain; offset (*Typ.*).

madame, *oft.* **M~** (madam) *f*, madam; Mrs.; mistress; lady.

madeleine (madlɛn) *f*, sponge cake.

mademoiselle, *oft.* **M~** (madmwazɛl) *f*, Miss; lady; waitress!

Madère (madɛːr) *f*, Madeira.

madone (madɔn) *f*, madonna.

madras (madrɑ[ːs]) *m*, madras (*fabric*).

madré, e (madre) *a*, speckled, spotted; bird's-eye (*maple*); crafty, deep.

madrépore (madrepoːr) *m*, madrepore.

madrier (madrie) *m*, plank.

madrigal (madrigal) *m*, madrigal.

mafflu, e (mafly) *a*, heavy-cheeked.

magasin (magazɛ̃) *m*, shop; store[s]; warehouse; magazine. ~ *à prix unique*, one-price shop; five and ten. ~ *à succursales multiples*, chain store. ~ *général*, bonded warehouse. *en ~*, in stock. **magasinage** (zinaːʒ) *m*, warehousing, storage. **magasinier** (nje) *m*, storekeeper, warehouseman. **magazine** (zin) *m*, magazine (*periodical*).

mages (maːʒ) *m.pl*, Magi.

magicien, ne (maʒisjɛ̃, ɛn) *n*, magician; wizard; sorcerer. **magie** (ʒi) *f*, magic, wizardry; witchery. ~ *noire*, black magic. b. art. **magique** (ʒik) *a*, magic(al).

magister (maʒistɛːr) *m*, pedagogue. **magistère** (tɛːr) *m*, dictatorship. **magistral, e†** (tral) *a*, magisterial; masterly; masterful. **magistrat** (tra) *m*, magistrate; judge. **magistrature** (tyːr) *f*, magistracy. ~ *assise*, bench. ~ *debout*, body of public prosecutors.

magnanerie (maɲanri) *f*, silkworm nursery; s. breeding.

magnanime† (maɲanim) *a*, magnanimous. **magnanimité** (mite) *f*, magnanimity.

magnat (magna) *m*, magnate (*Fin., etc.*).

magnésie (maɲezi) *f*, magnesia. **magnésium** (zjɔm) *m*, magnesium.

magnétique (maɲetik) *a*, magnetic; mesmeric. **magnétisation** (zasjɔ̃) *f*, magnetization (*Phys.*). **magnétiser** (ze) *v.t*, to mesmerize, magnetize (*fig.*). **magnétiseur** (zœːr) *m*, mesmerizer. **magnétisme** (tism) *m*, magnetism (*Phys. & fig.*); magnetics; mesmerism. **magnéto** (to) *f*, magneto. ~*-électrique, a*, magneto-electric.

magnétophone (maɲetɔfɔn) *m*, tape recorder.

magnificat (magnifikat) *m*, magnificat.

magnificence (maɲifisɑ̃ːs) *f*, magnificence; grandeur; (*pl.*) lavishness; (*pl.*) fine things. **magnifier** (fje) *v.t*, to magnify (*the Lord*). **magnifique†** (fik) *a*, magnificent, splendid, grand, fine; munificent.

magnolia (magnɔlja) *m*, magnolia.

magot (mago) *m*, magot (*ape &*

Chinese figure); Barbary ape; fright (*pers.*); hoard.

mahométan, e (maɔmetɑ̃, an) *n, & att,* Mohammedan, Moslem, Muslim. **mahométisme** (tism) *m,* Mohammedanism.

mai (mɛ) *m,* May (*month*); maypole.

maigre (mɛ:gr) *a,* lean; meager; scanty; thin; skinny; straggling (*beard*); poor; spare; meatless (*meal*); fast (*day*); vegetable (*soup*). ¶ *m,* lean. **maigrelet, te** (mɛgrəlɛ, ɛt) *a,* thinnish, slight. **maigrement** (grəmɑ̃) *ad,* meagerly, scantily. **maigreur** (grœ:r) *f,* leanness. **maigrir** (gri:r) *v.i,* to grow thin; (*v.t.*) to [make] thin.

maille (mɑ:j) *f,* stitch (*Knit., crochet, etc.*); mesh; speckle; bud; (*pl.*) mail (*armor*). ~ échappée, ~ perdue, run (*stocking*); dropped stitch (*Knit.*). ~ glissée, slip stitch (*Knit.*).

maillechort (majʃɔ:r) *m,* German silver.

maillet (majɛ) *m,* mallet. **mailloche** (jɔʃ) *f,* mallet, maul.

maillon (majɔ̃) *m,* link (*chain*); shackle.

maillot (majo) *m,* swaddling clothes (*baby*); tights, *or* any close-fitting woven garment, as bathing suit, football jersey, leotard. *le* ~ *jaune,* yellow jersey worn by Tour de France leader.

main (mɛ̃) *f,* hand; hand[writing]; handle (*drawer*); scoop; tendril; quire (*in Fr.* 25 *sheets*); trick (*cards*); lead (*cards*); deal (*cards*). ~ *courante,* handrail. ~-*d'œuvre,* workmanship; labor. ~-*forte,* assistance (to police).

mainmise (mɛ̃mi:z) *f,* hold (*influence*).

mainmorte (mɛ̃mɔrt) *f,* mortmain. *biens de* ~, property in mortmain.

maint, e (mɛ̃, ɛ̃:t) *a,* many a, many.

maintenant (mɛ̃tnɑ̃) *ad,* now. **maintenir** (tni:r) *v.t.ir,* to maintain, keep; uphold. *se* ~, to keep; hold one's own. **maintien** (tjɛ̃) *m,* maintenance, keeping; deportment, bearing.

maïolique (maɔlik) *f,* majolica.

maire (mɛ:r) *m,* mayor. **mairie** (mɛri) *f,* mayoralty; town hall, town clerk's office, registry [office].

mais (mɛ) *c. & ad,* but; why. ~ *non!* why no! not at all! ¶ *m,* but, objection.

maïs (mais) *m,* maize, Indian corn.

maison (mɛzɔ̃) *f,* house; home; household; firm; friary; convent. ~ *d'aliénés,* mental institution. ~ *d'arrêt,* prison, jail; lockup; guardhouse. ~ *d'éducation,* educational establishment. ~ *d'habitation,* dwelling house. ~ *de commerce,* business house, firm. ~ *de correction,* reformatory. ~ *de jeu,* gaming house. ~ *de plaisance,* weekend cottage. ~ *de rapport,* revenue-earning house. ~ *de retraite,* home for the aged. ~ *de santé,* nursing home. ~ *de ville,* town hall. ~ *des étudiants,* hostel. ~ *isolée,* detached house. ~ *jumelle,* semi-detached house. ~ *pour fournitures* (de sports, *etc.*), outfitter. *à la* ~, [at] home, indoors. **maisonnée** (zɔne) *f,* household, family. **maisonnette** (nɛt) *f,* bungalow.

maistrance (mɛstrɑ̃:s) *f,* petty officers (*Nav.*). **maître** (mɛ:tr) *m,* master; teacher; Mr. (*courtesy title of lawyers*); petty officer. ~-*autel,* high altar. ~ *chanteur,* blackmailer. ~-*coq,* cook (*ship's*). ~ *d'armes,* fencing master. ~ [*d'équipage*], boatswain; master of the hounds. ~ *d'hôtel,* [house] steward; headwaiter; superintendent (*restaurant*). ~ *de chapelle,* choirmaster. ~ *de conférences,* lecturer. ~ *de forges,* ironmaster. ~ *de timonerie,* quartermaster (*Naut.*). ~ *des cérémonies,* Master of the Ceremonies. ~ *drain,* main drain. ~ *homme,* masterful man. ~ *Jacques,* Jack of all work *or* trades. ~ *sot,* champion idiot. **maîtresse** (mɛtrɛs) *f,* mistress; paramour. ~ *de piano,* piano teacher. ~ *femme,* masterful woman. ~ *poutre,* main beam. **maîtrise** (tri:z) *f,* mastery; control; choir. **maîtriser** (trize) *v.t*, to [over]master; overpower; subdue; control.

majesté (maʒɛste) *f*, majesty; stateliness. *Sa M~*, His (*or* Her) Majesty. **majestueux, euse†** (tɥø, øːz) *a*, majestic; stately.

majeur, e (maʒœːr) *a*, major; greater. *être ~*, to come of [full] age (*law*). *le lac Majeur*, Lago Maggiore.

majolique (maʒɔlik) *f*, majolica.

major (maʒɔːr) (*Mil.*) *m*, adjutant; medical officer. *état~*, staff. **majoration** (ʒɔrasjɔ̃) *f*, increase (*price*); overvaluation; overcharge. **majordome** (dɔm), majordomo; comptroller of the Royal Household. **majorer** (re) *v.t*, to increase (*price*); overvalue; overcharge for *or* in. **majorité** (rite) *f*, majority.

Majorque (maʒɔrk) *f*, Majorca.

majuscule (maʒyskyl) *a. & f*, capital (letter).

mal (mal) *m*, evil; ill; wrong; harm; hurt; mischief; difficulty; damage; pain; ache; sore; ailment; trouble; disease; illness, sickness. *j'ai ~ au doigt*, I have a sore finger. *~ aux yeux*, *~ d'yeux*, eye trouble, sore eyes. *~ blanc*, gathering sore. *~ d'enfant*, labor [pains]. *~ de cœur*, sickness, qualms. *~ de dents*, *~ aux dents*, toothache. *~ de gorge*, sore throat. *~ de mer*, seasickness. *avoir le ~ de mer*, to be seasick. *~ de tête*, headache. *~ du pays*, homesickness. **¶** *ad*, ill; badly; evil; wrong; amiss. *~ famé, e*, ill-famed. *~ gérer*, to mismanage. *~ réussir*, to fail, turn out badly. *mal venu, e*, stunted; ill-advised. *de ~ en pis*, from bad to worse. *~ ¶ a. inv*, bad.

malachite (malakit) *f*, malachite.

malade (malad) *a*, ill, sick, unwell; diseased; bad, sore; in a bad way. **¶** *n*, sick person; invalid; patient. *~ du dehors*, outpatient. *~ interné, e*, in-patient. *faire le ~ ou simuler la maladie*, to malinger. **maladie** (di) *f*, illness, sickness, complaint, disease, disorder; obsession. *~ de lan-*

gueur, decline. *~ [des chiens]*, distemper. *~ du sommeil*, sleeping sickness. *~ professionnelle*, industrial disease. **maladif, ive** (dif, iːv) *a*, sickly; morbid.

maladresse (maladrɛs) *f*, awkwardness, clumsiness. **maladroit, e†** (drwa, at) *a. & n*, awkward, clumsy (person), maladroit.

malais, e (malɛ, ɛːz) *a. & M~, n*, Malay[an].

malaise (malɛːz) *m*, indisposition; uneasiness; straits. **malaisé, e** (leze) *a*, difficult; not easy; awkward. **malaisément** (mɑ̃) *ad*, with difficulty.

Malaisie (la) (malɛzi), Malaysia.

malandrin (malɑ̃drɛ̃) *m*, bandit.

malappris, e (malapri, iːz) *a. & n*, ill-bred (person).

malaria (malarja) *f*, malaria.

malart (malaːr) *m*, mallard.

malavisé, e (malavize) *a*, ill-advised; unwise.

malaxer (malakse) *v.t*, to mix; work up (*butter*).

malbâti, e (malbati) *a. & n*, misshapen (person).

malchance (malʃɑ̃ːs) *f*, ill luck; mischance. **malchanceux, euse** (ʃɑ̃sø, øːz) *a. & n*, unlucky (person).

maldonne (maldɔn) *f*, misdeal (*cards*); mistake, misunderstanding.

mâle (mɑːl) *m. & a*, male; he; cock; buck; bull; dog; man (*child*); masculine; manly, virile.

malédiction (malediksjɔ̃) *f*, malediction, curse.

maléfice (malefis) *m*, [evil] spell. **maléfique** (malefik) *a*, maleficent. *étoile ~*, unlucky star.

malencontreux, euse† (malɑ̃kɔ̃trø, øːz) *a*, untoward, unlucky, unfortunate.

mal-en-point (malɑ̃pwɛ̃) *ad*, in a bad way, in a sorry plight.

malentendu (malɑ̃tɑ̃dy) *m*, misunderstanding, misapprehension, misconception.

malfaçon (malfasɔ̃) *f*, bad workmanship.

malfaisant, e (malfəzɑ̃, ɑ̃ːt) *a*, malicious; injurious. **malfaiteur** (fɛtœːr) *m*, malefactor, evil-doer. ~ *public*, public menace (*pers.*).

malfamé, e (malfame) *a*, ill-famed.

malformation (malfɔrmasjɔ̃) *f*, malformation.

malgracieux, euse (malgrasjø, φ:z) *a*, ungracious, rude.

malgré (malgre) *pr*, in spite of, notwithstanding. ~ *tout*, for all that.

malhabile† (malabil) *a*, unskillful; tactless.

malheur (malœːr) *m*, misfortune; ill luck; unhappiness; evil days; woe. **malheureux, euse†** (lœrø, φ:z) *a*, unlucky; unfortunate; unhappy, miserable; woeful; sad; wretched; pitiful. ¶ *n*, unfortunate [person]; wretch.

malhonnête† (malɔnɛ:t) *a*, dishonest; rude, ill-mannered, unmannerly. **malhonnêteté** (nɛtte) *f*, dishonesty; rudeness.

malice (malis) *f*, malice, spite; artfulness; roguishness; practical joke. **malicieux, euse†** (sjø, φ:z) *a*, malicious, spiteful; roguish, arch.

malignité (maliɲite) *f*, malignity; maliciousness; mischievousness (*playful*). **malin, igne†** (lɛ̃, iɲ) *a. & n*, malicious; malignant; evil (*spirit*); mischievous, wicked, roguish; artful (person). *le malin* [*esprit*], the Evil One.

maline (malin) *f*, spring tide.

malines (malin) *f*, Mechlin [lace].

malingre (malɛ̃:gr) *a*, sickly, puny.

malintentionné, e (malɛ̃tɑ̃sjɔne) *a. & n*, evil-disposed (person).

malitorne (malitɔrn) *m*, lout.

mal-jugé (malʒyʒe) *m*, miscarriage of justice.

malle (mal) *f*, trunk; mail (*post*); mail steamer, m. boat, m. packet. ~*-armoire*, wardrobe trunk. ~ *de paquebot*, ~ *de cabine*, cabin t. ~*[-poste]*, mail [coach] (*stage*). *se faire la* ~, to take off on the sly.

malléable (malleabl) *a*, malleable.

malléole (malleɔl) *f*, ankle [bone].

malletier (maltje) *m*, trunk &

bag manufacturer. **mallette** (lɛt) *f*, suitcase; attaché c. ~ *garnie*, dressing c., fitted c.

malmener (malmøne) *v.t*, to abuse; maul, handle roughly.

malotru, e (malɔtry) *n*, ill-bred person.

malpeigné (malpɛɲe) *m*, unkempt fellow.

malpropre† (malprɔpr) *a*, dirty; indecent. **malpropreté** (prøte) *f*, dirtiness, etc.

malsain, e (malsɛ̃, ɛn) *a*, unhealthy; noisome; unwholesome; insanitary, unsanitary.

malséant, e (malseɑ̃, ɑ̃:t) *a*, unbecoming, unseemly.

malsonnant, e (malsɔnɑ̃, ɑ̃:t) *a*, offensive (*words*).

malt (malt) *m*, malt.

maltais, e (maltɛ, ɛ:z) *a. & M~, n*, Maltese. **Malte** (malt) *f*, Malta.

malterie (maltəri) *f*, malting, malt house.

maltôte (maltoːt) *f*, extortion (*taxes*).

maltraiter (maltrɛte) *v.t*, to maltreat, ill-treat, ill-use, misuse; wrong.

malveillance (malvɛjɑ̃:s) *f*, malevolence, ill will, spite. **malveillant, e** (jɑ̃, ɑ̃:t) *a. & n*, malevolent, ill-disposed (person).

malvenu, e (malvəny) *a*, stunted; ill-advised.

malversation (malvɛrsasjɔ̃) *f*, malpractice, embezzlement, peculation.

mamamouchi (mamamuʃi) *m*, panjandrum.

maman (ma- *ou* mɑ̃mɑ̃) *f*, mama.

mamelle (mamɛl) *f*, breast; udder. **mamelon** (ml5) *m*, nipple, teat; hummock, mamelon, pap.

mamel[o]uk (mamluk) *m*, Mameluke (*Hist.*); henchman, myrmidon.

mamillaire (mamillɛːr) *a*, mamillary.

mammifère (mamifɛːr) *m*, mammal, (*pl.*) mammalia.

mammouth (mamut) *m*, mammoth.

mamours (mamuːr) *m.pl*, caresses, billing & cooing.

manant (manɑ̃) *m*, boor, churl.

manche (mɑ̃:ʃ) *m*, handle, helve,

haft; stick (*umbrella*); neck (*violin*); knuckle [bone] (*mutton*). ~ *à balai*, broomstick. ¶ *f*, sleeve; hose (*pipe*); channel; game, hand (*cards*); set (*Ten.*). ~ *à air*, ~ *à vent*, ventilator (*ship*). ~ *de chemise*, shirt sleeve. **la M~**, the [English] Channel. **manchette** (mãʃɛt) *f*, cuff (*dress*); ruffle; headline (*news*). **manchon** (ʃɔ̃) *m*, muff (*ladies'*); coupling (*Mach.*); sleeve; socket; bush[ing]; mantle (*gas*). ~ *d'embrayage*, clutch.

manchot, e (mãʃo, ɔt) *a. & n*, one-handed *or* one-armed (person); (*m.*) penguin.

mandant (mãdã) *m*, principal, mandator.

mandarin (mãdarɛ̃) *m*, mandarin. **mandarine** (rin) *f*, mandarin[e] [orange], tangerine [orange].

mandat (mãda) *m*, mandate; order; instructions; trust; procuration, power [of attorney], proxy; order [to pay], money order, withdrawal notice; writ, warrant (*law*). ~[*-poste*], money order, postal o. **mandataire** (tɛːr) *m*, mandatary, -ory; agent; attorney; proxy. **mandater** (te) *v.t*, to authorize [the payment of]; commission.

mandement (mãdmã) *m*, charge, pastoral letter. **mander** (de) *v.t*, to tell; inform.

mandibule (mãdibyl) *f*, mandible; jaw.

mandoline (mãdɔlin) *f*, mandolin.

mandragore (mãdragoːr) *f*, mandrake.

mandrill (mãdril) *m*, mandrill (*Zool.*).

mandrin (mãdrɛ̃) *m*, mandrel, -il; spindle; arbor; chuck (*lathe*); drift[pin].

manège (manɛːʒ) *m*, training (*horses*); horsemanship, riding; r. school; horse gear; trick. ~ *de chevaux de bois*, merry-go-round.

mânes (mɑːn) *m.pl*, manes, shades.

manette (manɛt) *f*, handle, lever.

manganèse (mãganɛːz) *m*, manganese.

mangeable (mãʒabl) *a*, eatable. **mangeaille** (ʒɑːj) *f*, food, feed. **mangeoire** (ʒwaːr) *f*, manger, crib. **manger** (ʒe) *v.t. & abs*, to eat; feed; have one's meals, mess; eat up; devour; squander; clip (*one's words*). ~ *le morceau*, to turn stoolpigeon. ¶ *m*, food. **mangetout** (mãʒtu) *m*, spendthrift; skinless pea *or* bean. **mangeur, euse** (ʒœːr, øːz) *n*, eater, feeder. **mangeure** (ʒyːr) *f*, bite (*place bitten by worm, mouse*).

manglier (mãglie) *m*, mangrove. **mangouste** (mãgust) *f*, mongoose.

mangue (mãːg) *f*, mango. **manguier** (mãgje) *m*, mango [tree].

maniable (manjabl) *a*, supple; manageable; handy.

maniaque (manjak) *a*, maniac(al). ¶ *n*, maniac; faddist, crank. **manie** (ni) *f*, mania; craze; fad.

maniement (manimã) *m*, feeling; handling; management, conduct, care. ~ *des* (ou *d'*)*armes*, manual [exercise], rifle drill. **manier** (nje) *v.t*, to feel; handle; wield; work; ply; manage, conduct. *au* ~, by the feel.

manière (manjɛːr) *f*, manner, way, wise; sort, kind; mannerism; style; (*pl.*) manners (*bearing*). *par* ~ *d'acquit*, perfunctorily. ~ *noire*, mezzotint. **maniéré, e** (jere) *a*, affected, finical; mannered (*style, etc.*). **maniérisme** (rism) *m*, mannerism.

manieur (manjœːr) *m*, one who knows how to handle (*money, men*).

manifestant, e (manifɛstã, ãːt) *n*, demonstrator (*Pol., etc.*). **manifestation** (tasjɔ̃) *f*, manifestation; demonstration. **manifeste†** (fɛst) *a*, manifest, obvious, overt. ¶ *m*, manifesto; manifest (*Ship.*). **manifester** (te) *v.t*, to manifest, show; (*v.i.*) to demonstrate.

manigance (manigãːs) *f*, intrigue. **manigancer** (gãse). *v.t*, to concoct, plot.

manille (maniːj) *m*, Manila [cheroot]; (*f.*) shackle. **M~**, *f*, Manila (*Geog.*).

manioc (manjɔk) *m*, manioc.

manipuler (manipyle) *v.t*, to manipulate, handle.

manitou (manitu) *m*, big shot, boss (*slang*). *être le ~ de l'affaire*, to be in charge of the operation.

manivelle (manivɛl) *f*, crank; handle, winch.

manne (man) *f*, manna; basket, hamper.

mannequin (mankɛ̃) *m*, lay figure, manikin; dress stand; display figure, d. model; dummy; mannequin, model; puppet; basket.

manœuvre (manœːvr) *f*, working, handling, manipulation; shunting (*Rly.*); seamanship; maneuver; move; (*pl.*) field day; rope (*Naut.*); (*pl.*) rigging (*Naut.*); (*pl.*) scheming. *~s électorales*, electioneering. *~s frauduleuses*, swindling (*law*). ¶ *m*, laborer; hack [writer, etc.]. **manœuvrer** (nœvre) *v.t. & i*, to work, handle, manipulate; shunt; steer (*Ship.*); maneuver. **manœuvrier** (vrie) *m*, (*skillful*) seaman; maneuverer; tactician.

manoir (manwaːr) *m*, manor [house], country seat.

manomètre (manɔmɛtr) *m*, [pressure] gauge, manometer.

manquant, e (mɑ̃kɑ̃, ɑ̃ːt) *a*, missing; absent. ¶ *m*, deficiency, shortage. *~ à l'appel*, A.W.O.L. (*Mil.*). **manque** (mɑ̃ːk) *m*, want, lack, shortage, deficiency; breach; dropped stitch (*Knit.*); run. *~ de pose*, underexposure (*Phot.*). **manqué, e** (mɑ̃ke) *p.a*, missed; spoiled; misfit (*att.*); unsuccessful; abortive; wasted. *un peintre, etc., manqué*, a failure as a painter, etc. Cf. *garçon ~ & grand homme ~*. **manquer** (ke) *v.i*, to fail; miss; default; misfire, miss fire; be taken [away] (*die*); be wanting; be missing; be disrespectful; (*v.t.*) to miss; fail in. *~ de*, to want, lack, run short (*or* out) of; be out of stock of; to nearly . . . *~ de parole*, to break one's word.

mansarde (mɑ̃sard) *f*, dormer [window]; attic, garret.

mansuétude (mɑ̃sɥetyd) *f*, meekness; forbearance.

mante (mɑ̃ːt) *f*, mantle. **manteau** (mɑ̃to) *m*, coat, cloak, mantle, wrap. *~ de cheminée*, mantelpiece. *~ de cour*, court train. *~ de fourrure*, fur coat. *sous [le ~ de] la cheminée*, sub rosa, under the rose. *sous le ~ de la religion*, under the cloak of religion. **mantelet** (tlɛ) *m*, tippet; mantelet; port lid (*Nav.*). **mantille** (tiːj) *f*, mantilla.

Mantoue (mɑ̃tu) *f*, Mantua.

manucure (manykyːr) *n*, manicurist (*pers.*); (*f.*) manicure (*treatment*); m. set.

manuel, le† (manɥɛl) *a*, manual, hand (*as work*). ¶ *m*, manual, handbook; text book.

manufacture (manyfaktyːr) *f*, manufactory; staff. **manufacturier, ère** (tyrje, ɛːr) *a*, manufacturing. ¶ *m*, manufacturer.

manuscrit, e (manyskri, it) *a*, manuscript, written. ¶ *m*, manuscript.

manutention (manytɑ̃sjɔ̃) *f*, handling; commissary, post exchange; bakehouse (*Mil.*). *~s maritimes*, stevedoring.

mappemonde (mapmɔ̃ːd) *f*, map of the world in hemispheres. *~ céleste*, map of the heavens in hemispheres.

maquereau (makro) *m*, mackerel; pimp.

maquette (makɛt) *f*, model (*of statuary*); dummy (*publishing*).

maquignon (makiɲɔ̃) *m*, horse dealer; jobber (*shady*). **maquignonnage** (ɲɔnaːʒ) *m*, horse dealing; jobbery. **maquignonner** (ne) *v.t*, to bishop (*horses*); manipulate (*bad sense*).

maquillage (makijaːʒ) *m*, making up; makeup. **maquiller** (je) *v.t*, to make up (*face*); camouflage. **maquilleur, euse** (œːr, øːz) *n*, makeup artist.

maquis (maki) *m*, scrub; resistance (*war*).

marabout (marabu) *m*, marabout; marabou.

maraîcher (marɛʃe) *m*, truck gardener. **marais** (rɛ) *m*, marsh, swamp, bog, fen, morass. *~ salant*, saltern.

marasme (marasm) *m*, marasmus; stagnation.

marasquin (maraskɛ̃) *m*, maraschino.

marâtre (marɑːtr) f, [cruel] stepmother.

maraudage (maroda:ʒ) m. & **maraude** (ro:d) f, marauding, foray; pilfering. *en maraude*, cruising (*taxi*). **marauder** (rode) v.i, to maraud, raid; cruise (*taxi*). **maraudeur** (dœːr) m, marauder; petty thief; cabdriver in search of fares.

marbre (marbr) m, marble; [marble] slab *or* top; [imposing] stone; bed (*printing press*); [engineer's] surface plate; overset, overmatter (*newspaper work*). ~ *de foyer*, hearthstone. **marbrer** (bre) v.t, to marble; mottle. **marbrerie** (brəri) f, marble work; m. works. **marbreur** (brœːr) m, marbler. **marbrier** (brie) m, marble mason; monumental mason; marble merchant. **marbrière** (briɛːr) f, marble quarry. **marbrure** (bryːr) f, marbling.

marc (maːr) m, marc (*fruit refuse*); grounds (*coffee*); used leaves (*tea*). *au ~ le franc*, pro rata, proportionally, in proportion.

marcassin (markasɛ̃) m, young wild boar.

marcassite (markasit) f, marcasite.

marchand, e (marʃɑ̃, ɑ̃ːd) n, dealer, trader, merchant; shopkeeper, tradesman, -woman, vender; (*att.*) merchant[able], mercantile, commercial, market[able], salable, sale (*att.*) ~ *de journaux*, newsagent. ~ *de volaille*, poulterer. ~ *des quatre saisons*, fruit and vegetable pedlar. ~ *en magasin*, warehouseman. **marchandage** (ʃɑ̃da:ʒ) m, bargaining, haggling. **marchander** (de) v.t. & abs, to haggle (over), bargain, palter; grudge; (*v.i.*) to hesitate. **marchandeur, euse** (dœːr, øːz) n, haggler, bargainer. **marchandise** (diːz) f. oft. pl, goods, merchandise, wares; commodity; cargo. ~*s d'occasion*, job lot.

marche (marʃ) f, walk, walking; march, marching; procession; sailing; steaming; running; run; working; speed; motion; movement, move; journey, course; way, path; progress; step, stair; treadle. ~ *à suivre*, procedure. ~-*pied*, running board.

marché (marʃe) m, market; contract; bargain; dealing. ~ *aux bestiaux*, cattle market. ~ *commercial*, produce m. ~ *des valeurs*, ~ *des titres*, share m., stock m. ~ *aux puces*, flea market, thieves' market. *par-dessus le ~*, into the bargain.

marchepied (marʃəpje) m, [pair of] steps, stepladder; steps; footboard; stepping stone (*fig.*).

marcher (marʃe) v.i, to walk; tread; step; travel; tramp; march; be on the march; be driven (*Mach.*); sail; proceed, move on, advance, progress, go, go on; run, ply; work. *faire ~*, to spoof, put one over on. **marcheur, euse** (ʃœːr, øːz) n, walker; (*m.*) (*good, bad, fast*) sailer (*ship*).

marcotte (markɔt) f, layer (*Hort.*). **marcotter** (te) v.t, to layer.

mardi (mardi) m, Tuesday. *M~ gras*, Shrove Tuesday.

mare (maːr) f, pond, pool. **marécage** (mareka:ʒ) m, marsh, swamp, fen, bog. **marécageux, euse** (kaʒø, øːz) a, marshy, swampy, boggy.

maréchal (mareʃal) m: ~ *de France* (*Fr.*), Field Marshal (*Eng.*). ~ *des logis*, sergeant (*mounted troops*). ~ *des logis chef*, s. major. **maréchalat** (la) m, marshalship. **maréchalerie** (lri) f, farriery. **maréchalferrant** (fɛrɑ̃) m, farrier, shoeing smith.

marée (mare) f, tide, water; saltwater fish (*caught & fresh*); fresh sea fish, wet fish. ~ *noire*, oil slick.

marelle (marɛl) f, hopscotch.

mareyeur, euse (marɛjœːr, øːz) n, fish merchant & salesman, -woman.

margarine (margarin) f, margarine.

marge (marʒ) f, margin. **marger** (ʒe) v.t, to lay on, feed (*Typ.*); set a margin (*typing*). **marginal, e** (ʒinal) a, marginal.

margelle (marʒɛl) f, curb (*street*); lip (*well*).

margotin (margɔtɛ̃) m, bundle of firewood.

margouillis (marguʒi) *m*, mess.

marguerite (margərit) *f*, *(petite)* daisy; *(grande)* marguerite, ox-eye daisy; print wheel *(typewriter, etc.).* ~ *de la Saint-Michel,* Michaelmas daisy.

mari (mari) *m*, husband. **mariable** (rjabl) *a*, marriageable. **mariage** (rja:ʒ) *m*, marriage, matrimony, wedlock; match; wedding. **marié, e** (rje) *n*, bridegroom, bride. **marier** (rje) *v.t.* & se ~, to marry, wed; get married; match, unite. **marieur, euse** (rjœ:r, ø:z) *n*, matchmaker.

Marianne (marjan) *f*, the French Republic *(equivalent of Uncle Sam).*

marie-couche-toi-là (marikuʃtwala) *f*, slut, easy lay.

marie-jeanne (mariʒan) *f*, marijuana *(slang).*

marie-salope (marisaləp) *f*, slut; mud-dredger or barge; bloody Mary *(drink).*

marin, e (marɛ̃, in) *a*, marine; sea *(att.)*; nautical *(mile)*; sailor *(suit).* ¶ *m*, seaman, mariner, sailor; waterman, boatman. ~ *d'eau douce,* freshwater sailor, landlubber. **marine** (rin) *f*, marine, shipping, maritime navigation; seascape. ~ *[militaire],* ~ *de guerre,* navy. **mariné, e** (rine) *a*, sea-damaged. **mariner** (ne) *v.t,* to pickle; marinade.

maringouin (marɛ̃gwɛ̃) *m*, mosquito.

marinier (marinje) *m*, barge-man, bargee.

marionnette (marjɔnɛt) *f*, puppet, marionette.

marital, e† (marital) *a*, marital.

maritime (maritim) *a*, maritime, marine, sea *(att.)*; shipping *(att.)*; ship *(canal, broker, etc.)*; naval.

maritorne (maritɔrn) *f*, slut, slattern.

marivauder (marivode) *v.i,* to bandy flirtatious remarks.

marjolaine (marʒɔlɛn) *f*, [sweet] marjoram.

marmaille (marmɑ:j) *f.col,* children, brats.

Marmara (mer de) (marmara), Sea of Marmara.

marmelade (marməlad) *f*, preserve, marmalade. ~ *de pommes,* de prunes, stewed apples, plums. en ~, reduced to a pulp *(as cooked meat)*; to *(or* in) a jelly *(as face by blow).*

marmenteaux (marmɑ̃to) *m.pl,* ornamental trees.

marmitage (marmita:ʒ) *m*, shelling *(Artil.).* **marmite** (mit) *f*, boiler, pot; pot hole *(Geol.)*; heavy shell *(Artil.)* ~ *autoclave* steamer, steam cooker. **marmiter** (te) *v.t,* to shell. **marmiteux, euse** (tø, ø:z) *a.* & *n*, miserable *(wretch).* **marmiton** (tɔ̃) *m*, kitchen boy; scullion.

marmonner (marmɔne) *v.t,* to grumble about.

marmot, te (marmo, ɔt) *n*, youngster. *(f.)* marmot *(Zool.)*; kerchief. **marmotter** (mɔte) *v.t,* to mutter, mumble.

marmouset (marmuzɛ) *m*, little fellow; firedog.

marne (marn) *f*, marl. **marner** (ne) *v.t,* to marl. **marneux, euse** (nø, ø:z) *a*, marly. **marnière** (njɛ:r) *f*, marl pit.

Maroc (le) (marɔk), Morocco. **marocain, e** (kɛ̃, ɛn) *a.* & M~, *n*, Moroccan.

maronner (marɔne) *v.i,* to grumble.

maroquin (marɔkɛ̃) *m*, morocco [leather]. **maroquinerie** (kinri) *f*, fancy leather goods; f. l. shop.

marotique (marɔtik) *a*, archaic, quaint.

marotte (marɔt) *f*, bauble *(Hist.)*, cap & bells; milliner's dummy; hairdresser's dummy; pet theory, weakness, craze, [mono]mania.

marquant, e (markɑ̃, ɑ̃:t) *p.a,* prominent, outstanding; of note, leading. **marque** (mark) *f*, mark; stamp; brand; pit *(smallpox)*; score; bookmark; badge; token; tally. ~ *de commerce, de fabrique,* trademark. ~ *déposée,* registered t. m. ~ *typographique,* colophon. *de~,* branded, by well-known *(or* leading) maker(s); high-class. **marqué, e** (ke) *p.a,* marked; decided. **marquer** (ke) *v.t,* to mark; stamp; brand; score; show; *(v.i.)* to stand out. ~ *le pas,* to mark time. ~ *un but,* to kick *(or* score) a goal *(Foot.).*

marqueter (markəte) *v.t,* to

speckle, spot; inlay. **marqueterie** (kɛtri) *f*, marquetry, inlaid work; mosaic; patchwork.

marqueur, euse (markœːr, øːz) (*pers.*) *n*, marker; scorer.

marquis (marki) *m*, marquis, -quess. **marquise** (kiːs); *f*, marchioness; marquise; canopy (*Arch.*); awning.

marraine (marɛn) *f*, godmother, sponsor.

marrant, e (marã, ãt) *a*, side-splitting, funny. *il n'est pas* ~, he's a dull tool.

marre (maːr) *ad*, *en avoir* ~, to be fed up (*with it*). *se marrer* (səmare) *v*, to have fun, a good laugh.

marron (marɔ̃) *m*, chestnut; maroon (*firework*); marron (*glacé*); (*att.*) maroon (*color*). ~ *d'Inde,* horse chestnut.

marron, ne (marɔ̃, ɔn) *a*, [run] wild (*animal*); outside (*broker*); unlicensed; unqualified; pirate (*publisher*); chestnut-colored, maroon. *nègre marron, négresse marronne,* maroon. **marronnage** (rɔnaːʒ) *m*, running away (*slaves*).

marronnier (marɔnje) *m*, chestnut [tree]. ~ *d'Inde,* horse chestnut [tree].

marrube (maryb) *m*, hoarhound.

mars (mars) *m*, March. **M~,** Mars, warfare.

marseillais, e (marsɛjɛ, ɛːz) *a.* & **M~,** *n*, (*att.*) Marseilles. *la Marseillaise,* the Marseillais (*anthem*). **Marseille** (sɛːj) *f*, Marseilles.

marsouin (marswɛ̃) *m*, porpoise; colonial infantryman.

marsupial (marsypjal) *m*, marsupial.

marteau (marto) *m*, hammer. ~ *d'eau,* water h. ~ *de porte,* door knocker. ~~-*pilon,* power hammer. *être un peu* ~, to be a little cracked, nutty. **martel en tête** (tɛl) *m*, uneasiness, worry. **martelé, e** (təle) (*fig.*) *p.a,* labored; strongly stressed. **marteler** (le) *v.t. & abs,* to hammer. *se* ~ [*le cerveau*], to make oneself uneasy, worry oneself.

martial, e (marsjal) *a*, martial, warlike.

martinet (martinɛ) *m*, swift (*bird*); tilt hammer; scourge (*whip*).

martingale (martɛ̃gal) *f*, martingale (*harness, betting*); betting system.

martin-pêcheur (martɛ̃pɛʃœːr) ou **martinet-pêcheur** (tinɛ) *m*, kingfisher.

martre (martr) *f*, marten. ~ *zibeline,* sable (*Zool.*).

martyr, e (martiːr) *n*, martyr; victim. **martyre,** *m*, martyrdom; torment. **martyriser** (tirize) *v.t*, to martyr[ize]; torture. **martyrologe** (rɔlɔːʒ) *m*, martyrology (*list*).

mascarade (maskarad) *f*, masquerade.

mascaret (maskarɛ) *m*, [tidal] bore. *un* ~ *humain,* shoals of people.

mascaron (maskarɔ̃) *m*, mascaron, mask.

mascotte (maskɔt) *f*, mascot, charm.

masculin, e (maskylɛ̃, in) *a*, male; masculine. ¶ *m*, masculine [gender]. **masculinité** (linite) *f*, masculinity; male descent.

masque (mask) *m*, mask; blind; features; masker, -quer. ~ *à gaz,* gas mask, respirator. ¶ *f*, hussy, minx. **masquer** (ke) *v.t*, to mask; cover, conceal. *se* ~, to masquerade.

massacrant, e (masakrã, ãːt) *a*, very bad (*temper*). **massacre** (kr) *m*, massacre, slaughter. **massacrer** (kre) *v.t*, to massacre, slaughter; smash; murder; botch. **massacreur, euse** (krœːr, øːz) *n*, slaughterer; smasher; botcher.

massage (masaːʒ) *m*, massage.

masse (mas) *f*, mass, lump; solid; body; bulk; aggregate; funds; fund; sledge [hammer]; mace (*ceremonial*). ~ [*d'armes*], mace (*Hist.*). ~ *d'eau,* reed mace, bulrush. *à la* ~ (*Elec.*), grounded, connected to frame.

massepain (maspɛ̃) *m*, marzipan.

masser (mase) *v.t*, to mass; massage.

massette (masɛt) *f*, reed mace, bulrush.

masseur, euse (masœːr, øːz) *n*, masseur, euse.

massicot (masiko) *m*, lead ochre; guillotine (*for paper cutting*).

massier, ère (masje, ɛːr) *n*, treasurer; (*m.*) mace bearer.

massif, ive† (masif, iːv) *a*, massive; bulky; heavy; solid. ¶ *m*, [solid] mass; block; body; clump; massif.

massue (masy) *f*, club, bludgeon.

mastic (mastik) *m*, mastic; putty.

mastication (mastikasjɔ̃) *f*, mastication. **mastiquer** (ke) *v.t*, to masticate; putty.

mastoc (mastɔk) *a.inv*, lumpish.

mastodonte (mastɔdɔ̃ːt) *m*, mastodon; elephant[ine person].

mastoïde (mastɔid) *a*, mastoid.

masure (mazyːr) *f*, hovel, ruin.

mat, e (mat) *a*, mat (*color*), unpolished, lusterless, dead, flat, dull.

mat (mat) *a.m*, checkmated. faire ~, to [check]mate (*chess*).

mât (mɑ) *m*, mast; pole. ~ de charge, derrick (*ship's*). ~ de cocagne (kɔkaɲ), greasy pole. ~ de fortune, jury mast. ~ de hune, topmast. ~ de misaine, foremast. ~ de pavillon, flagstaff. ~ de pavoisement (pavwazmɑ̃), Venetian mast. ~ de signaux, signal post. ~ de tente, tent pole.

matador (matadɔːr) *m*, matador (*pers. & games*); magnate (*Fin., etc.*).

matamore (matamɔːr) *m*, swaggerer.

match (matʃ) *m*, match (*boxing, wrestling, tennis, football, chess, etc.*). ~ aller, first match. ~ nul, draw[n game]. ~ retour, return match.

matelas (matla) *m*, mattress. **matelasser** (lase) *v.t*, to stuff, pad. **matelassier, ère** (sje, ɛːr) *n*, mattress maker.

matelot (matlo) *m*, sailor, seaman. ~ coq, cook's mate. ~ de deuxième classe, able[-bodied] seaman. ~ de pont, deck hand. ~ de première classe, seaman first-class. ~ de troisième classe, ordinary s. [vaisseau] ~, consort (*Navy*).

mater (mate) *v.t*, to [check]mate (*chess*); mortify; humble.

mâter (mɑte) *v.t*, to mast (*a ship*); toss (*oars*).

matérialiser (materjalize) *v.t*, to materialize. **matérialisme** (lism) *m*, materialism. **matérialiste** (list) *n*, materialist. ¶ *a*, materialistic. **matériaux** (rjo) *m.pl*, materials. **matériel, le†** (rjɛl) *a*, material, physical, bodily. ¶ *m*, plant, material, stock; hardware (*computers*). ~ roulant, rolling stock.

maternel, le† (matɛrnɛl) *a*, maternal, motherly; mother's (*side*); mother, native (*tongue*). école ~, nursery school. **maternité** (nite) *f*, maternity, motherhood; maternity hospital.

mathématicien, ne (matematisjɛ̃, ɛn) *n*, mathematician. **mathématique†** (tik) *a*, mathematical. ~s, *f.pl*, mathematics. ~ spéciales, higher mathematics.

matière (matjɛːr) *f*, matter; material, stuff; type metal; subject; grounds; gravamen. ~ à réflexion, food for thought. ~s d'or & d'argent, bullion. ~ médicale, materia medica. ~s premières, raw material[s] (*used in trade*).

matin (matɛ̃) *m*, morning. un de ces ~s, one of these fine days. ¶ ad, early.

mâtin (mɑtɛ̃) *m*, mastiff; large watch dog; rascal.

matinal, e (matinal) *a*, [up] early, early riser (être = to be an); morning (att.).

mâtiné, e (mɑtine) *a*, mongrel, cross-bred; mixed.

matinée (matine) *f*, morning, forenoon; morning performance, matinée; dressing jacket. **matines** (tin) *f.pl*, matins. **matineux, euse** (nø, øːz) *a*, [up] early, early riser (être = to be an).

matir (matiːr) *v.t*, to mat, dull. **matité** (tite) *f*, dullness, deadness.

matois, e (matwa, aːz) *a. & n*, sly (person).

matou (matu) *m*, tom [cat]; lover (slang). un vilain ~, a nasty customer.

matraque (matrak) *f*, bludgeon, club, blackjack; repetition of "hit" song on radio.

matriarcat (matriarka) *m*, matriarchy. **matrice** (tris) *f*, womb; matrix; gangue; die; standard (*weight, measure*). ~ du rôle des contributions, assessment book (*taxes*). **matricule** (kyl) *f*, register, roll. [numéro] ~, *m*, army serial number. **matrimonial, e** (mɔnjal) *a*, matrimonial. **matrone** (trɔn) *f*, matron, dame.

maturation (matyrasjɔ̃) *f*, maturation, ripening.

mâture (mɑty:r) *f*, masts (*col.*); masting; mast[ing] house.

maturité (matyrite) *f*, maturity, ripeness.

maudire (modi:r) *v.t.ir*, to curse. **maudit, e** (di, it) *p.a*, [ac]cursed, confounded.

maugréer (mogree) *v.i*, to fume, bluster, curse.

Maure (mɔ:r) *m*, Moor. **m~, a**, Moorish. **mauresque** (mɔrɛsk) *a*, Moresque. ¶ *f*, Morisco, morris [dance].

Maurice [(l'île)] (mɔris) *f*, Mauritius.

mausolée (mozɔle) *m*, mausoleum.

maussade (mosad) *a*, sullen, peevish, disgruntled; dull, flat. **maussaderie** (dri) *f*, sullenness; sulks.

mauvais, e (movɛ, ɛ:z) *a*, bad; ill; evil; nasty; wrong; faulty; broken (*English, French, etc.*). **mauvais**, *comps:* ~ coucheur, quarrelsome fellow. ~ œil, evil eye. ~ pas, tight corner; scrape, fix (*fig.*). ~ plaisant, practical joker. ~ quart d'heure, bad time [of it], trying time. ~ service, disservice. ~ sujet, ne'er-do-well, scapegrace; bad boy (*Sch.*). ~ ton, bad form. **mauvaise**, *comps:* ~ action, ill deed. ~ gestion, mismanagement, maladministration. ~ herbe, weed. ~ honte, false shame; bashfulness. ~ langue, scandalmonger. **mauvais**, *ad*. & *m*, bad.

mauve (mo:v) *f*, mallow. ¶ *m*. & *att*, mauve.

mauviette (movjɛt) *f*, lark (*bird*); puny creature. **mauvis** (vi) *m*, red wing (*thrush*).

maxi (maksi) *m* or *f*, "new look" length skirt or coat.

maxillaire (maksillɛ:r) *a*, maxillary, jaw (*bone*).

maxime (maksim) *m*, maxim.

maximum, ma (maksimɔm, ma) *a*. & *m*, maximum, peak, top (*att.*). ~ de charge, burden, burthen (*ship*).

Mayence (majɑ̃:s) Mayence, Mainz.

mayonnaise (majɔnɛ:z) *f*. & *att*, mayonnaise.

mazette (mɑzɛt) *f*, weakling; duffer, rabbit (*at a game*).

mazout (mazu) *m*, oil fuel.

me, m' (mə, m) *pn*, me; [to] me; myself. ~ voici, here I am.

méandre (meɑ̃:dr) *m*, meander, winding.

mécanicien (mekanisjɛ̃) *m*, mechanician, mechanist; mechanic; engineman; engine driver; engineer (*ship*); (*att.*) mechanical (engineer). **mécanique†** (nik) *a*, mechanical; power (*att.*); clockwork (*train, motor car, or other toy*). ¶ *f*, mechanics; mechanism; brake [gear] (*carriage*). fait à la ~, machine-made. **mécaniser** (ze) *v.t*, to mechanize, motorize. **mécanisme** (nism) *m*, mechanism, machinery, gear; works (*as of a watch*); technique.

mécanographie (mekanɔgrafi) *f*, data processing; multicopy business, service.

mécène (mesɛn) *m*, patron (*as of the arts*).

méchant, e (meʃɑ̃, ɑ̃:t) *a*, wicked, evil; ill-natured; unkind; spiteful; mischievous, naughty; wretched, paltry, poor, sorry; unpleasant. ~ poète, poetaster. ¶ *n*, wicked, etc, person. **méchamment** (ʃamɑ̃) *ad*, wickedly, etc. **méchanceté** (ʃɑ̃ste) *f*, wickedness, etc.

mèche (mɛʃ) *f*, wick (*lamp*); tinder; fuse, match, cracker, snapper (*whip*); lock (*hair*); tassel; bit, drill; worm (*corkscrew*); tent (*Surg.*); secret, plot.

mécompte (mekɔ̃:t) *m*, miscalculation, disappointment.

méconnaissable (mekɔnesabl) *a*, unrecognizable. **méconnaître** (nɛ:tr) *v.t.ir*, to fail to recognize or diagnose, not to know; disown; disregard, ignore, misunderstand, slight.

mécontent, e (mekɔ̃tɑ̃, ɑ̃ːt) *a*, discontent[ed], dissatisfied, disgruntled. ¶ *m*, malcontent. **mécontentement** (tɑ̃tmɑ̃) *m*, discontent[ment], dissatisfaction. **mécontenter** (te) *v.t*, to dissatisfy, displease.

Mecque (la) (mɛk), Mecca.

mécréant, e (mekreɑ̃, ɑ̃ːt) *a*, unbelieving. ¶ *n*, unbeliever.

médaille (medaːj) *f*, medal; coin (*Greek, Roman*); badge (*porter's*). ~ **d'honneur**, prize medal. **médaillé, e** (daje) *a*, decorated (*Mil.*). ¶ *n*, medalist (*recipient*), prize winner. **médailler** (je) *v.t*, to award a medal (to). **médailleur** (œːr) *m*, medalist, medal maker. **médaillier** (je) *m*, coin (*or* medal) cabinet; collection of coins *or* medals. **médaillon** (jɔ̃) *m*, medallion; locket.

médecin (medsɛ̃) *m*, medical man, m. officer, physician, surgeon, doctor; (*of time*) healer. ~ **aliéniste** (aljenist), mental specialist. **médicine** (sin) *f*, medicine; surgery; physic. ~ **légale**, medical jurisprudence, forensic medicine.

médiateur, trice (medjatœːr, tris) *n*, mediator. **médiation** (sjɔ̃) *f*, mediation.

médical, e (medikal) *a*, medical. **médicament** (mɑ̃) *m*, medicament, medicine. **médicamenter** (te) *v.t*, to doctor, physic, dose. **médicamenteux, euse** (tø, øːz) *a*, medicinal, curative; medicated. **médicastre** (kastr) *m*, quack. **médication** (sjɔ̃) *f*, medication. **médicinal, e** (sinal) *a*, medicinal. **médico-légal, e** (kolegal) *a*, medico-judicial.

médiéval, e (medjeval) *a*, medieval. **médiéviste** (vist) *n*, medievalist.

médiocre (medjɔkr) *a*, mediocre, poor; middling, moderate. ¶ *m*, mediocrity (*pers. & quality*). **médiocrité** (krite) *f*, mediocrity (*quality*); moderate condition of life.

médire de (mediːr) *v.ir*, to speak ill of, slander. **médisance** (dizɑ̃ːs) *f*, slander, backbiting, scandal; scandalmongers. **médisant, e** (zɑ̃, ɑ̃ːt) *a*, slanderous. ¶ *n*, slanderer, scandalmonger.

méditatif, ive (meditatif, iːv) *a*, meditative. **méditation** (sjɔ̃) *f*, meditation. **méditer** (te) *v.t. & abs*, to meditate ([up]on), ponder, muse, pore; think; contemplate; plan.

méditerrané, e (mediterane) *a*, mediterranean, landlocked. **la** [*mer*] **Méditerranée**, the Mediterranean [sea]. **méditerranéen, ne** (neɛ̃, ɛn) *a*, Mediterranean.

médium (medjɔm) *m*, middle register (*Mus.*); medium (*spiritualism*).

médius (medjyːs) *m*, second finger, middle f.

médullaire (medyllɛːr) *a*, medullary.

méduse (medyːz) *f*, medusa, jellyfish, sea nettle. **la tête de M~** (*fig.*), a terrible shock. **méduser** (dyze) *v.t*, to petrify (*fig.*).

meeting (mitiŋ) *m*, meeting (*Pol., sport, social*).

méfait (mefɛ) *m*, misdeed, malpractice.

méfiance (mefjɑ̃ːs) *f*, mistrust, distrust. **méfiant, e** (jɑ̃, ɑ̃ːt) *a*, mis- *or* distrustful. **se méfier de** (fje), to mis- *or* distrust; beware of.

mégalomanie (megalɔmani) *f*, megalomania.

mégarde (par) (megard) *ad*, inadvertently.

mégère (meʒɛːr) *f*, termagant, virago, shrew.

mégie (meʒi) **& mégisserie** (sri) *f*, leather dressing, tawing.

mégot (mego) *m*, cigarette butt.

meilleur, e (mɛjœːr) *a*, better. **à meilleur marché**, cheaper. **le ~, la ~**, the better, the best. ¶ *m*, best.

Mein (le) (mɛ̃), the Main (*river*).

mélancolie (melɑ̃kɔli) *f*, melancholia; melancholy. **mélancolique†** (lik) *a*, melancholy, melancholic.

Mélanésie (la) (melanezi), Melanesia.

mélange (melɑ̃ːʒ) *m*, mixture; blending; medley; mash; (*pl.*) miscellany (*literary*); miscellaneous works. **mélanger** (lãʒe) *v.t*, to mix, mingle, blend. *laine mélangée*, wool mixture.

mélasse (melas) *f*, molasses, treacle; misfortune; poverty. *être dans la* ~, to be down on one's luck.

mêlé, e (mele) *p.a*, mixed, miscellaneous, medley. ¶ *f*, fight, mêlée, scrimmage, scramble. **mêler** (le) *v.t*, to mix, mingle; medley; shuffle (*cards*); mash. **se** ~, to interfere, meddle.

mélèze (mele:z) *m*, larch [tree].

mélodie (melɔdi) *f*, melody. **mélodieux, euse†** (djø, ø:z) *a*, melodious, tuneful.

mélodramatique (melɔdramatik) *a*, melodramatic. **mélodrame** (dram) *m*, melodrama.

melon (məlɔ̃) *m*, melon. **[chapeau]** ~, derby (*hat*).

membrane (mãbran) *f*, membrane; web (*bird's foot*). ~ *du tympan*, eardrum.

membre (mã:br) *m*, member; limb; rib (*ship*). **membré, e** (mãbre) *a*, -limbed. **membrure** (bry:r) *f*, limbs; frame; ribs (*ship*).

mémé (meme), **mémère** (mɛ:r) *f*, granny, grandma; old woman.

même (mɛ:m) *a*, same; like; very; self; itself. ¶ *m*, same [thing]. ¶ *ad*, even, indeed. à ~ *de*, in a position to, able to. *de* ~, *ad*, the same, likewise. **de** ~ **que**, *c*, [just] as, like.

mémento (memɛ̃to) *m*, memento, reminder, note; handbook.

mémoire (memwa:r) *f*, memory; recollection; fame; storage (*computers*). *de* ~, from memory, by heart. *de* ~ *d'homme*, within living memory. *pour* ~, as a memorandum, no[t] value[d] (*in account*). ~ *morte*, read only memory (*computers*). ~ *vive*, random access memory (*computers*). ~ *à ferrites*, core storage (*computers*). ¶ *m*, memorandum; paper (*learned*); bill, account; memoir. **mémorable** (mɔrabl) *a*, memorable. **mémorandum** (rãdɔm) *m*, memorandum; memorial (*State paper*). **mémorial** (rjal) *m*, memoirs.

menace (mənas) *f*, threat, menace. **menacer (se)** *v.t. & abs*, to threaten, menace.

ménade (menad) *f*, maenad.

ménage (mena:ʒ) *m*, housekeeping, housewifery; house[hold], establishment; household goods; home, family; housework. **[petit]** ~, miniature (*or* dolls') home set. ~ *à trois*, matrimonial triangle. **de** ~, household (*bread*); homespun; house *or* domestic (*as coal*); homemade (*as wine*). *faire des* ~s, to clean the house, do housekeeping work. *femme de* ~, cleaning woman. **ménagement** (naʒmã) *m. oft. pl*, care, stint; consideration, deference; tact. **ménager** (ʒe) *v.t*, to husband, manage, economize; save; take care of; look after; make the most of; keep; arrange; make; contrive; bring about; keep in with, humor; handle tactfully; spare. *sans* ~ *les termes*, without mincing one's words. **ménager, ère** (ʒe, ɛ:r) *a*, economical, thrifty; careful; sparing; domestic. ¶ *f*, housekeeper, housewife; cruet. **ménagerie** (ʒri) *f*, menagerie.

mendiant, e (mãdjã, ã:t) *n*, beggar; mendicant; (*att.*) mendicant; (*m.pl.*) dessert fruit & nuts. **mendicité** (disite) *f*, begging, mendicancy, mendicity; beggary. **mendier** (dje) *v.i. & t*, to beg; canvass.

meneau (məno) *m*, mullion; transom (*window*).

menée (məne) *f*, (*underhand*) intrigue; track (*Hunt.*). **mener** (ne) *v.t*, to lead, conduct; take, carry; drive; steer; partner (*lady at dance*). *mené par sa femme*, henpecked.

ménestrel (menɛstrel) *m*, minstrel (*Hist.*). **ménétrier** (netrie) *m*, (village) fiddler.

meneur, euse (mənœ:r, ø:z) *n*, leader; ringleader. ~ *de train*, pacemaker.

menhir (mɛni:r) *m*, menhir.

méninge (menɛ̃:ʒ) *f*, meninx (*Anat.*). *se creuser les* ~s, to rack one's brains.

méningite (menɛ̃ʒit) *f*, meningitis.

menotte (mənɔt) *f*, small hand; (*pl.*) handcuffs, manacles.

mensonge (mãsɔ̃:ʒ) *m*, lie, falsehood‚ untruth; fiction; vanity. ~ *innocent*, fib, story. ~ *pieux*, ~ *officieux*, white lie. **mensonger,** **ère†** (sɔ̃ʒe, ε:r) *a*, lying, mendacious; untrue, false, deceitful.

mensualité (mãsɥalite) *f*, monthly payment, drawing, salary, or like. **mensuel, le†** (sɥεl) *a*, monthly (*a*. & *ad*.). ¶ *m*, employee paid by month.

mensurable (mãsyrabl) *a*, measurable.

mensuration (mãsyrasjɔ̃) *f*, mensuration.

mental, e† (mãtal) *m*, mental. **mentalité** (lite) *f*, mentality.

menterie (mãtri) *f*, story, fib. **menteur, euse** (tœ:r, ø:z) *n*, liar. ¶ *a*, lying; deceptive.

menthe (mã:t) *f*, mint. ~ *poivrée*, peppermint. *pastille de* ~, peppermint [lozenge]. ~ *verte*, spearmint, garden mint. **menthol** (mãtɔl) *m*, menthol.

mention (mãsjɔ̃) *f*, mention, reference. **mentionner** (one) *v.t*, to mention, make reference to.

mentir (mãti:r) *v.i.ir*, to lie. *sans* ~, to tell the truth (*candidly*).

mentor (mɛ̃tɔ:r) *m*, mentor. (*ou en*) *galoche*, slipper chin. M~, Mentore (*Geog.*). **mentonnet** (tɔnε) *m*, latch catch.

mentor (mɛ̃tɔ:r) *m*, mentor.

menu, e (məny) *a*, small; slight; petty; minor (*repairs*); minute; fine. *le menu peuple*, the humbler classes. *menu plomb*, birdshot. *menue paille*, chaff. *menues herbes*, fine herbs (*fine in texture, as savory herbs*). *argent pour menus plaisirs*, pocket money. *menus propos*, small talk. **menu,** *ad*, small, fine. ¶ *m*, fare; menu, bill of fare. *par le* ~, in detail. **menuet** (nɥε) *m*, minuet. **menuiser** (nɥize) *v.i*, to carpenter. **menuiserie** (zri) *f*, joinery; cabinet making, c. work; woodwork. **menuisier** (zje) *m*, joiner; carpenter; cabinet maker; woodworker.

méphitique (mefitik) *a*, mephitic, noxious, dank.

méplat, e (mepla, at) *a*. & *m*, flat.

méprendre (se) (meprã:dr)

v.pr.ir, to be mistaken. *se* ~ *sur*, to mistake.

mépris (mepri) *m*, contempt, scorn. **méprisable** (zabl) *a*, contemptible, despicable, scurvy; disregardable. **méprisant, e** (zã, ã:t) *a*, contemptuous, scornful. **méprise** (pri:z) *f*, mistake; oversight. **mépriser** (prize) *v.t*, to despise, scorn; disregard, scoff at.

mer (mε:r) *f*, sea, ocean. ~ *du Nord*, North Sea. *Note.*—For other seas, see under proper name, e.g, *la mer Egée*, under *Egée*. *un homme à la* ~*!* [a] man overboard!

mercanti (mεrkãti) *m*, profiteer. **mercantile** (til) *a*, mercantile, mercenary. **mercantilisme** (lism) *m*, mercantilism, commercialism.

mercenaire (mεrsənε:r) *a*, mercenary. ¶ *m*, mercenary, hireling; [paid] worker.

mercerie (mεrsri) *f*, notions shop. **mercerisé, e** (ze) *a*, mercerized.

merci (mεrsi) *f*, mercy; (*m*.) thanks. ¶ *i*, thanks! thank you!; no, thank you! *Dieu* ~*!* thank God!

mercier, ère (mεrsje, ε:r) *n*, notions shopkeeper.

mercredi (mεrkrədi) *m*, Wednesday. *le* ~ *des Cendres*, Ash Wednesday.

mercure (mεrky:r) *m*, mercury, quicksilver. **mercuriale** (kyrjal) *f*, mercury (*Bot.*); reprimand; official list (*grain, etc, prices*). **mercuriel, e** (rjεl) *a*, mercurial, blue (*pill*).

merde (mεrd) *f*, excrement; shit; hash (*drug*); break a leg! (*Theat.*). ~*!*, damn it! *il ne se prend pas pour de la* ~, he's got a pretty good opinion of himself.

mère (mε:r) *f*, mother; parent (*lit.* & *fig.*); dam. *notre* ~ *commune*, mother earth. ~ *abeille*, queen bee. ~ *branche*, bough, limb. *la* ~ *Gigogne* (ʒiɡɔɲ), the Old Woman who lived in a shoe. *une* ~ *Gigogne*, the mother of many children. ~ *patrie*, parent state. *l'idée* ~, the main idea (*of book*).

méridien, ne (meridjɛ̃, εn) *a*,

meridian. ¶ *m*, meridian (*as of Greenwich*); (*f.*) siesta; couch. **méridional, e** (djɔnal) *a*, meridional, southern, south. ¶ (*pers.*) *n*, meridional, southerner.

meringue (mərɛ̃:g) *f*, meringue.

mérinos (merinɔs) *m*, merino.

merise (məri:z) *f*, wild cherry, merry. **merisier** (rizje) *m*, wild cherry [tree].

méritant, e (meritã, ã:t) *a*, deserving, meritorious. **mérite** (rit) *m*, merit, desert, worth. **mériter** (te) *v.t*, to merit, deserve; be worth; earn; require. **méritoire** (twa:r) *a*, meritorious.

merlan (mɛrlã) *m*, whiting (*fish*).

merle (mɛrl) *m*, blackbird; ouzel, ousel. *c'est le ~ blanc*, he is a strange mixture (*of qualities*). *je vous donnerai le* (ou *un*) *~ blanc*, I'll eat my hat (*if you can do that*). **merlette** (lɛt) *f*, [hen] blackbird.

merlin (mɛrlɛ̃) *m*, cleaving axe (*wood*); pole axe.

merluche (mɛrlyʃ) *f*, dried cod; dried hake. **merlus** (ly) *m*, hake.

merrain (mɛrɛ̃) *m*, stave wood.

merveille (mɛrvɛ:j) *f*, marvel, wonder. *à ~*, excellently; wonderfully; capitally. **merveilleux, euse†** (vɛjø, ø:z) *a*, marvelous, wonderful. *le ~*, the marvelous; the wonderful part. ¶ (*pers.*) (*Hist.*) *n*, fop.

mes see **mon**.

mésalliance (mezaljã:s) *f*, misalliance. **mésallier** (lje) *v.t*, to misally. *se ~*, to make a misalliance.

mésange (mezã:ʒ) *f*, tit[mouse]. *~ charbonnière*, tomtit.

mésaventure (mezavãty:r) *f*, misadventure, mishap.

mésentente (mezãtã:t) *f*, misunderstanding, disagreement.

mésestime (mezɛstim) *f*, disrepute. **mésestimer** (me) *v.t*, to undervalue, underestimate, underrate.

mésintelligence (mezɛ̃tɛliʒã:s) *f*, variance; misunderstanding.

mesquin, e† (mɛskɛ̃, in) *a*, mean, shabby; poky; stingy, niggardly; paltry; scanty. **mesquinerie** (kinri) *f*, meanness, etc.

mess (mɛs) *m*, mess (*officers'*).

message (mɛsa:ʒ) *m*, message; errand; TV commercial. **messager, ère** (saʒe, ɛ:r) *n*, messenger; (*m.*) carrier; harbinger. **messagerie** (ʒri) *f. oft. pl*, parcels [service]; mail, passenger & parcels service.

messe (mɛs) *f*, mass (*Eccl.*). *~ basse*, low m. *~ chantée*, high m.

messeoir (mɛswa:r) *v.i.ir*, to be unbecoming.

Messie (mɛsi) *m*, Messiah.

messieurs, *oft.* **M~** (mesjø), *pl.* of *monsieur*, messieurs, Messrs.

Messine (mɛsin) *f*, Messina.

mesurage (məzyra:ʒ) *m*, measurement. **mesure** (zy:r) *f*, measure; measurement; size; (*pl.*) mensuration; extent; meter (*Poet.*); time (*Mus.*); measure, (*& commonly but wrongly*) bar (*Mus.*); bounds; propriety. *à ~*, in proportion. *à ~ que*, [according] as. *en ~ de*, able to. *sur ~*, to measure, custom-made. **mesuré, e** (zyre) *a*, guarded (*language*). **mesurer** (re) *v.t*, to measure; weigh (*fig.*); proportion. *se ~ avec*, to cope with.

mésuser (mezyze) *v.t*, to misuse; abuse.

métairie (metɛri) *f*, farm worked on shares.

métal (metal) *m*, metal. *~ anglais*, britannia m. **métallifère** (tallifɛ:r) *a*, metalliferous. **métallique** (tallik) *a*, metallic; iron &/or steel; wire (*att.*); spring (*att.*). **métallurgie** (tallyrʒi) *f*, metallurgy. **métallurgiste** (ʒist) *m*, metallurgist.

métallo (metal[l]o) *m*, metalworker.

métamorphose (metamɔrfo:z) *f*, metamorphosis. **métamorphoser** (foze) *v.t*, to metamorphose.

métaphore (metafɔ:r) *f*, metaphor. *~ incohérente*, mixed m. **métaphorique†** (fɔrik) *a*, metaphorical.

métaphysicien (metafizisjɛ̃) *m*, metaphysician. **métaphysique** (zik) *f*, metaphysics. ¶ *a*, metaphysical.

métayage (metɛja:ʒ) *m*, cultivation on shares.

météore (meteɔ:r) *m*, meteor.

météorique (ɔrik) a, meteoric. **météorologie** (rɔlɔ3i) f, meteorology. **météorologique** (3ik) a, meteorologic(al); weather (*forecast, etc.*).

méthode (metɔd) f, method, way, system. **méthodique†** (dik) a, methodical. **méthodisme** (dism) m, methodism. **méthodiste** (dist) n, methodist.

méthyle (metil) m, methyl (*Chem.*).

méticuleux, euse† (metikylø, ø:z) a, meticulous, punctilious.

métier (metje) m, trade; craft; profession, business, calling, line; experience; loom; frame (*Need.*). ~ à broder, embroidery hoops; tambour frame. ~ de tailleur, tailoring. sur le ~ (fig.), in the works. faire son ~, to mind one's own business.

métis, se (metis) a, halfbred; crossbred; mongrel; hybrid (*Bot.*). ¶ n, halfbreed; cross; mongrel. **métissage** (tisa:3) m, crossbreeding.

métonymie (metɔnimi) f, metonymy.

métrage (metra:3) m, measurement, measuring; length (*in meters*); [quantity] surveying; footage (*cinema*). court ~, film short. long ~, feature film. **mètre** (mɛtr) m, meter (*verse*); meter = 39.370113 inches; meter measure or tape or stick (1 *meter long*). ~ carré, square meter = 10.7639 sq. feet. ~ cube, cubic meter = 35.3148 cub. feet. **métrer** (metre) v.t, to measure, survey. **métreur** (trœ:r) m, [quantity] surveyor. **métrique** (trik) a, metrical; metric. ¶ f, metrics, prosody.

métro (metro) m, subway.

métronome (metrɔnɔm) m, metronome.

métropole (metrɔpɔl) f, metropolis; mother country, home c. **métropolitaine, e** (litɛ̃, ɛn) a, metropolitan; mother (*church*); home, domestic.

mets (mɛ) m, dish, food, viand.

mettable (metabl) a, wearable. **metteur** (tœ:r) m: ~ en œuvre, stone (*gem*) setter; adapter (*pers., fig.*). ~ en scène, director (*cinema, TV*); producer (*Theat.*).

mettre (tr) v.t.ir, to put; place; lay; stake; set; poke; draw; make; bring; reduce; put on, wear; tear; take; throw. ~ à l'encre, to ink in. ~ à la retraite, to pension. ~ au point, to focus; adjust; tune up. ~ bas, to take off (*hat, etc.*); drop, foal, whelp. ~ dedans, to humbug, bamboozle. ~ en accusation, to arraign, commit for trial. ~ en commun, to pool. ~ en état, to enable. ~ les pouces, to knuckle under. se ~, to put oneself; sit [down]; lie [down]; begin; take to; dress; get; go; set. se ~ en habit pour dîner, to dress for dinner. se ~ sur deux rangs, to line up in twos.

meuble (mœbl) a, movable (*property*); light, loose, mellow (*earth*). ¶ m, piece of furniture; suite [of f.]; cabinet; (*pl.*) furniture; movables (*law*). ~-classeur, filing cabinet. ~ de famille, heirloom. **meublé** (ble) m, lodgings. **meubler** (ble) v.t, to furnish; stock, store (*fig.*).

meugler (møgle) v.i, to bellow, low.

meule (mø:l) f, grindstone, millstone; (*circular*) stack or rick (*hay*); round, wheel (*of cheese*). ~ [de moulin], millstone. ~ de dessous, ~ gisante, bedstone. ~ de dessus, ~ courante, runner. ~ en grès, grindstone. **meulière** (møljɛ:r) f, millstone grit; m. g. quarry. **meulon** (lɔ̃) m, cock (*hay*).

meunerie (mønri) f, milling (*flour*). **meunier, ère** (nje, ɛ:r) n, miller; (*m.*) chub (*fish*).

meurt-de-faim (mœrdəfɛ̃) m, starveling.

meurtre (mœrtr) m, murder; sin, shame (*vandalism*). **meurtrier, ère** (trie, ɛ:r) a, murderous; internecine; deadly. ¶ n, murderer, ess; (*f.*) loophole.

meurtrir (mœrtri:r) v.t, to bruise. **meurtrissure** (trisy:r) f, bruise.

meute (mø:t) f, pack (*hounds, enemies*).

mévente (mevã:t) f, slump [in trade], negligible sales (*enabling publisher to close account with author*).

mexicain, e (mɛksikɛ̃, ɛn) a. & M~, n, Mexican. **Mexico** (ko) *m*, Mexico [City]. **le Mexique** (sik), Mexico (*country*).

mezzo-soprano (mɛdzosɔsprano) *m*, mezzo-soprano.

mi (mi) *m*, E (*Mus.*). ¶ *word inv*, half, mid. *mi-bas*, *m.pl*, socks. *la mi-carême*, mid-lent. *à mi-chemin*, midway, halfway. *à mi-corps*, to the waist, waist-high *or* deep. *à mi-hauteur*, halfway up [the hill]. *mi-fil*, *m*, union (*linen & cotton thread*). *la mi-juin*, mid-June. *mi-lourd*, light-heavy (*Box.*). *mi-moyen*, welter (*Box.*). *mi-parti*, *e*, equally divided; half ... & half ... *la mi-temps*, half time (*Foot.*).

miasmatique (mjasmatik) *a*, malarial. **miasme** (asm) *m*, miasma.

miauler (mjole) *v.i*, to miaow, mew.

mica (mika) *m*, mica.

miche (miʃ) *f*, round loaf (*bread*); *pl*, buttocks. ¶ *m*, john (*prostitute's client*). **micheton** (tɔ̃) *m*, john (*prostitute's client*); hick who can easily be defrauded.

micheline (miʃlin) *f*, electric railway car.

micmac (mikmak) *m*, dirty work (*fig.*).

micro (mikro) *f*, mike.

microbe (mikrɔb) *m*, microbe.

micromètre (mikrɔmɛtr) *m*, micrometer.

micro-mioche (mikromjɔʃ) *n*, computer kid.

micro-onde (mikrɔɔ̃:d) *f*, microwave.

microphone (mikrɔfɔn) *m*, microphone.

microplaquette (mikrɔplakɛt) *f*, chip (*computers*).

microprogramme (mikrɔprogram) *m*, microprogram, **microprogrammer** (me) *v.t*, to microprogram.

microscope (mikrɔskɔp) *m*, microscope. **microscopique** (pik) *a*, microscopic(al).

microsillon (mikrɔsijɔ̃) *m*, microgroove; long-playing record.

midi (midi) *m*, noon, midday, noonday, twelve o'clock [in the day]; noontide; heyday (*of life*); south.

mie (mi) *f*, crumb (*bread*, opp. *crust*).

miel (mjɛl) *m*, honey. **mielleux, euse†** (lø, ø:z) *a*, bland; mealymouthed; honeyed; mawkish.

mien, ne (*with* **le, la, les**) (mjɛ̃, ɛn) *pn. & pr*, mine; my own.

miette (mjɛt) *f*, crumb (*broken bread, etc.*); bit, atom.

mieux (mjø) *ad. & a*, better; rather; more; best; better-looking. le ~, *ad*, the best. le ~, *m*, [the] best. *à qui* ~ ~, in competition.

mièvre (mjɛ:vr) *a*, [childishly] affected, finical.

mignard, e (miɲa:r, ard) *a*, mincing; girlish. **mignardise** (ɲardi:z) *f*, daintiness; affectation; (*pl.*) pretty ways; pink (*Bot.*). **mignon, ne** (ɲɔ̃, ɔn) *a*, dainty, petite; sweet; pet. ¶ *n*, pet, darling; (*m.*) minion. **mignonnette** (ɲɔnɛt) *f*, mignonette (*lace*); pink (*Bot.*); gimp nails; ground pepper; broken pebblestone.

migraine (migrɛn) *f*, migraine, bad headache.

migrateur, trice (migratœ:r, tris) *a*, migratory; migrant. **migration** (sjɔ̃) *f*, migration.

mijaurée (miʒore) *f*, affected woman.

mijoter (miʒote) *v.t*, to [let] simmer; (*v.i.*) to simmer. se ~, to be brewing.

mil (mil) *m*, mil[le] (*1000*); millet; Indian club. ¶ *a*, thousand (*dates*).

milan (milɑ̃) *m*, kite (*bird*).

Milan (milɑ̃) *m*, Milan. **milanais, e** (lanɛ, ɛ:z) *a. & M~, n*, Milanese.

mildiou (mildju) *m*, mildew (*on vines*).

milice (milis) *f*, militia. **milicien** (sjɛ̃) *m*, militiaman.

milieu (miljø) *m*, middle, midst, center; mean; medium; circle, milieu; underworld. *au ~ de*, in the midst of, amidst, among. *au ~ du navire*, amidships. *le juste ~*, the golden mean.

militaire† (milite:r) *a*, military. ¶ *m*, soldier, military man. *les ~s*, the military. **militant, e** (tɑ̃, ɑ̃:t) *a*, militant. ¶ *m*, fighter. **militariser** (tarize) *v.t*, to militarize. **militer** (te) *v.i*, to militate, tell.

mille (mil) *m. & a. inv,* (a *or* one) thousand; mile. *les M~ & une Nuits,* the Arabian nights. **millefeuille** *ou* **millefeuille** (fœːj) *f,* milfoil, yarrow; (*m.*) Genoese pastry, napoleon; female sex organ (*slang*). **millénaire** (milleneːr) *a. & m,* millenary (*a. & n.*); millennium (*n.*). **mille-pieds** (pje) *ou* **mille-pattes** (pat) *m,* centipede.

millésime (millezim) *m,* date, year.

millet (mijɛ) *m,* millet grass; millet. *~ des oiseaux,* canary seed.

milliard (miljaːr) *m,* billion, 1,000,000,000 francs. **milliardaire** (jardɛːr) *n. & a,* multi-millionaire.

milliasse (miljas) *f,* swarm[s].

millième (miljɛm) *a. & m,* thousandth. **millier** (je) *m,* thousand [or so]. **milligramme** (milligram) *m,* milligram = 0.015 grain. **millimètre** (millimɛtr) *m,* millimeter = 0.03937 inch.

million (miljɔ̃) *m,* million; 1,000,000 francs. **millionième** (jɔnjɛm) *a. & m,* millionth. **millionnaire** (nɛːr) *n,* millionaire.

mime (mim) *m,* mime; mimic. **mimer** (me) *v.t. & abs,* to mime; mimic. **mimétisme** (metism) *m,* mimicry (*Zool.*), mimesis. **mimique** (mik) *a,* mimic. ¶ *f,* mimicry.

mimosa (mimoza) *m,* mimosa.

minable (minabl) *a,* pitiable; wretched.

minauder (minode) *v.i,* to mince, simper, smirk. **minauderie** (dri) *f,* mincing, etc. **minaudier, ère** (dje, ɛːr) *a,* mincing, etc.

mince (mɛ̃ːs) *a,* thin, slender; slight. **minceur** (mɛ̃sœːr) *f,* thinness, etc.

mine (min) *f,* appearance, countenance, face, mien, look, looks. *de bonne ~,* good-looking.

mine (min) *f,* mine (*lit. & fig.*); mint (*fig.*); lead (*pencil*). *~ de plomb,* black lead. **miner** (ne) *v.t,* to mine; undermine; sap; hollow; wear; prey [up]on (*mind*). **minerai** (nrɛ) *m,* ore. **minéral, e** (neral) *a. & m,* mineral; inorganic (*chemistry*). **minéralogie** (lɔʒi) *f,* mineralogy. **minéralogique** (ʒik) *a,* minera-

logical. **minéralogiste** (ʒist) *m,* mineralogist.

minet, te (minɛ, ɛt) *n,* puss[y]; elegant young man or woman. *faire minette,* perform cunnilingus.

mineur (minœːr) *m,* miner; sapper (*Mil.*).

mineur, e (minœːr) *a,* minor; under age. ¶ *n,* minor (*pers.*); infant (*law*); (*m.*) minor (*Mus.*); (*f.*) minor premise (*Log.*).

miniature (minjatyːr) *f,* miniature. **miniaturiser** (tyrize) *v.t,* to miniaturize. **miniaturiste** (tyrist) *n,* miniaturist.

minidisque (minidisk) *m,* floppy disk (*computers*).

minier, ère (minje, ɛːr) *a,* mining (*att.*). ¶ *f,* gangue, matrix; surface mine, diggings.

minimarge (minimarʒ) *m,* discount store.

minime (minim) *a,* minute, trifling, trivial.

minimum, ma (minimɔm, ma) *a. & m,* minimum.

ministère (ministɛːr) *m,* department; ministry; office; secretaryship; board; agency, services, good offices, ministration. *M~ des Affaires étrangères,* State Department. *M~ des Finances,* Treasury Department. *M~ du Commerce,* Commerce Department. *~ public,* public prosecutor. **ministériel, le** (terjɛl) *a,* ministerial; State nominated (*officer*); Government (*organ*). **ministre** (tr) *m,* minister; secretary [of state]; clergyman, vicar. *~ de l'Intérieur,* Secretary of the Interior.

minium (minjɔm) *m,* minium; red lead.

minois (minwa) *m,* face, looks.

minon (minɔ̃) & **minou** (nu) *m,* puss[y].

minorité (minɔrite) *f,* minority; nonage; infancy (*law*).

Minorque (minɔrk) *f,* Minorca.

minoterie (minɔtri) *f,* [flour] milling; flour mill. **minotier** (tje) *m,* miller; flour merchant.

minuit (minɥi) *m,* midnight, twelve o'clock [at night].

minuscule (minyskyl) *a,* minute, tiny. ¶ *f,* small letter.

minute (minyt) *f,* minute; small

hand (*writing*); original; draft.
minuter (te) *v.t*, to minute, draw
[up], draft. **minuterie** (tri) *f*, time
switch.
minutie (minysi) *f*, trifle, (*pl.*)
minutiae; minuteness, great care.
minutieux, euse† (sjø, ∅:z) *a*,
meticulous; minute, thorough.
mioche (mjɔʃ) *m*, youngster, kid,
tot.
mirabelle (mirabɛl) *f*, mirabelle
[plum].
miracle (mirɑ:kl) *m*, miracle;
marvel; miracle [play], mystery
[play]. *à ~*, admirably. **miraculeux**, euse† (rakylø, ∅:z) *a*, mi-
raculous; marvelous.
mirage (mira:ʒ) *m*, mirage; testing, candling (*eggs*). **mire** (mi:r)
f, sight (*gun*); aiming stake.
mirer (mire) *v.t. & abs*, to aim
at, take aim; test, candle (*eggs*).
se ~, to look at oneself; see oneself reflected.
mirettes (mirɛt) *f.pl*, eyes, pee-
pers (*slang*).
mirifique (mirifik) *a*, marvelous.
mirliflore (mirliflɔ:r) *m*, spark,
dandy.
mirliton (mirlitɔ̃) *m*, mirliton
(*musical toy pipe*).
mirobolant, e (mirɔbɔlɑ̃, ɑ̃:t) *a*,
wonderful.
miroir (mirwa:r) *m*, mirror, [look-
ing] glass. *~ d'eau*, ornamental
lake. *~ déformant*, distorting
mirror. **miroiter** (rwate) *v.i*, to
flash, gleam, glisten, glint, sparkle. **miroiterie** (tri) *f*, mirror
trade. **miroitier** (tje) *m*, mirror
manufacturer *or* dealer.
misaine (mizɛn) *f*, foremast.
misanthrope (mizɑ̃trɔp) *m*, misanthrope, -pist. ¶ *~ &* **misanthropique** (pik) *a*, misanthropic.
mise (mi:z) *f*, putting, etc, as
mettre (*gaming*); bid (*auction*); get-up. *~ à prix*, reserve
[price], upset p. *~ à terre*, landing. *~ au point*, focusing; adjustment; tuning (*motor*). *~ [de
fonds*], putting up of money; investment; capital; stake. *~
[de]hors*, disbursement. *~ en accusation*, indictment. *~ en
marche*, starting. *~ en œuvre*, application. *~ en pages*, making up;
page proof. *~ en scène*, staging;

production; setting. *~ en train*,
starting; making ready (*Typ.*);
practice (*sport*). *de ~*, in fashion;
current; admissible. *être de ~*, to
be appropriate. **miser** (mize) *v.t.
& i*, to stake, bid.
misérable† (mizerabl) *a*, miserable; wretched; unfortunate;
worthless. ¶ *n*, unfortunate, poor
wretch; villain, scoundrel. **misère**
(ze:r) *f*, misery, wretchedness,
distress, destitution; misfortune;
trifle; misère (*cards*). *~ de santé*,
ailment. **miserere** (zerere) *m*,
miserere. **miséreux**, euse (zerø,
∅:z) *a. & n*, poverty-stricken
(person).
miséricorde (mizerikɔrd) *f*,
mercy; misericord. ¶ *i*, mercy on
us! good gracious! **miséricordieux**, euse† (djø, ∅:z) *a*, merci-
ful.
misogyne (mizɔʒin) *a*, misogynic.
¶ *m*, misogynist, woman hater.
missel (misɛl) *m*, missal.
mission (misjɔ̃) *f*, mission. **missionnaire** (ɔnɛ:r) *m*, missionary.
missive (si:v) *f*, missive.
mistral (mistral) *m*, mistral
(*wind*).
mitaine (mitɛn) *f*, mitten.
mite (mit) *f*, mite (*insect*); moth.
miteux, euse (tø, ∅:z) *a*, shabby.
mitiger (mitiʒe) *v.t*, to mitigate,
temper.
mitonner (mitɔne) *v.t. & i*, to
simmer.
mitoyen, ne (mitwajɛ̃, ɛn) *a*,
party (*wall, structure*). **mitoyen-
neté** (jɛnte) *f*, party rights.
mitraille (mitrɑ:j) *f*, grapeshot;
group firing. **mitrailleur** (tra-
jœ:r) *m*, machine gunner. **mitrailleuse** (jø:z) *f*, machine
gun.
mitre (mitr) *f*, miter; cowl
(*chimney*). **mitré**, e (tre) *a*, mi-
tered. **mitron** (trɔ̃) *m*, baker's
man.
mixage (miksaʒ) *m*, mixing (*cinema, TV*). *~ son*, sound mixing.
~ de pistes multiple, multi-track
mixing.
mixeur (miksœ:r) *m*, mixer; swiz-
zlestick.
mixte (mikst) *a*, mixed; composite; joint; promiscuous. **mix-**

tion (tjɔ̃) f, mixture (*medicinal*). **mixture** (ty:r) f, mixture; concoction.

mnémonique (mnemɔnik)· a, mnemonic. **la ~,** mnemonics.

mobile (mɔbil) a, movable; portable; mobile; changeable, fickle. ¶ m, moving body (*Mech.*); motive power; prime mover; motive, incentive. **mobilier, ère** (lje, ɛːr) a, personal, movable (*law*); transferable (*securities*). ¶ m, furniture, suite [of f.]. **mobilisation** (lizazjɔ̃) f, mobilization. **mobiliser** (ze) v.t. & abs, to mobilize. **mobilité** (te) f, mobility; fickleness.

moche (mɔʃ) a, ugly; lousy; rotten, etc.

modalité (mɔdalite) f, modality; method. **mode** (mɔd) f, mode, way; fashion, vogue; (*pl.*) millinery. **à la ~ & de ~,** in the fashion, fashionable, modish, stylish. **à la ~,** ad, fashionably, modishly, stylishly. ¶ m, mode; method; mood (*Gram.*). **~ d'emploi,** directions for use. **~ de circulation,** rule of the road.

modelage (mɔdlaːʒ) m, modeling; pattern making (*foundry*). **modèle** (dɛl) m, model, pattern; specimen; paragon; (*att.*) model, exemplary. **~ de broderie,** sampler. **modelé** (dle) m, modeling (*relief of forms*). **modeler** (dle) v.t. & abs, to model; pattern; mold, shape. **modeleur** (dlœːr) m, modeler; patternmaker.

Modène (mɔdɛːn) f, Modena.

modération (mɔderasjɔ̃) f, moderation; mitigation.· **modéré†, e** (re) a, moderate. **les modérés,** the moderates (*Pol.*). **modérer** (re) v.t, to moderate; check, curb; mitigate.

moderne (mɔdɛrn) a, modern; up to date; new. **les ~s,** m.pl, the moderns. **moderniser** (nize) v.t, to modernize.

modeste† (mɔdɛst) a, modest; quiet (*dress*). **modestie** (ti) f, modesty.

modicité (mɔdisite) f, moderateness; lowness.

modification (mɔdifikasjɔ̃) f, modification, alteration, varia-

tion. **modifier** (fje) v.t, to modify, alter, vary.

modique† (mɔdik) a, moderate (*price*); small (*sum, etc.*).

modiste (mɔdist) f, milliner, modiste.

modulation (mɔdylasjɔ̃) f, modulation. **module** (dyl) m, module; modulus. **moduler** (le) v.i. & t, to modulate.

moelle (mwal) f, marrow; pith. **~ épinière,** spinal cord. **moelleux, euse†** (lø, ø:z) a, marrowy; pithy; mellow; soft. ¶ m, softness; mellowness.

moellon (mwalɔ̃) m, quarry stone, rubble. **~ d'appareil,** ashlar.

mœurs (mœrs) f.pl, manners, habits; morals, morality. **les ~,** police vice squad.

mohair (mɔɛːr) m, mohair.

moi (mwa) pn, me; [to] me, I. **à ~! au secours!** help, help! ¶ m, self; ego. **~-même,** pn, myself.

moignon (mwaɲɔ̃) m, stump (*limb, tree*).

moindre (mwɛ̃:dr) a, less; lesser; lower; minor. **le, la, ~,** the least; the slightest. **[ne . . .] pas le moindrement** (mwɛ̃drəmɑ̃), not in the least.

moine (mwan) m, monk, friar; bed warmer. **~ bourru,** bugaboo, bugbear, goblin, bog[e]y; bear,' brute.

moineau (mwano) m, sparrow. **~ franc,** English sparrow. **un drôle de ~,** a queer bird (*person*).

moinerie (mwanri) f, monkhood, monkery.

moins (mwɛ̃) ad. & pr, less; not so [much]; fewer; under; minus; to (*of the hour*). **[signe] ~,** m, minus [sign]. **à ~ de,** for less than; barring; unless, without. **à ~ que,** unless. **au ~,** at least; however, above all. **le ~,** the least. **pas le ~ du monde,** not in the least.

moins-value (mwɛ̃valy) f, depreciation; deficit.

moire (mwaːr) f, moire, watering. **~ de soie** ou **soie moirée** (mware), watered silk, moiré, s. **moirer** (re) v.t, to water, moiré.

mois (mwa) m, month; month's pay, rent, or like.

moïse (mɔiːz) *m*, wicker cradle.
moise (mwaːz) *f*, brace (*Carp*.);
ledger (*Build*.). **moiser** (mwaze)
v.t, to brace.

moisi, e (mwazi) *p.p*, moldy,
mildewy; musty; frowsy. **moisir**
(ziːr) *v.t. & i, & se ~*, to mildew,
turn moldy. **moisissure** (zisyːr)
f. & **moisi** (zi) *m*, mildew, mold,
moldiness, mustiness.

moissine (mwasin) *f*, vine branch
with grapes hanging (*as ceiling
decoration*).

moisson (mwasɔ̃) *f*, harvest, reaping. **moissonner** (sɔne) *v.t. &
abs*, to reap, harvest; cut off
(*fig*.). **moissonneur, euse** (nœːr,
øːz) *n*, reaper, harvester (*pers*.);
(*f*.) reaping machine, reaper.
moissonneuse-batteuse, combine
harvester. *moissonneuse-lieuse*,
reaper-binder.

moite (mwat) *a*, moist, damp;
clammy. **moiteur** (tœːr) *f*, moist-
ness; clamminess.

moitié (mwatje) *f*, half, moiety;
better half (*wife*). ¶ *ad*, half,
partly. *à ~*, half, by half; on
half profits. *à ~ chemin*, halfway. *de ~*, by half. *être* (ou *se
mettre*) *de ~ avec*, to go halves
with.

Moka (mɔka) *m*, Mocha. *m~
ou café de M~*, mocha, M. coffee; coffee (*ordinary*).

mol *see* mou.

molaire (mɔlɛːr) *a. & f*, molar.

môle (moːl) *m*, mole, breakwater.

moléculaire (mɔlekylɛːr) *a*, molecular. **molécule** (kyl) *f*, molecule.

moleskine (mɔlɛskin) *f*, moleskin; oilcloth.

molester (mɔlɛste) *v.t*, to taunt.

moleter (mɔlte) *v.t*, to mill,
knurl. **molette** (lɛt) *f*, rowel;
muller; milled nut; knurl; milling tool; cutter wheel.

mollasse (mɔlas) *a*, flabby; flimsy;
spineless (*fig*.). **mollement** (lmɑ̃)
ad, softly; gracefully; feebly; vo-
luptuously. **mollesse** (lɛs) *f*, softness; mildness; feebleness; flabbiness; overindulgence; voluptuousness. **mollet, te** (lɛ, ɛt) *a*,
softish; soft-boiled (*eggs*); fancy
(*roll*). ¶ *m*, calf (*leg*). **molletière** (ltjɛːr) *f*, legging. **molle-**

ton (ltɔ̃) *m*, swansdown (*cloth*).

mollir (liːr) *v.i. & t*, to soften;
slacken; lull.

mollo (mɔlo) *ad*, gently, with care.
vas-y ~!, take it easy!

mollusque (mɔlysk) *m*, mollusc.

Moluques (les) (mɔlyk) *f.pl*, the
Moluccas.

môme (moːm) *n*, youngster.

moment (mɔmɑ̃) *m*, moment;
time; momentum. **momentané†,
e** (tane) *a*, momentary, temporary.

momerie (mɔmri) *f*, pose (*fig*.);
mummery.

momie (mɔmi) *f*, mummy; sleepyhead. **momifier** (fje) *v.t*, to mummify.

mon, ma, mes (mɔ̃, ma, me) *a*,
my. *oui, mon colonel, etc*, yes,
sir (*in the army*).

monacal, e† (mɔnakal) *a*, monastic, monkish.

monarchie (mɔnarʃi) *f*, monarchy. **monarchique** (ʃik) *a*, mo-
narchic(al). **monarchiste** (ʃist)
m. & att, monarchist. **monarque**
(nark) *m*, monarch.

monastère (mɔnastɛːr) *m*, monastery; convent. **monastique** (tik)
a, monastic.

monceau (mɔ̃so) *m*, heap, pile.

mondain, e (mɔ̃dɛ̃, ɛn) *a*,
worldly, mundane; (*att*.) society.
¶ *n*, society man, woman; worldling; police vice squad. **mondanité**
(danite) *f*, worldliness; (*pl*.) social
events (*news*). **monde** (mɔ̃:d) *m*,
world; people; company; set;
crowd; servants. *le ~ inanimé*,
inanimate nature. *tiers ~*, third
world. *tout le ~*, everybody. *elle
a du ~ au balcon*, she's got big
breasts (*slang*).

monder (mɔ̃de) *v.t*, to hull.

mondial, e (mɔ̃djal) *a*, world-
wide.

monétaire (mɔnetɛːr) *a*, monetary, money (*att*.).

mongol, e (mɔ̃gɔl) *a. & M~, n*,
Mongol[ian]. **la Mongolie** (li),
Mongolia.

moniteur (mɔnitœːr) *m*, adviser;
coach; (*name of many French
newspapers*).

monnaie (mɔnɛ) *f*, money; currency; coin; coinage; [small]
change. *~ de papier*, [converti-

ble] paper money. *faire de la ~*, to make or get change. *payer en ~ de singe*, to defraud. *la M~*, the mint. **monnayer** (neje) *v.t*, to coin, mint; commercialize (*fig.*). **monnayeur** (jœːr) *m*, minter. *faux ~*, counterfeiter.

monochrome (mɔnɔkroːm) *a*, monochrome. **monocle** (kl) *m*, monocle, eyeglass. **monocorde** (kɔrd) *m*, single-string instrument; monochord; monotonist (*pers.*). **monogamie** (gami) *f*, monogamy. **monogramme** (gram) *m*, monogram. **monographie** (grafi) *f*, monograph. **monolithe** (lit) *a*, monolithic. ¶ *m*, monolith. **monologue** (lɔg) *m*, monologue. **monologuer** (ge) *v.i*, to monologize, soliloquize. **monomanie** (mani) *f*, monomania. **monoplan** (plɑ̃) *m*, monoplane. **monopole** (pɔl) *m*, monopoly. **monopoliser** (lize) *v.t*, to monopolize. **monosyllabe** (silab) *m*, monosyllable. ¶ *~* & **monosyllabique** (bik) *a*, monosyllabic. **monotone** (tɔn) *a*, monotonous; humdrum. **monotonie** (ni) *f*, monotony, sameness. **monotype** (tip) *f*, monotype.

mons (mɔ̃ːs) *m*, Master (*so-&-so*) (*jocularly*). **monseigneur**, (oft. **M~** (mɛ̃sɛnœːr) *m*, His (or Your) Royal Highness; my lord, his (or your) lordship, his (or your) Grace; jimmy (*burglar's*). **monsieur**, oft. **M~** (məsjø) *m*, gentleman; Mr.; Esq.; sir; my (or the) master; man. *~ le juge*, your, his, Honor.

monstre (mɔ̃ːstr) *m*. & *att*, monster. **monstreux, euse†** (mɔ̃stryø, øːz) *a*, monstrous, freakish. **monstruosité** (ozite) *f*, monstrosity; freak [of nature].

mont (mɔ̃) *m*, mount, mountain; (*pl.*) Alps. *le ~ Blanc, etc.* See under *blanc, etc. par ~s & par vaux*, up hill & down dale. *~-de-piété*, pawnshop.

montage (mɔ̃taːʒ) *m*, raising; mounting; setting; erection; fit (*Mech.*); editing (*movie*). *~ des mailles*, casting on (*Knit.*). *~-son*, sound editing (*movie*).

montagnard, e (mɔ̃taɲaːr, ard) *a*, highland, mountain (*att.*). ¶ *n*, highlander, mountaineer. *les Montagnards*, the wild men (*Pol.*). **montagne** (taɲ) *f*, mountain; mountains. *~s russes*, scenic railway, switchback. **montagneux, euse** (ɲø, øːz) *a*, mountainous.

montant, e (mɔ̃tɑ̃, ɑ̃ːt) *a*, rising, ascending; incoming (*tide*); uphill; up (*train, etc.*); high; high-necked (*dress*); stand-up (*collar*). ¶ *m*, upright; post; stile; amount; total; tang. **monte** (mɔ̃ːt) *f*, covering (*of animals*); mount (*turf*); riding; jockey. **montecharge** (mɔ̃tʃarʒ) *m*, freight elevator, hoist. **montée** (mɔ̃te) *f*, ascent, rise, rising.

monténégrin, e (mɔ̃tenegrɛ̃, in) *a*. & **M~**, *n*, Montenegrin. *le Monténégro* (gro), Montenegro.

monter (mɔ̃te) *v.i*. & *t*, to go up, ascend; mount; climb; ride; command (*ship*); amount; raise, hoist, elevate; take up, carry up; set up, put up; erect; fit; set; string (*violin*); wind [up] (*spring*); turn up (*wick*); stage (*play*); cast on (*Knit.*); excite. *~ en amazone*, to ride side-saddle. *~ en graine*, to run to seed. *~ en voiture*, to take one's seat in a carriage. *~ sur un vaisseau, en avion*, to [go on] board a ship, a plane. *se ~*, to amount; equip oneself. **monteur** (tœːr) *m*, setter, mounter; fitter, erector.

monticule (mɔ̃tikyl) *m*, hillock, mound, knoll, hummock.

montjoie (mɔ̃ʒwa) *f*, cairn.

montoir (mɔ̃twaːr) *m*, horse block.

montrable (mɔ̃trabl) *a*, presentable. **montre** (mɔ̃ːtr) *f*, parade; show; display; [shop] window (*display*); sample; watch. *~-bracelet*, wristwatch. **montrer** (mɔ̃tre) *v.t*, to show; point [out]; teach. *~ du doigt*, to point at. **montreur** (trœːr) *m*, showman; exhibitor.

montueux, euse (mɔ̃tɥø, øːz) *a*, hilly.

monture (mɔ̃tyːr) *f*, mount (*animal*); mount[ing], setting; hook to gut (*Fish.*). *~ de rideaux*, cornice pole. *sans ~*, rimless (*glasses*).

monument (mɔnymɑ̃) *m*, monument, memorial; building (*public or historic*). ~ *aux morts [de la guerre]*, war memorial. ~ *historique*, national monument, building, etc, of historic interest. **monumental, e** (tal) *a*, monumental.

moquer (se) de (mɔke), to mock (at), deride, jeer at, laugh at, ridicule, make fun of. *s'en moquer*, not to care. **moquerie** (kri) *f*, mockery, jeer[s]. **moquette** (kɛt) *f*, moquette, velvet pile, saddle bag; Brussels carpet. **moqueur, euse** (kœːr, øːz) *n*, mocker, scoffer. ¶ *a*, mocking. [*oiseau*] *moqueur*, mocking bird.

moraillon (mɔrajɔ̃) *m*, hasp.

moraine (mɔrɛːn) *f*, moraine.

moral, e (mɔral) *a*, moral; mental. ¶ *m*, mind; moral[e]. **morale** (ral) *f*, morals (*ethics*); moral (*of story*). **moralement** (lmɑ̃) *ad*, morally. **moraliser** (lize) *v.i. & t*, to moralize; lecture. **moraliste** (list) *m*, moralist. **moralité** (te) *f*, morality (*principles, drama*); moral (*of fable*).

moratoire (mɔratwaːr) *a*, moratory; on overdue payments (*interest*); postponement of some social goals in favor of others. ¶ ~ & **moratorium** (tɔrjɔm) *m*, moratorium.

Moravie (la) (mɔravi), Moravia.

morbac (mɔrbak) *m*, crab (*body louse*); young child.

morbide (mɔrbid) *a*, morbid; unwholesome.

morceau (mɔrso) *m*, piece, bit; morsel; snack; lump, knob; scrap, fragment. ~*x choisis*, selections (*from writings*). ~ *d'ensemble*, part song, p. music. ~ *de concours*, test piece (*music, etc.*). *un* ~ *de femme*, a slip of a woman. ~ *honteux*, last piece (*left on dish*). *casser le* ~ *à quelqu'un*, to tell someone off. *casser un* ~, to have a bite to eat. *emporter le* ~, to win (*deal, argument, etc.*). **morceler** (sɔle) *v.t*, to parcel [out]; subdivide.

mordant, e (mɔrdɑ̃, ɑ̃ːt) *a*, mordant, biting; pungent. ¶ *m*, mordant; pungency; keenness; shrillness. **mordicus** (dikyːs) *ad*, dog-

gedly. **mordiller** (dije) *v.t*, to nibble.

mordoré, e (mɔrdɔre) *a*, reddish-brown; bronze (*shoes*).

mordre (mɔrdr) *v.t. & abs*, to bite, nip; nibble. *ça mord!* I have a bite! (*Fish.*). ~ *à*, to take to (*a study*). ~ *sur* (*fig.*), to find fault with. ~ *sur la latte*, to go over the mark (*Jump.*).

More (mɔːr) *m*, Moor. **m~**, *a*, Moorish.

morelle (mɔrɛl) *f*, nightshade.

moresque (mɔrɛsk) *a*, Moresque. ¶ *f*, Morisco, morris [*dance*].

morfil (mɔrfil) *m*, wire edge.

morfondre (mɔrfɔ̃ːdr) *v.t*, to chill. *se* ~, to be bored; to wait in vain, cool one's heels. **morfondu, e** (fɔ̃dy) *p.a*, [as if] frozen stiff.

morganatique† (mɔrganatik) *a*, morganatic.

morgeline (mɔrʒəlin) *f*, chickweed; pimpernel.

morgue (mɔrg) *f*, haughtiness; morgue.

moribond, e (mɔribɔ̃, ɔ̃ːd) *a. & n*, moribund, dying (man, woman).

moricaud, e (mɔriko, oːd) *n*, blackamoor.

morigéner (mɔriʒene) *v.t*, to take to task.

morne (mɔrn) *a*, gloomy, dismal, dreary, bleak, cheerless.

morose (mɔroːz) *a*, morose, sullen, moody. **morosité** (rozite) *f*, moroseness, etc.

Morphée (mɔrfe) *m*, Morpheus. **morphine** (fin) *f*, morphia, -phine. **morphinomane** (nɔman) *n*, morphinomaniac.

morphologie (mɔrfɔlɔʒi) *f*, morphology; accidence (*Gram.*).

mors (mɔːr) *m*, bit (*bridle*); jaw (*vise*).

morse (mɔrs) *m*, walrus, morse.

morsure (mɔrsyːr) *f*, bite; sting (*fig.*).

mort (mɔːr) *f*, death. *à* ~, to d.; to the d.; mortal (*strife*); mortally; deadly. ~ *& passion*, excruciating pains; agonies (*fig.*). **mort, e** (mɔːr, ɔrt) *a*, dead; still (*water, life*); spent (*shot*). *les morts*, the dead. *le jour des morts*, All Souls' Day. **mort**, *m*, dummy (*cards*).

mortaise (mɔrtɛːz) *f*, mortise, -ice; slot.

mortalité (mɔrtalite) *f*, mortality; death rate. **mort-aux-rats** (mɔrora) *f*, rat poison. **mort-bois** (mɔrbwɑ) *m*, underwood, brushwood. **morte-eau** (mɔrto) *f*, neap tide. **mortel, le†** (tɛl) *a*, mortal, deadly, lethal; fatal (*accident*). ¶ *n*, mortal. **morte-saison** (təsɛzɔ̃) *f*, dead season, off season.

mortier (mɔrtje) *m*, mortar (*plaster, vessel, Mil.*). ~ *de tranchée*, trench mortar.

mortifier (mɔrtifje) *v.t*, to mortify; make tender (*meat, game*). **mort-né, e** (mɔrne) *a*, stillborn. **mortuaire** (mɔrtɥɛːr) *a*, mortuary, [of] death; burial (*fees*). *le drap* ~, a pall.

morue (mɔry) *f*, cod[fish]. **morutier** (tje) *m*, cod fisher.

morve (mɔrv) *f*, mucus of the nose; glanders.

mosaïque (mɔzaik) *a*, Mosaic (*law*). ¶ *f*, mosaic, tessellated pavement.

Moscou (mɔsku) *m*, Moscow.

mosquée (mɔske) *f*, mosque.

mot (mo) *m*, word; saying; cell (*computers*); cue. ~ *à* ~ (motamo), ~ *pour* ~, word for word, verbatim. ~*s croisés* [-*énigmes*], crossword [puzzle]. ~ *d'ordre*, password; keynote. ~ *de l'énigme*, answer to the riddle. ~ *de passe*, password. ~ *de ralliement*, countersign (*Mil.*). *Note.*— In Fr., the ~ *de ralliement* is given in reply to the ~ *d'ordre*. ~ *en vedette*, word displayed in bold type, catchword. ~ *piquant*, quip. ~ *pour rire*, joke. ~ *de Cambronne*, shit (*reply of Napoleonic general to a demand for surrender*). ~ *de cinq lettres*, shit (*merde*). *gros* ~, swear word.

motard (mɔtaːr) *m*, motorcycle policeman.

moteur (mɔtœːr) *m*, engine, motor; mover. ~ *à essence*, gasoline engine. ~ *à gaz*, gas e. ~ *à pétrole*, oil e. ~*-fusée*, rocket e. **moteur, trice** (tœːr, tris) *att*, motive, driving. **motif** (tif) *m*, motive; reason; cause; (*pl.*) grounds; intentions (*matrimonial*); design, motif, traced article, (*pl.*) traced

goods; theme, motto (*Mus.*). **motion** (mosjɔ̃) *f*, motion (*proposal at meeting*). **motiver** (mɔtive) *v.t*, to state the reason for; justify.

motivation (mɔtivasjɔ̃) *f*, motivation. *études de* ~, motivational research.

motoculture (mɔtɔkylty:r) *f*, tractor farming, mechanized f. **motocyclette** (siklɛt), *abb.* **moto** (mɔto) *f*, motor [bi]cycle. **motocycliste** (klist) *n*, motorcyclist.

motoriser (mɔtrize) *v.t*, to motorize.

motte (mɔt) *f*, clod; turf, sod; roll (*butter*); mound.

motu proprio (mɔty prɔprio), of one's own accord.

motus (mɔtyːs) *i*, mum['s the word]!

mou, mol, molle (mu, mɔl) *a*, soft; lax; slack; inelastic (*Phys.*); limp, flabby; languid; muggy, close; indolent. **mou**, *m*, lights (*animal lungs*).

mouchard (muʃaːr) *m*, spy; police spy. **moucharder** (ʃarde) *v.t*, to spy.

mouche (muʃ) *f*, fly; patch, beauty spot; spot (*Bil.*); tuft (*on chin*); police spy; bull's-eye (*target*); bull (*shot*). ~ *à feu*, firefly. ~ *à miel*, honeybee. ~ *à viande*, meat fly, blowfly. ~ *bleue*, bluebottle. ~ *commune*, housefly. ~ *de mai*, May fly. ~ *noyée*, wet fly (*Fish.*). *poids* ~, fly weight (*Box.*). *prendre la* ~, to take offense.

moucher (muʃe) *v.t*, to wipe (*child's*) nose; snuff (*candle*); snub; tell off; beat up. *se* ~, to blow one's nose.

moucherolle (muʃrɔl) *f*, flycatcher (*bird*). **moucheron** (ʃrɔ̃) *m*, midge, gnat; whippersnapper; snuff (*candle*).

moucheté, e (muʃte) *a*, spotted, speckled; tabby (*cat*).

mouchettes (muʃɛt) *f.pl*, snuffers.

moucheture (muʃtyːr) *f*, spot, speckle.

mouchoir (muʃwaːr) *m*, handkerchief. ~ *de cou*, silk scarf.

moudre (mudr) *v.t. & abs. ir*, to grind, mill. *en* ~, to pedal hard (*bicycle*); to practice prostitution.

moue (mu) *f,* pout[ing]. *faire la ~,* to pout.

monette (mwɛt) *f,* [sea] gull, [sea] mew.

mouffette (mufɛt) *f,* skunk (*Zool.*).

moufle (mufl) *f,* pulley block, tackle b.; mitt[en]; (*m.*) pulley block, tackle b.; muffle (*Chem.*).

mouillage (muja:ȝ) *m,* wetting; watering (*wine, etc.*); mooring; moorings, anchorage, berth. **mouille-bouche** (mujbuʃ) *f,* bergamot (*pear*). **mouillée** (je) *p.a.f,* palat[al]ized (*consonant*). **mouiller** (je) *v.t. & abs,* to wet, moisten, damp; water; anchor, moor, berth. *~ quelqu'un,* to compromise someone. *se ~,* to take a risk. **mouillette** (jɛt) *f,* sippet. **mouilloir** (jwa:r) *m,* damper (*stamps, labels*). **mouillure** (jy:r) *f,* wetting; damp mark (*in books*).

mouise (mwi:z) *f,* poverty. *être dans la ~,* to be broke.

moulage (mula:ȝ) *m,* molding (*act*); casting. **moule** (mul) *m,* mold, (*f.*) mussel. **mouler** (le) *v.t,* to mold, cast; shape; print (*handwriting*). **mouleur** (lœ:r) *m,* molder.

moulin (mulɛ̃) *m,* mill; moulin (*glacier*). *~ à paroles,* chatterbox; windbag. *~ à prières,* prayer wheel. *~ à vent,* windmill. **mouliné, e** (line) *p.a. & p.p,* worm-eaten (*wood*); moth (*silk*). **moulinet** (nɛ) *m,* winch; reel (*Fish.*); turnstile (X *on post*). *faire le ~ avec,* to whirl, twirl. **moulu, e** (ly) *p.a: ~ de fatigue,* dead beat. *tout ~,* aching all over.

moulure (muly:r) *f,* molding (*ornamental strip*).

mourant, e (murɑ̃, ɑ̃:t) *a,* dying; languishing (*eyes*); faint (*voice*). **les mourants,** *m.pl,* the dying. **mourir** (ri:r) *v.i.ir,* to die, be dying; die away; d. out; d. down. *faire ~,* to execute (*criminal*). **se ~,** to be dying; fade out, give out.

mouron (murɔ̃) *m,* pimpernel. *~ [des oiseaux],* chickweed. *se faire du ~,* to get into a stew.

mousquet (muskɛ) *m,* musket. **mousquetaire** (kətɛ:r) *m,* musketeer; (*att.*) double (*cuffs*). **mous-**

queton (tɔ̃) *m,* carbine; snap hook.

mousse (mus) *m,* cabin boy; (*f.*) moss; froth; foam; lather; head (*on glass of beer*); mousse (*cream*).

mousseline (muslin) *f,* muslin; mousseline.

mousser (muse) *v.i,* to froth; foam; lather; effervesce, sparkle. *faire ~* (*fig.*), to make much of; advertise; make angry. **mousseux, euse** (sø, ø:z) *a,* mossy; moss (*rose*); frothy; foamy; sparkling (*wine*). *non mousseux,* still (*wine*).

mousson (musɔ̃) *f,* monsoon.

moussu, e (musy) *a,* mossy, moss-grown; moss (*rose*).

moustache (mustaʃ) *f,* mustache; whiskers (*animal*). *~ en brosse,* toothbrush m. *~ en croc,* turned up m. **moustachu, e** (ʃy) *a,* mustached.

moustiquaire (mustikɛ:r) *f,* mosquito net. **moustique** (tik) *m,* mosquito.

moût (mu) *m,* must, stum; wort.

moutard (muta:r) *m,* youngster, urchin.

moutarde (mutard) *f. & att,* mustard. *de la ~ après dîner,* too late to be useful. *la ~ lui est montée au nez,* he lost his temper. **moutardier** (dje) *m,* mustard pot; m. maker.

mouton (mutɔ̃) *m,* sheep; wether; mutton; sheep[skin]; lamb (*pers.*); spy (*on prisoner*); monkey; ram tup (*pile driving*); yoke, stock (*of bell*); (*pl.*) sheep; (*pl.*) whitecaps (*waves*); (*pl.*) fluff (*under furniture*). **moutonner** (tɔne) *v.i,* to [break into] foam (*sea*). *nuages moutonnés, ciel moutonné,* fleecy clouds, sky fleeced with clouds. **moutonneux, euse** (nø, ø:z) *a,* foamy; crested (*waves*). **moutonnier, ère** (nje, ɛ:r) *a,* sheeplike (*pers.*).

mouture (muty:r) *f,* milling; maslin.

mouvant, e (muvɑ̃, ɑ̃:t) *a,* moving, shifting, unstable; quick (*sand*). **mouvement** (vmɑ̃) *m,* motion; movement; progress; impulse; action, bustle, stir; life; arrangement (*Art.*); conformation (*of ground*); change; changes (*staff*); appointments & promotions; move (*Mil.*); burst (*oratory*); attack (*fever*); fluctuation; traffic; circulation; turnover; statistics (*population*); transaction; works (*Horol.*). ~ des navires, shipping intelligence, s. news, movements of ships. ~ populaire, civil commotion. ~ vissé, clockwise movement. ~ d'humeur, bad-tempered gesture or mood. dans le ~ (*fig.*), in the swim. de son propre ~, of one's own accord. **mouvementé, e** (te) *a*, lively, bustling, busy; eventful; stirring; broken (*ground*). **mouvoir** (vwa:r) *v.t.ir.* & se ~, to move; actuate; propel.

moyen, ne (mwajɛ̃, ɛn) *a*, middle; mean, average; medium; middling; intermediate (*course, Sch.*); doubtful (*virtue*). d'âge moyen, middle-aged (*pers.*). le ~ âge, the Middle Ages. du ~ âge, medieval. ~ terme, middle course (*conduct*). ~ [*terme*], middle [term] (*Log.*). moyen, *m*, means, way; help; (*pl.*) means (*pecuniary*); grounds (*law*). ~ de fortune, makeshift. **moyenâgeux, euse** (jɛnɑʒø̃, ø:z) *a*, medieval. **moyennant** (nɑ̃) *pr*, in consideration of; on; at; with the help of. **moyenne** (jɛn) *f*, average, mean. **moyennement** (nmɑ̃) *ad*, moderately, fairly.

moyeu (mwajø̃) *m*, nave; hub; boss. ~ arrière à roue libre & frein contre-pédalage, coaster hub.

mucilage (mysilɑ:ʒ) *m*, mucilage. **mucosité** (mykozite) *f*. & **mucus** (ky:s) *m*, mucus, phlegm.

mue (my) *f*, molt[ing]; slough[ing]; mew; [hen] coop; breaking (*voice*). **muer** (mɥe) *v.i*, to molt; slough; break; (*v.t.*) to change.

muet, te (mɥɛ, ɛt) *a*. & *n*, dumb (person); mute; speechless; silent. à la muette, without speaking.

muezzin (mɥɛzɛ̃) *m*, muezzin.

mufle (myfl) *m*, muzzle, muffle; cad. **muflier** (flie) *m*, antirrhinum, snapdragon.

muge (my:ʒ) *m*, gray mullet.

mugir (myʒi:r) *v.i*, to low; bellow; roar; whistle (*wind*).

muguet (mygɛ) *m*, lily of the valley.

mulâtre (mylɑ:tr) *a*. & *m*, **mulâtresse** (lɑtrɛs) *f*, mulatto. **mule** (myl) *f*, [she] mule; mule (*slipper*); slipper or toe (*of pope as kissed*). **mulet** (lɛ) *m*, [he] mule; mule (*pers.*); cross, hybrid, mule; gray mullet; test auto (*not mass produced*). **muletier** (ltje) *m*, muleteer; (*att.*) mule (*track*).

mulot (mylo) *m*, field mouse.

multicolore (myltikɔlɔ:r) *a*, multicolor[ed], many-colored.

multicopie (myltikɔpi) *f*, photocopy, Xerox, etc.

multiple (myltipl) *a*, multiple, manifold, multifarious. ¶ *m*, multiple. **multiplicande** (plikɔ̃:d) *m*, multiplicand. **multiplicateur** (katœ:r) *m*, multiplier. **multiplication** (sjɔ̃) *f*, multiplication; gear [ratio]. **multiplicité** (site) *f*, multiplicity. **multiplier** (plie) *v.t*. & *i*. & se ~, to multiply.

multiplet (myltiple) *m*, byte.

multitude (myltityd) *f*, multitude, crowd.

municipal, e (munisipal) *a*, municipal, town (*att.*). **municipalité** (lite) *f*, municipality; [municipal] corporation.

munificence (mynifisɑ̃:s) *f*, munificence, bounty.

munir (myni:r) *v.t*, to supply, provide, furnish; fortify. **munitions** (nisjɔ̃) *f.pl*, ammunition. ~ de bouche, provisions, food. ~ de guerre, war[like] stores, munitions.

muqueux, euse (mykø̃, ø:z) *a*, mucous. [**membrane**] **muqueuse**, *f*, m. membrane.

mur (my:r) *m*, wall.

mûr, e (my:r) *a*, ripe, mature; mellow; worn threadbare.

muraille (myrɑ:j) *f*, wall. **mural, e** (ral) *a*, mural, wall (*att.*).

mûre (my:r) *f*, mulberry. ~ sauvage, ~ de ronce, blackberry.

mûrement (myrmɑ̃) *ad*, closely, thoroughly.

murer (myre) *v.t*, to wall; w. up; screen (*fig*).

mûrier (myrje) *m*, mulberry [tree].

mûrir (myri:r) *v.i*. & *t*, to ripen, mature; mellow.

murmure (myrmy:r) *m*, murmur; grumbling; mutter; whisper; hum;

brawling; gurgle; soughing. **murmurer** (myre) *v.i. & t*, to murmur, etc.

mûron (myrɔ̃) *m*, blackberry; wild raspberry bush.

musaraigne (myzarɛɲ) *f*, shrew [mouse].

musarder (myzarde) *v.i*, to dawdle.

musc (mysk) *m*, musk; m. deer. [noix] **muscade** (kad) *f*, nutmeg. **muscadier** (dje) *m*, nutmeg [tree]. **muscat** (ka) *a. & m*, muscat (grape, wine).

muscle (myskl) *m*, muscle. **musclé, e** (kle) *a*, -muscled. **musculaire** (kylɛːr) & **musculeux, euse** (lø, øːz) *a*, muscular.

Muse (myːz) *f*, Muse.

museau (myzo) *m*, muzzle, snout.

musée (myze) *m*, museum.

museler (myzle) *v.t*, to muzzle. **muselière** (zəljɛːr) *f*, muzzle (*dog*).

muser (myze) *v.i*, to dawdle, moon [about].

musette (myzɛt) *f*, musette (*Mus.*); nosebag; haversack; bag.

muséum (myzeɔm) *m*, natural history museum.

musical, e† (myzikal) *a*, musical. **music hall** (myzik ɔl) *m*, music hall variety theater. **musicien, ne** (sjɛ̃, ɛn) *n*, musician; player; bandsman; (*att.*) musical. **musique** (zik) *f*, music; band; toy musical instrument; blackmail. *connaître la ~*, to have had the experience. *~ de chats*, caterwauling.

musoir (myzwaːr) *m*, pierhead.

musquer (myske) *v.t*, to [perfume with] musk.

musulman, e (myzylmɑ̃, an) *n. & att*, Mussulman.

mutabilité (mytabilite) *f*, mutability. **mutation** (sjɔ̃) *f*, mutation, change; transfer, conveyance (*law*). **muter** (te) *v.t*, to transfer (*official, soldier*).

mutilation (mytilasjɔ̃) *f*, mutilation, maiming; defacement. **mutilé de la guerre** (le) *m*, disabled soldier, disabled sailor. **mutiler** (le) *v.t*, to mutilate, etc.

mutin, e (mytɛ̃, in) *a. & n*, roguish (child), mischievous (child); mutinous; mutineer. **se mutiner**

(tine) *v.pr. & mutiner*, *v.abs*, to mutiny, rebel; be unruly. **mutinerie** (nri) *f*, mutiny; refractoriness; roguishness.

mutisme (mytism) *m*, dumbness, muteness.

mutualiste (mytɥalist) *n*, member of a mutual society *or* association. **mutualité** (te) *f*, mutuality; mutual association. *~ de crédit*, mutual loan association. **mutuel, le†** (tɥɛl) *a*, mutual.

mycélium (miseljɔm) *m*, mycelium, spawn.

myope (mjɔp) *a. & n*, shortsighted (person), nearsighted (person). **myopie** (pi) *f*, myopia.

myosotis (mjɔzɔtis) *m*, myosotis, forget-me-not.

myriade (mirjad) *f*, myriad. **myriagramme** (gram) *m*, myriagram = 10000 grams *or* 22.046 lbs. **myriapode** (pɔd) *m*, myriapod.

myrrhe (miːr) *f*, myrrh.

myrte (mirt) *m*, myrtle. **myrtille** (til) *f*, whortleberry, bilberry.

mystère (mistɛːr) *m*, mystery; m. [play], miracle [play]. *~ de la Passion*, passion play. **mystérieux, euse†** (terjø, øːz) *a*, mysterious. **mysticisme** (tisism) *m*, mysticism. **mysticité** (te) *f*, mysticalness. **mystificateur, trice** (fikatœːr, tris) *n*, hoaxer, humbug. **mystifier** (fje) *v.t*, to mystify; hoax, humbug. **mystique†** (tik) *a*, mystic(al). ¶ *n*, mystic (*pers.*); (*f.*) mystical theology; mysterious appeal (*as of the olden times*).

mythe (mit) *m*, myth. **mythique** (tik) *a*, mythic(al). **mythologie** (tɔlɔʒi) *f*, mythology. **mythologique** (ʒik) *a*, mythologic(al). **mythologue** (lɔg) *n*, mythologist.

N

nabab (nabab) *m*, nabob.

nabot, e (nabo, ɔt) (*pers.*) *n*, midget, shrimp, manikin.

nacelle (nasɛl) (*Avn.*) *f*, car, nacelle, gondola; cockpit; skiff; dinghy; pontoon boat.

nacre (nakr) *f*, mother of pearl. **nacré, e** (kre) *a*, pearly.

nadir (nadiːr) *m*, nadir.

nævus (nevy:s) *m*, birthmark, mole.

nage (na:ʒ) *f*, swimming; stroke. ~ [*d'aviron*], rowing. ~ *à la pagaie*, paddling. ~ *de côté*, sidestroke. ~ *en grenouille*, breaststroke. ~ *en couple*, sculling. *en* ~, bathed in perspiration. **nageoire** (naʒwa:r) *f*, fin (*fish*); flipper. **nager** (ʒe) *v.i*, to swim, float; welter, revel; row. ~ *debout*, to tread water; row standing up. ~ *en couple*, to scull. ~ *entre deux eaux*, to swim under water. **nageur, euse** (ʒœ:r, ø:z) *n*, swimmer; rower, oarsman.

naguère (nagɛ:r) *ad*, not long since.

naïade (najad) *f*, naiad, water nymph.

naïf, ïve (naif, i:v) *a*, artless, naïve, unaffected ingenuous; unsophisticated; simpleminded; green.

nain, e (nɛ̃, ɛn) *n. & att*, dwarf.

naissance (nɛsã:s) *f*, birth; descent; rise (*river*); spring[ing] (*Arch.*). ~*du jour*, dawn, break of day. **naissant, e** (sã, ã:t) *a*, dawning; budding; nascent. **naître** (nɛ:tr) *v.i.ir*, to be born; grow; bud; [a]rise, spring up. *à* ~, unborn.

naïvement (naivmã) *ad*, artlessly, etc. **naïveté** (vte) *f*, artlessness, etc.

nana (nana) *f*, woman (*slang*).

nankin (nãkɛ̃) *m*, nankeen.

nanti, e (nãti) *p.p*: ~ *de* (*fig.*), secured by. *homme* ~, man who has made his pile. **nantir** (ti:r) *v.t*, to secure; provide; register (*mortgage*). **nantissement** (smã) *m*, hypothecation, collateral security.

napel (napɛl) *m*, wolfsbane.

naphtaline (naftalin) *f*, naphthalene. **naphte** (naft) *m*, naphtha.

napolitain, e (napɔlitɛ̃, ɛn) *a. &* N~, *n*, Neapolitan.

nappe (nap) *f*, tablecloth; cloth; sheet (*water, flame*). **napperon** (prɔ̃) *m*, cloth (*tea, tray*).

narcisse (narsis) *m*, narcissus. ~ *des prés*, daffodil.

narcotique (narkɔtik) *a. & m*, narcotic, opiate.

narguer (narge) *v.t*, to flout.

narguilé, -ghileh (nargile) *m*, hookah.

narine (narin) *f*, nostril.

narquois, e (narkwa, a:z) *a*, sly, cunning, bantering.

narrateur, trice (narratœ:r, tris) *n*, narrator, storyteller. **narratif, ive** (tif, i:v) *a*, narrative. **narration** (sjɔ̃) *f*, narrative, story; narration; essay (*Sch.*). **narrer** (re) *v.t*, to narrate, relate, tell.

narval (narval) *m*, narwhal.

nasal, e (nazal) *a. & f*, nasal. **nasarde** (zard) *f*, fillip; snub. **naseau** (zo) *m*, nostril (*horse*). **nasiller** (zije) *v.i*, to speak through the nose, snuffle, twang.

nasse (nas) *f*, eel pot; lobster pot; net; trap.

natal, e (natal) *a*, native; natal. **natalité** (lite) *f*, birthrate, natality.

natation (natasjɔ̃) *f*, swimming, natation.

natif, ive (natif, i:v) *a*, native, inborn. **les natifs**, *m. pl*, the natives.

nation (nasjɔ̃) *f*, nation; people. **national, e** (ɔnal) *a*, national. **nationalisme** (lism) *m*, nationalism. **nationaliste** (list) *n. & a*, nationalist. **nationalité** (te) *f*, nationality. **nationaux** (no) *m.pl*, nationals.

nativité (nativite) *f*, nativity.

natte (nat) *f*, mat, matting; plait. **natter** (te) *v.t*, to mat; plait. *se* ~, to plait one's hair. **nattier** (tje) *m*, mat maker.

naturalisation (natyralizasjɔ̃) *f*, naturalization. **naturaliser** (ze) *v.t*, to naturalize; stuff (*animal*); preserve (*plant*). **naturaliste** (list) *m*, naturalist. ~ [*fourreur*], taxidermist. **nature** (ty:r) *f*, nature; life (*art*); life size; plain [-boiled]. ~ *morte*, still life. *en* ~, in kind. **naturel, le†** (tyrɛl) *a*, natural; native; unaffected; illegitimate. ¶ *m*, naturalness; nature, disposition; native (*pers.*).

naufrage (nofra:ʒ) *m*, wreck, shipwreck. *faire* ~, to be [ship]-wrecked. **naufragé, e** (fraʒe) *n*, shipwrecked person, castaway.

nauséabond, e (nozeabɔ̃, 5:d) *a*, nauseous, sickening, foul. **nau-**

sée (ze) *f*, nausea. **nauséeux, euse** (zeø, ø:z) *a*, neauseating.

nautile (notil) *ou* **nautilus** (ly:s) *m*, nautilus. **nautique** (tik) *a*, nautical; aquatic (*sports*). **nautonier, ère** (tonje, ɛ:r) (*Poet.*) *n*, mariner; ferryman.

naval, e (naval) *a*, naval, sea (*att.*); ship (*att.*).

navet (navɛ) *m*, turnip; bad painting; unsuccessful play. ~ *de Suède*, Swede turnip (*Agric.*).

navette (navɛt) *f*, rape (*oil seed plant*); incense box; shuttle. *faire la* ~, to go to & fro.

navigable (navigabl) *a*, navigable. **navigateur** (tœ:r) *m*, navigator; (*att.*) seafaring. **navigation** (sjɔ̃) *f*, navigation; sailing; shipping. **naviguer** (ge) *v.i*, to navigate, sail.

navire (navi:r) *m*, ship, vessel, boat, bottom. ~ *à vapeur*, steamship. ~*-citerne*, *m*, tank ship. ~ *de charge*, cargo boat. ~ *frère*, ~ *jumeau*, sister ship. ~ *de ligne* [*régulière*], liner. ~ *pose-mines*, mine layer.

navrant, e (navrɑ̃, ɑ̃:t) *a*, heartrending, heartbreaking, harrowing. **navrer** [**le cœur**] (vre) *v.t*, to break one's heart, harrow.

ne, n' (nə, n) *neg. particle*, used mostly with the words *pas* or *point*, not, n't. *n'importe!* no matter!

né, e (ne) *a*, born. *Je suis* ~, I was born.

néanmoins (neɑ̃mwɛ̃) *ad*, nevertheless, notwithstanding, yet, still.

néant (neɑ̃) *m*, nothing[ness], nought; nil, none.

nébuleux, euse (nebylø, ø:z) *a*, nebulous, cloudy; clouded. ¶ *f*, nebula (*Astr.*).

nécessaire† (nesɛsɛ:r) *a*, necessary, needful. ¶ *m*, necessary, -ries, needful; busybody; outfit, case. ~ *à ouvrage*, workbox, workbasket, needlework case. **nécessité** (site) *f*, necessity. **nécessiter** (te) *v.t*, to necessitate. **nécessiteux, euse** (tø, ø:z) *a*, necessitous, needy. *les* ~, *m.pl*, the needy, the destitute.

nécrologe (nekrɔlɔ:ʒ) *m*, necrology, obituary (*roll, book*). **nécrologie** (lɔʒi) *f*, deaths, obitu-

ary, necrology (*notice*). **nécromancie** (mɑ̃si) *f*, necromancy. **nécromancien, ne** (sjɛ̃, ɛn) *n*, necromancer. **nécropole** (pɔl) *f*, necropolis. **nécrose** (kro:z) *f*, necrosis.

nectaire (nɛktɛ:r) *m*, nectary. **nectar** (ta:r) *m*, nectar.

néerlandais, e (neɛrlɑ̃dɛ, ɛ:z) *a*, Netherlandish, Dutch. **N~**, *n*, Netherlander, Dutchman, -woman. **la Néerlande** (lɑ̃:d), the Netherlands.

nef (nɛf) *f*, nave (*church*); bark, ship (*Poet.*).

néfaste (nefast) *a*, luckless, illfated, ill-starred, disastrous.

nèfle (nɛfl) *f*, medlar. **néflier** (neflie) *m*, medlar [tree].

négatif, ive† (negatif, i:v) *a*, negative. ¶ *m*, negative (*Phot.*). **la négative**, the negative (*statement, etc.*). **négation** (sjɔ̃) *f*, negation; negative (*Gram.*).

négligé, e (negliʒe) *p.a*, neglected; unheeded; loose; slovenly; slipshod. ¶ *m*, undress, négligé; tea gown. **négligeable** (ʒabl) *a*, negligible. **négligemment** (ʒamɑ̃) *ad*, negligently, carelessly. **négligence** (ʒɑ̃:s) *f*, negligence, neglect, carelessness; default. **négligent, e** (ʒɑ̃, ɑ̃:t) *a*, negligent, careless, neglectful, remiss. **négliger** (ʒe) *v.t*, to neglect, slight. *se* ~, to neglect oneself; slack; be careless.

négoce (negɔs) *m*, trade; business. **négociable** (sjabl) *a*, negotiable; marketable. **négociant, e** (sjɑ̃, ɑ̃:t) *n*, trader, merchant. **négociateur, trice** (atœ:r, tris) *n*, negociâtor. **négociation** (sjɔ̃) *f*, negotiation; transaction; dealing; bargain. **négocier** (sje) *v.t*, to negotiate.

nègre (nɛ̃:gr) *a.m. & a.f.*, Negro. ¶ *m*, Negro; one who does the donkey work, underling (*vulg.*); ghost-writer, literary hack. **négresse** (negrɛs) *f*, Negress. **négrier** (grie) *m*, slaver, slave trader; s. driver (*hard employer*).

négritude (negrityd) *f*, overall cultural & spiritual values of people of black race.

neige (nɛ:ʒ) *f. oft. pl*, snow. *de la* ~ *fondue*, sleet; slush. *tomber* *de la* ~ *fondue,* to sleet. **neiger** (nɛʒe) *v.imp,* to snow. **neigeux, euse** (zø, ø:z) *a,* snowy.

Némésis (nemezi:s) *f,* Nemesis.

ne m'oubliez pas (nəmubliepɑ) *m,* forget-me-not.

nénuphar (nenyfa:r) *m,* water lily.

néologisme (neɔlɔʒism) *m,* neologism.

néon (neɔ̃) *m,* neon.

néophyte (neɔfit) *n,* neophyte.

néo-zélandais, e (neɔzelɑ̃dɛ, ɛ:z) *a,* New Zealand (*att.*). **Néo-Zélandais, e,** *n,* New Zealander.

népotisme (nepɔtism) *m,* nepotism.

Néréide (nereid) *f,* Nereid, sea nymph.

nerf (nɛ:r & nɛrf) *m,* nerve; band (*Bookb.*); sinews (*of war*); (*pl.*) thews; (*pl.*) nerves, hysterics; (*pl.*) tantrums.

nerveux, euse† (nɛrvø, ø:z) *a,* nervous; highly strung; hysterical; fidgety. **nervosité** (vozite) *f,* irritability. **nervure** (vy:r) *f,* rib, nerve, nervure, vein (*Bot., etc.*).

net, te (nɛt) *a,* clean; flawless; clear; sharp; empty; free; net. *mettre au net,* to make a clean copy of. **net,** *ad,* clean; plainly, flatly, outright. **nettement** (tmɑ̃) *ad,* clearly; frankly, plainly, flatly, downright. **netteté** (nɛtte) *f,* cleanness; clearness.

nettoiement (nɛtwamɑ̃) & **nettoyage** (ja:ʒ) *m,* cleaning, cleansing. **nettoyer** (je) *v.t,* to clean, cleanse; clear. ~ *à sec,* to dry-clean. **nettoyeur, euse** (jœ:r, ø:z) *n,* cleaner.

neuf (nœf & nœ & nœv) *a. & m,* nine; ninth. ~ *fois sur dix,* nine times out of ten.

neuf, euve (nœf, œ:v) *a,* new; in-experienced, raw.

neurasthénie (nørasteni) *f,* neurasthenia. **neurologiste** (rɔlɔʒist) *ou* **neurologue** (lɔg) *n,* nerve specialist, neurologist.

neutraliser (nøtralize) *v.t,* to neutralize. **neutralité** (te) *f,* neutrality. **neutre** (nø:tr) *a,* neutral; noncommittal; neuter; undenominational (*school*). ¶ *m,* neuter; neutral.

neuvième† (nœvjɛm) *a. & n,* ninth.

neveu (nəvø) *m,* nephew. *nos* ~*x,* posterity.

névralgie (nevralʒi) *f,* neuralgia. **névralgique** (ʒik) *a,* neuralgic; sore (*point*). **névrite** (vrit) *f,* neuritis. **névrose** (vro:z) *f,* neurosis. **névrosé, e** (vroze) *a,* neurotic.

nez (ne) *m,* nose; face; nosing (*stair*); scent (*dogs*). *à vue de* ~, at the first blush. *avoir un verre dans le* ~, to be tipsy. ~ *à* ~, face to face.

ni (ni) *c,* nor; or; neither. ~ *fleurs,* ~ *couronnes,* no flowers, by request. ~ *l'un* (*l'une*) *ni l'autre,* pn. & a, neither.

niable (njabl) *a,* deniable.

niais, e† (njɛ, ɛ:z) *a. & n,* silly. **niaiser** (ɛze) *v.i,* to play the fool. **niaiserie** (zri) *f,* silliness.

niche (niʃ) *f,* niche; trick, prank, practical joke. ~ *à chien,* dog kennel. **nichée** (ʃe) *f,* nest[ful]; brood. **nicher** (ʃe) *v.i,* to nest; (*v.t.*) to put, ensconce. **nichet** (ʃɛ) *m,* nestegg.

nichon (niʃɔ̃) *m,* breast (*slang*). *faux* ~*s,* falsies, gay deceivers.

nickel (nikɛl) *m,* nickel. **nickeler** (kle) *v.t,* to nickle.

nicodème (nikɔdɛːm) *m,* booby.

nicotine (nikɔtin) *f,* nicotine.

nid (ni) *m,* nest; den. ~ *d'hirondelle,* edible bird's nest. ~ *de pie,* crow's nest (*Naut.*). *il croit avoir trouvé la pie au* ~, he has found a mare's nest.

nièce (njɛs) *f,* niece.

nielle (njɛl) *f,* smut, blight (*Agric.*). ¶ *m,* niello.

nier (nje) *v.t,* to deny; repudiate; (*abs.*) to deny it. ~ *sa culpabilité,* to plead not guilty.

nigaud, e (nigo, o:d) *a,* silly. ¶ *n,* noodle, ninny, booby, nincompoop. **nigauder** (gode) *v.i,* to play the fool. **nigauderie** (dri) *f,* silliness.

nigelle de Damas (niʒɛl) *f,* love-in-a-mist.

nihiliste (niilist) *m,* nihilist.

Nil (le) (nil), the Nile.

nimbe (nɛ̃:b) *m,* nimbus, halo,

glory. **nimbus** (nɛ̃byːs) *m*, nimbus (*Meteor.*).

Ninive (niniːv) *f*, Nineveh.

nippes (nip) *f.pl*, old clothes; togs. **nipper** (pe) *v.t*, to rig out, outfit someone. *se ~ aux puces*, to buy one's clothes secondhand, at a flea market.

nitouche (sainte) (nituʃ) *f*, [prudish & demure] little hypocrite.

nitrate (nitrat) *m*, nitrate. **nitre** (tr) *m*, niter, saltpeter. **nitrique** (trik) *a*, nitric. **nitroglycérine** (trɔgliserin) *f*, nitroglycerin[e].

niveau (nivo) *m*, level. *~ à bulle d'air*, spirit l. *~ de vie*, standard of living. *de ~*, level, at grade. **niveler** (vle) *v.t*, to level. **niveleur** (vlœːr) *m*, leveler. **niveleuse** (løz) *f*, grader (*Build.*). **nivellement** (vɛlmɑ̃) *m*, leveling.

nobiliaire (nɔbiljɛːr) *a*, nobiliary. ¶ *m*, peerage (*book*). **noble†** (bl) *a*, noble. ¶ *n*, noble[man], noblewoman. **noblesse** (blɛs) *f*, nobility; nobleness; noblesse.

noce (nɔs) *f*, wedding festivities; wedding party; jollification, spree; (*pl.*) wedding, marriage, nuptials. *~s d'argent, d'or, de diamant*, silver, golden, diamond, wedding. **noceur, euse** (sœːr, øːz) *n*, reveler.

nocher (nɔʃe) (*Poet.*) *m*, boatman; ferryman.

nocif, ive (nɔsif, iːv) *a*, noxious.

noctambule (nɔktɑ̃byːl) *n*, sleepwalker. **nocturne** (tyrn) *a*, nocturnal, night (*att.*). ¶ *m*, nocturne.

Noël (nɔɛl) *m*, Christmas[tide], yule[tide]. *à la [fête de] ~, à ~*, at Christmas[tide], at yuletide. **n~**, [Christmas] carol.

nœud (nø) *m*, knot; node; cluster; crux; rub; tie, bond (*fig.*). *~ coulant*, slip knot, running k.; noose. *~ [de ruban]*, bow. *~ gordien* (gɔrdjɛ̃), Gordian knot. *~[-papillon]*, bow tie. *~ plat*, reef knot.

noir, e (nwaːr) *a*, black; dark; swarthy; brown (*bread*); black & blue (*bruised*); gloomy; drunk (*slang*). *noir sur blanc* [down] in black & white (*writing*). *la mer Noire*, the Black Sea. ¶ *m*,

black; b. mark (*bruise*); b. [man, boy], man of color; bull's eye (*target*). ¶ *f*, black [ball] (*gaming*); crotchet (*Mus.*). **noirâtre** (nwarɑːtr) *a*, blackish; darkish. **noiraud, e** (ro, oːd) *a. & n*, swarthy (man, woman). **noirceur** (sœːr) *f*, blackness; black spot; smudge, smut. **noircir** (siːr) *v.t. & i*, to blacken; black; blot (*paper with useless writing*). **noircissure** (sisyːr) *f*, smudge.

noise (nwaːz) *f*, quarrel.

noisetier (nwaztje) *m*, hazel (*bush*), nut tree. **noisette** (zɛt) *f*, hazelnut; nut; hazel (*color, eyes*); nut-brown. *les ~s*, testicles (*slang*).

noix (nwa) *f*, walnut; nut. *~ de coco*, coconut. *~ de galle*, nut gall. *~ vomique* (vɔmik), nux vomica.

nolis (nɔli) *m*, freight. **noliser** (ze) *v.t*, to freight, charter.

nom (nɔ̃) *m*, name; style; noun. *~ de baptême*, Christian name. *~ [de famille]*, *~ patronymique*, surname. *~ de plume*, assumed name, alias; stage n.; pen n. *~ de jeune fille*, maiden n. *~ de plume*, pen n. *~ de théâtre*, stage n. *~ & prénoms*, full n. *sous un ~ interposé*, in a nominee's n. *petit nom*, given n.

nomade (nɔmad) *a*, nomad(ic). ¶ *m*, nomad, wanderer.

nombre (nɔ̃ːbr) *m*, number. *les N~s* (*Bible*), Numbers. *~ des adhérents*, membership. *avoir du ~*, to be well-balanced (*phrase*). **nombrer** (nɔ̃bre) *v.t*, to number, count. **nombreux, euse** (brø, øːz) *a*, numerous; well-balanced (*style, prose*).

nombril (nɔ̃bri) *m*, navel; eye (*fruit*). *se prendre pour le ~ du monde*, to think oneself very important. **nombrilisme** (lism) *m*, navel gazing.

nomenclature (nɔmɑ̃klatyːr) *f*, nomenclature. **nominal, e†** (minal) *a*, nominal; face (*value*). *appel ~*, roll call. **nominatif, ive** (tif, iːv) *a*, nominal, of [the] names; registered (*securities*). ¶ *m*, nominative [case]. **nomination** (sjɔ̃) *f*, nomination; appointment; commissioning (*officer*);

gift (*of an office*); award (*at a show*). **nominativement** (tivmã) *ad,*. by name. **un nommé . . .** (me),. a man called . . ., one . . . [by name]. **nommément** (memã) *ad,* namely, to wit, by name. **nommer** (me) *v.t,* to name; call; nominate; appoint; commission; return, elect. **se ~,** to give one's name; be called. *je me nomme Adam,* my name is Adam.

non (nɔ̃) *neg. particle,* no; not. *ni moi ~ plus,* nor I either. ¶ *m,* no, nay.

non-activité (en) (nɔnaktivite) *f,* on the unemployed list (*Mil.*).

nonagénaire (nɔnaʒenɛːr) *a. & ' n,* nonagenarian.

non avenu, e (nɔnavny) *a,* void, non avenu.

nonce du Pape *ou* **nonce apostolique** (nɔ̃:s) *m,* papal nuncio.

nonchalamment (nɔ̃ʃalamã) *ad,* nonchalantly, listlessly. **nonchalance** (lã:s) *f,* nonchalance, listlessness. **nonchalant, e** (lã, ã:t) *a,* nonchalant, listless.

nonciature (nɔ̃sjatyːr) *f,* nunciature.

non-combat (nɔ̃kɔ̃ba) *m,* no contest (*Box.*). **non-combattant, e** (batã, ã:t) *a. & m,* noncombatant (*Mil.*).

non-conformiste (nɔ̃kɔ̃fɔrmist) *n. & att,* nonconformist.

non-être (nɔnɛːtr) (*Philos.*) *m,* nonentity, nonexistence.

non-intervention (nɔnɛ̃tervãsjɔ̃) . (*Pol.*) *f,* nonintervention, noninterference.

non-lieu (nɔ̃ljø) *m,* no case to answer (*law*).

nonne (nɔn) & **nonnain** (nɛ̃) *f,* nun.

nonobstant (nɔnɔpstã) *pr,* notwithstanding.

non-paiement (nɔ̃pɛmã) *m,* nonpayment; dishonor (*bill*).

non-sens (nɔ̃sãːs) *m,* nonsense. *un ~,* all nonsense, meaningless.

non-valeur (nɔ̃valœːr) *f,* unproductiveness; worthless security; valueless stock; (*pl.*) irrecoverable arrears (*taxes*); bad debt; noneffective (*Mil.*); useless person.

nord (nɔːr) *m,* north; (*att.*) north[ern]. *mer du N~,* North Sea. *perdre le ~,* to get confused. **nord-est** (nɔr[d]ɛst; *Naut.,* nɔrɛ) *m,* northeast; northeast wind; (*att.*) northeast[ern]. **nordique** (dik) *a,* Nordic. **nord-ouest** (nɔr[d]wɛst; *Naut.,* nɔrwa) *m,* northwest, northwest wind; (*att.*) northwest[ern].

normal, e† (nɔrmal) *a,* normal; standard; ordinary. **normalien, ne** (ljɛ̃, ɛn) *n,* student [of a normal school].

normand, e (nɔrmã, ã:d) *a,* Norman; noncommittal (*fig.*); evasive; feigned. *les îles Normandes,* the Channel Islands. *N~, n,* Norman. *un fin n~,* a shrewd crafty fellow. **la Normandie** (mãdi), Normandy.

norme (nɔrm) *f,* norm.

norois (l'ancien) (nɔrwa) *m,* Old Norse (*language*).

Norvège (la) (nɔrvɛːʒ), Norway. **norvégien, ne** (vɛʒjɛ̃, ɛn) *a. & N~, n,* Norwegian, Norseman. *le norvégien,* Norwegian, Norse (*language*).

nos, our, *possessive adjective plural, see* **notre.**

nostalgie (nɔstalʒi) *f,* nostalgia, homesickness; pining. **nostalgique** (ʒik) *a,* nostalgic, homesick.

nota [bene] (nɔta bene) (*abb.* N.B.) *m,* note, nota bene, N.B. **notabilité** (nɔtabilite) *f,* notability. **notable†** (bl) *a,* notable; especial; eminent, distinguished. ¶ *m,* person of distinction, notable.

notaire (nɔtɛːr) *m,* notary.

notamment (nɔtmã) *ad,* especially, notably.

notation (nɔtasjɔ̃) *f,* notation.

note (nɔt) *f,* note, memorandum; mark (*Sch.*); record (*of service*); bill, account; tune (*fig.*). *~ d'agrément,* grace note (*Mus.*). *~ de passage,* passing note (*Mus.*). *~ naturelle,* natural [note] (*Mus.*). **noter** (te) *v.t,* to note; note down; write down; mark (*pupil, etc.*). **notice** (tis) *f,* notice, account; review (*book*). **notifier** (tifje) *v.t,* to notify.

notion (nɔsjɔ̃) *f,* notion, smattering.

notoire† (nɔtwa:r) *a*, well-known. **notoriété** (tɔrjete) *f*, notoriety. ~ *publique*, common knowledge.

notre (nɔtr) *a*, our. *Notre-Dame*, Our Lady. *Notre-Seigneur*, our Lord. **le nôtre, la ~, les ~s** (no:tr) *pn*, ours; our own. *il est des nôtres*, he is one of us.

noue (nu) *f*, valley (*roof*); water meadow.

nouer (nwe) *v.t*, to tie; knot; knit (*fig.*); form. **noueux, euse** (nuø, ø:z) *a*, knotty; gnarled.

nougat (nugɑ) *m*, nougat.

nouilles (nu:j) *f.pl*, vermicelli.

nounou (nunu) *f*, nanny, nursy.

nourrain (nurɛ̃) *m*, fry (*fish*).

nourri, e (nuri) *p.p. & p.a*, fed; (*fig.*) copious; full; steeped; prolonged (*applause*); brisk (*fire, Mil.*). *mal ~, pas ~*, underfed, ill-fed. **nourrice** (ris) *f*, [wet] nurse. *être la ~ de*, to nurse, suckle. *mère ~*, nursing mother. **nourrir** (ri:r) *v.t*, to nourish; nurture, rear; suckle, nurse; feed; board, keep; foster, cherish, harbor, entertain. **nourrissage** (risa:ɜ) *m*, rearing (*cattle*). **nourrissant, e** (sɑ̃, ɑ̃:t) *a*, nourishing, nutritious. **nourrisseur** (sœ:r) *m*, dairy farmer; feed-roll (*Mech.*). **nourrisson** (sɔ̃) *m*, nurseling; suckling; foster child. **nourriture** (ty:r) *f*, food, nourishment, nutriment; sustenance; board; feeding; nurture.

nous (nu) *pn*, we; us, to us, ourselves; each other. *chez ~*, at our house. *à ~!* help! *~-mêmes*, ourselves.

nouveau, el, le (nuvo, ɛl) *a. & ad*, new; newly; recent; novel; fresh; another, further. *le Nouveau-Brunswick* (brɔ̃zvik), New Brunswick. *nouveau marié, nouvelle mariée*, bridegroom, bride (*about to be married or on marriage day*). *nouveaux mariés*, [newly] married couple; bride & bridegroom. *nouveau-né, e, n. & att*, newborn (child). *nouveau riche*, upstart. *nouveau venu, nouvelle venue*, newcomer. *la Nouvelle-Ecosse*, Nova Scotia. *la Nouvelle-Galles du Sud*, New South Wales. *la Nouvelle-Guinée*, New Guinea. *la Nouvelle-*

Orléans, New Orleans. *la Nouvelle-Zélande* (zelɑ̃:d), New Zealand. *la Nouvelle-Zemble* (ɜɑ̃:bl), Nova Zembla. *le nouveau*, *m*, the new, a novelty, something new. *le nouveau, la nouvelle*, the new boy, man, girl (*Sch., etc.*). *à nouveau*, anew, afresh; carried forward. *de nouveau*, again, afresh. **nouveauté** (te) *f*, newness; novelty; new thing, book, play, etc; innovation; (*pl.*) new styles, latest fashions; ladies' & children's wear; drapery.

nouvelle (nuvɛl) *f.*, *oft. pl. in sense of* news, [piece of] news; tidings, intelligence; tale, short story, novelette. *~s à la main* (*journalism*), today's gossip, looking at life.

nouvellement (nuvɛlmɑ̃) *ad*, newly, recently.

nouvelliste (nuvɛlist) *n*, newsmonger, intelligencer, quidnunc.

novateur, trice (nɔvatœ:r, tris) *n*, innovator.

novembre (nɔvɑ̃:br) *m*, November.

novice (nɔvis) *n*, novice; probationer; tyro; apprentice (*Naut.*). ¶ *a*, inexperienced, raw, fresh, green. **noviciat** (sja) *m*, noviciate; apprenticeship.

noyade (nwajad) *f*, drowning (*fatality*); noyade (*Hist.*).

noyau (nwajo) *m*, stone (*fruit*); kernel, core, center; nucleus; newel.

noyer (nwaje) *m*, walnut [tree, wood].

noyer (nwaje) *v.t*, to drown; flood, deluge; sink; swamp; play (*fish*). *un noyé* (je), a drowned man; a drowning man. *les noyés*, the [apparently] drowned.

nu (ny) *a*, naked, nude; bare; barebacked (*horse*); plain. *à l'œil nu*, with the naked eye. *~ comme un ver*, stark naked. *nu-pieds*, *inv.* ou *pieds nus*, barefoot[ed]. *nu-tête*, *inv.* ou *tête nue*, bareheaded. ¶ *m*, nakedness, nudity, nude; bareness. *le nu*, the nude. *les nus*, the naked. *à nu*, bare, naked; bareback[ed] (*riding*).

nuage (nya:ɜ) *m*, cloud; volume (*of smoke, etc.*); haze, mist (*fig.*);

suspicion. **nuageux, euse** (aʒø, ø:z) *a*, cloudy; hazy.

nuance (nyɑ̃:s) *f*, shade; hue; tinge; nuance; (*pl.*) lights & shades; sign of expression (*Mus.*) **nuancer** (ɑ̃se) *v.t*, to shade; mark (*or* observe) the signs of expression; execute with feeling.

Nubie (la) (nybi), Nubia. **nubien, ne** (bjɛ̃, ɛn) *a.* & **N~**, *n*, Nubian.

nubile (nybil) *a*, nubile, marriageable.

nucléaire (nykleɛ:r) *a*, nuclear. *centrale* ~, nuclear power plant. *rayonnement* ~, nuclear radiation.

nudité (nydite) *f*, nudity, nakedness; bareness; nude (*art*).

nue (ny) (*poetic*) *f*, high clouds. *oft. pl*, cloud, sky. **nuée** (nye) *f*, storm cloud, thunder cloud; cloud (*fig.*), host, swarm; shower.

nuire (nɥi:r) *v.i.ir.* & ~ à, to harm, hurt, injure, wrong, prejudice. **nuisible** (nɥizibl) *a*, harmful, hurtful, injurious, noxious, noisome.

nuit (nɥi) *f*, night; dark[ness]. *cette* ~, tonight; last night. *à [la]* ~ *close*, after dark. *à la* ~ *tombante*, at nightfall. ~ *américaine*, day-for-night shooting (*cinema*, *TV*). **nuitamment** (tamɑ̃) *ad*, by night, in the n.

nul, le (nyl) *a*, no; not any; null, nugatory, nil; of no account; drawn (*game*); dead (*heat*). *nul(le)* & *non avenu(e)* (avny), null & void. *nulle part, ad*, nowhere. **nul,** *pn*, no one, none. **nulle,** *f*, null (*in cipher*). **nullement** (lmɑ̃) *ad*, in no way, not at all, by no means, nowise. **nullité** (lite) *f*, nullity; emptiness; nonentity, cipher (*pers.*).

nûment (nymɑ̃) *ad*, openly, frankly, nakedly.

numéraire (nymerɛ:r) *a*, numerary. ¶ *m*, coin, cash, specie. **numéral, e** (ral) *a*, numeral. **numérateur** (tœr) *m*, numerator (*Arith.*). **numérique†** (rik) *a*, numerical; digital. **numéro** (ro) *m*, number; size; issue (*periodical*); turn (*music hall*). **numérotage** (rota:ʒ) *m*, numbering. **numéroter** (te) *v.t*, to number.

numismate (nymismat) *m*, numismatist. **numismatique** (tik) *f*, numismatics.

nuptial, e (nypsjal) *a*, nuptial, bridal, wedding (*att.*), marriage (*att.*).

nuque (nyk) *f*, nape (*of neck*).

nutritif, ive (nytritif, i:v) *a*, nutritive, nutritious. **nutrition** (sjɔ̃) *f*, nutrition.

nymphe (nɛ̃:f) *f*, nymph.

O

ô (o) *i*, O! oh!

oasis (oazis) *f*, oasis (*lit.* & *fig.*).

obédience (ɔbedjɑ̃:s) *f*, obedience (*Eccl.*). **obéir** (i:r) *v.i*, to obey. ~ à, to obey; submit to, yield to; comply with; respond to. **obéissance** (isɑ̃:s) *f*, obedience; allegiance; authority; compliance; submission. **obéissant, e** (sɑ̃, ɑ̃:t) *a*, obedient; dutiful; submissive.

obélisque (ɔbelisk) *m*, obelisk.

obérer (ɔbere) *v.t*, to encumber [with debts].

obèse (ɔbɛ:z) *a*, obese, fat. **obésité** (bezite) *f*, obesity, fatness.

obier (ɔbje) *m*, guelder rose.

objecter (ɔbʒɛkte) *v.t*, to object (*que* = that); o. to, o. against; allege. **objectif, ive†** (tif, i:v) *a.* & *m*, objective (*Philos.*). ¶ *m*, objective, aim. [*verre*] *objectif*, objective, object glass, lens. **objection** (ksjɔ̃) *f*, objection; demur. **objet** (ʒɛ) *m*, object; subject; article. ~ *d'art*, work of art.

objurgation (ɔbʒyrgasjɔ̃) *f*, objurgation.

oblation (ɔblasjɔ̃) *f*, oblation, offering (*Lit.*).

obligataire (ɔbligatɛ:r) *m*, bondholder, debenture h. **obligation** (sjɔ̃) *f*, obligation; bond; debenture: recognizance. **obligatoire** (twa:r) *a*, obligatory, compulsory, binding. *sens* ~, one-way street, road. **obligé, e** (ʒe) *a*, usual; obbligato (*Mus.*). ¶ *n*, debtor (*for services*). **obligeamment** . (ʒamɑ̃) *ad*, obligingly, kindly. **obligeant, e** (ʒɑ̃, ɑ̃:t) *a*, obliging, kind[ly]; complimentary. **obliger** (ʒe) *v.t*, to oblige, bind, compel; obligate. s'~, to bind oneself; undertake.

oblique† (ɔblik) a, oblique, slanting, skew; side (glance); crooked (fig.), underhand. **obliquer** (ke) v.i. to slant. **obliquité** (kite) f, obliquity; crookedness.

oblitérer (ɔblitere) v.t, to obliterate; cancel.

oblong, ongue (ɔblɔ̃, ɔ̃:g) a, oblong.

obnubiler (ɔbnybile) v.t, to cloud.

obole (ɔbɔl) f, [brass] farthing, stiver; mite.

obscène (ɔpsɛ:n) a, obscene. **obscénité** (senite) f, obscenity.

obscur, e (ɔpsky:r) a, dark; dim, murky, obscure. **obscurcir** (skyrsi:r) v.t, to darken; overcast, overshadow. **obscurément** (remã) ad, darkly, etc. **obscurité** (rite) f, dark[ness], etc.

obséder (ɔpsede) v.t, to worry; obsess.

obsèques (ɔpsɛk) f.pl, obsequies. **obséquieux, euse†** (sekjø, ø:z) a, obsequious. **obséquiosité** (kjozite) f, obsequiousness.

observance (ɔpsɛrvã:s) f, observance (Theol.). **observateur, trice** (vatœ:r, tris) n, observer; (att.) observant. **observation** (sjɔ̃) f, observance; observation; remark. **observatoire** (twa:r) m, observatory; observation post (Mil.). **observer** (ve) v.t, to observe; keep; watch; spot. **s'~,** to be careful, cautious.

obsession (ɔpsɛsjɔ̃) f, obsession.

obstacle (ɔpstakl) m, obstacle. faire ~ à, to stand in the way of.

obstétrical, e (ɔpstetrikal) a, obstetric(al). **obstétrique** (trik) f, obstetrics, midwifery.

obstination (ɔpstinasjɔ̃) f, obstinacy, stubbornness, wilfulness; doggedness. **obstiné†, e** (ne) a, obstinate, etc. **s'obstiner** (ne) v.pr, to persist.

obstruction (ɔpstryksjɔ̃) f, obstruction; stoppage; filibuster. **obstruer** (strye) v.t, to obstruct; block.

obtempérer à (ɔptãpere), to obey, comply with.

obtenir (ɔptəni:r) v.t.ir, to obtain, secure, get. j'ai obtenu de

. . ., I induced . . .; I managed to . . .

obturateur (ɔptyratœ:r) m, obturator, plug; shutter (Phot.). **obturer** (re) v.t, to stop [up].

obtus, e (ɔpty, y:z) a, obtuse.

obus (ɔby:s) m, shell. ~ à balles, shrapnel. **obusier** (byzje) m, howitzer.

obvier à (ɔbvje), to obviate, prevent.

ocarina (ɔkarina) m, ocarina.

occasion (ɔkazjɔ̃) f, opportunity; opening; occasion; bargain. d'~, second-hand, used; occasional (occupation). **occasionnel, le** (ɔnɛl) a, causative; occasional (Philos.). **occasionnellement** (lmã) ad, occasionally, now & then. **occasionner** (ne) v.t, to occasion.

occident (ɔksidã) m, west. **occidental, e** (tal) a, west[ern].

occiput (ɔksipyt) m, occiput.

occire (ɔksi:r) v.t, to slay.

occulte (ɔkylt) a, occult, hidden.

occupant (ɔkypã) m, occupant (law). **occupation** (pasjɔ̃) f, occupation; pursuit. **occupé, e** (pe) p.a, busy. **occuper** (pe) v.t, to occupy; hold. **s'~,** to occupy (or busy) oneself, be engaged; be interested in (with de).

occurrence (ɔkyrã:s) f, occurrence; emergency; juncture.

océan (ɔseã) m, ocean, sea. l'~ Atlantique, Pacifique, Indien, the Atlantic, Pacific, Indian, O. l'~ Glacial arctique, antarctique, the Arctic, Antarctic, O. **l'Océanie** (ani) f, Oceania.

ocre (ɔkr) f, ocher.

octave (ɔkta:v) f, octave. **octavon, ne** (tavɔ̃, ɔn) n, octaroon. **octobre** (tɔbr) m, October. **octogénaire** (ʒenɛ:r) a. & n, octogenarian. **octogone** (gɔn) a, octagonal. ¶ m, octagon.

octroi (ɔktrwa) m, octroi (duty on goods entering town). **octroyer** (trwaje) v.t, to grant.

oculaire (ɔkylɛ:r) a, ocular, eye (att.). témoin ~, eyewitness. [verre] ~, m, eyepiece, ocular. **oculiste** (list) m, oculist. médecin ~, eye doctor.

ode (ɔd) f, ode.

odeur (odœ:r) *f*, odor, smell, scent.

odieux, euse† (ɔdjø, ø:z) *a*, odious, hateful, heinous, outrageous; obnoxious; invidious. ¶ *m*, odium.

odorant, e (ɔdɔrɑ̃, ɑ̃:t) & **odoriférant, e** (riferɑ̃, ɑ̃:t) *a*, fragrant, [sweet-]scented, odoriferous. **odorat** (ra) *m*, [sense of] smell.

odyssée (ɔdise) *f*, Odyssey (*fig*.).

oé (oe) *i*, wo!, whoa!

œil (œ:j) *m*, eye; look; loop; hole; face (*Typ*.); luster; gloss. ~*-de-bœuf*, bull's eye (*window*). ~*-de-chat*, cat's-eye (*jewel*). ~*-de-perdrix*, soft corn (*foot*). *à l'~*, free of charge. *se rincer l'~*, to watch a sexy show. *coup d'~*, a glance. *faire de l'~*, to ogle. **œillade** (œjad) *f*, glance (*loving*); ogle. **œillère** (jɛ:r) *f*, blinker; eye bath. [*dent*] ~, eyetooth. **œillet** (jɛ) *m*, eyelet; e. hole; pink (*Bot*.). ~ [*des fleuristes*], carnation. ~ *de poète*, sweet-william. **œilleton** (jtɔ̃) *m*, sucker, offset (*Hort*.).

œsophage (ezɔfa:ʒ) *m*, oesophagus.

œstre (ɛstr) *m*, oestrum, oestrus, gad-fly.

œuf (œf) *m*, egg; (*pl, de poisson*) hard roe, spawn. ~ *à la coque*, soft-boiled egg. ~ *dur*, hard-boiled e. ~ *brouillé*, scrambled e. ~ *sur le plat*, fried e. ~*s coque*, very fresh eggs. ~*s au jambon*, ham & eggs. *tondre un* ~, to be miserly. **œuvé, e** (ve) *a*, hardroed.

œuvre (œ:vr) *f*, work; setting (*jewel*); (*pl*.) charity; (*pl*.) work (*social*). ¶ *m*, carcass, carcase (*of a building*); works (*of an artist*).

offensant, e (ɔfɑ̃sɑ̃, ɑ̃:t) *a*, offensive, obnoxious, objectionable, insulting. **offense** (fɑ̃:s) *f*, offense; trespass (*Theol*.). ~ *à la cour*, contempt of court. **offensé, e** (fɑ̃se) *n*, aggrieved party. **offenser** (se) *v.t*, to offend; trespass against; injure. **s'~**, to take offense. **offenseur** (sœ:r) *m*, offender. **offensif, ive†** (sif, i:v) *a*. & *f*, offensive (*attacking*).

offertoire (ɔfɛrtwa:r) *m*, offer-

tory (*Lit*.); voluntary (*organ, between credo & sanctus*).

office (ɔfis) *m*, office; service; worship; department (*government*). ~ *des morts*, burial service. *d'~*, official[ly]; arbitrary (*assessment*); as a matter of course. ¶ *f*, pantry, servants' hall. **officiel, le†** (sjɛl) *a*, official. ¶ *m*, official (*sport, etc*.). **officier** (sje) *v.i*, to officiate (*Eccl*.). ¶ *m*, officer. ~ *à la suite*, supernumerary o. ~ *d'ordonnance*, orderly o. ~ *de l'état civil*, registrar (*births, etc*.). ~ *de marine*, naval officer. ~ *du génie*, engineer (*Mil*.). **officieux, euse†** (sjø, ø:z) *a*, officious (*diplomacy*); informal, semiofficial, unofficial; white (*lie*). **officine** (sin) *f*, dispensary; hotbed (*fig*.); shady office, thieves' kitchen.

offrande (ɔfrɑ̃:d) *f*, offering. **le plus offrant** [& dernier enchérisseur] (frɑ̃), the highest bidder. **offre** (fr) *f*, offer; tender. ~ *d'emploi*, help wanted. *l'~ & la demande*, supply & demand. **offrir** (fri:r) *v.t.ir*, to offer, proffer, tender; bid; present; offer up. ~ *sa main*, to propose (*marriage to a man*). ~ *son nom*, to propose (*to a woman*).

offusquer (ɔfyske) *v.t*, to obfuscate, obscure; dazzle; offend.

ogive (ɔʒi:v) *f*, ogive, pointed arch.

ognon (ɔɲɔ̃) *m*, bulb (*Bot*.).

ogre, ogresse (ɔgr, grɛs) *n*, ogre, ogress.

oh (o) *i*, oh! O!

ohé (o[h]e) *i*, hi! hullo[a]!; ahoy!; wo! whoa!

oie (wa) *f*, goose.

oignon (ɔɲɔ̃) *m*, onion; bulb (*Bot*.); bunion. *personne qui se mêle des* ~*s des autres*, meddlesome person, meddler, officious person. **oignonière** (ɲɔɲɛ:r) *f*, onion bed.

oindre (wɛ̃:dr) *v.t.ir*, to anoint.

oiseau (wazo) *m*, bird, fowl; guy. ~ *de mauvais augure*, bird of ill omen. ~*-mouche*, humming bird. ~ *rare*, rare bird, rara avis. *à vol d'~*, as the crow flies. *vue à vol d'~*, bird's-eye view. **oiselet** (zlɛ) *m*, small bird. **oiseleur** (zlœːr) *m*, bird catcher, fowler. **oiselier** (zəlje) *m*, bird fancier. **oisellerie** (zɛlri) *f*, bird fancying; aviary.

oiseux, euse (wazø, øːz) *a*, idle (*words, etc.*). **oisif, ive†** (zif, iːv) *a*, idle (*pers., money*).

oisillon (wazijɔ̃) *m*, fledgling.

oisiveté (wazivte) *f*, idleness.

oison (wazɔ̃) *m*, gosling. ~ *bridé* (*fig.*), simpleton.

oléagineux, euse (ɔleaʒinø, øːz) *a*, oleaginous, oily; oil (*seed*).

oléandre (ɔleɑ̃ːdr) *m*, oleander.

oléoduc (ɔleɔdyk) *m*, pipeline.

olfactif, ive (ɔlfaktif, iːv) *a*, olfactory.

olibrius (ɔlibriyːs) *m*, conceited fool.

oligarchie (ɔligarʃi) *f*, oligarchy.

olivade (ɔlivàd) *f*, olive harvest. **olivaie** (vɛ) *f*, o. grove. **olivaison** (vɛzɔ̃) *f*, o. season; o. harvest. **olivâtre** (vɑːtr) *a*, olive (*complexion*). **olive** (liːv) *f*, olive. *couleur* [*d*]~, olive[-green]. **olivier** (livje) *m*, o. [tree]; o. [wood].

olympe (ɔlɛ̃ːp) *m*, Olympus (*fig.*). **olympique** (lɛpik) *a*, Olympic.

ombilic (ɔ̃bilik) *m*, umbilicus; navel.

omble[-chevalier] (ɔ̃ːbl) *m*, char (*fish*).

ombrage (ɔ̃braːʒ) *m*, [spread of] foliage; shade; umbrage. **ombragé, e** (braʒe) *p.a*, shady. **ombrager** (ʒe) *v.t*, to shade, overshadow. **ombrageux, euse** (ʒø, øːz) *a*, shy, skittish (*beast*); touchy. **ombre** (ɔ̃ːbr) *f*, shade; shadow; ghost. ~*s chinoises*, shadow play. ~ *portée*, cast shadow. ¶ *m*, grayling, umber (*fish*). ~*-chevalier*, char (*fish*). **ombrelle** (ɔ̃brɛl) *f*, sunshade, parasol. **ombrer** (bre) *v.t*, to shade (*art*). **ombreux, euse** brø, øːz) *a*, shady (*Poet.*).

oméga (ɔmega) *m*, omega.

omelette (ɔmlɛt) *f*, omelet[te]. ~ *aux confitures*, jelly o. ~ *aux fines herbes*, savory o.

omettre (ɔmɛtr) *v.t.ir*, to omit, leave out. **omission** (misjɔ̃) *f*, omission.

omnibus (ɔmnibyːs) *m*, [omni-bus; (*att.*) slow (*train, boat*).

omnipotence (ɔmnipɔtɑ̃ːs) *f*, omnipotence. **omnipotent, e** (tɑ̃, ɑ̃ːt) *a*, omnipotent.

omniscience (ɔmnisjɑ̃ːs) *f*, omniscience. **omniscient, e** (jɑ̃, ɑ̃ːt) *a*, omniscient.

omnivore (ɔmnivɔːr) *a*, omnivorous.

omoplate (ɔmɔplat) *f*, shoulder blade.

on (ɔ̃), *oft.* **l'on**, *pn*, one; a man, woman, etc; we; you; they; people; somebody; anybody. ~ *demande . . .*, wanted . . . (*advertisement*). ~ *dit*, it is said, they say. ~**-dit** (5di) *m*, hearsay, rumor. *on n'embauche pas*, no help wanted. *on ne passe pas*, no thoroughfare.

once (ɔ̃ːs) *f*, ounce (*Zool.*), snow leopard; grain, particle (*fig.*).

oncle (ɔ̃ːkl) *m*, uncle.

onction (ɔ̃ksjɔ̃) *f*, unction; rubbing [with oil]. **onctueux, euse†** (tɥø, øːz) *a*, unctuous; oily; greasy.

onde (ɔ̃ːd) *f*, wave, billow; (*Poet.*) sea, main; water; stream. *en* ~*s*, wavy (*hair*). ~ *sonore*, sound wave. **ondé, e** (5de) *a*, waved, wavy; grained (*wood*). **ondée** (de) *f*, heavy shower. **ondoyer** (dwaje) *v.i*, to undulate, wave; billow, surge. **ondulation** (dylasjɔ̃) *f*, undulation; wave. ~ *permanente*, permanent wave (*hair*). **ondulé, e** (le) *a*, undulating, wavy; corrugated (*iron*). **onduler** (le) *v.i*, to undulate; (*v.t.*) to wave (*hair*). *se faire onduler* [*les cheveux*], to have one's hair waved.

onéreux, euse (ɔnerø, øːz) *a*, onerous, burdensome.

ongle (ɔ̃ːgl) *m*, nail; claw; hoof. **onglée** (5gle) *f*, numbness [of the fingers]. **onglet** (glɛ) *m*, guard (*Bookb.*); tab; miter (*Carp.*). **onglier** (glie) *m*, manicure set. ~ [*en*] *écrin*, box m. s.

onguent (5gɑ̃) *m*, ointment, salve.

ongulé, e (5gyle) *a*, hoofed.

onomatopée (ɔnɔmatɔpe) *f*, onomatopoeia.

onyx (ɔniks) *m*, onyx.

onze (ɔ̃z) *a. & m,* eleven; eleventh. **onzième†** (ɔ̃zjɛm) *a. & n,* eleventh. (*Note.—Say* le onze, le onzième, *not* l'onze, l'onzième.)

oolithe (ɔɔlit) *m,* oolite.

opacité (ɔpasite) *f,* opacity.

opale (ɔpal) *f,* opal. **opalin, e** (lɛ̃, in) *a,* opaline.

opaque (ɔpak) *a,* opaque.

opéra (ɔpera) *m,* opera; o. [house]. ~ *bouffe,* comic opera, musical comedy. ~*-comique,* opera comique (*spoken dialogue*).

opérateur, trice (ɔperatœːr, tris) *n,* operator; cameraman (*film*). **opération** (sjɔ̃) *f,* operation; stage; working; transaction, dealing. **opéré, e** (re) *n,* surgical case (*pers.*). **opérer** (re) *v.t. & abs,* to operate, work, effect; make; do; act; deal; operate on (*Surg.*).

opérette (ɔperɛt) *f,* operetta, light opera, musical play.

ophtalmie (ɔftalmi) *f,* ophthalmia. **ophtalmique** (mik) *a,* ophthalmic.

opiacé, e (ɔpjase) *a,* opiated.

opinant (ɔpinɑ̃) *m,* speaker (*in debate*). **opiner** (ne) *v.i,* to opine; vote. ~ *du bonnet,* to say nothing but ditto to everything. **opiniâtre†** (njɑːtr) *a. & n,* [self-]opinionated; self-willed; obstinate, pertinacious, stubborn (person). **s'opiniâtrer** (ɑtre) *v.pr,* to persist. **opiniâtreté** (trəte) *f,* obstinacy, etc. **opinion** (njɔ̃) *f,* opinion; view; mind; vote.

opiomane (ɔpjɔman) *n,* opium addict. **opium** (jɔm) *m,* opium.

opossum (ɔpɔsɔm) *m,* opossum.

opportun, e (ɔpɔrtœ̃, yn) *a,* opportune, seasonable, timely, well-timed. **opportunément** (tynemɑ̃) *ad,* opportunely, etc. **opportunisme** (nism) *m,* opportunism. **opportuniste** (nist) *n,* opportunist, timeserver. **opportunité** (te) *f,* opportuneness; opportunity.

opposant, e (ɔpozɑ̃, ɑ̃ːt) *n,* opponent; (*att.*) opposing; opponent. **opposé, e** (ze) *a,* opposed; opposite. ¶ *m,* opposite, reverse, contrary. **opposer** (ze) *v.t. &*

g'~ à, to oppose. ~ *une exception,* to demur (*law*). **à l'opposite** (pozit) *ad,* opposite, facing. **opposition** (sjɔ̃) *f,* opposition; contrast; contradistinction; stop; objection.

oppresser (ɔprese) *v.t,* to oppress (*Med. & fig.*). **oppresseur** (sœːr) *m,* oppressor. **oppressif, ive** (sif, iːv) *a,* oppressive. **oppression** (sjɔ̃) *f,* oppression. **opprimer** (prime) *v.t,* to oppress.

opprobre (ɔprɔbr) *m,* disgrace, opprobrium.

opter (ɔpte) *v.i,* to choose.

opticien (ɔptisjɛ̃) *m,* optician.

optime (ɔptime) (*Latin word*), very well, all right. **optimisme** (mism) *m,* optimism. **optimiste** (mist) *a,* optimistic, hopeful, sanguine. ¶ *n,* optimist.

option (ɔpsjɔ̃) *f,* option.

optique (ɔptik) *a,* optic; optical. ¶ *f,* optics; perspective (*Theat.*).

opulence (ɔpylɑ̃ːs) *f,* opulence, affluence, wealth; buxomness. **opulent, e** (lɑ̃, ɑ̃ːt) *a,* opulent, etc.

opuscule (ɔpyskyl) *m,* short treatise, tract.

or (ɔːr) *c,* now. ~ *çà,* now then.

or (ɔːr) *m,* gold. ~ *laminé,* rolled g. ~ *moulu,* ormolu. **ni pour** ~ **ni pour argent,** for love or money. *d'~,* gold; golden.

oracle (ɔraːkl) *m,* oracle.

orage (ɔraːʒ) *m,* thunderstorm; storm. **orageux, euse†** (raʒø, øːz) *a,* stormy; thundery.

oraison (ɔrɛzɔ̃) *f,* prayer. ~ *dominicale,* Lord's prayer. ~ *funèbre,* funeral oration.

oral, e† (ɔral) *a,* oral, viva voce.

orange (ɔrɑ̃ːʒ) *f,* orange. ~ *amère,* Seville o. ~ *sanguine,* blood o. **orange, m. & a. & orangé, e** (rɑ̃ʒe) *a. & m,* orange (*color*). **orangeade** (ʒad) *f,* orangeade. **oranger** (ʒe) *m,* orange [tree]. **orangerie** (ʒri) *f,* orangery.

orang-outang (ɔrɑ̃utɑ̃) *m,* orangutan.

orateur (ɔratœːr) *m,* orator, speaker. **oratoire** (twaːr) *a,* oratorical; rhetorical, declamatory. *l'art* ~, oratory. ¶ *m,* oratory (*chapel*). **oratorio** (tɔrjo) *m,* oratorio.

orbe (ɔrb) *m*, orb (*heavenly body*). **orbite** (bit) *f*, orbit; socket (*eye*).

Orcades (**les**) (ɔrkad) *f.pl*, the Orkneys.

orchestral, e (ɔrkɛstral) *a*, orchestral. **orchestre** (tr) *m*, orchestra, band; orchestra seats (*Theat.*). **orchestrer** (tre) *v.t*, to orchestrate, score.

orchidée (ɔrkide) *f*, orchid. **orchis** (kis) *m*, orchis.

ordalie (ɔrdali) *f*, ordeal (*Hist.*).

ordinaire† (ɔrdinɛɪr) *a*, ordinary; common; customary; usual, everyday. ¶ *m*, wont; ordinary; [company] mess (*Mil.*).

ordinal (ɔrdinal) *a.m*, ordinal.

ordinateur (ɔrdinatœːr) *m*, computer, data processer. ~ *domestique*, home computer. **ordinogramme** (ɔgram) *m*, process chart (*computers*).

ordination (ɔrdinasjɔ̃) *f*, ordination (*Eccl.*); data processing, computing.

ordonnance (ɔrdɔnɑ̃ːs) *f*, ordering (*arrangement*); organization; regulation (*police*); [treasury] warrant; prescription (*Med.*). ¶ *f. or m*, orderly. **ordonnancer** (nɑ̃se) *v.t*, to pass for payment; schedule (*computers*). **ordonnateur, trice** (natœːr, tris) *n*, director; master of ceremonies. **ordonné, e** (ne) *p.a*, tidy, orderly (*pers.*). **ordonner** (ne) *v.t. & abs*, to order; organize; prescribe; ordain. **ordre** (dr) *m*, order; rate. ~ *d'exécution*, death warrant. ~ *du jour*, agenda, business [before the meeting]; order of the day. *numéro d'~*, serial number. ~ *public, law & order; peace; public policy. à l'~! order!; chair!

ordure (ɔrdyːr) *f*, filth, dirt, muck; refuse, dust; ordure; smut. **ordurier, ère** (dyrje, ɛːr) *a*, filthy; scurrilous; smutty.

orée (ɔre) *f*, verge, skirt (*of a wood*).

oreille (ɔrɛːj) *f*, ear; lug; wing (*nut*). *avoir l'~ dure*, to be hard of hearing. *avoir l'~ juste*, to have a good ear (*for music*). *~-d'ours*, bear's-ear, auricula. *~-*

de-souris, forget-me-not. **oreiller** (rɛje) *m*, pillow. **oreillette** (jɛt) *f*, auricle (*heart*); ear (*Bot.*). **oreillon** (jɔ̃) *m*, ear flap; ear (*Bot.*); (*pl.*) mumps.

orémus (ɔremyːs) *m*, prayer.

Orénoque (**l'**) (ɔrenɔk) *m*, the Orinoco.

ores (ɔːr) *ad*: *d'~ & déjà*, now & henceforth.

orfèvre (ɔrfɛːvr) *m*, goldsmith &/or silversmith. **orfèvrerie** (fɛvrəri) *f*, gold[smith's] &/or silver[smith's] work.

orfraie (ɔrfrɛ) *f*, osprey.

organdi (ɔrgɑ̃di) *m*, organdy; book muslin.

organe (ɔrgan) *m*, organ; spokesman; (*pl, Mach.*) parts, gear. **organique** (nik) *a*, organic. **organisateur, trice** (zatœːr, tris) *n*, organizer. **organisation** (zasjɔ̃) *f*, organization. **organiser** (ze) *v.t*, to organize. *une tête bien organisée, un cerveau organisé*, a level-headed person. **organisme** (nism) *m*, organism. **organiste** (nist) *n*, organist (*Mus.*).

orge (ɔrʒ) *f*, barley. ~ *perlé*, *m*, pearl barley. **orgeat** (ʒa) *m*, orgeat. **orgelet** (ʒəlɛ) *m*, stye (*eye*).

orgie (ɔrʒi) *f*, orgy; riot (*fig.*).

orgue (ɔrg) *m*, *the pl. is f*, organ; o. loft. ~ *de Barbarie*, barrel organ.

orgueil (ɔrgœːj) *m*, pride. **orgueilleux, euse†** (gœjø, øːz) *a. & n*, proud (*person*).

orient (ɔrjɑ̃) *m*, orient, east. l'O~ (*Geog.*), the Orient, the East. ~ *moyen*, the Middle East. **orientable** (tabl) *a*, adjustable; revolving, swiveling. **oriental, e** (tal) *a*, oriental, eastern. O~, *n*, Oriental, Eastern. **orientation** (tasjɔ̃) *f*, orientation; bearings; direction; aspect; trend; trimming (*sails, yards*). **orienter** (te) *v.t*, to orient[ate]; direct, point; trim (*sails, yards*). *s'~*, to get one's bearings.

orifice (ɔrifis) *m*, mouth, aperture, port, orifice.

oriflamme (ɔriflaɪm) *f*, oriflamme; banner.

originaire† (ɔriʒinɛːr) *a*, original. *être ~ de*, to come from, be a native of. **original, e†** (nal) *a*, original; first (*edition*); inventive; odd, queer. ¶ *m*, original; oddity. **originalité** (lite) *f*, originality. **origine** (ʒin) *f*, origin; beginning, outset. **originel, le†** (nɛl) *a*, original.

oripeaux (ɔripo) *m.pl*, tinsel; tawdry finery; rags.

Orléans (ɔrleɑ̃) *m. or f*, Orleans.

ormaie (ɔrmɛ) *ou* **ormoie** (mwa) *f*, elm grove. **orme** (ɔrm) & **ormeau** (mo) *m*, elm [tree]. *orme de montagne*, wych-elm. **ormille** (miːj) *f*, elm row.

orné, e (ɔrne) *p.a*, ornate. **ornemaniste** (nəmanist) *n*, ornamentalist. **ornement** (mɑ̃) *m*, ornament. *sans ~s*, unadorned. **ornemental, e** .(tal) *a*, ornamental. **ornementation** (tasjɔ̃) *f*, ornamentation. **orner** (ne) *v.t*, to ornament, adorn; grace.

ornière (ɔrnjɛːr) *f*, rut; groove.

ornithogale (ɔrnitɔgal) *m*, star of Bethlehem. **ornithologie** (lɔʒi) *f*, ornithology. **ornithologiste** (ʒist) *ou* **ornithologue** (lɔg) *n*, ornithologist.

orpailleur (ɔrpajœːr) *m*, gold washer (*pers.*).

orphelin, e (ɔrfəlɛ̃, in) *n. & att*, orphan. *~ de père*, fatherless. **orphelinat** (lina) *m*, orphanage.

orphéon (ɔrfeɔ̃) *m*, choral society.

orphie (ɔrfi) *f*, garfish.

orpin (ɔrpɛ̃) *m*, stonecrop.

orque (ɔrk) *f*, orc, grampus.

orteil (ɔrtɛːj) *m*, toe. *gros ~*, big toe.

orthodoxe (ɔrtɔdɔks) *a*, orthodox. **orthodoxie** (ksi) *f*, orthodoxy. **orthographe** (graf) *f*, orthography, spelling. **orthographie** (fi) *f*, orthography (*Arch.*). **orthographier** (fje) *v.t. & abs*, to spell. *mal ~*, to misspell. **orthographique** (fik) *a*, orthographic; spelling (*att.*). **orthopédie** (pedi) *f*, orthopedics. **orthopédique** (dik) *a*, orthopedic.

ortie (ɔrti) *f*, nettle. *~ brûlante*, *~ grièche* (griɛʃ), stinging nettle.

ortolan (ɔrtɔlɑ̃) *m*, ortolan.

orvet (ɔrvɛ) *m*, slowworm, blindworm.

orviétan (ɔrvjetɑ̃) *m*: *marchand d'~s*, quack.

os (ɔs, *pl*. o) *m*, bone. *~ à moelle*, marrow b. *tomber sur un ~*, to run into a problem).

osciller (ɔsile) *v.i*, to oscillate, swing, sway about; fluctuate; waver. **oscillation** (lasjɔ̃) *f*, oscillation, etc.

osé, e (oze) *p.a*, daring, bold.

oseille (ozɛːj) *f*, sorrel; money (*slang*). *la faire à l'~*, to pull a fast one.

oser (oze) *v.t*, to dare, d. to, 'venture, v. to.

oseraie (ozrɛ) *f*, osier bed.

oseur, euse (ozœːr, øːz) *n*, bold man, woman.

osier (ozje) *m*, osier, wicker.

osmium (ɔsmjɔm) *m*, osmium.

ossature (ɔsatyːr) *f*, frame[work]. **osselet** (slɛ) *m*, ossicle; (*pl.*) knuckle bones, dibs. **ossements** (smɑ̃) *m.pl*, bones (*dead*). **osseux, euse** (sø, øːz) *a*, bony, osseous. **ossifier** (sifje) *v.t*, to ossify. **ossu, e** (sy) *a*, big-boned, bony. **ossuaire** (sɥɛːr) *m*, ossuary.

Ostende (ɔstɑ̃ːd) *m*, Ostend.

ostensible† (ɔstɑ̃sibl) *a*, fit (*or* intended) to be shown; open. **ostensoir** (swaːr) *m*, ostensory, monstrance. **ostentateur, trice** (tatœːr, tris) & **ostentatoire** (twaːr) *a*, ostentatious, showy. **ostentation** (sjɔ̃) *f*, ostentation, show.

ostracisme (ɔstrasism) *m*, ostracism.

ostréiculture (ɔstreikyltyːr) *f*, oyster culture.

ostrogot[h], e (ɔstrɔgo, ɔt) (*fig.*) *n*, goth, barbarian.

otage (ɔtaːʒ) *m*, hostage.

otalgie (ɔtalʒi) *f*, earache.

otarie (ɔtari) *f*, otary, sea lion.

ôté (ote) *pr*, barring, except. **ôter** (te) *v.t*, to remove, take away; t. out; t. off, pull off; doff. *s'~*, to get out (*of. way, etc.*).

ottoman, e (ɔtɔmɑ̃, an) *a. &* **O~**, *n*, Ottoman. **ottomane**, *f*, ottoman.

ou (u) *c*, or; either. *~ bien*, or [else].

où (u) *ad*, where, whither; whence; how far; which; what; when; in. *d'~*, whence, where from. *par ~*, [by] which way, through which.

ouailles (waːj) *f.pl*, flock (*Christians*).

ouate (wat) *f*, wadding, cotton wool. **ouater** (te) *v.t*, to wad, pad; quilt.

oubli (ubli) *m*, forgetfulness; oblivion; neglect; oversight, lapse. **oublie** (bli) *f*, cone, cornet, wafer (*ice cream*). **oublier** (blie) *v.t. & abs*, to forget; neglect; overlook. **oubliettes** (ɛt) *f.pl*, oubliette. **oublieux, euse** (ø, øːz) *a*, forgetful, oblivious.

Ouessant (wesã) *m*, Ushant.

ouest (wɛst) *m*, west; (*att.*) west, western.

ouf (uf) *i*, oh! what a relief!

oui (wi) (*particle*), yes; ay; so. ¶ *m*, (*le ~, un ~*), yes; ay. *~-da, i*, [yes] indeed!

oui-dire (widiːr) *m*, hearsay. **ouïe** (wi) *f*, hearing; (*pl.*) sound holes (*Mus.*); (*pl.*) gills (*fish*).

ouiller (uje) *v.t*, to fill up (*ullaged cask*).

ouïr (wiːr) *v.t.ir*, to hear (*witness—law*).

ouragan (uragã) *m*, hurricane.

Oural (l') (ural) *m*, the Ural. *les monts Ourals*, the Ural Mountains.

ourdir (urdiːr) *v.t*, to warp (*yarn*); hatch (*fig.*); weave (*fig.*).

ourler (urle) *v.t*, to hem. *~ à jour*, to hemstitch. **ourlet** (lɛ) *m*, hem; rim. *~ à jour*, hemstitch. *~ piqué*, stitched hem.

ours (urs) *m*, bear. *~ blanc*, polar b. *~ grizzlé* (grizle), grizzly b. *~ [Martin]*, *~ de peluche*, teddy b. **ourse** (urs) *f*, [she-]bear; Bear (*Astr.*). **oursin** (sɛ̃) *m*, sea urchin; bearskin (*cap*). **ourson** (sɔ̃) *m*, bear's cub; bearskin (*cap*).

oust (ust) *i*, beat it! scram!

outarde (utard) *f*, bustard.

outil (uti) *m*, tool. **outillage** (tijaːʒ) *m*, tools; plant, machinery; equipment; outfit. *~ national*, national capital (*eco-*

nomics). **outiller** (je) *v.t*, to equip, fit out.

outrage (utraːʒ) *m*, outrage; insult; offense; ravages (*time*). **outrageant, e** (traʒã, ãːt) *a*, insulting, scurrilous. **outrager** (ʒe) *v.t*, to insult; outrage. **outrageux, euse†** (ʒø, øːz) *a*, insulting, scurrilous.

outrance (utrãːs) *f*, excess. *à ~*, to the death; mortal; internecine; desperately, to the bitter end; out & out. **outrancier, ère** (trãsje, ɛːr) *a*, extremist (*att.*), out & out.

outre (utr) *f*, leather bottle.

outre (utr) *pr. & ad*, beyond; further. *d'~ en ~*, through [& through]. *nos voisins d'~-Manche*, our neighbors across the Channel. *en ~*, moreover, besides, further[more]. *passer ~*, to go on; ignore. *~-mer, ad. & d'~-mer, a*, oversea[s].

outré, e (utre) *a*, excessive, far-fetched, overdone, fulsome, outré; carried away; disgusted.

outrecuidance (utrəkɥidãːs) *f*, presumptuousness. **outrecuidant, e** (dã, ãːt) *a*, overweening.

outremer (utrəmɛːr) *m*, ultramarine (*pigment*).

outrepasser (utrəpɑse) *v.t*, to go beyond, overstep.

outrer (utre) *v.t*, to overdo; overstrain; provoke.

ouvert, e† (uvɛːr, ɛrt) *p.a*, open; free; frank. **ouverture** (vɛrtyːr) *f*, opening; aperture; orifice; hole; port; gap; spread; overture; openness.

ouvrable (uvrabl) *a*, workable; business (*day*). **ouvrage** (uvraːʒ) *m*, work; doing (*fig.*). *~s d'agrément*, fancy work. *~s d'art*, permanent works, [p.] structures. *~s de dames*, fancy needlework, art n. *~s de ville*, job work (*Typ.*). **ouvragé, e** (vraʒe) *a*, [highly] worked, elaborated.

ouvre-boîte (uvrə) *m*, can opener. **ouvre-gants**, *m*, glove stretcher.

ouvrer (uvre) *v.i*, to work; (*v.t.*) to work; diaper.

ouvreur, euse (uvrœːr, øːz) *n*, opener; (*f.*) box attendant (*Theat.*).

ouvrier, ère (uvrie, ɛːr) *n*, workman; workwoman; worker; operative; factory hand; journeyman; laborer (*farm*). ~ *d'art*, handicraftsman. ¶ *a*, working, laboring (*class*); workmen's; labor (*troubles, etc.*).

ouvrir (uvriːr) *v.t. & abs. ir*, to open; unlock; disburden; open up; cut; propose; head (*as a list*); turn on, switch on; draw back (*curtains*); sharpen (*appetite*); (*v.i.ir.*) to open. *la maison reste ouverte pendant les travaux*, business as usual during alterations. *s'~*, to open; unburden oneself.

ouvroir (uvrwaːr) *m*, workroom (*convent*).

ovaire (ovɛːr) *m*, ovary.

ovale (ɔval) *a. & m*, oval. ~ [*de table*], doily.

ovation (ɔvasjɔ̃) *f*, ovation. **ovationner** (ne) *v.t*, to acclaim.

ovine (ɔvin) *a.f*, ovine.

ovipare (ɔvipaːr) *a*, oviparous.

oxhydrique (ɔksidrik) *a*, oxyhydrogen (*blowpipe, etc.*); lime (*light*).

oxyde (ɔksid) *m*, oxide. ~ *de carbone*, carbon monoxide. **oxyder** (de) *v.t*, to oxidize. **oxygène** (ʒɛn) *m*, oxygen.

ozone (ɔzɔn) *m*, ozone.

P

pacage (pakaːʒ) *m*, grazing; pasturage. **pacager** (kaʒe) *v.t*, to pasture, graze.

pachyderme (paʃidɛrm) *m*, pachyderm.

pacificateur, trice (pasifikatœːr, tris) *n*, peacemaker. ¶ *a*, pacifying. **pacifier** (fje) *v.t*, to pacify; appease. **pacifique†** (fik) *a*, pacific, peaceable; peaceful. le P~, the Pacific. **pacifiste** (fist) *n. & a*, pacificist, pacifist.

package (pakaʒ) *m*, software package.

pacotille (pakɔtiːj) *f*, barter goods; trash.

pacte (pakt) *m*, [com]pact, covenant. **pactiser avec** (tize), to compound with (*condone*); compound (*felony*).

Pactole (le) (paktɔl) (*fig.*), a gold mine.

Padoue (padu) *f*, Padua.

pæan (peɑ̃) *m*, paean.

paf (paf) *m*, penis (*obscene*). *beau comme un ~*, elegant (*ironic*). *tomber sur un ~*, to fail, suffer defeat.

pagaie (pagɛ) *f*, paddle (*canoe*).

pagaïe, pagaille (pagaːj) *f*, clutter, mess, disorder, etc.

paganisme (paganism) *m*, paganism, heathenism.

pagayer (pageje) *v.t*, to paddle (*canoe*). **pagayeur, euse** (jœːr, øːz) *n*, paddler.

page (paːʒ) *f*, page (*book*); chapter (*of one's life*). *à la ~*, up to date. ¶ *m*, page (*noble youth*); bellhop.

pagel (paʒɛl) *m*, [sea] bream.

paginer (paʒine) *v.t*, to page, paginate.

pagode (pagɔd) *f*, pagoda; mandarin (*toy*).

paie (pɛ) *f*, pay, wages; (*good, bad*) payer. **paiement** (mɑ̃) *m*, payment.

païen, ne (pajɛ̃, ɛn) *a. & n*, pagan, heathen.

paillard, e (pajaːr, ard) *a. & n*, lewd (*person*). **paillasse** (jas) *f*, straw mattress; drainboard; whore (*slang*). ¶ *m*, clown (*pagliaccio*). **paillasson** (sɔ̃) *m*, doormat; matting (*Hort.*); servile person; slut, easy lay (*slang*). **paille** (pɑːj) *f*, straw; flaw; (*fig.*) mote (*in eye*). ~ *de bois*, wood shaving. ~ *de fer*, steel wool. *une ~!*, a trifle! (*ironic*). [*couleur*] ~, straw-color[ed]. **pailler** (paje) (*fig.*) *m*, dunghill. ¶ *v.t*, to mulch; rush (*chair*). **paillet** (jɛ) *a.m*, pale (*red wine*). **paillet d'abordage**, *m*, collision mat. **pailleté, e** (jte) *a*, spangled. **paillette** (jɛt) *f*, spangle; flake; scale; chaff, window (*radar*). **pailleux** (jø) *a.m*, strawy; flawy. **paillis** (ji) *m*, mulch. **paillon** (jɔ̃) *m*, straw casing (*bottle*); spangle; foil; grain (*solder*). **paillote** (pajɔt) *f*, straw hut (*native*).

pain (pɛ̃) *m*, bread; loaf (*bread, sugar*); biscuit (*dog*); cake (*soap, fish, etc.*); tablet; pat (*butter*). ~

à cacheter, signet wafer. ~ *à chanter,* wafer (*Eccl.*). ~ *d'épice,* gingerbread. ~ *de bougie,* taper (*coiled*). ~ *de munition,* ration bread. ~ *de régime,* diet b. ~ *grillé,* ~ *rôti, toast.* ~ *complet,* whole wheat bread. ~ *de mie,* sandwich b.

pair (pɛːr) *a.m*; **paire,** *Arith. only, a.f*, equal, like; even (*number*). ¶ *m*, peer; equal; par, equality; mate (*bird*). *au ~,* (*engagement*) on mutual terms; room and board (*no salary*). *marcher de ~ avec,* to keep pace with; rank with.

paire (pɛːr) *f*, pair; brace; yoke (*oxen, etc.*).

pairesse (pɛrɛs) (*Eng.*) *f*, peeress. **pairie** (ri) (*Fr. Hist. & Eng.*) *f*, peerage.

paisible† (pɛzibl) *a*, peaceable, peaceful.

paître (pɛːtr) *v.t. & i. ir*, to graze, pasture, browse; feed; tend.

paix (pɛ) *f*, peace; pax (*Eccl.*). ¶ *i*, hush! be quiet!

pal (pal) *m*, pale, stake.

palabre (palaːbr) *f. or m*, palaver. **palabrer** (labre) *v.i*, to palaver.

paladin (paladɛ̃) *m*, paladin; knight errant (*fig.*).

palais (palɛ) *m*, palace; [law] courts; court; law; palate; roof of the mouth. ~ *dur,* hard palate, bony p. ~ *mou,* soft p.

palan (palɑ̃) *m*, pulley block; tackle, purchase. **palanche** (lɑ̃ːʃ) *f*, yoke (*for pails*).

palanque (palɑ̃ːk) *f*, stockade.

palatal, e (palatal) *a*, palatal.

palatine (palatin) *f*, fur cape, tippet.

pale (pal) *f*, shut-off; sluice gate; blade (*oar, air propeller*).

pâle (pɑːl) *a*, pale, pallid, wan; (*fig.*) colorless.

palée (pale) *f*, sheet piling.

palefrenier (palfrənje) *m*, groom, [h]ostler. **palefroi** (frwa) (*Poet.*) *m*, palfrey.

palémon (palemɔ̃) *m*, prawn.

paléographie (paleɔgrafi) *f*, paleography. **paléontologie** (3tɔlɔʒi) *f*, paleontology.

Palerme (palɛrm) *f*, Palermo.

paleron (palrɔ̃) *m*, shoulder blade (*horse, ox*).

palet (palɛ) *m*, quoit; quoits; puck (*ice hockey*).

paletot (palto) *m*, overcoat; greatcoat.

palette (palɛt) *f*, battledore; bat; palette; pallet; paddle.

palétuvier (paletyvje) *m*, mangrove.

pâleur (pɑlœːr) *f*, pallor, paleness.

palier (palje) *m*, landing (*stairs*); floor; bearings, plummer block; level.

palimpseste (palɛ̃psɛst) *m. & a*, palimpsest.

palinodie (palinɔdi) *f*, recantation.

pâlir (pɑliːr) *v.i. & t*, to pale, blanch; wane; fade.

palis (pali) *m*, pale, paling. **palissade** (sad) *f*, palisade, fence; stockade; hoarding (*street*). **palissader** (de) *v.t*, to palisade, fence.

palissandre (palisɑ̃ːdr) *m*, rosewood.

palladium (paladjɔm) *m*, palladium; safeguard.

palliatif, ive (palljatif, iːv) *a. & m*, palliative. **pallier** (pallje) *v.t*, to palliate.

palmarès (palmarɛːs) *m*, prize list, honors l. ~ *de la chanson,* hit parade (*popular song*).

palme (palm) *f*, palm [branch], p. [tree]; **palmé, e** (me) *a*, palmate[d]; webbed.

palmer (palmɛːr) *m*, micrometer.

palmeraie (palmərɛ) *f*, palm grove. **palmier** (mje) *m*, palm [tree]. **palmipède** (mipɛd) *a*, webfooted. **palmiste** (mist) *m*, cabbage tree.

palombe (palɔ̃ːb) *f*, ring dove, wood pigeon.

pâlot, te (pɑlo, ɔt) *a*, palish, wan.

palourde (palurd) *f*, clam (*Mol.*).

palpable (palpabl) *a*, palpable. **palpe** (palp) *f. or m*, palp[us], feeler. **palper** (pe) *v.t*, to feel, finger. **palpitation** (pitasjɔ̃) *f*,

palpitation, throbbing, fluttering.
palpiter (te) *v.i,* to palpitate, etc;
go pit-[a-]pat; thrill.
paltoquet (paltɔkɛ) *m,* churl.
paludéen, ne (palydeɛ̃, ɛn) *a,*
marshy; malarial. **paludisme**
(dism) *m,* malaria.
pâmer (pɑme) *v.i.* & se ~, to
swoon, faint; die *(of laughing,
etc.).*
pampas (pɑ̃pɑs) *f.pl,* pampas.
pamphlet (pɑ̃flɛ) *m,* lampoon.
pamphlétaire (fletɛ:r) *m,* lampooner.
pamplemousse (pɑ̃pləmus) *f,*
grapefruit.
pampre (pɑ̃:pr) *m,* vine branch.
pan (pɑ̃) *m,* skirt, flap; tail *(coat);*
face, side; pane, slab; frame. *à
6 ~s,* hexagonal. *à 8 ~s,* octagonal.
pan (pɑ̃) *onomatopoeia,* bang!
~! ~! rat-tat[-tat]!
panacée (panase) *f,* panacea,
nostrum.
panache (panaʃ) *m,* plume, tuft;
mettle, go, dash. *faire ~,* to have
a spill, turn right over. **panacher**
(ʃe) *v.t,* to plume, tuft; streak,
variegate, mix. *la bière panaché,*
shandy.
panais (panɛ) *m,* parsnip.
panama (panama) *m,* panama,
Panama hat.
Paname (panam) *m,* Paris *(slang).*
panaris (panari) *m,* whitlow.
pancarte (pɑ̃kart) *f,* placard,
bill, show card.
pancréas (pɑ̃kreɑ:s) *m,* pancreas.
pandémonium (pɑ̃demɔnjɔm)
m, pandemonium.
pandit (pɑ̃di) *m,* pundit.
pandour (pɑ̃dur) *m,* pandor,
brute *(pers.).*
panégyrique (paneʒirik) *m,*
panegyric, encomium.
paner (pane) *v.t,* to crumb
(Cook.).
panerée (panre) *f,* basketful.
panetière (pantjɛ:r) *f,* sideboard.
pangermanisme (pɑ̃ʒɛrma-
nism) *m,* pan-Germanism.
panier (panje) *m,* basket, hamper; pannier; straw hive; lobster
basket; basketful. ~ *à ouvrage,*
work basket. ~ *[à papiers],*

wastepaper b. ~ *à pêche,* creel. ~
à provisions, shopping basket;
luncheon b. ~ *roulant,* go-cart.
~ *à salade,* prison van, Black
Maria.
panique (panik) *a.* & *f,* panic,
scare.
panne (pan) *f,* lard; plush; purlin;
pane *(hammer);* breakdown, failure. *avoir une ~ d'essence ou une
~ sèche,* to run out of gas. *laisser
en ~,* to leave in the lurch. *mettre
en ~,* to heave to *(Naut.).* *en ~,*
out of order.
panneau (pano) *m,* panel; snare.
~-*réclame, m,* billboard.
panneton (pantɔ̃) *m,* bit, web
(key).
panonceau (panɔ̃so) *m,* medallion, tablet, sign.
panoplie (panɔpli) *f,* panoply,
trophy *(wall).*
panorama (panɔrama) *m,* panorama. **panoramique** *(mik) m,* pan
shot *(cinema, TV).* ~ *rapide, filé,*
whip pan, swish p. **panoramiquer**
(mike) *v.i,* to pan, tilt.
panse (pɑ̃:s) *f,* belly, paunch.
pansement (pɑ̃smɑ̃) *m,* dressing
(wound). **panser** (se) *v.t,* to
dress; groom *(horse).*
pansu, e (pɑ̃sy) *a,* corpulent.
pantagruélique (pɑ̃tagʁyelik)
a, sumptuous *(fare).*
pantalon (pɑ̃talɔ̃) *m,* [pair of]
trousers. **pantalonnade** (lɔnad)
f, comic turn; clownery; [tom-]
foolery; masquerade, sham.
pantelant, e (pɑ̃tlɑ̃, ɑ̃:t) *a,*
panting; twitching *(flesh).* **panteler** (le) *v.i,* to pant.
panthéisme (pɑ̃teism) *m,* pantheism.
panthéon (pɑ̃teɔ̃) *m,* pantheon.
panthère (pɑ̃tɛ:r) *f,* panther.
pantin (pɑ̃tɛ̃) *m,* *(toy)* jumping
jack; *(pers.)* monkey on a stick
(*gesticulator*); shallow-brained &
fickle person. *mener une vie de
~,* to run wild.
pantographe (pɑ̃tɔgraf) *m,*
pantograph.
pantois, e (pɑ̃twa, a:z) *a,* flabbergasted.
pantomime (pɑ̃tɔmim) *(pers.)*
n, pantomimist. ¶ *f,* pantomime,
dumb show.

pantoufle (pɑ̃tufl) f, slipper. ~s
en tapisserie, carpet s—s. en ~s,
in a free & easy way; informal.
panure (pany:r) f, [grated] bread
crumbs.
paon (pɑ̃) m, peacock; p. butterfly. **paonne** (pan) f, peahen. **paonneau** (pano) m, peachick.
papa (papa) m, papa, dad[dy]. à la
~, without hurrying, simply.
papal, e (papal) a, papal. **papauté**
(pote) f, papacy. **pape** (pap) m,
pope.
papegai (papgɛ) m, popinjay
(Hist.); clay bird (pigeon shooting).
papelard, e (papla:r, ard) a. & n,
sanctimonious (person).
paperasse (papras) f, useless old
paper. **papeterie** (pap[ɛ]tri) f,
paper mill; p. making; p. trade;
stationery store; stationery; s.
case, writing case. **papetier, ère**
(paptje, ɛ:r) n, paper maker;
stationer. **papier** (pje) m, paper;
bills (Fin.). ~ à calquer, ~-cal-
que, tracing paper. ~ à lettres,
note p., letter p. ~ autovireur
(otovirœ:r), self-toning p. ~ buvard, ~ brouillard, blotting p. ~
carbone, carbon [p.] (duplicating). ~ de Chine, rice p. ~ de
journal, newsprint. ~ de soie,
tissue p. ~ de verre, sandpaper.
~ hygiénique, toilet p. ~ imperméable à la graisse, ~ sulfurisé, grease-proof p. ~ indien,
India p. ~ machine, typewriting
p. ~ [peint]. ~-tenture, m, wallpaper. ~ pelure, tissue p. ~
quadrillé (kadrije), graph p., plot-
ting p., section[al] p. ~ tue-
mouches, fly p. ~ timbré, official
(stamped) p. ~ à en-tête, letter-
head p. ~ de brouillon, scrap p.
papillon (papijɔ̃) m, butterfly;
wing nut; bow (necktie); slip
(paper); parking ticket. ~s noirs,
gloomy ideas. ~ [de nuit], moth;
throttle (auto). **papillonner** (jɔne)
v.i, to flit about.
papillote (papijɔt) f, curl paper;
foiled chocolate. **papilloter** (te)
v.i, to flicker; blink; dazzle; slur
(Typ.).
papisme (papism) m, popery.
papiste (pist) n, papist. ¶ a,
popish.

papoter (papɔte) v.i, to gossip.
papule (papyl) f, pimple.
papyrus (papiry:s) m, papyrus.
pâque (pɑ:k) f, Passover. **Pâques**
(pɑ:k) m.s, Easter. **Pâques
fleuries,** f.pl, Palm Sunday.
paquebot (pakbo) m, passenger
&/or mail boat, liner, packet
[boat]. ~ à vapeur, passenger
steamer. ~ aérien, airship.
pâquerette (pɑkrɛt) f, daisy.
paquet (pakɛ) m, packet, package, bundle, pack; parcel, lot,
block; clincher; (att.) plump. un
~ de mer, a, [heavy] sea. **paquetage** (kta:ʒ) m, pack (soldier's).
par (par) pr, by; through; across;
via; out of; per; a; in; into; with;
on; about; over; from; for; at;
during. ~ an, per annum. ~-ci,
~-là, ad, here & there, hither &
thither; at odd times. ~-dessous,
~-dessus. See dessous, dessus. ~
ici, this way, through here. ~ là,
that way, through there; by that.
de ~ le monde, somewhere in the
world. ~ les présentes, hereby
(law). ~ où? which way? ~
trop, far too, too much, unduly.
parabole (parabɔl) f, parable;
parabola. **parabolique†** (lik) a,
parabolic(al) (Geom.).
parachever (paraʃve) v.t, to
finish [off], perfect.
parachute (paraʃyt) m, parachute.
parade (parad) f, parade; show;
parry[ing]; repartee. **parader** (de)
v.i, to parade; show off.
paradis (paradi) m, paradise;
top balcony (Theat.). le ~ [ter-
restre], [the earthly] paradise,
[the Garden of] Eden.
paradoxal, e (paradɔksal) a,
paradoxical. **paradoxe** (dɔks) m,
paradox.
parafe (paraf) m, initials; flourish;
paraph. **parafer** (fe) v.t, to initial.
paraffine (parafin) f, paraffin
[wax].
parage (para:ʒ) m, lineage; (pl.)
grounds (fishing, cruising), waters.
dans ces ~s, in these parts, here-
abouts.
paragraphe (paragraf) m, para-

graph; section mark (§).

paraître (parɛ:tr) *v.i.ir*, to appear; show; be published, come out; seem, look. *vient de*~, just out, published. ¶ *m*, seeming. *l'être & le* ~, the seeming & the real.

Paralipomènes (paralipɔmɛn) *m. pl*, Chronicles (*Bible*).

parallaxe (paralaks) *f*, parallax. **parallèle†** (lɛl) *a*, parallel. ¶ *f*, parallel (*Geom., Mil.*). ¶ *m*, parallel (*of latitude; comparison*). **parallélipipède** (lelipipɛd) *m*, parallelepiped. **parallélogramme** (lɔgram) *m*, parallelogram.

paralyser (paralize) *v.t*, to paralyze; cripple (*fig.*). **paralysie** (zi) *f*, paralysis. ~ *progressive*, creeping paralysis. **paralytique** (tik) *a. & n*, paralytic.

parangon (parãgɔ̃) *m*, paragon.

parapet (parapɛ) *m*, parapet.

paraphe (paraf) *m*, initials; flourish, paraph. **parapher** (fe) *v.t*, to initial.

paraphrase (parafrɑ:z) *f*, paraphrase; circumlocution. **paraphraser** (frɑze) *v.t. & abs*, to paraphrase; amplify.

parapluie (paraplɥi) *m*, umbrella.

parasitaire (parazitɛ:r) *a*, parasitic(al) (*Biol.*). **parasite** (zit) *m*, parasite; hanger-on; sponger. ~*s atmosphériques*, static (*radio*). ¶ *a*, parasitical; redundant.

parasol (parasɔl) *m*, sunshade, umbrella (*garden, beach, held over potentate*); tent umbrella.

paratonnerre (paratɔnɛ:r) *m*, lightning rod.

paravent (paravã) *m*, screen (*folding & fig.*).

paraverse (paravɛrs) *m*, raincoat.

parbleu (parblø) *i*, why, of course! to be sure!

parc (park) *m*, park; enclosure; yard; paddock; pen, fold; range, run; bed (*oyster*); playpen. ~ *à bestiaux* (cattle) & ~ *à matières* (materials), stockyard. ~ *à voitures*, car park. ~ *d'agrément*, pleasure grounds. **parcage** (ka:ʒ) *m*, parking; penning.

parcelle (parsɛl) *f*, particle, scrap; driblet; parcel, plot, patch.

parce que (pars[ə]kə) *c*, because.

parchemin (parʃəmɛ̃) *m*, parchment; (*fig.*) title; diploma.

parcimonie (parsimɔni) *f*, parsimony. **parcimonieux, euse†** (njø, ∅:z) *a*, parsimonious, penurious.

parcourir (parkuri:r) *v.t.ir*, to travel over, cover; perambulate; run through. **parcours** (ku:r) *m*, distance, stretch, run; haul; course. ~ *de 18 trous*, 18-hole course (*golf*).

pardessus (pardəsy) *m*, overcoat.

pardi (pardi) *i*, of course!

pardon (pardɔ̃) *m*, pardon, forgiveness. **pardonnable** (dɔnabl) *a*, pardonable. **pardonner** (ne) *v.t. & ~ à*, to pardon, forgive; excuse.

pare- (par) *prefix*: ~*battage*, *m*, fender (*Naut.*). ~*boue*, *m*, fender; ~*brise*, *m*, windshield. ~*chocs*, *m*, bumper. ~*étincelles*, *m*, fireguard.

parégorique (paregɔrik) *a*, paregoric.

pareil, le (parɛ:j) *a*, like, alike, similar, to match; equal; parallel; such. ¶ *n*, like, equal; parallel; match, fellow. *la* ~, the like (treatment). *sans pareil*, unequalled, matchless. **pareillement** (rɛjmã) *ad*, in like manner; also, likewise.

parement (parmã) *m*, facing; face; cuff (*coat*); cloth (*altar*); curbstone.

parent, e (parã, ã:t) *n*, relative, kinsman, -woman; relation; (*m. pl.*) parents, kin. **parenté** (rãte) *f*, relationship, kinship; relations.

parenthèse (parãtɛ:z) *f*, parenthesis; bracket (,). *par* ~, parenthetically.

parer (pare) *v.t. & i*, to adorn, deck; dress; ward [off], fend [off]; parry; guard.

paresse (parɛs) *f*, laziness, idleness, sloth; sluggishness. **paresser** (se) *v.i*, to idle; laze; loll, lounge. **paresseux, euse†** (sø, ∅:z) *a. & n*, idle, etc (person). ¶ *m*, sloth (*Zool.*).

parfaire (parfɛ:r) *v.t.ir*, to finish [off]; make up. **parfait, e** (fɛ, ɛt) *a*, perfect; thorough; capital. ¶ *m*, perfect [tense]. **parfaitement** (tmã) *ad*, perfectly; thoroughly;

quite; quite so, exactly.

parfiler (parfile) *v.t,* to unravel.

parfois (parfwa) *ad,* sometimes, at times, now & again.

parfum (parfœ̃) *m,* perfume, fragrance; scent; flavor. *être au ~,* to be in on it *(trick, scheme).* **parfumer** (fyme) *v.t,* to scent, perfume; wise someone up. **parfumerie** (mri) *f,* perfumery. **parfumeur,** euse (mœːr, øːz) n, perfumer; *(m.)* perfume distiller.

pari (pari) *m,* bet, wager.

paria (parja) *m,* outcaste, untouchable; pariah, outcast.

parier (parje) *v.t,* to bet, wager, lay. *~ sur,* to back *(horse). il y a à ~ que . . .,* the odds are that *. . .* **parieur,** euse (jœːr, øːz) n, bettor, backer.

parisien, ne (parizjɛ̃, ɛn), *a.* & P~, *n,* Parisian.

parité (parite) *f,* parity, equality, likeness; equivalent.

parjure (parʒyːr) *m,* perjury; breach of oath. ¶ *n,* perjurer. ¶ *a,* perjured, forsworn. se **parjurer** (ʒyre) *v.pr,* to perjure (*or* forswear) oneself.

parking (parkiŋ) *m,* parking lot.

parlant, e (parlɑ̃, ɑ̃ːt) *a,* speaking, talking *(film, eyes);* lifelike; talkative. **parlé** (le) *m,* spoken part *(opera);* patter *(in song).*

parlement (parləmɑ̃) *m,* parliament. **parlementaire** (tɛːr) *a,* parliamentary; of truce *(flag).* ¶ *m,* member of parliament; bearer of a flag of truce. **parlementer** (te) *v.i,* to parley.

parler (parle) *v.i.* & *abs.* & *v.t,* to speak, talk; t. about; tell, mention, say. *~ du nez,* to speak through the nose. ¶ *m,* way of speaking; speech; dialect. **parleur,** euse (lœːr, øːz) n, talker; *(att.)* talking *(bird).* **parloir** (lwaːr) *m,* parlor *(convent, school).* **parlote** (lɔt) *f,* debating society; gossip.

Parme (parm) *f,* Parma.

parmi (parmi) *pr,* among[st], amid[st].

parodie (parɔdi) *f,* parody. **parodier** (dje) *v.t,* to parody. **parodiste** (dist) *m,* parodist.

paroi (parwa) *f,* wall *(partition, etc.);* side; coat[ing] *(stomach, etc.).*

paroisse (parwas) *f,* parish; p. church. **paroissial,** e (sjal) *a,* parish *(att.),* parochial. **paroissien,** ne (sjɛ̃, ɛn) *n,* parishioner. ¶ *m,* prayer book.

parole (parɔl) *f,* word; utterance; delivery; speaking; speech; parole. *~ d'Évangile,* gospel [truth]. *avoir la ~,* to have the floor.

paroxysme (parɔksism) *m,* paroxysm.

parpaillot, e (parpajo, ɔt) *n,* heretic.

Parque (park) *f,* Fate *(Myth.).*

parquer (parke) *v.t,* to pen, fold; park.

parquet (parkɛ) *m,* floor, parquet; well *(of court);* central floor of Fr. *Bourse* reserved for use of *agents de change.* **parqueter** (kəte) *v.t,* to floor, parquet.

parrain (parɛ̃) *m,* godfather, sponsor; proposer, recommender. **parrainage** (rɛnaːʒ) *m,* sponsorship; recommendation.

parricide (parisid) *(pers.) n.* & *(act) m,* parricide; *(att.)* parricidal.

parsemer (parsəme) *v.t,* to strew, intersperse.

parsi (parsi) *m.* & **parse** (pars) *m.* & *a,* Parsee.

part (paːr) *(law) m,* child, birth.

part (paːr) *f,* share; part; portion; hand, side. *~ du lion,* lion's share. *à ~,* apart; aside; except, *autre ~,* elsewhere, somewhere else. *d'autre ~,* on the other hand *or* side. *de la ~ de,* on the part of, on behalf of, from. *de ~ en ~,* right through. *faire ~,* to share; acquaint, inform. *à ~ entière,* completely *(un français à part entière,* a full-fledged French citizen).

partage (partaːʒ) *m,* division, sharing; share, lot. *~ [des voix],* equality of votes. *~ de temps,* time-sharing *(computers).* **partagé,** e (taʒe) *p.a,* reciprocal, mutual *(love);* halved *(hole) (golf).* **partageable** (ʒabl) *a,* divisible. **partager** (ʒe) *v.t,* to divide, share, split.

partance (partã:s) *f*, sailing. en
~, about to sail, outward bound.
partant (tã) *ad*, hence, therefore.
¶ *m*, starter (*horse, runner*).

partenaire (partənɛ:r) *n*, partner. ~ *d'entraînement*, sparring
partner.

parterre (partɛ:r) *m*, bed (*garden*), plot, parterre; orchestra
pit (*Theat.*).

parti (parti) *m*, party, side; part;
course; decision; match (*marriage*). ~ *pris*, set purpose; prejudice, bias. *faire un mauvais* ~ *à*,
to ill-treat. *prendre* ~, to take
sides, to side. *tirer* ~ *de*, to make
use of, turn to account.

partial, e† (parsjal) *a*, partial,
biased, unfair. **partialité** (lite) *f*,
partiality.

participation (partisipasjɔ̃) *f*,
participation, sharing; partaking;
share; joint [ad]venture, joint account. ~ *aux bénéfices*, profit-
sharing. **participe** (sip) *m*, participle (*Gram.*). **participer** (pe) *v.i*, to
participate, share; partake.

particulariser (partikylarize)
v.t, to particularize. **particularité**
(te) *f*, particularity; peculiarity.
particule (kyl) *f*, particle; speck.
particulier, ère† (lje, ɛ:r) *a*, particular; peculiar; [e]special; private. ¶ *n*, [private] individual.

partie (parti) *f*, part; parcel, lot;
block; match, round, game; excursion, trip; line (*of business*);
party; client (*lawyer's*). ~ *de
trois*, threesome (*golf*). ~ *double*, doubles game (*Ten.*); four-
some (*golf*); double entry
(*Bkkpg.*) ~ *du discours*, part
of speech. ~ *civile*, plaintiff. ~
nulle, tie (*sports*). *prendre à*
~, to take to task.

partiel, le (parsjɛl) *a*, partial
(*not entire*). **partiellement** (lmã)
ad, partially, partly.

partir (parti:r) *v.i.ir*, to depart, set
out, start, go; leave; sail; go off;
emanate, proceed. *êtes-vous
prêts? partez!* are you ready? go!
à ~ *de*, from; on & after. *il est
parti*, he is drunk.

partisan (partizã) *m*, partisan,
henchman, follower, believer;
supporter; guerrilla (*soldier*).

partitif, ive (partitif, i:v) *a*, partitive (*Gram.*). **partition** (sjɔ̃) *f*,
score (*Mus.*).

partouse, partouze (partu:z) *f*,
orgy (*slang*).

partout (partu) *ad*, everywhere.
2, 3, jeux ~, 2, 3, all (*Ten.*). ~ *où*,
wherever.

parure (pary:r) *f*, adornment;
ornament; dress, attire; dressing (*meat*); set (*jewels, underclothing*).

parution (parysjɔ̃) *f*, publication,
appearance, issue (*book, maga-
-ine*).

parvenir (parvəni:r) *v.i. & abs.
ir*, to arrive; succeed. ~ *à*, to
arrive at, reach; attain [to]; manage to; succeed in. **parvenu, e**
(ny) *n*, upstart, parvenu.

parvis (parvi) *m*, parvis, square;
court.

pas (pɑ) *m*, step; pace; stride; gait;
walk; march; time (*Mil.*); dance,
pas; progress; precedence (*in
rank*); footfall; footprint; threshold; pass (*Phys. Geog.*); strait[s];
pitch, thread (*screw*). ~ *accéléré*, quick march. *P~ de Calais*,
Straits of Dover. ~ *de clerc*,
blunder. ~ *de la porte*, door-
step. *à* ~ *de tortue*, at a snail's
pace. ~ *seul*, solo dance. *au* ~,
drive slowly, dead slow (*traffic
sign*). *au* ~ *gymnastique*, at the
double (*Mil.*). *faux* ~, slip; mis-
step.

pas (pɑ) *neg. particle usually
coupled with* ne, not; no. ~ *libre*,
[I am] sorry, the line is busy.
(*Teleph.*). ~ *possible!* you don't
say so!

pascal, aux (paskal, ko) *a*, paschal; Easter.

pasquin (paskɛ̃) *m*, lampooner;
lampoon. **pasquinade** (kinad) *f*,
pasquinade, lampoon, squib.

passable† (pɑsabl) *a*, passable,
tolerable, fair, pretty good. **passade** (sad) *f*, passing fancy (*liaison*); passade. **passage** (sa:ʒ) *m*,
passage; passing; crossing; going;
transit; transition; pass; passageway, gangway, way, thoroughfare; arcade; ferry; right of way;
toll; run (*computers*). ~ *à niveau*,
grade crossing. ~ *clouté*, studded
crossing (*pedestrian crossing*). ~

d'escalier, stairway. ~ *interdit [au public]*, no thoroughfare. ~ *souterraine*, underground passage.

passager, ère (pɑsaʒe, ɛːr) *a*, passing, fleeting, transient, fugitive, short-lived, momentary. ¶ *n*, passenger; visitor, sojourner. ~ *clandestin*, stowaway. ~ *d'entrepont*, steerage passenger. **passagèrement** (ʒɛrmɑ̃) *ad*, in passing, for a short time. **passant, e** (pɑsɑ̃, ɑ̃ːt) *n*, passerby.

passavant (pɑsavɑ̃) *m*, gangway (*on ship*); permit.

passe (pɑːs) *f*, pass; passage; plight; way; thrust; cut; fairway, channel; brim (*hat*); passkey; passport. *mauvaise* ~, bad fix. ~ *étroite*, narrow[s] (*Naut.*).

passé, e (pɑse) *p.a*, past, [by]gone, last; over; faded. *passé maître*, a past master. ¶ *m*, past; p. [tense]; satin stitch (*Emb.*). **passé,** *pr*, after.

passe-droit (pɑsdrwa) *m*, injustice, invidious distinction.

passe-lacet (pɑslase) *m*, bodkin. *raide comme un* ~, stone broke.

passement (pɑsmɑ̃) *m*, lace, braid; gimp. **passementerie** (tri) *f*, passementerie, trimmings.

passe-partout (pɑspartu) *m*, master key.

passe-passe (pɑspɑs) *m*, sleight-of-hand. *tour de* ~, conjuring trick.

passe-plats (pɑspla) *m*, service hatch.

passepoil (pɑspwal) *m*, piping (*braid*).

passeport (pɑspɔːr) *m*, passport; clearance (*ship*).

passer (pɑse) *v.i. & t*, to pass; p. on; p. by; p. away; go; cross; spend; call, look in; ferry over; slip on; exceed; rank; enter, post; enter into; give, place; file (*a return at a registry*). ~ *à tabac*, to beat brutally (*slang*). ~ *l'arme à gauche*, to cash in one's chips, die. se ~ *de*, to do without, dispense with.

passereau (pɑsro) *m*, sparrow.

passerelle (pɑsrɛl) *f*, footbridge; bridge (*ship's*); gangway; catwalk (*Theat., cinema*).

passerose (pɑsroːz) *f*, hollyhock.

passe-temps (pɑstɑ̃) *m*, pastime.

passeur (pɑsœːr) *m*, ferryman.

passible (pɑsibl) *a*, liable. ~ *de droits*, dutiable.

passif, ive (pɑsif, iːv) *a*, passive. ¶ *m*, passive [voice]; liabilities.

passiflore (pɑsiflɔːr) *f*, passion flower.

passion (pɑsjɔ̃) *f*, passion. **passionnant, e** (onɑ̃, ɑ̃ːt) *a*, thrilling. **passionné†, e** (ne) *a*, passionate; impassioned. *il est* ~ *pour*, he is passionately fond of; his hobby is. **passionner** (ne) *v.t*, to impassion; enthral[l]. se ~, to become impassioned; become enamored.

passivement (pɑsivmɑ̃) *ad*, passively. **passiveté** (vite) *f*, passivity.

passoire (pɑswaːr) *f*, colander; strainer.

pastel (pɑstɛl) *m*, crayon; pastel; woad.

pastèque (pɑstɛk) *f*, watermelon.

pasteur (pɑstœːr) *m*, shepherd; pastor, minister.

pasteuriser (pɑstœrize) *v.t*, to pasteurize.

pastiche (pɑstiʃ) *m*, pastiche; imitation, copy.

pastille (pɑstiːj) *f*, lozenge, pastille, drop; patch (*tire*).

pastoral, e (pɑstɔral) *a*, pastoral. ¶ *f*, pastoral; pastorale.

pastoriser (pɑstɔrize) *v.t*, to pasteurize.

pat (pat) *m*, stalemate (*chess*); (*att.*) stalemated. *faire* ~, to stalemate.

patache (pɑtaʃ) *f*, rattletrap (*vehicle*).

pataquès (pɑtakɛːs) *m*, malaprop[ism].

patarafe (pɑtaraf) *f*, scrawl.

patard (pɑtaːr) *m*, coin of little value.

patate (pɑtat) *f*, sweet potato; potato.

patatras (pɑtatrɑ) *onomatopoeia*, crash!

pataud, e (pɑto, oːd) *a. & n*, clumsy (*person*). ¶ *m*, big-pawed puppy.

patauger (pɑtoʒe) *v.i*, to flounder, squelch; wade.

pâte (pɑːt) *f*, paste; dough; pulp;

impasto; pie (*printers'*). **pâté**
(pɑte) *m*, pie, pasty; pâté; mud
pie; blot; block (*houses*); pie
(*printers'*). **pâtée** (te) *f*, mash
(*poultry*); dog food.

patelin, e (patlɛ̃, in) *a*, wheedling.
¶ *m*, village.

patelle (patɛl) *f*, limpet.

patène (patɛn) *f*, paten.

patent, e (patɑ̃, ɑ̃:t) *a*, patent
(*obvious*). ¶ *f*, license. ~ *de santé*, bill of health.

Pater (patɛ:r) *m*, paternoster.

patère (patɛ:r) *f*, base, block (*on
wall*); hat peg.

paterne (patɛrn) *a*, patronizing.
paternel, le† (nɛl) *a*, paternal,
fatherly; father's (*side*). **paternité** (nite) *f*, paternity, father-
hood; authorship.

pâteux, euse (patø, ø:z) *a*, pasty,
clammy, thick.

pathétique† (patetik) *a*, pathetic.
¶ *m*, pathos.

pathologie (patɔlɔʒi) *f*, pathology. **pathologique** (ʒik) *a*, pathological. **pathologiste** (ʒist) *n*,
thologist.

pathos (patɔs) *m*, bathos.

patibulaire (patibylɛ:r) *a*, hang-
dog.

patiemment (pasjamɑ̃) *ad*, patiently. **patience** (sjɑ:s) *f*, patience; button stick (*Mil.*); patience (*cards*); dock (*Bot.*).
patient, e (sjɑ̃, ɑ̃:t) *a*, patient,
enduring. ¶ *n*, patient; sufferer.
patienter (ɑ̃te) *v.i*, to have patience.

patin (patɛ̃) *m*, skate; runner;
skid; shoe; flange. ~*s à glace*, (1)
à visser, (2) *à griffes*, iceskates,
(1) screw-on, (2) clamp-on. ~*s à
roulettes*, roller skates. ~*s de
course*, racing s. ~*s de figure*,
figure s. ~*s de hockey*, hockey s.
patinage (tinaːʒ) *m*, skating; skid-
ding, slipping. **patine** (tin) *f*, patina. **patiné, e** (ne) *p.p*, patinated;
fumed (*oak*). **patiner** (ne) *v.i*, to
skate; skid, slip. **patinette** (nɛt) *f*,
scooter. **patineur, euse** (nœːr, øːz)
n, skater. **patinoire** (waːr) *f*, skating rink.

pâtir (patiːr) *v.i*, to suffer. **pâtiras**
(tira) *m*, drudge.

pâtis (pati) *m*, grazing ground,
pasture.

pâtisser (patise) *v.i*, to make
pastry. **pâtisserie** (sri) *f*, pastry;
confectionery; bakery; tea shop.
pâtissier, ère (sje, ɛːr) *n*, pastry-
cook [*&/or* confectioner]. **pâtissoire** (swaːr) *f*, pastry board.

patois (patwa) *m*, dialect; jargon.

patouiller (patuje) *v.i*, to flounder.

patraque (patrak) *a*, out of sorts,
slightly sick; worn out, not working well. ¶ *f*, watch (*slang*).

pâtre (pɑːtr) *m*, herdsman.

patriarcal, e (patriarkal) *a*, patri-
archal. **patriarche** (arʃ) *m*, patriarch.

patrice (patris) *m.* **& patricien,
ne** (sjɛ̃, ɛn) *a.* & *n*, patrician.
patrie (tri) *f*, native land, [n.]
country, fatherland; home. [*petite*] ~, birthplace. **patrimoine**
(trimwan) *m*, patrimony; inheritance, heritage. **patriote** (ɔt) *n*,
patriot. ¶ ~*.* & **patriotique** (tik)
a, patriotic. **patriotisme** (tism)
m, patriotism. **patron, ne** (trɔ̃,
ɔn) *n*, patron, ess; patron saint;
employer, principal; master, mistress; governor; skipper; coxswain. ¶ *m*, pattern (*for dress,
etc.*); templet, template; stencil
[plate]. **dès patron-minet**, at early
dawn. **patronage** (trɔnaːʒ) *m*,
patronage; advowson; benevolence; guild, club (*church*). **patronal, e** (nal) *a*, patronal, patron
saint's (*day*); employer's, ers'
(*att.*). **patronat** (na) *m*, employers
(*col.*). Patronat (*Conseil National
du Patronat Français—CNPF*),
French employers' association.
patronner (ne) *v.t*, to patronize;
stencil. **dame patronnesse** (nɛs) *f*,
patroness (*fête, etc.*). **nom patronymique** (nimik) *m*, patronymic; surname.

patrouille (patruːj) *f*, patrol.
patrouiller (truje) *v.i*, to patrol.

patte (pat) *f*, paw; foot; leg;
claw; tab; strap, clip; clamp,
holdfast; fluke (*anchor*). *à quatre
~s,*.on all fours. ~*-d'oie*, *f*, multiple fork, crowsfoot [forking (*of
roads*); crow's-foot (*wrinkle*).

pâturage (pɑtyraːʒ) *m*, pasturage. **pâture** (tyːr) *f*, pasture;

food (*fig.*). **pâturer** (tyre) *v.i*, to pasture, graze.

paturon (patyrɔ̃) *m*, pastern.

paume (poːm) *f*, palm (*hand*); real tennis (*ancient game*).

paumer (pome) *v.t*, to slap; swipe; lose. **se faire ~**, to be caught, nabbed.

paupérisme (poperism) *m*, pauperism.

paupière (popjɛːr) *f*, eyelid.

pause (poːz) *f*, pause, stop; rest (*Mus.*).

pauvre† (poːvr) *a. & m*, poor (man); pauper; penurious; scanty, meager. **pauvresse** (povrɛːs) *f*, beggar woman. **pauvret, te** (vrɛ, ɛt) *n*, poor little thing (*pers.*). **pauvreté** (ˈvrəte) *f*, poverty; poorness; commonplace.

pavage (pavaːʒ) *m*, pavement; paving.

pavaner (se) (pavane) *v.pr*, to strut [about].

pavé (pave) *m*, paving stone, pavement; pavé; street(s) (*fig.*); 10,000 francs (*slang*). **sur le ~**, out of work. **pavement** (vmɑ̃) *m*, paving; pavement. **paver** (ve) *v.t*, to pave. **paveur** (vœːr) *m*, paver.

pavie (pavi) *f*, clingstone.

Pavie (pavi) *f*, Pavia (*Geog.*).

pavillon (pavijɔ̃) *m*, pavilion; lodge; box (*Hunt.*); summer house; house (*club*); flag, colors (*Naut. & Nav.*); flare; horn; earpiece. **~ de poupe**, ensign.

pavois (pavwa) *m*, bulwark (*ship's*); flags (*col.*). **pavoiser** (ze) *v.t*, to dress (*ship*); deck with flags; (*abs.*) to dress ship.

pavot (pavo) *m*, poppy. **~ somnifère**, opium poppy.

payable (pejabl) *a*, payable. **~ à la commande**, cash with order. **~ comptant**, pay cash. **payant, e** (jɑ̃, ɑ̃ːt) *a*, paying. ¶ *n*, payer. **paye** (pɛːj) *f*, pay, wages; (*good, bad*) payer. **payement** (pɛjˈmɑ̃) *m*, payment. **payer** (je) *v.t. & abs*, to pay; p. for; p. out; cash (*check*); stand (*drink*). **~ d'audace**, to brazen it out. **~ de sa personne**, to risk one's neck. **payeur, euse** (jœːr, øːz) *n*, payer; paymaster; drawee.

pays (pei) *m*, country, land; native place. **~ de cocagne** (kɔkaɲ), land of milk & honey, l. of plenty. **les Pays-Bas**, the Netherlands. **mal du ~**, homesickness. **paysage** (zaːʒ) *m*, landscape; l. painting; description of scenery; (*pl.*) scenery. **paysagiste** (zaʒist) *m*, landscape painter; (*att.*) landscape (*gardener*).

paysan, ne (peizɑ̃, an) *n. & att*, peasant, rustic. **les paysans**, the peasantry. **paysannerie** (zanri) *f*, portrait of peasant life.

péage (peaːʒ) *m*, toll; t. house. **péager** (aʒe) *m*, toll collector.

péan (peɑ̃) *m*, paean.

peau (po) *f*, skin, fell, pelt; scruff (*neck*); slough; leather; rind, peel; shell (*nut*); case (*sausage*). **~ de tambour**, drumhead. **P~ Rouge**, *m*, redskin, red Indian. **peausserie** (sri) *f*, skin dressing; skins, peltry. **peaussier** (sje) *m*, skin dresser. [*médecin*] **peaussier** ou [*médecin*] **peaucier** (sje) *m*, skin specialist.

pécari (pekari) *m*, peccary.

peccadille (pɛkadiːj) *f*, peccadillo, slip.

pêche (pɛːʃ) *f*, peach (*fruit*); fishing (*act & right*); fishery, catch. **~ à la crevette**, shrimping. **~ à la ligne**, line fishing, rod f., angling. **~ à la mouche noyée**, wet fly f. **~ à la mouche sèche**, dry fly f. **~ à traîner**, trolling. **~ au bord de la mer**, shore fishing. **~ au lancer**, casting. **~ au large, ~ hauturière** (otyrjɛːr), offshore fishing, deep-sea f. **~ au vif**, live-bait f. **~ chalutière** (ʃalytjɛːr), trawling. **~ côtière, ~ dans les eaux territoriales**, inshore fishing. **~ de fond**, ground angling, bottom fishing. **~ de grand sport**, big-game fishing. **~ de plage**, surf f., beach f. **~ en eaux douces, ~ d'eau douce**, freshwater f. **~ de** (ou, *en*) **mer**, sea f., salt-water f.

péché (peʃe) *m*, sin. **~ d'habitude**, besetting s. **~ mignon**, pet vice, weak point. **pécher** (ʃe) *v.i*, to sin; err; offend.

pêcher (pɛʃe) *m*, peach (tree). ¶ *v.t*, to fish for; fish; f. up; drag (*pond*); pick up, get hold of. ~ **à la ligne,** to angle. ~ **à la traîne,** to troll. **pêcherie** (ʃri) *f,* fishery, fishing ground. **pêcheur, euse** ʃœːr, øːz) *n,* fisherman, angler.

pécheur, eresse (peʃœːr, ʃrɛs) *n,* sinner.

péculat (pekyla) *m,* embezzlement (*public funds*). **pécule** (kyl) *m,* savings, nest egg; earnings (*of convict*); mustering-out money (*on discharge, Mil., Nav.*).

pécuniaire† (pekynjɛːr) *a,* pecuniary.

pédagogue (pedagɔg) *m,* pedagogue.

pédale (pedal) *f,* pedal; treadle; homosexual (*slang*). ~ *d'embrayage,* clutch (*auto*). ~ *forte,* loud p. ~ *sourde,* soft p. *lacher les* ~*s,* to renounce (*slang*). *perdre les* ~*s,* to lose one's head (*slang*). **pédaler** (le) *v.i,* to pedal; cycle. **pédalier** (lje) *m,* pedal [key]board; crank gear (*cycle*). **pédalo** (lo) *m,* pedal boats.

pédant, e (pedã, ãːt) *n,* pedant; prig; wiseacre. ¶ ~ & **pédantesque**† (dãtɛsk) *a,* pedantic, priggish. **pédanterie** (tri) *f.* & **pédantisme** (tism) *m,* pedantry.

pédé (pede) *m,* homosexual (*slang*).

pédestre (pedɛstr) *a,* pedestrian (*statue*). **pédestrement** (trəmã) *ad,* on foot.

pédicure (pedikyːr) *n,* chiropodist.

pedigree (pedigri) *m,* pedigree (*beast*).

Pégase (pegɑːz) *m,* Pegasus (*fig.*).

pègre (pɛːgr) *f,* underworld.

peignage (pɛɲaːʒ) *m,* combing, carding (*textiles*). **peigne** (pɛɲ) *m,* comb; card; pecten, scallop. ~ *à décrasser,* fin, scurf comb, [small] tooth c. ~ *coiffeur,* hair c. **peignée** (ɲe) *f,* drubbing, thrashing. **peigner** (ɲe) *v.t,* to comb; card; chase (*screws*). **peignier** (nje) *m,* comb maker. **peignoir** (nwaːr) *m,* dressing gown. ~ *de bain,* bathrobe. ~ *éponge,* toweling beach coat. **peignures** (ɲyːr) *f.pl,* combings.

peinard (pɛnaːrd) *a,* easygoing. *père* ~, easygoing fellow. *se tenir* ~, to behave cautiously. ¶ *m,* toiler (*archaic*); one who takes it easy.

peindre (pɛ̃ːdr) *v.t. & abs. ir,* to paint; depict, portray.

peine (pɛn) *f,* punishment, penalty, pain; sorrow; infliction; anxiety; pains, trouble; difficulty. *à* ~, hardly, scarcely, barely. *être en* ~ *de,* to be at a loss to. *valoir la* ~, to be worthwhile. **peiner** (ne) *v.t,* to pain, grieve; (*v.i.*) to labor, [toil &] moil; be difficult. ~ *en lisant un livre,* to wade through a book.

peintre (pɛ̃ːtr) *m,* painter; portrayer. ~ *d'enseignes,* sign writer. ~ *en bâtiments,* house painter. ~ *verrier,* stained glass artist. **peinture** (pɛ̃tyːr) *f,* painting; picture; paint, color; portrayal. **peinturlurer** (tyrlyrer) *v.t,* to daub.

péjoratif, ive (peʒɔratif, iːv) *a,* pejorative, disparaging, depreciatory.

Pékin (pekɛ̃) *m,* Peking (*Geog.*). p~, *m,* pekin (*fabric*); civilian. *être en* ~, to be in civilian clothes. **pékinois** (kinwa) *m,* Pekinese, peke (*dog*).

pelage (pəlaːʒ) *m,* coat, wool, fur.

pélargonium (pelargɔnjɔm) *m,* pelargonium.

pelé, e (pəle) *p.a,* bare, bald. **peler** (le) *v.t. & i,* to strip, peel, skin.

pêle-mêle (pɛlmɛl) *ad. & m,* pellmell, helter-skelter.

pèlerin, e (pɛlrɛ̃, in) *n,* pilgrim; fox (*pers.*). ¶ *f,* cape, pelerine. **pèlerinage** (lrinaːʒ) *m,* pilgrimage; place of pilgrimage.

pélican (pelikã) *m,* pelican.

pelisse (pəlis) *f,* pelisse.

pelle (pɛl) *f,* shovel; scoop. ~ *à poussière,* dustpan. ~ *à sel,* salt spoon. ~ *à tarte,* pastry server. ~-*bêche,* entrenching tool. **pelletée** (lte) *f,* shoveful, spadeful.

pelleterie (pɛltri) *f,* furriery; peltry. **pelletier, ère** (ltje, ɛːr) *n,* furrier.

pellicule (pɛllikyl) *f,* pellicle, skin; film; (*pl.*) dandruff, scurf. ~ *en bobine,* roll film (*Phot.*). *la* ~ *blanche et noire,* black-and-white film. *la* ~ *en couleurs,* color f.

pelote (plɔt) *f*, ball (*wool, string*); pincushion; pile (*money*); pelota. **peloter** (te) *v.i*, to knock the balls about (*Ten.*). ~ *en attendant partie*, to fill in time; caress (*slang*). **peloton** (tɔ̃) *m*, ball; knot, cluster; squad, party, platoon (*Mil.*). ~ *d'exécution*, firing squad. **pelotonner** (tɔne) *v.t*, to ball, wind. se ~, to curl up, snuggle.

pelouse (plu:z) *f*, lawn, green; public enclosures (*turf.*). ~ *d'arrivée*, putting green (*golf*).

peluche (plyʃ) *f*, plush. **pelucher** (ʃe) *v.i*, to fluff up. **pelucheux, euse** (ʃø, ø:z) *a*, fluffy.

pelure (ply:r) *f*, peel, skin, rind; onionskin paper.

pénal, e (penal) *a*, penal; criminal (*law*); penalty (*clause*). **pénalité** (lite) *f*, penalty.

pénates (penat) *m.pl*, home. *dieux* ~, Penates, household gods.

penaud, e (pəno, o:d) *a*, crestfallen; sheepish.

penchant, e (pɑ̃ʃɑ̃, ɑ̃:t) *a*, leaning; tottering. ¶ *m*, slope; brink; verge; leaning, inclination, bent, propensity, proclivity, fondness. **penché, e** (ʃe) *p.a*, leaning (*tower*); drooping (*looks*). **penchement** (ʃmɑ̃) *m*, bend[ing]; stoop[ing]. **pencher** (ʃe) *v.t. & i. & se* ~, to bend, incline, tilt; lean; bank; stoop; verge. *faire* ~ *la balance*, to turn the scale. *se* ~ *sur*, to make a study of.

pendable (pɑ̃dabl) *a*, [deserving of] hanging; outrageous. **pendaison** (dezɔ̃) *f*, [death by] hanging. **pendant, e** (dɑ̃, ɑ̃:t) *a*, hanging [down]; dangling; drooping; pendent, -ant; pending. ¶ *m*, drop (*ear*); frog (*sword*); counterpart, fellow, match. *les* [*deux*] ~*s*, the pair (*pictures, etc.*).

pendant (pɑ̃dɑ̃) *pr*, during, for. ~ *que*, while, whilst.

pendard, e (pɑ̃da:r, ard) (*jocular*) *n*, rascal; hussy; gallowsbird. **pendeloque** (pɑ̃dlɔk) *f*, drop (*ear, chandelier*). **pendentif** (dɑ̃tif) *m*, pendentive; pendant, -ent. **penderie** (dri) *f*, closet, wardrobe. **pendiller** (dije) *v.i*, to hang, dangle. **pendre** (dr) *v.t. & i*, to hang; h. up, h. out.

pendule (dyl) *m*, pendulum. ¶ ~ & **pendulette** (lɛt) *f*, timepiece, clock. *pendule à sonnerie & à carillon*, striking & chiming clock.

pêne (pɛ:n) *m*, bolt (*lock*).

pénétrant, e (penetrɑ̃, ɑ̃:t) *a*, penetrating, piercing, searching. **pénétration** (trasjɔ̃) *f*, penetration; insight. **pénétrer** (tre) *v.t. & i*, to penetrate, pierce; break into; permeate, pervade, sink in; fathom; see through; imbue.

pénible† (penibl) *a*, laborious, hard; painful.

péniche (peniʃ) *f*, barge, landing craft.

péninsulaire (penɛ̃syle:r) *a*, peninsular. **péninsule** (syl) *f*, peninsula.

pénitence (penitɑ̃:s) *f*, penitence; penance; punishment; penalty, forfeit (*at play*). **pénitencier** (tɑ̃sje) *m*, penitentiary, reformatory; convict prison. **pénitent, e** (tɑ̃, ɑ̃:t) *a. & n*, penitent. **pénitentiaire** (tɑ̃sjɛ:r) *a*, penitentiary.

penne (pɛn) *f*, quill [feather].

pénombre (penɔ̃:br) *f*, penumbra; twilight; background (*fig.*).

pensant, e (pɑ̃sɑ̃, ɑ̃:t) *a*, thinking; -minded (*bien* = right), -disposed (*mal* = ill). **pense-bête** (pɑ̃sbɛt) *m*, memory jogger. **pensée** (se) *f*, thought; thinking; meditation; mind; idea; pansy, heartsease. *arrière-*~, ulterior motive. **penser** (se) *v.i. & t. & abs*, to think; mean. ¶ *m*, thought (*Poet.*). **penseur** (sœ:r) *m*, thinker. **pensif, ive** (sif, i:v) *a*, pensive, thoughtful.

pension (pɑ̃sjɔ̃) *f*, room & board; boarding house; b. school; pension; annuity. ~ *alimentaire*, alimony. ~ *pour les chevaux*, livery stables. **pensionnaire** (ɔne:r) *n*, boarder; paying guest; inmate; pensioner. **pensionnat** (na) *m*, boarding school. **pensionner** (ne) *v.t*, to pension.

pensum (pɛ̃sɔm) *m*, extra work (*Sch.*).

Pen[n]sylvanie (la) (pɛ̃silvani), Pennsylvania.

Pentateuque (le) (pɛtatø:k), the Pentateuch.

pente (pɑ̃ːt) *f*, slope, incline, [downward] gradient; bent (*fig.*).

Pentecôte (la) (pɑ̃tkoːt), Whitsun[tide]; Pentecost.

penture (pɑ̃tyːr) *f*, hinge (*of hook & hinge*).

pénultième (penyltjɛm) *a*, penultimate.

pénurie (penyri) *f*, penury, scarcity, dearth, lack.

pépie (pepi) *f*, pip (*poultry*); thirst. **pépier** (pje) *v.i*, to peep, chirp.

pépin (pepɛ) *m*, pip (*fruit*); stone (*grape*); umbrella; accident; breakdown. *avoir le ~ pour quelqu'un*, to have the hots for someone. *avoir des ~s*, to be in trouble. *risquer le ~*, to risk trouble (*all slang*). **pépinière** (pinjɛːr) *f*, nursery (*Hort. & fig.*). [jardinier] **pépiniériste** (njerist) *m*, nurseryman.

pépite (pepit) *f*, nugget.

péplum (peplɔm) *m*, peplos, peplum (*ancient Greek costume*); historical movie epic.

perçant, e (pɛrsɑ̃, ɑ̃ːt) *a*, piercing; keen, sharp; shrill. **mettre en perce** (pɛrs), to broach, tap (*cask*). **percée (se)** *f*, opening; cutting. **perce-neige**, *f*, snowdrop. **perce-oreille**, *m*, earwig.

percepteur (pɛrsɛptœːr) *m*, collector (*tax*). **perceptible** (tibl) *a*, collectable, -ible; perceptible, discernible, noticeable. *~ à l'ouïe*, audible. **perception** (sjɔ̃) *f*, collection; collectorship; collector's office; perception.

percevoir (pɛrsəvwaːr) *v.t*, to collect; charge; perceive.

perche (pɛrʃ) *f*, pole; perch (*fish*). *~ d'étendoir*, clothes prop. **percher** (ʃe) *v.i*, to perch, roost. **perchoir** (ʃwaːr) *m*, perch, roost.

perchiste, perchman (pɛrʃist, man) *m*, boom operator, perchist, perchman (*TV & cinema*).

perclus, e (pɛrkly, yːz) *a*, crippled.

percussion (pɛrkysjɔ̃) *f*, percussion, impact. **percutant, e** (tɑ̃, ɑ̃ːt) *a*, percussive.

perdant, e (pɛrdɑ̃, ɑ̃ːt) *n*, loser. ¶ *a*, losing. **perdition** (disjɔ̃) *f*, perdition. *en ~*, in a sinking condition (*ship*). **perdre** (dr) *v.t. & abs*, to lose; waste; ruin. **perdu** (dy) *a*, lost; ruined; spent (*bullet*).

perdreau (pɛrdro) *m*, young partridge. **perdrix** (dri) *f*, partridge. *~ des neiges*, ptarmigan.

père (pɛr) *m*, father, parent; sire (*Poet. & beast*); senior. *le ~ Noël*, Santa Claus. *de ~ de famille*, safe (*investment*). *en bon ~ de famille*, with due & proper care.

pérégrination (peregrinasjɔ̃) *f*, peregrination.

péremptoire† (perɑ̃ptwaːr) *a*, peremptory.

péréquation (perekwasjɔ̃) *f*, equalization. *~ des prix*, standardization of charges (*freight, taxes*).

perfection (pɛrfɛksjɔ̃) *f*, perfection. **perfectionner** (ɔne) *v.t*, to perfect; improve.

perfide† (pɛrfid) *a. & n*, treacherous, perfidious (person). **perfidie** (di) *f*, treachery, perfidy.

perforateur (pɛrfɔratœːr) *m*, punch (*paper*). **perforatrice** (tris) *f*, drill (*rock, etc.*); card punch (*data processing*). **perforer** (re) *v.t*, to perforate; drill; punch.

perforeur, euse (pɛrfɔrœːr, øːz) *n*, card punch, key p.; card punch, key p. operator.

performance (pɛrfɔrmɑ̃ːs) *f*, performance (*sport*). *~ classée*, winning performance. **performant, e** (mɑ̃, ɑ̃t) *a*, capable of high performance; competitive.

pergola (pɛrgɔla) *f*, pergola.

péricliter (periklite) *v.i*, to be in danger.

péril (peril) *m*, peril. **périlleux, euse†** (rijø, øːz) *a*, perilous.

périmé, e (perime) *p.p*, out of date (*ticket, etc.*); exploded (*theory*). **périmer** (me) *v.i*, to lapse, expire.

périmètre (perimɛtr) *m*, perimeter; limit.

période (perjɔd) *f*, period, stage; spell; repetend; phrase (*Mus.*). ~ *radioactive*, radioactive halflife (*Phys.*). ¶ *m*, pitch; stage. **périodique†** (dik) *a*, periodic; periodical; recurrent, recurring. ¶ *m*, periodical.

péripétie (peripesi) *f*, sudden change; vicissitude.

périphérie (periferi) *f*, periphery.

périphrase (perifrɑːz) *f*, periphrasis.

périr (periːr) *v.i*, to perish, be lost; die; lapse.

périscope (periskɔp) *m*, periscope.

périssable (perisabl) *a*, perishable.

péristyle (peristil) *m*, peristyle.

péritonite (peritɔnit) *f*, peritonitis.

perle (pɛrl) *f*, pearl; bead; treasure (*fig.*). ~ *de culture*, cultured pearl. **perlé, e** (le) *a*, pearly; exquisitely done.

permanence (pɛrmanɑ̃ːs) *f*, permanence. *en* ~, without interruption. **permanent, e** (nɑ̃, ɑ̃ːt) *a*, permanent, standing; continuous; abiding; perennial.

permanganate (pɛrmɑ̃ganat) *m*, permanganate.

perméable (pɛrmeabl) *a*, permeable, pervious.

permettre (pɛrmɛtr) *v.t.ir*, to permit, to allow; may. *se* ~, to allow oneself, indulge in. *se* ~ *de*, to venture to. **permis** (mi) *m*, permit, license, order. ~ [*de circulation*], [free] pass (*Rly.*). ~ *de conduire* [*les automobiles*], driver's license. **permission** (sjɔ̃) *f*, permission; leave, pass (*Mil.*). **permissionnaire** (ɔnɛːr) *m. & a*, (soldier) on leave.

permutation (pɛrmytasjɔ̃) *f*, exchange (*of posts*); permutation; transposition.

pernicieux, euse† (pɛrnisjø, øːz) *a*, pernicious, baneful.

péroné (perɔne) *m*, fibula, splint [bone].

péronnelle (perɔnɛl) *f*, pert hussy.

péroraison (perɔrɛzɔ̃) *f*, peroration. **pérorer** (re) *v.i*, to hold forth, speechify.

Pérou (le) (peru), Peru. *ce n'est pas le* ~, it's not Eldorado, not a lot of money.

Pérouse (peruːz) *f*, Perugia.

peroxyde (perɔksid) *m*, peroxide.

perpendiculaire† (pɛrpɑ̃dikylɛːr) *a. & f*, perpendicular.

perpétrer (pɛrpetre) *v.t*, to perpetrate.

perpétuation (pɛrpetɥasjɔ̃) *f*, perpetuation. **perpétuel, le†** (tɥɛl) *a*, perpetual, permanent; for life. **perpétuer** (tɥe) *v.t*, to perpetuate. **perpétuité** (tɥite) *f*, perpetuity. *à* ~, in perpetuity; for life.

perplexe (pɛrplɛks) *a*, perplexed, puzzled; perplexing. **perplexité** (ksite) *f*, perplexity.

perquisition (pɛrkizisjɔ̃) *f*, search (*law*).

perron (pɛrɔ̃) *m*, front steps, perron.

perroquet (perɔkɛ) *m*, parrot; topgallant. **perruche** (ryʃ) *f*, parakeet; hen parrot; high-flown random talker (*woman*).

perruque (peryk) *f*, wig; old fogy. **perruquier** (kje) *m*, wigmaker.

pers, e (pɛːr, ɛrs) *a*, greenish-blue.

persan, e (pɛrsɑ̃, an) *a. & P~*, *n*, Persian (*modern*). *le persan*, Persian (*language*). **la Perse** (pɛrs), Persia. **perse** *a. & P~*, *n*, Persian (*ancient*). **perse**, *f*, chintz.

persécuter (pɛrsekyte) *v.t*, to persecute; bait; dun. **persécuteur, trice** (tœːr, tris) *n*, persecutor. **persécution** (sjɔ̃) *f*, persecution.

persévérance (pɛrseverɑ̃ːs) *f*, perseverance. **persévérer** (re) *v.i. & abs*, to persevere; persist.

persienne (pɛrsjɛn) *f*, shutter, persienne, Persian blind.

persiflage (pɛrsiflaːʒ) *m*, banter, persiflage. **persifler** (fle) *v.t*, to banter, chaff.

persil (pɛrsi) *m*, parsley. **persillé, e** (sije) *a*, blue-moldy (*cheese*).

persistance (pɛrsistɑ̃ːs) *f*, persistence, -ency. **persistant, e** (tɑ̃, ɑ̃ːt) *a*, persistent. **persister** (te) *v.i*, to persist.

personnage (pɛrsɔnaːʒ) *m*, personage; character; (*pl.*) dramatis personae. ~ *de carton*, figurehead. *être un* ~, to be somebody. **personnalité** (nalite) *f*, personality; (*pl.*) [well-known] people. **personne** (sɔn) *f*, person; self; (*pl.*) people. ~ *à charge*, dependent person; hanger-on. ~ *collante*, burr, sticker. ~ *interposée*, nominee. ~ *morale*, ~ *juridique*, ~ *civile*, body corporate, legal entity. ¶ *pn.m*, anybody, anyone; nobody, no one, none. **personnel, le†** (nɛl) *a*, personal; private; selfish. ¶ *m*, staff, personnel. **personnifier** (nifje) *v.t*, to personify; impersonate.

perspective (pɛrspɛktiːv) *f*, perspective; outlook, view, prospect; vista. *en* ~, in view.

perspicace (pɛrspikas) *a*, perspicacious. **perspicacité** (site) *f*, perspicacity.

persuader (pɛrsɥade) *v.t. & abs*, to persuade; prevail. **persuasif, ive** (zif, iːv) *a*, persuasive. **persuasion** (zjɔ̃) *f*, persuasion; belief.

perte (pɛrt) *f*, loss; leak[age]; waste; casualty (*Mil.*); ruin; swallow (*river*); discount (opp. *premium*). ~ *sèche*, dead loss. *à* ~, at a loss. *à* ~ *de vue*, as far as the eye can reach. *en* ~, out of pocket, to the bad, a loser. *en pure* ~, to no purpose.

pertinent, e (pɛrtinɑ̃, ɑ̃ːt) *a*, pertinent, apposite, relevant. **pertinemment** (namɑ̃) *ad*, pertinently, etc.

pertuis (pɛrtɥi) *m*, sluiceway; strait[s] (*Geog.*).

perturbateur, trice (pɛrtyrbatœːr, tris) *n*, disturber. **perturbation** (sjɔ̃) *f*, disturbance, perturbation.

péruvien, ne (peryvjɛ̃, ɛn) *a. &* **P~**, *n*, Peruvian.

pervenche (pɛrvɑ̃ːʃ) *f*, periwinkle (*Bot.*).

pervers, e (pɛrvɛːr, ɛrs) *a*, perverse. ¶ *m*, evil-doer, pervert. **perversion** (vɛrsjɔ̃) *f*, perversion.

perversité (site) *f*, perversity. **pervertir** (tiːr) *v.t*, to pervert.

pesade (pəzad) *f*, rearing (*horse*).

pesage (pəsaːʒ) *m*, weighing; (*turf*) w. in; w. in room; paddock. **pesamment** (zamɑ̃) *ad*, heavily; ponderously. **pesant, e** (zɑ̃, ɑ̃ːt) *a*, heavy, weighty; ponderous, unwieldy; ponderable. *son pesant d'or*, his, its, weight in gold. **pesant**, *ad*, in weight. **pesanteur** (zɑ̃tœːr) *f*, heaviness, weight; gravity (*Phys.*); dullness [*spirit*]. **pesée** (ze) *f*, weighing; prize, -se; wrench. **pèse-lettre** (pɛzlɛtr) *m*, letter scales. **peser** (pəze) *v.t*, to weigh; ponder; (*v.i.*) to weigh; lie heavy; bear, press; dwell. **peseur** (zœːr) *m*, weigher. **peson** (zɔ̃) *m*, balance (*spring, etc.*).

pessimisme (pɛsimism) *m*, pessimism. **pessimiste** (mist) *m*, pessimist. ¶ *a*, pessimistic.

peste (pɛst) *f*, plague, pestilence. ~ *bovine*, cattle plague, rinderpest. **pester** (te) *v.i*, to rail (*contre* = at). **pestiféré, e** (tifere) *a. & n*, plague-stricken (person). **pestilentiel, le** (lɑ̃sjɛl) *a*, pestilential.

pet (pɛ) *m*, fart. *ne pas valoir un* ~ *de lapin*, to be worthless. **péter** (te) *v.i*, to fart. ~ *dans la soie*, to be very rich. ~ *plus haut que le cul*, to show off; bite off more than one can chew (*both slang*).

pétale (petal) *m*, petal.

pétarade (petarad) *f*, sp[l]utter; frisking. **pétarader** (de) *v.i*, to sp[l]utter. **pétard** (taːr) *m*, shot, blast; detonator, fog signal; firecracker; scandal (*news*). **pétarder** (tarde) *v.t*, to blow up, blast.

pétaudière (petodjɛːr) *f*, bedlam, bear garden.

pète-sec (pɛtsɛk) *m*, martinet.

pétiller (petije) *v.i*, to crackle; sparkle; fizz[le]; bubble [over].

pétiole (pesjɔl) *m*, petiole, leaf stalk.

petiot, e (pətjo, ɔt) *a*, tiny, wee. ¶ *n*, dot, tot, chickabiddy. **petit, e** (ti, it) *a*, little, small; short; diminutive; young; junior; low, slow; lesser; minor; petty; slight;

light; mean; retail. **petit, comps:** *au ~ bonheur,* I'll risk it, come what may; hit or miss. *le P~ Chaperon rouge,* Little Red Riding Hood. ~ *chat,* kitten. ~ *chien,* pup[py]. ~ *comité,* select party, informal gathering. *le ~ commerce,* [the] small traders, tradespeople, the retail trade. ~ *commis,* office boy. *le ~ déjeuner,* coffee & rolls, early morning coffee. ~ *enfant,* little child, infant. ~*s-enfants,* grandchildren. ~*fils,* grandson, -child. *au ~ galop,* at a canter. ~*s jeux,* parlor games, forfeits. *le ~ jour,* daybreak. ~ *juif,* funny bone. ~*lait,* whey. ~ *lieu,* ~ *endroit,* privy. ~*maître,* fop, coxcomb. ~ *ménage,* miniature (*or* dolls') home set. *le ~ monde,* little people; the lower classes; the child world. *le ~Noël,* a Christmas present (*to a child*). ~ *nom,* Christian name. ~ *nom d'amitié,* pet name. ~ *pain,* roll. *le ~ peuple,* [the] common people. ~*s pois,* green peas. ~ *salé,* pickled pork. ~ *salon,* sitting room, parlor. ~ *trot,* jogtrot. **petite, comps:** ~ *chatte,* kitten. ~ *correspondance,* answers to correspondents. *la ~ épargne,* the small investor. ~*fille,* grand-daughter, grandchild. ~ *gorgée,* sip. ~ *guerre,* mimic war. *à ~s journées,* by easy stages. ~ *largeur,* single width (*cloth*). *à ~ mentalité,* mentally deficient. ~ *multiplication,* low gear. ~ *noblesse,* gentry. ~ *pédale,* soft pedal. *une ~ santé,* poor health. ~*s tables,* separate tables (*meal*). ~ *vérole,* smallpox. ~ *vérole volante,* chicken pox. *en ~ vitesse* (*Rly.*), by slow train; by freight train. **petit, e,** *n,* little boy, l. girl, l. one. **un petit,** a young one, cub, pup, whelp. **les petits,** the small, the little (*people*); little things. **petitement** (titmã) *ad,* meanly; pettily. **petitesse** (tɛs) *f,* littleness, smallness; shortness; pettiness.

pétition (petisjɔ̃) *f,* petition. ~ *de principe,* begging the question. *faire une ~ de principe,* to beg the question. **pétitionnaire** (sjɔnɛːr) *n,* petitioner. **pétition-**

ner (ne) *v.i,* to petition.

peton (pətɔ̃) *m,* tiny foot, tootsy [-wootsy].

pétoncle (petɔ̃:kl) *f,* scallop (*Mol.*).

pétrel (petrɛl) *m,* storm[y] petrel.

pétrification (petrifikasjɔ̃) *f,* petrification. **pétrifier** (fje) *v.t,* to petrify.

pétrin (petrɛ̃) *m,* kneading trough; fix, mess. **pétrir** (tri:r) *v.t,* to knead, work, make; shape; steep. **pétrissage** (trisa:ʒ) *m,* kneading, etc.

pétrochimie (petrɔʃimi) *f,* petrochemistry. **pétrochimique** (mik) *a,* petrochemical.

pétrole (petrɔl) *m,* petroleum, oil. ~ *à brûler.* ~ *lampant* (lãpã), paraffin [oil], kerosene. **pétrolier, ère** (lje, ɛːr) *a,* petroleum, oil (*att.*) [*navire*] **pétrolier,** tanker.

pétulant, e (petylã, ã:t) *a,* lively, impetuous.

pétunia (petynja) *m,* petunia.

peu (pø) *ad,* little, not much; few, not many; not very. ¶ *m,* little; bit; few; lack; little while. *à ~ [de chose] près,* about, nearly.

peulven (pølvɛn) *m,* menhir.

peuplade (pøplad) *f,* tribe. **peuple** (pl) *m,* people, nation; tribe. ¶ *a,* plebeian, common. **peupler** (ple) *v.t,* to people, populate; stock, plant; fill; (*v.i.*) to multiply.

peuplier (pøplie) *m,* poplar.

peur (pœːr) *f,* fear, fright. *avoir ~,* to be afraid. *faire ~,* to frighten. *de ~ que,* lest. **peureux, euse†** (pœrø, ø:z) *a,* timid, nervous.

peut-être (pøtɛːtr) *ad. & m,* perhaps, maybe, perchance, possibly.

phaéton (faetɔ̃) *m,* phaeton.

phalange (falã:ʒ) *f,* phalanx; host.

phalène (falɛn) *f,* moth.

phantasme (fãtasm) *m,* phantasm.

pharaon (faraɔ̃) *m,* Pharaoh; faro (*cards*).

phare (faːr) *m,* lighthouse; light; beacon; headlight, headlamp. ~ *anti-éblouissant,* ~*-code,* antidazzle lamp *or* light. ~ *antibrouillard,* fog light. ~ *de croise-*

ment, courtesy l. ~ *de roulement*, taxi l.

pharisaïque (farizaik) *a*, Pharisaic(al). **pharisien** (zjɛ̃) *m*, Pharisee.

pharmaceutique (farmasøtik) *a*, pharmaceutical. **pharmacie** (si) *f*, pharmacy; dispensary; drug store; medicine chest. **pharmacien, ne** (sjɛ̃, ɛn) *n*, druggist; pharmacist.

pharyngite (farɛ̃ʒit) *f*, pharyngitis, relaxed throat. **pharynx** (rɛ̃:ks) *m*, pharynx.

phase (fɑ:z) *f*, phase; stage.

phébus (feby:s) *m*, bombast, fustian.

phénicien, ne (fenisjɛ̃, ɛn) *a*, Phoenician.

phénix (feniks) *m*, phoenix; paragon.

phénol (fenɔl) *ou* **acide phénique** (nik) *m*, phenol, carbolic acid.

phénoménal, e (fenɔmenal) *a*, phenomenal. **phénomène** (mɛn) *m*, phenomenon; freak [of nature].

Philadelphie (filadɛlfi) *f*, Philadelphia.

philanthrope (filɑ̃trɔp) *n*, philanthropist. **philanthropie** (pi) *f*, philanthropy. **philanthropique** (pik) *a*, philanthropic.

philatélisme (filatelism) *m*, philately. **philatéliste** (list) *n*, philatelist.

philharmonique (filarmɔnik) *a*, philharmonic.

philippique (filipik) *f*, philippic.

philistin (filistɛ̃) *m*, Philistine.

philologie (filɔlɔʒi) *f*, philology. **philologue** (lɔg) *m*, philologist.

philosophe (filɔzɔf) *n*, philosopher; student in philosophy. ¶ *a*, philosophic(al) (*calm*). **philosopher** (fe) *v.i*, to philosophize. **philosophie** (fi) *f*, philosophy. **philosophique**† (fik) *a*, philosophic(al).

philtre (filtr) *m*, philter, love potion.

phlébite (flebit) *f*, phlebitis.

phlox (flɔks) *m*, phlox.

phobie (fɔbi) *f*, morbid fear, dread.

phonétique (fɔnetik) *a*, phonetic. ¶ *f*, phonetics. **phonographe** (nɔgraf) *m*, phonograph. ~*coffret*, tabletop phonograph.

phoque (fɔk) *m*, seal (*Zool.*).

phosphate (fɔsfat) *m*, phosphate. **phosphore** (fɔ:r) *m*, phosphorus. **phosphorescence** (fɔrɛ-(sɑ̃:s) *f*, phosphorescence. **phosphorescent, e** (sɑ̃, ɑ̃:t) *a*, phosphorescent.

photographe (fɔtɔgraf) *n*, photographer. ~ *de plateau*, still photographer (*cinema*). **photographie** (fi) *f*, photography; photograph. **photographier** (fje) *v.t*, to photograph. **photographique** (fik) *a*, photographic. **photogravure** (vy:r) *f*, photogravure. **photojumelle,** *f*, binocular camera.

phrase (frɑ:s) *f*, sentence; phrase. ~*s à effet*, claptrap. **phraséologie** (frazeɔlɔʒi) *f*, phraseology. **phraser** (ze) *v.i. & t*, to phrase.

phrénologie (frenɔlɔʒi) *f*, phrenology. **phrénologiste** (ʒist) *m*, phrenologist.

phtisie (ftizi) *f*, phthisis, consumption. **phtisique** (zik) *a. & n*, consumptive.

physicien, ne (fizisjɛ̃, ɛn) *n*, physicist.

physiologie (fizjɔlɔʒi) *f*, physiology.

physionomie (fizjɔnɔmi) *f*, physiognomy, face, countenance; aspect; character.

physique† (fizik) *a*, physical; bodily. ¶ *f*, physics. ¶ *m*, physique.

piaffer (pjafe) *v.i*, to paw the ground; prance.

piailler (pjɑje) *v.i*, to cheep; screech.

pianiste (pjanist) *n*, pianist. **piano** (no) *m*, piano[forte]. ~ *à demi-queue*, baby grand[piano]. ~ *à queue*, [concert] grand piano. ~ *droit*, upright piano. ~ *mécanique*, piano player, player piano; piano organ. ~ *oblique*, overstrung piano.

piaule (pjo:l) *f*, pad, digs, room, place (*where one lives*).

piauler (pjole) *v.i*, to cheep; whimper.

pic (pik) *m*, pick; peak; woodpecker. *à* ~, sheer, precipitous.

piccolo (pikɔlo) *m*, piccolo.

pichet (piʃɛ) *m*, pitcher; small jug.

pick-up (pikœp) *m*, phonograph.

picorer (pikɔre) *v.i*, to forage, peck.

picot (piko) *m*, splinter; barb; picot. **picoté de petite vérole** (kɔte), pockmarked. **picoter** (te) *v.t*, to prick; pit; peck; sting, make smart, make tingle; tease.

picotin (pikɔtɛ̃) *m*, peck.

picrate (pikrat) *m*, cheap wine (*slang*).

pictural, e (piktyral) *a*, pictorial.

pie (pi) *f*, magpie. ¶ *a*, piebald; charitable (*works*).

pièce (pjɛs) *f*, piece; bit; fragment; part; man (*chess*); head (*cattle*, *game*); joint (*meat*); document; paper; tip (*gratuity*); cask, barrel; puncheon; gun; room (*house*). [*la*] ~, *apiece*, each. ~ *à conviction*, exhibit (*criminal law*). ~ *à succès*, hit. ~ *à thèse*, problem play. ~ *d'artifice*, firework. ~ *d'eau*, ornamental lake. ~ [*coulée*], casting. ~ [*de monnaie*], coin. ~ *de rechange*, spare [part]. ~ [*de théâtre*], [stage] play. ~ *historique*, costume piece, c. play. ~ *justificative*, ~ *à l'appui*, exhibit (*civil law*); voucher (*Com.*). ~ *moulée*, molding, cast.

pied (pje) *m*, foot; trotter; base, bottom; leg (*chair*); stalk; footing; foothold; stand; standard. ~-*à-terre*, *m*, small apartment in town. ~ [*à trois branches*], tripod. ~*-d'alouette*, larkspur, delphinium. ~-*debiche*, claw [bar] forceps. ~-*droit*, pier (*of arch*). ~-*fumeur*, smoker's stand. *au* ~ *de la lettre*, literally. *avoir le* ~ *marin*, to have got one's sea legs. *mettre sur* ~, to establish. *sur* ~, on foot; standing (*crops*). *faire un* ~ *de nez*, to thumb one's nose. *prendre son* ~ (*slang*), to have an orgasm (*slang*). **piédestal** (pjedɛstal) *m*, pedestal.

pied-noir (pjenwaːr) *m & f*, Algerian-born French citizen (*generally one who has been repatriated*).

piège (pjɛːʒ) *m*, trap, snare, pit-

fall. **piéger** (e) *v.t*, to snare, entrap.

pie-grièche (pigriɛʃ) *f*, shrike; shrew (*pers.*).

Piémont (le) (pjemɔ̃), Piedmont.

pierraille (pjɛraːj) *f*, small stones. **pierre** (pjɛːr) *f*, stone. ~ *à aiguiser*, grindstone; hone. ~ [*à briquet*] & ~ *à fusil*, flint. ~ *à chaux*, ~ *calcaire*, limestone. ~ *à gué*, stepping stone. ~ *blanche*, hearthstone. ~ *d'achoppement* (aʃɔpmɑ̃), stumbling block, snag. ~ *d'aimant*, loadstone, lodestone. ~ *de lune*, moonstone. ~ *de taille*, freestone. ~ *de touche*, touchstone (*lit. & fig.*); test. ~ *philosophale* (filozɔfal), philosophers' stone. ~ *précieuse*, precious stone, gem [stone]. ~ *tombale* (tɔbal), ~ *tumulaire*.

pierrot (pjɛro) *m*, pierrot, clown; sparrow.

piété (pjete) *f*, piety, godliness; devotion.

piétiner (pjetine) *v.t*, to trample on, stamp on; tread; (*v.i.*) to dance (*with rage*). ~ *sur place*, to mark time (*fig.*). **piéton, ne** (tɔ̃, ɔn) *n*, pedestrian, foot passenger; walker.

piètre† (pjɛtr) *a*, wretched, poor, shabby.

pieu (pjø) *m*, stake, post; pile.

pieuvre (pjœːvr) *f*, octopus.

pieux, euse† (pjø, øːz) *a*, pious, godly; reverent.

pige (piːʒ) *f*, arbitrary measure; year (*of age, penal servitude*). **piger** (ʒe) *v.t*, to look at, admire; understand. *se faire* ~, to get caught.

pigeon, ne (piʒɔ̃, ɔn) *n*, pigeon, dove; greenhorn, gull. ~ *artificiel*, clay bird. ~ *grosse gorge*, pouter. ~ *ramier*, wood pigeon, ring dove. ~ *voyageur*, carrier pigeon, homing p. **pigeonneau** (ʒɔno) *m*, young pigeon, squab; gull, dupe. **pigeonnier** (nje) *m*, dovecote.

pigment (pigmɑ̃) *m*, pigment.

pignocher (piɲɔʃe) *v.i*, to pick at one's food.

pignon (piɲɔ̃) *m*, gable; pinion. ~ *de chaîne*, sprocket wheel.

pilastre (pilastr) *m*, pilaster; newel.

pile (pil) *f*, pile, heap; stack (*of wood*); pier (*bridge*); battery, cell (*Elec.*); reverse (*coin*); reactor (*nuclear*). ~ *ou face?* heads or tails?

piler (pile) *v.t*, to pound, pestle, grind.

pilier (pilje) *m*, pillar, column, post.

pillage (pija:ʒ) *m*, pillage, looting; pilfering. **piller** (je) *v.t*, to pillage, plunder, loot, sack, ransack; pilfer; seize, worry (*of dog*).

pilon (pilɔ̃) *m*, pestle; stamp (*ore*); rammer; hammer (*power*); drumstick (*fowl*). **pilonner** (ne) *v.t*, to pound; pulp; flatten (*military target*).

pilori (pilɔri) *m*, pillory. **pilorier** (rje) *v.t*, to pillory, gibbet.

pilotage (pilɔta:ʒ) *m*, pile work; piloting; attitude control. *bloc de* ~, automatic pilot. **pilote** (lɔt) *m*, pilot. ~ *d'essai*, test pilot. *industrie* ~, key industry. **piloter** (te) *v.t*, to pile; pilot; guide. ~ *dans*, to show (*pers.*) round (*town*). **pilotis** (ti) *m*, pile (*stake*); piling.

pilou (pilu) *m*, flannelette.

pilule (pilyl) *f*, pill.

pimbêche (pɛ̃bɛʃ) *f*, conceited woman.

piment (pimɑ̃) *m*, pimento, capsicum, allspice. **pimenter** (te) *v.t*, to spice.

pimpant, e (pɛ̃pɑ̃, ɑ̃:t) *a*, smart, spruce, spick & span.

pin (pɛ̃) *m*, pine [tree], fir [tree]. ~ *du Chili*, Chili pine, monkey puzzle.

pinacle (pinakl) *m*, pinnacle.

pince (pɛ̃:s) *f*, grip, hold; (*oft. pl.*) pliers, nippers; forceps; tweezers; tongs; (*s.*) clip; clamp; crowbar; claw, nipper (*crab, etc.*); pleat; hand (*slang*). ~*s à épiler*, eyebrow tweezers. ~*monseigneur, f*, jimmy (*burglar's*). ~*-nez, m*, eyeglasses. ~*sans-rire, m*, man of dry humor. **pincé, e** (pɛse) *a*, affected, prim; stiff; wry; pursed (*lips*).

pinceau (pɛ̃so) *m*, paintbrush;

brush; touch (*fig.*); pencil (*Opt.*). ~ *à barbe*, shaving brush.

pincée (pɛse) *f*, pinch (*snuff, etc.*). **pincer** (se) *v.t*, to pinch, nip, squeeze; purse (*lips*); pluck (*strings*); play (*harp, etc.*), twang; grip; catch. **pincettes** (sɛt) *f.pl*, tweezers; tongs (*fire*). **pinçon** (sɔ̃) *m*, mark, bruise (*left on the skin by a pinch*).

pine (pin) *f*, penis (*obscene*).

pineraie (pinrɛ) *f*, pine wood (*forest*).

pingouin (pɛ̃gwɛ̃) *m*, auk. ~ *royal*, king penguin.

pingre (pɛ̃:gr) *a*, stingy. ¶ *m*, skinflint.

pinnule (pinnyl) *f*, pinnule; sight [vane].

pinson (pɛ̃sɔ̃) *m*, finch; chaffinch.

pintade (pɛ̃tad) *f*, guinea fowl.

pioche (pjɔʃ) *f*, pick; pickaxe; mattock. **piocher** (ʃe) *v.t. & i*, to pick up; work hard, grind.

piolet (pjɔlɛ) *m*, ice axe.

pion (pjɔ̃) *m*, pawn (*chess*); man (*checkers*).

pionnier (pjɔnje) *m*, pioneer.

pipe (pip) *f*, pipe (*cask, tobacco*); cigarette (*slang*). *se fendre la* ~, to split one's side laughing. **pipeau** (po) *m*, [reed] pipe; lime twig; bird call. **pipée** (pe) *f*, bird catching. **piper** (pe) *v.t*, to lure (*birds*); dupe; load (*dice*); mark (*card*).

pipi[t] (pipi[t]) *m*, pipit, titlark.

piplet (piplɛ) *m*, concierge (*slang*).

piquant, e (pikɑ̃, ɑ̃:t) *a*, prickly; stinging; cutting; pointed; pungent; racy; piquant. ¶ *m*, prickle; sting; quill (*porcupine*); spike; pungency; point, zest, pith. **pique** (pik) *f*, pike (*weapon*); pique, spite; tiff; (*m.*) spade[s] (*cards*). ~*-nique* (nik) *m*, picnic. ~*-notes, m*, bill file. ~*-assiette* (asʃɛt) *m. & f*, freeloader. **piqué, e** (ke) *a*, quilted; padded; staccato (*notes*); crazy. ~ *des mouches*, flyblown. ~ *des vers*, worm-eaten, motheaten. ¶ *m*, quilting. **piquer** (ke) *v.t*, to prick; sting; bite; spur; goad; prod; nettle; pique; puncture; pit; lard; stitch; quilt; nibble (*fish*); stick; scale (*boiler*). ~ *du nez*, to nose dive (*Avn.*). se ~, to pride oneself; take offense; turn sour (*wine*). **piquet** (kɛ) *m*, peg, stake; picket; piquet (*cards*). **piqueter** (te) *v.t*, to stake out (*claim*); picket. **piqueur** (kœːr) *m*, whipper-in, huntsman; stud groom. **piqueuse** (kø:z) *f*, stitcher, sewer (*pers.*). **piqûre** (ky:r) *f*, injection; vaccination; prick; sting; bite; puncture; pit, hole; spot, speck; quilting.

pirate (pirat) *m*, pirate. **pirater** (te) *v.i*, to pirate. **piraterie** (tri) *f*, piracy.

pire (pi:r) *a*, worse. *le* ~, the worst.

Pirée (le) (pire), Piraeus.

pirogue (pirɔg) *f*, canoe. ~ *de barre*, surf boat. ~ *en écorce*, birch-bark canoe.

pirouette (pirwɛt) *f*, whirling; pirouette. **pirouetter** (te) *v.i*, to pirouette, twirl.

pis (pi) *m*, udder, dug.

pis (pi) *ad*, worse. *le* ~, the worst. ~ *aller*, *m*, last resource; makeshift. *au* ~ *aller*, at the worst.

pisciculture (pisikylty:r) *f*, pisciculture. **piscine** (sin) *f*, swimming pool.

Pise (pi:z) *f*, Pisa.

pissenlit (pisɑ̃li) *m*, dandelion. **pistache** (pistaʃ) *f*, pistachio [nut]. **pistachier** (ʃje) *m*, pistachio tree.

piste (pist) *f*, track (*running, racing*); run (*toboggan*); rink (*skating*); racecourse; runway (*Avn.*); track, trail, scent, clue; sound track (*cinema*). ~ *de cirque*, ring. ~ *en cendrée*, cinder track; dirt t. **pister** (te) *v.t*, to track; tail someone (*slang*).

pistil (pistil) *m*, pistil.

pistolet (pistɔlɛ) *m*, pistol.

piston (pistɔ̃) *m*, piston; cornet (*Mus.*); influence, pull (*slang*). **pistoner** (tɔne)*v.t*, to pull strings for someone.

pitchpin (pitʃpɛ̃) *m*, pitchpine.

piteux, euse† (pitø, ø:z) *a*, piteous, woeful, pitiable; sorry. **pitié** (tje) *f*, pity, mercy.

piton (pitɔ̃) *m*, screw eye; peak (*mountain*).

pitoyable† (pitwajabl) *a*, pitiable, pitiful; wretched, paltry.

pitre (pi:tr) *m*, clown; buffoon.

pittoresque† (pitɔrɛsk) *a*, picturesque, beauty (*spot*); quaint; graphic; pictorial (*magazine*). ¶ *m*, picturesqueness.

pituite (pityit) *f*, phlegm, mucus.

pivoine (pivwan) *f*, peony.

pivot (pivo) *m*, pivot, pin; tap root; crux. **pivoter** (vɔte) *v.i*, to pivot, turn, hinge; slew; wheel (*Mil.*).

piz (pi) (*Geog.*) *m*, pap, mamelon.

placage (plaka:ʒ) *m*, veneering; patchwork (*fig.*).

placard (plaka:r) *m*, wall cupboard; placard, poster, bill; galley [proof]. **placarder** (karde) *v.t*, to post (*bills*), placard.

place (plas) *f*, place; room; way; stead; seat, fare; berth; spot; patch; ground; town; market; square (*in town*); churchyard (*public square surrounding a church or cathedral*). ~ *aux dames!* ladies first! ~ *d'armes*, parade ground, drill g. ~ [*de voitures*], cabstand. ~*s debout seulement!* standing room only! ~ *dénudée d'herbes*, bare patch (*golf*). ~ *forte*, ~ *de guerre*, fortified place. **placement** (smɑ̃) *m*, placing; investment. *bureau de* ~, employment agency. **placer** (se) *v.t*, to place, put, set; dispose of; deposit; invest (*money*).

placer (plasɛ:r) (*Min.*) *m*, placer, diggings.

placide† (plasid) *a*, placid. **placidité** (dite) *f*, placidity.

placier (plasje) *m*, canvasser, salesman.

plafond (plafɔ̃) *m*, ceiling; maximum, peak [figure]. **plafonner** (fɔne) *v.t*, to ceil. **plafonnier** (nje) *m*, ceiling fixture (*light*).

plage (pla:ʒ) *f*, beach, shore; seaside resort; sands.

plagiaire (plaʒjɛ:r) *m*, plagiarist. **plagiat** (ʒja) *m*, plagiarism. **plagier** (ʒje) *v.t*, to plagiarize.

plaid (plɛd) *m*, plaid; traveling rug.

plaider (plɛde) *v.i. & t*, to plead, argue. **plaideur, euse** (dœːr, øːz) *n*, litigant; suitor. **plaidoirie** (dwari) *f*, pleading; counsel's speech. **plaidoyer** (dwaje) *m*, speech for the defense.

plaie (plɛ) *f*, wound, sore; evil; plague.

plaignant, e (plɛɲɑ̃, ɑ̃ːt) *n*, plaintiff, prosecutor.

plain, e (plɛ̃, ɛn) *a*, plain; open. **plain-chant**, *m*, plainsong. *de plain-pied*, on one floor, on a level.

plaindre (plɛ̃ːdr) *v.t.ir*, to pity, be sorry for. *se* ~, to complain; moan, groan.

plaine (plɛn) *f*, plain (*Phys. Geog.*).

plainte (plɛ̃ːt) *f*, moan, groan; complaint; action (*law*). **plaintif, ive†** (plɛ̃tif, iːv) *a*, plaintive, doleful; querulous.

plaire (plɛːr) *v.i.ir*, to please. *s'il vous plaît*, [if you] please. *plût au ciel que . . .*, would to heaven that . . . ~ *à*, to please (*v.t.*). *se* ~, to be pleased; like; thrive. **plaisamment** (plɛzamɑ̃) *ad*, funnily; ludicrously. **de plaisance** (zɑ̃ːs), pleasure (*boat*); weekend (*cottage*). **Plaisance,** *f*, Piacenza. **plaisant, e** (zɑ̃, ɑ̃ːt) *a*, funny, droll, jocular; comical; ludicrous; pleasant. ¶ *m*, wag, joker, fool; comical side. **plaisanter** (zɑ̃te) *v.i*, to joke, jest, trifle; (*v.t.*) to chaff. **plaisanterie** (tri) *f*, joke, jest; fun. **plaisir** (ziːr) *m*, pleasure, delight; treat; convenience; will; sake; amusement; enjoyment; cone, cornet, wafer (*ice cream*). *à* ~, gratuitously.

plan, e (plɑ̃, an) *a*, plane, even, level, flat. ¶ *m*, plane, level; ground (*of painting*); plan; map; table; project, scheme; shot (*cinema, TV*). ~ *américain*, medium close shot. ~ *d'archives*, stock s. ~ *cassé*, angle s. ~ *d'essai*, test s. ~ *moyen*, medium s. ~ *séquence*, deep-focus s. ~ *serré*, close-up s. ~ *de situation*, establishing s. *gros* ~, close-up. ~ *des support*, media planning.

planche (plɑ̃ːʃ) *f*, board; shelf; bed (*Hort.*); plate (*Typ.*). ~ *de salut*, sheet anchor (*fig.*). *faire la* ~, to float (*Swim.*). **planchéier** (plɑ̃ʃeje) *v.t*, to board; floor. **plancher** (ʃe) *m*, floor. *le* ~ *des vaches*, terra firma. **planchette** (ʃɛt) *f*, slat; plane table (*Surv.*).

plancton (plɑ̃ktɔ̃) *m*, plankton.

plane (plan) *m*, plane [tree]; (*f.*) drawing knife.

planer (plane) *v.t*, to smooth; plane; planish; (*v.i.*) to soar; hover; look down; glide (*Avn.*) fly (*drugs*).

planétaire (planetɛːr) *a*, planetary. ¶ *m*, planetarium, orrery. **planète** (nɛt) *f*, planet. *heureuse* ~, lucky star (*fig.*).

planeur (planœːr) *m*, planisher (*pers.*); glider (*Avn.*).

planification (planifikasjɔ̃) *f*, planning (*computers*). ~ *des naissances*, family planning. **planifier** (ifje) *v.i*, to plan (*political economy*).

plant (plɑ̃) *m*, sapling, set, slip; plantation. **plantage** (taːʒ) *m*, planting; plantation. **plantain** (tɛ̃) *m*, plantain (*Plantago*). **plantanier** (tanje) *m*, plantain (*banana*). **plantation** (sjɔ̃) *f*, planting; plantation. **plante** (plɑ̃ːt) *f*, sole (*foot*); plant (*Bot.*). ~ *annuelle*, annual. ~ *marine*, seaweed. ~ *potagère*, vegetable. ~ *vivace*, perennial. **planter** (plɑ̃te) *v.t*, to plant, set. **planteur, euse** (tœːr, øːz) *n*, planter; grower. **plantoir** (twaːr) *m*, dibble. **planton** (tɔ̃) (*Mil.*) *m*, orderly; o. duty.

planque (plɑ̃ːk) *f*, hiding place; sinecure (*slang*).

plantureux, euse† (plɑ̃tyrø, øːz) *a*, copious; fleshy; fertile.

planure (planyːr) *f*, shaving[s].

plaque (plak) *f*, plate; sheet; slab; plaque; tablet; badge. ~ *d'identité*, identity badge. ~ *minéralogique*, car license-plate. ~ *de gazon*, turf, sod. ~ *tournante*, turntable (*Rly.*). **plaqué** (ke) *m*, electroplate. **plaquer** (ke) *v.t*, to plate; veneer; lay on; cake; lay down (*turf*); jilt, leave flat. **pla-**

quette (kɛt) *f*, thin slab or plate; disc; booklet.

plastique (plastik) *a*, plastic.

plastron (plastrɔ̃) *m*, breast-plate; front (*shirt*); butt (*pers.*, *fig.*). **plastronner** (ne) *v.i*, to pose; put on the dog.

plat, e (pla, at) *a*, flat; level; lank, straight (*hair*); smooth (*sea*); dead (*calm*); dull, bald (*fig.*). à ~, flat. *à plat* [*ventre*], flat on one's face. ¶ *m*, flat; blade (*oar*); side, board (*book*); *pan* (*scale*); dish; mess; course (*dinner*). ~ *de quête*, collection plate. ~ *du jour*, special dish for the day.

platane (platan) *m*, plane [tree].

plat-bord (plabɔːr) *m*, gunwale, gunnel.

plate (plat) *f*, punt (*boat*).

plateau (plato) *m*, tray; salver; pan (*scale*); dish (*soap*); stage, platform (*Theat.*); plateau, table land; upland; plate, table; face plate, chuck (*lathe*). ~ *roulant*, service wagon.

plate-bande (platbãːd) (*Hort.*) *m*, border; bed.

platée (plate) *f*, dishful.

plate-forme (platfɔrm) *f*, platform, stage; flat roof.

platement (platmã) *ad*, flatly; dully.

platine (platin) *f*, plate, platen; stage (*microscope*); lock (*firearm*). ¶ *m*, platinum.

platitude (platityd) *f*, flatness (*fig.*), dullness; platitude.

platonique (platɔnik) *a*, Platonic.

plâtre (plɑːtr) *m*, plaster; p. cast. ~ *de moulage*, p. of Paris. **plâtrer** (plɑtre) *v.t*, to plaster. **plâtrier** (trie) *m*, plasterer. **plâtrière** (ɛːr) *f*, gypsum quarry.

plausible† (plozibl) *a*, plausible.

plébéien, ne (plebejɛ̃, ɛn) *a*, plebeian. **plébiscite** (bisit) *m*, plebiscite, referendum.

plein, e† (plɛ̃, ɛn) *a*, full; replete; fraught; whole; mid; high (*tide*, *seas*); solid; open; pregnant (*animals*). ~ *comme un œuf*, chock full. *en plein jour*, *en plein midi*, in broad daylight. *faire le* ~, fill it

up (*gas*, *water*, *etc.*). ¶ *m*, plenum; full; height; thick stroke, downstroke. **plénier, ère** (plenje, ɛːr) *a*, full; plenary. **plénipotentiaire** (nipɔtɑ̃sjɛːr) *m. & att*, plenipotentiary. **plénitude** (tyd) *f*, plenitude, fullness; repletion.

pléonasme (pleɔnasm) *m*, pleonasm.

pléthore (pletɔːr) *f*, plethora, glut.

pleur (plœːr) *m. usually pl*, tear. **pleurard, e** (plœraːr, ard) *n*, whimperer; (*att.*) whimpering; tearful; maudlin (*voice*). **pleurer** (re) *v.i. & t*, to weep; mourn; bewail; cry; water, run (*eyes*); drip; bleed.

pleurésie (plœrezi) *f*, pleurisy.

pleureur, euse (plœrœːr, øːz) *n*, whimperer; mute, [hired] mourner; (*att.*) weeping. **pleurnicher** (niʃe) *v.i*, to whimper, whine, snivel.

pleutre (pløtr) *m*, cad.

pleuvoir (plœvwaːr) *v.i.ir*, to rain; pour, shower.

plèvre (plɛːvr) *f*, pleura.

plexus (plɛksyːs) *m*, plexus.

pli (pli) *m*, fold; pleat; wrinkle, pucker, crease; bend; ply; cover, envelope. *mise en* ~, hairset, wave. *sous ce* ~, enclosed. **pliable** (abl) *a*, pliable. **pliant, e** (ã, ãːt) *a*, pliant; folding. ¶ *m*, camp stool.

plie (pli) *f*, plaice.

plier (plie) *v.t. & i*, to fold; strike (*tent*); bend; bow. ~ *bagage*, to pack up; decamp; die.

plinthe (plɛ̃ːt) *f*, plinth; skirting [board].

plisser (plise) *v.t. & i*, to pleat, fold; kilt; crease, crumple, wrinkle, crinkle, pucker.

plomb (plɔ̃), *m*, lead; shot; came; plumb, plummet; plomb (*Cust.*); sink; ballast (*fig.*). ~ [*fusible*], fuse (*Elec.*). *faire sauter un* ~, to blow a fuse. *à* ~, upright. **plombage** (baːʒ) *m*, plumbing; filling (*teeth*). **plombagine** (baʒin) *f*, plumbago, graphite, black lead. **plomber** (be) *v.t*, to lead, plumb; plomb; fill (*tooth*). **plomberie** (bri) *f*, plumbing; lead works. **plombier** (bje) *m*, plumber.

plombe (plɔ̃be) f, hour (slang). j'ai attendu trois ~s, I waited three hours.

plongée (plɔ̃ʒe) f, high-angle shot (cinema, TV).

plongeoir (plɔ̃ʒwaːr) m, diving board. **plongeon** (ʒɔ̃) m, diver (bird); dive, plunge. **plonger** (ʒe) v.i. & t, to plunge; dive; submerge; dip; duck; immerse; thrust. **plongeur, euse** (ʒœːr, øːz) n, diver (Swim.); (m.) diver (in diving dress); dishwasher (man); plunger (pump).

plot (plo) m, stud (Elec. contact).

ployer (plwaje) v.t. & i, to bend, bow; wrap up; give way.

pluie (plɥi) f, rain; shower; wet. ~ d'or, golden rain (fireworks).

plumage (plymaːʒ) m, plumage, feathers. **plumard** (aːr) m, feather duster; bed (slang). **plumasserie** (masri) f, feather trade. **plume** (plym) f, feather (bird & Box.); pen. ~ [à écrire], nib; bed. ~ d'oie, quill [pen]. sans ~s, unfledged, callow. **plumeau** (mo) m, feather duster; eiderdown quilt. **plumée** (me) f, penful, dip (ink). **plumer** (me) v.t, to pluck; fleece (fig.); (v.i.) to feather (rowing). **plumet** (mɛ) m, plume. **plumeux, euse** (mø, øːz) a, feathery, plumose. **plumier** (mje) m, pen tray, pencilcase. **plumitif** (mitif) m, minute book; quill driver.

plupart (la) (plypaːr), most, the generality, the majority.

plural, e (plyral) a, plural (vote). **pluralité** (lite) f, plurality; majority. **pluriel, le** (rjɛl) a. & m, plural (Gram.).

plus (ply) finally often plys; in liaison, plyz) ad, more; -er (suffix forming comparatives); longer; any l., anymore. **le ~,** the most; -est (suffix forming superlatives). [signe] ~ (plys) m, plus [sign]. **plusieurs** (zjœːr) a. & pn, several. **plusque-parfait** (plyskaparfɛ) m, pluperfect. **plus-value** (plyvaly) f, appreciation; surplus; [unearned] increment.

plutôt (plyto) ad, rather, sooner, instead.

pluvial, e (plyvjal) a, rain (water); rainy.

pluvier (plyvje) m, plover.

pluvieux, euse (plyvjø, øːz) a, rainy; wet.

pneumatique (pnømatik) (abb. **pneu**) m, [pneumatic] tire. ¶ a, pneumatic, air (att.); express letter (in Paris).

pneumonie (pnømɔni) f, pneumonia.

Pô (le) (po), the Po (river).

pochade (pɔʃad) f, rapid sketch.

pochard (pɔʃaːr) m, drunkard. **pocharder (de)** v.t, to make drunk. se ~, to get drunk.

poche (pɔʃ) f, pocket; sack; pouch; case; crop (bird); ladle; pucker. ~ rapportée, patch pocket. **pocher** (ʃe) v.t, to poach (eggs); black (eye); dash off (sketch). **pochette** (ʃɛt) f, pocket; pocket case, packet. ~ en soie, de couleur, silk colored handkerchief. **pochoir** (ʃwaːr) m, stencil [plate].

poêle (pwaːl) f, frying pan; pan. ¶ m, pall; canopy; stove, range. ~ à pétrole, oil heater. **poêlier** (pwalje) m, stove & range maker. **poêlon** (lɔ̃) m, saucepan, pipkin.

poème (pɔɛːm) m, poem. **poésie** (ezi) f, poetry; poem, piece of poetry. ~ enfantine, nursery rhyme. **poète** (ɛt) m, poet. **poétereau** (etro) m, poetaster. **poétesse** (tɛs) f, poetess. **poétique†** (tik) a, poetic; poetical.

pognon (pɔɲɔ̃) m, money, dough, bread (slang).

poids (pwɑ) m, weight; shot (in sport of putting the shot); heaviness; burden, brunt. ~ spécifique, specific gravity. ~lourd, heavy truck.

poignant, e (pwaɲɑ̃, ɑ̃ːt) a, poignant.

poignard (pwaɲaːr) m, dagger, dirk, poignard. **poignarder** (narde) v.t, to stab, knife. **poigne** (pwaɲ) f, grip; energy. **poignée** (ɲe) f, handful; handle, grip, hilt; hank. ~ de main, handshake. **poignet** (ɲɛ) m, wrist; wristband, cuff (soft).

poil (pwal) m, hair (on animal & body pers.); fur, coat; pile, nap; bristle; down (plant); energy.

~ *de chèvre d'Angora*, mohair. ~*follet*, down (*chin, etc.*). *à* ~, naked; bareback. *à* ~ *ras*, short-haired, smooth-haired (*dog*). *au* ~ *rude*, rough-haired, wirehaired (*dog*). **poilu, e** (ly) *a*, hairy, shaggy. ¶ *m*, French soldier.

poinçon (pwɛ̃sɔ̃) *m*, punch (*solid*); awl, point; stamp; puncheon. ~ *de contrôle*, hallmark. **poinçonner** (sɔne) *v.t*, to punch; stamp; hallmark.

poindre (pwɛ̃:dr) *v.i.ir*, to dawn, break; come up.

poing (pwɛ̃) *m*, fist, hand.

point (pwɛ̃) *m*, point; dot; speck; mark; tick; score (*games*); [full] stop, period; note; stitch; point [lace]; degree, extent; verge (*fig.*); focus. ~ *à terre*, landmark (*Naut.*). ~ *arrière*, backstitch. ~ *coupé*, cut openwork stitch. ~ *croisé*, herringboning. ~ *d'appui*, fulcrum. ~ *d'appui de la flotte*, naval station (*foreign*). ~ *d'éclair*, ~ *d'inflammabilité*, flash[ing] point. ~ *d'interrogation*, note of interrogation, question mark. ~ *d'ourlet*, hemming. ~ *de chaînette*, chain stitch. ~ *de côté*, stitch in the side (*Med.*). ~ *de croix*, cross-stitch. ~ *de fuite*, vanishing point. ~ *de languette*, ~ *de feston*, blanket stitch, buttonhole s. (*Emb.*). ~*de marque*, marking stitch. ~ *de mire*, aim; cynosure (*fig.*). ~ *de piqûre*, lockstitch. ~ *de repère*, reference mark, datum point; bench mark; landmark (*fig.*). ~ *de surjet*, oversewing stitch, seam s. ~ *de tige*, ~ *coulé*, crewel s. ~ *de vue*, point of view, standpoint. ~ *devant*, running stitch. ~ *du jour*, daybreak, dawn. ~ *& virgule* ou ~*-virgule*, *m*, semicolon. ~ *mort*, dead center; neutral (*auto*). ~ *chaud*, trouble spot. ~ *de non-retour*, point of no return. ~ *noir*, blackhead. *à* ~, [just] in time, to a turn. *à* ~ *nommé*, in the nick of time; at the right moment.

point (pwɛ̃) *ad*, no, not at all, [not] any.

pointage (pwɛta:ʒ) *m*, ticking [off], checking; timekeeping; timing; scoring; aiming, pointing, laying, training (*gun*).

pointe (pwɛ̃:t) *f*, point (*sharp end*); tip; head; top; peak; toe (*shoe, sock*); (*pl.*) toe dancing; center (*lathe*); nail, brad; touch; quip, quirk. ~ *de Paris*, wire nail, French n., sprig. ~ *de terre*, headland, foreland. ~ *du jour*, daybreak, dawn. *sur la* ~ *du pied*, on tiptoe. ~ *sèche*, drypoint (*engraving*).

pointeau (pwɛto) *m*, center punch.

pointer (pwɛte) *v.t*, to tick [off], check, tally; point, aim, level, lay, train; thrust; (*v.i.*) to soar; appear, sprout. *se* ~, to show up at a rendezvous (*slang*). **pointeur** (tœ:r) *m*, checker; timekeeper; marker, scorer; gun layer. **pointille** (ti:j) *f*, punctilio. **pointiller** (tije) *v.t*, to dot; stipple; bait; (*v.i.*) to cavil; split hairs. **pointillerie** (jri) *f*, captiousness, hair-splitting. **pointilleux, euse** (jø, ø:z) *a*, captious, touchy; fastidious, punctilious.

pointu, e (pwɛty) *a*, pointed; sharp; shrill.

pointure (pwɛty:r) *f*, size (*of shoes, gloves, etc.*).

poire (pwa:r) *f*, pear; bulb, ball; dupe; face (*slang*). **poire** (pware) *m*, perry.

poireau (pwaro) *m*, leek; wart; simpleton (*slang*). **poireauter** (te) *v.i*, to be kept waiting (*slang*).

poirier (pwarje) *m*, pear tree; pear wood.

pois (pwɑ) *m*, pea; dot (*Emb.*); spot (*as on tie*). ~ *cassés*, split peas. ~ *chinois*, soy[a] bean. ~ *de senteur*, sweet pea. *petit* ~, ~*verts*, green peas.

poison (pwazɔ̃) *m*, poison.

poissard, e (pwasa:r, ard) *a*, vulgar. ¶ *f*, fishwife.

poisse (pwas) *f*, bad luck. ¶ *m*, thief; pimp.

poisser (pwase) *v.t*, to pitch; wax (*thread*); make sticky. **poisseux, euse** (sø, ø:z) *a*, sticky.

poisson (pwasɔ̃) *m*, fish. *faire un* ~ *d'avril à*, to make an April fool of. ~ *de grand sport*, big-game fish. ~ *de mer*, salt-water fish, sea fish. ~ *rouge*, goldfish. *faire une queue de* ~, to cut sharply in front of another driver. **poisson-naille** (sɔnɑːj) f, fry. **poissonnerie** (nri) f, fish market; f. shop. **poissonneux, euse** (nø, øːz) a, full of fish. **poissonnier, ère** (nje, ɛːr) n, fishmonger. ¶ f, fish kettle (Cook.).

poitrail (pwatrɑːj) m, breast (horse). **poitrinaire** (trinɛːr) a. & n, consumptive. **poitrine** (trin) f, chest, breast; brisket.

poivre (pwaːvr) m, pepper. ~ de Cayenne (kajen), ~ rouge, Cayenne p., red p. **poivré, e** (pwavre) p.a, peppery; spicy (tale). **poivrer** (vre) v.t, to pepper. **poivrier** (vrie) m, pepper plant; p. box. **poivrière** (vriɛːr) f, pepper box. **poivron** (vrɔ̃) m, pimento.

poix (pwa) f, pitch; cobbler's wax.

polaire (pɔlɛːr) a, polar; pole (star). **pôle** (poːl) m, pole (Astr., Phys., etc.).

polar (pɔlar) m, detective novel (slang).

polémique (pɔlemik)ˋ a, polemic(al). ¶ f, polemic; polemics.

poli, e (pɔli) p.a, polished, bright; glossy, sleek; polite, mannerly; refined. ¶ m, polish, gloss.

police (pɔlis) f, policing; police regulations; police [force]; policy (Insce.), ~ de la circulation, traffic police, faire la ~, to keep order. **policer (se)** v.t, to control, organize, civilize. **policier** (je) m, policeman.

polichinelle (pɔliʃinel) m, Punch; buffoon. avoir un ~ dans le tiroir, to be pregnant (slang).

poliment (pɔlimɑ̃) ad, politely. **polir** (liːr) v.t, to polish; buff; smooth; refine. **polissoir** (swaːr) f, buffer.

polisson, ne (pɔlisɔ̃, ɔn) a, street child; rascal; scamp; immodest person; (att.) naughty, precocious, indecent. **polissonner** (sɔne) v.i, to run the streets (child); be lewd.

politesse (pɔlites) f, politeness; compliment.

politicien (pɔlitisjɛ̃) m, politician (as a trade). **politique†** (tik) a, political; politic. ¶ m, politician. ¶ f, policy; polity; politics. **politiquer** (ke) v.i, to talk politics.

polka (pɔlka) m, polka.
pollen (pɔllɛn) m, pollen.
polluer (pɔllɥe) v.t, to pollute, defile; profane. **pollution** (pɔllysjɔ̃) f, pollution.

polo (pɔlo) m, polo; polo cap.

Pologne (la) (pɔlɔɲ), Poland. **polonais, e** (ne, ɛːz) a, Polish. P~, n, Pole. le polonais, Polish (language). **polonaise**, f, polonaise.

poltron, ne (pɔltrɔ̃, ɔn) a, cowardly. ¶ n, poltroon, coward. **poltronnerie** (trɔnri) f, cowardice.

polycopier (pɔlikɔpje) v.t, to mimeograph, etc.

polygame (pɔligam) n, polygamist. ¶ a, polygamous. **polygamie** (mi) f, polygamy. **polyglotte** (glɔt) a. & n, polyglot. **polygone** (gɔn) m, polygon. la Polynésie (nezi), Polynesia. **polype** (lip) m, polyp; polypus. **polysyllabe** (silab) a, polysyllabic. ¶ m, polysyllable. **polytechnique** (teknik) a, polytechnic. **polytechnicien** (teknisjɛ̃) m, student or graduate of the École Polytechnique. **polythéisme** (teism) m, polytheism.

pommade (pɔmad) f, pomade; salve. passer de la ~, to butter up, flatter. **pommader (de)** v.t, to pomade.

pomme (pɔm) f, apple; cone (fir, pine); knob; head (stick, cabbage); head (person; slang). tomber dans les ~s, to faint (slang). ~ d'Adam (adɑ̃), Adam's pome. ~ de terre, potato. ~s de terre en robe [de chambre], jacket potatoes. ~ sauvage, crab [apple]. **pommé, e** (me) (fig.) p.a, downright. **pommeau** (mo) m, pommel. **pommelé, e** (mle) p.a, dapple[d]; mackerel (sky). **pommeraie** (mre) f, apple orchard. **pommette** (met) f, cheekbone. **pommier** (mje) m, apple tree. ~ sauvage, crab [apple tree].

pompe (pɔ̃ːp) f, pomp; pump. ~ à incendie, fire engine. ~ aspirante, suction pump. ~ foulante, force pump. ~ funèbre, funeral; (pl.) undertaking.

pomper (põpe) *v.t. & i,* to pump; suck up.

pompeux, euse† (põpø, ø:z) *a,* pompous; stately.

pompier (põpje) *m,* pump maker; fireman; conventionalist, formulist; (*att.*) conventional, formulistic. **pompiste** (pist) *m,* gas station attendant.

pompon (põpõ) *m,* pompon, tuft, tassel.

pomponner (põpɔne) *v.t,* to smarten or dress up.

ponce (põ:s) *f,* pumice; pounce (*art*).

ponceau (põso) *m,* culvert; poppy.

poncer (põse) *v.t,* to pumice; sandpaper; pounce. **poncif** (sif) (*fig.*) *m,* conventionalism.

ponction (põksjõ) (*Surg.*) *f,* puncture, tapping.

ponctualité (põktɥalite) *f,* punctuality.

ponctuation (põktɥasjõ) *f,* punctuation.

ponctuel, le† (põktɥɛl) *a,* punctual.

ponctuer (põktɥe) *v.t. & abs,* to punctuate; emphasize.

pondérable (põderabl) *a,* ponderable. **pondérer** (re) *v.t,* to balance.

pondre (põ:dr) *v.t. & abs,* to lay (*eggs*); be delivered of (*fig.*).

poney (pɔnɛ) *m,* pony.

pont (põ) *m,* bridge; platform; deck (*ship*). ~ *à bascule,* drawbridge. ~ *abri,* awning deck, hurricane d. ~ *de manœuvre,* hurricane deck. ~ *roulant,* traveling crane. ~ *suspendu,* suspension bridge. ~ *suspendu à chaînes,* chain bridge. ~ *tournant,* swing bridge. ~ *aérien,* airlift. *faire le* ~, to make a long holiday weekend. **pontage** (ta:3) *m,* bridging; bridge building; bypass (*Surg.*).

ponte (põ:t) *f,* laying (*eggs*); (*m.*) punt[er] (*cards, etc.*).

ponté, e (põte) *a,* decked. *non* ~, open (*boat*).

ponter (põte) *v.i,* to punt (*cards, etc.*).

pontife (põtif) *m,* pontiff; pundit. **pontifical, e†** (fikal) *a. & m,* pontifical. **pontificat** (ka) *m,* pontificate.

pont-levis (põləvi) *m,* drawbridge (*castle*).

ponton (põtõ) *m,* pontoon; hulk; landing stage.

popeline (pɔplin) *f,* poplin.

popote (pɔpɔt) *f,* canteen, mess (*Mil.*). *faire la* ~, to cook (*slang*).

popotin (pɔpɔtɛ̃) *m,* buttock, backside (*slang*).

populace (pɔpylas) *f,* populace, rabble. **populacier, ère** (sje, ɛ:r) *a,* vulgar. **populaire†** (lɛ:r) *a,* popular. **popularité** (larite) *f,* popularity. **population** (sjõ) *f,* population. **populeux, euse** (lø, ø:z) *a,* populous.

porc (pɔ:r) *m,* pig, swine; pork. ~ [*châtré*], hog.

porcelaine (pɔrsəlɛn) *f,* porcelain, china[ware]; cowrie. ~ *de Saxe,* Dresden china. **porcelainier, ère** (nje, ɛ:r) *n,* china manufacturer; china dealer.

porc-épic (pɔrkepik) *m,* porcupine.

porche (pɔrʃ) *m,* porch.

porcher, ère (pɔrʃe, ɛ:r) *n,* swineherd. **porcherie** (ʃəri) *f,* pigsty. **porcine** (sin) *a.f,* porcine, pig (*att.*).

pore (pɔ:r) *m,* pore. **poreux, euse** (pɔrø, ø:z) *a,* porous. **porosité** (rozite) *f,* porousness.

pornographe (pɔrnɔgraf) *m,* pornographer. **pornographie** (fi) *f,* pornography. **pornographique** (fik) *a,* pornographic.

porphyre (pɔrfi:r) *m,* porphyry.

port (pɔ:r) *m,* port, harbor, haven; carrying; wearing; carriage; postage; bearing; burden (*ship*). ~ *d'armes,* gun license. ~ *d'armement,* home port. ~ *d'attache,* port of registry. ~ *de guerre,* ~ *militaire,* naval port, n. station, n. base. ~ *de toute marée,* deep-water harbor. *à bon* ~, safe[ly]; to a happy issue. **portable** (pɔrtabl) *a,* wearable.

portail (pɔrtaːj) *m,* portal.

portant, e (pɔrtɑ̃, ɑ̃:t) *a,* bearing. *à bout* ~, pointblank. *bien* ~, in good health. *mal* ~, in bad h. ¶ *m,* chest handle, lifting h.;

outrigger (*for rowlocks*). **portatif, ive** (tatif, i:v) *a*, portable; small (*arms*).

porte (pɔrt) *f*, door, doorway; gate, gateway; arch. ~ *brisée*, folding door. ~ *charretière*, carriage entrance. ~ *cochère* (kɔʃɛːr), built-over carriage entrance. ~ *de service*, back door, tradesmen's entrance. ~*-fenêtre*, French window. ~ *matelassée*, baize door. ~ *à tambour*, revolving door. ~ *va-et-vient*, swing door.

porte- (pɔrt; *sometimes* pɔrtə *as noted*) *comps, all m*: ~*à faux*, overhang. ~*-avions*, aircraft carrier. ~*-bagages*, luggage carrier. ~*-bonheur*, charm. ~*-bouquet*, flower holder. ~*-bouteilles*, bottle rack; bin. ~*-cartes* (tɛkart), card case; map case. ~*-chapeaux*, hat & coat stand. ~*-cigare*, cigar holder. ~*-cigares*, c. case. ~*-clefs* (tɛkle), turnkey; key ring. ~*-couteau*, knife rest. ~*-crayon* (tɛkrɛjɔ̃), pencil case. ~*-en-dehors*, outrigger (*for rowlocks*). ~*-épée*, frog (*sword*). ~*-étendard*, standard bearer. ~*feuille*, billfold. ~*-jarretelles*, garter belt. ~*-malheur*, bringer of ill luck; bird of ill omen, Jonah. ~*-menu* (təmny), menu holder. ~*-monnaie*, purse. ~*-parapluies*, umbrella stand. ~*-parole*, spokesman, mouthpiece (*pers.*). ~*-potiche*, pedestal (*for vase*). ~*-queue* (tɛkø), train bearer. ~*-respect*, person of imposing appearance; weapon. ~*-serviettes*, towel rod, ring. ~*-trésor*, jewel case (*traveling*). ~*-vêtements*, clothes hanger. ~*-voix* (təvwa), megaphone.

porté, e (pɔrte) *p.a*, inclined, disposed, prone, apt; fond.

portée (pɔrte) *f*, bearing; litter (*of pups*); span; reach, range, radius, scope, compass, shot; significance, purport; stave, staff (*Mus.*). *à* ~ *de la voix*, within call.

portefaix (pɔrtəfɛ) *m*, porter (*street, etc.*); rough fellow.

portefeuille (pɔrtəfœ:j) *m*, portfolio; letter case, wallet; office

(*in ministry*). ~*-titres*, investments, securities, share holdings, stocks & shares.

portemanteau (pɔrtmɑ̃to) *m*, hat & coat stand, portemanteau.

porter (pɔrte) *v.t. & i*, to bear; carry; take; bring; lay; wear; have on; shoulder (*arms*); drink (*health*); deal, strike (*blow*); enter, put, mark; post (*Bkkpg.*); prompt, lead, incline; raise; rest; tell (*shot, word*); turn (*discussion*). ~ *à faux*, to overhang; miss the point (*fig.*). **se** ~, to go; be; do; stand. **porteur, euse** (tœːr, øːz) *n*, porter; carrier; (*m.*) bearer; holder. *porteurs des cordons du poêle*, pall bearers.

portier, ère (pɔrtje, ɛːr) *n*, porter, doorkeeper, caretaker. ¶ *f*, door (*carriage, car*); door curtain.

portion (pɔrsjɔ̃) *f*, portion, share, part; helping (*food*).

portique (pɔrtik) *m*, portico, porch; gantry; gallows (*Gym.*).

Porto (pɔrto) *m*, Oporto. **porto** *ou* **vin de Porto**, *m*, port [wine].

portrait (pɔrtrɛ) *m*, portrait, likeness; image; description. ~ *en buste*, half-length portrait. ~ *en pied*, full-length portrait.

portugais, e (pɔrtygɛ, ɛːz) *a. & P~, n*, Portuguese. *le portugais*, Portuguese (*language*). **le Portugal** (gal), Portugal.

posage (poza:ʒ) *m*, laying, fixing. **pose** (po:z) *f*, laying; pose, posture; lie (*golf ball*); exposure (*Phot.*). ~*mètre*, exposure meter. **posé†, e** (poze) *p.a*, staid, sedate; steady. **poser** (ze) *v.i*, to rest, lie; pose, sit (*portrait*); (*v.t.*) to place, put; p. down; lay; l. down; set; hang (*bells*); pose; post (*sentry*); state; grant. ~ *ses clous*, to down tools. **se** ~, to settle, alight; set up; pose. **poseur, euse** (zœːr, øːz) *n*, layer; setter; hanger (*bells*); affected person. *poseur de mines*, minelayer. *poseur de voie*, platelayer.

positif, ive† (pozitif, i:v) *a*, positive, real; practical, matter-of-fact. ¶ *m*, real[ity].

position (pozisjɔ̃) *f*, position; situation; book (*Stk Ex.*); posture; stance.

posologie (pozɔlɔʒi) f, dosage (*drugs, etc.*).

possédé, e (pɔsede) p.a, possessed (*mad*). ¶ n, one possessed.

posséder (de) v.t, to possess, own, have, hold; be master of. **posses-seur** (sɛsœːr) m, possessor, owner. **possession** (sjɔ̃) f, possession; tenure.

possibilité (pɔsibilite) f, possibility. **possible** (bl) a. & m, possible.

postal, e (pɔstal) a, postal, post, mail (*att.*).

postdater (pɔstdate) v.t, to postdate.

poste (pɔst) f, mail; post [office]. ~ *restante*, general delivery, to be called for. *aller un train de* ~, to go posthaste. **postier, ère** (je, jɛːr) n, post-office employee.

poste (pɔst) m, post, station; guard room; berth; radio (*slang*); head[ing]; item; shift (*men*). ~ *central*, exchange (*Teleph.*). ~ *de l'équipage*, forecastle, foc's'le. ~ *de police*, police station. ~ *de secours*, first-aid station. ~ *supplémentaire*, extension [line] (*Teleph.*). ~ *éloigné*, remote terminal (*computers*). **poster** (te) v.t, to post, station.

postérieur, e† (pɔsterjœːr) a, posterior, subsequent, later; hind-[er], back. ¶ m, posterior.

postérité (pɔsterite) f, posterity, issue.

posthume (pɔstym) a, posthumous.

postiche (pɔstiʃ) a, false, artificial; sham. *cheveux* ~s, wig.

postillon (pɔstijɔ̃) m, postillion.

post-scriptum (pɔstskriptɔm) (*abb.* P.-S.) m, postscript, P.S.

postulant, e (pɔstylɑ̃, ɑ̃ːt) n, candidate, applicant; postulant. **postuler** (le) v.t, to apply for; (*v.i.*) to act for (*client, law*).

posture (pɔstyːr) f, posture; position.

pot (po; *before* à, au, pɔt) m, pot, jug, ewer; tankard; can; jar. ~-*au-feu*, stock pot, soup p; beef and vegetables; (*att.*) stay-at-home (*pers.*). ~ *d'échappement*, muffler (*auto*). ~ *perdu*, no-de-

posit jar, bottle. *avoir du* ~, to be lucky. *manque de* ~, bad luck. *payer les* ~s *cassés*, to pay the damages. ~-*de-vin*, bribe. ~-*pourri*, hodgepodge; medley.

potable (pɔtabl) a, drinkable, drinking (*water*).

potache (pɔtaʃ) m, schoolboy (*slang*).

potage (pɔtaːʒ) m, soup. ~ *ou consommé?* thick or clear? (*at dinner*). *pour tout* ~, all told. **potager, ère** (taʒe, ɛːr) a, pot (*herb*); kitchen (*garden*). ¶ m, kitchen garden; dinner pail; kitchen stove, charcoal-fired cooker.

potasse (pɔtas) f, potash. **potas-sium** (sjɔm) m, potassium.

potasser (pɔtase) v.t, to study hard, cram (*slang*).

pote (pɔt) m, pal, buddy.

poteau (pɔto) m, post, pole. ~ [*d'arrivée*], [winning] post. ~ *de départ*, starting p. ~ *de signalisation* (siɲalizasjɔ̃), traffic sign. ~ *indicateur*, signpost.

potée (pɔte) f, potful, jugful; swarm. ~ *d'étain*, putty powder.

potelé, e (pɔtle) a, plump, chubby.

potelet (pɔtlɛ) m, stud (*scantling in wall*).

potence (pɔtɑ̃ːs) f, gallows, gibbet; bracket.

potentat (pɔtɑ̃ta) m, potentate.

potentiel, le (pɔtɑ̃sjɛl) a. & m, potential.

poter (pɔte) v.t, to putt (*golf*).

poterie (pɔtri) f, pottery, earthenware; ware. ~ *de grès*, stoneware.

poterne (pɔtɛrn) f, postern.

poteur (pɔtœːr) m, putter (*golf club*).

potiche (pɔtiʃ) f, vase (*Chinese, or like*).

potier (pɔtje) m, potter. ~ *d'étain*, pewterer.

potin (pɔtɛ̃) m, gossip; row, fuss.

potion (posjɔ̃) f, potion, draft.

potiron (pɔtirɔ̃) m, pumpkin.

pou (pu) m, louse.

pouah (pwa) i, ugh!

poubelle (pubɛl) f, garbage can, trash c.

pouce (pu:s) *m*, thumb.

pouding (pudiŋ) *m*, pudding.

poudre (pu:dr) *f*, powder; dust. ~ *à canon*, gunpowder. ~ *à lever*, baking powder. ~ *d'or*, gold dust. ~ *de mine*, blasting powder. ~ *de riz*, face powder, toilet powder. **poudrer** (pudre) *v.t*, to powder. **poudrerie** (drəri) *f*, powder mill. **poudreux, euse** (drø, ø:z) *a*, dusty. **poudrier** (drie) *m*, powder box; salt sifter. **poudrière** (ɛ:r) *f*, powder magazine.

pouf (puf) *m*, overstuffed footstool. **pouffiasse** (fjas) *f*, slut, slattern (*slang*).

pouffer [de rire] (pufe), to burst out laughing.

pouilleux, euse (pujø, ø:z) *a*, lousy.

poulailler (pulaje) *m*, hen house; poulterer; top balcony, cheap seats (*Theat.*).

poulain (pulɛ̃) *m*, colt, foal.

poulaine (pulɛn) *f*, bedroom slipper.

poularde (pulard) *f*, table fowl. **poule** (pul) *f*, hen, fowl; sweepstake[s]; round robin (*sports*); whore (*slang*). *chair de* ~, gooseflesh. ~ *d'eau*, moor hen. ~ *d'Inde*, turkey [hen]. ~ *faisane*, hen pheasant. ~ *mouillée*, milksop (*pers.*). **poulet** (lɛ) *m*, chicken, chick; policeman, cop (*slang*). **poulette** (lɛt) *f*, pullet; girl.

pouliche (pulif) *f*, filly, foal.

poulie (puli) *f*, pulley, block, sheave.

pouliner (puline) *v.i*, to foal. [**jument**] **poulinière** (njɛ:r) *f*, brood mare, breeder.

poulpe (pulp) *m*, octopus.

pouls (pu) *m*, pulse (*as in wrist*).

poumon (pumɔ̃) *m*, lung.

poupard, e (pupa:r, ard) *a*, chubby; baby (*face*). ¶ *m*, baby; baby doll.

poupe (pup) *f*, stern, poop.

poupée (pupe) *f*, doll; puppet; dummy; block. **poupin, e** (pɛ̃, in) *a*, doll-faced. **poupon, ne** (pɔ̃, ɔn) *n*, baby. **pouponner** (pɔne) *v.t*, to fondle, dandle, cuddle.

pouponnière (njɛ:r) *f*, day nursery.

pour (pu:r) *pr*, for; instead of; per; pro; as; on; to; (*money's*) worth. ~ *ainsi dire*, so to speak. ~ *cent*, percent. ~ *que*, in order that. *le* ~ *& le contre*, the pros & cons, for & against.

pourboire (purbwa:r) *m*, tip, gratuity.

pourceau (purso) *m*, hog, pig, swine.

pourcentage (pursãta:ʒ) *m*, percentage, rate.

pourchasser (purfase) *v.t*, to pursue; dun.

pourfendre (purfã:dr) *v.t*, to fend, cleave.

pourlécher (purlefe) *v.t*, to lick all over. *se* ~ *les babines*, to lick one's chops.

pourparlers (purparle) *m.pl*, parley; negotiations.

pourpre (purpr) *f*, purple (*robe*); crimson (*color*); (*m.*) purple (*color*); (*att.*) crimson (*color*). **pourpré, e** (pre) *a*, purple (*red—color*).

pourquoi (purkwa) *ad. & c*, why, wherefore, what. ¶ *m*, why.

pourri, e (puri) *p.a*, rotten. **pourrir** (ri:r) *v.i. & t*, to rot, **pourriture** (rity:r) *f*, rotting; rot; rottenness.

poursuite (pursɥit) *f*, pursuit, chase; tracking (*spacecraft*). (*oft. pl.*) lawsuit, proceedings; prosecution. **poursuivant** (vã) *m*, plaintiff, prosecutor; suitor, wooer. **poursuivre** (vr) *v.t.ir*, to pursue, chase; haunt; follow up; prosecute, sue.

pourtant (purtã) *ad*, yet, nevertheless, however.

pourtour (purtu:r) *m*, circumference; surround; precincts, close; gangway.

pourvoi (purvwa) *m*, appeal; petition. **pourvoir** (vwa:r) *v.i. & t. ir*, to provide, supply, furnish. **pourvoyeur** (vwajœ:r) *m*, purveyor, provider, caterer. **pourvu que** (vy) *c*, provided [that].

poussah (pusa) *m*, tumbler (*toy*); tub[by man].

pousse (pus) *f*, growth; cutting (*teeth*); shoot, sprout. **~-pousse**, *m*, ricksha[w]. **poussée (se)** *f*, push, shove; thrust; pressure; outburst; buoyancy. **pousser (se)** *v.t. & i*, to push, shove, thrust; drive; urge; utter, give; grow, shoot, spring up. ~ *à la perche*, ~ *du fond*, to punt (*boating*). ~ *au large*, to push off (*Naut.*).

poussette (pusɛt) *f*, stroller; shopping cart.

poussier (pusje) *m*, dust (*coal, etc.*). **poussière** (sjɛːr) *f*, dust. ~ *d'eau*, spray. *des* ~*s*, small change left after paying bill (*often left for waiter*). **poussiéreux, euse** (sjerø, ø:z) *a*, dusty.

poussif, ive (pusif, iːv) *a*, broken-winded; wheezy.

poussin (pusɛ̃) *m*, chick; spring chicken. **poussinière** (sinjɛːr) *f*, coop; incubator.

poussoir (puswaːr) *m*, push [button].

poutre (putr) *f*, beam; girder. **poutrelle** (trɛl) *f*, small beam; skid (*Artil.*).

pouvoir (puvwaːr) *m*, power; authority; power of attorney; proxy; (*pl.*) credentials. ¶ *v.i. & t. ir*, to be able; can; can do; may. **se** ~, to be possible. *cela se peut*, it may be.

prairie (prɛri) *f*, meadow; grassland; prairie.

praline (pralin) *f*, burnt almond, praline.

praticable (pratikabl) *a*, practicable, feasible; passable (*road*). **praticien** (sjɛ̃) *m*, practician; practitioner. **pratiquant** (pratikɑ̃) *a*, church-going. **pratique†** (tik) *a*, practical. ¶ *f*, practice; experience; observance; (*pl.*) dealings; pratique; custom; customer. **pratiquer** (ke) *v.t*, to practice; make; frequent. **se** ~, to be done; rule (*prices*).

pré (pre) *m*, meadow.

préalable† (prealabl) *a*, previous; preliminary. ¶ *m*, preliminary.

préambule (preɑ̃byl) *m*, preamble.

préau (preo) *m*, courtyard, quadrangle; playground (*covered*).

préavis (preavi) *m*, [previous] notice, warning. *avec* ~ *pour . . .*, person-to-person call for . . .

prébende (prebɑ̃ːd) *f*, prebend. **prébendier** (bɑ̃dje) *m*, prebendary.

précaire† (prekɛːr) *a*, precarious.

précaution (prekosjɔ̃) *f*, precaution; caution, wariness. **précautionner** (sjɔne) *v.t*, to caution, warn.

précédemment (presedamɑ̃) *ad*, previously. **précédent, e** (dɑ̃, ɑ̃:t) *a*, preceding, previous, before. ¶ *m*, precedent. **précéder** (de) *v.t*, to precede.

précepte (presɛpt) *m*, precept. **précepteur** (tœːr) *m*, tutor, teacher, preceptor. **préceptorat** (tɔra) *m*, tutorship.

prêche (prɛʃ) *m*, sermon. **prêcher** (ʃe) *v.t. & abs*, to preach; extol; exhort; lecture. **prêcheur** (ʃœːr) *m*, sermonizer.

précieux, euse† (presjø, ø:z) *a*, precious; valuable; affected.

précipice (presipis) *m*, precipice.

précipitamment (presipitamɑ̃) *a*, precipitately, headlong. **précipitation** (sjɔ̃) *f*, precipitancy, haste; precipitation. **précipité, e** (te) *a*, precipitate, hasty, hurried, headlong. ¶ *m*, precipitate. **précipiter** (te) *v.t*, to precipitate; hasten; plunge. **se** ~, to rush.

précis, e (presi, iːz) *a*, precise, exact; sharp (*hour*); definite. ¶ *m*, abstract, summary, précis. **précisément** (sizemɑ̃) *ad*, precisely, exactly. **préciser** (ze) *v.t*, to state precisely, specify. **précision** (zjɔ̃) *f*, precision, accuracy; (*pl.*) particulars.

précité, e (presite) *a*, aforesaid, above.

précoce (prekɔs) *a*, precocious; early, forward. **précocité** (site) *f*, precociousness, etc.

préconçu, e (prekɔ̃sy) *a*, preconceived.

préconiser (prekɔnize) *v.t*, to preconize; [re]commend, advocate.

précurseur (prekyrsœːr) *m*, precursor, forerunner; (*att.*) precursory, premonitory.

prédécès (predesɛ) *m*, predecease.

prédécesseur (predesɛsœːr) *m*, predecessor.

prédestination (predɛstinasjɔ̃) *f*, predestination.

prédicant (predikɑ̃) *m*, preacher.

prédicat (predika) *m*, predicate.

prédicateur (predikatœːr) *m*, preacher. **prédication** (sjɔ̃) *f*, preaching.

prédiction (prediksjɔ̃) *f*, prediction; forecast.

prédilection (predilɛksjɔ̃) *f*, predilection, partiality. *de ~*, favorite.

prédire (prediːr) *v.t.ir*, to predict, foretell.

prédisposer (predispoze) *v.t*, to predispose.

prédominer (predɔmine) *v.i*, to predominate, prevail.

prééminent, e (preeminɑ̃, ɑ̃ːt) *a*, preeminent.

préemption (preɑ̃psjɔ̃) *f*, preemption.

préfabriquer (prefabrike) *v.t*, to prefabricate.

préface (prefas) *f*, preface, foreword; preliminaries; forerunner.

préfecture (prefɛktyːr) *f*, prefecture; headquarters (*of police*).

préférable† (preferabl) *a*, preferable, better. **préférence** (rɑ̃ːs) *f*, preference. **préférer** (re) *v.t*, to prefer.

préfet (prefɛ) *m*, prefect. *~ de police*, police commissioner.

préfixe (prefiks) *m*, prefix. ¶ *a*, prefixed.

préhenseur (preɑ̃sœːr) *a.m*, prehensile.

préhistorique (preistɔrik) *a*, prehistoric.

préjudice (preʒydis) *m*, prejudice, detriment; injury. **préjudiciable** (sjabl) *a*, prejudicial, detrimental. **préjudicier** (sje) *v.i*, to be detrimental to. **préjugé** (ʒe) *m*, prejudice; presumption. **préjuger** (ʒe) *v.t*, to prejudge.

prélart (prelaːr) *m*, tarpaulin.

prélasser (se) (prelɑse) *v.pr*, to strut along; loll. **prélat** (la) *m*, prelate.

prélèvement (prelɛvmɑ̃) *m*, deduction, levy. *~ de sang*, blood

test. **prélever** (lve) *v.t*, to deduct, levy.

préliminaire (preliminɛːr) *a. & m*, preliminary.

prélude (prelyd) *m*, prelude; voluntary. **préluder** (de) *v.i*, to prelude (*Mus.*). *~ à*, to preface, lead up to.

prématuré†, e (prematyre) *a*, premature, untimely.

préméditation (premeditasjɔ̃) *f*, premeditation; malice aforethought, m. prepense. **préméditer** (te) *v.t*, to premeditate.

prémices (premis) *f.pl*, firstfruits; beginning.

premier, ère (prəmje, ɛːr) *a*, first; opening (*price*); leading; early; earliest; next; prime; primary; premier. **premier**, *comps*: *~ choix*, best quality, finest q. *~ garçon*, headwaiter. *~ ministre*, prime minister, premier. *~-né, m*, first-born. *de ~ order*, first-class, first-rate; gilt-edged (*securities*). *~ plan*, foreground; close-up (*Phot.*). *~ rôle*, leading part; l. man, l. lady. ¶ *m*, first. ¶ *f*, first; f. night; forewoman. *~ mondiale*, world premiere (*film*). *~s* [galeries], dress circle. **premièrement** (mjɛrmɑ̃) *ad*, first[ly].

prémisses (premis) *f.pl*, premis[s]es (*Log.*).

prémonitoire (premɔnitwaːr) *a*, premonitory.

prémunir (premyniːr) *v.t*, to forewarn. *se ~ contre*, to provide against.

prenable (prənabl) *a*, pregnable; corruptible. **prenant, e** (nɑ̃, ɑ̃ːt) *a*, taking; prehensile. **prendre** (prɑ̃ːdr) *v.t.ir*, to take; t. up; t. in; t. over; lay hold of; seize; clasp; catch; pick up; assume; acquire; come to; charge; put on; assume; wreak; (*v.i.ir*) to set; congeal; curdle; freeze; catch; take root, strike; take, catch on; bear (*to right, left*).*~ le large*, to sail out to sea. *à tout ~*, all in all. *se ~*, to catch; congeal; cling; clasp. *s'en ~ à*, to blame. *s'y ~*, to set about it. **preneur, euse** (prənœːr, øːz) *n*, taker; captor; buyer; lessee.

prénom (prenɔ̃) *m*, first name, Christian n.

préoccupation (preɔkypasjɔ̃) *f*, preoccupation. **préoccuper** (pe) *v.t*, to preoccupy.

préopinant (preɔpinɑ̃) *m*, previous speaker.

préparateur, trice (preparatœːr, tris) *n*, tutor, coach; assistant. **préparatis** (tif) *m.pl*, preparations. **préparation** (sjɔ̃) *f*, preparation. ~ *automatisée*, process automation (*data processing*). **préparatoire** (twaːr) *a*, preparatory. **préparer** (re) *v.t*, to prepare, make ready; lay (*fire*); coach (*pupil*); read for (*exam*). se ~, to prepare, get ready; brew (*storm*).

prépondérance (prepɔ̃derɑ̃ːs) *f*, preponderance. **prépondérant, e** (rɑ̃, ɑ̃ːt) *a*, preponderant; casting (*vote*).

préposé, e (prepoze) *n*, servant; officer; official; clerk. **préposer** (ze) *v.t*, to appoint.

préposition (prepozisjɔ̃) *f*, preposition.

prérogative (prerɔgatiːv) *f*, prerogative; privilege.

près (prɛ) *ad. & pr*, near; by; close; to. *à . . . ~*, save on, save in, except for; to a; within. *à peu ~*, nearly, about, pretty much.

présage (prezaːʒ) *m*, presage, omen, portent, foreboding, premonition. **présager** (zaʒe) *v.t*, to presage, portend, [fore]bode; augur.

pré-salé (presale) *m*, salt-meadow sheep; salt-meadow mutton.

presbyte (prɛzbit) *n. & att*, far-sighted (person).

presbytère (prɛzbitɛːr) *m*, presbytery; rectory, vicarage, parsonage. **presbytérien, ne** (terjɛ̃, ɛn) *n. & att*, Presbyterian.

prescience (presjɑ̃ːs) *f*, prescience, foreknowledge.

prescription (prɛskripsjɔ̃) *f*, prescription; bar of the statute of limitations; directions. **prescrire** (skriːr) *v.t.ir*, to prescribe, ordain. se ~, to be statute barred.

préséance (preseɑ̃ːs) *f*, precedence (*in rank*).

présence (prezɑ̃ːs) *f*, presence; attendance; sight. **présent, e** (zɑ̃, ɑ̃ːt) *a*, present; this (*letter, etc*.). ¶ *m*, present; gift. *à ~*, now. **présentable** (zɑ̃tabl) *a*, presentable. **présentation** (sjɔ̃) *f*, presentation; introduction. **présentement** (zɑ̃tmɑ̃) *ad*, at present, now; with immediate possession (*house*). **présenter** (te) *v.t*, to present; offer; pay (*respects*); produce, show; introduce. se ~, to sit for an exam, go for an interview, etc.

préservatif (prezɛrvatif) *m. & a*, preservative, preventive; contraceptive. **préservation** (sjɔ̃) *f*, preservation. **préserver** (ve) *v.t*, to preserve, keep.

présidence (prezidɑ̃ːs) *f*, presidency; chairmanship. **président, e** (dɑ̃, ɑ̃ːt) *n*, president; chairman; presiding judge. ~ *du conseil* [*des ministres*], premier. **présidentiel, le** (dɑ̃sjɛl) *a*, presidential. **les présidentielles**, *f.pl*, presidential elections. **présider** [à] (de) *v.t. & i*, to preside at, over; superintend.

présomptif, ive (prezɔ̃ptif, iːv) *a*, presumptive; (*heir*) apparent. **présomption** (sjɔ̃) *f*, presumption. **présomptueux, euse**† (tɥø, øːz) *a*, presumptuous.

presque (prɛsk) *ad*, almost, nearly, all but; scarcely, hardly (*ever*). **presqu'île** (kil) *f*, peninsula.

pressant, e (presɑ̃, ɑ̃ːt) *a*, pressing, urgent. **presse** (prɛs) *f*, press; clamp, cramp; squeezer; crowd, throng; pressure, congestion; hurry; newspapers, the press. *attaché de ~*, press agent. **presse-citron**, *m*, lemon squeezer. **presse-purée**, *m*, potato masher.

pressentiment (presɑ̃timɑ̃) *m*, presentiment, foreboding, misgiving. **pressentir** (tiːr) *v.t.ir*, to have a presentiment of; sound (*pers*.).

presse-papiers (prɛspapje) *m*, paperweight. **presser** (se) *v.t*, to press; squeeze; clasp; ply; hurry, push. se ~, to press, crowd, throng; hurry. **pression** (sjɔ̃) *f*, pressure. *bière à la ~*, draft beer. **pressoir** (swaːr) *m*, press (*wine, etc*.). **pressurer** (syre) *v.t*, to press (*grapes, etc*.); grind (*fig*.).

prestance (prɛstɑ̃ːs) *f*, presence, bearing, portliness.

prestation (prɛstasjɔ̃) *f*, provision; taking (*oath*).

preste† (prɛst) *a*, quick, nimble. **prestesse** (tɛs) *f*, quickness.

prestidigitateur (prɛstidiʒitatœːr) *m*, conjurer, juggler. **prestidigitation** (sjɔ̃) *f*, conjuring, sleight-of-hand, legerdemain.

prestige (prɛstiːʒ) *m*, marvel, magic, glamour; prestige. **prestigieux, euse** (tiʒjø, øːz) *a*, marvelous; influential.

présumer (prezyme) *v.t. & abs*, to presume, suppose.

présupposer (presypoze) *v.t*, to presuppose, take for granted.

présure (prezyːr) *f*, rennet.

prêt, e (prɛ, ɛːt) *a*, ready, prepared, game.

prêt (prɛ) *m*, loan; advance.

prêt-à-manger (prɛtamɑ̃ʒe) *m. & a*, fast food.

prêt-à-monter (prɛtamɔ̃te), *m*, do-it-yourself kit.

prêt-à-porter (prɛtaporte) *m*, ready-to-wear (*mass-produced garments*).

prêt-bail (prɛbaj) *m*, lend-lease.

prétendant, e (pretɑ̃dɑ̃, ɑ̃ːt) *n*, applicant; claimant; pretender; (*m.*) suitor, wooer. **prétendre** (tɑ̃ːdr) *v.t. & i*, to claim, require, pretend; assert; contend; aspire. **prétendu, e** (tɑ̃dy) *p.a*, alleged; would-be; so-called. ¶ *n*, intended (*in marriage*).

prête-nom (prɛtnɔ̃) *m*, dummy (*pers.*).

pretentaine (courir la) (prətɑ̃tɛn), to gad about.

prétentieux, euse (pretɑ̃sjø, øːz) *a*, pretentious. **prétention** (sjɔ̃) *f*, claim, pretension.

prêter (prɛte) *v.t*, to lend; give; take (*oath*); attribute. ~ *serment*, to take oath, swear.

prétérit (preterit) *m*, preterite.

prêteur, euse (pretœːr, øːz) *n*, lender. ~ *sur gages*, money lender; pawnbroker.

prétexte (pretɛkst) *m*, pretext, pretense, plea, excuse. **prétexter** (te) *v.t*, to plead.

prêtre (prɛːtr) *m*, priest. **prêtresse** (prɛtrɛs) *f*, priestess. **prêtrise** (triːz) *f*, priesthood, [holy] orders.

preuve (prœːv) *f*, proof; evidence; token. ~ *par l'absurde*, reductio ad absurdum. ~ *par présomption*, circumstantial evidence.

preux (prø) *a.m*, doughty, valiant.

prévaloir (prevalwaːr) *v.i.ir*, to prevail. **se ~ de**, to presume [up]on.

prévaricateur, trice (prevarikatœːr, tris) *n*, unjust judge; defaulter. **prévarication** (sjɔ̃) *f*, breach of trust, default. **prévariquer** (ke) *v.i*, to fail in one's duty; betray one's trust.

prévenance (prevnɑ̃ːs) *f*, [kind] attention. **prévenant, e** (vnɑ̃, ɑ̃ːt) *a*, attentive, kind, considerate, thoughtful; prepossessing. **prévenir** (vniːr) *v.t.ir*, to forestall, prevent; ward off; prepossess; prejudice, bias; [fore]warn, inform. **prévention** (vɑ̃sjɔ̃) *f*, prepossession, prejudice; imprisonment on suspicion, preventive arrest. **prévenu, e** (vny) *n*, accused, prisoner. **prévenu, a**, prejudiced; warned; accused.

prévision (previzjɔ̃) *f*, prevision, forecast, expectation. **prévoir** (vwaːr) *v.t. & abs. ir*, to foresee; forecast; provide for.

prévôt (prevo) *m*, provost.

prévoyance (prevwajɑ̃ːs) *f*, foresight, forethought; precaution. ~ *sociale*, state insurance. **prévoyant, e** (jɑ̃, ɑ̃ːt) *a*, provident; farsighted.

prie-Dieu (pridjø), *m*, prayer stool. **prier** (e) *v.t*, to pray (to); beg, ask, request, beseech, entreat; invite. *je vous en prie*, you're welcome, don't mention it. **prière** (ɛːr) *f*, prayer; request, entreaty. ~ *de . . .*, please . . . **prieur, e** (œːr) *n*, prior, ess. **prieuré** (œre) *m*, priory.

primage (primaːʒ) *m*, primage (*Ship.*).

primaire (primɛːr) *a*, primary; elementary (*Sch.*).

primat (prima) *m*, primate. **primatie** (si) *f*, primacy. **primauté**

(mote) *f*, primacy; lead (*cards, etc.*).

prime (prim) *a*, first; earliest. ¶ *f*, premium; bounty, bonus; gift (*for coupons*); option (*Stk Ex.*). **primé, e** (me) *p.a*, bounty-fed; prize (*bull, etc.*). **primer** (me) *v.t*, to surpass; override; award a prize to; (*v.i.*) to excel; rank before.

primesautier, ère (primsotje, εːr) *a*, impulsive.

primeur (primœːr) *f*, freshness, newness; early vegetable, early fruit.

primevère (primvεːr) *f*, primrose. ~ *des champs*, cowslip.

primitif, ive† (primitif, iːv) *a*, primitive, original; primeval; pristine; primary; crude.

primo (primo) *ad*, first[ly].

primogéniture (primɔʒenityːr) *f*, primogeniture.

primordial, e† (primɔrdjal) *a*, primordial, primary; primeval.

prince (prɛ̃ːs) *m*, prince. *bon ~*, a good fellow.

princeps (prɛ̃sεps) *a.inv*, first (*edition*).

princesse (prɛ̃sεs) *f*, princess. **princier, ère** (sje, εːr) *a*, princely.

principal, e† (prɛ̃sipal) *a*, principal, chief, head, main; staple (*product*); major (*planet*); senior. ¶ *m*, principal; chief; headmaster; main thing.

principauté (prɛ̃sipote) *f*, principality.

principe (prɛ̃sip) *m*, principle; beginning.

printanier, ère (prɛ̃tanje, εːr) *a*, vernal, spring (*att.*). **printemps** (tɑ̃) *m*, spring[time].

priorité (priɔrite) *f*, priority, precedence.

pris, p.p, prendre.

prise (priːz) *f*, taking; catch; hold, purchase, grip; setting (*cement*); prize (*Naut.*); pinch (*snuff*); dose; electric plug. ~ *d'eau*, intake of water, tapping; hydrant. ~ *de bec*, altercation, set-to. ~ *de courant*, wall socket. ~ *de corps*, arrest. ~ *de sang*, blood test. ~ *de tête à terre*, nelson (*wrestling*). ~ *de vues*, filming, shooting (*cin-*

ema, TV). *être aux ~s avec*, to struggle with.

prisée (prize) *f*, valuation. **priser** (ze) *v.t*, to appraise, value; prize; snuff up; (*abs.*) to take snuff. **priseur** (zœːr) *m*, appraiser; snuff taker.

prismatique (prismatik) *a*, prismatic. **prisme** (prism) *m*, prism.

prison (prizɔ̃) *m*, prison, jail; cells; imprisonment (*term*). **prisonnier, ère** (zɔnje, εːr) *n*, prisoner.

privation (privasjɔ̃) *f*, deprivation, loss; privation, hardship.

privatisation (privatizasjɔ̃) *f*, denationalization (*industry, public utility, etc.*).

privauté (privote) *f*, familiarity, liberty.

privé†, e (prive) *a*, private. ¶ *m*, privy, water closet.

priver (prive) *v.t*, to deprive, bereave.

privilège (privilεːʒ) *m*, privilege, prerogative; lien, charge. **privilégié, e** (leʒje) *p.a*, privileged; preferential. **privilégier** (ʒje) *v.t*, to privilege; charter.

prix (pri) *m*, price; value, worth, cost; consideration [money]; terms; rate; charge; fare; prize; stakes (*turf*). ~ *affiché*, posted price. ~ *courant*, market p. ~ *homologué*, established p. ~ *d'excellence*, class prize. ~ *de revient* (rəvjε̃), ~ *coûtant* (kutɑ̃), cost [price]. ~ *de sagesse*, good-conduct prize.

probabilité (prɔbabilite) *f*, probability, likelihood. **probable†** (bl) *a*, probable, likely.

probant, e (prɔbɑ̃, ɑ̃ːt) *a*, convincing, cogent. **probation** (basjɔ̃) *f*, probation (*Eccl.*). **probe** (prɔb) *a*, honest, upright. **probité** (bite) *f*, probity, honesty.

problématique (prɔblematik) *a*, problematic(al). **problème** (blεm) *m*, problem; puzzle; poser, teaser.

proboscide (prɔbɔsid) *f*, proboscis.

procédé (prɔsede) *m*, proceeding, dealing; behavior; process; tip

(*Bil. cue*). **procéder** (de) *v.i*, to proceed. ~ *à l'impression*, to go to press. **procédure** (dy₁r) *f*, procedure; proceedings. **procès** (sɛ) (*law*) *m*, proceedings, action, case. ~ *civil*, [*law*]suit. ~ *criminel*, [criminal] trial. **processif, ive** (sɛsif, i₁v) *a*, litigious. **procession** (sjɔ̃) *f*, procession. **processus** (sy₁s) *m*, process, course. **procès-verbal**, *m*, report; minutes.

prochain, e (prɔʃɛ̃, ɛn) *a*, nearest; next; near; proximate; forthcoming; coming; neighboring. ¶ *m*, neighbor, fellow creature. **prochainement** (ʃɛnmɑ̃) *a*, shortly, soon. **proche** (prɔʃ) *ad*, near, close. ¶ *a*, near, at hand. ~ *Orient*, Near East. ~*s* [*parents*] *m.pl*, near relations, next of kin.

proclamation (prɔklamasjɔ̃) *f*, proclamation. **proclamer** (me) *v.t*, to proclaim, publish; declare.

procrastination (prɔkrastinasjɔ̃) *f*, procrastination.

procréer (prɔkree) *v.t*, to procreate.

procuration (prɔkyrasjɔ̃) *f*, procuration, proxy, power of attorney. **procurer** (re) *v.t*, to procure, obtain, get. **procureur** (rœ₁r) *m*, proxy; attorney.

prodigalement (prɔdigalmɑ̃) *a*, lavishly. **prodigalité** (lite) *f*, prodigality, lavishness; wastefulness; (*pl.*) extravagance.

prodige (prɔdi₁ʒ) *m*, prodigy, wonder. **prodigieux, euse†** (di₃jø, ø₁z) *a*, prodigious, stupendous.

prodigue (prɔdig) *a*, prodigal, lavish, unsparing, profuse; wasteful. ¶ *n*, prodigal, spendthrift. **prodiguer** (ge) *v.t*, to lavish; squander.

prodrome (prɔdro₁m) *m*, premonitory symptom.

producteur, trice (prɔdyktœ₁r, tris) *n*, producer. ¶ ~ *& productif, ive* (tif, i₁v) *a*, producing, productive, bearing. **production** (sjɔ̃) *f*, production, output, yield; product. **produire** (dɥi₁r) *v.t.ir*, to produce, bring forth, bear, yield; show. ~ *dans le monde*, to introduce into society, bring

out. se ~, to occur, happen. **produit** (dɥi) *m*, product, produce, proceeds, yield; takings, receipts. ~ *pharmaceutique*, patent medicine.

proéminent, e (prɔeminɑ̃, ɑ̃₁t) *a*, prominent.

profanation (prɔfanasjɔ̃) *f*, profanation. **profane** (fan) *a*, profane; secular; unconsecrated (*ground*). ¶ *n*, layman; outsider; (the) profane. **profaner** (ne) *v.t*, to profane, desecrate.

proférer (prɔfere) *v.t*, to utter.

profès, esse (prɔfɛ, ɛs) *a*, professed. **professer** (se) *v.t*, to profess; teach. **professeur** (sœ₁r) *m*, professor; teacher; master, mistress; lecturer; instructor. **profession** (sjɔ̃) *f*, profession; occupation; calling, business, trade. **professionnel, le** (ɔnɛl) *a. & n*, professional. **professorat** (sɔra) *m*, professorship.

profil (prɔfil) *m*, profile, side face; contour, outline, section. ~ *de l'horizon*, skyline. **profiler** (le) *v.t*, to profile, streamline.

profit (prɔfi) *m*, profit, benefit. **profitable** (tabl) *a*, profitable. **profiter** (te) *v.i*, to benefit, profit; avail oneself (*de* = of); thrive. **profiteur, euse** (tœ₁r, ø₁z) *n*, profiteer.

profond, e (prɔfɔ̃, ɔ̃₁d) *a*, deep, profound; low (*bow*); sound (*sleep*). **profondément** (demɑ̃) *ad*, deeply, etc. **profondeur** (dœ₁r) *f*, depth; profundity.

profus, e (prɔfy, y₁z) *a*, profuse (*perspiration*). **profusément** (fyzemɑ̃) *ad*, profusely, lavishly. **profusion** (zjɔ̃) *f*, profusion, lavishness.

progéniture (prɔʒenity₁r) *f*, progeny, offspring.

progiciel (prɔʒisjl) *m*, package (*computers*).

prognathe (prɔgnat) *a*, prognathous.

programmathèque (prɔgramatek) *f*, program library (*computers*).

programmation (prɔgramasjɔ̃) *f*, programming (*computers, data processing, cinemas*).

programme (prɔgram) *m*, program; syllabus; platform (*Pol.*). ~ *d'études*, curriculum. ~ *des courses*, race card. ~ *d'arrière-plan, de coulisse,* background program (*computers*). ~ *en boîte,* computer software program. *feuilles de* ~, computer instruction manual. **programmer** (e) *v.i,* to program (*computers*). **programmeur, euse** (œːr, øz) *n,* programmer (*computers*).

progrès (prɔgrɛ) *m, oft. pl,* progress, [head]way. **progresser** (grɛse) *v.i,* to progress. **progressif, ive†** (sif, iːv) *a,* progressive, forward. **progression** (sjɔ̃) *f,* progression.

prohiber (prɔibe) *v.t,* to prohibit, forbid. **prohibitif, ive** (bitif, iːv) *a,* prohibitory; prohibitive. **prohibition** (sjɔ̃) *f,* prohibition. **prohibitionniste** (ɔnist) *m,* prohibitionist.

proie (prwa) *f,* prey; quarry.

projecteur (prɔʒɛktœːr) *m,* projector; searchlight; floodlight. ~ *orientable* (ɔrjɑ̃tabl), spotlight. **projectile** (til) *a. & m,* projectile, missile. **projection** (sjɔ̃) *f,* projection. **projet** (ʒɛ) *m,* project, scheme, plan; draft. ~ *de loi,* bill, measure. **projeter** (ʒte) *v.t,* to project, throw, cast; plan, contemplate.

prolétaire (prɔletɛːr) *m,* proletarian. **prolétariat** (tarja) *m,* proletariat. **prolétarien, ne** (rjɛ̃, ɛn) *a,* proletarian.

proliférer (prɔlifere) *v.t. & i,* to proliferate, spread.

prolifique (prɔlifik) *a,* prolific.

prolixe (prɔliks) *a,* prolix, long-winded.

prologue (prɔlɔg) *m,* prologue.

prolongation (prɔlɔ̃gasjɔ̃) *f. &* **prolongement** (lɔ̃ʒmɑ̃) *m,* prolongation; extension. **prolonge** (lɔ̃ːʒ) *f,* ammunition wagon. **prolonger** (lɔ̃ʒe) *v.t,* to prolong, protract, extend, lengthen.

promenade (prɔmnad) *f,* walking; walk, stroll; ride; drive; trip, outing, ramble; promenade. *sur la* ~ [*de la mer*], on the [sea] front. ~ *en bateau,* row; sail. ~ *militaire,* route march. **promener**

(mne) *v.t,* to take for a walk; pass, run, cast. ~ *par,* ~ *dans,* to show round. **se**~, to [go for a] walk, stroll. *allez vous* ~*!* be off with you! **promeneur, euse** (mnœːr, øːz) *n,* walker. **promenoir** (mnwaːr) *m,* promenade, walk; lounge.

promesse (prɔmɛs) *f,* promise. **prometteur, euse** (tœːr, øːz) *a,* promising. **promettre** (mɛtr) *v.t. & abs. ir,* to promise. *terre promise* (miːz), *terre de promission* (misjɔ̃), promised land, land of promise. **se** ~, to resolve.

promis (prɔmi) *a,* promised; intended. ¶ *m,* fiancé.

promiscuité (prɔmiskɥite) *f,* promiscuity.

promontoire (prɔmɔ̃twaːr) *m,* promontory.

promoteur, trice (prɔmɔtœːr, tris) *n,* promoter. **promotion** (sjɔ̃) *f,* promotion, preferment. ~ *des ventes,* sales promotion. **promotionel, le** (sjɔnɛl) *a,* relating to promotion. *vente* ~, special sale offer. **promouvoir** (muvwaːr) *v.t.ir,* to promote, prefer.

prompt e† (prɔ̃, ɔ̃ːt) *a,* prompt, ready, quick. **promptitude** (prɔ̃tityd) *f,* promptitude, dispatch.

promu, e (prɔmy) *a,* decorated, promoted. ¶ *n,* person who has been decorated or promoted.

promulguer (prɔmylge) *v.t,* to promulgate.

prône (proːn) *m,* sermon; homily. **prôner** (prone) *v.t,* to extoll; puff.

pronom (prɔnɔ̃) *m,* pronoun. **pronominal, e†** (nɔminal) *a,* pronominal.

prononcer (prɔnɔ̃se) *v.t. & abs,* to pronounce; utter; speak; mention; deliver (*speech*); pass (*sentence*). **se** ~, to declare oneself; be pronounced (*letter, syllable*). **prononciation** (sjasjɔ̃) *f,* delivery; passing; pronunciation.

pronostic (prɔnɔstik) *m,* prognostic[ation], forecast; selection (*betting*); omen. **pronostiquer** (ke) *v.t,* to prognosticate, forecast.

propagande (prɔpagɑ̃ːd) *f*, propaganda; advertising.

propager (prɔpaʒe) *v.t*, to propagate, spread.

propension (prɔpɑ̃sjɔ̃) *f*, propensity.

prophète, étesse (prɔfɛt, etɛs) *n*, prophet, ess, seer. **prophétie** (fesi) *f*, prophecy. **prophétique†** (tik) *a*, prophetic(al). **prophétiser** (ze) *v.t*, to prophesy.

propice (prɔpis) *a*, propitious, auspicious, lucky.

propitiation (prɔpisjasjɔ̃) *f*, propitiation. **propitiatoire** (twaːr) *m*, mercy seat.

proportion (prɔpɔrsjɔ̃) *f*, proportion, ratio, percentage. **proportionnel, le†** (ɔnɛl) *a*, proportional. **proportionner** (ɔne) *v.t*, to proportion.

propos (prɔpo) *m*, purpose; subject, matter; remark, (*pl.*) talk. ~ *de couloir, pl*, lobbying. **à ~**, *a. & ad*, to the point, apropos, opportune(ly); seasonable, -bly; apposite(ly); pertinent(ly); apt-(ly); by the way. **à ~ de**, *pr*, with regard to, about. **à tout ~**, at every turn. **de ~ délibéré**, deliberately, purposely. **proposer** (ze) *v.t*, to propose; move; propound; offer; put forward; recommend. **se ~**, to offer oneself; purpose, mean. **proposition** (zisjɔ̃) *f*, proposal, proposition; motion; clause (*Gram.*).

propre† (prɔpr) *a*, clean, neat; proper; peculiar; inherent; literal; own; appropriate, fit, suited. *un ~ à rien*, a good-for-nothing, a ne'er-do-well. *c'est du ~*, a nice thing, that is (*ironic*). ¶ *m*, characteristic, property; literal sense (*word*). **propret, te** (prɛ, ɛt) *a*, neat, tidy. **propreté** (prəte) *f*, cleanliness; neatness, tidiness.

propriétaire (prɔprietɛːr) *n*, proprietor, owner; landlord, -lady. **propriété** (te) *f*, ownership; property, estate, holding; rights; propriety. ~ *littéraire*], copyright.

propulseur (prɔpylsœːr) *m*, propeller; engine, jet, thruster. ~ *auxiliaire*, booster (*rocket, spacecraft*). **propulsion** (sjɔ̃) *f*, propulsion.

prorata (prɔrata) *m: au ~ de*, *pr*, in proportion to, pro rata to.

proroger (prɔrɔʒe) *v.t*, to prorogue; extend.

prosaïque† (prɔzaik) *a*, prosaic.

prosateur (prɔzatœːr) *m*, prose writer.

proscrire (prɔskriːr) *v.t.ir*, to proscribe, outlaw, banish; do away with. **proscrit, e** (skri, it) *n*, outlaw.

prose (proːz) *f*, prose.

prosélyte (prɔzelit) *n*, proselyte.

prosodie (prɔzɔdi) *f*, prosody.

prospecter (prɔspɛkte) *v.t*, to prospect (*Min.*). **prospecteur** (tœːr) *m*, prospector. **prospection** (sjɔ̃) *f*, prospecting.

prospectus (prɔspɛktyːs) *m*, prospectus; handbill.

prospère (prɔspɛːr) *a*, prosperous, thriving; favorable, kind. **prospérer** (pere) *v.i*, to prosper, thrive. **prospérité** (rite) *f*, prosperity.

prostate (prɔstat) *f*, prostate [gland].

prosternation (prɔstɛrnasjɔ̃) *f*, prostration; (*pl.*) bowing & scraping. **prosterné, e** (ne) *p.a*, prostrate, prone. **prosterner** (ne) *v.t*, to prostrate. **se ~**, to bow down (*before, etc.*)

prostituer (prɔstitɥe) *v.t*, to prostitute.

prostration (prɔstrasjɔ̃) *f*, prostration, break down. **prostré, e** (tre) *a*, prostrate[d].

protagoniste (prɔtagɔnist) *m*, protagonist.

protecteur, trice (prɔtɛktœːr, tris) *n*, protector; patron, ess; (*m.*) protector, shield, guard. ¶ *a*, protective; patronizing. **protection** (sjɔ̃) *f*, protection; patronage. **protectionniste** (ɔnist) *m. & att*, protectionist. **protectorat** (tɔra) *m*, protectorate. **protégé, e** (teʒe) *n*, protégé, e. **protéger** (ʒe) *v.t*, to protect, shield, guard; patronize.

protestant, e (prɔtɛstɑ̃, ɑ̃ːt) *n. & a*, Protestant. **protestation** (tasjɔ̃) *f*, protest[ation]. **protester** (te) *v.t. & i*, to protest; vow. **protêt** (tɛ) *m*, protest (*bill of exchange*).

protocole (protokɔl) *m*, proto-col; etiquette.

prototype (prototip) *m*, proto-type.

protubérance (protyberã:s) *f*, protuberance.

proue (pru) *f*, prow; nose (*Avn.*).

prouesse (pruɛs) *f*, prowess, valor; feat.

prouver (pruve) *v.t*, to prove; show.

provenance (provnã:s) *f*, origin, provenance; (*s. & pl.*) produce.

provende (provã:d) *f*, provender, fodder.

provenir (provni:r) *v.i.ir*, to pro-ceed, come, arise.

proverbe (provɛrb) *m*, proverb. **proverbial, e†** (bjal) *a*, proverb-ial.

providence (providã:s) *f*, provi-dence; godsend; good angel. **providentiel, le†** (dãsjɛl) *a*, provi-dential.

province (provɛ̃:s) *f*, province; provinces, country. **provincial, e** (vɛ̃sjal) *a*, provincial, country (*att.*).

proviseur (provizœ:r) *m*, head-master. **provision** (zjɔ̃) *f*, provi-sion, store, stock, supply; de-posit; funds; cover, margin (*Fin.*); consideration (*law*); re-tainer (*law*). **~s de bouche**, pro-visions, food. **~s de guerre**, mu-nitions. **provisionnel, le** (ɔnɛl) *a*, provisional. **provisoire†** (zwa:r) *a*, provisional, interim, pro tem; nisi (*decree*). **provisorat** (zɔra) *m*, headmastership.

provoquer (provoke) *v.t*, to pro-voke; challenge; incite, instigate; induce. **provocateur** (katœ:r) *m*, provoker; instigator; aggressor. **agent ~**, professional agitator. **provocation** (kasjɔ̃) *f*, provoca-tion.

proxénète (proksenɛt) *n*, pro-curer, procuress.

proximité (proksimite) *f*, prox-imity, nearness, propinquity, vi-cinity. **~ du sang**, near relation-ship.

prude (pryd) *a*, prudish. ¶ *f*, prude.

prudemment (prydamã) *ad*,

prudently. **prudence** (dã:s) *f*, prudence, discretion; wisdom. **prudent, e** (dã, ã:t) *a*, prudent.

pruderie (prydri) *f*, prudery, prudishness.

prud'homme (prydɔm) *m*, man of experience and integrity; mem-ber of conciliation board. **prud'-hommesque** (mɛsk) *a*, pompous & sententiously dull.

prune (pryn) *f*, plum. **pruneau** (no) *m*, prune; bullet; bruise; black eye. **prunelaie** (nlɛ) *f*, plum or-chard. **prunelle** (nɛl) *f*, sloe; pupil, apple (*eye*). [*liqueur de*] **~**, sloe gin. **prunellier** (lje) *m*, blackthorn, sloe tree. **prunier** (nje) *m*, plum [tree]. **~ de damas**, damson [tree].

prurit (pryrit) *m*, pruritus, itch-ing.

Prusse (la) (prys), Prussia. **prus-sien, ne** (sjɛ̃, ɛn) *a*. & **P~**, *n*, Prussian. **prussique** (sik) *a*, prussic.

psalmiste (psalmist) *m*, psalmist. **psalmodie** (mɔdi) *f*, psalmody; singsong. **psalmodier** (dje) *v.i. & t*, to intone, chant; drone. **psaume** (pso:m) *m*, psalm. **psau-tier** (psotje) *m*, psalter.

pseudonyme (psødɔnim) *m*, pseudonym.

psychanalyse (psikanali:z) *f*, psychoanalysis. **psyché** (ʃe) *f*, cheval glass, full-length mirror. **psychiatre** (kjɑ:tr) *m*, psychia-trist. **psychique** (ʃik) *a*, psychic-(al). **psychologie** (kɔlɔʒi) *f*, psychology. **psychologique** (ʒik) *a*, psychological. **psychologue** (lɔg) *m*, psychologist. **psychose** (ko:z) *f*, psychosis. **~ trauma-tique** (tromatik), shell shock.

ptomaïne (ptɔmain) *f*, ptomaine.

puant, e (pyã, ã:t) *a*, stinking; foul. **puanteur** (ãtœ:r) *f*, stink, stench.

puberté (pybɛrte) *f*, puberty.

public, ique† (pyblik) *a*, public; common; national (*debt*); civil (*service*). ¶ *m*, public. **publicain** (kɛ̃) *m*, publican (*Bible*); ex-tortioner. **publication** (kasjɔ̃) *f*, publication; publishing, issue.

publiciste (sist) *m*, publicist; advertising man. **publicité** (te) *f*, publicity, advertising. ~*sur les nuages*, sky writing. **publier** (e) *v.t*, to publish; proclaim; issue.

puce (pys) *f*, flea; chip (*computers*). *secouer les* ~*s*, to tell someone off. ¶ *a*, puce.

pucelle (pysεl) *f*, maid[en], virgin.

puceron (pysrɔ̃) *m*, plant louse.

pudding (pudiŋ) *m*, pudding.

puddler (pydle) *v.t*, to puddle (*iron*).

pudeur (pydœ:r) *f*, modesty, decency, shame. **pudibond, e** (dibɔ̃, ɔ̃:d) *a*, prudish. **pudique†** (dik) *a*, chaste, modest.

puer (pɥe) *v.i*, to stink, smell; (*v.t.*) to stink of, smell of.

puériculture (pɥerikylty:r) *f*, rearing of children. ~ *sociale*, child welfare. **puéril, e†** (ril) *a*, puerile, childish. **puérilité** (lite) *f*, puerility, childishness.

pugilat (pyʒila) *m*, pugilism; set-to. **pugiliste** (list) *m*, pugilist.

pugnace (pygnas) *a*, pugnacious.

puîné, e (pɥine) *a. & n*, younger (brother, sister).

puis (pɥi) *ad*, then, afterwards, next; besides.

puisard (pɥiza:r) *m*, sink, sump. **puisatier** (zatje) *m*, well-digger. **puiser** (ze) *v.t. & i*, to draw, derive.

puisque, puisqu' (pɥisk[ə]) *c*, since, as, seeing that.

puissamment (pɥisamɑ̃) *ad*, powerfully, mightily. **puissance** (sɑ̃:s) *f*, power; might; strength, force; authority, sway, ~ *lumineuse en bougies*, candlepower. **puissant, e** (sɑ̃, ɑ̃:t) *a*, powerful; mighty; strong; potent; weighty. *les puissants*, the mighty ones.

puits (pɥi) *m*, well, hole; shaft (*Min.*); cockpit (*Avn.*); fount (*fig.*).

pull (pul) *m*, pullover, sweater. **pull-over** (ɔvœ:r) *m*, pullover, sweater.

pulluler (pyllyle) *v.i*, to pullulate, swarm.

pulmonaire (pylmɔnε:r) *a*, pulmonary.

pulpe (pylp) *f*, pulp. **pulper** (pe) *v.t*, to pulp.

pulsation (pylsasjɔ̃) *f*, pulsation, throb[bing].

pulvériser (pylverize) *v.t*, to pulverize, powder; spray. **pulvérulent, e** (rylɑ̃, ɑ̃:t) *a*, powdery.

puma (pyma) *m*, puma, cougar.

punais, e (pynε, ε:z) *a*, foul-breathed.

punaise (pynε:z) *f*, bug; thumbtack.

punch (pɔ̃:ʃ) *m*, punch (*drink*).

punir (pyni:r) *v.t*, to punish; avenge. **punissable** (nisabl) *a*, punishable. **punition** (sjɔ̃) *f*, punishment.

pupille (pypil) *n*, ward. ¶ *f*, pupil (*eye*).

pupitre (pypitr) *m*, desk; stand (*music*); console (*TV, computers*). ~ *à clavier*, keyboard console. ~ *de mélange*, mixing c, audio-mixer, switcher. ~ *de régie*, control c. **pupitreur** (trœ:r) console operator.

pur, e† (py:r) *a*, pure; unalloyed; plain; mere; sheer; clear; neat (*unwatered*).

purée (pyre) *f*, mash; [thick] soup. ~ *de pommes de terre, de navets*, mashed potatoes, turnips.

pureté (pyrte) *f*, purity; clearness (*sky*).

purgatif, ive (pyrgatif, i:v) *a. & m*, purgative. **purgation** (sjɔ̃) *f*, purging; purge. **purgatoire** (twa:r) *m*, purgatory. **purger** (ʒe) *v.t*, to purge, cleanse, clear; redeem (*mortgage*). ~ *une peine*, to serve a prison sentence.

purifier (pyrifje) *v.t*, to purify, cleanse. **puriste** (rist) *n*, purist.

purin (pyrɛ̃) *m*, liquid manure.

puritain, e (pyritɛ̃, εn) *n*, Puritan. ¶ *a*, Puritan; puritanic(al).

purpurin, e (pyrpyrɛ̃, in) *a*, purplish.

purulent, e (pyrylɑ̃, ɑ̃:t) *a*, purulent, mattery. **pus** (py) *m*, pus, matter.

pusillanime (pyzillanim) *a*, pusillanimous.

pustule (pystyl) *f*, pustule, pimple.

putain (pytɛ̃) *f*, whore, prostitute; slut.

putatif, ive (pytatif, i:v) *a*, putative, reputed.

putois (pytwa) *m*, polecat.

putréfaction (pytrefaksjɔ̃) *f*, putrefaction. **putréfier** (fje) *v.t*, to putrefy. **putride** (trid) *a*, putrid.

puy (pɥi) *m*, mountain, peak.

pygmée (pigme) *m*, pygmy.

pyjama (piʒama) *m*, pajamas.

pylône (pilo:n) *m*, pylon, tower.

pyorrhée (pyɔre) *f*, pyorrhea.

pyramide (piramid) *f*, pyramid. **Pyrénées (les)** (pirene) *f.pl*, the Pyrenees.

pyrite (pirit) *f*, pyrites.

pyrogravure (pirɔgravy:r) *f*, poker work.

pyrotechnie (pirɔtɛkni) *f*, pyrotechnics.

python (pitɔ̃) *m*, python.

Q

quadrangulaire (kwadrãgylɛ:r) *a*, quadrangular.

quadrant (kwadrã) *m*, quadrant (*Math.*).

quadrupède (kwadrypɛd) *a*, quadruped (al), four-footed. ¶ *m*, quadruped.

quadruple (kwadrypl) *a. & m*, quadruple, fourfold. ~ *croche*, *f*, semi- *or* hemi-demisemiquaver.

quai (ke) *m*, quay, wharf; embankment (*river*); platform (*Rly*).

quaiche (kɛʃ) *f*, ketch.

qualifier (kalifje) *v.t*, to qualify; call, style; describe. **qualité** (te) *f*, quality; property; qualification, profession; capacity. ~ *d'amateur*, amateur status.

quand (kã) *c. & ad*, when; [al] though, even if. ~ *même*, all the same, notwithstanding, nevertheless.

quant à (kãta) *pr*, as for, as to, as regards, for. **quant-à-moi, quant-à-soi,** *m*, dignity, reserve, stand-offishness.

quantième (kãtjɛm) *m*, day of the month, date.

quantité (kãtite) *f*, quantity; amount; lots, a lot. ~ *de pluie* [*tombée*], rainfall.

quantum (kwãtɔm) *m*, quantum.

quarantaine (karãtɛn) *f*, [about] forty; quarantine; Lent. *mettre en ~*, to quarantine (*ship*); send (*pers.*) to Coventry. **quarante** (rã:t) *a*, forty. ¶ *m*, forty; 40th. **quarantième** (rãtjɛm) *a. & n*, fortieth.

quart (ka:r) *m*, quarter, fourth [part]; ¼ liter; watch (*Naut.*). ~ *d'heure*, quarter of an hour. ~ *de cercle*, quadrant (*Surv. instrument*). ~ [*de vent*], point [of the compass]. **quarte** (kart) *f*, fourth (*Mus.*).

quarteron, ne (kartərɔ̃, ɔn) *n*, quadroon.

quartier (kartje) *m*, quarter; portion, lump; haunch (*meat*); gammon (*bacon*); ward, district; neighborhood; quarters. ~ *général*, headquarters.

quartz (kwarts) *m*, quartz.

quasi (kazi) *ad*, almost, quasi. ~ *aveugle*, almost blind, purblind. ~ *-délit*, *m*, quasi-delict, technical offense. **Quasimodo** (kazimɔdo) *f*, Low Sunday.

quassia (kwasja) *m*, quassia (*bark*). **quassier** (sje) *m*, quassia (*tree*).

quatorze (katɔrz) *a. & m*, fourteen; 14th. **quatorzième†** (zjɛm) *a. & n*, fourteenth.

quatrain (katrɛ̃) *m*, quatrain.

quatre (katr) *a. & m*, four; 4th. *lac des Q~-Cantons*, Lake of Lucerne. ~ *jumeaux*, quadruplets. *à ~ pattes*, on all fours. ~*-vingt-dix* (trəvɛdi[s]) *a. & m*, ninety. ~ *-vingt-onze* (vɛ̃ɔ:z), 91. ~*-vingt-dixième* (zjɛm) *a. & n*, ninetieth. ~*-vingtième* (tjɛm) *a. & n*, eightieth. ~*-vingts & ~-vingt*, *a. & m*, eighty. ~*-vingt-un* (vɛ̃œ̃), 81. **quatrième†** (triɛm) *a. & n*, fourth.

quatuor (kwatyɔ:r) *m*, quartet.

que, qu' (kə, k) *c. & ad*, that; than; as; whether; how; but, only; lest; let, may. ¶ *pn*, whom; which; that; what. *qu'est-ce que?* (kɛskə) & *qu'est-ce qui* (ki)? what?

quel, le (kɛl) *a*, what; what a;

which; who. ~ *que*, whatever; whoever.

quelconque (kɛlkɔ̃ːk) *a*, any; some; ordinary, mediocre.

quelque (kɛlk[ə]) *a*, some, any; a few, ~ *chose*, *m*, something; anything. ~*fois*, *ad*, sometimes. ~ *part*, *ad*, somewhere.

quelqu'un, quelqu'une (kɛl-kœ̃, kyn) *pn*, somebody, someone, one, anybody, anyone. *quelques-uns, unes* (kəzœ̃, yn) *pl*, some [people], a few.

quémander (kemɑ̃de) *v.i*, to beg; (*v.t.*) to beg for, solicit.

qu'en-dira-t-on (le) (kɑ̃dira-tɔ̃) *m*, what people may say.

quenouille (kənuːj) *f*, distaff; bedpost.

querelle (kərɛl) *f*, quarrel, row. ~ *d'ivrognes*, drunken brawl. **quereller** (le) *v.t*, to quarrel with; scold nag. se ~, to quarrel, wrangle. **querelleur, euse** (lœːr, øːz) *n*, quarreler, wrangler; (*att.*) quarrelsome.

question (kɛstjɔ̃) *f*, question; query; point, matter, issue. ~ *d'intérêt secondaire*, side issue. **questionnaire** (onɛːr) *m*, list of questions. **questionner** (ne) *v.t*, to question.

quête (kɛːt) *f*, quest, search; collection, offertory. **quêter** (kɛte) *v.t*, to seek for; collect (*alms*).

queue (kø) *f*, tail; brush (*fox*); pigtail; stem; stalk; handle, shank; cue (*Bil.*); train; rear; queue, file; penis (*obscene*). ~ *d'aronde* (darɔ̃ːd) *f*, dovetail. ~*-de-morue* (dmɔry) ou ~*-de-pie* (dpi) *f*, [swallow] tails (*dress coat*). en ~, in the rear. *faire* ~, to wait in line. *faire une* ~ *de poisson*, to cut in front of another automobile. *finir en* ~ *de poisson*, to end badly. **queuter** (køte) *v.i*, to push the ball (*Bil.*).

qui (ki) *pn*, who; whom; which; that. ~ *vive?* who goes there?

quiconque (kikɔ̃ːk) *pn*, who[so]-ever.

quiétude (kɥietyd) *f*, quietude.

quignon (kiɲɔ̃) *m*, [c]hunk, hunch.

quille (kiːj) *f*, skittle, ninepin; keel. **quillier** (kije) *m*, skittle alley.

quincaillerie (kɛ̃kajri) *f*, hardware. **quincaillier** (je) *m*, hardware man.

quinconce (kɛ̃kɔ̃ːs) *m*, staggered arrangement.

quinine (kinin) *f*, quinine.

quinquennal, e (kɥɛ̃kɛnnal) *a*, quinquennial; five-year (*plan*).

quinquina (kɛ̃kina) *m*, Peruvian bark.

quintal [métrique] (kɛ̃tal) *m*, [metric] quintal = 100 kilos.

quinte (kɛ̃ːt) *f*, quint; fifth (*Mus.*); caprice, crotchet. ~ [*de toux*], fit of coughing.

quintessence (kɛ̃tɛsɑ̃ːs) *f*, quintessence.

quintette (kɥɛ̃tɛt) *f*, quintet[te].

quinteux, euse (kɛ̃tø, øːz) *a*, crotchety; fitful.

quintuple (kɛ̃typlə) *a*, quintuple, fivefold. ¶ *m*, fivefold.

quinzaine (kɛ̃zɛn) *f*, [about] fifteen; fortnight. **quinze** (kɛ̃ːz) *a. & m*, fifteen; 15th. ~ *jours*, fortnight. **quinzième†** (kɛ̃zjɛm) *a. & n*, fifteenth.

quiproquo (kiprɔko) *m*, mistake, misunderstanding (*mistaking one for another*).

quittance (kitɑ̃ːs) *f*, receipt. **quittancer** (tɑ̃se) *v.t*, to r. **quitte** (kit) *a*, quit, rid, free. ~ *à* ~, *ad*, quits. ~ *ou double*, double or quits. *nous sommes* ~*s*, we're even. **quitter** (te) *v.t. & i*, to leave, quit, vacate; give up; swerve from. *ne quittez pas!* hold on! hold the line! (*Teleph.*). **quitus** (kityːs) *m*, discharge.

qui-vive (kiviːv) *m*, challenge (*sentry's*); qui vive, look-out, alert.

quoi (kwa) *pn. & i*, what; which; that. ~ *qu'il en soit*, be that as it may. *de* ~, something; enough, the wherewithal.

quoique, quoiqu' (kwak[ə]) *c*, [al]though.

quolibet (kɔlibɛ) *m*, gibe; quibble.

quorum (kɔrɔm) *m*, quorum.

quota (kwɔta) *m*, quota. ~ *d'exploitation*, exhibitor's quota. *sondage par* ~, quota sampling.

quote-part (kɔtpaːr) *f*, share, quota.

quotidien, ne (kɔtidjɛ̃, ɛn) *a*, daily; everyday. **[journal] quotidien,** *m*, daily [paper]. **quotidiennement** (ɛnmɑ̃) *ad*, daily.

quotient (kɔsjɑ̃) *m*, quotient.

quotité (kɔtite) *f*, quota, share.

R

rabâchage (rabɑʃaːʒ) *m*, endless repetition. **rabâcher** (baʃe) *v.i*, to repeat over and over. *il rabâche toujours les mêmes choses*, he is always harping on the same string.

rabais (rabɛ) *m*, allowance, rebate. *adjudication au* ~, award to the lowest bidder. **rabaisser** (se) *v.t*, to lower; disparage, belittle.

rabat (raba) *m*, beating (*for game*). **~-joie,** *m*, killjoy. **rabatteur, euse** (tœːr, øːz) *n*, tout; (*m.*) beater. **rabattre** (tr) *v.t.ir*, to beat down, bring d., turn d., press d., lower; bate; take off; beat up (*hunting*). **se** ~, to turn off, change; come down.

rabbin (rabɛ̃) *m*, rabbi.

râble (rɑːbl) *m*, back; saddle (hare). **râblé** (ble) *a*, strong, sturdy, husky.

rabot (rabo) *m*, plane (*tool*). **raboter** (bɔte) *v.t*, to plane; polish (*fig.*). **raboteux, euse** (tø, øːz) *a*, rough, rugged; knotty.

rabougrir (rabugriːr) *v.t*, to stunt (*growth*).

rabouter (rabute) *ou* **raboutir** (tiːr) *v.t*, to join [up].

rabrouer (rabrue) *v.t*, to rebuff, snub; rebuke.

racaille (rakɑːj) *f*, rabble, riffraff.

raccommodage (rakɔmɔdaːʒ) *m*, mending, repairing. **raccommodement** (dmɑ̃) *m*, reconciliation. **raccommoder** (de) *v.t*, to mend, repair; reconcile. **se~,** to make it up. **raccommodeur, euse** (dœːr, øːz) *n*, mender, repairer.

raccord (rakɔːr) *m*, join; joint; connection, union, coupling; continuity shot (*cinema*). **raccorder** (kɔrde) *v.t*, to join, connect, couple, patch (*computers*).

raccourci (rakursi) *m*, abridgement; epitome; shortcut; foreshortening; bypass (*computers*). **raccourcir** (siːr) *v.t*, to shorten; abridge; curtail; foreshorten. **[se]** ~, to draw in (*days*).

raccroc (rakro) *m*, fluke, lucky stroke. **raccrocher** (krɔʃe) *v.t*, to hook up, hang up, replace. **se** ~, to clutch, catch; cling.

race (ras) *f*, race, descent, ancestry; strain, blood, breed, stock, tribe, species. *de* ~, thoroughbred. **racé, e** (se) *a*, thoroughbred.

rachat (raʃa) *m*, repurchase; redemption; ransom; surrender (*Insce*). **racheter** (ʃte) *v.t*, to repurchase, buy back; redeem; surrender; ransom; atone for.

rachitisme (raʃitism) *m*, rachitis, rickets.

racine (rasin) *f*, root; root, fang (*of tooth*); [silkworm] gut (*Fish.*). ~ *d'iris*, orris root. ~ *pivotante*, taproot.

raclée (rɑkle) *f*, thrashing, hiding. **racler** (kle) *v.t*, to scrape; rake; rasp; strike (*measure*). **racloir** (klwaːr) *m*, scraper; squeegee. **racloire** (klwaːr) *f*, strickle, strike (*grain*). **raclure** (klyːr) *f*, scrapings.

racoler (rakɔle) *v.t*, to recruit; tout for.

racontar (rakɔ̃taːr) *m*, gossip, scandal. **raconter** (te) *v.t*, to relate, recount, narrate, tell; (*abs.*) to tell a story (*well, etc.*). **en** ~, to tell tall tales.

racornir (rakɔrniːr) *v.t*, to harden; shrivel.

rade (rad) *f*, roadstead, roads (*Naut.*).

radeau (rado) *m*, raft.

radial, e (radjal) *a*, radial. **radiateur** (tœːr) *m*, radiator; fire (*gas, Elec.*). **radiation** (sj5) *f*, striking out; s. off; radiation.

radical, e† (radikal) *a. & m*, radical; root.

radier (radje) *v.t*, to strike out; s. off.

radieux, euse (radjø, ø:z) *a*, radiant, beaming.

radin (radɛ̃) *a*, stingy. ¶ *m*, miser, stingy person.

radio (radjo) *f*, radio; cablegram; X-ray; radio operator.

radioactif, ive (radjoaktif, i:v) *a*, radioactive. **radiodiffuser** (ɔdifyze) *v.t*, to broadcast. **radiodiffusion** (zjɔ̃) *f*, broadcasting. **radiogramme** (gram) *m*, radiogram. **radiographie** (fi) *f*, radiography. **radiotélégraphie** (telegrafi) *f*, radiotelegraphy. **radiothérapie** (terapi) *f*, X-ray treatment, radiotherapy.

radis (radi) *m*, radish. *sans un ~*, without a cent.

radium (radjɔm) *m*, radium.

radius (radjy:s) *m*, radius (*Anat.*).

radoter (radɔte) *v.i*, to drivel (*talk*), dote. **radoteur, euse** (tœ:r, ø:z) *n*, dotard.

radouber (radube) *v.t*, to repair (*ship*).

radoucir (radusi:r) *v.t*, to soften; make milder.

rafale (rafal) *f*, squall, gust. *~ de pluie*, cloudburst.

raffermir (rafɛrmi:r) *v.t*, to harden; strengthen.

raffinage (rafina:ʒ) *m*, refining. **raffiné, e** (ne) *p.a*, refined; subtle. **raffinement** (nmɑ̃) *m*, refinement, subtlety. **raffiner** (ne) *v.t. & abs*, to refine. **raffinerie** (nri) *f*, refinery.

raffoler de (rafɔle), to be very fond of, dote on.

rafistoler (rafistɔle) *v.t*, to patch up.

rafle (rɑ:fl) *f*, stalk (*grape*); cob (*corn*); clean sweep; raid; round up; swag, loot. **rafler** (rɑfle) *v.t*, to carry off; round up. *~ le tout*, to sweep the board.

rafraîchir (rafreʃi:r) *v.t. & abs. & i*, to cool, refresh, freshen; revive; trim (*hair, grass*). **rafraîchissements** (ʃismɑ̃) *m.pl*, [light] refreshments.

ragaillardir (ragajardi:r) *v.t*, to cheer up.

rage (ra:ʒ) *f*, rage; rabies, madness; mania. *~ de dents*, raging

toothache. **rager** (raʒe) *v.i*, to rage. **rageur, euse†** (ʒœ:r, ø:z) *a. & n*, passionate (person), spitfire.

ragot (rago) *m*, gossip, scandal.

ragoût (ragu) *m*, stew. *~ de mouton*, lamb stew. **ragoûtant, e** (tɑ̃, ɑ̃:t) *a*, tempting.

ragréer (ragree) *v.t*, to clean up; do up (*repair house, etc.*).

rai (rɛ) *m*, ray; spoke.

raid (rɛd) *m*, raid; endurance test.

raide (rɛd) *a*, stiff; stark; tight, taut, tense; steep. *être ~*, to be broke. ¶ *m*, 10-franc note (*slang*). **raideur** (dœ:r) *f*, stiffness. **raidir** (di:r) *v.t*, to stiffen; tighten.

raie (rɛ) *f*, line, stroke; streak; stripe; ridge (*Agric.*); part (*hair*); ray, skate (*fish*).

raifort (rɛfɔ:r) *m*, horseradish.

rail (rɑ:j) *m*, rail (*Rly. metal or transport*). *~ de courant*, live rail.

railler (rɑje) *v.t. & abs*, to jeer at, laugh at; joke. **raillerie** (jri) *f*, raillery, banter, joke, jesting.

rainure (rɛny:r) *f*, groove, slot. *~ de clavette*, keyway.

raire (rɛ:r) *v.i.ir*, to troat, bell.

raisin (rɛzɛ̃) *m*, grape, grapes. *~s de Corinthe*, currants (*dried*). *~ de serres*, hothouse grapes. *~s de Smyrne*, sultanas. *~ de treille*, dessert grapes. *~ de vigne*, wine grapes. *~s secs*, raisins. *~s secs muscats*, muscatels.

raison (rɛzɔ̃) *f*, reason, motive, ground; sanity, senses; sense; satisfaction; ratio, rate. *~ [sociale]*, firm [name], trade name. *avoir ~*, to be right. *à ~ de*, at the rate of. **raissonable†** (zɔnabl) *a*, reasonable; rational; fair, adequate. **raisonnement** (nmɑ̃) *m*, reasoning; argument. **raisonner** (ne) *v.i*, to reason; argue; (*v.t.*) to consider; reason with. **raisonneur, euse** (nœ:r, ø:z) *n*, reasoner, arguer; (*att.*) reasoning, argumentative.

rajeunir (raʒœni:r) *v.t*, to rejuvenate; make look younger; renovate.

rajouter (raʒute) *v.t*, to add more of something.

rajuster (raʒyste) *v.t*, to readjust; put straight; refit.

râle (rɑːl) *m*, rail (*bird*); rattle (*in throat*). **râler** (le) *v.i*, to rattle (*throat*); gasp one's last; grumble.

ralenti (ralɑ̃ti) *m*, slow motion (*cinema*). travail au ~, slowdown strike.

ralentir (ralɑ̃tiːr) *v.t. & i*, to slacken, slow down.

rallier (ralje) *v.t*, to rally; rejoin.

rallonge (ralɔ̃ːʒ) *f*, lengthening piece; leaf (*table*). **rallonger** (lɔ̃ʒe) *v.t*, to lengthen.

rallumer (ralyme) *v.t*, to relight, rekindle.

rallye (rali) *m*, race meeting, rally. ~-*paper* (pepœːr) *m*, paper chase, hare & hounds.

ramage (ramaːʒ) *m*, floral design; song (*of birds*).

ramas (ramɑ *m*, heap.

ramasse (ramɑs) *f*, sledge (*alpine*). ~-*couverts*, *m*, plate basket. ~-*miettes*, *m*, crumb tray. ~-*miettes automatique*, crumb sweeper. **ramassé, e** (se) *p.a*, thickset, stocky. **ramasser** (se) *v.t*, to gather, collect; pick up. **ramasseur, euse** (sœːr, øːz) *n*, collector, gatherer. **ramassis** (si) *m*, heap; set.

rame (ram) *f*, stick (*Hort.*); oar; ream (*500 sheets*); train (*of cars, etc.*). ~ *directe*, through portion (*Rly.*).

rameau (ramo) *m*, branch; bough; palm (*Eccl.*). dimanche des ~x, Palm Sunday. **ramée** (me) *f*, greenwood, arbor.

ramener (ramne) *v.t*, to bring back; reduce; restore; reset.

ramer (rame) *v.t*, to stick (*Hort.*); (*v.i.*) to row, pull (*oar*). ~ à rebours, to back water. **rameur, euse** (mœːr, øːz) *n*, rower, oarsman, -woman.

ramier (ramje) *m*, ring dove, wood pigeon.

ramification (ramifikasjɔ̃) *f*, ramification. **se ramifier** (fje) *v.pr*, to ramify. **ramilles** (miːj) *f.pl*, twigs.

ramolli, e (ramɔli) *p.a*, dull-witted. **ramollir** (liːr) *v.t*, to soften; enervate.

ramoner (ramɔne) *v.t*, to sweep (*chimney*). **ramoneur** (nœːr) *m*, chimney sweep[er].

rampant, e (rɑ̃pɑ̃, ɑ̃ːt) *a*, rampant; creeping; crawling; reptile; groveling. **rampe** (rɑ̃ːp) *f*, rise, slope; upgrade; rack; banisters, handrail; footlights; ramp. ~ *de lancement*, launching ramp (*missiles*). **ramper** (rɑ̃pe) *v.i*, to creep, crawl; cringe, truckle, fawn, grovel.

ramure (ramyːr) *f*, branches; antlers.

rancart (mettre au) (rɑ̃kaːr), to cast aside.

rance (rɑ̃ːs) *a*, rancid, rank. **rancir** (rɑ̃siːr) *v.i*, to become rancid.

rancœur (rɑ̃kœːr) *f*, rancor, bitterness.

rançon (rɑ̃sɔ̃) *f*, ransom. **rançonner** (sɔne) *v.t*, to ransom; fleece.

rancune (rɑ̃kyn) *f*, rancor, spite; grudge. **rancunier, ère** (nje, ɛːr) *a*, rancorous, spiteful.

randonnée (rɑ̃dɔne) *f*, circuit; trip, run.

rang (rɑ̃) *m*, row, line; tier; rank, station, place; rate, class. **rangé, e** (ʒe) *p.a*, tidy; steady (*man*); pitched (*battle*). **rangée** (ʒe) *f*, row, line; tier; array. **ranger** (ʒe) *v.t*, to arrange, marshal, array; tidy, put away; rank, range. **se** ~, to draw up; fall in, side; stand aside; sober down; veer. *rangés comme des harengs en caque*, packed like sardines (*people*).

ranimer (ranime) *v.t*, to revive; stir up; cheer.

rapace (rapas) *a*, rapacious.

rapatrier (rapatrie) *v.t*, to repatriate, send home.

râpe (rɑːp) *f*, rasp; grater (*nutmeg, etc.*) **râpé, e** (rɑpe) *p.a*, grated; threadbare, shabby. **râper** (pe) *v.t*, to rasp; grate; wear threadbare. **rapeux, euse** (pø, øːz) *a*, grating, harsh (*wine*).

rapetasser (raptase) *v.t*, to patch, cobble.

rapetisser (raptise) *v.t. & i*, to shorten; dwarf.

rapide† (rapid) *a*, rapid, fast,

swift; speedy; cursory; steep. ¶ *m*, rapid (*river*); fast train, express.

rapiécer (rapjese) *v.t*, to piece, patch.

rapin (rapē) *m*, art student; dauber.

rapine (rapin) *f*, rapine. **rapiner** (ne) *v.t. & i*, to pillage.

rappareiller (rapareje) & **rapparier** (rje) *v.t*, to match, pair.

rappel (rapɛl) *m*, recall; call[ing]; reminder; repeal. **rappeler** (ple) *v.t*, to recall; call (*to order, etc.*); summon; remind; r. of; remember; repeal. **se ~**, to recollect, remember.

rapport (rapɔːr) *m*, yield, return; report, account, statement; tale; relation, connection; regard; (*pl.*) terms; (*pl.*) intercourse; ratio. **~ à**, because of. **~s probables**, betting forecast. **rapporter** (pɔrte) *v.t. & abs*, to bring back; retrieve (*game*); yield; get; add; inset; report, state; tell tales; refer, ascribe; revoke. **se ~**, to agree, tally; refer, relate. **rapporteur, euse** (tœːr, øːz) *n*, talebearer; (*m.*) protractor.

rapprendre (raprãːdr) *v.t.ir*, to learn again.

rapprocher (raprɔʃe) *v.t*, to bring nearer; b. together; reconcile; compare.

rapt (rapt) *m*, abduction; kidnapping.

raquette (rakɛt) *f*, racket; battledore. **~ à neige**, snowshoe.

rare (rɑːr) *a*, rare; scarce; uncommon; unusual; sparse, thin. **raréfier** (rarefje) *v.t*, to rarefy. **rarement** (rarmã) *ad*, rarely, seldom. **rareté** (te) *f*, rarity; scarcity; curiosity.

ras, e (rɑ, ɑːz) *a*, close-cropped; c.-shaven; bare, naked, open. **à** (ou *au*) **ras de**, level with, flush with. **~ du cou**, crew-necked. **en avoir ~ le bol**, to be weary of something, have "had it." **rase campagne**, open country. **rasade** (rɑzad) *f*, bumper (*brimful glass*).

raser (rɑze) *v.t*, to shave; raze; graze, brush, skim. **se ~**, to be bored (*slang*). **rasoir** (zwaːr) *m*, razor; bore (*slang*).

rassasier (rasazje) *v.t*, to satisfy, satiate, sate, surfeit, cloy, glut.

rassembler (rasãble) *v.t*, to reassemble; assemble, muster, collect.

rasseoir (raswaːr) *v.t.ir*, to reseat; settle. **se ~**, to sit down again.

rasséréner (se) (raserene) *v.pr*, to clear [up] (*weather*); calm.

rassis, e (rasi, iːz) *p.a*, settled, calm, staid, sedate, sane; stale (*bread*).

rassortir (rasɔrtiːr) *v.t*, to match; restock.

rassurer (rasyre) *v.t*, to reassure, cheer, hearten; strengthen.

rat, (ra) *m*, rat; ballet girl. **un ~ dans la tête**, a bee in one's bonnet. **~ de bibliothèque** bookworm (*pers.*). **~ de cave**, exciseman; taper (*coiled*). **~ des champs**, field mouse. **~ musqué**, muskrat, musquash.

ratatiné, e (ratatine) *p.a*, shriveled, shrunken; wizened.

rate (rat) *f*, spleen, milt (*Anat.*); she-rat.

raté (rate) *m*, misfire; failure; flop.

râteau (rɑto) *m*, rake. **râteler** (tle) *v.t*, to rake up. **râtelier** (təlje) *m*, rack; denture.

rater (rate) *v.i*, to misfire; miscarry, fail; (*v.t.*) to miss; fail in; fail to obtain.

ratier (ratje) *m*, ratter (*dog*). **ratière** (tjɛːr) *f*, rattrap.

ratifier (ratifje) *v.t*, to ratify, confirm.

ration (rasjɔ̃) *f*, ration, allowance.

rationalisme (rasjɔnalism) *m*, rationalism. **rationnel, le†** (nɛl) *a*, rational; pure (*mechanics*).

rationner (rasjɔne) *v.t*, to ration; stint.

ratisser (ratise) *v.t*, to rake; scrape.

raton (ratɔ̃) *m*, young rat; darling; Arab (*pejorative*). **~ laveur**, raccoon. **ratonnade** (ad) *f*, brutal police raid.

rattacher (rataʃe) *v.t*, to refasten; bind; connect.

rattraper (ratrape) *v.t*, to recap-

ture; overtake, catch up; recover.
rature (raty:r) *f*, erasure. **raturer**
(tyre) *v.t*, to erase, scratch out.
rauque (ro:k) *a*, hoarse, raucous,
harsh.
ravage (rava:ʒ) *m. oft. pl*, ravage, havoc, devastation. **ravager**
(vaʒe) *v.t*, to ravage, devastate,
lay waste. *ravagé(e)* [*par les intempéries*], weather-beaten.
ravaler (ravale) *v.t*, to swallow
again; eat (*one's words*); disparage; rough-cast (*wall*). se ~,
to lower oneself, stoop (*fig*.).
ravauder (ravode) *v.t. & abs*,
to mend; darn.
rave (ra:v) *f*, rape, coleseed.
Ravenne (ravɛn) *f*, Ravenna.
ravi (ravi) *a*, entranced.
ravigoter (ravigɔte) *v.t*, to revive, enliven.
ravilir (ravili:r) *v.t*, to degrade.
ravin (ravɛ̃) *m*, **ravine** (vin) *f*,
ravine, gully. **raviner** (vine) *v.t*,
to gully; furrow.
ravir (ravi:r) *v.t*, to ravish, carry
off; delight, enrapture; surly.
raviser (se) (ravize) *v.pr*, to
change one's mind.
ravissant (ravisɑ̃) *a*, ravishing,
delightful; predatory; ravenous.
ravissement (mɑ̃) *m*, rapture; kidnapping; rape. **ravisseur** (œ:r)
m, ravisher; kidnapper.
ravitailler (ravitaje) *v.t*, to [re]-
victual.
raviver (ravive) *v.t*, to revive.
ravoir (ravwa:r) *v.t*, to get
(*something*) back.
rayer (reje) *v.t*, to scratch, score;
rule; stripe, streak; rifle; strike
out, delete.
ray-grass (rɛgrɑ:s) *m*, rye grass.
rayon (rejɔ̃) *m*, ray, beam; gleam;
radius; spoke; comb (*honey*);
drill, furrow, row; shelf; department; rayon, artificial silk. **rayonnant, e** (jɔnɑ̃, ɑ̃:t) *a*, radiant;
beaming. **rayonnement** (nmɑ̃)
m, radiation; radiance, effulgence.
rayonner (ne) *v.i*, to radiate,
beam, shine; (*v.t*.) to fit with
shelves.
rayure (rɛjy:r) *f*, scratch, etc., as
rayer.
raz de marée (rɑ) *m*, tide race,
bore; tidal wave.

razzia (razja) *f*, raid, foray. **razzier** (zje) *v.t*, to raid.
ré (re) *m*, D (*Mus*.).
réactif (reaktif) *m*, reagent
(*Chem*.). **réacteur** (tœ:r) *m*, jet engine; reactor; nuclear pile. ~ *à
fission*, fission reactor. ~ *producteur de matière fissile*, ~ *surrégénérateur*, breeder r. **réaction** (sjɔ̃)
f, reaction. *avion à* ~, jet plane.
réactionnaire (ɔnɛ:r) *a. & n*, reac-
tionary. **réagir** (ʒi:r) *v.i*, to react.
réalisateur (realizatœ:r) *m*, director (*cinema*). **réalisation**
(zasjɔ̃) *f*, direction (*cinema*).
réaliser (realize) *v.t*, to realize;
make (*profit*); close (*bargain*).
réaliste (list) *a. & n*, realist. **réalité**
(te) *f*, reality.
réanimer (reanime) *v.t*, to revive, resuscitate.
réapparition (reaparisjɔ̃) *f*, reappearance.
réassurer (reasyre) *v.t*, to reinsure.
rébarbatif, ive (rebarbatif, i:v)
a, grim; surly.
rebâtir (rəbɑti:r) *v.t*, to rebuild;
reconstruct.
rebattre (rəbatr) *v.t.ir*, to beat
again; reshuffle (*cards*); repeat.
rebattu, e (ty) *p.a*, beaten (*track*);
hackneyed.
rébecca (rebɛka) *m. & f*, rumpus,
row. *faire du* ~, kick up a fuss.
rebelle (rəbɛl) *a*, rebellious; refractory. ¶ *n*, rebel. **se rebeller**
(le) *v.pr*, to rebel. **rébellion** (re-
bɛljɔ̃) *f*, rebellion.
rebiffer (se) (rəbife) *v.pr*, to
show temper.
rebondi, e (rəbɔ̃di) *a*, rounded,
plump. **rebondir** (di:r) *v.i*, to rebound, bounce; crop up again.
rebondissement (dismɑ̃) *m*, rebound; repercussion.
rebord (rəbɔ:r) *m*, edge, rim;
hem; ledge; flange.
rebours (rəbu:r) *m*, wrong way;
contrary, reverse. *à* ~, the wrong
way; backward. *prendre à* ~, to
misconstrue.
rebouteur, euse (rəbutœ:r, ø:z)
n, bonesetter.
rebrousse-poil (à) (rəbruspwal)
ad, against the nap, the wrong

way. **rebrousser** (se) *v.t*, to rub the wrong way. ~ [*chemin*], to retrace one's steps.

rebuffade (rəbyfad) *f*, rebuff.

rébus (reby:s) *m*, picture puzzle; riddle.

rebut (rəby) *m*, waste, refuse, rubbish; dead letter (*Post.*); scum (*fig.*). **rebutant, e** (tã, ã:t) *a*, disheartening; repellent. **rebuter** (te) *v.t*, to rebuff, repulse; dishearten.

récalcitrant, e (rekalsitrã, ã:t) *a. & n*, recalcitrant; refractory.

recaler (rəkale) *v.t*, to set (*someone*) on his feet again; flunk, fail (*someone*) in examination.

récapituler (rekapityle) *v.t*, to recapitulate.

receler (rəsle) *v.t*, to conceal; harbor (*criminal*); receive (*stolen goods*). **receleur, euse** (slœ:r, φ:z) *n*, receiver, fence.

récemment (resamã) *ad*, recently, lately.

recensement (rəsãsmã) *m*, census, return; counting (*votes*); stocktaking. **recenser** (se) *v.t*, to take the census of; count.

récent, e (resã, ã:t) *a*, recent, late; fresh.

receper (rəsəpe) *v.t*, to cut back (*Hort.*).

récépissé (resepise) *m*, receipt. **réceptacle** (sɛptakl) *m*, receptacle; repository. **récepteur** (tœ:r) *m*, receiver (*Teleph.*, etc.). **réception** (sjɔ̃) *f*, receipt; reception; welcome; acceptance; party, at-home. **recette** (rəsɛt) *f*, receipts, takings; gate money; collectorship; recipe. **recevable** (səvabl) *a*, admissible. **receveur, euse** (vœ:r, φ:z) *n*, collector (*taxes*, etc.); conductor (*bus*); (*f.*) attendant (*Theat.*). ~ **des postes**, postmaster, -mistress. **recevoir** (vwa:r) *v.t. & abs*, to receive; admit; get; meet with; accept; welcome; take in (*boarders*); be at home (*to visitors*). **être reçu à**, to pass (*exam*).

récession (resɛsjɔ̃) *f*, recession (*economic*).

rechange (rəʃɑ̃:ʒ) *m*, change, spare. **pièce de** ~, spare part.

réchapper (reʃape) *v.i*, to escape; recover.

recharger (rəʃarʒe) *v.t*, to recharge; reload.

réchaud (reʃo) *m*, stove; ring (*gas*); heater; hot plate. **réchauffer** (ʃofe) *v.t*, to reheat, warm up; revive.

rêche (rɛʃ) *a*, rough, harsh.

recherche (rəʃɛrʃ) *f*, search, quest, pursuit; research, inquiry; prospecting; studied elegance. **recherché, e** (ʃe) *p.a*, sought after, in request; choice; studied; elaborate. **rechercher** (ʃe) *v.t*, to search for, seek.

rechigner (rəʃiɲe) *v.i*, to look sour. **en rechignant** (ɲã), with a bad grace.

rechute (rəʃyt) *f*, relapse, backsliding.

récidiver (residive) *v.i*, to relapse into crime. **récidiviste** (vist) *n*, person with previous convictions; old offender.

récif (resif) *m*, reef (*of rocks*).

récipiendaire (resipjãdɛ:r) *n*, new member. **récipient** (pjã) *m*, receiver, vessel.

réciproque (resiprɔk) *a*, reciprocal, mutual; inverse; converse. **réciproquement** (kmã) *ad*, reciprocally, etc; vice versa.

récit (resi) *m*, recital, account, narration, narrative; solo (*Mus.*). **récital** (tal) *m*, recital (*Mus.*). **récitatif** (tatif) *m*, recitative (*Mus.*). **récitation** (sjɔ̃) *f*, recitation. **réciter** (te) *v.t*, to recite; say (*lessons*).

réclamant, e (reklamã, ã:t) *n*, claimant. **réclamation** (masjɔ̃) *f*, claim; complaint, protest. **bureau de** ~, complaint department. **réclame** (klam) *f*, advertisement, blurb. **réclamer** (me) *v.i*, to complain, protest, object; (*v.t.*) to claim; crave; call for. ~ **à grands cris**, to clamor for.

reclus, e (rəkly, y:z) *n*, recluse. **réclusion** (reklyzjɔ̃) *f*, reclusion, seclusion; solitary imprisonment.

recoin (rəkwɛ̃) *m*, nook, recess.

récolte (rekɔlt) *f*, harvest[ing]; crop; vintaging; vintage; collection. **récolter** (te) *v.t*, to harvest; collect.

recommander (rəkɔmɑ̃de) *v.t.* to [re]commend; register (*mail*).

recommencer (rəkɔmɑ̃se) *v.t. & i,* to recommence; begin again.

récompense (rekɔ̃pɑ̃ːs) *f,* recompense, reward; retribution, requital. **récompenser** (pɑ̃se) *v.t,* to recompense.

réconcilier (rekɔ̃silje) *v.t,* to reconcile.

reconduire (rəkɔ̃dɥiːr) *v.t.ir,* to escort; see home; show out.

réconfort (rekɔ̃fɔːr) *m,* comfort, consolation; stimulant. **réconforter** (fɔrte) *v.t,* to strengthen; comfort.

reconnaissable (rəkɔnɛsabl) *a,* recognizable. **reconnaissance** (sɑ̃ːs) *f,* recognition; acknowledgment; gratitude, thankfulness; reconnaissance, exploration; pawn ticket. **reconnaissant, e** (sɑ̃, ɑ̃ːt) *a,* grateful, thankful. **reconnaître** (nɛːtr) *v.t.ir,* to recognize; tell; sight (*land*); acknowledge; be grateful for; reconnoiter, explore.

reconquérir (rəkɔ̃keriːr) *v.t.ir,* to reconquer; regain.

reconstituer (rəkɔ̃stitye) *v.t,* to reconstitute; reconstruct (*crime*); restore.

reconstitution (rəkɔ̃stitysjɔ̃) *f,* reconstruction (*fig.*).

reconstruction (rəkɔ̃stryksjɔ̃) *f,* rebuilding. **reconstruire** (strɥiːr) *v.t.ir,* to rebuild.

reconvention (rəkɔ̃vɑ̃sjɔ̃) *f,* counterclaim.

recopier (rəkɔpje) *v.t,* to recopy; revise; transcribe (*computers*).

record (rəkɔːr) *m,* record (*sports*). **recorder** (kɔrde) *v.t,* to con, go over; restring. **recors** (kɔːr) *m,* bailiff's man; minion (*of the law*).

recoupe (rəkup) *f,* middlings (*flour*); chips; clippings. **recoupement** (mɑ̃) *m,* cross-checking of information.

recourber (rəkurbe) *v.t,* to bend, crook.

recourir (rəkuriːr) *v.i.ir,* to run again; have recourse, resort. **recours** (kuːr) *m,* recourse, resort; appeal; remedy (*law*).

recouvrement (rəkuvrəmɑ̃) *m,*

recovery; cover[ing]; [over]lap; overlay (*computers*); (*pl.*) book debts. **recouvrer** (vre) *v.t,* to recover, regain.

recouvrir (rəkuvriːr) *v.t.ir,* to re-cover; cover.

récréation (rekreasjɔ̃) *f,* recreation; playtime.

récréer (rekree) *v.t,* to recreate, divert, entertain; enliven, refresh; re-create.

récrier (se) (rekrie) *v.pr,* to cry out, exclaim.

récrimination (rekriminasjɔ̃) *f,* recrimination. **récriminer** (ne) *v.i,* to recriminate; countercharge; retort.

récrire (rekriːr) *v.t.ir,* to re-write; write again; reply.

recroqueviller (se) (rəkrɔkvije) *v.pr,* to shrivel.

recrudescence (rəkrydɛsɑ̃ːs) *f,* recrudescence.

recrue (rəcry) *f,* recruit. **recruter** (te) *v.t,* to recruit.

recta (rɛkta) *ad,* on the nail, punctually.

rectangle (rɛktɑ̃ːgl) *a,* right-angled. ¶ *m,* rectangle. ~ [*de table*], doily. **rectangulaire** (tɑ̃gylɛːr) *a,* rectangular.

recteur (rɛktœːr) *m,* rector.

rectifier (rɛktifje) *v.t,* to rectify; amend; true, straighten.

rectiligne (rɛktiliɲ) *a,* rectilinear.

rectitude (rɛktityd) *f,* straightness; rectitude, soundness, sanity.

recto (rɛkto) *m,* recto, front, face.

rectum (rɛktɔm) *m,* rectum.

reçu (rəsy) *m,* receipt. *au ~ de,* on receipt of. ¶ *a,* received, accepted, customary. *être ~,* to pass (*examination*).

recueil (rəkœːj) *m,* collection; book. ~ *factice,* miscellany. **recueillement** (kœjmɑ̃) *m,* self-communion. **recueillir** (jiːr) *v.t.ir,* to collect, gather; pick up; reap. se ~, to collect one's thoughts.

recuire (rəkɥiːr) *v.t.ir,* to re-bake; reheat; anneal.

recul (rəkyl) *m,* recoil, kick; set-back. **reculade** (lad) *f,* backward movement; retreat. **reculé, e (le)**

p.a, distant, remote. **reculer** (le) *v.i. & t*, to draw back; move back; recede; retreat; back; recoil; kick; postpone. **à reculons** (l5) *ad*, backward[s].

récupérer (rekypere) *v.t*, to recover, recoup.

récurer (rekyre) *v.t*, to scour, clean.

récuser (rekyze) *v.t*, to challenge, object to. *se ~*, to disclaim competence.

recyclage (rəsikla:ʒ) *m*, reprocessing; recycling; retraining. **recycler** (le) *v.t*, to reprocess; recycle; retrain.

rédacteur, trice (redaktœ:r, tris) *n*, writer, drafter (*documents*). *~ en chef*, editor. **rédaction** (sjɔ̃) *f*, drafting, editing; editorial staff; newsroom.

reddition (rɛddisjɔ̃) *f*, surrender; rendering (*of accounts*).

redemander (rədmɑ̃de) *v.t*, to ask for again; ask for more; ask for back.

Rédempteur (redɑ̃[p]tœ:r) *m*, Redeemer. **rédemption** ([p]sjɔ̃) *f*, redemption (*Theol.*).

redescendre (rədɛsɑ̃:dr) *v.i*, to come down again; fall again (*barometer*); back (*wind*).

redevable (rədəvabl) *a*, indebted, beholden; liable. ¶ *n*, debtor. **redevance** (vɑ̃:s) *f*, rent[al]; royalty. **redevoir** (vwa:r) *v.t*, to still owe.

rédiger (rediʒe) *v.t*, to draw up, draft; write; edit.

redingote (rədɛ̃gɔt) *f*, frock coat (*man's*); coat (*woman's*).

redire (rədi:r) *v.t.ir*, to say again; repeat. *trouver à ~ à*, to find fault with. **redite** (dit) *f*, repetition.

redondant, e (rədɔ̃dɑ̃, ɑ̃:t) *a*, redundant.

redonner (redɔne) *v.t*, to give again; restore; (*v.i.*) to fall again; charge again.

redoubler (rəduble) *v.t*, to redouble; repeat (*a class*); reline (*clothing*).

redoutable (rədutabl) *a*, redoubtable, formidable.

redoute (rədut) *f*, redoubt; gala night (*at dance hall*).

redouter (rədute) *v.t*, to dread, fear.

redresser (rədrɛse) *v.t*, to reerect; straighten; redress; right.

réduction (redyksjɔ̃) *f*, reduction; reducing; cut. **réduire** (dɥi:r) *v.t.ir*, to reduce; boil down. **réduit** (dɥi) *m*, retreat, nook; redoubt.

rééditer (reedite) *v.t*, to republish, reissue.

réel, le† (reɛl) *a*, real; actual. ¶ *m*, real[ity].

réélection (reelɛksjɔ̃) *f*, reelection. **rééligible** (liʒibl) *a*, reeligible. **réélire** (li:r) *v.t.ir*, to reelect.

réer (ree) *v.i*, to troat, bell.

réexporter (reɛkspɔrte) *v.t*, to reexport.

refaire (rəfɛ:r) *v.t.ir*, to remake, do [over] again; do up, repair; recover. **refait** (fɛ) *m*, draw[n game]; new horns (*stag*). **réfection** (refɛksjɔ̃) *f*, restoration. **réfectoire** (twa:r) *m*, refectory.

refendre (rəfɑ̃:dr) *v.t*, to split; rip.

référence (referɑ̃:s) *f*, reference. **referendum** (referɛ̃dɔm) *m*, referendum. **référer** (fere) *v.t. & i. & se ~*, to refer; ascribe.

réfléchi, e (refleʃi) *p.a*, reflective; thoughtful; considered, deliberate; reflexive (*Gram.*). **réfléchir** (ʃi:r) *v.t. & i*, to reflect; think over, ponder, consider. **réflecteur** (flɛktœ:r) *m*, reflector. **reflet** (rəflɛ) *m*, reflection; reflex; shimmer, glint. *~s irisés*, play of colors. **refléter** (flete) *v.t*, to reflect; mirror. **réflexe** (reflɛks) *a. & m*, reflex. **réflexion** (ksjɔ̃) *f*, reflection; thought. *~ après coup*, afterthought.

refluer (rəflye) *v.i*, to flow back, ebb; surge. **reflux** (fly) *m*, reflux, ebb.

refondre (rəfɔ̃:dr) *v.t*, to recast, remodel. **refonte** (fɔ̃:t) *f*, recasting; recoinage; reorganization; reconstruction.

réformateur, trice (reformatœ:r, tris) *n*, reformer. **réformation** (sjõ) *f*, reformation. **réforme** (form) *f*, reform[ation]; discharge, retirement (*Mil.*, *Nav.*).

reformer (rəforme) *v.t*, to reform.

réformer (reforme) *v.t*, to reform, amend; discharge, retire; reverse (*law*).

refouler (rəfule) *v.t*, to drive back; stem; compress; ram home; repress; (*v.i*) to flow back, ebb. **refouloir** (lwa:r) *m*, rammer (*gun*).

réfractaire (refraktɛ:r) *a*, refractory; fire[-proof]. ¶ *m*, draft-dodger (*Mil.*).

réfracter (refrakte) *v.t*, to refract.

refrain (rəfrɛ̃) *m*, refrain; burden; theme. ~ *en chœur*, chorus.

refréner (rəfrene) *v.t*, to curb, bridle.

réfrigération (refriʒerasjõ) *f*, refrigeration, cooling, chilling.

refrogner (se) (rəfroɲe) *v.pr*, to frown, scowl, look sullen.

refroidir (rəfrwadi:r) *v.t. & t. & se* ~, to cool, chill; damp (*fig.*); get cold.

refuge (rəfy:ʒ) *m*, refuge, shelter; [street] refuge. **réfugié, e** (refyʒje) *n*, refugee. **se réfugier** (ʒje) *v.pr*, to take refuge.

refus (rəfy) *m*, refusal. ~ *d'obéissance*, insubordination; contempt of court. **refuser** (ze) *v.t*, to refuse, decline; deny; reject; flunk, fail (*exam*); disable (*computers*). *se* ~, to object, refuse, decline.

réfuter (refyte) *v.t*, to refute, confute, rebut, disprove.

regagner (rəgaɲe) *v.t*, to regain, win back, recover; make up for; get back to.

regain (rəgɛ̃) *m*, aftergrowth; renewal; new lease (*of life*).

régal (regal) *m*, feast; treat. **régaler** (le) *v.t*, to entertain, feast; treat; regale.

regard (rəga:r) *m*, look, gaze, glance, eye(s); attention, notice; peephole; manhole. ~ *appuyé*, stare. ~ *polisson*, leer. *en* ~, opposite, facing. **regardant, e**

(gardɑ̃, ɑ̃:t) *a*, close-fisted, mean.

regarder (de) *v.t. & abs*, to look (at, on), see, eye; consider, regard, mind, be one's business; face, front. ~ *fixement*, to stare at.

régate (regat) *f*, regatta. [*cravate*] ~, open-end tie.

régence (reʒɑ̃:s) *f*, regency.

régénérer (reʒenere) *v.t*, to regenerate.

régent, e (reʒɑ̃, ɑ̃:t) *n. & a*, regent. **régenter** (ʒɑ̃te) *v.t*, to dictate to; dominate; (*abs.*) to domineer.

régicide (reʒisid) *m*, regicide; (*att.*) regicidal.

régie (reʒi) *f*, administration (*of property*); State (*control*); excise.

regimber (rəʒɛ̃be) *v.i*, to kick, balk.

régime (reʒim) *m*, regime[n], rules, system, conditions; diet; object (*Gram.*); bunch, cluster (*bananas*, *etc.*). ~ *de faveur*, preference (*Cust.*).

régiment (reʒimɑ̃) *m*, regiment; swarm. **régimentaire** (tɛ:r) *a*, regimental.

région (reʒjõ) *f*, region, district. **régional, e** (onal) *a*, regional, district (*att.*); toll (*att.*, *Teleph.*).

régir (reʒi:r) *v.t*, to govern, rule, manage. **régisseur** (ʒisœ:r) *m*, manager, steward, bailiff (*farm*); stage manager. ~ *d'extérieur*, location m. (*cinema*). ~ *de plateau*, studio m. (*cinema*). ~ *général*, casting director.

registre (rəʒistr) *m*, register, book; record, note; damper (*flue*). ~ *des délibérations*, minute book.

règle (regl) *f*, rule; ruler; order. ~ *à calcul*, sliderule. *les* ~*s*, menses. **réglé, e** (regle) *p.a*, regular, steady; set, stated; ruled (*paper*). **règlement** (regləmɑ̃) *m*, settlement, adjustment; regulation, rule. **réglementaire** (tɛ:r) *a*, regulation (*att.*), prescribed. **réglementer** (te) *v.t*, to regulate. **régler** (regle) *v.t*, to rule; regulate; order; settle, adjust; set, time.

réglisse (reglis) *f*, licorice.

règne (rɛɲ) *m*, reign; sway; kingdom (*Nat. Hist.*). **régner** (ɲe) *v.i*, to reign, rule; obtain; prevail, be prevalent; extend, run.

regorger (rəgɔrʒe) *v.i. & t*, to overflow, brim, abound, teem; burst.

regrattier, ère (rəgratje, ɛːr) *n*, huckster.

régresser (regrɛse) *v.i*, to regress; diminish (*amount, intensity*).

regret (rəgrɛ) *m*, regret. *à ~*, reluctantly. **regrettable** (tabl) *a*, regrettable, unfortunate. **le (la) regretté, e . . . (te)**, the [late] lamented **. . . regretter** (te) *v.t*, to regret, be sorry (for); miss.

régulariser (regylarize) *v.t*, to regularize. **régularité** (te) *f*, regularity. **régulateur** (tœːr) *m*, regulator, governor. **régulier, ère†** (lje, ɛːr) *a*, regular; orderly, businesslike.

réhabiliter (reabilite) *v.t*, to rehabilitate, reinstate; discharge (*bankrupt*).

rehausser (rəose) *v.t*, to raise; enhance; heighten. **rehauts (o)** *m.pl*, highlights (*art*).

réimporter (reɛ̃pɔrte) *v.t*, to reimport.

réimposer (reɛ̃poze) *v.t*, to reimpose.

réimpression (reɛ̃prɛsjɔ̃) *f*, reprint[ing]. **réimprimer** (prime) *v.t*, to reprint.

Reims (rɛ̃ːs) *m*, Rheims.

rein (rɛ̃) *m*, kidney; (*pl.*) loins, back. *mal aux ~s*, backache.

reine (rɛn) *f*, queen (*pers. & chess*); belle (*of ball*). *~-claude* (kloːd), greengage. *~ des abeilles*, queen bee. *~-des-prés*, meadow-sweet. *~-marguerite*, China aster.

reinette (rɛnɛt) *f*, pippin, rennet. *~ grise*, russet (*apple*).

réinjection (reɛ̃ʒeksjɔ̃) *f*, feedback (*computers*).

réintégrer (reɛ̃tegre) *v.t*, to reinstate.

réitérer (reitere) *v.t*, to reiterate, repeat.

rejaillir (rəʒajiːr) *v.i*, to gush out; reflect, redound.

rejet (rəʒɛ) *m*, throwing out; rejection; shoot (*Hort.*). **rejeter** (ʒ[ə]te) *v.t*, to throw back; t. out; t. up; reject, set aside; negate; dismiss; disallow. **rejeton** (ʒtɔ̃) *m*, shoot, cane (*raspberry*); scion, offspring.

rejoindre (rəʒwɛ̃ːdr) *v.t. & abs. ir*, to re-join; rejoin (*one's regiment*).

rejouer (rəʒwe) *v.t. & i*, to replay; play again.

réjoui, e (reʒwi) *p.a*, jolly, joyous, jovial, merry. **réjouir** (ʒwiːr) *v.t. & se ~*, to rejoice, gladden, cheer; be glad; enjoy oneself. **réjouissance** (ʒwisɑ̃ːs) *f*, rejoicing; makeweight (*butcher's*).

relâche (rəlɑːʃ) *m*, respite, intermission, breathing space, relaxation; no performance, closed (*Theat.*); (*f.*) call[ing] (*Naut.*); port of call. **relâcher** (lɑʃe) *v.t. & i*, to loosen, slacken; relax; release; call, put in (*Naut.*).

relais (rəlɛ) *m*, relay; shift; stage, relay station; sand flats.

relancer (rəlɑ̃se) *v.t*, to throw back; return (*ball, Ten.*); badger. **relanceur, euse** (sœːr, øːz) *n*, receiver (*Ten.*).

relaps, e (rəlaps) *n*, apostate, backslider.

rélargir (relarʒiːr) *v.t*, to widen; let out.

relater (rəlate) *v.t*, to relate, state. **relatif, ive†** (tif, iːv) *a*, relative, relating. **relation** (sjɔ̃) *f*, relation, connection, intercourse; acquaintance; narrative.

relaxer (rəlakse) *v.t*, to relax; release.

relayer (rələje) *v.t*, to relay; change with; change horses. *se ~*, to take turns, shifts.

reléguer (rəlege) *v.t*, to relegate, consign; intern (*prisoner in Fr. colony*).

relent (relɑ̃) *m*, bad odor.

relevailles (rəlvaːj) *f.pl*, churching. **relève** (lɛːv) *f*, relief (*from turn of duty*). **relevé, e** (lve) *p.a*, high, exalted, lofty; strong (*flavor*). ¶ *m*, statement, abstract, return. ~ *de potage*, course after soup. ¶ *f*, afternoon. **relever** (lve) *v.t*, to raise, lift [up]; pick up; turn up; take up; restore; make out (*account*); take, read (*meter*); point out, note; set off, enhance, exalt; season; relieve; release; plot (*ground*); (*v.i.*) to depend, rest; recover. ~ *le menton* à, to chuck under the chin.

relief (rəljɛf) *m*, relief; (*pl.*) leftovers.

relier (rəlje) *v.t*, to [re]tie; unite; bind (*book*); [re]hoop (*cask*). **relieur, euse** (jœːr, ø:z) *n*, [book]-binder.

religieux, euse† (rəliʒiø, ø:z) *a*, religious; sacred (*song, etc.*); scrupulous. ¶ *m*, monk, friar. ¶ *f*, nun; cream puff. **religion** (ʒjɔ̃) *f*, religion; vows; bounden duty; sanctity (*oath*).

reliquaire (rəlikɛːr) *m*, reliquary, shrine.

reliquat (rəlika) *m*, balance, residue.

relique (rəlik) *f*, relic.

reliure (rəljyːr) *f*, [book]binding. ~ *amateur*, extra binding. ~ *pleine*, full b., whole b.

relogement (rələʒmɑ̃) *m*, re-housing.

relouer (rəlue) *v.t*, to relet; re-rent; sublet.

reluire (rəlɥiːr) *v.i.ir*, to shine, glitter; enjoy oneself; have an orgasm (*slang*). **reluisant, e** (lɥizɑ̃, ɑ̃:t) *a*, shining; creditable; brilliant.

reluquer (rəlyke) *v.t*, to ogle, covet.

remâcher (rəmɑʃe) *v.t*, to chew again; ruminate on, brood over, chew (*fig.*).

remanier (rəmanje) *v.t*, to re-handle; manipulate; relay; recast.

remarquable† (rəmarkabl) *a*, remarkable; noteworthy; conspicuous. **remarque** (mark) *f*, re-mark, note. **remarquer** (ke) *v.t*, to re-mark; remark, observe, notice, note, mark.

remballer (rɑ̃bale) *v.t*, to re-pack.

rembarquer (rɑ̃barke) *v.t. & i*, to reembark, reship.

remblai (rɑ̃blɛ) *m*, filling up (*with earth*); embankment. **remblayer** (je) *v.t*, to fill [up], [em]-bank.

remboîter (rɑ̃bwate) *v.t*, to [re]-set; recase.

rembourrer (rɑ̃bure) *v.t*, to stuff, pad, upholster.

rembourser (rɑ̃burse) *v.t*, to repay, pay off, return, refund; redeem; reimburse.

rembrunir (rɑ̃bryniːr) *v.t*, to darken, gloom.

rembucher (se) (rɑ̃byʃe) *v.pr*, to return to cover[t].

remède (rəmɛd) *m*, remedy, cure. ~ *de charlatan*, nostrum. **remédier** à (medje), to remedy, cure.

remembrer (rəmɑ̃bre) *v.t*, to re-group (*farmland*), reallocate. **re-membrement** (brəmɑ̃), *m*, re-grouping of farmland.

remémorer (se) (rəmemɔre) *v.pr*, to remember.

remerciement (rəmɛrsimɑ̃) *m*. *oft. pl*, thanks. **remercier** (sje) *v.t*, to thank; dismiss, fire.

réméré (remere) *m*, repurchase.

remettre (rəmɛtr) *v.t. & abs. ir*, to put back [again]; put on again; restore; remit, send [in]; hand [over], deliver; commend; put off, postpone; pardon; entrust; remember; calm; set (*bone*). ~ à *blanc*, à *zéro*, to clear (*computers*). *remettez-vous!* get a grip on yourself. se ~, to become well again, start off again.

remeubler (rəmœble) *v.t*, to re-furnish.

réminiscence (reminisɑ̃ːs) *f*, re-miniscence.

remise (rəmiːz) *f*, putting back; restoration; remittance; remission; delivery; postponement; allowance, discount; commission; coach house; shed; cover (*game*). ~ [*sur marchandises*], [trade] discount. *une voiture de* ~ *ou un* ~, a hired carriage. **remiser** (mize) *v.t*, to put up (*vehicle*). **remisier** (zje) *m*, intermediate broker.

rémission (remisjɔ̃) *f*, remission.

rem[m]aillage (rɑ̃majaːʒ) *m*, grafting (*Knit.*).

remmancher (rãmãʃe) v.t, to rehandle; resume.

remmener (rãmne) v.t, to take back.

remontant (rəmɔ̃tã) m, stimulant, tonic, pick-me-up. **remonte** (mɔ̃:t) f, remount[ing] (Mil.). ~-*pentes*, m, ski lift. **remonter** (mɔ̃te) v.i. & t, to [re]ascend; remount; go back; raise; rise; wind [up] (spring); restock, replenish; restage; veer (wind). **remontoir** (twa:r) m, winder, key; keyless watch. ~ à heures sautantes, jumping-hour watch.

remontrance (rəmɔ̃trã:s) f, remonstrance, expostulation. **remontrer** (tre) v.t. & abs, to show again; point out; remonstrate.

remords (rəmɔ:r) m, remorse.

remorque (rəmɔrk) f, tow[ing]; trailer. **remorquer** (ke) v.t, to tow, haul. **remorqueur** (kœ:r) m, tug [boat].

rémouleur (remulœ:r) m, [knife] grinder.

remous (rəmu) m, eddy, [back]-wash, swirl.

rempart (rãpa:r) m, rampart; bulwark (fig.).

remplaçant, e (rãplasã, ã:t) n, substitute. **remplacer** (se) v.t, to replace; take the place of; supersede.

rempli (rãpli) m, tuck. **remplier** (e) v.t, to tuck; turn over (paper wrapper—Bookb.).

remplir (rãpli:r) v.t, to fill up, refill, replenish; fill; swamp (boat); fulfil, comply with; perform.

remplumer (se) (rãplyme) v.pr, to get new feathers; put on flesh again; pick up again.

remporter (rãpɔrte) v.t, to take away; carry off, win, gain.

rempoter (rãpɔte) v.t, to repot.

remuant, e (rəmɥã, ã:t) a, restless. **remue-ménage** (mymena:ʒ) m, bustle, stir, upset. **remue-méninges** (menɛ̃:ʒ) m, brainstorming. **remuement** (mã) m, moving, removal; bustle, stir. **remuer** (mɥe) v.t. & i, to move; stir [up], rake up; shake, wag, swish; remove, shift.

rémunérateur, trice (remyneratœ:r, tris) a, remunerative, paying. ¶ m, rewarder. **rémunération** (sjɔ̃) f, remuneration, payment; consideration; return. **rémunérer** (re) v.t, to remunerate, pay for, reward.

renâcler (rənɑkle) v.t, to snort; hang back; refuse. ~ à la besogne, to shirk work.

renaissance (rənɛsã:s) f, rebirth; revival; renaissance. **renaître** (nɛ:tr) v.i.ir, to be born again; spring up again; revive.

renard (rəna:r) m, fox. ~ argenté, silver f. **renarde** (nard) f, vixen. **renardeau** (do) m, fox cub. **renardière** (djɛ:r) f, fox earth, fox's hole.

rencaisser (rãkɛse) v.t, to rebox; recash.

rencarder (rãkarde) v.t, to inform, wise up.

renchéri, e (rãʃeri) n, fastidious person. **renchérir** (ri:r) v.i, to get dearer, go up. ~ sur, to outbid, outdo, improve on.

rencogner (rãkɔɲe) v.t, to drive into a corner.

rencontre (rãkɔ̃:tr) f, meeting, encounter; occurrence; occasion; collision, clash; duel. ~ de front, head-on collision. **rencontrer** (kɔ̃tre) v.t, to meet, m. with, encounter, come across, strike; run into, collide with.

rendement (rãdmã) m, yield, return; output, capacity; efficiency. **rendez-vous** (devu) m, appointment; place of meeting; resort, haunt.

rendormir (rãdɔrmi:r) v.t, to send to sleep again. se ~, to go to sleep again.

rendre (rã:dr) v.t, to give back, return; restore; give up; render; give; pay; dispense; repay; yield; deliver; surrender; vomit; make; drive (one mad). ~ l'âme, to die. se ~, to make oneself; go; surrender, yield. **rendu** (rãdy) m, rendering (art); return (article, goods—Com.).

rêne (rɛn) f, rein.

renégat, e (rənega, at) n, renegade, turncoat.

renfermé (rɑ̃fɛrme) *m*, musty smell. **renfermer** (me) *v.t*, to shut up; confine; comprise, contain; restrict.

renflement (rɑ̃fləmɑ̃) *m*, swell-[ing]; bulge, boss. **renfler** (fle) *v.i*, to swell.

renflouer (rɑ̃flue) *v.t*, to refloat (*ship*).

renfoncement (rɑ̃fɔ̃smɑ̃) *m*, driving in; recess; inden[ta]tion (*Typ.*); punch (*blow*). **renfoncer** (se) *v.t*, to drive in; knock in; indent.

renforcé, e (rɑ̃fɔrse) *p.a*, stout, strong; out & out; arrant. **renforcer** (se) *v.t*, to reinforce; strengthen, brace; intensify (*Phot.*). **renfort** (fɔːr) *m*, reinforcement (*Mil.*). *à grand ~ de*, with plenty of.

renfrogner (se) (rɑ̃frɔɲe) *v.pr*, to frown, scowl, look sullen.

rengager (rɑ̃gaʒe) *v.t*, to re-engage; (*v.i.*) to reenlist.

rengaine (rɑ̃gɛːn) *f*, tag, story; catchword; hackneyed refrain.

rengainer (rɑ̃gene) *v.t*, to sheathe; suppress.

rengorger (se) (rɑ̃gɔrʒe) *v.pr*, to bridle [up]; strut, swagger.

reniement (rənimɑ̃) *m*, denial; disavowal.

renier (rənje) *v.t*, to disown, deny.

renifler (rənifle) *v.i. & t*, to sniff; snuffle; snort; tolerate. *je ne peux pas le ~* I can't bear him.

renne (rɛn) *m*, reindeer.

renom (rənɔ̃) *m*, renown, fame; repute. **renommé**, e (nɔme) *p.a*, renowned, famed, noted. ¶ *f*, fame, renown, name; rumor, report. **renommer** (me) *v.t*, to reappoint.

renonce (rənɔ̃ːs) (*cards*) *f*, renounce; revoke. **renoncement** (nɔ̃smɑ̃) *m*, renunciation, self-denial. **renoncer** (se) *v.i. & t. & ~ à*, to renounce, give up, forgo; disown, deny; revoke (*cards*). **renonciation** (sjasjɔ̃) *f*, renunciation, disclaimer. ✓

renoncule (rənɔ̃kyl) *f*, ranunculus, buttercup, crowfoot. *~ bulbeuse*, kingcup.

renouer (rənwe) *v.t*, to retie; renew, resume.

renouveau (rənuvo) *m*, renewal; return of spring. **renouveler** (vle) *v.t*, to renew, renovate; change; revive. **rénover** (renɔve) *v.t*, to renovate, restore.

renseignement (rɑ̃sɛɲmɑ̃) *m. oft. pl*, information, intelligence, particular; inquiry. **renseigner** (ɲe) *v.t*, to inform. *se ~*, to inquire.

rente (rɑ̃ːt) *f*, income; annuity; pension; interest; stock. *~ viagère*, life endowment, annuity. **renter** (rɑ̃te) *v.t*, to endow. **rentier**, **ère** (tje, ɛːr) *n*, stockholder, fundholder, investor; annuitant; person of independent means.

rentraire (rɑ̃trɛːr) *v.t.ir*, to fine-draw.

rentrant, **e** (rɑ̃trɑ̃, ɑ̃ːt) *a*, re-entrant; sunk. **rentré**, **e** (tre) *p.a*, suppressed (*rage, etc.*). ¶ *f*, return; reentry; reappearance; reopening; ingathering; collection, receipt. **rentrer** (tre) *v.i*, to re-enter; return; reappear; reopen; (*v.t.*) to bring in, house; indent (*Typ.*). *~ dans*, to recover; re-enter; return to, rejoin. **rentrez!** all in! (*Sch.*).

renverse (à la) (rɑ̃vɛrs) *ad*, backwards, on one's back. **renverser** (se) *v.t*, to throw down, overthrow, upset; invert, reverse; astound. *se ~ sur sa chaise*, to lean (*or* lie) back (*or* recline) in one's chair.

renvoi (rɑ̃vwa) *m*, return; dismissal; postponement; reference; caret; repeat (*Mus.*); alteration; eructation; countershaft. **renvoyer** (je) *v.t*, to send back, return; dismiss; put off, adjourn; refer. *~ à une autre audience*, to remand. *~ une page*, to page-out (*computers*).

réorganiser (reɔrganize) *v.t*, to reorganize.

réouverture (reuvɛrtyːr) *f*, reopening.

repaire (rəpɛːr) *m*, den, lair; nest; haunt.

repaître (rəpɛːtr) *v.t*, to feed, feast.

répandre (repɑ̃:dr) *v.t*, to pour out, spill, shed; spread, diffuse, waft, scatter, sprinkle. **répandu, e** (pɑ̃dy) *p.a*, widespread; well-known.

réparable (reparabl) *a*, reparable, repairable.

reparaître (rəparɛ:tr) *v.i.ir*, to reappear.

réparateur, trice (reparatœ:r, tris) *n*, repairer, mender. **réparation** (sjɔ̃) *f*, repair; reparation; amends, atonement, redress. **réparer** (re) *v.t*, to repair, mend; retrieve; make amends for; make up for; redress, rectify.

repartie (rəparti) *f*, repartee, retort, rejoinder. **repartir** (ti:r) *v.i.ir*, to retort; set out again.

répartir (reparti:r) *v.t*, to distribute, apportion, allot; assess; spread. **repartiteur** (tœ:r) *m*, assessor (*taxes*); dispatcher (*transport*). **répartition** (tisjɔ̃) *f*, distribution, etc.

repas (rəpɑ) *m*, meal, repast, spread. ~ **de corps**, regimental dinner. ~ **de noce**, wedding breakfast, w. banquet.

repasser (rəpɑse) *v.i. & t*, to repass; recross; come again; reexamine, con, go over, think over; grind, sharpen; set; strop; iron (*linen*); rerun (*computers*). **repasseur** (sœ:r) *m*, grinder; strop (*razor*). **repasseuse** (sø:z) *f*, ironer, laundress.

repêcher (rəpeʃe) *v.t*, to fish up, f. out; give a second chance to (*exam*).

repentir (rəpɑ̃ti:r) *m*, repentance. **se** ~, *v.pr.ir*, to repent. **se** ~ **de**, to repent (*v.t.*), to rue, be sorry for.

repercer (rəpɛrse) *v.t*, to retap (*cask*); pierce (*metal*).

répercussion (repɛrkysjɔ̃) *f*, repercussion. **répercuter** (te) *v.t*, to reverberate.

repère (rəpɛ:r) *m*, reference mark; bench mark. *point de* ~, guide-mark, landmark. **répertoire** (repɛrtwa:r) *m*, index, list, register; directory; repertory; repository (*fig.*). ~ *à onglets*, thumb index. **répertorier** (tɔrje) *v.t*, to index.

répéter (repete) *v.t. & abs*, to repeat; rehearse; claim back (*law*). **répétiteur, trice** (titœ:r, tris) *n*, assistant teacher; tutor, coach. **répétition** (sjɔ̃) *f*, repetition, recurrence; reproduction, replica, duplicate; rehearsal; private lesson; claiming back. ~ *générale*, dress rehearsal.

repeupler (rəpœple) *v.t*, to re-people; restock; replant.

repiquer (rəpike) *v.t*, to prick again; restitch; plant out.

répit (repi) *m*, respite.

replacer (rəplase) *v.t*, to replace; reinvest.

replanter (rəplɑ̃te) *v.t*, to replant.

replâtrer (rəplɑtre) *v.t*, to replaster; patch up.

replet, ète (rəplɛ, ɛt) *a*, stout (*pers.*). **réplétion** (replesjɔ̃) *f*, repletion, corpulence.

repli (rəpli) *m*, fold, crease; coil (*snake*); recess (*heart*); falling back (*Mil.*). **replier** (plie) *v.t*, to fold up. **se** ~, to fold up; coil up; fall back.

réplique (replik) *f*, retort, rejoinder, answer; cue (*Theat.*); replica. **répliquer** (ke) *v.t*, to retort, rejoin, answer [back].

répondant, e (repɔ̃dɑ̃, ɑ̃:t) *n*, respondent; surety; sponsor; bail[sman]. **repondeur** (dœ:r) *m*, telephone answering machine. **répondre** (pɔ̃:dr) *v.t. & i*, to answer, reply, respond; say in reply; write back (*in reply*); correspond; agree; answer for, guarantee. **réponds** (pɔ̃) *m*, response (*Lit.*). **réponse** (pɔ̃:s) *f*, answer, reply; response.

report (rəpɔ:r) *m*, carry forward; c. over. **reportage** (pɔrtaːʒ) *m*, reporting; report (*news*). **reporter** (te) *v.t*, to carry forward; bring forward; carry over (*Stk Ex.*). **se** ~, to refer; look back to. **reporter** (tœ:r) *m*, reporter (*news*).

repos (rəpo) *m*, rest, repose; quiet; ease; peace; pause (*Mus., Pros.*); half-cock (*gun*); resting place, seat; landing (*stairs*). *de tout* ~, safe, reliable. *valeur de tout* ~, gilt-edged security. **reposant, e** (zɑ̃, ɑ̃:t) *a*, restful. **reposé, e** (ze) *p.a*, refreshed; fresh. *à tête* ~, at leisure. ¶ *f*, lair. **reposer** (ze) *v.t*, to replace; re-lay; rest; refresh; order (*arms*); (*v.i.*) to lie; rest; sleep; be based. **se** ~, to rest, lie down, recline; rely.

repoussant, e (rəpusɑ̃, ɑ̃:t) *a*, repulsive, repellent. **repoussé, e** (se) *p.a*, embossed. **repoussement** (smɑ̃) *m*, rejection; recoil; kick. **repousser** (se) *v.t*, to push back; repel, repulse, reject; deny; spurn; (*v.i.*) to recoil; sprout again, grow again. **repoussoir** (swa:r) *m*, punch (*tool*); set-off, foil.

répréhensible (repreɑ̃sibl) *a*, reprehensible.

reprendre (rəprɑ̃:dr) *v.t. & i. ir*, to retake, recapture; take up [again]; take back; recover; resume; regain; pick up [again]; reprove, find fault with; reply; rejoin; take root again; set again; freeze again. ~ *de volée*, to volley (*Ten.*). ~ *sous œuvre*, to underpin; reconstruct (*fig.*).

représaille (rəprezɑ:j) *f. oft. pl*, reprisal, retaliation.

représentant, e (rəprezɑ̃tɑ̃, ɑ̃:t) *n*, representative; agent. **représentatif, ive** (tatif, i:v) *a*, representative. **représentation** (sjɔ̃) *f*, representation; production; [purchase] consideration; performance (*Theat.*). ~ *à bénéfice*, benefit performance. **représenter** (te) *v.t*, to present again; represent; produce, show; perform, act; personate; picture; (*abs.*) to bear oneself; (*abs.*) to entertain.

répression (reprɛsjɔ̃) *f*, repression.

réprimande (reprimɑ̃:d) *f*, reprimand, reproof, rebuke. **réprimander** (mɑ̃de) *v.t*, to reprimand, reprove, rebuke.

réprimer (reprime) *v.t*, to repress, curb; put down, quell.

repris de justice (rəpri) *m*, habitual criminal, old offender, jailbird. **reprisage** (za:ʒ) *m*, darning, mending (*stockings, etc.*). **reprise** (pri:z) *f*, retaking, recapture; recovery; rally; resumption, renewal; revival; repetition; occasion, time; round (*Box.*); bout (*Fenc.*); darn[ing]; repair; key

money (*for apartment*). ~ *perdue*, invisible mending. **repriser** (prize) *v.t*, to darn, mend.

réprobation (reprɔbasjɔ̃) *f*, reprobation.

reproche (rəprɔʃ) *m*, reproach, blame. **reprocher** (ʃe) *v.t*, to reproach, blame, upbraid; taunt, twit.

reproduction (rəprɔdyksjɔ̃) *f*, reproduction. **reproduire** (dɥi:r) *v.t.ir*, to reproduce. **se** ~, to recur; reproduce, breed.

reprographie (rəprɔgrafi) *f*, duplicating (*document, etc.*).

réprouvé, e (repruve) *n*, outcast; reprobate. **réprouver** (ve) *v.t*, to reprobate; reject, disapprove of, deprecate.

reptation (rɛptasjɔ̃) *f*, creeping, crawling. **reptile** (til) *m*, reptile.

repu (rəpy) *a*, satiated, glutted, full. ~ *de fatigue*, dog-tired.

républicain, e (repyblikɛ̃, ɛn) *a. & n*, republican. **république** (lik) *f*, republic; commonwealth; community.

répudier (repydje) *v.t*, to repudiate; renounce.

répugnance (repyɲɑ̃:s) *f*, repugnance; reluctance. **répugnant, e** (ɲɑ̃, ɑ̃:t), *a*, repugnant. **répugner** (ɲe) *v.i*, to feel repugnance, feel loath; be repugnant.

répulsif, ive (repylsif, i:v) *a*, repulsive, repellent. **répulsion** (sjɔ̃) *f*, repulsion.

réputation (repytasjɔ̃) *f*, reputation, repute; name; character. **réputé, e** (te) *p.a*, well-known; of repute. **réputer** (te) *v.t*, to repute, deem, hold.

requérant, e (rekerɑ̃, ɑ̃:t) *n*, applicant, plaintiff. **requérir** (ri:r) *v.t.ir*, to require; summon. **requête** (kɛ:t) *f*, request, suit, petition.

requiem (rekɥiɛm) *m*, requiem.

requin (rəkɛ̃) *m*, shark (*fish & preying pers.*).

requinquer (se) (rəkɛ̃ke) *v.pr*, to smarten oneself up.

requis (rəki) *a*, required, requisite. ¶ *m*, labor conscript (*WW II*).

réquisition (rekizisjɔ̃) *f*, requisition, levy. **réquisitionner**

(ɔne) *v.t*, to requisition, commandeer, impress. **réquisitoire** (twa:r) *m*, charge, indictment.

rescapé, e (rɛskape) *n*, survivor, saved [person].

rescision (rɛssizjɔ̃) *f*, rescission.

rescousse (à la) (rɛskus) to the rescue.

rescrit (rɛskri) *m*, rescript.

réseau (rezo) *m*, netting; network; system; area; plexus; tracery. ~ *de fils de fer*, wire entanglement (*Mil.*). ~ *banalisé*, shared network (*computers*).

réséda (rezeda) *m*, reseda, mignonette.

réservation (rezɛrvasjɔ̃) *f*, reservation. **réserve** (zɛrv) *f*, reservation; booking (*seats*); reserve; store; exception, qualification; preserve (*Hunt.*); sanctuary (*animals*). *sous* ~ *de*, subject to. *sous* ~ *que*, on condition that. **réservé, e** (ve) *a*, reserved; cautious, guarded; shy; coy. **réserviste** (vist) *m*, reservist. **réservoir** (vwa:r) *m*, reservoir, tank, cistern, well.

résidence (rezidɑ̃:s) *f*, residence, dwelling, abode. **résident, e** (dɑ̃, ɑ̃:t) *n. & a*, resident (*diplomatic*); settler (*colony*). **résider** (de) *v.i*, to reside, dwell, live; lie, rest. **résidu** (dy) *m*, residue.

résignation (reziɲasjɔ̃) *f*, resignation; submissiveness. **résigner** (ɲe) *v.t*, to resign.

résilier (rezilje) *v.t*, to cancel, annul.

résille (rezi:j) *f*, hairnet; cames.

résine (rezin) *f*, resin, rosin. **résineux, euse** (nø, ø:z) *a*, resinous.

résistance (rezistɑ̃:s) *f*, resistance; opposition; strength; toughness; endurance, stamina; underground army. **résistant, e** (tɑ̃, ɑ̃:t) *a*, resistant, strong, tough. **résister à** (te) *v.i*, to resist, withstand.

résolu†, e (rezɔly) *p.a*, resolute, determined. **résolution** (sjɔ̃) *f*, resolution; solution; cancelation; resolve.

résonance (rezɔnɑ̃:s) *f*, reso-

nance. **résonnant, e** (nɑ̃, ɑ̃:t) *a*, resonant. **résonner** (ne) *v.i*, to resound; ring; reecho; twang.

résorber (rezɔrbe) *v.t*, to reabsorb; absorb, imbibe.

résoudre (rezu:dr) *v.t.ir*, to resolve, solve; annul.

respect (rɛspɛ) *m*, respect, regard, deference. **respectable** (pɛktabl) *a*, respectable. **respecter** (te) *v.t*, to respect; spare. **respectif, ive†** (tif, i:v) *a*, respective, several. **respectueux, euse†** (tɥø, ø:z) *a*, respectful, dutiful. ~ *des lois*, law-abiding.

respiration (rɛspirasjɔ̃) *f*, respiration, breathing. **respirer** (re) *v.i. & t*, to breathe; respire; inhale; exhale.

resplendir (rɛsplɑ̃di:r) *v.i*, to be resplendent, shine, glitter. **resplendissant, e** (disɑ̃, ɑ̃:t) *a*, resplendent; aglow; glorious.

responsabilité (rɛspɔ̃sabilite) *f*, responsibility; liability; care. **responsable** (bl) *a*, responsible, answerable, liable. ¶ *m*, person in charge. **responsif, ive** (sif, i:v) *a*, in reply (*law*).

resquille (rɛski:j) *f*, [gate] crashing. **resquilleur, euse** (kijœ:r, ø:z) *n*, [gate] crasher.

ressac (rəsak) *m*, undertow; surf.

ressaisir (rəsɛzi:r) *v.t*, to recover.

ressasser (rəsase) *v.t*, to resift; repeat.

ressaut (rəso) *m*, projection, setoff.

ressemblance (rəsɑ̃blɑ̃:s) *f*, semblance, likeness. **ressemblant, e** (blɑ̃, ɑ̃:t) *a*, [a]like. **ressembler à** (ble) *v.t*, to resemble, be like, look like.

ressemeler (rəsəmle) *v.t*, to resole.

ressentiment (rəsɑ̃timɑ̃) *m*, resentment. **ressentir** (ti:r) *v.t*, to feel; resent. *se* ~, to feel.

resserre (rəsɛ:r) *f*, storeroom. **resserrer** (sɛre) *v.t*, to tighten; close up; bind; put away [again]; contract, narrow, confine, restrict; condense.

ressort (rəsɔ:r) *m*, spring; elasticity; buoyancy; incentive; province; purview; resort, appeal. ~ à boudin, spiral spring. à ~, spring (scale, etc.). **ressortir** (sɔrti:r) v.i, to be under the jurisdiction of; (v.i.ir.) to go out again; stand out (in relief); result, appear.

ressource (rəsurs) f, resource; expedient, shift, resort.

ressouvenir (rəsuvni:r) m, remembrance, memory. **se ~,** v.pr. ir, to remember.

ressuer (rəsɥe) v.i, to sweat (walls).

ressusciter (resysite) v.t, to resuscitate, revive; raise (the dead.)

restant, e (rɛstɑ̃, ɑ̃:t) a, remaining, left.

restaurant, e (rɛstɔrɑ̃, ɑ̃:t) a, restorative. ¶ m, restorative; restaurant, eating house. **restaurateur, trice** (ratœ:r, tris) n, restorer; restaurant keeper, caterer. **restauration** (sjɔ̃), f, restoration. **restaurer** (re) v.t, to restore, reestablish; refresh.

reste (rɛst) m, rest, remainder, remains; leavings, remnant. au, du ~, besides, moreover. ~s mortels, mortal remains. **rester** (te) v.i, to remain, be left; stay, stop, stand, sit, keep, stick; last; live.

restituer (rɛstitɥe) v.t, to restore, return. **restitution** (tysjɔ̃) f, restitution; restoration.

restoroute (rɛstɔrut) m, restaurant on turnpike, highway, etc.

restreindre (rɛstrɛ̃:dr) v.t.ir, to restrict, limit. **restriction** (triksjɔ̃) f, restriction; reservation.

résultat (rezylta) m, result, outcome. **résulter** (te) v.i, to result, follow, ensue.

résumé (rezyme) m, summary, abstract. ~ des débats, summing up. **résumer** (me) v.t, to summarize; sum up.

résurrection (rezyrɛksjɔ̃) f, resurrection.

retable (rətabl) m, reredos, altar piece.

rétablir (retabli:r) v.t, to reestablish, restore; retrieve; reinstate.

retaille (rətɑ:j) f, cutting, paring (snip, bit).

rétamer (retame) v.t, to replate, retin. être rétamé, to be drunk; exhausted; broke.

retaper (rətape) v.t, to do up; recast.

retard (rəta:r) m, delay. en ~, late, behind[hand]; overdue; in arrears; slow (clock). **retardataire** (tardatɛ:r) a, late, in arrears; overstaying pass (Mil.). ¶ n, latecomer. **retarder** (de) v.t, to retard, delay; hinder; put off; put back (clock); (v.i.) be slow; lag.

retâter (rətate) v.t. & i, to touch again; try again.

retenir (rətni:r) v.t.ir, to keep back, retain, withhold, stop; keep; engage; reserve, book; detain; hold; h. back; check, restrain; remember; carry (Arith.). se ~, to refrain; catch hold. **rétention** (retɑ̃sjɔ̃) f, retention.

retentir (rətɑ̃ti:r) v.i, to [re]sound, echo, ring. **retentissant** (tisɑ̃) a, resounding, echoing; sonorous.

retenu, e (rətny) a, cautious, discreet. ¶ f, stoppage (on pay, etc.); carry (Arith.); reserve, discretion. mettre en ~, to keep in (Sch.).

réticence (retisɑ̃:s) f, reticence; concealment.

réticule (retikyl) m, reticule; reticle.

rétif, ive (retif, i:v) a, restive; stubborn.

rétine (retin) f, retina.

retiré, e (rətire) p.a, solitary, secluded. **retirer** (re) v.t, to redraw; draw back; withdraw; retire (bill); take out; remove; extract; draw, get, derive; recall; reclaim (from vice). se ~, to retire, withdraw; stand down; recede; shrink.

retombée (rətɔ̃be) f, spring[ing] (arch); repercussions, consequences (bad); fallout (nuclear). **retomber** (be) v.i, to fall down [again]; relapse; fall [back], devolve; hang down.

rétorquer (retɔrke) v.t, to retort.

retors, e (rətɔːr, ɔrs) a, twisted; crafty.

retouche (rətuʃ) f, retouch[ing]; patch (computers). **retoucher** (ʃe) v.t. & ~ à, to retouch, touch up.

retour (rətuːr) m, turn; return; recurrence; reversion; reversal; decline (life), wane; ruse. ~ de flamme, backfire. ~ de manivelle, backfire [kick]. ~ en arrière, flashback (TV, cinema, literature, etc.). être de ~, to be back. **retourne** (turn) f, turn-up (card), trumps. **retournement** (nəmã) m, turning, reversal. ~ de bras, hammerlock (wrestling). **retourner** (ne) v.i. & t, to return; revert; turn (coat, etc.); t. over; t. up; mix (salad). ~ un plan, to retake a shot (cinema). se ~, to turn [round], veer (opinion).

retracer (rətrase) v.t, to retrace, recall. se ~, to recur.

rétracter (retrakte) v.t, to retract, recant.

retrait, e (rətrɛ, ɛt) p.a, shrunken. ¶ m, withdrawal; deprivation; shrinkage; recess. ¶ f, retreat; tattoo; withdrawal; retirement; superannuation; pension; retired pay; shelter; seclusion; shrinkage; offset (Arch.). ~ aux flambeaux, torchlight tattoo. prendre sa ~, to retire. **retraité, e** (te) a, pensioned off, superannuated. [officier] retraité, officer on the retired list.

retrancher (rətrãʃe) v.t, to cut off; c. out; take away; deduct; subtract; entrench.

rétrécir (retresiːr) v.t. & i, to narrow; shrink. se ~, to shrink.

retremper (rətrãpe) v.t, to retemper; brace.

rétribuer (retribɥe) v.t, to remunerate, pay. **rétribution** (bysjɔ̃) f, remuneration, salary, reward.

rétro (retrɔ) a, harking back to or imitating the past. ¶ m, return to the past (abbrev. of "rétrograde").

rétroactif, ive (retroaktif, iːv) a, retroactive. **rétroaction** (aksjɔ̃) f, feedback (computers).

rétrocéder (retrɔsede) v.i, to retrocede; recede; go back. **rétrocession** (sɛsjɔ̃) f, retrocession; recession.

rétrograde (retrɔgrad) a, retrograde, backward. **rétrograder** (de) v.i, to go back[wards]. (v.t.) to reduce to lower rank (Mil.).

rétrospectif, ive† (retrɔspɛktif, iːv) a, retrospective. ¶ f, retrospect.

retrousser (rətruse) v.t, to turn up; tuck up; curl (lip).

retrouver (rətruve) v.t, to find [again], recover; recognize; retrieve (computers). se ~, to meet again.

rétroviseur (retrɔvizœːr), m, rearview mirror (auto).

rets (rɛ) m, net; (pl.) toils (fig.).

réunion (reynjɔ̃) f, [re]union; assembly, gathering, function, meeting. **réunir** (niːr) v.t, to [re]unite; join; combine; lump. se ~, to meet, foregather.

réussi, e (reysi) p.a, successful. **réussir** (siːr) v.i, to succeed; prosper. **réussite** (sit) f, success; solitaire (cards).

revaloir (rəvalwaːr) v.t.ir, to pay (someone) out, be even with (someone).

revanche (rəvãʃ) f, revenge; return; requital, return match.

rêvasser (rɛvase) v.i, to have troubled dreams; muse. **rêve** (rɛːv) m, dream; day dream.

revêche (rəvɛʃ) a, cantankerous.

réveil (revɛj) m, waking, awakening; revival (Relig.); reveille; alarm clock. **réveille-matin** (vej) m, alarm clock; awakener. **réveiller** (veje) v.t, to awake[n], wake[n], call [a]rouse; revive. se ~, to wake [up]; revive. **réveillon** (jɔ̃) m, Christmas or New Year's Eve supper.

révélateur, trice (revelatœːr, tris) n, revealer; (m.) developer (Phot.). **révélation** (sjɔ̃) f, revelation; disclosure; eye-opener. **révéler** (le) v.t, to reveal, disclose; develop (Phot.).

revenant (rəvnã) m, ghost.

revenant-bon (rəvnãbɔ̃) m, perquisite.

revendeur, euse (rəvãdœːr, øːz) n, second-hand dealer; retailer; peddler.

revendication (rəvãdikasjɔ̃) f, demand; claim; claiming.

revendiquer (rəvɑ̃dike) *v.t*, to claim, assert.

revendre (rəvɑ̃:dr) *v.t*, to resell. *avoir à ~*, to have enough & to spare.

revenir (rəvni:r) *v.i.ir*, to come [back], return; come again, recur; revert; recover; cost; amount. *~ sur*, to retrace; go back on; reconsider; rake up (*past*). *je n'en reviens pas*, I can't believe it. *faire ~*, to sauté lightly.

revente (rəvɑ̃:t) *f*, resale.

revenu (rəvny) *m*, revenue, income. **revenue** (ny) *f*, new growth, young wood.

rêver (rɛve) *v.i. & t*, to dream; d. of; muse; ponder.

réverbère (revɛrbɛ:r) *m*, street lamp; reflector. **réverbérer** (bere) *v.t*, to reverberate.

reverdir (rəvɛrdi:r) *v.i*, to grow green again; grow young again.

révérence (reverɑ̃:s) *f*, reverence; bow, curtsy. **révérenciel, le** (rɑ̃sjɛl) *a*, reverential. **révérencieux, euse†** (sjø, øːz) *a*, obsequious; over-polite. **révérend, e** (rɑ̃, ɑ̃:d) *a*, reverend. **révérendissime** (rɑ̃disim) *a*, most reverend, right r. **révérer** (re) *v.t*, to revere, reverence.

rêverie (rɛvri) *f*, reverie, musing; idle fancy.

revers (rəvɛ:r) *m*, reverse; back; backhand [stroke, blow]; facing, lapel; turnover [top] (*stocking, etc.*).

reverser (rəvɛrse) *v.t*, to pour out again; pour back; transfer. **réversible** (revɛrsibl) *a*, reversible; revertible. **réversion** (sjɔ̃) *f*, reversion.

revêtement (rəvɛtmɑ̃) *m*, facing (*wall, etc.*); lining; revetment. **revêtir** (ti:r) *v.t*, to clothe, dress; don, put on; assume; provide; face, line; revet.

rêveur, euse (rɛvœ:r, øːz) *a*, dreaming; dreamy. ¶ *n*, dreamer.

revient (rəvjɛ̃) *m*, cost. *prix de ~*, cost price.

revigorer (rəvigɔre) *v.t*, to reinvigorate.

revirement (rəvirmɑ̃) *m*, change, turn; turnover; veering.

reviser (rəvize) *v.t*, to revise; review, reconsider; overhaul. **reviseur** (zœ:r) *m*, examiner; proof-reader. **revision** (jɔ̃) *f*, revision; review; proofreading; medical examination (*recruits*); overhaul (*engine, etc.*). *conseil de ~*, draft board.

revivifier (rəvivifje) *v.t*, to revivify, revive. **revivre** (vi:vr) *v.i.ir*, to live again, come to life again; revive.

révocation (revɔkasjɔ̃) *f*, revocation; repeal; dismissal, removal.

revoici (rəvwasi) *pr*, here . . . again. *le ~*, here he is again. **revoilà** (la) *pr*, there . . . again.

revoir (rəvwa:r) *v.t.ir*, to see again; meet again; revise; review. *au ~!* good-bye!

revoler (rəvɔle) *v.i*, to fly again; fly back.

révoltant, e (revɔltɑ̃, ɑ̃:t) *a*, revolting. **révolte** (vɔlt) *f*, revolt, rebellion, mutiny. **révolté, e** (te) *n*, rebel, insurgent, mutineer. **révolter** (te) *v.t*, to cause to revolt; shock. *se ~*, to revolt, rebel, mutiny.

révolu, e (revɔly) *a*, completed. **révolution** (sjɔ̃) *f*, revolution; revulsion. **révolutionnaire** (ɔnɛ:r) *a. & n*, revolutionary. **révolutionner** (ne) *v.t*, to revolutionize; upset. **revolver** (revɔlvɛ:r) *m*, revolver (*gun*); capstan, turret (*lathe*). *~ à six coups*, six-shooter.

revomir (rəvɔmi:r) *v.t*, to vomit [up, again].

révoquer (revɔke) *v.t*, to revoke, repeal; dismiss; recall.

revue (rəvy) *f*, review, inspection; magazine; revue.

révulsion (revylsjɔ̃) *f*, revulsion (*Med.*).

rez-de-chaussée (redʃose) *m*, ground floor.

rhabiller (rabije) *v.t*, to repair, mend, overhaul; dress again; reclothe.

rhapsodie (rapsɔdi) *f*, rhapsody (*all Eng. senses*).

rhénan, e (renɑ̃, an) *a*, Rhine (*att.*).

rhétorique (retɔrik) *f*, rhetoric. **Rhin** (le) (rɛ̃) the Rhine.

rhinocéros (rinɔserɔs) *m*, rhinoceros.

rhododendron (rɔdɔdɛ̃drɔ̃) *m*, rhododendron.

rhombe (rɔ̃:b) *m*, rhomb[us].

Rhône (le) (ro:n) the Rhone.

rhubarbe (rybarb) *f*, rhubarb.

rhum (rɔm) *m*, rum.

rhumatismal, e (rymatismal) *a*, rheumatic. **rhumatisme** (tism) *m*, rheumatism. **rhume** (*de cerveau, de poitrine*) (rym) *m*, cold (in the head, on the chest).

rhythme (ritm) *m*, rhythm. **rhythmique** (mik) *a*, rhythmic[al].

riant, e (riɑ̃, ɑ̃:t) *a*, smiling; cheerful.

ribambelle (ribɑ̃bɛl) *f*, string, swarm.

ribote (ribɔt) *f*, drunken bout.

ricaner (rikane) *v.i*, to snigger, sneer.

richard (riʃa:r) *m*, [rich] upstart. **riche†** (riʃ) *a*, rich, wealthy; copious; valuable; handsome. **richesse** (ʃɛs) *f*, wealth, riches; richness.

ricin (risɛ̃) *m*, castor oil plant.

ricocher (rikɔʃe) *v.i*, to ricochet. **ricochet** (ʃɛ) *m*, ricochet; (*pl.*) duck & drake.

rictus (rikty:s) *m*, grin.

ride (rid) *f*, wrinkle, line; puckering; ripple; lanyard. **rideau** (do) *m*, curtain; [drop] curtain; screen; veil (*fig.*). ~ *de fer*, safety curtain (*Theat.*); iron curtain. *lever de* ~, curtain raiser. **rider** (de) *v.t*, to wrinkle, line; shrivel; ripple; ruffle.

ridicule† (ridikyl) *a*, ridiculous. ¶ *m*, ridiculousness; ridicule. **ridiculiser** (lize) *v.t*, to ridicule.

rien (rjɛ̃) *pn.m*, anything; (*oft. with* ne) nothing. ~ *à* ~, love all (*Ten.*). *de* ~, don't mention it, you're welcome. ¶ *m*, trifle, mere nothing; (*pl.*) small talk.

rieur, euse (rjœ:r, ø:z) *n*, laugher; (*att.*) laughing.

riflard (rifla:r) *m*, jack plane; gamp.

rigide† (riʒid) *a*, rigid; stiff. **rigidité** (dite) *f*, rigidity, stiffness. ~ *cadavérique* (kadaverik), rigor mortis.

rigolade (rigɔlad) *f*, lark, nonsense; joke.

rigole (rigɔl) *f*, channel, ditch, trench.

rigoler (rigɔle) *v.i*, guffaw; furrow, channel. **rigolo** (lo) *a*, comic, funny.

rigoureux, euse† (rigurø, ø:z) *a*, rigorous, severe; strict. **rigueur** (gœ:r) *f*, rigor, severity; hardship; strictness. *à la* ~, if necessary. *de* ~, required.

rimailler (rimaje) *v.i*, to write bad verse. **rimailleur** (jœ:r) *m*, rhym[est]er. **rime** (rim) *f*, rhyme. **rimer** (me) *v.t*, to versify; (*v.i.*) to rhyme. **rimeur** (mœ:r) *m*, rhym[est]er.

rincer (rɛ̃se) *v.t*, to rinse; r. out. **rinçure** (sy:r) *f*, rinsings, slops.

ringard (rɛ̃ga:r) *m*, poker, rake.

ripaille (ripɑ:j) *f*, feasting, carousal.

riper (ripe) *v.t. & i*, to scrape; slide; shift (*cargo*).

ripopée (ripɔpe) *f*, slops; mishmash.

riposte (ripɔst) *f*, riposte, counter[stroke]; retort. **riposter** (te) *v.t*, to riposte.

rire (ri:r) *m*, laughter; laugh. *fou* ~, uncontrolled laughter. ~ *moqueur*, sneer. ¶ *v.i.ir*, to laugh, smile; joke. ~ *en dedans*, ~ *en dessous*, to laugh inwardly, snigger.

ris (ri) *m*, reef (*sail*). ~ *de veau*, sweetbread.

risée (rize) *f*, jeer, mockery; laughing stock, butt. **risible†** (zibl) *a*, ludicrous, laughable.

risque (risk) *m*, risk. **risquer** (ke) *v.t*, to risk, chance. ~ *le paquet*, to chance it.

rissole (risɔl) *f*, rissole. **rissoler** (le) *v.t*, to brown (*Cook.*).

ristourne (risturn) *f*, return, refund; discount.

rite (rit) *m*, rite. **rituel, le** (tyɛl) *a. & m*, ritual.

rivage (riva:ʒ) *m*, shore, foreshore, beach, strand; bank, side.

rival, e (rival) *n. & a*, rival. **rivaliser avec** (lize), to rival, vie with, emulate. **rivalité** (te) *f*, rivalry, emulation.

rive (ri:v) *f*, bank, side, shore.

river (rive) *v.t*, to rivet, clinch.

riverain, e (rivrɛ̃, ɛn) *a*, riparian, riverside, waterside; wayside.

rivet (rive) *m*, rivet; pin, bolt.

rivière (rivjɛ:r) *f*, river; rivière (*gems*); single openwork (*Need.*). ~ *à truites*, trout stream. *la R~ de Gênes*, the Riviera (*French & Italian*).

rixe (riks) *f*, scuffle, brawl, fight.

riz (ri) *m*, rice. **rizière** (zjɛ:r) *f*, rice field.

rob (rɔb) *m*, rubber (*cards*).

robe (rɔb) *f*, dress, gown, frock; robe; robe (*legal dress*); cloth (*clerical dress*); coat (*animal's*); skin (*onion, bean, etc.*); wrapper (*cigar*); color (*wine*). ~ *de chambre*, dressing gown. ~ *de mariée*, wedding dress. **robin** (bɛ̃) *m*, lawyer.

robert (rɔbɛ:r) *m*, breast (*vulgar*).

robinet (rɔbinɛ) *m*, cock, faucet. spigot.

robre (rɔbr) *m*, rubber (*cards*).

robuste† (rɔbyst) *a*, robust, lusty, sturdy, able-bodied; stout; hardy (*plant*). **robustesse** (tɛs) *f*, robustness, strength.

roc (rɔk) *m*, rock. **rocaille** (ka:j) *f*, rockwork. **rocailleux, euse** (kajø, ø:z) *a*, rocky, stony, rugged.

rocade (rɔkad) *m*, castling (*chess*). *ligne de ~*, castling base (*chess*). *voie de ~, chemin de fer de ~*, strategic road or railroad paralleling a military front.

rocambolesque (rɔkɑ̃bɔlɛsk) *a*, fantastic, incredible.

roche (rɔʃ) *f*, rock, stone, boulder. **rocher** (ʃe) *m*, rock, crag, cliff. ~ *artificiel*, rock garden. ~ *branlant*, rocking stone, logan [stone].

rochet (rɔʃɛ) *m*, ratchet; rochet (*surplice*).

rocheux, euse (rɔʃø, ø:z) *a*, rocky.

rococo (rɔkɔkɔ) *m. & att*, rococo.

roder (rɔde) *v.t*, to grind, lap; break in (*Motor.*).

rôder (rode) *v.i*, to prowl, hang about. **rôdeur** (dœ:r) *m*, prowler. ~ *de grève*, beachcomber.

rodomontade (rɔdɔmɔ̃tad) *f*, bluster.

rogations (rɔgasjɔ̃) *f.pl*, rogations.

rogatons (rɔgatɔ̃) *m.pl*, scraps (*food*); odds & ends.

Roger-Bontemps (rɔʒebɔ̃tɑ̃) *m*, happy-go-lucky fellow.

rogne (rɔɲ) *f*, itch, mange; scab; [bad] temper.

rogner (rɔɲe) *v.t*, to clip, trim, pare; cut down; cut (*edges of book*); (*v.i.*) to grumble, grouse.

rogneux, euse (rɔɲø, ø:z) *a*, mangy, scabby.

rognon (rɔɲɔ̃) *m*, kidney (*animal*); nodule.

rognonner (rɔɲɔne) *v.i*, to grumble.

rognure (rɔɲy:r) *f*, clipping, paring (*bit*).

rogue (rɔg) *a*, arrogant, haughty.

roi (rwa) *m*, king; champion. *fête des ~s*, Twelfth Night. ~ *de la nature*, lord of creation.

roide (rɛd & rwad) *a*, **roideur** (dœ:r) *f*, **roidir** (di:r) *v.t*. Same as *raide, etc.*

roitelet (rwatlɛ) *m*, kinglet; wren.

rôle (ro:l) *m*, roll, list, roster, rota; calendar (*prisoners for trial*); part, rôle. ~ *travesti*, man's part acted by a woman. *à tour de ~*, in rotation, in turn.

romain, e (rɔmɛ̃, ɛn) *a. & R~* (*pers.*) *n*, Roman. **romain**, *m*, roman (*Typ.*). **romaine**, *f*, romaine lettuce, cos l.; steelyard.

roman, e (rɔmɑ̃, an) *a. & m*, Romance (*language*); Romanesque (*Arch.*). ¶ *m*, novel; fiction; romance. ~ *à deux sous*, pulp novel. ~ *policier* (pɔlisje), detective story. **romance** (mɑ̃:s) *f*, song, ballad; sloppiness, maudlin[ism]. ~ *sans paroles*, song without words. ¶ *a*, sloppy, maudlin. **romancier, ère** (mɑ̃sje, ɛ:r) *n*, novelist. **romand, e** (mɑ̃, ɑ̃:d) *a*, French-speaking (*Switzerland*). **romanesque†** (manɛsk) *a*, romantic. **romanichel** (maniʃɛl) *m*, gypsy, romany. **romantique** (mɑ̃tik) *a*, romantic (*literature*).

romarin (rɔmarɛ̃) *m*, rosemary.

rompre (rɔ̃:pr) *v.t. & i*, to break; b. up; b. in; b. off; snap; rupture; disrupt; burst; interrupt, cut off; upset; cancel. ~ *charge*, to tran ship (*Rly.*). ~ *les chiens,* to call off the hounds; change the subject. *rompez!,* dismissed (*Mil.*). **rompu,** e (rɔ̃py) *p.a,* broken; b. in, used, inured. ~ [*de fatigue*], tired out. *à batons* ~s, by fits and starts.

romsteck (rɔmstɛk) *m,* rump steak.

ronce (rɔ̃:s) *f,* bramble; blackberry bush; barb[ed] wire; annoyance. ~ *de noyer,* walnut burr. ~*-framboise,* loganberry.

ronchonner (rɔʃɔne) *v.i,* to grumble.

rond, e (rɔ̃, ɔ̃:d) *a,* round; rounded; rotund; even (*money*); drunk; broke (*money*). ¶ *m,* round; circle; ring. ~*-de-cuir,* pen-pusher, bureaucrat; air cushion. ~ *de serviette,* napkin ring. ¶ *f,* round; beat; roundelay; round hand; semibreve. **rondelet,** te (rɔ̃dlɛ, ɛt) *a,* roundish. **rondelle** (dɛl) *f,* washer; ring (*umbrella*); disc. **rondement** (dmɑ̃) *ad,* roundly, briskly, bluntly. **rondeur** (dœ:r) *f,* roundness, rotundity; fullness; frankness. **rondin** (dɛ̃) *m,* billet, log. **rond-point** (rɔ̃pwɛ̃) *m,* traffic circle.

ronflant, e (rɔ̃flɑ̃, ɑ̃:t) (*fig.*) *a,* sonorous, highsounding. **ronfler** (fle) *v.i,* to snore; boom, roar, hum, whir, buzz.

ronger (rɔ̃ʒe) *v.t,* to gnaw, nibble; pick (*bone*); eat [away, into], corrode; undermine; fret; prey. **rongeur, euse** (ʒœ:r, ø:z) *a,* rodent, gnawing; corroding. ¶ *m,* rodent.

ronron (rɔ̃rɔ̃) *m,* purr[ing]; hum; drone.

roquer (rɔke) *v.t,* to castle (*chess*); roquet (*croquet*).

roquet (rɔkɛ) *m,* pug [dog]; cur, mongrel.

roquette (rɔkɛt) *f,* rocket (*Bot.*).

rosace (rozas) *f,* rosette; rose window. **rosacé,** e (se) rosaceous. ¶ *f.pl,* Rosaceae. **rosaire** (zɛ:r) *m,* rosary (*beads*).

rosbif (rɔzbif) *m,* roast beef; roast sirloin.

rose (ro:z) *f,* rose; rose window; rose diamond. ~ *des vents,* compass card. ~ *moussue,* moss rose. ~ *muscade,* musk r. ~ *thé,* tea r.

~ *trémière* (tremjɛ:r), hollyhock. ¶ *m. & a,* rose [color], pink. *le mont Rose,* Monte Rosa. **rosé,** e (roze), *a,* roseate, rosy.

roseau (rozo) *m,* reed; broken reed (*fig.*).

rosée (roze) *f,* dew.

roselet (rɔslɛ) *m,* ermine (*fur*).

roseraie (rɔzrɛ) *f,* rose garden, rosary, rosery. **rosette** (zɛt) *f,* rosette; bow (*ribbon*); red ink, r. chalk. **rosier** (zje) *m,* rose bush. ~ *grimpant,* rambler [rose]. **rosière** (jɛ:r) *f,* innocent girl.

rosse (rɔs) *f,* jade, sorry steed; nasty (*or* objectionable) person. **rosser** (se) *v.t,* to thrash, beat.

rossignol (rɔsiɲɔl) *m,* nightingale; picklock; whistle; unsalable article, white elephant.

rot (ro) *m.* belch.

rôt (ro) *m,* roast [meat]; roast meat course.

rotation (rɔtasjɔ̃) *f,* rotation. **rotatoire** (twa:r) *a,* rotary.

roter (rɔte) *v.i,* to belch.

rôti (roti) *m,* roast [meat]; r. m. course. ~ *de porc,* r. pork. **rôtie** (ti) *f,* [round of] roast. ~ *à l'anglaise,* ~ *au fromage,* Welsh rabbit, W. rarebit.

rotin (rɔtɛ̃) *m,* rattan; r. cane.

rôtir (roti:r) *v.t. & i,* to roast, broil; toast; scorch. **rôtisserie** (tisri) *f,* shop where one buys cooked meats. **rôtissoire** (tiswa:r) *f,* roaster, Dutch oven.

rotonde (rɔtɔ̃:d) *f,* rotunda; cloak. **rotondité** (tɔ̃dite) *f,* rotundity.

rotule (rɔtyl) *f,* knee cap, patella. ~ *sphérique,* ball & socket.

roture (rɔty:r) *f,* commonalty. **roturier, ère** (tyrje, ɛ:r) *n,* commoner.

rouage (rwa:ʒ) *m,* wheels, wheelwork, works; machinery (*fig.*).

rouan, ne (rwɑ̃, an) *a. & n,* roan (*animal*).

roucouler (rukule) *v.i,* to coo; bill & coo; (*v.t.*) to warble.

roue (ru) *f,* wheel. ~ *libre,* free w. *faire la* ~, to spread its tail (*peacock*); turn catherine wheels. ~ *de secours,* spare w. ~ *d'impression,* print w. **roué** (rwe) *m,* rake,

profligate. rouelle (rwɛl) *f*, round [slice]; fillet (*veal*).

rouennerie (rwanri) *f*, printed cotton goods.

rouer (rwe) *v.t*, to coil (*rope*); break upon the wheel. ~ **de coups**, to thrash. **rouerie** (ruri) *f*, trickery. **rouet** (rwɛ) *m*, spinning wheel; sheave.

rouflaquette (ruflakɛt) *f*, love-lock, earlock, cowlick.

rouge (ru:ʒ) *m*, red (*color & pers. in Pol.*); rouge; red wine. ¶ *a*, red; red-hot; blushing; glowing. **mer R~**, Red Sea. ~ **gorge**, *m*, [robin] redbreast. ~ *à lèvres*, *m*, lipstick. **rougeâtre** (ruʒɑːtr) *a*, reddish. **rougeaud, e** (ʒo, oːd) *a*, red-faced, ruddy. **rougeole** (ʒɔl) *f*, measles. **rouget** (ʒɛ) *m*, red mullet. **rougeur** (ʒœːr) *f*, redness; blush, flush; red spot (*skin*). **rougir** (ʒiːr) *v.t,. & i*, to redden; blush, flush.

rouille (ruːj) *f*, rust; mildew; blight (*Agric.*). **rouillé, e** (ruje) *a*, rusty; mildewed; out of practice. **rouiller** (je) *v.t*, to rust. **rouillure** (jyːr) *f*, rustiness.

roulade (rulad) *f*, roll (*down-hill*); roulade, run (*Mus.*). **roulage** (laːʒ) *m*, haulage. **roulant, e** (lɑ̃, ɑ̃ːt) *a*, rolling; traveling; circulating (*capital*). **rouleau** (lo) *m*, roller; roll; spool (*film ~Phot.*); scroll; twist (*tobacco*); coil (*rope*). **~de pâtissier**, rolling pin. **au bout de son ~**, at the end of one's rope, at one's wits' end. **roulement** (lmɑ̃) *m*, roll[ing]; working, running; r. gear; rumbling (*traffic*); bearings; turnover (*capital*); rotation. ~ *à billes*, ball bearings. **rouler** (le) *v.t*, to roll; r. up; coil; haul; (*v.i.*) to. roll; run, work; turn, rotate; travel, drive; rove, roam; circulate freely; fluctuate; fleece, cheat. *faire ~ la presse*, to machine (*Typ.*). **~[sur le sol]**, to taxi (*Avn.*). **roulette** (lɛt) caster, -or; roller; wheel; tape [measure] (*coiled*); roulette. **roulier** (lje) *m*, carter, waggoner. **roulis** (li) *m*, rolling (*ship*). **roulotte** (lɔt) *f*, caravan (*house on wheels*); trailer.

roumain, e (rumɛ̃, ɛn) *a & R~, n. & le roumain* (*language*), R[o]umanian. **la Roumanie** (mani), R[o]umania.

roupiller (rupije) *v.i*, to snooze. **rouspéter** (ruspete) *v.i*, to complain, protest; resist; gripe.

roussâtre (rusɑːtr) *a*, reddish. **rousseau** (so) *m. & att*, red-haired (person). **rousserolle** (srɔl) *f*, sedge warbler. **rousseur** (sœːr) *f*, redness. *tache de ~*, freckle. **roussi** (si) *m*, [smell of] burning. **roussir** (siːr) *v.t. & i*, to redden; brown (*meat*); scorch, singe.

route (rut) *f*, road, path, track; route, course, way; transit; journey. *grande ~*, ~ *nationale*, highway. ~ *départementale*, secondary road. ~ *déviée*, loopway. **routier** (tje) *ère* (tjɛ:r) *a*, road (*att.*). ¶ *m*, campaigner, stager. **routine** (tin) *f*, routine; rote; red tape.

rouvieux (ruvjø) *m*, mange; (*att.*) mangy.

rouvrir (ruvri:r) *v.t.ir*, to re-open.

roux, rousse (ru, rus) *a. & n*, russet; brown[ed]; red (*hair*); red-haired (person). ¶ *m*, russet (*color*); brown sauce.

royal, e ¶ (rwajal) *a*, royal, regal, kingly. **royaliste** (list) *a. & n*, royalist. **royaume** (jo:m) *m*, kingdom, realm. **royauté** (ote) *f*, royalty; kingship; dominance.

ruade (rɥad) *f*, lashing out; kick (*horse*).

ruban (rybɑ̃) *m*, ribbon; band; tape. ~ *perforé*, punched tape (*data processing*).

rubéole (rybeɔl) *f*, German measles.

rubicond, e (rybikɔ̃, ɔ̃:d) *a*, rubicund, florid.

rubis (rybi) *m*, ruby; jewel (*Horol.*).

rubrique (rybrik) *f*, red chalk; rubric; heading, section; column (*special subject news*); publisher's imprint (*place of publication*).

ruche (ryʃ) *f*, [bee]hive; ruche. **rucher** (ʃe) *m*, apiary.

rude† (ryd) *a*, rough; rugged; harsh; hard; severe; gruff; stiff; steep. **rudesse** (dɛs) *f*, roughness, etc.

rudiment (rydimɑ̃) *m*, rudiment. **rudimentaire** (tɛːr) *a*, rudimentary.

rudoyer (rydwaje) *v.t*, to use roughly, brow-beat.

rue (ry) *f*, street; rue (*Bot.*). ~ *à sens unique*, one-way street. ~ *piétonne*, pedestrian mall.

ruée (rɥe) *f*, rush, onrush, onslaught.

ruelle (rɥɛl) *f*, lane, alley; ruelle (*bedside*).

ruer (rɥe) *v.t*, to lash out, kick (*horse*). **se ~ sur**, to hurl oneself at, rush at.

rugir (ryʒiːr) *v.i*, to roar. **rugissement** (ʒismɑ̃) *m*, roar, roaring; howling (*storm*).

rugosité (rygozite) *f*, ruggedness, roughness; corrugation.

rugueux, euse (rygø, øːz) *a*, rough, rugged.

ruine (rɥin) *f*, ruin, [down]fall. **ruiner** (ne) *v.t*, to ruin. **ruineux, euse** (nø, øːz) *a*, ruinous.

ruisseau (rɥiso) *m*, stream[let], brook, rivulet, rill; gutter (*street & fig.*). **ruisseler** (sle) *v.i*, to stream, run down, trickle.

rumeur (rymœːr) *f*, hum (*voices, etc.*); uproar; rumor.

ruminant, e (rymināa, ɑ̃ːt) *a. & m*, ruminant. **ruminer** (ne) *v.t. & abs*, to ruminate; ponder.

rupture (ryptyːr) *f*, breaking; rupture; fracture; breaking off, breach.

rural, e (ryral) *a*, rural, country (*att.*).

ruse (ryːz) *f*, ruse, trick[ery], wile, dodge; stratagem. **rusé, e** (ryze) *a*, artful, crafty, wily. **ruser** (ze) *v.i*, to use cunning.

russe (rys) *a. & R~, n. & le russe* (*language*), Russian. **la Russie** (si), Russia.

rustaud, e (rysto, oːd) *a*, boorish, uncouth. ¶ *n*, boor. **rusticité** (tisite) *f*, rusticity; boorishness. **rustique†** (tik) *a*, rustic; country (*att.*); hardy (*plant*); crazy (*pavement*). **rustre** (str) *m*, boor, churl.

rustine (rystin) *f*, inner-tube patch.

rut (ryt) *m*, rut, heat (*animals*).

rutabaga (rytabaga) *m*, rutabaga.

rutilant (rytilā) *a*, glowing, gleaming red.

rythme (ritm) *m*, rhythm. **rythmique** (mik) *a*, rhythmic(al).

S

sa *see* **son**.

sabbat (saba) *m*, sabbath (*Jewish, witches'*); row, racket.

sable (saːbl) *m*, sand; gravel (*Med.*); sable (*fur, Her.*). ~ *mouvant*, quicksand. **sabler** (sɑble) *v.t*, to sand, gravel (*path*); swig, toss off. **sablier** (blie) *m*, hourglass, sand g. **sablière** (ɛːr) *f*, sand pit, gravel pit; wall plate. **sablon** (blɔ̃) *m*, fine sand. **sablonneux, euse** (blɔnø, øːz) *a*, sandy. **sablonnière** (njɛːr) *f*, sand pit.

sabord (saboːr) *m*, port [hole]. **saborder** (bɔrde) *v.t*, to scuttle (*ship*).

sabot (sabo) *m*, clog, sabot; shoe; skid; hoof; whipping top; tub (*bad ship*); rubbishy instrument *or* tool. **sabotage** (bɔtaːʒ) *m*, sabotage, foul play. **saboter** (te) *v.t*, to botch; damage wilfully, wreck. **sabotière** (tjɛːr) *f*, clog dance.

sabouler (sabule) *v.t*, to jostle; rate, scold.

sabre (saːbr) *m*, saber, sword, broadsword, cutlass; swordfish. **sabrer** (sɑbre) *v.t. & abs*, to saber; slash; slash about; cut down, blue-pencil.

sac (sak) *m*, sack, bag, pouch, sac; sackcloth (*Theol.*); sacking, pillage; 100-franc note (*slang*). ~ *à main*, handbag. ~ *à ouvrage*, work b. ~ *à provisions*, shopping b. ~ *à terre*, sand b. ~ *d'ordonnance* (*Mil.*), knapsack. ~ *de couchage*, sleeping bag. ~ *de touriste*, ~ *de montagne*, ~ *d'alpinisme*, rucksack. *vider son ~*, to get something off one's chest.

saccade (sakad) *f*, jerk, start. **saccadé, e** (de) *p.a*, jerky; irregular; staccato (*voice*).

saccager (sakaʒe) *v.t*, to sack, pillage; ransack; upset.

saccharin, e (sakarɛ̃, in) *a*, saccharine, sugary; sugar (*att.*). ¶ *f*, saccharin.

sacerdoce (saserdɔs) *m*, priesthood; ministry. **sacerdotal, e** (tal) *a*, sacerdotal, priestly.

sachée (saʃe) *f*, sackful, bagful. **sachet** (ʃɛ) *m*, bag. ~ *à parfums*, scent bag, sachet. **sacoche** (kɔʃ) *f*, saddlebag; courier's bag; tool b.

sacramental (sakramɑ̃tal) *m*, sacramental. **sacramentel, le†** (tɛl) *a*, sacramental, binding. **sacre** (kr) *m*, anointing, coronation; consecration (*bishop*). **sacré, e** (kre) *a*, holy, sacred, consecrated; damned, cursed. **sacrement** (krəmɑ̃) *m*, sacrament. **sacrer** (kre) *v.t*, to anoint, crown; consecrate; curse, swear. **sacrifice** (krifis) *m*, sacrifice; offering. **sacrifier** (fje) *v.t. & abs*, to sacrifice. **sacrilège** (lɛːʒ) *m*, sacrilege; (*att.*) sacrilegious.

sacripant (sakripɑ̃) *m*, rascal, bully.

sacristain (sakristɛ̃) *m*, sacristan. **sacristie** (ti) *f*, vestry, sacristy. **sacro-saint, e** (krɔsɛ̃, ɛ̃ːt) *a*, sacrosanct.

sadique (sadik) *a*, sadistic. ¶ *m*, sadist. **sadiste** (dist) *m*, sadist.

safran (safrɑ̃) *m*, saffron, crocus.

sagace (sagas) *a*, sagacious, shrewd. **sagacité** (site) *f*, sagacity, shrewdness.

sage† (saːʒ) *a*, wise, sage, sapient; judicious, prudent, sensible; well-behaved, good (*child*); chaste. ¶ *m*, sage, wise man. ~-*femme*, *f*, midwife. **sagesse** (ʒɛs) *f*, wisdom, etc; good conduct.

sagou (sagu) *m*, sago. **sagou[t]ier** ([t]je) *m*, sago palm.

sagouin (sagwɛ̃) *m*, saguin (*monkey*); sloven.

saignant, e (sɛɲɑ̃, ɑ̃ːt) *a*, bleeding; raw; rare (*meat*). **saignée** (ɲe) *f*, bleeding, blood letting; bend of the arm; trench; holocaust. **saigner** (ɲe) *v.i. & t*, to bleed; stick (*pig*); tap (*tree, etc.*); drain; rankle.

saillant, e (sajɑ̃, ɑ̃ːt) *a*, salient, projecting, prominent; striking, outstanding. **saillie** (ji) *f*, spurt, bound; projection; ledge; protrusion; sally; covering. **saillir** (jiːr) *v.i.ir*, to gush out; project; protrude; sally; (*v.t.ir.*) to service (*of animals*).

sain, e† (sɛ̃, ɛn) *a*, sound; wholesome; healthy, hale; sane. *sain & sauf*, safe & sound.

saindoux (sɛ̃du) *m*, lard.

saint, e (sɛ̃, ɛ̃ːt) *n*, saint, patron s. *le* ~ *des saints*, the holy of holies, sanctum. ¶ *a*, holy; sainted; saintly, godly; consecrated, hallowed. *saint-frusquin*, worldly goods. *Saint-Siège*, Holy See. *sainte table*, communion table. *la Sainte Vierge*, the Blessed Virgin. Saint, *comps*: *le* ~-*Esprit* (sɛ̃tɛspri), the Holy Ghost, the Holy Spirit. *la* ~-*Jean* (sɛ̃ʒɑ̃), Midsummer Day. *le* ~-*Laurent* (lɔrɑ̃), the St. Lawrence. *la* ~-*Martin* (martɛ̃), Martinmas. *la* ~-*Michel* (miʃel), Michaelmas. *la* ~-*Sylvestre* (silvɛstr), New Year's eve. **Sainte-Hélène** (sɛ̃telɛn) *f*, St. Helena. **saintement** (tmɑ̃) *ad*, holily, in a godly manner, righteously. **sainteté** (təte) *f*, holiness, saintliness; sanctity.

saisie (sɛzi) *f*, seizure; distraint, execution; distress (*law*); foreclosure (*mortgage*). **saisir** (ziːr) *v.t*, to seize, lay hold of, grasp; catch; snatch; distrain, attach; foreclose; startle; lay before (*court*). **saisissant, e** (zisɑ̃, ɑ̃ːt) *a*, piercing (*cold*); startling, striking; thrilling. **saisissement** (smɑ̃) *m*, shock; thrill.

saison (sɛzɔ̃) *f*, season, time (*of year*). *marchand des quatre-*~*s*, street vendor.

salade (salad) *f*, salad; jumble. *panier à* ~, Black Maria, police wagon. **saladier** (dje) *m*, salad bowl.

salage (salaːʒ) *m*, salting, curing.

salaire (salɛːr) *m*, wage[s], pay; hire; reward. ~ *de famine*, starvation wage.

salaison (salɛzɔ̃) *f*, salting, curing; (*pl.*) salt provisions.

salamalec (salamalɛk) *m*, salaam.

salamandre (salamɑ̃:dr) *f*, salamander. ~ *aquatique*, newt, eft.

Salamanque (salamɑ̃:k) *f*, Salamanca.

salant (salɑ̃) *a.m*, salt (*marsh*), saline.

salarié, e (salarje) *p.a*, wage-earning, paid. **salarier** (je) *v.t*, to pay a wage to.

salaud (salo) *m*, (*pers.*) skunk, bastard.

sale† (sal) *a*, dirty, unclean, filthy; foul; nasty; soiled (*linen*); messy.

salé, e (sale) *p.a*, salt, salted; corned (*beef*); briny; keen; broad (*story*); stiff (*price*). [*porc*] *salé, m*, salt pork. **saler** (le) *v.t*, to salt, pickle, cure, corn; overcharge (*someone*).

Salerne (salɛrn) *f*, Salerno.

saleté (salte) *f*, dirtiness; dirt, filth; mess; rubbish, trash[y goods].

salicole (salikɔl) *a*, salt (*industry*); saliferous. **salicoque** (kɔk) *f*, shrimp. **salière** (ljɛ:r) *f*, salt cellar; salt box. **salin, e** (lɛ̃, in) *a*, saline, briny, salt[y]. ¶ *f*, salt works; rock salt mine.

saligaud (saligo) *m*, bastard, swine (*person*).

salir (sali:r) *v.t*, to dirty, soil; foul; sully. **salissant** (lisɑ̃) *a*, dirtying; easily soiled. **salissure** (lisy:r) *f*, stain.

salive (sali:v) *f*, saliva, spittle. **saliver** (live) *v.i*, to salivate.

salle (sal) *f*, hall; room; ward (*hospital*); house (*Theat., etc.*); auditorium; office. ~ *à manger*, dining room; d. saloon (*ship*); coffee room (*hotel*); mess room (*Mil.*). ~ *de séjour*, living room. ~ *d'armes*, armory; fencing school. ~ *d'attente*, waiting room (*Rly.*). ~ *de bain*, bathroom. ~ *de classe*, schoolroom. ~ *de police*, guardroom (*Mil.*). ~ *des festins*, banqueting hall. ~ *des pas perdus*, waiting room (*Rly.*); lobby. ~ *de deuxième vision*, second-run movie theater. ~ *d'exclusivité*, first run m. t.

salmigondis (salmigɔ̃di) *m*, hodgepodge.

salon (salɔ̃) *m*, reception room; drawing room; parlor; saloon; room; salon, exhibition, show. ~ *d'exposition*, showroom. ~ *de l'automobile*, auto show. ~ *de l'aviation*, aircraft exhibition. ~ *de pose*, studio (*Phot.*).

Salonique (salɔnik) *f*, Salonica.

salope (salɔp) *f*, slattern, slut, saloperie (pri) *f*, filth, muck; trash. **salopette** (pɛt) *f*, overalls; dungarees, jeans.

salpêtre (salpɛ:tr) *m*, saltpeter, niter.

salsepareille (salsparɛ:j) *f*, sarsaparilla.

saltimbanque (saltɛ̃bɑ̃:k) *m*, showman, tumbler; mountebank.

salubre (salybr) *a*, salubrious, healthy; wholesome. **salubrité** (brite) *f*, salubrity; health (*public*).

saluer (salɥe) *v.t*, to salute, bow to; greet, hail.

salure (saly:r) *f*, saltness; tang.

salut (saly) *m*, safety, welfare; salvation; salutation, bow, greeting; salute; evening service (*Eccl.*). ¶ *i*, hail! greeting! **salutaire†** (tɛ:r) *a*, salutary, wholesome, beneficial. **salutation** (tasjɔ̃) *f*, salutation, greeting, bow.

salve (salv) *f*, salvo, salute; round (*applause*).

samedi (samdi) *m*, Saturday.

samovar (samɔva:r) *m*, urn (*for tea, coffee*).

sanatorium (sanatɔrjɔm) *m*, sanatorium.

sanctifier (sɑ̃ktifje) *v.t*, to sanctify, hallow. **sanction** (sjɔ̃) *f*, sanction, assent; penalty, punishment. **sanctionner** (ɔne) *v.t*, to sanction, approve. **sanctuaire** (tɥɛ:r) *m*, sanctuary; sanctum.

sandale (sɑ̃dal) *f*, sandal, shoe.

sandwich (sɑ̃dwitʃ) *m*, sandwich.

sang (sɑ̃) *m*, blood, gore; race, lineage, kinship. ~*-froid*, coolness, self-possession, nerve. [*homme de*] ~ *mêlé*, half-caste. *se faire des mauvais* ~, to worry, be uneasy. **sanglant, e** (glɑ̃, ɑ̃:t) *a*, bloody; sanguinary; deadly; cutting, scathing; outrageous.

sangle (sãːgl) *f*, strap, band, girth, webbing. **sangler** (sãgle) *v.t*, to strap; girth; lash. se ~, to lace oneself tight[ly].

sanglier (sãglje) *m*, wild boar.

sanglot (sãglo) *m*, sob. **sangloter** (glote) *v.i*, to sob.

sangsue (sãsy) *f*, leech; blood-sucker. **sanguin, e** (gẽ, in) *a*, sanguineous, blood (*att.*); full-blooded, sanguine. ¶ *f*, red chalk; bloodstone. **sanguinaire** (ginɛːr) *a*, sanguinary, bloody; bloodthirsty.

sanitaire (sanitɛːr) *a*, sanitary.

sans (sã) *pr*, without; but for; -less; -lessly; un-; no; non-. ~ *arrêt*, ~ *escale*, nonstop. ~ *cela*, ~ *quoi*, otherwise. ~ *date*, sine die; undated. ~ *empattement*, sanserif. [*perdu*] ~ *nouvelles*, missing (*ship*). ~ *que*, without. ~ *valeur déclarée*, uninsured (*Post*). ~ *un*, stone-broke.

sans-cœur (sãkœːr) *n*, heartless person.

sans-façon (sãfasɔ̃) *m*, straightforwardness, bluntness.

sans-fil (sãfil) *f*, wireless [telegraphy]; (*m.*) wireless [telegram].

sans-gêne (sãʒɛn) *m*, off-handedness, cheek.

sansonnet (sãsɔnɛ) *m*, starling (*bird*).

sans-souci (sãsusi) *n*, easy-going person, happy-go-lucky individual; (*m.*) unconcern.

sans-travail (les) (sãtravaːj) *m.pl*, the workless, the unemployed.

santal (sãtal) *m*, sandal[wood].

santé (sãte) *f*, health. ~ *de fer*, iron constitution. *la* ~, quarantine (*station*).

saoul *see* soûl.

sape (sap) *f*, sap (*Mil.*); undermining. **saper** (pe) *v.t*, to sap, etc. **sapeur** (pœːr) *m*, sapper. ~-*pompier*, fireman. *les sapeurs-pompiers*, the fire brigade.

saphir (safiːr) *m*, sapphire; phonograph needle.

sapin (sapẽ) *m*, fir [tree]; spruce [fir]. [*bois de*] ~, deal. *sentir le* ~, to smell approaching death. **sapinière** (pinjɛːr) *f*, fir plantation.

Saragosse (saragɔs) *f*, Saragossa.

sarbacane (sarbakan) *f*, pea shooter; blow gun, blowpipe, blow tube (*dart tube*).

sarcasme (sarkasm) *m*, sarcasm, taunt. **sarcastique** (tik) *a*, sarcastic.

sarcler (sarkle) *v.t*, to weed. **sarcleur, euse** (klœːr, øːz) *n*, weeder (*pers.*). **sarcloir** (klwaːr) *m*, weeding hoe, weeder.

sarcophage (sarkɔfaːʒ) *m*, sarcophagus.

Sardaigne (la) (sardɛɲ) Sardinia. **sarde** (sard) *a*. & **S~**, *n*, Sardinian.

sardine (sardin) *f*, pilchard; sardine.

sardoine (sardwan) *f*, sardonyx.

sardonique (sardɔnik) *a*, sardonic.

sarigue (sarig) *m*. & *f*, opossum, sarigue.

sarment (sarmã) *m*, vine shoot; bine.

sarrasin (sarazẽ) *m*, buckwheat; Saracen.

sarrau (saro) *m*, smock, overall.

sarriette (sarjɛt) *f*, savory (*Bot.*).

sas (sɑ) *m*, sieve. **sasser** (se) *v.t*, to sift.

Satan (satã) *m*, Satan. **satané, e** (tane) *a*, devilish. **satanique** (nik) *a*, satanic.

satellite (satɛllit) *m*, satellite; henchman.

satiété (sasjete) *f*, satiety, surfeit.

satin (satẽ) *m*, satin. **satiner** (tine) *v.t*, to satin; glaze (*paper, etc.*); burnish (*Phot.*). **satinette** (nɛt) *f*, sateen.

satire (satiːr) *f*, satire. **satirique†** (tirik) *a*, satiric, satirical. ¶ *m*, satirist. **satiriser** (ze) *v.t*, to satirize.

satisfaction (satisfaksjɔ̃) *f*, satisfaction, gratification, comfort; atonement (*Theol.*). **satisfaire** (fɛːr) *v.t.ir*, to satisfy, please, gratify, answer. ~ *à*, to satisfy; answer, meet; fulfill. **satisfaisant, e** (fəzã, ãːt) *a*, satisfactory.

saturer (satyre) *v.t*, to saturate.

saturnales (satyrnal) *f.pl*, saturnalia. **saturnisme** (nism) *m*, lead poisoning.

satyre (sati:r) *m*, satyr.
sauce (so:s) *f*, sauce. **saucer** (sose) *v.t*, to dip in the sauce; drench, souse. **saucière** (sjɛ:r) *f*, gravy boat.
saucisse (sosis) *f*, sausage (*fresh*); s. balloon; frankfurter. **saucisson** (sɔ̃sõ) *m*, smoked sausage.
sauf, sauve (sof, so:v) *a*, safe, unhurt, unscathed; saved. **sauf,** *pr*, save, saving, but, except[ed]; unless; subject; under. **~-conduit,** *m*, safe-conduct, pass.
sauge (so:ʒ) *f*, sage (*Bot., Cook.*).
saugrenu, e (sogrəny) *a*, absurd, preposterous.
saulaie (solɛ) *f*, willow plantation. **saule** (so:l) *m*, willow [tree].
saumâtre (soma:tr) *a*, brackish, briny.
saumon (somõ) *m*, salmon; ingot, pig (*metal*). **saumoneau** (mɔno) *m*, young salmon.
saumure (somy:r) *f*, [pickling] brine.
saunage (sona:ʒ) *m*, salt making; s. trade. **saunerie** (nri) *f*, salt works.
saupoudrer (sopudre) *v.t*, to sprinkle, dust, powder. **saupoudroir** (drwa:r) *m*, sifter.
saure (so:r) *a*, sorrel (*horse*). **saurer** (sore) *v.t*, to kipper.
saussaie (sosɛ) *f*, willow plantation.
saut (so) *m*, leap, jump, vault; hop; skip; bound; fall[s] (*water*). ~ à la perche, pole vault. ~-delit, dressing gown; bedside rug. ~ de mouton, buck (*of horse*); leapfrog. ~ en hauteur, high jump. ~ en longueur, long j. le ~ périlleux, a somersault; the plunge (*fig.*). par ~s & par bonds, by fits & starts, spasmodically. faire un ~, to make a quick visit, stop at. **saute** (so:t) *f*, shift, change; jump. **~-au-crac,** erotomaniac. **~-au-paf,** nymphomaniac. **~-mouton** (sotmutõ) *m*, leap-frog. **sauter** (sote) *v.i*, to leap, jump; skip; hop; bound, spring; vault; fly, fling oneself; explode, blow up; go smash; fall; shift, change (*wind*); (*v.t.*) to leap [over], jump [o.]; skip, leave out; drop (*stitch*); cover (*of animals*). **sauterelle**

(trɛl) *f*, grasshopper; locust; woman (*pejorative*). **saute-ruisseau** (sotrɥiso) *m*, errand boy.
sauteur, euse (tœ:r, ø:z) *n*, jumper, leaper; weathercock (*pers.*); (*f.*) sauté pan; jig saw. **sautiller** (tije) *v.i*, to hop, skip; trip along; jump about. **sautoir** (twa:r) *m*, saltire; kerchief; vaulting standard. en ~, crosswise, over the shoulder.
sauvage† (sova:ʒ) *a*, savage, uncivilized; wild; barbarous; unsociable, shy. ¶ *n*. & **sauvagesse** (vaʒɛs) *f*, savage; unsociable person. **sauvageon** (ʒõ) *m*, wild stock (*grafting*); wilding, seedling. **sauvagerie** (ʒri) *f*, savagery; unsociability, shyness. **sauvagin, e** (ʒɛ̃, in) *a*, fishy (*taste, smell, of flesh*).
sauvegarde (sovgard) *f*, safeguard, protection; safe-conduct. ~ des données, data safety (*computers*). **sauve-qui-peut** (kipø) *m*, stampede, headlong flight. **sauver** (ve) *v.t*, to save, rescue; salve, salvage. se ~, to escape; run away, be off. **sauvetage** (vta:ʒ) *m*, life saving, rescue; salvage. bateau de ~, lifeboat. ceinture de ~, lifebelt. **sauveur** (vœ:r) *m*, saver, deliverer. le Sauveur, the Savior.
savamment (savamɑ̃) *ad*, learnedly; knowingly. **savant, e** (vɑ̃, ɑ̃:t) *a*, learned, scholarly; skillful; performing (*dog*); knowing, precocious (*in vice*), sophisticated. ¶ *n*, scientist, scholar.
savate (savat) *f*, old shoe; boxing with the feet, head, & fists. en ~s, down at the heel, slipshod. **saveter** (vte) *v.t*, to botch. **savetier** (vtje) *m*, cobbler; botcher.
saveur (savœ:r) *f*, savor, flavor, taste; relish, zest.
Savoie (la) (savwa), Savoy.
savoir (savwa:r) *v.t.ir*, to know; be aware of, tell; be acquainted with, know of; understand; know how to; be able to; can. ~ [bon] gré à, to be grateful to. ~ mauvais gré à, to be annoyed with. ¶ *m*, knowledge, learning, scholarship. être payé pour ~, to know all too well. **~-faire** (vwarfɛ:r) *m*,

ability, tact, gumption, know-how. ~-**vivre**, *m*, good manners.

savon (savõ) *m*, soap. ~ *à barbe en bâton*, shaving stick. **savonner** (vɔne) *v.t*, to soap, wash; lather; reprimand severely (*slang*). **savonnerie** (nri) *f*, soap works; s. trade. **savonneux, euse** (nø, ø:z) *a*, soapy. **savonnier** (nje) *m*, soap maker.

savourer (savure) *v.t*, to taste; relish, enjoy. **savoureux, euse** (rø, ø:z) *a*, savory, tasty; enjoyable.

saxe (saks) *m*, Dresden china. **la Saxe**, Saxony.

saxhorn (saksɔrn) *m*, saxhorn.

saxon, ne (saksõ, ɔn) *a. & S~, n*, Saxon.

saxophone (saksɔfɔn) *m*, saxophone.

saynète (sɛnɛt) *f*, playlet, sketch.

sbire (zbi:r) *m*, sbirro; myrmidon.

scabieux, euse (skabjø, ø:z) *a*, scabious, scabby. ¶ *f*, scabious (*Bot.*).

scabreux, euse (skabrø, ø:z) *a*, rough; ticklish; scabrous, improper.

scalpel (skalpɛl) *m*, scalpel.

scalper (skalpe) *v.t*, to scalp.

scandale (skãdal) *m*, scandal, shame. **scandaleux, euse†** (lø, ø:z) *a*, scandalous, shameful. **scandaliser** (lize) *v.t*, to scandalize, shock.

scander (skãde) *v.t*, to scan (*verse*); stress (*Mus.*); syllabize (*articulate by syllables*).

scandinave (skãdina:v) *a. & S~, n*, Scandinavian. **la Scandinavie** (navi), Scandinavia.

scanner (skãne) *v.t*, to scan. **scanneur** (nœ:r) *m*, scanner.

scansion (skãsjõ) *f*, scansion, scanning.

scaphandre (skafã:dr) *m*, diving dress. **scaphandrier** (fãdrie) *m*, diver (*in diving dress*).

scarabée (skarabe) *m*, beetle; scarab.

scarifier (skarifje) *v.t*, to scarify.

scarlatine (skarlatin) *f*, scarlatina, scarlet fever.

scarole (skarɔl) *f*, endive.

sceau (so) *m*, seal; stamp (*fig.*).

scélérat, e (selera, at) *a*, villainous, wicked. ¶ *n*, villain, scoundrel, miscreant. **scélératesse** (tɛs) *f*, villainy, wickedness.

scellé (sɛle) *m*, seal (*official*). **sceller** (le) *v.t*, to seal; s. up.

scénario (senarjo) *m*, scenario. **scène** (sɛn) *f*, stage; scene; action; local[e]; shindy. **scénique** (senik) *a*, scenic, theatrical, stage (*att.*).

scepticisme (sɛptisism) *m*, skepticism. **sceptique** (tik) *a*, skeptical. ¶ *n*, skeptic.

sceptre (sɛptr) *m*, scepter.

Schaffhouse (ʃafu:z) *f*, Schaffhausen.

schampooing (ʃãpwɛ̃) *m*, shampoo.

schéma (ʃema) *ou* **schème** (ʃɛm) *m*, diagram, plan.

schisme (ʃism) *m*, schism.

schiste (ʃist) *m*, shale, schist.

schlitte (ʃlit) *f*, lumber sledge.

schooner (ʃunɛ:r) *m*, schooner (*Naut.*).

sciage (sja:ʒ) *m*, sawing.

sciatique (sjatik) *a*, sciatic. ¶ *f*, sciatica.

scie (si) *f*, saw; bore, nuisance; joke; catchword; catch phrase, gag. ~ *à chantourner*, jig saw. ~ *à métaux*, hack s. ~ *du jour*, hit tune. *jeu de la* ~, cat's cradle. *monter une* ~, to play a practical joke. *quelle* ~!, what a nuisance!

sciemment (sjamã) *ad*, knowingly, wittingly. **science** (sjã:s) *f*, knowledge, learning, lore; science. ~ *économique*, economics. **scientifique†** (ãtifik) *a*, scientific. ¶ *m*, scientifically-oriented person. **scientiste chrétien** (tist) *m*, Christian Scientist.

scier (sje) *v.t*, to saw; saw off; reap; bore (*weary*); (*v.i.*) to back water. **scierie** (siri) *f*, saw mill. **scieur** (sjœ:r) *m*, sawyer.

scinder (sɛde) *v.t*, to divide, split (*fig.*).

scintillation (sɛtillasjõ) *f*, scintillation; twinkling. **scintiller** (tije) *v.i*, to scintillate; twinkle.

scion (sjõ) *m*, shoot, scion (*Hort.*); top [joint] (*fishing rod*).

scission (sisjõ) *f*, scission, split, cleavage; secession.

sciure (sjy:r) *f*, sawdust.

sclérose (sklero:z) *f*, sclerosis.

scolaire (skɔlɛ:r) *a*, school (*att.*); academic (*year*); educational. **scolastique** (lastik) *a*, scholastic.

sconse (skɔ̃:s) *m*, skunk (*fur*).

scorbut (skɔrby) *m*, scurvy.

scorie (skɔri) *f. oft. pl*, slag, scoria; dross; scale.

scorpion (skɔrpjɔ̃) *m*, scorpion.

scotch (skɔtʃ) *m*, scotch whiskey; self-adhesive tape (*trademark used as generic term*).

scribe (skrib) *m*, scribe; copyist.

script (skript) *m*, scrip (*Fin.*); script (*TV & cinema*); continuity, script person (*cinema*).

scrofules (skrɔfyl) *f.pl*, scrofula. **scrofuleux, euse** (lø, ø:z) *a*, scrofulous.

scrupule (skrypyl) *m*, scruple, qualm. **scrupuleux, euse†** (lø, ø:z) *a*, scrupulous.

scrutateur (skrytatœ:r) *m*, scrutinizer; poll watcher. **scruter** (te) *v.t*, to scrutinize, scan; peer into; search. **scrutin** (tɛ̃) *m*, poll, ballot, voting, vote.

sculpter (skylte) *v.t*, to sculpt; carve. **sculpteur** (tœ:r) *m*, sculptor; carver. **sculpture** (ty:r) *f*, sculpture. ~ *sur bois*, wood carving.

se, s' (sə, s) *pn*, oneself; himself, herself, itself; themselves; each other, one another. *Note:* An English intransitive is often expressed in French by the pronominal form (se, s'); thus, to depreciate, *v.t*, déprécier, avilir; to depreciate, *v.i*, se déprécier, s'avilir. The pronominal form also serves to give to a transitive verb a passive meaning; as, lettre qui se prononce, letter which is pronounced.

séance (seɑ̃:s) *f*, seat (*at a council*); sitting, session, meeting; performance. ~ *de spiritisme*, seance. ~ *tenante*, during the sitting; forthwith, there & then, on the spot. **séant, e** (ɑ̃, ɑ̃:t) *p.a*, sitting (*à* = at), in session. ¶ *a*, becoming, seemly, proper. *sur son séant*, in a sitting posture, sitting up.

seau (so) *m*, pail, bucket; pailful. ~ *à biscuits*, biscuit barrel. ~ *à charbon*, coal scuttle. ~ *à ordures*, trashbin. ~ *de toilette*, slop pail.

sébile (sebil) *f*, wooden bowl.

sec, sèche (sɛk, sɛʃ) *a*, dry; dried; spare, gaunt, lean; curt; bald (*style*). sec, *ad*, drily (*answer coldly*); hard (*drinking*); neat (*drinking*). à sec, *ad*, [when] dry; dried up; broke. sec, *m*, dry; dry place; dry land; dry fodder.

sécateur (sekatœ:r) *m*, pruning shears.

sécession (sesɛsjɔ̃) *f*, secession.

sèchement (sɛʃmɔ̃) *ad*, drily, curtly; baldly. **sécher** (seʃe) *v.t. & i*, to dry; d. up; season (*wood*); wither, pine away. ~ *à un examen*, to flunk an exam. ~ *une classe*, to cut a class. **sécheresse** (ʃrɛs) *f*, dryness; drought; spareness, as *sec*. **séchoir** (ʃwa:r) *m*, drying room; drier; airer; towel bar.

second, e† (səgɔ̃, ɔ̃:d) *a*, second; junior (*partner*). *second plan*, *m*, middle distance; background (*fig.*). *seconde vue*, *f*, second sight, clairvoyance. *un second*, *une seconde*, another (*like*). ¶ *m*, second (*pers., floor*); first mate (*Naut.*). ¶ *f*, second (*class*); second (*time*). ~ [*épreuve*], revise (*Typ.*). **secondaire†** (gɔ̃dɛ:r) *a*, secondary; minor; side (*att.*). **seconder** (gɔ̃de) *v.t*, to second, support, back up, further.

secouer (səkwe) *v.t. & abs*, to shake; s. up; s. down; s. off; toss; buffet; jolt; rate, scold.

secourable (səkurabl) *a*, helpful, helping; relievable. **secourir** (ri:r) *v.t.ir*, to succor, help, relieve. **secours** (ku:r) *m*, help, succor, relief, aid. *au ~!* help! *de ~,* (*att.*) emergency; breakdown; relief, spare; backup (*computers*). *roue de ~,* spare wheel.

secousse (səkus) *f*, shake, jerk, jolt, shock.

secret, ète† (səkrɛ, ɛt) *a*, secret. ¶ *m*, secret; s. spring; secrecy; privacy; solitary confinement.

secrétaire (kretɛ:r) *m*, secretary, amanuensis; writing desk. ~ *de mairie*, town clerk. ~ *intime*, private s. **secrétariat** (tarja) *m*, secretaryship; secretariat. **sécréter** (sekrete) *v.t*, to secrete (*physiology*). **sécrétion** (sjɔ̃) *f*, secretion.

sectaire (sɛktɛ:r) *m*. & *att*, sectarian. **sectateur** (tatœ:r) *m*, follower, votary. **secte** (sɛkt) *f*, sect.

secteur (sɛktœ:r) *m*, sector; quadrant; district. **section** (sjɔ̃) *f*, section; division; fare zone (*bus*); platoon.

séculaire (sekylɛ:r) *a*, secular (*100*); time-honored. **séculier, ère†** (lje, ɛ:r) *a*, secular (*clergy, etc.*); laic; worldly (*life*). ¶ *m*, layman; (*pl.*) laity.

sécurité (sekyrite) *f*, security, reliability; safety. ~ *d'abord*, safety first. *de* ~, backup (*computers*).

sédatif, ive (sedatif, i:v) *a*. & *m*, sedative.

sédentaire (sedɑ̃tɛ:r) *a*, sedentary; fixed, stationary.

sédiment (sedimɑ̃) *m*, sediment, deposit.

séditieux, euse† (sedisjø, ø:z) *a*, seditious; mutinous. **sédition** (sjɔ̃) *f*, sedition; revolt.

séducteur, trice (sedyktœ:r, tris) *n*, tempter; seducer. **séduire** (dɥi:r) *v.t.ir*, to seduce, entice; [al]lure; bribe, suborn. **séduisant, e** (dɥizɑ̃, ɑ̃:t) *a*, seductive, tempting; fascinating.

segment (sɛgmɑ̃) *m*, segment; ring (*piston*).

ségrégation (segregasjɔ̃) *f*, segregation.

seiche (sɛʃ) *f*, cuttle fish.

séide (seid) *m*, blind supporter, henchman.

seigle (sɛgl) *m*, rye.

seigneur (sɛɲœ:r) *m*, lord; squire; noble[man]. *le Seigneur*, the Lord. **seigneurie** (nœri) *f*, lordship; manor.

seille (sɛ:j) *f*, pail, bucket.

sein (sɛ̃) *m*, breast; bosom; lap (*luxury*); bowels (*earth*); members; womb.

seine (sɛn) *f*, seine (*net*).

seing (sɛ̃) *m*, signature, signing.

séisme (seism) *m*, earthquake. **séismique** (mik) *a*, seismic.

seize (sɛ:z) *a*. & *m*, sixteen; 16th. **seizième†** (sɛzjɛm) *a*. & *n*, sixteenth.

séjour (seʒu:r) *m*, stay, sojourn; abode, regions; resort. ~ *linguistique*, a stay with family in foreign country (*to learn language*). **séjourner** (ʒurne) *v.i*, to stay, tarry, sojourn; lie.

sel (sɛl) *m*, salt; piquancy, wit. ~ *ammoniac* (amɔnjak), sal-ammoniac. ~ *fin*, table salt. ~ *gemme*, rock salt. ~*s pour bains*, bath salts. ~*s* [*volatils*] *anglais*, smelling salts.

sélection (selɛksjɔ̃) *f*, selection, choice. **sélectionner** (ɔne) *v.t*, to select.

selle (sɛl) *f*, saddle; seat; stool, motion (*Med.*). **seller** (le) *v.t*, to saddle. **sellerie** (lri) *f*, saddlery; harness room. **sellette** (lɛt) *f*, stool; pedestal (*vase*). *tenir, mettre, quelqu'un sur la* ~, to cross-examine someone. **sellier** (lje) *m*, saddler, harness maker.

selon (səlɔ̃) *pr*, [according] to. ~ *moi*, in my opinion. *c'est* ~, it all depends.

semailles (səmɑ:j) *f.pl*, seed time; sowing.

semaine (səmɛn) *f*, week; week's work, pay. *la* ~ *seulement*, weekdays only.

sémaphore (semafɔ:r) *m*, semaphore.

semblable† (sɑ̃blabl) *a*, [a]like, similar; such. ¶ *m*, fellow [man], like. **semblant** (blɑ̃) *m*, semblance, appearance, show. [*faux*] ~, pretence, sham. *un* ~ *de . . .*, an apology (*bad specimen*) for a . . . **sembler** (ble) *v.i*, to seem, appear, look, strike.

semelle (səmɛl) *f*, sole (*shoe, etc.*); foot (*stocking*); sock (*cork, loofa*); tread (*tire*).

semence (səmɑ̃:s) *f*, seed; brads. ~ *de perles*, seed pearls. **semer** (me) *v.t*, to sow; scatter, strew, spread; powder (*Emb.*); shake off (*somebody following*). ~ *la merde*, to create confusion (*vulgar*).

semestre (səmɛstr) *m*, semester,

term; half-year; 6 months' pay, duty, leave. **semestriel, le** (triɛl) *a*, half-yearly.

semeur, euse (səmœːr, ∅ːz) *n*, sower; spreader.

semi- (səmi) *prefix*, semi-, half-.

sémillant, e (semijɑ̃, ɑ̃ːt) *a*, sprightly, bright.

séminaire (seminɛːr) *m*, seminary, college.

semis (səmi) *m*, seed plot, seedlings; powdering (*Emb.*).

sémitique (semitik) *a*, Semitic.

semoir (səmwaːr) *m*, sowing machine, drill.

semonce (səmɔ̃ːs) *f*, call (*to a ship*); reprimand, scolding. **semoncer** (mɔ̃se) *v.t*, to call upon (*ship*); lecture, scold; summon.

semoule (səmul) *f*, semolina.

sénat (sena) *m*, senate. **sénateur** (tœːr) *m*, senator.

séné (sene) *m*, senna.

seneçon (sənsɔ̃) *m*, groundsel.

Sénégal (le) (senegal), Senegal.

sénestre (senɛstr) *a*, sinister (*Her.*).

sénevé (senve) *m*, mustard (*Bot.*); m. seed.

sénile (senil) *a*, senile. **sénilité** (lite) *f*, senility.

sens (sɑ̃ːs, sɑ̃) *m*, sense; judgment, understanding; opinion; meaning, import; direction, way. ~ *commun* (sɑ̃), [common] sense, senses. ~ *dessus dessous* (sɑ̃), upside down; topsy-turvy. ~ *devant derrière* (sɑ̃), back to front. ~ *interdit*, no entry, one way street. ~ *unique*, entry only, one way street. **sensation** (sɑ̃sasjɔ̃) *f*, sensation; feel[ing], sense. *à* ~ *& sensationnel, le* (sjɔnɛl) *a*, sensational, thrilling, exciting. **sensé†, e** (se) *a*, sensible, judicious. **sensibilité** (sibilite) *f*, sensitiveness; feeling. **sensible** (sibl) *a*, sensitive, susceptible, responsive, sensible, alive; sentient; sensitized (*Phot.*); tender, sore; appreciable, palpable, perceptible. **sensiblement** (bləmɑ̃) *a*, appreciably; deeply. **sensiblerie** (ri) *f*, sentimentality. **sensitif, ive** (tif, iːv) *a*, sensitive; sensory.

sensoriel, ielle (sɑ̃sɔrjɛl) *a*, sensorial, sensory.

sensualiste (sɑ̃sɥalist) *n*, sensualist. **sensualité** (te) *f*, sensuality; voluptuousness. **sensuel, le†** (sɥɛl) *a*, sensual.

sente (sɑ̃ːt) *f*, footpath.

sentence (sɑ̃tɑ̃ːs) *f*, maxim; sentence (*law*); award. **sentencieux, euse†** (tɑ̃sjø, ∅ːz) *a*, sententious.

senteur (sɑ̃tœːr) *f*, scent, odor, perfume. *pois de* ~, sweet pea (*Bot.*).

senti, e (sɑ̃ti) *p.a*, well-expressed, strong. *bien* ~, heartfelt (*words*). **sentier** (sɑ̃tje) *m*, footpath, path, track. ~ *pour cavaliers*, bridle path.

sentiment (sɑ̃timɑ̃) *m*, feeling, sensation; sense; sentiment; opinion. **sentimental, e** (tal) *a*, sentimental. **sentimentalité** (lite) *f*, sentimentality, gush.

sentine (sɑ̃tin) *f*, well (*ship*); sink (*iniquity*).

sentinelle (sɑ̃tinɛl) *f*, sentry, sentinel; guard, watch.

sentir (sɑ̃tiːr) *v.t. & abs. ir*, to feel; be conscious of; smell; scent; taste of; smell of; smack of; be redolent of. *se* ~, to feel.

seoir (swaːr) *v.i.ir*, to sit; be situated.

seoir (swaːr) *v.i.ir*, to suit, become.

séparation (separasjɔ̃) *f*, separation, parting, severance; dispersal; partition (*wall*). ~ *de l'Église & de l'État*, disestablishment [of the Church]. **séparé†, e** (re) *p.a*, separate, distinct; apart. **séparer** (re) *v.t. & se* ~, to separate, part; sever; divide; disband. **séparez! break!** (*Box.*).

sépia (sepja) *f*, sepia; sepia [drawing].

sept (sɛ; *alone & in liaison*, sɛt) *a. & m*, seven; 7th.

septembre (sɛptɑ̃ːbr) *m*, September.

septentrion (sɛptɑ̃triɔ̃) *m*, north. **septentrional, e** (ɔnal) *a*, northern. ¶ *n*, northerner.

septième† (sɛtjɛm) *a. & n*, seventh.

septique (sɛptik) *a*, septic.

septuor (sɛptɥɔːr) *m*, septet.

sépulcral, e (sepylkral) *a*, sepulchral. **sépulcre** (kr) *m*, sepulcher. **sépulture** (tyːr) *f*, burial; burial place, resting place; tomb.

séquelle (sekɛl) *f*, crew, gang; string.

séquence (sekɑ̃ːs) *f*, sequence, run (*cards*, *etc.*); film sequence.

séquestre (sekɛstr) *m*, sequestration.

sérail (seraːj) *m*, seraglio.

séraphin (serafɛ̃) *m*, seraph. **séraphique** (fik) *a*, seraphic.

serbe (sɛrb) *a.* & S~, *n*, Serb[ian]. **le serbe**, Serb[ian] (*language*). **la Serbie** (bi), Serbia.

serein, e (sərɛ̃, ɛn) *a*, serene, calm; halcyon. ¶ *m*, evening dew, evening damp.

sérénade (serenad) *f*, serenade.

sérénité (serenite) *f*, serenity; equanimity.

serf, serve (sɛrf, sɛrv) *n*, serf, thrall.

serfouir (sɛrfwiːr) *v.t*, to hoe.

serge (sɛrʒ) *f*, serge.

sergent (sɛrʒɑ̃) *m*, sergeant; cramp (*tool*). ~ **de ville**, policeman. ~ **instructeur**, drill sergeant.

sériciculture (serisikyltyːr) *f*, silkworm breeding.

série (seri) *f*, series; range; set; chapter (*accidents*); break (*Bil.*). **en ~**, standardized, mass-produced.

sérieux, euse† (serjø, øːz) *a*, serious; grave; sober (*dress*); earnest, genuine, bona fide. ¶ *m*, seriousness, gravity.

serin, e (s[ə]rɛ̃, in) *n*, canary; silly, noodle. **seriner** (rine) *v.t*, to teach (*bird*); din it into (*pers.*); drum (*à* = into).

seringa (s[ə]rɛ̃ga) *m*, syringa, seringa.

seringue (s[ə]rɛ̃ːg) *f*, syringe, squirt. ~ [à lavement], enema. ~ **de Pravaz** (pravɑ), hypodermic syringe. **seringuer** (rɛ̃ge) *v.t*, to syringe, squirt, inject.

serment (sɛrmɑ̃) *m*, oath.

sermon (sɛrmɔ̃) *m*, sermon; lecture (*scolding*). **sermonner** (mɔne)

v.t. & *abs*, to sermonize, lecture.

serpe (sɛrp) *f*, bill hook.

serpent (sɛrpɑ̃) *m*, serpent, snake. ~ **à sonnettes**, rattlesnake. ~ **caché sous les fleurs**, snake in the grass. **serpentaire** (tɛːr) *m*, secretary bird. **serpenteau** (to) *m*, young snake; squib (*firework*). **serpenter** (te) *v.i*, to wind, meander. **serpentin, e** (tɛ̃, in) *a*, serpentine. ¶ *m*, worm (*still*, *etc.*); coil; [paper] streamer. ¶ *f*, serpentine (*rock*).

serpette (sɛrpɛt) *f*, pruning knife; bill hook.

serpillière (sɛrpijɛːr) *f*, sacking; apron.

serpolet (sɛrpɔlɛ) *m*, wild thyme.

serrage (sɛraːʒ) *m*, tightening, application (*brake*). **serre** (sɛːr) *f*, greenhouse, glasshouse, conservatory; grip; claw, talon. ~ **à palmiers**, palm house. ~ **à vignes**, vinery. ~ **chaude**, hothouse. **serré, e** (sɛre) *p.a*, tight, close, serried; clenched. **serrefrein** (sɛrfrɛ̃) *m*, brakesman. **serre-joint**, *m*, cramp, clamp (*tool*). **serre-livres**, *m*, bookends. **serrement** (rmɑ̃) *m*, pressure; squeeze, shake (*hand*). ~ **de cœur**, pang. **serrer** (re) *v.t*, to press, squeeze; clasp, hug, wring, grip; clench; shake (*hand*); tighten; put on (*brake*); put away, stow away; furl (*sail*). ~ **sous clef**, to lock up. **serre-tête**, *m*, headband. **serrure** (ryːr) *f*, lock. ~ **à demi-tour**, latch. **trou de ~**, keyhole. **serrurerie** (ryrri) *f*, locksmithery; metal work, ironwork. **serrurier** (rje) *m*, locksmith; metal worker, ironworker.

sertir (sɛrtiːr) *v.t*, to set (gem); crease.

sérum (serɔm) *m*, serum.

servage (sɛrvaːʒ) *m*, serfdom, thraldom. **servant** (vɑ̃) *a.m*, lay (*brother*). ¶ *m*, gunner; server (*Ten.*). **servante** (vɑ̃ːt) *f*, [maid-]servant; waitress; service table; dumbwaiter. **serviable** (vjabl) *a*, obliging. **service** (vis) *m*, service; serve (*Ten.*); running; booking; supply; department; duty; attendance, waiting (*hotel, etc.*); course (*meal*); set (*utensils*). ~ *de table & dessert*, dinner service. ~ *par en bas*, underhand service (*Ten.*). ~ *par en haut*, overhand s. ~ *compris*, s. included. ~ *militaire*, military s. *en* ~, in opera tion. *libre* ~, self-service. **serviette** (vjɛt) *f*, dispatch case, document c. ~ [*de table*], [table] napkin. ~ [*de toilette*], towel. ~*éponge*, Turkish towel. ~ *hygiénique*, sanitary napkin.

serveur, euse (sɛrvœ:r, ø:z) *m*, barman, -woman; waiter, waitress; server (*Ten.*).

servile† (sɛrvil) *a*, servile, menial; slavish. **servilité** (lite) *f*, servility; slavishness.

servir (sɛrvi:r) *v.i. & t. & abs.* ir, to serve; be of use; wait (on); attend to; serve up. **se** ~ **chez**, to deal with (*tradesman*). **se** ~ **de**, to use. **serviteur** (vitœ:r) *m*, servant. **servitude** (tyd) *f*, servitude, slavery; easement (*law*). **ses** *see* **son.**

sésame (sezam) *m*, sesame (*Bot.*). **S~**, *ouvre-toi*, open sesame.

session (sɛsjɔ̃) *f*, session, sitting, term.

seuil (sœ:j) *m*, threshold, sill.

seul, e (sœl) *a*, alone, by oneself, solo; lonely; only; one, single; sole; mere, bare, very. **seulement** (lmɑ̃) *ad*, only; solely, merely.

sève (sɛ:v) *f*, sap (*plant*); vigor.

sévère† (sevɛ:r) *a*, severe, stern; hard; strict. **sévérité** (verite) *f*, severity, etc.

sévices (sevis) *m.pl*, maltreatment, cruelty (*in law*).

Séville (sevil) *f*, Seville.

sévir (sevi:r) *v.i*, to deal severely (*contre* = with); rage, be rife, be rampant.

sevrage (səvra:ʒ) *m*, weaning. **sevrer** (vre) *v.t*, to wean; deprive.

sexe (sɛks) *m*, sex; genitals.

sextant (sɛkstɑ̃) *m*, sextant.

sextuor (sɛkstɥɔ:r) *m*, sextet.

sexuel, le (sɛksɥɛl) *a*, sexual.

seyant, e (sɛjɑ̃, ɑ:t) *a*, becoming.

shake-hand (ʃɛkɑ̃:d) *m*, handshake.

si, s' (si, s) *c*, if, whether; how [much]; what if, suppose. ~ *le temps le permet*, weather permitting. **si**, *ad*, so; so much; such; however; yes. ~ *fait*, yes, indeed. ¶ *m*, if; B (*Mus.*).

Siam (le) (sjam), Siam. **siamois, e** (mwa, a:z) *a. & S~, n*, Siamese. **le siamois**, Siamese (*language*).

Sibérie (la) (siberi), Siberia. **sibérien, ne** (rjɛ̃, ɛn) *a. & S~, n*, Siberian.

sicaire (sikɛ:r) *m*, hired assassin.

siccatif (sikatif) *m*, drier[s] (*painter's*).

Sicile (la) (sisil), Sicily. **sicilien, ne** (ljɛ̃, ɛn) *a. & S~, n*, Sicilian.

sicle (sikl) *m*, shekel (*Bible*).

sidéral, e (sideral) *a*, sidereal.

sidéré (sidere) *a*, thunderstruck, flabbergasted.

siècle (sjɛkl) *m*, century; age, times; world. *les ~s d'ignorance*, the dark ages.

siège (sjɛ:ʒ) *m*, seat; bench; box (*driver's*); bottom (*chair*); see (*Eccl.*); siege (*Mil.*). ~ *arrière*, back seat; pillion. ~ *social*, head office. *Saint-Siège*, Holy See. **siéger** (eʒe) *v.i*, to have its headquarters; sit; be seated.

sien, ne (*with* le, la, les) (sjɛ̃, ɛn) *pn. & m*, his, hers; one's own. his own, her own.

Sienne (sjɛn) *f*, Sienna.

sieste (sjɛst) *f*, siesta, nap.

sieur (sjœ:r) *m*, Mr.

siffler (sifle) *v.i. & t*, to whistle; pipe; hiss; whirr, whizz; wheeze. **sifflet** (flɛ) *m*, whistle; pipe (*boatswain's*); hiss, catcall. [canard] **siffleur** (flœ:r) *m*, widgeon. **siffloter** (flɔte) *v.i*, to whistle softly.

sigle (sigl) *m*, set of initials often used as word. i.e. O.N.U. (*Organisation des Nations Unies*), U.N. (*United Nations*).

signal (siɲal) *m*, signal. **signalé, e** (le) *p.a*, signal; conspicuous; well-known. **signalement** (lmɑ̃) *m*, description. **signaler** (le) *v.t*, to signalize, point out; signal; notify. **signaleur** (lœ:r) *m*, signaler (*Mil.*); signalman (*Rly.*). **signalisation** (izasjɔ̃) *f*, signaling; road signs. ~ *routière internationale*, international road signs system.

signataire (siɲatɛ:r) *n*, signatory, signer. **signature** (ty:r) *f*, signing, signature. **signe** (siɲ) *m*, sign, token, mark; motion, wave (*hand*). ~ *d'omission*, caret. ~ [*de tête*], nod. ~ *des yeux*, wink. **signer** (ɲe) *v.t*, to sign. ~ *à*, to witness. se ~, to cross oneself. **signet** (ɲɛ) *m*, bookmark, signet.

significatif, ive (siɲifikatif, i:v) *a*, significant, meaning, of deep significance (*look*). **signification** (sjɔ̃) *f*, signification, meaning, sense, import; service (*writ*). **signifier** (fje) *v.t*, to signify, mean; notify, intimate; serve (*a notice*).

silence (silɑ̃:s) *m*, silence, stillness, hush; pause; rest (*Mus.*). **silencieux, euse†** (lɑ̃sjø, ø:z) *a*, silent, noiseless, still. ¶ *m*, silencer.

Silésie (la) (silezi), Silesia. **silésienne** (zjɛn) *f*, silesia (*fabric*).

silex (silɛks) *m*, silex, flint.

silhouette (silwɛt) *f*, silhouette.

silicate (silikat) *m*, silicate. **silice** (lis) *f*, silica.

sillage (sija:ʒ) *m*, wake, track; headway (*ship*). **sillet** (jɛ) *m*, nut (*violin*). **sillon** (jɔ̃) *m*, furrow; drill (*furrow*); (*pl.*, *Poet.*) fields; wrinkle; track, trail; streak; groove. **sillonner** (ɔne) *v.t*, to furrow; plow (*seas*); wrinkle; streak, groove.

silo (silo) *m*, silo.

simagrée (simagre) *f*. *oft. pl*, pretence; affectation.

simiesque (simjɛsk) *a*, apelike, apish.

similaire (similɛ:r) *a*, similar, like. **simili-** (li) *prefix*, imitation (*att.*), artificial. **similigravure** (ligravy:r) *f*, process engraving, halftone e. **similitude** (tyd) *f*, similitude, similarity; simile.

simonie (simɔni) *f*, simony.

simple† (sɛ̃:pl) *a*, simple; single; ordinary; private (*soldier*); plain; homely; mere; simple[-minded]; half-witted. ¶ *m*, single (*Ten.*); half-wit; (*pl.*) medicinal herbs. **simplicité** (séplisite) *f*, simplicity. **simplifier** (fje) *v.t*, to simplify.

simulacre (simylakr) *m*, simulacrum, image; dummy (*Mil.*); show. ~ *de combat*, sham fight, mock f. **simulé, e** (le) *p.a*, feigned, sham; bogus, fictitious. **simuler** (le) *v.t*, to simulate. ~ *la maladie*, to malinger.

simulie (simyli) *f*, sand fly.

simultané†, e (simyltane) *a*, simultaneous.

Sinaï (le mont) (sinai), Mount Sinai.

sinapisme (sinapism) *m*, mustard plaster.

sincère† (sɛ̃sɛ:r) *a*, sincere, candid, unfeigned, genuine. **sincérité** (serite) *f*, sincerity, candor.

sinécure (sineky:r) *f*, sinecure.

Singapour (sɛ̃gapu:r) *m*, Singapore.

singe (sɛ̃:ʒ) *m*, monkey, ape; copycat; winch; boss (*slang*). **singer** (sɛ̃ʒe) *v.t*, to ape, mock. **singerie** (ʒri) *f*, monkey house; grimace, grotesque imitation.

singulariser (sɛ̃gylarize) *v.t*, to make conspicuous. **singulier, ère†** (lje, ɛ:r) *a*, singular; peculiar; odd, queer, quaint; single (*combat*). ¶ *m*, singular (*Gram.*). **singularité** (larite) *f*, singularity, etc.

sinistre† (sinistr) *a*, sinister, ominous; grim; lurid, baleful. ¶ *m*, disaster, casualty; loss (*Insce.*). **sinistré** (tre) *m*, victim of a disaster (*fire, flood, bombing*). ¶ *a*, homeless, bombed-out, etc.

sinistrose (sinistro:z) *f*, conduct of person traumatized by accident, generally on the job.

sinon (sinɔ̃) *c*, otherwise, else; except, save.

sinueux, euse (sinɥø, ø:z) *a*, sinuous, winding. **sinuosité** (nɥozite) *f*, sinuosity, bend.

sinus (siny:s) *m*, sinus; sine.

sionisme (sjɔnism) *m*, Zionism.

siphon (sifɔ̃) *m*, siphon; trap (*drain*).

sire (si:r) *m*, sire (*to king*).

sirène (sirɛn) *f*, siren, mermaid; hooter.

sirop (siro) *m*, syrup. **siroter** (rote) *v.t*, to sip. **sirupeux, euse** (rypø, ø:z) *a*, syrupy.

sis, e (si, i:z) *p.p,* situated.

sismique (sismik) *a,* seismic. **sismographe** (mɔgraf) *m,* seismograph.

site (sit) *m,* site, location.

sitôt (sito) *ad,* as soon, so soon.

situation (sitɥasjɔ̃) *f,* situation, position; condition, state; statement, report. **situé, e** (tɥe) *p.p. & p.a,* situated.

six (si; *in liaison,* siz; *at end of phrase,* sis) *a. & m,* six; 6th. **sixième**† (sizjɛm) *a. & n,* sixth. **sixte** (sikst) *f,* sixth (*Mus.*).

ski (ski) *m,* ski. *~s de saut,* jumping skis.

slave (sla:v) *a. &* S*~, n,* Slav.

slip (slip) *m,* underpants; trunks.

sloughi (slugi) *m,* saluki.

smic (smik) *or* smig (ig) *m,* guaranteed minimum wage (*salaire minimum interprofessionnel de croissance, garanti*). *~ard,* *~arde* (kar, kard) *n,* person covered by *smic.*

smilax (smilaks) *m,* smilax (*Bot.*).

smoking (smɔkiŋ) *m,* tuxedo.

Smyrne (smirn) *f,* Smyrna.

snob (snɔb) *a,* snobbish. **snobisme** (bism) *m,* snobbishness, snobbery.

sobre† (sɔbr) *a,* sober, temperate, abstemious; sparing, chary. **sobriété** (briete) *f,* sobriety.

sobriquet (sɔbrikɛ) *m,* nickname.

soc (sɔk) *m,* plowshare.

sociable† (sɔsjabl) *a,* sociable; companionable, genial. **social, e** (sjal) *a,* social; corporate; registered (*capital, offices*); of the firm; company's. **socialisme** (lism) *m,* socialism. **socialiste** (list) *n. & a,* socialist. **sociétaire** (sjetɛ:r) *n,* member; stockholder. **société** (te) *f,* society; community; companionship, fellowship; club; company; firm; partnership. *~ anonyme,* corporation. S*~ des Nations,* League of Nations. *~ immobilière,* building society. *~ par actions,* joint-stock company. **sociologie** (sjɔlɔʒi) *f,* sociology.

socle (sɔkl) *m,* pedestal, stand.

socque (sɔk) *m,* clog, pattern. **socquettes** (kɛt) *f.pl,* ankle socks.

sodium (sɔdjɔm) *m,* sodium.

sœur (sœ:r) *f,* sister. *et ta ~?,* mind your own business. **sœurette** (sœrɛt) *f,* [dear] little sister.

sofa (sɔfa) *m,* sofa.

soffite (sɔfit) *m,* soffit.

software (sɔftwɛ:r) *m,* software (*computers*).

soi (swa) *& ~-même, pn,* oneself; himself, herself, itself. *~-disant* (dizɑ̃) *a.inv,* self-styled, would-be; so-called.

soie (swa) *f,* silk; bristle (*hog*); tang (*of tool*). *~ floche* (flɔʃ), floss silk. **soierie** (ri) *f,* silk goods, silks; silk mill; silk trade.

soif (swaf) *f,* thirst; craving, hankering. *avoir ~,* to be thirsty, to thirst.

soigné, e (swaɲe) *p.a,* carefully done; trim, neat. **soigner** (ɲe) *v.t,* to take care of, look after, attend to; tend; nurse; manicure. **soigneur** (ɲœ:r) *m,* minder; second (*Box.*). **soigneux, euse**† (ɲø, ø:z) *a,* careful, painstaking; tidy. **soin** (swɛ̃) *m. oft. pl,* care, attention, pains; nursing. *~ des mains,* manicure. *~ des pieds,* chiropody. *aux [bons] ~s de,* care of, c/o. *premiers ~s,* first aid.

soir (swa:r) *m,* evening; night; afternoon. **soirée** (sware) *f,* evening; [evening] party. *de ~,* evening (*dress, etc.*).

soit (swa) *c,* either; or; whether; suppose, let. *~ que,* whether. *~!* (swat), so be it! agreed! *tant ~ peu,* ever so little.

soixantaine (swasɑ̃tɛn) *f,* sixty [or so]. **soixante** (sɑ̃:t) *a. & m,* sixty. *~-dix* (sɑ̃tdis) *a. & m,* seventy. *~ & onze, ~-douze,* 71, 72. *~-dixième* (zjɛm) *a. & n,* seventieth. **soixantième** (tjɛm) *a. & n,* sixtieth.

soja (sɔja) *m,* soybean.

sol (sɔl) *m,* ground, earth; soil; G (*Mus.*).

solaire (sɔlɛ:r) *a,* solar, sun (*att.*). *cadran ~,* sun dial.

soldat (sɔlda) *m,* soldier. *~ de plomb,* tin soldier. *le S~ inconnu,* the Unknown Soldier. **soldatesque** (tɛsk) *f,* (*unruly*) soldiery.

solde (sɔld) *f,* pay (*Mil., Nav., etc.*). ¶ *m,* balance; settlement;

surplus stock, job lot; [clearance] sale. ~ *d'édition*, remainder (*books*). ~ *de dividende*, final dividend. *vente de* ~*s*, clearance sale. ~*s de dégriffés*, s. of clothes with labels removed. **solder** (de) *v.t*, to balance (*a/c*); pay off, settle; sell off, clear; remainder. **soldeuse** (dø:z) *f*, woman who buys everything at sales.

sole (sɔl) *f*, sole (*fish, hoof, bed plate*). ~ *limande*, lemon sole.

solécisme (sɔlesism) *m*, solecism.

soleil (sɔlɛːj) *m*, sun; sunshine; sunflower; catherine wheel (*fireworks*). ~ *couchant*, setting sun, sunset. *coup de* ~, sunstroke.

solennel, le† (sɔlanɛl) *a*, solemn; formal; state (*att.*); impressive. **solenniser** (nize) *v.t*, to solemnize, celebrate. **solennité** (te) *f*, solemnity; celebration.

solfège (sɔlfɛːʒ) *m*, sol-fa, solfeggio. **solfier** (fje) *v.t. & abs*, to sol-fa.

solidaire† (sɔlidɛːr) *a*, mutually responsible; interdependent; solidary. **solidariser** (lidarize) *v.t*, to make jointly responsible. **se** ~, to make common cause. **solide†** (lid) *a*, solid; strong; substantial; hefty; firm; fast (*color*); sound; sterling (*fig.*). ¶ *m*, solid; s. foundation, s. ground; main chance. **solidifier** (difje) *v.t*, to solidify. **solidité** (te) *f*, solidity; strength; soundness.

soliloque (sɔlilɔk) *m*, soliloquy.

soliste (sɔlist) *n*, soloist; solo (*violin*).

solitaire† (sɔlitɛːr) *a*, solitary, lonely. ¶ *m*, hermit; solitaire (*gem & game*). **solitude** (tyd) *f*, solitude, loneliness; wilderness, wild.

solive (sɔliːv) *f*, joist, beam, girder.

solliciter (sɔllisite) *v.t*, to solicit, ask for, apply for; canvass; entreat; urge; attract. **sollicitude** (tyd) *f*, solicitude; anxiety.

solo (sɔlo) *m*, solo (*Mus.*).

solstice (sɔlstis) *m*, solstice.

soluble (sɔlybl) *a*, soluble; solvable. **solution** (sjɔ̃) *f*, solution; break; discharge (*law*).

solvabilité (sɔlvabilite) *f*, solvency (*Fin.*). **solvable** (bl) *a*, solvent.

sombre (sɔ̃ːbr) *a*, dark, somber, gloomy; dim.

sombrer (sɔ̃bre) *v.i*, to founder, sink, go down.

sommaire† (sɔmɛːr) *a*, summary, compendious; scant. ¶ *m*, summary, synopsis.

sommation (sɔmasjɔ̃) *f*, summons, appeal.

somme (sɔm) *f*, sum, amount; burden. ~ *toute* ou *en* ~, [up] on the whole.

somme (sɔm) *m*, nap, snooze. **sommeil** (mɛːj) *m*, sleep, slumber; sleepiness. **sommeiller** (mɛje) *v.i*, to slumber, doze, nod.

sommelier (sɔmǝlje) *m*, wine waiter.

sommer (sɔme) *v.t*, to summon, call on; sum up.

sommet (sɔmɛ) *m*, summit, top; vertex, apex; acme.

sommier (sɔmje) *m*, pack animal; transom, lintel; dossier; register; bed mattress, spring m.

sommité (sɔmmite) *f*, summit, top; leading man, (*pl.*) leading people.

somnambule (sɔmnɑ̃byl) *n*, somnambulist, sleepwalker. **somnambulisme** (lism) *m*, somnambulism. **somnolent, e** (nɔlɑ̃, ɑ̃ːt) *a*, sleepy. **somnoler** (nɔle) *v.i*, to doze; drowse.

somnifère (sɔmnifɛːr) *m*, opiate; narcotic; sleeping pill.

somptueux, euse† (sɔ̃ptɥø, øːz) *a*, sumptuous. **somptuosité** (tɥozite) *f*, sumptuousness.

son, sa, ses (sɔ̃, sa, se) *a*, his, her, its, one's.

son (sɔ̃) *m*, sound; clang; tone; bran.

sonate (sɔnat) *f*, sonata.

sonde (sɔ̃ːd) *f*, [sounding] lead, plummet; probe; spit; drill (*Min.*); taster (*cheese*). **sonder** (sɔ̃de) *v.t*, to sound; probe; fathom. **sondeur** (dœːr) *m*, leadsman; driller.

songe (sɔ̃ːʒ) *m*, dream. ~-**creux**, *m*, dreamer, visionary. **songer** (sɔ̃ʒe) *v.i*, to dream, muse. ~ *à*,

to think of, intend. **songeur, euse**
(ʒœːr, ɸːz) *a*, dreamy; pensive.

sonnaille (sonaːj) *f*, cowbell. **sonnailler** (naje) *m*, bellwether. ¶ *v.i*,
to keep ringing [the bell]. **sonnant,
e** (nɑ̃, ɑ̃ːt) *a*, [re]sounding; hard
(*cash*). **sonné, e** (ne) *p.a*, past,
struck (*hour*); turned (*a certain
age*). **sonner** (ne) *v.i. & t*, to
sound; ring; r. for; toll; strike.
sonnerie (nri) *f*, ringing; bells;
bell; call (*trumpet, bugle*). **sonnet**
(nɛ) *m*, sonnet. **sonnette** (nɛt) *f*,
bell; pile driver. **sonneur** (nœːr)
m, bell ringer. **sonore** (nɔːr) *a*,
sonorous; loud (*laugh, cheers*);
sound (*att.*). **sonoriser** (nɔrize)
v.t, to add sound track to film.
sonorité (nɔrite) *f*, sonorousness,
volume [of sound].

sophisme (sofism) *m*, sophism;
fallacy. **sophistique** (tik) *f*, sophistry. **sophistiquer** (ke) *v.t. &
i*, to sophisticate.

soporifique (sɔpɔrifik) *a. & m*,
soporific.

soprano (sɔprano) *m*, soprano
(*voice & pers.*).

sorbet (sɔrbɛ) *m*, ices (*flavored*).
sorbetière (btjɛːr) *f*, ice-cream
freezer.

sorbier (sɔrbje) *m*, service tree,
sorb. ~ **des oiseaux**, mountain
ash.

sorcellerie (sɔrsɛlri) *f*, sorcery,
witchcraft. **sorcier, ère** (sje, ɛːr)
n, sorcerer, ess, wizard, witch;
hag. *sorcier guérisseur*, medicine
man, witch doctor. *ce n'est pas
sourcier*, it's not that difficult,
complicated.

sordide† (sɔrdid) *a*, sordid; filthy,
squalid.

sorgho (sɔrgo) *m*, sorghum.

Sorlingues (îles) (sɔrlɛ̃g) *f.pl*,
Scilly Islands, Scilly Isles.

sornettes (sɔrnɛt) *f.pl*, nonsense.

sort (sɔːr) *m*, lot, fate; spell.
sortable (sɔrtabl) *a*, suitable; eligible. **sortant** (tɑ̃) *a.m*, drawn,
winning (*number*); retiring, outgoing (*pers.*).

sorte (sɔrt) *f*, sort, kind; manner,
way. *en quelque* ~, in a way, as
it were.

sortie (sɔrti) *f*, going out; coming out; exit; issue; sally, sortie;
outlet; way out, egress. ~ **de bal**,
~ **de théâtre**, opera cloak, evening wrap.

sortilège (sɔrtilɛːʒ) *m*, witchcraft, spell.

sortir (sɔrtːr) *v.i.ir*, to go out;
come out; leave; emerge, issue,
spring; stand out; (*v.t.ir.*) to bring
out; take out; pull out. X. *sort*,
exit X. (*Theat.*). ~ *sur imprimante*, to print out (*computers*).

sosie (sozi) *m*, double (*pers.*).

sot, te† (so, ɔt) *a*, silly, foolish;
sheepish. ¶ *n*, fool. **sot-l'y-laisse**
(solilɛs) *m*, pope's nose. **sottise**
(sotiːz) *f*, silliness, foolishness,
folly; (*pl.*) nonsense; insult.

sou (su) *m*, sou = 5 centimes;
penny (*in sense of very little
money*).

soubassement (subɑsmɑ̃) *m*,
basement; base.

soubresaut (subrəso) *m*, start,
leap, jolt.

souche (suʃ) *f*, stump, stock,
stub; founder (*family*); shaft,
stack (*chimney*); counterfoil. *à
la* ~, unissued (*stocks, shares*).

souci (susi) *m*, care, concern;
worry; marigold. ~ **d'eau**, marsh
marigold, kingcup. **se soucier de**
(sje), to care for, mind. **soucieux, euse** (sjø, ɸːz) *a*, anxious.

soucoupe (sukup) *f*, saucer.

soudain, e† (sudɛ̃, ɛn) *a*, sudden.
soudain, *ad*, suddenly. **soudaineté** (dɛnte) *f*, suddenness.

soude (sud) *f*, soda; saltwort.

souder (sude) *v.t*, to solder; weld.

soudoyer (sudwaje) *v.t*, to hire;
bribe.

soudure (sudyːr) *f*, soldering;
solder; welding; joint; weld.

souffle (sufl) *m*, breath; puff, waft,
inspiration. *second* ~, second
wind. **souffler** (fle) *v.i. & t*, to
blow; b. up; b. out; pant; breathe;
prompt; prime, whisper. **soufflerie**
(fləri) *f*, bellows (*organ*). **soufflet**
(flɛ) *m*, bellows; hood (*carriage*);
box on the ear[s]; slap; snub.
souffleter (flɔte) *v.t*, to box (*someone's*) ears, slap. **souffleur** (flœːr)

m, blower; prompter. **soufflure** (fly:r) *f*, blowhole; flaw (*casting*).

souffrance (sufrã:s) *f*, sufferance (*law*); suffering; pain. **en ~,** in suspense, in abeyance, held over; unclaimed, on hand (*goods*); undeliverable (*parcel*). **souffrant,** **e** (frã, ã:t) *a*, suffering; ailing; unwell, poorly. **souffre-douleur** (frədulœ:r) *m*, butt; scapegoat. **souffreteux, euse** (tø, ø:z) *a*, sickly. **souffrir** (frir) *v.t. & i. ir,* to suffer; bear; endure, stand; undergo; allow.

soufre (sufr) *m*, sulfur, brimstone. **soufrière** (frie:r) *f*, sulfur mine.

souhait (swɛ) *m*, wish. **~s de bonne année,** New Year's wishes, season's greetings. **souhaitable** (tabl) *a*, desirable. **souhaiter** (te) *v.t,* to wish; w. for. **~ la (ou une bonne) fête à quelqu'un,** to wish someone many happy returns [of the day].

souille (su:j) *f*, wallow. **souiller** (suje) *v.t,* to soil, dirty; pollute, taint; stain, sully, besmirch. **souillon** (jõ) *n*, sloven; (*f.*) slut, slattern. **souillure** (jy:r) *f*, spot, stain; blot, blemish.

soûl, e (su, ul) *a*, drunk; gorged. ¶ *m*, fill. **soûlard, e** (la:r, ard) *n*, drunkard. **soûler** (le) *v.t,* to glut (*food, drink*); inebriate.

soulager (sulaʒe) *v.t,* to relieve, lighten, ease, alleviate; comfort. **souleur** (sulœ:r) *f*, shock (*startling emotion*).

soulèvement (sulɛvmã) *m*, rising; heaving; upheaval (*Geol.*); revolt. **soulever** (lve) *v.t,* to raise, lift; make heave; mood; rouse. **se ~,** to rise, heave; revolt. **soulier** (sulje) *m*, shoe; slipper. **souligner** (suliɲe) *v.t,* to underline; emphasize.

soulte (sult) *f*, balance (*in cash*).

soumettre (sumɛtr) *v.t.ir,* to subdue; submit; subject. **se ~,** to submit, yield, give in. **soumis, e** (mi, i:z) *p.a,* submissive, dutiful; subject, amenable; liable. **soumission** (misjõ) *f*, submission; submissiveness; tender; bond. **soumissionner** (ɔne) *v.t,* to tender for.

soupape (supap) *f*, valve; plug (*bath, etc.*). **~ d'échappement,** exhaust v. **~ de sécurité,** safety v.

soupçon (supsõ) *m*, suspicion; surmise; dash; touch. **soupçonner** (sɔne) *v.t,* to suspect; surmise. **soupçonneux, euse** (nø, ø:z) *a*, suspicious, distrustful.

soupe (sup) *f*, soup; food; chow (*Mil.*).

soupente (supã:t) *f*, loft.

souper (supe) *m*, supper. **~ assis,** sit-down supper. **~ debout,** buffet (*at a ball*). ¶ *v.i,* to have supper, sup.

soupeser (supəze) *v.t,* to feel the weight of.

soupière (supjɛ:r) *f*, soup tureen.

soupir (supi:r) *m*, sigh; breath; crotchet rest (*Mus.*). **soupirail** (pira:j) *m*, airhole, vent. **soupirant** (rã) *m*, suitor, wooer. **soupirer** (re) *v.i,* to sigh; yearn.

souple (supl) *a*, supple, pliant, pliable; lithe[some], lissom[e]; limp (*binding*); versatile. *feutre* **~,** soft felt (*hat*). **souplesse** (plɛs) *f*, suppleness.

source (surs) *f*, source, spring, fountainhead; well; rise; wellspring, fount. **sourcier, ère** (sje, ɛ:r) *n*, water diviner, dowser.

sourcil (sursi) *m*, eyebrow. **sourciller** (je) *v.i,* to frown; wince. **sourcilleux, euse** (jø, ø:z) *a*, beetling; frowning, anxious.

sourd, e (su:r, urd) *a*, deaf, dull; hollow (*voice*); mute[d]; muffled; underhand. ¶ *n*, deaf person. **sourdement** (surdəmã) *ad*, dully; secretly. **sourdine** (din) *f*, mute (*Mus.*); damper. **en ~,** on the sly. **sourd-muet, sourde-muette** (surmɥɛ, dmɥɛt) *a*, deaf & dumb. ¶ *n*, deaf-mute.

sourdre (surdr) *v.i,* to spring, well up.

souriant, e (surjã, ã:t) *a*, smiling.

souriceau (suriso) *m*, young mouse. **souricière** (sje:r) *f*, mousetrap; trap (*police*).

sourire (suri:r) *m*, smile. ¶ *v.i.ir,* to smile. **~ à,** to be attractive to, please.

souris (suri) *f*, mouse; knuckle end (*mutton*).

sournois, e† (surnwa, a:z) *a*, sly, underhand.

sous (su; *in liaison*, suz) *pr*, under[neath], beneath, below; in; by; with; within; on. **sous**, *comps*: **~-affermer**, *v.t*, to sublet. **~-bail**, *m*, sublease. **~-cutané, e**, *a*, subcutaneous. **~-entendre**, *v.t*, to understand, imply. **~-entendu**, *m*, implication; double entendre. *sous-estimer*, *v.t*, to underestimate, undervalue, underrate. *sous-jacent, e* (suʒɑsɑ̃, ɑ̃:t) *a*, underlying. **~-lieutenant**, *m*, second lieutenant. **~-locataire**, *n*, subtenant. **~-louer**, *v.t*, to sublet; rent (*as subtenant*). **~-marin, e, a. & m**, submarine. *en* **~-œuvre**, underpinned. **~-officier**, *m*, noncommissioned officer. **~-ordre**, *m*, subordinate, underling; sub-order. *en* **~-ordre**, subordinate(ly). **~-produit**, *m*, byproduct. **~-secrétaire**, *m*, undersecretary. **~-sol**, *m*, subsoil; basement. **~-titre**, *m*, subtitle, caption. **~-traitant** (trɛtɑ̃) *m*, subcontractor. **~-traité**, *m*, subcontract. **~-ventrière** (vɑ̃triɛ:r) *f*, bellyband; [saddle] girth. **~-vêtement**, *m*, undergarment; (*pl.*) underwear, underclothing.

souscripteur (suskriptœ:r) *m*, subscriber; applicant (*shares*); drawer (*bill*); underwriter (*Insce*). **souscription** (sjɔ̃) *f*, execution, signing (*deed*); signature; subscription; application; underwriting. **souscrire** (skri:r) *v.t. & i. ir*, to execute, sign; subscribe; draw; apply for; underwrite.

sous-développement (sudevlɔpmɑ̃) *f*, underdevelopment (*economics*).

sous-prolétariat (suprɔletarja) *m*, unemployables leading a marginal social life. Equivalent of German *Lumpenproletariat*.

soussigné, e (susiɲe) *a. & n*, undersigned.

soustraction (sustraksjɔ̃) *f*, abstraction; subtraction. **soustraire** (strɛ:r) *v.t.ir*, to abstract (*steal*), purloin; withdraw; screen; subtract (*Arith.*). *se* **~** *à*, to elude,

avoid. *se* **~** *à la justice*, to abscond.

soutache (sutaʃ) *f*, braid. **soutacher** (ʃe) *v.t*, to braid.

soutane (sutan) *f*, cassock; cloth (*clergy*).

soute (sut) *f*, storeroom (*Naut.*); magazine, bunker, locker; tank.

soutenable (sutnabl) *a*, bearable; tenable. **soutenir** (tni:r) *v.t.ir*, to sustain, support, hold up; uphold; keep, maintain; back [up]; stand, bear; afford. **soutenu, e** (tny) *p.a*, sustained; unremitting; lofty, rhetorical (*style*).

souterrain, e (sutɛrɛ̃, ɛn) *a*, underground, subterranean; underhand. ¶ *m*, tunnel; cavern.

soutien (sutjɛ̃) *m*, support; mainstay; upholder. **~** *de famille*, breadwinner. **~-gorge**, *m*, brassière.

soutirer (sutire) *v.t*, to draw off, rack [off] (*wine*); extract (*money*).

souvenance (suvnɑ̃:s) *f*, memories. **souvenir** (vni:r) *m*, remembrance, recollection, memory; memento; keepsake. *se* **~**, *v.pr. ir*, to remember, recollect.

souvent (suvɑ̃) *ad*, often.

souverain, e† (suvrɛ̃, ɛn) *a*, sovereign; supreme, superlative. ¶ *n*, sovereign. **souveraineté** (vrɛnte) *f*, sovereignty.

soviet (sɔvjɛt) *m*, soviet. **soviétique** (etik) *a*, soviet (*att.*).

soya (sɔja) *m*, soybean.

soyeux, euse (swajø, ø:z) *a*, silky.

spacieux, euse† (spasjø, ø:z) *a*, spacious, roomy, capacious.

spadassin (spadasɛ̃) *m*, ruffian.

sparadrap (sparadra) *m*, adhesive tape, court plaster.

sparte (spart) *m*, esparto [grass].

spartiate (sparsjat) *a. & n*, Spartan.

spasme (spasm) *m*, spasm. **spasmodique** (mɔdik) *a*, spasmodic (*Med.*).

spath (spat) *m*, spar.

spatial, aux (spasjal, o) *a*, relating to space; astounding (*slang*).

spatule (spatyl) *f*, spatula; spoonbill.

speaker (spikœ:r) *m*, announcer (*radio*); speaker.

spécial, e† (spesjal) *a*, special, particular. **se spécialiser dans** (lize), to specialize in. **spécialiste** (list) *n*, specialist. **spécialité** (te) *f*, specialty. ~ *pharmaceutique*, patent medicine.

spécieux, euse† (spesjø, ø:z) *a*, specious.

spécification (spesifikasjɔ̃) *f*, specification. **spécifier** (fje) *v.t*, to specify. **spécifique†** (fik) *a.* & *m*, specific.

spécimen (spesimɛn) *m*, specimen; free copy (*book*).

spectacle (spɛktakl) *m*, spectacle, sight, scene; play, entertainment, show. ~ *forain*, sideshow (*fair*). ~ *payant*, sideshow (*exhibition*). ~ *permanent*, continuous performance (*movies*). ~ *solo*, one-man show. **spectateur, trice** (tœ:r, tris) *n*, spectator, onlooker, bystander; (*m.pl.*) audience (*Theat.*).

spectral, e (spɛktral) *a*, spectral; ghostly, unearthly, eerie, -ry, weird. **spectre** (tr) *m*, specter, ghost; spectrum. **spectroscope** (trɔskɔp) *m*, spectroscope.

spéculateur, trice (spekylatœ:r, tris) *n*, speculator. **spéculatif, ive** (tif, i:v) *a*, speculative. **spéculation** (sjɔ̃) *f*, speculation. **spéculer** (le) *v.i*, to speculate.

spermatozoaire (spɛrmatɔzɔɛ:r) *m*, spermatozoon. **sperme** (spɛrm) *m*, sperm.

sphère (sfɛ:r) *f*, sphere, orb, globe. **sphérique** (sferik) *a*, spherical.

sphincter (sfɛ̃ktɛ:r) *m*, sphincter.

sphinx (sfɛ̃:ks) *m*, sphinx.

spinal, e (spinal) *a*, spinal.

spinelle (spinɛl) *m.* & *att*, spinel.

spiral, e (spiral) *a*, spiral. ¶ *m*, hairspring; (*f.*) spiral. **spire** (spi:r) *f*, turn, spire, whorl.

spirite (spirit) *n*, spiritualist (*psychics*). **spiritisme** (tism) *m*, spiritualism. **spiritualisme** (tɥalism) *m*, spiritualism (*Philos.*). **spiritualiste** (list) *n*, spiritualist. **spirituel, le†** (tɥɛl) *a*, spiritual; sacred (*concert*); witty. **spiri-**

tueux, euse (tɥø, ø:z) *a*, spirituous. ¶ *m.pl*, spirits.

Spitzberg (le) (spitsbɛrg), Spitzbergen.

spleen (splin) *m*, spleen, dumps, blues.

splendeur (splɑ̃dœ:r) *f*, splendor. **splendide†** (did) *a*, splendid, gorgeous.

spolier (spɔlje) *v.t*, to despoil, rob, rifle.

spongieux, euse (spɔ̃ʒjø, ø:z) *a*, spongy.

spontané†, e (spɔ̃tane) *a*, spontaneous; willing.

sporadique (spɔradik) *a*, sporadic.

spore (spɔ:r) *f*, spore.

sport (spɔ:r) *m*, sport, sports. **sportif, ive** (spɔrtif, i:v) *a*, fond of sport[s]; sporting; sports (*att.*); athletic (*meeting*); game (*fish, fishing, etc.*). **un sportif**, a sportsman.

square (skwa:r) *m*, park, square.

squelette (skəlɛt) *m*, skeleton; scrag (*pers.*).

stabilité (stabilite) *f*, stability. **stabiliser** (ze) *v.t*, to stabilize (*Fin.*). **stable** (bl) *a*, stable; lasting.

stade (stad) *m*, stadium; stage (*Med.*).

stage (sta:ʒ) *m*, probation; course; stage, period. **stagiaire** (staʒjɛ:r) *n*, probationer.

stagnant, e (stagnɑ̃, ɑ̃:t) *a*, stagnant; standing (*water*). **stagnation** (nasjɔ̃) *f*, stagnation.

stalactite (stalaktit) *f*, stalactite.

stalagmite (stalagmit) *f*, stalagmite.

stalle (stal) *f*, seat (*Theat.*); box (*horse*); garage.

stance (stɑ̃:s) *f*, stanza.

stand (stɑ̃:d) *m*, stand (*racetrack, exhibition*); shooting gallery, rifle range.

standing (stɑ̃diŋ) *m*, elevated standard of living; status. *immeuble de grand ~*, luxury apartment house.

station (stasjɔ̃) *f*, station; halt; stop (*bus*); stand (*cab*); resort. ~ *balnéaire*, spa, seaside resort. ~ *climat[ér]ique*, health resort. **stationnaire** (ɔnɛ:r) *a*, stationary.

stationnement (nmã) *m*, stopping, standing, halt; parking. ~ *interdit*, no parking. **stationner** (ne) *v.i*, to stop; stand; station; park.

station-aval (stasjɔ̃-aval) *f*, downrange station.

statique (statik) *a*, static(al). ¶ *f*, statics.

statisticien (statistisjɛ̃) *m*, statistician. **statisque** (tik) *a*, statistic(al). ¶ *f*, statistics, return[s]. ~ *militaire*, intelligence department.

statuaire (statyɛːr) *a*, statuary. ¶ *f*, [art of] statuary. ¶ *m*, statuary (*pers.*). **statue** (ty) *f*, statue; (*pl. col.*) statuary.

statuer (statye) *v.t*, to ordain. ~ *sur*, to decide, resolve on.

statuette (statyɛt) *f*, statuette.

stature (statyːr) *f*, stature, height (*of pers.*).

statut (staty) *m*, statute; (*pl.*) memorandum & articles [of association]; status. **statutaire** (tɛːr) *a*, statutory.

stéarine (stearin) *f*, stearin. **stéatite** (tit) *f*, steatite.

steeple-chase (stiplətʃɛs) *m*, hurdle race.

stellaire (stɛllɛːr) *a*, stellar.

sténodactylographe (stenɔdaktilɔgraf) *n*, shorthand-typist. **sténographe** (graf) *n*, stenographer. **sténographie** (fi), *f*, shorthand, stenography. **sténographier** (fje) *v.t*, to take down [in shorthand].

stère (stɛːr) *m*, stere = 1 cub. meter (*firewood*).

stéréoscope (stereɔskɔp) *m*, stereoscope.

stéréotyper (stereɔtipe) *v.t*, to stereotype.

stérile† (steril) *a*, sterile, barren; effete; unfruitful; fruitless. **stériliser** (lize) *v.t*, to sterilize. **stérilité** (te) *f*, sterility, etc.

stérilet (sterile) *m*, I.U.D., coil, loop (*contraceptive device*).

sterling (stɛrliɲ) *a.inv*, sterling.

sterne (stɛrn) *m*, tern (bird).

sternum (stɛrnɔm) *m*, sternum, breast bone.

stethoscope (stetɔskɔp) *m*, stethoscope.

stigmate (stigmat) *m*, stigma, brand. **stigmatiser** (tize) *v.t*, to stigmatize, brand.

stimulant (stimylɑ̃) *m*, stimulant; whet; stimulus. **stimuler** (le) *v.t*, to stimulate, exhilarate, whet.

stimulateur (stimylatœːr) *m*, pacemaker (*Med.*).

stipendiaire (stipɑ̃djɛːr) *a*, mercenary.

stipuler (stipyle) *v.t*, to stipulate.

stock (stɔk) *m*, stock (*goods, gold*).

stockfisch (stɔkfiʃ) *m*, stockfish.

stockiste (stɔkist) *m*, warehouseman (*trade goods*); accredited dealer.

stoïcien, ne (stɔisjɛ̃, ɛn) *a. & m*, Stoic. **stoïcisme** (sism) *m*, stoicism. **stoïque†** (ik) *a*, stoical.

stomacal, e (stɔmakal) *a*, stomachal; stomach (*pump*). **stomachique** (ʃik) *a. & m*, stomachic.

stop (stɔp) *i*, stop (*Naut., in telegrams*). **stoppage** (stɔpaːʒ) *m*, invisible mending. **stopper** (pe) *v.t. & i*, to stop (*ship*); reweave.

store (stɔːr) *m*, blind, shade, awning.

strangulation (strɑ̃gylasjɔ̃) *f*, strangulation.

strapontin (strapɔ̃tɛ̃) *m*, jumpseat.

Strasbourg (strazbuːr) *m*, Strasburg.

strasse (stras) *f*, floss silk.

stratagème (strataʒɛm) *m*, stratagem. **stratège** (tɛːʒ) *m*, strategist. **stratégie** (teʒi) *f*, strategy; generalship. **stratégique** (ʒik) *a*, strategic(al).

stratification (stratifikasjɔ̃) *f*, stratification.

strict, e† (strikt) *a*, strict.

strident, e (stridɑ̃, ɑ̃ːt) *a*, strident, shrill, grating.

strie (stri) *f*, stria, score; ridge. **strié, e** (e) *a*, striate[d]; fluted. **striure** (yːr) *f*, striation.

strophe (strɔf) *f*, stanza, verse.

structure (stryktyːr) *f*, structure, make.

strychnine (striknin) *f*, strychnine.

stuc (styk) *m*, stucco.

studieux, euse† (stydjø, øːz) *a*, studious.

stupéfiant (stypefjã) *m*, narcotic, drug. stupéfier (fje) *v.t*, to stupefy; amaze. stupeur (pœ:r) *f*, stupor; amazement. stupide† (pid) *a*, stupid. stupidité (dite) *f*, stupidity.

style (stil) *m*, style. styler (le) *v.t*, to train. stylet (lɛ) *m*, stiletto; stylet; probe.

stylo (stilɔ) *m*, fountain pen. ~ à bille, ball-point pen.

su (sy) *m*: *au ~ de*, to the knowledge of.

suaire (sɥɛ:r) *m*, shroud, winding sheet.

suant, e (sɥã, ã:t) *a*, sweating; sweaty.

suave† (sɥa:v) *a*, sweet, soft; suave, bland. suavité (avite) *f*, sweetness, suavity.

subalterne (sybaltɛrn) *a*, subordinate, minor. ¶ *m*, underling; subaltern.

subconscience (sybk5sjã:s) *f*, subconsciousness. subconscient, e (sjã, ã:t) *a*. & *m*, subconscious.

subdiviser (sybdivize) *v.t*, to subdivide.

subir (sybi:r) *v.t*, to undergo, submit to, suffer; serve (*a sentence*).

subit, e† (sybi, it) *a*, sudden. subito (to) *ad*, all of a sudden.

subjectif, ive† (syb3ɛktif, i:v) *a*. & *m*, subjective.

subjonctif (syb35ktif) *m*, subjunctive [mood].

subjuguer (syb3yge) *v.t*, to subjugate, subdue.

sublime† (syblim) *a*. & *m*, sublime. sublimer (me) *v.t*, to sublimate; refine. sublimité (mite) *f*, sublimity.

sublunaire (syblynɛ:r) *a*, sublunar[y].

submerger (sybmɛr3e) *v.t*, to submerge, flood, swamp. submersion (sj5) *f*, submersion; flooding; drowning (*of pers.*).

subodorer (sybɔdɔre) *v.t*, to scent [out], suspect.

subordonné, e (sybɔrdɔne) *a*. & *n*, subordinate. subordonner (ne) *v.t*, to subordinate.

suborner (sybɔrne) *v.t*, to suborn, tamper with.

subrécargue (sybrekarg) *m*, supercargo.

subreptice† (sybrɛptis) *a*, surreptitious.

subroger (sybrɔ3e) *v.t*, to subrogate.

subséquemment (sypsekamã) *ad*, subsequently. subséquent, e (kã, ã:t) *a*, subsequent, ensuing.

subside (sypsid) *m*, subsidy.

subsidiaire† (sypsidjɛ:r) *a*, subsidiary.

subsistance (sypsistã:s) *f*, subsistence, sustenance; (*pl.*) provisions, supplies. subsister (te) *v.i*, to subsist.

substance (sybstã:s) *f*, substance; gist, kernel (*fig.*). substantiel, le† (stãsjɛl) *a*, substantial. substantif (tif) *a.m*. & *m*, substantive.

substituer (sybstitɥe) *v.t*, to substitute; entail (*law*). substitut (ty) *m*, deputy; surrogate.

substruction (sybstryksj5) *f*, substructure.

subterfuge (syptɛrfy:3) *m*, subterfuge, shift.

subtil, e† (syptil) *a*, subtle; pervasive; keen; fine. subtiliser (lize) *v.t*, to filch; (*v.i.*) to subtilize. subtilité (te) *f*, subtlety.

suburbain, e (sybyrbɛ̃, ɛn) *a*, suburban.

subvenir à (sybvəni:r) *v.ir*, to come to the aid of; provide for. subvention (vãsj5) *f*, subsidy, subvention, grant. subventionner (ɔne) *v.t*, to subsidize.

subversif, ive (sybvɛrsif, i:v) *a*, subversive. subversion (sj5) *f*, subversion, overthrow.

suc (syk) *m*, juice; pith (*fig.*).

succédané (syksedane) *m*, substitute (*product*). succéder à (de), to succeed; s. to; follow; inherit. succès (sɛ) *m*, success; issue. ~ fou, smash hit. successeur (sɛsœ:r) *m*, successor. successif, ive (sif, i:v) *a*, successive, running. succession (sj5) *f*, succession, sequence; inheritance, estate. successivement (sivmã) *ad*, successively; seriatim.

succinct, e† (syksɛ̃, ɛ̃:kt) *a*, succinct; meager.

succion (syksjɔ̃) *f*, suction, sucking.

succomber (sykɔ̃be) *v.i*, to succumb; sink; yield; die.

succulent, e (sykylɑ̃, ɑ̃:t) *a*, succulent, juicy, luscious, toothsome.

succursale (sykyrsal) *f*, branch (*establishment*).

sucer (syse) *v.t*, to suck; imbibe. **sucette** (sεt) *f*, lollipop; pacifier. **suçoir** (swa:r) *m*, sucker (*of insect*).

sucre (sykr) *m*, sugar. ~ *cristallisé*, granulated s. ~ *d'orge*, barley s., ~ *en morceaux*, ~ *cassé*, lump s., cube s. ~ *en poudre*, powdered s. ~ *semoule*, granulated s. **sucré, e** (kre) *p.a*, sugared, sweet[ened]; sugary (*fig.*). *elle fait la sucrée*, butter wouldn't melt in her mouth. **sucrer** (kre) *v.t*, to sugar, sweeten; suppress or eliminate (*slang*). ~ *un texte*, to eliminate part of a text. *se faire* ~, to be arrested. **sucrerie** (krəri) *f*, sugar refinery; (*pl.*) candy. *aimer les* ~*s*, to have a sweet tooth. **sucrier, ère** (krie, ε:r) *a*, sugar (*att.*). ¶ *m*, sugar refiner; sugar bowl.

sud (syd) *m*, south; (*att.*) south-[ern]. ~*-africain, e*, South African. ~*-américain, e*, South American. ~*-est* (sydεst; *Naut.*, syε) *m*, southeast. ~*-ouest* (sydwεst; *Naut.*, syrwε) *m*, southwest. *le S~-Ouest africain*, South West Africa.

Suède (la) (syεd), Sweden. **suédois, e** (edwa, a:z) *a*. & (*language*) *m*, Swedish. **S~**, *n*, Swede (*pers.*).

suée (sye) *f*, sweat (*state*). **suer** (e) *v.i*. & *t*, to sweat, perspire, ooze; reek of, with. ~ *à grosses gouttes*, to sweat profusely. ~ *d'ahan* (a[h]ɑ̃), to toil & moil. *faire* ~, to annoy, irritate. **sueur** (œ:r) *f*, sweat, perspiration.

suffire (syfi:r) *v.i.ir*, to suffice, be enough, do. ~ *à*, to be equal to, satisfy, cope with. *suffit que*, suffice it to say that. **suffisamment** (fizamɑ̃) *ad*, sufficiently, enough, adequately. **suffisance** (zɑ̃:s) *f*, sufficiency, adequacy, enough; self-importance, bump-

tiousness. **suffisant, e** (zɑ̃, ɑ̃:t) *a*, sufficient, etc.

suffixe (syfiks) *m*, suffix. ¶ *a*, suffixed.

suffocation (syfɔkasjɔ̃) *f*, suffocation, choking. **suffoquer** (ke) *v.t. & i*, to suffocate, stifle, choke.

suffragant (syfragɑ̃) *a.m. & m*, suffragan.

suffrage (syfra:ʒ) *m*, suffrage, vote.

suffusion (syfysjɔ̃) *f*, suffusion.

suggérer (sygʒere) *v.t*, to suggest; prompt. **suggestion** (sygʒεstjɔ̃) *f*, suggestion, hint. **suggestionner** (ɔne) *v.t*, to affect by suggestion (*psychology*).

suicide (sɥisid) *m. &* **suicidé (de)** (*pers.*) *m*, suicide. *suicide du genre humain*, race suicide. **se suicider (de)** *v.pr*, to commit suicide.

suie (sɥi) *f*, soot.

suif (sɥif) *m*, tallow; (*mutton*) fat; candle grease; reprimand (*slang*). *chercher du* ~, to look for a quarrel. **suiffer** (fe) *v.t*, to tallow, grease.

suint (sɥε̃) *m*, grease (*in wool*). **suinter** (te) *v.i*, to ooze, run; leak.

suisse (sɥis) *a*, Swiss. ¶ *m*, Swiss (*man*); Swiss guard; beadle. *en suisse, faire suisse*, to eat or drink without inviting others present. *la S~*, Switzerland. **Suissesse** (sεs) *f*, Swiss (*woman*).

suite (sɥit) *f*, continuation; consequence, result, effect; sequence, series, succession, run; sequel; suite; attendants, retinue, train; set; coherence, consistency. *donner* ~ *a*, to deal with, carry out, decision or order. *la* ~ *au prochain numéro*, to be continued in our next. ~ *& fin*, concluded (*serial*). **suivant, e** (vɑ̃, ɑ̃:t) *a*, next, following, ensuing. ¶ *n*, follower, attendant; (*f.*) lady's maid. **suivant**, *pr*, along; according to, pursuant to. ~ *que*, according as. **suivi, e** (vi) *p.a*, coherent; consistent; steady; well-attended. **suivre** (sɥi:vr) *v.t.ir*, to follow; succeed; pursue; watch, observe; attend; practise. ~ *la balle*, to follow through. *à* ~, to be continued (*se-*

rial). **faire** ~, to forward, read-dress; run on (*Typ.*).

sujet, te (syʒε, εt) *a*, subject, amenable, liable, prone. ¶ *n*, sub-ject (*of a State*). ¶ *m*, subject, topic, matter, theme; cause, grounds; stock (*Hort.*); fellow. **sujétion** (ʒesjɔ̃) *f*, subjection, subservience; constraint; sedu-lousness.

sulfate (sylfat) *m*, sulfate. **sulfite** (fit) *m*, sulfite. **sulfure** (fy:r) *m*, sulfide. **sulfuré, e** (fyre) *a*, sulfur-reted. **sulfureux, euse** (rø, ø:z) *a*, sulfurous. **sulfurique** (rik) *a*, sulfuric.

sultan (syltɑ̃) *m*, sultan; silk-lined basket; sachet. **sultane** (tan) *f*, sultana (*pers.*).

sumac (symak) *m*, sumac. ~ *vé-néneux*, poison ivy, oak, sumac.

superbe† (syperb) *a*, superb, stately; vainglorious. ¶ *f*, vain-glory.

supercherie (syperʃəri) *f*, fraud, hoax.

superfétation (syperfetasjɔ̃) *f*, redundancy.

superficie (syperfisi) *f*, super-ficies, surface; area. **superficiel, le†** (sjel) *a*, superficial, shallow, skin-deep.

superfin, e (syperfɛ̃) *a*, super-fine.

superflu, e (syperfly) *a*, super-fluous. **superflu**, *m*. & **superfluité** (ite) *f*, superfluity.

supérieur, e (syperjœ:r) *a*, su-perior; upper; higher. ¶ *n*, supe-rior, chief; better (*pers.*). **supér-ieurement** (œrmɑ̃) *ad*, superla-tively, in a masterly way. ~ *à*, better than. **supériorité** (rjorite) *f*, superiority.

superlatif, ive (syperlatif, i:v) *a*, superlative (*Gram.*); consum-mate. ¶ (*Gram.*) *m*, superlative.

supermarché (sypεmarʃe) *m*, supermarket.

superposer (syperpoze) *v.t*, to super[im]pose; overlay (*comput-ers*).

superstitieux, euse† (syper-stisjø, ø:z) *a*, superstitious. **su-perstition** (sjɔ̃) *f*, superstition.

supplanter (syplɑ̃te) *v.t*, to sup-plant.

suppléance (sypleɑ̃:s) *f*, sub-stitution; deputyship; temporary term. **suppléant, e** (ɑ̃, ɑ̃:t) *n*. & *a*, substitute, deputy. **suppléer** (ee) *v.t*, to supply, make up for; deputize for; eke out. ~ *à*, to make up for; fill (*vacancy*). **sup-plément** (mɑ̃) *m*, supplement, ad-dition, excess, extra [charge, fare]. **supplémentaire** (tε:r) *a*, supple-mentary, additional, extra, fur-ther; relief (*train*).

suppliant, e (sypliɑ̃, ɑ̃:t) *a*. & *n*, suppliant. **supplication** (kasjɔ̃) *f*, supplication, entreaty. **supplice** (plis) *m*, punishment, torture, tor-ment; (*extreme*) penalty; rack (*fig.*). **supplier** (plie) *v.t*, to be-seech, entreat, implore, suppli-cate. **supplique** (plik) *f*, petition, prayer.

support (sypɔ:r) *m*, support, stay; rest, stand, holder. ~ *à chariot*, slide rest (*lathe*). **sup-portable** (portabl) *a*, supportable, bearable, endurable, tolerable. **supporter** (te) *v.t*, to support; en-dure, bear, suffer, stand. **sup-ports-chaussettes**, *m.pl*, garters (*men's*).

supposé, e (sypoze) *p.a*, sup-positititious; fictitious. **supposé que**, supposing [that]. **supposer** (ze) *v.t*, to suppose; assume, infer, take; imply; put forward as gen-uine (*what is false—law*). **sup-position** (zisjɔ̃) *f*, supposition, as-sumption. ~ *de personne*, imper-sonation (*law*).

suppôt (sypo) *m*, tool (*pers.*), myrmidon.

suppression (sypresjɔ̃) *f*, sup-pression; discontinuance (*train*); concealment. **supprimer** (prime) *v.t*, to suppress, do away with, cut out; discontinue; conceal.

suppurer (sypyre) *v.i*, to sup-purate.

supputer (sypyte) *v.t*, to com-pute, reckon.

suprématie (sypremasi) *f*, su-premacy. **suprême†** (prε:m) *a*, supreme; highest; crowning; par-amount.

sur (syr) *pr*, on, upon; over, above; by; after; in; about; as to; to; towards; out of. ~ *ce*, thereupon.

sur, e (sy:r) *a*, sour, tart.

sûr, e (sy:r) *a*, sure, safe, secure; reliable; settled (*weather*).

surabondant, e (syrabɔ̃dã, ã:t) *a*, superabundant.

suraigu, uë (syregy) *a*, high-pitched, shrill.

suralimenter (syralmãte) *v.t*, to overfeed (*person*); supercharge (*engine*).

suranné, e (syrane) *a*, out-of-date, antiquated, superannuated.

surboum (syrbum) *f*, surprise party, dance, celebration.

surcharge (syrʃarʒ) *f*, overload; excess weight (*luggage*); weight handicap; surcharge; correction, overprint. **surcharger** (ʒe) *v.t*, to overload; overtax; surcharge; correct, alter (*write over*).

surchauffer (syrʃofe) *v.t*, to overheat; superheat.

surcroît (syrkrwa) *m*, increase. *par ~*, in addition, to boot.

surdité (syrdite) *f*, deafness.

sureau (syro) *m*, elder [tree].

surélever (syrelve) *v.t*, to heighten; raise; tee (*golf*).

sûrement (syrmã) *ad*, surely, as *sûr*.

surenchère (syrãʃɛ:r) *f*, higher bid. **surenchérir sur** (ʃeri:r), to bid higher than, outbid.

surestaries (syrestari) *f.pl*, demurrage (*ship*).

surestimer (syrestime) *v.t*, to overestimate, overvalue, overrate.

sûreté (syrte) *f*, safety, security, safe keeping; sureness, reliability. *la S~ Nationale* (*Fr.*), equivalent of Federal Bureau of Investigation in the U.S.

surexciter (syreksite) *v.t*, to overexcite.

surface (syrfas) *f*, surface; area; standing, repute. *~ des étages*, floor space (*building*). *une grande ~*, supermarket, shopping center.

surfaire (syrfɛ:r) *v.t. & abs. ir*, to overcharge (for); overrate, overestimate.

surfin, e (syrfɛ̃, in) *a*, superfine.

surgelé (syrʒale) *a*, deep-frozen. *produits ~s*, frozen foods. **surgeler** *v.t*, to deep-freeze.

surgeon (syrʒɔ̃) *m*, sucker (*Hort.*).

surgir (syrʒi:r) *v.i*, to rise; arise; loom.

surhausser (syrose) *v.t*, to heighten, raise.

surhomme (syrɔm) *m*, superman.

surhumain, e (syrymɛ̃, ɛn) *a*, superhuman.

surimposer (syrɛ̃poze) *v.t*, to overtax, overassess.

surintendant, e (syrɛ̃tãdã, ã:t) *n*, superintendent, overseer, steward.

surjet (syrʒɛ) *m*, oversewing stitch, seam s.

sur-le-champ (syrləʃã) *ad*, there & then; out of hand, off-hand.

surlendemain (syrlãdmɛ̃) *m*, day after tomorrow.

surmener (syrməne) *v.t*, to overwork; overdrive, override (*horse*); jade.

surmonter (syrmɔ̃te) *v.t*, to surmount, [over]top; overcome.

surnager (syrnaʒe) *v.i*, to float [on the surface]; survive.

surnaturel, le† (syrnatyrɛl) *a. & m*, supernatural, preternatural.

surnom (syrnɔ̃) *m*, surname, family name; nickname. **surnommer** (nɔme) *v.t*, to [nick]name, call.

surnombre (syrnɔ̃:br) *m*, surplus.

surnuméraire (syrnymerɛ:r) *a. & m*, supernumerary.

suroît (syrwa) *m*, sou'wester (*wind, hat*).

surpasser (syrpɑse) *v.t*, to surpass, overtop, exceed, outdo; astonish.

surpayer (syrpɛje) *v.t*, to overpay.

surplis (syrpli) *m*, surpli̇.̇.̇

surplomb (syrplɔ̃) *m*, overhang. **surplomber** (be) *v.i. & t*, to overhang.

surplus (syrply) *m*, surplus, excess; rest. *au ~*, moreover, besides.

surprenant, e (syrprənã, ã:t) *a*, surprising. **surprendre** (prã:dr) *v.i.ir*, to surprise; catch [unawares]; overtake; intercept; detect; deceive; obtain by fraud. **surprise** (pri:z) *f*, surprise.

surproduction (syrprɔdyksjɔ̃) *f*, overproduction.

surrégénérateur (syrreʒeneratœr) *m*, breeder reactor.

surréservation (syrrezεrvasjɔ̃) *f*, overbooking.

sursaut (syrso) *m*, start, jump; burst (*energy*). **sursauter** (te) *v.i*, to start. **faire ~**, to startle.

surseoir à (syrswa:r) (*law*) *v.ir*, to suspend, delay, stay. ~ *l'exécution de*, to reprieve. **sursis** (si) *m*, stay [of proceedings]; reprieve, respite, postponement, or exemption, in many senses, e.g, *condamné à un an de prison avec* ~, means sentenced to a year's imprisonment but with suspended sentence.

surtaxe (syrtaks) *f*, surtax; surcharge; overassessment; fee; duty. **surtaxer** (kse) *v.t*, to surtax; surcharge; overassess.

surtout (syrtu) *ad*, above all, especially. ¶ *m*, centerpiece, epergne; overcoat, surtout.

surveillance (syrvεjɑ̃:s) *f*, supervision; watch. **surveillant, e** (jɑ̃, ɑ̃:t) *n*, supervisor, overseer. **surveiller** (je) *v.t.*, to supervise, superintend, watch [over], look after.

survenir (syrvəni:r) *v.i.ir*, to arrive unexpectedly; supervene; come upon one; befall.

survie (syrvi) *f*, survivorship; survival. **survivance** (vɑ̃:s) *f*, survival, outliving. ~ *du plus apte*, survival of the fittest. **survivant, e** (vɑ̃, ɑ̃:t) *n*, survivor. **survivre à** (vi:vr) *v.ir*, to survive, outlive. **se survivre**, to survive; live again.

survol (syrvɔl) *m*, overflight; panning (*cinema*).

sus (sy; *in liaison*, syz) *ad*, [up]on; come on! **en ~**, extra, to boot. **en ~ de**, over & above.

susceptibilité (sysεptibilite) *f*, susceptibility; touchiness. **susceptible** (bl) *a*, susceptible; capable; apt; sensitive; touchy.

susciter (sysite) *v.t*, to raise up; give rise to; stir up.

suscription (syskripsjɔ̃) *f*, superscription.

susdit, e (sysdi, it) *a. & n*, aforesaid. **susmentionné, e** (mɑ̃sjone) *a*, above-mentioned. **susnommé, e** (nɔme) *a*, above-named.

suspect, e (syspεkt) *a*, suspicious, questionable, doubtful, suspect. **suspecter** (te) *v.t*, to suspect, question.

suspendre (syspɑ̃:dr) *v.t*, to suspend, hang up; sling; stop; stay. **en suspens** (pɑ̃), in abeyance, outstanding. **suspension** (sjɔ̃) *f*, suspension, hanging; discontinuance. **suspensoir** (swa:r) *m*, suspensory bandage.

suspens (syspɑ̃) *a*, suspended. ¶ *m*, suspense.

suspicion (syspisjɔ̃) *f*, suspicion.

sustenter (systɑ̃te) *v.t*, to sustain, nourish.

susurrer (sysyre) *v.i. & t*, to murmur, whisper.

suture (syty:r) *f*, suture; join.

suzerain, e (syzrε̃, εn) *a*, paramount. ¶ *n*, suzerain. **suzeraineté** (rεnte) *f*, suzerainty.

svastika (svastika) *m*, swastika.

svelte (svεlt) *a*, slender, slim.

sybarite (sibarit) *m*, sybarite.

sycomore (sikɔmɔ:r) *m*, sycamore.

sycophante (sikɔfɑ̃:t) *m*, sycophant.

syllabaire (silabε:r) *m*, spelling book. **syllabe** (lab) *f*, syllable.

syllogisme (silɔʒism) *m*, syllogism.

sylphe (silf) *m*, **sylphide** (fid) *f*, sylph.

sylvestre (silvεstr) *a*, woodland (*att.*). **sylviculture** (vikylty:r) *f*, forestry.

symbole (sε̃bɔl) *m*, symbol. **le ~** [*des apôtres*], the [Apostles'] Creed. **symbolique** (lik) *a*, symbolic(al). **symboliser** (ze) *v.t*, to symbolize.

symétrie (simetri) *f*, symmetry. **symétrique**† (trik) *a*, symmetric(al).

sympa (sε̃pa) *a*, likable, attractive.

sympathie (sε̃pati) *f*, sympathy, fellow feeling; (*pl.*) (*one's*) likes.

sympathique (tik) *a*, sympathetic; congenial; likable; invisible (*ink*).
sympathiser (tize) *v.i*, to sympathize.
symphonie (sɛ̃fɔni) *f*, symphony.
symptôme (sɛ̃ptoːm) *m*, symptom.
synagogue (sinagɔg) *f*, synagogue.
synchrone (sɛ̃krɔn) *a*, synchronous.
syncope (sɛ̃kɔp) *f*, syncope; syncopation. **syncoper** (pe) *v.t*, to syncopate.
syndic (sɛ̃dik) *m*, syndic; trustee; assignee (*bankruptcy*); agent. **syndicaliste** (kalist) *m*, trade unionist. **syndicat** (ka) *m*, trusteeship; syndicate; association, federation; labor union. ~ *de placements*, pool (*Fin.*). ~ *d'initiative*, tourist information bureau. **syndicataire** (tɛːr) *m*, member of a syndicate; underwriter (*Fin.*). **syndiquer** (ke) *v.t*, to syndicate.
synode (sinɔd) *m*, synod.
synonyme (sinɔnim) *a*, synonymous. ¶ *m*, synonym.
syntaxe (sɛ̃taks) *f*, syntax.
synthèse (sɛ̃tɛːz) *f*, synthesis. **synthétique**† (tetik) *a*, synthetic(al).
Syrie (la) (siri), Syria. **syrien, ne** (rjɛ̃, ɛn) *a. & S~, n*, Syrian.
systématique† (sistematik) *a*, systematic; hidebound (*fig.*). **système** (tɛm) *m*, system; plan. *le ~ D* (*de la debrouillardise*), resourcefulness, ability to manage.

T

ta *see* **ton**.
tabac (taba) *m*, tobacco; tobacco shop. *passer à ~*, to beat up (*slang*). ~ *à priser*, snuff. **tabatière** (batjɛːr) *f*, snuffbox; skylight.
tabasser (tabase) *v.t*, to beat up (*slang*).
tabernacle (tabɛrnakl) *m*, tabernacle.
table (tabl) *f*, table; telephone switchboard; slab; tablet; list; index. ~ *à pied central*, pedestal table. ~ *à rallonge(s)*, leaf t. ~

alphabétique, alphabetical list; a. table; index (*book*). ~ *d'harmonie*, soundboard (*Mus.*). ~ *de jeu*, gaming table; card t. ~ *de nuit*, ~ *de chevet*, bedside t. ~ *des hors-texte*, list of plates. ~ *des matières*, contents (*book*). ~ *gigogne* (ʒigɔɲ), nested table, nest of 3 tables. ~ *rase*, tablet for inscription; open mind; clean sweep (*fig.*). *se mettre à ~*, to sit down to table; confess (*slang*). **tableau** (blo) *m*, board; picture; view; tableau; curtain!; scene; list, table; roll, rolls; panel; bag (*of game*). ~ *d'autel*, altarpiece. ~ *de bord*, dashboard. ~ *de commande, de connexions*, control panel (*computers*). ~ *de distribution*, switchboard. ~ *noir*, blackboard. **tablette** (blet) *f*, shelf; slab; cake, tablet, lozenge. ~ *de cheminée*, mantel-shelf. **tabletterie** (tri) *f*, fancy goods (*ivory, inlay*). **tablier** (blie) *m*, apron; board (*chess*); floor, deck (*of bridge*). ~ [*d'enfant*], pinafore.
tabou (tabu) *m*, taboo. *il est ~*, he, it, is taboo.
tabouret (taburɛ) *m*, stool; footstool; stocks (*Hist.*); shepherd's purse. ~ *de piano*, music stool, piano s.
tache (taʃ) *f*, stain, spot, speck, blot, blemish, stigma, taint. ~ *d'humidité*, damp mark (*in books*). ~ *de naissance*, birthmark. ~ *de rousseur*, freckle. ~ *de vin*, portwine mark, birthmark.
tâche (tɑːʃ) *f*, task; job. *à la ~*, piecework.
tacher (taʃe) *v.t*, to stain, spot; sully.
tâcher (tɑʃe) *v.i*, to try, endeavor; strive. **tâcheron** (ʃrɔ̃) *m*, jobber.
tacheter (taʃte) *v.t*, to spot, speckle.
tachymètre (takimɛtr) *m*, speedometer.
tacite† (tasit) *a*, tacit, implied.
taciturne (tasityrn) *a*, taciturn, silent.
tacot (tako) *m*, jalopy; has-been (*sports journalism*).
tact (takt) *m*, touch; tact.
tacticien (taktisjɛ̃) *m*, tactician.

tactile (taktil) *a*, tactile, tactual.
tactique (taktik) *a*, tactical. ¶ *f*,
tactics.
tadorne (tadɔrn) *m*, sheldrake.
taffetas (taftɑ) *m*, taffeta. ~
d'Angleterre, ~ *gommée*, court
plaster; adhesive tape.
tafia (tafja) *m*, tafia. ~ *de laurier*,
bay rum.
Tage (le) (ta:ʒ), the Tagus.
taïaut (tajo) *i*, tally-ho!
taie (tɛ) *f*, case, slip (*pillow*);
cover (*cushion*).
taillade (tajad) *f*, cut, slash, gash.
tailluder (de) *v.t*, to slash, slit,
gash; whittle.
taillanderie (tajɑ̃dri) *f*, edge
tools. **taillandier** (dje) *m*, tool-
maker. **taillant** (jɑ̃) *m*, [cutting]
edge. **taille** (tɑ:j) *f*, cutting; cut;
pruning; edge (*sword*); height,
stature; size; shape; waist; tally
[stick]. ~-*crayon*, *m*, pencil sharpener. ~-*douce*, *f*, copperplate
[engraving]. ~ *hors série*, outsize. ~-*mer*, *m*, cutwater (*bow*). *il
n'est pas de* ~, he's not up to it
(*job*, *etc.*). **tailler** (taje) *v.t*, to
cut; cut out; prune; trim; clip;
dress; hew; carve; sharpen,
point. ~ *une plume* or *une pipe*,
to practice fellatio (*obscene*). *se*
~, to take off, beat it, escape.
tailleur (tajœ:r) *m*, cutter; hewer;
tailor; tailored suit; (*att.*) tailormade, tailored. **taillis** (ji) *m*,
copse, coppice; brushwood, underwood. **tailloir** (tajwa:r) *m*,
trencher (*platter*).
tain (tɛ̃) *m*, silvering (*for mirror*),
foil.
taire (tɛ:r) *v.t.ir*, to say nothing
about; not to mention; leave unsaid; conceal. *faire* ~, to silence,
hush. *se* ~, to hold one's tongue,
be silent.
talc (talk) *m*, talc; French chalk;
talcum.
talent (talɑ̃) *m*, talent; faculty;
gift.
talion (taljɔ̃) *m*, talion, retaliation, eye for eye.
talisman (talismɑ̃) *m*, talisman.
talle (tal) *f*, sucker (*Hort.*).
taloche (talɔʃ) *f*, cuff, clout.
talon (talɔ̃) *m*, heel; butt (*cue*);

counterfoil; (*pl. fig.*) footsteps.
~ *rouge* (*fig.*), aristocratic. **talonner** (lɔne) *v.t*, to follow on
the heels of, dog; dun; spur on.
talonnette (nɛt) *f*, heel piece;
heel (*rubber*).
talus (taly) *m*, slope, batter; bank.
tamarin (tamarɛ̃) *m*, tamarind.
tambour (tɑ̃bu:r) *m*, drum;
drummer; barrel; tambour,
frame. ~ *de basque*, tambourine.
~-*major*, drum major. **tambouriner** (burine) *v.i*, to drum;
thrum; (*v.t.*) to cry (*news*); cry
up.
tamis (tami) *m*, sieve; sifter;
strainer; gauze.
Tamise (la) (tami:z), the Thames.
tamiser (tamize) *v.t*, to sift;
strain; subdue (*light*).
tampon (tɑ̃pɔ̃) *m*, plug; bung; tampion; rubber stamp; wad; pad;
buffer. **tamponner** (pɔne) *v.t*, to
plug; pad; dab; collide with.
tam-tam (tamtam) *m*, tomtom;
gong.
tan (tɑ̃) *m*, tan, bark (*tanners'*).
tancer (tɑ̃se) *v.t*, to scold.
tandem (tɑ̃dɛm) *m*, tandem (*carriage*, *cycle*).
tandis que (tɑ̃di[s]) *c*, while,
whilst; whereas.
tangage (tɑ̃ga:ʒ) *m*, pitching
(*ship*).
tangent, e (tɑ̃ʒɑ̃, ɑ̃:t) *a*, tangent[ial]. ¶ *f*, tangent.
Tanger (tɑ̃ʒe) *m*, Tangier.
tangible (tɑ̃ʒibl) *a*, tangible.
tango (tɑ̃go) *m*, tango.
tanguer (tɑ̃ge) *v.i*, to pitch (*ship*).
tanière (tanjɛ:r) *f*, den, lair; hole,
earth.
tannin (tanɛ̃) *m*, tannin. **tanne**
(tan) *f*, blackhead. **tanné, e** (ne)
p.a, tanned; tan[-colored]. **tanner** (ne) *v.t*, to tan, cure; tire,
bore. **tannerie** (nri) *f*, tannery,
tan yard. **tanneur** (nœ:r) *m*, tanner.
tant (tɑ̃) *ad*, so much; so many;
such; so; as much; as well [as]; as
long; as far. ~ *pis*, ~ *mieux*, so
much the worse, so much the better. ~ *soit peu*, ever so little. ~
s'en faut, far from it.
tantale (tɑ̃tal) *m*, tantalum.

tante (tã:t) *f,* aunt; homosexual (*pejorative*). ma ~, pawnshop (*slang*).

tantième (tãtjɛm) *m,* percentage.

tantinet (tãtinɛ) *m,* tiny bit, little bit, dash.

tantôt (tãto) *ad,* soon, presently, anon, by & by; in the afternoon; just now; sometimes, now.

taon (tã) *m,* gadfly, horsefly.

tapage (tapa:ʒ) *m,* noise, uproar, disturbance, row; fuss, ado, stir. **tapageur, euse** (paʒœ:r, ɸ:z) *a,* noisy, rowdy, uproarious; loud, flash[y], showy, garish. ¶ *n,* roisterer, rowdy, brawler.

tape (tap) *f,* tap, rap, pat, slap. **tapé, e** (pe) *p.a,* dried (*apples, etc, in rings*); smart (*answer*). **tapecul** (pky) *m,* jigger (*sail*); rattletrap. **tapée** (pe) *f,* heaps, swarm. **taper** (pe) *v.t. & abs,* to tap, smack, slap; beat; pat; type-[write]; stamp (*foot*).

tapette (tapɛt) *f,* bat; carpet beater; homosexual (*slang*).

tapin (tapɛ̃) *m,* prostitute, whore (*slang*).

tapinois (en) (tapinwa) *ad,* stealthily.

tapioca (tapjɔka) *m,* tapioca.

tapir (tapi:r) *m,* tapir.

tapir (se) (tapi:r) *v.pr,* to squat, crouch, cower; nestle.

tapis (tapi) *m,* carpet; tapis; cloth; cover. **~-brosse,** *m,* doormat. **~ de gazon,** [green]sward. **~ roulant,** assembly line. **~ vert,** green baize; gaming table. **tapisser (se)** *v.t,* to hang with tapestry; paper (*wall*); cover, line; carpet (*with flowers*). **tapisserie** (sri) *f,* tapestry, hangings, arras; tapestry work; rug work. *faire* ~, to be a wallflower (*dance*). **tapissier, ère** (sje, ɛ:r) *n,* tapestry maker; upholsterer. ¶ *f,* delivery truck.

tapon (tapõ) *m,* knot, tangle.

tapoter (tapɔte) *v.t,* to tap; strum, thrum.

taquet (takɛ) *m,* stop, block; cleat (*rope*).

taquin, e (takɛ̃, in) *n,* tease. **taquiner** (kine) *v.t. & i,* to tease, torment; worry.

tarabiscoter (tarabiskɔte) *v.t,* to groove (*moldings, etc.*); over-decorate.

tarabuster (tarabyste) *v.t,* to pester, worry, plague.

taraud (taro) *m,* (*screw*) tap. **taraudage** (da:ʒ) *m,* screw cutting, tapping, threading. **tarauder** (de) *v.t,* to tap, screw, thread.

tard (ta:r) *ad,* late; later. *sur le* ~, late in the day; late in life. **tarder** (tarde) *v.i,* to delay, be long; loiter; (*v.imp.*) to long. **tardif, ive†** (dif, i:v) *a,* tardy, belated; late; slow, sluggish; backward. **tardiveté** (divte) *f,* lateness, backwardness.

tare (ta:r) *f,* defect; taint; tare (*Com.*).

taré, e (tare) *p.a,* damaged, tainted; defective (*child*); depraved.

tarentelle (tarãtɛl) *f,* tarantella. **tarentule** (tyl) *f,* tarantula.

tarer (tare) *v.t,* to spoil, damage; tare (*Com.*).

targette (tarʒɛt) *f,* bolt (*door*).

targuer (se) de (targe), to pride oneself on, plume oneself on.

tarière (tarjɛ:r) *f,* auger.

tarif (tarif) *m,* tariff, rate, rates, scale; price list; fare. **tarifer** (fe) *v.t,* to tariff, rate, price.

tarin (tarɛ̃) *m,* siskin.

tarir (tari:r) *v.t. & i,* to dry up; stop. **tarissable** (sabl) *a,* likely to run dry, out.

Tarragone (taragɔn) *f,* Tarragona.

tarse (tars) *m,* tarsus.

tartan (tartã) *m,* tartan (*cloth, garment*).

tarte (tart) *f,* tart, pie; slap, smack. **tartine** (tin) *f,* slice of bread & butter; bread & jam; rigmarole, screed.

tartre (tartr) *m,* tartar; scale, fur. **tartrique** (trik) *a,* tartaric.

tartufe (tartyf) *m,* sanctimonious hypocrite.

tas (ta) *m,* heap, pile; pack; cock (*hay*); shock, mow; stake [anvil].

Tasmanie (la) (tasmani), Tasmania.

tasse (ta:s) *f,* cup; mug. **~ à café,**

coffee cup. ~ *de café*, cup of coffee.

tassé, e (tase) *p.a*, squat, dumpy.

tasseau (taso) *m*, strip, cleat.

tassement (tasmã) *m*, settling, sinking; setback. **tasser (se)** *v.t*, to press down; squeeze; (*v.i.*) to grow thick. **se ~**, to settle, sink; settle down; have a setback.

tâter (tate) *v.t*, to feel, touch; try; taste. *en ~*, to know how to go about it. **se ~**, to feel for a bruise, think it over.

tatillon, ne (tatijõ, ɔn) *n*, fusser; busybody. **tatillonner** (jɔne) *v.i*, to fuss, meddle.

tâtonnement (tatɔnmã) *m*, groping; tentative effort; (*pl.*) trial & error. **tâtonner (ne)** *v.i*, to grope; fumble. **à tâtons** (tõ) *ad*, gropingly; warily.

tatou (tatu) *m*, armadillo.

tatouage (tatwaːʒ) *m*, tattooing; tattoo (*on skin*). **tatouer** (twe) *v.t*, to tattoo.

taudis (todi) *m*, hovel; slum.

taule (toːl) *f*, prison, jail (*slang*).

taupe (toːp) *f*, mole (*Zool.*); moleskin. **taupière** (topjɛːr) *f*, mole trap. **taupinière** (pinjɛːr) *f*, molehill; mean dwelling, hovel.

taureau (tɔro) *m*, bull.

tauromachie (tɔrɔmaʃi) *f*, bullfighting.

tautologie (totɔlɔʒi) *f*, tautology.

taux (to) *m*, rate, price. *~ officiel [d'escompte]*, bank rate.

taverne (tavɛrn) *f*, tavern.

taxation (taksasjõ) *f*, taxation, rating; assessment; charges. **taxe** (taks) *f*, tax rate, duty, due; charge, fee. *~ de séjour*, visitors' tax. **taxer** (kse) *v.t*, to tax, rate, assess; charge with duty; charge [for]; fix the minimum price of; accuse.

taxi (taksi) *m*, taxi [cab].

tchécoslovaque (tʃekɔslɔvak) *a.* & T~, *n*, Czechoslovak. **Tchécoslovaquie** (ki) *f*, Czechoslovakia. **tchèque** (tʃɛk) *a.* & (*language*) *m.* & T~ (*pers.*) *n*, Czech.

te, t' (tə, t) *pn*, you, yourself, thee, thyself.

té (te) *m*, T, tee. *~ [à dessin]*, T square.

technique† (tɛknik) *a*, technical. ¶ *f*, technique. **technologie** (nɔlɔʒi) *f*, technology.

technocratie (tɛknɔkrasi) *f*, technocracy.

teck (tɛk) *m*, teak.

tégument (tegymã) *m*, tegument.

teigne (tɛɲ) *f*, moth; ringworm.

teindre (tɛ̃ːdr) *v.t.ir*, to dye; stain; tincture. **teint** (tɛ̃) *m*, dye, color; complexion. **teinte** (tɛ̃ːt) *f*, tint, shade, hue; tinge, touch, strain. **teinter** (tɛ̃te) *v.t*, to tint; tone (*paper*); fume (*wood*); tinge. **teinture** (ty:r) *f*, dyeing; dye; tinge; smattering; tincture. **teinturerie** (tyrri) *f*, dyeing; dye works. **teinturier, ère** (tyrje, ɛːr) *n*, dyer [& cleaner].

tek (tɛk) *m*, teak.

tel, telle (tɛl) *a*, such; like; as; so. ¶ *pn*, such a one, some. *un tel*, *une telle*, so-&-so. *tel que*, such, as. *~ quel*, as it is.

télécommande (telekɔmãːd) *f*, remote control. *dispositif de ~*, remote control system. **télécommander** (de) *v.t*, to telecommand.

télédétection (teledetɛksjõ) *f*, remote sensing.

télégramme (telegram) *m*, telegram, wire. **télégraphe** (graf) *m*, telegraph. **télégraphie** (fi) *f*, telegraphy. *~ sans fils*, (*abb.* T.S.F.), wireless t., radio. **télégraphier** (fje) *v.t.* & *abs*, to telegraph, wire. **télégraphique†** (fik) *a*, telegraphic, telegraph (*att.*).

téléguider (telegide) *v.t*, to radio-control; operate by remote control.

téléimprimeur (teleɛ̃primœːr) *m*, teleprinter, teletypewriter.

téléinformatique (teleɛ̃fɔrmatik) *f*, data communication.

télémètre (telemɛtr) *m*, range finder.

téléobjectif (teleɔbʒɛktif) *m*, telephoto lens, telelens.

télépathie (telepati) *f*, telepathy.

téléphone (telefɔn) *m*, telephone. *~ rouge*, "hot line" between White House & Kremlin. **téléphoner** (ne) *v.t.* & *abs*, to telephone. **téléphonie** (ni) *f*, telephony. **téléphonique** (nik) *a*, telephonic, telephone (*att.*).

télescope (teleskɔp) *m*, [reflecting] telescope. **se télescoper** (pe) *v.pr*, to telescope (*trains*). **télescopique** (pik) *a*, telescopic; minor (*planet*).

téléspectateur (telespɛktatœːr) *m*, televiewer.

télétraitement (teletrɛtmã) *m*, teleprocessing. *~ par lots*, remote batch processing (*computers*).

téléviser (televize) *v.t*, to televise. **téléviseur** (vizœr) *m*, television set. **télévision** (vizjɔ̃) *f*, television.

tellement (tɛlmã) *ad*, so, in such a way.

téméraire† (temerɛːr) *a*, rash, reckless, foolhardy. **témérité** (rite) *f*, temerity, rashness.

témoignage (temwaɲaːʒ) *m*, testimony, evidence, witness; mark, token. **témoigner** (ɲe) *v.i. & t*, to testify, bear witness, give evidence; evince, show, prove. **témoin** (mwɛ̃) *m*, witness; second (*duel*); telltale, pilot (*lamp, etc.*); baton (*relay race*). *~ à charge*, witness for the prosecution. *~ à décharge*, w. for the defense. *~ muet*, circumstantial evidence.

tempe (tãːp) *m*, temple (*Anat.*).

tempérament (tãperamã) *m*, temperament, constitution. *à ~*, installment buying.

tempérance (tãperãːs) *f*, temperance. **tempérant, e** (rã, ãːt) *a*, temperate.

température (tãperatyːr) *f*, temperature. **tempéré, e** (re) *a*, temperate; limited (*monarchy*). **tempérer** (re) *v.t*, to temper, moderate.

tempête (tãpɛːt) *f*, storm, tempest. *à la ~*, at stormy (*barometer*). **tempêter** (pɛte) *v.i*, to storm, fume. **tempétueux, euse** (petɥø, øːz) *a*, tempestuous, stormy; boisterous.

temple (tãːpl) *m*, temple; church.

temporaire† (tãpɔrɛːr) *a*, temporary. **temporel, le†** (rɛl) *a*, temporal. **temporiser** (rize) *v.i*, to temporize. **temps** (tã; *in liaison*, tãz) *m*, time; while; times, days;

age; season; weather; tense (*Gram.*); beat (*Mus.*); phase. *quel ~ fait-il?* what's the weather? *au ~!* as you were! *en ~ & lieu*, in due course. *~ mort*, idle time (*computers*). *~ réel*, real t. (*computers*). *~ de panne*, down t. (*computers*). *partage de ~*, timesharing (*computers*).

tenable (tənabl) *a*, tenable; bearable.

tenace (tənas) *a*, tenacious; adhesive; tough, stiff; stubborn; retentive. **ténacité** (tenasite) *f*, tenacity.

tenaille (tənɑːj) *f*, tongs; (*pl.*) pincers. **tenailler** (naje) *v.t*, to be gnawed at, racked by (*remorse, hunger*).

tenancier, ère (tənãsje, ɛːr) *n*, keeper; lessee. **tenant** (nã) *m*, champion, supporter.

tendance (tãdãːs) *f*, tendency, trend. **tendancieux, euse** (dãsjø, øːz) *a*, tendentious; leading (*question*).

tender (tãdɛːr) *m*, tender (*locomotive*).

tendeur (tãdœːr) *m*, layer (*carpets*); setter (*traps*); strainer, stretcher, tightener.

tendon (tãdɔ̃) *m*, tendon, sinew.

tendre (tãːdr) *v.t*, to stretch, tighten, strain; bend (*bow*); crane (*neck*); hold out (*hand, etc.*); pitch (*tent*); lay, spread, set; drape; (*v.i.*) to tend, lead, conduce.

tendre† (tãːdr) *a*, tender, soft; sensitive; new (*bread*); early (*youth*); fond. **tendresse** (tãdrɛs) *f*, tenderness, fondness, love; (*pl.*) caresses. **tendreté** (drəte) *f*, tenderness (*meat*). **tendron** (drɔ̃) *m*, tender shoot; gristle (*veal*); maiden.

tendu, e (tãdy) *p.a*, tense, taut, tight.

ténèbres (tenɛːbr) *f.pl*, dark[ness], gloom. **ténébreux, euse†** (nebrø, øːz) *a*, dark, murky; gloomy; obscure.

teneur, euse (tənœːr, øːz) *n*, holder. **teneur,** *f*, tenor, purport; terms; content[s], percentage; grade (*ore*).

ténia (tɛnja) *m*, tapeworm.

tenir (tənir) *v.t.ir*, to hold; h. on; keep; have; contain; take; t. up (*space*); consider; (*v.i.ir.*) to hold; last; cling; border on; owe; partake, savor, be like; be owing to; rest, lie; be anxious; sit. ~ *tête à*, to resist. se ~, to keep; stand; sit; stick; contain oneself. *à quoi s'en tenir*, what to believe in.

tennis (tɛnis) *m*, [lawn] tennis; t. court.

tenon (tənɔ̃) *m*, tenon.

ténor (tenɔr) *m*, tenor (*voice, singer*).

tension (tɑ̃sjɔ̃) *f*, tension; tightness; strain; pressure; voltage. ~ *artérielle*, blood pressure.

tentacule (tɑ̃takyl) *m*, tentacle, feeler.

tentateur, trice (tɑ̃tatœr, tris) *n*, tempter, temptress. **tentation** (sjɔ̃) *f*, temptation.

tentative (tɑ̃tativ) *f*, attempt, endeavor. ~ *d'assassinat*, attempted murder.

tente (tɑ̃t) *f*, tent; awning. ~ *conique*, bell tent. ~ *de plage*, bathing t. ~-*pavillon*, *f*, marquee. *dresser une* ~, to pitch a t.

tenter (tɑ̃te) *v.t*, to attempt, try; tempt.

tenture (tɑ̃tyr) *f*, hangings; wallpaper.

tenu, e (təny) *p.a*, (*well, ill*) kept; neat, trim; (*to be*) bound (*à* to); firm (*price*). ¶ *m*, hold (*Box.*). ¶ *f*, holding; keeping; bearing, carriage, behavior; seat (*on horse*); dress, clothes, uniform, order; firmness. ~ *de ville*, street dress.

ténu, e (teny) *a*, thin, slender, tenuous, fine; watery (*fluid*). **ténuité** (nɥite) *f*, thinness.

tercet (tɛrsɛ) *m*, tercet, triplet (*Pros., Mus.*).

térébenthine (terebɑ̃tin) *f*, turpentine.

tergiverser (tɛrʒivɛrse) *v.i*, to be shifty, beat around the bush.

terme (tɛrm) *m*, term, end; time; date; account, settlement (*Stk Ex.*); quarter (*year*), q.'s rent; installment. **terminaison** (minɛzɔ̃) *f*, termination, ending. **terminer**

(ne) *v.t*, to terminate, end, wind up. **terminus** (nyːs) *m*, terminus (*Rly.*).

termite (tɛrmit) *m*, termite, white ant.

terne (tɛrn) *a*, dull, lusterless, drab. **ternir** (niːr) *v.t*, to tarnish, dull; dim; sully.

terrain (tɛrɛ̃) *m*, ground, land; field; site; course, links (*golf*); court (*croquet*). ~ *d'aviation*, airfield.

terrasse (tɛras) *f*, terrace, bank; flat roof; [pavement] outside (*café*). **terrassement** (smɑ̃) *m*, earthwork. **terrasser** (se) *v.t*, to bank up; throw, floor. **terrassier** (sje) *m*, day laborer; earthwork contractor.

terre (tɛːr) *f*, earth; ground; land; soil; estate; loam; clay; shore (*Naut.*); world. ~ *battue*, hard court (*Ten.*). ~ *cuite*, terra-cotta. ~ *d'ombre*, umber. *la* T~ *de Feu*, Tierra del Fuego. ~ *de Sienne brûlée*, burnt sienna. ~ *à* ~, commonplace. *la* ~ *ferme*, the continent, the mainland; terra firma. T~ *Sainte*, Holy Land. *ventre à* ~, at full speed. **terreau** (tɛro) *m*, [vegetable] mold. ~ *de feuilles*, leaf m. **Terre-Neuve**, *f*, Newfoundland. **terre-neuve**, *m*, N. [dog]. **terreplein**, *m*, open space; roadbed (*Rly.*); terrace. **terrer** (tɛre) *v.t*, to earth up; (*v.i.*) to burrow. se ~, to burrow; entrench oneself. **terrestre** (tɛrɛstr) *a*, terrestrial; ground (*att.*); land (*att.*); earthy.

terreur (tɛrœr) *f*, terror, dread.

terreux, euse (tɛrø, øːz) *a*, earthy; dull.

terrible† (tɛribl) *a*, terrible, terrific; dreadful.

terrien, ne (tɛrjɛ̃, ɛn) *a*. & *n*, landed (*proprietor*); (*m.*) landsman. **terrier** (rje) *m*, burrow, hole; earth (*fox*); terrier (*dog*).

terrifier (tɛrifje) *v.t*, to terrify.

terrine (tɛrin) *f*, [earthenware] pot, pan; (*pl.*) potted meats. **terrinée** (ne) *f*, panful.

territoire (tɛritwaːr) *m*, territory. **territorial, e** (tɔrjal) *a*. & *m*, territorial. **terroir** (rwaːr) *m*, soil.

terroriser (tɛrɔrize) *v.t,* to terrorize.

tertre (tɛrtr) *m,* hillock, knoll, mound. **~ de départ,** teeing ground (*golf*).

tes *see* **ton.**

Tessin (le) (tɛsɛ̃), the Ticino.

tesson (tɛsɔ̃) *m,* piece of broken glass *or* earthenware, potsherd.

testament (tɛstamã) *m,* will, testament. **testamentaire** (tɛːr) *a,* testamentary. **testateur, trice** (tœːr, tris) *n,* testator, trix. **tester** (te) *v.i,* to make one's will.

testicule (tɛstikyl) *m,* testicle.

tétanos (tetanɔs) *m,* tetanus, lockjaw.

têtard (tɛtaːr) *m,* tadpole; pollard. **tête** (tɛːt) *f,* head; top; face; lead; brains; wits. **~-à-~,** *m,* private interview, p. conversation; 2-cup tea set; sofa. **~ de linotte,** feather-brained person. **~ forte, forte ~,** good head, strong-minded person. **faire la ~ à quelqu'un,** to frown at someone. **faire une ~,** to look unhappy. **faire à sa ~,** to have one's own way.

téter (tete) *v.t. & abs,* to suck (*of child*).

têtière (tɛtjɛːr) *f,* infant's cap; headstall; chair back.

tétin (tetɛ̃) *m,* nipple, pap, teat (*pers.*). **tétine** (tin) *f,* dug; nipple (*nursing bottle*). **téton** (tɔ̃) *m,* breast (*of woman*).

tétras (tetrɑ) *m,* grouse.

tette (tɛt) *f,* dug, teat (*animal*).

têtu, e (tety) *a,* stubborn, mulish.

teuton, ne (tøtɔ̃, ɔn) **& teutonique** (tɔnik) *a,* Teutonic.

texte (tɛkst) *m,* text. **~ [composé],** letterpress.

textile (tɛkstil) *a. & m,* textile.

textuel, le† (tɛkstɥel) *a,* textual.

texture (tɛkstyːr) *f,* texture; arrangement.

thaumaturge (tomatyrʒ) *n,* miracle worker; magician.

thé (te) *m,* tea; t. plant; t. party. **~ complet,** tea, roll & butter. **~ de viande,** beef tea.

théâtral, e† (teɑtral) *a,* theatrical; dramatic. **théâtre** (ɑːtr) *m,*

theater, playhouse; stage; drama; scene; seat (*as of war*).

théière (tejɛːr) *f,* teapot.

théisme (teism) *m,* theism.

thème (tɛm) *m,* theme; topic; exercise, composition (*Sch.*); stem (*Gram.*).

théodolite (teɔdɔlit) *m,* theodolite.

théologie (teɔlɔʒi) *f,* theology. **théologien, ne** (ʒjɛ̃, ɛn) *n,* theologian, divine. **théologique†** (ʒik) *a,* theological.

théorème (teɔrɛm) *m,* theorem. **théoricien** (risjɛ̃) *m,* theorist. **théorie** (ri) *f,* theory; procession (*poetic*). **théorique†** (rik) *a,* theoretic(al).

théosophie (teɔzɔfi) *f,* theosophy.

thérapeutique (terapøtik) *a,* therapeutic; apothecaries' (*measure, weight*). **¶** *f,* therapeutics.

thermal, e (tɛrmal) *a,* thermal, hot. **thermes** (tɛrm) *m.pl,* thermal baths.

thermomètre (tɛrmɔmɛtr) *m,* thermometer. **~ médical,** clinical thermometer.

thésauriser (tezɔrize) *v.i,* to hoard.

thèse (tɛːz) *f,* thesis, argument.

thon (tɔ̃) *m,* tuna.

thorax (tɔraks) *m,* thorax.

thune (tyn) *f,* 5-franc coin (*slang*).

thym (tɛ̃) *m,* thyme.

thyroïde (tirɔid) *a,* thyroid.

tiare (tjaːr) *f,* tiara.

tibia (tibja) *m,* tibia, shinbone; shin.

Tibre (le) (tibr), the Tiber.

tic (tik) *m,* tic; twitching; habit, mannerism, trick.

tic tac (tiktak) *m,* tick[-tack], pit[a-]pat.

tiède† (tjed) *a,* tepid, lukewarm. **tiédeur** (tjedœːr) *f,* tepidness, etc. **tiédir** (diːr) *v.i,* to become tepid.

tien, ne (*with* **le, la, les**) (tjɛ̃, ɛn) *pn. & m,* yours, thine, thy own.

tiens (tjɛ̃) *v. abs. imperative,* well! indeed!

tiercé (tjɛrse) *m,* three-horse bet.

tiers, tierce (tjɛːr, ɛrs) *a,* third. **¶** *m,* third person, t. party. **¶** *f,* third. **tiers arbitre,** *m,* referee.

tige (ti:ʒ) *f*, stem, stalk; trunk (*tree*); shaft; shank, leg (*boot, stocking*); rod.

tignasse (tiɲas) *f*, shock, mop (*hair*).

tigre, tigresse (tigr, grɛs) *n*, tiger, tigress. **le Tigre**, the Tigris. **tigré, e** (gre) *a*, striped, tabby.

tillac (tijak) *m*, deck (*ship*).

tille (ti:j) *f*, bast, bass. **tilleul** (tijœl) *m*, lime [tree], linden [tree]; lime blossom.

timbale (tɛ̃bal) *f*, kettledrum; cup (*metal*).

timbrage (tɛ̃bra:ʒ) *m*, stamping. **timbre** (tɛ̃:br) *m*, stamp; bell; gong; timbre; postmark. ~ *humide*, pad stamp, rubber s. ~ [-*poste*], *m*, [postage] s. ~*quittance*, *m*, receipt s. ~ *sec*, ~ *fixe*, embossed s., impressed s. **timbré, e** (tɛ̃bre) *p.a*, stamped; cracked, nuts (*pers.*). **timbrer** (bre) *v.t*, to stamp; postmark.

timide† (timid) *a*, timid; nervous; shy, bashful, diffident. **timidité** (dite) *f*, timidity.

timon (timɔ̃) *m*, pole (*carriage*); helm (*fig.*). **timonier** (mɔnje) *m*, helmsman; signalman (*Naut.*); quartermaster (*Naut.*).

timoré, e (timɔre) *a*, timorous.

tinctorial, e (tɛ̃ktɔrjal) *a*, dye (*stuffs, etc.*).

tine (tin) *f*, butt, cask; tub.

tintamare (tɛ̃tama:r) *m*, din, racket, noise.

tinter (tɛ̃te) *v.i. & t*, to ring, toll; tinkle; jingle; clink; chink; tingle, buzz. **tintement** (tmɑ̃) *m*, ringing, etc; singing (*ears*).

tintouin (tɛ̃twɛ̃) *m*, trouble, worry.

tipule (tipyl) *f*, daddy-longlegs, crane fly.

tique (tik) *f*, tick (*insect*). **tiquer** (ke) *v.i*, to twitch; wince.

tiqueté, e (tikte) *a*, speckled, variegated.

tir (ti:r) *m*, shooting; musketry; gunnery; fire, firing; rifle range; shooting gallery. ~ *à l'arc*, archery. *à ~ d'aile*, at full speed.

tirade (tirad) *f*, tirade; long speech (*Theat.*).

tirage (tira:ʒ) *m*, drawing; pull[ing]; draft; towing; tow[ing] path; extension (*camera*); printing; hard copy (*computers*); circulation (*news*). ~ *au sort*, drawing lots.

tiraillement (tirɑjmɑ̃) *m*, tugging; gnawing (*stomach*); wrangling. **tirailler** (je) *v.t*, to tug, pull; pester; (*v.i.*) to blaze away. **tirailleur** (jœ:r) *m*, skirmisher, sharpshooter, rifleman; freelance.

tirant (tirɑ̃) *m*, string, strap; tie; tag; stay; sinew (*meat*).

tire (tir) *comps, all m*: ~-*botte*, bootjack. ~-*bouchon*, corkscrew. ~-*bouton*, buttonhook. ~-*feu*, lanyard (*gun*). ~-*ligne*, drawing pen.

tiré, e (tire) *p.a*, drawn, pinched, haggard. ~ *à quatre épingles*, spick & span, dapper. ~ *par les cheveux*, farfetched.

tirelire (tirli:r) *f*, piggy bank.

tirer (tire) *v.t. & i*, to draw; pull; drag; tug; haul; get, derive; take; wreak; put out (*tongue*); raise; doff (*hat*); milk (*cow*); fire; shoot, let off; print, machine; incline, verge. ~ [*à pile ou face*], to toss a coin. se ~, to extricate oneself. *se ~ d'affaire*, to get over a difficulty. *s'en ~*, to make ends meet, get along.

tiret (tirɛ) *m*, dash (*line*); hyphen.

tirette (tirɛt) *f*, curtain or blind cord; leaf (*table*).

tireur, euse (tirœ:r, ø:z) *n*, drawer; marksman, shot. ~ *d'armes*, fencer. ~ *de cartes*, fortune-teller. ~ *isolé*, sniper.

tiroir (tirwa:r) *m*, drawer (*table, etc.*); slide; slide valve. ~ *de caisse*, till.

tisane (tizan) *f*, infusion, (*herb*) tea.

tison (tizɔ̃) *m*, brand, firebrand. **tisonner** (zɔne) *v.i*, to meddle with the fire. **tisonnier** (nje) *m*, poker.

tissage (tisa:ʒ) *m*, weaving. **tisser** (se) *v.t*, to weave. **tisserand** (srɑ̃) *m*, weaver. **tisseranderie** (dri) *f*, weaving [trade]. **tissu** (sy) *m*, texture, weave; textile, fabric, cloth, gauze; tissue. ~ *éponge*, toweling. **tissure** (sy:r) *f,* texture, tissue. **tistre** (tistr) *v.t.ir,* to weave.

titi (titi) *m,* street urchin.

titiller (titille) *v.t,* to titillate, tickle.

titre (titr) *m,* title; [title] deed, muniment, document; proof, evidence; status; title page; heading; certificate, scrip, warrant, bond, security, stock, share; holding; claim; fineness (*coins*); grade; strength (*solution*). *à ~ d'office,* ex officio. *à ~ de,* by right of, in virtue of, as. *au ~,* standard (*gold*). *en ~,* titular. **titré, e** (tre) *a,* titled; standard (*solution*). **titrer** (tre) *v.t,* to give a title to; titrate; assay.

tituber (titybe) *v.i,* to stagger, lurch.

titulaire (titylɛːr) *a,* titular. ¶ *n,* holder; occupant; incumbent.

toast (tɔst) *m,* toast (*health*); buttered toast.

toboggan (tɔbɔgɑ̃) *m,* toboggan.

toc (tɔk) *m,* fake, sham goods.

tocsin (tɔksɛ̃) *m,* alarm bell; tocsin, hue & cry.

toge (tɔːʒ) *f,* toga; gown, robe.

tohu-bohu (tɔybɔy) *m,* chaos; hurly-burly.

toi (twa) *pn,* you, thee, thou. *~-même,* yourself, thyself.

toile (twal) *f,* linen; cloth; canvas; gauze; curtain (*Theat.*); sail (*Naut.*); (*pl.*) toils (*Hunt.*); 10,000 francs (*slang*). *~ à calquer,* tracing cloth. *~ à matelas,* tick[ing]. *~ à voiles,* sailcloth, canvas. *~ cirée,* oilcloth. *~ d'araignée,* spider's web, cobweb. *~ de matelas,* tick. *~ de ménage,* homespun [linen]. *~ de sol,* ground sheet. *~ écrue, ~ bise,* unbleached linen. *~ huilée, vernie,* oilskin. *~ ouvrée,* huckaback. *~ peinte,* print[ed fabric].

toilette (twalɛt) *f,* toilet, washing, dressing; dress; dressing table; washstand; lavatory.

toilier, ère (twalje, ɛːr) *n,* linen draper.

toise (twaːz) *f,* height standard (*apparatus*); standard (*comparison*). **toiser** (twaze) *v.t,* to measure; look (*one*) up & down.

toison (twazɔ̃) *f,* fleece.

toit (twa) *m,* roof; housetop; shed. **toiture** (tyːr) *f,* roof[ing].

tôle (toːl) *f,* sheet; [sheet] iron; plate. *~ ondulée,* corrugated iron. *~ de blindage,* armor plate.

Tolède (tɔlɛd) *f,* Toledo.

tolérable (tolerabl) *a,* tolerable. **tolérance** (rɑ̃ːs) *f,* tolerance; toleration; sufferance; margin, limit. *maison de ~,* licensed brothel. **tolérant, e** (rɑ̃, ɑ̃ːt) *a,* tolerant. **tolérer** (re) *v.t,* to tolerate, bear, suffer.

toletière (tɔltjɛːr) *f,* rowlock.

tollé (tɔlle) *m,* outcry, hue & cry.

tomate (tomat) *f,* tomato.

tombe (tɔ̃ːb) *f,* tomb, grave; death (*fig.*). **tombeau** (tɔ̃bo) *m,* tomb, vault, monument; death.

tombée (tɔ̃be) *f,* fall. *~ de pluie,* downpour; rainfall. **tomber** (be) *v.i,* to fall; tumble; drop; crash; flag; crumble; lapse; hang [down]; (*v.t.*) to throw (*wrestling*); damn (*a play*). *~ d'accord,* to come to an agreement. *~ bien, ~ mal,* to come at right, wrong, time. **tombereau** (bro) *m,* [tip] cart; cartload; tumbril. **tombola** (bola) *f,* raffle.

tombeur (tɔ̃bœːr) *m,* professional wrestler; ladykiller.

Tombouctou (tɔ̃buktu) *m,* Timbuctoo.

tome (toːm) *m,* volume, tome.

ton, ta, tes (tɔ̃, ta, te) *a,* your, thy.

ton (tɔ̃) *m,* tone; tune (*fig.*); style; manners, breeding, form; [whole] tone (*in distinction from a semitone*); key (*Mus.*).

tondeur, euse (tɔ̃dœːr, øːz) *n,* shearer. ¶ *f,* shearing machine, shears; clippers; mower (*lawn*). **tondre** (tɔ̃ːdr) *v.t,* to shear, clip, crop, mow; fleece (*pers.*).

tonique (tonik) *a,* tonic. ¶ *m,* tonic (*Med.*). ¶ *f,* tonic (*Mus.*), keynote.

tonitruer (tɔnitrye) *v.i,* to thunder.

tonnage (tɔnaːʒ) *m,* tonnage; burden (*ship*); shipping. **tonne** (tɔn) *f,* tun; ton. Fr. **tonne** = 1000 kilos. **tonneau** (no) *m,* cask, barrel; tun; butt, tub; bin; drum; governess car[t]; tonneau (*auto*); roll (*Avn.*); ton (*Ship.——Fr.*

tonneau = 1000 *kilos*). ~ *d'arrosage*, water[ing] cart. **tonnelet** (nlɛ) *m*, keg. **tonnelier** (nəlje) *m*, cooper. **tonnelle** (nɛl) *f*, arbor, bower. **tonnellerie** (lri) *f*, cooperage.

tonner (tɔne) *v.i. & imp*, to thunder; boom; inveigh. **tonnerre** (nɛːr) *m*, thunder; thunderbolt; breech (*firearm*).

tonsure (tɔ̃syːr) *f*, tonsure. **tonsurer** (syre) *v.t*, to tonsure.

tonte (tɔ̃ːt) *f*, shearing; clipping; mowing.

tonton (tɔ̃tɔ̃) *m*, uncle (*children & slang*).

topaze (tɔpɑːz) *f*, topaz.

toper (tɔpe) *v.t*, to agree, consent.

topinambour (tɔpinɑ̃buːr) *m*, Jerusalem artichoke.

topique (tɔpik) *a*, topical (*Med.*); local; to the point; in point.

topographie (tɔpɔgrafi) *f*, topography.

toquade (tɔkad) *f*, craze, fancy.

toque (tɔk) *f*, cap; toque.

toqué, e (tɔke) *p.a*, crazy, cracked.

torche (tɔrʃ) *f*, torch; mat, pad. **torcher** (ʃe) *v.t*, to wipe. **torchère** (ʃɛːr) *f*, cresset; floor lamp. **torchis** (ʃi) *m*, loam; cob (*Build.*). **torchon** (ʃɔ̃) *m*, dishcloth, swab, duster; twist of straw. *coup de ~*, short but violent battle; police raid.

torcol (tɔrkɔl) *m*, wryneck (*bird*).

tordant (tɔrdɑ̃) *a*, howlingly funny.

tordre (tɔrdr) *v.t*, to twist; distort; wring; wrest. **se ~**, to writhe; be convulsed (*laughing*).

toréador (tɔreadɔːr) *m*, toreador.

tornade (tɔrnad) *f*, tornado.

toron (tɔrɔ̃) *m*, strand (*rope*).

torpeur (tɔrpœːr) *f*, torpor. **torpide** (pid) *a*, torpid.

torpille (tɔrpiːj) *f*, torpedo; mine (*war*). **torpiller** (pije) *v.t*, to torpedo; mine. **torpilleur** (jœːr) *m*, torpedo boat; t. man. *contre~*, destroyer.

torréfier (tɔrrefje) *v.t*, to roast.

torrent (tɔrɑ̃) *m*, torrent; flood, flow; stream; rush. **torrentiel, le** (rɑ̃sjɛl), *a*, torrential.

torride (tɔrid) *a*, torrid.

tors, e (tɔːr, ɔrs) *a*, twisted; contorted; crooked; wry. **torsade** (tɔrsad) *f*, twist, coil; bullion (*fringe*). **torse** (trs) *m*, torso, trunk. **torsion** (sjɔ̃) *f*, torsion.

tort (tɔːr) *m*, wrong; fault; mistake; injury, harm. *à ~*, wrongly. *à ~ & à travers*, at random. *faire ~ à*, to wrong.

torticolis (tɔrtikɔli) *m*, crick, stiff neck.

tortillage (tɔrtijaːʒ) *m*, involved language. **tortiller** (je) *v.t*, to twist; twirl; twiddle; kink; (*v.i.*) to shuffle. **se ~**, to wriggle; writhe. **tortillon** (jɔ̃) *m*, twist; pad (*for carrier's head*); bun (*hair*).

tortionnaire (tɔrsjɔnɛːr) *a*, torturous. *appareil ~*, instrument of torture. ¶ *m*, torturer.

tortu, e (tɔrty) *a*, crooked; tortuous.

tortue (tɔrty) *f*, tortoise; tortoise shell butterfly. *~ de mer*, turtle.

tortueux, euse† (tɔrtɥø, øːz) *a*, tortuous; winding; underhand; crooked.

torture (tɔrtyːr) *f*, torture; rack. **torturer** (tyre) *v.t*, to torture, strain. **se ~ l'esprit**, to rack, cudgel, one's brains.

toscan, e (tɔskɑ̃, an) *a. & T~, n*, Tuscan. **la Toscane**, Tuscany.

tôt (to) *ad*, soon; quickly; early, betimes. *~ ou tard*, sooner or later. *le plus ~ possible*, as soon as possible.

total, e† (tɔtal) *a. & m*, total, whole; (*a.*) utter. **totalis[at]eur** (liz[at]œːr) *m*, totalizer; adding machine. **totalité** (te) *f*, whole, totality.

toton (tɔtɔ̃) *m*, teetotum.

toubib (tubib) *m*, doctor (*slang*).

toucan (tukɑ̃) *m*, toucan.

touchant, e (tuʃɑ̃, ɑ̃ːt) *a*, touching, moving, affecting. **touchant**, *pr*, touching, concerning, about. **touchau[d]** (ʃo) *m*, touch needle. **touche** (tuʃ) *f*, touch; hit; nibble (*fish*); key (*piano, typewriter, etc.*); finger board (*violin*); fret (*guitar, etc.*). **touche-à-tout**, *a*, meddlesome, officious. ¶ *m*, meddler, busybody, officious person.

toucher (ʃe) *m*, touch; feel. ¶ *v.t. & i*, to touch; feel; finger; tap; hit; strike; whip; move, affect; concern; play (*piano, etc.*); ink up (*Typ.*); draw, receive, cash; test; touch on, allude to; meddle; adjoin. **toucheur** (ʃœːr) *m*, drover.

touer (twe) *v.t*, to tow, warp (*Naut.*). **toueur** (twœːr) *m*, tug.

touffe (tuf) *f*, tuft; wisp; clump; bunch. ~ *de gazon*, divot (*golf*).

touffeur (tufœːr) *f*, stifling heat (*of room*).

touffu, e (tufy) *a*, bushy, thick; overloaded.

toujours (tuʒuːr) *ad*, always, ever; still; anyhow. ~ *vert*, evergreen. *essayez* ~, try anyway.

toupet (tupɛ) *m*, tuft of hair, forelock; cheek, impudence. *avoir du* ~, to be impudent.

toupie (tupi) *f*, [peg] top. ~ *d'Allemagne*, humming t. **toupiller** (je) *v.i*, to spin round.

tour (tuːr) *f*, tower; castle, rook (*chess*); derrick. ¶ *m*, turn; revolution; round; stroll, walk; trip, tour; spell; bout; row (*stitches*); circumference; size, measurement; lathe; wheel (*potter's*); trick; feat. ~ *de Babel* (babɛl), babel (*fig.*). ~ *de bâton*; perquisites, pickings. ~ *de cartes*, card trick. ~ *de col*, collar (*fur, etc.*). ~ *de cou*, necklet, wrap. ~ *de main*, knack; trick of the trade. *en un* ~ *de main*, in a jiffy, in a trice. ~ *de nage*, swim. ~ *de passe-passe*, conjuring trick; juggle; clever trick. ~ *[de piste]*, lap. ~ *de reins*, strain in the back. ~*s & retours*, twists & turns. ~ *de lancement*, launching rail. ~ *de montage*, servicing tower. *un trente-trois* ~*s*, an LP record.

tourbe (turb) *f*, peat; rabble, mob. **tourbeux, euse** (bø, øːz) *a*, peaty, boggy. **tourbière** (bjɛːr) *f*, peat bog, peatery.

tourbillon (turbijɔ̃) *m*, whirlwind; whirl, swirl; whirlpool; vortex; bustle. **tourbillonner** (jɔne) *v.i*, to whirl, swirl, eddy.

tourelle (turɛl) *f*, turret; capstan (*lathe*).

touret (turɛ) *m*, wheel; reel.

tourie (turi) *f*, carboy.

tourillon (turijɔ̃) *m*, axle, trunnion, gudgeon, journal, pin, pivot.

tourisme (turism) *m*, touring, travel for pleasure. **touriste** (rist) *n*, tourist.

tourment (turmɑ̃) *m*, torment, torture; pain; pang; worry; plague. **tourmentant, e** (tɑ̃, ɑ̃ːt) *a*, tormenting; troublesome. **tourmente** (mɑ̃ːt) *f*, storm, gale; turmoil. ~ *de neige*, blizzard. **tourmenté, e** (mɑ̃te) *p.a*, distorted; broken; labored. **tourmenter** (te) *v.t*, to torment, torture, rack; worry; plague; overelaborate.

tournage (turnaːʒ) *m*, turning (*lathe*); shooting (*cinema*).

tournailler (turnɑje) *v.i*, to wander around. **tournant, e** (nɑ̃, ɑ̃ːt) *a*, turning, revolving; swing (*bridge*); winding. ¶ *m*, turning; t. space; t. point; bend; corner (*street*); eddy; shift. **tourné, e** (ne) *p.a*, turned; shaped; disposed; sour (*milk*). **tourne-à-gauche** (nagoːʃ) *m*, wrench; saw set. **tournebride** (nəbrid) *m*, roadhouse; roadside inn; somewhere to stay. **tournebroche** (nəbrɔʃ) *m*, turnspit. **tournée** (ne) *f*, round, tour; circuit. **tourner** (ne) *v.t. & i*, to turn; t. over; t. out; rotate; revolve; gyrate; swivel; hinge; swing; wind; belay; shoot (*film*); film. **tournesol** (nəsɔl) *m*, sunflower; litmus. **tourneur** (nœːr) *m*, turner. **tournevis** (nəvis) *m*, screwdriver. **tourniquet** (nikɛ) *m*, turnstile; swivel; tourniquet.

tourne-disque (turnədisk) *m*, record player; disk drive (*computers*).

tournoi (turnwa) *m*, tournament (*Hist., chess, etc.*); tourney. ~ *par élimination*, elimination tournament (*Ten.*). **tournoyer** (nwaje) *v.i*, to spin, whirl; wheel; swirl.

tournure (turnyːr) *f*, turn, course; cast; shape, figure; face.

tourte (turt) *f*, pie, tart. **tourteau** (to) *m*, oil cake.

tourtereau (turtəro) *m*, young

turtledove. **tourterelle** (tərɛl) f, turtledove.

tourtière (turtjɛːr) f, pie dish; baking tin.

Toussaint (la) (tusɛ̃), All Saints' day. *la veille de la* ~, Halloween.

tousser (tuse) v.i, to cough.

tout (tu) pn, all, everything. le ~, the whole, the lot. **tout, e** (tu, tut) a.s, **tous** (tu & tuːs) a.m.pl, all, the whole [of]; every; any; full; only, sole. *tout le monde*, everybody, everyone. *tout le monde descend!* everybody out! (*Rly.*). ¶ ad, quite; very; thoroughly; all; right; ready (*made, cooked*); wide; stark (*naked*); bolt (*upright*); just. ~ ... *que*, however, [al]though. **tout,** comps: ~ *à coup*, suddenly, all at once. ~ *à fait*, quite; altogether; perfectly. ~ *à l'heure*, presently, by & by; just now. ~ *à vous*, yours very truly. ~ *d'un coup*, suddenly. ~ *de suite*, at once, directly. ~ *en parlant*, while speaking. **tout-à-l'égout,** m, main drainage. **toute-épice,** f, allspice. **toute-fois,** ad, yet, however, nevertheless, still. **toute-puissance,** f, omnipotence. **tout-puissant, toute-puissante,** a, almighty, omnipotent; all-powerful; overpowering. *le Tout-Puissant*, the Almighty, the Omnipotent.

toutou (tutu) m, bowwow, doggie.

toux (tu) f, cough[ing].

toxine (tɔksin) f, toxin. **toxique** (ksik) a, toxic, poisonous, poison (*gas*). ¶ m, poison.

trac (trak) m, fright; stage fright.

tracas (trakɑ) m, worry, bother. **tracasser** (kase) v.t, to worry. **tracasserie** (sri) f, wrangling.

trace (tras) f, trace; trail; track; spoor; scent; print; footprint; [foot]step; mark; weal. **tracé** (se) m, outline; graph; traced pattern. **tracer** (se) v.t, to trace; lay out; mark out; map out; draw, sketch, outline.

trachée-artère (traʃeartɛːr) f, trachea, windpipe.

tractation (traktasjɔ̃) f, dealing; bargaining.

tracteur (traktœːr) m, tractor. **traction** (ksjɔ̃) f, traction, haulage, draft; drive (*auto*). ~ *avant*, front wheel drive.

tradition (tradisjɔ̃) f, tradition; folklore; delivery (*law*). **traditionnel, le†** (sjɔnɛl) a, traditional.

traducteur, trice (tradyktœːr, tris) n, translator. **traduction** (ksjɔ̃) f, translation; pony, crib. **traduire** (dɥiːr) v.t.ir, to summon; translate; express, interpret. *se* ~, to show.

trafic (trafik) m, traffic; trading; trade. **trafiquant** (kɑ̃) m, trader, trafficker. **trafiquer** (ke) v.i, to traffic, trade, deal.

tragédie (traʒedi) f, tragedy. **tragédien, ne** (djɛ̃, ɛn) n, tragedian, tragedienne. **tragi-comédie** (ʒikɔmedi) f, tragicomedy. **tragi-comique** (mik) a, tragicomic. **tragique†** (ʒik) a, tragic(al).

trahir (traiːr) v.t, to betray; reveal. **trahison** (izɔ̃) f, treachery; treason; betrayal.

train (trɛ̃) m, train, string; raft; set; suite; quarters (*horse*); pace, rate; progress; routine; mood. ~ *de paquebot*, boat train. le ~ [*des équipages*], the army service corps. ~ *militaire*, troop train. ~ *omnibus*, local t. ~-*poste*, m, mail t. ~ *d'atterissage*, landing gear (*Avn.*); undercarriage. *en* ~ *de*, in the process of.

traînant, e (trɛnɑ̃, ɑ̃ːt) a, trailing; shambling; listless, languid; singsong. **traînard** (naːr) m, straggler, laggard; slowcoach. **traînasser** (nase) v.t, to draw out; drag out; (*v.i.*) to loiter; laze. **traîne** (trɛːn) f, train (*of dress*). *à la* ~, in tow. **traîneau** (treno) m, sledge, sleigh. **traînée** (ne) f, trail; train; ground line (*Fish.*); streetwalker. **traîner** (ne) v.t. & i, to drag, draw, haul; trail; draggle; drawl; lag; flag, droop; straggle; loiter; loaf. ~ *la jambe*, to shuffle along. *ça traîne les rue*, it's not rare, not hard to find.

train-train (trɛ̃trɛ̃) m, jogtrot, routine.

traire (trɛːr) v.t.ir, to milk; draw.

trait (trɛ) m, pull[ing]; draft;

stretch; trace (*harness*); leash; arrow, dart; shot; beam; thunderbolt; dash (*Teleg.*); stroke; streak; line; flash; sally; gulp; feature; trait; touch; reference, bearing. ~ *d'union*, hyphen. ~ *de balance*, turn of the scale. ~ *d'esprit*, witticism. *tout d'un* ~, suddenly. traitable (tabl) *a*, tractable, manageable. traite (trɛt) *f*, stretch; stage (*journey*); trade, traffic; transport; trading; draft, bill; milking. *la* ~ *des noirs*, *la* ~ *des nègres*, the slave trade. traité (te) *m*, treatise; treaty; agreement. traitement (tmɑ̃) *m*, treatment; usage; salary, pay, stipend; processing, computing; adaptation (*cinema*). ~ *automatique des données*, automatic data processing. ~ *de l'information*, d. p. ~ *par lots*, batch processing (*computers*). ~ *de texte*, word p. ~ *d'inactivité*, pension. traiter (te) *v.t. & i*, to treat, use; entertain; deal; negotiate. ~ *de*, to treat of; call, dub. traiteur (tœ:r) *m*, caterer.

traître, traîtresse (trɛ:tr, trɛtrɛs) *n*, traitor, traitress; betrayer; villain (*Theat.*). ¶ *a*, treacherous, traitorous. **traîtreusement** (trøzmɑ̃) *ad*, treacherously. **traîtrise** (tri:z) *f*, treachery.

trajectoire (traʒɛktwa:r) *f*, trajectory; path (*storm*, *etc.*). **trajet** (ʒɛ) *m*, journey, passage, transit, trip, run, ride, course.

tramail (trama:j) *m*, trammel [net].

trame (tram) *f*, woof, weft; web; thread (*of life*); half-tone screen; plot. **tramer** (me) *v.t*, to weave; hatch (*plot*).

tramway (tramwɛ) *m*, streetcar, trolley car.

tranchant, e (trɑ̃ʃɑ̃, ɑ̃:t) *a*, cutting, sharp, keen; edge[d]; trenchant; peremptory; glaring. ¶ *m*, [cutting] edge. **tranche** (trɑ̃:ʃ) *f*, slice, cut; steak; rasher; slab; block, portion, set; edge (*book*, *coin*). *doré sur* ~, gilt-edged. ~*s rognées*, cut edges. **tranché, e** (trɑ̃ʃe) *a*, well-marked; distinct. **tranchée** (ʃe) *f*, trench; drain; cutting; (*pl.*) colic, gripes.

tranchefile (ʃfil) *f*, headband (*Bookb.*). **trancher** (ʃe) *v.t*, to slice; cut; chop off; cut short; settle; contrast. **tranchoir** (ʃwa:r) *m*, trencher, cutting board.

tranquille† (trɑ̃kil) *a*, tranquil, quiet, calm, peaceful, still, undisturbed, easy. **tranquilliser** (lize) *v.t*, to calm, soothe. **tranquillité** (te) *f*, tranquillity, peace.

transaction (trɑ̃zaksjɔ̃) *f*, transaction, dealing; compromise.

transatlantique (trɑ̃zatlɑ̃tik) *a*, transatlantic. ¶ *m*, deckchair; liner.

transborder (trɑ̃sbɔrde) *v.t*, to tranship. **transbordeur** (dœ:r) *m*, car ferry.

transcendant, e (trɑ̃sɑ̃dɑ̃, ɑ̃:t) *a*, transcendent.

transcription (trɑ̃skripsjɔ̃) *f*, transcript[ion]; copy; posting (*Bkkpg.*). **transcrire** (skri:r) *v.t*, ir, to transcribe; post.

transe (trɑ̃:s) *f*, fright, scare; trance.

transept (trɑ̃sɛpt) *m*, transept.

transférer (trɑ̃sfere) *v.t*, to transfer; translate (*bishop*); alter the date of (*function*). **transfert** (fɛ:r) *m*, transfer.

transfiguration (trɑ̃sfigyrasjɔ̃) *f*, transfiguration. **transfigurer** (re) *v.t*, to transfigure.

transformateur (trɑ̃sfɔrmatœ:r) *m*, transformer. **transformer** (me) *v.t*, to transform, change, convert.

transfuge (trɑ̃sfy:ʒ) *m*, deserter (*to enemy*); turncoat, rat.

transfuser (trɑ̃sfyze) *v.t*, to transfuse.

transgresser (trɑ̃sgrɛse) *v.t*, to transgress.

transhumer (trɑ̃zyme) *v.t*, to move flock to new pasture; transplant.

transiger (trɑ̃ziʒe) *v.i*, to compound, compromise.

transir (trɑ̃si:r) *v.t*, to chill; paralyze (*fig.*).

transit (trɑ̃zit) *m*, transit (*Cust.*).

transitif, ive† (trɑ̃zitif, i:v) *a*, transitive.

transition (trãzisjɔ̃) f, transition. **transitoire** (twa:r) a, transitory, transient.

translation (trãslasjɔ̃) f, translation (bishop); transfer, conveyance; alteration of date (function).

translucide (trãslysid) a, translucent.

transmetteur (trãsmɛtœ:r) m, transmitter. **transmettre** (tr) v.t. ir, to transmit; pass on; hand down; transfer, convey. **transmission** (misjɔ̃) f, transmission; drive, driving, shaft[ing] (Mech.).

transmuer (trãsmɥe) v.t, to transmute.

transparence (trãsparã:s) f, transparency. **transparent, e** (rã, ã:t) a, transparent. ¶ m, transparency (picture); black lines.

transpercer (trãspɛrse) v.t, to transfix, pierce.

transpirer (trãspire) v.i, to perspire; transpire.

transplanter (trãsplãte) v.t, to transplant.

transport (trãspɔ:r) m, transport, conveyance, carriage; visit (of experts, etc; law); transfer (law); troopship; rapture. ~ [au cerveau], light-headedness, delirium. **transportation** (pɔrtasjɔ̃) f, transportation. **transporter** (te) v.t, to transport, etc.

transposer (trãspoze) v.t, to transpose.

transsubstantiation (trãssypstãsjasjɔ̃) f, transubstantiation.

transvaser (trãsvaze) v.t, to decant.

transversal, e† (trãsvɛrsal) a, transverse, cross (att.).

trapèze (trapɛ:z) m, trapeze.

trappe (trap) f, trap, pitfall; trapdoor. **trappeur** (pœ:r) m, trapper.

trapu, e (trapy) a, thickset, dumpy, squat, stocky.

traque (trak) f, beating (game). **traquenard** (kna:r) m, trap. **traquer** (ke) v.t, to beat (game); surround; track down. **traqueur** (kœ:r) m, beater.

traumatiser (tromatize) v.t, to traumatize.

travail (trava:j) m. oft. pl, work; working; labor, toil; piece of work, job; employment; stress (Mech.); childbirth; workmanship. ~ d'artisan, craftsmanship. travaux forcés, hard labor. ~ en série, mass production. **travaillé, e** (vaje) (fig.) p.a, labored, elaborate. **travailler** (je) v.i, to work, labor, toil; be in stress; (v.t.) to torment; work; w. up; elaborate. ~ comme un pied, sabot, to work badly. ~ d'arrache-pied, w. hard. **travailleur, euse** (jœ:r, ø:z) n, worker; workman; laborer; toiler. ¶ f, workstand (lady's).

travée (trave) f, bay (Arch.); span (bridge, roof).

travelling (travəliŋ) m, dolly (cinema); dolly shot.

travers (travɛ:r) m, breadth; beam (ship), broadside; fault. à ~, through. de ~, askew, awry, amiss, wrong; askance. en ~, ad, across, athwart, cross[wise]. en ~ de, pr, across, athwart. **traverse** (vɛrs) f, shortcut; crossbar; crossbeam; crossroad; transom; sill; tie (rail track); hitch, setback. **traversée** (se) f, crossing, passage. ~ des piétons, pedestrian crossing. **traverser** (se) v.t, to traverse, cross, go through; thwart. **traversin** (sɛ̃) m, bolster (bed).

travestir (travɛsti:r) v.t, to disguise; travesty, burlesque; misrepresent.

trayon (trɛjɔ̃) m, dug, teat (cow, etc.).

trébucher (trebyʃe) v.i, to stumble, trip. **trébuchet** (ʃɛ) m, trap; balance (scales).

tréfiler (trefile) v.t, to wiredraw (metal).

trèfle (trɛfl) m, trefoil; clover; clubs (cards).

tréfonds (trefɔ̃) m, subsoil.

treillage (trɛja:ʒ) m, trellis, lattice. **treillis** (ji) m, trellis, lattice; netting; sackcloth. **treillisser** (se) v.t, to trellis, lattice.

treize (trɛ:z) a. & m, thirteen; 13th. ~ douze, baker's dozen. **treizième†** (trɛzjɛm) a. & n, thirteenth.

tréma (tremɑ) *m*, diaeresis.
tremblaie (trɑ̃blɛ) *f*, aspen plantation. **tremble** (trɑ̃:bl) *m*, asp[en].
tremblement (trɑ̃bləmɑ̃) *m*, trembling, trepidation, quavering, shaking; tremor. ~ *de terre*, earthquake. **tremblé, e** (ble) *p.a*, wavy, waved; shaky. **trembler** (ble) & **trembloter** (blɔte) *v.i*, to tremble, shake, vibrate, quake, quiver, quaver, quail, shiver, flutter, flicker.
trémie (tremi)*f*, hopper (*Mach.*).
tremolo (tremɔlo) *m*, tremolo (*Mus.*).
trémousser (se) (tremuse) *v.pr*, to fidget; flounce about; bestir oneself. *trémousser de l'aile*, to flutter, flap its wings.
trempe (trɑ̃:p) *f*, damping; tempering, hardening; temper; stamp, kidney (*fig.*). **tremper** (trɑ̃pe) *v.t*. & *i*, to steep, soak, dip; drench; damp, wet; temper; imbrue.
tremplin (trɑ̃plɛ̃) *m*, spring board, diving b.; ski jump; jumping-off ground (*fig.*).
trentaine (trɑ̃tɛn) *f*, thirty [or so]. **trente** (trɑ̃:t) *a*, thirty. ¶ *m*, thirty; 30th. ~ *et quarante*, rouge et noir. **T~,** *f*, Trent (*Italy*). **trentième** (trɑ̃tjɛm) *a*. & *n*, thirtieth. **le Trentin** (tɛ̃), the Trentino.
trépan (trepɑ̃) *m*, trepan; bit, chisel (*boring*). **trépaner** (pane) *v.t*, to trepan.
trépas (trepɑ) *m*, death, decease. **trépasser (se)** *v.i*, to die, pass away. **les trépassés (se)**, the dead, the departed.
trépidation (trepidasjɔ̃) *f*, tremor; vibration (*of machinery, car, ship*).
trépied (trepje) *m*, tripod; trivet (*stove*).
trépigner (trepiɲe) *v.i*, to stamp (*rage*).
trépointe (trepwɛ̃:t) *f*, welt (*shoe*).
très (trɛ; *in liaison*, trɛz) *ad*, very, most, [very] much.
trésor (trezɔ:r) *m*, treasure;

treasury. **trésorerie** (zɔrri) *f*, treasury; finances. **trésorier, ère** (zɔrje, ɛ:r) *n*, treasurer; paymaster.
tressaillir (trɛsaji:r) *v.i.ir*, to start; thrill; wince.
tressauter (trɛsote) *v.i*, to start, jump.
tresse (trɛs) *f*, plait, tress; braid; tape; gasket. **tresser** (se) *v.t*, to plait; braid; weave (*wicker, etc.*).
tréteau (treto) *m*, trestle, horse; (*pl.*) boards, stage.
treuil (trœ:j) *m*, winch, windlass, hoist.
trêve (trɛ:v) *f*, truce; respite.
Trèves (trɛ:v) *f*, Treves, Trier.
trévire (trevi:r) *f*, parbuckle.
tri (tri) & **triage** (a:ʒ) *m*, sorting.
triangle (triɑ̃:gl) *m*, triangle (*Geom.* & *Mus.*). **triangulaire** (ɑ̃gylɛ:r) *a*, triangular.
tribord (tribɔ:r) *m*, starboard.
tribu (triby) *f*, tribe.
tribulation (tribylasjɔ̃) *f*, tribulation, trial.
tribun (tribœ̃) (*pers.*) *m*, tribune (*Hist.*); demagogue. **tribunal** (bynal) *m*, tribunal; bench; court. **tribune** (byn) *f*, tribune; rostrum; platform; gallery; loft (*organ*); grandstand; discussion or debate (*TV*).
tribut (triby) *m*, tribute. **tributaire** (tɛ:r) *a*. & *m*, tributary (*pers., river*); dependent.
triceps (trisɛps) *a*. & *m*, triceps.
tricher (triʃe) *v.i*. & *t*, to cheat; trick; doctor. **tricherie** (ʃri) *f*, cheating; trickery. **tricheur, euse** (ʃœ:r, ø:z) *n*, cheat; trickster; sharper.
trichromie (trikrɔmi) *f*, three-color process.
tricot (triko) *m*, knitting (*art*); sweater; knitted garment; (*pl.*) knit[ted] wear. ~ *à l'envers*, purl knitting. **tricotage** (kɔta:ʒ) *m*, knitting (*act*). **tricoter** (te) *v.t*. & *abs*, to knit. **tricoteur, euse** (tœ:r, ø:z) *n*, knitter.
trictrac (triktrak) *m*, backgammon; b. board.
tricycle (trisikl) *m*, tricycle.

trident (tridã) *m*, trident; fish spear.

triennal, e (triɛnnal) *a*, triennial.

trier (trie) *v.t*, to sort; pick. **trieur, euse** (œːr, øːz) *n*, sorter; picker.

trigonométrie (trigɔnɔmetri) *f*, trigonometry.

trille (triːj) *m*, trill, shake (*Mus.*).

trillion (triljɔ̃) *m*, a million millions.

trimbaler (trɛ̃bale) *v.t*, to drag about.

trimer (trime) *v.i*, to slave, drudge.

trimestre (trimɛstr) *m*, quarter, 3 months; term (*Sch.*); quarter's rent, salary, etc. **trimestriel, le** (triɛl) *a*, quarterly.

tringle (trɛ̃ːgl) *f*, rod; curtain rod; chalk line (*mark*).

Trinité (la) (trinite), the Trinity; Trinidad.

trinquer (trɛ̃ke) *v.i*, to clink glasses; hobnob.

trio (trio) *m*, trio. **triolet** (ɔlɛ) *m*, triolet; triplet (*Mus.*).

triomphal, e† (triɔ̃fal) *a*, triumphal. **triomphe** (ɔ̃ːf) *f*, triumph; exultation. **triompher** (ɔ̃fe) *v.i*, to triumph; exult; excel; gloat.

tripaille (tripɑːj) *f*, garbage, offal.

tripe de velours (trip) *f*, velveteen.

triperie (tripri) *f*, tripe shop. **tripes** (trip) *f.pl*, tripe. **tripier, ère** (pje, ɛːr) *n*, tripe dealer.

triple† (tripl) *a. & m*, treble, triple, threefold, 3 times; triplicate. ~ *croche*, *f*, demisemiquaver. ~ *saut*, *m*, hop, step, & jump. **tripler** (ple) *v.t. & i*, to treble, triple. **triplicata** (plikata) *m*, triplicate.

tripoli (tripɔli) *m*, tripoli.

tripot (tripo) *m*, bawdy house; gambling den. **tripoter** (pɔte) *v.t. & abs*, muddle up; plot; job, rig; handle; gamble; meddle with. **tripoteur** (pɔtœːr) *m*, intriguer; shady speculator; mischiefmaker.

triptyque (triptik) *m*, triptych.

trique (trik) *f*, cudgel, bludgeon. *avoir la* ~, to have an erection (*obscene*).

triqueballe (trikbal) *m*, sling cart.

trisaïeul, e (trizajœl) *n*, greatgreat-grandfather, -mother.

triste† (trist) *a*, sad, sorrowful, woeful; dreary, gloomy, dismal; bleak, depressing, sorry, wretched. **tristesse** (tɛs) *f*, sadness.

triton (tritɔ̃) *m*, triton; merman; newt; eft.

triturer (trityre) *v.t*, to triturate, grind.

trivial, e† (trivjal) *a*, vulgar, coarse; not in decent use (*expression*); trite, hackneyed. **trivialité** (lite) *f*, vulgarity, etc; vulgarism.

troc (trɔk) *m*, truck, exchange, barter.

trochée (trɔʃe) *m*, head of shoots (*tree stump*).

troène (trɔɛn) *m*, privet (*Bot.*).

troglodyte (trɔglɔdit) *m*, troglodyte, cave dweller.

trognon (trɔɲɔ̃) *m*, core (*apple*); stump (*cabbage*).

trois (trwa; *in liaison*, trwaz) *a. & m*, three; third. ~ *fois*, three times, thrice. ~ *jumeaux*, triplets, ~-*mâts*, *m*, three-master. **troisième†** (zjɛm) *a*, third. ¶ *m*, third (*number*, *pers.*, *floor*). ¶ *f*, third (*class*). ~*s* [*galeries*], gallery (*Theat.*).

trolley (trɔlɛ) *m*, troll[e]y (*grooved wheel*).

trombe (trɔ̃ːb) *f*, waterspout. ~ *d'eau*, cloudburst. *entrer en* ~, to burst in.

trombone (trɔ̃bɔn) *m*, trombone; paper clip.

trompe (trɔ̃ːp) *f*, horn; hooter; trumpet; proboscis; trunk. ~ ~ *d'Eustache* (østaʃ), Eustachian tube.

trompe-l'œil (trɔ̃plœːj) *m*, stilllife deception; bluff, window dressing (*fig.*). **tromper** (pe) *v.t*, to deceive, delude; cheat; mislead; disappoint; outwit; beguile. *se* ~, to be mistaken, mistake. **tromperie** (pri) *f*, deceit, deception, imposture; illusion.

trompeter (trɔ̃pɛte) *v.t*, to trumpet (*secret*). **trompette** (pɛt) *f*, trumpet,-trump (*last, of doom*); whelk. ¶ *m*, trumpeter.

trompeur, euse (trɔ̃pœːr, øːz) *n*, deceiver, cheat. ¶ *a*, deceitful; deceptive.

tronc (trɔ̃) *m*, trunk; parent stock; frustum. ~ *des pauvres*, poor box. **tronçon** (sɔ̃) *m*, (*broken*) piece, stump; section; dock (*of tail*). **tronçonner** (sɔne) *v.t*, to cut up.

trône (troːn) *m*, throne. **trôner** (trone) *v.i*, to sit enthroned, sit in state.

tronquer (trɔ̃ke) *v.t*, to truncate; mutilate.

trop (tro; *in liaison,* trɔp) *ad. & m*, too; over-; too much, too many; too long; too well; excess. ~ *cuit, e*, overdone. *être de* ~, to be in the way, be unwelcome; superfluous.

trope (trɔp) *m*, trope.

trophée (trɔfe) *m*, trophy.

tropical, e (trɔpikal) *a*, tropical. **tropique** (pik) *m*, tropic.

trop-plein (trɔplɛ̃) *m*, overflow.

troquer (trɔke) *v.t*, to barter, exchange.

trot (tro) *m*, trot. **trotte** (trɔt) *f*, distance, step. **trotter** (te) *v.i. & t*, to trot; run (*in one's head*). **trotteur, euse** (tœːr, øːz) *n*, trotter (*horse*). **trottin** (tɛ̃) *m*, errand girl. **trottiner** (tine) *v.i*, to trot; toddle. **trottinette** (nɛt) *f*, scooter. **trottoir** (twaːr) *m*, pavement, footway, footpath. *bordure du* ~, curb. *faire le* ~, to walk the streets (*prostitute*).

trou (tru) *m*, hole; eye; blank ~ *barré*, stimy, stymie (*golf*). ~ *d'air*, air pocket (*Avn.*); ~ [*d' arrivée*], hole (*golf*). ~ *d'homme*, manhole. ~ *de sonde*, bore hole.

troubadour (trubaduːr) *m*, troubadour.

trouble (trubl) *a*, troubled, turbid, muddy, cloudy; dim, blurred, misty; overcast; confused. ¶ *m*, disorder; disturbance; trouble. ~-*fête* (bləfɛːt) *m*, spoilsport, killjoy. **troubler** (ble) *v.t*, to dis-

turb; muddy; dim; mar; hamper; upset.

trouée (true) *f*, gap. **trouer** (e) *v.t*, to pierce with holes.

troufion (trufjɔ̃) *m*, soldier, private (*slang*).

trouille (truːj) *f*, fear (*slang*). *avoir la* ~, to be afraid.

troupe (trup) *f*, troop, band; host; set, gang; troop; troupe; flock. **troupeau** (po) *m*, herd, drove; flock. **troupier** (pje) *m*, soldier, campaigner.

trousse (trus) *f*, truss; bundle; case; kit; outfit; roll. ~ *manucure*, manicure set. *aux* ~*s de*, at the heels of. **trousseau** (so) *m*, bunch (*keys*); outfit, kit; trousseau. **trousser** (se) *v.t*, to tuck up; turn up; truss; dispatch; polish off. ~ *bagage*, to pack up; decamp; die. **troussis** (si) *m*, tuck.

trouvaille (truvaːj) *f*, [lucky] find. **trouver** (ve) *v.t*, to find; discover; get; think; like; spare (*the time*). *objets trouvés*, lost and found. *enfant trouvé*, foundling. *se* ~, to be; feel; happen.

truc (tryk) *m*, knack; trick, dodge; gadget; platform car (*Rly.*).

truca (tryka) *m*, optical printer (*cinema*).

trucage (trykaːʒ) *m*, faking; camouflage; trick photography; gerrymandering.

truchement (tryʃmɑ̃) *m*, interpreter, spokesman.

truculent, e (trykylɑ̃, ɑ̃ːt) *a*, truculent.

trudgeon (trydʒɔ̃) *m*, trudgen (*Swim.*).

truelle (tryɛl) *f*, trowel. ~ *à poisson*, fish slice.

truffe (tryf) *f*, truffle.

truie (trɥi) *f*, sow.

truisme (tryism) *m*, truism.

truite (trɥit) *f*, trout. ~ *saumonée* (somɔne), salmon t. **truité, e** (te) *a*, speckled, mottled.

trumeau (trymo) *m*, pier (*Arch.*); pierglass; leg of beef.

truquage (trykaːʒ) *m*, fake; trick shot (*TV, cinema*). **truquer** (ke) *v.t*, to fake.

tu (ty) *pn*, you, thou.
tuant, e (tɥɑ̃, ɑ̃:t) *a*, killing; boring.
tuba (tyba) *m*, tuba.
tube (tyb) *m*, tube; telephone (*slang*); hit song (*slang*).
tubercule (tybɛrkyl) *m*, tuber; tubercle. **tuberculeux, euse** (lø, ø:z) *a*, tuberculous. ¶ *n*, consumptive. **tuberculose** (lo:z) *f*, tuberculosis.
tubéreuse (tyberø:z) *f*, tuberose.
tubulaire (tybylɛ:r) *a*, tubular.
tue-mouches (tymuʃ) *m*, flyswat[ter], flyflap. **tuer** (tɥe) *v.t*, to kill, slay; slaughter; swat (*fly*); bore. *tué à l'ennemi*, killed in action. *les tués*, the killed. *un tué, une tuée*, a fatality (*accident*). **tuerie** (tyri) *f*, slaughter, butchery, carnage. *à tue-tête*, at the top of one's voice. **tueur** (tɥœ:r) *m*, killer, slayer.
tuile (tɥil) *f*, tile; bad luck (*slang*). **tuilerie** (lri) *f*, tile works. **tuilier** (lje) *m*, tile maker.
tulipe (tylip) *f*, tulip. **tulipier** (pje) *m*, tulip tree.
tulle (tyl) *m*, tulle, net.
tumeur (tymœ:r) *f*, tumor.
tumulte (tymylt) *m*, tumult, uproar, turmoil; riot. **tumultueux, euse†** (tɥø, ø:z) *a*, tumultuous, riotous.
tumulus (tymyly:s) *m*, tumulus, barrow.
tungstène (tœ̃gstɛn) *m*, tungsten.
tunique (tynik) *f*, tunic; coat (*Anat., Bot.*).
Tunis (tynis) *m*, Tunis (*capital*). **la Tunisie** (zi), Tunis (*state*). **tunisien, ne** (zjɛ̃, ɛn) *a. & T~, n*, Tunisian.
tunnel (tynɛl) *m*, tunnel.
turban (tyrbɑ̃) *m*, turban.
turbin (tyrbɛ̃) *m*, work, grind (*slang*). *le ~ journalier*, the daily grind. **turbiner** (ne) *v.t*, to work hard; cram.
turbine (tyrbin) *f*, turbine.
turbot (tyrbo) *m*, turbot.
turbulence (tyrbylɑ̃:s) *f*, turbulence. **turbulent, e** (lɑ̃, ɑ̃:t) *a*, turbulent, unruly, restless; boisterous.

turc, turque (tyrk) *a*, Turkish. *être assis à la turque*, to sit cross-legged. **T~,** *n*, Turk. **le turc,** Turkish (*language*). **Turcoman** (kɔmɑ̃) (*pers.*) *m*, Turkoman.
turf (tyrf) *m*, racetrack, racecourse. *le ~*, the turf.
turgescent, e (tyrʒɛsɑ̃, ɑ̃:t) *a*, turgescent, turgid.
turlupin (tyrlypɛ̃) *m*, buffoon. **turlupiner** (pine) *v.i*, to play the fool. *v.t*, to bother, worry.
turpitude (tyrpityd) *f*, turpitude, baseness.
Turquie (tyrki) *f*, Turkey.
turquoise (tyrkwa:z) *f. & att*, turquoise.
tutélaire (tytelɛ:r) *a*, tutelar[y], guardian; (*m.*) prop (*Hort.*). **tutelage, guardianship; protection. tuteur, trice** (tœ:r, tris) *n*, guardian; (*m.*) prop (*Hort.*).
tutoyer (tytwaje) *v.t*, to address as "tu" and "toi." *se faire ~*, to be severely reprimanded.
tutu (tyty) *m*, ballet skirt.
tuyau (tɥijo) *m*, pipe; tube; hose; flue; stem; hint. *avoir des ~x*, to be in the know. *~ acoustique*, speaking tube. *~ d'arrosage*, garden hose. *~ d'échappement*, exhaust pipe. **tuyauter** (te) *v.t*, to flute, frill, plait; tip off. **tuyauterie** (tri) *f*, pipe system, p. factory.
tuyère (tɥjɛ:r) *f*, nozzle; pipe. *~ orientable*, swiveling nozzle.
tympan (tɛ̃pɑ̃) *m*, tympanum, ear drum; tympan. **tympanon** (panɔ̃) *m*, dulcimer.
type (tip) *m*, type (*model & Typ.*); standard; fellow, guy.
typhoïde (tifɔid) *a*, typhoid.
typhon (tifɔ̃) *m*, typhoon.
typhus (tify:s) *m*, typhus.
typique (tipik) *a*, typical.
typographie (tipɔgrafi) *f*, typography; printing works. **typographique** (fik) *a*, typographic(al).
tyran (tirɑ̃) *m*, tyrant. **tyrannie** (rani) *f*, tyranny. **tyrannique†** (nik) *a*, tyrannic(al); high-handed. **tyranniser** (nize) *v.t*, to tyrannize [over].
Tyrol (le) (tirɔl), the Tyrol.

tyrolien, ne (ljẽ, ɛn) *a. & T~, n,* Tyrolese.

tzigane (tsigan) *n. & a,* gipsy, zigane.

U

ubiquité (ybikɥite) *f,* ubiquity.

ulcération (ylserasjɔ̃) *f,* ulceration. **ulcère** (sɛːr) *m,* ulcer. **ulcérer** (sere) *v.t,* to ulcerate; embitter.

ultérieur, e (ylterjœːr) *a,* ulterior, later, subsequent. **ultérieurement** (œrmɑ̃) *ad,* later [on].

ultimatum (yltimatɔm) *m,* ultimatum. **ultime** (tim) *a,* final, ultimate.

ultra (yltra) *m,* ultraist, extremist. **~-violet, te,** *a,* ultraviolet.

ululer (ylyle) *v.i,* to hoot, ululate.

un (œ̃) *m,* one. **un, une** (œ̃, yn) *a,* one; a, an. **~ à ~,** one by one; one after another. **l'~,** each (*price of articles*). **l'~ l'autre, les uns** (*les unes*) **les autres,** one another, each other. **l'~ & l'autre,** both. **l'~ ou l'autre,** either. **ni l'~ ni l'autre,** neither. **une fois,** once. **une fois, deux fois,** [*trois fois*]; *adjugé!* going, going; gone! *une fois pour toutes,* once for all. **en une** [*seule*] **fois,** in a lump sum, outright (*opp. by installments*). *il y avait* (ou *il était*) *une fois,* once upon a time. **la une,** *the front page.*

unanime† (ynanim) *a,* unanimous. **unanimité** (mite) *f,* unanimity, consensus. **à l'~,** unanimously.

uni, e (yni) *p.a,* united; even; level; smooth; plain; uniform.

unième† (ynjɛm) *a,* first (*only after 20, 30, etc, e.g, vingt & ~,* 21st; *cent ~,* 101st).

unifier (ynifje) *v.t,* to unify, consolidate; standardize. **uniforme** (fɔrm) *a,* uniform, even. ¶ *m,* uniform; regimentals. **uniformément** (memɑ̃) *ad,* uniformly, evenly. **uniformité** (mite) *f,* uniformity.

unilatéral, e (ynilateral) *a,* unilateral; one-sided.

uniment (ynimɑ̃) *ad,* smoothly, evenly; plainly; simply.

union (ynjɔ̃) *f,* union; unity. *U~ des Républiques soviétiques socialistes,* Union of Soviet Socialist Republics. *U~ Sud-Africaine,* Union of South Africa.

unique (ynik) *a,* only; sole; single;, one; unique. *prix ~,* dime store.. *sens ~,* one way. **uniquement** (kmɑ̃) *ad,* solely, uniquely, only.

unir (yniːr) *v.t,* to unite, join; level, smooth. **unisson** (nisɔ̃) *m,* unison. **unitaire** (tɛːr) *a,* unitary; unit (*att.*). **unité** (te) *f,* unit; unity, one; oneness. *~ d'affichage,* display unit (*computers*).

univers (yniveːr) *m,* universe. **universalité** (versalite) *f,* universality. **universel, le†** (sɛl) *a,* universal; world[-wide]. **universitaire** (sitɛːr) *a,* university (*att.*). **université** (te) *f,* university.

Untel (œtɛl) *m, M.~,* Mr. So-and-so.

uranium (yranjɔm) *m,* uranium.

urbain, e (yrbɛ̃, ɛn) *a,* urban. **urbanisme** (banism) *m,* town planning. **urbanité** (te) *f,* urbanity.

urée (yre) *f,* urea. **urémie** (mi) *f,* uremia.

urètre (yrɛːtr) *m,* urethra.

urgence (yrӡɑ̃ːs) *f,* urgency. *d'~,* urgently; emergency (*as a brake*). **urgent, e** (ӡɑ̃, ɑ̃ːt) *a,* urgent.

urinal (yrinal) *m,* urinal (*vessel*). **urine** (rin) *f,* urine. **uriner** (ne) *v.i,* to urinate; (*v.t.*) to pass. **urinoir** (nwaːr) *m,* urinal (*place*). **urique** (rik) *a,* uric.

urne (yrn) *f,* urn. *~ électorale,* ballot box.

urticaire (yrtikɛːr) *f,* nettle rash.

us & coutumes (ys) *m.pl,* use & wont. **usage** (zaːӡ) *m,* use; purpose; wear; usage, custom, practice. *~* [*du monde*], ways of society. *article d'~,* serviceable article. *faire de l'~,* to wear well. *valeur d'~,* value as a going concern. **usagé, e** (zaӡe) *a,* used, secondhand. **usager** (ӡe) *m,* user. **usé, e** (ze) *a,* worn [out]; shabby. *~* [*jusqu'à la corde*], threadbare, hackneyed, stale. **user** (ze) *v.t,* to use; wear [out, away]; abrade. *~ de,* to use, exercise.

s'~, to wear [away]. *être d'un bon user*, to wear well.

usine (yzin) *f*, works; factory; mill; (*power*) station. **usiner** (ne) *v.t*, to machine, tool; exploit. **usinier** (nje) *m*, mill owner.

usité, e (yzite) *a*, used, in use. *peu usité*, rare (*word*).

ustensile (ystãsil) *m*, utensil; implement, tool.

usuel, le† (yzɥɛl) *a*, usual, customary.

usufruit (yzyfrɥi) *m*, usufruct.

usuraire† (yzyrɛ:r) *a*, usurious. **usure** (zy:r) *f*, usury; interest; wear [& tear], wearing; attrition. *guerre d'~*, war of attrition. **usurier, ère** (zyrje, ɛ:r) *n*, usurer.

usurpateur, trice (yzyrpatœ:r, tris) *n*, usurper. **usurpation** (sjɔ̃) *f*, usurpation; encroachment. **usurper** (pe) *v.t*, to usurp; (*v.i.*) to encroach.

ut (yt) *m*, C (*Mus.*).

utérin, e (yterɛ̃, in) *a*, uterine. **utérus** (ry:s) *m*, uterus.

utile† (ytil) *a*, useful, serviceable; effective; due, good (*time*). **utiliser** (lize) *v.t*, to utilize. **utilitaire** (tɛ:r) *a. & n*, utilitarian. **utilité** (te) *f*, utility, use[fulness]; utility [man] (*Theat.*).

utopie (ytɔpi) *f*, utopia. **utopique** (pik) *a. & utopiste* (pist) *a. & n*, utopian.

uvule (yvyl) *f*, uvula.

V

va *see* **aller.**

vacance (vakɑ:s) *f*, vacancy; (*pl.*) holiday[s]; vacation, recess; opening. **vacant, e** (kã, ã:t) *a*, vacant, unoccupied.

vacarme (vakarm) *m*, uproar, din, row.

vacation (vakasjɔ̃) *f*, attendance, sitting (*experts*); (*pl.*) fees (*lawyer's*); (*pl.*) recess (*courts*).

vaccin (vaksɛ̃) *m*, vaccine, lymph. **vaccination** (sinasjɔ̃) *f*, vaccination. **vaccine** (sin) *f*, cowpox. **vacciner** (ne) *v.t*, to vaccinate.

vache (vaʃ) *f*, cow; cowhide. ~ *à lait*, ~ *laitière*, milch cow; policeman (*pejorative*). *bouffer de la* ~

enragée, to endure a period of hard times. *mort aux* ~*s*, off the pigs. **vacher, ère** (ʃe, ɛ:r) *n*, cowherd, neatherd. **vacherie** (ʃri) *f*, cow house; dairy [farm].

vaciller (vasile) *v.i*, to be unsteady, wobble; vacillate, waver; flicker.

vacuité (vakɥite) *f*, vacuity, emptiness.

vadrouiller (vadruje) *v.i*, to roam the streets; knock about.

va-et-vient (vaevjɛ̃) *m*, come-&-go; to & fro; reciprocating motion; swing (*door*); ferry boat; two-way wiring (*Elec.*).

vagabond, e (vagabɔ̃, ɔ̃:d) *a*, vagabond, vagrant, roving; truant. ¶ *n*, vagabond, vagrant, tramp. **vagabondage** (bɔ̃da:ʒ) *m*, vagrancy; truancy. **vagabonder** (de) *v.i*, to rove, wander.

vagin (vaʒɛ̃) *m*, vagina. **vaginé** (ʒine) *a*, sheathed (*Anat.*). **vaginite** (ʒinit) *f*, vaginitis.

vagir (vaʒi:r) *v.i*, to wail, cry (*of baby*). **vagissement** (ʒismɑ̃) *m*, wailing (*infant*); squeaking (*hare*).

vague (va:g) *f*, wave, billow; surge.

vague† (va:g) *a*, vague; hazy; waste (*land*). ¶ *m*, vagueness; void. **vaguer** (vage) *v.i*, to wander [about].

vaguemestre (vagmɛtr) *m*, baggage master (*Mil.*); postman (*Mil.*).

vaillamment (vajamɑ̃) *ad*, valiantly, gallantly. **vaillance** (jɑ̃:s) *f*, gallantry, valor. **vaillant, e** (jã, ã:t) *a*, valiant, gallant. **vaillantise** (jãti:z) *f*, prowess.

vain, e† (vɛ̃, ɛn) *a*, vain; useless; conceited. *vaine pâture*, common [land]. *en vain*, in vain, fruitlessly.

vaincre (vɛ̃:kr) *v.t.ir*, to vanquish, conquer; beat; overcome. **les vaincus** (vɛ̃ky) *m.pl*, the vanquished. **vainqueur** (kœ:r) *m*, conqueror, victor; winner (*sport*).

vairon (vɛrɔ̃) *m*, minnow.

vaisseau (vɛso) *m*, vessel; ship; boat; body (*as nave of church*), main hall. ~ *amiral*, flagship. ~-*école*, training s. ~-*hôpital*, hospital s. ~ *rasé*, hulk. ~ *sanguin*, blood vessel. **vaisselier** (səlje) *m*, sideboard; dresser. **vaisselle** (sɛl) *f*, crockery, plates & dishes. *faire la* ~, to do the dishes.

val (val) *m*, vale, glen. *par monts & par vaux*, over hill & dale.

valable† (valabl) *a*, valid; good; available (*law*).

valence (valɑ̃:s) *f*, valence, -cy (*Chem.*).

Valence (valɑ̃:s) *f*, Valencia (*Spain*).

valet (valɛ) *m*, valet; man[servant]; groom (*stable*); stand; knave, jack (*cards*). ~ *de chambre*, valet. ~ *de charrue*, plowman. ~ *de ferme*, farmhand. ~ *de pied*, footman; flunkey. **valetaille** (lta:j) *f*, menials, flunkeydom. **faire valeter** (lte) to make (*someone*) fetch & carry.

Valette (la) (valɛt), Valetta.

valétudinaire (valetydinɛ:r) *a. & n*, valetudinarian.

valeur (valœ:r) *f*, value; worth; valor, gallantry; value [date], as at (*Com.*); security (*Fin.*); stock; share; investment; holding; asset; bill; paper; money. ~ *déclarée: fr.* —, insured for: —francs. *avec* ~ *déclarée*, insured (*parcel*). *sans* ~ *déclarée*, uninsured. ~*s mobilières*, stocks & shares, transferable securities. [*objet de*] ~, valuable [article], a. of value. *mettre en* ~, to emphasize; enhance; develop (*property, etc.*). **valeureux, euse†** (lœrø, ø:z) *a*, valorous.

valide† (valid) *a*, valid; available; ablebodied, fit for service (*pers.*). **valider** (de) *v.t*, to validate; enable (*computers*). **validité** (dite) *f*, validity.

valise (vali:z) *f*, portmanteau; suitcase, grip.

vallée (vale) *f*, valley. **vallon** (l5) *m*, dale, vale, glen.

valoir (valwa:r) *v.i. & t. ir*, to be worth; win; gain. *cela vaut la peine*, it is worth while. *il vaut mieux*, it is better to. *autant vaut*, one might as well. *à* ~ *sur*, on ac-

count of. *faire* ~, to turn to account, make the best of; develop; enforce.

valse (vals) *f*, waltz. **valser (se)** *v.i*, to waltz. **valseur, euse** (sœ:r, ø:z) *n*, waltzer. *m.pl*, buttocks. *f.pl*, testicles (*slang*).

valve (valv) *f*, valve.

vampire (vɑ̃pi:r) *m*, vampire.

vandale (vɑ̃dal) *m*, vandal. **vandalisme** (lism) *m*, vandalism, wanton destruction.

vandoise (vɑ̃dwa:z) *f*, dace.

vanille (vani:j) *f*, vanilla.

vanité (vanite) *f*, vanity, conceit. **vaniteux, euse** (tø, ø:z) *a*, vain, conceited.

vannage (vana:ʒ) *m*, winnowing; gating. **vanne** (van) *f*, sluice gate, floodgate; gate; shutter; unkind comment (*slang*). **vanneau** (no) *m*, lapwing, pewit. *œufs de* ~, plovers' eggs (*Cook.*). **vanner** (ne) *v.t*, to winnow, fan (*grain*). **vannerie** (nri) *f*, basket making; b. work, wicker work. **vanneur, euse** (nœ:r, ø:z) *n*, winnower. **vannier** (nje) *m*, basket maker.

vantail (vɑ̃ta:j) *m*, leaf (*door, shutter*).

vantard, e (vɑ̃ta:r, ard) *a*, boastful. ¶ *n*, boaster, braggart. **vantardise** (tardi:z) & **vanterie** (tri) *f*, boast[ing], brag[ging]. **vanter** (te) *v.t*, to praise, extol, cry up, vaunt. **se** ~, to boast, vaunt, brag.

va-nu-pieds (vanypje) *n*, ragamuffin.

vapeur (vapœ:r) *f*, vapor; fume; mist; steam. *à* ~, steam (*engine, boat*). ¶ *m*, steamer, steamship, steamboat. ~-*citerne*, tank steamer. ~ *de charge*, cargo boat. ~ *de ligne* [*régulière*], liner. **vaporeux, euse** (pɔrø, ø:z) *a*, vaporous, -ry; misty; hazy; filmy, gauzy. **vaporisateur** (rizatœ:r) *m*, spray[er]; atomizer. **vaporiser (ze)** *v.t*, to vaporize; spray.

vaquer (vake) *v.i*, to be vacant (*employ*); not to sit (*court*). ~ *à*, to attend to.

varech (varɛk) *m*, seaweed, wrack.

varenne (varɛn) *f*, waste pasturage.

vareuse (varø:z) *f*, jumper (*sailor's*); blouse (*Mil.*); cardigan [jacket] (*woman's*).

variable (varjabl) *a*, variable, changeable, unsettled. *au* ~, at change (*barometer*). **variante** (rjɑ̃:t) *f*, variant. **variation** (rjasjɔ̃) *f*, variation, change.

varice (varis) *f*, varicose vein.

varicelle (varisɛl) *f*, chicken pox.

varier (varje) *v.t. & i*, to vary, change; variegate, diversify; differ. **variété** (rjete) *f*, variety; diversity; (*pl.*) miscellany.

variole (varjɔl) *f*, smallpox. **varioleux, euse** (lø, ø:z) *n*, smallpox case (*pers.*).

varlet (varlɛ) *m*, varlet (*Hist.*).

varlope (varlɔp) *f*, plane (*Carp.*).

Varsovie (varsɔvi) *f*, Warsaw.

vasculaire (vaskylɛ:r) *a*, vascular.

vase (vɑ:z) *f*, mud, silt, slime, ooze. ¶ *m*, vessel, vase. ~ *à filtrations chaudes*, beaker. ~ *clos*, retort. ~ *de nuit*, chamber pot.

vaseline (vazlin) *f*, vaseline.

vaseux, euse (vazø, ø:z) *a*, muddy, slimy.

vasistas (vazistɑ:s) *m*, transom; casement window.

vasque (vask) *f*, ornamental basin (*fountain*); bowl.

vassal, e (vasal) *n*, vassal (*Hist.*).

vaste (vast) *a*, vast, spacious, wide.

va-tout (vatu) *m*, (*one's*) all.

vaudeville (vodvil) *m*, vaudeville.

vaudoise (vodwa:z) *f*, dace.

vau-l'eau (à) (*volo*) *ad*, downstream; to rack & ruin.

vaurien, ne (vorjɛ̃, ɛn) *n*, blackguard; rascal.

vautour (votu:r) *m*, vulture.

vautre (votr) *m*, boar hound.

vautrer (se) (votre) *v.pr*, to wallow; sprawl.

veau (vo) *m*, calf; veal; calf[skin]. ~ *d'or*, golden calf. ~ *gras*, fatted c. ~ *raciné* (rasine), tree calf.

vécés (vese) *m.pl*, W.C., john, toilet.

vecteur (vɛktœ:r) *m*, vector.

vécu, e (veky) *p.a*, true to life (*novel, etc.*).

vedette (vədɛt) *f*, mounted sentry; scout (*warship*); motor boat; leader; leading counter; star (*Theat., film*). *en* ~, prominent[ly], in the limelight; starred; displayed in bold type. **vedettariat** (tarja) *m*, stardom; overemphasis on "star" personalities.

végétal, e (veʒetal) *a*, plant (*life*); vegetable. ¶ *m*, plant. **végétarien, ne** (tarjɛ̃, ɛn) *a. & n*, vegetarian. **végétarisme** (rism) *m*, vegetarianism. **végétation** (sjɔ̃) *f*, vegetation; growth. ~*s* [*adénoïdes*], adenoids. **végéter** (te) *v.i*, to vegetate.

véhémence (veemɑ̃:s) *f*, vehemence. **véhément, e†** (mɑ̃, ɑ̃:t) *a*, vehement.

véhicule (veikyl) *m*, vehicle; medium. **véhiculer** (le) *v.t*, to cart; convey.

veille (vɛ:j) *f*, watch, vigil, staying up; lookout; wakeful night; eve; day before; brink; point. **veillée** (vɛje) *f*, evening; vigil; night nursing; wake. **veiller** (je) *v.i. & t*, to sit up, stay up, lie awake; watch. ~ *à*, to see that. ~ *sur*, to look after, take care of. **veilleur, euse** (jœ:r, ø:z) *n*, watchman; watcher; (*f.*) night-light. *mettre en veilleuse*, to douse lights, cut back production.

veinard, e (vɛnɑ:r) *a*, lucky, fortunate.

veine (vɛn) *f*, vein; tricklet (*water*); luck. **veiner** (ne) *v.t*, to vein, grain.

vêler (vɛle) *v.i*, to calve.

vélin (velɛ̃) *m*, vellum.

velléité (vɛlleite) *f*, (*irresolute*) intention.

vélo (velo) *m*, bike. **vélocipède** (lɔsipɛd) *m*, velocipede; cycle. **vélocité** (te) *f*, swiftness. **vélodrome** (drɔ:m) *m*, cycle track.

velours (vəlu:r) *m*, velvet. ~ *à* [*grosses*] *côtes*, ~ *côtelé*, corduroy. ~ *de coton*, velveteen. **velouté, e** (lute) *a*, velvet[y].

velu, e (vəly) *a*, hairy (*skin, caterpillar, leaf*).

venaison (vənɛzɔ̃) *f*, venison.

vénal, e† (venal) *a*, venal; market[able], sale (*value*). **vénalité** (lite) *f*, venality.

venant (vənɑ̃) *m*, comer.

vendable (vãdabl) *a*, salable, marketable.

vendange (vãdã:ʒ) *f*, grape gathering; vintage. **vendanger** (dãʒe) *v.t. & abs*, to gather. **vendangeur, euse** (ʒœ:r, ø:z) *n*, vintager.

vendetta (vɛ̃dɛtta) *f*, vendetta, feud.

vendeur, euse (vãdœ:r, ø:z) *n*, seller, vendor; salesman, -woman. **vendeur, eresse** (dœ:r, drɛs) *n*, vendor (*law*). **vendre** (dr) *v.t*, to sell, sell at; sell for.

vendredi (vãdrədi) *m*, Friday. *le ~ saint*, Good Friday.

vénéneux, euse (venenø, ø:z) *a*, poisonous, venomous (*plant, food*).

vénérable (venerabl) *a*, venerable. **vénération** (sjɔ̃) *f*, veneration. **vénérer** (re) *v.t*, to venerate; worship (*saints, relics*).

vénerie (venri) *f*, hunting (*science*).

vénérien, ne (venerjɛ̃, ɛn) *a*, venereal.

Vénétie (la) (venesi), Venetia.

veneur (vənœ:r) *m*, huntsman.

vengeance (vãʒã:s) *f*, vengeance; revenge. **venger** (ʒe) *v.t*, to avenge, revenge. **vengeur, eresse** (ʒœ:r, ʒrɛs) *n*, avenger. ¶ *a*, avenging, vengeful.

véniel, le† (venjɛl) *a*, venial.

venimeux, euse (vənimø, ø:z) *a*, venomous, poisonous (*bite, animal, & fig.*). **venin** (nɛ̃) *m*, venom, poison.

venir (vəni:r) *v.i.ir*, to come; strike (*idea*); occur, happen; hail (*de =* from); grow. *en ~ aux mains,* to come to blows. *je viens de . . . ,* I have just . . .

Venise (vəni:z) *f*, Venice. **vénitien, ne** (venisjɛ̃, ɛn) *a. & V~, n*, Venetian.

vent (vã) *m*, wind; air; blast; draft; scent (*hunting*); inkling; windage; flatus. *~ coulis,* draft. *en plein ~,* in the open air. *îles du V~,* Windward Islands. *îles sous le V~,* Leeward Islands.

vente (vã:t) *f*, sale, selling. *~ à tempérament, ~ par abonnement,* installment plan. *~ aux*

enchères, auction sale. *~ de blanc,* white sale. *~ de charité,* [charity] bazaar.

venter (vãte) *v.imp*, to be windy, blow. **venteux, euse** (tø, ø:z) *a*, windy; breezy. **ventilateur** (tilatœ:r) *m*, fan, ventilator. **ventilation** (sjɔ̃) *f*, ventilation, airing; apportionment, analysis. **ventiler** (le) *v.t*, to ventilate, etc.

ventouse (vãtu:z) *f*, cupping glass; air hole; sucker (*of leech*); boring or leechlike person. *voiture ~,* car parked in same spot for long time. **ventouser** (tuze) *v.t*, to cup (*Surg.*).

ventral, e (vãtral) *a*, ventral. **ventre** (vã:tr) *m*, belly, abdomen; womb; bulge; bilge (*cask*). *faire [le] ~,* to bulge, belly. **ventrée** (vãtre) *f*, litter (*pups, etc.*).

ventricule (vãtrikyl) *m*, ventricle.

ventriloque (vãtrilɔk) *n*, ventriloquist. **ventriloquie** (ki) *f*, ventriloquism, -quy.

ventru, e (vãtry) *a*, paunchy.

venu, e (vəny) *n*, comer; (*f.*) coming; appearance; inrush; occurrence; growth. ¶ *a*, come. *le premier ~,* the first to come; anybody. *mal ~,* displeasing; unwelcome.

vêpres (vɛ:pr) *f.pl*, vespers, evensong.

ver (vɛ:r) *m*, worm; grub; maggot; moth. *~ à soie,* silkworm. *~ luisant,* glowworm. *~ rongeur,* canker[worm]; remorse. *~ solitaire,* tapeworm.

véracité (verasite) *f*, veracity, truthfulness.

véranda (verãda) *f*, veranda.

verbal, e† (vɛrbal) *a*, verbal. **verbaliser** (lize) *v.i*, to take particulars; draw up a report. **verbe** (vɛrb) *m*, verb; [tone of] voice. *le Verbe,* the Word (*Theol.*). **verbeux, euse** (bø, ø:z) *a*, verbose, prosy; wordy. **verbiage** (bja:ʒ) *m*, verbiage. **verbosité** (bozite) *f*, verbosity, wordiness, prosiness.

verdal (vɛrdal) *m*, pavement light.

verdâtre (vɛrdɑ:tr) *a*, greenish.

verdelet, te (dəlɛ, ɛt) *a*, tartish (*wine*); hale. **verdet** (dɛ) *m*, verdigris. **verdeur** (dœːr) *f*, greenness; unripeness; tartness.

verdict (vɛrdikt) *m*, verdict.

verdier (vɛrdje) *m*, greenfinch. **verdir** (diːr) *v.t. & i*, to green. **verdoyant, e** (dwajɑ̃, ɑ̃ːt) *a*, verdant. **verdoyer** (je) *v.i*, to green. **verdure** (dyːr) *f*, verdure; greenery; greenness; greensward; greens.

véreux, euse (verø, øːz) *a*, wormy, maggoty, grubby; shady, bogus, fishy; bad (*debt*).

verge (vɛrʒ) *f*, rod; wand, verge; beam (*scales*); shank (*anchor*); (*vulgar*) penis; (*pl.*) birch [rod]. **vergé** (ʒe) *a*, laid (*paper*). **verger** (ʒe) *m*, orchard. **vergeture** (ʒətyːr) *f*, weal.

verglas (vɛrglɑ) *m*, glazed frost, silver thaw.

vergne (vɛrɲ) *m*, alder [tree].

vergogne (sans) (vɛrgɔɲ), shameless.

vergue (vɛrg) *f*, yard (*Naut.*).

véridique† (veridik) *a*, truthful, veracious. **vérificateur** (fikatœːr) *m*, examiner, inspector; gauge; calipers. ~ *comptable*, auditor. **vérification** (sjɔ̃) *f*, verification, inspection, examination, checking, vouching, audit[ing]. ~ *de testament*, probate. **vérifier** (fje) *v.t*, to verify.

vérin (verɛ̃) *m*, jack (*Mach.*); actuator, control (*Avn.*). ~ *d'escamotage*, retraction actuator.

véritable† (veritabl) *a*, true; real; veritable; regular. **vérité** (te) *f*, truth, verity; fact.

vermeil, le (vɛrmɛːj) *a*, vermillion; ruby, rosy. ¶ *m*, silver gilt.

vermicelle (vɛrmisɛl) *m*, vermicelli; v. soup.

vermillon (vɛrmijɔ̃) *m*, vermillion.

vermine (vɛrmin) *f*, vermin. **vermoulu, e** (muly) *a*, wormeaten. **vermoulure** (lyːr) *f*, wormhole; dust from wormholes.

vermouth (vɛrmut) *m*, vermouth.

vernal, e (vɛrnal) *a*, vernal, spring (*att.*).

verne (vɛrn) *m*, alder [tree].

verni, e (vɛrni) *a*, varnished, as *vernir*; patent (*leather*), patent leather (*shoes*). ¶ *m.pl*, patent leather shoes; dress shoes.

vernier (vɛrnje) *m*, vernier.

vernir (vɛrniːr) *v.t*, to varnish; japan; gloss over. **vernis** (ni) *m*, varnish; japan; glaze; veneer (*fig.*). ~ *à l'alcool*, spirit varnish. ~ *gras*, oil varnish. **vernissage** (nisaːʒ) *m*, varnishing, varnishing day, private viewing (*art exhibit*). **vernisser** (se) *v.t*, to glaze (*pottery*).

vérole (verɔl) *m*, syphilis. *petite* ~, smallpox. *quelle* ~, what a pain in the ass.

Vérone (verɔn) *f*, Verona.

véronique (verɔnik) *f*, speedwell, veronica.

verrat (vera) *m*, boar.

verre (vɛːr) *m*, glass. ~ *à vin*, wineglass. ~ *de vin*, glass of wine. ~ *soluble*, water glass. ~ *pilé*, ground g. ~ *perdu*, nondeposit bottle. **verrerie** (verri) *f*, glass making; g. works; glass[ware]. **verrier** (rje) *m*, glass maker. **verrière** (rjɛːr) *f*, stained-glass window. **verroterie** (rɔtri) *f*, [small] glassware; [glass] beads.

verrou (veru) *m*, bolt. *sous les* ~*s*, under lock & key, locked up. **verrouiller** (ruje) *v.t*, to bolt; lock up (*prisoner*).

verrue (very) *f*, wart. **verruqueux, euse** (kø, øːz) *a*, warty.

vers (vɛːr) *m*, verse, line (*poetry*). ~ *blancs*, blank verse. ¶ *pr*, towards; to; about.

versant (vɛrsɑ̃) *m*, side, slope (*hill*).

versatile (vɛrsatil) *a*, fickle. **versatilité** (lite) *f*, fickleness.

verse (vɛrs) *f*, laying, lodging (*corn*). *à* ~, fast, hard (*rain*). **versé(e) dans** (se), versed in, conversant with. **versement** (səmɑ̃) *m*, payment, paying in; p. up; remittance; installment; call; deposit (*savings bank*); pouring; spilling, etc. **verser** (se) *v.t. & i*, to pour [out]; shed, spill; tip;

overturn, upset, capsize; pay; p. in, p. up; deposit; issue (*Bible*). **verset** (sɛ) *m*, verse (*Bible*); **versicle** (*Lit.*). **verseuse** (sø:z) *f*, coffeepot.

versificateur (versifikatœ:r) *m*, versifier. **versifier** (fje) *v.i. & t*, to versify. **version** (sjɔ̃) *f*, version; translation. ~ *originale*, film shown in original language.

verso (verso) *m*, verso, back. *au* ~, overleaf.

vert, e (vɛ:r, ɛrt) *a*, green; verdant; unripe; unseasoned; callow; raw; sour; sharp; fresh; hale; smutty. *donner le feu* ~, to authorize. ¶ *m*, green; grass. **vert-degris** (verdəgri) *m*, verdigris.

vertébral, e (vɛrtebral) *a*, vertebral; spinal (*column*). **vertèbre** (tɛ:br) *f*, vertebra. **vertébré, e** (tebre) *a. & m*, vertebrate; (*m. pl.*) Vertebrata.

vertement (vɛrtəmɑ̃) *ad*, sharply, soundly.

vertical, e (vɛrtikal) *a*, vertical, upright. ¶ *f*, vertical. **verticalement** (lmɑ̃) *ad*, vertically; down (*crossword clues*).

verticille (vɛrtisil) *m*, verticil, whorl.

vertige (vɛrti:ʒ) *m*, dizziness; giddiness; vertigo. **vertigineux, euse** (tiʒinø, ø:z) *a*, dizzy, giddy. **vertigo** (go) *m*, staggers (*Vet.*).

vertu (vɛrty) *f*, virtue. *en* ~ *de*, in (*or* by) v. of; in pursuance of. **vertueux, euse†** (tɥø, ø:z) *a*, virtuous; righteous.

verve (vɛrv) *f*, verve.

verveine (vɛrvɛn) *f*, verbena.

vesce (vɛs) *f*, vetch, tare.

vésicatoire (vezikatwa:r) *m*, blister (*plaster*). **vésicule** (kyl) *f*, vesicle, bladder. ~ *biliaire*, gall b.

vespasienne (vɛspazjɛn) *f*, urinal (*street*).

vessie (vɛsi) *f*, bladder. *prendre des* ~*s pour des lanternes*, not to know which end is up.

vestale (vɛstal) *f*, vestal [virgin].

veste (vɛst) *f*, jacket (*short, usually waiter's, etc.*). **vestiaire** (tjɛ:r) *m*, cloakroom; dressing room; locker r.

vestibule (vɛstibyl) *m*, vestibule, [entrance] hall, lobby.

vestige (vɛsti:ʒ) *m*, footprint, track, trace; (*pl.*) vestiges, remains.

veston (vɛstɔ̃) *m*, jacket (*man's*); lounge coat. ~ *d'intérieur*, smoking jacket.

Vésuve (le) (vezy:v) Vesuvius. **vésuvien, ne** (zyvjɛ̃, ɛn) *a*, Vesuvian.

vêtement (vɛtmɑ̃) *m*, garment; vestment; (*pl.*) clothes, clothing. ~ *de dessous*, undergarment (*woman's*); (*pl.*) underclothing, underwear (*women's*).

vétéran (veterɑ̃) *m*, veteran; long-service man (*Mil.*). **vétérance** (rɑ̃:s) *f*, long service.

vétérinaire (veterinɛ:r) *a*, veterinary. [*médecin*] ~, *m*, veterinary [surgeon].

vétille (veti:j) *f*, trifle. **vétilleux, euse** (tijø, ø:z) *a*, finical, ticklish.

vêtir (veti:r) *v.t.ir*, to clothe, dress.

veto (veto) *m*, veto.

vêture (vɛty:r) *f*, taking the habit, taking the veil (*Eccl.*).

vétusté (vetyste) *f*, decay, [old] age.

veuf, veuve (vœf, vœ:v) *a*, widowed; deprived, bereft. ¶ *m*, widower. ¶ *f*, widow, relict.

veuillez *see* **vouloir.**

veule (vœ:l) *a*, slack, flabby.

veuvage (vœva:ʒ) *m*, widowerhood, widowhood.

vexatoire (vɛksatwa:r) *a*, vexatious. **vexer** (kse) *v.t*, to vex, provoke.

viabilité (vjabilite) *f*, good condition (*of roads*); viability. **viable** (bl) *a*, viable.

viaduc (vjadyk) *m*, viaduct.

viager, ère (vjaʒe, ɛ:r) *a*, life (*att.*), for life. *rente* ~*e*, life annuity.

viande (vjɑ̃:d) *f*, meat. ~ *de boucherie*, butcher's meat. ~ *de cheval*, horseflesh.

viatique (vjatik) *m*, provision for journey; viaticum.

vibration (vibrasjɔ̃) *f*, vibration (*Phys.*). **vibrer** (bre) *v.i*, to vibrate (*Phys. & fig.*).

vicaire (vikɛ:r) *m*, vicar; curate. **vicariat** (karja) *m*, vicariate; curacy.

vice (vis) *m*, vice; defect, fault, flaw.

vice (vis) *prefix*, vice: ~-*président*, *e*, *n*, vice- (*or* deputy) chairman *or* president. ~-*roi*, *m*, viceroy.

vicelard, e (visla:r, ard) *a*, vicious, cunning; depraved. ¶ *n*, depraved person.

Vicence (visã:s) *f*, Vicenza.

vicier (visje) *v.t*, to vitiate, foul. **vicieux, euse**† (sjø, ø:z) *a*, vicious; faulty; unsound. *locution vicieuse*, faulty expression (*Gram.*).

vicinal, e (visinal) *a*, parish, local (*road*).

vicissitude (visisityd) *f*, vicissitude.

vicomte (vikõ:t) *m*, viscount. **vicomtesse** (vikõtes) *f*, viscountess.

victime (viktim) *f*, victim; casualty; sufferer.

victoire (viktwa:r) *f*, victory; win. **victoria** (tɔrja) *f*, victoria (*carriage*). **victorieux, euse**† (rjø, ø:z) *a*, victorious, triumphant.

victuailles (viktɥa:j) *f.pl*, victuals.

vidange (vidã:ʒ) *f*, emptying; clearing; ullage; (*pl.*) night soil. *en* ~, ullaged (*cask*). **vidanger** (dãʒe) *v.t*, to empty. **vidangeur** (ʒœ:r) *m*, nightman. **vide** (vid) *a*, empty, void; idle. ¶ *m*, void; vacuum; space; gap; vacancy; empty (*case*). *à* ~, [when] empty. ~-*pomme*, *m*, apple corer. ~-*poche*, *m*, pin tray; glove compartment (*auto*). ~-*vite*, *m*, fuel jettison apparatus. **vider** (de) *v.t*, to empty, vacate (*les lieux* = the premises); settle (*dispute*); thresh out; bore (*cannon*); draw (*fowl*); gut (*fish*); stone (*fruit*); core (*apple, etc.*); dump (*computers*).

viduité (vidɥite) *f*, widowhood.

vie (vi) *f*, life; lifetime; living, livelihood. *la* ~ *à trois*, the eternal triangle. *à* ~, for life.

vieil, vieille *see* vieux.

vieillard (vjeja:r) *m*, old man. *les* ~*s*, the aged (*either sex*). **vieilleries** (jri) *f.pl*, old things. **vieillesse** (jɛs) *f*, [old] age. **vieilli, e** (ji) *a*, antiquated; obsolete, archaic; aged. **vieillir** (ji:r) *v.i*, to grow old, age, become obsolete;

(*v.t.*) to age, make [look] old[er]. **vieillissant, e** (jisã, ã:t) *a*, aging; obsolescent. **vieillot, te** (jo, ɔt) *a*, oldish, quaint. ¶ *n*, little old man, little old woman.

Vienne (vjɛn) *f*, Vienna. **viennois, e** (nwa, a:z) *a*. & **V**~, *n*, Viennese.

vierge (vjɛrʒ) *f*, virgin, maid. ¶ *a*, virgin; blank (*page*); free; unexposed (*Phot.*).

vieux, vieil, vieille (vjø, vjɛ:j) *a*, old; stale; obsolete, archaic. *vieille fille*, old maid. **vieux, vieille**, *n*, old man, old woman. *le vieux*, the old (*opp.* the new). *les vieux*, the old (*either sex*).

vif, vive (vif, i:v) *a*, alive; live; living; quick; lively; sprightly; brisk; smart; sharp; vital; keen; crisp, tangy; hasty; spirited; vivid; bright; spring (*water, tide*). *de vive force*, by main (*or* sheer) force. *de vive voix*, by word of mouth, viva voce. *le vif*, the quick (*flesh, etc.*); the heart (*of a matter*); life (*art*). **vif-argent**, *m*, quicksilver.

vigie (viʒi) *f*, lookout; lookout [man]; vigia.

vigilance (viʒilã:s) *f*, vigilance, watchfulness. **vigilant, e** (lã, ã:t) *a*, vigilant, watchful. **vigile** (ʒil) *f*, vigil, eve (*Eccl.*).

vigne (viɲ) *f*, vine, vineyard. ~ *vierge*, Virginia creeper. **vigneron, ne** (ɲərõ, ɔn) *n*, winegrower. **vignette** (ɲɛt) *f*, vignette; cut; ornamental border; revenue label; car license (*special auto tax*). **vignoble** (ɲɔbl) *m*, vineyard.

vigogne (vigɔɲ) *f*, vicugna, vicuña.

vigoureux, euse† (vigurø, ø:z) *a*, vigorous, strong, forceful; stout, sturdy, robust, lusty; plucky (*Phot.*). **vigueur** (gœ:r) *f*, vigor, strength. *mettre en* ~, to put in force, enforce.

vil, e† (vil) *a*, vile, base, mean. *à vil prix*, dirt-cheap. **vilain, e**† (lɛ̃, ɛn) *a*, ugly; wretched; nasty; scurvy; naughty. ¶ *n*, villain, villein (*Hist.*); naughty boy, girl, villain; scurvy fellow.

vilebrequin (vilbrəkɛ̃) *m*, brace, bit stock; wimble; crank shaft.

vilenie (vilni) *f*, meanness; dirty trick; abuse. **vileté** (lte) *f*, cheapness; worthlessness. **vilipender** (lipãde) *v.t*, to vilify.

villa (vila) *f*, villa. **village** (vila:ʒ) *m*, village. **villageois, e** (laʒwa, a:z) *n*, villager; (*att.*) rustic, country. **ville** (vil) *f*, town, city. ~ *d'eaux,* watering place, spa. *hôtel de* ~, town hall, city h. **villégiature** (leʒjaty:r) *f*, stay in the country; holiday.

vin (vɛ̃) *m*, wine. ~ *blanc du Rhin,* hock. ~ *ordinaire,* table wine. ~ *de liqueur,* sweet dessert wine. ~ *du cru,* wine of the country. ~ *en cercles,* wine in the wood. ~ *de marque,* vintage wine. ~ *mousseux,* sparkling wine. **vinage** (vina:ʒ) *m*, fortification (*of wine*). **vinaigre** (nɛgr) *m*, vinegar. **vinaigrer** (nɛgre) *v.t*, to vinegar. **vinaigrette** (nɛgrɛt) *f*, oil & vinegar dressing. **vinaigrerie** (grəri) *f*, vinegar works.

vindas (vɛ̃da:s) *m*, crab [capstan]; giant['s] stride.

vindicatif, ive (vɛ̃dikatif, i:v) *a*, vindictive, revengeful; avenging. **vindicte** (dikt) *f*, (*public*) prosecution (*of crime*).

vinée (vine) *f*, vintage (*crop*). **viner** (ne) *v.t*, to fortify (*wine*). **vineux, euse** (nø, ø:z) *a*, vinous; winy; full-bodied (*wine*); rich in vineyards; rich in wines.

vingt (vɛ̃) *a*, twenty. ¶ *m*, twenty; 20th. ~*deux!* watch it! look out! **vingtaine** (tɛ:n) *f*, score, twenty [or so]. **vingtième** (tjɛm) *a.* & *n*, twentieth.

vinicole (vinikɔl) *a*, wine-growing. **vinosité** (nozite) *f*, vinosity.

viol (vjɔl) *m*, rape, ravishment. **violacé, e** (vjɔlase) *a*, violaceous. **violacées,** *f.pl*, Violaceae.

violariacée (vjɔlarjase) *f*, viola (*Bot.*); (*pl.*) Viola (*genus*).

violateur, trice (vjɔlatœ:r, tris) *a*, violator; transgressor. **violation** (sjɔ̃) *f*, violation, transgression, breach; desecration.

violâtre (vjɔla:tr) *a*, purplish.

viole (vjɔl) *f*, viol; jackscrew.

violemment (vjɔlamɑ̃) *ad*, violently. **violence** (lɑ̃:s) *f*, violence;

duress; stress. **violent, e** (lɑ̃, ɑ̃:t) *a*, violent. **violenter** (lɑ̃te) *v.t*, to do violence to. **violer** (le) *v.t*, to violate, transgress, break; rape, ravish; desecrate.

violet, te (vjɔlɛ, ɛt) *a*, violet, purple. **violet,** *m*, violet (*color*). **violette,** *f*, violet (*Bot.*). ~ *de chien,* dog v. ~ *de Parme,* Parma v. ~ *odorante,* sweet v. **violier** (lje) *m*, stock. ~ *jaune,* wallflower.

violon (vjɔlɔ̃) *m*, violin, fiddle; lockup, clink. **violoncelle** (sɛl) *m*, violoncello, [']cello. **violoncelliste** (list) *n*, [violon]cellist. **violoniste** (lɔnist) *n*, violinist.

vipère (vipɛ:r) *f*, viper, adder.

virage (vira:ʒ) *m*, turning, slewing, swinging; tacking (*Naut.*); turn, bend, corner; toning (*Phot.*).

virago (virago) *f*, amazon (*forceful woman*).

virement (virmɑ̃) *m*, turning; tacking (*Naut.*); bank transfer; transfer (*Bkkpg.*). **virer** (re) *v.i*, to turn; bank (*Avn.*); heave (*Naut.*); (*v.t.*) to transfer; tone (*Phot.*). ~ *de bord,* to tack (*Naut.*).

vireux, euse (virø, ø:z) *a*, noxious.

virginal, e† (virʒinal) *a*, virginal, maiden[ly]. **virginie** (ni) *m*, Virginia [tobacco]. **la V~,** Virginia (*Geog.*). **virginité** (te) *f*, virginity, maidenhood.

virgule (virgyl) *f*, comma. ~ [*décimale*], decimal point. *Note:* — The decimal point is indicated in French by a comma.

viril, e (viril) *a*, virile, manly. **virilité** (lite) *f*, virility, manliness; manhood.

virole (virɔl) *f*, ferrule.

virtuel, le (virtɥɛl) *a*, virtual. **virtuellement** (lmɑ̃) *ad*, virtually, to all intents & purposes.

virtuose (virtɥo:z) *n*, virtuoso. **virtuosite** (ozite) *f*, virtuosity.

virulence (virylɑ̃:s) *f*, virulence. **virulent, e** (lɑ̃, ɑ̃:t) *a*, virulent. **virus** (ry:s) *m*, virus.

vis (vis) *f*, screw. ~ *ailée,* wing s. ~ *d'Archimède* (arʃimɛd), Archimedean s. ~ *sans fin,* worm.

visa (viza) *m*, visa; initials, signature.

visage (viza:ʒ) *m*, face, visage; aspect. *à ~ découvert*, barefacedly.

vis-à-vis (vizavi) & *~ de*, *pr.* & *ad*, opposite, o. to; face to face; facing; vis-à-vis; towards. ¶ *m*, person opposite; vis-à-vis.

viscères (visɛ:r) *m.pl*, viscera.

viscose (visko:z) *f*, viscose. **viscosité** (kozite) *f*, viscosity, stickiness.

visée (vize) *f*, sight[ing], observation, aim; (*pl.*), aims, designs, ambition. **viser** (ze) *v.t*, to aim at; sight; cater for; visa; initial, sign; refer to; have in view; certify. *~ à*, to aim at. **viseur** (zœ:r) *m*, [view]finder (*Phot.*); dial (*calculating mach.*). *~ redresseur*, collapsible viewfinder. **visibilité** (zibilite) *f*, visibility. **visible**† (bl) *a*, visible; obvious; at home. *pas ~*, engaged; not accessible. **visière** (zjɛ:r) *f*, peak (*cap*); eyeshade; visor (*Hist.*). **vision** (zjɔ̃) *f*, vision, sight; seeing; fantasy; hallucination. **visionnaire** (zjɔnɛ:r) *a*. & *n*, visionary.

visioconférence (vizjɔkɔ̃ferɑ̃:s) *f*, videoconference.

visitation (vizitasjɔ̃) *f*, visitation (*Eccl.*). **visite** (zit) *f*, visit, call; attendance; inspection, examination, survey. **visiter** (te) *v.t*, to visit. **visiteur, euse** (tœ:r, ø:z) *n*, visitor, caller; inspector, examiner.

vison (vizɔ̃) *m*, mink (*Zool.* & *fur*).

visqueux, euse (viskø, ø:z) *a*, viscous, sticky, tacky.

visser (vise) *v.t*, to screw [on, down, up].

Vistule (la) (vistyl) , the Vistula.

visu (vizy) *f*, display device (*computers*).

visuel, le (vizɥɛl) *a*, visual, (*line, etc.*) of sight. ¶ *m*, display device (*computers*).

vital, e (vital) *a*, vital. **vitalité** (lite) *f*, vitality. **vitamine** (min) *f*, vitamin.

vite (vit) *a*, swift, quick, fast. ¶ *ad*, quick[ly], fast.

vitesse (vitɛs) *f*, speed, velocity, quickness. *première ~*, low gear.

viticole (vitikɔl) *a*, viticultural. **viticulteur** (kyltœ:r) *m*, viticultur[al]ist, winegrower. **viticulture** (ty:r) *f*, viticulture.

vitrage (vitra:ʒ) *m*, glazing; windows, glass work; glass door; curtain net, vitrage. **vitrail** (tra:j) *m*, leaded window. *vitraux peints*, stained glass. **vitre** (tr) *f*, [window] pane. **vitrer** (tre) *v.t*, to glaze (*window*). **vitrerie** (trəri) *f*, glaziery. **vitreux, euse** (trø, ø:z) *a*, vitreous, glassy; lackluster. **vitrier** (trie) *m*, glazier. **vitrifier** (fje) *v.t*, to vitrify. **vitrine** (trin) *f*, glass case, showcase; display cabinet, china cabinet; curio cabinet; shop window.

vitriol (vitriɔl) *m*, vitriol.

vitupération (vityperasjɔ̃) *f*, abuse. **vitupérer** (pere) *v.t*, to abuse. *v.i*, to protest against.

vivable (vivabl) *a*, livable.

vivace (vivas) *a*, long-lived; inveterate; perennial (*Bot.*). **vivacité** (site) *f*, vivacity, liveliness; heat; hastiness; petulance; vividness.

vivandier, ère (vivɑ̃dje, ɛːr) *n*, sutler, canteen-keeper.

vivant, e (vivɑ̃, ɑ̃:t) *a*, alive; living; lifelike; live; modern (*language*); lively; vivid. ¶ *m*, living being; lifetime, life. **vivat** (vat) *i*. & *m*, hurrah, -ray!; cheer. **vive-eau**, *f*, spring tide. **vivement** (vmɑ̃) *ad*, briskly; sharply; keenly; warmly. **viveur** (vœ:r) *m*, gay man, fast liver, rake. **vivier** (vje) *m*, fish pond. **vivifier** (vifje) *v.t*, to vivify, quicken; vitalize; invigorate, brace. **vivipare** (pa:r) *a*, viviparous. **vivisection** (sɛksjɔ̃) *f*, vivisection. **vivoter** (vivɔte) *v.i*, to scrape by; live from hand to mouth. **vivre** (vi:vr) *v.i.* & *t. ir*, to live; be alive; subsist; endure; behave. ¶ *m*, living; food; (*pl.*) provisions, victuals; rations. *le ~* & *le couvert*, room & board.

vizir (vizi:r) *m*, vizier.

vocable (vɔkabl) *m*, vocable. **vocabulaire** (bylɛ:r) *m*, vocabulary. **vocal, e** (kal) *a*, vocal. **vocaliser**

(lize) *v.t.* to vocalize. **vocatif** (katif) *m,* vocative [case]. **vocation** (sjɔ̃) *f,* vocation, calling; call (*divine*).

vociférer (vɔsifere) *v.i.* to vociferate, shout, bawl, yell.

vœu (vø) *m,* vow; wish; prayer.

vogue (vɔg) *f,* fashion, vogue; request; run. *vogue la galère!,* come what may! **voguer** (ge) *v.i,* to row; sail.

voici (vwasi) *pr,* here is, here are; here; this is. *me ~!* here I am.

voie (vwa) *f,* way; road; route; track; line; duct; scent; means; course; process. *~ de départ,* aircraft runway. *~ d'eau,* leak; waterway. *~s de fait,* assault [& battery]; blows, violence, force. *~ de garage,* siding. *~ ferrée,* railway. *~ lactée,* Milky Way, galaxy. *~ navigable,* waterway. *~ publique,* public thoroughfare, highway. *~ à double sens,* two-way street.

voilà (vwala) *pr,* there is, there are; that is.

voile (vwal) *f,* sail, canvas. ¶ *m,* veil; velum; cloth; voile; mist; fog; mask; blind. **voiler** (le) *v.t,* to veil; cloak; muffle; fog; [en]shroud; buckle. **voilerie** (lri) *f,* sail loft; sailmaking. **voilier** (lje) *m,* sail maker; sailing ship; (*good, bad*) sailer (*ship*). **voilure** (ly:r) *f,* sails (*col.*); buckling.

voir (vwa:r) *v.t. & abs. ir,* to see; look [at, on]; behold; sight; understand; examine; visit. *faire ~,* to show.

voire (vwa:r) *ad,* nay; even. *~ même,* & even, indeed.

voirie (vwari) *f,* highways committee; refuse dump.

voisin, e (vwazɛ̃, in) *a,* neighboring; aking; next. ¶ *n,* neighbor. **voisinage** (zina:ʒ) *m,* neighborhood; vicinity. **voisiner** (ne) *v.i,* to border on, be near.

voiture (vwaty:r) *f,* conveyance; carriage; coach; car; wagon; cart; van. *en ~!* all aboard! *~ cellulaire,* patrol wagon. *~ d'enfant,* baby carriage. *~ de course,* racing car. *~ d'occasion,* second hand c. *~ hors série,* custom-built

c. **voiturer** (tyre) *v.t,* to convey, carry, cart. **voiturette** (rɛt) *f,* trap; light car, runabout. **voiturier** (rje) *m,* carter; carrier.

voix (vwa) *f,* voice; register; speech; word; dictate[s]; opinion; say; vote. *~ de stentor* (stɑ̃tɔ:r), stentorian voice. *de vive ~,* by word of mouth.

vol (vɔl) *m,* flying, flight; wing; flock (*birds*). *~ à voile,* gliding (*Avn.*). *à ~ d'oiseau,* as the crow flies. *~ piqué,* dive (*Avn.*).

vol (vɔl) *m,* theft, stealing, robbery. *~ à l'américaine,* confidence trick. *~ à l'étalage,* shoplifting. *~ à la tire,* pocket, picking; bag snatching. *~ à main armée,* armed robbery. *~ de grand chemin,* highway robbery. *~ [de nuit avec effraction],* burglary.

volage (vɔla:ʒ) *a,* fickle, inconstant.

volaille (vɔla:j) *f,* poultry, fowls; police (*pejorative*).

volant, e (vɔlɑ̃, ɑ̃:t) *a,* flying; loose; portable. *soucoupe ~e,* flying saucer. ¶ *m,* shuttlecock; leaf (*opp.* counterfoil); flywheel; sail (*windmill*); flounce. [*jeu de*] *~,* battledore & shuttlecock. *feuille ~e,* looseleaf. *~ au filet,* badminton. *~ de direction,* steering wheel.

volatil, e (vɔlatil) *a,* volatile. **volatile** (til) *m,* winged creature. **volatiliser** (lize) *v.t,* to volatilize. *se~,* to volatilize; vanish.

volcan (vɔlkɑ̃) *m,* volcano. **volcanique** (kanik) *a,* volcanic.

volée (vɔle) *f,* flight; wing; flock; volley; peal (*bells*); rank (*class*); splinter bar, swingle-tree; chase (*gun*). *~ de coups,* drubbing. *à la ~,* in the air; on the wing; promptly; broadcast; at random. **voler** (le) *v.i,* to fly; (*v.t.*) to chase, fly at (*hawking*); steal, rob. **volerie** (lri) *f,* hawking (*falconry*); thieving.

volet (vɔlɛ) *m,* shutter; volet; sorting board; flap (*Avn.*); wipe (*cinema*).

voleter (vɔlte) *v.i,* to flutter; flit; skip.

voleur, euse (vɔlœ:r, ø:z) *n,*

thief, robber; (att.) thievish (pers.). ~ à la tire, pickpocket; bag snatcher. ~ de grand chemin, highwayman.

volière (vɔljɛːr) f, aviary; run (pheasants, etc.).

volige (vɔliːʒ) f, batten; lath.

volition (vɔlisjɔ̃) f, volition.

volontaire† (vɔlɔ̃tɛːr) a, voluntary; wilful, wayward. ¶ m, volunteer (Mil.). volonté (te) f, will; (pl.) whims. dernières ~s, last will & testament. volontiers (tje) ad, willingly, gladly; fain; apt, rather.

volt (vɔlt) m, volt. voltage (taːʒ) m, voltage. voltaïque (taik) a, voltaic.

volte-face (vɔltəfas) f, about-face; change of front.

voltige (vɔltiːʒ) f, trick riding & similar circus gymnastics. voltiger (tiʒe) v.i, to fly about, flit, hover; flutter, flap; perform on horseback; perform on the slack rope.

voltmètre (vɔltmɛtr) m, voltmeter.

volubile (vɔlybil) a, twining (Bot.); voluble, glib (speaker). volubilis (lis) m, convolvulus. volubilité (lite) f, volubility, glibness.

volume (vɔlym) m, volume; tome; bulk; measurement. volumineux, euse (minø, øːz) a, voluminous, bulky.

volupté (vɔlypte) f, voluptuousness, pleasure, delight. voluptueux, euse† (tɥø, øːz) a, voluptuous. ¶ n, voluptuary.

volute (vɔlyt) f, volute, scroll.

vomir (vɔmiːr) v.t. & abs, to vomit, spew, belch out. vomissement (mismɑ̃) m, vomiting; vomit. vomitif (mitif) m, emetic, vomitory.

vorace† (vɔras) a, voracious. voracité (site) f, voracity.

vos see votre.

votant (vɔtɑ̃) m, voter. votation (tasjɔ̃) f, voting. vote (vɔt) m, vote, poll. voter (te) v.i. & t, to vote; pass, carry. ~ à main levée, to vote by a show of hands. votif, ive (tif, iːv) a, votive.

votre, pl. vos (vɔtr, vo) a, your.

~ affectionné, e, yours affectionately. vôtre (voːtr) a, yours. le vôtre, la vôtre, les vôtres, yours, your own.

vouer (vwe) v.t, to vow; dedicate; devote.

vouloir (vulwaːr) m, will. ¶ v.t.ir, to will; want; wish; like; [be] please[d to]; mean; intend; require, need. en ~ à, to bear ill will. s'en ~ de, to be angry with oneself for. veuillez agréer, please accept. voulu, e (ly) p.a, required, requisite; deliberate, intentional; studied. en temps ~, in due time.

vous (vu) pn, you; ye; to you; yourself, yourselves; each other. ~-même, ~-mêmes, yourself, yourselves.

voussoir (vuswaːr) m, voussoir, arch stone. voûte (vut) f, vault, arch; dome; canopy. ~ palatine, ~ du palais, roof of the mouth. voûté, e (te) p.a, vaulted; arched; stooping, bent, round-shouldered. voûter (te) v.t, to vault, arch; bow.

voyage (vwajaːʒ) m, journey, voyage, trip, tour. voyager (jaʒe) v.i, to travel; journey; migrate. voyageur, euse (ʒœːr) øːʒ) n, traveler; passenger, fare.

voyant, e (vwajɑ̃, ɑ̃ːt) a, seeing; gaudy, garish; showy; conspicuous. ¶ n, clairvoyant.

voyelle (vwajɛl) f, vowel.

voyer (vwaje) m, surveyor (roads).

voyou (vwaju) m, guttersnipe; hooligan.

vrac (en) (vrak), in bulk; loose.

vrai, e (vrɛ) a, true, truthful; real, genuine; right; downright, thorough, arrant. vrai & vraiment (mɑ̃) ad, truly, really; indeed. vrai, m, truth. vraisemblable† (sɑ̃blabl) a, probable, likely. vraisemblance (blɑ̃ːs) f, probability, likelihood, verisimilitude.

vrille (vriːj) f, tendril; gimlet, tailspin (Avn.). vriller (vrije) v.t, to bore; (v.i.) to kink, corkscrew. vrillette (jɛt) f, deathwatch [beetle].

vrombir (vrɔ̃biːr) v.i, to buzz; throb; purr; whirr; hum. vrom-

bissement (bismã) *m*, buzzing, hum, etc.

vu (vy) *m*, sight, inspection. ¶ *pr*, considering, seeing. ~ *que*, seeing that; whereas.

vue (vy) *f*, [eye]sight; eyes, eye; view; sight; prospect, outlook; slide; window, light. ~ *cavalière*, ~ *à vol d'oiseau*, bird's-eye view. ~*s fondantes*, dissolving views. *à* ~ *d'œil*, at a rough estimate; visibly. *à* ~ *de nez*, a rough guess. *prise de* ~*s*, shooting (*cinema, TV*). ~ *en coupe*, sectional drawing.

vulcain (vylkẽ) *m*, red admiral (*butterfly*).

vulcaniser (vylkanize) *v.t*, to vulcanize.

vulgaire† (vylgɛːr) *a*, vulgar; common; low; everyday; vernacular. **le** ~, the common people, the vulgar [herd]. **vulgariser** (garize) *v.t*, to popularize; vulgarize. **vulgarité** (te) *f*, vulgarity. **la Vulgate** (gat), the Vulgate.

vulnérable (vylnerabl) *a*, vulnerable.

W

wagon (vagɔ̃) (*Rly.*) *m*, carriage, coach, car; wagon, truck. ~*-lit*, sleeping car. ~ *de marchandise*, freight car. ~*-poste*, mail car. ~*-restaurant*, restaurant car, dining car. ~*-salon*, observation car, parlor c. ~*-citerne*, tank c.

wagonnet (vagɔnɛ) *m*, dump truck.

warrant (warãːt) *m*, warrant (*dock, warehouse*).

waters (watɛːr) *pl.m*, toilet, lavatory, john.

watt (wat) *m*, watt.

Westphalie (la) (vɛstfali), Westphalia.

whisky (wiski) *m*, whiskey.

whist (wist) *m*, whist (*cards*). ~ *à trois avec un mort*, dummy w. ~ *de Gand*, solo w.

X

xénophobe (ksenɔfɔb) *a*, xeno-

phobic. ¶ *m*, xenophobe. **xénophobie** (fɔbi) *f*, xenophobia.

xérès (kerɛs) *m*, sherry.

xylophone (ksilɔfɔn) *m*, xylophone.

Y

y (i) *ad*, there; here; at home. ¶ *pn*, of it, him, etc; to it; about it; at it; by it; in it; it. *ça* ~ *est!* it's done! that's it! *il* ~ *a*, there is, there are. *je n'* ~ *suis pour rien*, I had nothing to do with it. ~ *compris*, including.

yacht (jɔt) *m*, yacht. *Note.*—le yacht, *not* l'yacht.

yaourt (jaurt) *m*, yogurt.

yeuse (jøːz) *f*, ilex, holm oak.

yeux *see* œil.

yole (jɔl) *f*, gig, skiff, yawl, *Note:* —la yole.

yougoslave (jugɔslaːv) *a. & Y~*, *n*, Yugoslav. **la Yougoslavie** (slavi) Yugoslavia.

youpin, e (jupẽ, in) *n*, Jew, Jewess (*pejorative*).

ypérite (iperit) *f*, mustard gas.

Z

zazou (zazu) *m*, zoot-suiter; snappy dresser (*WW II*).

zèbre (zɛbr) *m*, zebra; individual, type, guy. *faire le* ~, to play the fool. *un drôle de* ~, a peculiar fellow. **zébré, e** (zebre) *a*, striped.

zélateur, trice (zelatœːr, tris) *n*, zealot. **zèle** (zɛːl) *m*, zeal. *faire du* ~, to be unnecessarily zealous. **zélé, e** (zele) *a*, zealous.

zénith (zenit) *m*, zenith.

zéphyr (zefiːr) *m*, zephyr.

zeppelin (zɛplẽ) *m*, zeppelin.

zéro (zero) *m*, cipher, nought, 0; love (*Ten.*); zero (See *centigrade* Fr.-Eng.); nobody. ~ *partout*, love-all (*Ten.*).

zeste (zɛst) *m*, woody partitions (*walnut*); peel (*orange, lemon*); straw (*fig*). ~ *confit*, candied peel.

zézayer (zezeje) *v.i*, to lisp.

zibeline (ziblin) *f*, sable (*Zool., fur*).

zigzag (zigzag) *m*, zigzag. *disposé en ~*, staggered.

zizi (zizi) *m*, penis (*children's slang*).

zinc (zɛ̃:g) *m*, zinc, spelter; bar, counter. **zincogravure** (zɛ̃kɔgravy:r) *f*, zincography. **zingueur** (gœ:r) *m*, zinc worker.

zircon (zirkɔ̃) *m*, zircon.

zizanie (zizani) *f*, discord.

zob (zɔb) *m*, penis (*slang*).

zodiaque (zɔdjak) *m*, zodiac.

zone (zo:n) *f*, zone; belt; area. *~ des calmes*, doldrums. *~ bleue*,

limited parking area. *~ crépusculaire*, gray area (*statistics*). *citoyen de seconde ~*, second-class citizen. *la Z~*, slum, shantytown; city outskirts.

zoologie (zɔɔlɔʒi) *f*, zoology. **zoologique** (ʒik) *a*, zoological. **zoologiste** (ʒist) *n*, zoologist.

zoulou (zulu) *a*. & **Z~**, *n*, Zulu.

zozo (zozo) *m*, idiot, clod, fool.

zozoter (zɔzɔte) *v.i*, to lisp (*slang*).

zut (zyt) *i*, darn it! go to the devil!

Zuyderzée (**le**) (zɥidɛrze), the Zuyder Zee.

Order of tenses & parts:

(1) = Indicative Present
(2) =   "   Imperfect
(3) =   "   Preterit
(4) =   "   Future
(5) = Conditional Present
(6) = Imperative
(7) = Subjunctive Present
(8) =   "   Imperfect
(9) = Participle Present
(10) =   "   Past

Prefixed verbs not included in the list, such as **abattre, sourire, désapprendre, satisfaire,** follow the second or last element (**battre, rire, prendre, faire**).

absoudre.—(1) j'absous, tu absous, il absout, nous absolvons, vous absolvez, ils absolvent. (2) j'absolvais. (4) j'absoudrai. (5) j'absoudrais. (6) absous, absolvons, absolvez. (7) que j'absolve. (9) absolvant. (10) absous, oute.

abstraire.—*like* **traire,** *but only in* (1) (2) *and compound tenses.*

accroître.—*like* **croître,** *but* (10) accru, *no circumflex accent.*

acquérir.—(1) j'acquiers, tu acquiers, il acquiert, nous acquérons, vous acquérez, ils acquièrent. (2) j'acquérais. (3) j'acquis. (4) j'acquerrai. (5) j'acquerrais. (6) acquiers, acquérons, acquérez. (7) que j'acquière. (8) que j'acquisse. (9) acquérant. (10) acquis, e.

aller.—(1) je vais, tu vas, il va, nous allons, vous allez, ils vont. (2) j'allais. (3) j'allai. (4) j'irai. (5) j'irais. (6) va (*but* vas-y), allons, allez. (7) que j'aille. (8) que j'allasse. (9) allant. (10) allé, e.

s'en aller.—*like* **aller.** *The auxiliary* être *is used in the compound tenses and is placed between* en *and* allé; *thus,* je m'en suis allé. (6) va-t-en, allons-nous-en, allez-vous-en.

apparaître.—*like* **connaître.**

assaillir.—(1) j'assaille, tu assailles, il assaille, nous assaillons, vous assaillez, ils assaillent. (2) j'assaillais. (3) j'assaillis. (4) j'assaillirai. (5) j'assaillirais. (6) assaille, assaillons, assaillez. (7) que j'assaille. (8) que j'assaillisse. (9) assaillant. (10) assailli, e.

asseoir.—(1) j'assieds, tu assieds, il assied, nous asseyons, vous asseyez, ils asseyent. (2) j'asseyais. (3) j'assis. (4) j'assiérai *ou* j'asseyerai. (5) j'assiérais *ou* j'asseyerais. (6) assieds, asseyons, asseyez. (7) que j'asseye. (8) que j'assisse. (9) asseyant. (10) assis, e. *This verb is sometimes conjugated in maintaining throughout the* oi *of the radical; thus,* (1) j'assois, nous assoyons. (2) j'assoyais, etc.

astreindre.—*like* **atteindre.**

atteindre.—(1) j'atteins, tu atteins, il atteint, nous atteignons, vous atteignez, ils atteignent. (2) j'atteignais. (3) j'atteignis. (4) j'atteindrai. (5) j'atteindrais. (6) atteins, atteignons, atteignez. (7) que j'atteigne. (8) que j'atteignisse. (9) atteignant. (10) atteint, e.

avoir.—(1) j'ai, tu as, il a, nous avons, vous avez, ils ont. (2) j'avais. (3) j'eus. (4) j'aurai. (5) j'aurais. (6) aie, ayons, ayez. (7) que j'aie. (8) que j'eusse. (9) ayant. (10) eu, e.

battre.—(1) je bats, tu bats, il bat, nous battons, vous battez, ils battent. (2) je battais. (3) je battis. (4) je battrai. (5) je battrais. (6) bats, battons, battez. (7) que je batte. (8) que je battisse. (9) battant. (10) battu, e.

boire.—(1) je bois, tu bois, il boit, nous buvons, vous buvez, ils boivent. (2) je buvais. (3) je bus. (4) je boirai. (5) je boirais. (6) bois, buvons, buvez. (7) que je boive. (8) que je busse. (9) buvant. (10) bu, e.

bouillir.—(1) je bous, tu bous, il bout, nous bouillons, vous bouillez, ils bouillent. (2) je bouillais. (3) je bouillis. (4) je bouillirai. (5) je bouillirais. (6) bous, bouillons, bouillez. (7) que je bouille. (8) que je bouillisse. (9) bouillant. (10) bouilli, e.

braire.—*like* **traire** *but seldom used except in infinitive & in 3rd persons of* (1) (4) & (5).

bruire.—*Seldom used except in infinitive and in 3rd person s.* of (1) il bruit, and in *3rd persons* of (2) il bruissait, ils bruissaient.

ceindre.—*like* **atteindre.**

choir.—(10) chu, e. *Others not used.*

circoncire.—*like* **confire,** *but* (10) circoncis, e.

circonscrire.—*like* **écrire.**

clore.—(1) je clos, tu clos, il clôt. (4) je clorai, etc. (6) clos. (7) que je close, etc. (10) clos e. *Other forms not, or very seldom, used.*

comparaître.—*like* **connaître,** *but* (10) comparu (*inv.*).

conclure.—(1) je conclus, tu conclus, il conclut, nous concluons, vous concluez, ils concluent. (2) je concluais. (3) je conclus. (4) je conclurai. (5) je conclurais. (6) conclus, concluons, concluez. (7) que je conclue. (8) que je conclusse. (9) concluant. (10) conclu, e.

conduire.—(1) je conduis, tu conduis, il conduit, nous conduisons, vous conduisez, ils conduisent. (2) je conduisais. (3) je conduisis. (4) je conduirai. (5) je conduirais. (6) conduis, conduisons, conduisez. (7) que je conduise. (8) que je conduisisse. (9) conduisant. (10) conduit, e.

confire.—(1) je confis, tu confis, il confit, nous confisons, vous confisez, ils confisent. (2) je confisais. (3) je confis. (4) je confirai. (5) je confirais. (6) confis, confisons, confisez. (7) que je confise. (8) que je confisse. (9) confisant. (10) confit, e.

connaître.—(1) je connais, tu connais, il connaît, nous connaissons, vous connaissez, ils connaissent. (2) je connaissais. (3) je connus. (4) je connaîtrai. (5) je connaîtrais. (6) connais, connaissons, connaissez. (7) que je connaisse. (8) que je connusse. (9) connaissant. (10) connu, e.

conquérir.—*like* **acquérir.**

construire.—*like* **conduire.**

contraindre.—*like* **craindre.**

contredire.—*like* **dire,** *except* (1) vous contredisez. (6) contredisez.

coudre.—(1) je couds, tu couds, il coud, nous cousons, vous cousez, ils cousent. (2) je cousais. (3) je cousis. (4) je coudrai. (5) je coudrais. (6) couds, cousons, cousez. (7) que je couse. (8) que je cousisse. (9) cousant. (10) cousu, e.

courir.—(1) je cours, tu cours, il court, nous courons, vous courez, ils courent. (2) je courais. (3) je courus. (4) je courrai. (5) je courrais. (6) cours, courons, courez. (7) que je coure. (8) que je courusse. (9) courant. (10) couru, e.

couvrir.—*like* **ouvrir.**

craindre.—(1) je crains, tu crains, il craint, nous craignons, vous craignez, ils craignent. (2) je craignais. (3) je craignis. (4) je craindrai. (5) je craindrais. (6) crains, craignons, craignez. (7) que je craigne. (8) que je craignisse. (9) craignant. (10) craint, e.

croire.—(1) je crois, tu crois, il croit, nous croyons, vous croyez, ils croient. (2) je croyais. (3) je crus. (4) je croirai. (5) je croirais. (6) crois, croyons, croyez. (7) que je croie. (8) que je crusse. (9) croyant. (10) cru, e.

croître.—(1) je croîs, tu croîs, il croît, nous croissons, vous croissez, ils croissent. (2) je croissais. (3) je crûs. (4) je croîtrai. (5) je croîtrais. (6) croîs, croissons, croissez. (7) que je croisse. (8) que je crûsse. (9) croissant. (10) crû, crue (*pl.* crus, crues).

cueillir.—(1) je cueille, tu cueilles, il cueille, nous cueillons, vous cueillez, ils cueillent. (2) je cueillais. (3) je cueillis. (4) je cueillerai. (5) je cueillerais. (6) cueille, cueillons, cueillez. (7) que je cueille. (8) que je cueillisse. (9) cueillant. (10) cueilli, e.

cuire.—*like* **conduire.**

déchoir.—(1) je déchois, tu déchois, il déchoit. (3) je déchus. (4) je décherrai. (7) que je déchoie. (8) que je déchusse. (10) déchu, e.

déconfire.—(10) déconfit, e.

découvrir.—*like* **ouvrir.**

décrire.—*like* **écrire.**

décroître.—*like* **croître,** *except* (10) décru, e.

dédire.—*like* **dire,** *except* (1) vous dédisez. (6) dédisez.

déduire.—*like* **conduire.**

défaillir.—(1) nous défaillons, vous défaillez, ils défaillent. (2) je défaillais, etc. (3) je défaillis, etc. (9) défaillant. *Other forms seldom used.*

démentir.—*like* **sentir.**

dépeindre.—*like* **atteindre.**

dépourvoir.—(10) dépourvu, e.

déteindre.—*like* **atteindre.**

détruire.—*like* **conduire.**

devoir.—(1) je dois, tu dois, il doit, nous devons, vous devez, ils doivent. (2) je devais. (3) je dus. (4) je devrai. (5) je devrais. (6) dois, devons, devez. (7) que je doive. (8) que je dusse. (9) devant. (10) dû, due (*pl.* dus, dues).

dire.—(1) je dis, tu dis, il dit, nous disons, vous dites, ils disent. (2) je disais. (3) je dis. (4) je dirai. (5) je dirais. (6) dis, disons, dites. (7) que je dise. (8) que je disse. (9) disant. (10) dit, e.

disparaître.—*like* **connaître.**

dissoudre.—*like* **absoudre.**

dormir.—(1) je dors, tu dors, il dort, nous dormons, vous dormez, ils dorment. (2) je dormais. (3) je dormis. (4) je dormirai. (5) je dormirais. (6) dors, dormons, dormez. (7) que je dorme. (8) que je dormisse. (9) dormant. (10) dormi (*inv.*).

échoir.—(1) il échoit *ou* il échet. (4) il écherra. (9) échéant. (10) échu, e. *Other forms hardly ever used.*

éclore.—(1) il éclôt, ils éclosent. (4) il éclora. (5) il éclorait. (7) qu'il éclose. (10) éclos, e.

écrire.—(1) j'écris, tu écris, il écrit, nous écrivons, vous écrivez, ils écrivent. (2) j'écrivais. (3) j'écrivis. (4) j'écrirai. (5) j'écrirais. (6) écris, écrivons, écrivez.

(7) que j'écrive. (8) que j'écrivisse. (9) écrivant. (10) écrit, e.

élire.—*like* **lire.**

embatre.—*like* **battre,** *but with* one t *only.*

empreindre.—*like* **atteindre.**

enceindre.—*like* **atteindre.**

enduire.—*like* **conduire.**

enfreindre.—*like* **atteindre.**

enquérir.—*like* **acquérir.**

épreindre.—*like* **atteindre.**

éteindre.—*like* **atteindre.**

être.—(1) je suis, tu es, il est, nous sommes, vous êtes, ils sont. (2) j'étais. (3) je fus. (4) je serai. (5) je serais. (6) soyons, soyez. (7) que je sois. (8) que je fusse. (9) étant. (10) été (*inv.*).

étreindre.—*like* **atteindre.**

exclure.—*like* **conclure.**

faillir.—(1) il faut (*in* s'en faut). (3) je faillis, etc. (10) failli, e. *Seldom used in other forms.*

faire.—(1) je fais, tu fais, il fait, nous faisons, vous faites, ils font. (2) je faisais. (3) je fis. (4) je ferai. (5) je ferais. (6) fais, faisons, faites. (7) que je fasse. (8) que je fisse. (9) faisant. (10) fait, e.

falloir.—(1) il faut. (2) il fallait. (3) il fallut. (4) il faudra. (5) il faudrait. (7) qu'il faille. (8) qu'il fallût. (10) fallu (*inv.*).

feindre.—*like* **atteindre.**

forclore.—(10) forclos, e.

frire.—(1) je fris, tu fris, il frit, nous faisons frire, vous faites frire, ils font frire. (2) je faisais frire. (4) je frirai. (5) je frirais. (6) fris. (10) frit, e.

fuir.—(1) je fuis, tu fuis, il fuit, nous fuyons, vous fuyez, ils fuient. (2) je fuyais. (3) je fuis. (4) je fuirai. (5) je fuirais. (6) fuis, fuyons, fuyez. (7) que je fuie. (8) que je fuisse. (9) fuyant. (10) fui, e.

geindre.—*like* **atteindre.**

gésir.—(1) je gis, tu gis, il gît, nous gisons, vous gisez, ils gisent. (2) je gisais, etc. (9) gisant. *Other forms not used.*

inclure.—*like* **conclure.**

induire.—*like* **conduire.**

inscrire.—*like* **écrire.**

instruire.—*like* **conduire.**

interdire.—*like* **dire,** *except* (1) vous interdisez. (6) interdisez.

introduire.—*like* **conduire.**

joindre.—(1) je joins, tu joins, il joint, nous joignons, vous joignez, ils joignent. (2) je joignais. (3) je joignis. (4) je joindrai. (5) je joindrais. (6) joins, joignons, joignez. (7) que je joigne. (8) que je joignisse. (9) joignant. (10) joint, e.

lire.—(1) je lis, tu lis, il lit, nous lisons, vous lisez, ils lisent. (2) je lisais. (3) je lus. (4) je lirai. (5) je lirais. (6) lis, lisons, lisez. (7) que je lise. (8) que je lusse. (9) lisant. (10) lu, e.

luire.—*like* **conduire,** *except* (10) lui. (*inv.*) & *no* (3) *or* (8).

maudire.—(1) je maudis, tu maudis, il maudit, nous maudissons, vous maudissez, ils maudissent. (2) je maudissais. (3) je maudis. (4) je maudirai. (5) je maudirais. (6) maudis, maudissons, maudissez. (7) que je maudisse. (8) que je maudisse. (9) maudissant. (10) maudit, e.

méconnaître.—*like* **paraître.**

médire.—*like* **dire,** *except* (1) vous médisez. (6) médisez.

mentir.—*like* **sentir.**

messeoir.—*like* **seoir,** *in sense to suit.*

mettre.—(1) je mets, tu mets, il met, nous mettons, vous mettez, ils mettent. (2) je mettais. (3) je mis. (4) je mettrai. (5) je mettrais. (6) mets, mettons, mettez. (7) que je mette. (8) que je misse. (9) mettant. (10) mis, e.

moudre.—(1) je mouds, tu mouds, il moud, nous moulons, vous moulez, ils moulent. (2) je moulais. (3) je moulus. (4) je moudrai. (5) je moudrais. (6) mouds, moulons, moulez. (7) que je moule. (8) que je moulusse. (9) moulant. (10) moulu, e.

mourir.—(1) je meurs, tu meurs, il meurt, nous mourons, vous mourez, ils meurent. (2) je mourais. (3) je mourus. (4) je mourrai. (5) je mourrais. (6) meurs, mourons, mourez. (7) que je meure. (8) que je mourusse. (9) mourant. (10) mort, e.

mouvoir.—(1) je meus, tu meus, il meut, nous mouvons, vous mouvez, ils meuvent. (2) je mouvais. (3) je mus. (4) je mouvrai. (5) je mouvrais. (6) meus, mouvons, mouvez. (7) que je meuve. (8) que je musse. (9) mouvant. (10) mû, mue (*pl.* mus, mues).

naître.—(1) je nais, tu nais, il naît, nous naissons, vous naissez, ils naissent. (2) je naissais. (3) je naquis. (4) je naîtrai. (5) je naîtrais. (6) nais, naissons, naissez. (7) que je naisse. (8) que je naquisse. (9) naissant. (10) né, e.

nuire.—*like* **conduire,** *except* (10) nui (*inv.*).

offrir.—*like* **ouvrir.**

oindre.—*like* **joindre.**

ouïr.—(10) ouï, ïe.

ouvrir.—(1) j'ouvre, tu ouvres, il ouvre, nous ouvrons, vous ouvrez, ils ouvrent. (2) j'ouvrais. (3) j'ouvris. (4) j'ouvrirai. (5) j'ouvrirais. (6) ouvre, ouvrons, ouvrez. (7) que j'ouvre. (8) que j'ouvrisse. (9) ouvrant. (10) ouvert, e.

paître.—(1) je pais, tu pais, il paît, nous paissons, vous paissez, ils paissent. (2) je paissais. (4) je paîtrai. (5) je paîtrais. (6) pais, paissons, paissez. (7) que je paisse. (9) paissant.

paraître.—*like* **connaître,** *but* (10) paru (*inv.*).

partir.—(1) je pars, tu pars, il part, nous partons, vous partez, ils partent. (2) je partais. (3) je partis. (4) je partirai. (5) je partirais. (6) pars, partons, partez. (7) que je parte. (8) que je partisse. (9) partant. (10) parti, e.

peindre.—*like* **atteindre.**

plaindre.—*like* **craindre.**

plaire.—(1) je plais, tu plais, il plaît, nous plaisons, vous plaisez, ils plaisent. (2) je plaisais. (3) je plus. (4) je plairai. (5) je plairais. (6) plais, plaisons, plaisez. (7) que je plaise. (8)

que je plusse. (9) plaisant. (10)
plu (*inv.*).

pleuvoir.—(1) il pleut. (2) il
pleuvait. (3) il plut. (4) il pleu-
vra. (5) il pleuvrait. (7) qu'il
pleuve. (8) qu'il plût. (9) pleu-
vant. (10) plu (*inv.*).

poindre.—*like* joindre, *but seldom used except in infinitive &
(4).*

pourvoir.—(1) je pourvois, tu
pourvois, il pourvoit, nous pourvoyons, vous pourvoyez, ils pour-
voient. (2) je pourvoyais. (3)
je pourvus. (4) je pourvoirai. (5)
je pourvoirais. (6) pourvois,
pourvoyons, pourvoyez. (7) que
je pourvoie. (8) que je pour-
vusse. (9) pourvoyant. (10)
pourvu, e.

pouvoir.—(1) je peux *ou* je puis,
tu peux, il peut, nous pouvons,
vous pouvez, ils peuvent. (2) je
pouvais. (3) je pus. (4) je pour-
rai. (5) je pourrais. (7) que je
puisse. (8) que je pusse. (9)
pouvant. (10) pu (*inv.*).

prédire.—*like* dire, *except* (1)
vous prédisez. (6) prédisez.

prendre.—(1) je prends, tu
prends, il prend, nous prenons,
vous prenez, ils prennent. (2) je
prenais. (3) je pris. (4) je
prendrai. (5) je prendrais. (6)
prends, prenons, prenez. (7) que
je prenne. (8) que je prisse. (9)
prenant. (10) pris, e.

prescrire.—*like* écrire.

prévaloir.—*like* valoir, *but* (7)
que je prévale.

prévoir.—*like* voir, *except* (4)
je prévoirai. (5) je prévoirais.

produire.—*like* conduire.

promouvoir.—*like* mouvoir, *but
seldom used except in infinitive
& (10) promu, e (no circumflex
accent).*

proscrire.—*like* écrire.

raire.—*like* traire, *but the only
forms in common use are* (1)
il rait, ils raient.

reclure.—(10) reclus, e.

reconquérir.—*like* acquérir.

reconstruire.—*like* conduire.

recouvrir.—*like* ouvrir.

récrire.—*like* écrire.

recuire.—*like* conduire.

réduire.—*like* conduire.

réélire.—*like* lire.

reluire.—*like* luire.

renaître.—*like* naître, *but no*
(10) *or compound tenses.*

reparaître.—*like* paraître.

repentir (se).—*like* sentir.

reproduire.—*like* conduire.

requérir.—*like* acquérir.

résoudre.—(1) je résous, tu résous, il résout, nous résolvons,
vous résolvez, ils résolvent. (2)
je résolvais. (3) je résolus. (4)
je résoudrai. (5) je résoudrais.
(6) résous, résolvons, résolvez. (7)
que je résolve. (8) que je ré-
solusse. (9) résolvant. (10) résolu, e.

restreindre.—*like* atteindre.

rire.—(1) je ris, tu ris, il rit, nous
rions, vous riez, ils rient. (2) je
riais. (3) je ris. (4) je rirai.
(5) je rirais. (6) ris, rions, riez.
(7) que je rie. (8) que je risse.
(9) riant. (10) ri (*inv.*).

rouvrir.—*like* ouvrir.

saillir.—*like* assaillir.

savoir.—(1) je sais, tu sais, il
sait, nous savons, vous savez, ils
savent. (2) je savais. (3) je sus.
(4) je saurai. (5) je saurais. (6)
sache, sachons, sachez. (7) que
je sache. (8) que je susse. (9)
sachant. (10) su, e.

séduire.—*like* conduire.

sentir.—(1) je sens, tu sens, il
sent, nous sentons, vous sentez,
ils sentent. (2) je sentais. (3)
je sentis. (4) je sentirai. (5) je
sentirais. (6) sens, sentons, sentez. (7) que je sente. (8) que
je sentisse. (9) sentant. (10)
senti, e.

seoir.—*In sense to sit,* (9) séant.
(10) sis, e. *In sense to suit,* (1)
il sied, ils siéent. (2) il seyait, ils
seyaient. (4) il siéra, ils siéront.
(7) qu'il siée, qu'ils siéent. (9)
séant *ou* seyant. *No other forms.*

servir.—(1) je sers, tu sers, il sert,
nous servons, vous servez, ils ser-
vent. (2) je servais. (3) je ser-
vis. (4) je servirai. (5) je ser-
virais. (6) sers, servons, servez.
(7) que je serve. (8) que je
servisse. (9) servant. (10) servi,
e.

sortir.—(1) je sors, tu sors, il
sort, nous sortons, vous sortez,

ils sortent. (2) je sortais. (3) je sortis. (4) je sortirai. (5) je sortirais. (6) sors, sortons, sortez. (7) que je sorte. (8) que je sortisse. (9) sortant. (10) sorti, e.

souffrir.—*like* **ouvrir.**

souscrire.—*like* **écrire.**

suffire.—*like* **confire.**

suivre.—(1) je suis, tu suis, il suit, nous suivons, vous suivez, ils suivent. (2) je suivais. (3) je suivis. (4) je suivrai. (5) je suivrais. (6) suis, suivons, suivez. (7) que je suive. (8) que je suivisse. (9) suivant. (10) suivi, e.

surseoir.—(1) je sursois, tu sursois, il sursoit, nous sursoyons, vous sursoyez, ils sursoient. (2) je sursoyais. (3) je sursis. (4) je surseoirai. (5) je surseoirais. (6) sursois, sursoyons, sursoyez. (7) que je sursoie. (8) que je sursisse. (9) sursoyant. (10) sursis, e.

taire.—*like* **plaire,** *except* (1) il tait (*no circumflex*) & (10) tu, e.

teindre.—*like* **atteindre.**

tenir.—(1) je tiens, tu tiens, il tient, nous tenons, vous tenez, ils tiennent. (2) je tenais. (3) je tins. (4) je tiendrai. (5) je tiendrais. (6) tiens, tenons, tenez. (7) que je tienne. (8) que je tinsse. (9) tenant. (10) tenu, e.

tistre.—*Used only in* (10) tissu, e, *and compound tenses.*

traduire.—*like* **conduire.**

traire.—(1) je trais, tu trais, il trait, nous trayons, vous trayez, ils traient. (2) je trayais. (4) je trairai. (5) je trairais. (6) trais, trayons, trayez. (7) que je traie. (9) trayant. (10) trait, e.

transcrire.—*like* **écrire.**

tressaillir.—*like* **assaillir.**

vaincre.—(1) je vaincs, tu vaincs, il vainc, nous vainquons, vous vainquez, ils vainquent. (2) je vainquais. (3) je vainquis. (4)

je vaincrai. (5) je vaincrais. (6) vaincs, vainquons, vainquez. (7) que je vainque. (8) que je vainquisse. (9) vainquant. (10) vaincu, e.

valoir.—(1) je vaux, tu vaux, il vaut, nous valons, vous valez, ils valent. (2) je valais. (3) je valus. (4) je vaudrai. (5) je vaudrais. (6) vaux, valons, valez. (7) que je vaille. (8) que je valusse. (9) valant. (10) valu, e.

venir.—(1) je viens, tu viens, il vient, nous venons, vous venez, ils viennent. (2) je venais. (3) je vins. (4) je viendrai. (5) je viendrais. (6) viens, venons, venez. (7) que je vienne. (8) que je vinsse. (9) venant. (10) venu, e.

vêtir.—(1) je vêts, tu vêts, il vêt, nous vêtons, vous vêtez, ils vêtent. (2) je vêtais. (3) je vêtis. (4) je vêtirai. (5) je vêtirais. (6) vêts, vêtons, vêtez. (7) que je vête. (8) que je vêtisse. (9) vêtant. (10) vêtu, e.

vivre.—(1) je vis, tu vis, il vit, nous vivons, vous vivez, ils vivent. (2) je vivais. (3) je vécus. (4) je vivrai. (5) je vivrais. (6) vis, vivons, vivez. (7) que je vive. (8) que je vécusse. (9) vivant. (10) vécu (*inv.*).

voir.—(1) je vois, tu vois, il voit, nous voyons, vous voyez, ils voient. (2) je voyais. (3) je vis. (4) je verrai. (5) je verrais. (6) vois, voyons, voyez. (7) que je voie. (8) que je visse. (9) voyant. (10) vu, e.

vouloir.—(1) je veux, tu veux, il veut, nous voulons, vous voulez, ils veulent. (2) je voulais. (3) je voulus. (4) je voudrai. (5) je voudrais. (6) veuille & veux, veuillons & voulons, veuillez & voulez. (7) que je veuille. (8) que je voulusse. (9) voulant. (10) voulu, e.

In French, words are divided into syllables according to the following rules.

(1) *A consonant between two vowels begins a new syllable:*
ca-pi-tal, ca-pi-ta-li-ser, ca-pi-ta-lis-me, ca-pi-ta-lis-te, li-bé-ra-toi-re, dé-sa-bon-ne-ment, a-rith-mé-ti-que, pri-vi-lè-ge, su-bor-don-né, é-ti-que-ta-ge, e-xa-men, e-xer-ci-ce, i-ne-xac-te-ment, to-xi-que, i-nu-ti-le, u-ne, u-na-ni-me-ment, vi-gueur, vi-gou-reux, vi-gou-reu-se, paie-ment, em-pla-ce-ment, vé-hi-cu-le, pa-ral-lé-li-pi-pè-de. *Note:*—In order not to misrepresent the pronunciation of certain prefixes, there are a few exceptions to this rule, and collaterally to rule 3 also; such as sur-é-le-ver, sur-en-ché-rir, and the like; in-ter-o-cé-a-ni-que, in-ter-ur-bain, and the like.

(2) *Two adjoining consonants (except Rule 4 digraphs) between two vowels separate into two syllables:*
ac-com-mo-der, at-ter-ris-sage, bail-le-res-se, chan-geant, chan-gean-te, cor-res-pon-dan-ce, des-cen-dre, di-a-phrag-me, ex-cep-ti-on-nel-le-ment, ex-pé-di-ti-on-nai-re, in-nom-ma-ble, em-bar-ras-sant, in-ter-val-le, ir-res-pon-sa-bi-li-té, os-cil-ler, fais-ceau, ras-seoir, re-con-nais-san-ce, res-ti-tu-er, sub-di-vi-ser, sur-taux, veil-le, el-les, mal-heur, in-hé-rent, ex-hi-ber, mo-les-ki-ne.

(3) *A vowel can only begin a syllable, other than an initial syllable, when preceded by another vowel:*
ac-cue-il-lir, a-é-ro-pla-ne; po-è-me, a-gré-er, an-ci-en, ar-ri-è-re, bé-né-fi-ci-ai-re, ca-mi-on, ca-out-chouc, co-as-so-ci-é, co-ef-fi-ci-ent, coïn-ci-der, dé-pou-il-le-ment, ex-tra-or-di-nai-re, feu-il-le, li-er, mi-eux, na-ti-on, ou-est, ré-u-ni-on, vic-tu-

ail-les, vi-e-il-lir, ré-é-li-re, voi-li-er, pay-a-ble, ba-lay-u-res, en-voy-er, voy-a-ge, roy-au-me, en-nuy-eux.

(4) *The following digraph consonants are inseparable:*
bl, cl, fl, gl, pl: a-bla-taf, pu-bli-que, (*Exception:* sub-lu-nai-re); é-clec-tis-me, ex-clu-sif; ré-fle-xe, ré-fle-xi-on; é-glan-ti-ne, rè-gle-ment; é-plu-cher.

br, cr, dr, fr, gr, pr, tr, vr: a-bri-cot, su-bré-car-gue, (*Exception:* sub-ro-ger & *derivatives*); é-cri-tu-re, ma-nus-crit, pres-cri-re, sous-cri-re, des-crip-ti-ve; a-dres-ser; re-frain; a-gri-co-le; a-près; a-tro-ce; a-vril, ou-vri-er.

ch, dh, ph, rh: é-choir, re-cher-che; ré-dhi-bi-toi-re; té-lé-pho-ne, pho-no-gra-phe; en-rhu-mer, ar-rhes.

gn: en-sei-gne-ment, si-gnal, es-pa-gnol, i-gna-re (*but* mag-nat, mag-no-li-a, di-ag-nos-ti-que, ig-né, *because here* gn *is not palatalized; in other words, the* g *is hard*).

ng: ving-ti-è-me (*but* sin-gu-li-er, *because here* ng *is not digraph, i.e., expressing one sound*).

pt: lé-pi-do-pte-res.

(5) (*a*) ns, bs, *and* rs *are separable if followed by a vowel:*
con-sa-crer, con-seil-ler, con-si-dé-rer, in-sé-rer, in-sol-va-ble, in-suf-fi-sant, tran-sac-ti-on, tran-sat-lan-ti-que, tran-si-tif; ab-sor-ber, ob-ser-ver; per-su-a-der.
 (*b*) ns, bs, *and* rs *are inseparable if followed by a consonant:*
cons-pi-rer, cons-ta-ter, cons-ti-tu-er, ins-pec-ter, ins-tal-ler, trans-cen-dant, trans-fè-re-ment, trans-port; no-nobs-tant, obs-ta-cles, subs-tan-ce; in-ters-ti-ce, pers-pec-ti-ve.
 (*c*) ns *and* bs *are inseparable if followed by a consonant coupled with* r:
cons-trui-re, ins-cri-re, trans-cri-

re, trans-gres-ser; abs-trac-ti-
on, obs-truc-ti-on.
(d) *ns and* bs *are separable
before* ci:
con-sci-en-ci-eux, in-sci-em-ment;
ab-scis-se.

(6) (a) mp *and* nc *followed by* t
are inseparable:
a-comp-te, comp-ta-ble, es-comp-
ter, pré-emp-ti-on; fonc-ti-on,
sanc-ti-on.

(b) *In all other combinations*
mp *and* nc *are separable:*
em-ploy-er, em-prun-ter, im-por-
tant; a-van-cer, fran-çais, franche, fran-co.

(7) *In writing or in print no syllable is separable which does
not include a vowel; thus,* tri-
graph consonants are inseparable initially: scru-tin, *but may
be separable medially:* ins-cru-
ta-ble.

ENGLISH-FRENCH DICTIONARY

A

A, *letter*, (*Mus.*) la, *m*; (*house number*) bis, **a**, *indefinite art.* or *a*, un, une. *what ~ . . . l*, quel! quelle! *such ~ . . .*, tel, telle. *2 or 3 times ~ day*, 2 ou 3 fois par jour.

aback, *ad*: *taken ~*, interloqué, déconcerté.

abacus, *n*, abaque, *m*.

abaft, *ad*, vers l'arrière. ¶ *pr*, sur l'arrière de.

abandon, *v.t*, abandonner, délaisser. **~ment**, *n*, abandon, délaissement, *m*.

abase, *v.t*, abaisser, humilier.

abash, *v.t*, décontenancer, confondre.

abate, *v.t*, diminuer, rabattre; (*v.i.*) [se] calmer; (*weather, etc.*) s'apaiser. **abatement**, *n*, diminution, *f*; rabais, *m*.

abbess, *n*, abbesse, *f*. **abbey**, *n*, abbaye, *f*. **abbot**, *n*, abbé, *m*.

abbreviate, *v.t*, abréger. **abbreviation**, *n*, abréviation, *f*.

A B C, *n*, A b c, abécédaire, alphabet, *m*; enfance, *f*.

abdicate, *v.t. & i*, abdiquer. **abdication**, *n*, abdication, *f*.

abdomen, *n*, abdomen, ventre, *m*. *lower part of the ~*, bas-ventre, *m*. **abdominal**, *a*, abdominal. *~ belt*, ceinture ventrière, *f*.

abduct, *v.t*, détourner, enlever.

abeam, *ad*, par le travers.

abed, *ad*, au lit, couché.

aberration, *n*, aberration, *f*, égarement, *m*.

abet, *v.t*, soutenir, encourager, exciter.

abeyance, (*law*) *n*, vacance, *f*. *in ~*, en suspens, en souffrance.

abhor, *v.t*, abhorrer, haïr, avoir en horreur. **abhorrence**, *n*, horreur, haine, *f*. **abhorrent**, *a*, répugnant.

abide, *v.i. & t*. *ir*, demeurer, rester; souffrir, supporter. *to ~ by* (*laws*), s'en tenir à. **abiding**, *a*, durable, permanent.

ability, *n*, capacité, habileté, *f*, talent, savoir-faire, *m*.

abject, *a*, abject. **~ion**, *n*, abjection, *f*.

abjure, *v.t*, abjurer, renoncer.

ablative [**case**], *n*, ablatif, *m*.

ablaze, *ad*, en feu, en flammes.

able, *a*, capable, habile; efficace. **~-bodied**, robuste, valide. **~-**[*-bodied*] *seaman*, matelot de deuxième classe, *m*. *to be ~ to*, pouvoir, savoir, être en mesure (*ou* à même) de, suffire a. **ably**, *ad*, habilement, bravement.

abnegation, *n*, abnégation, *f*.

abnormal†, *a*, anormal. **~ity**, *n*, anormal, *m*.

aboard, *ad*, à bord. ¶ *pr*, à bord de.

abode, *n*, domicile, *m*, demeure, habitation, *f*; séjour, *m*.

abolish, *v.t*, abolir, supprimer.

abominable†, *a*, abominable. **abominate**, *v.t*, abominer. **abomination**, *n*, abomination, *f*.

aboriginal, *a. & n*, aborigène, *a. & m*. **aborigines**, *n.pl*, aborigènes, *m.pl*.

abortion, *n*, avortement; (*creature*) avorton, *m*. **abortive**, *a*, abortif; (*fig.*) avorté, manqué.

abound, *v.i*, abonder, foisonner, fourmiller, affluer.

about, *pr*, autour de; auprès de; pour; dans; en; par; vers; sur; à propos de, touchant. ¶ *ad*, autour, çà & là; environ, à peu [de chose] près. *to be ~ to*, être sur le point de, aller. *what is it all ~?* de quoi s'agit-il?

above, *pr*, au-dessus de; sur; plus de; en amont de; en contrehaut. ¶ *ad*, en haut; là-haut; au-dessus; ci-dessus. *from ~*, d'en haut. *~ all*, surtout, avant tout. *~-board*, franc, cartes sur table. *~-mentioned*, susmentionné, ci-dessus. *~-named*, susnommé.

abrade, *v.t*, user; (*skin*) écorcher. **abrasion**, *n*, (*Phys.*) attrition; (*skin*) écorchure, *f*.

abreast, *ad*, de front; (*Naut.*) par le travers. *~ of*, à la hauteur de.

abridge, *v.t*, abréger, raccourcir. **abridgment**, *n*, abrégé, raccourci, *m*.

abroad, *ad*, à l'étranger, à l'extérieur; au large. *from ~*, de l'étranger, de l'extérieur. *there is* *a rumor ~ that . . .*, le bruit court que . . .

abrogate, *v.t,* abroger. **abrogation,** *n,* abrogation, *f.*

abrupt, *a,* abrupt; brusque. *to treat ~ly,* brusquer. **~ly,** *ad,* brusquement. **~ness,** *n,* brusquerie, *f.*

abscess, *n,* abcès, *m.*

abscond, *v.i,* s'enfuir, se soustraire à la justice.

absence, *n,* absence, *f,* éloignement; défaut, *m.* ~ *of mind,* absence [d'esprit], distraction, *f. leave of ~,* permission, *f;* congé, *m.* **absent,** *a,* absent, manquant. **~minded,** distrait. ¶ *~ oneself,* s'absenter. **absentee,** *n,* absent; (*Mil.*) insoumis, *m.* **absently,** *ad,* distraitement.

absinthe, *n,* absinthe, *f.*

absolute, *a,* absolu. **~ly,** *ad,* absolument.

absolution, *n,* absolution, *f.* **absolve,** *v.t,* absoudre.

absorb, *v.t,* absorber. **absorbent, absorbing,** *a,* absorbant; (*cotton wool*) hydrophile. **absorption,** *n,* absorption, *f.*

abstain, *v.i,* s'abstenir. **~er,** *n,* abstème, *m.f.* **abstemious,** *a,* abstème, sobre. **abstention,** *n,* abstention, *f.* **abstinence,** *n,* abstinence, *f.*

abstract, *a,* abstrait. ¶ *n,* extrait, relevé, résumé, *m.* the ~ (opp. *concrete*), l'abstrait, *m.* ¶ *v.t,* abstraire; relever; (*steal*) distraire, soustraire, détourner. **abstraction,** *n,* abstraction; distraction, soustraction, *f,* détournement, *m.*

abstruse, *a,* abstrus.

absurd†, *a,* absurde. the ~, an absurdity, l'absurde, *m,* une absurdité.

abundance, *n,* abondance, *f.* **abundant,** *a,* abondant. **~ly,** *ad,* abondamment.

abuse, *n,* abus; excès; *m;* injures, insultes, *f.pl,* abuser de; injurier, malmener, maltraiter. **abusive†,** *a,* abusif; injurieux.

abutment (*Arch.*) *n,* culée, butée, *f.*

abyss, *n,* abîme, abysse, gouffre, *m.*

Abyssinia, *n,* l'Abyssinie, *f.* **Abyssinian,** *a,* abyssinien, abyssin. ¶ *n,* Abyssinien, ne, Abyssin, e.

acacia, *n,* acacia, *m.*

academic(al†), *a,* académique; (*year*) scolaire. **academician,** *n,*

académicien, ne. **academy,** *n,* académie, *f.*

accede, *v.i,* accéder.

accelerate, *v.t,* accélérer. **accelerator,** *n,* accélérateur, *m.*

accent, *n,* accent, *m.* **accent & accentuate,** *v.t,* accentuer.

accept, *v.t,* accepter, agréer; (*a sport record*) homologuer. **~able,** *a,* acceptable; de mise; agréable. **~ance,** *n,* acceptation; réception, *f.* **~ation,** *n,* acception, *f.* ~*ed term,* terme consacré, *m.* **~or,** *n,* accepteur, *m.* ~ *for honor* (*Com.*), intervenant, *m.*

access, *n,* accès, abord, *m,* entrée, *f.* (*computers*) *direct ~,* accès direct; *serial ~,* accès séquentiel, *m.* **~ible,** *a,* accessible, abordable. **~ion,** *n,* accession, *f,* avènement, *m.*

accessory†, *a,* accessoire. ¶ *n,* accessoire, *m;* (*law*) complice, *m.f.*

accidence (*Gram.*) *n,* morphologie, *f.*

accident, *n,* accident; sinistre, *m.* [*personal*] ~ *insurance,* assurance contre les accidents [corporels] *f.* **accidental†,** *a,* accidentel, fortuit. ¶ (*Mus.*) *n,* accident, *m.*

acclaim, *v.t,* acclamer. **acclamation,** *n,* acclamation, *f.*

acclimatization, *n,* acclimatation, *f,* acclimatement, *m.* **acclimatize,** *v.t,* acclimater.

acclivity, *n,* montée, *f.*

accommodate, *v.t,* arranger; contenir; loger. ~ *oneself to,* s'accommoder à. **accommodating,** *p.a,* accommodant, complaisant, coulant, débonnaire. **accommodation,** *n,* accommodation, *f;* aménagement; logement, *m.* ~ *paper,* billet de complaisance, *m.*

accompaniment, *n,* accompagnement, *m.* **accompanist,** *n,* accompagnateur, trice. **accompany,** *v.t,* accompagner.

accomplice, *n,* complice, *m.f.*

accomplish, *v.t,* accomplir. **~ed,** *a,* accompli, achevé, émérite. **~ment,** *n,* accomplissement, *m;* (*pl.*) arts d'agrément, *m.pl.*

accord, *n,* accord, *m. of one's own ~,* de son propre mouvement, de son plein gré, d'office. *with one ~,* d'un commun accord. ¶ *v.t,* accorder; (*v.i.*) s'a. **~ance,** *n,* conformité, *f.* **according as,** à mesure que, selon que, suivant que. **according to**, selon, suivant; conforme à, conformément à; conséquemment à; d'après; à. **accordingly**, *ad*, par conséquent; en conséquence; conséquemment.

accordion, *n*, accordéon, *m*.

accost, *v.t*, accoster, aborder.

account, *n*, compte, *m*; (*pl.*) écritures [comptables] *f.pl*; (*pl.*) comptabilité, *f*; (*pl.*) inventaire; exercice; état, exposé, mémoire, *m*, note, *f*; récit, *m*, relation, notice, *f*, historique; (*Stk Ex.*) terme, *m*, liquidation, *f. of no ~*, nul. *on ~* (*Com.*), à compte, à valoir. *on ~ of*, à cause de; (*Com.*) pour le compte de, à l'acquit de. *on no ~*, en aucune manière, aucunement. *~ book*, livre de comptabilité, *m.* ¶ *~ for*, rendre compte de; expliquer. *~able*, *a*, comptable; responsable. *~ancy*, *n*, comptabilité, *f.* *~ant*, *n*, comptable, *m,f*, agent comptable, *m. ~ing*, *n*, comptabilité, *f. ~ machine*, machine comptable, *f. ~ period*, exercice, *m*.

accoutre, *v.t*, équiper; harnacher. *~ment*, *n*, équipement, *m*.

accredit, *v.t*, accréditer. *~ed*, *p.a*, accrédité, attitré. *~ dealer*, stockiste, *m*.

accrue, *v.i*, courir, accroître, s'acquérir. *~d interest*, intérêt couru, *m*, intérêts accrus, *m.pl. accruing interest*, intérêts à échoir.

accumulate, *v.t*, accumuler, amonceler; (*v.i.*) s'accumuler, s'amonceler. **accumulation**, *n*, accumulation, *f*, amoncellement, *m*. **accumulator**, *n*, accumulateur, *m*.

accuracy, *n*, exactitude, justesse, *f*. **accurate†**, *a*, exact, juste.

accursed, *a*, maudit.

accusation, *n*, accusation, *f*. **accusative [case]**, accusatif, *m*. **accuse**, *v.t*, accuser; taxer. *the ~d*, l'accusé, e, l'inculpé, e. **accuser** *n*, accusateur, trice. **accusing**, *a*, accusateur.

accustom, *v.t*, accoutumer, habituer, familiariser, faire. *~ed*, *a*, accoutumé, coutumier, habituel. *to get ~ to*, s'accoutumer à.

ace, *n*, as, *m. within an ~ of*, à deux doigts de.

acerbity, *n*, âpreté, aigreur, *f*.

acetate, *n*, acétate, *m.* **acetic**, *a*, acétique.

acetylene, *n*, acétylène, *m.* *~ lamp*, lampe à acétylène, *f*.

ache, *n*, mal, *m*, douleur, *f.* ¶ *v.i*, faire mal; souffrir. *my head aches*, j'ai mal à la tête.

achieve, *v.t*, accomplir, exécuter. *~ment*, *n*, accomplissement, exploit, *m*.

aching, *a*, endolori. *~ all over*, tout moulu.

acid, *a. & n*, acide, *a. & m.* *~ity*, *n*, acidité *f.* **acidulate**, *v.t*, aciduler.

acknowledge, *v.t*, reconnaître, avouer, s'accuser de, confesser. *~ receipt of*, accuser réception de. **acknowledgment**, *n*, reconnaissance, *f*; accusé de réception; reçu, *m*; (*pl.*) remerciements, *m.pl*.

acme, *n*, apogée, comble, sommet, *m*.

acne, *n*, acné, couperose, *f*.

acolyte, *n*, acolyte, *m*.

acorn, *n*, gland, *m.* *~ crop*, glandée, *f*.

acoustic, *a*, acoustique. *~s*, *n.pl*, acoustique, *f*.

acquaint, *v.t*, faire connaître, faire savoir, faire part, informer. *to get ~ed with*, faire la connaissance de. *~ance*, *n*, connaissance, relation, *f*.

acquiesce, *v.i*, acquiescer. **acquiescence**, *n*, acquiescement, *m*.

acquire, *v.t*, acquérir; prendre. *~ments*, *n.pl*, acquis, *m.s. & m.pl*, connaissances, *f.pl*. **acquisition**, *n*, acquisition, *f*.

acquit, *v.t*, acquitter. **acquittal**, *n*, acquittement, *m*.

acre, *n*, acre, arpent, *m*.

acrid, *a*, âcre. *~ity*, *n*, âcreté, *f*.

acrimonious, *a*, acrimonieux. **acrimony**, *n*, acrimonie, *f*.

acrobat, *n*, acrobate, *m,f*. **acrobatic**, *a*, acrobatique. *~s*, *n.pl*, acrobatie, *f*.

across, *ad*, en travers; (*crossword clues*) horizontalement. ¶ *pr*, en travers de, par. *our neighbors ~ the Channel*, nos voisins d'outre-Manche.

acrostic, *n*, acrostiche, *m*.

act, *n*, acte, *m*, action, *f*, fait, *m.* *~ [of the legislature]*, loi [votée] *f. in the [very] ~*, sur le fait; en flagrant délit. ¶ *v.t*, jouer, représenter; faire; (*v.i.*) agir; fonctionner; opérer. *~ as*, faire fonction de. *~ for* (client, *law*), postuler. **acting** (*Theat.*) *n*, jeu, *m*.

~*manager*, directeur intérimaire, *m*. ~ *partner*, commandité, *m*.

action, *n*, action, *f*; effet; mouvement; geste, *m*; scène, *f*; combat; procès, *m*, plainte, *f*.

active†, *a*, actif, agissant, agile, allant, énergique. *in* ~ *service*, en activité [de service]. ~ *voice*, voix active, *f*, actif, *m*. **activity**, *n*, activité, agilité, *f*, allant, *m*.

actor, tress, *n*, acteur, trice, comédien, ne.

actual, *a*, actuel, réel, effectif, véritable; de fait. ~**ity**, *n*, actualité, réalité, *f*. ~**ly**, *ad*, réellement, en effet.

actuary, *n*, actuaire, *m*.

actuate, *v.t* actionner, animer, mouvoir.

acumen, *n*, flair, *m*.

acute, *a*, aigu; vif, poignant. ~*-angled*, acutangle. ~**ly**, *ad*, vivement. ~**ness**, *n*, acuité; finesse, subtilité; vivacité, *f*.

A.D. (*Anno Domini*), ap. J.C.

adage, *n*, adage, *m*.

adamant (to be), être inflexible.

Adam's apple, pomme d'Adam, *f*.

adapt, *v.t*, adapter, accommoder, approprier. ~**ation**, *n*, adaptation, *f*. ~**er**, *n*, (*Phot.*) adaptateur; (*pers. fig.*) metteur en œuvre, *m*.

add, *v.t*, ajouter; joindre; additionner. (*part*) **added** (*to a building*), hors-d'œuvre, *e.g, an added room*, un cabinet hors-d'œuvre.

adder, *n*, vipère, *f*.

addict, *n*, toxicomane, camé, *m*.

addict oneself to (to), s'adonner à, se livrer à.

addition, *n*, addition, *f*; suppément; (*to a building*) hors-d'œuvre, *m*. ~**al**, *a*, additionnel, supplémentaire.

addled, *a*, couvi; pourri. **addle-headed**, *a*, écervelé.

address, *n*, adresse; allocution, *f*. ¶ *v.t*, adresser; s'adresser à. ~**ee**, *n*, destinataire, *m,f*.

adduce, *v.t*, alléguer, fournir.

adenoids, *n.pl*, végétations [adénoïdes] *f.pl*.

adept, *a*, habile, versé, expérimenté. ¶ *n*, adepte, *m,f*.

adequate, *a*, suffisant; efficace; raisonnable. ~**ly**, *ad*, suffisamment, raisonnablement; dignement.

adhere, *v.i*, adhérer, s'en tenir. **adherence**, *n*, adhésion, *n*, **adhesiveness**, *n*, adhérence, adhésion, ténacité, *f*. **adhesive**, *a*, ad-

hésif, tenace. ~ *stamp*, timbre mobile, *m*. ~ *tape*, bande gommée, *f*; sparadrap, *m*.

adieu, *i*. & *n*, adieu, *i*. & *m*.

adipose, *a*, adipeux.

adit, *n*, galerie à flanc de coteau, *f*.

adjacent, *a*, adjacent, contigu.

adjectival, *a*. & **adjective**, *n*, adjectif, *a.m*. & *m*.

adjoin, *v.i*, joindre, être contigu à, toucher. ~**ing**, *a*, contigu, attenant, adjacent, joignant [à].

adjourn, *v.t*, ajourner, renvoyer, remettre. ~**ment**, *n*, ajournement, renvoi, *m*, remise, *f*.

adjudge, adjudicate, *v.t*, adjuger. **adjudication**, *n*, adjudication, *f*.

adjunct, *n*, accessoire, *m*.

adjure, *v.t*, adjurer.

adjust, *v.t*, ajuster, régler, mettre au point. ~**able wrench**, clef à molette, *f*. ~**ment**, *n*, ajustement, règlement, réglage, *m*, mise au point, *f*.

adjutant, *n*, adjudant major, *m*.

administer, *v.t*, administrer, gérer; (*oath*) déférer. **administration**, *n*, administration, gestion; régie, *f*. **administrative**, *a*, administratif. **administrator, trix**, *n*, administrateur, trice; curateur, trice; cadre, *m*.

admirable†, *a*, admirable.

admiral, *n*, amiral, *m*. ~ *of the fleet*, a. commandant d'escadre. **Admiralty**, *n*, (*Eng.*) Amirauté, *f*; (*Fr.*) Conseil supérieur de la Marine, *m*. ~ [*Office*], Ministère de la Marine, *m*.

admiration, *n*, admiration, *f*. **admire**, *v.t*, admirer. **admirer**, *n*, admirateur, trice. **admiringly**, *ad*, avec admiration.

admissible, *a*, admissible; recevable. **admission**, *n*, admission, entrée, *f*; aveu, *m*. **admit**, *v.t*, admettre, reconnaître; (*as member*) recevoir, agréger. ~ *bearer*, laissez passer. **admittance**, *n*, admission, entrée, *f*.

admixture, *n*, dosage, *m*.

admonish, *v.t*, admonester. **admonition**, *n*, admonition, admonestation, *f*.

ado, *n*, façons, *f.pl*, cérémonie, *f*; aria, bruit, tapage, *m*.

adolescence, *n*, adolescence, *f*. **adolescent**, *a*. & *n*, adolescent, e.

Adonis, *n*, adonis, beau, *m*.

adopt, *v.t,* adopter; prendre. **adopted, adoptive** (*of pers.*) *a,* adoptif. **adoption,** *n,* adoption; prise, *f.*

adorable, *a,* adorable. **adoration,** *n,* adoration, *f.* **adore,** *v.t,* adorer. **adorer,** *n,* adorateur, trice.

adorn, *v.t,* parer, orner, agrémenter, empanacher; (*of pers.*) faire l'ornement de. *to ~ oneself,* se parer. **~ment,** *n,* parure, *f,* ornement, *m.*

Adriatic, *a. & n,* Adriatique, *a. & f.*

adrift, *ad,* en (*ou* à la) dérive.

adroit†, *a,* adroit. **~ness,** *n,* dextérité, *f.*

adulate, *v.t,* aduler. **adulation,** *n,* adulation, *f.* **adulatory,** *a,* adulateur.

adult, *a. & n,* adulte. *a. & m,f.*

adulterate, *v.t,* falsifier, frelater, sophistiquer, altérer. **adulteration,** *n,* falsification, *f,* frelatage, *m,* sophistication, altération, *f.*

adulterer, ess, *n,* adultère, *m,f.* **adulterous,** *a,* adultère. **adultery,** *n,* adultère, *m.*

advance, *n,* avance; anticipation; hausse, *f;* prêt, *m. in ~,* en avance, d'a., par a., à l'a. ¶ *v.t,* avancer; hausser; (*v.i.*) [s']avancer, cheminer. **~ment,** *n,* avancement, *m.*

advantage, *n,* avantage, bénéfice, *m. ~* [*game*] (*Ten.*), avantage [de jeu]. *~ in,* a. dedans, a. au servant. **~ous†,** *a,* avantageux.

advent, *n,* venue, apparition, *f;* (*of Christ*) avènement; (*Eccl.*) l'avent, *m.*

adventure, *n,* aventure, expédition, *f.* ¶ *v.t,* aventurer. **adventurer,** *n,* aventurier, chercheur d'aventures, chevalier d'industrie, *m.* **adventuress,** *n,* aventurière, *f.* **adventurous,** *a,* aventureux.

adverb, *n,* adverbe, *m. ~ of number,* a. de quantité. **adverbial†,** *a,* adverbial.

adversary, *n,* adversaire, *m.* **adverse,** *a,* adverse; contraire; déficitaire. **adversity,** *n,* adversité, infortune, *f.*

advert, *v.i,* faire allusion.

advertise, *v.t,* annoncer, publier; afficher; (*v.i.*) faire une annonce (des annonces), faire de la publicité. *~ for,* demander par voie d'annonces. **~ment,** *n,* annonce; réclame. *f. ~ billboard,*

panneau-réclame, *m.* **advertiser,** *n,* annonceur, *m.* **advertising,** *n,* publicité, réclame, *f. ~ agency,* agence de publicité, *f.*

advice, *n,* avis, conseil, *m.* **advisable,** *a,* à conseiller, expédient, convenable. **advise,** *v.t,* conseiller; engager; aviser. **advisedly,** *ad,* de propos délibéré, en connaissance de cause. **adviser,** *n,* conseiller, ère, moniteur, *m.* **advisory,** *a,* consultatif.

advocate, *n,* avocat, défenseur; partisan, *m.* ¶ *v.t,* préconiser.

adze, *n,* herminette, *f.*

Aegean Sea (the), la mer Égée.

aegis, *n,* égide, *f.*

Aeolian, *a,* éolien.

aerate, *v.t,* aérer; gazéifier. *~d water,* eau gazeuse, *f.* **aeration,** *n,* aération, *f.*

aerial, *a,* aérien. ¶ (*radio*) *n,* antenne, *f.*

aerie, *n,* aire, *f.*

aerodynamic, *a. & ~s, n,* aérodynamique, *a. & f.*

aerolite, *n,* aérolithe, météorite, *m.*

aeronaut, *n,* aéronaute, *m,f.* **~ic(al),** *a,* aéronautique. **~ics,** *n,* aéronautique, *f.*

aerospatial, *a,* aérospatial.

afar, *ad,* loin, au loin. *from ~,* de loin.

affability, *n,* affabilité, *f.* **affable,** *a,* affable. **affably,** *ad,* avec affabilité.

affair, *n,* affaire, *f.*

affect, *v.t,* affecter, concerner, atteindre, impressionner; toucher, émouvoir, attendrir. **~ation,** *n,* affectation, afféterie, *f,* apprêt, *m.* **~ed,** *a,* affecté, affété, précieux, apprêté, maniéré, pincé. **~edly,** *ad,* avec affectation. **~ing,** *p.a,* touchant. **affection,** *n,* affection, *f.* **~ate†,** *a,* affectueux, aimant, affectionné.

affiance, *n,* confiance, foi, *f;* fiançailles, *f.pl.* ¶ *v.t,* fiancer.

affidavit, *n,* déclaration sous serment, *f.*

affiliate, *v.t,* affilier. ¶ *n,* compagnie associée, *f.*

affinity, *n,* affinité, *f.*

affirm, *v.t,* affirmer, assurer. **~ation,** *n,* affirmation, *f.* **~ative†,** *a,* affirmatif. ¶ *n,* affirmative, *f.*

affix, *n,* affixe, *m.* ¶ *v.t,* apposer. **~ture,** *n,* apposition, *f.*

afflict, *v.t,* affliger, chagriner. **~ion,** *n,* affliction, *f,* chagrin, *m.*

affluence, *n*, affluence; opulence, aisance, *f*. **affluent**, *a*, affluent, tributaire; opulent, aisé. ¶ *n*, affluent, *m*.

afford, *v.t*, donner, fournir, accorder. *can ~ to*, avoir les moyens de, pouvoir.

afforest, *v.t*, boiser. **~ation**, *n*, boisement, *m*.

affray, *n*, échauffourée, rixe, *f*.

affront, *n*, affront, *m*, avanie, *f*. ¶ *v.t*, offenser.

Afghan, *a*, afghan. ¶ *n*, Afghan, e.

afield, *ad*: *far ~*, très loin.

afire, *ad*, en feu, embrasé, brûlant.

afloat, *ad. & a*, à flot, sous voile, flottant; (*fig.*) sur pied, en circulation.

afoot, *ad*, à pied; sur pied; en cours; en route.

aforesaid, *a*, susdit, précité. ¶ *n*, susdit, e.

afraid, *a*, craintif. *to be ~ of*, avoir peur de, craindre.

afresh, *ad*, de nouveau, à nouveau.

Africa, *n*, l'Afrique, *f*, **African**, *a*, africain. ¶ *n*, Africain, e.

aft, *a*, arrière. ¶ *ad*, sur l'arrière, derrière.

after, *ad*, après; suivant; passé; à l'issue de. ¶ *c*, après que. ¶ *pr*, après, passé; d'après; à; sur. *~ all*, après tout, au bout du compte. *~ the event*, après coup.

aftermath, *n*, regain, *m*; répercussions, conséquences.

afternoon, *n*, après-midi, *m*.

aftertaste (*nasty*) *n*, arrière-goût, déboire, *m*.

afterthought, *n*, réflexion après coup, *f*.

afterwards, *ad*, après, ensuite, puis, plus tard.

again, *ad*, encore, de nouveau. *~ & ~*, mille [& mille] fois. *never ~*, jamais plus. *now and ~*, de temps à autre. **again** *after a verb is often expressed by the prefix* re- *as, to set out again*, repartir.

against, *pr*, contre, contraire à; sauf. *~ the grain*, à contre-fil, à rebours. *~ the light*, à contre-jour.

agate, *n*, agate, *f*.

age, *n*, âge; siècle; temps, *m*; époque; (*old age*) vieillesse; (*decay*) vétusté, *f*. *10 years of ~* or *~d 10*, âgé de 10 ans. *he is not of* (or *is under*) *~*, il n'est pas en âge. *to come of* [*full*] *~*,

être majeur, e. *it is ~s since*, il y a belle lurette que. ¶ *v.i*, vieillir.

aged (*of an advanced age*) *a*, âgé. *he has ~ considerably*, il a bien vieilli. *the ~* (either sex), les vieillards, *m.pl*.

agency, *n*, action; entremise, *f*, ministère, *m*; (*Com.*) agence, *f*, bureau; comptoir, *m*; factorerie; représentation, *f*.

agenda, *n*, ordre du jour, agenda, *m*.

agent, *n*, agent, commissionnaire, *m*; représentant, e; stockiste, *m*; mandataire, *m,f*; régisseur, *m*.

agglomerate, *v.t*, agglomérer.

agglutinate, *v.t*, agglutiner.

aggravate, *v.t*, aggraver. **aggravation**, *n*, aggravation, *f*.

aggregate, *a*, global, d'ensemble. ¶ *n*, total global; ensemble, *m*, masse, *f*. **aggregation**, *n*, agrégation, *f*.

aggression, *n*, agression, *f*. **aggressive**, *a*, agressif. **aggressor**, *n*, agresseur, *m*.

aggrieve, *v.i*, chagriner; léser. **aggrieved party**, offensé, e.

aghast, *a*, épouvanté, ébahi.

agile†, *a*, agile. **agility**, *n*, agilité, *f*.

agitate, *v.t*, agiter, remuer. **agitation**, *n*, agitation, *f*. **agitator**, *n*, agitateur, *m*.

aglow, *a*, resplendissant.

ago, *ad. & a*, passé, écoulé. *many years ~*, il y a de nombreuses années.

agog, *a*, en branle-bas; animé; impatient.

agonizing, *a*, déchirant, cuisant. **agony**, *n*, douleur déchirante, d. cuisante, (*pl.*) mort & passion; (*death pangs*) agonie, *f*.

agrarian, *a*, agraire.

agree, *v.t*, faire accorder, faire concorder, faire cadrer, apurer; (*v.i.*) s'accorder, s'arranger, s'entendre, cadrer, concorder, convenir. *~ to*, consentir à, souscrire à, s'engager à. *quite ~ with*, abonder dans le sens de. *meat does not ~ with me*, je ne digère pas la viande. **~able†**, *a*, agréable, amène; conforme. **~d** *price*, prix convenu, [prix à] forfait, *m*. **~ment**, *n*, accord, *m*, entente, convention, concordance, conformité, *f*; acte, contrat, marché, traité, *m*. *to be in ~*, être d'accord.

agricultural, *a*, agricole, aratoire. *~ implements*, instruments

aratoires, *m.pl.* ~ *show*, concours (*ou* comice) agricole, *m.*
agricultur[al]ist, *n,* agriculteur, cultivateur, *m.* **agriculture,** *n,* agriculture, *f.*
agronomist, *n,* agronome, *m.* **agronomy,** *n,* agronomie, *f.*
aground, *ad. & a,* échoué. **to run** ~, *v.i. & t,* [s']échouer.
ague, *n,* fièvre paludéenne, *f.*
ahead, *ad,* en avant, devant. **go** ~*l* en avant!
ahoy, *i,* ho!, ohé! *ship* ~*l* ho! du navire.
aid, *n,* aide, assistance, *f,* secours, *m.* ¶ *v.t,* aider, assister, secourir.
aide-de-camp, *n,* aide de camp, *m.*
ail, *v.t. & i,* avoir, souffrir. ~**ing,** *a,* maladif, souffrant. ~**ment,** *n,* mal, malaise, *m.*
aim, *n,* point de mire, *m,* visée, *f;* but, objectif, *m,* fin, *f.* ¶ *v.t,* pointer, coucher en joue. ~ *at,* viser [à], ajuster, coucher (*ou* metter) en joue. ~**less,** *a,* ~**less-ly,** *ad,* sans but.
air, *n,* air; vent; ciel, *m. to give oneself* ~*s,* faire l'important, e. ~*craft carrier,* porte-avions, *m.* ~ *craft exhibition,* salon de l'aviation. *m.* ~ *current,* courant d'air, *m.* ~ *cushion,* coussin à air, *m.* ~*field,* terrain d'aviation, *m.* ~ *gun,* fusil à air comprimé, f., à vent, *m.* ~*hole,* aspirail, soupirail, évent, *m;* soufflure, *f.* ~*line,* ligne aérienne, ligne d'avion, *f.* ~*liner,* avion de ligne régulière, *m.* ~*lock,* bouchon de vapeur, *m.* ~*mail,* poste aérienne, poste-avion, *f. by* ~*mail,* par avion. ~*man,* aviateur, *m.* ~ *mechanic,* mécanicien d'avions, *m.* ~*minded,* tourné vers l'aviation. ~ *parcel,* colis-avion, *m.* ~*plane,* avion, *m.* ~ *pocket,* trou d'air, *m.* ~*port,* aéroport, .*m.* ~ *pump,* (*Phys:*) machine pneumatique, *f.* ~ *race,* course d'avions, *f.* ~ *raid,* raid aérien, *m.* ~*shaft* (Min.), puits d'aérage, *m.* ~*ship,* dirigeable, paquebot aérien, *m.* ~*tight,* [à fermeture] hermétique, imperméable à l'air. ~*way* (Min.) galerie d'aérage. ¶ *v.t,* aérer, ventiler; donner de l'air à; éventer; chauffer, sécher; étaler. ~**ing,** *n,* aérage, *m,* aération, ventilation, *f.* ~**less,** *a,* sans

air, privé d'air. ~**y,** *a,* ventilé, aéré; en l'air; vain.
air-condition, *v.t,* climatiser. ~**ed,** *a,* climatisé. ~**er,** *n,* climatiseur, *m.*
aisle, *n,* aile, *f,* bas-côté, *m.*
ajar, *a,* entrebâillé, entrouvert. *be* ~, bâiller.
akimbo, *ad: to set one's arms* ~, faire le pot à deux anses. *with arms* ~, les mains sur les hanches.
akin, *a,* apparenté, voisin.
alabaster, *n,* albâtre, *m.*
alacrity, *n,* empressement, *m.*
alarm, *n,* alarme, alerte, *f;* avertisseur, *m.* ~ *clock,* réveille-matin, réveil, *m.* ¶ *v.t.* alarmer. ~**ing,** *a,* alarmant.
alas, *i,* hélas!
alb, *n,* aube, *f.*
albatross, *n,* albatros, *m.*
albino, *n,* albinos, *m,f.*
album, *n,* album, *m.*
albumen, *n,* albumen, *m.* **albumin,** *n,* albumine, *f.*
alchemist, *n,* alchimiste, *m.* **alchemy,** *n,* alchimie, *f.*
alcohol, *n,* alcool, *m.* ~**ic,** *a. & n,* alcoolique, *a. & m,f.*
alcove, *n,* alcôve, *f.*
alder, *n,* aune, ver[g]ne, *m.*
ale, *n,* bière, ale, *f.*
alert, *a,* alerte. *on the* ~, en alerte, en éveil, sur le qui-vive.
Alexandria, *n,* Alexandrie, *f.* **Alexandrian & Alexandrine,** *a,* alexandrin.
alfresco, *a. & ad,* en plein air.
algebra, *n,* algèbre, *m.*
Algeria, *n,* l'Algérie, *f.* **Algerian,** *a,* algérien. ¶ *n,* Algérien, ne. **Algiers,** *n,* Alger, *m.*
alias, *ad,* alias, autrement dit. ¶ *n,* faux nom; nom de guerre, *m.*
alibi, *n,* alibi, *m.*
alien, *a,* étranger. ¶ *n,* étranger, ère.
alienate, *v.t,* aliéner. (*Theat.*) *alienation effect,* distanciation, *f.*
alight, *a,* allumé. ¶ *v.i,* descendre, débarquer; atterrir; se poser. ~ [*on the water*] (seaplane), amerrir.
align, *v.t,* aligner. ~**ment,** *n,* alignement, *m.*
alike, *a,* semblable, pareil; ressemblant. ¶ *ad,* également; à la fois. *to be* ~, se ressembler.
alimentary, *a,* alimentaire. **alimony,** *n,* pension alimentaire, *f.*

alive, *a,* en vie, vivant, vif, au monde, animé; sensible; éveillé, dégourdi. *to be* ~ *with vermin,* grouiller de vermine.

alkali, *n,* alcali, *m.* **alkaline,** *a,* alcalin.

all, *a,* tout. ~ *the year* [*round*], [*pendant*] toute l'année. ~ [*those*] *who,* tous ceux qui, toutes celles qui. *at* ~ *hours,* à toute heure. *on* ~ *occasions,* en toute occasion. ¶ *ad,* tout; entièrement. ~ *at once,* tout à coup. ~ *but,* presque, à peu près. ~ *right!* très bien! c'est bien! à la bonne heure! ~ *the better,* tant mieux. ~ *the same,* tout de même, quand même. ¶ *n,* tous, *m.pl.*; tout; avoir, *m.* ~ *of us,* nous tous. *that is* ~, c'est tout, voilà tout. *that is not* ~, il s'en faut de beaucoup. *is that* ~? est-ce là tout? n'est-ce que cela? *one's* ~, tout son avoir, son tout, son va-tout. ~ *clear* (*Mil.*), fin d'alerte. ~ *in,* fatigué. ~ *told* or *in* ~, tout compte fait, pour tout potage.

allay, *v.t,* calmer, apaiser, adoucir.

allegation, *n,* allégation, *f.* **allege,** *v.t,* alléguer, prétendre, objecter.

allegiance, *n,* fidélité, obéissance, *f,* loyalisme, *m.*

allegoric(al†), *a,* allégorique. **allegory,** *n,* allégorie, *f.*

allergy, *n,* allergie, *f.*

alleviate, *v.t,* alléger, soulager, adoucir. **alleviation,** *n,* allégement, soulagement, adoucissement, *m.*

alley, *n,* ruelle, *f,* passage, *m.* *blind* ~, impasse, *f.*

All Fools' Day, le jour des poissons d'avril.

alliance, *n,* alliance, *f.*

allied, *a,* allié; parent.

alligator, *n,* alligator, *m.*

all-important, *ad,* de toute importance.

allocate, *v.t,* allouer. **allocation,** *n,* allocation, *f.*

allot, *v.t,* attribuer, répartir; destiner. ~**ment,** *n,* attribution, répartition, distribution, *f;* lopin de terre, allotissement, *m.* **allotee,** *n,* attributaire, *m,f.*

allow, *v.t,* permettre, autoriser; admettre; souffrir; laisser; allouer, accorder, faire, bonifier. ~**ance,** *n,* allouance, allocation; ration; pension; tolérance; boni-

fication, remise, déduction, *f,* rabais, décompte, *m,* ristourne, indemnité, *f.*

alloy, *n,* alliage, *m.* ¶ *v.t,* allier.

all-powerful, *a,* tout-puissant.

all-round, *a,* complet.

All Saints' Day, la Toussaint.

All Souls' Day, le jour des morts.

allspice, *n,* toute-épice, *f,* piment, *m.*

allude to (to), toucher.

allure, *v.t* amorcer, allécher, affrioler, affriander, appâter. ~**ment,** *n,* amorce, *f,* allèchement, appât, *m.* ~**ing,** *a,* séduisant.

allusion, *n,* allusion, *f.*

alluvion, alluvium, *n,* alluvion, *f.*

ally, *n,* allié, e. ¶ *v.t,* allier, apparenter.

almanac, *n,* almanach, *m.*

almighty, *a,* tout-puissant. *the Almighty,* le Tout-Puissant.

almond, *n,* amande, *f.* ~ *eyes,* des yeux en amande, des yeux bridés, *m.pl.* ~ [*tree*], amandier, *m.*

almost, *ad,* presque.

alms, *n.s. & pl,* aumône, l'aumône, charité, *f.* ~*giving,* distribution des aumônes, charité, *f.*

aloe, *n,* aloès; (*pl.*) [suc d']aloès, *m.*

aloft, *ad,* en haut; dans la mâture.

alone, *a,* seul; isolé. *to let* (or *leave*) ~, laisser tranquille. ¶ *ad,* seulement.

along, *pr. & ad,* le long de; suivant. ~*side of* (*pers.*), côte à côte avec. ~*side* [*the ship*], le long [du bord]. *to come* ~*side,* accoster. *come* ~! venez donc! *all* ~, tout du long; tout le temps.

aloof, *ad,* à l'écart, en dehors, isolé (*from* = de). ¶ *a,* distant.

aloud, *ad,* à haute voix, tout haut.

alpaca, *n,* alpaga, *m.*

alpha, *n,* alpha, *m.* **alphabet,** *n,* alphabet, *m.* ~**ical†,** *a,* alphabétique.

Alpine, *a,* alpin; alpestre. **the Alps,** les Alpes, *f.pl,* les monts, *m.pl.*

already, *ad,* déjà.

Alsace, *n,* l'Alsace, *f.* **Alsatian,** *a,* alsacien. ¶ *n,* (*pers.*) Alsacien, ne; (*dog*) chien-loup, *m.*

also, *ad,* aussi, également, pareillement.

altar, *n,* autel, *m.* ~ *cloth,* nappe

d'a., *f.* ~ *piece*, tableau d'a.; retable, *m.*

alter, *v.t*, changer, modifier; surcharger; (*v.i.*) [se] changer. ~ *the date of* (function, etc.), transférer. ~**ation**, *n*, changement, *m*, modification; surcharge, *f*, renvoi [en marge], *m.*

altercation, *n*, altercation, prise de bec, *f.*

alternate†, *a*, alternatif. ~ *months* (newspaper appearing), bimensuel. ¶ *v.i.* & *t*, alterner. **alternating**, *p.a*, alternatif. **alternative**, *a*, alternatif. ¶ *n*, alternative, *f.*

although, *c*, quoique, bien que, encore que, quand, tout . . . que.

altitude, *n*, altitude, élévation, hauteur, *f.*

alto, *n.* & ~ *saxhorn*, alto, *m.* ~ *clef*, clef d'ut, *f.*

altogether, *ad*, tout à fait; en tout; grandement.

altruist, *n.* & ~**ic**, *a*, altruiste, *m.f.* & *a.*

alum, *n*, alun, *m.*

aluminum, *n*, aluminium, *m.*

always, *ad*, toujours.

amalgam, *n*, amalgame, *m.* ~**ate**, *v.t*, amalgamer, fusionner.

amanuensis, *n*, secrétaire, *m.*

amass, *v.t*, amasser.

amateur, *n*, amateur; dilettante, *m.* ~ *status*, qualité d'amateur, *f*, statut d'a., *m.* **amatory**, *a*, galant, érotique.

amaze, *v.t*, étonner, stupéfier. ~**ment**, *n*, étonnement, *m*, stupeur, *f.*

Amazon, *n*, amazone; virago, *f.* the ~ (*river*), l'Amazone, *m*, le fleuve des Amazones.

ambassador, **dress**, *n*, ambassadeur, drice.

amber, *n*, ambre, *m.* ~**gris**, *n*, ambre gris, *m.*

ambiguity, *n*, ambiguïté, équivoque, *f.* **ambiguous**†, *a*, ambigu, équivoque.

ambition, *n*, ambition, *f.* **ambitious**†, *a*, ambitieux.

amble along (**to**), aller son petit train.

ambrosia, *n*, ambroisie, *f.*

ambulance, *n*, ambulance, *f.*

ambuscade, **ambush**, *n*, embuscade, *f*, guetapens, *m. to place in* ~, embusquer. **ambush**, *v.i*, s'embusquer.

ameliorate, *v.t*, améliorer. **amelioration**, *n*, amélioration, *f.*

amen, *i.* & *n*, amen, *i.* & *m.*

amenable, *a*, sujet, soumis; susceptible; justiciable; docile.

amend, *v.t*, amender; réformer; rectifier; changer. ~**s**, *n*, réparation, *f. make* ~ *for*, réparer, corriger, racheter.

amenity, *n*, aménité, *f*; agrément, *m.*

America, *n*, l'Amérique, *f.* **American**, *a*, américain. ¶ *n*, Américain, e.

amethyst, *n*, améthyste, *f.*

amiability, *n*, amabilité, *f.* **amiable**, *a*, aimable, accort. **amiably**, *ad*, avec amabilité.

amicable†, *a*, amical, amiable.

amid, **amidst**, *pr*, au milieu de, parmi. **amidships**, *ad*, au milieu du navire.

amiss, *ad.* & *a*, de travers; mal, en mal, en mauvaise part. *to take* ~, prendre mal.

ammonia, *n*, ammoniaque, *f.*

ammunition, *n*, munitions, *f.pl.* ~ *wagon*, prolonge, *f.*

amnesia, *n*, amnésie, *f.*

amnesty, *n*, amnistie, *f.*

among, **amongst**, *pr*, parmi, entre, dans; au milieu de; au nombre de; chez. ~ *strangers*, dépaysé.

amorous†, *a*, amoureux.

amorphous, *a*, amorphe.

amortization, *n*, amortissement, *m.* **amortize**, *v.t*, amortir.

amount, *n*, montant, *m*, somme, *f*, chiffre, *m*, quantité, *f.* ¶ *v.i*, monter, se chiffrer, s'élever; revenir. ~*ing to*, à concurrence de.

ampere, *n*, ampère, *f.*

amphibian, *n*, amphibie, *m.* **amphibious**, *a*, amphibie.

amphitheater, *n*, amphithéâtre, *m.*

ample†, *a*, ample. ~**ness**, *n*, ampleur, *f.* **amplifier** (*radio*) *n*, amplificateur, *m.* **amplify**, *v.t.* & *i*, amplifier; développer; paraphraser. **amplitude**, *n*, amplitude, *f.*

amputate, *v.t*, amputer.

amulet, *n*, amulette, *f.*

amuse, *v.t*, amuser, divertir, distraire. ~**ment**, *n*, amusement, plaisir, divertissement, *m*, distraction, *f.*

amusing, *a*, amusant.

an, *indefinite art.* or *a*, un, une.

anachronism, *n*, anachronisme, *m.*

anagram, *n*, anagramme, *f.*

analogous, *a*, analogue. **analogy**, *n*, analogie, *f*.

analyze, *v.t*, analyser; (*Bkkpg.*) dépouiller, ventiler. **analysis**, *n*, analyse; ventilation, *f*. **analyst**, *n*, analyste, *m*. **analytic**(**al**†), *a*, analytique.

anarchic(**al**), *a*, anarchique. **anarchist**, *n*, anarchiste, *m.f*. **anarchy**, *n*, anarchie, *f*.

anatomical†, *a*, anatomique. **anatomy**, *n*, anatomie, *f*.

ancestor, *n*, ancêtre, *m*. **ancestral**, *a*, ancestral. **ancestry**, *n*, race, *f*, ascendants, *m.pl*.

anchor (*all senses*), *n*, ancre, *f*. ¶ (*Naut.*) *v.t. & i*, mouiller; (*Build. & fig.*) *v.t*, ancrer. **~age** (*Naut.*) *n*, mouillage, *m*.

anchoret, **anchorite**, *n*, anachorète, *m*.

anchovy, *n*, anchois, *m*. **~ paste**, beurre d'anchois, *m*.

ancient†, *a*, ancien; antique. ¶ *n*, ancien, *m*. **~ness**, *n*, ancienneté, antiquité, *f*.

and, *c*. (*abb. &*), et, &. **~ even**, voire même. **~ so on** or **~ so forth**, et ainsi de suite. **~ so on**, **~ so forth**, et patati, et patata. **go ~ see**, allez voir. **more ~ more**, de plus en plus. **two ~ two**, deux à deux. **steak ~ potatoes**, bifteck aux pommes.

andiron, *n*, chenet, *m*.

anecdote, *n*, anecdote, historiette, *f*.

anemia, *n*, anémie, *f*. **anemic**, *a*, anémique.

anemone, *n*, anémone, *f*.

aneroid [**barometer**], baromètre anéroïde, *m*.

anesthetic, *a. & n*, anesthetique, *a. & m*. ¶ *v.t*, **anesthetize**, insensibiliser.

anew, *ad*, à nouveau, de nouveau.

angel, *n*, ange, *m*. **~ic**(**al**†), *a*, angélique. **angelus** [**bell**], Angélus, *m*.

anger, *n*, colère, *f*, courroux, *m*. ¶ *v.t*, mettre en colère, fâcher, courroucer, irriter.

angina, *n*, angine, *f*. **~ pectoris**, angine de poitrine.

angle, *n*, angle, *m*. **~** [*iron*], fer cornière, *m*, cornière, *f*.

angle, *v.i*, pêcher à la ligne. **angler**, *n*, pêcheur à la ligne, *m*.

Anglicism, *n*, anglicisme, *m*.

angling, *n*, pêche à la ligne, *f*. **~ at set pitches**, pêche au coup.

Anglomania, *n*, anglomanie, *f*.

Anglophil[**e**], *a. & n*, anglophile,

a. & m.f. **Anglophobe**, *a. & n*, anglophobe, *a. & m.f*. **Anglo-Saxon**, *a*, anglo-saxon. ¶ *n*, Anglo-Saxon, ne.

angrily, *ad*, avec colère. **angry**, *a*, en colère, fâché, irrité. *to get* (or *be*) **~**, se fâcher. *to be* **~ with oneself** *for*, s'en vouloir de.

anguish, *n*, angoisse, *f*. ¶ *v.i*, angoisser.

angular, *a*, angulaire.

aniline, *n*, aniline, *f*. **~ dye**, teinture d'aniline, *f*.

animal, *a*, animal. ¶ *n*, animal, *m*.

animate, *a*, animé, doué de vie. ¶ *v.t*, animer. **animation**, *n*, animation, *f*.

animosity, **animus**, *n*, animosité, *f*.

aniseed, *n*, anis, *m*, graine d'anis, *f*.

ankle, *n*, cheville [du pied], malléole, *f*.

annals, *n.pl*, annales, *f.pl*, fastes, *m.pl*.

anneal, *v.t*, recuire. **~ing**, *n*, recuit, *m*, recuite, *f*.

annex, *v.t*, annexer. **~ation**, *n*, annexion, *f*. **annex**[**e**], *n*, annexe, dépendance, *f*.

annihilate, *v.t*, anéantir, annihiler. **annihilation**, *n*, anéantissement, *m*, annihilation, *f*.

anniversary, *a. & n*, anniversaire, *a. & m*.

annotate, *v.t*, annoter.

announce, *v.t*, annoncer. **~ment**, *n*, annonce, *f*. **announcer** (*radio*) *n*, speaker; annoncier, *m*.

annoy, *v.t*, agacer, tracasser, contrarier, ennuyer. *to be* **~ed with**, savoir mauvais gré à. **~ance**, *n*, agacement, *m*, tracasserie, contrariété; fâcherie, *f*. **~ing**, *a*, agaçant, contrariant.

annual†, *a*, annuel. ¶ *n*, plante annuelle, *f*; (*book*) annuaire, *m*. **annuitant**, *n*, rentier, ère. **annuity**, *n*, annuité, rente [à terme], *f*.

annul, *v.t*, annuler, annihiler.

annular, *a*, annulaire.

annum, *n*: *per* **~**, par an.

Annunciation (**the**), l'Annonciation, *f*.

anode, *n*, anode, *f*.

anodyne, *a*, anodin. ¶ *n*, anodin, *m*.

anoint, *v.t*, oindre, sacrer. **~ed**, *a. & n*, oint, *a.m. & m*.

anomalous, *a*, anomal. **anomaly**, *n*, anomalie, *f*.

anon, *ad*, tantôt, tout à l'heure.

anonymous, *a*, anonyme.

another, *n*, un (une) autre; autre; encore un, encore une; nouveau; un (une) second, e.

answer, *n*, réponse; réplique, *f*. ~s to correspondents, petite correspondance, *f*. ~ to the riddle, mot de l'énigme, *m*. ¶ *v.t*, répondre à: ~ [*back*], répliquer. ~ for, répondre pour, de. **~able**, *a*, responsable.

ant, *n*, fourmi, *f*. **~eater**, fourmilier, *m*. **~hill**, fourmilière, *f*.

antagonism, *n*, antagonisme, *m*. **antagonist**, *n*, antagoniste, *m*. **antagonize**, *v.t*, rendre hostile.

antarctic, *a*, antarctique. the A~ Ocean, l'océan Glacial antarctique, *m*.

antecedent, *a*. & *n*, antécédent, *a*. & *m*.

antechamber, *n*, antichambre, *f*.

antedate, *v.t*, antidater.

antediluvian, *a*, antédiluvien.

antelope, *n*, antilope, *f*.

ante meridiem (*abb*. a.m.), avant midi; du matin.

antenna, *n*, antenne, *f*.

anterior†, *a*, antérieur.

anteroom, *n*, antichambre, *f*.

anthem, *n*, antienne, *f*; (*national*) hymne, *m*.

anther, *n*, anthère, *f*.

anthology, *n*, anthologie, *f*.

anthracite, *n*, anthracite, *m*.

anthrax (*Med.*) *n*, anthrax, *m*.

antiaircraft, *a*, anti-aérien, contre-avions.

antibiotic, *n*, antibiotique, *m*.

antibody, *n*, anticorp, *m*.

anti-British, *a*, anglophobe.

antic, *n*, (*pl.*) gambades, *f.pl*.

antichrist, *n*, antéchrist, *m*. the A~, l'A.

anticipate, *v.t*, anticiper, prévenir, escompter. **anticipation**, *n*, anticipation, prévision, *f*.

anticlimax, *n*, gradation descendante, *f*.

anticyclone, *n*, anticyclone, *m*.

antidote, *n*, antidote, contre-poison, *m*.

antifreeze, *n*, antigel, *m*.

anti-French, *a*, gallophobe.

antiglare, *a*, anti-aveuglant.

antimony, *n*, antimoine, *m*.

antipathetic, *a*, antipathique. **antipathy**, *n*, antipathie, *f*.

antipodes, *n.pl*, antipodes, *m.pl*.

antiquary, antiquarian, *n*, antiquaire, *m,f*. **antiquated**, *a*, suranné, vieilli. **antique**, *a*, antique. ¶ *n*, (*style*) antique, *m*;

(*relic*) antique, *f*. **antiquity**, *n*, antiquité; ancienneté, *f*.

antiseptic, *a*. & *n*, antiseptique, *a*. & *m*.

antithesis, *n*, antithèse, *f*.

antler, *n*, andouiller, *m*, (*pl.*) bois, *m.pl*.

Antwerp, *n*, Anvers, *m*.

anus, *n*, anus, *m*.

anvil, *n*, enclume, *f*.

anxiety, *n*, anxiété, inquiétude; sollicitude, *f*. **anxious**, *a*, anxieux, inquiet; soucieux; désireux, jaloux. **~ly**, *ad*, avec anxiété.

any, *a*, *ad*. & *pn*, quelque; quelconque; de; du, de la, des; aucun; tout; plus; quelqu'un. has he ~? en a-t-il? I don't have ~, je n'en ai pas. ~ farther, ~ further, plus loin. ~ more, encore; (*neg.*) plus. **~way**, n'importe comment; en tout cas.

anybody, anyone, *n*. & *pn*, quelqu'un; on; personne; aucun; tout le monde; le premier venu.

anyhow, *ad*, de toute façon; en tout cas, toujours; n'importe comment; à l'abandon, à la débandade.

anything, *pn*. & *n*, quelque chose, *m*; (*neg.*) rien, *m*; quoi que ce soit; n'importe quoi.

anywhere, *ad*, n'importe où; quelque part; (*neg.*) nulle part.

aorta, *n*, aorte, *f*.

apace, *ad*, à grands pas.

apart, *ad*, à part; de côté; séparément. ~ from, abstraction faite de. to move ~, se séparer, s'écarter. to tell ~, distinguer.

apartment, *n*, appartement, logement, *m*, salle, pièce, *f*. ~ house, maison de rapport, *f*.

apathetic, *a*, apathique, indolent. **apathy**, *n*, apathie, indolence, *f*.

ape, *n*, singe (sans queue), *m*. ¶ *v.t*, singer.

aperture, *n*, ouverture, *f*, orifice, *m*.

apex, *n*, sommet, faîte, *m*.

aphorism, *n*, aphorisme, *m*.

apiary, *n*, rucher, *m*.

apiece, *ad*, [la] pièce.

apish, *a*, simiesque.

apogee, *n*, apogée, *m*.

apologetic, *a*, apologétique. **apologize**, *v.i*, faire ses excuses. **apology**, *n*, apologie, *f*; excuses, *f.pl*; semblant, *m*.

apoplectic, *a*. & *n*, apoplectique, *a*. & *m*. ~ fit, attaque d'apoplexie, *f*, coup de sang, *m*. **apoplexy**, *n*, apoplexie, *f*.

apostasy, *n*, apostasie, *f*. **apostate**, *n*. & *a*, apostat, *m*. & *att*, relaps, e.

apostle, *n*, apôtre, *m*. the [*A~s'*] *Creed*, le symbole [des apôtres]. **apostolate, apostleship**, *n*, apostolat, *m*. **apostolic**(al†), *a*, apostolique.

apostrophe, *n*, apostrophe, *f*. **apostrophize**, *v.t*, apostropher.

apothecaries' measure, mesure pharmaceutique, *f*.

apotheosis, *n*, apothéose, *f*.

appall, *v.t*, épouvanter. **appalling**, *a*, épouvantable.

apparatus, *n*, appareil, attirail, *m*.

apparel, *n*, habillement, *m*, vêtements, *m.pl*.

apparent, *a*, apparent; (*heir*) présomptif. **~ly**, *ad*, apparemment.

apparition, *n*, apparition, *f*.

appeal, *n*, appel; pourvoi; recours; attrait, *m*. ¶ *v.i*, en appeler; faire appel; appeler.

appear, *v.i*, paraître, sembler; apparaître; figurer, ressortir; comparaître. **~ance**, *n*, apparition; apparence, venue, *f*, semblant, aspect, *m*; mine; comparution, *f*; (*pl*.) apparences, *f.pl*, dehors, *m.pl*.

appease, *v.t*, apaiser, adoucir; pacifier. **~ment**, *n*, apaisement, *m*, conciliation, *f*.

appellation, *n*, surnom, *m*; désignation, *f*.

append, *v.t*, apposer. **~age**, appendix, *n*, appendice, *m*. **appendicitis**, *n*, appendicite, *f*.

appertain, *v.i*, appartenir.

appetite, *n*, appétit, *m*. **appetizer**, *n*, apéritif, *m*. **appetizing**, *a*, appétissant.

applaud, *v.t*, applaudir [à]. **applause**, *n*, applaudissement[s] *m*. [*pl*.].

apple, *n*, pomme, *f*; (*eye*) prunelle, *f*. ~ *corer*, vide-pomme, *m*. ~ *orchard*, pommeraie, *f*. ~ *pie*, tourte aux pommes, *f*. ~ *tree*, pommier, *m*.

appliance, *n*, engin, appareil; (*pl*.) attirail, *m*.

applicant, *n*, demandeur, euse; postulant, e; souscripteur, *m*. **application**, *n*, application; contention; affectation; demande, réclamation; souscription; mise en œuvre, *f*; (*brake*) serrage, *m*. on

~, sur demande. **applied** (*of sciences*) *a*, appliqué. **appliqué** lace, [dentelle d']application, *f*. **appliqué** [**work**] (*metal*), applique, *f*. **appliqué** (*or applied*) **work** (*Emb*.), broderie-application, *f*. **apply**, *v.t*, appliquer, affecter; (*brake*) serrer. ~ *for*, solliciter, postuler, demander, réclamer; souscrire. ~ *to*, s'adresser à.

appoint, *v.t*, nommer, instituer, constituer, désigner, préposer. **~ment**, *n*, nomination, désignation, constitution, *f*; rendezvous; (*pl*.) aménagement, emménagement, *m*.

apportion, *v.t*, répartir, ventiler.

apposite, *a*, à propos, pertinent.

apposition, *n*, apposition, *f*.

appraise, *v.t*, priser. **~ment**, *n*, prisée, *f*. **appraiser**, *n*, priseur, *m*.

appreciable, *a*, appréciable, sensible. **appreciably**, *ad*, sensiblement. **appreciate**, *v.t*, apprécier; améliorer; (*v.i.*) s'améliorer. **appreciation**, *n*, appréciation; amélioration, plus-value, *f*.

apprehend, *v.t*, appréhender; redouter; saisir. **apprehension**, *n*, appréhension, *f*. **apprehensive**, *a*, inquiet.

apprentice, *n*, apprenti, e; (*Naut.*) novice, *m*. ¶ *v.t*, mettre en apprentissage. **~ship**, *n*, apprentissage; noviciat, *m*.

apprise, *v.t*, prévenir, informer.

approach, *n*, approche, *f*; accès, abord, *m*. ¶ *v.t*, [s']approcher de, aborder; (*v.i.*) [s']approcher. **~able**, *a*, abordable, accessible.

approbation, *n*, approbation, *f*.

appropriate†, *a*, propre, convenable, approprié. to be ~, être de mise. ¶ *v.t*, s'approprier; consacrer, distraire, affecter. **appropriation**, *n*, somme affectée, destination, *f*.

approval, *n*, approbation, *f*, agrément, *m*, sanction, *f*. on ~, à condition. **approve**, *v.t*, approuver, agréer, sanctionner.

approximate†, *a*, approximatif. ¶ *v.t*, rapprocher, approcher. **approximation**, *n*, approximation, *f*.

apricot, *n*, abricot, *m*. ~ *tree*, abricotier, *m*.

April, *n*, avril, *m*. to make an ~ *fool of*, donner un poisson d'avril à.

apron, *n*, tablier, *m*.

apropos, *ad*, à propos.

apse, *n,* abside, *f.*

apt, *a,* enclin, sujet, disposé, porté; à propos; apte. **~ly,** *ad,* à propos. **~ness,** *n,* àpropos, *m.* **aptitude,** *n,* aptitude, facilité, *f,* dispositions, *f.pl.*

aqua-fortis, eau-forte, *f.* **aquamarine,** *n,* aigue-marine, *f.* **aqua-regis,** eau régale, *f.*

aquarium, *n,* aquarium, *m.*

aquatic, *a,* (*plant*) aquatique; (*sport*) nautique.

aqueduct, *n,* aqueduc, *m.*

aqueous, *a,* aqueux.

aquiline, *a,* aquilin.

Arab, *a,* arabe. ¶ *n,* Arabe, *m,f.* **arabesque,** *n,* arabesque, *f.* **Arabia,** *n,* l'Arabie, *f.* **Arabian,** *a,* arabe. *the ~ Nights,* les Mille & une Nuits. ¶ *n,* Arabe, *m,f.* **Arabic** (*language*) *n,* l'arabe, *m.* **Arabic numerals,** chiffres arabes, *m.pl.*

arable, *a,* arable, labourable.

arbiter, *n,* arbitre, *m.* **arbitrage** & **arbitrament,** *n,* arbitrage, *m.* **arbitrary†,** *a,* arbitraire; conventionnel; d'office. **arbitrate,** *v.t,* arbitrer. **arbitration,** *n,* arbitrage, *m.* *~ clause,* clause compromissoire, *f.* **arbitrator,** *n,* arbitre; (*law*) amiable compositeur, *m.*

arbor, *n,* arbre, mandrin, *m,* broche, *f.*

arbor, *n,* tonnelle, *f,* verger, *m.*

arc, *n,* arc, *m.* *~ lamp,* lampe à arc, *f.*

arcade, *n,* arcades, *f.pl,* galerie, *f,* passage, bazar, *m.*

arch, *a,* espiègle, malicieux. ¶ *n,* voûte, *f,* arceau, *m,* arcade, arche; porte, *f*; arc, cintre, *m.* *~ support* (for foot in shoe), cambrure-support, *f.* ¶ *v.t,* cintrer, arquer, cambrer, voûter.

archaeologic(al), *a,* archéologique. **archaeologist,** *n,* archéologue, *m.* **archaeology,** *n,* archéologie, *f.*

archaic, *a,* archaïque, vieux, vieilli.

archangel, *n,* archange, *m.*

archbishop, *n,* archevêque, *m.* **archbishopric,** *n,* archevêché, *m.*

archdeacon, *n,* archidiacre, *m.*

archer, *n,* archer, *m.* **~y,** *n,* tir à l'arc, *m.*

Archimedean screw, vis d'Archimède, limace, *f.*

archipelago, *n,* archipel, *m.*

architect, *n,* architecte; (*fig.*) artisan, *m.* **architectural,** *a,* ar-chitectural. **architecture,** *n,* ar-chitecture, *f.*

archives, *n.pl,* archives, *f.pi.*

archly, *ad,* malicieusement. **archness,** *n,* espièglerie, *f.*

archway, *n,* arcade, *f,* passage voûté; portail, *m.*

arctic, *a,* arctique. *the A~ Ocean,* l'océan Glacial arctique, *m.*

ardent, *a,* ardent. **~ly,** *ad,* ardemment. **ardor,** *n,* ardeur, *f,* zèle, *m.*

arduous, *a,* ardu, pénible, laborieux.

are *see* be.

area, *n,* aire, superficie, surface; zone, étendue, *f*; réseau, *m.*

arena, *n,* arène, *f.*

argentine, *a,* argentin. **A~** (*Geog.*) *a,* argentin. ¶ *n* (*pers.*), Argentin, e. *the ~,* l'Argentine, *f.*

argue, *v.i. & t,* argumenter, raisonner, discuter, débattre, prétendre, plaider. **argument,** *n,* argument, raisonnement, *m,* thèse, *f.* **~ation,** arguing, *n,* argumentation, *f.* **~ative,** *a,* raisonneur.

aria (*Mus.*) *n,* air, *m.*

arid, *a,* aride. **~ity,** *n,* aridité, *f.*

aright, *ad,* bien, justement.

arise, *v.i.ir,* s'élever, surgir, naître, survenir.

aristocracy, *n,* aristocratie, *f.* **aristocrat,** *n,* aristocrate, *m,f.* **aristocratic(al†),** *a,* aristocratique.

arithmetic, *n,* arithmétique, *f,* calcul, *m.* **~al†,** *a,* arithmétique. **~ian,** *n,* arithméticien, ne.

ark, *n,* arche, *f.* *the A~ of the Covenant,* l'arche d'alliance, *f.*

arm, *n,* (*limb*) bras; (*of cross*) croisillon, *m*; (*weapon*) arme, *f*; (*pl., Her.*) armes, armoiries, *f.pl,* blason, *m*; (*rest*) bras, accotoir, accoudoir, *m.* *~ in ~,* bras dessus, bras dessous. *to be up in ~s,* se gendarmer. *~chair,* fauteuil, *m.* **~hole,** emmanchure, *f.* **~pit,** aisselle, *f.* *~s race,* course aux armements, *f.* ¶ *v.t,* armer; (*v.i.*) [s']armer.

armadillo, *n,* tatou, *m.*

armament, *n,* armement, *m.*

armature, *n,* (*Phys.*) armature, armure, *f*; (*dynamo*) induit, *m.*

Armenia, *n,* l'Arménie, *f.* **Armenian,** *a,* arménien. ¶ *n,* Arménien, ne.

armful, *n,* brassée, *f.*

armistice, *n*, armistice, *m*. A~ Day, la fête [de l'anniversaire] de l'Armistice, le jour anniversaire de l'Armistice.

armlet, *n*, brassard, *m*.

armor, *n*, armure; (*sheathing*) armature, cuirasse, *f*. ~ *plate*, plaque de blindage, *f*. ~ *plating*, blindage, *m*. ~ed, *a*, armé; blindé, cuirassé, protégé. ~ *car*, automobile blindée, *f*. ~er, *n*, armurier, *m*. ~y, *n*, salle d'armes, *f*. **armorial,** *a*. & *n*, armorial, *a*. & *m*. ~ *bearings*, armoiries, armes, *f.pl*, blason, *m*.

army, *n*, armée, *f*. ~ *contractor*, fournisseur de l'armée, *m*.

arnica, *n*, arnica, *m*.

aroma, *n*, arôme; bouquet, *m*. **aromatic,** *a*, aromatique.

around, *ad*, autour, alentour. ¶ *pr*, autour de.

arouse, *v.t*, réveiller; provoquer.

arpeggio, *n*, arpège, *m*.

arraign, *v.t*, accuser; traduire en justice. ~ment, *n*, mise en accusation, *f*.

arrange, *v.t*, arranger, disposer, agencer, ménager; distribuer; accommoder; débattre, arbitrer. ~ment, *n*, arrangement, *m*, disposition, *f*, agencement, mouvement, *m*; économie; distribution, *f*; accommodement; dispositif, *m*.

arrant, *a*, franc, insigne, fieffé, achevé, fier.

arras, *n*, tapisserie, *f*.

array, *n*, ordre; appareil, *m*; série, rangée, *f*. ¶ *v.t*, ranger; ajuster; revêtir.

arrears, *n.pl*, arrérages, *m. in arrear[s]*, en arrière, arriéré en retard, retardataire; en demeure.

arrest, *n*, arrestation, prise de corps, *f*; arrêt, *m*. *under* ~, (*civil*) en état d'arrestation; (*Mil.*) aux arrêts. ¶ *v.t*, arrêter; appréhender. ~er (*Elec.*, *etc.*) *n*, déchargeur, *m*.

arrival, *n*, arrivée, *f*; arrivage, *m*. **arrive,** *v.i*, arriver; parvenir. ~ *unexpectedly*, survenir.

arrogance, *n*, arrogance, *f*. **arrogant,** *a*, arrogant, rogue. ~ly, *ad*, arrogamment. **to arrogate** [to oneself], s'arroger.

arrow, *n*, flèche, *f*, trait, *m*.

arsenal, *n*, arsenal, *m*.

arsenic, *n*, arsenic, *m*. ~al, *a*, arsenical.

arson, *n*, incendie volontaire, *m*.

art, *n*, art; artifice, *m*. ~ *school*, école des beaux-arts, *f*.

arterial (*Anat.*) *a*, artériel. ~ *road* (*Eng.*), route nationale de grand itinéraire, *f*. (= in Fr. *a widened main road*). **artery,** *n*, artère, *f*.

artesian, *a*, artésien. ~ *well*, puits artésien, *m*.

artful†, *a*, artificieux, astucieux, rusé. ~ *dodger*, fin matois, finaud, *m*. ~ness, *n*, artifice, art, *m*, astuce, finauderie, finasserie, ruse, malice, *f*.

arthritis, *n*, arthrite, *f*.

artichoke, *n*, artichaut, *m*. *Jerusalem* ~, topinambour, *m*.

article, *n*, article, objet, envoi; (*pl.*) stage, apprentissage; (*pl.*) contrat; (*pl.*—ship's) rôle d'équipage, rôle d'armement, *m*. ~s [*of association*], statuts, *m.pl*. (*newspaper*) *lead* ~, article de fond, *m*.

articulate, *v.t*, articuler; (*v.i.*) [s']articuler. **articulation,** *n*, articulation, *f*.

artifice, *n*, artifice, art, *m*.

artificer, *n*, [mécanicien] adjusteur, serrurier mécanicien; (*fig.*) artisan, *m*.

artificial†, *a*, artificiel, factice, simili-, postiche.

artillery, *n*, artillerie, *f*. ~man, *n*, artilleur, *m*.

artisan, *n*, artisan, *m*.

artist, & **artiste,** *n*, artiste, *m,f*. **artistic,** *a*, artistique; artiste. ~ *novelties*, articles de Paris, *m.pl*. ~ally, *ad*, artistiquement, avec art.

artless†, *a*, sans art, naturel; innocent; naïf, ingénu.

Aryan, *a*, aryen.

as, *ad*. & *c*, comme; ainsi que; de même que; parce que; puisque, aussi; que; à titre de; pour. ~ *also*, ainsi que. ~ [& *when*], au fur & à mesure que. ~ [& *when*] *required*, au fur & à mesure des besoins. ~ *before*, comme par le passé. ~ *for*, ~ *to*, ~ *regards*, quant à. ~ *if*, comme si. ~ *in* (like, equal to), à l'instar de. ~ *it were*, en quelque sorte. ~ *per*, suivant, dont. ~ *well* ~, aussi bien que, en même temps que. ~ *you were!* au temps!

asbestos, *n*, asbeste, *m*.

ascend, *v.t*. & *i*, [re]monter, faire l'ascension de. ~ancy, ~ency, & ~ant, ~ent, *n*, ascendant, *m*. **ascension,** *n*, ascension, *f*. A~

Day, l'Ascension. **ascent**, *n*, ascension; montée, *f*.

ascertain, *v.t*, constater, reconnaître, se rendre compte de.

ascetic, *a*, ascétique. ¶ *n*, ascète, *m,f*.

ascribe, *v.t*, attribuer, imputer, rapporter.

ash, *n. oft. pl*, cendre, *f. oft. pl*. ~ **blonde** (color), blond cendré, *m*. ~ **pit**, fosse aux cendres, *f*. ~**tray**, cendrier [de fumeur] *m*. ~ [**tree**], frêne, *m*. **A~ Wednesday**, le mercredi (*ou* le jour) des Cendres.

ashamed, *a* honteux. **to be ~**, avoir honte, rougir.

ashen, **ashy** (*ash-colored*) *a*, cendré.

ashlar, *n*, moellon d'appareil, *m*.

ashore, *ad*, à terre.

Asia, *n*, l'Asie, *f*. ~ *Minor*, l'Asie Mineure. **Asiatic**, *a*, asiatique. ¶ *n*, Asiatique, *m,f*.

aside, *ad*, de côté; à part; à l'écart; en aparté. ¶ *n*, aparté, *m*.

ask, *v.t*, demander, prier, inviter, interroger, solliciter; poser; s'enquérir. ~ *not to come* (guests), désinviter, décommander.

askance, *ad*, de travers, de biais.

askew, *ad*, en biais, de travers, de guingois.

aslant, *ad*, en biais, obliquement.

asleep, *a*, endormi. **to fall ~**, s'endormir.

asp, *n*, (*serpent*) aspic; (*tree*) tremble, *m*.

asparagus, *n*, asperge, *f*; asperges, *f.pl*. ~ *tongs*, pince à asperges, *f*.

aspect, *n*, aspect, *m*; face, *f*, visage, *m*; exposition, orientation, *f*.

aspen, *n*, tremble, *m*. ~ *plantation*, tremblaie, *f*.

asperity, *n*, aspérité, âpreté, *f*.

asperse, *v.t*, asperger; diffamer, calomnier, noircir. **aspersion**, *n*, aspersion; diffamation, calomnie, *f*.

asphalt, *n*, asphalte, bitume, *m*. ¶ *v.t*, bitumer.

asphyxia, *n*, asphyxie, *f*. **asphyxiate**, *v.t*, asphyxier.

aspirant, *n*, aspirant, e. **aspirate**, *v.t*, aspirer. **aspiration**, *n*, aspiration, *f*. **to aspire to**, aspirer à, prétendre à, affecter, ambitionner, briguer.

aspirin, *n*, aspirine, *f*.

ass, *n*, âne, *m*, (*she*) ânesse, *f*. *ass's foal*, ânon, *m*. *ass's* (*or*

asses') *milk*, lait d'ânesse, *m*.

assail, *v.t*, assaillir. ~**ant**, *n*, assaillant, *m*.

assassin, *n*, assassin, e. ~**ate**, *v.t*, assassiner. ~**ation**, *n*, assassinat, *m*.

assault, *n*, assaut; attentat, *m*, (*law*) agression, *f*. ~ [& *battery*], voies de fait, *f.pl*. ¶ *v.t*, assaillir, attaquer.

assay, *n*, essai, *m*. ~ *office* (government), bureau de garantie, *m*. ¶ *v.t*, essayer; (*v.i.*) titrer. ~**er**, *n*, essayeur, *m*.

assemblage, *n*, assemblage, *m*. **assemble**, *v.t*, [r]assembler, réunir. **assembly**, *n*, assemblée, réunion, *f*.

assent, *n*, assentiment; consentement, *m*, sanction, *f*. **to ~ to**, donner son assentiment à.

assert, *v.t*, soutenir; affirmer; prétendre; revendiquer. **assertion**, *n*, assertion, *f*; dire, *m*.

assess, *v.t*, coter, imposer. évaluer, taxer. ~**ment**, *n*, cote, cotisation, imposition, répartition, taxation, *f*.

asset, *n*, valeur [active] *f*; (*pl.*) actif, *m*, capitaux, *m.pl*. ~**s nil**, carence, *f*. ~**s transferred** *or* *taken over*, apport[s] *m.[pl.]*.

assiduity, *n*, assiduité, *f*. **assiduous**, *a*, assidu. ~**ly**, *ad*, assidûment.

assign, *v.t*, assigner; céder; apporter; affecter, destiner. ~**ation**, *n*, assignation, *f*. ~**ment**, *n*, assignation; cession, *f*; apport, *m*; (*Sch.*) devoir, *m*.

assimilate, *v.t*, assimiler.

assist, *v.t*, assister, aider, secourir. ~**ance**, *n*, assistance, aide, *f*, secours; concours, *m*; (*to police*) main-forte, *f*. ~**ant**, *n*, aide, *m,f*, adjoint, e, assistant, auxiliaire, *m*.

assize, *n*, **assizes**, *n.pl*, assises, *f*. *pl*.

associate, *n*, associé, e. ¶ *v.t*, associer, adjoindre; (*v.i.*) s'associer, frayer. **association**, *n*, association, société, *f*; syndicat, *m*; caisse, *f*.

assort, *v.t*, assortir. ~**ment**, *n*, assortiment, classement, *m*.

assuage, *v.t*, apaiser, adoucir.

assume, *v.t*, prendre, affecter, revêtir; assumer; s'arroger; supposer; (*name*) emprunter. **assuming**, *a*, prétentieux, arrogant. **assumption**, *n*, supposition; arrogance, *f*. **A~** (*Eccl.*) *n*, assomption, *f*.

assurance, n, assurance, f. **assure,** v.t, assurer. **assuredly,** ad, assurément, à coup sûr.

Assyria, n, l'Assyrie, f. **Assyrian,** a, assyrien. ¶ n, Assyrien, ne.

aster, n, aster, m.

asterisk, n, astérisque, m, étoile, f.

astern, ad, derrière, en arrière, à (ou sur) l'arrière.

asteroid, n, astéroïde, m.

asthma, n, asthme, m. **asthmatic,** a, asthmatique.

astigmatic, a, astigmate.

astir, ad. & a, en mouvement, en branle-bas; agité, en émoi.

astonish, v.t, étonner, émerveiller, surprendre. **~ingly,** ad, étonnamment. **~ment,** n, étonnement, m, surprise, f.

astound, v.t, ébahir.

astray, ad. & a, hors du [bon] chemin; égaré. to go ~, s'égarer.

astride, astraddle, ad. & a, à califourchon, à cheval, affourché, jambe deçà, jambe delà.

astringent, a. & n, astringent, a. & m.

astrologer, n, astrologue, m. **astrology,** n, astrologie, f.

astronaut, n, astronaute, m.

astronomer, n, astronome, m. **astronomic(al†),** a, astronomique. **astronomy,** n, astronomie, f.

astute, a, fin, rusé; astucieux.

asunder, ad, en deux; éloigné l'un de l'autre.

asylum, n, asile, hospice, m.

at, pr, à; en; dans; de; par; contre; chez; moyennant. ~ a loss, profit, à perte, profit. ~ all, du tout. ~ first, d'abord. ~ hand, à portée [de la main]. ~ home, chez soi, chez moi, chez lui, chez nous, chez vous, etc; à la maison; au logis; visible; en famille; à son aise. ~ last, ~ length, enfin. ~ least, au moins. ~ once, tout de suite; à la fois, incessamment. ~ sea, en mer. ~ the same time, en même temps. ~ war, en guerre.

Athanasian Creed (the), le symbole attribué à saint Athanase.

atheism, n, athéisme, m. **atheist,** n, athée, m. **atheistic,** a, athée.

Athenian, a, athénien. ¶ n, Athénien, ne. **Athens,** n, Athènes, f.

athirst, ad, altéré; avide.

athlete, n, athlète, m. **athletic,** a, athlétique. **athletics,** n.pl, athlétisme, m.

at-home, n, réception, f. her ~ day, son jour [de réception].

athwart, ad, en travers. ¶ pr, en travers de.

Atlantic, a, atlantique. ~ liner, [paquebot] transatlantique, m. the A~ [Ocean], l'[océan] Atlantique, m.

atlas, n, atlas, m.

atmosphere, n, atmosphère, f. **atmospheric(al),** a, atmosphérique.

atoll, n, atoll, m.

atom, n, atome, m; miette, f. **~ic(al),** a, atomique. **~ize,** v.t, atomiser, pulvériser. **~izer,** n, vaporisateur, m.

atone for (to), expier, racheter. **atonement,** n, expiation, réparation, satisfaction, f.

atrocious†, a, atroce. **atrocity,** n, atrocité, f.

atrophy, n, atrophie, f. ¶ v.i, atrophier.

attach, v.t, attacher; atteler; annexer, joindre; (law) saisir. **attaché,** n, attaché, m. ~ case, mallette, f. **attachment,** n, attachement, m, inclination; attache, f; attelage; appareil, m; (law) saisie, f.

attack, n, attaque, f; accès, m, crise, f. ¶ v.t, attaquer, s'attaquer à.

attain, v.t, atteindre, parvenir à. **~der,** n, condamnation, f. **~ment,** n, atteinte, f; (pl.) acquis, m.s. & pl, connaissances, f.pl.

attar, n, essence de roses, f.

attempt, n, tentative, f, essai, coup, jet; (criminal) attentat, m. to make an ~ on, attenter à. ¶ v.t, tenter, essayer, tâcher. ~ed murder, tentative d'assassinat, f. ~ed suicide, faux suicide, m.

attend, v.t, accompagner; assister à, suivre; soigner; visiter. ~ to, faire attention à, écouter; s'occuper de; soigner, servir. **~ance,** n, présence; assistance; visite, f; service, m. **~ant,** n, suivant, e; (pl.) suite, f; gardien, m; (Theat.) receveuse; (Theat. box) ouvreuse, f. **attention,** n, attention, f; soin; regard, m; prévenance, f. to pay ~, faire attention. ~! (Mil.) garde-à-vous! **attentive†,** a, attentif, empressé; prévenant.

attenuate, v.t, atténuer.

attest, *v.t*, attester, constater. **~ation**, *n*, attestation, constatation, *f*.

Attic, *a*, attique.

attic, *n*, mansarde, *f*, grenier, *m*.

attire, *n*, vêtement, costume, *m*; parure, *f*. ¶ *v.t*, vêtir; parer.

attitude, *n*, attitude, posture, pose, *f*.

attorney, *n*, avoué, *m*, mandataire, *m.f*; procureur, *m*. ~ *general*, procureur de la République, *m*.

attract, *v.t*, attirer; solliciter. **attraction**, *n*, attraction; attirance, *f*; (*pl.*) attraits, appas, charmes, *m.pl*. **attractive**, *a*, attrayant, attirant; (*Phys.*) attractif.

attributable, *a*, attribuable. **attribute**, *n*, attribut, emblème, *m*. ¶ *v.t*, attribuer; prêter. **attribution**, *n*, attribution, *f*. **attributive adjective**, adjectif épithète, *m*. **attributively** (*Gram.*) *ad*, adjectivement; en apposition.

attrition, *n*, attrition; usure, *f*.

attune, *v.t*, accorder, harmoniser.

auburn hair, cheveux blond ardent, *m.pl*.

auction, *n*, enchère[s] *f.[pl.]*. ~ *bridge*, bridge aux enchères, *m*. ~ *mart*, ~ *rooms*, hôtel des ventes, *m*. ¶ *v.t*, vendre aux enchères. **~eer**, *n*, commissaire priseur, *m*.

audacious†, *a*, audacieux. **audacity**, *n*, audace, *f*.

audible, *a*, perceptible à l'ouïe, intelligible.

audience, *n*, (*hearing*) audience; (*pers.*) assistance, *f*; spectateurs, *m.pl*.

audit, *v.t*. vérifier. **~[ing]**, *n*, vérification [comptable] *f*. **audition**, *n*, audition, *f*. **auditor**, *n*, vérificateur comptable, censeur; auditeur, *m*. **auditorium**, *n*, salle, *f*.

auger, *n*, tarière, *f*, laceret, *m*.

aught, *n*, quelque chose, rien, *m*.

augment, *v.t*, augmenter.

augur, *n*, augure, *m*. ¶ *v.t*, augurer. **~y**, *n*, augure, présage, *m*.

august, *a*, auguste. **A~**, *n*, août, *m*.

auk, *n*, pingouin, *m*.

aunt, *n*, tante, *f*.

aureole, *n*, auréole, *f*.

auricle (*heart*) *n*, oreillette, *f*. **auricula**, *n*, oreille-d'ours, *f*. **auricular**, *a*, auriculaire.

auriferous, *a*, aurifère.

aurora, *n*, aurore, *f*. ~ *borealis*, a. boréale.

auspice, *n*, (*usually pl.*) auspice, *m*. *under the* ~*s of*, sous les auspices de. **auspicious**, *a*, propice, favorable, de bon augure.

austere†, *a*, austère, sévère. **austerity**, *n*, austérité, *f*.

austral, *a*, austral. **Australasia**, *n*, l'Australasie, *f*. **Australia**, *n*, l'Australie, *f*. **Australian**, *a*, australien. ¶ *n*, Australien, ne.

Austria, *n*, l'Autriche, *f*. **Austrian**, *a*, autrichien. ¶ *n*, Autrichien, ne.

authentic, *a*, authentique. **~ity**, *n*, authenticité, *f*.

author, *n*, (*lit. & fig.*) auteur; (*fig. only*) artisan, inventeur, *m*. **authoritative**, *a*, autoritaire; d'autorité. **~ly**, *ad*, avec autorité, en maître. **authority**, *n*, autorité, puissance; source, *f*. *to be regarded as an* ~, faire autorité. *the authorities*, les autorités, *f.pl*, l'administration, *f*.

authorization, *n*, autorisation, *f*. **authorize**, *v.t*, autoriser, mandater.

authorship, *n*, métier d'auteur, *m*; paternité, *f*.

autobiography, *n*, autobiographie, *f*.

autocracy, *n*, autocratie, *f*. **autocrat**, *n*, autocrate, trice. **autocratic(al)**, *a*, autocratique.

autogenous, *a*, autogène.

autograph, *n. & a*, autographe, *m. & a*. ~ *book*, livre de signatures, *m*.

auto, automobile, *n*, auto, automobile, *f*.

automatic(al)†, *a*, automatique. **automaton**, *n*, automate, *m*.

autonomous, *a*, autonome. **autonomy**, *n*, autonomie, *f*.

autopsy, *n*, autopsie, *f*.

autumn, *n*, automne, *f*. **~al**, *a*, automnal.

auxiliary, *a. & n*, auxiliaire, *a. & m*.

avail, *n*, effet, *m*. *to* ~ *oneself of*, profiter de. *to* ~ *oneself of the services of*, jouir de. **~able**, *a*, disponible; libre.

avalanche, *n*, avalanche, *f*.

avarice, *n*, avarice, *f*. **avaricious†**, *a*, avare, avaricieux.

avenge, *v.t*, venger, punir. **avenger**, *n*, vengeur, eresse. **avenging**, *a*, vengeur.

avenue, *n*, avenue, *f*, boulevard, cours, *m*.

aver, *v.t*, soutenir, affirmer.

average, *a*, moyen; commun.

¶ *n*, moyenne, *f*; (*marine law*) avarie[s] *f*.[*pl*.]. ¶ *v.t*, établir la moyenne de.

averse to, ennemi de. *I am ~*, il me répugne de. **aversion**, *n*, aversion, répugnance, *f*, dégoût, *m*.

avert, *v.t*, détourner; écarter.

aviary, *n*, volière, oisellerie, *f*.

aviation, *n*, aviation, *f*. **aviator**, *n*, aviateur, trice.

avid†, *a*, avide. **~ity**, *n*, avidité, *f*.

avocations, *n.pl*, occupations, *f.pl*, travaux, *m.pl*.

avoid, *v.t*, éviter, se soustraire à, fuir. **~able**, *a*, évitable.

avow, *v.t*, avouer, s'accuser de. **~al**, *n*, aveu, *m*.

await, *v.t*, attendre.

awake, *a*, réveillé; vigilant. ¶ *v.t.ir*, réveiller; (*v.i.*) se réveiller. **awaken**, *v.t*, réveiller. **~ing**, *n*, [r]éveil, *m*.

award, *n*, décision, sentence; (*at a show*) nomination, *f*. ¶ *v.t*, décerner; adjuger. *~ a medal to*, médailler. *~ a prize to*, couronner; primer. *~ the contract for*, adjuger.

aware, *a: to be ~ of*, savoir, connaître, ne pas ignorer. *not to be ~ of*, ignorer.

away, *ad*, d'ici; de là. *~* [*from home*], absent. *right ~*, tout de suite. *to go ~*, s'en aller. *to keep ~*, se tenir à l'écart. *~ with you!* allez-vous-en!

awe, *n*, crainte, *f*. **~struck**, saisi de crainte. ¶ *v.t*, imposer à.

awful†, *a*, effroyable, terrible; redoutable; solennel.

awhile, *ad*, un instant, un peu.

awkward, *a*, incommode, embarrassant, malaisé; gauche, maladroit, emprunté. *the ~ age*, l'âge ingrat, *m*. *~ incident*, contretemps, *m*.

awl, *n*, alène, *f*, poinçon, *m*.

awn, *n*, barbe, arête, *f*.

awning, *n*, tente, banne, *f*, tendelet, *m*. *~ deck*, pont abri, *m*.

awry, *ad*. & *a*, de travers, de guingois.

axe, *n*, hache, cognée, *f*.

axiom, *n*, axiome, *m*.

axis, *n*, axe, *m*.

axle, *n*, arbre, essieu, *m*. **axletree**, *n*, essieu, *m*.

ay, *i*. & *n*, oui, *particle & m*.

azalea, *n*, azalée, *f*.

azimuth, *n*, azimut, *m*.

Azores (the), les Açores, *f.pl*.

azure, *a*, azur. ¶ *n*, azur, *m*.

B

B (*Mus.*) letter, si, *m*.

baa, *v.i*, bêler. **baa[ing]**, *n*, bêlement, *m*.

babble, *n*, babil, *m*. ¶ *v.i*, babiller; (*stream*) gazouiller; (*of hound*) clabauder.

Babel (*fig.*) *n*, tour de Babel, *f*.

baboon, *n*, babouin, *m*.

baby, *n*, bébé, enfant, petit, *m*. *~ carriage*, landau [pour enfant] *m*. *~ face*, physionomie pouparde, *f*. *~ grand*, piano à demi-queue, crapaud, *m*. *~hood*, *n*, première enfance, *f*. *~ish*, *a*, enfantin.

Babylonian, *a*, babylonien.

babysitter, *n*, gardienne d'enfant, *f*. **babysitting**, *n*, garde d'enfants, *m*. (*supermarket*, *dept. store*) *~ facility*, *n*, halte-garderie, *m*.

Bacchanalia, *n.pl*, bacchanales, *f.pl*. **Bacchic**, *a*, bachique.

bachelor, *n*, célibataire, garçon, *m*; (*science, etc.*) bachelier, ère, licencié, e. *~ flat*, garçonnière, *f*. *~ girl*, garçonne, *f*.

back, *ad*, en arrière; en retour. *Note:—After a verb* back *is sometimes expressed by* re- *as*, *to come back*, revenir. ¶ *n*, dos; derrière; arrière; revers; envers; dossier; fond; verso; dessus, *m*; reins, *m.pl*; (*book*) dos, *m*. *~ to front*, sens devant derrière. *to ~ up*, faire marche arrière. *with one's ~ to the light*, à contrejour. ¶ *v.t*, [faire] reculer; adosser; épauler; appuyer, soutenir, seconder; (*betting*) parier sur, jouer; (*v.i.*) reculer; (*of wind*) redescendre.

backache, *n*, mal de reins, *m*.

backbite, *v.i*, clabauder. **backbiting**, *n*, médisance, *f*, cancans, *m.pl*.

backbone, *n*, épine dorsale, échine; énergie, *f*.

back door, porte de derrière, p. de service, *f*.

backer, *n*, partisan; (*betting*) parieur, *m*. *financial ~*, bailleur de fonds, *m*.

backfire, retour de flamme, *m*. *backfire* [*kick*], retour de manivelle, *m*.

backgammon, *n*. & *~ board*, trictrac, *m*.

background, *n*, arrière-plan,

fond, enfoncement, second plan, m; pénombre, f.
backhand, n, arrière-main, revers, m.
back number (*news*), vieux numéro, m.
back-pedal, v.i, contre-pédaler.
backsight (*gun*) n, hausse, f.
backslider, n, relaps, e. **backsliding**, n, rechute, f.
backstay (*Naut.*) n, galhauban, m.
backstitch, n, point arrière, arrière-point, m.
back tooth, dent du fond, f.
backup, n, (*computers*) de secours, m, de sécurité, f.
backward, a, peu avancé, tardif; rétrograde; (*child*) arriéré. ¶ ~, ~s, ad, en arrière; à reculons; à la renverse; à rebours. **~ness**, n, tardiveté; répugnance, f.
backwash, n, remous, m.
backwater (to), scier, ramer à rebours. ¶ n, eau arrêtée, f, ressac, m.
bacon, n, lard, bacon, m.
bacteria, n.pl, bactéries, f.pl.
bad, a, mauvais; mal, malade; grave; fort; irrégulier; véreux. to go ~ (meat), s'avarier. ~ language, gros mots, m.pl. ~ time [of it], mauvais quart d'heure, m. in a ~ way, mal-en-point, malade. ~ workmanship, malfaçon, f. too ~! tant pis! ¶ n, mauvais, m. from ~ to worse, de mal en pis. to the ~ (out of pocket), en perte.
badge, n, insigne, m, marque; plaque, médaille, f; brassard; symbole, m; livrée, f.
badger, n, blaireau, m. ¶ v.t, harceler, relancer.
badly, ad, mal; gravement.
badminton, n, badminton, volant au filet, m.
badness, n, mauvais état, m; méchanceté, f.
baffle, v.t, déjouer, déconcerter, frustrer; défier, échapper à. ~ [plate] n, chicane, f.
bag, n, sac, m; bourse; valise, f; (of game) tableau, m. ~snatcher, voleur à la tire, m. ¶ v.t, ensacher; empocher, chiper; (v.i, trousers) goder. **~ful**, n, sachée, f.
bagatelle, n, (trifle) bagatelle, f. ~ (game) ~ board, billard japonais, m.
baggage, n, bagage; attirail, m.

~ car, fourgon, m. ~ check, bulletin de bagages, m.
baggy, a, avachi, flottant.
bagpipe[s], n, cornemuse, f.
bail, n, caution, f, cautionnement, m. **bail[sman]**, n, caution, f, répondant, e. ¶ v.t, cautionner. ~ [out] (boat) v.t, écoper, vider. **~er**, n, écope, épuisette, f.
bailiff, n, huissier; intendant, régisseur, m.
bait, n, amorce, f, appât; hameçon (fig.) m. ¶ v.t, amorcer, appâter; (pers.) harceler, pointiller, persécuter.
baize, n, bayette, f, tapis, drap, m. ~ door, porte matelassée, f.
bake, v.t, cuire [au four]; (v.i.) cuire. **~house**, n, fournil, m; (Mil.) manutention, f. **baker**, n, boulanger, ère. **~y**, n, boulangerie, f. **baking**, n, cuisson; cuite; boulangerie, f. ~ powder, poudre à lever, f. ~ pan, tourtière, f.
balance, n, balance, f; peson; équilibre; solde, reliquat, surplus, m; soulte, f. ~ of power (Pol.), équilibre, m. ~ sheet, bilan, m. ~ sheet & schedules, inventaire, m. ~ weight, contrepoids, m. ~ wheel (Horol.), balancier, m. ¶ v.t. & i, balancer, équilibrer, pondérer; solder. **~d** lever, bascule, f. **balancing**, n, balancement, m. ~ pole (tightrope), balancier, m.
balcony, n, balcon, m.
bald, a, chauve; nu, pelé; (style) plat, sec, décharné.
balderdash, n, galimatias, m.
baldness, n, calvitie; nudité, f.
bale, n, balle, f, ballot, m. ¶ v.t, emballer.
baleful, a, sinistre, funeste.
balk, n, tronc d'arbre équarri, m, poutre, f. ¶ v.t, frustrer; (horse) se dérober.
Balkan, a, balkanique; (states, peninsula) des Balkans. **the ~s**, les Balkans, m.pl.
ball, n, balle; bille; boule, f; boulet; ballon; (eye, lightning) globe, m; (thumb) éminence; (pendulum) lentille; (wool, string) pelote, f, peloton, m; (Danc.) bal, m. ~ & socket, rotule sphérique, f. ~ bearings, roulement à billes, m. ~ cartridge, cartouche à balle, f. ~ cock, robinet à flotteur, m. ~ frame, boulier, m. (pen) ~ point,

bic, *m.* ~ *room*, salle de bal, *f.*
¶ *v.t*, pelotonner; mettre en
boule.

ballad, *n*, (*poem*) ballade; (*song*)
chanson, romance, complainte, *f.*

ballast, *n*, (*road*, *Rly.*) ballast,
m; (*Build.*) blocaille, *f*; (*Naut.*,
Avn.) lest; (*fig.*) plomb, *m.*
¶ *v.t*, lester.

ballet, *n*, ballet, *m.* ~ *dancer*,
danseur, euse, figurant, e, ballerine, *f.* ~ *skirt*, tutu, *m.*

ballistics, *n*, balistique, *f.*

balloon, *n*, ballon; aérostat, *m.*
~ *fabric*, toile d'avion, *f.* ~ed
(*dress*) *p.a*, ballonné. ~ing, *n*,
aérostation, *f.* ~ist, *n*, aérostier,
m.

ballot, *n*, [tour de] scrutin, *m.* ~
box, urne électorale, *f.* ~ *paper*,
bulletin de vote, *m.* ¶ *v.i*, voter
au scrutin.

balm, *n*, baume, *m.* ~y, *a*, em-
baumé, balsamique.

balsam, *n*, baume, *m*; (*garden
plant*) balsamine, *f.* ~ [*tree*],
baumier, balsamier, *m.* ~ic, *a*,
balsamique.

Baltic [sea] (the), la [mer] Baltique.

baluster, *n*, balustre, *m.* **balustrade**, *n*, balustrade, *f.*

bamboo, *n*, bambou, *m.*

bamboozle, *v.t*, enjôler, mettre
dedans.

ban, *n*, ban, *m*; interdiction, *f.*
¶ *v.t*, interdire.

banana, *n*, banane, *f.* ~ [*plant
or tree*], bananier, *m.*

band, *n*, bande; frette; courroie, *f*;
ruban; (*Bookb.*) nerf, *m*; musique, *f*, orchestre, *m.* harmonie,
f. ~*box*, carton de modiste, *m.* ~
brake, frein à ruban, *f.* à bande,
m. ~ *saw*, scie à ruban, *f.* ~*master*, chef de musique, *m.* (*CB
radio*) *citizen's* ~, canal banalisé,
m. ¶ *v.t*, lier, fretter; (*v.i.*) se liguer.

bandage, *n*, bandage, bandeau,
m, bande, *f.* ¶ *v.t*, bander. **bandeau**, *n*, bandeau, *m.*

bandit, *n*, bandit, *m.*

bandoleer, *n*, bandoulière, *f.*

bandy, *v.t*, ballotter, se renvoyer.
~ *words with*, faire assaut de
paroles avec. ~[-*legged*], *a*, bancal.

bane (*fig.*) *n*, fléau, *m.* ~ful, *a*,
pernicieux, funeste.

bang, *n*, battement, *m*; détonation, *f.* ¶ *i*, pan! ¶ *v.t.* & *i*, frapper, faire battre; battre, cogner.

bangle, *n*, bracelet; porte-bonheur, *m.*

banish, *v.t*, bannir.

banishment, *n*, exile, *m.*

banister, *n*, balustre, *m*; (*pl.*)
rampe, *f.*

bank, *n*, rive, berge, *f*, bord; talus;
banc, *m*; (*Fin.*) banque, caisse,
f, crédit, *m.* ~ *note*, billet de
banque, *m.* ~ [*pass*] *book*, carnet de banque, c. de compte, *m.*
~ *rate*, taux officiel [d'escompte]
m. ~ *transfer*, virement, *m.*
¶ *v.t*, terrasser, remblayer; verser
à la banque; (*v.i.*) virer, pencher.
~ *on*, compter sur. ~er, *n*, banquier, *m.* ~ing, *n*, banque, *f.*

bankrupt, *n*, banqueroutier, ère;
failli, *m. to go* ~, faire banqueroute; faire faillite. ~cy, *n*,
banqueroute; faillite, *f.*

banner, *n*, bannière, *f*; pavillon,
m; oriflamme, *f.*

banns, *n.pl*, bans de mariage,
m.pl.

banquet, *n*, banquet, festin, *m.*
~*ing hall*, salle des festins, *f.*

bantam weight (*Box.*), poids
coq, *m.*

banter, *n*, badinage, *m.* ¶ *v.t*,
badiner.

baptism, *n*, baptême, *m.* ~al, *a*,
baptismal. **baptist[e]ry**, *n*, baptistère, *m.* **baptize**, *v.t*, baptiser.

bar, *n*, barre, *f*, barreau, *m*, barrette; bille, brique; barrière, *f*;
fer, *m*; (*Mus., vertical line*) barre;
(*commonly but incorrectly, portion between two bar lines*) mesure, *f*; (*window*) croisillon,
(*counter*) comptoir, *m*, buvette,
f, bar, *m.* ~ *bell*, barre à sphères,
f. ~ *iron*, fer en barre, *m.* ¶ *v.t*,
barrer.

barb, *n*, barbe, *f*; picot, *m.* ~[*ed*]
wire, fil de fer barbelé, *m*, ronce,
f. ¶ *v.t*, barbeller; barder.

Barbados, *n*, la Barbade.

barbarian, *a. & n*, barbare, *a. &
m.* **barbaric**, **barbarous**, *a*, barbare. **barbarism**, *n*, barbarie, *f*;
(*Gram.*) barbarisme, *m.* **barbarity**, *n*, barbarie, *f.*

Barbary ape, magot, *m.*

barbecue, *n*, (*grill*) barbecue, *m.*

barber, *n*, barbier, *m.*

Barcelona, *n*, Barcelone, *f.*

bard, *n*, (*poet*) barde; chantre, *m.*

the Bard of Avon, le chantre d'Avon.

bare, *a*, nu; à nu; chenu; découvert; pelé; simple, seul; *(majority)* faible. **~back[ed]** *(riding)*, à nu, à poil, à cru. **~back horse,** cheval nu, *m*. **~faced,** éhonté, effronté. **~facedly,** à visage découvert. **~foot[ed],** nu-pieds, pieds nus, déchaussé. **~headed,** nu-tête, tête nue. ¶ *v.t*, mettre à nu, dénuder, dépouiller, découvrir, déchausser. **~ly,** *ad*, à peine, juste, tout au plus; ne . . . guère. **~ness,** *n*, nudité, *f*.

bargain, *n*, marché, *m*, négociation, affaire; occasion; emplette, *f*. *into the* **~,** pardessus le marché. ¶ *v.i*, marchander. **~er,** *n*, marchandeur, euse.

barge, *n*, chaland, *m*, gabare, allège, péniche, *f*. **bargee, bargeman,** *n*, batelier, marinier, *m*.

baritone, *n*. & **~ saxhorn,** baryton, *m*.

bark, *n*, *(tree)* écorce; *(left on felled tree)* grume, *f*; *(dog)* aboiement, *m*; *(boat)* barque, *f*; *(Poet.)* nef, *f*. ¶ *v.t*, écorcer, décortiquer, peler; *(v.i.)* aboyer. **~ing,** *n*, *(tree)* décortication, *f*; *(dog)* aboiement, *m*.

barley, *n*, orge, *f*. **~ sugar,** sucre d'orge, *m*. **~ water,** eau d'orge, *f*.

barm, *n*, levure, *f*, levain, *m*.

barman, *n*, barman, serveur, *m*.

barn, *n*, grange, *f*. **~ owl,** effraie, fresaie, *f*. **~yard,** basse-cour, *f*.

barnacle, *n*, *(Crust.)* bernacle, *f*, cravan, *m*.

barometer, *n*, baromètre, *m*. **barometric(al),** *a*, barométrique.

baron, **ess,** *n*, baron, ne.

barque, *n*, barque, *f*.

barrack, *n*. oft. pl, caserne, *f*. **~ room,** chambrée [militaire], *f*. ¶ *v.t*, caserner.

barrage, *n*, barrage, *m*.

barrel, *n*, baril, fût, *m*, futaille, pièce, *f*, tonneau, *m*, caque, *f*; corps, cylindre, tambour, canon, *m*. **~ organ,** orgue de Barbarie, *m*. ¶ *v.t*, mettre en baril, entonner, [en]caquer.

barren, *a*, stérile, aride. **~ness,** *n*, stérilité, aridité, *f*.

barricade, *n*, barricade, *f*. ¶ *v.t*, barricader.

barrier, *n*, barrière, *f*; barrage, *m*; digue, *f*.

barring, *pr*, ôté, sauf, à part, hormis, excepté, à moins de.

barrow, *n*, brouette; *(peddler's)* baladeuse, *f*; *(mound)* tumulus, *m*.

barter, *n*, échange, troc, *m*. **~ goods,** pacotille, *f*. ¶ *v.t*, échanger, troquer.

basal, *a*, basique.

basalt, *n*, basalte, *m*.

bascule bridge, pont à bascule, *m*.

base, *a*, bas, vil, ignoble, **~ metal,** bas métal, métal vil, m. pauvre. *m*. ¶ *n*, base, assiette, *f*, fondement[s] *m.[pl.]*; soubassement; culot, *m*. **launching ~,** base de lancement, *f*. ¶ *v.t*, asseoir, fonder. **~less,** *a*, sans fondement, **~ly,** *ad*, bassement, lâchement. **~ment,** *n*, soubassement, soussol, *m*. **~ness,** *n*, bassesse, *f*.

bashful, *a*, timide. **~ness,** *n*, timidité, fausse honte, mauvaise honte, *f*.

basic, *a*, fondamental; *(Chem.)* basique.

basil, *n*, *(Bot.)* basilic, *m*; *(hide)* basane, *f*.

basilica, *n*, basilique, *f*.

basilisk, *n*, basilic, *m*.

basin, *n*, bassin; bol, *m*; cuvette, *f*.

basis, *n*, base, assiette, *f*, fondement[s] *m.[pl.]*.

bask, *v.i*, se chauffer.

basket, *n*, panier, *m*, corbeille; manne; benne; bourriche, *f*. **~ ball,** basket-ball, ballon au panier, *m*. **~ maker,** vannier, *m*. **~ making,** **~ work,** vannerie, *f*. **~ful,** *n*, panier, *m*, panerée, *f*.

bas-relief, *n*, bas-relief, *m*.

bass, *n*, *(fish)* bar, *m*. **~ [voice, singer, string, tuba],** basse, *f*. **~ clef,** clef de fa, *f*. **~ drum,** grosse caisse, *f*.

bassinet, *n*, bercelonnette, *f*.

bassoon, *n*, basson, *m*.

bast, *n*, tille, *f*.

bastard, *a*, bâtard. ¶ *n*, bâtard, e. **~y,** *n*, bâtardise, *f*.

baste, *v.t*, *(Need.)* bâtir, baguer, faufiler; *(meat)* arroser; *(beat)* bâtonner.

bat, *n*, bat, *m*; batte; palette, *f*; *(Zool.)* chauve-souris, *f*.

batch, *n*, fournée, *f*; groupe, *m*.

bate, *v.t*, rabattre.

bath, *n*, bain, *m*; *(tub)* baignoire, *f*. **~ attendant,** baigneur, euse. **B~ chair,** fauteuil roulant, *m*.

~ *robe*, peignoir de bain, *m.*
~*man*, baigneur, *m.* ~*mat*, tapis de bain, *m.* ~*room*, salle de bain, *f.* ~ *salts*, sel pour bain, *m.* ~*tub*, baignoire, *m.* **bathe**, *v.t.* baigner; (*v.i.*) baigner, se b.; s'abreuver. **bather**, *n*, baigneur, euse. **bathing**, *n*, bains, *m.pl*; bain, *m.* ~ *cap*, bonnet de bain, *m.* ~ *suit*, maillot (*ou* costume) de bain, *m.* ~ *place*, baignade, *f.* ~ *resort*, station balnéaire, *f.*

bathos, *n*, pathos, *m.*

baton, *n*, bâton, *m*; (*relay race*) témoin, *m.*

battalion, *n*, bataillon, *m.*

batten, *n*, [latte] volige, *f.* ~ *down* (*Naut.*), condamner. ~ *on*, s'engraisser de.

batter, pâte, *f.* ¶ *v.t.* battre, bossuer, bosseler, cabosser. ~*ing-ram*, *n*, bélier, *m.* ~*y*, *n*, batterie, pile, *f.*

battle, *n*, bataille, *f*, combat, *m.* ~*axe*, hache d'armes, *f.* ~ *cruiser*, croiseur cuirassé de combat, *m.* ~*field*, champ de bataille, *m.* ~*ship*, [navire] cuirassé, *m.* ¶ *v.i.* lutter; batailler.

battledore, *n*, palette, raquette, *f*, battoir, *m.* ~ & *shuttlecock*, [jeu de] volant, *m.*

battlement, *n*, créneau, *m.* ~*ed*, *a*, crénelé.

bauble, *n*, babiole, *f*, brimborion, *m*; (*fool's*) marotte, *f.*

Bavaria, *n*, la Bavière. **Bavarian**, *a*, bavarois. ¶ *n*, Bavarois, e.

bawl, *v.i*, brailler, beugler.

bawl out, *v.t*, engueuler. *to be* ~*ed out*, se faire engueuler.

bay, *a*, bai. ¶ *n*, (*horse*) bai, *m*; (*Geog.*) baie, *f*; golfe, *m*; (*Arch.*) travée, *f.* B~ *of Biscay*, golfe de Gascogne, *m.* ~ *rum*, tafia de laurier, *m.* ~[*tree*], laurier, *m.* ~ *window*, fenêtre baie. *f.* *at* ~, aux abois. ¶ *v.i*, aboyer. ~*ing*, *n*, aboiement, *m.*

bayonet, *n*, baïonnette, *f.*

bazaar, *n*, bazar, *m*; vente de charité, *f.*

B.C. (*before Christ*), av. J.C.

be, *v.i.ir*, être; exister; avoir; faire; se faire; aller, se trouver, se porter; y avoir. ~ *that as it may*, quoi qu'il en soit. *it is . . . since*, il y a . . . que. *there is* (*are*) *some*, il y en a. *there is none left*, il n'y en a plus. *I am leaving*, je vais partir, je pars. *a man to be feared*, un homme à crain-

dre. *not to be confused with . . .*, à ne pas confondre avec . . . *to be off*, s'en aller, filer, se sauver. *be off with you!* allez vous promener!

beach, *n*, plage, grève, *f*, rivage, *m.* ~*comber*, rôdeur de grève, *m.* ~ *fishing*, pêche de plage, *f.* ~*head*, tête de pont, *f.* ¶ *v.t.* & *i.* échouer; tirer à sec.

beacon, *n*, balise, *f*; phare, *m.* ¶ *v.t.* baliser.

bead, *n*, perle, *f*, grain, *m*; goutte; (*Arch.*) baguette, *f.* [*glass*] ~*s*, verroterie, *f.* [*string of*] ~*s*, chapelet, *m.*

beadle, *n*, appariteur; bedeau, suisse, *m.*

beak, *n*, bec, *m.* ~*er*, *n*, buire, *f*; vase à filtrations chaudes, *m.*

beam, *n*, (*timber*) poutre; (*plow*) flèche, haie, *f*, timon; (*Mach.*) balancier; (*scale*) fléau, *m*, verge, *f*; (*ship's timber*) bau, *m*; (*ship's breadth*) largeur, *f*, travers; (*ray*) rayon, trait; (*rays*) faisceau, *m.* ~ *radio*, signal par radio. ¶ *v.i.* rayonner.

bean, *n*, fève, *f*; haricot; (*coffee*) grain, *m.*

bear, *n*, ours, e; (**B**~, *Astr.*) ourse, *f*; (*pers.*) bourru, dogue, *m*; (*Mach.*) poinçonneuse, *f*; (*Stk Ex.*) baissier, *m.* ~*s cub*, ourson, *m.* ~*skin* (*cap*) oursin, ourson, *m.* ¶ *v.t.* & *i. ir*, porter; supporter, souffrir, tolérer, endurer, compatir; appuyer, peser; produire, rapporter; enfanter; (*to right*, *left*) prendre. *to* ~ *out*, confirmer. *to* ~ *up*, résister. ~*able*, *a*, supportable, tenable.

beard, *n*, barbe; (*Bot.*) barbe, arête, *f.* ~*ed*, *a*, barbu, à barbe, chevelu. ~*less*, *a*, imberbe.

bearer, *n*, porteur, euse; (*Fin.*) porteur, *m.* ~ *of a flag of truce*, parlementaire, *m.* *stretcher*~, brancardier, *m.* **bearing**, *n*, portée, *f*; rapport, trait; aspect; (*Naut.*) gisement, *m*; (*pl. fig.*) orientation, *f*; (*gait*) port, *m*, mine, tenue, démarche, contenance, *f*, maintien, *m*; conduite, *f*; (*Mech., oft. pl.*) coussinet, *m.* *oft. pl*; palier; dé; roulement, *m*; chape, *f*; (*pl. Her.*) armes, armoiries, *f.pl.* ~ *rein*, fausse rêne, *f.* ~ *surface*, surface portante, s. de portée, *f.*

beast, *n*, bête, *f*; animal; abruti,

m. ~ of burden, bête de somme. ~ly, a, bestial; dégoûtant.

beat, n, battement; coup; temps, m; tournée, ronde; (*Hunt.*) battue, f. ¶ v.t. & i. ir, battre; taper; assommer, bâtonner, brosser; fourrer; fouetter; (*Hunt.*) rabattre, traquer; vaincre; l'emporter sur, enchérir sur. ~ back, ~ off, repousser. ~en path, chemin [re]battu, c. frayé, m. ~er, n, batteur, battoir, m, batte, f; (*Hunt.*) rabatteur, traqueur, m.

beatify, v.t, béatifier.

beating, n, battement, battage, m; batterie; brossée; défaite, f; (*Hunt.*) rabattage, m, traque, f. ~ rain, pluie battante, f.

beau, n, amoureux, galant, m.

beautiful, a, beau; magnifique. ¶ n, beau, m. **beautify,** v.t, embellir. **beauty,** n, beauté; belle, f. B~ & the Beast, la Belle & la Bête. ~ parlor, institut de beauté, m. ~ spot, site pittoresque, m; (*patch on face*) mouche, f; (*mole*) grain de beauté, m.

beaver, n, castor, m.

becalmed, a, encalminé, pris par le calme.

because, c, parce que; car. ~ of, à cause de.

beck, n, signe, m; ordres, m.pl. **beckon,** v.i, faire signe.

become, v.i.ir, devenir. With p.p. often rendered by pronominal form of verb, as, to become accustomed, s'accoutumer; (v.t.ir.) convenir à. **becoming,** a, convenable; [bien]séant, seyant; assortissant, décent.

bed, n, lit, m, couche, f; coucher, m; assise, assiette, fondation, plate-forme, f; banc, gisement, gîte; (*oyster*) parc; (*Hort.*) carré, m, plate-bande, planche, f, parterre, m. to go to ~, [aller] se coucher. ~bug, punaise, f. ~clothes, draps & couvertures. ~fellow, camarade de lit. ~pan, bassin [de garde-robe], b. pour malade, b. de lit, m. ~post, quenouille, f. ~ridden, alité, grabataire. ~room, chambre [à coucher] f. ~side, chevet, m. ~side carpet, descente de lit, f. a good ~side manner, une bonne manière professionnelle. ~side table, table de chevet, t. de nuit, f. ~spread, couvrelit, dessus de lit, jeté de l., m. ~stead, bois de lit; lit, m. ~time, l'heure du coucher, f. ¶ v.t, coucher; asseoir; [faire] précipiter. **bedding,** n, coucher, m, literie, garniture de lit; stratification, f.

bedeck, v.t, parer, chamarrer.

bedew, v.t, arroser, humecter.

bedizen, v.t, attifer, chamarrer.

bedlam, n, maison de fous; (*fig.*) pétaudière, f.

bedraggle, v.t, traîner dans la boue.

bee, n, abeille, f. ~ eater, guêpier, m. ~hive, ruche, f. ~ keeping, apiculture, f. a ~ in one's bonnet, un rat dans la tête.

beech [tree], n, hêtre, m. ~ marten, fouine, f. ~mast, faînes, f.pl. ~nut, faîne, f.

beef, n, bœuf, m. ~ steak, bifteck, m. ~ tea, thé de viande, bouillon de bœuf, m. corned ~, bœuf salé, m.

beer, n, bière, f. ~pump, pompe à b., f.

beet, n, bette; betterave, f. ~ sugar, sucre de betterave, m. **beetroot,** n, betterave, f.

beetle, n, coléoptère, scarabée; escarbot, m; (*rammer*) dame, demoiselle, hie, f, pilon, m. ¶ v.t, pilonner. **beetling brows,** sourcils fournis, m.pl. **beetling crag,** rocher qui surplombe, m.

befall, v.i.ir, arriver, advenir, survenir.

befit, v.t, convenir à. **befitting,** a, convenable.

before, ad, devant; avant; auparavant; en avant; déjà; jusqu'ici; précédent. ¶ c, avant que. ¶ pr, devant; avant; pardevant; avant [que] de. ~ you could say Jack Robinson, crac! ~hand, ad, à l'avance, d'a., en a., par a.

befriend, v.t, favoriser; secourir.

beg, v.t. & i, mendier, quémander, chercher, gueuser; demander, prier; (*Com.*) avoir l'honneur de; (*dog*) faire le beau. I ~ your pardon, je vous demande pardon. ~ for, solliciter, quémander. ~ the question, faire une pétition de principe.

beget, v.t.ir, engendrer; faire naître.

beggar, n, mendiant, m. ¶ v.t, appauvrir, ruiner. ~ly, a, gueux; misérable. ~y, n, mendicité, gueuserie, misère, f. reduced to ~, réduit à la besace.

begin, v.t. & i. ir, commencer; débuter; entamer, amorcer; ouvrir; se mettre. ~ *again*, recommencer. **beginner**, n, commençant, e, débutant, e. **beginning**, n, commencement, début, m; amorce; ouverture; origine, f; prémices, f.pl.

begone, i, va-t-en! allez-vous-en!

begonia, n, bégonia, m.

begrudge, v.t, envier.

beguile, v.t, tromper; séduire; charmer, amuser.

behalf of (on), de la part de; à l'acquit de; pour le compte de.

behave, v.i. & *reflexive*, se comporter, se conduire, vivre. [*properly*]! (to child), tiens-toi bien! **behavior**, n, conduite, f, manières, f.pl, tenue, f, procédé, m.

behead, v.t, décapiter. ~**ing**, n, décapitation, f.

behest, n, commandement, ordre, m.

behind, ad, derrière, en arrière. ¶ pr, derrière, en arrière de. ~**hand**, ad, en arrière, arriéré, en retard.

behold, v.t. & i. ir, voir. ¶ i, voyez! ~*en to*, à charge à, redevable à. ~**er**, n, spectateur, trice.

behoof, n, profit, m. **behove**, v.t.imp, incomber, convenir à.

being, n, être, m; existence, f. *for the time* ~, actuel; actuellement.

belabor, v.t, charger de coups, bourrer, rosser, échiner.

belated, a, attardé; tardif.

belay, v.t, tourner, amarrer.

belch[ing], n, rot, m; crudité, éructation, f. **belch**, v.i, roter; éructer; (v.t, fig.) vomir.

beldam[e], n, vieille sorcière, f.

beleaguer, v.t, assiéger.

belfry, n, beffroi, clocher, m.

Belgian, a, belge. ¶ n, Belge, m.f. **Belgium**, n, la Belgique.

belie, v.t, démentir.

belief, n, croyance, foi; persuasion, f. **believable**, a, croyable. **believe**, v.t. & i, croire. *to make . . .* ~, faire [ac]croire à . . . **believer**, n, croyant, e; partisan, m.

belittle, v.t, décrier, rabaisser, déprécier.

bell, n, cloche; clochette, sonnette, sonnerie, f, timbre; (*globular*) grelot, m. ~*boy*, groom d'hôtel, m. ~ [*flower*], campanule, clochette, f. ~ *glass* & ~ *jar*, cloche, f. ~ *push*, bouton de sonnette,

m. ~ *ringer*, sonneur, carillonneur, m. ~ *tent*, tente conique, f. ~ *tower*, campanile, m. ~ *turret*, clocheton, m. ~*wether*, sonnailler, m. ¶ v.i, bramer, raire, réer.

belladonna, n, belladone, f.

belle, n, beauté, reine, f.

bellicose, a, belliqueux. **belligerent**, a. & n, belligérant, e.

bellow, v.i, beugler, mugir. ¶ n, mugissement, m.

bellows, n.pl, soufflet, m; soufflerie, f.

belly, n, ventre, m, panse, f; bombement, m. ~ *band*, sous-ventrière; sangle, f. ¶ v.i, faire [le] ventre, bomber.

belong, v.i, appartenir, dépendre, être. ~**ings**, n.pl, effets, m.pl.

beloved, a. & n, bien-aimé, e, chéri, e.

below, ad, en bas; au-dessous; dessous; ci-dessous; ci-après; là-bas; en contrebas. ¶ pr, sous; au-dessous de; en aval de.

belt, n, ceinture, f; ceinturon, m; (*Mech.*) courroie; bande; (*Geog.*) zone, f. fan ~, courroie de ventilateur, f. safety ~, ceinture de sécurité, f. ¶ v.t, ceindre. ~**ing**, n, courroies [de transmission] f.pl.

belvedere, n, belvédère, m.

bemoan, v.t, déplorer; pleurer.

bench, n, banc, m; banquette, f; établi; siège, m; cour; magistrature, assise, f, tribunal, m. ~ *mark*, [point de] repère, m.

bend, n, coude, m; courbe, courbure, f; pli, m; inflexion, f; tournant, virage; (*knot*) nœud, m. ~ *of the arm*, saignée, f. ~ *of the knee*, jarret, m. ¶ v.t. & i. ir, courber, se c.; couder; bander; tendre; cintrer; fléchir, plier, ployer; fausser, se f., gauchir. on ~*ed knees*, à genoux.

beneath, ad, dessous; par-dessous; en bas. ¶ pr, au-dessous de, sous.

benediction, n, bénédiction, f.

benefaction, n, bienfait, m. **benefactor, tress**, n, bienfaiteur, trice.

benefice, n, bénéfice, m.

beneficence, n, bienfaisance, f. **beneficent**, a, bienfaisant.

beneficial, a, avantageux, profitable, salutaire. **beneficiary**, n, bénéficiaire, m.f. **benefit**, n, bénéfice, bienfait, avantage, fruit, profit; secours, *m*; (*Theat.*) représentation à bénéfice, *f.* ~ *society*, société de secours mutuels, *f.* ¶ *v.t*, faire du bien à, avantager; (*v.i.*) profiter, bénéficier.

benevolence, *n*, bienfaisance, *f*; patronage, *m.* **benevolent**, *a*, bienfaisant.

Bengal, *n*, le Bengale. ~ *light*, feu de bengale, *m*, flamme de b., *f.* **Bengali, -lee**, *a*, bengali, *inv.* ¶ *n*, (*pers.*) Bengali, (*bird*) bengali, *m.*

benighted, *a*, (*fig.*) ignorant; plongé dans les ténèbres.

benign, benignant, *a*, bénin. **benignly, benignantly**, *ad*, bénignement.

bent, *a*, courbé, coudé; faussé, gauchi. ~ *lever*, levier coudé, *m.* ~*wood furniture*, meubles en bois courbé, *m.pl.* ¶ *n*, penchant, *m*, pente, *f*, biais, génie, attrait, *m.* ¶ *to be* ~ *on*, s'aheurter à, se buter à, s'acharner à.

benumb, *v.t*, engourdir, morfondre.

benzine, benzoline, *n*, benzine, *f.*

benzoin, *n*, benjoin, *m.*

benzol[e], benzene, *n*, benzol, *m.*

bequeath, *v.t*, léguer. **bequest**, *n*, legs, *m.*

bereave, *v.t.ir*, priver; enlever, ravir. ~**ment**, *n*, deuil, *m.*

beret, *n*, béret [basque] *m.*

bergamot, *n*, (*orange, pear*) bergamote; (*pear*) mouille-bouche, *f.* ~ *oil*, essence de bergamote, *f.* ~ [*tree*] (orange), bergamotier, *m.*

Bermudas (the), les Bermudes, *f.pl.*

berry, *n*, baie, *f*; (*coffee*) grain, *m.*

berth, *n*, poste de mouillage, mouillage, emplacement, poste, *m*, place; couchette, *f.*

beryl, *n*, béryl, *m.*

beseech, *v.t.ir*, supplier, adjurer, implorer.

beset, *v.t.ir*, entourer, assiéger. *besetting sin*, péché d'habitude, *m.*

beside, *pr*, à côté de; auprès de; hors de; excepté. ~ *oneself*, hors de soi. **besides**, *ad. & pr*, d'ailleurs, du reste, de plus, d'autre part, en outre, puis.

besiege, *v.t*, assiéger. **besieger**, *n*, assiégeant, *m.*

besmear, *v.t*, barbouiller.

besmirch, *v.t*, souiller.

besom, *n*, balai [de bouleau] *m.*

besotted, *a*, abruti.

bespangle, *v.t*, pailleter; parsemer.

bespatter, *v.t*, éclabousser, crotter.

bespeak, *v.t.ir*, retenir; commander; stipuler.

besprinkle, *v.t*, arroser.

best, *a*, [le] meilleur; le mieux; le plus beau *ou* grand *ou* fort. ~ *man* (wedding), garçon d'honneur, *m.* ~ *quality*, premier choix, *m.* ~*seller*, livre à succès, l. à grand tirage, *m.* ¶ *ad*, mieux, le mieux; plus. ¶ *the* ~, le mieux. *the* ~ *of it*, le meilleur de l'affaire; le plus beau de l'histoire; le dessus. *in one's* [*Sunday*] ~, endimanché. *do the* ~ *you can!* arrangez-vous!

bestial†, *a*, bestial.

bestir oneself (to), se remuer, s'empresser.

bestow, *v.t*, accorder, gratifier, déférer; impartir, donner.

bestride, *v.t.ir*, enjamber, enfourcher.

bet, *n*, pari, *m.* ¶ *v.t*, parier; gager.

betake oneself (to), *v.reflexive ir*, se livrer, recourir; se rendre.

bethink oneself (to), *v.reflexive ir*, s'aviser.

betide, *v.t*, arriver à. *whate'er* ~, arrive (*ou* advienne) que pourra.

betimes, *ad*, de bonne heure, tôt.

betoken, *v.t*, présager; désigner; dénoter; annoncer.

betray, *v.t*, trahir; tromper; révéler, accuser. ~ *one's trust*, prévariquer. ~**al**, *n*, trahison, *f.* ~**er**, *n*, traître, traîtresse.

betroth, *v.t*, fiancer. ~**al**, *n*, fiançailles, *f.pl.* ~**ed**, *n. & a*, fiancé, e.

better, *a*, meilleur; préférable. *my* ~ *half* (wife), ma [chère] moitié. ~*-looking*, mieux. *to be* ~ (health), se porter (*ou* aller) mieux. *it is* ~ *to*, il vaut mieux. ¶ *ad*, mieux. *so much the* ~, tant mieux. ¶ (*pers.*) *n*, supérieur, e. ¶ *v.t*, améliorer. ~**ment**, *n*, amélioration, *f.*

better, bettor, *n*, parieur, euse. **betting**, *n*, pari, *m*; (*odds*) cote, *f.* ~ *system*, martingale, *f.* ~ *with bookmakers*, pari à la cote.

between, *pr*, entre; de; à. ~ *now & then*, d'ici là. ~ *this & . . .*, d'ici à . . . ~ [*times*], dans l'intervalle. **~-decks**, *n*, entrepont, *m*.

bevel, *n*, biseau, *m*. **~** [*square*], fausse équerre, sauterelle, *f*. **~** *gear*, roue d'angle, *f*. ¶ *v.t*, biseauter.

beverage, *n*, breuvage, *m*, boisson, *f*.

bevy, *n*, compagnie; volée; troupe, *f*.

bewail, *v.t*, pleurer, déplorer, se lamenter sur.

beware, *v.i*, se garder, se méfier, se défier, prendre garde. **~** *of pickpockets!* méfiez-vous des voleurs!

bewilder, *v.t*, égarer, désorienter; ahurir. **~ment**, *n*, affolement, *m*.

bewitch, *v.t*, ensorceler, envoûter, enchanter. **~ing**, *a*, ensorcelant, enchanteur. **~ingly**, *ad*, à ravir.

beyond, *ad*, au-delà, plus loin. ¶ *pr*, au-delà de, par-delà, delà; hors; au-dessus de; sans; outre. *the* **~** (*future life*), l'au-delà, *m*.

bezel, *n*, chaton, *m*.

bias, *n*, biais; (*fig.*) penchant, parti pris, *m*, partialité, *f*. ¶ *v.t*, influencer, détourner; biaiser. **biased**, *p.a*, partial.

bib, *n*, bavoir, *m*, bavette, *f*.

Bible, *n*, Bible, *f*. **~** *Society*, Société biblique, *f*. **biblical**, *a*, biblique.

bibliography, *n*, bibliographie, *f*. **bibliophile**, *n*, bibliophile, *m*.

bibulous, *a*, absorbant; adonné à la boisson.

biceps, *n*, biceps, *m*.

bicker, *v.i*, disputailler, se chamailler.

bicycle, *n*, bicyclette, *f*; bicycle, *m*. **bicyclist**, *n*, cycliste, *m.f*.

bid, *n*, (*Stk Ex.*) demande; (*auction*) enchère, mise, *f*. *to make a* **~** *for*, vouloir capter. ¶ *v.t. & i. ir*, commander, ordonner; (*adieu*) dire; offrir; enchérir, miser; (*Stk Ex.*) demander. **~** *higher than*, surenchérir sur. **bidder**, *n*, enchérisseur, *m*.

bide one's time (to), attendre son heure, se réserver.

biennial, *a*, biennal, bisannuel.

bier, *n*, civière, *f*.

bifurcation, *n*, bifurcation, *f*.

big, *a*, gros; grand; fort; considérable; haut; (*pregnant*) grosse, enceinte, (*animals*) pleine. **~-boned**, ossu. *to talk* **~**, le prendre de haut.

bigamist, *n*, bigame, *m.f*. **bigamous**, *a*, bigame. **bigamy**, *n*, bigamie, *f*.

bight, *n*, golfe, enfoncement; (*rope*) double, *m*.

bigness, *n*, grosseur; grandeur, *f*.

bigot, *n.* & **~ed**, *a*, bigot, e. **~ry**, *n*, bigoterie, *f*.

bigshot, *n*, grosse légume, *f*.

bigwig, *n*, gros bonnet, *m*.

bike, *n*, vélo, *m*.

bilberry, *n*, airelle, myrtille, *f*.

bile, *n*, bile, *f*.

bilge, *n*, (*ship*) fond de cale; (*cask*) bouge, ventre, *m*. **~** *water*, eau de cale, *f*.

bilious, *a*, bilieux.

bilk, *v.t*, frustrer; flouer.

bill, *n*, (*bird*) bec, *m*; (*notice*) affiche, pancarte, *f*, placard; écriteau; prospectus; programme; (*legislative*) projet de loi, *m*; (*account*) note, *f*, mémoire, *m*; addition; facture, *f*; (*Fin.*) effet, billet, mandat, *m*, échéance, traite, remise, lettre, valeur, *f*; (*pl.*) portefeuille[-effets], papier, *m*. **~** *file*, pique-notes, *m*. *to settle a* **~**, régler une note. **~** *head[ing]*, en-tête de facture, *m*. **~hook**, croissant, *m*, serpe, serpette, *f*. **~** *of exchange*, lettre de change, traite, *f*; **~** *of fare*, carte de restaurant; carte du jour, *f*, menu, *m*. **~** *of health*, patente de santé, *f*. **~** *of lading*, connaissement, *m*. **~** *payable*, *receivable*, effet à payer, à recevoir, *m*. **~poster**, **~sticker**, afficheur, colleur, *m*. ¶ *v.t*, afficher, placarder; facturer; (*v.i.*) se becqueter. **~** & *coo*, faire des mamours, roucouler.

billet, *n*, (*Mil.*) billet de logement; (*pl.*) cantonnement, *m*; (*log*) bûche, *f*, rondin, *m*. ¶ *v.t*, cantonner; (*on householder*) loger.

billiard: **~** *ball*, bille [de billard] *f*. **~** *room*, salle de billard, *f*, billard, *m*. **~** *table*, table de billard, *f*, billard, *m*. **~s**, *n.pl*, billard, *m*.

billingsgate, *n*, langage de poissarde, l. des halles, *m*.

billion, *n*, milliard, *m*.

billow, *n*, vague, lame, onde, *f*, flot, *m*. ¶ *v.i*, ondoyer. **~y**, *a*, houleux.

billy goat, bouc, *m*.

bimonthly, *a*, (*in alternate months*) bimestriel; (*½ monthly*) semi-mensuel.

bin, *n,* huche, *f;* tonneau, tonnelet, *m;* trémie, case, *f,* casier, caisson, coffre; porte-bouteilles, *m.*

binary, *a,* binaire.

bind, *v.t.ir,* lier, attacher, ligoter; (*sheaf*) [en]gerber; bander; assujettir; serrer; enchaîner; astreindre; border; engager, obliger; (*books*) relier; (*paper covers*) brocher; (*with metal*) ferrer; (*Med.*) resserrer, constiper. *I'll be bound,* j'en réponds. **~er,** *n,* (*sheaf, pers.*) lieur, *m;* (*Mach.*) lieuse, *f;* (*book*) relieur, euse; brocheur, euse; (*tie*) lien, *m,* attache, *f;* (*papers*) biblorhapte. *m.* **~ing,** *a,* obligatoire. ¶ *n,* reliure, *f;* brochage, *m,* brochure; bordure, *f,* galon, *m,* tresse, *f.*

bindweed, *n,* liseron, liset, *m.*

bine, *n,* sarment, *m.*

binnacle, *n,* habitacle, *m.*

binocular, *n,* jumelle, *f.*

biographer, *n,* biographe, *m.* **biography,** *n,* biographie, *f.*

biologist, *n,* biologiste, biologue, *m.* **biology,** *n,* biologie, *f.*

biped, *n,* bipède, *m.* **~[al],** *a,* bipède.

biplane, *n,* biplan, *m.*

birch, *n,* (*tree*) bouleau, *m;* (*rod*) verges, *f.pl.* **~bark** [*canoe*] pirogue en écorce, *f.* **~ broom,** balai de bouleau, *m.* ¶ *v.t,* frapper de verges. **~ing,** *n,* (des) coups de verges, *m.pl.*

bird, *n,* oiseau, (*small*) oiselet, *m.* **~ call,** appeau, pipeau, *m.* **~ catcher,** oiseleur, *m.* **~lime,** *n,* glu, *f;* (*v.t.*) engluer. **~ of ill omen,** oiseau de mauvais augure, porte-malheur, *m.* **~ of paradise,** oiseau de paradis. **~'s-eye view,** vue à vol d'oiseau, *f.* **~ shot,** menu plomb, *m,* dragée, *f.*

birth, *n,* naissance; extraction, *f;* enfantement, *m;* (*childbed*) couches, *f.pl.* **~ certificate,** acte de naissance, *m.* **~ control,** limitation des naissances, *f.* **~day,** jour de naissance, anniversaire de ma (de sa, etc.) naissance, *m,* fête, *f.* **~mark,** tache de naissance, envie, *f,* nævus, *m.* **~place,** lieu de naissance, *m,* [petite] patrie, *f.* **~ rate,** natalité, *f,* pourcentage des naissances, *m.* **~ right,** droit d'aînesse; droit du sang, *m.*

biscuit, *n,* biscuit, *m.*

bisect, *v.t,* diviser en deux parties égales. **bisection,** *n,* bissection, *f.*

bishop, *n,* évêque, *m;* (*chess*) fou, *m.* **~'s house** & **bishopric,** *n,* évêché, *m.*

bismuth, *n,* bismuth, *m.*

bison, *n,* bison, *m.*

bit, *n,* morceau, fragment, *m,* pièce, miette, *f;* bout, brin; peu; (*bridle*) mors, frein; (*borer*) foret, *m,* mèche, *f;* (*key*) panneton; (*iron of plane, etc.*) fer, *m;* (*computers*) bit, *m.*

bitch, *n,* chienne; (*woman*) garce, *f.* **~ fox,** renarde, *f.* **~ wolf,** louve, *f.*

bite, *n,* morsure, *f,* coup de dents; mordant, *m;* (*sting*) piqûre; (*to eat*) bouchée; (*place bitten by worm, mouse*) mangeure, *f.* *I have a ~!* (*Fish.*), ça mord! ¶ *v.t. & i. ir,* mordre; piquer. **biting,** *a,* mordant, piquant; (*cold*) cuisant.

bitter, *a,* amer; aigre; cuisant; cruel; acharné. **~ pill** (*fig.*), couleuvre, *f.* **~sweet,** *a,* aigre-doux; (*n. Bot.*) douce-amère, *f.* **~ly,** *ad,* amèrement; aigrement; (*cold*) extrêmement. *cry ~,* pleurer à chaudes larmes. **~ness,** *n,* amertume, *f,* amer, fiel, *m.* **~s,** *n,* amers, *m.pl.*

bittern, *n,* butor, *m.*

bitumen, *n,* bitume, *m.* **bituminous,** *a,* bitumineux.

bivalve, *a.* & *n,* bivalve, *a.* & *m.*

bivouac, *n,* bivouac, *m.* ¶ *v.i,* bivouaquer.

blab, *v.t,* divulguer; (*v.i.*) bavarder, jaser.

black, *a,* noir. **~ & blue,** meurtri, noir. [*down*] **in ~ & white,** noir sur blanc. **~ball** (*voting*), boule noire, *f.* **~beetle,** blatte, *f,* cafard, *m.* **~berry,** mûre sauvage, *m.* de ronce, *f.* **~berry bush,** ronce, *f.* **~bird,** merle, *m,* (*hen*) merlette, *f.* **~board,** tableau [noir] *m.* **~-bordered envelope,** enveloppe deuil, *f.* **~ currant(s)** & **~ currant bush** & **~ currant cordial,** cassis, *m.* **~ eye,** œil poché, pochon, *m. to give someone a ~ eye,* pocher l'œil à quelqu'un. *B ~ Forest,* Forêt-Noire, *f.* **~guard,** canaille, *f,* goujat, *m.* **~head,** point noir, *m,* tanne, *f.* **~jack,** assommoir, *m,* matraque, *f.* **~ lead,** mine de plomb, plombagine, *f,* graphite, *m.* **~list,** *n,* index, *m;* (*v.t.*)

mettre à l'i. ~ *magic*, ~ *art*, magie noire, *f*. ~*mail*, *n*, chantage, *m*; (*v.t.*) faire chanter. ~*mailer*, maître chanteur, *m*. ~ *mark* (bruise), noir, *m*. ~ *market*, marché noir, *m*. ~ *out*, black-out, *m*. B~ *Sea*, mer Noire, *f*. ~ *sheep* (fig.), brebis galeuse, *f*. ~*smith*, forgeron, *m*. ~*thorn*, épine noire, *f*, prunellier, *m*. ¶ *n*, (*color, man*) noir, *m*; (*ball—gaming*) noire, *f*. ¶ *v.t*, noircir; charbonner; mâchurer; (*boots*) cirer.

blackamoor, *n*, moricaud, e; noir, e.

blacken, *v.t* noircir. **blacking**, *n*, noircissement; (*boots*) cirage; cirage pour chaussures, *m*. ~ *brush*, brosse à cirer, b. à étendre, *f*. **blackish**, *a*, noirâtre. **blackness**, *n*, noirceur, *f*.

bladder, *n*, vessie, *f*. (*Bot.*) vésicule, *f*.

blade, *n*, (*grass*) brin, *m*; (*knife*) lame, feuille; (*vane*) aile, aube; (*propeller*) palette; (*oar*) pale, *f*, plat, *m*.

blame, *n*, blâme, reproche, *m*, faute, *f*. ¶ *v.t* blâmer, reprocher, accuser, s'en prendre à. ~*less*, *a*, innocent. ~*worthy*, *a*, digne de blâme.

blanch, *v.t. & i*, blanchir, faire pâlir, pâlir.

bland, *a*, doux, suave, doucereux, mielleux. ~*ishment*, *n*, flatterie, chatterie, *f*.

blank, *a*, blanc, vierge. ~ *cartridge*, cartouche à blanc, *f*. ~ *verse*, vers blancs, *m.pl*. ¶ *n*, blanc, *m*; lacune, *f*, trou, *m*; (*lottery*) billet perdant; (*for coin*) flan, *m*.

blanket, *n*, couverture [en laine], couverte, *f*. ~ *stitch* (*Emb.*), point de languette, p. de feston, *m*.

blare, *n*, flonflon, *m*. ¶ *v.i*, retentir.

blarney, *n*, blague, *f*.

blaspheme, *v.i. & t*, blasphémer, jurer. **blasphemer**, *n*, blasphémateur, trice. **blasphemous**, *a*, blasphématoire. **blasphemy**, *n*, blasphème, *m*.

blast, *n*, vent, coup de vent, courant d'air, souffle, *m*, chasse d'air, *f*; coup; coup [de mine], pétard, *m*, mine, *f*. ~ *furnace*, haut fourneau, *m*. ¶ *v.t*, faire sauter, pétarder; foudroyer; (*blight*) brouir, flétrir. ~*ing*, *n*, travail

aux explosifs (*ou* à la poudre), *m*. ~ *powder*, poudre de mine, *f*.

blatant, *a*, bruyant, criard.

blaze, *n*, flambée, *f*; éclat, *m*. in a ~, en flammes. ¶ *v.i*, flamber; flamboyer; (*v.t, tree*) griffer. ~ *a trail*, frayer un chemin. ~ *away*, tirailler. **blazing**, *a*, flambant, flamboyant, ardent, d'enfer; éclatant.

blazon, *v.t*, blasonner, armorier, proclamer. ~*ry*, *n*, blason, *m*.

bleach, *v.t*, blanchir. ~*er*, *n*, blanchisseur, euse, buandier, ère; (*pl.*) (*seats*) gradins, *m.pl*. ~*ery*, *n*, blanchisserie, *f*. ~*ing*, *n*, blanchiment, *m*.

bleak, *a*, morne, triste.

blear-eyed, *a*, chassieux.

bleat, *v.i*, bêler; (*goat & fig.*) chevroter. **bleat[ing]**, *n*, bêlement, *m*.

bleed, *v.t. & i. ir*, saigner; pleurer. ~*ing*, *n*, saignement, *m*; saignée, *f*

blemish, *n*, tache, tare, défectuosité, *f*, défaut, *m*. ¶ *v.t*, tacher; ternir.

blench, *v.i*, reculer; fuir; broncher.

blend, *n*, assortiment, *m*. ¶ *v.t.ir* assortir; fondre; confondre; incorporer; (*wines*) mélanger, couper; (*v.i.ir.*) [s']assortir, se confondre, s'apparenter. ~*ing* (*wines*) *n*, mélange, coupage, *m*.

bless, *v.t*, bénir; (*bell, etc.*) baptiser; favoriser. **blessed, blest**, *a*, béni; heureux; bienheureux. *the Blessed Virgin* [*Mary*], la Sainte Vierge. *to be ~ with*, avoir le bonheur d'avoir, de posséder; jouir de. **blessedness**, *n*, béatitude; félicité, *f*. **blessing**, *n*, bénédiction, *f*; bonheur; (*grace*) bénédicité, *m*.

blight, *n*, brouissure, nielle, rouille, *f*. ¶ *v.t*, brouir, nieller, rouiller; flétrir.

blind, *a*, aveugle; borgne. ~ *alley*, impasse, *f*, cul-de-sac, *m*. ~ *man, woman*, aveugle, *m.f*. *the* ~, les aveugles, *m.pl*. ~*man's buff*, colin-maillard, *m*. ~*worm*, orvet, *m*. ¶ *n*, store, *m*; jalousie; (*shop*) banne, *f*; (*fig.*) voile, masque, faux-semblant, *m*. ¶ *v.t*, aveugler. ~*fold*, *v.t*, bander [les yeux à, de]. ~*ly*, *ad*, aveuglément, à l'aveuglette. ~*ness*, *n*, cécité, *f*; (*fig.*) aveuglement, *m*.

blink, n, clign[ot]ement. m. ¶ v.i,
clign[ot]er, ciller; vaciller, papilloter; (v.t.) se cacher. ~er, n,
œillère, f.

bliss, n, béatitude, félicité, f.
~ful, a, heureux; bienheureux;
béat.

blister, n, ampoule, bulle, cloque,
f; (plaster) vésicatoire, m. ¶ v.t,
faire venir des ampoules à. I ~
easily, il me vient facilement des
ampoules.

blithe, a, gai, joyeux.

blizzard, n, tourmente de neige,
f.

bloat, v.t, bouffir. **bloater,** n. or
bloated herring, hareng bouffi,
m.

block, n, bloc, massif, m; motte,
f; paquet, m; partie, tranche, f,
ensemble; (chopping) billot, m;
(shape) forme, poupée, f;
(houses) pâté, îlot, m; (pulley)
moufle, poulie, f; (stoppage) embarras, encombrement, embouteillage, m. ~ letters (e.g, child's
writing), lettres moulées, f.pl.
in ~ letters (as on coupon), en
caractères d'imprimerie. ~ writing, la lettre moulée. ¶ v.t, obstruer, encombrer; embouteiller;
bloquer; (Bookb.) dorer. ~ up
(door), condamner.

blockade, n, blocus. m. ¶ v.t,
bloquer.

blockhead, n, bûche, f, imbécile,
m,f.

blockhouse, n, blockhaus, m.

blond, as applied to a woman
blonde, a, blond (blonde, f.).
¶ n, (color) blond, m; (pers.)
blond, e.

blood, n, sang, m; race, f; (dandy)
petit-maître, élégant, m. ~ heat,
température du sang, f. ~hound,
limier, m. ~ letting, saignée, f.
~ orange, orange sanguine, f. ~
poisoning, empoisonnement du
sang, m. ~ pressure, tension artérielle, f. ~ red, rouge sang, m.
~ relationship, consanguinité, f.
~shed, effusion de sang, f; carnage, m. ~shot, injecté [de
sang], éraillé. ~stone, jaspé sanguin, héliotrope, m, sanguine, f.
~sucker, sangsue, f. ~ test, prise
de sang, f, prélèvement de s., m.
~thirsty, altéré de sang, sanguinaire. ~ vessel, vaisseau sanguin, m. ~y Mary, marie-salope,
f. ~less, a, exsangue; non sanglant. ~y, a, ensanglanté, sanglant, en sang; sanguinaire.

bloom, n, fleur; fraîcheur, f. ¶ v.i,
fleurir. ~ing, a, fleurissant; (fig.)
florissant. ¶ n, floraison, f.

blossom, n, fleur, f. ¶ v.i, fleurir.
~ing, n, floraison, f.

blot, n, pâté, m, tache, f. ¶ v.t,
faire un pâté sur, tacher; (paper
with useless writing) noircir;
(with blotting paper) éponger.
~ out, effacer.

blotch, n, pustule; tache, f. ¶ v.t,
tacher.

blotting: ~ case, ~ pad, **blotter,**
n, buvard, sous-main, m. ~
paper, papier buvard, papier
brouillard, m.

blouse, n, chemisette, blouse, f.
~ front, guimpe, f.

blow, n, coup, m; at-
teinte, f; (pl.) voies de fait, f.pl;
échec, m. ~fly, mouche à viande,
f. ~ gun, ~pipe, ~ tube, (dart
tube), sarbacane, f. ~[hole],
soufflure, f, bouillon, m. ~out,
crevaison, f. ~pipe, chalumeau,
m. ¶ v.t.ir, souffler; (wind instrument) souffler dans, emboucher;
(to puff, to wind) essouffler;
(v.i.ir) souffler; venter; (flower)
s'épanouir; (fuse) fondre, jouer.
~ a horn, corner. ~ one's brains
out, se brûler la cervelle. ~ one's
nose, se moucher. ~ out, souffler. ~ up, v.t, souffler; faire
sauter, pétarder; (v.i.) sauter.
~er, n, souffleur, m.

blubber, n, graisse, f, lard, m.
¶ v.i, sangloter.

bludgeon, n, assommoir, gourdin, m, trique, massue, f.

blue, a, bleu. Bluebeard, Barbe-
Bleue, m. ~bell, jacinthe des
bois, f. ~bottle, mouche bleue,
f. ~eyed, aux yeux bleus.
~jacket, marin de l'État, m. ~
mark (bruise), bleu, m. ~
moldy (cheese), persillé. ~pen-
cil, v.t, marquer au crayon bleu;
sabrer, barrer. ~ peter, pavillon de partance, m. ~print, bleu,
m. ~stocking, bas-bleu. m. out
of the ~, soudainement. to feel
~, avoir le cafard. ¶ n, bleu;
(pl.) spleen, m. ¶ v.t, bleuir.

blueberry, n, airelle, f.

bluff, a, brusque; franc; escarpé.
¶ n, cap à pic; trompe-l'œil, m.
¶ v.t, leurrer, ~er, n, faiseur, m.

bluish, a, bleuâtre.

blunder, n, bévue, bourde, ignorance, f, impair, m ¶ v.i, faire

des bévues, gaffer. **~er,** *n,* gaffeur, maladroit, *m.*

blunt, *a,* émoussé; contondant; brusque, cru. ¶ *v.t,* émousser, épointer. **~ly,** *ad,* brusquement, crûment, rondement. **~ness,** *n,* état émoussé; sans-façon, *m;* brusquerie, *f.*

blur, *n,* tache, *f;* embrouillement, *m.* ¶ *v.t,* tacher, barbouiller; [em]brouiller.

blurb, *n,* réclame, publicité, *f.*

blurred, *p.a,* trouble. **blurry,** *a,* flou.

blurt out, *v.t,* lâcher, laisser échapper.

blush, *n,* rougeur; fleur, *f.* at the first **~,** à vue de nez. ¶ *v.i,* rougir. **~ing,** *p.a,* rougissant, rouge.

bluster, *n,* fracas, *m;* fanfaronnade, rodomontade, *f.* ¶ *v.i,* tempêter; maugréer. **~er,** *n,* fanfaron, *m.*

boa (wrap) *n,* boa, *m.* **~** constrictor, boa constrictor, *m.*

boar, *n,* verrat; (wild) sanglier; (young wild) marcassin, *m.* **~** hound, vautre, *m.* **~** hunting, chasse au sanglier, *m.* **~'s head,** hure de sanglier, *f.* **~** spear, épieu, *m.*

board, *n,* planche, *f,* ais; plat; tableau; tablier; (notice) écriteau, *m,* enseigne, *f;* (Naut.) bord, *m;* bordée, *f.* on **~,** à bord. room & **~,** pension complète. **~** [of directors], conseil [d'administration] *m,* administration, *f.* **~** of examiners, jury d'examen, *m.* ¶ *v.t,* planchéier; (ship) monter sur, aborder; (train, car) monter dans; (feed) nourrir. **~** up (window), condamner. **~er,** *n,* pensionnaire; [élève] interne, *m,f.* **~ing,** *n,* planchéiage, *m.* **~** house, pension, *f.* **~~in,** internat, *m.* **~** school, pensionnat, internat, *m,* pension, *f.*

boast, *n,* vanterie; gloire, *f.* ¶ *v.t,* vanter; (v.i.) se vanter. **~er,** *n,* vantard, e, fanfaron, ne. **~ful,** *a,* vantard.

boat, *n,* bateau, canot, *m,* embarcation, barque, *f;* navire, bâtiment, vaisseau, *m.* **~** deck, pont des embarcations, *m.* **~** fishing, pêche en bateau, *f.* **~** hook, gaffe [pour l'amarrage des bateaux] *f,* croc [de batelier] *m.* **~house,**

garage [des bateaux] *m.* **~load,** batelée, *f.* **~man,** marin, canotier, *m.* **~** train, train de paquebot, *m.* ¶ *v.i,* canoter. **~ing,** *n,* canotage, *m.* **boatswain,** *n,* maître [d'équipage] *m;*

bob, *n,* secousse, *f;* révérence, *f;* lentille, poire, *f;* plomb; poids, *m.* ¶ *v.i,* balloter, branler. bob[bed hair], coiffure à la Ninon, coiffure à la Jeanne d'Arc, *f.*

bobbin, *n,* bobine, canette, *f.*

bobsleigh, *n,* traîneau, bobsleigh, *m.*

bobtail, *n,* queue écourtée, *f.*

bode, *v.t,* présager.

bodice, *n,* corps, corsage, *m.*

bodily, *a,* corporel; physique; matériel; (fear) pour sa personne. ¶ *ad,* corporellement; en masse.

bodkin, *n,* passe-lacet, *m,* aiguille à passer, *f.*

body, *n,* corps, *m;* carcasse, *f;* vaisseau; massif, *m;* masse, *f;* gros, *m;* (water) masse; (vehicle) carrosserie, *f.* **~** belt, gaine, *f.* **~** corporate, personne morale, p. juridique, p. civile, *f.*

bog, *n,* marais, marécage, *m,* fondrière, *f.* ¶ *v.t,* embourber.

bogey [man], *n,* croque-mitaine, *m.*

boggle, *v.i,* reculer, hésiter.

boggy, *a,* marécageux, tourbeux.

bogus, *a,* faux, simulé; véreux.

Bohemia (fig.) *n,* la bohème. **Bohemian** (fig.) *n.* & *a,* bohème, *m,f.* & *a.*

boil (Path.) *n,* furoncle, clou, *m.*

boil, *v.t,* faire bouillir; cuire [à l'eau]; (v.i.) bouillir; bouillonner. **~** down, condenser, réduire. **~ed,** *p.a:* **~** beef, bœuf bouilli, *m.* **~** egg, œuf à la coque, *m.* **~** potatoes, pommes de terre à l'eau, p—s de t. nature, p—s de t. vapeur, *f.pl.* **~er,** *n,* (steam) chaudière, *f;* (pot) marmite, *f.* **~** maker, chaudronnier, *m.* **~** making & **~** works, [grosse] chaudronnerie, *f.* **~** plate, tôle de chaudière, *f.* **~** room, chambre de chauffe, chaufferie, *f.* double **~,** bain-marie, *m.* **~ing,** *n,* ébullition, *f;* bouillonnement, *m.* **~** point, point d'ébullition, *m.* (212° F. or 100° C.).

boisterous†, *a*, bruyant, turbulent.

bold, *a*, hardi, osé, audacieux, téméraire, assuré; net. *~-faced* (type), gras. *displayed in ~ type*, en vedette. *~ly*, *ad*, hardiment, audacieusement; hautement, franchement. *~ness*, *n*, hardiesse, audace; fierté (*de touche*) *f*.

Bolivia, *n*, la Bolivie. **Bolivian**, *a*, bolivien. ¶ *n*, Bolivien, ne.

bollard, *n*, canon d'amarrage, poteau d'a., *m*.

Bologna, *n*, Bologne, *f*.

bolster, *n*, traversin, chevet; coussin, *m*. *~ up*, *v.t*, (*doctrine*) étayer; (*pers.*) soutenir.

bolt, *n*, boulon, *m*, cheville, *f*; (*door*) verrou; (*lock*) pêne, *m*; (*thunder*) foudre; (*flight*) fugue, *f*. ¶ *v.t*, boulonner; cheviller; verrouiller; (*sift*) bluter; (*food*) expédier, gober; (*v.i.*) (*horse*) s'emporter, s'emballer; (*pers.*) prendre la poudre d'escampette. **bolt upright**, tout droit.

bolus, *n*, bol, *m*.

bomb, *n*, bombe, *f*. *~proof*, à l'épreuve des b—s. *~shell* (*fig.*), bombe, *f*. *~thrower*, lance-bombe, *m*. ¶ *v.t*, (*Avn.*) bombarder; (*Mil.*) lancer des bombes à. **bombard**, *v.t*, bombarder, canonner; fusiller (*fig.*). *~ier*, *n*, bombardier, *m*. *~ment*, *n*, bombardement, *m*.

bombast, *n*, emphase, *f*, phébus, *m*. *~ic*, *a*, emphatique, ampoulé, boursouflé, bouffi.

bomber, *n*, (*Avn.*) bombardier; (*pers.*) grenadier, *m*.

bond, *n*, lien, *m*, attache, *f*; nœud, *m*; liaison; chaîne, *f*; agglutinant; (*Fin.*) bon, *m*; obligation, *f*; titre, *m*, valeur, *f*; (*law*) acte, contrat; cautionnement; compromis, *m*; soumission, *f*. *bond[ed ware-house*], entrepôt [légal *ou* de douane] *m*. *in bond[ed ware-house*], en (*ou* à l')entrepôt. **bond**, *v.t*, entreposer; (*masonry*) liaisonner. **bondage**, *n*, captivité, servitude, *f*, esclavage, *m*.

bone, *n*, os, *m*; (*fish*) arête, *f*; (*pl*, *dead*) ossements, *m.pl*; (*casta-nets*) cliquettes, *f.pl*. *~ of con-tention*, pomme de discorde, *f*. *~setter*, rebouteur, euse. ¶ *v.t*, désosser; ôter les arêtes de.

bonfire, *n*, feu de joie, bûcher, *m*.

bonnet, *n*, chapeau; (*auto*) capot, *m*, capote, *f*.

bonny, *a*, joli; bien portant; gai.

bonus, *n*, gratification, prime, indemnité, *f*. *~ shares*, actions gratuites, *f.pl*.

bony, *a*, osseux; (*big-boned*) ossu. *~ palate*, palais dur, *m*.

boo, *v.t*, huer, conspuer.

booby, *n*, nigaud, e, benêt, dadais, *m*, huître, *f*. *~ prize*, fiche de consolation, *f*. *~ trap*, attrape-nigaud, *m*.

book, *n*, livre; livret; carnet; registre; journal; cahier; recueil; album; (*old & of little value*) bouquin, *m*. *~binder*, relieur, euse. *~binding*, reliure, *f*. *~case*, bibliothèque, *f*; serre-livres, *m*. *~keeper*, teneur de livres, *m*, comptable, *m,f*. *~keeping*, tenue de[s] livres, comptabilité, *f*. *~ lover*, biblio-phile, *m*. *~maker*, bookmaker, *m*. *~mark[er]*, signet, *m*, marque, *f*. *~matches*, allumettes en carnet, *f.pl*. *~muslin*, organdi, *m*. *~plate*, ex-libris, *m*. *~rest*, pupitre, *m*. *~seller*, libraire, *~seller & publisher*, libraire-éditeur, *m*. *~[seller's] shop*, li-brairie, *f*. *~shelf*, rayon, *m*. *~stall*, bibliothèque, *f*; kiosque, *m*. *~ value*, valeur comptable, *f*. *~worm* (*pers.*), rat de biblio-thèque, *m*. *~ work* (*Typ.*), labeur, *m*. ¶ *v.t*, enregistrer; en-gager, retenir, louer; réserver; demander; (*v.i.*) prendre un billet, des billets. **booking**, *n*, en-registrement; engagement, *m*, lo-cation; réserve, *f*; transport, voyage, service, *m*. **booklet**, *n*, brochure, *f*, livret, *m*.

Boolean, *a*, booléen, ne. *~ alge-bra*, algèbre booléen. *~ opera-tion*, opération booléenne.

boom, *n*, (*harbor*) estacade; (*crane*) flèche, *f*; (*prices*) emballe-ment [à la hausse]; (*noise*) grondement, *m*. (*cinema*) *~ op-erator*, perchiste, *m*. ¶ *v.i*, gron-der, bourdonner, ronfler, tonner.

boon, *a*, gai, joyeux. *~ compa-nion*, bon compagnon; camarade de bouteille, *m*. ¶ *n*, beinfait, *m*, faveur, *f*.

boor, *n*, rustre, manant, *m*, rus-taud, e. *~ish*, *a*, rustaud, gros-sier. *~ishness*, *n*, rusticité, gros-sièreté, *f*.

boost, n, poussée; augmentation, f. ~er, n, (rocket, spacecraft) propulseur auxiliaire, m. ¶ v.t, pousser; augmenter; (Elec.) doper.

boot, n, chaussure [montante]; bottine, botte, f; brodequin. ~ & shoe repairer, cordonnier, m. ~ & shoe trade, cordonnerie, f. ~black, cireur de bottes, m. ~jack, tire-botte, m. ~lace, lacet de chaussure, m. ~maker, bottier, m. ~tree, embouchoir, embauchoir, m. ¶ v.t, chausser; botter. ~ee, n, chausson, m.

booth, n, baraque, boutique, échoppe, f.

bootless, a, inutile, vain, futile.

booty, n, butin, m.

booze, v.i, riboter, godailler.

boracic, a, borique. **borax,** n, borax, m.

border, n, bord, m, bordure; frontière; lisière, f; cordon, m; (garden) plate-bande, f. ~ land, pays limitrophe, m. ¶ v.t, border. ~ [up]on, avoisiner, côtoyer, friser.

bore, n, alésage, calibre; (Min.) sondage, forage, m; (tidal) barre d'eau, f, mascaret, m; (nuisance) scie, f; (pers.) raseur, euse, endormeur, casse-pieds, m, scie, f, crampon, m. ~ core, témoin, f, carotte, f. ~hole, trou de sonde, m. ¶ v.t, percer, forer, vriller; aléser, vider; (fig.) ennuyer, embêter, scier, assommer, tuer, assassiner, ~dom, n, ennui, m.

boric, a, borique.

born, p.p. & a, né; issu; de naissance. ~ blind, aveugle de naissance, aveugle-né. to be~, naître.

borough, n, bourg, m.

borrow, v.t, emprunter. ~er, n, emprunteur, euse. ~ing, n, emprunt, m. oft. pl.

borzoi, n, lévrier russe, m.

bosom, n, sein, m; gorge, f; (church) sein, giron, m. ~ friend, ami de cœur, m.

Bosphorus (the), le Bosphore.

boss, n, bosse, f; moyeu; (pers.) patron, chef, m.

botanic(al), a, botanique. ~ gardens, jardin des plantes, m. **botanist,** n, botaniste, m. **botanize,** v.i, herboriser. **botany,** n, botanique, f.

botch, n, bousillage, m. ¶ v.t, bousiller, gâcher, massacrer.

both, a. & ad, tous [les] deux, deux; l'un(e) & l'autre; (at the same time) à la fois . . . et . . .

bother, n, tracas, aria, m. ¶ v.t, tracasser.

bottle, n, bouteille; canette, f; flacon; bocal, m; burette, f. ~ brush, rince-bouteille, m. ~ neck, embouteillage, goulot d'étranglement, m. ¶ v.t, mettre en bouteille(s), embouteiller. ~ up (block), embouteiller.

bottom, n, fond, bas, m, base, f, pied, bout; dessous; derrière, cul; (of chair) siège; (of lowland) bas-fond; (ship) navire, m; (of ship) carène, f. ¶ a, inférieur; de fond; de dessous; le plus bas. ~less, a, sans fond.

bough, n, mère branche, f; rameau, m.

boulder, n, roche, f, gros galet, caillou, m.

bounce, n, bond, m; vanterie, blague, f. ¶ v.i, bondir; se vanter, faire le fanfaron.

bound, n, borne, limite, f; bond, saut, rebond, m. to exceed all ~s, dépasser la mesure. ¶ v.t, borner, limiter; (v.i.) bondir, sauter. ~ for (ship), à destination de. to be ~ to, être tenu(e) de (ou à), être obligé(e) de. **boundary,** n, limite, borne, f. **boundless,** a, illimité, sans bornes, immense.

bounteous†, a, généreux. **bountiful†,** a, généreux, libéral, bienfaisant; fécond. **bounty,** n, générosité, munificence, largesse; prime, f.

bouquet, n, bouquet; (wine) bouquet, fumet, m.

bourn, n, ruisseau, m.

bout, n, tour, assaut, m, partie, reprise, f.

bovine, a, bovin.

bow, n, (knot) nœud, nœud de ruban; (necktie) nœud[-papillon]; (curve) arc; (fiddle) archet; (saddle) arçon, m; (padlock) anse, f. ~ compasses, compas à balustre, m. ~ window, bow-window, m.

bow, n, salut, coup de chapeau, m, inclination, révérence, f; (ship) avant, m. ¶ v.t. & i, courber, incliner, fléchir, plier. ~ &

scrape, faire des courbettes. ~ *to*, saluer; s'incliner devant.

bowdlerize, *v.t*, expurger.

bowels, *n.pl*, entrailles, *f.pl*, intestins, *m.pl*; tripes, *f.pl*.

bower, *n*, tonnelle, *f*, berceau, cabinet de verdure, *m*.

bowing & scraping, prosternations, *f.pl*.

bowl, *n*, bol, bassin, *m*, écuelle, coupe, cuvette, jatte, sébile *f*; plateau; (*pipe*) fourneau, *m*; (*game*) boule, *f*. [*game of*] ~*s*, boules, *f.pl*, jeu de boules, *m*. ~**ful**, *n*, écuellée, *f*.

bowlegged, *a*, bancal.

bowler [*hat*], *n*, [chapeau] melon; (*player*) joueur, *m*.

bowling: ~ *alley*, jeu de boules couvert, *m*. ~ *green*, jeu de boules découvert.

bowman, *n*, archer; (*boat*) brigadier, *m*.

bowsprit, *n*, beaupré, *m*.

bow-wow, *n*, toutou, *m*.

box, *n*, boîte; caisse, *f*; coffre; coffret; tronc; boîtier; (*cardboard*) carton; (*driver's*) siège, *m*; (*jury*) banc, *m*; (*Theat.*) loge, *f*. ~ *office*, bureau [de location], contrôle, *m*. ~ *on the ear*[*s*], soufflet, *m*. ~*spring mattress*, sommier élastique, *m*. ~ [*tree*] & ~*wood*, buis, *m*. ¶*v.t*, encaisser; (*someone's ears*) squffleter, frotter; (*fight*) boxer; (*v.i.*) boxer. ~*er*, *n*, boxeur, *m*. ~*ing*, *n*, boxe, *f*. ~ *match*, combat de b., assaut de b., match de b., *m*.

boy, *n*, garçon, garçonnet, enfant, gars, *m*. ~ *scout*, boy-scout, éclaireur, scout, *m*. ~*hood*, *n*, jeunesse, *f*. ~*ish*, *a*, enfantin, puéril.

boycott, *n*, boycottage, *m*. ¶*v.t*, boycotter.

brace, *n*, (*strut, stay*) entretoise, *f*, étrésillon; arc-boutant, *m*, contre-fiche; bielle, *f*; tirant, *m*; moise; (*tool*) vilebrequin; cliquet; (*pair*) couple, paire. ¶ *v.t*, renforcer, armer; moiser; fortifier, retremper; bander; accolader.

bracelet, *n*, bracelet, *m*.

bracing, *a*, fortifiant, vivifiant.

bracken, *n*, fougère [à l'aigle] *f*.

bracket, *n*, console, potence, applique, *f*; (*Typ.*) [,], crochet, *m*;

(,), parenthèse; {, }, accolade, *f*. ¶*v.t*, accoler.

brackish, *a*, saumâtre.

brad, *n*, pointe, *f*. ~*awl*, *n*, poinçon, *m*.

brag, *n*, vanterie, hâblerie, blague, fanfaronnade, *f*. ¶ *v.i*, se vanter.

braggart, *n*, vantard, e, hâbleur, euse, fanfaron, ne.

brahmin, *n*, brahmane, *m*.

braid, *n*, tresse, soutache, *f*, bordé, galon; passement, *m*. ¶*v.t*, tresser, soutacher, galonner, passementer.

brain, *n*. & ~*s*, *pl*, cerveau, *m*, cervelle, tête, *f*; (*pl. Cook.*) cervelle[s]. ~ *fatigue*, fatigue cérébrale, *f*. ~ *fever*, fièvre cérébrale, *f*. ~*storming*, remue-méninges, *m*. to rack one's ~*s*, se creuser les méninges. ~*less*, *a*, sans cervelle.

braise, *v.t*, braiser.

brake, *n*, (*on wheel*) frein; (*waggonette*) break, *m*; (*bracken*) fougère [à l'aigle] *f*; (*thicket*) fourré, *m*. ~ [*gear*] timonerie des freins; (*carriage*) mécanique, *f*. ¶*v.t*, enrayer. *to put on* (or *apply*) *the* ~*s*, freiner, serrer les freins. **brakeman**, *n*, serre-frein, garde-frein, *m*.

bramble, *n*, ronce, *f*.

bran, *n*, son, *m*.

branch, *n*, branche, *f*; rameau; embranchement; (*Elec.*) branchement, *m*. ~ [*line*] (*Rly*), ligne (*ou* voie) secondaire, *f*. ~ [*office*], succursale, *f*; comptoir, *m*. ¶*v.t*, brancher; (*v.i.*) se ramifier. ~ *off*, *v.t*, embrancher; (*v.i.*) fourcher.

brand, *n*, (*fire*) tison, brandon, *m*; (*fig.*) flétrissure, *f*, stigmate; (*Poet.*) glaive, *m*; (*Com. & hot iron*) marque, *f*. **brand new**, battant (*ou* tout flambant) neuf. ¶*v.t*, marquer [à chaud]; flétrir, stigmatiser. **brandish**, *v.t*, brandir.

brandy, *n*, eau-de-vie, *f*, cognac, *m*. ~ *& soda*, fine à l'eau, *f*.

brass, *n*, laiton, cuivre [jaune]; (*Poet.*) airain; (*bearing*) coussinet, *m*; (*cheek*) effronterie, *f*, toupet, *m*. the ~*es* (*Mus.*), les cuivres. ~ *band*, fanfare, *f*. ~ *foundry*, fonderie de cuivre, robinetterie, *f*. ~*wares*, dinanderie, *f*.

brassière, *n*, soutien-gorge, *m*.

brassy, *a*, cuivré.

brat, *n*, gamin, e, marmot, *m*, gosse, *m*,*f*, (*pl*, *col*.) marmaille, *f*.

bravado, *n*, bravade, *f*. **brave†**, *a*, brave. ~*man*, [homme] brave, *m*. ¶ *v.t*, braver, affronter, défier. ~**ry**, *n*, bravoure, *f*. **bravo**, *i*, bravo!

brawl, *a*, mêlée, bagarre, rixe, querelle, *f*; tapage, *m*. ¶ *v.i*, se chamailler; (*stream*) murmurer. ~**er**, *n*, tapageur, euse, casseur d'assiettes, *m*.

brawn, *n*, hure, *f*, fromage de porc, *m*; (*fig*.) force musculaire, *f*. ~**y**, *a*, charnu, musculeux.

bray, *v.i*, braire. ~[**ing**], *n*, braiment, *m*.

braze, *v.t*, braser. **braze** (*joint*) & **brazing**, *n*, brasure, *f*.

brazen, *a*, d'airain. ~[-*faced*], effronté. *to* ~ *it out*, crâner, faire le crâne.

brazier, *n*, (*pers*.) chaudronnier; dinandier; (*pan*) brasero, *m*.

Brazil, *n*, le Brésil. **Brazilian**, *a*, brésilien. ¶ *n*, Brésilien, ne.

breach, *n*, brèche; infraction, violation, contravention, *f*. ~ *of faith*, manque de foi, *m*. ~ *of promise*, violation de promesse de mariage, *f*. ~ *of trust*, infidélité, prévarication, forfaiture, *f*, abus de confiance, *m*.

bread, *n*, pain, *m*; (*money*) pognon, *m*. ~ *crumbs* (*Cook*.), panure, chapelure, *f*. ~ *knife*, couteau à pain, *m*. ~ *winner*, soutien de famille, *m*. *sandwich* ~, pain de mie. *whole wheat* ~, pain complet.

breadth, *n*, largeur; envergure, *f*; travers, *m*; (*of stuffs*) largeur, *f*, lé, *m*.

break, *n*, rupture, cassure, brisure; solution; (*gap*) trouée, *f*; (*day*) point, *m*; (*voice*) mue; (*prices*) dérobade, *f*; (*Bil*.) série, *f*. ¶ *v.t.ir*, casser, briser; fracturer; fragmenter; rompre; crever; fendre; concasser; enfreindre, violer; (*the bank*, *gaming*) faire sauter; (*a set*) dépareiller; (*news*) faire part de; (See also *broken*); (*v.i.ir*.) [se] casser, se briser, etc; (*voice*) muer; (*dawn*) poindre; (*waves*) déferler. ¶ (*Box*.), séparez! ~ *cover* (*Hunt*.), débucher. ~ *down*, *v.t*,

abattre; (*v.i*.) avoir une panne. ~ *into*, envahir; pénétrer; entamer. ~ *loose*, se déchaîner. ~ *of the habit*, déshabituer, désaccoutumer. ~ *one's arm*, se casser le bras. ~ *one's back*, s'échiner. ~ *one's word*, manquer de parole. ~ *open*, enfoncer. ~ *out*, (*fire*) éclater, se déclarer; (*fig*.) déborder, se débonder. ~ *their engagement* (marriage), se désaccorder. ~ *through*, percer. ~ *upon the wheel*, rouer. **breakable**, *a*, fragile. **breakage**, *n*, casse, rupture, *f*, bris, *m*. **breakaway**, *n*, dislocation; dérive, *f*. **breakdown**, *n*, (*failure*) fiasco, *m*; (*car*, *etc*.) panne; (*health*) prostration, *f*. **breaker**, *n*, (*pers*.) casseur; démolisseur; (*wave*) brisant, *m*. **breakfast**, *n*, déjeuner [du matin] *m*. ¶ *v.i*, déjeuner. **breaking**, *n*, rupture, fracture, *f*, brisement, *m*; (*holy bread*) fraction; (*voice*) mue, *f*. **breakneck**, *n*, casse-cou, *m*. **breakwater**, *n*, brise-lames, brisant, môle, *m*.

bream, *n*, brème, *f*; (*sea*) pagel, *m*.

breast, *n*, sein, *m*; poitrine, *f*; (*horse*) poitrail; (*fowl*) blanc, *m*. *at the* ~, à la mamelle. ~*bone*, sternum, *m*. ~*high*, à hauteur d'appui. ~*stroke* (Swim.), brasse, nage en grenouille, *f*.

breath, *n*, haleine, *f*; souffle; soupir, *m*. **breathe**, *v.i*. & *t*, respirer; souffler; soupirer. **breathing**, *n*, respiration, *f*. ~ *space*, temps de respirer, relâche, *m*. **breathless**, *a*, inanimé; haletant, essoufflé, à bout de souffle.

breech, *n*, derrière, *m*; (*gun*) culasse, *f*, tonnerre, *m*. ~*loading*, se chargeant par la culasse. **breeches**, *n.pl*, culotte, *f*.

breed, *n*, race, *f*. ¶ *v.t.ir*, élever; engendrer; (*v.i.ir*.) multiplier, se reproduire. ~**er** (*stock*) *n*, éleveur, *m*. ~**ing**, *n*, (*animals*) élevage, *m*; (*pers*.) éducation, *f*, ton, *m*.

breeze, *n*, (*wind*) brise, *f*. **breezy**, *a*, venteux; frais.

Bremen, *n*, Brême, *f*.

brethren, *n.pl*, frères, *m.pl*.

breviary, *n*, bréviaire, *m*.

brevity, *n*, concision; brièveté, *f*.

brew, *v.t*, brasser; (*tea*) faire infuser; (*v.i.*) faire de la bière; (*storm*) couver, se préparer; (*fig.*) couver, se tramer, se mijoter. ~**er**, *n*, brasseur, *m.* ~**ery**, *n*, brasserie, *f.* ~**ing**, *n*, brassage, *m.*

briar, *n*, églantier, *m*; (*pipe wood*) bruyère, *f.*

bribe, *n*, pot-de-vin, *m.* ¶ *v.t*, corrompre, séduire, soudoyer. ~**ry**, *n*, corruption, *f.*

brick, *n*, brique, *f.* ~ *kiln*, four à briques, *m.* ~*layer*, maçon, *m.* ~**maker**, briquetier, *m.* ~ *paving*, carrelage en briques, *m.* ~**work**, briquetage, *m.* ~**yard**, briqueterie, *f.*

bridal, *a*, nuptial; de mariée. **bride**, *n*, nouvelle mariée; (*about to be married* or *on marriage day*) mariée, *f.* ~ *& ~***groom**, nouveaux mariés, *m.pl.* ~**groom**, nouveau marié; marié, *m.* **bridesmaid**, demoiselle d'honneur, *f.*

bridge, *n*, pont, *m*; (*foot & ship's*) passerelle, *f*; (*violin*) chevalet; (*nose*) dos; (*cards*) bridge, *m.* ~**head**, tête de pont, *f.* ¶ *v.t*, jeter un pont sur; franchir.

bridle, *n*, bride, *f.* ~ *path*, sentier pour cavaliers, *m*, piste cavalière, *f.* ¶ *v.t*, brider; refréner; (*v.i.*) se rengorger.

brief, *a*, bref, concis; de courte durée. ¶ *n*, cause, *f*, dossier, *m.* ~**case**, serviette, *f.* ¶ *v.t*, confier une cause à, constituer. ~**ly**, *ad*, brièvement, bref, en abrégé.

brier, églantier, *m*; (*pipe wood*) bruyère, *f.*

brig, *n*, brick, *m.*

brigade, *n*, brigade, *f*; corps, *m.* ¶ *v.t*, embrigader.

brigand, *n*, brigand, *m.* ~**age**, *n*, brigandage, *m.*

bright, *a*, brillant, éclatant, luisant; vif; beau; gai; poli; lumineux, clair; encourageant; intelligent. ~ *interval* (*Meteor.*), éclaircie, *f.* ~**en**, *v.t*, faire briller; polir; éclaircir; aviver, animer. ~**ly**, *ad*, brillamment, clairement. ~**ness**, *n*, brillant, éclat, *m*; bonne orientation, *f.*

brill, *n*, barbue, *f.*

brilliance, *n*, éclat, brillant, *m.* **brilliant**, *a*, brillant, éclatant. ¶ *n*, brillant, *m.* ~**ine**, *n*, brillantine, *f.* ~**ly**, *ad*, brillamment.

brim, *n*, bord, *m.* ¶ ~ *over*, déborder. ~**ful**, *a*, plein jusqu'aux bords, à pleins bords.

brimstone, *n*, soufre, *m.*

brindled, *a*, tacheté.

brine, *n*, saumure; (*Poet.*) onde amère, *f*; larmes, *f.pl.*

bring, *v.t.ir*, apporter; amener; conduire; faire; mettre; porter. ~ *about*, déterminer; ménager. ~ *an action against*, intenter une action à, actionner, attaquer en justice. ~ *back*, rapporter; ramener. ~ *forth*, mettre au monde; produire. ~ *forward* (*Bkkpg*), reporter. ~ *in* (house), rentrer. ~ *up*, élever, bercer, nourrir; (*food*) rendre. ~ *up the rear*, fermer la marche. ~**ing up**, éducation, *f.*

brink, *n*, bord; penchant, *m*; veille, *f.*

briny, *a*, saumâtre; (*Poet.*) amer.

briquet[te], *n*, briquette, *f*, aggloméré, *m.*

brisk†, *a*, vif, actif, animé, allègre. ~ *fire* (*Mil.*), feu nourri, *m.*

brisket, *n*, poitrine, *f.*

briskness, *n*, vivacité; activité, *f.*

bristle, *n*, soie, *f*; poil, *m.* ¶ *v.t*, hérisser; (*v.i.*) [se] hérisser. **bristling**, *p.a.* & **bristly**, *a*, hérissé.

Bristol Channel (the), le canal de Bristol.

Britain, *n*, la Grande-Bretagne. *Britannia metal*, métal anglais, *m.* **British**, *a*, britannique; anglais. ~ *ambassador*, ambassadeur d'Angleterre, *m.* ~ *consul*, consul britannique, *m.* ~ *Isles*, îles Britanniques, *f.pl.*

Brittany, *n*, la Bretagne.

brittle, *a*, cassant, fragile. ~**ness**, *n*, fragilité, *f.*

broach, *n*, (*spit*) broche, *f*; (*Mech.*) alésoir, *m.* ¶ *v.t*, (*cask*) percer; (*bore*) aléser; (*fig.*) entamer, aborder.

broad, *a*, grand; gros; ample; plein; (*accent*) prononcé; (*ribald*) libre, cru, gras; (*hint*) peu voilé, assez clair. ~ *bean*, fève de marais, *f.* ~**brimmed hat**, chapeau à grands bords, *m.* in ~ *daylight*, au grand jour, en plein jour, en plein midi. ~**minded**, à l'esprit large. ~**shouldered**, large d'épaules. ~**side** (*Naut.*) flanc, travers, côté, *m*; (*guns, fire*) bordée, *f*; (*fig.*) jeu de massacre, *m.* ~**sword**, sabre, *m.* ~**en**, *v.t*, élargir. ~**ly**, *ad*, largement, ouvertement; èn gros. ~ness, *n*, largeur; grossièreté, *f*; accent prononcé, *m*.

broadcast, *v.t.* (*radio & TV*) diffuser, émettre. ¶ *n*, émission, radio-diffusion, *f*. live ~, émission en direct. *pre-recorded* ~, é. en différée, é. pre-enregistrée, *f*. *broadcasting station*, station émettrice, *f*.

brocade, *n*, brocart, *m*.

broil, *n*, bagarre, *f*; tumulte, *m*. ¶ *v.t*, brasiller, griller. ~er, *n*, gril, *m*. **broiling**, *a*, brûlant.

broke (*hard up*), *a*, aux abois, fauché; raide.

broken, *a*, (*country*) tourmenté, accidenté, mouvementé; (*health*) délabrée, caduque, *f*; (*speech, sleep, etc.*) entrecoupé; (*English, French*) mauvais. *to be ~-down* (car), être (*ou* rester) en panne. *to be ~-hearted*, avoir le cœur navré (*ou* serré de douleur). ~ *winded*, poussif.

broker, *n*, courtier, ère; agent; banquier, *m*. ~age, *n*, courtage, *m*. ~ *fees*, commissions de courtier, *f.pl*.

bromide, *n*, bromure, *m*.

bronchia, *n.pl*, bronches, *f.pl*. **bronchitis**, *n*, bronchite, *f*.

bronze, *n*, bronze, *m*. ~ *shoes*, souliers mordorés, *m.pl*. ¶ *v.t*, bronzer.

brooch, *n*, broche; (*bar shaped*) barrette, *f*.

brood, *n*, couvée; nichée, engeance, *f*. ~ *hen*, couveuse, *f*. ~ *mare*, [jument] poulinière, *f*. ¶ *v.i*, couver; ruminer. ~ing time, couvaison, *f*.

brook, *n*, ruisseau, *m*. ¶ *v.t*, digérer, tolérer. ~let, *n*, ruisselet, *m*.

broom, *n*, balai; (*Bot.*) genêt, *m*. ~stick, manche à balai, *m*.

broth, *n*, bouillon; potage, *m*.

brothel, *n*, bordel, *m*.

brother, *n*, frère; confrère, *m*. ~-in-law, beau-frère. ~hood, fraternité, confrérie; confraternité, *f*. ~ly, *a*, fraternel.

brow, *n*, sourcil; (*forehead & cliff*) front; (*hill*) sommet, *m*. ~beat, *v.t*, rudoyer.

brown, *a*, brun; (*bread—light*) bis; (*bread—dark*) noir; (*sunburnt*) bruni. ~ *crust* (in pot), gratin, *m*. ~ *hair*, cheveux châtains, *m.pl*. ~ *owl*, chat-huant,

m. ~ *study*, rêverie, *f*. ~ *sugar*, cassonade, *f*. ¶ *n*, brun, *m*. ¶ *v.t*, brunir; (*meat*) roussir, rissoler. ~ish, *a*, brunâtre.

brownie, *n*, elfe, *m*.

browse, *n*, brout, *m*. ¶ *v.i. & t*, brouter, paître.

bruise, *n*, contusion, meurtrissure, *f*, pinçon, *m*; (*dent*) bosse, *f*. ¶ *v.t*, contusionner, meurtrir, froisser; bossuer, bosseler. ~d, *p.a*, meurtri, contus.

brunette, *a*, brun, brunet. ¶ *n*, femme brune, *f*.

brunt, *n*, poids; choc, *m*.

brush, *n*, brosse, *f*; pinceau; coup de brosse; (*Elec.*) balai, *m*; (*fox*) queue; (*affray*) échauffourée, *f*. ~ *maker*, brossier, ère. ~ *making*, brosserie, *f*. ~wood, broussailles, *f.pl*, [bois] taillis, mortbois, *m*. ¶ *v.t*, brosser; (*mud off*) décrotter; (*graze*) raser, effleurer, frôler. ~ *one's hair, teeth*, se brosser la tête, les dents. ~ *up* (*fig.*), repolir, dérouiller. ~ *aside*, écarter.

brusque, *a*, brusque.

Brussels, *n*, Bruxelles, *f*. ~ *carpet*, tapis de moquette, *m*, moquette, *f*. ~ *sprout*, chou de Bruxelles, *m*.

brutal†, *a*, brutal. ~ity, *n*, brutalité, *f*. ~ize, *v.t*, abrutir. **brute**, *n*, brute, *f*, animal, *m*. ~ *beast*, bête brute, *f*. *the* ~ *creation*, l'espèce animale, *f*. ~ *force*, force brute, *f*. **brutish**†, *a*, brutal, abruti.

bubble, *n*, bulle, *f*; bouillon; projet en l'air, *m*. ¶ *v.i*, bouillonner; pétiller. **bubbly**, *a*, mousseux, pétillant.

buccaneer, *n*, boucanier, *m*.

buck, *n*, (*deer*) daim; (*jump*) saut de mouton; (*pers.*) luron, gaillard, *m*. ~ *rabbit*, lapin mâle, bouquin, *m*. ~skin, peau de daim, *f*, daim, *m*; (*pl.*) culotte de peau, *f*. ~shot, chevrotine, *f*. ¶ *v.i*, ruer.

bucket, *n*, seau, *m*, seille, *f*; godet, *m*, auge, *f*, auget; baquet, *m*; benne, *f*. ~ *shop*, maison de contrepartie, *f*. ~ful, *n*, seau, *m*; augée, *f*.

buckle, *n*, boucle, *f*. ¶ *v.t*, boucler. (*v.i.*) se boucler; se corber. ~ *down to*, s'appliquer à.

buckram, *n*, bougran, *m*.

buckthorn, *n*, nerprun, *m*.

buckwheat, n, [blé-]sarrasin, blé noir, m.

bucolic, a, bucolique.

bud, n, bourgeon, bouton, m, gemme, f; (fig.) germe, m. ¶ v.i, bourgeonner; naître.

buddhist, a, bouddhique. ¶ n, bouddhiste, m.

budding (fig.) a, naissant; en herbe.

buddy, n, copain, m.

budge, v.i, bouger.

budget, n, budget, m. ~ for, porter au b.

buff (color) a. & n, fauve, a. & m. ~ [leather], buffle, m, peau de buffle, f. ¶ v.t, polir. **buffalo,** n, buffle, m.

buffer, n, tampon [de choc], heurtoir, butoir, m. ~ state, état tampon, m.

buffet, n, (blow) soufflet; (sideboard) buffet; (at a ball) souper debout, m. ~ car, wagon-restaurant, m. ¶ v.t, secouer.

buffoon, n, bouffon, ne, pitre, m. ~ery, n, bouffonnerie, f.

bug, n, punaise, f. ~bear, n, loup-garou, croque-mitaine, épouvantail, cauchemar, m.

bugle, n, clairon, m; (Bot.) bugle, f. ~ call, sonnerie, f. **bugler,** n, clairon, m.

build, n, construction, f. of sturdy ~ or well built (man), bien charpenté. ¶ v.t.ir, bâtir, construire. ~ up, édifier, échafauder. ~er, n, constructeur, entrepreneur [de bâtiments] m. ~ing, n, construction, f, bâtiment, édifice; monument, m. ~ materials, matériaux de construction, m.pl. ~ site, terrain à bâtir, m.

bulb, n, (Bot.) bulbe, f, o[i]gnon, m; (Anat.) bulbe, m; (lamp, thermometer) ampoule, f; (Chem.) ballon, m; (rubber) poire, f. ~ous, a, bulbeux.

Bulgaria, n, la Bulgarie. **Bulgarian,** a, bulgare. ¶ n, Bulgare, m,f.

bulge, n, bombement, ventre, m. ¶ v.i. & t, bomber, boucler, bouffer, faire [le] ventre.

bulk, n, volume; gros, m; masse, f. in ~ (Ship.), en vrac, en grenier. ~head, cloison, f. ~y, a, volumineux, massif; encombrant.

bull, n, taureau, m; (Pope's) bulle, f; (incongruity) prudhommerie,

f, contresens, m; (Stk Ex.) haussier, m. ~ calf, veau mâle, taurillon, m. ~dog, bouledogue, m. ~fight, course de taureaux, f. ~'s-eye (target) noir, m, mouche, f; (window) œil-de-bœuf, m. ~'s-eye [lantern], lanterne avec projecteur à lentille faisant saillie, f.

bulldozer, n, bouteur, m.

bullet, n, balle, f.

bulletin, n, bulletin, m.

bullfinch, n, bouvreuil, m.

bullion, n, or en barres, m.

bullock, n, bœuf, m.

bully, n, bravache, brutal, m. ¶ v.t, malmener, brutaliser.

bulrush, n, jonc, m; (reed mace) massette, masse d'eau, f.

bulwark, n, rempart; boulevard; (ship's) pavois, m.

bum, n, vagabond, m.

bumblebee, n, bourdon, m.

bump, n, bosse, f; cahot, heurt, m. ¶ v.t. & i, cogner, heurter, se heurter; cahoter.

bumper, n, (brimful glass) rasade, f, rouge bord; (auto) pare-chocs, m.

bumpkin, n, rustre, lourdaud, m.

bumptious, a, suffisant. ~ness, n, suffisance, f.

bun (hair) n, torpillon, m.

bunch, n, bouquet, m; botte, f; (keys) trousseau, m; (grapes) grappe, f; (bananas, etc.) régime, m. ¶ v.t, botteler.

bundle, n, paquet; faisceau, m; botte, f; fagot, m; liasse, f. ¶ v.t, empaqueter; botteler; fagoter; mettre en liasse.

bung, n, bondon, m, bonde, f, bouchon, tampon, m. ~[hole], bonde, f. ¶ v.t, bondonner, boucher.

bungalow, n, maisonnette, f.

bungle, n, bousillage, f, mauvaise besogne, f. ¶ v.t, bousiller, barbouiller, massacrer. **bungler,** n, bousilleur, euse, fagoteur, m.

bunion, n, oignon, m.

bunk, n, couchette, f.

bunker, n, soute, f; caisson, m; (golf) banquette, f. ~ coal, charbon de soute, m.

bunkum, n, blague, f.

bunt, v.t, pousser, encorner.

bunting, n, (stuff) étamine à pavillon, f; (flags) draperie, f; (bird) bruant, m.

buoy, n, bouée, f. ¶ v.t, baliser.

~ *up*, soutenir. ~**ancy**, *n*, flottabilité; poussée, *f*; (*fig.*) ressort, *m*. ~**ant**, *a*, flottant; élastique; vif, animé.

burden, *n*, fardeau, *m*, charge, *f*; poids, faix; (*ship*) port, maximum de charge, tonnage; (*song*) refrain, *m*. ¶ *v.t*, charger; grever. ~**some**, *a*, onéreux.

burdock, *n*, bardane, *f*.

bureau, *n*, bureau; cabinet, *m*. *weather* ~, office de météorologie, *m*.

bureaucracy, *n*, bureaucratie, *f*. **bureaucrat,** *n*, bureaucrate, *m*.

burglar, *n*, cambrioleur, *m*. ~ *alarm*, appareil avertisseur contre le vol, *m*. ~**y,** *n*, cambriolage, vol [de nuit avec effraction] *m*. ~ *insurance*, assurance contre le vol, *f*. **burgle,** *v.t*, cambrioler.

burgundy, *n*, bourgogne, vin de B., *m*.

burial, *n*, enterrement, *m*. ~ *ground*, cimetière, *m*. ~ *place*, lieu de sépulture, *m*. ~ *service*, office des morts, *m*.

burlap, *n*, serpillière, *f*.

burlesque, *a*. & *n*, burlesque, *a*. & *m*. ¶ *v.t*, travestir.

burly, *a*, solidement bâti; corpulent.

Burma, *n*, la Birmanie. **Burmese,** *a*, birman. ¶ *n*, Birman, e.

burn, *n*, brûlure, *f*. ¶ *v.t*. & *i.ir*, brûler; incendier; calciner; (*of sun*) hâler. *I have burned my arm*, je me suis brûlé le bras. *to burn one's fingers* (*fig.*), s'échauder. ~**er,** *n*, brûleur, bec, *m*. ~**ing,** *a*, brûlant, en feu, enflammé; ardent; cuisant. ¶ *n*, combustion; ignition; cuisson, cuite, *f*; (*smell*) brûlé, roussi, graillon, *m*.

burnish, *v.t*, (*metal, etc.*) brunir; (*paper, etc.*) satiner. ~**ing,** *n*, brunissage; satinage, *m*.

burnout, *n*, (*nuclear*) arrêt par épuisement, *m*.

burnt, *p.a*: ~ *almond*, praline, *f*. ~ *offering*, holocauste, *m*. ~ *Sienna*, terre de Sienne brûlée, *f*.

burnup, *n*, (*nuclear*) combustion, *f*.

burr, *n*, barbes, *f.pl*; (*speech*) grasseyement, *m*. ¶ (*speaking*) *v.i*, grasseyer.

burrow, *n*, terrier, clapier, *m*. ¶ *v.i*, terrer; se terrer; fouiller.

bursar, *n*, économe, *m*, dépensier,

ère. ~'s *office* & ~**ship,** *n*, économat, *m*.

burst, *n*, éclat, jet; (*light*) coup; (*speed*) emballement; (*eloquence*) mouvement; (*passion, etc.*) transport, élan, *m*. ¶ *v.t.ir*, faire éclater, [faire] crever; rompre; (*v.i.ir*) éclater; crever; se précipiter. ~**ing,** *n*, éclatement, *m*, crevaison, *f*.

bury, *v.t*, enterrer, ensevelir.

bus, *n*, autobus, bus, *m*.

bush, *n*, buisson, arbuste, *m*; (*scrub*) brousse; (*Mach.*) coquille, bague, *f*, manchon, *m*.

bushel, *n*, boisseau, *m*.

bushy, *a*, touffu, fourni; embroussaillé; buissonneux.

busily, *ad*, activement.

business, *n*, affaires, *f.pl*, commerce, négoce, *m*; affaire, entreprise, *f*; fonds [de commerce] *m*; qualité, *f*, métier, *m*; délibérations, questions [à délibérer] *f.pl*; ordre du jour; (*right*) droit; (*fuss*) aria, *m*. ~ *as usual during alterations*, la maison reste ouverte pendant les travaux. ~ *card*, bristol, *m*, carte d'adresse, *f*. ~ *day*, jour non férié, *m*. ~ *hours*, heures d'affaires, heures d'ouverture, *f.pl*; régulier; pratique, entendu. ~**man,** homme d' (*ou* dans les) affaires, *m*. ~ *premises*, locaux commerciaux, *m.pl*, immeuble commercial, *m*. ~ *quarter*, quartier commerçant, *m*. ~ *world*, monde des affaires, *m*.

buskin, *n*, brodequin; cothurne, *m*.

bust, *n*, buste, *m*; gorge, *f*, corsage, *m*. ~ *measurement*, [con]tour de poitrine, *m*.

bustard, *n*, outarde, *f*.

bustle, *n*, mouvement; remueménage, *m*; animation, *f*, tourbillon, *m*. ¶ *v.i*, se remuer.

busy, *a*, occupé, affairé, embesogné; industrieux; mouvementé; actif; empressé; diligent. ~ *bee*, abeille industrieuse, *f*. ~ *man*, *woman*, affairé, e. ~**body,** touchent-à-tout, *m*, commère, *f*, tatillon, ne, nécessaire, *m*.

but, *c*, mais; que; or. ~ *for*, sans. ¶ *ad*. & *pr*, hormis, excepté; seulement; ne ... que. ¶ *n*, mais, *m*.

butcher, *n*, boucher, *m*. ~'s *shop*, boucherie, *f*. ¶ *v.t*, massacrer. ~**y,** *n*, carnage, *m*.

butler, *n,* sommelier; maître d'hôtel, *m.*

butt, (*cask*) tonneau, *m;* (*pl., behind target*) butte; (*cigarette*) mégot, *m;* (*rifle*) crosse, *f;* (*cue*) talon; (*pers.*) plastron, bouffon, *m,* cible, risée, *f,* souffre-douleur; (*ram, etc.*) coup de corne, coup de tête, *m.* ¶ *v.i. & t,* cosser; heurter de la tête; buter.

butter, *n,* beurre, *m.* ~ *dish,* beurrier, *m.* ~**milk,** lait de beurre, babeurre, *m.* ¶ *v.t,* beurrer. ~*ed toast,* rôties au beurre, *f.pl,* toast, *m.*

buttercup, *n,* bassinet, bouton d'or, *m.*

butterfly, *n,* papillon [diurne] *m.*

buttock, *n,* fesse, *f;* (*beef*) cimier, *m.*

button, *n,* bouton, *m.* ~**hole,** boutonnière, *f.* ~**hole stitch** (*Emb.*), point de languette, p. de feston, *m.* ~**hole** (detain), cueillir. ~**hook,** tire-bouton, *m.* ¶ *v.t,* boutonner. ~ *oneself up,* se b.

buttress, *n,* contrefort, éperon; (*flying*) arc-boutant, *m.* ¶ *v.t,* arc-bouter; soutenir.

buxom, *a,* opulent, plantureux, rondelet & de bonne mine. ~**ness,** *n,* opulence, *f.*

buy, *v.t.ir,* acheter, acquérir. ~ *back,* racheter. ~*out,* désintéresser. ~ *up,* enlever, accaparer. ~**er,** *n,* acheteur, euse, acquéreur, preneur, *m.* ~**ing,** *n,* achat, *m,* acquisition, *f.*

buzz, *v.i,* bourdonner, ronfler, tinter.

buzzard, *n,* buse, *f.*

by, *pr,* par; à; sur; sous; en; près. ¶ *ad,* près, à part. ~ & ~, tantôt. ~ *the* ~, ~ *the way,* à propos, en passant.

bylaw, *n,* règlement, *m.*

by-election, *n,* élection de remplacement, *f.*

bygone, *a,* passé, ancien, d'autrefois.

bypass, *n,* route d'évitement; (*gas*) veilleuse, *f;* (*computers*) raccourci, *m;* (*Surg.*) pontage, *m.*

bypath, *n,* chemin écarté, sentier détourné, *m.*

by-product, *n,* sous-produit, *m.*

bystander, *n,* assistant, e, spectateur, trice, curieux, *m.*

byte, *n,* (*computers*) multiplet, *m.*

byway, *n,* chemin détourné, *m.*

byword, *n,* dicton, *m;* risée, fable, *f.*

C

C (*Mus.*) letter, ut, do, *m.* ~ *clef,* clef d'ut, *f.*

cab, *n,* taxi, fiacre, *m,* voiture [de place], *f;* (*locomotive*) abri, *m.* ~**man,** cocher, chauffeur, *m.* ~**stand,** station de taxis, *f.*

cabal, *n,* cabale, *f.*

cabaret [**show**], *n,* attractions, *f.pl.*

cabbage, *n,* chou, *m.* ~ *lettuce,* laitue pommée, *f.* ~ *tree,* palmiste, *m.*

cabin, *n,* cabine, chambre; cabane, case; guérite, *f.* ~ *boy,* mousse, *m.* ~ *passenger,* passager (ère) de cabine. ~ *trunk,* malle de paquebot, malle de cabine, *f.*

cabinet, *n,* cabinet, *m;* armoire, *f,* meuble, *m.* ~ *council,* Conseil des ministres, C. de Cabinet, *m.* ~**maker,** menuisier, ébéniste, *m.* ~**making & ~work,** menuiserie, ébénisterie, *f.* ~ *minister,* ministre d'État, *m.*

cable, *n,* câble, *m.* ~ *railway,* [chemin de fer] funiculaire, *m.* *feeder* ~, coaxial, *m.* ¶ (*Teleg.*) *v.t,* câbler.

cacao, *n,* cacao, *m.* ~ [*tree*], cacaoyer, cacaotier, *m.*

cachet, *n,* cachet, *m.*

cachou, *n,* cachou, *m.*

cackle, *n,* caquet, *m.* ¶ *v.i,* caqueter.

cactus, *n,* cactus, *m.*

cad, *n,* canaille, *f,* goujat, pleutre, mufle, *m.*

caddie (*golf*) *n,* cadet, te.

caddy, *n,* boîte [à thé] *f.*

cadence, *n,* cadence, *f.*

cadet, *n,* cadet; élève (*de l'école navale*), *m.*

cadge, *v.t,* écornifler. **cadger,** *n,* écornifleur, euse.

Cadiz, *n,* Cadix, *m.*

cafeteria, *n,* restaurant de libre service, *m.*

cage, *n,* cage; cabine; loge, *f.* ~ *bird,* oiseau de volière, *m.* ¶ *v.t,* encager.

cairn, *n,* montjoie, *f.*

Cairo, *n,* le Caire.

caisson, *n,* caisson; (*dock*) bateau-porte, *m.*

cajole, *v.t,* cajoler, amadouer. ~**ry,** *n,* cajolerie, *f.*

cake, *n,* gâteau; (*soap*) pain; (*oilseed*) tourteau, *m.* ¶ *v.i,* se cailler, faire croûte.

calabash, *n,* calebasse, *f.*

calamitous, *a,* calamiteux. **calamity,** *n,* calamité, *f.*

calcareous, *a,* calcaire.

calcine, *v.t,* calciner.

calcium, *n,* calcium, *m.*

calculate, *v.t,* calculer; (*v.i.*) compter. ~**d to,** propre à, de nature à. **calculating machine,** machine à calculer, *f.* **calculation & calculus** (*Med.*) *n,* calcul, *m.* **calculator,** *n,* (*small*) calculateur, *m,* (*large*) calculatrice, *f.*

caldron, *n,* chaudron, *m.*

calendar, *n,* calendrier; (*prisoners for trial*) rôle, *m.* ~ **year,** année civile, *f.*

calender, *n,* calandre, *f.* ¶ *v.t,* calandrer, cylindrer.

calf, *n,* veau; (*leg*) mollet, gras de la jambe, *m.* ~[*skin*], peau de veau, *f,* [cuir de] veau, *m.*

caliber, *n,* calibre, *m.* **calibrate,** *v.t,* calibrer.

calico, *n,* calicot, *m.*

California, *n,* la Californie. **Californian,** *a,* californien. ¶ *n,* Californien, ne.

caliper, *n,* calibre; (*pl.*) compas [de calibre] *m.* ¶ *v.t,* calibrer.

caliph, *n,* calife, *m.*

call, *n,* appel; rappel, *m;* demande; (*trumpet, bugle*) sonnerie; visite; communication; (*Relig.*) vocation; (*to a ship*) semonce; (*of a ship*) escale; relâche, *f;* (*Fin.*) appel [de fonds], versement; terme, *m;* option, faculté; (*cards*) invite, *f.* ~ **of the blood** (fig.), force du sang, *f.* ~ **to arms,** appel aux armes. ¶ *v.t. & i,* appeler; héler; rappeler; convoquer; faire venir; prendre; réveiller; qualifier; traiter de; nommer; surnommer; intituler; passer, s'arrêter; faire; (*ship*) faire escale; relâcher. ~ **back,** rappeler. ~ **for,** demander, réclamer; (*trumps*) inviter; exiger. ~ **off,** contremander, décommander; (*hounds*) rompre. ~ **out,** appeler, crier. ~ [**up**]**on,** sommer, invoquer. **caller,** *n,* visiteur, euse. **calling,** *n,* appel, *m;* convocation; vocation, profession, *f,* métier, *m.*

callosity & callus, *n,* callosité,

f, cal, durillon, *m.* **callous,** *a,* endurci, insensible; (*skin*) calleux.

callow, *a,* sans plumes. ~ **youth,** la verte jeunesse; jeune homme imberbe, blanc-bec, *m.*

calm, *a,* calme. ¶ *v.t,* calmer. ~**ly,** *ad,* tranquillement. ~[**ness**], *n,* calme, *m,* tranquillité, *f.*

calorie, *n,* calorie, *f.*

calumniate, *v.t,* calomnier. **calumny,** *n,* calomnie, *f.*

Calvary (*place*) *n,* Calvaire, *m.* **calvary** (*representation*) *n,* calvaire, *m.*

calve, *v.i,* vêler.

calyx, *n,* calice, *m.*

cam, *n,* came, *f,* excentrique, *m.*

camber, *n,* bombement, *m,* cambrure, *f.*

cambric, *n,* batiste, *f.*

came, *n,* plomb, *m,* (*pl.*) résille, *f.*

camel, *n,* chameau, *m.* ~ **driver,** chamelier, *m.*

camellia, *n,* camélia, *m.*

cameo, *n,* camée, *m.*

camera, *n,* appareil photographique, *m.* ~**man** (*cinema*) cadreur, *m.* ~ **obscura** (*Opt.*), chambre noire, c. obscure, *f. in* ~, à huit clos.

camisole, *n,* cache-corset, *m.*

camomile, *n,* camomille, *f.*

camouflage, *n,* camouflage, *m.* ¶ *v.t,* camoufler, maquiller.

camp, *n,* camp, *m.* ~ **bed,** lit de camp, *m.* ~ **stool,** [siège] pliant, *m.* ¶ *v.i. & t,* camper. ~ **out,** bivouaquer.

campaign, *n,* campagne, *f.* ~**er,** *n,* routier, troupier, *m.*

campanula, *n,* campanule, *f.*

camper, *n,* (*mobile home*) autocaravane, *f.*

camphor, *n,* camphre, *m.* ~**ate,** *v.t,* camphrer.

camping, *n,* camping, *m. to go* ~, faire le camping.

can, *n,* bidon, *m;* burette; boîte, *f;* pot, *m.* ~ **opener,** ouvre-boîtes. *m.* ¶ *v.t,* mettre en boîte(s), m. en conserve. **canned salmon,** saumon en boîte(s), *m.*

can, *v.aux.ir,* pouvoir; savoir.

Canada, *n,* le Canada. **Canadian,** *a,* canadien. ¶ *n,* Canadien, ne.

canal, *n,* canal, *m.* ~**ize,** *v.t,* canaliser.

canary, *n,* serin, e, canari, *m.* ~ *seed,* graine des canaris, *f,* millet des oiseaux, *m. the C*~

Islands, the Canaries, les [îles] Canaries, *f.pl.*

cancel, *n,* (*Typ.*) carton; (*Mus.*) bécarre, *m.* ¶ *v.t,* biffer, effacer; oblitérer; annuler, résilier, rompre; décommander.

cancer (*Med.*) *n,* cancer, *m.* ~**ous,** *a,* cancéreux.

candelabrum, *n,* candélabre, *m.*

candid†, *a,* sincère, franc, désintéressé.

candidacy, *n,* candidature, *f.*

candidate, *n,* candidat, e, postulant, e, aspirant, e, prétendant, e.

candied peel, zeste confit, *m.*

candle, *n,* chandelle, bougie, *f;* cierge, *m.* ~ *grease,* suif, *m.* ~ *power,* puissance (*ou* intensité) lumineuse en bougies, *f. a 60 c.p. lamp,* une lampe de 60 bougies. ~*stick,* bougeoir; chandelier; flambeau, *m.* ¶ (*eggs*) *v.t,* mirer. **candling,** *n,* mirage, *m.*

candor, *n,* sincérité, franchise, *f.*

candy, *v.i,* se candir. ¶ *n,* bonbon, candi, *m.* ~ *shop,* confiserie, *f.*

cane, *n,* canne; badine; (*Sch.*) férule, *f;* jonc, *m.* ~ *sugar,* sucre de canne, *m.* ¶ *v.t,* donner de la férule à; (*chair*) canner.

canine, *a,* canin.

canister, *n,* boîte [métallique] *f.*

canker, *n,* (*lit. & fig.*) chancre, *m.* ~*worm,* ver rongeur, *m.* ¶ *v.t,* gangrener.

canned goods, conserves [en boîtes] *f.pl.*

cannibal, *n. & a,* cannibale, *m,* anthropophage, *m. & a.*

cannon, *n,* canon; (*Bil.*) carambolage, *m.* ~ *ball,* boulet, *m.* ~ *shot,* coup de canon, *m.* ~**ade,** *n,* canonnade, *f.* ¶ *v.i,* canonner.

canny, *a,* fin, sagace; avisé; rusé.

canoe, *n,* canoë, *m;* périssoire; (*dugout*) pirogue, *f.*

canon, *n,* (*Eccl. rule*) canon; (*pl, taste*) code; (*pers.*) chanoine, *m.* ~ *law,* droit canon, *m.* **canonicate, canonry,** *n,* canonicat, *m.* **canonize,** *v.t,* canoniser.

canopy, *n,* dais; baldaquin; ciel, *m;* voûte, calotte, *f,* dôme, *m;* (*Arch.*) marquise, *f.*

cant, *n,* argot; jargon, *m;* hypocrisie, *f;* (*slope*) devers, *m,* inclinaison, *f.* ¶ *v.t,* incliner.

cantaloupe, *n,* melon cantaloup, *m.*

cantankerous, *a,* revêche, har-

gneux. ~ *fellow,* mauvais coucheur, *m.*

cantata, *n,* cantate, *f.*

canteen, *n,* cantine, *f;* (*bottle*) bidon, *m.* ~ *keeper,* cantinier, ère.

canter, *n,* petit galop, *m;* (*pers.*) cafard, e, tartufe, *m.*

Canterbury bell, campanule à grandes fleurs, *f.*

canticle, *n,* cantique, *m.*

cantilever, *n,* encorbellement, *m.*

canto, *n,* chant, *m.* **cantor,** *n,* chantre, *m.*

canvas, *n,* canevas, *m,* toile; toile à voiles; voile, *f.* ~ *shoe with hempen sole,* espadrille, *f.*

canvass, *v.t,* débattre; solliciter; solliciter des suffrages; s. des commandes; faire (*the town =* la place). ~**er,** *n,* solliciteur, euse; placier, démarcheur, *m.*

canyon, cañon, *n,* canon, *m.*

cap, *n,* bonnet, chapeau, *m;* (*peaked*) casquette, *f,* képi, *m;* toque; calotte, *f;* culot, *m;* chape; coiffe, *f;* couvercle; chapiteau, bouchon; bout; (*bullet*) détonateur, *m,* capsule, amorce, *f.* ~ *& bells* (*Hist.*), marotte, *f.* ~ *case* (*Typ.*), haut de casse, *m.* ¶ *v.t,* coiffer; couronner.

capability, *n,* capacité, *f.* **capable,** *a,* capable; apte, susceptible. **capacious,** *a,* spacieux. **capacitate,** *v.t,* rendre capable; (*law*) habiliter. **capacity,** *n,* capacité, *f;* rendement, débit, *m;* qualité; habilité, *f.*

caparison, *v.t,* caparaçonner.

cape, *n,* (*Phys. Geog.*) cap, *m;* (*dress*) pèlerine, *f.* **C~** *Colony,* la colonie du Cap. *the C~ of Good Hope,* le cap de Bonne-Espérance. **C~** *Verde,* le cap Vert.

caper, *n,* cabriole, gambade, *f,* entrechat, *m;* (*Bot.*) câpre, *f.* ¶ *v.i,* cabrioler.

capillary, *a,* capillaire.

capital†, *a,* capital; admirable, fameux, parfait, chic; ¶ *n,* (*country, province*) [ville] capitale, *f;* (*county, department*) chef-lieu, *m;* (*letter*) [lettre] majuscule, [lettre] capitale, *f;* (*Arch.*) chapiteau, *m;* (*Fin.*) capital, *m,* capitaux, *m.pl;* fonds, *m.s. & pl,* mise [de fonds] *f;* (*brought in*) apport, *m.* **C~** *& Labor,* le capital & le travail. ~ *expenditure,* immobilisations, *f.pl*, établissement, *m*. ~ *stock & ~ sum*, capital, *m*. ~ *value*, valeur en capital, *f*. ~**ist**, *n*, capitaliste, *m,f*; (*financial "whiz"*) fonceur, *m*. ~**ize**, *v.t*, capitaliser; immobiliser; écrire avec une majuscule.

capitulate, *v.i*, capituler.

capon, *n*, chapon, *m*.

caprice, *n*, caprice, *m*. **capricious**, *a*, capricieux.

capsicum, *n*, piment, *m*.

capsize, *v.t*, [faire] chavirer; (*v.i.*) chavirer, capoter, faire capot.

capstan, *n*, cabestan, *m*; (*lathe*) revolver, *m*, tourelle, *f*.

capsule, *n*, capsule, *f*.

captain, *n*, (*Mil., Naut., sport*) capitaine; (*Nav.*) capitaine de vaisseau, *m*. ~ *of merchant ship*, capitaine marchand.

caption, *n*, sous-titre, *m*; légende, *f*.

captious, *a*, captieux, difficultueux.

captivate, *v.t*, captiver. **captive**, *a*, captif. ¶ *n*, captif, ive. **captivity**, *n*, captivité, *f*. **capture**, *n*, capture, prise, *f*. ¶ *v.t*, capturer.

Capuchin friar, nun, capucin, e.

car, *n*, voiture, auto, *f*; wagon; char, chariot, *m*. ~ *park*, parking, *m*. *custom-built* ~, voiture hors serie, *f*. *dining* ~, wagon-restaurant, *m*. *racing* ~, voiture de course, *f*. *second-hand* ~, v. d'occasion, *f*.

caramel, *n*, caramel, *m*.

carapace, *n*, carapace, *f*.

carat, *n*, carat, *m*.

caravan, *n*, caravane; (*house on wheels*) roulotte, *f*. **caravanserai**, *n*, caravansérail, *m*.

caraway, *n*, carvi, *m*. ~ *seed*, graine de c., *f*.

carbide, *n*, carbure, *m*.

carbine, *n*, carabine, *f*, mousqueton, *m*.

carbolic acid, acide phénique, phénol, *m*.

carbon, *n*, (*Chem.*) carbone; (*Elec.*) charbon, *m*. ~ [*copy*], double, *m*. ~ *monoxide*, oxyde de carbone, *m*. ~ [*paper*] (duplicating), papier-carbone, *m*. **carbonate**, *n*, carbonate, *m*. **carbonic**, *a*, carbonique. **carboniferous**, *a*, carbonifère, houiller. **carbonize**, *v.t*, carboniser; (*v.i.*) [se] charbonner.

carboy, *n*, tourie, *f*.

carbuncle, *n*, (*jewel*) grenat cabochon; (*Med.*) charbon, anthrax, *m*.

carburetor, *n*, carburateur, *m*.

carcass, *n*, carcasse, *f*, cadavre, *m*; (*ship*) carcasse; (*building*) bâtisse, *f*, œuvre, *m*.

card, *n*, carte; (*loose index*) fiche, *f*; (*textiles*) peigne, *m*. ~*board*, carton, *m*. ~ *case*, porte-cartes, *m*. ~ *index & ~ index* [*cabinet*], fichier, *m*. ~ *sharper*, bonneteur, *m*. ~ *table*, table de jeu, *f*. ~ *trick*, tour de cartes, *m*. *punched* ~, carte perforée, *f*. (*car*) *registration* ~, carte grise, *f*. ¶ *v.t*, peigner.

cardigan [**jacket**], *n*, vareuse, *f*, gilet, *m*.

cardinal, *a*, cardinal. ¶ *n*, cardinal, *m*.

cardiogram, *n*, cardiogramme, *m*. **cardiographer**, *n*, cardiograph, *m*. **cardiologist**, *n*, cardiologue, *m*.

care, *n*, soin, *m*. oft. pl, attention; précaution; garde, *f*; souci, *m*; responsabilité; charge; tenue; conservation, *f*; maniement, *m*, manutention, gestion, *f*, gouvernement, *m*. *with due & proper* ~, en bon père de famille. ~ *of*, c/o, chez, aux [bons] soins de. ~**taker**, gardien, ne, portier, ère. ~**worn**, miné (*ou* rongé) par les soucis. *to take* ~ *of*, avoir soin de. ¶ *v.i*, se soucier, s'inquiéter.

careen, *v.t*, caréner.

career, *n*, carrière; profession; course, *f*. ¶ *v.i*, galoper.

careful†, *a*, soigneux, attentif; ménager. ~**ness**, *n*, soin, *m*, attention, *f*. **careless**, *a*, insouciant; négligent. ~**ly**, *ad*, négligemment. ~**ness**, *n*, négligence, inattention, incurie, *f*, laisser-aller, *m*.

caress, *n*, caresse, *f*; (*pl.*) mamours, *f.pl*. only. ¶ *v.t*, caresser.

caret, *n*, signe d'omission, renvoi, *m*.

cargo, *n*, cargaison, *f*, chargement, *m*, charge, *f*; marchandises, (*Insce.*) facultés, *f.pl*. ~ *boat, steamer*, cargo; navire, vapeur, de charge, *m*.

Caribbean Sea (the), la mer des Antilles.

caricature, *n*, caricature, charge, *f*. ¶ *v.t*, caricaturer, charger.

carload, *n,* chargement d'un wagon, *m.*

Carmelite, *n,* (*friar*) carme, *m;* (*nun*) carmélite, *f.*

carmine, *n,* carmin, *m.*

carnage, *n,* carnage, *m.*

carnal†, *a,* charnel.

carnation (*Bot.*) *n,* œillet [des fleuristes] *m.*

carnelian, *n,* cornaline, *f.*

carnival, *n,* carnaval, *m.*

carnivorous, *a.* & **carnivore,** *n,* carnassier, carnivore, *a.* & *m.*

carob [bean], *n,* caroube, *f.*

carol, *n,* chant, chanson, cantique, *m.* [*Christmas*] ~, noël. *m.* ¶ *v.i,* chanter; (*lark*) grisoller.

carousal, *n,* orgie, débauche, ripaille, *f.* **carouse,** *v.i,* faire [la] débauche.

carp (*fish*) *n,* carpe, *f.* ~ **at,** chicaner.

Carpathians (the), les Carpathes, *m.pl.*

carpenter, *n,* charpentier, menuisier, *m.* ¶ *v.t,* charpenter; (*v.i.*) menuiser. **carpentry,** *n,* charpenterie, *f.*

carpet, *n,* tapis, *m.* ~ *slippers,* pantoufles en tapisserie, *f.pl.* ~ *sweeper,* balai, *m,* (*ou* balayeuse, *f.*) mécanique. ¶ *v.t,* recouvrir d'un tapis; (*with flowers, etc.*) tapisser.

carriage, *n,* voiture, *f;* wagon; équipage; (*gun*) affût; (*Mach.*) chariot, *m;* démarche, allure, tenue, *f;* transport, port; prix du transport (*ou* de la voiture) *m.* ~ *entrance,* porte charretière, *f.* *baby* ~, voiture d'enfant, *f.*

carrier, *n,* porteur; messager, voiturier, transporteur, entrepreneur de transports (*ou* de roulage); (*Mach.*) chariot, *m;* porte-, *e.g, luggage* ~, porte-bagage, *m.* ~ *pigeon,* pigeon voyageur, *m.* *airplane* ~, porte-avions, *m.*

carrion, *n,* charogne, *f.*

carrot, *n,* carotte, *f.* ~ *y hair,* des cheveux [rouge] carotte, *m.pl.*

carry (*Arith.*) *n,* retenue, *f.* ¶ *v.t,* porter; emporter; transporter; véhiculer; mener; conduire; charrier, voiturer; (*Arith.*) retenir; adopter; prendre; voter. ~ *away,* enlever, emporter, entraîner; emballer, enthousiasmer. ~ *forward* (*Bkkpg*) reporter. ~ *on,*

poursuivre, opérer. ~ *out,* exécuter, effectuer; suivre.

cart, *n,* charrette; voiture; cariole, *f;* tombereau, *m.* ~ *horse,* cheval de charrette, *m.* ~ *load,* charretée, *f;* tombereau, *m.* ¶ *v.t,* charrier, charroyer, voiturer, camionner. ~ *age,* *n,* charroi, roulage; camionnage; factage; prix du transport, *m.* ~ *er,* *n,* charretier, voiturier, camionneur, *m.*

Carthusian [monk], *n,* chartreux, *m.* ~ *monastery,* chartreuse, *f.*

cartilage, *n,* cartilage, *m.*

carton, *n,* carton, *m.*

cartoon, *n,* carton; dessin, *m;* caricature, *f.* *animated* ~, dessin, *m.* ~ *ist,* *n,* dessinateur, trice; caricaturiste, *m,f;* (*cinema*) animateur, trice, *m,f.*

cartouche, *n,* cartouche, *m.* **cartridge,** *n,* cartouche, *f;* (*cannon*) gargousse, *f.* ~ *belt,* ceinture cartouchière, *f.* ~ *pouch,* sac à cartouches, *m,* cartouchière, *f.*

carve, *v.t,* sculpter; tailler; (*meat*) découper. **carver** (*pers.*) *n,* sculpteur, *m;* découpeur, euse. **carving,** *n,* sculpture, *f;* découpage, *m.* ~ *knife,* couteau à découper, *m.* ~ *tool,* outil de sculpteur, *m.*

cascade, *n,* cascade, cascatelle, *f.*

case, *n,* cas; état, *m;* question, *f;* exemple, *m;* cause, affaire, *f,* procès, *m;* caisse, boîte; mallette, *f;* sac; étui; écrin, *m;* gaine, *f;* trousse; pochette, poche, cassette, *f,* nécessaire; fourreau; boîtier; portefeuille, *m;* douille; chemise; enveloppe; (*for firework*) cartouche; (*sausage*) peau; (*precision balance*) cage, *f;* (*piano*) coffre, *m;* (*Typ.*) casse, *f.* ~ *opener,* ciseau à déballer, *m.* *in any* ~, en tout cas. ¶ *v.t,* encaisser, envelopper, [en]gainer; (*Min.*) cuveler.

caseharden, *v.t,* aciérer, cémenter. ~ *ed* (*fig.*) *p.a,* bronzé, cuirassé.

casemate, *n,* casemate, *f.*

casement, *n,* châssis de fenêtre. ~ [window], fenêtre [ordinaire], croisée, *f.* ~ *stay,* entrebâilleur de fenêtre, *m.*

cash, *n,* espèces, *f.pl,* numéraire, argent, *m,* finances, *f.pl;* comptant, *m;* caisse, encaisse, *f,* fonds, *m.pl.* ~ *book,* livre de caisse, *m.* ~ *box,* coffret à monnaie, *m;* caisse, *f.* ~ *discount,* escompte

de caisse (*ou* au comptant) *m.*
~ *down* or *in* ~ & *for* ~, [au] comptant. ~ *in hand*, [en]caisse, fonds (*ou* espèces) en caisse. ~ *on delivery*, envoi contre remboursement, *m.* ~ *register*, caisse enregistreuse (*ou* contrôleuse). ~ *with order*, payable à la commande. ¶ *v.t.* encaisser; (*check*) toucher; escompter, payer. ~**ier**, *n*, caissier, ère. ¶ *v.t.* destituer, casser.

cashmere, *n*, cachemire, *m.*

casing, *n*, enveloppe, *f*; bâti, dormant, *m.*

cask, *n*, tonneau, *m*, barrique, *f*, baril, fût, *m*, futaille, pièce, *f.*

casket, *n*, cassette, *f*, écrin; (*coffin*) cercueil, *m.*

Caspian Sea (the), la mer Caspienne.

casserole, *n*, casserole, *f.*

cassette, *n*, (*magnetic tape*) cassette, *f.*

cassia, *n*, casse, *f*. ~ *tree*, cassier, *m.*

cassock, *n*, soutane, *f.*

cast, *n*, jet, *m*, coulée; pièce moulée, *f*; coup de filet, *m*; addition; (*Theat.*) distribution, *f*. ~ *of features*, physionomie, *f*, facies, *m*. ~ *of mind*, tournure d'esprit, mentalité, *f*. ¶ *v.t.ir*, jeter, lancer; promener; fondre, couler, mouler; additionner; distribuer. *to* ~ *lots*, tirer au sort. ~ *iron*, fonte [de fer] *f*, fer de fonte, *m*; (*att., fig.*) rigide. ~ *its skin*, se dépouiller. ~ *net*, épervier, *m.* ~ *off*, (*Typ.*) évaluer; (*Knit.*) faire une chaîne de mailles. ~-*off clothing*, défroque, *f.* ~ *on* (*Knit.*), monter. ~ *out*, chasser, rejeter. ~ *steel*, acier coulé, *m*, fonte d'acier, *f*. [*crucible*] ~ *steel*, acier fondu [au creuset], *m. to have a* ~ *in the eye*, loucher.

castanet, *n*, castagnette, *f.*

castaway, *n*, réprouvé, e; naufragé, e.

caste, *n*, caste, *f.*

castellated, *a*, crénelé.

castigate, *v.t*, châtier. **castigation**, *n*, châtiment, *m.*

casting, *n*, jet, *m*; coulée, fonte; pièce [coulée], *f*, moulage, coulé, *m*; pêche au lancer, *f.* ~ *off*, (*Typ.*) évaluation, *f*; (*Knit.*) chaîne de mailles, *f.* ~ *on* (*Knit.*), montage des mailles, *m.* ~ *rod*, canne à lancer, *f. to give*

the ~ *vote*, départager les voix.

castle, *n*, château, *m*; (*chess*) tour, *f*. ¶ (*chess*) *v.i*, roquer.

castor, *n*, (*bottle*) saupoudroir, *m*; (*roller*) roulette, *f*, galet [pivotant] *m*; (*beaver*) castor, *m.* **castor oil**, huile de ricin, *f. castor oil plant*, ricin, *m.*

castrate, *v.t*, châtrer. **castration**, *n*, castration, *f.*

casual†, *a*, casuel, accidentel, fortuit; sans cérémonie; (*remark*) en passant. ¶ *n*, indigent(e) de passage. ~**ty**, *n*, sinistre, *m*; (*pers.*) victime; (*Mil.*) perte, *f.*

casuistry, *n*, casuistique, *f.*

cat, *n*, chat, te. ~ *burglar*, cambrioleur chat, *m*. ~'**s** *call*, sifflet, *m.* ~'*calling*, sifflerie, aubade, *f.* ~'**s** *cradle*, jeu de la scie, *m.* ~'*s eye* (jewel), œil-de-chat, *m.* ~'*s paw* (fig.), patte du chat, *f. to be someone's* ~'*s paw*, tirer les marrons du feu pour quelqu'un.

cataclysm, *n*, cataclysme, *m.*

catacomb, *n*, catacombe, *f.*

catafalque, *n*, catafalque, *m.*

catalog, *n*, catalogue, *m.* ¶ *v.t*, cataloguer.

catapult, *n*, (*Hist. & Avn.*) catapulte; (*boy's*) fronde, *f.* ¶ *v.t.* & *abs*, fronder; (*Avn.*) lancer.

cataract (*falls & Med.*) *n*, cataracte, *f.*

catarrh, *n*, catarrhe, *m.*

catastrophe, *n*, catastrophe, *f.*

catch, *n*, prise; (*fish*) prise, pêche, *f*, coup de filet, jet, *m*; (*trick*) attrape, *f*, leurre; (*Mech.*) arrêt, mentonnet, cran; (*window*) loqueteau, *m.* ~ *phrase*, scie, *f.* ~*word*, rengaine, scie, *f.* ¶ *v.t.* & *i. ir*, attraper; saisir; accrocher; s'engager; gagner; capturer; capter; happer; prendre; se p.; surprendre; frapper. ~ *up again*, rattraper. ~-[*as*-~-]*can*, lutte libre, *f.* ~ *fire*, prendre feu, s'enflammer; (*Cook.*) graillonner. ~ *on*, prendre; comprendre. ~**er**, *n*, preneur, chasseur, *m.* ~**ing**, *a*, contagieux; séduisant.

catechism, *n*, catéchisme, *m.* **catechize**, *v.t*, catéchiser.

categorical†, *a*, catégorique. **category**, *n*, catégorie, *f.*

cater, *v.i*, donner à manger. ~ *for*, pourvoir à; s'adresser à, viser. **caterer**, *n*, restaurateur, trice, cafetier, ère, traiteur; pourvoyeur, *m.*

caterpillar, *n*, chenille, *f*; tracteur, *m*.

caterwaul, *v.i*, miauler. ~**ing**, *n*, miaulement, *m*, musique de chats, *f*.

catgut, *n*, corde à boyau, *f*.

cathead, *n*, bossoir, *m*.

cathedral, *n*, cathédrale, *f*.

catherine wheel, soleil, *m*. *to turn* ~ ~**s**, faire la roue.

cathode, *n*, cathode, *f*.

catholic, *a. & n*, catholique, *a. & m,f.* ~**ism**, *n*, catholicisme, *m*.

cattle, *n*, bétail, *m*, bestiaux, *m.pl.* ~ *market*, marché aux bestiaux, *m.* ~*show*, concours (*ou* comice) agricole, *m*.

catwalk, *n*, (*Theat. & cinema*) passerelle, *f*.

Caucasian, *a*, caucasien. ¶ *n*, Caucasien, ne. *the Caucasus*, le Caucase.

caucus, *n*, cabale, *f*.

cauldron, *n*, chaudron, *m*.

cauliflower, *n*, chou-fleur, *m*.

caulk, *v.t*, calfater.

causative, *a*, occasionnel; (*Gram.*) causal. **cause**, *n*, cause, raison, *f*, sujet, motif; cas, *m*. ¶ *v.t*, causer, occasionner, provoquer, entraîner; faire, *e.g*, *to* ~ *to vary*, faire varier.

causeway, *n*, chaussée, levée, *f*.

caustic, *a. & n*, caustique, *a. & m*. **cauterize**, *v.t*, cautériser. **cautery**, *n*, cautère, *m*.

caution, *n*, prudence, précaution, *f*; avertissement, *m*. ¶ *v.t*, prémunir, précautionner, avertir. **cautious**, *a*, prudent, réservé, retenu, sur ses gardes, en garde. ~**ly**, *ad*, avec circonspection. ~**ness**, *n*, prudence, *f*.

cavalcade, *n*, cavalcade, *f*.

cavalier†, *a*, cavalier. ¶ *n*, cavalier, *m*.

cavalry, *n*, cavalerie, *f*.

cave, *n*, caverne, *f*, antre, *m*. ~ *dweller*, troglodyte, *m*. ~ **in**, *v.i*, s'effondrer, ébouler; céder.

cavern, *n*, caverne, *f*, souterrain, *m*. ~**ous**, *a*, caverneux.

caviar, *n*, caviar, *m*.

cavil, *n*, chicane, argutie, *f*. ¶ *v.i*, chicaner, ergoter.

cavity, *n*, cavité, *f*, creux, *m*.

caw, *v.i*, croasser.

Cayenne pepper, poivre de Cayenne, *m*.

cease, *v.i. & t*, cesser. *without* ~,

sans cesse. ~**less**, *a*, incessant. ~**lessness**, *n*, continuité, *f*.

cedar, *n*, cèdre, *m*. ~ *of Lebanon*, cèdre du Liban.

cede, *v.t*, céder.

ceil, *v.t*, plafonner. ~**ing**, *n*, plafond, *m*.

celebrate, *v.t. & i*, célébrer; solenniser; fêter. ~**d**, *p.a*, célèbre, fameux, renommé. **celebrity**, *n*, célébrité; illustration, *f*.

celery, *n*, céleri, *m*.

celestial, *a*, céleste.

celibacy, *n*, célibat, *m*. **celibate**, *n*, célibataire, *m,f*.

cell, *n*, cellule, *f*; cachot, *m*; pile électrique, *f*. ~ *jar*, bac d'éléments, *m*.

cellar, *n*, cave, *f*, caveau, *m*. ¶ *v.t*, encaver. ~**er**, *n*, cellérier, *m*.

cellist, *n*, violoncelliste, *m*. [?] **cello**, *n*, basse, *f*, violoncello, *m*.

cellular, *a*, cellulaire. **celluloid**, *n*, celluloïd, *m*. **cellulose**, *a, n*, cellulose, *f*.

Celt, *n*, Celte, *m,f*. **Celtic**, *a. & (language) n*, celtique, *a. & m*.

cement, *n*, ciment, *m*. ¶ *v.t*, cimenter; (*metal*) cémenter. *reinforced* ~, ciment armé, *m*.

cemetery, *n*, cimetière, *m*.

cenotaph, *n*, cénotaphe, *m*.

cense, *v.t*, encenser. **censer**, *n*, encensoir, *m*.

censor, *n*, censeur, *m*. ~**ious**, *a*, critique. ~**ship** & [*vote of*] **censure**, *n*, & [*board of*] **censors**, censure, *f*. **censure**, *v.t*, censurer.

census, *n*, recensement, dénombrement, *m*.

cent, *n*, (¹⁄₁₀₀ *of a dollar*) sou, *m*. *without a* ~, sans un sou.

centaur, *n*, centaure, *m*.

centenarian, *n*, centenaire, *m,f*. **centenary**, *n*, centenaire, *m*.

centigrade, *a*, centigrade. (*See note in French-English section.*)

centipede, *n*, scolopendre, *f*.

center, *n*, centre, milieu; noyau; (*Arch.*) cintre, *m*; (*lathe*) pointe, *f*. ¶ *v.t*, centrer; (*fig.*) concentrer. **central**, *a*, central. C~ *America*, l'Amérique Centrale, *f*. ~ *heating*, chauffage central, *m*. ~**ize**, *v.t*, centraliser; canaliser. **centrifugal**, *a*, centrifuge. **centripetal**, *a*, centripète.

century, *n*, siècle, *m*.

ceramics, *n*, céramique, *f*.

cereal, *a. & n*, céréale, *a.f. & f*.

ceremonial, *n*, cérémonial, *m*.

¶ *a*, de cérémonie. **ceremonious†**, *a*, cérémonieux, façonnier. **ceremony**, *n*, cérémonie; façon, *f. oft. pl.*

certain†, *a*, certain. **~ty**, *n*, certitude, *f. for a ~*, à coup sûr.

certificate, *n*, certificat; diplôme; brevet; acte, *m*; attestation; déclaration, *f*; extrait; titre, *m*. **~d**, *p.a*, diplômé. **certify**, *v.t*, certifier; viser; attester; déclarer.

certitude, *n*, certitude, assurance, *f*.

cessation, *n*, arrêt, *m*, suspension, *f*.

cesspool, *n*, fosse [d'aisances] *f*; cloaque, *m*.

Ceylon, *n*, Ceylan, *m*.

chafe, *v.t*, frictionner; écorcher; (*v.i.*) s'écorcher; s'irriter.

chaff, *n*, balle; glume; menue paille, *f*; badinage, *m*. ¶ *v.t*, plaisanter, gouailler, berner.

chaffinch, *n*, pinson, *m*.

chafing dish, chauffe-plats, *m*.

chagrin, *n*, chagrin, *m*. ¶ *v.t*, chagriner.

chain, *n*, chaîne; chaînette, *f*. ~ *bridge*, pont suspendu à chaînes, *m*. ~ *stitch*, point de chaînette, *m*. ~ *store*, magasin à succursales multiples, *m*. ¶ ~ & ~ *up*, *v.t*, enchaîner.

chair, *n*, chaise; (*Univ.*) chaire, *f*; (*at meeting*) fauteuil [de la présidence], *m*. **chairman**, *n*, président, e. **~ship**, *n*, présidence, *f*.

chalcedony, *n*, calcédoine, *f*.

chalice, *n*, calice, *m*, coupe, *f*.

chalk, *n*, craie, *f*; (*Bil.*) blanc, *m*. ~ *pit*, carrière de craie, *f*. *French ~*, talc, *m*. ¶ *v.t*, marquer à la craie. **~y**, *a*, crayeux.

challenge, *n*, défi, cartel, *m*, provocation, *f*; (*auditing*) sondage; (*Mil.*) qui-vive; (*sport*) challenge, *m*. ~ *cup*, coupe challenge, *f*, challenge, *m*. ~ *match*, match défi, *m*. ¶ *v.t*, défier, provoquer, contester; récuser; incriminer.

chamber, *n*, chambre, *f*; (*pl.*) cabinet, *m*, étude, *f*. ~ *maid*, femme de chambre, *f*. ~ *music*, musique de chambre, *f*. ~ [*pot*], vase de nuit, *m*. *air ~*, chambre à air, *f*.

chameleon, *n*, caméléon, *m*.

chamois, *n*, chamois, *m*. ~ [*leather*], peau de chamois, *f*, chamois, *m*.

champ, *v.t*, ronger, mâcher.

champagne, *n*, champagne, vin de Champagne, *m*. ~ *glass*, coupe à c., *f*.

champion, *n*, champion, *m*. ¶ *v.t*, défendre, protéger. **~ship**, *n*, championnat, *m*.

chance, *a*, de hasard; de fortune; d'occasion, fortuit, aléatoire. ¶ *n*, chance; fortune, *f*; hasard, aléa, *m*. *to ~ it*, risquer le paquet, brusquer l'aventure.

chancel, *n*, chœur, *m*.

chancellery, *n*, chancellerie, *f*. **chancellor**, *n*, chancelier, *m*.

chancre, *n*, chancre, *m*.

chandelier, *n*, lustre, *m*.

chandler, *n*, chandelier, *m*; épicier, ère.

change, *n*, changement; mouvement, *m*; altération; mutation; variation, *f*; revirement, *m*; saute; vicissitude; (*money*) monnaie, *f*; appoint, *m*; (*exchange*) bourse, *f*. *at ~* (barometer), au variable. *make or give ~*, faire de la monnaie. ~ *of clothes*, vêtements de rechange, *m.pl*. ¶ *v.t.' & i*, changer; c. de; se c., convertir; altérer; sauter. ~ *here for . . .*, on change de train pour . . . ~ *one's mind*, *one's linen*, changer d'avis, de linge. ~ *the subject*, quitter le sujet, rompre les chiens. **~able**, *a*, changeant; mobile; variable, inconstant.

channel, *n*, chenal, *m*, passe, *f*; canal, *m*, rigole; manche; cannelure; (*fig.*) voie, entremise; (*television*) chaîne, *f*. *the* [*English*] *C~*, la Manche. *the C~ Islands*, les îles [Anglo-]Normandes, *f.pl*. ¶ *v.t*, raviner, canneler. **channeling**, *n*, cannelure, *f*.

chant, *n*, chant, *m*. ¶ *v.i. & t*, chanter, psalmodier. **chanty**, *n*, chanson [de bord] *f*.

chaos, *n*, chaos, *m*. **chaotic**, *a*, chaotique.

chap, *n*, garçon; gaillard, *m*; (*pl.*) (*on the skin*) crevasses, gerçures, *f.pl*; (*animal*) babines, bajoues; (*vice*) mâchoires, *f.pl*. ¶ *v.t. & i*, crevasser, gercer, se gercer.

chapel, *n*, chapelle, *f*. ~ *of ease*, [église] succursale, *f*.

chaperon, *n*, chaperon, *m*. ¶ *v.t*, chaperonner.

chaplain, *n,* aumônier; chapelain, *m.*

chaplet, *n,* guirlande, *f;* (*beads*) chapelet, *m.*

chapter, *n,* chapitre, *m;* (*fig.*) page; série, *f.*

char (*fish*) *n,* omble[-chevalier], ombre-chevalier, *m.* ¶ *v.t.* carboniser; (*v.i.*) [se] charbonner.

character, *n,* caractère, *m;* nature, allure; réputation; cote, *f;* rôle; personnage; certificat, *m.* **characteristic,** *a,* caractéristique. ¶ *n,* caractéristique, *f,* caractère propre, *m;* (*pl, of map*) légende, *f.* **characterize,** *v.t,* caractériser.

charade, *n,* charade, *f.*

charcoal, *n,* charbon [de bois] *m.* ~ *burner* (*pers.*), charbonnier, *m.* ~ *drawing,* [dessin au] fusain, *m.* ~ [*pencil*], fusain, charbon à dessin, *m.*

charge, *n,* charge, *f;* soin, *m,* garde; accusation, inculpation, *f;* privilège, *m;* affectation; assignation; imputation, *f;* (*bishop's*) mandement; prix, *m,* taxe, *f,* frais, *m.pl,* dépense; redevance, *f.* ~ *account,* compte dans un magasin. ¶ *v.t,* charger; foncer sur; demander; prendre; mettre à [la] charge; taxer; percevoir; imputer; inculper; affecter; appliquer; accuser. ~**able,** *a,* à la charge; imputable; affectable; applicable.

charger (*horse*) *n,* cheval de bataille; (*Poet.*) coursier, *m.*

charily, *ad,* prudemment; chichement.

chariot, *n,* char, *m.*

charitable†, *a,* charitable, bienfaisant. **charity,** *n,* charité; bienfaisance, assistance, *f,* œuvres [pies] *f.pl,* aumône, l'aumône, *f.*

charlatan, *n,* charlatan, banquiste, *m.*

charm, *n,* charme, enchantement, agrément, *m;* (*pl.*) appas, attraits, *m.pl;* (*trinket*) breloque, amulette; mascotte, *f,* fétiche, *m.* ¶ *v.t,* charmer, enchanter. ~**er,** *n,* charmeur, euse, enchanteur, teresse.

charnel house, charnier, ossuaire, *m.*

chart, *n,* carte, *f;* graphique, diagramme, *m.* ¶ *v.t,* porter sur la carte, le graphique, etc.

charter, *n,* charte, *f.* ¶ *v.t,* [af]fréter, prendre à fret; privilégier.

~**er,** *n,* affréteur, *m.* ~**ing,** *n,* affrètement, *m.*

chary, *a,* prudent; avare, chiche, sobre.

chase, *n,* chasse, poursuite; (*gun*) volée, *f;* (*Typ.*) châssis, *m.* ¶ *v.t,* chasser, poursuivre; (*hawking*) voler; (*metals*) ciseler; (*screws*) peigner. **chaser** (*Nav.*) *n,* chasseur, *m.*

chasm, *n,* abîme, gouffre, *m.*

chassé, *n,* chassé, *m.* ¶ *v.t,* chasser.

chassis, *n,* châssis, *m.*

chaste†, *a,* chaste, pudique.

chasten & chastise, *v.t,* châtier. **chastisement,** *n,* châtiment, *m.*

chastity, *n,* chasteté, pudicité, *f.*

chasuble, *n,* chasuble, *f.*

chat, *n,* causerie, causette, *f.* ¶ *v.i,* causer, deviser.

chattel, *n,* chose, *f;* (*pl.*) biens, effets, *m.pl.*

chatter, *n,* babil, *m,* jaserie, *f.* ¶ *v.i,* babiller, jaser; jacasser; (*teeth*) claquer; (*tool*) brouter. ~**box,** moulin à paroles, *m,* babillard, e.

chauffeur, *n,* chauffeur, *m.*

cheap, *a,* (*article, etc.*) [à] bon marché; (*ticket, etc.*) à prix réduit; (*price*) bas. ~ *edition,* édition à bon marché, *f.* ~**er,** *a,* [à] meilleur marché, moins cher. ~[*ly*], *ad,* à bon marché, à peu de frais. ~**ness,** *n,* bon marché, *m,* vileté, *f.*

cheat (*pers.*) *n,* fourbe, *m, f;* tricheur, euse. ¶ *v.t. & i,* tromper; frauder; friponner, tricher, filouter. ~[*ing*], *n,* fourberie; tromperie; tricherie, *f.*

check, *n,* échec, *m;* bride, *f,* frein; contrôle, pointage; chèque bancaire; bulletin; (*design*) dessin à carreaux, *m;* (*fabric*) étoffe à carreaux, é. en damier; (*restaurant*) addition, *f;* (*att.*) de contrôle, contradictoire, témoin, ~**book,** carnet de chèques, *m.* ~**erboard,** damier, *m.* ¶ *v.t,* brider, enrayer, modérer; contrôler, vérifier; pointer. ¶ (*chess*) *i,* échec! ~**mate,** *n,* échec & mat, *m;* (*v.t.*) mater, faire [échec &] mat; (*fig.*) faire échec à.

Cheddar [*cheese*], *n,* chester, *m.*

cheek, *n,* joue; impudence, *f,* front, toupet, sans-gêne, *m.* ~**bone,** pommette, *f.* ~**y,** *a,* impudent, hardi, effronté.

cheep, *v.i,* piailler, piauler.

cheer, n, (*food*) chère; consolation, f; applaudissement, vivat, hourra, bravo, m. ¶ v.t, réjouir, égayer, rassurer, consoler; applaudir. ~ up, ragaillardir. ~ up! [du] courage! ~ful†, a, gai, joyeux, riant, allègre. ~fulness, n, gaieté, allégresse, f. ~less, a, triste, morne.

cheese, n, fromage, m. ~ knife, couteau à dessert, m.

cheetah, n, guépard, m.

chemical†, a, chimique. ¶ n, produit chimique, m.

chemise, n, chemise de jour, f.

chemist, n, chimiste, m.f. ~ry, n, chimie, f.

cherish, v.t, chérir, bercer, caresser, nourrir, choyer.

cherry, n, cerise, f. ~ orchard, cerisaie, f. ~-red, a. & n, cerise, a. & m. ~ stone, noyau de cerise, m. ~ [tree], cerisier; (wild) merisier, m.

cherub, n, chérubin, m.

chervil, n, cerfeuil, m.

chess, n, échecs, m.pl. ~board, échiquier, m. ~men, pièces, f.pl, échecs, m.pl.

chest, n, (Anat.) poitrine, f; (box) coffre, m, caisse, boîte, f; bahut, m. ~ measurement, grosseur de poitrine, f. ~ of drawers, commode, f.

chesterfield, n, (overcoat) pardessus chesterfield; (couch) canapé-divan, m.

chestnut, n, châtaigne, f, marron, m. ~-brown, châtain. ~ [tree], châtaignier, marronnier, m.

cheval dressing table, coiffeuse psyché, f. **cheval glass,** psyché, f.

chew, v.t. & i, mâcher; (tobacco) chiquer; (fig.) remâcher. ~ the cud, ruminer. ~ing, n, mastication, f. ~ gum, gomme à mâcher, f.

chiaroscuro, n, clair-obscur, m.

chicane, v.t. & i, chicaner. ~ry, n, chicane[rie] f.

chick, n, poussin, poulet, m. **chick-pea,** n, pois chiche, m. **chicken,** n, poulet, te. ~ heart (pers.) poule mouillée, f, poltron, ne. ~-hearted, poltron. ~ pox, varicelle, f.

chickweed, n, mouron [des oiseaux] m, morgeline, f.

chicory, n, chicorée; endive, f.

chide, v.t. & i.ir, gronder.

chief, a, premier, principal; en

chef. ~ attraction, clou de la fête, m. to be ~ mourner, conduire (ou mener) le deuil. ¶ n, chef; supérieur, m. ~ly, ad, principalement, surtout. **chieftain,** n, chef, m.

chiffon, n, chiffon, m. **chiffonier,** n, chiffonnier, m.

chilblain, n, engelure, f.

child, n, enfant, m.f. from a ~, dès l'enfance. with ~, enceinte. ~-bed, couches, f.pl. ~-birth, travail [d'enfant], accouchement, m. ~'s play, un jeu d'enfant, jeu d'e., m. ~hood, n, enfance, f. ~ish, a, enfantin; puéril. ~ishly, ad, puérilement. ~ishness, n, enfantillage, m, puérilité, f. ~less, a, sans enfant. ~like, a, comme un enfant, en enfant. **children,** n.pl, enfants, m.pl.

Chile, n, le Chili. **Chilean, -lian,** a, chilien. ¶ n, Chilien, ne.

chill, a, froid, glacé. ¶ n, froid, frisson, aigre, m, fraîcheur, f; coup d'air, c. de froid, m; (fig., of age) glaces, f.pl. to take the ~ off (water) faire dégourdir; (wine) chambrer. ¶ v.t, refroidir, glacer, transir, morfondre. **chilliness,** n, froideur, f, froid, m. **chilly,** a, froid; frisquet; (pers.) frileux.

chime[s], n.[pl.], carillon, m. ¶ v.i, carillonner. ~ in, placer son mot. **chiming clock,** pendule à carillon, f.

chimera, n, chimère, f. **chimerical,** a, chimérique.

chimney, n. & ~ piece, cheminée, f. ~ corner, coin du feu, m. ~ pot, cheminée, f. ~ sweep[er], ramoneur, m.

chimpanzee, n, chimpanzé, m.

chin, n, menton, m. ~ strap, jugulaire, f.

china & ~ware, n, porcelaine, faïence [fine] f. ~ cabinet, vitrine, armoire vitrée, f. ~ clay, terre à porcelaine, f, kaolin, m. ~ manufacturer & ~ dealer, porcelainier, ère. ~ shop, magasin de porcelaines, m.

China (Geog.) n, la Chine. ~ aster, reinemarguerite, f.

chine, n, échine; (Cook.) échinée, f.

Chinese, a, chinois. ~ curio, chinoiserie, f. ~ lantern, lanterne vénitienne, f, lampion [en papier] m. ~ puzzle (fig.), casse-tête

chinois, m. ¶ n, (*language*) chinois, m; (*pers.*) Chinois, e.
chink, n, lézarde, fente, crevasse, f. ¶ v.t, fendiller.
chints, n, perse, f.

chip, n, copeau, éclat, m, écaille, écornure, f; (*computers*) microplaquette, pastille, "puce," f. ~ *off the old block*, fils de son père, m. ¶ v.t, tailler par éclats; buriner; écorner; ébrécher; (*v.i.*) s'écorner.
chipmunk, n, tamia, m.
chiropodist, n, pedicure, m,f. chiropody, n, soin des pieds, m.
chiropractic, n, chiropraxie, f. chiropractor, n, chiropracteur, m, chiropracticien, ne.
chirp, n, pépiement, guilleri; (*insect*) cri, cricri, m. ¶ v.i, pépier; crier.
chisel, n, ciseau, burin, m. ¶ v.t, ciseler, buriner.
chit, n, marmot, te; [petit] bout, m. ~ *of a girl*, petite fille, f.
chitchat, n, causerie, f; commérage, m.
chivalrous, a, chevaleresque. chivalry, n, chevalerie, f.
chive, n, cive[tte], ciboulette, f.
chivy, v.t, chasser.
chlorate, n, chlorate, m. chloride, n, chlorure, m. ~ *of lime*, c. de chaux. chlorinate, v.t, javelliser. chlorine, n, chlore, m. chloroform, n, chloroforme, m. ¶ v.t, chloroformer.
chocolate, n, chocolat, m; (*pl.*) bonbons au c., m.pl. ~ *box*, bonbonnière, f. ~ *cream*, crème chocolatée, f. ~ *creams*, chocolats fourrés à la crème, m.pl. ~ *éclair*, éclair au chocolat, m. ~ *manufacturer* or *seller*, chocolatier, ère. ~ *pot*, chocolatière, f.
choice, a, choisi, de [grand] choix; fin; recherché. ¶ n, choix, m; élite, fleur, f. ~ness, n, excellence, f.
choir, n, chœur, m. ~ *boy*, enfant de chœur, m. ~ *master*, maître de chapelle, m.
choke, v.t, suffoquer, étouffer, étrangler; engorger; bourrer. ¶ n, (*auto*) obturateur, m.
cholera, n, choléra, m.
choose, v.t.ir, choisir; élire; (*v.i.ir.*) opter.
chop, n, coup, m; côtelette, f; (*pl.*)

babines, bajoues, f.pl. ¶ v.t, (*meat*) hacher; (*firewood*) débiter. ~ *off*, couper, trancher. chopper, n, couperet, m. chopping block, hachoir, billot, m. chopping board, hachoir, m. choppy (*sea*) a, clapoteuse.
chopstick, n, bâtonnet, m.
choral, a, choral. ~ *society*, [société] chorale, f, orphéon, m.
chord, n, corde, f; (*Mus.*) accord, m.
chore, n, besogne, f.
choreography, n, chorégraphie, f.
chorister, n, choriste, m,f; enfant de chœur, m. chorus, n, chœur; refrain en c.; concert, m. ~ *singer* (opera), choriste, m,f. *to* [*repeat in*] ~, faire chorus. *to join in the* ~, faire chœur au refrain.
Christ, n, le Christ. christen, v.t, baptiser. Christendom, n, chrétienté, f. christening, n, baptême, m. Christian, a, chrétien, ~ *name*, nom de baptême, petit nom, prénom, m. ~ *Science*, le culte des scientistes chrétiens. ¶ n, chrétien, ne. Christianity, n, christianisme, m. christianize, v.t, christianiser. christianly, ad, chrétiennement.
Christmas & ~tide (*abb.* Xmas) n, Noël, m. *at* ~, à la [fête de] Noël, à Noël. ~ *present. In Fr., presents are given on or about Jan. 1 and called* étrennes, f.pl. *a* ~ *present* (to child), le petit Noël. ~ *eve*, nuit de Noël, f. ~ *pudding*, pudding de Noël, plum-pudding, m.
chromate, n, chromate, m.
chromatic, a, chromatique.
chrome, n, chrome, m; (*att., steel, leather*) chromé; (*yellow*) de chrome. chromium, n, chrome, m; (*att., steel*) chromé. ~*-plated*, chromé.
chronic, a, chronique.
chronicle, n, chronique, f. C~s (*Bible*) pl, Paralipomènes, m.pl. ¶ v.t, enregistrer, consigner. chronicler, n, chroniqueur, m.
chronological†, a, chronologique. chronology, n, chronologie, f.
chronometer, n, chronomètre, m.
chrysalis, n, chrysalide, f.

chrysanthemum, n, chrysan-thème, m.

chub (*fish*) n, chabot, meunier, m.

chubby, a, joufflu, potelé.

chuck (*lathe*) n, mandrin, plateau, m. ¶ (*throw*), v.t, flanquer. ~ *out*, flanquer à la porte. ~ *under the chin,* relever le menton à.

chuckle, v.i, glousser, rire sous cape.

chum, n, camarade, m,f, copain, m.

chump, n, bûche, f; lourdaud, m.

chunk, n, quignon, chanteau, m.

church, n, église, f; temple, m. *the C~ of England,* l'Église anglicane. ~ *service,* office divin, m. ~*warden,* marguillier, m. ~*yard,* cour de l'église, f; jardin de l'église; champ du repos, cimetière, m; (*public square surrounding a church*) place, f, e.g, la Place de la Madeleine.

churl, n, manant, bourru, rustre, m. ~**ish,** a, bourru, aigre.

churn, n, baratte, f. ~ *dash[er],* batte à beurre, f, babeurre, m. ¶ v.t, baratter, battre.

chute, n, glissière, f. *garbage* ~, vide-ordures, m.

cider, n, cidre, m.

cigar, n, cigare, m. ~ *case,* porte-cigares, m. ~ *cutter,* coupe-cigares, m. ~ *holder,* porte-cigare, fume-cigare, m.

cigarette, n, cigarette, f. ~ *box,* coffret à c~s, m. ~ *case,* étui à c~s, m. ~ *holder,* porte-cigarette, fume-cigarette, m.

cinch, n, sangle, f. ¶ v.t, sangler.

cinder[s], n.[*pl.*], escarbille[s], f.[*pl.*], fraisil, m, braise, f; scorie[s], f.[*pl.*]; cendrée, f. *burnt to a* ~ (meat), en charbon. ~ *sifter,* tamis à escarbilles, m. ~ *track,* piste en cendrée, f.

Cinderella, n, Cendrillon, f.

cinema, n, cinéma, cinématographe, m.

cinerary, a, cinéraire, f.

Cingalese, a, cingalais. ¶ n, Cingalais, e.

cinnabar, n, cinabre, m.

cinnamon, n, cannelle, f.

cipher, n, chiffre; zéro, m; nullité, f, comparse, m. *word in* ~, mot en chiffre, m. ¶ v.t. & i, chiffrer.

circle, n, cercle; milieu, m. ¶ v.t, ceindre, cerner. **circlet,** n, couronne, f. **circuit,** n, circuit, tour,

m; tournée, f. ~**ous,** a, détourné.

circular†, a. & n, circulaire, a. & f. **circulate,** v.t, faire circuler, répandre; (v.i.) circuler, rouler.

circulating, a, circulant; roulant. ~ *decimal,* fraction périodique, f. ~ *library,* bibliothèque circulante, f. **circulation,** n, circulation, f; mouvement, m; (*newspaper*) tirage, m.

circumcise, v.t, circoncire.

circumference, n, circonférence, f, tour, m.

circumflex, a. & n, circonflexe, a. & m.

circumlocution, n, circonlocution, f, circuit de paroles, m, paraphrase, f.

circumscribe, v.t, circonscrire.

circumspect, a, circonspect, mesuré, avisé. ~**ly,** ad, avec circonspection.

circumstance, n, circonstance, f; état; cas, m; cérémonie, f. *in easy* ~s, à son aise. *in straitened* (or *reduced*) ~s, dans la gêne. ~s *permitting,* sauf imprévu. *under no* ~s, en aucun cas. **circumstantial,** a: ~ *account,* relation circonstanciée, f. ~ *evidence,* témoin muet, m, preuve par présomption, f.

circumvent, v.t, circonvenir.

circus, n, cirque; hippodrome, f.

cirrhosis, n, cirrhose, f.

cirrus (*Meteor.*), n, cirrus, m.

cistern, n, fontaine, f; réservoir, m; citerne; (*barometer*) cuvette, f.

citadel, n, citadelle, f.

citation, n, citation; mention, f.

cite, v.t, citer, alléguer; assigner.

citizen, n, citoyen, ne, citadin, e. ~**ship,** n, droit de cité, m.

citric, a, citrique. **citron,** n, cédrat, citron, m.

city, n, ville; cité, f. ¶ a, urbain; municipal. ~ *hall,* la mairie, f.

civet [*cat*], n, civette, f.

civic, a, civique.

civil†, a, civil; honnête. ~ *engineering,* génie civil, m. ~ *servant,* employé(e) d'administration, fonctionnaire public, m, fonctionnaire publique, f. ~ *service,* administration publique, f. ~**ian,** n, civil, m. ~**ity,** n, civilité, f.

civilization, n, civilisation, f. **civilize,** v.t, civiliser. **civilizing,** a, civilisateur.

clack, n. claquement; caquet, m. ~ [*valve*], clapet, m.

claim, n. réclamation, revendication, f. recours; titre, m, prétention, exigence, demande, demande d'indemnité; indemnité, f. ¶ v.t. réclamer, revendiquer, prétendre [à], demander, s'attribuer. ~ant, n. réclamant, e, prétendant, e.

clairvoyance, n. seconde vue, f. **clairvoyant**, n. voyant, e.

clam (*Mol.*) n. palourde, peigne, f.

clamber [up], v.i. & t. gravir, grimper.

clamminess, n. moiteur, f. **clammy**, a. moite, pâteux.

clamorous, a. bruyant, criard. ~ly, ad. à cor & à cri. **clamor**, n. clameur, f. ¶ v.i. crier, vociférer. ~ for, réclamer à grands cris.

clamp, n. bride [de serrage], presse, happe, f. serre-joint[s], crampon, m; pince, f. ¶ v.t. brider, cramponner, bloquer.

clan, n. clan, m.

clandestine†, a. clandestin.

clang, n. son, m. ¶ v.i. retentir.

clank, n. cliquetis, m. ¶ v.t. cliqueter.

clap, n. coup; battement, m. ~trap, phrases à effet, f.pl. boniment, m. ¶ v.t. & i. claquer; battre. **clapper**, n. claquet, claquoir, m. claquette, f; (*bell*) battant, m. **clapping**, n. battement [de mains] m.

claret, n. bordeaux [rouge], vin de Bordeaux, m.

clarify, v.t. clarifier.

clarion, n. clairon, m. **clarinet**, n. clarinette, f.

clarity, n. clarté, lumière, f.

clash, n. choc, m. rencontre, collision, f; fracas; cliquetis; conflit, m. ¶ v.i. s'entrechoquer; être en conflit; jurer.

clasp, n. agrafe, f. fermoir, m; étreinte, f. serrement, m. ~ knife, couteau à virole, c. à cran d'arrêt, m. ¶ v.t. agrafer; prendre, se prendre; presser, étreindre, serrer.

class, n. classe; catégorie; cote, f; cours, m. ~consciousness, l'esprit de caste, m. ~mate, camarade de classe, c. de promotion, m.f. ~room, [salle de] classe, f. ~ war, guerre sociale,

f. ¶ v.t. classer; coter. **classic** & **classical**†, a. classique. **classic**, n. classique, m. **classification**, n. classification, f. **classify**, v.t. classer. **classing**, n. classement, m.

clatter, n. fracas, tapage, m. ¶ v.i. claquer, carillonner.

clause, n. clause, f. article, m; (*Gram.*) proposition, f. ·

claustral, a. claustral.

claw, n. griffe, serre, patte, f. ongle, m; pince, f. pied-de-biche, m. ¶ v.t. griffer, s'agriffer à; égratigner.

clay, n. argile; glaise; terre, f. ~ pigeon, pigeon artificiel, papegai, m. ~ pipe, pipe en terre, f. ~ pit, carrière d'argile, glaisière, f. **clayey**, a. argileux.

clean, a. propre; blanc; net; pur; sain; sans réserves; (*Typ. proof*) peu chargée. ~shaven, glabre, entièrement rasé. ~ slate (*fig.*), coup d'éponge, m. ~ sweep (*fig.*), table rase; rafle, f. ¶ v.t. nettoyer; blanchir; dégraisser; débourber. ~er, n. nettoyeur, euse; femme de ménage, femme de journée, f. ~ing, n. nettoyage; dégraissage; curage, f. **cleanliness**, n. propreté, netteté, f. **cleanse**, v.t. assainir, purger; [é]curer;

clear, a. clair; limpide; pur; net; distinct; libre; franc. ~ soup, consommé, m. ~sighted, clairvoyant. ¶ v.t. éclaircir; débarrasser; dégager; franchir; évacuer; déblayer; défricher; purger; (*table*) desservir; (*computers*) remettre à blanc, à zéro; (*letter box*) [re]lever; (*check*) compenser; (*shop goods*) solder; (*Cust.—goods*) dédouaner; (*a ship inwards*) faire l'entrée [en douane]; (*a ship outwards*) expédier [en douane]. ~ up, v.t. éclaircir, tirer au clair, mettre au net, débrouiller; (v.i.) s'éclaircir, se raséréner. ~ance, n. (*Mech.*) jeu, m. chasse, f; (*goods through Cust.*) dédouanement, m; (*ship through Cust.*) expédition, f; (*foreign ship leaving French port*) passeport; (*French ship leaving French port*) congé, m. ~ papers (ship's), expéditions, f.pl. ~ sale, solde, m. ~ing (*glade*) n. éclaircie, clairière, f. ~ house (*bank-*

ing), chambre de compensation, *f*. ~**ly**, *ad*, clair[ement], nettement, bien. ~**ness**, *n*, clarté, netteté; pureté, *f*.

cleat, *n*, tasseau, *m*, languette, *f*; taquet, *m*.

cleavage, *n*, fendage; (*Miner.*) clivage; *m*; (*fig.*) scission, *f*. **cleave**, *v.t.ir*, fendre, refendre; cliver; (*v.i.ir*.) se fendre; se cliver; se coller, s'attacher. **cleaver**, *n*, fendoir, couperet, *m*.

clef, *n*, clef, clé, *f*.

cleft, *n*, fente, fissure, *f*. ~ *stick*, piquet fourchu, *m*.

clematis, *n*, clématite, *f*.

clemency, *n*, clémence, *f*. **clement**, clément.

clench, *v.t*, crisper; serrer.

clergy, *n*, clergé, *m*, gens d'Église, *m.pl*. ~**man**, *n*, ecclésiastique; ministre, *m*. **cleric**, *n*, ecclésiastique, *m*. ~**al**, *a*, d'employé, de commis; (*of clergy*) ecclésiastique, clérical. ~ *error*, erreur (*ou* faute) de plume (*ou* de copiste) *f*; (*law*) vice (*ou* pas) de clerc, *m*. ¶ *n*, clérical, *m*.

clerk, *n*, employé, e, commis [de bureau], *m*, préposé, e; (*law & Eccl.*) clerc; (*court*) greffier, *m*.

clever†, *a*, habile; adroit. ~ *move*, adresse, *f*. ~**ness**, *n*, dextérité, habileté, *f*.

clew, *n*, fil, *m*.

cliché, *n*, banalité, *f*, cliché, *m*.

click, *n*, cliquetis, tic tac; (*Mech.*) cliquet, déclic, *m*, détente, *f*. ¶ *v.i*, cliqueter, faire tic tac. ~ *heels*, claquer talons.

client, *n*, client, e; partie, *f*. **clientele**, *n*, clientèle, *f*.

cliff, *n*, (*coast*) falaise, *f*; (*inland*) rocher [en escarpement] *m*.

climacteric, *a*, critique, climatérique.

climate, *n*, climat; ciel, *m*. **climatic**, *a*, climatérique, climatique.

climax, *n*, (*Rhet.*) gradation [ascendante] *f*; point culminant; bouquet, *m*.

climb, *n*, ascension, montée, *f*. ¶ *v.t. & i*, gravir, monter, faire l'ascension de, grimper. ~ *over*, escalader. ~**er**, *n*, grimpeur, alpiniste, *m*; plante grimpante, *f*. ~**ing** boots, bottines d'escalade, *f.pl*.

clime (*Poet.*) *n*, terre, *f*; ciel, *m*.

clinch (*Box.*) *n*, corps à corps, *m*. ¶ *v.t*, river; (*fig.*) conclure.

cling, *v.i.ir*, se cramponner, s'attacher, s'agriffer, se coller, s'aheurter, tenir.

clinic, *n*, clinique, *f*. ~**al**, *a*, clinique; (*thermometer*) médical. ~**ian**, *n*, clinicien, *m*.

clink, *n*, (*glasses*) choc; (*jail*) violon, *m*. ¶ *v.t*, choquer, trinquer; (*v.i.*) tinter.

clinker, *n*, mâchefer, *m*.

clip, *n*, pince, serre, griffe, attache, patte [d'attache], *f*; (*paper*) trombone, *m*. ¶ *v.t*, cisailler; tailler; tondre; rogner; (*ticket*) poinçonner; (*words*) estropier, manger. **clippers**, *n.pl*, ciseaux, *m.pl*, tondeuse, *f*. **clippings**, *n.pl*, rognures; (*newspaper*) coupures de journal, *f.pl*.

clique, *n*, clique, coterie, *f*.

cloak (*lit. & fig.*) *n*, manteau, *m*. ~ *room*, vestiaire, *m*. ¶ *v.t*, voiler, masquer.

clock, *n*, (*big*) horloge; (*small*) pendule, pendulette, *f*; (*on stocking*) baguette, *f*. ~ *& watch maker*, horloger, *m*. ~*work* [*movement*], mouvement d'horlogerie, *m*. alarm ~, reveille-matin, *m*.

clod, *n*, motte, *f*. ~[*hopper*], rustre, rustaud, lourdaud, *m*.

clog, *n*, sabot, socque, *m*, galoche, *f*; (*fig.*) entrave[s] *f.[pl.]*. ~ *dance*, sabotière, *f*. ¶ *v.t*, encrasser; engorger; charger; entraver.

cloister, *n*, cloître, *m*. ¶ *v.t*, cloîtrer. **cloistral**, *a*, claustral.

close, *a*, clos; fermé; étroit; serré; dense; [r]enfermé; lourd, mou; minutieux; vif; intime; près, proche; appliqué; jointif; soutenu. ~*fitting garment*, vêtement collant; (*woven*) maillot, *m*. ~ *season*, temps prohibé, *m*, période d'interdiction, *f*. ~*shaven*, rasé de près, ras. ¶ *ad*, près, de près; auprès. ~*up*, premier plan, gros plan, *m*. ¶ *n*, fin; clôture; levée, *f*. the ~ *of day*, la chute du jour. ¶ *v.t*, fermer; clore; arrêter; régler; lever; liquider, réaliser; serrer; barrer; boucher; (*v.i.*) fermer, se f.; clore; chômer. ~**d** (*Theat.*), relâche. ~**ly**, *ad*, de près; attentivement; strictement; étroitement. ~**ness**, *n*, compacité; intimité; proximité, *f*; manque d'air, *m*; lourdeur, *f*. **closet**, *n*, cabinet, *m*. ¶ *v.t*, chambrer, claquemurer. **closing**, *n*, fermeture, clôture, *f*; liquidation. *f*. ~ *date*, date de clôture, *f*. ~ *price*, dernier cours, c. de clôture, *m*. **closure**, *n*, clôture, *f*.

clot, *n*, caillot, grumeau, *m*. ¶ *v.i*, se cailler, se grumeler.

cloth, *n*, drap, *m*; toile; étoffe, *f*; voile; tissu; linge; tapis, *m*; nappe, *f*; parement, *m*; couverture, *f*; napperon; torchon, *m*; robe, soutane, *f*. ~ *trade*, draperie, *f*. **clothe**, *v.t.ir*, habiller, vêtir; revêtir. **clothes**, *n.pl*, habits, vêtements, *m.pl*, tenue, *f*, entretien, *m*; (*worn*) hardes, *f.pl*. ~ *brush*, brosse à habits, *f*. ~ *hanger*, porte-vêtements, cintre, *m*. ~ *line*, étendoir, *m*, corde à linge, *f*, (*pl.*) étendage, *m*. ~ *pin*, pince à linge, *f*. **clothier**, *n*, drapier, *m*; confectionneur, euse. **clothing**, *n*, habillement, vêtement, *m*. *ready-to-wear* ~, prêt-à-porter, *m*.

cloud, *n*, nuage, *m*; (*fig.*) nuée; (*Poet.*) nue, *f*. ~ *burst*, trombe d'eau, rafale de pluie, *f*. *in the* ~*s* (*fig.*), dans le bleu. ¶ *v.t*, couvrir de nuages; obscurcir, voiler, obnubiler; assombrir. ~**less**, *a*, sans nuage. ~**y**, *a*, nuageux, nébuleux, couvert, chargé, bas; terne, trouble, louche.

clout, *n*, torchon; chiffon, *m*; (*blow*) gifle, *f*.

clove, *n*, [clou de] girofle, *m*. ~ *of garlic*, gousse d'ail, *f*.

cloven hoof, pied fourchu, *m*.

clover, *n*, trèfle, *m*. *in* ~ (*fig.*), dans l'abondance.

clown, *n*, paillasse, pierrot, clown, Gille, pitre, baladin, bouffon, *m*. ¶ *v.i*, faire le clown. ~**ery**, *n*, bouffonnerie, clownerie, pantalonnade, *f*. ~**ish**, *a*, bouffon.

cloy, *v.t*, rassasier (*with* = de).

club, *n*, massue, casse-tête, *f*, gourdin, *m*; (*golf*) crosse, *f*, club, *m*. (Clubs such as brassie, mashie, niblick are named the same in French and are *m*.); (*people*) club, cercle, *m*, société; *f*; (*church*) patronage; (*cards*, *s. & pl.*) trèfle, *m*. ~ *foot*, pied

bot, *m*. ~ *together*, se cotiser. ¶ *v.t*, frapper, assommer.

cluck, *n*, gloussement, *m*. ¶ *v.i*, glousser.

clue, *n*, indication; clef, piste, *f*.

clump, *n*, masse; motte; botte; touffe, *f*, massif, bouquet, *m*.

clumsiness, *n*, gaucherie, maladresse, *f*. **clumsy†**, *a*, gauche, maladroit, empoté, pataud; incommode. ~ *fellow*, maladroit, pataud, *m*.

cluster, *n*, faisceau, nœud, bouquet, peloton, groupe, *m*, grappe, *f*, régime, *m*. ¶ *v.i*, se grouper.

clutch, *n*, griffe; (*eggs*) couvée, *f*; (*Mech.*) [manchon d']embrayage, *m*. ¶ *v.t. & i*, empoigner, [a]gripper; se raccrocher. *to let out the* ~, débrayer.

clutter, *n*, désordre, *m*; confusion, *f*. ¶ *v.t*, mettre en désordre.

coach, *n*, voiture, *f*, wagon; carrosse, coche; (*tutor*) répétiteur, préparateur; (*sport*) entraîneur, instructeur; (*boating*) capitaine d'entraînement, *m*. ~ *horse*, carrossier, *m*. ~ *house*, remise, *f*. ~**man**, cocher, *m*. ¶ *v.t*, préparer; entraîner; endoctriner.

coagulate, *v.t*, coaguler; (*v.i.*) se coaguler.

coal, *n*, charbon [de terre] *m*, houille, *f*; (*pl.*) charbon[s]. ~ *mine*, mine de charbon (*ou* de houille), houillère, *f*. ~ *miner*, houilleur, mineur de houille, *m*. ~ *scuttle*, seau à charbon, *m*. ~ *tar*, goudron de houille, coaltar, *m*. ~ *yard*, chantier (*ou* parc) à charbon, *m*, charbonnerie, *f*. ¶ *v.i*, faire du charbon.

coalesce, *v.i*, se confondre. **coalition**, *n*, coalition, *f*, bloc, cartel, *m*.

coarse†, *a*, grossier, gros; rude; brutal. ~**ness**, *n*, grossièreté, rudesse, *f*.

coast, *n*, côte[s] *f.[pl.]*, littoral, *m*, bord[s] *m.[pl.]*. ¶ *v.i*, côtoyer; (*auto & fig.*) débrayer.

coat, *n*, habit, *m*; (*man's*) pardessus; manteau; (*woman's*) redingote, *f*; (*long*) manteau, *m*; (*short*) jaquette, *f*; (*woolly*) gilet, *m*; (*Mil.*) tunique; (*animal's*) robe, *f*, poil, pelage, *m*; (*Anat.*) paroi; tunique; (*layer*) couche, *f*, enduit, *m*. ~ *hanger*, porte-manteau, *m*. ~ *of arms*,

armes, armoiries, *f.pl*, blason, *m*.
~ *of mail*, cotte de mailles, *f*.
¶ *v.t*, enduire, revêtir.

coax, *v.t*, enjôler, amadouer.

cob, *n*, (*horse*) bidet; (*corn*) épi,
m, rafle, *f*. ~[*nut*], grosse noisette, aveline, *f*.

cobalt, *n*, cobalt, *m*.

cobble [stone], *n*, galet, pavé, *m*.
¶ *v.t*, saveter, rapetasser. **cob-**
bler, *n*, savetier, *m*. ~'s *wax*,
poix, *f*.

cobra, *n*, cobra, *m*.

cobweb, *n*, toile d'araignée, *f*.

cocaine, *n*, cocaïne, *f*.

cochineal, *n*, cochenille, *f*.

cock, *n*, coq; (*tap*) robinet; (*hay*)
meulon; (*of gun*) chien, *m*.
~-*a-doodle-doo*, coquerico, cocorico, *m*. ~-*&-bull story*, coq-
à-l'âne, *m*, contes en l'air, *m.pl*.
~*crow*[ing], chant du coq, *m*.
~ *of the walk*, coq du village,
m. ~ *pheasant*, [coq] faisan, *m*.
safety ~, cran d'arrêt, *m*. ¶ *v.t*,
relever, [re]dresser; (*gun*) armer.
~*ed hat*, chapeau à cornes, *m*.

cockade, *n*, cocarde, *f*.

cockatoo, *n*, cacatoès, *m*.

cockchafer, *n*, hanneton, *m*.

cockerel, *n*, cochet, *m*.

cockle, *n*, (*Mol.*) clovisse, coque;
(*Bot.*) ivraie, *f*.

cockpit, *n*, arène, *f*; (*Avn.*) nacelle, *f*.

cockroach, *n*, cafard, cancrelat,
m, blatte, *f*.

cockscomb, *n*, crête de coq;
(*Bot.*) crête-de-coq, *f*.

cocktail (*drink*) *n*, cocktail, *m*. ~
bar, bar-cocktail, *m*. ~ *shaker*,
shaker, *m*. ~ *snack*, amuse-
gueules, *m.pl*.

cocky, *a*, impertinent, insolent.

cocoa, *n*, cacao, *m*.

coco[*nut*], *n*, coco, *m*, noix de c.,
f. ~ *palm*, cocotier, *m*.

cocoon, *n*, cocon, *m*.

cod[*fish*], *n*, morue, *f*, cabillaud,
m; (*dried*) merluche, *f*. ~ *fisher*,
morutier, *m*. ~ *liver oil*, huile
de foie de morue, *f*.

coddle, *v.t*, dorloter, câliner,
choyer.

code, *n*, code, *m*. ~ *word*, mot
convenu, *m*. ¶ *v.t*, chiffrer, codicil, *n*, codicille, *m*; avenant, *m*.
codify, *v.t*, codifier.

coefficient, *n*, coefficient, *m*.

coerce, *v.t*, contraindre.

coffee, *n*, café; moka, *m*. ~ *cup*,

tasse à café, *f*. ~ *pot*, cafetière,
f. ~ *spoon*, cuiller à café, c. à
moka, *f*. ~ *table*, guéridon, *m*.
~ *tree* & ~ *planter*, caféier, *m*.

coffer, *n*, coffre, *m*, caisse, *f*.

coffin, *n*, cercueil, *m*, bière, *f*.

cog, *n*, dent, *f*; alluchon, *m*.
~*wheel*, roue dentée, *f*. ¶ *v.t*,
[en]denter.

cogency, *n*, force, *f*. **cogent**, *a*,
convaincant, probant.

cogitate, *v.i*, méditer, réfléchir.

cognate, *a*, de même origine.

cognizance, *n*, connaissance, *f*.
cognizant of, instruit de.

cognomen, *n*, surnom, *m*.

cohabit, *v.i*, cohabiter.

cohere, *v.i*, adhérer. **coherence**,
n, cohérence; suite, *f*. **coherent**,
a, cohérent; suivi. ~*ly*, *ad*, avec
cohérence, *f*. **cohesion**, *n*, cohésion, *f*. **cohesive**, *a*, cohérent.

cohort, *n*, cohorte, *f*.

coil, *n*, rouleau, (*contraceptive de-*
vice) stérilet, *m*; (*Elec.*) bobine, *f*. ¶ *v.t*, lover.

coin, *n*, pièce, [pièce de] monnaie,
f; numéraire, *m*, espèces [mon-
nayées] *f.pl*; (*ancient*) médaille,
f. ~ *machine*, appareil à sous, *m*.
¶ *v.t*, monnayer, frapper, battre;
(*fig.*) forger, inventer; fabriquer.
~*age*, *n*, monnayage, *m*, frappe,
f; monnaie[s] *f.*[*pl*.], numéraire,
m.

coincide, *v.i*, coïncider. **coinci-**
dence, *n*, coïncidence, *f*.

coir, *n*, fibre de coco, *f*.

coke, *n*, coke, *m*.

colander, *n*, passoire, *f*.

cold†, *a*, froid; à froid. *in* ~ *blood*
or ~*blooded*, de sang-froid, à
froid. ~*blooded* (*animal*), à
sang froid. ~ *chisel*, burin (*ou*
ciseau) à froid, *m*. ~ *snap*, coup
de froid, *m*. ~ *steel*, arme
blanche, *f*. ¶ *n*, froid, *m*, froidure, *f*; (*Path.*) rhume, coup
d'air, *m*. ~ *on the chest, in the*
head, rhume de poitrine, de
cerveau.

coleopter[*an*], *n*, coléoptère, *m*.
coleopterous, *a*, coléoptère.

colic, *n*, colique, *f*, tranchées, *f.pl*.

collaborate, *v.i*, collaborer. **col-**
laborator, *n*, collaborateur, trice.

collapse, *n*, effondrement, écroulement; affaissement, *m*; chute,
débâcle, *f*. ¶ *v.i*, s'effondrer,
crouler, s'écrouler, s'affaisser.
collapsible, *a*, pliant.

collar, *n,* collier, collet; col; frette, bague, *f.* [*shirt*] ~ (detached), faux col, *m.* *attached* ~ (to shirt), col tenant. ~ *bone,* clavicule, *f.* ~ *size, n,* encolure, *f.* ~ *button,* bouton de col, *m.* ¶ *v.t,* colleter.

collate, *v.t,* collationner; (*computers*) interclasser. **collation,** *n,* (*computers*) interclassement, *m.* **collator,** *n,* (*computers*) interclasseuse, *f.*

collateral, *a,* collatéral. ~ *security,* nantissement, *m.*

collation, *n,* collationnement, *m;* (*snack*) collation, *f.*

colleague (*Bot.*) *n,* collègue, *m.*

collect, *n,* collecte, *f.* ¶ *v.t,* recueillir, rassembler, réunir; retirer, enlever; [re]lever; capter; collectionner; recouvrer, récupérer; percevoir; encaisser; quêter. ~*ed,* *p.a,* recueilli, calme. ~*ion, n,* rassemblement, recueil, *m;* réunion, *f;* captage; recouvrement, *m;* récupération, perception, rentrée; levée, *f,* relevage; encaissement; enlèvement, apport, *m;* quête, collecte, *f;* cabinet, *m.* ~ *of coins* or *medals,* médaillier, *m.* ~*ive†, a,* collectif. ~*or, n,* collecteur, receveur, percepteur; collectionneur, fureteur, curieux, ramasseur, euse.

college, *n,* collège, *m;* faculté, académie, *f.* **collegian,** *n,* collégien, ne. **collegiate,** *a,* collégial.

collide, *v.i,* s'aborder, se rencontrer, se tamponner. ~ *with,* aborder, rencontrer, tamponner.

collier, *n,* (*pers.*) houilleur; (*ship*) charbonnier, *m.* ~*y, n,* houillière, *f;* (*col. pl.*) charbonnage, *m.*

collision, *n,* abordage, *m,* collision, rencontre, *f,* tamponnement, *m.* ~ *mat,* paillet d'abordage, *m.*

colloquial†, *a,* de la conversation; (*words, phrases*) familier. ~*ism, n,* expression familière, *f.* **colloquy,** *n,* colloque, *m.*

collusion, *n,* collusion, *f.*

Colombia, *n,* la Colombie.

colon, *n,* deux-points; (*Anat.*) côlon, *m.*

colonel, *n,* colonel, *m.*

colonial, *a,* colonial. **colonist,** *n,* colon, *m.* **colonize,** *v.t,* coloniser.

colonnade, *n,* colonnade, *f.*

colony, *n,* colonie, *f.*

colophon, *n,* marque (typographique) *f,* chiffre, fleuron, *m.*

color, *n,* couleur, *f;* teint; coloris, *m;* peinture, *f;* (*pl.*) couleurs, *f.pl,* drapeaux, *m.pl;* pavillon, *m.* *under* ~ *of* (*fig.*), sous couleur de. ~ *bar,* distinction sociale (*ou* légale) entre la race blanche & la race noire, *f.* ~*blind,* daltonien. ~ *blindness,* cécité pour les c—s, *f.* ¶ *v.t,* colorer, colorier; enluminer. ~*ed, p.a. & p.p:* ~ *dress,* robe de couleur, *f.* ~ *sketch,* croquis en couleurs, *m.* ~*ing, n,* coloris, *m.* ~*less, a,* sans couleur, incolore, pâle.

colossal†, *a,* colossal. **colossus,** *n,* colosse, *m.*

colt, *n,* poulain, *m.* **coltsfoot** (*Bot.*) *n,* pas-d'âne, tussilage, *m.*

columbine (*Bot.*) *n,* ancolie, *f.*

column, *n,* colonne, *f;* pillier, *m;* (*news on special subject*) rubrique, *f.* ~*ist, n,* journaliste, *m.*

coma (*Med.*) coma, *m;* (*Bot. & comet*) chevelure, *f.* **comatose,** *a,* comateux.

comb, *n,* peigne, *m;* (*crest*) crête, *f;* (*honey*) rayon, gâteau, *m,* gaufre, *f.* ¶ *v.t,* peigner. ~ *out* (*fig.*), éliminer.

combat, *n,* combat, *m.* ¶ *v.t,* combattre. ~*ant, n,* combattant, *m.* ~*ive, a,* batailleur. ~*iveness, n,* combativité, *f.*

combination, *n,* combinaison, *f.* **combine,** *n,* coalition; combine; (*Agric.*) batteuse, *f.* ¶ *v.t,* combiner, réunir; joindre; (*v.i.*) se combiner; se coaliser.

combings, *n.pl,* peignures, *f.pl.*

combustible, *a,* combustible. **combustion,** *n,* combustion, *f.* ~ *chamber* (motor), chambre d'explosion, *f.*

come, *v.i.ir,* venir; provenir; arriver; se présenter; se faire; entrer; être. ~ *along!,* ~ *on!* allons!, venez!, marchons! ~ *about,* se faire. ~ *across,* rencontrer. ~ *back,* revenir. ~ *down,* descendre. ~ *for,* venir chercher. ~ *from* (be a native of), être originaire de. ~ *home,* rentrer; revenir; porter coup. ~ *in!* entrez! ~ *now!* enfin!, ah! çà. ~ *off,* se détacher; (*ink*) décharger. ~ *off on* (dye), déteindre sur. ~ *out,* sortir; débuter; (*book, etc.*) paraître. ~ *to,* se monter à; revenir à; (*decision*) prendre.

~ *to an agreement,* tomber d'accord. ~ *to blows,* en venir aux mains. ~ *to light,* se découvrir. ~ *to pass,* arriver, advenir. ~ *to terms,* s'arranger. ~ *undone,* se défaire. ~ *up* (sprout), poindre. ~ *upon,* tomber sur. ~ *what may,* arrive (*ou* advienne) que pourra, au petit bonheur.

comedian, *n,* comédien, ne; farceur, *m.* **comedy,** *n,* comédie, *f,* comique, *m.*

comeliness, *n,* beauté, grâce, bonne mine, *f.* **comely,** *a,* beau, gracieux, avenant.

comer, *n,* venant, *m;* venu, e. ~*s & goers,* allants & venants, *m.pl.*

comet, *n,* comète, *f.*

comfort, *n,* consolation, satisfaction, aise, *f,* [ré]confort, *m.* ¶ *v.t,* consoler, réconforter, soulager. ~**able**†, *a,* aisé, confortable. ~**er,** *n,* consolateur, trice; (*blanket*) couvre-pied, *m.*

comic & comical, *a,* comique; humoristique, cocasse; plaisant, bouffon, bouffe, burlesque. ~ *actor,* comique, *m.* ~ *opera,* opéra bouffe, *m.* ~ *song,* chanson burlesque, chansonnette, *f.* ~ *turn,* pantalonnade, *f.*

coming, *p.a,* à venir; d'avenir; futur. ¶ *n,* venue, arrivée, *f;* (*of Christ*) avènement, *m.* [*I am*] ~*l* j'y vais! on y va! voilà! ~ *& going,* allées & venues, *f.pl.* ~ *out* (in society), début, *m,* entrée dans le monde, *f.*

comma, *n,* virgule, *f. Note:—* Sets of three figures, separated in Eng. by commas, are separated in Fr. either by points or by spaces.

command, *n,* commandement, *m;* ordre[s] *m.[pl.];* empire, *m;* facilité, *f.* (*computers*) ~ *key,* touche de commande, *f.* ¶ *v.t,* commander; monter; ordonner; avoir à sa disposition; (*a view of*) donner sur. ~**ant,** *n,* commandant, chef, *m.*

commandeer, *v.t,* réquisitionner.

commander, *n,* commandant, chef; (*Nav.*) capitaine de frégate, *m. commanding officer,* commandant, chef, *m.*

commandment, *n,* commandement, *m.*

commemorate, *v.t,* commémorer.

commence, *v.t. & i,* commencer, entamer. ~**ment,** *n,* commencement, début, *m.*

commend, *v.t,* recommander; applaudir à, préconiser; remettre. ~**able,** *a,* recommandable, louange; recommandation, *f.*

commensurate, *a,* proportionné.

comment & commentary, *n,* commentaire, *m,* glose, *f.* **to comment on,** commenter [sur].

commentator, *n,* commentateur.

commerce, *n,* commerce, négoce, *m.* **commercial,** *a,* commercial, commerçant, marchand, de commerce, d'affaires. ~**ism,** *n,* mercantilisme, *m.* ~**ize,** *v.t,* achalander, monnayer. ~**ly,** *ad,* commercialement.

commiserate, *v.t,* plaindre.

commissariat, *n,* intendance militaire, *f.*

commission, *n,* commission, remise, *f;* courtage, *m;* (*shop*) guelte, *f;* (*officer's*) lettre[s] de service, *f.[pl.].* ~ *agent,* commissionaire, *m.* ¶ *v.t,* commissioner, mandater; (*officer*) nommer; (*ship*) armer. ~**ed work,** ouvrage de commande, *m.* **commissioner,** *n,* commissaire, *m.*

commit, *v.t,* commettre, faire; livrer; confier; renvoyer. ~ *for trial,* mettre en accusation. ~ *oneself,* s'engager; se compromettre. ~ *to prison,* ordonner l'incarcération de. ~ *to writing,* coucher (*ou* mettre) par écrit. ~**ment** (*Com.*) *n,* engagement, *m.*

committee, *n,* comité; bureau, *m.*

commode, *n,* chaise [percée] *f.*

commodious, *a,* commode. ~**ly,** *ad,* commodément. ~**ness,** *n,* commodité, *f.*

commodity, *n,* produit, *m,* denrée, marchandise, matière [première] *f,* article, *m;* ressource, *f.*

commodore, *n,* chef d'escadre, *m.*

common, *a,* commun; général; coutumier; ordinaire; vulgaire; peuple; banal; simple; type; public. ~ [*land*], communal, *m,* champs communs, *m.pl,* vaine pâture, *f.* ~ *law,* droit coutumier, *m.* [*the*] ~ *people,* les gens du commun, *m.pl,* le petit peuple, le vulgaire. ~ *sense*, sens commun, bon sens, m. *the ~ weal*, la chose publique. *in, out of the*, ~, en, hors du, commun. ~*ly*, *ad*, communément, couramment. ~*ness*, *n*, fréquence, *f*. ~*place*, *a*, banal, commun; (*n*.) banalité; pauvreté, *f*, (*pl*.) lieux communs, *m.pl.* ~*wealth*, *n*, république; communauté, *f*.

commonalty, *n*, roture, *f*. **commoner**, *n*, roturier, ère.

commotion, *n*, commotion, *f*, mouvement, *m*.

communal, *a*, communal. **commune**, *v.i*, converser. **communicant**, *n*, communiant, e. **communicate**, *v.t. & i*, communiquer; correspondre; (*Eccl*.) communier. **communication**, *n*, communication, *f*. ~ *cord*, corde de signal d'alarme, *f*. ~ *trench*, branche de tranchée, *f*, boyau de t., *m*. **communicative**, *a*, communicatif. **communion**, *n*, communion, *f*. ~ *cup*, calice, *m*. ~ *service*, office du saint sacrement, *m*. ~ *table*, sainte table, *f*. **communism**, *n*, communisme, *m*. **communist**, *n*, communiste, *m.f*. **community**, *n*, communauté; société, république, *f*. ~ *singing*, chansons en chœur, *f.pl.* *bedroom* ~, cité-dortoire, *f*.

commutation, *n*, commutation; substitution, *f*; replacement; échange, *m*. ~ *ticket*, carte d'abonnement au chemin de fer, *f*.

commutator, *n*, commutateur, *m*.

commute, *v.t*, commuer. ~*r*, *n*, abonné des chemins de fer, *m*.

Como (Lake), le lac de Côme.

compact, *a*, compact. ¶ *n*, pacte, *m*; (*powder*) poudrier, *m*; (*auto*) voiture compact, *f*. ~*ness*, *n*, compacité, *f*.

companion, *n*, compagnon, *m*, compagne, *f*, camarade, *m.f*; (*thing*) pendant, *m*. [*lady*] ~, dame, demoiselle, de compagnie. ~*able*, *a*, sociable. ~*ship*, *n*, compagnie, société, *f*, fréquentations, *f.pl.*

company, *n*, compagnie; société; bande; troupe, *f*; groupe; équipage; monde, *m*.

comparable, *a*, comparable. **comparative**†, *a*, comparatif; (*sciences*) comparé. ¶ (*Gram*.)

n, comparatif, *m*. **compare**, *v.t*, comparer, assimiler; rapprocher, collationner; conférer. **comparison**, *n*, comparaison, *f*, rapprochement, *m*.

compartment, *n*, compartiment, *m*; case, *f*.

compass, *n*, cadre, *m*, étendue, portée; (*magnetic*) boussole, *f*; compas; (*voice*) diapason; (*musical*) clavier, *m*. ~ *card*, rose des vents, *f*. **compass[es]**, *n.[pl.]*, compas, *m*. *compasses with pen point*, *with pencil point*, compas à tire-ligne, à porte-crayon. **compass**, *v.t*, cerner, ceindre.

compassion, *n*, compassion, *f*. ~*ate*, *a*, compatissant.

compatible, *a*, compatible.

compatriot, *n*, compatriote, *m.f*.

compeer, *n*, égal, e, pair, *m*.

compel, *v.t*, contraindre, astreindre, obliger, forcer.

compendious, *a*, sommaire. **compendium**, *n*, compendium, *m*.

compensate, *v.t*, compenser, indemniser, dédommager. **compensation**, *n*, compensation, indemnité, *f*, dédommagement, *m*.

compete for, concourir pour, à. ~ *with*, faire concurrence à.

competence, **-cy**, *n*, aisance; compétence; aptitude, *f*. **competent**, *a*, compétent, apte.

competition, *n*, concurrence; compétition, *f*; concours, *m*. **competitor**, *n*, concurrent, e, compétiteur, trice.

compile, *v.t*, compiler.

complacency, *n*, contentement, *m*. **complacent**, *a*, content de soi. ~*ly*, *ad*, avec un air suffisant.

complain, *v.i*, se plaindre; réclamer, gémir. ~ *of* (medically), accuser. ~*ant*, *n*, plaignant, e. **complaint**, *n*, plainte, doléance, réclamation, *f*, grief; gémissement, *m*; (*Med*.) affection, maladie, *f*. ~ *department*, bureau de reclamation, *m*.

complaisance, *n*, complaisance, *f*. **complaisant**, *a*, complaisant.

complement, *n*, complément, effectif, *m*. ~*ary*, *a*, complémentaire.

complete†, *a*, complet, au complet. ¶ *v.t*, compléter. ~*d* (*time, age*) *p.p*, révolus. **completion**, *n*, complètement, achèvement, *m*.

complex, *a. & n*, complexe, *a. & m*.

complexion, *n*, (*of face*) teint; (*fig.*) caractère, aspect, *m*.
complexity, *n*, complexité, *f*.
compliance, *n*, conformité, *f*. **compliant**, *a*, facile, complaisant.
complicate, *v.t*, compliquer. **complication**, *n*, complication, *f*.
complicity, *n*, complicité, *f*.
compliment, *n*, compliment, *m*; (*pl.*) compliments, *m.pl*, civilités, politesses, *f.pl*, hommages, *m.pl*, choses, *f.pl*. ~s of the season, souhaits de bonne année, *m.pl*. ¶ *v.t*, complimenter. **~ary**, *a*, flatteur; (*free*) gratis.
comply, *v.i.abs*, se soumettre. ~ *with*, se conformer à, condescendre à, observer, obéir à, remplir, respecter. *not complied with* (rule), inobservée.
component, *a*, constituant; composant. ¶ *n*, composant, *m*. ~ [*part*], pièce détachée, *f*.
compose, *v.t*, composer. *to be~d of*, se c. de. ~ *oneself*, se calmer. ~**d**, *p.p*, composé, calme. **composer** (*Mus.*) *n*, compositeur, trice, auteur, *m*. *composing stick* (*Typ.*), composteur, *m*. **composite**, *a*, composé, mixte. **composition**, *n*, composition; constitution, *f*; thème, *m*. **compositor** (*Typ.*) *n*, compositeur, trice.
composure, *n*, calme, sang-froid, *m*.
compound, *a*, composé; (*steam*) compound. ~ *interest*, intérêt[s] composé[s] *m.[pl.]*. ¶ *n*, composé; combiné, corps composé, *m*. ¶ *v.t*, composer; pactiser avec (*a felony* = un crime); (*v.i.*) transiger; pactiser.
comprehend, *v.t*, comprendre. **comprehension**, *n*, compréhension, *f*. **comprehensive**, *a*, compréhensif.
compress, *n*, compresse, *f*. ¶ *v.t*, comprimer, refouler. ~**ion**, *n*, compression, *f*. ~**or**, *n*, compresseur, *m*.
comprise, *v.t*, comprendre, renfermer, contenir.
compromise, *n*, compromis, accommodement, *m*, transaction, *f*. ¶ *v.t. & i*, compromettre, transiger; capituler. ~ *oneself*, se compromettre.
comptroller, *n*, contrôleur, *m*.
compulsion, *n*, contrainte, *f*. **compulsorily**, *ad*, forcément. **compulsory**, *a*, forcé, obligatoire.

compunction, *n*, componction, *f*.
computation, *n*, supputation, *f*.
compute, *v.t*, supputer, computer.
computer, *n*, ordinateur, *m*. ~ *kid*, micro-mioche, *m. & f.* ~ *network*, réseau informatique, *m*. ~ *process chart*, ordinogramme, *m*. ~ *training course*, cours d'informatique, *m*. *home* ~, ordinateur domestique, *m*. ~**ize**, *v.t*, informatiser.
comrade, *n*, camarade, *m.f*. ~**ship**, *n*, camaraderie, *f*.
concatenation, *n*, caténation, *f*.
concave, *a*, concave. **concavity**, *n*, concavité, *f*.
conceal, *v.t*, cacher; celer; dérober; dissimuler; supprimer; taire; receler. ~**ment**, *n*, réticence; dissimulation; suppression, *f*; recèlement, *m*.
concede, *v.t*, accorder, concéder.
conceit, *n*, vanité, suffisance, *f*. ~**ed**, *a*, vain, vaniteux, suffisant.
conceivable, *a*, concevable. **conceive**, *v.t. & i*, concevoir.
concentrate, *v.t*, concentrer; canaliser. **concentration**, *n*, concentration, *f*.
concentric, *a*, concentrique.
concept, *n*, concept, *m*; idée, *f*. ~**ion**, *n*, conception, *f*.
concern, *n*, affaire, *f*; souci, *m*, sollicitude, inquiétude; entreprise, exploitation; boutique, *f*. ¶ *v.t*, concerner, intéresser, regarder, toucher, appartenir. ~**ing**, *pr*, concernant, touchant, à l'égard de.
concert, *n*, concert, *m*; audition, *f*. ~ *grand* [*piano*], piano à queue, *m*. ¶ *v.t*, concerter. **concerto**, *n*, concerto, *m*.
concession, *n*, concession, *f*. **concessionaire**, *n*, concessionnaire, *m.f*.
conch, *n*, conque, *f*; coquillage, *m*. ~**ology**, *n*, conchyliogie, *f*.
conciliate, *v.t*, concilier. **conciliation**, *n*, conciliation, *f*. ~ *board*, conseil de prud'hommes, *m*.
concise, *a*, concis; (*edition*) compacte. ~**ness**, *n*, concision, *f*.
conclave, *n*, conclave, *m*; assemblée, *f*.
conclude, *v.t. & i*, conclure; arrêter, clore. **conclusion**, *n*, conclusion; décision, *f*. **conclusive**, *a*,

démonstratif; concluant; décisif.
concoct, *v.t*, confectionner; (*fig.*) cuisiner, machiner, tramer. **concoction**, *n*, mixture; machination, *f*.

concomitant, *n*, accompagnement, *m*.

concord, *n*, concorde, *f*; accord, *m*; concordance, *f*. **~ance**, *n*, concordance, *f*.

concourse, *n*, concours, *m*, affluence, *f*.

concrete, *a*, concret. **the concrete** (opp. *abstract*), le concret. ¶ *n*, béton, *m*.

concubine, *n*, concubine, *f*.

concupiscence, *n*, concupiscence, *f*.

concur, *v.i*, concourir. **concurrence**, *n*, concours, *m*.

concussion, *n*, ébranlement, *m*. **~ of the brain**, commotion au cerveau, *f*.

condemn, *v.t*, condamner. **~ed man, woman**, condamné(e) à mort. **condemnation**, *n*, condamnation, *f*.

condensation, *n*, condensation, *f*. **condense**, *v.t*, condenser; resserrer. **~d milk**, lait condensé, l. concentré, l. conservé, *m*. **condenser**, *n*, (*Phys.*, *Elec.*, *Opt.*) condensateur; (*steam*) condenseur, *m*.

condescend, *v.i*, condescendre. **condescension**, *n*, condescendance, *f*.

condiment, *n*, condiment, assaisonnement, *m*.

condition, *n*, condition, *f*; état, *m*. **on ~ that**, à condition que, à [la] charge de, sous réserve que. ¶ *v.t*, conditionner. **~al†**, *a*, conditionnel.

condole with, exprimer ses condoléances à. **condolence**, *n*, condoléance, *f*.

condone, *v.t*, passer sur, fermer les yeux sur.

conduce, *v.t*, contribuer, conduire, tendre.

conduct, *n*, conduite, *f*; maniement, *m*. ¶ *v.t*, conduire, guider, gérer, manier, mener. **~ed tour**, excursion accompagnée, *f*. **conductor, tress**, *n*, conducteur, trice; guide, *m*; receveur, euse, chef d'orchestre, *m*.

conduit, *n*, conduit; caniveau, *m*.

cone, *n*, (*Geom.*) cône, *m*; (*fir*, *pine*) pomme; (*ice cream*) cornet de glace, *m*.

confectioner, *n*, confiseur, euse; pâtissier, ère, glacier, *m*. **~'s shop**, confiserie, pâtisserie, *f*. **~y**, *n*, confiserie, *f*, bonbons, *m.pl*, sucreries, *f.pl*; pâtisserie, *f*.

confederacy, *n*, confédération, *f*. **confederate**, *n*, compère, *m*, complice, *m,f*, (*pl.*) consorts, *m.pl*. ¶ *v.i*, se confédérer. **confederation**, *n*, confédération, *f*.

confer, *v.t*, conférer; accorder; (*v.i.*) conférer. **~ence**, *n*, conférence, *f*.

confess, *v.t*, confesser, avouer, s'accuser de; (*v.i.*) se confesser. **~edly**, *ad*, de son propre aveu. **confession**, *n*, confession, *f*, aveu, *m*; confesse, *f*. **~al**, *n*, confessional, *m*. **confessor**, *n*, confesseur, *m*.

confidant, e, *n*, confident, e. **confide**, *v.t*, confier, livrer; (*v.i.*) se confier. **confidence**, *n*, confiance; assurance; (*secret*) confidence, *f*. **~ trick**, vol à l'américaine, *m*. **~ man**, escroc, *m*. **confident**, *a*, confiant, assuré. **confidential**, *a*, (*of things*) confidentiel; (*of pers.—in good sense*) de confiance; (*bad sense*) affidé. **~ly**, *ad*, confidentiellement, confidemment. **confiding**, *p.a*, confiant.

confine, *v.t*, confiner, borner; chambrer, enfermer, renfermer, resserrer; retenir, faire garder. **~ oneself to, within**, se borner à, dans, se cantonner dans. **~ [to barracks]**, consigner. **to be ~d** (woman), accoucher, faire ses couches. **~ment**, *n*, détention, *f*; (woman) couches, *f.pl*, accouchement, *m*. **~ to barracks**, consigne, *f*. **confines**, *n.pl*, confins, *m.pl*.

confirm, *v.t*, confirmer; ratifier; approuver, adopter. **~ation**, *n*, confirmation; ratification, approbation, adoption, *f*. **~ed**, *p.a*, invétéré, acharné, fieffé, émérite. **~ invalid**, incurable, *m,f*.

confiscate, *v.t*, confisquer. **confiscation**, *n*, confiscation, *f*.

conflagration, *n*, embrasement, *m*; conflagration, *f*.

conflict, *n*, conflit, *m*. ¶ *v.i. & abs*, se contredire. **~ing**, *p.a*, en conflit; contradictoire.

confluence, *n*, confluent; concours, *m*.

conform, *v.t*, conformer; (*v.i.*)

se c. ~**able,** *a,* conforme. ~**ably,**
ad, conformément. ~**ation,** *n,*
conformation, *f.* ~**ity,** *n,* conformité, *f.*
confound, *v.t,* confondre. ~**ed,**
p.a, maudit.
confraternity, *n,* confraternité;
(*pers.*) confrérie, *f.*
confront, *v.t,* affronter; confronter; faire face à.
confuse, *v.t,* confondre, mêler;
embrouiller. **confused,** *a,* confus.
~**ly,** *ad,* confusément. **confusion,**
n, confusion, *f,* désarroi, *m.*
confute, *v.t,* réfuter.
congeal, *v.t,* congeler, geler, figer;
(*v.i.*) se congeler; prendre, se
prendre.
congenial, *a,* sympathique; agréable.
congenital, *a,* congénital.
conger [eel], *n,* congre, *m.*
congest (*Med.*) *v.t,* congestionner, engorger. ~**ion,** *n,* (*Med.*)
congestion, *f,* engorgement;
(*traffic, etc.*) encombrement, *m,*
presse, *f.* ~ **of the blood, of the
brain, of the lungs,** congestion
sanguine, cérébrale, pulmonaire.
~ **of the liver,** engorgement au
foie.
conglomerate, *n,* conglomérat,
m.
congratulate, *v.t,* féliciter, complimenter. ~ *oneself,* se féliciter,
s'applaudir. **congratulation,** *n,*
félicitation, *f,* compliment, *m.*
congregate, *v.t,* rassembler; (*v.i.*)
se r., s'assembler. **congregation,**
n, assemblage, *m*; (*of pers.*)
assemblée, *f.*
congress, *n,* congrès, *m.* **member of the** (*or* a) ~, congressiste,
m,f.
congruity, *n,* convenance, *f.*
congruous, *a,* congru. ~**ly,** *ad,*
congrûment.
conic(al), *a,* conique.
conifer, *n,* conifère, *m.* ~**ous,** *a,*
conifère.
conjectural†, *a,* conjectural.
conjecture, *n,* conjecture, *f.*
¶ *v.t,* conjecturer.
conjoin, *v.t,* conjoindre. **con-
joint†,** *a,* conjoint.
conjugal†, *a,* conjugal.
conjugate, *v.t,* conjuguer. **conjugation,** *n,* conjugaison, *f.*
conjunction, *n,* conjonction, *f.*
conjuncture, *n,* conjoncture, *f.*

conjure, *v.t,* (*adjure*) conjurer;
(*enchant*) ensorceler; (*v.i.*) escamoter. ~ *away,* escamoter.
~ [*up*], évoquer, se forger. **conjurer, -or,** *n,* escamoteur, prestidigitateur, *m.* **conjuring,** *n,* escamotage, *m,* prestidigitation, *f.*
~ *trick,* tour de passe-passe, *m.*
connect, *v.t,* relier, raccorder,
joindre, réunir; lier; (*Elec.*)
[ac]coupler. ~**ed,** *p.a,* suivi; apparenté. *connecting rod,* bielle, *f.*
connection, *n,* connexion; liaison;
relation, *f*; raccord; contact; rapport, *m*; correspondance, *f*; parent, e; clientèle, *f,* achalandage,
m. travel ~, liaison, correspondance, *f.*
conning tower, blockhaus;
(*submarine*) kiosque, *m.*
connivance, *n,* connivence, *f.*
connive at, être de connivence
pour.
connoisseur, *n,* connaisseur,
euse; gourmet, *m.*
connubial, *a,* conjugal, matrimonial.
conquer, *v.t,* vaincre, conquérir.
conqueror, conqueress, *n,* vainqueur, *m,* conquérant, e. *William
the Conqueror,* Guillaume le
Conquérant. **conquest,** *n,* conquête, *f.*
consanguinity, *n,* consanguinité, *f.*
conscience, *n,* conscience, *f,* for
intérieur, *m.* ~ *money,* restitution anonyme, *f.* *to be*
~-*stricken,* avoir une conscience
bourrelée de remords. **consci-
entious†,** *a,* consciencieux. ~**ness,**
n, conscience, *f.*
conscious, *a*: *to be* ~, avoir sa
connaissance. *to be* ~ *of,* avoir
conscience de, être conscient de,
sentir. ~**ly,** *ad,* sciemment.
~**ness,** *n,* connaissance; conscience, *f.*
conscript, *n,* conscrit, *m.* ~**ion,**
n, conscription, *f.*
consecrate, *v.t,* consacrer; bénir;
sacrer. ~**d,** *p.a,* bénit; sacré;
saint. **consecration,** *n,* consécration; bénédiction, *f*; sacre, *m.*
consecutive†, *a,* consécutif.
consensus, *n,* unanimité, *f.*
consent, *n,* consentement, accord,
agrément, aveu, *m.* ¶ *v.i,* consentir, accéder, entendre (*to* = à).
consequence, *n,* conséquence,
suite; importance, *f.* **consequent,**
a, conséquent. *consequential*

damages, dommages indirects, *m.pl.* **consequently,** *ad,* conséquemment, par conséquent, aussi.

conservation, *n,* conservation, préservation, *f.*

conservative, *a,* conservateur. ¶ *n.* & **conservator,** *n,* conservateur, trice. **conservatory,** *n,* serre, *f.*

consider, *v.t,* considérer, regarder; délibérer sur; (*v.i.* & *abs.*) songer, réfléchir. **~able†,** *a,* considérable. **~ate,** *a,* prévenant. **~ation,** *n,* considération, *f;* égard, *m;* délibération, *f;* ménagements, *m.pl;* (*law*) provision, cause, *f. in ~ of* (value received), moyennant. (matter) *under ~,* sur le bureau. *without due ~,* à la légère. **~ing,** *pr,* attendu, vu, eu égard à.

consign, *v.t,* livrer; confier; remettre, expédier; reléguer; (*goods*) consigner. **~ee,** *n,* consignataire, destinataire, réceptionnaire, *m.* **~ment,** *n,* consignation; expédition, *f;* envoi, chargement, *m.* (goods) *on ~,* en consignation. **~or,** *n,* consignateur, *m.*

consist, *v.i,* consister, se composer. **~ence, -cy,** *n,* consistance; suite, *f.* **~ent,** *a,* conséquent, compatible; qui ne se dément point; suivi. **~ently with,** conséquemment à. **~ory,** *n,* consistoire, *m.*

consolation, *n,* consolation, *f. ~ prize,* prix de c., *m.* **console,** *v.t,* consoler. ¶ *n,* console, *f;* (*computers & TV*) pupitre, *m. ~ operator,* pupitreur, *m. keyboard ~,* pupitre à clavier, *m. control ~,* p. de régie, *m. mixing ~,* p. de mélange, *m.*

consolidate, *v.t,* consolider; unifier. **consolidation,** *n,* consolidation; unification, *f.*

consonance, *n,* consonance, *f.* **consonant,** *a,* (*Mus., words*) consonant. *~ with,* en rapport avec. ¶ *n,* consonne, *f.*

consort, *n,* époux, ouse, (*Naut.*) conserve, *f,* navire d'escort; (*prince*) consort, *m.* ¶ *v.i,* s'associer.

conspicuous, *a,* voyant, en évidence; insigne, signalé, remarquable. *to make oneself ~,* se faire remarquer, se singulariser.

conspiracy, *n,* conspiration, conjuration, *f.* **conspirator,** *n,* conspirateur, trice, conjuré, *m.* **conspire,** *v.i.* & *t,* conspirer, conjurer.

constancy, *n,* constance, *f.* **constant,** *a,* constant. ¶ *n,* constante, *f. ~ly,* *ad,* constamment.

constellation, *n,* constellation, *f.*

consternation, *n,* consternation, *f.*

constipate, *v.t,* constiper. **constipation,** *n,* constipation, *f.*

constituency, *n,* circonscription électorale, *f,* collège électoral, *m;* électeurs, *m.pl.* **constituent,** *a,* constituant, composant. ¶ *n,* composant; ingrédient, *m;* (*pl.*) électeurs, commettants, *m.pl.* **constitute,** *v.t,* constituer. **constitution,** *n,* constitution, *f;* tempérament, *m.* **~al†,** *a,* constitutionnel.

constrain, *v.t,* contraindre, gêner, forcer. **constraint,** *n,* contrainte, gêne, sujétion, *f.*

construct, *v.t,* construire, établir. **~ion,** *n,* construction; interprétation; explication, *f.* **~ional,** *a,* de construction. **~ive,** *a,* constructif. **~or,** *n,* constructeur, *m.*

construe, *v.t,* construire; expliquer.

consul, *n,* consul, *m.* **~ar,** *a,* consulaire. **~ate** & **~ship,** *n,* consulat, *m.*

consult, *v.t,* consulter. **~ation,** *n,* consultation, *f.* **consulting,** *p.a:* *~ engineer,* ingénieur-conseil, *m. ~ physician,* médecin consultant, *m. ~ room,* cabinet de consultation, salon de c., *m.*

consume, *v.t,* consumer, dévorer; (*use*) consommer. **consumer,** *n,* consommateur, *m.*

consummate, *a,* consommé, fini, superlatif. ¶ *v.t,* consommer. **consummation,** *n,* consommation, *f.*

consumption, *n,* (*destruction*) consomption; (*Med.*) consomption, phtisie; (*use*) consommation, dépense, *f.* **consumptive,** *a.* & *n,* tuberculeux, euse, poitrinaire, phtisique, *a.* & *m,f.*

contact, *n,* contact; attouchement; frottement, *m.* ¶ *v.t,* être en relations avec, être en contact avec.

contagion, *n,* contagion, *f.* **contagious,** *a,* contagieux. **~ness,** *n,* contagion, *f.*

contain, *v.t.,* contenir, tenir, renfermer. ~**er**, *n*, conténant; recipient; container *ou* conteneur, *m*. ~**ization**, *n*, conteneurisation, *f*. ~**ize**, *v.t*, conteneuriser.

contaminate, *v.t*, contaminer, souiller. **contamination**, *n*, contamination, souillure, *f*.

contemplate, *v.t*, contempler; méditer; projeter; envisager; (*v.i.*) méditer. **contemplation**, *n*, contemplation, *f. in* ~, en vue. **contemplative**, *a*, contemplatif.

contemporaneous & contemporary, *a*, contemporain. **contemporary**, *n*, contemporain, e.

contempt, *n*, mépris, *m*. *oft. pl*, dédain, *m*. ~ *of court*, offense à la cour, *f*; refus d'obéissance, *m*. ~**ible**, *a*, méprisable. **contemptuous**, *a*, méprisant, dédaigneux.

contend, *v.t. & i:* ~ *that*, prétendre que. ~ *with*, combattre; lutter contre; disputer.

content, *a*, content. ¶ *n*, contentement, *m*; (*holding*) contenance; teneur, *f*; titre; (*pl.*) contenu, *m*; table des matières, *f*. ¶ *v.t*, contenter. ~*ed with*, satisfait de. ~**edly**, *ad*, content.

contention, *n*, démêlé, *m*; dispute, discorde, *f*. *my* ~ *is that* . . ., ce que je prétends, c'est que . . . **contentious**, *a*, litigieux; contentieux.

contentment, *n*, contentement, *m*.

contest, *n*, lutte, *f*, combat; concours, *m*, joute, dispute, *f*. ¶ *v.t*, contester; disputer.

context, *n*, contexte, *m*.

contexture, *n*, contexture, *f*.

contiguity, *n*, contiguïté, *f*. **contiguous**, *a*, contigu.

continence, *n*, continence, *f*. **continent**, *a*, continent. ¶ *n*, continent, *m*; terre ferme, *f. the C~* (*Europe*), le continent. ~**al**, *a*, continental.

contingency, *n*, contingence, éventualité, *f*, imprévu, *m*. ~ *fund*, fonds de prévoyance, *m*. **contingent**, *a*, contingent, aléatoire, éventuel. ¶ *n*, contingent; évènement fortuit, *m*.

continual†, *a*, continuel. **continuance**, *n*, continuation, *f*. **continuation**, *n*, continuation, suite, *f*. **continue**, *v.t. & i*, continuer; prolonger. **to be** ~**d** (*serial*), à suivre,

la suite au prochain numéro. **continuity**, *n*, continuité, *f*. (*cinema*), ~ *shot*, raccord, *m*. **continuous**, *a*, continu. (*movies*) ~ *performance*, spectacle permanent, *m*. ~**ly**, *ad*, continûment.

contort, *v.t*, contourner. ~**ed**, *p.a*, tors. **contortion**, *n*, contorsion, *f*. ~**ist**, *n*, homme-caoutchouc, homme-serpent, *m*; femme-caoutchouc, femme-serpent, *f*.

contour, *n*, contour; profil, tracé, galbe, *m*. ~ *line*, courbe de niveau, *f*. ~ *map*, carte en courbes de niveau, *f*.

contraband, *n*, contrebande, *f*; (*att.*) de c.

contrabass, *n*, contrebasse, *f*.

contraceptive, *a*, contraceptif. ¶ *n*, préservatif, (*slang*) capote anglaise, *f*.

contract, *n*, contrat, *m*, convention, *f*, acte, traité, *m. on* ~ *or by* ~, à l'entreprise, à forfait, forfaitaire; par contrat. ~ *bridge*, bridge plafond, b. contrat, *m*. ¶ *v.t*, (*shrink*) contracter, [r]étrécir, resserrer; (*law*) contracter; [entre]prendre; (*v.i. or abs.*) contracter, s'étrécir, se rétrécir, se resserrer; (*law*) contracter. ~**ant** (*pers.*) *n*, contractant, e. ~**ing**, *a*, contractant. ~**ion**, *n*, contraction, *f*, [r]étrécissement, resserrement, *m*; abréviation, *f*. ~**or**, *n*, entrepreneur, euse; fournisseur, euse; adjudicataire, *m,f*. **contractual**, *a*, contractuel, forfaitaire.

contradict, *v.t*, contredire, démentir. ~**ion**, *n*, contredit, démenti, *m*. ~**ory**, a, contradictoire.

contradistinction, *n*, opposition, *f*.

contralto, *n*, contralto, *m*.

contrariety, *n*, contrariété, *f*. **contrarily & contrary**, *ad*, contrairement. **contrary**, *a*, contraire; opposé; inverse. ¶ *n*, contraire, opposé, rebours; contre-pied, *m*; contrepartie, *f. on the* ~, au contraire.

contrast, *n*, contraste, *m*, opposition, *f*. ¶ *v.t. & i*, mettre en contraste; contraster, trancher. ~**y**, *a*, heurté.

contravene, *v.t*, contrevenir à, enfreindre. **contravention**, *n*, contravention, infraction, *f*.

contribute, *v.t*, contribuer; (*v.i.*) contribuer à, collaborer à. ~ *to* (journal), collaborer à. **contribution**, *n*, contribution, *f*; apport, fournissement, *m*, cote, cotisation, *f. to lay under* ~, mettre à contribution. **contributor** (*to journal*) *n*, collaborateur, trice.

contrite, *a*, contrit. **contrition**, *n*, contrition, *f*, brisement de cœur, *m*.

contrivance, *n*, combinaison, *f*, dispositif; artifice, *m*. **contrive**, *v.t*, combiner; ménager. ~ *to*, faire en sorte que, s'ingénier à.

control, *n*, contrôle, *m*; commande, *f*; empire, *m*, maîtrise, *f*. ¶ *v.t*, contrôler, contenir; maîtriser; policer. **controller**, *n*, contrôleur, *m*.

controversial, *a*, de controverse. **controversy**, *n*, controverse, *f*. **controvert**, *v.t*, discuter.

contumacy, *n*, contumace, *f*.

contumely, *n*, outrage; opprobre, *m*.

contuse, *v.t*, contusionner. **contusion**, *n*, contusion, *f*.

conundrum, *n*, devinette, énigme, *f*.

convalesce, *v.i*, entrer en convalescence. **convalescence**, *n*, convalescence, *f*. **convalescent**, *a. & n*, convalescent, e.

convene, *v.t*, convoquer.

convenience, *n*, commodité, convenance; aise, *f*; (*toilet*) commodités, *f.pl.* **convenient**, *a*, commode, convenable. ~**ly**, *ad*, commodément.

convent, *n*, couvent, *m*. ~ *school*, couvent, *m*.

convention, *n*, convention, *f*. ~**al**, *a*, conventionnel, de convention; pompier. ~**alism**, *n*, poncif, *m*, le style pompier. ~**alist**, *n*, pompier, *m*.

converge, *v.i*, converger. **convergent**, *a*, convergent.

conversant, *a*, versé, ferré.

conversation, *n*, conversation, *f*; colloque, *m*. ~**al**, *a*, de, de la, conversation. ~[**al**]**ist**, *n*, causeur, euse.

converse, *a.. & n*, contraire, *a. & m*; converse, *a.f. & f*, réciproque, *a.. & f*. ¶ *v.i*, converser, causer.

conversion, *n*, conversion, *f*, convertissement (*Fin.*) *m*; transformation, *f*. **convert**, *n*, converti, e. ¶ *v.t*, convertir, transformer.

~*ed goal*, but de transformation, *m. to become* ~*ed* (*Relig.*), se convertir. ~**er**, *n*, convertisseur, *m*; adapteur, *m*. ~**ible**, *a*, convertible; (*stocks*) convertissable. ¶ *n*, (*auto*) décapotable, *m*.

convex, *a*, convexe. ~**ity**, *n*, convexité, *f*.

convey, *v.t*, [trans]porter, véhiculer, conduire, charrier, voiturer; (*law, etc.*) transmettre; communiquer, exprimer. ~**ance**, *n*, transport, charriage, *m*; voiture; (*law*) translation, transmission, mutation, *f*; (*deed*) acte de transmission, acte translatif de propriété, *m*.

convict, *n*, condamné, e, forçat, *m*. ~ *prison*, bagne, *m*. ¶ *v.t*, convaincre; condamner. ~**ion**, *n*, conviction; condamnation, *f. person with previous* ~*s*, récidiviste, *m.f.*

convince, *v.t*, convaincre. **convincing**, *p.a*, convaincant.

convivial, *a*: ~ *gathering*, joyeuse compagnie, *f*. ~ *person*, joyeux convive, bon c., *m*.

convocation, *n*, convocation, *f*. **convoke**, *v.t*, convoquer.

convolvulus, *n*, convolvulus, volubilis, *m*, belle-de-jour, *f*.

convoy, *n*, convoi, *m*; escorte, *f*. ¶ *v.t*, convoyer, escorter.

convulse, *v.t*, bouleverser. *to be* ~*d* (laughing), se tordre. **convulsion**, *n*, convulsion, *f*, bouleversement, *m*. **convulsive**†, *a*, convulsif.

cony, *n*, lapin, *m*.

coo, *n*, roucoulement, *m*. ¶ *v.i*, roucouler.

cook, *n*, cuisinier, ère; (*ship's*) [maître-]coq, *m*. ~**book**, livre de cuisine, *m*. ~*'s mate*, matelot coq, *m*. ¶ *v.t*, [faire] cuire; (*fig.*) cuisiner, falsifier; (*v.i.*) cuisiner. **cookery**, *n*, cuisine, *f*. **cookie**, *n*, petit gateau, biscuit, *m*. **cooking**, *n*, cuisine; cuisson, *f*. ~ *apples*, pommes à cuire, *f.pl*.

cool†, *a*, frais; froid; calme; hardi; sans gêne. ~*-headed*, à l'esprit calme. ¶ *n*, frais, *m*, fraîcheur, *f*. ¶ *v.t*, attiédir; rafraîchir; refroidir; (*v.i.*) s'attiédir, se refroidir. ~ *down*, se calmer, caler [la voile]. ~ *one's heels*, se morfondre; ~**er**, *n*, rafraîchisseur; refroidisseur, *m*; prison, *f*. ~**ness**, *n*, fraîcheur; froideur, *f*, froid; calme, sang-froid, flegme; sans-gêne, *m*.

coop, *n*, cage [à poulets], mue, *f*, poulailler, *m*. **~[up],** *v.t*, claque-murer.

cooper, *n*, tonnelier, *m*. **~age,** *n*, tonnellerie, *f*.

cooperate, *v.i*, coopérer. **co-operation,** *n*, coopération, *f*. **cooperative,** *a*, coopératif. **~ society,** [société] coopérative, *f*.

coordinate, *v.t*, coordonner. ¶ *a*, coordonné.

coot, *n*, foulque, *f*.

cope, *n*, chape, *f*. ¶ *v.i*, lutter. **~ with,** tenir tête à, suffire à.

Copenhagen, *n*, Copenhague, *f*.

coping, *n*, chaperon, couronnement, *m*.

copious†, *a*, copieux, riche, plantureux; nourri.

copper, *n*, cuivre [rouge] *m*. **~ [coin],** cuivre, *m*, monnaie de cuivre, *f*, billon, *m*. **~ beech,** hêtre rouge, *m*. **~-colored,** cuivré. **~plate,** planche de cuivre, *f*, cuivre, *m*. **~plate [engraving],** gravure sur cuivre, taille-douce, *f*. **~smith,** chaudronnier, *m*. ¶ *v.t*, cuivrer.

copperas, *n*, couperose, *f*.

coppice, copse, *n*, taillis, *m*.

copulation, *n*, copulation, *f*.

copy, *n*, copie; transcription, *f*; calque, exemplaire; exemple, *m*. **~book,** cahier d'écriture, livre d'exemples, *m*. **~cat,** singe, *m*. ¶ *v.t*, copier; transcrire; calquer.

copying, *n*, transcription, *f*.

copyist, *n*, copiste, *m,f*.

copyright, *n*, droit d'auteur, *m*, propriété [littéraire] *f*. **~ by so-&-so,** tous droits de reproduction, de traduction, d'adaptation & d'exécution réservés pour tous pays.

coquet, *v.i*, coqueter. **~ry,** *n*, coquetterie, *f*. **coquettish,** *a*, coquet.

coral, *n*, corail, *m*. **~ fisher,** corailleur, *m*. **~ reef,** banc corallifère, *m*.

corbel, *n*, corbeau, *m*.

cord, *n*, corde; cordelette, *f*; cordon; câble, *m*; (braided) ganse, *f*. **spinal ~,** moelle épinière, *f*. ¶ *v.t*, corder. **~age,** *n*, cordages, *m.pl*.

cordial†, *a*, cordial, chaleureux. ¶ *n*, cordial, *m*. **~ity,** *n*, cordialité, *f*.

corduroy, *n*, velours côtelé, *m*.

core, *n*, cœur, trognon; noyau, *m*; âme, *f*. (computers) **~ storage,** mémoire à ferrites, m. à tores (magnétiques), *f*. ¶ *v.t*, vider (une pomme, etc.).

co-respondent, *n*, complice en adultère, *m,f*.

Corinth, *n*, Corinthe, *f*. **Corinthian,** *a*, corinthien. ¶ *n*, Corinthien, ne.

cork, *n*, liège; bouchon [en liège] *m*. **~ jacket,** brassière de sauvetage, *f*. **~screw,** tire-bouchon, *m*. **~screw curl,** boudin, *m*. **~screw,** *v.i*, vriller. **~-tipped** (cigarettes), à bouts de liège. **~ tree,** chêne-liège, *m*. ¶ *v.t*, boucher. **~y,** *a*, liégeux. **~ taste,** goût de bouchon, *m*.

cormorant, *n*, cormoran, *m*.

corn, *n*, maïs; (on feet) cor, (soft) œil-de-perdrix, *m*. **~ cob,** épi de maïs, *m*, rafle, *f*. **~flower,** bleuet, *m*.

corned beef, *n*, bœuf salé, *m*.

corner, *n*, coin, angle; tournant, virage, *m*; encoignure, *f*; recoin, (Com.) accaparement, *m*. (att.) cornier, d'angle; d'encoignure, de coin, du coin. **~ cupboard,** encoignure, *f*. **~stone,** pierre angulaire, *f*. ¶ *v.t*, acculer, rencogner; (monopolize) accaparer.

cornet, *n*, (cone) cornet; (Mus.) cornet à pistons, piston; (ice cream wafer) plaisir, *m*, oublie, *f*.

cornice, *n*, corniche, *f*.

Cornish, *a*, de Cornouailles.

cornucopia, *n*, corne d'abondance, *f*.

Cornwall, *n*, la Cornouailles.

corolla, *n*, corolle, *f*.

corollary, *n*, corollaire, *m*.

corona, *n*, couronne, *f*. **coronation,** *n*, couronnement, sacre, *m*. **coronet,** *n*, couronne, *f*.

coroner, *n*, coroner, *m*.

corporal† & corporeal†, *a*, corporel. **corporal,** *n*, caporal; (cavalry) brigadier, *m*. **corporate,** *a*, social. ¶ *v.i*, faire corps. **corporation,** *n*, société, corporation, *f*.

corps, *n*, corps, *m*.

corpse, *n*, cadavre, corps [mort] *m*. **~like,** cadavéreux.

corpulence, -ency, *n*, corpulence, *f*, embonpoint, *m*, réplétion, *f*. **corpulent,** *a*, corpulent, ventru.

Corpus Christi, la Fête-Dieu.
corpuscle, n, corpuscule, m.
corral, n, enclos, m. ¶ v.t, enfermer dans un enclos.
correct†, a, correct; exact, juste. ¶ v.t, corriger; rectifier, redresser; surcharger. ~ed copy, corrigé, m. ~ion, n, correction; rectification, f, redressement, m; surcharge, f. ~ional†, a, correctionnel. ~ive, n, correctif, m. ~ness, n, correction, exactitude, justesse, f. ~or, n, correcteur, trice.
correlate, v.t, (statistics) corréler; relier, mettre en relation. correlation, n, corrélation, f. correlative, a, corrélatif, ive.
correspond, v.i, correspondre; répondre. ~ence, n, correspondance, f; intelligences, f.pl. ~ent, n, correspondant, e. ~ing, p.a, correspondant.
corridor, n, couloir, corridor, m.
corroborate, v.t, corroborer.
corrode, v.t, corroder; ronger; miner. **corrosion**, n, corrosion, f. **corrosive**, a. & n, corrosif, a. & m.
corrugate, v.t, canneler, strier; onduler. ~d [sheet] iron & ~d iron sheet, tôle ondulée, f.
corrupt, v.t, corrompre, débaucher, vicier, gâter, gangrener. ~ible, a, corruptible; prenable. ~ion, n, corruption, f.
corsair, n, corsaire, m.
corset, n, corset, m. ~ maker, corsetier, ère. ¶ v.t, corseter.
Corsica, n, la Corse. **Corsican**, a, corse. ¶ n, Corse, m,f.
corundum, n, corindon, m.
coruscate, v.i, scintiller.
cos, n. or **Cos lettuce**, [laitue] romaine, f.
cosily, ad, à son aise, confortablement.
cosmetic, a. & n, cosmétique, a. & m.
cosmic(al), a, cosmique.
cosmopolitan & cosmopolite, a. & n, cosmopolite, a. & m.
cost, n, coût, prix, m; frais, m.pl, dépense, f. at all ~s, coûte que coûte, à toute force. ~ of living bonus, indemnité de vie chère, f. ~ of living figure, indice du coût de la vie, m. ~ [price], prix de revient, p. coûtant, p. d'acquisition, m. ¶ v.i.ir, coûter; revenir.
costive, a, constipé. ~ness, n, constipation, f.

costliness, n, cherté; somptuosité, f. **costly**, a, coûteux, dispendieux; somptueux.
costume, n, costume, m. ~ piece, ~ play, pièce historique, f. **costum[i]er**, n, costumier, m.
cot, n, lit d'enfant; lit pliant, lit de camp, m.
coterie, n, coterie, chapelle, f. ~ of wits, bureau d'esprit, m.
cottage, n, chaumière; habitation ouvrière, f; cottage, chalet; (fig.) chaume, m.
cotter, n, clavette, f. ~ pin, goupille, f.
cotton, n, coton, m; (thread) fil à coudre, m. ~ [cloth], cotonnade, toile de coton, f. absorbent ~, coton hydrophile, m. ~ goods, cotonnade, f. ~ mill, filature de coton, f. ~ plant, cotonnier, m. ~ waste, bourre de coton, f. ~ wool, ouate [de coton] f, coton [en laine] m. ~y, a cotonneux.
couch, n, couche; chaise longue, f; canapé, m. ¶ v.i, se coucher; se tapir, se blottir. ~ed in these terms, ainsi conçu. ~ [grass] n, chiendent, m.
cough, n, toux, f. ~ mixture, sirop, m, (ou potion, f.) pour la toux. ~ drop, pastille pour la t., f. whooping ~, coqueluche, f. ¶ v.i, tousser; ~ up, expectorer.
council, n, conseil; (Eccl.) concile, m. **councillor**, n, conseiller, ère.
counsel, n, conseil, m; délibération, f; (pers.) avocat, conseil, défenseur, m. ¶ v.t, conseiller. **counselor**, n, conseiller, ère.
count, n, compte, (pers.) comte, m. ~down, compte à rebours, m. ~ of indictment, chef d'accusation, m. ¶ v.t. & i, compter; nombrer; (votes) recenser, dépouiller.
countenance, n, contenance; physionomie, figure, mine, f. ¶ v.t, approuver; encourager.
counter, n, riposte, f; (play) jeton, m, fiche, f; (shop) comptoir, m; (cashier's) caisse, f, guichet, m. ¶ v.t, riposter. to run ~ to, aller à l'encontre de.
counteract, v.t, contrecarrer.
counterattack, n, contre-attaque, f.
counterbalance, n, contrepoids, m. ¶ v.t, contrebalancer, équilibrer.

counterclaim, *n,* reconvention, *f.*

counterfeit, *a,* contrefait, faux. ¶ *n,* contrefaçon, *f.* ¶ *v.t,* contrefaire. ~er, *n,* contrefacteur, faux monnayeur, *m.*

counterfoil, *n,* souche, *f,* talon, *m.*

counter instructions, contrordre, *m.*

countermand, *v.t,* contremander; (*Com.*) décommander. ¶ *n,* contrordre, *m.*

counterpane, *n,* couverture [de lit] *f.*

counterpart, *n,* contrepartie, *f;* (*pers.*) pendant; (*deed*) double, *m.*

counterpoint, *n,* contrepoint, *m.*

counterpoise, *n,* contrepoids, *m.* ¶ *v.t,* contrebalancer, équilibrer.

countershaft, *n,* arbre secondaire, a. de renvoi, *m.*

countersign, (*Mil.*) *n,* mot de ralliement, *m.* ¶ *v.t,* contresigner.

countersink, *n,* fraisure, *f.* ~ [*bit*], fraise, *f.* ¶ *v.t,* fraiser.

counterstroke, *n,* riposte, *f.*

counterweight, *n,* contrepoids, *m.*

countess, *n,* comtesse, *f.*

counting, *n,* compte; recensement, *m.* **countless,** *a,* innombrable.

country, *n,* pays, *m;* contrée; campagne; province; patrie, *f;* corps électoral, *m.* ~ *club,* country-club, *m.* ~ *house,* maison de campagne, *f.* ~ *life,* vie champêtre, v. rurale, *f.* ~*man,* -*woman,* campagnard, e. [*fellow*] ~*man,* -*woman,* compatriote, *m.f.,* ~*side,* campagne, *f.* ~ *town,* ville de province, *f.* open ~, rase campagne, *f.*

county, *n,* comté, *m.* ~ *seat,* chef-lieu, *m.*

couple, *n,* (*things*) couple, *f;* (*pers., Mech.*) couple, *m.* ¶ *v.t,* coupler, accoupler; atteler. **couplet,** *n,* distique, *m.* **coupling,** *n,* accouplement; manchon; attelage, *m.*

coupon, *n,* coupon, *m.*

courage, *n,* courage, *m.* ~ous†, *a,* courageux.

courier, *n,* courrier, *m.*

course, *n,* cours; courant, *m;* carrière; route; direction, *f;* chenal; trajet, *m;* marche, *f;* processus; parti; stage; (*meal*) service, plat, *m;* (*Build.*) assise; couche, *f;* (*ground*) champ; terrain; parcours, *m. in due ~,* en temps & lieu. *of ~,* naturellement, bien entendu, certainement. *why, of ~l* parbleu! ¶ *v.t* & *i,* chasser, courir. **courser** (*Poet.*) *n,* coursier, *m.* **coursing,** *n,* chasse au lévrier, *f.*

court, *n,* cour, *f;* tribunal; conseil, *m;* chambre; audience, *f;* (*Ten.*) court, jeu, tennis; (*croquet*) terrain, *m.* ~ *house,* palais de justice, *m.* ~ *martial,* conseil de guerre, *m.* ~ *plaster,* taffetas d'Angleterre, *m.* ~*yard,* cour, *f;* préau, *m.* ¶ *v.t,* faire sa cour à, courtiser; (*favor*) briguer; (*disaster*) inviter.

courteous†, *a,* courtois, honnête.

courtesan, *n,* courtisane, hétaïre, *f.* **courtesy,** *n,* courtoisie, honnêteté, *f.* **courtier,** *n,* courtisan, *m;* (*pl.*) gens de cour, *m.pl.* **courtly,** *a,* courtois. **courtship,** *n,* cour, *f.*

cousin, *n,* cousin, e. *first ~,* cousin germain, *m.*

cove (*bay*) *n,* anse, *f,* accul, *m.*

covenant, *n,* convention, *f,* pacte, *m.* ¶ *v.i,* s'engager.

Coventry (**to send to**) (*fig.*), mettre en quarantaine.

cover, *n,* couverture; enveloppe, *f;* tapis; pli, *m;* gaine, *f;* couvercle; capot, *m;* chape, *f,* chapeau; plateau, *m;* chemise, *f;* étui; fourreau; couvert; abri; fourré, *m,* remise, *f;* masque, voile, *m;* provision, marge, *f,* acompte, *m;* prévision, *f.* ¶ *v.t,* couvrir, recouvrir, envelopper, revêtir, tapisser; masquer; parcourir. ~*ed walk,* allée en berceau, *f.* ~*ing,* *n,* couverture, *f;* vêtement, *m.* ~*let,* *n,* couverture pour berceau, *f.*

covert, *a,* voilé, indirect.

covet, *v.t,* convoiter, reluquer. ~*ous,* *a,* convoiteux, cupide. ~*ousness,* *n,* convoitise, *f.*

covey, *n,* compagnie, *f.*

cow, *n,* vache, *f;* (*att., of elephants, etc.*) femelle. ~ *bell,* clarine, sonnaille, *f.* ~*herd,* vacher, ère. ~ *hide,* [peau de] vache, *f,* cuir de v., *m.* ~ *shed,* étable à vaches, vacherie, *f.* ~*lick* (*hair*), épi, *m.* ~*pox,* vaccine, *f.* ¶ *v.t,* intimider.

coward, *n,* poltron, ne, lâche,

couard, *m.* ~ice, *n,* poltronnerie, lâcheté, couardise, *f.* ~ly, *a,* poltron, lâche, couard.

cower, *v.i,* se blottir, se tapir, s'accroupir.

cowl, *n,* capuchon, *m,* capote, *f,* champignon, *m,* mitre, *f.*

cowrie, *n,* porcelaine, *f.*

cowslip, *n,* coucou, *m,* primevère des champs, *f.*

coxcomb, *n,* fat, freluquet, *m.*

coxswain (*abb.* cox) *n,* barreur, patron, *m.*

coy, *a,* réservé, farouche. ~ness, *n,* réserve, *f.*

cozen, *v.t,* duper; séduire.

cozy, *a,* confortable; douillet.

crab, *n,* (*Crust.*) crabe, cancre; (*hoisting*) treuil, *m.* ~ [*apple*], pomme sauvage, *f.* ~ [*apple tree*], pommier sauvage, *m.* ~ [*louse*], morpion, *m.* **crabbed,** *a,* acariâtre, revêche, grincheux, bourru. ~ *handwriting*, écriture de pattes de mouche, *f.*

crack, *n,* fente, fissure, crevasse, fêlure; craquelure, *f;* (*noise*) craquement; claquement; coup sec, crac, *m,* cric crac, flic flac. ~ *of doom*, dernier jugement, *m.* ¶ *v.t,* fendre; fêler; fendiller; gercer; crever; (*nuts*) casser; (*open a bottle*) décoiffer. ~ed (*daft*) *p.a,* timbré, toqué.

cracker, *n,* (*food*) craquelin, (*petroleum*) craqueur, *m.*

crackle, *v.i,* craque[te]r, crépiter; pétiller. **crackling,** *n,* friton, gratton, *m.*

Cracow, *n,* Cracovie, *f.*

cradle, *n,* berceau, moïse; (*Surg.*) arceau, cerceau, *m.* ¶ *v.t,* bercer.

craft, *n,* adresse, *f;* artifice, *m;* astuce, *f;* métier, *m;* (*Naut.*) embarcation, allège, *f.* **craftily,** *ad,* artificieusement. **craftsman,** *n,* homme de métier, artisan, *m.* ~ship, *n,* travail d'artisan, *m.* **crafty,** *a,* artificieux, rusé, futé, cauteleux, retors.

crag, *n,* rocher, *m.* **craggy,** *a,* anfractueux.

cram, *v.t,* bonder, bourrer, fourrer; farcir; (*poultry*) gaver; (*exam*) potasser, gaver, chauffer.

cramp, *n,* crampe, colique, *f.* ¶ *v.t,* resserrer, entraver, gêner; cramponner.

cranberry, *n,* canneberge, *f.*

crane, *n,* (*bird & hoist*) grue, *f.* ¶ *v.t,* tendre le cou.

cranium, *n,* crâne, *m.*

crank, *n,* (*Mach.*) manivelle, *f,* coude; (*pers.*) excentrique, original, *m,* maniaque, *m,f;* (*whim*) marotte, *f.* ~ *gear* (cycle), pédalier, *m.* ~ *pin,* bouton de manivelle, *m.* ~ *shaft,* arbre à manivelle, arbre coudé, vilebrequin, *m.* ~ *tool,* [outil à] crochet, *m.* ¶ *v.t,* couder.

cranny, *n,* fente, crevasse, *f.*

crash, *n,* fracas, écrasement; krach, *m,* débâcle, chute, *f.* ¶ *i,* patatras! ¶ *v.i,* s'abattre; tomber, s'écraser (*sur le sol, la chaussée, etc.*).

crass, *a,* crasse (*a.f.*), grossier.

crate, *n,* caisse à claire-voie, harasse, *f.*

crater, *n,* cratère; (*mine, Mil.*) entonnoir, *m.*

crave, *v.t,* implorer. ~ *for,* appéter.

craven, *a,* poltron, lâche.

craving, *n,* ardent désir, *m,* soif, appétence, fringale, *f.*

crawl, *n,* (*Swim.*) crawl, *m.* ¶ *v.i,* ramper, se traîner.

crayfish, *n,* (*river*) écrevisse; (*sea*) langouste, *f.*

crayon, *n,* [crayon] pastel, *m.*

craze, *n,* folie, fureur, toquade, marotte, manie, *f.* **crazy,** *a,* délabré; dément, détraqué, toqué, piqué. *to drive someone* ~, rompre la cervelle à quelqu'un.

creak, *v.i,* grincer, crier, craquer. ¶ *n,* grincement, crissement, *m.*

cream, *n,* crème, *f;* (*of story*) bon, *m.* ¶ *v.t,* écrémer, battre en crème. ~ *cheese,* fromage blanc, *m.* ~-colored, couleur crème. ~ *jug,* crémier, *m.* ~ery, *n,* crémerie, *f.* ~y, *a,* crémeux.

crease, *n,* pli, faux pli, godet, *m.* ¶ *v.t,* plisser; (*v.i.*) [se] plisser. ~less, *a,* infroissable.

create, *v.t,* créer; faire, produire; provoquer. **creation,** *n,* création, *f.* **creative,** *a,* créateur. **creator,** tress, *n,* créateur, trice. **creature,** *n,* créature, *f,* être; animal, *m,* bête, *f.* ~ *comforts,* aises, *f.pl.*

credence, *n,* créance, *f.* **credentials,** *n.pl,* lettres de créance; l—s d'introduction, *f.pl;* pouvoirs, *m.pl.* **credibility,** *n,* crédibilité, *f.* **credible,** *a,* croyable; digne de foi. **credibly,** *ad,* de bonne source.

credit, *n,* croyance, foi, créance, consistance, *f;* honneur; crédit, avoir, *m. do ~ to,* honorer. *~ balance,* solde créditeur, *m.* ¶ *v.t,* ajouter foi à; créditer, bonifier. **~able,** *a,* reluisant. **~s,** *n. (cinema)* générique, *m.* **~or,** *n,* créancier, ère, créditeur, *m.*

credo, *n,* credo, symbole, *m.*

credulity, *n,* crédulité, bonhomie, *f.* **credulous,** *a,* crédule.

creed, *n,* credo, symbole; culte, *m,* croyance, *f.*

creek, *n,* crique, *f.*

creel, *n,* panier à pêche, *m.*

creep, *v.i.ir,* ramper; cheminer. *it makes one's flesh ~,* cela fait venir la chair de poule. **~er,** *n,* plante grimpante, *f; (grapnel)* grappin, *m.* **~ing paralysis,** paralysie progressive, *f.* '

cremate, *v.t,* incinérer. **cremation,** *n,* crémation, incinération, *f.* **crematorium,** *n,* four crématoire, *m.*

Cremona, *n,* Crémone, *f.*

creole, *n. & a,* créole, *m.f. & a.*

creosote, *n,* créosote, *f.*

crepitate, *v.i,* crépiter.

crescendo, *ad. & n,* crescendo, *ad. & m.*

crescent, *n,* croissant, *m; (of buildings)* demilune, *f.*

cresset, *n,* torchère, *f.*

crest, *n,* crête; huppe, *f;* cimier, *m.* **~fallen,** penaud. **~ed,** *a,* crêté, huppé, aigretté; *(sea)* moutonneuse.

Crete, *n,* la Crète.

cretonne, *n,* cretonne, *f.*

crevasse, *n,* crevasse [glaciaire] *f.* **crevice,** *n,* crevasse, fente, lézarde, *f.*

crew, *n, (ship)* équipage, *m; (boat)* équipe, *f; (set, gang)* bande, *f.*

crewel stitch *(Emb.),* point de tige, point coulé, *m.*

crib, *n,* crèche, mangeoire; cabane; couchette, *f;* larcin, *m.* ¶ *v.t,* chiper.

cribbage, *n,* cribbage, *m.*

crick *(in neck) n,* torticolis, *m.*

cricket, *n,* grillon, criquet, cricri; *(game)* cricket, *m.*

crier, *n,* crieur, *m.*

crime, *n,* crime, forfait, *m.*

Crimea (the), la Crimée.

criminal†, *a,* criminel. *~ law,* droit pénal, *m.* ¶ *n,* criminel, le. **criminate,** *v.t,* incriminer, charger.

crimp, *v.t,* friser, crêper; fraiser, gaufrer.

crimson, *a,* cramoisi, pourpre. *~ clover,* trèfle incarnat, farouch[e] *m.* ¶ *n,* cramoisi, *m,* pourpre, *f.* ¶ *v.t,* empourprer.

cringe, *v.i,* faire le chien couchant. **cringing,** *p.a,* servile.

crinkle, *n,* plissement, *m.* ¶ *v.t. & i,* plisser.

cripple, *n,* impotent, e, estropié, e. ¶ *v.t,* estropier; *(fig.)* paralyser. **~d,** *a,* impotent, estropié, éclopé, perclus; *(ship)* incommodé.

crisis, *n,* crise, *f.*

crisp, *a,* cassant, croquant; *(air)* vivifiant, vif; *(hair)* frisé; *(style)* concis. ¶ *v.t,* crêper.

crisscross, *v.i,* s'entrecroiser.

criterion, *n,* critère, critérium, *m.*

critic, *n,* critique; censeur; frondeur, *m.* **~al,** *a,* critique; décisif. **criticism,** *n,* critique, glose, *f.* **criticizable,** *a,* critiquable. **criticize,** *v.t,* critiquer; censurer.

croak, *v.i, (raven)* croasser; *(frog)* coasser.

crochet, *n, & ~ hook,* crochet, *m.*

crockery, *n,* faïence, vaisselle, *f.*

crocodile, *n,* crocodile, *m.* *~ tears,* larmes de crocodile, *f.pl.*

crocus, *n,* crocus, safran, *m.*

Croesus, *n,* Crésus, *m.*

crone, *n,* vieille femme momifiée, *f.*

crony, *n,* compère, *m.*

crook, *n,* crochet, *m;* houlette, crosse, *f; (pers.)* escroc, *m.* ¶ *v.t,* recourber. **~ed,** *a,* crochu, tortu, tors; gauche; de travers; *(legs)* cagneux; *(fig.)* tortueux, oblique, indirect. **~edly,** *ad,* de travers; tortueusement. **~edness,** *n,* guingois, *m.*

crop, *n,* récolte; cueillette, *f; (bird)* jabot, *m,* poche; *f; (whip)* cravache, *f.* ¶ *v.t,* tondre, bretauder; *(ears)* essoriller, écourter. *~ up,* surgir. *~ up again,* rebondir.

croquet, *n,* croquet, *m.* *~ court,* terrain de croquet, *m.* ¶ *v.t,* croquer.

crosier, *n,* crosse, *f.*

cross, *a,* de méchante humeur. ¶ *comps:* **~bar,** **~beam,** traverse, *f.* **~belt,** bandoulière, *f;* baudrier, *m.* **~-bred,** métis, mâtiné. **~-breed,** race croisée, *f,* métis, se. **~breeding,** croisement, métissage, *m.* *(informa-*

tion) ~-checking, recoupement, _m._ ~-_country running, race,_ cross-country, _m._ ~-_examine someone,_ faire subir à quelqu'un un interrogatoire; tenir qqn sur la sellette. ~-_eyed,_ louche. ~_piece,_ entretoise, _f. to be at_ ~-_purposes,_ se contrecarrer. ~ _reference,_ référence croisée, _f._ ~_road,_ chemin de traverse, _m._ traverse, _f; (pl.)_ carrefour, _m._ ~ _section,_ coupe en travers, _f,_ profil transversal, _m._ ~-_stitch,_ point de croix, _m._ ~_word [puzzle],_ mots croisés [-énigmes], _m.pl._ ¶ _n,_ croix; _(fig.)_ croix, _f,_ calvaire; croisement; croisillon, _m; (on a letter t)_ barre, _f._ ¶ _v.t,_ croiser; traverser, couper, passer, franchir; _(a "t")_ barrer; contrarier, contrecarrer. ~ _oneself,_ se signer. ~ _out,_ rayer, radier, biffer, barrer.

crossing, _n,_ croisement, _m;_ traversée, _f,_ passage, _m._

crotchet, _n, (Mus.)_ noire, _f; (whim)_ boutade, lubie, quinte, _f._ ~ _rest (Mus.),_ soupir, _m._ ~**y,** _a,_ quinteux.

crouch, _v.i,_ se tapir, se blottir, s'accroupir.

croup _(Med.) n,_ croup, _m._

croup _(rump) n,_ croupe, _f._

crow, _n,_ corbeau, _m,_ corneille, _f; (cock's)_ chant, _m._ ~-_[bar],_ pince [à levier] _f._ ~-_foot (Bot.),_ renoncule, _f._ ~'_s-foot (wrinkle),_ patte-d'oie, _f._ ~'_s-nest (Naut.),_ nid de pie, _m;_ 'hune de vigie, _f. as the_ ~ _flies,_ à vol d'oiseau. ¶ _v.i.ir,_ chanter. ~ _over,_ chanter victoire sur.

crowd, _n,_ foule, presse, _f,_ rassemblement, monde, _m,_ cohue, _f._ ~ _round,_ se presser autour de, assiéger. ~**ed,** _p.a,_ fréquenté, comble.

crown, _n,_ couronne, _f; (head, arch)_ sommet; _(hat)_ fond, _m._ ¶ _v.t,_ couronner; _(checkers)_ damer. ~**ing,** _n,_ couronnement, _m._ ¶ _a,_ suprême.

crucial, _a,_ décisif, critique.

crucible, _n,_ creuset, pot, _m._

crucifix, _n,_ crucifix, christ, _m._ ~**ion,** _n,_ crucifiement, _m,_ crucifixion, _f._ **crucify,** _v.t,_ crucifier.

crude, _a,_ cru, brut; informe; indigeste; primitif. ~**ly,** _ad,_ crûment. ~**ness,** _n,_ crudité, _f._

cruel†, _a,_ cruel. ~**ty,** _n,_ cruauté, _f; (in law)_ sévices, _m.pl._

cruet, _n,_ ménagère, _f,_ huilier, _m; (Eccl.)_ burette, _f._

cruise, _n,_ croisière; campagne, _f._ ¶ _v.i,_ croiser; _(for sexual partner)_ draguer. **cruiser,** _n,_ croiseur, _m._ **cruising:** ~ _fleet &_ ~ _ground,_ croisière, _f._ ~ _taxicab,_ taxi en maraude, _m._

crumb, _n,_ miette; _(opp. crust)_ mie, _f._ ¶ _(Cook.) v.t,_ paner.

crumble, _v.t,_ émietter; _(v.i.)_ s'émietter; crouler, tomber. **crumbly,** _a,_ friable.

crumple, _v.t,_ chiffonner; _(v.i.)_ se c. ~ _up,_ s'écraser.

crunch, _v.t. & i,_ croquer, craquer. ¶ _i,_ crocl

crupper, _n,_ croupe; _(harness)_ croupière, _f._

crusade, _n,_ croisade, _f._ ¶ _v.i,_ entreprendre une croisade. **crusader,** _n,_ croisé, _m._

crush, _(crowd) n,_ cohue, _f._ ¶ _v.t,_ écraser; froisser; broyer, concasser. ~**er,** _n,_ broyeur, concasseur, _m._

crust, _n,_ croûte; croustille; _(earth's)_ écorce, croûte, _f;_ morceau de pain, _m._

crustacean, _a. & n,_ crustacé, _a._ & _m._

crusted, _a,_ encroûté. **crusty,** _a, (bread)_ croustillant; _(fig.)_ irritable, bourru. **crust[y]** _end_ (bread), croûton, grignon, _m._

crutch, _n,_ béquille, _f._

crux, _n,_ pivot, nœud, _m._

cry, _n,_ cri, _m._ ~ _baby,_ pleurnicheur, _m. to be in full_ ~, aboyer. ¶ _v.i,_ crier, s'écrier; pleurer; _(v.t.)_ crier, chanter; tambouriner. ~ _out,_ crier; s'écrier. ¶ _n,_ cri[s] _m.[pl.]._

crypt, _n,_ crypte, _f._

crystal, _n,_ cristal, _m._ ¶ _a,_ de cristal. ~ _gazing,_ cristallomancie, _f._ ~ _[glass],_ cristal, _m._ ~ _glass[ware] making or works,_ cristallerie, _f._ **crystalline,** _a,_ cristallin. ~ _lens (eye),_ cristallin, _m._ **crystalize,** _v.t,_ cristalliser; _(v.i.)_ [se] cristalliser. _crystalized fruits,_ fruits candis, _m.pl._

cub, _n,_ petit, _m._

Cuban, _a,_ cubain. ¶ _n,_ Cubain, e.

cube, _n,_ cube, _m._ ~ _root,_ racine cubique, _f._ cube, _f._ ~ _sugar,_ sucre en morceaux, s. cassé, _m._ ¶ _v.t,_ cuber. **cubic,** _a,_ cube; cubique. ~ _foot,_ pied cube, _m._ = 0.028317 cubic meter. ~ _inch,_

pouce cube, *m.* = 16.387 cubic centimeters. ~ *yard,* yard cube, *m.* = 0.764553 cubic meter. ~**al,** *a,* cubique.
cubicle, *n,* alcôve de dortoir, *f.*
cubism, *n,* cubisme, *m.* **cubist,** *n,* cubiste, *m.f.*
cuckoo, *n,* coucou, *m.* ~ *clock,* pendule à coucou, *f;* coucou, *m.*
cucumber, *n,* concombre, *m.*
cud, *n,* aliment ruminé, *m.*
cuddle, *v.t,* câliner, pouponner, serrer dans ses bras. ~ *up,* se pelotonner, se blottir.
cudgel, *n,* bâton, gourdin, *m,* trique, *f.* ¶ *v.t,* bâtonner; (*one's brains*) torturer. **cudgeling,** *n,* bastonnade, *f.*
cue, *n,* (*Theat.*) réplique; (*Bil.*) queue, *f.*
cuff, *n,* (*blow*) calotte, taloche, *f;* (*shirt*) manchette, *f;* poignet; (*coat*) parement, *m.* ~ *links,* boutons de manchettes, *m.pl.* ¶ *v.t,* calotter.
cuirass, *n,* cuirasse, *f.* ~**ier,** *n,* cuirassier, *m.*
culinary, *a,* culinaire.
cull, *v.t,* cueillir; recueillir.
culminate, *v.i,* atteindre sa plus grande hauteur; aboutir; (*Astr.*) culminer. **culminating,** *a,* culminant.
culpability, *n,* culpabilité, *f.* **culpable,** *a,* coupable. **culprit,** *n,* coupable, *m.f.*
cultivate, *v.t,* cultiver. **cultivation,** *n,* culture, *f.* **cultivator,** *n,* cultivateur, trice. **culture,** *n,* culture, *f.* ~**d** (*pers., pearl*) *p.a,* de culture.
culvert, *n,* ponceau, *m.*
cumber, *v.t,* embarrasser, encombrer. ~**some, cumbrous,** *a,* embarrassant, encombrant.
cumulative, *a,* cumulatif.
cumulus, *n,* cumulus, *m.*
cuneiform, *a,* cunéiforme.
cunning, *a,* rusé, artificieux; habile. ¶ *n,* finesse, finasserie, ruse, *f.*
cup, *n,* tasse; coupe; timbale, *f;* calice, bol, *m.* ~ *bearer,* échanson, *m.* ~**board,** armoire, *f;* buffet; (*wall*) placard, *m.* ¶ (*Surg.*) *v.t,* ventouser.
cupel, *n,* coupelle, *f.* ¶ *v.t,* coupeller.
Cupid, *n,* Cupidon, *m.*
cupidity, *n,* cupidité, *f.*
cupola, *n,* coupole, *f.*
cupping glass, ventouse, *f.*

cur, *n.* roquet, *m.*
curable, *a,* curable.
curacy, *n,* vicariat, *m.* **curate,** *n,* vicaire, *m.*
curative, *a,* curatif, médicamenteux.
curator, *n,* conservateur, trice.
curb, *n,* (*harness*) gourmette; (*street*) bordure, margelle, *f;* (*fig.*) bride, *f,* frein, *m.* ¶ *v.t,* (*horse*) gourmer; (*street*) border; (*fig.*) brider, modérer.
curd[s], *n.[pl.],* caillé, *m,* caillebotte, *f.* **curdle,** *v.t,* cailler; (*fig.*) glacer.
cure, *n,* guérison; cure, *f;* remède, *m;* (*souls*) charge, *f.* ¶ *v.t,* guérir; remédier à; (*salt*) saler; (*smoke*) fumer; (*herrings*) caquer.
curfew, *n,* couvre-feu, *m.*
curiosity & curio, *n,* curiosité, rareté, *f,* bibelot, *m.* **curio cabinet,** vitrine, table vitrée, *f.* **curious†,** *a,* curieux. **the ~ part** or **thing,** le curieux. ~ **person,** curieux, euse.
curl, *n,* boucle, *f,* frison, *m.* (*pl.*) frisure; spirale, *f.* ¶ *v.t,* friser, boucler, bichonner; (*lip*) retrousser. ~ *up,* se mettre en boule, se pelotonner. **curler** (*hair*) *n,* épingle [à friser] *f;* (*leather*) bigoudi [à friser] *m.*
curlew, *n,* courlis, courlieu, *m.*
curliness, *n,* frisure, *f.* **curling,** *n,* frisure, *f.* ~ *tongs,* fer à friser, *m.* **curly,** *a,* frisé, bouclé.
curmudgeon, *n,* bourru; ladre, pingre, *m.*
currant, *n,* (*red, white*) groseille [à grappes] *f;* (*black*) cassis; (*dried*) raisin de Corinthe, *m.* ~ *bush,* groseillier [à grappes]; cassis, *m.*
currency, *n,* cours, *m,* circulation; monnaie, *f.* [*foreign*] ~, devise [étrangère], monnaie étrangère, *f.* **current,** *a,* courant, en cours; de mise. ~ *events,* actualités, *f.pl.* ~ *liabilities,* exigibilités, *f.pl.* ¶ *n,* courant, *m.* peak ~, courant de pointe, *m.*
curriculum, *n,* programme d'études, *m.*
curry (*Cook.*) *n,* cari, kari, *m.* ¶ *v.t,* (*leather*) corroyer; (*horse*) étriller. ~ *favor with,* se faufiler dans les bonnes grâces de. ~**comb,** étrille, *f.* ~**ing,** *n,* corroi; étrillage, *m.*

curse, n, malédiction, imprécation, f; fléau, m. ¶ v.t, maudire; affliger; (v.i.) blasphémer, jurer. **cursed,** a, maudit.

cursor, n, (computers) curseur, m.

cursory, a, hatif, rapide.

curt, a, bref, sec, cassant, brusque.

curtail, v.t, raccourcir, écourter; (output) contingenter.

curtain, n, rideau; brise-bise, m; toile, f; tableau! ~ **holder,** embrasse, f. ~ **net,** vitrage, m. ~ **raiser,** lever de rideau, m. ~ **rod,** tringle de rideau; tringle de brise-bise, f.

curtly, ad, brusquement.

curtsy, n, révérence, f.

curvature, n, courbure, f. ~ **of the spine,** déviation de la colonne vertébrale, f.

curve, n, courbe, f. ¶ v.t, courber, cintrer. **curvet,** n, courbette, f. ¶ v.i, faire des courbettes. **curvilinear,** a, curviligne.

cushion, n, coussin; coussinet; bourrelet; carreau, m; (Bil.) bande, f. ¶ v.t, amortir. ~ **cover,** dessus de coussin, m, taie de coussin, f.

custard, n, flan, m; crème, f.

custodian, n, gardien, ne. **custody,** n, garde, charge; arrestation, f.

custom, n, usage, m, coutume; pratique, f; achalandage, m. **~ary,** a, usuel, d'usage, ordinaire; coutumier. **~er,** n, client, e; chaland, e; (at café) consommateur, m; (at bank) déposant, e.

customization, adaptation à l'usager, f.

customs, n.pl, douane[s] f.[pl.]. ~ **or** custom house, douane, f. ~ [duty], douane, f, droit[s] de douane, m.[pl.]. ~ **agent,** agent en douane, m. ~ **officer,** agent de la douane, douanier, m.

cut, n, coupure, coupe, entaille, saignée; fouille, f, déblai, m; taille, passe; taillade, balafre, f; coup, m, atteinte, f, affront; morceau, m, tranche; réduction, compression, f; dégrèvement, m; vignette; gravure, f. short~, raccourci, m. ¶ v.t.ir, couper; tailler; entailler; entamer; découper; trancher; rogner; fendre; cingler; (teeth) faire; graver. have one's hair ~, se faire couper les che-veux. ~ a class, sécher une classe. ~ & dried **or** dry, tout taillé, tout fait. ~ **back** (Hort.) receper. ~ [crystal] **glass,** cristal taillé, m. ~ **down,** abattre; moissonner; rogner; sabrer. ~ **off,** couper; retrancher; amputer; intercepter; isoler; moissonner. ~ **out,** découper, couper, tailler; retrancher; supprimer. ~ **short,** écourter; trancher. **~throat,** coupe-jarret, escarpe, m. ~ **up,** découper, dépecer; débiter; tronçonner.

cutaneous, a, cutané.

cute, a, attirant; fin, rusé.

cuticle, n, cuticule, f.

cutlass, n, sabre, m.

cutler, n, coutelier, ère. **cutlery,** n, coutellerie, f.

cutlet, n, côtelette, f.

cutter, n, (clothes, etc.) coupeur, euse; (gems, stone, files) tailleur; (price) gâte-métier, m; (tool) lame, f, couteau, m; fraise; molette, f; (boat) cotre; canot, m. ~ **wheel,** molette, f. **cutting,** p.a, coupant, tranchant; piquant, caustique, acéré. ~ **board,** tranchoir, m. ~ **edge,** tranchant, coupant, fil, m. ¶ n, taille; coupe; (teeth) pousse; (newspaper) coupure; tranchée, f, déblai, m; percée, f; copeau, m; rognure, f; (snip of cloth) chanteau, m, retaille; (plant) bouture, f. ~ **out** (clothes), coupe, f.

cuttle fish, seiche, f.

cutwater, n, (bow) taille-mer; (bridge) bec, m.

cyanide, n, cyanure, m.

cyclamen, n, cyclamen, m.

cycle, n, cycle, m; bicyclette, f; vélocipède, m. ~ **track,** vélodrome, m. ¶ v.i, aller à bicyclette, pédaler. **cycling,** n, cyclisme, m. **cyclist,** n, [bi]cycliste, m,f.

cyclone, n, cyclone, m.

cygnet, n, jeune cygne, m.

cylinder, n, cylindre; corps; barillet; fourreau, m. **cylindrical,** a, cylindrique.

cymbals, n.pl, cymbales, f.pl.

cynic, n, cynique, m. ¶~ **& cynical†,** a, cynique. **cynicism,** n, cynisme, m.

cynosure (fig.) n, pointe de mire, m.

cypress, n, cyprès. m.

Cyprus, n, Chypre, f.

cyst (*Med.*) *n*, kyste, *m*.
Czech, *a.* & (*language*) *n*, tchèque, *a.* & *m.* ¶ (*pers.*) *n*, Tchèque, *m,f.* **Czechoslovak,** *n*,
Tchécoslovaque, *m,f.* **Czechoslovakia,** *n*, Tchécoslovaquie, *f.*

D

D (*Mus.*) *letter*, ré, *m*.
dab, *n*, coup de tampon, d'éponge,
de mouchoir, etc; petit tas mou,
m; (*fish*) limande, *f.* ¶ *v.t*, tamponner; éponger. **dabber,** *n*,
tampon, *m*.
dabble, *v.i*, barboter, patauger.
~ *on the stock exchange*, boursicoter.
dace, *n*, vandoise, vaudoise, *f*,
dard, *m*.
dachshund, *n*, basset allemand,
m.
dad[dy], *n*, papa, *m*.
daddy longlegs, *n*, tipule, *f*.
dado, *n*, lambris d'appui, *m*.
daffodil, *n*, narcisse des prés, *m*.
daft, *a*, timbré.
dagger, *n*, poignard, *m*; (*Typ.*)
croix, *f. at* ~*s drawn*, à couteaux
tirés.
dahlia, *n*, dahlia, *m*.
daily, *a*, quotidien, journalier. ~
[*paper*], [journal] quotidien, *m*.
¶ *ad*, journellement, quotidiennement.
dainties, *n.pl*, friandises, chatteries, douceurs, *f.pl.* **daintily,** *ad*,
délicatement. **daintiness,** *n*, délicatesse, chatterie, *f.* **dainty,** *a*,
friand, délicat; mignon.
dairy, *n*, laiterie, crémerie, *f.* ~
[*farm*], vacherie, *f.* ~*maid*, fille
de ferme, *f.* ~*man*, laitier, crémier, *m*.
dais, *n*, estrade, *f*.
daisy, *n*, marguerite, pâquerette,
f.
dale, *n*, vallon, val, *m*, combe, *f*.
dally, *v.i*, s'amuser, batifoler;
tarder.
Dalmatia, *n*, la Dalmatie. **Dalmatian,** *a*, dalmate.
dam, *n*, barrage, *m*, digue; (*animal*) mère, *f.* ¶ *v.t*, barrer, endiguer.
damage, *n*, dommage, dégât, *m*,
avarie, *f*, mal, *m*; (*pl., law*)
dommages-intérêts, *m.pl.* ¶ *v.t*,
endommager, avarier. ~ *wilfully*,
saboter.
damascene, *v.t*, damasquiner.

Damascus, *n*, Damas, *m.* **damask,** *n*, damas, *m*.
damn, *v.t*, damner; (*a play*)
tomber. ~**able,** *a*, damnable,
maudit. ~**ation,** *n*, damnation,
f. ~**ed,** *a*, damné, maudit; sacré.
the ~, les damnés. ~**ing,** *p.a*,
accablant, écrasant.
damp, *a*, humide; moite. ~ *mark*
(*in books*), tache d'humidité,
mouillure, *f.* ¶ *n*, humidité, *f.*
¶ *v.t*, humecter, mouiller, tremper; (*fig.*) refroidir; (*shock*)
amortir. ~**er,** *n*, (*piano*) étouffoir; (*furnace*) registre; (*radio*)
amortisseur, *m*, sourdine, *f*;
(*stamps, labels*) mouilloir, *m*.
~**ness,** *n*, humidité, *f*.
damsel, *n*, demoiselle, jeune fille,
f.
damson, *n*, damas, *m*. ~ [*tree*],
prunier de damas, *m*.
dance, *n*, danse, *f*; bal; pas, *m*.
~ *hall*, salle de bal, *f*, bal, *m*. *D*~
of Death, *D*~ *Macabre*, Danse
macabre. ¶ *v.i.* & *t*, danser;
faire danser. ~ *attendance* (*on*),
s'empresser (auprès de); faire le
pied de grue. **dancer,** *n*, danseur,
euse. **dancing,** *n*, la danse. ~
master, maître de danse, *m*.
dandelion, *n*, pissenlit, *m*.
dandle, *v.t*, bercer, dodeliner,
pouponner.
dandruff, *n*, pellicules, *f.pl*.
dandy, *n*, dandy, gandin, élégant,
m.
Dane, *n*, Danois, e.
danger, *n*, danger, *m. this patient is out of* ~, ce malade est
hors d'affaire. ~**ous†,** *a*, dangereux.
dangle, *v.i*, pendiller, brimballer;
(*v.t.*) brandiller.
Danish, *a*, danois. ¶ (*language*)
n, le danois.
dank, *a*, méphitique.
dapper, *a*, tiré à quatre épingles;
bellot.
dappled, *p.a*, pommelé.
dare, *v.i.i.ir*, oser, s'aviser; (*v.t.ir*)
défier, braver, oser. ¶ *i*, *I* ~ *you!*
chiche! ~*devil*, casse-cou, *m*.
daring†, *a*, audacieux, osé, hardi.
¶ *n*, audace, hardiesse, *f*.
dark, *a*, obscur; sombre; noir;
ténébreux; foncé; brun; sourd.
the ~ *ages*, les siècles d'ignorance, *m.pl.* ~ *horse*, outsider,
m. ~ *man*, ~ *boy*, brunet, *m*.
~ *room* (*Phot.*), chambre noire,
f. ~ *woman*, ~ *girl*, brunette, *f*.

¶*n*, obscurité, nuit, *f*, ténèbres, *f.pl. after ~*, à [la] nuit close. *in the ~* (*fig.*), à l'aveuglette. **~en**, *v.t*, obscurcir; assombrir, embrumer, rembrunir. **~ish**, *a*, noirâtre. **~ly**, *ad*, obscurément; sourdement. **~ness**, *n*, obscurité, nuit, *f*, ténèbres, *f.pl*; teinte foncée, *f*.

darling, *a*, chéri, bien-aimé, favori. ¶*n*, chéri, e, bien-aimé, e, bijou, *m*, mignon, ne, câlin, e, chou[chou]; coco, *m*, cocotte, *f*, Benjamin, *m*; favori, ite, coqueluche, *f*.

darn, *n*, reprise, *f*. ¶*v.t*, repriser. **~ing**, *n*, reprisage, *m*, reprise, *f*. ~ *needle*, aiguille à repriser, *f*.

dart, *n*, élan; dard, trait, *m*; fléchette, *f*; (*pl.*) jeu de fléchettes, *m*. ¶*v.t*, darder, lancer; (*v.i.*) s'élancer.

dash, *n*, élan, *m*, fougue, *f*, panache, entrain; grain, tantinet, filet, soupçon; (*Teleg.*) trait; (*Typ.*) tiret, *m*. *to make a ~ at*, *for*, s'élancer sur, vers. ~ *board*, tableau de bord, *m*. ¶*v.t*, heurter, jeter; briser, abattre; confondre. **~ing**, *a*, fougueux; pimpant.

dastard, *n*, lâche, *m*. **~ly**, *a*, lâche.

data, *n.pl*, données, *f.pl*. ~ *bank*, banque de données, *f*. ~ *communication*, téléinformatique, *f*. ~ *processing*, informatique, traitement, *f*. ~ *safety*, sauvegarde des données, *f*. ~ *set*, ensemble de données, *m*. ~ *sheet*, feuille-document, *f*. *automatic ~ processing*, traitement automatique des données, *m*.

date, *n*, date, *f*; échéance; époque; (*with pers.*) rendez-vous; (*fruit*) datte, *f*. *to ~*, à ce jour. *up to ~*, à jour. ~ *palm*, dattier, *m*. ~ *stamp*, timbre à date, *m*. ¶*v.t*, dater.

dative [*case*], *n*, datif, *m*.

datum, *n*, donnée, *f*; repère, *m*.

daub, *n*, barbouillage, *m*; (*painting*) croûte, *f*; (*for walls*) bousillage, *m*. ¶*v.t*, barbouiller, peinturlurer; bousiller.

daughter, *n*, fille, *f*. ~*-in-law*, belle-fille, *f*.

daunt, *v.t*, intimider, décourager. **~less**, *a*, intrépide.

davit, *n*, bossoir, *m*.

dawdle, *v.i*, flâner, muser, lambiner.

dawn, *n*, aube, *f*, point du jour, *m*, naissance du jour, (*of day & fig.*) aurore, *f*. ¶*v.i*, poindre; naître. **~ing**, *a*, naissant.

day, *n*, jour, *m*; journée, *f*. *the ~ after*, le lendemain. *the ~ after the morrow*, le surlendemain. *the ~ after tomorrow*, après-demain. *the ~ before*, la veille. *the ~ before yesterday*, avant-hier. *one of these fine ~s*, un de ces matins. ~ *boarder*, demi-pensionnaire, *m,f*. **~break**, point du jour, *m*, pointe du j., *f*, le petit jour. **~dream**, rêve, *m*. ~ *laborer*, journalier, *m*. **~light**, jour, *m*. ~ *nursery*, crèche, garderie, pouponnière, *f*. ~ *of atonement*, jour des propitiations. ~*'s journey*, journée de chemin, *f*. ~*'s pay* & ~*'s work*, journée, *f*. ~*time*, heures de jour, *f.pl*, jour, *m*, journée, *f*.

daze, *v.t*, ahurir, hébéter; étourdir. ¶*n*, étourdissement, *m*; confusion, *f*.

dazzle, *n*, éblouissement, *m*. ¶*v.t*, éblouir, offusquer; (*v.i.*) papilloter. **dazzling**, *a*, éblouissant.

deacon, *n*, diacre, *m*.

dead, *a.* & *ad*, mort; terne; éteint (*fire*). ~ *beat*, ~ *tired*, éreinté, fourbu, moulu de fatigue, flapi. ~ *calm*, calme plat, *m*. ~ *center*, point mort, *m*. ~ *drunk*, ivre mort. ~ *end*, impasse, rue borgne, *f*. **~fall**, assommoir, *m*. ~ *heat*, épreuve nulle, course nulle, c. à égalité, *f*. ~ *letter*, (*post*) rebut, *m*; (*fig.*) lettre morte, *f*. ~*-letter office*, bureau des rebuts, *m*. ~ *lock*, impasse, *f*. ~ *loss*, perte sèche, *f*. ~ *reckoning* (*Naut.*), estime, estimation, *f*. *D~ Sea*, mer Morte, *f*. ~ *season*, morte-saison, *f*. ~ *wire*, fil hors courant, *m*. *the ~*, les morts, les trépassés, *m.pl*. **~en**, *v.t*, amortir; étourdir. **~ly**, *a*, mortel, à mort; léthifère; funeste, meurtrier. ~ *nightshade*, belladone, *f*. ~ *sins*, péchés capitaux, *m.pl*.

deaf, *a*, sourd. ~ & *dumb*, sourd-muet. **~mute**, sourd-muet, *m*, sourde-muette, *f*. **~en**, *v.t*, assourdir. **~ening**, *a*, assourdissant. **~ness**, *n*, surdité, *f*.

deal, *n*, (*cards*) donne, main, *f*; [bois de] sapin, *m*. *a great ~*,

a good ~, beaucoup, bien. ¶
v.t.ir, (*cards*) donner, faire; (*blow*) porter, assener; (*v.i.ir*) traiter; faire les cartes. ~ *out*, distribuer. ~ *with* (shop), se servir chez. ~**er**, *n*, marchand, e, débitant, e, fournisseur, *m*; (*cards*) donneur, euse. ~**ing**, *n*, affaire, opération, négociation, *f*; procédé; (*pl.*) commerce, *m*, pratique, *f*, intelligences, accointances, *f.pl.*

dean, *n*, doyen, ne. ~**ery**, *n*, (*office*) doyenné, décanat; (*house*) doyenné, *m*.

dear, *a. & ad*, cher. *my* ~, ma chère. *my* ~ *fellow*, mon cher. *O* ~/aïe!, oh là [là]! *O dear no!* ma foi non! ~**est** (*pers.*), mon chéri, ma chérie. ~**ly**, *ad*, chèrement, cher. ~**ness** (*price*) *n*, cherté, *f*.

dearth, *n*, disette, *f*.

death, *n*, mort, *f*; décès, trépas, *m*; (*pl., obituary*) nécrologie, *f*. ~**bed**, lit de mort, *m*. ~ *blow*, coup mortel, *m*. ~ *certificate*, extrait mortuaire, *m*. ~ *knell*, glas funèbre, *m*. ~ *rate*, mortalité, *f*, taux de la m., *m*. ~ *trap*, casse-cou, *m*. ~ *warrant*, ordre d'exécution; (*fig.*) arrêt de mort, *m*. ~*watch* [*beetle*], horloge de la mort, vrillette, *f*. ~**less**, *a*, immortel.

debar, *v.t*, exclure, priver. ~ *by time* (*law*), forclore. ~**ment by time**, forclusion, *f*.

debase, *v.t*, avilir; altérer, falsifier.

debatable, *a*, discutable, contestable, en litige. **debate**, *n*, débat, *m*, discussion, *f*. ¶ *v.t*, débattre, discuter, agiter.

debauch, *v.t*, débaucher. ~**ee**, *n*, débauché, e. ~[**ery**], *n*, débauche, crapule, *f*.

debenture, *n*, obligation, *f*. ~ *holder*, obligataire, *m,f*.

debilitate, *v.t*, débiliter, déprimer. **debility**, *n*, débilité, *f*.

debit, *n*, débit, doit, *m*. ¶ *v.t*, débiter. **debt** [**due by the trader**] *n*, dette [passive] *f*. **debt** [**due to the trader**] *n*, créance, dette [active] *f*. *debt collector*, agent de recouvrements, *m*. *in debt*, endetté. *involve in debt*, endetter. *run into debt*, s'endetter. **debtor**, *n*, débiteur, trice; redevable, *m,f*; obligé, e. ~ [*side*], débit, doit, *m*.

debug, *v.t*, (*computers*) épurer.

decade, *n*, décade, decennie, *f*.

decadence, *n*, décadence, *f*. **decadent**, *a*, décadent.

decaffeinate, *v.t*, décaféiner. ~**d**, *a*, décaféiné.

decagon, *n*, décagone, *m*.

decamp, *v.i*, décamper, plier bagage.

decant, *v.t*, décanter, transvaser. ~**er**, *n*, carafe, *f*, (*small*) carafon, *m*.

decapitate, *v.t*, décapiter.

decay, *n*, décadence; carie, *f*. ¶ *v.i*, dépérir; se carier.

decease, *n*, décès, trépas, *m*. ¶ *v.i*, décéder. ~**d**, *n*, défunt, e.

deceit, *n*, tromperie, *f*. ~**ful**, *a*, trompeur, mensonger. **deceive**, *v.t*, tromper, décevoir, abuser. **deceiver**, *n*, trompeur, euse.

decelerate, *v.t*, ralentir.

December, *n*, décembre, *m*.

decency, *n*, décence, *f*.

decennial, *a*, décennal.

decent, *a*, décent; honnête. ~**ly**, *ad*, décemment; honnêtement.

decentralize, *v.t*, décentraliser.

deception, *n*, tromperie, *f*. **deceptive**, *a*, trompeur, décevant, menteur.

decibel (*Phys.*) *n*, décibel, *m*.

decide, *v.t*, décider; statuer sur; (*v.i.*) [se] décider. **decided**, *a*, décidé, arrêté, marqué. ~**ly**, *ad*, décidément.

deciduous, *a*, décidu.

decimal, *a*, décimal. ~ *point*, virgule [décimale] *f*. *Note:*—The decimal point is indicated in French by a comma. ¶ *n*, décimale, *f*.

decimate, *v.t*, décimer.

decipher, *v.t*, déchiffrer.

decision, *n*, décision; délibération, *f*; parti, *m*. ~ *in one's favor*, gain de cause, *m*. **decisive†**, *a*, décisif.

deck, *n*, pont, tillac, *m*; (*of bridge*) tablier, *m*. ~ *cabin, chair*, cabine, chaise, de pont, *f*. ~ *hand*, matelot de p., *m*. ~ *tennis*, deck-tennis, *m*. *flight* ~, pont d'envol, *m*. ¶ *v.t*, parer, orner; (*ship*) ponter. ~ *with flags*, pavoiser. ~ *with flowers*, fleurir.

declaim, *v.i*, déclamer. **declamatory**, *a*, (*bad sense*) déclamatoire; (*good sense*) oratoire.

declaration, *n*, déclaration, *f*. **declare**, *v.t*, déclarer, constater; proclamer, dénoncer.

declension (*Gram.*) *n*, déclinaison, *f*.

decline, *n*, déclin; retour, *m*; maladie de langueur; baisse, *f*. ¶ *v.i.* & *t*, décliner; pencher; baisser; refuser.

declivity, *n*, déclivité, pente, *f*.

decoction, *n*, décoction, *f*.

decode, *v.t*, déchiffrer.

decompose, *v.t*, décomposer.

decorate, *v.t*, décorer; garnir; orner. **decoration**, *n*, décoration, *f*; décor, *m*. **decorative**, *a*, décoratif. **decorator**, *n*, décorateur, *m*.

decorous†, *a*, convenable, bienséant. **decorum**, *n*, décorum, *m*.

decoy, *n*, (*bait*) leurre, *m*; (*place*) canardière, *f*; (*pers.*) mouton, *m*. ~ *bird*, appelant, *m*. ¶ *v.t*, leurrer.

decrease, *n*, décroissement, *m*, décroissance, *f*. ¶ *v.i*, décroître.

decree, *n*, décret, arrêt; jugement, *m*. ¶ *v.t*, décréter; édicter.

decrepit, *a*, décrépit, caduc. **decrepitude**, *n*, décrépitude, caducité, *f*.

decry, *v.t*, décrier.

dedicate, *v.t*, dédier, [dé]vouer, consacrer. **dedication**, *n*, consécration, dédicace, *f*; envoi, *m*.

deduce, *v.t*, déduire.

deduct, *v.t*, déduire, retrancher, défalquer, rabattre. ~**ion**, déduction, défalcation, *f*.

deed, *n*, action, *f*; acte; fait; exploit; contrat; titre, *m*.

deem, *v.t*, juger, estimer, considérer. ~**ed**, *p.p*, censé, réputé.

deep, *a*, profond; creux; (*in depth*) de (*ou* en) profondeur; (*colors*) foncé, gros; (*mourning*) grand; (*sound*) grave. ~*-sea fishing*, pêche au large, p. hauturière; (*whale & cod*) grande pêche, *f*. ~*-sea navigation* & ~*-sea voyage*, long cours, *m*. ~*-seated*, profond, foncier. ~*-water harbor*, port de toute marée, *m*. ¶ *n*, profondeur; fosse, *f*. ~**en**, *v.t*, approfondir, creuser. ~[**ly**], *ad*, profondément, avant; sensiblement, fortement.

deer, *n*, daim; cerf, *m*; (*col.*) bêtes fauves, *f.pl*, fauves, *m.pl*. ~*skin*, peau de daim, *f*. ~ *stalking*, chasse au cerf à l'affût, *f*.

deface, *v.t*, défigurer, mutiler. ~**d**, *p.a*, fruste.

defalcate, *v.i*, commettre des détournements. **defalcation**, *n*, détournement de fonds, *m*.

defamation, *n*, diffamation, *f*. **defamatory**, *a*, diffamatoire, diffamant, infamant. **defame**, *v.t*, diffamer.

default, *n*, défaut, *m*, défaillance, négligence, *f*. *in* ~ *of*, à défaut de, faute de. ¶ *v.i*, manquer. ~**er**, *n*, défaillant; délinquant, *m*.

defeat, *n*, défaite, *f*. ¶ *v.t*, défaire; frustrer.

defecate, *v.t*. & *i*, déféquer.

defect, *n*, défaut, *m*, défectuosité, *f*, vice, *m*, tare, *f*. ~**ion**, *n*, défection; apostasie, *f*. ~**ive**†, *a*, défectueux; (*Gram.*) défectif.

defense, *n*, défense, *f*. self-~, légitime défense, *f*. ~*less*, *a*, sans défense. **defend**, *v.t*, défendre. ~**ant**, *n*, défendeur, eresse. ~**er**, *n*, défenseur, *m*. **defensible**, *a*, défendable. **defensive**, *a*, défensif. ¶ *n*, défensive, *f*.

defer, *v.t*, & *i*, différer, remettre, arriérer, éloigner; (*submit*) déférer. ~**ence**, *n*, déférence, *f*, respect, *m*, ménagements, *m*. *pl*. **deferential**, *a*, déférent.

defiance, *n*, défi, *m*. **defiant**, *a*, de défi.

deficiency, *n*, défaut, *m*, insuffisance, *f*; déficit, manquant, *m*. **deficient**, *a*, défectueux; insuffisant. *to be* ~ *in*, manquer de. **deficit**, *n*, déficit, *m*, moins-value, *f*.

defile, *n*, défilé, *m*. ¶ *v.i*, défiler; (*v.t.*) souiller. ~**ment**, *n*, souillure, *f*.

definable, *a*, définissable. **define**, *v.t* définir. **definite**, *a*, défini; déterminé; précis. ~**ly**, *ad*, décidément. **definition**, *n*, définition, *f*. **definitive**†, *a*, définitif.

deflate, *v.t*, dégonfler, désenfler. **deflation**, *n*, dégonflement, *m*; (*Fin.*) déflation, *f*.

deflect, *v.t*, défléchir, détourner, dévier; (*v.i.*) dévier. **deflection**, *n*, déviation; flexion, *f*.

defloration, *n*, (*ravishment*) défloration; (*stripping of flowers*) défloraison, *f*. **deflower**, *v.t*, (*ravish*) déflorer; (*strip of flowers*) défleurir, déflorer.

deforest, *v.t*, déboiser.

deform, *v.t*, déformer, contrefaire. ~**ed**, *a*, difforme, contrefait. ~**ity**, *n*, difformité, *f*.

defraud, *v.t*, frauder, frustrer.

defray, *v.t,* défrayer.

defrost, *v.t,* dégivrer. ~*ing device,* dégivreur, *m.*

deft†, *a,* adroit. ~**ness,** *n,* adresse, *f.*

defunct, *a,* défunt. ¶ *n,* défunt, e.

defy, *v.t,* défier, braver.

degeneracy & degeneration, *n,* dégénérescence, dégénération, *f,* abâtardissement, *m.* **degenerate,** *v.i,* dégénérer, s'abâtardir. ¶ *n,* dégénéré, *m.* ¶ *a,* dégénéré.

degradation, *n,* dégradation, *f;* avilissement, *m.* **degrade,** *v.t,* dégrader; déclasser; [r]avilir.

degree, *n,* degré; point; (*Univ.*) diplôme, grade, *m.*

dehydrate, *v.t,* déshydrater.

deify, *v.t,* déifier, diviniser.

deign to (to), daigner, condescendre à.

deity, *n,* divinité, déité, *f.*

dejected, *a,* abattu, découragé. **dejection,** *n,* abattement, accablement, *m.*

delay, *n,* retard, délai, sursis, *m.* ¶ *v.t,* différer, retarder, atermoyer; (*v.i.*) tarder.

delectation, *n,* délices, *f.pl.*

delegate, *n,* délégué, e, député, *m.* ¶ *v.t,* déléguer. **delegation,** *n,* délégation, *f.*

delete, *v.t,* effacer, biffer, rayer.

deleterious, *a,* délétère.

deliberate, *a,* réfléchi; délibéré; lent. ¶ *v.i,* délibérer. ~**ly,** *ad,* délibérément. **deliberation,** *n,* délibération, *f.*

delicacy, *n,* délicatesse; friandise, chatterie, *f.* **delicate**†, *a,* délicat; fin.

delicious†, *a,* délicieux. **delight,** *n,* délice, enchantement, *m;* jouissance; volupté, *f.* ¶ *v.t,* délecter, charmer, enchanter, ravir.

delimit[ate], *v.t,* délimiter.

delineate, *v.t,* tracer; [dé]peindre. **delineation,** *n,* délinéation; peinture, *f.*

delinquency, *n,* faute; négligence, *f,* méfait, *m.* **delinquent,** *n,* délinquant, e.

deliquescence, *n,* déliquescence, *f.*

delirious, *a,* délirant. *to be* ~, délirer. **delirium,** *n,* délire, *m.*

deliver, *v.t,* délivrer; livrer; remettre; rendre; distribuer; (*Med.*) accoucher; (*ball, Ten., etc.*) lancer; (*speech, etc.*) pro-

noncer; (*pump*) refouler. *to be* ~*ed of,* accoucher de; (*fig.*) pondre. ~**ance,** *n,* délivrance, *f.* ~**er,** *n,* libérateur, trice. ~**y,** *n,* délivrance; livraison; remise; distribution; tradition, *f;* accouchement, *m;* prononciation, déclamation; diction, parole, *f,* débit; refoulement, *m.* ~ *man,* ~ *boy,* ~ *girl,* livreur, euse. ~ *truck,* voiture de livraison, *f.*

dell, *n,* vallon, *m.*

delouse, *v.t,* épouiller.

delphinium, *n,* pied-d'alouette, *m.*

delta, *n,* delta, *m.*

delude, *v.t,* tromper, abuser.

deluge, *n,* déluge, *m.* ¶ *v.t,* inonder, noyer.

delusion, *n,* illusion, *f.* **delusive**†, *a,* illusoire.

delve, *v.t,* fouir, sonder.

demagogue, *n,* démagogue, *m.*

demand, *n,* demande, *f;* débit, *m;* exigence, *f. on* ~, *sur demande,* à vue, à bureau ouvert, à guichet ouvert, à présentation. ¶ *v.t,* demander; exiger. ~**ing,** *a,* exigeant.

demarcation, *n,* démarcation, *f.*

demean oneself (to) (*behave*), se comporter; (*misbehave*) s'abaisser. **demeanor,** *n,* allure, *f,* maintien, *m.*

demented, *p.p,* dément. **dementia,** *n,* démence, *f.*

demerit, *n,* démérite, *m.*

demesne, *n,* domaine, *m.*

demigod, *n,* demi-dieu, *m.*

demijohn, *n,* dame-jeanne, *f.*

demise, *n,* mutation, *f;* décès, *m.* ¶ *v.t,* transmettre; léguer.

demisemiquaver, *n,* triple croche, *f.*

demobilize, *v.t,* démobiliser.

democracy, *n,* démocratie, *f.* **democrat,** *n,* démocrate, *m.* ~**ic,** *a,* démocratique.

demolish, *v.t,* démolir. **demolition,** *n,* démolition, *f;* (*pl.*) démolitions, *f.pl,* abattis, *m,* abats, décombres, *m.pl.*

demon, *n,* démon, *m.*

demonetize, *v.t,* démonétiser.

demoniac, *n,* démoniaque, *m,f.* ~(**al**), *a,* démoniaque.

demonstrate, *v.t,* démontrer; (*v.i.*) manifester. **demonstration,** *n,* démonstration; (*political, etc.*) manifestation, *f.* **demonstrative,** *a,* démonstratif. **demon-**

strator, *n,* manifestant, e; (*Sch.*) démonstrateur, *m.*

demoralize, *v.t,* démoraliser.

demur, *n,* objection, *f.* ¶ *v.i,* opposer des objections; (*law*) opposer une exception.

demure, *a,* composé; (*look*) de sainte nitouche; (*woman*) qui fait la sucrée.

demurrage, *n,* surestaries, *f.pl.*

demurrer, *n,* exception péremptoire, *f.*

demy, *n,* carré, *m;* coquille, *f.*

den, *n,* antre, repaire, *m,* tanière, caverne, *f;* bouge; nid; cabinet, *m.*

denationalization, *n,* privatisation, *f.*

denature, *v.t,* dénaturer.

denial, *n,* dénégation, *f,* démenti; refus; reniement, *m.*

denizen, *n,* habitant, hôte, *m.*

Denmark, *n,* le Danemark.

denominate, *v.t,* dénommer. **denomination,** *n,* dénomination; (*sect*) communion; (*unit*) coupure, *f.* ~**al,** *a,* confessionnel. **denominator,** *n,* dénominateur, *m.*

denote, *v.t,* dénoter.

denounce, *v.t,* dénoncer.

dense†, *a,* dense, compact, épais. **density,** *n,* densité, épaisseur, *f.*

dent, *n,* bosse, *f.* ¶ *v.t,* bossuer, bosseler, cabosser.

dental, *a,* (*Anat.*) dentaire, dental; (*Gram.*) dental. ~ *surgeon,* chirurgien dentiste, *m.* ¶ (*Gram.*) *n,* dentale, *f.* **dentate,** *a,* denté. **dentist,** *n,* dentiste, *m.* ~**ry,** *n,* l'art dentaire, *m.* **dentition,** *n,* dentition, *f.* **denture,** *n,* dentier, *m. permanent* ~, dentier définitif, *m. removable* ~, d. amovible, *m.*

denude, *v.t,* dénuder, mettre à nu.

denunciation, *n,* dénonciation, *f.*

deny, *v.t,* nier, dénier, se défendre de; renier; refuser. *to* ~ *it,* nier.

deodorize, *v.t,* désodoriser, désinfecter.

depart, *v.i,* partir; s'éloigner. ~ *this life,* quitter la vie, q. ce monde, trépasser. ~**ed,** *n,* défunt, e, trépassé, e.

department, *n,* département, *m;* division, *f;* service; rayon; office, *m.* ~ *store,* grand magasin, *m.* ~**al,** *a,* départemental.

departure, *n,* départ, *m,* sortie, *f;*

(*lapse*) manquement, *m;* innovation, *f.*

depend, *v.i,* dépendre, s'appuyer, compter. ~**ant,** ~**ent,** *n,* personne à charge, *f.* ~**ence,** *n,* dépendance; confiance, *f.* ~**ency,** *n,* dépendance; (*country*) annexe, *f.* ~**ent,** *a,* dépendant. *to be* ~ *on,* être à la charge de; être tributaire de.

depict, *v.t,* dépeindre, peindre.

depilate, *v.t,* épiler. **depilatory,** *a,* dépilatoire. ¶ *n,* dépilatoire, *m.*

deplete, *v.t,* amoindrir; épuiser.

deplorable†, *a,* déplorable, lamentable. **deplore,** *v.t,* déplorer, se lamenter sur.

deploy, *v.t,* déployer. ~**ment,** *n,* déploiement, *m.*

depoliticization, *n,* dépolitisation, *f.* **depoliticize,** *v.t,* dépolitiser.

deponent (*pers.*) *n,* déposant, e.

depopulate, *v.t,* dépeupler. **depopulation,** *n,* (*action*) dépeuplement, *m;* (*state*) dépopulation, *f.*

deport, *v.t,* déporter. ~**ation,** *n,* déportation, *f.*

deportment, *n,* maintien, *m,* tenue, *f,* manières, *f.pl.*

depose, *v.t,* déposer.

deposit, *n,* dépôt, *m;* consignation, *f;* (*bottles, etc.*) consigne, *f;* versement; cautionnement, *m;* provision [de garantie] *f;* arrhes, *f.pl,* (*Geol.*) dépôt, gîte, gisement, *m. non*~ *bottle, jar,* verre, pot, perdu, *m.* ¶ *v.t,* déposer; consigner; verser; placer, mettre; fournir. ~**ary,** *n,* dépositaire, *m.f.* ~**ion,** *n,* déposition, *f;* dépôt, *m.* ~**or,** *n,* déposant, e. ~**ory,** *n,* dépôt, *m;* (*fig.*) répertoire, *m.* **depot,** *n,* dépôt, *m;* gare, *f.*

depravation & depravity, *n,* dépravation, *f.* **deprave,** *v.t,* dépraver. ~**d,** *p.a,* dépravé, taré, vicelard. ~ *person,* vicelard, e.

deprecate, *v.t,* réprouver.

depreciate, *v.t,* déprécier, avilir; amortir. **depreciation,** *n,* dépréciation, moins-value, *f,* avilissement; amortissement, *m.* **depreciatory,** *a,* péjoratif.

depredation, *n,* déprédation, *f.*

depress, *v.t,* déprimer. ~**ing,** *p.a,* décourageant; triste. ~**ion,** *n,* dépression, f; enfoncement, m; (*economic*) crise, f.

deprivation, n, privation, interdiction, f, retrait, m. **deprive**, v.t, priver, dépourvoir, sevrer; (*Eccl.*) interdire.

depth, n, profondeur; hauteur, f; fond; (*winter*) cœur, fort, m; (*color*) intensité; (*sound*) gravité, f. ~ *charge*, grenade sousmarine, f.

deputation, n, députation, délégation, f. **depute**, v.t, députer, déléguer. **deputize for**, suppléer, faire l'intérim de. **deputy**, n, député, m; délégué, e; suppléant, e, substitut, m. ~ *chairman*, vice-président, e. ~ *governor*, sousgouverneur, m.

derail, v.i, dérailler. ~**ment**, n, déraillement, m.

derange, v.t, déranger, fausser; aliéner, détraquer.

derelict, a, abandonné. ¶ n, navire abandonné, m, épave, f; (*pers.*) clochard, m. ~**ion**, n, abandon; manquement, m.

deride, v.t, se moquer de. **derision**, n, dérision, f. **derisive**, a, de dérision. **derisory**, a, dérisoire.

derivation, n, dérivation, f. **derivative**, n, dérivé, m. **derive**, v.t, tirer, retirer, puiser. to be ~d *from*, dériver de.

dermatology, n, dermatologie, f.

derogate, v.t, déroger. **derogatory** (*disparaging*) a, dénigrant.

derrick, n, grue, f, derrick, m; (*ship's*) mât de charge, m.

dervish, n, derviche, dervis, m.

descant, v.i, disserter, discourir, s'étendre.

descend, v.i. & t, descendre. ~**ed** *from*, issu de. ~**ant**, n, descendant, e. **descent**, n, descente; (*lineage*) descendance, naissance, race, f.

describe, v.t, décrire, définir, qualifier. **description**, n, description, f, libellé[s], m.[pl.]; signalement, m; qualités, f.pl, profession; espèce, f, genre, m. **descriptive**, a, descriptif; (*catalog*) raisonné.

descry, v.t, découvrir, apercevoir.

desecrate, v.t, profaner, violer.

desert, a, désert, désertique. ¶ n, désert; mérite, m. ¶ v.t. & i, déserter; abandonner, délaisser.

~**ed**, a, abandonné, désert, ~**er**, n, déserteur, m. ~**ion**, n, désertion, f; abandon, délaissement, m.

deserve, v.t, mériter. **deservedly**, ad, à juste titre. **deserving**, a, méritant; digne (*of* = de). ~ *of praise*, louable.

desiccate, v.t, dessécher. **desiccation**, n, dessèchement, m, dessiccation, f.

desideratum, n, desideratum, m.

design, n, dessein; modèle; dessin; motif, m. ¶ v.t, destiner, affecter; projeter, se proposer; dessiner. **designate**, v.t, désigner. **designation**, n, désignation, f.

designedly, ad, à dessein. **designer**, n, dessinateur, trice; auteur, m. **designing**, a, intrigant.

desirable, a, désirable, à désirer, souhaitable. **desire**, n, désir; appétit, m; envie; demande; prière, f. ¶ v.t, désirer. **desirous**, a, désireux. to be ~ *of*, désirer.

desist, v.i, se départir.

desk, n, pupitre; bureau, m; chaire, f.

desolate, a, désert; désolé. ¶ v.t, désoler. **desolation**, n, désolation, f.

despair, n, désespoir, m. to drive to ~ & ~, v.t, désespérer.

desperado, n, apache, escarpe, m. **desperate**, a, désespéré; acharné; éperdu. ~**ly**, ad, désespérément; à outrance; éperdument. **desperation**, n, désespoir; acharnement, m.

despicable, a, méprisable, lâche. **despise**, v.t, mépriser, dédaigner.

despite, n, dépit, m.

despoil, v.t, dépouiller, spolier.

despond, v.i, perdre courage, se décourager. ~**ency**, n, abattement, découragement, m. ~**ent**, a, abattu, découragé.

despot, n, despote, m. ~**ic**†, a, despotique. ~**ism**, n, despotisme, m.

dessert, n, dessert, m. ~ *fruit & nuts*, mendiants, m.pl. ~ *spoon*, cuiller à dessert, c. à entremets, f.

destination, n, destination, f. **destine**, v.t, destiner. **destiny**, n, destin, m, destinée, f.

destitute, a, dans le dénuement; dépourvu, dénué (*of* = de). the ~, les nécessiteux, m.pl. **destitution**, n, dénuement, délaissement, m, misère, f.

destroy, v.t. détruire. ~er, n, destructeur, trice; (ship) contre-torpilleur, destroyer, m. destruction, n, destruction, f; ravages, m.pl. destructive, a, destructif, destructeur. ~ person, brise-tout, m. destructor, n, incinérateur, m.

desultorily, ad, à bâtons rompus. desultory, a, décousu.

detach, v.t, détacher; isoler. ~able, a, amovible, rapporté. ~ed house, maison isolée, f. ~ment, n, détachement, m.

detail, n, détail, m. ¶ v.t, détailler; circonstancier; (Mil.) détacher.

detain, v.t, détenir, retenir, empêcher de partir; arrêter.

detect, v.t, découvrir; surprendre. ~ion, n, découverte, f. ~ive, n, détective, m. ~ story, roman policier, polar, m. ~or, n, détecteur, m.

detent, n, détente, f, chien, m. ~ion, n, détention, f; arrêt, m; (Sch.) retenue, colle, f, arrêt, m.

deter, v.t, détourner; décourager.

detergent, n, détersif, m.

deteriorate, v.i, se détériorer.

determinate, a, déterminé. determination, n, détermination; résolution, f. determine, v.t, déterminer, décider, définir, résoudre. ~d, a, déterminé, résolu.

deterrent, n, détersif, m. military ~, arme de dissuasion, f.

detest, v.t, détester, abhorrer. ~able, a, détestable.

dethrone, v.t, détrôner.

detonate, v.i, détoner; (v.t.) faire détoner. detonation, n, détonation, f. detonator, n, détonateur, pétard, m.

detour, v.i, prendre un détour. ¶ n, détour, m.

detoxicate, v.t, désintoxiquer.

detract from, rabaisser, dénigrer. detractor, n, détracteur, m.

detrain, v.i, débarquer.

detriment, n, détriment, préjudice, m. ~al, a, préjudiciable. be ~ to, préjudicier.

detritus, n, détritus, m.

deuce, n, diantre, diable; (cards, dice) deux, m.

Deuteronomy, n, Deutéronome, m.

devaluation, n, dévaluation, f.

devastate, v.t, dévaster, ravager.

devastator, n, dévastateur, trice.

develop, v.t, développer; faire valoir; (Min.) tracer. ~er (Phot.) n, révélateur, m. ~ing bath, bain de développement, bain révélateur, m. ~ment, n, développement; traçage, m.

deviate, v.i, dévier; s'écarter. deviation, n, déviation, f; écart, m.

device, n, moyen, expédient; dispositif, m; (emblem) devise, f.

devil, n, diable, démon, m. the ~l diable! ~ish†, a, diabolique, diable de, satané. ~ment, n, malice; verve endiablée; diablerie, f. ~ry, n, diablerie, f.

devious, a, détourné.

devise, v.t, combiner, inventer, imaginer; (law) léguer.

devoid, a, dépourvu, dénué.

devolve, v.i, échoir, incomber, retomber.

devote, v.t, dévouer, consacrer, dédier, vouer; livrer. devotee, n, dévot, e, fervent, e, fanatique, m.f. devotion, n, (Relig.) dévotion; piété, f; (zeal) dévouement, attachement, m. ~al, a, dévot, de dévotion, de piété.

devour, v.t, dévorer, avaler, manger.

devout†, a, dévot; sincère. ~ness, n, dévotion, f.

dew, n, rosée, f. ~drop, goutte de r., f.

dewlap, n, fanon, m.

dewy, a, couvert de rosée.

dexterity, n, dextérité, adresse, f. dextrous†, dexterous†, a, adroit.

dextrin, n, dextrine, f.

diabetes, n, diabète, m.

diabolic(al)†, a, diabolique.

diacritical, a, diacritique.

diadem, n, diadème, m.

diaeresis, n, tréma, m.

diagnose, v.t, diagnostiquer. diagnosis, n, diagnostic, m.

diagonal†, a, diagonal. ¶ n, diagonale, f.

diagram, n, diagramme; graphique; abaque; schéma, m; épure, f.

dial, n, (plate) cadran; (calculating mach.) viseur; (Teleph.) disque [d'appel] m; (compass) boussole, f. ¶ v.t, composer un numéro.

dialect, n, dialecte, parler, idiome, patois, m.

dialectics, n, dialectique, f.

dialogue, n, dialogue, m.

diameter, *n,* diamètre, *m.* **diametric†,** *a,* diamétral.

diamond, *n,* diamant; (*Geom.*) losange, rhombe; (*pl., cards*) carreau, *m.* baseball ~, terrain de base-ball, *m.* ~ *wedding,* noces de diamant, *f.pl.*

diaper, *n,* étoffe diaprée *f;* linge ouvré, *m;* (*infant*) couche, *f.*

diaphanous, *a,* diaphane.

diaphragm, *n,* diaphragme, *m.*

diarrhea, *n,* diarrhée, courante, *f.*

diary, *n,* agenda; livre; (*of one's life*) journal, *m.*

diatonic, *a,* diatonique.

diatribe, *n,* diatribe, *f,* factum, *m.*

dibble, *n,* plantoir, *m.*

dice, *n.pl,* dés, *m.pl.* ~ *box,* cornet [à dés] *m.*

dicker, *v.i,* marchander.

dictate, *v.t. & abs,* dicter. ~ *to,* régenter. ~[s], *n.*[*pl.*], voix, *f.* **dictation,** *n,* dictée, *f.* **dictator,** *n,* dictateur, *m.* ~**ial,** *a,* dictatorial. ~**ship,** *n,* dictature, *f;* magistère, *m.*

diction, *n,* diction, *f.* ~**ary,** *n,* dictionnaire, *m.*

dictum, *n,* dicton, *m.*

didactic, *a,* didactique.

die, *n,* dé [à jouer]; (*Mech.*) dé, *m;* filière, *f;* coussinet, *m;* lunette; matrice, *f.* ~ *sinker,* graveur en creux, *m.*

die, *v.i.ir,* mourir, trépasser, succomber; périr; s'éteindre; (*animals*) crever; (*of laughing, etc.*) mourir, [se] pâmer. ~ *away,* ~ *down,* mourir, s'assoupir. ~*hard,* intransigeant, *m.*

diet, *n,* diète, *f,* régime [alimentaire] *m.* ¶ *v.t,* mettre à la diète; (*v.i.*) suivre un régime. ~**ary,** *n,* régime diététique, *m.* ~ *bread,* pain de régime, *m.*

differ, *v.i,* différer, varier, s'éloigner. ~**ence,** *n,* différence, *f,* écart; différend, *m.* ~**ent,** *a,* différent. **differential,** *a,* différentiel. **differentiate,** *v.t,* différencier. **differently,** *ad,* différemment, autrement.

difficult, *a,* difficile, malaisé ~ *to catch,* insaisissable. ~**y,** *n,* difficulté; peine, *f;* embarras, mal, *m.* *with* ~, difficilement, malaisément. (*ship in*) **difficulties** (*Nav.*), incommodité, *f.*

diffidence, *n,* défiance de soi-même; timidité, *f.* **diffident†,** *a,* timide.

diffuse, *v.t,* diffuser; répandre. ¶ *a,* diffus, filandreux. ~**d,** *a,* diffus. **diffusion,** *n,* diffusion, *f.*

dig, *n,* coup; (*fig.*) coup de patte, *m.* ¶ *v.t. & i. ir,* creuser; bêcher; fouiller. ~ *up,* déterrer; arracher.

digest, *v.t. & i,* digérer. ¶ *n,* compilation, *f.* digeste, *m.* ~**ible,** *a,* digestible. ~**ion,** *n,* digestion, *f.* ~**ive,** *a. & n,* digestif, *a. & m.*

digit, *n,* doigt, *m.* *a* ~ (0–9), un [seul] chiffre. **digitalis** (*Phar.*) *n,* digitale, *f.*

dignified, *a,* digne. **dignify,** *v.t,* ennoblir; investir; honorer, décorer. **dignitary,** *n,* dignitaire, *m.* **dignity,** *n,* dignité, *f.*

digress, *v.i,* divaguer. ~**ion,** *n,* digression, divagation, *f,* écart, hors-d'œuvre, *m.* **digressive,** *a,* hors d'œuvre.

dike, *n,* digue, *f;* (*Geol. & Min.*) filon d'injection, *m.* ¶ *v.t,* endiguer.

dilapidate, *v.t,* dégrader, délabrer, détériorer. ~*d state* (*building*), caducité, *f.*

dilate, *v.t,* dilater; (*v.i.*) se d.; s'étendre.

dilatoriness, *n,* lenteur, *f.* **dilatory,** *a,* lent, dilatoire.

dilemma, *n,* dilemme, *m.*

dilettante, *n,* dilettante, *m.*

diligence, *n,* diligence, *f.* **diligent,** *a,* diligent. ~**ly,** *ad,* diligemment.

dilly-dally, *v.i,* lanterner, barguigner.

dilute, *v.t,* étendre, diluer, détremper, délayer, couper, (*wine*) baptiser. **dilution,** *n,* dilution, *f.*

diluvial, *a,* diluvien.

dim, *a,* obscur, sombre; indistinct; vague; trouble. ¶ *v.t,* obscurcir; ternir; offusquer; (*auto lights*) mettre en code. **dimmed lights,** éclairage code, *m.*

dimension, *n,* dimension, *f;* échantillon, *m.*

dime store, *n,* prix unique, Prisunic, Monoprix, *m.*

diminish, *v.t. & i,* diminuer. **diminution,** *n,* diminution, *f.* **diminutive,** *a,* exigu; fort petit; (*Gram.*) diminutif. ¶ (*Gram.*) *n,* diminutif, *m.*

dimness, *n,* obscurcissement, *m;* obscurité, *f.*

dimple, *n,* fossette, *f.* ~d, *a,* à fossettes.

din, *n,* bruit, tintamarre, *m.* ¶ *v.t,* assourdir.

dine, *v.i,* dîner. ~ *out,* dîner en ville. **diner,** *n,* dîneur, euse.

dinghy, *n,* canot, youyou, *m.*

dingy, *a,* terne; sale; borgne.

dining: ~ *car,* wagon-restaurant, *m.* ~ *room,* salle à manger, *f.* ~ *table,* table de salle à manger, *f.* **dinner,** *n,* dîner, *m. at* ~ à table. ~ *jacket,* smoking, *m. give a* ~ [*party*], donner à dîner. ~ *plate,* assiette plate, *f.* ~ *service,* service de table & dessert, *m.* ~ *time,* heure du dîner, *f.*

dint, *n,* bosse, *f. by* ~ *of,* à force de.

diocesan, *a,* diocésain. **diocese,** *n,* diocèse, *m.*

diopter, *n,* dioptrie, *f.* **dioptric,** *a,* dioptrique.

dip, *n,* plongement, *m,* plongée; baignade, *f;* pendage, *m,* inclinaison; flèche; (*ink*) plumée, *f. dipper switch,* basculeur de phares, *m.* ¶ *v.t,* plonger, tremper, immerger; (*auto headlights*) faire basculer; (*v.i.*) plonger; s'incliner.

diphtheria, *n,* diphtérie, *f.*

diphthong, *n,* diphtongue, *f.*

diploma, *n,* diplôme, *m;* (*fig.*) parchemin, *m.*

diplomacy, *n,* diplomatie, *f;* doigté, *m.* **diplomatic,** *a,* diplomatique. **diplomat[ist],** *n,* diplomate, *m.*

dipper, *n,* écope, *f.*

dipstick, *n,* jauge à huile, *f.*

dire, *a,* (*distress*) dernière, extrême; (*necessity*) dure.

direct, *a,* direct; immédiat. ~ *current* (*Elec.*), courant continu, *m.* ~ *trade,* commerce direct, *m.* ¶ *ad,* directement. ¶ *v.t,* diriger; administrer, conduire; charger; adresser; acheminer; orienter. *to* ~ *me to . . .,* m'indiquer le chemin pour aller à . . . ~ion, *n,* direction; administration; conduite; orientation; (*Theat. & Cinema*) réalisation; *f,* sens, côté, *m;* a-dresse, *f;* (*pl.*) instructions, *f.pl,* charge, prescription, *f.* ~s *for use,* mode d'emploi, *m.* **directly,**

ad, directement; immédiatement, à l'instant, aussitôt.

director, *n,* (*of company*) administrateur, trice; (*manager*) directeur, trice; ordonnateur, trice; (*Theat. & cinema*) metteur en scène, réalisateur, *m. casting* ~, régisseur général, *m.* ~ate, *n,* administration, *f.*

directory, *n,* (*Teleph.*) annuaire; répertoire, *m.*

direful, *a,* terrible; sinistre.

dirge, *n,* chant, funèbre, chant de mort, *m.*

dirigible, *a. & n,* dirigeable, *a. & m.*

dirk, *n,* dague, *f,* poignard, *m.*

dirt, *n,* saleté, crasse, ordure, immondice, crotte, boue; terre, *f.* ~-*cheap,* à vil prix. ~ *track,* piste en cendrée, *f.* **dirtily,** *ad,* salement. **dirtiness,** *n,* saleté, *f.* **dirty,** *a,* sale, malpropre, crasseux; crotté, boueux. ~ *pig,* cochon, *m.* ~ *trick,* vilain tour, croc-en-jambe, *m,* vilenie, goujaterie, saleté, *f.* ~ *work* (*fig.*), sale besogne, *f,* micmac, *m.* ¶ *v.t,* salir, souiller; crotter, barbouiller.

disable, *v.t,* rendre incapable; rendre hors de combat; (*ship*) désemparer. ~d *soldier,* ~d *sailor,* mutilé de la guerre, *m.* ~ment & **disability,** *n,* incapacité, invalidité, *f.*

disabuse, *v.t,* désabuser.

disadvantage, *n,* désavantage, *m. place at a* ~, désavantager. ~ous†, *a,* désavantageux.

disaffection, *n,* désaffection, *f.*

disagree, *v.i,* n'être pas d'accord, être en désaccord; ne pas convenir. ~able†, *a,* désagréable. ~ment, *n,* désaccord, *m,* discordance, *f;* dissentiment, *m.*

disallow, *v.t,* rejeter.

disappear, *v.i,* disparaître. ~ance, *n,* disparition, *f.*

disappoint, *v.t,* désappointer; tromper, décevoir. *don't* ~ *me,* ne manquez pas à votre parole, à v. promesse. ~ment, *n,* désappointement, *m,* déception, *f,* mécompte, démenti, déboire, *m.* ~ *in love,* déception, *f,* (*ou* chagrin, *m.*) d'amour.

disapprobation & **disapproval,** *n,* désapprobation, improbation, *f.* **disapprove,** *v.t.* &

~ **of**, désapprouver, réprouver, improuver.

disarm, v.t. désarmer. **disarmament,** n, désarmement, m.

disarrange, v.t. déranger, désajuster. ~ (someone's hair) décoiffer.

disarray, n, désarroi, m.

disaster, n, désastre, sinistre; cataclysme, m. **disastrous,** a, désastreux, néfaste.

disavow, v.t. désavouer. ~**al,** n, désaveu, m.

disband, v.t. licencier; (v.i.) se séparer.

disbelief, n, manque de foi, m. **disbelieve,** v.t. ne pas croire.

disbud, v.t. ébourgeonner, éborgner.

disburden, v.t. décharger.

disburse, v.t. débourser. ~**ment,** n, déboursement, débours, déboursé, m, mise [de]hors, f.

disc, n, disque, plateau, m; rondelle, f. ~ jockey, animateur, m.

discard, v.t. laisser de côté; (cards) écarter.

discern, v.t. discerner. ~**ible,** a, perceptible. ~**ing,** a, judicieux. ~**ment,** n, discernement, jugement, m.

discharge, n, décharge, f; déversement, m; évacuation, f; débit, m; (Med.) écoulement, m, suppuration, f; libération, f, acquit[tement] m, quittance, f, quitus; renvoi, congé, m; (Mil., Navy) réforme; (bankrupt) réhabilitation, f. ¶ v.t. & i, décharger; déverser; débiter; (wound) suppurer; débarquer; libérer, [ac]quitter; liquider; renvoyer, congédier; réformer; réhabiliter. to get (obligation) discharged, apurer.

disciple, n, disciple, m. **disciplinarian,** n, disciplinaire, m. **disciplinary,** a, disciplinaire; de discipline. **discipline,** n, discipline, f. ¶ v.t. discipliner.

disclaim, v.t. désavouer; dénier. ~**er,** n, dénégation, f; désaveu, m; renonciation, f.

disclose, v.t. révéler, divulguer, dévoiler. **disclosure,** n, révélation, divulgation, f.

discoloration, n, décoloration, f. **discolour,** v.t. décolorer.

discomfit, v.t. confondre. ~**ure,** n, déconvenue, f.

discomfort, n, incommodité, f, malaise, m, gêne, f.

discompose, v.t. troubler. **discomposure,** n, trouble, m.

disconcert, v.t. déconcerter, interdire, désorienter.

disconnect, v.t. désassembler; (Mech.) débrayer; (Elec.) rompre. ~**ed,** a, détaché; isolé, incohérent.

disconsolate, a, désolé.

discontent[ed], a, p.p. mécontent. **discontent[ment],** n, mécontentement, m.

discontinuance, n, cessation, suspension; suppression, f. **discontinue,** v.t. discontinuer; (a train) supprimer. ~ one's subscription, se désabonner.

discord, n, discorde, f; (Mus.) désaccord, m, dissonance, f. ~**ance,** n, discordance, f. ~**ant,** a, discordant, dissonant.

discount, n, escompte, m; remise, f; rabais, m; (opp. premium) perte, f. ¶ v.t. escompter.

discountenance, v.t. s'opposer à.

discounter, n, escompteur, m. **discounting,** n, escompte, m.

discourage, v.t. décourager. ~**ment,** n, découragement, m.

discourse, n, discours, m. ¶ v.i. discourir.

discourteous, a, discourtois. **discourtesy,** n, discourtoisie, f.

discover, v.t. découvrir. ~**er,** n, inventeur, m. ~**y,** n, découverte, f.

discredit, n, discrédit, m. ¶ v.t. discréditer, déconsidérer, démonétiser. ~**able,** a, déshonorant.

discreet†, a, discret, retenu.

discrepancy, n, contradiction, f.

discrete, a, discret.

discretion, n, discrétion, retenue, prudence, f. ~**ary,** a, discrétionnaire. full ~ power, carte blanche, f.

discriminate, v.t. distinguer, discerner, faire le départ. **discrimination,** n, discernement, m, discrimination, f.

discursive, a, discursif.

discus, n, disque, m.

discuss, v.t. discuter, débattre, agiter. ~**ion,** n, discussion, f, débat, m.

disdain, n, dédain, m. ¶ v.t. dédaigner. ~**ful†,** a, dédaigneux.

disease, *n*, maladie, *f*; mal, *m*.
~d, *a*, malade; (*meat*) provenant d'animaux malades.
disembark, *v.t. & i*, débarquer.
~ation, *n*, débarquement, *m*.
disembody, *v.t*, désincorporer.
disembowel, *v.t*, éventrer.
disenchant, *v.t*, désenchanter.
disencumber, *v.t*, désencombrer; (*Fin.*) dégrever.
disengage, *v.t*, dégager; (*Mech.*) débrayer. ~d, *a*, libre.
disentangle, *v.t*, démêler, débrouiller.
disestablishment [of the Church] *n*, séparation de l'Eglise & de l'Etat, *f*.
disfavor, *n*, défaveur, *f*.
disfigure, *v.t*, défigurer, enlaidir.
~ment, *n*, enlaidissement, *m*.
disforest, *v.t*, déboiser.
disgorge, *v.t*, dégorger.
disgrace, *n*, disgrâce; honte, *f*; déshonneur, opprobre, *m*. ¶ *v.t*, disgracier; déshonorer. ~ful†, *a*, honteux, ignominieux.
disgruntled, *a*, maussade, mécontent.
disguise, *n*, déguisement, *m*; dissimulation, *f*. ¶ *v.t*, déguiser, camoufler; travestir; contrefaire.
disgust, *n*, dégoût, *m*. ¶ *v.t*, dégoûter; (*slang*) débecter, débecqueter. ~ing, *a*, dégoûtant.
dish, *n*, plat, *m*; (*food*) mets, *m*. ~es, vaisselle, *f*. ~cloth, torchon [de cuisine] *m*, lavette, *f*. ~ warmer, chauffe-plats, *m*. ~ washer, laveur de vaisselle, plongeur, *m*. ~ up, *v.t*, dresser, servir. ~ed, *a*, à cuvette. ~ful, *n*, platée, *f*.
dishabille, *n*, déshabillé, *m*.
dishearten, *v.t*, décourager, rebuter.
disheveled, *a*, échevelé, ébouriffé.
dishonest†, *a*, malhonnête, infidèle, déloyal. ~y, *n*, malhonnêteté, infidélité, *f*.
dishonor, *n*, déshonneur, *m*. ¶ *v.t*, déshonorer. ~able, *a*, peu honnête, déshonorant.
disillusion, *n*, désillusion, *f*. ¶ *v.t*, désillusionner, dégriser, désenchanter.
disinclination, *n*, éloignement, *m*. **disincline**, *v.t*, éloigner.
disinfect, *v.t*, désinfecter. ~ant, *n*, désinfectant, *m*. ~ion, *n*, désinfection, *f*.

disingenuous, *a*, peu sincère.
disinherit, *v.t*, déshériter.
disintegrate, *v.t*, désagréger, effriter.
disinter, *v.t*, déterrer, exhumer.
disinterested, *a*, désintéressé. ~ness, *n*, désintéressement, *m*.
disinterment, *n*, exhumation, *f*.
disjoin, *v.t*, disjoindre.
disjoint, *v.t*, désassembler. ~ed, *a*, décousu.
disk, *n*, disque, plateau, *m*; rondelle, *f*. (*computers*) ~ drive, tourne-disque, *m*. (*computers*) floppy ~, minidisque, *m*, disquette, *f*.
diskette, *n*, disquette, *f*, minidisque, *m*.
dislike, *n*, dégoût, éloignement, *m*, aversion, antipathie, grippe, *f*. ¶ *v.t*, ne pas aimer, avoir en aversion, avoir de l'aversion pour (*ou* contre), prendre en grippe.
dislocate, *v.t*, disloquer, luxer, démettre, déboîter, démancher.
dislocation, *n*, dislocation, luxation, *f*.
dislodge, *v.t*, déchausser, débusquer, disloquer.
disloyal†, *a*, déloyal, infidèle. ~ty, *n*, déloyauté, infidélité, *f*.
dismal†, *a*, lugubre, morne, sombre.
dismantle, *v.t*, démanteler, dégarnir.
dismast, *v.t*, démâter.
dismay, *n*, consternation, *f*. ¶ *v.t*, consterner.
dismember, *v.t*, démembrer.
dismiss, *v.t*, renvoyer, congédier, remercier, destituer; chasser; rejeter. ~al, *n*, renvoi, congé, *m*, destitution, *f*.
dismount, *v.i*, descendre; (*v.t.*) démonter.
disobedience, *n*, désobéissance, *f*. **disobedient**, *a*, désobéissant. **disobey**, *v.t*, désobéir à; (*v.i.*) désobéir.
disoblige, *v.t*, désobliger. **disobliging**, *a*, désobligeant. ~ness, *n*, désobligeance, *f*.
disorder, *n*, désordre; trouble, *m*; maladie, *f*. ¶ *v.t*, dérégler. ~ly, *a*, désordonné.
disorganize, *v.t*, désorganiser.
disorient, *v.t*, déorienter, déphaser.
disown, *v.t*, désavouer, renier, méconnaître.

disown, v.t, désavouer, renier, méconnaître.

disparage, v.t, dénigrer, rabaisser, déprécier, ravaler. **~ment**, n, dénigrement, m. **disparaging**, a, dénigrant; péjoratif.

disparate, a, disparate. **disparity**, n, disparité, f.

dispassionate; a. & **~ly**, ad, sans passion; sans parti pris.

dispatch, n, expédition, f, envoi, acheminement, m; diligence, célérité, promptitude, rapidité; (*message*) dépêche, f. ~ *case*, serviette, f. ¶ v.t, expédier, envoyer, acheminer; dépêcher, brasser. **~er**, n, (*transport*) répartiteur, m.

dispel, v.t, dissiper, chasser.

dispensary, n, officine, pharmacie, f; (*charitable*) dispensaire, m. **dispensation**, n, (*of Providence*) disposition; (*exemption*) dispense, f. **dispense**, v.t, dispenser; départir; rendre; (*Med.*) préparer [& débiter]. ~ *with*, se passer de; supprimer. **dispenser**, n, dispensateur, trice; (*Med.*) pharmacien, ne.

dispersal & **dispersion**, n, dispersion, séparation, f. **disperse**, v.t, disperser; dissiper.

dispirit, v.t, décourager, déprimer.

displace, v.t, déplacer; (*from office*) destituer; (*securities, Fin.*) déclasser. **~ment**, n, déplacement, m; destitution, f; déclassement, m.

display, n, montre, parade, f; étalage, m. ~ *cabinet*, vitrine, armoire vitrée, f. ~ *model*, mannequin, m. (*computers*) ~ *unit*, unité d'affichage, f. ¶ v.t, exposer, étaler; faire preuve de. ~*ed in bold type*, en vedette.

displease, v.t, déplaire à; mécontenter. **displeasure**, n, déplaisir, mécontentement, m.

disposable, a, disponible. **disposal**, n, disposition; expédition, f. **dispose**, v.t, disposer. ~ *of*, disposer de; placer; expédier. *well, ill,* **~d** *towards*, bien, mal, disposé pour, envers. **disposition**, n, disposition, f; naturel, m.

dispossess, v.t, déposséder.

disproof, n, réfutation, f.

disproportion, n, disproportion, f. **~ate**, a, disproportionné.

disprove, v.t, réfuter.

dispute, n, dispute, contestation, f, litige, m. ¶ v.t. & i, disputer, contester. ~ *every inch of the ground* (*Mil.*), chicaner le terrain.

disqualification, n, disqualification, f. **disqualified** (*law*) p.p. & p.a, indigne. **disqualify**, v.t, disqualifier; (*law*) frapper d'incapacité.

disquiet, v.t, inquiéter. **~[ude]**, n, inquiétude, f.

disquisition, n, dissertation, f.

disrate, v.t, déclasser.

disregard, n, indifférence, f; dédain, m. ¶ v.t, négliger; mépriser.

disrelish, n, dégoût, m.

disreputable, a, peu honorable; de mauvaise réputation. **disrepute**, n, discrédit, décri, m.

disrespect, n, manque de respect, m, irrévérence, f. **~ful†**, a, irrespectueux, irrévérencieux.

disrobe, v.t, déshabiller.

disrupt, v.t, rompre.

dissatisfaction, n, mécontentement, m. **dissatisfied**, p.a, mécontent.

dissect, v.t, disséquer. **~ion**, n, dissection, f.

dissemble, v.t. & i, dissimuler. **dissembler**, n, dissimulateur, trice.

disseminate, v.t, disséminer.

dissension, n, dissension, f. **dissent**, n, dissentiment, m; dissidence, f. ¶ v.i, s'opposer. **~er** & **dissentient**, n, dissident, e. **~ing** & **dissentient**, a, dissident.

dissertation, n, dissertation, f.

disservice, n, mauvais service, m.

dissidence, n, dissidence, f. **dissident**, a, dissident.

dissimilar, a, dissemblable, dissimilaire. **~ity**, n, dissemblance, f.

dissimulate, v.t. & i, dissimuler. **dissimulation**, n, dissimulation, duplicité, f.

dissipate, v.t, dissiper. **dissipation**, n, dissipation, f.

dissociate, v.t, dissocier.

dissolute, a, dissolu. **~ness**, n, dissolution, f.

dissolution, n, dissolution, f. **dissolve**, v.t, dissoudre, fondre. **dissolvent**, a. & n, dissolvant, a. & m. *dissolving views*, vues fondantes, f.pl.

dissonance, n, dissonance, f. **dissonant**, a, dissonant.

dissuade, *v.t,* dissuader, déconseiller.

dissyllable, *n,* dissyllabe, *m.*

distaff, *n,* quenouille, *f.*

distance, *n,* distance, *f;* éloignement; écart; lointain, *m;* trotte, *f.* keep one's ~ garder ses distances. ~ *apart* or *between,* écartement, *m.* ¶ *v.t,* éloigner; distancer. **distant,** *a,* éloigné, reculé, lointain; distant.

distaste, *n,* dégoût, *m.* ~**ful,** *a,* désagréable au goût.

distemper, *n,* maladie [des chiens]; *(paint)* détrempe, *f,* badigeon, *m.* ¶ *v.t,* peindre à la détrempe, badigeonner.

distend, *v.t,* distendre, ballonner. **distension,** *n,* distension, *f,* ballonnement, *m.*

distil, *v.t,* distiller. **distillate** & **distillation,** *n,* distillation, *f.* **distiller,** *n,* distillateur, *m.* ~**y,** *n,* distillerie, *f.*

distinct†, *a,* distinct; tranché. ~**ion,** *n,* distinction, *f.* ~**ive,** *a,* distinctif. **distinctness,** *n,* netteté, *f.* **distinguish,** *v.t,* distinguer. *to be* ~**able** *from,* se distinguer de. ~**ed,** *a,* distingué, de distinction, éminent, notable, insigne.

distort, *v.t,* déformer; défigurer, dénaturer, tordre. ~*ing mirror,* miroir déformant, *m.* ~**ion,** *n,* déformation; distorsion, *f;* *(fig.)* travestissement, *m.*

distract, *v.t,* distraire, détourner; déchirer. ~**ed†,** *p.a,* éperdu, affolé. ~**ion,** *n,* distraction, *f;* affolement, *m;* folie, fureur, *f.*

distrain upon, *(pers.)* exécuter, contraindre par saisie de biens; *(goods)* saisir. ~**able,** *a,* saisissable. *not* ~, insaisissable. **distraint,** *n,* saisie, exécution, *f.*

distress, *n,* détresse; misère; *(law)* saisie, *f.* ¶ *v.t,* affliger, désoler, angoisser. ~**ing,** *a,* affligeant, désolant, angoissant.

distribute, *v.t,* distribuer, répartir. **distribution,** *n,* distribution, répartition, *f.*

district, *n,* district, *m;* région, *f;* quartier, *m.*

distrust, *n,* défiance; méfiance, *f.* ¶ *v.t,* se défier de; se méfier de. ~**ful,** *a,* défiant; méfiant, soupçonneux.

disturb, *v.t,* troubler, déranger; remuer; inquiéter. ~**ance,** *n,* dérangement, trouble, *m;* perturbation, *f;* tapage, *m;* émeute, *f.*

disunion, *n,* désunion, *f.* **disunite,** *v.t,* désunir.

disuse, *n,* désuétude, *f.* ~**d,** *p.a,* hors d'usage.

ditch, *n,* fossé; canal, *m;* rigole; douve, *f.*

ditto, *n,* dito, idem *(ad.).* *to say nothing but* ~ *to everything,* opiner du bonnet.

ditty, *n,* chanson, chansonnette, *f.*

divan, *n,* divan, *m.*

dive, *n,* plongeon; *(Avn.)* vol piqué, *m;* *(seamy café)* caboulot, *m.* ¶ *v.i,* plonger; fouiller; *(Avn.)* piquer. **diver,** *n,* *(Swim.)* plongeur, euse; *(in diving dress)* plongeur, scaphandrier; *(bird)* plongeon, *m.*

diverge, *v.i,* diverger. **divergence,** *n,* divergence, *f.* **divergent,** *a,* divergent.

diverse†, *a,* divers, varié. **diversify,** *v.t,* diversifier, varier. **diversion,** *n,* diversion, *f;* divertissement, *m.* **diversity,** *n,* diversité, variété, *f.* **divert,** *v.t,* détourner, dériver, écarter; *(amuse)* divertir.

Dives, *n,* riche; *(Bible)* le mauvais riche, *m.*

divest, *v.t,* dépouiller.

divide, *v.t,* diviser; scinder; partager; répartir. ~*d skirt,* jupeculotte, *f.* **dividend,** *n,* dividende, *m;* répartition, *f.* **dividers,** *n.pl,* *(instrument)* compas à pointes sèches, *m.*

divination, *n,* divination, *f.* **divine†,** *a,* divin. ¶ *n,* théologien, *m.* ¶ *v.t,* deviner. **diviner,** *n,* devin, *m,* devineresse, *f.*

diving: ~ *bell,* cloche à plongeur, *f.* ~ *board,* plongeoir, tremplin, *m.* ~ *suit,* scaphandre, *m.*

divining rod, baguette divinatoire, *f.*

divinity, *n,* divinité; *(science)* théologie, *f.*

divisible, *a,* divisible; partageable. **division,** *n,* division, *f;* partage, *m;* section; coupe; séparation; case, *f.* **divisor,** *n,* diviseur, *m.*

divorce, *n,* divorce, *m.* ¶ *v.t,* divorcer d'avec.

divot *(golf) n,* touffe de gazon, *f.*

divulge, *v.t,* divulguer.

dizziness, *n,* vertige, *m.* **dizzy,** *a,* vertigineux.

do, *v.t.ir,* faire; opérer; *(v.i.ir.)* faire; agir; s'acquitter; aller; se trouver, se porter; convenir, faire l'affaire; suffire. ~ *away with*, supprimer, abolir. ~*-it-yourselfer*, bricoleur, *m*. [*please*] *do not touch*, défense de toucher. ~*nothing*, *a*, fainéant. ~ *odd jobs*, bricoler. ~ *one's hair*, se coiffer. ~ *one's utmost to*, s'efforcer de. ~ *over again*, refaire. ~ *without*, se passer de. *I have done*, j'ai fini. *that will* ~, cela suffit. *well-to-*~, aisé, cossu.

docile†, *a*, docile. **docility**, *n*, docilité, *f*.

dock, *n*, (*tail*) tronçon, *m*; (*Bot.*) patience, *f*; (*court*) banc des prévenus; (*Naut.*) bassin, dock, *m*; forme, cale, *f*. *dry* ~, cale seche, *f*. ~ *company*, compagnie des docks, *f*. ~ *strike*, grève des travailleurs des docks, *f*. ~ *warehouse*, dock[-entrepôt] *m*. *naval* ~*yard*, arsenal maritime, *m*. ¶ *v.t*, (*wages*) diminuer; rogner; faire entrer en bassin; (*v.i.*) entrer en bassin. ~**er**, *n*, docker, déchargeur, débardeur, *m*.

docket, *n*, étiquette, *f*. ¶ *v.t*, étiqueter.

docking, *n*, accostage, amarrage, *m*.

doctor, *n*, médecin, docteur, *m*; (*slang*) toubib, *m*. ¶ *v.t*, médicamenter; soigner; (*falsify*) frelater; (*patch up*) tricher. ~**ate**, *n*, doctorat, *m*.

doctrinaire, *n*. & *a*, doctrinaire, *m*. & *a*. **doctrine**, *n*, doctrine, *f*.

document, *n*, document, écrit, *m*, pièce, *f*; acte, titre, *m*. ~ *cabinet*, cartonnier, *m*. ~ *case*, serviette, *f*. ¶ *v.t*, documenter. ~**ary**, *a*, documentaire.

dodder (*Bot.*) *n*, cuscute, *f*. ¶ *v.i*, brandiller [de] la tête.

dodge, *n*, biais; détour; truc, *m*; ruse, *f*. ¶ *v.t*, esquiver, éviter; (*v.i.*) biaiser. **dodger**, *n*, biaiseur, euse. *artful* ~, finassier, rusé compère, *m*.

doe, *n*, (*deer*) daine; (*hare*) hase; (*rabbit*) lapine, *f*. ~**skin**, *n*, peau de daim, *f*, daim, *m*.

doer, *n*, faiseur, euse.

doff, *v.t*, ôter, tirer.

dog, *n*, chien, *m*; (*fire*) chenet, *m*. ~ *biscuit*, pain de chien, *m*. ~ *cart*, charrette anglaise, *f*. ~ *days*, canicule, *f*. ~ *fish*, chien

de mer, *m*. ~ *Latin*, latin de cuisine, *m*. ~ *racing* or *dogs*, courses de lévriers, *f.pl*. ~ *rose*, rose de chien, églantine, *f*; (*bush*) églantier, rosier sauvage, *m*. ~['s] *ear*, corne, *f*; (*v.t.*) [é]corner. ~ *show*, exposition canine, *f*. ~ *violet*, violette de chien, *f*. ¶ *v.t*, talonner. **dogged**, *a*, tenace. ~**ly**, *ad*, mordicus. ~**ness**, *n*, obstination, *f*.

doggerel, *n*, méchants vers, *m.pl*.

doggy or **doggie**, *n*, toutou, *m*.

dogma, *n*, dogme, *m*. **dogmatic**(**al**)†, *a*, dogmatique. **dogmatize**, *v.i*, dogmatiser.

doily, *n*, rond, ovale, rectangle [de table] *m*.

doings, *n.pl*, faits & gestes; (*underhand*) agissements, *m.pl*. *your doing* (fig.), votre ouvrage.

do-it-yourselfer, *n*, bricoleur, *m*.

doldrums (*Naut.*) *n.pl*, calmes, *m.pl*, zone des calmes, *f*. *to be in the* ~ (fig.), broyer du noir.

dole, *n*, charité; indemnité de chômage, *f*. ~ *out*, distribuer parcimonieusement. ~**ful**†, *a*, plaintif, dolent.

doll, *n*, poupée, *f*. ~*-faced*, poupin. ~*s house*, maison de poupée, *f*.

dollar, *n*, dollar, *m*.

dolly, *n*, chariot, diabolo, *m*. ~ *shot*, travelling, *m*.

dolphin, *n*, (*porpoise*) dauphin, *m*; (*dorado*) dorade, *f*; (*mooring*) corps mort, *m*.

dolt, *n*, lourdaud, e.

domain, *n*, domaine, *m*.

dome, *n*, dôme, *m*, coupole, voûte, *f*.

domestic, *a*, domestique; (*coal, or like*) de ménage; (*trade*) intérieur, métropolitain. ¶ *n*, domestique, *m,f*. **domesticate**, *v.t*, domestiquer. **domesticated**, (*pers.*) *a*, d'intérieur. **domesticity**, *n*, domesticité, *f*.

domicile, *n*, domicile, *m*. ¶ *v.t*, domicilier.

dominant, *a*, dominant. **dominate**, *v.t*. & *i*, dominer, régenter. **domination**, *n*, domination, *f*. **domineer**, *v.t*, dominer; (*v.i.*) régenter. ~**ing**, *a*, dominateur.

Dominican, *n*, dominicain, e.

dominion, *n*, domination, *f*, empire, *m*. *D~ of Canada*, of New

Zealand, Dominion du Canada, de la Nouvelle-Zélande, *m.*

domino, *n,* domino, *m.*

don, *v.t,* mettre, endosser, revêtir.

donate, *v.i. & t,* donner, accorder. **donation,** *n,* don, *m,* donation; (*pl.*) bienfaisance, *f.*

done, *p.p,* fait; (*Cook.*) cuit.

donee, *n,* donataire, *m,f.*

donkey, *n,* âne, baudet, grison, *m,* bourrique, *f.* ~ *driver,* ânier, ère. ~ *engine,* petit cheval, *m.* ~ *pump,* pompe alimentaire, *f.*

donor, *n,* donneur, euse; (*law*) donateur, *m,* donatrice, *f.*

doom, *n,* destin; jugement, *m.* ¶ *v.t,* condamner. **doomsday,** *n,* jour du jugement [dernier] *m.*

door, *n,* porte; fermeture; (*carriage, car*) portière, *f;* (*peephole*) regard, *m.* ~ *curtain,* portière, *f.* ~*keeper,* concierge, *m, f,* portier, ère, gardien, ne. ~*mat,* essuie-pieds, *m.* ~*step,* pas de la porte, *m.* ~*way,* [baie de] porte, *f.*

dope, *n,* stupéfiant, *m.* ¶ *v.t,* droguer; doper.

Doric, *a. & n,* dorique, *a. & m.*

dormant, *a,* dormant, endormi.

dormer [*window*]*, n,* mansarde, lucarne, *f.* **dormitory,** *n,* dortoir, *m.* **dormouse,** *n,* loir, *m.*

dosage, *n,* posologie, *f.* **dose,** *n,* dose, prise, *f.* ¶ *v.t,* medicamenter; doser.

dot, *n,* point; (*Emb.*) pois, *m.* ¶ *v.t,* marquer d'un point, mettre un p. sur; (*Mus.*) pointer; pointiller; jalonner, parsemer. *dotted line,* ligne pointillée, *f.*

dotage, *n,* enfance, *f;* radotage, *m.* **dotard,** *n,* radoteur, euse; (*of comedy*) grime, *m.* **dote** *or* **doat,** *v.i,* radoter. ~ *on,* être fou, folle, de, raffoler de.

double, *a,* double. ~*-acting,* à double effet. ~*-barreled gun,* fusil à deux coups, *m.* ~ *bass,* contrebasse, *f.* ~ *bed,* lit à deux places, *m.* ~*[-bedded] room,* chambre à deux lits, *f.* ~*-breasted,* croisé. ~*-dealing,* duplicité, *f;* (*a.*) double. ~*-entry bookkeeping,* tenue des livres en partie double, *f.* ~*-faced,* à double face. ~*-fronted* (house), à deux façades. ~ *meaning or* ~ *entendre,* mot à double entente, *m,* phrase à d. e., *f.* ~ *width* (cloth), grande largeur, *f.*

¶ *ad,* double. ¶ *n,* double; (*person*) sosie, *m.* ~ *or nothing,* quitte ou double. *the* ~ (*Mil.*), au pas gymnastique. ~*s game* (*Ten.*), partie double, *f.* ¶ *v.t. & i,* doubler. **doubly,** *ad,* doublement.

doubt, *n,* doute, *m.* ¶ *v.i,* douter; (*v.t.*) douter de. ~*ful*†, *a,* douteux; suspect; (*virtue*) moyenne. ~*less,* *a,* sans doute.

dough, *n,* pâte, *f.*

doughty, *a,* preux. ~ *deeds,* hauts faits, *m.pl,* prouesses, *f.pl.*

dour, *a,* froid & sévère; peu démonstratif.

douse, *v.t,* éteindre; tremper.

dove, *n,* colombe, *f;* pigeon, *m.* ~*cot[e],* colombier, pigeonnier, *m.* ~*tail,* queue d'aronde, *f.*

dowager, *n,* douairière, *f.*

dowdy, *a,* [mal] fagoté.

dowel, *n,* goujon, *m.* ¶ *v.t,* goujonner.

dower, dowry, *n,* dot, *f;* don, *m.* ¶ *v.t,* doter.

down, *a,* descendant. ~*grade,* pente, *f.*

down, *ad,* en bas; à bas; bas; à terre; par terre; en aval; (*prices*) en baisse; (*sun, moon*) couché, e; (*crossword clues*) verticalement. *to walk with the head* ~, *the hands* ~, marcher la tête basse, les mains basses. ~ *at heel,* en savates. ~ *there,* ~ *below,* là-bas. ~ *to,* jusqu'à, jusque.

down, *comps:* ~*cast,* *a,* baissé; abattu. ~*fall,* *n,* chute, *f,* effondrement, *m,* ruine, *f.* ~*-hearted, a,* découragé, abattu. ~*hill, a,* en pente; (*ad.*) en descendant. ~*pour, n,* tombée de pluie, *f,* déluge, *m.* ~*right, a,* franc, fieffé, pommé, vrai; (*ad.*), franchement, nettement. ~*stairs, ad,* en bas. ~*stream, ad,* en aval, à vau-l'eau. ~*stroke, n,* (*piston*) course descendante, *f;* (*writing*) jambage, plein, *m.* ~*trodden, a,* foulé [aux pieds]. ~*ward, a,* descendant; de baisse, à la baisse. ~*ward[s], ad,* en bas, en contrebas.

down, *i,* à bas! ~ *with . . .,* à bas . . .! conspuez . . .!

down, *n,* duvet, poil follet; poil, *m;* bourre, *f;* coton, *m;* (*sand hill*) dune, *f.* ~ *quilt,* couvrepied, *m.*

down, *pr*, en bas de, au bas de; en aval de.

down, *v.t*, abattre; baisser; renverser.

downy, *a*, duveté, douillet, follet, cotonneux, bourru.

dowral, *a*, dotal. **dowry**, *n*, dot, *f*.

dowser, *n*, sourcier, ère, hydroscope, *m*. **dowsing**, *n*, hydroscopie, *f*. ~ **rod**, baguette divinatoire, *f*.

doze, *v.i*, sommeiller, s'assoupir. **to have a** ~, faire un somme.

dozen, *n*, douzaine, *f*. **by the** ~, à la d.

drab, *a*, gris brun; terne.

drachm, *n*, *(apothecaries' measure)* = 3.552 milliliters; *(a—'s weight)* = 3.888 grams.

drachma, *n*, drachme, *f*.

draft, *n*, vent, courant d'air; vent coulis; appel d'air; aérage; tirage; tirant d'eau; trait, coup; breuvage, *m*; potion, *f*; coup de filet, *m*, pêche, prise, *f*; tracé, plan, *m*, *(outline)* projet, ébauche, *f*; *(Mil.)* conscription, *f*. ~ **animal**, animal de trait, *m*. ~ **beer**, bière au tonneau; b. à la pompe, *f*. ~ **board**, conseil de revision, *m*. ¶ *v.t*, ébaucher, tracer; *(writings)* minuter. **draftsman**, *n*, dessinateur, traceur; *(writings)* rédacteur, *m*. **drafty**, *a*, exposé aux courants d'air.

draftee, *n*, conscrit, *m*.

drag, *n*, drague, *f*; sabot [d'enrayage]; tirage, *m*; résistance, *f*. ~**net**, traîneau, *m*, drague, *f*. ¶ *v.t*, traîner; arracher; *(wheel)* enrayer; *(pond)* draguer, pêcher; *(anchor)* chasser; *(v.i.)* se traîner; languir; chasser. ~ **about**, *v.t*, trimbaler.

draggle, *v.t. & i*, traîner.

dragon, *n*, dragon, *m*. ~**fly**, libellule, demoiselle, *f*. ~**'s blood**, sang-[de-]dragon, *m*.

dragoon, *n*, dragon, *m*. ¶ ~ **into**, forcer à embrasser.

drain, *n*, drain, *m*; tranchée, *f*; égout; *(demand)* drainage, *m*. ~**pipe**, tuyau de drainage; drain, *m*. ~ ¶ *v.t*, drainer, assécher, dessécher, saigner, épuiser, [faire] égoutter, faire écouler; purger. ~ [*away*], s'écouler; s'égoutter. ~**age**, *n*, drainage, assèchement, dessèchement, épuisement, écoulement, *m*; purge, *f*; *(surplus water)* égout, *m*. ~**er**, *n*. & ~**ing rack**, égouttoir, *m*.

drake, *n*, canard, *m*.

dram, *n*, *(avoirdupois)* = 1.772 grams; *(draft)* goutte, *f*.

drama, *n*, drame, *m*. **the** ~, le théâtre. **dramatic**†, *a*, dramatique; théâtral. **dramatis personae**, personnages, *m.pl*, rôle scénique, *m*, **dramatist**, **dramaturge**, *n*, auteur dramatique, dramatiste, *m*, dramaturge, *m,f*. **dramatize**, *v.t*, dramatiser.

drape, *v.t*, draper; tendre. **draper**, *n*, *(cloth)* drapier; *(general)* marchand de nouveautés, *m*. ~**y**, *n*, draperie, *f*; nouveautés, *f.pl*.

drastic, *a*, drastique, extrême.

draw, *n*, tirage, *m*; loterie, *f*; attrait, *m*, attraction, *f*; appât, *m*; *(game)* partie nulle, *f*, match nul, refait, *m*.

draw, *v.t.ir*, tirer; retirer; attirer; traîner; entraîner; remorquer; *(Min.)* remonter; *(metal)* étirer; arracher; extraire; puiser; aspirer; *(so much water—ship)* caler; dessiner; tracer; *(wages)* toucher; *(fowl)* vider; *(v.i.ir.)* tirer; *(tea)* [s']infuser. ~ [*a game*], faire match nul, **f**, partie nulle. ~ **aside**, tirer à l'écart. ~ **back**, reculer; *(curtains)* ouvrir. ~ **down**, faire descendre, baisser. ~ **in** *(days)*, [se] raccourcir. ~ **near**, approcher. ~ **off**, tirer; soutirer. ~ **on**, mettre à contribution. ~ **out** *(days)*, croître. ~ **up**, *(writing)* dresser, rédiger, formuler; *(carriage)* s'arrêter.

drawback, *n*, désavantage, inconvénient, *m*.

drawbridge, *n*, pont levant; pont à bascule; *(Hist.)* pont-levis, *m*.

drawee, *n*, tiré, payeur, *m*. **drawer**, *n*, tireur, euse; *(of bill, check)* tireur, souscripteur, *m*; *(receptacle)* tiroir; carton, *m*; *(pl., chest)* commode, *f*; *(pl., dress)* caleçon, *m*.

drawing, *n*, dessin; *(lottery)* tirage, *m*. ~ **board**, planche à dessin, *f*. ~ **knife**, plane, *f*. ~ **pen**, tire-ligne, *m*. ~ **room**, [grand] salon, *m*.

drawl, *v.t*, traîner.

drawn: ~ **battle**, bataille indécise, *f*. ~ **face**, visage tiré, v. hagard, *m*. ~ **game**, partie nulle, p. indécise, p. remise, *f*. ~ **number**, numéro sortant, *m*. **with** ~ **sword**, sabre au clair.

dray, *n*, haquet, *m*. ~**horse**, cheval de h., *m*.

dread, *a*, redouté. ¶ *n*, terreur, crainte; phobie, *f*. ¶ *v.t*, redouter, craindre. ~**ful**†, *a*, terrible, épouvantable, affreux. **dreadnought** (*Nav.*) *n*, dreadnought, *m*; (*cloth*) ratine, *f*.

dream, *n*, rêve, songe, *m*; rêverie, *f*. ¶ *v.i. & t. ir*, rêver, songer. ~ *of*, rêver. ~**er**, *n*, rêveur, euse; songe-creux, *m*. ~**y**, *a*, rêveur, songeur.

drear[y], *a*, triste, morne. **dreariness**, *n*, tristesse, *f*, aspect morne, *m*.

dredge, *n*, drague, *f*. ¶ *v.t*, draguer; (*sprinkle*) saupoudrer. **dredger**, *n*, dragueur; saupoudroir, *m*. **mud-~**, marie-salope, *f*. **dredging**, *n*, dragage, *m*.

dregs, *n.pl*, lie, *f*.

drench, *v.t*, tremper; · saucer; abreuver. ~**ing rain**, pluie battante, *f*.

Dresden, *n*, Dresde, *f*. ~ **china**, porcelaine de Saxe, *f*, saxe, *m*.

dress, *n*, habillement; entretien; costume, *m*; robe; mise; toilette; tenue; parure, *f*; chiffons, *m.pl*. ~ **circle**, premières [galeries] *f.pl*, [premier] balcon, *m*. ~ **coat**, habit de soirée, *m*. ~**maker**, couturière; entrepreneuse de confection, *f*. ~**making**, confections pour dames, *f.pl*. ~ **rehearsal**, avant-première, répétition générale, *f*. ~ **shirt**, chemise de soirée, *f*. ¶ *v.t*, habiller, [re]vêtir; (*in fancy dress*) costumer; orner, parer; (*ship with flags*) pavoiser; (*wound*) panser; (*food*) apprêter; (*salad*) assaisonner; (*materials*) dresser, tailler, corroyer; (*Mil.*) aligner. ~ [*oneself*], s'habiller, se mettre, se vêtir. ~ *for dinner*, se mettre en habit pour dîner. ~ *the window*(*s*), faire l'étalage. **dressing**, *n*, habillement, *m*; toilette, *f*; (*of wound*) pansement; (*on wound*) appareil; (*food*) apprêt, *m*; (*meat*) parure, *f*; (*salad*) assaisonnement, *m*. ~ *gown*, robe de chambre, *f*, peignoir, saut de lit, *m*. ~ *room*, cabinet de toilette, *m*; (*Theat.*) loge, *f*. ~ *table*, [table de] toilette, coiffeuse, *f*.

dribble, *n*, goutte; (*slaver*) bave, *f*. ¶ *v.i*, dégoutter; baver; (*v.t*, *Foot.*) dribbler. **dribbling** (*Foot.*) *n*, dribbling, *m*. **in driblets**, par parcelles.

dried, *p.a*, séché; (*raisins*, *fruits*,

fish, *etc.*) sec; (*apples*, *etc.*, *in rings*) tapé. **drier**, *n*, séchoir; (*s. or pl*, *for paint*) siccatif, *m*.

drift, *n*, poussée, tendance, portée, *f*; laisser-faire, *m*, inaction; déviation, *f*; (*snow*) amas, *m*; (*Naut. & fig.*) dérive; (*Min.*) galerie, *f*; (*Geol.*) apport[s] *m*. [*pl*.]. ~*wood*, bois flotté, *m*. ¶ *v.t*, charrier, entraîner; apporter; chasser; amonceler; (*Mech.*) brocher; (*v.i.*) chasser; (*Naut.*) dériver, aller en dérive; s'amonceler. ~**er** (*boat*) *n*, cordier, *m*.

drill, *n*, foret, *m*, mèche; (*Min.*, *etc.*) perforatrice, foreuse, perceuse, sonde, *f*; (*furrow*) sillon; (*Agric. mach.*) semoir; (*Mil.*) exercice, *m*, école, *f*; (*fabric*) coutil, *m*. ~ *ground*, champ de manœuvres, *m*, place d'armes, *f*. ~[*holder*], porte-foret, porte-mèche, *m*. ~ *sergeant*, [sergent] instructeur, *m*. ¶ *v.t*, percer, forer, perforer; (*Mil.*) exercer, faire faire l'exercice à; (*v.i.*) faire l'exercice. **drilling**, *n*, perçage, percement, *m*, perforation, *f*; forage, sondage; (*Mil.*) exercice, *m*. ~ *machine*, machine à percer, perceuse; foreuse, *f*.

drink, *n*, boisson; consommation, *f*; breuvage, *m*; liqueur, *f*. *to have a* ~, boire un coup. ¶ *v.t. & i. ir*, boire; consommer. ~**able**, *a*, buvable, potable. ~**er**, *n*, buveur, euse. ~**ing**, *att*: ~ *fountain*, fontaine publique, *f*. ~ *song*, chanson à boire, c. bachique, *f*, air à boire, *m*. ~ *straw*, chalumeau, *m*. ~ *trough*, abreuvoir, *m*. ~ *water*, eau potable, *f*.

drip, *n*, goutte, *f*. ~[*stone*], larmier, *m*. ¶ *v.i*, [dé]goutter, découler, pleurer, ruisseler. **dripping**, *n*, graisse de rôti, *f*. ~ *pan*, lèchefrite, *f*. ~ *wet*, tout trempé, saucé.

drive, *n*, promenade; avenue; allée; initiative; (*Hunt.*) battue; (*Mach.*) commande, transmission; (*golf*) crossée, *f*; (*Ten.*) drive, *m*; (*Min.*) galerie, *f*. *front-wheel* ~, traction avant, *f*. ¶ *v.t.ir*, chasser, pousser, forcer; (*horse*, *car*) conduire, mener; (*golf*) driver; (*Ten.*) chasser; (*Mach.*) actionner, commander; (*Min.*) chasser, percer [en direction]; (*nail*) enfoncer; forcer, contraindre; faire; (*one mad*) rendre;

(*v.i.ir.*) aller (*ou* se promener) en voiture, rouler. ~ *ashore* (ship), dériver à la côte. ~ *away*, chasser. ~ *back*, refouler. ~ *into a corner*, acculer, rencogner. ~ *out*, ~ *off*, chasser, débusquer. ~ *slowly* (traffic sign), au pas. *what are you* ~*ing at?* où voulez-vous en venir?

drivel, *n*, bave, *f*. ¶ *v.i*, baver; (*fig.*) radoter.

driver, *n*, conducteur; cocher; chauffeur; (*Rly*) mécanicien, *m*; (*golf*) grand-crosse, *f*. ~*'s license*, permis de conduire [les automobiles] *m*. **driving**, *n*, conduite; commande, transmission; *f*; serrage; percement; (*nails, piles*) enfoncement; (*piles*) battage, *m*. ~ *iron* (*golf*), grand-fer, *m*. ~ *rain*, pluie battante, *f*. ~ *shaft*, arbre moteur, arbre de couche, *m*.

drizzle, *n*, bruine, *f*. ¶ *v.imp*, bruiner.

droll, *a*, drôle, cocasse, plaisant. ~*ery*, *n*, drôlerie, *f*. **drolly**, *ad*, drôlement.

dromedary, *n*, dromadaire, *m*.

drone, *n*, ronron; (*Mus.*) bourdon, *m*. ~ [*bee*], [faux] bourdon, *m*. ¶ *v.i*, ronronner, bourdonner; (*v.t.*) psalmodier.

droop, *v.i*, pendre, traîner; (*wilt*) s'étioler. ~*ing*, *p.a*, pendant, tombant. ~ *looks*, airs penchés, *m.pl.* ~ *spirits*, forces défaillantes. *f.pl.*

drop, *n*, goutte; larme; chute; baisse; pastille, *f*; pendant, *m*; pendeloque, *f*. ~ *curtain*, rideau, *m*. ~*-forged*, estampé. ¶ *v.t*, laisser tomber goutte à goutte; laisser tomber, lâcher; lancer; (*letter in mail*) jeter; (*a line*) envoyer; (*a stitch*) sauter; (*her young*) mettre bas; (*v.i.*) tomber. *dropped stitch* (*Knit.*), manque, *m*, maille échappée, *m*. perdue, *f*. **dropper**, *n*, compte-gouttes, *m*. **droppings** (*dung*) *n.pl*, fiente, crotte, *f*.

dropsical, *a*, hydropique. **dropsy**, *n*, hydropisie, *f*.

dross, *n*, écume, crasse, scorie, chiasse, *f*.

drought, *n*, sécheresse; disette d'eau, *f*.

drove, *n*, troupeau, *m*. **drover**, *n*, conducteur [de bestiaux], toucheur, *m*.

drown, *v.t*, noyer; (*sounds*) couvrir; (*v.i.*) boire. ~ *oneself*, se noyer. ~*ing*, *n*, submersion; (*fatality*) noyade, *f*. *a* ~ *man*, un noyé.

drowse, *v.i*, sommeiller; somnoler.

drowsiness, *n*, assoupissement. *m*. **drowsy**, *a*, endormi, ensommeillé. *to make* ~, assoupir.

drub, *v.t*, [b]rosser, frotter, etriller. **drubbing**, *n*, [b]rossée, frottée, peignée, volée de coups, *f*.

drudge, *n*, souffre-douleur, cheval de bât, pâtiras, *m*. ¶ *v.i*, trimer. ~*ry*, *n*, besognes fastidieuses, *f.pl*, corvée, *f*, collier de misère, *m*.

drug, *n*, drogue; *f*; stupéfiant, narcotique, *m*. ~ *addict*, toxicomane, *m. & f*. ~ *traffic*, trafic des stupéfiants, *m*. ~ *store*, pharmacie, *f*. ¶ *v.t*, narcotiser.

drugget, *n*, droguet, *m*.

druggist, *n*, pharmacien; (*wholesale*) droguiste, *m*.

Druid, *n*, druide, *m*.

drum, *n*, tambour, *m*, caisse, *f*; (*ear*) tympan; cylindre, barillet; tonneau, fût, *m*. ~*s & bugles* (*Mil. band*), clique, *f*. ~*head*, peau de tambour, *f*. ~*head court-martial*, cour martiale, *f*. ~ *major*, tambour-major, *m*. ~*stick*, baguette de tambour, *f*; (*fowl*) pilon, *m*. ¶ *v.i*, tambouriner. ~ *into*, seriner à. **drummer**, *n*, tambour, *m*.

drunk, *a*, ivre, soûl. *to get* ~, s'enivrer. ~*ard*, *n*, ivrogne, *m*. ~*en*, *a*, ivrogne. ~ *bout*, débauche de boisson, ribote, *f*. ~ *brawl*, querelle d'ivrognes, *f*. ~*enness*, *n*, ébriété ivresse; (*habitual*) ivrognerie, *f*.

dry, *a*, sec; à sec; desséché; tari. ~*-clean*, nettoyer à sec. ~ *dock*, cale sèche, *f*, bassin [à] sec, *m*, forme de radoub, *f*. ~ *fly fishing*, pêche à la mouche sèche, *f*. ~ *measure*, mesure de capacité pour les matières sèches, *f*. ~ *nurse*, nourrice sèche, *f*. ~ *rot*, carie sèche, *f*. ¶ *v.t. & i*, sécher; assécher. ~ *up*, tarir, dessécher.

dryad, *n*, dryade, *f*.

drying, *n*, séchage; assèchement, *m*. ~ *room*, séchoir, *m*. **dryly**, *ad*, (*answer coldly*) sèchement, sec. **dryness**, *n*, sécheresse, aridité, *f*.

drymounting, *n*, (*Phot.*) collage à sec, *m*.

dual, *a*, double. ~**ity**, *n*, dualité, *f*.

dub, *v.t*, (*knight*) armer; (*nickname*) baptiser; (*movies*) doubler.

dubious†, *a*, douteux, incertain; équivoque; interlope.

ducal, *a*, ducal. **duchess**, *n*, duchesse, *f*. **duchy**, *n*, duché, *m*.

duck, *n*, canard, *m*, cane, *f*, barboteur; (*dip*) plongeon; (*cloth*) coutil, *m*. ~ & *drake* (game), ricochets, *m.pl*. ~ *decoy* & ~ *pond*, canardière, *f*. ~'*s egg*, œuf de cane, *m*. ~*weed*, lentille d'eau, l. de marais, *f*. ¶ *v.t*, plonger; (*v.i.*) faire le plongeon, éviter de la tête, faire une courbette. ~**ling**, *n*, canneton, *m*, canette, *f*.

duct, *n*, canal, conduit, *m*, voie, *f*.

ductile, *a*, (*metals*) ductile; (*pers.*) docile, souple.

dudgeon (in), en haine.

due, *a*, dû; échu; régulier; requis, voulu, utile. *the train is* ~ *at* . ., le train arrive (*ou* doit arriver) à . . *in* ~ *course*, en temps & lieu. ~ *date*, échéance, *f*. ¶ *ad*, droit; directement. ¶ *n*, dû, *m*; (*duty*) droit, *m*; taxe, *f*.

duel, *n*, duel, *m*, rencontre, *f*. **duelist**, *n*, duelliste, *m*.

duenna, *n*, duègne, *f*.

duet, *n*, duo, *m*.

duffer, *n*, cancre, *m*, ganache, *f*, imbécile, *m,f*; (*at a game*) mazette, *f*.

dug, *n*, trayon, pis, *m*, tétine, *f*.

dugout, *n*, pirogue; cagna, *f*; abri [de bombardement] *m*.

duke, *n*, duc, *m*. ~**dom**, *n*, duché, *m*.

dulcet, *a*, doux.

dulcimer, *n*, tympanon, *m*.

dull, *a*, lourd; obtus; assoupissant, assommant, fastidieux; fade; maussade; inactif; atone; plat; terne; mat; sombre; gris; sourd; émoussé. ¶ *v.t*, ternir; émousser; hébéter. ~**ard**, *n*, lourdaud, e. ~**ness**, *n*, pesanteur, *f*, appesantissement; ennui, *m*; inactivité, atonie; platitude; ternissure; matité, *f*.

duly, *ad*, dûment; régulièrement; bien. ~ *authorized representative*, fondé de pouvoir(s) *m*.

dumb†, *a*, muet. ~ *animals*, animaux, *m. pl*. ~*bell*, haltère, *m*. ~ *show*, jeu muet, *m*, pantomime, *f*.

dumbfound, *v.t*, ébahir, atterrer.

dumbness, *n*, mutisme, *m*.

dumbwaiter, *n*, monte-plat, *m*.

dummy, *a*, feint; faux. ~ *book* (for bookshelf), livre feint, *m*. ¶ *n*, prête-nom; mannequin, *m*; poupée; fausse boîte; (*publisher's blank book*) maquette, *f*; (*Mil.*) simulacre; (*cards*) mort, *m*.

dump, *n*, chantier de dépôt, *m*. ~ *core*, impression de mémoire, *f. to be in the* ~*s*, avoir le spleen. ¶ *v.t*, culbuter, chavirer; (*computers*) vider. ~**ing** (*economy*) *n*, dumping, *m*. ~**y**, *a*, trapu, boulot, courtaud.

dun, *a*, fauve gris. ¶ *n*, fauve gris; créancier importun; agent de recouvrements, *m*. ¶ *v.t*, importuner, pourchasser, assiéger, persécuter.

dunce, *n*, ignorant, e, cancre, âne, *m*. ~ *cap*, bonnet d'âne, *m*.

dunderhead, *n*, imbécile, *m*.

dune, *n*, dune, *f*.

dung, *n*, fiente, *f*; crottin, *m*; bouse; crotte, *f*. ~ *beetle*, escarbot, *m*. ~*hill*, fumier; (*fig.*) pailler, *m*. ¶ *v.t*, fumer.

dungeon, *n*, cachot, *m*.

dunk, *v.t*, tremper.

Dunkirk, *n*, Dunkerque, *m*.

dunnage, *n*, fardage, grenier, chantier [d'arrimage] *m*.

dupe, *n*, dupe, *f*. ¶ *v.t*, duper, blouser, piper. ~**ry**, *n*, duperie, *f*.

duplicate, *a*, double; (*tools, parts*) de rechange. ¶ *n*, double, duplicata, *m*, ampliation; pièce de rechange; répétition, *f*. ¶ *v.t*, faire le double de; (*train*) dédoubler. **duplication**, *n*, double emploi, *m*. **duplicity**, *n*, duplicité, *f*.

durable, *a*, durable. **duration**, *n*, durée, *f*.

duress, *n*, violence, *f*.

during, *pr*, pendant, durant, par, dans.

dusk, *n*, la brune. *at* ~, sur (*ou* à) la brune, entre chien & loup. ~**y**, *a*, brun.

dust, *n*, poussière, *f*; poussier, *m*; poudre, *f*; cendres; ordures, *f.pl*. ~*coat*, cache-poussière, *m*. ~ *cover* (*furniture*) housse, *f*. ~ *jacket* (*book*) couvre-livre, *m*. ~*pan*, pelle à poussière, *f. saw* ~, sciure, *f*. ¶ *v.t*, épousseter; hous-

ser; (*sprinkle*) saupoudrer. ~er,
n, essuie-meuble, *m*. ~y, *a*, poussiéreux, poudreux.

Dutch, *a*, hollandais, de Hollande,
néerlandais. ~ *cheese*, fromage
de Hollande, *m*. ~ *courage*,
courage arrosé, *m*. ~*man*, *-woman*, Hollandais, e, Néerlandais,
e. ~ *oven*, rôtissoire, *f*. ¶ (*language*) *n*, le hollandais.

dutiable, *a*, passible de droits,
sujet à des droits, imposable.

dutiful† & **duteous**†, *a*, obéissant,
soumis, respectueux. **duty**, *n*, devoir, *m*; charge, fonction, *f*, office; service; droit, *m*, taxe, *f*,
impôt, *m*, surtaxe, *f*. *on* ~, de
service, de garde. ~*-free*, *a*, exempte d'impôt.

dwarf, *n*. & *a*, nain, e. ¶ *v.t*, rapetisser.

dwell, *v.i.ir*, habiter, demeurer;
insister, peser. ~*er*, *n*, habitant,
e. ~*ing*, *n*, habitation, demeure,
f, logis, *m*. ~ *house*, maison
d'habitation, *f*.

dwindle, *v.i*, dépérir. **dwindling**,
n. dépérissement, *m*.

dye, *n*, teinture, *f*. ~ *stuffs*, matières tinctoriales, *f.pl. of the
deepest* ~ (*fig*.), de la plus belle
eau, fieffé. ¶ *v.t*, teindre. ~*ing*,
n, teinture; teinturerie, *f*. **dyer**
[& **cleaner**] *n*, teinturier, ère.

dying, *a*, mourant; à l'agonie,
agonisant; moribond. *the* ~, les
mourants, *m.pl. to be* ~, [*se*]
mourir. ~ *words*, dernières paroles, *f.pl*.

dynamic(al), *a*, dynamique. **dynamics**, *n*, dynamique, *f*.

dynamite, *n*, dynamite, *f*.

dynamo, *n*, dynamo, *f*.

dynasty, *n*, dynastie, *f*.

dysentery, *n*, dysenterie, *f*.

dyspepsia, *n*, dyspepsie, *f*.

E

E (*Mus.*) *letter*, mi, *m*.

each, *a*. & *pn*, chaque; chacun, e;
l'un, l'une, [la] pièce. ~ *one*,
chacun, e. ~ *other*, l'un (l'une)
l'autre, les uns (les unes) les
autres; se, nous, vous.

eager, *a*, ardent, assoiffé, acharné,
avide, empressé. *to be* ~ *for*,
ambitionner. ~*ly*, *ad*, ardemment, avidement. ~*ness*, *n*,

ardeur, avidité, *f*, empressement,
m.

eagle, *n*, (*bird*) aigle, *m,f*; (*standard*) aigle, *f*. **eaglet**, *n*, aiglon, ne.

ear, *n*, oreille, *f*. ~*ache*, douleur
d'oreille, otalgie, *f*. ~*drum*,
membrane du tympan, *f*, tympan,
m. ~ *flap*, oreillon, *m*. ~*mark*,
affecter. ~*phones*, casque, *m*.
~*ring*, boucle [d'oreille] *f*. ~
trumpet, cornet acoustique, *m*.

earliness, *n*, heure peu avancée;
précocité, *f*. **early**, *a*, peu avancé;
prématuré; avancé; précoce; hâtif; premier; (*youth*) tendre; ancien. ~ *fruits*, ~ *vegetables*,
primeurs, *f.pl. to be* [*up*] ~, *to
be an* ~ *riser*, être matinal, être
matineux. ¶ *ad*, de bonne heure,
tôt, matin.

earn, *v.t*, gagner, acquérir; mériter.

earnest, *a*, sérieux; ardent, fervent. ¶ *n*, gage; (*fig*.) avant-goût,
m. ~*ly*, *ad*, sérieusement; ardemment; instamment. ~*ness*, *n*,
ardeur, ferveur, instance, *f*.

earning, *n*, acquisition, *f*; (*pl*.)
gain[s] *m.[pl.]*.

earth, *n*, terre, *f*; sol; (*of fox*) terrier, *m*, tanière, *f*. ~*quake*, tremblement de t., *m*. ~*work*, terrassement, *m*. ¶ *v.t*, (*Hort.*)
butter, chausser, terrer. ~*en*, *a*
de terre. ~*enware*, *n*, poterie
[de terre], faïence, *f*. ~*ly*, *a*, ter
restre. ~*y*, *a*, terreux.

earthquake, *n*, tremblement de
terre, séisme, *m*.

earwig, *n*, perce-oreille, *m*.

ease, *n*, aise, aisance; facilité, *f*,
repos; soulagement, *m*. ¶ *v.t*,
adoucir; soulager; décharger;
(*v.i.*) mollir.

easel, *n*, chevalet, *m*.

easement, *n*, soulagement, *m*.

easily, *ad*, aisément, facilement;
doucement. *not* ~, malaisément.

east, *n*, est; levant; orient, *m*.
from ~ *to west*, du levant au
couchant. *the E~* (*Geog.*), l'
Orient. ¶ *a*, d'est, de l'est; oriental. *Near* ~, Proche-Orient.
Far ~, Extrême-Orient.

Easter, *n*, Pâques, *m.s*. ~ *egg*,
œuf de P.

easterly, *a*, d'est. **eastern**, *a*, de
l'est; oriental; (*question, etc.*)
d'Orient.

easy, *a*, facile, aisé; doux; commode; coulant; tranquille; désinvolte. ~ *chair*, fauteuil, *m.* ~-*going person*, personne commode, *f*, sans-souci, *m.f. by ~ stages*, à petites journées. ~ *to get on with* (*pers.*), d'un commerce agréable. *it's* ~, c'est du gâteau (*slang*).

eat, *v.t. & i. ir*, manger. ~ *away*, ~ *into*, ronger. ~ *up*, dévorer. ~**able**, *a*, mangeable. ~**ables**, *n.pl*, comestibles, *m.pl.* ~**er**, *n*, mangeur, euse. ~**ing:** ~ *apples*, pommes à couteau, *f.pl.*

eaves, *n.pl*, avant-toit, *m.* **eavesdrop**, *v.i*, écouter aux portes. **eavesdropper**, *n*, écouteur (euse) aux portes.

ebb, *n*, jusant, reflux, *m.* ~ *tide*, courant de jusant, *m. the* ~ *and flow*, le flux et le reflux. ¶ *v.i*, refluer, refouler.

ebonite, *n*, ébonite, vulcanite, *f.*

ebony *n*, ébène, *f*; (*tree*) ébénier, *m.*

ebullition, *n*, ébullition, *f.*

eccentric, *a. &* (*Mech.*) *n*, excentrique, *a. & m.* ~**ity**, *n*, excentricité, *f.*

Ecclesiastes, *n*, l'Ecclésiaste, *m.* **ecclesiastic**, *n. & *~**al**† , *a*, ecclésiastique, *m. & a.* **Ecclesiasticus**, *n*, l'Ecclésiastique, *m.*

echo, *n*, écho, *m.* ¶ *v.i*, faire écho, retentir; (*v.t.*) se faire l'écho de.

eclectic, *a*, éclectique. **eclecticism**, *n*, éclectisme, *m.*

eclipse, *n*, éclipse; défaillance, *f.* ¶ *v.t*, éclipser. *to become* ~*d*, s'éclipser. **ecliptic**, *a. & n*, écliptique, *a. & f.*

ecological, *a*, écologique. **ecology**, *n*, écologie, *f.*

economic, *a*, économique. ~(**al**)† , *a*, économique; économe, ménager. ~**s**, *n.pl*, science économique, *f.* **economist**, *n*, économiste, *m.* **economize**, *v.t. & i*, économiser, ménager. **economy**, *n*, économie, *f. planned* ~, dirigisme économique.

ecstasy, *n*, extase, *f. to go into ecstasies*, s'extasier. **ecstatic**, *a*, extatique.

Ecuador, *n*, l'Équateur, *m.*

eczema, *n*, eczéma, *m.*

eddy, *n*, remous, tournant, *m.* ¶ *v.i*, tourbillonner.

edelweiss, *n*, edelweiss, *m.*

Eden (*fig.*) *n*, éden, *m.* [*the Garden of*] ~, l'Eden, le paradis [terrestre].

edge, *n*, bord, rebord, *m*, bordure; lisière; arête, *f*; tranche, *f*; tranchant, coupant, taillant, *m.* ~**ways**, ~**wise**, *ad. or on* ~, de chant. ¶ *v.t*, border. **edging**, *n*, bordure, *f*, bord, *m.* ~ *knife*, hache coupe-gazon, *f.*

edible, *a*, comestible.

edict, *n*. édit, *m.*

edifice, *n*, édifice. *m.* **edify**, *v.t*, édifier.

Edinburgh, *n*, Édimbourg, *m.*

edit, *v.t*, éditer, rédiger. ~**ion**, *n*, édition, *f.* **editor**, *n*, rédacteur (trice) en chef. **editorial**, *a*, de la rédaction; (*n.*) article, *m*, (*ou* note, *f.*) [émanant] de la rédaction. ~ *staff*, rédaction, *f.*

educate, *v.t*, élever, instruire, éduquer. **education**, *n*, éducation, *f*; enseignement *m*; instruction, *f.* ~**al**, *a*, d'éducation; scolaire; (*book*) classique. ~ *establishment*, maison d'éducation, *f.* **educator**, *n*, éducateur, trice.

educe, *v.t*, tirer; dégager.

eel, *n*, anguille, *f.* ~ *pot*, nasse, *f.*

eerie, -y, *a*, fantastique.

efface, *v.t*, effacer. ~**able**, *a*, effaçable.

effect, *n*, effet, *m*; suite; action, *f*; (*pl.*) effets, *m.pl.* ¶ *v.t*, effectuer, faire, opérer; contracter. ~**ive**† , *a*, effectif; utile. ¶ *n*, effectif, *m.*

effectual† , *a*, efficace.

effeminacy, *n*, caractère efféminé, *m.* **effeminate**, *a*, efféminé. *to* [*make*] ~, efféminer. ~ *[man]*, *n*, efféminé, *m*, femmelette, *f.*

effervesce, *v.i*, être en effervescence; faire e.; mousser. **effervescence, -ency**, *n*, effervescence, *f.* **effervescent**, *a*, effervescent. **effervescing** (*drink*) *p.a*, gazeux.

effete, *a*, épuisé.

efficacious† , *a*, efficace.

efficiency, *n*, efficacité, *f*; rendement, *m.* **efficient**† , *a*, efficace; capable.

effigy, *n*, effigie, *f.*

effloresce, *v.i*, [s']effleurir. **efflorescence**, *n*, efflorescence, *f.*

effluence, *n*, émanation, *f.*

effluvium, *n*, effluve, *m.*

efflux, *n*, dépense; émanation, *f.*

effort, *n*, effort, *m.*

effrontery, *n*, effronterie, *f.*

effulgence, *n*, rayonnement, *m.*

effusion, *n*, effusion, *f*, épanchement, *m*. **effusive**, *a*, expansif. **~ness**, *n*, effusion, *f*.

eft, *n*, triton, *m*, salamandre aquatique, *f*.

egg, *n*, œuf, *m*; (*pl.*, silkworm) graine, *f*. **~ cup**, coquetier, *m*. **~plant**, aubergine, *f*. **~shell**, coquille d'œuf, *f*. **boiled ~**, œuf à la coque. **fried ~**, œuf sur le plat. **scrambled ~s**, œufs brouillés. **~ on**, *v.t*, pousser.

eglantine, *n*, églantine odorante, *f*.

ego, *n*, moi, *m*. **egoism**, *n*, égoïsme, *m*. **egoist**, *n*, égoïste, *m,f*. **egoistic(al)**, *a*, égoïste. **egotism**, *n*, égotisme, *m*. **egotist**, *n*, égotiste, *m,f*. **egotistic(al)**, *a*, égotiste.

egregious, *a*, insigne, énorme, grossier, lourd; fieffé.

egress, *n*, sortie, issue, *f*.

egret (*bird & tuft*) *n*, aigrette, *f*.

Egypt, *n*, l'Égypte, *f*. **Egyptian**, *a*, égyptien. ¶ *n*, Égyptien, ne. **Egyptologist**, *n*, égyptologue, *m*. **Egyptology**, *n*, égyptologie, *f*.

eh, *i*, eh! hein!

eider [**duck**], *n*, eider, *m*. **~down**, édredon, *m*.

eight, *a. & n*, huit, *a. & m*. **eighteen**, *a. & n*, dix-huit, *a. & m*. *18-hole course*, parcours (*ou* golf) de 18 trous, *m*. **eighteenth**, *a. & n*, dix-huitième, *a. & m,f*; dix-huit, *m*. **eighth**, *a. & n*, huitième, *a. & m,f*; huit, *m*. **~ly**, *ad*, huitièmement. **eightieth**, *a. & n*, quatre-vingtième, *a. & m,f*. **eighty**, *a. & n*, quatre-vingts, quatre-vingt, *a. & m*. *81, etc*, quatre-vingt-un, etc.

either, *pn*, l'un (l'une) ou l'autre; l'un d'eux, l'une d'elles; un, une; chaque. ¶ *c*, ou; soit. ¶ *ad*, non plus. *nor I ~*, ni moi n. p.

ejaculate, *v.t. & abs*, lancer; faire; (*fluid*) éjaculer. **ejaculation**, *n*, interjection, exclamation; (*fluid*) éjaculation, *f*.

eject, *v.t*, expulser. **~ion**, *n*, expulsion, *f*.

eke out, *v.t*, allonger; suppléer.

elaborate, *a*, travaillé; étudié; recherché. ¶ *v.t*, élaborer; travailler.

elapse, *v.i*, s'écouler, [se] passer.

elastic, *a*, élastique. ¶ *n*, élastique, caoutchouc, *m*. **~ band**, bande

en caoutchouc, *f*. **~ity**, *n*, élasticité, *f*, ressort, *m*.

elate, *v.t*, enivrer; enorgueillir.

Elba (**the Island of**), l'île d'Elbe, *f*.

Elbe (**the**) (*river*), l'Elbe, *m*.

elbow, *n*, coude, *m*. *to rest on one's ~(s)*, s'accouder. **~ grease** (*fig.*), huile de coude, *f*. **~ room**, coudées franches, *f.pl*. ¶ *v.t*, coudoyer. *to ~ one's way*, jouer des coudes.

elder, *a*, aîné, plus âgé. ¶ *n*, aîné, e; (*Eccl.*) ancien; (*Bot.*) sureau, *m*. *our ~s*, nos aînés. **~ berry**, baie de sureau, *f*. **~ly**, *a*, d'un certain âge. **eldest**, *n. & a*, aîné, e.

El Dorado, *n*, eldorado, *m*.

elect, *v.t*, élire, nommer. *the ~* (*Relig.*), les élus, *m.pl*. **~ed member**, élu, e. **election**, *n*, élection, *f*. **electioneering**, *n*, manœuvres électorales, *f.pl*. **elector**, *n*, électeur, trice. **~ate**, *n*, corps électoral, *m*.

electric, *a*, électrique. **~ eel**, gymnote, *m*. **~ sign**, enseigne (*ou* affiche) lumineuse, *f*. **~al**, *a*, électrique. **~ engineer**, ingénieur électricien, *m*. **~ally**, *ad*, par l'électricité. **~ian**, *n*, électricien, *m*. **~ity**, *n*, électricité, *f*. **electrify**, *v.t*, électriser; (*Rly, etc.*) électrifier. **electrocute**, *v.t*, électrocuter. **electrode**, *n*, électrode, *f*. **electrolysis**, *n*, électrolyse, *f*. **electromagnet**, *n*, électroaimant, *m*. **electron**, *n*, électron, *m*. **electroplate**, *n*, plaqué, *m*. ¶ *v.t*, argenter. **electrotype** (*printing*) *n*, galvano, *m*.

elegance, *n*, élégance, *f*. **elegant**, *a*, élégant. **~ly**, *ad*, élégamment.

elegy, *n*, élégie, *f*.

element, *n*, élément; facteur; (*Chem.*) corps simple; (*voltaic*) couple, *m*. **~ary**, *a*, élémentaire; (*Sch.*) primaire.

elephant, *n*, éléphant, *m*. **~[ine person]**, mastodonte, *m*.

elevate, *v.t*, élever; [re]monter. **elevation**, *n*, élévation; altitude, hauteur, *f*. **elevator**, *n*, ascenseur; (*Surg.*) élévatoire, *m*; (*in shoe*) hausse, *f*.

eleven, *a. & n*, onze, *a. & m*. **eleventh†**, *a. & n*, onzième, *a. & m,f*; onze, *m*.

elf, *n*, elfe, lutin, *m*. **elfin**, *a*, des elfes. **elfish**, *a*, des elfes; lutin, espiègle.

elicit, *v.t,* tirer, soutirer.

elide, *v.t,* élider.

eligible, *a,* éligible; sortable.

eliminate, *v.t,* éliminer. **elimination,** *n,* élimination, *f.*

elision, *n,* élision, *f.*

elixir, *n,* élixir, *m.*

elk, *n,* élan, *m.*

ellipse & ellipsis, *n,* ellipse, *f.* **elliptic(al)†,** *a,* elliptique.

elm [tree], *n,* orme, ormeau, *m.* ~ **grove,** ormaie, ormoie, *f.* ~ **row,** ormille, *f.*

elocution, *n,* élocution; déclamation, *f.*

elongate, *v.t,* allonger.

elope, *v.i,* se faire enlever (*with* = par); s'enfuir. ~**ment,** *n,* enlèvement, *m,* fugue, *f.*

eloquence, *n,* éloquence, *f.* **eloquent,** *a,* éloquent. ~**ly,** *ad,* éloquemment.

else, *ad,* autre; autrement, sinon, encore. *everything* ~, tout le reste. ~**where,** *ad,* autre part, ailleurs.

Elsinore, *n,* Elseneur, *f.*

elucidate, *v.t,* élucider, dégager.

elude, *v.t,* éluder, se soustraire à, se dérober à. **elusive,** *a,* insaisissable; flottant.

Elysian, *a,* élyséen. **Elysium,** *n,* élysée, *f.* (*Myth.*) Élysée, *m.*

emaciated, *p.p,* émacié, décharné, étique, hâve.

emanate, *v.i,* émaner.

emancipate, *v.t,* émanciper, affranchir.

emasculate, *v.t,* émasculer.

embalm, *v.t,* embaumer.

embank, *v.t,* remblayer, terrasser, encaisser. ~**ment,** *n,* remblai, encaissement; quai, *m;* levée, *f.*

embargo, *n,* embargo, *m.*

embark, *v.t,* embarquer. ~**ation,** *n,* embarquement, *m.*

embarrass, *v.t,* embarrasser. ~**ment,** *n,* embarras, *m.*

embassy, *n,* ambassade, *f.*

embattle, *v.t,* ranger en bataille; (*Arch.*) créneler.

embed, *v.t,* encastrer.

embellish, *v.t,* embellir.

ember days, Quatre-Temps, *m.pl.*

embers, *n.pl,* braise, *f,* charbon, *m;* cendre[s] *f.[pl.].*

embezzle, *v.t,* détourner. ~**ment,** *n,* détournement, *m,* malversation, *f;* péculat, *m.*

embitter, *v.t,* envenimer, enfieller, aigrir.

emblazon, *v.t,* blasonner.

emblem, *n,* emblème, *m.* ~**atic(al),** *a,* emblématique.

embodiment, *n,* incarnation, *f.* embody, *v.t,* incarner; englober.

embolden, *v.t,* enhardir.

embolism, *n,* embolie, *f.*

emboss, *v.t,* graver en relief; estamper, gaufrer; bosseler. ~**ed stamp,** timbre sec, timbre fixe, *m.*

embrace, *n,* embrassement, *m,* étreinte, *f.* ¶ *v.t,* embrasser.

embrasure, *n,* embrasure, *f.*

embrocation, *n,* embrocation, *f.*

embroider, *v.t,* broder. ~**er,** ~**ess,** *n,* brodeur, euse. ~**y,** *n,* broderie, *f.* ~ *cotton,* coton à broder, *m.* ~ *hoops,* métier à broder, *m.*

embroil, *v.t,* [em]brouiller.

embryo, *n,* embryon, *m. in* ~ (*fig.*), en e., en herbe. **embryonic,** *a,* embryonnaire.

emend, *v.t,* corriger. ~**ation,** *n,* correction, *f.*

emerald, *n,* émeraude, *f.*

emerge, *v.i,* émerger, déboucher. **emergence,** *n,* émergence, *f.*

emergency, *n,* urgence, *f;* événement [inattendu] *m,* occurrence, *f.* ~ *brake,* frein d'urgence, *m.* ~ *exit,* sortie de secours, *f.*

emeritus, *a,* émérite.

emery, *n,* émeri, *m.* ~ *cloth,* toile d'é., *f.*

emetic, *a. & n,* émétique, *a. & m.*

emigrant, *n,* émigrant, e. **emigrate,** *v.i,* émigrer. **emigration,** *n,* émigration, *f.* ~ *officer,* commissaire d'émigration, *m.*

eminence, *n,* éminence, *f. His E*~ (cardinal), son Éminence, *f.* **eminent,** *a,* éminent; notable, considérable. ~**ly,** *ad,* éminemment.

emir, *n,* émir, *m.*

emissary, *n,* émissaire, *m.* **emission** *n,* émission, *f.* **emit,** *v.t,* émettre; dégager.

emollient, *a. & n,* émollient, *a. & m.*

emoluments, *n.pl,* émoluments, *m.pl.*

emotion, *n,* émotion, *f,* émoi, *m.* ~**al,** *a,* facile à émouvoir.

empanel a jury, former une liste de jurés, former un tableau.

emperor, *n,* empereur, *m.*

emphasis, *n,* emphase; énergie, *f. to lay* ~ *upon* or **emphasize,** *v.t,* appuyer sur, souligner, accentuer, ponctuer. **emphatic**†, *a*, emphatique; énergique.

empire, *n*, empire, *m*.

empiric(al)†, *a*, empirique. **empiricism**, *n*, empirisme, *m*. **empiric[ist]**, *n*, empirique, *m*.

employ, *v.t*, employer; se servir de. *he is in my* ~, je l'emploie. ~**ee**, *n*, employé, e. ~**er**, *n*, patron, ne, employeur, euse. ~**ment**, *n*, emploi, travail, *m*. ~ **agency**, bureau de placement, *m*.

emporium, *n*, entrepôt; grand magasin, *m*.

empower, *v.t*, autoriser, investir du pouvoir.

empress, *n*, impératrice, *f*.

emptiness, *n*, vacuité, *f*; vide, *m*; nullité, *f*. **empty**, *a*, vide; à vide; à blanc; net; désert; creux; vain; en l'air. ~*-headed*, les mains vides. *to be* ~*-headed*, avoir la tête vide. *on an* ~ *stomach*, à jeun. ¶ (*case, etc.*) *n*, vide, *m*. ¶ *v.t*, vider, vidanger, épuiser, décharger.

empyrean, *n*, empyrée, *m*.

emulate, *v.t*, rivaliser avec. **emulation**, *n*, émulation, rivalité, *f*. **emulator**, *n*, émule, *m*.

emulsion, *n*, émulsion, *f*.

enable, *v.t*, mettre à même; permettre; (*law*) habiliter; (*computers*) valider.

enact, *v.t*, décréter, édicter. ~**ment**, *n*, loi, *f*, décret, *m*.

enamel, *n*. & ~ *ware*, émail, *m*. ¶ *v.t*, émailler, laquer. **enameling**, *n*, émaillage, *m*.

enamored, *p.p*, épris, amoureux.

encage, *v.t*, encager.

encamp, *v.i*. & *t*, camper. ~**ment**, *n*, campement, *m*.

encase, *v.t*, encaisser, enrober.

encash, *v.t*, encaisser.

encaustic, *a*. & *n*, encaustique, *a*. & *f*.

enchain, *v.t*, enchaîner.

enchant, *v.t*, enchanter. ~**er**, ~**ress**, *n*, enchanteur, eresse. ~**ing**, *p.a*, enchanteur. ~**ment**, *n*, enchantement, *m*.

encircle, *v.t*, encercler, ceindre, cerner.

enclave, *n*, enclave, *f*.

enclose, *v.t*, enfermer; [en]clore, enceindre; (*in letter*) inclure, joindre. ~**d**, *p.p*, ci-inclus, ci-joint. **enclosure**, *n*, enceinte, clôture, *f*, [en]clos, parc, *m*; (*in letter*) [pièce] annexe, pièce jointe, *f*.

encode, *v.t*, encoder. ~**r**, *n*, (*computers, etc.*) encodeur, *m*. **encoding**, *n*, encodage, *m*.

encomium, *n*, panégyrique, éloge, *m*.

encompass, *v.t*, entourer, ceindre.

encore, *i*. & *n*, bis, *ad*. & *m*. ¶ *v.t*, bisser.

encounter, *n*, rencontre, *f*. ¶ *v.t*, rencontrer.

encourage, *v.t*, encourager.

encroach on (**to**), empiéter sur, envahir; anticiper sur. ~**ment**, *n*, empiètement, envahissement, *m*.

encumber, *v.t*, embarrasser, encombrer; grever, obérer. **encumbrance**, *n*, embarras, *m*; charge, *f*.

encyclic(al), *a*. & *n*, encyclique, *a*. & *f*.

encyclopedia, *n*, encyclopédie, *f*.

end, *n*, fin, *f*, terme, *m*; extrémité; issue, *f*; bout; but, *m*. *no* ~ *of*, une infinité de. *on* ~, debout; (*hair*) hérissés; (*fig.*) d'arraché-pied. ~ *paper*, [feuille de] garde, *f*. ¶ *v.t*, finir, achever, terminer; (*v.i*) finir, prendre fin; aboutir.

endanger, *v.t*, mettre en danger.

endear, *v.t*, rendre cher. ~**ment**, *n*, caresse, *f*.

endeavor, *n*, effort, *m*, tentative, *f*. ¶ *v.i*, s'efforcer, tâcher, travailler.

ending, *n*, fin, *f*; dénouement, *m*; (*Gram.*) terminaison, désinence, *f*.

endive, *n*, scarole, endive, *f*.

endless, *a*. & ~**ly**, *ad*, sans fin.

endorse, *v.t*, endosser; (*fig.*) souscrire à. ~**ment**, *n*, (*bill, check, etc.*) endos, endossement; (*Insce*) avenant, *m*. **endorser**, *n*, endosseur, *m*.

endow, *v.t*, renter, doter; douer, avantager. ~**ment**, *n*, dotation, *f*.

endue, *v.t*, revêtir; douer.

endurable, *a*, supportable. **endurance**, *n*, endurance; résistance, *f*. ~ *test*, épreuve d'endurance, *f*, raid, *m*. **endure**, *v.t*, endurer, supporter; (*v.i*) vivre.

enema, *n*, (*instrument*) irrigateur, *m*; (*action*) lavement, *f*.

enemy, *n*. & *a*, ennemi, e.

energetic†, *a*, énergique. ~**s** (*Phys.*) *n.pl*, énergétique, *f*. en-

ergize, *v.t*, infuser de l'ardeur dans; (*Elec.*) amorcer. **energy**, *n*, énergie; poigne, *f*; travail, *m*.

enervate, *v.t*, énerver, [r]amollir.

enfeeble, *v.t*, affaiblir.

enfilade, *n*, enfilade, *f*. ¶ *v.t*, enfiler.

enfold, *v.t*, envelopper; étreindre.

enforce, *v.t*, imposer; faire valoir; mettre en vigueur, exécuter. **~able**, *a*, exécutoire. **~ment**, *n*, contrainte; exécution, *f*.

enfranchise, *v.t*, affranchir; accorder le droit de vote à.

engage, *v.t*, engager, retenir; embaucher; arrêter; prendre; (*Mech.*) engrener; embrayer; (*v.i.*) s'engager, se mettre; engager le combat. ¶ *v.t*, **~ment**, *n*, engagement; (*Mech.*) engrenage, *f*; fiançailles, *f.pl*. **~ ring**, bague de fiançailles, *f*. **engaging**, *p.a*, engageant, attrayant, attachant.

engender, *v.t*, engendrer.

engine, *n*, machine, *f*, moteur, *m*; (*Rly*) locomotive, *f*; (*of war*) engin, *m*; (*jet*) réacteur, *m*. **~ driver**, **~man**, mécanicien, *m*. **engineer**, *n*, ingénieur; (*maker*) ingénieur constructeur; (*ship*) mécanicien; (*Mil.*) officier du génie; soldat du génie, *m*. ¶ *v.t*, provoquer. **engineering**, *n*, l'art (*m.*) (*ou* la science) de l'ingénieur; construction, *f*; génie, *m*. **engineless**, *a*, sans moteur.

England, *n*, l'Angleterre, *f*. **English**, *a*, anglais. the **~ Channel**, la Manche. **~man**, **~woman**, Anglais, e. ¶ (*language*) *n*, l'anglais, *m*.

engrave, *v.t*, graver; buriner. **engraver**, *n*, graveur, *m*. **engraving**, *n*, gravure, estampe, *f*.

engross, *v.t*, absorber; s'emparer de; (*law*) grossoyer. **~ment** (*law*) *n*, grosse, *f*.

engulf, *v.t*, engouffrer, engloutir.

enhance, *v.t*, rehausser; augmenter.

enigma, *n*, énigme, *f*. **enigmatic(al)**†, *a*, énigmatique.

enjoin, *v.t*, enjoindre.

enjoy, *v.t*, jouir de, savourer, goûter. **~ oneself**, s'amuser, se réjouir. **~able**, *a*, agréable, savoureux. **~ment**, *n*, jouissance, *f*; plaisir, *m*.

enlarge, *v.t*, agrandir, augmenter, élargir. **~ upon**, s'étendre sur.

~ment, *n*, agrandissement, *m*. **enlarger** (*Phot.*) *n*, agrandisseur, *m*.

enlighten, *v.t*, éclairer, édifier.

enlist, *v.t*, enrôler, engager. **~ment**, *n*, enrôlement, engagement, *m*.

enliven, *v.t*, [r]animer, vivifier, égayer.

enmity, *n*, inimitié, *f*.

ennoble, *v.t*, anoblir; (*fig.*) ennoblir.

enormity, *n*, énormité, *f*. **enormous**, *a*, énorme. **~ly**, *ad*, énormément. **~ness**, *n*, énormité, *f*.

enough, *a*, assez de; assez; suffisant. ¶ *ad*, assez; suffisamment. ¶ *n*, suffisance, *f*, assez, de quoi. to have **~** & to spare, avoir à revendre.

enquire, *etc*. Same as *inquire*, etc.

enrage, *v.t*, rendre furieux, faire enrager.

enrapture, *v.t*, enchanter, ravir, enthousiasmer.

enrich, *v.t*, enrichir.

enroll, *v.t*, enrôler, immatriculer, embrigader, enrégimenter. **enrollment**, *n*, enrôlement, *m*.

ensconce, *v.t*, camper, nicher.

enshrine, *v.t*, enchâsser.

enshroud, *v.t*, envelopper; voiler.

ensign, *n*, (*banner, flag*) enseigne, *f*; (*Naut.*) pavillon de poupe; (*pers.*) enseigne, *m*.

enslave, *v.t*, asservir, enchaîner.

ensnare, *v.t*, attraper.

ensue, *v.i*, s'ensuivre, résulter. **ensuing**, *p.a*, suivant, subséquent.

ensure, *v.t*, assurer.

entablature, *n*, entablement, *m*.

entail, *v.t*, entraîner; (*law*) substituer.

entangle, *v.t*, empêtrer, emmêler, embarrasser.

enter, *v.t*, entrer dans; pénétrer; engager; (*names, etc.*) inscrire, enregistrer; (*v.i.*) entrer; pénétrer; s'engager. **~ into** (*bargain, contract*) faire, passer, souscrire, contracter, intervenir dans. **~ X.** (*Theat.*), X. entre [en scène].

enterprise, *n*, entreprise, *f*; esprit entreprenant, *m*. **enterprising**, *a*, entreprenant.

entertain, *v.t*, recevoir, héberger; régaler, fêter; (*abs.*) traiter; représenter; amuser, divertir, défrayer; (*idea*) concevoir, nourrir; accueillir favorablement. **~ment**, *n*, amusement, divertissement;

spectacle, *m*. ~ *tax*, taxe sur les spectacles, *f*.

enthrall, *v.t*, captiver, enchaîner; passionner.

enthrone, *v.t*, introniser. **~ment**, *n*, intronisation, *f*.

enthusiasm, *n*, enthousiasme, *m*. **enthusiast**, *n*, enthousiaste, *m,f*, fervent, e. **~ic**, *a*, enthousiaste. **~ically**, *ad*, avec enthousiasme.

entice, *v.t*, allécher; séduire. **~ment**, *n*, allèchement, *m*, séduction, *f*. **enticing**, *p.a*, alléchant, acquinant, séduisant.

entire†, *a*, entier, intégral. **~ty**, *n*, entier, *m*; intégralité, *f*.

entitle, *v.t*, intituler; donner droit à.

entity, *n*, entité, *f*.

entomb, *v.t*, ensevelir.

entomologist, *n*, entomologiste, *m*. **entomology**, *n*, entomologie, *f*.

entr'acte (*Theat.*) *n*, entracte, *m*.

entrails, *n.pl*, entrailles, *f.pl*.

entrain, *v.t*, embarquer.

entrance, *n*, entrée; porte, *f*. ~ [*fee*], cotisation d'admission, *f*; droit d'entrée, *m*.

entrance, *v.t*, jeter en extase; ravir.

entrap, *v.t*, attraper.

entreat, *v.t*, supplier, prier instamment. **~y**, *n*, supplication, prière, *f*, (*pl.*) instances, *f.pl*.

entrench, *v.t*, retrancher. **~ing tool**, pellebêche, *f*.

entrust, *v.t*, confier, charger, remettre.

entry, *n*, entrée, *f*; engagement, *m*; inscription, *f*, enregistrement, *m*.

entwine, *v.t*, enlacer, entortiller.

enumerate, *v.t*, énumérer.

enunciate, *v.t*, énoncer.

envelope, *n*, enveloppe, *f*, pli, *m*. ¶ *v.t*, envelopper.

envenom, *v.t*, envenimer.

enviable, *a*, enviable. **envious**, *a*, envieux.

environ, *v.t*, environner. **~ment**, *n*, entourage, milieu, *m*, ambiance, *f*. **environs**, *n.pl*, environs, entours, *m.pl*.

envisage, *v.t*, envisager.

envoy, *n*, envoyé, *m*.

envy, *n*, envie, *f*. ¶ *v.t*, envier.

epaulet, *n*, épaulette, *f*.

epergne, *n*, surtout [de table] *m*, girandole, *f*.

ephemeral, *a*, éphémère.

epic, *a*, épique. ¶ *n*, épopée, *f*.

epicure, *n*, gourmet, *m*, friand, e. **epicurean**, *a*. & *n*, épicurien, *a*. & *m*.

epidemic, *n*, épidémie, *f*. ~(al) *a*, épidémique.

epidermis, *n*, épiderme, *m*.

epiglottis, *n*, épiglotte, *f*.

epigram, *n*, épigramme, *f*.

epigraph, *n*, (*prefixed to book or chapter*) épigraphe; (*on stone*) inscription, *f*.

epilepsy, *n*, épilepsie, *f*. **epileptic**, *a*. & *n*, épileptique, *a*. & *m,f*.

epilogue, *n*, épilogue, *m*.

Epiphany, *n*, Épiphanie, *f*.

episcopal, *a*, épiscopal. **episcopate** & **episcopacy**, *n*, épiscopat, *m*.

episode, *n*, épisode, *m*.

epistle, *n*, épître, *f*. **epistolary**, *a*, épistolaire.

epitaph, *n*, épitaphe, *f*.

epithet, *n*, épithète, *f*.

epitome, *n*, épitomé, abrégé, raccourci, *m*. **epitomize**, *v.t*, abréger; personnifier.

epoch, *n*, époque, ère, *f*.

epsom salt[s], sel d'Epsom, *m*.

equable†, *a*, égal. **equal†**, *a*, égal, pareil; pair. ~ *to* (*task*), à la hauteur de. ¶ *n*, égal, e, pareil, le, pair, *m*. ¶ *v.t*, égaler. **~ity**, *n*, égalité, *f*, pair, *m*; (*rights*) concurrence, *f*, concours; (*votes*) partage, *m*. **~ize**, *v.t*, égaliser, égaler.

equanimity, *n*, sérénité, *f*.

equation, *n*, équation, *f*.

equator, *n*, équateur, *m*. **~ial**, *a*, équatorial.

equerry, *n*, écuyer, *m*.

equestrian, *a*, équestre. ¶ *n*, cavalier, ère; écuyer, ère [de cirque].

equilibrate, *v.t*, équilibrer. **equilibrium**, *n*, équilibre, *m*.

equine, *a*, chevalin, hippique.

equinoctial, *a*, équinoxial. **equinox**, *n*, équinoxe, *m*.

equip, *v.t*, équiper, armer, outiller. **~age**, *n*, équipage, *m*. **~ment**, *n*, équipement, armement, outillage; fourniment, *m*.

equipoise, *n*, équilibre, *m*.

equitable†, *a*, équitable. **equity**, *n*, équité, *f*.

equivalent, *a*. & *n*, équivalent, *a*. & *m*; parité, *f*. *to be* ~, équivaloir.

equivocal, *a*, équivoque. equivocate, *v.i*, équivoquer. equivocation, *n*, équivoques, *f.pl*.

era, *n*, ère, époque, *f*.

eradicate, *v.t*, déraciner, extirper.

erase, *v.t*, raturer, gratter, effacer. eraser, *n*, (*knife*) grattoir, *m*; (*rubber*) gomme [à effacer] *f*. erasure, *n*, rature, *f*, grattage, *m*, effaçure, *f*.

ere, *c*, avant que. ~ long, sous peu.

Erebus, *n*, l'Érèbe, *m*.

erect, *a*, droit; debout, *ad*; dressé. ¶ *v.t*, ériger; construire; élever; monter; dresser; hérisser. ~ion, *n*, érection; construction, *f*; montage; dressage. *m*. to have an ~, bander (*obscene*).

Erie (Lake), le lac Érié.

ermine, *n*, hermine, *f*.

erode, *v.t*, éroder. erosion, *n*, érosion, *f*.

erotic, *a*, érotique.

err, *v.i*, errer, pécher.

errand, *n*, commission, ambassade, course, *f*, message, *m*. ~ boy, garçon de course, (*law office*) saute-ruisseau, *m*.

errant, *a*, errant.

erratic, *a*, irrégulier; (*Geol., Med.*) erratique.

erratum, *n*, erratum, *m*. erroneous, *a*, erroné, faux. ~ly, *ad*, par erreur. error, *n*, erreur, faute, *f*, mécompte; écart, *m*.

eructation, *n*, éructation, *f*.

erudite, *a*, érudit. erudition, *n*, érudition, *f*.

eruption, *n*, éruption, *f*.

escalation, *n*, (*Mil.*) escalade, *f*.

escalator, *n*, escalier roulant, *m*.

escallop, *n*, pétoncle, *m*.

escapade, *n*, escapade; équipée, frasque, *f*.

escape, *n*, fuite; évasion, *f*; échappement, *m*; issue, *f*. fire~, échelle de sauvtage, *f*. ¶ *v.i*, s'échapper; échapper; fuir; s'enfuir; se sauver; s'évader; se débonder; (*v.t.*) échapper à; échapper de; échapper. escaped prisoner, évadé, *m*. ~ment, *n*, échappement, *m*.

escarpment, *n*, escarpement, *m*.

escheat, *n*, déshérence, *f*. ¶ *v.i*, tomber en déshérence; (*v.t.*) confisquer.

eschew, *v.t*, éviter, fuir.

escort, *n*, escorte, *f*; cavalier, *m*.

¶ *v.t*, escorter, reconduire, accompagner.

escutcheon, *n*, écusson, *m*.

espagnolette, *n*, espagnolette, crémone, *f*.

espalier, *n*, espalier, *m*.

especial, *a*, notable, digne d'être signalé, qui mérite une mention particulière; particulier; tout spécial. ~ly, *ad*, surtout; notamment; particulièrement. ~ as, d'autant que.

espionage, *n*, espionnage, *m*.

esplanade, *n*, esplanade, *f*.

espousal, *n*, adoption, adhésion, *f*. espouse, *v.t*, épouser; embrasser.

espy, *v.t*, apercevoir, aviser, découvrir.

esquire, (*Hist.*) *n*, écuyer, *m*. Esquire, *n*. (*abb.* Esq.), Monsieur, *m*. (*Note.—As a form of address on envelope or in letter, Monsieur should not be abbreviated.*)

essay, *n*, essai, *m*, composition, dissertation, narration, *f*. ¶ *v.t*, essayer. ~ist, *n*, essayiste, *m,f*.

essence, *n*, essence, *f*. essential†, *a*, essentiel; capital. ¶ *n*, essentiel, *m*.

establish, *v.t*, établir; créer; asseoir; constater. the ~ed Church, l'Église d'Etat, *f*. ~ment, *n*, établissement, *m*; création; fondation; constatation, *f*; ménage, *m*.

estate, *n*, bien[s] *m*.[pl.], propriété[s] *f*.[pl.]; domaine, fonds, *m*, terre; succession, *f*. real ~ agency, agence immobilière, *f*.

esteem, *n*, estime, *f*. ¶ *v.t*, estimer; considérer (*ou* regarder) comme.

Esthonia, *n*, l'Estonie, *f*.

estimate, *n*, estimation, appréciation, évaluation, prisée, *f*; état (*ou* devis) estimatif; (*pl.*) budget, *m*. ¶ *v.t*, estimer, apprécier, évaluer, priser. ~d, *p.a*, estimatif. estimation, *n*, jugement, *m*, estime, *f*.

estrange, *v.t*, éloigner, aliéner.

estuary, *n*, estuaire, *m*.

etch, *v.t*, graver à l'eau-forte. ~er, *n*, graveur à l'eau-forte, aquafortiste, *m*. ~ing, *n*, [gravure à l']eau-forte, *f*.

eternal†, *a*, éternel. the ~ triangle, la vie à trois. etern[al]ize, *v.t*, éterniser. eternity, *n*, éternité, *f*.

ether, *n,* éther, *m.* **ethereal,** *a,* éthéré.

ethical, *a,* éthique. **ethics,** *n.pl,* éthique, *f.*

Ethiopia, *n,* l'Éthiopie, *f.* **Ethiopian,** *a,* éthiopien. ¶ *n,* Éthiopien, ne.

ethnic, *a,* ethnique.

ethnography, *n,* ethnographie, *f.* **ethnologic(al),** *a,* ethnologique. **ethnologist,** *n,* ethnologue, *m.* **ethnology,** *n,* ethnologie, *f.*

ethyl, *n,* éthyle, *m.*

etiolate, *v.t,* étioler.

etiquette, *n,* étiquette, *f,* décorum, protocole, *m.*

etymologic(al), *a,* étymologique. **etymology,** *n,* étymologie, *f.*

eucalyptus, *n,* eucalyptus, *m.*

Eucharist, *n,* Eucharistie, *f.*

eugenic, *a,* eugénique. **~s,** *n.pl,* eugénie, *f.*

eulogistic†, *a,* élogieux. **eulogize,** *v.t,* faire l'éloge de. **eulogy,** *n,* éloge, *m.*

eunuch, *n,* eunuque, *m.*

euphemism, *n,* euphémisme, *m.* **euphemistic,** *a,* euphémique.

euphonic & euphonious, *a,* euphonique. **euphony,** *n,* euphonie, *f.*

Euphrates (the), l'Euphrate, *m.*

Europe, *n,* l'Europe, *f.* **European,** *a,* européen. ¶ *n,* Européen, ne.

eustachian tube, trompe d'Eustache, *f.*

euthanasia, *n,* euthanasie, *f.*

evacuate, *v.t,* évacuer.

evade, *v.t,* éviter, éluder, esquiver; frauder.

evaluate, *v.t,* évaluer.

evanescent, *a,* évanescent.

evangelic(al)†, *a,* évangélique. **evangelist,** *n,* évangéliste, *m.*

evaporate, *v.t,* [faire] évaporer; (*v.i.*) s'évaporer. **evaporation,** *n,* évaporation, *f.*

evasion, *n,* échappatoire, *f,* fauxfuyant, subterfuge, *m,* défaite, *f,* atermoiement, *m.* ~ **of tax,** la fraude fiscale. **evasive†,** *a,* évasif; flottant; normand.

eve, *n,* veille, *f.* **even** (*Poet.*) *n,* soir, *m.* ~**song,** vêpres, *f.pl.* ~**tide,** chute du jour, *f.*

even, *a,* uni; plan; égal; uniforme; pair; (*games*) but à but. ~ **money,** compte rond, *m.* ~ **number,** nombre pair, *m.* **to be** ~ **with** (someone), revaloir. ¶ *ad,* même; jusque. ~ **if,** ~ **though,**

même si, quand, lors même que. ¶ *v.t,* égaliser; aplanir.

evening, *n,* soir, *m;* soirée; veillée, *f;* (*fig.*) déclin, *m.* ~ **dew,** ~ **damp,** serein, *m.* ~ **dress,** (*man*) tenue de soirée; (*woman*) toilette de s., *f.* ~ **gown,** robe du soir, *f.*

evenly, *ad,* uniment; uniformément. **evenness,** *n,* égalité; uniformité, *f.*

event, *n,* événement; cas, *m;* (*sport*) épreuve, *f.* ~**ful,** *a,* plein d'événements; mouvementé, accidenté.

eventual†, *a,* éventuel. ~**ity,** *n,* éventualité, *f.* **eventuate,** *v.i,* aboutir.

ever, *ad,* jamais; toujours. **for** ~, à (*ou* pour) jamais (*ou* toujours). ~ **so little,** tant soit peu. **hardly** ~, presque jamais. **if** ~, si jamais.

evergreen, *n,* arbre toujours vert, *m.*

everlasting†, *a,* éternel; immortel.

evermore, *ad,* toujours. **for** ~, à tout jamais.

every, *a,* chaque; tout, e; tous (toutes) les. ~**body, everyone, every one** (every person), tout le monde, chacun, *m. only.* ~**day,** *a,* quotidien; vulgaire; ordinaire. ~**day clothes,** vêtements ordinaires, habits de tous les jours, *m.pl.* ~ **one** (each), chacun, e. ~**thing,** *n,* tout, *pn.* ~**where,** *ad,* partout.

evict, *v.t,* évincer, expulser. ~**ion,** *n,* éviction, *f.*

evidence, *n,* évidence; preuve, *f;* témoignage, *m;* déposition, *f;* titre, *m.* **to give** ~, témoigner. ¶ *v.t,* constater. **evident,** *a,* évident. ~**ly,** *ad,* évidemment.

evil, *a,* mauvais; méchant; malin, malfaisant. ~**-minded** (*person*), *a.* & *n,* malintentionné, e. ~ **doer,** malfaiteur, *m.* ~ **eye,** mauvais œil, *m.* **the E**~ **One,** le malin [esprit], l'esprit malin, *m.* ~ **speaking,** médisance, *f.* ~ **spirit,** esprit malin, malin esprit, *m.* ¶ *ad,* mal. ¶ *n,* mal, *m,* plaie, *f.*

evince, *v.t,* manifester, témoigner.

eviscerate, *v.t,* éventrer.

evocation, *n,* évocation, *f.* **evoke,** *v.t,* évoquer.

evolution, *n,* déroulement, *m;* (*Biol., etc.*) évolution, *f;* (*Geom.*)

développement; (*Chem.*) dégagement, *m.* **evolve**, *v.t,* élaborer; dégager; (*v.i.*) évoluer.

ewe, *n,* brebis, *f.* ~ **lamb**, agneau femelle, *m.*

ewer, *n,* pot à eau, broc de toilette, *m;* aiguière, *f.*

ex-, *prefix:* ~-*professor*, ex-professeur, ancien professeur, *m.* ~-*serviceman*, ancien combattant, *m.*

exacerbate, *v.t,* exacerber.

exact, *a,* exact, précis. ¶ *v.t,* exiger. ~**ing**, *p.a,* exigeant. ~**ion**, *n,* exaction, *f.* ~**ly**, *ad,* exactement, au juste, précisément, parfaitement. ~**ness, exactitude**, *n,* exactitude, *f.*

exaggerate, *v.t.* & *abs,* exagérer, grossir.

exaggeration, *n,* exagération, *f.*

exalt, *v.t,* exalter, relever.

examination, *n,* examen, *m;* inspection; visite, *f;* concours; interrogatoire, *m;* instruction; expertise, *f.* **examine**, *v.t,* examiner; interroger; inspecter; visiter; (*documents*) compulser. **examinee**, *n,* candidat, e. **examiner**, *n,* examinateur, trice; interrogateur, trice; inspecteur, trice; visiteur; vérificateur; contrôleur, *m.*

example, *n,* exemple, *m.*

exasperate, *v.t,* exaspérer, énerver, indigner.

excavate, *v.t,* creuser, fouiller. **excavation**, *n,* excavation, fouille, *f,* déblai, *m.* **excavator** (*Mach.*) *n,* excavateur, *m.*

exceed, *v.t,* excéder, [dé]passer, outrepasser. ~**ingly**, *ad,* excessivement, extrêmement.

excel, *v.i,* exceller, primer; (*v.t.*) surpasser. **excellence**, *n,* excellence, *f.* His Excellency, Son Excellence, *f.* **excellent**, *a,* excellent. ~**ly**, *ad,* excellemment, à merveille.

except, *c,* sinon. ~ & ~**ing**, *pr,* excepté, à l'exception de, hors, hormis, sauf, ôté, à part. ¶ *v.t,* excepter. ~**ion**, *n,* exception; réserve, *f.* to take ~ to, se formaliser de. ~**ionable**, *a,* récusable; critiquable. ~**ional**†, *a,* exceptionnel, hors ligne.

excerpt, *n,* extrait, *m,* bribe, *f.* ¶ *v.t,* extraire.

excess, *n,* excès; excédent; surplus, trop, *m;* outrance, *f;* débordement, *m;* intempérance, *f.*

~ *profits*, surplus des bénéfices. ~ *weight*, excédent de poids, *m,* surcharge, *f.* ~**ive**†, *a,* excessif, immodéré, outré.

exchange, *n,* échange; change; troc, *m;* permutation, *f;* (*Teleph.*) bureau [central], poste central, *m.* ~ *rates*, cote des changes, *f.* stock ~, Bourse, *f.* ¶ *v.t,* échanger; changer; troquer.

exchequer, *n,* trésor, *m,* trésorerie, *f;* (*Eng.*) échiquier, *m;* (*of pers.*) finances, *f.pl.*

excise, *n,* (*Fr.*) régie; (*Eng.*) accise, *f.*

excite, *v.t,* exciter, provoquer; irriter, exalter; agacer. ~**ment**, *n,* excitation; exaltation; émotion, *f.*

exclaim, *v.i,* s'écrier, se récrier, s'exclamer. ~ *against, abs,* s'exclamer. **exclamation**, *n,* exclamation, *f.*

exclude, *v.t,* exclure. **exclusion**, *n,* exclusion, *f.* **exclusive**†, *a,* exclusif. ~ *right*(*s*), droit[s] exclusif[s] *m.*[*pl.*], exclusiveté, *f.*

excommunicate, *v.t,* excommunier.

excoriate, *v.t,* écorcher.

excrement, *n,* excrément, *m.*

excrescence, *n,* excroissance, *f.*

excruciating†, *p.a,* atroce.

exculpate, *v.t,* disculper.

excursion, *n,* excursion; partie; promenade, *f.* ~ *ticket*, billet d'excursion, *m.* ~**ist**, *n,* excursionniste, *m,f.*

excusable, *a,* excusable.

excuse, *n,* excuse, *f,* prétexte, *m.* ¶ *v.t,* excuser, pardonner; exempter, dispenser de; faire remise de. ~ *me*, excusez-moi; pardon!

execrable†, *a,* exécrable. **execrate**, *v.t,* exécrer.

execute, *v.t,* exécuter; effectuer; (*document*) souscrire; exécuter [à mort], faire mourir. **execution**, *n,* exécution, *f;* jeu, *m;* souscription; saisie[-exécution] *f.* ~**er**, *n,* bourreau, *m.* **executive**, *n,* bureau; État-major, *m.* **executor, -trix**, *n,* exécuteur (trice) testamentaire. **executory**, *a,* exécutoire.

exemplary, *a,* exemplaire, modèle. **exemplify**, *v.t,* éclaircir par un exemple, des exemples.

exempt, *a,* exempt. ¶ *v.t,* exempter. ~**ion**, *n,* exemption, franchise, *f.*

exercise, n, exercice; (Sch.) devoir; thème, m. ~ book, cahier, m. ¶ v.t, exercer, user de; (Stk Ex. option) consolider, lever; (v.i.) prendre de l'exercice.

exert, v.t, exercer. ~ oneself, s'évertuer, faire un effort. ~ion, n, effort, m.

exfoliate, v.i, s'exfolier.

exhalation, n, (act) exhalation; (mist) exhalaison, f. **exhale,** v.t, exhaler, respirer.

exhaust, n, échappement, m. ¶ v.t, épuiser; aspirer. ~ion, n, épuisement, m; aspiration, f. ~ive, a, approfondi. ~ively, ad, à fond, mûrement.

exhibit, n, objet exposé, produit [à présenter] m; (law, civil) pièce justificative, p. à l'appui; (criminal) p. à conviction, f. ¶ v.t, exposer; exhiber. ~ion, n, exposition, f; salon, m; exhibition. **exhibitor,** n, exposant, e; montreur, m.

exhilarate, v.t, émoustiller, égayer, stimuler.

exhort, v.t, exhorter, prêcher [à].

exhume, v.t, exhumer, déterrer.

exigence, -cy, n, exigence, f.

exile, n, exil, m; (pers.) exilé, e. ¶ v.t, exiler.

exist, v.i, exister. ~ence, n, existence, f.

exit, n, sortie, issue, f, dégagement, m. ~ X. (Theat.), X. sort.

exodus, n, exode, m. E~ (Bible), l'Exode.

exonerate, v.t, exonérer.

exorbitance, n, extravagance, f. **exorbitant,** a, exorbitant. ~ly, ad, exorbitamment.

exorcise, v.t, exorciser.

exotic, a, exotique. ¶ n, plante exotique, f.

expand, v.t, étendre; déployer; dilater. **expanse,** n, étendue; envergure, f. **expansion,** n, expansion; dilatation; détente, f. **expansive,** a, expansif.

expatiate, v.i, s'étendre.

expatriate, v.t, expatrier.

expect, v.t, attendre, s'attendre à; espérer. ~ancy, n, expectative, f. ~ant, a, expectant. ~ mother, femme enceinte, f. ~ation, n, attente, expectative; espérance, prévision, f.

expectorate, v.t. & abs, expectorer.

expedience, -cy, n, convenance, f. **expedient,** a, expédient, con-

venable. ¶ n, expédient, m, ressource, f. **expedite,** v.t, expédier; hâter. **expedition,** n, expédition, f. ~ary, a, expéditionnaire. **expeditious,** a, expéditif, diligent.

expel, v.t, expulser, chasser, bannir.

expend, v.t, dépenser. **expenditure,** n, dépense[s] f.[pl.]. **expense,** n, frais, m.pl, dépense, charge, f, dépens, m.pl. at the ~ of, aux frais (ou dépens) (ou crochets) de; à la charge de. **incidental ~s,** faux frais. **expensive†,** a, cher, coûteux, dispendieux.

experience, n, expérience, pratique, f, métier, m, acquis, m.s. & pl. ~d, a, expérimenté, expert. ¶ v.t, éprouver, faire l'expérience de. **experiment,** n, expérience, f. ¶ v.i, expérimenter. ~ on, faire des expériences sur. ~al†, a, expérimental.

expert, a. & n, expert, a. & m. ~ness, n, habileté, f.

expiate, v.t, expier.

expiration, n, expiration, échéance, déchéance, f. **expire,** v.t. & abs, expirer; (v.i.) expirer, échoir, périmer.

explain, v.t, expliquer, exposer. ~able, a, explicable. **explanation,** n, explication, f. **explanatory,** a, explicatif.

expletive (Gram.) a, explétif. ¶ n, mot explétif, m, (in verse) cheville, f; (oath) gros mot, juron, m.

explicit†, a, explicite; clair.

explode, v.t, faire explorer, f. éclater; f. sauter; (fig.) démolir; (v.i.) exploser, éclater, faire explosion. ~d theory, théorie périmée, f.

exploit, n, exploit, m. ¶ v.t, exploiter. ~ation, n, exploitation, f.

explore, v.t, explorer, reconnaître. **explorer,** n, explorateur, trice.

explosion, n, explosion, f. **explosive,** n, explosif, m.

exponent, n, exposant; interprète, m; (Math.) exposant, m.

export, v.t, exporter. ~[ation], n, exportation, f. ~er, n, exportateur, m.

expose, v.t, exposer, mettre à nu; (Phot.) [ex]poser. **exposition,** n, exposition, f.

expostulate, *v.i,* faire des remontrances. **expostulation,** *n,* remontrance, *f.*

exposure, *n,* exposition, mise à nu; (*Phot.*) pose, exposition, *f.*

expound, *v.t,* exposer.

express, *a,* exprès, formel. ¶ (*Post, etc.*) *n,* exprès, *m.* ~ [*train*], [train] express, *m.* ¶ *v.t,* exprimer; énoncer; traduire. ~ion, *n,* expression, *f.* ~ive, *a,* expressif. **expressly,** *ad,* expressément.

expropriate, *v.t,* exproprier.

expulsion, *n,* expulsion, *f.*

expunge, *v.t,* rayer, effacer.

expurgate, *v.t,* expurger.

exquisite, *a,* exquis; vif. ~**ly,** *ad,* exquisément. ~**ness,** *n,* exquis, *m.*

extant (to be), exister.

extempore, *a,* improvisé, impromptu. ¶ *dd,* d'abondance, impromptu. **extemporize,** *v.t.* & *i,* improviser.

extend, *v.t,* étendre; prolonger. **extension,** *n,* extension, *f,* prolongement, *m;* prolongation, *f;* (*Teleph.*) poste supplémentaire, *m.* ~ *ladder,* échelle à coulisse, *f.* ~ *tripod,* trépied extensible, *m.* **extensive,** *a,* étendu, large. ~**ly,** *ad,* largement. **extensor** (*muscle*) *n,* extenseur, *m.* **extent,** *n,* étendue; importance, *f;* degré, point, *m,* mesure, *f.*

extenuate, *v.t,* atténuer.

exterior†, *a,* extérieur, externe. ¶ *n,* extérieur; dehors, *m;* enveloppe (*fig.*) *f.*

exterminate, *v.t,* exterminer.

external, *a,* externe, extérieur. ~**ly,** *ad,* extérieurement.

extinct, *a,* éteint. ~**ion,** *n,* extinction, *f.* **extinguish,** *v.t,* éteindre. ~**er,** *n,* (*light*) éteignoir; (*fire*) extincteur, *m.*

extirpate, *v.t,* extirper.

extol, *v.t,* exalter; vanter; prôner.

extort, *v.t,* extorquer, arracher. ~**ion,** *n,* extorsion; maltôte, *f.* ~**ionate,** *a,* exorbitant. ~**ioner,** *n,* écorcheur, euse, *m.*

extra, *a,* supplémentaire, supplément de, en sus, hors d'œuvre. ~ *fare,* supplément [de taxe] *m.* ¶ *ad,* extra. ¶ *n,* extra, supplément, *m,* plus-value, *f;* hors-d'œuvre, *m;* (*movies*) figurant,

m; (*newspaper*) édition spéciale, *f.*

extract, *n,* extrait, *m.* ¶ *v.t,* extraire; arracher; [sou]tirer, retirer. ~**ion,** *n,* extraction, *f.*

extradite, *v.t,* extrader. **extradition,** *n,* extradition, *f.*

extraneous, *a,* étranger.

extraordinary†, *a,* extraordinaire; insolent. ¶ *n,* extraordinaire, *m.*

extraterritoriality, *n,* exterritorialité, *f.*

extravagance, *n,* extravagance, *f;* dévergondage (*fig.*) *m;* (*money*) folles dépenses, *f.pl,* dissipation [s] *f.*[*pl.*], prodigalités, *f.pl.* **extravagant,** *a,* extravagant; (*of pers.*) dépensier; (*price*) exorbitant. ~**ly,** *ad,* follement.

extreme†, *a.* & *n,* extrême, *a.* & *m.* ~ *penalty,* dernier supplice, *m.* ~ *unction,* extrême-onction, *f.* **extremist,** *n,* extrémiste, *m,f,* ultra, *m;* (*att.*) outrancier. **extremity,** *n,* extrémité, *f,* bout, *m.*

extricate, *v.t,* dégager, débarrasser, débarbouiller, dépêtrer, tirer.

extrinsic, *a,* extrinsèque.

exuberance, *n,* exubérance, *f.* **exuberant,** *a,* exubérant.

exude, *v.i,* exsuder; (*v.t.*) distiller.

exult, *v.i,* exulter, triompher. ~**ation,** *n,* exaltation, *f.*

eye, *n,* œil, *m;* paupière; vue, *f;* (*needle, etc.*) œil, chas, trou; (*fruit*) nombril; (*potato*) germe, *m;* boucle, *f;* regard, *m;* porte, *f.* ~*ball,* globe de l'œil, *m;* prunelle, *f.* ~ *bath,* œillière, *f.* ~*brow,* sourcil, *m.* ~*brow pencil,* crayon pour les yeux, *m.* ~*brow tweezers,* pinces à épiler, *f.pl.* ~ *doctor,* médecin oculiste. *m.* ~*s front!* (*Mil.*) fixe! ~*glass,* monocle, *m;* (*pl.*) binocle, lorgnon, pince-nez, *m.* ~*lash,* cil, *m.* ~*lid,* paupière, *f.* ~*opener,* révélation, *f.* ~*piece,* [verre] oculaire. *m.* ~*shade,* visière, *f,* garde-vue, *m.* ~*sight,* vue, *f.* ~*sore,* objet qui choque la vue, *m.* ~*tooth,* [dent] œillère, *f.* ~*trouble,* mal aux (*ou* d') yeux, *m.* ~*witness,* témoin oculaire, *m.* to keep an ~ on, ne pas perdre de vue. to make ~s at, faire les yeux doux à. ¶ *v.t,* regarder; lorgner. **eyelet,** *n,* œillet, *m.*

eyrie, *n,* aire (*de l'aigle*) *f.*

F

F (*Mus.*) letter, fa, *m*. ~ *clef*, clef de fa, *f*.

fable, *n*, fable, *f*. ~d, *p.p*, légendaire, fabuleux.

fabric, *n*, tissu, *m*, étoffe, *f*. ~ate, *v.t*, fabriquer. ~ation, *n*, fabrication; fantasmagorie, *f*. ~ator, *n*, fabricateur, trice.

fabulist, *n*, fabuliste, *m*. **fabulous†**, *a*, fabuleux.

façade, *n*, façade, *f*.

face, *n*, face, *f*; visage, *m*, figure, *f*; mine; grimace; tournure, *f*; parement; pan; recto; (*cloth*) endroit; (*cards*) dessous; (*of type*) œil, *m*. ~ *lifting*, chirurgie esthétique du visage, *f*. ~ *massage*, massage facial, *m*. ~ *powder*, poudre de riz, *f*. ~ *to* ~, vis-à-vis. ~ *value* (*Fin.*), valeur nominale, *f*. *to about* ~, faire demi-tour. *to lose* ~, perdre contenance. ¶ *v.t*, faire face à; affronter; braver; donner sur, être exposé à; dresser. ~d with (silk), à revers de.

facet, *n*, facette, *f*. ¶ *v.t*, facetter.

facetious, *a*, facétieux.

facial, *a*, facial.

facile, *a*, facile. **facilitate**, *v.t*, faciliter. **facility**, *n*, facilité, *f*.

facing, *n*, revers; parement, revêtement, *m*. ¶ *ad. & pr*, en face (de), face à, vis-à-vis (de), à l'opposite (de).

facsimile, *n*, fac-similé, *m*.

fact, *n*, fait, *m*; vérité; chose, *f*.

faction, *n*, faction, brigue, *f*. **factious**, *a*, factieux. **factitious**, *a*, factice.

factor, *n*, facteur; (*pers.*) commissionnaire, *m*.

factoring, *n*, (*Fin.*) affacturage, *m*.

factory, *n*, manufacture, fabrique, usine, *f*. ~ *hand*, ouvrier (ère) [de fabrique]. ~ *inspector*, inspecteur du travail, *m*.

factotum, *n*, factotum, *m*.

faculty, *n*, faculté; aptitude, *f*, talent, *m*.

fad, *n*, dada, *m*, marotte, lubie, vogue, manie, *f*. **faddist**, *n*, maniaque, *m,f*.

fade, *v.i*, se faner, se défraîchir, déteindre, se flétrir, pâlir. ~

away, s'évanouir. ~ *out*, se mourir. ~d, *p.a*, fané, défraîchi, passé. **fading**, *n*, (*radio, sound, etc.*) évanouissement, *m*.

fade-in, *n*, (*TV & cinema*) fondu ouvert, *m*.

fadeout, *n*, (*TV & cinema*) fondu, *m*.

fagot, *n*, fagot, cotret, *m*. ¶ *v.t*, fagoter.

Fahrenheit, *a*, Fahrenheit. See note under *centigrade* in French-English section.

fail, *v.i*, manquer, faire défaut, défaillir, échouer, mal réussir, rater, chavirer; faillir; (*Com.*) faire faillite; (*v.t.*) manquer à. ~ *in one's duty*, manquer à son devoir, prévariquer. *without* ~, sans faute. ~ing, *n*, faible, *m*; défaillance, *f*. ¶ *pr*, à défaut de, faute de. ~ure, *n*, défaut, insuccès, échec, *m*, chute, *f*, coup manqué; four, fiasco, *m*; (*Elec.*) panne; (*Com.*) faillite, *f*.

fain, *a. & ad*: *to be* ~ *to*, être amené par nécessité à, être réduit à. *I would* ~ *be* . . ., je serais volontiers . . . *I would* ~ *have* . . ., j'aurais bien voulu . . .

faint, *a*, faible; mourant; défaillant. ~*hearted*, lâche. ¶ *v.i*, s'évanouir, défaillir, [se] pâmer. ~ing [fit], évanouissement, *m*, défaillance, *f*.

fair, *a*, beau; (*skin*) blanche; (*hair*) blonds; juste, équitable, loyal, honnête, raisonnable; passable. *at* ~ (barometer), au beau. ~*haired*, aux cheveux blonds. ~*haired person*, blond, e. *by* ~ *means or foul*, de gré ou de force. ~ *play*, franc jeu, *m*, de bonne guerre; traitement honnête, *m*. *not* ~, pas du (*ou* de) jeu. ~ *sex*, beau sexe, *m*. ~*spoken*, bien-disant. ~*way*, chenal, *m*, passe, *f*. ¶ *n*, foire, *f*. ~*ly*, *ad*, à juste titre; bel & bien; loyalement; assez; moyennement. ~*ness*, *n*, beauté, *f*; teint blond, *m*; équité; loyauté, honnêteté, *f*.

fairy, *n*, fée, *f*. *Fairyland*, féerie, *f*. ~*like*, féerique. ~ *ring*, cercle des fées, *m*. ~ *tale*, conte de fées, conte bleu, *m*.

faith, *n*, foi; confiance; croyance, communion, *f*. ~*ful†*, *a*, fidèle. *the* ~, les fidèles, les croyants, *m.pl*. fulness, *n*, fidélité, *f*. ~*less*, *a*, sans foi, infidèle. **~lessness**, *n*, infidélité, *f*.

fake, *n*, truquage, *m*. ¶ *v.t*, truquer.

fakir, *n*, fakir, *m*.

falcon, *n*, faucon, *m*. **~er**, *n*, fauconnier, *m*. **falconry**, *n*, fauconnerie, *f*.

fall, *n*, chute; tombée; descente; (*prices*) baisse, *f*; abaissement, *m*; culbute; ruine, *f*; éboulement; éboulis, *m*; cascade, *f,m*; (*pl.*) chute, *f*; automne; (*government*) renversement, *m*. ¶ *v.i.ir*, tomber; descendre; baisser; s'abaisser. ~ *back*, se replier. ~ *down*, tomber [par terre]. ~ *due*, échoir. ~ *in* (*cave in*) ébouler; (*Mil.*) se mettre en rangs; à vos rangs! ~ *in love*, s'enamourer, s'éprendre. ~ *in with* (opinion), se ranger à. ~ *off*, tomber [à bas] de; (*business, etc.*) ralentir. ~ *out with*, ~ *foul of*, se brouiller avec. ~ *through* (fail), échouer.

fallacious, *a*, fallacieux. **fallacy**, *n*, erreur, *f*; (*Log.*) sophisme, *m*.

fallen angel, ange déchu, *m*. **fallen leaves**, feuilles tombées, fanes, *f.pl*, fanage, *m*.

fallibility, *n*, faillibilité, *f*. **fallible**, *a*, faillible.

falling star, étoile tombante, é. filante, *f*.

fallout, *n*, (*nuclear*) retombée, *f*. *nuclear* ~, les retombées radioactives.

fallow, *a*, (*color of deer*) fauve; (*land*) en jachère, en friche. ~ *deer*, daim, *m*. *to lie* ~, rester en friche, chômer. ¶ *v.t*, jachérer.

false, *a*, faux; mensonger; postiche; feint. ~ *bottom*, double fond, faux f., *m*. ~ *shame*, fausse honte, mauvaise h., *f*. ¶ *ad*, faux. **~hood**, *n*, mensonge, *m*. **~ly**, *ad*, faussement. **~ness**, *n*, fausseté, *f*. **falsetto**, *n*, fausset, *m*. **falsify**, *v.t*, falsifier, fausser. **falsity**, *n*, fausseté, *f*.

falter, *v.i*, chanceler, défaillir; hésiter; (*speech*) ânonner, bégayer.

fame, *n*, renommée, *f*, renom, *m*, gloire, mémoire, *f*. **~d**, *a*, renommé.

familiar†, *a*, familier. ~ *face*, figure de connaissance, *f*. ¶ *n*, familier, *m*. **~ity**, *n*, familiarité; privauté, *f*. **~ize**, *v.t*, familiariser.

family, *n*, famille, *f*; ménage, *m*; maisonnée, *f*. ~ *likeness*, air de famille, *m*. ~ *life*, vie de f., v. familiale, *f*. ~ *man*, père de famille; homme de foyer, *m*. ~ *tree*, arbre généalogique, *m*.

famine, *n*, famine, *f*. **famish**, *v.t*, affamer. *to be* ~*ing*, avoir la fringale.

famous†, *a*, fameux, célèbre, renommé. ~ *case* (*law*), cause célèbre, *f*.

fan, *n*, éventail; ventilateur, *m*. ~ *light*, vasistas, *m*. ~ *tail*, pigeon paon, *m*. ¶ *v.t*, éventer; (*grain*) vanner; (*fire*, & *fig.*) souffler; exciter, attiser.

fanatic, *n*, fanatique, *m,f*. **~(al)**, *a*, fanatique. **fanaticism**, *n*, fanatisme, *m*. **fanaticize**, *v.t*, fanatiser.

fancied, *p.a*, imaginaire. **fancier**, *n*, grand amateur (de . . .) *m*. **fanciful**, *a*, de fantaisie; fantastique, chimérique. **fancy**, *n*, fantaisie; envie; toquade; boutade, *f*, caprice, *m*; imagination; idée, *f*. ~ *dress*, déguisement, *m*. ~*dress ball*, bal costumé, b. travesti, *m*. ~ *leather goods* or *shop*, maroquinerie, *f*. ~ *needlework*, ouvrages de dames, *m.pl*. ~ *work*, ouvrages d'agrément, *m.pl*. ¶ *v.t*, imaginer; s'imaginer; se figurer. ~ *oneself*, se complaire.

fang, *n*, croc, *m*.

fantasia, *n*, fantaisie, *f*. **fantastic**, *a*, fantastique; *fantaisiste*. **fantasy**, *n*, vision; fantaisie, *f*.

far, *ad*, loin, au loin; avant; beaucoup; bien. *from* ~, de loin. *how* ~ *is it to* . . .*?* combien y a-t-il d'ici à . . .? ~ & *wide*, au long & au large. *as* ~ *as*, jusqu'à; autant que. *as* ~ *as the eye can reach*, à perte de vue. *by* ~, de beaucoup. ~*fetched*, tiré par les cheveux, forcé, outre. ~ *into the night*, fort avant dans la nuit. ~ *off*, lointain. ~*reaching*, étendu. ~*sighted*, prévoyant. ~ *too*, par trop. ¶ *a*, éloigné. *the F~ East*, l'Extrême-Orient, *m*.

farce, *n*, farce, *f*. **farcical**, *a*, burlesque, bouffon.

fare, *n*, prix [de la place], prix de passage, tarif, *m*, place; course, *f*; voyageur, euse; chère, *f*, menu, *m*. ¶ *v.i*, aller. *to* ~ (feed) *well*, faire bonne chère. ~*well*, *i*. & *n*, adieu, *i*. & *m*.

farina, *n,* farine; fécule, *f.* **farinaceous,** *a,* farineux, farinacé.

farm, *n,* ferme, *f.* ~ **hand,** valet de ferme, *m.* ~**house,** ferme, *f.* ~ **products,** produits agricoles, *m.pl.* ~**yard,** cour de f., basse-cour, *f.* ¶ *v.t,* exploiter, cultiver; (*lease*) affermer. ~ **out,** amodier. ~**er,** *n,* fermier, ère, cultivateur, trice, agriculteur, *m.* ~**ing,** *n,* exploitation [d'une ferme], agriculture, culture, *f;* (*att.*) aratoire.

faro (*cards*) *n,* pharaon, *m.*

farrago, *n,* farrago, salmigondis, *m.*

farrow, *n,* cochonnée, *f.* ¶ *v.i,* cochonner.

fart, *n,* pet, *m.*

farther, *ad,* plus loin, [plus] en delà. **farthest,** *a,* le plus éloigné. ¶ *ad,* le plus loin.

farthing, *n,* farthing, *m.* = ¼ penny; (*fig.*) liard, *m,* obole, *f.*

fasces (*Hist.*) *n.pl,* faisceaux, *m.pl.*

fascinate, *v.t,* fasciner. **fascinating,** *a,* fascinateur. **fascination,** *n,* fascination, *f.*

fascine, *n,* fascine, *f.*

fascism, *n,* fascisme, *m.* **fascist,** *n,* fasciste, *m.*

fashion, *n,* façon; mode, *f.* genre, *m.* after a ~, tant bien que mal. ~ **plate,** gravure de mode, *f.* ¶ *v.t,* façonner. ~**able,** *a,* à la mode, élégant. ~ **society,** le beau monde. ~**ably,** *ad,* à la mode.

fast, *a,* fixe; fidèle; (*dissipated*) léger; rapide, vite; express, de grande vitesse; (*of clock*) en avance. ~ *asleep,* profondément endormi. ~ *color,* bon teint, t. solide, *m.* ~ *cruiser* (speedboat), glisseur de croisière, *m.* ¶ *ad,* ferme; bien; vite; (*rain*) à verse. *to hold* ~, tenir bon. *to make* ~, amarrer, *f.* ¶ *v.i,* jeûner. ~**ing,** *n,* jeûne, *m;* (*Naut.*) amarre, *f.* ¶ *v.i,* jeûner. ~**ing,** *ad* à jeun. ~[**ing**] **day,** jour de jeûne, j. maigre, *m.*

fasten, *v.t,* fixer; assujettir; attacher; agrafer. ~ *off* (*Need.*), arrêter. ~**er** & ~**ing,** *n,* attache; armature; fermeture; agrafe, *f.*

fastidious (**to be**), être pointilleux, faire le (*of woman*) la) dégoûté(e), f. le difficile, f. le délicat, f. le (la) renchéri(e).

fat, *a,* gras; obèse; (*land*) fertile. ~**head,** lourdaud, e; couillon, *m.* ~ *profits,* profits substantiels,

m.pl. ¶ *n,* gras, *m;* graisse, *f;* lard; suif, *m. to live on the* ~ *of the land,* vivre grassement.

fatal†, *a,* fatal, funeste; mortel. ~**ism,** *n,* fatalisme, *m.* ~**ist,** *n,* fataliste, *m,f.* ~**ity,** *n,* fatalité, *f;* accident mortel, *m;* tué, e.

fate, *n,* destin, sort, *m,* fatalité, *f. the Fates* (*Myth.*), les Parques, *f.pl. to be* ~d *to,* être destiné à. ~**ful,** *a,* fatal.

father, *n,* père, *m.* ~*-in-law,* beau-père, *m.* ~**land,** patrie, *f.* ~*'s side* (family), côté paternel, *m.* ~**hood,** *n,* paternité, *f.* ~**less,** *a,* sans père, orphelin de père. ~**ly,** *a,* paternel, de père. ¶ *v.t,* patronner. ~ *upon,* attribuer à.

fathom, *n,* brasse, *f.* (Eng. *fathom* = 6 feet; Fr. *brasse marine* = 1 meter 62). ¶ *v.t,* sonder, pénétrer. ~**less,** *a,* insondable.

fatigue, *n,* fatigue; (*Mil.*) corvée, *f.* ¶ *v.t,* fatiguer. **fatiguing,** *a,* fatigant.

fatness, *n,* obésité; fertilité, *f. fatted calf,* veau gras, *m.* **fatten,** *v.t,* engraisser. **fattish,** *a,* grasset. **fatty,** *a,* gras, graisseux, adipeux.

fatuity, *n,* imbécillité, *f.* **fatuous,** *a,* imbécile.

fauces, *n.pl,* arrière-bouche, *f.*

faucet, *n,* robinet, fausset, *m;* douille, *f.*

fault, *n,* faute, *f;* tort; défaut, vice; dérangement, *m;* (*Geol.*) faille, *f. to find* ~ *with,* trouver à redire à, reprendre, mordre sur, censurer, fronder, gloser [sur]. ~ *finder,* critiqueur, frondeur, *m.* ~**less,** *a,* sans faute; sans défaut; irréprochable. ~**y,** *a,* fautif, vicieux, défectueux, mauvais.

faun, *n,* faune, *m.* **fauna,** *n,* faune, *f.*

favor, *n,* faveur, grâce, *f;* plaisir, *m.* ¶ *v.t,* favoriser, avantager, honorer. **favorable†,** *a,* favorable; prospère. **favorite,** *a,* favori. ~ *author,* auteur de prédilection, *m.* ~ *book,* livre de chevet, *m.* ¶ *n,* favori, ite. *the* ~, le [cheval] favori. **favoritism,** *n,* favoritisme, *m,* cote d'amour, *f.*

fawn, *n,* faon, chevrotin; (*color*) fauve, *m.* ~[*-colored*], fauve. ¶ (*of deer*) *v.i,* faonner. ~ [*up*]*on,* flagorner, courtiser, ramper devant. ~**ing,** *n,* servilité, flatterie, *f.*

fear, n, crainte, peur, frayeur, f;
danger, m. ¶ v.t. & i, craindre,
redouter. ~ful†, a, affreux, épouvantable; craintif. ~less, a, sans
peur, intrépide. ~lessness, n, intrépidité, f.

feasibility, n, praticabilité, f.
feasible, a, faisable, praticable.

feast, n, fête, f; festin, régal, m.
¶ v.i. & t, festiner, festoyer, régaler; (fig.) repaître. ~ing, n,
bombance, f.

feat, n, fait, exploit; tour, m, prouesse, f.

feather, n, plume, f; (pl.) plumage, m; penne; (Carp. & Mach.)
languette, f. ~ bed, lit de plume,
m. ~brained person, tête de linotte, f, évaporé, e. ~ duster,
plumeau, houssoir, m. ~ stitch,
point de plume, m. ~weight
(Box.), poids plume, m. ¶ (rowing) v.i, plumer. to ~ one's nest,
s'enrichir. ~ed, p.a: ~ game,
gibier à plume, m. ~ hat, chapeau orné de plumes, m. ~y, a,
plumeux.

feature, n, trait, linéament, m;
caractéristique, f. ¶ v.i, mettre
en vedette.

February, n, février, m.

fecund, a, fécond. ~ate, v.t, féconder. ~ity, n, fécondité, f.

federal, a, fédéral. **federate,** v.t,
fédérer. **federation,** n, fédération,
f; syndicat, m.

fee, n. oft. pl, honoraires, m.pl;
frais, m.pl; cotisation, f; droit,
m; taxe; surtaxe, f. admission
~, droit d'entrée, m.

feeble†, a, faible, débile.

feed, n, nourriture; mangeaille;
pâture, f; (of oats) picotin, m;
alimentation, f; (Mach.) avancement, entraînement, m. ~ pump,
pompe alimentaire, f. ¶ v.t.ir,
nourrir; [re]paître; alimenter;
(v.i.ir.) manger. ~ forcibly, gaver. ~er, n, mangeur, euse; appareil d'alimentation, m; (stream,
Rly) affluent, m; (Elec.) artère,
f. ~ing bottle, biberon, m.

feedback, n, (computers) rétroaction, réinjection, f.

feel, n, manier, toucher, tact, m.
¶ v.t. & i. ir, tâter, palper, manier,
toucher; sentir; se s., ressentir, se
r., éprouver; se trouver. to ~
one's way, avancer à tâtons. to
~ like, avoir envie de. ~er, n,

antenne, f, palpe, f. or m; (fig.)
ballon d'essai, m. **feeling,** a,
sensible, touchant, tendre. ¶ n,
maniement, m; sensation; sensibilité, f; (pL) cœur; sentiment;
esprit, m. ~ly, ad, avec émotion.

feign, v.t, feindre, simuler, jouer.
feint, n, feinte, f. ¶ v.i, feindre.

felicitous, a, heureux, à propos.
felicity, n, félicité, f.

feline, a. & n, félin, a. & m.

fell, n, peau, f; abat[tis] m. ¶ v.t,
abattre; assommer. ~er, n, abatteur, m. ~ing, n, abattage, m.

fellow, n, compagnon, m, camarade, m.f; pareil, pendant; garçon, gaillard, individu, sujet, m.
~ boarder, commensal, e. ~ citizen, concitoyen, ne. ~ countryman, -woman, compatriote, m.f.
~ creature, ~ man, semblable,
prochain, m. ~ feeling, sympathie, f. ~ passenger, ~ traveler,
compagnon de voyage, m, compagne de voyage, f. ~ student,
camarade de collège, m, f, condisciple, m. ~ sufferer, camarade
de malheur, compagnon de ma-
leur, compagne de malheur. good
~, chic type, m. ~ship, n, société; camaraderie, f; situation
universitaire, f.

felon, n, criminel, le. ~ious, a,
criminel. ~y, n, crime, m.

felt, n, feutre, m. ~ [hat], [cha-
peau de] feutre, m. ¶ v.t, feutrer.

female, a, femelle; de femme;
(pers.) féminin. ¶ n, (animal)
femelle; (pers.) femme, f. **feminine,** a, & n, féminin, a. & m.
feminism, n, féminisme, m. **feminist,** a. & n, féministe, a. & m.f.
feminize, v.t, féminiser.

femur, n, fémur, m.

fen, n, marais, marécage, m.

fence, n, clôture, barrière, palissade, f; (Mach.) guide, m; (pers.)
receleur, euse. to be on the ~,
être indécis. ¶ v.t, palissader;
(v.i.) faire (ou tirer) des armes.
~ in, enclore. ~ off, barrer.
fencer, n, tireur d'armes, m. **fencing,** n, clôture, enceinte; (foils)
escrime, f. ~ master, maître
d'armes, m. ~ school, salle d'-
armes, s. d'escrime, f.

fend [off], v.t, parer. ~ for oneself, se suffire. ~er, n, garde-

cendre; (*Naut.*) parebattage; (auto) pare-boue, *m.*

fennel, *n*, & ~ *seed*, fenouil, *m.*

ferment, *n*, ferment, *m*; (*fig.*) fermentation, effervescence, *f.* ¶ *v.i*, fermenter; (*v.t.*) faire f. **~ation,** *n*, fermentation, *f.*

fern, *n*, fougère, *f.*

ferocious, *a*, féroce. **ferocity,** *n*, férocité, *f.*

ferret, *n*, furet, *m.* ¶ *v.i.* & *t*, fureter. ~ *about*, fureter. ~ *out*, dénicher.

ferrous, *a*, ferreux.

ferrule, *n*, virole, bague, frette, *f*, [em]bout, *m.* ¶ *v.t*, mettre une virole, etc., à.

ferry, *n*, passage, *m.* ~[*boat*], bateau de passage, bac, *m.* ~*man*, passeur, *m.* car ~, transbordeur, *m.* ~ over, passer [l'eau].

fertile, *a*, fertile, fécond, plantureux. **fertility,** *n*, fertilité, fécondité, *f.* **fertilize,** *v.t*, fertiliser. **fertilizer,** *n*, engrais fertilisant, *m.*

fervent & **fervid,** *a*, fervent, ardent. **fervently** & **fervidly,** *ad*, avec ferveur, ardemment. **fervor** & **fervency,** *n*, ferveur, ardeur, *f.*

fester, *v.i*, s'ulcérer. ¶ *n*, ulcère, *m*; suppuration, *f.*

festival, *n*, fête, *f*; (*musical*) festival, *m.* **festive,** *a*, de fête. **festivity,** *n*, fête, *f.*

festoon, *n*, feston, *m.* ¶ *v.t*, festonner.

fetch, *v.t*, apporter; aller chercher. ~ *it!* (to dog), apporte!

fete, *n*, fête; kermesse; (*at a fair*) fête foraine, *f.* ¶ *v.t*, fêter.

fetid, *a*, fétide. **~ness,** *n*, fétidité, *f.*

fetish, *n*, fétiche, *m.* **fetishism,** *n*, fétichisme, *m.*

fetlock, *n*, fanon, *m.*

fetter, *n. oft. pl*, entrave, *f*, fer, *m*, chaîne, *f.* ¶ *v.t*, entraver, enchaîner.

fettle, *n*, état, *m*, forme, *f.*

fetus, *n*, fœtus, *m.*

feud, *n*, guerre, vendetta, *f*; (*Hist.*) fief, *m.* **~al,** *a*, féodal. **~alism** & **~ality,** *n*, féodalité, *f.*

fever, *n*, fièvre, *f.* ~ *case* (*pers.*), fiévreux, euse. *scarlet* ~, scarlatine, *f.* **~ish†,** *a*, fiévreux; fébrile.

few, *a.* & *n*, peu de; peu, *m*; quelques; quelques-uns, -unes. ~ & *far between*, clairsemé. **~er,** *a*, moins; moins de.

fez, *n*, fez, *m.*

fiasco, *n*, fiasco, four, *m.*

fiat, *n*, décret, *m.*

fib, *n*, mensonge innocent, *m*, menterie, *f.* ¶ *v.i*, débiter des bourdes. **fibber,** *n*, menteur, *m.*

fiber, *n*, fibre, *f*; crin. *m.* **fibril,** *n*, fibrille, *f.* **fibrous,** *a*, fibreux.

fickle, *a*, volage, changeant, mobile, versatile, inconstant. **~ness,** *n*, inconstance, mobilité, versatilité, *f.*

fiction, *n*, fiction, *f*, mensonge, *m*; (*prose*) le roman, les romans. **fictitious†,** *a*, fictif, supposé. **fictive,** *a*, imaginaire.

fiddle, *n*, violon, crincrin, *m.* ~ *stick*, archet, *m*; (*pl., i.*) chansons, chansons! ¶ *v.i*, jouer du violon; (*fig.*) baguenauder. **fiddler,** *n*, ménétrier, *m.*

fidelity, *n*, fidélité, *f.*

fidget, *v.i*, remuer, frétiller, se trémousser. **~s,** *n.pl*, impatiences, crispations, *f.pl.* **~y,** *a*, inquiet, nerveux.

fiduciary, *a*, fiduciaire.

fie, *i*, fi!

fief (*Hist.*) *n*, fief, *m.*

field, *n*, champ, *m*; (*pl.*) campagne, *f*; (*pl., poet.*) sillons, *m.pl*; terrain, *m*; (*Mil.*) campagne, *f*; (*Her.*) champ, *m*, table d'attente, *f.* ~ *artillery*, artillerie de campagne, *f.* ~ *day*, manœuvres, *f.pl*; (*fig.*) grand jour; débat important, *m.* ~ *geology*, géologie sur le terrain, *f.* ~ *glass*[es], jumelle de campagne, *f.* ~ *mouse*, rat des champs, mulot, *m.* ~ *sports*, la chasse, la pêche, & sports analogues. (*TV* & *cinema*) depth of ~, profondeur de champ, *m.* *landing* ~, terrain d'atterrissage, *m.*

fiend, *n*, démon, *m*; enragé, e. **~ish,** *a*, diabolique.

fierce, *a*, féroce, farouche, acharné. **~ly,** *ad*, avec férocité. **~ness,** *n*, férocité, *f.*

fiery, *a*, de feu; ardent, bouillant, fougueux.

fife & **fifer,** *n*, fifre, *m.*

fifteen, *a*, & *n*, quinze, *a.* & *m.* **~th†,** *a*, & *n*, quinzième, *a.* & *m.f*; quinze, *m.* **fifth†,** *a*, cinquième. ¶ *n*, cinquième, *m.f*; cinq, *m*; (*Mus.*) quinte, *f.* **fiftieth,** *a.* & *n*, cinquantième, *a.* & *m.f.* ~ *anniversary*, cinquantenaire, *m.* **fifty,**

fig 523 **fine**

a. & n, cinquante, *a. & m.* ~ [*or so*], une cinquantaine.

fig, *n*, figue, *f*; (*fig.*) fétu, *m*. ~ *leaf*, feuille de figuier; (*Art*) feuille de vigne, *f*. ~ *tree*, figuier, *m*.

fight, *n*, combat, *m*; lutte, joute, bataille, mêlée, batterie, *f*. *air* ~, combat aérien, *m*. *hand-to-hand* ~, corps-à-corps, *m*. ¶ *v.i.r.* se battre, combattre, lutter, batailler; (*v.t.ir.*) se battre avec, combattre, lutter contre; (*a battle*) livrer; (*one's way*) se frayer. ~**er**, *n*, combattant; batailleur; militant, avion de combat, *m*.

figment, *n*, fiction, *f*.

figurative, *a*, figuratif. ~ *sense*, [sens] figuré, *m.* ~**ly**, *ad*, figurativement; (*sense*) figurément, au figuré. **figure,** *n*, figure; (*bodily shape*) taille, tournure, *f*; (*Arith.*) chiffre, *m.* ~ *dance*, danse figurée, *f.* ~**head**, (*ship*) figure de proue, *f*; personnage de carton, *m.* ~ *of speech*, figure de mots, figure de rhétorique. ~ *skates*, patins de figure, *m.pl.* ¶ *v.t. & i*, chiffrer; gaufrer; figurer; (*Mus.*) chiffrer.

filament, *n*, filament; fil; filet, *m*.

filbert, *n*, aveline, *f.* ~ [*tree*], avelinier, *m*.

filch, *v.t*, escamoter, subtiliser, filouter.

file, *n*, (*rank*) file; (*of people*) file, queue, *f*; (*for letters*) classeur, *m*; (*bundle*) liasse; collection; (*tool*) lime, *f*; (*computers*) fichier, *m.* ~ *card*, fiche, *f*. ¶ *v.t*, classer; déposer; passer; enregistrer; limer. ~ *past*, défiler.

filial†, *a*, filial. **filiation,** *n*, filiation, *f*.

filigree [**work**], *n*, filigrane, *m*. ~**d,** *a*, façonné en filigrane.

filing, *n*, classement; dépôt; limage, *m*; (*pl.*) limaille, *f*. ~ *cabinet,* [meuble-]classeur, *m*.

fill, *n*, suffisance, *f*, content, soûl, *m*. ¶ *v.t*, [r]emplir; combler; charger; peupler; suppléer à; (*tooth*) plomber. ~ *in*, insérer, remplir. ~ *in time*, peloter en attendant partie. (*gas, water*) *to* ~ *it up*, faire le pleine. ~ *up*, remplir.

fillet, *n*, filet; (*Arch.*) congé, *m.* ~ *of veal*, rouelle de veau, *f*. ~**ed** *sole*, filets de sole, *m.pl*.

filling, *n*, remplissage, chargement; (*tooth*) plombage, *m.* ¶ *a*, (*food*) bourratif.

fillip, *n*, chiquenaude, *f*; (*fig.*) coup de fouet, *m*.

fillister, *n*, feuillure, *f*.

filly, *n*, pouliche, *f*.

film, *n*, pellicule, *f*; film, *m*; (*movies*) bande, *f*; (*fig.*) voile, *m.* ~ *library*, cinémathèque, *f*. ~*maker*, cinéaste, *m.* ~ *pack*, bloc-film, *m.* ~ *projector*, ciné-projecteur, *m.* ~ *rights*, droits d'adaption au cinématographe, *m.pl.* ~ *serial*, ciné-roman, *m.* ~ *short*, court métrage, *m.* ~ *star*, vedette de l'écran, v. de cinéma, *f. feature* ~, long métrage, *m. silent* ~, film muet, *m.* ¶ *v.t*, mettre à l'écran, tourner. ~**y**, *a*, vaporeux.

filter, *n*, filtre; (*Phot.*) écran, *m*. ¶ *v.t. & i*, filtrer.

filth, *n*, immondice, fange, ordure, crasse, saleté, *f*. **filthiness,** *n*, saleté, *f*. **filthy†,** *a*, sale, crasseux; crapuleux, fangeux, ignoble.

fin, *n*, nageoire, *f*, (*Avn.*) aileron, *m*.

final†, *a*, final, dernier, fatal. ~ [*heat*], (épreuve) finale, *f*. **finale** (*Mus.*) *n*, final[e] *m.* **finality,** *n*, finalité, *f*.

finance, *n*, finance; commandite, *f*; (*pl.*) finances, *f.pl*, trésorerie, *f.* ¶ *v.i*, financer; (*v.t.*) commanditer. **financial†,** *a*, financier. **financier,** *n*, financier, *m*.

finch, *n*, pinson, *m*.

find, *n*, trouvaille, découverte, *f*. ¶ *v.t.ir*, trouver, retrouver; découvrir; rechercher; s'apercevoir; reconnaître; procurer, se procurer; fournir. ~ *out*, découvrir, se rendre compte. ~**er,** *n*, inventeur; (*camera*) viseur, *m*; (*telescope*) lunette de repère, *f*. ~**ing** (*jury*) *n*, déclaration, *f*.

fine, *a*, beau; fin; délicat; bon; menu; ténu; joli; magnifique. ~ *arts*, beaux-arts, *m.pl. one of these* ~ *days, one* ~ *day*, un de ces matins, un beau matin. ~ *speaking*, bien-dire, *m.* ~ *things*, objets magnifiques, *m.pl*, magnificences, *f.pl.* ¶ *n*, amende, *f*. ¶ *v.t*, mettre (*ou* condamner) à l'amende; (*wine*) coller, clarifier. ~**ly**, *ad*, finement; joliment. ~**ness,** *n*, finesse; ténuité; *f*; (*gold*, *etc.*) titre, *m.* **finery**, *n,* chiffons, colifichets, affiquets, atours, *m.pl.* **finesse**, *n,* finesse, *f.* ¶ *v.t,* finasser. *finest quality,* premier choix, *m.*

finger, *n,* doigt, *m.* ~ *board,* touche, *f.* ~ *bowl,* bol rince-doigts, *m.* ~ *print,* empreinte digitale, *f. middle* ~, médius, *m. ring* ~, annulaire, *m.* ¶ *v.t,* toucher, palper; (*Mus.*) doigter. ~*ing* (*Mus.*) *n,* doigté, *m.*

finical, *a,* dégoûté, difficile, maniéré, vétilleux, mièvre.

finis, *n,* fin, *f.* **finish**, *n,* fini, *m*; (*end*) fin, *f,* bout, *m.* ¶ *v.t. & abs. & i,* finir; en finir; achever; parachever, parfaire. *to ~ speaking,* finir de parler. ~*ing stroke,* coup de grâce, *m.* ~*ing touches,* dernière main, *f.*

finite, *a,* fini; (*Gram.*) défini.

Finland, *n,* la Finlande. **Finn, Finlander**, *n,* Finnois, e, Finlandais, e. **Finnish**, *a,* finnois, finlandais. ¶ (*language*) *n,* le finnois.

fir [**tree**], *n,* sapin, pin, *m.* ~ *plantation,* sapinière, *f.*

fire, *n,* feu; incendie; tir, *m*; fougue, *f.* (*house, etc, on*) ~*l* au feu! ~ *alarm,* avertisseur d'incendie, *m.* ~*arms,* armes à feu, *f.pl.* ~*box,* foyer, *m*; boîte à feu, *f.* ~*brand,* tison, brandon, boutefeu, *m.* ~*brick,* brique réfractaire, *f.* ~ *brigade,* sapeurs-pompiers, *m.pl.* ~*clay,* argile réfractaire, *f.* ~*damp,* grisou, *m.* ~ *dog,* chenet, *m.* ~ *engine,* pompe à incendie, *f.* ~ *escape,* échelle de sauvetage, *f.* ~ *extinguisher,* extincteur d'incendie, *m.* ~*fly,* mouche à feu, luciole, *f.* ~*guard,* garde-feu, pare-étincelles, *m.* ~ *hydrant,* ~ *plug,* bouche d'incendie, *f.* ~ *insurance,* assurance contre l'incendie, *f.* ~ *irons,* garniture de foyer, *f.* ~ *lighter,* allume-feu, *m.* ~*man,* pompier, sapeur-pompier; (*stoker*) chauffeur, *m.* ~*place,* cheminée, *f,* âtre, *m.* ~*proof, a,* ignifuge, incombustible, à l'épreuve du feu; (*v.t.*) ignifuger. ~*side,* coin du feu, foyer, *m.* ~*side chair,* chauffeuse, *f.* ~ *station,* poste d'incendie, p. de pompiers, *m.* ~*wood,* bois à brûler, b. de chauffage, *m.* ~ *work,* feu d'artifice, *m,* pièce d'a., *f.* ¶ *v.t,* enflammer, embraser, mettre le feu à; incen-

dier; allumer; chauffer; (*shot*) tirer, lâcher, lancer; (*v.i.*) prendre feu; (*gun*) tirer, faire feu. ~*l* (*Mil.*), feu! **firing**, *n,* chauffage, *m,* chauffe, *f*; combustible; (*Mil.*) feu, tir, *m.*

firm†, *a,* ferme; solide; consistant; tenu. ¶ *n,* maison [de commerce], société [en nom collectif] *f.* ~ [*name*], raison [sociale] *f.* ~*'s capital,* capital social, *m.*

firmament, *n,* firmament, *m.*

firmness, *n,* fermeté, assiette, solidité; consistance; tenue, *f.*

first, *a,* premier; (*after 20, 30, etc.*) unième; (*cousins*) germain. ~ *aid,* premiers soins, *m.pl.* ~ *appearance & ~ work, or ~ book,* début, *m. to make one's ~ appearance,* débuter. ~ *attempt,* coup d'essai, *m.* ~ *born,* premier-né, *m. 1st class,* 1re classe, *f. the ~ comer,* le premier venu, la première venue. ~ *edition,* édition originale, é. princeps, *f.* ~ *finger,* index, *m.* ~ [*floor*], premier [étage] *m.* ~ *fruits,* prémices, *f.pl.* ~*rate,* de premier ordre; fameux. (*movie*) ~*run,* en exclusivité. ¶ *ad,* premièrement, primo. ~, *at ~,* ~ *of all,* [tout] d'abord, de premier abord, de prime abord. ~ *& foremost,* en premier. *the first,* le premier, la première. *the 1st January,* le 1er janvier. ~*ly, ad,* premièrement, primo.

firth, *n,* estuaire, *m.*

fiscal, *a,* fiscal. ~ *system,* fiscalité, *f.* ~ *year,* année budgétaire, *f.*

fish, *n,* poisson, *m.* ~*bone,* arête, *f.* ~*bowl,* bocal, *m.* ~ *glue,* colle de poisson, *f.* ~*hook,* hameçon, *m.* ~ *kettle,* poissonnière, *f.* ~ *market,* halle aux poissons, poissonnerie, *f.* [*wet*] ~*monger,* poissonnier, ère. ~ *out of water* (*pers.*), déraciné, e. ~ *pond,* vivier, *m.* ~ *shop,* poissonnerie, *f.* ~ *slice,* truelle à poisson, *f.* ~ *spear,* fouine, *f,* trident, *m.* ~*wife,* poissarde, harengère, *f.* ¶ *v.i. & t.* ~ *for,* pêcher. ~ *out, ~ up,* [re]pêcher. ~[**plate**], *v.t,* éclisser. ~**erman**, *n,* pêcheur, euse. ~**ery**, *n,* pêche; (*ground*) pêcherie, *f.* ~**ing** (*act or right*) *n,* pêche, *f.* ~ *boat,* bateau de pêche, *m.* ~ *ground,* parage de

pêche, *m*, pêcherie, *f*. ~ *rod*,
canne à pêche, gaule, *f*. ~ *tackle*,
engins de pêche, *m.pl*, harnais
de p., *m*. ~y, *a*, sauvagin; (*fig*.)
véreux.

fission, *n*, fission, *f*.

fissure, *n*, fissure, fente, *f*. ¶ *v.t*,
fendiller.

fist, *n*, poing, *m*. **fisticuffs,** *n.pl*,
coup[s] de poing, *m*.[*pl*.].

fistula, *n*, fistule, *f*.

fit, *a*, propre, bon, apte, convenable, approprié, à propos; capable; dispos, frais. ~ *for service*,
valide. ¶ *n*, accès, *m*, attaque,
crise, boutade, bouffée, *f*; (*Mech*.)
montage, *m*. ~ *of coughing*,
quinte [de toux] *f*. *by* ~*s &
starts*, par sauts & par bonds, par
boutades, à bâtons rompus. ¶
v.t, ajuster, adapter, agencer,
aménager, cadrer; monter, épouser [la forme de]; chausser; botter; coiffer; (*v.i*.) s'ajuster; aller.
~ *in*, emboîter, enclaver. ~ *out*,
équiper, armer, outiller. ~ *tightly*, coller. **fitful,** *a*, changeant;
agité; saccadé; quinteux. **fitly,**
ad, convenablement. **fitness,** *n*,
convenance, aptitude, *f*. **fitter,** *n*,
ajusteur, monteur, appareilleur,
m; (*clothes*) essayeur, euse. **fit-
ting†,** *a*, convenable. ~**s,** *n.pl*,
armature, *f*; garnitures; ferrures,
f.pl; appareillage, *m*. ~ [*& fixtures*], agencement, *m*.

five, *a. & n*, cinq, *a. & m*. ~*-finger
exercise*, exercice de doigté, *m*.
~ *year plan*, plan quinquennal, *m*.

fix, *n*, impasse, *f*, embarras, pétrin,
m. ¶ *v.t*, fixer, assujettir, asseoir;
ancrer; arrêter. ~**ed†,** *a*, fixe; à
demeure. ~ *salary*, fixe, *m*. ~**ing,**
n, fixage, *m*, fixation, pose, *f*. ~
& toning bath, bain de virage-
fixage, *m*. ~ [*solution*] (*Phot*.),
fixateur, *m*. **fixture,** *n*, pièce fixe,
p. à demeure, *f*; engagement, *m*.
~**s & fittings,** agencement, *m*.

fizz[le], *v.i*, pétiller. *fizzle out*,
n'aboutir à rien.

flabbergast, *v.t*, atterrer, ébahir.

flabbiness & flaccidity, *n*, flaccidité, mollesse, *f*. **flabby & flaccid,** *a*, flasque, mollasse, avachi,
mou, veule.

flag, *n*, drapeau, pavillon; (*pl*.) pavois; (*Bot*.) iris des marais, *m*. ~
at half-mast, drapeau en berne,
m. ~ *of truce*, (*Mil*.) drapeau parlementaire; (*Nav*.) pavillon p.

~*ship*, [vaisseau] amiral, *m*. ~
staff, mât de pavillon, *m*.
~[*stone*], dalle, *f*. ¶ *v.t*, daller;
pavoiser; faire des signaux; (*v.i*.)
fléchir; faiblir, languir; tomber;
traîner.

flagellate, *v.t*, flageller.

flageolet, *n*, flageolet, *m*.

flagitious, *a*, scélérat, infâme.

flagon, *n*, flacon, *m*, bouteille [len-
ticulaire] (pour le vin) *f*.

flagrant, *a*, flagrant.

flail, *n*, fléau, *m*.

flair, *n*, aptitude, *f*, dispositions,
f.pl.

flake, *n*, (*snow*) flocon, *m*; écaille;
lame; lamelle; feuille; paillette;
flammèche, *f*. ¶ *v.i*, floconner;
s'écailler. **flaky,** *a*, floconneux;
écailleux; feuilleté; laminé.

flame, *n*, flamme, *f*, feu, *m*. ~
thrower, lance-flamme, *m*. ¶ *v.i*,
flamber, flamboyer; s'enflammer;
(*v.t*.) flamber.

flamingo, *n*, flamant, *m*.

Flanders, *n*, la Flandre.

flange, *n*, bride, *f*; boudin; rebord;
bourrelet; patin, *m*; aile, *f*. ¶ *v.t*,
border.

flank, *n*, flanc, *m*. ¶ *v.t*, flanquer.

flannel, *n*, flanelle, *f*. ~**ette,** *n*,
flanelle de coton, *f*, pilou, *m*.

flap, *n*, coup; clapet; bord; pan;
abattant, *m*; trappe; patte; oreille,
f. ¶ *v.t. & i*, battre, voltiger.

flare, *n*, feu, *m*, flamme, *f*; évase-
ment, pavillon, *m*. ¶ *v.i*, flamber,
flamboyer; (*lamp*) filer; (*bell-
mouth*) s'évaser. *to* ~ *up*, (*anger*) s'emporter.

flash, *a*, tapageur. ¶ *n*, éclair;
éclat; feu; trait, *m*; saillie, *f*.
~*back*, retour en arrière, *m*. ~ *in
the pan* (*fig*.), feu de paille. ~
light, lampe de poche. ~ *of light*
& ~ *of lightning*, éclair, *m*.
~[*ing*] *point*, point d'éclair, p.
d'inflammabilité, *m*. ¶ *v.i*, étinceler; miroiter; éclater; jaillir; flamboyer. ~**y,** *a*, voyant, tapageux.

flask, *n*, bouteille; gourde, *f*; flacon, *m*; bidon, *m*; fiole, *f*.

flat, *a*, plat; méplat; aplati; (*nose*)
épaté; à plat; plan; géométral;
couché; net, formel, catégorique,
direct; fade, éventé; maussade,
inactif; mat; (*Mus*.) bémol. ~
iron, fer à repasser, *m*. ~*roof*,
toit en terrasse, *m*, terrasse, plate-
forme, *f*. ¶ *ad*, à plat. ~ *on one's*

face, à plat [ventre]. *to sing* ~, détonner. ¶ *n*, plat; méplat; (*rooms*) appartement; (*plain, shoal*) bas-fond, haut-fond, *m*, basse, *f*; (*Theat.*) châssis; (*Mus.*) bémol, *m*. ~**ly**, *ad*, platement; nettement; [tout] net, carrément. ~**ness**, *n*, aplatissement; (*liquor*) évent, *m*; fadeur, platitude, *f*. **flatten**, *v.t*, aplatir; éventer; affadir.

flatter, *v.t*, flatter, caresser. ~**er**, *n*, flatteur, euse. ~**ing**, *a*, flatteur. ~**y**, *n*, flatterie, *f*.

flatulence, -**cy**, *n*, flatulence, *f*. **flatus**, *n*, flatuosité, *f*, gaz, vent, *m*.

flaunt, *v.t*, étaler, faire parade de.

flautist, *n*, flûtiste, *m.f*.

flavor, *n*, saveur, *f*, goût, *m*. ¶ *v.t*, assaisonner. ~**ing**, *n*, assaisonnement, *m*. ~**less**, *a*, insipide, fade.

flaw, *n*, paille, *f*, défaut, *m*, défectuosité; glace, *f*, crapaud; vice, *m*. ¶ *v.t*, rendre défectueux. ~**less**, *a*, sans défaut, net. ~**y**, *a*, pailleux.

flax, *n*, lin, *m*. ~ *field*, linière, *f*. ~**en**, *a*. & *n*, blond, *a*. & *m*.

flay, *v.t*, écorcher.

flea, *n*, puce, *f*. ~ *bite*, piqûre de puce, *f*.

fleck, *n*, tache, moucheture, *f*.

fledged (**to be**), avoir sa plume. **fledgling**, *n*, oisillon, *m*.

flee, *v.i*. & *t. ir*, fuir, s'enfuir.

fleece, *n*, toison, *f*. ¶ *v.t*, tondre, plumer, écorcher, étriller. **fleecy**, *a*, floconneux. ~ *clouds, sky fleeced with clouds*, nuages moutonnés, *m.pl*, ciel moutonné, *m*.

fleet, *n*, flotte, *f*. ~ *of foot*, léger (ère) à la course. ~**ing**, *a*, passager, fugitif, fugace.

Fleming, *n*, Flamand, e. **Flemish**, *a*. & (*language*) *n*, flamand, *a*. & *m*.

flesh, *n*, chair, *f*; chairs *f.pl*; charnure, *f*; (*meat*) viande, *f*; embonpoint, *m*. ¶ ~**y**, *a*, charnu; plantureux. ~ *part of the arm*, gras du bras, *m*.

flexible, *a*, flexible, souple. *to make* ~, assouplir. **flexor**, *a*. & *n*, fléchisseur, *a.m*. & *m*.

flick, *n*, chiquenaude, *f*; (*sound*) flic flac, *m*.

flicker, *v.i*, papilloter, trembler, vaciller.

flier, *n*, aviateur, *m*.

flight, *n*, fuite, *f*; vol, envol, *m*, volée; envolée, *f*, essor; élan;

exode, *m*; bande, *f*; écart, *m*. ~ *of stairs*, volée d'escalier, *f*. ~**y**, *a*. volage, léger, étourdi, frivole.

flimsy, *a*, sans consistance, mollasse; frivole. ¶ *n*, (*tissue*) papier pelure, *m*.

flinch, *v.i*, défaillir, broncher.

fling, *n*, coup; trait, *m*. ¶ *v.t.ir*, jeter, lancer, darder. ~ *away* & ~ *off*, rejeter.

flint, *n*, silex; caillou, *m*; pierre à fusil; pierre [à briquet] *f*. ~ & *steel*, briquet, *m*. ~ *glass*, flintglass, *m*. ~**y**, *a*, siliceux; caillouteux; de pierre.

flip, *v.t*, voleter.

flippant, *a*, léger, désinvolte.

flipper, *n*, nageoire, *f*.

flirt (*pers.*) *n*, coquet, te. ¶ *v.i*, coqueter, flirter. ~**ation**, *n*, coquetterie, *f*, flirt, *m*.

flit, *v.i*, voleter, voltiger; fuir. ~ *about*, papillonner.

float & ~**er**, *n*, flotte, *f*; flotteur; bouchon, *m*. ~[*board*], aube, palette, *f*, aileron, *m*. ~**plane**, hydravion à flotteurs, *m*. ¶ *v.t*, faire flotter; mettre à flot, renflouer; (*Fin.*) lancer; (*v.i.*) flotter; [sur]nager; (*Swim.*) faire la planche. ~**ation**, (*Fin.*) *n*, lancement, *m*. ~**ing**, *a*, flottant.

flock, *n*, troupeau; vol. *m*, bande, troupe, *f*; ouailles, *f.pl*; (*wool, etc.*) flocon, *m*; bourre, *f*. ¶ *v.i*, s'assembler [en troupe]; affluer.

floe, *n*, banquise, *f*; glaçon, *m*.

flog, *v.t*, fouetter, fustiger, cravacher. *a flogging*, le fouet.

flood, *n*, inondation, *f*, déluge; flot; torrent, *m*; crue, *f*; (*of the tide*) flux, *m*. ~ *gate*, vanne; (*fig.*) écluse, *f*. ~ *lighting*, éclairage par projection, *m*, illumination par p., *f*. ~ *tide*, marée de flot, *f*, flot, *m*. ¶ *v.t*, inonder, noyer, submerger.

floor, *n*, plancher; parquet; carreau; carré, *m*; aire, *f*; plateau; chantier; tablier; (*story*) étage, palier, *m*. *on one* ~ (rooms), de plain-pied. *to take the* ~, prendre la parole. ~ *lamp*, lampe à pied, torchère, *f*. ~ *polisher* (*pers.*) frotteur, *m*; (*Mach.*) cireuse, *f*. ~ *space*, surface des étages, *f*; encombrement, *m*. ¶ *v.t*, planchéier; parqueter; jeter par terre; terrasser, désarçonner.

flora, *n*, flore, *f*. **floral**, *a*, floral;

fleuriste. ~ *design*, ramage, *m.*
florid, *a*, fleuri; rubicond. **Florida**, *n*, la Floride. **florist**, *n*, fleuriste, *m,f.*
floss, *n*, bourre, *f.* ~ *silk*, soie floche, filoselle, strasse, *f.*
flotation (*Fin.*) *n*, lancement, *m.*
flotilla, *n*, flottille, escadrille, *f.*
flotsam, *n*, épaves [flottantes] *f.pl.*
flounce, *n*, volant, *m.* ¶ *v.t*, garnir de volants. ~ *about*, se trémousser.
flounder, (*fish*) *n*, flet, *m.* ¶ *v.i*, se débattre; barboter, patauger, patouiller.
flour, *n*, farine, *f.* ~ *mill*, moulin à farine, *m*, minoterie, *f.*
flourish, *n*, floriture, *f*; parafe, *m*; fanfare, *f*; (*of hand*) geste; (*with stick*) moulinet, *m.* ¶ *v.t*, brandir; (*v.i.*) fleurir; faire le moulinet. ~**ing**, *a*, florissant.
floury, *a*, farineux.
flout, *v.t*, narguer. ~ *at*, se railler de.
flow, *n*, écoulement; cours; *m*; coulée, *f*; débit; flux; torrent, *m*. ~ *of words*, flux de paroles, *m*, faconde, *f.* ¶ *v.i*, couler, s'écouler, affluer.
flower, *n*, fleur, *f.* ~ *garden*, jardin fleuriste, *m.* ~ *girl*, bouquetière, *f.* ~ *holder*, porte-bouquet, *m.* ~ *market*, marché aux fleurs, *m.* ~ *pot*, pot à fleurs, *m.* ~ *show*, exposition de fleurs, e. florale, *f.* ~ *stand*, jardinière, *f.* ~ *wire*, fil carcasse des fleuristes, *m.* ¶ *v.i*, fleurir. ~**et**, *n*, fleurette, *f.* ~**ing**, *a*, à fleurs. ¶ *n*, floraison, *f.* ~**y**, *a*, fleuri.
flowing, *a*, coulant, fluide; flottant, tombant.
flu, *n*, grippe, *f.*
fluctuate, *v.i*, osciller; flotter. **fluctuation**, *n*, fluctuation, oscillation, *f*, mouvement, *m.*
flue, *n*, tuyau; carneau; aspirail, *m.*
fluency, *n*, facilité, *f.* **fluent**, *a*, facile, disert. ~**ly**, *ad*, couramment.
fluff, *n*, bourre, *f*; coton, *m*; (*under furniture*) moutons; (*hair*) cheveux follets, *m.pl.* ~ *to* ~ *up*, pelucher. ~**y**, *a*, duveté; follet; cotonneux; pelucheux.
fluid, *a*, fluide. ¶ *n*, (*imponderable*) fluide; (*ponderable*) liquide, *m.* ~**ity**, *n*, fluidité, *f.*
fluke, *n*, (*anchor*) patte, *f*; coup de hasard, raccroc, *m.*
flummery, *n*, fadaises, *f.pl.*

flunk, *v.t*, échouer; être recalé.
flunkey, *n*, laquais, valet de pied, larbin, *m.* ~**dom**, *n*, valetaille, *f.*
fluorescent, *a*, fluorescent. **fluorine**, *n*, fluor, *m.* **fluorspar**, spath fluor, *m.*
flurry, *n*, ahurissement; coup de vent, *m.* ¶ *v.t*, ahurir.
flush, *a*, à fleur, au ras, de niveau; noyé; lisse; bien pourvu. ¶ *n*, accès, transport; flot de sang, *m*; bouffée; rougeur; fleur; chasse [d'eau] *f*; (*cards*) flux, *m.* ¶ *v.t*, affleurer; laver à grande eau; (*hunting*) faire lever; (*v.i.*) rougir. ~ed *face*, face injectée, *f.*
Flushing, *n*, Flessingue, *f.*
fluster, *v.t*, ahurir, troubler; (*with drink*) griser.
flute, *n*, flûte; (*groove*) cannelure, *f.* ~ [*glass*], flûte, *f.* **flutist**, *n*, flûtiste, *m,f.*
flutter, *n*, battement; émoi, *m.* ¶ *v.i. & t*, voleter; voltiger; palpiter.
fluty, *a*, flûté.
fluvial, **fluviatile**, *a*, fluvial, fluviatile.
flux, *n*, flux; (*Chem. & Metall.*) fondant, *m.*
fly, *n*, mouche; (*trouser*) braguette, *f.* ~ *blown*, piqué des mouches. ~ *catcher* (bird), gobemouches, *m*, moucherolle, *f.* ~ *fishing*, pêche à la mouche, *f.* ~ *leaf*, garde blanche, *f.* ~ *paper*, papier tue-mouches, *m.* ~ *speck*, chiure, *f.* ~ *swat*[*ter*], tue-mouches, *m.* ~ *trap* (plant), gobemouches, *m.* ~ *weight* (*Box.*), poids mouche, *m.* ~ *wheel*, volant, *m.* ~ *whisk*, chasse-mouches, émouchoir, *m.* ¶ *v.i.ir*, voler, s'envoler; [s'en]fuir; dénicher; éclater; sauter; jaillir; (*v.t.ir*) fuir; (*flag*) battre; (*kite*) lancer. ~ *about*, voltiger. ~ *at*, s'élancer sur; sauter à; s. sur; apostropher; voler. ~ *open*, s' ouvrir en coup de vent. ~**ing**, *n*, vol, *m*; aviation, *f.* ~ *ace*, as de l'aviation, *m.* ~ *buttress*, arcboutant, *m.* ~ *field*, champ d' aviation, *m.* ~ *fish*, poisson volant, *m.* ~ *squad*, brigade (*de police*) mobile, *f.* ~ *start*, départ lancé, *m.* ~ *visit*, camp volant, *m.*
foal, *n*, poulain, *m*, pouliche, *f*; (*ass's*) ânon, *m.* ¶ *v.i*, pouliner, mettre bas.
foam, *n*, écume, mousse, *f.* ¶ *v.i*,

écumer, mousser; (*sea*) moutonner. **~y**, *a*, écumeux, mousseux; (*sea*) moutonneuse.

focal, *a*, focal. **focus**, *n*, foyer, *m*. ¶ *v.t*, mettre au point; canaliser (*fig.*).

fodder, *n*, fourrage, *m*, provende, *f*.

foe, *n*, ennemi, e, adversaire, *m*.

fog, *n*, brouillard, *m*, brume, *f*; (*Phot.*) voile, *m*. **~ dispersal**, dénébulation, *f*. **~-dispersal device**, dénébulateur, *m*. **~ horn**, trompe de brume, *f*. **~ light**, phare antibrouillard, *m*. ¶ *v.t*, embrumer; (*Phot.*) voiler. **foggy**, *a*, brumeux.

fog[e]y, *n*, or **old ~**, croûton, *m*, [vieille] ganache, [vieille] perruque, *f*. **fogyish**, *a*, encroûté.

foible, *n*, faible, *m*.

foil, *n*, (*tinsel*) feuille, *f*, clinquant; paillon; tain; (*Fenc.*) fleuret; (*fig.*) repoussoir, lustre, *m*. ¶ *v.t*, déjouer; dépister.

foist, *v.t*, glisser; colloquer; attribuer.

fold, *n*, pli, repli; parc, *m*, bergerie, *f*; (*Relig.*) bercail, *m*. ¶ *v.t*, plier; (*arms*) [se] croiser; (*hands*) joindre; (*sheep*) parquer. **~ up**, *v.t*, [re]plier; (*v.i.*) se replier. **~er**, *n*, plieur, euse; chemise [pour dossier] *f*; (*publicity*) dépliant, *m*. **~ing**, *p.a*: **~ door**, porte brisée, *f*. **~ machine**, machine à plier, plieuse, *f*. **~ stool**, pliant, *m*.

foliaceous, *a*, foliacé. **foliage**, *n*, feuillage, *m*, frondaison, *f*, ombrage, *m*, chevelure, *f*. **foliate**, *a*, feuillé. **foliation**, *n*, foliation, feuillaison, frondaison, *f*.

folio, *n*, folio, *m*; (*book*) n. & a., in-folio, *m*. & *a*. ¶ *v.t*, folioter.

folklore, *n*, folk-lore, *m*, tradition, *f*.

folks, *n.pl*, gens, *m.pl*. & *f.pl*.

follicle, *n*, follicule, *m*, crypte, *f*.

follow, *v.t*, suivre; (*cards*) fournir de; (*v.i.*) s'ensuivre, résulter. **~ suit**, (*cards*) fournir [à] la couleur demandée; (*fig.*) faire de même. **~ through**, suivre la balle. **~ up**, [pour]suivre. **~ [shot]** (*Bil.*) *n*, coulé, *m*. **~er**, *n*, suivant, e; disciple, partisan, sectateur, *m*; suite [de lettre] *f*. **~ing** (*day, etc.*) *a*, suivant. **in the ~ manner**, & voici comment. **the ~ [persons]**, les personnes dont

les noms suivent. **the ~ story**, l'histoire que voici. ¶ *n*, partisans, *m.pl*.

folly, *n*, folie; sottise, bêtise, *f*.

foment, *v.t*, fomenter; étuver. **~ation**, *n*, fomentation, *f*.

fond†, *a*, tendre, affectueux. **to be ~ of**, aimer; affectionner; être friand de, ê. gourmand de; ê. porté pour; ê. amateur de.

fondle, *v.t*, caresser, câliner, pouponner.

fondness, *n*, affection, tendresse, *f*; penchant, goût, *m*.

font, *n*, (*Eccl.*) fonts, *m.pl*; (*Typ.*) fonte, *f*.

food, *n*, nourriture, *f*, aliment, *m*, vivres, *m.pl*; mangeaille, *f*, mets, *m*; table, cuisine; pâture, *f*. **~ & drink**, le boire & le manger. **~ for thought**, matière à réflexion, *f*. **~ stuff**, matière d'alimentation, denrée alimentaire, *f*. **fast ~**, prêt-à-manger, *m*.

fool, *n*, sot, te; bête, *f*; imbécile, *m,f*, idiot, e; paltasan, *m*; (*Hist., court*) fou, *m*. **to play the ~**, faire l'imbécile, nigauder, niaiser. **~hardiness**, témérité, *f*. **~hardy**, téméraire. ¶ *v.t*, duper; jouer; amuser. **~ [about]**, *v.i*, baguenauder. **~ery**, *n*, farce, *f*, vains propos, *m.pl*, pantalonnade, *f*, calembredaines, *f.pl*, bouffonnerie, *f*; badinage, *m*, gaminerie, *f*. **~ish†**, *a*, sot bête, benêt. **~ishness**, *n*, folie, sottise, *f*. **~proof**, *a*, indéréglable.

foot, *n*, pied, *m*; patte; semelle; base, *f*; bas, *m*; (*Meas.*) pied = 0.30480 meter. **~ & mouth disease**, fièvre aphteuse, *f*. **~ball**, ballon de football; (*game*) football, *m*. **~ bath**, bain de pieds, *m*. **~bridge**, passerelle, *f*. **~fall**, pas, *m*. **~ fault** (*Ten.*), faute de pied, *f*. **~hold**, assiette pour le pied, *f*, pied, *m*. **~lights**, rampe, *f*. **~man**, valet de pied, laquais, *m*. **~note**, apostille, *f*. **~path**, sentier, *m*, sente, *f*; (*street*) trottoir, *m*. **~print**, empreinte de pas, e. du pied, *f*, pas, vestige, *m*; trace, *f*. **~ race**, course à pied, *f*. **~sore**, éclopé. **~step**, pas, *m*. **~stool**, tabouret [de pied] *m*. **~ warmer**, chauffepieds, *m*, chaufferette, bouillotte, *f*. **~wear**, chaussures, *f.pl*. **~ work**, jeu de jambes,

on ~, à pied. ~ing, *n*, pied, *m*;
assiette pour le pied, *f*.
fop, *n*, fat, *m*. **foppish,** *a*, fat.
for, *pr*, pour; par; à; de; à cause
de; pendant; il y a; depuis; malgré. ~ *all that*, malgré cela,
malgré tout. ~ & *against*, le
pour & le contre. ¶ *c*, car.
forage, *n*, fourrage, *m*. ¶ *v.i*, fourrager; (*bird*) picorer. **forager,**
n, fourrageur, *m*.
forasmuch, *c*, étant donné.
foray, *n*, incursion, maraude, *f*.
forbear, *v.i.ir*, s'abstenir, s'empêcher. ~ance, *n*, indulgence,
longanimité, mansuétude, *f*.
forbid, *v.t.ir*, défendre, interdire.
God ~! à Dieu ne plaise! **for-
bidden,** *a*, interdit. **forbidding,** *a*,
rebutant, repoussant.
force, *n*, force, *f*; effort; effectif,
m; armée, *f*. ~ *of circumstances*,
force des choses. *by* ~, à main
armée. *in* ~, en vigueur. ~
pump, pompe foulante, *f*. ¶ *v.t*,
forcer; hâter; se frayer. **forced,**
p.a, forcé; factice. *by* ~ *marches*,
à grandes journées. **forcedly,** *ad*,
forcément. **forceful**†, *a*, vigoureux. **forcemeat,** *n*, farce, *f*.
forceps, *n.s*. & *pl*, (*Surg.*) pince,
f; (*dental*) davier; (*obstetrical*)
forceps, *m*, fers, *m.pl*.
forcible, *a*, énergique, corsé. ~
feeding, gavage, *m*. **forcibly,** *ad*,
énergiquement; de force.
ford, *n*, gué, *m*. ¶ *v.t*, guéer.
~able, *a*, guéable.
fore, *a*, de devant, *e.g.* ~*paw*,
patte de devant, *f*; (*Naut.*) de
l'avant. ¶ *ad*, à l'avant. ~ & *aft*,
de l'avant à l'arrière. ¶ (*golf*)
i, attention!, hep!, balle! ¶ *n*,
devant; (*Naut.*) avant, *m*.
forearm, *n*, avant-bras, *m*. ¶ *v.t*,
prémunir.
forebode, *v.t*, présager. **foreboding,** *n*, présage, pressentiment, *m*.
forecast, *n*, prévision, *f*, pronostic, *m*. *weather* ~, prévision météorologique, *f*. ¶ *v.t*, pronostiquer, prédire.
forecastle *or* **foc's'le,** *n*, gaillard d'avant; poste de l'équipage,
m.
foreclose, *v.t*, saisir. **foreclosure,**
n, saisie, *f*.
forecourt, *n*, (*house*) cour de devant; (*castle, palace*), avant-
cour, *f*.
forefathers, *n.pl*, aïeux, *m.pl*.

forefinger, *n*, index, *m*.
foregoing, *p.a*, précédent. *the*
~, ce qui précède. *foregone conclusion*, décision prise d'avance,
f.
foreground, *n*, premier plan, *m*,
devants, *m.pl*.
forehand [stroke] (*Ten.*) *n*,
[coup d']avant-main, *m*.
forehead, *n*, front, *m*.
foreign, *a*, étranger; extérieur;
exotique. ~ *exchange rates*
(table), cote des changes, *f*. ~
service, service diplomatique, *m*.
~er, *n*, étranger, ère.
foreknowledge, *n*, prescience,
f.
foreland, *n*, cap, *m*, pointe [de
terre] *f*.
forelock (*hair*) *n*, toupet, *m*.
foreman, *n*, contremaître, chef
d'équipe, chef, *m*. ~ *of the jury*,
chef du jury.
foremast, *n*, mât de misaine, *m*.
foremost (*the*), le plus avancé;
le tout premier.
forenoon, *n*, matinée, *f*.
forensic, *a*, de palais; (*medicine*)
légale.
forerunner, *n*, avant-coureur,
précurseur, *m*, préface, *f*.
foresee, *v.t.ir*, prévoir.
foreshadow, *v.t*, annoncer.
foreshore, *n*, rivage, *m*.
foreshorten, *v.t*, raccourcir.
foresight, *n*, prévoyance, *f*.
forest, *n*, forêt, *f*; (*att.*) forestier.
forestall, *v.t*, anticiper; prévenir;
devancer.
forester, *n*, (*officer*) forestier;
habitant de la forêt, *m*. **forestry,**
n, sylviculture, *f*.
foretaste, *n*, avant-goût, *m*.
foretell, *v.t.ir*, prédire, annoncer.
forethought, *n*, prévoyance;
préméditation, *f*.
forewarn, *v.t*, prévenir, prémunir, avertir.
forewoman, *n*, première, *f*.
foreword, *n*, avant-propos, *m*,
préface, *f*.
forfeit, *n*, dédit, *m*, pénalité, *f*; (*at
play*) gage, *m*, pénitence, *f*; (*pl.*)
gages, jeux innocents, petits jeux,
m.pl. ¶ *v.t*, déchoir de; (*honor*)
forfaire à. ~ure, *n*, perte; (*rights*)
déchéance; forfaiture, *f*.

forgather, *v.i*, se réunir.
forge, *n*, forge, *f*. ¶ *v.t*, (*metal &
fig.*) forger; falsifier, contrefaire.
~d, *p.a*, faux. **forgeman,** *n*, for-

geur, *m.* **forger,** *n,* faussaire, *m,f.* fabricateur, trice. **forgery,** *n,* faux; crime de faux, *m;* contrefaçon, *f.*

forget, *v.t.ir,* oublier. **~-me-not,** ne m'oubliez pas, myosotis, *m,* oreille-de-souris, *f.* **~ oneself,** s'échapper, s'émanciper. **~ful,** *a,* oublieux. **~fulness,** *n,* oubli, *m.*

forgive, *v.t.ir,* pardonner; (*pers.*) pardonner à; faire grâce à, remettre. **~ness,** *n,* pardon, *m;* rémission; remise, *f.*

forgo, *v.t.ir,* s'abstenir de; renoncer à.

fork, *n,* fourche; (*table, etc.*) fourchette, *f;* (*tree*) fourchon, *m;* (*road, etc.*) bifurcation, *f.* **tuning ~,** diapason, *m.* ¶ *v.i,* fourcher, bifurquer. **~ed,** *a,* fourchu. **~ lightning,** éclair ramifié, *m.*

forlorn, *a,* délaissé; désolé, inconsolé. **~ hope,** vague espoir, *m.*

form, *n,* forme, *f,* ton, *m;* (*paper*) formule, *f,* bulletin, *m;* (*seat*) banc; (*hare*) gîte, *m.* ¶ *v.t,* former; façonner; constituer; nouer; faire; se faire, se former. **~ single file,** dédoubler les rangs. **~al†,** *a,* formel; de forme; dans les formes; cérémonieux; solennel; formaliste. **~ality,** *n,* formalité, *f.* **~ation,** *n,* formation; constitution, *f.* **form** (*Typ.*) *n,* forme, *f.*

former, *a,* ancien; passé; précédent. *the ~,* celui-là. **~ly,** *ad,* autrefois, jadis, anciennement, cidevant.

formidable†, *a,* formidable.

Formosa, *n,* Formose, *f.*

formula, *n,* formule, *f.* **~ry,** *n,* formulaire, *m.* **formulate,** *v.t,* formuler. **formulism,** *n,* le style pompier. **formulist,** *n.* & **~ic,** *a,* pompier, *m.* & *att.*

fornication, *n,* fornication, *f.*

forsake, *v.t.ir,* délaisser, abandonner.

forsooth, *ad,* en vérité, ma foi.

forswear, *v.t.ir,* abjurer. **~ oneself,** se parjurer.

fort, *n,* fort, (*small*) fortin, *m.* **forte** (*Mus.*) *ad,* forte. ¶ (*strong point*) *n,* fort, *m.*

forth, *ad,* en avant. **~coming,** *a,* [prêt] à paraître; à venir; prochain. **~with,** *ad,* incessamment, sur-le-champ, séance tenante.

fortieth, *a.* & *n,* quarantième, *a.* & *m,f.*

fortification, *n,* fortification, *f;* (*wine*) vinage, *m.* **fortify,** *v.t,* fortifier; munir; corser; viner. *fortified place,* place forte, p. de guerre, *f.* **fortitude,** *n,* force d'âme, *f,* courage, *m.*

fortnight, *n,* quinze jours, *m.pl,* quinzaine, *f.* **~ly,** *ad,* tous les quinze jours.

fortress, *n,* forteresse, *f.*

fortuitous†, *a,* fortuit.

fortunate, *a,* heureux, fortuné. **~ly,** *ad,* heureusement, par bonheur. **fortune,** *n,* fortune, *f;* horoscope, *m. to tell ~s,* dire la bonne aventure. **~-teller,** diseur (euse) de bonne aventure; tireur (euse) de cartes, cartomancien, ne.

forty, *a.* & *n,* quarante, *a.* & *m.*

forum, *n,* forum, *m.*

forward, *a,* avancé; d'avance; avant; progessif; précoce, hâtif; hardi, indiscret; (*Com.*) à terme, à livrer. **~[s],** *ad,* [en] avant. ¶ *n,* (*Foot.*) avant, *m.* ¶ *v.t,* avancer; hâter; expédier, acheminer; faire suivre, transmettre. **~ing agent,** commissionnaire de transport[s], expéditeur, *m.* **~ness,** *n,* précocité; hardiesse, *f.*

fossil, *a.* & *n,* fossile, *a.* & *m.*

foster, *v.t,* encourager; favoriser; nourrir. ¶ *a,* adoptif. **~ brother,** frère de lait, *m.* **~ child,** nourrisson, *m.*

foul, *a,* sale; crasseux; immonde; mauvais, vilain; infect; vicié; fétide; puant; infâme; (*words*) gros. **~-mouthed,** mal embouché. **~ play,** vilain tour; sabotage, *m.* ¶ *n,* faute, *f;* coup déloyal, *m.* ¶ *v.t,* salir, souiller, encrasser; vicier; fausser; (*Naut., rope, etc.*) engager; (*ship*) entrer en collision; (*sports*) violer la règle. **~ness,** *n,* fétidité; noirceur, *f.*

found, *v.t,* fonder, créer; (*metal*) fondre, mouler. **foundation,** *n,* fondation, *f;* fondement; établissement, *m;* assiette; assise, *f.* **~ stone,** pierre fondamentale, première p., *f.* **founder,** *n,* fondateur, créateur; (*race*) auteur, *m;* (*family*) souche, *f;* (*metal*) fondeur, *m.* ¶ *v.i,* sombrer, couler, c. à fond, c. à pic, c. bas.

foundling, *n,* enfant trouvé, *m.*

foundress, *n,* fondatrice, créatrice, *f.*

foundry, *n,* fonderie, *f.*

fount, *n,* fontaine, *f;* puits; *m;*

(*Typ.*) fonte, *f.* **fountain**, *n,* fontaine, source, *f;* jet d'eau, *m;* (*pl.*) [grandes] eaux, *f.pl.* ~**head**, source, *f.* ~ *of youth*, fontaine de Jouvence. ~ *pen,* stylographe, porte-plume [à] réservoir, *m.*

four, *a. & n,* quatre, *a. & m.* ~*fold,* quadruple. ~*footed,* quadrupède. ~*poster,* lit à colonnes, *m.* ~*score,* *a. & n,* quatre-vingts, quatre-vingt, *a. & m.* ~*some* (*golf*), partie double, *f.* ~*wheeled,* à quatre roues. *on all* ~*s,* à quatre pattes. **fourteen,** *a. & n,* quatorze, *a. & m.* ~**th**†, *a. & n,* quatorzième, *a. & m,f;* quatorze, *m.* **fourth**†, *a,* quatrième. ~ *finger,* petit doigt, [doigt] auriculaire, *m.* ¶ *n,* quatrième, *m,f;* quatre, *m;* (*part*) quart, *m;* (*Mus.*) quatre, *f.*

fowl, *n,* oiseau; o. de basse-cour, *m;* volaille; poule; poularde, *f.* ~**er,** *n,* oiseleur, *m.* ~**ing,** *n,* chasse aux oiseaux, *f.* ~ *piece,* canardière, *f.*

fox, *n,* renard, *m.* ~ *cub,* renardeau, *m.* ~*'s hole,* renardière, *f.* ~*glove,* gantelée, digitale, *f.* ~*hound,* foxhound, *m.* ~ *hunting,* chasse au renard, *f.* ~ *terrier,* fox-terrier, *m.* ~*trot,* foxtrot, *m.* ~**y** (*fig.*) *a,* rusé.

foyer, *n,* foyer [du public] *m.*

fraction, *n,* fraction, *f.* ~**al,** *a,* fractionnaire.

fractious, *a,* hargneux.

fracture, *n,* fracture; cassure, rupture, *f.* ¶ *v.t,* fracturer.

fragile, *a,* fragile. **fragility,** *n,* fragilité, *f.*

fragment, *n,* fragment, morceau, éclat, *m.* ~**ary,** *a,* fragmentaire.

fragrance, *n,* bonne odeur, *f,* parfum, *m.* **fragrant,** *a,* odoriférant, odorant.

frail, *a,* frêle; fragile; caduc. ¶ *n,* cabas, *m;* bourriche, *f.* ~**ty,** *n,* fragilité; infirmité, *f.*

frame & ~**work,** *n,* cadre; bâti; châssis, *m;* charpente; membrure; ossature; carcasse; armature; monture; châsse, *f;* pan, *m;* case, *f;* (*Need.*) métier, *m.* ~ *of mind,* état d'esprit, *m,* disposition, *f.* ¶ *v.t,* former; charpenter; (*picture, etc.*) encadrer; (*cinema*) cadrer. **framing** (*act*) *n,* encadrement, *m;* (*cinema*) cadrage, *m.*

France, *n,* la France.

franchise, *n,* droit électoral, électorat, *m.*

Franciscan, *n,* franciscain, *m.*

Francophil[e], *a. & n,* francophile, *a. & m,f.* **Francophobe,** *a. & n,* francophobe, *a. & m,f.*

frank†, *a,* franc, ouvert, en dehors. ~**ness,** *n,* franchise, rondeur, *f.*

Frankfort, *n,* Francfort, *m.*

frankfurter, *n,* saucisse, *f.*

frankincense, *n,* encens mâle, *m.*

frantic†, *a,* frénétique; effréné, fou.

fraternal†, *a,* fraternel. **fraternity,** *n,* fraternité, *f.* **fraternize,** *v.i,* fraterniser. **fratricide,** *n, &* **fratricidal,** *a,* fratricide, *m. & a.*

fraud, *n,* fraude; supercherie, *f.* **fraudulent**†, *a,* frauduleux.

fraught with, plein de, gros de.

fray, *n,* lutte, rixe, bagarre; bataille, *f.*

fray, *v.t,* érailler, effranger, effilocher.

freak, *n,* caprice, *m.* ~ [*of nature*], monstruosité, *f,* jeu [bizarre] de la nature, phénomène, *m.* ~**ish**†, *a,* capricieux; bizarre; hétéroclite; monstrueux.

freckle, *n,* tache de rousseur, lentille, éphélide, *f.* ¶ *v.t,* tacheter de rousseurs.

free, *a,* libre; ouvert; large; débarrassé; dépourvu; exempt; privé; gratuit; net; indépendant; quitte; dégagé, désinvolte. ~ *allowance of luggage* or *weight allowed* ~, franchise de bagages, *f.* de poids, *f.* ~ *& easy,* sans gêne, bohème, cavalier. ~ *& easy manner,* désinvolture, *f.* ~ *hand* (*fig.*), carte blanche, *f.* ~*hand drawing,* dessin à main levée, *m.* ~*lance,* franc-tireur, tirailleur, *m.* ~*mason,* franc-maçon, *m.* ~*pass,* billet de faveur; (*Rly*) permis de circulation, *m.* ~*stone,* pierre franche, *f.* ~*thinker,* m. ~*thinking,* ~ *thought,* libre pensée, *f.* ~ *trade,* libre-échange, *m.* ~*trader,* abolitioniste, *m.* ~ *verse,* vers libres, *m.pl.* ~ *wheel,* roue libre, *f.* ~ *will,* [plein] gré; (*Philos.*) libre (*ou* franc) arbitre, *m.* ¶ *ad,* gratis; gracieusement; franco; en franchise. ¶ *v.t,* libérer, affranchir; dégager; exempter. **freedom**, *n*, liberté; exemption; franchise; aisance, *f*. *free[dom of] speech*, libre parole, liberté de parler, *f*. **freely**, *ad*, librement; franchement; largement.

freeway, *n*, autoroute, *f*.

freeze, *v.t.ir*, geler, glacer, congeler, réfrigérer; (*v.i.ir*.) geler; se g., [se] glacer, prendre. ¶ *n*, (*diplomacy*) gel, *m*; (*price &/or wage*) blocage, *m*. **freezer**, *n*, glacière; sorbetière, *f*. *freezing point*, température de congélation, *f*. (thermometer) *at freezing*, à glace.

freeze-dry, *v.t*, lyophiliser.

Freiburg (*Baden*) *n*, Fribourg-en-Brisgau, *m*.

freight, *n*, fret, *m*. ~ *train*, train de merchandises, *m*. ¶ *v.t*, fréter.

French, *a*, français. ~ *ambassador, consul*, ambassadeur, consul, de France, *m*. ~ *chalk*, talc, *m*. ~ *fries*, frites, *f.pl*. ~ *horn*, cor d'harmonie, *m*. ~ *to take* ~ *leave*, filer à l'anglaise. ~ *lesson, master*, leçon, *f*, professeur, *m*, de français. ~*man*, ~*woman*, Français, e. ~ *polish*, *n*, vernis au tampon, *m*; (*v.t.*) vernir au t. ~*speaking Switzerland*, la Suisse romande. ~ *window*, porte-fenêtre, *f*. ¶ (*language*) *n*, le français. the ~, *pl*, les Français, *m.pl*. **Frenchify**, *v.t*, franciser.

frenzied, *p.p*, frénétique; délirant.

frenzy, *n*, frénésie, fureur, ivresse, *f*.

frequency, *n*, fréquence, *f*. **frequent**, *a*, fréquent. ¶ *v.t*, fréquenter, pratiquer, hanter, courir. ~**er**, *n*, habitué, e, coureur, euse. ~**ly**, *ad*, fréquemment.

fresco, *n*, fresque, *f*.

fresh, *a*, frais; récent, vert; reposé; nouveau; novice. ~ *from the wash*, blanc de lessive. ~ *water*, eau fraîche; (*not salt*) e. douce, *f*. ~*water fishing*, pêche en eaux douces, p. d'eau douce, *f*. ~**en**, *v.t. & i* (*Naut.*) fraîchir. ~**et**, *n*, crue, *f*, grandes eaux, *f.pl*. ~**ly** & ~, *ad*, fraîchement; (*with p.p.*) frais, aîche, *e.g, fresh[ly] gathered roses*, des roses fraîches cueillies. ~**ness**, *n*, fraîcheur; nouveauté; primeur, *f*.

fret, *n*, (*on guitar*) touche; (*Arch.*, *Her.*) frette, *f*. ~*saw*, *n*, scie à découper, *f*; (*v.t. & i.*) découper. ~*work*, découpure, *f*. ¶ *v.i*, s'irriter, se chagriner, geindre; (*v.t.*) ronger; chagriner, tracasser. ~**ful**, *a*, chagrin, geignard.

friable, *a*, friable.

friar, *n*, moine, frère, religieux, *m*.

friction, *n*, friction, *f*, frottement, *m*.

Friday, *n*, vendredi, *m*. *Good* ~, vendredi saint.

fried fish, poisson frit, *m*, friture, *f*.

friend, *n*, ami, e; cousin, e. ~**less**, *a*, sans ami. ~**liness**, *n*, bienveillance, *f*. ~**ly**, *a*, ami, amical, amiable. ~**ship**, *n*, amitié, camaraderie, *f*.

Friesland, *n*, la Frise.

frieze, *n*, frise, *f*.

frigate, *n*, frégate, *f*.

fright, *n*, frayeur, épouvante, peur, *f*, effroi, *m*, transe, *f*; (*pers.*) horreur, *f*, magot, *m*. ~**en**, *v.t*, effrayer, épouvanter. ~**ful**†, *a*, effrayant, épouvantable, affreux.

frigid†, *a*, glacial, froid. ~**ity**, *n*, frigidité, froideur, *f*.

frill, *n*, ruche, *f*; jabot, *m*. ~*s & furbelows*, fanfreluches, *f.pl*. ¶ *v.t*, rucher.

fringe, *n*, frange, crépine, *f*, effilé; bord, *m*. ¶ *v.t*, franger; border.

frippery, *n*, friperie, *f*, falbalas, colifichets, *m.pl*.

Frisian, *a*, frison. ¶ *n*, Frison, ne.

frisk, *n*, gambade, *f*. ¶ *v.i*, gambader, fringuer, frétiller; (*search*) palper.

frisky, *a*, frétillant, fringant.

fritter (*Cook.*) *n*, beignet, *m*. ~ *away*, éparpiller, dissiper, fricasser.

frivolity, *n*, frivolité, *f*. **frivolous**, *a*, frivole, léger.

frizzle, *v.t*, crêper, friser. **frizzle** (*bacon, etc.*) *v.t*, faire se recoquiller.

frock, *n*, robe, *f*, costume, *m*; (*smock*) blouse, *f*; (*monk's*) froc, *m*. ~ *coat*, redingote, *f*.

frog, *n*, grenouille, *f*; (*horse*) fourchette, *f*; (*Rly*) croisement; (*sword*) porte-épée, pendant, *m*.

frolic, *v.i*, folâtrer. ~**some**, *a*, follet.

from, *pr*, de; d'avec; de chez; depuis; dès; à; d'après; à partir de, à dater de; de la part de; par. ~ *that point of view*, à ce point de vue. ~ *what you do*, d'après ce que vous faites. ~ *the beginning*, dès le commencement. *the train ~ Paris*, le train de Paris.

frond, *n*, fronde, *f*.

front, *a*, de devant; d'avant; de front; de tête; de face; premier. ~ *[line]* (*Mil.*), front, *m*, première ligne, *f*. ¶ *n*, devant; avant, *m*, tête; devanture; face; façade, *f*; front; recto, *m*; (*shirt*) plastron, *m*. *in ~ & in ~ of*, devant. *on the [sea] ~*, en bordure de la mer; sur la promenade [de la mer]; (*hotel*) sur la mer. ¶ *v.t*, affronter, faire face à; donner sur; ~**age**, *n*, devant, *m*; (*extent*) face; façade; exposition, *f*. ~**al**, *a*, de front; (*Anat.*) frontal.

frontier, *n. & att*, frontière, *f. & att*.

frontispiece, *n*, (*book*) frontispice, *m*; (*Arch.*) façade, *f*.

frost, *n*, gelée, *f*; (*degrees of*) froid, *m*; (*fig., of age*) glaces, *f.pl*. ~**bite**, congélation, *f*. ~**bitten**, gelé. ~**ed glass**, verre dépoli, *m*. ~**y**, *a*, glacial, de glace.

froth, *n*, écume; mousse, *f*. ¶ *v.i*, écumer; mousser. ~**y**, *a*, écumant; mousseux; frivole.

frown, *n*, froncement des sourcils, *m*. ¶ *v.i*, froncer le[s] sourcil[s], sourciller, se re[n]frogner. ~ *[up]on*, regarder d'un mauvais œil, désapprouver.

frowzy, *a*, moisi; borgne.

frozen, *p.a*, gelé, glacé; glacial; (*meat, etc.*) frigorifié; (*credit*) gelé. *[as if]* ~ *stiff*, morfondu.

fructify, *v.i*, fructifier; (*v.t.*) féconder.

frugal†, *a*, frugal. ~**ity**, *n*, frugalité, *f*.

fruit, *n*, fruit, *m*. ~ *bowl*, coupe à fruits, *f*, compotier, *m*. ~ *salad*, macédoine de fruits, salade de f—s, *f*. ~ *store*, fruiterie, *f*. ~ *tree*, arbre fruitier, *m*. à fruit, *m*. **fruitful**†, *a*, fertile, fécond; fructueux (*fig. & poet.*). ~**ness**, *n*, fertilité, fécondité, *f*. **fruition**, *n*, jouissance; réalisation, *f*. **fruitless**, *a*, sans fruit; (*fig.*) infructueux; vain. ~**ly**, *ad*, en vain.

frump, *n*, femme mal fagotée, *f*.

frustrate, *v.t*, frustrer, déjouer. **frustration**, *n*, insuccès, renversement, *m*.

frustum, *n*, tronc, *m*.

fry, *n*, (*fish*) fretin, frai, alevin, nourrain, *m*, poissonnaille, blanchaille; (*Cook.*) friture, *f*. *French fries*, pommes frites, *f.pl*. ¶ *v.t*, [faire] frire; (*v.i.*) frire. ~**ing**, *n*, & ~ *oil* or *fat*, friture, *f*. ~ *pan*, poêle [à frire] *f*.

fuchsia, *n*, fuchsia, *m*.

fuddle, *v.t*, griser. ~**d**, *p.a*, gris.

fuel, *n*, combustible; (*fig.*) aliment, *m*. ~ *oil*, pétrole combustible, *m*. ¶ *v.t*, alimenter; chauffer.

fugitive, *a*, fugitif, passager. ¶ *n*, fugitif, ive, fuyard, e.

fugleman, *n*, chef de file; meneur; porteparole, *m*.

fugue, *n*, fugue, *f*.

fulcrum, *n*, [point d']appui, *m*.

fulfil, *v.t*, remplir, accomplir; satisfaire à, exécuter. ~**ment**, *n*, accomplissement, *m*, exécution, *f*.

full, *a*, plein; comble; rempli; complet; au complet; entier; plénier; tout; copieux; nourri; intégral; germain. ~**blooded**, sanguin. ~**bodied** (wine), vineux, corsé. ~ *dress*, grande tenue, tenue de cérémonie; grande toilette, *f*. ~**grown**, fait. ~ *length mirror*, psyché, *f*. ~ *length portrait*, portrait en pied, *m*. ~ *name*, (*pers.*) nom & prénoms; (*stock, etc.*) désignation détaillée, *f*. ~ *of fish* (river, lake), poissonneux. ~ *orchestra*, grand orchestre, *m*. ~**page illustration**, gravure en pleine page, *f*. ~ *size*, grandeur naturelle, *f*. *I am ~*, je suis rassasié. *in ~*, in extenso. *Also = fully.* ¶ *n*, plein, *m*.

full, *v.t*, fouler. ~**er**, *n*, foulon, *m*. ~**'s earth**, terre à foulon, *f*.

fully, *ad*, pleinement; complètement; entièrement; intégralement; bien; en toutes lettres.

fulminate, *v.i. & t*, fulminer.

fullness, *n*, plénitude; ampleur; rondeur, abondance, *f*. **fulsome**, *a*, outré, excessif, exagéré, écœurant.

fumble, *v.i*, [far]fouiller, tâtonner.

fume, *n*, fumée, vapeur, bouffée, buée; colère, *f*. ¶ *v.i. & t*, fumer; enrager, maugréer. ~**d** (*oak*) *a*, patiné, teinté.

fumigate, *v.t*, faire des fumigations dans.

fun, *n*, amusement, *m*; plaisanterie, drôlerie, *f*. *in ~*, pour rire. *to make ~ of*, se moquer de, se divertire aux dépens de.

function, *n,* fonction, *f,* office, *m;* réunion, *f.* ¶ *v.i.* fonctionner; opérer. **~al,** *a,* fonctionnel. **~ary,** *n,* fonctionnaire, *m,f.*

fund, *n,* fonds, *m,* caisse, masse *f;* (*pl.*) fonds, deniers, *m.pl;* fonds, *m,* masse, provision, *f.* sinking ~, caisse d'amortissement, *f.* ¶ *v.t.* consolider.

fundament, *n,* fondement, *m.* **—al†,** *a,* fondamental, foncier.

funeral, *n,* enterrement, *m,* (*elaborate*) funérailles, *f. pl;* convoi, *m,* pompe funèbre, *f.* ¶ *a,* funéraire; funèbre. ~ *oration,* oraison funèbre, *f.* **funereal,** *a,* funèbre, d'enterrement.

fungous, *a,* fongueux; transitoire. **fungus,** *n,* fongus; champignon [vénéneux] *m.*

funicular, *a.* & *n,* funiculaire, *a.* & *m.*

funnel, *n,* entonnoir, *m;* (*Naut.*) cheminée, *f.*

funny, *a,* comique, drôle, plaisant. ~ *bone,* petit juif, *m.* ~ *little* (*pers.*), falot, *a.* ~ *man,* comique de la troupe, loustic, *m.* a ~ (queer) *man,* un drôle. the ~ *part,* le comique.

fur, *n,* fourrure, *f,* poil; pelage; dépôt, tartre, *m,* incrustation, *f.* ~ *coat,* manteau de fourrure, *m.* **~-lined,** fourré. ~ *lining,* fourrage, *m.* ~ *trade,* pelleterie, *f.*

furbelows, *n.pl,* falbalas, *m.pl.*

furbish, *v.t,* fourbir.

furious†, *a,* furieux, acharné.

furl, *v.t,* serrer, ferler.

furlong, *n,* furlong, *m.* = ⅛ mile or 201.168 meters.

furlough, *n,* (*Mil.*) permission, *f.*

furnace, *n,* four; fourneau; foyer, *m;* fournaise, *f.* blast ~, haut fourneau, *m.*

furnish, *v.t,* fournir; pourvoir; garnir; meubler. **~ed** *apartments* or *rooms,* [appartement] meublé hôtel meublé, *m.* **furniture,** *n,* meubles, *m.pl;* ameublement, mobilier, *m;* garniture, *f,* accessoires, *m.pl.* ~ *polish,* encaustique pour meubles, *f.* ~ *warehouse,* garde-meuble, *m.*

furore, *n,* fureur, *f.*

furred (*tongue*) *p.a,* chargée.

furier, *n,* fourreur, pelletier, *m.* **~y,** *n,* pelleterie, *f.*

furrow, *n,* sillon, *m.* ¶ *v.t,* sillonner; raviner.

furry, *a,* à fourrure; (*tongue*) chargée.

further, *a,* supplémentaire, nouveau; plus éloigné. ¶ *ad,* plus loin; au-delà; [plus] en delà; [en] outre, de plus; encore, davantage. ¶ *v.t,* avancer, seconder. **~ance,** *n,* avancement, *m.* **~more,** *ad,* de plus, d'ailleurs, en outre. **furthest,** *a,* le plus éloigné. ¶ *ad,* le plus loin.

furtive†, *a,* furtif.

fury, *n,* furie, fureur, *f,* acharnement, *m;* (*pers.*) furie, forcenée, *f.* F~ (*Myth.*), Furie, *f.*

furze, *n,* ajonc, genêt épineux, *m.*

fuse, *n,* fusée; mèche; étoupille, *f;* (*Elec.*) plomb [fusible] *m. to blow* a ~, faire sauter un plomb. ¶ *v.t.* & *i,* fondre.

fusee (*Horol.*) *n,* fusée, *f.*

fuselage, *n,* fuselage, *m.*

fusible, *a,* fusible.

fusillade, *n,* fusillade, *f.*

fusion, *n,* fusion, *f.*

fuss, *n,* bruit, tapage, *m,* cérémonies, façons, histoires, *f. pl.* ¶ *v.i,* tatillonner, faire des histoires. **~y,** *a,* façonnier, difficultueux.

fustian, *n,* futaine; (*fig.*) emphase, *f,* phébus, *m.*

fusty, *a,* qui sent le renfermé; moisi.

futile, *a,* futile. **futility,** *n,* futilité, *f.*

future, *a,* futur; d'avenir; à venir; (*Com.*) à terme. ¶ *n,* avenir; futur; (*pl.,* *Com.*) livrable, *m.* ~ [*tense*], futur [simple] *m.* ~ *perfect,* futur antérieur. **futurity,** *n,* futur, *m.*

fuzzy, *a,* (*hair*) crépu; (*image*) flou.

G

G (*Mus.*) *letter,* sol, *m.* ~ *clef,* clef de sol, *f.*

gabble, *v.t,* débiter trop vite; (*v.i.*) caqueter, babiller.

gable, *n,* pignon, *m.* ~ *roof,* comble sur pignon(s), *m.*

gad about, courir çà & là, c. la pretentaine. **gadabout,** *n,* coureur, euse.

gadfly, *n,* œstre, taon, *m.*

gadget, *n,* machine, *f,* truc, bidule, gadget, *m.*

gaff, *n,* (*spear*) gaffe; (*spar*) corne, *f.*

gag, *n*, bâillon, *m*; *(actor's)* scie, cascade, *f*. ¶ *v.t*, bâillonner.

gage, *n*, gage, *m*; assurance, *f*. See also *gauge*.

gaiety, *n*, gaieté, joie; gaillardise, *f*. **gaily**, *ad*, gaiement.

gain, *n*, gain, *m*. ¶ *v.t*, gagner; remporter; valoir; *(v.i.)* profiter; *(clock)* avancer. ~ *admittance*, s'introduire. *to be the gainer (by)*, gagner (à).

gainsay, *v.t*, contredire, disconvenir de.

gait, *n*, démarche, allure, *f*, pas, *m*.

gaiter, *n*, guêtre, *f*.

gala, *n*, gala, *m*; *(att., day, night, dress, performance)* de gala. ~ *night*, soirée de gala, *f*.

galaxy, *n*, (Astr.) voie lactée; *(fig.)* constellation, *f*.

gale, *n*, coup de vent, *m*.

gall, *n*, fiel; amer, *m*; écorchure, *f*. ~*bladder*, vésicule biliaire, *f*. ~ *[nut]*, [noix de] galle, *f*. ¶ *v.t*, écorcher, blesser.

gallant, *a*, vaillant, brave; *(to women)* galant. ¶ *n*, galant, *m*. ~*ly*, *ad*, vaillamment; galamment. ~*ry*, *n*, vaillance; galanterie, *f*.

galleon (*Hist.*) *n*, galion, *m*.

gallery, *n*, galerie; tribune, *f*; *(Theat.)* troisième [galeries], dernières galeries, *f.pl*, poulailler, paradis, *m*.

galley, *n*, *(boat)* galère; *(cook's)* cuisine; *(Typ.)* galée, *f*. ~ *[proof]*, épreuve en placard, *f*. ~ *slave*, galérien, *m*.

Gallic, *a*, gaulois. **Gallican**, *a*. & *n*, gallican, e. **gallicism**, *n*, gallicisme, *m*. **gallicize**, *v.t*, franciser.

gallipot, *n*, pot de faïence, *m*.

gallon, *n*, gallon, *m*.

gallop, *n*, galop, *m*. ¶ *v.i*, galoper. ~*ing consumption*, phtisie galopante, *f*.

Gallophile, *a*. & *n*, francophile, *a*. & *m,f*. **Gallophobe**, *a*. & *n*, gallophobe, *a*. & *m,f*.

gallows, ~ *n,pl*. & *s*, potence, *f*, gibet. ~ *bird*, gibier de potence, *m*, pendard, e.

galop *(dance)* *n*, galop, *m*.

galore, *ad*, à foison.

galosh, *n*, caoutchouc, *m*.

galvanic, *a*, galvanique. **galvanism**, *n*, galvanisme, *m*. **galvanize**, *v.t*, galvaniser.

Gambia, *n*, la Gambie.

gambit, *n*, gambit, *m*.

gamble, *n*, spéculation de hasard, *f*. ¶ *v.i*, jouer, agioter. ~ *away*, perdre au jeu. **gambler**, *n*, joueur, euse; agioteur, *m*. **gambling**, *n*, jeu[x], *m.[pl*.]; agiotage, *m*. ~ *den*, tripot, *m*.

gamboge, *n*, gomme-gutte, *f*.

gambol, *n*, gambade, *f*. ¶ *v.i*, gambader.

game, *n*, jeu, *m*; partie; *(dodge)* ficelle, *f*; *(Hunt.)* gibier, *m*. ~ *bag*, carnassière, *f*, carnier, *m*, gibecière, *f*. ~ *cock*, coq de combat, *m*. ~*keeper*, garde-chasse, *m*. ~ *of skill*, jeu d'adresse, *m*. ¶ *a*, courageux; prêt; sportif. ~ *fishing*, pêche sportive, *f*. *to have a* ~ *leg*, être estropié de la jambe. ¶ *v.i*, jouer. ~*ster*, *n*, joueur, euse. **gaming**, *n*, jeu. *m*. ~ *house*, maison de j., *f*. ~ *table*, table de j., *f*, tapis vert, *m*.

gamut, *n*, gamme, *f*.

gamy, *a*, giboyeux; *(Cook.)* faisandé.

gander, *n*, jars, *m*.

gang, *n*, bande; brigade, équipe, *f*.

Ganges (the), le Gange.

ganglion, *n*, ganglion, *m*.

gangrene, *n*, gangrène, *f*. ¶ *v.t*, gangrener.

gangster, *n*, bandit, gangster, *m*.

gangue, *n*, gangue, matrice, *f*.

gangway, *n*, passage; pourtour; *(on ship)* passavant, *m*; *(to shore)* passerelle, *f*.

gannet, *n*, fou [de Bassan] *m*.

gantry, *n*, portique; beffroi, *m*.

gap, *n*, brèche, trouée, ouverture, *f*, intervalle, vide, *m*, lacune, *f*.

gape, *v.i*, bâiller. ~ *[at the moon]*, bayer aux corneilles. **gaper**, *n*, gobe-mouches, *m*, badaud, e.

garage, *n*, garage, *m*. ~ *space*, box, *m*. ¶ *v.t*, garer.

garb, *n*, costume, habit, accoutrement, *m*.

garbage, *n*, rebuts, *m.pl*; ordures, *f.pl*. ~ *can*, poubelle, *f*.

garble, *v.t*, altérer, tronquer.

garden, *n*, jardin; *(small)* jardinet, *m*. ~ *flower*, fleur de jardin, *f*. ~ *hose*, tuyau d'arrosage, *m*. ~ *mint*, menthe verte, *f*. *the G*~ *of Eden*, Éden, *m*, le paradis [terrestre]. ~ *party*, garden-party, *f*. ~ *plant*, plante jardinière, *f*. ~ *plots*, jardinage, *m*. ~ *tools*, outils de jardinage, *m.pl*. ¶ *v.i*, jardiner. ~*er*, *n*, jardinier, ère.

gardenia, *n*, gardénia, *m*.

gardening, n, jardinage, m, horticulture, f.

garfish, n, orphie, f.

gargle, n, gargarisme, m. ¶ v.i, se gargariser.

gargoyle, n, gargouille, f.

garish, a, éblouissant; voyant, tapageur, cru.

garland, n, guirlande, f.

garlic, n, ail, m.

garment, n, vêtement, m.

garner, n, grenier, m. ¶ v.t, engranger; rassembler.

garnet, n, grenat, m.

garnish, n, garniture, f. ¶ v.t, garnir

garret, n, mansarde, f.

garrison, n, garnison, f. ~artillery, artillerie de place, f.

garrulous, a, bavard, loquace.

garter, n, jarretière, f. ~ belt, porte-jarretelles, m.

gas, n, gaz, m; (gasoline) essence, f. ~ burner, bec de gaz, m. ~ lighting, éclairage au gaz, m. ~ man, employé du gaz, m. ~ mask, (war) masque à g.; (fire) casque respiratoire, m. ~ meter, compteur à gaz, m. ~ pipe, tuyau de g., m. ~ shell, obus à g., m. ~ station attendant, pompiste, m. ~ works, usine à gaz, f. tear ~, gaz lacrymogène, m. ¶ v.t, asphyxier; (war) gazer. ~eous, a, gazeux.

gash, n, balafre, estafilade, f. ¶ v.t, balafrer.

gasket, n, garcette, f, raban, m; tresse; garniture, f.

gasogene, n, gazogène, m. **gasometer,** n, gazomètre, m.

gasoline, n, essence, f.

gasp, n, halètement; souffle coupé; hoquet, m. to ~ for breath, haleter.

gassy, a, gazeux; verbeux.

gastropod, n, gastéropode, m. **gastric,** a, gastrique. **gastritis,** n, gastrite, f. **gastronome,** n, gastronome, m. **gastronomic(al),** a, gastronomique. **gastronomy,** n, gastronomie, f.

gate, n, porte; barrière; (sluice) vanne, f. ~-crasher, resquilleur, euse. ~-crashing, resquille, f. ~-keeper, portier, ère; (level crossing) garde-barrière, m.f. ~-money, recette, f. ~way, porte, f.

gather, n, fronce, f. ¶ v.t, [r]assembler; [r]amasser; [re]cueillir;

récolter; vendanger; inférer; (Need.) froncer. ~er, n, ramasseur, euse. ~ing, n, rassemblement, m; accumulation; cueillette; réunion, f; (Med.) mal blanc, abcès, m.

gating (Hyd.) n, vannage, m.

gaudy, a, fastueux, voyant, tapageur.

gauge, n, calibre, m; jauge, f; gabarit; (Rly. track) écartement, m, voie, largeur, f; manomètre; indicateur, m. ¶ v.t, calibrer; jauger; cuber.

gaunt, a, décharné, sec.

gauntlet, n, gantelet; (fig.) gant, m.

gauze, n, gaze; toile, f, tissu, tamis, m. **gauzy,** a, vaporeux.

gavotte, n, gavotte, f.

gawky, a, dégingandé.

gay, a, gai.

gaze, n, regard, m. to ~ at, contempler, couver des yeux.

gazelle, n, gazelle, f.

gazette, n, gazette, f, journal, m; journal officiel; moniteur, m.

gazetteer, n, dictionnaire géographique, m.

gear, n, appareil[s] m.[pl.]; engins; organes; agrès, m.pl; mécanisme; dispositif; harnais, m; armature, f; gréement, m; (toothed) engrenage[s] m.[pl.]; (ratio) multiplication, f; (bicycle) développement, m. ~ box, boîte à engrenages; boîte de changement de vitesse, f. ~ case, carter; couvre-engrenages, m. ~ ratio, multiplication, f. ~-shift, changement de vitesse, m. ~ wheel, roue d'engrenage, f. ¶ v.t, engrener.

gee-gee, n, dada, m. **gee up,** i, hue!

gehenna, n, géhenne, f.

gelatin, n, gélatine, f. **gelatinous,** a, gélatineux.

geld, v.t, châtrer, hongrer. ~ing, n, castration, f; [cheval] hongre, m.

gem, n, pierre précieuse, [pierre] gemme, f; bijou, m; (pl.) pierreries, f.pl.

gender, n, genre, m.

genealogical, a, généalogique. **genealogy,** n, généalogie, f.

general, a, général, d'ensemble; commun; collectif. ~ effect, ensemble, m. ~ expenses, frais divers, m.pl. ~ post office, hôtel des postes, *m. the ~ public*, le grand public. *to become ~*, se généraliser. ¶ *n*, général en chef, chef, *m*. **~ity**, *n*, généralité; plupart, *f*. **~ize**, *v.t. & i*, généraliser. **~ly**, *ad*, généralement; communément. **~ship**, *n*, généralat, *m*; stratégie, *f*.

generate, *v.t*, engendrer; produire. **generating**, *p.a*, générateur. **generation**, *n*, génération, *f*. **generator**, *n*, générateur, *m*.

generic, *a*, générique.

generosity, *n*, générosité, *f*. **generous†**, *a*, généreux, donnant.

genesis, *n*, genèse, *f*. **G~** (*Bible*), la Genèse.

genet (*civet*) *n*, genette, *f*.

geneva (*gin*) *n*, genièvre, *m*. **G~** (*Geog.*), Genève, *f*. *Lake of G~*, lac de Genève, lac Léman, *m*.

genial, *a*, bienfaisant; chaleureux; joyeux; sociable. **~ity**, *n*, bonhomie, *f*.

genital, *a*, génital.

genitive [case], *n*, génitif, *m*.

genius, *n*, génie; démon, *m*.

Genoa, *n*, Gênes, *f*. **Genoese**, *a*, génois. ¶ *n*, Génois, e.

genteel, *a*, distingué, de bon ton.

gentian, *n*, gentiane, *f*.

gentile, *n*, gentil, *m*.

gentle, *a*, doux. *of ~ birth*, de qualité. **~folk[s]**, gens de qualité, *m.pl*. **~man**, monsieur; galant homme; homme de qualité, gentilhomme, gentleman; cavalier, *m*. **~man *farmer***, gentilhomme campagnard, *m*. **~manliness**, savoir-vivre, *n*, gentilhommerie, *f*. **~manly**, comme il faut; distingué; gentleman. **~woman**, femme de qualité, *f*. **~ness**, *n*, douceur, *f*. **gently**, *ad*, doucement, bellement. **gentry**, *n*, petite noblesse, *f*.

genuflexion, *n*, génuflexion, *f*.

genuine, *a*, vrai; authentique; sincère; sérieux. **~ness**, *n*, authenticité; sincérité, *f*.

genus, *n*, genre, *m*.

geodesy, *n*, géodésie, *f*. **geognosy**, *n*, géognosie, *f*. **geographer**, *n*, géographe, *m*. **geographic(al)†**, *a*, géographique. **geography**, *n*, géographie, *f*. **geologic(al)**, *a*, géologique. **geologist**, *n*, géologue, *m*. **geology**, *n*, géologie, *f*. **geometer** & **geometrician**, *n*, géomètre, *m*. **geometric(al)†**, *a*,

géométrique. **geometry**, *n*, géométrie, *f*.

Georgia, *n*, (*U.S.A.*) la Georgie; (*Asia*) la Géorgie.

geranium, *n*, géranium, *m*.

germ, *n*, germe, *m*.

german, *a*, germain.

German, *a*, allemand; d'Allemagne. *~ measles*, rubéole, *f*. ¶ *n*, (*pers.*) Allemand, e; (*language*) l'allemand, *m*.

germander (*Bot.*) *n*, germandrée, *f*.

germane to, se rapportant à.

Germany, *n*, l'Allemagne, *f*.

germinate, *v.i*, germer. **germination**, *n*, germination, *f*.

gerund, *n*, gérondif, *m*.

gestation, *n*, gestation, *f*.

gesticulate, *v.i*, gesticuler.

gesture, *n*, geste, *m*.

get, *v.t.ir*, obtenir; gagner; acquérir; procurer; se *f*; se faire; se mettre; tirer; recevoir; retirer; trouver; avoir; (*v.i.ir*.) aller; arriver; parvenir; devenir; se faire; se trouver. *Often rendered by se, e.g, ~ an opinion into one's head*, se chausser d'une opinion. *~ away*, s'échapper; se sauver. *~ back*, *v.t*, ravoir; (*v.i.*) revenir. *~ down*, descendre. *~ hold of*, s'emparer de; saisir. *~ in*, entrer, s'introduire; (*grain*) engranger. *~ married*, se marier. *~ on*, s'arranger; s'entendre; réussir. *~ out*, sortir. *~ out of the way*, s'ôter, de là, se garer. *~ over*, franchir; surmonter. *~ ready*, préparer; se préparer. *~ rid of*, se débarrasser de. *~ round* (*someone*), entortiller. *~ up*, se lever. *~ up steam*, chauffer.

getup, *n*, mise, *f*; affiquets, *m.pl*.

gewgaw, *n*, colifichet, *m*.

geyser, *n*, (*spring*) geyser, *m*.

ghastly, *a*, de spectre, de déterré; macabre; blême, livide; affreux.

Ghent, *n*, Gand, *m*.

gherkin, *n*, cornichon, *m*.

ghetto, *n*, ghetto, *m*, juiverie, *f*.

ghost, *n*, esprit, *m*; fantôme, spectre, revenant, *m*, ombre, *f*. *~ story*, histoire de revenants, *f*. *~ writer*, nègre, *m*. **~ly**, *a*, spectral, fantomatique.

ghoul, *n*, goule, *f*.

giant, *a*, géant. **giant**, ess, *n*, géant, e, colosse, *m*. *giant['s] stride*, pas de géant, vindas, *m*.

gibber, *v.i*, baragouiner. **~ish**, *n*, baragouin, galimatias, *m*.

gibbet, n, gibet, m, potence, f.
¶ (fig.) v.t, pilorier.

gibe, n, brocard, quolibet, lardon,
m. ¶ v.i, lancer des brocards ou
des lardons (at = à).

giblets, n.pl, abattis, m. & m.pl.

giddiness, n, vertige, étourdissement, m. **giddy,** a, (height) vertigineux; (flighty) écervelé. it
makes me feel ~, cela me donne
le vertige.

gift, n, don; cadeau, m; donation;
(for coupons) prime; (of an
office) nomination, f; talent, m.
the ~ of the gab, du bagou. ~ed,
a, doué, de talent.

gig, n, cabriolet, m; (boat) yole, f.

gigantic, a, gigantesque.

giggle, v.i, rire bêtement, glousser.

gild, v.t.ir, dorer. ~er, n, doreur,
euse. ~ing, n, dorure, f.

gill, n. (fish) ouïe, branchie, f.

gilt, n, dorure, f. ¶ p.a, doré.
~-edged, (book, bill of exchange)
doré sur tranche; (investment, security) de premier ordre. ~-tool-
ing, fers dorés, m.pl. ~ top, tête
dorée, f.

gimcrack, n, bibelot, m; pacotille,
patraque, f. ¶ a, de camelote;
délabré.

gimlet, n, vrille, f.

gimp, n, ganse, f, galon, bordé,
passement, m.

gin, n, (snare) trébuchet, m;
(hoist) chèvre, f; treuil, m; (cotton) égreneuse, f; (spirit) gin, m.
¶ v.t, égrener.

ginger, n, gingembre, m. ~-bread,
pain d'épice, m. ~ nut, non-
nette, f. ~ly, ad, en tâtonnant.

gingham, (fabric) n, guingan,
m.

giraffe, n, girafe, f.

girandole, n, girandole, f.

girasol[e] (opal) n, girasol, m.

gird, v.t.ir, [en]ceindre. ~er, n,
poutre; solive; ferme, f. ~le, n,
ceinture, f. ¶ v.t, ceindre.

girl, n, fille, jeune fille, fillette, enfant, demoiselle, f. ~ friend,
amie, copine, f. ~hood, n, jeunesse, f. ~ish, a, de jeune fille;
mignard.

girth, n, sangle; sous-ventrière;
circonférence, f.

gist, n, substance, f.

give, v.t. & i. ir, donner; accorder;
prêter; apporter; passer; rendre;
fournir; (cry) pousser. ~ & take,
donnant donnant. ~ back, ren-

dre. ~ one's name, décliner son
nom, se nommer. ~ in, céder.
~ oneself away, s'enferrer soi-
même. (lamp, etc.) se mourir. ~
someone a piece of one's mind,
dire son fait à quelqu'un. ~ up,
renoncer à; livrer; abandonner,
quitter; céder; (patient) condamner. ~ way, céder; fléchir;
s'effondrer. **given to,** adonné à;
enclin à. **giver,** n, donneur, euse.

gizzard, n, gésier, m.

glacé kid gloves, gants de peau
glacée, m.pl.

glacial, a, glacial; (Geol.) glaciaire. **glacier,** n, glacier, m.

glad, a, [bien] aise; content;
heureux; joyeux. **gladden,** v.t, réjouir.

glade, n, clairière, f.

gladiator, n, gladiateur, m.

gladiolus, n, glaïeul, m.

gladly, ad, volontiers. **gladness,**
n, joie, f.

glamour, n, enchantement; éclat;
prestige, m.

glance, n, coup d'œil, regard, m;
(loving) œillade, f. ¶ v.i, effleurer.
~ at, jeter un coup d'œil sur.

gland, n, glande, f.

glanders, n.pl, morve, f.

glare, n, éclat; éblouissement; regard perçant; r. furieux, m.
¶ v.i, éblouir. ~ at (pers.) lancer
un regard furieux à. **glaring,** a,
éclatant, éblouissant; grossier; flagrant; criant; tranchant.

glass, n, verre, m; vitre, f; miroir,
m; lunette, f; (pl.) lunettes, f.pl;
jumelle, f. ~[,with care], fragile.
~ beads, verroterie, f. ~ case, vitrine, f. ~ cutter, diamant de
vitrier; (wheel) coupe-verre à
molette, m. ~ door, porte vitrée,
f, vitrage, m. ~ maker, verrier,
m. ~ making & ~ works, verrerie, f. ~ of beer, bock, m,
chope, f. ~[ware], verrerie,
(small) verroterie, f. field~, jumelles, f.pl. magnifying ~, loupe,
f. shatterproof ~, verre incassable, m. ~y, a, vitreux.

glaucous, a, glauque.

glaze, n, émail, vernis, m; couverte, f; lustre, m. ¶ v.t, (window)
vitrer; émailler, vernir, vernisser;
lustrer; satiner; glacer; dorer;
(v.i.) se glacer. ~d frost, verglas,
m. **glazier,** n, vitrier, m. ~y, n,
vitrerie, f.

gleam, n, lueur, f, rayon, m. ¶ v.i,
luire, miroiter.

glean, *v.t*, glaner; (*grapes*) grappiller. **~er**, *n*, glaneur, euse. **~ing**, *n*, glanage, *m*, glane; (*pl.*) glanure, *f*.

glebe, *n*, glèbe; terre d'église, *f*.

glee, *n*, joie, gaieté; chanson à plusieurs voix, *f*.

gleet, *n*, écoulement, *m*.

glen, *n*, vallon, val, *m*.

glib, *a*, (*pers.*) volubile; (*tongue*) déliée.

glide, *n*, glissement; (*Danc.*) glissé, *m*. ¶ *v.i*, glisser; couler. **glider** (*Avn.*) *n*, planeur, *m*. **gliding** (*Avn.*) *n*, vol à voile, *m*.

glimmer, *n*, lueur, *f*. ¶ *v.i*, jeter une faible lueur.

glimpse, *n*, lueur, *f*; coup d'œil, *m*; échappée [de vue] *f*. *catch a ~ of*, entrevoir.

glint, *n*, reflet, *m*. ¶ *v.i*, étinceler, miroiter.

glisten, glitter, *v.i* briller, reluire, miroiter. **glitter**, *n*, brillant, *m*.

gloaming, *n*, crépuscule, *m*, brune, *f*.

gloat over, triompher de; couver des yeux.

globe, *n*, globe, *m*, sphère, *f*; (*fish bowl*) bocal, *m*. **globular**, *a*, globulaire, globuleux. **globule**, *n*, globule, *m*.

gloom, *v.t*, rembrunir. **~[iness]**, *n*, obscurité, *f*, ténèbres, *f.pl*; air sombre, *m*, tristesse, *f*. **~y**, *a*, sombre, ténèbreux, triste, morne, noir, lugubre.

glorify, *v.t*, glorifier. **glorious†**, *a*, glorieux; resplendissant. **glory**, *n*, gloire, *f*; nimbe, *m*. **~ in**, se glorifier de, se faire gloire de.

gloss, *n*, luisant, lustre, poli, œil, *m*; (*comment*) glose, *f*. ¶ *v.t*, lustrer; glacer; (*text*) gloser. ~ [*over*], vernir, farder. **~ary**, *n*, glossaire, *m*. **~y**, *a*, luisant; lustré; brillant.

glottis, *n*, glotte, *f*.

glove, *n*, gant, *m*. ~ *trade*, ganterie, *f*. ¶ *v.t*, ganter. *to put on one's ~s*, se ganter. **glover**, *n*, gantier, ère.

glow, *n*, incandescence, *f*; embrasement, *m*; chaleur, *f*; élan, *m*; (*pleasant, in the body*) moiteur, *f*. **~worm**, ver luisant, lampyre, *m*, luciole, *f*. ¶ *v.i*, briller d'un vif éclat. *~ing with health*, rouge de santé.

glower at, regarder d'un air féroce.

glucose, *n*, glucose, *f*.

glue, *n*, colle forte; colle; (*marine*) glu, *f*. ~ *pot*, pot à colle, *m*. ¶ *v.t*, coller. **~y**, *a*, gluant.

glum, *a*, morose, chagrin.

glut, *n*, pléthore, *f*; encombrement, *m*. ¶ *v.t*, gorger, rassasier; encombrer.

gluten, *n*, gluten, *m*. **glutinous**, *a*, glutineux.

glutton, *n*, glouton, ne, gourmand, e. **~ous†**, *a*, glouton, gourmand. **~y**, *n*, gloutonnerie, gourmandise, *f*.

glycerin[e], *n*, glycérine, *f*.

gnarl, *n*, broussin, *m*. **~ed**, *a*, noueux.

gnash one's teeth, grincer des (*ou* les) dents.

gnat, *n*, moucheron, *m*.

gnaw, *v.i*, ronger. **~ing**, *n*, rongement; tiraillement, *m*.

gnome, *n*, gnome, *m*.

gnostic, *n*, gnostique, *m*.

go, *n*, entrain, allant, panache, *m*; mode, vogue, *f*; jet, *m*. ¶ *v.i. & t. ir*, aller; se rendre, se porter; se mettre; marcher; passer; partir; s'en aller; faire; tourner; devenir. *are you ready? go!* êtes-vous prêts? partez! *who goes there?* qui vive? ~ *astray*, s'égarer; se dévoyer. ~ *away*, s'en aller; partir. ~ *back*, retourner. **~between** intermédiaire, *m*; entremetteur, euse. ~ *by*, passer. **~cart**, chariot, panier roulant, *m*. ~ *down*, descendre; baisser; (*sun, moon*) se coucher; (*ship*) sombrer; couler; (*swelling*) désenfler. ~ *for*, aller chercher; a. faire; a. prendre. ~ *in*, entrer; monter. ~ *off*, partir. ~ *on*, aller; avancer; continuer. ~ *on!* allons donc! ~ *on board a ship, an airplane*, monter sur un navire, en avion. ~ *out*, sortir; (*light*) s'éteindre. ~ *over*, passer sur; traverser; parcourir; (*Jump.*) dépasser; mordre sur (*the mark* = la latte). ~ *through*, passer par, traverser, parcourir; dépouiller. ~ *to press*, procéder à l'impression. ~ *to sleep*, s'endormir. ~ *up*, monter; remonter; renchérir. ~ *with*, accompagner. ~ *without*, se passer de.

goad, *n*, aiguillon, *m*. ¶ *v.t*, aiguillonner, piquer.

goal, *n*, but, *m*. ~ *keeper, kick, post*, gardien, coup [de pied], poteau, de b., *m*.

goat, *n,* chèvre, *f;* *(he)* bouc, *m.*
~*herd,* chevrier, ère. ~*ee, n,*
barbe de bouc, barbiche, *f.*
gobble, *v.t,* manger goulûment;
(v.i, of turkey) glouglouter.
goblet, *n,* gobelet, *m;* coupe, *f.*
goblin, *n,* lutin, follet, farfadet,
gobelin, *m.*
God, *n,* Dieu, *m.* ~*child,* filleul, e.
~*daughter,* filleule, *f.* ~*father,*
parrain, *m.* ~*head,* divinité, *f.*
~*mother,* marraine, *f.* ~*send,*
providence, aubaine, chapechute,
f. ~*son,* filleul, *m.* **goddess,** *n,*
déesse, *f.* **godless,** *a,* sans Dieu;
impie, **godlike,** *a,* divin. **godli-**
ness, *n,* piété, *f.* **godly,** *a,* pieux,
saint, de Dieu.
goffer, *n,* tuyau, *m.* ¶ *v.t,* gaufrer,
tuyauter.
goggles, *n,pl,* lunettes, *f.pl.*
going, *n,* aller, *m.* ~ & *coming,*
allées & venues, *f.pl.* ~ *back to*
school, rentrée des classes, *f.* ~
concern, affaire roulante, *f. value*
as a ~ *concern,* valeur d'usage, *f.*
~, ~, *gonel* une fois, deux fois,
[trois fois]; adjugé! ~*s-on,* pro-
cédés; agissements, *m.pl.*
goiter, *n,* goitre, *m.*
gold, *n,* or, *m.* ~*-beater's skin,*
baudruche, *f. the G*~ *Coast,* la
Côte de l'Or, ~*-digger,* chercheur
d'or, *m.* ~*field,* champ aurifère,
m. ~*finch,* chardonneret, *m.*
~*fish,* poisson rouge, *m,* dorade,
f. ~ *mine,* mine d'or, *f.* ~*smith*
&/or *silversmith,* orfèvre, *m.*
~*[smith's]* &/or *silver[smith's]*
work, orfèvrerie, *f.* ~ *standard,*
étalon d'or, *m.* ¶ *a,* d'or, en or. ~
francs, francs-or, *m.pl.* ~*en, a,*
d'or; doré; *(hair)* blond doré. ~
calf, veau d'or, *m.* ~ *mean,* juste
milieu, *m.* ~ *rain,* pluie d'or, *f.* ~
wedding, noces d'or, *f.pl,* cinquantaine, *f.*
golf, *n,* golf, *m.* ~ *club (pers. &*
stick) club de g, *m.* ~ *course,*
~ *links,* [terrain de] golf, *m.* ~*er,*
n, joueur (euse) de golf.
golosh, *n,* caoutchouc, *m.*
gondola, *n,* gondole, *f; (Avn.)* nacelle, *f.* **gondolier,** *n,* gondolier,
m.
gong, *n,* gong, tam-tam; timbre, *m.*
good, *a,* bon; beau; de bien; brave;
(of a child) sage; avantageux;
valable; utile. ~ *angel,* bon ange,
m; providence, *f.* ~ *breeding,*

politesse, *f,* savoir-vivre, *m.* ~*bye,*
i. & n, adieu, *i. & m;* au revoir!
a ~ *ear (*for music), l'oreille juste.
~ *evening!* ~ *night!* bonsoir!
bonne nuit! *(a)* ~*-for-nothing,*
n. & a, (un) propre à rien. *G*~
Friday, le vendredi saint. ~
gracious! miséricorde! ~*-looking,*
joli, de bonne mine. *my* ~ *man,*
mon brave. ~ *morning!* ~ *after-*
noon! ~ *day!* bonjour! ~ *nature,*
bonhomie, *f,* bon naturel, *m.*
~*-natured,* *(pers.)* bon enfant;
(laugh) jovial. ~ *offices,* ministère, *m. the* ~ *old days,* le bon
vieux temps. ~*will,* bienveillance,
bonne volonté, faveur, *f;* fonds
[de commerce] *m,* clientèle, *f.* ¶
i, bon!, bien! ¶ *n,* bien, *m.* *for*
~, pour de bon. *it's no* ~ . . .,
inutile de . . . *to the* ~, en gain.
goodies, *n.pl,* [du] nanan, *m.*
goodness, *n,* bonté, *f.* *for* ~
sake, de grâce.
goods, *n.pl,* marchandises, *f.pl;*
biens; effets, *m.pl.*
goose, *n,* oie, *f.* ~*flesh (fig.),* chair
de poule, *f.* ~ *step,* pas de l'oie,
m.
gooseberry, *n,* groseille verte, g.
à maquereau, *f.* ~ *bush,* groseillier à maquereau, *m.*
Gordian knot, nœud gordien,
m.
gore, *n,* sang [caillé] *m.* ¶ *v.t,* percer de coups de corne.
gorge, *n,* gorge, *f.* ¶ *v.t,* gorger.
gorgeous†, *a,* magnifique, splendide.
gorilla, *n,* gorille, *m.*
gormandize, *v.i,* goinfrer, bâfrer.
gorse, *n,* ajonc, genêt épineux, *m.*
gory, *a,* sanglant, ensanglanté.
goshawk, *n,* autour, *m.*
gosling, *n,* oison, *m.*
gospel, *n,* Évangile; credo, *m.* ~
[truth], parole d'Évangile, *f.*
gossamer, *n,* fils de la Vierge,
m.pl, filandres, *f.pl.*
gossip, *n,* commérage, bavardage
de commères, racontar, *m;*
(pers.) commère, *f.* ~ *columnist,*
échotier, *m.* ¶ *v.i,* commérer, bavarder.
goth *(fig.)* *n,* ostrogot[h], e.
Gothic, *a,* gothique.
gouache *(Art)* *n,* gouache, *f.*
gouge, *n,* gouge, *f.*
gourd, *n,* courge, calebasse, *f.*
gourmand, *a. & n,* gourmand, e.
gourmet, *n,* gourmet, *m.*

gout, *n*, goutte, *f*. ~**y**, *a*, goutteux.
govern, *v.t*, gouverner, régir; (*Gram.*) régir. ~**ess**, *n*, gouvernante, *f*. ~**ment**, *n*, gouvernement; État, *m*. ~ *in power*, gouvernants, *m.pl*. ~ *organ*, journal ministériel, *m*. ~**or**, *n*, gouverneur; (*Mach.*) régulateur, *m*.
gown, *n*, robe, *f*. *dressing* ~, peignoir, *m*. *night*~, chemise de nuit, *f*.
grab, *v.t*, empoigner, agripper.
grace, *n*, grâce, *f*; (*before meal*) le bénédicité; (*after*) les grâces, *f.pl*. ~ *note*, note d'agrément, *f*. *the G*~*s*, les [trois] Grâces. *his G*~, monseigneur, *m*. *your G*~, Votre Grandeur, *f*. ¶ *v.t*, orner; honorer. ~**ful**†, *a*, gracieux.
gracious†, *a*, gracieux. ~**ness**, *n*, graciuseté, *f*.
gradation, *n*, gradation, *f*. **grade**, *n*, grade, degré, *m*; teneur, *f*; titre, *m*. ¶ *v.t*, classer; graduer; régulariser. **gradient**, *n*, (*up*) rampe; (*down*) pente; (*up or down*) inclinaison, *f*. **gradual**†, *a*, graduel. **graduate**, *v.t*, graduer; (*v.i.*) prendre ses grades. ¶ *n*, gradué, e. **graduation**, *n*, graduation; gradation; (*Univ.*) licence, grade, *f*.
graft, *n*, (*Hort.*) greffe, ente; (*Surg.*) greffe; (*spoils*) gratte, *f*. ¶ *v.t*, greffer; enter. ~**ing** (*Knit.*) *n*, remmaillage, *m*.
grain, *n*, (*wheat, etc.*) céréales, *f.pl*; grain, *m*; (*wood*) fil; (*weight*) grain, *m*; (*pl, brewer's*) drèche, drague, *f*. *against the* ~, à rebours. ¶ *v.t*, grener, greneler; veiner. ~**ed**, *p.a*, (*leather*) grenu; (*wood*) ondé. ~**ing**, *n*, grenu, *m*.
gram, *n*, gramme, *m*.
grammar, *n*, grammaire, *f*. ~**ian**, *n*, grammairien, ne. **grammatical**†, *a*, grammatical.
grampus, *n*, épaulard, *m*, orque, *f*.
Granada (*Spain*) *n*, Grenade, *f*.
granary, *n*, grenier, *m*.
grand†, *a*, grand; magnifique. ~**child**, ~**son**, ~**daughter**, petit-fils, *m*, petite-fille, *f*. ~**children**, petits-enfants, *m.pl*. ~**father**, grand-père, aïeul, *m*. ~**father's clock**, horloge de parquet, *f*. ~**mamma**, grand-maman, bonne maman, *f*. ~**mother**, grand-mère, aïeule, *f*. ~ *piano*, piano à queue, *m*. ~ *staircase*, escalier d'honneur, *m*. ~ *stand*, tribune, *f*. ~ *total*, somme toute, *f*. **grandee**, *n*, grand, *m*. **grandeur**, *n*, grandeur, majesté; splendeur, *f*.
grandiloquence, *n*, grandiloquence, *f*. **grandiloquent**, *a*, grandiloquent, doctoral.
grandiose, *a*, grandiose.
granite, *n*, granit, *m*.
granny, *n*, grand-maman, bonne maman, *f*.
grant, *n*, concession; allocation; subvention, *f*. ¶ *v.t*, accorder; concéder; octroyer; admettre; poser. *to take for* ~*ed*, présupposer. ~**ee**, *n*, concessionnaire, *m,f*; impétrant, e. ~**or**, *n*, cédant, e.
granulate, *v.t*, grener; granuler. ~*d sugar*, sucre semoule, *m*. **granule**, *n*, granule, *m*.
grape, *n*, grain de raisin, *m*; (*pl*.) raisin[s] *m.*[*pl.*]. ~*fruit*, pamplemousse, *f*. ~*shot*, mitraille, *f*.
graph, *n*, graphique, tracé, *m*. ~**ic**†, *a*, graphique; pittoresque. ~**ics**, *n*, graphie; (*computers*) infographie, *f*. ¶ *v.t*, tracer un graphique, faire un diagramme.
graphite, *n*, graphite, *m*, plombagine, *f*.
grapnel, *n*, grappin, *m*. **grapple**, *v.t*, accrocher. ~ *with*, s'attaquer à; colleter.
grasp, *n*, prise; étreinte; poigne; poignée; portée, *f*. ¶ *v.t*, saisir, empoigner; serrer. ~ *round the body*, ceinturer. ~**ing**†, *p.a*, avide, cupide, âpre [au gain].
grass, *n*, herbe, *f*, herbage; gazon, *m*; verdure, *f*; vert, *m*. ~*hopper*, sauterelle; cigale, *f*. ~*land*, prairie, *f*. ~ *snake*, couleuvre à collier, *f*. ~ *widow*, veuve à titre temporaire, *f*. ~**y**, *a*, herbeux, herbu.
grate, *n*, grille, *f*. ¶ *v.t*, griller; râper; (*teeth*) grincer [de]; (*ears*) écorcher, blesser. ~*d bread crumbs*, panure, chapelure, *f*.
grateful†, *a*, reconnaissant; agréable. *to be* ~ *to*, savoir [bon] gré à. ~**ness**, *n*, reconnaissance, *f*.
grater, *n*, râpe, *f*.
gratification, *n*, satisfaction, *f*, plaisir, *m*. **gratify**, *v.t*, satisfaire; contenter.
gratin, *n*, gratin, *m*. ~**ate**, *v.t*, gratiner.
grating, *n*, grille, *f*; grillage; gril, *m*; claire-voie; crapaudine, *f*. ¶ *p.a*, strident.

gratis, *ad*, gratis, gratuitement.

gratitude, *n*, reconnaissance, gratitude, *f*.

gratuitous†, *a*, gratuit, gracieux; sans motif. **~ness**, *n*, gratuité, *f*. **gratuity**, *n*, gratification, *f*, pourboire, *m*.

gravamen, *n*, matière, *f*.

grave†, *a*, grave, sérieux. ¶ *n*, fosse; tombe, *f*, tombeau, *m*. **~-digger**, fossoyeur, *m*. **~stone**, pierre tombale, tombe, *f*. **~yard**, cimetière, *m*. ¶ *v.t*, (*ship*) radouber.

gravel, *n*, gravier[s] *m.[pl.]*; (*Med.*) graviers, *m.pl*, gravelle, *f*, sable, *m*. **~ path**, **~walk**, allée sablée, *f*. **~ pit**, gravière, *f*. **~ly**, *a*, graveleux.

graver, *n*, burin, ciselet, *m*.

graving dock, forme de radoub, *f*.

gravitate, *v.i*, graviter. **gravitation**, *n*, gravitation, *f*. **gravity**, *n*, (*Phys.*) gravité, pesanteur, *f*, poids, *m*; (*fig.*) gravité, *f*; sérieux, *m*.

gravy, *n*, jus, *m*. **~ boat**, saucière, *f*. **~ spoon**, cuiller à ragoût, *f*.

gray, *a*, gris. ¶ *v.t*, grisailler. **~ish**, *a*, grisâtre. **~ness**, *n*, couleur grise, *f*.

graze, *n*, écorchure, *f*. ¶ *v.t. & i*, effleurer, raser, friser, frôler; écorcher; (*sea bottom*) labourer; (*cattle*) paître, pâturer, pacager. **grazier**, *n*, éleveur, *m*.

grease, *n*, graisse, *f*; (*in wool*) suint, *m*. **~ box**, boîte à graisse, *f*. **~ paint**, fard, *m*. **~-proof paper**, papier imperméable à la graisse, p. sulfurisé, *m*. ¶ *v.t*, graisser; suiffer. **greasiness**, *n*, onctuosité, *f*. **greasy**, *a*, graisseux, gras, onctueux. **~ pole**, mât de cocagne, *m*.

great, *a*, grand; gros; fort. **~ aunt**, grand-tante, *f*. **~ bell**, bourdon, *m*. **G~ Britain**, la Grande-Bretagne. **~coat**, pardessus, *m*; (*Mil.*) capote, *f*. **~ Dane**, grand danois, *m*. **a ~ deal**, **a ~ many**, beaucoup. **~-grandchildren**, arrière-petits-enfants, *m.pl*. **~-granddaughter**, **-son**, arrière-petite-fille, *f*, a.-petit-fils, *m*. **~-grandfather**, **-mother**, arrière-grand-père, *m*, a.-grand-mère, *f*, bisaïeul, e. **~-~-grandfather**, **-mother**, trisaïeul, e. **~ toe**, gros doit du pied, orteil, *m*. **~ uncle**,

grand-oncle, *m*. **the ~** (*fig.*), le grand. **the ~ ones**, les grands (*de la terre*). **~ly**, *ad*, grandement; fort. **~ness**, *n*, grandeur, *f*.

grebe, *n*, grèbe, *m*.

Grecian, *a*, grec. **Greece**, *n*, la Grèce.

greed[iness], *n*, avidité, âpreté; gourmandise, *f*. **greedy†**, *a*, avide; gourmand, goulu.

Greek, *a*, grec. **~ fret** (*Arch.*), grecque, *f*. ¶ *n*, (*pers.*) Grec, ecque; (*language*) le grec; (*fig.*) du grec, de l'hébreu (*to me =* pour moi).

green, *a*, vert; en herbe; novice; naïf. **~ baize**, tapis vert, drap v., *m*. **~finch**, verdier, *m*. **~fly**, puceron, *m*. **~gage**, [prune de] reine-claude, *f*. **~horn**, novice, conscrit, pigeon, *m*. **~house**, serre, *f*. **~ peas**, petits pois, pois verts, *m.pl*. **greens**, *n.pl*, herbages, légumes verts, *m.pl*, verdure, *f*. **~sward**, tapis de gazon, *m*, herbette, verdure, *f*; (*roadside*) accotement, *m*. **~wood**, feuillée, ramée, *f*. ¶ *n*, vert, *m*; (*grass plot & golf*) pelouse, *f*. **through the ~** (*golf*), à travers le parcours. ¶ *v.t. & i*, verdir, verdoyer. **~ery**, *n*, verdure, *f*. **~ish**, *a*, verdâtre.

Greenland, *n*, le Groenland.

greenness, *n*, verdure; verdeur; naïveté, *f*.

greet, *v.t*, saluer; accueillir. **~ing**, *n*, salutation, *f*, salut, *m*.

gregarious, *a*, grégaire.

Gregorian, *a*, grégorien.

Grenada (*W. Indies*) *n*, la Grenade. **grenade**, *n*, grenade, *f*. **grenadine**, *n*, (*cordial, fabric*) grenadine, *f*; (*Cook.*) grenadin, *m*.

greyhound, *n*, lévrier, *m*, levrette, *f*. **~ racing**, courses de lévriers, *f.pl*.

grid, *n*, grille, *f*. **~iron**, gril; (*sports*) terrain de football, *m*.

griddle, *n*, gril, *m*.

grief, *n*, chagrin, *m*, douleur, peine, affliction, *f*. **grievance**, *n*, grief, *m*. **grieve**, *v.t*, chagriner, affliger, peiner, fâcher. **grievous†**, *a*, grave; cruel.

griffin, **griffon**, *n*, griffon, *m*.

grill, *n*, gril, *m*; (*meat*) grillade, *f*. ¶ *v.t*, [faire] griller.

grille, *n*, (*grating*) grille, *f*.

grim, *a*, farouche, rébarbatif; macabre.

grimace, *n,* grimace, *f,* rictus, *m.*
¶ *v.i,* grimacer.

grime, *n,* crasse, *f.* ¶ *v.t,* encrasser, noircir. **grimy,** *a,* crasseux, noir.

grin, *n,* grimace, *f.* ¶ *v.i,* grimacer.

grind, *v.t.ir,* moudre; broyer; (*knife*) aiguiser, affûter, repasser; roder; grincer [de]; pressurer, opprimer; jouer. ~ *at,* piocher. ~*stone,* meule en grès, ~*ery,* *n,* crépins, *m.pl.* ~*ing* (*grain*) *n,* mouture, *f.*

grip, *n,* prise, pince, serre; poigne; étreinte; poignée; griffe, *f.* ¶ *v.t,* saisir, empoigner, serrer, étreindre; pincer, agripper.

gripes, *n.pl,* tranchées, *f.pl;* colique, *f.*

grippe, *n,* grippe, *f.*

grisly, *a,* effrayant, horrible, affreux.

grist, *n,* blé à moudre, *m.*

gristle, *n,* cartilage, *m.* **gristly,** *a,* cartilagineux.

grit, *n,* graviers, *m.pl,* sable; grès, *m;* (*fig.*) courage, *m.* **gritty,** *a,* graveleux; pierreux.

grizzled, *a,* grison. *grizzly bear,* ours grizzly, ours grizzlé, *m.*

groan, *n,* gémissement, *m.* ¶ *v.i,* gémir.

groats, *n.pl,* gruau; gruau d'avoine, *m.*

grocer, *n,* épicier, ère. ~*'s shop* & **grocery,** *n,* épicerie, *f.*

grog, *n,* grog, *m.* **groggy,** *a,* ivre; aviné; chancelant.

groin, *n,* aine; (*Arch.*) arête, *f.*

groom, *n,* palefrenier, *m.* ¶ *v.t,* panser.

groove, *n,* rainure; cannelure, *f;* sillon, *m;* gorge; ornière, *f.* ¶ *v.t,* canneler; sillonner.

grope, *v.t.* & *i,* fouiller, tâtonner. *to* ~ *for,* chercher à tâtons.

grosbeak, *n,* gros-bec, *m.*

gross†, *a,* grossier; gros; (*Com.*) brut. ¶ (*144*) *n,* grosse, *f.* ~*ness,* *n,* grossièreté, *f.*

grotesque†, *a.* & ~[*ness*] *n,* grotesque, *a.* & *m.* ¶ (*Art*), *n,* grotesque, *f.*

grotto, *n,* grotte, *f.*

grouch, *n,* ronchon, *m.* ¶ *v.i,* ronchonner.

ground, *n,* terre, *f;* sol; terrain; champ, *m;* place, *f;* fond; plan; sujet, lieu, *m,* raison, (*pl.*) cause, *f,* lieu, *m,* matière, *f;* (*pl, law*) motifs, moyens, *m.pl;* (*pl, dregs*)

marc, *m;* effondrilles, *f.pl;* sédiment, *m;* (*of mansion*) dehors, *m.pl,* parc, *m;* (*fishing, cruising*) parages, *m.pl.* ~ *floor,* rez-de-chaussée, *m.* ~ *game,* gibier à poil, *m.* ~ *ivy,* lierre terrestre, *m.* ~ *line* (*Fish.*), ligne de fond, traînée, *f.* ~*nut,* arachide, cacahuète, *f.* ~ *rent,* redevance foncière, *f.* ~*sheet,* toile de sol, *f.* ~ *swell,* houle de fond, *f.* ~*work,* base, *f;* canevas, *m. stand one's* ~, tenir bon. ¶ *p.p,* en poudre; moulu; (*rice, etc.*) farine de . . .; (*glass*) dépoli. ¶ *v.t.* & *i,* mettre à terre; (*Elec.*) m. à la terre; fonder; (*ship*) échouer, engraver. ~*less,* *a.* & ~*lessly,* *ad,* sans fondement; en l'air.

groundsel, *n,* seneçon, *m.*

group, *n,* groupe, *m.* ~ *firing* (*Artil.*), feu concentré, *m,* mitraille, *f.* ¶ *v.t,* grouper.

grouse, *n,* petit coq de bruyère, tétras, *m,* grouse, *f,* (*young*) grianneau, *m.* ¶ *v.i,* grogner.

grout[ing] (*Build.*) *n,* coulis, *m.*

grove, *n,* bocage, bosquet, *m.*

grovel, *v.i,* ramper.

grow, *v.i.ir,* croître; pousser; venir; grandir; [s']accroître; devenir, se faire; *often expressed by* se, *e.g,* ~ *cold,* se refroidir; (*v.t.ir.*) cultiver. ~ *green again* & ~ *young again,* reverdir. ~*er,* *n,* cultivateur, trice, planteur, euse. ~*ing crops,* récoltes sur pied, *f.pl.*

growl, *n,* grondement, *m.* ¶ *v.i,* gronder.

grown-up, grand. **grown-up,** *a.* & *n,* adulte, *a.* & *m,f,* grande personne, *f.* **growth,** *n,* croissance; venue; pousse; végétation, *f;* (*vintage*) cru; développement, *m.*

grub, *n,* larve, *f,* ver, *m.* **grubby,** *a,* (*wormy*) véreux; (*dirty*) crasseux.

grudge, *n,* rancune, *f.* ¶ *v.t,* marchander, reprocher à.

gruel, *n,* gruau, *m,* bouillie, *f.*

gruesome, *a,* macabre.

gruff, *a,* rude, brusque, bourru.

grumble, *v.i,* murmurer, gronder, grogner. ~ *at,* ~ *about,* grommeler, marmonner. **grumpy,** *a,* bourru.

grunt, *n,* grognement, *m.* ¶ *v.i,* grogner.

guano, *n,* guano, *m.*

guarantee, -ty, *n,* garantie; caution, *f;* aval, *m.* ¶ *v.t,* garantir;

cautionner; avaliser. **guarantor;** *n*, garant, e, caution, *f*.

guard, *n*, garde; sentinelle, *f*; protecteur, *m*; (*pers.*) garde; (*Bookb.*) onglet, *m*. **on ~,** en faction; sur le qui-vive. **~house,** **~room,** corps de garde, poste, *m*, salle de police, *f*. ¶ *v.t.* & *i*, [se] garder; se prémunir; parer. **~ed,** *p.a,* mesuré; réservé. **guardian,** *n*, gardien, ne; curateur, trice, tuteur, trice, correspondant, e; (*att.*) gardien, tutélaire. **~ship,** *n*, garde; (*law*) tutelle, curatelle, *f*.

guava, *n*, goyave, *f*; (*tree*) goyavier, *m*.

gudgeon, *n*, goujon; tourillon, *m*.

guelder rose, boule de neige, *f*, obier, *m*.

guerrilla, *n*, guérilla, *f*, partisan, guérillero, *m*. **~ war[fare],** guerre de guérillas, g. de partisan, *f*.

Guernsey, *n*, Guernesey, *f*.

guess, *n*, conjecture, *f*. ¶ *v.t.* & *i*, deviner, conjecturer.

guest, *n*, convive, *m,f*, convié, e; hôte, esse, invité, e. **~ room,** chambre d'ami, *f*. **~ of honor,** invité(e) d'honneur.

guffaw, *v.i*, rigoler.

Guiana, *n*, la Guyane.

guidance, *n*, direction; gouverne, *f*. **guide,** *n*, guide; cicerone, *m*. **~ [book],** guide; indicateur, *m*. **~ post,** poteau indicateur, *m*. **~ rope,** câble-guide; (*Avn.*) guiderope, *m*. ¶ *v.t*, guider, conduire. **guiding principle,** idée directrice, *f*.

guild, *n*, corps de métier, *m*, corporation; association, *f*; (*church*) patronage, *m*.

guile, *n*, ruse, astuce, *f*, artifice, *m*. **~less,** *a*, innocent, candide; naïf.

guillotine, *n*, guillotine, *f*. ¶ *v.t*, guillotiner.

guilt, *n*, culpabilité, *f*. **~less,** *a*, innocent. **~y,** *a*, coupable, criminel.

guinea (21/-) *n*, guinée, *f*. **~ fowl,** pintade, *f*. **~ pig,** cochon, d'Inde, cobaye, *m*. **G~** (*Geog.*), la Guinée.

guise, *n*, apparence, *f*.

guitar, *n*, guitare, *f*.

gules (*Her.*), *n*, gueules, *m*.

gulf, *n*, golfe; gouffre, abîme, *m*. **G~ Stream,** Gulf-Stream, *m*.

gull, *n*, (*sea*) mouette, *f*, goéland, *m*; (*pers.*) dupe, *f*. ¶ *v.t*, duper.

gullet, *n*, gosier, *m*, gorge, *f*.

gullible, *a*, crédule.

gully, *n*, ravine, *f*, ravin; (*gutter*) caniveau, *m*.

gulp, *n*, goulée, gorgée, *f*, trait, *m*. **to ~ down,** gober.

gum, *n*, gomme; (*Anat.*) gencive, *f*. **~ arabic,** gomme arabique. **~boil,** abcès aux gencives, *m*. **~ tree,** gommier, *m*. ¶ *v.t*, gommer. **gummy,** *a*, gommeux.

gumption, *n*, entregent, savoirfaire, *m*.

gun, *n*, fusil; canon, *m*, pièce, *f*. **~boat,** [chaloupe] canonnière, *f*. **~ carriage,** affût, *m*. **~cotton,** coton-poudre, fulmicoton, *m*. **~ license,** port d'armes, *m*. **~ metal,** bronze [industriel] *m*. **~powder,** poudre à canon, *f*. **~shot,** coup de fusil, c. de canon, *m*. **~shot wound,** blessure d'arme à feu, *f*. **~smith,** armurier, *m*. **gunner,** *n*, artilleur, canonnier, *m*. **~y,** *n*, tir, *m*, artillerie, *f*, canonnage, *m*.

gunwale, gunnel, *n*, plat-bord, *m*.

gurgle, *n*, glouglou, *m*. ¶ *v.i*, faire glouglou; gargouiller.

gurnard, *n*, trigle, grondin, rouget, *m*.

gush, *n*, jaillissement, bouillon, *m*; sentimentalité, *f*. ¶ *v.i*, jaillir.

gusset, *n*, gousset, *m*.

gust, *n*, coup, *m*, bourrasque, rafale, bouffée, *f*.

gusto, *n*, entrain, *m*.

gusty, *a*, (*wind*) impétueux; (*day*) de grand vent.

gut, *n*, boyau; intestin; (*Fish.*) crin, florence, *m*, racine, *f*; (*Naut.*) goulet, *m*. **he has ~s,** il a du cran. ¶ *v.t*, vider, étriper.

gutta-percha, *n*, gutta-percha, *f*.

gutter, *n*, (*roof*) gouttière, *f*, chéneau; (*street*) ruisseau; (*conduit*) caniveau; chenal, *m*; rigole, *f*; (*book*) blancs de petit fond, *m.pl*.; (*fig.*) ruisseau; carrefour, *m*, crasse, fange, crotte, *f*. **~ language,** langage de carrefour, *m*. **~snipe,** voyou, *m*. ¶ *v.i*, couler.

guttural, *a*, guttural. ¶ *n*, gutturale, *f*.

guy, *n*, (*rope*) hauban, *m*; (*pers.*) type, *m*. **hefty ~,** costaud, *m*. **laid-back ~,** type décontracté, *m*.

guzzle, *v.i,* bâfrer, goinfrer.

gymnasium, *n,* gymnase, *m.*
gymnast, *n,* gymnaste, gymnasiarque, *m.* ~**ic**, *a.* & *n,* gymnastique, *a.* & *f.* ~**ics**, *n.pl,* gymnastique, gymnique, *f.*

gynecology, *n,* gynécologie, *f.*

gypseous, *a,* gypseux. **gypsum**, *n,*
gypse, *m.* ~**quarry**, plâtrière, *f.*

gypsy, *n,* gitan, e.

gyrate, *v.i,* tourner. **gyration**, *n,*
giration, *f.* **gyratory**, *a,* giratoire.
gyroscope, *n,* gyroscope, *m.*

H

haberdasher, *n,* chemisier, mercier, *m.* ~**y**, *n,* mercerie, chemiserie, *f.*

habiliment, *n,* attirail; *(pl.)*
habillement, *m.*

habit, *n,* habitude, coutume, *f;*
(pl.) mœurs, *f.pl;* tic; *(dress)*
habit, *m. to be in the ~ of doing
so,* être coutumier (ère) du fait.
~**able**, *a,* habitable. **habitat**, *n,*
habitat, *m.* **habitation**, *n,* habitation, *f.* **habitual**†, *a,* habituel, familier. ~ *criminal,* repris de
justice, *m.* **habituate**, *v.t,* habituer.

hack, *n,* entaille, *f;* cheval de
louage; c. de selle, *m; (jade)*
rosse, *f.* ~ *saw,* scie à métaux, *f.*
~ *[writer],* écrivailleur, *m.* ¶ *v.t,*
écharper, hacher, charcuter.

hackneyed, *p.p,* banal, rebattu,
usé jusqu'à la corde. ~ *phrase,*
cliché, *m.* ~ *refrain,* rengaine, *f.*

haddock, *n,* aigrefin, *m.*

Hades, *n,* les enfers, *m.pl.*

haft, *n,* manche, *m,* poignée, *f.*

hag, *n,* sorcière, *f.*

haggard, *a,* hagard, tiré.

haggle, *v.i,* marchander, barguigner, chipoter.

Hague (the), la Haye.

hail, *n,* grêle, *f,* grésil, *m. to damage by ~,* grêler. ~*stone,* grain de
grêle, *(big)* grêlon, *m.* ~ *storm,*
orage [accompagné] de grêle, *m,*
giboulée, *f.* ¶ *i,* salut! ~ *fellow
well met,* de pair à compagnon.
H~ Mary, Ave Maria. ¶ *v.i.imp,*
grêler, grésiller; *(v.t.)* faire pleuvoir; saluer; héler; acclamer. ~
from, venir de. *within ~,* à portée
de la voix.

hair, *n,* (un) cheveu, *m; (des)*

cheveux, *m.pl;* chevelure, *f;* poil;
crin, *m;* soie; bourre, *f.* ~**brush,**
brosse à cheveux, b. à tête, *f.* ~
comb, peigne coiffeur, *m.* ~
curler, bigoudi, *m.* ~**cut,** coupe
de cheveux, *f.* ~**dresser,** coiffeur,
euse. ~ *drier,* appareil à douche
d'air, *m.* ~ *maitress,* matelas de
crin, *m.* ~ *net,* filet à cheveux, *m,*
résille, *f.* ~ *oil,* huile pour les
cheveux, *f.* ~**pin,** épingle à
cheveux, *f.* ~**pin bend,** virage en
é. à c., *m.* ~ *shirt,* haire, *f.* ~**splitting,** pointillerie, argutie, *f.* ~**less,**
a, sans poils; glabre. ~**y,** *a,* velu;
poilu; chevelu.

Haiti, *n,* Haïti, *m.*

hake, *n,* merlus, *m; (dried)* merluche, *f.*

halation *(Phot.) n,* halo, *m.*

halberd *(Hist.) n,* hallebarde, *f.*

halcyon days, jours alcyoniens;
(fig.) jours sereins, *m.pl.*

hale, *a,* sain, vert, verdelet, frais.
~ *& hearty,* frais & gaillard, frais
& dispos.

half, *n,* moitié; demie, *f;* demi;
(Rly ticket) coupon, *m.* ~ *by ~,*
à moitié; de moitié. *to go halves
with,* être (*ou* se mettre) de moitié
avec. *No 29½ (house),* N° 29 bis.
¶ *a,* demi-. ¶ *ad,* moitié; à moitié;
à mi-; à demi. ~ *a cup,* la moitié
d'une tasse, une demi-tasse. ~ *an
hour,* une demi-heure. ~**back**
(Foot.), demi, *m.* ~**breed,** métis,
métisse. ~**brother,** demi-frère, *m.*
~**caste,** [homme de] sang mêlé,
m. ~ *fare,* ~ *price,* demi-place, *f.*
~ *holiday,* demi-congé, *m.* ~
light, demi-jour, *m. at* ~**mast**
(flag), en berne. ~**open,** *a,* entrouvert, entrebâillé; *(v.t.)* entrouvrir. ~ *past twelve,* midi &
demi; minuit & demi. ~ *past two,*
deux heures & demie. *on* ~ *pay,*
en demi-solde. ~**sister,** demi-
sœur, *f.* ~ *time (Foot.),* la
mi-temps. ~**title,** faux titre,
m. ~**way,** à mi-chemin, à
moitié chemin. ~**witted,** simple.
~**yearly,** *a,* semestriel; *(ad.)* par
semestre.

halibut, *n,* flétan, *m.*

hall, *n,* vestibule; hall, *m;* salle;
enceinte, *f;* château, *m.* ~**mark,**
n, [poinçon de] contrôle, *m;*
(v.t.) contrôler, poinçonner. ~
porter, concierge, *m. town ~,*
hôtel de ville, *m.*

hallelujah, *n,* Alléluia, *m.*

hallo[a], *i*, holà!, hé! ~ *there!* hé là-bas! **halloo**, *n*, cri [d'appel] *m*. ¶ *v.i*, crier, huer; (*v.t*, *dogs*) houper, encourager. ~ *to*, appeler à grands cris.

hallow, *v.t*, sanctifier, consacrer. ~ed, *p.a*, saint. *Hallowe'en*, vigile de la Toussaint, *f*.

hallucination, *n*, hallucination, vision, *f*.

halo, *n*, halo, *m*, auréole, *f*, nimbe, *m*.

halt, *n*, halte, station, *f*; stationnement, *m*. ¶ *i*, halte[-là]! ¶ *v.i*, faire halte; stationner; (*waver*) balancer; (*limp*) boiter.

halter, *n*, (*harness*) licou, *m*; (*hanging*) corde, *f*.

halting, *a*, boiteux.

halve, *v.t*, partager en deux, p. par la moitié.

halyard, *n*, drisse, *f*.

ham, *n*, (*in man*) jarret; (*hog*, *boar*) jambon, *m*. ~ *& eggs*, œufs au jambon, *m.pl*.

Hamburg, *n*, Hambourg, *m*.

hames, *n.pl*, attelles, *f.pl*.

hamlet, *n*, hameau, *m*.

hammer, *n*, marteau; (*power*) pilon; (*gun*) chien, *m*. ~lock (*wrestling*), retournement de bras, *m*. ¶ *v.t*, marteler, battre.

hammock, *n*, hamac, *m*.

hamper, *n*, [gros] panier, *m*, manne; malle en osier, *f*; (*impedimenta*) bataclan. ¶ *v.t*, empêtrer; troubler.

hand, *n*, main, *f*; poing, *m*; (*pointer*) aiguille; écriture; signature, *f*; (*side*) côté, *m*, part; (*cards*) main, *f*, jeu, *m*; (*horse*) = 4 inches *or* 10.16 centimeters; (*pl*, *men*) bras, hommes, *m.pl*; (*att.*) à main, à bras; à la main; manuel. *on the other* ~, de l'autre côté, d'autre part. ~*bag* (*lady's, etc.*), sac à main, *m*. ~*bill*, prospectus, imprimé; (*political, etc.*) tract, *m*. ~*book*, manuel, livret, aide-mémoire, guide-âne, mémento, *m*. ~*cuff*, *v.t*, mettre les menottes à; (*n.pl.*) menottes, *f.pl*. ~*kerchief*, mouchoir, *m*; (*silk*) pochette, *f*. ~*s off!* bas les mains! ~*rail*, main courante, rampe, *f*, garde-fou, *m*. ~*shake*, poignée de main, *f*; *shake-hand*, *m*. ~ *to* ~ (*fight*), corps à corps. *from* ~ *to mouth*, au jour le jour. ~*s up!* haut les mains! ~*writing*, écriture, *f*. *get the upper* ~, prendre le dessus.

¶ *v.t*, passer. ~ *down* (*fig.*) transmettre. ~ *in*, déposer. ~ [*over*], remettre, délivrer. ~ *over* (to justice), remettre, déférer. ~ful, *n*, poignée, *f*.

handicap, *n*, (*sport*) handicap; (*fig.*) désavantage, *m*. ¶ *v.t*, handicaper; désavantager. **handicapper**, *n*, handicapeur, *m*.

handicraft, *n*, industrie d'art, *f*. *handicraftsman*, ouvrier d'art, *m*.

handle, *n*, manche, *m*; poignée; (*umbrella*) poignée; main; manivelle; manette, *f*; bras; fût, *m*; (*basket*) anse; queue; branche; boucle, *f*; (*door*) bouton, *m*. ~*bar* (cycle), guidon, *m*. *to fly off the* ~, sortir de ses gonds. ¶ *v.t*, manier; manipuler; traiter; filer; emmancher. *one who knows how to* ~ (money, men), manieur, *m*. *to* ~ *roughly*, malmener. **handling**, *n*, manutention, *f*, maniement, *m*, manipulation, *f*. **hand-made**, *a*, fait à la main.

handsome, *a*, beau; riche. ~ly, *ad*, joliment, généreusement, grassement. ~ness, *n*, beauté, *f*.

handy, *a*, sous la main; commode; maniable; adroit; (*man*) à tout faire.

hang, *v.t. & i.ir*, pendre; suspendre; [r]accrocher; tomber; tapisser, tendre; poser. ~ *about*, rôder. ~ *back*, hésiter. ~ *heavy* (time), durer. ~ *out* (washing), étendre. ~*dog*, *a*, patibulaire. ~*man*, bourreau, *m*. ~*nail*, envie, *f*.

hangar, *n*, hangar, *m*.

hanger, *n*, crochet, *m*. ~*on*, personne à charge, *f*; parasite, *m*. **hanging**, *p.a*, suspendu. ~ *committee* (Art), jury d'admission, *m*. ~ *garden*, jardin suspendu, *m*. ~ *lamp*, baladeuse, *f*. ~ *matter*, cas pendable, *m*. [*death by*] ~, pendaison, mort par suspension, *f*. **hangings**, *n.pl*, tapisserie, *f*.

hank, *n*, écheveau, *m*, poignée, *f*.

hanker *after*, soupirer après, avoir soif de.

Hanover, *n*, Hanovre, *m*; (*province*) le H.

haphazard, *ad*, au hasard, à l'aventure.

hapless, *a*, infortuné.

happen, *v.i*, arriver; advenir, venir, se passer, se trouver. ~**ing**, *n*, événement, *m*.

happiness, *n*, bonheur, *m*; félicité, *f*. **happy†**, *a*, heureux. ~*-go-lucky person*, sans-souci, *m,f*. *to a* ~ *issue*, à bon port. ~ *medium*, juste milieu, *m*. *a* ~ *New Year*, la bonne année.

harangue, *n*, harangue, *f*. ¶ *v.t. & i*, haranguer.

harass, *v.t*, harceler, fouler.

harbinger, *n*, avant-coureur, messager, fourrier, *m*.

harbor, *n*, port; refuge, *m*. ~ *master*, capitaine de port, *m*. ¶ *v.t*, héberger; nourrir; garder; (*criminal*) receler.

hard, *a*, dur; rude; rigoureux; ardu, laborieux, pénible; (*water*) crue. ~ & *fast*, absolu, immuable. ~*-bitten sailor*, loup de mer, *m*. ~*-boiled* (egg), dur. ~ *cash*, espèces sonnantes, *f.pl*. ~ *court* (*Ten.*) terre battue, *f*. ~ *labor*, travail disciplinaire, *m*. ~ *luck*, mauvais sort, *m*. ~ *palate*, palais dur, *m*. ~ *roe*, œufs, *m.pl*. ~ *tack*, biscuit de mer, *m*. ~ *to please*, exigeant. ~*ware*, quincaillerie; (*computers*) 'hardware, *m*. (*builder's*) serrurerie, *f*. ~*wearing* & *for* ~ *wear*, inusable. ~*working*, laborieux. ¶ *ad*, dur; durement; fort; fortement; (*drink*) sec; (*look*) fixement; (*raining*) à verse. ~ *up*, à sec, aux abois.

harden, *v.t*, durcir, endurcir; (*to temper metal*) tremper. **hardihood**, *n*, hardiesse, *f*. **hardly**, *ad*, durement; à peine; ne ... guère; presque. **hardness**, *n*, dureté; rigueur; (*water*) crudité, *f*. ~ *of hearing*, dureté d'oreille. **hardship**, *n*, privation; rigueur, *f*. **hardy**, *a*, hardi; (*plant*) robuste, rustique.

hard copy, *n*, (*computers*) tirage, *m*.

hare, *n*, lièvre, (*young*) levraut, *m*. ~ & *hounds*, rallye-paper, *m*. ~*bell*, campanule, clochette, *f*. ~*brained*, écervelé. ~*lip*, bec-de-lièvre, *m*.

harem, *n*, harem, *m*.

haricot beans (*dried*), haricots secs, *m.pl*.

hark, *i*, écoute!, écoutez!

harlequin, *n*, arlequin, *m*. ~*ade*, *n*, arlequinade, *f*.

harlot, *n*, prostituée, *f*.

harm, *n*, mal; tort, *m*. ¶ *v.t*, faire du mal à; nuire à. ~*ful*, *a*, nuisible, pernicieux. ~*less*, *a*, inoffensif, innocent, anodin. ~*lessness*, *n*, innocuité; innocence, *f*.

harmonic†, *a. & n*, harmonique, *a. & m*. **harmonica**, *n*, harmonica, *m*. **harmonious†**, *a*, harmonieux. **harmonium**, *n*, harmonium, *m*. **harmonize**, *v.t*, harmoniser. **harmony**, *n*, harmonie, *f*; ensemble, *m*.

harness, *n*, harnais; harnachement, *m*. *die in* ~, mourir debout. ~ *maker*, bourrelier; sellier, *m*. ¶ *v.t*, harnacher; (*waterfall*) aménager.

harp, *n*, harpe, *f*. *to be always* ~*ing on the same string*, chanter toujours la même antienne, rabâcher toujours les mêmes choses. ~*ist*, *n*, harpiste, *m,f*.

harpoon, *n*, harpon, *m*. ¶ *v.t*, harponner.

harpsichord, *n*, clavecin, *m*.

harpy, *n*, harpie, *f*.

harrow, *n*, herse, *f*. ¶ *v.t*, herser; (*fig.*) déchirer, navrer. ~*ing*, *a*, déchirant.

harry, *v.t*, harceler; dévaster.

harsh†, *a*, dur; rude; âpre; aigre. ~*ness*, *n*, dureté; rudesse; âpreté; aigreur, *f*.

hart, *n*, cerf, *m*. **hartshorn**, *n*, liqueur d'ammoniaque, *f*.

harum-scarum, *n*, hurluberlu, *m*.

harvest, *n*, moisson; récolte, *f*. ~ *festival*, fête de la moisson, *f*. ~*man* (insect), faucheur, faucheux, *m*. ¶ *v.t*, moissonner; récolter. ~*er*, *n*, moissonneur, euse; (*Mach.*) moissonneuse, *f*.

hash, *n*, hachis, *m*, capilotade, *f*. ¶ *v.t*, hacher.

hasp, *n*, moraillon, *m*.

hassock, *n*, agenouilloir; carreau, coussin, *m*.

haste, *n*, hâte; précipitation, *f*. *to* [*make*]~ & **hasten**, *v.i*, se dépêcher, se hâter, s'empresser. **hasten**, *v.t*, hâter, presser, précipiter. **hasty†**, *a*, hâtif, à la hâte, précipité; vif, emporté.

hat, *n*, chapeau, *m*. ~ & *coat stand*, portechapeaux, portemanteau, *m*. ~*box*, boîte à chapeau(x), *f*. ~ *brush*, brosse à chapeaux, *f*. ~ *peg*, patère, *f*. ~ *shop* & ~ *trade*, chapellerie, *f*. ~*s off!*, chapeaux bas! (*In student circles* *the cry "chapeau!" warns offender to remove his/her hat.).*

hatch (*brood*) *n,* couvée, *f.* ~[*way*], *n,* panneau, *m,* écoutille, *f.* ¶ *v.i.* (*eggs*) éclore; (*v.t.*) faire éclore; (*fig.*) couver, ourdir, tramer; (*engrave*) hacher.

hatchet, *n,* hache à main, *f.* ~ *face,* figure en lame de couteau, *f.*

hatching, *n,* éclosion; (*engraving*) hachure, *f.*

hatchment, *n,* écusson; blason funèbre, *m.*

hate, *n,* haine, *f.* ¶ *v.t,* haïr; détester. ~fult, *a,* haïssable; odieux. **hatred,** *n,* haine, *f. full of* ~, haineux.

hatter, *n,* chapelier, *m.*

haughtily, *ad,* avec hauteur, d'une manière hautaine. **haughtiness,** *n,* hauteur, morgue, *f.* **haughty,** *a,* hautain, altier, arrogant.

haul, *n,* coup de filet; parcours, trajet, *m;* acquisition, *f.* ¶ *v.t,* haler; traîner, tirer, remorquer; transporter.

haunch, *n,* hanche, *f;* (*meat*) quartier, cuissot, cimier; (*Arch.*) rein, *m.*

haunt, *n,* rendez-vous, lieu fréquenté (*of* = par); repaire, *m,* caverne, *f,* liteau, *m.* ¶ *v.t,* hanter, fréquenter; poursuivre.

hautboy (*Mus.*), *n,* hautbois, *m.*

Havana, *n,* la Havane. ~ [*cigar*], cigare de la Havane, havane, *m.*

have, *v.t.ir,* avoir; posséder; jouir de; tenir; prendre; faire. ~ *on* (*wear*), porter, avoir. *I* ~ *come,* je suis venu. *I* ~ *been had,* on m'a eu.

haven, *n,* havre, port; (*fig.*) asile, *m.*

haversack, *n,* musette, *f,* sac, *m.*

havoc, *n,* ravage[s] *m.*[*pl.*], dégâts, *m.pl.*

Havre, *n,* le Havre.

haw (*Bot.*) *n,* cenelle, *f.* ~*finch,* gros-bec, *m.* ¶ *v.i,* ânonner.

Hawaii, *n,* Hawaï, *m.* ~*an, a,* hawaïen.

hawk, *n,* faucon, *m.* ¶ *v.i,* chasser au faucon; (*throat*) graillonner; (*v.t.*) colporter. ~*er, n,* colporteur, *m;* crieur, euse; camelot, *m.* ~*ing* (*falconry*) *n,* volerie, *f.*

hawser, *n,* haussière, amarre, *f,* grelin, *m.*

hawthorn, *n,* aubépine, *f.*

hay, *n,* foin, *m.* oft. pl. ~*cock,* tas de foin, *m.* ~ *fever,* fièvre des foins, *f.* ~*loft,* fenil, m. ~*maker,* faneur, euse. ~*making,* fenaison, *f.* ~*stack,* meule de foin, *f.*

hazard, *n,* hasard, *m;* (*golf*) hasard, accident, *m.* ¶ *v.t,* hasarder. ~*ous*†, *a,* hasardeux, chanceux.

haze, *n,* brume, *f,* brouillard; nuage, *m.*

hazel, *n,* noisetier, coudrier, *m;* (*att., color, eyes*) [de] noisette. ~*nut,* noisette, *f.*

hazy, *a,* brumeux; nuageux; vaporeux; vague; flou.

he, *pn,* il; lui; celui; ce, c'. ¶ *n. & att,* mâle, *m. it is* ~, c'est lui. *there* ~ *is,* le voilà.

head, *n,* tête, *f;* cerveau, *m;* [*of hair*] chevelure, *f;* chef; titre; haut; fond; chapeau; cap, *m;* pointe; pomme; rubrique, *f,* poste, chapitre; en-tête; (*bed*) chevet, *m;* (*on glass of beer*) mousse; (*coin*) face; (*book page*) tête, tranche supérieure, *f;* (*deer*) bois, *m;* (*game*) pièce; (*boar, etc.*) hure, *f;* (*lathe*) poupée, *f;* (*spear*) fer, *m.* ~*s or tails?* pile ou face? ~*ache,* mal de tête, *m.* ~*band,* bandeau, serre-tête, *m;* (*Bookb.*) tranchefile, comète, *f.* ~ *cook,* chef [de cuisine] *m.* ~*dress,* ~*gear,* coiffure, coiffe, *f,* couvre-chef, *m.* ~*land,* pointe de terre, *f,* cap, *m.* ~*light,* feu d'avant, fanal de tête; (*auto*) phare, *m.* ~*line,* (*book*) titre courant, *m;* (*news*) manchette, *f.* ~*long, a,* précipité; (*ad.*) précipitamment. ~*master,* directeur; principal; proviseur. ~*mistress,* directrice, *f.* ~ *office,* siège [principal], siège social, *m.* ~*on collision,* rencontre de front, *f.* ~*phones,* casque, *m.* ~*quarters,* quartier général; (*staff*) État-major; chef-lieu, *m;* préfecture, *f.* ~*room,* échappée, *f.* ~*sman,* bourreau, *m.* ~*stone,* pierre tombale, tombe, *f.* ~*strong,* entêté, entier. ~*waiter,* maître d'hôtel, premier garçon, chef de salle, *m.* ~ *waters,* amont, *m.* ~*way,* chemin, progrès, *m;* (*Naut.*) erre, *f.* ~ *wind,* vent debout, *m.* ¶ *v.t,* être (*ou* se mettre) à la tête de. ~ *the procession,* ouvrir la marche. ~*ed* (*paper*) *p.a,* à en-tête. ~*ing,* *n,* titre; en-tête, *m.* ~*y* (*liquor*) *a,* capiteux.

heal, *v.t,* guérir; (*v.i.*) [se] g. ~*er,*

n, guérisseur, euse; (*of time*) médecin, *m.* ~**ing,** *n,* guérison, *f.*
health, *n,* santé; salubrité; hygiène, *f.* ~**y,** *a,* sain; salubre; hygiénique.

heap, *n,* tas, amas, monceau, *m.* ¶ *v.t,* entasser, amonceler, amasser.

hear, *v.t. & i. ir,* entendre; écouter; (*witness—law*) ouïr; (*learn*) apprendre; (*prayer*) exaucer. ~ *from,* lire. ~**er,** *n,* auditeur, trice. ~**ing,** *n,* ouïe; oreille; audition; audience, *f*; débats, *m.pl. to be hard of* ~, avoir l'ouïe (*ou* l'oreille) dure. ~**say,** on-dit, ouï-dire, *m.*

hearse, *n,* corbillard, char [funèbre], char de deuil, *m.*

heart, *n,* cœur, *m*; âme, *f*; entrailles, *f.pl*; fond, vif, *m. by* ~, par cœur, de mémoire. ~ *attack,* crise cardiaque, *f.* ~ *& soul* (*fig.*), tout son cœur. ~**beat,** battement de cœur, *m.* ~**break,** brisement de cœur, *m.* ~**breaking, ~rending,** désespérant, navrant, déchirant. ~**burn,** ardeur d'estomac, *f.* ~ *case* (pers.), cardiaque, *m,f.* ~ *disease,* maladie de cœur, *f. in one's* ~ *of* ~*s,* au fond du cœur. ~**en,** *v.t,* encourager, rassurer. ~**felt,** *a,* bien senti. *to be* ~*less,* n'avoir point de cœur. ~*less person,* sans-cœur, *m,f.* **heartsease** (*Bot.*) *n,* pensée, *f.*

hearth, *n,* âtre; foyer; feu; (*smith's*) bâti, *m.* ~ *brush,* balai d'âtre, *m.* ~ *rug,* tapis de foyer, t. de cheminée, *m.* ~**stone,** pierre de foyer, *f,* [marbre de] foyer, *m*; (*whitening*) pierre blanche, *f.*

heartily, *ad,* cordialement; franchement. **hearty,** *a,* cordial; (*fit*) dispos; (*laugh*) gros; (*meal*) solide, copieux.

heat, *n,* chaleur, *f*; calorique, *m*; température; chauffe; fièvre; vivacité, ardeur, *f,* feu, *m*; (*sport*) épreuve, *f*; (*animals*) rut, *m.* ~ *lightning,* éclair[s] de chaleur, *m.[pl.]*, fulguration, *f.* ~*stroke,* coup de chaleur, *m.* ~ *wave,* vague de c., *f.* ¶ *v.t,* chauffer, échauffer. ~**er,** *n,* calorifère; radiateur; réchaud, *m.*

heath, *n,* (*land*) bruyère, brande, lande; (*shrub*) bruyère, brande, *f.* ~**cock,** coq de bruyère, *m.*

heathen, *n,* païen, ne. ~[**ish**], *a,* païen. ~**ism,** *n,* paganisme, *m.*

heather, *n,* bruyère, brande, *f.*

heating, *n,* chauffage; échauffement, *m.* ~ *engineer,* fumiste, *m.* ~ *surface,* surface de chauffe, *f.*

heave, *v.t.ir,* soulever; pousser; jeter; lancer; haler; virer; (*v.i.ir*) palpiter; (*retch*) faire des haut-le-cœur. ~ *to* (*Naut.*), mettre en panne.

heaven, *n,* ciel, *m,* cieux, *m.pl.* ~**ly,** *a,* céleste. **heavily,** *ad,* lourdement, pesamment. **heaviness,** *n,* pesanteur, *f,* poids, *m*; lourdeur, *f.* **heavy,** *a,* lourd; pesant; massif; fort; chargé; grave; gros; grand. ~ *shell* (*Artil.*), marmite, *f.* ~ *weight,* (*for lifting*) gueuse [d'athlétisme] *f*; (*for throwing*) gros boulet; (*Box.*) poids lourd, *m.*

Hebraic & Hebrew, *a,* hébraïque. **Hebrew** (*language*) *n,* l'hébreu, *m.*

hecatomb, *n,* hécatombe, *f.*

heckle, *v.t,* harceler [de questions].

hectic (*fever*) *a,* hectique.

hector, *n,* bravache, fanfaron, *m.*

hedge, *n,* haie, *f.* ~**hog,** hérisson, *m.* ~**row,** haie, *f.* ~ *sparrow,* fauvette des haies, *f,* mouchet, *m.* ¶ *v.t,* entourer d'une haie. (*v.i.*) chercher des échappatoires; (*Fin.*) faire un arbitrage, se couvrir. ~ *in,* [r]enfermer.

heed, *n,* attention; garde, *f.* ¶ *v.t,* faire attention à. ~**less,** *a,* insoucieux.

heel, *n,* talon, *m*; (*rubber*) talonnette; (*Naut.*) bande, *f. at the* ~*s of,* aux trousses de. *down at the* ~*s,* dans la dèche.

hefty, *a,* solide.

hegemony, *n,* hégémonie, *f.*

heifer, *n,* génisse, *f.*

height, *n,* hauteur, élévation, altitude, *f*; comble, plein, apogée, *m*; (*stature*) taille, *f*; (*of summer*) cœur, fort, *m.* ~**en,** *v.t,* rehausser, surélever.

heinous†, *a,* odieux; atroce.

heir, *n,* ess, *n,* héritier, ère, hoir, *m.* ~*loom,* bijou de famille, meuble de famille, *m.* ~**ship,** *n,* hérédité, *f.*

helical, *a,* en hélice, hélicoïdal.

helicopter, *n,* hélicoptère, *m.* **heliport,** *n,* héliport, *m.* ~ *terminal,* héligare, *f.*

heliotrope, n, héliotrope, m.

helium, n, hélium, m.

helix, n, hélice, f; (ear) hélix, m.

hell, n, enfer, m; géhenne, f. ~cat, harpie, f.

Hellenism, n, hellénisme, m.

hellish, a, infernal.

hello (Teleph.) i, allô!

helm, n, barre, f; (fig.) gouvernail, timon, m, helmsman, timonier, homme de barre, m.

helmet, n, casque, m.

helot, n, ilote, m. ~ism, n, ilotisme, m.

help, n, aide, assistance, f, moyen, secours; remède, m. ¶ v.t. & i, aider, assister, secourir. I can't ~ saying, je ne peux m'empêcher de dire. ~ one another, s'entraider. ~ yourself, servez-vous. ~! au secours! à l'aide! à moi! à nous! ~er, n, aide, m,f. ~ful & ~ing, a, utile; serviable. ~ing (food) n, portion, f. ~less, a, impuissant; impotent.

helter-skelter, ad. & n, pêle-mêle, ad. & m.

helve, n, manche, m.

hem, n, ourlet; [re]bord, m, bordure, f. ¶ v.t, ourler; border; (v.i.) ânonner. ~ in, cerner.

hematite, n, hématite, f.

hemidemisemiquaver, n, quadruple croche, f.

hemisphere, n, hémisphère, m.

hemlock, n, ciguë, f.

hemorrhage, n, hémorragie, f. **hemorrhoids,** n.pl, hémorroïdes, f.pl.

hemming, n, point d'ourlet, m.

hemp, n, chanvre, m. ~ seed, chènevis, m. ~[en], a, de chanvre.

hemstitch, n, ourlet à jour, m. ¶ v.t, ourler à jour.

hen, n, poule, f. ~ coop, cage à poulets, mue, f. ~ house, poulailler, m. ~ partridge, perdrix femelle, f. ~pecked, mené par sa femme. ~ pheasant, [poule] faisane, f. ~ roost, juchoir, m.

hence, ad, d'ici; de là; dans; partant; donc. ~forth, ~forward, ad, désormais, dorénavant, dès maintenant.

henchman, n, partisan, satellite, séide. mamel[o]uk, m.

henna, n, henné, m.

her, pr, elle; la; lui; son, sa, ses.

herald, n, (Hist.) héraut; (fig.) avant-coureur, m. ¶ v.t, annoncer. ~ic, a, héraldique. ~ry, n, blason, m. héraldique, f.

herb, n, herbe, f. ~aceous, a, herbacé. ~age, n, herbage, m. ~al, n, herbier, m. ~alist, n, herboriste, m,f. ~arium, n, herbier, m. ~ivorous, a. & ~ animal, herbivore, a. & m. **herborize,** v.i, herboriser.

Herculean, a, herculéen. a Hercules, un hercule.

herd, n, troupeau, m; (deer) harde, f. the [common] ~, le vulgaire. the ~ instinct, le sentiment grégaire. ~ together, vivre en troupe. ~ed together, empilé. **herdsman,** n, bouvier, pâtre, m.

here, ad, ici; que voici; y; présent! ~ a little & there a little, de bric & de broc. ~ & there, ici & là; [de]çà & [de]là; par-ci, par-là. ~ below, ici-bas. ~ I am, me voici! ~ is, ~ are, voici. ~ lies (grave), ci-gît, ici repose. [look] ~! tenez! **hereabout[s],** ad, ici près, dans ces parages. **hereafter,** ad, désormais, à l'avenir; dans la vie future. **hereby** (law) ad, par les présentes.

hereditary†, a, héréditaire. **heredity,** n, hérédité, f.

herein (law) ad, dans les présentes. **hereinafter,** ad, ci-après. **heresy,** n, hérésie, f. **heretic,** n, hérétique, m,f. ~al, a, hérétique.

hereunder, ad, ci-dessous; de ce chef. **hereupon,** ad, sur ces entrefaites. **herewith,** ad, ci-joint, ci-inclus.

heritage, n, héritage, patrimoine, m.

hermaphrodite, n, hermaphrodite, m.

hermetic†, a, hermétique.

hermit, n, ermite, solitaire, m. ~ arab, bernard-l'ermite, m. ~age, n, ermitage, m.

hernia, n, hernie, f.

hero, n, héros, m. ~ worship, culte des héros, m. ~ic†, a, héroïque. ~icomic, a, héroï-comique. ~ine, n, héroïne, f. ~ism, n, héroïsme, m.

heron, n, héron, m. ~ry, n, héronnière, f.

herpes, n, herpès, m.

herring, n, hareng, m. ~ boat, harenguier, m. ~-boning (Need.), point croisé, m. ~ fishery & ~ season, harengaison, f. **red ~,** hareng saur, m.

hers, *pn,* le sien, la sienne, les siens, les siennes; ses; à elle. **herself,** *pn,* elle même; elle; soi, soimême; se.

hesitate, *v.i,* hésiter, balancer, marchander. **hesitation,** *n,* hésitation, *f.*

heterodox, *a,* hétérodoxe. **~y,** *n,* hétérodoxie, *f.*

heterogeneous, *a,* hétérogène.

hew, *v.t.ir, (tree)* abattre, couper; *(stone)* tailler.

hexagon, *n,* hexagone, *m.* **~al,** *a,* hexagone. **~ nut,** écrou à 6 pans, *m.* **hexameter,** *n,* hexamètre, *m.*

heyday of life, fleur de l'âge, *f.*

hi, *i,* ohé!

hiatus, *n,* fissure; lacune, *f; (Gram.)* hiatus, *m.*

hibernate *(Zool.) v.i,* hiberner.

hiccup, *n,* hoquet, *m.* ¶ *v.i,* avoir le h.

hickory, *n, (tree, wood)* noyer d'Amérique, *m.*

hidden, *p.p,* caché; dérobé; occulte; latent. **hide,** *v.t.ir,* cacher. **~** *[oneself],* se cacher. **~-&-seek,** cache-cache, *m.*

hide, *n,* peau, *f,* cuir, *m.* ***a, ~bound,*** à l'esprit étroit.

hideous†, *a,* hideux.

hiding *(thrashing) n,* raclée, *f.*

hiding place, cache[tte] *f,* affût, *m.*

hierarchy, *n,* hiérarchie, *f.*

hieroglyph, *n,* hiéroglyphe, *m.*

higgledy-piggledy, *ad,* pêlemêle.

high, *a,* haut; plein; élevé; grand; gros; fort; *(dear)* cher; *(meat)* avancé; *(game)* faisandé; *(in height)* de haut, haut de. **~ altar,** maître-autel, grand autel, *m.* **~ & dry** *(Naut.),* échoué à sec. **~born,** de haute naissance. **~class,** de marque; *(wine)* grand; haut; perfectionné. **~ collar,** faux col montant, *m.* **~ dive,** plongeon d'une grande hauteur, *m.* **~flown,** ampoulé. **~handed,** arbitraire; tyrannique. **~ hat,** chapeau haut de forme, *m.* **~ jump,** saut en hauteur, *m.* **~lights** *(Art),* rehauts, *m.pl.* **~ mass,** grand-messe, messe chantée, *f.* **~necked dress,** robe montante, *f.* **~ priest,** grand prêtre, *m.* **~ society, ~ life,** le grand monde. **~ tide,** marée haute, pleine mer, *f.* **to be ~waisted** *(dress),* avoir la taille haute. **~**

water mark, grand de l'eau, *m,* laisse de haute mer, *f; (fig.)* apogée, *m.* **~way,** grand chemin, *m,* grand-route, grande route; voie publique, *f.* **~way code,** code de la route, *m.* **~wayman,** voleur de grand chemin, *m.* **~way robbery,** vol de grand chemin, brigandage, *m.* ¶ *ad,* haut. **~er,** *a,* plus haut; supérieur. **~ bid,** surenchère, *f.* **~ education,** haut enseignement, *m.* **~ mathematics,** mathématiques spéciales, *f.pl.* **~ notes** *(Mus.),* haut, *m.* **the ~est bidder,** le plus offrant [& dernier enchérisseur]. **~ly,** *ad,* hautement; fortement, éminemment. **~ amusing,** désopilant, impayable. **~ paid,** très bien payé. **~ strung,** nerveux. **~ness,** *n,* hauteur; *(title)* altesse, *f.*

hiker, *n,* excursionniste à pied, *m,f.*

hilarious, *a,* hilare. **hilarity,** *n,* hilarité, *f.*

hill, *n,* colline, *f,* coteau, *m,* côte, hauteur, *f.* **~side,** flanc de coteau. **~top,** cime, *f.* **up ~ & down dale,** par monts & par vaux. ¶ *(Hort.) v.t,* butter, chausser. **hillock,** *n,* monticule, tertre, *m,* butte, *f.* **hilly,** *a,* montueux; accidenté.

hilt, *n,* poignée; garde, *f.*

him, *pn,* le; lui. **himself,** *pn,* luimême; lui; soi, soi-même; se.

hind *(deer) n,* biche, *f.*

hind, *a,* de derrière; [d']arrière.

hinder, *v.t,* empêcher, gêner, entraver.

hindmost, *a,* dernier.

hindrance, *n,* empêchement, *m.* **without ~,** sans encombre.

Hindu, -doo, *a,* hindou. ¶ *n,* Hindou, e. **Hindustani,** *n,* l'hindoustani, *m.*

hinge, *n,* charnière; fiche; penture, *f;* gond, *m. (fig.)* pivot, *m.* ¶ *v.i,* tourner, pivoter. **~d,** *p.a,* à charnière(s).

hinny, *n,* petit mulet, bardot, *m.*

hint, *n,* allusion; suggestion, *f;* mot [couvert] *m.* ¶ *v.t,* laisser entendre. **~ at,** insinuer.

hip, *n,* hanche, *f; (Arch.)* arête, croupe, *f.* **~ bath,** bain de siège, *m.* **~ bone,** os iliaque, *m.* **~ measurement,** [con]tour de hanches, *m.*

hippodrome, *n,* hippodrome, *m.*

hippopotamus, *n,* hippopotame, *m.*

hire, *n*, louage, *m*, location, *f*; loyer, *m*. ¶ *v.t*, louer; (*assassin, etc.*) soudoyer. ~**d**, *p.p*, de louage; à gages; mercenaire. ~**ling**, *n*, mercenaire, *m.f*. **hirer**, *n*, loueur, euse.

hirsute, *a*, hirsute.

his, *pn*, le sien, la sienne, les siens, les siennes; son, sa, ses; à lui; de lui.

hiss, *v.t. & i*, siffler; chuter. ~[**ing**,] *n*, sifflement; sifflet, *m*.

historian, *n*, historien, *m*. **historic** & ~**al**†, *a*, historique; d'histoire. **history**, *n*, histoire, *f*; his-torique, *m*.

histrion, *n*, histrion, *m*. ~**ic**, *a*, du théâtre.

hit, *n*, coup, *m*; pièce à succès; touche; balle au but, balle mise, *f*, coup au but, *m*. ~ & *run driver*, chauffard, *m*. ~ *or miss*, au petit bonheur. (*slang*) ~ *song*, tube, *m*. *smash* ~, succès fou. ¶ *v.t.ir*, frapper; toucher; atteindre; attra-per.

hitch, *n*, accroc, contretemps, *m*. ¶ *v.t*, accrocher. ~**hiking**, auto-stop, *m*.

hither *ad*, ici, y. ~ & *thither*, çà & là; par-ci, par-là. ~**to**, *ad*, jusqu'à présent, jusqu'ici.

hive, *n*, ruche, *f*.

hives, *n*, urticaire, *m*.

hoard, *n*, amas; magot, *m*. ¶ *v.t*, amasser; (*v.i.*) thésauriser.

hoarding, *n*, clôture en planches, *f*, palissade, *f*.

hoarfrost, gelée blanche, *f*, givre, *m*.

hoarhound, *n*, marrube, *m*.

hoarse, *a*, enroué, éraillé; rauque. ~**ness**, *n*, enrouement, *m*.

hoary, *a*, blanc; blanchi.

hoax, *n*, mystification; attrape, *f*; canard, *m*; supercherie, *f*. ¶ *v.t*, mystifier; attraper. ~**er**, *n*, mysti-ficateur, trice.

hob, *n*, plaque de cheminée, *f*; des-sus [de fourneau] *m*.

hobble, *v.i*, clocher, clopiner, boi-ter; (*v.t.*) entraver. **hobbledehoy**, *n*, [garçon] godiche, *m*. **hobbling along**, clopin-clopant.

hobby, *n*, (*bird*) hobereau, *m*. (*an art, collecting, gardening*) is his ~, il est [grand] amateur de . . ., . . . est sa folie, . . . est sa distraction. (*a sport*) is his ~,

il est passionné pour le . . . ~ *horse*, cheval de bois; dada, *m*.

hobgoblin, *n*, esprit follet, *m*.

hobnail, *n*, caboche, *f*, gros clou, *m*. ~**ed**, *p.a*, ferré.

hobnob with, être à tu & à toi avec; trinquer avec.

hobo, *n*, clochard, *m*.

Hobson's choice (*it is*), c'est à prendre ou à laisser.

hock, *n*, vin blanc du Rhin; (*horse*) jarret, *m*.

hockey, *n*, hockey, *m*. ~ *skates*, patins de h., *m.pl*. ~ *stick*, crosse de h., canne de h., *f*, bâton de h., *m*.

hocus, *v.t*, mystifier, attraper. ~ *pocus*, *n*, tour de passe-passe, *m*.

hod, *n*, oiseau [de maçon] *m*.

hodgepodge, *n*, méli-mélo, *m*.

hoe, *n*, houe; binette, *f*; sarcloir, *m*. ¶ *v.t*, houer; biner; serfouir.

hog, *n*, cochon, pourceau, porc [châtré] *m*. ~**backed**, en dos d'âne. **hoggish**, *a*, bestial.

hogshead, *n*, barrique, *f*, bou-caut, *m*.

hoist, *n*, treuil; monte-charge, *m*. ¶ *v.t*, [re]monter; lever; hisser; guinder; (*flag*) arborer.

hold, *n*, prise; pince; emprise, mainmise, *f*; (*Box.*) tenu; empire, *m*; (*ship*) cale, *f*. ¶ *v.t.ir*, tenir; retenir; détenir; occuper; con-tenir; posséder, avoir; réputer; célébrer. ~ *back*, *m*, in, retenir. ~*fast*, crampon, *m*; patte, *f*; va-let, *m*. ~ *forth*, pérorer. ~ *on*, tenir [bon], t. sa position. ~ *on! ~ the line!* (*Teleph.*), ne quittez pas! ~ *one's own*, se maintenir. ~ *one's nose*, se boucher le nez. ~ *one's tongue*, se taire. ~ *out*, tendre; présenter; durer. ~ *up*, soutenir. ~**er**, *n*, support, *m*; porte- *always m*, *e.g. tool* ~, porte-outil, *m*; douille, *f*; (*pers.*) détenteur, trice; titulaire, *m,f*; porteur, *m*. ~**ing**, *n*, tenue; dé-tention; possession; propriété, *f*; avoir, *m*; valeur, *f*; portefeuille, *m*.

hole, *n*, trou; orifice, *m*; ouverture, *f*; (*fox's*) tanière; fosse, *f*, puits; œil, *m*; lumière, *f*; creux, *m*; pi-qûre, *f*; (*golf*) trou [d'arrivée] *m*. ¶ *v.t*, trouer, percer; (*golf*) jouer dans le trou.

holiday, *n*, jour de fête; jour fé-rié, *m*; fête, *f*; vacances, *f.pl*; [jour de] congé, *m*.

holily, *ad*, saintement. **holiness**, *n*, sainteté, *f*.

Holland (*Geog.*) *n*, la Hollande. **h~**, *n*, toile écrue, toile bise, *f*.

hollo, *v.t*, houper. See *hallo*.

hollow, *a*, creux; cave; caverneux; (*voice*) sourde. *to beat* ~, battre à plate couture. ¶ *n*, creux; enfoncement; entonnoir, *m*; cavité, *f*. ~ [out], *v.t*, creuser; évider; caver.

holly, *n*, houx, *m*. ~ *berry*, cenelle, *f*.

hollyhock, *n*, rose trémière, passerose, *f*.

holocaust, *n*, holocauste, *m*; (*fig.*) immolation saignée, *f*.

holster, *n*, (*pistol*) etui, *m*, (*saddle*) fonte, *f*.

holy, *a*, saint; sacré; (*bread, water*) bénit, e; (*day*) férié. *Holy Ghost*, Saint-Esprit, *m*. *H~ Land*, Terre Sainte, *f*. ~ *orders*, ordres sacrés, *m.pl*. *H~ See*, Saint-Siège, *m*. ~-*water basin*, bénitier, *m*. ~-*water sprinkler*, aspersoir, goupillon, *m*. *H~ Writ*, l'Ecriture sainte, *f*. ~ *year*, année jubilaire, *f*.

homage, *n*, hommage[s] *m.[pl.]*.

home, *n*, foyer familial, foyer [domestique]; chez-moi; chez-soi; intérieur; logis, *m*; maison, *f*; gîte, *m*; ménage, *m*; pays, *m*; patrie, *f*; asile; hospice, *m*. ~ *for the aged*, maison de retraite. *at* ~. See *under at*. ¶ *ad*, chez soi; à la maison; juste; à fond; à bloc. ¶ *a*, domestique; de famille; indigène; intérieur; métropolitain. ~*land*, terre natale, *f*. ~ *life*, vie d'intérieur, *f*. ~-*sick*, nostalgique. ~-*sickness*, mal du pays, *m*, nostalgie, *f*. ~ *truths*, vérités bien senties, bonnes vérités, *f.pl*. ~-*work*, (*Sch.*) devoirs [à faire à la maison] *m.pl*. ~*less*, *a*, sans foyer, sans asile. **homelessness**, *n*, sans façon, *m*. **homely**, *a*, simple, sans façon, bourgeois.

homeopath[ist], *n*, homéopathe, *m*. **homeopathic**, *a*, homéopathique. **homeopathy**, *n*, homéopathie, *f*.

Homeric, *a*, homérique.

homespun, *n*, toile de ménage, *f*.

homestead, *n*, ferme, *f*, manoir, *m*. **homeward**, *a*. & *ad*, de retour; en r. ~ *bound*, en retour, effectuant son voyage de retour. ~*s*, *ad*, en retour.

homicidal, *a*, homicide. **homicide**, *n*, (*pers.*) homicide, *m,f*; (*act*) homicide, *m*.

homily, *n*, homélie, *f*, prône, *m*.

homing pigeon, pigeon voyageur, *m*.

homogeneous, *a*, homogène.

homonym, *n*, homonyme, *m*.

homosexual, *n*, (*slang*) folle, *f*, pédé, *m*.

hone, *n*, pierre à aiguiser, *f*. ¶ *v.t*, (*razor*) repasser; affiler.

honest†, *a*, honnête, probe, droit, intègre; brave, de bien. ~*y*, *n*, honnêteté, probité, intégrité.

honey, *n*, miel; (*pers.*) chou[chou] *m*. ¶ *v.t*, sucrer. ~ *bee*, mouche à miel, *f*. ~*comb*, *n*, gâteau de miel; rayon de m., *m*. ~*moon*, lune de miel, *f*. ~*suckle*, chèvrefeuille, *m*. ~*ed*, *a*, [em]miellé; mielleux.

honk, *n*, coup de klaxon, *m*. ¶ *v.i*, klaxoner.

honor, *n*, honneur, *m*. ¶ *v.t*, honorer; faire honneur à, accueillir. ~*able†*, *a*, honorable. ~*ed*, *p.a*, honoré; respecté.

honorarium, *n*, honoraires, *m.pl*. **honorary**, *a*, honoraire; honorifique; sans rétribution. ~ *membership*, honorariat, *m*.

hood, *n*, capuchon; chapeau; (*auto*) capot, *m*; capote; cape; capeline, *f*; dais; soufflet, *m*; hotte, *f*. ~*wink*, éberluer.

hoof, *n*, sabot, *m*. ~*ed*, *a*, ongulé.

hook, *n*, crochet; croc; gond, *m*; agrafe, *f*; (*Fish.*) hameçon; (*Box.*) crochet, *m*. ~ & *eye*, agrafe & porte. ~ & *hinge*, gond & penture. *by* ~ *or by crook*, de façon ou d'autre. ¶ *v.t*, accrocher; agrafer. ~[*ed*] (*nose*) *a*, aquilin.

hooky [*to play*] *v.i*, faire l'école buissonnière.

hookah, *n*, narghileh, *m*.

hooligan, *n*, apache, voyou, *m*.

hoop, *n*, cercle; cerceau, *m*; frette, *f*; arceau, *m*. ~ *iron*, feuillard de fer, *m*. ~ *ring*, jonc, *m*. ¶ *v.t*, [en]cercler; relier; fretter.

hoopoe, *n*, huppe, *f*.

hoot, *v.t*, huer, conspuer; (*v.i.*) (*owl*) chuinter. ~[*ing*] (*boo[ing]*) *n*, huée[s] *f.[pl.]*.

hop, *n*, saut; (*pl.*) houblon, *m*. ~

[*plant*], houblon, *m*. ~ *field*, houblonnière, *f*. ~*scotch*, marelle, *f*. ~, *step*, & *jump*, triple saut, *m*. ¶ *v.t*, houblonner; (*v.i.*) sauter à cloche-pied; (*like a sparrow*) sautiller. ~ *about*, s'ébattre.

hope, *n*, espérance, *f*; espoir, *m*. ¶ *v.t. & i*, espérer. ~*ful*, *a*, plein d'espoir; encourageant; confiant; optimiste; (*lad*) de grandes espérances. ~*less*, *a*, sans espoir, désespéré; incorrigible. ~*less-ness*, *n*, désespérance, *f*.

hopper, *n*, (*insect*) sauteur, *m*; (*Mach*.) trémie, *f*.

horde, *n*, horde, *f*.

horehound, *n*, marrube, *m*.

horizon, *n*, horizon, *m*. **horizontal**†, *a*, horizontal.

hormonal, *a*, hormonal, aux. **hormone**, *n*, hormone, *f*.

horn, *n*, corne, *f*; (*pl, deer*) bois, *m.pl*; (*insect*) antenne, *f*; cor; cornet, *m*; trompe, *f*. ~ *of plenty*, corne d'abondance, *f*.~*rimmed spectacles*, lunettes en écaille, *f.pl*. *horned cattle*, bêtes à cornes, bêtes cornues, *f.pl*.

hornet, *n*, frelon, *m*. ~*'s nest* (*fig*.), guêpier, *m*.

horny, *a*, corné; (*hands*) calleuses.

horology, *n*, horlogerie, *f*.

horoscope, *n*, horoscope, *m*.

horrible† & **horrid**†, *a*, horrible. **horror**, *n*, horreur, *f*. **horrify**, *v.t*, horrifier.

horse, *n*, cheval, *m*; (*pl*.) cavalerie, *f*; (*trestle*) chevalet, *m*, chèvre, *f*. *on* ~*back*, à cheval. ~ *bean*, féverole, *f*. ~ *box*, wagon-écurie, *m*. ~~*chestnut*, marron d'Inde; (*tree*) marronnier d'I., *m*. ~ *dealer*, marchand de chevaux, maquignon, *m*, ~*fly*, taon, *m*. ~*hair*, crin, *m*. ~*man*, cavalier, écuyer, *m*. ~*manship*, équitation, *f*, manège, *m*. ~ *play*, jeux de main, *m.pl*. ~*pond*, abreuvoir, *m*. ~ *power*, cheval [vapeur] *m*, force de cheval, f. en chevaux, *f*. *a* 10 ~ [*power*] *car*, une [automobile de] 10 chevaux. ~ *race*, course de chevaux, *f*. ~ *racing*, les courses, *f.pl*. ~*radish*, raifort, *m*. ~*shoe*, fer à cheval, *m*. ~ *show*, concours hippique, *m*. ~*tail plume*, crinière, *f*. ~*whip*, *n*, cravache, *f*; (*v.t.*) cravacher. ~*woman*, cavalière, écu-

yère, amazone, *f*. ~*y*, *a*, de cheval, chevalin.

horticultural, *a*, horticole. **horticulture**, *n*, horticulture, *f*. **horticulturist**, *n*, horticulteur, *m*.

hosanna, *n*, hosanna, *m*.

hose, *n*, (*dress*, col. as *pl*.) bas, *m.pl*; (*pipe*) tuyau, boyau, *m*, manche, *f*. **hosier**, *n*, chemisier, bonnetier, *m*. ~*y*, *n*, chemiserie, bonneterie, *f*.

hospitable, *a*, hospitalier. **hospital**, *n*, hôpital, *m*. ~ *attendant*, ~ *nurse*, infirmier, ère. ~ *ship*, vaisseau-hôpital, *m*. **hospitality**, *n*, hospitalité, *f*. **hospitalize**, *v.t*, hospitaliser.

host, *n*, (*pers*.) hôte, *m*; armée, *f*, bataillon, *m*, troupe, nuée, phalange; (*Eccl.*) hostie, *f*. ~*ess*, *n*, hôtesse, *f*.

hostage, *n*, otage; (*fig*.) gage, *m*.

hostel, *n*, auberge, *f*, foyer d'étudiants, *m*, maison des étudiants, auberge de jeunesse, *f*; hospice, *m*, institution, *f*. ~*ry* (*archaic*) *n*, hôtellerie, *f*.

hostile†, *a*, hostile. **hostility**, *n*, hostilité, *f*.

hostler, *n*, garçon d'écurie, palefrenier, *m*.

hot, *a*, chaud; à chaud; ardent; brûlant. *to get* ~ chauffer. ~*bed*, (*Hort.*) couche [de fumier] *f*; (*fig*.) foyer, *m*. *in* ~ *haste*, en toute hâte, au [grand] galop. ~*head*, cerveau brûlé, *m*, échauffé, e. ~*headed*, bouillant, impétueux. ~*house*, serre chaude, *f*. ~*house grapes*, raisin de serres, *m*. ~ *plate*, réchaud, *m*. ~ *spring*, source thermale, *f*. ~ *water bottle*, boule d'eau chaude, *f*.

hotchpotch, *n*, (*Cook*.) hochepot, (*Cook*. & *fig*.) salmigondis, pot pourri. *m*.

hotel, *n*, hôtel, *m*. ~ *keeper*, hôtelier, ère.

hot line, *n*, téléphone rouge, *m*, ligne r., *f*.

hotly, *ad*, chaleureusement.

hound, *n*, chien courant, c. de chasse, chien, *m*; (*bitch*) lice, *f*. ~ *out*, chasser.

hour, *n*, heure, *f*. ~*glass*, sablier, *m*. ~ *hand*, petite aiguille, *f*. *office* ~*s*, heures de bureau, *f.pl*. ~*ly*, *a*, par heure; (*ad*.) d'heure en heure.

house, *n*, maison, *f*; logis, *m*; habitation, *f*; hôtel; pavillon, *m*; bâtiment; ménage, *m*; (*Theat.*) salle, *f*. neither ~ nor home, ni feu ni lieu. ~ boat, bateau d'habitation, *m*. ~breaking, effraction, *f*, cambriolage, *m*. ~ fly, mouche commune, *f*. ~ full (*Theat.*), complet. ~hold, ménage, *m*; (*staff*) maison, domesticité, *f*. ~hold gods, dieux familiers, dieux pénates, *m.pl.* ~hold goods, ménage, *m*. ~hold linen, linge de maison, *m*. ~keeper, femme de charge; ménagère, *f*. ~keeping, ménage, *m*; économie domestique, *f*. ~maid, fille de service, servante, *f*. ~ martin, hirondelle de fenêtre, *f*. ~ number, numéro d'habitation, *m*. ~ painter, peintre en bâtiments, *m*. ~ top, toit, *m*. to give a ~warming, pendre la crémaillère. ~wife, maîtresse de maison; ménagère, *f*. ~wifery, ménage, *m*. ~work, ménage, *m*. ¶ *v.t*, loger; mettre à l'abri; (*carp., etc.*) encastrer, emboîter; (*harvest*) rentrer, engranger. housing, *n*, logement, *m*. ~problem, crise du logement, *f*.

hovel, *n*, taudis, bouge, *m*, baraque, *f*.

hover, *v.i*, planer, voltiger; se balancer.

hovercraft, *n*, aéroglisseur, *m*.

how, *ad*, comment; comme; que. any~, de toute façon. ~ are you?, ça va? ~ long? combien de temps? ~ much? ~ many? combien?

however, *ad*, de quelque manière que; quelque . . . que, si . . . que; tout . . . que; pourtant.

howitzer, *n*, obusier, *m*.

howl, *n*, hurlement, *m*. ¶ *v.i*, hurler; (*wind*) gronder. ~er, *n*, bévue, gaffe, *f*.

hoyden, *n*, gamine bruyante, *f*, garçon manqué, *m*.

hub, *n*, moyeu; (*fig.*) centre, *m*.

hubbub, *n*, brouhaha, charivari, *m*.

hubcap, *n*, enjoliveur, *m*.

huckaback, *n*, toile ouvrée, *f*. ~ towel, serviette nid d'abeilles, *f*.

huckster, *n*, agent de publicité, marchande des quatre-saisons, colporteur, *m*. ¶ *v.t*, colporter; marchander.

huddle, *v.t*, entasser; (*v.i.*) se blottir.

hue, *n*, teinte; nuance, *f*.

hue & cry, haro, tocsin, tollé, *m*.

huff, *v.i*, souffler; (*anger*) s'emporter; malmener. he is in a ~, il a pris la mouche.

hug, *n*, étreinte, *f*, embrassement, *m*, accolade, *f*. ¶ *v.t*, serrer, étreindre, embrasser; (*the wind*, *Naut.*) pincer le vent; (*the shore*) côtoyer; (*an error*) chérir.

huge, *a*, énorme, immense, démesuré. ~ly, *ad*, énormément, immensément, démesurément.

hulk, *n*, vaisseau rasé; ponton, *m*. ~ing, *a*, balourd.

hull, *n*, (*husk*) cosse; (*ship*) coque, *f*, corps, *m*. ¶ *v.t*, monder.

hullabaloo, *n*, hourvari, *m*.

hullo[a], *i*, hél, ohé! tiens!

hum, *v.i. & t*, (*bee, etc.*) bourdonner; (*top*) ronfler; (*tune*) fredonner, chantonner. ¶ *n*, fredon, *m*. ¶ *i*, heml, hom!

human†, *a*, humain. **humane**†, *a*, humain. **humanitarian**, *a. & n*, humanitaire, *a. & m*. **humanity**, *n*, humanité, *f*. **humanize**, *v.t*, humaniser.

humble†, *a*, humble. ¶ *v.t*, humilier, abaisser, mater. ~ness, *f*, humilité; (*birth*) bassesse, *f*. the humbler classes, le menu peuple.

humbug, *n*, blague; mystification, *f*; (*pers.*) blagueur, euse; mystificateur, trice; imposteur, *m*. ¶ *i*, chansons! chansons! ¶ *v.t*, mystifier; lanterner, enjôler; mettre dedans.

humdrum, *a*, monotone; banal; assoupissant.

humerus, *n*, humérus, *m*.

humid, *a*, humide. ~ity, *n*, humidité, *f*.

humiliate, *v.t*, humilier. **humiliation**, *n*, humiliation, *f*. **humility**, *n*, humilité, *f*.

humming bird, oiseau-mouche, colibri, *m*.

humming top, toupie d'Allemagne, *f*.

hummock, *n*, mamelon; monticule, *m*.

humorist, *n*, humoriste, *m*; farceur, euse. **humorous**, *a*, humoriste; humoristique; drôle, drolatique. ~ly, *ad*, avec humour; par facétie. **humor**, *n*, (*mood*) humeur, disposition, *f*; (*jocosity*) humour, *m*. ¶ *v.t*, complaire à, flatter; ménager.

hump, *n*, bosse, *f*. ~back, *n*. & ~backed, *a*, bossu, e.

humph, *i,* heml, homl

hunch, *n,* bosse, *f;* (*chunk*) chanteau, *m;* (*feeling*) presentiment, *m.* ~ back, *n.* & ~backed, *a,* bossu, e.

hundred, *a.* & *n,* cent, *a.* & *m.* ~ [*or so*], centaine, *f.* ~fold, *n,* centuple, *m.* ~th, *a.* & *n,* centième, *a.* & *m.*

Hungarian, *a,* hongrois. ¶ *n,* Hongrois, e; (*language*) le hongrois. **Hungary,** *n,* la Hongrie.

hunger, *n,* faim, fringale, *f.* ~ strike, grève de la faim, *f.* ~ striker, gréviste de la faim, *m,f.* ~ after, être affamé de, avoir une fringale de. **hungrily,** *ad,* d'un œil affamé; avidement. **hungry,** *a,* affamé. to be ~, very ~, avoir faim, grand-faim.

hunk, *n,* chanteau, (*bread*) guignon, *m.*

hunt, *n,* chasse; (*riding to hounds*) chasse à courre, *f;* équipage de chasse, *m.* ¶ *v.t.* & *i,* chasser, courir. ~ for, chercher. ~er, *n,* chasseur; cheval de chasse; (*curios*) dénicheur, *m.* **hunting,** *n,* chasse; c. à courre; (*science*) vénerie, *f.* **huntress,** *n,* chasseuse, *f.* **huntsman,** *n,* chasseur; (*man in charge*) veneur, piqueur, *m.*

hurdle, *n,* claie; haie, *f.* ~ fence, échalier, *m.* ~ race, course de haies, *f;* steeple-chase, *m.*

hurl, *v.t,* lancer, darder, projetor.

hurly-burly, *n,* tohu-bohu, *m.*

hurrah, -ray, *i,* hourra, hosanna, *m.* ¶ *i,* bravo! vivat!

hurricane, *n,* ouragan, *m.* ~ deck, pont de manœuvre; pont abri, *m.* ~lamp, lanterne-tempête, *f.*

hurry, *n,* précipitation, hâte; presse, *f.* ¶ *v.t,* presser, hâter, précipiter; (*v.i.*) se hâter. ~ up, se dépêcher. be in a ~, avoir 'hâte.

hurt, *n,* mal, *m;* blessure; lésion, *f;* tort, *m.* ¶ *v.t.ir,* faire [du] mal à; blesser; nuire à.

husband, *n,* mari, époux, *m.* ¶ *v.t,* ménager.

husbandman, *n,* cultivateur, *m.* **husbandry,** *n,* économie rurale, agronomie, *f.*

hush, *n,* silence, *m.* ~ money, prix du silence, *m.* ¶ *i,* silence! chut!; motus!; paix! ¶ *v.t,* faire taire. ~ up, étouffer.

husk, *n,* cosse, *f;* (*walnut*) brou,

m; (*grain*) balle, *f.* ¶ *v.t,* (*corn*) éplucher; (*barley*) monder; écosser. ~y, (*hoarse*) *a,* enroué, éraillé.

hussy, -zzy, *n,* coquine, friponne, drôlesse, masque, *f.*

hustle, *v.t,* bousculer.

hut, *n,* hutte, cabane, baraque, *f.*

hutch, *n,* cabane, *f,* clapier, *m.*

hyacinth, *n,* jacinthe, hyacinthe, *f.*

hybrid, *a,* hybride, métis. ¶ *n,* hybride, mulet, *m.*

hydra, *n,* hydre, *f.*

hydrangea, *n,* hortensia, *m.*

hydrant, *n,* bouche [d'eau], prise d'eau, *f.*

hydrate, *n,* hydrate, *m.*

hydraulic, *a.* & ~s, *n.pl,* hydraulique, *a.* & *f.*

hydrocarbon, *n,* hydrocarbure, *m.* **hydrochloric,** *a,* chlorhydrique. **hydrofoil,** *n,* hydroptère, *m.* **hydrogen,** *n,* hydrogène, *m.* **hydropathic,** *a,* hydrothérapique. ¶ *n,* établissement hydrothérapique, *m.* **hydropathy,** *n,* hydrothérapie, *f.* **hydrophobia,** *n,* hydrophobie, *f.* **hydroplane,** *n,* hydravion, hydroglisseur, *m.*

hyena, *n,* hyène, *f.*

hygiene & **hygienics,** *n,* hygiène, *f.* **hygienic(al)**†, *a,* hygiénique.

hymen, *n,* hymen, hyménée, *m.*

hymenoptera, *n.pl,* hyménoptères, *m.pl.*

hymn, *n,* hymne, *m;* (*in church*) hymne, *f,* cantique, *m.* ~ book, recueil d'hymnes, *m.*

hyperbola & hyperbole, *n,* hyperbole, *f.*

hyphen, *n,* trait d'union, tiret, *m;* (*end of line*) division, *f.*

hypnotism, *n,* hypnotisme, *m.* **hypnotize,** *v.t,* hypnotiser.

hypochondriac, *a.* & *n,* hypochondriaque, *a.* & *m,f.* **hypocrisy,** *n,* hypocrisie, *f.* **hypocrite,** *n,* hypocrite, *m,f.* **hypocritical**†, *a,* hypocrite. **hypodermic,** *a,* hypodermique. ~ syringe, seringue de Pravaz, *f.* **hypothecation,** *n,* nantissement, *m.* **hypothesis,** *n,* hypothèse, *f.* **hypothetic(al)**†, *a,* hypothétique.

hysteria, *n,* hystérie, *f.* **hysteric(al),** *a,* hystérique; nerveux. **hysterics,** *n.pl,* crise de nerfs, nerfs, *m.pl.*

I

I, *pn,* je; moi.
iambic, *a,* ïambique. ¶ *n,* ïambe,
m.
ibex, *n,* bouquetin, *m.*
ibis, *n,* ibis, m.
ice, *n,* glace, *f.* oft. pl. ~ *age,* période glaciaire, *f.* ~ *berg,* iceberg,
m. ~*bucket,* seau à glace, *m.* ~
cream, glace, *f.* ~ *cream freezer,*
sorbetière, *f.* ~ *cream pop,* esquimau, *m.* ~ *cream vender,* glacier,
m. ~ *cube,* glaçon, *m.* ~ *hockey,*
hockey sur glace, *m.* ~ *pack,*
banquise, *f.* ~*pick,* piolet, *m.* ~
skates, patins à glace, *m.pl.* ¶ *v.t,*
glacer; (*wine*) frapper [de glace].
Iceland, *n,* l'Islande, *f.* ~**er,** *n,*
Islandais, e. ~**ic,** *a.* & (*language*)
n, islandais, *a.* & *m.*
ichthyology, *n,* ichtyologie, *f.*
icicle, *n,* glaçon, *m.* **icing,** (*sugar*)
n, glace, *f.*
icon, *n,* icône, *f.* **iconoclast,** *n,*
iconoclaste, démolisseur, *m.*
icy, *a,* glacé, glacial.
idea, *n,* idée, pensée; image, *f.* ~
man, concepteur, *m.* **ideal†,** *a.* &
n, idéal, *a.* & ~*ism,* *n,* idéa-
lisme, *m.* ~*ist,* *n,* idéaliste, *m,f.*
identical†, *a,* identique. **identification,** *n,* identification, *f.* **identify,** *v.t,* identifier. **identity,** *n,*
identité, *f.*
idiocy, *n,* idiotie, *f.*
idiom, *n,* (*dialect*) idiome; (*phrase*)
idiotisme, *m.*
idiosyncrasy, *n,* idiosyncrasie, *f.*
idiot, *n.* & ~**ic,** *a,* idiot, e.
idle, *a,* oisif; paresseux; fainéant;
inoccupé; désœuvré; de loisir;
sans affaires; futile; oiseux, en
l'air. ~ *fancy,* rêverie, *f.* ¶ *v.i,* paresser, fainéanter; (*motor*) tourner au ralenti. ~**ness,** *n,* oisiveté; paresse, *f*; chômage, *m.*
idler, *n,* oisif, ive, paresseux,
euse, fainéant, e; badaud, e. **idly,**
ad, dans l'oisiveté.
idol, *n,* idole, *f*; amour, *m.* **idolater, tress,** *n,* idolâtre, *m,f.* **idolatrous,** *a,* idolâtre, idolâtrique.
idolatry, *n,* idolâtrie, *f.* **idolize,**
v.t, idolâtrer.
idyll, *n,* idylle, *f.* **idyllic,** *a,* idyl-
lique.

if, *c,* si, s'. ~ *not,* sinon.
igneous, *a,* igné. ignis fatuus, *n,*
feu follet, *m.* **ignite,** *v.t,* enflammer; allumer. **ignition,** *n,* ignition;
inflammation, *f*; allumage, *m.* ~
key, clef de contact, *m.* ~ *lock,*
antivol, *m.* to switch off the ~,
couper l'allumage.
ignoble†, *a,* ignoble.
ignominious†, *a,* ignominieux.
ignominy, *n,* ignominie, *f.*
ignoramus, *n,* ignorant, e, ignare,
m,f. **ignorance,** *n,* ignorance, *f.*
ignorant, *a,* ignorant, ignare. to
be ~ of, ignorer.
ignore, *v.t,* méconnaître; ne faire
aucune attention à.
iguana, *n,* iguane, *m.*
ill, *n,* mal, *m.* speak ~ of, médire
de. ¶ *a,* malade, souffrant; mauvais; méchant. ¶ *ad,* mal; peu.
~*advised,* malavisé; malvenu,
mal venu. ~*assorted,* disparate.
~*bred,* mal élevé, malappris,
sans éducation. ~*famed,* malfamé, mal famé. ~*fated,* ~*
starred,* néfaste. ~ *feeling,* inimitié, *f.* ~*gotten gains,* biens
mal acquis, *m.pl.* ~ *humor,* humeur, *f.* ~ *luck,* mauvaise
chance, malchance, *f*; malheur,
m. ~*mannered,* malhonnête. ~*
natured* (*person*), méchant, e. ~*
omened,* de mauvis augure, funèbre. ~*temper,* humeur [cha-
grin] *f.* ~*tempered,* d'h. c., revêche, hargneux. ~*timed,* intempestif, déplacé. ~*treat,* ~*
use,* maltraiter, faire un mauvais
parti à. ~ *will,* malveillance, *f.*
to bear ~ will, en vouloir à.
illegal†, *a,* illégal.
illegible†, *a,* illisible.
illegitimacy, *n,* illégitimité, *f.*
illegitimate†, *a,* illégitime.
illicit†, *a,* illicite.
illiterate, *a,* illettré.
illness, *n,* maladie, *f*, mal, *m.*
illogical, *a,* illogique. ~**ity,** *n,*
illogisme, *m.*
illuminate, *v.t,* éclairer; (*festively*) illuminer, embraser; (*MS.*)
enluminer, historier. **illumination,** *n,* éclairage, *m*; illumination,
f; embrasement; *m*; enluminure,
f. **illumine,** *v.t,* éclairer.
illusion, *n,* illusion, tromperie, *f.*
illusive, illusory, *a,* illusoire.
illustrate, *v.t,* illustrer. ~*d price*

list, tarif-album, *m*. **illustration**, *n*, illustration; gravure, *f*; exemple, *m*. **illustrious**, *a*, illustre. *to make* ~, illustrer.

image, *n*, image, *f*. ~**ry**, *n*, images, *f.pl.* **imaginary**, *a*, imaginaire. **imagination**. *n*, imagination, *f*. **imagine**, *v.t. & i*, imaginer; s'imaginer; se figurer.

imbecile, *a*, imbécile. ¶ *n*, idiot, e.

imbibe, *v.t*, absorber; s'imbiber de; boire, sucer.

imbricate, *v.t*, imbriquer.

imbroglio, *n*, imbroglio, *m*.

imbrue, *v.t*, tremper.

imbue, *v.t*, impregner, (*fig*.) pénétrer. ~**d**, *p.p*, imbu, inspiré.

imitate, *v.t*, imiter; contrefaire. **imitation**, *n*, imitation; contrefaçon, *f*; (*att*.) [d']imitation, simili-; faux. **imitator**, *n*, imitateur, trice.

immaculate, *a*, immaculé. *the I~ Conception*, l'Immaculée Conception, *f*.

immanent, *a*, immanent.

immaterial, *a*, immatériel; sans importance.

immature, *a*, prématuré; pas mûr.

immeasurable, *a*, immensurable.

immediate†, *a*, immédiat.

immemorial, *a*, immémorial.

immense, *a*, immense. ~**ly**, *ad*, immensément. **immensity**, *n*, immensité, *f*.

immerse, *v.t*, immerger, plonger. **immersion**, *n*, immersion, *f*.

immigrant, *n*, immigrant, *m*. **immigrate**, *v.i*, immigrer.

imminence, *n*, imminence, *f*. **imminent**, *a*, imminent.

immobile, *a*, immobile. **immobility**, *n*, immobilité, *f*. **immobilization**, *n*, immobilisation, *f*. **immobilize**, *v.t*, immobiliser.

immoderate†, *a*, immodéré.

immodest†, *a*, immodeste.

immolate, *v.t*, immoler.

immoral, *a*, immoral. ~**ity**, *n*, immoralité, *f*.

immortal†, *a. & n*, immortel, *a. & m*. ~**ity**, *n*, immortalité, *f*. ~**ize**, *v.t*, immortaliser. **immortelle**, *n*, immortelle, *f*.

immovable†, *a*, inébranlable, immobile; (*feelings*) insensible.

immunity, *n*, immunité; exemption; franchise, *f*.

immunize, *v.t*, immuniser.

immure, *v.t*, claquemurer, cloîtrer.

immutable†, *a*, immuable.

imp, *n*, diablotin, lutin, démon, *m*.

impact, *n*, choc, *m*; percussion, *f*.

impair, *v.t*, détériorer; endommager; altérer; compromettre.

impale, *v.t*, embrocher; (*Hist*.) empaler.

impalpable, *a*, impalpable.

impanel a jury, former une liste de jurés, former un tableau.

impart, *v.t*, impartir; imprimer; faire part de.

impartial†, *a*, impartial. ~**ity**, *n*, impartialité, *f*.

impassable, *a*, impraticable, infranchissable.

impassible & impassive, *a*, impassible.

impassioned, *p.p*, passionné.

impasto, *n*, empâtement de couleurs, *m*.

impatience, *n*, impatience, *f*. **impatient**, *a*, impatient. *to grow* ~, s'impatienter. ~**ly**, *ad*, impatiemment.

impeach, *v.t*, accuser. ~**ment**, *n*, accusation, *f*.

impecunious, *a*, besogneux.

impede, *v.t*, entraver, empêcher. **impediment**, *n*, empêchement, obstacle, *m*. ~ *of speech*, ~ *in one's speech*, empêchement (*ou* embarras) de la langue, *m*. **impedimenta**, *n.pl*, impedimenta, *m.pl*.

impel, *v.t*, pousser, animer.

impending, *p.a*, imminent.

impenetrable, *a*, impénétrable.

impenitence, *n*, impénitence, *f*. **impenitent**, *a*, impénitent.

imperative†, *a. & n*, impératif, *a. & m*.

imperceptible†, *a*, imperceptible, insaisissable.

imperfect†, *a. &* ~ [*tense*], *n*, imparfait, *a. & m*. ~**ion**, *n*, imperfection, *f*.

imperial, *a*, impérial; (*weights & measures*) *anglais*. ¶ (*beard*) *n*, impériale, *f*. ~**ist**, *n. &* ~**istic**, *a*, impérialiste, *m. & a*.

imperil, *v.t*, mettre en danger.

imperious†, *a*, impérieux.

imperishable, *a*, impérissable.

impermeable, *a*, imperméable.

impersonal†, *a*, impersonnel.

impersonate, v.t, personnifier. **impersonation**, n, personnification; (Theat.) création; (law) supposition de personne, f.
impertinence, n, impertinence, f. **impertinent**, a, impertinent. ~ly, ad, impertinemment.
imperturbable†, a, imperturbable.
impervious, a, imperméable, impénétrable.
impetuous†, a, impétueux.
impetus, n, impulsion, f, élan, branle, m.
impiety, n, impiété, f.
impinge [up]on, venir en contact avec; empieter sur.
impious, a, impie.
impish, a, lutin, espiègle.
implacable†, a, implacable.
implant, v.t, implanter.
implement, n, instrument, ustensile, m. ¶ v.t, rendre effectif; ajouter.
implicate, v.t, impliquer. not ~d, désintéressé. **implication**, n, implication, f; sous-entendu, m. **implicit†**, a. & **implied**, p.a, implicite, tacite.
implore, v.t, implorer, supplier.
imply, v.t, impliquer; insinuer; sous-entendre.
impolite†, a, impoli. ~ness, n, impolitesse, f.
impolitic, a, impolitique.
imponderable, a. & n, impondérable, a. & m.
import, n, (meaning) portée, signification, f, sens, m; (Com., etc.) importation, f. ~ duty, droit d'entrée, m, entrée, f. ¶ v.t, signifier; (Com., etc.) importer.
importance, n, importance, f. **important**, a, important.
importation, n, importation, f. **importer**, n, importateur, m.
importunate, a, importun. **importune**, v.t, importuner. **importunity**, n, importunité, f.
impose, v.t, imposer; (fine) frapper. ~ [up]on someone, en faire accroire à (ou en imposer à) quelqu'un. person of imposing appearance, porte-respect, m. **imposition**, n, imposition; imposture, f.
impossibility, n, impossibilité, f, l'impossible, m. **impossible**, a, impossible.
impost (Arch.) n, imposte, f.

impostor, n, imposteur, m. **imposture**, n, imposture, f.
impotence, -cy, n, impotence; (sexual) impuissance, f. **impotent**, a, impotent; (sexual) impuissant.
impound, v.t, mettre à la fourrière; enfermer; confisquer.
impoverish, v.t, appauvrir.
impracticable, a, infaisable, impraticable.
imprecation, n, imprécation, f.
impregnable, a, imprenable, inexpugnable.
impregnate, v.t, imprégner; féconder. ~d (wood) p.a, injecté.
impresario, n, impresario, m.
impress, n, empreinte, impression, f. ¶ v.t, imprimer, empreindre; graver; impressionner; réquisitionner. ~ion, n, impression; empreinte, f; (Typ.) foulage, m. to be under the ~, avoir dans l'idée. ~ionism, n, impressionnisme, m. **impressive**, a, impressionnant; solennel.
imprint, n, empreinte; marque de l'editeur, f. ¶ v.t, imprimer, empreindre.
imprison, v.t, emprisonner. ~ment, n, emprisonnement, m; prison, f.
improbability, n, improbabilité, invraisemblance, f. **improbable**, a, improbable, invraisemblable. **improbably**, ad, invraisemblablement.
impromptu, ad. a. & n, impromptu, ad. a.inv. & m.
improper, a, impropre, abusif; inconvenant, incongru; vice de . . .; faux. ~ly, ad, improprement; abusivement. **impropriety**, n, inconvenance, incongruité; impropriété, f.
improve, v.t, améliorer; perfectionner; bonifier; amender. ~ on, renchérir sur. ~ on acquaintance, gagner à être connu. ~ment, n, amélioration, f; perfectionnement, m; bonification, f; embellissement, m.
improvidence, n, imprévoyance, f. **improvident**, a, imprévoyant.
improvise, v.t, improviser.
imprudence, n, imprudence, f. **imprudent**, a, imprudent. ~ly, ad, imprudemment.
impudence, n, impudence, f, toupet, m. **impudent**, a, impu-

dent. ~**ly**, *ad*, impudemment.
impudicity, *n*, impudicité, *f*.
impugn, *v.t*, attaquer.
impulse & **impulsion**, *n*, impulsion, *f*; mouvement; branle, *m*. **impulsive**, *a*, impulsif; primesautier.
impunity, *n*, impunité, *f*. with ~, impunément.
impure†, *a*, impur. **impurity**, *n*, impureté, *f*.
imputation, *n*, imputation, *f*. **impute**, *v.t*, imputer.
in, *pr*, dans; en; à; au; entre; chez; auprès de; sur; sous; par; de; pour; à la. ¶ *ad*, dedans; chez, y; arrivé. ~ *between*, entre deux. ~ *demand*, demandé. ~ *fashion*, à la mode, de mode, de mise. ~ *print*, imprimé, disponible. ~ *there*, là-dedans. **ins & outs**, détours; êtres, *m.pl.*
inability, *n*, incapacité, *f*.
inaccessible, *a*, inaccessible, inabordable.
inaccuracy, *n*, inexactitude, infidélité, *f*. **inaccurate**†, *a*, inexact, infidèle.
inaction, *n*, inaction, *f*. **inactive**, *a*, inactif.
inadequate, *a*, insuffisant. ~**ly**, *ad*, insuffisamment.
inadmissible, *a*, inadmissible.
inadvertently, *ad*, par inadvertance, par mégarde.
inalienable, *a*, inaliénable, incessible.
inane, *a*, inepte, absurde.
inanimate, *a*, inanimé. ~ *nature*, le monde inanimé. **inanition**, *n*, inanition, *f*.
inanity, *n*, inanité, ineptie, *f*.
inapplicable, *a*, inapplicable.
inapposite, *a*, hors de propos.
inappreciable, *a*, inappréciable.
inappropriate†, *a*, impropre, qui ne convient pas, peu en situation.
inapt, *a*, inapte. **inaptitude**, *n*, inaptitude, *f*.
inarticulate, *a*, inarticulé.
inasmuch, *ad*, étant donné. ~ *as*, vu que.
inattentive, *a*, inattentif.
inaudible†, *a*, imperceptible [à l'ouïe].
inaugurate, *v.t*, inaugurer.
inauspicious, *a*, défavorable.
inborn & **inbred**, *a*, inné, infus, naturel, natif.
incalculable, *a*, incalculable.
incandescence, *n*, incandes-

cence, *f*. **incandescent**, *a*, incandescent; (*lamp, etc.*) à incandescence.
incantation, *n*, incantation, *f*.
incapable, *a*, incapable; inhabile; non-susceptible. **incapably**, *ad*, inhabilement. **incapacitate**, *v.t*, rendre incapable. **incapacity**, *n*, incapacité; impéritie, *f*.
incarcerate, *v.t*, incarcérer.
incarnate, *a*, incarné. **incarnation**, *n*, incarnation, *f*.
incautious, *a*, imprudent.
incendiarism, *n*, incendie volontaire, *m*. **incendiary**, *a*. & *n*, incendiaire, *a*. & *m,f*.
incense, *n*, encens, *m*. ~ *burner*, brûle-parfum, *m*. ¶ *v.t*, (*perfume*) encenser; (*enrage*) courroucer.
incentive, *n*, aiguillon; mobile, ressort, *m*.
inception, *n*, commencement, *m*.
incessant, *a*, incessant. ~**ly**, *ad*, incessamment.
incest, *n*, inceste, *m*. **incestuous**, *a*, incestueux.
inch, *n*, pouce, *m* = 2.54 (about 2½) centimeters.
incidence, *n*, incidence, *f*. **incident**, *n*, incident, événement, *m*. ¶ *a*, incident. ~**al**, *a*, incident. ~ *expenses*, faux frais, *m.pl.* ~**ally**, *ad*, incidemment.
incinerate, *v.t*, incinérer. **incinerator**, *n*, incinérateur, *m*.
incipient, *a*, naissant.
incise, *v.t*, inciser. **incision**, *n*, incision, *f*. **incisive**, *a*, incisif. **incisor**, *n*, [dent] incisive, *f*.
incite, *v.t*, inciter, provoquer; exciter. ~**ment**, *n*, incitation; excitation, *f*.
incivility, *n*, incivilité, *f*.
inclemency, *n*, inclémence, *f*. **inclement**, *a*, inclément.
inclination, *n*, inclination, *f*; penchant; attrait, *m*; inclinaison, *f*. **incline**, *n*, plan incliné, *m*; (*down*) pente; (*up*) rampe, *f*. ¶ *v.t*. & *i*, incliner; pencher; porter; (*color*) tirer. **inclined**, *p.a.* & *p.p*, (*plane*) incliné; (*fig.*) enclin, porté.
include, *v.t*, comprendre, englober, renfermer. *the tip is* ~*d*, le service est compris. **including**, *participle*, y compris. *not* ~, non compris. **inclusive**, *a*, tout compris; (*sum*) globale; (*dates*) inclusivement. ~ *of*, y compris. ~**ly**, *ad*, inclusivement.

incognito, *ad. & n,* incognito, *ad. & m.*

incoherence, *n,* incohérence, *f.* **incoherent,** *a,* incohérent.

incombustible, *a,* incombustible.

income, *n,* revenu, *m.* oft. *pl*; rapport, *m*; rente, *f.* oft. *pl.* ~ **tax,** impôt sur le revenu, *m,* impôt[s] cédulaire[s], *m.[pl.].* ~ **tax return,** déclaration de revenu, *f.*

incoming, *a,* à l'arrivée; d'arrivée; d'entrée; à échoir; (*tide*) montante.

incommensurable, *a,* incommensurable. **incommensurate with,** hors de proportion avec.

incommode, *v.t,* incommoder.

incomparable†, *a,* incomparable.

incompatibility, *n,* incompatibilité, *f.* ~ **of temper,** incompatibilité d'humeurs. **incompatible,** *a,* incompatible.

incompetence, -cy, *n,* incompétence, incapacité, *f.* **incompetent,** *a,* incompétent, incapable, insuffisant.

incomplete†, *a,* incomplet. **incompletion,** *n,* imperfection, *f.*

incomprehensible, *a,* incompréhensible.

inconceivable, *a,* inconcevable.

inconclusive, *a,* non-concluant.

incongruity, *n,* incongruité, disparate, *f.* **incongruous,** *a,* incongru, disparate. ~**ly,** *ad,* incongrûment.

inconsequent[ial], *a,* inconséquent.

inconsiderable, *a,* sans importance.

inconsiderate†, *a,* inconsidéré.

inconsistency, *n,* inconséquence; inconsistance, *f.* **inconsistent,** *a,* inconséquent; inconsistant.

inconsolable†, *a,* inconsolable, inguérissable.

inconspicuous, *a,* peu (*ou* pas) en évidence.

inconstancy, *n,* inconstance, *f.* **inconstant,** *a,* inconstant, volage; journalier.

incontinent, *a,* incontinent.

incontrovertible, *a,* incontestable.

inconvenience, *n,* incommodité, *f*; inconvénient, *m.* ¶ *v.t,* incommoder. **inconvenient,** *a,* incommode.

incorporate, *v.t,* incorporer; enencadrer; enchâsser; (*a company*) s'incorporer, former une société.

incorrect†, *a,* incorrect; inexact. ~**ness,** *n,* incorrection; inexactitude, *f.*

incorrigible†, *a,* incorrigible, indécrottable.

incorruptible, *a,* incorruptible.

increase, *n,* augmentation, *f,* accroissement, *m,* majoration, *f.* ¶ *v.t,* augmenter, accroître; aggraver, majorer. **increasing,** *p.a.,* croissant. ~**ly,** *ad,* de plus en plus.

incredibility, *n,* incrédibilité, *f.* **incredible†,** *a,* incroyable. **incredulity,** *n,* incrédulité, *f.* **incredulous,** *a,* incrédule.

increment, *n,* accroissement, *m*; plus-value, *f.*

incriminate, *v.t,* incriminer, charger.

incrust, *v.t,* incruster.

incubate, *v.t. & i,* couver. **incubation,** *n,* incubation, *f.* **incubator,** *n,* couveuse artificielle; poussinière, *f.*

incubus, *n,* cauchemar; faix, *m.*

inculcate, *v.t,* inculquer.

inculpate, *v.t,* inculper.

incumbent, *n,* bénéficier, titulaire, *m.* **to be ~ on,** incomber à.

incur, *v.t,* encourir; courir; s'attirer.

incurable†, *a. & n,* incurable, *a. & m,f.*

incursion, *n,* incursion, *f.*

indebted, *a,* redevable. ~**ness,** *n,* dette; créance, *f*; dettes & créances, *f.pl.*

indecency, *n,* indécence, malpropreté, *f.* **indecent,** *a,* indécent, malpropre. ~**ly,** *ad,* indécemment, malproprement.

indecision, *n,* indécision, *f.*

indecorous, *a,* inconvenant.

indeed, *ad,* vraiment, en effet; certes; bien, voire même, même. ¶ *i,* vraiment!, tiens!

indefatigable†, *a,* infatigable.

indefensible, *a,* indéfendable.

indefinable, *a,* indéfinissable. **indefinite†,** *a,* indéfini; (*leave*) illimité.

indelible, *a,* indélébile.

indelicacy, *n,* indélicatesse, *f.* **indelicate†,** *a,* indélicat.

indemnify, *v.t,* indemniser, dédommager. **indemnity,** *n,* indemnité; caution, *f.*

indent, v.t, denteler, échancrer; (Typ.) renfoncer, [faire] rentrer. **indentation**, n, dentelure, échancrure, f; (Typ.) renfoncement, m. **indention**, n, renfoncement, m. **indenture**, n, acte, contrat; (pl.) brevet, m.

independence, n, indépendance, f. **independent**, a, indépendant. to be ~, (financially) avoir une fortune indépendante. person of ~ means, rentier, ère. ~ly, ad, indépendamment.

indescribable, a, indescriptible, indicible.

indestructible, a, indestructible.

indeterminate, a, indéterminé.

index, n, indice, m; table; table alphabétique, f; index; répertoire, m. ~ expurgatorius, index expurgatoire. ¶ v.t, dresser la table [alphabétique] de, répertorier.

India, n, l'Inde, f. ~ paper, papier indien, m. **Indian**, a, indien. ~ Archipelago, archipel Indien, m, Insulinde, f. ~ club, massue en bois, f, mil, m. ~ corn, blé de Turquie, maïs, m. ~ ink, encre de Chine, f. ~ Ocean, océan Indien, m, mer des Indes, f. ¶ n, Indien, ne.

indicate, v.t, indiquer, désigner. **indication**, n, indication, f; indice, m. **indicative**, a, indicatif. ~ [mood], n, [mode] indicatif, m. **indicator**, n, indicateur, m.

indict, v.t, accuser. ~ment, n, acte d'accusation, réquisitoire, m.

Indies (the) n.pl, les Indes, f.pl.

indifference, n, indifférence; indolence, f. **indifferent**, a, indifférent; indolent; sans gêne. ~ly, ad, indifféremment.

indigence, n, indigence, f.

indigenous, a, indigène.

indigent, a, indigent.

indigestible, a, indigeste, cru [à l'estomac]. **indigestion**, n, indigestion, f.

indignant, a, indigné. ~ly, ad, avec indignation. **indignation**, n, indignation, f. **indignity**, n, indignité, f.

indigo, n, indigo, m. ~ blue, [bleu d'Jinde, m. ~ plant, indigotier, m.

indirect†, a, indirect.

indiscreet†, a, indiscret. **indiscretion**, n, indiscrétion; imprudence, f.

indiscriminate, a, sans aucun

discernement; confus. ~ly, ad, indistinctement, sans distinction.

indispensable†, a, indispensable.

indisposed, p.p, indisposé. **indisposition**, n, indisposition, f, malaise, m; disposition peu favorable, f.

indisputable†, a, indiscutable.

indissoluble†, a, indissoluble.

indistinct†, a, indistinct.

indite, v.t, rédiger; composer.

individual†, a, individuel. ¶ n, individu; particulier, m. ~ity, n, individualité, f.

indivisible†, a, indivisible.

Indochina, n, l'Indochine, f.

indoctrinate, v.t, endoctriner.

indolence, n, indolence, f. **indolent**, a, indolent, mou. ~ly, ad, indolemment.

indomitable, a, indomptable; (will) irréductible.

indoor, a, d'intérieur; de cabinet; (games) de société. ~s, ad, à la maison; à l'abri.

indorse, v.t, endosser; adopter; confirmer; garantir. ~ment, m, endossement, endos, m; souscription; adhésion; garantie, m.

indubitable†, a, indubitable.

induce, v.t, porter; décider; engager; induire; provoquer. ~ment, n, mobile, motif, m; tentation, f.

induct, v.t, installer; introduire. ~ion, n, induction; (Eccl.) installation, f.

indulge, v.t, gâter; caresser. ~ in, se permettre. **indulgence**, n, indulgence, f. **indulgent**, a, indulgent.

indurate, v.t, [en]durcir.

industrial†, a, industriel. ~ disease, maladie professionnelle, f. ~ism, n, industrialisme, m. ~ist, n, industriel, m. ~ize, v.t, industrialiser. **industrious**, a, industrieux, diligent, travailleur, assidu. **industriously**, ad, industrieusement, diligemment. **industry**, n, industrie; diligence, f.

inebriate, a, ivre. ¶ n, ivrogne, m, ivrognesse, f. ¶ v.t, enivrer.

ineffable, a, ineffable.

ineffaceable, a, ineffaçable.

ineffective† & **ineffectual**† & **inefficacious**†, a, inefficace.

inefficient, a, incapable.

inelastic, a, sans élasticité; sans souplesse.

inelegant, *a*, inélégant.
ineligible, *a*, inéligible.
inept, *a*, inepte. **ineptitude**, *n*. ineptie, *f*.
inequality, *n*, inégalité, *f*.
inequitable†, *a*, injuste.
ineradicable, *a*, indéracinable.
inert, *a*, inerte. **inertia**, *n*, inertie, *f*.
inestimable, *a*, inestimable.
inevitable†, *a*, inévitable.
inexact†, *a*, inexact. **inexactitude**, *n*, inexactitude, *f*.
inexcusable, *a*, inexcusable.
inexecutable, *a*, inexécutable.
inexhaustible†, *a*, inépuisable, intarissable.
inexorable†, *a*, inexorable.
inexpedient, *a*, pas expédient.
inexpensive, *a*, peu coûteux.
inexperience, *n*, inexpérience, *f*. ~**d**, *a*, inexpérimenté, novice, neuf.
inexplicable, *a*, inexplicable.
inexplicit, *a*, pas explicite.
inexpressible, *a*, inexprimable.
inextinguishable, *a*, inextinguible.
inextricable, *a*, inextricable.
infallible†, *a*, infaillible, impeccable.
infamous, *a*, infâme; (*law*) infamant. **infamy**, *n*, infamie, *f*.
infancy, *n*, enfance, *f*; bas âge, *m*; (*law*) minorité, *f*. **infant**, *n*, [petit] enfant, *m,f*; (*law*) mineur, e. ~ *mortality*, mortalité infantile, *f*. ~ *prodigy*, enfant prodige. **infanticide**, *n*, infanticide (*act*) *m*; (*pers*.) *m,f*. **infantile**, *a*, enfantin; (*Med*.) infantile.
infantry, *n*, infanterie, *f*. ~**man**, fantassin, *m*.
infarct, *n*, infarctus, *m*.
infatuate, *v.t*, affoler, embéguiner. *to become* ~**d**, s'infatuer, s'engouer. **infatuation**, *n*, infatuation, *f*, engouement, *m*.
infect, *v.t*, infecter, empester. ~**ion**, *n*, infection, *f*. ~**ious**, *a*, infectieux; contagieux.
infer, *v.t*, inférer, conclure, supposer, déduire. ~**ence**, *n*, inférence, conclusion, déduction, *f*. **inferential**, *a*, déductif. ~**ly**, *ad*, par déduction.
inferior†, *a. & n*, inférieur, *a. & m*. ~**ity**, *n*, infériorité, *f*. ~ *complex*, complexe d'i., *m*.

infernal, *a*, infernal. **inferno**, *n*, enfer, *m*.
infertile, *a*, infertile.
infest, *v.t*, infester.
infidel, *a. & n*, infidèle, *a. & m,f*. ~**ity**, *n*, infidélité, *f*.
infighting (*Box*.) *n*, combat de près, *m*.
infiltrate, *v.i*, s'infiltrer.
infinite†, *a*, infini. the ~, l'infini, *m*. **infinitesimal**, *a*, infinitésimal. **infinitive** [mood], *n*, [mode] infinitif, *m*. **infinitude & infinity**, *n*, infinité; immensité, *f*. **infinity** (*Math*., *Phot*.) *n*, l'infini, *m*.
infirm, *a*, infirme. ~**ary**, *n*, infirmerie, *f*. ~**ity**, *n*, infirmité, *f*.
inflame, *v.t*, enflammer; exalter. **inflammable**, *a*, inflammable. **inflammation**, *n*, inflammation, *f*.
inflate, *v.t*, gonfler; (*fig*.) enfler; grossir; charger. ~**d** (*fig*.) *p.p*, enflé, ampoulé, boursouflé. **inflation**, *n*, gonflement, *m*; enflure; (*Fin*.) inflation, *f*. *runaway* ~, flambée des prix, *f*.
inflect, *v.t*, infléchir. ~**tion**, *n*, inflexion; flexion, *f*. **inflexible†**, *a*, inflexible.
inflict, *v.t*, infliger. ~**ion**, *n*, infliction, *f*; châtiment, *m*; peine, *f*.
influence, *n*, influence, *f*; crédit, *m*; cote d'amour, *f*. ¶ *v.t*, influer sur; influencer. **influential**, *a*, influent, prestigieux.
influenza, *n*, grippe, *f*.
influx, *n*, venue; invasion, *f*.
inform, *v.t*, informer, instruire, renseigner, faire part, mander, prévenir. ~**al**, *a*, sans cérémonie; officieux; (*law*) informe. ~**ality**, *n*, vice de forme, *m*. ~**ant**, *n*, informateur, trice, auteur, *m*. ~**ation**, *n*, renseignement[s], *m*. [*pl*.], indication[s] *f*.[*pl*.]; (*law*) dénonciation, *f*. ~**er**, *n*, délateur, trice, indicateur, trice.
infraction, *n*, infraction, *f*.
infrequent, *a*, peu fréquent, rare.
infringe, *v.t*, enfreindre, contrevenir à; contrefaire. ~**ment**, *n*, infraction, contravention; contrefaçon, *f*. ~ *of copyright*, contrefaçon littéraire, c. de librairie.
infuriate, *v.t*, faire enrager.
infuse, *v.t*, infuser. **infusible**, *a*, infusible. **infusion**, *n*, infusion; tisane, *f*.
ingenious†, *a*, ingénieux. **ingenuity**, *n*, ingéniosité, industrie, *f*.

ingenuous†, *a*, ingénu, naïf, candide.

inglenook, coin du feu, *m*.

inglorious†, *a*, honteux, ignominieux; obscur.

ingoing, *a*, entrant.

ingot, *n*, lingot, saumon, *m*.

ingrained, *a*, enraciné, invétéré.

ingratiate oneself with, s'insinuer dans les bonnes grâces de.

ingratitude, *n*, ingratitude, *f*.

ingredient, *n*, ingrédient, *m*.

ingress, *n*, entrée, *f*.

ingrowing (*nail*) *a*, incarné.

inhabit, *v.t* habiter. **~able**, *a*, habitable. **~ant**, *n*, habitant, e.

inhale, *v.t*, inhaler, aspirer, respirer, humer.

inherent, *a*, inhérent; propre.

inherit, *v.t. & abs*, hériter, succéder à. **~ance**, *n*, héritage, patrimoine, *m*, succession; (*right*) hérédité, *f*.

inhibit, *v.t*, interdire, réprimer. **~ed**, *a*, (*psychologically*) refoulé. **~ion**, *n*, interdiction, inhibition, *f*.

inhospitable, *a*, inhospitalier.

inhuman†, *a*, inhumain. **~ity**, *n*, inhumanité, *f*.

inimical, *a*, ennemi, hostile.

inimitable, *a*, inimitable.

iniquitous†, *a*, inique. **iniquity**, *n*, iniquité, *f*.

initial, *a*, initial. ¶ *n*, initiale, *f*; (*pl.*) parafe, *m*, initiales, *f.pl*. ¶ *v.t*, parafer, viser.

initiate, *n*, initié, e. ¶ *v.t*, prendre l'initiative de; (*pers.*) initier; entamer, lancer. **initiation**, *n*, initiation, *f*. **initiative**, *n*, initiative, *f*.

inject, *v.t*, injecter; seringuer. **~ion**, *n*, injection, *f*. **~or**, *n*, injecteur, *m*.

injudicious, *a*, peu judicieux.

injunction, *n*, injonction, *f*.

injure, *v.t*, léser; nuire à; offenser; endommager; blesser. ~ *fatally*, blesser à mort. **injurious**†, *a*, nuisible; malfaisant; préjudiciable; injurieux. **injury**, *n*, injure, *f*; préjudice, tort, *m*; lésion, blessure, *f*.

injustice, *n*, injustice, *f*; passe-droit, *m*.

ink, *n*, encre, *f*. ~ *eraser*, gomme pour l'encre, *f*. **~well**, encrier, *m*. ¶ *v.t*, encrer; tacher d'encre. ~ *in*, mettre à l'encre. ~ *up* (*Typ.*), toucher.

inkling, *n*, indication, idée, *f*.

inlaid, *p.a*: ~ *linoleum*, linoléum incrusté, *m*. ~ *work*, incrustation; marqueterie, *f*.

inland, *a*, intérieur. ¶ *ad*, dans l'intérieur [du pays].

inlay, *v.t.ir*, incruster; marqueter.

inlet, *n*, crique; entrée; arrivée, *f*.

inmate, *n*, habitant, e; hôte, esse; (*paying*) pensionnaire, *m,f*; (*asylum*) interné, e; hospitalisé, e.

inmost, *a*, le plus intime.

inn, *n*, auberge, *f*. **~keeper**, aubergiste, *m,f*.

innate, *a*, inné, infus. **~ness**, *n*, innéité, *f*.

inner, *a*, intérieur, interne. ~ *harbor*, arrière-port, *m*. *the* ~ *man*, l'homme intérieur. ~ *tube* (tiré), chambre à air, *f*.

innermost, *a*, le plus intime.

innings, *n*, tour, *m*.

innocence, *n*, innocence, *f*. **innocent**, *a. & n*, innocent, *a. & m*. **~ly**, *ad*, innocemment.

innocuous, *a*, inoffensif.

innovation, *n*, innovation, nouveauté, *f*. **innovator**, *n*, novateur, trice.

innuendo, *n*, insinuation, allusion, *f*.

innumerable, *a*, innombrable.

inobservance, *n*, inobservance, inobservation, *f*.

inoculate, *v.t*, inoculer. **inoculation**, *n*, inoculation, *f*.

inodorous, *a*, inodore.

inoffensive, *a*, inoffensif.

inoperative, *a*, inopérant.

inopportune, *a*, inopportun. **~ly**, *ad*, mal à propos, à contre-temps.

inordinate†, *a*, démesuré.

inorganic, *a*, (*matter*) inorganique; (*body*) brut; (*chemistry*) minérale.

inpatient, *n*, malade interné, e, hospitalisé, e.

input-output, *n*, (*computers*) entrée-sortie, *f*.

inquest, *n*, enquête, *f*.

inquire, *v.t. & i*, demander; s'informer (de); s'enquérir (de); se renseigner; s'adresser; enquêter. **inquirer**, *n*, chercheur, euse; demandeur de renseignements, *m*. *inquiring mind*, [esprit] chercheur, *m*. **inquiry**, *n*, demande, *f*; renseignements, *m.pl*; informations, *f.pl*; recherche; enquête, *f*;

informé, *m.* ~ *office*, bureau de renseignements, *m.*

nquisition, *n*, inquisition, *f.* **inquisitive**, *a*, inquisiteur; curieux.

nroad & inrush, *n*, incursion; irruption, venue, *f.*

nsane, *a*, fou; insensé. **insanity**, *n*, démence, aliénation d'esprit; (*folly*) insanité, *f.*

nsanitary, *a*, insalubre, malsain.

nsatiable†, *a*, insatiable.

nscribe, *v.t*, inscrire; graver; dédier. **inscription**, *n*, inscription; dédicace, *f.*

nscrutable, *a*, inscrutable, impénétrable.

nsect, *n*, insecte, *m.* ~ *powder*, poudre insecticide, *f.* **insectivora**, *n.pl*, insectivores, *m.pl.* **insectivorous**, *a*, insectivore.

nsecure, *a*, mal assuré. **insecurity**, *n*, insécurité, *f.*

nsensate, *a*, insensé. **insensible†**, *a*, insensible; sans connaissance. **insensitive**, *a*, insensible.

nseparable†, *a. & n*, inséparable, *a. & m,f.*

nsert (*Bookb.*) *n*, encart, *m.* ¶ *v.t*, insérer; (*Bookb.*) encarter. **~ion**, *n*, insertion, *f*; intercolage; ajout, *m.*

nset, *n*, pièce rapportée, *f.* ¶ *v.t.ir*, rapporter, encarter.

nshore, *a*, côtier. ~ *fishing*, pêche côtière, pêche dans les eaux territoriales, *f.*

nside, *n*, dedans; intérieur, *m.* ¶ *a*, intérieur; d'i. ¶ *ad*, [en] dedans, à l'intérieur; (*Meas.*) dans œuvre, *m.* ~ *out*, à l'envers.

nsidious†, *a*, insidieux.

nsight, *n*, pénétration, *f*. aperçu, *m.*

nsignia, *n.pl*, insignes, *m.pl.*

nsignificant, *a*, insignifiant, infime.

nsincere, *a*, qui n'est pas sincère; faux; dissimulé. **insincerity**, *n*, absence de sincérité, dissimulation *f.*

nsinuate, *v.t*, insinuer, faufiler.

nsipid, *a*, insipide, fade, fadasse.

nsist, *v.i*, insister. **~ence**, *n*, insistance, *f.*

nsobriety, *n*, intempérance, *f.*

nsolation, *n*, insolation, *f.*

nsolence, *n*, insolence, *f.* **insolent**, *a*, insolent. **~ly**, *ad*, insolemment.

nsoluble, *a*, insoluble.

nsolvency, *n*, insolvabilité, carence, faillite; déconfiture, *f.* **insolvent**, *a*, insolvable. ¶ *n*, failli, *m.*

insomnia, *n*, insomnie[s] *f.[pl.]*.

inspect, *v.t*, inspecter, visiter, contrôler; (*excise*) exercer. **~ion**, *n*, inspection, visite, *f*, contrôle; exercice, *m*; revue; *f.* ~ *committee*, comité de surveillance, *m.* **~or**, *n*, inspecteur, trice; visiteur; contrôleur; (*weights*) vérificateur, *m.* **~orship**, *n*, inspection, *f.*

inspiration, *n*, inspiration; aspiration; illumination, *f*, souffle, *m.* **inspire**, *v.t*, inspirer; aspirer.

inspirit, *v.t*, animer. **~ing**, *a*, entraînant.

instability, *n*, instabilité, *f.*

install, *v.t*, installer, emménager. **~ation**, *n*, installation, *f.*

installment, *n*, acompte, paiement à compte; versement; terme; fascicule, *m.* ~ *plan*, vente à tempérament, *f*; facilités de paiement, *f.pl.*

instance, *n*, cas, *m*; demande; (*law*) instance, *f*. *for* ~, par exemple. ¶ *v.t*, citer. **instant**, *a*, instant; (*month*) courant. ¶ *n*, instant, *m.* **instantaneous**, *a*, instantané. **~ly**, *ad*, instantanément.

instead, *ad*, plutôt. ~ *of*, au lieu de, à la place de, pour.

instep, *n*, cou-de-pied, *m.*

instigate, *v.t*, provoquer, inciter. **instigation**, *n*, instigation, *f.*

instill, *v.t*, instiller; (*fig.*) inculquer, infuser, faire pénétrer.

instinct, *n*, instinct, *m.* ¶ *a*, doué, animé. **~ive†**, *a*, instinctif.

institute, *n*, institut, *m.* ¶ *v.t*, instituer; intenter. **institution**, *n*, institution, *f*; institut, établissement, *m.*

instruct, *v.t*, instruire; charger; (*counsel*) constituer. **~ion**, *n*, instruction, *f*; (*pl.*) instructions, indications, *f.pl*, charge, *f*, mandat, *m.* **~ive**, *a*, instructif. **instructor**, *n*, professeur; (*Mil.*) instructeur; (*Mil. gym.*) moniteur, *m.* **instructress**, *n*, professeur, *m.*

instrument, *n*, instrument; (*law*) instrument, acte, *m.* ~ *board*, tableau de bord, *m.* **~al**, *a*, instrumental. **~alist**, *n*, instrumentiste, *m,f.* **~ality**, *n*, intermédiaire, *m.*

insubordinate, *a*, insubordonné.

insufferable†, *a*, insupportable.
insufficiency, *n*, insuffisance, *f*. **insufficient**, *a*, insuffisant. **~ly**, *ad*, insuffisamment.
insular, *a*, insulaire. **~ity**, *n*, insularité, *f*.
insulate, *v.t*, isoler. **insulation**, *n*, isolement, *m*. **insulator**, *n*, isolateur, *m*.
insult, *n*, insulte, injure, *f*, outrage, *m*. ¶ *v.t*, insulter, outrager. **~ing**†, *a*, injurieux, offensant, outrageant, outrageux.
insuperable, *a*, insurmontable.
insupportable†, *a*, insupportable.
insurance, *n*, assurance, *f*; (*mail*) chargement, *m*. ~ *company*, compagnie d'assurance[s] *f*. **insure**, *v.t*, assurer, faire a.; (*mail*) charger; (*v.i.*) s'assurer, se faire assurer. **~d** (*pers.*) *n*, assuré, e. ~*d package*, colis avec valeur déclarée, colis chargé, *m*. **insurer**, *n*, assureur, *m*.
insurgent, *n. & a*, insurgé, e, révolté, e.
insurmountable, *a*, insurmontable.
insurrection, *n*, insurrection, *f*.
intact, *a*, intact.
intaglio, *n*, intaille, *f*.
intake, *n*, prise, admission, *f*, appel, *m*.
intangible, *a*, intangible.
integer, *n*, [nombre] entier, *m*. **integral**†, *a*, intégral. **integrate**, *v.t*, intégrer. **integrity**, *n*, intégrité, *f*.
intellect, *n*, intellect, *m*, intelligence, *f*, cerveau, *m*. **intellectual**†, *a. & n*, intellectuel, *a. & m*.
intelligence, *n*, intelligence, *f*, entendement, *m*; nouvelles, *f.pl*; chronique, *f*, courrier, *m*. ~ *department*, service des renseignements, *m*, statistique militaire, *f*. **intelligent**, *a*, intelligent. **~ly**, *ad*, intelligemment. **intelligible**†, *a*, intelligible.
intemperance, *n*, intempérance, *f*. **intemperate**, *a*, intempérant.
intend, *v.t*, se proposer, avoir l'intention, compter; vouloir; destiner. **~ed**, *n*, prétendu, e, futur, e.
intense, *a*, intense. **~ly**, *ad*, extrêmement. **intensifier** (*Phot.*) *n*, renforçateur, *m*. **intensify**, *v.t*, intensifier; (*Phot.*) renforcer. **intensity**, *n*, intensité, *f*.

intent, *a*, fixe. ~ *on*, tout entier à. ¶ *n*, intention, *f*, but, *m*. *to all* ~*s & purposes*, virtuellement. **~ion**, *n*, intention, *f*, but; motif, *m*. **~ional**†, *a*, intentionnel, voulu. **-intentioned**, *a*, intentionné. **intentness**, *n*, contention, *f*.
inter, *v.t*, enterrer, inhumer.
intercalate, *v.t*, intercaler.
intercede, *v.i*, intercéder.
intercept, *v.t*, intercepter, surprendre.
intercession, *n*, intercession, *f*. **intercessor**, *n*, intercesseur, *m*.
interchange, *n*, communication, *f*, échange, *m*. **~able**, *a*, interchangeable.
intercom, *n*, interphone, *m*.
intercourse, *n*, commerce, *m*; relations, *f.pl*; rapports, *m.pl*.
interdict, *v.t*, interdire. ¶ *v.t*, interdire. **~ion**, *n*, interdiction, *f*.
interest, *n*, intérêt, *m*; intérêts, *m.pl*; arrérages, *m.pl*; usure; commandite, *f*. *to take no further* ~ *in*, se désintéresser de. ~ *on overdue payments*, intérêts moratoires. ~ *payable* (date), jouissance. ¶ *v.t*, intéresser. **~ed**, *p.a*, intéressé; curieux. ~ *party*, intéressé, e. **~ing**, *p.a*, intéressant; attachant. *in an* ~ *condition* (pregnant), dans une situation intéressante.
interfere, *v.i*, intervenir, s'immiscer, s'ingérer. ~ *with* (hinder), contrarier, gêner. **interference**, *n*, intervention, immixtion, ingérence; (*Phys.*) interférence, *f*; (*radio*) brouillage, *m*.
interim, *n*, intérim, *m*. ~ *dividend*, acompte de dividende, dividende intérimaire, dividende provisoire, *m*.
interior†, *a. & n*, intérieur, *a. & m*.
interject, *v.t*, placer. **~ion**, *n*, interjection, *f*.
interlace, *v.t*, entrelacer.
interlard, *v.t*, entrelarder.
interleave, *v.t*, interfolier.
interline, *v.t*, écrire dans l' (*ou* en.) interligne. **interlinear**, *a*, interlinéaire. **interlineation**, *n*, entre-ligne, *m*.
interlock, *v.i*, s'engrener, s'entrelacer.

interlocutor, tress or trix, *n*, interlocuteur, trice.

interloper, *n*, intrus, e.

interlude, *n*, intervalle, intermède; (*Mus.*) interlude, *m*.

intermarriage, *n*, mariage entre individus de tribus diverses (*ou* de races différentes), *m*, alliance, *f*. **intermarry**, *v.i*, se marier entre eux, s'allier.

intermeddle, *v.i*, se mêler, s'immiscer.

intermediary, *n. & a*, intermédiaire, *m. & a*. **intermediate**, *a*, intermédiaire. ~ *course*, (*Sch.*), cours moyen, *m*.

interment, *n*, enterrement, *m*, inhumation, *f*.

intermezzo, *n*, intermède, *m*.

interminable, *a*, interminable.

intermingle, *v.t*, entremêler.

intermission, *n*, (*Theat.*) entracte; relâche, intermédiaire, *m*. **intermittent**, *a*, intermittent.

intermix, *v.t*, entremêler.

intern, *v.t*, interner. ¶ *n*, interne, *m*.

internal, *a*, interne; intérieur; intestin. ~**ly**, *ad*, intérieurement.

international, *a*, international. ~**ist**, *n. & a*, internationaliste, *m,f. & a*.

internecine, *a*, meurtrier, à outrance.

internment, *n*, internement, *m*. ~ *camp*, (*civil*) camp de concentration; (*Mil.*) camp de prisonniers, *m*.

interplanetary, *a*, interplanétaire.

interpolate, *v.t*, interpoler.

interpose, *v.t*, interposer; (*v.i.*) s'interposer.

interpret, *v.t*, interpréter; traduire. ~**ation**, *n*, interprétation, *f*. ~**er**, *n*, interprète, *m,f*.

interregnum, *n*, interrègne, *m*.

interrogate, *v.t*, interroger. **interrogation**, *n*, interrogation, *f*. **interrogative**†, *a*, interrogatif. **interrogatory**, *n*, interrogatoire, *m*.

interrupt, *v.t*, interrompre; couper. ~**er**, *n*, (*pers.*) interrupteur, trice; (*Elec.*) rupteur, *m*. **interruption**, *n*, interruption, *f*.

intersect, *v.t*, couper; entrecouper. ~**ion**, *n*, intersection, *f*.

intersperse, *v.t*, entremêler; émailler.

interstice, *n*, interstice, *m*.

intertwine, *v.t*, entrelacer.

interval, *n*, intervalle, entretemps, *m*.

intervene, *v.i*, intervenir. **intervention**, *n*, intervention, *f*.

interview, *n*, entretien, *m*, entrevue, *f*; (*for news*) interview, *m*. ¶ *v.t*, interviewer.

interweave, *v.t.ir*, entrelacer. *interwoven pattern* (fabrics), brochure, *f*.

intestate, *a*, intestat (*inv.*).

intestinal, *a*, intestinal. **intestine**, *a. & n*, intestin, *a. & m*.

intimacy, *n*, intimité, familiarité, *f*. **intimate**†, *a. & n*, intime, *a. & m*, lié, *a*, familier, *a. & m*. ¶ *v.t*, faire entendre, signifier. **intimation**, *n*; indication, premonition, *f*.

intimidate, *v.t*, intimider.

into, *pr*, dans; en; à; entre; par; par-dessus.

intolerable†, *a*, intolérable. **intolerance**, *n*, intolérance, *f*. **intolerant**, *a*, intolérant.

intonation, *n*, intonation, *f*. **intonate**, **intone**, *v.t*, entonner.

intoxicate, *v.t*, enivrer. ~**d**, *a*, ivre, enivré. **intoxication**, *n*, ivresse, *f*.

intractable, *a*, intraitable, indocile.

intransitive†, *a*, intransitif.

intrench, *v.t*, retrancher.

intrepid†, *a*, intrépide. ~**ity**, *n*, intrépidité, *f*.

intricacy, *n*, complication; *f*; embrouillement, *m*. **intricate**, *a*, compliqué, embrouillé.

intrigue, *n*, intrigue, brigue, *f*. ¶ *v.i*, intriguer, briguer, cabaler; (*v.t.*) intriguer. **intriguer**, *n. &* **intriguing**, *a*, intrigant, e.

intrinsic†, *a*, intrinsèque.

introduce, *v.t*, introduire; insinuer; présenter. ~ *into society*, produire dans le monde. ~ *oneself*, se présenter, se faire connaître. **introducer**, *n*, introducteur, trice. **introduction**, *n*, introduction; présentation, *f*.

introit, *n*, introït, *m*.

introspection, *n*, introspection, *f*.

intrude, *v.i*, s'introduire [contre le droit *ou* la forme], se faufiler. **intruder**, *n*, intrus, e, importun, e. **intrusion**, *n*, intrusion, *f*.

intuition, *n*, intuition, *f*. **intuitive**, *a*, intuitif. ~**ly**, *ad*, par intuition.

inundate, *v.t*, inonder. **inundation**, *n*, inondation, *f*.

inure, *v.t*, aguerrir, accoutumer; habituer.

invade, *v.t*, envahir. **invader**, *n*, envahisseur, *m*.

invalid, *a*, malade, infirme, invalide; (*law*) invalide; non valable. ¶ *n*, malade, infirme, *m,f*, invalide, *m*. ¶ *v.t*, réformer. ~**ate**, *v.t*, invalider, casser. **invalided**, *p.a*, invalide, réformé. **invalidity**, *n*, invalidité, *f*.

invaluable, *a*, inestimable, impayable.

invariable†, *a*, invariable.

invasion, *n*, invasion, *f*, envahissement, *m*.

invective, *n*, invective, *f*. **inveigh**, *v.i*, invectiver, tonner.

inveigle, *v.t*, enjôler.

invent, *v.t*, inventer, imaginer. ~**ion**, *n*, invention, *f*. ~**ive**, *a*, inventif, original. **inventor**, **tress**, *n*, inventeur, trice, *m*.

inventory, *n*, inventaire, *m*, description, *f*. ¶ *v.t*, inventorier.

inverse†, *a*, inverse, réciproque. **inversion**, *n*, inversion, *f*; renversement, *m*. **invert**, *v.t*, renverser; invertir.

invertebrate, *a. & n*, invertébré, *a. & m*.

invest, *v.t*, revêtir; investir; cerner; (*money*) placer, investir.

investigate, *v.t*, rechercher, examiner. **investigation**, *n*, investigation, enquête, *f*. **investigator**, *n*, investigateur, trice.

investiture, *n*, investiture, *f*.

investment, *n*, placement, *m*; valeur, *f*; portefeuille, *m*; mise [de fonds] *f*; (*Mil.*) investissement, *m*. **investor**, *n*, personne qui place ses fonds, *f*.

inveterate, *a*, invétéré, acharné, vivace.

invidious, *a*, méchant; odieux. ~ **distinction**, distinction contre le droit & l'usage ordinaire, *f*, passe-droit, *m*.

invigorate, *v.t*, fortifier, vivifier.

invincible†, *a*, invincible.

inviolable†, *a*, inviolable. **inviolate**, *a*, inviolé.

invisible†, *a*, invisible. ~ **mending**, reprise perdue, *f*, stoppage, *m*.

invitation, *n*, invitation, *f*; appel, *m*. **invite**, *v.t*, inviter, prier;

convier; appeler, faire appel à. **inviting**, *p.a*, engageant.

invocation, *n*, invocation, *f*.

invoice, *n*, facture, *f*. ¶ *v.t*, facturer.

invoke, *v.t*, invoquer.

involuntary†, *a*, involontaire.

involve, *v.t*, envelopper; entraîner; impliquer; empêtrer. ~**d**, *p.a*, compliqué, embrouillé. ~ **language**, tortillage, *m*.

invulnerable, *a*, invulnérable.

inward, *a*, intérieur; interne; intime; d'entrée. ~ **bound**, en retour; effectuant son voyage de retour. ~[**s**] & ~**ly**, *ad*, intérieurement, en dedans. ~**s**, *n.pl*, entrailles, *f.pl*.

iodine, *n*, iode, *m*.

ion, *n*, ion, *m*.

Ionian, **Ionic**, *a*, ionien, ionique.

iota, *n*, iota, *m*.

ipecac, *n*, ipéca, *m*.

irascible, *a*, irascible. **irate**, *a*, irrité, en colère. **ire**, *n*, courroux, *m*.

Iraq, *n*, Irak, *m*.

Iraqi, *n*, Irakien, enne.

Ireland, *n*, l'Irlande, *f*.

iridescence, *n*, irisation, *f*. **iridescent**, *a*, irisé, chatoyant.

iridium, *n*, iridium, *m*.

iris, *n*, iris, *m*.

Irish, *a*, irlandais. ~**man**, ~**woman**, Irlandais, e. ~ **Sea**, mer d'Irlande, *f*. ¶ (*language*) *n*, l'irlandais, *m*.

irksome, *a*, ennuyeux, fastidieux.

iron, *n*, (*metal for linen, golf, etc.*) fer, *m*; (*cast, pig*) fonte; (*sheet*) tôle, *f*. ¶ *a*, en fer, de fer; en (*ou* de) fonte. ~ **constructional work**, charpente métallique, *f*. ~ [*or* *steel*] **bridge**, pont métallique, *m*. ~ & **steel shares**, valeurs sidérurgiques, v—s du groupe forges & fonderies, *f.pl*. ~**clad**, [navire] cuirassé, *m*. ~ **constitution**, santé de fer, *f*. ~**master**, maître de forges, *m*. ~**monger**, (*small*) quincaillier; (*big*) ferronnier; (*builders*') serrurier, *m*. ~**mongery**, quincaillerie; ferronnerie; serrurerie, *f*. **scrap** ~, ferraille, *f*. ~**shod**, ferré. ~**work**, ferrement, *m*; ferrure; serrurerie; (*girders*, *etc.*) charpente en fer, *f*. ~**worker**, ferronnier; serrurier; charpentier en fer, *m.* ~*works*, ferronnerie, *f*; forge[s] *f*.[*pl*.]; usine sidérurgique, *f*. *wrought* ~, fer forgé, *m*. ¶ *v.t*, ferrer; (*linen*) repasser. ~ *out*, défroncer, déplisser. ~er, *n*, repasseuse, *f*. ~ing, *n*, repassage, *m*.

ironic(al)†, *a*, ironique. **irony**, *n*, ironie, *f*.

irradiation, *n*, irradiation, *f*.

irrational, *a*, irrationnel, irraisonnable.

irreclaimable†, *a*, (*pers*.) incorrigible; (*land*) indéfrichable.

irreconcilable, *a*, irréconciliable; inconciliable.

irrecoverable, *a*, irrécouvrable. ~ *arrears* (taxes), non-valeurs, *f.pl*.

irredeemable, *a*, irrachetable.

irredentism, *n*, irrédentisme, *m*.

irreducible, *a*, irréductible.

irrefutable†, *a*, irréfutable.

irregular†, *a*, irrégulier; saccadé. ~ity, *n*, irrégularité, *f*; déréglement, *m*.

irrelevant, *a*, hors de propos, non pertinent, étranger; (*law*) impertinent.

irreligious†, *a*, irréligieux, indévot.

irremediable†, *a*, irrémédiable.

irremovable, *a*, inamovible: immuable.

irreparable†, *a*, irréparable.

irrepressible, *a*, irrépressible; (*laughter*) inextinguible.

irreproachable†, *a*, irréprochable.

irresistible†, *a*, irrésistible.

irresolute, *a*, irrésolu.

irrespective of, indépendamment de, sans égard à.

irresponsible, *a*, irresponsable, inconscient.

irretrievable†, *a*, irréparable.

irreverent, *a*, irrévérent.

irrevocable†, *a*, irrévocable.

irrigate, *v.t*, irriguer. **irrigation**, *n*, irrigation, *f*. **irrigator**, *n*, irrigateur, *m*.

irritable, *a*, irritable. **irritate**, *v.t*, irriter; agacer. **irritation**, *n*, irritation, *f*; agacement, *m*.

irruption, *n*, irruption, *f*.

isinglass, *n*, colle de poisson, *f*.

Islam, *n*, Islam, *m*.

island, *n*, île, *f*; (*houses*) îlot, *m*. ~er, *n*, insulaire, *m.f*. **isle**, *n*, île, *f*. **islet**, *n*, îlot, *m*.

isolate, *v.t*, isoler. **isolation**, *n*, isolement, *m*. ~ *hospital*, hôpital de contagieux, *m*.

Israeli, *a.* & *n*, Israélien, ienne. **Israelite**, *n*, israélite, *m.f*.

issue, *n*, issue, *f*; événement, *m*; distribution; délivrance; sortie, *f*; succès, *m*; (*money*) émission; impression; publication, *f*; (*newspaper*) numéro, *m*; lignée, postérité; (*law*) question, *f*. ¶ *v.i*, sortir; découler; émaner; (*v.t*.) lancer; émettre; publier; distribuer; délivrer.

isthmus, *n*, isthme, *m*.

it, *pn*, il, elle; le, la; lui, elle; ce, c', ç'; cela; y. ~ *is said that* . . ., on dit que . . . *about* ~, en; y. *at* ~, y. *by* ~, y; en. *for* ~, en; *from* ~, en. *of* ~, en; y. *to* ~, y; lui.

Italian, *a*, italien. ¶ *n*, (*pers*.) Italien, ne; (*language*) l'italien, *m*.

italic, *a.* & ~s, *n.pl*, italique, *a.* & *m*.

Italy, *n*, l'Italie, *f*.

itch, *v.i*, démanger. *my arm itches*, le bras me démange. *I am* ~*ing to*, j'ai grande envie de. ~[ing], *n*, démangeaison, *f*, prurit, *m*, gale, *f*. ~y, *a*, galeux.

item, *n*, article, poste, chapitre, *m*. ¶ *ad*, item.

itinerant, *a*, ambulant. **itinerary**, *n*, itinéraire, *m*.

its, *pn*, son, sa, ses; en.

itself, *pn*, lui[-même], elle[-même], soi[-même]; même; se.

ivory, *n*, ivoire, *m*. *the I~ Coast*, la Côte d'Ivoire.

ivy, *n*, lierre, *m*. *poison* ~, sumac vénéneux, *m*.

J

jab, *v.t*, piquer. ¶ *n*, (*Box*.) coup sec; coup de canif, *m*.

jabber, *v.i*. & *t*, jaboter, bredouiller, jargonner.

jacinth, *n*, jacinthe, *f*.

jack, *n*, (*Mach*.) vérin; (*auto*) cric, *m*; chèvre, *f*; (*spit*) tourne-broche; (*fish*) brochet; (*cards*) valet, *m*. ~*ass*, âne, baudet, *m*. ~*boots*, bottes à genouillère, *f.pl*. ~*daw*, choucas, *m*. ~*-in-the-box*, boîte à surprise, *f*. ~ *knife*, couteau à virole, c. à cran d'arrêt,

m. J~ *of all trades* or *work,*
homme à tout faire, maître Jacques, *m. before you could say*
J~ *Robinson,* crac!; en moins
d'un instant.

jackal, *n,* chacal, *m.*

jackanapes, *n,* fat, *m.*

jackass, *n,* (*animal*) âne; (*person*) sot, *m.*

jacket, *n,* (*lounge*) veston, *m;*
(*short*) veste, *f;* (*cardigan*) gilet;
(*book*) couvre-livre, *m;* (*steam,
water*) chemise, *f.*

jacobin, *n,* jacobin, *m.*

jade, *n,* (*horse*) rosse, haridelle;
(*woman*) coquine, *f;* (*Miner.*)
jade, *m.* ~d, *p.p,* surmené.

jag, *v.t,* ébrécher, denteler, déchiqueter. **jagged,** *a,* dentelé.

jaguar, *n,* jaguar, *m.*

jail, *n,* prison, geôle, *f;* ~*bird,*
cheval de retour, *m.* ~**er,** *n,*
geôlier, *m.*

jalopy, *n,* bagnole, *f,* tacot, *m.*

jam, *n,* (*fruit*) confiture, *f.* oft. *pl;*
(*squeeze*) coincement; (*traffic*)
embouteillage; (*radio*) brouillage,
m. ~ *pot,* pot à confitures, *m.*
¶ *v.t,* coincer. ~**mer,** *n,* (*radio*)
brouilleur, *m.*

Jamaica, *n,* la Jamaïque.

jamb, *n,* jambage, *m.*

jangle, *n,* ébranlement, *m.* ¶ *v.t,*
ébranler.

janitor, *n,* concierge, *m.*

January, *n,* janvier, *m.*

japan, *n,* laque [de Chine], vernis
[japonais] *m.* ¶ *v.t,* laquer, vernir. **Japan,** *n,* le Japon. **Japanese,** *a,* japonais. ~ *curio,* japonerie, *f.* ~ *paper* & ~ *porcelain,*
Japon, *m.* ¶ *n,* (*pers.*) Japonais,
e; (*language*) le japonais.

jar, *n,* secousse, *f,* battement; pot,
m, jarre, bouteille, *f,* bocal, *m.*
¶ *v.i,* détoner, jurer; (*shake*) secouer. ~ *upon,* agacer.

jardinière, *n,* (*stand*) jardinière,
f; (*pot*) cachepot, *m.*

jargon, *n,* jargon, baragouin,
patois, *m.*

jarring, *a,* discordant.

jasmine, *n,* jasmin, *m.*

jasper, *n,* jaspe, *m.*

jaundice, *n,* jaunisse, *f,* ictère, *m.*

jaunt, *n,* course, promenade, *f.*
~**y†,** *a,* insoucieux, crâne.

Java, *n,* Java, *m.* **Javanese,** *a,*
javanais. ¶ *n,* Javanais, e.

javelin, *n,* javelot, *m.*

jaw, *n,* mâchoire; mandibule, *f;*
mors, bec, *m;* (*pl, of death*) bras,
m.pl. ~ *bone,* [os] maxillaire, *m.*

jay (*bird*) *n,* geai, *m.*

jealous†, *a,* jaloux. ~**y,** *n,* jalousie, *f.*

jeer, *n,* risée, moquerie, *f.* ¶ *v.i,*
goguenarder. ~ *at,* insulter à, se
moquer de; (*pers.*) railler, se
moquer de, dauber [sur].

jejune, *a,* maigre; exigu.

jelly, *n,* gelée, *f. to* (or *in*) *a* ~
(as face by blow), en marmelade,
en compote. ~*fish,* méduse, *f.*

jeopardize, *v.t,* mettre en danger.

jeopardy, *n,* danger, *m.*

jerboa, *n,* gerboise, *f.*

jeremiad, *n,* jérémiade, *f.*

jerk, *n,* à-coup, *m,* saccade, secousse, *f.* ¶ *v.t,* donner un à-
coup, des secousses, à. ~**y,** *a,*
saccadé.

jerry-build, *v.t,* bousiller. ~**er,**
n, bousilleur, *m.* ~**ing,** *n,* bâtisse,
f. **jerry-built,** *a,* de carton, fait
de boue & de crachat. **jerry-
work,** *n,* bousillage, *m.*

jersey, *n,* maillot; jersey, *m.* **Jersey**
(*Geog.*), *n,* Jersey, *f.* J~ *cow,*
vache jersiaise, *f.*

Jerusalem, *n,* Jérusalem, *f.*

jest, *n,* plaisanterie, *f.* ¶ *v.i,* plaisanter, badiner. ~**er,** *n,* plaisant,
m, bouffon, ne; (*court*) fou, *m.*

Jesuit, *n,* jésuite, *m.* ~**ical,** *a,*
jésuitique.

Jesus, *n,* Jésus, *m. Jesus Christ,*
Jésus-Christ, *m.*

jet, *n,* jet; bec; (*lignite*) jais; avion
à réaction, *m.* ~[-*black*], noir
comme [du] jais. ~ *stream,* cou-
rant-jet, *m.* ¶ *v.t,* jeter.

jetsam, *n,* épaves [rejetées] *f.pl.*
jettison, *n,* jet [à la mer] *m.* ¶ *v.t,*
jeter [à la mer].

jetty, *n,* jetée, estacade, *f.*

Jew, *n,* juif, israélite, *m;* (*woman*)
juive, *f.* ~*'s harp,* guimbarde, *f.*
~**ish,** *a,* juif, israélite.

jewel, *n,* bijou, joyau; (*Horol.*)
rubis, *m.* ~ *case,* ecrin [à bijoux]
m. **jeweler,** *n,* bijoutier, ère, joaillier, ère. **jewelry,** *n,* bijouterie,
joaillerie, *f.*

jib, *n,* (*sail*) foc, *m;* (*crane*) volée,
flèche, *f.* ¶ *v.i,* regimber, se cabrer, s'acculer.

jiffy, *n,* tour de main, instant, *m.*

jig, *n,* (*Mus., dance*) gigue, *f.*
~*saw,* sauteuse, scie à chantour-

ner, *f.* ~*saw puzzle*, jeu de patience, *m.*

jiggle, *v.t. & i*, sautiller, gigoter.

jilt, *v.t.* délaisser, lâcher.

jingle, *n*, tintement; cliquetis, *m.* ¶*v.i. & t*, tinter.

jingoism, *n*, chauvinisme, *m.*

job, *n*, tâche; besogne; *f*; travail; emploi, *m*; affaire, *f.* ~ *lot*, marchandises d'occasion, *f.pl*, solde, *m.*

jockey (*turf*) *n*, jockey, *m.* J~ *Club*, Jockey-Club, *m.*

jocose, *a*, badin.

jocular, *a*, enjoué, facétieux, plaisant. ~*ly*, *ad*, en plaisantant.

jocund, *a*, joyeux.

jog, *v.t*, secouer, pousser. ~ *along*, aller son chemin. ~ *on*, aller cahin-caha. ~ *trot*, petit trot; (*fig.*) train-train, *m.*

joggle, *n*, secousse, *f*; (*Carp.*) embrèvement; goujon, *m.* ¶*v.t*, embrever.

John Dory, *n*, dorée, *f.*

join, *v.t*, joindre; assembler; [ré]unir; raccorder; rabouter, raboutir; relier; rejoindre. ~ *in*, faire chorus. ~*er*, *n*, menuisier, *m.* **joint**, *n*, joint, *m*; jointure; articulation, *f*; assemblage; (*fishing rod*) brin, *m*; (*meat*) pièce, *f.* to *put out of* ~, démettre, disloquer. ~ *owners, tenants*, copropriétaires, *m.pl.* ¶*v.t*, articuler; assembler. ¶†, *a*, conjoint; indivis; co-; (*commission*) mixte. ~ *manager*, codirecteur, cogérant, *m.* ~-*stock company*, société par actions, *f.*

joist, *n*, solive, *f*; soliveau, *m*; poutrelle; lambourde, *f.*

joke, *n*, plaisanterie, facétie, *f*, mot pour rire, *m*; (le) comique de l'histoire. ¶*v.i*, plaisanter, rire, railler. **joker**, *n*, farceur, euse, plaisant, *m.*

jollification & jollity, *n*, jubilation, noce, gaillardise, gaieté, *f.* **jolly**†, *a*, gaillard, jovial, gai.

jolt, *n*, cahot, *m.* ¶*v.i. & t*, cahoter.

Jonah (*fig.*) *n*, porte-malheur, *m.*

jonquil, *n*, jonquille, *f.*

Jordan (*river*) *n*, le Jourdain, *m*; (*country*) la Jordanie, *f.*

jostle, *v.t*, coudoyer, bousculer.

jot, *n*, iota, *m.* ~ *down*, tenir note (*ou* registre) de.

journal, *n*, journal; livre; (*shaft*) tourillon, *m*; (*axle*) fusée, *f.* ~*ism*, *n*, journalisme, *m.* ~*ist*, *n*, journaliste, *m.*

journey, *n*, voyage, *m*; marche; route, *f*; trajet; parcours, *m.* on *the* ~, en route. to *take a* ~, faire un voyage.

joust, *n*, joute, *f.* ¶*v.i*, jouter.

jovial†, *a*, jovial, réjoui. ~*ity*, *n*, jovialité, *f.*

jowl, *n*, joue; (*fish*) hure, *f.*

joy, *n*, joie, *f.* ~*ful*† & ~*ous*†, *a*, joyeux. ~*fulness*, *n*, allégresse, *f.*

jubilation, *n*, jubilation, *f.*

jubilee, *n*, jubilé, *m.* ~ *year*, année jubilaire, *f.*

Judaic, *a*, judaïque.

judo, *n*, judo, *m.*

judge, *n*, juge; magistrat; arbitre, *m.* ¶*v.t. & i*, juger. **judgment**, *n*, jugement; arrêt; avis; sens; coup d'œil, *m.* **Judges** (*Bible*) *n.pl*, les Juges, *m.pl.*

judicature, *n*, justice, *f.* **judicial**†, *a*, judiciaire.

judicious†, *a*, judicieux, sage, sensé.

jug, *n*, cruche, *f*, broc, pot, *m*; carafe, *f.* ~*ful*, *n*, potée, *f.*

juggle, *v.i*, jongler; escamoter. ~ & ~*ry*, *n*, tour de passepasse, *m*, jonglerie, *f*; escamotage, *m.* **juggler**, *n*, jongleur; escamoteur, *m.*

jugular [**vein**], *n*, [veine] jugulaire, *f.*

juice, *n*, jus; suc, *m.* **juicy**, *a*, juteux; succulent; fondant.

ju-jitsu, *n*, jiu-jitsu, *m.*

jujube, *n*, jujube, *m*; pastille, *f.* ~ [*shrub*], jujubier, *m.*

julep, *n*, julep, *m.*

July, *n*, juillet, *m.*

jumble, *n*, pêle-mêle, fouillis, fatras, *m*, salade, *f.* ~ *sale*, vente au déballage, *f.* ~ *shop*, capharnaüm, *m.* ¶*v.t*, brouiller; jeter pêle-mêle.

jump, *n*, saut; sursaut; haut-le-corps, *m.* ¶*v.i. & t*, sauter; se jeter. ~ *over*, sauter, franchir. ~*er*, *n*, (*pers.*) sauteur, euse; (*sailor's*) vareuse; (*woman's*) casaque, *f.* ~*ing*: ~ *jack*, pantin, *m.* ~-*off ground* (*fig.*), tremplin, *m.* ~ *skis*, skis de saut, *m.pl.*

junction, *n*, jonction; (*Rly line, etc.*) bifurcation, *f*, embranchement, *m*; (*Rly station*) gare de bifurcation, gare d'embranchement, *f.* **juncture,** *n,* jonction; occurrence, *f.*

June, *a,* juin, *m.*

jungle, *n,* jungle, *f.*

junior, *a,* cadet; (*partner*) second, dernier; (*clerk*) petit. ¶ *n,* cadet, te; [le] jeune; (*son*) fils; (*sports*) junior, *m.* ~ *event,* épreuve pour juniors, *f.*

juniper, *n,* (*genus*) genévrier; (*common*) genièvre, *m.*

junk, *n,* (*Chinese*) jonque; (*tow*) étoupe, *f.*; (*refuse*) rebut, *m.* ¶ *v.t,* mettre au rebut.

junket, *v.i,* faire bombance.

juridical†, *a,* juridique. **jurisdiction,** *n,* juridiction; compétence, *f.* **jurist,** *n,* juriste, jurisconsulte, *m.*

juror, juryman, *n,* juré, *m.* **jury,** *n,* jury, *m.*

just, *a,* juste; équitable. ¶ *ad,* juste; justement; ne . . . que; tout. ~ *as,* de même que. ~ *out,* vient de paraître. *I have ~ . . ,* je viens de . . . ~**ice,** *n,* justice, *f*; (*as to a meal*) honneur; (*pers.*) juge, *m.*

justifiable, *a,* justifiable; (*homicide*) excusable. **justification,** *n,* justification, *f*; gain de cause, *m.* **justify,** *v.t,* justifier; motiver.

justly, *ad,* justement, équitablement. **justness,** *n,* justice, *f.*

jut [out], *v.i,* faire saillie, [s']-avancer.

jute, *n,* jute, *m.*

juvenile, *a,* juvénile; jeune; (*books*) pour la jeunesse. ¶ *n,* jeune personne, *f.*

juxtapose, *v.t,* juxtaposer.

K

kale, *n,* chou frisé, *m.*

kaleidoscope, *n,* kaléidoscope, *m.*

kangaroo, *n,* kangourou, *m.*

kedge [anchor], *n,* ancre à jet, *f.*

keel, *n,* quille, *f.* **keelson,** *n,* carlingue, *f.*

keen, *a,* acéré; tranchant; vif; fin; mordant; (*sportsman, etc.*) ardent, déterminé. *a ~ disappointment,* un crève-cœur. ~**ly,** *ad,* vivement, ~**ness,** *n,* acuité, finesse, *f*; mordant; flair, *m.*

keep, *n,* entretien; (*castle*) donjon, *m.* ¶ *v.t.ir,* tenir; maintenir; garder; retenir; ménager; entretenir;

hanter; nourrir; conserver; garantir; préserver; avoir; faire; observer; (*v.i.ir.*) se tenir; se conserver; rester. ~ *a saint's day,* chômer une fête. ~ *away,* s'absenter. ~ *back,* retenir. ~ *from,* s'abstenir de; empêcher de. ~ *in* (*Sch.*) mettre en retenue. ~ *off,* s'éloigner; au large! [*please*] ~ *off the grass,* ne marchez pas sur les pelouses, défense de circuler sur l'herbe. ~ [*on*], continuer. ~ *one's hand in,* s'entretenir la main. ~ *oneself to,* se cantonner dans. ~**er,** *n,* garde, *m*; gardien, ne; concierge, *m,f*; conservateur, *m.* ~**ing,** *n,* garde; conservation; tenue, *f.* *in* ~ *with,* en harmonie avec, à l'avenant de.

keepsake, *n,* souvenir, *m.*

keg, *n,* caque, *f*; baril[let], tonnelet, *m.*

ken, *n,* connaissance, *f.*

kennel, *n,* niche, cabane, *f*; (*hounds*) chenil, *m.*

Kenya, *n,* Kénia, *m.*

kerchief, *n,* fichu, carré, foulard, *m.*

kernel, *n,* (*of nut, stone-fruit, seed*) amande, *f*; (*nucleus*) noyau, *m*; (*gist*) substance, *f.*

kerosene, *n,* pétrole à brûler, p. lampant, *m,* huile de pétrole, *f.*

kestrel, *n,* crécerelle, *f,* émouchet, *m.*

ketch, *n,* quaiche, *f.*

kettle, *n,* bouilloire, bouillotte, *f,* coquemar, *m.* ~**drum,** timbale, *f.* ~**drummer,** timbalier, *m.*

key, *n,* clef, clé, *f*; (*winder*) remontoir, *m*; (*piano*) touche, *f*; (*to school book*) corrigé; (*Mus.*) ton, *m*; (*Mech.*) clavette; cale, *f*; coin, *m.* ~**board,** clavier, *m.* ~ *chain,* châtelaine, *f.* ~**hole,** trou de serrure, *m.* ~**hole saw,** scie à guichet, *f.* ~ *industry,* industrie-clef, *f.* ~ *money,* denier à Dieu, *m*; reprise, *f.* ~ *note,* [note] tonique, *f*; (*fig.*) mot d'ordre, *m.* ~ *ring,* [anneau] porte-clefs, *m.* ~ *signature* (*Mus.*), armature, *f.* ~**stone,** clef de voûte, *f.* ¶ *v.t,* caler; coincer; harmoniser. ~**ed,** *p.a,* à clef.

khaki, *n,* kaki, *m.*

Khedive, *n,* khédive, *m.*

kick, *n,* coup de pied, *m*; (*horse*) ruade, *f*; (*gun*) recul, *m.* ~**off**

(*Foot.*), coup [de pied] d'envoi, *m.* ¶ *v.t,* donner un coup (des coups) de pied à; (*a goal*) marquer; (*v.i.*) (*horse*) ruer, regimber; (*gun*) reculer. ~ *about,* gigoter. ~ *at* (*fig.*), regimber contre. ~er, *n,* rueur, euse.

kid, *n,* chevreau, *m,* chevrette, *f,* cabri; (*child*) gosse, *m.* ~ *gloves,* gants de [peau de] chevreau, g—s de chevrotin, *m.pl.*

kidnap, *v.t,* enlever, kidnapper. **kidnapper,** *n,* kidnappeur, *m.* **kidnapping,** *n,* rapt, kidnapping, *m.*

kidney, *n, (Anat.)* rein; (*meat*) rognon; (*fig.*) acabit, *m,* trempe, *f.* ~ *bean,* haricot, *m.*

kill, *n,* chasse, *f;* abattis, *m.* ¶ *v.t,* tuer, assassiner; abattre. *to nearly* ~, assommer. *killed in action,* tué à l'ennemi. *the killed,* les tués, *m.pl.* ~*joy,* rabat-joie, trouble-fête, *m.* ~er, *n,* tueur, *m.* ~ing, *n,* tuerie, *f;* abattage, *m.* ¶ *a,* tuant, assommant.

kiln, *n,* four, *m.* ~*-dry,* sécher au four.

kilogram, *n,* kilogramme, *m.*
kilometric(al), *a,* kilométrique.
kilowatt, *n,* kilowatt, *m.*
kilt, *v.t,* plisser.
kimono, *n,* kimono, saut de lit, *m.*
kin, *n,* parents, *m.pl;* parenté, *f.*
kind, *a,* bon; aimable; gentil; bienveillant, obligeant; prospère. ~ *regards,* amitiés, *f.pl;* compliments, *m.pl.* ¶ *n,* genre, *m;* espèce; sorte; manière; (*of wood*) essence, *f. in* ~, en nature.

kindergarten, *n,* jardin d'enfants, *m.*

kindle, *v.t,* allumer.
kindliness, *n,* bienveillance; bénignité, *f.* **kindly,** *a,* bienveillant, obligeant; ami. ¶ *ad,* aimablement. **kindness,** *n,* bonté; amabilité; attention, *f.*

kindred, *n,* parenté, *f.* ¶ *a,* de la même famille.

kinescope, *n,* cinégramme, cinéscope, *m.*

king, *n,* roi, *m;* (*checkers*) dame, *f.* ~*bolt,* cheville ouvrière, *f.* ~*post,* poinçon, *m.* ~*fisher,* martin-pêcheur, martinet-pêcheur, *m. oil, steel,* ~, roi des pétroles, de l'acier. ~*dom,* *n,* royaume; (*Nat. Hist.*) règne, *m.* ~*ly,* *a,* royal.

kink, *v.t,* tortiller; (*v.i.*) vriller. ~*y,* *a,* noué; crépu.

kinship, *n,* parenté, *f,* sang, *m.* **kinsman,** ~*woman,* *n,* parent, e.

kiosk, *n,* kiosque; édicule, *m.*

kipper, *n,* hareng salé & fumé, *m.* ¶ *v.t,* saler & fumer, saurer.

kiss, *n,* baiser, *m.* ¶ *v.t,* embrasser; baiser (*see note under this word*). ~ & *cuddle,* baisoter.

kit, *n,* équipement; trousseau, *m;* trousse; (*Mil.*) musette, fourbi, *f. mess* ~, cantine, *f.* ~ & *caboodle,* tout le fourbi. *do-it-yourself* ~, prêt-à-monter, *m. repair* ~, lot de réparation, *m. survival* ~, équipement de survie, *m.*

kitchen, *n,* cuisine, *f.* ~ *garden,* [jardin] potager, *m.* ~ *maid,* fille de cuisine, *f.*

kite, *n,* (*bird*) milan; (*toy*) cerf-volant, *m.*

kith & kin, amis & parents, *m.pl.*

kitten, *n,* chaton, petit chat, *m,* petite chatte, *f.*

kleptomania, *n,* cleptomanie, *f.* **kleptomaniac,** *n,* cleptomane, *m,f.*

knack, *n,* don, coup; truc, tour de main, *m. to have a* ~ *for,* avoir la bosse de.

knapsack, *n,* sac; havresac, *m.*

knave, *n,* fripon, coquin, fourbe; (*cards*) valet, *m.* ~*ry,* *n,* friponnerie, coquinerie, fourberie, fourbe, *f.* **knavish,** *a,* fourbe.

knead, *v.t,* pétrir.

knee, *n,* genou, *m.* ~ *breeches,* culotte, *f,* ~*cap,* (*Anat.*) rotule; (*pad*) genouillère, *f.* ~*hole desk,* bureau ministre, *m.*

kneel [down], *v.i.ir,* [s']agenouiller.

knell, *n,* glas, *m.*

knickerbockers & knickers, *n.pl,* culotte, *f.*

knick-knack, *n,* colifichet, brimborion, *m.*

knife, *n,* couteau, *m.* ~*edge,* couteau, *m.* ~, *fork,* & *spoon,* couvert, *m.* ~ *grinder,* rémouleur, *m.* ~ *rest,* porte-couteau, *m. pocket* ~, canif, *m.* ¶ *v.t,* poignarder.

knight, *n,* chevalier; (*chess*) cavalier, *m.* ~*errant,* chevalier errant; (*fig.*) paladin, *m.* ~*errantry,* chevalerie errante, *f.* ~*hood,* *n,* chevalerie, *f.* ~*ly,* *a,* chevaleresque.

knit, *v.t.* & *i. ir,* tricoter; (*brow*)

froncer; (*fig.*) lier, nouer. **knitted** (*vest, etc.*) *p.a,* de tricot. ~ *garment,* tricot, *m.* **knitter,** *n,* tricoteur, euse. **knitting,** *n,* tricotage; tricot, *m.* ~ *needle,* aiguille à tricoter, *f.* **knitwear,** *n,* tricots, *m.pl.*

knob, *n,* bouton, *m;* pomme, *f.*

knock, *n,* coup; (*at the door*) coup de marteau, *m,* ¶ *v.t. & i,* frapper; heurter; cogner; taper. *to* ~ *about,* vadrouiller. ~ *down,* assommer; terrasser; abattre; (*auction*) adjuger. ~*kneed,* cagneux. ~er (*door*), *n,* marteau, *m.*

knoll, *n,* monticule, tertre, *m,* butte, *f.*

knot, *n,* nœud, *m;* (*cluster*) peloton; (*tangle*) tapon, *m.* ¶ *v.t,* nouer. **knotty,** *a,* noueux, raboteux; (*fig.*) épineux.

know, *v.t. & i. ir,* connaître; savoir. ~ *how to,* savoir. *let me* ~, faites-moi savoir. *not to* ~, ignorer. ~**ing,** *a,* savant. ~**ingly,** *ad,* savamment, sciemment, à bon escient. **knowledge,** *n,* connaissance; intelligence; science, *f;* savoir, *m;* notoriété, *f. to my* ~, à mon su. *without my* ~, à mon insu. **known,** *n,* connu, *m.*

knuckle, *n,* jointure, articulation; *f;* (*veal*) jarret, *m.* ~ *fighting,* boxe à poings nus, *f.* ~ [*joint*] (*Mech.*), genouillère, *f. knuckle under* or *down,* mettre les pouces, caler [la voile].

knurl, *n,* molette, *f.* ¶ *v.t,* moleter.

kohlrabi, *n,* chou-rave, *m.*

Koran, *n,* Coran, *m.*

Korea, *n,* la Corée.

kosher, *a,* kascher.

kudos, *n,* gloriole, *f.*

L

label, *n,* étiquette, *f.* ¶ *v.t,* étiqueter.

labial, *a,* labial. ¶ *n,* labiale, *f.*

laboratory, *n,* laboratoire, *m.*

labor, *n,* main-d'œuvre, *f;* travail; labeur, *m;* peine; façon, *f.* ~ *market,* marché du travail, *m.* ~ [*pains*], mal d'enfant, *m.* ~*saving, a,* économisant la main-d'œuvre. ~ *troubles,* troubles ouvriers, *m.pl.* ¶ *v.i. & t,* travailler, peiner; (*ship*) fatiguer. ~**ed** (*fig.*) *p.a,* travaillé, martelé,

tourmenté, laborieux. ~**er,** *n,* manœuvre, homme de peine; ouvrier, *m.* **laborious†,** *a,* pénible; laborieux.

laburnum, *n,* faux ébénier, cytise, *m.*

labyrinth, *n,* labyrinthe, dédale, *m.*

lace, *n,* dentelle, *f;* point; passement; (*shoe*) lacet, cordon, *m;* (*leather*) lanière, *f.* ~ *boots,* bottines (*or if high,* bottes) à lacets (*ou* à lacer), *f.pl,* brodequins, *m.pl.* ~ *insertion,* entretoile, *f.* ¶ *v.t,* galonner; (*fasten*) lacer.

lacerate, *v.t,* déchirer, lacérer.

lack, *n,* manque, défaut, *m,* pénurie, disette, *f,* peu, *m.* ¶ *v.t,* manquer de. ~*ing in,* destitué de. ~*luster, a,* atone; vitreux.

lackadaisical, *a,* languissant; indolent, apathique, gnangnan.

lackey, *n,* laquais, *m.*

laconic†, *a,* laconique.

lacquer, *n. & ~ work,* laque, *m.* ¶ *v.t,* laquer.

lacrosse, *n,* la crosse canadienne.

lacteal, *a,* lacté.

lacuna, *n,* lacune, *f.*

lacustrine, *a,* lacustre.

lad, *n,* garçon; enfant, gars, *m.*

ladder, *n,* échelle, *f.*

laden, *a,* chargé.

ladle, *n,* louche, *f.* ~**ful,** *n,* cuillerée, *f.*

lady, *n,* dame; madame; mademoiselle, *f. Ladies & Gentlemen!* Mesdames, Messieurs! *ladies first!* place aux dames! ~**bird,** coccinelle, bête à bon Dieu, *f.* *L~ chapel,* chapelle de la Vierge, *f. L~ Day,* fête de l'Annonciation, *f;* le 25 mars. ~**killer,** bourreau des cœurs, homme à bonnes fortunes, *m. his (my)* ~*love,* la dame de ses (de mes) pensées. ~ *of the manor,* châtelaine, *f.* ~*s maid,* fem☐ de chambre, *f.* ~*s* (*or ☐ies'*) *man,* homme galant, h. à femmes, *m.* ~*like,* de dame, comme il faut.

lag, *v.i,* traîner; lambiner; (*v.t.*) garnir. ¶*n,* décalage, *m.*

lager [beer], *n,* bière, *f.*

lagoon, *n,* lagune, *f.*

laic, *n. &* **laic(al),** *a,* laïque, séculier, *m. & a.*

laid paper, papier vergé, *m.* **laid up** (*in bed*) alité; (*ship*) désarmé.

lair, *n,* tanière, *f;* repaire, **antre,** *m.*

laity, *n,* laïques, *m.pl.*

lake, *n,* lac, *m.* ~ *dwelling,* habitation lacustre, *f.*

lama, *n,* lama, *m.*

lamb, *n,* agneau; (*pers.*) agneau, mouton, *m.* ¶ *v.i,* agneler. ~**kin,** *n,* agnelet, *m.*

lambent, *a,* [doucement] radieux, lumineux.

lame, *a,* boiteux, éclopé, estropié; (*fig.*) qui cloche. ¶ *v.t,* estropier.

lamé, *a. & n,* lamé, *a. & m.*

lameness, *n,* claudication; boiterie, *f.*

lament, *n,* lamentation, *f;* chant funèbre, *m.* ¶ *v.i,* se lamenter. ~**able**†, *a,* lamentable. ~**ation,** *n,* lamentation, *f.* **the** [late] ~**ed** . . ., le (la) regretté, e . . .

lamina, *n,* lamelle, lame, *f,* feuillet, *m.* **laminate,** *v.t,* laminer.

lamp, *n,* lampe; lanterne, *f;* fanal; feu; (*street*) réverbère, *m.* ~ *black,* noir de fumée, *m.* ~ *man,* lampiste, *m.* ~ *oil,* huile d'éclairage, h. de lampe, *f.* ~ *post,* poteau de réverbère; lampadaire, *m.* ~ *shade,* abat-jour, *m.* *kerosine* ~, lampe à pétrole, *f.*

lampoon, *n,* satire, *f,* libelle, pasquin, pamphlet, *m.* ¶ *v.t,* chansonner, écrire une satire contre. ~**er,** *n,* faiseur de pasquinades, pamphlétaire, *m.*

lamprey, *n,* lamproie, *f.*

lance, *n,* lance, *f.* ¶ (*Surg.*) *v.t,* inciser, percer, ouvrir. **lancers** (*Danc.*) *n.pl,* lanciers, *m.pl.* **lancet,** *n,* lancette, *f.*

land, *n,* terre, *f;* terrain; pays, *m.* ~*-locked property,* enclave, *f.* ~*lord,* ~*lady,* propriétaire, *m,f;* logeur, euse; aubergiste, *m,f.* ~*lubber,* marin d'eau douce, *m.* ~*mark,* borne, *f;* point à terre, amer; point de repère, *m.* ~ *of milk & honey,* ~ *of plenty,* pays de cocagne. ~*owner,* propriétaire foncier, *m,f,* terrien, ne. ~*scape & ~scape painting,* paysage, *m.* ~*scape garden,* jardin anglais, *m.* ~*scape gardener,* dessinateur de jardins, architecte (*ou* jardinier) paysagiste, *m.* ~*scape painter,* [peintre] paysagiste, *m.* ~*slide,* éboulement de terres, *m.* ~*slide* (*Pol.*) débâcle, *f.* ¶ *v.t,* mettre à terre, débarquer; (*blow*) flanquer; (*v.i.*) débarquer;

aborder; (*Avn.*) atterrir; (*on moon*) alunir.

landed property, propriété foncière, *f,* biensfonds, *m.pl.*

landing, *n,* mise à terre, *f,* débarquement; atterrissage; (*stairs*) palier, repos, *m.* (*Avn.*) ~ *gear,* train d'atterrissage, *m.* ~ *place,* embarcadère, débarcadère, ponton, *m.* ~ *ticket,* carton de débarquement, *m.*

lane, *n,* chemin, *m;* allée; ruelle; clairière, *f;* (*running*) couloir, *m.*

language, *n,* langage, *m;* langue, *f.*

languid, *a,* mou; languissant; traînant. **languish,** *v.i,* languir. ~**ing,** *a,* languissant, mourant. **langor,** *n,* langueur, *f.* ~**ous,** *a,* langoureux.

lank, *a,* efflanqué; (*hair*) plats. ~**y,** *a,* efflanqué.

lantern, *n,* lanterne, *f;* falot, *m.* ~*-jawed,* aux joues de lanterne.

lanyard, *n,* (*Naut.*) ride, *f;* (*gun*) tire-feu, *m.*

lap, *n,* (*of pers.*) giron, *m,* genoux, *m.pl;* (*of luxury*) sein; (*of dress*) pan; (*overlap*) recouvrement, *m;* (*layer*) couche, *f;* (*sport*) tour [de piste]. ~*dog,* chien de salon, *m,* bichon, ne. ~ *scorer,* contrôleur des tours, *m.* ¶ *v.t,* envelopper; (*grind*) roder. ~ *over,* *v.i.* chevaucher, croiser. ~ [*up*], *v.t,* laper.

lapel, *n,* revers, *m.*

lapidary, *a. & n,* lapidaire, *a. & m.*

lapis lazuli, *n,* lapis[-lazuli] *m.* **Lapland,** *n,* la Laponie. **Lapp,** *a,* lapon. **Lapp, Laplander,** *n,* Lapon, ne.

lapse, *n,* lapsus; oubli, *m;* (*moral*) défaillance, incartade; (*expiration*) déchéance, *f;* (*time*) laps, *m.* ¶ *v.i,* périmer, périr, devenir caduc; (*time*) s'écouler; tomber.

lapwing, *n,* vanneau, *m.*

larceny, *n,* larcin, *m.*

larch, *n,* mélèze, larix, *m.*

lard, *n,* saindoux, *m.* ¶ *v.t,* (*Cook.*) larder, piquer; (*fig.*) larder, chamarrer. ~**er,** *n,* garde-manger, *m.*

large, *a,* gros; grand; fort; considérable; large. **at** ~, en liberté; [tout] au long; en général. ~**ly,** *ad,* grandement; en grande partie. ~**ness,** *n,* grandeur, *f.*

largess[e], *n,* largesse, *f.*

lark, *n,* (*bird*) alouette; mauviette;

(frolic) équipée, escapade, *f.*
~spur, pied-d'alouette, *m.*

larva, *n,* larve, *f.*

laryngitis, *n,* laryngite, *f.* **larynx,**
n, larynx, *m.*

lascivious†, *a,* lascif.

lash, *n,* *(of whip)* lanière; *(cut
with a whip)* coup de fouet;
(eye) cil; *(Mech.)* jeu, *m;* *(fig.)*
férule, *f.* ¶ *v.t,* cingler, sangler,
fouetter; hier; ligoter; *(Naut.)* amarrer.
~ out, ruer.

lass[ie], *n,* [jeune] fille, fillette, *f.*

lassitude, *n,* lassitude, *f.*

lasso, *n,* lasso, *m.* ¶ *v.t,* prendre
au lasso.

last, *a,* dernier; final; *(honors)*
suprêmes. **~ but one,** *a. & n,*
avant-dernier, ère. **~ night,** cette
nuit; hier [au] soir. **~ piece** *(left
on dish),* morceau honteux, *m.*
~ resort, pis aller, *m.* **~ straw,**
comble (de nos maux) *m.* **~
week,** la semaine dernière, la s.
passée. **~ will & testament,** acte
de dernière volonté, *m.* **the ~
word,** le dernier [mot], le fin mot.
the ~ word in (as elegance), le
nec plus ultra de. ¶ *ad,* pour la
dernière fois; en dernier lieu.
¶ *n,* dernier, ère; fin; *(shoe)*
forme, *f.* **at ~,** enfin. ¶ *v.i,*
durer, tenir. **~ing,** *a,* durable,
stable. **~ly,** *ad,* en dernier lieu,
enfin.

latch, *n,* *(gate)* loquet, *m;* *(door)*
serrure à demi-tour, *f.* **~ key,**
clef de maison, *f.*

late, *a,* tardif; en retard, retardataire; avancé; récent; dernier;
ancien, ex-; *(deceased)* feu;
défunt. **~-comer,** retardataire,
m,f. **~ season,** arrière-saison, *f.*
¶ *ad,* tard; en retard. **~ in the
day & ~ in life,** sur le tard. **~ly,**
ad, dernièrement; récemment.
~ness, *n,* tardiveté, *f.* **the ~ of
the hour,** l'heure tardive, *f.*

latent, *a,* latent; caché.

later, *a,* postérieur, ultérieur. **~
[on],** *ad,* plus tard, ultérieurement.

lateral†, *a,* latéral.

latest, *a,* dernier; fatal. **~ style**
(in dress), dernière mode;
[haute] nouveauté, *f.* **~ [thing
out],** dernier cri, *m.*

latex, *n,* latex, *m.*

lath, *n,* latte; volige; *(blind)* lame,
f. ¶ *v.t,* latter; voliger.

lathe, *n,* tour, *m.*

lather, *n,* mousse; écume, *f.* ¶ *v.i,*
mousser; *(v.t.)* savonner.

lathing, *n,* lattis, *m.*

Latin, *a. & n,* latin, *a. & m.*

latitude, *n,* latitude, *f.*

latrine, *n,* lieux [d'aisance] *m.pl.*

latter (the), ce dernier, cette
dernière; celui-ci, celle-ci, ceux-
ci, celles-ci. **~ly,** *ad,* dernièrement.

lattice, *n,* treillis, treillage, *m.*
¶ *v.t,* treillisser.

Latvia, *n,* la Lettonie. **Latvian,**
a, letton. ¶ *n,* Letton, ne.

laud, *v.t,* louer. **~** [to the skies],
louanger. **~able,** *a,* louable.
laudatory, *a,* laudatif.

laugh, *n,* rire, *m.* ¶ *v.i,* rire; se r.,
se moquer. **~ derisively,** ricaner.
~ heartily, rire aux éclats.
~able†, *a,* risible; dérisoire. *it is
no ~ing matter,* il n'y a pas [là]
de quoi rire. **~ing stock,** risée, *f.*

laughter, *n,* rire[s] *m.* [*pl.*], hilarité, *f.*

launch, *n,* chaloupe, *f;* grand
canot, *m.* ¶ *v.t,* lancer; *(Mil.)* déclencher. **~[ing],** *n,* lancement,
m. **~ pad,** aire de lancement, *f.* **~
ramp,** rampe de l., *f.*

launder, *v.t,* blanchir. **laundress,**
n, blanchisseuse [de fin], repasseuse [de linge fin] *f.* **laundry,**
n, blanchisserie; buanderie, *f.*

laureate, *a,* lauréat, *a.m.*

laurel, *n,* laurier, *m;* *(pl, fig.)*
lauriers, *m.pl.*

lava, *n,* lave, *f.*

lavatory, *n,* lavabo, *m.*

lavender, *n,* lavande, *f.*

lavish, *a,* prodigue. ¶ *v.t,* prodiguer. **~ly,** *ad,* prodigalement.
~ness, *n,* prodigalité, magnificences, *f.pl.*

law, *n,* loi, *f;* droit, *m;* justice; jurisprudence, *f;* palais, *m.* **~-abid-
ing,** respectueux des lois. **~ &
order,** ordre public, *m.* **~ case,**
affaire contentieuse, *f.* **~ costs,**
frais de justice; dépens, *m.pl.* **~
courts,** cours de justice, *f.pl,* tri-
bunaux, *m.pl;* palais [de justice]
m. **~ department,** [service du]
contentieux, *m.* **~-giver,** législateur, *m.* **~ suit,** procès civil, *m,*
affair, *f.* **commercial ~,** droit
commercial, *m.* **~ful†,** *a,* légale;
légitime; licite. **~fulness,** *n,* léga-

lité, légitimité, *f.* ~**less,** *a,* sans loi; déréglé.

lawn, *n,* pelouse, *f,* gazon, boulingrin; (*linen*) linon, *m.* ~ **mower,** tondeuse, *f.* ~ **tennis,** le [lawn-] tennis.

lawyer, *n,* homme de loi; avoué; légiste, juriste, jurisconsulte, *m.*

lax†, *a,* lâche; relâché; mou. ~**ative,** *a. & n,* laxatif, *a. & m.* ~**ity,** *n,* relâchement, *m.*

lay, *a:* ~ **brother,** frère lai, *f.* convers, *f.* servant, frater, *m.* ~**man,** laïque, séculier; profane, *m.* ~ **sister,** sœur converse, *f.* ¶ *n,* chanson, *f;* chant, *m;* complainte; (*of ground*) configuration, *f.* ¶ *v.t.ir,* mettre; poser; dresser; porter; déposer; abattre; coucher; imposer; (é]tendre; (*fire*) préparer; (*gun*) pointer; (*eggs*) pondre; (*a wager*) faire; (*to bet*) parier. ~ **bare,** mettre à nu, déshabiller. ~ **before** (court), saisir. ~ **down,** [dé]poser; plaquer. ~ **hold of,** saisir, s'agripper à, agripper. ~ **in** [*a stock of*], approvisionner de. ~ **out,** disposer; aménager; ajuster; tracer; débourser. ~ **waste,** dévaster.

lay day (*Ship.*) *n,* jour de planche, *m.*

layer, *n,* (*stratum, bed*) couche, *f,* lit, *m;* (*Hort.*) marcotte, *f.*

laying, *n,* mise; pose; (*eggs*) ponte, *f.*

layout, *n,* disposition, *f;* tracé, *m.*

laze, *v.i,* paresser, traînasser. **lazily,** *ad,* paresseusement; indolemment. **laziness,** *n,* paresse, *f.* **lazy,** *a,* paresseux. ~**bones,** paresseux, euse, fainéant, e, cagnard, e.

lea (*Poet.*) *n,* pré, *m,* prairie, *f.*

leach, *v.t. & i,* lessiver; filtrer.

lead, *n,* plomb, *m;* (*for pencils*) mine [de plomb]; (*Typ.*) interligne, *f;* (*Naut.*) plomb [de sonde] *m,* sonde, *f.* ~ **poisoning,** intoxication par le plomb, *f,* saturnisme, *m.* ¶ *v.t,* plomber; (*Typ.*) interligner.

lead, *n,* direction, conduite; avance; tête, *f;* exemple, *m;* (*cards*) main, primauté, *f;* (*Elec.*) conducteur principal; (*Elec. service*) branchement, *m;* (*leash*) laisse, *f.* ~ **rope** (attached to halter), longe, *f.* ¶ *v.t. & i. ir,* mener; conduire; diriger; amener; aboutir; induire; porter;

tendre; (*cards*) débuter. ~ **astray,** égarer, dérouter, fourvoyer; débaucher. ~ **back,** reconduire. ~ **up to** (*fig.*), amener, préluder à.

leaden, *a,* de plomb; (*sky*) de plomb, plombé.

leader, *n,* directeur; meneur; chef de file, *m,* vedette, *f;* (*political*) leader; (*violin, chorus*) chef d'attaque; (*horse*) cheval de volée; (*Anat.*) tendon, *m;* (*Typ.*) points conducteurs, *m.pl;* (*tape, etc.*) amorce, *f.* ~**ship,** *n,* direction; autorité, *f.* **leading,** *a,* principal; premier; marquant. ~ **lady** (*Theat.*) premier rôle, *m;* vedette, *f.* ~ **man,** premier rôle, *m.* ~ **part** (*Theat.*), premier rôle, *m.* ~ **question,** question tendancieuse, *f.*

leadsman, *n,* sondeur, *m.*

leaf, *n,* feuille, *f;* feuillet; volant; (*door*) battant, vantail, *m;* (*table*) rallonge, *f.* ~ **mold,** terreau de feuilles, *m.* ~ **stalk,** pétiole, *m.* ~ **table,** table à rallonge(s) *f.* ~**age,** *n,* feuillage, *m.* ~**less,** *a,* dénudé. ~**let,** *n,* dépliant, imprimé, tract, *m.* ~**y,** *a,* feuillu, feuillé.

league, *n,* ligue; (*of Nations*) société; (*Meas.*) lieue, *f.* ¶ *v.t,* liguer.

leak & ~age, *n,* fuite, perte, *f,* échappement, coulage, *m;* voie d'eau, *f.* ¶ *v.i,* fuir, perdre, s'échapper, couler, faire eau. ~**y,** *a,* qui perd, qui fuit; qui fait eau.

lean, *a,* maigre; sec. ¶ *n,* maigre, *m.* ¶ *v.t.ir,* appuyer, accoter, adosser; (*v.i.ir*) (*rest*) s'appuyer; (*slope*) pencher. ~ **back in,** se renverser sur. ~ **on one's elbow(s),** s'accouder. ~**ing** (*fig.*) *n,* penchant, *m.* ~ **tower** (Pisa), tour penchée, *f.* ~**ness,** *n,* maigreur, *f.* ~**to,** *n,* appentis, *m.*

leap, *n,* saut, bond; soubresaut, *m.* **by ~s & bounds,** par sauts & par bonds. ¶ *v.t. & i. ir,* sauter, bondir. ~**frog,** saute-mouton, saut de mouton, *m.* ~ **year,** année bissextile, *f.* **leaper,** *n,* sauteur, euse.

learn, *v.t. & i.ir,* apprendre. ~**ed,** *a,* savant, érudit, docte, instruit; (*profession*) libérale. ~**edly,** *ad,* savamment, doctement. ~**er,** *n,* apprenti, e; commençant, e. ~**ing,** *n,* érudition, connaissances, *f.pl,* savoir, *m,* science, *f.*

lease, n, bail, m; ferme, f. ¶ v.t, (grant) donner à bail, affermer, arrenter; (take) prendre à bail; amodier. ~holder, locataire, m.f. leasing, n, (land, fishing rights, etc.) amodiation, f.

leash, n, laisse, [ac]couple, attache, f, trait, m; (set of dogs) harde, f. ¶ v.t, harder.

least (the), a, le moindre; le plus petit. ¶ ad. & n, le moins. at ~, au moins; du moins. not in the ~, pas le moins du monde, [ne . . .] pas le moindrement.

leather, n, cuir, m, peau, f. ~ dressing, mégie, mégisserie, f. ~ette, n, similicuir, m. ~y, a, coriacé.

leave, n, permission; autorisation; faculté, liberté, f; congé, m. by your ~l attentionl on ~, en permission, permissionnaire. sick ~, congé de convalescence, m. ¶ v.t. ir, laisser, abandonner; partir de, sortir de, quitter; léguer; (v.i.ir.) partir; déloger. ~ off, cesser; laissez doncl ~ out, omettre, on leaving, à l'issue de.

leaven, n, levain; ferment, m. ¶ v.t, faire lever; (fig.) assaisonner.

leavings, n.pl, restes, m.pl, bribes, f.pl.

lecherous†, a, débauché, lascif.

lectern, n, lutrin, pupitre, m.

lecture, n, leçon; conférence; (scolding) semonce, mercuriale, f, sermon, m. ¶ v.t, sermonner, chapitrer, moraliser. ~ on, faire une leçon, une conférence, sur. lecturer, n, professeur, m; conférencier, ère, maître de conférences, m.

ledge, n, rebord; appui, m; saillie, f.

ledger, n, grand livre, m; (Build.) moise, f. ~ line (Mus.), ligne supplémentaire, f.

lee [side], n, côté sous le vent, m.

leech, n, sangsue, f.

leek, n, poireau, m.

leer, n, regard polisson, m. to ~ at, lorgner.

lees, n.pl, lie, f.

leeward, a, sous le vent. L~ Islands, îles sous le Vent, f.pl. leeway, n, dérive, f.

left, a. & n, gauche, a. & f. the ~ (Box.), le [poing] gauche. ¶ ad,

à gauche. ~-handed, a. (pers. or player) n, gaucher, ère.

left (to be), rester. left-overs, n.pl, (food, etc.) restes, m.pl; bribes, f.pl.

leg, n, jambe; (birds, insects, etc.) patte; (fowl) cuisse, f; (mutton) gigot; (table, etc.) pied, m; (compass, etc.) branche; (boot, stocking) tige, f. ~ lock (wrestling), croc-en-jambe, m. on one ~, à cloche-pied.

legacy, n, legs, m.

legal†, a, légal; judiciaire. ~ aid, assistance judiciaire, f. ~ charges, frais de contentieux, m.pl. ~ entity, personne morale, p. juridique, p. civile, f. ~ maxim, adage de droit, m. ~ tender [currency], (value) pouvoir libératoire, m; (money) monnaie légale, f. ~ize, v.t, légaliser.

legate, n, légat, m. legatee, n, légataire, m.f. legation, n, légation, f.

legend, n, légende, f. ~ary, a, légendaire.

legerdemain, n, prestidigitation, f.

leggings, n.pl, molletières; jambières, f.pl.

Leghorn, n, Livourne, f.

legible†, a, lisible.

legion, n, légion, f. their name is ~, ils s'appellent légion.

legislate, v.i, faire les lois; légiférer. legislation, n, législation, f. legislator, n, législateur, m. legislature, n, législature, f. legist, n, légiste, m.

legitimacy, n, légitimité, f. legitimate†, a, légitime. legitim[at]ize, v.t, légitimer.

legwarmer, n, jambière, f.

leisure, n, loisir[s] m.[pl.]. at ~, à loisir. a ~ly man, un homme lambin. [in a] ~ly [way], ad, sans se presser, sans hâte, avec lenteur.

leitmotiv, -if, n, leitmotiv, m.

lemon, n, citron, m. ~ squash, citron pressé, m. ~ squeezer, presse-citron, m. ~ tree, citronnier, m. ~ade, n, limonade, citronnade, f.

lend, v.t.ir, prêter. ~er, n, prêteur, euse. ~ing, n, prêt, m, prestation, f. ~ library, bibliothèque de prêt, f, cabinet de lecture, m.

lend-lease, n, prêt-bail, m.

length, n, longueur, f, long, m; étendue; durée; (*piece of a stuff*) coupe, f. *at* ~, au long; à la fin. ~*en,* v.t, [r]allonger; prolonger. ~*ening piece,* [r]allonge, f. ~*ways,* ~*wise,* ad, en long. ~y, a, long.

lenient, a, indulgent, clément; de douceur.

Leningrad, n, Léningrad, m.

lens, n, lentille; loupe, f; (*camera, microscope, etc.*) objectif, m. telephoto ~, télé-objectif, m.

Lent, n, carême, m. ~*en,* a, de carême.

lenticular, a, lenticulaire.

lentil, n, lentille, f.

leonine, a, léonin.

leopard, n, léopard, m. ~*ess,* n, l. femelle, m.

leper, n, lépreux, euse. ~ *hospital,* léproserie, f.

leprosy, n, lèpre, f. **leprous,** a, lépreux.

lesbian, n, lesbienne, (*slang*) gouine, f.

lesion, n, lésion, f.

less, a, moindre; inférieur. ~, *suffix,* sans; in-. ¶ ad, moins, m. de. ¶ n, moins, m. ~*en,* v.t. & i, diminuer, amoindrir.

lessee, n, preneur, euse; fermier, ère; tenancier, ère.

lesser, a, plus petit; moindre; petit.

lesson, n, leçon, f.

lessor, n, bailleur, eresse.

lest, c, de peur que . . . [ne].

let, v.t. & aux. ir, laisser; permettre; faire; louer. *to [be]* ~, à louer. ~ *down,* [a]baisser; (*fail pers. at need*) lâcher, laisser en panne. ~ *go* (hold), lâcher prise, démordre; larguer. ~ *have,* céder. ~ *loose,* déchaîner. ~ *in,* faire entrer. ~ *off,* faire grâce à; (*gun*) tirer; (*epigram*) décocher. ~ *out,* laisser sortir; l. échapper; lâcher; (*clothes*) [r]élargir.

lethal, a, léthifère, mortel. ~ *chamber,* chambre de [mise à] mort, f. ~ *weapon,* assommoir, m.

lethargic, a, léthargique. **lethargy,** n, léthargie, f. **Lethe,** n, Léthé, m.

letter, n, lettre; épître; cote, f. ~ *box,* boîte aux lettres, f. ~ *head,*

en-tête, m. ~ *opener,* ouvre-lettre[s] m. ~ *paper,* papier à lettres, m. ~*press,* texte [composé] m. ~*press printing,* impression typographique, f. ~ *scales,* pèse-lettre, m. ~ *writer,* (*pers.*) épistolier, ère, m. ~*ing,* n, lettrage, m.

lettuce, n, laitue, f.

letup, n, détente, f.

Levant, n, Levant, m. **Levantine,** a, levantin; (*ports*) du Levant. ¶ n, Levantin, e.

level, a, de niveau; en palier; plat; plan; uni; égal. a ~*headed person,* une tête bien organisée, un cerveau organisé. ~ *with,* à fleur de, à ras de. ¶ n, niveau; plan, m; hauteur, f; palier, m; (*Min.*) galerie, f. ¶ v.t, niveler; aplanir; égaliser; unir; (*gun, etc.*) pointer. **leveling,** n, nivellement, m.

lever, n, levier, m; manette, f. ~ [*up*] v.t, soulever au moyen d'un levier. ~*age,* n, force de levier, f; (*fig.*) avantage, m.

leveret, n, levraut, m.

leviathan, n, léviathan, m.

Levite, n, lévite, m. **Leviticus,** n, le Lévitique.

levity, n, légèreté, f.

levy, n, levée, réquisition, f; prélèvement, m. ¶ v.t, [pré]lever; imposer, frapper.

lewd†, a, impudique, crapuleux. ~*ness,* n, impudicité, f.

lewis, n, louve, f.

lexicographer, n, lexicographe, m.

lexicon, n, lexique, m.

Leyden, n, Leyde, f.

liability, n, obligation, f; engagement, m; responsabilité, f; (*pl, Fin.*) passif, m. **liable,** a, tenu; soumis; sujet; passible; responsable; solidaire.

liaison officer, agent de liaison, m.

liar, n, menteur, euse.

lias, n, lias, m. **liassic,** a, liasique.

libation, n, libation, f.

libel, n, libelle, m; diffamation, f. ~ *action,* action en diffamation, f. ¶ v.t, diffamer. ~*ous,* a, diffamatoire.

liberal†, a, libéral; large. ¶ n, libéral, m. ~*ism,* n, libéralisme, m. ~*ity,* n, libéralité, f.

liberate, v.t, libérer; affranchir; lâcher; (*from complexes*) défouler.

libertine, *a. & n,* libertin, *a. & m.*

liberty, *n,* liberté; faculté; privauté, *f. at ~,* libre.

librarian, *n,* bibliothécaire, *m,f.*

library, *n,* bibliothèque, *f.*

librettist, *n,* librettiste, *m.* **libretto,** *n,* livret, *m.*

license, *n,* licence, *f;* permis, *m;* dispense, *f;* brevet; bon; acte, *m;* concession, *f. ~ plate,* plaque matricule, de contrôle, *f. ~ to sell,* droit de vendre; *(tobacco, spirits)* débit, *m.* driver's ~, permis de conduire, *m.* **license,** *v.t,* accorder un permis à; breveter. **licentious†,** *a,* licencieux, dévergondé, décolleté. ~ness, *n,* licence, *f,* dévergondage, *m.*

lichen, *n,* lichen, *m.*

licit†, *a,* licite.

lick, *v.t,* lécher. *~ one's chops,* se pourlécher les babines. *~ up,* laper.

licorice, *n,* réglisse, *f;* jus de réglisse, *m.*

lictor, *n,* licteur, *m.*

lid, *n,* couvercle, *m; (eye)* paupière, *f.*

lie, *n,* mensonge; démenti, *m. give the ~ to,* démentir. ¶ *v.i,* mentir.

lie, *n, (of ground)* disposition, configuration; *(Naut.)* gisement, *m.* ¶ *v.i.ir,* coucher, reposer; gésir; séjourner, stationner; résider, tenir. *~ dormant,* dormir. *~ down,* se coucher. *~ idle,* chômer. *~ in wait,* se tenir en embuscade, s'embusquer.

liege, *a,* lige. ¶ *n,* vassal lige, *m.*

lien, *n,* privilège; droit de rétention, *m.* de gage, *m.* ~or, *n,* créancier gagiste, *m.*

lieu of (in), au lieu de.

lieutenant, *n,* lieutenant; *(naval)* l. de vaisseau, *m. ~ colonel,* lieutenant-colonel, *m. ~ commander,* capitaine de corvette, *m. ~ general,* général de corps d'armée, *m.*

life, *n,* vie; existence, *f;* vivant, *m;* durée, *f;* mouvement, *m. for ~,* à vie, viager; perpétuel, à perpétuité. *from ~ (Art),* d'après nature, au vif, sur le vif. *to the ~,* au naturel. *2 lives lost,* 2 personnes ont péri. *~ & property (law),* corps & biens. *~ [& soul] (of the party),* boute-entrain, *m. ~ annuity,* rente viagère, *f,* viager, *m. ~ belt,* ceinture de sauvetage, *f. ~ boat,* bateau de s., *m. ~ buoy,* bouée de s., *f. ~-giving,* fécond. *~ insurance,* assurance sur la vie, *f. ~ jacket,* brassière de sauvetage, *f;* gilet de s., *m. ~-saving,* sauvetage, *m. ~ size,* en grand, grandeur naturelle, nature, *f. ~time,* vivant, *m. ~less, a,* sans vie; inanimé. *~like, a,* vivant; parlant. *~long, a,* de toute la vie.

lift, *n,* coup d'épaule; *(of the hand)* geste, *m.* ¶ *v.t,* lever; soulever; élever; enlever; relever.

liftoff, *n, (aircraft, etc.)* décollage, *m.* ¶ *v.i. (aircraft)* décoller.

ligament, *n,* ligament, *m.* **ligature,** *n,* ligature, *f.*

light, *a,* léger; faible; petit; *(ship unladen)* lège; *(Rly engine)* haut le pied; *(color)* clair; *(earth)* meuble. *~-headed,* délirant. *~-headedness,* transport, *m. ~ lager,* bière blanche, b. blonde, *f. ~ meal,* collation, *f. ~ opera,* opérette, *f. ~ reading,* livres d'agrément, *m.pl. ~ refreshments,* rafraîchissements, *m.pl. ~ weight (Box.),* poids léger, *m.* ¶ *n,* lumière, *f;* jour; éclairage, *m;* vue; clarté, *f,* clair; feu, fanal, phare, *m;* flamme, *f. against the ~,* à contre-jour. *~s out (Mil.),* extinction des feux, *f,* couvre-feu, *m. ~ & shade, (Art)* clair-obscur, *m. ~house,* phare, *m. ~ meter,* cellule, *f. ~-ship,* bateau-feu, *m. do you have a ~?* avez-vous du feu? ¶ *v.t.ir,* allumer; éclairer. *~ up,* illuminer. *~ [up]on,* tomber sur.

lighten, *v.t,* alléger; soulager; éclairer; *(v.imp.)* éclairer, faire des éclairs.

lighter, *a,* plus léger.

lighter, *n, (pers.)* allumeur; *(pipe, etc.)* briquet, *m; (boat)* allège, gabare, *f,* chaland, *m.* **lighting,** *n,* éclairage, *m.*

lightly, *ad,* légèrement; à la légère. **lightness,** *n,* légèreté, *f.*

lightning, *n,* éclair, *m.* oft. pl, foudre, *f. ~ rod,* paratonnerre, *m.*

lights *(animal lungs) n.pl,* mou, *m.*

ligneous, *a,* ligneux. **lignite,** *n,* lignite, *m.* **lignum vitae,** [bois de] gaïac, *m.*

likable, *a,* sympathique. **like,** *a,*

pareil; pair; semblable; analogue; approchant; ressemblant; même; tel; à l'égal de. to be ~, ressembler, approcher de, imiter. to look ~, avoir l'air de, ressembler. ¶ n, pareil, le; semblable, m. ~s & dislikes, sympathies & antipathies, f.pl. ¶ pr, ad, comme; de même que; tel que; à l'instar de; en. ¶ v.t. & i, aimer; affectionner; vouloir; se plaire à; trouver; goûter.

likelihood, n, probabilité; apparence; vraisemblance, f. likely, a, probable, vraisemblable. very ~, vraisemblablement.

liken, v.t, comparer, assimiler.

likeness, n, ressemblance; parité, f; air, m; image, f; portrait, m.

likewise, ad, pareillement, également, aussi, de même.

liking, n, goût; gré, m; affection, f.

lilac, n. & a, lilas, m. & att.

Lilliputian, a, lilliputien.

lily, n, lis, m. ~ of the valley, muguet, m.

limb, n, membre, m; (tree) mère branche, f; (Math., etc.) limbe, m. -limbed, a, membré.

limber, a, souple. ¶ n, avanttrain, m. ~ up, mettre l'avanttrain.

limbo, n, les limbes, m.pl.

lime, n, chaux, f; (citrus) limon, m. ~ burner, chaufournier, m. ~ juice, jus de limon, m. ~ kiln, four à chaux, chaufour, m. ~ light, lumière oxhydrique, f. to be in the ~light, être sous les feux de la rampe; (fig.) être en vedette. ~stone, pierre à chaux, p. calcaire, f, calcaire, m. ~ [tree], (citrus) limonier; (linden) tilleul, m. ~ twig, gluau, pipeau, m. ¶ v.t, (Agric.) chauler; (twig) engluer.

limit, n, limite, borne, f; périmètre, m. ¶ v.t, limiter, borner. ~ation, n, limitation, f. limited, p.p. & p.a, limité, borné, étroit; (monarchy) tempérée; (edition) à tirage restreint. ~ partnership, [société en] commandite, f.

limousine, n, limousine, f.

limp, a, flasque, mou; (binding) souple. ¶ n, claudication, f, boitement, clochement, m. ¶ v.i, boiter, clocher.

limpet, n, lépas, m, patelle, f.

limpid, a, limpide. ~ity, n, limpidité, f.

linchpin, n, clavette d'essieu, esse, f.

linden, n, tilleul, m.

line, n, ligne; file; haie; voie, f; trait, m; raie; ride; (Teleph.) ligne, f, poste; (Poet.) vers; câble, m; corde, f; cordeau, m; amarre, f; genre; métier; emploi; département; ressort, m; partie; juridiction, f. ~ cut, cliché, m. ~ engraving, taille-douce; gravure au trait, f. plumb ~, fil à plomb, m. wait in ~, faire queue. ¶ v.t, (clothes) doubler; tapisser; garnir; revêtir; rider, sillonner; border. ~ one's stomach, se lester l'estomac. lineage, n, descendance, f, parage, m. lineal, a, linéaire; (pers.) en ligne directe. lineament, n, linéament, trait, m. linear, a, linéaire.

linen, n, toile [de lin] f; [tissu de] lin; linge, m. ~ [thread], fil [de lin] m. ~ trade, industrie linière, toilerie, f.

liner, n, (ship) transatlantique, paquebot; (aircraft) avion de transport, m.

ling, n, (fish) grande morue barbue; (Bot.) bruyère, brande, f.

linger, v.i, s'attarder; traîner. ~ing death, mort lente, f.

lingerie, n, lingerie [fine] f.

lingo, n, jargon, baragouin, m.

lingual, a, lingual. ¶ n, linguale, f. linguist, n, linguiste, m. ~ics, n, linguistique, f.

liniment, n, liniment, m.

lining, n, doublure; garniture; chemise; (hat) coiffe, f; revêtement, m.

link, n, chaînon, maillon, anneau, m; (Mach.) coulisse, f; (fig.) lien, m. ¶ v.t, articuler; enchaîner. ~ up, raccorder.

links, n.pl. & s, lande, f; (golf) terrain, m.

linnet, n, linotte, f, linot, m.

linoleum, n, linoléum, m.

linotype, n. & att, linotype, f. & a.

linseed, n, graine de lin, f. ~ oil, huile de [graine de] lin, f.

lint, n, charpie, f.

lintel, n, linteau, sommier, m, traverse, f.

lion, ess, n, lion, ne. ~ cub, ~ whelp, lionceau, m. ~'s share, part du lion, f.

lip, *n*, lèvre; babine, *f*; bec, *m*. ~**stick**, rouge à lèvres, *m*.

liquefaction, *n*, liquéfaction, *f*. **liquefy,** *v.t*, liquéfier.

liqueur, *n*, liqueur [de dessert] *f*. ~ **brandy**, fine champagne, *f*.

liquid, *a*, liquide; (*Com., Fin.*) liquide, disponible; (*fig.*) coulant, doux. ~ **ammonia**, liqueur d'ammoniaque, *f*. ~ **assets**, disponibilités, *f.pl*. ¶ *n*, liquide, *m*; (*phonetics*) liquide, *f*.

liquidate, *v.t*, liquider. **liquidation,** *n*, liquidation, *f*. **liquidator,** *n*, liquidateur, *m*.

liquor, *n*, liquide, *m*, boisson; liqueur, *f*.

Lisbon, *n*, Lisbonne, *f*.

lisp, *v.i*, zézayer. ¶ *n*, zézeiements, *m*.

lissom[e], *a*, souple.

list, *n*, liste, *f*; bordereau, *m*; feuille, *f*; rôle; tableau, *m*; table, *f*; inventaire; bulletin; catalogue, *m*; côte, *f*; (*Naut.*) bande; (*selvage*) lisière, *f*; (*pl.*) lice, arène, barrière, *f*. ~ **of plates,** table des hors-texte. ¶ *v.t*, cataloguer; inventorier; (*door*) calfeutrer; (*computers*) lister. (*v.i, Naut.*) donner [de] la bande. ~**ing,** *n*, (*computers*) listage, *m*.

listen, *v.i. & ~ in* (*radio*), écouter. ~**er,** *n*, (*hearer & radio*) auditeur, *m*; (*spy*) écouteur, euse.

listless†, *a*, nonchalant, distrait, traînard.

litany, *n*, litanies, *f.pl*.

literal†, *a*, littéral. ~ [*error*], coquille, *f*. ~ *sense,* (*passage*) sens littéral; (*word*) [sens] propre, *m*.

literary, *a*, littéraire. ~ *man,* homme de lettres, littérateur, *m*. **literate,** *a*, qui sait lire; lettré. **literature,** *n*, littérature, *f*.

litharge, *n*, litharge, *f*.

lithe, *a*, souple, agile.

lithia, *n*, lithine, *f*. **lithium,** *n*, lithium, *m*.

lithograph & ~**y,** *n*, lithographie, *f*. ¶ *v.t*, lithographier. ~**er,** *n*, lithographe, *m*. ~**ic,** *a*, lithographique.

Lithuania, *n*, la Lit[h]uanie. **litigant,** *n*, plaideur, euse. **litigation,** *n*, litige, *m*. **litigious,** *a*, litigieux, processif.

litmus, *n*, tournesol, *m*. ~ *paper,* papier tournesol, *m*.

litter, *n*, (*palanquin*) litière, civière, *f*, brancard, *m*; (*straw & dung*) litière, *f*, fumier, *m*; (*young*) portée, ventrée; (*pigs*) cochonnée, *f*; encombrement, fouillis, *m*; immondices, *f.pl*; détritus, débris, *m.pl*. ¶ *v.t*, encombrer; joncher.

little, *a*, petit. ~ *devil,* diablotin, *m*. ~ *finger,* petit doigt, [doigt] auriculaire, *m*. ~ *ones,* petits enfants; (*cubs*) petits, *m.pl*. *L*~ *Red Riding Hood,* le Petit Chaperon Rouge. *a* ~ [*while*] *longer,* un peu. ¶ *ad*, peu; ne ... guère. ¶ *n*, peu, *m*. ~**ness,** *n*, petitesse *f*.

livable, *a*, vivable; supportable; habitable.

live, *a*, vif; vivant; (*coal*) ardent; (*axle*) tournant; (*Elec.*) en charge; (*shell*) chargé. ~*-bait fishing,* pêche au vif, *f*. ~ *stock,* animaux vivants, *m.pl*. ~ *rail,* rail conducteur, *m*.

live, *v.i. & t*, vivre; durer; se nourrir (*on milk, etc.* = de); demeurer, habiter.

livelihood, *n*, subsistance, *f*, gagne-pain, *m*.

liveliness, *n*, vivacité, animation, *f*, entrain, *m*. **lively,** *a*, vif, vivant, animé, mouvementé; allègre, fringant, émerillonné.

liver (*Anat.*) n, foie, *m*.

livery, *n*, livrée, *f*. ~ *stables,* pension pour les chevaux, *f*.

livid, *a*, livide. ~**ity,** *n*, lividité, *f*.

living, *a*, vivant; en vie; (*force*) vive. ~ *being,* vivant, *m*. ~ *wage,* minimum vital, *m. within* ~ *memory,* de mémoire d'homme. ¶ *n*, vie, *f*, vivre, *m*; (*fare*) chère, *f*; (*Eccl.*) bénéfice, *m*. ~ *expenses,* dépense de bouche, *f*. ~**-in,** internat, *m*. ~ *room,* salon, *m*; salle de séjour, *f. the* ~, les vivants, *m.pl. to earn a* ~, gagner sa vie.

lizard, *n*, lézard, *m*.

llama, *n*, lama, *m*.

loach, *n*, loche, *f*.

load, *n*, charge, *f*; fardeau, *m*. ~ [*water*] *line,* ligne de [flottaison en] charge, *f*. ¶ *v.t*, charger; combler; couvrir; (*dice*) piper; (*v.i.*) prendre charge. ~**ed,** *p.p*, chargé. ~**er,** *n*, chargeur, *m*. ~**ing,** *n*, charge, *f*; chargement, *m*. [*now*] ~ (*ship*), en charge.

loaf, *n.* & ~ *of bread*, pain, *m*; (*round loaf*) miche, *f.*

loaf, *v.i*, fainéanter, battre le pavé. ~**er**, *n*, fainéant, batteur de pavé, *m*.

loam, *n*, terre grasse; terre, *f.*

loan, *n*, prêt; emprunt, *m*. ~*shark*, usurier, *m*.

loath (to be), ne vouloir pas, répugner. **loathe**, *v.t*, haïr, abhorrer. **loathing**, *n*, dégoût, *m*. **loathsome**, *a*, dégoûtant.

lob (*Ten.*) *n*, chandelle, *f.*

lobby, *n*, vestibule; couloir, *m*. ¶ *v.i*, faire les couloirs. ~**ing**, *n*, propos de couloir, *m.pl.*

lobe, *n*, lobe, *m.*

lobelia, *n*, lobélie, *f.*

lobster, *n*, homard, *m*. ~ *pot*, ~ *basket*, nasse, *f*, panier, *m.*

local, *a*, local; topique; de clocher; (*custom*) de place, des lieux. ~[e], *n*, scène, *f*. ~**ity**, *n*, localité, *f*. ~**ize**, *v.t*, localiser. ~**ly**, *ad*, localement; sur place.

locate, *v.t*, fixer [l'emplacement de]; repérer; rechercher.

lock, *n*, serrure; (*canal*) écluse; (*hair*) boucle, mèche; (*pl.*) chevelure; (*gun*) platine, *f*. *under* ~ & *key*, sous clef. ~*jaw*, tétanos, *m*. ~*nut*, contre-écrou, *m*. ~*out*, lockout, *m*, grève patronale, *f*. ~*smith*, serrurier, *m*. ~ *stitch*, point de piqûre, *m*. ~*up*, (*police*) violon; (*att.*) fermant à clef. ¶ *v.t*, fermer [à clef]; bloquer. ~ *out*, fermer la porte à clef sur; (*workmen*) renvoyer en masse. ~ *up*, fermer à clef; mettre (*ou* serrer) sous clef; verrouiller, enfermer, coffrer, boucler; (*Fin.*) immobiliser, bloquer.

locker, *n*, case, *f*; caisson, *m*; soute, *f.*

locket, *n*, médaillon, *m.*

locksmith, *n*, serrurier, *m.*

locomotion, *n*, locomotion, *f.* **locomotive**, *a*, locomoteur. ¶ *n*, locomotive, *f.* **locomotor ataxy**, ataxie locomotrice, *f.*

loculus, *n*, loge, *f.*

locust, *n*, sauterelle, locuste, *f*, criquet, *m*. ~ [*bean*], caroube, *f.*

locution, *n*, façon de s'exprimer, *f*, tour de langage, idiotisme, *m.*

lode, *n*, filon, *m*. ~*star*, étoile polaire, *f*. ~*stone*, pierre d'aimant, *f.*

lodge, *n*, loge, *f*; pavillon, *m.*

¶ *v.t*, loger; déposer; [re]mettre; fournir; (*appeal*) interjeter; (*v.i*.) [se] loger, camper. **lodger**, *n*, locataire, *m.f.* **lodging**, *n*, logement, *m*, chambre, *f*, le couvert; (*pl.*) meublé *m*.

loft, *n*, grenier, *m*; soupente; (*organ*) tribune, *f.* ¶ (*golf*) *v.t*, enlever. **loftiness**, *n*, élévation, hauteur, *f*. **lofty**, *a*, élevé; relevé; fier; hautain, altier; (*style*) soutenu.

log, *n*, bûche, *f*; (*Naut.*) loch, *m*. (*computers*) transmission ~, journal des transmissions, *m*. ~ [*book*], livre de loch; journal de bord, *m*. ~ *cabin*, ~ *hut*, cabane de bois, *f*. ~*wood*, [bois de] campêche, *m.*

loganberry, *n*, ronce-framboise, *f.*

logarithm, *n*, logarithme, *m.*

loggerheads (at), en bisbille.

logic, *n*, logique, *f*. ~**al†**, *a*, logique. ~**ian**, *n*, logicien, *m.*

loin, *n*, (*veal*) longe, *f*; (*mutton*) filet, *m*; (*pl.*) reins, lombes, *m.pl.* ~ *chop*, côtelette de filet, *f*. ~ *cloth*, pagne, *m.*

loiter, *v.i*, s'attarder, traîner, s'amuser. ~**er**, *n*, traînard, *m.*

loll, *v.i*, se prélasser; (*tongue*) pendre.

lollipop, *n*, sucette, *f.*

Lombardy, *n*, la Lombardie.

London, *n*, Londres, *m*; (*att.*) londonien. ~**er**, *n*, Londonien, ne.

loneliness, *n*, solitude, *f*, isolement, *m*. **lonely** & **lone**[**some**], *a*, solitaire, isolé, esseulé. *lone cottage*, chartreuse, *f.*

long, *a*, long; grand; allongé; (*Meas.*) de long. ~*boat*, chaloupe, *f*. ~*distance race*, course de fond, *f*. ~*drawn*, filandreux. ~*haired*, chevelu. ~*legged* (man), bien fendu. ~*lived*, vivace. ~ *service*, vétérance, *f*. ~*shoreman*, débardeur, *m*. *a* ~ *while*, un long temps, longtemps; *ad.* ~*winded*, prolixe, diffus. ¶ *ad*, longtemps; le long de. ~ *ago*, il y a longtemps. *not* ~ *since*, naguère. ~*suffering*, longanimité, *f.* ¶ *n*: *the* ~ & *the short of it*, le fin mot. ¶ *v.i*: *I* ~ *to*, il me tarde de, je brûle de, je grille de. ~ *for*, languir pour, soupirer après. *to be* ~ (delay), tarder.

longest way round, chemin des écoliers, *m.*

longevity, *n*, longévité, *f.*

longing, *n*, [grande] envie, démangeaison, *f.*

longitude, *n*, longitude, *f:* **longitudinal**†, *a*, longitudinal.

look, *n*, regard; coup d'œil; œil; air, *m*; mine; apparence, *f*, aspect, *m.* ~*out*, veille, vigie, *f*, qui-vive, *m*; (*post*) guérite, *f*; (*man*) guetteur, *m*; affaire, *f.* ¶*v.i*, regarder; avoir l'air; sembler; paraître. ~ *after*, veiller à, soigner, ménager, gouverner. ~ *at*, regarder. ~ *down* (from on high), planer. ~ *down* [*up*]*on*, mépriser. ~ *for*, chercher; s'attendre à. ~ *into*, examiner. ~ *like*, ressembler à, jouer. ~ *on*, regarder; envisager; (*front*) donner sur. ~ *out!* attention!, gare!, alerte!, vingt-deux! ~ *out for*, chercher; s'attendre à. ~ *out of the window*, regarder par la fenêtre. ~ *over*, parcourir; repasser. ~ *up a word in the dictionary*, chercher un mot dans le dictionnaire. *to translate by looking up every other word in the dictionary*, traduire à coups de dictionnaire. ~*ing glass*, glace, *f*, miroir, *m.*

loom, *n*, métier [à tisser] *m.*

loom, *v.i*, se dessiner, émerger, surgir.

loop, *n*, boucle; coque, *f*; œil; *m*; ganse, *f.* ~*hole*, meurtrière, *f*, créneau, *m*; (*fig.*) échappatoire, *f.* ¶*v.t*, boucler. ~ *the* ~, boucler la boucle.

loose, *a*, mobile; volant; branlant; flottant; coulant; large; lâche; (*pulley*) folle; libre; négligé; desserré; décousu; (*in bulk*) en vrac. *at a* ~ *end*, désœuvré. **loose**[n], *v.t*, [re]lâcher; délier; desserrer.

loot, *n*, butin, *m.* ¶*v.t. & i*, piller.

lop, *v.t*, élaguer, ébrancher. ~*-ear* [*ed rabbit*], lapin bélier, *m.* ~*-sided*, de guingois; (*boat*) bordier.

loquacious, *a*, loquace. **loquacity**, *n*, loquacité, *f.*

lord, *n*, seigneur; (*Eng.*) lord, *m.* ~ *of creation*, roi de la nature, *m.* ~ *of the manor*, châtelain, *m.* *the Lord* (God), le Seigneur. *Lord's Prayer*, oraison dominicale, *f. Lord's Supper*, communion, Cène, *f:* ~ *it over*, faire le maître avec. ~*ly*, *a*, hautain;

altier, fier. ~*ship*, *n*, seigneurie, *f. Your L*~, Votre grandeur, *f.*

lore, *n*, science, *f.*

lorgnette, *n*, face à main, *f.*

lose, *v.t. & i. ir*, perdre; (*train*) manquer; (*clock*) retarder. ~ *heart*, se décourager. **loser**, *n*, perdant, e; (*good, bad*) joueur, euse. **loss**, *n*, perte; déperdition, *f*; déchet[s] *m.*[pl.]; sinistre, *m.* ~ *of appetite*, inappétence, *f.* ~ *of voice*, extinction de voix, *f. at a* ~, à perte; (*fig.*) empêché. *dead* ~, perte sèche. **lost**, *p.p. & p.a*, perdu; égaré; dépaysé; (*in thought*) absorbé, abîmé; (*motion*) rejetée. ~ *& found office*, bureau des objets trouvés, *m.*

lot, *n*, lot, *m*; partie, *f*; paquet; partage; sort, destin, *m*, destinée, *f. the* ~, le tout. *to draw* ~*s*, tirer au sort.

lotion, *n*, lotion, *f.*

lottery, *n*, loterie, *f.*

lotto, *n*, loto, *m.*

lotus, *n*, lotus, lotos, *m.*

loud, *a*, haut; fort; grand; gros; sonore; bruyant; tapageur. ~ *cheers*, vivats sonores, *m.pl.* ~ *pedal*, grande pédale, p. forte, *f.* ~*speaker*, haut-parleur, *m.* ~[*ly*], *ad*, [tout] haut; fort.

Louisiana, *n*, la Louisiane.

lounge, *n*, (*hotel, etc.*) hall; (*music hall, etc.*) promenoir; canapé, *m.* ¶*v.i*, flâner, paresser. **lounger**, *n*, flâneur, batteur de pavé, *m.*

louse, *n*, pou, *m.* **lousy**, *a*, pouilleux.

lout, *n. & ~ish*, *a*, rustre, rustaud, *m. & a.*

lovable, *a*, aimable. **love**, *n*, amour, *m*; inclination; tendresse, *f*; chéri, e, bijou, *m.* ~ *for* ~ *or money*, ni pour or ni pour argent. *in* ~, amoureux, épris. *fall in* ~, s'enamourer, s'éprendre. *make* ~ *to*, faire la cour à. *play for* ~, jouer pour l'honneur. ~ *all* (*Ten.*), zéro partout, égalité à rien, rien à rien. ~ *at first sight*, coup de foudre, *m.* ~ *bird*, inséparable, *m. ou f.* ~ *knot*, lacs d'amour, *m.* ~ *letter*, billet doux, *m.* ~*lock* (as worn by a man) rouflaquette, *f*; (*by a woman*) accroche-cœur, *m.* ~ *match*, mariage d'amour, mariage d'inclination, *m.*

~ *potion*, philtre, *m*. ~*-sick*, qui languit d'amour. ~ *story*, roman d'amour, *m*. ¶ *v.t. & i*, chérir. ~ *one another*, s'entr'aimer.

loveliness, *n*, beauté, *f*. **lovely**, *a*, beau; adorable; du nanan.

lover, *n*, amant, *m*; amoureux, euse; galant; ami, e; amateur, *m*. ~ *of old books*, bouquineur, *m*.

loving†, *a*, affectueux, aimant.

low, *a*, bas; petit; faible; (*fever, speed*) lente; (*bow*) profonde; vulgaire. L~ *Countries*, Pays-Bas, *m.pl.* ~ *gear*, première vitesse, *f*. ~ *mass*, messe basse, petite m., *f*. ~ *relief*, bas-relief, *m*. L~ *Sunday*, Quasimodo, *f*. ~*water mark*, (*sea*) laisse de basse mer, *f*; (*river*) étiage, *m*. ¶ *ad*, bas; profondément. ~*necked* (*dress*), décolleté, a. & m. ~*-spirited*, abattu. *to be* ~*waisted* (*dress*), avoir la taille basse.

low, *v.i*, mugir, beugler.

lower, *a*, plus bas; inférieur; bas; moindre. ~ *register* (*Mus.*), grave, *m*. ~ *tooth*, dent de dessous, *f*. ¶ *v.t*, [a]baisser; rabattre; descendre, avaler. ~ *oneself* (*fig.*), se ravaler. *award, etc., to the lowest tenderer*, adjudication, *etc.*, au rabais, *f*.

lowlands, *n.pl*, basses terres, *f.pl*.

lowliness, *n*, humilité, *f*. **lowly**, *a*, humble.

lowness, *n*, peu de hauteur, *m*; (*price, etc.*) modicité; (*vileness*) bassesse, *f*.

lox, *n*, saumon fumé, *m*.

loyal†, *a*, loyal, fidèle. ~*ism*, *n*, loyalisme, *m*. ~*ist*, *n. & att*, loyaliste, *m,f. & a*. ~*ty*, *n*, loyauté, *f*; (*to sovereign*) loyalisme, *m*.

lozenge, *n*, pastille, tablette, *f*; (*Geom.*) losange, *m*.

lubber, *n*, lourdaud, mastoc, *m*.

lubricate, *v.t*, graisser, lubrifier. *lubricating oil*, huile à graisser, *f*. **lubricator**, *n*, graisseur, *m*.

Lucca, *n*, Lucques, *f*.

Lucerne (**Lake of**), lac des Quatre-Cantons, *m*.

lucid, *a*, lucide. ~*ity*, *n*, lucidité, *f*.

luck, *n*, chance, *f*, hasard, *m*; veine; fortune, *f*; bonheur, *m*. ~*less*, *a*, malheureux, néfaste. ~*y†*, *a*, heureux, chanceux, for-

tuné, bien loti; propice. ~ *star*, bonne étoile, *f*.

lucrative, *a*, lucratif. **lucre**, *n*, lucre, gain, *m*.

lucubration, *n*, élucubration, *f*.

ludicrous†, *a*, risible, comique; plaisant.

luff, *n*, lof, *m*. ¶ *v.t*, lofer.

lug, *n*, oreille, *f*, ergot, *m*. ¶ *v.t*, traîner.

luggage, *n*, bagage[s] *m.[pl.]*. ~ *carrier*, porte-bagages, *m*.

lugger, *n*, lougre, *m*.

lugubrious†, *a*, lugubre.

lukewarm, *a*, tiède. ~*ness*, *n*, tiédeur, *f*.

lull, *n*, accalmie, embellie, *f*. ¶ *v.t*, bercer; mollir; assoupir. **lullaby**, *n*, berceuse, *f*.

lumbago, *n*, lumbago, *m*. **lumbar**, *a*, lombaire.

lumber, *n*, bois [de charpente] *m*. ~*man*, bûcheron, *m*.

luminary, *n*, luminaire, astre, *m*; (*pers.*) lumière, *f*. **luminous†**, *a*, lumineux. ~ *dial* (*watch*), cadran lumineux, *m*.

lump, *n*, [gros] morceau, *m*, masse, *f*, bloc, *m*, motte, *f*. ~ *sugar*, sucre en morceaux, s. cassé, *m*. ~ *sum* (opp. *by installments*), en une [seule] fois. ¶ *v.t*, bloquer, réunir. ~*ish*, *a*, balourd, mastoc (*inv.*).

lunacy, *n*, aliénation d'esprit, aliénation mentale, démence, *f*.

lunar, *a*, lunaire.

lunatic, *n*, aliéné, e. ~ *asylum*, hospice (*ou* asile) d'aliénés, *m*.

lunch & luncheon, *n*, déjeuner [de midi], lunch, *m*. *lunch[eon] basket*, panier-repas, *m*. **lunch**, *v.i*, déjeuner.

lung, *n*, poumon, *m*.

lunge, *n*, (*fencing*) botte, *f*; coup porté, *m*. ¶ *v.i*, (*fencing*) porter une botte; allonger un coup [à].

lupus (*Med.*) *n*, lupus, *m*.

lurch, *n*, embardée, *f*. *leave in the* ~, camper là, planter là, laisser en panne. ¶ *v.i*, tituber.

lure, *n*, leurre, *m*. ¶ *v.t*, leurrer; (*birds*) piper.

lurid, *a*, blafard; cuivré, fauve; sinistre.

lurk, *v.i*, se cacher; se dissimuler.

luscious, *a*, succulent; fondant.

lush, *a*, luxuriant.

lust, *n*, luxure, convoitise, *f*. ~

after, convoiter. ~**ful**, *a*, luxurieux.
luster, *n*, lustre, éclat, *m*. ¶ *v.t*, lustrer. ~**less**, *a*, terne.
lusty†, *a*, vigoureux, robuste.
lute, *n*. (*Mus.*) luth; (*cement*) lut, *m*. ¶ *v.t*, luter.
Lutheran, *a*. & *n*, luthérien, ne.
Luxembourg, *n*, Luxembourg, *m*.
luxuriance, *n*, exubérance, *f*.
luxuriant, *a*, luxuriant, exubérant.
luxurious, *a*, luxueux; voluptueux.
luxury, *n*, luxe; délice, *m*.
lye, *n*, lessive, *f*.
lying, *a*, mensonger, menteur. ¶ *n*, mensonge, *m*.
lymph, *n*, lymphe, *f*.
lynch, *v.t*, lyncher.
lynx, *n*, lynx; (*common*) loupcervier, *m*.
Lyons, *n*, Lyon, *m*.
lyre, *n*, lyre, *f*. ~**bird**, oiseaulyre, *m*.
lyric & ~**al**, *a*, lyrique. **lyricism**, *n*, lyrisme, *m*.

M

macadam, *n*, macadam, *m*. ~**ize**, *v.t*, macadamiser.
macaque, *n*, macaque, *m*.
macaroni, *n*, macaroni, *m*.
macaroon, *n*, macaron, *m*.
macaw, *n*, ara, *m*.
mace, *n*, masse, *f*; (*spice*) macis, *m*. ~ **bearer**, massier, *m*.
macerate, *v.t*, macérer.
Machiavellian, *a*, machiavélique.
machination, *n*, machination, *f*.
machine, *n*, machine, *f*. ~**cut**, taillé à la machine. ~ *gun*, fusil mitrailleur, *m*, mitrailleuse, *f*. ~ *gunner*, [fusilier] mitrailleur, *m*. ~**made**, fait à la mécanique. ~ *oil*, huile pour machine, *f*. ~ *tool*, machine-outil, *f*. ¶ *v.t*, usiner, façonner. **machinery**, *n*, machinerie, *f*, machines, *f.pl*, outillage; (*fig.*) rouage, *m*. **machinist**, *n*, machiniste, mécanicien, *m*.
mackerel, *n*, maquereau, *m*. ~ *sky*, ciel pommelé, *m*.
mackintosh, *n*, imperméable, caoutchouc, *m*.
mad, *a*, fou; insensé; furieux (*pers. & bull*); enragé (*pers. & dog*). ~**cap**, écervelé, e, cerveau brûlé, *m*. ~**man**, -**woman**, fou, *m*, folle,

f, insensé, e, forcené, e, désespéré, e, enragé, e.
madam, *n*, madame, *f*.
madden, *v.t*, rendre fou; affoler; faire enrager. ~**ing**, *p.a*, enrageant.
madder, *n*, garance, *f*.
Madeira, *n*, Madère, *f*.
madly, *ad*, follement, en fou.
madness, *n*, folie; démence; (*dog's*) rage, *f*.
madonna, *n*, madone, *f*.
madras (*fabric*) *n*, madras, *m*.
madrepore, *n*, madrépore, *m*.
madrigal, *n*, madrigal, *m*.
magazine, *n*, magasin, *m*; (*warehouse*) soute; (*periodical*) revue, *f*, magazine, *m*.
Maggiore (Lago), le lac Majeur.
maggot, *n*, ver; asticot, *m*. ~**y**, *a*, véreux.
Magi, *n.pl*, mages, *m.pl*.
magic, *a*, magique. ¶ *n*, magie, *f*; enchantement; prestige, *m*. ~**al**, *a*, magique. ~**ally**, *ad*, d'une façon magique. ~**ian**, *n*, magicien, ne.
magisterial, *a*, de magistrat; (*fig.*) magistral. ~**ly**, *ad*, en magistrat; magistralement. **magistracy**, *n*, magistrature, *f*. **magistrate**, *n*, magistrat; juge, *m*.
magnanimity, *n*, magnanimité, *f*. **magnanimous**†, *a*, magnanime.
magnate, *n*, magnat, gros bonnet, *m*.
magnesia, *n*, magnésie, *f*. **magnesium**, *n*, magnésium, *m*. ~ *light*, lumière magnésique, *f*.
magnet, *n*, aimant, *m*. ~**ic**, *a*, magnétique; (*bar*, *needle*) aimanté, e; (*fig.*) attirant. ~**ics**, *n*. & ~**ism**, *n*, magnétisme, *m*. ~**ize**, *v.t*, aimanter; (*fig.*) magnétiser. **magneto**, *n*, magnéto, *f*. ~**electric**, *a*, magnéto-électrique.
magnificat, *n*, magnificat, *m*.
magnificence, *n*, magnificence, *f*. **magnificent**†, *a*, magnifique.
magnify, *v.t*, grossir, grandir; (*the Lord*) magnifier. *magnifying glass*, loupe, *f*.
magniloquence, *n*, emphase, *f*. **magniloquent**, *a*, emphatique.
magnitude, *n*, grandeur; importance, *f*.
magnolia, *n*, magnolia, *m*.
magot (*Chinese figure & ape*), *n*, magot, *m*.
magpie, *n*, pie, *f*.

mahogany, *n,* acajou, *m.*

mahout, *n,* cornac, *m.*

maid, *n,* fille; vierge, pucelle, *f.* ~[*servant*], fille [de service], bonne, domestique, servante, *f.* *maid of all work,* bonne à tout faire. *maid of honor,* demoiselle d'honneur, *f.* *maid's room,* chambre de domestique, *f.*

maiden, *n,* vierge, fille; pucelle, *f.* ~[*lady*], demoiselle, *f.* ¶ *a,* virginal; (*speech*) de début, premier; (*trip*) premier. ~*hair* [*fern*], capillaire, *m.* ~ *name,* nom de jeune fille, *m.* ~**hood,** *n,* virginité, *f.* ~**ly,** *a,* de jeune fille, virginal.

mail, *n,* (*armor*) mailles, *f.pl* (*post*) poste, *f,* courrier, *m.* *air* ~, poste aérienne, *f.* ~ *bag,* sac à dépêches, *m.* ~ *boat,* ~ *steamer,* paquebot-poste, *m.* ~ *box,* boîte aux lettres, *f.* ~ *man,* facteur, *m.* ~ *order business,* affaires par correspondance, *f.pl.* ~ [*train*], train-poste, *m.*

maim, *v.t,* estropier, mutiler.

main, *a,* principal; grand; maître, esse. ~ [*portion of*] *building,* corps de logis, c. de bâtiment, *m.* ~ *deck,* pont principal, *m.* ~ *drain,* maître drain, d. collecteur, *m. by* ~ *force,* de vive force. ~ *hall* (body of building), vaisseau, *m. the* ~ *idea* (of a book), l'idée mère. ~ *issue* (law), fond, *m.* ~*land,* continent, *m,* terre ferme, *f.* ~ *line* (Rly), ligne principale, grande l., *f.* ~*mast,* grand mât, *m. the* ~ *point,* le point principal, l'essentiel, *m.* ~ *road,* grand chemin, *m,* grand-route, *f.* ~*sail,* grand-voile, *f.* ~*spring,* grand ressort, *m*; (*fig.*) cheville ouvrière, *f,* mobile, *m.* ~*stay* (*fig.*), âme, *f*; soutien, *m. the* ~ *thing,* le principal, l'important, *m.* ~ *walls,* gros murs, *m.pl.* ¶ *n,* (*pipe*) conduite [maîtresse]; (*pl.*) canalisation, *f*; (*Elec.*) conducteur principal, *m*; (*sea, Poet.*) onde, *f. in the* ~, en général. **the M**~ (river), le Mein. ~**ly,** *ad,* principalement.

maintain, *v.t,* maintenir, soutenir; entretenir. **maintenance,** *n,* maintien, soutien; entretien, *m.*

Mainz, *n,* Mayence, *f.*

maize, *n,* maïs, *m.*

majestic†, *a,* majestueux. **majesty,** *n,* majesté, *f. His, Her,* **M~,** Sa Majesté.

majolica, *n,* majolique, maïolique, *f.*

major, *a,* majeur; (*prophet, etc.*) grand; (*pers.*) aîné. ~ *planet,* planète principale, *f.* ~ *road,* route de priorité, *f.* ¶ (*Mil.*) *n,* commandant, chef de bataillon, *m.* ~ *general,* général de division, *m.*

Majorca, *n,* Majorque, *f.*

majority, *n,* majorité; pluralité, (la) plupart, *f.*

make, *n,* façon; fabrication, *f.* ~*-believe,* feinte, frime, *f.* ~*shift,* moyen de fortune, pis aller, *m.* ~*up,* maquillage, fard, *m.* ~*weight,* complément de poids, *m*; (*butcher's*) réjouissance, *f*; (*fig.*) remplissage, *m.* ¶ *v.t.ir,* faire; dresser; pratiquer; fabriquer; confectionner; créer; rendre; forcer; réaliser; mettre; (*inquiries*) prendre; (*v.i.ir.*) se diriger [vers]; contribuer [à]; faire [comme si]. ~ *away with,* se défaire de; détourner. ~ *faces,* grimacer. ~ *hay,* faire les foins. ~ *it up,* se raccommoder. ~ *light of,* faire peu de cas de. ~ *money,* s'enrichir. ~ *much of,* faire mousser. ~ *off,* filer, décamper. ~ *one's will,* tester. ~ *out,* distinguer; déchiffrer; comprendre; dresser. ~ *the most of,* ménager. ~ *up,* (*quarrel*) se réconcilier; confectionner; (*face*) se farder, se maquiller; (*Theat.*) se grimer; (*Typ.*) mettre en pages. ~ *up for,* suppléer [à]. ~ *up one's mind,* se décider, se déterminer. **maker,** *n,* créateur, trice; faiseur, euse; fabricant; constructeur, *m.* **making,** *n,* création; fabrication; construction; confection, *f.*

malachite, *n,* malachite, *f.*

maladjusted, *a,* mal ajusté; inadapté. ¶ *n,* (*person*) inadapté, e.

maladministration, *n,* mauvaise gestion, *f.*

maladroit†, *a,* maladroit.

malady, *n,* maladie, *f.*

Malagasy, *a,* malgache. ¶ *n,* Malgache, *m,f.*

malaprop[ism], *n,* incongruité, *f,* pataquès, *m.*

malaria, *n,* paludisme, *m,* malaria, *f.* **malarial,** *a,* paludéen; miasmatique.

Malay[an], *a,* malais. ¶ *n,* (*pers.*) Malais, e; (*language*) le malais.

Malaysia, *n,* la Malaisie; Malaysia.

malcontent, *a. & n,* mécontent, *a. & m.*

male, *n,* mâle, *m.* ¶ *a,* mâle; masculin. ~ *descent,* masculinité, *f.* ~ *nurse,* infirmier, *m.*

malediction, *n,* malédiction, *f.*

malefactor, *n,* malfaiteur, *m.*

malevolent, *a,* malveillant.

malformation, *n,* malformation, *f,* vice de conformation, *m.*

malice, *n,* malice, rancune, *f.* ~ *aforethought,* préméditation, *f.*

malicious†, *a,* malicieux.

malign, *v.t,* diffamer, calomnier. **malign†, malignant†,** *a,* malin.

malinger, *v.i,* faire le malade, simuler la maladie.

mallard, *n,* malart, *m.*

malleable, *a,* malléable.

mallet, *n,* maillet, *m,* mailloche, batte, *f.*

mallow, *n,* mauve, *f.*

malnutrition, *m,* sous-alimentation, *f.*

malpractice, *n,* incurie; malfaçon, *f.*

malt, *n,* malt, *m.* ¶ *v.t,* convertir en malt. ~**ing,** *n,* malterie, *f.* ~**ster,** *n,* malteur, *m.*

Malta, *n,* Malte, *f.* **Maltese,** *a,* maltais. ~ *cross,* croix de Malte, *f.* ~ [*dog, bitch*], chien(ne) de Malte, bichon, ne. ¶ *n,* (*pers.*) Maltais, e; (*language*) le maltais.

maltreat, *v.t,* maltraiter, brutaliser. ~**ment,** *n,* mauvais traitements; sévices, *m.pl.*

mamillary, *a,* mamillaire.

mama, *n,* maman, *f.*

mammal, *n,* mammifère, *m.* **mammalia,** *n.pl,* mammifères, *m.pl.*

mammoth, *n,* mammouth, *m.*

man, *n,* homme; monsieur; cavalier; employé; ouvrier; valet, *m*; (*checkers*) pion, *m.* (*chess*) pièce, *f.* ~ *& wife,* mari & femme. ~ *child,* enfant mâle, *m.* ~-*eater,* mangeur d'hommes, *m.* ~ *Friday,* factotum, *m.* ~-*hole,* (*Mach.*) trou d'homme; (*sewer, etc.*) regard, *m.* the ~ *in the street,* l'homme de la rue. ~ *of all work,* homme à tout faire. ~ *of fashion,* élégant, *m.* ~ *of substance,* homme, calé. ~-*of-war,* bâtiment de guerre, *m.* ~'s *estate,* l'âge viril, *m.* ~[*servant*], domestique, valet, *m.* ~**slaughter,**

homicide involontaire, *m.* ¶ *v.t,* (*boat, etc.*) armer; équiper. ~**hood,** ~**kind,** ~**ly,** *etc.* See below.

manacle, *v.t,* mettre des menottes à; (*fig.*) enchaîner. ~**s,** *n.pl,* menottes, *f.pl,* fers, *m.pl.*

manage, *v.t,* diriger, administrer; gérer; conduire; manier; ménager; (*v.i.*) s'arranger; (*slang*) démerder. ~ *to,* parvenir à; obtenir de. ~**ment,** *n,* direction, administration; gérance, gestion; conduite; économie, *f*; maniement, *m. joint* ~, cogestion, *f.* **manager,** ess, *n,* directeur, trice, gérant, e; chef; (*ship's*) armateur, *m.* (*cinema*) *location* ~, régisseur d'exterieur, *m. managing director,* administrateur délégué, a. directeur, a. gérant, *m.*

manatee, *n,* lamantin, *m.*

Manchuria, *n,* la Mandchourie. **Manchu[rian],** *a,* mandchou. ¶ *n,* Mandchou, e.

mandarin, *n,* mandarin, *m.*

mandatory, *n,* mandataire, *m.* **mandate,** *n,* mandat, *m.* ~*d territory,* pays sous mandat, **mandator,** *n,* mandant, *m.*

mandible, *n,* mandibule, *f.*

mandolin[e], *n,* mandoline, *f.*

mandrake, *n,* mandragore, *f.*

mandrel, -il (*lathe*) *n,* mandrin, arbre, *m.*

mandrill (*baboon*) *n,* mandrill, *m.*

mane, *n,* crinière, *f,* crins, *m.pl.*

manege, -ège, *n,* manège, *m.*

manes, *n.pl,* mânes, *m.pl.*

maneuver, *n,* manœuvre, *f.* ¶ *v.i. & t,* manœuvrer, évoluer.

manfully, *ad,* en homme, courageusement.

manganese, *n,* manganèse, *m.*

mange, *n,* gale, rogne, *f,* rouvieux, *m.*

mangel[-wurzel] *or* **mangold** [-wurzel], *n,* betterave fourragère, *f.*

manger, *n,* mangeoire, crèche, *f.*

mangle, *n,* calandre, *f.* ¶ *v.t,* mutiler; (*linen*) calandrer.

mango, *n,* mangue, *f.* ~ [*tree*], manguier, *m.*

mangrove, *n,* manglier, palétuvier, *m.*

mangy, *a,* galeux, rogneux, rouvieux.

manhandle, *v.t,* malmener.

manhood, *n,* virilité, *f;* âge viril, *m.*

mania, *n,* manie; folie; rage; marotte, *f.* **maniac,** *n.* & ~**(al),** *a,* maniaque, *m,f.* & *a.*

manicure, *n,* soin des mains, *m,* manucure, *f.* ~ **set,** onglier, *m,* manucure, *f.* ~ *the hands,* soigner les. mains, faire de la manucure. **manicurist,** *n,* manucure, *f,m.*

manifest†, *a,* manifeste. ¶ *(ship.) n,* manifeste, *m.* ¶ *v.t,* manifester.

manifesto, *n,* manifeste, *m.*

manifold, *a,* multiple. ~ *book,* carnet genre manifold, cahier de copie, *dit* manifold, *m.*

manikin, *n,* [petit] bout d' homme; mannequin, *m.*

Manila, *n,* (*Geog.*) Manille, *f;* (*cheroot*) manille, *m.*

manioc, *n,* manioc, *m.*

manipulate, *v.t,* manœuvrer, manipuler; (*pers.*) empaumer.

mankind, *n,* le genre humain, l'espèce humaine; les hommes. **manliness,** *n,* virilité, *f.* **manly,** *a,* mâle, viril; (*woman*) hommasse.

manna, *n,* manne, *f.*

mannequin, *n,* mannequin, *m.*

manner, *n,* manière; façon, *f;* air; genre, *m;* (*pl.*) manières, formes, mœurs, *f.pl,* ton, *m. he has no* ~*s,* il n'a pas de savoir-vivre. ~**ed** (*style, etc.*) *a,* maniéré. ~**ism,** *n,* maniérisme, *m,* manière, *f,* tic, *m.* ~**ly,** *a,* poli.

mannish, *a,* garçonnier, hommasse.

manometer, *n,* manomètre, *m.*

manor, *n,* manoir, château, *m,* seigneurie, *f.*

mansard roof, comble brisé, *m.*

mansion, *n,* hôtel [particulier]; château; (*pl.*) immeuble à appartements, *m.*

manslaughter, *n,* homicide involontaire, *m.*

mantelpiece, *n,* manteau de cheminée, *m,* cheminée, *f.* **mantelshelf,** *n,* tablette de cheminée, *f.*

mantilla, *n,* mantille, *f.*

mantle, *n,* manteau; (*gas*) manchon, *m.* ~ *maker,* couturier, *m.* ¶ *v.t,* couvrir.

Mantua, *n,* Mantoue, *f.*

manual†, *a,* manuel, à bras. ~ [*exercise*] (*Mil.*), maniement des

(*ou* d') armes, *m.* ¶ *n,* manuel, guide-âne; (*organ*) clavier, *m.*

manufacture, *n,* fabrication, industrie, *f.* **manufacturer,** *n,* industriel, fabricant, manufacturier, *m.* ~*'s price,* prix de fabrique, *m.* **manufacturing,** *p.a,* manufacturier.

manure, *n,* fumier; engrais, *m.* ¶ *v.t,* engraisser; fumer.

manuscript, *n.* & *a,* manuscrit, *m.* & *a.*

Manx, *a,* de l'île de Man.

many, *a,* beaucoup; bien des; force; grand; maint, divers. ~ *a,* plus d'un, maint. *how* ~? combien? ~*-colored,* multicolore. ~*-sided,* complexe. *a great* ~, un grand nombre (de). *as* ~, autant. *so* ~, tant. *the* ~, la multitude. *too* ~, trop.

map, *n,* carte, *f;* plan, *m.* ~ *case,* porte-cartes, *m.* ~ *of the heavens.* carte céleste, *f.* ~ *of the world in hemispheres,* mappemonde, *f.* ~ *producer,* cartographe, *m.* ~ *road* ~, carte routière, *f.* ¶ *v.t,* dresser (*ou* faire) la carte de. ~ *out,* tracer.

maple, *n,* érable, *m.*

mar, *v.t,* gâter; troubler.

marabou & **marabout,** *n,* marabout, *m.*

maraschino, *n,* marasquin, *m.*

marasmus, *n,* marasme, *m.*

marathon [*race*], *n,* course de Marathon, *f.*

maraud, *v.t,* marauder. ~**er,** *n,* maraudeur, *m.* ~**ing,** *n,* maraudage, *m,* maraude, *f.*

marble, *n,* marbre, *m;* (*games*) bille, *f.* ~ *mason* & ~ *merchant,* marbrier, *m.* ~ *quarry,* marbrière, *f.* ~ *work* & ~ *works,* marbrerie, *f.* ¶ *v.t,* marbrer. **marbler,** *n,* marbreur, *m.* **marbling,** *n,* marbrure, *f.*

marc (*fruit refuse*) *n,* marc, *m.*

marcasite, *n,* marcassite, *f.*

March, *n,* mars, *m.*

march, *n,* marche, *f;* pas, *m.* ¶ *v.i,* marcher. ~ *in,* entrer. ~ *off,* se mettre en marche. ~ *out,* sortir. ~ *past,* défiler. ~*ing,* *n,* marche, *f.* ~ *song,* chanson de route, *f.*

marchioness, *n,* marquise, *f.*

mare, *n,* jument, *f. he has found a* ~*'s nest,* il croit avoir trouvé la pie au nid.

margarine, *n,* margarine, *f.*

margin, *n,* marge; (*book page*) marge, *f,* blanc; bord, *m;* provision; tolérance, *f.* ~**al,** *a,* marginal.

marguerite, *n,* grande marguerite, *f.*

marigold, *n,* souci, *m.*

marine, *a,* maritime; marin. ~ **glue,** glu marine, *f.* ~ **stores,** fournitures pour navires, f—s maritimes, *f.pl.* ¶ *n,* (*shipping*) marine, *f;* (*pers.*) soldat d'infanterie de marine, fantassin de la flotte, fusillier marin, *m.* **mariner,** *n,* marin, *m.* ~'**s compass,** boussole marine, *f.*

marionette, *n,* marionnette, *f.*

marital, *a,* marital.

maritime, *a,* maritime.

marjoram, *n,* marjolaine, *f.*

mark, *n,* marque, *f;* point; signe; repère, *m;* trace, *f;* but, *m;* estampille; cote, *f;* témoignage, (*Sch.*) point, *m,* note, *f.* ~ *of origin,* estampille, *f.* *question* ~, point d' interrogation, *m.* ¶ *v.t,* marquer; indiquer; porter [la mention]; noter; estampiller; coter; remarquer; faire attention à; (*card*) piper. ~ *out,* tracer; borner. ~ *time,* marquer le pas; piétiner sur place. ~ *my words,* écoutez-moi bien. ~**ed,** *p.a,* marqué, prononcé, sensible; (*man*) noté; (*cards*) biseautées. ~**er,** *n,* pointeur; repère; indicateur, *m.*

market, *n,* marché, *m;* place; bourse; (*covered*) halle, *f;* débouché; débit, *m.* ~ *town,* ville à marché, *f,* bourg, *m.* ~ *value,* valeur marchande, v. vénale, *f.* ¶ *v.t,* mettre en vente. ~**able,** *a,* marchand; de vente; vénal; négociable. ~**ing,** *n,* mise en vente, *f.*

marking, *n,* marquage, *m;* cote, *f.* ~ *ink,* encre à marquer le linge, *f.*

marksman, *n,* [bon] tireur, *m.*

marl, *n,* marne, *f.* ~ *pit,* marnière, *f.* ¶ *v.t,* marner.

marline, *n,* lusin, *m.* ~ *spike,* marlinspike, épissoir, *m.*

marly, *a,* marneux.

marmalade, *n,* confitures (*d'oranges*) *f.pl;* marmelade, *f.*

Marmora (Sea of), mer de Marmara, *f.*

marmot (*Zool.*) *n,* marmotte, *f.*

maroon, *a,* marron. ¶ *n,* couleur marron, *f;* (*pers.*) nègre marron, *m,* négresse marronne, *f.*

marquee, *n,* tente-pavillon, *f.*

marquetry, *n,* marqueterie, *f.*

marquis, -quess, *n,* marquis, *m.*

marriage, *n,* mariage, *m;* noces, *f.pl.* ~ *license,* dispense de bans, *f.* ~ *of convenience,* mariage de raison, m. de convenance. ~ *portion,* dot, *f.* ~ *settlement,* constitution de dot, *f.* ~ *tie,* lien conjugal, *m.* *cousin by* ~, cousin par alliance. ~**able,** *a,* mariable, nubile. ~ *daughter,* fille à marier, *f.* **married,** *p.a,* marié. [*newly*] ~ *couple,* nouveaux mariés, *m.pl.* ~ *life,* vie conjugale, *f. get* ~, se marier.

marrow, *n,* moelle; (*vegetable*) courge à la moelle, *f.* ~**bone,** os à moelle, *m.* ~*fats,* pois carrés, *m.pl.* ~**y,** *a,* moelleux.

marry, *v.t,* marier; épouser; (*v.i.*) se marier; s'allier. ~ *a third, time,* convoler en secondes, en troisièmes, noces. ~ *again,* se remarier, convoler. ~ *into,* s'apparenter à.

Marseilles, *n,* Marseille, *f. the Marseillaise* (*anthem*), la Marseillaise.

marsh, *n,* marais, marécage, *m.* ~ *marigold,* souci d'eau, *m.*

marshal, *n,* (*Mil.*) maréchal. ¶ *v.t,* classer; ranger; trier. ~**ship,** *n,* maréchalat, *m.*

marshmallow, *n,* guimauve, *f.*

marshy, *a,* marécageux, paludéen.

marsupial, *n,* marsupial, *m.*

mart, *n,* centre des affaires; marché, *m.*

marten, *n,* martre; fouine, *f.*

martial, *a,* martial; (*pers.*) guerrier. ~ *law* (in a town), état de siège, *m.*

martin, *n,* hirondelle de fenêtre, *f.*

martinet, *n,* gendarme, pète-sec, *m.*

martingale, (*harness, betting*) *n,* martingale, *f.*

Martinmas, *n,* la Saint-Martin.

martyr, *n,* martyr, e. ~**dom,** martyre, *m.* ~**[ize]** *v.t,* martyriser. ~**ology** (*list*) *n,* martyrologe, *m.*

marvel, *n,* merveille, *f;* prestige, miracle, *m.* ¶ *v.i,* s'émerveiller, s'étonner. **marvelous†,** *a,* merveilleux, prestigieux.

marzipan, *n,* massepain, *m.*

mascot, n, mascotte, f, porte-bonheur, fétiche, m.

masculine, a, masculin, mâle; (woman) hommasse, garçonnier. ~ [gender], [genre] masculin, m. **masculinity,** n, masculinité, f.

mash, n, mélange; (cattle) barbotage, m; (poultry) pâtée; (Cook.) purée, f. ¶ v.t, mélanger, brasser; réduire en purée. ~ed potatoes, turnips, purée de pommes de terre, de navets, f.

mask, n, masque; (Arch.) mascaron, m; (Phot.) cache, f. ¶ v.t, masquer, cacher. ~ed ball, bal masqué, m. **masker, -quer** (pers.) n, masque m.

maslin, n, mouture, f.

mason, n, maçon, m. ¶ v.t, maçonner. ~ic, a, maçonnique. ~ry, n, maçonnerie, f; maçonnage, m.

masquerade, n, mascarade; (fig.) mascarade, pantalonnade, f. ¶ v.i, se masquer, se déguiser.

mass, n, masse, f; amas, m; (Relig.) messe, f. ~ production, production en masse, fabrication en série, f. ¶ v.t, masser.

massacre, n, massacre, m. ¶ v.t, massacrer.

massage, n, massage, m. ¶ v.t, masser. **masseur, euse,** n, masseur, euse.

massive†, a, massif; en amas; en masses.

mast, n, mât, m; (pl.) mâture, f; (beech) faînes, f.pl; (oak) glands, m.pl, glandée, f. ¶ v.t, mâter.

master, n, maître; professeur; directeur; chef; patron; capitaine, m. be ~ of, posséder. be one's own ~, s'appartenir. ~ key, passepartout, m. ~ mind, cheville ouvrière, f. ~ of the hounds, maître d'équipage. ~piece, chef-d'œuvre, m. ~ stroke, coup de maître, m. ¶ v.t, maîtriser. ~ful, a, (tone) magistral. ~ man, woman, maître homme, maîtresse femme. ~ly, a, de maître, magistral. in a ~ way, magistralement, supérieurement. ~y, n, maîtrise, f, empire; dessus, m.

mastic, n, mastic, m. ~ [tree], lentisque, m.

masticate, v.t, mâcher, mastiquer. **mastication,** n, mastication, f.

mastiff, n, mâtin, m.

mastodon, n, mastodonte, m.

mastoid, a, mastoïde.

mat, a, mat. ¶ n, natte, f; paillasson; tapis; (plate) dessous, m. ~ maker, nattier, m. ¶ v.t, natter. **matted hair,** cheveux embroussaillés, m.pl.

matador, n, matador, m.

match, n, (light) allumette; alliance, f, parti, m; assortiment; pendant; (pers.) pareil, le; (Ten., etc.) partie, f, match; (Box., wrestling) combat, match, m. ~board, planche bouvetée, f. ~box, boîte à allumettes, f. ~maker, marieur, euse. ~ play (golf), concours par trous, m. ¶ v.t, allier; marier; égaler; assortir; [r]appareiller; [r]apparier. to ~, pareil. ~less, a, sans pareil.

mate, n, camarade, m,f, compagnon, m, compagne, f; aide, m,f; (bird) pair; (Naut.) second, lieutenant; (chess) mat, m. ¶ v.t, appareiller, accoupler; (chess) faire mat, mater.

material†, a, matériel; essentiel. ¶ n, matière, f; matériel, m; étoffe, f; (pl.) matières, f.pl; matériaux, m.pl; fournitures, f.pl; articles, m.pl. raw ~, matière première, f. ~ism, n, matérialisme, m. ~ist, n. & ~istic, a, matérialiste. ~ize, v.t, matérialiser; (v.i.) se m.; aboutir.

maternal†, a, maternel. **maternity,** n. & ~ hospital, maternité, f. ~ doctor, accoucheur, m.

mathematical†, a, mathématique; (precise) géométrique; (instruments) de mathématiques. **mathematician,** n, mathématicien, ne. **mathematics,** n.pl, mathématiques, f.pl.

matinée, n, matinée, f. **matins,** n.pl, matines, f.pl.

matriarchy, n, matriarcat, m.

matriculate, v.i, prendre des (ses) inscriptions. **matriculation,** n, inscription, f.

matrimonial†, a, conjugal; (law, agent, etc.) matrimonial. ~ triangle, ménage à trois, m. **matrimony,** n, mariage, m, vie conjugale, f.

matrix, n, matrice; gangue, f.

matron, n, matrone; (hospital, etc.) infirmière en chef, f. ~ly, a, de matrone.

matter, n, matière; affaire; chose; question, f; propos; cas; sujet; article; chapitre; (Med.) pus, m.

as a ~ of course, comme une chose toute naturelle *ou* qui va de soi. *as a ~ of fact*, dans (*ou* par) le fait, en fait. *~-of-fact*, positif. *~ of history*, fait historique, *m. what's the ~?* qu'avez-vous? ¶ *v.i.* importer, faire. *no ~!* n'importe!

Matterhorn (the), le mont Cervin.

mattery, *a*, purulent.

matting, *n*, natte[s] *f*.[*pl.*], paillasson; abrivent, *m*.

mattins, *n.pl.* matines, *f.pl.*

mattock, *n*, pioche-hache, *f*; hoyau, *m*.

mattress, *n*, matelas; sommier, *m*. *~ maker*, matelassier, ère.

mature†, *a*, mûr. ¶ *v.i. & t*, mûrir; (*Com.*) échoir. **maturity**, *n*, maturité; échéance, *f*.

maudlin, *a*, bêtement sentimental; ivre à pleurer; pleurard, larmoyant. **~[ism]**, *n*, romance, *f*.

maul, *v.t*, malmener. *~stick*, appui-main, *m*.

Mauritius, *n*, [l'île] Maurice, *f*.

mausoleum, *n*, mausolée, *m*.

mauve, *n. & a*, mauve, *m. & att*.

mawkish†, *a*, mielleux, doucereux, fade.

maxim, *n*, maxime, sentence, *f*; adage, *m*.

maximum, *n*, maximum; plafond, *m*. ¶ *a*, maximum.

May (*month*) *n*, mai, *m. May Day*, le premier mai. *May fly*, mouche de mai, *f*, éphémère, *m. maypole*, mai, *m*.

may (*Bot.*) *n*, fleurs d'aubépine, *f.pl. ~* [*bush*], aubépine, épine blanche, *f*.

may, *v. aux. ir*, pouvoir; permettre; que. *it ~ be*, cela se peut. *~be*, *ad*, peut-être.

mayonnaise, *n. & att*, mayonnaise, *f. & att*.

mayor, *n*, maire, *m. ~alty*, *n*, mairie, *f*.

maze, *n*, labyrinthe, dédale, *m*.

mazurka, *n*, mazurka, *f*.

me, *pn*, me; moi.

meadow & (*Poet.*) **mead**, *n*, pré, *m*, prairie, *f. meadowsweet*, reine des prés, *f*.

meager†, *a*, maigre, pauvre. **~ness**, *n*, maigreur, pauvreté, *f*.

meal, *n*, repas, *m*; (*grain*) farine, *f. ~ time*, l'heure du repas, *f. at ~ times*, aux heures de repas. **~y**, *a*, farineux. **~mouthed**, mielleux, doucereux.

mean†, *a*, bas; vil; abject; chétif; mesquin; ladre; chiche; petit; (*average*) moyen. *in the ~ time* (*or while*) or **~time**, **~while**, *ad*, en attendant; entretemps, cependant. ¶ *n*, milieu, *m*; (*Math.*) moyenne, *f*; (*pl.*) moyen, *m*; moyens, *m.pl*, facultés, *f.pl*. *by no ~s*, nullement. *private ~s*, fortune personnelle, *f*. ¶ *v.t. & i. ir*, se proposer; avoir l'intention de; vouloir; compter; penser; vouloir dire; signifier; entendre; destiner; faire exprès. *~ well*, avoir de bonnes intentions.

meander, *n*, méandre, *m*. ¶ *v.i*, cheminer, serpenter.

meaning, *n*, signification, *f*, sens, *m*; intention, *f*. **-meaning**, *a*, intentionné. **~less**, *a*, sans aucun sens, un non-sens.

meanness, *n*, bassesse, abjection, ladrerie, vilenie, *f*.

measles, *n.pl*, rougeole, *f*.

measurable, *a*, mesurable à, appréciable. **measure**, *n*, mesure; dose; démarche; (*tape*) mesure, *f*; mètre; centimètre, *m*; (*bill*) projet de loi, *m*; (*pl, Geol.*) étage, *m*, série, *f*, terrain, *m. to ~* (*clothes*), sur mesure. ¶ *v.t. & i*, mesurer; métrer; arpenter; jauger; cuber; toiser; (*the body*) mensurer; (*for fitting*) prendre mesure à; avoir. *~ out*, doser. **~d**, *a*, mesuré, modéré. **~ment**, *n*, mesurage, *m*; mesure; grosseur, *f*; volume; arpentage; jaugeage, *m*.

meat, *n*, viande; chair, *f. ~ break-fast*, déjeuner à la fourchette, *m. ~ day* (*Eccl.*), jour gras, *m. ~y*, *a*, charnu; (*food*) carné.

Mecca, *n*, la Mecque.

mechanic, *n*, [ouvrier] mécanicien, mécanique, *m. ~al†*, *a*, mécanique; (*fig.*) machinal. *~ dentistry*, prothèse dentaire, *f. ~ drawing*, dessin industriel, *m. ~ engineer*, ingénieur mécanicien, *m. ~ engineering*, l'art de la mécanique, *m*; construction mécanique, *f*. **mechanician** & **mechanist**, *n*, mécanicien, *m*. **mechanics**, *n.pl*, mécanique, *f*. **mechanism**, *n*, mécanisme, *m*, mécanique, *f*, organes, *m.pl*. **mechanization**, *n*, mécanisme, *m*. **mechanize**, *v.t*, mécaniser.

Mechlin [**lace**], *n*, malines, *f*.

medal, *n*, médaille, *f. ~ cabinet & collection of ~s*, médaillier, *m.* ~ *maker* or **medalist**, *n,* médailleur. *m. award a* ~ *to,* médailler. **medaled**, *a,* médaillé. **medallion**, *n,* médaillon, *m.* **medalist** (*recipient*) *n,* médaillé, *e.*

meddle, *v.i,* se mêler, s'immiscer, s'ingérer; toucher. **meddler**, *n,* or **meddlesome person,** touche-à-tout, *m,* personne qui se mêle des oignons des autres, *f.* **meddling**, *n,* immixtion, ingérence, *f.*

median, *a,* médian; moyen.

mediate, *v.i,* s'interposer. **mediation**, *n,* médiation, *f.* **mediator, trix**, *n,* médiateur, trice.

medical, *a,* médical; (*school, etc.*) de médecine; (*student*) en médecine. ~ *examination* (recruits), revision, *f.* ~ *jurisprudence,* médecine légale, *f.* ~ *man,* ~ *officer,* médecin, *m.* **medicament**, *n,* médicament, *m.* **medicated**, *p.a,* médicamenteux. **medicinal**, *a,* médicinal; médicamenteux. **medicine**, *n,* médecine, *f;* médicament, *m.* ~ *cabinet,* ~ *chest,* pharmacie; caisse à médicaments, *f.* ~ *man,* [sorcier] guérisseur, *m.* **medico-judicial**, *a,* médico-légal.

medieval, *a,* médiéval, moyenâgeux.

mediocre, *a,* médiocre. **mediocrity**, *n,* (*quality*) médiocrité, *f,* médiocre, *m;* (*pers.*) médiocre, *m.*

meditate ([up]on), *v.t. & i,* méditer (sur), contempler. **meditation**, *n,* méditation, *f,* pensées, *f.pl.* **meditative**, *a,* méditatif.

mediterranean, *a,* méditerrané. M~, *a,* méditerranéen. **the M~** [Sea], la [mer] Méditerranée.

medium, *a,* moyen. ¶ *n,* milieu; agent; véhicule, *m;* (*ether*) atmosphère; (*agency*) entremise, *f,* intermédiaire; (*spiritualism*) médium, *m.*

medlar, *n,* nèfle, *f.* ~ [*tree*], néflier, *m.*

medley, *n,* mélange, bariolage, (*Mus.*) pot pourri, *m.* ¶ *a,* mêlé. ¶ *v.t,* mêler; bigarrer.

medullary, *a,* médullaire.

medusa (*jelly fish*) *n,* méduse, *f.*

meek, *a,* doux; débonnaire. ~**ly**, *ad,* avec douceur. ~**ness**, *n,* douceur, mansuétude, *f.*

meerschaum, *n,* écume de mer, *f.*

meet (Hunt.) *n,* assemblée, *f.* ¶ *v.t,r,* rencontrer; trouver; faire face à; accueillir; honorer;

(*v.i.ir.*) se rencontrer; confluer; s'assembler; se réunir. ~ *with,* éprouver, essuyer. ~**ing**, *n,* rencontre; jonction, *f;* confluent, *m;* entrevue; assemblée; réunion, *f;* meeting; concours, *m;* séance, *f.* (*of engagements, bills of exchange*) bonne fin, *f.*

megaphone, *n,* porte-voix, *m.*

melancholia & melancholy, *n,* mélancolie, *f.* **melancholic & melancholy**, *a,* mélancolique.

Melanesia, *n,* la Mélanésie.

mellow, *a,* mûr; moelleux; (*earth*) meuble. ¶ *v.t,* mûrir.

melodious†, *a,* mélodieux. **melody**, *n,* mélodie, *f,* chant, *m.*

melon, *n,* melon, *m.*

melt, *v.t. & i. ir,* fondre; attendrir; s'a. *that* ~*s in the mouth* (as a pear), fondant. ~**er**, *n,* fondeur, *m.* ~**ing**, *n,* fonte, fusion, *f.* ~ *point,* point de fusion, *m.* ~ *pot,* creuset, pot, *m.*

member, *n,* membre, *m,* adhérent, e, associé, e; représentant, *m.* ~ *of a conciliation board,* prud'homme, *m.* ~ *of a* (or *the*) *congress,* congressiste, *m,f.* ~ *of legislature,* représentant à la Chambre, *m.* ~**ship**, *n,* qualité [de membre]; adhésion; charge; (*legislature*) députation, *f;* nombre des adhérents, *m.*

membrane, *n,* membrane, *f.*

memento, *n,* mémento; souvenir, *m.*

memoir, *n,* mémoire, *m;* (*pl, book*) mémorial, *m.*

memorable, *a,* mémorable. **memorandum**, *n,* mémorandum, *m,* note, *f,* mémoire, *m. as a* ~, pour mémoire. ~ *book,* carnet, calepin, *m.* **memorial**, *n,* mémorial, monument, *m.* **memorize**, *v.t,* apprendre par cœur. **memory**, *n,* mémoire, *f;* souvenir, *m;* (*pl.*) souvenances, *f.pl.* ~ *from* ~, de mémoire. (*computers*) *read only* ~, mémoire morte, *f. random access* ~, m. vive, *f.*

menace, *n,* menace, *f. public* ~ (*pers.*), malfaiteur public, *m.* ¶ *v.t,* menacer.

menagerie, *n,* ménagerie, *f.*

mend, *v.t,* raccommoder, réparer; repriser; améliorer; réformer. ~ *one's ways,* changer de conduite.

mendacious, *a,* mensonger. **men-**

dacity, *n*, l'habitude du mensonge, *f*.

mender, *n*, raccommodeur, euse, réparateur, trice.

mendicancy & mendicity, *n*, mendicité, *f*. **mendicant**, *a*. *& n*, mendiant, e.

mending, *n*, raccommodage, *m*, réparation; reprise, *f*.

menhir, *n*, menhir, peulven, *m*.

menial, *a*, servile. ¶ *n*, laquais, *m*.

meningitis, *n*, méningite, *f*.

menopause, *n*, ménopause, *f*. menses, *n*, règles, *f.pl*.

mensuration, *n*, mesure, *f*; (*science*) mesures, *f.pl*; (*of the body*) mensuration, *f*.

mental, *a*, mental; moral. ~ *arithmetic*, calcul mental, *m*. ~ *institution*, maison d'aliénés, *f*, asile d'a—s, *m*. ~ *patient*, aliéné, e. ~ *reservation*, restriction mentale, arrière-pensée, *f*. ~**ity**, *n*, mentalité, *f*. ~**ly**, *ad*, mentalement. ~ *deficient*, à petite mentalité.

menthol, *n*, menthol, *m*.

mention, *n*, mention; constatation, *f*. ~ *in dispatches*, citation à l'ordre de l'armée, *f*. ¶ *v.t*, mentionner, parler de, prononcer; indiquer; citer; constater. *don't ~ it!* il n'y a pas de quoi, du tout!

Mentone, *n*, Menton, *m*.

menu, *n*, menu, *m*; carte du jour, *f*. ~ *holder*, porte-menu, *m*.

meow, *n*, miaulement, *m*. ¶ *v.i*, miauler.

mercantile, *a*, marchand, commercial, de commerce; (*mercenary*) mercantile.

Mercator's projection, projection de Mercator, *f*.

mercenary, *a*, mercenaire, stipendiaire, vénal, mercantile. ¶ *n*, mercenaire, *m*.

mercer, *n*, marchand de soieries, *m*. ~**ized**, *a*, mercerisé.

merchandise, *n*, marchandise, *f*. *oft. pl.* **merchant**, *n*, négociant, e, commerçant, e; marchand, e. ~ *marine*, marine marchande, *f*.

merciful†, *a*, miséricordieux, clément. **merciless†**, *a*, impitoyable.

mercurial, *a*, (*Chem.*) mercuriel; (*barometer, etc.*) à mercure; (*fig.*) vif. **mercury**, *n*,

(*metal*) mercure, *m*; (*Bot.*) mercuriale, *f*.

mercy, *n*, miséricorde, merci, clémence, grâce, *f*, bienfait, bien, *m*; pitié, *f*. *at the ~ of*, à la merci de; *au gré de*. ~ *on us!* miséricorde!

mere†, *a*, simple, pur, seul. *a ~ nothing*, un rien. ¶ *n*, lac, *m*.

meretricious, *a*, de courtisane; factice.

merge, *v.t*, fusionner; se fondre; s'amalgamer.

meridian, *n. & a*, méridien, *m. & a*. **meridional**, *a. & n*, méridional, e.

meringue, *n*, meringue, *f*.

merino, *n*, mérinos, *m*.

merit, *n*, mérite, *m*. ¶ *v.t*, mériter. **meritorious**, *a*, méritoire; (*of pers.*) méritant.

merlin (*bird*) *n*, émerillon, *m*.

mermaid, *n*, sirène, *f*. **merman**, *n*, triton, *m*.

merrily, *ad*, gaiement, joyeusement. **merriment**, *n*, gaieté, joie, hilarité, *f*. **merry**, *a*, gai, joyeux; jovial. *a ~ Christmas!* joyeux Noël! *make ~*, se réjouir, s'égayer. *make ~ over*, se divertir [aux dépens] de. ~**-go-round**, manège de chevaux de bois, carrousel, *m*. ~**making**, réjouissances, *f.pl*.

mesh, *n*, maille, *f*. *in ~* (*Mech.*), en prise. ¶ *v.t*, s'engrener.

mesmeric, *a*, magnétique. **mesmerism**, *n*, magnétisme, *m*. **mesmerist**, *n*, magnétiseur, *m*. **mesmerize**, *v.t*, magnétiser.

mess, *n*, (*Mil., Nav.*) popote, gamelle, *f*; ordinaire; plat; (*fig.*) gâchis, margouillis, pétrin, *m*; saleté, *f*. ~ *kit*, gamelle, *f*. ~**mate**, camarade de plat, *m,f*, commensal, e. ¶ *v.t*, salir; (*v.i.*) manger. ~ *about*, tripoter. ~ *up*, gâcher.

message, *n*, message, *m*; dépêche, *f*. **messenger**, *n*, messager, ère; envoyé, e; courrier; commissionnaire; porteur; chasseur; garçon de bureau, *m*.

Messiah, *n*, Messie, *m*.

Messina, *n*, Messine, *f*.

messy, *a*, sale, graisseux.

metal, *n*, métal, *m*. ~ *saw*, scie à métaux, *f*. **metallic**, *a*, métallique; (*voice*) cuivrée. **metalliferous**, *a*, métallifère. **metallurgist**, *n*, métallurgiste, *m*. **metallurgy**, *n*, métallurgie, *f*.

metamorphose, *v.t*, métamor- phoser. **metamorphosis**, *n*, méta- morphose, *f*.

metaphor, *n*, métaphore, *f*. **~ical**†, *a*, métaphorique.

metaphysical, *a*, métaphysique. **metaphysician**, *n*, métaphysicien, *m*. **metaphysics**, *n.pl*, méta- physique, *f*.

mete [out], *v.t*, mesurer, doser.

meteor, *n*, météore, *m*. **~ic**, *a*, météorique. **~ite**, *n*, aérolithe, *m*. **~ologic(al)**, *a*, météorologique. **~ology**, *n*, météorologie, *f*.

meter, *n*, (*Meas.*) mètre; (*Poet.*) mesure, mètre; (*gasoline*) jaug- eur; compteur, *m*.

method, *n*, méthode, *f*, mode, *m*, modalité, *f*. **~ical**†, *a*, métho- dique. **~ism**, *n*, méthodisme, *m*. **~ist**, *n*, méthodiste, *m,f*.

methyl (*Chem.*), *n*, méthyle, *m*. **~ated spirit**, alcool dénaturé, alcool à brûler, *m*.

meticulous†, *a*, méticuleux.

metric & metrical, *a*, métrique. **metrics** (*Poet.*) *n*, métrique, *f*.

metronome, *n*, métronome, *m*.

metropolis, *n*, capitale; métro- pole, *f*. **metropolitan**, *a*, de la capitale; métropolitain.

mettle, *n*, fougue, *f*, panache, cran; honneur, *m*. **~some**, *a*, fougueux.

mew, *n*, (*sea gull*) mouette; (*cage for hawks*) mue, *f*. ¶ *v.i*, miauler. **~[ing]**, *n*, miaulement, *m*. **mews**, *n*, écuries, *f.pl*.

Mexican, *a*, mexicain. ¶ *n*, Mexi- cain, e. **Mexico** (*country*) *n*, le Mexique. **~** [City], Mexico, *m*.

mezzanine [floor], *n*, entresol, *m*. **mezzo-relievo**, *n*, demi-relief, *m*. **mezzo-soprano**, *n*, mezzo- soprano, *m*. **mezzotint**, *n*, ma- nière noire; gravure à la m. n., *f*.

miasma, *n*, miasme, *m*.

mica, *n*, mica, *m*.

Michaelmas, *n*, la Saint-Michel. **~ daisy**, marguerite de la Saint- Michel, *f*.

microbe, *n*, microbe, *m*.

microgroove, *n*, microsillon, *m*. **micrometer**, *n*, micromètre, palmer, *m*. **microphone**, *n*, micro- phone, *m*. **microprocessing**, *n*, microtraitement, *m*, micro-infor- matique, *f*. **microprocessor**, *n*, mi- croprocesseur, *m*. **microscope**, *n*, microscope, *m*.

microprogram, *v.t*, micropro-

grammer. ¶ *n*, microprogramme, *m*.

microwave, *n*, micro-onde, *f*.

mid, *a*: **in ~ air**, *Channel*, au milieu de l'air, de la Manche. **~day**, midi, *m*. **~iron** (*golf*), fer moyen, *m*. **~ lent**, la micarême. **~night**, minuit, *m*. **~shipman**, aspirant [de marine] *m*. **~sum- mer**, milieu de l'été. **Midsummer Day**, la Saint-Jean; le 24 juin. **~way**, *ad*, à moitié chemin, à mi- chemin. **~wife**, sage-femme, *f*. **in ~ winter**, en plein hiver.

middle, *a*, du milieu; moyen. **~-aged**, d'âge moyen, entre deux âges. **M~ Ages**, moyen âge, *m*. **~ class[es]**, classe moyenne, bourgeoisie, *f*. **~-class house**, maison bourgeoise, *f*. **~-class man, woman**, bourgeois, e. **~ course** (conduct), moyen terme, *m*. **~ distance**, second plan, *m*. **the M~ East**, Moyen-Orient, *m*. **~ finger**, doigt du milieu, médius, *m*. **~man**, intermédiaire, *m*. **~ register** (*Mus.*), médium, *m*. **~ [term]** (*Log.*), moyen [terme] *m*. **~weight** (*Box.*), poids moyen, *m*. ¶ *n*, milieu; centre, *m*; (*waist*) ceinture, *f*.

middling†, *a*, moyen; médiocre. ¶ *ad*, assez bien, entre deux, comme ci, comme ça, cahin-caha. **~s** (*flour*) *n.pl*, recoupe, *f*.

midge, *n*, moucheron, cousin, *m*.

midget, *n*, nabot, e, [petit] bout d'homme, *m*.

midnight, midshipman, *etc.* See under *mid*.

midst, *n*, milieu, sein, *m*.

mien, *n*, mine, *f*, air, *m*.

might, *n*, puissance; force, *f*. **with ~ & main**, de toutes ses forces. **one ~ as well**, autant vaut. **a ~-have-been**, un grand homme manqué. **mightiness**, *n*; puissance; grandeur, *f*. **mighty**†, *a*, puissant. **the ~ ones**, les puis- sants, *m.pl*.

mignonette, *n*, (*Bot.*) réséda, *m*; (*lace*) mignonnette, *f*.

migrant, *a*, migrateur. **migrate**, *v.i*, émigrer. **migration**, *n*, migra- tion *f*. **migratory**, *a*, migrateur, voyageur, de passage.

Milan, *n*, Milan, *m*. **~ese**, *a*, milanais. ¶ *n*, Milanais, e.

milch cow, vache à lait, vache laitière; (*fig.*) vache à lait, *f*.

mild†, *a*, doux; bénin; anodin.

mildew, *n*, moisi, *m*, moisissure; (*blight on plants*) rouille, *f*; (*on vines*) mildiou, *m*. ¶*v.t*, moisir; (*v.i.*) [se] moisir.

mildness, *n*, douceur, *f*.

mile, *n*, mille [anglais] *m.* = 1.6093 kilometers (*Note:—To convert miles to kilometers, approximately, multiply miles by 8 and divide by 5*); (*long way*) lieue, *f*. *a* ~ *off*, d'une lieue. ~*stone*, pierre milliaire; (*Fr.*) borne kilométrique, *f*.

militant, *a. & n*, militant, *a. & m*. **militarize**, *v.t*, militariser. **military**†, *a. & ~ man*, militaire, *a. & m. the* ~, les militaires, *m.pl.* ~ *pageant*, scène militaire à grand spectacle, *f*. **militate**, *v.i*, militer. **militia**, *n*, milice, *f*. ~*man*, milicien, *m*.

milk, *n*, lait, *m*. ~ *chocolate*, chocolat lacté, c. au lait, *m*. ~ *diet*, régime lacté, *m*, diète lactée, *f*. ~ *fever*, fièvre de lait, *f*. ~ *food*, laitage, *m*. ~*maid*, fille de ferme, *f*. ~*man*, ~*woman*, laitier, ère. ~*sop* (*pers.*), poule mouillée, *f*. ~ *tooth*, dent de lait, *f*. ~ *train*, wagon-laitière. *m*. ¶*v.t*, traire, tirer. ~**er**, *n*, trayeur, euse; (*cow*) laitière, *f*. ~**ing**, *n*, traite, mulsion, *f*. **milky**, *a*, laiteux. M~ *Way*, voie lactée, *f*.

mill, *n*, moulin, *m*; fabrique; usine, *f*; atelier, *m*. ~*board*, carton [épais] *m*. ~*hand*, ouvrier (ère) d'usine. ~*owner*, industriel, usinier, *m*. ~*stone*, meule de moulin, *f*. ~*stone grit & ~stone grit quarry*, meulière, *f*. *textile* ~, usine de textiles, *f*. ¶*v.t*, moudre; (*ore*, *etc.*) bocarder, broyer; (*cloth*) fouler; (*to knurl*) moleter, (*to slot*) fraiser; (*a coin*) créneler. ~*ed edge*, cordon[net], crénelage, *m*.

millenary, *a. & n*, millénaire, *a. & m*. **millennium**, *n*, millénaire; (*fig.*) bonheur sans mélange, paradis terrestre, *m*.

millepede, *n*, mille-pieds, mille-pattes, *m*.

miller, *n*, meunier, ère, minotier, *m*; farinier, ère.

millet, *n*, millet, mil, *m*. ~ *grass*, millet, *m*.

milliner, *n*, modiste, *f*; marchand(e) de modes; chapelier, *m*. ~*'s head*, marotte, *f*. ~**y**, *n*, modes, *f.pl*, articles de modes, *m. pl*; chapeaux, *m.pl*.

milling, *n*, (*flour*) meunerie, minoterie, *f*; (*ore*) broyage; (*cloth*) foulage; (*metal*) fraisage; (*coins*) crénelage, grènetis, *m*. fraise, *f*. ~ *machine*, machine à fraiser, *f*.

million, *n*, million, *m. the* ~*s*, la multitude, la masse du peuple. **millionaire**, *n*, millionnaire, *m.f*. **millionth**, *a. & n*, millionième, *a. & n*.

milt, *n*, (*in mammals*) rate; (*in fish*) laitance, laite, *f*. ¶*v.t*, féconder.

mime, *n*, mime, *m*. ¶*v.i*, mimer. **mimic**, *a*, mimique, imitateur. ¶*n*, mime, *m*, imitateur, trice. ¶*v.t*, mimer, imiter, contrefaire. **mimicry**, *n*, mimique, *f*. **mimicry or mimesis** (*Zool.*) *n*, mimétisme, *m*.

mimosa, *n*, mimosa, *m*.

mince, *n*, hachis, *m*. ~*meat*, hachis, *m*. ¶*v.t*, (*meat*) hacher [menu]; (*v.i.*) minauder. ~ *one's words*, ménager les termes; parler avec affectation. *not to* ~ *matters*, ne pas le mâcher. **mincer**, *n*, hachoir, *m*. **mincing** (*fig.*) *n*, minauderie, *f*. ¶*a*, minaudier, mignard, affété, grimacier.

mind, *n*, esprit, *m*; âme, *f*; moral; cerveau, *m*, cervelle, *f*; envie, idée, pensée, *f*; avis, *m*, opinion, *f. go out of one's* ~, perdre la raison. ¶*v.t*, faire attention à; se soucier de; regarder à; garder. *I don't* ~, cela m'est égal. *bear in* ~, tenir compte de. *make up one's* ~, se décider. ~ *your own business! mêlez-vous de vos affaires!* ~**ed**, *a*, disposé, porté, pensant, enclin. ~**ful**, *a*, attentif.

mine, *pn*, le mien, la mienne, les miens, les miennes; à moi. *a friend of* ~, un de mes amis, un ami à moi.

mine, *n*, mine; (*fig.*) mine, *f*, filon, *m*; (*war*) mine, torpille, *f*. ~ *crater*, entonnoir, *m*. ~ *layer*, poseur de mines. *m*. ~ *sweeper*, dragueur de mines, *m*. ¶*v.t. & i*, exploiter; abattre; fouiller; miner; caver; torpiller. **miner**, *n*, mineur, *m*. **mineral**, *a. & n*, minéral, *a. & m*. ~ *water*, eau minérale [naturelle] *f*. ~ [*water*], eau minérale [artificielle] *f*. **mineralogical**, *a*, minéralogique. **mineralogist**, *n*, minéralogiste, *m*. **mineralogy**, *n*, minéralogie, *f*.

mingle, *v.t*, mélanger, mêler, confondre.

miniature, n, miniature, f; diminutif, m. ~ *golf,* golf miniature, m. **miniaturist,** n, miniaturiste, m,f. **miniaturize,** v.t, miniaturiser.

minimize, v.t, atténuer. **minimum,** n. & a, minimum, m. & a.

mining, n, exploitation [de mines] f; (att.) minier. ~ *engineer,* ingénieur [civil] des mines, m.

minion, n, mignon, favori, m. ~*s of the law,* recors de la justice, m.pl.

minister, n, ministre; pasteur, m. ~ *to,* pourvoir à; servir; (Eccl.) desservir. ~**ial,** a, ministériel. ~*ing angel,* ange de bonté, m; sœur de charité, f. **ministration,** n, ministère, m. **ministry,** n, ministère; département; sacerdoce, m.

miniver, n, petit-gris, m.

mink (Zool. & fur) n, vison, m.

minnow, n, vairon, m.

minor, a, petit; secondaire, subalterne; moindre; peu important; peu grave; mineur; (repairs) menues; (planet) télescopique; (pers.) jeune, cadet; (poet) de second ordre. ¶ n, (pers.) mineur, e; (Mus.) mineur, m.

Minorca, n, Minorque, f.

minority, n, minorité, f.

minster, n, église de monastère, é. abbatiale; cathédrale, f.

minstrel, n, (Hist.) ménestrel; chanteur, musicien; acteur comique, m.

mint, n, Monnaie, f, hôtel de la Monnaie, h. des Monnaies, m; (fig.) mine; (Bot.) menthe, f. a ~ *of money,* un argent fou. ¶ v.t, monnayer, frapper. ~**er,** n, monnayeur, m.

minuet, n, menuet, m.

minus, pr, moins. ~ *quantity,* déficit, m. ~ [sign] n, [signe] moins, m.

minute, a, menu, minime, minuscule; minutieux. ¶ n, minute, f, (pl.) procès-verbaux, m. ~ *book,* registre des délibérations, r. des procès-verbaux, plumitif, m. ~ *hand,* aiguille des minutes, f. ¶ v.t, minuter; constater par procès-verbal. ~**ly,** ad, minutieusement. ~**ness** & **minutia,** n, minutie, f.

minx, n, coquine, friponne, masque, f.

miracle, n, miracle, m. ~ [play],

miracle, mystère, m. **miraculous†,** a, miraculeux.

mirage, n, mirage, m.

mire, n, fange, boue, f. ¶ v.t, embourber.

mirror, n, miroir, m, glace, f. *rearview* ~, rétroviseur, m. ¶ v.t, refléter.

mirth, n, joie, gaieté, f. ~**ful†,** a, joyeux, gai.

miry, a, fangeux, boueux.

misadventure, n, mésaventure, f.

misalliance, n, mésalliance, f. *make a* ~, se mésallier. **misally,** v.t, mésallier.

misanthrope, -pist, n, misanthrope, m. **misanthropic(al),** a, misanthropique, misanthrope.

misapply, v.t, mal appliquer; détourner.

misapprehend, v.t, mal comprendre. **misapprehension,** n, malentendu, m.

misappropriate, v.t, détourner, dilapider.

misbehave [oneself], se comporter mal. **misbehavior,** n, mauvaise conduite, inconduite, f.

miscalculate, v.i, se tromper. **miscalculation,** n, erreur de calcul, f, mécompte, m.

miscarriage, n, (letter, etc.) égarement, m; (Med.) fausse couche, f; (failure) avortement, insuccès, m. ~ *of justice,* erreur judiciaire, f. **miscarry,** v.i, s'égarer; (Med.) faire une fausse couche; (fail) avorter, échouer, rater.

miscellaneous, a, divers; mêlé. ~ *works* or **miscellany** or **miscellanea,** n, mélanges, m.pl, variétés, f.pl, recueil factice, m.

mischance, n, infortune, fatalité, f.

mischief, n, mal; (playful) espièglerie, f. ~ *maker,* boutefeu, m. **mischievous†,** a, méchant; espiègle.

misconceive, v.i, mal concevoir. **misconception,** n, malentendu, m.

misconduct, n, déportements, m.pl., inconduite, f. ~ *oneself,* se conduire mal.

misconstruction, n, contresens, m. **misconstrue,** v.t, prendre à rebours.

miscreant, n, gredin, scélérat, m.

miscue, n, faux coup de queue, m.

misdeal (cards) n, maldonne, f.

misdeed, n, méfait, m.

misdeliver, v.t, livrer par erreur.

misdemeanant, n, délinquant, e. **misdemeanor,** n, délit, m.

misdirect, v.t, mal diriger; (a letter) se tromper d'adresse sur.

miser, n, avare, m,f, harpagon, m.

miserable†, a, misérable, malheureux; chétif.

miserere, n, miserere, m.

misericord, n, miséricorde, f.

miserly, a, avare.

misery, n, misère, f; souffrances, f.pl.

misfire, n, raté [d'allumage] m. ¶ v.i, rater, manquer.

misfit, n, vêtement mal ajusté, v. manqué, m; chaussure manquée, f.

misfortune, n, malheur, m, infortune, adversité, disgrâce, misère, f.

misgiving, n, doute; pressentiment, m.

misgovern, v.t, mal gouverner. ~ment, n, mauvais gouvernement, m.

misguide, v.t, égarer; abuser. **misguided,** p.p, mal dirigé, dévoyé.

mishap, n, contretemps, m, mésaventure, f.

misinform, v.t, mal renseigner.

misinterpretation, n, contresens, m.

misjudge, v.t, mal juger.

mislay, v.t, égarer.

mislead, v.t, égarer, fourvoyer, abuser; induire en erreur; tromper. ~ing, p.a, décevant, fallacieux.

mismanage, v.t, mal faire, mal gérer. ~ment, n, mauvaise gestion, f.

misnamed, p.p, mal nommé.

misnomer, n, erreur de nom, f.

misogynist, n, misogyne, m.

misplace, v.t, mal placer.

misprint, n, faute d'impression, erreur typographique, coquille, f.

mispronounce, v.t, mal prononcer. **mispronunciation,** n, vice de prononciation, m.

misquotation, n, citation inexacte, f. **misquote,** v.t, citer à faux.

misrepresent, v.t, représenter mal, travestir, dénaturer. ~ation, n, travestissement, m; déclaration inexacte, f.

misrule, n, mauvaise administration, f.

miss, n, manque [à toucher] m; demoiselle, f. M~, mademoiselle; Mademoiselle, f. ¶ v.t. & i, manquer; rater; regretter; sauter. ~ fire, rater, manquer. ~ the point, porter à faux.

missal, n, missel, m.

misshapen, a, contrefait, biscornu, difforme, malbâti.

missile, n, projectile, m.

missing, a, manquant; (ship) [perdu] sans nouvelles. ~ link, chaînon manquant, m. m. the ~ (Mil.), les disparus, m.pl. be ~, manquer.

mission, n, mission, f. ~ary, n, missionnaire, m. **missive,** n, missive, f.

misspell, v.t, mal orthographier. ~ing, n, faute d'orthographe, f.

misstatement, n, déclaration inexacte, f.

mist, n, brouillard, m, brume; brouillasse; vapeur, f, nuage, voile, m.

mistake, n, erreur, faute, bévue; méprise, f, quiproquo, tort, m. ¶ v.t.ir, se méprendre sur, se tromper de, confondre. **mistaken,** a, erroné. ~ identity, erreur de (ou sur la) personne, f. ~ kindness, indulgence mal comprise, f. be ~, se tromper.

mister, n, monsieur, m.

mistletoe, n, gui, m.

mistranslation, n, contresens, m.

mistreat, v.t, maltraiter.

mistress, n, maîtresse; patronne; institutrice, f; professeur, m; madame, f. be one's own ~, s'appartenir.

mistrust, n, méfiance, défiance, f. ¶ v.t, se méfier de, se défier de. ~ful, a, méfiant, défiant.

misty, a, brumeux; vaporeux; trouble.

misunderstand, v.t.ir, mal comprendre, méconnaître. ~ing, n, malentendu, m; mésintelligence, brouille, f; quiproquo, m. **misunderstood** (pers.) p.a, incompris.

misuse, n, abus, m. ¶ v.t, abuser de; maltraiter; mésuser.

mite, n, (farthing) obole, f, denier, m; (child) petit, e; (insect) mite, f, acare, ciron, m.

miter, n, (bishop's) mitre, f; (Carp.) onglet, m. ~ed, a, mitré; (Carp.) à onglet.

mitigate, *v.t*, atténuer; mitiger; modérer.

mitt[en], *n*, moufle, mitaine, *f.*

mix, *v.t*, mêler, mélanger, malaxer; *(salad)* retourner. **mixed**, *a*, mêlé; mixte; hétérogène. ~ *bathing*, bain mixte, *m.* ~ *double* *(Ten.)*, double mixte, *m.* ~ *metaphor*, métaphore incohérente, *f.* **mixing** *(TV & cinema)* mixage, *m.* **mixture**, *n*, mélange, *m*; mixture, *f*; ambigu, *m*; *(Med.)* mixtion, *f*; *(fodder)* farrago; *(cloth)* drap mélangé, *m. wool ~*, laine mélangée, *f.*

miz[z]en [sail], *n. & miz[z]en mast*, artimon, *m.*

mizzle, *n*, bruine, *f.* ¶ *v.imp*, bruiner.

mnemonic, *a*, mnémonique. ~*s*, *n.pl*, la mnémonique.

moan, *n*, gémissement, *m*, plainte, *f.* ¶ *v.i*, gémir, se plaindre.

moat, *n*, fossé, *m*, douve, *f.*

mob, *n*, foule; canaille, populace, *f.* ~ *law*, la loi de la populace, *f.* ¶ *v.t*, houspiller.

mobile, *a*, mobile. **mobility**, *n*, mobilité, *f.*

mobilization, *n*, mobilisation, *f.* **mobilize**, *v.t*, mobiliser.

mocha, *n*, moka, *m. mocha coffee* or *mocha*, *n*, café de Moka, moka, *m.*

mock, *v.t*, se moquer de; singer. ¶ *a*, faux, imité. ~ *fight*, simulacre de combat, *m.* ~*-heroic*, héroï-comique. ~*er*, *n*, moqueur, euse. ~*ery*, *n*, moquerie, *f.* ~*ing bird*, [oiseau] moqueur, *m.*

mode, *n*, *(way, fashion)* mode, *f*; *(form, method)* mode, *m.*

model, *n*, modèle, *m*; maquette, *f*; mannequin, *m*; *(att.)* modèle. ¶ *v.t*, modeler. ~*er*, *n*, modeleur, *m.* ~*ing*, *n*, modelage; modelé, *m.*

moderate, *a*, modéré; *(price)* modique. ¶ *v.t*, modérer, tempérer. ~*ly*, *ad*, modérément, moyennement. ~*ness*, *n*, modicité, *f.* **moderation**, *n*, modération, *f.*

modern, *a. & n*, moderne, *a. & m.* ~ *language*, langue vivante, *f.* ~*ize*, *v.t*, moderniser.

modest†, *a*, modeste. ~*y*, *n*, modestie, *f.*

modicum, *n*, petite quantité; légère dose, *f*, grain, *m.*

modification, *n*, modification, *f.* **modify**, *v.t*, modifier.

modish, *a*, à la mode, de mode. ~*ly*, *ad*, à la mode.

modulate, *v.t*, moduler. **modulation**, *n*, modulation, *f.* **module & modulus**, *n*, module, *m.*

mohair, *n*, poil de chèvre d'Angora, mohair, *m.*

Mohammedan, *n. & a*, mahométan, e. ~*ism*, *n*, mahométisme, *m.*

moiety, *n*, moitié, *f.*

moil, *v.i*, peiner.

moire, *n*, moire, *f.* **moiré**, *v.t*, moirer. ~ *silk*, moire de soie, soie moirée, *f.*

moist, *a*, humide; moite. ~*en*, *v.t*, humecter; mouiller. ~*ness &* ~*ure*, *n*, humidité; moiteur; buée, *f.*

molar, *a. & n*, molaire, *a. & f.*

molasses, *n*, mélasse, *f.*

mold, *n*, moule, creux, *m*; *(Typ.)* empreinte, *f*, flan; *(vegetable)* terreau, humus; *(ship)* gabarit; *(decay)* moisi, *m*, moisissure, *f.* ¶ *v.t*, mouler; modeler; *(Typ.)* prendre l'empreinte de. ~*er*, *n*, mouleur, *m.* ~*er [away]*, *v.i*, tomber en poussière. **moldiness**, *n*, moisissure, *f*, moisi, *m.* **molding**, *n*, *(act)* moulage, *m*; *(ornamental strip)* moulure, *f.* **moldy**, *a*, moisi. *turn ~*, [se] moisir.

mole, *n*, nævus, *m*, couenne, *f*, grain de beauté; *(jetty)* môle, *m*; *(Zool.)* taupe, *f.* ~*hill*, taupinière, *f.* ~*skin*, [fourrure de] taupe; moleskine, *f.* ~ *trap*, taupière, *f.*

molecular, *a*, moléculaire. **molecule**, *n*, molécule, *f.*

molest, *v.t*, tourmenter, inquiéter, importuner. ~*ation*, *n*, importunité, *f.*

mollify, *v.t*, amollir; adoucir.

mollusk, *n*, mollusque, *m.*

molt, *v.i*, se déplumer.

molten, *p.p*, fondu, en fusion, en bain.

Moluccas (the), les Moluques, *f.pl.*

moment, *n*, moment; instant, *m*; importance, *f. a ~ ago*, à l'instant. ~*ary†*, *a*, momentané, passager. ~*ous*, *a*, de la dernière importance. **momentum**, *n*, *(Mech.)* moment; *(impetus)* élan, *m.*

monarch, *n*, monarque, *m.* ~*ic(al)*, *a*, monarchique. ~*ist*, *n*, monarchiste, *m.* ~**y**, *n*, monarchie, *f.*

monastery, *n*, monastère, couvent, *m.* **monastic**, *a*, monastique, monacal. **monastically, **ad*, monacalement.

Monday, *n*, lundi, *m.*

monetary, *a*, monétaire. **monetize,** *v.t*, transformer en monnaie. **money,** *n*, argent, *m*; monnaie, *f*; numéraire, *m*; fonds, *m.pl*; capital, *m*, capitaux, *m.pl*; valeurs; finances, *f.pl*; deniers, *m.pl*. ~ *changer*, changeur, *m.* ~ *box*, tirelire; cassette, grenouillère, *f.* ~ *grubber* grippesou, *m.* ~**lender**, bailleur de fonds, *m.* ~ *order*, mandat [de poste] *m.* ~**ed**, *a*, fortuné.

Mongolia, *n*, la Mongolie. **Mongol[ian]**, *a*, mongol. ¶ *n*, Mongol, e.

mongoose, *n*, mangouste, *f.*

mongrel, *a*, métis, bâtard, mâtiné. ¶ *n*, métis, se, bâtard, e; (*cur*) roquet, *m.*

monk, *n*, moine, religieux, *m.* ~'*s hood* (*Bot.*), aconit, napel, *m.* ~**ery** & ~**hood**, *n*, moinerie, *f.* ~**ish**, *a*, monacal.

monkey, *n*, singe, *m*, (*she*) guenon, guenuche, *f*; (*pile driving*) mouton, *m.* ~ *house*, singerie, *f.* ~ *trick*, singerie, *f.* ~ *wrench*, clef anglaise, *f.*

monochord, *n*, monocorde, *m.* **monochrome,** *a*, monochrome. **monocle,** *n*, monocle, *m.* **monogamy,** *n*, monogamie, *f.* **monogram,** *n*, monogramme, chiffre, *m.* **monograph,** *n*, monographie, *f.* **monolith,** *n.* & ~**ic**, *a*, monolithe, *m.* & *a.* **monologize,** *v.i*, monologuer. **monologue,** *n*, monologue, *m.* **monomania,** *n*, monomanie, *f.* **monoplane,** *n*, monoplan, *m.* **monopolist,** *n*, accapareur, euse. **monopolize,** *v.t*, monopoliser, accaparer, s'emparer de. **monopoly,** *n*, monopole, *m.* **monosyllabic,** *a*, monosyllabique, monosyllable. **monosyllable,** *n*, monosyllabe, *m.* **monotonist** (*pers.*) *n*, monocorde, *m.* **monotonous,** *a*, monotone. **monotony,** *n*, monotonie, *f.* **monotype,** *n*, monotype, *f.*

monster, *n.* & *a*, monstre, *m.* & *att.*

monstrance, *n*, ostensoir, *m.*

monstrosity, *n*, monstruosité, *f.* **monstrous†**, *a*, monstrueux.

Mont Blanc, le mont Blanc. **Montenegrin,** *a*, monténégrin. ¶ *n*, Monténégrin, e. **Montenegro,** *n*, le Monténégro. **Monte Rosa,** le mont Rosa.

month, *n*, mois, *m.* ~'*s pay, rent, or like*, mois, *m.* ~**ly**, *a*, mensuel; au mois. ~ *payment, drawing, salary, or like*, mensualité, *f.* ~ *statement* (*Com.*), relevé de fin de mois, *m.* ¶ *ad*, mensuellement, par mois. ¶ *n*, revue mensuelle, *f.*

monument, *n*, monument; (*tombstone*) tombeau, *m.* ~**al**, *a*, monumental.

moo, *v.i*, beugler. ¶ *n*, beuglement, *m.*

mood, *n*, humeur, *f*, train; (*Gram.*) mode, *m.* ~**y**, *a*, morose, chagrin.

moon, *n*, lune, *f.* ~**beam,** rayon de l., *m.* ~**light,** clair de l., *m.* ~**lit,** éclairé par la l. ~**shine,** contes en l'air, *m.pl.* ~**stone,** pierre de lune, *f.* ~**struck,** toqué. ~ [*about*], muser.

moor & ~**land**, *n*, lande, brande, bruyère, *f.* ~**cock,** coq de bruyère *m.* ~**hen,** poule d'eau, *f.*

Moor (*pers.*) *n.* More, Maure, *m.*

moor, *v.t*, amarrer, mouiller. ~**ing,** *n*, amarrage, mouillage; (*pl.*) mouillage, *m.*

Moorish, *a*, more, maure.

moose, *n*, élan, *m.*

moot, *a*, discutable, contestable. ¶ *v.t*, soulever.

mop, *n*, balai à laver; (*Naut.*) écouvillon, *m*; (*of hair*) tignasse, *f.* ¶ *v.t*, éponger. ~ *up*, essuyer, éponger.

mope, *v.i*, languir.

moraine, *n*, moraine, *f.*

moral†, *a*, moral. ¶ *n*, (*of story, of fable*) morale, moralité, *f*; (*pl, manners*) mœurs, *f.pl*; (*pl, ethics*) morale, *f.* ~[**e**], *n*, moral, *m.* ~**ist,** *n*, moraliste, *m.* ~**ity,** *n*, moralité, *f*; [bonnes] mœurs, *f.pl.* ~**ize,** *v.i.* & *t*, moraliser.

morass, *n*, fondrière, *f*, marais, marécage, *m.*

moratorium, *n*, moratorium, moratoire, *m.*

Moravia, *n*, la Moravie.

morbid, *a*, morbide, maladif. ~**ness,** *n*, état maladif, *m.*

mordant, *a.* & *n*, mordant, *a.* & *m.*

more, *a*, plus de; plus. ¶ *ad*, plus; davantage; encore; de plus. *all the* ~, d'autant plus. *never* ~, jamais plus. ~ *and* ~, de plus en plus. ~**over**, *ad*, d'ailleurs, aussi bien, en outre, du reste, encore.

moresque, *a*, moresque, mauresque.

morganatic†, *a*, morganatique.

moribund, *a*, moribond.

morning & (*Poet.*) **morn**, *n*, matin, *m*; matinée; aurore, *f*. ~ *star*, étoile du matin, é. matinière, *f*.

Moroccan, *a*, marocain. ¶ *n*, Marocain, e. **Morocco**, *n*, le Maroc. *morocco* [*leather*], maroquin, *m*.

morose, *a*, morose. ~**ness**, *n*, morosité, *f*.

Morpheus, *n*, Morphée, *m*. **morphia, -phine**, *n*, morphine, *f*.

morrow (the) & **on the** ~, le lendemain.

morsel, *n*, morceau, *m*.

mortal†, *a*, mortel; (*strife*) à mort, à outrance. ¶ *n*, mortel, le. ~**ity**, *n*, mortalité, *f*.

mortar (*plaster, vessel, Mil.*) *n*, mortier, *m*.

mortgage, *n*, hypothèque, *f*. ¶ *v.t*, hypothéquer; engager. **mortgagee**, *n*, créancier hypothécaire, *m*. **mortgagor**, *n*, débiteur h., *m*.

mortification, *n*, mortification, *f*. **mortify**, *v.t*, mortifier, affliger, mater.

mortise, *n*, mortaise, *f*. ¶ *v.t*, emmortaiser.

mortmain, *n*, mainmorte, *f*. *property in* ~, biens de mainmorte, *m.pl*.

mortuary, *a*, mortuaire. ¶ *n*, institut médico-légal; établissement de pompes funèbres, *m*.

Mosaic (*of Moses*) *a*, mosaïque.

mosaic, *n*, mosaïque, marqueterie, *f*.

Moscow, *n*, Moscou, *m*.

Moslem, *n*. & *a*, mahométan, e.

mosque, *n*, mosquée, *f*.

mosquito, *n*, moustique; maringouin, *m*. ~ *net*, ~ *curtain*, moustiquaire, *f*.

moss, *n*, mousse, *f*. ~**y**, *a*, mousseux; moussu.

most, *a*, le plus de; la plupart de. ~ *eminent*, éminentissime. ~ *illustrious*, illustrissime. ~ *reverend*, révérendissime. ¶ *ad*, le plus; plus; très. ~**ly**, *ad*, pour la plupart.

mote, *n*, (*dust*) atome, *m*; (*in eye, fig.*) paille, *f*.

moth, *n*, papillon [de nuit] *m*; teigne, gerce, *f*, artison; ver, *m*, mite, *f*. ~**ball**, boule de naphtaline, *f*. ~**eaten**, mangé aux mites, artisonné.

mother, *n*, mère, *f*. ~ *church*, église métropolitaine, *f*. ~ *earth*, notre mère commune. ~**hood**, maternité, *f*. ~**in-law**, belle-mère, *f*. ~**of-pearl**, nacre, *f*. ~'*s side* (*family*), côté maternel, *m*. ~ *superior*, mère supérieure, *f*. ~ *tongue*, (*native*) langue maternelle; (*original*) l. mère, *f*. ~ *wit*, esprit naturel, *m*. ¶ *v.t*, servir de mère à; (*fig.*) couver. ~**less**, *a*, sans mère. ~**ly**, *a*, maternel, de mère.

motif, *n*, (*art, Need.*) motif, *m*; (*literary*) donnée, *f*. **motion**, *n*, mouvement, *m*, marche, *f*; signe, *m*; (*proposal*) motion; proposition, *f*. ¶ *v.i*, faire signe. ~**less**, *a*, sans mouvement, immobile. **motive**, *a*, moteur, *m*. ~ *power*, force motrice, *f*, mobile, *m*. ¶ *n*, raison, *f*; motif; mobile, *m*.

motley, *a*, bariolé, bigarré; mêlé. ¶ *n*, bariolage; habit d'arlequin, *m*.

motor, *n*, moteur, *m*. ~ [*bi*]*cycle*, motocyclette, moto, *f*; cyclomoteur, *m*. ~ *boat*, canot automobile, *m*. vedette, *f*. ~ *bus*, autobus, *m*. ~ [*car*], automobile, auto, *f*. ~ *coach*, autocar, *m*. ~ *cyclist*, motocycliste, *m,f*. ~**man**, machiniste, *m*. ~ *road*, autoroute, *f*. ~ *show*, salon de l'automobile, *m*. ¶ *v.i*, aller en auto. ~**ing**, *n*, automobilisme, *m*. ~**ist**, *n*, automobiliste, *m,f*. ~**ize**, *v.t*, mécaniser; motoriser.

mottled, *a*, marbré.

motto, *n*, devise; (*prefixed to book or chapter*) épigraphe, *f*.

mound, *n*, monticule, *m*, butte, *f*, tertre, *m*, bosse, motte, *f*.

mount, *n*, (*as Etna*) le mont; carton [pour montage photographique] *m*; (*horse, etc.*) monture; (*horse racing*) monte, *f*. ¶ *v.i*. & *t*, monter.

mountain, *n*, montagne, *f*. ~ *ash*, sorbier des oiseaux, *m*. ~ *sickness*, mal de montagne, *m*. ~**eer**, *n*, (*dweller*) montagnard, e; (*climber*) alpiniste, ascensionniste, *m,f*. ~**eering**, *n*, l'alpinisme,

m. ~ous, *a*, montagneux; énorme.
mountebank, *n*, saltimbanque;
baladin, *m*.
mounted, *p.a*, à cheval; monté.
mounter, *n*, monteur, *m*. **mounting,** *n*, montage, *m*; monture; ferrure, *f*.
mourn, *v.t. & i*, pleurer. **the ~ers,**
le deuil. [hired] ~er, pleureur,
euse. ~ful†, *a*, douloureux.
~ing, *n*, deuil, *m*. ~ **band,** brassard de d., *m*.
mouse, *n*, souris, *f*; (*young*) souriceau, *m*. ~trap, souricière, *f*.
moustache, *n*, moustache, *f*. ~d,
a, moustachu.
mouth, *n*, bouche; embouchure;
(*vulgar*) gueule, *f*; bec; orifice;
trou, *m*; entrée, *f*. ~ **organ,** harmonica à bouche, *m*. ~piece, embouchure, *f*; bec; (*pers.*) organe,
porte-parole, *m*. ~wash, eau dentifrice, *f*. ~ful, *n*, bouchée, goulée, gorgée, *f*.
movable, *a*, mobile; (*law*) meuble, mobilier. **move,** *n*, mouvement, *m*; manœuvre, *f*; (*chess,
etc.*) coup, *m*. *whose ~ is it?* à qui
à jouer? ¶ *v.t*, [faire] mouvoir;
remuer; déplacer; jouer; affecter;
toucher, émouvoir, attendrir;
proposer; (*v.i.*) se mouvoir;
bouger; déloger. ~ **along,** cheminer. ~ **back,** reculer. ~ **in**
(*house*), emménager. ~ **off,**
s'éloigner, s'ébranler. ~ **on!** circulez! ~ [**out**] (*house*), déménager. ~ment, *n*, mouvement, *m*,
marche, *f*; geste, *m*. **moving,** *a*,
mouvant; touchant.
movie, *n*, cinéma, film, *m*. ~ *camera*, camera, *m*.
mow, *v.t.tr*, faucher; tondre. ~
down, faucher. ~er, *n*, (*pers.*)
faucheur, *m*; (*Mach.*) faucheuse;
(*lawn*) tondeuse, *f*.
Mr, Monsieur, M.; (*partner in
firm*) sieur; (*courtesy title of
lawyers*) maître, *m*. **Mrs,** Madame, Mme; (*law*) la dame.
much, *a. & ad*, beaucoup (de);
grand-chose (*usually with neg.*);
bien (de); très; cher. *as ~,* autant
(de). *as ~ as,* autant que. *how
~?* combien? *so ~,* [au]tant (de).
too ~, trop. *very ~,* beaucoup.
mucilage, *n*, mucilage, *m*.
muck, *n*, fumier, *m*; fange; cochonnerie; saloperie, *f*.
mucous, *a*, muqueux. ~ *membrane,* [membrane] muqueuse, *f*.

mucus, *n*, mucosité, *f*, mucus, *m*;
pituite, morve, *f*.
mud, *n*, boue, *f*. oft. *pl*, crotte,
bourbe, fange; (*river*) vase, *f*,
limon, *m*. ~ **bath,** brain de boue
[s minérales] *m*. ~guard, garde-
boue, *m*. ~lark, barboteur, *m*.
~ *pie,* pâté, *m*. ~ **spring,** source
boueuse, *f*.
muddle, *n*, [em]brouillamini; fouillis, *m*. ¶ *v.t*, [em]brouiller, emmêler; (*with drink*) griser. ~ *up,*
tripoter. **muddler,** *n*, barboteur,
euse, fatrassier, ère, brouillon, ne.
muddy, *a*, boueux, crotté, bourbeux, fangeux; vaseux, limoneux;
trouble. ¶ *v.t*, embouer.
muezzin, *n*, muezzin, *m*.
muff, *n*, manchon; (*pers.*) serin,
m, jobard, e, huître, *f*. **muffle**
(*Chem.*) *n*, moufle, *m*. ¶ *v.t*, assourdir; (*drum*) voiler. ~ *up,* embéguiner, emmitoufler. ~d *p.a*,
sourd. **muffler,** *n*, cache-nez;
(*auto*) amortisseur de son; pot
d'échappement, *m*.
mufti (**in**), en civil, en bourgeois.
mug, *n*, timbale, tasse, *f*, pot, *m*.
muggy, *a*, mou.
mulatto, *n*, mulâtre, *m*, mulâtresse, *f*. ¶ *a*, mulâtre.
mulberry, *n*, mûre, *f*. ~ [*tree*],
mûrier, *m*.
mulch, *n*, paillis, *m*. ¶ *v.t*, pailler.
mulct, *v.t*, frapper d'une amende.
mule, *n*, (*he & pers.*) mulet, *m*,
(*she*) mule, *f*; (*pl, slippers*)
mules, babouches, *f.pl*. ~ *track,*
piste muletière, *f*. **muleteer,** *n*,
muletier, *m*. **mulish,** *a*, têtu.
mulled wine, vin brûlé, *m*.
muller (*grinding*), *n*, molette, *f*.
mullet, *n*, (*gray*) mulet, muge;
(*red*) rouget, *m*.
mullion, *n*, meneau, *m*.
multicolor[ed], *a*, multicolore.
multifarious, *a*, multiple.
multimillionaire, *n. & a*, milliardaire, *m,f. & a*.
multiple, *n. & a*, multiple, *m. &
a*. **multiplicand,** *n*, multiplicande,
m. **multiplication,** *n*, multiplication, *f*. **multiplicity,** *n*, multiplicité, *f*. **multiplier,** *n*, multiplicateur, *m*. **multiply,** *v.t*, multiplier;
(*v.i.*) [se] m.; peupler.
multitude, *n*, multitude, *f*.
mum[['s the word], motus!, bouche close!

mumble, *v.i*, marmotter, balbutier, barboter.

mummer, *n*, cabotin, e. ~**y**, *n*, momerie, *f.*

mummify, *v.t*, momifier. **mummy**, *n*, momie; (*mother*) maman, *f.*

mumps, *n*, (*Med.*) oreillons, *m.pl.*

munch, *v.i*, croquer.

mundane, *a*, du monde, de ce m.; mondain.

municipal, *a*, municipal. ~**ity**, *n*, municipalité, *f.*

munificence, *n*, munificence, *f.* **munificent**, *a*, magnifique.

muniment, *n*, acte, titre, *m.*

munitions, *n.pl*, provisions de guerre, munitions de guerre, *f.pl.*

mural, *a*, mural.

murder, *n*, meurtre, assassinat, *m.* ~**!** à l'assassin! ¶ *v.t*, assassiner; (*fig.*) massacrer; (*language*) estropier, écorcher. ~**er**, ~**ess**, *n*, meurtrier, ère, assassin, e. ~**ous**, *a*, meurtrier.

murky, *a*, sombre, obscur, ténébreux.

murmur, *n*, murmure, *m.* ¶ *v.i. & t*, murmurer; bruire.

murrain, *n*, peste, *f.*

muscat [grape, wine], [raisin, vin] muscat, *m.* **muscatels**, *n.pl*, raisins secs muscats, *m.pl.*

muscle, *n*, muscle, *m.* -**muscled**, *a*, musclé. **muscular**, *a*, (*force*) musculaire; (*pers.*) musculeux.

Muse, *n*, Muse, *f*; génie, *m.*

muse, *v.i*, méditer; rêver, rêvasser.

museum, *n*, musée; (*natural history*) muséum, *m.*

mush, *n*, bouillie, *f.*

mushroom, *n*, champignon [comestible] *m*; (*att.*) éphémère, d'un jour. ~ **bed**, champignonnière, *f.*

music, *n*, musique, *f.* ~ *case*, porte-musique, *m.* ~ *hall*, music-hall, *m.* ~ *master*, professeur de musique, *m.* ~ *stand*, pupitre à m., *m.* **musical**, *a*, musical; chantant; (*pers.*) musicien. ~ *box*, boîte à musique, *f.* ~ *chairs*, chaises musicales, *f.pl.* ~ *clock*, horloge à carillon, *f.* ~ *comedy*, opéra bouffe, *f.* ~ *director*, directeur musical, chef de théâtre, *m.* ~ *ear*, oreille pour la musique, *f.* ~ *instrument*, instrument de musique, *m*; (*toy*) musique, *f.* ~ *instrument maker*, luthier, *m.* ~ *interlude*, entracte de musique, *m.* ~ *play*, opérette, *f.* ~**e**, soirée

musicale, *f.* **musician**, *n*, musicien, ne.

musing, *n*, rêverie, *f.*

musk, *n*, musc, *m.* ~ *deer*, [porte-] musc, chevrotin, *m.* ~*rat*, rat musqué, *m.* ~ *rose*, rose muscade, *f.* to [*perfume with*] ~, musquer.

musket, *n*, mousquet, *m.* ~**eer** (*Hist.*) *n*, mousquetaire, *m.* ~**ry** (*Mil.*) *n*, tir, *m*, exercices de tir, *m.pl.*

Muslim, *n. & a*, mahométan, e.

muslin, *n*, mousseline, *f.*

musquash, *n*, rat musqué; (*fur*) castor du Canada, *m.*

muss, *v.t*, déranger.

mussel, *n*, moule, *f.*

Mussulman, *n. & a*, musulman, e, *m.f. & att.*

must, *v.aux.ir*, falloir; devoir.

must, *n*, (*grapes*) moût, *m.*

mustard, *n*, moutarde; (*Bot.*) moutarde, *f*, sénevé, *m.* ~ *gas*, gaz moutarde, *m*, ypérite, *f.* ~ *maker & ~ pot*, moutardier, *m.* ~ *plaster*, sinapisme, *m.* ~ *sauce*, sauce moutarde, *f.* ~ *seed*, graine de m., *f*, sénevé, *m.* ~ *spoon*, cuiller à m., pelle à m., *f.*

muster, *n*, appel [nominal] *m.* ~ *roll*, feuille d'appel, *f.* ¶ *v.t*, faire l'appel de; rassembler. ~ *out*, démobiliser.

musty, *a* moisi; (*smell*) de renfermé.

mutability, *n*, mutabilité, *f.* **mutation**, *n*, mutation, *f.*

mute, *a*, muet; sourd. ¶ *n*, muet, te; (*Mus.*) sourdine, *f.* ~**d**, *p.a*, sourd; en sourdine. ~**ly**, *ad*, en silence.

mutilate, *v.t*, mutiler. **mutilation**, *n*, mutilation, *f.*

mutineer, *n*, mutin, révolté, *m.* **mutinous**, *a*, mutin. **mutiny**, *n*, mutinerie, révolte, *f.* ¶ *v.i*, [se] mutiner, se révolter.

mutter, *v.i*, murmurer [entre ses dents], marmotter; (*of thunder*) gronder.

mutton, *n*, mouton, *m.* ~ *chop*, côtelette de mouton, *f.*

mutual†, *a*, mutuel; réciproque, partagé. ~ *association*, mutualité, *f.* ~ *loan association*, mutualité de crédit. on ~ *terms* (engagement), au pair. ~**ity**, *n*, mutualité; réciprocité, *f.*

muzzle, *n*, (*animal*) museau, *m*; (*gun*) bouche, gueule; (*for dog*)

muselière, *f*. ~*loading*, se chargeant par la bouche. ¶ *v.t*, museler.
my, *a*, mon, ma, mes.
myopia, *n*, myopie, *f*. **myopic**, *a*, myope.
myriad, *n*, myriade, *f*. e, *m*.
myriapod, *n*, myriapode, *m*.
myrmidon, *n*, suppôt, *m*.
myrrh, *n*, myrrhe, *f*.
myrtle, *n*, myrte, *m*. ~ *berry*, baie de m., *f*.
myself, *pn*, moi-même; moi; me.
mysterious†, *a*, mystérieux. **mystery**, *n*, mystère, *m*. ~ [*play*], mystère, miracle, *m*. **mystic** (*pers.*) *n*, mystique, *m,f*. ~(al)†, *a*, mystique. **mysticalness**, *n*, mysticité, *f*. **mysticism**, *n*, mysticisme, *m*. **mystify**, *v.t*, mystifier.
myth, *n*, mythe, *m*. ~ic(al), *a*, mythique. ~ologic(al), *a*, mythologique. ~ologist, *n*, mythologue, *m,f*. ~ology, *n*, mythologie, *f*.

N

nab, *v.t*, saisir, arrêter. *to be nabbed*, se faire paumer.
nabob, *n*, nabab, *m*.
nadir, *n*, nadir, *m*.
nag, *n*, bidet, *m*. ~ (*at*), *v.t. & i*, criailler (après), quereller. **nagging**, *p.a*, hargneux.
naiad, *n*, naïade, *f*.
nail, *n*, (*finger, toe*) ongle; (*metal*) clou, *m*; pointe, *f*. *hit the ~ on the head*, tomber juste. ~ *brush*, brosse à ongles, *f*. ~ *extractor*, arrache-clou, *m*. ~ *file*, lime à ongles, *f*. ~ *maker*, cloutier, *m*. ~ *scissors*, ciseaux à ongles, *m. pl*. ~ [*up*], *v.t*, clouer.
naïve†, *a*, naïf. **naïvety**, *n*, naïveté, *f*.
naked, *a*, nu; à nu; ras. *with the ~ eye*, à l'œil nu. ~ly (*fig.*) *ad*, nûment. ~**ness**, *n*, nudité, *f*.
namby-pamby, *a*, fade.
name, *n*, nom, *m*; dénomination; raison, *f*; intitulé, *m*; renommée; réputation, *f. by ~*, (*to mention*) nommément; (*be called on*) nominativement. *Christian ~*, nom de baptême, *m. my ~ is Adam*, je m'appelle Adam, je me nomme A. *given ~*, petit nom, *m. ~ plate*, plaque de porte, *f*. ~*sake*,

homonyme, *m. nick~*, sobriquet, *m*. ¶ *v.t*, nommer; dénommer; intituler. ~*less*, *a*, sans nom. ~*ly*, *ad*, [à] savoir; (*of pers.*) nommément.
nankeen, *n*, nankin, *f*.
nanny, *n*, (*nursemaid*) nounou, *f*. ~ [*goat*], chèvre, bique, *f*.
nap, *n*, (*sleep*) somme, *m*, sieste, *f*; (*pile*) poil; duvet, *m. to catch napping*, prendre au dépourvu. ¶ *v.i*, sommeiller.
nape [*of the neck*], *n*, nuque, *f*.
naphtha, *n*, naphte, *m*. **naphthalene**, *n*, naphtaline, *f*.
napkin, *n*, serviette [de table]. ~ *ring*, rond de serviette, *m*.
narcissus, *n*, narcisse, *m*.
narcotic, *a*, narcotique. ¶ *n*, narcotique, stupéfiant, *m*.
narrate, *v.t*, narrer, raconter. **narration & narrative**, *n*, narration, *f*, récit, *m*. **narrative**, *a*, narratif. **narrator**, *n*, narrateur, trice, conteur, euse.
narrow†, *a*, étroit, resserré. *to have a ~ escape*, l'échapper belle. ~*gauge railway*, chemin de fer à voie étroite, *m*. ~*-minded*, à l'esprit étroit. ¶ *n*, (*Naut.*) (*pl.*) détroit, *m*. ¶ *v.t*, [r]étrécir; reserrer, étrangler. ~**ness**, *n*, étroitesse, *f*.
nasal, *a*, nasal. ¶ (*Gram.*) **n**, nasale, *f*.
nascent, *a*, naissant.
nastiness, *n*, saleté; méchanceté, *f*.
nasturtium, *n*, capucine, *f*.
nasty†, *a*, sale; désagréable; villain; rosse. *be in a ~ situation*, être dans les beaux draps.
natal, *a*, natal.
natation, *n*, natation, *f*.
nation, *n*, nation, *f*, peuple, *m*. ~*al*, *a*, national; public. ~ *capital* (*economics*), outillage national, *m*. ~ *monument*, monument historique, *m*. **nationalism**, *n*, nationalisme; étatisme, *m*. **nationalist**, *n. & att*, nationaliste, *m, f. & a*. **nationality**, *n*, nationalité, *f*, nationalize, *v.t*, nationaliser. **nationals**, *n.pl*, nationaux, *m.pl*.
native, *a*, naturel; natif; natal; originaire; indigène; maternel. ~ *land*, ~ *country*, patrie, *f*. ¶ *n*, natif, ive; indigène, *m,f*; naturel, *m*. **nativity**, *n*, nativité; naissance, *f*.

natty, *a,* chic, coquet, propret.

natural†, *a,* naturel. ¶ *n,* idiot, e;
(*Mus.*) (*note*) note naturelle, *f;*
(*cancel sign*) bécarre, *m.* ~ *history museum,* muséum [d'histoire
naturelle] *m.* ~**ist,** *n,* naturaliste,
m. ~**ization,** *n,.* naturalisation, *f.*
~ *papers,* lettres de n., *f.pl.* ~**ize,**
v.t, naturaliser. ~**ness,** *n,* naturel,
m. **nature,** *n,* nature, *f;* naturel,
caractère, acabit, *m.* ~**natured,** *a,*
d'un (*bon, mauvais*) naturel.

naught, *n,* rien; (*Arith.*) zéro, *m.*

naughtiness, *n,* méchanceté, *f.*
naughty†, *a,* méchant, vilain, laid;
(*indecent*) polisson, croustilleux,
graveleux, gras.

nausea, *n,* nausée, *f.* **nauseate,**
v.t, écœurer. **nauseating,** *a,* nauséeux. **nauseous,** *a,* nauséabond.

nautical, *a,* (*science, almanac*)
nautique; (*mile*) marin.

nautilus, *n,* nautile, nautilus, *m.*

naval, *a,* naval; maritime; de marine; de la m. ~ *cadet,* élève de
l'école navale, *m.* ~ *dockyard,*
arsenal maritime, *m.* ~ *officer,*
officier de marine, *m.* ~ *station,*
port de guerre, p. militaire; point
d'appui de la flotte, *m.*

nave, *n,* (*wheel*) moyeu, *m;*
(*church*) nef, *f.*

navel, *n,* nombril, *m.*

navigable, *a,* navigable. **navigate,** *v.i,* naviguer; (*v.t.*) naviguer sur, faire naviguer. **navigation,** *n,* navigation, *f.* **navigator,**
n, navigateur, *m.*

navy, *n,* marine [militaire], m. de
guerre, *f.* ~ *blue,* bleu marine, *m.*

nay, *neg. particle,* & qui plus est,
voire. ¶ *n,* non, *m.*

Neapolitan, *a,* napolitain. ¶ *n,*
Napolitain, e,

neap tide, morte-eau, *f.*

near, *a,* proche; près de; rap-
proché; intime. *the N~ East,* le
Proche Orient. ~ *relations,*
proches [parents] *m.pl.* ~ *relationship,* proximité du sang, *f.*
~*sighted* (*person*), myope, *a.* &
m,f. ¶ *ad,* près; proche; auprès;
de près. ¶ *pr,* près de; auprès de.
¶ *v.i,* s'approcher de. ~**ly,** *ad,* de
près; à peu [de chose] près;
presque. *he ~ fell,* il a manqué
de tomber. *I ~ missed the train,*
j'ai failli manquer le train. ~**ness,**
n, proximité, *f.*

neat†, *a,* propre; soigné; bien tenu;
(*drink*) pur, sec; adroit. ~*herd,*

bouvier, ère, vacher, ère, pâtre,
m. ~*'s foot oil,* huile de pied de
bœuf, *f.* ~**ness,** *n,* propreté, *f.*

nebula (*Astr.*) *n,* nébuleuse, *f.*
nebulous, *a,* nébuleux.

necessarily, *ad,* nécessairement,
forcément. **necessary,** *a,* nécessaire. *if ~,* s'il est n., au besoin.
¶ *n.* & **necessaries,** *n.pl,* le nécessaire. **necessitate,** *v.t,* nécessiter.
necessitous, *a,* nécessiteux. **necessity,** *n,* nécessité, *f.*

neck, *n,* cou, *m;* gorge; encolure,
f; col; collet; goulot; (*violin*)
manche, *m.* ~*band,* bande de col,
brisure, *f.* ~*lace,* collier, *m.* ~
measurement, ~ *size,* encolure, *f.*
~*tie,* cravate, *f.* stiff ~, torticolis,
m: to win by a ~, gagner par une
encolure. **neckerchief,** *n,* fichu, *m.*

necrology, *n,* (*notice*) nécrologie, *f;* (*roll, book*) nécrologe, *m.*
necromancer, *n,* nécromancien,
ne. **necromancy,** *n,* nécromancie,
f. **necropolis,** *n,* nécropole, *f.* **necrosis,** *n,* nécrose, *f.*

nectar, *n,* nectar, *m.* ~**ine,** *n,*
brugnon, *m.* ~**y,** *n,* nectaire, *m.*

need, *n,* besoin, *m.* ¶ *v.i.* & *t,*
avoir b. (de); vouloir. ~**ful,** *a.* &
n, nécessaire, *m.* & *m.* ~**iness,** *n,*
besoin, *m,* gêne, indigence, *f.*

needle, *n,* aiguille, *f.* ~*point lace,*
dentelle au point à l'aiguille, *f.*
~*woman,* couturière, *f.* ~*work,*
travail à l'aiguille, *m,* couture, *f.*
to do ~work, travailler à l'a.,
chiffonner. ~**ful,** *n,* aiguillée, *f.*

needless†, *a,* inutile. **needs,** *ad,*
nécessairement. **needy,** *a,* nécessiteux, besogneux.

ne'er (*Poet.*) *ad,* ne . . . jamais.
a ~do-well, un mauvais sujet,
un propre à rien.

nefarious†, *a,* inique, abominable.

negation, *n,* négation, *f.* **nega-
tive†,** *a,* négatif. ¶ *n,* la négative; (*Gram.*) négation, *f;* (*Phot.*)
cliché, négatif, *m.*

neglect, *v.t,* négliger, oublier. **neglect** & **negligence,** *n,* négligence,
f, oubli, *m.* **neglectful†** & **negli-
gent†,** *a,* négligent. **negligible,** *a,*
négligeable.

negotiable, *a,* négociable. ~ *instrument,* effet de commerce, *m.*
negotiate, *v.t.* & *i,* négocier, traiter, trafiquer. **negotiation,** *n,* négociation, *f;* (*pl.*) pourparlers,

m.pl. by ~, de gré à gré. **nego-tiator, tress** *or* **trix,** *n,* négociateur, trice.

Negro, *n,* nègre, *m;* (*woman*) nègresse *f.* ¶ *a,* nègre, *a.m.,* & *a.f.*

neigh, *v.i,* hennir. ~[**ing**] *n,* hennissement, *m.*

neighbor, *n,* voisin, e; prochain, *m.* ~**hood,** *n,* voisinage, *m,* environs, *m.pl;* quartier, *m.* ~**ing,** *a,* voisin, avoisinant, prochain. *in a ~ly way,* en bon voisin.

neither, *pn. & a,* ni l'un (l'une) ni l'autre. ¶ *c,* ni; ne . . . pas non plus. ¶ *ad,* non plus.

nelson (*wrestling*) *n,* prise de tête à terre, *f.*

Nemesis, *n,* Némésis, *f.*

neologism, *n,* néologisme, *m.*

neon, *n,* néon, *m.* ~ *light,* lumière néon, *f.*

neophyte, *n,* néophyte, *m.f.*

nephew, *n,* neveu, *m.*

nepotism, *n,* népotisme, *m.*

Nereid, *n,* néréide, *f.*

nerve, *n,* nerf, *m;* (*Bot.*) nervure, *f;* (*fig.*) audace, *f,* courage, sangfroid, *m.* ~ *specialist,* neurologiste, neurologue, *m.f.* **nervous**†, *a,* nerveux; peureux, timide. ~ *breakdown,* prostration nerveuse, *f.* ~**ness,** *n,* timidité, *f.*

nest, *n,* nid; faisceau; (*fig.*) repaire, *m.* ~ *egg,* nichet; (*savings*) pécule, *m.* ~ *of drawers,* casier, *m.* ~ *of* (insect's) *eggs,* couvain, *m.* ¶ *v.i,* nicher. ~*ed table* or ~ *of 3 tables,* table gigogne, *f.* ~[**ful**], *n,* nichée, *f.* **nestle,** *v.i,* se blottir, se tapir. **nestling,** *n,* petit oiseau au nid, *m.*

net, *n,* filet; rets; tulle, *m;* résille; *f.* ~ *maker,* fileur, euse. ~ *sinker,* ~ *weight* (*Fish.*), gousse de plomb, *f.* ~*work,* réseau; lacis, *m.* ¶ (*Com.*) *a,* net. ¶ (*catch*) *v.t,* prendre au filet.

nether, *a,* inférieur, bas. ~ *regions,* enfers, *m.pl.* **Netherlander,** *n,* Néerlandais, e. **Netherlandish,** *a,* néerlandais. **the Netherlands,** les Pays-Bas, *m.pl,* la Néerlande. **nethermost,** *a,* (le) plus bas.

netting, *n,* filet, *m,* filoche, *f;* (*wire*) treillis, treillage, grillage, réseau, *m.*

nettle, *n,* ortie, *f.* ~ *rash,* urticaire, *f.* ¶ *v.t,* piquer.

network, *n,* lacis; réseau, *m*

(*computers*) *shared* ~, réseau banalisé.

neuralgia, *n,* névralgie, *f.* **neuralgic,** *a,* névralgique. **neurasthenia,** *n,* neurasthénie, *f.* **neuritis,** *n,* névrite, *f.* **neurologist,** *n,* neurologiste, -logue, *m.f.* **neurosis,** *n,* névrose, *f.* **neurotic,** *a,* névrosé.

neuter, *a. & n,* neutre, *a. & m.* **neutral,** *a. & n,* neutre, *a. & m.* ~**ity,** *n,* neutralité, *f.* ~**ize,** *v.t,* neutraliser.

never, *ad,* jamais; ne . . . jamais; ne . . . pas. ~*-ending,* éternel. ~ *mind,* cela ne fait rien. ~*more,* jamais plus. **nevertheless,** *ad. & c,* néanmoins; cependant; toutefois; pourtant, quand même.

new, *a,* neuf; nouveau; récent; frais, tendre. ~*-born* (*child*), nouveau-né, e. ~*-comer,* nouveau venu, *m,* nouvelle venue, *f. Newfoundland* [*dog*], terre-neuve, *m.* ~ *growth* (*forestry*), revenue, *f.* ~*-laid,* frais [pondu]. ~ *lease on life,* regain de vie, *m.* ~ *member* (of a society), récipiendaire, *m.f.* ~ *par*[*agraph*], alinéa, *m.* N~ *Testament,* Nouveau Testament, *m.* N~*Year's day,* le jour de l'an. N~*Year's eve,* veille du j. de l'a., *f,* la Saint-Sylvestre. N~*Year's wishes,* souhaits (*ou* vœux) de bonne année, *m.pl.*

New (*Geog.*) *a:* ~ *Brunswick,* le Nouveau-Brunswick. ~*foundland,* Terre-Neuve, *f.* ~ *Guinea,* la Nouvelle-Guinée. ~ *Orleans,* la Nouvelle-Orléans. ~ *South Wales,* la Nouvelle-Galles du Sud. ~ *York,* New York, *m.* ~ *Zealand,* la Nouvelle-Zélande; (*att.*) néo-zélandais. ~ *Zealander,* Néo-Zélandais, e.

newel, *n,* noyau; pilastre, *m.*

newly, *ad,* nouvellement, fraîchement. **newness,** *n,* nouveauté; primeur, *f.*

news, *n,* nouvelle, *f. oft. pl;* courrier; bruit, *m;* (*reel*) actualités, *f.pl.* ~ *agency,* agence, d'information, presse, *f.* ~ *boy,* vendeur de journaux, *m.* ~ [*bulletin*] (*radio*), informations, *f.pl.* ~*paper,* journal, *m.*

newt, *n,* triton, *m,* salamandre aquatique, *f.*

next, *a,* voisin; d'à côté; prochain; plus prochain; suivant; (*world*) autre. *the ~ day*, le lendemain. *the ~ day but one*, le surlendemain. ¶ *ad*, après; ensuite; puis. *~ to*, [au]près de; à côté de; presque. ¶ *~ of kin*, plus proche parent, e, proches [parents] *m.pl.*

nib, *n*, plume [à écrire], *f*, bec, *m*.

nibble (*Fish.*) *n*, touche, *f*. ¶ *v.t. & i*, grignoter, chipoter, mordiller; (*grass*) brouter; (*fish*) piquer, mordre.

nice, *a*, bon; agréable; friand; délicat; beau; joli; gentil. **~ly**, *ad*, bien; joliment; gentiment.

Nicene Creed (**the**), le symbole de Nicée.

nicety, *n*, précision; subtilité, *f*. *to a ~*, à point.

niche, *n*, niche, *f*.

nick, *n*, [en]coche, hoche, entaille, *f*, cran, *m*, saignée, fente, *f*. *in the ~ of time*, à point nommé. ¶ *v.t*, encocher, entailler, hocher, fendre.

nickel, *n*, nickel, *m*. ¶ *v.t*, nickeler.

nickname, *n*, sobriquet, surnom, *m*. ¶ *v.t*, baptiser; surnommer.

nicotine, *n*, nicotine, *f*.

niece, *n*, nièce, *f*.

niggard, *n*, ladre, *m.f*. **~ly**, *a*, ladre, mesquin, chiche.

nigh, *a*, proche. ¶ *ad*, près; presque.

night, *n*, nuit, *f*; soir, *m*. *at ~*, la nuit, le soir; (*hour*) du soir. *by ~*, de nuit, nuitamment. *the ~ before last*, avant-hier soir. **~club**, boîte de n., *f*. **~gown**, chemise de nuit, *f*. **~fall**, la tombée de la nuit, la chute du jour. *at ~fall*, à la nuit tombante. **~lamp & ~light**, veilleuse, *f*. **~mare**, cauchemar, *m*. **~ nurse**, veilleuse de nuit, *f*. **~nursing**, veillée, *f*. **~shade**, morelle, *f*. **~shirt**, chemise de nuit, *f*. **~ soil**, vidanges, *f.pl*, gadoue, *f*.

nightingale, *n*, rossignol, *m*.

nightly, *a*, de nuit. ¶ *ad*, toutes les nuits; tous les soirs.

nihilist, *n*, nihiliste, *m*.

nil, *n*, rien, néant, *m*, nul, *a*.

Nile (**the**), le Nil.

nimble†, *a*, agile, leste, preste, ingambe. **~ness**, *n*, agilité, prestesse, *f*.

nimbus, *n*, nimbe; (*Meteor.*) nimbus, *m*.

nincompoop, *n*, nigaud, e.

nine, *a. & n*, neuf, *a. & m*. *9-hole course*, parcours (*ou* golf) de 9 trous, *m*. **~pins**, quilles, *f.pl*. *~ times out of ten*, neuf fois sur dix. **nineteen**, *a. & n*, dix-neuf, *a. & m*. **nineteenth**, *a. & n*, dix-neuvième, *a. & m,f*; dix-neuf, *m*. **ninetieth**, *a. & n*, quatre-vingt-dixième, *a. & m,f*. **ninety**, *a. & n*, quatre-vingt-dix, *a. & m*. *91, 92, etc.*, quatre-vingt-onze, -douze, *etc*.

Nineveh, *n*, Ninive, *f*.

ninny, *n*, nigaud, e, dadais, *m*.

ninth, *a. & n*, neuvième, *a. & m,f*; neuf, *m*. **~ly**, *ad*, neuvièmement.

nip, *n*, (*liquor*) doigt, *m*; (*bite*) morsure, *f*. ¶ *v.t*, pincer; serrer; mordre; brûler. **nipper**, *n*, (*boy*) gamin, *m*; (*of crustacean*) pince, *f*; (*pl.*) pinces [de serrage], tenailles, *f. pl*.

nipple, *n*, mamelon, bout du sein, *m*; (*nursing bottle*) tétine, *f*.

nit, *n*, lente, *f*.

nitrate, *n*, nitrate, azotate, *m*. **niter**, *n*, nitre, salpêtre, *m*. **nitric**, *a*, azotique, nitrique. **nitrogen**, *n*, azote, *m*. **nitroglycerin[e]**, *n*, nitroglycérine, *f*. **nitrous**, *a*, azoteux.

no, *ad*, non; pas. ¶ *n*, non, *m*. ¶ *a*, aucun; nul; ne ... pas de; pas de; pas moyen de. *~ admittance [except on business]*, entrée interdite, défense d'entrer [sans autorisation]. *~ contest* (*Box.*), non-combat. *~ doubt*, sans doute. *~ entry*, [*one way street*], sens interdit. *~ flowers, by request*, ni fleurs, ni couronnes. *~ matter!* n'importe! *~ occupation*, sans profession. *~ one*, personne, *m*, aucun, e. *~ parking*, stationnement interdit. *~ performance*, relâche. *~ smoking*, défense de fumer. *~ thoroughfare*, défense de passer, passage interdit [au public].

Noah's ark, l'arche de Noé, *f*.

nobility, *n*, noblesse; grandeur, *f*. **noble†**, *a*, noble; grand. **~[man]**, noble, seigneur, gentilhomme, *m*. **~woman**, noble, *f*. **~ness**, *n*, noblesse, *f*.

nobody, *n*, personne, *pn.m*. *a ~*, un zéro; un (une) inconnu, e.

nocturnal, *a. & nocturne**, *n*, nocturne, *a. & m*.

nod, *n*, signe [de tête] *m*, inclination de t., *f.* ¶ *v.i*, s'incliner; s'assoupir.

node, *n*, nœud, *m*. nodule, *n*, rognon, *m*.

noggin, *n*, godet, *m*; (*Meas.*) ½ pint.

noise, *n*, bruit; fracas, tapage, vacarme; (*in ears*) tintement; (*fig.*) éclat, retentissement, *m*. ~*abroad*, *v.t*, ébruiter, carillonner, claironner. ~**less**†, *a*, silencieux.

noisome, *a*, nuisible; malsain.

noisy†, *a*, bruyant; tapageur.

nomad, *n*. & ~**(ic)**, *a*, nomade, *m. & a.*

nomenclature, *n*, nomenclature, *f.*

nominal†, *a*, nominal; (*of* [*the*] *names, as a list*) nominatif. **nominate,** *v.t*, nommer, désigner. **nomination,** *n*, nomination, désignation, *f*. **nominative** [**case**], nominatif, *m*. **nominee,** *n*, personne nommée; personne interposée, *f. in a ~'s name*, sous un nom interposé.

non, *prefix*: ~*alcoholic drinks*, liqueurs fraîches, *f.pl*. ~*combatant, n. & att*, noncombattant; *civil, m. & a.* ~*commissioned officer*, sous-officier, gradé, *m*. ~*committal*, qui n'engage à rien, normand. *to be* ~*committal*, rester neutre. ~*existence*, inexistence, *f*; (*Philos.*) non-être, *m*. ~*existent*, inexistant. ~*interference*, ~*intervention*, non-intervention, *f*, laissez-faire, *m*. ~*payment*, nonpaiement, *m*. ~*performance*, inexécution, *f*. ~*skid*, *a*, antidérapant. ~*stop*, *a*, sans arrêt, s. escale. ~*vintage wine*, vin sans année, v. non-millésimé, *m*.

nonage, *n*, minorité, *f*.

nonagenarian, *a. & n*, nonagénaire, *a. & m,f*.

nonce, *n*, circonstance, *f*; (*att.*) de c.

nonchalance, *n*, nonchalance, *f*. **nonchalant,** *a*, nonchalant. ~**ly**, *ad*, nonchalamment.

nonconformist, *n. & att*, nonconformiste, *m,f. & att*.

nondescript, *a*, indéfinissable.

none, *a. & pn*, aucun; nul; pas un; pas; personne, *pn.m.*

nonentity, *n*, (*Philos.*) non-être, *m*; (*pers.*) nullité *f*, homme nul, *m*.

nonplus, *n*, embarras, *m*. ¶ *v.t*, embarrasser, dérouter, démonter.

nonsense, *n*, non-sens, *m*, absurdité, insanité, *f*, sottises, bêtises,

lanternes, sornettes; chinoiseries, *f.pl. all ~*, un non-sens. ¶ *i*, allons donc!; chansons, chansons!

nonsuit, *v.t*, débouter.

noodle, *n*, (*food*) nouille, *f*. nigaud, e, bêta, *m*.

nook, *n*, recoin, réduit, *m*.

noon & noonday & noontide, *n*, midi, *m*.

noose, *n*, nœud coulant; lacet, *m*.

nor, *c*, ni; ne . . . pas non plus.

Nordic, *a*, nordique.

norm, *n*, norme, *f*. **normal**†, *a*, normal.

Norman, *a*, normand. ¶ *n*, Normand, e. **Normandy,** *n*, la Normandie.

Norse, *a. & n. &* ~**man,** *n*, norvégien, *a. & m*. *Old Norse* (language), l'ancien norois, *m*. **north,** *n*, nord; septentrion, *m*. ¶ *ad*, au nord. ¶ *a*, [du] nord; septentrional. *N~ Africa*, l'Afrique septentrionale, *f*. *N~ America*, l'Amérique du Nord, *f*. ~*east*, *n*, nord-est, *m*. *N~ pole*, pôle nord, *m*. *N~ Sea*, mer du Nord, *f*. *N~ Star*, étoile polaire, *f*. ~*west*, *n*, nord-ouest, *m*. ~*wester* (wind) *n*, galerne, *f*. **northerly,** *a*, du nord. **northern,** *a*, [du] nord, boréal. ~*lights*, aurore boréale, *f*. **northerner,** *n*. septentrional, e. **northward[s],** *ad*, vers le nord.

Norway, *n*, la Norvège. **Norwegian,** *a*, norvégien. ¶ *n*, (*pers.*) Norvégien, ne; (*language*) le norvégien.

nose, *n*, nez; (*beast*) museau; (*tool*) bec; (*scent*) flair, *m*. *to blow one's* ~, se moucher. ~ *cone*, coiffe, *f*. ~*dive*, *v.i*, piquer du nez. ~*gay*, bouquet, *m*. ~ *about*, fouiner. ~ [*out*], *v.t*, flairer. **nosing,** *n*, (*of step*) nez; (*of locomotive*) lacet, *m*.

nostalgia, *n*, nostalgie, *f*. **nostalgic,** *a*, nostalgique.

nostril, *n*, narine, *f*; (*horse*) naseau, *m*.

nostrum, *n*, remède de charlatan, *m*, drogue; panacée, *f*.

not, **n't**, *ad*, ne . . . pas, ne . . . point, ne, n'; non; pas non pas. ~ *at all*, pas du tout, point du tout, nullement, mais non, aucunement. ~ *at home*, absent. *not competing* [*for prize*], hors concours. ~ *exceeding*, jusqu'à concurrence de, ne dépassant pas.

~ *guilty*, innocent. *to find* ~ *guilty*, innocenter. ~ *negotiable (check)*, non négociable. ~ *to be confused with* . . ., à ne pas confondre avec . . .
notability, *n*, notabilité, *f*. **notable†**, *a*, notable.
notary, *n*, notaire, *m*.
notation, *n*, notation, *f*.
notch, *n*, [en]coche, entaille, hoche, *f*, cran, *m*. ¶ *v.t*, [en]cocher, entailler, hocher.
note, *n*, note, *f*, mémento, *m*; remarque, *f*; billet, *m*; lettre, *f*; bulletin; bordereau; *m*; facture, *f*; bon; permis, *m*; (*Mus.*) note, *f*; (*please observe*) nota [bene]. (*pers.*) *of* ~, de marque. ~*book*, carnet, calepin, *m*. ~ *of hand*, billet à ordre. ~ *paper*, papier à lettres, *m*. ~*worthy*, digne de remarque, remarquable. ¶ *v.t*, noter; relever; constater; remarquer. **noted**, *p.p*, renommé, célèbre.
nothing, *n*, rien; rien de; néant; zéro, *m*. ~ *at all*, rien du tout. ~*ness*, *n*, néant, *m*.
notice, *n*, observation, *f*; regard, *m*; attention, garde, *f*; avis; préavis; avertissement, *m*; notice, *f*; écriteau, *m*. at short ~, à bref délai; (*loan*) à court terme. *until further* ~, jusqu'à nouvel avis. ~ *of meeting*, avis de convocation, *m*, convocation d'assemblée, *f*. ~ [*to quit*], congé, *m*. ¶ *v.t*, observer, remarquer, faire attention à. ~*able*, *a*, digne d'attention; perceptible. *to become more* ~, s'accentuer, *v.i*. **notify**, *v.t*, notifier, avertir, signaler, aviser, intimer.
notion, *n*, notion, idée, *f*.
notoriety, *n*, notoriété, *f*. **notorious†**, *a*, notoire; insigne, fameux.
notwithstanding, *pr*, malgré, nonobstant. ¶ *ad*, néanmoins, quand même.
noun, *n*, nom, substantif, *m*.
nourish, *v.t*, nourrir. ~*ing*, *a*, nourrissant. ~*ment*, *n*, nourriture, *f*.
nous, *n*, esprit, *m*; savoir-faire, *m*.
Nova Scotia, la Nouvelle-Écosse.
novel, *a*, nouveau, inédit. ¶ *n*, roman, *m*. ~*ette*, *n*, nouvelle, *f*. ~*ist*, *n*, romancier, ère. ~*ty*, *n*, nouveauté, *f*.
November, *n*, novembre, *m*.

novice, *n*, novice, *m,f*, apprenti, e.
noviciate, *n*, noviciat, *m*.
now, *ad*, maintenant, à présent, actuellement; tantôt. ¶ *c*, or. ¶ *n*, [moment] présent, *m*. ¶ *i*, voyons! ~ *then!* eh bien!, ah! çà, or çà! ~ *& again*, de temps à autre, à diverses reprises, parfois, occasionnellement. ~ *& henceforth*, d'ores & déjà. *between* ~ *& then*, d'ici là. [*every*] ~ *& then*, de temps en temps. *from* ~, d'ici. *from* ~ *onward*, dorénavant. *right* ~, tout de suite.
nowadays, *ad*, de nos jours, aujourd'hui; par le temps qui court.
nowhere, *ad*, nulle part, en aucun lieu. **nowise**, *ad*, nullement, aucunement.
noxious, *a*, nocif, malsain, nuisible. ~*ness*, *n*, nocivité, *f*.
nozzle, *n*, ajutage, bec, jet, *m*; tuyère, buse, *f*.
Nubia, la Nubie. **Nubian**, *a*, nubien. ¶ *n*, Nubien, ne.
nubile, *a*, nubile.
nuclear, *a*, nucléaire. ~ *fission*, fission n., *f*. ~ *power plant*, centrale n., *m*. ~ *radiation*, rayonnement n., *m*.
nucleus, *n*, noyau, *m*.
nude, *a. & n*, nu, *a. & m*.
nudge, *n*, coup de coude, *m*. ¶ *v.t*, donner un coup de coude à, pousser du coude.
nudity, *n*, nudité, *f*; nu, *m*.
nugatory, *a*, futile; inefficace; nul.
nugget, *n*, pépite, *f*.
nuisance, *n*, ennui, embêtement, *m*, contrariété, scie; (*law, etc.*) incommodité, *f*; (*pers.*) gêneur, *m*, importun, e, brebis galeuse, *f*; (*child*) tourment, *m*.
null, *a*, nul. ~ *& void*, nul(le) & non avenu(e). ¶ *n*, nulle, *f*. **nullify**, *v.t*, annuler. **nullity**, *n*, nullité, caducité, *f*.
numb, *a*, engourdi, gourd, transi. ¶ *v.t*, engourdir, transir. ~*ness*, *n*, engourdissement, *m*.
number, *n*, nombre; numéro, chiffre, *m*, cote, *f*; (*publication*) livraison, *f*. N~*s* (*Bible*), les Nombres. ¶ *v.t*, compter; nombrer; numéroter, chiffrer; coter. ~*ing*, *n*, numérotage, *m*. ~*less*, *a*, innombrable.
numeral, *a*, numéral. ¶ *n*, chiffre, *m*. **numerary**, *a*, numéraire. **nu-**

merator (*Arith.*) *n*, numérateur, *m*. **numerical**, *a*, numérique. **numerous**, *a*, nombreux.

numismatics, *n*, numismatique, *f*. **numismatist**, *n*, numismate, *m*.

numskull, *n*, lourdaud, e.

nun, *n*, religieuse, nonne, *f*.

nunciature, *n*, nonciature, *f*. **nuncio**, *n*, nonce, *m*.

nunnery, *n*, couvent, *m*.

nuptial, *a*, nuptial. ~s, *n.pl*, noces, *f.pl*.

nurse, *n*, nourrice, *f*; infirmier, ère; gardemalades, *m.f*. ~[maid] bonne [d'enfant] *f*. ¶ *v.t*, nourrir, allaiter; soigner; dorloter. **nursery**, *n*, nursery, chambre d'enfants; (*Hort. & fig.*) pépinière, *f*. ~ *language*, langage enfantin. ~man, [jardinier] pépiniériste, *m*. ~ *rhyme*, poésie enfantine, *f*, conte rimé, *m*. ~ *school*, école maternelle, *f*. ~ *tale*, conte de nourrice, conte de fées, *m*. **nursing**, *n*, allaitement, *m*; soins, *m.pl*. ~ *home*, maison de santé, clinique, *f*. ~ *mother*, mère nourrice, *f*. **nursling**, *n*, nourrisson, *m*.

nurture, *n*, éducation; nourriture, *f*. ¶ *v.t*, nourrir.

nut, *n*, noix; noisette, *f*; (*violin, etc.*) sillet; (*for bolt*) écrou, *m*; (*pl, coal*) gaillette, *f*, gailletin, *m*. ~chest~, châtaigne, *f*. ~-brown, noisette. ~crackers, casse-noisettes, casse-noix, *m*. ~shell, coquille de noix, *f*. ~tree, noisetier, *m*.

nutmeg, *n*, [noix] muscade, *f*. ~ [tree], muscadier, *m*.

nutriment, *n*, aliment, *m*. **nutrition**, *n*, nutrition, *f*. **nutritious** & **nutritive**, *a*, nourrissant, nutritif.

nutty, *a*, (*taste, smell*) qui sent la noisette.

nuzzle, *v.i. & t*, fouiller; se blottir.

nylon, *n*, Nylon, *m*. ~s, (*stockings*) des nylons.

nymph, *n*, nymphe; bergère, *f*.

O

O, *i*, ô! (*of pain*), aïe!

oaf, *n*, enfant disgracié par la nature; lourdaud, *m*,

oak [tree], *n*, chêne, *m*. ~ [wood or timber] [bois de] chêne, *m*. ~

apple, pomme de chêne, *f*. ¶ *att.* & ~en, *a*, de chêne.

oakum, *n*, étoupe, *f*.

oar, *n*, rame, *f*, aviron, *m*. ~ *lock*, porte-rame, *m*. **oarsman**, *n*, rameur, nageur, canotier, *m*. **oarswoman**, *n*, rameuse, *f*.

oasis (*lit. & fig.*) *n*, oasis, *f*.

oat, *n*, (*pl.*) avoine, *f*. ~meal, farine d'avoine, *f*, gruau d'avoine, *m*. *sow one's wild* ~s, jeter sa gourme.

oath, *n*, serment; (*profane*) juron, *m*.

obdurate *a*, endurci; impénitent.

obedience, *n*, obéissance, soumission; (*Eccl.*) obédience, *f*. **obedient**, *a*, obéissant, soumis. ~ly, *ad*, avec obéissance, avec soumission. **obeisance**, *n*, révérence, *f*.

obelisk, *n*, obélisque, *m*; (*Typ.*) croix, *f*.

obese, *a*, obèse. **obesity**, *n*, obésité, *f*.

obey, *v.t*, obéir à; (*v.i.*) obéir.

obfuscate, *v.t*, offusquer, obscurcir.

obituary, *n*, nécrologie, *f*.

object, *n*, objet; but, *m*; (*Gram.*) régime, *m*. ~ *lesson* leçon de choses; (*fig.*) application pratique, *f*. ¶ *v.t. & i* objecter; réclamer. **objection**, *n*, objection, *f*; mais, *m*; opposition, *f*. ~able, *a*, susceptible d'objections; indésirable; offensant, rosse. **objective†**, *a*, objectif. ¶ (*aim, Opt.*) *n*, objectif, *m*. ~ [*case*], régime direct, *m*. *the* ~ (*Philos.*), l'objectif, *m*.

objurgation, *n*, objurgation, *f*.

oblation, *n*, oblation, offrande, *f*.

obligate, *v.t*, obliger. **obligation**, *n*, obligation, *f*. **obligatory**, *a*, obligatoire. **oblige**, *v.t*, obliger. **obliging**, *a*, obligeant, serviable, arrangeant. ~ly, *ad*, obligeamment.

oblique, *a*, oblique. ~ly, *ad*, en biais. **obliquity**, *n*, obliquité, *f*.

obliterate, *v.t*, oblitérer, effacer.

oblivion, *n*, oubli, *m*; (*Pol.*) amnistie, *f*. **oblivious**, *a*, oublieux.

oblong, *a*, oblong. ¶ *n*, figure oblongue, *f*, carré long, *m*.

obloquy, *n*, reproche; dénigrement, *m*.

obnoxious, *a*, offensant, odieux.

oboe, n, hautbois, m. **oboist,** n, hautboïste, m.

obscene, a, obscène. **obscenity,** n, obscénité, f.

obscure, a, obscur, ténébreux, fumeux. ¶ v.t, obscurcir, offusquer. **~ly,** ad, obscurément. **obscurity,** n, obscurité, f.

obsequies, n.pl, obsèques, f.pl. **obsequious†,** a, obséquieux. **~ness,** n, obséquiosité, f.

observance, n, observation; (Theol.) observance; (religious) pratique, f. **observant,** a, observateur. **observation,** n, observation, f. ~ post (Mil.) & **observatory,** n, observatoire, m. **observe,** v.t, observer; remarquer; suivre. **observer,** n, observateur, trice.

obsess, v.t, obséder. to be ~ed by, with, être obsédé par, être fanatique de, s'aheurter à. **~ion,** n, obsession, aheurtement, dada, m, hantise, f.

obsolescent, a, vieillissant. **obsolete,** a, vieux, vieilli, inusité, désuet.

obstacle, n, obstacle, m. ~ race, course d'obstacles, f.

obstetric(al), a, obstétrical. **obstetrics,** n.pl, obstétrique, f.

obstinacy, n, obstination, opiniâtreté, f, entêtement; acharnement, m. **obstinate,** a, obstiné, opiniâtre, entêté; acharné; rebelle. **~ly,** ad, obstinément, opiniâtrement.

obstreperous, a, turbulent.

obstruct, v.t, obstruer, boucher; (v.i.) fronder. **~ion,** n, obstruction; (fig.) obstruction, f.

obtain, v.t, obtenir, procurer; (v.i.) régner, prévaloir, avoir cours.

obtrude, v.t, forcer, imposer; (v.i.) s'introduire de force; être importun.

obtuse, a, obtus.

obverse (coin) n, avers, m, face, f.

obviate, v.t, obvier à.

obvious†, a, évident, manifeste, visible.

ocarina, n, ocarina, m.

occasion, n, occasion; circonstance; cause, raison, f; sujet, m. ¶ v.t, occasionner, donner lieu à; causer. **~al,** a, par occasion; (occupation) d'occasion; de circonstance; de temps en temps; (cause, Philos.) occasionnelle.

~ally, ad, occasionnellement, parfois.

occidental, a. & n, occidental.

occiput, n, occiput, m.

occult, a, occulte. **~ism,** n, occultisme, m.

occupant, n, habitant, e; occupant, m; titulaire, m,f. **occupation,** n, occupation; profession, f, état, m, qualités, f.pl. **occupy,** v.t, occuper; habiter.

occur, v.i, [sur]venir, se présenter, s'offrir; arriver, advenir. **occurrence,** n, occurrence, venue, f, fait, événement, m.

ocean, n, océan, m, mer, f. **~[-going],** a, au long cours. **Oceania,** n, l'Océanie, f.

ocher, n, ocre, f.

o'clock, heure(s).

octagon, n. & **~al,** a, octogone, m. & a. **~al nut,** écrou à 8 pans, m. **octave,** n, octave, f. **octavo,** a. & n. (abb. 8vo), in-octavo, in-8°, a.m. & m. **October,** n, octobre, m. **octogenarian,** a. & n, octogénaire, a. & m,f. **octopus,** n, poulpe, m, pieuvre, f. **octoroon,** n, octavon, ne.

ocular, a. & n, oculaire, a. & m. **oculist,** n, oculiste, m.

odd, a, (number) impair; & quelques; & quelque chose; (pair or set) dépareillé; singulier, étrange, bizarre, baroque, original, drôle. ~ jobs, bricoles, f.pl. at ~ times, par-ci, par-là. **~ity,** n, singularité, bizarrerie, f; (pers.) original, drôle de corps, m. **~ly,** ad, étrangement, bizarrement. **~ments,** n.pl, articles dépareillés, m.pl. **~ness,** n, imparité; singularité, f. **odds,** n.pl, chances; forces supérieures, f.pl; avantage, m; différence; (turf) cote, f. to lay ~ of 3 to 1, parier 3 contre 1. the ~ are that . . ., il y a à parier que . . . ~ & ends, bribes, f.pl, rogatons, m.pl.

ode, n, ode, f.

odious†, a, odieux. **odium,** n, haine, f; odieux, m.

odoriferous, a, odoriférant, odorant. **odor,** n, odeur, f. **~less,** a, inodore. **~ous,** a, odorant.

Odyssey (fig.) n, odyssée, f.

of, pr, de; en; parmi; entre; d'entre; à; chez.

off, pr, éloigne de; au large de; de dessus; de là. ~ and on, de temps à autre. **~hand,** a. & ad, im-

promptu; sur-le-champ; sans cérémonie; cavalier; brusque. ~-
handedness, sans-gêne, *m.* ~-
peak hours, heures creuses. ~
season, morte-saison, *f.* ~*shore
fishing,* pêche au large, p. hauturière, *f.* ¶ *ad,* de distance; d'ici.
to be ~, s'en aller; partir.

offal, *n,* issues, *f.pl,* tripaille, *f.*

offend, *v.t,* offenser, blesser, choquer, offusquer; (*v.i.*) pécher.
~**er,** *n,* offenseur, *m;* coupable,
m,f; délinquant, e. **offense,** *n,*
offense, blessure, *f,* outrage; délit; crime, *m;* infraction, contravention, *f. to take* ~, s'offenser,
se formaliser. **offensive,** *a,* offensant, blessant, choquant; malsonnant; (*attacking*) offensif.

offer, *n,* offre, *f.* ¶ *v.t,* offrir; proposer; présenter. ~ *up,* offrir.
~**ing,** *n,* offrande; oblation, *f;*
sacrifice, *m.* ~**tory,** *n,* (*Lit.*) offertoire, *m;* (*collection*) quête, *f.*

office, *n,* charge, *f,* office, exercice, *m,* fonction, *f.* oft. *pl,* place,
f, ministère; portefeuille; bureau;
cabinet, *m,* étude; salle, *f,* siège;
comptoir, *m;* caisse, recette, *f.* ~
boy, petit commis, *m.* main ~,
siège social, *m.* **officer,** *n,* officier,
m; fonctionnaire, *m,f;* agent, *m,*
préposé, e. ¶ *v.t,* encadrer. **offi-
cial†,** *a,* officiel; d'office. ~ *statement* (to press), communiqué,
m. ¶ *n,* fonctionnaire, *m,f,* préposé, e; (*sport, etc.*) officiel, *m.*
~**dom** & ~**ism,** *n,* fonctionna-
risme, *m.* **officiate,** *v.i,* officier, *f,* (*Eccl.*)
officier; exercer les fonctions (*as*
= de). **officious,** *a,* touche-à-
tout; (*diplomacy*) officieux. ~
person, touche-à-tout, *m,* personne qui se mêle des oignons
des autres, *f.*

offing, *n,* large, *m. in the* ~, au
l., dehors.

off-line, *a,* (*computers*) autonome.

offscourings, (*fig.*) *n.pl,* lie, *f,*
bas-fonds, *m.pl.*

offset, *n,* compensation, *f;* (*Hort.*)
rejeton, œilleton; (*Arch.*) ressaut, *m.* ~ *process,* offset, *m.*

offshoot, *n,* rejeton, *m.*

offspring, *n,* rejeton, *m;* progéniture, *f.*

often & (*Poet.*) **oft,** *ad,* souvent.
how often? combien de fois?

ogee, *n,* doucine, *f.* **ogive,** *n,*
ogive, *f.*

ogle, *n,* œillade, *f.* ¶ *v.t,* lorgner,
reluquer.

ogre, ogress, *n,* ogre, *m,* ogresse,
f.

oh, *i,* oh!; ô!; ah!

oil, *n,* huile, *f;* pétrole, *m;* essence,
f. ~ *can,* (*storage*) bidon à huile,
m; (*nozzled*) burette à h., *f.*
~*cloth,* (*table, etc.*) toile cirée,
moleskine, *f,* (*floor*) linoléum,
m. ~ *color,* ~ *paint,* couleur à
l'huile, *f.* ~ *engine,* moteur à pétrole, *m.* ~ *field,* champ de pétrole, *m.* ~ *fuel,* mazout, pétrole
combustible, *m.* ~ *heater,* poêle
à pétrole, *m.* ~ *hole,* trou de
graissage, *m,* lumière, *f.* ~ *painting,* peinture à l'huile, *f.* ~
shares, valeurs de pétrole, *f.pl.* ~
skin, toile huile, *f;* (*garment*) ciré,
m. ~ *slick,* marée noire, *f.* ~
stone, pierre à huile, *f.* ~ *stove,*
fourneau à pétrole, *m.* ~ *varnish,*
vernis gras, *m.* ~ *well,* puits à pétrole, *m.* ¶ *v.t,* graisser [à l'huile],
huiler. ~**y,** *a,* huileux; onctueux;
oléagineux.

ointment, *n,* onguent, *m.*

okay, o.k., *i,* d'accord, d'ac, dac;
très bien.

old, *a,* vieux; ancien. *how* ~ *is
he? he is 10 years* ~, quel âge
a-t-il? il a 10 ans. *the* ~, (*opp.
new*) le vieux; (*people*) les vieux,
m.pl. ~ & *young,* grands & petits.
of ~, jadis, anciennement. ~ *age,*
la vieillesse; (*decay*) vétusté, *f.*
~ *age pension fund,* caisse de retraites pour la vieillesse, *f.* ~
clothes, vieilles hardes, nippes, *f.
pl.* ~*-established,* fort ancien. ~
fashioned, à l'ancienne mode;
passé de mode, démodé; arriéré;
gothique. ~ *gold,* vieil or, *m.* ~
guard (*Mil.*), garde descendante,
f. ~ *maid,* vieille fille, *f.* ~ *man,*
vieillard, vieux; (*in comedy*) géronte, *m.* ~ **master** (*art*), ancien
maître, *m.* ~ *offender,* récidiviste,
m,f, repris de justice, cheval de
retour, *m.* ~ *salt* (sailor), loup
de mer, *m. the same* ~ *story,* la
même histoire, la même guitare.
O~ *Testament,* Ancien Testament, *m.* ~ *things,* vieilleries,
f.pl. the good ~ *times,* le bon
vieux temps. ~ *woman,* vieille

[femme] *f. the O~ Woman who lived in a shoe,* la mère Gigogne. **in the ~en time,** au temps jadis. **~ish,** *a,* vieillot.

oleaginous, *a,* oléagineux.

oleander, *n,* laurier-rose, oléandre, *m.*

olfactory, *a,* olfactif.

oligarchy, *n,* oligarchie, *f.*

olive, *n,* olive, *f.~ [tree, wood],* olivier, *m. ~ (complexion) a,* olivâtre. **~[-green],** vert olive, couleur [d']olive. **~ grove,** olivaie, *f. ~ oil,* huile d'olive, *f.*

Olympic games, jeux olympiques, *m.pl.* **Olympus** *(fig.) n,* olympe, *m.*

omega, *n,* oméga, *m.*

omelet, *n,* omelette, *f.*

omen, *n,* augure, présage, auspice, pronostic, *m.* **ominous,** *a,* de mauvais augure; sinistre; menaçant.

omission, *n,* omission, *f.* **omit,** *v.t,* omettre.

omnibus, *n,* omnibus, *m.*

omnipotence, *n,* omnipotence, toute-puissance, *f.* **omnipotent,** *a,* omnipotent, tout-puissant. *the Omnipotent,* le Tout-Puissant. **omniscience,** *n,* omniscience, *f.* **omniscient,** *a,* omniscient.

omnivorous, *a,* omnivore.

on, *pr,* sur; à; de; en; après; par; pour; sous. **~ & after,** à partir de, à dater de. **~ hand,** *(orders)* en carnet, en portefeuille; *(cash)* en caisse, disponible. **~ leave,** en congé. **¶ ad,** dessus; en avant. **~ that,** là-dessus.

once, *ad,* une fois; une seule fois. **at ~,** tout de suite; à la fois. **~ again,** **~ more,** encore une fois, encore un coup. **~ for all,** une fois pour toutes. **~ upon a time,** il y avait *(ou* il était) une fois, autrefois.

one, *a,* un; seul; unique. **~-act play,** pièce en un acte, *f,* acte, *m,* **~-armed & ~-handed** *(person),* manchot, ote. **~-eyed,** borgne. **~-man band,** homme-orchestre, *m.* **~-price shop,** magasin à prix unique, *m.* **~-self,** soi, soi-même. **~-sided,** unilatéral; *(fig.)* léonin. **~-way street,** rue à sens unique, *f.* **~-way traffic,** circulation à s. u., *f.* **¶ n,** un, *m;* unité, *f.* **¶ pn,** celui, celle; quelqu'un, e; on; un(e) nommé(e), un(e) certain(e). **~ & all,** tous sans ex-

ception. **~ another,** l'un(e) l'autre; les uns (les unes) les autres; se. **~ by ~** *or* **~ after another,** un à un, une à une. **he is ~ of us,** il est des nôtres. **~ness,** *n,* unité, *f.*

onerous, *a,* onéreux.

one's, *pn,* son, sa, ses. **oneself,** *pn,* soi-même; soi; se; son individu.

onion, *n,* oignon, *m. ~ bed,* oignonière, *f. ~ sauce,* sauce à l'oignon, *f. ~ skin,* *~ peel,* pelure d'oignon, *f.*

on-line, *a,* *(computers)* en direct, en ligne, connecté.

onlooker, *n,* assistant, e, spectateur, trice, curieux, *m.*

only, *a,* seul, unique, tout. **¶ ad,** seulement, rien que, ne . . . guère; uniquement.

onomatopoeia, *n,* onomatopée, *f.*

onset, onrush, onslaught, *n,* attaque, ruée, *f,* assaut, choc, *m.*

onus, *n,* charge, *f. ~ of proof,* charge de la preuve.

onward, *a,* progressif. **~[s],** *ad,* en avant; plus loin.

onyx, *n,* onyx, *m.*

ooze, *n,* vase, *f,* limon; suintement, *m.* **¶ v.i,** suinter, suer. **~ out,** transpirer.

opacity, *n,* opacité, *f.*

opal, *n,* opale, *f.* **~ine,** *a,* opalin.

opaque, *a,* opaque. **~ness,** *n,* opacité, *f.*

open, *v.t,* ouvrir; percer; entamer; écarter; découvrir; exposer; inaugurer; *(bottle)* déboucher; *(oysters)* écailler; *(Med.)* débonder; *(v.i.)* ouvrir; s'o.; *(flowers)* s'épanouir. **~ sesame,** Sésame, ouvre-toi. **¶ a,** ouvert; découvert, à découvert; exposé; ostensible; libre; franc; *(boat)* non ponté. **in the ~ [air],** en plein air, au grand air, à ciel ouvert. *the ~ [country],* la pleine campagne, la rase c. **in the open** *(publicly),* au grand jour. **~handed,** libéral. **~hearted,** franc. **~ house,** table ouverte, *f.* **~-mouthed,** bouche béante, b. bée. **in the ~ sea,** en pleine *(ou* haute) mer, au large. **~ space,** terre-plein, franc-bord, *m. ~ warfare,* guerre de mouvement, *f.* **~[work],** *att,* à jour, ajouré, à claire-voie. **~work** *(Need.) n,* (les) jours, *m.pl.* **~er,**

n, ouvreur, euse. **~ing**, *n*, ouverture; percée; éclaircie; (*neck*) débouché, *m*; occasion, *f*. ¶ *a*, initial; d'ouverture; de début; préliminaire; premier. **~ly**, *ad*, ouvertement; ostensiblement; hautement; franchement. **~ness**, *n*, franchise, candeur, *f*.

opera, *n*. & ~ *house*, opéra, *m*. ~ *cloak*, sortie de bal, s. de théâtre, *f*. ~ *glass[es]*, jumelle[s] de théâtre, lorgnette[s] de spectacle, *f*.[*pl.*]. ~ *hat*, [chapeau] claque, *m*.

operate, *v.t*, opérer; exploiter; (*v.i.*) opérer, agir; jouer. ~ *on* (*Surg.*), opérer.

operatic, *a*, d'opéra; lyrique.

operating room *or* **theater**, salle d'opération, *f*. **operation,** *n*, opération; exploitation, *f*. **operative,** *n*, ouvrier, ère, artisan, e. ¶ *a*, actif, efficace. **operator,** *n*, opérateur, trice.

operetta, *n*, opérette, *f*.

ophthalmia, *n*, ophtalmie, *f*. **ophthalmic,** *a*, ophtalmique.

opiate, *n*, narcotique. *m*. **~d**, *a*, opiacé.

opine, *v.i*, opiner. **opinion,** *n*, opinion, voix, *f*; sentiment, avis, sens, *m*; (*legal*) consultation, *f*. **~ated**, *a*, opiniâtre.

opium, *n*, opium, *m*. ~ *addict*, opiomane, *m.f*. ~ *den*, fumerie, *f*. ~ *poppy*, pavot somnifère, *m*.

opossum, *n*, opossum, *m*; sarigue, *m.f*.

opponent, *n*, opposant, e, adversaire, antagoniste, *m*. ¶ *a*, opposant.

opportune, *a*, opportun, à propos. **~ly**, *ad*, opportunément, à propos. **~ness**, *n*, opportunité, *f*, à-propos, *m*. **opportunism,** *n*, opportunisme, *m*. **opportunist,** *n*, opportuniste, *m.f*. **opportunity,** *n*, occasion; opportunité, *f*.

oppose, *v.t*, opposer, s'opposer à; combattre. **~d**, *p.p*, opposé, contraire. **opposing,** *p.a*, opposant, adverse. **opposite,** *n*, opposé, contraire, contre-pied, *m*. ~ (*to*), *a*, *pr*, *ad*, opposé; en face (de), vis-à-vis (de), en regard (de), contraire (à); (*sex*) opposé. **opposition,** *n*, opposition; résistance, *f*.

oppress, *v.t*, opprimer; oppresser (*Med.* & *fig.*). **~ion**, *n*, oppres-

sion, *f*. **~ive**, *a*, oppressif, assommant. **~or**, *n*, oppresseur, *m*.

opprobrious, *a*, infamant, injurieux. **opprobrium,** *n*, opprobre, *m*.

optic, *a*, optique. **~al**, *a*, optique (*glass*, *instruments*, *illusion*), d'optique. **optician,** *n*, opticien; lunetier, *m*. **optics,** *n*, optique, *f*.

optimism, *n*, optimisme, *m*. **optimist,** *n*. & **~(ic)**, *a*, optimiste, *m.f*. & *a*.

option, *n*, option; alternative, *f*, choix, *m*; (*Stk Ex.*) prime, *f*. **~al†**, *a*, facultatif.

opulence, *n*, opulence, *f*. **opulent,** *a*, opulent.

or, *c*, ou; soit; (*neg.*) ni. ~ *else*, ou bien, autrement. *2 ~ 3 times a day*, de 2 à 3 fois par jour.

oracle, *n*, oracle, *m*.

oral†, *a*, oral. ~ *examination*, examen oral, *m*.

orange, *n*, orange, *f*; (*color*) orange, *m*, orangé, *m*. ¶ *a*, orange, orangé. ~ [*tree*], oranger, *m*. ~ *blossom*, fleurs d'oranger, *f.pl*. ~ *marmalade*, confitures d'oranges, *f.pl*. ~ *peel*, pelure d'orange, écorce d'o., *f*. **~ade**, *n*, orangeade, *f*. **~ry**, *n*, orangerie, *f*.

orangutan, *n*, orang-outang, *m*.

oration, *n*, discours, *m*; (*funeral*) oraison, *f*. **orator,** *n*, orateur, *m*. **~ical**, *a*, oratoire. **oratorio,** *n*, oratorio, *m*. **oratory,** *n*, l'art oratoire, *m*, éloquence, *f*; (*chapel*) oratoire, *m*.

orb, *n*, globe, *m*, sphère, *f*, orbe, *m*. **orbit,** *n*, orbite, *f*.

orc, *n*, orque, *f*, épaulard, *m*.

orchard, *n*, verger, *m*.

orchestra, *n*, orchestre, *m*. ~ *seat*, fauteuil d'orchestre, *m*. **orchestral,** *a*, orchestral. **orchestrate,** *v.t*, orchestrer.

orchid, *n*, orchidée, *f*.

ordain, *v.t*, ordonner; décréter; prescrire.

ordeal, *n*, épreuve; (*Hist.*) ordalie, *f*.

order, *n*, ordre, *m*; règle, *f*; état, *m*; classe, *f*; classement, *m*; commande, *f*; mandat, bon, permis; arrêté, *m*; décoration; (*pl*, *Mil.*) ordres, *m.pl*, consigne, *f*. ~! à l'ordre! *in ~ that*, afin que, pour que. *in ~ to*, afin de. ~ *book*, livre (*ou* carnet) de commandes, *m*. ~ *form*, bon (*ou* bulletin) de commande, *m.* out of ~, (*Mach.*) en panne. ¶ *v.t*, ordonner; statuer; régler; charger; (*goods*) commander; (*arms, Mil.*) reposer. ~ing, *n,* ordonnance, disposition, *f.* ~ly, *a,* ordonné, rangé, régulier. ¶ *n,* (*Mil.*) ordonnance, *f.* or *m,* planton, *m;* (*hospital*) infirmier, *m.* on ~ duty, de planton. ~ officer, officier d'ordonnance, *m.* ~ room, salle du rapport, *f.*

ordinal [**number**] *n,* nombre ordinal, *m.*

ordinance, *n,* décret, *m;* (*law*) ordonnance, *f.*

ordinary†, *a,* ordinaire; commun; normal. ~ seaman, simple matelot, matelot de troisième classe, *m.*

ordination, *n,* ordination, *f.*

ordnance, *n,* artillerie, *f;* matériel de guerre, *m.* ~ [*survey*] *map,* carte d'État-major, *f.*

ore, *n,* mineral, *m.*

organ, *n,* organe; (*Mus.*) orgue, *m.* ~ grinder, joueur d'orgue de Barbarie, *m.* ~ loft, tribune d'orgues, *f.* ~ pipe, tuyau d'orgue, *m.*

organdie, *n,* organdi, *m.*

organic, *a,* organique. **organism**, *n,* organisme, *m.* **organization**, *n,* organisation; (*fête*) ordonnance, *f.* **organize**, *v.t,* organiser; ordonner; policer. **organizer**, *n,* organisateur, trice; ordonnateur, trice.

orgy, *n,* orgie, *f.*

orient, *n,* orient, *m. the O~* (*Geog.*), l'O. ~al, *a,* oriental. O~, *n,* Oriental, e. ~[ate], *v.t,* orienter.

orifice, *n,* orifice, *m,* ouverture, *f.*

oriflamme, *n,* oriflamme, *f.*

origin, *n,* origine; provenance, *f.* ~al†, *a,* (*not copied*) original; (*primitive*) originaire, originel. ¶ *n,* original, *m.* ~ality, *n,* originalité, *f.* ~ate, *v.t,* prendre l'initiative de; (*v.i.*) tirer son origine, dériver. **originator**, *n,* auteur, *m.*

oriole (*bird*) *n,* loriot, *m.*

Orleans, *n,* Orléans, *m.* or *f.*

ormolu, *n,* or moulu, *m.*

ornament, *n,* ornement, *m;* parure, *f.* ¶ *v.t,* orner, agrémenter. ~al, *a,* ornemental; d'ornement; d'agrément. **ornamentation**, *n,* ornementation, *f.* **ornate**, *a,* orné; imagé.

ornithologist, *n,* ornithologiste,

ornithologue, *m,f.* **ornithology**, *n,* ornithologie, *f.*

orphan, *n.* & *a,* orphelin, e. ~age (*asylum*) *n,* orphelinat, *m.*

orrery, *n,* planétaire, *m.*

orris root, racine d'iris, *f.*

orthodox, *a,* orthodoxe; catholique. ~y, *n,* orthodoxie, *f.* **orthography**, *n,* orthographe, *f.* **orthopedic**, *a,* orthopédique. **orthopedy**, *n,* orthopédie, *f.*

ortolan, *n,* ortolan, *m.*

oscillate, *v.i,* osciller; (*v.t.*) faire osciller. **oscillation**, *n,* oscillation, *f.*

osier, *n,* osier, *m.* ~ bed, oseraie, *f.*

osmium, *n,* osmium, *m.*

osprey, *n,* orfraie, *f.*

osseous, *a,* osseux. **ossicle**, *n,* osselet, *m.* **ossify**, *v.t,* ossifier. **ossuary**, *n,* ossuaire, charnier, *m.*

Ostend, *n,* Ostende, *f.*

ostensible, *a,* avoué. **ostensibly**, *ad,* en apparence, sous prétexte. **ostensory**, *n,* ostensoir, *m.* **ostentation**, *n,* ostentation, *f,* faste, *m.* **ostentatious**, *a,* ostentateur, ostentatoire, fastueux.

ostracism, *n,* ostracisme, *m.* **ostracize**, *v.t,* frapper d'ostracisme.

ostrich, *n,* autruche, *f.* ~ feather, plume d'autruche, *f.*

other, *a.* & *pn,* autre. every ~ day, tous les deux jours. *the* ~ side (opinion, pers.), la contrepartie. on the ~ side or hand, de l'autre côté. ~s, ~ people, les autres, d'autres, autrui. ~wise, *ad,* autrement, sinon, sans quoi, sans cela.

otter, *n,* loutre, *f.*

Ottoman, *a,* ottoman. ¶ *n,* Ottoman, e. o~, *n,* ottomane, *f.*

oubliette, *n,* oubliettes, *f.pl.*

ought, *v.aux.ir,* devoir; falloir.

ounce, *n,* (*Zool.*) once; (*Meas.*) once, *f:* (*avoirdupois*) = 28.350 grams; (*troy & apothecaries' weight*) = 31.1035 grams; (*apothecaries' measure*) = 2.84123 centiliters.

our, *a,* notre, nos, *pl. Our Lady,* Notre-Dame, *f. Our Lord,* Notre-Seigneur, *m.* ~s, *pn,* le nôtre, la nôtre, les nôtres; nos; à nous; de nous. **ourselves**, *pn,* nous-mêmes; nous.

oust, *v.t,* débusquer, dégommer; évincer, déposséder.

out, *ad.* & *pr.* dehors; hors; sorti,

absent, en course; en fleur; paru; éteint. ~ & *out*, franc, fieffé, achevé, renforcé, à tous crins, à outrance, outrancier. ~ *loud*, tout haut. ~[, *see copy*] (*Typ.*), bourdon, *m.* ~ *there*, là-dehors. **out of**, *comps*: ~ *action*, hors de combat. ~ *bounds*, hors des limites. ~ *breath*, à bout de souffle. ~ *date*, suranné, démodé; (*ticket, etc.*) périmé. ~ *doors*, dehors, au grand air. ~ *fashion*, passé de mode, démodé. ~ *hand*, sur-le-champ; échappé à tout contrôle. ~ *one's element*, hors de son élément, dépaysé. ~ *one's reckoning*, loin de compte. ~ *order*, (*Mech.*) en panne. ~ *place* (*fig.*), déplacé, hors de propos. ~ *pocket*, en perte. ~ *practice*, rouillé. ~ *print*, épuisé. ~ *shape*, avachi. ~ *sight*, hors de vue. ~ *sorts*, indisposé, dolent. *to be* ~ *stock of*, être à court de, manquer de. ~ *the common*, hors ligne. *out-of-the-way*, *a*, écarté, retiré, isolé. ~ *tune*, faux. *to be out* [*of work*], être sans travail, chômer. **out**, *i*, dehors! hors d'ici! (*Box.*) dehors! ~ *with him!* à la porte! ~ *with it!* achevez donc!

outbid, *v.t.ir*, [r]enchérir sur, surenchérir sur.

outboard, *ad*, hors bord. ~ *motor*, propulseur amovible, *m.*

outbreak, *n*, début, *m*; (*riot*) émeute; (*disease*) épidémie, *f.* ~ *of fire*, incendie, *m.* *at the* ~ *of war*, quand la guerre éclata.

outbuilding, *n*, dépendance, *f.*

outburst, *n*, débordement, emportement, déchaînement, élan, accès, *m*, poussée, explosion; incartade, *f.*

outcast, *n*, déclassé, e, réprouvé, e, paria, homme sans aveu, *m*

outcaste, *n*, paria, *m.*

outcome, *n*, conséquence, issue, *f*, résultat, *m.*

outcry, *n*, cri, *m*, clameur, *f.*

outdistance, *v.t*, distancer.

outdo, *v.t.ir*, surpasser; l'emporter sur; devancer.

outdoor, *a*, en plein air, au grand air, de plein air.

outer, *a*, extérieur. ~ *harbor*, avant-port, *m.*

outfall, *n*, décharge, *f*; (*mouth*) débouché, *m.*

outfit, *n*, équipement, équipage, nécessaire, trousseau, *m*, trousse,

f. **outfitter**, *n*, maison pour fournitures (*de sports, etc.*) *f*; confectionneur, euse.

outflank, *v.t*, déborder.

outflow, *n*, écoulement, *m*, décharge, *f.*

outgoing, *a*, sortant, de sortie, de départ, au départ; (*tide*) descendante. ~s, *n.pl*, débours, déboursés, *m.pl.*

outgrow, *v.t.ir*, devenir trop grand pour; se guérir de.

outhouse, *n*, dépendance, *f*; appentis, *m.*

outing, *n*, course, excursion, promenade, *f.*

outlandish, *a*, bizarre.

outlast, *v.t*, durer plus longtemps que.

outlaw, *n*, proscrit, e. ¶ *v.t*, proscrire, mettre hors la loi. ~ry, *n*, proscription, *f.*

outlay, *n*, débours, déboursés, *m.pl.*

outlet, *n*, issue, sortie, *f*; débouché, *m.*

outline, *n*, contour, tracé, crayon, galbe, canevas, aperçu, *m*, esquisse, ébauche, *f.* ~ *drawing*, dessin au trait, *m.* ¶ *v.t*, établir les grandes lignes de, tracer, dessiner, crayonner, esquisser.

outlive, *v.t*, survivre à, enterrer.

outlook, *n*, perspective, vue, *f*; avenir, *m.*

outlying, *a*, éloigné; avancé; excentrique.

outmaneuver, *v.t*, déjouer.

outnumber, *v.t*, surpasser en nombre.

outpatient, *n*, malade du dehors, *m,f.*

outpost, *n*, avant-poste, *m.*

outpouring, *n*, épanchement, *m*, effusion, *f.*

output, *n*, rendement, *m*, production, *f.*

outrage, *n*, outrage, *m*, indignité, *f*; attentat, *m.* ¶ *v.t*, outrager, faire outrage à; violer. ~ous, *a*, indigne; odieux; pendable; sanglant; énorme.

outrider, *n*, piqueur, *m.*

outrigger, *n*, (*boat*) outrigger; (*for rowlocks*) porte-en-dehors, *m.*

outright, *a*, fieffé. ¶ *ad*, net, carrément; (*opp. by installments*) en une [seule] fois.

outrival, *v.t*, devancer.

outrun, *v.t*, dépasser à la course.

outset, *n,* début, *m,* origine, *f.*

outshine, *v.t.ir,* éclipser.

outside, *a,* extérieur. ¶ *ad,* [en] dehors, là-dehors, à l'extérieur. ¶ *n,* extérieur, dehors, *m;* (*café*) terrasse, *f.* at the ~, tout au plus. **outsider,** *n,* (*pers.*) profane, *m,f;* (*horse*) outsider, *m.*

outsize, *n,* taille hors série, *f.*

outskirts, *n.pl,* environs, entours, *m.pl;* banlieue, *f.*

outspoken, *a,* franc. ~**ness,** *n,* franchise, liberté [de langage], liberté de parole, *f.*

outspread, *a,* étendu.

outstanding, *a,* (*Fin.*) à payer; arriéré; en suspens; marquant, saillant.

outstretched, *a,* étendu.

outstrip, *v.t,* devancer.

outward†, *a,* extérieur; d'aller; de sortie. ~ *bound,* en partance; effectuant son voyage d'aller. ~[s], *ad,* en dehors.

outwit, *v.t,* déjouer, circonvenir, tromper.

oval, *a.* & *n,* ovale, *a.* & *m.*

ovary, *n,* ovaire, *m.*

ovation, *n,* ovation, *f.*

oven, *n,* four, *m;* (*fig.*) étuve, *f.*

over, *ad,* dessus; par-dessus; au-dessus; davantage, en sus; trop; fini; passé. ~ *again,* de nouveau, encore une fois. ~ & *above,* en sus de. ~ *there,* là-bas. ¶ *pr,* sur; par-dessus; au-dessus de; plus de; en sus de; de l'autre côté de; par. ~ *all* (*Meas.*), hors tout.

overact, *v.t,* charger.

overalls, *n,* salopette, *f.*

overarm stroke, coupe, *f.*

overassess, *v.t,* surimposer, surtaxer. **overassessment,** *n,* surimposition, surtaxe, *f.*

overawe, *v.t,* intimider.

overbalance, *v.i,* perdre l'équilibre.

overbearing, *a,* insolent, arrogant, excédent.

overboard (*Naut.*) *ad,* par-dessus bord. [a] *man* ~*l* un homme à la mer!

overbooking, *n,* (*hotel, airline*) surréservation, *f.*

overburden, (*Min.*) *n,* terrains de couverture, *m.pl.* ¶ *v.t,* surcharger.

overcast, *a,* couvert, chargé, trouble. ¶ *v.t.ir,* obscurcir. ¶ (*Emb.*) *n,* cordonnet, *m.*

overcautious, *a,* prudent à l'excès.

overcharge, *n,* majoration, *f.* ¶ *v.t.* & *i,* surcharger; faire payer trop cher, écorcher; (*weapon*) charger trop.

overcoat, *n,* pardessus, *m;* (*Mil.*) capote, *f.*

overcome, *v.t.ir,* surmonter, vaincre; accabler.

overcrowd, *v.t,* encombrer.

overdo, *v.t.ir,* outrer, charger. **overdone,** *a,* exagéré, outré; (*Cook.*) trop cuit.

overdose, *n,* trop forte dose, *f.*

overdraft, *n,* découvert, *m,* avance à découvert, *f.* **overdraw,** *v.t.ir,* mettre à découvert; tirer un chèque sans provisions.

overdrive, *v.t.ir,* surmener.

overdue, *a,* arriéré, en retard.

overelaborate, *v.t,* tourmenter, fignoler, lécher.

overestimate, *v.t,* surestimer, surfaire, majorer.

overexcite, *v.t,* surexciter.

overexposure (*Phot.*) *n,* surexposition, *f.*

overfeed, *v.t.ir,* trop nourrir; suralimenter.

overflow, *n,* débordement; trop-plein, *m.* ¶ *v.i,* [se] déborder; surabonder.

overgrow, *v.t.ir,* envahir. **overgrown,** *p.a,* couvert, encombré; trop grand. **overgrowth,** *n,* surcroissance, *f.*

overhang, *n,* surplomb, porte à faux, *m.* ¶ *v.i.* & *t.ir,* surplomber.

overhaul, *n,* (*engine, etc.*) revision, *f.* ¶ *v.t,* reviser; visiter; examiner; remettre à point.

overhead, *a,* aérien; de plafond; au-dessus; en haut. ~*charges,* frais généraux, *m.pl.* ¶ *ad,* au-dessus de la tête; en haut, en l'air, au ciel.

overhear, *v.t.ir,* entendre par hasard.

overheat, *v.t,* surchauffer.

overindulgence, *n,* excès d'indulgence, *m,* mollesse; gâterie, *f.*

overjoyed, *p.p,* comblé de joie, ravi.

overladen, *p.p,* surchargé.

overland, *ad.* & *a,* par terre, de terre.

overlap, *v.t.* & *i,* chevaucher, recouvrir, déborder, imbriquer.

overleaf, *ad,* au verso.

overload, *v.t,* surcharger.

overlook, *v.t,* donner sur; dominer; laisser échapper; oublier, négliger.

overmantel, *n*, étagère de cheminée, *f*.

overmatter (*newspaper work*) *n*, marbre, *m*.

overmuch, *ad*, [par] trop, à l'excès.

overnight, *ad*, pendant la nuit; la veille au soir.

overpay, *v.t.ir*, surpayer, trop payer.

over-polite, *a*, révérencieux.

overpower, *v.t*, maîtriser; accabler. ~**ing**, *a*, accablant; tout-puissant.

overprint, *v.t*, surimprimer, surcharger. ¶ *n*, surimpression, surcharge, *f*.

overproduction, *n*, surproduction, *f*.

overrate, *v.t*, surestimer, surfaire.

overreach, *v.t*, dépasser; circonvenir.

override, *v.t.ir*, surmener; primer.

overripe, *a*, trop mûr, blet.

overrule, *v.t*, écarter; l'emporter sur; gouverner.

overrun, *v.t.ir*, envahir; infester; (*Typ.*) remanier.

oversea[s], *a*, d'outre-mer. ¶ *ad*, outre-mer.

overseer, *n*, surveillant, inspecteur, *m*.

oversewing stitch, [point de] surjet, *m*.

overshadow, *v.t*, ombrager; obscurcir, éclipser.

overshoe, *n*, caoutchouc, *m*.

overshoot, *v.t.ir*, dépasser.

oversight, *n*, inadvertance, *f*, oubli, *m*, méprise; surveillance, *f*.

overspread, *v.t.ir*, se répandre sur.

overstate, *v.t*, exagérer.

overstaying pass (*Mil.*), retardataire, *a*.

overstep, *v.t*, outrepasser, franchir.

overstock, *v.t*, encombrer [de].

overstrain, *v.t*, outrer; surmener.

overtraining, *n*, surentraînement, *m*.

overt₁, *a*, manifeste.

overtake, *v.t.ir*, rattraper, surprendre, atteindre, gagner; (*auto*) doubler.

overtax, *v.t*, surtaxer, surimposer; surcharger.

overthrow, *v.t.ir*, renverser, bouleverser, subvertir.

overtime, *n*, heures supplémentaires, *f.pl*.

overtop, *v.t*, surpasser, surmonter.

overture, *n*, ouverture, *f*.

overturn, *v.t*, [ren]verser, [faire] chavirer; (*auto*) capoter.

overvalue, *v.t*, surestimer, surfaire, majorer.

overweening, *a*, outrecuidant.

overweight, *n*, poids fort, excédent de poids, *m*.

overwhelm, *v.t*, accabler, atterrer, assommer; combler.

overwork, *v.t*, surmener, forcer.

ovine, *a*, ovine, *a.f*.

oviparous, *a*, ovipare.

owe₂ *v.t*, devoir, être redevable de. **owing**, *a*, dû, échu; arriéré.

owl, *n*, hibou, *m*, chouette, *f*.

own, *a*, propre; (*brother, sister*) germain, e. *not my* ~, pas à moi, pas le mien. *one's* ~, son [propre]; à soi. ¶ *v.t*, posséder; reconnaître; avouer. **owner**, *n*, propriétaire, *m,f*, possesseur; (*ship's manager*) armateur; (*ship's proprietor*) propriétaire, *m*. ~**-driver**, propriétaire-conducteur, *m*. ~**ship**, *n*, propriété, *f*.

ox, *n*, bœuf, *m*. ~**eye daisy**, grande marguerite, *f*. **oxford**, *n*, (*shoe*) richelieu, *m*.

oxide, *n*, oxyde, *m*. **oxidize**, *v.t*, oxyder. **oxygen**, *n*, oxygène, *m*. **oxyhydrogen** (*blowpipe, etc.*) att, oxhydrique.

oyster, *n*, huître, *f*. ~ *bed*, banc d'h—s; parc à h—s, *m*. ~ *culture*, ostréiculture, *f*. ~*man*, ~*woman*, écailler, ère.

ozone, *n*, ozone, *m*.

P

pace, *n*, pas, *m*; allure, *f*; train, *m*. *to keep* ~ *with*, marcher du même pas que; (*fig.*) marcher de pair avec. ~*maker*, meneur de train, entraîneur, *m*. ¶ *v.t*, arpenter; entraîner.

pachyderm, *n*, pachyderme, *m*.

pacific, *a*, pacifique. **P**~ [Ocean], [océan] Pacifique, *m*. **pacificist**, **pacifist**, *n*. & att, pacifiste, *m,f*. & *a*. **pacify**, *v.t*, pacifier. **pacifying**, *p.a*, pacificateur.

pack, *n*, ballot, *m*, paquet; (*soldier's*) paquetage, *m*; bande, *f*, tas, *m*; (*hounds*) meute, *f*; (*cards*) jeu, *m*; (*ice*) banquise, *f*. ~*horse*, cheval de bât, *m*. ~*saddle*, bât, *m*. ~*thread*, ficelle, *f*. ¶ *v.t*, emballer, empaqueter; (*hounds*) ameuter. ~ [*up*], plier (*ou* trousser) bagage, faire ses malles. ~*age*, *n*, colis; envoi, (*computers*), progiciel, *m*. ~*ed*, *p.a*, ~*like sardines* (*people*), rangés comme des harengs en caque. ~*er*, *n*, emballeur, *m*. ~*et*, *n*, paquet; envoi, *m*; pochette, *f*. ~ [*boat*], paquebot, *m*. ~*ing*, *n*, emballage, *m*; garniture, *f*. ~ *case*, caisse d'emballage, *f*.

pact, *n*, pacte; contrat, *m*; convention, *f*.

pad, *n*, coussinet; bourrelet; (*for carrier's head*) tortillon; (*stamp*) tampon; (*blotting*) sous-main; (*writing*) bloc-notes, bloc de correspondance, *m*. ¶ *v.t*, [rem]-bourrer, matelasser, feutrer, ouater; tamponner; (*verses*) cheviller. *padded cell*, cabanon, *m*.
padding, *n*, [rem]bourrage, *m*; bourre, *f*.

paddle (*canoe*) *n*, pagaie, *f*. ~ *wheel*, roue à aubes, *f*. ¶ *v.i*, pagayer; (*splash about*) barboter.

paddock, *n*, enclos, paddock, *m*; (*turf*) enceinte du pesage, *f*, pesage, *m*.

padlock, *n*, cadenas, *m*. ¶ *v.t*, cadenasser.

Padua, *n*, Padoue, *f*.

paean, *n*, péan, pæan, *m*.

pagan, *a*. & *n*, païen, ne. ~*ism* & ~*dom*, *n*, paganisme, *m*.

page, *n*, (*book*) page, *f*; (*Hist., noble youth*) page, *m*. ~ [*boy*], chasseur, *m*. ~ *proof*, mise en pages, *f*. *the front* ~, la Une. ¶ *v.t*, paginer; (*have called*) envoyer chercher par un chasseur.

pageant, *n*, scène à grand spectacle, *f*; cortège [à spectacle] *m*, cavalcade, *f*. ~*ry*, *f*, faste, *m*.

paid, *p.p*, payé; versé; [pour] acquit; salarié, à gages. ~ *up*, (*capital*) versé, effectif, réel; (*shares*) libérées.

pail, *n*, seau, *m*. ~[*ful*], *n*, seau, *m*.

pain, *n*, douleur, souffrance, *f*, mal, *m*; peine, *f*. *in* ~, souffrant. *to take* ~*s*, se donner du mal. ~*killer*, antalgique, *m*. ¶ *v.t*, faire mal à; angoisser, peiner, fâcher.

~*ful*†, *a*, douloureux; dolent; pénible; cruel. ~*less*, *a*, sans douleur, indolent, indolore. **pains**, *n.pl*, peine, *f*, soin, *m*, frais, *m.pl*. ~*taking*, *a*, soigneux.

paint, *n*, peinture, couleur, *f*; (*face*) fard, *m*. ~*brush*, brosse à peindre, pinceau, *m*. ¶ *v.t*, peindre; (*face*) farder. *to* ~ *the town red*, faire la bombe. ~*er*, *n*, peintre, *m*; (*boat*) bosse, *f*. ~*ing*, *n*, peinture, *f*.

pair, *n*, paire, *f*; couple, *m*. ~ *of scissors*, ciseaux, *m.pl*. ~ *of trousers*, pantalon, *m*. *the* ~ (*pictures, etc.*), les [deux] pendants, *m.pl*. ¶ *v.t*, apparier, appareiller, accoupler, jumeler.

pajamas, *n.pl*, pyjama, *m*.

pal, *n*, copain, *m*.

palace, *n*, palais, *m*.

paladin, *n*, paladin, *m*.

palatable, *a*, agréable [au goût], bon. **palatal**, *a*, palatal. **palate**, *n*, palais, *m*.

palatial, *a*, vaste & somptueux.

palaver, *n*, palabre, *f*. *or m*. ¶ *v.i*, palabrer.

pale, *a*, pâle; blafard, blême; clairet, paillet. ¶ *n*, palis; pal, *m*. ¶ *v.i*, pâlir, blêmir. ~*ness*, *n*, pâleur, *f*.

paleography, *n*, paléographie, *f*.

paleontology, *n*, paléontologie, *f*.

Palermo, *n*, Palerme, *f*.

palette, *n*, palette, *f*. ~ *knife*, couteau à palette, *m*.

paling, *n*, palis, *m*; clôture à claire-voie, *f*.

palisade, *n*, palissade, *f*. ¶ *v.t*, palissader.

palish, *a*, pâlot.

pall, *n*, poêle, drap mortuaire, *m*. ~ *bearers*, porteurs des cordons du poêle, *m.pl*. ¶ *v.t*. & *i*, s'affadir; rendre insipide.

pallet, *n*, palette, *f*; (*bed*) grabat, *m*.

palliasse, *n*, paillasse, *f*.

palliate, *v.t*, pallier. **palliative**, *a*. & *n*, palliatif, *a*. & *m*.

pallid, *a*, pâle, blafard, blême. **pallor**, *n*, pâleur, *f*.

palm (*hand*) *n*, paume, *f*. ~ [*branch*], palme, *f*. ~ [*tree*], palmier, *m*, palme, *f*. ~ *grove*, palmeraie, *f*. ~ *oil*, huile de palme, *f*. *P*~ *Sunday*, dimanche des Rameaux, *m*. ~ *off*, faire passer. ~*ist*, *n*, chiromancien, ne.

~**istry**, *n*, chiromancie, *f*. ~**y days**, beaux jours, *m.pl.*

palpable, *a*, palpable, sensible. **palpitate**, *v.i*, palpiter. **palpitation**, *n*, palpitation, *f*.

palter, *v.i*, tergiverser; marchander; se jouer. **paltry**, *a*, mesquin, méchant, chétif, pitoyable.

pampas, *n.pl*, pampas, *f.pl.*

pamper, *v.t*, gâter; dorloter.

pamphlet, *n*, brochure, *f*, pamphlet, *m*.

pan, *n*, poêle; terrine; casserole; bassine, *f*; (*scale*) bassin, plateau, plat, *m*; cuvette, *f*. (*cinema*) ~ **shot**, panoramique, survol, *m*.

panacea, *n*, panacée, *f*.

panama, *n*. or *Panama hat*, panama, *m*.

pancake, *n*, crêpe, *f*.

pancreas, *n*, pancréas, *m*.

pandemonium, *n*, pandémonium; tumulte, *m*.

pander to, se faire le ministre complaisant de.

Pandora's box, la boîte de Pandore.

pane, *n*, (*glass*) carreau, *m*, vitre, *f*; (*side or face*) pan, *m*.

panegyric, *n*, panégyrique, *m*.

panel, *n*, panneau, *f*; (*wall*) lambris; tableau, *m*, liste, *f*. (*computers*) *control* ~, tableau de commande, *m. jury* ~, liste des jurés, *f*, jury, *m*. ¶ *v.t*, lambrisser.

pang, *n*, serrement de cœur, tourment, *m*, angoisse, *f*; (*pl.*)affres, *f.pl.*

panic, *n*, [terreur] panique, *f*. ¶ *a*, de panique.

panjandrum, *n*, mamamouchi, *m*.

pannier, *n*, panier, *m*; (*on back*) hotte, *f*.

pannikin, *n*, petit pot, *m*.

panoply, *n*, panoplie, *f*.

panorama, *n*, panorama, *m*.

pansy, *n*, pensée, *f*.

pant, *v.i*, haleter, panteler. ~**ing**, *p.a*, haletant, pantelant.

pantheism, *n*, panthéisme, *m*.

pantheon, *n*, panthéon, *m*.

panther, *n*, panthère, *f*.

pantograph, *n*, pantographe, *m*.

pantomime (*dumb show*), *n*, pantomime, *f*. **pantomimist**, *n*, pantomime, *m.f.*

pantry, *n*, office, *f*, garde-manger, *m*.

pants, *n,pl*, pantalon, *m*.

pantyhose, *n*, collant, *m*.

pap, *n*, bouillie; pulpe, *f*; mamelon, *m*.

papa, *n*, papa, *m*.

papacy, *n*, papauté, *f*. **papal**, *a*, papal. ~ *nuncio*, nonce du Pape, n. apostolique, *m*.

paper, *n*, papier, *m*; pièce, *f*; bulletin; (*news*) journal, *m*, feuille, *f*; (*learned*) mémoire, *m*; (*Sch.*) composition, copie, *f*. ~**back book**, livre de poche, *m*. ~ *clip*, ~ *fastener*, attache [de bureau] *f*. ~**hanger**, colleur, *m*. ~ *knife*, coupe-papier, *m*. ~ *lantern* (Chinese, Japanese), lampion en papier, *m*, lanterne vénitienne, *f*. ~ *maker*, papetier, ère. ~ *making* & ~ *trade*, papeterie, *f*. ~ *money*, (*convertible*) monnaie de papier, *f*; (*inconvertible*) papier-monnaie, *m*. ~ *streamer*, serpentin, *m*. ~ *weight*, presse-papiers, *m*. ¶ *v.t*, tapisser.

papist, *n*, papiste, *m,f.*

papyrus, *n*, papyrus, *m*.

par, *n*, pair, *m*. ~ *value*, valeur au pair, *f*.

parable & **parabela**, *n*, parabole, *f*. **parabolic(al)**†, *a*, en paraboles; (*Geom.*) parabolique.

parachute, *n*, parachute, *m*. ~ *drop*, largage, *m*.

parade, *n*, parade, *f*; défilé; cortège, *m*. ~ *ground*, place d'armes, *f*, champ de manœuvres, *m*.

paradise, *n*, paradis, *m*; (*Eden*) le paradis [terrestre].

paradox, *n*, paradoxe, *m*. ~**ical**, *a*, paradoxal.

paraffin [oil], *n*, huile de pétrole, *f*, pétrole à brûler, pétrole lampant, *m*. ~ [wax], *n*, paraffine, *f*.

paragon, *n*, parangon, modèle, phénix, *m*.

paragraph (*abb*. par) *n*, paragraphe; alinéa; entrefilet, *m*. *new* ~, à la ligne.

parallax, *n*, parallaxe, *f*.

parallel†, *a*, parallèle; (*drill shank, etc.*) cylindrique; (*fig.*) pareil. ~ *bars*, barres parallèles, *f.pl.* ~ *ruler*, règle à tracer des parallèles, *f*. ¶ *n*, (*Geom., Mil.*) parallèle, *f*; (*of latitude*) parallèle, *m*; (*comparison*) parallèle, pareil, *m*. **parallelepiped**, *n*, parallélipipède, *m*. **parallelogram**, *n*, parallélogramme, *m*.

paralyze, *v.t*, paralyser; transir.
paralysis, *n*, paralysie, *f*. **paralytic**, *a*. & *n*, paralytique, *a*. & *m*, *f*. ~ *stroke*, attaque de paralysie, *f*.

paramount, *a*, suprême; suzerain.

paramour, *n*, amant, *m*, maîtresse, *f*.

parapet, *n*, parapet, *m*.

paraphernalia, *n.pl*, attirail, bataclan, *m*.

paraphrase, *n*, paraphrase, *f*. ¶ *v.t*. & *i*, paraphraser.

parasite, *n*, parasite, *m*. **parasitic(al)**, *a*, parasite; parasitaire.

parasol, *n*, ombrelle, *f*.

parboil, *v.t*, fair bouillir à demi.

parbuckle, *n*, trévire, *f*. ¶ *v.t*, trévirer.

parcel, *n*, colis; envoi; *m*; paquet, *m*, parcelle, *f*. ~ *post*, service des colis postaux, *m*. *by* ~ *post*, par colis postal. ~ [*out*], *v.t*, morceler, lotir.

parch, *v.t*, brûler; dessécher.

parchment, *n*, parchemin, *m*.

pardon, *n*, pardon, *m*; grâce, *f*. ¶ *v.t*, pardonner; pardonner à; gracier. ~**able**, *a*, pardonnable, excusable.

pare, *v.t*, rogner; éplucher; peler.

paregoric, *a*, parégorique.

parent, *n*, père, *m*, mère; (*fig.*) mère, *f*; (*pl.*) parents, *m.pl*; (*att.*) mère. ~**age**, *n*, extraction, *f*. ~**al**, *a*, de père, de mère, des parents.

parenthesis, *n*, parenthèse, *f*. **parenthetic(al)**, *a*, entre parenthèses. **parenthetically**, *ad*, par parenthèse.

pariah, *n*, paria, *m*.

paring, *n*, rognure; retaille; épluchure, *f*.

parish, *n*, (*civil*) commune; (*Eccl.*) paroisse, *f*; (*att.*) communal; paroissial. ~ *church*, église paroissiale, paroisse, *f*. **parishioner**, *n*, habitant (e) de la commune; paroissien, ne.

Parisian, *a*, parisien. ¶ *n*, Parisien, ne.

parity, *n*, parité, *f*.

park, *n*, parc; bois, *m*. ¶ *v.t*, parquer; garer; (*v.i.*) stationner. ~**ing**, *n*, stationnement, parcage, *m*. *no* ~, défense de stationner. *squeeze into a* ~ *space*, faire un créneau. ~ *lot*, parking, *m*.

parlance, *n*, langage, *m*, termes, *m.pl*.

parley, *n*, pourparlers, *m.pl*. ¶ *v.i*, parlementer.

parliament, *n*, parlement, *m*. ~**ary**, *a*, (*government*) parlementaire; (*election*) législative; (*candidate*) à la députation.

parlor, *n*, [petit] salon; (*convent, school*) parloir, *m*. *beauty* ~, salon de coiffure, *m*. ~ *games*, jeux de salon; jeux innocents, petits jeux, *m.pl*. ~**maid**, femme de chambre (*servant à table*) *f*.

Parma, *n*, Parme, *f*. ~ *violet*, violette de Parme, *f*.

parochial, *a*, (*civil*) communal; (*Eccl.*) paroissial; (*fig.*) de clocher.

parodist, *n*, parodiste. *m*. **parody**, *n*, parodie, *f*. ¶ *v.t*, parodier.

parole, *n*, parole, *f*. ¶ *v.t*, libérer sur parole.

paroxysm, *n*, paroxysme, *m*.

parquet, *n*, parquet, *m*. ¶ *v.t*, parqueter.

parrakeet, *n*, perruche, *f*.

parricidal, *a*, parricide. **parricide**, *n*; (*pers.*) parricide, *m,f*; (*act*) parricide, *m*.

parrot, *n*, perroquet, *m*, (*hen*) perruche, *f*.

parry, *v.t*, parer; esquiver. ¶ *n*, parade, *f*.

parse, *v.t*, analyser.

parsimonious†, *a*, parcimonieux. **parsimony**, *n*, parcimonie, *f*.

parsing, *n*, analyse grammaticale, *f*.

parsley, *n*, persil, *m*.

parsnip, *n*, panais, *m*.

parson, *n*, curé; ecclésiastique, *m*. ~*'s nose*, croupion, as de pique, sot-l'y-laisse, *m*. ~**age**, *n*, presbytère, *m*.

part, *n*, partie, part, portion; (*hair*) raie, *f*; endroit, parage, *m*; pièce, *f*, organe; (*Theat.*) rôle, emploi; (*book*) fascicule, *m*, livraison, *f*. ~ *time*, mi-temps, *f*. *spare* ~*s*, pièces de rechange, *f.pl*. ¶ *v.t*, diviser; séparer; (*metals*) départir; (*v.i.*) se séparer; se décoller. ~ *with*, se défaire de; céder.

partake, *v.i.ir*, participer.

partial†, *a*, (*biased*) partial; (*not entire*) partiel. *to be* ~ *to*, avoir un faible pour. ~**ity**, *n*, partialité; prédilection, *f*, faible *m*.

participate, *v.i*, participer.
participial adjective, *(present)* adjectif verbal; *(past)* participe passé employé *(ou* pris) adjectivement, *m*. **participle**, *n*, participe, *m*.
particle, *n*, particule, parcelle; *(Gram.)* particule, *f*.
particolored, *a*, bigarré, bariolé.
particular†, *a*, particulier; spécial; exigeant; méticuleux. ¶ *n*, particularité, *f*, point, détail, *m*; *(pl.)* détails, *m.pl*, indications, *f.pl*, libellé, *m*, renseignements, *m.pl*, précisions, *f.pl*. **~ity**, *n*, particularité, *f*. **~ize**, *v.t*, particulariser.
parting, *n*, séparation, *f*; décollement; entredeux, *m*; adieu, *m*.
partisan, *n*, partisan, *m*.
partition, *n*, séparation; cloison, *f*. **~ off**, cloisonner. **partitive** *(Gram.)* *a*, partitif.
partly, *ad*, [en] partie; moitié; partiellement.
partner, *n*, *(Com.)* associé, e; *(sports, games, Danc., & husband)* partenaire, *m,f*; *(wife)* compagne, *f*; *(Danc.)* danseur, euse, cavalier, *m*, dame, *f*. ¶ *(a lady, Danc.)* *v.t*, mener. **~ship**, *n*, société, association, *f*. to enter into ~ with, s'associer avec.
partridge, *n*, perdrix, *f*, *(young)* perdreau, *m*.
party, *n*, *(body united in cause)* parti, *m*; *(united in pleasure)* partie, *(young people's)* surboum, *f*; complice *(to* = de); groupe, *m*; réception; soirée, *f*. to give a ~, recevoir du monde, donner une soirée.
paschal, *a*, pascal.
pass, *n*, passage, *m*; passe, *f*; col; pas; laissez-passer, sauf-conduit; permis, *m*; *(Mil.)* permission, *f*. ~ *book*, carnet de compte, c. de banque, *m*. **~word**, mot de passe; *(Mil.)* mot d'ordre, *m*. ¶ *v.i. & t*, passer; admettre, être reçu à; prononcer; faire; adopter, prendre, approuver; voter; dépasser, franchir; croiser, *(auto)* doubler. ~ *by*, passer. ~ *for payment*, ordonnancer. ~ *on*, transmettre; passer *[son chemin]*; p. outre. ~ *out*, *(faint)* s'évanouir. **~able†**, *a*, passable; *(road, etc.)* practicable. **~age**, *n*, passage, *m*; traversée, *f*; trajet; canal; couloir,

corridor, *m*. ~ *money*, prix de passage, p. de voyage, *m*.
passenger, *n*, *(land, sea, or air)* voyageur, euse; *(sea or air)* passager, ère. ~ *elevator*, ascenseur, *m*. ~ *ship*, paquebot, *m*. ~ *train*, train de voyageurs, *m*, grande vitesse, *f*.
passerby, *n*, passant, e, *(pl.)* allants & venants, *m.pl*. **passing**, *n*, passage, *m*; adoption, *f*, *in* ~, en passant, passagèrement. ~ *events*, actualités, *f.pl*. ~ *fancy*, caprice, *m*; *(liaison)* passade, *f*. ~ *note (Mus.)*, note de passage, *f*.
passion, *n*, passion; flamme; fureur; colère, *f*. ~ *flower*, fleur de la Passion, passiflore, *f*. ~ *play*, mystère de la Passion. ~ **ate**, *a*, emporté, rageur; passionné, ardent. **~ately**, *ad*, rageusement; passionnément, ardemment, à la folie. ~ *fond of*, fou de.
passive†, *a*, passif. ~ **[voice]**, *n*, passif, *m*. **passivity**, *n*, passivité, *f*.
Passover, *n*, la Pâque.
passport, *n*, passeport, *m*.
past, *n*, passé, *m*. ¶ *a. & p.p*, passé. *a* ~ *master*, passé maître, *m*. ~ *[tense]*, [temps] passé, *m*. it is ~ ten, il est dix heures sonnées.
paste, *n*, pâte; colle [de pâte]; pierre d'imitation, p. factice, *f*, faux brillant, *m*. **~board**, carton [de collage] *m*. ¶ *v.t*, coller.
pastel, *n*, pastel, *m*. ~ **ist**, *n*, pastelliste, *m,f*.
pasteurize, *v.t*, pasteuriser, pastoriser.
pastil[le], *n*, pastille, *f*.
pastime, *n*, passe-temps, jeu, *m*.
pastor, *n*, pasteur, *m*. **~al**, *a*, pastoral. **~al & ~ale**, *n*, pastorale, *f*.
pastry, *n*, pâtisserie, *f*. ~ *board*, pâtissoire, *f*. ~ *cook* [& *confectioner*], pâtissier, ère.
pasturage, *n*, pâturage, pacage, gagnage, *m*. **pasture**, *n*, pâture, *f*, pâtis; *(uncut)* herbage, *m*. ¶ *v.t*, faire paître, pacager.
pasty, *a*, pâteux. ¶ *n*, pâté, *m*, bouchée, *f*.
pat, *a. & ad*, à propos, tout juste. ¶ *n*, tape, *f*; *(butter)* rond de beurre, *m*. ¶ *v.t*, taper, tapoter; *(an animal)* flatter, caresser. ~

oneself on the back, se complaire.

patch, *n*, (*ground*) lopin, coin; (*cabbages, etc.*) caré, *m*; (*face*) mouche; (*tire*) pastille, (*inner-tube*) rustine, *f*; (*computers*) retouche, *f*. ~ *pocket*, poche rapportée, *f*. ~*-work*, rapiéçage, *m*; marqueterie, *f*, placage, *m*. ¶ *v.t*, rapiécer; (*computers*) raccorder. ~ *up*, replâtrer, rafistoler.

pate, *n*, caboche, *f*.

paten, *n*, patène, *f*.

patent, *a*, breveté; (*obvious*) patent. ~ *leather*, cuir verni, *m*; (*att.*) verni. ~ *medicine*, spécialité pharmaceutique, *f*. ¶ *v.t*, brevet [d'invention] *m*. ¶ *v.t*, [faire] breveter.

paternal†, *a*, paternel. **paternity**, *n*, paternité, *f*. **paternoster**, *n*, Pater, *m*.

path, *n*, sentier, chemin, *m*; allée; (*storm, etc.*) trajectoire, *f*.

pathetic†, *a*, pathétique.

pathological, *a*, pathologique. **pathologist**, *n*, pathologiste, *m,f*. **pathology**, *n*, pathologie, *f*.

pathos, *n*, pathétique, *m*.

patience, *n*, patience; constance; (*cards*) réussite, patience, *f*. *to put out of* ~, impatienter. **patient**†, *a*, patient, endurant. ¶ *n*, malade, *m,f*, patient, e, client, e.

patina, *n*, patine, *f*. **patinated**, *a*, patiné.

patriarch, *n*, patriarche, *m*. ~*al*, *a*, patriarcal.

patrician, *a. & n*, patricien, ne.

patrimony, *n*, patrimoine, *m*.

patriot, *n*, patriote, *m,f*. ~*ic*, *a*, patriotique; patriote. ~*ism*, *n*, patriotisme, *m*.

patrol, *n*, patrouille, *f*. ¶ *v.i*, patrouiller; (*v.t.*) patrouiller sur.

patron, *n*, patron, protecteur, mécène, *m*; (*shop*) chaland, e, client, *m*. ~ [*saint*], patron, ne, saint, e. ~ *saint's day*, fête patronale, *f*. ~*age*, *n*, patronage, *m*, protection, *f*; (*shop*) achalandage, *m*. ~*ess*, *n*, patronne, protectrice; (*fête, etc.*) dame patronnesse, *f*. **patronize**, *v.t*, patronner, protéger. ~*d* (*shop*) *p.p*, achalandé. **patronizing**, *a*, paterne, protecteur.

patronymic, *n*, nom patronymique, *m*.

patten, *n*, socque, patin, *m*.

patter, *n*, bruit [des pas, des sabots]; (*in song*) parlé; (*showman's*) boniment, *m*. ¶ *v.i*, trottiner; (*rain*) crépiter. *a* ~*ing of feet*, un bruit de pas précipités.

pattern, *n*, modèle; échantillon; calibre, gabarit; patron; dessin, *m*. ~ *maker* (*foundry*) modeleur, *m*. ~ *making*, modelage, *m*. ¶ *v.t*, modeler.

patty, *n*, bouchée, *f*.

paunch, *n*, panse, *f*.

pauper, *n*, indigent, e, pauvre, *m*. ~*ism*, *n*, paupérisme, *m*.

pause, *n*, pause, *f*; silence; repos, *m*. ¶ *v.i*, faire une pause.

pave, *v.t*, paver; (*fig.*) frayer. ~*ment*, *n*, pavage; pavement; pavé; dallage; trottoir, *m*; (*outside café*) terrasse, *f*. ~ *light*, ~ *glass*, verdal, *m*. **paver**, **pavior**, *n*, paveur, *m*.

Pavia, *n*, Pavie, *f*.

pavilion, *n*, pavillon, *m*.

paving, *n*, pavage, pavement, *m*. ~ *stone*, pavé; grès à paver, *m*.

paw, *n*, patte, *f*. *to* ~ *the ground*, piaffer.

pawl, *n*, cliquet, chien, *m*.

pawn, *n*, gage, *m*; pension (*Fin.*) *f*; (*chess*) pion, *m*. ~*broker*, prêteur sur gages, *m*. ~*shop*, mont-de-piété, *m*. ¶ *v.t*, engager.

pay, *n*, paie, paye, *f*, salaire, traitement, *m*, gages, *m.pl*; solde, *f*. (*computers*) ~*load*, charge utile, *f*. ~*master*, payeur, trésorier; commissaire, *m*. ~ *roll*, état de paiements, *m*. *severance* ~, indemnité de licenciement, *f*. ¶ *v.t. & i*. *ir*, payer; verser; solder, gager; rémunérer; rapporter; (*visit*) faire; (*respects*) présenter; (*homage*) rendre. ~ *back*, rembourser, rendre. ~ *for*, payer, rémunérer. ~ *in*, verser. ~ *off*, solder; désintéresser; casser aux gages, congédier; (*mortgage*) purger. ~ *out*, payer, verser; (*cable*) filer. ~ *up*, (*v.t.*) libérer; (*v.i.*) se libérer, s'exécuter. ~*able*, *a*, payable; exigible; à payer; à la charge; exploitable. ~*ee*, *n*, bénéficiaire, *m, f*. ~*er*, *n*, payeur, euse, payant, e; (*good, bad*) paie, paye, *f*. ~*ing*, *a*, payant, rémunérateur. ~ *guest*, pensionnaire, *m,f*. ~*ment*, *n*, paiement, payement; versement, *m*; rémunération, *f.* advance ~, à valoir, *m.*

pea, *n,* pois, *m.* green ~s, petits pois, *m.pl.* ~chick, paonneau, *m;* ~cock, paon, *m.* ~hen, paonne, *f.* ~nut, cacahuète, *f.* ~ shooter, sarbacane, *f.* ~ soup, purée de pois, *f.*

peace, *n,* paix; tranquillité, *f,* repos; ordre public, *m.* ~maker, pacificateur, trice. ~ablet & ~fult, *a,* paisible, pacifique; tranquille.

peach, *n,* pêche, *f.* ~ [tree], pêcher, *m.*

peak, *n,* cime, *f,* sommet; piton, pic, *m,* dent; (cap) visière; pointe, *f,* maximum, plafond, *m.* ~hours, heures de pointe, *f.pl.* ~load, charge de pointe, *f.*

peal, *n,* carillon, *m,* volée, *f;* (laughter) éclat; coup, *m.*

pear, *n,* poire, *f.* ~ tree & ~ wood, poirier, *m.*

pearl, *n,* perle, *f.* mother-of-~, nacre, *f.* ~ button, bouton de nacre, *m.* ~ barley, orge perlé, *m.* ~ oyster, huître perlière, *f.* ~y, *a,* de perle, perlé, nacré.

peasant, *n. & att,* paysan, ne. ~ry, *n,* les paysans, *m.pl.*

peat, *n,* tourbe, *f.* ~ bog, ~ery, *n,* tourbière, *f.* ~y, *a,* tourbeux.

pebble, *n,* caillou; galet, *m.*

peccadillo, *n,* peccadille, *f.*

peccavi, *n,* meâ-culpâ, *m.*

peck, *n,* coup de bec, *m.* ¶ *v.t,* becqueter, picoter; (v.i.) picorer. to be ~ish, (hunger) avoir la fringale.

peculate, *v.t,* détourner. **peculation,** *n,* détournement, *m,* malversation, *f.*

peculiart†, *a,* particulier; propre; singulier, bizarre. ~ity, *n,* particularité, singularité, *f.*

pecuniary†, *a,* pécuniaire.

pedagogue, *n,* pédagogue, magister, *m.*

pedal, *n,* pédale, *f.* ~ [key]board, pédalier, *m.* ¶ *v.i,* pédaler.

pedant, *n,* pédant, e. ~ict, *a,* pédant; pédantesque. ~ry, *n,* pédanterie, *f,* pédantisme, *m.*

peddle, *v.i. & t,* baguenauder; détailler; colporter. **peddler,** *n,* colporteur, *m.*

pedestal, *n,* piédestal, pied, socle, *m,* gaine; sellette, *f,* porte-potiche, *m.* ~ desk, bureau-

ministre, *m.* ~ table, table à pied central, *f.*

pedestrian, *n,* piéton, *m.* ~ crossing, traversée des piétons, *f.* ~ mall, rue piétonne, *f.* ¶ *a,* à pied; (statue) pédestre.

pedigree, *n,* généalogie, *f;* pedigree, *m.*

pediment, *n,* fronton, *m.*

pedometer, *n,* podomètre, compte-pas, *m.*

peel, *n,* peau, pelure, écorce, *f;* zeste, *m.* ¶ *v.t,* peler, éplucher, écorcer, décortiquer. ~ [off], *v.i,* se peler, s'écailler. ~ings, *n.pl,* épluchures, *f.pl.*

peep, *n,* regard [furtif] *m;* échappée [de vue] *f.* ~hole, regard, judas, *m.* ¶ *v.i,* regarder; regarder sans faire semblant, guigner; émerger; (chirp) pépier. ~ at, guigner.

peer, *n,* pair, *m.* ~ into, scruter; fouiller. ~age, *n,* pairie, *f;* (book) nobiliaire, *m.* ~ess, pairesse, *f.* ~less, *a,* sans pair, introuvable.

peevish, *a,* maussade.

peewit, *n,* vanneau, *m.*

peg, *n,* cheville; fiche, *f;* jalon; (degree) cran, *m.* ¶ *v.t,* cheviller; jalonner. ~ [away], persister.

Pegasus (fig.) *n,* Pégase, *m.*

pekin (fabric) *n,* pékin, *m.* **Pekinese** or **peke** (dog) *n,* pékinois, *m.* **Peking** (Geog.) *n,* Pékin, *m.*

pelf, *n,* lucre, gain, *m.*

pelican, *n,* pélican, *m.*

pelisse, *n,* pelisse, *f.*

pellet, *n,* boulette, *f;* grain de plomb, *m.*

pellicle, *n,* pellicule, *f.*

pell-mell, *ad. & n,* pêle-mêle, *ad. & m.*

pellucid, *a,* limpide.

pelt, *n,* peau, *f.* ¶ *v.t,* lapider, assaillir à coups (with = de). ~ing rain, pluie battante, *f.* ~ry, *n,* peausserie; pelleterie, *f.*

pelvis, *n,* bassin, *m.*

pen, *n,* plume, *f;* parc; (cattle, etc.) enclos, *m.* ballpoint ~, pointe-bille, *f.* ~ & ink drawing, dessin à la plume, *m.* ~holder, porte-plume, *m.* ~knife, canif, *m.* ~manship, calligraphie, *f.* ~name, nom de plume, n. de guerre, pseudonyme, *m.* ¶ *v.t,* écrire, composer; parquer.

penal, *a,* pénal. ~ty, *n,* pénalité, peine, sanction; pénitence, *f,* dédit, m. ~ area (*Foot.*), surface de réparation, *f*. ~ clause, clause pénale, *f*. ~ kick, coup de réparation, c. de pénalité, *m*. **penance**, *n*, pénitence, *f*.

pencil, *n*, crayon; pinceau, *m*. ~ case, porte-crayon. ~ sharpener, taille-crayon, *m*. ¶ *v.t*, crayonner.

pendant, *n*, pendentif, *m*; (*Nav.*) flamme, *f*. **pendant**, *a*, pendant. **pendentive** (*Arch.*) *n*, pendentif, *m*. **pending**, *a*, pendant. ¶ *pr*, en attendant. **pendulum**, *n*, pendule; (*Horol.*) balancier, *m*.

penetrate, *v.t*. & *i*, pénétrer; percer.

penguin, *n*, manchot, *m*.

peninsula, *n*, péninsule, presqu'île, *f*. **peninsular**, *a*, péninsulaire.

penis, *n*, pénis, *m*; (*slang*) bite, queue, *f*, zob, *m*.

penitence, *n*, pénitence, *f*. **penitent**, *a*. & *n*, pénitent, e. **penitentiary**, *a*, pénitentiaire. ¶ *n*, pénitencier, *m*, maison de correction, *f*.

pennant, *n*, flamme, *f*; guidon, *m*.

penniless, *a*, sans le sou.

pennon, *n*, flamme, *f*.

Pennsylvania, *n*, la Pen[n]sylvanie.

penny, *n*, penny, = 1/100 of a dollar; (*very little money*) sou, *m*. ~royal, pouliot, *m*. ~weight, *Meas.* = 1.5552 grams.

pension, *n*, pension, rente, *f*. ¶ *v.t*, pensionner. ~ off, retraiter. ~er, *n*, pensionnaire, *m,f*; (*Mil.*) invalide, *m*.

pensive, *a*, pensif, songeur.

pentagon, *n*, pentagone, *m*.

Pentateuch (the), le Pentateuque.

Pentecost, *n*, la Pentecôte.

penthouse, *n*, appentis, auvent, *m*.

penultimate, *a*, pénultième.

penumbra, *n*, pénombre, *f*.

penurious†, *a*, pauvre. **penury**, *n*, pénurie, disette d'argent, *f*.

peony, *n*, pivoine, *f*.

people, *n*, peuple, *m*; nation, *f*; gens, *m.pl*. & *f.pl*; personnes; personnalités, *f.pl*; population, *f*; monde, *m*; famille, *f*. ~ say, on dit. ¶ *v.t*, peupler.

pepper, *n*, poivre, *m*. ~corn, grain de poivre, *m*. ~mint, menthe poivrée, *f*. ~mint [*lozenge*], pastille de menthe, *f*. ~shaker,

poivrière, *f*. ~ plant, poivrier, *m*. ¶ *v.t*, poivrer; (*shot*) canarder; (*questions*) harceler. ~y, *a*, poivré; irascible, colérique.

per, *pr*, par; pour. ~ annum, par an, l'an. ~ cent, pour cent. ~ contra, en contrepartie, porté ci-contre.

perambulate, *v.t*, parcourir. **perambulator**, *n*, voiture d'enfant, *f*, landau [pour e.], *m*.

perceive, *v.t*, apercevoir; s'apercevoir de; (*Philos.*) percevoir.

percentage, *n*, pourcentage, tant pour cent, *m*; proportion, *f*.

perceptible, *a*, perceptible. **perception**, *n*, perception, *f*.

perch, *n*, (*bird's*) perchoir, bâton; (*fig.*) haut, *m*; (*fish*) perches, *f*; *Meas.* = 25.293 sq. meters. ¶ *v.i*, percher, jucher, brancher.

perchance, *ad*, peut-être.

percolate, *v.i*. & *t*, filtrer.

percussion, *n*, percussion, *f*. ~ cap, capsule, amorce, *f*. ~ instruments, instruments de percussion, *m*. *pl*, batterie, *f*. **percussive**, *a*, percutant.

perdition, *n*, perdition, *f*.

peregrination, *n*, pérégrination, *f*. **peregrine** [*falcon*], *n*, faucon pèlerin, *m*.

peremptory†, *a*, péremptoire; tranchant, absolu.

perennial, *a*, permanent, intarissable; vivace. ¶ *n*, plante vivace, *f*.

perfect†, *a*, parfait; achevé; vrai. ¶ *v.t*, [par]achever; perfectionner. ~ion, *n*, perfection, *f*. ~ly sweet (*pers.*), gentil à croquer.

perfidious†, *a*, perfide. **perfidy**, *n*, perfidie, *f*.

perforate, *v.t*, perforer.

perforce, *ad*, forcément.

perform, *v.t*. & *i*, faire; exécuter; accomplir; jouer, donner, représenter. ~ance, *n*, exécution, *f*, accomplissement, *m*; (*sport*) performance; (*Theat.*) représentation; (*movies*, *etc.*) séance, *f*. ~er, *n*, exécutant, e; joueur, euse; concertant, e; artiste, *m,f*. ~ing dog, chien savant, *m*.

perfume, *n*, parfum, *m*. ~ distiller, parfumeur, *m*. ¶ *v.t*, parfumer; embaumer. **perfumer**, *n*, parfumeur, euse. ~y, *n*, parfumerie, *f*.

perfunctory, *a*, fait par manière d'acquit.

pergola, *n,* pergola, *f.*

perhaps, *ad,* peut-être.

peril, *n,* péril. *m.* **~ous†,** *a,* périlleux.

perimeter, *n,* périmètre, *m.*

period, *n,* période; époque, *f;* terme; exercice; *(punctuation)* point, *m; (menses)* les règles, *f.pl.* *to have one's* ~, avoir ses règles. **~ic** & **~ical†,** *a,* périodique. **~ical,** *n,* périodique, *m.*

periphery, *n,* périphérie, *f.*

periphrasis, *n,* périphrase, *f.*

periscope, *n,* périscope, *m.*

perish, *v.i,* périr. **~able,** *a,* périssable.

peristyle, *n,* péristyle, *m.*

peritonitis, *n,* péritonite, *f.*

periwinkle, *n,* (Mol.) bigorneau, *m; (Bot.)* pervenche, *f.*

perjure oneself, se parjurer. **~d,** *p.a,* parjure. **perjurer,** *n,* parjure, *m.f; (law)* faux témoin. **perjury,** *n,* faux témoignage; parjure, *m.*

perky, *a,* éveillé; dégagé.

permanence, *n,* permanence, *f.* **permanent,** *a,* permanent; perpétuel. ~ *wave,* indéfrisable, *f.* **~ly,** *ad,* de façon permanente.

permanganate, *n,* permanganate, *m.*

permeable, *a,* perméable. **permeate,** *v.t,* pénétrer; saturer.

permissible, *a,* loisible. **permission,** *n,* permission, *f.* **permit,** *n,* permis, *m.* ¶ *v.t,* permettre.

pernicious†, *a,* pernicieux.

peroration, *n,* péroraison, *f.*

peroxide, *n,* peroxyde, *m.*

perpendicular†, *a.* & *n,* perpendiculaire, *a.* & *f.*

perpetrate, *v.t,* perpétrer, commettre; faire. **perpetrator** *(crime)* *n,* auteur, *m.*

perpetual†, *a,* perpétuel. **perpetuate,** *v.t,* perpétuer. **perpetuity,** *n,* perpétuité, *f.*

perplex, *v.t,* embarrasser. **~ed** & **~ing,** *a,* perplexe, **~ity,** *n,* perplexité, *f,* embarras, *m.*

perquisite, *n,* revenant-bon, *m,* *(pl.)* casuel, *m.*

persecute, *v.t,* persécuter. **persecution,** *n,* persécution, *f.* **persecutor,** *n,* persécuteur, trice.

perseverance, *n,* persévérance, constance, *f.* **persevere,** *v.i,* persévérer.

Persia *(Iran),* *n,* la Perse. **Per-**

sian *(modern)* *a,* persan. ~ *carpet,* tapis de Perse, *m.* ~ *cat,* chat persan, [c.] angora, *m.* ~ *Gulf,* golfe Persique, *m.* ¶ *n,* (pers.) Persan, e; *(language)* le persan. **Persian** *(ancient)* *a,* perse. ¶ *n,* Perse, *m.f.*

persist, *v.i,* persister, s'obstiner, s'opiniâtrer; persévérer. **~ence,** **~ency,** *n,* persistance, constance, *f.* **~ent,** *a,* persistant.

person, *n,* personne, *f.* ~ *of independent means,* rentier, ère. ~ *opposite,* vis-à-vis, *m.* **~age,** *n,* personnage, *m.* **~al†,** *a,* personnel; mobilier, meuble. **~ality,** *n,* personnalité, *f.* **~alty,** *n,* biens meubles, *m.pl.* **personify,** *v.t,* personnifier.

perspective, *n,* perspective; *(Theat.)* optique, *f.*

perspicacious, *a,* perspicace. **perspicacity,** *n,* perspicacité, *f.* **perspicuous†,** *a,* clair, net.

perspiration, *n,* transpiration, sueur, *f. bathed in* ~, en nage. **perspire,** *v.i,* transpirer, suer.

persuade, *v.t,* persuader; décider. **persuasion,** *n,* persuasion; croyance, communion, *f.* **persuasive,** *a,* persuasif.

pert†, *a,* insolent; hardi; impertinent.

pertain, *v.i,* appartenir; avoir rapport.

pertinacious†, *a,* opiniâtre. **pertinacity,** *n,* opiniâtreté, *f.*

pertinent, *a,* pertinent, à propos. **~ly,** *ad,* à propos.

pertness, *n,* hardiesse; impertinence, *f.*

perturb, *v.t,* troubler, agiter. **~ation,** *n,* perturbation, agitation, *f.*

Peru, *n,* le Pérou.

Perugia, *n,* Pérouse, *f.*

perusal, *n,* lecture, *f.* **peruse,** *v.t,* lire attentivement.

Peruvian, *a,* péruvien. ~ *bark,* quinquina, *m.* ¶ *n,* Péruvien, ne.

pervade, *v.t,* pénétrer. **pervasive,** *a,* pénétrant, subtil.

perverse, *a,* pervers. **perversion,** *n,* perversion, *f.* **perversity,** *n,* perversité, *f.* **pervert** *n,* pervers, vicieux, *m.* ¶ *v.t,* pervertir; dénaturer; fausser.

pervious, *a,* perméable.

pessimism, *n,* pessimisme, *m.* **pessimist,** *n.* & **~ic,** *a,* pessimiste, *m.* & *a.*

pest, n, peste, f.

pester, v.t, tourmenter, importuner.

pestilence, n, peste, f. **pestilential**, a, pestilentiel.

pestle, n, pilon, m. ¶ v.t, piler.

pet, n, accès de mauvaise humeur; animal favori, m; favori, ite, mignon, ne, chéri, e, chouchou, m. ~ argument, cheval de bataille, m. ~ aversion, bête noire, f. ~ dog, chien favori, m. ~ name, petit nom d'amitié, m. ~ scheme, plan favori, m. ~ subject, sujet favori, dada, m. ~ theory, marotte, f. ~ vice, péché mignon, m. ¶ v.t, câliner, choyer

petal, n, pétale, m.

petiole, n, pétiole, m.

petition, n, pétition, supplique; requête, f. ¶ v.t, adresser une requête à; (v.i.) pétitionner. ~er, x, pétitionnaire, m,f; requérant, e, demandeur, euse.

petrel, n, pétrel, m.

petrifaction, n, pétrification, f. **petrify**, v.t, pétrifier; méduser.

petroleum, n, pétrole, m. **petrochemical**, a, pétrochimique. **petrochemistry**, n; pétrochimie, f.

petticoat, n, jupon, cotillon, m, cotte, f.

pettifoggery, n, avocasserie; chicane[rie] f.

pettiness, n, petitesse, f.

pettish, a, maussade.

petty, a, petit; menu. ~ officer, maître, m; (pl, col.) maistrance, f. ~ cash, argent pour menus frais, m.

petulance, n, vivacité [de caractère], humeur, f.

petunia, n, pétunia, m.

pew, n, banc [d'église] m.

pewit, n, vanneau, m.

pewter, m, étain, m. ~er, n, potier d'é., m.

phaeton, n, phaéton, m.

phalanx, n, phalange, f.

phantasm, n, phantasme, m, illusion, f. **phantasy**, n, vision, f. **phantasmagoria**, n, fantasmagorie, f. **phantom**, n, fantôme, m.

Pharaoh, n, pharaon, m.

Pharisaic(al), a, pharisaïque. **Pharisee**, n, pharisien, m.

pharmaceutical, a, pharmaceutique. **pharmacy**, n, pharmacie, f.

pharyngitis, n, pharyngite, f.

pharynx, n, pharynx, m.

phase, n, phase, f; temps, m. ~ displacement, déphasage, m. (engine) out of ~, décalé.

pheasant, n, faisan, e, (young) faisandeau, m.~ry, n, faisanderie, f.

phenomenal, a, phénoménal. **phenomenon**, n, phénomène, m.

phial, n, fiole; ampoule, f.

Philadelphia, n, Philadelphie, f.

philander, v.i, faire le galant. ~er, n, galant, m.

philanthropic, a, philanthropique. **philanthropist**, n, philanthrope, m,f. **philanthropy**, n, philanthropie, f.

philatelist, n, philatéliste, m,f. **philately**, n, philatélisme, m.

philharmonic, a, philharmonique.

philippic, n, philippique, f.

Philistine, n, philistin, m.

philologist, n, philologue, m. **philology**, n, philologie, f.

philosopher, n, philosophe, m. ~s' stone, pierre philosophale, f. **philosophic(al)**†, a, philosophique; (calm) philosophe. **philosophize**, v.i, philosopher. **philosophy**, n, philosophie, f.

philter, n, philtre, m.

phlebitis, n, phlébite, f.

phlegm, n, mucosité, pituite, f; (fig.) flegme, m. ~atic, a, flegmatique.

phlox, n, phlox, m.

phoenix, n, phénix, m.

phonetic, a, phonétique. ~s, n.pl, phonétique, f.

phonograph, n, phonographe, m. ~ needle, saphir, m. ~ record, disque, m. ~-record dealer, disquaire, m.

phosphate, n, phosphate, m. **phosphorescence**, n, phosphorescence, f. **phosphorescent**, a, phosphorescent. **phosphorus**, n, phosphore, m.

photocopy, n, multicopie, f.

photograph, n, photographie, f. ~ frame, porte-photographie, m. ¶ v.t, photographier. ~er, n, photographe, m,f. still ~, photographe de plateau, m. ~ic, a, photographique. ~y, n, photographie, f. **photogravure**, n, photogravure, f.

phrase, n, locution, expression,

phrase; (*Mus.*) phrase, période, *f.*
¶ *v.t*, phraser. **phraseology**, *n*,
phraséologie, *f.*
phrenologist, *n*, phrénologiste,
m. **phrenology**, *n*, phrénologie, *f.*
phthisis, *n*, phtisie, *f.*
physic, *v.t*, médicamenter. **~al**†,
a, physique; matériel. **~ian**, *n*,
médecin, *m.* **~ist**, *n*, physicien,
ne. **~s**, *n.pl*, physique, *f.*
physiognomy, *n*, physionomie,
f.
physiology, *n*, physiologie, *f.*
physique, *n*, physique, *m.*
Piacenza, *n*, Plaisance, *f.*
pianist, *n*, pianiste, *m,f.* **piano-**
[**forte**], *n*, piano, *m.* ~ *stool*,
tabouret de piano, *m.* ~ *wire*,
corde à piano, *f.*
piccolo, *n*, piccolo, *m.*
pick, *n*, pic, *m*, pioche, *f*; choix,
m; élite, fleur, *f*; (*of the basket*)
dessus, *m.* **~axe**, pioche, *f.* ~
lock, crochet [de serrurier], rossignol, *m.* **~me-up**, remontant,
m. the ~ *of the bunch*, la fleur des
pois. **~pocket**, voleur à la tire,
pickpocket, *m.* ¶ *v.t*, cueillir;
trier; choisir; (*bone*) ronger;
(*lock*) crocheter; (*teeth*) curer;
(*quarrel*) chercher; (*peck*) becqueter. ~ *at one's food*, pignocher. ~ *up*, relever; ramasser;
(*passengers*) prendre; (*news*) écumer.
picked, *p.a*, choisi, de choix;
d'élite. **picker**, *n*, cueilleur, euse;
trieur, euse.
picket, *n*, piquet; jalon, *m.* ¶ *v.t*,
piqueter.
picking, *n*, cueillette, *f*; triage,
m; (*pl.* pilferings) gratte, *f*; tour
de bâton, *m.*
pickle, *n*, (*brine*) saumure, *f*;
(*plight*) arroi, *m*; (*pl.*) conserves
au vinaigre, *f.pl.* ¶ *v.t*, mariner,
saler; conserver [au vinaigre].
~d, *a*, (*vegetables*) au vinaigre;
(*meat*) salé. ~ *cucumbers*, cor-
nichons, *m.pl.*
picnic, *n*, pique-nique, *m*, partie
de plaisir, *f.* ~ *basket*, panier
pique-nique, *m.* ¶ *v.i*, pique-
niquer.
pictorial, *a*, pictural; en images;
(*journal*) illustré, pittoresque;
(*plan, map*) figuratif, figuré. **pic-**
ture, *n*, tableau, *m*, peinture;
image, *f.* ~ *book*, livre d'images,
album d'images pour enfants, *m.*

~ *gallery*, galerie de tableaux, *f.*
~ *postcard*, carte postale illustrée, *f.* ~ *writing*, écriture figurative, *f.* ¶ *v.t*, dépeindre, figurer,
représenter. ~ *to oneself*, se figurer. **picturesque**†, *a*, pittoresque, imagé. **~ness**, *n*, pittoresque, *m.*
pie, *n*, (*meat*) pâté, *m*; (*fruit*)
tourte, *f*; (*printers'*) pâté, *m*,
pâte, *f.* ~ *dish*, tourtière, *f.*
piebald, *a*, pie.
piece, *n*, morceau; fragment; tronçon, *m*; pièce, *f.* ~ *of business*,
affaire, *f.* ~ *of furniture*, meuble,
m. ~ *of ice*, glaçon, *m.* ~
of impertinence, impertinence, *f.*
~ *of news*, nouvelle, *f.* ~ *of ord-*
nance, bouche à feu, *f.* ~ *of*
poetry, poésie, *f.* ~ *of work*,
travail, *m*; besogne, *f.* **~work**,
travail à la tâche, *m.* ¶ *v.t*, rapiécer. ~ *together* (*fig.*), coudre
ensemble. **piecemeal**, *ad*, en
morceaux; par degrés.
pied, *a*, bigarré, bariolé.
Piedmont, *n*, le Piémont.
pier, *n*, jetée; jetée promenade;
pile, *f*; pied-droit; jambage, trumeau, *m.* **~head**, musoir, *m.*
pierce, *v.t. & i*, percer; repercer;
pénétrer. **piercing**, *p.a*, perçant;
(*cold*) saisissant.
piety, *n*, piété, *f.*
pig, *n*, cochon, porc, pourceau;
(*child*) goret, *m*; (*metal*) gueuse,
f, saumon, *m.* ~ *breeding*, l'industrie porcine, *f.* **~headed**,
têtu comme un mulet. ~ [*iron*],
fonte en gueuses, *f.* en saumons,
[gueuse de] fonte, *f.* ~ *meat*,
charcuterie, *f.* **~skin**, peau de
porc, *f*, cuir de p., *m.* **~sty** or
piggery, *n*, étable à pourceaux,
m, porcherie, *f.* **~tail** (hair),
queue, *f.*
pigeon, *n*, pigeon, ne; (*young*)
pigeonneau, *m.* **~hole**, boulin,
m; (*in desk*) case, *f.* [*set of*] ~
holes, casier, *m.* **~ry**, *n*, pigeonnier, *m.*
piglet, *n*, goret, *m.*
pigment, *n*, pigment, *m.*
pigmy, *n*, pygmée, *f.*
pike, *n*, pique, *f*; (*fish*) brochet,
m.
pilaster, *n*, pilastre, *m.*
pilchard, *n*, sardine, *f.*
pile, *n*, pile, *f*, monceau, amas,
tas, *m*; pelote, *f*; (*mass of build-*

ings) amas; (*wood*) bûcher; (*arms*) faisceau; (*stake*) pieu, pilotis; (*nap*) poil, m; (*Elec.*) pile, *f*. *man who has made his* ~, homme nanti, *m*. ~ [up], *v.t*, empiler, entasser, amonceler, amasser.

piles (*Med.*) *n.pl*, hémorroïdes, *f.pl*.

pilfer, *v.t*, piller.

pilgrim, *n*, pèlerin, e. ~**age**, *n*. & *place of pilgrimage*, pèlerinage, *m*.

piling (*pile work*) *n*, pilotis, *m*.

pill, *n*, pilule, *f*.

pillage, *n*, pillage, *m*. ¶ *v.t*, piller.

pillar, *n*, pilier, *m*, colonne, *f*.

pillory, *n*, pilori, *m*. ¶ *v.t*, pilorier, draper.

pillow, *n*, oreiller; chevet; coussin, *m*. ~ *case*, taie d'oreiller, *f*. ~ *lace*, dentelle aux fuseaux, *f*.

pilot, *n*, pilote, *m*. *automatic* ~, bloc de pilotage, *m*. ~ *boat*, bateau-pilote, *m*. ~ *lamp*, lampe témoin, *f*. ¶ *v.t*, piloter.

pimpernel, *n*, mouron, *m*, morgeline, *f*.

pimple, *n*, bouton, bourgeon, *m*, pustule, *f*. *to break out in* ~s, boutonner, bourgeonner.

pin, *n*, épingle; (*peg*) cheville, *f*, boulon, *m*; goupille; clavette; broche; fiche, *f*; (*fig.*) épingle, *f*, fétu, *m*. ~s & *needles* (*fig.*), fourmis, *f.pl*. ~*cushion*, pelote [à épingles] *f*. ~ *money*, argent de poche, *m*. ~ *prick*, piqûre d'épingle, *f*, coup d'é., *m*. ¶ *v.t*, épingler; cheviller; clouer.

pinafore, *n*, tablier [d'enfant] *m*.

pincers, *n.pl*, tenailles; (*smith's*) tricoises, *f.pl*.

pinch, *n*, (*of salt*) pincée; (*snuff*) pincée, prise, *f*; pincement, *m*. *in a* ~, au besoin. ¶ *v.t*, pincer; blesser, brider, gêner. ~**ed**, *p.a*, tiré.

pine, *v.t*, languir; dépérir, sécher. ¶ *n*, pin, *m*.

pineapple, *n*, ananas, *m*.

ping-pong, *n*, ping-pong, tennis de table, *m*. ~ *set*, jeu de p.-p., jeu de t. de t., *m*.

pining, *n*, dépérissement, *m*; nostalgie, *f*.

pinion, *n*, aileron; (*Mech.*) pignon, *m*. ¶ *v.t*, couper les ailes à; (*pers.*) garrotter.

pink, *a*, rose, incarnat. ¶ *n*, rose; (*Bot.*) œillet, *m*, mignardise, *f*.

pinnace, *n*, grand canot, *m*.

pinnacle, *n*, pinacle, *m*.

pioneer, *n*, pionnier, *m*.

pious†, *a*, pieux.

pip, *n*, (*seed*) pépin; (*dominoes*) point, *m*; (*disease*) pépie, *f*.

pipe, *n*, tuyau, conduit, *m*, conduite, *f*; canal; (*key*) canon, *m*, forure; (*tobacco*) pipe, *f*; (*flute*) pipeau, chalumeau; (*boatswain's*) sifflet, *m*. ~ *clay*, terre de pipe, *f*; blanc de terre à pipe, *m*. ~ *line*, canalisation, *f*. ¶ *v.i. & t*, siffler. **piping** (*braid*) *n*, passepoil, liséré, *m*. ~ *hot*, bouillant.

pipkin, *n*, poêlon, *m*, huguenote, *f*.

pippin, *n*, reinette, *f*.

piquancy, *n*, goût piquant; (*fig.*) piquant, sel, *m*. **piquant**, *a*, piquant. **pique**, *n*, pique, *f*. ¶ *v.t*, piquer. **piquet**, *n*, piquet, *m*.

piracy, *n*, piraterie; contrefaçon, *f*. **pirate**, *n*, pirate; forban, *m*. ~ *publisher*, éditeur marron, *m*. ¶ *v.t*, contrefaire; (*v.i*) pirater.

Piraeus, *n*, le Pirée.

pirouette, *n*, pirouette, *f*. ¶ *v.i*, pirouetter.

Pisa, *n*, Pise, *f*.

pisciculture, *n*, pisciculture, *f*.

pistachio, *n*, (*nut*) pistache, *f*; (*tree*) pistachier, *m*.

pistil, *n*, pistil, dard, *m*.

pistol, *n*, pistolet, *m*. *a* ~ [*held*] *at one's head* (*fig.*), un couteau à la gorge.

piston, *n*, piston, *m*. ~ *rod*, tige, *f*.

pit, *n*, fosse, fouille, *f*, creux, puits, *m*; carrière; (*in metal*) piqûre; (*pock*) marque, couture, *f*. ~*fall*, trappe, *f*. piège; (*fig.*) écueil, *m*. ~ *saw*, scie de long, *f*. ¶ *v.t*, marquer, couturer; piquer; mettre aux prises; (*fruit*) denoyauter.

pit-[a-]pat (to go), faire tic tac, palpiter.

pitch, *n*, poix, *f*; brai, bitume; point, degré, *m*, période; inclinaison, pente, *f*; (*Mus.*) diapason, *m*, hauter [musicale] *f*; (*Mech.*) pas; (*Naut.*) coup de tangage; (*angler's*) coup, *m*. ~ *dark*, noir comme poix. ~*fork*, fourche à faner, fouine, *f*. ~*fork someone into an office*, bombarder quelqu'un à une place. ~*pine*, pitchpin, *m*. ~ *pipe*, diapason à bouche, *m.* ¶ *v.t*, poisser; jeter, lancer; dresser, tendre, asseoir; (*v.i.*) plonger; (*ship*) tanguer, canarder. *~ed battle*, bataille rangée, *f.*

pitcher, *n*, cruche, *f,* broc; (*baseball*) lanceur, *m.*

piteous†, *a*, piteux, pitoyable.

pith, *n*, moelle; (*palm tree*) cervelle; (*fig.*) moelle, *f*, suc; (*of a story*) piquant, *m.* *~ helmet,* casque en moelle, *m.* *~y, a,* moelleux; (*fig.*) plein de moelle.

pitiable† & **pitiful**†, *a*, piteux, à faire pitié, pitoyable, lamentable. **pitiless**†, *a,* impitoyable, sans pitié.

pittance, *n*, maigre revenu, revenu dérisoire, *m*; faible portion, *f.*

pity, *n*, pitié, *f*; (*regret*) dommage, *m. to move to ~*, apitoyer. ¶ *v.t,* plaindre, avoir pitié de.

pivot, *n*, pivot, *m.* ¶ *v.i,* pivoter.

pixie, *n*, elfe, lutin, *m*; fée, *f.*

placard, *n*, placard, *m*, affiche, pancarte, *f.* ¶ *v.t,* placarder, afficher.

place, *n*, place, *f*; endroit; lieu, *m*; localité, *f.* *hiding ~,* cachette, *f. to take ~,* avoir lieu, se passer. ¶ *v.t,* placer; mettre; déposer; poser.

placer (*Min.*) *n*, placer, *m.*

placid†, *a*, placide. *~ity, n,* placidité, *f.*

plagiarism, *n*, plagiat, larcin, *m.* **plagiarist,** *n*, plagiaire. *m.* **plagiarize,** *v.t,* plagier.

plague, *n*, peste, plaie, *f*; fléau; tourment, *m*, brebis galeuse, *f.* *~-stricken* (*person*), pestiféré, e, *a. & n.* ¶ (*fig.*) *v.t,* tourmenter, assassiner; (*tease*) lutiner.

plaice, *n*, plie, *f*, carrelet, *m.*

plaid, *n*, plaid, tissu écossais, *m.*

plain, *a*, uni; lisse; plat; simple; (*cigarettes*) ordinaires; clair, évident; distinct; nu; au naturel; laid. *~ cooking,* cuisine bourgeoise, *f.* *~ dealing,* franchise, *f. in ~ figures,* en chiffres connus. *~ girl,* jeune fille laide, *f*, laideron, *m.* *~ language* (*Teleg.*), [langage] clair, *m.* *~-song,* plain-chant, *m.* ¶ *n,* plaine, *f.* *~ly, ad,* simplement; clairement; distinctement; nettement; net, bonnement. *~ness, n,* simplicité; clarté; netteté; laideur, *f.*

plaintiff, *n*, demandeur, eresse,

plaignant, e. **plaintive**†, *a,* plaintif.

plait, *n*, natte, tresse, *f.* ¶ *v.t,* natter, tresser. *to ~ one's hair,* se natter.

plan, *n*, plan; projet, dessein, *m*, batterie, *f.* ¶ *v.t,* dresser le plan de; projeter, méditer, concerter; (*political economy*) planifier. *~ing, n,* (*computers*) planification, *f. family ~,* planification des naissances.

plane, *a*, plan. ¶ *n,* plan, *m*, surface plane, *f*; (*tool*) rabot; avion, aéroplane, *m.* *~ [tree]*, platane, plane, *m.* ¶ *v.t,* raboter; planer.

planet, *n*, planète, *f.* **planetarium,** *n*, planétaire, *m.* **planetary,** *a,* planétaire.

plank, *n*, planche, *f*, madrier, *m.*

plankton, *n*, plancton, *m.*

plant, *n*, plante, herbe, *f*, végétal; (*factory*) usine, *f*; matériel, outillage, appareil, *m.* *~ life,* vie végétale, *f.* ¶ *v.t,* planter; poser.

plantain, *n*, plantain; (*banana*) plantanier, *m.*

plantation, *n*, plantation, *f*, plantage, plant, *m.* **planter,** *n*, planteur, euse.

plaque, *n*, plaque, *f.*

plasma, *n*, plasma, *m.*

plaster, *n*, platre; (*Med.*) emplâtre, *m.* *~ cast,* plâtre, *m.* *~ of paris,* plâtre de moulage, gypse, *m.* ¶ *v.t,* plâtrer. *~er, n,* plâtrier, *m.*

plastic, *a,* plastique. *~ity, n,* plasticité, *f.*

plate, *n*, (*eating*) assiette, *f*; (*collection*) plat, bassin, *m*; (*Phot.*) plaque; (*book*) planche, *f*, hors-texte, *m*; (*turf*) coupe; (*metal*) plaque, *f.* *~s & dishes,* vaisselle, *f.* *~ glass,* glace de vitrage, *f.* *~ glass insurance,* assurance contre le bris de glaces, *f.* *~ holder* (*Phot.*), châssis négatif, c. porte-plaque(s) *m.* ¶ *v.t,* plaquer; argenter; (*ship*) border. *~[ful], n,* assiettée, assiette, *f.*

plateau, *n*, plateau, *m.*

platen (*Typ.*) *n*, platine, *f.*

platform, *n*, plate-forme; estrade; tribune, *f*; pont; (*Rly.*) quai, débarcadère, embarcadère; (*Pol.*) programme, *m.* *~ scales,* bascule romaine, *f.* *~ ticket,* billet de quai, *m.*

platinotype, *n*, platinotypie, *f.*

platinum, *n,* platine, *m.* ~ *blonde* (color), blond platine, *m.*
platitude, *n,* platitude, *f.*
Platonic, *a,* platonique.
platoon, *n,* peloton, *m.*
plaudit, *n,* applaudissement, *m.*
plausible†, *a,* plausible.
play, *n,* jeu, *m;* récréation, *f;* essor, *m,* carrière; pièce [de théâtre] *f;* spectacle; (*Mech.*) jeu, *m,* chasse, *f.* ~*fellow,* ~*mate,* camarade de jeu, *m,f.* ~*goer,* coureur (euse) de spectacles. ~*ground,* cour de récréation, *f,* (*covered*) préau, *m.* ~ *of colors,* reflets irisés, *m.pl.* ~ *of features,* jeux de physionomie, *m.pl.* ~ *of light,* jeu de lumière, chatoiement, *m.* ~ *on words,* jeu de mots, *m.* ~ *pen,* parc d'enfant, *m.* ~*thing,* jouet, joujou, *m,* amusette, babiole, *f.* ~*time,* récréation, *f.* ~*wright,* auteur dramatique, dramatiste, *m,* dramaturge, *m,f.* ¶ *v.i,* jouer; (*v.t.*) jouer; j. de; faire; (*harp, etc.*) pincer; (*a fish*) noyer. ~*er,* *n,* joueur, euse; musicien, ne; acteur, trice, comédien, ne. ~ *piano,* piano mécanique, *m.* ~*ful,* *a,* folâtre, enjoué, badin. ~*fulness,* *n,* enjouement, *m. playing cards,* cartes à jouer, *f.pl.*
plea, *n,* prétexte, *m;* (*law*) défenses, *f.pl;* exception, *f;* (*pl.*) conclusions, *f.pl.* **plead,** *v.t.* & *i,* plaider, alléguer, prétexter. ~ *guilty,* s'avouer coupable, s'accuser soi-même. ~ *not guilty,* nier sa culpabilité. ~*ing* (*law*) *n,* (*oral advocacy*) plaidoirie; (*preparatory formalities*) instruction; (*pl, statement*) instruction par écrit, *f.*
pleasant†, *a,* agréable, aimable; commode. ~*ness,* *n,* agrément, *m.* ~*ry,* *n,* plaisanterie, *f.* **please,** *v.t,* plaire à, agréer à; sourire à; flatter; accommoder; (*abs.*) plaire. ¶ *imperative,* s'il vous plaît; veuillez; prière de . . .; de grâce! ~**d,** *p.a,* content, heureux, aise. **pleasing†,** *a,* agréable, amène; gracieux. **pleasurable†,** *a,* agréable. **pleasure,** *n,* plaisir; agrément, *m;* douceur; jouissance; volupté, *f;* honneur; gré, *m.* ~ *boat,* bateau de plaisance, *m.* ~ *trip,* voyage d'agrément, *m.*

pleat, *n,* pli, *m,* pince, *f.* ¶ *v.t,* plisser.
pledge, *n,* gage, engagement, *m,* plébiscite, *n,* plébiscite, *m.*
pledge, *n,* gage, engagement, *m,* assurance, *f.* ¶ *v.t,* engager; boire à la santé de.
plenary, *a,* plénier. **plenipotentiary,** *a.* & *n,* plénipotentiaire, *a.* & *m.* **plenitude,** *n,* plénitude, *f.* **plenteous†** & **plentiful†,** *a,* abondant. *to be plentiful,* foisonner. **plenty,** *n,* abondance; foison, *f.* ~ *of,* force. *with* ~ *of,* à grand renfort de. **plenum,** *n,* plein, *m.*
pleonasm, *n,* pléonasme, *m.*
plethora, *n,* pléthore, *f.*
pleura, *n,* plèvre, *f.* **pleurisy,** *n,* pleurésie, *f.*
plexus, *n,* plexus, réseau, lacis, *m.*
pliable, *a,* pliable, pliant, flexible, souple. **pliancy,** *n,* flexibilité, souplesse, *f.*
pliers, *n.pl,* pince, *f,* pinces, *f.pl. flat-nosed* ~, bec-de-cane, *m.*
plight, *n,* état, *m,* passe, *f,* arroi, *m.* ¶ *v.t,* engager.
plinth, *n,* plinthe, *f.*
plod on, along, *v.i,* avancer péniblement. **plodder,** *n,* bûcheur, euse.
plot, *n,* parcelle, *f,* lopin, coin; complot, *m,* conspiration, trame, intrigue; (*novel, play*) intrigue, *f.* ¶ *v.t.* & *i,* (*curve, etc.*) tracer; comploter, conspirer, machiner. **plotter,** *n,* conspirateur, trice.
plow, *n,* charrue, *f.* ~ *land,* terre labourable, *f.* ~*man,* laboureur, valet de charrue, *m.* ~*share,* soc, *m.* ¶ *v.t.* & *i,* labourer; (*fig.*) sillonner. ~*ing,* *n,* labourage, labour, *m.*
pluck, *n,* courage, estomac, cran, *m;* (*butchery*) fressure, *f.* ¶ *v.t,* arracher; [dé]plumer, dépiler; cueillir; (*Mus. strings*) pincer. ~*y†,* *a,* courageux, crâne.
plug, *n,* tampon, bouchon, obturateur, *m;* (*Elec.*) prise de courant, *f;* (*twist of tobacco*) carotte, *f.* ¶ *v.t,* tamponner, boucher. ~ *in,* brancher.
plum, *n,* prune, *f;* (*dried*) pruneau, *m.* ~ *orchard,* prunelaie, *f.* ~ *pudding,* plum-pudding, *m.* ~ [*tree*], prunier, *m.*
plumage, *n,* plumage, *m.*
plumb, *a,* droit, vertical. ¶ *ad,* à plomb, d'aplomb. ¶ *n,* plomb, *m.*

~ *line*, fil à plomb, *m.* ¶ *v.t*, plomber. **plumbago**, *n*, plombagine, *f*; graphite, *m*. **plumber**, *n*, plombier, fontainier, *m*. **plumbing**, *n*, plombage, *m*; plomberie, *f*.

plume, *n*, plumet, panache, *m*, aigrette, *f*. ¶ *v.t*, empanacher. ~ *its feathers*, s'éplucher. ~ *oneself on*, se piquer de, se targuer de.

plummet, *n*, plomb; fil à plomb, *m*; sonde, *f*.

plump, *a*, rebondi, dodu, potelé, en chair, paquet; (*chicken*) gras. ~**ness**, *n*, embonpoint, *m*.

plunder, *n*, pillage; butin, *m*. ¶ *v.t*, piller, butiner. ~**er**, *n*, pillard, e.

plunge, *n*, plongeon; (*Swim.*) plongeon sans élan, *m*. *to take the* ~ (*fig.*), faire le saut périlleux, sauter le fossé. ¶ *v.t*, plonger, immerger; ensevelir; (*v.i.*) [se] plonger. **plunger**, *n*, plongeur, *m*.

pluperfect, *n*, plus-que-parfait, *m*.

plural, *a*, plural; (*Gram.*) pluriel. ¶ *n*, pluriel, *m*. ~**ity**, *n*, pluralité, *f*; (*of offices*) cumul, *m*.

plus, *pr*, plus. *he is 10, 12,* ~, il a 10, 12, ans révolus. ~**-fours**, culotte pour le golf, *f*. ~ [*sign*], [signe] plus, *m*.

plush, *n*, peluche, *f*.

ply, *n*, pli, *m*, épaisseur, *f*. ~**wood**, [bois] contreplaqué, *m*. ¶ *v.t*, (*tool*) manier; (*questions*) presser (*with* = de); (*trade*) exercer; (*v.i.*) faire le service, marcher.

pneumatic, *a*, pneumatique; à air comprimé. ~ [*tire*], [bandage] pneumatique, pneu, *m*.

pneumonia, *n*, pneumonie, *f*.

Po (the), le Pô.

poach, *v.t*, pocher; (*v.i.*) braconner. ~**er**, *n*, braconnier, *m*.

pocket, *n*, poche, *f*; (*vest*) gousset, *m*; (*Bil.*) blouse, *f*. *air* ~, trou d'air, *m*. ~ *money*, argent de poche, *m*. *in one's* ~ (*fig.*), en poche. ¶ *v.t*, empocher. ~**ful**, *n*, pleine poche, *f*.

pocketbook, *n*, sac à main; (*publishing*) livre de poche; (*wallet*) portefeuille; (*small purse*) portemonnaie, *m*.

pocketknife, *n*, canif, *m*.

pockmarked, *a*, marqué (*ou* picoté) de petite vérole, grêlé.

pod, *n*, cosse, gousse. *f*.

poem, *n*, poème, *m*, poésie, *f*. **poet**, *n*, poète, *m*. ~**aster**, *n*, poétereau, *m*. ~**ess**, *n*, poétesse, femme poète, *f*. ~**ic**, ~**ical†**, *a*, poétique. ~**ry**, *n*, poésie, *f*.

poignant, *a*, poignant, empoignant.

point, *n*, point; fait, *m*; pointe, *f*; poinçon; bec, *m*; (*Rly.*) aiguille, *f*; piquant, *m*; température; question, *f*. ~**-blank**, *ad*, de but en blanc, à bout portant, à brûle-pourpoint. ~ *lace*, point, *m*. ~ *of the compass*, aire de vent, *f*, quart de ~, *m*. 6, 8, ~ [*size*] (*Typ.*), corps 6, 8; corps de 6, de 8, points, *m*. *to the* ~, à propos. ¶ *v.t*, pointer; appointer, époiner, tailler [en pointe]; (*masonry*) jointoyer; (*v.t. & abs.,* of *dog*) arrêter. ~ *at*, montrer du doigt. ~ *out*, signaler, indiquer, désigner. ~**ed**, *a*, pointu; piquant; peu voilé, peu équivoque. ~**er**, *n*, (*rod*) baguette, *f*; index; chien d'arrêt, *m*.

poise, *n*, balance, *f*, équilibre, *m*. ¶ *v.t*, balancer, équilibrer.

poison, *n*, poison, toxique, *m*. ~ *gas*, gaz toxique, *m*. ¶ *v.t*, empoisonner, intoxiquer. ~**er**, *n*, empoisonneur, euse. ~**ing**, *n*, empoisonnement, *m*, intoxication, *f*. ~**ous**, *a*, toxique; vénéneux; venimeux. *substance which is* ~, substance qui empoisonne.

poke, *n*, coup, *m*. ¶ *v.t*, fourrer; mettre; (*fire*) attiser, fourgonner. ~ *about*, fourgonner. **poker**, *n*, tisonnier, fourgon; (*cards*) poker, *m*. **poky**, *a*, resserré, étroit, mesquin.

Poland, *n*, la Pologne.

polar, *a*, polaire. ~ *bear*, ours blanc, *m*. **pole**, *n*, poteau, *m*, perche, gaule, *f*, mât; bâton; (*carriage*) timon; (*Astr., Phys., etc.*) pôle, *m*; Meas. = 25.293 sq. meters. **P**~, *n*, Polonais, e. ~**axe**, *n*, merlin, assommoir, *m*; (*Hist.*) hache d'armes, *f*. ~**cat**, putois, *m*. ~ *jump*, saut à la perche, *m*. ~ *star*, étoile polaire, *f*. ¶ *v.t*, échalasser.

polarization, *n*, polarisation, *f*. **polarize**, *v.t*, polariser.

polemic(al), *a*, polémique. polemic, *n*. & ~**s**, *n.pl*, polémique, *f*.

police, *n,* police, *f.* ~ *court,* tribunal de simple police, *m.* ~ *department,* préfecture de police, *f.* ~ *headquarters,* commissariat, *m.* ~*man,* agent de police, gardien de la paix, sergent de ville, *m.* ~ *records,* casier judiciarie, *m.* ~ *station,* bureau de police, poste de p, *m.* ~ *wagon,* panier à salade, *m. motorcycle* ~*man,* motard, *m.*

policy, *n,* politique, *f;* (*public*) ordre, *m;* (*Insce*) police, *f.*

Polish, *a,* polonais. ¶ *n,* le polonais.

polish, *n,* poli; vernis, *m;* pâte à polir, *f.* ¶ *v.t,* polir; vernir; cirer; faire reluire; frotter; encaustiquer. ~*ing brush* (*shoes*), brosse à reluire, *f.*

polite, *a,* poli. **politely,** *ad,* poliment. ~**ness,** *n,* politesse; (*to women*) galanterie, *f.*

politic & ~al†, *a,* politique. ~**ian,** *n,* [homme] politique; (*as a trade*) politicien, *m.* ~**s,** *n.pl. & polity,** *n,* politique, *f.* *to talk politics,* politiquer.

polka, *n,* polka, *f.*

poll, *n,* scrutin, vote, *m.* ~ *tax,* capitation, *f.* ~*ing station,* bureau de scrutin, *m.*

pollard, *n,* têtard, *m.* ¶ *v.t,* étêter.

pollen, *n,* pollen, *m.*

pollute, *v.t,* polluer, souiller.

polo, *n. & ~ cap,* polo, *m.*

polonaise, *n,* polonaise, *f.*

poltroon, *n,* poltron, ne.

polyanthus, *n,* primevère des jardins, *f.* **polygamist,** *n. & polygamous,** *a,* polygame, *m,f. & a.* **polygamy,** *n,* polygamie, *f.* **polyglot,** *a. & n,* polyglotte, *a. & m,f.* **polygon,** *n,* polygone, *m.* **Polynesia,** *n,* la Polynésie. **polyp & polypus,** *n,* polype, *m.* **polysyllabic,** *a. & polysyllable,** *a. & m.* **polytechnic,** *a,* polytechnique. **polytheism,** *n,* polythéisme, *m.*

pomade, *n,* pommade, *f.* ¶ *v.t,* pommader.

pomegranate, *n,* grenade, *f.* ~ [*tree*], grenadier, *m.*

Pomeranian [*dog*], *n.* or **pom,** *abb,* loulou [de Poméranie] *m.*

pommel, *n,* pommeau, *m.* ¶ *v.t,* rosser, frotter, gourmer.

pomp, *n,* pompe, *f,* faste, apparat, attirail, *m.*

Pompeii, *n,* Pompéi, *f.*

pomposity, *n,* emphase, *f.* **pompous†,** *a,* pompeux; emphatique; doctoral.

pond, *n,* étang, *m,* mare, *f;* (*of canal*) bief, *m.*

ponder, *v.i,* réfléchir, méditer, rêver; (*v.t.*) peser, ruminer. ~**able,** *a,* pondérable, pesant. ~**ous†,** *a,* pesant.

pontiff, *n,* pontife, *m.* **pontifical†,** *a. & n,* pontifical, *a. & m.* **pontificate,** *n,* pontificat, *m.*

pontoon, *n,* ponton, caisson, *m.* ~ *bridge,* pont de bateaux, *m.*

pony, *n,* poney, *m.*

poodle, *n,* caniche, *m,f.*

pooh, *i,* bah!, baste! **pooh-pooh,** *v.t,* faire fi de, repousser avec mépris.

pool, *n,* (*swimming*) piscine; mare, *f,* étang, *m;* (*cards*) poule, cagnotte, *f;* (*fencing, shooting, ice hockey*) poule, *f;* (*Com.*) pool; (*Fin.*) syndicat de placement, groupement, *m.* ~ *betting,* pari mutuel, *m.* ¶ *v.t,* mettre en commun.

poop, *n. & ~ deck,* dunette, *f.*

poor, *a,* pauvre; indigent; maigre; méchant. ~ *box,* tronc des pauvres, *m.* ~ *health,* une santé médiocre, une petite santé. ~ *house,* hospice, *m.* ~ *little thing* (*pers.*), pauvret, te. *the* ~, les pauvres, les indigents, *m.pl.* ~**ly,** *ad,* pauvrement. ¶ *a,* indisposé, incommodé, souffrant. ~**ness,** *n,* pauvreté, *f.*

pope, *n,* pape, *m.* ~**ry,** *n,* papisme, *m.*

popinjay (*Hist.*) *n,* papegai, *m.*

popish, *a,* papiste.

poplar, *n,* peuplier, *m.*

poplin, *n,* popeline, *f.*

poppy, *n,* pavot; coquelicot, ponceau, *m.*

populace, *n,* populace, *f.* **popular†,** *a,* populaire; (*treatise*) de vulgarisation. ~**ity,** *n,* popularité, *f.* ~**ize,** *v.t,* vulgariser. **populate,** *v.t,* peupler. **population,** *n,* population, *f.* **populous,** *a,* populeux.

porcelain, *n,* porcelaine, *f.*

porch, *n,* porche, portique, *m.*

porcupine, *n,* porc-épic, *m.*

pore, *n,* pore, *m.* ~ *over,* s'absorber dans la lecture de; méditer sur.

pork, *n*, porc, *m*; charcuterie, *f*. ~ **butcher**, charcutier, *m*. ~**er**, *n*, cochon; goret, *m*.

pornographer, *n*, pornographe, *m*. pornographic, *a*, pornographique, porno. **pornography**, *n*, pornographie, porno, *f*.

porosity, *n*, porosité, *f*. **porous**, *a*, poreux.

porphyry, *n*, porphyre, *m*.

porpoise, *n*, marsouin, *m*.

porridge, *n*, bouillie, *f*. **porringer**, *n*, écuelle, *f*.

port, *n*, port; (*side*) bâbord, *m*. *free* ~, port franc, *m*. ~ [*hole*], hublot, *m*. ~ *of call*, escale; relâche, *f*. ~ *of registry*, port d'attache. ~ [*wine*], porto, vin de Porto, *m*.

portable, *a*, portatif, mobile.

portage, *n*, portage, *m*.

portal, *n*, portail, *m*.

portcullis, *n*, herse, *f*.

portend, *v.t*, présager. **portent**, *n*, présage, *m*. **portentous**, *a*, de mauvais présage; prodigieux.

porter, *n*, concierge, portier; porteur; portefaix; commissionaire; facteur, *m*. ~**age**, *n*, portage, factage, *m*.

portfolio, *n*, portefeuille, *m*, serviette, *f*.

portico, *n*, portique, *m*.

portion, *n*, portion, part, *f*, quartier, *m*; (*of Rly. train*) rame; (*marriage*) dot, *f*. ¶ *v.t*, partager; doter.

portland cement, chaux-limite, *f*.

portliness, *n*, corpulence; prestance, *f*. **portly**, *a*, corpulent, gros; d'un port noble.

portmanteau, *n*, valise, *f*.

portrait & ~**ure**, *n*, portrait, *m*. **portray**, *v.t*, [dé]peindre. **portrayal**, *n*, peinture, *f*.

portress, *n*, concierge, portière, *f*.

Portugal, *n*, le Portugal. **Portuguese**, *a*, portugais. ¶ *n*, (*pers.*) Portugais, *e*; (*language*) le portugais.

pose, *n*, pose; affectation, *f*. ¶ *v.i*. & *t*, poser. **poser**, *n*, problème, *m*. **position**, *n*, position, situation; posture; condition, *f*; emplacement; classement, *m*. ¶ *v.t*, classer.

positive†, *a*, positif; absolu.

posse, *n*, brigade, *f*.

possess, *v.t*, posséder. ~**ed**, *p.p*, possédé; *as if* ~, endiablé. *one* ~, possédé, e. ~**ion**, *n*, possession; jouissance, *f*; (*pl.*) possessions, *f.pl*, avoir, bien, *m. with immediate* ~, présentement. ~**ive**, *a*, possessif. ~**or**, *n*, possesseur, *m*.

possibility, *n*, possibilité, *f*. **possible**, *a*. & *n*, possible, *a*. & *m*. *to be* ~, se pouvoir. **possibly**, *ad*, peut-être. *he cannot* ~ . . ., il est impossible qu'il . . .

post, *n*, (*upright*) poteau; (*door*) montant; pieu; étai, *m*; (*bed*) colonne, *f*; (*place*) poste, *m*; (*P.O.*) poste, *f*; (*letters*) courrier, *m*. ~**card**, carte postale, *f*. *to go* ~**haste**, accourir dare-dare. ~**man**, facteur [des postes] *m*. ~**mark**, *n*, timbre, *m*; (*v.t.*) timbrer. ~**master, mistress**, maître (maîtresse) de poste, receveur (euse) des postes. ~**master general**, directeur général des postes, télégraphes & téléphones, *m*. ~ *office*, bureau de poste, *m*, poste, *f*. ~ *office guide*, indicateur universel des P.T.T., *m*. ~ *office order*, mandat[-poste] *m*. ¶ *v.t*, mettre à la poste; afficher, placarder; mettre au courant; (*Bkkpg.*) [re]porter; (*men*) [a]poster, poser. ~**age**, *n*, port, *m*. ~ *stamp*, timbre-poste, *m*. ~**al**, *a*, postal. ~ *order*, mandat [-poste] *m*. **postpaid**, *ad*, affranchi, post payé.

postdate, *n*, postdate, *f*. ¶ *v.t*, postdater.

poster, *n*, affiche, *f*, placard, *m*.

posterior†, *a*. & *n*, postérieur, *a*. & *m*.

posterity, *n*, postérité, *f*.

postern, *n*, poterne, *f*.

posthumous, *a*, posthume.

postillion, *n*, postillon, *m*.

posting, *n*, mise à la poste, *f*; affichage; (*Bkkpg.*) report, *m*; (*sentry*) pose, *f*.

post meridiem (*abb.* p.m.), après midi; de l'après-midi, du soir.

post mortem, *n*, autopsie, *f*.

postpone, *v.t*, remettre, renvoyer, différer, ajourner.

postscript (*abb.* P.S.) *n*, postscriptum, P.-S., *m*.

postulant, *n*, postulant, e.

posture, *n,* posture, pose, attitude, *f;* état, *m.*

postwar, *a,* d'après-guerre.

posy, *n,* fleur, *f.*

pot, *n,* pot, *m;* marmite, *f;* chaudron, *m;* terrine, *f;* creuset, *m;* (*cards*) cagnotte, *f.* ~ *bellied,* ventru. ~ *boiler,* besogne alimentaire, *f.* ~ *herb,* herbe potagère, *f.* ~*hole,* excavation, marmite, *f.* ~*holder,* attrape-plats, *m.* ~*hook,* crémaillère, *f;* (*writing*) jambage, *m.* to take ~ luck, dîner à la fortune du pot. ¶ *v.t,* empoter. ~*ful,* *n,* potée, *f.*

potable, *a,* potable.

potash, *n,* potasse, *f.* **potassium,** *n,* potassium, *m.*

potato, *n,* pomme de terre, *f.* sweet ~, patate, *f.*

potency, *n,* force, *f.* **potent†,** *a,* puissant; fort. **potentate,** *n,* potentat, *m.* **potential,** *a.* & *n,* potentiel, *a.* & *m.*

potion, *n,* potion, *f.*

potted, *p.a,* en pot, en terrine.

potter, *n,* potier, *m.* ~'s wheel, tour de potier, *m.* ~**y,** *n,* poterie; faïence; faïencerie, *f.*

pouch, *n,* poche, *f,* sac, *m,* bourse; (*cartridge*) cartouchière, giberne; gibecière; (*tobacco*) blague, *f.*

pouf, *n,* pouf, *m.*

poulterer, *n,* marchand de volaille, *m.*

poultice, *n,* cataplasme, *m.*

poultry, *n,* volaille, *f.* ~ *farming,* aviculture, *f.* ~ *yard,* basse-cour, *f.*

pounce, *n,* ponce, *f.* ¶ *v.t,* poncer. ~ *on,* fondre sur.

pound, *n,* (*for cattle*) fourrière; (£) livre; (*avoirdupois weight*) livre [poids] *f.* = 0.45359243 kilogram. ¶ *v.t,* piler.

pour, *v.t,* verser; couler, jeter; répandre; épancher; (*oil on waves*) filer. *it is* ~*ing,* il pleut à verse. ~*ing rain,* pluie battante, *f.*

pout, *v.i,* faire la moue, faire la lippe. ~*er,* *n,* pigeon grosse gorge, *m.*

poverty, *n,* pauvreté, *f.* ~*stricken* (*person*), miséreux, euse.

powder, *n,* poudre, *f.* ~ *box,* boîte à poudre, *f;* poudrier, *m.* ~ *magazine,* poudrière, *f.* ~ *puff,* houppe à poudrer, *f.* ¶ *v.t,* pulvériser; poudrer; saupoudrer. ~**y,** *a,* poudreux, pulvérulent.

power, *n,* puissance, *f;* pouvoir, *m;* énergie; force; faculté; autorité, *f;* (*att.*) mécanique; marchant au moteur. ~ *hammer,* marteau-pilon, *m.* ~ *house,* ~ *station,* usine de force motrice, *f.* ~*ful†,* *a,* puissant; fort; énergique. ~**less,** *a,* impuissant.

practicable, *a,* praticable, faisable, exécutable. **practical†,** *a,* pratique; (*pers.*) positif. ~ *joke,* farce, fumisterie; brimade, *f.* ~ *joker,* farceur, euse, fumiste, *m.*

practice, *n,* pratique; habitude, *f;* usage, *m;* coutume, *f;* exercice; tir, *m;* (*sport*) mise en train, *f;* quelques coups d'essai, quelques échanges, *m.pl;* clientèle; charge; étude, *f,* cabinet, *m.* **practician,** *n,* praticien, *m.* **practice,** *v.t,* pratiquer; exercer; suivre; s'exercer à; user de. **practitioner,** *n,* praticien, *m.*

prairie, *n,* prairie, *f.*

praise, *n,* louange, *f;* éloge, *m.* ¶ *v.t,* louer; glorifier; prôner, vanter. ~*worthy,* digne d'éloges, louable.

prance, *v.i,* piaffer.

prank, *n,* escapade, espièglerie, *f.*

prate, *v.i,* bavarder.

pratique, *n,* [libre] pratique, *f.*

prattle, *n,* babil, gazouillement, *m.* ¶*v.i,* babiller, gazouiller.

prawn, *n,* crevette rouge, *f.*

pray, *v.t.* & *i,* prier. ¶ (*form of address*), je vous prie, veuillez; de grâce; je vous le demande. **prayer,** *n,* prière; supplique, *f,* orémus, *m.* ~ *book,* livre d'église, l. de prières, *m;* l. d'office, paroissien, *m.* ~ *wheel,* moulin à prières, *m.*

preach, *v.t.* & *i,* prêcher. ~*er,* *n,* prédicateur; (*protestant*) prédicant, *m.* ~*ing,* *n,* prédication, *f.*

preamble, *n,* préambule, *m.*

prearranged, *p.a,* arrangé d'avance.

prebend, *n,* prébende, *f.* ~*ary,* *n,* prébendier, *m.*

precarious†, *a,* précaire.

precast, *a,* préfabriqué; précontraint.

precaution, *n,* précaution, prévoyance, *f.* ~*ary,* *a,* de précaution, de prévoyance.

precede, *v.t,* précéder, devancer. **precedence,** *n,* priorité; préséance, *f,* pas, *m.* **precedent,** *n.* & **preceding,** *a,* précédent, *m.* & *a.*

precentor, *n,* grand chantre, *m.*
precept, *n,* précepte, *m.* ~or, *n,* précepteur, *m.*
precinct, *n,* enceinte, *f;* (*pl.*) pourtour, *m.*
precious†, *a,* précieux.
precipice, *n,* précipice, *m.* **precipitancy & precipitation,** *n,* précipitation, *f.* **precipitate,** *v.t. & i,* précipiter; brusquer. ¶ *a.* & *n,* précipité, *a.* & *m.* ~ly, *ad,* précipitamment. **precipitous,** *a,* escarpé, à pic.
precise, *a,* précis; formaliste. ~ly, *ad,* précisément. *to state* ~, préciser. **precision,** *n,* précision, *f.*
preclude, *v.t,* empêcher de.
precocious, *a,* précoce; (*too knowing*) savant; (*in vice*) polisson. ~ness, *n,* précocité, *f.*
preconceived, preconcerted, *a,* préconçu, arrêté.
precursor, *n.* & ~y, *a,* précurseur, *m.* & *a.m.*
predatory, *a,* rapace; de proie.
predecease, *n,* prédécès, *m.* ¶ *v.i,* prédécéder.
predecessor, *n,* prédécesseur, *m,* devancier, ère.
predestination, *n,* prédestination, *f.*
predicament, *n,* [mauvaise] passe, situation difficile; (*Log.*) catégorie, *f.*
predicate (*Log.* & *Gram.*) *n,* attribut, prédicat, *m.* ¶ *v.t,* attribuer; affirmer (*ou* énoncer) un rapport (*of* = entre). **predicative adjective,** adjectif attribut, *m.*
predict, *v.t,* prédire. ~ion, *n,* prédiction, *f.*
predilection, *n,* prédilection, *f.*
predispose, *v.t,* prédisposer.
predominance, *n,* prédominance, *f.* **predominate,** *v.i,* prédominer.
preeminent, *a,* prééminent. ~ly, *ad,* par excellence.
preemption, *n,* préemption, *f.*
preen, *v.t,* éplucher. ~ *its feathers,* s'éplucher.
prefab, *a,* préfabriqué. **prefabrication,** *n,* préfabrication, *f.*
preface, *n,* préface, *f,* avant-propos, *m.* ¶ *v.t,* préluder à. **prefatory,** *a,* liminaire; à titre de préface.
prefect, *n,* préfet, *m.* ~ure, *n,* préfecture, *f.*

prefer, *v.t,* préférer, aimer mieux; promouvoir; (*charges*) déposer. ~able†, *a,* préférable. ~ence, *n,* préférence, *f;* (*Cust.*) régime de faveur, *m,* préférence, *f.* **preferred stock,** actions de priorité, *a—s* privilégiées, *f.pl.* **preferential,** *a,* de préférence, privilégié. **preferment,** *n,* promotion, *f.*
prefix, *n,* préfixe. *m.* ¶ *v.t,* joindre à titre de préface; joindre comme préfixe. ~ed (*Gram.*) *p.a,* préfixe.
pregnable, *a,* prenable.
pregnancy, *n,* grossesse, *f.* **pregnant,** *a,* enceinte, grosse; (*animal*) pleine; (*fig.*) gros, plein. *to become* ~, engrossir. *to make* ~, engrosser.
prehensile, *a,* préhenseur, *a.m.* ~ *tail,* queue prenante, *f.*
prehistoric, *a,* préhistorique.
prejudge, *v.t,* préjuger. **prejudice,** *n,* préjudice, détriment; préjugé, *m,* prévention, *f,* parti pris, *m. without* ~ *to,* sans préjudice de. ¶ *v.t,* prévenir; nuire à. **prejudicial,** *a,* préjudiciable; attentatoire.
prelacy, *n,* prélature, *f.* **prelate,** *n,* prélat, *m.*
preliminary, *a,* préliminaire, préalable. ~ *expenses* (company), frais de constitution, *m. pl.* **preliminaries,** *n.pl,* préliminaires, *m.pl,* préface, *f;* (*book, abb.* **prelims**) pièces liminaires, *f.pl.*
prelude, *n,* prélude. *m.* ¶ *v.i,* préluder.
premature†, *a,* prématuré; (*childbirth*) avant terme.
premeditate, *v.t,* préméditer. **premeditation,** *n,* préméditation, *f.*
premier, *a,* premier. ¶ *n,* président du conseil [des ministres], premier ministre, *m.* ~ship, *n,* présidence du conseil, *f.*
premise, *v.t,* faire remarquer d'avance. ~s, *n.pl,* immeuble, *m,* locaux, lieux, *m.pl;* (*deed*) intitulé, *m.* **premises** (*Log.*) *n.pl,* prémisses, *f.pl.*
premium, *n,* prime; récompense, *f.*
premonition, *n,* présage, *m.* **premonitory,** *a,* prémonitoire, avant-coureur, précurseur. ~ *symptom,* prodrome, *m.*

preoccupation, *n,* préoccupation, *f.* **preoccupy,** *v.t,* préoccuper.

preparation, *n,* préparation; *(Sch.)* étude, *f;* *(pl.)* préparatifs, apprêts, *m.pl.* **preparatory,** *a,* préparatoire. ~ **work** *(Min.),* dispositifs de mines, *m.pl.* **prepare,** *v.t,* préparer; apprêter. **~d** *(ready)* *p.a,* prêt.

prepay, *v.t,* payer d'avance; affranchir.

preponderance, *n,* prépondérance, *f.* **to preponderate over,** l'emporter sur.

preposition, *n,* préposition, *f.*

prepossess, *v.t,* prévenir. **~ing,** *a,* prévenant, avenant. **~ion,** *n,* prévention, *f.*

preposterous†, *a,* déraisonnable, absurde, saugrenu.

prerequisite, *a,* requis. ¶ *n,* nécessité préalable, *f.*

prerogative, *n,* prérogative, *f,* privilège, *m.*

presage, *n,* présage, *m.* ¶ *v.t,* présager.

Presbyterian, *n. & a,* presbytérien, ne.

prescience, *n,* prescience, *f.*

prescribe, *v.t,* prescrire; *(Med.)* ordonner. **prescription,** *n,* prescription; *(Med.)* ordonnance, prescription, formule, *f.*

presence, *n,* présence; prestance, *f.* ~ **of mind,** présence d'esprit, *f.* **present,** *a,* présent; actuel; courant. ¶ *n,* présent; *(gift)* cadeau, present, *m.* **at** ~, présentement. ¶ *v.t,* présenter; offrir. **~able,** *a,* présentable; montrable. **presentation,** *n,* présentation, *f.* ~ **copy,** exemplaire en hommage, *m.*

presentiment, *n,* pressentiment, *m.* **to have a** ~ **of,** pressentir.

presently, *ad,* tantôt, tout à l' heure.

preservation, *n,* conservation; préservation, *f.* **preservative,** *n. & a,* préservatif; *(for food)* antiseptique, *m. & a.* **preserve,** *n,* conserve, *f,* confiture, *f.* oft. pl, marmelade; réserve, *(pl.)* chasse gardée, c. réservée, *f;* *(fig.)* fief, *m;* *(pl.)* conserves, *f.pl.* ¶ *v.t,* préserver; conserver; confire; *(plant)* naturaliser.

preside, *v.i,* présider. ~ **at, over,** présider [à]. **presidency,** *n,* présidence, *f.* **president,** *n,* président, e.

press, *n,* presse, *f;* pressoir, *m;* armoire, *f;* journalisme, *m;* *(of sail)* force, *f.* **the** ~ *(newspapers),* la presse. **in the** ~, sous presse. ~ **agency,** agence d'information, *f.* *(book)* exemplaire de presse, e. de publicité, *m.* ~ **cutting,** coupure de journal, *f.* **~man,** *(Typ.)* pressier, *m.* ¶ *v.t. & i,* presser; serrer; pressurer; fouler; activer; appuyer; peser. **~ing,** *a,* pressant, pressé, urgent; *(debt)* criarde. **pressure,** *n,* pression, *f;* serrement, *m;* presse, *f;* accablement, *m;* *(Mech.)* poussée; tension, *f.* **blood** ~, tension artérielle, *f.* ~ **cooker,** autocuiseur, *m,* cocotte-minute, *f.* ~ **gauge,** manomètre, *m.*

prestige, *n,* prestige, *m.*

presume, *v.t. & i,* présumer. ~ *[up]on,* se prévaloir de. **presumption,** *n,* présomption, *f;* préjugé, *m.* **presumptuous,** *a,* présomptueux. **~ness,** *n,* outrecuidance, *f.*

presuppose, *v.t,* présupposer.

pretence, *n,* [faux] semblant, *m,* feinte, *f,* prétexte, *m.* **pretend,** *v.t. & i,* faire semblant; prétexter; feindre; prétendre. **~er,** *n,* prétendant, e. **pretension,** *n,* prétention, *f.* **pretentious,** *a,* prétentieux.

preterite, *n,* prétérit, *m.*

preternatural†, *a,* surnaturel.

pretext, *n,* prétexte, *m.*

prettiness, *n,* gentillesse, *f.* **pretty†,** *a,* joli, gentil, bellot. ¶ *ad,* assez. ~ **good,** passable, passablement bon. ~ **much,** à peu près. ~ **well,** assez bien.

prevail over, prévaloir sur, l'emporter sur. **prevail** *[up]on,* décider, persuader à. **prevailing,** *p.a,* dominant, régnant; général. **prevalence,** *n,* fréquence, prédominance, *f.* **prevalent,** *a,* régnant, prédominant. **to be** ~, régner.

prevaricate, *v.i,* tergiverser, équivoquer. **prevarication,** *n,* tergiversation, équivoque, *f.*

prevent, *v.t,* empêcher, obvier à, prévenir. **~ion,** *n,* empêchement, *m;* défense préventive, *f.* **society for the** ~ **of cruelty to animals,** société protectrice des animaux, *f.* **~ive,** *n,* préservatif, *m.*

previous†, *a*, précédent, antérieur, préalable. ~ *speaker*, préopinant, *m*.

prevision, *n*, prévision, *f*.

prewar, *a*, d'avant-guerre.

prey, *n*, proie, *f*. ~ [*up*]*on*, faire sa proie de; (*the mind*) miner, ronger.

price, *n*, prix; cours; taux, *m*; cote, *f*. *all at the same* ~, au choix. ~ *list*, prix courant, tarif, *m*. ¶ *v.t*, tarifer. ~**less**, *a*, sans prix, inappréciable, inestimable, impayable.

prick, *n*, piqûre, *f*; coup; (*conscience*) reproche, *m*. ¶ *v.t*, piquer; (*conscience*) bourreler. ~ *up* (ears), dresser. **prickle**, *n*, aiguillon, piquant, *m*. **prickly**, *a*, épineux, piquant. ~ *pear*, figue de Barbarie, *f*.

pride, *n*, orgueil, *m*, fierté, gloire, *f*; amour-propre, *m*; (*collection of animals*) troupe, *f*. ~ *oneself* [*up*]*on*, s'enorgueillir de, se faire gloire de, se piquer de, se targuer de.

priest, *n*, prêtre, *m*. ~**ess**, *n*, prêtresse, *f*. ~**hood**, *n*, prêtrise, *f*, sacerdoce; clergé, *m*. ~**ly**, *a*, sacerdotal.

prig, *n*, pédant, e. **priggish**, *a*, pédant.

prim, *a*, pincé, affecté, collet monté.

primacy, *n*, primatie, primauté, *f*.

primary†, *a*, primitif; premier; primordial; primaire. **primate**, *n*, primat, *m*. **prime**, *a*, premier; primordial; de première qualité. ~ *minister*, président du conseil [des ministres], premier ministre, *m*. ~ *mover*, mobile, *m*; cheville ouvrière, *f*. ~ *of life*, fleur de l'âge, force de l'âge, *f*. ¶ *v.t*, (*pump, blasting*) amorcer; (*with paint*) imprimer; (*pers.*) souffler. **primer**, *n*, premier livre de lecture, alphabet, A b c, abécédaire, *m*. **primeval**, *a*, primitif. **priming**, *n*, amorce; (*paint*) impression, *f*. **primitive†**, *a*, primitif; primordial. **primogeniture**, *n*, primogéniture, *f*. **primordial**, *a*, primordial. **primrose**, *n*, primevère, *f*.

prince, *n*, prince, *m*. ~**ly**, *a*, princier. **princess**, *n*, princesse, *f*.

principal†, *a*, principal; capital. ¶ *n*, principal; chef, *m*; directeur, trice; proviseur; patron, ne; mandant, commettant, donneur d'ordre; (*of debt*) capital, principal, *m*. ~**ity**, *n*, principauté, *f*.

principle, *n*, principe, *m*.

prink, *v.t*, éplucher.

print, *n*, empreinte; impression; (*Phot.*) épreuve [positive]; gravure; estampe, *f*; (*type*) caractères, *m.pl*. *out of* ~, épuisé. ¶ *v.t*, imprimer; tirer; (*with pen*) mouler. ~**er**, *n*, imprimeur, *m*; (*computers*) imprimante, *f*. ~*'s error*, faute d'impression, erreur typographique, *f*. ~*'s imprint*, indication de nom & de lieu de résidence de l'imprimeur, *f*. *high-speed* ~, imprimante à grande vitesse, *f*. *optical* ~, truca, *m*. ~**ing**, *n*, impression, *f*; tirage, *m*; (*art*) imprimerie, *f*. ~ *frame* (*Phot.*), châssis-presse, *m*. ~ *ink*, encre d'imprimerie, *f*. ~ *plant*, imprimerie, typographie, *f*. ~*-out paper* (*Phot.*), papier à image directe, papier à noircissement direct, *m*.

printout, *n*, (*computers*) copie en clair, *f*. ¶ *v.i*, (*computers*) sortir sur imprimante.

prior, *a*, antérieur. ¶ *n*, prieur, *m*. ~**ess**, *n*, prieure, *f*. ~**ity**, *n*, priorité, antériorité, *f*. **priory**, *n*, prieuré, *m*.

prism, *n*, prisme, *m*. ~**atic**, *a*, prismatique.

prison, *n*, prison, *f*. ~ *breaking*, bris de p., *m*. ~**er**, *n*, prisonnier, ère, détenu, e; prévenu, e. ~*'s base*, jeu de barres, *m*, barres, *f.pl*.

pristine, *a*, primitif.

privacy, *n*, secret, *m*. **private**, *a*, privé; particulier; personnel; intime; bourgeois; simple; (*on door*) défense d'entrer. ~ [*soldier*], [simple] soldat, *m*. *by* ~ *treaty*, à l'amiable, de gré à gré. *in* ~, en particulier. ~ *means*, fortune personnelle, *f*. ~ *view* (*art*), avant-première, *f*. **privateer**, *n*, corsaire, *m*. **privateering**, *n*, course, *f*. **privately**, *ad*, en particulier; dans le privé; privément.

privation, *n*, privation, *f*. **privative** (*Gram.*) *a*. & *n*, privatif, *a*. & *m*.

privet, *n*, troène, *m*.

privilege, *n*, privilège, *m*; prérogative, *f*. ¶ *v.t*, privilégier.

privily, *ad*, en secret. **privy**, *a*, privé. ~ *to*, instruit de. ¶ *n*, privé, *m*, lieux [d'aisance] *m.pl*.

prize, *n*, prix, *m*; (*Nav.*) prise, *f*; (*lottery*) lot, *m*; (*leverage*) levier, *m*, pesée, *f*. ~ *bull*, taureau primé, *m*. ~ *fight[ing]*, combat de boxe professionnel, *m*. ~ *fighter*, boxeur professionnel, professionnel de la boxe, *m*. ~ *giving*, distribution de prix, *f*. ~ *medal*, médaille d'honneur, *f*. ~ *winner*, médaillé, e, lauréat, e. ¶ *v.t*, (*value*) estimer, priser; (*lever*) forcer.

pro, *pr*, pour. *the ~s & cons*, le pour & le contre.

probability, *n*, probabilité, vraisemblance, *f*. **probable**†, *a*, probable, vraisemblable.

probate, *n*, vérification de testament, *f*.

probation, *n*, stage, *m*; (*Eccl.*) probation, *f*. ~**er**, *n*, stagiaire, novice, *m.f*.

probe, *n*, (*instrument*) sonde, *f*, stylet, *m*. ¶ *v.t*, sonder.

probity, *n*, probité, *f*.

problem, *n*, problème, *m*. ~ *play*, pièce à thèse, *f*, ~**atic(al)**, *a*, problématique.

proboscis, *n*, trompe; proboscide, *f*.

procedure, *n*, marche à suivre; (*law*) procédure, *f*. **proceed**, *v.i*, procéder; provenir; découler; partir; cheminer; s'acheminer; se rendre; marcher; continuer. ~ *against*, (*law*) poursuivre. ~**ing**, *n*, procédé, *m*; (*pl.*) actes, *m.pl*; démarches; délibérations, *f.pl*; débats, *m.pl*; procédure, *f*; poursuites, *f.pl*. **proceeds**, *n.pl*, produit, *m*.

process, *n*, cours; procédé; processus, *m*. *in the ~ of*, en train de.

procession, *n*, procession, *f*, défilé, *m*, marche, *f*, cortège, convoi, *m*.

processor, *n*, (*computers*) processeur, *m*. *word ~*, machine de traitement de texte, *f*. **processing**, *n*, traitement, *m*. *data ~*, traitement de l'information, *m*. *word ~*, t. de texte, *m*.

proclaim, *v.t*, proclamer; publier; annoncer; déclarer; dénoncer;

afficher. **proclamation**, *n*, proclamation; déclaration, *f*.

proclivity, *n*, penchant, *m*.

procrastinate, *v.i*, aller de délai en délai, atermoyer. **procrastination**, *n*, procrastination, *f*, atermoiement, *m*.

procreate, *v.t*, procréer.

proctor (*Univ.*) *n*, censeur, *m*.

procuration, *n*, procuration, *f*, mandat, *m*. **procure**, *v.t*, procurer. ~**ment**, *n*, obtention, *f*; approvisionnement, *m*.

procurer, *n*, proxénète, *m*. **procuress**, *n*, entremetteuse, *f*.

prod, *v.t*, piquer.

prodigal, *a. & n*, prodigue, *a. & m,f*. ~ *son*, enfant p., *m*. ~**ity**, *n*, prodigalité, *f*.

prodigious†, *a*, prodigieux. **prodigy**, *n*, prodige, *m*.

produce, *n*, produit[s] *m.[pl.]*; provenances, denrées, *f.pl*. ¶ *v.t*, produire; rapporter, fournir; exhiber, [re]présenter, communiquer. **producer**, *n*, producteur, trice; (*movies*) metteur en scène, *m*. **product**, *n*, produit, *m*, production, *f*. ~**ion**, *n*, production; exhibition; (*Theat.*) [re]présentation; mise en scène, *f*. ~**ive**, *a*, productif.

profanation, *n*, profanation, *f*. **profane**, *a*, profane; blasphémateur. ¶ *v.t*, profaner. **profanity**, *n*, irrévérence, *f*; blasphème, *m*.

profess, *v.t*, professer. ~**ed**, *a*, profès, déclaré. ~**ion**, *n*, profession, *f*; état, métier, *m*. ~**ional**, *a. & n*, professionnel, le. ~ *jealousy*, jalousie de métier, *f*. ~**or**, *n*, professeur, *m*. ~**orship**, *n*, professorat, *m*, chaire, *f*.

proficient, *a*, versé, expert.

profile, *n*, profil, *m*. ¶ *v.t*, profiler.

profit, *n*, profit, bénéfice, gain, *m*. ~*-sharing*, participation aux bénéfices, *f*. ¶ *v.i*, profiter, bénéficier. ~**able**, *a*, rémunérateur, profitable, fructueux. ~**ably**, *ad*, fructueusement. ~**eer**, *n*, profiteur, mercanti, *m*.

profligacy, *n*, dérèglement; *m*. **profligate**, *a*, dissolu, débauché. ¶ *n*, dévergondé, e.

profound, *a*, profond, approfondi. ~**ly**, *ad*, profondément. **profundity**, *n*, profondeur, *f*.

profuse, *a*, abondant; prodigue; profus. ~**ly**, *ad*, abondamment;

profusément. **profusion**, n, profusion, f, luxe, m.

progenitor, n, auteur, m. our ~s, les auteurs de nos jours.

progeny, n, descendants, m.pl; progéniture, couvée, f.

prognathous, a, prognathe.

prognosticate, v.t, pronostiquer. **prognostic[ation]**, n, pronostic, m.

program, n, programme, m. ~ library, programmathèque, f. ¶ v.t, (computers) programmer. ~ed instruction, enseignement programmé, m. ~mer, n, programmeur, m. ~ming, n, (computers, cinema) programmation, f.

progress, n, progrès, m. oft. pl, essor, m, marche, f, mouvement, train, m. in ~, en cours. ¶ v.i, s'avancer, progresser, faire des progrès. ~ion, n, progression, f. ~ive†, a, progressif.

prohibit, v.t, défendre, interdire, prohiber. ~ion, n, défense, interdiction, prohibition, f. ~ionist, n, prohibitionniste, m. ~ive & ~ory, a, prohibitif.

project, n, projet, plan, dessein, m. ¶ v.t, projeter; (v.i.) se p., faire saillie, saillir, avancer. ~ile, n. & a, projectile, m. & a. ~ing, p.a, en saillie, saillant, avancé. ~ion, n, projection; (protruding) saillie, avance, f; ressaut, m. film ~, projection cinématographique, f. ~or (Opt.) n, projecteur, m.

proletarian, a, prolétarien. ¶ n, prolétaire, m. **proletariat**, n, prolétariat, m.

proliferate, v.t. & i, proliférer.

prolific, a, prolifique; fécond, fertile.

prolix, a, prolixe. ~ity, n, prolixité, f.

prologue, n, prologue, m.

prolong, v.t, prolonger. ~ation, n, prolongation, f; prolongement, m. **prolonged applause**, applaudissements nourris, m.pl.

promenade, n, promenade, f; promenoir, m. ~ deck, pontpromenade, m.

prominence, n, proéminence; saillie, f. **prominent**, a, proéminent; saillant; éminent; en vedette.

promiscuity, n, promiscuité, f. **promiscuous**, a, confus; débauché. ~ly, ad, pêle-mêle.

promise, n, promesse, f; espérances, f.pl, avenir, m. ¶ v.t. & i, promettre; s'engager. ~d land, terre promise, t. de promission, f. **promising**, a, prometteur. promissory note, billet à ordre, m. that's promising, ça s'annonce bien.

promontory, n, promontoire, m.

promote, v.t, encourager, favoriser; avancer, promouvoir; lancer. **promoter**, n, promoteur, trice; lanceur, m, fondateur, trice. **promotion**, n, promotion, f; avancement; (of a public company, pers.) lancement, m; (sales) promotion des ventes.

prompt†, a, prompt. ~ cash, [argent] comptant, m. ¶ v.t, porter; suggérer, inspirer; (Theat.) souffler. ~ book, exemplaire du souffleur, m. ~er, n, souffleur, m. ~itude, n, promptitude, f.

promulgate, v.t, promulguer.

prone, a, couché sur le ventre; prosterné; sujet, enclin, porté. ~ness, n, inclination, f, penchant, m.

prong, n, dent, branche, f, fourchon, m.

pronominal†, a, pronominal. **pronoun**, n, pronom, m.

pronounce, v.t. & i, prononcer. **pronunciation**, n, prononciation, f; accent, m.

proof, n, preuve, f; titre; gage, m; épreuve, f. in ~ of which, à telles enseignes que. ~ against, à l'épreuve de; cuirassé contre. ~reader, correcteur d'imprimerie, reviseur, m. ~reading, correction des épreuves, revision, f. water~, a, imperméable.

prop, n, étai, m; chandelle, f; échalas; tuteur, m. ¶ v.t, étayer; échalasser.

propaganda, n, propagande, f.

propagate, v.t, propager.

propel, v.t, donner l'impulsion à, mouvoir. **propellant**, n, ergol, m. **propeller**, n, propulseur, m.

propensity, n, propension, f, penchant, m.

proper†, a, propre; bon; bien; convenable; [bien]séant, décent; (behavior) comme il faut. ~ty, n, propriété, f, bien, m, oft. pl, avoir; domaine, m; chose; faculté, qualité, f, caractère, propre, *m*; (*pl. Theat.*) accessoires, *m.pl.* (*Theat.*) ~ man, accessoiriste, *m.* ~ *tax*, impôt foncier, *m.*

prophecy, *n*, prophétie, *f.* **prophesy**, *v.t.* & *i*, prophétiser. **prophet**, *n*, prophète; augure, *m.* ~**ess**, *n*, prophétesse, *f.* ~**ic(al)**†, *a*, prophétique.

propinquity, *n*, proximité, *f.*

propitiate, *v.t*, rendre propice. **propitious**, *a*, propice.

proportion, *n*, proportion, *f. out of* ~, disproportionné. ¶ *v.t*, proportionner, mesurer. ~**al**†, *a*, proportionnel.

proposal, *n*, proposition; demande, *f.* **propose**, *v.t.* & *i*, proposer; (*toast*) porter; (*marriage to woman*) offrir son nom, (*to man*) offrir sa main. **proposer**, *n*, parrain, *m.* **proposition**, *n*, proposition, affaire, *f.*

propound, *v.t*, proposer.

proprietary, *a*, (*rights*) de propriété. **proprietor**, **tress**, *n*, propriétaire, *m.f.* **propriety**, *n*, décence, bienséance, convenance, mesure; correction, propriété, *f.*

propulsion, *n*, propulsion, *f.*

prorogue, *v.t*, proroger.

prosaic†, *a*, prosaïque.

proscenium, *n*, avant-scène, *f.*

proscribe, *v.t*, proscrire.

prose, *n*, prose, *f.* ~ *writer*, prosateur, *m.*

prosecute, *v.t*, poursuivre. **prosecution**, *n*, poursuites, *f.pl*, vindicte, *f.* **prosecutor**, **trix**, *n*, poursuivant, e, plaignant, e.

proselyte, *n*, prosélyte, *m.f.*

prosiness, *n*, verbosité, *f.*

prosody, *n*, prosodie, *f.*

prospect, *n*, vue; perspective, *f*, avenir, *m.* ¶ *v.t*, prospecter. ~**ing**, *n*, prospection, *f*, recherches, *f.pl.* ~**ive**, *a*, en perspective. ~**or**, *n*, prospecteur, *m.*

prospectus, *n*, prospectus, *f.*

prosper, *v.i*, prospérer, réussir. ~**ity**, *n*, prospérité, *f.* ~**ous**, *a*, prospère, fortuné, florissant, heureux.

prostate [gland], *n*, prostate, *f.*

prostitute, *v.t*, prostituer. ¶ *n*, prostituée, putain, *f.*

prostrate, *a*, prosterné; prostré, anéanti. ¶ *v.t*, prosterner; anéantir. ~ *oneself*, se prosterner

prostration, *n*, prosternation; (*Med.*) prostration, *f.*

prosy, *a*, verbeux, ennuyeux.

protagonist, *n*, protagoniste, *m.*

protect, *v.t*, protéger, garder, défendre, préserver. ~**ion**, *n*, protection, garde, défense, préservation, sauvegarde, *f.* ~**ionist**, *n.* & *att*, protectionniste, *m.* & *att.* ~**ive**, *a*, protecteur. **protector**, **tress**, *n*, protecteur, trice. ~**ate**, *n*, protectorat, *m.*

protein, *n*, protéine, *f.*

protest, *n*, protestation, réclamation, *f.* ¶ *v.t.* & *i*, protester; crier. ~**ant**, *n.* & *a*, protestant, e.

protocol, *n*, protocole, *m.*

prototype, *n*, prototype, *m.*

protoplasm, *n*, protoplasme, *m.*

protract, *v.t*, prolonger. ~**or**, *n*, rapporteur, *m.*

protrude, *v.i*, faire saillie.

protuberance, *n*, protubérance, *f.*

proud†, *a*, fier; orgueilleux; glorieux. ~ *flesh*, chairs baveuses, *f. pl.*

prove, *v.t*, prouver, faire la preuve de, vérifier, justifier [de]; démontrer; constater; éprouver; (*will*) homologuer.

provender, *n*, fourrage, *m*, provende, *f.*

proverb, *n*, proverbe. *m.* ~**ial**†, *a*, proverbial.

provide, *v.t*, pourvoir, fournir, munir; prescrire, stipuler, prévoir. ~ *against*, se prémunir contre. ~*d* [*that*], pourvu que. **providence**, *n*, prévoyance; providence; (*God*) Providence, *f.* **provident**, *a*, prévoyant. ~**ial**†, *a*, providentiel. **provider**, *n*, pourvoyeur, *m.*

province, *n*, province; (*pl.*) province; (*sphere*) compétence, *f*, ressort, domaine, département, *m*, juridiction, *f.* **provincial**, *a*, provincial; de province.

provision, *n*, provision; prestation; disposition; (*pl.*) provisions de bouche, munitions de b. *f.pl*, vivres, comestibles, *m.pl*, subsistances, *f.pl.* ¶ *v.t*, approvisionner. ~**al**†, *a*, provisoire; provisionnel.

proviso, *n*, clause provisionnelle, *f.*

provocation, *n*, provocation; agacerie, *f.* **provoke**, *v.t*, provoquer, agacer, contrarier, vexer, impatienter.

provost, *n*, prévôt; recteur, *m*.

prow, *n*, proue, *f*.

prowess, *n*, prouesse, vaillantise, *f*.

prowl, *v.i*, rôder. **~er**, *n*, rôdeur, *m*.

proximate†, *a*, prochain; immédiat. **proximity**, *n*, proximité, *f*.

proxy, *n*, procuration, *f*; mandataire, *m*, fondé de pouvoir(s), *m*. **by ~**, par procuration.

prude, *n*, prude, *f*.

prudence, *n*, prudence, sagesse, *f*. **prudent†**, *a*, prudent, sage, avisé. **~ial**, *a*, de prudence.

prudery, *n*, pruderie, bégueulerie, *f*. **prudish**, *a*, prude, pudibond, bégueule.

prune, *n*, pruneau, *m*. ¶ *v.t*, tailler, émonder, élaguer. **pruning**, *n*, taille, *f*, émondage, élagage, *m*; (*pl.*) élagage, *m*, émondes, *f.pl*. **~ hook**, serpe, *f*, croissant, *m*. **~ knife**, serpette, *f*. **~ shears**, sécateur, *m*.

pruriency, *n*, sensualité, *f*. **prurient**, *a*, sensuel, lascif.

Prussia, *n*, la Prusse. **Prussian**, *a*, prussien. **~ blue**, bleu de Prusse, *m*. ¶ *n*, Prussien, ne. **prussic**, *a*, prussique.

pry, *v.i*, fureter, fouiller; soulever avec un levier. **~ing**, *a*, indiscret, curieux.

psalm, *n*, psaume, *m*. **~ist**, *n*, psalmiste, *m*. **psalter**, *n*, psautier, *m*.

pseudonym, *n*, pseudonyme, *m*.

psychiatrist, *n*, psychiatre, *m*. **psychic(al)**, *a*, psychique. **psychoanalysis**, *n*, psychanalyse, *f*. **psychological**, *a*, psychologique. **psychologist**, *n*, psychologue, *m*. **psychology**, *n*, psychologie, *f*. **psychosis**, *n*, psychose, *f*. **psychosomatic**, *a*, psychosomatique.

ptarmigan, *n*, perdrix des neiges, *f*.

ptomaine, *n*, ptomaïne, *f*. **~ poisoning**, empoisonnement par les ptomaïnes, *m*.

puberty, *n*, puberté, *f*.

public†, *a*, public. **~ spirited**, dévoué au bien public. ¶ *n*, public, *m*; clientèle, *f*. **~an**, *n*, (*Bible*) publicain, *m*. **~ation**, *n*, publication, *f*. **~ist**, *n*, publiciste, *m*. **~ity**, *n*, publicité, *f*. **publish**, *v.t*,

publier; éditer; faire paraître; proclamer. **to be ~ed** (book), vient de paraître. **~er**, *n*, éditeur, *m*. **~'s imprint**, indication de nom (*ou* de firme) de l'éditeur; (*place only*) rubrique, *f*. **~ing**, *n*, publication, édition, *f*. **~ house**, maison d'édition, librairie, *f*.

puce, *a*, puce.

puck, *n*, lutin, [esprit] follet; (*ice hockey*) palet, puck, *m*.

pucker, *n*, poche, fronce, *f*, godet, pli, *m*. ¶ *v.t*, froncer, plisser; (*v.i.*) goder, [se] plisser.

pudding, *n*, pudding, pouding, *m*.

puddle, *n*, flaque, *f*. ¶ *v.t*, (*clay*) corroyer; (*Metall.*) puddler.

puerile†, *a*, puéril.

puff, *n*, souffle, *m*; bouffée, réclame, *f*; (*powder*) houppe, *f*. ¶ *v.t. & i*, souffler; bouffer; époumoner; prôner. **~ one's goods**, faire l'article.

puffin, *n*, macareux, *m*.

puffy, *a*, bouffi, soufflé.

pug (*clay*) *n*, corroi, *m*. **~ [dog]**, carlin, roquet, *m*. **~ nose**, nez camus, *m*. ¶ *v.t*, corroyer; hourder.

pugilism, *n*, pugilat, *m*. **pugilist**, *n*, pugiliste, *m*. **pugnacious**, *a*, pugnace, batailleur.

pule, *v.i*, piauler.

pull, *n*, traction, *f*; effort [de traction] *m*; (*drink*) lampée; (*Typ.*) feuille de tirée, *f*; (*bell*) cordon; (*fig.*) avantage, *m*. **~ over**, pullover, *m*. ¶ *v.t. & i*, tirer; arracher; (*trigger*) presser. **~ down**, démolir. **~ wires for** (*fig.*), intriguer pour; pistonner. **~ to one side** (traffic), se garer. **~ to pieces**, mettre en pièces; (*fig.*) éreinter.

pullet, *n*, poulette, *f*.

pulley, *n*, poulie, *f*. **~ block**, moufle, *f. or m*.

Pullman [car], *n*, voiture Pullman, *f*.

pullover, *n*, pull-over, pull, *m*.

pullulate, *v.i*, pulluler.

pulmonary, *a*, pulmonaire.

pulp, *n*, pulpe; chair; (*paper making*) pâte; bouillie, *f*. ¶ *v.t*, pulper.

pulpit, *n*, chaire [du prédicateur] *f*.

pulsate, *v.i*, battre. **pulsation**, *n*, pulsation, *f*, battement, *m*. **pulse**, *n*, (*Anat.*) pouls, *m*; légumi-

neuse, *f.* ~ *rate*, force du pouls,*f.*
pulverize, *v.t*, pulvériser.
puma, *n*, puma, couguar, *m.*
pumice [stone], *n*, [pierre] ponce,
f. ¶ *v.t*, poncer.
pump, *n*, pompe, *f*; (*dress shoe*)
escarpin, *m.* **gasoline** ~, pompe
à essence, *f.* ~ *handle*, levier de
pompe, *m*, brimbale, *f.* ~ *room*
(*at spa*), buvette, *f.* ¶ *v.t. & i*,
pomper; (*fig.*) sonder, cuisiner.
~ *up* (*tire*), gonfler.
pumpkin, *n*, citrouille, courge, *f*,
potiron, *m.*
pun, *n*, calembour, jeu de mots, *m.*
¶ *v.i*, faire des calembours, jouer
sur le(s) mot(s).
punch, *n*, coup de poing, renfoncement, *m*, gourmade,*f*; (*tool*)
poinçon; emporte-pièce; (*drink*)
punch, *m.* ~ *bowl*, bol à punch,
m. P~, *n*, polichinelle, *m.* ~ *&
Judy* [*show*], guignol, *m.* ¶ *v.t*,
poinçonner; découper; (*hit*)
battre; (*Rly. ticket*) composter.
[*Note: this must be done before
boarding train.*]
puncheon, *n*, poinçon, *m*; pièce,
f.
punching bag, ballon de boxe,
m.
punctilio, *n*, pointille, *f.* **punctilious**, *a*, pointilleux, méticuleux.
punctual†, *a*, ponctuel, exact. ~
ity, *n*, ponctualité, exactitude, *f.*
punctuate, *v.t. & abs*, ponctuer.
punctuation, *n*, ponctuation, *f.*
puncture, *n*, piqûre; (*Surg.*)
ponction; (*tire*) crevaison, *f.* ¶
v.t. & i, piquer; ponctionner; crever.
pundit, *n*, pandit, pontife, *m.*
pungency, *n*, piquant, *m*; âcreté,
f; mordant, *m.* **pungent**, *a*, piquant; âcre; mordant.
punish, *v.t*, punir. ~**able**, *a*, punissable. ~**ment**, *n*, punition;
peine, sanction, pénitence, *f*; supplice, *m.*
punster, *n*, faiseur de calembours, *m.*
punt, (*boat*) *n*, bachot, *m*, plate,
f. ¶ *v.i*, (*cards*) ponter; (*boating*) pousser du fond; (*v.t.*) pousser (*un bateau*) à la perche.
puny, *a*, chétif, malingre.
pup, *n*, petit chien, *m.* ¶ *v.i*, mettre
bas.
pupa, *n*, chrysalide, *f.*
pupil, *n*, (*eye*) pupille, prunelle,

f; (*scholar*) élève, *m,f*, écolier,
ère; pupille, *m,f.*
puppet, *n*, marionnette, poupée, *f*,
mannequin, fantoche, *m.*
puppy, *n*, chiot; (*pers.*) freluquet,
m.
purblind, *a*, quasi aveugle.
purchase, *n*, achat, *m*, acquisition; (*shopping*) emplette; (*hold*)
prise, *f*; (*tackle*) palan, *m.* ¶ *v.t*,
acheter, acquérir. **purchaser**, *n*,
acheteur, euse, acquéreur, *m.*
pure†, *a*, pur. ~ *mechanics*, mécanique rationnelle, *f.* ~**ness**, *n*,
pureté, *f.*
purgative, *a. & n*, purgatif, *a. &
m.* **purgatory**, *n*, purgatoire, *m.*
purge, *v.t*, purger. **purge**, **purging**, *n*, purge, purgation, *f.*
purify, *v.t*, purifier; épurer. **purist**, *n*, puriste, *m,f.* **Puritan**, *n. &
a. & puritanic(al)**, *a*, puritain, e.
purity, *n*, pureté, *f.*
purl, *v.i*, murmurer, gazouiller. ~
knitting, tricot à l'envers, *m.*
purlieus, *n.pl*, environs, entours,
m.pl.
purloin, *v.t*, soustraire.
purple, *n*, pourpre, *m*; (*robe*)
pourpre, *f.* ¶ *a*, violet. ~ *red*,
rouge pourpré, *m.* **purplish**, *a*,
purpurin, violâtre.
purport, *n*, teneur, portée, *f.* ¶
v.t, signifier, vouloir dire; sembler, paraître.
purpose, *n*, but, *m*, fin; intention,
f; propos; dessein; effet; usage,
m. *to no* ~, en pure perte. ¶ *v.t*,
se proposer. ~**ly**, *ad*, à dessein,
exprès.
purr, *n*, ronron, *m.* ¶ *v.i*, faire
ronron.
purse, *n*, porte-monnaie, *m*,
bourse, *f.* ¶ (*lips*) *v.t*, pincer.
purser, *n*, commissaire [de la marine marchande] *m.*
pursuant to, **in pursuance
of**, en vertu de, suivant. **pursue**,
v.t, [pour]suivre, chasser. **pursuit**, *n*, poursuite, chasse; recherche; occupation, *f.* ~ *plane*,
avion de chasse, *m.*
purulent, *a*, purulent.
purvey, *v.t*, pourvoir. ~**or**, *n*,
pourvoyeur, *m.*
purview, *n*, ressort; (*law*) dispositif, *m.*
pus, *n*, pus, *m.*
push, *n*, poussée; initiative, *f.* ~
[*button*], poussoir, *m.* ¶ *v.t*,

pousser; presser; avancer. ~
about, bousculer. ~ *aside*, écarter. ~ *back*, repousser, reculer.
~ *off* (*Naut.*), pousser au large.
~**ing**, *a*, entreprenant.

pusillanimous, *a*, pusillanime.

puss[y], *n*, minet, te, minon, minou, *m*. *Puss in Boots*, le Chat
botté.

pustule, *n*, pustule, *f*.

put, *v.t.ir*, mettre; placer; porter;
poser; apposer; appliquer; faire.
~ (*things*) *away*, ranger, serrer.
~ *down*, réprimer; baisser. ~
forward, avancer; proposer. ~
in, insérer; (*Naut.*) relâcher. ~
off, remettre; différer. ~ *on*, mettre; revêtir; prendre; avancer;
(*brake*) serrer. ~ *out*, éteindre;
(*tongue*) tirer. ~ *out of joint*,
démettre, disloquer. ~ *out of
order*, dérégler, déranger. ~ *out
of tune*, désaccorder. ~ *up*,
(*money*) faire mise de; (*money
at cards*) caver [de]; (*at hotel*)
descendre. ~*up job*, coup
monté, *m*. ~ *up with*, supporter.

putt, (*golf.*) *n*, coup [roulé] *m*. ¶
v.t, poter.

putrefaction, *n*, putréfaction, *f*.
putrefy, *v.t*, putréfier; (*v.i.*) se p.
putrid, *a*, putride.

puttee, *n*, bande molletière, *f*.

putter (*club*) *n*, poteur, *m*. ¶ *v.i*,
bricoler. **putting green**, pelouse
d'arrivée, *f*. **putting the shot**,
lancement du poids, *m*.

putty, *n*, mastic, *m*. ~ *powder*,
potée d'étain, *f*. ¶ *v.t*, mastiquer.

puzzle, *n*, casse-tête; problème, *m*;
énigme, *f*. *crossword* ~, mots
croisés, *m.pl*. ¶ *v.t*, intriguer,
alambiquer. ~**d**, *p.a*, perplexe;
empêché.

pygmy, *n*, pygmée, *m*.

pylon, *n*, pylône, *m*.

pyorrhoea, *n*, pyorrhée, *f*.

pyramid, *n*, pyramide, *f*.

pyre, *n*, bûcher, *m*.

Pyrenees (the), les Pyrénées, *f.pl*.

pyrethrum, *n*, pyrèthre, *m*.

pyrites, *n*, pyrite, *f*.

pyrotechnics, *n.pl*, pyrotechnie,
f. **pyrotechnist**, *n*, artificier, *m*.

python, *n*, python, *m*.

Q

quack [**doctor**], *n*, charlatan,
médicastre, *m*, guérisseur, euse.
~**ery**, *n*, charlatanisme, *m*.

quadrangle, *n*, figure quadrangulaire, *f*; préau, *m*; cour d'honneur, *f*.

quadrant, *n*, quadrant; quart de
cercle; secteur, *m*.

quadroon, *n*, quarteron, ne.

quadruped, *n*. & *a*, quadrupède,
m. & *a*.

quadruple, *a*. & *n*, quadruple,
a. & *m*. **quadruplets**, *n.pl*, quatre
jumeaux, *m.pl*.

quaff, *v.t*, boire.

quagmire, *n*, fondrière, *f*, bourbier, *m*.

quail, *n*, caille, *f*. ¶ *v.i*, trembler.

quaint, *a*, vieillot; pittoresque;
baroque; étrange; curieux. ~**ness**,
n, étrangeté; curiosité, *f*.

quake, *v.i*, trembler. ¶ *n*, tremblement, *m*.

qualification, *n*, qualité; capacité, aptitude, *f*. **qualified**, *p.a*,
qualifié; capable, apte; sous réserve. **qualify**, *v.t*, qualifier; adoucir. **qualitative**, *a*, qualitatif, ive.
quality, *n*, qualité, *f*; choix; aloi,
m.

qualms, *n.pl*, mal de cœur, *m*;
scrupules, *m.pl*.

quandary, *n*, embarras, *m*.

quantity, *n*, quantité, *f*.

quantum, *n*, quantum, *m*.

quarantine, *n*, quarantaine, *f*;
(*station*) la santé. ¶ *v.t*, mettre
en quarantaine.

quarrel, *n*, querelle, *f*. ¶ *v.i*, se
quereller. ~**some**, *a*, querelleur.

quarry, *n*, (*marble, etc.*) carrière;
proie, *f*. ¶ *v.t*, extraire.

quarter, *n*, quartier; (¼ *th*) quart;
(*3 months*) trimestre; terme, *m*;
(*28 lbs*) = 12.70 kilos; (*8 bushels*)
= 2.909 hectoliters; (*pl.*) logement; cantonnement, *m*; quar-
tiers, *m.pl*; (*horse*) train, *m*. *a*
~ *of an hour*, un quart d'heure.
~ *deck*, gaillard d'arrière, *m*.
~**master**, (*Mil.*) fourrier; (*Naut.*)
maître de timonerie, *m*. ~ *past*,
un quart, et quart. ¶ *v.t*, diviser
en quatre parties; écarteler; loger; cantonner. ~**ly**, *a*, trimestriel; (*ad.*) par trimestre.

quartet[te], *n*, quatuor, *m*.

quartz, *n*, quartz, *m*.

quash, *v.t*, casser, annuler, infirmer.

quasi, *c*. & **quasi-**, *prefix*, quasi
(*ad.*), quasi-.

quassia, *n*, (*tree*) quassier; (*bark*)
quassia, *m*.

quatrain, *n,* quatrain, *m.*
quaver (*Mus.*) *n,* croche, *f.* ¶ *v.i,* chevroter, trembler.
quay, *n,* quai, *m.*
queen, *n,* reine; (*cards, chess*) dame, reine, *f.* ~ *bee,* reine des abeilles, mère abeille, *f.* ¶ (*chess*) *v.t,* damer. ~**ly,** *a,* de reine.
queer†, *a,* étrange, bizarre, singulier, original, drôle; indisposé. *a* ~ *fellow,* un drôle de corps.
quell, *v.t,* réprimer, étouffer, apaiser.
quench, *v.t,* éteindre; (*thirst*) étancher, apaiser.
querulous†, *a, plaintif.*
query, *n,* question, interrogation, *f.* **quest,** *n,* quête, recherche, *f.*
question, *n,* question; demande; interrogation, *f.* ~ *mark,* point d'interrogation, *m.* ¶ *v.t,* questionner, interroger; contester, mettre en question, suspecter. **questionable,** *a,* contestable; suspect, équivoque. **questionnaire,** *n,* questionnaire, *m.*
queue, *n,* file, *f. v.i,* faire la queue.
quibble, *n,* chicane, argutie, *f.* ¶ *v.i,* chicaner, ergoter.
quick, *a,* vif; rapide; prompt; preste. ~*-change artist,* acteur à transformations, *m.* ~*lime,* chaux vive, *f.* ~*sand,* sable mouvant, *m.* ~*silver,* mercure, *m.* ~*step,* pas accéléré, *m;* en avant marche! ~*-tempered,* emporté, vif. ¶ *ad,* vite, prestement. *be* ~*l* vite!; dépêchez-vous! ¶ *n,* vif, *m.* ~**en,** *v.t,* vivifier, animer; accélérer, activer. ~**ly,** *ad,* vite, tôt, promptement. ~**ness,** *n,* promptitude, prestesse, *f.*
quid (*tobacco*) *n,* chique, *f.*
quiescent, *a,* en repos. **quiet†,** *a,* tranquille; calme; doux; modeste. ¶ *v.t,* calmer, apaiser. ~**[ness],** *n,* tranquillité, *f,* repos, calme, *m,* quiétude, *f.*
quietus, *n,* (*Jur.*) quitus, *m;* (*death*) mort, *f;* coup de grâce, *m.*
quill, *n,* (*porcupine*) piquant, *m;* (*bird*) plume, *f.* ~ *driver,* gratte-papier, rond-de-cuir, plumitif, *m.* ~ [*feather*], penne, *f.* ~ [*pen*], plume d'oie, *f.*
quilt, *n,* couvre-pied, *m.* ¶ *v.t,* ouater, piquer, capitonner.
quince, *n,* coing, *m.* ~[*tree*], cognassier, *m.*
quinine, *n,* quinine, *f.*
quinquennial, *a,* quinquennal.

quinsy, *n,* angine, *f.*
quintessence, *n,* quintessence, *f.*
quintet[te], *n,* quintette, *m.*
quintuple, *a,* quintuple. ¶ *n,* quintuple, *m.* **quintuplet,** *n,* quintuplet, *m.*
quip, *n,* pointe, *f,* mot piquant, *m.*
quire, *n,* main, *f.* (*in Fr. 25 sheets*).
quirk, *n* (*quip*), pointe, *f;* caprice; (*Join.*) carré, *m.*
quit, *a,* quitte. ¶ *v.t,* renoncer à; cesser de; quitter.
quite, *ad,* tout à fait; tout, e; bien; complètement; parfaitement.
quits, *a,* quitte à quitte; quittes.
quiver (*for arrows*) *n,* carquois, *m.* ¶ *v.i,* trembler, frémir; frissonner. ~[**ing**], *n,* tremblement, frisson[nement] *m.*
Quixote, *n,* Don Quichotte, *m.* **quixotic,** *a,* de D. Q. ~**ally,** *ad,* en D. Q.
quiz, *v.t,* interroger; (*mock*) berner. ¶ *n,* examen, *m.* **quizzical,** *a,* (*mocking*) narquois.
quoin, *n,* coin; (*Typ.*) bois de corps, *m.*
quoit, *n.* & ~**s,** *n.pl,* palet, *m.*
quondam, *a,* ancien.
quorum, *n,* quorum, *m.*
quota, *n,* quote-part, quotité, cote, cotisation, *f,* contingent, quota, *m.* ~ *sampling,* sondage par quota, *m.*
quotation, *n,* citation; épigraphe; (*Com., Fin.*) cote, *f,* cours, prix, *m;* (*in Stk Ex. list*) inscription, *f.* ~ *marks,* guillemets, *m.pl.* **quote,** *v.t,* citer; alléguer; guillemeter, coter, faire; inscrire.
quotient, *n,* quotient, *m.*

R

rabbet, *n,* feuillure, *f.* ~ *plane,* guillaume, *m.*
rabbi, *n,* rabbin, *m.*
rabbit, *n,* lapin, e, (*young*) lapereau, *m;* (*pers. at game*) mazette, *f.* ~ *burrow,* ~ *hole,* terrier de lapin, clapier, *m.* ~ *hutch,* clapier, *m.*
rabble, *n,* canaille, populace, *f.*
rabid, *a,* acharné; enragé. **rabies,** *n,* la rage, hydrophobie, *f.*
racoon, *n,* raton laveur, *m.*
race, *n,* (*tribe*) race, *f;* sang, *m;* (*contest*) course, *f;* (*sea*) raz, *m.* ~*horse,* cheval de course, *m.* ~ *suicide,* suicide du genre hu-

main, m. ~*track*, champ de courses, m, piste, f. ~[*way*], bief, canal, chenal, m. ¶ *v.i,* courir; (*v.t.*) (*horses*) faire courir.

racer, n, coureur, euse; cheval de course, m; bicyclette de course, f. **racial,** a, de race. **racing,** n, courses; (*horse*) les courses, f.pl. ~ *calendar,* calendrier des courses, m. ~ *cyclist,* coureur cycliste, m.

rack, n, râtelier, m; rampe, f; caster, m; (*luggage, Rly.*) filet; supplice, m, torture, f, hat ~, porte-chapeau, m. to ~ & ruin, à vau-l'eau. to ~ one's brains, se torturer l'esprit, se casser la tête, se creuser le cerveau.

racket, n, tapage; bacchanal; m; raquette, f. ~ *press,* presse à raquette, f.

racy (*fig.*) a, piquant.

radial, a, radial. **radiance** & **radiation,** n, rayonnement, m. **radiancy,** n, éclat, m. **radiant,** a, rayonnant; radieux. **radiate,** v.i, rayonner. **radiator,** n, radiateur, m. ~ *cap,* bouchon de r., m.

radical†, a. & n, radical, a. & m.

radio, n, radio, T.S.F., f. ~ *broadcast,* radiodiffusion, f. ¶ *v.t.* & *i,* émettre, radiodiffuser.

radioactive, a, radioactif. **radiogram,** n, radiogramme, m. **radiography,** n, radiographie, f. **radiology,** n, radiologie, f. **radiotelegraphy,** n, radiotélégraphie, f. **radiotherapy,** n, radiothérapie, f.

radish, n, radis, m.

radium, n, radium, m.

radius, n, rayon, m; portée, f; (*Anat.*) radius, m.

raffle, n, loterie, tombola, f. ¶ *v.t,* mettre en loterie.

raft, n, radeau, m, drome, f; train [de bois] m.

rafter, n, chevron, m.

rag, n, chiffon; lambeau; haillon, m, loque, guenille; (*pl, for paper making*) drille; (*newspaper*) feuille de chou, f, canard; (*Sch.*) chahut, m. ~*picker,* ~ *merchant,* ~ [& *bone*] *man,* chiffonnier, ère. ~*tag* [& *bobtail*], canaille, f. ~*wort,* jacobée, f.

ragamuffin, n, petit va-nu-pieds, m.

rage, n, rage, fureur; colère, f, courroux, m. ¶ *v.i,* faire rage; (*of war*) sévir. to be the ~, être du dernier cri; faire fureur.

ragged, a, déguenillé, loqueteux.

raging, a, furieux. ~ *fever,* fièvre ardente, f. ~ *toothache,* rage de dents, f.

raid, n, incursion, descente, razzia, f, raid, m; rafle; attaque, f. air ~, raid aérien, m. ¶ *v.t,* razzier; marauder; faire une descente dans.

rail, n, barre, f; barreau, m; traverse; rampe, f, garde-fou, accoudoir, m; (*ship's*) lisse, f, garde-corps; (*Rly.*) rail; (*bird*) râle, m. ¶ *v.t,* barrer. ~ *at,* invectiver contre, pester contre. ~**ing,** n, grille, balustrade, f, balustre, garde-fou, m.

raillery, n, raillerie, f.

railway & **railroad,** n, chemin de fer, m, voie ferrée, f. ~*man,* employé de chemin de fer, cheminot, m. ~ *station,* gare, f. ~ *strike,* grève d'agents de chemins de fer, f.

raiment, n, vêtement, habillement, m.

rain, n, pluie, eau, f. ~*bow,* arc-en-ciel; (*halo*) iris, m. ~ *coat,* imperméable, m. ~*fall,* quantité de pluie [tombée] f. ~*water,* eau de pluie, f, eaux pluviales, f.pl. ¶ *v.i,* pleuvoir; (*v.t.*) faire pleuvoir. ~**y,** a, pluvieux, pluvial; (*day*) de pluie.

raise, v.t, lever; soulever; relever; remonter; [sur]élever; hausser; exhausser; augmenter; porter; (*hat*) tirer; (*flag*) arborer; cultiver; faire naître; produire; (*money for some purpose*) procurer; (*money for oneself*) se procurer; (*the dead*) ressusciter. ¶ n, hausse, augmentation, f. **raised,** p.a, en relief; saillant.

raisin, n, raisin sec, m.

rake, n, râteau; (*fire*) fourgon, ringard, m; inclinaison, f; libertin, débauché, roué, coureur, m. ¶ *v.t,* ratisser, râteler; enfiler. ~ *up,* remuer; revenir sur. *raking fire,* feu d'enfilade, m. *raking shore,* arc-boutant, m, contre-fiche, f. **rakish,** a, libertin.

rally, n, ralliement, m; reprise, f; (*Ten.*) long échange; (*race meeting*) rallye, m. ¶ *v.t,* rallier; (*v.i.*) se rallier; [se] reprendre.

ram, n, bélier; (*pile driving*) mouton, pilon; piston; (*battleship*) éperon, m. ¶ *v.t,* damer, battre; bourrer; refouler.

ramble, *n*, excursion, promenade, *f*. ¶ *v.i*, errer; (*rave*) divaguer.
rambler, *n*, rosier grimpant, *m*.
rambling, *a*, errant; (*discourse*) décousu, incohérent.
ramification, *n*, ramification, *f*.
ramify, *v.i*, se ramifier.
rampant (Her.) *a*, rampant. **to be ~**, sévir, courir.
rampart, *n*, rempart, *m*.
ramrod, *n*, baguette, *f*.
ramshackle, *a*, délabré.
ranch, *n*, ranch, *m*.
rancid, *a*, rance. **~ness**, *n*, rancidité, *f*.
rancorous, *a*, rancunier, fielleux.
rancor, *n*, rancune, rancœur, *f*, fiel, *m*.
random, *a. & at ~*, au hasard, à l'aventure, à l'abandon, à la volée, à coup perdu.
range, *n*, étendue; portée; distance, *f*; champ, *m*; série; gamme, *f*; (*voice*) diapason; (*musical*) clavier, *m*; (*hills*) chaîne, *f*; fourneau; parc, *m*. **gas ~**, fourneau à gaz, *m*. **within ~**, à portée de. **~ finder**, télémètre, *m*. ¶ *v.t*, étager; aligner; parcourir; ranger; (*v.i.*) s'aligner; varier. **ranger**, *n*, conservateur; garde, *m*.
Rangoon, *n*, Rangoun, Rangoon, *m*.
rank, *n*, rang; grade, *m*; dignité; (*cab*) station, place, *f*. **~ & file**, les hommes de troupe, gradés & soldats. ¶ *v.t*, ranger; (*v.i.*) prendre rang; marcher de pair. ¶ *a*, luxuriant; rance; grossier; insigne, fieffé.
rankle, *v.i*, saigner.
ransack, *v.t*, saccager, piller; fouiller.
ransom, *n*, rançon, *f*, rachat, *m*. ¶ *v.t*, rançonner, racheter.
rant, *n*, divagation, *f*. ¶ *v.i*, déclamer.
ranunculus, *n*, renoncule, *f*.
rap, *n*, coup, *m*, tape, *f*. ¶ *v.t. & i*, taper, frapper, donner des petits coups secs. *I don't give a ~*, je m'en moque.
rapacious, *a*, rapace. **rape**, *n*, (*sexual*) viol; (*kidnapping*) enlèvement, *m*; (*oil seed plant*) navette; (*colerape*) rave, *f*.
rapid†, *a*, rapide; (*pulse*) fréquent. ¶ *n*, rapide, *m*. **~ity**, *n*, rapidité, *f*.
rapier, *n*, rapière, *f*.

rapine, *n*, rapine, *f*.
rapt, *a*, ravi, en extase. **rapture**, *n*, ravissement, enthousiasme, *m*, ivresse, *f*. **rapturous**, *a*, extatique.
rare†, *a*, rare; (*word*) peu usité; fameux; (*meat*) saignante. **rarefy**, *v.t*, raréfier. **rareness**, *n*, rareté, *f*.
rascal, *n*, coquin, e, fripon, ne; canaille, *f*. **~ity**, *n*, coquinerie, friponnerie, *f*. **~ly**, *a*, canaille.
rash†, *a*, téméraire, hardi. ¶ *n*, éruption, *f*. **~ness**, *n*, témérité, *f*.
rasher, *n*, tranche, *f*.
rasp, *n*, râpe, *f*. ¶ *v.t*, râper; racler. **~ing**, *a*, rugueux.
raspberry, *n*, framboise, *f*. **~ bush**, framboisier, *m*.
rat, *n*, rat, e, (*young*) raton; (*pers.*) gâtemétier; (Pol.) transfuge, *m*. **~ catcher**, preneur de rats, *m*. **~ poison**, mort aux rats, *f*. **~ trap**, ratière, *f*. ¶ *v.i*, tuer des rats; (Pol.) tourner casaque.
rate, *n*, taux; pourcentage; cours; prix; tarif; ordre, rang, *m*, classe; raison, *f*; train, *m*; taxe, contribution, *f*, impôt, *m*. **at any ~**, quoi qu'il en soit. ¶ *v.t*, évaluer; tarifer; imposer; taxer.
rather, *ad*, un peu; assez; plutôt; mieux. **~ nice**, gentillet. **~ slowly** (Mus.), gravement. **~ than**, plutôt que.
ratification, *n*, ratification, *f*. **ratify**, *v.t*, ratifier.
rating, *n*, classement; (Naut.) grade, *m*.
ratio, *n*, rapport, *m*, raison, proportion, *f*.
ration, *n*, ration, *f*, (*pl.*) vivres, *m.pl*. ¶ *v.t*, rationner. **~al†**, *a*, rationnel, raisonnable; conséquent; raisonné. **rationalism**, *n*, rationalisme, *m*. **rationalization**, *n*, organisation rationnelle, *f*. **rationing**, *n*, rationnement, *m*.
rattan, *n. & ~ cane*, rotin, *m*.
rat-tat[-tat], *n*, pan! pan!
ratter, *n*, [chien] ratier, *m*.
rattle, *n*, crécelle, *f*; (*baby's*) hochet; ballottement, claquement; (*throat*) râle, *m*. **~snake**, serpent à sonnettes, *m*. **~trap**, patraque, *f*; (*vehicle*) guimbarde, patache, *f*, tapecul, *m*. ¶ *v.i*, & *t*, ballotter; cliqueter.
raucous, *a*, rauque.
ravage, *v.t*, ravager. **~s**, *n.pl*, ravages, *m.pl*; (*of time*) injure[s], *f.[pl.]*, outrage, *m*.

rave, *v.i,* être en délire; extravaguer.

raven, *n,* corbeau, *m.*

Ravenna, *n,* Ravenne, *f.*

ravenous†, *a,* vorace; dévorant.

ravine, *n,* ravin, *m,* ravine, *f.*

raving, *n,* délire, *m.* ~ *mad,* fou à lier.

ravish, *v.t,* ravir; violer. **ravishing,** *a,* ravissant. **ravishingly,** *ad,* à ravir.

raw, *a,* cru; brut; (*silk*) grège; (*meat, wound*) saignante; (*Sienna*) naturelle; (*material*) première; (*fig.*) vert; novice; imberbe; (*weather*) humide & froid. **~ness,** *n,* crudité, *f.*

ray, *n,* rayon, *m;* (*fish*) raie, *f.*

rayon, *n,* rayon, *m,* soie artificielle, *f.*

raze, *v.t,* raser. **razor,** *n,* rasoir, *m.*

reach, *n,* portée; atteinte; étendue, *f.* *within* ~ *of,* à portée de. ¶ *v.t,* atteindre [à]; arriver à, parvenir à; s'élever à. ~ [*out*], étendre.

react, *v.i,* réagir. **~ion,** *n,* réaction, *f;* contrecoup, *m.* **~ionary,** *a. & n,* réactionnaire. *a. & m.f.*

reactor, *n,* (*nuclear*) réacteur, *m. breeder* ~, r. producteur de matière fissile, surrégénérateur, *m. fission* ~, r. à fission, *m.*

read, *v.t. & i. ir,* lire; (*report*) donner lecture de; (*meter*) relever. ~ *over,* collationner. **~able†,** *a,* lisible.

reader, *n,* lecteur, trice; liseur, euse; livre de lecture, *m.*

readiness, *n,* promptitude, *f;* empressement, *m;* facilité, *f.*

reading, *n,* lecture; leçon; cote, *f.* ~ *desk,* pupitre; (*church*) lutrin, *m.* ~ *glass,* loupe à lire, *f.* ~ *stand,* liseuse, *f.* ~ *lamp,* lampe de travail, *f.* ~ *room,* salle de lecture, *f;* cabinet de l., *m.*

readjust, *v.t. & i,* rajuster. **~ment,** *n,* rajustement, *m.*

ready†, *a,* prêt; prompt; facile. **~made,** tout fait (*f.* toute faite), confectionné. **~-to-wear,** prêt-à-porter. ~ *money,* [argent] comptant, *m.*

reagent, *n,* réactif, *m.*

real†, *a,* réel; positif; véritable; vrai; effectif; (*law*) immeuble, immobilier. ~ *estate,* propriété immobilière, *f.* **~ist,** *n. & a,* réaliste, *m.f. & a.* **~ity,** *n,* réalité, *f,* le réel; positif, *m.* **~ize,** *v.t,* réaliser.

realm, *n,* royaume, *m.*

realty, *n,* biens immeubles, *m.pl.*

ream, *n,* rame, *f.* (*In Fr. 500 sheets.*) ¶ *v.t,* aléser. **~er,** *n,* alésoir, *m.*

reanimate, *v.t,* réanimer. reanimation, *n,* réanimation, *f.*

reap, *v.t.,* moissonner, recueillir (*fig.*). **reaper,** *n,* moissonneur, *m;* (*machine*) moissonneuse, *f.* ~ & *binder,* moissonneuse-lieuse, *f.* **reaping,** *n,* moisson, *f.*

reappear, *v.i,* reparaître, réapparaître. **~ance,** *n,* réapparition, *f.*

reappoint, *v.t,* renommer.

rear, *n,* arrière, *m;* queue, *f.* ~ *admiral,* contre-amiral, *m.* ~ *guard,* arrière-garde, *f.* ~ *rank,* dernier rang, *m.* ¶ *v.t,* élever, nourrir; (*v.i.*) se cabrer, se dresser. **~ing of children,** puériculture, *f.*

reason, *n,* raison; cause, *f;* motif, *m. to state the* ~ *for,* motiver. ¶ *v.i,* raisonner. ~ *with,* raisonner, catéchiser. **~able†,** *a,* raisonnable; honnête. **~er,** *n,* raisonneur, euse. **~ing,** *n,* raisonnement, *m.*

reassure, *v.t,* rassurer.

rebate, *n,* rabais, *m,* ristourne; (*Join.*) feuillure, *f.*

rebel, *n,* rebelle, *m.f,* révolté, e. ¶ *v.i,* se rebeller, se révolter. **rebellion,** *n,* rébellion, révolte, *f.* **rebellious,** *a,* rebelle.

rebind, *v.t.ir,* relier de nouveau.

rebirth, *n,* renaissance, *f.*

rebound *n,* [second] bond; contrecoup, *m.* ¶ *v.i,* rebondir.

rebuff, *n,* rebuffade, *f.* ¶ *v.t,* rebuter.

rebuild, *v.t.ir,* rebâtir, reconstruire.

rebuke, *n,* réprimande, *f.* ¶ *v.t,* réprimander.

rebut, *v.t,* réfuter.

recalcitrant, *a. & n,* récalcitrant, e.

recall, *n,* rappel. *m.* ¶ *v.t,* rappeler; retracer; révoquer; (*recollect*) se rappeler.

recant, *v.t,* rétracter. **~ation,** *n,* rétractation, palinodie, *f.*

recapitulate, *v.t,* récapituler.

recapture, *n,* reprise, *f.* ¶ *v.t,* reprendre.

recast, *v.t.ir,* refondre; remanier.

recede, *v.i,* reculer; se retirer; fuir.

receding (*forehead*, *chin*) *p.a*, fuyant.

receipt, *n*, réception, *f*; reçu, *m*; quittance, *f*, acquit, *m*; récépissé, *m*; (*pl.*) recette, *f*. *oft. pl.* ¶ *v.t*, acquitter, quittancer. **receive**, *v.t*, recevoir; accueillir; (*money*) toucher; (*stolen goods*) receler. **receiver**, *n*, destinataire, *m,f*; receleur, euse; (*Teleph.*) écouteur; (*vessel*) récipient, *m*.

recent†, *a*, récent, nouveau, frais.

receptacle, *n*, réceptacle, *m*. **reception**, *n*, réception, *f*; accueil, *m*. ~ *room*, salon, *m*.

recess, *n*, [r]enfoncement, retrait, *m*, retraite, enclave; embrasure; (*Sch.*) récréation, *f*; (*pl. heart*) replis, *m.pl.* ¶ *v.t*, défoncer; suspendre les séances.

recession, *n*, (*economic*) récession, *f*.

recipe, *n*, recette; (*Phar.*) formule, *f*.

recipient, *n*, destinataire, *m,f*.

reciprocal†, *a*, réciproque; inverse; partagé. **reciprocate**, *v.t*, payer de retour. **reciprocating**, *p.a*, alternatif, de va-et-vient. **reciprocity**, *n*, réciprocité, *f*.

recital, *n*, récit, *m*; énumération, *f*; (*Mus.*) récital, *m*; audition, *f*. **recitation**, *n*, récitation, *f*. **recitative**, *n*, récitatif, *m*. **recite**, *v.t*, réciter; déclamer; énumérer.

reckless, *a*, téméraire; insouciant. ~ *driver*, chauffard, *m*. ~**ly**, *ad*, témérairement; à corps perdu.

reckon, *v.t. & i*, compter, calculer, chiffrer; estimer. ~**ing**, *n*, compte, calcul, *m*; carte à payer; addition, *f*, écot, *m*.

reclaim, *v.t*, ramener dans la bonne voie; (*from vice*) retirer; (*uncultivated land*) défricher; (*submerged land*) aménager.

recline, *v.i*, se renverser, se reposer.

recluse, *n*, reclus, e. **reclusion**, *n*, réclusion, *f*.

recognition, *n*, reconnaissance, *f*. **recognizable**, *a*, reconnaissable. **recognizance**, *n*, obligation, *f*. **recognize**, *v.t*, reconnaître.

recoil, *n*, recul, repoussement, *m*. ¶ *v.i*, reculer, repousser.

recoin, *v.t*, refondre, refrapper.

recollect, *v.t*, se rappeler. ~**ion**, *n*, souvenir, *m*, mémoire, *f*.

recommence, *v.t. & i*, recommencer.

recommend, *v.t*, recommander; préconiser; proposer. ~**ation**, *n*, recommendation; proposition, *f*; (*for election*) parrainage, *m*. ~**er**, *n*, parrain, *m*.

recompense, *n*, récompense, *f*. ¶ *v.t*, récompenser.

reconcile, *v.t*, réconcilier, [r]accommoder; concilier. **reconciliation**, *n*, réconciliation; résignation, *f*.

recondite, *a*, abstrus, obscure.

reconnoiter, *v.t*, reconnaître.

reconsider, *v.t*, revenir sur, reviser.

reconstitute, *v.t*, reconstituer.

reconstruct, *v.t*, reconstruire; (*fig.*) constituer de nouveau, reprendre sous œuvre. ~**ion**, *n*, reconstruction; (*fig.*) reconstitution, *f*.

record, *n*, registre, *m*; note, *f*; dossier, *m*; (*pl.*) archives, *f.pl*; (*pl.*) historique; (*sport*) record; (*phonograph*) disque, *m*. *off the* ~, à titre confidentiel. ~ *player*, pick-up, tourne-disque, *m*. ¶ *v.t*, enregistrer; consigner; constater. ~**er**, *n*, enregistreur; compteur de sport, *m*. *flight* ~, enregistreur de vol.

re-count, *v.t*, recompter.

recount, *v.t*, raconter.

recoup, *v.t*, récupérer; dédommager.

recourse, *n*, recours, *m*.

re-cover, *v.t*, recouvrir.

recover, *v.t*, recouvrer; rattraper; (*v.i.*) se rétablir; [se] reprendre, se relever. ~**y**, *n*, recouvrement, *m*; reprise, *f*.

recreant, *a. & n*, lâche; apostat, *a. & m*.

re-create, *v.t*, recréer.

recreate, *v.t*, récréer. **recreation**, *n*, récréation, *f*, délassement, *m*.

recrimination, *n*, récrimination, *f*.

recrudescence, *n*, recrudescence, *f*.

recruit, *n*, recrue, *f*. ¶ *v.t*, recruter, racoler; (*v.i.*) se rétablir. ~**ing sergeant**, sergent recruteur, *m*.

rectangle, *n*, rectangle, carré long, *m*. **rectangular**, *a*, rectangulaire.

rectify, *v.t*, rectifier; redresser.

rectilinear, *a*, rectiligne.

rectitude, *n*, rectitude; droiture, *f*.

rector, *n*, recteur; curé, *m*. ~**ship**, *n*, cure, *f*. ~**y**, *n*, presbytère, *m*, cure, *f*.

rectum, *n*, rectum, *m*.

recumbent, *a*, couché. ~ *figure* (statue), gisant, e.

recuperate, *v.i*, se récupérer.

recur, *v.i*, revenir, se reproduire, se retracer. **recurrence**, *n*, retour, *m*, répétition, *f*.

recycle, *v.t*, recycler. **recycling**, *n*, recyclage, *m*.

red, *a*. & *n*, rouge, *a*. & *m*; (hair) roux, *a. the* ~*s* (Pol.), les rouges, *m.pl*. ~*breast*, rouge-gorge, *m. the R~ Cross*, la Croix Rouge. ~*faced* (person), rougeaud, e. ~*haired* (person), roux, rousse, rousseau, *m*. & *att*. ~*handed*, sur le fait, en flagrant délit. ~ *herring*, hareng saur, *m*. ~*hot*, (chauffé au) rouge; tout chaud. ~ *Indian* or ~*skin*, Peau Rouge, *m*. ~ *lead*, minium, *m*. *to be a* ~*letter day*, faire époque. ~ *mullet*, rouget, *m*. ~ *pepper*, poivre rouge, p. de Cayenne, *m. R~ Sea*, mer Rouge, *f*. ~ *tape*, chinoiseries, *f.pl*, routine, *f*. ~*wood*, sequoia, *m*. **redden**, *v.t*. & *i*, rougir; roussir. **reddish**, *a*, rougeâtre; roussâtre; blond hasardé.

redeem, *v.t*, racheter; rembourser; amortir; dégager; purger; s'acquitter de. **Redeemer**, *n*, Rédempteur, *m*. **redemption**, *n*, rachat; remboursement; amortissement; dégagement, *m*; (mortgage) purge, *f*; (Relig.) rachat, *m*, rédemption, *f*.

redness, *n*, rougeur; rousseur, *f*.

redolent of, qui sent le, la.

redouble, *v.t*, redoubler.

redoubt, *n*, redoute, *f*, réduit, *m*.

redoubtable, *a*, redoutable.

redound, *v.i*, rejaillir.

redress, *n*, redressement, *m*, réparation, *f*. ¶ *v.t*, redresser, réparer.

reduce, *v.t*, réduire; diminuer; ramener; affaiblir. ~ *to lower rank* (Mil.), rétrograder. ~ *to the ranks*, casser, réduire à la condition de simple soldat. **reduction**, *n*, réduction; diminution, *f*; (tax) dégrèvement, *m*. ~ *to the absurd* or *reductio ad absurdum*, démonstration (*ou* preuve) par l'absurde, *f*. ~ *to the ranks*, cassation, *f*.

redundant, *a*, redondant.

reecho, *v.i*, résonner.

reed, *n*, roseau; (pipe) chalumeau, *m*; (Mus.) anche; (Arch.) baguette, *f*.

reef, *n*, récif, écueil, banc, brisant; (*in sail*) ris, *m*.

reek, *n*, odeur fétide; exhalaison pestilentielle, *f*. ~ *with*, *of*, exhaler; suer. ~*ing with*, fumant de.

reel, *n*, dévidoir, *m*, bobine, *f*; touret; (Fish.) moulinet, *m*. ¶ *v.t*, dévider, bobiner; (*v.i.*) chanceler; (*when drunk*) festonner.

reelect, *v.t*, réélire. ~*ion*, *n*, réélection, *f*. **reeligible**, *a*, rééligible.

reembark, *v.t*, rembarquer; (*v.i*) [se] r.

reengage, *v.t*, rengager.

reenlist, *v.i*, [se] rengager.

reenter, *v.i*, rentrer; (*v.t.*) rentrer dans. **reentrant**, *a*, rentrant. **reentry**, *n*, rentrée, *f*.

reestablish, *v.t*, rétablir, restaurer.

reeve (Naut.) *v.t.ir*, passer.

reexamine, *v.t*, repasser, revoir.

reexport, *v.t*, réexporter.

refectory, *n*, réfectoire, *m*.

refer, *v.t*, référer; renvoyer; déférer. ~ *to*, se référer à, se reporter à; renvoyer à, consulter. ~*ee*, *n*, arbitre; tiers arbitre; (Box.) [arbitre] directeur de combat, *m*. ¶ *v.t*, arbitrer. **reference**, *n*, renvoi, *m*; référence; mention, *f*; trait, *m*. ~ *library*, bibliothèque où les livres se consultent sur place; b. d'ouvrages à consulter, *f*. ~ [mark], [guidon de] renvoi, *m*. ~ *point*, point de repère, *m*. *with* ~ *to*, à l'égard de. **referendum**, *n*, referendum, plébiscite, *m*.

refill, *v.t*. & *i*, remplir; réapprovisionner.

refine, *v.t*, affiner; raffiner; épurer; polir; (*v.i.*) raffiner. ~**d**, *p.a*, raffiné, distingué; poli; délicat. ~**ment** (fig.) *n*, raffinement, *m*. **refiner**, *n*, affineur; raffineur, *m*. **refinery**, *n*, raffinerie, *f*.

reflect, *v.t*. & *i*, réfléchir; refléter; rejaillir. ~**ion**, *n*, réflexion; image, *f*; reflet, *m*; atteinte, *f*.

~**ive,** *a,* réfléchi. ~**or,** *n,* réflecteur, *m.* **reflex,** *a,* réflexe. ¶ *n,* reflet; réflexe, *m.* **reflexive** (*Gram.*) *a,* réfléchi.

refloat (*ship*) *v.t,* renflouer.

reflux, *n,* reflux, *m.*

re-form, *v.t,* reformer.

reform, *n,* réforme, *f.* ¶ *v.t,* réformer. ~**ation,** *n,* réformation; réforme, *f.* ¶ *v.t,* ~**atory,** *n,* maison de correction, *f,* pénitencier, *m.* ~**er,** *n,* réformateur, trice.

refract, *v.t,* réfracter. ~**ing** *telescope,* lunette [d'approche] *f.* **refractoriness,** *n,* mutinerie, *f.* **refractory,** *a,* réfractaire.

refrain, *n,* refrain, *m.* ¶ *v.i,* se retenir; s'abstenir.

refresh, *v.t,* rafraîchir; restaurer; délasser, reposer, récréer. **refreshment,** *n,* rafraîchissement, *m.* ~ *bar,* ~ *room,* buvette, *f,* buffet, *m.*

refrigerate, *v.t,* frigorifier. **refrigeration,** *n,* réfrigération, *f.* **refrigerator,** *n,* réfrigérateur, *m.*

refuge, *n,* refuge, *m.* *to take* ~, se réfugier. **refugee,** *n,* réfugié, e, émigré, e.

refulgent, *a,* éclatant.

refund, *v.t,* rembourser.

refurnish, *v.t,* remeubler.

refusal, *n,* refus, *m.* refuse, *n,* rebut, déchet, *m.* oft. *pl;* immondices, *f.pl,* ordure, *f.* ~ *dump,* dépotoir, *m.* ¶ *v.t. & i,* refuser, se r. ~ *admittance,* consigner à la porte.

refutation, *n,* réfutation, *f.* refute, *v.t,* réfuter.

regain, *v.t,* regagner; reconquérir.

regal†, *a,* royal.

regale, *v.t,* régaler.

regalia, *n,* insignes de la royauté; décors, *m. pl.*

regard, *n,* égard, *m;* considération, *f;* respect; rapport, *m.* with ~ *to,* ~**ing,** à l'égard de, à propos de, quant à, à l'endroit de. ¶ *v.t,* regarder; considérer. ~**less,** *a,* insoucieux, sans se soucier.

regatta, *n,* régate, *f.* oft. *pl.*

regency, *n,* régence, *f.*

regenerate, *v.t,* régénérer. **regeneration,** *n,* régénération, *f.*

regent, *n. & a,* régent, e.

regicidal, *a. & regicide, n,* régicide, *a. & m.*

regild, *v.t.ir,* redorer.

regime, *n,* régime, *m.* **regiment,** *n,* régiment, *m.* **regimental,** *a,*

régimentaire. ~ *records,* historique du régiment, *m.*

region, *n,* région, contrée, *f.* ~**al,** *a,* régional.

register, *n,* registre, livre, journal; grand livre; répertoire, *m;* matricule; voix, *f;* (*book mark*) signet, *m.* ~ *of voters,* liste électorale, *f.* ¶ *v.t,* enregistrer, inscrire, immatriculer; (*design, etc.*) déposer; recommander. **registrar,** *n,* greffier; archiviste, *m.* **registration,** *n,* inscription, immatriculation; recommandation, *f.* **registry** [office], *n,* (*marriage*) mairie, *f;* (*servants*) bureau de placement, *m.*

regress, *v.i,* régresser.

regret, *n,* regret, *m. to send* ~**s,** envoyer des excuses. ¶ *v.t,* regretter.

regular†, *a,* régulier; réglé; assidu; véritable; franc, fieffé. ~ *channel[s]* (*fig.*), filière, *f.* ~**ity,** *n,* régularité, *f.* ~**ize,** *v.t,* régulariser. **regulate,** *v.t,* régler; réglementer. **regulation,** *n,* réglementation, *f;* règlement, *m,* ordonnance, *f;* (*att.*) réglementaire. **regulator,** *n,* régulateur, *m.*

rehabilitate, *v.t,* réhabiliter.

rehandle, *v.t,* remmancher.

rehearsal, *n,* répétition, *f.* **rehearse,** *v.t,* répéter; énumérer.

rehousing, *n,* relogement, *m.*

reign, *n,* règne, *m.* ¶ *v.i,* régner. ~**ing,** *a,* régnant.

reimburse, *v.t,* rembourser.

reimport, *v.t,* réimporter.

reimpose, *v.t,* réimposer.

rein, *n,* rêne, guide, bride, *f.* ¶ *v.t,* guider, refréner.

reindeer, *n,* renne, *m.*

reinforce, *v.t,* renforcer; (*concrete*) armer. ~**ment,** *n,* renforcement, *m;* armature, *f;* (*men*) renfort, *m.*

reinstate, *v.t,* réintégrer, rétablir, réhabiliter.

reinsure, *v.t,* réassurer.

reinvest (*Fin.*) *v.t,* replacer.

reinvigorate, *v.t,* redonner de la vigueur à, revigorer.

reissue (*book*) *n,* réédition, *f.*

reiterate, *v.t,* réitérer.

reject, *v.t,* rejeter; repousser; refuser. ~**ion,** *n,* rejet; repoussement, *m.*

rejoice, *v.t,* réjouir; (*v.i.*) se r. **rejoicing,** *n,* réjouissance, *f.*

re-join, *v.t,* rejoindre.

rejoin, v.t, répliquer; (one's regiment) rejoindre, rallier. **rejoinder,** n, réplique, repartie, f.

rejuvenate, v.t, rajeunir.

rekindle, v.t, rallumer.

relapse, n, (Med.) rechute, f; (Fin.) recul, m; (crime) récidive, f. ¶ v.i, retomber; reculer. ~ into crime, récidiver.

relate, v.t, raconter, narrer, relater; (v.i.) se rapporter, avoir rapport. ~d to, parent avec, apparenté à. **relation,** n, relation, f; rapport, m; parent, e; allié, e; (pl.) parenté, f. ~ship, n, parenté; filiation, f. **relative†,** a, relatif. ¶ n, parent, e. **relativism,** n, relativisme, m. **relativity,** n, relativité, f.

relax, v.t, relâcher; détendre, débander; délasser; (Med.) [re]lâcher. ~ation, n, relâchement, f; relâche, délassement, m.

re-lay, v.t.ir, reposer.

relay, n, relais, m. ~ race, course de (ou à) relais, f. ¶ v.t, relayer.

release, n, relaxation, f, élargissement; (pigeons) lancer, m; libération; délivrance, f; (Mech.) déclic; (Phot.) déclencheur, m. ¶ v.t, relaxer, élargir; lancer; libérer; lâcher; délivrer; délier.

relegate, v.t, reléguer.

relent, v.i, fléchir. ~less†, a, impitoyable, acharné.

relet, v.t.ir, relouer. **reletting,** n, relocation, f.

relevant, a, pertinent; qui se rapporte à.

reliability, n, sûreté, sécurité, f; fidélité; (test) fiabilité, f. **reliable†,** a, sûr; de tout repos; de confiance. **reliance,** n, confiance, foi, f.

relic, n, relique, f; reste, m.

relief, n, soulagement; secours, m, assistance, f; (tax) dégrèvement; (for dependants, Inc. tax) abattement; (art) relief, m; (Mil.) relève, f. ~ fund, caisse de secours, f. ~ train, train supplementaire, m. **relieve,** v.t, soulager, secourir, assister; relever; débarrasser.

relight, v.t, rallumer.

religion, n, religion, f. **religious†,** a, religieux; (book) dévot, de dévotion. ~ness, n, religiosité, f.

relinquish, v.t, abandonner.

reliquary, n, reliquaire, m.

relish, n, goût, m; saveur, f; as-saisonnement, m. ¶ v.t, goûter; savourer.

reluctance, n, répugnance, f. **I am reluctant to,** il me répugne de, je me fais conscience de. **reluctantly,** ad, à contrecœur, à regret.

rely, v.i, compter, se reposer, faire fond.

remain, v.i, rester; demeurer. **remainder,** n, reste, restant; solde d'édition, m. ~ sale, soldes, m.pl. ¶ v.t, solder. **remains,** n.pl, restes, vestiges, débris, m.pl; dépouille, f.

remake, v.t.ir, refaire.

remand, v.t, renvoyer à une autre audience.

remark, n, remarque, observation, f, propos, m. **remark** & remark, v.t, remarquer. ~able†, a, remarquable.

remarriage, n, remariage, m. **remarry,** v.t, remarier.

remedy, n, remède; (law) recours, m. ¶ v.t, remédier à.

remember, v.t, se [res]souvenir de; se rappeler, retenir. **remembrance,** n, [res]souvenir, m; mémoire, f.

remind of, faire penser à, rappeler à. **you ~ me of someone,** vous me rappelez quelqu'un. ~er, n, mémento; rappel, m.

reminiscence, n, réminiscence, f.

remiss†, a, négligent. ~ion, n, rémission; remise, f. **remit,** v.t, remettre; envoyer. **remittance,** n, remise, f; envoi, m.

remnant, n, reste; coupon; lambeau, m; épave, f.

remodel, v.t, remodeler; refondre.

remonstrance, n, remontrance, f. **remonstrate,** v.i, faire des remontrances, [en] remontrer (with = à).

remorse, n, remords, m. ~less, a, & ~lessly, ad, sans remords.

remote, a, éloigné, écarté; (antiquity) reculée, haute. ~ control, télécommande, f. ~ness, n, éloignement, m.

remount, n, remonte, f. ¶ v.t, re-monter.

removable, a, amovible. **removal,** n, déplacement; éloignement; déménagement; enlèvement, m; (of officer) destitution, f. **remove,** v.t, déplacer; éloigner; enlever; lever; destituer.

remunerate, *v.t*, rémunérer, rétribuer. **remuneration**, *n*, rémunération, rétribution, *f*.

renaissance, *n*, renaissance, *f*.

rename, *v.t*, débaptiser.

rend, *v.t.ir*, déchirer; (*the air*) fendre.

render, *v.t*, rendre; expliquer; interpréter; (*plaster*) enduire. ~ *void*, frapper de nullité. ~**ing**, *n*, (*accounts*) reddition, *f*; (*art*) rendu, *m*; explication; interprétation, *f*; (*plaster*) enduit, *m*.

renegade, *n*, renégat, e.

renew, *v.t*, renouveler. ~**al**, *n*, renouvellement, *m*; rénovation; reprise, *f*.

rennet, *n*, présure; (*apple*) reinette, *f*.

renounce, *v.t*, renoncer à, répudier, abjurer.

renovate, *v.t*, renouveler, rénover, rajeunir.

renown, *n*, renommée, *f*, renom, *m*. ~**ed**, *a*, renommé.

rent, *n*, (*tear*) déchirure, *f*; accroc; (*periodical payment*) loyer; fermage, *m*; redevance, *f*. ¶ *v.t*, louer; sous-louer. ~**al**, *n*, prix de location, *m*; redevance; valeur locative, *f*. ~**er**, *n*, locataire, *m,f*.

renunciation, *n*, renonciation, répudiation, *f*, renoncement, *m*.

reopen, *v.t*, rouvrir; (*v.i.*) se r.; rentrer. ~**ing**, *n*, réouverture; rentrée, *f*.

reorganize, *v.t*, réorganiser.

repack, *v.t*, remballer.

repair, *n*, état, *m*; réparation, *f*. *beyond* ~, irréparable. *under* ~, en réparation. ¶ *v.t*, réparer; raccommoder; (*v.i.*) se rendre. ~**able** & **reparable**, *a*, réparable. **reparation**, *n*, réparation, *f*.

repartee, *n*, repartie, *f*.

repast, *n*, repas, *m*.

repatriate, *v.t*, rapatrier.

repay, *v.t.ir*, rembourser; rendre. ~**ment**, *n*, remboursement, *m*.

repeal, *n*, rappel, *m*, révocation, *f*. ¶ *v.t*, rappeler, révoquer.

repeat (*Mus.*) *ad*, bis. ¶ (*Mus.*) *n*, renvoi, *m*. ¶ *v.t*, répéter, redire. ~**edly**, *ad*, fréquemment, à plusieurs reprises. ~**ing** (*rifle, watch*) *p.a*, à répétition.

repel, *v.t*, repousser. **repellent**, *a*, rebutant, repoussant; (*Phys.*) répulsif.

repent, *v.i*, se repentir; (*v.t.*) se

repentir de. ~**ance**, *n*, repentir, *m*.

repeople, *v.t*, repeupler.

repercussion, *n*, répercussion, *f*.

repertory, *n*, répertoire, *m*.

repetend, *n*, période, *f*. **repetition**, *n*, répétition; redite; reprise, *f*.

repine, *v.i*, se chagriner.

replace, *v.t*, replacer; reposer; remplacer. ~**ment**, *n*, remplacement, *m*.

replant, *v.t*, replanter.

replate, *v.t*, rétamer.

replay, *v.t*, rejouer.

replenish, *v.t*, remplir; remonter. **replete**, *a*, plein. **repletion**, *n*, plénitude; réplétion, *f*.

replica, *n*, reproduction, *f*, facsimilé, *m*.

reply, *n*, réponse, *f*. ~ *paid*, avec réponse payée. *in* ~ (*law*), responsif. ¶ *v.t*. & *i*, répondre.

report, *n*, rapport; reportage; bulletin; compte rendu; procès-verbal, *m*; expertise, *f*; bruit, *m*, renommée; détonation, *f*. ¶ *v.t*, rendre compte de, rapporter. ~**er** (*news*) *n*, reporter, chroniqueur, journaliste d'information, *m*. ~**ing**, *n*, reportage, *m*.

repose, *n*, repos, *m*. ¶ *v.i.* se reposer.

repository, *n*, dépôt, magasin; réceptacle; (*fig.*) répertoire, *m*.

repot, *v.t*, rempoter.

repoussé work, travail de repoussé, *m*.

reprehend, *v.t*, reprendre, censurer. **reprehensible**, *a*, répréhensible.

represent, *v.t.*, représenter. ~**ation**, *n*, représentation, *f*. ~**ative**, *a*, représentatif. ¶ *n*, représentant, e.

repress, *v.t*, réprimer, refouler, comprimer. ~**ion**, *n*, répression, compression, *f*.

reprieve, *n*, sursis, *m*. ¶ *v.t*, surseoir à l'exécution de, gracier.

reprimand, *n*, réprimande, semonce, mercuriale, *f*; blâme, *m*. ¶ *v.t*, réprimander, chapitrer; blâmer.

reprint, *n*, réimpression, *f*. ¶ *v.t*, réimprimer.

reprisal, *n*, représaille, *f*.

reproach, *n*, reproche, *m*; honte, *f*. ¶ *v.t*, faire des reproches à; reprocher. ~**ful**, *a*, de reproche. ~**fully**, *ad*, d'un ton de reproche.

reprobate, n, réprouvé, m. ¶ v.t, réprouver. **reprobation**, n, réprobation, f.

reproduce, v.t, reproduire. **reproduction**, n, reproduction; répétition, f.

reproof, n, réprimande, f. **reprove**, v.t, reprendre.

reptile, n, reptile, m.

republic, n, république, f. ~**an**, a. & n, républicain, e.

republish, v.t, publier de nouveau.

repudiate, v.t, répudier, [re]nier.

repugnance, n, répugnance, f. **repugnant**, a, répugnant. to be ~ to, répugner à.

repulse, n, échec, m. ¶ v.t, repousser, rebuter. **repulsion**, n, répulsion, f. **repulsive**, a, repoussant; (Phys.) répulsif.

repurchase, n, rachat, m. ¶ v.t, racheter.

reputable, a, honorable. **reputation & repute**, n, réputation, renommée, f, renom, crédit, m. of repute, réputé. **reputed**, p.p, réputé; censé; putatif.

request, n, demande, prière, requête, instance, f. by ~, on ~, sur demande. ¶ v.t, demander, prier, inviter.

requiem, n, requiem, m.

require, v.t, exiger; requérir; demander; réclamer; vouloir; avoir besoin de; falloir. ~**ment**, n, exigence, f; besoin, m. **requisite**, a, requis, voulu. ¶ n, article, m; fourniture, f. **requisition**, n, réquisition, f. ¶ v.t, réquisitionner.

requital, n, récompense; revanche, f. **requite**, v.t, récompenser.

reredos, n, retable, m.

rerun, v.t, (computers) repasser.

resale, n, revente, f.

rescind, v.t, annuler. **rescission**, n, rescision, f.

rescript, n, rescrit, m.

rescue, n, délivrance, f; sauvetage, m. to the ~, à la rescousse. ¶ v.t, délivrer; sauver.

research, n, recherche, f. ~ worker, chercheur, euse. motivational ~, études de motivation, f.pl.

reseat, v.t, rasseoir; remettre un fond à.

resemblance, n, ressemblance, f. **resemble**, v.t, ressembler à, approcher de, imiter.

resent, v.t, s'indigner contre, ressentir. ~**ment**, n, ressentiment, m.

reservation, n, réserve, réservation; (mental) restriction, arrière-pensée; (seats) location, f. **reserve**, n, réserve, provision; retenue, f. ¶ v.t, réserver; retenir, louer. ~**d seat ticket**, billet garde-place, billet de location de place, m. **reservist**, n, réserviste, m. **reservoir**, n, réservoir, m.

reset, v.t.ir, remonter; remettre; (Typ.) recomposer. **resetting** (Typ.) n, recomposition, f.

reship, v.t, rembarquer.

reshuffle, v.t, rebattre.

reside, v.i, résider, demeurer. **residence**, n, résidence, f; séjour, m; demeure, f, domicile, m; habitation, f. **resident**, n, habitant, e; (diplomatic) résident, m.

residuary legatee, légataire universel, m. **residue**, n, résidu; reliquat, m.

resign, v.t, résigner, se démettre de; (v.i.) démissionner. **resignation**, n, résignation, démission; (submission) résignation, f.

resilient, a, élastique.

resin, n, résine; (for violin) colophane, f. ~**ous**, a, résineux.

resist, v.t, résister à; (v.i.) résister. ~**ance**, n, résistance, f.

resole, v.t, ressemeler.

resolute†, a, résolu, déterminé. **resolution**, n, résolution; détermination; délibération; décision; proposition, f. **resolve**, n, détermination, f. ¶ v.t, résoudre, déterminer. ~ on, statuer sur, décider.

resonance, n, résonance, f. **resonant**, a, résonnant.

resort, n, recours; ressort, m, ressource, f; rendez-vous; séjour, m; station, f, centre, m. as a last ~, en dernier ressort. **seaside** ~, station balnéaire, f. ~ **to**, recourir à; se rendre à; fréquenter.

resound, v.i, résonner, retentir.

resource, n, ressource, f; expédient, m. ~**ful**, a, de ressources; débrouillard. ¶ n, (person), débrouillard, m.

respect, n, respect; rapport, égard, m; acception, f. in all ~s, à tous égards. ¶ v.t, respecter. ~**able**, a, respectable, honorable, honnête. ~**ably**, ad, honorablement. ~**ful†**, a, respectueux.

~ing, *pr*, concernant. ~ive†, *a*, respectif.

respiration, *n*, respiration, *f*. **re**-spiratory, *a*, respiratoire.

respite, *n*, répit, relâche, *m*, trêve, *f*; sursis, *m*.

resplendent, *a*, resplendissant.

respond, *v.i*, répondre; obéir. ~ent, *n*, répondant, e; (*law*) défendeur, eresse. **response**, *n*, réponse, *f*; (*Eccl.*) répons, *m*. **responsibility**, *n*, responsabilité, *f*. **responsible**, *a*, responsable; solidaire. **responsive**, *a*, sensible, liant.

rest, *n*, repos; (*Mus.*) silence, *m*, pause, *f*; support; appui; (*Bil., etc.*) chevalet; (*remainder*) reste, *m*. & all the ~ of it, & toute la lyre. ¶ *v.i*, se reposer; reposer; poser; s'appuyer; porter; tenir; résider; incomber; (*v.t.*) reposer, appuyer.

restage, *v.t*, remonter.

restaurant, *n*, restaurant, *m*. ~ keeper, restaurateur, trice.

restful, *a*, reposant. **resting place**, repos, *m*; sépulture, *f*.

restitch, *v.t*, repiquer.

restitution, *n*, restitution, *f*.

restive, *a*, rétif.

restless, *a*, inquiet; agité; remuant; turbulent.

restoration, *n*, restauration; réfection, *f*; rétablissement, *m*; restitution, *f*. **restorative**, *a*. & *n*, restaurant, *a*. & *m*. **restore**, *v.t*, restaurer; rénover; rétablir; ramener; rendre; restituer. **restorer**, *n*, restaurateur, trice.

restrain, *v.t*, retenir, contenir, comprimer, contraindre. **restraint**, *n*, contrainte, *f*. *to place* (lunatic) *under ~*, interner.

restrict, *v.t*, restreindre, borner, renfermer. ~ion, *n*, restriction, *f*.

restring, *v.t.ir*, recorder.

result, *n*, résultat, *m*; suite, *f*. ¶ *v.i*, résulter.

resume, *v.t*, reprendre; renouer. resumption, *n*, reprise, *f*.

resurrection, *n*, résurrection, *f*.

resurvey, *n*, contre-expertise, *f*.

resuscitate, *v.t*, resusciter.

retail, *n*, [commerce de] détail; petit commerce, *m*. ¶ *v.t*, détailler, débiter. ~er, *n*, détaillant, e.

retain, *v.t*, retenir; arrêter. ~er, *n*, (*fee*) provision, *f*; (*pl.*) gens, *m.pl.*

retake, *v.t.ir*, reprendre.

retaliate, *v.i*, user de représailles (*upon* = envers). **retaliation**, *n*, représailles, *f.pl*, talion, *m*. **retaliatory**, *a*, de représailles.

retard, *v.t*, retarder.

retch, *v.i*, avoir des haut-le-cœur, vomir.

retention, *n*, rétention, *f*. **retentive**, *a*, tenace, fidèle.

reticence, *n*, réticence, *f*. *to be reticent*, se taire à dessein.

reticle & **reticule**, *n*, réticule, *m*.

retina, *n*, rétine, *f*.

retinue, *n*, suite, *f*, cortège, *m*.

retire, *v.t*, retirer; mettre à la retraite, prendre sa retraite; (*officer*) réformer; (*v.i.*) se retirer. ~d, *p.p*, retiré; en retraite. ~ment, *n*, retraite, *f*. **retiring**, *p.a*, retiré en lui-même, qui fuit la société; (*manners*) effacées; (*director*) sortant; (*pension*) de retraite.

retort, *n*, réplique, riposte; (*Chem.*) cornue, *f*, vase clos, *m*. ¶ *v.t*. & *i*, rétorquer, répliquer, riposter.

retouch, *v.t*, retoucher, retoucher à. ~[ing], *n*, retouche, *f*.

retrace, *v.t*, retracer; revenir sur, rebrousser. ~ *one's steps*, rebrousser chemin.

retract, *v.t*, rétracter; (*v.i.*) se rétracter.

retreat, *n*, retraite; reculade; (*glacier*) décrue, *f*. ¶ *v.i*, se retirer, reculer.

retrench, *v.t*, retrancher, restreindre. ~ment, *n*, retranchement, *m*.

retribution, *n*, récompense, *f*.

retrieve, *v.t*, rétablir, réparer; (*game*) rapporter; (*computers*), retrouver. **retriever** (*dog*) *n*, retriever, *m*. *a good ~*, un chien qui rapporte bien.

retroactive, *a*, rétroactif.

retrograde, *a*, rétrograde.

retrospect, *n*, revue rétrospective, *f*. ~ive†, *a*, rétrospectif; (*effect of a law*) rétroactif.

return, *n*, retour, *m*; rentrée; restitution, revanche, *f*; remboursement; renvoi; rendu; état, relevé, *m*; déclaration; statistique; rémunération, *f*; rapport, rendement; (*pl.—books, newspapers*) bouillon, *m*. ~ *address*,

adresse de l'expéditeur, *f*. ~
match, revanche, *f*, match retour, *m. by ~ mail,* par retour
du courrier. ¶ *v.t,* rendre; restituer; renvoyer; retourner; rembourser; déclarer; élire, nommer;
(Ten.) relever *(le service); (v.i.)*
retourner; revenir; rentrer. ~
able, *a,* restituable. *~ed letter,*
lettre renvoyée, *f*.
reunion, *n,* réunion, *f*. **reunite,**
v.t, réunir.
reveal *(Arch.) n,* jouée, *f*. ¶ *v.t,*
révéler.
reveille, *n,* réveil, *m,* diane, *f*.
revel, *n. oft. pl,* réjouissance, *f*.
oft. pl; ripaille, *f*. ¶ *v.i,* ripailler,
faire bombance. ~ *in,* nager
dans.
revelation, *n,* révélation, *f*. R~
(Bible), Apocalypse, *f*.
reveler, *n,* noceur, euse. **revelry,**
n, ripaille, *f*.
revenge, *n,* vengeance; revanche,
f. ~ **oneself,** se venger. ~**ful,** *a,*
vindicatif.
revenue, *n,* revenu; rapport; fisc,
m. ~ *stamp,* timbre fiscal, *m*.
(law) réformer.
reverberate, *v.t. & i,* réverbérer. **reverberation,** *n,* réverbér-
ation, *f*.
revere, *v.t,* révérer. **reverence,** *n,*
révérence, *f*. ¶ *v.t,* révérer. **reverend,** *a,* révérend. **reverent†,** *a,*
pieux. **reverential,** *a,* révérenciel.
reverentially, *ad,* avec révérence.
reverie, *n,* rêverie, *f*.
reversal, *n,* retournement; retour,
m, inversion, *f*. **reverse,** *n,* revers; envers; inverse; contraire,
opposé; rebours; *(of coin, of
medal)* revers, *m,* pile, *f*. ¶ *v.t,*
renverser; inverser, invertir;
(law) réformer. **reversible,** *a,* réversible. **reversion,** *n,* réversion,
f; retour, *m*. **revert,** *v.i,* revenir,
retourner.
revet, *v.t,* revêtir. ~**ment,** *n,* revêtement, *m*.
revictual, *v.t,* ravitailler.
review, *n,* revue; revision; *(book)*
compte rendu, *m,* notice, critique [littéraire] *f*. ¶ *v.t,* revoir,
reviser; *(Mil.)* passer en revue;
(book) faire le compte rendu de.
~**er,** *n,* critique [littéraire] *m*.
revile, *v.t,* injurier.
revise *(Typ.) n,* seconde [épreuve]
f. ¶ *v.t,* revoir, reviser. **revision,**
n, revision, *f*.

revival, *n,* reprise; renaissance, *f*;
rétablissement; *(Relig.)* réveil,
m. revive, v.t, ranimer; raviver;
réveiller.
revive, *v.t, (reanimate)* réanimer;
(film, play) reprendre.
revoke, *v.t,* révoquer; *(v.i, cards)*
renoncer.
revolt, *n,* révolte, *f,* soulèvement,
m. ¶ *v.i,* se révolter, se soulever.
~**ing,** *a,* révoltant.
revolution, *n,* révolution, *f*; tour,
m. ~**ary,** *a. & n,* révolutionnaire,
a. & m,f. ~**ize,** *v.t,* révolutionner;
modifier entièrement. **revolve,**
v.t. & i, tourner.
revolver, *n,* révolver, *m*.
revue, *n,* revue, *f*.
revulsion, *n,* révolution; *(Med.)*
révulsion, *f*.
reward, *n,* récompense, *f*. ¶ *v.t,*
récompenser; couronner.
rewrite, *v.t.ir,* récrire.
rhapsody, *n,* rhapsodie, *f*.
Rheims, *n,* Reims, *m*.
rhetoric, *n,* rhétorique, *f*. ~**al,** *a,*
oratoire soutenu.
rheumatic, *a,* rhumatismal.
rheumatism, *n,* rhumatisme, *m*.
Rhine (the), le Rhin. ¶ *att,*
rhénan; *(wine)* du Rhin. *the ~
land,* les pays rhénans.
rhinoceros, *n,* rhinocéros, *m*.
rhododendron, *n,* rhododendron, *m*.
rhomb[us], *n,* rhombe, losange,
m.
Rhone (the) le Rhône.
rhubarb, *n,* rhubarbe, *f*.
rhyme, *n,* rime, *f*. ¶ *v.i,* rimer.
rhym[est]er, *n,* rim[aill]eur, *m*.
rhythm, *n,* rythme, *m,* cadence,
f. ~**ic(al),** *a,* rythmique, cadencé.
rib, *n,* côte; nervure; *(ship)* côte,
f, membre, *m*; *(umbrella)* baleine, *f*. ~ *steak,* entrecôte, *f*.
ribald, *a,* gaillard, égrillard, licencieux.
ribbed, *a,* côtelé, à côtes; à ner-
vure(s).
ribbon or **riband,** *n,* ruban;
cordon, *m*. ~ *maker,* rubanier,
ère. ~ *trade,* rubanerie, *f*.
rice, *n,* riz, *m*. ~ *field,* rizière, *f*.
~ *paper,* papier de Chine, *m*.
rich†, *a,* riche; *(food)* gras. *the
~,* les riches, *m.pl.* **riches,** *n.pl*,
richesse, *f. oft. pl.* **richness,** *n,*
richesse, *f*.
rick, *n, (hay)* meule, *f*; *(strain)*
effort, *m*.

rickets, *n*, rachitisme, *m*. **rickety,** *a*, rachitique; boiteux, bancal.

ricksha[w], *n*, pousse-pousse, *m*.

ricochet, *n*, ricochet, *m*. ¶ *v.i*, ricocher.

rid, *v.t.ir*, débarrasser. **riddance,** *n*, débarras, *m*.

riddle, *n*, énigme, devinette, *f*; rébus; (*sieve*) crible, *m*. ¶ *v.t*, cribler.

ride, *n*, promenade; chevauchée; cavalcade, *f*; trajet, *m*. ¶ *v.t. & i. ir*, monter; chevaucher; aller. ~ *sidesaddle*, monter en amazone. ~ *to death* (*fig.*), enfourcher, revenir sans cesse à. **rider,** *n*, cavalier, ère; écuyer, ère; (*document*) codicille; (*Com.*) allonge, *m*.

ridge, *n*, arête; strie; (*roof*) crête; (*hill*) croupe; (*Agric.*) raie, *f*; (*left by plow*) billon, *m*. ~ *pole*, faîtage, *m*; (*tent*) faîtière, *f*. ¶ (*Agric.*) *v.t*, butter.

ridicule, *n*, ridicule, *m*. ¶ *v.t*, ridiculiser. **ridiculous†,** *a*, ridicule. **~ness,** *n*, ridicule, *m*.

riding, *n*, équitation, *f*; manège; chevauchement, *m*; (*turf*) monte, *f*. ~ *boots*, bottes à l'écuyère, *f.pl*. ~ *breeches*, culotte de cheval, *f*. ~ *habit*, amazone, *f*. ~ *school*, école d'équitation, *f*, manège, *m*. ~ *whip*, cravache, *f*.

rife (to be), courir, sévir.

riffraff, *n*, canaille, racaille, *f*.

rifle, *n*, fusil, *m*; carabine, *f*. ~ *drill*, maniement des (*ou* d') armes, *m*. ~*man*, fusilier, carabinier, *m*. ~ *range*, [champ de] tir; (*gallery*) tir, stand, *m*. ¶ *v.t*, (*rob*) dévaliser, spolier; (*groove*) rayer, canneler.

rift, *n*, crevasse; éclaircie, *f*; (*fig.*) fossé, *m*.

rig, *v.t*, équiper; accoutrer, harnacher; (*ship*) gréer. **rigging,** *n*, gréement, *m*, agrès, *m.pl*. ~ *the market*, tripotage de bourse, *m*.

right, *a*, droit; bon; bien; juste; vrai; qu'il faut. ~*-angled*, rectangle. ~*-handed person* or *player*, droitier, ère. ~*-minded*, bien pensant. *at the* ~ *moment*, à point nommé. ~ *side* (fabric), endroit, dessus, *m*. *to be* ~, avoir raison. ¶ *ad*, tout droit; bien; tout. *all* ~, très bien, ça va. ~ *away*, tout de suite. ~ *& left*, *ad*, à droite & à gauche. ~ *through*, de part en part; en entier. ¶ *n*, droit, *m*; faculté; raison, *f*; chef; gain de cause, *m*; (*side*) droite; (*pl.*) justice, *f*. ~ *of way*, [droit de] passage, *m*. *by* ~*s*, en toute justice. ¶ *v.t*, redresser.

righteous, *a*, vertueux; juste. ~*ly*, *ad*, droitement. ~*ness*, *n*, justice, *f*.

rightful†, *a*, légitime. **rightly,** *ad*, justement, bien; à juste titre.

rigid†, *a*, rigide. ~*ity*, *n*, rigidité, *f*.

rigmarole, *n*, litanie, kyrielle, tartine, *f*.

rigorous†, *a*, rigoureux. **rigor,** *n*, rigueur, *f*.

rill, *n*, ruisseau, *m*.

rim, *n*, [re]bord, *m*, bordure, *f*, ourlet, *m*; (*wheel*) jante; (*watch*) lunette, *f*. ~ *brake*, frein sur jantes, *m*. ¶ *v.t*, border. ~**less** (*glasses*) *a*, sans monture.

rime, *n*, givre, frimas, *m*.

rind, *n*, écorce, peau; (*cheese*) pelure, croûte; (*bacon*) couenne, *f*.

rinderpest, *n*, peste bovine, *f*.

ring, *n*, cercle; anneau, *m*; bague; boucle; frette, *f*; rond; segment; collier; cerne, *m*; couche; enceinte; arène; piste de cirque; coalition; bande, *f*; coup de sonnette; coup de téléphone, *m*. ~ *bolt*, boucle d'amarrage, *f*. ~ *finger*, [doigt] annulaire, *m*. ~*leader*, meneur; chef d'émeute, *m*. ~*s under the eyes*, les yeux cernés, *m.pl*. ~*worm*, teigne, *f*. ¶ *v.t. & i. ir*, sonner; corner; tinter; résonner; retentir; cerner; (*bull*) boucler. ~ *a peal*, carillonner. ~ *for*, sonner.

ringlet, *n*, boucle, *f*.

rink, *n*, patinoir, *f*.

rinse & ~ out, *v.t*, rincer. **rinsings,** *n.pl*, rinçure, *f*.

riot, *n*, émeute, *f*; tumulte, *m*; (*fig.*) orgie, débauche, *f*. ¶ *v.i*, prendre part à une émeute; ripailler. ~*er*, *n*, émeutier, *m*. ~*ous†,** *a*, tumultueux.

rip, *n*, déchirure, *f*. ¶ *v.t*, fendre; déchirer; refendre; découdre; éventrer. ~ *off*, arracher. ~ *saw*, scie à refendre, *f*.

riparian, *a*, riverain.

ripe, *a*, mûr. **ripen,** *v.t. & i*, mûrir. **ripeness,** *n*, maturité, *f*. **ripening,** *n*, maturation, *f*.

ripple, *n*, ride, *f*. ¶ *v.t*, rider; (*v.i.*) se r.

riposte, *n*, riposte, *f*. ¶ *v.t*, riposter.

rise, *n*, élévation; montée; rampe, *f*; lever, *m*; crue; naissance; source; hausse; augmentation; (*of a step*) hauteur de marche, *f*. ¶ *v.i.ir*, se lever; se relever; se soulever; s'élever; monter; naître; croître; augmenter; hausser; (*dead*) ressusciter. **rising**, *n*, lever, *m*; ascension, *f*; soulèvement, *m*. ¶ *p.a*: ~ *generation*, jeune génération, *f*. ~ *sun*, soleil levant, *m*. ~ *tide*, marée montante, *f*.

risk, *n*, risque; hasard, *m*. ¶ *v.t*, risquer; hasarder. *I'll* ~ *it*, au petit bonheur. **~y**, *a*, hasardeux, chanceux.

rite, *n*, rite, *m*. **ritual**, *a*. & *n*, rituel, *a*. & *m*.

rival, *a*, rival. ¶ *n*, rival, e, émule, *m,f*. ¶ *v.t*, rivaliser avec. **~ry**, *n*, rivalité, *f*.

rive, *v.t.ir*, fendre; (*v.i.ir*.) se fendre.

river, *n*, rivière, *f*; fleuve, *m*; (*att.*) de rivière, fluvial. ~*side*, bord de l'eau, *m*; (*att.*) riverain.

rivet, *n*, rivet, *m*. ¶ *v.t*, river; enchaîner, attacher. **~ing**, *n*, rivure, *f*; rivetage, *m*.

Riviera (**the**), la Rivière de Gênes, la Côte d'Azur.

rivulet, *n*, ruisseau, *m*.

roach (*fish*) *n*, gardon, *m*.

road, *n*, route; voie, *f*; chemin, *m*. ~ *mender*, cantonnier, *m*. ~ *map*, carte routière, *f*. ~ *race*, course sur route, *f*. ~*side*, bord de la route, *m*; (*att.*) sur le b. de la r. ~ *stones*, cailloutis, *m*. winding ~, route en lacets, *f*.

roam, *v.i*, rouler, errer.

roan, *a*, (*animal*) rouan; (*shoes*) rouges. ¶ *n*, (*animal*) rouan, e; (*sheepskin*) basane, *f*.

roar, *v.i*. & *t*, rugir; mugir; gronder; ronfler; éclater. ¶ *n*, rugissement, *m*.

roast, *v.t*. & *i*, rôtir; cuire [au four]; brûler; griller; torréfier. ~ *beef*, bœuf rôti, rosbif, *m*. ~ [*meat*], rôti, *m*.

rob, *v.t*, voler, dérober, dévaliser, filouter. **robber**, *n*, voleur, euse, brigand, *m*. **~y**, *n*, vol, *m*; filouterie, *f*. *armed* ~, vol à main armée.

robe, *n*, robe; toge, *f*. *lap* ~, plaid, *m*.

robin [**redbreast**], *n*, rougegorge, *m*.

robust, *a*, robuste, vigoureux.

rock, *n*, rocher; roc, *m*; roche, *f*. ~ *crystal*, cristal de roche, *m*. ~ *garden*, jardin de rocaille, jardin alpestre, *m*. ~ *salt*, sel gemme, *m*. ~*work*, rocaille, *f*. ¶ *v.t*, balancer; bercer. **~er**, *n*, bascule; (*pers.*) berceuse, *f*. **~ery**, *n*, rocher artificiel, *m*. **~et**, *n*, fusée; (*Bot.*) roquette, *f*. ~ *engine*, moteur-fusée, *m*. **~ing**, *n*, balancement; bercement, *m*. ~ *chair*, fauteuil à bascule, *m*, berceuse, *f*. ~ *horse*, cheval à bascule, *m*. ~ *stone*, rocher branlant, *m*. **~y**, *a*, rocailleux; rocheux. *R*~ *Mountains*, montagnes Rocheuses, *f.pl*.

rococo, *n*. & *a*, rococo, *m*. & *att*.

rod, *n*, baguette, verge; barre; tige; (*curtain*) tringle; (*piston*) bielle; (*fishing*) canne, *f*.

rodent, *n*. & *a*, rongeur, *m*. & *a*.

roe, *n* (*fish*) œufs de poisson, *m.pl*. ~*buck*, chevreuil, *m*. ~*doe*, chevrette, *f*.

rogations, *n.pl*, rogations, *f.pl*.

rogue, *n*, coquin, e, fripon, ne; espiègle, *m,f*. **roguish**, *a*, fripon; espiègle, mutin, malicieux. **roguishness** & **roguery**, *n*, friponnerie; espièglerie, malice, *f*.

roisterer, *n*, tapageur, euse.

roll, *n*, rouleau; cylindre, *m*; (*downhill*) roulade; (*package*) trousse; (*butter*) motte, *f*; petit pain; rôle, *m*; matricule, *f*, tableau; (*pl.*) tableau, *m*. ~ *call*, appel [nominal] *m*. ~ *of the drum*, batterie de tambour, *f*. ¶ *v.t*. & *i*, rouler; cylindrer; laminer. ~*top desk*, bureau américain, b. à rideau, *m*. ~ *up*, rouler. ~*ed gold*, or laminé, *m*, doublé or. **roller**, *n*, rouleau; cylindre, *m*; roulette, *f*; galet, *m*; (*Mech.*) tambour, *m*. ~ *skates*, patins à roulettes, *m.pl*. ~ *skating*, patinage à r—s, *m*. ~ *towel*, essuie-main à rouleau, *m*.

rollick, *v.i*, faire la fête. **~ing**, *a*, bruyant.

rolling, *n*, roulement; laminage; (*ship*) roulis, *m*. ~ *mill*, laminoir, *m*. ~ *pin*, rouleau de pâtissier, *m*. ~ *stock*, matériel roulant, *m*.

Roman, *a*, romain; (*nose*) aquilin. ~ *candle*, chandelle romaine, *f.* ~ *Catholic*, *a. & n*, catholique, *a. & m,f.* ~ *Catholicism*, catholicisme, *m.* ¶ *n*, (*pers.*) Romain, e; (*Typ.*) romain, *m.*

Romania, *n*, la Roumanie. **Romanian**, *a*, roumain. ¶ *n*, (*pers.*) Roumain, e; (*language*) le roumain.

romance, *n*, roman, *m*; romance, idylle, *f.* R~, *a. & n*, roman, *a. & m.* ¶ *v.i*, en raconter.

Romanesque, *a*, roman.

romantic, *a*, romanesque; (*literature*) romàntique.

romp, *n*, jeu bruyant, *m*; gamine bruyante, *f*, garçon manqué, *m.* ¶ *v.i*, folâtrer, batifoler. ~**ers** (*child's*) *n.pl*, barboteuse, combinaison, *f.*

rood, *n*, croix, *f.*

roof, *n*, toit; comble, *m*; voûte, *f.* ~ *garden*, jardin sur le toit, *m.* ~ *of the mouth*, voûte palatine, voûte du palais, *f*, palais, *m.* ¶ *v.t*, couvrir. ~**ing**, *n*, toiture, couverture, *f*, faîtage, *m.*

rook, *n*, freux, *m*, corneille; (*chess*) tour, *f.* ~**ery**, *n*, colonie de freux; c. de miséreux, *f.*

room, *n*, pièce; chambre, *f*; cabinet; (*pl.*) appartement; salon, *m*; salle; soute; place, *f*; large, espace, *m.* ~**mate**, compagnon de chambre, *m.* ~**ful**, *n*, chambrée, *f.* ~**y**, *a*, spacieux.

roost, *n*, juchoir, perchoir, *m.* ¶ *v.i*, [se] jucher, percher. ~**er**, *n*, coq, *m.*

root, *n*, racine, *f*; radical, *m.* ¶ *v.i*, s'enraciner; fouiller. ~ *out*, déraciner, extirper, dénicher.

rope, *n*, corde, *f*, cordage; câble, *m*; manœuvre, *f*; chapelet, *m*, glane, *f.* ~ *dancer*, danseur (euse) de corde. ~ *end*, garcette, *f.* ~ *maker*, cordier, *m.* ~ *making & ~ works*, corderie, *f.* ~ *walker*, funambule, *m,f.* ¶ *v.t*, corder. **ropiness** (*wine*) *n*, graisse, *f.* **ropy**, *a*, (*liquid*) filant; (*wine*) gras.

roquet (*croquet*) *v.t*, roquer.

rosary, *n*, rosaire, *m*; (*rose garden*) roseraie, *f.* **rose**, *n*, rose, *f*; (*color*) rose, *m*; (*ceiling*) rosace; (*can*) pomme, *f*; (*pipe*) crépine, *f.* ~ *bud*, bouton de rose, *m.* ~**bush**, rosier, *m.* ~ *grower*, ro-

siériste, *m.* ~ *window*, rose, rosace, *f.* ~**wood**, palissandre, *m.* **roseate**, *a*, rosé, incarnat. **rosemary**, *n*, romarin, *m.* **rosery**, *n*, roseraie, *f.* **rosette**, *n*, rosette; cocarde; (*Arch.*) rosace, *f.*

rosin, *n*, résine; (*for violin*) colophane, *f.*

roster, *n*, contrôle, rôle, *m.*

rostrum, *n*, tribune, *f.*

rosy, *a*, [de] rose, rosé, incarnat, vermeil.

rot, *n*, pourriture; carie, *f.* ¶ (*v.i.*) pourrir; se carier; (*v.t.*) faire pourrir; carier.

rota, *n*, rôle, *m.* **rotary**, *a*, rotatoire, tournant. **rotate**, *v.t. & i*, tourner; rouler. **rotation**, *n*, rotation, *f*; (*in office*) roulement; (*crops*) assolement, *m.* in ~, à tour de rôle, par roulement.

rote, *n*, routine, *f.* by ~, par cœur.

rotten, *a*, pourri; carié; (*egg, etc.*) gâté. ~**ness**, *n*, pourriture; carie, *f.*

rotund, *a*, rond, arrondi; pompeux. **rotunda**, *n*, rotonde, *f.* **rotundity**, *n*, rondeur, rotondité, *f.*

rouge, *n*, rouge, *m.* ~ *et noir*, trente et quarante. ¶ *v.i*, mettre du rouge.

rough†, *a*, grossier; brut; rude; brutal; bourru; raboteux; rugueux; âpre; (*sea*) agitée. in a ~ & ready fashion, à coups de hache, à la serpe, à coups de serpe. ~**cast** (*walls*) *n*, crépi, *m*; (*v.t*) crépir, hourder, ravaler. ~ *draft*, brouillon, *m.* ~ *estimate,* aperçu, *m.* at (or on) a ~ estimate, à vue d'œil, par aperçu. ~**rider**, casse-cou, *m.* ~**shod** (*horse*) ferré à glace. to ride ~*shod* over, fouler aux pieds, traiter avec rudesse. ¶ *n*, apache, *m.* the ~ (*golf*), l'herbe longue, *f.* ~**,** ~ **down,** ~ **out,** ~**hew,** *v.t*, dégrossir, ébaucher. ~**ness,** *n*, aspérité; rudesse; grossièreté; âpreté, *f.*

round, *a*, rond. ~**-shouldered**, voûté. ~ *trip*, aller & retour. ¶ *n*, rond, *m*; (*slice*) rouelle, *f*; (*rung*) échelon, *m*; (*tour*) ronde, tournée; (*applause*) salve, *f*; (*lap*) circuit, *m*; (*sport*) partie; (*Box.*) round, *m.* ~ [*of ammunition*], cartouche, *f.* ¶ *ad*, autour. ~ *about*, alentour. ¶ *pr*, autour de, alentour de. ¶ *v.t*, arrondir. ~ *up*, rafler. **roundabout**, *a*, détourné. **roundelay**, *n*, ronde, *f*. **roundish**, *a*, rondelet. **roundly**, *ad*, rondement. **roundness**, *n*, rondeur, *f*. **roundsman**, *n*, livreur, *m*.

rouse, *v.t*, [r]éveiller; exciter.

rout, *n*, déroute, débandade, *f*. ¶ *v.t*, mettre en déroute, défaire.

route, *n*, route, voie, *f*. ~ *march*, promenade militaire, *f*. ¶ *v.t*, acheminer.

routine, *n*, routine, *f*, train, *m*.

rove, *v.i*, rouler, errer, vagabonder; (*v.t*.) écumer. **rover**, *n*, coureur; (*sea*) forban; (*croquet*) corsaire, *m*. **roving**, *a*, vagabond.

row, *n*, rang, *m*, rangée, *f*; (*of stitches*, *Knit.*, etc.) tour, *m*; haie, *f*; cordon; bruit; tapage, fracas, potin, *m*; promenade en bateau, *f*. *a* ~ *of houses*, une rangée de maisons, des maisons en enfilade, *f.pl*. ¶ *v.i*, ramer, aller à la rame, canoter, nager, voguer. ~[*ing*] *boat*, bateau à rames; bateau de promenade, *m*.

rowdy, *n. & a*, tapageur, *m. & a*.

rowel, *n*, molette, *f*.

rower, *n*, rameur, euse, nageur, canotier, *m*. **rowing**, *n*, canotage, *m*, nage [d'aviron] *f*, l'aviron, *m*.

royal†, *a*, royal. *His*, *Your*, *R~ Highness*, monseigneur, son, votre, altesse royale. ~**ist**, *n. & att*, royaliste, *m,f. & a*. ~**ty**, *n*, royauté; (*rent*) redevance, *f*; (*author's*) droit d'auteur, *m*.

rub, *n*, (*with a cloth*) coup de chiffon; (*fig.*) hic, nœud, *m*, enclouure, *f*. ~ *of the green* (*golf*), risque de jeu, *m*. ¶ *v.t. & i*, frotter; frictionner; (*inscription*) estamper. ~ *down* (*horse*), épousseter, bouchonner. ~ *one's hands*, se frotter les mains. ~ *out*, effacer. ~ *shoulders with*, se frotter à, frayer avec. **rubber**, *n*, frottoir; (*cards*) rob[re] *m*; (*3rd game*) belle, *f*; caoutchouc, *m*; gomme [élastique] *f*. ~ *stamp*, timbre en c., t. humide, *m*. **rubbing**, *n*, frottement, *m*; friction, *f*. *oft. pl*; (*with oil*) onction, *f*; (*copy*) frottis, *m*.

rubbish, *n*, décombres, *m.pl*, détritus, *m*; (*dirt*) immondice; (*trash*) camelote, saleté; (*nonsense*) blague, *f*, fadaises, *f.pl*.

rubble[stone], *n*, blocaille, *f*, moellon, *m*.

rubicund, *a*, rubicond.

rubric, *n*, rubrique, *f*.

ruby, *n*, rubis, *m*. ¶ (*lips*) *a*, vermeilles.

ruck, *n*, pli, godet, *m*.

rucksack, *n*, sac de touriste, s. de montagne, s. d'alpinisme, *m*.

rudder, *n*, gouvernail, *m*.

ruddy, *a*, coloré, rougeaud, rubicond.

rude†, *a*, grossier, malhonnête, malgracieux; rude. ~**ness**, *n*, grossièreté, rudesse, *f*.

rudiment, *n*, rudiment, *m*; (*pl, of a science*, *an art*) éléments, *m.pl*. ~**ary**, *a*, rudimentaire.

rue (*Bot.*) *n*, rue, *f*. ¶ *v.t*, se repentir de. ~**ful**†, *a*, triste.

ruff (*Hist.*, *dress*) *n*, fraise, *f*.

ruffian, *n*, bandit, *m*. ~**ly**, *a*, de brigand.

ruffle, *n*, ruche, *f*. ¶ *v.t*, rider; froisser, chiffonner; (*hair*) ébouriffer.

rug, *n*, tapis de pied, *m*; carpette; descente de lit; (*traveling*) couverture, *f*, plaid, *m*. ~ *work*, tapisserie, *f*.

rugged, *a*, raboteux; rugueux; rocailleux; rude. ~**ness**, *n*, aspérité; rudesse, *f*.

ruin, *n*, ruine, perte, *f*. ¶ *v.t*, ruiner, perdre, abîmer. ~**ous**, *a*, ruineux.

rule, *n*, règle; domination, *f*; empire; (*Typ.*) filet, *m*. *as a* ~, ordinairement. ~ *of thumb*, procédé empirique, *m*; (*att.*) empirique. *by* ~ *of thumb*, empiriquement. ¶ *v.t*, régler; rayer; gouverner; régir; (*v.i.*) gouverner; régner; (*prices*) se pratiquer. **ruler**, *n*, gouvernant; dominateur, *m*; (*for lines*) règle, *f*. **ruling**, *p.a*, dominant; (*price*) pratiqué. ~ *passion*, passion dominante, épée de chevet, *f*. ¶ *n*, réglage, *m*, réglure; décision; (*law*) sentence, *f*.

rum, *n*, rhum, *m*.

rumble, *v.i*, gronder; rouler; (*bowels*) gargouiller. ¶ *n*, grondement, grouillement, *m*.

ruminant, *n. & a*, ruminant, *m. & a*. **ruminate**, *v.i. & t*, ruminer.

rummage, *v.t. & i*, fouiller, farfouiller.

rumor, *n*, rumeur, renommée, *f*,

bruit, on-dit, *m. it is ~ed· that,* le bruit court que.

rump, *n,* croupe, *f; (bird)* croupion, *m; (beef)* culotte. *f.* **~steak,** romsteck, *m.*

rumple, *v.t,* chiffonner, froisser.

rumpus, *n,* potin, chahut, *m;* rébecca, *m. & f. to create a ~,* faire du rébecca.

run, *n,* course; marche; campagne, *f;* cours; parcours, trajet, *m;* roulade; coulée; suite; séquence; *(stocking)* maille, *f;* commun, *m;* descente, ruée; volière, *f;* parc, *m. in the long ~,* à la longue. *~-off (from dead heat),* course de barrage, *f. ~[-up] (Jump.),* course d'élan, *f,* élan, *m.* ¶ *v.i.ir,* chiffonner; accourir; affluer; fonctionner; marcher; *(stockings)* se démailler; circuler; trotter; couler; pleurer, suinter; tourner; rouler; aller; être; *(v.t.ir.)* faire; faire courir; faire marcher; actionner; conduire; [en]courir. *~ about,* faire des allées & venues. *~ against,* heurter. *~ aground,* échouer. *~ along,* longer, border, côtoyer. *~ away,* s'enfuir, se sauver. *~ into,* rencontrer. *~ out of (stock),* manquer de, être à court de. *~ out of gas,* avoir une panne d'essence *ou* une p. sèche. *~ over,* parcourir; déborder. *to be ~ over,* être écrasé. *~ through,* parcourir; feuilleter; transpercer, enferrer, embrocher. *~ to earth,* dépister. *~ up against (pers.),* coudoyer. **runabout,** *n,* coureur, euse; voiturette. *f.* **runaway,** *n. & a,* fugitif, ive, fuyard, e, échappé, e. **rundown,** *a,* épuisé.

rung, *n,* échelon; barreau, *m.*

runner, *n,* coureur, euse; courrier; agent de transmission; *m; (Hort., Bot.)* coulant; *(slider of sledge)* patin, *m.* **running,** *n,* courses, *f.pl;* marche, *f;* roulement; service, *m.* ¶ *p.a,* courant; coulant; cursif; successif, de suite. *~ dive,* plongeon avec élan, *m. ~ water,* eau courante, *f.*

runt, *n,* nabot, *m.*

runway, *n,* piste, *f.*

rupee, *n,* roupie, *f.*

rupture, *n,* rupture; *(Med.)* hernie, *f.* ¶ *v.t,* rompre. *to be ~d,* avoir une hernie.

rural, *a,* rural, champêtre.

ruse, *n,* ruse, *f.*

rush, *n,* jonc, *m;* élan, *m;* ruée; bousculade; presse; chasse, *f;* flot, torrent, *m. ~ chair,* chaise paillée, *f. ~ hours,* heures d'affluence, *f.pl. (TV & cinema) ~es,* épreuves de tournage, *f.pl.* ¶ *v.t,* brusquer; *(v.i.)* se précipiter, se ruer, accourir, foncer.

rusk, *n,* biscotte, *f.*

russet, *a,* roux. ¶ *n,* roux, *m; (apple)* reinette grise, *f.*

Russia, *n,* la Russie. **Russian,** *a,* russe. ¶ *n (pers.)* Russe, *m,f; (language)* le russe.

rust, *n,* rouille, *f. to rub off the ~ from,* dérouiller. ¶ *v.t,* rouiller; *(v.i.)* se r. **rustiness,** *n,* rouillure, *f.* **rustproof,** *a,* inoxydable.

rustic, *a,* rustique, agreste, paysan. ¶ *n,* rustre, paysan, *m.* **rusticate,** *v.i,* être en villégiature.

rustle, *v.i,* frémir, bruire; *(dress)* faire frou-frou.

rusty, *a,* rouillé.

rut, *n, (groove)* ornière, *f; (of animals)* rut, *m.*

ruthless, *a,* impitoyable, acharné, âpre.

rye, *n,* seigle, *m. ~ bread,* pain de seigle, *m.*

S

S, *n. & S hook,* esse, *f,* S, *m.*

sabbath, *n,* sabbat; dimanche, *m.*

sable, *n, (Zool.)* [martre] zibeline; *(fur)* zibeline, *f,* sable; *(Her.)* sable, *m.*

saber, *n,* sabre, *m.* ¶ *v.t,* sabrer.

sabotage, *n,* sabotage, *m.* ¶ *v.t,* saboter. **saboteur,** *n,* saboteur, euse.

saccharin, *n,* saccharine, *f.*

sacerdotal, *a,* sacerdotal.

sachet, *n,* sachet à parfums, sultan, *m.*

sack, *n,* sac, *m.* **~cloth,** *sacking,* toile à sacs, *f,* treillis, *m,* serpillière, *f; (Theol.)* sac, *m. in ~cloth & ashes,* sous le sac & la cendre. *~ race,* course en sacs, *f.* ¶ *v.t,* ensacher; saccager; mettre à sac. **~ful,** *n,* sachée, *f.*

sacrament, *n,* sacrement, *m,* communion, *f.* **~alt,** *a,* sacramentel. **~al,** *n,* sacramental, *m.*

sacred, *a,* sacré; saint; inviolable;

(*song*) religieux; (*concert*) spirituel; (*to the memory of*) consacré. **sacrifice,** *n,* sacrifice, *m.* ¶ *v.t. & i,* sacrifier, immoler. **sacrificial,** *a,* du sacrifice. **sacrilege,** *n. &* **sacrilegious,** *a,* sacrilège, *m. & a.* **sacristy,** *n,* sacristie, *f.* **sacrosanct,** *a,* sacro-saint.

sad, *a,* triste, douloureux, fâcheux. **sadden,** *v.t,* attrister, contrister.

saddle, *n,* selle; (*lathe*) cuirasse, *f;* (*mountain*) col, *m.* ~-backed, ensellé. ~bag, sacoche, *f.* ~bow, arçon, *m.* ~ *horse,* cheval de selle, *m.* ¶ *v.t,* seller; (*pack animal*) embâter; (*fig.*) grever, charger. **saddler,** *n,* sellier, *m.* **saddlery,** *n,* sellerie, *f.*

sadism, *n,* sadisme, *m.* **sadist,** *n,* sadique, *m. & f.* **sadistic,** *a,* sadique. **sadomasochism,** *n,* sadomasochisme, *m.* **sadomasochist,** *a. & n,* sadomasochiste, *m. & f.*

sadly, *ad,* tristement; cruellement. **sadness,** *n,* tristesse, *f.*

safe, *a,* sauf; sûr; sans danger; assuré; de sécurité; (*investment*) sûr, de tout repos, de père de famille; (*arrival*) bonne, heureuse. ~ *& sound,* sain & sauf, bagues sauves. ~ *conduct,* sauf-conduit, *m.* sauvegarde, *f.* ~ *custody,* garde [en dépôt] *f.* ~ *keeping,* sûreté, *f.* ¶ *n,* coffrefort, *m.* ~ *deposit box,* coffre, *m.* ~guard, *n,* sauvegarde, garantie, *f,* palladium, *m;* (*v.t.*) garantir. ~ly, *ad,* en sûreté; sûrement; sans danger; sans accident; (*arrival*) à bon port. ~ty, *n,* sûreté; sécurité, *f;* salut, *m.* ~ *catch,* cran d'arrêt, *m.* ~ *first,* sécurité d'abord. ~ *pin,* épingle de sûreté, é. de nourrice, é. anglaise, *f.* ~ *razor,* rasoir de sûreté, *m.* ~ *valve* (*lit. & fig.*), soupape de sûreté, *f.*

saffron, *n,* safran, *m.*

sag, *n,* fléchissement, *m.* ¶ *v.i,* fléchir, donner.

sagacious, *a,* sagace. **sagacity,** *n,* sagacité, *f.*

sage, *n,* (*pers.*) sage, *m;* (*herb*) sauge, *f.* ¶ *a,* sage.

sago, *n,* sagou, *m.* ~ *palm,* sagou[t]ier, *m.*

said (the) (*law*) *p.a,* ledit.

sail, *n,* voile, toile, (*pl.*) voilure, *f;* (*windmill*) volant, *m;* promenade en bateau, *f.* ~boat, voilier, *m.* ~ *cloth,* toile à voiles, *f.* ~ *maker,* voilier, *m.* ¶ *v.i,* faire voile; naviguer; voguer; marcher, courir; partir; (*v.t.*) faire naviguer; naviguer sur. ~er, *n,* voilier, marcheur, *m.* ~ing, *n,* navigation [à voile] *f;* départ, *m;* partance; marche, *f.* ~ *ship,* navire à voiles, voilier, *m.* ~or, *n,* marin; matelot, *m.* ~ *suit,* costume marin, *m.*

saint, *a,* saint. ¶ *n,* saint, e. ~'s *day,* fête, *f. St. Bernard dog,* chien de Saint-Bernard, *m. Saint Helena,* Sainte-Hélène, *f. Saint Lawrence,* Saint-Laurent, *m. St. Vitus's dance,* danse de Saint-Guy, chorée, *f.* ¶ *v.t,* canoniser. ~ed, *p.p,* saint, canonisé. **saintliness,** *n,* sainteté, *f.* **saintly,** *a,* saint.

sake, *n,* cause, *f;* amour; plaisir; égard, *m. for God's* ~, pour l'amour de Dieu.

sal, *n,* sel, *m.* ~ *ammoniac,* sel ammoniac. ~ *volatile,* alcool ammon aromatique, spiritus aromaticus, *m.*

salaam, *n,* salamalec, *m.*

salable, *a,* vendable, de vente; marchand, vénal.

salacious, *a,* lascif, lubrique.

salad, *n,* salade, *f.* ~ *bowl,* saladier, *m.* ~ *oil,* huile de table, h. comestible, *f.*

Salamanca, *n,* Salamanque, *f.*

salamander, *n,* salamandre, *f.*

salaried, *p.a,* appointé. **salary,** *n,* appointements, *m.pl;* traitement; cachet, *m;* indemnité, *f. to put on a* ~ *basis,* appointer.

sale, *n,* vente, *f;* débit; solde, *m;* liquidation; enchère, *f. for* ~, à vendre. *on* ~, en vente.

Salerno, *n,* Salerne, *f.*

salesman, -woman, *n,* vendeur, euse; (*market*) facteur (de la halle) *m.* ~ship, l'art de vendre, *m.*

Salic law, loi salique, *f.*

salient, *a. & n,* saillant, *a. & m.*

saline, *a,* salin.

saliva, *n,* salive, *f.* **salivate,** *v.i,* saliver.

sallow, *a,* jaunâtre.

sally, *n,* (*Mil.*) sortie, saillie; (*wit*) saillie, *f,* trait d'esprit, *m,* boutade, *f.*

salmon, *n,* saumon, (*young*) saumoneau, *m.* ~ *pink*, rose saumon, *m.* ~ *trout*, truite saumonée, *f.*

Salonica, *n*, Salonique, *f.*

saloon, *n*, bar, estaminet, *m.*

salt, *n*, sel, *m.* ~*cellar*, salière, *f.* ~ *lake*, lac salé, *m.* ~ *pork*, [porc] salé, *m.* ~ *provisions*, salaisons, *f.pl.* ~ *spoon*, pelle à sel, *f.* ~ *water*, eau salée, e. saline, *f.* ~*water fish*, poisson de mer, *m*; (*caught & fresh*) marée, *f.* ~*water fishing*, pêche en mer, *f. smelling* ~*s*, sels volatiles, *m.pl.* ¶*v.t*, saler. ~*ing*, *n*, salage, *m*; salaison, *f.* **saltern**, *n*, marais salant, *m.* **saltpeter**, *n*, salpêtre, nitre, *m.* **salty**, *a*, salé.

salubrious, *a*, salubre.

salutary†, *a*, salutaire. **salutation**, *n*, salutation, *f*, salut, *m.* **salute**, *n*, salut; (*guns*) salut, *m*, salve, *f.* ¶*v.t*, saluer.

salvage, *n*, sauvetage, *m.* ¶*v.t*, sauver. **salvation**, *n*, salut, *m.* *S*~ *Army*, Armée du Salut, *f.* **salve**, *n*, onguent, *m*; pommade, *f.* ¶ (*fig.*) *v.t*, calmer.

salver, *n*, plateau, *m.*

salvo, *n*, salve, *f.*

Salzburg, *n*, Salzbourg, *m.*

same, *a*, même. *it's all the* ~ *to me*, cela m'est égal. ~*ness*, *n*, identité; monotonie, *f.*

sample, *n*, échantillon, *m.* ¶*v.t*, échantillonner; (*taste wines*) déguster. **sampler**, *n*, modèle de broderie, *m.*

sanatorium, *n*, sanatorium, *m.*

sanctify, *v.t*, sanctifier. **sanctimonious**†, *a*, béat, cagot, papelard. **sanction**, *n*, sanction; consécration, *f.* ¶*v.t*, sanctionner; consacrer. **sanctity**, *n*, sainteté; religion, *f.* **sanctuary**, *n*, sanctuaire; asile; réserve, *f.* **sanctum**, *n*, le saint des saints; sanctuaire, *m.*

sand, *n*, sable; sablon, *m*; (*pl.*) plage, *f.* ~ *bag*, sac à terre, *m.* ~ *bank*, banc de sable, ensablement, *m.* ~ *blast*, jet de sable, *m.* ~ *flats*, relais, *m.* ~ *fly*, simulie, *f.* ~ *glass*, sablier, *m*, horloge de sable, *f.* ~ *hill*, dune, *f.* ~*paper*, *n*, papier de verre, *m*; (*v.t.*) *v.t*, ~*piper*, bécasseau, *m.* ~ *pit*, sablière; sablonnière, *f.* ~*stone*, grès, *m.* ~*stone quarry*, gresserie, *f.* ¶*v.t*, sabler.

sandal, *n*, sandale, *f.* ~ [*wood*], [bois de] santal, *m.*

sandwich, *n*, sandwich, *m.* ~ *man*, homme-sandwich, *m.*

sandy, *a*, sablonneux. ~ *hair*, chevelure blond roux, *f.*

sane, *a*, sain, rassis.

sanguinary, *a*, sanguinaire. **sanguine**, *a*, optimiste; plein d'espérance; (*full-blooded*, *Hist.*) sanguin.

sanitary, *a*, sanitaire; hygiénique. ~ *inspector*, inspecteur sanitaire, *m.* ~ *napkin*, serviette hygiénique, *f.* **sanitate**, *v.t*, assainir. **sanitation**, *n*, assainissement, *m*; hygiène, *f.*

sanity, *n*, raison, *f*; bon sens, *m*; rectitude, *f.*

sanserif, *a*, sans empattement.

Santa Claus, le père Noël, le bonhomme Noël.

sap, *n*, sève; lymphe; (*Mil.*) sape, *f.* ~*wood*, aubier, *m.* ¶*v.t*, saper. **sapling**, *n*, plant, *m.* **sapper**, *n*, [sapeur] mineur, *m.*

sapphire, *n*, saphir, *m.*

sappy, *a*, plein de sève.

Saragossa, *n*, Saragosse, *f.*

Saratoga [*trunk*], *n*, [malle] chapelière, *f.*

sarcasm, *n*, sarcasme, *m.* **sarcastic**, *a*, sarcastique.

sarcophagus, *n*, sarcophage, *m.*

sardine, *n*, sardine, *f.*

Sardinia, *n*, la Sardaigne. **Sardinian**, *a*, sarde. ¶*n*, Sarde, *m,f.*

sardonic, *a*, sardonique.

sarsaparilla, *n*, salsepareille, *f.*

sarsenet, *n*, florence, *m.*

sash, *n*, ceinture; écharpe, *f*; (*window*) châssis, *m.* ~ *window*, fenêtre à guillotine, *f.*

Satan, *n*, Satan, *m.* ~**ic**, *a*, satanique.

satchel, *n*, cartable, *m*; gibecière, sacoche, *f.*

sate, *v.t*, rassasier.

sateen, *n*, satinette, *f.*

satellite, *n*, satellite, *m.*

satiate, *v.t*, rassasier. **satiety**, *n*, satiété, *f.*

satin, *n*, satin, *m.* ~ *stitch* (*Emb.*), passé, *m.* ~ *wood*, bois de satin, *m.* ~**y**, *a*, satiné.

satire, *n*, satire, *f.* **satiric & ~al**, *a*, satirique. **satirist**, *n*, satirique, *m.* **satirize**, *v.t*, satiriser.

satisfaction, *n*, satisfaction; raison, *f.* **satisfactorily**, *ad*, d'une

manière satisfaisante. **satisfactory**, *a*, satisfaisant. **satisfy**, *v.t*, satisfaire, satisfaire à; contenter.
saturate, *v.t*, saturer.
Saturday, *n*, samedi, *m*.
saturnalia, *n.pl*, saturnales, *f.pl*.
saturnine, *a*, sombre; (*Chem.*) saturnin.
satyr, *n*, satyre, *m*.
sauce, *n*, sauce, *f*. ~ *boat*, saucière, *f*. ~ *ladle*, cuiller à sauce, *f*. ~*pan*, casserole, *f*; poêlon, *m*. **saucer**, *n*, soucoupe, *f*. *flying* ~, s. volante, *f*. **saucy** *a*, gamin; impertinent.
sauerkraut, *n*, choucroute, *f*.
saunter, *v.i*, flâner. ~**ing**, *n*, flânerie, *f*.
sausage, *n*, (*fresh*) saucisse, *f*; (*smoked*) saucisson, *m*. ~ *skin*, ~ *case*, peau à saucisses, *f*.
savage†, *a*, sauvage; féroce, farouche. ¶*n*, sauvage, *m,f*, sauvagesse, *f*, cannibale, *m*. ~**ry**, *n*, sauvagerie; férocité, *f*.
savant, *n*, savant, *m*.
save, *v.t*, sauver; épargner; ménager; économiser; gagner; capter; (*v.i.*) économiser. ¶*pr*, sauf sinon, hormis, près. **saving**, *n*, épargne; économie, *f*. ~*s bank*, caisse d'épargne, *f*. **the Saviour**, le Sauveur.
savory (*Bot.*) *n*, sarriette, *f*. **savor**, *n*, saveur, *f*. **to** ~ **of**, tenir de, sentir le, la. **savory**, *a*, savoureux. ~ *herbs*, fines herbes, *f.pl*. ~ *omelet*, omelette aux fines herbes, *f*.
Savoy, *n*, la Savoie. *s*~, chou de Milan, *m*.
saw, *n*, scie, *f*; dicton, adage, *m*. *hand*~, égoïne, *f*. *power*~, scie mécanique, *f*. ~*dust*, sciure, *f*. ~*mill*, scierie, *f*. ¶*v.t.ir*, scier; débiter. ~ *off*, scier. ~**ing**, *n*, sciage, *m*.
saxhorn, *n*, saxhorn, *m*.
saxifrage, *n*, saxifrage, *f*.
Saxon, *a*, saxon. ¶*n*, Saxon, ne. **Saxony**, *n*, la Saxe.
saxophone, *n*, saxophone, *m*.
say, *n*, mot, *m*; voix, *f*. ¶*v.t. & i. ir*, dire; réciter; parler. *as they* ~, comme on dit. *you don't* ~ *sol* pas possible! **saying**, *n*, mot, dire; dicton, adage, *m*. ~*s & doings*, faits & dits, *m.pl*.
scab, *n*, croûte, *f*; (*Vet.*) gale; (*Hort.*) rogne, *f*.
scabbard, *n*, fourreau, *m*.

scabby, *a*, scabieux, galeux, rogneux.
scaffold, *n*, échafaud, *m*. ~**ing**, *n*, échafaudage, *m*.
scald, *n*, brûlure, *f*. ¶*v.t*, échauder, ébouillanter; blanchir.
scale, *n*, échelle; (*Mus.*) gamme, *f*; barême; tarif; (*pan*) plateau, bassin, *m*; (*pl*, *lancet*) châsse; écaille, paillette; incrustation; (*s. or pl.*) balance; bascule, *f*. ~ *maker*, balancier, *m*. ¶*v.t*, (*wall*) escalader; (*boiler*) piquer; (*v.i.*) s'écailler. **scaly**, *a*, écailleux.
scallion, *n*, ciboule, *f*.
scallop, *n*, (*Mol.*) pétoncle; coquillage, (*edging*) feston, *m*. ¶*v.t*, festonner.
scalp, *n*, cuir chevelu, *m*; (*trophy*) chevelure, *f*. ~ *massage*, friction, *f*. ¶*v.t*, scalper.
scalpel, *n*, scalpel, *m*.
scamp, *n*, chenapan, vaurien, polisson, [mauvais] garnement, *m*. ¶*v.t*, brocher, bâcler.
scamper away, s'enfuir en courant, détaler.
scan, *v.t*, scruter, éplucher; (*verse*) scander; scanner. ~**ner**, *n*, scanneur, *m*.
scandal, *n*, scandale, éclat, *m*; honte; médisance, *f*, cancan, la contar; pétard, *m*. ~*monger*, médisant, e; mauvaise langue, *f*. ~**ize**, *v.t*, scandaliser. ~**ous†**, *a*, scandaleux.
Scandinavia, *n*, la Scandinavie. **Scandinavian**, *a*, scandinave. ¶*n*, Scandinave, *m,f*.
scansion, *n*, scansion, *f*.
scant[y], *a*, exigu; étriqué; maigre; faible; pauvre; mesquin; (*attire*) sommaire.
scape (*Bot.*) *n*, hampe, *f*. ~*goat*, bouc émissaire, souffre-douleur, *m*. ~*grace*, [mauvais] garnement, mauvais sujet, *m*.
scar, *n*, cicatrice, couture, balafre, *f*. ¶*v.t*, cicatriser, couturer, balafrer.
scarab, *n*, scarabée, *m*.
scarce, *a*, rare; (*time*) cher. ~**ly**, *ad*, à peine; presque. **scarcity**, *n*, rareté; disette, *f*.
scare, *n*, panique, transe, *f*. ¶*v.t*, épouvanter, effrayer, effarer. ~*crow*, *n*, épouvantail, *m*.
scarf, *n*, écharpe, *f*, cache-nez, *m*.
scarify, *v.t*, scarifier.
scarlatina, *n*. or scarlet fever,

[fièvre] scarlatine, *f.* **scarlet**, *n.* & *a,* écarlate, *f.* & *a.*

carp, *n,* escarpe, *f.*

catheless, *a,* indemne. **scathing,** *a,* cinglant, sanglant. ~ *attack* (*fig.*), jeu de massacre, *m.*

scatter, *v.t,* disperser, éparpiller; semer. ~**brained,** *a,* écervelé.

scavenge, *v.t,* balayer. **scavenger,** *n,* boueux, balayeur; animal qui se nourrit de charogne, *m.*

scenario, *n,* scénario, *m.* **scene,** *n,* scène, *f;* spectacle; tableau; théâtre, *m. behind the* ~*s,* dans la coulisse. ~ *painter,* peintre de décors, décorateur, *m.* ~ *shifter,* machiniste, *m.* ~ *shifting,* changement de décor[ation] *m.* **scenery,** *n,* paysages, *m.pl;* (*Theat.*) décors, *m.pl,* décoration, *f.* **scenic,** *a,* scénique. ~ *railway,* montagnes russes, *f.pl.*

scent, *n,* parfum, *m;* odeur; senteur, *f;* flair, fumet, nez; vent, *m,* piste, voie, *f.* ~ *bottle,* flacon à odeur, *m. to throw off the* ~, dépister. ¶ *v.t,* parfumer, embaumer; flairer, subodorer. ~**ed,** *a,* parfumé, odorant.

scepter, *n,* sceptre, *m.*

Schaffhausen, *n,* Schaffhouse, *f.*

schedule, *n,* horaire; (*work*) plan, (*price*) tarif, *m;* annexe, *f;* bordereau, *m.*

scheme, *n,* projet, plan; cadre, *m,* combinaison, *f.* ¶ *v.t,* projeter; machiner; (*v.i.*) former des projets; intriguer. **schemer,** *n,* homme à projets, *m;* intrigant, *e.* **scheming,** *n,* manœuvres, *f.pl.*

schism, *n,* schisme, *m.*

schist, *n,* schiste, *m.* ~**ose,** *a,* schisteux.

scholar, *n,* écolier, ère; savant, érudit, *m.* ~**ly,** *a,* savant, érudit. ~**ship,** *n,* savoir, *m,* érudition; bourse, *f.* **scholastic,** *a,* scolastique. **school,** *n,* école; classe, *f;* collège; conservatoire; (*of fish*) banc, *m.* ~ *boarding* ~, pensionnat, *m.* ~ *book,* livre de classe, l. classique, l. scolaire, *m.* ~**boy,** ~**girl,** écolier, ère, lycéen, ne, collégien, ne. ~**fellow,** camarade d'école, *m,f,* condisciple, *m.* ~**master,** ~**mistress,** instituteur, trice. ~ *room,* [salle de] classe, *f.* **schooling,** *n,* instruction, *f.*

schooner, *n,* schooner, *m,* goélette, *f.*

sciatic, *a.* & **sciatica,** *n,* sciatique, *a.* & *f.*

science, *n.* science, *f.* **scientific**†, *a,* scientifique; (*instruments*) de précision. **scientist,** *n,* savant, homme de science, *m.*

Scilly Islands *or* **Isles,** îles Scilly, îles Sorlingues, *f.pl.*

scimitar, *n,* cimeterre, *m.*

scintillate, *v.i,* scintiller.

scion, *n,* (*Hort.*) scion; (*pers.*) rejeton, *m.*

scissors, *n.pl,* ciseaux, *m.pl. with* ~ & *paste* (*fig.*), à coups de ciseaux.

sclerosis, *n,* sclérose, *f.*

scoff at, se railler de; mépriser. **scoffer,** *n,* moqueur, euse, railleur, euse. **scoffing,** *n,* moquerie, *f.*

scold, *n,* grondeuse, mégère, *f.* ¶ *v.t,* gronder, tancer, semoncer, quereller; (*v.i.*) criailler.

scoop, *n,* pelle; main; cuiller; casse; écope, *f;* (*journalism*) article en exclusivité, *m.* ~ *out,* caver, vider; écoper.

scope, *n,* étendue, *f,* champ, *m;* latitude, *f;* cadre, *m,* portée; carrière, *f;* essor, *m.*

scorch, *v.t,* brûler, rôtir, roussir.

score, *n,* coche; strie, *f;* écot; point, *m,* marque, *f;* compte des points; c. des coups, *m;* (*Mus.*) partition; vingtaine, *f.* ¶ *v.t,* cocher; rayer; (*game*) marquer; (*Mus.*) orchestrer. **scorer,** *n,* marqueur, euse; pointeur, *m.*

scoria, *n,* scorie, *f.*

scoring, *n,* pointage, *m;* orchestration, *f.*

scorn, *n,* mépris, dédain, *m.* ¶ *v.t,* mépriser, dédaigner. ~**er,** *n,* contempteur, trice. ~**ful**†, *a,* dédaigneux.

scorpion, *n,* scorpion, *m.*

Scotch, *a,* écossais; d'Écosse. ~**man,** -**woman,** Écossais, e. *the* ~, les Écossais, *m.pl.* ~ *mist,* brouillasse, *f.*

scot-free, *a,* indemne; impuni.

Scotland, *n,* l'Écosse, *f.* **Scottish,** *a,* écossais.

scoundrel, *n,* scélérat, e, gredin, e.

scour, *n,* chasse [d'eau] *f.* ¶ *v.t,* donner une chasse à; dégraisser, décaper; (*seas*) écumer; (*country*) battre.

scourge, *n*, (*whip*) martinet; (*plague*) fléau, *m*. ¶ *v.t*, flageller.

scout, *n*, éclaireur; (*boy*) scout, *m*; (*warship*) vedette, *f*. ~ *master*, chef éclaireur, c. scout, *m*. ~ *mistress*, cheftaine, *f*. ¶ *v.i*, aller à la découverte; (*v.t.*) repousser avec mépris.

scowl, *v.i*, froncer le sourcil. ¶ *n*, froncement de sourcils, *m*.

scrag, *n*, (*mutton*) collet; (*pers.*) squelette, *m*. ~ *end*, bout saigneux, *m*. **scraggy**, *a*, décharné.

scramble, *n*, mêlée; (*for place, etc.*) curée, *f*. ~*d eggs*, œufs brouillés, *m.pl*. **scrambler**, *n*, (*code*) brouilleur, *m*.

scrap, *n*, bout, morceau; chiffon, *m*; (*metal*) déchets, débris, *m.pl*; (*pl.*) restes, *m.pl*. ~*book*, album, *m*. ~ *iron*, ferraille, *f*. ¶ *v.t*, mettre au rebut; se débarrasser de.

scrape, *v.t*, gratter; racler; décrotter; (*golf*) érafler. ¶ *n*, embarras, *m*. **scraper**, *n*, grattoir; racloir, *m*; curette, *f*; (*mat*) décrottoir, *m*. **scrapings**, *n.pl*, raclure; (*savings*) gratte, *f*.

scratch, *n*, égratignure, *f*; coup de griffe, *m*; rayure, *f*; (*sport*) scratch, *m*. ¶ *v.t*, gratter; rayer; effleurer; (*sport*) rayer de l'épreuve. ~ *out*, gratter, raturer.

scrawl, *n*, griffonnage, *m*, patarafe, *f*. ¶ *v.t*, & *i*, griffonner.

scream & **screech**, *n*, cri, *m*. ¶ *v.i*. & *t*, crier. **screech** *owl*, chat-huant, *m*.

screed, *n*, tartine, *f*.

screen, *n*, écran; paravent; rideau; (*choir*) clôture, grille, *f*; crible, *m*, claie, *f*. ~ *door*, contreporte, *f*. ~*writer*, dialogiste, *m*. *on* ~, dans le champs. ¶ *v.t*, abriter; murer; soustraire; cribler; (*movies*) présenter à l'écran.

screw, *n*, vis; hélice. ~*-capped bottle*, flacon à couvercle vissé, *m*. ~*driver*, tournevis, *m*. ~ *eye*, piton, *m*. ¶ *v.t*, visser.

screwball, *n*, loufoque, *m*. ¶ *a*, loufoque, maboul, e.

scribble, *n*, griffonnage, *m*. ¶ *v.t*, griffonner; (*v.i*, *of author*) écrivailler. **scribbler**, *n*, griffonneur, euse; écrivassier, ère, folliculaire, *m*. **scribe**, *n*, scribe, *m*.

scrimmage, *n*, mêlée; bousculade, *f*.

scrip, *n*, titre provisoire; titre, *m*.

script, *n*, scénario, *m*. *shooting* ~, découpage, *m*. ~*writer*, *n* scénariste, *m*.

Scripture, *n. oft. pl*, l'Écriture, *f oft. pl*.

scrofula, *n*, scrofules, *f.pl*. **scrofulous**, *a*, scrofuleux.

scroll, *n*, rouleau, *m*; volute, *f*.

scrub (*bush*) *n*, broussailles, *f.pl*. ¶ *v.t*, brosser; laver, lessiver. *scrubbing brush*, brosse à laver, *f*.

scruff of the neck, peau du cou *f*, collet, *m*.

scrunch, *v.t*, croquer. ¶ *i*, croc!

scrummage, *n*, mêlée; bousculade, *f*.

scruple, *n*, scrupule, *m*. ~ *to*, se faire scrupule de. **scrupulous†**, *a*, scrupuleux, religieux.

scrutineer, *n*, scrutateur, *m*. **scrutinize**, *v.t*, scruter. **scrutiny**, *n*, examen, *m*.

scuffle, *n*, rixe, bagarre, batterie *f*. ¶ *v.i*, se bousculer; se battre.

scull, *n*, aviron de couple, *m*; (*stern oar*) godille, *f*. ¶ *v.t*, godiller; (*v.i.*) ramer en couple, nager en couple. ~*er*, *n*, rameur de couple, *m*.

scullery, *n*, lavoir [de cuisine] *m*

scullion, *n*, marmiton fouille-au-pot, *m*.

sculptor, *n*, sculpteur, *m*. **sculptress**, *n*, femme sculpteur, *f*. **sculpture**, *n*, sculpture, *f*. ¶ *v.t*, sculpter.

scum, *n*, écume, crasse; (*fig.*) écume, lie, *f*.

scumble, *n*, frottis, glacis, *m*. ¶ *v.t*, frotter, glacer.

scupper, *n*, dalot, *m*.

scurrilous, *a*, outrageant, ordurier.

scurvy, *n*, scorbut, *m*. ¶ *a*, vilain, méprisable.

scutcheon, *n*, écusson, *m*.

scuttle, *n*, (*coal*) seau; (*Naut.*) hublot, *m*. ¶ *v.t*, saborder.

scythe, *n*, faux, *f*.

sea, *n*, mer, *f*. *on the high* ~*s*, sur la haute mer. *open* ~, pleine mer ~*board*, littoral, *m*. ~*coast*, côte de la mer, *f*. ~ *cow*, lamantin, *m* ~*farer*, homme de mer, *m*. ~*faring people*, peuple navigateur, *m*

~ *fishing*, pêche en mer, *f.* ~*go-ing* (ship), de mer. ~ *gull*, mouette, *f*, goéland, *m.* ~ *horse*, cheval marin, hippocampe, *m.* to have got one's ~ *legs*, avoir le pied marin. ~ *level*, niveau de la mer, *m.* ~ *lion*, lion marin, *m*, otarie, *f.* ~*man*, marin, homme de mer, matelot; (*skilful*) manœuvrier, *m.* in a ~*manlike manner*, en bon marin. ~ *nymph*, nymphe de la mer, Néréide, *f.* ~ *plane*, hydravion, *m.* ~ *scape*, marine, *f.* ~*shore*, rivage de la mer, *m.* ~*sickness*, mal de mer, *m.* to be ~*sick*, avoir le m. de m. ~*side*, bord de la mer, *m.* ~*side resort*, plage, station balnéaire, *f.* ~ *urchin*, oursin, hérisson de mer, *m.* ~ *wall*, digue, *f.* ~*weed*, plante marine, algue, *f*, varech, goémon, *m.* ~*worthy*, en [bon] état de navigabilité.

seal, *n*, sceau; cachet, *m*; (*bottle*) capsule, *f*; (*Zool.*) phoque, *m.* ~*skin*, peau de phoque, *f.* ¶ *v.t*, sceller; cacheter; boucher. ~*ed book* (*fig.*), lettre close, *f.* ~*ing wax*, cire à cacheter, *f.*

seam, *n*, couture; (*Geol.*) couche, *f*, gisement, *m.* ~ *stitch* (*Need.*), [point de] surjet, *m.* ¶ *v.t*, couturer. ~*less*, *a*, sans couture. **seamstress**, *n*, couturière, *f.* *seamy side* (lit. & fig.), envers, *m.*

seance, *n*, séance de spiritisme, *f.*

seaplane, *n*, hydravion, *m.* ~ *base*, hydrobase, *f.*

sear, *a*, desséché, fané. ¶ *v.t*, brûler; cautériser.

search, *n*, recherche, *f*. oft. pl; (*law*) perquisition, *f.* ~*light*, projecteur, *m*; lampe de poche, *f.* ~ *warrant*, mandat de perquisition, *m.* ¶ *v.t*, scruter. ~ *for*, [re]chercher. ~*er*, *n*, chercheur, euse, fouilleur, *m.* ~*ing*, *a*, pénétrant; scrutateur.

season, *n*, saison, *f*, temps, *m.* ~ *ticket*, carte d'abonnement, *f.* *slack* ~, saison creuse, *f.* ¶ *v.t*, assaisonner, relever; (*wood*) sécher; (*fig.*) aguerrir. ~*able*, *a*, de saison; opportun. ~*ably*, *ad*, à propos. ~*ing* (*Cook.*) *n*, assaisonnement, *m*; (*of a salad*) garniture, fourniture, *f.*

seat, *n*, siège, *m*; place; place assise; stalle, *f*; chef-lieu, *m*; charge; séance, *f*; office; foyer;

château; banc, *m*; banquette; chaise, *f*; repos; (*trousers chair*) fond, *m*; assiette; (*on horse*) tenue, *f.* ¶ *v.t*, asseoir.

secede, *v.i*, faire scission, faire sécession.

secluded, *p.a*, retiré. **seclusion**, *n*, retraite; réclusion, *f.*

second†, *a*, second; deuxième; deux; (*cousin*) issu(e) de germain. ~ *finger*, doigt du milieu, médius, *m.* ~*hand* (*d'occasion*; de seconde main. ~*hand bookseller*, bouquiniste, *m.* ~*hand dealer*, revendeur, euse, brocanteur, euse. ~ *lieutenant*, sous-lieutenant, *m.* one's ~ *self*, un autre soi-même. on ~ *thoughts*, réflexion faite. [on] the ~ *of September*, le deux septembre. ¶ *n*, second, *m*; deuxième, *m,f*; (*Box.*) second, soigneur; (*duel*) témoin, *m*; (*time*) seconde, *f.* ~ *hand*, aiguille des secondes, *f.* ¶ *v.t*, seconder; appuyer. ~*ary*, *a*, secondaire. ~ *school*, école secondaire, *f*, lycée, *m.*

secrecy, *n*, secret, *m*; discrétion, *f.* **secret**, *a*, secret; caché; dérobé. ¶ *n*, secret, *m.* **secretary**, *n*, secrétaire, *m.* ~ *bird*, serpentaire, secrétaire, *m.* ~*ship* & **secretariat**, *n*, secrétariat; ministère, *m.* **secrete**, *v.t*, cacher; (*physiology*) sécréter. **secretion**, *n*, sécrétion, *f.* **secretive**, *a*, dissimulé, cachottier. **secretly**, *ad*, secrètement, en cachette; sourdement.

sect, *n*, secte, *f.* ~*arian*, *n.* & *a*, sectaire, *m.* & *att.*

section, *n*, section; coupe, *f*; profil; fer; tronçon; article, *m*, rubrique, *f.* ~*al*, *a*, démontable; (*iron*) profilé; (*view*) en coupe. **sector**, *n*, secteur, *m.*

secular†, *a*, séculier; profane; (*100*) séculaire.

secure†, *a*, sûr; à l'abri. ¶ *v.t*, mettre à l'abri; assurer; garantir; asseoir; fixer; obtenir. **security**, *n*, sécurité; sûreté; assiette; garantie; assurance; caution, *f*; cautionnement; titre, *m*; valeur, *f.*

sedan, *n*, (*auto*) berlin; (*chair*) chaise à porteurs, *f.*

sedate†, *a*, posé, rassis. **sedative**, *n.* & *a*, sédatif, calmant, *m.* & *a.* **sedentary**, *a*, sédentaire.

sedge, *n*, laîche, *f.*

sediment, *n*, sédiment, dépôt, *m.*

sedition, n, sédition, f. **seditious**†, a, séditieux.

seduce, v.t, séduire. ~ *from duty*, débaucher. **seducer,** n, séducteur, trice. **seduction,** n, séduction, f. **seductive,** a, séduisant.

sedulous, a, assidu. ~**ly,** ad, assidûment.

see, n, siège [épiscopal] m, chaire, f, évêché, m.

see, v.t. & i. ir, voir; regarder; reconduire; s'occuper; veiller. ~ *about*, s'occuper de. ~ *home*, reconduire. ~ *through*, pénétrer. ¶ (*vide*) v.imperative, voir, voyez.

seed, n, semence; graine, f; grain; (*fig.*) germe, m. ~ *pearls*, semence de perles. ~ *time*, semailles, f.pl. ¶ v.i, grener, s'égrener. ~ *the players* (*Ten.*), sélectionner les têtes de séries. ~**ling,** n, jeune plant, sauvageon, (*pl.*) semis, m. **seedsman,** n, grainier, ère.

seeing, n, vision, f. ~ *that*, vu que, attendu que, puisque.

seek, v.t. & i. ir, chercher, rechercher. ~**er,** n, chercheur, euse.

seem, v.i, sembler, paraître. **seeming,** n, paraître, m. *the* ~ & *the real*, l'être & le paraître. ¶ p.a, apparent. **seemingly,** ad, en apparence. **seemly,** a, [bien]séant.

seer, n, prophète, m.

seep, v.i, suinter; filtrer.

seesaw, n, bascule, balançoire, f. ¶ v.i, basculer, se balancer.

seethe, v.i, bouillonner; grouiller.

segment, n, segment, m.

segregate, v.t, séparer. **segregation,** n, ségrégation, f.

seine (*net*) n, seine, f.

seismic, a, sismique. **seismograph,** n, sismographe, m.

seize, v.t, saisir, arrêter, prendre, s'emparer de; (v.i, *Mach.*) gripper. **seizure,** n, saisie, f; arrêt, m; attaque de paralysie, f.

seldom, ad, rarement.

select, a, chosi; bien composé. ~ *party*, petit comité, m. ¶ v.t, choisir; (*sport*) sélectionner. ~**ion,** n, choix, m; sélection, f; recueil, m; (*pl. from writings*) morceaux choisis, m.pl.

self, n, personne, f; moi-même; moi, m; -même. ~-*centered,* ego-centriste. ~-*contained*, indépendant. ~-*control,* empire sur soi-même, m, maîtrise de soi, f. ~-*defense,* légitime défense, f. ~-*denial,* abnégation, f, renoncement, m. ~-*esteem,* amour-propre, m. ~-*government,* autonomie, f. ~-*importance,* suffisance, f. ~-*made man,* fils de ses œuvres, m. ~-*possession,* sang-froid, aplomb, m, ~-*reliance,* confiance en soi, f. ~-*respect,* amour-propre, m. ~-*sacrifice,* dévouement, m. ~-*satisfied,* béat. ~-*service,* libre service, m. ~-*styled,* soi-disant, a.inv. ~-*taught,* autodidacte. ~-*willed,* entier, opiniâtre, volontaire.

selfish†, a, égoïste, intéressé, personnel. ~**ness,** n, égoïsme, m.

sell, v.t.ir, vendre; débiter; (v.i.ir,) se vendre, s'écouler. ~ *off*, liquider, solder. **seller,** n, vendeur, euse.

seltzer, n, eau de Seltz, f.

selvage, -edge, n, lisière, f.

semaphore, n, sémaphore, m.

semblance, n, semblant, m, apparence, f.

semi, prefix: ~*breve,* ronde, f. ~*circle,* demi-cercle, m. ~*colon,* point & virgule, point-virgule, m. ~*demisemiquaver,* quadruple croche, f. ~*detached,* jumelle. ~*final,* demi-finale, f. ~*official,* semi-officielle, officieux. ~*quaver,* double croche, f. ~*tone,* demi-ton, m. ~*weekly,* a, bihebdomadaire.

seminary, n, séminaire, m.

Semitic, a, sémitique.

semolina, n, semoule, f.

senate, n, sénat, m. **senator,** n, sénateur, m.

send, v.t. & i. ir, envoyer; expédier; remettre. ~ *away* & ~ *back*, renvoyer. ~ *for*, envoyer chercher, faire appeler. ~ *to sleep*, endormir. ~**er,** n, envoyeur, euse, expéditeur, trice.

Senegal, n, le Sénégal.

senile, n, sénile. ~ *decay*, décrépitude, caducité, f. **senility,** n, sénilité, f.

senior, a, aîné; ancien; principal; chef. ¶ n, aîné, e; père, m; doyen, ne; (*sports*) senior, m. ~**ity,** n, aînesse; ancienneté, f.

senna, n, séné, m.

sensation, n, sensation; impression, f. ~**al,** a, sensationnel. ~ *affairs*, drame, m. **sense,** n, sens;

sentiment, *m*; sensation, *f*; esprit, *m*; raison, *f*; bons sens, sens commun, *m*; acception, part, *f*. ¶ *v.t*, entrevoir. ~less, *a*, insensé; sans connaissance. **sensibility**, *n*, sensibilité, *f*. **sensible**, *a*, sensé, sage; sensible. **sensibly**, *ad*, sensément. **sensitive**, *a*, sensible; sensitif; tendre; susceptible; chatouilleux. **sensitivity**, *n*, sensibilité, *f*. **sensitized** (*Phot.*) *a*, sensible.

sensory, *a*, sensoriel, ielle.

sensual†, *a*, sensuel, charnel. ~ist, *n*, sensualiste, *m.f*. ~ity, *n*, sensualité, *f*.

sentence, *n*, sentence, *f*, jugement, *m*; (*Gram.*) phrase, *f*. *death* ~, peine capitale, *f*. ¶ *v.t*, condamner. **sententious†**, *a*, sentencieux.

sentient, *a*, sensible; conscient. **sentiment**, *n*, sentiment, *m*. ~al†, *a*, sentimental. ~ality, *n*, sentimentalité, sensiblerie, *f*.

sentinel, *n*, sentinelle, *f*. **sentry**, *n*, sentinelle, *f*, factionnaire, *m*; (*mounted*) vedette, *f*. ~ *box*, guérite, *f*. ~ *duty*, faction, *f*.

separate†, *a*, séparé; distinct; à part. ~ *cell system*, emprisonnement cellulaire, *m*. *at* ~ *tables* (meal), par petites tables. ¶ *v.t*, séparer. **separation**, *n*, séparation, *f*. **separatism**, *n*, séparatisme, *m*. **separatist**, *n*, séparatiste, *m. & f*.

sepia, *n*, sépia, *f*.

September, *n*, septembre, *m*.

septet[te], *n*, septuor, *m*.

septic, *a*, septique. ~ *tank*, fosse s., *f*.

septum, *n*, cloison, *f*.

sepulchral, *a*, sépulcral. **sepulcher**, *n*, sépulcre, *m*.

sequel, *n*, suite; conséquence, *f*. **sequence**, *n*, suite, succession; (*cards*) séquence, *f*.

sequestered, *p.p*, retiré, écarté. **sequestration** (*law*) *n*, séquestre, *m*.

seraglio, *n*, sérail, *m*.

seraph, *n*, séraphin, *m*. ~ic, *a*, séraphique.

Serbia, *n*, la Serbie. **Serb[ian]**, *a*, serbe. ¶ *n*. (*pers.*) Serbe, *m,f*; (*language*) le serbe. **Serbo-Croatian**, *n*, (*language*) serbo-croate, *m*.

sere, *a*, desséché, fané.

serenade, *n*, sérénade, *f*. ¶ *v.t*, donner une sérénade à.

serene, *a*, serein. **serenity**, *n*, sérénité, *f*.

serf, *n*, serf, *m*, serve, *f*. ~dom, *n*, servage, *m*.

serge, *n*, serge, *f*.

sergeant, *n*, sergent; (*cavalry*) maréchal des logis; (*police*) brigadier, *m*. ~ *major*, adjudant; maréchal des logis chef, *m*.

serial, *a*, en série. ~ *rights*, droits de reproduction dans les journaux & périodiques, *m.pl*. ~ [*story*], [roman] feuilleton, *m*. ~ *number*, numéro matricule. *m*. **seriatim**, *ad*, successivement. **series**, *n*, série, suite, *f*.

serif, *n*, empattement, *m*.

seringa, *n*, seringa, *m*.

serious†, *a*, sérieux; grave. ~ness, *n*, sérieux, *m*; gravité, *f*.

sermon, *n*, sermon; prône; prêche, *m*. ~ize, *v.t*, sermonner. ~izer, *n*, prêcheur, *m*.

serpent, *n*, serpent, *m*. **serpentine**, *a*, serpentin. ¶ *n*, serpentine, *f*.

serration, *n*, dentelure; dent, *f*. **serrate[d]**, *a*, denté en scie, dentelé, en dents de scie.

serried, *a*, serré.

serum, *n*, sérum, *m*.

servant, *n*, employé, e; serviteur, *m*; domestique, *m,f*; bonne; (*pl.*) domesticité, livrée, *f*, gens, *m.pl*. ~ *girl*, fille de service, *f*. **serve** *v.t. & i*, servir; desservir; (*a sentence*) subir; (*a notice*) signifier; faire le service militaire; suffire. ~ *up*, servir. ¶ (*Ten.*) *n*, service, *m*. **server** (*Ten.*) *n*, servant, *m*. **service**, *n*, service, *m*; desserte; démarche, *f*, ministère; office, *m*; (*domestic*) domesticité, condition, *f*; (*china, etc.*) service, *m*; (*of writ*) signification, *f*. *to grow old in the* ~, blanchir sous le harnois. ~ *hatch*, passe-plats, *m*. ~ *station*, poste d'essence, *f*. ~ *tree*, sorbier, *m*. ~able, *a*, d'usage; utile. **servicing**, *n*, entretien, *m*; réparation, *f*.

servile†, *a*, servile. **servility**, *n*, servilité, *f*. **servitude**, *n*, servitude, *f*.

sesame, *n*, sésame, *m*.

session, *n*, session; séance; bourse, *f*.

set, *n*, série, *f*; jeu; assortiment; train, *m*; batterie; suite; garniture; trousse, *f*; (*Math.*) tranche;

parure, *f;* ensemble; service, *m;*
(*fixity*) assiette; (*of saw*) voie,
chasse, *f;* (*Theat.*) décor, *m;*
(*Ten.*) manche, *f,* set, *m.* ~ *of*
(artificial) *teeth,* dentier, *m.* ~-
back, recul, tassement; décalage, *m,* traverse, *f.* ~*off,* compensation, *f;* (*foil*) repoussoir;
(*Arch.*) ressaut, *m;* (*Typ.*) macu-
lature; (*law*) reconvention, *f.* ~-*to,*
prise de bec; bagarre, *f;* pugilat,
m. ¶ *v.t.ir,* mettre; poser; placer;
aposter; fixer; planter; asseoir;
assurer; (*bone*) remettre, remboîter; (*dog on, fashion, etc.*)
lancer; (*gem*) sertir, enchâsser,
monter; (*hen*) mettre couver; (*a
sail*) établir; (*saw*) donner la
voie à; (*seal*) apposer; (*shutter*
—*Phot.*) armer; (*task, example*)
donner; (*tools*) affiler, repasser;
(*trap*) tendre, dresser; (*type*)
composer; (*watch*) régler; (*v.i.
ir.*) se figer, prendre; (*sun*) se
coucher. ~ *about it,* s'y prendre.
~ *down in writing,* coucher par
écrit. ~ *off,* (*figure*) dégager. ~
on (*pers.*), lapider. ~ *out,* partir.
~ *up,* monter; ériger; établir.
¶ *p.a:* ~ *purpose,* parti pris, *m.*
~ *smile,* sourire figé, *m.* ~
speech, discours d'apparat, *m.*

settee, *n,* divan, *m,* causeuse, *f.*

setter, *n,* poseur, euse; tendeur;
monteur; metteur; compositeur;
chien couchant, *m.* **setting,** *n,*
entourage, encadrement, *m;* (*cement*) prise; (*gem*) enchâssure,
œuvre, *f,* chaton; (*sun*) coucher,
m; (*type*) composition, *f.* ~
aside, abstraction faite de. ~ *sun,*
soleil couchant, *m.*

settle, *n,* banc, *m.* ¶ *v.t,* régler;
arranger; accommoder; trancher;
liquider; établir, installer; emménager; (*property*) constituer;
(*v.i.*) se fixer; s'établir; (*alight*)
se poser; (*matter*) se déposer;
(*ground*) [se] tasser. ~**d,** *p.a,*
décidé, arrêté; (*weather*) sûr.
~**ment,** *n,* règlement, *m;* constitution, *f;* (*Stk Ex.*) terme, *m,* liquidation; colonie, colonie de peu-
plement, *f.* **settler,** *n,* colon, *m,*
résident, e.

seven, *a. & n,* sept, *a. & m.* **seventeen,** *a. & n,* dix-sept, *a. & m.*
seventeenth, *a. & n,* dix-septième,
a. & m,f; dix-sept, *m.* ~**ly,** *ad,* en
dix-septième lieu. **seventh,** *a. &
n,* septième, *a. & m,f;* sept, *m.*

~**ly,** *ad,* septièmement. **seventieth,**
a. & n, soixante-dixième, *a. &
m,f.* **seventy,** *a. & n,* soixante-dix,
a. & m. 71, 72, soixante et onze,
soixante-douze.

sever, *v.t,* séparer. ~**al†,** *a,* divers,
plusieurs; respectif; individuel.
~**ance,** *n,* séparation, distraction,
f.

severe†, *a,* sévère; rigoureux;
rude; grave. **severity,** *n,* sévérité;
rigueur; gravité, *f.*

Seville, *n,* Séville, *f.* ~ *orange,*
bigarade, orange amère, *f.*

sew, *v.t.ir,* coudre. ~**er,** *n,* couseur, euse, piqueuse, *f.* ~**ing,** *n,*
couture, *f.* ~ *machine,* machine à
coudre, *f.*

sewer, *n,* égout, *m.* sew[er]**age,** *n,*
eaux d'égout, eaux-vannes, *f.pl.*

sex, *n,* sexe, *m.* ~ *appeal,* sex-ap-
peal, *m.*

sextant, *n,* sextant, *m.*

sextet[te], *n,* sextuor, *m.*

sexton, *n,* sacristain, *m.*

sexual, *a,* sexuel. ~**ity,** *n,* sexu-
alité, *f.*

shabby, *a,* usé, râpé, miteux; mesquin.

shack, *n,* hutte, cabane, *f.*

shackle, *n,* boucle; manille, *f;*
maillon; *m;* (*fig.*) entrave, *f.* ¶
v.t, entraver.

shade, *n,* ombre, *f;* ombrage, *m;*
(*pl, spirits*) mânes, *m.pl;* nuance,
f; (*lamp*) abat-jour; écran; globe
protecteur, *m.* ¶ *v.t,* ombrager;
(*art*) ombrer; (*v.i.*) passer. ~
off, dégrader. **shadow,** *n,* ombre,
f. ~ *boxing,* boxe contre son
ombre, *f.* ¶ *v.t,* filer. **shady,** *a,*
ombragé; (*Poet.*) ombreux; (*disreputable*) louche, véreux. *to be
on the* ~ *side of* 40, avoir dépassé
la quarantaine.

shaft, *n,* flèche, *f,* trait, *m;* (*spear*)
hampe; (*of chimney*) souche, *f;*
(*cart*) limon, brancard; (*Arch.*)
fût, *m,* tige, *f;* (*Mech.*) arbre, *m,*
transmission, *f;* (*Min.*) puits, *m;*
(*elevator*) cage, *f.* ~ *horse,* brancardier, timonier, *m.*

shaggy, *a,* poilu, hirsute.

shagreen, *n,* chagrin, *m.*

shah, *n,* shah, chah, *m.*

shake, *n,* secousse, *f;* (*head*)
hochement; (*hand*) serrement,
m, poignée; (*timber*) gerçure, *f,*
éclat; (*Mus.*) trille, *m.* ¶ *v.t.ir,*

secouer; agiter; [é]branler; hocher; serrer; (v.i.ir.) trembler;
s'ébranler; ballotter; flageoler,
chevroter. **shaky,** a, branlant;
chancelant; chevrotant; tremblé.
shale, n, schiste, m. ~ oil, huile de
s., f.
shall, v.aux.ir, is expressed in Fr.
by future tense. Also by falloir.
shallot, n, échalot, f.
shallow, a, peu profond, bas; faible; creux; frivole; superficiel.
~s, n.pl, bas-fond, m.
sham, n, feinte, f, [faux-]semblant,
m. ¶ a, feint; simulé; fictif. ~
fight, simulacre de combat, m.
¶ v.t. & i, feindre, simuler.
shambles, n, décombres, m.pl,
ruines, f.pl.
shambling, p.a, traînant.
shame, n, honte; pudeur, f; scandale, m. for ~! fi donc! ¶ v.t,
faire honte à. ~faced, a, honteux,
penaud. ~ful†, a, honteux; scandaleux. ~less, a, éhonté, dévergondé, impudent. ~lessly, ad,
sans vergogne, impudemment.
shampoo, n, (wet) schampooing,
m; (dry) friction, f. ¶ v.t, faire
un schampooing à; faire une friction à.
shamrock, n, trèfle, m.
shank, n, jambe; queue; tige, f.
shanty, n, baraque, bicoque, f.
~town, bidonville, m.
shape, n, forme; figure; taille,
tournure; carcasse, f; profil, m.
¶ v.t, former; façonner; mouler;
modeler; pétrir. ~less, a, informe. ~ly, bien tourné.
share, n, part; quote-part, quotité,
f; écot, m; (Fin.) action, valeur,
f; titre; (plow) soc, m. ~holder,
actionnaire; sociétaire, m,f. ¶
v.t. & i, partager, participer (à).
shark (fish & rapacious pers.) n,
requin, m.
sharp, a, tranchant; aigu; acéré;
fin; net; vif; perçant; (acid) aigre;
(rebuke) verte. ~ practices, pro-
cédés indélicats, m.pl. ~shooter,
tirailleur, m. ¶ ad. (hour), pré-
cise. look ~! dépêchez-vous! vite!
¶ (Mus.) n, dièse, m. ~en, v.t,
aiguiser; affûter; repasser; tailler
[en pointe]; (wits) déniaiser. ~ly,
ad, vivement; nettement. ~ness,
n, acuité; finesse; âcreté; netteté,
f.
shatter, v.t, briser, fracasser.

shave, v.t, raser; (v.i.) se raser,
se faire la barbe. to have a close
~, l'échapper belle. **shaving,** n, la
barbe; (chip) copeau, m; rognure,
planure, f. ~ brush, pinceau à
barbe, blaireau, m. ~ soap, savon
à barbe, m.
shawl, n, châle, m.
she, pn, elle; celle; ce, c', ç'; (of
ship) il. ¶ n, femelle, f. ~-ass,
ânesse, bourrique, f. ~-bear,
ourse, f. ~-camel, chamelle, f.
~-devil, diablesse, f. ~-goat,
chèvre, chevrette, f. ~-monkey,
guenon, guenuche, f. ~-wolf,
louve, f.
sheaf, n, gerbe, f; faisceau, m.
¶ v.t, [en]gerber.
shear, v.t.ir, tondre; cisailler. ~er,
n, tondeur, euse. ~ing, n, tonte,
f. ~ machine, tondeuse, f. **shears,**
n. pl, cisailles, forces, f.pl; ciseaux,
m.pl, tondeuse, f.
sheath, n, gaine, f; fourreau, m.
sheathe, v.t, [r]engainer; recouvrir.
sheave, n, poulie, f, rouet, m.
shed, n, hangar; garage, m;
baraque; remise; étable, f. ¶
v.t.ir, verser, répandre; se dépouiller de. **shedding** (blood) n,
effusion, f.
sheen, n, éclat; lustre, m.
sheep, n, mouton, m; brebis, f.
black ~, brebis galeuse, f. ~ dog,
chien de berger, m. ~fold, bergerie, f. ~like (pers.), moutonnier. ~[skin], peau de mouton, f,
basane, f. ~ish, a, penaud, sot,
honteux.
sheer, a, pur; (force) vive; abrupt,
à pic.
sheet, n, feuille; lame; nappe;
couche; bâche; tôle, plaque;
(Naut.) écoute, f; (bed) drap, m.
~ anchor, ancre de veille; (fig.)
a. de salut, planche de s., f. ~
glass, verre à vitres, m. ~ iron,
tôle [de fer] f. ~ lead, plomb en
feuilles, m. ~ lightning, éclair
diffus, é. en nappes, m.
sheik[h], n, cheik, m.
shekel (Bible) n, sicle, m.
sheldrake, n, tadorne, m.
shelf, n, planche, tablette, f,
rayon; (Naut.) écueil, m. [set of]
shelves, étagère, f.
shell, n, coquille; coque; carapace; cosse; écale; peau, f; coquillage, m; écaille; chape, f;

(*Artil.*) obus, *m.* ~*fish*, coquillage, *m.* ~ *hole*, entonnoir, *m.* ~ *shock*, commotion, psychose traumatique, *f.* ¶ *v.t*, écaler, écosser, égrener, cerner; bombarder, canonner, battre.

shellac, *n*, laque en écailles, gomme laque, *f.*

shelter, *n*, abri, *m*, le couvert, asile, refuge; édicule, *m.* ¶ *v.t*, abriter.

shelve, *v.i*, aller en pente; (*v.t.*) mettre de côté.

shepherd, *n*, berger; pasteur, *m.* ~*s crook*, houlette, *f.* ~*'s-purse*, bourse à pasteur, *f*, tabouret, *m.* ~**ess**, *n*, bergère, *f.*

sherbet, *n*, sorbet, *m.*

sheriff, *n*, shérif, *m.*

sherry, *n*, xérès, vin de Xérès, *m.*

shield, *n*, bouclier; protecteur; (*armor*) bouclier, écu; (*Her.*) écusson, *m*; blindage, *m.* (*atomic physics*) *heat* ~, bouclier thermique, *m.* ¶ *v.t.* abriter; défendre; protéger; garantir.

shift, *n*, déplacement; changement, *m*; (*Naut., of wind*) saute; équipe, *f*, poste; expédient, tournant, *m*, ressource, *f*; subterfuge, biais, *m. gear* ~, changement de vitesse, *m.* ¶ *v.t. & i*, déplacer; se d.; changer; changer de place; sauter; (*cargo*) riper; biaiser. ~*ing*, *p.a*, changeant; (*sand*) mouvant. ~**y**, *a*, fuyant.

shilling (½0 of a £) *n*, shilling, *m.* (*In Fr. pronounced* ʃələ̃).

shilly-shally, *v.i*, lanterner, barguigner.

shimmer, *v.i*, chatoyer.

shin, *n*, tibia; (*beef*) jarret, *m.* ~ *bone*, tibia, *m.*

shindy, *n*, chahut, tapage, *m*; (*dance*) sauterie, *f.*

shine, *n*, brillant; luisant, *m.* ¶ *v.i.ir*, luire; briller; rayonner; reluire.

shingle, *n*, galets, *m.pl*, galet; (*Build.*) bardeau, *m.* (*pl.*) (*Med.*) zona, *m.* ¶ (*Metall.*) *v.t*, cingler. ~[*d hair*], nuque rasée, *f.*

shining & shiny, *a*, [re]luisant; brillant.

ship, *n*, navire; vaisseau; bâtiment, bateau; bord, *m.* ~*building*, construction navale, *f.* ~*mate*, camarade de bord, *m.* ~*owner*, armateur, *m.* ~*shape*, à sa place. ~*wreck*, naufrage, *m.* to be

~*wrecked*, faire naufrage. ~*wright*, constructeur de navires; charpentier de vaisseau, *m.* ~*yard*, chantier naval, *m.* ¶ *v.t*, charger; embarquer; expédier; (*oars*) border. **shipment**, *n*, chargement; embarquement, *m*; expédition, *f.* **shipper**, *n*, chargeur, expéditeur, *m.* **shipping**, *n*, navigation, *f*; transport maritime, *m*; marine, *f*; tonnage; armement, *m.* ~ *agent*, agent maritime, commissionnaire chargeur, *m.* ~ *charges*, frais d'expédition, *m.pl.* ~ *clerk*, expéditionnaire, *m.*

shirk, *v.t*, éluder, se soustraire à; (*v.i.*) s'embusquer. ~[**er**], *n*, embusqué, fricoteur, *m.*

shirt, *n*, chemise, *f.* ~ *collar*, col de chemise; faux col, *m.* ~ *maker*, chemisier, ère. ~*ing*, *n*, toile à chemises, *f*, shirting, *m.*

shiver, *v.t*, briser, fracasser; (*v.i.*) frissonner, grelotter.

shoal, *n*, (*sand, fish*) banc; (*shallow*) haut-fond, *m.* ~*s of people*, un mascaret humain.

shock, *n*, choc; coup; saisissement, ébranlement, à-coup, *m*, secousse; (*hair*) tignasse, forêt, *f*; (*corn*) tas, *m.* ~ *absorber*, amortisseur, *m.* ¶ *v.t*, heurter, choquer; (*fig.*) choquer, scandaliser, révolter, blesser.

shoddy, *a*, de camelote.

shoe, *n*, soulier, *m*, chaussure, *f*; chausson; (*horse*) fer; sabot; patin, *m.* ~ *brush*, brosse à souliers, *f.* ~ *horn*, chausse-pied, *m.* ~*lace*, lacet de soulier, *m.* ~*maker*, cordonnier, *m.* ~ *polish*, cirage, *m*, crème à chaussure, *f.* ¶ *v.t.ir*, chausser; ferrer; saboter. **shoeing**, *n*, ferrage, *m.*

shoot, *n*, chasse, *f*, tiré, *m*; rejeton; couloir, *m.* ¶ *v.t.ir*, tirer; lancer; darder; chasser; blesser [d'un coup de fusil, d'une flèche]; tuer [d'un coup de fusil, *etc.*]; (*spy, deserter*) fusiller; (*tip*) culbuter; (*rapids*) franchir; (*v.i.ir*.) tirer; chasser [au fusil]; (*grow*) pousser, germer; (*Foot.*) shooter; (*pain*) élancer. ~ *a movie*, tourner un film. **shooting**, *n*, tir, (*TV & cinema*) tournage, *m*; chasse [au tir] *f.* ~ *gallery*, tir, stand, *m.* ~ *pains*, douleur lancinante, *f*, élancement, *m.pl.* ~ *star*, étoile filante, *f.*

shop, *n*, magasin, *m*, boutique, *f*; débit; atelier, *m.* ~ *foreman*, chef d'atelier, *m.* ~*front*, devanture de magasin, *f.* ~*keeper*, marchand, e, boutiquier, ère. ~*lifting*, vol à l'étalage, *m.* ~*walker*, inspecteur, *m.* ~ *window*, vitrine, montre, *f.* ~*worn*, défraîchi. *duty-free* ~, boutique franche, *f.* ¶ *v.i*, faire des emplettes. **shopping**, *n*, achat, *m. to go* ~, aller faire des courses. ~ *basket*, panier à provisions. ~ *cart*, pousette, *f.*

shore, *n*, rivage, bord; étai; accore, *m.* ~ *fishing*, pêche au bord de la mer, *f. on* ~, à terre. ¶ *v.t*, étayer; chevaler; accorer.

short, *a*, court; petit; bref; déficitaire; cassant. ~ *circuit*, court-circuit, *m.* ~*coming*, manquement, *m.* ~*cut*, raccourci, *m.* ~*haired* (dog), à poil ras. ~*hand*, sténographie, *f.* ~*handtypist*, sténodactylographe, *m,f.* ~*hand writer*, sténographe, *m,f.* ~*lived*, passager, fugitif, sans lendemain. . . . *are* ~*lived*, . . . ne vivent pas longtemps. ~*sighted*, myope; à courtes vues; imprévoyant. ~ *story*, conte, *m*, nouvelle, *f.* ~ [*syllable*], [syllabe] brève, *f.* ¶ *n.pl*, ~*s*, caleçon; short, *m.* ¶ *ad*, [tout] court. *in* ~, bref, enfin. ~*age*, *n*, manque; déficit, *m*, crise, *f.* ~*en*, *v.t*, [r]accourcir. ~*ly*, *ad*, bientôt, prochainement, sous peu; peu de temps (*avant*, *après*); brièvement. ~*ness*, *n*, brièveté; courte durée; petitesse, *f.* ~ *of breath*, courte haleine, *f.*

shot, *n*, coup de feu; coup; trait; boulet, *m*; balle, *f*; plomb, *m*; grenaille, *f*; (*putting the shot*) poids, *m*; portée, *f*; tireur, *m*; (*TV & cinema*) plan, champ, *m*, prise de vues, *f.* ~ *gun*, fusil de chasse, *m. close-up* ~, plan serré, *m. continuity* ~, raccord, *m. high-angle* ~, plongée, *f. low-angle* ~, contre-plongée, *f. stock* ~, plan d'archives, *m. trick* ~, trucage, truquage, *m.*

shot (*fabrics*) *p.p*, changeant, chatoyant.

should, *v.aux*, *is expressed in Fr.*

by conditional mood. Also by devoir, falloir.

shoulder, *n*, épaule, *f*; (*Carp.*) épaulement, *m.* ~ *blade*, plat de l'épaule, *m*, omoplate, *f*; (*horse*, *ox*) paleron, *m.* ~ *strap*, bretelle; épaulette, *f.* ¶ *v.t*, pousser de l'épaule; prendre sur ses épaules; (*arms*) porter; (*fig.*) endosser.

shout, *n*, cri; éclat, *m.* ¶ *v.t. & i*, crier; vociférer.

shove, *n*, poussée, *f.* ¶ *v.t. & i*, pousser. ~ *off*, pousser au large.

shovel, *n*, pelle, *f.* ¶ *v.t*, remuer à la pelle. ~*ful*, *n*, pelletée, *f.*

show, *n*, semblant, simulacre; étalage; déballage, *m*; parade; représentation, *f*, spectacle, *m*; exposition, *f*, concours, salon, *m.* ~ *case*, vitrine, *f.* ~*down*, épreuve de force, *f.* ~*man*, forain; montreur, *m.* ~ *room*, salon d'exposition, *m.* ¶ *v.t.ir*, montrer; manifester; enseigner; accuser; [re]présenter; constater; prouver; (*v.i.ir.*) se montrer; paraître. ~ *in*, faire entrer, introduire. ~ *off*, faire parade (de); (*abs.*) parader. ~ *out*, reconduire. ~ *round*, piloter dans, promener par, promener dans. ~ *the white feather*, caner. ~ *up*, démasquer, afficher.

shower, *n*, ondée; averse; giboulée; pluie; grêle; nuée; avalanche, *f.* ~ *bath*, douche [en pluie] *f.* ¶ *v.t*, faire pleuvoir; combler.

showy, *a*, ostentateur, ostentatoire, fastueux, voyant.

shrapnel, *n*, obus à balles, *m.*

shred, *n*, lambeau, *m*; (*pl.*) charpie, *f.* ¶ *v.t*, déchiqueter.

shrew, *n*, mégère, *f.* ~ [*mouse*], musaraigne, *f.*

shrewd, *a*, sagace, clairvoyant; adroit. ~*ness*, *n*, sagacité, clairvoyance; adresse, *f.*

shriek, *n*, cri, *m.* ¶ *v.i*, crier.

shrike, *n*, pie-grièche, *f.*

shrill, *a*, aigu, perçant, strident. ~*ness*, *n*, acuité, *f*; (*voice*) mordant, *m.*

shrimp, *n*, crevette, *f*; (*pers.*) gringalet, *m.* ~*ing*, *n*, pêche à la crevette, *f.*

shrine, *n*, châsse, *f*, reliquaire; sanctuaire, *m.*

shrink, *v.i.ir*, [se] rétrécir; se retirer; (*v.t.ir.*) rétrécir. ~*age*, *n*, rétrécissement; **retrait,** *m,* retraite, *f.*

shrivel, *v.t,* rider, grésiller, ratatiner, racornir.

shroud, *n,* linceul, suaire; *(Naut.)* hauban, *m.* ¶ *v.t,* envelopper; embrumer.

Shrovetide, *n,* les jours gras, *m.pl.* **Shrove Tuesday,** mardi gras, *m.*

shrub, *n,* arbrisseau, *m.* **shrubbery,** *n,* plantation d'arbrisseaux, *f;* bosquet, *m.*

shrug, *n,* haussement d'épaules, *m.* ¶ *v.t,* hausser.

shudder, *v.i,* frissonner, frémir.

shuffle, *v.t,* *(cards)* battre; *(v.i.)* biaiser, tortiller, tergiverser. ~ **along,** traîner la jambe. ¶ *(excuse) n,* défaite, *f.* **shuffling gait,** pas traînant, *m.*

shun, *v.t,* éviter, fuir.

shunt *(Elec.) n,* dérivation, *f;* *(Surg.)* pontage, *m.* ¶ *v.t,* *(Rly.)* garer, manœuvrer; *(Elec.)* dériver.

shut, *v.t.ir,* fermer; *(v.i.)* [se] f. ~ **in,** enfermer. ~ **out,** fermer la porte à; exclure. ~ **up,** fermer; enfermer; clouer la bouche à. **shutter,** *n,* volet; contrevent; *(Phot.)* obturateur, *m.*

shutdown, *n,* arrêt, *m.* **emergency** ~, arrêt d'urgence.

shuttle, *n,* navette, *f.* ~**cock,** volant, *m.*

shy†, *a,* timide, sauvage, réservé, farouche, ombrageux. ¶ *v.i,* faire un écart; *(v.t.)* lancer. ~**ness,** *n,* timidité, sauvagerie, *f.*

Siam, *n,* le Siam. **Siamese,** *a,* siamois. ~ **cat,** chat de Siam, *m.* ¶ *n,* *(pers.)* Siamois, e; *(language)* le siamois.

Siberia, *n,* la Sibérie. **Siberian,** *a,* sibérien. ¶ *n,* Sibérien, ne.

Sicilian, *a,* sicilien. ¶ *n,* Sicilien, ne. **Sicily,** *n,* la Sicile.

sick, *a,* malade; dégoûté. **to be** ~, être malade; *(stomach)* avoir mal au cœur. **the** ~, les malades, *m,f.pl.* ~ **& tired,** excédé. ~ **bed,** lit de douleur, *m.* ~ **headache,** mal de tête accompagné de nausées, *m.* ~ **leave,** congé de maladie, c. de convalescence, *m.* ~ **list,** état des malades, *m.* ~ **room,** chambre de malade; *(Sch., etc.)* infirmerie, *f.* ~**en,**

v.i, tomber malade; *(v.t.)* écœurer.

sickle, *n,* faucille, *f.*

sickly, *a,* maladif, souffreteux, malingre; chétif; doucereux, fadasse. **sickness,** *n,* maladie, *f;* *(stomach)* mal de cœur, *m.*

side, *n,* côté; flanc; bord, *m,* rive, *f;* versant; plat, *m;* face; part, *f;* parti; camp, *m.* ~ **by** ~, côte à côte. ~**board,** buffet, dressoir, *m,* panetière, crédence, *f.* ~ **car,** side-car, *m.* ~ **dish,** entremets, *m.* ~ **door,** porte latérale, *f.* ~ **glance,** regard oblique, *m.* ~ **issue,** question d'intérêt secondaire, *f.* ~**long,** de côté; *(glance)* en coulisse. ~ **saddle,** selle de dame, *f.* ~ **show,** spectacle payant; *(fair)* spectacle forain, *m.* ~**slip,** déraper. ~**step,** faire un écart. ~ **stroke,** nage de côté, *f.* ~**walk,** trottoir, *m.* ~**ways,** de côté. ~**whiskers,** favoris, *m.pl.* ~ **with,** se ranger du côté de.

sidereal, *a,* sidéral.

siding, *n,* voie de garage, *f;* *(private)* embranchement, *m.*

sidle in, entrer de guingois.

siege, *n,* siège, *m.*

Sienna, *n,* Sienne, *f.*

siesta, *n,* sieste, méridienne, *f.*

sieve, *n,* tamis, sas, crible, *m.* **sift,** *v.t,* tamiser, sasser, cribler; bluter; *(question)* éplucher. **siftings,** *n.pl,* criblure, *f.*

sigh, *n,* soupir, *m.* ¶ *v.i,* soupirer.

sight, *n,* vue; vision, *f;* aspect, *m;* présence; *(Surv.)* visée, *f,* coup [de lunette] *m;* *(gun)* mire, *f;* spectacle, *m;* curiosité; caricature, *f.* **at** ~, à première vue; *(reading)* à livre ouvert; *(Com.)* à vue. **by** ~, de vue. ¶ *v.t,* viser; voir; *(land)* reconnaître.

sign, *n,* signe, *m.* ~**[board],** enseigne, *f;* panonceau, *m.* ~ **of expression** *(Mus.),* nuance, *f.* ~ **post,** poteau indicateur, *m.* ¶ *v.t. & i,* signer; *(in the margin)* émarger; faire signe. ~ **[on],** engager.

signal *n,* signal, *m.* ~ **box,** cabine à signaux, *f.* ~**man** *(Rly)* signaleur, *m.* ¶ *a,* signalé, insigne. ¶ ~ **& ~ize,** *v.t,* signaler. **signaler,** *n,* *(Mil.)* signaleur; *(Naut.)* timonier, *m.* **signatory** **or signer,** *n,* signataire, *m,f.* **signature,** *n,* signature; souscription; *(Mus.)* armature; *(Typ.)*

signature, *f.* **signet**, *n*, cachet, *m*.
~ **ring**, [bague à la] chevalière, *f.*
significance, *n*, portée, *f.* *look of
deep ~*, regard [fort] significatif,
r. d'intelligence, *m.* **significant**,
a, significatif. **signify**, *v.t.* & *i*,
signifier; importer.

silence, *n*, silence, *m.* ¶ *v.t*, faire
taire; (*enemy's fire*) éteindre.
silencer, *n*, silencieux; amortisseur de bruit, *m.* **silent**†, *a*, silencieux, taciturne; (*Gram.*) muet.
~ *partner*, commanditaire, *m. to
be ~*, se taire.

Silesia, *n*, la Silésie. **s~**, *n*, silésienne, *f.*

silhouette, *n*, silhouette, *f.*

silica, *n*, silice, *f.* **silicate**, *n*, silicate, *m.* **silicon**, *n*, silicone, *m.*

silk, *n*, soie, *f.* ~ *goods* or *silks*,
soierie, *f.* ~ *hat*, chapeau de
soie, *m.* **silkworm**, *n*, ver à soie,
m. ~ *breeding*, magnanerie, sériciculture, *f.* ~*'s eggs*, graine, *f.*
silky, *a*, soyeux.

sill, *n*, (*door*) seuil; (*window*) rebord, *m.*

silliness, *n*, niaiserie, bêtise, *f.*
silly, *a*, niais, sot, bête.

silo, *n*, silo, *m.* ¶ *v.t*, ensiler.

silt, *n*, vase, *f*, limon, *m.* ~ *up*,
s'envaser.

silver, *n*, argent, *m.* ~ *birch*,
bouleau blanc, *m.* ~ *fox*, renard
argenté, *m.* ~*-gilt*, vermeil, argent doré. ~ *mine*, mine d'argent, *f.* ~ *plate*, n, argenterie, *f*;
(*v.t.*) argenter. ~ *side*, gîte à
la noix, *m.* ~*smith*, orfèvre, *m.*
~[*smith's*] *work*, orfèvrerie, *f.*
~ *wedding*, noces d'argent, *f.pl.*
¶ *v.t*, argenter; (*mirror*) étamer.
~*ing* (*for mirror*) *n*, tain, *m.* ~**y**,
a, argenté; argentin.

simian, *a*, qui appartient au singe.

similar, *a*, semblable, pareil, similaire. ~*ity* & **similitude**, *n*, similitude, *f.* ~**ly**, *ad*, semblablement.
simile, *n*, comparaison, similitude, *f.*

simmer, *v.i.* & *t*, mijoter, cuire à
petit feu.

simony, *n*, simonie, *f.*

simoom, **simoon**, *n*, simoun, *m.*

simper, *n*, sourire affecté, *m.* ¶ *v.i*,
minauder.

simple†, *a.* & *n*, simple. *a.* & *m.*
~*-minded*, simple, naïf. **simpleton**, *n*, niais, e, gogo, *m*, innocent,
e. **simplicity**, *n*, simplicité; bon-

homie, *f.* **simplify**, *v.t*, simplifier.

simulacrum, *n*, simulacre, *m.*

simulate, *v.t*, simuler, feindre.

simultaneous†, *a*, simultané.

sin, *n*, péché, *m*; iniquité, *f.* ¶ *v.i*,
pécher.

Sinai (Mount), le mont Sinaï.

since, *ad.* & *pr*, depuis. ¶ *c*, depuis
que; que; puisque, comme.

sincere†, *a*, sincère. **sincerity**, *n*,
sincérité, *f.*

sine, *n*, sinus, *m.*

sinecure, *n*, sinécure, *f.*

sinew, *n*, tendon; (*in meat*) tirant;
(*pl. of war*) nerf, *m.*

sinful, *a*, coupable.

sing, *v.t.* & *i. ir*, chanter. ~ *to
sleep*, endormir en chantant.

Singapore, *n*, Singapour, *m.*

singe, *v.t*, flamber, brûler; roussir.

singer, *n*, chanteur, euse; cantatrice, *f.* **singing**, *n*, chant; (*ears*)
tintement, *m*; (*att.*) de chant;
(*kettle*) à sifflet.

single, *a*, unique; seul; simple.
~ *bed*, lit à une place, *m.* ~
blessedness, le bonheur du célibat. ~*-breasted*, droit. ~ *combat*, combat singulier, *m.* ~*-
handed*, tout seul, à moi seul.
a ~ *life*, le célibat. ~ *man*, célibataire, garçon, *m.* ~ *out*, distinguer. **singly**, *ad*, isolément;
un(e) à un(e).

singsong, *a*, chantant, traînant.
¶ *n*, psalmodie, *f.*

singular†, *a.* & *n*, singulier, *a.* &
m.

sinister, *a*, sinistre; (*Her.*) sénestre.

sink, *n*, évier; plomb; puisard;
(*fig.*) cloaque, *m*, sentine, *f.*
¶ *v.i.ir*, [s']enfoncer; s'affaisser;
se tasser; crouler; s'abaisser;
baisser; descendre; succomber;
(*ship*) couler [à fond], c. bas;
(*v.t.ir*) enfoncer; noyer; foncer,
creuser; couler; (*die*) graver en
creux; (*money, a fortune*) enterrer (*in* = en); (*loan, national
debt*) amortir. ~ *in[to*], pénétrer; s'imbiber. *in a sinking condition* (ship), en perdition.
sinking fund, fonds d'amortissement, *m*, caisse d'amortissement,
f. ~**er**, *n*, plomb de ligne, *m.*

sinless, *a*, innocent. **sinner**, *n*,
pécheur, *m*, pécheresse, *f.*

sinuous, *a*, sinueux.

sinus, *n*, sinus, *m.*

sip, *n*, petite gorgée; goutte, *f*.
¶ *v.t.* & *i*, siroter, humer, buvoter.

siphon, *n*, siphon, *m*.

sir, *n*, monsieur, *m*; (*title*) sir. *no*,
~, (*army*) non, mon colonel, etc.;
(*navy*) non, amiral, etc.; (*but to
any officer in command of a
ship*) non, commandant. **sire**, *n*,
père; (*to kings*) sire, *m*. ¶ *v.t*,
engendrer.

siren (*Myth. & hooter*) *n*, sirène, *f*.

sirloin, *n*, aloyau, *m*. *a roast* ~,
un rosbif.

sister, *n*, sœur, *f*. ~*-in-law*, belle-
sœur, *f*. ~ [*ship*], [navire] frère,
n. jumeau, *m*. ~*hood*, confrérie;
communauté, *f*. ~**ly**, *a*, de sœur.

sit, *v.i.ir*, s'asseoir; rester; [se]
tenir; (*portrait*) poser; (*court*)
siéger; (*hen*) couver. ~ *down*,
s'asseoir. ~ *for* (portrait), poser
pour. ~ *enthroned* & ~ *in state*,
trôner. ~ *on* (eggs), couver. ~
out, faire galerie. ~ *out a dance*,
causer une danse. ~ *up*, se tenir
droit; veiller.

site, *n*, emplacement; terrain; site,
m; assiette, *f*.

sitting, *n*, séance; audience; pose,
f. ~ *hen*, couveuse, *f*. ~ *posture*,
séant, *m*. ~ *room*, petit salon,
m. ~ *time*, couvaison, *f*.

situated, *a*, situé; sis; placé; dans
une position. **situation**, *n*, situation, assiette, position; place, *f*.
~ *wanted*, demande d'emploi, *f*.

sitz bath, bain de siège, *m*.

six, *a*. & *n*, six, *a*. & *m*. **sixteen**, *a*.
& *n*, seize, *a*. & *m*. **sixteenth**†, *a*.
& *n*, seizième, *a*. & *m,f*; seize, *m*.
sixth†, *a*. & *n*, sixième, *a*. & *m,f*;
six, *m*; (*Mus.*) sixte, *f*. **sixtieth**, *a*.
& *n*, soixantième, *a*. & *m,f*, **sixty**,
a. & *n*, soixante, *a*. & *m*.

size, *n*, dimension, *f*. *oft. pl*; grandeur; grosseur; mesure; taille;
pointure, *f*; numéro; format; calibre, *m*; (*glue, etc.*) colle, *f*, encollage, *m*. ¶ *v.t*, classer en grosseur; [en]coller. ~ *up* (*pers.*),
jauger.

skate, *n*, patin, *m*; (*fish*) raie, *f*.
¶ *v.i*, patiner. **skater**, *n*, patineur,
euse. *skating rink*, patinoire, *f*.

skedaddle, *v.i*, prendre la poudre
d'escampette.

skein, *n*, écheveau, *m*.

skeleton, *n*, squelette, *m*; carcasse, *f*; canevas, *m*. ~ *in the*

cupboard, secret de la famille,
m. ~ *key*, crochet [de serrurier]
m.

skeptic, *n*, sceptique, *m*, *f*. ¶ *a*,
sceptique. ~**al**, *a*, sceptique.
skepticism, *n*, scepticisme, *m*.

sketch, *n*, esquisse, *f*, croquis, dessin, crayon, canevas, *m*; (*playlet*)
saynète, *f*. ~ *book*, album de
dessin, cahier de dessin, *m*. ¶ *v.t*,
esquisser, croquer, crayonner,
dessiner, tracer.

skew, *a*, biais, oblique. ¶ *n*, biais,
m.

skewer, *n*, brochette, *f*.

ski, *n*, ski, *m*. ~ *pole*, bâton de ski,
m. ¶ *v.i*, faire du ski. **skiing**, *n*,
courses en ski, *f.pl*.

skid, *n*, enrayure, *f*, sabot; (*Avn.*)
patin; (*slip*) dérapage, *m*. ¶ *v.t*,
enrayer; (*v.i.*) patiner; déraper.

skiff, *n*, skiff, esquif, *m*, yole, *f*.

skill, *n*, habileté, adresse, *f*. ~**ed**,
a, expérimenté, expert. ~**ful**†, *a*,
habile, adroit.

skim, *v.t*, écumer, dégraisser, écrémer; effleurer, raser. ~ *milk*,
lait écrémé, *m*. **skimmer**, *n*,
écumoire; écrémoire, *f*. **skimmings**, *n.pl*, écume, *f*.

skimp, *v.t*, étriquer.

skin, *n*, peau; (*pl.*) peausserie;
fourrure; dépouille, *f*; cuir, *m*;
pelure; écorce; enveloppe, *f*.
~*-deep*, superficiel. ~ *disease*,
maladie cutanée, *f*. ~ *dresser*,
peaussier, *m*. ~ *specialist*, spécialiste des maladies de peau,
[médecin] peaussier, [médecin]
peaucier, *m*. ¶ *v.t*, écorcher; dépouiller; peler. ~*flint*, *n*, grippe-
sou, *m,f*, pingre, *m*. ~*less pea*
or bean, mange-tout, *m*. **skinny**,
a, décharné, maigre.

skip, *n*, saut, *m*. ¶ *v.i*. & *i*, sauter;
voleter. ~ *about*, gambiller, frin-
guer. **skipper**, *n*, patron; capitaine, *f*. *skipping rope*, corde à
sauter, *f*.

skirmish, *n*, escarmouche, *f*.
¶ *v.i*, escarmoucher. ~**er**, *n*, tirailleur, *m*.

skirt, *n*, jupe; basque, *f*; (*of a
wood*) lisière, orée, *f*. ¶ *v.t*,
longer.

skit, *n*, sketch comique, *m*. **skittish**, *a*, (*horse*) ombrageux,
écouteux; folâtre; coquet.

skittle, *n*, quille, *f*. ~ *alley*, quillier, *m*.

skulk, *v.i,* se dissimuler.

skull, *n,* crâne, *m.* ~ *cap,* calotte, *f.*

skunk, *n,* mouffette, *f;* (*fur*) sconse; (*pers.*) ladre, *m.*

sky, *n,* ciel, *m;* (*pl, Poet.*) nues, *f.pl.* ~ *blue,* bleu de ciel, b. céleste, *m.* ~*lark,* alouette des champs, *f.* ~*light,* [fenêtre à] tabatière, *f.* ~ *line,* profil de l'horizon, *m.* ~ *rocket,* fusée volante, *f.* ~*scraper,* gratte-ciel, *m.* ~ *writing,* publicité sur les nuages, *f.*

slab, *n,* dalle, plaque, table, tranche, *f,* pan, *m;* tablette, *f;* (*Typ.*) marbre, *m.*

slack†, *a,* lâche; mou; faible. ~ *season,* morte saison, *f.* ~ *water* (*Naut.*), mer étale, *f,* l'étale de la marée, *m.* ¶ ~ & ~**en,** *v.t. &* *i,* détendre; se d.; relâcher; se r.; ralentir.

slag, *n,* scorie, *f,* laitier, *m.*

slake, *v.t,* éteindre.

slam (*cards*) *n,* chelem, *m.* ¶ (*bang*) *v.i. & t,* claquer.

slander, *v.t,* médire de, calomnier; diffamer. ~**ous,** *a,* médisant.

slang, *n,* argot, *m.*

slant, *n,* inclinaison, *f.* ¶ *v.i. & t,* incliner.

slap, *n,* gifle, tape, claque, *f,* soufflet, *m.* ¶ *v.t,* frapper, taper, claquer, souffleter, gifler.

slash, *v.t,* taillader; balafrer. ~ *about,* ferrailler.

slat, *n,* latte; planchette; (*blind*) lame, *f.*

slate, *n,* ardoise, *f.* ~*colored* ardoisé. ~ *pencil,* crayon d'ardoise, *m.* ~ *quarry,* ardoisière, *f.* ¶ *v.t,* couvrir d'ardoises.

slattern, *n,* souillon, salope, maritorne, *f.*

slaughter, *n,* tuerie, *f,* massacre, carnage, *m.* ~ *house,* abattoir, *m.* ~ *man,* abatteur, *m.* ¶ *v.t,* massacrer, égorger; (*cattle*) abattre.

Slav, *a,* slave. ¶ *n,* Slave, *m,f.*

slave, *n,* esclave, *m,f.* ~ *bangle,* bracelet esclave, *m.* ~ *driver &* ~ *trader,* négrier, *m.* ~ *trade,* traite des noirs, *f.* **slave,** *v.i,* s'échiner, trimer.

slaver, *n,* bave, *f.* ¶ *v.i,* baver.

slavery, *n,* esclavage, *m.* **slavish†,** *a,* servile. ~**ness,** *n,* servilité, *f.*

slay, *v.t.ir,* immoler. ~**er,** *n,* tueur, *m.*

sleazy, *a,* mal soigné, mal tenu.

sledge, *n,* traîneau, *m;* (*man-guided, in the Alps*) ramasse, *f.* ~[*hammer*], masse, *f.* **sledging,** *n,* traînage, *m.*

sleek, *a,* lisse, poli.

sleep, *n,* sommeil, *m.* ~*walker,* somnambule, *m,f.* ¶ *v.i. & t. ir,* dormir; reposer; coucher. ~ *like a log,* dormir comme une souche. ~ *out,* découcher. ~**er,** *n,* dormeur, euse; (*Rly. track*) traverse, *f,* wagon-lit, *m.* **sleepiness,** *n,* envie de dormir, somnolence, *f,* sommeil, *m.* **sleeping,** *p.a,* endormi. ~ *bag,* sac de couchage, *m. the* S~ *Beauty,* la Belle au bois dormant. ~ *car,* wagon-lit, *m.* ~ *pill,* soporifique, *f.* ~ *sickness,* maladie du sommeil, *f.* **sleepless,** *a,* sans dormir. ~**ness,** *n,* insomnie, *f.* **sleepy,** *a,* ensommeillé, somnolent.

sleet, *n,* grésil, *f.* ¶ *v.i,* grésiller.

sleeve, *n,* manche, *f;* (*Mach.*) manchon, *m. to laugh up one's* ~, rire sous cape. ~**less,** *a,* sans manches.

sleigh, *n,* traîneau, *m.* ~**ing,** *n,* traînage, *m.*

sleight-of-hand, *n,* prestidigitation, *f.*

slender, *a,* mince; délié; fluet; grêle; gracile, svelte; faible.

sleuth hound, (*dog & fig.*) limier, *m.*

slew, *v.t,* faire pivoter.

slice, *n,* tranche, tartine, *f.* ~ *of bread & butter,* beurrée, tartine, *f.* ¶ *v.t,* trancher; (*ball*) couper.

slide, *n,* glissade; glissoire; débâcle; coulisse, *f;* tiroir; coulant; curseur; (*microscope*) porte-objet, *m;* (*Phot.*) diapositive, *f.* ~ *changer,* diapositif passe-vues, *m.* ~ *rule,* règle à calcul, *f.* ~ *valve,* tiroir, *m.* ¶ *v.i.ir,* glisser; couler. **sliding,** *p.a:* ~ *roof,* toit découvrable, *m.* ~ *scale,* échelle mobile, *f.*

slight†, *a,* léger; mince; faible; petit; menu, maigrelet. ¶ *n,* affront, *m.* ¶ *v.t,* négliger; faire un affront à. *the* ~*est,* le moindre, la moindre.

slim, *a,* svelte, gracile, élancé.

slime, *n*, bave; vase, *f*, limon, *m*, boue, *f*. **slimy**, *a*, baveux; visqueux; vaseux.

sling, *n*, fronde; écharpe; bretelle; élingue, *f*. ¶ *v.t.ir*, (*throw*) lancer; suspendre. *slung* [*over the shoulders*], en bandoulière.

slink away, *v.i.ir*, se dérober.

slip, *n*, glissement, *m*, glissade, *f*; faux pas; lapsus, *m*, erreur; peccadille; bande; fiche; feuille, *f*; papillon, *m*, (*woman's*) combinaison, *f*; (*Hort.*) plant, *m*, bouture; (*Naut.*) cale, *f*. ~*cover*, housse, *f*. ~ *knot*, nœud coulant, *m*. ~*shod*, en savates; négligé. ~ *stitch*, maille glissé, *f*. ¶ *v.i.* & *t*, glisser; couler; patiner; échapper; (*rope*) larguer. ~ *in*, *v.t*, faufiler. ~ *on* (*garment*), *v.t*, passer. **slipper**, *n*, pantoufle, *f*; chausson, *m*; mule, *f*. **slippery**, *a*, glissant.

slit, *n*, fente, *f*. ¶ (*dress*) *p.a*, taillade. ¶ *v.t.ir*, fendre.

slither, *v.i*, se glisser.

slobber, *n*, bave, *f*. ¶ *v.i*, baver.

sloe, *n*, prunelle, *f*. ~ *gin*, [liqueur de] prunelle, *f*. ~ [*tree*], prunellier, *m*.

slogan, *n*, devise publicitaire, *f*.

sloop, *n*, sloop, *m*.

slop [*over*], *v.i*, déborder. *slop pail*, seau de toilette, *m*.

slope, *n*, pente; rampe, *f*; talus, *m*. ¶ *v.i*, s'incliner, aller en pente.

sloppiness, *n*, état détrempé, *m*.

sloppy, *a*, débraillé, mal ajusté.

slops, *n.pl*, rinçure, *f*; eaux ménagères, *f.pl*; (*thin soup*) lavasse, *f*; (*liquid diet*) bouillon, *m*.

slot, *n*, mortaise, rainure, (*of a slot machine*) fente, *f*. ~ *machine*, appareil à jetons, *m*.

sloth, *n*, paresse, indolence, *f*; (*Zool.*) paresseux, *m*. ~**ful**, *a*, paresseux, indolent.

slouch, *v.i*, donner un air disloqué à sa taille, à son attitude, à sa marche. ~ *hat*, chapeau rabattu, *m*.

slough, *n*, bourbier, *m*; (*snake*) dépouille, peau, mue; (*Med.*) escarre, *f*. ¶ *v.i*, se dépouiller, muer.

sloven, *n*, sagouin, e, souillon, *m,f*. ~**ly**, *a*, négligé.

slow†, *a*, lent; tardif; lambin; (*train*) omnibus, de petite vitesse; (*clock*) en retard. *to be*

~ (*tedious*), manquer d'entrain. ~*-motion picture*, cinéma au ralenti, *m*. ¶ *ad*, lentement. ~ **down**, ralentir. **slowness**, *n*, lenteur, *f*.

slow-worm, *n*, orvet, *m*.

sludge, *n*, (*mud*) boue; (*snow*) neige fondue, *f*; (*oil*) cambouis, *m*.

slug, *n*, limace, loche, *f*; (*bullet* & *Typ.*) lingot, *m*.

sluggard, *n*, paresseux, euse. **sluggish†**, *a*, paresseux; inerte; tardif.

sluice, *n*, canal, *m*. ~ *gate*, vanne, *f*.

slum, *n*, taudis, *m*. ~ *area*, zône des taudis, *f*.

slumber, *n*, sommeil, *m*. ¶ *v.i*, sommeiller.

slump, *n*, (*in prices*) effondrement, *m*, dégringolade; (*in trade*) mévente; crise, *f*. ¶ *v.i*, s'effondrer.

slur, *n*, atteinte; (*Mus.*) liaison, *f*. ¶ *v.t*, (*Mus.*) lier. ~ *over*, glisser sur.

slush, *n*, de la neige fondue, *f*.

slut, *n*, garce, souillon, salope, *f*.

sly, *a*, sournois; rusé. ~*boots*, cachottier, ère, finaud, e. *on the* ~, à la dérobée.

smack, *n*, claque; (*boat*) barque, *f*, bateau, *m*. ¶ *v.t*, claquer; taper; (*tongue*) clapper. *to* ~ *of*, sentir le, la. *to* ~ *one's lips*, se lécher les babines.

small, *a*, petit; faible; modique; menu; fin; (*intestine*) grêle; (*arms*, *Mil.*) portatives. ~ *fry* (*fig.*), fretin, *m*. ~*pox*, petite vérole, variole, *f*. ~*pox case* (*pers.*), varioleux, euse. ~ *stones*, pierraille, *f*. ~ *talk*, menus propos, *m.pl*, conversation banale, *f*, choses indifférentes, *f.pl*, (*dire*) des riens. ¶ ~ *of the back*, chute des reins, *f*. ~*ness*, *n*, petitesse, *f*, peu d'importance, *m*.

smart, *n*, cuisson, *f*. ¶ *v.i*, picoter, cuire. ¶ *†a*, vif; fin; beau, chic, pimpant, coquet, huppé. *the* ~ *set*, les gens huppés. ~*en oneself up*, se requinquer. ~*ing*, *n*, cuisson, *f*. ¶ *p.a*, cuisant. ~*ness*, *n*, finesse, *f*; chic, *m*.

smash, *n*, accident, *f*. (*Fin.*) krach; (*Ten.*) smash, *m*. *to go* ~ (*bank*), sauter. ¶ *v.t*, briser, fracasser, massacrer; (*atom*) désintegrer.

smattering, *n*, teinture, *f*.
smear, *v.t*, enduire; barbouiller.
smell, *n*, odorat, *m*; odeur, *f*. ¶ *v.t*. & *i. ir*, sentir, fleurer; flairer; puer; *smelling bottle*, flacon à odeur, *m. smelling salts*, sels [volatils] anglais, *m.pl.*
smelt, *n*, éperlan, *m*.
smelt, *v.t*, fondre. ~*ing works*, fonderie, *f*.
smilax, *n*, smilax, *m*.
smile, *n*, sourire, *m*. ¶ *v.i*, sourire. **smiling**, *a*, [sou]riant.
smirch, *v.t*, salir.
smirk, *n*, sourire affecté, *m*. ¶ *v.i*, minauder.
smite, *v.t.ir*, frapper. (Cf. *smitten*.)
smith, *n*, forgeron, *m*. ~*'s hearth*, bâti de forge, *m*. ~*y*, *n*, forge, *f*.
smitten, *p.p*, (*remorse*) pris; (*love*) epris, féru.
smock [**frock**], *n*, blouse, *f*, sarrau, *m*. **smocking**, *n*, fronces smock, *f.pl*.
smoke, *n*, fumée, *f*. ~ *screen*, écran de fumée, *m*. ~*stack*, cheminée, *f*. ¶ *v.i*. & *t*, fumer; enfumer; (*lamp*) charbonner. ~*d sausage*, saucisson, *m*. ~*less*, *a*, sans fumée. **smoker**, *n*, fumeur, euse. **smoking**, *n*, l'habitude de fumer, *f*. ~ *compartment*, compartiment pour fumeurs, *m*. ~ *room*, fumoir, *m*. ~ *strictly prohibited*, défense expresse de fumer. **smoky**, *a*, fumeux.
smolder, *v.i*, couver.
smooth, *a*, lisse; uni; doux; (*sea*) unie, plate. ~*bore*, à canon lisse. ~*haired* (*dog*), à poil ras. ~*tongued*, mielleux, doucereux. ¶ *v.t*, lisser; polir; unir; planer; aplanir; adoucir; défroncer. ~*ly*, *ad*, uniment; doucement. ~*ness*, *n*, égalité; douceur, *f*.
smother, *v.t*, étouffer.
smudge, *n*, noirceur, *f*. ¶ *v.t*, barbouiller, mâchurer.
smug†, *a*, béat.
smuggle, *v.t*, passer en contrebande; (*v.i.*) faire la contrebande. ~ *in*, *v.t*, entrer en fraude. **smuggler**, *n*, contrebandier, ère.
smut, *n*, noirceur, *f*, (*Agric.*) nielle, *f*. **smutty**, *a*, noirci; niellé; (*obscene*) graveleux.
Smyrna, *n*, Smyrne, *f*.
snack, *n*, morceau [sur le pouce], *m*, cassecroûte, *m*, collation, *f*. *to have a* ~, collationner.

snag, *n*, (*stump*) chicot; (*fig.*) accroc, *m*.
snail, *n*, [co]limaçon; (*edible*) escargot, *m*. *at a* ~*'s pace*, à pas de tortue.
snake, *n*, serpent, (*young*) serpenteau, *m*. *there is a* ~ *in the grass*, le serpent est caché sous les fleurs.
snap, *n*, crac; cric crac!; coup sec, *m*; (*fastening*) agrafe, *f*, fermoir, *m*. ~*dragon*, muflier, *m*, gueule-de-loup, *f*. ~ *fastener*, fermeture pression, *f*. ~ [*shot*], instantané, *m*. ¶ *v.t*, casser, rompre; faire claquer. ~ *at*, bourrer. ~ *up*, happer; enlever. **snappy**, (*surly*) *a*, hargneux.
snare, *n*, piège; (*drum*) timbre, *m*. ~ *drum*, caisse claire, *f*. ¶ *v.t*, attraper.
snarl, *v.i*, gronder. (*v.t.*) s'enchevêtrer. ~*ing*, *p.a*, hargneux.
snatch (*scrap*) *n*, fragment, *m*, bribe, *f*. ¶ *v.t*, empoigner; enlever; arracher; dérober; (*kiss*) cueillir.
sneak, *n*, sournois, e; (*Sch.*) capon, ne. ~ *away*, s'en aller à la dérobée. *a* ~*ing fondness for*, du (*ou* un) faible pour.
sneakers, *pl.n*, chaussures de tennis, *f.pl*, baskets, *m.pl*.
sneer, *n*, rire moqueur, *m*. ¶ *v.i*, goguenarder. ~ *at*, railler.
sneeze, *v.i*, éternuer; (*animals*) s'ébrouer.
sniff, *v.i*. & *t*, renifler.
snigger, *v.i*, rire en dedans, rire en dessous.
snip, *n*, coup de ciseaux; bout, *m*. ¶ *v.t*, cisailler.
snipe, *n*, bécassine, *f*. ¶ *v.t*, canarder. **sniper**, *n*, tireur isolé, franc-tireur, *m*.
snivel, *v.i*, pleurnicher.
snob, *n*, snob, *m*. ~*ishness*, *n*, snobisme, *m*.
snooze, *n*, somme, *m*. ¶ *v.i*, roupiller, pioncer.
snore, *v.i*, ronfler.
snort, *v.i*, renifler, renâcler, s'ébrouer.
snout, *n*, museau; (*pig*) groin; (*boar*) boutoir, *m*.
snow, *n*, neige, *f*. oft. *pl*. ~*ball*, boule de neige, *f*. ~*blindness*, cécité des neiges, *f*. ~ *boots*, chaussures pour la n., *f.pl*. ~*capped*,

chenu. ~ *drift*, congère, *f*. ~*drop*, perce-neige, clochette d'hiver, *f*. ~*flake*, flocon de n, *m*. ~ *line*, limite des neiges éternelles, *f*. ~*man*, bonhomme de n., *m*. ~ *plow*, chasse-neige, *m*. ~ *shoes*, raquettes à n., *f.pl*. ~ *squall*, chasse-neige, *m*. ~ *storm*, tempête de n., *f*. ~*suit*, esquimau, *m*. ¶ *v.i*, neiger. ~y, *a*, neigeux.

snub, *n*, affront, soufflet, *m*, nasarde, *f*. ~*-nosed*, camus, camard. ¶ *v.t*, rabrouer, mépriser.

snuff, *n*, tabac à priser, *m*. *to take* ~, prendre du tabac, priser. ~*box*, tabatière, *f*. ~ *taker*, priseur, euse. ¶ *v.t*, moucher.

snuffle, *v.i*, renifler, nasiller. ~*s*, *n.pl*, enchifrènement, *m*.

snug, *a*, confortable.

snuggle, *v.i*, se pelotonner, se blottir.

so, *ad. c. & pn*, ainsi; aussi; donc; si; oui; tellement; tel, telle; tant; le. ~*-&-~*, un tel, une telle. ~*called*, soi-disant, *a.inv*, prétendu. ~ *as to*, de manière à; afin de. ~ *~*, comme ci, comme ça; couci-couça. ~ *that*, de sorte que; afin que. ~ *to speak*, pour ainsi dire.

soak, *v.t*, imbiber, [dé]tremper; (*dirty linen*) essanger. ~ *up*, absorber.

so-and-so, *n*, Untel, *m*. Mr. ~, M. Untel.

soap, *n*, savon, *m*. ~ *dish*, plateau à s., *m*. ~ *maker*, savonnier, *m*. ~ *opera*, mélo radiodiffusé, *m*. ~*stone*, pierre de savon, *f*. ~ *suds*, eau de s., *f*. ¶ *v.t*, savonner, ~y, *a*, savonneux.

soar, *v.i*, pointer, planer, prendre son essor.

sob, *n*, sanglot, *m*. ~ *story*, drame pleureur, *m*. ¶ *v.i*, sangloter.

sober†, *a*, sobre; sérieux; pas en état d'ébriété. *he is never ~*, il ne désenivre point, il ne dessoule jamais. ¶ *v.t*, désenivrer, dégriser. ~*ness*, *n*, sobriété, *f*.

soccer, *n*, football, *m*.

sociable†, *a*, sociable, liant. **social**, *a*, social. ~ *events* (news), mondanités, *f.pl*. ~*ism*, *n*, socialisme, *m*. ~*ist*, *n. & a*, socialiste, *m,f. & a*. **society**, *n*, société, association; (*fashionable world*) société, *f*, le monde, le grand monde; (*att.*) mondain. ~ *man, woman*, mondain, e. **sociology**, *n*, sociologie, *f*.

sock, *n*, chaussette, *f*. ¶ *v.t*, frapper.

socket, *n*, douille, *f*, manchon, *m*; (*eye*) orbite, *f*; (*tooth*) alvéole, *m*; (*lamp*) bec, *m*; (*bone*) glène, *f*. ¶ *v.t*, emboîter.

sod, *n*, gazon, *m*; plaque de gazon, motte, *f*.

soda, *n*, soude, *f*; (*washing*) cristaux de soude, *m.pl*. ~ [*water*], soda, *m*, eau de Seltz, *f*. *baking* ~, bicarbonate de soude, *m*.

sodden, *a*, détrempé.

sodium, *n*, sodium, *m*.

sofa, *n*, canapé, sofa, *m*.

soffit, *n*, soffite; intrados, *m*.

soft†, *a*, mou; doux; tendre; moelleux; (*fruit*) blet. ~*-boiled* (eggs), mollet. ~ *collar*, col souple, *m*. ~ *corn*, œil-de-perdrix, *m*. ~ *felt* (hat), feutre souple, feutre mou, *m. a ~ job*, un fromage. ~ *palate*, palais mou, *m*. ~ *pedal*, petite pédale, p. sourde, *f*. ~ *soap* (*fig.*), flagornerie, *f*; (*v.t.*) amadouer. ~ *solder*, soudure tendre, *f*. ~*en*, *v.t*, [r]amollir; adoucir; attendrir. ~*ening of the brain*, ramollissement du cerveau, *m*. ~*ish*, *a*, mollet. ~*ness*, *n*, mollesse, *f*; moelleux, *m*; douceur; tendresse, *f*.

soft copy, *n*, (*computers*) image d'écran, *f*.

software, *n*, (*computers*) logiciel, *m*.

soil, *n*, sol, *m*, terre, *f*, terroir, *m*, glèbe, *f*. ¶ *v.t*, salir, souiller. ~*ed*, *p.a*, (linen) sale; (*shop goods*) défraîchi.

sojourn, *n*, séjour, *m*. ¶ *v.i*, séjourner.

solace, *n*, consolation, *f*. ¶ *v.t*, consoler.

solar, *a*, solaire. ~ *plexus*, plexus s., *m*.

solder & ~ing, *n*, soudure, *f*. ¶ *v.t*, souder. ~*ing iron*, fer à souder, *m*.

soldier, *n*, soldat, militaire, troupier, *m*. ~*y*, *n*, militaires, *m.pl*; (*unruly*) soldatesque, *f*.

sole†, *a*, seul; unique; tout; exclusif. ¶ *n*, (*foot*) plante; (*shoe*) semelle; (*hoof, plate, fish*) sole, *f*. ¶ (*shoes*) *v.t*, ressemeler.

solecism, *n,* solécisme, *m.*

solemn†, *a,* solennel; grave. **~ity,** *n,* solennité; gravité, *f.* **~ize,** *v.t,* solenniser; (*wedding, etc.*) célébrer.

solicit, *v.t,* solliciter, quémander; briguer. **~ous,** *a,* désireux; inquiet; jaloux. **~ude,** *n,* sollicitude, *f.*

solid†, *a,* solide; ferme; (*gold*) massif; plein. **~ rock,** roc vif, *m.* **¶***n,* solide, *m.* **~ify,** *v.t,* solidifier. **~ity,.** *n,* solidité, *f.*

soliloquize, *v.i,* monologuer. **soliloquy,** *n,* soliloque, *m.*

soling, *n,* ressemelage, *m.*

solitaire (*gem, game*) *n,* solitaire, *m.* **solitary†,** *a,* solitaire; retiré. **~ confinement,** secret, *m.* **~ imprisonment,** réclusion, *f.* **solitude,** *n,* solitude, *f.*

solo, *n,* solo; récit, *m.* **~ dance,** pas seul, *m.* **~ist,** *n,* soliste, *m.f.*

solstice, *n,* solstice, *m.*

soluble, *a,* soluble. **solution,** *n,* solution; résolution; issue; dissolution, liqueur, *f.* **solve,** *v.t,* résoudre. **solvency,** *n,* solvabilité, *f.* **solvent,** *a,* dissolvant; (*Com.*) solvable. **¶** *n,* dissolvant, *m.*

somber, *a,* sombre.

some, *a,* quelque, quelques; du, de la, des; certain. **¶** *pn,* quelques-uns, -unes; certains, certaines; les uns, les unes; en. **somebody** & **someone,** *n,* quelqu'un, *m;* on, *pn.* **~ else,** quelqu'un d'autre. **to be somebody,** être un personnage. **somehow** [or **other**], *ad,* d'une manière ou d'une autre; tant bien que mal.

somersault, *n,* culbute, *f,* (le) saut périlleux.

something, *n,* quelque chose, *m;* q. c. de; de quoi. **~ in the wind,** quelque anguille sous roche. **sometimes,** *ad,* quelquefois; parfois; tantôt. **somewhat,** *ad,* quelque peu, un peu, tant soit peu. **somewhere,** *ad,* quelque part. **~ else,** ailleurs, autre part. **~ in the world,** de par le monde. **~ to stay,** pied-à-terre, tournebride, *m.*

somnambulism, *n,* somnambulisme, *m.* **somnambulist,** *n,* somnambule, *m.f.* **somnolent,** *a,* somnolent.

son, *n,* fils; garçon, *m.* **~-in-law,** gendre, *m.* **step~,** beau-fils, *m.*

sonata, *n,* sonate, *f.*

song, *n,* chant, *m;* chanson; romance, *f;* air; cantique; (*of birds*) chant, ramage; (*mere trifle*) morceau de pain, *m.* **~bird,** oiseau chanteur, *m.* **~ book,** chansonnier, *m.* **~ thrush,** grive chanteuse, *f.* **~ without words,** romance sans paroles. **~ writer,** chansonnier, *m.*

sonnet, *n,* sonnet, *m.*

sonorous, *a,* sonore; ronflant.

soon, *ad,* bientôt; tôt. **as ~ as,** [aus]sitôt que, dès que. **as ~ as possible,** le plus tôt possible. **see you soon,** à tout à l'heure. **~er,** *ad,* plus tôt; (*rather*) plutôt. **~ or later,** tôt ou tard. **no ~ said than done,** aussitôt dit, aussitôt fait.

soot, *n,* suie, *f.* **~y,** *a,* noir de suie.

soothe, *v.t,* adoucir, calmer. **soothing,** *a,* calmant.

soothsayer, *n,* devin, *m,* devineresse, *f.*

sop, *n,* trempette, *f;* (*fig.*) os à ronger, *m.* **sopping wet,** être trempé comme une soupe.

sophism, *n,* sophisme, *m.* **sophisticate,** *v.t,* sophistiquer. **~d,** *p.a,* savant. **sophistry,** *n,* sophistique, *f.*

soporific, *a.* & *n,* soporifique, *a.* & *m.*

soprano (*voice & pers.*) *n,* soprano, *m.*

sorcerer, ess, *n,* sorcier, ère, magicien, ne. **sorcery,** *n,* sorcellerie, *f.*

sordid†, *a,* sordide. **~ness,** *n,* vilenie, *f.*

sore†, *a,* douloureux, meurtri; malade; sensible; endolori; affligé; cruel. **I have a ~ finger,** j'ai mal au doigt. **~ eyes,** mal aux (ou d') yeux. **~ point,** endroit sensible, *m.* **~ throat,** mal à la gorge. **¶** *n,* plaie, *f.*

sorrel, *n,* oseille, *f.* **¶** *a,* saure.

sorrily, *ad,* tristement. **sorrow,** *n,* chagrin, *m,* douleur, peine, *f.* **¶** *v.i,* s'affliger. **~ful,** *a,* chagrin; triste. **~fully,** *ad,* tristement. **sorry,** *a,* fâché; triste; méchant, mauvais, pauvre, piteux. **I am ~,** je regrette. **to be ~ for,** être fâché de; plaindre; se repentir de. **in a ~ plight,** mal-en-point. **~! pardon!**

sort, *n,* sorte, *f,* genre, *m,* espèce, nature; manière, *f;* (*pl, Typ.*) as-

sortiment, *m. all* ~*s of*, of toute sorte de. *of the same* ~, de même acabit. ¶ *v.t*, trier; classer. ~**er**, *n*, trieur, euse.

sortie, *n*, sortie, *f*.

sot, *n*, ivrogne, *m*, ivrognesse, *f*. **sottish**, *a*, abruti.

sough, *v.i*, bruire, murmurer.

sought after, recherché.

soul, *n*, âme, *f*. ~**less**, *a*, sans âme.

sound†, *a*, sain; bon; solide; (*sleep*) profond. ¶ *n*, son; (*Geog.*) bras de mer, détroit, *m*; (*probe*) sonde, *f*. ~[*ing*] *board*, abat-voix, *m*; (*Mus.*) table d'harmonie, *f*. ~-*effects man*, bruiteur, *m*. (*TV & cinema*) ~ *track*, piste sonore, *f*. ~*proof*, *a*, insonore. ¶ *v.t*, faire sonner; sonner; sonder; pressentir; (*Med.*) ausculter; (*v.i.*) sonner, résonner. ~**ness**, *n*, solidité; rectitude, *f*.

soup, *n*, potage, bouillon, *m*; soupe, purée, *f*. ~ *kitchen*, fourneau philanthropique, *m*. ~ *ladle*, cuiller à potage, louche, *f*. ~ *plate*, assiette creuse, *f*. ~ *tureen*, soupière, *f*.

sour, *a*, aigre, sur, acide, vert; (*milk, etc.*) tourné. ¶ *v.t*, aigrir, enfieller. ~**ish**, *a*, aigrelet, suret. ~**ly**, *ad*, aigrement. ~**ness**, *n*, aigreur, acidité, *f*.

source, *n*, source, *f*.

south, *n*, sud; midi, *m*. ¶ *ad*, au sud. ¶ *a*, du sud; méridional; austral. S~ *Africa*, l'Afrique du Sud *ou* australe *ou* méridionale, *f*. S~ *African*, sud-africain. S~ *America*, l'Amérique du Sud, *f*. S~ *American*, sud-américain. ~*east*, sud-est, *m*. S~ *Pole*, pôle sud, *m*. S~ *Sea Islands*, îles du Pacifique, *f.pl*. ~*west*, sud-ouest, *m*. S~ *West Africa*, le Sud-Ouest africain, *m*. **southern**, *a*, [du] sud; méridionale; austral. ~**er**, *n*, méridional, e. **southward[s]**, *ad*, vers le sud.

souvenir, *n*, souvenir, *m*.

sou'wester (*wind, hat*) *n*, suroît, *m*.

sovereign, *a. &* (*pers.*) *n*, souverain, e; (£) souverain, *m*. ~**ty**, *n*, souveraineté, *f*.

soviet, *n*, soviet, *m*; (*att.*) soviétique.

sow, *n*, truie, coche; (*wild*) laie, *f*.

sow, *v.t. & i. ir*, semer; ensemencer.

~**er**, *n*, semeur, euse. **sowing**, *n*, ensemencement, *m*, semailles, *f.pl*. ~ *machine*, semoir, *m*, semeuse, *f*. ~ *time*, temps des semailles, *m*, semailles, *f.pl*.

soy[*a*] **bean**, soya, soja, pois chinois, *m*.

spa, *n*, ville d'eaux, *f*, eaux, *f.pl*, bains, *m.pl*.

space, *n*, espace; intervalle; entre-deux; vide, creux; (*Mus.*) interligne, *m*; (*on printed form*) case; (*Typ.*) espace, *f*. ~ *between lines*, interligne, *m*. *outer* ~, espace cosmique, extra-atmospherique, *m*. ¶ *v.t*, espacer. **spacious**, *a*, spacieux.

spacecraft, *n*, astronef, *m*.

spade, *n*, bêche, *f*; (*pl, cards*) pique, *m*. ¶ *v.t*, bêcher. ~**ful**, *n*, pelletée, *f*.

Spain, *n*, l'Espagne, *f*.

span, *n*, (*wings*) envergure; portée, travée, ouverture, *f*. ¶ *v.t*, franchir, chevaucher.

spandrel, *n*, tympan, *m*.

spangle, *n*, paillette, *f*. ~**d**, *p.p*, pailleté.

Spaniard, *n*, Espagnol, e. **spaniel**, *n*, épagneul, e. **Spanish**, *a*, espagnol; d'Espagne. ~ *fly*, cantharide, *f*. ~ *onion*, oignon doux d'Espagne, *m*. ¶ *n*, l'espagnol, *m*.

spank, *v.t*, fesser. ~**ing**, *n*, fessée, *f*.

spar, *n*, (*Naut.*) espar; (*Miner.*) spath, *m*. ¶ *v.i*, boxer; s'entraîner à la boxe.

spare, *a*, maigre, sec; disponible; libre; de rechange. ~ [*bed*]*room*, chambre d'ami, *f*. ~ [*part*], pièce de rechange, *f*. ~ *time*, loisir, *m*, *oft. pl*, heures dérobées, *f.pl*. ~ *tire*, pneu de secours, *m*. ¶ *v.t*, épargner; ménager; accorder; se passer de; respecter; faire grâce de; trouver. *to have enough & to* ~, avoir à revendre. **sparing**, *p.a*, économe, ménager; chiche, avare.

spark, *n*, étincelle; flammèche, *f*; brandon; gendarme, *m*; lueur, *f*; (*pers.*) mirliflore, galant, *m*. ~ *plug*, bougie d'allumage, *f*. **sparkle**, *v.i*, étinceler, briller, miroiter; pétiller; mousser. **sparkling**, *a*, étincelant; émerillonné; (*wine*) mousseux.

sparring, *n*, entraînement, *m*. ~ *match*, assaut de démonstration, *m.* ~ *partner,* partenaire d'entraînement, *m.*

sparrow, *n,* moineau, passereau, pierrot, *m.* ~ *hawk,* épervier, *m.*

sparse, *a,* peu dense, clairsemé, rare.

Spartan, *a.* & *n,* spartiate, *a.* & *m,f.*

spasm, *n,* spasme, *m.* **spasmodic,** *a,* saccadé; (*Med.*) spasmodique. ~**ally,** *ad,* par saccades, par sauts & par bonds.

spate, *n,* grandes eaux, *f.pl,* crue, *f.*

spats, *n. pl,* guêtres de ville, *f.pl.*

spatter, *v.t,* éclabousser.

spatula, *n,* spatule, *f.*

spawn, *n,* (*fish*) frai; (*mushroom*) blanc, mycélium, *m.* ¶ *v.i,* frayer.

speak, *v.i.* & *t. ir,* parler; dire; prononcer; prendre la parole; (*ship*) héler. ~ *one's mind,* se déboutonner. ~**er,** *n,* opinant; orateur, *m. loud*~, haut-parleur, *m.* **speaking,** *n,* parole, *f*; parler, *m.* X. ~ (*Teleph.*), ici X. *without* ~, à la muette. *we are not on* ~ *terms,* nous ne nous parlons pas.

spear, *n,* lance, *f.* ~ *head,* fer de lance, *m.* ~*mint,* menthe verte, *f.* ¶ *v.t,* percer; darder.

special†, *a,* spécial; particulier; extraordinaire. ~ *correspondent,* envoyé spécial, *m.* ~ *dish for the day,* plat du jour, *m.* ~**ist,** *n,* spécialiste, *m,f.* ~**ity,** *n,* spécialité, *f.* ~*ize in,* se spécialiser dans.

specie, *n,* espèces, *f.pl,* numéraire, *m.*

species, *n,* espèce, *f.*

specific†, *a,* spécifique; déterminé. ~ *gravity,* poids spécifique, *m.* ¶ *n,* spécifique, *m.* ~**ation,** *n,* spécification; énonciation, *f*; devis; cahier des charges, *m.* **specify,** *v.t,* spécifier; énoncer; préciser. **specimen,** *n,* spécimen; échantillon; modèle; exemplaire, *m.* **specious†,** *a,* spécieux.

speck, *n,* point, *m*; petite tache, *f*; grain, *m,* particule; piqûre, *f.* ~**le,** *v.t,* tacheter, moucheter.

spectacle, *n,* spectacle, *m*; (*pl.*) lunettes, *f.pl.* ~ *case,* étui à l—s, *m.* **spectacular,** *a,* à [grand] spectacle. **spectator,** *n,* spectateur, trice.

spectral, *a,* spectral. **specter,** *n,* spectre, *m.* **spectroscope,** *n,* spec-troscope, *m.* **spectrum,** *n,* spectre, *m.*

speculate, *v.i,* spéculer; jouer, agioter. **speculation,** *n,* spéculation, *f*; jeu, *m.* **speculative,** *a,* spéculatif; de spéculation. **speculator,** *n,* spéculateur, trice; agioteur, *m,* joueur, euse.

speech, *n,* parole, *f*; langage, *m*; langue, *f*; parler; discours, *m,* allocution, harangue, *f.* ~**ify,** *v.i,* pérorer. ~**less,** *a,* sans voix, muet.

speed, *n,* vitesse; célérité; rapidité, *f. at full* ~, à toute allure. ~*way,* autostrade, *f.* ¶ *v.i.ir,* se hâter, faire de la vitesse. ~ *up,* activer. **speedometer,** *n,* compteur de vitesse, *m.* **speedwell** (*Bot.*) *n,* véronique, *f.* **speedy,** *a,* rapide.

spell, *n,* charme, enchantement; sort; maléfice; tour, *m*; période, échappée, *f.* ~*bound,* fasciné. ¶ *v.t.* & *i. ir,* épeler; orthographier. **spelling,** *n,* orthographe; épellation, *f.* ~ *bee,* concours orthographique, *m.* ~ *book,* abécédaire, syllabaire, *m.*

spelter, *n,* zinc, *m.*

spend, *v.t.* & *i. ir,* dépenser; passer. ~*thrift,* n. & att, dépensier, ère, prodigue, *m,f.* & *a. spent bullet,* balle morte, *f.*

sperm, *n,* sperme, *m.* ~ *oil,* huile de spermaceti, *f.* ~ *whale,* cachalot, *m.* **spermaceti,** *n,* blanc de baleine, *m.* **spermatozoon,** *n,* spermatozoaire, *m.*

spew, *v.t.* & *i,* vomir.

sphere, *n,* sphère, *f.* **spherical,** *a,* sphérique.

sphincter, *n,* sphincter, *m.*

sphinx, *n,* sphinx, *m.*

spice, *n,* épice, *f*; (*fig.*) grain, *m.*

spick & **span,** tiré à quatre épingles, pimpant.

spicy, *a,* épicé, poivré.

spider, *n,* araignée, *f.* ~['s] *web,* toile d'a., *f.*

spigot, *n,* fausset, *m.*

spike, *n,* broche; cheville, *f,* crampon; (*pl, on wall*) chardon, artichaut; piquant; (*of flower*) épi, *m.* ¶ *v.t,* (*gun*) enclouer.

spill (*pipe light*) *n,* fidibus, *m.* *to have a* ~, faire panache. ¶ *v.t.ir,* répandre, renverser; verser.

spin, *n,* tournoiement, *m*; effet, *m*; (*Avn.*) vrille, *f.* ¶ *v.t.ir,* filer; (*top*) faire tourner, faire aller; (*v.i.*) tournoyer, toupiller. ~ *out,*

délayer. ~ yarns, débiter des histoires.

spinach, *n,* épinard, *m;* (*Cook.*) épinards, *m.pl.*

spinal, *a,* spinal; (*column*) vertébrale. ~ **cord,** moelle épinière, *f.*

spindle, *n,* fuseau, *m;* broche, *f;* mandrin; arbre, *m.* ~ **tree,** fusain, *m.*

spindrift, *n,* embrun, *m.*

spine, *n,* (*Bot.*) épine; (*Anat.*) é. dorsale, *f;* (*of book*) dos, *m.* **~less** (*fig.*) *a,* mollasse.

spinel, *n. & att,* spinelle, *m. & a.*

spinner, *n,* fileur, euse, filateur, trice; (*owner*) filateur, *m;* (*Fish.*) hélice, *f.*

spinney, *n,* bosquet, *m.*

spinning, *n,* filature; pêche à la [ligne] volante, *f.* ~ **mill,** filature, *f.* ~ **wheel,** rouet, *m.*

spinster, *n,* vieille fille, *f.*

spiny, *a,* épineux. ~ **lobster,** langouste, *f.*

spiral, *a,* spiral; hélicoïdal; (*spring*) à boudin; (*stairs*) tournant. ¶ *n,* spirale, *f.*

spire, *n,* flèche; (*whorl*) spire, *f.*

spirit, *n,* esprit, *m;* âme, *f;* génie; entrain, *m;* fougue; essence, *f;* alcool, *m;* liqueur [spiritueuse] *f,* (*pl.*) spiritueux, *m.pl.* ~ **lamp,** lampe à alcool, *f.* ~ **level,** niveau à bulle d'air, *m.* ~ **away,** faire disparaître comme par enchantement, escamoter. **~ed,** *a,* vif, animé; ardent, fougueux; courageux. **~less,** *a,* sans courage.

spiritual†, *a,* spirituel. **spiritualism,** *n,* (*psychics*) spiritisme; (*Philos.*) spiritualisme, *m.* **spiritualist,** *n,* (*psychics*) spirite; (*Philos.*) spiritualiste, *m,f.* **spirituous,** *a,* spiritueux.

spirt, *n,* jet, *m.* ¶ *v.i,* jaillir, gicler.

spit, *n,* (*roasting*) broche; (*Geog.*) flèche littorale, *m.* ¶ *v.t,* embrocher; sonder.

spit, *v.i. & t. ir,* cracher. ¶ *n,* crachat, *m.*

spite, *n,* dépit, *m,* malveillance, rancune, pique, *f.* **in ~ of,** en dépit de, malgré. ¶ *v.t,* dépiter. **~ful†,** *a,* malicieux, malveillant, rancunier, méchant.

spitfire, *n,* rageur, euse.

spittle, *n,* salive, *f.* **spittoon,** *n,* crachoir, *m.*

Spitzbergen, *n,* le Spitzberg.

splash, *n,* (*of water*) gerbe d'eau,

f; (*into water*) floc, *m;* (*mud*) éclaboussure; (*color*) goutte, *f.* ¶ *v.t,* faire jaillir; éclabousser; (*v.i.*) gicler; (*tap*) cracher. ~ **about,** s'agiter.

splay, *v.t,* couper en sifflet, ébraser; (*dislocate*) épauler.

spleen, *n,* (*Anat.*) rate, *f;* (*dumps*) spleen; (*spite*) dépit, *m.*

splendid†, *a,* splendide, magnifique; brillant. **splendor,** *n,* splendeur, magnificence, *f.*

splice, *n,* épissure, *f.* ¶ *v.t,* épisser.

splicer, *n,* (*film*) colleuse, *f.* **splicing,** *n,* (*film*) collage, *m.*

splint, *n,* éclisse, attelle, *f.* ~ [*bone*] péroné, *m.*

splinter, *n,* éclat, *m,* écharde; (*bone*) esquille, *f.* ¶ *v.t,* faire éclater; (*v.i.*) éclater.

split, *n,* fente; fêlure; (*fig.*) scission, *f.* **to do the ~,** faire le grand écart. ¶ *v.t.ir,* fendre; refendre; fractionner; (*ears with noise*) déchirer; (*v.i.*) se fendre, éclater; crever. ~ **hairs,** fendre un cheveu en quatre, pointiller. ~ **peas,** pois cassés, *m.pl.* ~ **the atom,** désintégrer l'atome. **splitting headache,** mal de tête affreux, *m.*

splutter, *n,* pétarade, *f.* ¶ *v.i,* pétarader; bredouiller.

spoil, *n,* dépouille, *f,* butin, gâteau, *m.* ¶ *v.t,* gâter, gâcher, abîmer; corrompre. **~sport,** trouble-fête, *m.*

spoke, *n,* rayon, *m.* ¶ *v.t,* enrayer.

spokesman, *n,* porte-parole, *m.*

spoliation, *n,* spoliation, *f.*

sponge, *n,* éponge, *f.* ~ **cake,** biscuit de Savoie, *m.* ~ **cloth,** tissu éponge, *m.* ¶ *v.t,* éponger. **sponger,** *n,* pique-assiette, *m.* **spongy,** *a,* spongieux.

sponsor, *n,* répondant, e; (*Eccl.*) parrain, *m,* marraine, *f.*

spontaneous†, *a,* spontané.

spook, *n,* fantôme, spectre, *m.*

spool, *n,* bobine, *f;* rouleau, *m.* ¶ *v.t,* bobiner.

spoon, *n,* cuiller, cuillère, *f.* **~bill,** spatule, *f.* **~ful,** cuillerée, *f.*

spoonerism, *n,* contre-petterie, *f.*

spoor, *n,* trace, *f,* erres, *f.pl.*

sporadic, *a,* sporadique.

spore, *n,* spore, *f.*

sport, *n,* jeu; (*s. & pl.*) sport, *m.* **~s editor,** rédacteur sportif, *m.* **~s ground,** terrain de jeux, *m.*

sportsman, n, sportif, amateur de sports, m.

spot, n, tache; macule; piqûre, f; goutte; place, f, endroit, site, lieu, m, lieux, m.pl; (Bil.) mouche, f; (Com.) disponible; comptant, m. on the ~, sur [la] place; séance tenante. ~light, projecteur orientable, m. weak ~, point faible, m. ¶ v.t, tacher; observer, repérer. **spotted,** p.p, tacheté, moucheté. **spotless,** a, sans tache.

spouse, n, époux, m, épouse, f.

spout, n, goulotte, f; bec; jet, m. ¶ v.i. & t, jaillir; déclamer, dégoiser.

sprain, n, entorse, foulure, f. to ~ one's . . ., se fouler le, la . . .

sprat, n, sprat, m.

sprawl, v.i, s'étaler, se vautrer.

spray, n, poussière [d'eau], gerbe [d'eau] f; (sea) embrun; (jewels) épi, m; (flowers) gerbe, chute; (Need.) chute, f; (squirt) vaporisateur, m. ¶ v.t, pulvériser, vaporiser. ~er, n, vaporisateur, m. arroseuse, f.

spread, n, développement, m; envergure; ouverture; propagation, f; (food) repas, m. ¶ v.t.ir, [é]tendre; déployer; répandre, semer; propager; échelonner, répartir, étager.

spree, n, noce, bamboche, f.

sprig, n, brin, m, brindille; pointe, f.

sprightly, a, vif, sémillant, éveillé; gai.

spring, n, élan, bond; ressort, m; élasticité; source, fontaine; (arch) naissance, retombée, f; (season) printemps, m; (att.) printanier. ~board, tremplin, m. ~ cleaning, grand nettoyage, m. ~ tide, grande marée, vive-eau, maline, f. ¶ v.i.ir, s'élancer, bondir; sourdre; dériver. ~ up, naître. ~y, a, élastique.

sprinkle, v.t, répandre; arroser; asperger; saupoudrer; (book edges) jasper. **sprinkler,** n, arrosoir, m.

sprint, n, course de vitesse, f. ~er, n, coureur de vitesse, m.

sprite, n, [esprit] follet, farfadet, m.

sprocket wheel, pignon de chaîne, m.

sprout, n, pousse, f, germe, m.

Brussels ~s, choux de Bruxelles, m.pl. ¶ v.i, pointer, germer.

spruce, a, pimpant, bien mis. ¶ n, sapin, m.

sprue, n, jet [de coulée] m.

sprung (provided with springs) p.a, à ressorts.

spur, n, éperon; (bird) ergot; (mountain) contrefort; (Build.) arc-boutant; (fig.) aiguillon, m. on the ~ of the moment, sous l'impulsion du moment. railway ~, embranchement, m. ¶ v.t, éperonner, talonner, piquer; aiguillonner.

spurious, a, faux, falsifié, contrefait, illégitime.

spurn, v.t, repousser, repousser du pied.

spurt, v.i, jaillir, gicler; (price) bondir, sauter. ¶ n, jet; bond, saut; (running) emballage; (rowing) enlevage, m.

sputter, n, pétarade, f. ¶ v.i, pétarader; bredouiller.

spy, n, espion, ne; (police) mouchard, m. ~glass, longue-vue, f. ¶ v.t. & i, espionner; moucharder; épier.

squab, n, pigeonneau, m.

squabble, n, querelle, f. ¶ v.i, se chamailler.

squad, n, escouade; brigade, f; peloton, m. **squadron,** n, (cavalry) escadron, m; (navy) escadre; (air) escadrille, f.

squalid, a, crasseux, sordide.

squall, n, grain, m, rafale, bourrasque, f. ¶ v.i, brailler. ~y, à grains, à rafales.

squalor, n, crasse, f.

squander, v.t, prodiguer, gaspiller, manger.

square, a, carré. ~ foot, pied carré, m. ~ inch, pouce carré, m. ~ meal, ample repas, m. ~ measure, mesure de surface, f. ~ mile, mille carré, m. ~ root, racine carrée, f. ~-shouldered, carré des épaules. ~ yard, yard carré, m. ¶ n, carré, m; (instrument & at right angles) équerre; (town) place, f; (parvis) parvis, m; (chessboard) case, f. ¶ v.t, carrer; équarrir; régler. ~[ly], ad, carrément.

squash, v.t, écraser, écarbouiller; aplatir. ¶ n, courge, courgette, f.

squat, v.i, s'accroupir; se blottir, se tapir. ¶ a, ragot, boulot, tassé, écrasé.

squatter, n, squatter, m.

squawk, n, cri rauque, m.

squeak, n, cri, m. ¶ v.i, crier, piailler.

squeal, n, cri [perçant] m. ¶ v.i, crier, piailler.

squeamish, a, dégoûté.

squeegee, n, racloir, m.

squeeze, n, compression, f; serrement, m. ¶ v.t, presser; serrer; pincer. ~ out, exprimer; (fig.) arracher de.

squelch, v.i, déconcerter; (revolt) étouffer.

squib, n, serpenteau, m; (fig.) pasquinade, f.

squid, n, calmar, m.

squint, v.i, loucher.

squirm, v.i, se tortiller.

squirrel, n, écureuil, m.

squirt, n, seringue, f. ¶ v.t, seringuer; (v.i.) jaillir.

stab, n, coup (de poignard) m. ¶ v.t, percer; poignarder.

stability, n, stabilité; consistance, f. **stabilize**, v.t, rendre stable; (Fin.) stabiliser. **stable**, a, stable. ¶ n, écurie; cavalerie, f. ¶ v.t, loger; établer.

staccato, a, (note) piquée; (voice) saccadée.

stack, n, (Agric.) meule; (heap) pile, f; (arms) faisceau, m; (chimney) souche, f. ¶ v.t, empiler; mettre en meule.

stadium, n, stade, m.

staff, n, bâton; (pilgrim's) bourdon, m; (Mus.) portée, f; personnel; atelier; (Mil.) État-major, m. ~ officer, officier d'É.-m., m.

stag, n, cerf, (young) hère m. ~ beetle, cerf-volant, m.

stage, n, estrade, f; échafaud, m; scène, f; théâtre, m; tréteaux, m.pl; platine, f; degré; stade, m; période, f. & m; phase; opération, f; relais, m; étape, traite; section, f. ~ door, entrée des artistes, f. ~ effect, effet scénique, artifice de théâtre, m. ~ fright, trac, m. ~hand, machiniste, m. ~ manager, régisseur, m. ~ name, nom de théâtre, m. ~ trick, jeu de scène, coup de théâtre, m. ~ whisper, aparté, m. ¶ v.t, mettre en scène, monter.

stagger, v.i, chanceler, tituber; (v.t.) consterner, ébouriffer; décaler.

stagnant, a, stagnant; (foul) croupissant. **stagnation**, n, stagnation, f, marasme, m.

staid, a, posé, rassis.

stain, n, tache; macule; souillure; couleur, f. ¶ v.t, tacher, souiller; colorer; mettre en couleur, teindre. stained glass, verre coloré, m; (church) vitraux peints, m. pl. stained-glass artist, peintre verrier, m. stained-glass window, verrière, f. **stainless**, a, sans tache; (steel) inoxydable.

stair, n, marche, f, degré, m. ~ carpet, tapis d'escalier, m. ~case & ~[s], escalier, m. ~ rail, rampe d'e., f.

stake, n, pieu, poteau, piquet, jalon; bûcher; intérêt; enjeu, m; mise, f; (pl, turf) prix, m. ¶ v.t, (bet) parier; garnir de pieux; (measure) jalonner. ~ one's reputation, jouer sa réputation.

stalactite, n, stalactite, f.

stalagmite, n, stalagmite, f.

stale, a, (bread) rassis; défraîchi; (liquor) éventé; vieilli.

stalemate (chess) n, pat, m. ¶ v.t, faire pat. ~d, p.a, pat.

stalk, n, tige, queue, f; pied, m. ¶ v.t, chasser à l'affût.

stall, n, stalle; chaise, f; kiosque; étalage, étal, m, échoppe, boutique, f. ¶ v.t, établer; (motor) caler.

stallion, n, étalon, m.

stalwart, a, robuste, vigoureux.

stamina, n, résistance, f, fond, m.

stammer, v.i. & t, bégayer. ~er, n, bègue, m,f.

stamp, n, poinçon; coin; pilon; bocard, m; marque; estampille, f; (postage, etc.) timbre, m; griffe; trempe, empreinte, f, cachet, sceau, m. rubber ~, timbre en caoutchouc, m. ¶ v.t. & i, frapper; piétiner, taper, trépigner; poinçonner; bocarder; marquer; étamper; estamper; estampiller; timbrer; affranchir. ~ed addressed envelope, enveloppe affranchie pour la réponse, f.

stampede, n, saùve-qui-peut, m.

stance, n, positition, f.

stanch, v.t, étancher.

stanchion, n, étançon, m; (ship) épontille, f.

stand, n, place; station, f; support; établi; pied; socle; affût; (music) lutrin; (exhibition) stand, *m*; (*stall*) étalage, *m*. (*cinema*) ~-*in*, doublure, *f*. ~*point*, point de vue, *m*. ~*still*, arrêt, *m*. ¶ *v.i.ir*, se tenir; se tenir debout; rester debout; se soutenir; stationner; se placer; se mettre; s'arrêter; se porter; tenir; durer; rester; reposer; (*v.t.ir.*) supporter, soutenir; subir; résister à; souffrir; (*drink*) payer. ~ *aside*, se ranger. ~ *back!* rangez-vous! ~ *fast*, tenir bon. ~ *in the way of*, faire obstacle à. ~ *on end* (hair), [se] hérisser. ~ *out*, [res]sortir, se détacher, marquer. ~ *up*, se tenir debout; se lever; se dresser.

standard, *n*, étendard; (*values*) étalon, *m*; (*weight, measure*) matrice, *f*; (*gold*) titre, *m*; (*of coin*) loi, *f*; critère, criterium; niveau, *m*; toise; classe, *f*; pied; arbre de plein vent; (*vaulting*) sautoir, *m*. ~ *bearer*, porte-étendard, *m*. ¶ *att*, étalon; type; classique; (*gauge*) normale; (*edition*) définitive; (*charge*) forfaitaire; (*gold*) au titre; (*solution*) titrée. ~*ize*, *v.t*, standardiser; unifier; (*Chem*.) titrer.

standing, *n*, place, pose, *f*; rang, *m*. *of long* ~, de longue date, ancien. ¶ *a*, debout; (*crops*) sur pied; (*Naut*.) dormant; (*water*) stagnante; (*orders*) permanent, e; (*expenses*) généraux; (*jump, dive*) sans élan; (*start*) arrêté. ~ *room only!* places debout seulement! ~ *type*, conservation, *f*.

standoffish, *a*, distant, réservé. ~*ness*, *n*, quant-à-moi, quant-à-soi, *m*.

stanza, *n*, stance, strophe, *f*.

staple, *n*, (*wall*) crampon; (*wire*) cavalier, *m*; (*lock*) gâche; (*to fasten papers*) agrate, *f*. ~ [*product*], produit principal, *m*, production principale, *f*. ~*s*, articles de première nécessité, *m.pl*. **stapler**, *n*, agrafeuse, *f*.

star, *n*, étoile, *f*; astre, *m*; (*lucky*) étoile, planète, *f*; (*Theat*.) vedette, *f*; (*Typ*.) astérisque, *m*. ~*fish*, étoile de mer, *f*. ~*gaze*, bayer aux corneilles. *shooting* ~, étoile filante, *f*.

starboard, *n*, tribord, *m*.

starch, *n*, amidon, *m*; fécule, *f*; (*paste*) empois, *m*. ¶ *v.t*, empeser, amidonner. ~*y* (*food*) *a*, féculent.

stare, *n*, regard appuyé, *m*. ¶ *v.i*, écarquiller les yeux. ~ *at*, regarder fixement, dévisager.

stark, *a*, raide. ~ *mad*, fou à lier. ~ *naked*, tout nu, nu comme un ver.

starling (*bird*) *n*, sansonnet, étourneau, *m*.

starry, *a*, étoilé.

start, *n*, tressaillement, sursaut, soubresaut, haut-le-corps; commencement, début; départ, *m*; avance, *f*. ¶ *v.i*, tressaillir; partir; commencer; débuter; démarrer; (*v.t*.) commencer; amorcer; mettre en marche; lancer; (*quarry*) lancer, débûcher. ~ *out*, se mettre en route. ~*er*, *n*, (*auto*) démarreur; (*signal giver*) starter; (*horse, runner*) partant, *m*. ~*ing line*, ligne de départ, *f*. ~*ing point*, point de d. ~*ing post*, poteau de d. *m*, barrière, *f*.

startle, *v.t*, faire tressaillir, effrayer, effaroucher, alarmer. **startling**, *p.a*, alarmant; saisissant.

starvation, *n*, inanition, faim, famine, *f*. ~ *diet*, diète absolue, *f*. ~ *wage*, salaire de famine, *m*. **starve**, *v.t*, priver de nourriture, affamer; (*v.i*.) mourir de faim. ~*ling*, *n*, affamé, e, meurt-de-faim, *m*. **starving**, *p.a*, affamé.

state, *n*, état, *m*; disposition, *f*; apparat; (*stage of engraved or etched plate*) état, *m*. *to lie in* ~ (of body), être exposé sur un lit de parade. ~ *controlled*, ~ *managed*, en régie. ~*room*, cabine, *f*. S~ *socialism*, étatisme, *m*. ¶ *v.t*, énoncer; déclarer; relater; annoncer; poser. ~*liness*, *n*, majesté, *f*. ~*ly*, *a*, majestueux, pompeux, superbe; fier. ~*ment*, *n*, énoncé, *m*, déclaration, *f*; relevé, état, exposé; bordereau, *m*. **statesman**, *n*, homme d'État, *m*.

static(al), *a*. & **statics**, *n*, statique, *a*. & *f*. *radio static*, perturbation atmosphérique, *f*.

station, *n*, station, *f*, poste, *m*; gare, *f*; rang, *m*. *filling* ~, poste d'essence, *m*. *police* ~, poste de police, *m*. ~*s of the Cross*, chemin de la croix, *m*. ~ *master*, chef de gare, *m*. ¶ *v.t*, [a]poster. ~*ary*, *a*, stationnaire; fixe, à demeure.

stationer, *n*, papetier, ère, ~*y*,

n, papeterie, *f*; papier à lettres, *m*.

stationwagon, *n*, break, *m*.

statistic(al), *a*, statistique. **statistician**, *n*, statisticien, *m*. **statistics**, *n*, statistique, *f*; mouvement, *m*.

statuary, *a*, statuaire. ¶ *n*, statues, *f.pl*; (*art*) statuaire, *f*; (*pers*.) statuaire, *m*. **statue**, *n*, statue, *f*. **statuette**, *n*, statuette, figurine, *f*.

stature, *n*, stature, taille, *f*.

status, *n*, statut, titre, état, *m*, qualité, *f*, standing, *m*. (*For example, "un immeuble de grand standing" = a luxury apartment house*.)

statute, *n*, loi, *f*; statut, *m*. ~ book, code, *m*. **statutory**, *a*, légal.

staunch, *a*, étanche; ferme; dévoué.

stave, *n*, douve; (*Mus*.) portée, *f*. ~ in, *v.t.ir*, enfoncer, défoncer. ~ off, parer.

stay, *n*, séjour; support; étai; tirant; hauban; (*pl*.) corset; (*law*) sursis, *m*. ~ in the country, villégiature, *f*. ¶ *v.i*, rester; demeurer; séjourner; attendre; s'arrêter; (*v.t*.) suspendre; (*law*) surseoir à; étayer. ~-at-home, *a*. & *n*. casanier, ère, pot-au-feu, *a*. ~ away, s'absenter. ~ up, veiller.

stead, *n*, lieu, *m*, place, *f*.

steadfast, *a*, constant, ferme. ~ly, *ad*, avec constance. ~ness, *n*, constance, *f*.

steady, *a*, ferme; stable; rangé; posé; réglé; suivi. ¶ *i*, fermel ¶ *v.t*, fixer, affermir.

steak, *n*, tranche, *f*; (*beef*) bifteck, *m*, entrecôte, *f*.

steal, *v.t*. & *i*. *ir*, voler, dérober. ~ away, se dérober. ~ in, se glisser dans. ~ing, *n*, vol, *m*. by stealth, à la dérobée. **stealthy**†, *a*, furtif.

steam, *n*, vapeur; fumée; buée, *f*; (*att*.) à vapeur. ~ engine, machine à vapeur, *f*. ~ room (bath), étuve humide, *f*. ¶ *v.t*, (*Cook*.) mettre à l'étuvée; (*v.i*.) marcher [à la vapeur]; fumer. ~er or ~boat or ~ship, *n*, vapeur, *m*, bateau à v., navire à v., steamer, *m*. ~ing (*Cook*.) *n*, étuvée, étouffée, estouffade, *f*.

steed, *n*, coursier, *m*.

steel, *n*, acier; (*of tinder box*) briquet; (*sharpener*) fusil, *m*; (*corset*) baleine, *f*; (*att*.) d'acier, en acier; métallique. ~ wool, paille de fer, *f*. ~ works, aciérie, *f*. ¶ *v.t*, acérer; aciérer; (*fig*.) cuirasser.

steep, *a*, raide, escarpé, ardu, fort, rapide. ¶ *v.t*, tremper, baigner. ~ed in (*fig*.), pétri de. **steeple**, *n*, clocher [pointu] *m*. ~chase, course d'obstacles, *f*. **steepness**, *n*, raideur, *f*, escarpement, *m*.

steer, *n*, bouvillon, *m*. ¶ *v.t*. & *i*, diriger, conduire, guider; gouverner. ~ clear of, éviter. **steerage**, *n*, avant, *m*. ~ passenger, passager de l'a., *m*. **steering**, *n*, direction; (*Naut*.) gouverne, *f*. ~ compass, compas de route, *m*. ~ wheel (auto) volant, *m*.

stellar, *a*, stellaire.

stem, *n*, tige; queue, *f*; (*ship*) étrave, *f*; (*Gram*.) thème, *m*. ~ stitch, point de tige, p. coulé, *m*. ¶ *v.t*, arrêter, refouler.

stench, *n*, puanteur, infection, *f*.

stencil, *n*, patron, pochoir; caractère à jour; (*typing*) stencil, *m*. ¶ *v.t*, patronner.

stenographer, *n*, sténographe, *m,f*. **stenography**, *n*, sténographie, *f*.

stentorian, *a*, de stentor.

step, *n*, pas, *m*; trotte; marche, *f*, degré; gradin; échelon, *m*; démarche; mesure; cadence, *f*; acheminement; (*pl*.) marchepied, *m*, échelle double, *f*. ~brother, demi-frère, *m*. ~daughter, belle-fille, *f*. ~father, beau-père, *m*. ~ladder, échelle double, *f*. ~mother, belle-mère; (*cruel*) marâtre, *f*. ~sister, demi-sœur, *f*. ~son, beau-fils, *m*. to take ~s, prendre des mesures. ¶ *v.i*, faire un pas; marcher; aller; venir; monter. ~ in, entrer. *stepping stone*, pierre à gué, *f*; (*fig*.) marchepied, échelon, *m*.

stereoscope, *n*, stéréoscope, *m*.

stereotype, *n*, cliché, *m*. ¶ *v.t*, clicher, stéréotyper.

sterile, *a*, stérile. **sterility**, *n*, stérilité, *f*. **sterilize**, *v.t*, stériliser.

sterling, *a*, (*Eng. money*) sterling, *a.inv*.; (*fig*.) de bon aloi; solide. ¶ *n*, la livre.

stern†, *a*, sévère; austère. ¶ *n*, ar-

rière, *m*; poupe, *f.* ~*post*, étambot, *m.* **sternness**, *n*, sévérité;
austérité, *f.*

sternum, *n*, sternum, *m.*

stet (*Typ.*), bon. ❡ *v.t*, donner son
bon à.

stethoscope, *n*, stéthoscope, *m.*

stevedore, *n*, déchargeur, débardeur, arrimeur, *m.*

stew, *n*, ragoût. *m.* ~*pan*, casserole, braisière, *f*, fait-tout, *m.*
❡ *v.t*, étuver; (*abs.*) fricoter.
stewed fruit, compote de fruits,
f.

steward, *n*, maître d'hôtel; intendant; régisseur; commissaire;
économe; garçon de cabine;
commis aux vivres; délégué, *m.*
~'s *mate* (*ship*), cambusier, *m.*
~'s *room*, dépense; (*ship*) cambuse, *f.*

stick, *n*, bâton, *m*; canne, *f*; (*umbrella*) manche, *m*; baguette, *f*;
cotret, *m*, (*pl.*) du bois. ❡ *v.t.ir*,
piquer; ficher; coller; (*Hort.*)
ramer; (*pig*) saigner; (*v.i.ir.*)
s'attacher; [se] coller, adhérer;
rester, tenir. ~ *in the mud*, s'embourber. **stickiness**, *n*, viscosité,
f.

stickleback, *n*, épinoche, *f.*

sticky, *a*, collant, gluant, visqueux.

stiff, *a*, raide; fort; rigide; tenace;
(*strained*) empesé, guindé; (*price*)
salé. ~ *collar*, faux col rigide,
m. ~ *neck*, torticolis, *m.* ~*en*,
v.t, raidir. ~*ness*, *n*, raideur; (*in
the joints of the body*) courbature, *f.*

stifle, *v.t*, étouffer, suffoquer.

stigma, *n*, stigmate, *m*, flétrissure,
tache, *f.* **stigmatize**, *v.t*, stigmatiser.

stile, *n*, échalier; (*door*) montant,
m.

stiletto, *n*, stylet, *m.*

still, *a*, calme, tranquille; silencieux; immobile, en repos; (*water*) dormante, morte; (*wine*)
non mousseux; (*lemonade*) non
gazeuse. ~*born*, mort-né. ~ *life*
(*art*), nature morte, *f.* ❡ *ad*, encore, toujours; cependant, néanmoins, toutefois. ❡ *n*, calme;
alambic, *m*, cornue, *f.* ❡ *v.t*,
calmer, apaiser, tranquilliser.
~*ness*, *n*, calme, *m*, tranquillité,
f, silence, *m.*

stilt, *n*, échasse, *f.* ~*ed*, *a*, guindé.

stimulant, *n*, stimulant, remontant, réconfort, *m.* **stimulate**, *v.t*,

stimuler. **stimulus**, *n*, stimulant,
aiguillon, *m.*

sting, *n*, aiguillon, dard, *m*,
piqûre; (*fig.*) morsure, *f.* ❡ *v.t.
& i. ir*, piquer; (*of conscience*)
bourreler. **stinging**, *p.a*, piquant.
~ *nettle*, ortie brûlante, ortie
grièche, *f.*

stingy, *a*, avare, pingre, mesquin,
chiche.

stink, *n*, puanteur, *f.* ❡ *v.i.ir*, puer.

stint, *v.t*, épargner; rationner.
~ *oneself*, se priver; se rationner.
without ~, sans réserve.

stipend, *n*, traitement, *m.*

stipple, *n*, pointillé, grené, *m.*
❡ *v.t*, pointiller.

stipulate, *v.t*, stipuler.

stir, *n*, remue-ménage, tapage;
mouvement, *m*. *make a* ~, faire
florès. ❡ *v.t*, remuer; agiter;
(*fire*) attiser; (*the blood*) fouetter;
(*v.i.*) remuer, bouger. ~ *up*,
exciter, susciter, émouvoir. **stirring**, *p.a*, émouvant; vibrant.

stirrup, *n*, étrier, *m.* ~ *cup*,
coup de l'étrier, *m.* ~ *leather*,
étrivière, *f.*

stitch, *n*, point [de couture] *m*;
(*Knit.*, *crochet*) maille, *f.* ~ *in
the side* (*Med.*), point de côté.
❡ *v.t*, coudre; (*leather*) piquer;
(*books*) brocher. ~ *together*,
appointer. ~*ed hem*, ourlet piqué, *m.* ~*er*, *n*, piqueuse, *f.*
~*ing*, *n*, point piqué, *m.*

stoat, *n*, hermine, *f.*

stock, *n*, (*descent*) race, lignée;
(*tree, etc.*) souche, *f*; estoc;
(*rifle, plane*) fût, bois, *m*; (*Hort.*)
sujet, porte-greffe, (*wild*) sauvageon; (*vine*) cep, *m*; (*flower*)
girofiée, *f*, violier, *m*; (*Com.*)
stock, *m*, provision; approvisionnement; matériel, *m*; (*Fin.*)
valeur, *f*. *oft. pl*, titre, *m*. *oft. pl*;
effets, fonds, *m.pl*; actions, *f.pl*;
(*Cook.*) consommé, *m*; (*pl*,
Naut.) chantier, *m*, cale [de
construction] *f*; (*pl*, *Hist.*) ceps,
m.pl, tabouret, *m. in* ~, en
magasin. ~*s & shares*, valeurs
mobilières, *f.pl.* ~*broker*, agent
de change; banquier en valeurs,
m. ~ *exchange*, bourse [des
valeurs] *f.* ~*fish*, stockfisch, *m.*
~*holder*, détenteur de titres, *m*;
actionnaire, sociétaire, *m,f*, rentier, ère. ~ *in trade*, existence
en magasin. ~ *phrase*, cliché, *m.*
~ *pot*, pot-au-feu, *m.* ~ *solution*

(*Phot.*), solution fondamentale, *f.* ~*-still*, sans mouvement. ~ *taking*, inventaire; recensement, *m.* ~ *yard*, (*cattle*) parc à bestiaux; (*materials*) parc à matières, *m.* ¶ *v.t.* approvisionner; assortir; tenir; peupler; meubler; empoissonner.

stockade, *n*, palissade, palanque, *f.*

stocking, *n*, bas, *m.*

stocky, *a*, trapu, ramassé, étoffé.

Stoic, *n. & att*, stoïcien, *m. & a.* **stoical†**, *a*, stoïque. **stoicism**, *n*, stoïcisme, *m.*

stoke, *v.t*, chauffer. ~*hole*, ~*hold*, chaufferie, chambre de chauffe, *f.* **stoker**, *n*, chauffeur; (*mechanical*) chargeur, *m.*

stole, *n*, étole; écharpe, *f.*

stolid, *a*, flegmatique. ~**ity**, *n*, flegme, *m.*

stomach, *n*, estomac; (*fig.*) cœur, *m.* ~ *ache*, mal d'estomac, *m.* ~ *pump*, pompe stomacale, *f.* ¶ *v.t*, digérer, avaler.

stone, *n*, pierre; roche, *f*; caillou; (*fruit*) noyau; (*grape*) pépin; (*building*) moellon, *m.* *grind*~, meule, *f.* ~ *dead*, raide mort. ~ (gem) *setter*, metteur en œuvre, *m.* ~'*s throw*, jet de pierre, *m.* ~*ware*, poterie de grès, *f.* grès, *m*, gresserie, *f.* ~*work*, maçonnerie, *f.* ¶ *v.t*, (*to death*) lapider. **stony**, *a*, pierreux; caillouteux; (*heart*) de pierre, de roche[r]; (*look*) glacé.

stool, *n*, tabouret; escabeau, *m*; sellette; (*Med.*) selle, *f. folding* ~, pliant, *m.*

stoop, *v.i*, se pencher; s'abaisser.

stop, *n*, arrêt, *m*; halte; station; pause; opposition, *f*; (*buffer*) butoir, *m*; (*Mech.*) butée, *f*; (*organ*) jeu; (*Phot.*) diaphragme; (*Typ.*) point, *m. to put a* ~ *to*, faire cesser. ~*cock*, robinet [d'arrêt] *m.* ~*gap*, bouche-trou, *m.* ~*watch*, chronographe; compteur de sport, *m.* ¶ *v.t*, arrêter; (*Naut.*) stopper; interrompre; suspendre; mettre opposition sur; cesser; (*wages*) retenir; (*leak*) boucher, aveugler; (*v.i.*) s'arrêter; stationner; rester; cesser. ~ *up*, boucher. ¶ *i*, halte[-là]! (*Naut.*, in telegrams) stop.

stope (*Min.*) *n*, gradin, *m.*

stoppage, *n*, arrêt; chômage, *m*;

retenue; obstruction, *f.* **stopper**, *n*, bouchon, *m.* ¶ *v.t*, boucher.

storage, *n*, [em]magasinage, *m.* **store**, *n*, approvisionnement, *m*, provision, fourniture; réserve; resserre, boutique, *f*, magasin, dépôt; entrepôt; économat, *m. department* ~, magasin de nouveautés, bazar, *m.* ~*keeper*, boutiquier, *m.* ¶ *v.t*, approvisionner; (*fig.*) meubler; emmagasiner; mettre en dépôt. ~ *up*, accumuler.

stork, *n*, cigogne, *f.*

storm, *n*, orage, *m*; tempête, tourmente, *f.* ~ *cloud*, nuée, *f.* ~ *of abuse*, algarade, *f.* ¶ *v.t*, donner l'assaut à; (*v.i.*) tempêter. **stormy**, *a*, orageux, tempétueux. *at* ~ (barometer), à la tempête.

story, *n*, histoire, *f*; conte, *m*; narration; fable; menterie, *f*; (*floor*) étage, *m.* ~ *book*, livre de contes, *m.* ~ *teller*, conteur, euse; narrateur, trice.

stout†, *a*, fort, vigoureux; robuste; renforcé; brave; gros, corpulent, replet. ¶ (*beer*) *n*, stout, *m.* ~**ness** (*of body*) *n*, embonpoint, *m.*

stove, *n*, poêle; fourneau; réchaud, *m*; étuve, *f.*

stow (*Naut.*) *v.t*, arrimer. ~ *away*, *v.t*, serrer; (*v.i.*) s'embarquer clandestinement. ~*away*, *n*, passager (ère) clandestin(e), *m.*

straddle, *v.t. & i*, chevaucher.

strafe, *v.t*, mitrailler.

straggle, *v.i*, traîner. **straggler**, *n*, traînard, *m.* **straggling**, *a*, (*houses*) éparses; (*village*) aux maisons éparses; (*beard*) maigre.

straight, *a*, droit; (*hair*) plats; (*respectable*) honnête. *go* ~ *ahead*, allez tout droit. ¶ *ad*, [tout] droit; directement. ¶ *n*, ligne droite, *f.* ~*en*, *v.t*, [re]dresser, rectifier. **straightforward**, *a*, droit. **straightforwardly**, *ad*, sans détour; carrément. **straightforwardness**, *n*, droiture, *f*; sans-façon, *m.* **straightness**, *n*, rectitude, *f.*

strain, *n*, (*molecular*) tension; (*Mech.*) déformation; (*overstrain*) fatigue, *f*; (*Med.*) effort; (*Vet.*) écart, *m*; (*descent*) race; (*dash*) teinte, *f*; (*pl.*) accents, *m.pl.* ~ *in the back*, tour de reins, *m.* ¶ *v.t*, tendre; déformer; fatiguer; torturer; (*Med.*) fouler;

(*filter*) passer, filtrer, tamiser. ~ed (*fig.*) *p.a*, guindé. ~er, *n*, passoire, couloire, *f*, tamis, *m*; crépine, *f*.

trait, *n*, (*s. & pl.*) détroit, pertuis, *m*; (*pl.*) gêne, détresse, *f*, malaise, embarras, *m*. S—s of Dover, [détroit du] Pas de Calais, *m*. S—s of Gibraltar, détroit de Gibraltar. **straitjacket**, *n*, camisole de force, *f*. **straitlaced**, *a*, collet monté, bégueule. **in straitened circumstances**, dans la gêne.

trand, *n*, rivage; (*rope*) cordon, toron, brin, *m*. ¶ *v.t. & i*, échouer; jeter à la côte.

trange†, *a*, étrange; étranger; bizarre. **stranger**, *n*, étranger, ère; inconnu, e. **strangeness**, *n*, étrangeté; bizarrerie, *f*.

trangle, *v.t.*, etrangler, juguler. ~s (*V et.*) *n.pl*, gourme, *f*. **strangulation**, *n*, etranglement, *m*, strangulation, *f*.

trap, *n*, courroie; sangle; bande, *f*; bracelet; tirant; lien, *m*. ¶ *v.t*, sangler.

tratagem, *n*, stratagème, *m*, ruse, *f*. **strategic(al)†**, *a*, stratégique. **strategist**, *n*, stratège, *m*. **strategy**, *n*, stratégie, *f*.

tratified, *p.p*, stratifié. **stratum**, *n*, couche, *f*, gisement, *m*.

tratosphere, *n*, stratosphère, *f*.

traw, *n*, paille, *f*; fétu; (*drinking*) chalumeau; (*fig.*) fétu, *m*. the last ~, le comble [de nos maux]. ~board, carton-paille, *m*. ~ hat, chapeau de paille, *m*. ~ hut (*native*), paillote, *f*. ~ mattress, paillasse, *f*.

trawberry, *n*, fraise, *f*. ~ plant, fraisier, *m*.

tray, *v.i*, errer; s'écarter. ¶ *a*, égaré; errant; épave. ~ cat, chat de gouttières, *m*. ¶ *n*, épave, *f*.

treak, *n*, trait, sillon, *m*, raie, bande, *f*. ¶ *v.t*, rayer, sillonner. ~y (*meat*) *a*, entrelardée.

tream, *n*, cours d'eau; ruisseau; flot; jet; filet; cours; torrent, *m*. ~lined, profilé, fuselé, aérodynamique. ~lining, aérodynamisme, *m*. ¶ *v.i*, ruisseler. ~er, *n*, flamme, *f*; (*paper*) serpentin, *m*.

treet, *n*, rue, *f*; (*s. & pl. fig.*) pavé, *m*. back ~, rue détournée, *f*. main ~, artère principale, *f*. ~ lamp, réverbère, *m*. ~ musician, musicien de carrefour, *m*.

streetcar, *n*, tramway, *m*.
streetcleaner, *n*, éboueur, *m*.
strength, *n*, force; puissance; résistance; robustesse; intensité, *f*; (*of a solution*) titre; (*men*) effectif, *m*. ~en, *v.t*, renforcer; consolider; fortifier.

strenuous†, *a*, énergique; (*life*) intense.

streptomycin, *n*, streptomycine, *f*.

stress, *n*, effort; travail, *m*; charge; fatigue; (*weather*) violence, *f*; accent, appui, *m*. to be in ~ (*Mech.*), travailler. ¶ *v.t*, charger; fatiguer; appuyer sur; accentuer; (*Mus.*) scander.

stretch, *n*, trait, *m*; étendue, traite; (*of person's arms*) envergure, *f*; parcours; (*Mech.*) allongement, *m*. ¶ *v.t*, étendre, étirer; allonger; tendre. ~ oneself, s'étirer. **stretcher**, *n*, brancard, *m*; civière, *f*; raidisseur; (*for painter's canvas*) châssis, *m*. ~ bearer, brancardier, *m*.

strew, *v.t.ir*, répandre; joncher; [par]semer.

stria, *n*, strie, *f*. **striate[d]**, *a*, strié, striation, *n*, striure, *f*.

strickle, *n*, racloire, *f*.

strict†, *a*, strict; formel; rigoureux; sévère; exact. ~ness, *n*, rigueur; sévérité, *f*. ~ure, *n*, critique, *f*; (*Med.*) rétrécissement, *m*.

stride, *n*, enjambée, *f*, pas, *m*; (*pl.*) essor, *m*. ~ along, *v.i.ir*, marcher à grands pas.

strident, *a*, strident.

strife, *n*, guerre, *f*; conflit, *m*.

strike, *n*, (*coin*) frappe; (*labor*) grève, *f*. wildcat ~, grève sauvage, *f*. ¶ *v.t.ir*, frapper; assener; porter; choquer; (*match*) frotter; rencontrer; atteindre; battre; (*clock*) sonner; (*root, v.t. & abs.*) jeter, prendre; (*tent*) plier; (*sail*) caler; (*colors*) amener; (*a balance*) établier, faire; (*fish*) ferrer; (*v.i.ir.*) frapper; sonner; (*labor*) se mettre en grève. it ~s me, il me semble, il me vient l'idée. without striking a blow, sans coup férir. ~ down, abattre. ~ out, effacer, rayer, radier, biffer. ~ up (*tune*) entonner. **striker**, *n*, gréviste, *m,f*. **striking**, *p.a*, frappant, saisissant; marquant; saillant;

(*labor*) en grève. ~ *clock*, pendule à sonnerie, *f.*

string, *n,* ficelle; corde; cordelette; *f;* cordon; tirant; filet, *m;* fibre; filandre, *f;* chapelet; attirail; train, *m;* enfilade, *f;* (*Bil.*) boulier, *m.* the ~s (*Mus.*), les cordes. ~ *band,* orchestre à cordes, *m.* ¶ *v.t,* order; enfiler; (*violin*) monter. ~**ed,** *p.a,* à cordes.

stringbean, *n,* haricot vert, *m.*

stringent, *a,* rigoureux.

stringy, *a,* fibreux; filandreux.

strip, *n,* bande, *f;* ruban, *m.* ¶ *v.t,* dépouiller; dégarnir; (*v.i.*) se déshabiller.

stripe, *n,* raie, barre, *f,* liteau; (*N.C.O.'s, Navy*) galon, *m.* ~**d,** *a,* rayé, à raies; tigré, zébré.

strive, *v.i.ir,* s'efforcer, tâcher; combattre.

stroke, *n,* coup, *m;* atteinte, *f;* battement, *m;* course, *f;* trait, *m;* raie, barre; attaque, *f,* coup de sang, *m;* (*Swim.*) nage; brassée; brasse, *f;* (*rowing*) chef de nage, *m.* sun ~, coup de soleil, *m.* ¶ *v.t,* caresser.

stroll, *n,* tour, *m,* promenade, *f.* ¶ *v.i,* se promener; errer; flâner. **stroller,** *n,* flaneur, *m;* (*baby carriage*) pousette, *f.* **strolling,** *p.a,* ambulant.

strong†, *a,* fort; puissant; vigoureux; énergique; renforcé; résistant; solide; (*flavor*) relevé; (*wind*) carabiné; (*language*) corsé; (*well up in*) calé. ~ *box,* coffre-fort, *m.* ~ *drink,* liqueurs fortes, *f.pl.* ~*hold,* citadelle, *f,* fort, *m.* ~ *man* (professional), hercule, *m.* ~*-minded person,* tête forte, forte tête, *f.* ~ *point,* fort, *m.* ~ *room,* cave forte; (*ship*) chambre des valeurs, *f.*

strop, *n,* cuir [à rasoir], affiloir; (*safety blade*) repasseur, *m.* ¶ *v.t,* repasser [sur le cuir, etc.].

structural, *a,* (*steel, etc.*) de construction; (*repairs*) grosses. **structure,** *n,* structure; construction; formation, *f;* édifice; ouvrage d'art; (*fig.*) échafaudage, *m.*

struggle, *n,* lutte, *f.* ¶ *v.i,* lutter, batailler.

strum, *v.t,* tapoter.

strut, *n,* entretoise; contre-fiche; bielle, *f.* ¶ *v.i,* se pavaner, se rengorger, se carrer.

strychnine, *n,* strychnine, *f.*

stub, *n,* souche, *f,* chicot; bout; (*check*) talon, *m.*

stubble, *n,* chaume, *m,* éteule, *f*

stubborn†, *a,* obstiné, entêté; têtu; tenace. ~**ness,** *n,* obstination, opiniâtreté; ténacité, *f.*

stucco, *n,* stuc, *m.* ¶ *v.t,* enduire de stuc.

stuck-up, *a,* fier.

stud, *n,* clou; crampon, *m;* pointe, *f;* goujon; bouton; plot [de contact]; (*scantling in wall*) potelet, *m;* (*horses*) écurie, *f;* (*breeding*) haras, *m.* ~ *book,* livre généalogique, stud-book, *m.* ~ *farm,* haras, *m.* ~ *horse,* étalon, *m.* ¶ *v.t,* clouter; parsemer; émailler; hérisser. *studded crossing* (pedestrian), passage clouté, *m,* les clous, *m.pl.*

student, *n,* élève, *m,f;* étudiant, e; normalien, ne. **studied,** *p.p,* étudié; recherché; (*deliberate*) voulu. ~ *elegance,* recherche, *f.* **studio,** *n,* atelier; théâtre; studio; salon de pose, *m.* **studious†,** *a,* studieux, appliqué. **study,** *n,* étude, *f;* cabinet de travail, *m* ¶ *v.t. & i,* étudier.

stuff, *n,* matière; étoffe, *f;* (*fig.*) bois, *m.* ~ *& nonsense,* fadaises, *f.pl.* ¶ *v.t,* rembourrer; fourrer; bourrer; (*dead animal*) empailler; (*Cook.*) farcir. ~**ing,** *n,* bourre; (*Cook.*) farce, *f.* ~**y,** *a,* étouffant.

stultify, *v.t,* neutraliser.

stumble, *v.i,* broncher, trébucher [s']achopper. *stumbling block,* pierre d'achoppement, *f.*

stump, *n,* tronçon; moignon; chicot, *m;* souche, *f;* trognon; bout, *m;* (*art*) estompe, *f.* ~ *orator,* déclamateur, *m.* ¶ *v.t,* faire une campagne électorale, marcher en clopinant.

stun, *v.t,* étourdir. *stunning blow,* coup de massue, *m.*

stunt, *n,* acrobatie, *f,* tour de force, *m.* ~*man,* cascadeur, *m* ¶ *v.t,* rabougrir.

stunted, *p.p,* rabougri, avorté; malvenu, chétif.

stupefy, *v.t,* hébéter; (*narcotize*) stupéfier.

stupendous†, *a,* prodigieux.

stupid†, *a,* stupide; bête. ~**ity,** *n* stupidité; bêtise, *f.* **stupor,** *n* stupeur, *f.*

sturdy†, *a,* vigoureux, robuste.

sturgeon, *n,* esturgeon, *m.*

stutter, *v.i.* & *t,* bégayer ~**er,** *n,* bègue, *m,f.*

sty, *n,* étable à porcs; porcherie, *f.*

sty[e] (*on the eye*) *n,* orgelet, compère-loriot, *m.*

style, *n,* style, *m;* manière, *f,* genre, goût; chic; nom, *m;* (*firm name*) raison [sociale] *f.* ~ *of hairdressing,* coiffure, *f.* ¶ *v.t,* qualifier; donner le titre de.

stymie (*golf*) *n,* trou barré, *m.*

stylish†, *a,* élégant, galant, à la mode; chic; coquet.

suave†, *a,* suave. **suavity,** *n,* suavité, *f.*

sub-acid, *a,* aigre-doux.

subaltern, *n,* [officier] subalterne, *m.*

subcommittee, *n,* sous-comité, *m.*

subconscious, *a.* & *n,* subconscient, *a.* & *m.* ~**ness,** *n,* subconscience, *f.*

subcontract, *n,* sous-traité, *m.* ~**or,** *n,* sous-traitant, *m.*

subcutaneous, *a,* sous-cutané.

subdivide, *v.t,* subdiviser, morceler.

subdue, *v.t,* subjuguer, soumettre, assujettir; maîtriser; adoucir; (*light*) adoucir, tamiser.

subject, *n,* sujet; propos, *m;* (*pers.*) sujet, te. ~ *catalog,* catalogue par ordre de matières, *m.* ¶ *v.t,* soumettre, assujettir. ¶ ~ *to,* sujet(te) à; soumis(e) à; sous [le] bénéfice de; sous réserve de; sauf à. ~**ion,** *n,* sujétion, *f,* assujettissement, *m;* dépendance, *f.* ~**ive†,** *a.* & *n,* subjectif, *a.* & *m.*

subjoined, *p.p,* ci-joint.

subjugate, *v.t,* subjuguer.

subjunctive [mood], *n,* subjonctif, *m.*

sublet, *v.t.ir,* sous-louer, relouer.

sublimate, *v.t,* sublimer.

sublime†, *a.* & *n,* sublime, *a.* & *m.* **sublimity,** *n,* sublimité, *f.*

sublunar[y], *a,* sublunaire.

submachine gun, *n,* mitraillette, *f.*

submarine, *a.* & *n,* sous-marin, *a.* & *m.*

submerge, *v.t,* submerger; (*v.i.*) plonger.

submission, *n,* soumission, *f.* **submissive,** *a,* soumis, obéissant. ~**ness,** *n,* soumission, résignation, *f.* **submit,** *v.t,* soumettre. ~ *to,* se soumettre à, obéir à, subir.

suborder, *n,* sous-ordre, *m.*

subordinate, *a,* subordonné, subalterne, en sous-ordre. ¶ *n,* subordonné, e, sous-ordre, *m.* ¶ *v.t,* subordonner.

suborn, *v.t,* suborner, séduire. ~**er,** *n,* suborneur, euse.

subpoena, *n,* citation, assignation, *f.* ¶ *v.t,* citer, assigner, ajourner.

subscribe, *v.t.* & *i,* souscrire; s'abonner; se cotiser. **subscriber,** *n,* souscripteur, *m;* abonné, e. **subscription,** *n,* souscription; cotisation, *f;* abonnement, *m.*

subscript, *n,* indice inférieur, *m.*

subsection, *n,* alinéa, *m.*

subsequent†, *a,* subséquent, postérieur.

subservience, *n,* sujétion, *f.* **subservient,** *a,* auxiliaire, subalterne; servile.

subside, *v.i,* baisser; s'affaisser; [se] calmer. **subsidence,** *n,* baisse, *f;* affaissement, effondrement, *m.*

subsidiary†, *a,* subsidiaire; auxiliaire. ~ [*company*], [société] filiale, *f.*

subsidize, *v.t,* subventionner. **subsidy,** *n,* subvention, *f;* subside, *m.*

subsist, *v.i,* subsister; vivre. ~**ence,** *n,* subsistance, *f.*

subsoil, *n,* sous-sol; (*law*) tréfonds, *m.*

substance, *n,* substance, *f;* fond; corps; bien, *m.* **substantial,** *a,* substantiel; solide; (*lunch*) dînatoire. ~**ly,** *ad,* substantiellement, en substance. **substantiate,** *v.t,* établir.

substantive, *a.* & *n,* substantif, *a.* & *m.*

substitute, *n,* succédané, *m;* (*pers.*) remplaçant, e; suppléant, e. ¶ *v.t,* substituer.

substratum, *n,* fond, *m.*

substructure, *n,* substruction, *f.*

subtenant, *n,* sous-locataire, *m,f.*

subterfuge, *n,* subterfuge, *m.*

subterranean, *a,* souterrain.

subtilize, *v.t.* & *i,* subtiliser.

subtitle, *n,* sous-titre, *m.*

subtle†, *a,* subtil, raffiné, fin. ~**ty,** *n,* subtilité, *f,* raffinement, *m.*

subtract, *v.t,* soustraire, retrancher. ~**ion,** *n,* soustraction, *f.*

suburb, *n,* faubourg, *m,* (*pl.*) banlieue, *f.* ~**an,** *a,* suburbain; de banlieue.

subvention, *n,* subvention, *f.*

subversive, *a*, subversif. **subvert**, *v.t*, renverser.

subway, *n*, passage souterrain; (*train*) métropolitain, métro, *m*.

succeed, *v.t*, succéder à; suivre; (*v.i.*) succéder; (*prosper*) réussir, succéder; arriver; parvenir. ~**ing**, *p.a*, suivant. **success**, *n*, succès, *m*, réussite, *f*. ~**ful†**, *a*, heureux; réussi. **succession**, *n*, succession; suite, *f*. **successive†**, *a*, successif. **successor**, *n*, successeur, *m*.

succinct†, *a*, succinct. ~**ness**, *n*, concision, *f*.

succor, *n*, secours, *m*. ¶ *v.t*, secourir.

succulent, *a*, succulent.

succumb, *v.i*, succomber.

such, *a*, tel; pareil; semblable. ~ *as*, tel que; comme.

suck, *v.t. & i*, sucer; téter; aspirer. ~ *in*, humer. ~ *up*, pomper. ~**er**, *n*; (*of insect*) suçoir, *m*; (*of leech*) ventouse, *f*; (*Hort.*) drageon, surgeon, *m*, talle, *f*, œilleton, *m*; branche gourmande, *f*; (*fig.*) poire, *f*. ~**le**, *v.t*, allaiter; nourrir. ~**ling**, *n*, enfant à la mamelle; nourrisson, *m*. **suction**, *n*, succion; aspiration, *f*. ~ *pump*, pompe aspirante, *f*.

sudden†, *a*, soudain, subit; brusque. ~ *turn* (road), crochet, *m*. *all of a* ~, tout à coup. ~**ness**, *n*, soudaineté, *f*.

suds, *n.pl*, eau de savon, *f*.

sue, *v.t*, (*legal*) traduire en justice, poursuivre, actionner.

suede, *n*, suède, daim, *m*.

suet, *n*, graisse de rognon de bœuf, de mouton, *f*.

suffer, *v.t*, supporter; subir; éprouver; tolérer; (*v.i.*) souffrir; pâtir. ~**able†**, *a*, supportable. ~**ance**, *n*, souffrance; tolérance, *f*. ~**er**, *n*, victime, *f*; patient, e. ~**ing**, *n*, souffrance, *f*. ~**ing**, *p.a*, souffrant.

suffice, *v.i*, suffire. ~ *it to say that*, suffit que. **sufficiency**, *n*, suffisance; aisance, *f*. **sufficient†**, *a*, suffisant.

suffix, *n*, suffixe, *m*. ~**ed**, *p.a*, suffixe.

suffocate, *v.t*, suffoquer; asphyxier. **suffocation**, *n*, suffocation; asphyxie, *f*.

suffragan, *a. & n*, suffragant, *a.m. & m*.

suffrage, *n*, suffrage, *m*. **suffragette**, *n*, suffragette, *f*.

suffuse, *v.t*, se répandre sur; baigner. **suffusion**, *n*, suffusion, *f*.

sugar, *n*, sucre, *m*. ~ *almond*, dragée, *f*. ~ *bowl*, sucrier, bol à sucre, *m*. ~ *beet*, betterave à s., *f*. ~ *candy*, sucre candi, *m*. ~ *cane*, canne à s., *f*. ~ *refinery*, sucrerie, *f*. ~ *sifter*, saupoudroir à sucre, *m*. ~ *tongs*, pinces à s., *f.pl*. *granulated* ~, sucre semoule, *m*. *lump* ~, s. en morceaux, *m*. *maple* ~, s. d'érable, *m*. ¶ *v.t*, sucrer. ~**y**, *a*, sucré; saccharin.

suggest, *v.t*, suggérer, dicter. ~**ion**, *n*, suggestion, *f*. ~**ive**, *a*, suggestif.

suicide, *n*, suicide, *m*; (*pers.*) suicidé, *m*. *to commit* ~, se suicider.

suit, *n*, procès civil; complet; habit; costume, (*slang*) costard, *m*; (*cards*) couleur, *f*. ~**case**, valise, *m*. ~ *of armor*, armure complète, *f*. ~ *of clothes*, complet. ~ *to measure*, complet sur mesure. ¶ *v.t*, adapter; approprier; assortir; aller à; convenir à; accommoder; (*v.i.*) cadrer; convenir. ~**ability**, *n*, convenance; adaptation, *f*. ~**able†**, *a. & ~ed*, *p.p*, convenable, sortable, adapté, approprié, assortissant; propre.

suite, *n*, suite, *f*, train, *m*; enfilade, *f*. ~ *[of furniture]*, ameublement; mobilier, *m*. ~ *[of rooms]*, appartement, *m*, chambres en enfilade, *f.pl*.

suitor, *n*, (*law*) plaideur; (*wooer*) aspirant, prétendant, soupirant, poursuivant, *m*.

sulfate, *n*, sulfate, *m*. **sulfide**, *n*, sulfure, *m*. **sulfite**, *n*, sulfite, *m*. ~ *pulp*, pâte au bisulfite, *f*. **sulfur**, *n*, soufre, *m*. ~ *bath*, bain sulfureux, *m*. ~ *mine*, soufrière, *f*.

sulk, *v.i*, bouder; (*slang*) faire la gueule. ~**y**, *a*, boudeur.

sullen, *a*, renfrogné, maussade, morose. ~**ness**, *n*, maussaderie, *f*.

sully, *v.t*, souiller, tacher, ternir.

sultan, *n*, sultan, *m*. **sultana**, *n*, sultane, *f*.

sultry, *a*, étouffant, lourd, caniculaire.

sum, *n*, somme, *f*; calcul; comble,

m. ~ *total*, somme totale, *f*, montant global, *m.* ~ *up*, résumer; résumer les débats. **summarize**, *v.t*, résumer. **summary†**, *a*, sommaire. ¶ *n*, sommaire, résumé, *m*.

summer, *n*, été, *m.* ~ *house*, pavillon [de jardin], kiosque de j., *m.* ~ *lightning*, éclair[s] de chaleur, *m.*[pl.]. ~ *resort*, station estivale, *f.* ~ *vacation*, grandes vacances, *f.pl.* Indian ~, été de la Saint-Martin, *m.* ¶ *v.i,* passer l'été; (*v.t.*) estiver.

summing up, résumé des débats, *m.*

summit, *n*, sommet, *m*, cime, *f*, faîte, comble, *m*.

summon, *v.t*, citer, assigner; sommer; convoquer. ~ *back* & ~ *up*, rappeler. **summons**, *n*, sommation; citation, *f.* ¶ *v.t*, citer.

sump, *n*, puisard, *m*.

sumptuous†, *a*, somptueux; (*fare*) pantagruélique. **~ness**, *n*, somptuosité, *f*, luxe, *m*.

sun, *n*, soleil, *m.* **~bath**, bain de s., *m.* **~bathing**, bains de s., *m.pl.* **~beam**, rayon de s., *m.* **~burn**, hâle, *m.* to get **~burnt**, se hâler. **~dial**, cadran solaire, *m.* **~flower**, soleil, tournesol, *m.* **~light**, lumière du s., *f.* **~lit**, ensoleillé. **~rise**, lever du s., *m.* **~set**, coucher de s., s. couchant, *m.* at **~set** or at **~down**, au coucher du s. **~shine**, soleil, *m.* **~shiny day**, jour de s., *m.* **~spot**, tache du s., t. solaire, macule, *f.* **~stroke**, insolation, *f*, coup de s., *m.* ¶ *v.t*, ensoleiller. ~ *oneself*, se chauffer au soleil, lézarder.

Sunday, *n*, dimanche, *m.* to put on one's ~ *best*, s'endimancher.

sunder, *v.t*, séparer.

sundries, *n.pl*, [articles] divers, *m.pl.* **sundry**, *a*, divers.

sunken, *p.a*, creux; cave; noyé.

sunless, *a*, sans soleil. **sunny**, *a*, ensoleillé.

sup, *v.i*, souper.

superabundant†, *a*, surabondant.

superannuated, *p.p*, suranné.

superb†, *a*, superbe.

supercargo, *n*, subrécargue, *m*.

supercilious†, *a*, dédaigneux, hautain.

superficial†, *a*, superficiel. **superficies**, *n*, superficie, *f*.

superfine, *a*, superfin, surfin.

superfluity, *n*, superfluité, *f*, superflu, embarras, *m.* **superfluous**, *a*, superflu.

superheat, *v.t*, surchauffer.

superhuman, *a*, surhumain.

superimpose, *v.t*, superposer.

superintend, *v.t*, surveiller; présider à. **~ence**, *n*, surveillance, *f.* **~ent**, *n*, surveillant, e; surintendant, e; chef; (*police*) commissaire; (*restaurant*) maître d'hôtel, *m*.

superior†, *a*. & *n*, supérieur, e. **~ity**, *n*, supériorité, *f*.

superlative†, *a*, souverain; (*Gram.*) superlatif. ¶ *n*, superlatif, *m*.

superman, *n*, surhomme, *m*.

supermarket, *n*, supermarché, (*outsized*) hypermarché, *m*.

supernatural†, *a*. & *n*, surnaturel, *a*. & *m*.

supernumerary, *a*. & *n*, surnuméraire, *a*. & *m.* ¶ (*Theat.*) *n*, figurant, e, comparse, *m,f*.

superscript, *n*, indice supérieur, *m*.

superscription, *n*, suscription, *f*.

supersede, *v.t*, remplacer.

supersonic, *a*, supersonique.

superstition, *n*, superstition, *f.* **superstitious†**, *a*, superstitieux.

superstructure, *n*, superstructure, *f*.

supervene, *v.i*, survenir.

supervise, *v.t*, surveiller, contrôler. **supervision**, *n*, surveillance, *f*, contrôle, *m.* **supervisor**, *n*, surveillant, e, contrôleur, *m*.

supine, *a*, couché sur le dos; indolent; léthargique.

supper, *n*, souper, *m.* to have ~, souper. ~ *time*, heure du s., *f.* **~less**, *a*, sans s.

supplant, *v.t*, supplanter.

supple, *a*, souple. to make ~, assouplir.

supplement, *n*, supplément, *m.* ¶ *v.t*, augmenter. **~ary**, *a*, supplémentaire.

suppleness, *n*, souplesse, *f*.

suppliant, *a*. & *n*, suppliant, e. **supplicate**, *v.t*, supplier. **supplication**, *n*, supplication, *f*.

supplier, *n*, fournisseur, euse. **supply**, *n*, provision, fourniture, *f*, approvisionnement, *m*; (*pl*, *food*) vivres, *m.pl.* ~ & *demand*, l'offre & la demande. ¶ *v.t*, fournir, approvisionner; pourvoir; assortir de; alimenter; suppléer.

support, *n,* support; soutien; appui; entretien, *m.* ¶ *v.t,* supporter; soutenir; appuyer; entretenir. ~**er,** *n,* partisan, tenant, *m,* adhérent, e.

suppose, *v.t,* supposer; présumer. supposing [*that*], supposé que. **supposition,** *n,* supposition, *f.* **supposititious,** *a,* supposé.

suppository, *n,* suppositoire, *m.*

suppress, *v.t,* supprimer. ~*ed rage,* rage rentrée, *f.* ~**ion,** *n,* suppression, *f.*

suppurate, *v.i,* suppurer.

supremacy, *n,* suprématie, *f.* **supreme†,** *a,* suprême; souverain.

surcharge, *v.t,* surcharger, surtaxer.

sure†, *a,* sûr; certain; assuré, immanquable. to make ~ of, s'assurer de. ~**ness,** *n,* sûreté, *f.* ~**ty,** *n,* sûreté; caution, *f.*

surf, *n,* ressac, *m,* brisants, *m.pl.* ~*board,* aquaplane, *m.* ~ *boat,* pirogue de barre, *f.* ~ *fishing,* pêche de plage, *f.* ~*riding,* sport de l'aquaplane, *m.*

surface, *n,* surface; superficie, *f.* ~ *plate,* marbre, *m.* ¶ *v.t,* aplanir; (*Naut.*) remonter à la surface.

surfeit, *n,* satiété, *f.* ¶ *v.t,* rassasier; blaser.

surge, *n,* houle, *f.* ¶ *v.i,* refluer, ondoyer.

surgeon, *n,* chirurgien; médecin, *m.* **surgery,** *n,* chirurgie; médecine, *f;* cabinet de consultation, *m,* clinique, *f.* **surgical,** *a,* chirurgical. ~ *case* (*pers.*), opéré, e.

surging, *p.a,* houleux.

surly, *a,* rébarbatif, bourru, maussade.

surmise, *n,* conjecture, supposition, *f.* ¶ *v.t,* soupçonner.

surmount, *v.t,* surmonter.

surname, *n,* nom [de famille] *m.*

surpass, *v.t,* surpasser. ~**ing,** *a,* supérieur; suprême.

surplice, *n,* surplis, *m.*

surplus, *n,* surplus, excédent, *m.*

surprise, *n,* surprise, *f;* étonnement, *m.* ~ *attack,* attaque faite à l'improviste, *f,* coup de main, *m.* ¶ *v.t,* surprendre; étonner. **surprising,** *a,* surprenant, étonnant. ~**ly,** *ad,* étonnamment.

surrender, *n,* reddition, *f;* abandon; (*Insce.*) rachat, *m.* ¶ *v.t,* rendre, livrer; abandonner, ab-

diquer, céder; (*insurance policy*) racheter; (*v.i.*) se rendre.

surreptitious†, *a,* subreptice.

surrogate, *n,* substitut, *m.*

surround, *v.t,* entourer, enceindre, encadrer. ¶ *n,* pourtour, *m.* ~**ing,** *p.a,* environnant; ambiant. ~**ings,** *n.pl,* alentours, *m.pl.*

surtax, *n,* surtaxe, *f;* impôt général (*ou* global) sur le revenu, *m.* ¶ *v.t,* surtaxer.

survey, *n,* étude; visite; expertise, *f;* levé [de plans]; arpentage; cadastre; métrage, *m.* ¶ *v.t,* étudier; expertiser; (*land*) arpenter; cadastrer; métrer. ~**or,** *n,* inspecteur; expert; (*land*) arpenteur, géomètre; (*quantity*) métreur; (*roads*) [agent] voyer, *m.*

survival, *n,* survivance, survie, *f.* ~ *of the fittest,* survivance du plus apte. **survive,** *v.t,* survivre à; (*v.i.*) se survivre. **survivor,** *n,* survivant, e; rescapé, e. ~**ship,** *n,* survie, *f.*

susceptible, *a,* susceptible, sensible.

suspect, *a,* suspect, interlope. ¶ *n,* suspect, *m.* ¶ *v.t,* suspecter; se douter de.

suspend, *v.t,* suspendre. ~**er,** *n,* bretelle, *f.* **suspense,** *n,* incertitude, *f. in* ~, en suspens, en souffrance. **suspension,** *n,* suspension, *f.* ~ *bridge,* pont suspendu, *m.*

suspicion, *n,* soupçon, *m;* (*law*) suspicion, *f.* **suspicious†,** *a,* soupçonneux; suspect; louche.

sustain, *v.t,* soutenir; sustenter; éprouver. ~**ing,** *p.a,* (*power*) soutenant; (*food*) qui soutient. **sustenance,** *n,* subsistance, nourriture, *f.*

sutler, *n,* vivandier, ère.

suture, *n,* suture, *f.*

suzerain, *n,* suzerain, e. ~**ty,** *n,* suzeraineté, *f.*

swab, *n,* torchon; (*Naut.*) faubert; (*Med.*) écouvillon, *m.*

swaddling clothes (*lit. & fig.*), langes, *m.pl.*

swage, *n,* étampe, *f.* ¶ *v.t,* étamper.

swagger, *v.i,* se rengorger, se carrer; faire le fanfaron. ~**er,** *n,* fanfaron, bravache, *m.*

swain, *n,* galant, *m.*

swallow, *n,* hirondelle, *f;* gorgée, *f;* (*river*) perte, *f.* ~*tail* (*coat*), queue-de-morue, queue-de-pie, *f.*

¶ *v.t*, avaler; engloutir; ingurgiter.

swamp, *n*, marais, marécage, *m*, grenouillère, *f*. ¶ *v.t*, remplir d'eau, submerger; engloutir, noyer. be ~ed (*work*), débordé de travail. ~y, *a*, marécageux.

swan, *n*, cygne, *m*. ~'s-down, duvet de cygne; (*cloth*) molleton, *m*. ~ song, chant du cygne, *m*.

sward, *n*, [tapis de] gazon, *m*, herbette, *f*.

swarm, *n*, (*bees*) essaim; (*multitude*) essaim, *m*, nuée, milliasse, potée, *f*. ¶ *v.i*, (*bees*) essaimer; pulluler, fourmiller, foisonner.

swarthy, *a*, noir; noiraud, basané.

swash, *v.i*, clapoter.

swastika, *n*, svastika, *m*.

swat (*fly*) *v.t*, tuer.

swath, *n*, javelle, *f*; (*path cut*) andain, *m*.

sway, *n*, balancement; empire, *m*; domination, puissance, *f*. ¶ *v.t*, balancer; influencer.

swear, *v.i. & t. ir*, jurer; prêter serment; (*witness*) assermenter. ~ at, maudire.

sweat, *n*, sueur; suée, *f*. ¶ *v.i. & t*, suer; ressuer; exploiter. ~ *profusely*, suer à grosses gouttes. ~y, *a*, suant.

sweater, *n*, pull-over, pull, chandail, *m*.

Swede, *n*, Suédois, e. s~, *n*, navet de Suède, rutabaga, *m*. **Sweden,** *n*, la Suède. **Swedish,** *a*, suédois. ¶ *n*, le suédois.

sweep, *n*, coup de balai; coup, mouvement; (*pers.*) ramoneur, *m*; boucle, courbe; étendue, *f*. ¶ *v.t. & i. ir*, balayer; (*chimney*) ramoner; (*Naut.*) draguer. ~ *away*, enlever. ~ *the board*, rafler le tout. ~er, *n*, balayeur, euse; (*Mach.*) balayeuse, *f*. ~ing gesture, geste large, *m*. ~ings, *n.pl*, balayures, *f.pl*. ~stake[s], *n*, sweepstake, *m*, loterie, *f*.

sweet†, *a*, doux; sucré; (*wine*) liquoreux; suave; charmant; gentil, mignon. ~bread, ris de veau, *m*. ~briar, églantine odorante, *f*; (*bush*) églantier odorant, *m*. ~heart, amoureux, euse. ~ herbs, herbes fines, *f.pl*. ~meat, sucrerie, *f*, bonbon, *m*. ~ pea, pois de senteur, *m*. ~ potato, patate, *f*. ~[-*scented*], odorant, odoriférant. to have a ~ tooth,

aimer les sucreries. ~-william, œillet de poète, *m*. the ~ (*opp.* the bitter), le doux. ~en, *v.t*, sucrer; adoucir. ~ish, *a*, douceâtre. ~ness, *n*, douceur; suavité, *f*; charme, *m*.

sweet-talk, *v.i. & t*, baratiner. ¶ *n*, baratin, *m*.

swell, *n*, bombement; renflement, *m*; (*sea*) houle, *f*; (*pers.*) élégant, e. ¶ *a*, chic. ¶ *v.t. & i. ir*, enfler, s'e.; gonfler; se g.; renfler; grossir; dilater; bouffer, gondoler. **swelling,** *n*, enflure, grosseur, fluxion, *f*; gonflement; renflement, *m*.

swelter, *v.i*, étouffer de chaleur.

swerve, *n*, crochet, *m*, embardée, *f*. ¶ *v.i*, faire une embardée; s'écarter, se départir.

swift†, *a*, rapide, vite. ~-footed, au pied léger. ¶ *n*, martinet, *m*. ~ness, *n*, rapidité, célérité, vélocité, *f*.

swig, *v.t*, lamper, sabler.

swill, *v.t*, laver à grande eau, lessiver; (*drink*) lamper; (*v.i.*) (*food & drink*) boustifailler.

swim, *n*, tour de nage, *m*. in the ~, dans le mouvement. ¶ *v.i. & t. ir*, nager. ~ *across*, passer à la nage. ~ *under water*, nager entre deux eaux. **swimming,** *n*, natation, *f*. ~ *pool*, piscine, *f*. **swimsuit,** maillot de bain, *m*.

swindle, *n*, escroquerie, *f*. ¶ *v.t*, escroquer. **swindler,** *n*, escroc, filou, *m*.

swine, *n*, pourceau, porc, cochon, *m*. ~herd, porcher, ère.

swing, *n*, oscillation, *f*, balancement; branle, *m*; (*playground*) balançoire, escarpolette, *f*. in full ~, en pleine activité. ~ bridge, pont tournant, *m*. ~ door, porte va-et-vient, *f*. ¶ *v.t. & i. ir*, balancer se b.; osciller; branler; basculer; tourner.

swingletree, *n*, volée, *f*.

swirl, *n*, tourbillon; remous, *m*. ¶ *v.i*, tourbillonner, tournoyer.

swish, *n*, sifflement; frou-frou, *m*. ¶ *v.t*, cingler; (*whip*) faire siffler; susurrer; remuer.

Swiss, *a*, suisse. ~ guard, suisse, *m*. ¶ *n*, Suisse, *m*, Suissesse, *f*.

switch, *n*, badine, houssine; (*Rly.*) aiguille, *f*; (*Elec.*) interrupteur, *m*. ~back, montagnes russes, *f.pl*. ~ board, tableau de distribution;

(Tele.) standard, *m.* ¶ *v.t,* *(whip)* houssiner. ~ *off,* couper, mettre hors circuit; *(light)* éteindre. ~ *on,* mettre en circuit; *(light)* allumer.

Switzerland, *n,* la Suisse.

swivel, *n,* émerillon; tourniquet, *m.* ¶ *v.i,* pivoter, tourner.

swollen glands, des glandes au cou, *f.pl.*

swoon, *n,* évanouissement, *m,* défaillance, *f.* ¶ *v.i,* s'évanouir, [se] pâmer.

swoop down on, fondre sur.

sword, *n,* épée, *f;* sabre; *(Poet.)* glaive, *m;* *(in fun)* flamberge, *f.* ~ *belt,* ceinturon, *m.* ~*fish,* espadon, *m.* ~ *rattler,* ferrailleur, *m.* **swordsman,** *n,* lame, *f.* **swordsmanship,** *n,* escrime, *f.*

Sybarite, *n,* sybarite, *m.*

sycamore, *n,* sycomore, *m.*

sycophant, *n,* sycophante, *m.*

syllabize, *v.t,* scander. **syllable,** *n,* syllabe, *f.*

syllabus, *n,* programme; *(Eccl.)* syllabus, *m.*

syllogism, *n,* syllogisme, *m.*

sylph, *n,* sylphe, *m,* sylphide, *f.*

sylvan, *a,* champêtre, bocager.

symbol, *n,* symbole, *m.* ~**ic(al),** *a,* symbolique. ~**ize,** *v.t,* symboliser.

symmetric(al)†, *a,* symétrique. **symmetry,** *n,* symétrie, *f.*

sympathetic, *a,* sympathique. **sympathize,** *v.i,* sympathiser, compatir. **sympathy,** *n,* sympathie, *f.*

symphony, *n,* symphonie, *f.*

symptom, *n,* symptôme, *m.* ~**atic,** *a,* symptomatique.

synagogue, *n,* synagogue, *f.*

synchronize, *v.t,* synchroniser.

synchronous, *a,* synchrone.

syncopate, *v.t,* syncoper. **syncopation & syncope,** *n,* syncope, *f.*

syndicate, *n,* syndicat, *m.* ¶ *v.t,* syndiquer.

synod, *n,* synode, *m.* ~**ic(al),** *a,* synodique.

synonym, *n.* & **synonymous,** *a,* synonyme, *m.* & *a.*

synopsis, *n,* argument, sommaire, *m.*

syntax, *n,* syntaxe, *f.*

synthesis, *n,* synthèse, *f.* **synthetic(al)†,** *a,* synthétique.

syphilis, *n,* vérole, *m.*

Syria, *n,* la Syrie, *f.* **Syrian,** *a,* syrien. ¶ *n,* Syrien, ne.

syringe, *n,* seringue, *f.* ¶ *v.t,* seringuer.

syrup, *n,* sirop, *m.* ~**y,** *a,* sirupeux.

system, *n,* système; régime; réseau, *m.* *communications* ~, réseau de transmissions, *m.* *(computers) dedicated* ~, ensemble spécialisé, *m.* ~**atic†,** *a,* systématique. ~**atize,** *v.t,* systématiser.

T

T, *n, T,* té, *m.* ~ *square,* té [à dessin] *m. to a* ~, tout craché.

tab, *n,* étiquette, *f;* *(index)* onglet, *m. to keep* ~*s on,* ne pas perdre de vue.

tabby cat, chat moucheté, chat tigré, *m.*

tabernacle, *n,* tabernacle, *m.*

table, *n,* table; tablette, *f;* bureau; plateau; tableau; plan; décompte, *m. card* ~, table à jeu, *f.* ~ *cloth,* nappe [de t.] *f.* ~ *companion,* convive, *m,f.* ~ *napkin,* serviette de t., *f.* ~ *salt,* sel fin, *m.* ~*spoon,* cuiller à bouche, c. à soupe, *f.* ~*spoonful,* cuillerée à bouche, *f.*~ *talk,* propos de t., *m.pl.* ¶ *v.t,* déposer sur le bureau. **tableau,** *n.* & *i,* tableau, *m.* & *i.* **tablet,** *n,* table, tablette, plaque, *f;* pain, *m.*

taboo, *n,* tabou, *m.* *he, it, is* ~, il est tabou. ¶ *v.t,* déclarer tabou.

tabular, *a,* en forme de tableau. **tabulate,** *v.t,* dresser en forme de tableau.

tachometer, *n,* tachymètre, compte-tours, *m.*

tacit†, *a,* tacite. **taciturn,** *a,* taciturne. ~**ity,** *n,* taciturnité, *f.*

tack, *n,* *(s. & pl.)* broquette, *(pl.)* semence; *(Naut.)* bordée, *f,* bord, *m;* *(of sail)* amure, *f.* ¶ *v.t,* clouer avec de la broquette, de la semence; *(Need.)* bâtir; *(fig.)* coudre; *(v.i.)* virer de bord, louvoyer.

tackle, *n,* engin, *m.* *oft. pl;* appareil, *m. oft. pl;* harnais, *m;* agrès, *m.pl;* treuil; palan; *(Foot.)* arrêt, *m.* ~ *block,* moufle, *f. or m. fishing* ~, articles de pêche, *m. pl.* ¶ *v.t,* s'attaquer à; *(Foot.)* plaquer; *(pers., fig.)* entreprendre.

tacky, *a,* collant, visqueux.

tact, *n,* tact, doigté, savoir-faire, *m,* ménagements, *m.pl.* **~ful,** *a,* [plein] de tact. **~less,** *a,* dépourvu de tact, malhabile.

tactical, *a,* tactique. **tactician,** *n,* tacticien, manœuvrier, *m.* **tactics,** *n.pl,* tactique, *f.*

tactile, *a,* tactile.

tadpole, *n,* têtard, *m.*

taffeta, *n,* taffetas, *m.*

taffrail, *n,* couronnement, *m.*

tag, *n,* ferret; *(stock phrase)* cliché, *m; (label)* étiquette, *f;* [jeu du] chat, *m.* ¶ *v.t, (label)* marquer, attacher une fiche; ferrer.

Tagus (the), le Tage.

Tahiti, *n,* Taïti, Tahiti, *m.*

tail, *n,* queue, *f;* arrière; aval; derrière; *(coat)* pan, *m,* basque; *(coin)* pile; *(book page)* queue, tranche inférieure, *f.* ~ *coat* or *tails,* *(evening)* queue-de-morue, queue-de-pie; *(morning)* jaquette, *f.* **~piece,** cul-de-lampe, *m.* ~ *spin,* vrille, *f.* ~ *stock* (lathe), contre-pointe, *f.*

tailor, *n,* tailleur, *m.* **~-made** or **~ed,** [fait par] tailleur. **~ing,** *n,* métier de tailleur, *m.*

taint, *n,* infection; tache, tare, *f.* ¶ *v.t,* corrompre, infecter; souiller. **~ed** *(meat) p.a,* gâté, faisandé.

take, *v.t.ir,* prendre; porter; conduire, mener; faire; mettre; relever; tirer; tenir; supposer; falloir; *(v.i.)* prendre. ~ *away,* emmener; ôter; [r]emporter. ~ *back,* ramener; reprendre. ~ *cover,* se garer. ~ *down,* descendre; décrocher; démonter. ~ *down* [*in shorthand*], sténographier. ~ *in,* prendre; recevoir; faire; embrasser; attraper. ~ *off,* ôter; rabattre; *(a pers.)* contrefaire; *(Avn.)* décoller, prendre son vol. ~ *on* (workers), embaucher. ~ *out,* ôter; retirer; arracher; sortir; *(Insce policy)* contracter. ~ *over,* prendre. ~ *shape,* se dessiner. ~ *to,* s'appliquer à; s'adonner à, mordre à. ~ *to pieces,* désassembler, démonter. ~ *to task,* prendre à partie, morigéner. ~ *up,* relever; lever; monter; s'occuper de; occuper, tenir; prendre; *(option)* lever, consolider. ~ *your seats!* (in carriage), en voiture! **taker,** *n,* preneur, euse. **taking,** *a,*

séduisant, avenant. ¶ *n,* prise, *f; (pl.)* recette, *f.* oft. *pl,* produit, *m.* ~ *off* (Avn.), décollage, envol, *m.*

talc, *n,* talc, *m.*

tale, *n,* conte, *m,* histoire, nouvelle, *f.* **~-bearer,** rapporteur, euse. *tall* ~, *canular, m.*

talent, *n,* talent, *m.* **~ed,** *a,* de talent.

talisman, *n,* talisman, *m.*

talk, *n,* conversation, causerie, *f,* entretien; discours, *m;* propos, *m.pl;* bavardage, *m.* ¶ *v.i. & t,* parler; causer; converser; bavarder. ~ *into,* persuader de. ~ *out of,* dissuader de. **~ative,** *a,* parlant, causeur, loquace. **~er,** *n,* parleur, euse, causeur, euse; bavard, e. **~ing,** *a,* parlant.

tall, *a,* grand; haut. **~ness,** *n,* (pers.) haute taille; (steeple) hauteur, *f.* how ~ *are you?* quelle taille avez-vous?

tallow, *n,* suif, *m.* ¶ *v.t,* suifer.

tally, *n,* (stick) taille; marque, *f; (check)* pointage, *m; (label)* étiquette, *f.* ¶ *v.i,* concorder, correspondre, cadrer, se rapporter. **~ho,** *i,* taïaut!

talon, *n,* serre, *f; (counterfoil)* talon, *m.*

talus, *n,* talus, *m.*

tamarind, *n,* tamarin, *m.*

tambour, *n,* tambour, métier [à broder] *m.* **~ine,** *n,* tambour de basque, *m.*

tame, *a,* apprivoisé; *(fig.)* anodin. ¶ *v.t,* apprivoiser, dompter. **tamer,** *n,* dompteur, euse.

tam-o'-shanter, *n,* béret écossais, *m.*

tamp, *v.t,* bourrer; damer, pilonner.

tamper with, falsifier; *(witness)* suborner.

tampion, *n,* tampon, *m.*

tan, *n,* tan; *(sunburn)* hâle, *m.* ¶ *v.t,* tanner; brunir, hâler, basaner. ¶ *a,* jaune-brun, hâlé.

tandem, *n,* tandem, *m.* ¶ *a. & ad,* en tandem.

tang, *n,* goût; montant, *m;* salure; *(shank)* queue, *f. there is a* ~ *in the air,* l'air est vif.

tangent, *n,* tangente, *f.* **~[ial],** *a,* tangent.

tangerine, *n,* mandarine, *f.*

tangible, *a,* tangible, palpable.

Tangier, *n,* Tanger, *m.*

tangle, *n,* enchevêtrement, *m.* ¶ *v.t,* enchevêtrer, emmêler.

tango, n, tango, m.

tank, n, réservoir, m, citerne; bâche; cuve; caisse à eau, soute, f; (Mil.) char d'assaut, tank, m. gasoline ~, réservoir à essence, m. **tanker,** n, bateau-citerne, m, (oil) pétrolier, m.

tankard, n, pot (d'étain) m.

tanner, n, tanneur, m. **~y,** n, tannerie, f. **tannin,** n, tanin, tannin, m.

tantalize, v.t, mettre au supplice. **tantalum,** n, tantale, m.

tantamount to (to be), équivaloir à.

tantrums, n.pl, nerfs, m.pl, bourrasques, f.pl.

tap, n, tape, f, coup; (water) robinet; (screw) taraud, m. ~ dance, claquettes, f.pl. **~root,** racine pivotante, f, pivot, m. ¶ v.t. & i, taper; toucher; frapper; (screw) tarauder; (cask) mettre en perce; (tree) saigner; (Surg.) faire une ponction à.

tape, n, ruban, (adhesive) scotch, m; tresse; bande, f. insulating ~, chatterton, m. punched ~, ruban perforé, m. red ~, bolduc, m. ~ measure, mesure à ruban, f; mètre à r.; centimètre, m; roulette, f. ~ recorder, magnétophone, m. **~worm,** ver solitaire, ténia, m.

taper, n, bougie filée; (coiled) bougie de poche, f, pain de bougie, rat de cave; (church) cierge, cône, m. ¶ v.t, diminuer, fuseler; (v.i.) aller en diminuant; se terminer en pointe. **~[ing],** a, conique, fuselé.

tapestry, n. & ~ work, tapisserie, f.

tapioca, n, tapioca, m.

tapir, n, tapir, m.

tar, n, goudron; brai; (pers.) loup de mer, m. **~paper,** carton goudronné, m. ¶ v.t, goudronner. ~ & feather, emplumer.

tarantella, n, tarentelle, f. **tarantula,** n, tarentule, f.

tardy†, a, tardif.

tare, n, vesce; (pl, fig.) ivraie; (Com.) tare, f.

target, n, cible, f, but m. ~ practice, tir à la cible, m.

tariff, n, tarif, m. ¶ v.t, tarifer.

tarnish, v.t, ternir; (v.i.) se ternir.

tarpaulin, n, bâche goudronnée, f, prélart, m.

tarragon, n, estragon, m.

Tarragona, n, Tarragone, f.

tarry, v.i, séjourner; tarder; attendre.

tarsus, n, tarse, m.

tart†, a, aigre, âcre, acide. ¶ n, (open) tarte; (covered) tourte; (woman) grue, f.

tartan, n, tartan, m.

tartar, n, tartre, m. **~ic,** a, tartrique.

tartness, n, aigreur, âcreté, acidité, f.

task, n, tâche; besogne, f; devoir, m. to take to ~, prendre à partie, morigéner. ¶ v.t, mettre à l'épreuve; fatiguer.

tassel, n, gland, m, houppe, f.

taste, n, goût; gré; échantillon, m. ¶ v.t. & i, goûter; g. de; (tea, wine) déguster. ~ of, sentir le, la, les. **~ful,** a, de bon goût. **~less,** a, sans goût, fade, insipide. **taster,** n, dégustateur, m; (device) sonde, f. **tasting,** n, gustation; dégustation, f. **tasty,** a, savoureux.

tatter, n, haillon, lambeau, m. **~ed,** a, déguenillé; en lambeaux.

tatting, n, frivolité, f.

tattle, n, babil[lage] m. ¶ v.i, babiller. **tattler,** n. & **tattling,** a, babillard, e.

tattoo, n, tatouage, m; (Mil.) retraite, f. ¶ v.t, tatouer; (v.i.) tambouriner.

taunt, n, sarcasme, m. ¶ v.t, houspiller, molester. ~ with, reprocher à.

taut, a, raide, tendu. **~en,** v.t, raidir.

tautologic(al), a, tautologique. **tautology,** n, tautologie, f.

tavern, n, taverne, f, cabaret, m. ~ with gardens & dance hall, guinguette, f.

tawdriness, n, faux éclat, m. **tawdry,** a, qui a un faux éclat. ~ finery, oripeaux, m.pl.

tawny, a, fauve; basané. ~ owl, chat-huant, m, hulotte, f.

tax, n, impôt, m, taxe, contribution, imposition, f. excise ~, droit de régie, m. income ~, impôt sur le revenu, m. ~ collector, percepteur, collecteur d'impôts, m. ~ dodger, fraudeur (euse) des droits du fisc. ~ free, net d'impôts. **~payer,** contribuable, m,f. ¶ v.t, imposer; taxer.

~able, *a*, imposable. **~ation**, *n*, taxation, *f*, impôts, *m.pl.*

taxi (*Avn.*) *v.i*, rouler [sur le sol]. **~** [*cab*], taxi, *m.* **~** *driver*, chauffeur de taxi, conducteur de taxi, *m.* **~meter**, compteur, *m.*

taxidermist, *n*, naturaliste [fourreur] *m*, empailleur, euse. **taxidermy**, *n*, empaillage, empaillement, *m.*

tea, *n*, thé, *m*; infusion, tisane, *f.* **~** *cosy*, couvre-théière, *m.* **~** *cup*, tasse à thé, *f.* **~** *party*, thé, *m.* **~pot**, théière, *f.* **~**, *roll, & butter*, thé complet. **~** *room*(*s*), **~** *shop*, salon de thé, *m.* pâtisserie, *f.* **~** *rose*, rose thé, *f.* **~spoon**, cuiller à thé, *f.* **~** *time*, l'heure du thé, *f.*

teach, *v.t. & i. ir*, enseigner, instruire; apprendre; professer; montrer à; (*bird*) seriner. **~** *someone a lesson*, donner une leçon à quelqu'un. **~** *someone manners*, donner à quelqu'un une leçon de politesse. **~er**, *n*, instituteur, trice; professeur; précepteur, *m*; maître, esse. **~ing**, *n*, enseignement, *m*; instruction, *f.*

teak, *n*, teck, tek, *m.*

teal, *n*, sarcelle, *f.*

team, *n*, attelage, *m*; équipe, *f.* **~** *spirit*, esprit de corps, *m.* **~work**, travail d'équipe, *m.*

tear, *n*, déchirure, *f*; accroc, *m.* ¶ *v.t.ir*, déchirer; arracher. **~** *one another to pieces*, s'entre-déchirer.

tear, *n*, larme, *f*, pleur, *m.* **~** *gas*, gaz lacrymogène, *m.* **~ful**, *a*, éploré, larmoyant.

tease, *v.t*, taquiner, lutiner; tourmenter. ¶ (*pers.*) *n*, taquin, e.

teaser, *n*, (*pers.*) taquin, e; problème, casse-tête, *m.* **teasing**, *n*, taquinerie, *f.*

teat, *n*, bout du sein, mamelon, tétin, *m.*

technical†, *a*, technique; d'ordre t. **~** *offense*, quasi-délit, *m.* **~** *school*, école pratique, *f.* **technique**, *n*, technique, *f*, faire, mécanisme, *m.* **technocracy**, *n*, technocratie, *f.* **technology**, *n*, technologie, *f.*

Teddy bear, ours [martin], o. de peluche, *m.*

tedious†, *a*, ennuyeux, fastidieux, fatigant. **~ness & tedium**, *n*, ennui, *m.*

tee, *n*, té, T; (*golf*) dé, *m.* *to a* **~**, tout craché. ¶ (*golf*) *v.t*, surélever. **~ing ground** (*golf*), tertre de départ, *m.*

teem with, fourmiller de, regorger de.

teenager, *n*, adolescent, e.

teethe, *v.i*, faire ses dents. **teething**, *n*, dentition, *f.*

teetotal, *a*, antialcoolique. **~ism**, *n*, antialcoolisme, *m.* **teetotaller**, *n*, abstinent, e.

teetotum, *n*, toton, *m.*

tegument, *n*, tégument, *m.*

telegram, *n*, télégramme, *m*, dépêche, *f.* **telegraph**, *n*, télégraphe, *m.* **~** *office*, [bureau du] télégraphe, *m.* ¶ *v.t. & i*, télégraphier. **~ese**, *n*, style télégraphique, *m.* **~ic†**, *a*, télégraphique. **~y**, *n*, télégraphie, *f.*

telepathy, *n*, télépathie, *f.*

telephone, *n*, téléphone, *m.* ¶ *v.t. & i*, téléphoner. ¶ *att. & **telephonic***, *a*, téléphonique. **~** *answering machine*, répondeur, *m.* **~** *booth*, cabine téléphonique, *f.* **~** *number*, numéro de téléphone, *m. person-to-person* **~** *call for*, avec préavis pour.

teleprinter, *n*, téléimprimeur, *m.*

teleprocessing, *n*, télétraitement, *m.*

telescope, *n*, (*reflecting*) télescope, *m.* (*refracting*) lunette; (*spy-glass*) longue-vue, *f.* ¶ *v.i*, se télescoper. **telescopic**, *a*, télescopique; (*sliding*) à coulisse.

televiewer, *n*, téléspectateur, *m.*

televise, *v.t*, téléviser. **television**, *n*, télévision, *f.* **~** *set*, téléviseur, *m.*

tell, *v.t. & i. ir*, dire; [ra]conter; narrer; apprendre; savoir; reconnaître; (*of remark*) porter; (*in one's favor*) militer. **~er**, *n*, (*voting*) scrutateur; (*bank*) caissier, *m.* (*banks*) *automatic* **~** *machine*, guichet automatique, *m.* **~ing**, *a*, qui porte. **~tale**, *n*, (*pers.*) rapporteur, euse.

temerity, *n*, témérité, *f.*

temper, *n*, caractère, *m*; humeur; trempe; colère, *f. to lose one's* **~**, s'emporter. ¶ *v.t*, (*metal*) tremper; (*mortar*) gâcher; (*fig.*) tempérer, mitiger. **temperament**, *n*, tempérament, *m*. ~**al**, *a*, constitutionnel; capricieux, fantasque. **temperance**, *n*, tempérance, *f*. **temperate**, *a*, tempérant, sobre; (*climate, speech*) tempéré. **temperature**, *n*, température, *f*. ~ *chart*, feuille de température, *f*.

tempest, *n*, tempête, *f*. **tempestuous**, *a*, tempétueux.

template, -plet, *n*, gabarit, calibre, *m*.

temple, *n*, temple, *m*; (*Anat.*) tempe, *f*.

temporal†, *a*, (*secular*) temporel. **temporary†**, *a*, temporaire, momentané. **temporize**, *v.i*, temporiser.

tempt, *v.t*, tenter; inviter; affriander. ~**ation**, *n*, tentation, *f*. **tempter, tress**, *n*, tentateur, trice, séducteur, trice. **tempting**, *a*, tentant, séduisant; (*food*) appétissant, ragoûtant.

ten, *a*, dix. ¶ *n*, dix, *m*; dizaine, *f*. ~**fold**, *a*. & *n*, décuple, *a* & *m*. *to increase* ~, décupler.

tenable, *a*, tenable; soutenable. **tenacious**, *a*, tenace. ~**ly**, *ad*, avec ténacité.

tenancy, *n*, location, *f*. **tenant**, *n*, locataire, *m,f*; (*farm*) fermier, ère. ~ *farmer*, fermier, ère. ~**able**, *a*, logeable.

tench, *n*, tanche, *f*.

tend, *v.t*, garder; soigner; (*v.i.*) tendre; conspirer. ~**ency**, *n*, tendance; disposition, *f*. **tendentious**, *a*, tendancieux. **tender**, *n*, soumission; offre; (*boat*) annexe, *f*; (*Naut.*) transbordeur, *m*. (*Rly.*) tender, *m*. ¶ *v.t*, offrir; donner. ~ *for*, soumissionner.

tender†, *a*, tendre; sensible; délicat. ~**ness**, *n*, tendresse; délicatesse; (*eatables*) tendreté, *f*.

tendon, *n*, tendon, *m*.

tendril, *n*, vrille, main, *f*.

tenement, *n*, habitation, *f*, logement, *m*, maison de rapport, *f*.

tenet, *n*, dogme, *m*, doctrine, *f*.

tennis, *n*, tennis, *m*. ~ *court*, jeu de tennis, [court de] tennis, *m*.

tenon, *n*, tenon, *m*. ~ *saw*, scie à t., *f*.

tenor, *n*, teneur; (*bill*) échéance, *f*; (*voice, singer*) ténor, *m*. ~ *clef*, clef d'ut, *f*.

tense, *a*, tendu, raide. ¶ *n*, temps, *m*. **tension**, *n*, tension, *f*.

tent, *n*, tente; (*Surg.*) mèche, *f*. ~ *pole*, mât de t., *m*.

tentacle, *n*, tentacule, *m*.

tentative [**effort**], tâtonnement, *m*.

tenterhook, *n*, crochet [du fabricant de drap]; clou à crochet, *m*. *on* ~*s*, sur des charbons [ardents], sur le gril, au supplice.

tenth†, *a*, dixième. ¶ *n*, dixième, *m,f*; dix, *m*.

tenuity, *n*, ténuité, *f*. **tenuous**, *a*, ténu.

tenure, *n*, possession; jouissance, *f*; mode de possession; exercise, *m*. *during his* ~ *of office*, pendant l'exercise de ses fonctions.

tepid†, *a*, tiede. ~**ness**, *n*, tiédeur, *f*.

term, *n*, terme, *m*; clause; durée; session, *f*; trimestre, *m*; (*pl.*) conditions, *f.pl*; prix, *m*; (*pl, opp.* [*for*] *cash*) à crédit; (*pl.*) rapports, *m.pl*, intelligence; teneur, *f*; accommodement, *m*. *to come to* ~*s*, conclure un arrangement. (*loan, etc.*) *short* ~, à courte écheance. ¶ *v.t*, appeler.

termagant, *n*, mégère, *f*, dragon, *m*.

terminable, *a*, résoluble. **terminal**, *a*, terminal; de tête de ligne. ¶ *n*, borne; extrémité, *f*; (*computers*) terminal, *m*. *remote* ~, poste éloigné, *m*. **terminate**, *v.t*, terminer; resoudre. **termination**, *n*, terminaison; fin, *f*. **terminus**, *n*, terminus, *m*.

termite, *n*, termite, *m*, fourmi blanche, *f*.

tern, *n*, sterne, *m*.

terrace, *n*, terrasse, *f*. ¶ *v.t*, étager.

terracotta, *n*, terre cuite, *f*.

terrain, *n*, terrain, *m*.

terrestrial, *a*, terrestre.

terrible†, *a*, terrible.

terrier, *n*, [chien] terrier, *m*.

terrific†, *a*, terrible. **terrify**, *v.t*, terrifier.

territorial, *a*. & *n*, territorial, *a*. & *m*. **territory**, *n*, territoire, *m*.

terror, *n*, terreur, *f*. ~**ism**, *n*, terrorisme, *m*. ~**ist**, *n*, terroriste, *m*. & *f*. ~**ize**, *v.t*, terroriser.

terse, *a*, concis. ~**ness**, *n*, concision, *f*.

tessellated pavement, mosaïque, *f*.

test, *n*, épreuve, *f*, essai, *m*; pierre

de touche, *f.* **blood ~**, prise de sang, *f.* **~ tube**, éprouvette, *f.* ¶ *v.t,* essayer, éprouver; expérimenter; contrôler.

testament, *n,* testament, *m.* **~ary,** *a,* testamentaire. **testator, trix,** *n,* testateur, trice. **testify,** *v.t, & i,* témoigner. **testimonial,** *n,* attestation, *f;* certificat, *m.* **testimony,** *n,* témoignage, *m.*

testicle, *n,* testicule, *m.*

testy, *a,* irritable, irascible.

tetanus, *n,* tétanos, *m.*

tether, *n,* longe, *f. at the end of one's ~,* au bout de son rouleau. ¶ *v.t,* mettre au piquet.

Teutonic, *a,* teutonique, teuton.

text, *n,* texte, *m.* **~book,** manuel, *m.*

textile, *n,* textile, tissu, *m.* ¶ *a,* textile.

textual†, *a,* textuel; *(error)* de texte.

texture, *n,* texture, tissure, *f,* tissu, *m,* contexture, *f.*

Thames (the), la Tamise.

than, *c. & pr,* que; de.

thank, *v.t,* remercier; bénir. **~ God!** Dieu merci! **~ Heaven!** grâce au ciel! **~ you! & no ~ you!** merci! **~ful,** *a,* reconnaissant. **~fully,** *ad,* avec reconnaissance. **~fulness,** *n,* reconnaissance, gratitude, *f.* **~less,** *a,* ingrat. **thanks,** *n.pl,* remerciements, *m.pl.* ¶ *i,* merci! **~ to,** grâce à. **thanksgiving,** *n,* action[s] de grâce, *f.[pl.].*

that, *a. & pn,* ce, cet, cette; ce . . ., etc., -là, celui, celle; cela, ça; ce, c', ç'; qui; que; là. **~ is all,** c'est tout; voilà tout. **~ is to say,** c'est-à-dire. **~ will do,** cela suffit. ¶ *c,* que; afin que; pour que.

thatch, *n,* chaume, *m.* ¶ *v.t,* couvrir en c. **~ed cottage,** chaumière, *f.* **~er,** *n,* couvreur en chaume, *m.*

thaw, *n,* dégel, *m.* ¶ *v.t, & i,* dégeler; se d.; *(fig.)* dégeler; se dégeler, se déraidir.

the, *art,* le, l', m, la, l', *f,* les, *m,f.pl. from ~, of ~,* du, de l', de la, des. **to ~, at ~,** au, à l', à la, aux.

theater, *n,* théâtre, *m.* **theatrical†,** *a,* de théâtre, du théâtre; théâtral, scénique. **theatricals,** *n.pl,* comédie, *f.*

thee, *pn,* te; toi.

theft, *n,* vol, *m.*

their, *a,* leur, leurs *(pl.).* **theirs,**

pn, le leur, la leur, les leurs; à eux, à elles.

theism, *n,* théisme, *m.* **theistic(al),** *a,* théiste.

them, *pn,* eux, elles; les; leur; ceux, celles. **~selves,** eux[-mêmes], elles[-mêmes]; se.

theme, *n,* thème; sujet; *(Mus.)* motif, *m.* **~ song,** leitmotif, leitmotiv, *m.*

then, *ad,* alors; ensuite, puis; donc; lors. **thence,** *ad,* de là. **thenceforth, thenceforward,** *ad,* dès lors.

theodolite, *n,* théodolite, *m.*

theologian, *n,* théologien, *m.* **theological†,** *a,* théologique. **theology,** *n,* théologie, *f.*

theorem, *n,* théorème, *m.* **theoretic(al†),** *a,* théorique. **theorist,** *n,* théoricien, *m.* **theory,** *n,* théorie, *f.*

theosophy, *n,* théosophie, *f.*

therapeutic, *a. & ~s,* n.pl, thérapeutique, *a. & f.*

there, *ad,* là; y; là-bas; il. **~ & back,** aller & retour. **~ & then,** séance tenante, sur-le-champ, tout de go. **~ is, ~ are,** il y a. **~about, ~abouts,** près de là; environ. **~by,** de ce fait. **~fore,** c'est pourquoi; donc, aussi, par conséquent. **~on,** là-dessus. **~upon,** sur ce, là-dessus.

thermal, *a,* thermal. **thermometer,** *n,* thermomètre, *m.*

thermonuclear, *a,* thermonucléaire.

thermostat, *n,* thermostat, *m.*

these, *pn,* ces; ces . . . -ci; ceux-ci, celles-ci.

thesis, *n,* thèse, *f.*

thews, *n.pl,* nerfs, *m.pl.*

they, *pn,* ils, elles; eux, elles; ceux, celles; il; ce, c'; on.

thick, *a,* épais; dense; puissant; gros; gras; dru; fourni; touffu; *(with someone)* lié. **~ or clear (soup)?** potage ou consommé? **~-lipped,** lippu. **~set,** trapu, ramassé; dru. **~[ly],** *ad,* épais; dru. **in the ~ of,** au fort de. **through ~ & thin,** envers & contre tous. **~en,** *v.t,* épaissir; *(sauce)* lier. **~ening,** *n,* épaississement *m; (for sauce)* liaison, *f.* **~et,** *n,* fourré; bosquet, *m.* **~ness,** *n,* épaisseur; puissance, *f.*

thief, *n,* voleur, euse, larron, *m.* **thieve,** *v.t,* voler. **thievish,** *a,* de voleur; *(pers.)* voleur.

thigh, *n,* cuisse, *f.* ~ *bone,* os de la c., *m.* ~ *boots,* bottes cuissardes, *f.pl.*

thill, *n,* limon, brancard, *m.*

thimble, *n,* dé [à coudre] *m;* (*Naut.*) cosse, *f.* ~*rigger,* joueur de gobelets, *m.* ~*ful,* *n,* doigt, *m.*

thin, *a,* mince; maigre; délié, ténu; faible; clair; (*hair, grass*) rare; (*legs, voice*) grêle. to be ~ skinned (*fig.*), avoir l'épiderme sensible. ~ *slice,* mince tranche, lèche, *f.* ¶ *v.t,* amincir, amenuiser; éclaircir; amaigrir.

thine, *pn,* le tien, la tienne, les tiens, les tiennes; à toi.

thing, *n,* chose; affaire, *f;* (*pers.*) être, *m;* (*pl.*) effets, *m.pl.* the ~ (in fashion), de mise.

think, *v.t. & i. ir,* penser; songer; juger; réfléchir; croire; trouver; s'imaginer. ~*er,* *n,* penseur, *m.* **thinking,** *a,* pensant. ¶ *n,* pensée; réflexion; *f;* avis, *m.*

thinly, *ad,* clair. ~ *sown,* semé clair, clairsemé. **thinness,** *n,* minceur, ténuité; maigreur; rareté, *f.* **thinnish,** *a,* maigrelet.

third†, *a,* troisième; tiers. ~ *finger,* [doigt] annulaire, *m.* ~ *person,* tiers, *m,* tierce personne, *f.* (*Gram.*) troisième personne, *f.* T~ *World,* tiers monde, *m.* ¶ *n,* tiers, *m;* tierce, *f;* troisième, *m,f;* trois, *m.*

thirst, *n,* soif, *f.* ~*creating,* altérant. ~ *for,* avoir soif de. **thirsty,** *a,* altéré; (*country*) de la soif. to be ~, avoir soif.

thirteen, *a. & n,* treize, *a & m.* ~*th†,* *a. & n,* treizième, *a. & m,f;* treize, *m.*

thirtieth, *a. & n,* trentième, *a. & m,f;* trente, *m.* **thirty,** *a. & n,* trente, *a. & m.*

this, *a. & pn,* ce, cet, cette; ce . . ., -ci; celui-ci, celle-ci; ceci; présent. ~ *way!* par ici! ~ *way & that,* çà & là.

thistle, *n,* chardon, *m.* ~*down,* duvet du chardon, *m.*

thong, *n,* lanière, *f.*

thorax, *n,* thorax, *m.*

thorn & ~ [*bush*] *n,* épine, *f.* ~*y,* *a,* épineux.

thorough, *a,* achevé; accompli; approfondi; minutieux; parfait. ~*bred* [*horse*], cheval pur sang, c. de race, c. racé, *m.* ~*fare,*

voie, *f,* passage, *m;* rue [passante]; artère, *f.* ~*ly,* *ad,* à fond, foncièrement; mûrement; complètement; parfaitement.

those, *pn,* ces; ces . . . -là; ceux, celles; ceux-là, celles-là; ce.

thou, *pn,* tu; toi. ¶ *v.t,* tutoyer.

though, *c,* quoique, bien que, quand; cependant, tout . . . que. as ~, comme si.

thought, *n,* pensée; réflexion; idée, *f.* ~*ful,* *a,* pensif, réfléchi. ~*less†,* *a,* étourdi; irréfléchi. ~*lessness,* *n,* étourderie; irréflexion, *f.*

thousand, *a,* mille; mil. ¶ *n,* mille; millier, *m.* ~*th,* *a. & n,* millième, *a. & m.*

thraldom, *n,* servage; esclavage, *m.* **thrall,** *n,* serf, *m,* serve, *f;* esclave, *m,f.*

thrash, *v.t,* battre, rosser. ~*ing,* *n,* peignée, *f.*

thread, *n,* fil, *m;* corde, *f;* filament, filé; (*screw*) filet; (*of life*) trame, *f.* ~*bare,* usé jusqu'à la corde, râpé; usé. ¶ *v.t,* enfiler; (*screw*) fileter.

threat, *n,* menace, *f.* ~*en,* *v.t,* menacer.

three, *a. & n,* trois, *a. & m.* ~*color process,* trichromie, *f.* ~*-master,* trois-mâts, *m.* ~*-ply* [*wood*], contreplaqué en trois, bois plaqué triplé, *m.* ~*some,* partie de trois, *f.* ~*-speed gear,* dispositif à 3 vitesses, *m.* ~*fold,* *a,* triple.

thresh, *v.t,* battre, dépiquer. ~ *out,* vider. ~*er* (*pers.*) *n,* batteur en grange, *m.* ~*ing machine,* batteuse, *f.*

threshold, *n,* seuil, pas, *m.*

thrice, *ad,* trois fois.

thrift, *n,* économie, épargne, *f.* ~*less,* *a,* prodigue, dépensier. ~*y,* *a,* économe, ménager.

thrill, *n,* tressaillement, saisissement, frisson, *m,* vive émotion, *f.* ¶ *v.t,* électriser; empoigner; (*v.i.*) tressaillir, palpiter. ~*ing,* *a,* passionnant, palpitant, empoignant.

thrive, *v.i.ir,* prospérer; (*plant*) se plaire. *not to* ~, se défraire. **thriving,** *a,* florissant, prospère.

throat, *n,* gorge, *f;* gosier, *m.*

throb, *v.i,* battre, palpiter; (*Med.*) élancer.

throe, *n,* douleur, *f;* (*pl.*) affres, *f.pl.*

throne, *n,* trône, *m;* (*bishop's*) chaire, *f.*

throng, *n,* foule, presse, *f.* ¶ *v.t,* accourir en foule à; assiéger; (*v.i.*) se presser.

throstle, *n,* grive chanteuse, *f.*

throttle, *n,* gosier; régulateur; (*Mech.*) étrangleur, *m.* ¶ *v.t,* étrangler.

through, *pr,* à travers; au t. de; par; à cause de. ~ *thick & thin,* envers & contre tous. ¶ *ad,* à travers; au t.; de part en part, à jour; jusqu'au bout; d'un bout à l'autre; directement. ¶ *a,* direct; à forfait, forfaitaire. ~ *ticket,* (*to final destination*) billet direct; (*sea-land-sea*) billet global, *m.* ~out, *pr,* par tout; pendant tout; (*ad.*) complètement, jusqu'au bout.

throw, *n,* jet, *m;* (*Mech.*) excentricité, *f.* ¶ *v.t.ir,* jeter; lancer; démonter; terrasser; tomber; mettre. ~ *away,* jeter. ~ *back,* rejeter. ~ *down,* ~ *over,* renverser. ~ *open,* ouvrir. ~ *out,* chasser; rejeter. ~ *up,* jeter en l'air; vomir. ~ing, *n,* lancement, *m.*

thrum, *v.t,* tapoter (*on* = sur); (*v.i.*) tambouriner.

thrush, *n,* grive; (*Med.*) aphte, *f.*

thrust, *n,* coup, *m;* (*Fenc.*) botte, estocade; (*Mech.*) poussée, butée, *f.* ¶ *v.t.ir,* pousser; plonger; (*sword*) pointer; (*Fenc.*) estocader; imposer. ~ *aside,* repousser. ~ *at* (*Fenc.*), porter une botte à.

thud, *n,* coup sourd, son mat, floc, *m.*

thug, *n,* étrangleur, *m.*

thumb, *n,* pouce, *m.* ~ *index,* répertoire à onglets, *m.* ~*screw,* écrou à oreilles, papillon, *m.* ~*tack,* punaise, *f.* ¶ *v.t,* feuilleter. ~ *one's nose,* faire un pied de nez.

thump, *n,* coup sourd, *m;* bourrade, *f,* horion, *m.* ¶ *v.t,* cogner; sonner lourdement.

thunder, *n,* tonnerre, *m,* foudre, *f.* ~*bolt,* foudre, *f,* coup de foudre, tonnerre, *m;* (*pl, Jove's*) foudres, traits, *m.pl.* ~*clap,* coup de tonnerre, *m.* ~*cloud,* nuée, *f.* ~*storm,* orage, *m.* ~*struck,* foudroyé. ¶ *v.i. & t,* tonner; fulminer. ~y, *a,* orageux.

Thursday, *n,* jeudi, *m.*

thus, *ad,* ainsi, de cette façon. ~ *far,* jusqu'ici.

thwack, *n,* coup, *m.* ¶ *v.t,* frapper.

thwart, *n,* banc [de nage] *m.* ¶ *v.t,* croiser, contrecarrer, traverser.

thy, *a,* ton, ta, tes.

thyme, *n,* thym; (*wild*) serpolet, *m.*

thyroid, *a,* thyroïde.

thyself, *pn,* toi-même; toi; te.

tiara, *n,* tiare, *f.*

Tiber (the), le Tibre.

tibia, *n,* tibia, *m.*

tic, *n,* tic, *m.*

Ticino (the), le Tessin.

tick, *n,* coutil, *m,* (*ticking*) toile à matelas; (*insect*) tique, *f,* acare; tic tac; point, *m;* seconde, *f.* ~*tack,* tic tac, *m.* ¶ *v.i,* battre; (*v.t.*) pointer.

ticket, *n,* billet; bulletin; cachet, *m;* entrée; carte; étiquette; (*auto*) contravention, *f.* ~ *collector,* contrôleur, *m.* ~ *window,* guichet [de distribution des billets] *m.* ¶ *v.t,* étiqueter.

tickle, *v.t. & i,* chatouiller. **ticklish,** *a,* chatouilleux; critique; délicat, scabreux.

tidal, *a:* ~ *basin,* bassin de marée, *m.* ~ *water,* eaux à m., *f.pl.* ~ *wave,* flot de la marée, raz de m., *m,* barre de flot, *f.* **tide,** *n,* marée, *f;* courant, *m.* ebb ~, marée descendante, *f.* flood ~, marée montante, *f.* to ~ over a difficulty, se tirer d'affaire.

tidiness, *n,* propreté, *f,* bon ordre, *m.*

tidings, *n.pl,* nouvelles, *f.pl.*

tidy, *a,* bien tenu, rangé; (*pers.*) ordonné. ¶ *v.t,* ranger. ~ *oneself up,* s'ajuster, faire un bout de toilette.

tie, *n,* lien, *m;* attache, *f;* tirant, *m;* cravate, *f,* nœud, *m;* (*Mus.*) liaison; (*voting*) égalité de voix; (*sport*) égalité de points, *f.* ~ *clip,* fixe-cravate, *m.* ~ *pin,* épingle de cravate, *f.* ¶ *v.t.ir,* lier; attacher; clouer; (*knot*) faire; (*v.i.*) (*sport*) arriver à égalité; (*exams*) être [classé] ex æquo. ~ *down,* lier; astreindre. ~ *up,* lier; bander; mettre à l'attache.

tier, *n,* rangée, *f,* rang, étage, gradin, *m.*

tierce, *n,* tierce, *f.*

Tierra del Fuego, la Terre de Feu.

tiff, *n*, fâcherie, pique, difficulté, *f*.

tiger, *n*, tigre, *m*. ~ **cat**, chat-tigre, *m*. ~ **lily**, lis tigré, *m*.

tight, *a*, serré; tendu; raide; étroit, juste; collant; étanche. ~ **corner**, coin étranglé; mauvais pas, *m*. ~**wad**, grippe-sou, *m*. ~**en**, *v.t*, [res]serrer, tendre, raidir. ~[ly], *ad*, serré; étroitement. ~**ness**, *n*, tension, raideur; étroitesse; étanchéité, *f*.

tigress, *n*, tigresse, *f*.

Tigris (the), le Tigre.

tile, *n*, tuile, *f*; carreau, *m*; (*pl, roof*) gouttières, *f.pl*. ~ **floor[ing]**, carrelage, *m*. ~ **maker**, tuilier, *m*. ~ **works**, tuilerie, *f*. ¶ *v.t*, couvrir de tuiles; carreler.

till, *n*, caisse, *f*, tiroir de c., *m*. ¶ *v.t*, labourer. ¶ *pr*, jusqu'à; jusque; avant; à. ¶ *c*, jusqu'à ce que; en attendant que. **tillage**, *n*, labourage, *m*. **tiller**, *n*, laboureur, *m*; barre [du gouvernail] *f*.

tilt, *n*, bâche; joute; inclinaison, *f*. ¶ *v.t*, incliner; culbuter; (*v.i.*) s'incliner; jouter. **tilting** (*Hist.*) *n*, joute, *f*.

timber, *n*, bois [de charpente]; (*ship*) couple, *m*. ~ **tree**, arbre de haute futaie, *m*. ~**tree forest**, futaie, *f*. ~**work**, charpente [en bois] *f*. ¶ *v.t*, boiser; charpenter.

timbre, *n*, timbre, *m*.

Timbuctoo, *n*, Tombouctou, *m*.

time, *n*, temps; moment, *m*; époque; saison, *f*; siècle, *m*; heure; fois, reprise, *f*; terme, *m*; mesure; cadence, *f*; pas, *m. at* ~**s**, parfois. [*just*] *in* ~, à point. ~ *fuse*, fusée à temps, *f*. ~**honored**, séculaire. ~**keeper** (*pers.*), pointeur, contrôleur; (*sport*) chronométreur, *m*. ~**piece**, pendule, *f*. ~**server**, opportuniste, *m,f*, caméléon, *m*, complaisant, e. (*computers*) ~**sharing**, partage de temps, *m*. ~ **sheet**, feuille de présence, *f*. ~**table**, (*book*) indicateur; (*placard & scheme of work*) horaire, *m. at any* ~, n'importe quand. (*computers*) *down* ~, temps de panne, *m. from* ~ *to* ~, de temps en temps. (*computers*) *idle* ~, temps mort, *m. next* ~, la prochaine fois. ¶ *v.t*, (*watch*) régler; (*sport*) chronomé-

trer. ~**ing**, *n*, pointage, *m*. **timeliness**, *n*, opportunité, *f*. **timely**, *a*, opportun.

timid†, *a*, timide, peureux. ~**ity**, *n*, timidité, *f*. **timorous**, *a*, timoré.

tin, *n*, étain; (*can*) bidon, *m*; boîte [métallique] *f*. ~ **foil**, feuille d'étain, *f*. ~ [*plate*], fer-blanc, *m*. ~ **soldier**, soldat de plomb, *m*. ~**smith**, ferblantier, *m*. ~**ware**, ferblanterie, *f*. ¶ *v.t*, étamer; mettre en boîte(s), *m*. en conserve.

tincture, *n*, teinture, *f*. ¶ *v.t*, teindre.

tinder, *n*, amadou, *m*. ~ **box**, briquet, *m*.

tine, *n*, dent, branche, *f*; (*deer*) andouiller, *m*.

tinge, *n*, teinte, nuance, *f*. ¶ *v.t*, teinter.

tingle, *v.i*, picoter; fourmiller; (*ears*) tinter.

tinker, *n*, chaudronnier ambulant, *m*.

tinkle, *v.i*, tinter. ¶ *n*, tintement, *m*. ~*l* ~*l* drelin-drelin!

tinsel, *n*, clinquant, *m*, oripeaux, *m.pl*; (*fig.*) faux brillant, *m*.

tint, *n*, teinte, *f*, ton, *m*. ¶ *v.t*, teinter.

tiny, *a*, minuscule, petiot, infime. ~ *bit*, tantinet, tout petit peu, *m*. ~ *drop*, gouttelette, *f*.

tip, *n*, bout; bec, *m*; pointe; extrémité, *f*; (*wing*) fouet; (*Bil. cue*) procédé; (*gratuity*) pourboire, *m*, pièce, *f*; (*information*) tuyau, *m*. ¶ *v.t*, embouter; basculer; culbuter; verser; donner un pourboire à; donner un tuyau à. ~*cart*, tombereau, *m*.

tippet, *n*, palatine, *f*, mantelet, *m*.

tipple, *v.i*, buvoter, chopiner. **tippler**, *n*, biberon, ne.

tipster, *n*, donneur de tuyaux, *m*.

tipsy, *a*, ivre. *a* ~ *walk*, une démarche avinée.

tiptoe (on), sur la pointe du pied.

tiptop, *n*, comble, *m*. ¶ *a*, excellent, parfait.

tirade, *n*, tirade, incartade, *f*.

tire, *n*, bandage; pneu[matique], caoutchouc, *m. flat* ~, pneu crevé, *m. nonskid* ~, p. antidérapant, *m. snow* ~, p. neige, *m. spare* ~, p. de rechange, *m*.

tire, *v.t*, fatiguer, lasser, excéder; (*v.i.*) se fatiguer, se lasser. ~*d out*, rompu [de fatigue]. ~**less**, a, infatigable. ~some, a, fatigant; ennuyeux, fâcheux.

tissue, n, tissu, m; tissure, f. ~ paper, papier de soie, m.

tit (bird) n, mésange, f. ~ for tat, donnant donnant; un prêté [pour un] rendu.

titbit, n, bonne bouche, f.

tithe, n, dîme, f. not a ~, pas un dixième.

titillate, v.t, titiller, chatouiller.

titivate, v.t, bichonner.

title, n, titre; intitulé; parchemin, m. ~ [deed], titre, m. ~ page, page du titre, f, titre, frontispice, m. ~d, a, titré.

titmouse, n, mésange, f.

titter, v.i, rire bêtement, glousser.

tittle, n, iota, m.

titular, a, titulaire, en titre.

to, pr, à; de; pour; afin de; en; dans; envers; vers; jusqu'à; chez; auprès de, près; sur; contre; (of the hour) moins. to go ~ & fro, aller de long en large, aller deçà, delà; aller & venir, faire la navette. ~ be called for, bureau restant, poste restante; télégraphe restant; gare restante, en gare. ~ be kept cool, dry or in a cool, dry, place, craint la chaleur, l'humidité. ~ be taken after meals, à prendre après les repas. ~ boot, en sus, par surcroît, avec ça. ~ match, pareil. ~ measure, sur mesure. ~ wit, savoir; (of pers.) nommément.

toad, n, crapaud, m. ~ hole, crapaudière, f. ~stone, crapaudine, f. ~stool, champignon [vénéneux] m. **toady,** n, flagorneur, euse, chien couchant, m. ~ to, flagorner. ~ism, n, flagornerie, f.

toast, n, pain grillé, m, rôtie, f; (buttered) toast; (health) toast, m. ¶v.t, griller, rôtir; (health) porter un toast à. ~er, n, grille-pain, m. ~ing fork, fourchette à griller le pain, f.

tobacco, n, tabac, m. ~ pouch, blague à t., f. **tobacconist,** n, débitant de t., m. ~'s shop, débit de t., bureau de t., m.

toboggan, n, toboggan, m. ~ run, piste de toboggan, f.

today, ad. & n, aujourd'hui, ad. & m. ~'s gossip, nouvelles à la main, f.pl.

toddle, v.i, trottiner.

to-do, n, cérémonies, f.pl; aria, m.

toe, n, doigt [de pied], orteil, m;

(shoe, sock) pointe, f. ~ dancing, pointes, f.pl. ~ nail, ongle d'orteil, m.

toga, n, toge, f.

together, ad, ensemble; à la fois. ~ with, avec, en compagnie de, ainsi que.

toil, n, travail, labeur, m; (pl.) lacets, lacs, rets, m.pl, toiles, f.pl. ¶v.i, peiner. ~ & moil, suer d'ahan, peiner. ~er, n, travailleur, euse.

toilet, n, toilette, f. ~ paper, papier hygiénique, m.

toilsome, a, pénible, laborieux.

token, n, signe, témoignage, m, preuve, marque, f; gage, hommage; jeton, m.

Toledo, n, Tolède, f.

tolerable, a, tolérable; passable. **tolerably,** ad, passablement. **tolerance & toleration,** n, tolérance, f. **tolerate,** v.t, tolérer.

toll, n, péage, passage, m. ~ call (Teleph.), communication régionale, f. ~ bridge, pont payant, m. ~ gate, barrière de péage, f. ¶ v.t. & i, tinter, sonner. ~ing, n, tintement funèbre, m.

tom: ~boy, garçon manqué, m. ~ [cat], matou, chat, m. ~foolery, farce, pantalonnade, gaminerie, f. ~tit, mésange charbonnière, f.

tomato, n, tomate, f. ~ sauce, sauce t., f.

tomb, n, tombe, f, tombeau, m, sépulture, f. ~stone, pierre tombale, f.

tome, n, tome, volume, m.

tomorrow, ad. & n, demain, ad. & m. ~ morning, demain matin. ~ night, ~ evening, demain soir.

tomtom, n, tam-tam, m.

ton, n, tonne, f; tonneau, m.

tone, n, ton; son; accent, m; gamme, f; dispositions, f.pl. ¶ (v.t, Phot.) virer; (v.i.) s'harmoniser. ~ down, adoucir, assourdir, estomper.

tongs, n.pl, pince, tenaille, f, pincettes, f.pl.

tongue, n, langue; (strip, slip) languette, f. ~tied, la langue liée.

Tonkin, le Tonkin.

tonic, a, tonique; remontant. ~ sol-fa, tonic-sol-fa, m. ¶ n, (Med. & drink) tonique, remontant, m; (Mus.) tonique, f.

tonight, ad. & n, ce soir, cette nuit.

toning (*Phot.*) *n*, virage, *m*.

tonnage, *n*, tonnage, *m*; jauge, *f*.

tonsil, *n*, amygdale, *f*. **tonsilitis**, *n*, amygdalite, *f*.

tonsure, *n*, tonsure, couronne, *f*. ¶ *v.t*, tonsurer.

too, *ad*, trop; aussi; également; de même; encore. ~ *long*, (*length*) trop long; (*time*) trop [longtemps]. ~ *much*, ~ *many* & ~ *well*, trop.

tool, *n*, outil; instrument; ustensile; (*pers.*) suppôt, *m*, âme damnée, *f*. ~ *box*, boîte à outils, *f*. ~ *maker*, fabricant d'outils, taillandier, *m*. ¶ *v.t*, (*Mach.*) travailler; (*Bookb.*) gaufrer.

tooth, *n*, dent, *f*. ~*ache*, mal de dents, *m*, (*violent*) rage de dents, *f*. ~ *brush*, brosse à dents, *f*. ~ *brush moustache*, moustache en brosse, *f*. ~*paste*, pâte dentifrice, *f*, dentifrice, *m*. ~*pick*, cure-dents, *m*. ~ *powder*, poudre dentifrice, *f*, dentifrice, *m*. ¶ *v.t*, [en]denter, créneler. ~*some*, *a*, succulent.

top, *n*, haut; sommet, *m*; cime, *f*; faîte; comble; dessus, *m*; tête, pointe, *f*; (*bus*) impériale; (*Naut.*) hune; (*turnip, etc.*) fane; (*book page*) tête, tranche supérieure; (*toys*) toupie, *f*, sabot, *m*. *at the* ~ *of one's voice*, à tue-tête. *on* ~ *of*, par-dessus, sur. ~ *boots*, bottes à revers, *f.pl*. ~*coat*, pardessus, *m*. ~ *figure*, chiffre maximum, *m*. ~*gallant*, perroquet, *m*. ~ *hat*, chapeau haut de forme, *m*. ~*-heavy*, trop lourd du haut. ~*mast*, mât de hune, *m*. ~*sail*, hunier, *m*. ¶ *v.t*, couronner; surpasser; dépasser; être à la tête de; (*tree*) étêter.

topaz, *n*, topaze, *f*.

topic, *n*, sujet, thème, *m*. ~*al song*, chanson de circonstance, *f*.

topographic(al), *a*, topographique. **topography**, *n*, topographie, *f*.

topple, *v.i*, dégringoler. ~ *over*, faire culbuter, renverser.

topsyturvy, *ad*, sens dessus dessous.

torch, *n*, flambeau, *m*, torche, *f*. ~ *bearer*, porte-flambeau, *m*. *by* ~*light*, à la lueur des flambeaux, aux flambeaux.

toreador, *n*, toréador, *m*.

torment, *n*, tourment, supplice, *m*. ¶ *v.t*, tourmenter; travailler; taquiner. **tormentor**, *n*, bourreau, *m*.

tornado, *n*, tornade, *f*.

torpedo, *n*, torpille, *f*. ~ *boat*, [bateau] torpilleur, *m*. ~ *launcher*, lance-torpille, *f*. ¶ *v.t*, torpiller.

torpid, *a*, torpide. **torpor**, *n*, torpeur, *f*.

torrent, *n*, torrent, *m*. *in* ~*s*, à torrents, à flots. ~*ial*, *a*, torrentiel, diluvien.

torrid, *a*, torride.

torsion, *n*, torsion, *f*.

torso, *n*, torse, *m*.

tort (*law*) *n*, acte dommageable, *m*.

tortoise, *n*, tortue, *f*. ~*shell*, écaille [de t.] *f*. ~*shell butterfly*, tortue, *f*. ~*shell cat*, chat d'Espagne, *m*.

tortuous†, *a*, tortueux, tortu.

torture, *n*, torture, *f*, tourment, supplice, *m*. *instrument of* ~, instrument de torture, appareil tortionnaire, *m*. ¶ *v.t*, torturer, tourmenter. **torturer**, *n*, tortionnaire, bourreau, *m*. **torturous**, *a*, tortionnaire.

toss, *v.t. & i*, jeter; ballotter; cahoter; secouer; (*head*) hocher; (*oars*) mâter. ~ *off* (*drink*), lamper, sabler. ~ [*up*] (*coin*), tirer [à pile où face].

tot, *n*, (*child*) petiot, e; (*rum, etc.*) boujaron, *m*.

total†, *a*, total; global; complet. ¶ *n*, total; montant, *m*. **totalitarian**, *a*, totalitaire. **totalizer**, **totalizator**, *n*, totaliseur, totalisateur, *m*.

totter, *v.i*, chanceler; s'ébranler.

toucan, *n*, toucan, *m*.

touch, *n*, toucher; tact, *m*; touche, *f*; contact, *m*; communication, *f*; coup; (*art*) pinceau; soupçon, *m*; pointe, *f*. ~*stone*, pierre de touche, *f*. ~*wood*, amadou, *m*. ¶ *v.t. & i*, toucher; t. à; se t.; tâter; effleurer. *to keep in* ~, garder le contact. ~ *up*, retoucher; chatouiller. ~*ed* (*crazy*), *p.p*, toqué, timbré. ~*iness*, *n*, susceptibilité, *f*. ~*ing*, *a. & pr*, touchant. ~*y*, *a*, susceptible, chatouilleux.

tough†, *a*, dur; résistant; tenace; coriace. ¶ *n*, voyou, dur. ~*en*, *v.t*, durcir. ~*ness*, *n*, dureté; ténacité, résistance, *f*.

tour, *n*, tour, voyage, *m*, tournée, *f*. ~**ing**, *n*, tourisme, *m*. ~**ist**, *n*, touriste, *m,f*. ~ *agency*, agence de tourisme, *f*.

tournament, *n*, tournoi; concours, *m*.

tourniquet, *n*, tourniquet, garrot, *m*.

tousle, *v.t*, ébouriffer.

tow, *n*, filasse, étoupe, *f*; (*boat*) remorqué, *m*. *in* ~, à la remorque, à la traîne. ¶ *v.t*, remorquer; haler, touer. ~[*ing*] *path*, chemin de halage, tirage, *m*.

toward[s], *pr*, vers; envers; vis-à-vis de, à l'endroit de; sur.

towel, *n*, serviette [de toilette] *f*, essuie-mains, *m*. **toweling**, *n*, tissu éponge, *m*.

tower, *n*, tour, *f*; pylône, *m*. ~ *above*, dominer. ~*ing rage*, colère bleue, *f*.

town, *n*, ville; place, *f*. ~ *clerk*, secrétaire de mairie, *m*. ~ *crier*, crieur public, *m*. ~ *hall*, hôtel de ville, *m*, maison de ville, mairie, *f*. ~ *house*, hôtel, *m*. ~ *planning*, urbanisme, *m*. **townsman**, *n*, citadin, *m*.

toxic, *a*, toxique. **toxin**, *n*, toxine, *f*.

toy, *n*, jouet, joujou, *m*, babiole, *f*. ~ *balloon*, ballon d'enfant, *m*. ¶ *v.i*, jouer, badiner.

trace, *n*, trace, *f*; (*harness*) trait; (*Fish*.) bas de ligne avec émerillons, *m*. ~ *horse*, [cheval] côtier, cheval de renfort, *m*. ¶ *v.t*, tracer; calquer; suivre la trace de; suivre à la trace. ~ *back*, faire remonter. ~*d pattern*, tracé, *m*. ~**ry**, *n*, réseau, *m*, dentelle, *f*.

trachea, *n*, trachée-artère, *f*.

tracing, *n*, calque, *m*. ~ *paper*, papier calque, *m*.

track, *n*, trace; piste; voie, *f*; chemin, sentier, *m*; route, *f*; sillage; sillon, *m*. ~ *race*, course sur piste, *f*. ¶ *v.t*, suivre à la piste. ~ *down*, (*game*) dépister; (*criminal*) traquer.

tract, *n*, étendue, *f*; (*leaflet*) opuscule, *m*. ~**able**, *a*, traitable. **traction**, *n*, traction, *f*. ~ *engine*, machine routière; locomobile, *f*. **tractor**, *n*, tracteur, *m*.

trade, *n*, commerce; négoce; trafic, *m*, traite, *f*; métier, *m*; industrie, *f*. ~ *discount*, remise [sur marchandises] *f*. ~*mark*, marque de commerce, *m*. de fabrique, appellation, *f*. ~ *union*, syndicat ouvrier, *m*. ~ *unionist*, syndicaliste, syndiqué, *m*. ~ *winds*, vents alizés, *m.pl*. ¶ *v.i*, trafiquer (*in* = en), faire [le] commerce (*in* = de). **trader**, *n*, commerçant, e; trafiquant, *m*; (*col. pl.*) le commerce. **trading**, *n*, commerce, *m*; traite, *f*; exercice, *m*. ~ *account*, compte d'exploitation, *m*. **tradesman**, *n*, marchand; boutiquier; fournisseur, *m*. *tradesmen's entrance*, porte de service, *f*.

tradition, *n*, tradition, *f*. ~**al**†, *a*, traditionnel.

traduce, *v.t*, calomnier. ~**er**, *n*, diffamateur, *m*.

traffic, *n*, trafic, *m*, traite, *f*; mouvement, *m*; circulation, *f*. ~ *jam*, embouteillage, *m*. ~ *lights*, signaux lumineux de circulation, feux de c., *m.pl*. ~ *police*, police de la circulation, *f*. ~ *circle*, rond-point, *m*. ~ *sign*, poteau de signalisation, *m*. **trafficker**, *n*, trafiquant, *m*.

tragedian, *n*, [auteur] tragique, *m*. ~, *tragedienne*, tragédien, ne. **tragedy**, *n*, tragédie, *f*; drame, *m*. **tragic**(**al**†), *a*, tragique. **tragicomedy**, *n*, tragi-comédie, *f*. **tragicomic**, *a*, tragi-comique.

trail, *n*, piste, trace; traînée, *f*, sillon, *m*; (*gun carriage*) flèche, *f*. ~ *rope* (*Avn*.), guiderope, *m*. ¶ *v.t*, suivre à la piste; traîner. ~**er**, *n*, remorque, *f*; (*cinema*) film-annonce, *m*.

train, *n*, train; convoi, *m*; suite, *f*; cortège, *m*; (*dress*) traîne, queue, *f*; (*comet*) queue; (*powder*) traînée, *f*; (*events*) enchaînement, *m*. ~ *ferry*, bac transbordeur, *m*. ¶ *v.t*, former, styler; instruire; dresser, éduquer; entraîner; (*gun*) diriger, pointer. ~**er**, *n*, dresseur; entraîneur, *m*. **training**, *n*, éducation; école; instruction, *f*; enseignement; dressage, manège; entraînement, *m*, haleine, *f*. ~ *ship*, vaisseau-école, *m*.

trait, *n*, trait, *m*.

traitor, **tress**, *n*, traître, *m*, traîtresse, *f*. ~**ous**, *a*, traître. ~**ously**, *ad*, en traître.

trajectory, *n*, trajectoire, *f*.

trammel, *n*, (*net*) tramail, *m*;

(*pl.*) entraves, *f.pl.* ¶*v.t*, entraver.

tramp, *n*, bruit de pas, *m*; (*horses*) battue; promenade [à pied] *f*; (*pers.*) chemineau, *m*, vagabond, e. ¶*v.i*, marcher pesamment; cheminer; marcher; (*v.t.*) arpenter. ~ *up & down*, courir.

trample [**on**] [**down**], *v.t*, fouler, piétiner.

trance, *n*, extase; (*hypnotic*) transe, *f*.

tranquil†, *a*, tranquille. **tranquility**, *n*, tranquillité, *f*.

transact, *v.t*, traiter, faire; délibérer sur. ~**ion**, *n*, négociation; affaire, transaction; délibération, *f*; (*pl.*) actes, *m.pl.*

transatlantic, *a*, transatlantique.

transcend, *v.t*, dépasser; surpasser. ~**ent**, *a*, transcendant.

transcribe, *v.t*, transcrire. **transcript & transcription**, *n*, transcription, *f*.

transept, *n*, transept, *m*.

transfer, *n*, transmission; cession, *f*; apport; (*law*) transfert; transport; virement, *m*; (*for china & as toy*) décalcomanie; (*bus*) billet de correspondance, *m*. ~ [*deed*], transfert, *m*, feuille de t., *f*. ¶*v.t*, transmettre; céder; apporter; transférer; transporter; virer; décalquer. ~**able**, *a*, cessible; mobilier.

transfiguration, *n*, transfiguration, *f*.

transfix, *v.t*, transpercer.

transform, *v.t*, transformer. ~**ation**, *n*, transformation, *f*. ~**er**, *n*, transformateur, *m*.

transfuse, *v.t*, transfuser. **transfusion**, *n*, transfusion, *f*.

transgress, *v.t*, transgresser, contrevenir à. ~**or**, *n*, violateur, trice; pécheur, eresse.

transient†, *a*, transitoire, passager.

transit, *n*, transit; passage; transport, *m. in* ~, en transit; en cours de route. ~**ion**, *n*, transition, *f*, passage, *m*. ~**ive**†, *a*, transitif. ~**ory**†, *a*, transitoire.

translate, *v.t*, traduire; (*bishop*) transférer. **translation**, *n*, traduction; version; (*bishop*) translation, *f*. **translator**, *n*, traducteur, trice.

translucent, *a*, translucide.

transmigration, *n*, transmigration, *f*.

transmission, *n*, transmission; (*auto*) boîte de vitesse; (*radio*) émission, *f*.

transmit, *v.t*, transmettre; émettre. **transmitter**, *n*, transmetteur; (*radio*) émetteur, *m*.

transmute, *v.t*, transmuer.

transom, *n*, vasistas, *m*; traverse, *f*.

transparency, *n*, transparence, *f*; transparent, *m*; diapositive, *f*. **transparent**, *a*, transparent.

transpire, *v.i*, transpirer.

transplant, *v.t*, transplanter, dépiquer.

transport, *n*, transport, *m*. ¶*v.t*, transporter. ~**ation**, *n*, transportation, *f*. *piggyback* ~, ferroutage, *m*.

transpose, *v.t*, transposer.

transubstantiation, *n*, transubstantiation, *f*.

transverse†, *a*, transversal.

trap, *n*, trappe, *f*, traquenard, piège; guetapens, *m. mouse* ~, souricière, *f*. ~*door*, trappe, *f*. ¶*v.t*, prendre au piège, attraper.

trapeze, *n*, trapèze, *m*.

trapper, *n*, trappeur, *m*.

trappings, *n.pl*, harnachement, *m*; (*fig.*) parure, *f*.

trash, *n*, camelote, pacotille, saloperie, saleté, *f*; (*worthless contents of book*) futilités, *f.pl.*

traumatic, *a*, traumatique. **traumatism**, *n*, traumatisme, *m*. **traumatize**, *v.t*, traumatiser.

travel, *n*, voyage, *m*. ¶*v.i*, voyager; marcher; rouler. ~ *over*, parcourir. **traveler**, *n*, voyageur, euse; placier, *m*. **traveling**, *p.a*, ambulant.

traverse, *v.t*, traverser.

travesty, *n*, travestissement, *m*. ¶*v.t*, travestir.

trawl [**net**], *n*, chalut, *m*, traille, *f*. ¶*v.i*, pêcher au chalut, p. à la traille. ~**er**, *n*, [bateau] chalutier, *m*. ~**ing**, *n*, pêche chalutière, *f*.

tray, *n*, plateau, *m*.

treacherous†, *a*, perfide, traître. **treachery**, *n*, traîtrise, perfidie, trahison, *f*.

treacle, *n*, mélasse, *f*.

tread, *n*, pas; (*of stair step*) giron, *m*. ¶*v.i.ir*, marcher; (*v.t. ir.*) fouler. ~ *water*, nager debout. ~**le**, *n*, marche, pédale, *f*.

treason, *n*, trahison, *f*, crime d'État, *m*.

treasure, *n. & ~ trove*, trésor, *m*.

¶ *v.t*, garder précieusement. **treasurer,** *n*, trésorier, ère. **treasury,** *n*, trésor, *m*, trésorerie, caisse, *f*; fisc, *m*.

treat, *n*, régal; plaisir, *m*; débauche, *f*. ¶ *v.t. & i*, traiter; régaler. **treatise,** *n*, traité, *m*. **treatment,** *n*, traitement, *m*; (*music, art*) facture, *f*. **treaty,** *n*, traité, *m*. *by private ~*, à l'amiable.

treble†, *a*, triple. ¶ *n*, triple; (*Mus.*) dessus, *m*; (*crochet*) bride, *f*. *~ clef*, clef de sol, *f*. ¶ *v.t*, tripler.

tree, *n*, arbre, *m*. *~top*, cime d'un arbre, *f*. *~less*, *a*, sans arbre.

trefoil, *n*, trèfle, *m*.

trellis, *n*, treillis, treillage, *m*. ¶ *v.t*, treillisser.

tremble, *v.i*, trembler. **trembling,** *n*, tremblement, *m*.

tremendous, *a*, énorme, formidable, effroyable, furieux, fou.

tremolo, *n*, tremolo, *m*. **tremor,** *n*, tremblement, *m*, trépidation, *f*. **tremulous,** *a*, tremblant.

trench, *n*, tranchée, *f*, fossé, *m*. *~ coat*, trench-coat, *m*. *~ mortar*, mortier de tranchée, *m*. *~ warfare*, guerre de tranchées, g. de position, *f*. ¶ *v.t*, creuser; (*Mil.*) faire des tranchées. *~ant*, *a*, tranchant, à l'emporte-pièce. **trencher,** *n*, tranchoir, tailloir, *m*. **trencherman,** *n*, mangeur, *m*.

trend, *n*, direction; tendance, *f*. ¶ *v.i*, se diriger.

Trent, *n*, Trente, *f*. **the Trentino,** le Trentin.

trepan, *n*, trépan, *m*. ¶ *v.t*, trépaner.

trepidation, *n*, tremblement, *m*.

trespass, *n*, intrusion; offense, *f*. ¶ *~ against*, offenser. *~ on*, s'introduire sans droit dans; (*fig.*) empiéter sur, abuser de. *~er*, *n*, intrus, e. *~s will be prosecuted*, défense d'entrer sous peine d'amende.

tress, *n*, tresse, *f*.

trestle, *n*, tréteau, chevalet, *m*.

Treves, *n*, Trèves, *f*.

trial, *n*, essai, *m*, épreuve; tribulation, *f*, procès; jugement, *m*; débats, *m.pl. to bring to ~*, mettre en jugement. *~ & error*, tâtonnements, *m.pl. ~ balance*, balance de vérification, b. d'ordre, *f*. *~ trip*, voyage d'essai, *m*.

triangle (*Geom. & Mus.*) *n*, triangle, *m*. **triangular,** *a*, triangulaire.

tribe, *n*, tribu; race, *f*.

tribulation, *n*, tribulation, *f*.

tribunal, *n*, tribunal, *m*. **tribune,** *n*, tribune, *f*; (*Hist. pers.*) tribun, *m*.

tributary, *a*, tributaire. ¶ *n*, tributaire; affluent, *m*. **tribute,** *n*, tribut; hommage, *m*.

trice, *n*, clin d'œil, *m*.

triceps, *a. & n*, triceps, *a. & m*.

trick, *n*, tour, jeu, *m*; ruse; ficelle; jonglerie, *f*; truc, *m*; (*cards*) levée, *f*; (*habit*) tic, *m*. *~ riding*, voltige, *f*. ¶ *v.t*, tricher, duper. *~ery*, *n*, tricherie, finasserie, *f*.

trickle, *n*, filet, *m*. ¶ *v.i*, [dé]couler, ruisseler.

trickster, *n*, tricheur, euse, finassier, ère, jongleur, *m*. **tricky,** *a*, adroit à s'évader; délicat.

tricycle, *n*, tricycle, *m*.

trident, *n*, trident, *m*.

triennial, *n*, triennal.

trifle, *a*, bagatelle, vétille, *f*, rien, *m*; misère; futilité, *f*. ¶ *v.i*, s'amuser à des riens; baguenauder. *~ with*, se jouer de. **trifler,** *n*, baguenaudier, homme futile, *m*. **trifling,** *a*, insignifiant, minime; futile.

triforium, *n*, triforium, *m*.

trigger, *n*, détente, *f*; déclic, *m*.

trigonometry, *n*, trigonométrie, *f*.

trill, *n*, trille, *m*. ¶ *v.t*, orner de trilles.

trillion, *n*, billion, *m*.

trim, *a*, soigné, bien tenu; coquet. ¶ *n*, ornement, *m*; assiette, allure, *f*; arrimage, *m*. ¶ *v.t*, tailler; parer; agrémenter; garnir; (*edges*) rogner; (*book edges*), ébarber; (*hair*) tailler, rafraîchir; (*wood*) dresser; (*ship*) arrimer; (*sails*) orienter. **trimmings,** *n.pl*, passementerie; garniture, *f*, fourniture, *f*. oft. pl; (*Cook.*) garniture, *f*.

trimonthly, *a*, trimestriel.

Trinidad, *n. & the Trinity,** la Trinité.

trinket, *n*, colifichet, bibelot, *m*.

trio, *n*, trio, *m*.

trip, *n*, (*fall*) croc-en-jambe; tour, voyage, *m*, excursion, *f*. *~ [up]*, *v.t*, faire trébucher, donner un croc-en-jambe à; (*Mech.*) déclencher; (*anchor*) déraper; (*v.i.*) trébucher. ~ *along*, sautiller.

tripe, *n*, tripes, *f.pl.*

triplet†, *a*, triple. ¶ *v.t. & i*, tripler. **triplet**, *n*, triolet, tercet, *m*; (*pl.*) trois jumeaux, *m.pl.* **triplicate**, *n*, triplicata, triple, *m*.

tripod, *n*, trépied, *m*.

tripoli, *n*, tripoli, *m*.

triptych, *n*, triptyque, *m*.

trite†, *a*, banal. ~**ness**, *n*, banalité, *f*.

triton, *n*, triton, *m*.

triumph, *n*, triomphe, *m*. ¶ *v.i*, triompher. ~**al**, *a*, triomphal, de triomphe. ~**ant**, *a*, triomphant, victorieux. ~**antly**, *ad*, triomphalement.

trivet, *n*, trépied, *m*, chevrette, *f*.

trivial, *a*, insignifiant, minime; frivole.

troglodyte, *n*, troglodyte, *m*.

Trojan, *a*, troyen; (*war*) de Troie.

troll (*Fish.*) *v.i*, pêcher à la traîne.

trolley, *n*, tramway, trolley, *m*. ~ *bus*, autobus à trolley.

trolling, *n*, pêche à traîner, *f*.

trombone, *n*, trombone, *m*.

troop, *n*, troupe; bande, *f*. ~ *ship*, transport, *m*. ~ *train*, train militaire, *m*. ~**er**, *n*, cavalier, *m*.

trope, *n*, trope, *m*.

trophy, *n*, trophée, *m*; panoplie, *f*.

tropic, *n*, tropique, *m*. ~ *of Cancer, of Capricorn*, tropique du Cancer, du Capricorne. ~**al**, *a*, tropical.

trot, *n*, trot, *m*. ¶ *v.i. & t*, trotter.

troth, *n*, foi, *f*.

trotter, *n*, trotteur, euse; (*pl.*) (*pigs' feet*) pieds, *m.pl.*

troubadour, *n*, troubadour, *m*.

trouble, *n*, peine, *f*; chagrin; ennui; mal; trouble, *m. engine* ~, panne de moteur, *f*. ~*shooter*, dépanneur, *m*. ~ *spot*, point chaud, *m*. ¶ *v.t*, inquiéter, tourmenter, chagriner; déranger. ~**d**, *p.a*, agité, inquiet. ~ *waters* (*fig.*), eau trouble, *f*. ~*some*, *a*, fâcheux; difficultueux; gênant; (*child*) tourmentant.

trough, *n*, bac, baquet, *m*, auge; huche, *f*; (*of wave*) creux; (*sea*) entre-deux, *m*.

trounce, *v.t*, rosser, étriller.

troupe, *n*, troupe, *f*.

trouser, *n*, (*pl.*) pantalon, *m*.

trousseau, *n*, trousseau, *m*.

trout, *n*, truite, *f*. ~ *fishing*,

pêche à la t., *f*. ~ *stream*, rivière à truites, *f*.

trowel, *n*, truelle; (*Hort.*) houlette, *f*, déplantoir, *m*.

truancy, *n*, vagabondage, *m*. **truant**, *a*, vagabond. *to play* ~, faire l'école buissonnière.

truce, *n*, trêve, *f*.

truck, *n*, (*Rly.*) wagon; chariot, camion; (*hand*) diable; (*engine*) bogie, *m*. ~ *load*, wagon complet. *dump* ~, camion à benne basculante, *m. tow* ~, dépanneuse, *f*. ¶ *v.t*, rouler.

truckle, *v.i*, ramper.

truculent, *a*, truculent.

trudge, *v.i*, cheminer, clopiner.

true, *a*, vrai; véritable; loyal; fidèle; juste; conforme; rectiligne. *in one's* ~ *colors*, en déshabillé. [*certified*] *a* ~ *copy*, pour copie conforme, pour ampliation. ~*love[r's] knot*, lacs d'amour, *m*. ~ *to life*, vécu. ¶ *v.t*, dégauchir, rectifier, [re]dresser.

truffle, *n*, truffe, *f*.

truism, *n*, truisme, *m*. **truly**, *ad*, vraiment, véritablement; fidèlement.

truly, *ad*, vraiment, sincèrement. *yours* ~, sincèrement vôtre.

trump, *n*, trompette, *f*. ~[*card*], *n*. *&* ~*s*, *n.pl*, atout, *m*, retourne, *f*. ~ *up*, fabriquer, inventer.

trumpery, *n*, friperie; camelote; blague, *f*. ¶ *a*, de pacotille; frivole.

trumpet, *n*, trompette, *f*. ~ *call*, sonnerie de t., *f*. ¶ *v.t. & i*, (*fig.*) trompeter, corner; (*elephant*) barrir; (*Mus.*) sonner de la trompette. ~**er**, *n*, trompette, *m*.

truncate, *v.t*, tronquer.

truncheon, *n*, bâton, *m*.

trundle, *n*, roulette, *f*. ¶ *v.t*, rouler.

trunk, *n*, tronc, *m*; tige, *f*; torse, *m*; (*elephant*) trompe; malle, *f*, coffre; bahut, *m*; (*pl.*) caleçon court, *m*. (*pl*, *Teleph.*) l'inter, *m*. ~ *call*, communication interurbaine, *f*. ~ *line*, grande artère, *f*.

trunnion, *n*, tourillon, *m*.

truss, *n*, trousse, botte, *f*; bandage [herniaire], brayer, *m*; (*Build.*) ferme, *f*. ¶ *v.t*, (*fowl*) trousser; (*hay*) botteler; (*Build.*) armer.

trust, *n*, confiance; créance, foi,

f, credit, *m*; charge, *f*; mandat; (*oil, steel*) trust, *m*. ~ **deed**, acte de fidéicommis, *m*. ¶ *v.t. & i*, se fier à; croire; faire crédit à; espérer. ~**ed**, *p.a*, de confiance. ~**ee**, *n*, curateur, trice; dépositaire, *m,f*, consignataire; syndic, *m*. **board of** ~**s**, conseil d'administration, *m*. ~**ful**, *a*, confiant. ~**worthy**, *a*, digne de confiance, croyable, fidèle. ~**y**, *a*, loyal, fidèle, sûr.

truth, *n*, vérité, *f*, vrai, *m*. ~**ful**, *a*, vrai, véridique. ~**fulness**, *n*. véracité, *f*.

try, *n*, essai, coup, *m*. ¶ *v.t. & i*, essayer; éprouver; expérimenter; goûter; tenter; tâter; chercher; (*law case*) juger; (*patience*) exercer. ~ **on**, essayer. ~**ing**, *a*, difficile; contrariant. ~ *time*, mauvais quart d'heure, *m*.

tub, *n*, cuve, *f*, baquet; tub; tonneau, *m*; caisse, *f*; (*bad ship*) sabot, *m*. *tub[by man]*, poussah, *m*.

tuba, *n*, tuba, *m*.

tube, *n*, tube, *m*; (*anatomy*) conduit, *m*; (*radio*) lampe, *f*.

tuber & **tubercle**, *n*, tubercule, *m*. **tuberculosis**, tuberculose, *f*. **tuberculous**, *a*, tuberculeux. **tuberous**, *n*, tubéreuse, *f*.

tubular, *a*, tubulaire. ~ [*tire*], boyau, *m*.

tuck, *n*, rempli, troussis, *m*. ¶ *v.t*, remplier. ~ *in*, border. ~ *up*, [re]trousser.

Tuesday, *n*, mardi, *m*.

tuft, *n*, touffe, *f*; bouquet; panache, *m*; huppe; houppe; (*on chin*) mouche, *f*. ~**ed**, *a*, touffu; aigretté, huppé, houppé.

tug, *n*, tiraillement; coup de collier; (*boat*) remorqueur, toueur, *m*. ~ **of war**, lutte à la corde, *f*; (*fig.*) effort suprême, *m*. ¶ *v.t*, tirer.

tuition, *n*, (*fees*) droit d'inscriptions, *m.pl*; enseignement, *m*.

tulip, *n*, tulipe, *f*.

tulle, *n*, tulle, *m*.

tumble, *n*, chute, dégringolade, culbute, *f. take a* ~, ramasser une bûche. ~ **down**, tomber, dégringoler, culbuter, débouler. ~**down**, *a*, délabré. **tumbler**, *n*, (*pers.*) acrobate; (*pigeon*) culbutant; (*toy*) poussah; (*glass*) [verre] gobelet, *m*. **tumbrel, -il**, *n*, tombereau, *m*.

tumor, *n*, tumeur, glande, *f*.

tumult, *n*, tumulte, *m*. **tumultuous†**, *a*, tumultueux, houleux.

tumulus, *n*, tumulus, *m*.

tun, *n*, tonneau, foudre, *m*.

tuna, *n*, thon, *m*.

tune, *n*, air; accord, *m*; (*fig.*) cadence; (*fig.*) note, *f*, ton, *m*, gamme, *f*. ¶ *v.t*, accorder, mettre d'accord. **tuner**, *n*, accordeur, *m*. **tuneful†**, *a*, harmonieux, mélodieux.

tungsten, *n*, tungstène, *m*.

tunic, *n*, tunique, *f*.

tuning, *n*, accordage, *m*; (*motor*) mise au point, *f*. ~ **fork**, diapason à branches, *m*.

Tunis, *n*, Tunis, *m*. **Tunisia**, *n*, la Tunisie. **Tunisian**, *a*, tunisien.

tunnel, *n*, tunnel, souterrain, *m*. ¶ *v.t*, percer un tunnel sous.

turban, *n*, turban, *m*.

turbid, *a*, trouble.

turbine, *n*, turbine, *f*.

turbot, *n*, turbot, (*young*) turbotin, *m*.

turbulence, *n*, turbulence, *f*. **turbulent**, *a*, turbulent.

tureen, *n*, soupière, *f*.

turf, *n*, gazon, *m*; plaque de g., motte, *f. the* ~ (*racing*), le turf. ¶ *v.t*, gazonner.

turgid, *a*, turgescent, boursouflé.

Turk, *n*, Turc, *m*, Turque, *f*. **Turkey**, *n*, la Turquie. *t*~ [*cock*], dindon, coq d'Inde, *m*. *t*~[*hen*], dinde, poule d'Inde, *f*. **turkish**, *a*, turc. ~ *bath*, bain turc, *m*. ~ *carpet*, tapis de Turquie, *m*. ~ *towel*, serviette-éponge, *f*. ¶ (*language*) *n*, le turc.

turmeric, *n*, safran des Indes, *m*.

turmoil, *n*, ébullition, tourmente, *f*, tumulte, *m*.

turn, *n*, tour; retour; détour, *m*; tournure, *f*; revirement; (*tide*) changement, renversement, *m*. ~ *of the scale*, trait de balance, *m. at every* ~, à tout propos. *in* ~, tour à tour, à tour de rôle. *to a* ~, à point. ¶ *v.t. & i*, tourner; se t.; retourner; se r.; virer; pivoter; transformer; convertir; changer; (*discussion*) porter (*on* = sur). ~ *aside*, écarter; détourner; se d. ~ *back*, rebrousser chemin. ~ *off*, (*tap*) fermer; (*water*) couper; (*light*) éteindre. ~ *on*, (*tap*) ouvrir, lâcher; (*water*) faire couler, ouvrir le robinet de; (*light*) allumer. ~ *out & ~ over*, [re]tourner. ~ *out badly*, mal réussir. ~ *right over*, faire panache. ~ *round*, se retourner. ~ *the scale*, faire pencher la balance. ~ *up*, [re]tourner; [re]trousser; ~*ed-up moustache*, moustache en croc, *f.* take ~*s*, se relayer.

turncoat, *n*, transfuge, rénégat, *m.*

turncock, *n*, fontainier, *m.*

turned (*a certain age*) *p.p*, dépassé, franchi, (*tant d'ans*) sonnés.

turnip, *n*, navet, *m.* ~ *tops*, fanes de navets, *f.pl.*

turnkey, *n*, porte-clefs, guichetier, *m.*

turnout (*Rly.*) *n*, branchement, *m.*

turnover, *n*, revirement; (*Fin.*) chiffre d'affaires, roulement; (*Cook.*) chausson; (*stocking, etc.*) revers, *m.*

turnpike, *n*, autoroute, *f.* ~ *tollgate*, pont à péage, *m*, barrière à p., *f.*

turnstile, *n*, (X *on post*) moulinet; (*admission*) tourniquet [-compteur] *m.*

turntable, *n*, plaque tournante, *f*; (*phonograph*) plateau, *m.*

turpentine, *n*, térébenthine, *f.*

turpitude, *n*, turpitude, *f.*

turquoise, *n. & att*, turquoise, *f. & att.*

turret, *n*, tourelle, *f.* ~ *lathe*, tour à revolver, *m.* ~ *ship*, navire à tourelles, *m.*

turtle, *n*, tortue de mer, *f.* ~ *dove*, tourterelle, *f.* (*young*) tourterau, *m.* ~*neck*, col roulé, *m.*

Tuscan, *a*, toscan. ~*y*, *n*, la Toscane.

tusk, *n*, défense, *f*; croc, *m.*

tussle, *n*, lutte, *f.*

tutelage, *n*, tutelle, *f.* **tutelar[y]**, *a*, tutélaire. **tutor**, *n*, précepteur, répétiteur, préparateur, *m.* ¶ *v.t*, instruire. **tutorship**, *n*, préceptorat, *m.*

tuxedo, *n*, smoking, *m.*

twaddle, *n*, balivernes, *f.pl*, babil, *m.*

twang, *n*, nasillement; son aigre, *m.* ¶ *v.i*, nasiller; résonner. ~ [*on*] (stringed instrument), pincer de.

tweak, *v.t*, pincer, tirer.

tweed, *n*, tweed, *m.*

'tween-decks, *n*, entrepont, *m.*

tweezers, *n.pl*, brucelles, pincettes, pinces, *f.pl.*

twelfth†, *a. & n*, douzième, *a. & m,f*; douze, *m*. T~ *Night*, soir de l'Épiphanie, *m.* **twelve**, *a. & n*, douze, *a. & m.* ~ *o'clock* [*in the day*] midi; [*at night*] minuit, *m.*

twentieth, *a. & n*, vingtième, *a. & m,f*; vingt, *m.* **twenty**, *a. & n*, vingt, *a. & m.*

twice, *ad*, deux fois. ~ *as much*, deux fois autant.

twiddle, *v.t*, tourner, tortiller.

twig, *n*, brindille, *f*, (*pl.*) ramilles, broutilles, *f.pl.*

twilight, *n*, crépuscule, *m*, pénombre, *f*, demi-jour, *m.* ~ *sleep*, anesthésie à la reine, *f.*

twill, *n*, croisé, *m.* ¶ *v.t*, croiser.

twin, *a*, jumeau; conjugué. ¶ *n*, jumeau, elle; (*pl.*) deux jumeaux, deux jumelles; (*crystal*) macle, *f.* ~ *beds*, lits jumeaux, *m.pl.*

twine, *n*, ficelle, *f.* ¶ *v.t*, enlacer; cordonner.

twinge, *n*, élancement, *m.*

twining (*Bot.*) *p.a*, volubile.

twinkle, *v.i*, scintiller, clignoter. *in the twinkling of an eye*, en un clin d'œil. ¶ *n*, scintillement, clignement, *m.*

twirl, *v.t*, faire tournoyer; (*stick*) faire le moulinet avec; (*moustache*) tortiller; (*v.i.*) pirouetter.

twist, *n*, torsade, *f*, tortillon, *m*; torsion, *f*; cordon, *m*; contorsion, *f*; (*of straw*) torchon, *m*; (*tobacco*) carotte, *f*, rouleau, *m.* ~*s & turns*, tours & retours, *m.pl.* ¶ *v.t*, tordre; [en]tortiller; cordonner. ~**ed**, *p.p. & p.a*, tordu; [re]tors.

twit, *v.t*, reprocher.

twitch, *v.i*, avoir un tic, tiquer; palpiter; (*v.t.*) arracher, crisper. ~**ing**, *p.a*, pantelant. ~**ing**, *n*, tic, *m.*

twitter, *v.i*, gazouiller.

two, *a. & n*, deux, *a. & m.* ~ *days before*, l'avant-veille, *f.* ~~*footed*, ~~*legged*, bipède. ~~*piece set*, ensemble deux pièces, *m.* ~~*way switch*, commutateur va-et-vient, *m.* ~*fold*, *a*, double.

tympan & tympanum, *n*, tympan, *m.*

type, *n*, type; genre; (*Typ.*) caractère [d'imprimerie], type, *m.* ~ *founder*, fondeur en caractères, *m.* ~ *metal*, matière, *f.* ~ *setting*, composition, *f.* ~[**write**], *v.t*, écrire à la machine, taper [à la m.]. ~*writer*, machine à écrire, *f.* ~*writing*, écriture à la machine, dactylographie, *f.* ~*written*, [écrit] à la machine.

typhoid [**fever**], *n*, fièvre typhoïde, *f.*

typhoon, *n*, typhon, *m.*

typhus, *n*, typhus, *m.*

typical, *a*, typique.

typist, *n*, dactylographe, *m,f.*

typographic(al), *a*, typographique. **typography**, *n*, typographie, *f.*

tyrannic(al†), *a*, tyrannique. **tyrannize [over]**, tyranniser. **tyranny**, *n*, tyrannie, *f.* **tyrant**, *n*, tyran, *m.*

tyro, *n*, novice, *m,f.*

Tyrol (the), le Tyrol. **Tyrolese**, *a*, tyrolien. ¶ *n*, Tyrolien, ne.

U

ubiquity, *n*, ubiquité, *f.*

udder, *n*, mamelle, *f*, pis, *m.*

ugh, *i*, pouah! fi!

ugliness, *n*, laideur, *f.* **ugly**, *a*, laid; vilain. [*as*] ~ *as sin*, laid comme un crapaud.

ulcer, *n*, ulcère, *m.* ~**ate**, *v.i*, s'ulcérer.

ulterior†, *a*, ultérieur. ~ *motive*, arrière-pensée, *f.*

ultimate†, *a*, final; définitif. **ultimatum**, *n*, ultimatum, *m.*

ultramarine, *n*, outremer, *m.*

ultraviolet, *a*, ultra-violet.

umber, *n*, terre d'ombre, *f.*

umbrage, *n*, ombrage, *m.*

umbrella, *n*, parapluie; (*garden, beach, held over potentate*) parasol, *m.* ~ *ring*, rondelle de parapluie, *f.* ~ *stand*, porte-parapluies, *m.* ~*-sunshade*, en-[tout-] cas, *m.*

umpire, *n*, arbitre, *m.* ¶ *v.t*, arbitrer.

unabated, *a*, sans diminution.

unable, *a*, incapable. *to be* ~ *to*, ne pouvoir [pas].

unabridged, *a*, complet.

unacceptable, *a*, inacceptable.

unaccompanied, *a*, non accompagné.

unaccountable, *a*, inexplicable.

unaccustomed, *a*, peu habitué; inaccoutumé.

unacknowledged, *a*, non reconnu; sans réponse.

unacquainted with (to be), être ignorant de; ne pas connaître.

unadorned, *a*, sans ornements.

unadulterated, *a*, non falsifié; sans mélange.

unaffected, *a*, naturel, naïf; inaltérable (*by* = à).

unafraid, *a*, sans peur.

unalloyed, *a*, sans alliage.

unalterable, *a*, inaltérable.

unambiguous, *a*, non équivoque, précis.

unambitious, *a*, sans ambition; sans prétentions.

unanimous, *a*, unanime. ~**ly**, *ad*, à l'unanimité, unanimement.

unanswerable, *a*, sans réplique.

unappreciated, *a*, inapprécié, incompris.

unapproachable, *a*, inabordable.

unarmed, *a*, sans armes, désarmé.

unasked, *a*, sans être invité.

unassailable, *a*, inattaquable, hors d'atteinte.

unassuming, *a*, sans prétentions.

unattached (Mil.**)** *a*, en disponibilité.

unattainable, *a*, impossible à atteindre.

unattended, *a*, sans suite; sans garde.

unattractive, *a*, peu attrayant; peu séduisant.

unavailable, *a*, indisponible. **unavailing**, *a*, inutile, vain.

unavoidable†, *a*, inévitable.

unaware of (to be), ignorer. **unawares**, *ad*, à l'improviste, au dépourvu; par mégarde.

unbalanced, *a*, déséquilibré; (*Mech.*) non compensé.

unballast, *v.t*, délester.

unbandage, *v.t*, débander.

unbearable†, *a*, insupportable.

unbecoming, *a*, inconvenant, malséant; qui ne va pas. *to be* ~, messeoir.

unbelief, *n*, incrédulité, *f.* **unbeliever**, *n*, incrédule, *m,f.*

unbend, *v.t.ir*, détendre; débander. ~**ing**, *a*, inflexible.

unbiased, *a*, sans prévention; impartial.

unbind, *v.t.ir*, délier, détacher.

unbleached, *a*, écru.

unblemished, *a*, sans tache, intact.

unblock, v.t, (passage, finances, etc.) débloquer.

unblushing, a, éhonté.

unbolt, v.t, déverrouiller.

unborn, a, à naître.

unbosom oneself, s'ouvrir.

unbound (book) a, non relié.

unbounded, a, sans bornes, illimité.

unbreakable, a, incassable.

unbridled, a, débridé; effréné.

unbroken, a, intact; ininterrompu; (horse) non dressé.

unbuckle, v.t, déboucler.

unbuilt on, non bâti, non construit.

unburden oneself, s'ouvrir.

unburied, a, sans sépulture.

unbusinesslike, a, incorrect.

unbutton, v.t, déboutonner.

uncalled for remark, observation déplacée, f.

uncanny, a, fantastique.

uncap, v.t, décalotter.

uncapsizable, a, inversable.

uncared for, à l'abandon.

unceasing, a, incessant. ~ly, ad, incessamment, sans cesse.

unceremoniously, ad, sans cérémonie.

uncertain, a, incertain. ~ty, n, incertitude, f.

unchain, v.t, déchaîner.

unchangeable†, a, immuable, invariable.

uncharitable, a, peu charitable; critique.

unchaste†, a, impudique, incontinent.

unchecked, a, sans frein.

uncircumcised, a, incirconcis.

uncivil†, a, incivil. ~ized, a, sauvage.

unclad, a, nu.

unclaimed, a, non réclamé; en souffrance.

unclassified, a, non classé.

uncle, n, oncle, (children's slang) tonton, m.

unclean, a, sale; impur, immonde.

unclothed, a, nu.

unclouded, a, sans nuages.

uncock (gun) v.t, désarmer.

uncoil, v.t, dérouler.

uncomely, a, peu avenant.

uncomfortable, a, incommode; (of pers.) mal à son aise.

uncommon†, a, rare; singulier.

uncommunicative, a, taciturne.

uncomplaining, a, résigné. the

~ **poor,** les pauvres honteux, m. pl.

uncompleted, a, inachevé.

uncompromising, a, intransigeant.

unconcerned, a, indifférent, insouciant.

unconditional, a. & ~ly, ad, sans condition.

unconfirmed, a, non confirmé.

unconnected (desultory) a, décousu.

unconquerable†, a, invincible.

unconscious†, a, inconscient; (dead faint) sans connaissance. ~ness, n, inconscience, f; une perte de connaissance.

unconsecrated ground, terre profane, f.

unconstitutional†, a, inconstitutionnel.

unconstrained, a, dégagé. **unconstraint,** n, désinvolture, f, abandon, laisser-aller, m.

uncontested, a, incontesté.

uncontrollable, a, ingouvernable; indomptable; inextinguible.

unconventional, a, sans gêne, original; affranchi, libre.

unconvincing, a, peu vraisemblable.

uncork, v.t, déboucher.

uncorrected, a, non corrigé.

uncouple, v.t, découpler.

uncouth, a, grossier, rude, rustaud.

uncover, v.t, découvrir; (v.i.) se découvrir.

uncreated, a, incréé.

unction, n, onction, f. **unctuous†,** a, onctueux.

uncultivated & **uncultured,** a, inculte.

uncurbed, a, indompté.

uncurl, v.t, défriser; dérouler.

uncustomary, a, inusité.

uncut, a, (gem) brut; (cake) non entamé. ~ **edges** (book), tranches non rognées, f.pl.

undamaged, a, non endommagé; non avarié.

undated, a, sans date, non daté.

undaunted, a, intrépide.

undeceive, v.t, détromper, désillusionner.

undecided, a, indécis; incertain.

undecipherable, a, indéchiffrable.

undefended, a, sans défense; sans défenseur; (law case) non contestée; (*heard ex parte*) jugée par défaut.

undefiled, *a*, sans souillure.

undefined, *a*, indéfini.

undeliverable, *a*, en souffrance.

undelivered, *a*, non livré; non distribué.

undeniable, *a*, indéniable, incontestable.

undenominational, *a*, laïque, neutre.

under, *pr*, sous; dessous; au-dessous de; en; à; sauf. ~ *there*, là-dessous. ~ *water*, entre deux eaux. ¶ *ad*, dessous; au-dessous.

underassessment, *n*, insuffisance d'imposition, *f*.

underclothing, *n*, (*women's*) [vêtements de] dessous; (*men's*) sous-vêtements, *m.pl*.

undercurrent, *n*, courant de fond; courant sous-marin; (*in air*) courant inférieur; (*fig*.) courant secret, fond, *m*.

undercut (*meat*) *n*, filet, *m*.

underdeveloped, *a*, sous-développé. **underdevelopment**, *n*, sous-développement, *f*.

underdone, *a*, pas [assez] cuit; peu cuit, saignant.

underestimate, *v.t*, sous-estimer, mésestimer.

underexposure (*Phot*.) *n*, manque de pose, *m*.

underfed, *a*, sous-alimenté.

undergarment, *n*, (*men's*) sous-vêtement; (*women's*) vêtement de dessous, *m*.

undergo, *v.t.ir*, subir, souffrir.

underground, *a*, souterrain. ¶ *n*, (*war*) Résistance, *f*. ¶ *ad*, en souterrain.

undergrowth, *n*, broussailles, *f.pl*.

underhand, *a*, clandestin, souterrain, sournois, sourd; (*Ten. service*) par en bas. ¶ *ad*, sous main, clandestinement.

underline, *v.t*, souligner.

underling, *n*, employé subalterne, *m*.

underlying, *a*, sous-jacent.

undermentioned, *a*, ci-dessous.

undermine, *v.t*, miner, affouiller, caver.

undermost, *a*, le plus bas.

underneath, *ad*, dessous; au-dessous. ¶ *pr*, sous.

underpay, *v.t.ir*, payer trop peu.

underpin, *v.t*, reprendre en sous-œuvre.

underrate, *v.t*, mésestimer, déprécier.

underscore, *v.t*, souligner.

undersea, *a*, sous-marin.

undersecretary, *n*, sous-secrétaire, *m*.

undersell, *v.t.ir*, vendre moins cher que.

undershirt, *n*, maillot, *m*; chemisette, *f*.

underside, *n*, dessous, *m*.

undersigned, *a*. & *n*, soussigné, e.

understand, *v.t*. & *i*. *ir*, comprendre, voir; entendre; s'e. à; apprendre; sous-entendre. ~*ing*, *n*, intelligence, *f*; entendement, sens, *m*; compréhension; entente, *f*.

understudy, *n*, doublure, *f*. ¶ *v.t*, doubler.

undertake, *v.t.ir*, entreprendre; se charger de; s'engager, se faire fort. **undertaker**, *n*, entrepreneur de pompes funèbres, *m*. **undertaking**, *n*, engagement, *m*; entreprise, *f*; pompes funèbres, *f.pl*.

undertone (**in an**), à demi-voix.

undertow, *n*, ressac, *m*.

undervalue, *v.t*, mésestimer, déprécier.

underwear, *n*. See *underclothing*.

underwood, *n*, [bois] taillis, mort-bois, *m*, broussailles, *f.pl*.

underworld, *n*, pègre, *f*; enfers; bas-fonds de la société, *m.pl*; milieu, *m*.

underwrite, *v.t.ir*, (*Insce*.) souscrire, s. pour; (*Fin*.) garantir. **underwriter**, *n*, souscripteur, assureur; (*Fin*.) syndicataire, *m*. **underwriting**, *n*, souscription; garantie, *f*.

undeserved, *a*, immérité. **undeserving**, *a*, peu méritant; indigne (*of* = de).

undesirable, *a*. & *n*, indésirable, *a*. & *m,f*.

undetermined, *a*, indéterminé.

undeveloped, *a*, en friche.

undigested, *a*, non digéré; (*fig*.) indigeste.

undignified, *a*, sans dignité.

undisciplined, *a*, indiscipliné.

undiscoverable, *a*, introuvable.

undiscovered, *a*, non découvert.

undiscriminating, *a*, sans discernement.

undismayed, *a*, sans être découragé.

undisputed, *a*, incontesté.

undisturbed, *a*, tranquille.

undo, *v.t.ir*, défaire, détacher; (*knitting*) démailler. ~**ing**, *n*, ruine, *f*. **come undone**, se défaire.

undoubted†, *a*, indubitable.

undress, *n*, déshabillé, négligé, *m*; (*Mil., Nav.*) petite tenue, *f*. ¶ *v.t*, déshabiller; (*v.i.*) se déshabiller.

undrinkable, *a*, imbuvable.

undue, *a*, exagéré, excessif; inexigible.

undulate, *v.i*, onduler, ondoyer. **undulating**, *a*, ondulé. **undulation**, *n*, ondulation, *f*.

unduly, *ad*, indûment; par trop.

undutiful, *a*, qui manque à ses devoirs.

undying, *a*, impérissable, immortel.

unearned, *a*, non acquis; immérité. ~ *increment*, plus-value, *f*.

unearth, *v.t*, déterrer. ~**ly**, *a*, spectral, fantomatique.

uneasiness, *n*, malaise, *m*, inquiétude, *f*, martel en tête, *m*. **uneasy**†, *a*, inquiet.

uneatable, *a*, immangeable.

uneducated, *a*, sans instruction.

unemployable (the), les incapables, *m.pl*. **unemployed**, *a*, inemployé; (*pers.*) sans travail, en chômage. *the* ~, les sans-travail, les chômeurs, *m.pl*. **unemployment**, *n*, manque de travail; chômage [involontaire] *m*. ~ *benefit*, indemnité de chômage, *f*. ~ *insurance*, assurance contre le chômage, *f*.

unending, *a*, sans fin.

unenterprising, *a*, sans initiative.

unenviable, *a*, peu enviable.

unequal†, *a*, inégal. ~ *to* (task), pas à la hauteur de, incapable de. **unequaled**, *a*, sans égal, sans pareil.

unequivocal, *a*, non équivoque.

unerring†, *a*, infaillible; sûr.

uneven†, *a*, inégal; (*number*) impair. ~**ness**, *n*, inégalité; (*number*) imparité, *f*.

unexceptionable, *a*, irrécusable.

unexpected, *a*, inattendu; inespéré.

unexpired, *a*, non expiré; non couru; non échu; non périmé.

unexplained, *a*, inexpliqué.

unexplored, *a*, inexploré.

unexpurgated, *a*, intégral.

unfailing, *a*, infaillible; (*spring*) intarissable.

unfair†, *a*, injuste; déloyal; partial. ~**ness**, *n*, injustice; déloyauté; partialité, *f*.

unfaithful†, *a*, infidèle. ~**ness**, *n*, infidélité, *f*.

unfamiliar, *a*, étranger.

unfasten, *v.t*, dégrafer, défaire.

unfathomable, *a*, insondable, abyssal.

unfavorable†, *a*, défavorable, contraire. ~ *light*, contre-jour, *m*.

unfeasible, *a*, irréalisable, impraticable, infaisable.

unfeeling, *a*, insensible.

unfeigned†, *a*, sincère.

unfenced, *a*, sans clôture.

unfettered, *a*, sans entraves.

unfinished, *a*, inachevé, imparfait.

unfit, *a*, impropre; hors d'état; inapte; incapable. *the* ~, les inaptes, *m.pl*. ~**ness**, *n*, inaptitude; incapacité, *f*. **unfitting**, *a*, inconvenant.

unflagging, *a*, soutenu.

unfledged, *a*, sans plumes.

unflinching, *a*, à toute épreuve.

unfold, *v.t*, déployer; dérouler.

unforeseen, *a*, imprévu.

unforgettable, *a*, inoubliable.

unforgivable, *a*, impardonnable. **unforgiving**, *a*, implacable.

unfortified, *a*, non fortifié; (*town*) ouverte.

unfortunate†, *a*, malheureux, infortuné; regrettable. *the* ~, les malheureux, les infortunés, *m.pl*.

unfounded, *a*, sans fondement.

unfrequented, *a*, infréquenté.

unfriendly, *a*, inamical; hostile.

unfrock, *v.t*, défroquer.

unfruitful, *a*, stérile. ~**ness**, *n*, stérilité, *f*.

unfulfilled, *a*, non accompli.

unfurl, *v.t*, déferler, déployer.

unfurnished, *a*, non meublé.

ungainly, *a*, dégingandé.

ungathered, *a*, non cueilli.

ungenerous, *a*, peu généreux.
ungodliness, *n*, impiété, *f*. **un-godly**, *a*, impie.
ungovernable, *a*, ingouvernable; indomptable.
ungraceful, *a*, disgracieux.
ungracious, *a*, malgracieux, dis-gracieux.
ungrafted, *a*, franc.
ungrammatical, *a*, contre la grammaire. **~ly**, *ad*, incorrecte-ment.
ungrateful, *a*, ingrat. **~ness**, *n*, ingratitude, *f*.
ungrudgingly, *ad*, de bon cœur.
unguarded, *a*, sans défense; in-discret.
unhair (*skins*) *v.t*, dépiler, dé-bourrer.
unhallowed, *a*, profane.
unhappiness, *n*, malheur, *m*. **unhappy**†, *a*, malheureux.
unharmed, *a*, indemne.
unharness, *v.t*, déharnacher.
unhatched, *a*, non éclos.
unhealthiness, *n*, insalubrité, *f*. **unhealthy**, *a*, insalubre; malsain.
unheard of, inouï.
unheeded, *a*, négligé.
unhesitatingly, *ad*, sans hésita-tion.
unhewn, *a*, non taillé.
unhindered, *a*, sans empêche-ment.
unhinge, *v.t*, démonter; troubler, aliéner.
unholiness, *n*, impiété, *f*. **un-holy**, *a*, impie.
unhonored, *p.a*, méconnu.
unhook, *v.t*, décrocher.
unhoped for, inespéré.
unhorse, *v.t*, démonter, désar-çonner.
unhurt, *a*, indemne, sauf.
unicorn, *n*, licorne, *f*.
uniform, *a*, uniforme; uni. ¶ *n*, uniforme, *m*, tenue, *f*. **~ity**, *n*, uniformité, *f*. **~ly**, *ad*, uniformé-ment. **unify**, *v.t*, unifier.
unilateral, *a*, unilatéral.
unimaginable, *a*, inimaginable.
unimpeachable, *a*, irrécusable.
unimpeded, *a*, sans entraves.
unimportant, *a*, insignifiant.
uninflammable, *a*, ininflam-mable.
uninhabitable, *a*, inhabitable.
uninhabited, *a*, inhabité.
uninhibited, *a*, (*psychology*) défoulé.

uninitiated person, profane, *m.f*.
uninjured, *a*, indemne.
uninstructed, *a*, ignorant.
uninsured, *a*, non assuré; (*mail*) sans valeur déclarée, non chargé.
unintelligent, *a*, inintelligent. **unintelligible**, *a*, inintelligible.
unintentional†, *a*, involontaire.
uninterested, *a*, indifférent. **un-interesting**, *a*, sans intérêt.
uninterrupted, *a*, interrompu. **~ly**, *ad*, sans interruption.
uninvited, *a*, sans invitation. **un-inviting**, *a*, peu attrayant; peu appétissant.
union, *n*, (*labor*) syndicat, *m*; union; alliance, *f*; (*Mech.*) raccord; (*pipe*) mi-fil, *m*. **U~** *of South Africa*, Union Sud-Africaine. **U~** *of Soviet So-cialist Republics*, Union des Ré-publiques soviétiques socialistes.
unique, *a*, unique.
unison, *n*, unisson, *m*.
unissued (*stocks, shares*) *a*, à la souche.
unit, *n*, unité, *f*; élément, *m*. **~ bookcase**, bibliothèque trans-formable, *f*. **~ price**, prix uni-taire, *m*. **unite**, *v.t*, unir; joindre; réunir; allier; marier. **united**, *a*, uni; joint; réuni. **U~** *Kingdom* [*of Great Britain and Northern Ireland*], Royaume-Uni [de Grande-Bretagne et Irlande du Nord] *m*. **U~** *States* [*of Amer-ica*], États-Unis [d'Amérique] *m.pl*. **unity**, *n*, unité; union, *f*; ensemble, *m*.
universal†, *a*, universel. **~ity**, *n*, universalité, *f*. **universe**, *n*, uni-vers, *m*. **university**, *n*, université, *f*; (*att.*) universitaire.
unjust†, *a*, injuste. **~** *judge*, [juge] prévaricateur, *m*. **unjustifiable**, *a*, injustifiable.
unkempt, *a*, mal peigné, inculte.
unkind, *a*, désobligeant; méchant. **~ness**, *n*, désobligeance; mé-chanceté, *f*.
unknown, *a*, inconnu; ignoré. **~** *person*, inconnu, e. **~** [*quantity*], [quantité] inconnue, *f*. **~** *to*, à l'insu de. *the* **~**, l'inconnu, *m*. *the U~ Soldier*, le Soldat in-connu.
unlace, *v.t*, délacer.
unlawful†, *a*, illégal, illicite. **~** *assembly*, attroupement, *m*. **~-ness**, *n*, illégalité, *f*.

unlearn, *v.t*, désapprendre. **~ed**, *a*, illettré.

unleavened, *a*, sans levain; (*Bible*) azyme.

unless, *c*, à moins que . . . [ne]; à moins de; si . . . ne . . . pas; sauf.

unlettered, *a*, illettré.

unlicensed, *a*, marron.

unlicked cub, ours mal léché, *m*.

unlike, *a*, dissemblable. ¶ *pr*, dissemblable à. **unlikelihood**, *n*, invraisemblance; improbabilité, *f*. **unlikely**, *a*, invraisemblable; improbable.

unlimber, *v.i*, décrocher l'avant-train.

unlimited, *a*, illimité.

unlined, *a*, non doublé.

unload, *v.t*, décharger; (*Fin.*) se défaire de.

unlock, *v.t*, ouvrir; (*Typ.*) desserrer.

unlooked for, *a*, inattendu.

unloose, *v.t*, lâcher.

unlovely, *a*, disgracieux.

unlucky†, *a*, malheureux, malchanceux, malencontreux.

unmake, *v.t.ir*, défaire.

unman, *v.t*, ôter tout courage de.

unmanageable, *a*, intraitable; impossible à conduire.

unmanly, *a*, lâche; efféminé.

unmannerly, *a*, grossier.

unmanufactured, *a*, brut.

unmarketable, *a*, invendable.

unmarried, *a*, non marié; célibataire. **unmarry**, *v.t*, démarier.

unmask, *v.t*, démasquer.

unmentionable, *a*, dont on ne parle pas.

unmerciful†, *a*, impitoyable.

unmerited, *a*, immérité.

unmethodical, *a*, non méthodique, incorrect.

unmindful, *a*, inattentif, oublieux.

unmingled, *a*, sans mélange, pur.

unmistakable†, *a*, évident, manifeste; immanquable.

unmitigated, *a*, fieffé, insigne; non adouci.

unmixed, *a*, sans mélange, pur.

unmolested, *a*, en paix.

unmoor, *v.t*, démarrer.

unmounted, *a*, non monté; (*gem*) hors d'œuvre; (*pers.*) à pied.

unmoved, *a*, immobile; impassible.

unmusical, *a*, inharmonieux.

unmuzzle, *v.t*, démuseler.

unnamable, *a*, innommable. **unnamed**, *a*, innomé; anonyme.

unnatural, *a*, dénaturé; contre nature.

unnavigable, *a*, non navigable, impropre à la navigation.

unnecessary†, *a*, inutile.

unneighborly way (in an), en mauvais voisin.

unnerve, *v.t*, ôter tout courage de.

unnoticed, unobserved, *a*, inaperçu. **unobservant**, *a*, inattentif.

unobstructed, *a*, non obstrué; (*view*) dégagée.

unobtainable, *a*, impossible à se procurer.

unobtrusive, *a*, effacé; discret. **~ly**, *ad*, discrètement.

unoccupied, *a*, inoccupé; libre, disponible.

unoffending, *a*, inoffensif.

unofficial, *a*, non officiel; (*information*) officieux.

unopened, *a*, non ouvert.

unopposed, *a*, sans opposition.

unorganized, *a*, non organisé.

unorthodox, *a*, hétérodoxe.

unostentatious, *a*. & **~ly**, *ad*, sans ostentation.

unpack, *v.t*, dépaqueter, déballer, décaisser. **~ed**, *a*, à découvert.

unpaid, *a*, (*bill*) impayé; (*capital*) non verse; (*letters*) non affranchi; (*no salary*) gratuit.

unpalatable, *a*, désagréable au goût.

unparalleled, *a*, sans pareil.

unpardonable, *a*, impardonnable.

unparliamentary, *a*, peu parlementaire.

unpatriotic, *a*, antipatriotique.

unperceived, *a*, inaperçu.

unphilosophical, *a*, peu philosophique.

unpin, *v.t*, enlever les épingles de.

unpleasant†, *a*, désagréable, méchant. **~ness**, *n*, désagrément, *m*.

unpleasing, *a*, déplaisant, ingrat.

unpoetic(al), *a*, peu poétique.

unpolished, *a*, non poli; mat; brut; rude.

unpolluted, *a*, non souillé.

unpopular, *a*, impopulaire. **~ity**, *n*, impopularité, *f*.

unpractical, *a*, peu pratique.

unpractised, *a*, inexercé; novice.

unprecedented, *a*, sans précédent(s).

unprejudiced, a, sans préjugés, impartial.

unpremeditated, a, sans préméditation.

unprepared, a, sans être préparé, au dépourvu.

unprepossessing, a, peu engageant.

unpretentious, a, sans prétentions; modeste, discret.

unprincipled, a, sans principes.

unprintable, a, impubliable.

unprocurable, a, impossible à se procurer.

unproductive, a, improductif.

unprofessional, a, contraire aux usages de sa profession.

unprofitable, a, peu lucratif; inutile; ingrat. unprofitably, ad, sans profit; inutilement.

unpromising, a, qui ne promet guère; ingrat.

unpronounceable, a, non prononçable. ~ name, nom à coucher dehors, m.

unpropitious, a, peu propice.

unprotected, a, découvert, à découvert.

unprovided, a, dépourvu (with = de).

unprovoked, a, sans provocation, gratuit.

unpublished (book) a, inédit.

unpunctual†, a, inexact. ~ity, n, inexactitude, f.

unpunished, a, impuni.

unqualified, a, sans les qualités requises; marron; formel; sans réserve.

unquenchable, a, inextinguible.

unquestionable†, a, indiscutable.

unravel, v.t, démêler, débrouiller, parfiler; dénouer.

unread, a, illettré; sans être lu. ~able (writing, insupportable book) a, illisible.

unreal, a, irréel. ~ity, n, irréalité, f.

unrealizable, a, irréalisable.

unreasonable†, a, déraisonnable, intraitable. ~ness, n, déraison, f. unreasoning, a, irraisonnable.

unrecognizable, a, méconnaissable.

unredeemable, a, irrachetable.

unredeemed, a, (stock) non amorti; (pledge) non dégagé.

unrefined, a, non épuré; brut; grossier.

unrefuted, a, irréfuté.

unregistered, a, non enregistré; (mail) non recommandé; (trademark) non déposée.

unrelenting†, a, inexorable, implacable, acharné.

unreliable, a, peu sûr; inexact; sujet à caution.

unremitting†, a, incessant, soutenu.

unremunerative, a, peu lucratif.

unrepealed, a, non abrogé.

unrepentant, a, impénitent.

unreservedly, ad, sans réserve.

unresponsive, a, froid, difficile à émouvoir.

unrest, a, agitation, effervescence, f.

unrestrained, a, immodéré; effréné.

unrestricted, a, sans restriction.

unretentive (memory) a, fugace.

unrewarded, a, sans récompense.

unrighteous†, a, injuste. ~ness, n, injustice, f.

unripe, a, verte; en herbe. ~ness, n, verdeur, f.

unrivaled, a, sans rival.

unrivet, v.t, dériver.

unroll, v.t, dérouler.

unruffled, a, imperturbable; calme, tranquille.

unruly, a, indiscipliné; turbulent.

unsaddle, v.t, desseller; (pack animal) débâter.

unsafe, a, peu sûr, mal assuré.

unsalable, a, invendable.

unsalaried, a, sans rétribution.

unsalted, a, non salé.

unsanitary, a, malsain, insalubre.

unsatisfactorily, ad, d'une manière peu satisfaisante. unsatisfactory, a, peu satisfaisant; défectueux.

unsavory, a, peu savoureux.

unsay, v.t.ir, se dédire de. to leave unsaid, taire.

unscathed, a, indemne, sauf.

unscientific, a, peu scientifique.

unscrew, v.t, dévisser. to come ~ed, se d.

unscrupulous, a, peu scrupuleux, indélicat. ~ly, ad, sans scrupule.

unseal, v.t, desceller; (letter) décacheter.

unseasonable, a, hors de saison; hors de propos, inopportun. unseasonably, ad, mal à propos,

inopportunément. **unseasoned**
(*wood*) *a*, vert.

unseat, *v.t*, invalider; (*rider*)
désarçonner.

unseaworthy, *a*, en mauvais état
de navigabilité.

unseemly, *a*, malséant, inconvenant, folichon.

unseen, *a*, inaperçu, invisible; occulte.

unselfish, *a*, désintéressé. ~ness,
n, désintéressement, *m*.

unserviceable, *a*, inutilisable.

unsettle, *v.t*, déranger; (*pers.*)
bouleverser. ~d, *a*, (*weather*)
incertain; variable; (*question*)
indécise.

unshakable†, *a*, inébranlable.

unshapely, *a*, difforme.

unshaven, *a*, non rasé.

unsheathe, *v.t*, dégainer.

unsheltered, *a*, sans abri; non
protégé.

unship, *v.t*, débarquer; (*oars*)
déborder.

unshoe (*horse*) *v.t.ir*, déferrer.

unshrinkable, *a*, irrétrécissable.

unsightliness, *n*, laideur, *f*.
unsightly, *a*, laid.

unsigned, *a*, non signé.

unsinkable, *a*, insubmersible.

unskillful, *a*, malhabile, maladroit. ~ness, *n*, maladresse, *f*.
unskilled, *a*, inexpérimenté.

unslaked lime, chaux vive, *f*.

unsociable, *a*, insociable.

unsocial, *a*, antisocial.

unsold, *a*, invendu.

unsolicited, *a*, non sollicité,
spontané.

unsolved, *a*, non résolu.

unsophisticated, *a*, non frelaté;
naïf, ingénu.

unsought, *a*, sans qu'on le
cherche.

unsound, *a*, vicieux; défectueux.
of ~ mind, ne . . . pas sain
d'esprit.

unsparing, *a*, prodigue; impitoyable.

unspeakable, *a*, indicible; ineffable.

unspent, *a*, non dépensé; non
épuisé.

unspotted, *a*, sans tache.

unstable, *a*, instable; mouvant.

unstained, *a*, non teint; sans
tache.

unstamped, *a*, non timbré;
(*paper with no revenue stamps*

on) libre; (*letter*) non affranchie.

unsteadiness, *n*, instabilité; vacillation, *f*. **unsteady**, *a*, instable,
chancelant; vacillant.

unstinting, *a*, prodigue.

unstitch, *v.t*, découdre.

unstop, *v.t*, débourrer.

unstressed (*Gram.*) *a*, atone.

unstudied, *a*, naturel.

unsubdued, *a*, insoumis, indompté.

unsubstantial, *a*, sans substance; immatériel.

unsuccessful, *a*, sans succès,
manqué; infructueux. ~ly, *ad*,
sans succès.

unsuitable†, *a*, impropre. **unsuited**, *a*, mal adapté; peu fait.

unsullied, *a*, sans tache.

unsupported, *a*, en porte à faux;
sans appui.

unsurpassed, *a*, non surpassé.

unsuspected, *a*, non soupçonné.
unsuspecting & **unsuspicious**, *a*,
peu soupçonneux; exempt de
soupçon. **unsuspectingly**, *ad*, sans
défiance.

unsweetened, *a*, non sucré;
(*wine*) brut.

unswerving, *a*, inébranlable.

unsymmetrical, *a*, dissymétrique.

untack (*Need.*) *v.t*, débâtir.

untainted, *a*, non corrompu, non
gâté; sans tache.

untamable, *a*, indomptable. **untamed**, *a*, indompté.

untarnished, *a*, non terni.

untaught, *a*, ignorant; inculte.

untenable, *a*, (*position*, *etc.*) intenable; (*assertion*, *etc.*) insoutenable.

untenanted, *a*, inhabité.

unthinkable, *a*, inimaginable.
unthinking, *a*, irréflechi.

unthread, *v.t*, désenfiler.

untidiness, *n*, désordre, *m*. **untidy**†, *a*, malpropre, désordonné;
mal tenu.

untie, *v.t*, délier, détacher; dénouer.

until, *pr*, jusqu'à; jusque; avant
à. ¶ *c*, jusqu'à ce que; en attendant que. *not ~*, ne . . . pas
avant de, ne . . . pas avant que.

untimely, *a*, intempestif, prématuré; (*hour*) indue.

untiring†, *a*, infatigable, inlassable.

untold, *a*, indicible; inimaginable; innombrable.

untouchable, *n*, paria, *m*. untouched, *a*, intact; sans y toucher; non ému.

untoward, *a*, malencontreux, fâcheux.

untrained, *a*, inexpérimenté; (*animal*) non dressé.

untranslatable, *a*, intraduisible.

untraveled, *a*, (*country*) non parcouru; (*pers.*) qui n'a jamais voyagé.

untried, *a*, non essayé, non éprouvé.

untrimmed, *a*, sans garniture; non rogné.

untrodden, *a*, non frayé, non battu.

untroubled, *a*, calme, paisible, tranquille.

untrue, *a*, faux; mensonger; infidèle. untruly, *ad*, faussement.

untrustworthy, *a*, indigne de confiance.

untruth, *n*, contrevérité; fausseté, *f*, mensonge, *m*. ~ful, *a*, peu véridique, menteur.

untutored, *a*, inculte.

untwist, *v.t*, détordre, détortiller.

unused, *a*, non employé; non utilisé; peu habitué. unusual, *a*, peu commun, inaccoutumé, insolite, rare. ~ly, *ad*, extraordinairement.

unutterable, *a*, indicible, ineffable.

unvarnished, *a*, non verni; pur & simple.

unvarying, *a*, uniforme, invariable.

unveil, *v.t*, dévoiler; inaugurer.

unventilated, *a*, non aéré; mal aéré.

unversed in, peu versé dans.

unwarily, *ad*, sans précaution.

unwarlike, *a*, peu belliqueux.

unwarrantable, *a*, inexcusable, njustifiable.

unwary, *a*, peu circonspect.

unwashed, *a*, non lavé; crasseux.

unwavering, *a*, inébranlable.

unweaned, *a*, non sevré.

unwearied, *a*, infatigable.

unwelcome, *a*, importun; de trop; désagréable.

unwell, *a*, indisposé, souffrant.

unwholesome, *a*, malsain; morbide.

unwieldy, *a*, lourd, pesant; incommode.

unwilling, *a*, peu disposé, mal disposé. ~ly, *ad*, à contre-cœur. ~ness, *n*, mauvaise volonté; répugnance, *f*.

unwind, *v.t.ir*, dévider, dérouler.

unwisdom, *n*, manque de sagesse, *m*. unwise, *a*, peu sage, malavisé. ~ly, *ad*, follement.

unwittingly, *ad*, sans y penser.

unwonted, *a*, inaccoutumé, insolite.

unworkable, *a*, inexécutable, impraticable. unworked, *a*, inexploité. in an unworkmanlike manner, en mauvais ouvrier.

unworn, *a*, non usé.

unworthiness, *n*, indignité, *f*. unworthy, *a*, indigne.

unwounded, *a*, non blessé.

unwrap, *v.t*, développer; découvrir.

unwrinkled, *a*, sans rides.

unwritten, *a*, non écrit. ~ law, droit coutumier, *m*.

unwrought, *a*, non travaillé, non ouvré.

unyielding, *a*, inflexible, inébranlable.

unyoke, *v.t*, dételer.

up, *a*, montant. ~grade, montée, côte, *f*. ¶ *ad*, en haut; au haut; haut; en amont; debout, sur pied; (*prices*) en hausse; (*risen*) levé, *a*. ~ & down, en haut & en bas; de long en large. ~stairs, en haut. ~stream, *ad*, en amont. ~ there, là-haut. ~ to, jusqu'à [concurrence de]. ~ to date, à la page; (*Fin.*) à jour; (*att.*) moderne. well ~ in (subject), fort en, calé en. ¶ ups & downs, hauts & bas, *m.pl.* ¶ up! debout! alerte! levez-vous!

upbraid, *v.t*, reprocher.

upheaval, *n*, (*Geol.*) soulèvement; (*fig.*) bouleversement, *m*, convulsion, *f*.

uphill, *a*, montant; ardu. ¶ *ad*, en montant.

uphold, *v.t.ir*, soutenir, maintenir. ~er, *n*, soutien, *m*.

upholster, *v.t*, tapisser, rembourrer. ~er, *n*, tapissier, ère. ~y, *n*, tapisserie, *f*.

upkeep, *n*, entretien, *m*.

upland, *n*, [haut] plateau, *m*.

uplift, *v.t,* ennoblir.
upon, *pr,* sur; dessus.
upper, *a,* supérieur; haut; de dessus. ~ *case* (*Typ.*), haut de casse, *m.* *the* ~ *classes,* les hautes classes, *f.pl.* ~ *deck,* pont supérieur, *m;* (*bus*) impériale, *f.* *the* ~ *hand* (*fig.*), le dessus; l'avantage, *m.* ~ *register* (*Mus.*), aigu, *m.* ~ *tooth,* dent de dessus, *f.* ~**most,** *a,* le plus haut, le plus élevé; le plus fort.
upright, *a. & ad,* droit; debout; vertical; d'aplomb; intègre, honnête. ~ *piano,* piano droit, *m.* ~**ness,** *n,* perpendicularité; droiture, intégrité, *f.*
uprising, *n,* soulèvement, *m.*
uproar, *n,* tumulte, vacarme, tapage, bacchanal, *m.* ~**ious†,** *a,* bruyant, tapageur.
uproot, *v.t,* déraciner, arracher.
upset, *n,* remue-ménage, *m.* ¶ *v.t,* renverser; verser; chavirer; déranger; bouleverser, rompre.
upshot, *n,* issue, *f,* fin mot; dénouement, *m.*
upside down, *ad,* sens dessus dessous.
upstart, *n,* parvenu, e.
upstroke, *n,* (*piston*) course montante, *f;* (*writing*) délié, *m.*
up-to-date, *a,* à la page; (*records*) mis à jour.
upward, *a,* ascendant; ascensionnel; jeté vers le haut. ~[s], *ad,* en haut, en contre-haut; en montant; au-dessus. ~*s of,* plus de.
Ural (the), l'Oural, *m. the* ~ *Mountains,* les monts Ourals, *m.pl.*
uranium, *n,* uranium, *m.*
urban, *a,* urbain. ~ *planner,* aménageur, *m.* **urbane,** *a,* courtois, poli. ~**ly,** *ad,* avec urbanité.
urchin, *a,* gamin, galopin, moutard, *m.*
urethra, *n,* urètre, *m.*
urge, *n,* démangeaison, *f.* ¶ *v.t,* pousser, presser, solliciter; exhorter; alléguer. **urgency,** *n,* urgence, *f.* **urgent,** *a,* urgent, pressant, instant. ~**ly,** *ad,* instamment.
uric, *a,* urique. **urinal,** *n,* urinoir, *m;* vespasienne, *f;* (*vessel*) urinal, *m.* **urinate,** *v.i,* uriner. **urine,** *n,* urine, *f.*
urn, *n,* urne, *f;* (*tea*) samovar, *m.*
us, *pn,* nous.

usage, *n,* usage; traitement, *m*
usance, *n,* usance, *f.* **use,** *n* usage; emploi; emprunt, *m* jouissance; utilité; habitude; cor sommation, *f. to be of* ~, servir *to make* ~ *of,* se servir de. ¶ *v.* se servir de, employer, emprun ter; consommer; user de; traiter *to get* ~*d to,* s'habituer. ~ *n* *hooks,* ne pas se servir de cro chets. ~**d,** *p.a,* usité; accoutumé rompu; ayant déjà servi; usagé d'occasion. ~ *car,* voiture d'occa sion, *f.* ~**ful†,** *a,* utile. ~**fulness** *n,* utilité, *f.* ~**less†,** *a,* inutile vain. ~ *person,* non-valeur, *f* ~ *things,* inutilités, *f.pl.* ~**less ness,** *n,* inutilité, *f.* **user,** *n* usager, *m.*
Ushant, *n,* Ouessant, *m.*
usher, *n,* (*court*) huissier, (*Theat* ouvreur, euse. ~**in,** introduir annoncer; (*fig.*) inaugurer.
usual†, *a,* usuel; habituel; oblige ordinaire.
usufruct, *n,* usufruit, *m.*
usurer, *n,* usurier, ère, fesse mathieu, *m.* **usurious†,** *a,* usu raire.
usurp, *v.t,* usurper. ~**ation,** *n* usurpation, *f.* ~**er,** *n,* usurpateu trice.
usury, *n,* usure, *f.*
utensil, *n,* ustensile; vase, *m.*
uterine, *a,* utérin. **uterus,** *n* utérus, *m.*
utilitarian, *a.& n,* utilitaire, *a.* *m,f.*
utility, *n,* utilité, *f.* **utilize,** *v.* utiliser.
utmost, *a,* extrême, dernier. *one* [*very*] ~, [tout] son possible l'impossible, *m. to the* ~, outrance.
utopia, *n,* utopie, *f.* **utopian,** *a* utopique, utopiste. ¶ *n,* utc piste, *m,f.*
utter†, *a,* complet; total; extrêm grand. ¶ *v.t,* proférer, prononce dire, débiter; (*cry*) pousse (*money*) passer. ~**ance,** *n,* a ticulation; parole, *f;* débit, *n* ~**most,** *a,* extrême; le plus recul
uvula, *n,* luette, uvule, *f.*

V

vacancy, *n,* vacance, *f;* vide, *n* **vacant,** *a,* vacant; libre; inoc cupé; distrait. **vacate**, *v.t*, (*office*) quitter; (*premises*) vider. **vacation**, *n*, vacances, *f.pl.*

ccinate, *v.t*, vacciner. **vaccination**, *n*, vaccination, *f*. **vaccine**, *n*, vaccin, *m*.

cillate, *v.i*, vaciller. **vacillation**, *n*, vacillation, *f*.

cuity, *n*, vacuité, *f*. **vacuous**, a, insignifiant. **vacuum**, *n*, vide, *m*. ~ *cleaner*, aspirateur [de poussières] *m*.

gabond, *n. & a*, vagabond, e.

gary, *n*, caprice, *m*, lubie, *f*.

gina, *n*, vagin; (*slang*) abricot, *m*, chatte, *f*.

grancy, *n*, vagabondage, *m*. **vagrant**, *n*, vagabond, e, clochard, e. ¶ *a*, vagabond,

guet†, *a*, vague, imprécis. ~**ness**, *n*, vague, *m*, imprécision, *f*.

in†, *a*, vain, vaniteux. ~**glorious**, *a*, vaniteux, glorieux, superbe. ~**glory**, *n*, gloriole, superbe, *f*.

lance, *n*, pente, *f*.

le, *n*, vallon, val, *m*.

ledictory, *a*, d'adieu.

lence (*Chem.*) *n*, valence, *f*.

lencia, *n*, Valence, *f*.

let, *n*, valet [de chambre] *m*. ¶ *v.t*, faire office de valet à.

letudinarian, *a. & n*, valétudinaire, *a. & m.f.*

liant†, *a*, vaillant, brave.

lid†, *a*, valide; (*ticket*) valable. ~**ate**, *v.t*, valider. ~**ity**, *n*, validité, *f*.

lise, *n*, valise, *f*.

lley, *n*, vallée; (*of roof*) noue, *f*.

lorous†, *a*, valeureux. **valor**, *n*, valeur, vaillance, bravoure, *f*.

luable, *a*, de valeur, de prix, riche; précieux. ~**s**, *n.pl*, valeurs, *f.pl*, objets de valeur, *m.pl*. **valuation**, *n*, évaluation, *f*. **value**, *n*, valeur, *f*; prix, *m. food* ~, valeur nutritive, *f. market* ~, v. marchande, *f*. ¶ *v.t*, évaluer; apprécier; faire cas de. ~**less**, *a*, sans valeur.

lve, *n*, soupape; valve, *f*. *exhaust* ~, soupape d'échappement, *f. safety* ~, s. de sécurité, *f*.

mp (*shoe*), *n*, empeigne, *f*. ¶ *v.t. & i*, improviser.

mpire, *n*, vampire, *m*.

n, *n*, voiture; tapissière, *f*;

wagon; fourgon, *m*. ~[*guard*], avant-garde, *f*.

vanadium, *n*, vanadium, *m*.

vandal, *n*, vandale, *m*. ¶ *a*, de vandale. ~**ism**, *n*, vandalisme, *m*.

vane, *n*, girouette; (*turbine*) aube; aile; (*technical*) pinnule, *f*.

vanilla, *n*, vanille, *f*.

vanish, *v.i*, s'évanouir, disparaître, devenir invisible; s'éclipser, se volatiliser, fuir. ~*ing point*, point de fuite, *m*.

vanity, *n*, vanité, *f*.

vanquish, *v.t*, vaincre. *the* ~*ed*, les vaincus, *m.pl*.

vantage, *n*, avantage, *m*.

vapid, *a*, insipide, fade, plat.

vaporize, *v.t*, vaporiser. **vaporizer**, *n*, vaporisateur, *m*. **vaporous**, -**ry**, *a*, vaporeux. **vapor**, *n*, vapeur, *f*.

variable, *a*, variable; changeant. *at variance*, en désaccord, en mésintelligence. **variant**, *n*, variante, *f*. **variation**, *n*, variation, *f*; changement, *m*; modification, *f*.

varicose vein, varice, *f*.

variegate, *v.t*, varier, bigarrer, panacher, diaprer. **variety**, *n*, variété, diversité; variation, *f*.

various†, *a*, différent, divers.

varlet (*Hist.*) *n*, varlet, *m*.

varnish, *n*, vernis, *m*. ¶ *v.t*, vernir. ~*ing*, *n*, vernissage, *m*.

vary, *v.t. & i*, varier; diversifier; modifier.

vascular, *a*, vasculaire.

vase, *n*, vase, *m*.

vaseline, *n*, vaseline, *f*.

vassal (*Hist.*) *n*, vassal, e.

vast, *a*, vaste, immense. ~**ly**, *ad*, grandement. ~**ness**, *n*, immensité, *f*.

vat, *n*, cuve, *f*, bac, *m*. ¶ *v.t*, encuver.

vaudeville, *n*, vaudeville, *m*.

vault, *n*, voûte; cave, *f*; caveau; tombeau; (*leap*) saut, *m*; chambre forte, *f*. ¶ *v.t*, voûter; (*v.i.*) sauter. ~*ing horse*, cheval de bois, *m*.

vaunt, *n*, vanterie, *f*. ¶ *v.t*, vanter; (*v.i.*) se vanter.

veal, *n*, veau, *m*. ~ *cutlet*, côtelette de v., *f*.

vector, *n*, vecteur, *m*.

veer, *v.i*, (*wind*) se ranger, remonter; (*opinion*) se retourner. ¶ *n*, virage, *m*. ~*ing* (*opinion*) *n*, revirement, *m*.

vegetable, *n*, légume, *m*, plante potagère, *f*. ¶ *a*, végétal. ~ *dish*, légumier, *m*. ~ *marrow*, courge à la moelle, *f*. **vegetarian**, *a*. & *n*, végétarien, ne. **vegetarianism**, *n*, végétarisme, *m*. **vegetate**, *v.i*, végéter. **vegetation**, *n*, végétation, *f*.

vehemence, *n*, véhémence, *f*. **vehement†**, *a*, véhément.

vehicle, *n*, (*carriage*) véhicule, *m*, voiture, *f*; (*medium*) véhicule, *m*. **vehicular traffic**, circulation des voitures, *f*.

veil, *n*, voile, *m*; voilette, *f*; (*fig.*) voile, rideau, bandeau, *m*. ¶ *v.t*, voiler.

vein, *n*, veine; (*leaf*) nervure, *f*. ¶ *v.t*, veiner.

vellum, *n*, vélin, *m*.

velocipede, *n*, vélocipède, *m*.

velocity, *n*, vitesse, *f*.

velour, *n*, feutre velours, *m*.

velum (*Anat.*) *n*, voile, *m*.

velvet, *n*, velours, *m*. ~ *pile*, moquette, *f*. **velveteen**, *n*, velours de coton, *m*, tripe de velours, *f*. **velvet[y]**, *a*, velouté.

venal†, *a*, vénal. ~**ity**, *n*, vénalité, *f*.

vendor, *n*, vendeur, euse; marchand, e; (*law*) vendeur, eresse; (*law*) apporteur, *m*. ~'*s assets*, valeurs d'apport, *f.pl*.

veneer, *n*, bois de placage, *m*, feuilles de p., *f.pl*; (*fig.*) vernis, *m*. ¶ *v.t*, plaquer; (*fig.*) donner du vernis à.

venerable, *a*, vénérable. **venerate**, *v.t*, vénérer. **veneration**, *n*, vénération, *f*.

venereal, *a*, vénérien.

Venetia, *n*, la Vénétie. **Venetian**, *a*, vénitien. ~ *blind*, jalousie, *f*. ¶ *n*, Vénitien, ne.

vengeance, *n*, vengeance, *f*. **vengeful**, *a*, vengeur.

venial†, *a*, véniel.

Venice, *n*, Venise, *f*.

venison, *n*, venaison, *f*.

venom, *n*, venin, *m*. ~**ous**, *a*, venimeux; vénéneux.

vent, *n*, évent, aspirail, soupirail, *m*; lumière; cheminée, *f*; libre cours, *m*, carrière, *f*. ¶ *v.t*, exhaler; donner libre cours à, évaporer. **ventilate**, *v.t*, aérer, donner de l'air à, ventiler. **ventilation**, *n*, aérage, *m*, aération, ventilation, *f*. **ventilator**, *n*, ventilateur; *m*; (*ship*) manche à air, manche à vent, *f*.

ventral, *a*, ventral.

ventricle, *n*, ventricule, *m*.

ventriloquism, -quy, *n*, ventriloquie, *f*. **ventriloquist**, *n*, ventriloque, *m,f*.

venture, *n*, aventure, entreprise, spéculation, *f*; hasard, *m*. ~ *ca[pital]*, capital-risque, *m*. ¶ *v.t*, aventurer, hasarder. ~ *to*, oser, se permettre de. ~**some**, *a*, aventureux; hasardeux.

veracious†, *a*, véridique. **verac[ity]**, *n*, véracité, *f*.

veranda[h], *n*, véranda, *f*.

verb, *n*, verbe, *m*. **verbal†**, *a*, verbal. **verbatim**, *ad*. & *a*, mot à mot, *m*. pour m. **verbiage**, *n*, verbiage, *m*. **verbose**, *a*, verbeux. **verbosity**, *n*, verbosité, *f*.

verdant, *a*, verdoyant; naïf.

verdict, *n*, verdict, *m*.

verdigris, *n*, vert-de-gris, verdet, *m*.

verdure, *n*, verdure, *f*.

verge, *n*, bord, *m*; orée, *f*; (*road*) accotement; (*fig.*) penchant, point, *m*; (*rod*) verge, *f*. ¶ ~ *on*, tirer à; pencher vers.

verification, *n*, vérification, *f*. **verify**, *v.t*, vérifier. **verisimili[tude]**, *n*, vraisemblance, *f*. **veri[table†]**, *a*, véritable. **verity**, *n*, vérité, *f*.

vermicelli, *n*, vermicelle, *m*, nouilles, *f.pl*.

vermilion, *n*, vermillon, *m*. ¶ *a*, vermeil.

vermin, *n*, vermine, *f*; animaux nuisibles, *m.pl*. ~**ous**, *a*, couvert de vermine.

vermouth, *n*, vermouth, *m*.

vernacular, *a*, vulgaire. ¶ *n*, langue vulgaire, *f*.

vernal, *a*, printanier; (*equinox*) de printemps.

vernier, *n*, vernier, *m*.

Verona, *n*, Vérone, *f*.

veronica, *n*, véronique, *f*.

versatile, *a*, souple. **versatility**, *n*, souplesse d'esprit, *f*.

verse, *n*, vers, *m*; vers, *m.pl*; verset, couplet, *m*, strophe, *f*. **versed in**, versé dans, ferré en. **versicle** (*Lit.*) *n*, verset, *m*. **versifier**, *n*, versificateur, *m*. **versify**, *v.t*, versifier, rimer. **version**, *n*, version, *f*. **verso**, *n*, verso, *m*.

versus, *pr*, contre.

vertebra, *n*, vertèbre, *f*. **vertebral**, *a*, vertébral. **vertebrate**, *a*. & *m*, vertébré, *a*. & *m*.

rtex, *n*, sommet, *m*. **vertical,** *a*, vertical. ¶ *n*, verticale, *f*. **~ity,** *a*, verticalité, *f*. **~ly,** *ad*, verticalement. **~ strung piano,** piano à cordes droites, *m*.

rtiginous, *a*, vertigineux. **vertigo,** *n*, vertige, *m*.

rve, *n*, verve, *f*.

ry, *a*, même; seul. ¶ *ad*, très; fort; bien; tout. **~ much,** beaucoup.

sicle, *n*, vésicule, *f*.

spers, *n.pl*, vêpres, *f.pl*.

ssel, *n*, vase, récipient; (*blood*) vaisseau; (*ship*) vaisseau, bâtiment, navire, *m*.

st, *n*, (*man's*) gilet, *m*; (*woman's*) chemise, camisole; *f*. ¶ *v.t*, investir; confier. **~ed rights,** droits acquis, *m.pl*.

sta, *n*, allumette, *f*.

stal [virgin], *n*, vestale, *f*.

stibule, *n*, vestibule, *m*.

stige, *n*, vestige, *m*, trace, *f*.

stment, *n*, vêtement, *m*.

stry, *n*, sacristie; (*council*) fabrique, *f*.

suvian, *n*, vésuvien. **Vesuvius,** *n*, le Vésuve.

teran, *n*, vétéran; ancien combattant, *m*. ¶ *a*, qui a vieilli dans sa profession; de longue date; depuis longtemps sous les drapeaux.

terinary, *a*, vétérinaire. **~ surgeon],** [médecin] vétérinaire, *n*.

to, *n*, veto, *m*. ¶ *v.t*, mettre le [son] v. à.

x, *v.t*, contrarier, chagriner, exer. **~ation,** *n*, contrariété, *f*; désagrément, *m*; vexation, *f*. **~atious,** *a*, contrariant, vexatoire. **vexed** (*question*) *p.a*, controversé, longuement débattue.

a, *pr*, par la voie [de], par.

ability, *n*, viabilité, *f*. **viable,** *a*, viable.

aduct, *n*, viaduc, *m*.

al, *n*, fiole, *f*.

and, *n*, mets, *m*.

brate, *v.i*, (*Phys. & fig.*) vibrer; (*machinery, car*) trembler. **vibration,** *n*, vibration; trépidation, *f*.

car, *n*, vicaire; curé; ministre, *m*. **~age,** *n*, cure, *f*; presbytère, *m*. **~ship,** *n*, cure, *f*.

ce, *n*, (*depravity*) vice, *m*.

ce-, *prefix*, vice-. **~chairman,** **~president,** vice-president, e. **~principal** (college), censeur,

m. **~reine,** vice-reine, *f*. **~roy,** vice-roi, *m*.

Vicenza, *n*, Vicence, *f*.

vice versa, *ad*, vice versa, réciproquement.

vicinity, *n*, voisinage, *m*, proximité, *f*.

vicious†, *a*, vicieux. **~ circle,** cercle vicieux, *m*. **~ness,** *n*, nature vicieuse, *f*.

vicissitude, *n*, vicissitude, péripétie, *f*, cahot, *m*.

victim, *n*, victime, *f*. **~ize,** *v.t*, rendre victime.

victor, *n*, vainqueur, *m*. **victorious†,** *a*, victorieux. **victory,** *n*, victoire, *f*.

victual, *v.t*, ravitailler. **~s,** *n.pl*, vivres, *m.pl*, victuailles, *f.pl*.

vicuña, *n*, vigogne, *f*.

video, *a*, vidéo. ¶ *n*, vidéo, *m*. **~ tape,** bande **~,** *f*. **~ conference,** visioconférence, *f*.

vie, *v.i*, rivaliser; lutter; faire assaut.

Vienna, *n*, Vienne, *f*. **Viennese,** *a*, viennois. ¶ *n*, Viennois, e.

view, *n*, vue; perspective, *f*, coup d'œil; tableau, *m*; idée, opinion, *f*. **to have in ~,** viser. **~finder,** viseur, *m*. ¶ *v.t*, contempler; envisager.

vigil, *n*, veille; veillée; (*Eccl.*) vigile, *f*. **~ance,** *n*, vigilance, *f*. **~ant,** *a*, vigilant. **~antly,** *ad*, avec vigilance.

vignette, *n*, vignette, *f*. ¶ *v.t*, dégrader. **vignetter,** *n*, dégradateur, *m*.

vigor, *n*, vigueur; sève, *f*. **vigorous†,** *a*, vigoureux.

vile, *a*, vil; abject. **~ness,** *n*, bassesse; abjection, *f*. **vilify,** *v.t*, vilipender.

villa, *n*, villa, *f*. **village,** *n*, village, *m*; bourgade, *f*; (*att.*) villageois, de village, de clocher. **villager,** *n*, villageois, e.

villain, *n*, scélérat, e, misérable, *m,f*, bandit; (*Theat.*) traître, *m*; (*Hist.*) vilain, e. **~ous,** *a*, scélérat. **~y,** *n*, scélératesse, *f*. **villein,** *n*, vilain, e.

vindicate, *v.t*, justifier. **vindication,** *n*, justification, *f*.

vindictive, *a*, vindicatif.

vine, *n*, vigne, *f*. **~ shoot,** sarment, *m*. **vinegar,** *n*, vinaigre, *m*. **~ works,** vinaigrerie, *f*. ¶ *v.t*, vinaigrer. **vinery,** *n*, serre à vignes, *f*. **vineyard,** *n*, vigne, *f*; vignoble, *m*.

vinosity, *n,* vinosité, *f.* **vinous,**
a, vineux. **vintage,** *n,* (*growth*)
cru, *m,* cuvée; (*season*) vendange; (*crop*) récolte, vinée, *f.*
~ *wine,* vin millésimé, *m.* ~ *year,*
année à millésime, *f.* **vintager,** *n,*
vendangeur, euse.

viola, *n,* (*Mus.*) alto, *m;* (*Bot.*)
violariacée, *f.* **violaceous,** *a,* violacé.

violate, *v.t,* violer. **violation,** *n,*
violation, *f;* (*rape*) viol, *m.* **violator,** *n,* violateur, trice. **violence,** *n,* violence, *f.* do ~ to,
violenter. **violent†,** *a,* violent.

violet, *n,* (*Bot.*) violette, *f;* (*color*)
violet, *m.* ¶ *a,* violet.

violin, *n,* violon, *m.* ~**ist,** *n,* violoniste, *m,f.* **violoncellist,** *n,* violoncelliste, *m,f.* **violoncello,** *n,*
violoncelle, *m.*

viper, *n,* vipère, *f.*

virago, *n,* dragon, *m,* mégère, *f.*

virgin, *n,* vierge; pucelle, *f.* ¶ *a,*
vierge. ~**al†,** *a,* virginal. **Virginia** (*Geog.*) *n,* la Virginie, *f.*
~ *creeper,* vigne vierge, *f.* ~ [*tobacco*], virginie, *m.* **virginity,** *n,*
virginité, *f.*

virile, *a,* viril, mâle. **virility,** *n,*
virilité, *f.*

virtual†, *a,* virtuel. **virtue,** *n,*
vertu, *f.* **virtuosity,** *n,* virtuosité,
f. **virtuoso,** *n,* virtuose, *m,f.* **vir-
tuous†,** *a,* vertueux.

virulence, *n,* virulence, *f.* **virulent,** *a,* virulent. **virus,** *n,* virus,
m.

visa, *n,* visa, *m.* ¶ *v.t,* viser.

visage, *n,* visage, *m,* figure, *f.*

viscera, *n.pl,* viscères, *m.pl.*

viscid & **viscous,** *a,* visqueux.
viscose, *n,* viscose, *f.* **viscosity,**
n, viscosité, *f.*

viscount, *n,* vicomte, *m.* ~**ess,** *n,*
vicomtesse, *f.*

vise, *n,* étau, *m.*

visibility, *n,* visibilité, *f.* **visible,**
a, visible. **visibly,** *ad,* visible-
ment; à vue d'œil.

vision, *n,* vision, *f.* ~**ary,** *a,* visionnaire; chimérique. ¶ *n,* visionnaire, *m,f;* illuminé, *m.*

visit, *n,* visite, *f.* ¶ *v.t,* visiter; voir;
(*Cust.*) arraisonner. ~**ation,** *n,*
visite; (*Eccl.*) visitation, *f.* ~**ing
card,** carte de visite, *f.* ~**or,** *n,*
visiteur, euse; hôte, esse; passager, ère. ~'*s tax,* taxe de séjour, *f.*

visor, *n,* visière, *f.*

vista, *n,* échappée [de vue]; pe[r]
spective, *f.*

Vistula (the), la Vistule.

visual, *a,* visuel. ~**ize,** *v.t,* s[e]
représenter.

vital, *a,* vital; (*fig.*) vif. ~**ity,** *n*[,]
vitalité, *f.* ~**ize,** *v.t,* vivifier. ~[s,]
n.pl, parties vitales, *f.pl.* **vit[a-]
min,** *n,* vitamine, *f.*

vitiate, *v.t,* vicier. **vitiation,** *n*[,]
viciation, *f.*

viticultural, *a,* viticole. **viticul[-]
tur[al]ist,** *n,* viticulteur, *m.* **vit[i-]
culture,** *n,* viticulture, *f.*

vitreous, *a,* vitreux; (*humor*[)]
vitrée. **vitrify,** *v.t,* vitrifier. **vitr[i-]
ol,** *n,* vitriol, *m.* ~**ic** *a,* vitrioliqu[e.]

vituperate, *v.t,* injurier, viliper[n-]
der. **vituperation,** *n,* injures, *f.p*[l.]

vivacious, *a,* enjoué. *to be* ~[,]
avoir de la vivacité. ~**ly,** *ad,* ave[c]
vivacité. **viva voce,** *ad,* de viv[e]
voix. ¶ *a,* oral. ¶ *n,* examen ora[l.]
m. **vivid,** *a,* vif, vivant. **vividnes**[s,]
n, vivacité, *f.* **vivify,** *a,* vivifie[r.]
viviparous, *a,* vivipare. **vivise[c-]
tion,** *n,* vivisection, *f.*

vixen, *n,* renarde; (*woman*) mé[-]
gère, f.

viz, *ad. abb,* c'est-à-dire, [à] savoi[r.]

vizier, *n,* vizir, *m.*

vocable, *n,* vocable, *m.* **vocabu[-]
lary,** *n,* vocabulaire, *m.* **vocal,** *a*[,]
vocal. ~**ist,** *n,* chanteur, eus[e,]
cantatrice, *f.* ~**ize,** *v.t,* vocalise[r.]
vocation, *n,* vocation, *f.* **vocati[ve]**
[*case*], *n,* vocatif, *m.*

vociferate, *v.i,* vociférer. **voci[f-]
erous,** *a,* bruyant. ~**ly,** *ad,* bruy[-]
amment.

vogue, *n,* vogue, mode, *f.*

voice, *n,* voix, *f.* ¶ *v.t,* exprime[r.]
~**less,** *a,* aphone.

void, *a,* vide; nul. ¶ *n,* vide; vagu[e,]
m. ¶ *v.t,* évacuer; annuler.

voile (*textile*) *n,* voile, *m.*

volatile, *a,* volatil. **volatilize,** *v*[.t,]
volatiliser.

volcanic, *a,* volcanique. **volcan**[o,]
n, volcan, *m.*

volition, *n,* volition, *f.*

volley, *n,* volée; décharge, *f.* ~[-]
ball, volleyball, *m.* ~ *firing,* fe[u]
de peloton, *m.* ¶ (*Ten.*) *v.t*[:]
[re]prendre à la (*ou* de) volé[e;]
(*abs.*) jouer à la (*ou* de) volé[e.]

volplane, *n,* vol plané, *m.* ¶ *v*[.i,]
descendre en vol plané, planer.

volt, *n,* volt, *m.* ~**age,** *n,* voltag[e,]
m, tension, *f.* *high* ~, haut[e]

tension, *f.* **voltaic,** *a,* voltaïque.
voltmeter, *n,* voltmètre, *m.*
olubility, *n,* volubilité, *f.* **voluble,** *a,* volubile, fécond en paroles.
olume, *n,* volume; tome; (*of smoke, etc.*) nuage, *m.* **voluminous,** *a,* volumineux.
oluntary†, *a,* volontaire; bénévole. ¶ (*organ*) *n,* (*before service*) prélude; (*during*) interlude, *m;* (*after*) sortie, *f;* (*between credo & sanctus*) offertoire, *m.*
volunteer, *n,* volontaire, *m.*
oluptuary, *n,* voluptueux, euse. **voluptuous†,** *a,* voluptueux. **~ness,** *n,* volupté, sensualité, mollesse, *f.*
olute, *n,* volute, *f.*
omit, *n,* vomissement, *m.* ¶ *v.t, & i,* vomir, revomir.
oracious, *a,* vorace. **~ly,** *ad,* avec voracité. **~ness, voracity,** *n,* voracité, *f.*
ortex, *n,* tourbillon, *m.*
otary, *n,* adorateur, trice; sectateur, *m.* **vote,** *n,* vote, scrutin; suffrage, *m,* voix, opinion, *f.* ¶ *v.t. & i,* voter, donner sa voix, opiner. *~ by a show of hands,* voter à main levée. **voter,** *n,* votant, *m.* **voting,** *n,* votation, *f. ~ paper,* bulletin de vote, *m.*
votive, *a,* votif.
ouch, *v.t,* attester; vérifier. *~ for,* répondre de, garantir. **~er,** *n,* pièce justificative, *f;* bon, bulletin, *m.* **~safe,** *v.t,* accorder; daigner.
ow, *n,* vœu, *m.* ¶ *v.t,* vouer; (*v.i.*) faire vœu; jurer.
owel, *n,* voyelle, *f.*
oyage, *n,* voyage, *m.* ¶ *v.i,* voyager.
ulcanite, *n,* caoutchouc vulcanisé, *m,* ébonite, *f.* **vulcanize,** *v.t,* vulcaniser.
ulgar†, *a,* vulgaire; populacier; trivial, commun, bas. *the ~ [herd],* le vulgaire. **~ism,** *n,* expression vulgaire, trivialité, *f.* **~ity,** *n,* vulgarité, trivialité, *f.* **~ize,** *v.t,* vulgariser; banaliser. *the Vulgate,* la Vulgate.
ulnerable, *a,* vulnérable.
ulture, *n,* vautour, *m.*

W

wad, *n,* bourre, *f;* tampon, *m;* (*banknotes*) liasse, *f.* ¶ *v.t,* ouater. **wadding,** *n,* ouate, *f.*

waddle, *n,* dandinement, déhanchement, *m.* ¶ *v.i.* marcher comme une cane, se dandiner.
wade, *v.i,* se mettre à l'eau sans nager; patauger, barboter. *~ through* (ford), passer à gué. *~ through a book,* peiner en lisant un livre. **wader,** *n,* (*bird*) échassier, *m;* (*pl.*) bottes cuissardes, *f.pl.*
wafer, *n,* (*flat biscuit*) gaufrette; (*cornet biscuit*) oublie, *f,* plaisir; (*Eccl.*) hostie, *f.*
waffle, *n,* gaufre, *f. ~ irons,* gaufrier, *m.*
waft, *n,* souffle, *m.* ¶ *v.t,* flotter, transporter; (*v.i.*) flotter dans l'air, sur l'eau.
wag, *n,* plaisant, loustic, farceur, *m.* ¶ *v.t,* (*tail*) agiter, frétiller de; (*head*) branler, dodeliner de (*la tête*).
wage, *n, oft. pl,* salaire, *m,* paie, *f,* gages, loyers, *m.pl. ~ earner,* salarié, e. *minimum ~,* smig ou smic (salaire minimum interprofessionel garanti, de croissance), *m. to ~ war,* faire la guerre, guerroyer.
wager, *n,* pari, *m,* gageure, *f.* ¶ *v.t,* parier.
wagon, *n,* voiture, *f,* fourgon, chariot, *m.* **~load,** charretée, *f.*
waggish, *a,* facétieux, badin.
waggle, *v.t. & i,* branler.
wagtail, *n,* hochequeue, *m,* bergeronnette, *f.*
waif, *n,* enfant abandonné, e, *m,f.*
wail, *n,* lamentation, *f.* ¶ *v.i,* se lamenter; (*of baby*) vagir.
wain, *n,* chariot, *m.*
wainscot, *n,* lambris, *m.* ¶ *v.t,* lambrisser.
waist, *n,* ceinture, taille, *f.* **~band,** ceinture, *f.* **~coat,** gilet, *m. ~ measurement,* tour de taille, *m,* grosseur de ceinture, *f.*
wait, *n,* attente, *f. to lie in ~,* se tenir en embuscade, s'embusquer. ¶ *v.t. & i,* attendre. **~-&-see,** *a,* expectant. *~ [up]on,* servir; se présenter chez. **waiter,** *n,* garçon, *m. ~! garçon!* **waiting,** *n,* attente, *f. ~ room,* salon d'attente, *m;* (*Rly*) salle d'a., *f.* **waitress,** *n,* servante, bonne, serveuse, *f. ~! mademoiselle!*
waive, *v.t,* renoncer à, se désister de.
wake, *n,* sillage, *m,* eaux, *f.pl;* (*fu-*

neral) veillée mortuaire, *f.* *follow in the* ~ *of* (*Naut. & fig.*), marcher dans les eaux de. ¶ *v.t.ir. & waken, v.t,* [r]éveiller; (*v.i.*) s'éveiller. ~**ful,** *a,* privé de sommeil; vigilant. ~**fulness,** *n,* insomnie, *f.*

Wales, *n,* le pays de Galles.

walk, *n,* marche; promenade [à pied] *f,* tour; pas, *m;* allure, démarche; allée, *f;* promenoir, *m.* ~ *of life,* carrière, profession, *f.* ~ *over,* (*sport*) walk-over, *m;* (*fig.*) victoire facile, *f.* ¶ *v.t. & i,* marcher; cheminer; aller à pied; aller au pas. ~ *about,* se promener. ~ *in,* entrer. ~ *off,* s'en aller. ~ *out,* sortir. **walker,** *n,* marcheur, euse; piéton, ne; promeneur, euse. **walking,** *n,* marche; promenade [à pied] *f.* ¶ *p.a. or att,* ambulant; (*boots*) de marche. ~ *stick,* canne, *f.* ~ *tour,* excursion à pied, *f.*

wall, *n,* mur, *m,* muraille; paroi, *f;* haut du pavé, *m.* ~ *cupboard,* placard, *m.* to be a ~*flower,* faire tapisserie. ~ *map,* carte murale, *f.* ~ *paper,* papier peint, papier-tenture, *m,* tenture, *f.*

wallet, *n,* sacoche, *f;* portefeuille, *m.*

wallow, *n,* souille, *f.* ¶ *v.i,* se vautrer; croupir.

walnut, *n,* noix, *f;* (*tree, wood*) noyer, *m.*

walrus, *n,* morse, *m.*

waltz, *n,* valsé, *f.* ¶ *v.i,* valser. ~**er,** *n,* valseur, euse.

wan, *a,* blême, blafard; (*face*) hâve.

wand, *n,* baguette, *f.*

wander, *v.i,* errer, vagabonder, vaguer; s'écarter; divaguer. ~ *around,* tournailler. ~**er,** *n,* coureur, nomade, *m.* *the Wandering Jew,* le Juif errant.

wane, *n,* déclin, retour, *m.* ¶ *v.i,* décroître; décliner.

want, *n,* besoin; manque, défaut, *m,* gêne, *f.* ¶ *v.t,* avoir besoin de; manquer de; désirer; falloir; vouloir. ~**ed** (*Advt*), on demande.

wanton, *a,* folâtre; folichon; licencieux; lascif; gratuit, sans motif. ~ *destruction,* vandalisme, *m.* *out of sheer* ~*ness,* de gaieté de cœur.

war, *n,* guerre, *f;* (*elements*) combat, *m.* ~ *dance,* danse guerrière, *f.* ~ *horse,* cheval de bataille, *m.* W~ *loan,* emprunt de la

Défense nationale, *m.* ~ *memorial,* monument aux morts [de la guerre] *m.* ~ *of attrition,* guerre d'usure. ~*ship,* vaisseau de guerre, *m.* ¶ *v.i,* faire la guerre, guerroyer.

warble, *v.i,* gazouiller; (*v.t.*) roucouler. **warbler** (*bird*) *n,* fauvette, *f.*

ward, *n,* pupille, *m,f;* (*prison*) quartier; arrondissement, *m;* (*hospital*) salle; (*lock*) garde, *f.* ~*room,* carré des officiers, *m;* [*off*], *v.t,* parer. ~**en,** *n,* gardien; gouverneur, *m.* **wardrobe,** *n,* armoire; garde-robe, *f;* vêtements, *m.pl.* ~ *trunk,* malle-armoire, *f.*

warehouse, *n,* magasin; dépôt; entrepôt; dock, *m.* ~ *keeper* (bonded), entreposeur, *m.* ~*man,* magasinier; marchand en magasin, stockiste, *m.* ¶ *v.t,* emmagasiner; entreposer.

wares, *n.pl,* marchandise, *f,* articles, *m.pl.*

warily, *ad,* avec circonspection, à tâtons. **wariness,** *n,* précaution, *f.*

warlike, *a,* guerrier, belliqueux; martial.

warm†, *a,* chaud; (*fig.*) chaleureux. *it is* ~, il fait chaud. *I am* ~, j'ai chaud. ¶ *v.t,* chauffer; réchauffer; échauffer. ~*ing pan,* bassinoire, *f,* chauffe-lit, *m.* ~**th,** *n,* chaleur, *f.*

warn, *v.t,* avertir, prévenir, ~**ing,** *n,* avertissement, préavis, *m.*

warp, *n,* chaîne, lice, lisse, *f.* ¶ *v.t,* déjeter; (*yarn*) ourdir; (*Naut.*) touer; (*v.i.*) se déjeter, gauchir, gondoler.

warrant, *n,* autorisation; ordonnance, *f;* garant; mandat; warrant, bulletin de gage; titre, *m.* ¶ *v.t,* garantir; justifier. ~**able,** *a,* justifiable. ~**y,** *n,* garantie, *f.*

warren, *n,* garenne, *f.*

warrior, *n,* guerrier, ère.

Warsaw, *n,* Varsovie, *f.*

wart, *n,* verrue, *f,* poireau, *m.* ~**y,** *a,* verruqueux.

wary, *a,* circonspect; défiant.

wash, *n,* (linen) lessive, *f;* (*art*) lavis, *m;* (*mouth*) eau, *f;* (*ship*) remous, *m;* (*slops*) lavasse, *f.* ~*basin,* cuvette, *f.* ~*cloth,* gant de toilette, *m.* ~ *drawing,* [dessin

au] lavis, *m.* ~*house*, lavoir, *m*,
laverie, buanderie, *f.* ~*stand*, lavabo, *m.* ~*tub*, cuvier, *m.* ¶ *v.t.*
& *i*, laver; se l.; blanchir; baigner.
~ *away*, emporter, entraîner; affouiller. ~ *the dishes*, laver la
vaisselle. ~**able**, *a*, lavable.
washed overboard, enlevé par la
mer. **washer**, *n*, (*pers.*) laveur,
euse; (*ring*) rondelle, *f.* ~*woman*,
laveuse de linge, blanchisseuse, *f.*
washing, *n*, lavage; blanchissage,
m; lessive; toilette; ablution; lotion, *f.* ~ *machine*, machine à
laver, *f.*

wasp, *n*, guêpe, *f.* ~*s' nest*, guêpier, *m*.

waste, *a*, (*land*) inculte, vague;
(*gas, heat*) perdu; (*matter*) de
rebut. *to lay* ~, dévaster, ravager.
¶ *n*, gaspillage, *m*; perte, *f*; déchet;
rebut, *m.* ¶ *comps:* ~ *paper*,
papier de rebut, *m*; papiers inutiles, *m.pl.* ~ *paper basket*, corbeille à papiers, *f.* ~ *pipe*, tropplein, *m.* ~ *water*, eaux-vannes,
f.pl. ¶ *v.t*, gaspiller; perdre; consumer. ~ *away*, se consumer;
s'atrophier. ~*d life*, vie manquée,
f. **wasteful**, *a*, dissipateur, prodigue. **wastefulness**, *n*, prodigalité, *f*.

watch, *n*, veille; garde, sentinelle,
f; (*Naut.*) quart, *m*, bordée; *f*;
(*Horo.*) montre, *f. on the* ~,
aux aguets, à l'affût. ~ *chain*,
chaîne de montre, *f.* ~*dog*, chien
de garde, *m.* ~ *fire*, feu de bivouac, *m.* ~*maker*, horloger, *m.*
~*man*, veilleur, garde, *m. wrist*~,
montre-bracelet, *f.* ¶ *v.t.* & *i*, veiller; surveiller; observer; guetter;
suivre. ~**er**, *n*, veilleur, euse.
~**ful**†, *a*, vigilant. ~**fulness**, *n*,
vigilance, *f*.

water, *n*, eau, *f*; eaux, *f.pl*; (*tide*)
marée, *f*, eaux, *f.pl*; (*pl.*) eaux,
f.pl, parages, *m.pl. fresh* ~, eau
douce, *f.* ~ *closet*, cabinets,
m.pl, cabinet [d'aisance] *m.*
~*color*, aquarelle, *f.* ~*cress*,
cresson [de fontaine] *m.* ~*fall*,
chute d'eau; cascade, *f.* ~*fowl*,
oiseau aquatique, *m.* ~*glass*,
verre soluble, *m.* ~ *hazard* (*golf*),
douve, *f.* ~ *jug*, pot à eau, *m.* ~
jump (*turf*), douve, *f.* ~ *level*, niveau d'eau, *m.* ~ *lily*, nénuphar,
m. ~ *line*, ligne de flottaison, *f.*

~*logged*, imbibé d'eau; (*boat*) engagé. ~*mark*, (*tidal*) laisse, *f*;
(*paper*) filigrane, *m.* ~*melon*,
melon d'eau, *m*, pastèque, *f.* ~
meter, compteur à eau, *m.* ~ *mill*,
moulin à eau, *m.* ~ *nymph*,
naïade, *f.* ~ *on the brain*, hydrocéphalie, *f.* ~ *on the knee*,
épanchement de synovie, *m.* ~
pipe, tuyau d'eau, *m.* conduite
d'eau, *f.* ~*power*, force hydraulique, houille blanche, *f.* ~*proof*,
a, imperméable [à l'eau]; (*v.t.*)
imperméabiliser. ~ *polo*, waterpolo, *m.* ~ *rat*, rat d'eau, *m.*
~*shed*, ligne de faîte, *f.* ~*side*,
bord de l'eau, *m*; (*att.*) riverain.
~*spout*, (*rain*) gargouille; (*Meteor.*) trombe, *f.* ~*tight*, étanche
[à l'eau]. ~ *tower*, château d'eau,
m. ~*way*, voie navigable, v.
d'eau, *f*; (*bridge*) débouché, *m.*
~*wheel*, roue hydraulique, *f.* ~*works*, usine hydraulique, *f.* ¶ *v.t*,
(*garden*) arroser; (*horse*) abreuver; (*drink*) couper, baptiser;
(*stock, Fin.*) diluer; (*silk*) moirer;
(*v.i.*) (*eyes*) pleurer, larmoyer;
(*take in water*) faire de l'eau. *it
makes one's mouth* ~, cela fait
venir l'eau à la bouche. ~*ed silk*,
moire de soie, soie moirée, *f.*
~*ing*, *n*, arrosement; arrosage;
abreuvage, *m*; moire, *f.* ~ *place*,
abreuvoir, *m*; ville d'eaux, *f*,
eaux, *f.pl*; bains, *m.pl*, station
balnéaire, *f.* ~*less*, *a*, dépourvu
d'eau. ~*y*, *a*, aqueux; humide;
(*fluid*) ténu.

watt, *n*, watt, *m*.

wattle, *n*, (*rods & twigs*) claie;
(*bird*) barbe, caroncule, *f*, fanon,
m; (*fish*) barbe, *f.* ¶ *v.t*, clayonner.

wave, *n*, vague, *f*; flot, *m*; lame, *f*;
coup de mer, *m*; onde; ondulation, *f*; (*hand*) signe, geste;
(*wand*) coup, *m.* ~*length*, longueur d'onde, *f. cold, heat* ~,
vague de chaleur, de froid, *f. permanent* ~, indéfrisable, *f. shock*
~, onde de choc, *f. short* ~,
ondes courtes, *f.pl.* ¶ *v.i*, flotter;
ondoyer; (*v.t.*) agiter; faire signe
de; onduler. *to have one's hair*
~*d*, se faire onduler [les cheveux]. **waver**, *v.i*, hésiter, va-

ciller, flotter, chanceler. **wavy,** a,
onduleux, ondé, en ondes; (line)
tremblée.

wax, n, cire; (cobbler's) poix, f.
~**works,** figures de cire, f.pl. ¶
v.t, cirer; (v.i.) croître; devenir.
~**ed thread,** fil poissé, m. ~**y,** a,
comme cire.

way, n, chemin, m, route; voie;
distance, f; passage, m; place, f;
progrès, m; marche; direction, f;
côté; sens, m; manière, façon,
sorte, f; genre; moyen, m; allure,
f, air; usage, m; guise, f; cours,
m; passe; (Naut.) erre, f. by
the ~, (fig.) à propos. half~, à
mi-chemin. in the ~, encombrant, gênant. to lose one's ~,
s'égarer. ~**bill,** feuille de route,
f. ~**farer,** voyageur, euse. ~ **in,**
entrée, f. ~**lay,** tendre une embûche à. ~ **out,** sortie; issue, f.
~**side,** bord de la route, m; (att.)
sur le b. de la r.; riverain; (Rly
station) de passage, d'escale.

wayward†, a, capricieux, volontaire, libertin. ~**ness,** n, libertinage, m.

we, pn, nous; on.

weak†, a, faible; débile; (tea) léger. ~ **spot** (fig. of pers.), côté
faible, m. ~**en,** v.t, affaiblir;
atténuer; (v.i.) faiblir. ~**ling,** n,
faiblard, e. ~**ly,** a, débile, faiblard. ~**ness,** n, faiblesse, f;
faible, m.

weal, n, bien, m. (Cf. the common
~); vergeture, trace d'un coup,
f.

wealth, n, richesses, f.pl, opulence, f, biens, m.pl. ~**y,** a, riche,
opulent.

wean, v.t, sevrer. ~**ing,** n, sevrage, m.

weapon, n, arme, f; porte-respect,
m. ~**less,** a, sans armes.

wear, n, usage, m; usure, f. the
worse for ~, patraque. ¶ v.t. &
i. ir, user; s'u.; miner; porter;
mettre. ~ **out,** user; épuiser, exténuer. ~ **well,** être d'un bon
user. ~**able,** a, mettable, portable.

weariness, n, fatigue, lassitude, f.

wearing, n, usure, f; port, m.

wearisome, a, endormant, assommant; fastidieux. ~**ness,** n,
ennui, m. **weary,** a, fatigué, las.
¶ v.t, fatiguer, lasser; ennuyer.
~ **for,** languir après.

weasel, n, belette, f.

weather, n, temps, m; intempéries, f.pl. ~~**-beaten,** ravagé [par
les intempéries]; hâlé. ~**cock,** girouette, f, coq, m; (fig.) girouette, f, sauteur, arlequin, m. ~
forecast, bulletin météorologique, m. ~ **permitting,** si le
temps le permet. ~**stripping,** m,
calfeutage, m. ¶ v.t, résister à;
(Geol.) altérer, désagréger.

weave, n, tissu, m. ¶ v.t.ir, tisser;
(basket) tresser; (fig.) ourdir,
tramer, **weaver,** n, tisserand, m.
weaving, n, tissage, m; tisseranderie, f.

web, n, toile; (bird's foot) membrane; (girder) âme, f; (key)
panneton, m; (of life) trame, f.
spider's ~, toile d'araignée, f.
~**-footed,** palmipède. **webbed,** a,
palmé. **webbing,** n, sangle, f.

wed, v.t, épouser; marier; (v.i.)
se m. **wedded,** a, conjugal; (to
opinion) attaché. **wedding,** n,
noces, f.pl, mariage, m. ~ **break-**
fast, repas de noce, m. ~ **cake,**
gâteau de noce, m. ~ **day,** jour
de mariage, m. ~ **dress,** robe de
mariée, f. ~ **festivities &** ~
party, noce, f. ~ **march,** marche
nuptiale, f. ~ **present,** cadeau
de noce, m; (bridegroom's) corbeille [de mariage] f. ~ **ring,**
alliance, f, anneau nuptial, m.

wedge, n, coin, m; cale; hausse, f.
¶ v.t, coincer; caler.

wedlock, n, mariage, m.

Wednesday, n, mercredi, m.

wee, a, petiot, tout petit.

weed, n, mauvaise herbe, f. ¶ v.t,
sarcler. ~ **out,** éliminer, épurer.
~**er,** n, (pers.) sarcleur, euse;
(hoe) sarcloir, m.

week, n, semaine; (e.g; Friday to
Friday) semaine, huitaine, f, huit
jours, m.pl. ~ **day,** jour de semaine, m. ~ **days only,** la semaine seulement. ~**end,** weekend, m. long ~**end,** weekend pro-
longé, m. ~**ly,** a, hebdomadaire.

weep, v.i. & t. ir. & ~ **for,** pleurer.
~**er,** n, pleureur, euse. **weeping,**
n, pleurs, m.pl, larmes, f.pl. ¶ a,
qui pleure, éploré; (tree) pleureur.

weevil, n, charançon, m. ~**y,** a,
charançonné.

weft, n, trame, f.

weigh, v.t, peser; mesurer; (an-

chor) lever; (*v.i.*) peser; farder.
~ *down*, appesantir, affaisser. *to
get under* ~, appareiller. ~*er*,
n, peseur, *m.* **weighing**, *n*, pesage, *m*; pesée, *f.* ~ *in & ~ in
room*, pesage, *m.* ~ *machine*,
[balance à] bascule, *f.* **weight**,
n, poids, *m*; pesanteur; gravité;
importance, *f. net* ~, poids net,
m. ~ *allowed free*, franchise de
poids, f. de bagages, *f. his, its,
~ in gold*, son pesant d'or. ~*y†*,
a, pesant; puissant; grave.

weir, *n*, barrage; déversoir; (*Fish.*)
gord, *m.*

weird, *a*, fantastique.

welcome, *a*, bienvenu; libre.
you're ~, de rien. ¶ *n*, bienvenue,
f, [bon] accueil, *m*, réception, *f.*
¶ *v.t*, bien accueillir, recevoir.

weld, *n*, soudure, *f.* ¶ *v.t*, souder,
corroyer.

welfare, *n*, bien-être, bonheur;
(*public*) salut, *m*, chose, *f.*

well, *n*, puits, *m*; source, fontaine,
f; réservoir, *m*; (*of ship*) sentine,
f; (*of court*) parquet, *m.* ~
sinker, puisatier, fontainier, *m.*
~*spring*, source, *f.* ¶ *v.i*, sourdre,
jaillir.

well, *a*, bien; dispos, bien portant,
en bonne santé. *he is* ~, il va
bien. ¶ *ad*, bien. ~*-advised*, bien
conseillé. ~ *& good*, à la bonne
heure. ~*-attended*, suivi. ~*-bal-
anced*, bien équilibré; (*style,
prose*) nombreux. *to be* ~ *balanced* (phrase), avoir du nombre. ~*-behaved*, sage. ~*-being*,
bien-être, *m.* ~*-beloved*, *a. & n*,
bien-aimé, e, bienaimé, e. ~*-
bred*, bien élevé, bien appris, de
bonne compagnie, honnête. ~*-
built*, ~*-knit*, bien charpenté.
~*-disposed & ~-meaning*, bien
intentionné. ~*-done* (*Cook.*),
bien cuit. ~ *done!* bravo! ~*-in-
formed*, calé. ~*-known*, bien
connu, réputé, signalé, répandu.
~ *off & ~-to-do*, à son aise, aisé,
au large, fortuné, calé, cossu.
~*-read*, instruit, lettré. ~*-spoken*,
bien-disant. ~*-timed*, opportun.

Wellingtons, *n.pl*, bottes montant aux genoux, *f.pl.*

Welsh, *a*, gallois; du pays de Galles. ¶ *n*, le gallois. ~*man*,
~*woman*, Gallois, e. ~ *rabbit*,
~ *rarebit*, rôtie à l'anglaise, r.
au fromage, *f.*

welt, *n*, (*shoe*) trépoint, *f*; (*strap*)
couvre-joint, *m*, fourrure, *f.*
wide ~ (shoe), semelle débor-
dante, *f.*

welter, *v.i*, nager, se baigner, s'a-
bîmer. ~ *weight* (*Box.*), poids
mi-moyen, *m.*

wen, *n*, loupe, *f*, goitre, *m.*

wench, *n*, donzelle, *f.*

wend, *v.i*, poursuivre.

werewolf, *n*, loup-garou, *m.*

west, *n*, ouest; (le) couchant; occident, *m.* ¶ *a*, de l'ouest, d'ouest,
occidental. *W~ Africa*, l'Afrique
occidentale, *f. the W~ Indies*,
les Indes occidentales, les Antilles, *f.pl.* **westerly**, *a*, d'ouest.
western, *a*, de l'ouest; occidental;
d'Occident.

Westphalia, *n*, la Westphalie.

wet, *a*, mouillé; humide; pluvieux;
(*goods*) liquide; (*paint, ink*)
fraîche. ~ *blanket*, rabat-joie,
m. ~ *fly fishing*, pêche à la
mouche noyée, *f.* ~ *nurse*, nourrice, *f.* ~ *through*, trempé. **wet
& ~ness**, *n*, humidité, *f. out in the
~*, dans la pluie. ¶ *v.t*, mouiller; imbiber; humecter; arroser.

whack, *n*, coup, *m.* ¶ *v.t*, battre.

whale, *n*, baleine, *f.* ~*boat*, baleinière, *f.* ~*bone*, fanon de
baleine, *m*, baleine, *f.* ~ *calf*,
baleineau, *m.* **whaler**, *n*, baleinier, *m.*

wharf, *n*, quai, appontement, débarcadère, embarcadère, *m.*
wharfinger, *n*, propriétaire de
quai, *m.*

what, *pn*, *a*, *& ad*, quoi; qu'est-ce
qui; qu'est-ce que; que; quel,
quelle; ce qui; ce que, tant;
comment. ~ *a*, quel, quelle. ~
a relief! ouf! ~ *for?* pourquoi?
~ *people may say*, le qu'en-dira-
t-on. **whatever**, *pn. & a*, tout ce
qui; tout ce que; quelque . . .
qui; quelque . . . que; quelconque; quoi que; quel(le) que.

whatnot, *n*, étagère, *f.*

wheat, *n*, froment, blé, *m.* ~*en*,
a, de froment.

wheedle, *v.t*, cajoler, enjôler.

wheel, *n*, roue, *f*; volant; disque;
galet, *m*; roulette; (*emery, etc.*)
meule; (*helm*) barre; (*Mil.*) conversion, *f.* (*typewriter, etc.*) *print
~*, marguerite, *f. spare* ~, roue
de rechange, *f.* ~*barrow*,
brouette, *f.* ~*base*, écartement des

essieux, empattement, *m.*
~*chair*, fauteuil roulant, *m.* ¶ *v.t,*
rouler; (*v.i.*) (*birds*) tournoyer. ~-
wheeled, *a,* à . . . roues.

wheeze, *v.i,* siffler. **wheezy,** *a,*
sifflant; (*pers.*) poussif.

whelk, *n,* buccin, *m.*

when, *ad,* quand, lorsque; alors
que, après que. **whence,** *ad,* d'où.
whenever, *ad,* toutes les fois que.

where, *ad,* où; là où; à l'endroit
où. **whereabouts,** *ad,* où. *one's*
~, où on est. **whereas,** *ad,* tandis que, au lieu que; attendu que,
vu que. **whereat,** *ad,* sur quoi.
whereby, *ad,* par où, par lequel.
wherefore, *ad,* pourquoi. **where-
in,** *ad,* en quoi. **whereof,** *ad,*
dont. **where[up]on,** *ad,* sur quoi.
wherever, *ad,* partout où, où
que. *the* **wherewithal,** de quoi,
les moyens, *m.pl.*

wherry, *n,* bachot, *m.* ~**man,** ba-
choteur, *m.*

whet, *n,* stimulant, *m.* ¶ *v.t,* (*tools*)
repasser, aiguiser; (*appetite*) aiguiser, stimuler. ~*stone,* pierre
à aiguiser, *f.*

whether, *c,* soit; soit que; que; si.

whey, *n,* petit-lait, *m.*

which, *pn. & a,* qui; que; lequel,
laquelle; ce qui; ce que; ce dont;
quel, quelle. ~ *way?* par où?
whichever, *pn,* n'importe quel,
n'importe quelle.

whiff, *n,* bouffée, *f.*

while, *n,* temps, *m. it is worth* ~,
cela vaut la peine. **while** &
whilst, *c,* tandis que, pendant
que; [tout] en. *while away,*
(faire) passer; charmer, tromper.

whim, *n,* caprice, *m,* fantaisie;
boutade, *f;* (*Mach.*) treuil, cabestan, *m.*

whimper, *v.i,* pleurnicher, piauler, geindre. ~**er,** *n,* pleureur,
euse, pleurard, e.

whimsical†, *a,* capricieux, fantasque, lunatique.

whin, *n,* ajonc, genêt épineux, *m.*

whine, *v.i,* pleurnicher, piauler,
geindre.

whinny, *n,* hennissement, *m.* ¶
v.i, hennir.

whip, *n,* fouet, *m.* ~*cord,* [fil de]
fouet, *m.* ~ *hand* (*fig.*), dessus,
m. ¶ *v.t. & i,* fouetter; toucher.
whipper-in, *n,* piqueur, *m.*
whipper-snapper, *n,* moucheron,
freluquet, *m.* **whipping,** *n,* fusti-

gation, *f,* le fouet; (*Need.*)
point roulé, *m.* ~ *top,* sabot, *m.*

whir, *v.i,* siffler, ronfler.

whirl, *n,* ébullition, *f;* tourbillon,
m. ¶ *v.i,* tournoyer, tourbillonner. ~*pool,* tourbillon, *m.* ~-
wind, tourbillon, *m.* **whirligig,**
n, pirouette, *f;* carrousel, *m.*

whisk, *n,* (*brush, broom*) balayette, *f,* houssoir, *m;* (*egg*)
fouet, *m.* ¶ *v.t,* (*dust*) épousseter;
(*eggs*) fouetter.

whiskers, *n.pl,* favoris, *m.pl;*
(*cat*) moustache, *f.*

whiskey, *n,* whisky, *m.*

whisper, *n,* chuchotement; murmure, *m.* ¶ *v.i. & t,* chuchoter;
murmurer. ~**er,** *n,* chuchoteur,
euse. ~**ing,** *n,* chuchoterie, *f.* ~
gallery, galerie à écho, *f.*

whist (*cards*) *n,* whist, *m.*

whistle, *n,* sifflet; coup de sifflet,
m. ¶ *v.t. & i,* siffler; (*wind*) mugir. **whistler,** *n,* siffleur, euse.

whit, *n,* iota, *m.*

white, *a,* blanc. ~ *ant,* fourmi
blanche, *f,* termite, *m.* ~*bait,*
blanchaille, *f.* ~*caps,* moutons,
m.pl. ~ *heat,* incandescence, *f.*
~*hot,* chauffé à blanc, incandescent. ~ *lead,* blanc de céruse,
m, céruse, *f.* ~ *lie,* mensonge
pieux, *m.* officieux, *m.* ~*wash,*
n, blanc de chaux, *m;* (*v.t.*)
blanchir à la chaux; (*fig.*) blanchir. ¶ *n,* (*color, man*) blanc,
m; (*ball, woman*) blanche, *f.* ~
of egg, blanc d'œuf, *m,* glaire,
f. ~ *sale,* vente de blanc, *f.*
white[n], *v.t,* blanchir. **whiteness,** *n,* blancheur, *f.*

whither, *ad,* où.

whiting, *n,* blanc de craie; (*fish*)
merlan, *m.*

whitish, *a,* blanchâtre.

Whitsuntide, *n,* la Pentecôte.
Whit Sunday, dimanche de la
Pentecôte, *m.*

whittle, *v.t,* taillader.

whiz, *n,* sifflement, *m.* ¶ *v.i,* siffler.

who, *pn,* qui. ~ *goes there?* qui
vive?

whoa, *i,* oé! ohé!

whoever, *pn,* quiconque.

whole, *a,* tout; entier; intégral; intact; complet; total; plein. ¶ *n,*
tout, *m,* totalité, intégralité, *f.*
[up]on the ~, à tout prendre,
en somme. **wholesale,** *a,* en
masse. ~ [*trade*], [commerce de
(*ou* en)] gros; (*small*) demi-

gros, *m.* **wholesome†**, *a,* sain; salubre; salutaire. **wholly,** *ad,* entièrement; intégralement; complètement; en totalité.

whom, *pn,* que; qui; lequel, laquelle, lesquels, lesquelles. **whomsoever,** *pn,* quiconque.

whoop, *n,* huée, *f,* cri, *m.* ¶ *v.i,* huer, crier. **~ing cough,** coqueluche, *f.*

whore, *n,* prostituée, *f.*

whorl, *n,* verticille, *m,* spire, *f.*

whortleberry, *n,* airelle, myrtille, *f.*

whose, *pn,* dont; de qui; à qui? **whosoever,** *pn,* quiconque.

why, *ad. & n,* pourquoi, *ad, c, & m.* ¶ *i,* mais!, comment!

wick, *n,* mèche, *f.*

wicked†, *a,* méchant, mauvais. **~ness,** *n,* méchanceté, *f.*

wicker, *n,* osier, *m.* ~ **cradle,** moïse, *m.* **~work,** vannerie, *f.* ¶ *v.t,* clisser.

wicket, *n,* guichet; (*croquet*) arceau, *m.*

wide, *a,* large; vaste; grand; ample; étendu; (*Meas.*) large de, de largeur. **to be ~ awake,** être tout(e) éveillé(e). **~-awake,** *n,* éveillé, dégourdi, déluré, en éveil. ~ **of the mark,** loin de compte. **~spread,** [largement] répandu. **~ly,** *ad,* largement. **widen,** *v.t,* [r]élargir; étendre. **in a wider sense,** par extension.

widgeon, *n,* [canard] siffleur, *m.*

widow, *n,* veuve, *f.* **the ~'s mite,** le denier de la v. ~'**s weeds,** deuil de v., *m.* **~ed,** *p.p,* veuf. **~er,** *n,* veuf, *m.* **~hood,** *n,* veuvage, *m,* viduité, *f.*

width, *n,* largeur; (*cloth*) largeur, laize, *f,* lé, *m.*

wield, *v.t,* manier; (*power*) exercer.

wife, *n,* femme; épouse, *f.*

wig, *n,* perruque, *f.* ~ **maker,** perruquier, *m.*

wight, *n,* hère, *m.*

wild, *a,* sauvage; farouche; inculte; fou; endiablé; égaré, hagard. ~ **beast,** bête féroce, b. sauvage, *f,* (*pl.*) bêtes fauves, *f.pl,* fauves, *m.pl.* ~ **boar,** sanglier, (*young*) marcassin, *m.* ~ **cherry,** merise, *f;* (*tree*) merisier, *m.* ~ **flowers,** fleurs des bois, f—s des champs, f—s des prés, f—s sauvages, *f.pl.* ~ **goose chase,** folle entreprise, *f.* **to sow one's**

~ **oats,** jeter sa gourme, faire ses farces. ~ **rabbit,** lapin de garenne, *m.* ~ **rose,** églantine, rose de chien, *f;* (*bush*) rosier sauvage, églantier, *m.* **wild & wilderness,** *n,* lieu sauvage, *m,* solitude, *f,* désert, *m.* **~ly,** *ad,* d'un air effaré; follement. **~ness,** *n,* état sauvage; égarement, *m.*

wile & wiliness, *n,* ruse, astuce, (*pl.*) finasserie, *f.*

wilful, *a,* volontaire, intentionnel. ~ **misrepresentation,** dol, *m.* ~ **murder,** homicide volontaire, assassinat, *m.* **~ly,** *ad,* volontairement; avec préméditation. **~ness,** *n,* obstination, *f.*

will, *n,* volonté; intention, *f;* vouloir; gré; plaisir; testament, *m.* ¶ *v.t, regular & ir,* vouloir; léguer par [son] testament; (*v.aux, is expressed in Fr. by future tense. Also by* will). **willing,** *a,* volontaire, spontané; (*hands*) de volontaires; complaisant. **to be ~,** vouloir [bien]. **~ly,** *ad,* volontiers. **~ness,** *n,* bonne volonté, complaisance, *f.*

will-o'-the-wisp, *n,* feu follet, ardent, *m.*

willow, *n,* saule, *m.* ~ **plantation,** saulaie, saussaie, *f.*

willynilly, *ad,* bon gré, mal gré.

wilt, *v.t,* flétrir; (*v.i.*) se f., se faner, s'étioler.

wily, *a,* rusé, finaud, astucieux.

wimple, *n,* guimpe, *f.*

win, *n,* victoire, *f.* ¶ *v.t.ir,* gagner; concilier; acquérir; (*prize*) remporter; valoir.

wince, *v.i,* sourciller; cligner; tiquer; tressaillir.

winch, *n,* moulinet; treuil, *m;* manivelle, *f.*

wind, *n,* vent, *m;* haleine; flatuosité, *f.* **~bag,** moulin à paroles, *m.* **~fall,** fruit tombé, *m;* [bonne] aubaine, chapechute, *f.* **~mill,** moulin à vent, *m.* **~pipe,** trachéeartère, *f.* ~ **row,** andain, *m.* **~shield,** pare-brise, *m.* **~shield wiper,** essuie-glace, *m.* **to get ~ of,** éventer. **second ~,** second souffle, *m.* ¶ *v.t,* essouffler.

wind, *v.t.ir,* enrouler, dévider, bobiner, pelotonner; (*Min.*) [re]monter; (*v.i.*) serpenter, tourner. ~ **up,** [re]monter; terminer; liquider. **~ing,** *a,* tournant; sinueux, anfractueux, tortueux.

¶ *n,* détour, *m,* sinuosité, *f,* lacet, méandre, *m.* ~ *sheet,* linceul, suaire, *m.* **windlass,** *n,* treuil, *m.*

window, *n,* fenêtre, *f;* (*pl. col.*) fenêtrage, vitrage, *m;* (*casement*) croisée, *f;* (*leaded*) vitrail, *m;* (*carriage*) glace; (*shop*) vitrine, devanture, montre, *f,* étalage, *m.* ~ *box,* jardin de fenêtre, *m.* ~ *dresser,* étalagiste, *m,f.* ~ *enve-lope,* enveloppe à fenêtre, e. à panneau, *f.* ~ *glass,* verre à vitres, *m.* ~*pane,* vitre, *f.* ~*shop-ping,* lèche-vitrines, *m.* ~*sill,* appui de fenêtre, *m.* rear ~, lu-nette arrière, *f.*

windward, *n,* coté du vent, *m;* (*a.*) au vent. W~ *Islands,* îles du Vent, *f.pl.* **windy,** *a,* venteux; (*day*) de grand vent. to be ~, ven-ter.

wine, *n,* vin, *m;* liqueur, *f.* ~ *glass,* verre à vin, *m.* ~ *grapes,* raisin de vigne, *m.* ~ *grower,* vig-neron, ne, viticulteur, *m.* ~ *growing,* *a,* vinicole, viticole. ~ *list,* carte des vins, *f.* ~ *of the country,* vin du cru, *m.* ~ *waiter,* sommelier, *m. table* ~, vin ordi-naire, *m.*

wing, *n,* aile, *f;* vol, essor, *m;* (*pl, Theat.*) coulisses, *f.pl.* ~ *collar,* faux col cassé, *m.* ~ *nut,* écrou à oreilles, [é.] papillon, *m.* ~ *spread,* ~ *span,* envergure, *f.* ~*ed,* *a,* ailé. ~ *creature,* volatile, *m.*

wink, *n,* clin d'œil, signe des yeux, clignement, *m.* ¶ *v.i,* cligner.

winkle (*Crust.*) *n,* bigorneau, *m.*

winner, *n,* gagnant, e; vainqueur, *m.* **winning,** *a,* gagnant; (*num-ber*) sortant; attrayant, attachant.

winnow, *v.t,* vanner. ~**ing,** *n,* vannage, *m.*

winsome, *a,* agréable.

winter, *n,* hiver, *m.* ¶ *v.i. & t,* hi-verner. ¶ ~, *att. &* **wintry,** *a,* d' hiver, hivernal, hiémal.

wipe, *n,* coup de chiffon, de mou-choir; (*cinema*) volet, *m.* ~ [up], *v.t,* essuyer; torcher; (*joint*) ébar-ber. ~ *off* (debt), apurer. ~ *out,* effacer.

wire, *n,* fil; câble, *m;* dépêche [té-légraphique] *f.* ~ *cutter,* bec-de-corbeau, *m.* ~ *entanglement,* ré-seau de fils de fer, *m.* ~ *fence,*

clôture en fil de fer, *f.* ~*haired* (dog), au poil rude. ~ *netting,* treillis métallique, grillage, *m.* ~ *puller,* intrigant, *m.* ~ *rope,* câble métallique, *m.* ¶ *v.t,* (*house,* Elec.) poser des fils dans; télégra-phier.

wisdom, *n,* sagesse; prudence, *f.* ~ *tooth,* dent de sagesse, *f.* **wise**†, *a,* sage. ~*acre,* sot qui se donne un air de sage, *m. the Three W~ Men,* les trois rois mages.

wish, *n,* désir; gré; souhait; vœu, *m.* ¶ *v.t. & i,* désirer; vouloir; souhaiter. ~ *someone many hap-py returns* [*of the day*], souhaiter la [ou une bonne] fête à quel-qu'un. ~*ful,* *a,* désireux. ~*bone,* lunette, fourchette, *f.* ~*ing cap,* bonnet magique, *m.*

wisp, *n,* bouchon, *m,* touffe, *f.*

wistaria, *n,* glycine, *f.*

wistful, *a,* désenchanté, pensif, de regret. ~*ly,* *ad,* avec envie.

wit, *n,* esprit; sel; (*pers.*) bel esprit, diseur de bons mots, *m;* (*pl.*) in-telligence, *f,* esprit, *m;* tête, *f. at one's* ~*s' end,* au bout de son rouleau, aux abois. *to lose one's* ~*s,* perdre la tête. ~*less,* *a,* sans esprit.

witch, *n,* sorcière, *f.* ~*craft,* sor-cellerie, *f,* sortilège, *m.* ~ *doctor,* sorcier guérisseur, *m.* ~ *hazel,* hamamelis, *m.* ~*hunt,* chasse aux sorcières, *f.* ~*ery,* *n,* magie, fascination, *f.*

with, *pr,* avec; à coups de; à; par; de; en; dans; sous; auprès de.

withdraw, *v.t.ir,* retirer; se désis-ter de; (*v.i.*) se retirer; se can-tonner; (*candidature*) se désister. ~*al,* *n,* retrait, *m;* retraite, *f;* dé-sistement, *m.*

wither, *v.t,* dessécher; (*v.i.*) se dessécher, dépérir. ~*ing* (*look*) *a,* foudroyant.

withers, *n.pl,* garrot, *m.*

withhold, *v.t.ir,* retenir.

within, *pr,* dans; en; en dedans de; là-dedans; à; sous. ~ *call,* à portée de la voix. *from* ~, de dedans.

without, *pr,* sans; sans que; en dehors de; là-dehors. *from* ~, de dehors. *to do* ~, se passer de.

withstand, *v.t.ir,* résister à.

witness, *n,* témoin; témoignage, *m;* foi, *f.* ~*box,* barre des té-moins, *f.* ~ *for the defense,* témoin à décharge. ~ *for the prosecution*, t. à charge. ¶ *v.t*, être témoin de; assister à; attester; signer à; certifier.

witticism, *n*, trait d'esprit, jeu d'esprit, *m*.

wittingly, *ad*, sciemment, à bon escient.

witty†, *a*, plein d'esprit; spirituel.

wizard, *n*, sorcier, magicien, *m*. **~ry**, *n*, magie, *f*.

wizened, *a*, ratatiné.

wo, *i*, oé!, ohé!

wobble, *v.i*, brimbaler; vaciller.

woe, *n*, douleur, *f*; malheur, *m*. **~begone** or **~ful†**, *a*, triste; malheureux; lamentable.

wolf, *n*, loup, *m*, louve, *f*. ~ *cub* (*Zool.*) louveteau, *m*. **~sbane**, napel, *m*.

wolfram, *n*, wolfram, *m*.

woman, *n*, femme, *f*. ~ *doctor*, femme médecin, f. docteur, *f*. ~ *driver*, chauffeuse, *f*. ~ *hater*, misogyne, *m*. ~ *of fashion*, élégante, *f*. **~ish**, *a*, efféminé; (*voice*) féminine. **~ly**, *a*, de femme.

womb, *n*, ventre, sein, flanc, *m*.

wonder, *n*, étonnement, *m*; merveille, *f*; prodige, *m*. ¶ *v.i*, s'étonner (*at* = de); se demander (*why* = pourquoi). **~ful†**, *a*, étonnant; merveilleux; admirable.

wont, *n*, coutume, *f*, ordinaire, *m*. **~ed**, *a*, habituel.

woo, *v.t*, faire la cour à.

wood, *n*, bois, *m*. *in the* ~ (*wine*), en cercles. **~bine**, chèvrefeuille, *m*. ~ *carver*, sculpteur sur bois, *m*. **~cock**, bécasse, *f*. **~cut**, gravure sur bois, *f*. **~land**, pays de bois, *m*; (*att.*) des bois; sylvestre. ~ *louse*, cloporte, *m*. **~man**, bûcheron, *m*. ~ *nymph*, nymphe bocagère, *f*. ~ *owl*, chat-huant, *m*, hulotte, *f*. **~pecker**, pic, *m*. ~ *pigeon*, [pigeon] ramier, *m*, palombe, *f*. **~shed**, bûcher, *m*. *the* **~**[*winds*], les bois, *m.pl*. **~work**, menuiserie; boiserie, *f*. **~worker**, artisan en bois, *m*. **~ed**, *a*, boisé, fourré. **~en**, *a*, de bois, en b. **~y**, *a*, ligneux.

wooer, *n*, prétendant, soupirant, poursuivant, *m*.

woof, *n*, trame, *f*.

wool, *n*, laine, *f*; (*animal's coat*) pelage, *m*. **woolen**, *a*, de laine; lainier. ~ *goods* or **~s**, *n.pl*, lainage, *m. oft. pl.* ~ *manufacturer*,

lainier, *m*. ~ *mill*, lainerie, *f*. ~ *trade*, industrie lainière, lainerie, *f*. **woolly**, *a*, laineux; (*fruit, style*) cotonneux; (*hair*) crépus; (*outline, sound*) flou.

word, *n*, mot, *m*; parole, *f*; terme, *m*. *by* ~ *of mouth*, de vive voix. *the Word* (*Theol.*), le Verbe. ~ *processing*, traitement de text, *m*. ¶ *v.t*, libeller, concevoir. **wordiness**, *n*, verbosité, *f*. **wording**, *n*, libellé, *m*, termes, *m.pl*. **wordy**, *a*, verbeux.

work, *n*, travail, *m*, *oft. pl*; fonctionnement; ouvrage; *m*; besogne; œuvre, *f*; (*social*) œuvres, *f.pl*; (*of art*) œuvre, *f*, objet; (*col. pl, of an artist*) œuvre, *m*; (*pl.*) rouage, *m. oft. pl*, mécanisme, mouvement, *m*; (*pl. & s.*) usine, fabrique, *f*; atelier, *m*. ~ *bag*, sac à ouvrage, *m*. ~ *box*, nécessaire à o., *m*. **~man, ~woman**, ouvrier, ère. **~manlike**, en bon ouvrier. **~manship**, main-d'œuvre, façon, facture, *f*, travail, *m*. **~men's compensation insurance**, assurance contre les accidents du travail, *f*. **~room**, atelier; (*convent*) ouvroir, *m*. **~shop**, atelier, *m*. ¶ *v.t*, travailler; faire t.; manœuvrer; opérer; actionner; exploiter; ouvrer; faire; se f.; (*v.i.*) travailler; fonctionner; jouer; marcher; aller; rouler; agir; fermenter. ~ *hard*, travailler à force, piocher. ~ *loose*, prendre du jeu. ~ *out*, *v.t*, élaborer; épuiser; décompter; (*v.i.*) se chiffrer. ~ *up*, travailler; malaxer. **~able**, *a*, exécutable; exploitable. **~er**, *n*, travailleur, euse; ouvrier, ère. *blue-collar* ~, col-bleu, *m*. *white-collar* ~, col-blanc, *m*. ~ *bee*, abeille ouvrière, *f*. **~ing**, *n*, travail, *m*; exploitation, *f*; fonctionnement, *m*; manœuvre; marche, *f*; jeu, *m*. ~ *capital*, capital de roulement, fonds de r., *m*. ~ *class*, classe ouvrière, c. laborieuse, *f*. ~ *clothes*, habits de fatigue, *m.pl*. ~ *day*, jour ouvrable, *m*; journée de travail, *f*. ~ *hours*, heures de travail, *f.pl*.

world, *n*, monde; siècle, *m*. ~ [-*wide*] *a*, mondial, universel. *Third W*~, tiers monde, *m*. **worldliness**, *n*, mondanité, *f*. **worldling**, *n*. &

worldly, *a,* mondain, e. *all one's worldly goods,* tout son [saint-] frusquin.

worm, *n,* ver; *(screw)* filet, *m;* *(corkscrew)* mèche; *(Mach.)* vis sans fin, *f;* *(still)* serpentin, *m.* **~-eaten,** rongé des vers, vermoulu. ~ *fishing,* pêche au ver, *f.* ¶ *v.i,* *(secret)* soutirer; se faufiler; se tortiller. **~y,** *a,* véreux.

worry, *n,* ennui, tourment, tracas, souci, *m.* ¶ *v.t,* ennuyer, tourmenter, tracasser, harceler; *(of dog)* piller.

worse, *a,* pire; plus mauvais; plus mal. *(machine)* the ~ *for wear,* patraque, *f.* & *a.* ¶ *ad,* pis. *grow* ~, s'empirer. *make* ~, empirer.

worship, *n,* culte, *m;* adoration, *f;* office, *m.* ¶ *v.t.* & *i,* *(God, gods)* adorer; *(saints, relics)* vénérer. **worshipper,** *n,* adorateur, trice.

worst, *a,* pire, plus mauvais. ¶ *ad,* pis. ¶ *n,* pis, pire, *m. at the ~,* au pis aller. ¶ *v.t,* vaincre.

worsted, *n,* laine peignée, estame, *f.*

wort, *n,* *(of beer)* moût, *m;* *(plant)* herbe, *f.*

worth, *n,* valeur, *f;* prix, *m;* mérite, *m;* *(money's)* pour. ¶ *a,* qui mérite; digne de. *to be ~,* valoir; mériter. **~less,** *a,* sans valeur; misérable; *(check)* sans provision. **~lessness,** *n,* vileté, *f.* **~y†,** *a,* digne.

would, *v.aux, is expressed in Fr. by conditional mood. Also by* vouloir. ~ *to heaven that . . ,* plût au ciel que . . . **~-be,** *a,* soidisant, *inv,* prétendu, e.

wound, *n,* blessure; plaie, *f.* ¶ *v.t,* blesser. *the ~ed,* les blessés, *m.pl.*

wrangle, *n,* querelle, *f.* ¶ *v.i,* se quereller, se disputer. **wrangling,** *n,* tiraillement, *m.*

wrap, *n,* manteau; châle, *m.* ~ *[up],* *v.t,* envelopper; enrouler; entortiller; ployer. **~[oneself]** *up,* s'empaqueter, se couvrir. **wrapper,** *n,* enveloppe; chemise; toilette; *(newspaper)* bande; *(cigar)* robe, *f.* ~ *wrapping paper,* papier d'emballage, *m.*

wrath, *n,* courroux, *m,* fureur, *f.* **~ful,** *a,* courroucé.

wreak, *v.t,* tirer, prendre *(vengeance).*

wreath, *n,* guirlande, couronne; couronne mortuaire, *f; (smoke)* panache, *m.* **wreathe,** *v.t,* enguirlander; ceindre.

wreck, *n,* naufrage; sinistre; délabrement, *m.* ~**[age],** *n,* débris, *m.pl,* épave, *f,* bris, *m.* **wreck,** *v.t,* causer le naufrage de; saboter; bouleverser. *to be ~ed,* faire naufrage.

wren, *n,* roitelet, *m.*

wrench, *n,* *(Med.)* entorse, foulure; *(twist)* pesée; *(tool)* clef, *f,* tourne-à-gauche; *(fig.)* crève-cœur, *m.* ¶ *v.t,* fouler, bistourner. ~ *open,* forcer.

wrest, *v.t,* tordre; arracher.

wrestle, *v.i,* lutter. **wrestler,** *n,* lutteur, catcheur, *m.* **wrestling,** *n,* lutte, *f.* ~ *match,* match de lutte, *m.*

wretch, *n,* malheureux, euse, misérable, *m.f,* hère, *m.* **~ed,** *a,* malheureux, misérable; pitoyable, méchant, piètre. **~edness,** *n,* misère, *f.*

wriggle, *v.i,* s'agiter, frétiller, se débattre.

wring, *v.t.ir,* tordre; étreindre; serrer; arracher; extorquer; *(linen)* essorer. **~er,** *n,* essoreuse, *f.* **~ing wet,** mouillé à tordre.

wrinkle, *n,* ride, *f.* pli, sillon; *(tip)* tuyau, *m.* ¶ *v.t,* rider, sillonner, plisser. **~proof,** *a,* infroissable.

wrist, *n,* poignet, *m.* **~band,** poignet, *m,* brisure, *f.* ~ *strap,* bracelet de force, *m.* **~watch,** montre-bracelet, *f.*

writ, *n,* exploit; mandat, *m;* assignation, *f.*

write, *v.t.* & *i. ir,* écrire; inscrire; rédiger. ~ *back,* répondre; *(Bkkpg)* contrepasser. ~ *for (journal),* écrire dans, collaborer à. ~ *off,* amortir. ~ *out,* tracer; rédiger; formuler. **writer,** *n,* écrivain; auteur, *m.*

writhe, *v.i,* se tordre, se tortiller.

writing, *n,* écriture, *f;* écrit, *m;* inscription, *f. in ~,* par écrit. ~ *materials,* de quoi écrire. ~ *pad,* bloc-notes, bloc de correspondance, *m.* **written,** *p.p,* par écrit, manuscrit.

wrong, *a,* faux; mauvais; mal; erroné; inexact. ~ *font,* lettre d'un autre œil, *f.* ~ *side* (fabric), envers, dessous, *m.* ~ *side up,*

sens dessus dessous. *the* ~ *way,
ad,* à rebours; à contresens; à
contre-poil, à rebrousse-poil. *they
are* ~, ils ont tort. ¶ *ad,* mal; de
travers. ¶ *n,* mal; tort, préjudice,
m. ¶ *v.t,* faire [du] tort à, léser,
maltraiter, nuire à. ~**ful**†, *a,* injuste. ~**ly,** *ad,* à tort; à faux.

wrought iron, fer [forgé] *m.*

wry, *a,* (*neck*) tors; (*smile*) pincé.
~ *face,* grimace, *f.* ~*neck* (bird),
torcol, *m.* ~**ness,** *n,* guingois, *m.*

X

xenophobia, *n,* xénophobie, *f.*
Xmas, *abb.* See *Christmas.*
Xrays, *n.pl,* rayons X, *m.pl. to
x-ray,* radiographier.
xylonite, *n,* celluloïd, *m.*
xylophone, *n,* xylophone, *m.*

Y

yacht, *n,* yacht, *m.* ~**ing,** *n,* promenade en yacht, *f.*
yam, *n,* igname, *f.*
yap, *v.i,* glapir, japper.
yard, *n,* cour, *f;* parc, chantier,
m; (*Naut.*) vergue, *f;* yard, *f;
Meas.* = 0.914399 meter. ~ *arm,*
bout de vergue, *m.*
yarn, *n,* (*thread*) fil, *m;* (*tale*) histoire, *f.*
yaw, *n,* embardée, *f.* ¶ *v.i,* faire
une e.; (*Avn.*) gouverner.
yawl, *n,* yole, *f.*
yawn, *v.i,* bâiller. ~**ing,** *a,* béant.
ye, *pn,* vous.
year, *n,* année, *f;* an; (*Fin.*) exercice, *m.* ~*book,* annuaire, *m.* ~*s
of discretion,* l'âge de raison, *m.
leap* ~, année bissextile, *f.* ~**ly,**
a, annuel; (*ad.*) annuellement.
yearn for, soupirer après. **yearning,** *n,* aspiration, *f;* élancements,
m.pl.
yeast, *n,* levure, *f,* levain, *m.*
yell, *n,* hurlement, *m.* ¶ *v.i,* hurler.
yellow, *a. & n,* jaune, *a. & m. Y~
Sea,* mer Jaune, *f.* ¶ *v.t. & i,*
jaunir. ~**ish,** *a,* jaunâtre.
yelp, *v.i,* glapir, japper.
yeoman, *n,* (*Naut.*) commis aux
écritures.
yes, *particle,* oui; si. ¶ *n,* oui, *m.*
yesterday, *n,* hier, *m. yesteryear,* antan, *m.*

yet, *c,* cependant, toutefois, pourtant. ¶ *ad,* encore.
yew (tree), *n,* if, *m.*
yield, *n,* rendement, rapport, *m.*
¶ *v.t,* rendre, rapporter; (*v.i.*)
céder; obéir; succomber.
yodel, *v.i,* iouler, yodler. ¶ *n,*
ioulement, *m.* yodler, *n,* iouleur,
m.
yoga, *n,* yoga, *m.* yogi, *n,* yogi, *m.*
yogurt, *n,* yaourt, *m.*
yoke, *n,* joug, *m;* paire, couple, *f,*
attelage, *m;* (*for pail*) palanche, *f;*
(*dress*) empiècement, *m,* épaulette, *f.* ~ *elm,* charme, *m.* ¶ *v.t,*
atteler.
yokel, *n,* rustre, *m.*
yolk, *n,* jaune (d'œuf) *m.*
yonder, *a,* ce . . . -là. ¶ *ad,* là-bas.
yore (of), d'autrefois, jadis.
you, *pn,* vous, tu; on.
young, *a,* jeune; petit. ~ *lady,*
demoiselle, jeune personne, *f.* ~
one, petit, e. ¶ (*animals*) *n,*
petits, *m.pl.* ~*er, a,* [plus] jeune,
cadet. ~ *brother, sister,* puîné,
e. *to make look* ~, rajeunir.
~**ster,** *n,* gamin, moutard, *m,*
môme, *m,f.*
your, *a,* votre, vos; ton, ta, tes.
yours, *pn. & your own,* le vôtre,
la vôtre, les vôtres; à vous; de
vous. ~ *affectionately,* votre
affectionné, e. ~ *truly,* agréez
(*ou* recevez), monsieur, mes
salutations empressées. **yourself,**
yourselves, *pn,* vous-même, vous-
mêmes; vous.
youth, *n,* jeunesse; adolescence, *f;*
jeune homme adolescent, *m.*
~**ful**†, *a,* jeune; juvénile; de
jeunesse.
Yugoslav, *n,* Yougoslave, *m. & f.*
Yugoslavia, *n,* la Yougoslavie.
yule[**tide**], *n,* Noël, *m,* la [fête de]
Noël. *yule log,* bûche de Noël, *f.*

Z

zeal, *n,* zèle, *m.* **zealot,** *n,* zélateur,
trice. **zealous,** *a,* zélé, empressé.
~**ly,** *ad,* avec zèle.
zebra, *n,* zèbre, *m.*
zenith, *n,* zénith; (*fig.*) zénith,
faîte, apogée, *m.*
zephyr, *n,* zéphyr, *m.*
zeppelin, *n,* zeppelin, *m.*
zero, *n,* zéro, *m.* ~ *hour,* heure
H, *f.*

zest, *n,* piquant, *m;* ardeur, *f.*
zigzag, *n,* zigzag, *m.* ¶ *v.i,* aller en zigzag.
zinc, *n,* zinç, *m.* ~ *worker,* zingueur, *m.* **zincography,** *n,* zincogravure, *f.*
Zion, *n,* Sion, *f.* ~**ism,** *n,* sionism *m.* ~**ist,** *a.* & *n,* sioniste.
zipper, *n,* fermeture éclair, *f.*
zircon, *n,* zircon, *m.*
zither, *n,* cithare, *f.*

zodiac, *n,* zodiaque, *m.* ~**al,** *a,* zodiacal.
zone, *n,* zone, *f.*
zoo, *n,* zoo, jardin zoologique, *m.*
zoological, *a,* zoologique. **zoologist,** *n,* zoologiste, *m,f.* **zoology,** *n,* zoologie, *f.*
zoom, *v.i,* bourdonner, vrombir.
Zulu, *a,* zoulou. ¶ *n,* Zoulou, *m,f.*
Zuyder Zee (the), le Zuyderzée.

APPENDICES

TREACHEROUS LOOK-ALIKES

The list of words given below is intended to flag some of the pitfalls that can cause trouble for anyone who assumes too close a relation between English and French. Many of the words are cognates, but some are not, and so we have preferred to call them all "look-alikes." Occasionally, an English word will have the same meaning as its French cognate, but only in a restricted sense. For example, the French *une audience* is best translated by "a hearing," but it can be translated by "an audience" if by that we mean "a hearing."

In the lefthand column the French word is given in italics and its most usual translation listed below in roman. In the righthand column its English look-alike is given and below it, in italics, its most usual French translation. Needless to say, not all possible translations are covered.

French / English	English / French	French / English	English / French
abuser to deceive to misguide to misuse	to abuse *injurier* *dénigrer*	*audience* hearing	audience (people) *auditoire* *assistance*
actuel present existent	actual (real) *véritable* *réel*	*auditeur* listener hearer	auditor *vérificateur de* *comptes*
advertisement warning	advertisement *réclame* *announce*	*bail* lease	bail *caution*
affronter to confront	to affront *insulter*	*banquette* bench	banquet *banquet*
alienation insanity transfer	alienation *brouille* *éloignement*	*baraque* shack booth	barrack *caserne*
aliéné lunatic	alien *étranger*	*blesser* to wound	to bless *bénir*
annonceur advertiser	announcer *speaker*	*blindé* armored	blinded *aveuglé*
apparat pomp show	apparatus *appareil*	*blouse* smock overall	blouse *chemisier*
appareil apparatus	apparel *vêtements*	*bosse* bump hump	boss *patron*
appointer to put on salary to sharpen to a point	to appoint *nommer*	*bribe* morsel	bribe *un pot de vin*
arguer to indicate to infer	to argue *argumenter*	*cake* fruitcake	cake *gâteau*
asparagus asparagus-fern	asparagus *asperge*	*caméra* movie camera	camera *appareil*
attendre to await to expect	to attend *assister à*	*candeur* credulousness naïveté	candor *franchise*
		cantine PX or post exchange	canteen *bidon de soldat*

742

French / English	English / French
capon	capon
coward	*chapon*
tattletale	
car	car
intercity bus	*voiture* / *auto*
cargo	cargo
cargo ship	*cargaison*
caution	caution
guarantee	*précaution*
bail	
chance	chance
luck	*hasard* / *sort*
chandelier	chandelier
candlestick	*lustre*
candlemaker	
chipie	chippy
bad-tempered woman	*femme de mœurs faciles*
clairvoyant	clairvoyant
perspicacious	*voyant*
combine	combine
scheme	*corporation*
racket	*trust*
complainte	complaint
ballad, lay	*plainte*
concussion	concussion
misappropriation	*commotion cérébrale*
extortion	
contrôler	to control
to check	*maîtriser*
to supervise	
corsage	corsage
blouse	*garniture de costume*
crucial	crucial
crosslike	*critique*
cure	cure
treatment	*guérison* / *remède*
débonnaire	debonair
meek	*gai*
easy-going	*élégant*
déception	deception (trickery)
disappointment	*tromperie*

French / English	English / French
défendeur	defender
defendant	*défenseur*
défiance	defiance
distrust	*défi*
déjection	dejection
evacuation (bowels)	*abattement*
délayer	to delay
to dilute	*tarder*
to drag out (speech)	*retarder*
demander	to demand
to request	*exiger*
to ask	
dépression	depression (economic)
dejection	*krach* / *récession*
déranger	to derange (make insane)
to disturb	*détraquer*
dérider	to deride
to smoothe	*railler*
to unwrinkle	*se moquer de*
destitué	destitute
removed from office	*misérable* / *dépourvu*
déterrer	to deter
to dig up	*décourager*
to unearth	
détonner	to detonate
to sing or play out of tune	*détoner*
dilapider	to become dilapidated
to waste	*détérior*
dissemblance	dissemblance
dissimilarity	*dissimulation*
droguerie	drugstore
housewares store	*pharmacie*
drugstore	drugstore
variety store	*pharmacie*
écrou	screw
bolt nut	*vis*
éditeur	editor
publisher	*rédacteur*

French English	English *French*	*French* English	English *French*
éduquer to bring up (children)	to educate (formally) *instruire*	*impotent* crippled helpless	impotent (sexual) *impuissant*
engin device	engine *moteur* *locomotive*	*improuver* to disapprove of	to improve *améliorer*
engrosser to make pregnant	to engross *absorber* *accaparer*	*incontrôlé* not verified	uncontrolled *effréné* *independant*
estampe print	stamp *timbre* *trépignement*	*ingénuité* ingenuousness	ingenuity *ingéniosité*
exténuer to exhaust to tire	to extenuate *atténuer* *diminuer*	*inhabité* uninhabited	inhabited *habité*
extravagant strange excessive	extravagant (money) *dépensier* *exorbitant*	*injurier* to insult to abuse to revile	to injure *blesser* *nuire à* *leser*
fabrique factory	fabric (cloth) *étoffe*	*journée* day day's pay	journey *voyage*
fade insipid	faded *fané*	*labourer* to plow	to labor *travailler* *peiner*
fastidieux tiresome	fastidious *difficile*	*laboureur* plowman	laborer *travailleur*
forgerie smithy	forgery *contrefaçon*	*large* broad generous	large *grand* *gros*
génial ingenious full of genius	genial *jovial* *cordial*	*librairie* bookstore	library *bibliothèque*
gentil nice	gentle *doux*	*licencier* to fire to disband	to license *autoriser* *breveter*
gourmander to scold	to gormandize *faire le glouton*	*location* renting hiring	location *emplacement* *situation*
grâcier to pardon	to grace *honorer* *embellir*	*luxure* lust	luxury *luxe*
gratification tip (money)	gratification *satisfaction*	*luxurieux* lustful sensual	luxurious *luxueux*
grossesse pregnancy	grossness *grossièreté*	*machin* thingamajig	machine *machine*
idiome language	idiom *idiotisme*	*magasin* store powder magazine	magazine *revue* *magazine*
idiotisme idiomatic expression	idiocy *idiotie*		
ignorer not to know	to ignore *faire semblant de ne pas voir*	*malicieux* mischievous naughty	malicious *malveillant* *méchant*

French / English	English / French	French / English	English / French
manéger to train (horse)	to manage *administer* *s'en tirer*	*prêtendre* to claim to intend	to pretend (simulate) *feindre* *faire semblant de*
marin sailor	marine *soldat de la marine*	*prévention* prejudice	prevention *empêchement*
ménagère housekeeper	manager *directeur*	*procureur* proxy attorney	procurer *entremetteur*
meurtrir to bruise	to murder *assassiner*	*propreté* cleanliness	property *biens* *propriété*
muser to dawdle to loiter	to muse *rêvasser*	*provençal* from Provence	provincial *provincial de province*
négociant merchant	negotiator *négociateur*	*prune* plum	prune *pruneau sec*
nouvelle short story	novel *roman*	*rafle* raid (police) clean sweep	raffle *tombola* *loterie*
office pantry	office *bureau*	*raisin* grape	raisin *raisin sec*
(le) pair peer equal	pair *(la) paire*	*récipient* receptacle vessel	recipient *celui qui reçoit*
pamphlet lampoon	pamphlet *brochure* *opuscule*	*rente* income	rent *loyer*
parents relatives— including mother & father	parents *le père et la mère*	*repli* fold recess	reply *réponse*
passer un examen to undergo (have) an examination	to pass an exam *être reçu*	*reporter* to carry back	to report *rapporter* *rendre compte de*
pétulant lively	petulant *grincheux*	*retenue* reserve discretion	retinue *suite*
phrase sentence	phrase *locution*	*retraiter* to pension off	to retreat *se retirer*
physicien physicist	physician *médecin*	*rude* rough hard	rude (behavior) *impoli*
piler to pound to grind	to pile *empiler* *entasser*	*saucière* gravy boat	saucer *soucoupe*
plain level flat	plain *simple* *sans charme*	*sentence* sentence (judicial)	sentence (grammar) *phrase*
portemanteau hat & coat stand	portmanteau *valise*	*sot* fool dolt	sot *ivrogne*

French	English	*French*	English
English	*French*	English	*French*
stoppage	stoppage	*vicieux*	vicious
darning	*arrêt*	depraved	*méchant*
mending	*obstruction*	defective	*haineux*
translation	translation	*vilain*	villain
transfer	(language)	bondsman	*scélérat*
removal	*traduction*	serf	
trépasser	to trespass	*zeste*	zest
to die	*empiéter sur*	peel (orange,	*piquant*
	s'introduire	lemon)	*saveur*
	sans droit		*verve*

FRENCH ALPHABET SOUP:
ABBREVIATIONS IN THE NEWS

A.C., Action Catholique.

A.C.F., Automobile Club de France.

A.C.P.G., Anciens Combattants et Prisoniers de Guerre (veterans association).

A.D.A.C., avion à décollage et atterissage courts (STOL: short takeoff and landing aircraft).

A.D.A.V., avion à décollage et atterissage verticaux (VTOL: vertical takeoff and landing aircraft).

A.d.S., Académie des Sciences.

A.E.L.E., Association Européenne de Libre-Échange (E.F.T.A.: European Free Trade Association).

A.F., allocations familiales (government family subsidy).

A.F.N.O.R., Association Française de Normalisation (French equivalent of A.N.S.I.: American National Standards Institute).

A.F.P., Agence France-Presse (news service, equivalent of Associated Press).

A.I.E.A., Agence Internationale de l'Énergie Atomique (I.A.E.A.: International Atomic Energy Association).

A.M., Arts et Métiers (university training for engineers).

A.P., Assistance Publique (government welfare administration).

A.S.L.V., assurance sur la vie (life insurance).

A.T., assurance contre les accidents du travail (workmen's compensation insurance).

B.D., bande dessinée (comic strip).

B.F., Banque de France (Bank of France).

B.N., Bibliothèque Nationale.

B.N.P., Banque Nationale de Paris.

B.Rh., Bas-Rhin.

Bx-A., Beaux-Arts.

c.-à-d., c'est-à-dire (that is to say).

C.A.P., certificat d'aptitude professionnelle (training certificate).

C.C.P., compte courant (chèque) postal (postal checking account).

C.-du-N., Côtes-du-Nord.

C.E.E., Communauté Économique Européenne (E.E.C.: European Economic Community).

C.E.N., Centre d'Études Nucléeaires (Center for Nuclear Studies).

C.E.P., Certificat d'Études Primaires (elementary school certificate).

C.G.T., Confédération Générale du Travail (France's largest labor confederation, Communist in orientation).

C.F.D.T., Confédération Française Démocratique du Travail (major rival of the C.G.T., it is Socialist in orientation).

C.N.P.F., Conseil National du Patronat Français (French employers' association known as the *Patronat*).

C.N.R.S., Centre National de la Recherche Scientifique.

C.R.F., Croix Rouge Française (French Red Cross).

C.R.S., Compagnies Républicaines de Sécurité (special riot police responsible for security).

D.C.A., défense contre avions (anti-aircraft defense).

D.E.U.G., Diplôme d'Études Universitaires Générales (certificate of study given after two years).

D.M., Docteur en Médecine (M.D.: Doctor of Medicine).

D.P., Défense Passive (C.D.: Civil Defense).

E.C.G., électrocardiogramme (EKG: electrocardiogram).

E.D.F., Électricité de France (nationalized in 1946).

E.N.A., École Nationale d'Administration (trains government civil service administrators; graduates known as *énarques*).

E.N.S., École Normale Supérieure (one of the Grandes Écoles; its graduates—*normaliens*—have dominated the intellectual life of France).

E.-U., États-Unis (U.S.: United States).

F.O., Force Ouvrière (a major labor union, reformist in orientation).

F.S.M, Fédération Syndical Internationale (W.F.T.U.: World Federation of Trade Unions).

F.M.I., Fonds Monétaire Internationale (I.M.F.: International Monetary Fund).

F.T.A., forces terrestre antiaériennes (anti-aircraft defense forces).

Gar., Garonne.

G.B., Grande Bretagne (G.B.: Great Britain).

G.D.F., Gaz de France (state-owned gas company).

G.E.P.A.N., Groupe d'Études des Phénomènes Aérospatiaux (Study Group for Aerospatial Phenomena).

Gir., Gironde.

H.-G., Haute-Garonne.

H.-L., Haute-Loire.

H.L.M., habitation à loyer modéré (subsidized low-cost government housing).

H.-M., Haute-Marne.

H.-P., Hautes-Pyrénées.

H.Q., [ouvriers] hautement qualifiés (highly trained workers, generally at foreman's level).

H.-Rh., Haut-Rhin.

H.S., hors de service (unfit for or out of service).

H.T., haute tension (high voltage).

H.V., Haute-Vienne.

I.D.H.E.C., Institut des Hautes Études Cinématographiques.

I.-et-L., Indre-et-Loire.

I.-et-V., Ille-et-Vilaine.

I.F.O.P., Institute Français d'Opinion Publique (French Institute of Public Opinion; surveys questions of public interest).

I.G.F., impôts sur les grandes fortunes (tax on private wealth, instituted by the controversial law of May 10, 1981).

I.N.S.E.A.D., Institut National des Sciences Économiques et de l'Administration (important business administration school at Fontainebleau).

I.R.C.A.M., Institut de Recherche et de Co-ordination Acoustique/Musique (research center for modern music set up in 1977 under Pierre Boulez).

J.O., *Journal Officiel* (reports on new laws and government regulations; issues publications similar to those of the Government Printing Office in the United States).

L.-et-C., Loire-et-Cher.

L.-et-G., Lot-et-Garonne.

M.-et-L., Maine-et-Loire.

M.-et-M., Meurthe-et-Moselle.

M.G., médecin de médecine générale (G.P.: general practitioner).

Mgr, Monseigneur (Mgr.: Monsignor).

M.L.F., Mouvement pour la Libération des Femmes (Women's Liberation Movement).

M.R.P., Mouvement Républicain Populaire (political party).

M.S.B.S., mer-sol-balistique-stratégique (underwater-to-land ballistic missile).

N.D.E., note de l'éditeur (publisher's note).

N.D.L.R., note de la rédaction (editor's note).

N.F., nouveau franc (the "new franc" was introduced in 1960, when it was substituted for 100 *anciens francs*; many older people still tend to give the prices of real estate, housing, etc., in *anciens francs,* which can be disconcerting).

N.R.F., *Nouvelle Revue Française* (along with *Les Temps Modernes,* for many years one of France's most important intellectual periodicals; the initials are also used as a logo for Gallimard, a prestigious publishing house).

O.A.A., Organisation pour l'Alimentation et l'Agriculture (F.A.O.: Food and Agriculture Organization).

O.C.D.E., Organisation de Coopération et de Développement Économique (O.E.C.D.: Organization for Economic Cooperation and Development).

O.E.A., Organisation des États Américains (O.A.S.: Organization of American States).

O.E.C.E., Organisation Européenne de Coopération Économique (O.E.E.C.: Organization for European Economic Cooperation).

O.I.P.C., Organisation Internationale de Police Criminelle (Interpol).

O.I.R., Organisation Internationale pour les Réfugiés (I.R.O.: International Refugee Organization).

O.I.T., Organisation Internationale du Travail (I.L.O.: International Labor Organization).

O.M.S., Organisation Mondiale de la Santé (W.H.O.: World Health Organization).

O.N.U., Organisation des Nations Unies (U.N.: United Nations).

O.P., ouvriers professionnels (workers having a C.A.P., *q.v.*).

O.R.T.F., Office de la Radiodiffusion et Télévision Françaises (government bureau controlling broadcasting, which is subject to control of party in power).

O.S., ouvriers spécialisés (semi-skilled workers).

O.T.A.N., Organisation du Traité de l'Atlantique Nord (NATO: North Atlantic Treaty Organization).

O.T.A.S.E., Organisation du Traité de l'Asie du Sud-Est (S.E.A.T.O.: South-East Asia Treaty Organization).

O.V.N.I., objet volant non identifié (U.F.O.: unidentified flying object).

P.-B., Pays-Bas (The Netherlands).

P.C.E.M., premier cycle d'études médicales.

P.C.F., Parti Communiste Français (French Communist Party; as often as not referred to simply as P.C.).

P.C.V., paiement contre vérification (collect phone call).

P.D.G., président directeur général (chairman, sometimes given as *pédégé*).

P.-de-C., Pas-de-Calais.

P.-de-D., Puy-de-Dôme.

P. et C., Ponts et Chausées (government department responsible for bridges and highways).

P.G., prisonnier de guerre (P.O.W.: prisoner of war).

P.J., Police Judiciaire (C.I.D.: Criminal Investigation Division).

P.-O., Pyrénées-Orientales.

P.S.U., Parti Socialiste Unifié.

P.T.T., Poste, Télégraphes et Téléphones (government post office, which also controls telephone and telegraph communications).

R.A.T.P., Régie Autonome des Transports Parisiens (Paris' equivalent of New York's M.T.A.).

R.A.U., République Arabe Unie (U.A.R.: United Arab Republic).

R.D.A., République Démocratique Allemande (G.D.R.: German Democratic Republic—East Germany).

R.E.R., Réseau Express Régional (suburban extension of the Paris Métro system).

R.F., République Française (French Republic).

R.F.A., République Fédérale Allemande (F.R.G.: Federal Republic of Germany–West Germany).

R.P.F., Rassemblement du Peuple Français (Reunion—or Rally—of the French People; political party founded by Charles de Gaulle in 1947).

r.g., rive gauche (left bank of Paris).

R.N.P., Rassemblement National Populaire (political party).

R.P., Révérend Père (Reverend Father).

S.A., société anonyme (Inc.).

S.-et-L., Saône-et-Loire.

S.-et-M., Seine-et-Marne.

S.-et-O., Seine-et-Oise.

S.M.I.C., or S.M.I.G., salaire minimum interprofessionnel de croissance, garanti (guaranteed minimum wage; those who come under its provisions are known as *smicards*).

S.N.C.F., Société Nationale des Chemins de Fer Français (French National Railways).

S.A.F.E.R.s., Sociétés d'Aménagements Foncier et d'Établissement Rural (regional societies empowered to acquire available farmland, improve and resell it).

S.I.C.A.s., Sociétés d'Intérêt Collectif Agricole (state-assisted farmers' marketing groups).

S.I.D.A., Syndrome d'Immunodéficience Acquise (AIDS: Acquired Immunity Deficiency Syndrome).

S.N.I.A.S., Société Nationale Industrielle Aérospatiale.

S.P.A., Société Protectrice des Animaux (French equivalent of the A.S.P.C.A.).

T.C.F., Touring Club de France.

T.E.P. Théâtre de l'Est Parisien (theater group founded by Guy Rétoré in Ménilmontant suburb to bring "serious"—and generally leftist —theater to popular audiences).

T.G.V., train à grande vitesse ("bullet train" destined to link Paris and Marseilles; first section went into operation in 1981; capable of speeds of up to 185 m.p.h.).

T.-et-G., Tarn-et-Garonne.

T.M.G., temps moyen de Greenwich (G.M.T.: Greenwich Mean Time).

T.N.P., Théâtre National Populaire (subsidized theater founded by Jean Vilar in 1951).

T.V.A., taxe sur la valeur ajoutée (value-added tax; in shops this is always included in the marked price).

U.R.S.S., Union des Républiques Socialistes Soviétiques (U.S.S.R.: Union of Soviet Socialist Republics).

FRENCH/AMERICAN CLOTHING SIZE EQUIVALENTS*

WOMEN

Dresses, suits, coats	F.	38	40	42	44	46	48	50
	USA	8	10	12	14	16	18	20
Knitwear, blouses	F.	38	40	42	44	46	48	48
	USA	32	34	36	38	40	42	42
Stockings	F.	0	1	2	3	4	5	
	USA	8	8½	9	9½	10	10½	
Shoes	F.	36	36½	37	37½	38	39	
	USA	4½	5	5½	6	6½	7½	

MEN

Suits	F.	34	36	38	40	42	44	46	48
	USA	34	35	36	37	38	39	40	42
Sweaters	F.	36–38	40–42	44–46	48–50				
	USA	S	M	L	XL				
Shirts	F.	36	37	38	39	40	41	42	43
	USA	14	14½	15	15½	16	16½	17	17½
Shoes	F.	39	40	41	42	43	44	45	46
	USA	6½–7	7½	8	8½	9–9½	10–10½	11–11½	12–12½

* Because sizing, especially in women's clothing, is not really standardized either in the United States, or, to a lesser degree, in France, these equivalencies are only approximate.